Organization and Governance in Higher Education

Sixth Edition

ASHE Reader Series

Edited by
M. Christopher Brown II

Associate Editors
Jason E. Lane
Eboni M. Zamani-Gallaher

Foreword by
Edward St. John

Series Editors
Lenoar Foster, Washington State University
Jerlando F. L. Jackson, University of Wisconsin

Learning Solutions

New York   Boston   San Francisco
London   Toronto   Sydney   Tokyo   Singapore   Madrid
Mexico City   Munich   Paris   Cape Town   Hong Kong   Montreal

Cover Art: *Dream Visions #1*, by Michelle Muhlbaum Aviksis

Pearson Learning Solutions, 501 Boylston Street, Suite 900, Boston, MA 02116
A Pearson Education Company
www.pearsoned.com

Printed in the United States of America

8 9 10 V0CR 15 14 13 12

000200010270570151

SB/SD

ISBN 10: 0-558-84952-0
ISBN 13: 978-0-558-84952-8

TABLE OF CONTENTS

DEDICATION

The Sixth Edition of Organization and Governance in Higher Education: An ASHE Reader
is dedicated to the memory of
Dr. Lenoar "Len" Foster
who served as Editor of the ASHE Reader Series at the time this project began.

Len was born December 18, 1951 and died April 3, 2009. He earned his bachelor's degree from Xavier University in New Orleans, Louisiana. After graduation, Len moved to Reno, Nevada. Len became a member of the Brothers of the Holy Rosary. He later earned both a master and doctorate degree from the University of Nevada. He served on the faculties of the University of Montana, San Diego State University, and Washington State University (WSU). In 2003, Len was appointed Associate Dean of Administration, Research, and Graduate Studies in the College of Education at WSU. And for one week preceding his death he served as Interim Dean of the College.

"An important and contemporary aggregate of effectiveness for institutions of higher education in the United States is the degree to which graduates have attained academic, social, economic, and political readiness for a society that is increasingly multicultural and global. Accreditation bodies have enjoined American higher education institutions to evaluate the success of their students and graduates against mission statements and leadership direction that clearly delineate institutional prioritization of resources and strategic planning. In short, when institutional benchmarks of mission, teaching, research, and service are supported by an infrastructure of leadership and dedicated resources, students mirror the success of colleges and universities from which they have graduated through a number of quantifiable measures. Among these measures are the rank and caliber of the graduate schools to which they have been accepted; the internship and job opportunities they have garnered at Fortune 500 and other top-ranked business conglomerates; the notoriety of their post-graduate accomplishments; the importance and significance of the corridors of power through which they have become associated as a result of their talent, achievement, and political, social, and economic affiliation; and, the innovations and contributions they are positioned to make in a variety of endeavors."

Lenoar Foster (2008)
Foreword to *Ebony Towers in Higher Education*

ADVISORY BOARD FOR THE SIXTH EDITION

ACKNOWLEDGMENTS REPORT

Grateful acknowledgment is made to the following sources for permission to reprint material copyrighted or controlled by them:

Copyright Acknowledgments

"Foundations of the Theory of Organization," by Philip Selznick, reprinted from *American Sociological Review* 13 (1948).

"Central Perspectives and Debates in Organization Theory," by W. Graham Astley and Andrew H. Van de Ven, reprinted from *Administrative Science Quarterly* 28 (1983).

"The Bases and Use of Power in Organizational Decision Making: The Case of a University," by Gerald R. Salancik and Jeffery Pfeffer, reprinted from *Administrative Science Quarterly* 19 (1974).

"The Professional Bureaucracy," by Henry Mintzberg, reprinted from *The Structuring of Organizations* (1979), Prentice-Hall, Inc.

"Educational Organizations as Loosely Coupled Systems," by Karl E. Weick, reprinted from *Administrative Science Quarterly* 21, no. 1 (1976).

"A Garbage Can Model of Organization," by Michael D. Cohen, James G. March, and Johan P. Olsen, reprinted from *Administrative Science Quarterly* 17, no. 1 (1972).

"Administrative and Professional Authority," by Amitai Etzioni, reprinted from *Modern Organizations* (1964), Prentice-Hall, Inc.

"Evolution of University Organization," by E. D. Duryea, reprinted from *The University as an Organization*, edited by J. A. Perkins (1973), the McGraw-Hill Companies.

"The Organizational Conception," by Burton R. Clark, reprinted from *Perspectives on Higher Education: Eight Disciplinary and Comparative Views*, edited by Burton R. Clark (1984), University of California Press.

"Emerging Developments in Postsecondary Organization Theory and Research: Fragmentation or Integration," by Marvin W. Peterson, reprinted from *Educational Research* 14, no. 3 (March 1985), American Educational Research Association.

"Organizational Concepts Underlying Governance and Administration," by Ellen Earle Chaffee, reprinted from *Key Resources in Higher Education Governance, Management, and Leadership: A Guide to the Literature*, edited by Marvin W. Peterson and Lisa A. Mets (1987), Jossey-Bass Publishers, Inc.

"A Comparison of Private and Public Educational Organizations," by Daniel C. Levy, reprinted from *The Nonprofit Sector: A Research Handbook*, edited by Walter W. Powell (1987), Yale University Press.

"Statements on Government of Colleges and Universities," reprinted from *Academe* 52, no. 4 (December 1966), American Association of University Professors.

"Alternative Models of Governance on Higher Education," by J. Victor Baldridge et al., reprinted from *Governing Academic Organizations* (1977), McCutchan Publishing Group.

"The Academic Life: Small Worlds, Different Worlds," by Burton R. Clark, reprinted from *Faculty Authority* (1987), University of California Press.

"The Latent Organizational Functions of the Academic Senate: Why Senates Do Not Work But Will Not Go Away," by Robert Birnbaum, reprinted from *Journal of Higher Education* 60, no. 4 (July/August 1989).

"Statement on Board Responsibility for Institutional Governance," Association of Governing Boards of Universities and Colleges, March 26, 2010.

"Higher Education Boards of Trustees," by Benjamin E. Hermalin, reprinted from *Governing Academia: Who Is in Charge at the Modern University?*, edited by Ronald G. Ehrenberg (2004), Cornell University Press.

"The Organizational Saga in Higher Education," by Burton R. Clark, reprinted from *Administrative Science Quarterly* 17, no. 2 (June 1972).

"The Effect of Institutional Culture on Change Strategies in Higher Education: Universal Principles or Culturally Responsive Concepts," by Adrianna Kezar and Peter D. Eckel, reprinted from *The Journal of Higher Education* 73, no. 4 (July/August 2002).

"Enhancing Campus Climates for Racial/Ethnic Diversity: Educational Policy and Practice," by Sylvia Hurtado et al., reprinted from *The Review of Higher Education* 73, no. 3 (1998), Association for the Study of Higher Education.

"An Integrative Model of Organizational Trust," by Robert C. Mayer, James H. Davis, and F. David Schoorman, reprinted from *Academy Management Review* 20, no. 3 (1995), Academy of Management Review.

"Organizational Culture in Higher Education: Defining the Essentials," by William G. Tierney, reprinted from *The Journal of Higher Education* 59, no. 1, Journal of Higher Education.

"The Importance of Acknowledging Context in Institutional Research," by Jason E. Lane; M. Christopher Brown II, reprinted from *New Directions for Institutional Research,* no. 124 (winter 2004), Wiley-Interscience.

"Leadership in an Organized Anarchy," by Michael D. Cohen and James G. March, reprinted from *Leadership and Ambiguity: The American College President* (March 1986), Harvard Business School Press.

"The Ambiguity of Leadership," by Jeffery Pfeffer, reprinted from *The Academy of Management Review* 12, no. 1 (1974).

"Symbolism and Presidential Perceptions of Leadership," by William G. Tierney, reprinted from *Review of Higher Education* 12, no. 2 (1989).

"Organizational Learning and Communities-of-Practice: Toward a Unified View of Working, Learning, and Innovation," by John Seely Brown and Paul Duguid, reprinted from *Organization Science* 2, no. 1(February 1991), Institute for Operations Research and the Management Sciences.

"Academic Leaders as Thermostats," by Jouni Kekale, reprinted from *Tertiary Education and Management* 9 (2003), Kluwer Academic Publishers.

"Jazz as a Process of Organizational Innovation," by David T. Bastien and Todd J. Hostager, reprinted from *Communication Research* 15 (1988), Sage Publications, Inc.

"Three Models of Strategy," by Ellen Earle Chaffee, reprinted from *Academy of Management Review* 10, no. 1 (1985).

"The Fall and Rise of Strategic Planning," by Henry Mintzberg, reprinted from *Harvard Business Review* 72 (1994).

"A Memo from Machiavelli," by Daniel J. Julius, Victor Baldridge, and Jeffrey Pfeffer, reprinted from *The Journal of Higher Education* 70, no. 2 (March/April 1999).

"An Organizational Learning Framework: From Intuition to Institution," by Henry W. Lane and Roderick E. White, reprinted from *Academy of Management Review* 24, no. 3 (1999).

"The Life Cycle of Academic Management Fads," by Robert Birnbaum, reprinted from *Journal of Higher Education* 71, no. 1 (2000).

"The Applicability of Institutional Goals to the University Organisation," by Glenys Patterson, reprinted from *Journal of Higher Education Policy and Management* 23, no. 2 (2001), Routledge Publishing, Inc.

"Performance and Paralysis: The Organizational Context of the American Research University," by Daniel Alpert, reprinted from *The Journal of Higher Education* 56, no. 3 (May/June 1985).

"The Role of Shared Governance in Institutional Hard Decisions: Enable or Antagonist," by Peter D. Eckel, reprinted from *Review of Higher Education* 24, no. 1(Fall 2000), Association for the Study of Higher Education.

"Academic restructuring: Organizational change and institutional imperatives," by Patricia J. Gumport, reprinted from *Higher Education* 39 (2000), Kluwer Academic Publishers.

"Experiences of Academic Unit Reorganization: Organizational Identity and Identification in Organizational Change," by Michael Mills et al., reprinted from *The Review of Higher Education* 28, no. 4 (summer 2005), Association for the Study of Higher Education.

"Managing Productivity in an Academic Institution: Rethinking the Whom, Which, What and Whose of Productivity," by Gary Rhoades, reprinted from *Research in Higher Education* 42, no. 5 (2001), Human Sciences Press.

"Who's Doing it Right? Strategic Activity in Public Research Universities," by Gary Rhoades, reprinted from *The Review of Higher Education* 24, no. 1 (fall 2000), Association for the Study of Higher Education.

"The Nature of Administrative Behavior in Higher Education," by David D. Dill, reprinted from *Educational Administration Quarterly* 20, no. 3 (1984), Sage Publications, Inc.

"The Bureaucratisation of Universities," by Ase Gornitza, Svein Kyvik, and Ingvild Marheim Larsen, reprinted from *Minerva* 36 (1998), Kluwer Academic Publishers.

"Trust, Markets and Accountability in Higher Education: A Comparative Perspective," by Martin Trow, reprinted from *Higher Education Policy* 9, no. 4 (1996), Palgrave Publishers, Ltd.

"A Case of Bureaucratic Accretion: Context and Consequences," by Patricia Gumport and Brian Pusser, reprinted from *The Journal of Higher Education* 66, no. 5 (September/October 1995).

"A Game-Theoretic Explanation of the Administrative Lattice in Institutions of Higher Learning," by Andreas Ortmann and Richard Squire, reprinted from *Journal of Economic Behavior and Organization* 43, no. 3 (2000), Elsevier Science.

"Adam Smith Goes to College: An Economist Becomes an Academic Administrator," by Ronald G. Ehrenberg, reprinted from *Journal of Economic Perspectives* 13, no. 1 (winter 1999).

"After globalization: emerging politics of education," by Simon Marginson, reprinted from *Journal of Education Policy* 14, no. 1 (1999), Routledge, Ltd.

"The Political Context of Higher Education," by Marilyn Gittell and Neil Scott Kleiman, reprinted from *American Behavioral Scientist* 43, no. 7 (2000), Sage Publications, Inc.

"Universities and Markets," by Roger L. Geiger, reprinted from *Knowledge & Money: Research Universities and the Paradox of the Marketplace* (2004), Stanford University Press.

"Interests, Information, and Incentives in Higher Education: Principle-Agent Theory and Its Potential Applications to the Study of Higher Education Governance," by Jason E. Lane and Jussi A. Kivisto, reprinted from *Higher Education: Handbook of Theory and Research*, edited by J. C. Smart, Springer Science + Business Media.

"How to Survive in Postindustrial Environments: Adam Smith's Advice for Today's Colleges and Universities," by Andreas Ortmann, reprinted from *The Journal of Higher Education* 68, no. 5 (September/October 1997).

"Beyond Baldridge: Extending the Political Model of Higher Education Organization and Governance," by Brian Pusser, reprinted from *Educational Policy* 17, no. 121 (2003), Sage Publications, Inc.

"Tribal Colleges and Universities in an Era of Dynamic Development," by Michael Pavel, Ella Inglebret, and Susan Rae Banks, reprinted from *Peabody Journal of Education* 26, no. 1 (2001), Routledge, Ltd.

"The Historically Black College as Social Contract, Social Capital, and Social Equalizer," by James Earle Davis, reprinted from *Peabody Journal of Education* 76, no. 1 (2001), Routledge, Ltd.

"Hispanic-Serving Institutions: Myths and Realities," by Berta Vigil Laden, reprinted from *Peabody Journal of Education* 76, no. 1 (2001), Routledge, Ltd.

"The Confluence of Race, Gender and Class Among Community College Students: Assessing Attitudes Toward Affirmative Action in College Admissions," by Eboni M. Zamani-Gallaher, reprinted from *Equity & Excellence in Education* (2007), Taylor & Francis.

"Achieving Equitable Educational Outcomes with All Students: The Institution's Roles and Responsibilities," by Georgia L. Bauman et al., reprinted from *Making Excellence Inclusive* (2005), Association of American Colleges & Universities.

"When and Where Interests Collide: Policy, Research, and the Case of Managing Campus Diversity," by T. Elon Dancy II, reprinted from *Managing Diversity: (Re)Visioning Equity on College Campuses* (2010), Peter Lang Publishing Inc.

"The Campus Racial Climate Contexts of Conflict," by Sylvia Hurtado, reprinted from *Journal of Higher Education* 63, no. 5 (1992).

"Racism in Higher Education: An Organizational Analysis," by Mark A. Chesler and James Crowfoot, reprinted from *The Working Paper Series; Center for research on Social Organization* (1989), Center for Research on Social Organization.

"The Emperor Has No Clothes: Rewriting "Race in Organizations," by Stella M. Nkomo, reprinted from *Academy of Management Review* 17, no. 3.

"E Plurbis Unum? Academic Structure, Culture, and the Case of Feminist Scholarship," by Patricia J. Gumport, reprinted from *The Review of Higher Education* 15, no. 1 (1991), Association for the Study of Higher Education.

"Deconstructing Organizational Taboos: The Suppression of Gender Conflict in Organizations," by Joanne Martin, reprinted from *Organization Science* 1, no. 4 (1990), Institute for Operations Research and the Management Sciences.

"The Challenge of Cultural Diversity: Harnessing a Diversity of Views to Understand Multiculturalism," by Patricia L. Netmetz and Sandra L. Christensen, reprinted from *Academy of Management Review* 21, no. 2 (1996).

"Postmodernism and Higher Education," by Harland G. Bloland, reprinted from *Journal of Higher Education* 66, no. 5 (1995).

"Understanding Radical Organizational Change," by Royston Greenwood and C. R. Hinings, reprinted from *Academy of Management Review* 21, no. 4 (1996).

"The Invisible Workers," by Judy Szekeres, reprinted from *Journal of Higher Education Policy and Management* 26, no. 1, Routledge, Ltd.

"Responding to Organizational Identity Threats: Exploring the Role of Organizational Culture," by Davide Ravasi and Majken Schultz, reprinted from *Academy of Management Journal* 49, no. 3 (2006).

"The Power of Symbolic Constructs in Reading Change in Higher Education," by Hasan Simsek, reprinted from *Journal of Higher Education* 33, no. 3.

"Balancing Corporation, Collegium, and Community," by James Downey, reprinted from *Innovative Higher Education* 21, no. 2 (winter 1996), Institute of Higher Education.

Organization and Governance in Higher Education: Foreword to the Sixth Edition

Edward P. St. John
University of Michigan

Every decade or so, higher education in the United States seems reach a crisis. In the 1960s, colleges could not expand fast enough for the baby boom generation, but in the early 1970s there was a "new depression" caused by plans for growth exceeding budget capacity (Cheit, 1971). Fast forwarding to the present, we are confronted by a major global, economic recession. Global competition is changing the landscape of higher education across the nation and world. One recent observer, Mark C. Taylor (2010), describes the convergence of globalization of universities and the economic crisis as an "education bubble," akin to an economic crash within higher education. In my view, the notion to the economic bubble does not quite hold up because of the great diversity of institutions, the ways they are financed, and the meaning postsecondary leaders will make out of the way they navigate through the puzzles of economic conditions and professional life in academic organizations. But the criterion of what holds up over time is a better indicator of the lasting importance of theory and research than are opinions at any particular point in time.

Each generation's crisis leaves an imprint on the organizations involved and on the literature that describes what happened. The explanations and theories that hold up and have lasting value in the study of colleges become "canonical," as M. Christopher Brown II, Jason E. Lane, and Eboni M. Zamani-Gallaher and his colleagues so aptly describe in their introduction. This volume provides an excellent primer on an extraordinarily fascinating field of study. It is crucial to have an understanding of the deeply rooted views of universities as organizations. Such knowledge prepares the aspiring academic or administrator to prepare for the professional life in academe. Understanding organizations and the ways they work is essential to successfully steering a career through these complicated but wonderfully dynamic institutions. I start this foreword by commending M. Christopher Brown and his associate editors on compiling an excellent volume.

While some of my peers may not agree, I am convinced that colleges and universities in the U.S. are remarkably adaptive organizations. Arguments about crises tend to focus on failure to develop according to plans (e.g. Taylor, 2010), rather than dynamic changes that happen occasionally in spite of the best laid plans. The creation of corporate boards as an artifact of the Supreme Court's Dartmouth decision (Thelin, 2004) rather than a plan or policy decision by state government gave U.S. higher education this decentralized model, still unique among national systems. While many experts predicted massive closings of liberal arts colleges in the 1980s, these institutions adapted and became more competitive in the 1990s, a development that occurred as the public colleges began raising tuition in response to declining support from their states. As Brown and colleagues so aptly describe in the introduction, one of the key concepts that emerged from the period was the concept of "strategy": institutional leaders learned they could alter their course by bringing internal direction-setting into play to combat the external forces that create "demography as destiny" (Norris & Poulton, 1987) Throughout the 1980s, many talented authors wrote about strategic planning and developed guides to inform practice. This current compilation highlights some of the excellent texts that have dealt with this complex turn of events from a grounded perspective.

There have been many points in the history of higher education that external events and internal maneuvering by college and university leaders have created new organizational forms within higher education. From the late 1800s until the 1960s, the concept of collegial governance was widely held by faculty to be the central organizational principal of academic communities (Goodman, 1962). In fact, much of the early scholarship in the field focused on the role of faculty governance, especially the U.C. Berkeley Center for Research and Development of Higher Education (e.g., McConnell & Mortimer, 1970). While many of the early scholars of organizations focused on governance, more modern concepts like "management" and "strategy" won out, as universities adapted to new and more difficult circumstances in the past few decades. However, let's hope that the concept of faculty governance is not left behind entirely in the scholarship on and practice of higher education leadership. In my view, the capacity of faculty members to have civil dialogues about the critical issues we face as professors is paramount to our ability to function as communities of scholars serving the public good (St. John, 2009).

Take, for instance, the problem of diversity within academic communities. In the U.S., historically black colleges and universities are an artifact of an earlier period of *de jure* segregation; we now also have predominantly Hispanic colleges and universities as a consequence of *de facto* segregation. We can still litigate against de jure segregation in some circumstances (Conrad & Weerts, 2004), but it has been difficult to litigate against de jure segregation in higher education because students have the right to choose their own college. Of course, financial and other policy factors influence patterns of enrollment, especially in four-year colleges (St. John, 2003), but the problems of inequality in access are not just about money. In this period of our history, when there are direct assaults on affirmative action in many states, it is important we learn to have conversations about underlying issues of fairness and the complex concept of inequality and how it relates to real or perceived reverse discrimination. The chapters on diversity and campus climate in this volume can help prepare aspiring academics and administrators to engage in these difficult but necessary conversations. It is better to communicate than to litigate if it is possible to do so within universities as organizations sometimes governed by heavy managerial hands.

The newer challenges of globalization are no less complex than the lingering ones related to diversity and desegregation. We have entered a period of global competition for talent, a "brain race" (Wildavsky, 2010). Major U.S. research universities are opening campuses abroad, the European Community has pushed for regional exchange at the same time diverse European nations are pushing to get more of their own universities to the top group in terms of international rankings, and nations in Asian and the Middle East are investing substantially in new universities. The argument that the U.S. can be the world's brain trust for decades to come, a conception that still has some saliency in the workforce planning literature (e.g., Commission on the Skills of the American Workforce, 2007), no longer seems as certain. There are many competitors aiming to provide quality education and to rise in the rankings, adding substantially to the complexity of academic leadership in our times. Fortunately, this volume includes a section on globalization with some very thoughtful papers on the topic.

The ASHE volumes are important for many reasons, not the least of which is that they provide the foundation, through a common set of readings, for discourse in the field. Of course, these common readings should be supplemented by other texts on core issues[1] when course syllabi are crafted. However, given the ASHE reader's central role in the academic discourse in higher education, graduate students who read these texts as part of their graduate courses can be assured they are better prepared for the conversations of professional life in academe. Compiling a volume of readings of this type and quality is a difficult task that can go without sufficient recognition; many research universities don't place much weight on this type of work. The value of the work is related

---

[1]Marybeth Gasman and I are developing a set of books on core issues in higher education (with Routledge Press) that will make additional contemporary voices of scholarship available to professors and graduate students in the field. We hope professors will explore ways of combining texts in their classes as part of the ongoing process of moving our field forward through an active interchange of ideas about core concepts. For example, my own book on college organization (St. John, 2009), a model for the series, and a forth coming book by Kathleen Manning were written to give professors options in ways of constructing courses on organizations.

to the community of scholars itself. Being a contributing member of this extended, now global, community of learners is a great experience. M. Christopher Brown II has taken on today's challenges with great style at a time when he has also been an engaged scholar doing meaningful academic work and a nationally recognized academic leader. The Association for the Study of Higher Education is fortunate to have now Executive Vice President and Provost Brown and others continue this important work. ASHE, the Reader's Editors, and the Series Editors should all be commended for this fine compilation of readings.

References

Cheit, E.F. (1971). *The new depression in higher education.* New York: Mc-Graw Hill.

Commission on the Skills of the American Workforce (2007). *Tough choices, tough times: The report of the new commission on skills of the American workforce.* Washington, DC: National Center on Education and the Economy.

Conrad, C. F., & Weerts, D. J. (2004). Federal involvement in higher education desegregation: An unfinished agenda. In E. P. St. John & M. D. Parsons (Eds.), *Public funding of higher education: Changing contexts and new rationales* (pp. 60–74). Baltimore: Johns Hopkins University Press.

Goodman, P. (1962). *The community of scholars.* New York: Random House. McConnell, T. R., & Mortimer, K. P. (1970). *The faculty in university governance.* Berkeley: Center for Research and Development in Higher Education, University of California.

Norris, D. M., & Poulton, N. L. (1987). *A guide for new planners.* Ann Arbor, MI: Society for College and University Planning.

St. John, E. P. (2003). *Refinancing the college dream: Access, equal opportunity, and justice for taxpayers.* Baltimore, MD: Johns Hopkins University Press.

St. John, E. P. (2009) *College organization and professional development: Integrating moral reasoning and reflective practice.* NY: Routledge-Taylor.

Taylor, M. C. (2010), *Crisis on campus: A bold plan for reforming our colleges and universities.* New York: Knopf.

Thelin, J. R. (2004). *A history of American higher education.* Baltimore: Johns Hopkins University Press.

Wildvasky, B. (2010). *The great brain race: How global universities are reshaping the world.* Princeton, NJ: Princeton University Press.

INTRODUCTION

Canonical and Emergent Scholarship on Organization and Governance in Higher Education: An Introduction to the Sixth Edition

M. CHRISTOPHER BROWN II, JASON E. LANE, AND EBONI M. ZAMANI-GALLAHER

The organization and governance of colleges and universities is the historically central theme of research and commentary on higher education. Academic management is often described as higher education administration, academic leadership, collegiate management, or a host of other words, clauses, or phrases that attempt to capture the complex series of issues, activities, and considerations that relate to the organization and governance of both traditional and now virtual institutions of higher learning. Higher education as a field of study has expanded its portfolio of themes to include research on students, faculty, curriculum, history, and policy. Notwithstanding, academic management and its twin dimensions—organization and governance—remain the cornerstone of the field as we have known it, engage it, and will come to experience it in the forthcoming years.

The question "what is a university?" is deceptively simple. There is no single, substantive, or sufficient answer that can cogently capture the wide array of types, issues, or functions that are critical to our understanding of institutions of higher education. Great scholars and practitioners such as Adam Smith, John Henry Newman, and Thorstein Veblen have all contributed to the discussion, debating the role of teaching, research, curriculum, knowledge creation, and knowledge dissemination. The reality is that colleges and universities are large and complex organizations. Their organizational structures tend not to be of purposeful design, rather the culmination of a decades- or centuries-long evolutionary process. The modern university retains vestiges of its medieval origins; however, it remains fluid in absorbing new roles and responsibilities. The complex and long history of colleges and universities as a cohort makes the study of their operation, governance, decision-making processes, and leadership difficult, even with all of the tools provided by organizational scholars.

Writings about higher education administration can be traced to the turn of the last century. However, Marvin Peterson, who edited an early version of this reader, observed that the infancy of the scholarly literature studying the organization of the postsecondary institution continued until the early 1960s, maturing rapidly since that time (Peterson, 1985). In his review of the literature, Peterson found fewer than 200 research-based articles dealing with the subject had been published at the time. More than twenty years later, in a paper presented at the 2008 ASHE conference, Michael Bastedo and his colleagues found that five core higher education journals in the United States (i.e., *Review of Higher Education*, *Research in Higher Education*, the *Journal of Higher Education*, the *Journal of College Student Development*, and *Higher Education*), published 327 organizational themed articles between 1990 and 2007 (Bastedo, Molina, & Barnharat, 2008). This does not include the numerous books, book chapters, reports, dissertations, conference papers, and articles in other journals written on the topic.

The research and scholarship that explores the organization and governance of academic management is as varied and extensive as the landscape of institutions available for examination. The specifics of how colleges and universities are organized and governed can differ by institutional designation (public versus private); national context, enrollment size, and mission (e.g., research intensive versus liberal arts focused). These basic differences are further complicated when considering the array of institutional types (Brown & Lane, 2003; Lane & Brown, 2004).

In the nearly four centuries since the founding of Harvard, the number and type of postsecondary institutions have grown significantly. As a matter of perspective, the U.S. Department of Education reports that more than 4,200 postsecondary institutions operate in the United States as of 2010. These organizations include community colleges, liberal art colleges, and research universities, regional comprehensive universities, training institutes, professional schools, and several other types. Some of these institutions are public, some private; some for-profit, some not-for-profit; some operate brick and mortar campuses while others exist almost entirely in cyberspace. It is simply not possible to provide an in-depth understanding of each institutional type. The best effort of a student, researcher, or practitioner is to understand the differences and similarities among such educational organizations.

Structure of Colleges and Universities in the United States

In many ways, the study of colleges and universities is very much the study of history. In order to understand and appreciate the current configuration of higher education institutions, one needs to understand the origins of the organization. Colleges and universities have not always been the large, complex "multiversities" that now epitomize higher education such as the University of Illinois, Penn State or UC-Berkley. In addition to their teaching and learning functions, these colleges and universities run hospitals, hotels (in addition to residence halls), research laboratories, nuclear reactors, major sports complexes, and some even operate airports. Each of the expanded and extensive academic portfolios of structures and activities within the United States can be traced back to Harvard College as the national matriarch of all institutions. Harvard College was founded in 1636 with a handful of students, and a president (principal) that served as teacher, registrar, bursar, as well as performing all the duties now relegated to other officers of the university (Morison, 1936).

As complex as higher education has now become, several characteristics reflect on our nation's first college and its medieval progenitors, such as graduations, academic regalia, and academic titles like dean, provost, rector, and chancellor. However, American colleges and universities primarily take the form of a corporate organization in which authority is vested with a lay governing board. That governing board (which can take one of several names in the United States, such as Board of Regents, Board of Trustees, or Board of Visitors) serves as the legal embodiment of the institution, having responsibility primarily for the financial stability of the institution, hiring and firing the president and setting policy. Even so, two different types of bureaucracies have developed within many institutions. Academics have created departments, schools, colleges, and senates to deal with academic affairs, while a separate bureaucracy has evolved to handle all of the other business, administrative, and support functions.

Much of the current configurations of academic administration is guided and influenced by academic freedom. The modern concept of academic freedom traces its origins to the influence of Germany during the middle of the 19th century, the leading academic nation of the time. One of the ideas that came across the Atlantic was that of *Lehrfrieheit*—the freedom to teach as one see fits. This concept slowly expanded to include research as well. Academic Freedom and tenure became formal beliefs in the academic community during the early 20th century. After several perceived violations of academic freedom, in which faculty were believed to have been terminated for scholarly pursuits, John Dewey (Columbia University) and A. O. Lovejoy (Johns Hopkins) issued a call for a meeting to create comprehensive professional organization for academic faculty. Out of this meeting of 867 professors from sixty institutions was born the American Association of University Professors and the first statement on academic freedom and tenure. A report referred to as the "intellectual declaration of principles by a committee of senior scholars convened by the new organization AAUP" characterized the university as an "intellectual experiment station, where new ideas may germinate and where their fruit, though still distasteful to the community as a whole, may be allowed to ripen until finally, perchance, it may become part of the accepted intellectual food of this nation and the world."

The basic tenets of academic freedom were codified in the 1940 Statement on Academic Freedom. It is important for scholars and administrators to note that Academic Freedom is not a legal right (although the courts have provided some deference to academic freedom) nor does it cover all actions by faculty. The three basic tenets are as follows. First, university faculty have the freedom to pursue research interests and publish findings. Second, university faculty have the freedom to teach and discuss a subject as they see best fit, although they should avoid controversial content which is unrelated to their academic discipline. Third, university faculties have freedom of speech as a citizen without fear or repercussion; however, they must be restrained that they do not assert for the institution, accurate in the declaration of facts, and respectful of the diversity of opinions on any given matter. This liberty of verbal and written speech is conjoined with the pursuit and receipt of academic tenure—a termless offer of employment designed to protect academic freedom.

Academic tenure is generally awarded to faculty upon their promotion from the rank of assistant professor to associate professor pursuant to having demonstrated success in the tripartite areas of research, teaching, and service. In addition to faculty constructions of academic freedom and academic tenure, college and university faculty are typically organized into units called departments or divisions, which are often, led by department chairs or division heads. The manner of selection and appointment vary, as do the roles and responsibilities contingent upon type of appointment, institutional culture, and departmental/division bylaws. Academic departments often are grouped into schools or colleges, which are likely to be managed by an academic dean (not to be confused with administrative deans—Dean of Admission or Dean of Students). The academic dean often holds both a faculty and administrative appointment. This is an important distinction as academic freedom and tenure apply to the academic appointment, not the administrative appointment. Typically, the dean and other senior academic leaders serve at the will or pleasure of the president and can be removed from their administrative office. This is complicated by the question of whether the academic dean holds a tenured academic appointment, as well as the presence of a faculty union that has collectively bargained for rules regarding administrative employment. Academic deans generally report to a provost (sometimes called a vice president for academic affairs)—the senior academic officer charged with organizing, governing, and managing curricular and faculty issues. It is important to note that occasionally, the academic deans of professional schools may report directly to the president, as does the provost.

In parallel to academic affairs are structures to manage business affairs and student life outside of the classroom. In fact, the formalization of student affairs as an administrative role within the university began in the nineteenth century "when President Charles Elliot at Harvard asked LeBaron Russell Briggs, a young English professor, to assume a newly established dean's position in the college in 1890, Briggs had no job description and no staff. His assignment was vaguely described as 'looking after the needs of the student' (Sandeen, 2001, p. 181)." Presently, colleges and universities employ individuals to oversee a wide range of student-centered functions such as athletics, residential housing, campus activities, and spiritual concerns. Beyond academic affairs and student affairs, colleges, and universities also have organizational components that resemble civic municipalities, including police forces, maintenance and janitorial services, and campus motor pool and transportation divisions. It is typical for an institution of higher education to have one or more athletic/recreational facilities, cafeterias/dining halls, bookstores, and the other auxiliary units. Each of these entities, like the students who attend and the academic units (both faculty and curriculum) comprise the organizational composite of colleges and universities and must be managed for effectiveness and efficiency. To this end, academic managers must possess an array of knowledge bases and employ a vast skill set matched to the organization and requisite for the governance of institutions of higher education (Dill, 1984; Katz, 1973; Mintzberg, 1979). Colleges and universities as mammoth academic enterprises that require contextual knowledge of organization, business acumen on a given structure's political realities, and careful observation of the diversity of the academic community and its constituent stakeholders.

Contextual Considerations in Academic Governance

The organizational culture of institutions of higher education is central to how malleable colleges and universities are to their constituencies and community. The overall effectiveness of academic leaders is often described in relationship to their ability to advance institutional aims with effective management of the community and constituent interests. This skill set is even more crucial when and if a college or university desires to change, transform, or modify one or more of the dimensions of its mission, staffing, activities, or locations (Simsek & Louis, 1994). While organizational culture as a construct emerged from the field of business shaped by management and organizational studies (e.g., Schein, 1985, 1990) its application to colleges and universities is central to the literature base of the higher education field. Organizational culture provides a constructive framework through which we can examine the organizational beliefs, experiences, and ideas of people and groups in college settings. Institutions of higher education are therefore quasi-microcosms of the extant hierarchies of business, with stakeholders and responsibilities central to the organizational/institutional mission.

In *The Academic Life: Small Worlds, Different Worlds*, Burton Clark (1987), the famed sociologist of higher education describes the internal operations of colleges and universities, focusing on the professional bureaucracies engaged in both informal and formal self-governance. Clark provides the reader with a fascinating exploration of the various types of "faculty," suggesting there are often interrelationships among institutional types, disciplinary background, faculty perceptions, and governance (see Barnaul, 1989 for a further discussion of these interrelationships). While Clark does not directly address how governance differs, he proffers how differences in faculty expectations can affect governance. Clark reminds the reader that context and culture have significant import for the organization and governance of colleges and universities.

Researchers such as Brint and Karabel (1989) frame the academic enterprise in higher education as an "organizational field" in which there is differential affinity for organizations given the variation of climate and culture across institutional type. Therefore, organizational life is nuanced and the organizational culture may or may not be congruent with an individual on different levels. The conceptual underpinnings of their study further our understanding of the importance of institutional type in shaping campus climate and culture to be more inclusive, collegial, and infused with strategies that facilitate positive prevailing change that fosters a sense of agency across groups. This theme anchors the investigation of colleges and university in an environmental context that was once homogenous by now includes a diversity of students, faculty, staff, and administrators holding multiple group memberships (Aragon & Zamani, 2002; Zamani-Gallaher, Green, Brown, & Stovall, 2009).

In the article "Enhancing Campus Climates for Racial/Ethnic Diversity: Educational Policy and Practice," Hurtado, Milem, Clayton-Pedersen, and Allen (1998), offer a framework for furthering our understanding of the challenges and opportunities that portend from the rapid diversification of American higher education. Hurtado and colleagues assert that as complex social systems, colleges have to attend more comprehensively to the issue of climate. They further assert that academic management is responsible for this academic environment and possesses considerable influence on collegiate climates for students, staff, and stakeholders. Similarly, work of Petersen and Spencer (1990) in "Understanding academic culture and climate," highlights how the institutional environment relates to not only organizational effectiveness but also bears important influence on individual performance as one makes sense of the established norms and their identity within the organizational context. Petersen and Spencer find that the collegiate climate is distinctive from the culture of an institution. The former is the interactive pattern of organizational dynamics and the latter is the normative context developed on time in the institution's academic management and mission. Hence, the study of academic management in higher education remains complicated by its panoply of institutional types, sizes, and purposes.

Among the aims of the scholarship on organization and governance in higher education is the establishment of consensus of disparate ideas, achieving continuity among differing goals, and to disentangle the functional aspects of academic management. The responsibility of each of the above is given to the academic leader whatever her or his title might be. The varying definitions of leadership allude to organizing the persons of a structure and governing the tasks assigned to them (Kekäle, 2003, p. 282). Academic leaders are responsible for sense making as it pertains to contextual considerations vital to the strategic management of the enterprise (Kezar & Eckel, 2002).

Further, academic leaders are essential in reconceptualizing ambiguities that threaten the effective and efficient operation of the organization. How leaders complete this task extends from authoritative realities to symbolic gestures—each of which aids in framing the academic unit's realities (Tierney, 1989).

Taken as a composite of its myriad dimensions, the academic leadership of colleges and universities is synergistic and multidimensional. Academic leadership, therefore like the word university, lacks an acceptable standard definition. Notwithstanding, the collective scholarship evinces the role of the academic leader as the responsible party for both understanding and leading operations and change in college settings. It is likely then that effective academic leaders possess the administrative prowess and contextual keenness necessary for understanding the disparate structures, missions, and potential outputs of the academic unity. She or he is the catalyst and manager of the individual components of the enterprise. They have the ability to foster and/or constrain members in the organization in order to affect a given aspiration.

In "Leadership in an Organized Anarchy," Cohen & March (1974) underscore that leading an academic institution is a major endeavor resulting from all of the ambiguities associated with being in charge of a college or university. Despite perceptions of power and prominence, Cohen and March found presidential leadership to be particularly tenuous given the absence of a direct and consistent relationship between the office's positional authority and the realization of institutional ambitions. Pfeffer (1977) confirms the sundry challenges associated with the nebulous definition and imprecise assessment of academic leadership. The conclave of college and university leaders defy consensus as they are of heterogeneous backgrounds, experiences, and personalities. The competencies of the individuals possessing positions of academic leadership are not correlative to the achievements or failures of the academic units under their charge. The role, while both authoritative and symbolic, is but one component of the organization; perennially present are the dynamics incident to context, climate, culture, and constituencies. These dynamics are particularly present when an academic leader endeavors to change one or more realities of a college or university.

Strategic Change and Management in the Academy

A quote attributed to Greek philosopher Heraclitus states, "The only constant is change." Change in higher education is inevitable and a core component of academic management and leadership. As such, colleges and universities have been drawing on management and planning techniques developed in the business realm for more than half a century (Birnbaum, 1990). Pascale (1990) noted that there have been more than two dozen management strategies developed between 1950 and 1990 that have import for higher education organization, governance, administration, leadership, and management. Of particularly note, are collegiate adaptations of Reengineering (Hammer & Champy, 1993), Six Sigma (Breyfogle, 1999), and the Blue Oceans Strategy (Kim & Mauborgne, 2003). Interestingly, Marchese (1991) observed that the application of business research on organizational management "arrive at higher education's doorstep five years after their trial in business, often just as corporations are discarding them" (p. 7). In an analysis of the extrapolation of business applications in higher education, Birnbaum (2000) presents the five stages of the life cycle of management fads. He concludes that despite the ebb and flow of particularistic business strategies in the academic enterprise, the quest for guidance and techniques to assist the academic leader in managing the complexities of the campus organization is worthy of attention and investigation.

With one notable exception (i.e., strategic planning), all of the management fads reviewed by Birnbaum have lost their prominence in higher education management. Strategic planning is notable as it was introduced to higher education more than two decades ago (see e.g., Kotler & Murphy, 1981) and continues to be used widely by colleges and universities, leading some to argue that it has significantly deterred the advancement of higher education management in the past ten years. Indeed, Mintzberg (1994) critiques strategic planning as a managerial heuristic that precludes, delimits, and impedes the strategic thinking. In a different approach, Chaffee (1985) assesses the use of the term "strategy." In addition to reviewing the early research literature addressing the concept, Chaffee describes three strategy models: linear, adaptive, and interpretive. The linear model, which seems to have been most popular in the late 1960s and early 1970s focuses on a proscribed and sequential planning process in which a centralized action plan is agreed to and carried out by the management. Adaptive strategy is much more iterative and responsive to changing with environmental needs. Interpretative strategy focuses on the internal operations of the organization by using metaphors and shared stories to unite employees in collectively pursuing the goals of the organization. While each makes important contributions to our understanding of change management in organizations, they are united in declaring the importance of and academic leaders acknowledging the roles of management, strategy, and change in collegiate settings generally and higher education administration specifically (Austin, 1990).

In the seminal text *The Fifth Discipline*, Peter Senge (1990) describes a learning organization as a place where people are continually discovering how they establish a shared reality. Senge emphasizes that successful organizations create structures that allow the organization to learn about itself and how to improve. Moreover, it describes an organization as a complex system of interrelated parts. The strategies provided by Senge are useful for academic leaders as they help identify the discrete structures that underlie their complex institutional contexts, as well as the interrelationships endemic to management and change. Arguably, organizational learning is an important component of strategic initiatives for role maintenance or mission transformation. Therefore, academic leaders must attend not only to context, but also simultaneously to change as central markers of governing the academic enterprise (Baldridge, 1971, 1972).

The complex nature of higher education institutions affirms the importance of academic leaders to understanding the role of context in the administration and governance of colleges and universities. Acknowledgment of the role of the environment in understanding organizations posits that colleges and universities are amalgamations of interdependent parts that are both fixed and intangible. Hence identifying the boundaries of what does and does not fall under academic management is difficult to discern. Becker (1997) described four different types of boundaries that may exist in organizations: physical, linguistic, systemic, and psychological. Physical boundaries are those that physically exclude people from the organization, which could include fences, walls, roads, or structures. Linguistic boundaries exist when people are excluded from an organization based upon specialized jargon employed by those within the organization. Systemic boundaries are those that separate people based upon rules, roles, and responsibilities. Psychological boundaries are those that restrict communication based on perceptual differences among people or units. These boundaries help define what is within and outside of an organizational structure. The academic leader of a college or university setting is deemed the boundary spanner and is responsible for engaging the contextual and political realities, which aid or inhibit effective functioning of the academic enterprise.

Institutions of higher education exist in an environment where they are concomitantly bounded and unbounded within contexts with structural, political, and symbolic significance (Bowman & Deal, 2003). Given the range of responsibilities charged to the academic leader it is possible to gloss over the importance of political and cultural understanding, however in recent years the study of the politics of higher education has grown significantly with a range of scholars borrowing on theoretical frameworks employed within the political science and economics disciplines (Lane & Kivisto, 2008). The effort to understand colleges and universities in the light of their political landscape demonstrate the ways in which organization and governance for academic leaders and their assigned can govern the constituents, stakeholders, and communities regarding their institution and its activities and ambitions.

Institutional Context and Organizational Considerations

Colleges and universities as organizations and their academic leaders continually grapple with the shifting terrain of student enrollment, faculty composition, geographic realities, and political climates. Even more as increasing numbers of people of color and women in society writ large occupy placement in the preceding, the complexities of culture, language, and context on college campuses provide the foreground for the institutional diversity in its myriad forms in the organization and governance of higher education (Yates, 2000; Zamani-Gallaher, Green, Brown, & Stovall, 2009). The nuanced role that context proffers to academic governance and management portends to the ways in which academic leaders understand, retrench, and expand institutional missions on college campuses (Bensimon, 2004).

The convergence of diverse entities, people, and context structure the internal and external institutional dynamics. Hence, the organizational structure is the visible scaffold upon which invisible layers of academic climate and community manifest. The culture of academic units and the overall institutional climate can be difficult for academic leaders to identify or discern, much less to govern, or manage. Kezar (2000), in "Pluralistic Leadership: Incorporating Diverse Voice," explores the assumptions of positionality theory in shaping the varying perspectives and standpoints leaders have due to their membership in multiple cultural groups (e.g., race/ethnicity, gender, social class). Kezar discusses the importance of power relations to the conceptualization of divergent leadership styles. The findings of this study show that individual leadership perspectives are related to one's positionality and are influenced by all aspects of social identity.

With all of the variation in institutional types and organizational formats, it is important to acknowledge and seek to understand the distinctive features across colleges and to discern the unique patterns of participation across constituencies. Hence, the various intersections between college access, mission, and outcomes across institution types inform academic leadership and university governance. Further, college and universities campuses must comport and comply with the legislative and judicial mandates that contour the academic landscape. Legal issues ranging from affirmative action to intellectual property rights require academic leaders to both govern and manage the academic enterprise in differing ways. For that reason, Lane and Brown (2004) emphasize the importance of acknowledging institutional context incident to the organization and governance of colleges and universities.

In order to understand the myriad contexts among, between, and across institutional types, careful consideration to the historic development, traditional composition, emergent dynamics, and political histories are critical for the academic leader. Ideally, these considerations illuminate the particularistic organization and the contextual dimensions that govern the role of academic management. To the extent that there is congruence between the academic leader and the institution, governance in higher education exists as an opportunity rather than a challenge on a campus (Kuh, 2001). Bloland (1995) argues that this contextual capital is critical in order for an academic leader to be effective in the efficient governance of the academic organization.

In as much as globalization continues to transform society, higher education governance and management must adapt to the opportunities and complications inherent in innovation, creativity, and production. Cultural expansion in the civic and social space provides academic leaders with a secondary lens for understanding the governance of colleges and universities. Greenwood and Hinings (1996) call this "new institutionalism." They posit that new institutionalism (i.e., neoinstitutional theory) will mandate organizational change and modification to governance systems in order to account for the technological, political, and regulatory realities that are relevant to our institutional contexts. Over time, the normative contexts within organizations will converge with new archetypes and nomenclatures that evince the exiting realities of institutions of higher education. It will become imperative for colleges and universities to understand and engage these new communities, constituents, and stakeholders. Contemporary organizational life within and surrounding colleges and universities across the nation will require critical reexamination of the organizational behavior and politics of the past with an intention of projecting new behaviors and politics for the future (Aronowitz & Giroux, 2000; Pusser, 2003; Scott, 1995).

Higher education as a collection of institutions and a systemic enterprise is challenged by the mandate to continually reconsider what constitutes institutional boundaries, as well as redefine the parameters of diversity and globalization within the academic space (Marginson, 2006). The organization and governance of colleges and universities is complex and contextual. Moreover, it is the epigenetic manifestation of multi-layered internal and external factors engaging the academic enterprise.

Ravasi and Schultz (2006) conducted a grounded theory, longitudinal study on organizational identity and culture focusing on the external images shaping responses to identity threats. The authors empirically tested what accounts for culture-identity dynamics by examining the characteristics' identity in correspondence with the social actor and social constructionist perspectives. In contrasting the two perspectives, the authors state that the social actor perspective stemming from institutional theory whereby the views of the organization shape the perspectives of its members are explicit, distinctive, stable, and allow for "sense-giving" within the organization. Conversely, the social constructionist perspective suggests that the collective perceptions of members regarding organizational identity are not static and evolve in response to the internal and external dynamics that may alter the institutional environment. Emergent and impending organizational dynamics provide new and important considerations for any academic leader without respect to institutional context.

The future of research on and practice in the areas of organization and governance in higher education will be weighted by issues of composition, changing definitions of positional power, and developing norms on the shifting structure and stratification of academic leaders in the academy. As historic conventions of power relations yield to new understandings of society in general, institutions of higher education will be forced to envision blended organizational models that acknowledge the order of the day (Minor & Tierney, 2005; Simsek & Louis, 1994). In order for the academic environment to respond to shifting paradigms, academic leaders will be required to shift from the collegiate origins to an organizational reality that both considers and captures the contributions and contexts endemic to its constituents, stakeholders, and communities.

Conclusion

The Sixth Edition of *Organization and Governance in Higher Education* provides an intentional and ordered collection of readings that aid students, faculty, researchers, administrators, policymakers, and stakeholders with understanding the infinite nuances of how colleges and universities are organized, governed, led, administered, and managed. Colleges and universities are complex organizations of tremendous diversity in mission and scope of typologies. Consequently, they remain among the most challenging of all entities to understand. Given the expanse of reach and focus across institutions, this volume seeks to expose the reader to the complex nature of postsecondary institutions, rather than to engage the specific paradigms and phenomena related to any one type of institution, governance structure, or collection of environmental realities.

In the pages that follow, the editors of this volume purpose to reify the canonical readings of organization and governance in higher education while concomitantly expanding the literature base to include emergent topics critical to our understanding of academic management. To this end, we present readings that describe the nature of the university as an organization and provide and understanding of the historical development of colleges and universities. Although the volume centers on the national realities of governing institutions, we understand that confluence of power, authority, and influence is not bounded upon the domestic shores of the United States. The themes of institutional structure, administrative behavior, campus culture/climate, as well as principles of management can be extrapolated and extended to other contexts with proper consideration to the appropriate particularities within the international higher education community.

This book explores the frameworks for approaching higher education governance, examines the considerable diversity among institutions, and establishes the knowledge base extant to the management paradigms and governance practices of colleges and universities across the nation. Without question, the myriad implications of organization and governance will remain central to the research and practice of higher education as a field of study. Despite the challenges of constituency, climate, and change, the effective and efficient functioning of colleges and universities stand as immutable topics for scholars and administrators interesting in the academic enterprise.

We introduce this Sixth Edition of *Organization and Governance in Higher Education* with a quote from *University Administration* written by Charles W. Eliot (1908) over a century ago. Eliot, the esteemed president of Harvard University from 1869 to 1909, observed the following about the unique nature of postsecondary organizations:

Anyone who makes himself familiar with all the branches of university administration in its numerous departments of teaching, in its financial and maintenance departments, its museums, laboratories, and libraries, in its extensive grounds and numerous buildings for very various purposes, and in its social organization, will realize that the institution is properly named the university.

References

AAUP/ACE/AGB (1966). Statement on governance of colleges and universities. *Academe*, 52(4), 375–379.

Aragon, S. R., & Zamani, E. M. (2002). Promoting access and equity through minority-serving institutions. In M. C. Brown and K. Freeman (Eds.), *Equity and access in higher education: New perspectives for the new millennium* (Readings on Equal Education, Volume 18, pp. 23–50). New York: AMS Press.

Aronowitz, S. & Giroux, H. A. (2000). The corporate university and the politics of education. *The Educational Forum*, 64(4), 332–339.

Baldridge, J. V. (1971). *Power and Conflict in the University*. New York. Wiley.

Baldridge, J. V. (1972). Organizational change: The human relations perspective versus the political systems perspective. *Educational Researcher*, 1, 4–10, 15.

Bastedo, Michael N., Danielle K. Molina, and Cassie K. Barnhardt. 2008. "The Big 'O' in Higher Education: An Empirical Analysis of Organizations Research in Field Journals, 1990–2006." Paper presented at the annual meeting of the Association for the Study of Higher Education, Jacksonville, FL, November 7–10, 2008.

Bensimon, E. M. (January/February 2004). The diversity scorecard. *Change*, 36(1), 44–52.

Birnbaum, R. (1988). Problems of governance, management, and leadership in academic institutions. In, *How colleges work: The cybernetics of academic organization and leadership*. (pp. 3–29). San Francisco: Jossey-Bass

Birnbaum, R. (1989). The latent organizational functions of the academic senate: Why senates do not work but will not go away. *Journal of Higher Education*, 60(4), 423–443.

Birnbaum, R. (2000). Life cycle of management fads. *Journal of Higher Education*, 71(1), 1–16.

Bloland, H. (1995). Postmodernism and higher education. *Journal of Higher Education*, 66(5), 521–559.

Bolman, L. G., & Deal, T. E. (2003). *Reframing Organizations: Artistry, choice, and leadership*. San Francisco, CA: Jossey-Bass.

Breyfogle, F. W. III (1999). *Implementing Six Sigma: Smarter Solutions Using Statistical Methods*. New York, NY: John Wiley & Sons.

Brint, S. & Karabel, J. (1989). *The diverted dream. Community colleges and the promise of educational opportunity in America, 1900–1985*. New York: Oxford University Press.

Brown, M. C., & Lane, J. E. (Eds.). (2003). *Studying diverse institutions: Contexts, challenges and considerations* (New Directions in Institutional Research, volume 118). San Francisco: Jossey-Bass.

Chaffee, E. (1985). Three models of strategy. *Academy of Management Review*, 10(1), 89–98.

Clark, B. R. (Ed.). (1987). The academic life: Small worlds, different worlds. In *Faculty Authority* (pp. 147–186). Berkeley, CA: University of California Press.

Cohen, M., & March, J. (1974). Leadership in an organized anarchy. In *Leadership and ambiguity: The American college president* (pp. 195–229). Boston, MA: Harvard Business School Press.

Dill, D. D. (1984). The nature of administrative behavior in higher education. *Educational Administration Quarterly*, 20(3), 69–99.

Eliot, C. W. (1908). *University administration*. Boston: Houghton Mifflin.

Greenwood, R., & Hinings, C. R. (1996). Understanding radical organizational change: Bringing together the old and new institutionalism. *Academy of Management Review*, 21(4), 1022–1054.

Hurtado, S., Milem, J. F., Clayton-Pedersen, A. R., & Allen, W. R. (1998). Enhancing campus climates for racial/ethnic diversity through educational policy and practice. *The Review of Higher Education*, 21(3), 279–302.

Kekäle, J. (2003). Academic leaders as thermostats. *Tertiary Education and Management*, 9(4), 281–298.

Kezar, A. (2000). Pluralistic leadership: Incorporating diverse voices. *Journal of Higher Education*, 71(6), 722–743.

Kezar, A., & Eckel, P. (2002). The effect of institutional culture on change strategies in higher education: Universal principles or culturally responsive concepts. *Journal of Higher Education*, 73(4), 443–460.

Kim, W. C., & Mauborgne, R. (2005). *Blue Ocean Strategy: How to create uncontested market space and make the competition irrelevant*. Boston: Harvard Business School Press.

Kotler, P., & Murphy, P. E. (1981). Strategic planning for higher education. *The Journal of Higher Education, 52*(5), 470–489.

Kuh, G. D. (2001). Organizational culture and student persistence: Prospects and puzzles. *Journal of College Student Retention: Research, Theory and Practice, 3*(1), 23–39.

Lane, J. E., & Brown II, M. C. (2004). The importance of acknowledging context in institutional research. *New Directions for Institutional Research, 124*, 93-103.

Lane, J. E., & Kivisto, J. A. (2008). Interests, information, and incentives in higher education: A review of principal-agent theory in higher education governance. *Higher Education: Handbook of Theory and Research, 23*, 141–180.

Marginson, S. (2006). Putting the 'public' back in to the public university. *Thesis Eleven, 84*, 44–59.

Minor, J. T., & Tierney, W. G. (2005). The danger of deference: A case of polite governance. *Teachers College Record, 107*(1), 137–156.

Mintzberg, H. (1979). The professional bureaucracy. In *The Structuring of Organizations* (pp. 348–379). Englewood Cliffs, NJ: Prentice-Hall.

Mintzberg, H. (1994). The fall and rise of strategic planning. *Harvard Business Review, 72*, 107–114.

Morison, S. E. (1936). *Three centuries of Harvard*. Cambridge: Harvard University Press.

Peterson, M. W. (1985). Emerging developments in postsecondary organization theory and research: Fragmentation or integration. Educational Research, 14(3), 5–12.

Pfeffer, J. (1977). The ambiguity of leadership. *The Academy of Management Review, 12*(1), 104–112.

Pusser, B. (2003). Beyond Baldridge: Extending the political model of higher education organization and governance. *Educational Policy, 17*(1), 121–140.

Ravasi, D., & Schultz, M. (2006). Responding to organizational identity threats: Exploring the role of organizational culture. *Academy of Management Journal, 49*(3), 433–458.

Schein, E. H. (1985). *Organizational culture and leadership*. San Francisco: Jossey Bass.

Schein, E. H. (1990). Organizational Culture. *American Psychologist 45*, 109–119.

Scott, W. R. (1995). *Institutions and organizations*. Thousand Oaks, CA: Sage Publications.

Simsek, H., & Louis, K. S. (1994). Organizational change as a paradigm shift: Analysis of the change process in a large, public university. *The Journal of Higher Education, 65* (6), 670–695.

Tierney, W. (1989). Symbolism and presidential perceptions of leadership. *Review of Higher Education, 12*(2), 153–166.

Yates, E. L. (2000). Survey shows support for diversity in colleges and business. *Black Issues in Higher Education, 17*(2), 17.

Zamani-Gallaher, E. M., Green, D. O., Brown, M. C., & Stovall, D. O. (2009). *The case for affirmative action on campus: Concepts of equity, considerations for practice*. Sterling, VA: Stylus Publishing.

PART I

ORGANIZATIONAL THEORY

FOUNDATIONS OF THE THEORY OF ORGANIZATION

PHILIP SELZNICK

UNIVERSITY OF CALIFORNIA, LOS ANGELES

Trades unions, governments, business corporations, political parties, and the like are formal structures in the sense that they represent rationally ordered instruments for the achievement of stated goals. "Organization," we are told, "is the arrangement of personnel for facilitating the accomplishment of some agreed purpose through the allocation of functions and responsibilities."[1] Or, defined more generally, formal organization is "a system of consciously coordinated activities or forces of two or more persons."[2] Viewed in this light, formal organization is the structural expression of rational action. The mobilization of technical and managerial skills requires a pattern of coordination, a systematic ordering of positions and duties which defines a chain of command and makes possible the administrative integration of specialized functions. In this context *delegation* is the primordial organizational act, a precarious venture which requires the continuous elaboration of formal mechanisms of coordination and control. The security of all participants, and of the system as a whole, generates a persistent pressure for the institutionalization of relationships, which are thus removed from the uncertainties of individual fealty or sentiment. Moreover, it is necessary for the relations within the structure to be determined in such a way that individuals will be interchangeable and the organization will thus be free of dependence upon personal qualities.[3] In this way, the formal structure becomes subject to calculable manipulation, an instrument of rational action.

But as we inspect these formal structures we begin to see that they never succeed in conquering the non-rational dimensions of organizational behavior. The latter remain at once indispensable to the continued existence of the system of coordination and at the same time the source of friction, dilemma, doubt, and ruin. This fundamental paradox arises from the fact that rational action systems are inescapably imbedded in an institutional matrix, in two significant senses: (1) the action system—or the formal structure of delegation and control which is its organizational expression—is itself only an aspect of a concrete social structure made up of individuals who may interact as *wholes,* not simply in terms of their formal roles within the system; (2) the formal system, and the social structure within which it finds concrete existence, are alike subject to the pressure of an institutional environment to which some over-all adjustment must be made. The formal administrative design can never adequately or fully reflect the concrete organization to which it refers, for the obvious reason that no abstract plan or pattern can— or may, if it is to be useful—exhaustively describe an empirical totality. At the same time, that which is not included in the abstract design (as reflected, for example, in a staff-and-line organization chart) is vitally relevant to the maintenance and development of the formal system itself.

Organization may be viewed from two standpoints which are analytically distinct but which are empirically united in a context of reciprocal consequences. On the one hand, any concrete organizational system is an *economy*; at the same time, it is an *adaptive social structure.* Considered as an economy, organization is a system of relationships which define the availability of scarce resources and which may be manipulated in terms of efficiency and effectiveness. It is the economic aspect of organization which commands the attention of management technicians and, for the most part, students of public as well as private administration.⁴ Such problems as the span of executive control, the role of staff or auxiliary agencies, the relation of headquarters to field offices, and the relative merits of single or multiple executive boards are typical concerns of the science of administration. The coordinative scalar, and functional principles, as elements of the theory of organization, are products of the attempt to explicate the most general features of organization as a "technical problem" or, in our terms, as an economy.

Organization as an economy is, however, necessarily conditioned by the organic states of the concrete structure, outside of the systematics of delegation and control. This becomes especially evident as the attention of leadership is directed toward such problems as the legitimacy of authority and the dynamics of persuasion. It is recognized implicitly in action and explicitly in the work of a number of students that the possibility of manipulating the system of coordination depends on the extent to which that system is operating within an environment of effective inducement to individual participants and of conditions in which the stability of authority is assured. This is in a sense the fundamental thesis of Barnard's remarkable study, *The Functions of the Executive.* It is also the underlying hypothesis which makes it possible for Urwick to suggest that "proper" or formal channels in fact function to "confirm and record" decisions arrived at by more personal means.⁵ We meet it again in the concept of administration as a process of education, in which the winning of consent and support is conceived to be a basic function of leadership.⁶ In short, it is recognized that control and consent cannot be divorced even within formally authoritarian structures.

The indivisibility of control and consent makes it necessary to view formal organizations as *cooperative* systems, widening the frame of reference of those concerned with the manipulation of organizational resources. At the point of action, of executive decision, the economic aspect of organization provides inadequate tools for control over the concrete structure. This idea may be readily grasped if attention is directed to the role of the individual within the organizational economy. From the standpoint of organization as a formal system, persons are viewed functionally, in respect to their *roles*, as participants in assigned segments of the cooperative system. But in fact individuals have a propensity to resist depersonalization, to spill over the boundaries of their segmentary roles, to participate as *wholes.* The formal systems (at an extreme, the disposition of "rifles" at a military perimeter) cannot take account of the deviations thus introduced, and consequently break down as instruments of control when relied upon alone. The whole individual raises new problems for the organization, partly because of the needs of his own personality, partly because he brings with him a set of established habits as well, perhaps, as commitments to special groups outside of the organization.

Unfortunately for the adequacy of formal systems of coordination, the needs of individuals do not permit a single-minded attention to the stated goals of the system within which they have been assigned. The hazard inherent in the act of delegation derives essentially from this fact. Delegation is an organizational act, having to do with formal assignments of functions and powers. Theoretically, these assignments are made to roles or official positions, not to individuals as such. In fact, however, delegation necessarily involves concrete individuals who have interests and goals which do not always coincide with the goals of the formal system. As a consequence, individual personalities may offer resistance to the demands made upon them by the official conditions of delegation. These resistances are not accounted for within the categories of coordination and delegation, so that when they occur they must be considered as unpredictable and accidental. Observations of this type of situation within formal structures are sufficiently commonplace. A familiar example is that of delegation to a subordinate who is also required to train his own replacement. The subordinate may resist this demand in order to maintain unique access to the "mysteries" of the job, and thus insure his indispensability to the organization.

In large organizations, deviations from the formal system tend to become institutionalized, so that "unwritten laws" and informal associations are established. Institutionalization removes such deviations from the realm of personality differences, transforming them into a persistent structural aspect of formal organizations.⁷ These institutionalized rules and modes of informal cooperation are normally attempts by participants in the formal organization to control the group relations which form the environment of organizational decisions. The informal patterns (such as cliques) arise spontaneously, are based on personal relationships, and are usually directed to the control of some specific situation. They may be generated anywhere within a hierarchy, often with deleterious consequences for the formal goals of the organization, but they may also function to widen the available resources of executive control and thus contribute to rather than hinder the achievement of the stated objectives of the organization. The deviations tend to force a shift away from the purely formal system as the effective determinant of behavior to (1) a condition in which informal patterns buttress the formal, as through the manipulation of sentiment within the organization in favor of established authority; or (2) a condition wherein the informal controls effect a consistent modification of formal goals, as in the case of some bureaucratic patterns.[8] This trend will eventually result in the formalization of erstwhile informal activities, with the cycle of deviation and transformation beginning again on a new level.

The relevance of informal structures to organizational analysis underlines the significance of conceiving of formal organizations as cooperative systems. When the totality of interacting groups and individuals becomes the object of inquiry, the latter is not restricted by formal, legal, or procedural dimensions. The *state of the system* emerges as a significant point of analysis, as when an internal situation charged with conflict qualifies and informs actions ostensibly determined by formal relations and objectives. A proper understanding of the organizational process must make it possible to interpret changes in the formal system—new appointments or rules or reorganizations—in their relation to the informal and unavowed ties of friendship, class loyalty, power cliques, or external commitment. This is what it means "to know the score."

The fact that the involvement of individuals as whole personalities tends to limit the adequacy of formal systems of coordination does not mean that organizational characteristics are those of individuals. The organic, emergent character of the formal organization considered as a cooperative system must be recognized. This means that the *organization* reaches decisions, takes action, and makes adjustments. Such a view raises the question of the relation between organizations and persons. The significance of theoretical emphasis upon the cooperative *system* as such is derived from the insight that certain actions and consequences are enjoined independently of the personality of the individuals involved. Thus, if reference is made to the "organization-paradox"—the tension created by the inhibitory consequences of certain types of informal structures within organizations—this does not mean that individuals themselves are in quandaries. It is the nature of the interacting consequences of divergent interests within the organization which creates the condition, a result which may obtain independently of the consciousness or the qualities of the individual participants. Similarly, it seems useful to insist that there are qualities and needs of leader*ship*, having to do with position and role, which are persistent despite variations in the character or personality of individual leaders themselves.

Rational action systems are characteristic of both individuals and organizations. The conscious attempt to mobilize available internal resources (e.g., self-discipline) for the achievement of a stated goal—referred to here as an economy or a formal system—is one aspect of individual psychology. But the personality considered as a dynamic system of interacting wishes, compulsions, and restraints defines a system which is at once essential and yet potentially deleterious to what may be thought of as the "economy of learning" or to individual rational action. At the same time, the individual personality is an adaptive structure, and this, too, requires a broader frame of reference for analysis than the categories of rationality. On a different level, although analogously, we have pointed to the need to consider organizations as cooperative systems and adaptive structures in order to explain the context of and deviations from the formal systems of delegation and coordination.

To recognize the sociological relevance of formal structures is not, however, to have constructed a theory of organization. It is important to set the framework of analysis, and much is accomplished along this line when, for example, the nature of authority in formal organizations is reinterpreted to emphasize the factors of cohesion and persuasion as against legal or coercive sources.[9] This redefinition is logically the same as that which introduced the conception of the self as social. The latter helps make possible, but does not of itself fulfill, the requirements for a dynamic theory of personality. In the same way, the definition of authority as conditioned by sociological factors of sentiment and cohesion—or more generally the definition of formal organizations as cooperative systems—only sets the stage, as an initial requirement, for the formulation of a theory of organization.

Structural-Functional Analysis

Cooperative systems are constituted of individuals interacting as wholes in relation to a formal system of coordination. The concrete structure is therefore a resultant of the reciprocal influences of the formal and informal aspects of organization. Furthermore, this structure is itself a totality, an adaptive "organism" reacting to influences upon it from an external environment. These considerations help to define the objects of inquiry; but to progress to a system of predicates *about* these objects it is necessary to set forth an analytical method which seems to be fruitful and significant. The method must have a relevance to empirical materials, which is to say, it must be more specific in its reference than discussions of the logic or methodology of social science.

The organon which may be suggested as peculiarly helpful in the analysis of adaptive structures has been referred to as "structural-functional analysis."[10] This method may be characterized in a sentence: *Structural-functional analysis relates contemporary and variable behavior to a presumptively stable system of needs and mechanisms.* This means that a given empirical system is deemed to have basic needs, essentially related to self-maintenance; the system develops repetitive means of self-defense; and day-to-day activity is interpreted in terms of the function served by that activity for the maintenance and defense of the system. Put thus generally, the approach is applicable on any level in which the determinate "states" of empirically isolable systems undergo self-impelled and repetitive transformations when impinged upon by external conditions. This self-impulsion suggests the relevance of the term "dynamic," which is often used in referring to physiological, psychological, or social systems to which this type of analysis has been applied.[11]

It is a postulate of the structural-functional approach that the basic need of all empirical systems is the maintenance of the integrity and continuity of the system itself. Of course, such a postulate is primarily useful in directing attention to a set of "derived imperatives" or needs which are sufficiently concrete to characterize the system at hand.[12] It is perhaps rash to attempt a catalogue of these imperatives for formal organizations, but some suggestive formulation is needed in the interests of setting forth the type of analysis under discussion. In formal organizations, the "maintenance of the system" as a generic need may be specified in terms of the following imperatives:

1. *The security of the organization as a whole in relation to social forces in its environment.* This imperative requires continuous attention to the possibilities of encroachment and to the forestalling of threatened aggressions or deleterious (though perhaps unintended) consequences from the actions of others.

2. *The stability of the lines of authority and communication.* One of the persistent reference-points of administrative decision is the weighing of consequences for the continued capacity of leadership to control and to have access to the personnel or ranks.

3. *The stability of informal relations within the organization.* Ties of sentiment and self-interest are evolved as unacknowledged but effective mechanisms of adjustment of individuals and subgroups to the conditions of life within the organization. These ties represent a cementing of relationships which sustains the formal authority in day-to-day operations and widens opportunities for effective communication.[13] Consequently, attempts to "upset" the informal structure, either frontally or as an indirect consequence of formal reorganization, will normally be met with considerable resistance.

4. *The continuity of policy and of the sources of its determination.* For each level within the organization, and for the organization as a whole, it is necessary that there be a sense that action taken in the light of a given policy will not be placed in continuous jeopardy. Arbitrary or unpredictable changes in policy undermine the significance of (and therefore the attention to) day-to-day action by injecting a note of capriciousness. At the same time, the organization will seek stable roots (or firm statutory authority or popular mandate) so that a sense of the permanency and legitimacy of its acts will be achieved.

5. *A homogeneity of outlook with respect to the meaning and role of the organization.* The minimization of disaffection requires a unity derived from a common understanding of what the character of the organization is meant to be. When this homogeneity breaks down, as in situations of internal conflict over basic issues, the continued existence of the organization is endangered. On the other hand, one of the signs of "healthy" organization is the ability to effectively orient new members and readily slough off those who cannot be adapted to the established outlook.

This catalogue of needs cannot be thought of as final, but it approximates the stable system generally characteristic of formal organizations. These imperatives are derived, in the sense that they represent the conditions for survival or self-maintenance of cooperative systems of organized action. An inspection of these needs suggests that organizational survival is intimately connected with the struggle for relative prestige, both for the organization and for elements and individuals within it. It may therefore be useful to refer to a *prestige-survival motif* in organizational behavior as a shorthand way of relating behavior to needs, especially when the exact nature of the needs remains in doubt. However, it must be emphasized that prestige-survival in organizations does not derive simply from like motives in individuals. Loyalty and self-sacrifice may be individual expressions of organizational or group egotism and self-consciousness.

The concept of organizational need directs analysis to the *internal relevance* of organizational behavior. This is especially pertinent with respect to discretionary action undertaken by agents manifestly in pursuit of formal goals. The question then becomes one of relating the specific act of discretion to some presumptively stable organizational need. In other words, it is not simply action plainly oriented internally (such as in-service training) but also action presumably oriented externally which must be inspected for its relevance to internal conditions. This is of prime importance for the understanding of bureaucratic behavior, for it is of the essence of the latter that action formally undertaken for substantive goals be weighed and transformed in terms of its consequences for the position of the officialdom.

Formal organizations as cooperative systems on the one hand, and individual personalities on the other, involve structural-functional homologies, a point which may help to clarify the nature of this type of analysis. If we say that the individual has a stable set of needs, most generally the need for maintaining and defending the integrity of his personality or ego; that there are recognizable certain repetitive mechanisms which are utilized by the ego in its defense (rationalization, projection, regression, etc.); and that overt and variable behavior may be interpreted in terms of its relation to these needs and mechanisms—on the basis of this logic we may discern the typical pattern of structural-functional analysis as set forth above. In this sense, it is possible to speak of a "Freudian model" for organizational analysis. This does not mean that the substantive insights of individual psychology may be applied to organizations, as in vulgar extrapolations from the individual ego to whole nations or (by a no less vulgar inversion) from strikes to frustrated workers. It is the *logic*, the *type* of analysis which is pertinent.

This homology is also instructive in relation to the applicability of generalizations to concrete cases. The dynamic theory of personality states a set of possible predicates about the ego and its mechanisms of defense, which inform us concerning the propensities of individual personalities under certain general circumstances. But these predicates provide only tools for the analysis of particular individuals, and each concrete case must be examined to tell which operate and in what degree. They are not primarily organs of prediction. In the same way, the predicates within the theory of organization will provide tools for the analysis of particular cases. Each organization, like each personality, represents a resultant of complex forces, an empirical entity which no single relation or no simple formula can explain. The problem of analysis becomes that of selecting among the possible predicates set forth in the theory of organization those which illuminate our understanding of the materials at hand.

The setting of structural-functional analysis as applied to organizations requires some qualification, however. Let us entertain the suggestion that the interesting problem in social science is not so much why men act the way they do as why men in certain circumstances *must* act the way they do. This emphasis upon constraint, if accepted, releases us from an ubiquitous attention to behavior in general, and especially from any undue fixation upon statistics. On the other hand, it has what would seem to be the salutary consequence of focusing inquiry upon certain necessary relationships of the type "if . . . then," for example: If the cultural level of the rank and file members of a formally democratic organization is below that necessary for participation in the formulation of policy, then there will be pressure upon the leaders to use the tools of demagogy.

Is such a statement universal in its applicability? Surely not in the sense that one can predict without remainder the nature of all or even most political groups in a democracy. Concrete behavior is a resultant, a complex vector, shaped by the operation of a number of such general constraints. But there is a test of general applicability: it is that of noting whether the relation made explicit must be *taken into account* in action. This criterion represents an empirical test of the significance of social science generalizations. If a theory is significant it will state a relation which will either (1) be taken into account as an element of achieving control; or (2) be ignored only at the risk of losing control and will evidence itself in a ramification of objective or unintended consequences.[14] It is a corollary of this principle of significance that investigation must search out the underlying factors in organizational action, which requires a kind of intensive analysis of the same order as psychoanalytic probing.

A frame of reference which invites attention to the constraints upon behavior will tend to highlight tensions and dilemmas, the characteristic paradoxes generated in the course of action. The dilemma may be said to be the handmaiden of structural-functional analysis, for it introduces the concept of *commitment* or *involvement* as fundamental to organizational analysis. A dilemma in human behavior is represented by an inescapable commitment which cannot be reconciled with the needs of the organism or the social system. There are many spurious dilemmas which have to do with verbal contradictions, but inherent dilemmas to which we refer are of a more profound sort, for they reflect the basic nature of the empirical system in question. An economic order committed to profit as its sustaining incentive may, in Marxist terms, sow the seed of its own destruction. Again, the anguish of man, torn between finitude and pride, is not a matter of arbitrary and replaceable assumptions but is a reflection of the psychological needs of the human organism, and is concretized in his commitment to the institutions which command his life; he is in the world and of it, inescapably involved in its goals and demands; at the same time, the needs of the spirit are compelling, proposing modes of salvation which have continuously disquieting consequences for worldly involvements. In still another context, the need of the human organism for affection and response necessitates a commitment to elements of the culture which can provide them; but the rule of the super-ego is uncertain since it cannot be completely reconciled with the need for libidinal satisfactions.

Applying this principle to organizations we may note that there is a general source of tension observable in the split between "the motion and the act." Plans and programs reflect the freedom of technical or ideal choice, but organized action cannot escape involvement, a commitment to personnel or institutions or procedures which effectively qualifies the initial plan. *Der Mensch denkt, Gott lenkt.* In organized action, this ultimate wisdom finds a temporal meaning in the recalcitrance of the tools of action. We are inescapably committed to the mediation of human structures which are at once indispensable to our goals and at the same time stand between them and ourselves. The selection of agents generates immediately a bifurcation of interest, expressed in new centers of need and power, placing effective constraints upon the arena of action, and resulting in tensions which are never completely resolved. This is part of what it means to say that there is a "logic" of action which impels us forward from one undesired position to another. Commitment to dynamic, self-activating tools is of the nature of organized action; at the same time, the need for continuity of authority, policy, and character are pressing, and require an unceasing effort to master the instruments generated in the course of action. This generic tension is specified within the terms of each cooperative system. But for all we find a persistent relationship between *need* and *commitment* in which the latter not only qualifies the former but unites with it to produce a continuous state of tension. In this way, the notion of constraint (as reflected in tension or paradox) at once widens and more closely specifies the frame of reference for organizational analysis.

For Malinowski, the core of functionalism was contained in the view that a cultural fact must be analyzed in its setting. Moreover, he apparently conceived of his method as pertinent to the analysis of all aspects of cultural systems. But there is a more specific problem, one involving a principle of selection which serves to guide inquiry along significant lines. Freud conceived of the human organism as an adaptive structure, but he was not concerned with all human needs, nor with all phases of adaptation. For his system, he selected those needs whose expression is blocked in some way, so that such terms as repression, inhibition, and frustration became crucial. All conduct may be thought of as derived from need, and all adjustment represents the reduction of need. But not all needs are relevant to the systematics of dynamic psychology; and it is not adjustment as such but reaction to frustration which generates the characteristic modes of defensive behavior.

Organizational analysis, too, must find its selective principle; otherwise the indiscriminate attempts to relate activity functionally to needs will produce little in the way of significant theory. Such a principle might read as follows: *Our frame of reference is to select out those needs which cannot be fulfilled within approved avenues of expression and thus must have recourse to such adaptive mechanisms as ideology and to the manipulation of formal processes and structures in terms of informal goals.* This formulation has many difficulties, and is not presented as conclusive, but it suggests the kind of principle which is likely to separate the quick and the dead, the meaningful and the trite, in the study of cooperative systems in organized action.[15]

The frame of reference outlined here for the theory of organization may now be identified as involving the following major ideas: (1) the concept of organizations as cooperative systems, adaptive social structures, made up of interacting individuals, sub-groups, and informal plus formal relationships; (2) structural-functional analysis, which relates variable aspects of organization (such as goals) to stable needs and self-defensive mechanisms; (3) the concept of recalcitrance as a quality of the tools of social action, involving a break in the continuum of adjustment and defining an environment of constraint, commitment, and tension. This frame of reference is suggested as providing a specifiable *area of relations* within which predicates in the theory of organization will be sought, and at the same time setting forth principles of selection and relevance in our approach to the data of organization.

It will be noted that we have set forth this frame of reference within the over-all context of social action. The significance of events may be defined by their place and operational role in a means-end scheme. If functional analysis searches out the elements important for the maintenance of a given structure, and that structure is one of the materials to be manipulated in action, then that which is functional in respect to the structure is also functional in respect to the action system. This provides a ground for the significance of functionally derived theories. At the same time, relevance to control in action is the empirical test of their applicability or truth.

Cooptation as a Mechanism of Adjustment

The frame of reference stated above is in fact an amalgam of definition, resolution, and substantive theory. There is an element of *definition* in conceiving of formal organizations as cooperative systems, though of course the interaction of informal and formal patterns is a question of fact; in a sense, we are *resolving* to employ structural-functional analysis on the assumption that it will be fruitful to do so, though here, too, the specification of needs or derived imperatives is a matter for empirical inquiry; and our predication of recalcitrance as a quality of the tools of action is itself a *substantive theory*, perhaps fundamental to a general understanding of the nature of social action.

A theory of organization requires more than a general frame of reference, though the latter is indispensable to inform the approach of inquiry to any given set of materials. What is necessary is the construction of generalizations concerning transformations within and among cooperative systems. These generalizations represent, from the standpoint of particular cases, possible predicates which are relevant to the materials as we know them in general, but which are not necessarily controlling in all circumstances. A theory of transformations in organization would specify those states of the system which resulted typically in predictable, or at least understandable, changes in such aspects of organization as goals, leadership, doctrine, efficiency, effectiveness, and size. These empirical generalizations would be systematized as they were related to the stable needs of the cooperative system.

Changes in the characteristics of organizations may occur as a result of many different conditions, not always or necessarily related to the processes of organization as such. But the theory of organization must be selective, so that explanations of transformations will be sought within its own assumptions or frame of reference. Consider the question of size. Organizations may expand for many reasons—the availability of markets, legislative delegations, the swing of opinion—which may be accidental from the point of view of the organizational process. To explore changes in size (as of, say, a trades union) as related to changes in non-organizational conditions may be necessitated by the historical events to be described, but it will not of itself advance the frontiers of the theory of organization. However, if "the innate propensity of all organizations to expand" is asserted as a function of "the inherent instability of incentives"[16] then transformations have been stated within the terms of the theory of organization itself. It is likely that in many cases the generalization in question may represent only a minor aspect of the empirical changes, but these organizational relations must be made explicit if the theory is to receive development.

In a frame of reference which specifies needs and anticipates the formulation of a set of self-defensive responses or mechanisms, the latter appear to constitute one kind of empirical generalization or "possible predicate" within the general theory. The needs of organizations (whatever investigation may determine them to be) are posited as attributes of all organizations, but the responses to disequilibrium will be varied. The mechanisms used by the system in fulfillment of its needs will be repetitive and thus may be described as a specifiable set of assertions within the theory of organization, but any given organization may or may not have recourse to the characteristic modes of response. Certainly no given organization will employ all of the possible mechanisms which are theoretically available. When Barnard speaks of an "innate propensity of organization to expand" he is in fact formulating one of the general mechanisms, namely, expansion, which is a characteristic mode of response available to an organization under pressure from within. These responses necessarily involve a transformation (in this case, size) of some structural aspect of the organization.

Other examples of the self-defensive mechanisms available to organizations may derive primarily from the response of these organizations to the institutional environments in which they live. The tendency to construct ideologies, reflecting the need to come to terms with major social forces, is one such mechanism. Less well understood as a mechanism of organizational adjustment is what we may term *cooptation*. Some statement of the meaning of this concept may aid in clarifying the foregoing analysis.

Cooptation is the process of absorbing new elements into the leadership or policy-determining structure of an organization as a means of averting threats to its stability or existence. This is a defensive mechanism, formulated as one of a number of possible predicates available for the interpretation of organizational behavior. Cooptation tells us something about the process by which an institutional environment impinges itself upon an organization and effects changes in its leadership and policy. Formal authority may resort to cooptation under the following general conditions:

1. When there exists a hiatus between consent and control, so that the legitimacy of the formal authority is called into question. The "indivisibility" of consent and control refers, of course, to an optimum situation. Where control lacks an adequate measure of consent, it may revert to coercive measures or attempt somehow to win the consent of the governed. One means of winning consent is to coopt elements into the leadership or organization, usually elements which in some way reflect the sentiment, or possess the confidence of the relevant public or mass. As a result, it is expected that the new elements will lend respectability or legitimacy to the organs of control and thus reestablish the stability of formal authority. This process is widely used, and in many different contexts. It is met in colonial countries, where the organs of alien control reaffirm their legitimacy by coopting native leaders into the colonial adminis-

tration. We find it in the phenomenon of "crisis-patriotism" wherein normally disfranchised groups are temporarily given representation in the councils of government in order to win their solidarity in a time of national stress. Cooptation is presently being considered by the United States Army in its study of proposals to give enlisted personnel representation in the court-martial machinery—a clearly adaptive response to stresses made explicit during the war, the lack of confidence in the administration of army justice. The "unity" parties of totalitarian states are another form of cooptation; company unions or some employee representation plans in industry are still another. In each of these cases, the response of formal authority (private or public, in a large organization or a small one) is an attempt to correct a state of imbalance by *formal* measures. It will be noted, moreover, that what is shared is the *responsibility* for power rather than power itself. These conditions define what we shall refer to as *formal cooptation.*

2. Cooptation may be a response to the pressure of specific centers of power. This is not necessarily a matter of legitimacy or of a general and diffuse lack of confidence. These may be well established; and yet organized forces which are able to threaten the formal authority may effectively shape its structure and policy. The organization in respect to its institutional environment—or the leadership in respect to its ranks—must take these forces into account. As a consequence, the outside elements may be brought into the leadership or policy-determining structure, may be given a place as a recognition of and concession to the resources they can independently command. The representation of interests through administrative constituencies is a typical example of this process. Or, within an organization, individuals upon whom the group is dependent for funds or other resources may insist upon and receive a share in the determination of policy. This form of cooptation is typically expressed in informal terms, for the problem is not one of responding to a state of imbalance with respect to the "people as a whole" but rather one of meeting the pressure of specific individuals or interest-groups which are in a position to enforce demands. The latter are interested in the substance of power and not its forms. Moreover, an open acknowledgement of capitulation to specific interests may itself undermine the sense of legitmacy of the formal authority within the community. Consequently, there is a positive pressure to refrain from explicit recognition of the relationship established. This form of the cooptative mechanism, having to do with the sharing of power as a response to specific pressures, may be termed *informal cooptation.*

Cooptation reflects a state of tension between formal authority and social power. The former is embodied in a particular structure and leadership, but the latter has to do with subjective and objective factors which control the loyalties and potential manipulability of the community. Where the formal authority is an expression of social power, its stability is assured. On the other hand, when it becomes divorced from the sources of social power its continued existence is threatened. This threat may arise from the sheer alienation of sentiment or from the fact that other leaderships have control over the sources of social power. Where a formal authority has been accustomed to the assumption that its constituents respond to it as individuals, there may be a rude awakening when organization of those constituents on a non-governmental basis creates nuclei of power which are able effectively to demand a sharing of power.[17]

The significance of cooptation for organizational analysis is not simply that there is a change in or a broadening of leadership, and that this is an adaptive response, but also that *this change is consequential for the character and role of the organization.* Cooptation involves commitment, so that the groups to which adaptation has been made constrain the field of choice available to the organization or leadership in question. The character of the coopted elements will necessarily shape (inhibit or broaden) the modes of action available to the leadership which has won adaptation and security at the price of commitment. The concept of cooptation thus implicity sets forth the major points of the frame of reference outlined above: it is an adaptive response of a cooperative system to a stable need, generating transformations which reflect constraints enforced by the recalcitrant tools of action.

Notes

1. John M. Gaus, "A Theory of Organization in Public Administration," in *The Frontiers of Public Administration* (Chicago: University of Chicago Press, 1936), p. 66.
2. Chester I. Barnard, *The Functions of the Executive* (Cambridge: Harvard University Press, 1938), p. 73.
3. Cf. Talcott Parsons' generalization (after Max Weber) of the "law of the increasing rationality of action systems," in *The Structure of Social Action* (New York: McGraw-Hill, 1937), p. 752.
4. See Luther Gulick and Lydall Urwick (editors), *Papers on the Science of Administration* (New York: Institute of Public Administration, Columbia University, 1937); Lydall Urwick, *The Elements of Administration* (New York, Harper, 1943); James D. Mooney and Alan C. Reiley, *The Principles of Organization* (New York: Harper, 1939); H. S. Dennison, *Organization Engineering* (New York: McGraw-Hill, 1931).
5. Urwick, *The Elements of Administration, op. cit.*, p. 47.
6. See Gaus, *op. cit.* Studies of the problem of morale are instances of the same orientation, having received considerable impetus in recent years from the work of the Harvard Business School group.
7. The creation of informal structures within various types of organizations has received explicit recognition in recent years. See F. J. Roethlisberger and W. J. Dickson, *Management and the Worker* (Cambridge: Harvard University Press, 1941), p. 524; also Barnard, *op. cit.*, c. ix; and Wilbert E. Moore, *Industrial Relations and the Social Order* (New York: Macmillan, 1946), chap. xv.
8. For an analysis of the latter in these terms, see Philip Selznick, "An Approach to a Theory of Bureaucracy," *American Sociological Review*, Vol. VIII, No. 1 (February, 1943).
9. Robert Michels, "Authority," *Encyclopedia of the Social Sciences* (New York: Macmillan, 1931), pp. 319ff.; also Barnard, *op. cit.*, c. xii.
10. For a presentation of this approach having a more general reference than the study of formal organizations, see Talcott Parsons, "The Present Position and Prospects of Systematic Theory in Sociology," in Georges Gurvitch and Wilbert E. Moore (ed.), *Twentieth Century Sociology* (New York: The Philosophical Library, 1945).
11. "Structure" refers to both the relationships within the system (formal plus informal patterns in organization) and the set of needs and modes of satisfaction which characterize the given type of empirical system. As the utilization of this type of analysis proceeds, the concept of "need" will require further clarification. In particular, the imputation of a "stable set of needs" to organizational systems must not function as a new instinct theory. At the same time, we cannot avoid using these inductions as to generic needs, for they help us to stake out our area of inquiry. The author is indebted to Robert K. Merton who has, in correspondence, raised some important objections to the use of the term "need" in this context.
12. For "derived imperative" see Bronislaw Malinowski, *The Dynamics of Culture Change* (New Haven: Yale University Press, 1945), pp. 44ff. For the use of "need" in place of "motive" see the same author's *A Scientific Theory of Culture* (Chapel Hill: University of North Carolina Press, 1944), pp. 89–90.
13. They may also *destroy* those relationships, as noted above, but the need remains, generating one of the persistent dilemmas of leadership.
14. See R. M. MacIver's discussion of the "dynamic assessment" which "brings the external world selectively into the subjective realm, conferring on it subjective significance for the ends of action." *Social Causation* (Boston: Ginn, 1942), chaps. 11, 12. The analysis of this assessment within the context of organized action yields the implicit knowledge which guides the choice among alternatives. See also Robert K. Merton, "The Unanticipated Consequences of Purposive Social Action," *American Sociological Review*, I, 6 (December, 1936).
15. This is not meant to deprecate the study of organizations as *economies* or formal systems. The latter represent an independent level, abstracted from organizational structures as cooperative or adaptive systems ("organisms").
16. Barnard, *op. cit.*, pp. 158–9.
17. It is perhaps useful to restrict the concept of cooptation to formal organizations, but in fact it probably reflects a process characteristic of all group leaderships. This has received some recognition in the analysis of class structure, wherein the ruling class is interpreted as protecting its own stability by absorbing new elements. Thus Michels made the point that "an aristocracy cannot maintain an enduring stability by sealing itself off hermetically." See Robert Michels, *Umschichtungen in den herrschenden Klassen nach dem Kriege* (Stuttgart: Kohlhammer, 1934), p. 39; also Gaetano Mosca, *The Ruling Class* (New York: McGraw-Hill, 1939), p. 413ff. The alliance or amalgamation of classes in the face of a common threat may be reflected in formal and informal cooptative responses among formal organizations sensitive to class pressures. In a forthcoming volume, *TVA and the Grass Roots*, the author has made extensive use of the concept of cooptation in analyzing some aspects of the organizational behavior of a government agency.

Central Perspectives and Debates in Organization Theory

W. Graham Astley and Andrew H. Van de Ven

The diverse schools of organizational thought are classified according to micro and macro levels of organizational analysis and deterministic versus voluntaristic assumptions of human nature to yield four basic perspectives: system-structural, strategic choice, natural selection, and collective-action views of organizations. These four views represent qualitatively different concepts of organizational structure, behavior, change, and managerial roles. Six theoretical debates are then identified by systematically juxtaposing the four views against each other, and a partial reconciliation is achieved by bringing opposing viewpoints into dialectical relief. The six debates, which tend to be addressed singly and in isolation from each other in the literature, are then integrated at a metatheoretical level. The framework presented thus attempts to overcome the problems associated with excessive theoretical compartmentalization by focusing on the interplay between divergent theoretical perspectives, but it also attempts to preserve the authenticity of distinctive viewpoints, thereby retaining the advantages associated with theoretical pluralism.

In recent years there has been a growing theoretical pluralism in the organizational literature, which reflects partly a growing awareness of the complexity of organizations and partly a refinement of the interests and preoccupations of organization theorists. On the one hand, this theoretical pluralism should be encouraged so that researchers will uncover novel aspects of organizational life and sharpen their critical inquiry. But on the other hand, this pluralism encourages excessive theoretical compartmentalization, and it becomes easy to lose sight of the ways in which various schools of thought are related to each other. It is the interplay between different perspectives that helps one gain a more comprehensive understanding of organizational life, since any one school of thought invariably offers only a partial account of reality. Moreover, the juxtaposition of different schools of thought brings into focus the contrasting world views that underlie the major debates that characterize contemporary organization theory.

Consequently, this paper examines six debates on the nature and structuring of organizations that currently permeate the literature. They revolve around the following questions:

1. Are organizations functionally rational, technically constrained systems, or are they socially constructed, subjectively meaningful embodiments of individual action?

2. Are changes in organizational forms explained by internal adaptation or by environmental selection?

3. Is organizational life determined by intractable environmental constraints, or is it actively created through strategic managerial choices?

4. Is the environment to be viewed as a simple aggregation of organizations governed by external economic forces, or as an integrated collectivity of organizations governed by its own internal social and political forces?

5. Is organizational behavior principally concerned with individual or collective action?

6. Are organizations neutral technical instruments engineered to achieve a goal, or are they institutionalized manifestations of the vested interests and power structure of the wider society?

Though these issues have, to a degree, been debated in the literature, no satisfactory resolutions have emerged—nor is such resolution likely. The problem is that different schools of thought tend to focus only on single sides of issues and use such different logics and vocabularies that they do not speak to each other directly. As Poggi (1965: 284) said, "A way of seeing is a way of not seeing." Some integration would thus be desirable, but at the same time, it must be an integration that preserves the distinctiveness of the different analytical perspectives involved. We contend that such integration is possible if it is recognized that different perspectives can present quite different pictures of the same organizational phenomenon without nullifying each other. This is achieved simply by using different analytical lenses to examine opposite or contradictory sides of the same issue. In this paper, rather than proclaiming certain points of view as "correct," we reconcile contradictions between contrasting theories by bringing together a variety of dialectical interpretations of organizational life. Such reconciliations preserve the authenticity of "incompatible" theories, but, at the same time, achieve some measure of integration by highlighting sources of dialectical tension between the theories.

This approach is applied to each of the above debates within the context of a metatheoretical scheme that is sufficiently broad to link the different debates together. Treating the six debates as interdependent brings into relief both points of contrast and tangency between most of the major theoretical approaches to the study of organizations. The intention is not only to refine and sharpen current theory, but also to further understanding of the underlying structures of thought that generate particular theories. We thus attempt integration not only within debates, but across debates at a metatheoretical level. In this respect, the ultimate aim is analogous to Rank's (1941) call that comparisons between "different psychologies" be replaced by a "psychology of difference." While we distinguish differences in organizational theories, we hope to contribute to a theory of difference between them based on an explicit awareness of the contrasting metatheoretical assumptions that underlie them. Put differently, we attempt to identify the paradigmatic underpinnings of the field's extant theoretical metaphors (Morgan, 1980).

Central Perspectives in Organization Theory

Figure 1 outlines a metatheoretical scheme for classifying the major schools of thought in organization and management theory into four basic views. The four views are based on two analytical dimensions: (1) the level of organizational analysis and (2) the relative emphasis placed on deterministic versus voluntaristic assumptions about human nature.

A number of authors have recently distinguished between organizational theories by using the classical duality between social determinism and free will—the view that human beings and their institutions are either determined by exogenous forces or are autonomously chosen and created by human beings (Weeks, 1973; Driggers, 1977; Burrell and Morgan, 1979; Van de Ven and Astley, 1981). Seen from the voluntaristic orientation, individuals and their created institutions are autonomous, proactive, self-directing agents; individuals are seen as the basic unit of analysis and source of change in organizational life. The deterministic orientation focuses not on individuals, but on the structural properties of the context within which action unfolds, and individual behavior is seen as determined by and reacting to structural constraints that provide organizational life with an overall stability and control.

Historically, the exchange of views between voluntaristic and deterministic approaches to organization analysis has been intertwined with a further distinction between the levels of organization analysis that are used. Traditionally, single organizations have been the primary focus; however, a number of recent theorists have raised the level of analysis to study total populations of organizations, under the assumption that populations exhibit distinctive properties and dynamics of their own that are not discernible in individual organizations. The major reason for our making this micro-macro distinction is to focus on the part-whole relations existing in all organizational

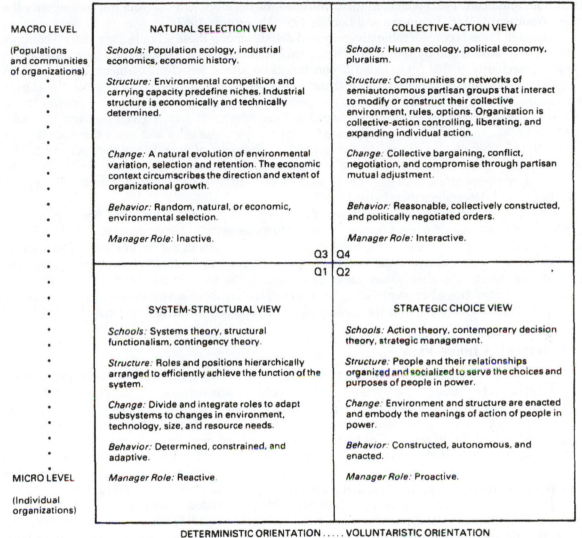

Figure 1   Four views of organization and management.

phenomena. Discussions about appropriate levels of analysis have overlapped the voluntarism-determinism argument, but this does not erase the analytical distinction between the two dimensions on which these debates are based.

Classifying schools of thought by these two dimensions yields four basic perspectives: system-structural, strategic choice, natural selection, and collective-action views of organizations. We contend that most, if not all, schools of thought can be classified in terms of these dimensions, whether authors refer to the dimensions explicitly or not. As the figure indicates, these four perspectives represent qualitatively different views of organization structure, behavior, change, and managerial roles. They provide a repertoire of ways to approach and understand organization theory.

The System-Structural View

At the level of individual organizations, structural functionalism and systems theory have been the dominant schools of organization thought (Silverman, 1970). These schools influenced classical management theory (Gulick and Urwick, 1937; Fayol, 1949) and the theory of bureaucracy (Merton,

1940; Blau and Scott, 1962) which, in turn, preceded the development of structural contingency theories (Woodward, 1965; Lawrence and Lorsch, 1967; Thompson, 1967).

Although there is considerable diversity and debate among these schools, they share a common deterministic orientation by which organizational behavior is seen to be shaped by a series of impersonal mechanisms that act as external constraints on actors. Structural elements are assumed to be interrelated in such a way that they instrumentally serve the achievement of organizational goals and are therefore "functional." The basic components of structure are roles. These predefine the set of behavioral expectations, duties, and responsibilities associated with a given position. It is roles, not individuals, that are structured; human beings occupy these roles and must therefore be carefully selected, trained, and controlled to meet the requirements of the position they occupy. Shared organizational goals impose a need for conformity and coherence. Individuals are thereby immersed as component parts of an interdependent collectivity—a structured, interlocking system that shapes and determines their behavior.

According to the system-structural view, the manager's basic role is a reactive one. It is a technician's role of fine-tuning the organization according to the exigencies that confront it. Change takes the form of "adaptation"; it occurs as the product of exogenous shifts in the environment. The manager must perceive, process, and respond to a changing environment and adapt by rearranging internal organizational structure to ensure survival or effectiveness. The focus of managerial decision making, therefore, is not on choice but on gathering correct information about environmental variations and on using technical criteria to examine the consequences of responses to alternative demands.

The Strategic Choice View

Critiques of the system-structural approach have emerged in the form of an "action frame of reference," advocated by those who adhere to a more voluntaristic orientation (Silverman, 1970). This viewpoint is used to attack system and structural-functional approaches for inferring the existence of self-regulating mechanisms that serve the "needs" and "functions" of the system. This is the problem of reification. In contrast, according to action theory, organizations are continuously constructed, sustained, and changed by actors' definitions of the situation—the subjective meanings and interpretations that actors impute to their worlds as they negotiate and enact their organizational surroundings. It is in this vein that a variety of approaches—exchange (Blau, 1964), symbolic (Feldman and March, 1981), interaction (Goffman, 1961), negotiated order (Strauss et al., 1963), phenomenological (Weick, 1979), and ethnomethodological (Bittner, 1965)—have come to the fore.

Action theory in organizational analysis has mainly been applied to "strategic choice" in decision-making situations (Child, 1972). According to this view, choice is available in the design of organizational structure, which may be fashioned more in accordance with political considerations than technical criteria. Decision theorists have emphasized that ambiguity is sufficiently widespread in organizations to afford the opportunity frequently to engineer such an outcome (March and Olsen, 1976). Strategic choice also extends to the organization's environment. Thus, strategic management and resource-dependence theorists argue that the environment is not to be viewed as a set of intractable constraints; it can be changed and manipulated through political negotiation to fit the objectives of top management (Pfeffer and Salancik, 1978; Lorange, 1980).

As the figure outlines, the strategic choice view draws attention to individuals, their interactions, social constructions, autonomy, and choices, as opposed to the constraints of their role incumbency and functional interrelationships in the system. Both environment and structure are enacted to embody the meanings and actions of individuals—particularly those in power. Managers are regarded as performing a proactive role; their choices are viewed as autonomous, and their acts are viewed as energizing forces that shape the organizational world.

The Natural Selection View

A more macro view of organization-environment relations that contrasts with both system-structural and strategic choice approaches has emerged in the form of a natural selection view that focuses not on single organizations, but on the structural and demographic characteristics of total populations of organizations or industries. Those who adopt this perspective include population ecologists, industrial economists, and economic historians.

The population ecology model is based on the notion that environmental resources are structured in the form of "niches" whose existence and distribution across society are relatively intractable to manipulation by single organizations. Consequently, this view emphasizes, rather deterministically, that there are definite limits to the degree to which autonomous strategic choice is available (Aldrich, 1979; Ch. 6). At the same time, organizations are seen as severely limited in their ability to adapt their internal "forms" to different niches. As a result, organizations are placed at the mercy of their environments, since they either fortuitously "fit" into a niche or are "selected out" and fail (Hannan and Freeman, 1977). This view also implies a population level of analysis, since whole species of organizations are seen to survive or fail regardless of the actions taken by single organizations within them.

A parallel to the population ecologist's concept of niche can be found in the industrial economist's notion of industrial structure, defined as the relatively stable economic and technical dimensions of an industry that provide the context within which competition occurs. Industrial structure inhibits movement between markets through "entry barriers" and sharply delimits the economic feasibility and appropriateness of different strategic alternatives for particular industrial contexts (Caves and Porter, 1977). Traditionally understood, "market conduct," or a firm's strategy, merely reflects the environment (Porter, 1981).

Moreover, economic historians such as Chandler (1977) and institutional economists such as Williamson (1975) contend that industrial structure evolves in determinate ways. The general thesis is that a competitive economy driven by market transactions among many small traditional enterprises has evolved into a regulated economy dominated by the internal, hierarchical transactions of big business. This has occurred as a response to changing environmental forces over which individual organizations have little control. In the view of those authors, structural transformations of the modern industrial environment are governed by impersonal economic laws and the dictates of administrative efficiency, not contrived through management strategy. Big business prevails not because it has succeeded in amassing and exploiting market power, but because it is a more efficient instrument than the market for minimizing transaction costs (Williamson, 1975) or for coordinating the flow of goods and services in the economy (Chandler, 1977).

In summary, in the natural selection view, the evolution of corporate society and its economic infrastructure is driven by environmental forces. Change is explained in terms of a natural drift of resources through the economy, rather than in terms of internal managerial action. Primacy is ascribed to the environment, which inhibits choice by channeling organizations in predetermined directions. In this sense, the managerial role can be described as inactive (see Figure 1) or, at most, symbolic (Pfeffer and Salancik, 1978: 263).

The Collective-Action View

Instead of conceiving of corporate society as subject to an environmentally determined evolution, it is possible to conceive of it as guided and constructed by collective purpose and choice. This point has been made by social ecologists (Emery and Trist, 1973), human ecologists (Hawley, 1950, 1968), and social planning theorists (Vickers, 1965; Schon, 1971; Michael, 1973; Ackoff, 1974; Warren, Rose, and Bergunder, 1974). They contend that contemporary societal conditions are, or should be, regulated by purposeful (voluntary) action taking place at a collective level. Rather than view organizations as pitched in a competitive battle for survival through a direct confrontation with the natural, or exogenous, environment, these authors emphasize collective survival, which is achieved by collaboration between organizations through the construction of a regulated and controlled social environment that mediates the effects of the natural environment.

The key notion involved in the idea of collective survival is that of the interorganizational network. A network is an interlocking system of exchange relationships negotiated between members of different organizations as they jointly shape their environments (Cook, 1977). This network consists of a social action system of symbiotically interdependent organizations that, over time, take on specialized roles within a framework of normative expectations that define rights and conduct (Van de Ven, Emmett, and Koenig, 1974; Benson, 1975). These norms—what Commons (1950) described as the "working rules of collective action"—permit the network to act as a unit and make decisions to attain the collective and individual interests of its member organizations.

The internal political structure of interorganizational networks has been represented in different ways: both as a pluralistic system of interaction (Schon, 1971; Metcalfe, 1974; Trist, 1979), and as a political economy (Benson, 1975), embodied in structures of domination or "hegemonic control" (Clegg, 1981; Perrow, 1981). But, in either case, change is understood to be actively produced by political negotiation and social definition rather than determined by neutral economic and environmental forces.

The collective-action view focuses on networks of symbiotically interdependent, yet semiautonomous organizations that interact to construct or modify their collective environment, working rules, and options. The manager's role is an interactive one. He transacts with others through collective bargaining, negotiation, compromise, political maneuver, and so on. Movements toward solutions are guided by norms, customs, and laws, which are the working rules of collective action.

Central Debates in Organization Theory

Each of these four perspectives represents only a partial view of reality, so that together they provide a repertoire of complementary ways to quadrangulate on organizational phenomena. This suggests the desirability of systematically juxtaposing the four perspectives to provide a more comprehensive understanding of organizations. At the same time, each of the perspectives contradicts the others in key respects, since each presents its own distinctive interpretation of reality. This suggests the desirability of systematically counterposing the four perspectives to bring points of divergence into dialectical relief. Consequently, we now turn to an analysis of the six debates that are generated from an interplay of the four perspectives.

System versus Action: Q1 vs. Q2[1]

Are organizations functionally rational, technically constrained systems, or are they socially constructed, subjectively meaningful embodiments of individual action? This debate is concerned with the interplay between what Dawe (1970) referred to as "the two sociologies": one views individual action as the derivative of the social system, and the other views the social system as the derivative of individual action.

In organization theory, Crozier and Friedberg (1980) have addressed this debate, contrasting a "systemic argument" (the system-structural view) and a "strategic argument" (the strategic choice view). The systemic argument begins analysis with the organization as a whole and locates individual action according to its place and function within the system. The individual is only a component of the system, an irritant that must be controlled so that overall functional integration can be maintained (see Howton, 1969).

The strategic argument, on the other hand, begins with the individual and proceeds to find the system only as the aggregated outcome of individual acts. It criticizes the functional explanation, claiming that the latter attempts to account for behavior indirectly, by reference to its supposed consequences, rather than directly, by reference to the specific acts that cause it (Silverman, 1970). To avoid reifying the organization, the strategic argument thus treats subjectively meaningful individual action as the central force of organizational behavior. In this view the organization is no longer a functionally cohesive monolith; it becomes a shifting coalition (March, 1962; Georgiou, 1973; Keeley, 1980), a loosely coupled system (Weick, 1976), or even organized anarchy (Cohen, March, and Olsen, 1972).

A dialectical reconciliation that escapes the one-sided subjectivism of action theory while resisting functional determinism must recognize that individual action is always, in some measure, curbed to avoid total disintegration of the system. But the system is never totally integrated into a perfectly cohesive body, either. Organizations do maintain a degree of cohesion, but this must always be contrived through a partial suppression of internal antagonism. For Crozier and Friedberg (1980), this balancing and managing of complex internal tensions is like playing a "game." The game has rules that must be obeyed so that collective association can continue. Within the rules, however, several different strategies are always possible. Moreover, the rules can be broken, but only to a limited extent. The player remains free, but if he wants to win he must adopt a strategy in reasonable conformance with the rules, since a complete abandonment of the game cannot serve his interests.

A parallel debate has emerged over discussions of rationality in decision making. Conventional, structural-functional approaches contend that decision making is mostly rational in that it exhibits goal-directed, functional behavior. An objective logic of effectiveness based on "technical rationality" (Thompson, 1967: 14) is presumed to operate. The decision-making process is represented as an exercise in engineering; it is governed by laws inferred from a cost-benefit calculus, a "logic of cost and efficiency" (Roethlisberger and Dickson, 1939) that underlies managerial action.

For contemporary decision theorists employing an action frame of reference, such "rationality" is only a mystifying gloss that obscures the pervasive nonrational elements in decision making. March and Olsen (1976) and Weick (1979) suggested that decision making is best conceived not as rationally contrived toward the instrumental attainment of organizational goals; rather, events simply unfold for one reason or another, be it accident, habit, or personal preference and expediency. In reality, actions may precede goals. Goals may be imaginative reconstructions that impute order and rationality to acts and decisions after they have occurred. Organizational arrangements should not, therefore, be misinterpreted as functionally or logically required. They become indispensable only by virtue of our conscious reflections, which superimpose the quality of logic on the already established order. Here is the dialectic: Is the system rationally planned and constructed, or does action just emerge, to be subsequently rationalized?

The system/action debate is also present in the tension between contingency theory, on the one hand, and strategic management and resource-dependency theory, on the other hand. Contingency theory assumes that contextual constraints have binding effects on organizational operations. In other words, context has causal primacy; management merely responds in the technically appropriate manner. Strategic management and resource-dependence theorists, in contrast, point to the extent to which management has the leeway to create and define the organization's context. Managers proactively choose from their environment what will be important and what will be the relevant operating context for them. There may well be costs involved in ignoring certain contextual factors, but these are only costs to be weighed against alternative costs; they are not determinants.

Child (1972) has attempted to reconcile these views by pointing out that, while a "goodness of fit" between organization context and structure may have performance implications that constrain managers, such performance constraints are themselves socially defined; they may be set at levels low enough to allow for the pursuit of other non-performance-related goals. Economic performance, in other words, may be only one of multiple points of reference influencing decision making. While managers still experience constraint, they do so only in the sense that they have chosen what will act as a constraint for them. Again, we see that the two sides of the argument are at once complementary, contradictory, and convergent.

Adaptation versus Selection: Q1 vs. Q3

Are changes in organizational forms explained by internal adaptation or by environmental selection? The first of these explanations, the internal adaptation view, has historically dominated organization theory. Drawing from systems theorists who analyze social organizations as "complex adaptive systems" (Buckley, 1968), contingency theorists have emphasized that organizations respond to change by modifying or elaborating their internal structures to maintain an isomorphic relationship with the environment. For example, environmental heterogeneity must be matched by internal differentiation and integration if organizational performance is not to suffer (Lawrence and Lorsch, 1967).

Population ecologists have reacted to this adaptation perspective, arguing that it exaggerates the degree to which managers of organizations can flexibly adjust their structural forms (Aldrich and Pfeffer, 1976). Sunk costs, historical precedent, political resistance to change, and so on, are held responsible for inducing a "structural inertia" (Hannan and Freeman, 1977). Given this inertia, if the niche that an organization occupies no longer continues to attract sufficient resources to sustain a particular organizational form, that form becomes obsolete and is "selected out." At the same time, resources transfer into new areas, creating niches that are sufficiently novel that limited adaptations of existing organizations cannot provide adequate degrees of fitness. Thus, entirely new organizational forms must be "selected in." Environmental selection thus replaces internal adaptation as the major vehicle of change.

Both the adaptation and selection perspectives share a deterministic orientation, in that the ultimate source of change is the environment. But they differ with respect to their level of analysis (McKelvey, 1979). In the adaptation view, organizations respond to change by fine-tuning themselves to the contingencies of their local task environments. The analysis is strictly unit-based. But in the selection view, no amount of fine-tuning within the localized confines of an organization's niche is adequate since, in the long run, the niche for a particular type of organization may disappear altogether. Thus, the focus shifts to entire species or populations of organizations that come and go in "waves" as whole industries are born and extinguished (Aldrich, 1979).

Population ecologists admit, however, that the natural selection model works much better for small, powerless organizations operating in environments with dispersed resources than for large, politically well-connected organizations operating in environments with concentrated resources (Aldrich, 1979: 111–112). This suggests a possible reconciliation between the selection and adaptation perspectives. The problem here is that large organizations are selected out only very infrequently (Edwards, 1979: 84–85).[2] For this reason, Lawrence (1981) contended that the natural selection perspective needs to be supplemented by an adaptation-by-learning perspective. He argued that if an organization survives environmental selection in the early stages of growth and expands along any one of several lines (e.g., product mix, geographical area), it may be better able to adapt to subsequent environmental changes that would have been fatal at an earlier stage.

The explanation for this may lie in the fact that small organizations experience greater risk of being selected out because they are typically locked into a single niche, whereas large organizations increasingly span many niches and thereby entrench their positions through geographical expansion and diversification (Pennings, 1980). Given that forces of institutionalization invariably induce structural inertia (Kimberly, 1980), however, it remains to be explained how small organizations can successfully change into larger ones without first being selected out. This may occur as institutionalization inhibits small-scale, short-term adaptation and leads to a build-up of tension as the organization becomes increasingly mismatched to its environment. Then, this tension is eventually resolved, not by "change within the system" but by "change of the system" (Parsons, 1961). This explains the "metamorphic" transformations (Starbuck, 1965, 1968) organizations undertake as their operations spill over into new product-market locations (Chandler, 1962). Once having gained a foothold in one or more niches, the organization can avoid being selected out by adjusting its portfolio, transferring resources away from areas of decline into more munificent spheres of operation. While a myopic focusing of activity may still induce structural inertia within niche-bound subunits, the organization can retain its overall buoyancy at the corporate level.

While this explanation of the adaptability of large organizations complements the population ecology view by overcoming one of the latter's major deficiencies, it does little to challenge the adequacy of another perspective that focuses specifically on large organizations while remaining consistent with the natural selection view. This is the "market failures" framework offered by Williamson (1975). This framework qualifies as a natural selection view in the sense that it deals with how the economic environment "selects in" a new and important breed of organization—what Chandler (1977) described as "the modern multiunit enterprise."

The general thesis is that "markets" are supplanted by "hierarchies" when markets cease to function properly because of "information impactedness," an asymmetrical distribution of information that interferes with the optimal allocation of resources through market exchange. An organization's superior monitoring and control capabilities overcome this problem: they reduce "transaction costs" and restore efficiency. The growth of large hierarchical organizations is therefore determined economically in the sense that internal organization reestablishes the natural operation of economic rationality when markets are no longer able to perform this function. At the same time, this economic rationality operates at a population level of analysis, since it governs the operation of the total market or industry. The shift from markets to hierarchies is explained as a triumph of the interests of the economic "system" as a whole over the opportunistic tendencies of its constituent members (Williamson, 1975: 27). Optimization of efficiency in allocating resources throughout the total economy is the salient force in operation.

While the market-failures framework plausibly extends the natural selection view to large corporations, it too is open to dialectical reinterpretation by the system-structural view. Thompson had a quite different account of how markets are supplanted by hierarchies as "organizations under norms of rationality seek to place their boundaries around those activities which if left to the task environment would be crucial contingencies" (Thompson, 1967: 39). In Thompson's explanation of this phenomenon, it is not the rational workings of an economic system that matter, but the norms of technical rationality that govern the internal operations of particular organizations. It is the interests of the focal organization that are at stake, not those of the economic marketplace. Hierarchies are not by-products of market failure that act simply as alternative mechanisms for allocating economic resources for society's benefit; rather, they are managerial contrivances for controlling, reducing, or removing contingencies that threaten the organization's technical functioning. In this view, internalization represents an absorption of external threat, not a market failure. It embodies the logic of organizational adaptation, not the logic of environmental evolution. It is technological determinism applied to single organizations, not economic determinism applied to populations of organizations in a market system.[3] Here again we see a dialectical tension; the subject matter is the same, it is the camera angle that shifts.

Constrained Niches versus Enacted Domains: Q2 vs. Q3

Is organizational life determined by intractable environmental constraints, or is it actively created through strategic managerial choices? This debate has been highlighted recently by Porter's (1981) discussion of the relationship between industrial economics and strategic management. In a systematic contrast of the two fields, Porter points to differences in orientation that pertain directly to the two dimensions of the figure. First, while industrial economists have been able to take the industry as a whole as their unit of analysis by assuming that all firms in the industry will react in identical ways to the same economic context, strategic management theorists have been interested in the problems of the individual firm as a unique entity with unique strengths and weaknesses. Second, industrial economists have presented a rather deterministic view because of their static, structural analysis of industries, while "the policy field has a long tradition of emphasizing the insight, creativity, and even vision that some firms have exhibited in finding unique ways to change the rules of the game in their industries" (Porter, 1981: 613).

Given these contrasting orientations, it is not surprising that Aldrich (1979: Ch. 6) relied heavily on the industrial economics literature to circumscribe the extent to which strategic choice is available within organizations. This argument centers around the postulated existence of niches, distinct combinations of resources and other constraints in the environment. The concept of niche implies a focus on populations of organizations rather than single organizations, since distributions of economic and other resources that form niches provide support for whole species of organizations. The fate of each single organization is tied to its membership in a particular population type because it cannot easily adapt to different niches. The macroeconomic, social, and political forces underlying the emergence and dissolution of niches overwhelm strategic managerial action in the long run, since only a few powerful and politically well-connected organizations can significantly counteract these forces.

By contrast, strategic choice theorists view the environment as a "domain" that managers enact, define, and otherwise influence (Levine and White, 1961). Rumelt (1979) has thus reacted to the natural selection position, arguing that a capacity for adaptation to new niches is reflected in the particular strategic posture adopted by managers of single organizations. The presence of idiosyncratic strategies produces variation in performance between organizations that are members of the same species but that nevertheless, carve out their own distinctive product-market niches. Thus, it is the particular transactions that managers of organizations engage in that alter their environmental position "without altering the environment itself" (Rumelt, 1979). Other theorists have argued that even the macro-structure of the environment changes in response to corporate strategy. Caves and Porter (1977) and Salop (1979), for example, have shown how managers can affect or even deter entry of their firms into industries by carefully choosing their strategies. Such observations require that the traditional industrial economics assumption that industry structure is relatively constant and is the primary determinant of strategy be counterbalanced by a "theory of dynamic industry structures" that, instead of regarding structure solely as an independent variable determining firm behavior, also treats market structure as a dependent variable that over time comes to reflect the past strategies of firms in the industry (Brock, 1981, Ch. 2).

The contrast between natural selection and strategic choice views is crystallized in Weick's (1979) modification of the variation-selection-retention model used by population ecologists (e.g., Aldrich, 1979), which he relabels an "enactment-selection-retention" model. Weick's substitution of enactment for variation is meant to emphasize that "managers construct, rearrange, single out, and demolish many 'objective' features of their surroundings" as they literally define and create their own constraints (Weick, 1979: 164). Selection criteria are not so much embodied in external environmental conditions as they are lodged in organizational members themselves. Selection takes place as individuals impose meaning upon, and make sense out of, their enacted raw data. Those patterns of data that fit their interpretation schemes and cognitive repertoires are selected in, while the rest is edited out. Selection criteria are thus specific to the particular individuals of particular organizations rather than being transmitted to whole species of organizations as niche constraints. Again, the retention process inheres not in features of the environment, but in "cause maps" built up out of individuals' past experience. These cause maps feed back to the enactment and selection processes, providing them with cues, attention patterns, and processes for scanning and monitoring, all of which play an active role in constructing an "artificial" environment out of the objective environment. Weick consequently insists that meaningful environments are outputs of organizing, not inputs to it, as population ecologists would contend. The variation-selection-retention model thus appears equally compatible with both natural selection and strategic choice views.

The fact that there is nothing inherent in the variation-selection-retention model that biases it toward a deterministic orientation suggests that the population ecologist's success in ascribing causal primacy to the environment relies more than anything else on the characteristic adoption of a population level of analysis. The actions of single organizations are held to count for little in the face of long-term demographic trends that affect whole populations. If it is true, however, that the successful application of the population ecology model to environmental selection rests on its level of analysis (Aldrich, 1979: 107), then the theoretical conclusions of population ecology that emphasize the importance of external environmental constraint are based on an analytical conflation of the two dimensions of the figure.

In other words, the population ecology model attributes to the environment what a population level of analysis actually achieves. If one focuses on populations of organizations, the strategic choices of single organizations must assume minimal importance. This is so, simply because the switch in level of analysis is designed to achieve just that effect. By seeking to understand the dynamics underlying aggregate distributions of organizations across environmental conditions, one takes a macro focus on the population, thereby automatically foregoing a micro view of the activities of single organizations. But to conclude from this restricted focus that the environment has primacy and that it is "the environment that selects" (Hannan and Freeman, 1977) incorrectly underplays the role of voluntarism in organizational life. Though it is still true to say that the actions of small, single organizations count for little in the face of long-run trends discerned at a population level of analysis, one should not be seduced into representing this fact in terms of vague natural forces and external constraints residing in a faceless environment. This is borne out by the fact that it is quite possible to employ a population level of analysis in conjunction with a voluntaristic orientation, as the following contrast of natural selection and collective-action views illustrates.

Economic Aggregates versus Political Collectivities: Q3 vs. Q4

Is the environment to be viewed as a simple aggregation of organizations governed by external economic forces, or viewed as an integrated collectivity of organizations governed by its own internal social and political forces? At the population level of analysis, the voluntarism-determinism dialectic between theories of ecology focuses on two issues: (1) the definition of "population," itself and (2) whether populations of organizations are driven by economic or by social and political dynamics. These two interrelated issues will be separated for analytical clarity.

In the population ecology view, a population is defined as an "aggregate" of organizations that are "relatively homogeneous" (Hannan and Freeman, 1977). All organizations within the population share certain "key elements" that constitute their "common form." Consequently, they also share a mutual "vulnerability" to the environment. This common vulnerability explains the occurrence and distribution of different species of organizations across differing environmental conditions.

In contrast, human ecologists (Hawley, 1950, 1968; Duncan, 1964; Boulding, 1978) define a population not in terms of common susceptibility to the environment, but in terms of the internal patterning of relationships between its constituent members. For human ecologists, the population is not an incoherent agglomeration, but a coherent organization—an "integrated system having some degree of unit character" (Hawley, 1968). Internal "organization" is the very attribute that transforms an assemblage of organizations into a collectivity with distinctive properties of its own.

The human ecologist's conception of collective behavior thus extends beyond Hannan and Freeman's notion of single-species populations. These single-species populations are comprised of a homogeneous set of organizations that share a competitive, "intraspecific" relationship known as "commensalism." For human ecologists, a population emerges only when the quality of corporate unity or internal cohesion can be attributed to it. Such cohesion derives from the functional interdependence that develops on the basis of complementary differences between heterogeneous units, especially units sharing an "interspecific relationship" known as "symbiosis."

In the human ecology view, adaptation takes place through the mechanism of network closure. Symbiosis results from the fact that some organizations become functionally specialized in obtaining needed resources directly from the environment, while others secure these resources indirectly through boundary-spanning organizations. The internal functioning of the population is thereby shielded from environmental effects, and this represents a creative, collective effort by the population to manage and control its existence, partially free from the need to react to environmental intrusions. "The symbiotic union enhances the efficiency of production or creative effort; the commensal union, since its parts are homogeneous, can only react and is suited, therefore, only to protective or conservative actions" (Hawley, 1968: 332).

Through its focus on populations of homogeneous organizations that are commensalistically related (i.e., indirectly related because of common dependence on the environment), the natural selection view draws attention to the open-system condition, where each member of the population interacts directly with the environment and is therefore directly influenced by it. Environmental influence is highlighted by defining the population in terms of its shared environmental vulnerability. By definition, the greater this vulnerability, the greater the population effect.

Through its focus on symbiotic interdependence and the movement toward network closure, which removes most parts of the population from direct contact with the environment, the human ecology view automatically plays down the effects of the environment while highlighting the social constructions of collective action. By definition, the greater the insulation from environmental influence through system closure, the greater the population effect.

In summary, population ecology focuses attention on a "natural" environment comprised of forces beyond the organization's control. Organizations can vie for environmental resources with other organizations in a competitive bid for survival, but ultimately their fortunes are environmentally determined. In contrast, human ecology focuses attention on the active construction of a protective "social" environment that displaces the natural environment as the critical influence. In effect, organizational parties symbiotically collude to ensure the continued existence of the interorganizational network as a whole.

This contrasting focus on "natural" versus "social" environments also carries implications for each view's assessment of what constitutes the essential dynamic underlying organizational activity. Thus, for population ecologists, "environmental pressures make competition for resources the central force in organizational activities" (Aldrich, 1979: 27–28), and the population ecology model is held to work best in environments with "dispersed resources" (Aldrich, 1979: 111), that is, in environments that approximate perfectly competitive markets.[4] The whole notion that relationships between organizations are mediated indirectly through natural environmental processes implies that something akin to Adam Smith's (1937) "invisible hand" is operating. The dynamic is essentially that of economic competition.

On the other hand, the human ecologist's emphasis on socially constructed and regulated environments tends to highlight the importance of social and political rather than economic forces. Power begins to play an explicit role as those units responsible for obtaining resources directly from the "natural" environment are able to regulate the conditions essential to the functioning of other units in the network that have only indirect relations with this environment. While some degree of power is held by all units, this power varies inversely with the number of steps that a unit is removed from direct environmental contact, with the result that power relationships between organizations grow ever more elaborate as interorganizational networks attain greater closure (Hawley, 1968). As this occurs, political negotiation plays an increasingly important role in regulating the flow of economic resources throughout the network. Though such resource flows may still be characterized as economic exchanges, to the extent that powerful members of the network are able to define their own terms of exchange and impose these on others, a political-economic analysis is required. Benson (1975) has consequently contended that the process of resource acquisition in interorganizational networks is inevitably linked to the distribution of power and must, accordingly, be analyzed as a "political economy."

Another aspect of this same emerging debate between industrial economists on the one hand and political economists on the other relates to the growing dominance of big business at the core of interorganizational networks. The construction of an artificial social environment among a community of organizations is one way to ensure immunity from the harsh realities of competition in the natural environment. An equally important way is to control the natural environment by absorbing it within the corporate boundaries of single enterprises. Galbraith (1967) and Edwards (1979) have pointed to this elimination of market exchange as a principal method of promoting control of the economy by an elite of giant corporations. Edwards (1979: 83) provides supporting evidence, noting that consolidations that control less than 50 percent of their markets fail nearly three times more often than firms with greater market control, while the latter earn roughly 30 percent higher profits than the former.

While these authors highlight the political rather than the economic significance of this phenomenon, others have incorporated it within a natural selection framework. As we noted earlier, Williamson (1975) argued that the growth of big business occurs when markets fail to allocate resources efficiently, so that a hierarchical monitoring of transactions becomes necessary to restore economic rationality by reducing costs. Similarly, Chandler (1977) argued that administrative efficiencies underlie the growth of big business because the latter provides superior scheduling and coordination of standardized products in high-volume industries. In other words, economic forces (especially the economic advantages of vertical integration) have led to the emergence of large-scale enterprise, since those firms that did not adjust to changing market and technological conditions by internalizing the environment were unable to compete and were selected out.

Perrow (1981) has criticized this neutral efficiency explanation for failing to take into account the possibility that vertical integration takes place for the somewhat more nefarious purpose of cutting off competitors' supplies or dominating available distribution outlets, rather than simply reducing economic costs. While he agreed that economic factors provide the necessary conditions that permit vertical integration to take place (since not all industries do, or can, vertically integrate), it is power and market control rather than economic efficiency that provides the essential motivation for such growth. Thus, the dialectic emerges again: industrial concentration is hegemonic power; economic success is political domination; corporate organization is social control.

Individual versus Collective Action: Q2 vs. Q4

Is organizational behavior principally concerned with individual or collective action? This question focuses on the basic tension between self versus collective frames of reference as these are exhibited in micro and macro levels of organizational analysis. In the main, organization and management theories have embraced a self-interest orientation by adhering to the rational model of administrative behavior. In contrast, the collective-interest problem remains largely ignored.

The basic axiom of rational behavior is to "maximize," or at least "satisfice," self-interests (Simon, 1976). A consistent preference ordering is assumed, in which individuals or organizations have a clearly specified objective function by which they can select the best from a set of alternatives. "As long as we assume that organizations have goals and that those goals have some classical properties of stability, precision, and consistency, we can treat an organization as some kind of rational actor" (March, 1981: 215). Indeed, the entire theory of rational organizational behavior relies on the premise that participants share common goals, for without it cooperative "teamwork" would not be possible (Simon, 1976).

But organizational stakeholders often have conflicting goals, particularly under conditions of scarcity. Then the rational model transforms into either a competitive theory of games with probability pay-off matrices for each participant, or attempts are made to alter the preferences of dissenting parties into a consensus so that "teamwork" can again prevail. Classical theories of the firm handle this problem in two stages. First, conflicting demands are converted into prices by having each individual negotiate the terms needed to agree to pursue another's preferences. Second, managers or entrepreneurs impose their goals on the organization in exchange for the negotiated wages paid to employees (March, 1981). In addition to these wage negotiations, organizations use elaborate systems of motivation, promotion, reward, and control to maintain order and consensus among organizational participants. Thus, the employment contract is reinforced by a system of inducements that provides management with a means of securing employee consensus toward organizational goals.

It is along these lines that Mancur Olson (1965) argued that because of the "free rider problem" there is no rational justification for individuals to contribute to "collective goods." In small groups, or oligarchies, individuals may be willing to contribute voluntarily to obtain collective goods because of a common norm of reciprocity, interpersonal trust, friendship, social pressure, or an altruistic concern for the welfare of the group as a whole. For large groups, these inducements diminish, however, and the problem of generating collective action becomes increasingly acute. For Olson (1965: 51), "only a separate and 'selective' incentive will stimulate a rational individual in a latent group to act in a group-oriented way."

Reacting to this individualistic thrust of classical economists, for whom "the human individual acted somewhat like an atom," Commons (1950: 36) argued "that individuals are not self-sufficient, independent entities; and society is not the summation of the individual members" (Commons, 1950: 14). Individual freedom is not an innate right; it is a collective achievement. The only way individual freedom can be obtained is through a collective adherence to "duties" that define and protect individual "rights" for everyone. Rights and duties are not individually determined; they come from norms, customs, and laws that are enforced by a sovereignty. Commons referred to these norms, customs, and laws as the "working rules of collective action," a notion he based on the legal concept of a "reasonable man." The reasonable man follows a very different logic from the rational man (Van de Ven and Freeman, 1983). In law, the reasonable man must meet some uniform, collective standard of conduct. This standard is determined with reference to a community valuation and must be the same for all persons, "since the law can have no favorites" (Prosser, 1971: 150).

Reasonable behavior, however, does not deny rational behavior; it provides an institutional framework within which it can work. Clearly, individuals do pursue their own goals and do attempt to maximize their self-interests as best they can under given conditions. Consequently, conflict and disruption are as ever-present and important as consensus and order, a fact that is recognized in the pluralistic perspective of Lindblom (1965), Wilson (1973), and Dahl and Lindblom (1976). These authors analyze collective action as an incremental process emerging from mutual adjustments among multiple, partisan interest groups. While partisan actors pursue their own interests, however, they do so within limits and must negotiate with others to find compromises that are acceptable from a collective point of view. This is the function served by the working rules of collective action: they embody an institutional order that defines limits within which individuals may exercise their own wills.

This individual-versus-collective-action debate is clearly evident in the literature dealing with organization-environment relationships. Again, the individual-as-rational-actor perspective has prevailed, a fact that is reflected in the tendency of authors to adopt the point of view of a focal organization. For example, resource dependence theory (Pfeffer and Salancik, 1978) contends that astute managers seek to increase their power over critical sources of dependence in the environment by, on the one hand, striking favorable bargains with their exchange partners, and, on the other hand, avoiding costly entanglements with them. Necessary resources must be acquired, but only in a way that guards against the organization's surrendering too much autonomy and becoming overly dependent on external parties (Thompson and McEwen, 1958). The resulting interaction is viewed as a kind of game: managers strategically counteract each others' maneuvers. Even apparent instances of collaboration are analyzed from a game-theoretic viewpoint. Thus, joint ventures, coalitions, informal agreements, and so on, are seen as mixed-motive games. They are alliances put together for expedient purposes, but they are temporary alliances that are adhered to only insofar as, and so long as, they serve each coalition partner's self-interests.

On the other hand, a genuinely collective orientation has also begun to emerge in the organization-environment literature. Thus, Benson (1975) and Pfeffer and Salancik (1978: 147) have outlined some of the norms (or working rules of collective action) that operate in interorganizational networks. Such norms stabilize the collective functioning of interdependent systems of organizations, and yet they do not completely suppress autonomy, the pursuit of localized interest, or the emergence of conflict between organizations. Instead, they facilitate mutual adjustment among multiple partisan interests in a pluralistic system that is neither individualistic and anarchic nor totalitarian. As Metcalfe (1974) and Van de Ven (1980) have indicated, pluralistic participation can reconcile both sectional interest and collective well-being in interorganizational relations.

But a problem remains: if organizations represent sectional interests, why do they voluntarily adhere to collective working rules at all—particularly those that are not legally enforceable—instead of relentlessly seeking to exploit each others' dependencies? The answer lies in the understanding that as representatives of organizations interact, their relationships become infused with shared values that turn sectional orientations into collective orientations. As expedient patterns of acting are discovered through trial and error, they tend to be repeated. Eventually, managers who continually interact come to share the idea that "these are the ways things should be done." With this development, norms become dissociated from the specific situations from which they first arose and are generalized to cover broad areas of collective activity. As such, they take on the character of autonomous social forces, directing and regulating collective action. This is the function that Warren, Rose, and Bergunder's (1974) "institutionalized thought structures" and Useem's (1982) "classwide rationality" serve in interorganizational networks.

Normative patterns of interorganizational interaction thus become infused by what Durkheim (1933) referred to as "the moral basis of social contracts." That is, norms become imbued with a sense of morality, rather than sheer pragmatism, so that organizational decision makers feel compelled to abide by them. Moral obligation should not, however, be interpreted as external constraint, since for Commons and Durkheim it is a liberating force. By making stable patterns of collective association possible, it frees organizations from the need to contrive new patterns of acting in each situation they encounter. Compliance with norms is voluntary rather than coerced. It signifies the adoption of a collective orientation with which managers and their organizations identify.

In summary, organizational parties are both independent actors and involved members of a larger collectivity. On the one hand, they act autonomously so as to maximize their chances of obtaining whatever goals they seek individually, apart from those of the collectivity. On the other hand, they adhere to unifying patterns of cultural and social order as they take on responsibilities as part of a larger social entity. In other words, the manager acts both as gamesman and statesman. The need to establish a balance between these opposing pressures underlies what Thompson (1967: 48) described as "the paradox of administration." The existence of this paradox produces not only contradictions in the practice of everyday organizational life, but also, as we have seen, a dialectical tension in theorizing.

Organization versus Institution: Q1 vs. Q4

Are organizations neutral technical instruments engineered to achieve a goal, or are they institutionalized manifestations of the vested interests and power structure of the wider society? The point of departure for this debate is Selznick's (1957) distinction between "organizations" and "institutions." According to Selznick, "organizations" are designed according to a "logic of efficiency"; they are "technical instruments" for mobilizing activity toward set goals. They can be regarded as "expendable tools" or "rational instruments engineered to do a job." "Institutions," on the other hand, are "infused with value beyond the technical requirements of the task at hand." They are "responsive-adaptive organisms," a product of the "social needs and pressures" that mold and shape them. As such, they embody a response to vested interests residing in their environments. As Meyer and Rowan (1977) indicate, institutions are significant less for their technical attributes than for the roles they play in the wider society; they merely reflect the institutional structures in which they are embedded.

There is little doubt that an image of the organization as a tool has dominated the history of organization theory, as Gouldner's (1959) prevailing "Rational Model" has shown. But there has been a contemporary reaction to this school of thought since Child (1972) attacked contingency theory's explanation of organizational behavior by reference to functional imperatives rather than to political action. This critique has gained force particularly from the work of radical, Marxist, and political economy theorists (Marglin, 1974; Stone, 1974; Clegg, 1975, 1979, 1981; Benson, 1977a; Goldman and Van Houten, 1977; Salaman, 1978; Burawoy, 1979; Edwards, 1979; Clegg and Dunkerley, 1980; Clawson, 1980). Those authors rejected the idea that organizational structure is designed on the basis of a neutral logic of technical effectiveness. Instead of viewing structural constraints as functional necessities whose existence is justified by reference to related ideals of "efficiency" and "rationality," they drew attention to the sectional advantages and functions of ostensibly neutral organizational elements and exposed efficiency and rationality as ideologies that buttress, disguise, and justify the inegalitarian nature of organizational structure. Political domination, rather than technical efficiency, is held to underlie the design of organizational structure.

The conventional argument that capitalist methods of production are more productive than earlier forms of work organization because they are more efficient is usually countered by the question, "efficient for whom?" (Perrow, 1980). The criticism here is that efficiency is defined in a way that is biased toward management's interests. A neutral definition would measure the efficiency of a transformation process by the ratio of outputs to inputs: the higher this ratio, the more efficient the transformation process. It is charged, however, that where capitalism is more productive than earlier modes of production, this is not because its transformation process is technically superior; rather, it is because its system of control has enabled managers to extract from workers a greater value of production than they needed to expend on the purchase of labor power. In other words, higher productivity results from increased labor input rather than from a more efficient transformation process. Of course, this makes capitalist production appear efficient to management, but it is only efficient from management's point of view (Clawson, 1980). For workers, it represents only exploitation and domination.

In this view, the capitalist form of organization is driven not by immutable laws of technical efficiency, but by the socially fashioned interests of managerial elites. Moreover, such domination is held to be rooted in factors emanating from beyond the particular circumstances of the shop floor, insofar as it occurs within a broader social context. For example, Edwards (1979) explained capitalist exploitation by reference to developments in the labor force at large: the proletarianization of the work force, the shift from agriculture to industry, the declining importance of workers' skills, and the segmentation of labor markets. It is thus that Burrell (1981) described contemporary organizational conditions as "epiphenomena" of forces that permeate society. Political domination in the workplace is one reflection of the larger dynamics of capitalism. Events seemingly far removed from the workplace itself impose important constraints on workplace relations. In this light, the worker-management struggle in organizations is to be seen, simply, as a microcosm of the wider arena of class conflict.

Thus, the focus shifts from the "problematic of rational structuring" (Benson, 1979) inherent in the system-structural view, to the socially and politically defined network relationships of the collective-action view. The proper unit of analysis becomes the structure of the wider societal environment itself (M. Meyer, 1978). Organizational structure and functioning must be seen in terms of the priorities of the "host" society rather than as a consequence of particular forms of work process or technology (Salaman, 1978). The organization comes to reflect its own distinctive history (Stinchcombe, 1965; Meyer and Brown, 1977) through an assimilation of values and demands thrust upon it by a multitude of vested interests in society (J. Meyer, 1978; Perrow, 1979). The political domination argument thus requires that we shift our analytical focus away from the determinism of efficiency considerations, internal to the organization, toward broad social dynamics that unfold at a collective level of analysis.

Discussion

By comparing and contrasting four basic views of organization theory (see Figure 1), six debates pervading the literature have been addressed.[5] These debates provide much insight for understanding the dialectical tensions of organizational life. Throughout the debates, the tensions focus on structural forms versus personnel action (debates 1 and 4) and on part-whole relationships (debates 2 and 5), as well as on the interaction of these two sources of organizational tension (debates 3 and 6). In conclusion, we speculate about the importance of these two overall dialectical tensions for directing future organizational theory and research. Benson's (1977b) "principles of dialectical analysis" are particularly relevant to this discussion.

Benson's (1977b) first principle was "social construction/production." Briefly, it asserted that "an organization, as part of the social world, is always in a state of becoming." Consequently, attention must be focused on the mechanisms through which an established organizational form is constructed, maintained, reproduced, and continuously reconstructed. This is the task to which theories located on the right-hand side of Figure 1 are committed. But Benson (1977b) also indicated that the processes that explain organizational emergence and dissolution occur within an existing social structure that constrains organizational action. The analysis of these constraining forces distinguishes the theories located on the left-hand side of Figure 1. These two sets of opposing forces are discussed below in terms of an interplay between "structural forms" and "personnel action."

The second principle of dialectical analysis is referred to by Benson (1977b) as the principle of "totality." This principle "expresses a commitment to study social arrangements as complex, interrelated wholes with partially autonomous parts." Thus, on the one hand, organizations are seen as intricately tied to the societal context in which they are located: they are regarded as constituent parts of the wider patterns and forces that unfold in society at large. But on the other hand, organizations are also capable of partially autonomous action in their own right, and this produces tensions between the parts and the whole. This source of tension is captured by the interplay between the lower and upper halves of Figure 1 and is discussed below.

Structural Forms and Personnel Action

Structural forms and personnel action are central issues of interest to organization and management theory. While determinism and voluntarism are useful for classifying organization theories, they have the limitation of easily misdirecting the inquiry by implying that deterministic views of organization structure and voluntaristic views of personnel action are mutually exclusive. In fact, both views are jointly necessary for developing a dynamic appreciation of organizations.

Organizations, after all, are neither purely objective nor purely subjective phenomena. They are objective systems insofar as they exhibit structures that are only partially modifiable through personnel actions, but they are subjective insofar as these structures are populated by individuals who act on the basis of their own perceptions and act in unpredictable as well as predictable ways. The interesting questions and problems, then, turn on how structural forms and personnel actions interrelate and produce tensions that stimulate changes over time.

For example, at the individual level are the problems of selecting, socializing, and controlling individuals for positions or jobs in the structure, on the one hand, and, on the other hand, examining how the actions of people over time restructure these positions. Over the years, tensions and misfits arise between the changing personal aspirations, needs, and growth of individuals and the changing career options for promotion and mobility among positions in the organizational structure. At the group level, an ongoing tension is produced as the structural division and integration of labor and resources among subunits both influence and are influenced by the social-psychological emergence of different norms, interaction patterns, conflict, and power relations within and between groups. At the organizational level is the question of how organizational structure is both a cause and consequence of environmental shifts and strategic choices of powerful individuals within and outside the organization. Finally, at the population level are questions about how organizational niches or market structures are both the product and constraint of collective action, arrived at through a long series of political contests and bargains among partisan groups as well as through societal norms and culture.

These questions are interesting because they (1) admit to both deterministic and voluntaristic views of organizational life; (2) juxtapose these views by reciprocally relating structural forms and personnel actions at comparable levels of analysis; and (3) focus on how these relationships unfold over time in complementary and contradictory ways. Unfortunately, the interesting aspects of these questions are often destroyed when attempts are made to represent these observable patterns in theoretical models. Because of training, socialization, and cognitive limits, theorists tend to reduce these observed complexities to unidirectional causal models among a limited set of factors that are viewed in isolation from other variables.

Such models are too constricting. As Weick (1979: 52) stated, "When any two events are related interdependently, designating one of those two 'cause' and the other 'effect' is an arbitrary designation." Most theorists and "managers get into trouble because they forget to think in circles. . . . Problems persist because managers (and theorists) continue to believe that there are such things as unidirectional causation, independent and dependent variables, origins, and terminations" (Weick, 1979: 52). Moreover, in efforts to identify ultimate causes and effects, the most interesting parts of the above questions tend to be ignored—namely, an investigation of the process by which the loops in the circular relationships unfold. To say that A causes B and B causes A is predictive, but it is intellectually sterile until one can explain the processes by which the reciprocal relationship unfolds over time.

It is these reciprocal relations between structural forms and personnel actions that make tension and conflict a pervasive characteristic of organizational life. As Gomberg (1964) pointed out, the very concept of organization implies conflict. This conflict can be interpreted in terms of the Hegelian dialectic, in which existing structural forms provide the thesis and contradictory personnel actions provide the antithesis ultimately leading to a synthesis:

> The structuring of an organization is identified with the thesis. The resulting hierarchy spawns the seed of its own opposition, the antithesis. The need for revision is generated within the womb of the organization by the activity of the old hierarchy. The needs for new and revised functions grow until they challenge the existing hierarchy. This antithesis, when fully developed, challenges the existing structural hierarchy. Out of this clash emerges either decline or a new hierarchy and set of relationships which we identify as the new temporary synthesis. This synthesis now emerges as the thesis in a new cycle of conflict and thus the process repeats itself as innovating organizers or entrepreneurial

managers pursue their satisfactions from the continuous building up of tension in order to savor their subsequent release. The history of management can be interpreted as this kind of dynamic process. (Gomberg, 1964: 52–53)

Part-Whole Relationships

Many problems apparent at one level of organization manifest themselves in different and contradictory ways at the other levels. At the micro level one focuses on the characteristics of positions, jobs, and subunits as well as the skills, orientations, preferences, and actions of individuals. At the macro level the focus is on the global structural configuration and domain of the organization and the relationships among collectives of decision makers within and outside the organization. The frame of reference, however, is substantially altered when the focus is on the relationships between the parts and the whole, or between these micro and macro levels of analysis.

For example, relying on the concept of requisite variety, Weick (1979) argued that with increasing environmental complexity, uncertainty, and variety, the overall structure of the organization becomes more complex, loosely coupled, decentralized, particularistic, and anarchic. If this is so, then the structure of the individual parts or groups within the organization will become more simple, tightly coupled, hierarchical, universalistic, and cohesive—all the factors that lead to nonadaptiveness, narrowness, and inflexibility. Although Weick clearly did not intend to write about this consequence, it is the result of a basic principle of opposite part-whole relations established in 1908 by Georg Simmel. "The elements of differentiated social circles are undifferentiated, those of undifferentiated ones are differentiated" (Blau, 1964: 284). Conant and Ashby's (1970) principle of requisite variety at the macro level turns out to be a law of requisite simplicity at the micro level.

Gouldner's (1959) notions concerning "functional interdependence" and "functional autonomy" are valuable in underscoring this point. Gouldner pointed out that the preoccupation of systems theorists with functional interdependence focuses attention on the constraints imposed by joint collaboration in the pursuit of systemic objectives. He argued, however, that such interdependence is never totally constraining and that it imposes different degrees of constraint at different points in the system. Thus, it makes as much sense to emphasize degrees of functional autonomy as functional interdependence. What appears as constraint from the point of view of the system appears as freedom from the point of view of its parts.

Blau (1964) further refined Gouldner's concept by noting that the dependence of subunits on their encompassing social structures directly conflicts with their autonomy. "The conflict is inevitable, since both some centralized coordination and some autonomy of parts are necessary for organized collectivities" (Blau, 1964: 303). Relationships between groups and collectivities are manifest in their interdependence, in the mobility of individuals acting as representatives of their groups, and in their roles as group members, whether this involves actions in the pursuit of collective or individual ends. Since individuals can simultaneously belong to many groups, Blau's image of part-whole relations is not one of concentric circles with mutually exclusive memberships at each level. Instead, it is one of intersecting circles, because social networks that define group structure are interpenetrating and overlapping and the boundaries between them are neither sharp nor fixed. "Groups expand and contract with the mobility of members in and out of them" (Blau, 1964: 284).

This kind of dialectical relationship between parts and wholes of organizations is not adequately taken into account by many organizational theories. This is unfortunate because it can be shown that any macro theory of order and consensus includes a micro theory of conflict and coercion, and vice versa. For example, structural-functional theories of organizations have been attacked by radical (Burrell and Morgan, 1979) and action (Silverman, 1970) theorists alike for their inability to explain change because of the emphasis on order, consensus, and unity. While this is true at the macro-organizational level, at the micro level it is only possible because of coercion, domination, and control of disruptive tendencies. If this were not so, there would be no need for rules, indoctrination, socialization, and control mechanisms in organizations; these are central concepts in structuralist views of organizations. On the other hand, radical-change theories (Burrell and Morgan, 1979) overemphasize conflict, coercion, and disruptive tendencies in organizations without admitting that these tendencies can only occur by having order, consensus, and unity at the micro level. Thus, it can be seen that while Marx posited conflict and struggle between classes, he failed to give due recognition to the forces of cohesion and unity within the classes. As Coser (1956) suggested, "out-group conflict" is associated with "in-group cohesion."

In summary, to properly study organizations across levels of analysis is to understand the dialectical relations between forces of conflict, coercion, and disruption at one level of organization, and forces of consensus, unity, and integration at another level—forces that are prerequisites and reciprocals of each other.

Conclusion

To have an adequate appreciation of organization theory, one must pay attention to the field's basic antithetical nature. We have focused on two general sources of antithesis manifested in structure-action and part-whole dialectics. The widespread existence of tensions generated by these opposing modes of analysis partly explains the ongoing theoretical debates and contradictions in organization theory. Benson's third principle of dialectical analysis, the principle of contradiction, addressed this point. He called attention to the "ruptures, inconsistencies, and incompatibilities in the fabric of social life" (Benson, 1977b). Because contradictions are pervasive in organizations, the theories that capture and reflect discrete segments of organizational life must also inevitably be contradictory and can be reconciled only dialectically.

But organization theory not only reflects organizational reality, it also produces that reality. As Albrow (1980) indicated, organization theory shares a dialectical relationship with organizational life. Like other social sciences, it helps to structure its own subject matter. By giving accounts of organizational phenomena, theory helps to give objectivity to the practices to which it refers. This reflexivity between theory and practical events is captured in a fourth and final principle of dialectical analysis formulated by Benson (1977b)—the principle of praxis, or the creative reconstruction of social arrangements on the basis of reasoned analysis.

This understanding gives an added significance to the analysis of this paper. It suggests that the interplay of organization theories is in reality a contest over the future shaping of the organizational world. In consequence, an awareness of the underlying values and biases upon which theory is constructed becomes essential. These values and biases act as assumptions, taken for granted, in the world views that guide theorizing, and they constitute paradigms that channel attention in specific directions and preclude the investigation of alternative theoretical, ideological, and practical spheres. Even when organizational theorists claim to be free from values, they invariably imply and contribute to value commitments through the construction of partial views of reality. This is why Ritzer (1980: 12) contended that "multiple paradigm sciences" like organization theory fulfill essentially political functions. The proponents of each paradigm are engaged in political efforts to gain dominance within the discipline as a means of imposing their own conceptions of reality on the practical events of social life.

Notes

1. The abbreviations Q1, Q2, Q3, and Q4 will be used throughout the paper to denote the numbered quadrants of the figure.
2. Indeed, turnover among large corporations has declined markedly throughout the twentieth century (Scherer, 1980: 54–56), probably because large corporations are in the best position to take advantage of institutional adaptations (Meyer and Rowan, 1977; J. Meyer, 1978).
3. While the corporate absorption of contingencies is a contrived adaptation of the organization to its environment, Thompson makes it clear that this adaptation is determined by technical rationality. Expansion of operations into the environment takes place in the direction of crucial contingencies and these are determined by technology and task considerations. Thus, long-linked technologies encourage expansion through vertical integration, while mediating technologies encourage geographical expansion (Thompson, 1967: 40–42). In other words, absorption of environmental elements is a defensive reaction, a way of buffering the technical core. It does not represent, for example, an attempt

to increase the organization's market dominance. That, of course, would be the kind of explanation that the voluntarism of the strategic choice view would offer in regard to this same phenomenon.

4. Despite the fact that the latter half of Aldrich's (1978) book is littered with examples that point to "non-natural" social and political aspects of the environment, these examples are not generated by, nor do they reflect, statements such as the ones quoted here that are central to his formal model of natural selection.

5. It should be recognized, though, that while we have classified the works of various authors into one view rather than another, this is not meant to imply any inflexibility of outlook on the part of those authors. Many of the authors referenced have written much more broadly and adopted a more balanced orientation than perhaps the discussion indicates. Thus, for example, we would not wish to label authors as "determinists" or as "reductionists" because of the particular analytical perspective they adopt on a particular occasion. As is well known, most authors adopt unique perspectives for specific, limited purposes and circumstances.

References

Ackoff, Russell. 1974. *Redesigning the Future.* New York: Wiley.

Albrow, Martin. 1980. "The dialectic of science and values in the study of organizations." In Graeme Salaman and Kenneth Thompson (eds.), *Control and Ideology in Organizations,* 278–296. Cambridge, MA: MIT Press.

Aldrich, Howard. 1979. *Organizations and Environments.* Englewood Cliffs, NJ: Prentice-Hall.

Aldrich, Howard, and Jeffrey Pfeffer. 1976. "Environments of organizations." In Alex Inkeles (ed.), *Annual Review of Sociology,* 11: 79–105. Palo Alto, CA: Annual Reviews, Inc.

Benson, J. Kenneth. 1975. "The interorganizational network as a political economy." *Administrative Science Quarterly,* 20: 229–249.

_____. 1977a. "Innovation and crisis in organizational analysis." *Sociological Quarterly,* 18: 3–16.

_____. 1977b. "Organizations: A dialectical view." *Administrative Science Quarterly,* 22: 1–21.

_____. 1979. "Recent theories of organizations: A dialectical critique." Address given at the Annual Meeting of the American Psychological Association, Industrial Psychology Section, New York City, September.

Bittner, Egon. 1965. "The concept of organization." *Social Research,* 32(3): 239–255.

Blau, Peter M. 1964. *Exchange and Power in Social Life.* New York: Wiley.

Blau, Peter M., and Richard Scott. 1962. *Formal Organizations.* San Francisco: Chandler.

Boulding, Kenneth E. 1978. *Ecodynamics: A New Theory of Societal Evolution.* Beverly Hills, CA: Sage.

Brock, Gerald W. 1981. *The Telecommunications Industry: The Dynamics of Market Structure.* Cambridge, MA: Harvard University Press.

Buckley, Walter. 1968. "Society as a complex adaptive system." In Walter Buckley (ed.), *Modern Systems Research for the Behavioral Scientist,* 490–513. Chicago: Aldine.

Burawoy, Michael. 1979. *Manufacturing Consent.* Chicago: University of Chicago Press.

Burrell, Gibson. 1981. "Towards a radical organization theory." Paper presented at the 41st Annual Academy of Management Meeting, San Diego.

Burrell, Gibson, and Gareth Morgan. 1979. *Sociological Paradigms and Organizational Analysis.* Exeter, NH: Heinemann.

Caves, Richard E., and Michael E. Porter. 1977. "From entry barriers to mobility barriers: Conjectural decisions and contrived deterrence to new competition." *Quarterly Journal of Economics,* 91: 241–462.

Chandler, Alfred. 1962. *Strategy and Structure.* Cambridge, MA: MIT Press.

_____. 1977. *The Visible Hand.* Cambridge, MA: Harvard University Press.

Child, John. 1972. "Organization structure, environment and performance: The role of strategic choice." *Sociology,* 6: 1–22.

Clawson, Daniel. 1980. "Class structure and the rise of bureaucracy." In David Dunkerly and Graeme Salaman (eds.), *The International Yearbook of Organization Studies,* 1–15. Boston: Routledge & Kegan Paul.

Clegg, Stewart. 1975. *Power, Rule and Domination: A Critical and Empirical Understanding of Power in Sociological Theory and Everyday Life.* Boston: Routledge & Kegan Paul.

_____. 1979. *The Theory of Power and Organization.* Boston: Routledge & Kegan Paul.

_____. 1981. "Organization and control." *Administrative Science Quarterly*, 26: 545–562.

Clegg, Stewart, and David Dunkerly. 1980. *Organization, Class and Control*. Boston: Routledge & Kegan Paul.

Cohen, Michael D., James G. March, and Johan P. Olsen. 1972. "A garbage can model of organizational choice." *Administrative Science Quarterly*, 17: 1–25.

Commons, John R. 1950. *The Economics of Collective Action*. Madison, WI: University of Wisconsin Press.

Conant, R. C., and R. W. Ashby. 1970. "Every good regulator of a system must be a model of the system." *International Journal of Systems Science*, 122: 89–97.

Cook, Karen S. 1977. "Exchange and power in networks of interorganizational relations." In J. Kenneth Benson (ed.), *Organizational Analysis: Critique and Innovation*, 64–84. Beverly Hills, CA: Sage.

Coser, Lewis A. 1956. *The Functions of Social Conflict*. New York: Free Press.

Crozier, Michel, and Erhard Friedberg. 1980. *Actors and Systems: The Politics of Collective Action*. Chicago: University of Chicago Press.

Dahl, Robert A., and Charles E. Lindblom. 1976. *Politics, Economics and Welfare*. Chicago: University of Chicago Press.

Dawe, Alan. 1970. "The two sociologies." *British Journal of Sociology*, 21: 207–218.

Driggers, Preston F. 1977. "Theoretical blockage: A strategy for the development of organization theory." In J. Kenneth Benson (ed.), *Organizational Analysis: Critique and Innovation*, 145–160. Beverly Hills, CA: Sage.

Duncan, Otis Dudley. 1964. "Social organization and the ecosystem." In Robert E. L. Faris (ed.), *Handbook of Modern Sociology*, 36–82. Chicago: Rand McNally.

Durkheim, Emile. 1933. *The Division of Labor in Society*. New York: Macmillan.

Edwards, Richard. 1979. *Contested Terrain: The Transformation of the Workplace in the Twentieth Century*. New York: Basic Books.

Emery, Fred E., and Eric L. Trist. 1973. *Towards a Social Ecology: Contextual Appreciations of the Future in the Present*. New York: Plenum.

Fayol, Henry. 1949. *General and Industrial Management*. London: Pitman.

Feldman, Martha S., and James G. March. 1981. "Information in organizations as signal and symbol." *Administrative Science Quarterly*, 26: 171–186.

Galbraith, John Kenneth. 1967. *The New Industrial State*. Boston: Houghton Mifflin.

Georglou, Petro. 1973. "The goal paradigm and notes toward a counter paradigm." *Administrative Science Quarterly*, 18: 291–310.

Goffman, Erving. 1961. *Asylums: Essays on the Social Situation of Mental Patients and Other Inmates*. New York: Doubleday.

Goldman, Paul, and Donald R. Van Houten. 1977. "Managerial strategies and the worker: A Marxist analysis of bureaucracy." In J. Kenneth Benson (ed.), *Organizational Analysis: Critique and Innovation*, 110–127. Beverly Hills, CA: Sage.

Gomberg, William. 1964. "Entrepreneurial psychology of facing conflict in organizations." In G. Fisk (ed.), *The Frontiers of Management Psychology*, 50–67. New York: Harper and Row.

Gouldner, Alvin. 1959. "Organizational analysis." In R. Merton, L. Broom, and L. Cottrell (eds.), *Sociology Today*, 400–428. New York: Harper and Row.

Gulick, Luther, and L. Urwick (eds.). 1937. *Papers on the Science of Administration*. New York: Institute of Public Administration, Columbia University.

Hannan, Michael, and John Freeman. 1977. "The population ecology of organizations." *American Journal of Sociology*, 82: 929–964.

Hawley, Amos. 1950. *Human Ecology: A Theory of Community Structure*. New York: Ronald Press.

_____. 1968 "Human ecology." In David L. Sills, (ed.), *The International Encyclopedia of the Social Sciences*, 4: 328–337. New York: Crowell-Collier and Macmillan.

Howton, F. William. 1969. *Functionaries*. Chicago: Quadrangle Books.

Keeley, Michael. 1980. "Organizational analogy: A comparison of organismic and social contract models." *Administrative Science Quarterly*, 25: 337–362.

Kimberly, John R. 1980. "The life cycle analogy and the study of organizations: Introduction." In John R. Kimberly and Robert H. Miles (eds.), *The Organizational Life Cycle, Issues in the Creation. Transformation, and Decline of Organizations*. San Francisco: Jossey-Bass.

Lawrence, Paul R. 1981. "The Harvard Organization and Environment Research Program." In Andrew H. Van de Ven and William Joyce (eds.), *Perspectives on Organization Design and Behavior,* 311–337. New York: Wiley Interscience.

Lawrence, Paul R., and Jay Lorsch. 1967. *Organization and Environment.* Cambridge, MA: Harvard University Press.

Levine, S., and Paul E. White. 1961. "Exchange as a conceptual framework for the study of interorganizational relationships." *Administrative Science Quarterly,* 5: 583–601.

Lindblom, Charles E. 1965. *The Intelligence of Democracy.* New York: Free Press.

Lorange, Peter. 1980. *Corporate Planning: An Executive Viewpoint.* Englewood Cliffs, NJ: Prentice-Hall.

March, James G. 1962. "The business firm as a political coalition." *Journal of Politics,* 24: 662–678.

_____. 1981 "Decisions in organizations and theories of choice." In Andrew Van de Ven and William F. Joyce (eds.), *Perspectives on Organization Design and Behavior,* 205–244. New York: Wiley Interscience.

March, James G., and Johan P. Olsen. 1976. *Ambiguity and Choice in Organizations.* Bergen, Norway: Universitetsforlaget.

Marglin, Steven A. 1974. "What do bosses do?—The origins and functions of hierarchy in capitalist production." *Review of Radical Political Economics,* 6: 60–112.

McKelvey, Bill. 1979. "Comment on the biological analog in organizational science, on the occasion of Van de Ven's review of Aldrich." *Administrative Science Quarterly,* 24: 488–493.

Merton, Robert K. 1940. "Bureaucratic structure and personality." *Social Forces,* 18: 560–568.

Metcalfe, J. L. 1974. "Systems models, economic models and the causal texture of organizational environments: An approach to macro-organization theory." *Human Relations,* 27: 639–663.

Meyer, John W. 1978. "Strategies for further research: Varieties of environmental variation." In Marshall W. Meyer (ed.), *Environments and Organizations,* 352–368. San Francisco: Jossey-Bass.

Meyer, John W., and Brian Rowan. 1977. "Institutionalized organizations: Formal structure as myth and ceremony." *American Journal of Sociology,* 83: 340–363.

Meyer, Marshall (ed.). 1978. *Environments and Organizations.* San Francisco: Jossey-Bass.

Meyer, Marshall, and M. Craig Brown. 1977. "The process of bureaucratization." *American Journal of Sociology,* 83: 364–385.

Michael, Donald. 1973. *On Learning to Plan—Planning to Learn.* San Francisco: Jossey-Bass.

Morgan, Gareth. 1980. "Paradigms, metaphors, and puzzle solving in organization theory." *Administrative Science Quarterly,* 25: 605–622.

Olson, Mancur, Jr. 1965. *The Logic of Collective Action.* Cambridge, MA: Harvard University Press.

Parsons, Talcott. 1961. "Some considerations on the theory of social change." *Rural Sociology,* 26: 219–239.

Pennings, Johannes M. 1980. "Environmental influences on the creation process." In John R. Kimberly and Robert H. Miles (eds.), *The Organizational Life Cycle: Issues in the Creation, Transformation, and Decline of Organizations,* 134–163. San Francisco: Jossey-Bass.

Perrow, Charles. 1979. *Complex Organizations: A Critical Essay,* 2d ed. Glenview, IL: Scott, Foresman.

_____. 1980. " 'Zoo story' or 'life in the organizational sandpit.' " In Graeme Salaman and Kenneth Thompson (eds.), *Control and Ideology in Organizations,* 259–277. Cambridge, MA: MIT Press.

_____. 1981. "Markets, hierarchies and hegemony." In Andrew H. Van de Ven and William Joyce (eds.), *Perspectives on Organization Design and Behavior,* 371–386. New York: Wiley Interscience.

Pfeffer, Jeffrey, and Gerald R. Salancik. 1978. *The External Control of Organizations: A Resource Dependence Perspective.* New York: Harper and Row.

Poggi, Gianfranco. 1965. "A main theme of contemporary sociological analysis: Its achievements and limitations." *British Journal of Sociology,* 16: 283–294.

Porter, Michael E. 1981. "The contributions of industrial organization to strategic management." *Academy of Management Review,* 6: 609–620.

Prosser, W. L. 1971. *Law of Torts,* 4th ed. St. Paul, MN: West Publishing.

Rank, Otto. 1941. *Beyond Psychology.* New York: Dover.

Ritzer, George. 1980. *Sociology: A Multiple Paradigm Science,* rev. ed. Boston: Allyn and Bacon.

Roethlisberger, F. J., and William J. Dickson. 1939. *Management and the Worker.* Cambridge, MA: Harvard University Press.

Rumelt, Richard P. 1979. "Strategic fit and the organization-environment debate." Paper presented at the Annual Meeting of the Western Regional Academy of Management, Portland, OR.

Salaman, Graeme. 1978. "Towards a sociology of organizational structure." *The Sociological Review,* 519–553.

Salop, S. C. 1979. "Strategic entry deterrence." *American Economic Review,* 69: 335–338.

Scherer, F. M. 1980. *Industrial Market Structure and Economic Performance.* Chicago: Rand McNally.

Schon, Donald. 1971. *Beyond the Stable State.* New York: Basic Books.

Selznick, Philip. 1957. *Leadership in Administration.* Evanston, IL: Row, Peterson.

Silverman, David. 1970. *The Theory of Organizations.* Exeter, NH: Heinemann.

Simon, Herbert A. 1976. *Administrative Behavior,* 3d ed. New York: Free Press.

Smith, Adam. 1937. *Wealth of Nations.* New York: Modern Library.

Starbuck, William H. 1965. "Organizational growth and development." In James G. March (ed.), *Handbook of Organizations,* 451–522. New York: Rand McNally.

_____. 1968. "Organizational metamorphosis." In R. W. Millman and M. P. Hottenstein (eds.), *Promising Research Directions,* 113–122. Atlanta, GA: Academy of Management.

Stinchcombe, Arthur L. 1965. "Social structure and organization." In James G. March (ed.), *Handbook of Organizations,* 142–193. Chicago: Rand McNally.

Stone, Katherine. 1974. "The origins of job structures in the steel industry." *Review of Radical Political Economics,* 6: 60–112.

Strauss, Anselm, Leonard Schatzman, Danuta Erlich, Rue Bucher, and Melvin Sabshin. 1963. "The hospital and its negotiated order." In Eliot Friedson (ed.), *The Hospital in Modern Society,* 147–169. New York: Free Press.

Thompson, James D. 1967. *Organizations in Action.* New York: McGraw-Hill.

Thompson, James D., and William McEwen. 1958. "Organizational goals and environment: Goal setting as an interaction process." *American Sociological Review,* 23: 23–31.

Trist, Eric. 1979. "Referent organizations and the development of interorganizational domains." Paper presented as Distinguished Lecture, Organization and Management Theory Division, 39th Annual Convention, Academy of Management, Atlanta.

Useem, Michael. 1982. "Classwide rationality in the politics of managers and directors of large corporations in the United States and Great Britain." *Administrative Science Quarterly,* 27: 199–226.

Van de Ven, Andrew H. 1980. "Problem solving, planning and innovation: Part II, Speculations for theory and practice." *Human Relations,* 33 (11): 757–779.

Van de Ven, Andrew H., and W. Graham Astley. 1981. "Mapping the field to create a dynamic perspective on organization design and behavior." In Andrew H. Van de Ven and William F. Joyce (eds.), *Perspectives on Organization Design and Behavior,* 427–468. New York: Wiley Interscience.

Van de Ven, Andrew H., D. Emmett, and R. Koenig, Jr. 1974. "Frameworks for interorganizational analysis." *Organization and Administrative Sciences Journal,* 5: 113–129.

Van de Ven, Andrew H., and Edward Freeman. 1983. "Three R's of administrative behavior: Rational, random and reasonable." Unpublished manuscript, School of Management, University of Minnesota.

Vickers, Sir Geoffrey. 1965. *The Art of Judgment.* New York: Basic Books.

Warren, Roland, Stephen Rose, and Ann Bergunder. 1974. *The Structure of Urban Reform.* Lexington, MA: D. C. Heath.

Weeks, David R. 1973. "Organization theory—Some themes and distinctions." In Graeme Salaman and Kenneth Thompson (eds.), *People and Organizations,* 375–395. London: Longmans.

Weick, Karl E. 1976. "Educational organizations as loosely coupled systems." *Administrative Science Quarterly,* 21: 1–19.

_____. 1979 *The Social Psychology of Organizing,* 2d ed. Reading, MA: Addison-Wesley.

Williamson, Oliver E. 1975. *Markets and Hierarchies.* New York: Free Press.

Wilson, James Q. 1973. *Political Organization.* New York: Basic Books.

Woodward, Joan. 1965. *Industrial Organization: Theory and Practice.* London: Oxford University Press.

The Bases and Use of Power in Organizational Decision Making: The Case of a University

Gerald R. Salancik and Jeffrey Pfeffer

The effects of subunit power on organizational decision making and the bases of subunit power are examined in a large midwestern state university. It is hypothesized that subunits acquire power to the extent that they provide resources critical to the organization and that power affects resource allocations within organizations in so far as the resource is critical to the subunits and scarce within the organization. Departmental power is found to be most highly correlated with the department's ability to obtain outside grants and contracts, with national prestige and the relative size of the graduate program following closely in importance. Power is used most in the allocation of graduate university fellowships, the most critical and scarce resource, and is unrelated to the allocation of summer faculty fellowships, the least critical and scarce resource.

Power in social systems may be vertical or horizontal. It may also be interpersonal or involve relations between organizational units. Social science research has been dominated historically with a concern for vertical interpersonal power—the influence of one person over another, usually in a superior-subordinate relationship (Cartwright, 1959; French and Raven, 1968; Leavitt, 1965; Tannenbaum, 1968). Milburn (1972) criticized this emphasis on vertical power in a review of behavioral science contributions to the literature on conflict and power and Perrow (1970) criticized the emphasis on interpersonal power, noting that this preoccupation has created a lack of attention to the important issue of power differences among subunits in organizations.

This article reports a study of the bases and use of power in decisions concerning resource allocations in a large American university. The focus is on subunit horizontal power differences, the factors which lead to those differences, and on the conditions under which power is used to affect the resource allocation process. Horizontal power is the use of influence among coacting peers to obtain benefits for themselves. It is an important mechanism used within and between organizations in allocating resources.

It has been argued that subunit power is an important determinant of budget allocations within organizations (Pfeffer and Salancik, 1974). An examination of the use and determination of organizational power is made here in detail. It is hypothesized that power is used in organizations to influence decisions concerning the allocation of resources which are critical to the subunit using the power and scarce within the organization. Further, it is argued that subunits will acquire power in the organization to the extent they contribute critical resources, including knowledge, to the organization; in return, other participants in the organization will respond to the demands of a subunit as some function of its power. In brief, a subunit instrumental in obtaining critical resources for the organization is in a better position to obtain the critical and scarce resources of the organization.

Background

In this examination of power in organizations, the organization is viewed as a coalition, as suggested by Cyert and March (1963; March, 1962). Simon's (1959) criticism of economic rationality as an explanation of decision making provided the foundation for this conceptualization. Simon, Cyert, and March explicitly rejected the notion that organizations operate as if they were individuals, resolving conflicts with the use of economic incentives to finally create an ordering of preferences that is shared by all organizational participants. Rather, the coalitional view of organizations emphasizes the differences in objectives and preferences of subunits and participants and seeks to describe the process by which conflicting preferences and beliefs are resolved. Thompson and Tuden (1959) argued that computational, bureaucratic forms of decision making could be employed only when there was agreement both about goals and about the causal connections between actions and the results of those actions. When there are differences and uncertainties about the appropriateness of actions, judgment and compromise become necessary to reach a decision.

The question of whose preferences and whose opinions are to prevail raises the possibility that subunit power may partially determine decisions. When there is disagreement about priorities and disagreement about the consequences of possible actions, decisions cannot be rationalized. Wildavsky speaks to this point in discussing budget decisions:

> The crucial aspect of budgeting is whose preferences are to prevail in disputes about which activities are to be carried on and to what degree, in the light of limited resources. The problem is not only "How shall budgetary benefits be maximized?" as if it made no difference who received them, but also "Who shall receive budgetary benefits and how much?" [1961: 184]

Political decision making is not limited to governmental budget disputes. Stagner (1969) reported that business executives said that the decisions of their organizations were frequently determined by considerations of power rather than what action was optimal for the total organization. Baldridge (1971) argued that a coalition model of decision making more accurately described decision making at New York University than either a bureaucratic or collegial model. The coalition model developed by Baldridge emphasizes power and conflict and de-emphasizes maximization and the use of bureaucratic, universal rules and procedures.

Organizations tend to operate as coalitions and subunit power affects decisions not because organizational participants are necessarily intentionally political, prone to conflict, or interested in self-aggrandizement. Rather, nonbureaucratic decision mechanisms are required to resolve differences in preferences and beliefs about what actions will produce what outcomes. Even the most objective indicators are open to different interpretation. When organizational participants derive different meanings from the same set of details, no bureaucratic decision procedures will unambiguously decide the issue. As Wildavsky noted, it is not just whether or not to do more or better, but who shall receive the benefits.

Bases of Subunit Power

Perrow (1970) suggested that despite protestations to the contrary, not all organizational subunits were equally influential within the organization. The question then arises as to what distinguishes some organizational subunits such that they become more powerful than others. Several answers have been provided in the literature. Crozier (1964), in a study of a French factory, noted that power accrued to the plant's maintenance engineers because they possessed the knowledge relevant to the repair of the equipment, the breakdown of which was the only remaining area of uncertainty affecting the operations of the plant. From this finding, Crozier has argued that uncertainty critical to the organization's functioning determines the distribution of power across organizational subunits. Thompson (1967) proposed a similar hypothesis by suggesting that power is held by those subunits that can cope with critical organizational contingencies. Perrow (1970), surveying persons in 12 industrial firms about the relative power of departments, argued that "the most critical function tends to have the most power" (1970: 66). He found that the marketing departments were consistently perceived as more powerful and suggested that this was because of the position of marketing in reducing the organization's most critical area of uncertainty.

Hickson *et al.* (1971) developed a theory of relative subunit power also based on the idea of coping with critical contingencies. Their model hypothesized that power was a function of (a) the ability to cope with organizational uncertainty, (b) the substitutability of subunits in their capacity to cope with uncertainty; and (c) the centrality of the subunit in the organization's workflow, a measure of the criticality or importance of the uncertainty to the organization. Hickson and his colleagues (1972) attempted to test their theory in a study of five breweries and one container company in Canada. They found that measures of perceived subunit power were correlated with measures suggested by their theory (Hinings *et al.*, 1974).

Critical organizational contingencies can arise either within the organization (Crozier, 1964) or from its environment. One persistent and critical area of organizational uncertainty for universities, and for other organizations as well, is the provision of resources required for continued operations. Organizations as open social systems depend on a cycle of resource acquisition, throughout, and output for their survival. Resource acquisition is so important and fundamental that Yuchtman and Seashore (1967) have suggested it as a measure of organizational effectiveness.

Organizational subunits may contribute resources to the organization that are of lesser or greater importance and may be more or less successful than other subunits in these pursuits. It was hypothesized in this study that subunits will possess relatively more power to the extent they provide resources for the organization and to the extent that the resources provided are critical, important, or valued by the organization. Ensuring an adequate flow of resources into the organization deals with one kind of uncertainty and, consequently, this hypothesis is a specific example of the general proposition. One advantage of this specific empirical referent is that it is more easily and unambiguously measured than the more generalized concept of uncertainty. By being less inclusive, however, it may account for less of the critical and observed variance in certain instances. If the acquisition of important resources for the organization is a source of subunit power, it is likely to be a more important source of power to the extent that the resource acquisition process itself becomes increasingly uncertain and problematic for the organization.

Data and Methods

The examination of the sources and use of power in organizational decision making uses data from the University of Illinois at Urbana-Champaign. This is a large state university which had 34,000 students in 1972, including 8,000 graduate students. Many of its departments have achieved national prominence (Roose and Andersen, 1970) and it is a major center for federally funded research projects.

Within the university, 29 departments or subunits were studied. The departments are listed in Table 1. These departments cover several, but not all, of the colleges. Because one department chairman chose not to participate in the study, the number of data points in any given analysis varies from 29 to 28, depending upon whether the analysis involves interview data or not. This slight variation in sample size has virtually no effect on any statistical tests, nor on the substantive conclusions reached.

To test the hypothesis that variations in departmental power are explained by variations in the extent to which departments provide scarce and important resources for the university, data were required on (a) the dependent variable, subunit power, and (b) the independent variable, the extent to which the subunit provides resources to the organization and the importance of the resources provided.

Measurement of Subunit Power

Social power is a concept with more intuitive appeal than empirical precision. March (1966), among others, has questioned its usefulness, particularly because of measurement difficulties. For this reason, particular care was taken to develop an adequate measure of subunit power. This involved developing multiple measures of the concept, seeing if the measures correlated as expected with hypothesized outcomes of power, and checking whether the measures correlated with other attributes of the subunits.

The first procedure for measuring subunit power was to interview each of the department heads, or their close assistants, and ask for their rating of the power of each of the subunits, including their own, on a 7-point scale ranging from a great deal to very little power. A column for a don't know response was also included. Respondents were told that power was the ability of the department to affect decisions so that they conformed more closely to what the department wanted. The departments were listed in random order. This interview-based measure of power corresponds to the measure used by Perrow (1970) in his study of power in industrial firms.

The second measure of subunit power was the subunit's representation on important university committees. As Cyert and March (1963) have noted, functions are allocated in organizations and this allocation contains information about the relative importance and power of various persons and functions. Because some of the committees had actual impact on resource allocation within the university, membership on the committee would provide the subunit with some power. Thus, committee membership may be both a source of power or an outcropping indicating the relative influence of organizational subunits or some combination thereof. Subunit representation on important university committees during the period 1958–1970 was thus the second indicator of subunit power. The committees employed in the analysis are listed in Table 1.

TABLE 1

Departments and University Committees Included in the Study

Departments	Committees
Economics	Nonrecurring Appropriations
History	Building Program
Psychology	University Research Board
Anthropology	Budget
Political Science	Student Affairs
Sociology	Senate Coordinating Council
Electrical Engineering	Educational Policy
Mechanical Engineering	
Physics	Executive committees of:
Chemistry	College of Liberal Arts and Sciences
Mathematics	College of Commerce and Business Administration
Civil Engineering	College of Engineering
Aeronautical and Astronautical Engineering	College of Agriculture
Geology	College of Physical Education
Computer Science	College of Fine and Applied Arts
Classics	
English	
Spanish and Italian	
French	
Germanic	
Dairy Science	
Home Economics	
Accounting	
Finance	
Architecture and Fine Arts	
Health Education	
Business Administration	
Animal Science	
Geography	

As reported elsewhere (Pfeffer and Salancik, 1974), these measures of subunit power are valid. The interview-based measure of power with don't know responses omitted is highly correlated with the interview-based measure of power with don't know responses coded to indicate very little power ($r=.96, p < .001$). More important, the interview-based measure of power is significantly correlated with total subunit membership on all committees ($r=.61, p < .001$), with membership on the University Research Board, probably the most influential committee ($r=.62, p < .001$), with membership on the respective college executive committees ($r=.60, p < .001$), and with membership on the budget committee ($r=.46, p < .01$). Thus, the interview-based measure of power and the committee-representation measures are correlated, indicating some convergent validity.

One possibility is that all the measures of subunit power are spuriously correlated with each other because they are all indicators of subunit size. This does not appear to be the case, however. Two measures of subunit size can be considered: the number of student-hours—instructional units—taught and the number of full-time equivalent teaching faculty. The proportion of total instructional units taught by the department is correlated $r=.46$ ($p < .01$) with proportional membership on the Research Board, $r=.30$ ($p < .10$) with the interview-based measure of power, and $r=.16$ (not significant) with the proportional membership on all committees. The correlations of the proportion of full-time equivalent teaching faculty are .56 ($p < .001$) with membership on the Research Board, .31 ($p < .10$) with membership on all committees, and .32 ($p < .10$) with the interview-based measure of power. While there are significant correlations with some measures of subunit size, it is also the case that the correlations are generally smaller than the intercorrelations among the power measures themselves, providing some evidence for the discriminant validity of the measures.

Finally, both measures of subunit power are significantly correlated with the budget allocations received by subunits, even when indicators of subunit size are statistically controlled (Pfeffer and Salancik, 1974). Since power should affect resource allocation and the measures of power do indicate this effect, even when competing explanations for allocations are statistically controlled, it can be said that the measures achieve a reasonable degree of construct validity as well.

Measurement of Resource Importance

Two ways of assessing the importance of resources to the total organization were employed. First, the department heads were asked to rank six dimensions in order of importance in terms of the effect each should have in allocating budgets to departments. The six bases for allocating the budget, ranked from 1 for the most important to 6 for the least important, were (1) the number of graduate students, (2) the number of undergraduate students, (3) national rank or prestige of the department, as assessed, for example, by the American Council on Education, (4) administrative and service contributions to the university, (5) amount of outside grants and contracts, and (6) public visibility of the department. The average ranking of each dimension was taken to be the consensual opinion concerning the importance of that dimension as a preferred basis of resource allocation within the university.

The respondents were also asked directly to assess the importance of resources departments provided to the total university. The following question was asked:

> Departments do not just get resources from the university, they also provide resources for the university. Below we list 7 resources which departments bring into the university in 1 way or another. We would like to get an idea as to how important these resources are to the university as a whole. Please rank from 1 (most important) to 7 (least important) the following for their importance to the overall operation of the university.

The resources, ranked in order of importance as assessed by this question, were (1) number of graduate students, (2) national rank or prestige of the department, (3) number of undergraduate students, (4) amount of outside grants or contracts, (5) public visibility of the department, (6) administrative and service contributions to the university, and (7) business and professional contacts.

Measurement of Subunit's Contribution

Two methods were used to assess the extent to which the subunit actually contributed a particular resource to the organization. First, for some resources, historical measures were available. From archival records, the proportion of total grants and contracts a particular department received—restricted funds in the budget categories—and the proportion of undergraduate and graduate students taught were obtained for the 13-year period, 1958–1970. For the 17 departments in which rankings were available, data on national prestige were obtained from the studies conducted by the American Council on Education (Cartter, 1966; Roose and Andersen, 1970).

Second, each department head interviewed was asked to assess the extent to which his department contributed each of the seven resources compared to other departments in the university. The scale used for this question was a 5-point rating scale, ranging from 1 for much more than average to 5 for much less than average.

For those four resources which are measured both from the interviews and from archival data, the extent to which the department heads accurately perceived their relative standing in terms of their provision of each resource can be assessed. The correlations between the proportion of each resource accounted for by a given department and the department heads' ratings of their relative position for that resource were .66 ($p < .001$) for the graduate instructional units taught, .70 ($p < .001$) for outside grants and contracts, .67 ($p < .001$) for national prestige, and .24 ($p < .15$) for the proportion of undergraduate instructional units taught. The department heads knew their relative position compared to other departments least accurately for undergraduate teaching, which they had rated as the second most important basis for allocating the budget.

Results

Table 2 presents the average responses to the question asking how the budget should be allocated and the responses to the question asking the importance of various resources the departments bring into the organization. The department heads' most preferred basis of budget allocation was the number of graduate students, with the number of undergraduate students being second, and the department's national reputation third. Considering the rankings of the importance of resources provided to the university, graduate students were the most important, with national prestige second, and undergraduate students third. The department's acquisition of outside grants and contracts ranked fifth as a desired determinant of budget allocation and fourth in terms of the importance of the resource to the university.

These rankings place surprisingly low emphasis on the importance of obtaining outside funds. While graduate students are important in a graduate-oriented university such as Illinois, much of the support for training graduate students is obtained from outside research grants. Indeed, 40 percent of the university's budget was in the form of grants and contracts for research. These funds, through the provision of overhead dollars, are a major source of discretionary resources providing organizational slack for the university. This would suggest that outside funding should be the most

TABLE 2

**Average Rankings of Criteria as a Preferred Basis for Allocating the Budget
and for Importance of a Resource to the University**

Criteria and Resources	Average Preference Rank	Average Importance Rank
Number of graduate students	2.12	2.22
Number of undergraduate students	2.44	2.94
National rank or prestige of the department	2.97	2.85
Amount of outside grants and contracts	4.33	3.88
Public visibility of departments	4.92	4.42
Administrative and service contributions to the university	4.18	5.68
Business and professional contacts	*	5.95

* This criteria or resource was not included in the preference measure.

important resource which departments provide and should be highly related to subunit power within the organization.

Determinants of Subunit Power

The three measures of subunit power, the interview-based measure, the membership on the University Research Board, and representation on all the committees considered were used as dependent variables to measure power.

In Table 3 correlations between the three indicators of subunit power and objective measures assessing possible bases for this power are displayed. Except for the national rank of the department, the number of observations is 28. For national rank, only the 17 departments covered by the American Council on Education were used. For all three indicators of subunit power, the best predictor was the proportion of faculty supported by restricted funds. Contrary to the results obtained from the interviews, the most important determinant of subunit power was the subunit's provision of outside funds to the organization. Closely following outside funds as a predictor of subunit power was the relative proportion of graduate students, with that followed closely by the department's national rank. Less important as a determinant of subunit power was the relative proportion of undergraduates taught by the department.

Much as the common folklore has it, graduate education and research were empirically found to be the best predictors of subunit power within the organization. Undergraduate instruction holds a distinctly secondary position.

The various measures of graduate education, national rank, and amount of outside funding are themselves intercorrelated. Two sets of multiple regressions were therefore obtained, one for the set of 28 departments and the other for the set of 17 ranked departments, to assess more precisely the relative contribution of each variable to predicting subunit power. These results are displayed in Table 4. The coefficients are the standardized regression coefficients (beta) and the numbers in parentheses are the t-values of the respective regression coefficients.

TABLE 3

Correlations between Measures of Subunit Power and Indicators of Determinants of Subunit Power

Determinants of Subunit Power	Representation on the University Research Board	Interview-based Measure of Power	Representation on All Committees
Proportion of restricted funds received	.62*	.72*	.36***
Proportion of faculty supported by restricted funds	.77*	.76*	.44**
Number of graduate students	.66*	.62*	.38***
Number of advanced graduate student instructional units	.66*	.56*	.26****
National rank in 1969, adjusted for number of contending departments	.47	.66*	.43**
Number of undergraduate instructional units taught	.38***	.14	.03
Total instructional units	.46**	.30***	.16

*p < .001.

**p < .01.

***p < .05.

****p < .10.

The results for the three measures of power, with national rank included or excluded from the equation, all indicate that outside funding was the best predictor of subunit power. In all the regressions, faculty funded by restricted funds—grants and contracts—is statistically significant and, in all equations, the beta weight for this variable is larger than for the other explanatory factors.

In addition to relating the measures of subunit power to the objective measures of the subunit's provision of resources, the measures of power can also be related to the subunit's own assessment of its relative standing in the university with respect to seven resources. Department heads were asked to assess how much of a given resource his department contributed compared with other departments within the university. Table 5 presents the correlations between the measures of subunit power and the extent to which the heads estimated their departments provided each of the seven resources.

TABLE 4

Regression Equations Explaining Variations in Subunit Power

Dependent Variable	Constant	Proportion of Graduate Instructional Units Taught	Proportion of Total FTE Faculty Supported by Restricted Funds	National Rank	r^2
		N = 29			
Interview measure of power	4.34	.222 (1.48)	.641 (4.29)		.61
Membership on University Research Board	−.008	.348 (2.61)	.594 (4.45)		.70
Representation on all committees	.027	.048 (.22)	.416 (1.95)		.19
		N = 17			
Membership on University Research Board	−.042	.247 (1.53)	.867 (4.80)	.234 (1.38)	.79
Interview measure of power	3.94	.203 (1.03)	.562 (2.56)	−.179 (.862)	.71
Representation on all committees	.022	−.069 (.258)	.706 (2.36)	−.006 (.002)	.38

TABLE 5

Correlations between Measures of Subunit Power and Department Head's Assessment of Subunit's Relative Contribution of Resources

Variables	Representation on the University Research Board	Interview-based Measure of Power	Representation on All Committees
Number of graduate students	.37***	.48**	.07
Outside grants and contracts	.44**	.80*	.39****
Undergraduate students	.26****	.31***	.01
National prestige	.38***	.33***	.15
Public image and visibility	.14	.19	.38***
Administrative expertise	.24	.37***	.08
Business and professional contacts	.24	.36***	.29****

*p < .001.
**p < .01.
***p < .05.
****p < .10.

As with the preceding analyses, the most highly correlated resource for all three measures of subunit power was the department's relative standing in the university in terms of its bringing in grants and contracts. This tended to be closely followed by the number of graduate students and the department's national prestige. Because of the consistency in the results over the two types of analysis, the acquisition of outside funds can more confidently be attributed as the major source of subunit power.

Analysis of Favored Bases of Budget Allocation

Department heads, on the average, judged graduate students and national prestige to be more important resources than outside grants and contracts. Empirical analysis indicated, however, that outside research funds were the best predictor of subunit power. This discrepancy in the findings suggests that either (1) the hypothesis is incorrect and subunit power is not related to the subunit's relative contribution of important resources or (2) the averaged assessments of the department heads provided biased or incorrect information concerning the relative importance of various resources to the total organization.

It is possible that the department head's judgments concerning the preferred bases of budget allocation and the importance of various resources provided to the total organization reflect their desire to use criteria which favor their own departments. One use of organizational power may be to influence the criteria used in organizational decision making. If this is the case, the procedure employed of averaging all department heads would overemphasize factors favored by subunits with lower power in the organization.

There is support in the data for the idea that when asked what the criteria for budget allocations should be respondents replied with criteria that tended to favor the relative position of their own organizational subunit. The correlation between the proportion of restricted funds obtained and the ranking of grants and contracts as a preferred basis for budget allocation was .27 ($p < .10$), while the correlation with the department head's assessment of his department's obtaining grants and contracts was .52 ($p < .005$). To the extent the department head perceived a comparative advantage in terms of his department's obtaining grants and contracts and to the extent his department actually did receive more restricted funds, the department head tended to favor grants and contracts as a basis of budget allocation.

Preferences for basing budget allocation on the number of undergraduate students was correlated .34 ($p < .05$) with the proportion of total undergraduate instructional units taught by the department and was correlated .24 ($p < .15$) with the department head's assessment of his department's position in terms of the relative number of students taught. Preferences for basing budget allocations on the national rank of the department were correlated .43 ($p < .05$) with the national rank of the department in 1969, but were correlated only .13 with the department head's assessment of his department's standing in the university in terms of national prestige. Preferences for basing budget allocations on graduate students were unrelated to the department's relative position in this respect. This result may have occurred because the graduate emphasis in the university is so pervasive and generally accepted that it is favored by persons regardless of how well their department ranks on this particular criterion.

The data indicate that departments with a comparative advantage in a particular area favored basing budget allocations more on this criterion. Given the bias to overvalue those resources which your department possesses and the fact that the ability to support graduate students is, in part, affected by the ability to obtain outside research support, it is not as surprising that the department's provision of outside funds has become an important predictor of subunit power within the university.

The Use of Power in Organizations

In considering the conditions under which power will be used in the allocation of resources within organizations, it is assumed that organizational subunits on the same horizontal level in the organizational hierarchy possess differential power within the organization. Defining power as potential influence (Lewin, 1951), the study focuses on the allocation of resources within the organization and addresses the issue of under what circumstances subunits will attempt to influence the allocation of these resources for their benefit.

It is hypothesized that power is used in the allocation of an organizational resource to the extent that the resource is scarce within the organization.

Hypothesis 1. The scarcer the resource, the more power is used to allocate it among subunits.

In the limiting case of no scarcity, every subunit can obtain all of the resource it desires, which presumably would be based on perceptions of its needs, as evidenced by objectively based criteria. As long as there is no scarcity, there is no problem of resource allocation and no reason for subunits to use their differential influence within the organization. With increasing scarcity, resource allocation becomes problematic; every subunit will vie for resources according to its needs and demands, but not all will be able to completely satisfy their demands. If a subunit is to obtain resources, it must overcome the pressures of other subunits for the same contested resource. In short, the subunit must have power to affect the outcome greater than the power of other subunits. A testable implication of the first hypothesis appears in the following revised version:

Hypothesis 1a. The more scarce an organizational resource becomes, the less objective criteria will be used in its allocation and the more power will be used. The amount of variance explained by objective criteria in resource allocation will be an inverse function of the scarcity of the resource.

While resource allocation becomes problematic only when resources are scarce, resource allocation is a problem only when the subunit wants the resource. It is therefore argued that

Hypothesis 2. The more critical the resource for the survival or effective operation of an organizational subunit, the more the subunit will make attempts to acquire it.

A corollary of this hypothesis is that the more critical a resource becomes to the effective operation of an organizational subunit, the more the subunit will use its power to acquire it; the less critical, the less power will be used in allocating the resource.

The use of power has costs; it requires resources to attempt to influence organizational decisions. Decisions to use power should depend, therefore, on the criticality of the resource to the subunit. It is unlikely that a subunit will attempt to use its power to acquire an unimportant, or less critical, resource. From the preceding arguments, two additional hypotheses can be derived,

Hypothesis 3. For a resource critical to most subunits, the scarcer it becomes, the more power will be used as the basis of its allocation in the organization.

Since the resource is critical or important, subunits will desire to acquire it. As this critical resource becomes more and more scarce, the total requirements of all subunits will be less satisfied and subunits will have to contend with each other to a greater degree for the resource. It is under these conditions that power is more likely to become used as the organization's basis for resource allocation.

On the other hand, given that the use of influence has its costs and that those costs increase with scarcity, subunits would be less likely to use power to acquire scarce, noncritical resources. Therefore,

Hypothesis 4. For a noncritical resource, the scarcer it becomes, the less power will be used for its allocation.

Implicit in the description of the use of power by organizational subunits is the notion that resource allocations decisions within organizations are not constrained by either organizational or extraorganizational sanctions against the use of power. In fact, power is exercised only when there is discretion in the allocation of resources. The greater the external constraint on the decision, the less power will be used in the allocation decisions. With scarcity, the use of power becomes necessary and with criticality, it becomes desirable. Without discretion, however, there is no opportunity to use subunit power. Discretion is missing when (a) there is no resource to allocate at all and (b) when the allocation process is determined by law, strongly held norms, or by some external agency affecting the organization. If, for instance, the state legislature were to pass a law that a university's department budget must be some multiplier of its instructional units taught, there will be no opportunity to use power in the allocation of the budget. It is likely, however, that such a law would have the effect of shifting the focus of power to the acquisition of students so that budget could be acquired.

Data and Methods

Data on the allocation of graduate university fellowships, summer faculty fellowships, University Research Board grants for faculty research, and appointments to the Center for Advanced Study were obtained from archival records for the 29 departments listed in Table 1 for the period 1958–1970, except for the Center for Advanced Study which did not start its fellows program until 1962. To control for inflation and growth, allocated resources were defined proportionally. Thus, in the analyses of graduate fellowships, the departmental allocations are represented as proportions allocated to each of the 29 departments in a given year.

Graduate university fellowships are fellowships allocated to the departments by the Graduate College and are provided by the general resources of the university. Fellowship support derived from outside grants, contracts, or direct contributions to the department are not subject to university discretionary allocation and are therefore not included. The summer faculty fellowship program is one in which primarily junior faculty submit brief proposals for a study to be conducted during the summer. The university provides $900 in tax-free support. The program provides some support for research activities for faculty without outside funding during the summer and also provides summer money for faculty who either do not want or do not have the opportunity to teach in the summer session. The Center for Advanced Study is an organizational subunit that administers programs to recognize outstanding junior and senior faculty, both at the University of Illinois and at other universities. Persons may be brought in to spend their sabbatical at the Center or, most frequently, if on the campus, may be appointed to the Center for either a semester or a full year. The Center reimburses the faculty member's department for the loss of his services. Appointment to the Center is considered an honor and provides the faculty member with time to study and to do research. The University Research Board provides small internally-funded research grants to faculty on the basis of proposals received. Support is typically in the form of research assistants or computer money.

Measurement of Resource Scarcity

As part of the interviews, department heads were asked to rank seven resources in terms of how scarce they were. They were told that scarcity implies that there is not enough of the resource for every department to get all it would like and is defined by the amount of the resource available divided by the amount requested. The rankings proceed from 1 for the most scarce to 7 for the least scarce. Included in the list of seven were the four resources examined in this study and, in addition, computer money for faculty research, computer money for instructional use, and new courses.

The best measure of resource scarcity would be to have an exact measure of the amount of the resource requested and the amount available and divide the amount requested by the amount available. Unfortunately, data on requests for the resources were not available. Even it if were, it is not clear that requests that are actually made are good estimates of anything except availability. Department heads may adjust their requests according to what they expect to receive or to what they have received in the past. Davis, Dempster, and Wildavsky (1966) illustrate this with respect to the budget requests of federal agencies. If requests are determined by the expected outcome of the request, requests compared to availability is not an ideal measure of resource scarcity. The department head's judgments were used as estimates of the scarcity of the resources and it is assumed that in averaging the individual responses, an accurate ranking of relative scarcity will be obtained.

Measurement of Criticality and Subunit Power

In the same interview, the department heads were asked to rank the same seven resources in terms of their criticality, from 1 for the most critical resource to 7 for the least critical. Criticality was defined as the extent to which the resource is absolutely necessary for the effective operation of the department.

The measures of subunit power were the same as were explained above in the analysis of the determinants of subunit power and as presented in a study of budget allocations (Pfeffer and Salancik, 1974).

Objective Criteria

It has been argued that resources can be allocated based on subunit power or on more universalistic bureaucratic criteria. One possible use of power is to ensure that criteria favoring the powerful departments are employed. For this analysis of the use of power, it is necessary to also obtain indicators of objective criteria for allocating the four resources. These criteria were obtained from discussions with persons involved in the allocation decisions and represent the ones they articulated as being reasonable bases for allocation. These criteria represent quantity indicators of a department's need for a resource independent of its assessment of the criticality of the resource.

Allocations of summer faculty fellowships and appointments to the Center for Advanced Study are made to faculty members. The principal criterion listed for eligibility is that a person be a member of the faculty. Thus, an objective indicator of a department's allocation of the resource would be the number of full-time equivalent faculty in the department. If strict proportionality were used in the decision making, the proportion of fellowships and appointments would be equivalent to the proportion of the faculty. Quality, of course, is also taken into account. It is difficult to compare individuals or departments in different fields. While no perfect solution is available, the quality of the department as assessed through its ratings by the American Council on Education was employed as the indicator of quality.

Allocations of university fellowships to graduate students should be based on (a) the number of graduate students and (b) the relative quality of those students. Since there were no tests or measures available that could compare graduate students across the departments studied, the department's national ranking was used. The assumption was that more highly rated departments would attract better graduate students. In place of the actual number of graduate students, the proportion of advanced graduate instructional units taught was used. This variable, highly correlated with the number of graduate students, is slightly more highly correlated with graduate fellowship allocations. It therefore is a slightly more powerful controlling variable.

Research Board allocations for faculty research should be based on the number of persons needing such funds and their relative abilities. The departmental need for research money was represented by the proportion of total graduate units taught by the department, since need for research funds and research activity were assumed to be related to graduate education. Again, the indicator of quality is the departments' national rank in 1969 (Roose and Andersen, 1970).

Results

The average assessment of the criticality and scarcity of the four resources being examined is displayed in Table 6. The lower the number, the more critical or the more scarce the resource was

TABLE 6

Average Rankings of Criticality and Scarcity of 4 Resources

Resource	Average Criticality	Average Scarcity
University graduate fellowships	2.46	2.45
Research Board grants for faculty research	3.00	3.20
Summer faculty fellowships	5.36	4.37
Appointments to the Center for Advanced Study	5.75	3.89

thought to be. Department heads showed significant agreement about the rankings. Kendall's coefficient of concordance (Siegel, 1956) was .33 ($p < .001$) for criticality rankings and .22 ($p < .001$) for scarcity.

Table 6 suggests that the four resources perceived as most scarce on the average were also perceived as most critical. The similarity in the overall rankings, however, is not due to a confounding of the separate concepts themselves by the respondents. The correlations between the criticality and scarcity rankings based on the department head's responses were .26 ($p < .10$) for appointments to the Center for Advanced Study, .20 (n.s.) for Research Board grants for faculty research, .20 (n.s.) for university graduate fellowships, and –.07 (n.s.) for summer faculty fellowships.

One phenomenon discovered during the interviewing was that persons tended to adjust to the realities of their situation. Thus, if a department found it difficult to obtain a resource, the department head was likely to say that the resource was not critical. The point is that organizations and organizational subunits adapt to the constraints of their situations. If the subunit cannot obtain an important resource, the subunit is likely to redefine its activity, find substitutes for the resource in question, or in some other way cope with the situation it confronts. The situation of a resource being both important and difficult to obtain is not likely to be stable. Either the subunit will ensure adequate provision of the critical resource or else the subunit will alter its preferences and beliefs about resource criticality.

Use of Power in Resource Allocation

It has been hypothesized that the use of power in resource allocation will become more prominent the more scarce the resource (Hypothesis 1) and the more critical the resource (Hypothesis 2). Thus, power would be expected to be most used in the allocation of graduate fellowships, since this is the most scarce and most critical resource, and would be used least in the allocation of summer faculty fellowships. Simple correlations between the three measures of power and the proportional allocations of the four resources are presented in Table 7. All three measures of power yield the same result: power is most highly correlated with the allocation of university graduate fellowships, is next most highly correlated with the allocation of grants for faculty research, and is least highly correlated with the allocations of summer faculty fellowships. The rank ordering of the relative use of power follows perfectly the rank ordering of the relative scarcity of the resources and follows almost perfectly the rank ordering of the criticality of the resources also.

Given that resource allocations may be based on both subunit power and objective factors, a more refined analysis requires computing partial correlations between power and allocations, controlling for the objective bases of resource allocation. The criterion used in the case of appointments to the Center for Advanced Study and summer faculty fellowships is the proportion of full-time equivalent instructional faculty, while in the case of graduate fellowships and grants for faculty research, it is the proportion of advanced graduate instructional units taught by the department. These results are displayed in Table 7. The pattern of results is again generally consistent with the argument.

Finally, partial correlations can be computed controlling for both the basic factors introduced in Table 7 and for the national ranking of the department, a rough indicator of quality. These partial correlations are also displayed in Table 7. As only 17 departments in the sample represent disciplines rated by the American Council on Education, this analysis includes only these 17. Once again, it appears that power is used most to allocate graduate university fellowships and is used least to allocate summer faculty fellowships. Research Board grants for faculty research are second in terms of being allocated by power, while appointments to the Center for Advanced Study are third. Looking at either the simple correlations or either set of partial correlations, the results are the same: power is more highly correlated with the allocation of resources which are more critical and more scarce.

It has been argued that a subunit within an organization will vie for a resource to the extent that resource is critical and the subunit's probability of obtaining the resource will depend upon its power relative to other subunits also contending for the resource. This suggests a hypothesis concerning the allocation of a resource which is differentially viewed as critical by different subunits. If

TABLE 7

Correlations of Measures of Subunit Power with Allocations of 4 Resources

Resource	Measures of Power		
	Membership on Research Board	Membership on All Committees	Interview-based Measure of Power
Simple correlations			
Graduate fellowships	.90*	.44**	.58**
Research Board grants	.85*	.35***	.56**
Appointments to the Center for Advanced Study	.74*	.32***	.36***
Summer faculty fellowships	.31***	.01	.15
Partial correlations, controlling for objective criteria			
Graduate fellowships	.83*	.38***	.25****
Research Board grants	.72*	.22	.32
Appointments to the Center for Advanced Study	.57*	.10	.18
Summer faculty fellowships	−.21	−.37***	−.60*
Partial correlations, controlling for objective criteria and national ranking			
Graduate fellowships	.90*	.40****	.26
Research Board grants	.86*	.27	.32
Appointments to the Center for Advanced Study	.65**	.04	.00
Summer faculty fellowships	.04	−.41****	−.52***

* $p < .001$.

** $p < .01$.

*** $p < .05$.

**** $p < .10$.

a given resource is viewed as critical by low-power subunits and simultaneously viewed as noncritical by high-power departments, the resource allocations should be negatively related to power. This is the case in the allocation of summer faculty fellowships. Across all departments, there was a negative correlation between power and the ranking of the criticality of the resource, with a correlation of .33 ($p < .05$) between Research Board membership and ranking of criticality for the summer faculty fellowships. Because of this, power itself is negatively correlated with the allocation of this resource when objective bases of allocation are controlled. Since power has been seen to be related to the obtaining of outside funds, it is likely that faculty in high-power departments find sources of other support and have less need for these university faculty fellowships.

Another way to indicate the relative effects of the objective criteria and subunit power on allocations is to present the multiple regressions accounting for the variation in the average proportional allocation of the four resources over the 13-year period. These results, presented in Table 8, are consistent with the previously presented analyses, and indicate that the formulation is able to explain a substantial portion of the variance, particularly in the case of the more critical and more scarce resources.

Discussion

Subunit power accrues to those departments that are most instrumental in bringing in or providing resources which are highly valued by the total organization. In turn, this power enables these

TABLE 8

Regression Equations Explaining Variations in Allocation of Resources to Departments

$$GRADFEL = .006 + .624\ RESBD + .413\ GRADIU$$
$$(7.60)\qquad\quad (6.62)$$
$r^2 = .90$

$$RESEARCH\$ = .01 + .717\ RESBD + .198\ GRADIU$$
$$(5.36)\qquad\quad (1.49)$$
$r^2 = .74$

$$CAS = .003 + .437\ RESBD + .529\ FTETEACH$$
$$(3.52)\qquad\quad (4.30)$$
$r^2 = .73$

$$SUMMERFAC = -.006 - .168\ RESBD + .839\ FTETEACH$$
$$(1.08)\qquad\quad (5.37)$$
$r^2 = .57$

GRADFEL is the proportion of graduate university fellowships.
RESEARCH $ is the proportion of university-funded research dollars.
CAS is the proportion of appointments to the Center for Advanced Study.
SUMMERFAC is the proportion of summer faculty fellowships.
RESBD is the proportional membership on the University Research Board.
GRADIU is the proportion of graduate instructional units taught.
FTETEACH is the proportion of full-time equivalent teaching faculty.

Numbers in parentheses are the standard errors of the regression coefficients.

Coefficients displayed are the standardized regression coefficients.

subunits to obtain more of those scarce and critical resources allocated within the organization. Stated succinctly, power derived from acquiring resources is used to obtain more resources, which in turn can be employed to produce more power—the rich get richer. In the specific instance examined, this leads to some strange results. For example, power is most highly correlated with the allocation of graduate research fellowships, accounting for approximately 80 percent of the variance. Yet power is predicted by the acquisition of outside grants, which are often used to provide graduate support. So, those subunits with the most outside support also tend to obtain the most internal support. Instead of compensating for the differential access to outside resources, the internal resource allocation system actually exacerbates resource inequalities. This same effect holds for the Research Board's allocations of grants for faculty research.

These results have a logical foundation. It might be argued that since outside grants and contracts, with their associated overhead funds, provide discretionary resources for the organization, in order to encourage departments to obtain these outside funds, and perhaps for fairness, those subunits most responsible for acquiring these discretionary resources should receive the largest portion of them.

These results on funding are consistent in some respects with Lodahl and Gordon's (1973) findings concerning differences between physical and social sciences. These authors reported that internal allocations tended to reinforce the disparities in funding created by the differential availability of outside money. This result obtains because acquisition of outside resources tends to provide power within the organization and this power can then be used to favorably influence allocations of internal resources. Most important, however, this result suggests how external organizational factors may affect internal organizational decisions.

An intriguing empirical question is the extent to which subunit power is based on dimensions that are important to groups or organizations outside of the organization as well, such as legislators or alumni, or other organizations or groups in the organization-set (Evan, 1966). It is quite possible that in some universities, and in general in other types of organizations that may have been buffered or isolated from the environment, those contingencies or resources that come to be defined within the organization as strategic or important may not be so perceived outside of the organization. Indeed, one might hypothesize that organizations will be successful only to the extent that the bases for subunit power within the organization are functional from the point of view of the organization's dealings with its environment. By functional we mean that the important resources or contingencies as defined by the social reality within the organization are indeed those resources or contingencies which are most critical to the organization's ability to obtain resources and transact with its environment. Since organizational decisions are partially based on subunit power, then to the extent power is based on contingencies or resources that are actually not as critical, the organization is likely to make maladaptive or incorrect decisions. This is particularly true since subunits once in power are likely to take actions to maintain that power.

If the preceding reasoning is essentially correct, then explaining and analyzing organizational power systems has implications for understanding the organization's ability to respond and cope with changing environments. It is likely that organizations that are relatively more insulated, due to their source of funding or due to their monopoly position, are more likely to be social units in which subunit power is based on less important, or less externally-based criteria. One effect of the environment is in constraining and providing feedback on organizational decisions (Thompson and McEwen, 1958). Subunit power will be based on environmental contingencies or important resources only to the extent that such feedback and constraint are perceived and recognized.

These arguments can be illustrated in a hypothesis specific to universities. Universities will fare relatively better at the hands of their state legislatures of alumni to the extent that the bases for subunit power within the organization more closely correspond to the relative importance of the criteria as held by the external organizations. It is possible, in other words, that through the influence of discretionary resources, organizations can come to jeopardize other significant portions of their input.

While the empirical results presented in this article are strong, there is the question of the extent to which they are generalizable. While Illinois is probably typical of large prestigious state universities, the results would not necessarily hold for universities with less of a research orientation or perhaps for private universities. In universities without extensive research or graduate programs, it is obvious that obtaining research funds and having a large, prestigious graduate program cannot be a predictor of subunit power. Similarly, organizations may vary in the extent to which internal resource allocations are mandated by external organizations. Yet, while the specific measures might change, the importance of providing resources to the organization as a source of power is likely to be generalizable, since it is derived from the more general concept of coping with critical organizational contingencies (Thompson, 1967; Crozier, 1964; Hickson *et al.*, 1971).

An even more basic question is the extent to which these analyses of subunit power are generalizable to other types of organizations. Universities are unique in that they exhibit primarily pooled interdependence (Thompson, 1967: 54). The interdependence between what happens in the History Department and what happens in the French Department is probably minimal compared to the interdependence between marketing and production in an industrial firm. Second, it may be maintained that university organizations are more collegial and less bureaucratic than other forms and particularly differ in the extent to which authority is wielded through collegial committees rather than through a hierarchy of authority. However, Perrow (1972: 32–35) has argued that universities are more hierarchical and less collegial than is often admitted. He maintained that "any group with a division of labor, professional or not, will be hierarchically structured" (Perrow, 1972: 35).

The form of interdependence found in the organization probably affects the extent to which subunits will go in their contest for resources, but not the basic propositions concerning the conditions that may create power or cause it to be used. Even in the university, as loosely coupled as it is, most departments stop before the point at which they advocate taking all of everyone else's resources and becoming a one subunit organization. To the extent that their activities were more interdependent, they would face additional internal constraints in terms of their contest for power and resources. While universities may be somewhat different from organizational forms, this is a difference in degree, rather than of form, and thus the basic arguments would still hold.

At the same time, however, too much cannot be claimed for this single study of a single institution. It is clear that the propositions presented were not disconfirmed when confronted with the data and some competing explanations and, further, the propositions are reasonably grounded in the literature on organizations. With the paucity of empirical studies of resource allocation within organizations noted by Pondy (1970), however, the propositions and their generalizability must await additional empirical work. Indeed, as important as the substantive results is the fact that this study has indicated how unobtrusive archival data can be used to assess and empirically examine power and resource allocation in social systems.

References

Baldridge, J. Victor. 1971. *Power and Conflict in the University.* New York: Wiley.

Cartter, Allan M. 1966. An Assessment of Quality in Graduate Education. Washington, D.C.: American Council on Education.

Cartwright, Dorwin. 1959. "A field theoretical conception of power." In Dorwin Cartwright (ed.), *Studies in Social Power,* 183–220. Ann Arbor, Mich.: Institute for Social Research.

Crozier, Michel. 1964. *The Bureaucratic Phenomenon.* Chicago: University of Chicago Press.

Cyert, Richard M., and James G. March. 1963. *A Behavioral Theory of the Firm.* Englewood Cliffs, N.J.: Prentice-Hall.

Davis, Otto A., M. A. H. Dempster, and Aaron Wildavsky. 1966. "A theory of the budgetary process." *American Political Science Review,* 60: 529–547.

Evan, William M. 1966. "The organization set: toward a theory of interorganizational relations." In James D. Thompson (ed.), *Approaches to Organizational Design,* 173–191. Pittsburgh: University of Pittsburgh Press.

French, John R. P., Jr., and Bertram Raven. 1968. "The bases of social power." In Dorwin Cartwright and Alvin Zander (eds.), *Group Dynamics,* 259–269. New York: Harper and Row.

Hickson, D. J., C. R. Hinings, C. A. Lee, R. E. Schneck, and J. M. Pennings. 1971. "A strategic contingencies' theory of intraorganizational power." *Administrative Science Quarterly,* 16: 216–229.

Hickson, D. J., C. R. Hinings, J. M. Pennings, and R. E. Schneck. 1972. *Contingencies and Conditions in Intraorganizational Power.* Paper presented at the Conference on Conflict and Power in Complex Organizations, Kent State University, Kent, Ohio.

Hinings, C. R., D. J. Hickson, J. M. Pennings, and R. E. Schneck. 1974. "Structural conditions of intraorganizational power." *Administrative Science Quarterly,* 19: 22–44.

Leavitt, Harold J. 1965. "Applied organizational change in industry: structural, technological and humanistic approaches." In James G. March (ed.), *Handbook of Organizations,* 1144–1170. Chicago: Rand McNally.

Lewin, Kurt. 1951. *Field Theory in Social Science.* New York: Harper.

Lodahl, J. B., and G. Gordon. 1973. "Funding sciences in university departments." *Educational Record,* 54: 74–82.

March, James G. 1962. "The business firm as a political coalition." *Journal of Politics,* 24: 662–678.

_____. 1966. "The power of power." In David Easton (ed.), *Varieties of Political Theory,* 39–60. Englewood Cliffs, Prentice-Hall.

Milburn, Thomas W. 1972. "Buried Treasures," a review of Conflict Resolution: Contributions to the Behavioral Sciences. *Contemporary Psychology,* 17: 596–598.

Perrow, Charles. 1970. "Departmental power and perspective in industrial firms." In Mayer N. Zald (ed.), *Power in Organizations,* 59–89. Nashville: Vanderbilt University Press.

_____. 1972. *Complex Organizations: A Critical Essay.* Glenview, Ill.: Scott, Foresman.

Pfeffer, Jeffrey, and Gerald R. Salancik. 1974. "Organizational decision making as a political process: the case of a university budget." *Administrative Science Quarterly,* 19: 135–151.

Pondy, Louis R. 1970. "Toward a theory of internal resource-allocation." In Mayer N. Zald (ed.), *Power in Organizations,* 270–311. Nashville: Vanderbilt University Press.

Roose, K. D., and C. J. Andersen. 1970. *A Rating of Graduate Programs.* Washington, D.C.: American Council on Education.

Siegel, Sidney. 1956. *Nonparametric Statistics for the Behavioral Sciences.* New York: McGraw-Hill.

Simon, Herbert A. 1959. "Theories of decision-making in economics and behavioral science." *American Economic Review,* 49: 253–283.

Stagner, Ross. 1969. "Corporate decision making: an empirical study." *Journal of Applied Psychology,* 53: 1–13.

Tannenbaum, Arnold S. 1968. *Control in Organizations.* New York: McGraw-Hill.

Thompson, James D. 1967. *Organizations in Action.* New York: McGraw-Hill.

Thompson, J. D., and W. J. McEwen. 1958. "Organizational goals and environment." *American Sociological Review,* 23: 23–31.

Thompson, James D., and Arthur Tuden. 1959. "Strategies, structures, and processes of organizational decision." In J. D. Thompson, P. B. Hammond, R. W. Hawkes, B. H. Junker, and A. Tuden (eds.), *Comparative Studies in Administration,* 195–216. Pittsburgh: University of Pittsburgh Press.

Wildavsky, Aaron. 1961. "Political implications of budgetary reform." *Public Administration Review,* 21: 183–190.

Yuchtman, Ephraim, and Stanley E. Seashore. 1967. "A system resource approach to organizational effectiveness." *American Sociological Review,* 32: 891–903.

THE PROFESSIONAL BUREAUCRACY

HENRY MINTZBERG

Prime Coordinating Mechanism:	Standardization of skills
Key Part of Organization:	Operating core
Main Design Parameters:	Training, horizontal job specialization, vertical and horizontal decentralization
Contingency Factors:	Complex, stable environment, nonregulating, non-sophisticated technical system, fashionable

We have seen evidence at various points in this book that organizations can be bureaucratic without being centralized. Their operating work is stable, leading to "predetermined or predictable, in effect, standardized" behavior, but it is also complex, and so must be controlled directly by the operators who do it. Hence, the organization turns to the one coordinating mechanism that allows for standardization and decentralization at the same time, namely the standardization of skills. This gives rise to a structural configuration sometimes called *Professional Bureaucracy*, common in universities, general hospitals, school systems, public accounting firms, social work agencies, and craft production firms. All rely on the skills and knowledge of their operating professionals to function; all produce standard products or services.

The Basic Structure

The Work of the Operating Core

Here again we have a tightly knit configuration of the design parameters. Most important, *the Professional Bureaucracy relies for coordination on the standardization of skills and its associated design parameter, training and indoctrination. It hires duly trained and indoctrinated specialists—professionals—for the operating core, and then gives them considerable control over their own work. In effect, the work is highly specialized in the horizontal dimension, but enlarged in the vertical one.*

Control over his own work means that the professional works relatively independently of his colleagues, but closely with the clients he serves. For example, "Teacher autonomy is reflected in the structure of school systems, resulting in what may be called their structural looseness. The teacher works alone within the classroom, relatively hidden from colleagues and superiors, so that he has a broad discre-

---

"The Professional Bureaucracy," by Henry Mintzberg, reprinted from *The Structuring of Organizations—A Synthesis of the Research,* 1979, Prentice-Hall, Inc.

tionary jurisdiction within the boundaries of the classroom" (Bidwell, 1965, pp. 975–976). Likewise, many doctors treat their own patients, and accountants maintain personal contact with the companies whose books they audit.

Most of the necessary coordination between the operating professionals is then handled by the standardization of skills and knowledge, in effect, by what they have learned to expect from their colleagues. ". . . the system works because everyone knows everyone else knows roughly what is going on" (Meyer quoted in Weick, 1976, p. 14). During an operation as long and as complex as open-heart surgery, "very little needs to be said [between the anesthesiologist and the surgeon] preceding chest opening and during the procedure on the heart itself: lines, beats and lights on equipment are indicative of what everyone is expected to do and does—operations are performed in absolute silence, particularly following the chest-opening phase" (Gosselin, 1978). The point is perhaps best made in reverse, by the cartoon that shows six surgeons standing around a patient on the operating table with one saying, "Who opens?" Similarly, the policy and marketing courses of the management school may be integrated without the two professors involved ever having even met. As long as the courses are standard, each knows more or less what the other teaches.

Just how standardized complex professional work can be is illustrated in a paper read by Spencer (1976) before a meeting of the International Cardiovascular Society. Spencer notes that "Becoming a skillful clinical surgeon requires a long period of training, probably five or more years" (p. 1178). An important feature of that training is "repetitive practice" to evoke an "automatic reflex" (p. 1179). So automatic, in fact, that Spencer keeps a series of surgical "cookbooks" in which he lists, even for "complex" operations, the essential steps as chains of thirty to forty symbols on a single sheet, to "be reviewed mentally in sixty to 120 seconds at some time during the day preceding the operation" (p. 1182).

But no matter how standardized the knowledge and skills, their complexity ensures that considerable discretion remains in their application. No two professionals—no two surgeons or teachers or social workers—ever apply them in exactly the same way. Many judgments are required, as Perrow (1970) notes of policemen and others:

> There exist numerous plans: when to suspend assistance, when to remove a gun from its holster, when to block off an area, when to call the FBI, and when to remove a child from the home. The existence of such plans does not provide a criterion for choosing the most effective plan . . . Instead of computation the decision depends upon human judgment. The police patrolman must decide whether to try to disperse the street corner gang or call for reinforcements. The welfare worker must likewise decide if new furniture is an allowable expense, and the high school counselor must decide whether to recommend a college preparatory or vocational program. Categories channel and shape these human judgments but they do not replace them (p. 216).

Training and indoctrination is a complicated affair in the Professional Bureaucracy. The initial training typically takes place over a period of years in a university or special institution. Here the skills and knowledge of the profession are formally programmed into the would-be professional. But in many cases that is only the first step, even if the most important one. There typically follows a long period of on-the-job training, such as internship in medicine and articling in accounting. Here the formal knowledge is applied and the practice of the skills perfected, under the close supervision of members of the profession. On-the-job training also completes the process of indoctrination, which began during the formal teaching. Once this process is completed, the professional association typically examines the trainee to determine whether he has the requisite knowledge, skills, and norms to enter the profession. That is not to say, however, that the individual is examined for the last time in his life, and is pronounced completely full, such that "After this, no new ideas can be imparted to him," as humorist and academic Stephen Leacock once commented about the Ph.D., the test to enter the profession of university teaching. The entrance examination only tests the basic requirements at one point in time; the process of training continues. As new knowledge is generated and new skills develop, the professional upgrades his expertise. He reads the journals, attends the conferences, and perhaps also returns periodically for formal retraining.

The Bureaucratic Nature of the Structure

All of this training is geared to one goal—the internalization of standards that serve the client and coordinate the professional work. In other words, *the structure of these organizations is essentially bureaucratic, its coordination—like that of the Machine Bureaucracy—achieved by design, by standards that predetermine what is to be done.* How bureaucratic is illustrated by Perrow's (1970) description of one well-known hospital department:

> . . . obstetrics and gynecology is a relatively routine department, which even has something resembling an assembly (or deassembly?) line wherein the mother moves from room to room and nurse to nurse during the predictable course of her labor. It is also one of the hospital units most often accused of impersonality and depersonalization. For the mother, the birth is unique, but not for the doctor and the rest of the staff who go through this many times a day (p. 74).

But the two kinds of bureaucracies differ markedly in the source of their standardization. *Whereas the Machine Bureaucracy generates its own standards—its technostructure designing the work standards for its operators and its line managers enforcing them—the standards of the Professional Bureaucracy originate largely outside its own structure, in the self-governing associations its operators join with their colleagues from other Professional Bureaucracies.* These associations set universal standards which they make sure are taught by the universities and used by all the bureaucracies of the profession. *So whereas the Machine Bureaucracy relies on authority of a hierarchical nature—the power of office—the Professional Bureaucracy emphasizes authority of a professional nature—the power of expertise* (Blau, 1967–68). Thus, although Montagna (1968) found internal as well as external rules in the large public accounting firms he studied, the latter proved more important. These were imposed by the American Institute of Certified Public Accountants and included an elaborate and much revised code of ethics, a newly codified volume of principles of accounting, and revised auditing standards and procedures.

> These rules serve as a foundation for the firms' more specific internal rules, a few of which are more stringent, others of which merely expand on the external rules. Nearly to a man, the total sample [of accountants questioned] agreed that compared with internal rules, the external rules were the more important rules for their firms and for the profession as a whole (p. 143).

Montagna's findings suggest that the other forms of standardization are difficult to rely on in the Professional Bureaucracy. The work processes themselves are too complex to be standardized directly by analysts. One need only try to imagine a work study analyst following a cardiologist on his rounds or observing a teacher in a classroom in order to program their work. Similarly, the outputs of professional work cannot easily be measured, and so do not lend themselves to standardization. Imagine a planner trying to define a cure in psychiatry, the amount of learning that takes place in the classroom, or the quality of an accountant's audit. Thus, Professional Bureaucracies cannot rely extensively on the formalization of professional work or on systems to plan and control it.

Much the same conclusion can be drawn for the two remaining coordinating mechanisms. Both direct supervision and mutual adjustment impede the professional's close relationships with his clients. That relationship is predicated on a high degree of professional autonomy—freedom from having not only to respond to managerial orders but also to consult extensively with peers. In any event, the use of the other four coordinating mechanisms is precluded by the capacity of the standardization of skills to achieve a good deal of the coordination necessary in the operating core.

The Pigeonholing Process

To understand how the Professional Bureaucracy functions in its operating core, it is helpful to think of it as a repertoire of standard programs—in effect, the set of skills the professionals stand ready to use—which are applied to predetermined situations, called contingencies, also standardized. As Weick (1976) notes of one case in point, "schools are in the business of building and maintaining categories" (p. 8). The process is sometimes known as *pigeonholing*. In this regard, *the professional has two basic tasks: (1) to categorize the client's need in terms of a contingency, which indicates which standard program to use, a task known as diagnosis, and (2) to apply, or execute, that program.* Pigeonholing simplifies matters enormously. "People are categorized and placed into pigeonholes because it would take enormous resources to treat every case as unique and requiring thorough analysis. Like stereotypes, categories allow us to move through the world without making continuous decisions at every moment" (Perrow, 1970, p. 58). Thus, a psychiatrist examines the patient, declares him to be manic-depressive, and initiates psychotherapy. Similarly, a professor finds 100 students registered in his course and executes his lecture program; faced with 20 instead, he runs the class as a seminar. And the management consultant carries his own bag of standard acronymical tricks—MBO, MIS, LRP, PERT, OD. The client with project work gets PERT, the one with managerial conflicts, OD. Simon (1977) captures the spirit of pigeonholing with his comment that "The pleasure that the good professional experiences in his work is not simply a pleasure in handling difficult matters; it is a pleasure in using skillfully a well-stocked kit of well-designed tools to handle problems that are comprehensible in their deep structure but unfamiliar in their detail" (p. 98).

It is the pigeonholing process that enables the Professional Bureaucracy to decouple its various operating tasks and assign them to individual, relatively autonomous professionals. Each can, instead of giving a great deal of attention to coordinating his work with his peers, focus on perfecting his skills. As Spencer (1976) notes in the case of vascular surgery, "with precise diagnosis and expert operative technique excellent results could almost always be obtained" (p. 1177).

The pigeonholing process does not deny the existence of uncertainty in servicing a client. Rather, it seeks to contain it in the jobs of single professionals. As Bidwell (1965) notes, "The problem of dealing with variability in student abilities and accomplishments during a school year . . . is vested in the classroom teacher, and one important component of his professional skill is ability to handle day-to-day fluctuations in the response to instruction by individual students and collectively by the classroom group" (p. 975). The containment of this uncertainty—what Simon characterizes as unfamiliarity in detail in the job of the single professional—is one of the reasons why the professional requires considerable discretion in his work.

In the pigeonholing process, we see fundamental differences among the Machine Bureaucracy, the Professional Bureaucracy, and the Adhocracy. The Machine Bureaucracy is a single-purpose structure: presented with a stimulus, it executes its one standard sequence of programs, just as we kick when tapped on the knee. No diagnosis is involved. In the Professional Bureaucracy, diagnosis is a fundamental task, but it is circumscribed. The organization seeks to match a predetermined contingency to a standard program. Fully open-ended diagnosis—that which seeks a creative solution to a unique problem—requires a third structural configuration, which we call Adhocracy. No standard contingencies or programs exist in that structure.

Segal (1974) refers to these three as "chain-structured," "mediatively-structured," and "adaptively-structured" organizations. The chain-structured organization relates to only a small part of the environment and accepts inputs only at one end; once ingested, these are processed through a fixed sequence of operations. The mediatively-structured organization—our Professional Bureaucracy—is designed "to channel external dissimilarity into uniform organizational categories" (p. 215). Segal cites the example of the welfare department:

> A glance at the telephone numbers individuals must call to initiate contact with the welfare department indicates that the potential client cannot simply need help, he must need help as defined by the organization—aging, adoption, children in trouble, landlord-tenant complaints, etc. (p. 215).

In other words, the welfare department leaves part of the diagnosis to the client. The adaptively-structured organization, or Adhocracy, "is not structured to screen out heterogeneity and uncertainty" (p. 217). It adapts to its client's individual problem rather than trying to fit it into one of its own categories. Segal provides an example of each of these three types of organizations from the field of mental health:

1. The chain-structured custodial unit responds to the pressure in the environment to keep mental patients out of the public eye and in physical captivity. The chain-structured custodial unit is thus designed to achieve the singular purpose of custodial behavior.

2. The individual treatment structure responds to other pressure in the environment by arranging its units and care to help each patient to fit into a *category* of behavior defined by society.

This facility is thus categorically responsive as staff attempts to change patients' behavior so that it fits their own standards of "normality."

3. The adaptively-structured milieu treatment ward responds to a more relativistic environmental pressure. In this instance, units and roles are arranged so that the very definition of normality is a product of interaction between staff and patients (p. 218).[1]

It is an interesting characteristic of the Professional Bureaucracy that its pigeonholing process creates an equivalence in its structure between the functional and market bases for grouping. *Because clients are categorized—or, as in the case of the welfare recipients above, categorize themselves—in terms of the functional specialists who serve them, the structure of the Professional Bureaucracy becomes at the same time both a functional and a market-based one.* Two illustrations help explain the point. A hospital gynecology department and a university chemistry department can be called functional because they group specialists according to the knowledge, skills, and work processes they use, or market-based because each unit deals with its own unique types of clients—women in the first case, chemistry students in the second. Thus, the distinction between functional and market bases for grouping breaks down in the special case of the Professional Bureaucracy.

Focus on the Operating Core

All the design parameters that we have discussed so far—the emphasis on the training of operators, their vertically enlarged jobs, the little use made of behavior formalization or planning and control systems—suggest that *the operating core is the key part of the Professional Bureaucracy. The only other part that is fully elaborated is the support staff, but that is focused very much on serving the operating core.* Given the high cost of the professionals, it makes sense to back them up with as much support as possible, to aid them and have others do whatever routine work can be formalized. For example, universities have printing facilities, faculty clubs, alma mater funds, building and grounds departments, publishing houses, archives, bookstores, information offices, museums, athletics departments, libraries, computer facilities, and many, many other support units.

The technostructure and middle line of management are not highly elaborated in the Professional Bureaucracy. In other configurations (except Adhocracy), they coordinate the work of the operating core. But in the Professional Bureaucracy, they can do little to coordinate the operating work. The need for planning or the formalizing of the work of the professionals is very limited, so there is little call for a technostructure (except, as we shall see, in the case of the nonprofessional support staff). In McGill University, for example, an institution with 17,000 students and 1200 professors, the only units that could be identified by the author as technocratic were two small departments concerned with finance and budgeting, a small planning office, and a center to develop the professors' skills in pedagogy (the latter two fighting a continual uphill battle for acceptance).

Likewise, the middle line in the Professional Bureaucracy is thin. With little need for direct supervision of the operators, or mutual adjustment between them, the operating units can be very large, with few managers at the level of first-line supervisor, or, for that matter, above them. The McGill Faculty of Management at the time of this writing has fifty professors and a single manager, its dean.

Thus, Figure 1 shows the Professional Bureaucracy, in terms of our logo, as a flat structure with a thin middle line, a tiny technostructure, and a fully elaborated support staff. All these features are reflected in the organigram of McGill University, shown in Figure 2.

Decentralization in the Professional Bureaucracy

Everything we have seen so far tells us that *the Professional Bureaucracy is a highly decentralized structure, in both the vertical and horizontal dimensions.* A great deal of the power over the operating work rests at the bottom of the structure, with the professionals of the operating core. Often each works with his own clients, subject only to the collective control of his colleagues, who trained and indoctrinated him in the first place and thereafter reserve the right to censure him for malpractice.

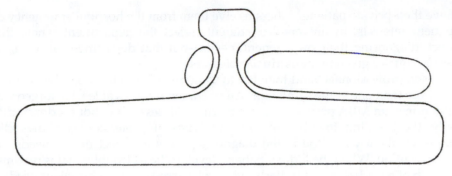

Figure 1 The Professional Bureaucracy.

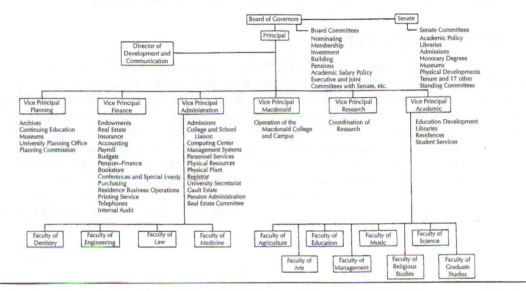

Figure 2 Organigram of McGill University (circa 1978, used by permission).

The professional's power derives from the fact that not only is his work too complex to be supervised by managers or standardized by analysts, but also that his services are typically in great demand. This gives the professional mobility, which enables him to insist on considerable autonomy in his work. The professional tends to identify more with his profession than with the organization where he practices it. Thus, Perrow (1965, p. 959) talks of the "stronger grip" of the medical profession on its members than the specific hospital, while Beyer and Lodahl (1976) note in academia that "Many faculty members receive an important part of their rewards—recognition—from their scientific communities, and this reward is only secondarily reinforced by their universities" (p. 124). In these organizations, even "promotion is not related to the climbing of an administrative ladder but to professional progress, or the ability to handle more and more complex professional problems" (SIAR, 1975, p. 62). Thus, when the professional does not get the autonomy he feels he requires, he is tempted to pick up his kit bag of skills and move on.

One is inclined to ask why professionals bother to join organizations in the first place. There are, in fact, a number of good reasons. For one thing, professionals can share resources, including support services, in a common organization. One surgeon cannot afford his own operating theater, so he shares it with others, just as professors share laboratories, lecture halls, libraries, and printing facilities. Organizations also bring professionals together to learn from each other, and to train new recruits.

Some professionals must join the organization to get clients. The clients present themselves to an organization that houses many different kinds of professionals, depending on it to diagnose their problem and direct them to the individual professional who can best serve them. Thus, while some physicians, have their private patients, others receive them from the hospital emergency department or from in-patient referrals. In universities, students select the department where they wish to study—in effect, diagnosing their own general needs—but that department, in turn, helps direct them into specific courses given by individual professors.

Another reason professionals band together to form organizations is that the clients often need the services of more than one at the same time. An operation requires at least a surgeon, an anesthesiologist, and a nurse; an MBA program cannot be run with less than about a dozen different specialists. Finally, the bringing together of different types of professionals allows clients to be transferred between them when the initial diagnosis proves incorrect or the needs of the client change during execution. When the kidney patient develops heart trouble, that is no time to change hospitals in search of a cardiologist. Similarly, when a law student finds his client needs a course in moral ethics, or an accountant finds his client needs tax advice, it is comforting to know that other departments in the same organization stand ready to provide the necessary service.

The Administrative Structure

What we have seen so far suggests that the Professional Bureaucracy is a highly democratic structure, at least for the professionals of the operating core. In fact, *not only do the professionals control their own work, but they also seek collective control of the administrative decisions that affect them,* decisions, for example, to hire colleagues, to promote them, and to distribute resources. Controlling these decisions requires control of the middle line of the organization, which professionals do by ensuring that it is staffed with "their own." Some of the administrative work the operating professionals do themselves. Every university professor, for example, carries out some administrative duties and serves on committees of one kind or another to ensure that he retains some control over the decisions that affect his work. Moreover, full-time administrators who wish to have any power at all in these structures must be certified members of the profession, and preferably be elected by the professional operators or at least appointed with their blessing. What emerges, therefore, is a rather democratic administrative structure. The university department chairmen, many of them elected, together with the deans, vice-presidents, and president—all of them necessarily academics—must work alongside a parallel hierarchy of committees of professors, many of them elected, ranging from the departmental curriculum committee to the powerful university senate (shown with its own subcommittees in Figure 2). This can be seen clearly in Figure 3, the organigram of a typical university hospital. The plethora of committees is shown on the right side, reporting up from the medical departments through the Council of Physicians and Dentists directly to the Board of Trustees, bypassing the managerial hierarchy entirely. (Notice also the large number of support services in the organization and the relative absence of technocratic units.)

The nature of the administrative structure which itself relies on mutual adjustment for coordination—indicates that the liaison devices, while uncommon in the operating core, are important design parameters in the middle line. Standing committees and ad hoc task forces abound, as was seen in Figure 3; a number of positions are designated to integrate the administrative efforts, as in the case of the ward manager in the hospital; and some Professional Bureaucracies even use matrix structure in administration.

Because of the power of their operators, Professional Bureaucracies are sometimes called "collegial" organizations. In fact, some professionals like to describe them as inverse pyramids, with the professional operators at the top and the administrators down below to serve them—to ensure that the surgical facilities are kept clean and the classrooms well supplied with chalk. Thus comments Amitai Etzioni (1959), the well-known sociologist:

> . . . in professional organizations the staff-expert line-manager correlation, insofar as such a correlation exists at all, is reversed. . . . Managers in professional organizations are in charge of secondary activities; they administer *means* to the major activity carried out by experts. In other words, if there is a staff-line relationship at all, experts constitute the line (major authority) structure and managers the staff. . . . The final internal decision is, functionally speaking, in the hands of various professionals and their decision-making bodies. The professor decides what research he is going to undertake and

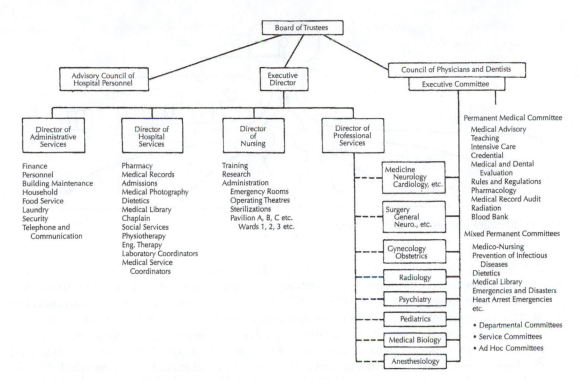

Figure 3   Organigram of a university hospital Board of Trustees.

to a large degree what he is going to teach; the physician determines what treatment should be given to the patient (p. 52).

Etzioni's description may underestimate the power of the *professional* administrator—an issue we shall return to shortly—but it seems to be an accurate description of the nonprofessional one, namely the administrator who manages the support units. For the support staff—often much larger than the professional one, but charged largely with doing nonprofessional work-there is no democracy in the Professional Bureaucracy, only the oligarchy of the professionals. Support units, such as housekeeping or kitchen in the hospital, printing in the university, are as likely as not to be managed tightly from the top. They exist, in effect, as machine bureaucratic constellations within the Professional Bureaucracy.

What frequently emerge in the Professional Bureaucracy are parallel administrative hierarchies, one democratic and bottom up for the professionals, and a second machine bureaucratic and top down for the support staff. As Bidwell (1965) notes: "The segregation of professional and nonprofessional hierarchies in school systems presumably permit this differentiation of modes of control" (p. 1016; see also Blau, 1967–68).

In the professional hierarchy, power resides in expertise; one has influence by virtue of one's knowledge and skills. In other words, a good deal of power remains at the bottom of the hierarchy, with the professional operators themselves. That does not, of course, preclude a pecking order among them. But it does require the pecking order to mirror the professionals' experience and expertise. As they gain experience and reputation academics move through the ranks of lecturer, and then assistant, associate, and full professor; and physicians enter the hospital as interns and move up to residents before they become members of the staff.

In the nonprofession hierarchy, power and status reside in administrative office; one salutes the stripes, not the man. The situation is that Weber originally described: "each lower office is under the control and supervision of a higher one" (cited in Blau, 1967–68, p. 455). Unlike the professional structure, here one must practice administration, not a specialized function of the organization, to attain status.

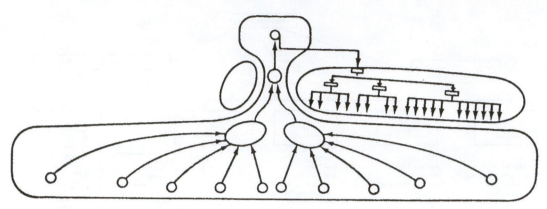

Figure 4   Parallel hierarchies in the Professional Bureaucracy.

But "research indicates that a professional orientation toward service and a bureaucratic orientation toward disciplined compliance with procedures are opposite approaches toward work and often create conflict in organizations" (Blau, 1967–68, p. 456). Hence, these two parallel hierarchies are kept quite independent of each other. The two may come together at some intermediate level, as when a university dean oversees both the professional and secretarial staff. But often, as shown in Figure 4, they remain separate right up to the strategic apex. The hospital medical staff, as shown in Figure 3, does not even report to the executive director—the chief executive officer—but directly to the board of trustees. (Indeed, Charns, [1976] reports that 41 percent of physicians he surveyed in academic medical centers claimed they were responsible to no one!)

The Roles of the Professional Administrator

Where does all this leave the administrators of the professional hierarchy, the executive directors and chiefs of the hospitals and the presidents and deans of the universities? Are they as powerless as Etzioni suggests? Compared with their peers in the Simple Structure and the Machine Bureaucracy, they certainly lack a good deal of power. But that is far from the whole story. While the professional administrator may not be able to control the professionals directly, he does perform a series of roles that gives him considerable indirect power in the structure.

First, *the professional administrator spends much time handling disturbances in the structure.* The pigeonholing process is an imperfect one at best, leading to all kinds of jurisdictional disputes between the professionals. Who should teach the statistics course in the MBA program, the mathematics department or the business school? Who should perform mastectomies in hospitals, surgeons who specialize in operations or gynecologists who specialize in women? Seldom, however, can a senior administrator impose a solution on the professionals or units involved in a dispute. Rather the unit managers—chiefs, deans, or whoever—must sit down together and negotiate a solution on behalf of their constituencies. Coordination problems also arise frequently between the two parallel hierarchies, and it often falls to the professional administrator to resolve them.

Second, *the professional administrators—especially those at higher levels—serve key roles at the boundary of the organization, between the professionals inside and interested parties—governments, client associations, and so on—on the outside.* On one hand, the administrators are expected to protect the professionals' autonomy, to "buffer" them from external pressures. "The principal is expected to 'back the teacher up'—support her authority in all cases of parental 'interference' "(Melcher, 1976, p. 334). So, too, the executive director of the hospital is supposed to keep the government or the trustees from interfering in the work of the physicians. On the other hand, the administrators are expected to woo these outsiders to support the organization, both morally and financially. ". . .teachers consider it a prime responsibility of the administrator to secure for them the greatest possible amount of resources" (Hills, quoted in Melcher, 1976, p. 333), as do professors in universities and physicians in hospitals. Thus, the external roles of the manager—maintaining liaison contacts, acting as figurehead and spokesman in a public relations capacity, negotiating with outside agencies—emerge as primary ones in the job of the professional administrator.

Some view the roles professional administrators are called upon to perform as signs of weakness. Like Etzioni, they see these people as the errand boys of the professionals, or else as pawns caught in various tugs of war—between one professional and another, between support staffer and professional, between outsider and professional. In fact, however, these roles are the very sources of administrator power. Power is, after all, gained at the locus of uncertainty. And that is exactly where the professional administrators sit. The administrator who succeeds in raising extra funds for his organization gains a say in how these are distributed. Similarly, the one who can reconcile conflicts in favor of his unit or who can effectively buffer the professionals from external influence becomes a valued—and therefore powerful—member of the organization. The professionals well know that "Without the 'superb politician,' metropolitan school systems, urban governments, universities, mental hospitals, social work systems, and similar complex organizations would be immobilized" (Thompson, 1967, p. 143).

Ironically, *the professional becomes dependent on the effective administrator.* The professional faces a fundamental dilemma. Frequently, he abhors administration, desiring only to be left alone to practice his profession. But that freedom is gained only at the price of administrative effort—raising funds, resolving conflicts, buffering the demands of outsiders. That leaves the professional two choices: to do the administrative work himself, in which case he has less time to practice his profession, or to leave it to administrators, in which case he must surrender some of his power over decision making. And that power must be surrendered, it should further be noted, to administrators who, by virtue of the fact that they no longer wish to practice the profession, probably favor a different set of goals. Damned if he does and damned if he doesn't. Take the case of the university professors oriented to research. To ensure the fullest support for research in his department, he should involve himself in committees where questions of the commitment to teaching versus research are decided. But that takes time, specifically time away from research. What is the use of spending time protecting what one has no time left to do. So the professor is tempted to leave administration to full-time administrators, those who have expressed a disinterest in research by virtue of seeking fulltime administrative office.

We can conclude that *power in these structures does flow to those professionals who care to devote the effort to doing administrative instead of professional work*—a considerable amount of power, in fact, to those who do it well, especially in complex professional organizations, such as the modern hospital (Perrow, 1967). *But that, it should be stressed, is not laissez-faire power: the professional administrator keeps his power only as long as the professionals perceive him to be serving their interests effectively.* The managers of the Professional Bureaucracy may be the weakest among those of the five structural configurations, but they are far from impotent. *Individually*, they are usually more powerful than individual professionals—the chief executive remaining the single most powerful member of the Professional Bureaucracy—even if that power can easily be overwhelmed by the *collective* power of the professionals.

Strategy Formulation in the Professional Bureaucracy

A description of the strategy formulation process in the Professional Bureaucracy perhaps best illustrates the two sides of the professional administrator's power. At the outset it should be noted that strategy takes on a very different form in these kinds of organizations. Since their outputs are difficult to measure, their goals cannot easily be agreed upon. So *the notion of a strategy—a single, integrated pattern of decisions common to the entire organization—loses a good deal of its meaning in the Professional Bureaucracy.*

Given the autonomy of each professional—his close working relationships with his clients, and his loose ones with his colleagues—it becomes sensible to think in terms of a personal strategy for each professional. In many cases, each selects his own clients and his own methods of dealing with them—in effect, he chooses his own product-market strategy. But professionals do not select their clients and methods at random. They are significantly constrained by the professional standards and skills they have learned. That is, the professional associations and training institutions outside the organization play a major role in determining the strategies that the professionals pursue. Thus, to an important extent all organizations in a given profession exhibit similar strategies, imposed on them from the outside. These strategies—concerning what clients to serve and how—are inculcated in the professionals during their formal training and are modified as new needs emerge and the new methods developed to cope with them gain acceptance by the professional associations. In medicine, for example, researchers develop new forms of treatment and test them experimentally. They publish their results in the medical journals, these publications leading to more experimentation and elaboration until the methods are considered sufficiently safe to pass into standard practice—that is, to become part of the repertoire of programs of all hospitals. And this whole process is overseen by the professional associations, which pass judgments on acceptable and unacceptable practices, and through whose journals, newsletters, conferences, and training programs information on new practices is disseminated. This control of strategy can sometimes be very direct: in one of the McGill studies, a hospital that refused to adopt a new method of treatment was, in effect, censured when one of the associations of medical specialists passed a resolution declaring failure to use it tantamount to malpractice.

We can conclude, therefore, that *the strategies of the Professional Bureaucracy are largely ones of the individual professionals within the organization as well as of the professional associations on the outside.* Largely, but not completely. There are still degrees of freedom that allow each organization within the profession to adapt the basic strategies to its own needs and interests. There are, for example, mental hospitals, women's hospitals, and veterans' hospitals; all conform to standard medical practice, but each applies it to a different market which it has selected.

How do these organizational strategies get made? It would appear that *the Professional Bureaucracy's own strategies represent the cumulative effect over time of the projects, or strategic "initiatives," that its members are able to convince it to undertake*—to buy a new piece of equipment in a hospital, to establish a new degree program in a university, to develop a new specialty department in an accounting firm. Most of these initiatives are proposed by members of the operating core—by "professional entrepreneurs" willing to expend the efforts needed to negotiate the acceptance of new projects through the complex administrative structure (and if the method is new and controversial, through outside professional associations as well, and also through outside funding agencies if the project is an expensive one). A proposal for a new Ph.D. program in management at McGill University was worked out by an ad hoc committee and then approved within the Faculty of Management by its Graduate Program Committee, Academic Committee, and Faculty Council; from there it went to the Executive Committee and the Council of the Faculty of Graduate Studies; then it moved on to the Academic Policy Committee of the Senate of the University and then to the full Senate itself; from there it went to the University Programs Committee of the Quebec government Ministry of Education and then into the Ministry itself, and then back and forth between these bodies and the university administration a few more times until it was finally approved (as a joint program of four universities).

What is the role of the professional administrator in all this? Certainly far from passive. As noted earlier, administration is neither the forte nor the interest of the operating professional (for good reason, as should be clear from the example above!). So he depends on the full-time administrator to help him negotiate his project through the system. For one thing, the administrator has time to worry about such matters—after all, administration is his job; he no longer practices the profession. For another, the administrator has a full knowledge of the administrative committee system as well as many personal contacts within it, both of which are necessary to see a project through it. The administrator deals with the system every day; the professional entrepreneur may promote only one new project in his entire career. Finally, the administrator is more likely to have the requisite managerial skills, for example, those of negotiation and persuasion.

But the power of the effective administrator to influence strategy goes beyond helping the professionals. Every good manager seeks to change his organization in his own way, to alter its strategies to make it more effective. In the Professional Bureaucracy, this translates into a set of strategic initiatives that the administrator himself wishes to take. But in these structures—in principle bottom up—the administrator cannot impose his will on the professionals of the operating core. Instead, he must rely on his informal power, and apply it subtly. Knowing that the professionals want nothing more than to be left alone, the administrator moves carefully—in incremental steps, each one hardly discernible. In this way, he may achieve over time changes that the professionals would have rejected out of hand had they been proposed all at once.

To conclude, we have seen again that while the weak administrator of the Professional Bureaucracy may be no more than the errand boy of the professionals, the strong one—a professional himself, politically adept and fully aware of the power system of his organization—can play a major role in changing its strategies.

Conditions of the Professional Bureaucracy

This third structural configuration appears wherever the operating core of an organization is dominated by skilled workers—professionals—who use procedures that are difficult to learn yet are well defined. This means an environment that is both complex and stable—complex enough to require the use of difficult procedures that can be learned only in extensive formal training programs, yet stable enough to enable these skills to become well defined, in effect, standardized. Thus, the environment is the chief contingency factor in the use of the Professional Bureaucracy.

In contrast, the factors of age and size are of less significance. Larger professional organizations tend to be somewhat more formalized (Holdaway et al., 1975; Bidwell, 1965, p. 1017)[2] and to have more fully developed staff support structures (Bidwell, 1965, p. 977). But that does not preclude the existence of small Professional Bureaucracies, or, for that matter, of young ones as well. The Machine Bureaucracy has a start-up time because the standards need to be worked out within the organization. Thus, it passes through a period of Simple Structure before its procedures become routinized. In the Professional Bureaucracy, in contrast, the skilled employees bring the standards into the organization with them when they join. So there is little start-up time. Put a group of doctors in a new hospital or a group of lawyers in a new law office and in no time they are functioning as if they had been there for years. Size would seem to be a relatively minor contingency factor for the same reason, and also because the professionals to a large extent work independently. One accountant working on his own adheres to the same professional standards as 2000 working in a giant firm. Thus, Professional Bureaucracies hardly pass through the stage of Simple Structure in their formative years.

Technical system is an important contingency factor, at least for what it is not in the Professional Bureaucracy—neither highly regulating, sophisticated, nor automated. The professional operators of this structural configuration require considerable discretion in their work. It is they who serve the clients, usually directly and personally. So the technical system cannot be highly regulating, certainly not highly automated. As Heydebrand and Noell (1973) point out, the professional resists the rationalization of his skills—their division into simply executed steps—because that makes them programmable by the technostructure, destroys his basis of autonomy, and drives the structure to the machine bureaucratic form.

Nor can the technical system be sophisticated. That would pull the professional into a closer working relationship with his colleagues and push him to a more distant one with his clients, driving the organization toward another structural configuration—the adhocratic form. The surgeon uses a scalpel, the accountant a pencil. Both must be sharp, but are otherwise simple and commonplace instruments; yet both allow their users to perform independently what can be exceedingly complex functions. More sophisticated instruments—such as the computer in the accounting firm or the coronary care unit in the hospital—reduce the professional's autonomy by forcing him to work in multidisciplinary teams, as he does in the Adhocracy. These teams are concerned in large part with the design, modification, and maintenance of the equipment; its operation, because that tends to be regulating, and often automated, impersonalizes the relationship between the professional and his clients. Thus, *in the pure form of the Professional Bureaucracy, the technology of the organization—its knowledge base—is sophisticated but its technical system—the set of instruments it uses to apply that knowledge base—is not.*

Thus, the prime example of the Professional Bureaucracy is the *personal service organization,* at least the one with complex, stable work. Schools and universities, consulting firms, law and accounting offices, social work agencies all rely on this structural configuration as long as they concentrate not on innovating in the solution of new problems, but on applying standard programs to well-defined ones. The same is true of hospitals, at least to the extent that their technical systems are simple. (In those areas that call for more sophisticated equipment—apparently a growing number, especially in teaching institutions—the hospital is driven toward a hybrid structure, with characteristics of the Adhocracy. The research function would also seem to drive it, and the university as well, toward the same hybrid, research being oriented more than clinical practice and teaching to innovation.[3] The same effect results from dynamic environmental conditions—again increasingly common in teaching hospitals. But all these forces are strongly mitigated by the hospital's overriding concern with safety. Only the tried and true can be used on regular patients. Institutions entrusted with the lives of their clients have a natural aversion to the looser, organic structures such as Adhocracy.)

A good deal of the service sector of contemporary society in fact applies standard programs to well-defined problems. Hence, the Professional Bureaucracy structure tends to predominate there. And with the enormous growth of this sector in the last few decades, we find that the Professional Bureaucracy has emerged as a major structural configuration.

So far, all of our examples have come from the service sector. But Professional Bureaucracies are found in manufacturing too, notably where the environment demands work that is complex yet stable, and the technical system is neither regulating nor sophisticated. This is the case of the *craft enterprise*, an important variant of the Professional Bureaucracy. Here the organization relies on skilled craftsmen who use relatively simple instruments to produce standard outputs. The very term "craftsman" implies a kind of professional who learns traditional skills through long apprentice training and then is allowed to practice them free of direct supervision. Craft enterprises seem typically to have tiny administrations—no technostructures and few managers, many of whom, in any event, work alongside the craftsmen.

Many craftsmen were eliminated by the Industrial Revolution. Their jobs—for example, the making of shoes—were rationalized, and so control over them passed from the workers who did them to the analysts who designed them. Small craft enterprises metamorphosed into large Machine Bureaucracies. But some craft industries remain, for example, fine glasswork and handmade pottery, portrait photography, and gastronomic cuisine.[4] In fact, as these examples indicate, the term "craft" has today come to be associated with functional art, handmade items that perform a function but are purchased for their aesthetic value.

There is at least one major industry that has remained largely in the craft stage, and that is construction. In a paper entitled "Bureaucratic and Craft Administration of Production: A Comparative Study," Stinchcombe (1959–60) contrasts mass production and construction firms, describing the latter much as we have described Professional Bureaucracy. He notes that professionalization of the labor force in the construction industry serves the same functions as bureaucratic administration in mass production industries" (p. 169). In construction, "work processes [are] governed by the worker in accordance with the empirical lore that makes up craft principles" (p. 170). As a result, few clerks are needed (20 percent of the administrative personnel, versus 53 percent in mass production, where they are used, Stinchcombe explains, to effect machine bureaucratic control), the communication system is less formalized, and less emphasis is placed on the hierarchy of authority. Stinchcombe also cites another study of the construction industry that noted "the low development of distinctly bureaucratic production control mechanisms, such as cost accounting, detailed scheduling, regularized reporting of work process, and standardized inspection of specific operations" (p. 182).[5]

The markets of the Professional Bureaucracy are often diversified. As noted earlier, these organizations often bring together groups of professionals from different specialties who serve different types of clients. The hospital includes gynecologists to serve women, pediatricians to serve children, and so on, while the university has its philosophy professors to teach those interested in general knowledge and its management professors for those in search of specific career skills. Hypothesis 11 would lead us to the conclusion that such market diversity encourages the use of the market basis for grouping the professionals. In fact, we have already seen this to be the case (although we also saw that the market basis for grouping turns out to be equivalent to the functional one in Professional Bureaucracies, as a result of the way in which professional services are selected).

Sometimes the markets of Professional Bureaucracies are diversified geographically, leading to a variant we call the *dispersed professional bureaucracy*. Here the problem of maintaining loyalty to the organization becomes magnified, since the professionals do their autonomous work in remote locations, far from the administrative structure. The Royal Canadian Mounted Police, for example, were dispersed across the Canadian west and north late last century to bring order to what were then lawless districts of the country. Once sent out, each Mountie was on his own. The same situation exists today in intelligence (spy) agencies, forest ranger services, and international consulting firms. As a result, these organizations must rely extensively on training and indoctrination, especially the latter. The employees are selected carefully, trained extensively, and indoctrinated heavily—often by the organization itself—before they are sent out to the remote areas to perform their work. Thus, even on their own, the Mounties carried the norms and skills of the R.C.M.P. with them and so served it resolutely. Moreover, the employees of the dispersed professional bureaucracy are frequently brought back to the central headquarters for a fresh dose of indoctrination, and they are often rotated in their jobs to ensure that their loyalty remains with the organization and does not shift to the geographical area they serve. The U.S. Forest Rangers, for example, are recruited largely from the forestry schools—having already demonstrated a commitment to forests and a love of the outdoors—and are then further trained and indoctrinated, and, once on the job, are rotated from post to post. Both the rotation and indoctrination "facilitate communication between headquarters and the field by keeping loyalties and career interests centrally directed" as well as keeping "the foresters independent of private interests in the regions or communities in which they serve . . ." (Wilensky, 1967, pp. 59–60; see also Kaufman, 1960).

This chapter has stressed the role of training in the Professional Bureaucracy more than indoctrination. Indoctrination only emerged as important in this last variant. But there is another variant, the *missionary organization*—common in religious orders, charitable foundations (Sills, 1957), and the like, and sometimes found also in business firms (Perrow, 1970, pp. 166–170)—where indoctrination replaces training as the key design parameter. Because this organization has an attractive mission, and perhaps a distinguished history as well, its members also share a strong ideology—a set of norms about the goals and strategies the organization pursues. The members may come by this naturally, or they may have been indoctrinated into the ideology when they first joined. In any event, because every member of the organization can be trusted to pursue its main goals and strategies, there can be an extensive decentralization to the level of the single individual, resulting in a structure that in some ways resembles the Professional Bureaucracy.

The Professional Bureaucracy is also occasionally found as a hybrid structure. In our discussion of hospitals earlier, we alluded to a possible combination with characteristics of the Adhocracy which we can call the *professional bureaucracy/adhocracy*. Another hybrid—the *simple professional bureaucracy*—occurs when highly trained professionals practicing standard skills nevertheless take their lead from a strong, sometimes even autocratic, leader, as in the Simple Structure. Consider, for example, the following description of a symphony orchestra, an organization staffed with highly skilled musicians who play standard repertoires:

> An orchestra is not a democracy but a dictatorship. The interpretation and presentation of this complex repertoire cannot be pieced together as a kind of consensus among the musicians.
>
> Such a system has been tried out, notably in Russia in the 1920's, but the famous conductorless orchestra, Persimfans, lasted only a few years. There were countless long rehearsals while the musicians argued about the treatment of every passage, and any one of the members was given the democratic right, in turn, to lay down his instrument and listen to the effect from the hall.
>
> It was finally decided that it would be much more efficient, and less costly, to allow one man of recognized ability to impose his ideas upon the rest of the orchestra, a conclusion the rest of the European orchestras had reached more than a century earlier . . .
>
> I think it was one of Szell's musicians who was quoted as saying: "He's a sonovabitch, but he makes us play beyond ourselves."[6]

Finally, we might note briefly the effects of the contingency factors of power, notably fashion and the influence of the operators. Professionalism is a popular word among all kinds of identifiable specialists today; as a result, *Professional Bureaucracy is a highly fashionable structure*—and for good reason, since it is a very democratic one. Thus, it is to the advantage of every operator to make his job more professional—to enhance the skills it requires, to keep the analysts of the technostructure from rationalizing those skills, and to establish associations that set industry-wide standards to protect those skills. In these ways, the operator can achieve what always escapes him in the Machine Bureaucracy—control of his work and the decisions that affect it.

Some Issues Associated with Professional Bureaucracy

The Professional Bureaucracy is unique among the five structural configurations in answering two of the paramount needs of contemporary men and women. It is democratic, disseminating its power directly to its workers (at least those who are professional). And it provides them with extensive autonomy, freeing them even of the need to coordinate closely with their peers, and all of the pressures and politics that entails. Thus, the professional has the best of both worlds: he is attached to an organization, yet is free to serve his clients in his own way, constrained only by the established standards of his profession.

As a result, professionals tend to emerge as responsible and highly motivated individuals, dedicated to their work and the clients they serve. Unlike the Machine Bureaucracy that places barriers between the operator and the client, this structure removes them, allowing a personal relationship to develop. Here the technical and social systems can function in complete harmony.

Moreover, *autonomy allows the professionals to perfect their skills, free of interference.* They repeat the same complex programs time after time, forever reducing the uncertainty until they get them just about perfect, like the Provençal potter who has spent his career perfecting the glazes he applies to identical pots. The professional's thought processes are "convergent"—vascular surgeon Spencer (1976) refers to them as deductive reasoning. Spencer quotes approvingly the bridge aficionado who stood behind champion Charles Goren during a three-day tournament and concluded: "He didn't do anything I couldn't do, except he didn't make any mistakes" (p. 1181). That captures nicely the secure feelings of professionals and their clients in Professional Bureaucracies. The Provençal potter expects few surprises when he opens his kiln; so, too, do Dr. Spencer's patients when they climb on to his operating table. They know the program has been executed so many times—by this surgeon as well as by the many whose experiences he has read about in the journals—that the possibility of mistakes has been minimized. Hospitals do not even get to execute new programs on regular patients until they have been thoroughly tested and approved by the profession. So the client of the Professional Bureaucracy can take satisfaction in the knowledge that the professional about to serve him will draw on vast quantities of experience and skill, will apply them in a perfected, not an experimental procedure, and will likely be highly motivated in performing that procedure.

But in these same characteristics of democracy and autonomy lie all the major problems of the Professional Bureaucracy. *For there is virtually no control of the work outside the profession, no way to correct deficiencies that the professionals themselves choose to overlook.* What they tend to overlook are the major problems of coordination, of discretion, and of innovation that arise in these structures.

Problems of Coordination

The Professional Bureaucracy can coordinate effectively only by the standardization of skills. Direct supervision and mutual adjustment are resisted as direct infringements on the professional's autonomy, in one case by administrators, in the other by peers. And standardization of work processes and of outputs are ineffective for this complex work with its ill-defined outputs. But *the standardization of skills is a loose coordinating mechanism at best, failing to cope with many of the needs that arise in the Professional Bureaucracy.*

There is, first of all, the need for coordination between the professional and the support staff. To the professional, that is simply resolved: he gives the orders. But that only catches the support staffer between two systems of power pulling in different ways, the vertical power of line authority above him, and the horizontal power of professional expertise to his side.

Perhaps more severe are the coordination problems between the professionals themselves. Unlike Machine Bureaucracies, Professional Bureaucracies are not integrated entities. They are collections of individuals who join to draw on the common resources and support services but otherwise want to be left alone. As long as the pigeonholing process works effectively, they can be. But that process can never be so good that contingencies do not fall in the cracks between the standard programs. The world is a continuous intertwined system. Slicing it up, although necessary to comprehend it, inevitably distorts it. Needs that fall at the margin or that overlap two categories tend to get forced—artificially—into one category or another. In contemporary medicine, for instance, the human body is treated not so much as one integrated system with interdependent parts, as a collection of loosely coupled organs that correspond to the different specialties. For the patient whose malady slots nicely into one of the specialties, problems of coordination do not arise. For others—for example, the patient who falls between psychiatry and internal medicine—it means repeated transfers in search of the right department, a time-consuming process when time is critical. In universities the pigeonholing process can be equally artificial, as in the case of the professor interested in the structure of production systems who fell between the operations and organizational behavior departments of his business school and so was denied tenure.

The pigeonholing process, in fact, emerges as the source of a great deal of the conflict of the Professional Bureaucracy. Much political blood is spilled in the continual reassessment of contingencies, imperfectly conceived, in terms of programs, artificially distinguished.

Problems of Discretion

The assumption underlying the design of the Professional Bureaucracy is that the pigeonholing process contains all of the uncertainty in single professional jobs. As we saw above, that assumption often proves false to the detriment of the organization's performance. But even where it works, problems arise. For it focuses all the discretion in the hands of single professionals, whose complex skills, no matter how standardized, require the exercise of considerable judgment. That is, perhaps, appropriate for professionals who are competent and conscientious. Unfortunately not all of them are; and *the professional bureaucratic structure cannot easily deal with professionals who are either incompetent or unconscientious.*

No two professionals are equally skilled. So the client who is forced to choose among them—to choose in ignorance, since he seeks professional help precisely because he lacks the specialized knowledge to help himself—is exposed to a kind of Russian Roulette, almost literally so in the case of medicine, where single decisions can mean life or death. But that is inevitable: little can be done aside from using the very best screening procedures for applicants to the training schools.

Of greater concern is the unconscientious professional—the one who refuses to update his skills after graduation, who cares more for his income than his clients, or who becomes so enamored with his skills that he forgets about the real needs of his clients. This last case represents a means-ends inversion common in Professional Bureaucracies, different from that found in Machine Bureaucracies but equally serious. In this case, the professional confuses the needs of his clients with the skills he has to offer them. He simply concentrates on the program that he favors—perhaps because he does it best or simply enjoys doing it most—to the exclusion of all the others. This presents no problem as long as only those clients in need of that favorite program are directed his way. But should other clients slip in, trouble ensues. Thus, we have the psychiatrists who think that all patients (indeed, all people) need psychoanalysis, the consulting firms prepared to design the same planning system for all their clients, no matter how dynamic their environments, the professors who use the lecture method for classes of 500 students or 5, the social workers who feel the compulsion to bring power to the people even when the people do not want it.

Dealing with this means-ends inversion is impeded by the difficulty of measuring the outputs of professional work. When psychiatrists cannot even define the words "cure" or "healthy," how are they to prove that psychoanalysis is better for manic-depressives than chemical therapy would be? When no one has been able to measure the learning that takes place in the classroom, how can it be demonstrated with reliability that lectures are better or worse than seminars or, for that matter, than staying home and reading. That is one reason why the obvious solution to the problems of discretion—censure by the professional association—is seldom used. Another is that professionals are notoriously reluctant to act against their own, to wash their dirty linen in public, so to speak. In extreme cases, they will so act—certain behavior is too callous to ignore. But these instances are relatively rare. They do no more than expose the tip of the iceberg of misguided discretion.

Discretion not only enables some professionals to ignore the needs of their clients; it also encourages many of them to ignore the needs of the organization. Professionals in these structures do not generally consider themselves part of a team. To many, the organization is almost incidental, a convenient place to practice their skills. They are loyal to their profession, not to the place where they happen to practice it. But the organization has need for loyalty, too—to support its own strategies, to staff its administrative committees, to see it through conflicts with the professional association. Cooperation, as we saw earlier, is crucial to the functioning of the administrative structure. Yet, as we also saw earlier, professionals resist it furiously. Professors hate to show up for curriculum meetings; they simply do not wish to be dependent on each other. One can say that they know each other only too well!

Problems of Innovation

In these structures, major innovation also depends on cooperation. Existing programs can be perfected by individual specialists. But new ones necessarily cut across existing specialties—in essence, they require a rearrangement of the pigeonholes—and so call for interdisciplinary efforts. As a result, the reluctance of the professionals to work cooperatively with each other translates itself into problems of innovation.

Like the Machine Bureaucracy, the Professional Bureaucracy is an inflexible structure, well suited to producing its standard outputs but ill-suited to adapting to the production of new ones. All bureaucracies are geared to stable environments; they are performance structures designed to perfect programs for contingencies that can be predicted, not problem solving ones designed to create new programs for needs that have never before been encountered.

The problems of innovation in the Professional Bureaucracy find their roots in convergent thinking, in the deductive reasoning of the professional who sees the specific situation in terms of the general concept. In the Professional Bureaucracy this means that new problems are forced into old pigeonholes. The doctoral student in search of an interdisciplinary degree—for, after all, isn't the highest university degree meant to encourage the generation of new knowledge—inevitably finds himself forced back into the old departmental mode. "It must be a D.B.A. or a D.Ed.; we don't offer educational administration here." Nowhere are the effects of this deductive reasoning better illustrated than in Spencer's (1976) comments that "All patients developing significant complications or death among our three hospitals . . . are reported to a central office with a narrative description of the sequence of events, with reports varying in length from a third to an entire page," and that six to eight of these cases are discussed in the one-hour weekly "mortality-morbidity" conferences, including presentation of it by the surgeon and "questions and comments" by the audience (p. 1181). An "entire" page and ten minutes of discussion for cases with "significant complications"! Maybe enough to list the symptoms and slot them into pigeonholes; hardly enough even to begin to think about creative solutions. As Lucy once told Charlie Brown, great art cannot be done in half an hour; it takes at least forty-five minutes!

The fact is that great art and innovative problem solving require *inductive* reasoning, that is, the induction of new general concepts or programs from particular experiences. That kind of thinking is *divergent*—it breaks away from old routines or standards rather than perfecting existing ones. And that flies in the face of everything the Professional Bureaucracy is designed to do.

So it should come as no surprise that Professional Bureaucracies and the professional associations that control their procedures tend to be conservative bodies, hesitant to change their well-established ways. Whenever an entrepreneurial member takes up the torch of innovation, great political clashes inevitably ensue. Even in the Machine Bureaucracy, once the managers of the strategic apex finally recognize the need for change, they are able to force it down the hierarchy. In the Professional Bureaucracy, with operator autonomy and bottom-up decision making, and in the professional association with its own democratic procedures, power for strategic change is diffuse. Everybody must agree on the change, not just a few managers or professional representatives. So change comes slowly and painfully, after much political intrigue and shrewd maneuvering by the professional and administrative entrepreneurs.

As long as the environment remains stable, the Professional Bureaucracy encounters no problem. It continues to perfect its skills and the given system of pigeonholes that slots them. But dynamic conditions call for change—new skills, new ways to slot them, and creative, cooperative efforts on the part of multidisciplinary teams of professionals.

Dysfunctional Responses

What responses do the problems of coordination, discretion, and innovation evoke? Most commonly, those outside the profession—clients, nonprofessional administrators, members of the society at large and their representatives in government—see the problems as resulting from a lack of external control of the professional, and his profession. So they do the obvious: try to control the work with one of the other coordinating mechanisms. Specifically, they try to use direct supervision, standardization of work processes, or standardization of outputs.

Direct supervision typically means imposing an intermediate level of supervision, preferably with a narrow "span of control"—in keeping with the tenets of the classical concepts of authority—to watch over the professionals. That may work in cases of gross negligence. The sloppy surgeon or the professor who misses too many classes can be "spoken to" or ultimately perhaps fired. But specific professional activities—complex in execution and vague in results—are difficult to control by anyone other than the professionals themselves. So the administrator detached from the work and bent on direct supervision is left nothing to do except engage in bothersome exercises. As in the case of certain district supervisors who sit between one Montreal school board and its schools and, according to the reports of a number of principals, spend time telephoning them at 4:59 on Friday afternoons to ensure they have not left early for the weekend. The imposition of such intermediate levels of supervision stems from the assumption that professional work can be controlled, like any other, in a top-down manner, an assumption that has proven false again and again.

Likewise, the other forms of standardization, instead of achieving control of the professional work, often serve merely to impede and discourage the professionals. And for the same reasons—the complexity of the work and the vagueness of its outputs. Complex work processes cannot be formalized by rules and regulations, and vague outputs cannot be standardized by planning and control systems. Except in misguided ways, which program the wrong behaviors and measure the wrong outputs, forcing the professionals to play the machine bureaucratic game—satisfying the standards instead of serving the clients. Back to the old means-ends inversion. Like the policeman in Chicago who described to Studs Terkel (1972) the effects of various such standards on his work:

> My supervisor would say, "We need two policy arrests, so we can be equal with the other areas." So we go out and hunt for a policy operator. . . .

> A vice officer spends quite a bit of time in court. You learn the judges, the things they look for. You become proficient in testifying. You change your testimony, you change the facts. You switch things around 'cause you're trying to get convictions. . . .

> Certain units in the task force have developed a science around stopping your automobile. These men know it's impossible to drive three blocks without committing a traffic violation. We've got so many rules on the books. These police officers use these things to get points and also hustle for money. The traffic law is a fat book. He knows if you don't have two lights on your license plate, that's a violation. If you have a crack in your windshield, that's a violation. If your muffler's dragging, that's a violation. He knows all these little things.

> So many points for a robbery, so many points for a man having a gun. When they go to the scene and the man with the gun has gone, they'll lock up somebody anyway, knowing he's not the one. The record says, "Locked up two people for UUW"—unlawful use of weapons. The report will say, "When we got there, we saw these guys and they looked suspicious." They'll get a point even if the case is thrown out of court. The arrest is all that counts (pp. 137–140).

Graphic illustrations of the futility of trying to control work that is essentially professional in nature. Similar things happen when accountants try to control the management consulting arms of their firms—"obedience is stressed as an end in itself because the CPA as administrator is not able to judge the non-accountant expert on the basis of that expert's knowledge" (Montagna, 1968:144). And in school systems when the government technostructure believes it can program the work of the teacher, as in that of East Germany described proudly to this author by a government planner, where each day every child in the country ostensibly opens the same book to the same page. The individual needs of the students—slow learners and fast, rural and urban—as well as the individual styles of the teachers have to be subordinated to the neatness of the system.

The fact is that complex work cannot be effectively performed unless it comes under the control of the operator who does it. Society may have to control the overall expenditures of its Professional Bureaucracies—to keep the lid on them—and to legislate against the most callous kinds of professional behavior. But too much external control of the professional work itself leads, according to Hypothesis 14, to centralization and formalization of the structure, in effect driving the Professional Bureaucracy to Machine Bureaucracy. The decision-making power flows from the operators to the managers, and on to the analysts of the technostructure. The effect of this is to throw the baby out with the bathwater. Technocratic controls do not improve professional-type work, nor can they distinguish between responsible and irresponsible behavior—they constrain both equally. That may, of course, be appropriate for organizations in which responsible behavior is rare. But where it is not—presumably the majority of cases—*technocratic controls only serve to dampen professional conscientiousness.* As Sorensen and Sorensen (1974) found, the more machine bureaucratic the large public accounting firms, the more they experienced conflict and job dissatisfaction.

Controls also upset the delicate relationship between the professional and his client, a relationship predicated on unimpeded personal contact between the two. Thus, Cizanckas, a police chief, notes that the police officer at the bottom of the pecking order in the "paramilitary structure is more than willing, in turn, to vent his frustration on the lawbreaker" (paraphrased by Hatvany, 1976, p. 73). The controls remove the responsibility for service from the professional and place it in the administrative structure, where it is of no use to the client. It is not the government that teaches the student, not even the school system or the school itself; it is not the hospital that delivers the baby, not the police force that apprehends the criminal, not the welfare department that helps the distraught family. These things are done by the individual professional. If that professional is incompetent, no plan or rule fashioned in the technostructure, no order from an administrator can ever make him competent. But such plans, rules, and orders can impede the competent professional from providing his service effectively. At least rationalization in the Machine Bureaucracy leaves the client with inexpensive outputs. In the case of professional work, it leaves him with impersonal, ineffective service.

Furthermore, the incentive to perfect, even to innovate—the latter weak in the best of times in professional bureaucracy—can be reduced by external controls. In losing control over their own work, the professionals become passive, like the operators of the Machine Bureaucracy. Even the job of professional administrator—never easy—becomes extremely difficult with a push for external control. In school systems, for example, the government looks top-down to the senior managers to implement its standards, while the professionals look bottom-up to them to resist the standards. The strategic apex gets caught between a government technostructure hungry for control and an operating core hanging on to its autonomy for dear life. No one gains in the process.

Are there then no solutions to a society concerned about its Professional Bureaucracies? Financial control of Professional Bureaucracies and legislation against irresponsible professional behavior are obviously necessary. But beyond that, must the professional be left with a blank check, free of public accountability? Solutions are available, but they grow from a recognition of professional work for what it is. *Change in the Professional Bureaucracy does not sweep in from new administrators taking office to announce major reforms, nor from government technostructures intent on bringing the professionals under control. Rather, change seeps in, by the slow process of changing the professionals—changing who can enter the profession, what they learn in its professional schools (ideals as well as skills and knowl-edge), and thereafter how willing they are to upgrade their skills.* Where such changes are resisted, society may be best off to call on the professionals' sense of responsibility to serve the public, or, failing that, to bring pressures on the professional associations rather than on the Professional Bureaucracies.

Notes

1. For an excellent related example—a comparison of the prison as a Machine Bureaucracy (custodial-oriented) and as a Professional Bureaucracy (treatment-oriented)—see Cressey (1958; or 1965, pp. 1044–1048). Van de Ven and Delbecq (1974) also discuss this trichotomy in terms of "systematized" programs, which specify both means and ends in detail, "discretionary" programs, which specify ends and a repertoire of means but require the operator to select the means in terms of the ends, and "developmental" programs, for highly variable tasks, which may specify general ends but not the means to achieve them.

2. Boland (1973) finds them also to be more democratic, which seems to stem from their being more formalized: "The faculty in the larger institutions are much more likely to develop a strong faculty government. Those in the smaller institutions, on the other hand, are more often subject to the decrees of administrative officials" (p. 636). This seems akin to the situation Crozier described, where the operators of large bureaucratic organizations force in rules to protect their interests. But that seems to work more to the operators' advantage in Professional rather than in Machine Bureaucracies, in the former case the rules setting up the means for true self-government, in the latter, serving only to protect the workers from the arbitrary whims of their bosses.

3. However, Kuhn's (1970) description of the practice of scientific research gives the distinct impression that most of the time—namely during periods of what he calls "normal" science, when the researchers are essentially elaborating and perfecting a given "paradigm"—the professional bureaucratic structure might be equally appropriate. Only during scientific "revolutions" should the adhocratic one clearly be more relevant.

4. Restaurants can be viewed as falling into the manufacturing or service sectors, depending on whether one focuses on the preparation of the food or on the serving of it.

5. Stinchcombe also ascribes some of these structural characteristics to the dynamic nature of the construction industry's environment, which pushes the firms to adopt the organic features of Simple Structure or Adhocracy.

6. From "MSD Crisis Plus ça change" by E. McLean, Canada Wide Feature Service in the *Montreal Star*, December 4, 1976. Used with permission.

EDUCATIONAL ORGANIZATIONS AS LOOSELY COUPLED SYSTEMS

KARL E. WEICK

In contrast to the prevailing image that elements in organizations are coupled through dense, tight linkages, it is proposed that elements are often tied together frequently and loosely. Using educational organizations as a case in point, it is argued that the concept of loose coupling incorporates a surprising number of disparate observations about organizations, suggests novel functions, creates stubborn problems for methodologists, and generates intriguing questions for scholars. Sample studies of loose coupling are suggested and research priorities are posed to foster cumulative work with this concept.

Imagine that you're either the referee, coach, player or spectator at an unconventional soccer match: the field for the game is round; there are several goals scattered haphazardly around the circular field; people can enter and leave the game whenever they want to, they can throw balls in whenever they want; they can say "that's my goal" whenever they want to, as many times as they want to, and for as many goals as they want to; the entire game takes place on a sloped field; and the game is played as if it makes sense (March, personal communication).

If you now substitute in that example principals for referees, teachers for coaches, students for players, parents for spectators and schooling for soccer, you have an equally unconventional depiction of school organizations. The beauty of this depiction is that it captures a different set of realities within educational organizations than are caught when these same organizations are viewed through the tenets of bureaucratic theory.

Consider the contrast in images. For some time people who manage organizations and people who study this managing have asked, "How does an organization go about doing what it does and with what consequences for its people, processes, products, and persistence?" And for some time they've heard the same answers. In paraphrase the answers say essentially that all organization does what it does because of plans, intentional selection of means that get the organization to agree upon goals, and all of this is accomplished by such rationalized procedures as cost-benefit analyses, division of labor, specified areas of discretion, authority invested in the office, job descriptions, and a consistent evaluation and reward system. The only problem with that portrait is that it is rare in nature. People in organizations, including educational organizations, find themselves hard pressed either to find actual instances of those rational practices or to find rationalized practices whose outcomes have been as beneficent as predicted, or to feel that those rational occasions explain much of what goes on within the organization. Parts of some organizations are heavily rationalized but many parts also prove intractable to analysis through rational assumptions.

It is this substantial unexplained remainder that is the focus of this paper. Several people in education have expressed dissatisfaction with the prevailing ideas about organizations supplied by organizational theorists. Fortunately, they have also made some provocative suggestions about

"Educational Organizations as Loosely Coupled Systems," by Karl E. Weick, reprinted with permission from *Administrative Science Quarterly*, Vol. 26, No. 1, March 1976.

newer, more unconventional ideas about organizations that should be given serious thought. A good example of this is the following observation by John M. Stephens (1967: 9–11):

> (There is a) remarkable constancy of educational results in the face of widely differing deliberate approaches. Every so often we adopt new approaches or new methodologies and place our reliance on new panaceas. At the very least we seem to chorus new slogans. Yet the academic growth within the classroom continues at about the same rate, stubbornly refusing to cooperate with the bright new dicta emanating from the conference room . . . [These observations suggest that] we would be making a great mistake in regarding the management of schools as similar to the process of constructing a building or operating a factory. In these later processes deliberate decisions play a crucial part, and the enterprise advances or stands still in proportion to the amount of deliberate effort exerted. If we must use a metaphor or model in seeking to understand the process of schooling, we should look to agriculture rather than to the factory. In agriculture we do not start from scratch, and we do not direct our efforts to inert and passive materials. We start, on the contrary, with a complex and ancient process, and we organize our efforts around what seeds, plants, and insects are likely to do anyway. . . . The crop, once planted, may undergo some development even while the farmer sleeps or loafs. No matter what he does, *some* aspects of the outcome will remain constant. When teachers and pupils foregather, some education may proceed even while the Superintendent disports himself in Atlantic City.

It is crucial to highlight what is important in the examples of soccer and schooling viewed as agriculture. To view these examples negatively and dismiss them by observing that "the referee should tighten up those rules," "superintendents don't do that," "schools are more sensible than that," or "these are terribly sloppy organizations" is to miss the point. The point is although researchers don't know what these kinds of structures are like but researchers do know they exist and that each of the negative judgments expressed above makes sense only if the observer assumes that organizations are constructed and managed according to rational assumptions and therefore are scrutable only when rational analyses are applied to them. This paper attempts to expand and enrich the set of ideas available to people when they try to make sense out of their organizational life. From this standpoint, it is unproductive to observe that fluid participation in schools and soccer is absurd. But it can be more interesting and productive to ask, how can it be that even though the activities in both situations are only modestly connected, the situations are still recognizable and nameable? The goals, player movements, and trajectory of the ball are still recognizable and can be labeled "soccer." And despite variations in class size, format, locations, and architecture, the results are still recognized and can be labeled "schools." How can such loose assemblages retain sufficient similarity and permanence across time that they can be recognized, labeled, and dealt with? The prevailing ideas in organization theory do not shed much light on how such "soft" structures develop, persist, and impose crude orderliness among their elements.

The basic premise here is that concepts such as loose coupling serve as sensitizing devices. They sensitize the observer to notice and question things that had previously been taken for granted. It is the intent of the program described here to develop a language for use in analyzing complex organizations, a language that may highlight features that have previously gone unnoticed. The guiding principle is a reversal of the common assertion, "I'll believe it when I see it" and presumes an epistemology that asserts, "I'll see it when I believe it." Organizations as loosely coupled systems may not have been seen before because nobody believed in them or could afford to believe in them. It is conceivable that preoccupation with rationalized, tidy, efficient, coordinated structures has blinded many practitioners as well as researchers to some of the attractive and unexpected properties of less rationalized and less tightly related clusters of events. This paper intends to eliminate such blindspots.

The Concept of Coupling

The phrase "loose coupling" has appeared in the literature (Glassman, 1973; March and Olsen, 1975) and it is important to highlight the connotation that is captured by this phrase and by no other. It might seem that the word coupling is synonymous with words like connection, link, or interdependence, yet each of these latter terms misses a crucial nuance.

By loose coupling, the author intends to convey the image that coupled events are responsive, *but* that each event also preserves its own identity and some evidence of its physical or logical separateness. Thus, in the case of an educational organization, it may be the case that the counselor's office is loosely coupled to the principal's office. The image is that the principal and the counselor are somehow attached, but that each retains some identity and separateness and that their attachment may be circumscribed, infrequent, weak in its mutual affects, unimportant, and/or slow to respond. Each of those connotations would be conveyed if the qualifier loosely were attached to the word coupled. Loose coupling also carries connotations of impermanence, dissolvability, and tacitness all of which are potentially crucial properties of the "glue" that holds organizations together.

Glassman (1973) categorizes the degree of coupling between two systems on the basis of the activity of the variables which the two systems share. To the extent that two systems either have few variables in common or share weak variables, they are independent of each other. Applied to the educational situation, if the principal-vice-principal-superintendent is regarded as one system and the teacher-classroom-pupil-parent-curriculum as another system, then by Glassman's argument if we did not find many variables in the teacher's world to be shared in the world of a principal and/or if the variables held in common were unimportant relative to the other variables, then the principal can be regarded as being loosely coupled with the teacher.

A final advantage of coupling imagery is that it suggests the idea of building blocks that can be grafted onto an organization or severed with relatively little disturbance to either the blocks or the organization. Simon (1969) has argued for the attractiveness of this feature in that most complex systems can be decomposed into stable subassemblies and that these are the crucial elements in any organization or system. Thus, the coupling imagery gives researchers access to one of the more powerful ways of talking about complexity now available.

But if the concept of loose coupling highlights novel images heretofore unseen in organizational theory, what is it about these images that is worth seeing?

Coupled Elements

There is no shortage of potential coupling elements, but neither is the population infinite.

At the outset the two most commonly discussed coupling mechanisms are the technical core of the organization and the authority of office. The relevance of those two mechanisms for the issue of identifying elements is that in the case of technical couplings, each element is some kind of technology, task, subtask, role, territory and person, and the couplings are task-induced. In the case of authority as the coupling mechanism, the elements include positions, offices, responsibilities, opportunities, rewards, and sanctions and it is the couplings among these elements that presumably hold the organization together. A compelling argument can be made that *neither* of these coupling mechanisms is prominent in educational organizations found in the United States. This leaves one with the question what *does* hold an educational organization together?

A short list of potential elements in educational organizations will provide background for subsequent propositions. March and Olsen (1975) utilize the elements of intention and action. There is a developing position in psychology which argues that intentions are a poor guide for action, intentions often follow rather than precede action, and that intentions and action are loosely coupled. Unfortunately, organizations continue to think that planning is a good thing, they spend much time on planning, and actions are assessed in terms of their fit with plans. Given a potential loose coupling between the intentions and actions of organizational members, it should come as no surprise that administrators are baffled and angered when things never happen the way they were supposed to.

Additional elements may consist of events like yesterday and tomorrow (what happened yesterday may be tightly or loosely coupled with what happens tomorrow) or hierarchical positions, like, top and bottom, line and staff, or administrators and teachers. An interesting set of elements that lends itself to the loose coupling imagery is means and ends. Frequently, several different means lead to the same outcome. When this happens, it can be argued that any one means is loosely coupled to the end in the sense that there are alternative pathways to achieve that same end. Other elements that might be found in loosely coupled educational systems are teachers-materials, voters-schoolboard, administrators-classroom, process-outcome, teacher-teacher, parent-teacher, and teacher-pupil.

While all of these elements are obvious, it is not a trivial matter to specify which elements are coupled. As the concept of coupling is crucial because of its ability to highlight the identity and separateness of elements that are momentarily attached, that conceptual asset puts pressure on the investigator to specify clearly the identity, separateness, and boundaries of the elements coupled. While there is some danger of reification when that kind of pressure is exerted, there is the even greater danger of portraying organizations in inappropriate terms which suggest an excess of unity, integration, coordination, and consensus. If one is nonspecific about boundaries in defining elements then it is easy—and careless—to assemble these ill-defined elements and talk about integrated organizations. It is not a trivial issue explaining how elements persevere over time. Weick, for example, has argued (1974: 363–364) that elements may appear or disappear and may merge or become separated in response to need-deprivations within the individual, group, and/or organization. This means that specification of elements is not a one-shot activity. Given the context of most organizations, elements both appear and disappear over time. For this reason a theory of how elements become loosely or tightly coupled may also have to take account of the fact that the nature and intensity of the coupling may itself serve to create or dissolve elements.

The question of what is available for coupling and decoupling within an organization is an eminently practical question for anyone wishing to have some leverage on a system.

Strength of Coupling

Obviously there is no shortage of meanings for the phrase loose coupling. Researchers need to be clear in their own thinking about whether the phenomenon they are studying is described by two words or three. A researcher can study "loose coupling" in educational organizations or "loosely coupled systems." The shorter phrase, "loose coupling," simply connotes things, "anythings," that may be tied together either weakly or infrequently or slowly or with minimal interdependence. Whether those things that are loosely coupled exist in a system is of minor importance. Most discussions in this paper concern loosely coupled systems rather than loose coupling since it wishes to clarify the concepts involved in the perseverance of sets of elements across time.

The idea of loose coupling is evoked when people have a variety of situations in mind. For example, when people describe loosely coupled systems they are often referring to (1) slack times—times when there is an excessive amount of resources relative to demands; (2) occasions when any one of several means will produce the same end; (3) richly connected networks in which influence is slow to spread and/or is weak while spreading; (4) a relative lack of coordination, slow coordination or coordination that is dampened as it moves through a system; (5) a relative absence of regulations; (6) planned unresponsiveness; (7) actual causal independence; (8) poor observational capabilities on the part of a viewer; (9) infrequent inspection of activities within the system; (10) decentralization; (11) delegation of discretion; (12) the absence of linkages that should be present based on some theory—for example, in educational organizations the expected feedback linkage from outcome back to inputs is often nonexistent; (13) the observation that an organization's structure is not coterminus with its activity; (14) those occasions when no matter what you do things always come out the same—for instance, despite all kinds of changes in curriculum, materials, groupings, and so forth the outcomes in an educational situation remain the same; and (15) curricula or courses in educational organizations for which there are few prerequisites—the longer the string of prerequisites, the tighter the coupling.

Potential Functions and Dysfunctions of Loose Coupling

It is important to note that the concept of loose coupling need not be used normatively. People who are steeped in the conventional literature of organizations may regard loose coupling as a sin or something to be apologized for. This paper takes a neutral, if not mildly affectionate, stance toward the concept. Apart from whatever affect one might feel toward the idea of loose coupling, it does appear a priori that certain functions can be served by having a system in which the elements are loosely coupled. Below are listed seven potential functions that could be associated with loose coupling plus additional reasons why each advantage might also be a liability. The dialectic generated by each of these oppositions begins to suggest dependent variables that should be sensitive to variations in the tightness of coupling.

The basic argument of Glassman (1973) is that loose coupling allows some portions of an organization to persist. Loose coupling lowers the probability that the organization will have to—or be able to—respond to each little change in the environment that occurs. The mechanism of voting, for example, allows elected officials to remain in office for a full term even though their constituency at any moment may disapprove of particular actions. Some identity and separateness of the element "elected official" is preserved relative to a second element, "constituency," by the fact of loosely coupled accountability which is measured in two, four, or six year terms. While loose coupling may foster perseverance, it is not selective in what is perpetuated. Thus archaic traditions as well as innovative improvisations may be perpetuated.

A second advantage of loose coupling is that it may provide a sensitive sensing mechanism. This possibility is suggested by Fritz Heider's perceptual theory of things and medium. Heider (1959) argues that perception is most accurate when a medium senses a thing and the medium contains many independent elements that can be externally constrained. When elements in a medium become either fewer in number and/or more internally constrained and/or more interdependent, their ability to represent some remote thing is decreased. Thus sand is a better medium to display wind currents than are rocks, the reason being that sand has more elements, more independence among the elements, and the elements are subject to a greater amount of external constraint than is the case for rocks. Using Heider's formulation metaphorically, it could be argued that loosely coupled systems preserve many independent sensing elements and therefore "know" their environments better than is true for more tightly coupled systems which have fewer externally constrained, independent elements. Balanced against this improvement in sensing is the possibility that the system would become increasingly vulnerable to producing faddish responses and interpretations. If the environment is known better, then this could induce more frequent changes in activities done in response to this "superior intelligence."

A third function is that a loosely coupled system may be a good system for localized adaptation. If all of the elements in a large system are loosely coupled to one another, then any one element can adjust to and modify a local unique contingency without affecting the whole system. These local adaptations can be swift, relatively economical, and substantial. By definition, the antithesis of localized adaptation is standardization and to the extent that standardization can be shown to be desirable, a loosely coupled system might exhibit fewer of these presumed benefits. For example, the localized adaptation characteristic of loosely coupled systems may result in a lessening of educational democracy.

Fourth, in loosely coupled systems where the identity, uniqueness, and separateness of elements is preserved, the system potentially can retain a greater number of mutations and novel solutions than would be the case with a tightly coupled system. A loosely coupled system could preserve more "cultural insurance" to be drawn upon in times of radical change than in the case for more tightly coupled systems. Loosely coupled systems may be elegant solutions to the problem that adaptation can preclude adaptability. When a specific system fits into an ecological niche and does so with great success, this adaptation can be costly. It can be costly because resources which are useless in a current environment might deteriorate or disappear even though they could be crucial in a modified environment. It is conceivable that loosely coupled systems preserve more diversity in responding than do tightly coupled systems, and therefore can adapt to a considerably wider range of changes in the environment than would be true for tightly coupled systems. To appreciate the possible problems associated with this abundance of mutations, reconsider the dynamic outlined in the preceding discussion of localized adaptation. If a local set of elements can adapt to local idiosyncrasies without involving the whole system, then this same loose coupling could also forestall the spread of advantageous mutations that exist somewhere in the system. While the system may contain novel solutions for new problems of adaptation, the very structure that allows these mutations to flourish may prevent their diffusion.

Fifth, if there is a breakdown in one portion of a loosely coupled system then this breakdown is sealed off and does not affect other portions of the organization. Previously we had noted that loosely coupled systems are an exquisite mechanism to adapt swiftly to local novelties and unique problems. Now we are carrying the analysis one step further, and arguing that when any element misfires or decays or deteriorates, the spread of this deterioration is checked in a loosely coupled system. While this point is reminiscent of earlier functions, the emphasis here is on the localization of trouble rather than the localization of adaptation. But even this potential benefit may be problematic. A loosely coupled system can isolate its trouble spots and prevent the trouble from spreading, but it should be difficult for the loosely coupled system to repair the defective element. If weak influences pass from the defective portions to the functioning portions, then the influence back from these functioning portions will also be weak and probably too little, too late.

Sixth, since some of the most important elements in educational organizations are teachers, classrooms, principals, and so forth, it may be consequential that in a loosely coupled system there is more room available for self-determination by the actors. If it is argued that a sense of efficacy is crucial for human beings, then a sense of efficacy might be greater in a loosely coupled system with autonomous units than it would be in a tightly coupled system where discretion is limited. A further comment can be made about self-determination to provide an example of the kind of imagery that is invoked by the concept of loose coupling.

It is possible that much of the teacher's sense of—and actual—control comes from the fact that diverse interested parties expect the teacher to link their intentions with teaching actions. Such linking of diverse intentions with actual work probably involves considerable negotiation. A parent complains about a teacher's action and the teacher merely points out to the parent how the actions are really correspondent with the parent's desires for the education of his or her children. Since most actions have ambiguous consequences, it should always be possible to justify the action as fitting the intentions of those who complain. Salancik (1975) goes even farther and suggests the intriguing possibility that when the consequences of an action are ambiguous, the stated *intentions* of the action serve as surrogates for the consequences. Since it is not known whether reading a certain book is good or bad for a child, the fact that it is intended to be good for the child itself becomes justification for having the child read it. The potential trade-off implicit in this function of loose coupling is fascinating. There is an increase in autonomy in the sense that resistance is heightened, but this heightened resistance occurs at the price of shortening the chain of consequences that will flow from each autonomous actor's efforts. Each teacher will have to negotiate separately with the same complaining parent.

Seventh, a loosely coupled system should be relatively inexpensive to run because it takes time and money to coordinate people. As much of what happens and should happen inside educational organizations seems to be defined and validated outside the organization, schools are in the business of building and maintaining categories, a business that requires coordination only on a few specific issues—for instance, assignment of teachers. This reduction in the necessity for coordination results in fewer conflicts, fewer inconsistencies among activities, fewer discrepancies between categories and activity. Thus, loosely coupled systems seem to hold the costs of coordination to a minimum. Despite this being an inexpensive system, loose coupling is also a nonrational system of fund allocation and therefore, unspecifiable, unmodifiable, and incapable of being used as means of change.

When these several sets of functions and dysfunctions are examined, they begin to throw several research issues into relief. For example, oppositions proposed in each of the preceding seven points suggest the importance of contextual theories. A predicted outcome or its opposite should emerge depending on how and in what the loosely coupled system is embedded. The preceding oppositions also suggest a fairly self-contained research program. Suppose a researcher starts with the first point made, as loose coupling increases the system should contain a greater number of anachronistic practices. Loosely coupled systems should be conspicuous for their cultural lags. Initially, one would like to know whether that is plausible or not. But then one would want to examine in more fine-grained detail whether those anachronistic practices that are retained hinder the system or impose structure and absorb uncertainty thereby producing certain economies in responding. Similar embellishment and elaboration is possible for each function with the result that rich networks of propositions become visible. What is especially attractive about these networks is that there is little precedent for them in the organizational literature. Despite this, these propositions contain a great deal of face validity when they are used as filters to look at educational organizations. When compared, for example, with the bureaucratic template mentioned in the introduction, the template associated with loosely coupled systems seems to take the observer into more interesting territory and prods him or her to ask more interesting questions.

Methodology and Loose Coupling

An initial warning to researchers: the empirical observation of unpredictability is insufficient evidence for concluding that the elements in a system are loosely coupled. Buried in that caveat are a host of methodological intricacies. While there is ample reason to believe that loosely coupled systems can be seen and examined, it is also possible that the appearance of loose coupling will be nothing more than a testimonial to bad methodology. In psychology, for example, it has been argued that the chronic failure to predict behavior from attitudes is due to measurement error and not to the unrelatedness of these two events. Attitudes are said to be loosely coupled with behavior but it may be that this conclusion is an artifact produced because attitudes assessed by time-independent and context-independent measures are being used to predict behaviors that are time and context dependent. If both attitudes and behaviors were assessed with equivalent measures, then tight coupling might be the rule.

Any research agenda must be concerned with fleshing out the imagery of loose coupling—a task requiring a considerable amount of conceptual work to solve a few specific and rather tricky methodological problems before one can investigate loose coupling.

By definition, if one goes into an organization and watches which parts affect which other parts, he or she will see the tightly coupled parts and the parts that vary the most. Those parts which vary slightly, infrequently, and periodically will be less visible. Notice, for example, that interaction data—who speaks to whom about what—are unlikely to reveal loose couplings. These are the most visible and obvious couplings and by the arguments developed in this paper perhaps some of the least crucial to understand what is going on in the organization.

An implied theme in this paper is that people tend to overrationalize their activities and to attribute greater meaning, predictability, and coupling among them than in fact they have. If members tend to overrationalize their activity, then their descriptions will not suggest which portions of that activity are loosely and tightly coupled. One might, in fact, even use the presence of apparent over-rationalization as a potential clue that myth making, uncertainty, and loose coupling have been spotted.

J. G. March has argued that loose coupling can be spotted and examined only if one uses methodology that highlights and preserves rich detail about context. The necessity for a contextual methodology seems to arise, interestingly enough, from inside organization theory. The implied model involves cognitive limits on rationality and man as a single channel information processor. The basic methodological point is that if one wishes to observe loose coupling, then he has to see both what is and is not being done. The general idea is that time spent on one activity is time spent away from a second activity. A contextually sensitive methodology would record both the fact that some people are in one place generating events and the fact that these same people are thereby absent from some other place. The rule of thumb would be that a tight coupling in one part of the system can occur only if there is loose coupling in another part of the system. The problem that finite attention creates for a researcher is that if some outcome is observed for the organization, then it will not be obvious whether the outcome is due to activity in the tightly coupled sector or to inactivity in the loosely coupled sector. That is a provocative problem of interpretation. But the researcher should be forewarned that there are probably a finite number of tight couplings that can occur at any moment, that tight couplings in one place imply loose couplings elsewhere, and that it may be the *pattern* of couplings that produces the observed outcomes. Untangling such intricate issues may well require that new tools be developed for contextual understanding and that investigators be willing to substitute nonteleological thinking for teleological thinking (Steinbeck, 1941: chapter 14).

Another contextually sensitive method is the use of comparative studies. It is the presumption of this methodology that taken-for-granted understandings—one possible "invisible" source of coupling in an otherwise loosely coupled system—are embedded in and contribute to a context. Thus, to see the effects of variations in these understandings one compares contexts that differ in conspicuous and meaningful ways.

Another methodological trap may await the person who tries to study loose coupling. Suppose one provides evidence that a particular goal is loosely coupled to a particular action. He or she says in effect, the person wanted to do this but in fact actually did that, thus, the action and the intention are loosely coupled. Now the problem for the researcher is that he or she may simply have focused on the wrong goal. There may be other goals which fit that particular action better. Perhaps if the researcher were aware of them, then the action and intention would appear to be tightly coupled. Any kind of intention-action, plan-behavior, or means-end depiction of loose coupling may be vulnerable to this sort of problem and an exhaustive listing of goals rather than parsimony should be the rule.

Two other methodological points should be noted. First, there are no good descriptions of the kinds of couplings that can occur among the several elements in educational organizations. Thus, a major initial research question is simply, what does a map of the couplings and elements within an educational organization look like? Second, there appear to be some fairly rich probes that might be used to uncover the nature of coupling within educational organizations. Conceivably, crucial couplings within schools involve the handling of disciplinary issues and social control, the question of how a teacher gets a book for the classroom, and the question of what kinds of innovations need to get clearance by whom. These relatively innocuous questions may be powerful means to learn which portions of a system are tightly and loosely coupled. Obviously these probes would be sampled if there was a full description of possible elements that can be coupled and possible kinds and strengths of couplings. These specific probes suggest, however, in addition that what holds an educational organization together may be a small number of tight couplings in out-of-the-way places.

Illustrative Questions for a Research Agenda

Patterns of Loose and Tight Coupling: Certification versus Inspection

Suppose one assumes that education is an intrinsically uninspected and unevaluated activity. If education is intrinsically uninspected and unevaluated then how can one establish that it is occurring? One answer is to define clearly who can and who cannot do it and to whom. In an educational organization this is the activity of certification. It is around the issues of certification and of specifying who the pupils are that tight coupling would be predicted to occur when technology and outcome are unclear.

If one argues that "certification" is the question "who does the work" and "inspection" is the question "how well is the work done," then there can be either loose or tight control over either certification or inspection. Notice that setting the problem up this way suggests the importance of discovering the distribution of tight and loosely coupled systems within any organization. Up to now the phrase loosely coupled systems has been used to capture the fact that events in an organization seem to be temporally related rather than logically related (Cohen and March, 1974). Now that view is being enriched by arguing that any organization must deal with issues of certification (who does the work) and inspection (how well is the work done). It is further being suggested that in the case of educational organizations there is loose control on the work—the work is intrinsically uninspected and unevaluated or if it is evaluated it is done so infrequently and in a perfunctory manner—but that under these conditions it becomes crucial for the organization to have tight control over who does the work and on whom. This immediately suggests the importance of comparative research in which the other three combinations are examined, the question being, how do these alternative forms grow, adapt, manage their rhetoric and handle their clientele. Thus it would be important to find organizations in which the controls over certification and inspection are both loose, organizations where there is loose control over certification but tight control over inspection, and organizations in which there is tight control both over inspection and over certification. Such comparative research might be conducted among different kinds of educational organizations within a single country (military, private, religious schooling in the United States), between educational and noneducational organizations within the same country (for example, schools versus hospitals versus military versus business organizations) or between countries looking at solutions to the problem of education given different degrees of centralization. As suggested earlier, it may not be the existence or nonexistence of loose coupling that is a crucial determinant of organizational functioning over time but rather the patterning of loose and tight couplings. Comparative studies should answer the question of distribution.

If, as noted earlier, members within an organization (and researchers) will see and talk clearly about only those regions that are tightly coupled, then this suggests that members of educational organizations should be most explicit and certain when they are discussing issues related to certification for definition and regulation of teachers, pupils, topics, space, and resources. These are presumed to be the crucial issues that are tightly controlled. Increasing vagueness of description should occur when issues of substantive instruction—inspection—are discussed. Thus, those people who primarily manage the instructional business will be most vague in describing what they do, those people who primarily manage the certification rituals will be most explicit. This pattern is predicted *not* on the basis of the activities themselves—certification is easier to describe than inspection—but rather on the basis of the expectation that tightly coupled subsystems are more crucial to the survival of the system and therefore have received more linguistic work in the past and more agreement than is true for loosely coupled elements.

Core Technology and Organizational Form

A common tactic to understand complex organizations is to explore the possibility that the nature of the task being performed determines the shape of the organizational structure. This straightforward tactic raises some interesting puzzles about educational organizations. There are suggestions in the literature that education is a diffuse task, the technology is uncertain.

This first question suggests two alternatives: if the task is diffuse then would not any organizational form whatsoever be equally appropriate *or* should this directly compel a diffuse form of organizational structure? These two alternatives are not identical. The first suggests that if the task is diffuse then any one of a variety of quite specific organizational forms could be imposed on the organization and no differences would be observed. The thrust of the second argument is that there is one and only one organizational form that would fit well when there is a diffuse task, namely, a diffuse organizational form (for instance, an organized anarchy).

The second question asks if the task in an educational organization is diffuse then why do all educational organizations look the way they do, and why do they all look the same? If there is no clear task around which the shape of the organization can be formed then why is it that most educational organizations do have a form and why is it that most of these forms look identical? One possible answer is that the tasks of educational organizations does not constrain the form of the organization but rather this constraint is imposed by the ritual of certification and/or the agreements that are made in and by the environment. If any of these nontask possibilities are genuine alternative explanations, then the general literature on organizations has been insensitive to them.

One is therefore forced to ask the question, is it the case within educational organizations that the technology is unclear? So far it has been argued that loose coupling in educational organizations is partly the result of uncertain technology. If uncertain technology does not generate loose coupling then researchers must look elsewhere for the origin of these bonds.

Making Sense in/of Loosely Coupled Worlds

What kinds of information do loosely coupled systems provide members around which they can organize meanings, that is, what can one use in order to make sense of such fleeting structures? (By definition loosely coupled events are modestly predictable at best.) There is a rather barren structure that can be observed, reported on, and retrospected in order to make any sense. Given the ambiguity of loosely coupled structures, this suggests that there may be increased pressure on members to construct or negotiate some kind of social reality they can live with. Therefore, under conditions of loose coupling one should see considerable effort devoted to constructing social reality, a great amount of face work and linguistic work, numerous myths (Mitroff and Kilmann, 1975) and in general one should find a considerable amount of effort being devoted to punctuating this loosely coupled world and connecting it in some way in which it can be made sensible. Loosely coupled worlds do not look as if they would provide an individual many resources for sense making—with such little assistance in this task, a predominant activity should involve constructing social realities. Tightly coupled portions of a system should not exhibit nearly this preoccupation with linguistic work and the social construction of reality.

Coupling as a Dependent Variable

As a general rule, any research agenda on loose coupling should devote equal attention to loose coupling as a dependent and independent variable. Most suggestions have treated loose coupling as an independent variable. Less attention has been directed toward loose coupling as a dependent variable with the one exception of the earlier argument that one can afford loose coupling in either certification or inspection but not in both and, therefore, if one can locate a tight coupling for one of these two activities then he can predict as a dependent variable loose coupling for the other one.

Some investigators, however, should view loose coupling consistently as a dependent variable. The prototypic question would be, given prior conditions such as competition for scarce resources, logic built into a task, team teaching, conflict, striving for professionalism, presence of a central ministry of education, tenure, and so forth, what kind of coupling (loose or tight) among what kinds of elements occurs? If an organization faces a scarcity of resources its pattern of couplings should differ from when it faces an expansion of resources (for instance, scarcity leads to stockpiling leads to decoupling). Part of the question here is, what kinds of changes in the environment are the variables of tight and loose coupling sensitive to? In response to what kinds of activities or what kinds of contexts is coupling seen to change and what kinds of environments or situations, when they change, seem to have no effect whatsoever on couplings within an organization? Answers to these questions, which are of vital importance in predicting the outcomes of any intervention, are most likely to occur if coupling is treated as a dependent variable and the question is, under what conditions will the couplings that emerge be tight or loose?

Assembling Loosely Connected Events

Suppose one assumes that there is nothing in the world except loosely coupled events. This assumption is close to Simon's stable subassemblies and empty world hypothesis and to the idea of cognitive limits on rationality. The imagery is that of numerous clusters of events that are tightly coupled within and loosely coupled between. These larger loosely coupled units would be what researchers usually call organizations. Notice that organizations formed this way are rather unusual kinds of organizations because they are neither tightly connected, nor explicitly bounded, but they are stable. The research question then becomes, how does it happen that loosely coupled events which remain loosely coupled are institutionally held together in one organization which retains few controls over central activities? Stated differently, how does it happen that someone can take a series of loosely coupled events, assemble them into an organization of loosely coupled systems, and the events remain both loosely coupled but the organization itself survives? It is common to observe that large organizations have loosely connected sectors. The questions are, what makes this possible, how does it happen? What the structure in school systems seems to consist of is categories (for example, teacher, pupil, reading) which are linked by understanding and legitimated exogenously (that is, by the world outside the organization). As John Meyer (1975) puts it, "the system works because everyone knows everyone else knows roughly what is to go on. . . . Educational organizations are holding companies containing shares of stock in uninspected activities and subunits which are largely given their meaning, reality, and value in the wider social market." Note the potential fragility of this fabric of legitimacy.

It remains to be seen under what conditions loosely coupled systems are fragile structures because they are shored up by consensual anticipations, retrospections, and understanding that can dissolve and under what conditions they are resilient structures because they contain mutations, localized adaptation, and fewer costs of coordination.

Separate Intending and Acting Components

Intention and action are often loosely coupled within a single individual. Salancik (1975) has suggested some conditions under which dispositions within a single individual may be loosely coupled. These include such suggestions as follows. (1) If intentions are not clear and unambiguous, then the use of them to select actions which will fulfill the intentions will be imperfect. (2) If the consequences of action are not known, then the use of intention to select action will be imperfect. (3) If the means by which an intention is transformed into an action are not known or in conflict, then the coupling of action to intention will be imperfect. (4) If intentions are not known to a person at the time of selecting an action, then the relationships between action and intention will be imperfect. This may be more common than expected because this possibility is not allowed by so-called rational models of man. People often have to recall their intentions after they act or reconstruct these intentions, or invent them. (5) If there exists a set of multiple intentions which can determine a set of similar multiple actions, then the ability to detect a relationship between any one intention and any one action is likely to be imperfect. To illustrate, if there is an intention A which implies selecting actions X and Y, and there is also an intention B which implies selecting actions X and Y, then it is possible that under both presence and absence of intention A, action X will be selected. Given these circumstances, an observer will falsely conclude that this relationship is indeterminate.

The preceding list has the potential limitation for organizational inquiry in that it consists of events within a single person. This limitation is not serious *if* the ideas are used as metaphors or if each event is lodged in a different person. For example, one could lodge intention with one person and action with some other person. With this separation, then all of the above conditions may produce loose coupling between these actors but additional conditions also come into play given this geographical separation of intention from action. For example, the simple additional requirement that the intentions must be communicated to the second actor and in such a way that they control his actions, will increase the potential for error and loose coupling. Thus any discussion of separate locations for intention and action within an organization virtually requires that the investigator specify the additional conditions under which the intending component can control the acting component. Aside from the problems of communication and control when intention and action are separated there are at least two additional conditions that could produce loose coupling.

1. If there are several diverse intending components all of whom are dependent on the same actor for implementing action, then the relationship between any one intention and any one action will be imperfect. The teacher in the classroom may well be the prototype of this condition.

2. The process outlined in the proceeding item can become even more complicated, and the linkages between intention and action even looser, if the single acting component has intentions of its own.

Intention and action are often split within organizations. This paper suggests that if one were to map the pattern of intention and action components within the organization these would coincide with loosely coupled systems identified by other means. Furthermore, the preceding propositions begin to suggest conditions under which the same components might be at one moment tightly coupled and at the next moment loosely coupled.

Conclusion: A Statement of Priorities

More time should be spent examining the possibility that educational organizations are most usefully viewed as loosely coupled systems. The concept of organizations as loosely coupled systems can have a substantial effect on existing perspectives about organizations. To probe further into the plausibility of that assertion, it is suggested that the following research priorities constitute a reasonable approach to the examination of loosely coupled systems.

1. Develop Conceptual Tools Capable of Preserving Loosely Coupled Systems

It is clear that more conceptual work has to be done before other lines of inquiry on this topic are launched. Much of the blandness in organizational theory these days can be traced to investigators applying impoverished images to organizational settings. If researchers immediately start stalking the elusive loosely coupled system with imperfect language and concepts, they will perpetuate the blandness of organizational theory. To see the importance of and necessity for this conceptual activity the reader should reexamine the 15 different connotations of the phrase "loose coupling" that are uncovered in this paper. They provide 15 alternative explanations for any researcher who claims that some outcome is due to loose coupling.

2. Explicate What Elements Are Available in Educational Organizations for Coupling

This activity has high priority because it is essential to know the practical domain within which the coupling phenomena occur. Since there is the further complication that elements may appear or disappear as a function of context and time, this type of inventory is essential at an early stage of inquiry. An indirect benefit of making this a high priority activity is that it will stem the counterproductive suspicion that "the number of elements in educational organizations is infinite." The reasonable reply to that comment is that if one is precise in defining and drawing boundaries around elements, then the number of elements will be less than imagined. Furthermore, the researcher can reduce the number of relevant elements if he has some theoretical ideas in mind. These theoretical ideas should be one of the outcomes of initial activity devoted to language and concept development (Priority 1).

3. Develop Contextual Methodology

Given favorable outcomes from the preceding two steps, researchers should then be eager to look at complex issues such as patterns of tight and loose coupling keeping in mind that loose coupling creates major problems for the researcher because he is trained and equipped to decipher predictable, tightly coupled worlds. To "see" loosely coupled worlds unconventional methodologies need to be developed and conventional methodologies that are underexploited need to be given more attention. Among the existing tools that should be refined to study loose coupling are comparative studies and longitudinal studies. Among the new tools that should be "invented" because of their potential relevance to loosely coupled systems are nonteleological thinking (Steinbeck, 1941), concurrence methodology (Bateson, 1972: 180–201), and Hegelian, Kantian, and Singerian inquiring systems (Mitroff, 1974). While these latter methodologies are unconventional within social science, so too is it unconventional to urge that we treat unpredictability (loose coupling) as our topic of interest rather than a nuisance.

4. Promote the Collection of Thorough, Concrete Descriptions of the Coupling Patterns in Actual Educational Organizations

No descriptive studies have been available to show what couplings in what patterns and with what strengths existed in current educational organizations. This oversight should be remedied as soon as possible.

Adequate descriptions should be of great interest to the practitioner who wants to know how his influence attempts will spread and with what intensity. Adequate description should also show practitioners how their organizations may be more sensible and adaptive than they suspect. Thorough descriptions of coupling should show checks and balances, localized controls, stabilizing mechanisms, and subtle feedback loops that keep the organization stable and that would promote its decay if they were tampered with.

The benefits for the researcher of full descriptions are that they would suggest which locations and which questions about loose coupling are most likely to explain sizeable portions of the variance in organizational outcomes. For example, on the basis of good descriptive work, it might be found that both tightly and loosely coupled systems "know" their environments with equal accuracy in which case, the earlier line of theorizing about "thing and medium" would be given a lower priority.

5. Specify the Nature of Core Technology in Educational Organizations

A surprisingly large number of the ideas presented in this paper assume that the typical coupling mechanisms of authority of office and logic of the task do not operate in educational organizations. Inquiry into loosely coupled systems was triggered partly by efforts to discover what *does* accomplish the coupling in school systems. Before the investigation of loose coupling goes too far, it should be established that authority and task are not prominent coupling mechanisms in schools. The assertions that they are not prominent seem to issue from a combination of informal observation, implausibility, wishful thinking, looking at the wrong things, and rather vague definitions of core technology and reward structures within education. If these two coupling mechanisms were defined clearly, studied carefully, and found to be weak and/or nonexistent in schools, *then* there would be a powerful justification for proceeding vigorously to study loosely coupled systems. Given the absence of work that definitively discounts these coupling mechanisms in education and given the fact that these two mechanisms have accounted for much of the observed couplings in other kinds of organizations, it seems crucial to look for them in educational organizations in the interest of parsimony.

It should be emphasized that if it *is* found that substantial coupling within educational organizations is due to authority of office and logic of the task, this does not negate the agenda that is sketched out in this paper. Instead, such discoveries would (1) make it even more crucial to look for patterns of coupling to explain outcomes, (2) focus attention on tight and loose couplings within task and authority induced couplings, (3) alert researchers to keep close watch for any coupling mechanisms other than these two, and (4) would direct comparative research toward settings in which these two coupling mechanisms vary in strength and form.

6. Probe Empirically the Ratio of Functions to Dysfunctions Associated with Loose Coupling

Although the word "function" has had a checkered history, it is used here without apology—and without the surplus meanings and ideology that have become attached to it. Earlier several potential benefits of loose coupling were described and these descriptions were balanced by additional suggestions of potential liabilities. If one adopts an evolutionary epistemology, then over time one expects that entities develop a more exquisite fit with their ecological niches. Given that assumption, one then argues that if loosely coupled systems exist and if they have existed for some time, then they bestow some net advantage to their inhabitants and/or their constituencies. It is not obvious, however, what these advantages are. A set of studies showing how schools benefit and suffer given their structure as loosely coupled systems should do much to improve the quality of thinking devoted to organizational analysis.

7. Discover How Inhabitants Make Sense Out of Loosely Coupled Worlds

Scientists are going to have some big problems when their topic of inquiry becomes low probability couplings, but just as scientists have special problems comprehending loosely coupled worlds so too must the inhabitants of these worlds. It would seem that quite early in a research program on loose coupling, examination of this question should be started since it has direct relevance to those practitioners who must thread their way through such "invisible" worlds and must concern their sense-making and stories in such a way that they don't bump into each other while doing so.

References

Bateson, Mary Catherine. *Our Own Metaphor,* New York: Knopf, 1972.

Cohen, Michael D., and James G. March. *Leadership and Ambiguity.* New York: McGraw-Hill, 1974.

Glassman, R. B. "Persistence and Loose Coupling in Living Systems." *Behavioral Science,* 1973,18; 83–98.

Heider, Fritz. "Thing and medium." *Psychological Issues,* 1959, 1 (3); 1–34.

March, J. G., and J. P. Olsen, *Choice Situations in Loosely Coupled Worlds.* Unpublished manuscript, Stanford University, 1975.

Meyer, John W., *Notes on the Structure of Educational Organizations.* Unpublished manuscript, Stanford University, 1975.

Mitroff, Ian I., *The Subjective Side of Science.* New York: Elsevier, 1974.

Mitroff, Ian I., and Ralph H. Kilmann, *On Organizational Stories: An Approach to the Design and Analysis of Organizations Through Myths and Stories.* Unpublished manuscript. University of Pittsburgh, 1975.

Salancik, Gerald R., *Notes on Loose Coupling: Linking Intentions to Actions.* Unpublished manuscript. University of Illinois, Urbana–Champaign, 1975.

Simon, H. A., "The architecture of complexity." *Proceedings of the American Philosophical Society,* 106, 1969; 467–482

Steinbeck, John, *The Log from the Sea of Cortez.* New York: Viking, 1941.

Stephens, John M., *The Process of Schooling.* New York: Holt, Rinehart, and Winston, 1967.

Weick, Karl E., "Middle range theories of social systems." *Behavioral Science,* 1974, 19; 357–367.

A Garbage Can Model
of Organizational Choice

Michael D. Cohen, James G. March, and Johan P. Olsen

Organized anarchies are organizations characterized by problematic preferences, unclear technology, and fluid participation. Recent studies of universities, a familiar form of organized anarchy, suggest that such organizations can be viewed for some purposes as collections of choices looking for problems, issues and feelings looking for decision situations in which they might be aired, solutions looking for issues to which they might be an answer, and decision makers looking for work. These ideas are translated into an explicit computer simulation model of a garbage can decision process. The general implications of such a model are described in terms of five major measures on the process. Possible applications of the model to more narrow predictions are illustrated by an examination of the model's predictions with respect to the effect of adversity on university decision making.

Consider organized anarchies. These are organizations—or decision situations—characterized by three general properties.[1] The first is problematic preferences. In the organization it is difficult to impute a set of preferences to the decision situation that satisfies the standard consistency requirements for a theory of choice. The organization operates on the basis of a variety of inconsistent and ill-defined preferences. It can be described better as a loose collection of ideas than as a coherent structure; it discovers preferences through action more than it acts on the basis of preferences.

The second property is unclear technology. Although the organization manages to survive and even produce, its own processes are not understood by its members. It operates on the basis of simple trial-and-error procedures, the residue of learning from the accidents of past experience, and pragmatic inventions of necessity. The third property is fluid participation. Participants vary in the amount of time and effort they devote to different domains; involvement varies from one time to another. As a result, the boundaries of the organization are uncertain and changing; the audiences and decision makers for any particular kind of choice change capriciously.

These properties of organized anarchy have been identified often in studies of organizations. They are characteristic of any organization in part—part of the time. They are particularly conspicuous in public, educational, and illegitimate organizations. A theory of organized anarchy will describe a portion of almost any organization's activities, but will not describe all of them.

To build on current behavioral theories of organizations in order to accommodate the concept of organized anarchy, two major phenomena critical to an understanding of anarchy must be investigated. The first is the manner in which organizations make choices without consistent, shared goals. Situations of decision making under goal ambiguity are common in complex organizations. Often problems are resolved without recourse to explicit bargaining or to an explicit price system market— two common processes for decision making in the absence of consensus. The second phenomenon is the way members of an organization are activated. This entails the question of how occasional members become active and how attention is directed toward, or away from, a decision. It is important to understand the attention patterns within an organization, since not everyone is attending to everything all of the time.

Additional concepts are also needed in a normative theory of organizations dealing with organized anarchies. First, a normative theory of intelligent decision making under ambiguous circumstances (namely, in situations in which goals are unclear or unknown) should be developed. Can we provide some meaning for intelligence which does not depend on relating current action to known goals? Second, a normative theory of attention is needed. Participants within an organization are constrained by the amount of time they can devote to the various things demanding attention. Since variations in behavior in organized anarchies are due largely to questions of who is attending to what, decisions concerning the allocation of attention are prime ones. Third, organized anarchies require a revised theory of management. Significant parts of contemporary theories of management introduce mechanisms for control and coordination which assume the existence of well-defined goals and a well-defined technology, as well as substantial participant involvement in the affairs of the organization. Where goals and technology are hazy and participation is fluid, many of the axioms and standard procedures of management collapse.

This article is directed to a behavioral theory of organized anarchy. On the basis of several recent studies, some elaborations and modifications of existing theories of choice are proposed. A model for describing decision making within organized anarchies is developed, and the impact of some aspects of organizational structure on the process of choice within such a model is examined.

The Basic Ideas

Decision opportunities are fundamentally ambiguous stimuli. This theme runs through several recent studies of organizational choice.[2] Although organizations can often be viewed conveniently as vehicles for solving well-defined problems or structures within which conflict is resolved through bargaining, they also provide sets of procedures through which participants arrive at an interpretation of what they are doing and what they have done while in the process of doing it. From this point of view, an organization is a collection of choices looking for problems, issues and feelings looking for decision situations in which they might be aired, solutions looking for issues to which they might be the answer, and decision makers looking for work.

Such a view of organizational choice focuses attention on the way the meaning of a choice changes over time. It calls attention to the strategic effects of timing, through the introduction of choices and problems, the time pattern of available energy, and the impact of organizational structure.

To understand processes within organizations, one can view a choice opportunity as a garbage can into which various kinds of problems and solutions are dumped by participants as they are generated. The mix of garbage in a single can depends on the mix of cans available, on the labels attached to the alternative cans, on what garbage is currently being produced, and on the speed with which garbage is collected and removed from the scene.

Such a theory of organizational decision making must concern itself with a relatively complicated interplay among the generation of problems in an organization, the deployment of personnel, the production of solutions, and the opportunities for choice. Although it may be convenient to imagine that choice opportunities lead first to the generation of decision alternatives, then to an examination of their consequences, then to an evaluation of those consequences in terms of objectives, and finally to a decision, this type of model is often a poor description of what actually happens. In the garbage can model, on the other hand, a decision is an outcome or interpretation of several relatively independent streams within an organization.

Attention is limited here to interrelations among four such streams.

Problems. Problems are the concern of people inside and outside the organization. They might arise over issues of lifestyle; family; frustrations of work; careers; group relations within the organization; distribution of status, jobs, and money; ideology; or current crises of mankind as interpreted by the mass media or the nextdoor neighbor. All of these require attention.

Solutions. A solution is somebody's product. A computer is not just a solution to a problem in payroll management, discovered when needed. It is an answer actively looking for a question. The creation of need is not a curiosity of the market in consumer products; it is a general phenomenon of processes of choice. Despite the dictum that you cannot find the answer until you have formulated the question well, you often do not know what the question is in organizational problem solving until you know the answer.

Participants. Participants come and go. Since every entrance is an exit somewhere else, the distribution of "entrances" depends on the attributes of the choice being left as much as it does on the attributes of the new choice. Substantial variation in participation stems from other demands on the participants' time (rather than from features of the decision under study).

Choice opportunities. These are occasions when an organization is expected to produce behavior that can be called a decision. Opportunities arise regularly and any organization has ways of declaring an occasion for choice. Contracts must be signed; people hired, promoted, or fired; money spent; and responsibilities allocated.

Although not completely independent of each other, each of the streams can be viewed as independent and exogenous to the system. Attention will be concentrated here on examining the consequences of different rates and patterns of flows in each of the streams and different procedures for relating them.

The Garbage Can

A simple simulation model can be specified in terms of the four streams and a set of garbage processing assumptions.

Four basic variables are considered; each is a function of time.

A stream of choices. Some fixed number, m, of choices is assumed. Each choice is characterized by (a) an entry time, the calendar time at which that choice is activated for decision, and (b) a decision structure, a list of participants eligible to participate in making that choice.

A stream of problems. Some number, w, of problems is assumed. Each problem is characterized by (a) an entry time, the calendar time at which the problem becomes visible, (b) an energy requirement, the energy required to resolve a choice to which the problem is attached (if the solution stream is as high as possible), and (c) an access structure, a list of choices to which the problem has access.

A rate of flow of solutions. The verbal theory assumes a stream of solutions and a matching of specific solutions with specific problems and choices. A simpler set of assumptions is made and focus is on the rate at which solutions are flowing into the system. It is assumed that either because of variations in the stream of solutions or because of variations in the efficiency of search procedures within the organization, different energies are required to solve the same problem at different times. It is further assumed that these variations are consistent for different problems. Thus, a solution coefficient, ranging between 0 and 1, which operates on the potential decision energies to determine the problem solving output (effective energy) actually realized during any given time period is specified.

A stream of energy from participants. It is assumed that there is some number, v, of participants. Each participant is characterized by a time series of energy available for organizational decision making. Thus, in each time period, each participant can provide some specified amount of potential energy to the organization.

Two varieties of organizational segmentation are reflected in the model. The first is the mapping of choices onto decision makers, the decision structure. The decision structure of the organization is described by D, a v-by-m array in which d_{ij} is 1 if the ith participant is eligible to participate in the making of the jth choice. Otherwise, d_{ij} is 0. The second is the mapping of problems onto choices, the access structure. The access structure of the organization is described by A, a w-by-m array in which a_{ij} is 1 if the jth choice is accessible to the ith problem. Otherwise, a_{ij} is 0.

In order to connect these variables, three key behavioral assumptions are specified. The first is an assumption about the additivity of energy requirements, the second specifies the way in which energy is allocated to choices, and the third describes the way in which problems are attached to choices.

Energy additivity assumption. In order to be made, each choice requires as much effective energy as the sum of all requirements of the several problems attached to it. The effective energy devoted to a choice is the sum of the energies of decision makers attached to that choice, deflated, in each time period, by the solution coefficient. As soon as the total effective energy that has been expended on a choice equals or exceeds the requirements at a particular point in time, a decision is made.

Energy allocation assumption. The energy of each participant is allocated to no more than one choice during each time period. Each participant allocates his energy among the choices for which he is eligible to the one closest to decision, that is the one with the smallest energy deficit at the end of the previous time period in terms of the energies contributed by other participants.

Problem allocation assumption. Each problem is attached to no more than one choice each time period, choosing from among those accessible by calculating the apparent energy deficits (in terms of the energy requirements of other problems) at the end of the previous time period and selecting the choice closest to decision. Except to the extent that priorities enter in the organizational structure, there is no priority ranking of problems.

These assumptions capture key features of the processes observed. They might be modified in a number of ways without doing violence to the empirical observations on which they are based. The consequences of these modifications, however, are not pursued here. Rather, attention is focused on the implications of the simple version described. The interaction of organizational structure and a garbage can form of choice will be examined.

Organizational Structure

Elements of organizational structure influence outcomes of a garbage can decision process (a) by affecting the time pattern of the arrival of problems choices, solutions, or decision makers, (b) by determining the allocation of energy by potential participants in the decision, and (c) by establishing linkages among the various streams.

The organizational factors to be considered are some that have real-world interpretations and implications and are applicable to the theory of organized anarchy. They are familiar features of organizations, resulting from a mixture of deliberate managerial planning, individual and collective learning, and imitation. Organizational structure changes as a response to such factors as market demand for personnel and the heterogeneity of values, which are external to the model presented here. Attention will be limited to the comparative statics of the model, rather than to the dynamics produced by organizational learning.

To exercise the model, the following are specified: (a) a set of fixed parameters which do not change from one variation to another, (b) the entry times for choices, (c) the entry times for problems, (d) the net energy load on the organization, (e) the access structure of the organization, (f) the decision structure of the organization, and (g) the energy distribution among decision makers in the organization.

Some relatively pure structural variations will be identified in each and examples of how variations in such structures might be related systematically to key exogenous variables will be given. It will then be shown how such factors of organizational structure affect important characteristics of the decisions in a garbage can decision process.

Fixed Parameters

Within the variations reported, the following are fixed: (a) number of time periods—twenty, (b) number of choice opportunities—ten, (c) number of decision makers—ten, (d) number of problems—twenty, and (e) the solution coefficients for the 20 time periods—0.6 for each period.[3]

Entry Times

Two different randomly generated sequences of entry times for choices are considered. It is assumed that one choice enters per time period over the first ten time periods in one of the following orders: (a) 10, 7, 9, 5, 2, 3, 4, 1, 6, 8, or (b) 6, 5, 2, 10, 8, 9, 7, 4, 1, 3.

Similarly, two different randomly generated sequences of entry times for problems are considered. It is assumed that two problems enter per time period over the first ten time periods in one of the following orders: (a) 8, 20, 14, 16, 6, 7, 15, 17, 2, 13, 11, 19, 4, 9, 3, 12, 1, 10, 5, 18, or (b) 4, 14, 11, 20, 3, 5, 2, 12, 1, 6, 8, 19, 7, 15, 16, 17, 10, 18, 9, 13.

Net Energy Load

The total energy available to the organization in each time period is 5.5 units. Thus, the total energy available over twenty time periods is $20 \times 5.5 = 110$. This is reduced by the solution coefficients to 66. These figures hold across all other variations of the model. The net energy load on the organization is defined as the difference between the total energy required to solve all problems and the total effective energy available to the organization over all time periods. When this is negative, there is, in principle, enough energy available. Since the total effective energy available is fixed at 66, the net load is varied by varying the total energy requirements for problems. It is assumed that each problem has the same energy requirement under a given load. Three different energy load situations are considered.

Net energy load 0: light load. Under this condition the energy required to make a choice is 1.1 times the number of problems attached to that choice. That is, the energy required for each problem is 1.1. Thus, the minimum total effective energy required to resolve all problems is 22, and the net energy load is $22 - 66 = -44$.

Net energy load 1: moderate load. Under this condition, the energy required for each problem is 2.2. Thus, the energy required to make a choice is 2.2 times the number of problems attached to that choice, and the minimum effective energy required to resolve all problems is 44. The net energy load is $44 - 66 = -22$.

Net energy load 2: heavy load. Under this condition, each problem requires energy of 3.3. The energy required to make a choice is 3.3 times the number of problems attached to that choice. The minimum effective energy required to resolve all problems is 66, and the net energy load is $66 - 66 = 0$.

Although it is possible from the total energy point of view for all problems to be resolved in any load condition, the difficulty of accomplishing that result where the net energy load is zero—a heavy load—is obviously substantial.

Access Structure

Three pure types of organizational arrangements are considered in the access structure (the relation between problems and choices).

Access structure 0: unsegmented access. This structure is represented by an access array in which any active problem has access to any active choice.

$$
A_0 =
\begin{matrix}
1111111111 \\
1111111111 \\
1111111111 \\
1111111111 \\
1111111111 \\
1111111111 \\
1111111111 \\
1111111111 \\
1111111111 \\
1111111111 \\
1111111111 \\
1111111111 \\
1111111111
\end{matrix}
$$

1111111111
1111111111
1111111111
1111111111
1111111111
1111111111
1111111111

Access structure 1: hierarchical access. In this structure both choices and problems are arranged in a hierarchy such that important problems—those with relatively low numbers—have access to many choices, and important choices—those with relatively low numbers—are accessible only to important problems. The structure is represented by the following access array:

$$
A_1 = \begin{matrix}
1111111111 \\
1111111111 \\
0111111111 \\
0111111111 \\
0011111111 \\
0011111111 \\
0001111111 \\
0001111111 \\
0000111111 \\
0000111111 \\
0000011111 \\
0000011111 \\
0000001111 \\
0000001111 \\
0000000111 \\
0000000111 \\
0000000011 \\
0000000011 \\
0000000001 \\
0000000001
\end{matrix}
$$

Access structure 2: specialized access. In this structure each problem has access to only one choice and each choice is accessible to only two problems, that is, choices specialize in the kinds of problems that can be associated to them. The structure is represented by the following access array:

$$
A_2 = \begin{matrix}
1000000000 \\
1000000000 \\
0100000000 \\
0100000000 \\
0010000000 \\
0010000000 \\
0001000000 \\
0001000000 \\
0000100000 \\
0000100000 \\
0000010000
\end{matrix}
$$

```
0000010000
0000001000
0000001000
0000000100
0000000100
0000000010
0000000010
0000000001
0000000001
```

Actual organizations will exhibit a more complex mix of access rules. Any such combination could be represented by an appropriate access array. The three pure structures considered here represent three classic alternative approaches to the problem of organizing the legitimate access of problems to decision situations.

Decision Structure

Three similar pure types are considered in the decision structure (the relation between decision makers and choices).

Decision structure 0: unsegmented decisions. In this structure any decision maker can participate in any active choice opportunity. Thus, the structure is represented by the following array:

$$
D_0 = \begin{array}{l}
1111111111 \\
1111111111 \\
1111111111 \\
1111111111 \\
1111111111 \\
1111111111 \\
1111111111 \\
1111111111 \\
1111111111 \\
1111111111
\end{array}
$$

Decision structure 1: hierarchical decisions. In this structure both decision makers and choices are arranged in a hierarchy such that important choices—low numbered choices—must be made by important decision makers—low numbered decision makers—and important decision makers can participate in many choices. The structure is represented by the following array:

$$
D_1 = \begin{array}{l}
1111111111 \\
0111111111 \\
0011111111 \\
0001111111 \\
0000111111 \\
0000011111 \\
0000001111
\end{array}
$$

0000000111

0000000011

0000000001

Decision structure 2: specialized decisions. In this structure each decision maker is associated with a single choice and each choice has a single decision maker. Decision makers specialize in the choices to which they attend. Thus, we have the following array:

$$D_2 = \begin{matrix} 1000000000 \\ 0100000000 \\ 0010000000 \\ 0000100000 \\ 0000010000 \\ 0000001000 \\ 0000000100 \\ 0000000010 \\ 0000000001 \end{matrix}$$

As in the case of the access structure, actual decision structures will require a more complicated array. Most organizations have a mix of rules for defining the legitimacy of participation in decisions. The three pure cases are, however, familiar models of such rules and can be used to understand some consequences of decision structure for decision processes.

Energy Distribution

The distribution of energy among decision makers reflects possible variations in the amount of time spent on organizational problems by different decision makers. The solution coefficients and variations in the energy requirement for problems affect the overall relation between energy available and energy required. Three different variations in the distribution of energy are considered.

Energy distribution 0: important people—less energy. In this distribution important people, that is people defined as important in a hierarchical decision structure, have less energy. This might reflect variations in the combination of outside demands and motivation to participate within the organization. The specific energy distribution is indicated as follows:

Decision Maker	Energy	
1	0.1	
2	0.2	
3	0.3	
4	0.4	
5	0.5	$= E_0$
6	0.6	
7	0.7	
8	0.8	
9	0.9	
10	1.0	

The total energy available to the organization each time period (before deflation by the solution coefficients) is 5.5.

Energy distribution 1: equal energy. In this distribution there is no internal differentiation among decision makers with respect to energy. Each decision maker has the same energy (0.55) each time period. Thus, there is the following distribution:

Decision Maker	Energy	
1	0.55	
2	0.55	
3	0.55	
4	0.55	
5	0.55	$= E_1$
6	0.55	
7	0.55	
8	0.55	
9	0.55	
10	0.55	

The total energy available to the organization each time period (before deflation by the solution coefficients) is 5.5.

Energy distribution 2: important people—more energy. In this distribution energy is distributed unequally but in a direction opposite to that in E_0. Here the people defined as important by the hierarchical decision structure have more energy. The distribution is indicated by the following:

Decision Maker	Energy	
1	1.0	
2	0.9	
3	0.8	
4	0.7	
5	0.6	$= E_2$
6	0.5	
7	0.4	
8	0.3	
9	0.2	
10	0.1	

As in the previous organizations, the total energy available to the organization each time period (before deflation by the solution coefficients) is 5.5.

Where the organization has a hierarchical decision structure, the distinction between important and unimportant decision makers is clear. Where the decision structure is unsegmented or specialized, the variations in energy distribution are defined in terms of the same numbered decision makers (lower numbers are more important than higher numbers) to reflect possible status differences which are not necessarily captured by the decision structure.

Simulation Design

The simulation design is simple. A Fortran version of the garbage can model is given in the appendix, along with documentation and an explanation. The $3^4 = 81$ types of organizational situations obtained by taking the possible combinations of the values of the four dimensions of an organization (access structure, decision structure, energy distribution, and net energy load) are studied here under the four combinations of choice and problem entry times. The result is 324 simulation situations.

Summary Statistics

The garbage can model operates under each of the possible organizational structures to assign problems and decision makers to choices, to determine the energy required and effective energy applied to choices, to make such choices and resolve such problems as the assignments and energies indicate are feasible. It does this for each of the twenty time periods in a twenty-period simulation of organizational decision making.

For each of the 324 situations, some set of simple summary statistics on the process is required. These are limited to five.

Decision Style

Within the kind of organization postulated, decisions are made in three different ways.

By resolution. Some choices resolve problems after some period of working on them. The length of time may vary, depending on the number of problems. This is the familiar case that is implicit in most discussions of choice within organizations.

By oversight. If a choice is activated when problems are attached to other choices and if there is energy available to make the new choice quickly, it will be made without any attention to existing problems and with a minimum of time and energy.

By flight. In some cases choices are associated with problems (unsuccessfully) for some time until a choice more attractive to the problems comes along. The problems leave the choice, and thus it is now possible to make the decision. The decision resolves no problems; they having now attached themselves to a new choice.

Some choices involve both flight and resolution—some problems leave, the remainder are solved. These have been defined as resolution, thus slightly exaggerating the importance of that style. As a result of that convention, the three styles are mutually exclusive and exhaustive with respect to any one choice. The same organization, however, may use any one of them in different choices. Thus, the decision style of any particular variation of the model can be described by specifying the proportion of completed choices which are made in each of these three ways.

Problem Activity

Any measure of the degree to which problems are active within the organization should reflect the degree of conflict within the organization or the degree of articulation of problems. Three closely related statistics of problem activity are considered. The first is the total number of problems not solved at the end of the twenty time periods; the second is the total number of times that any problem shifts from one choice to another, while the third is the total number of time periods that a problem is active and attached to some choice, summed over all problems. These measures are strongly correlated with each other. The third is used as the measure of problem activity primarily because it has a relatively large variance; essentially the same results would have been obtained with either of the other two measures.

Problem Latency

A problem may be active, but not attached to any choice. The situation is one in which a problem is recognized and accepted by some part of the organization, but is not considered germane to any available choice. Presumably, an organization with relatively high problem latency will exhibit somewhat different symptoms from one with low latency. Problem latency has been measured by the total number of periods a problem is active, but not attached to a choice, summed over all problems.

Decision Maker Activity

To measure the degree of decision maker activity in the system, some measure which reflects decision maker energy expenditure, movement, and persistence is required. Four are considered: (a) the total number of time periods a decision maker is attached to a choice, summed over all decision makers, (b) the total number of times that any decision maker shifts from one choice to another, (c) the total amount of effective energy available and used, and (d) the total effective energy used on choices in excess of that required to make them at the time they are made. These four measures are highly intercorrelated. The second was used primarily because of its relatively large variance; any of the others would have served as well.

Decision Difficulty

Because of the way in which decisions can be made in the system, decision difficulty is not the same as the level of problem activity. Two alternative measures are considered: the total number of choices not made by the end of the twenty time periods and the total number of periods that a choice is active, summed over all choices. These are highly correlated. The second is used, primarily because of its higher variance; the conclusions would be unchanged if the first were used.

Implications of the Model

An analysis of the individual histories of the simulations shows eight major properties of garbage can decision processes.

First, resolution of problems as a style for making decisions is not the most common style, except under conditions where flight is severely restricted (for instance, specialized access) or a few conditions under light load. Decision making by flight and oversight is a major feature of the process in general. In each of the simulation trials there were twenty problems and ten choices. Although the mean number of choices not made was 1.0, the mean number of problems not solved was 1.2.3. The results are detailed in Table 1. The behavioral and normative implications of a decision process which appears to make choices in large part by flight or by oversight must be examined. A possible explanation of the behavior of organizations that seem to make decisions without apparently making progress in resolving the problems that appear to be related to the decisions may be emerging.

Second, the process is quite thoroughly and quite generally sensitive to variations in load. As Table 2 shows, an increase in the net energy load on the system generally increases problem activity,

TABLE 1

Proportion of Choices That Resolve Problems under Four Conditions of Choice and Problem Entry Times, by Load and Access Structure

		Access Structure			
		All	Unsegmented	Hierarchical	Specialized
Load	Light	0.55	0.38	0.61	0.65
	Moderate	0.30	0.04	0.27	0.60
	Heavy	0.36	0.35	0.23	0.50
	All	0.40	0.26	0.37	0.58

TABLE 2

Effects of Variations in Load under Four Conditions of Choice and Problem Entry Times

		Mean Problem Activity	Mean Decision Maker Activity	Mean Decision Difficulty	Proportion of Choices by Flight or Oversight
Load	Light	114.9	60.9	19.5	.45
	Moderate	204.3	63.8	32.9	.70
	Heavy	211.1	76.6	46.1	.64

decision maker activity, decision difficulty, and the uses of flight and oversight. Problems are less likely to be solved, decision makers are likely to shift from one problem to another more frequently, choices are likely to take longer to make and are less likely to resolve problems. Although it is possible to specify an organization that is relatively stable with changes in load, it is not possible to have an organization that is stable in behavior and also has other desirable attributes. As load changes, an organization that has an unsegmented access structure with a specialized decision structure stays quite stable. It exhibits relatively low decision difficulty and decision maker activity, very low problem latency, and maximum problem activity. It makes virtually all decisions placed before it, uses little energy from decision makers, and solves virtually no problems.

Third, a typical feature of the model is the tendency of decision makers and problems to track each other through choices. Subject to structural restrictions on the tracking, decision makers work on active problems in connection with active choices; both decision makers and problems tend to move together from choice to choice. Thus, one would expect decision makers who have a feeling that they are always working on the same problems in somewhat different contexts, mostly without results. Problems, in a similar fashion, meet the same people wherever they go with the same result.

Fourth, there are some important interconnections among three key aspects of the efficiency of the decision processes specified. The first is problem activity, the amount of time unresolved problems are actively attached to choice situations. Problem activity is a rough measure of the potential for decision conflict in the organization. The second aspect is problem latency, the amount of time problems spend activated but not linked to choices. The third aspect is decision time, the persistence of choices. Presumably, a good organizational structure would keep both problem activity and problem latency low through rapid problem solution in its choices. In the garbage can process such a result was never observed. Segmentation of the access structure tends to reduce the number of unresolved problems active in the organization but at the cost of increasing the latency period of problems and, in most cases the time devoted to reaching decisions. On the other hand, segmentation of the decision structure tends to result in decreasing problem latency, but at the cost of increasing problem activity and decision time.

Fifth, the process is frequently sharply interactive. Although some phenomena associated with the garbage can are regular and flow through nearly all of the cases, for example, the effect of overall load, other phenomena are much more dependent on the particular combination of structures involved. Although high segmentation of access structure generally produces slow decision time, for instance, a specialized access structure, in combination with an unsegmented decision structure, produces quick decisions.

Sixth, important problems are more likely to be solved than unimportant ones. Problems which appear early are more likely to be resolved than later ones. Considering only those cases involving access hierarchy where importance is defined for problems, the relation between problem importance and order of arrival is shown in Table 3. The system, in effect, produces a queue of problems in terms of their importance, to the disadvantage of late-arriving, relatively unimportant problems, and particularly so when load is heavy. This queue is the result of the operation of the model. It was not imposed as a direct assumption.

TABLE 3

Proportion of Problems Resolved under Four Conditions of Choice and Problem Entry Times, by Importance of Problem and Order of Arrival of Problem (for Hierarchical Access)

		Time of Arrival of Problem	
		Early, First 10	Late, Last 10
Importance of problem	High, first 10	0.46	0.44
	Low, last 10	0.48	0.25

TABLE 4

**Proportion of Choices That Are Made by Flight or Oversight under Four Conditions
of Choice and Problem Entry Times, by Time of Arrival and Importance
of Choice (for Hierarchical Access or Decision Structure)**

		Time of Arrival of Choice	
		Early, First 5	Late, Last 5
Importance of choice	High, first 5	0.86	0.65
	Low, last 5	0.54	0.60

Seventh, important choices are less likely to resolve problems than unimportant choices. Important choices are made by oversight and flight. Unimportant choices are made by resolution. These differences are observed under both of the choice entry sequences but are sharpest where important choices enter relatively early. Table 4 shows the results. This property of important choices in a garbage can decision process can be naturally and directly related to the phenomenon in complex organizations of important choices which often appear to just happen.

Eighth, although a large proportion of the choices are made, the choice failures that do occur are concentrated among the most important and least important choices. Choices of intermediate importance are virtually always made. The proportion of choice failures, under conditions of hierarchical access or decision structures is as follows:

Three most important choices	0.14
Four middle choices	0.05
Three least important choices	0.12

In a broad sense, these features of the process provide some clues to how organizations survive when they do not know what they are doing. Much of the process violates standard notions of how decisions ought to be made. But most of those notions are built on assumptions which cannot be met under the conditions specified. When objectives and technologies are unclear, organizations are charged to discover some alternative decision procedures which permit them to proceed without doing extraordinary violence to the domains of participants or to their model of what an organization should be. It is a hard charge, to which the process described is a partial response.

At the same time, the details of the outcomes clearly depend on features of the organizational structure. The same garbage can operation results in different behavioral symptoms under different levels of load on the system or different designs of the structure of the organization. Such differences raise the possibility of predicting variations in decision behavior in different organizations. One possible example of such use remains to be considered.

Garbage Cans and Universities

One class of organization which faces decision situations involving unclear goals, unclear technology, and fluid participants is the modern college or university. If the implications of the model are applicable anywhere, they are applicable to a university. Although there is great variation among colleges and universities, both between countries and within any country, the model has general relevance to decision making in higher education.

General Implications

University decision making frequently does not resolve problems. Choices are often made by flight or oversight. University decision processes are sensitive to increases in load. Active decision makers and problems track one another through a series of choices without appreciable progress in solving problems. Important choices are not likely to solve problems.

Decisions whose interpretations continually change during the process of resolution appear both in the model and in actual observations of universities. Problems, choices, and decision makers arrange and rearrange themselves. In the course of these arrangements the meaning of a choice can change several times, if this meaning is understood as the mix of problems discussed in the context of that choice.

Problems are often solved, but rarely by the choice to which they are first attached. A choice that might, under some circumstances, be made with little effort becomes an arena for many problems. The choice becomes almost impossible to make, until the problems drift off to another arena. The matching of problems, choices, and decision makers is partly controlled by attributes of content, relevance, and competence; but it is also quite sensitive to attributes of timing, the particular combinations of current garbage cans, and the overall load on the system.

Universities and Adversity

In establishing connections between the hypothetical attributes of organizational structure in the model and some features of contemporary universities, the more detailed implications of the model can be used to explore features of university decision making. In particular, the model can examine the events associated with one kind of adversity within organizations, the reduction of organizational slack.

Slack is the difference between the resources of the organization and the combination of demands made on it. Thus, it is sensitive to two major factors: (a) money and other resources provided to the organization by the external environment, and (b) the internal consistency of the demands made on the organization by participants. It is commonly believed that organizational slack has been reduced substantially within American colleges and universities over the past few years. The consequences of slack reduction in a garbage can decision process can be shown by establishing possible relations between changes in organizational slack and the key structural variables within the model.

Net energy load. The net energy load is the difference between the energy required within an organization and the effective energy available. It is affected by anything that alters either the amount of energy available to the organization or the amount required to find or generate problem solutions. The energy available to the organization is partly a function of the overall strength of exit opportunities for decision makers. For example, when there is a shortage of faculty, administrators, or students in the market for participants, the net energy load on a university is heavier than it would be when there is no shortage. The energy required to find solutions depends on the flow of possible problem solutions. For example, when the environment of the organization is relatively rich, solutions are easier to find and the net energy is reduced. Finally, the comparative attractiveness and permeability of the organization to problems affects the energy demands on it. The more attractive, the more demands. The more permeable, the more demands. Universities with slack and with relatively easy access, compared to other alternative arenas for problem carriers, will attract a relatively large number of problems.

Access structure. The access structure in an organization would be expected to be affected by deliberate efforts to derive the advantages of delegation and specialization. Those efforts, in turn, depend on some general characteristics of the organizational situation, task, and personnel. For example, the access structure would be expected to be systematically related to two features of the organization: (a) the degree of technical and value heterogeneity, and (b) the amount of organizational slack. Slack, by providing resource buffers between parts of the organization, is essentially a substitute for technical and value homogeneity. As heterogeneity increases, holding slack constant, the access structure shifts from an unsegmented to a specialized to a hierarchical structure. Similarly, as slack decreases, holding heterogeneity constant, the access structure shifts from an unsegmented to a specialized to a hierarchical structure. The combined picture is shown in Figure 1.

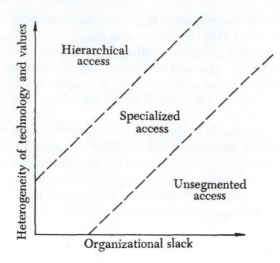

Figure 1   Hypothesized relationship between slack, heterogeneity, and the access structure of an organization.

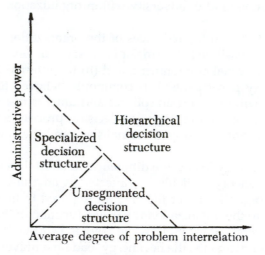

Figure 2   Hypothesized relationship between administrative power, interrelation of problems, and the decision structure of an organization.

Decision structure. Like the access structure, the decision structure is partly a planned system for the organization and partly a result of learning and negotiation within the organization. It could be expected to be systematically related to the technology, to attributes of participants and problems, and to the external conditions under which the organization operates. For example, there are joint effects of two factors: (a) relative administrative power within the system, the extent to which the formal administrators are conceded substantial authority, and (b) the average degree of perceived interrelation among problems. It is assumed that high administrative power or high interrelation of problems will lead to hierarchical decision structure, that moderate power and low interrelation of problems leads to specialized decision structures, and that relatively low administrative power, combined with moderate problem interrelation, leads to unsegmented decision structures. The hypothetical relations are shown in Figure 2.

Energy distribution. Some of the key factors affecting the energy distribution within an organization are associated with the alternative opportunities decision makers have for investing their time. The extent to which there is an active external demand for attention affects the extent to which decision makers will have energy available for use within the organization. The stronger the relative

Figure 3 Hypothesized relationship between exit opportunities and the distribution of energy within an organization.

outside demand on important people in the organization, the less time they will spend within the organization relative to others. Note that the energy distribution refers only to the relation between the energy available from important people and less important people. Thus, the energy distribution variable is a function of the relative strength of the outside demand for different people, as shown in Figure 3.

Within a university setting it is not hard to imagine circumstances in which exit opportunities are different for different decision makers. Tenure, for example, strengthens the exit opportunities for older faculty members. Money strengthens the exit opportunities for students and faculty members, though more for the former than the latter. A rapidly changing technology tends to strengthen the exit opportunities for young faculty members.

Against this background four types of colleges and universities are considered: (a) large, rich universities, (b) large, poor universities, (c) small, rich colleges, and (d) small, poor colleges.

Important variations in the organizational variables among these schools can be expected. Much of that variation is likely to be within-class variation. Assumptions about these variables, however, can be used to generate some assumptions about the predominant attributes of the four classes, under conditions of prosperity.

Under such conditions a relatively rich school would be expected to have a light energy load, a relatively poor school a moderate energy load. With respect to access structure, decision structure, and the internal distribution of energy, the appropriate position of each of the four types of schools is marked with a circular symbol on Figures 4, 5, and 6. The result is the pattern of variations indicated below:

	Load	Access Structure	Decision Structure	Energy Distribution
Large, rich	Light 0	Specialized 2	Unsegmented 0	Less 0
Large, poor	Moderate 1	Hierarchical 1	Hierarchical 1	More 2
Small, rich	Light 0	Unsegmented 0	Unsegmented 0	More 2
Small, poor	Moderate 1	Specialized 2	Specialized 2	Equal 1

With this specification, the garbage can model can be used to predict the differences expected among the several types of school. The results are found in Table 5. They suggest that under conditions of prosperity, overt conflict (problem activity) will be substantially higher in poor schools than

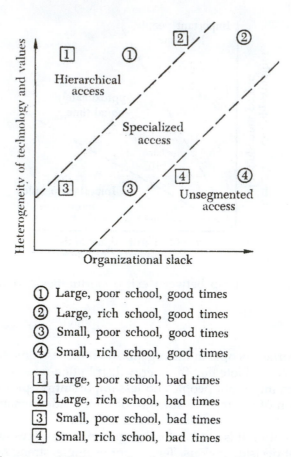

① Large, poor school, good times
② Large, rich school, good times
③ Small, poor school, good times
④ Small, rich school, good times

1 Large, poor school, bad times
2 Large, rich school, bad times
3 Small, poor school, bad times
4 Small, rich school, bad times

Figure 4 Hypothesized location of different schools in terms of slack and heterogeneity.

in rich ones, and decision time will be substantially longer. Large, rich schools will be characterized by a high degree of problem latency. Most decisions will resolve some problems.

What happens to this group of schools under conditions of adversity—when slack is reduced? According to earlier arguments, slack could be expected to affect each of the organizational variables. It first increases net energy load, as resources become shorter and thus problems require a larger share of available energy to solve, but this effect is later compensated by the reduction in market demand for personnel and in the relative attractiveness of the school as an arena for problems. The market effects also reduce the differences in market demand for important and unimportant people. The expected results of these shifts are shown by the positions of the square symbols in Figure 6.

At the same time, adversity affects both access structure and decision structure. Adversity can be expected to bring a reduction in slack and an increase in the average interrelation among problems. The resulting hypothesized shifts in access and decision structures are shown in Figures 4 and 5.

Table 5 shows the effects of adversity on the four types of schools according to the previous assumptions and the garbage can model. By examining the first stage of adversity, some possible reasons for discontent among presidents of large, rich schools can be seen. In relation to other schools they are not seriously disadvantaged. The large, rich schools have a moderate level of problem activity, a moderate level of decision by resolution. In relation to their earlier state, however, large, rich schools are certainly deprived. Problem activity and decision time have increased greatly; the proportion of decisions which resolve problems has decreased from 68 percent to 21 percent; administrators are less able to move around from one decision to another. In all these terms, the relative deprivation of the presidents of large, rich schools is much greater, in the early stages of adversity, than that of administrators in other schools.

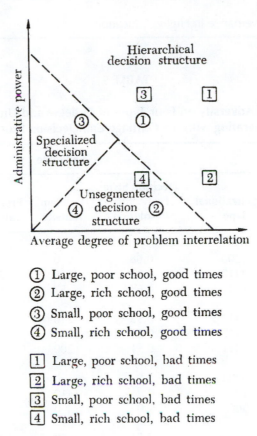

Figure 5 Hypothesized location of different schools in terms of administrative power and perceived interrelation of problems.

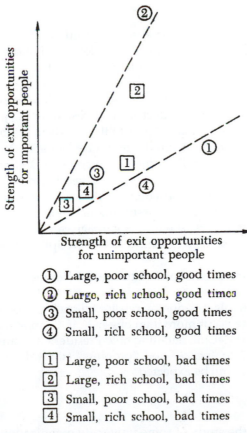

Figure 6 Hypothesized location of different schools in terms of exit opportunities.

TABLE 5

**Effect of Adversity on Four Types of Colleges and Universities
Operating within a Garbage Can Decision Process**

Type of School/ Type of Situation	Organizational Type	Outcome					
		Decision Style Proportion Resolution	Problem Activity	Problem Latency	Decision Maker Activity	Decision Time
Large, rich universities						
Good times	0200	0.68	0	154	100	0
Bad times, early	1110	0.21	210	23	58	34
Bad times, late	0111	0.65	57	60	66	14
Large, poor universities						
Good times	1112	0.38	210	25	66	31
Bad times, early	2112	0.24	248	32	55	38
Bad times, late	1111	0.31	200	30	58	28
Small, rich colleges						
Good times	0002	1.0	0	0	100	0
Bad times, early	1002	0	310	0	90	20
Bad times, late	0001	1.0	0	0	100	0
Small, poor colleges						
Good times	1221	0.54	158	127	15	83
Bad times, early	2211	0.61	101	148	73	52
Bad times, late	1211	0.62	78	151	76	39

The large, poor schools are in the worst absolute position under adversity. They have a high level of problem activity, a substantial decision time, a low level of decision maker mobility, and a low proportion of decisions being made by resolution. But along most of these dimensions, the change has been less for them.

The small rich schools experience a large increase in problem activity, an increase in decision time, and a decrease in the proportion of decisions by resolution as adversity begins. The small, poor schools seem to move in a direction counter to the trends in the other three groups. Decision style is little affected by the onset of slack reduction, problem activity, and decision time decline, and decision-maker mobility increases. Presidents of such organizations might feel a sense of success in their efforts to tighten up the organization in response to resource contraction.

The application of the model to this particular situation among American colleges and universities clearly depends upon a large number of assumptions. Other assumptions would lead to other interpretations of the impact of adversity within a garbage can decision process. Nevertheless, the derivations from the model have some face validity as a description of some aspects of recent life in American higher education.

The model also makes some predictions of future developments. As adversity continues, the model predicts that all schools, and particularly rich schools, will experience improvement in their position. Among large, rich schools decision by resolution triples, problem activity is cut by almost three-fourths, and decision time is cut more than one-half. If the model has validity, a series of articles in the magazines of the next decade detailing how President X assumed the presidency of large, rich university Y and guided it to "peace" and "progress" (short decision time, decisions without problems, low problem activity) can be expected.

Conclusion

A set of observations made in the study of some university organizations has been translated into a model of decision making in organized anarchies, that is, in situations which do not meet the conditions for more classical models of decision making in some or all of three important ways: preferences are problematic, technology is unclear, or participation is fluid. The garbage can process is one in which problems, solutions, and participants move from one choice opportunity to another in such a way that the nature of the choice, the time it takes, and the problems it solves all depend on a relatively complicated intermeshing of elements. These include the mix of choices available at any one time, the mix of problems that have access to the organization, the mix of solutions looking for problems, and the outside demands on the decision makers.

A major feature of the garbage can process is the partial uncoupling of problems and choices. Although decision making is thought of as a process for solving problems, that is often not what happens. Problems are worked upon in the context of some choice, but choices are made only when the shifting combinations of problems, solutions, and decision makers happen to make action possible. Quite commonly this is after problems have left a given choice arena or before they have discovered it (decisions by flight or oversight).

Four factors were specified which could be expected to have substantial effects on the operation of the garbage can process: the organization's net energy load and energy distribution, its decision structure, and problem access structure. Though the specifications are quite simple their interaction is extremely complex, so that investigation of the probable behavior of a system fully characterized by the garbage can process and previous specifications requires computer simulation. No real system can be fully characterized in this way. Nonetheless, the simulated organization exhibits behaviors which can be observed some of the time in almost all organizations and frequently in some, such as universities. The garbage can model is a first step toward seeing the systematic interrelatedness of organizational phenomena which are familiar, even common, but which have previously been regarded as isolated and pathological. Measured against a conventional normative model of rational choice, the garbage can process does appear pathological, but such standards are not really appropriate. The process occurs precisely when the preconditions of more normal rational models are not met.

It is clear that the garbage can process does not resolve problems well. But it does enable choices to be made and problems resolved, even when the organization is plagued with goal ambiguity and conflict, with poorly understood problems that wander in and out of the system, with a variable environment, and with decision makers who may have other things on their minds.

There is a large class of significant situations in which the preconditions of the garbage can process cannot be eliminated. In some, such as pure research, or the family, they should not be eliminated. The great advantage of trying to see garbage can phenomena together as a process is the possibility that that process can be understood, that organizational design and decision making can take account of its existence and that, to some extent, it can be managed.

Appendix

Version five of the Fortran program for the garbage can model reads in entry times for choices, solution coefficients, entry times for problems, and two control variables, NA and IO. NA controls various combinations of freedom of movement for decision makers and problems. All results are based on runs in which NA is 1. Comment cards included in the program describe other possibilities. The latter variable, IO, controls output. At the value 1, only summary statistics are printed. At the value 2, full histories of the decision process are printed for each organizational variant.

The following are ten summary statistics:

1. (KT) Problem persistence, the total number of time periods a problem is activated and attached to a choice, summed over all problems.
2. (KU) Problem latency, the total number of time periods a problem is activated, but not attached to a choice, summed over all problems.
3. (KV) Problem velocity, the total number of times any problem shifts from one choice to another.
4. (KW) Problem failures, the total number of problems not solved at the end of the twenty time periods.

5. (KX) Decision maker velocity, the total number of times any decision maker shifts from one choice to another.

6. (KS) Decision maker inactivity, the total number of time periods a decision maker is not attached to a choice, summed over all decision makers.

7. (KY) Choice persistence, the total number of time periods a choice is activated, summed over all choices.

8. (KZ) Choice failures, the total number of choices not made by the end of the twenty time periods.

9. (XR) Energy reserve, the total amount of effective energy available to the system but not used because decision makers are not attached to any choice.

10. (XS) Energy wastage, the total effective energy used on choices in excess of that required to make them at the time they are made.

In its current form the program generates both the problem access structure and the decision structure internally. In order to examine the performance of the model under other structures, modification of the code or its elimination in favor of Read statements to take the structures from cards will be necessary.

Under IO = 2, total output will be about ninety pages. Running time is about two minutes under a Watfor compiler.

APPENDIX TABLE

Fortran Program for Garbage Can Model, Version Five

```
C     THE GARBAGE CAN MODEL. VERSION 5
C     ***
C     IO IS 1 FOR SUMMARY STATISTICS ONLY
C     IO IS 2 FOR SUMMARY STATISTICS PLUS HISTORIES
C     ***
C     NA IS 1 WHEN PROBS AND DMKRS BOTH MOVE
C     NA IS 2 WHEN DMKRS ONLY MOVE
C     NA IS 3 WHEN PROBS ONLY MOVE
C     NA IS 4 WHEN NEITHER PROBS NOR DMKRS MOVE
C     ***
C     IL IS A FACTOR DETERMINING PROB ENERGY REQ
C     ***
C     VARIABLES
C        ***
C        NUMBERS
C           COUNTERS   UPPER LIMITS      NAME
C              ***
C                 I         NCH          CHOICES
C                 J         NPR          PROBLEM
C                 K         NDM          DECMKRS
C                 LT        NTP          TIME
C        ***
C        ARRAYS
C           CODE          DIMEN         NAME
C              ***
C           ICH           NCH           CHOICE ENTRY TIME
C           ICS           NCH           CHOICE STATUS
C           JET           NPR           PROB. ENTRY TIME
C           JF            NPR           PROB. ATT. CHOICE
C           JFF           NPR           WORKING COPY JF
C           JPS           NPR           PROB. STATUS
C           KDC           NDM           DMKR. ATT. CHOICE
```

(continued)

Appendix Table (Continued)

```
C                    KDCW           NDM         WORKING COPY KDC
C                    XEF            MCH         ENERGY EXPENDED
C                    XERC           NCH         CHOICE EN. REQT.
C                    XERP           NPR         PROB. EN. REQT.
C                    XSC            NTP         SOLUTION COEFFICIENT
C             ***
C             2-DIMENSIONAL ARRAYS
C                    ***
C                    CODE           DIMEN       NAME
C                    ***
C                    IKA            NCH.NDM     DECISION STRUCTURE
C                    JIA            NPR.NCH     ACCESS STRUCTURE
C                    XEA            NDM.NTP     ENERGY MATRIX
C             ***
C             ***
C             ***
C          ***
C          SUMMARY STATISTICS FOR EACH VARIANT
C                    COL 1: KZ: TOTAL DECISIONS NOT MADE
C                    COL 2: KY: TOTAL NUMBER ACTIVE CHOICE PERIODS
C                    COL 3: KX: TOTAL NUMBER CHANGES BY DECISION MAKERS
C                    COL 4: KW: TOTAL PROBLEMS NOT SOLVED
C                    COL 5: KV: TOTAL NUMBER CHANGES BY PROBLEMS
C                    COL 6: KU: TOTAL NUMBER LATENT PROBLEM PERIODS
C                    COL 7: KT: TOTAL NUMBER ATTACHED PROBLEM PERIODS
C                    COL 8: KS: TOTAL NUMBER PERIODS DMKRS RESTING
C                    COL 9: XR: TOTAL AMOUNT OF UNUSED ENERGY
C                    COL 10:XS: TOTAL AMOUNT OF WASTED ENERGY
C          ***
C          INPUT BLOCK. READ-IN AND INITIALIZATIONS.
           DIMENSION ICH(20),JF(20),XERC(20),XEE(20),XSC(20),JFF(20),XERP(20
          *),JET(20),JPS(20),ICS(20),KDC(20),KDCW(20),JIA(20,20),IKA(20,20),
           CXEA(20,20),KABC(20,20),KBBC(20,20),KCBC(20,20)
1001       FORMAT(5(I3,1X))
1002       FORMAT(10(I3,1X))
1003       FORMAT(25(I1,1X))
1004       FORMAT(10F4.2)
           NTP=20
           NCH=10
           NPR=20
           NDM=10
8          READ(5,1002)(ICH(I),I=1,NCH)
           READ(5,1004)(XSC(LT),LT=1,NTP)
           READ(5,1002)(JET(J),J=1,NPR)
           READ(5,1003) NA,IO
           WRITE(6,1050) NA
1050       FORMAT('1       DEC.MAKER MOVEMENT CONDITION (NA). IS   ',I1/)
           DO 998 IL=1,3
           IB=IL-1
           DO 997 JAB=1,3
           JA=JAB-1
           DO 996 JDB=1,3
           JD=JDB-1
           DO 995 JEB=1,3
           JE=JEB-1
           XR=0.0
           XS=0.0
           KS=0
           DO 10 I=1,NCH
           XERC(I)=1.1
           XEE(I)=0.0
```

(continued)

Appendix Table (Continued)

```
10      ICS(I)=0
        DO 20 K=1,NDM
        KDC(K)=0
20      KDCW(K)=KDC(K)
        DO 40 J=1,NPR
        XERP(J)=IL*1.1
        JF(J)=0
        JFF(J)=0
40      JPS(J)=0
C       SETTING UP THE DECISION MAKERS ACCESS TO CHOICES.
        DO 520 I=1,NCH
        DO 510 J=1,NDM
        IKA(I,J)=1
        IF(JD.EQ.1) GO TO 502
        IF(JD.EQ.2) GO TO 504
        GO TO 510
502     IF(I.GE.J) GO TO 510
        IKA(I,J)=0
        GO TO 510
504     IF(J.EQ.I) GO TO 510
        IKA(I,J)=0
510     CONTINUE
520     CONTINUE
C       SETTING UP THE PROBLEMS ACCESS TO CHOICES.
        DO 560 I=1,NPR
        DO 550 J=1,NCH
        JIA(I,J)=0
        IF(JA.EQ.1) GO TO 532
        IF(JA.EQ.2) GO TO 534
        JIA(I,J)=1
        GO TO 550
532     IF ((I-J).GT.(I/2)) GO TO 550
        JIA(I,J)=1
        GO TO 550
534     IF(I.NE.(2*J))   GO TO 550
        JIA(I,J)=1
        JIA(I-1,J)=1
550     CONTINUE
560     CONTINUE
        DO 590 I=1,NDM
        DO 580 J=1,NTP
        XEA(I,J)=0.55
        IF(JF.EQ.1)GO TO 580
        XXA=I
        IF(JE.EQ.0)GO TO 570
        XEA(I,J)=(11.0-XXA)/10.0
        GO TO 580
570     XEA(I,J)=XXA/10.0
580     CONTINUE
590     CONTINUE
C       *** FINISH READ   INITIALIZATION
        DO 994 LT=1,NTP
1006    FORMAT(2X,6HCHOICE,2X,I3,2X,6HACTIVE )
C       CHOICE ACTIVATION
        DO 101   I=1,NCH
        IF(ICH(I).NE.LT)GO TO 101
        ICS(I)=1
101     CONTINUE
C       PROB. ACTIVATION
        DO 110 J=1,NPR
        IF(JET(J).NE.LT)GO TO 110
        JPS(J)=1
```

(continued)

Appendix Table (Continued)

```
 110   CONTINUF
C      FIND MOST ATTRACTIVE CHOICE FOR PROBLEM J
       DO 120 J=1,NPR
       IF (JPS(J).NE.1) GO TO 120
       IF(NA.EQ.2)GO TO 125
       IF(NA.EQ.4)GO TO 125
       GO TO 126
 125   IF(JF(J).NE.0)GO TO 127
 126   S=1000000
       DO 121 I=1,NCH
       IF (ICS(I).NE.1) GO TO 121
       IF(JIA(J,I).EQ.0)GO TO 121
       IF(JF(J).EQ.0)GO TO 122
       IF(JF(J).EQ.I)GO TO 122
       IF((XERP(J)+XERC(I)-XEE(I)).GE.S)GO TO 121
       GO TO 123
 122   IF((XERC(I)-XEE(I)).GE.S)GO TO 121
        S=XERC(I)-XEE(I)
       GO TO 124
 123   S=XERP(J)+XERC(I)-XEE(I)
 124   JFF(J)=I
 121   CONTINUE
       GO TO 120
 127   JFF(J)=JF(J)
 120   CONTINUE
       DO 130 J=1,NPR
 131   JF(J)=JFF(J)
 130   JFF(J)=0
       LTT=LT-1
       IF(LT.EQ.1)LTT=1
C      FIND MOST ATTRACTIVE CHOICE FOR DMKR K
       DO 140 K=1,NDM
       IF(NA.EQ.3)GO TO 145
       IF(NA.EQ.4) GO TO 145
       GO TO 146
 145   IF(KDC(K).NE.0)GO TO 147
 146   S=1000000
       DO 141 I=1,NCH
       IF (ICS(I).NE.1) GO TO 141
       IF(IKA(I,K).EQ.0)GO TO 141
       IF(KDC(K).EQ.0)GO TO 142
       IF(KDC(K).EQ.I)GO TO 142
 148   IF((XFRC(I)-XEE(I)-(XEA(K,LTT)*XSC(LTT))).GE.S)GO TO 141
       GO TO 143
 142   IF((XERC(I)-XEE(I)).GE.S)GO TO 141
       S=XERC(I)-XEE(I)
       GO TO 144
 143   S=XERC(I)-XEE(I)-XEA(K,LTT)*XSC(LTT)
 144   KDCW(K)=I
 141   CONTINUE
       GO TO 140
 147   KDCW(K)=KDC(K)
 140   CONTINUF
       DO 150 K=1,NDM
 151   KDC(K)=KDCW(K)
       IF(KDC(K).NE.0)GO TO 150
       XR=XR+(XEA(K,LT)*XSC(LT))
       KS=KS+1
 150   KDCW(K)=0
C      ESTABLISHING THE ENERGY REQUIRED TO MAKE EACH CHOICE.
       DO 199 I=1,NCH
       IF(ICS(I).EQ.0)GO TO 199
```

(continued)

Appendix Table (Continued)

```
        XERC(I)=0.0
        DO 160 J=1,NPR
        IF (JPS(J).NE.1) GO TO 160
        IF(JF(J).NE.I)GO TO 160
        XERC(I)=XERC(I)+XERP(J)
160     CONTINUE
        DO 170 K=1,NDM
        IF(IKA(I,K).EQ.0)GO TO 170
        IF(KDC(K).NE.I)GO TO 170
        XEE(I)=XEE(I)+XSC(LT)*XEA(K,LT)
170     CONTINUE
199     CONTINUE
C       MAKING DECISIONS
        DO 299 I=1,NCH
        IF (ICS(I).NE.1) GO TO 299
        IF(XERC(I).GT.XEE(I))GO TO 299
        XS=XS+XEE(I)-XERC(I)
        ICS(I)=2
        DO 250 J=1,NPR
        IF(JF(J).NE.I)GO TO 250
        JPS(J)=2
250     CONTINUE
        IF(NA.EQ.3)GO TO 261
        IF(NA.EQ.4)GO TO 261
        GO TO 299
261     DO 262 K=1,NDM
        IF(KDC(K).NE.I)GO TO 262
        KDCW(K)=1
262     CONTINUE
299     CONTINUE
        DO 200 I=1,NCH
200     KABC(LT,I)=ICS(I)
        DO 210 K=1,NDM
        KBBC(LT,K)=KDC(K)
        IF(KDCW(K).EQ.0)GO TO 210
        KDC(K)=0
210     KDCW(K)=0
        DO 220 J=1,NPR
        KCBC(LT,J)=JF(J)
        IF(JPS(J).EQ.0) GO TO 230
        IF(JPS(J).EQ.1) GO TO 220
        KCBC(LT,J)=1000
        GO TO 220
230     KCBC(LT,J)=-1
220     CONTINUE
994     CONTINUE
C       FINISH TIME PERIOD LOOP. BEGIN ACCUMULATION OF 10 SUMMARY STATISTI
        KZ=0
        KY=0
        KX=0
        KW=0
        KV=0
        KU=0
        KT=0
        DO 310 I=1,NTP
        DO 320 J=1,NCH
        IF(KABC(I,J).NE.1)GO TO 320
        KY=KY+1
        IF(I.NE.NTP)GO TO 320
        KZ=KZ+1
320     CONTINUE
```

(continued)

```
310   CONTINUE
      DO 330 I=2,NTP
      DO 340 J=1,NDM
      IF(KBBC(I,J).EQ.KBBC(I-1,J))GO TO 340
      KX=KX+1
340   CONTINUE
330   CONTINUE
      DO 350 I=1,NTP
      DO 360 J=1,NPR
      IF(KCBC(I,J).EQ.0)GO TO 351
      IF(KCBC(I,J).EQ.-1) GO TO 360
      IF(KCBC(I,J).EQ.1000) GO TO 352
      KT=KT+1
      GO TO 360
351   KU=KU+1
      GO TO 360
352   IF(I.NE.NTP)GO TO 360
      KW=KW+1
360   CONTINUE
350   CONTINUE
      KW=NPR-KW
      DO 370 I=2,NTP
      DO 380 J=1,NPR
      IF(KCBC(I,J).EQ.KCBC(I-1,J))GO TO 380
      KV=KV+1
380   CONTINUE
370   CONTINUE
C     BEGIN WRITEOUT OF MATERIALS FOR THIS ORGANIZATIONAL VARIANT.
1000  FORMAT(1H1)
1019  FORMAT(2X,'LOAD=',I1,' PR.ACC.=',I1,' DEC.STR.=',I1,' EN.DIST.=',
     BI1,2X,'STATS 1-10',3X,8I5,1X,2F6.2/)
      WRITE(6,1019)IB,JA,JD,JE,KZ,KY,KX,KW,KV,KU,KT,KS,XR,X5
      IF(IO.EQ.1) GO TO 995
2000  FORMAT(' CHOICE ACTIVATION HISTORY',34X,'DEC.MAKER ACTIVITY HISTOR
     BY'/' 20 TIME PERIODS,10 CHOICES',33X,'20 TIME PERIODS,10 DEC. MAKE
     CRS'/' 0=INACTIVE,1=ACTIVE,2=MADE',33X,'0=INACTIVE,X=WORKING ON CHO
     DICE X'//9X,'  1 2 3 4 5 6 7 8 9 10',30X,'1 2 3 4 5 6 7 8 9 10'/)
      WRITE(6,2000)
2001  FORMAT( 5X,I2,3X,10I2,25X,I2,3X,10I2)
      WRITE(6,2001)(LT,(KABC(LT,J),J=1,NCH),LT,( KBBC(LT,J),J=1,NDM),
     B LT=1,NTP )
2002  FORMAT(/' PROBLEM HISTORY:ROWS=TIME,COLS=PROBS., -1=NOT ENTERED,,
     B0=UNATTACHED,X=ATT.TO CH.X,**=SOLVED'/10X,
     C' 1  2  3  4  5  6  7  8  9 10 11 12 13 14 15 16 17 18 19 20'/)
      WRITE(6,2002)
2003  FORMAT(20(5X,I2,3X,20(1X,I2)/))
      WRITE(6,2003)(LT,(KCBC(LT,J),J=1,NPR),LT=1,NTP)
      WRITE(6,1000)
995   CONTINUE
996   CONTINUE
997   CONTINUE
998   CONTINUE
      STOP
      END
```

```
******   DATA AS FOLLOWS  (AFTER GUIDE CARDS)    **********


0         1         2         3         4         5         6         7
1234567890123456789012345678901234567890123456789012345678901234567890123456789012

008.005.006.007.004.009.002.010.003.001
1.000.900.700.300.100.100.300.700.901.00
0.600.600.600.600.600.600.600.600.600.60
009.005.008.007.010.003.003.001.007.009
006.008.005.002.004.002.004.010.006.001
1 2
```

Notes

1. We are indebted to Nancy Block, Hilary Cohen, and James Glenn for computational, editorial, and intellectual help; to the Institute of Sociology, University of Bergen, and the Institute of Organization and Industrial Sociology, Copenhagen School of Economics, for institutional hospitality and useful discussions of organizational behavior; and to the Ford Foundation for the financial support that made our collaboration feasible. We also wish to acknowledge the helpful comments and suggestions of Søren Christensen, James S. Coleman, Harald Enderud, Kåre Rommetveit, and William H. Starbuck.
2. We have based the model heavily on seven recent studies of universities: Christensen (1971), Cohen and March (1972), Enderud (1971), Mood (1971), Olsen (1970, 1971), and Rommetveit (1971). The ideas, however, have a broader parentage. In particular, they obviously owe a debt to Allison (1969), Coleman (1957), Cyert and March (1963), Lindblom (1965), Long (1958), March and Simon (1958), Schilling (1968), Thompson (1967), and Vickers (1965).
3. The model has also been exercised under conditions of a set of solution coefficients that varies over the time periods. Specifically, the following series has been used: 1, 0.9, 0.7, 0.3, 0.1, 0.1, 0.3, 0.7, 0.9, 1, 0.6, 0.6, 0.6, 0.6, 0.6, 0.6, 0.6, 0.6, 0.6, 0.6. This simulation, using only one combination of choice and problem entry times, gives results consistent with all of the conclusions reported in the present article.

References

Allison, Graham T. 1969. "Conceptual models and the Cuban missile crises." *American Political Science Review,* 63: 689–718.

Christensen, Søren. 1971. Institut og laboratorieorganisation på Danmarks tekniske Højskole. Copenhagen: Copenhagen School of Economics.

Cohen, Michael D., and James G. March. 1972. *The American College President.* New York: McGraw-Hill, Carnegie Commission on the Future of Higher Education.

Coleman, James S. 1957. *Community Conflict.* Glencoe: Free Press.

Cyert, Richard M., and James G. March. 1963. *Behavioral Theory of the Firm.* Englewood Cliffs: Prentice-Hall.

Enderud, Harald. 1971. Rektoratet og den centrale administration på Danmarks tekniske Højskole. Copenhagen: Copenhagen School of Economics.

Lindblom, Charles E. 1965. *The Intelligence of Democracy.* New York: Macmillan.

Long, Norton. 1958. "The local community as an ecology of games." *American Journal of Sociology,* 44: 251–261.

March, James G., and Herbert A. Simon. 1958. *Organizations.* New York: John Wiley.

Mood, Alexander (ed.). 1971. *More Scholars for the Dollar.* New York: McGraw-Hill, Carnegie Commission on the Future of Higher Education.

Olsen, Johan P. 1970. *A Study of Choice in an Academic Organization.* Bergen: University of Bergen.

_____. 1971. *The Reorganization of Authority in an Academic Organization.* Bergen: University of Bergen.

Rommetveit, Kåre. 1971. Framveksten av det medisinske fakultet ved Universitetet i Tromsø. Bergen: University of Bergen.

Schilling, Warner R. 1968. "The H-bomb decision: how to decide without actually choosing." In W. R. Nelson (ed.), *The Politics of Science.* London: Oxford University Press.

Thompson, James D. 1967. *Organizations in Action.* New York: McGraw-Hill.

Vickers, Geoffrey. 1965. *The Art of Judgment.* New York: Basic Books.

PART II

ORGANIZATIONAL EVOLUTIONS IN HIGHER EDUCATION

Part II

ADMINISTRATIVE AND PROFESSIONAL AUTHORITY

AMITAI ETZIONI

The ultimate source of the organizational dilemmas reviewed up to this point is the incomplete matching of the personalities of the participants with their organizational roles. If personalities could be shaped to fit specific organizational roles, or organizational roles to fit specific personalities, many of the pressures to displace goals, much of the need to control performance, and a good part of the alienation would disappear. Such matching is, of course, as likely as an economy without scarcity and hence without prices. But even if all the dilemmas which result from the incomplete articulation of personality and organization were resolved, there still would remain those which are consequences of conflicting tendencies built into the organizational structure.

Probably the most important structural dilemma is the inevitable strain imposed on the organization by the use of knowledge. All social units use knowledge, but organizations use more knowledge more systematically than do other social units. Moreover, most knowledge is created in organizations and passed from generation to generation—i.e., preserved—by organizations. It is here that Weber overlooked one necessary distinction: He viewed bureaucratic or administrative authority as based on technical knowledge or training; the subordinates, he thought, accept rules and orders as legitimate because they consider being rational being right, and regard their superiors as more rational.[1] One is not "stretching" Weber much to suggest that he thought that the higher the rank of an official the better equipped he tends to be either in terms of formal education e.g., academic degrees or in terms of merit and experience. Examinations and promotion according to merit, Weber pointed out, help to establish such association between rank and knowledge. To a degree, this conception is valid. There is considerable evidence that persons who have only a high-school education will be more frequently found in lower ranks, and college-educated persons in the higher ones. There is probably some correlation between IQ and rank, in the sense that on the average the IQ of the top third of an organization is likely to be higher than that of the lowest third. One could argue that when the superiority-of-knowledge requirement is not fulfilled, when the higher in rank knows less or has a lower IQ than the lower in rank, his orders might still be followed because of his power to enforce them; but Weber would counter that such orders would not be considered legitimate and hence the official would have power but not authority.

Still the reader is correct in his intuition that there is something fundamentally wrong with the notion of viewing the bureaucracy as a hierarchy in which the more rational rule the less rational. There are two reasons. First, by far most of the trained members of the organization are found not in the highest but in the middle ranks, and not in the regular line or command positions but around them. Depending on the type of organization, they are referred to as experts, staff, professionals, specialists, or by the names of their respective professions. Second, the most basic principle of administrative authority and the most basic principle of authority based on knowledge—or professional authority—not only are not identical but are quite incompatible.

"Administrative and Professional Authority," by Amitai Etzioni, reprinted from *Modern Organizations*, 1964, Prentice-Hall, Inc.

Administrative vs. Professional Authority

Administration assumes a power hierarchy. Without a clear ordering of higher and lower in rank, in which the higher in rank have more power than the lower ones and hence can control and coordinate the latter's activities, the basic principle of administration is violated; the organization ceases to be a coordinated tool. However, knowledge is largely an individual property; unlike other organization means, it cannot be transferred from one person to another by decree. Creativity is basically individual and can only to a very limited degree be ordered and coordinated by the superior in rank. Even the application of knowledge is basically an individual act, at least in the sense that the individual professional has the ultimate responsibility for his professional decision. The surgeon has to decide whether or not to operate. Students of the professions have pointed out that the autonomy granted to professionals who are basically responsible to their consciences (though they may be censured by their peers' and in extreme cases by the courts) is necessary for effective professional work. Only if immune from ordinary social pressures and free to innovate, to experiment, to take risks without the usual social repercussions of failure, can a professional carry out his work effectively. It is this highly individualized principle which is diametrically opposed to the very essence of the organizational principle of control and coordination by superiors—i.e., the principle of administrative authority. In other words, the ultimate justification for a professional act is that it is, to the best of the professional's knowledge, the right act. He might consult his colleagues before he acts, but the decision is his. If he errs, he still will be defended by his peers. The ultimate justification of an administrative act, however, is that it is in line with the organization's rules and regulations, and that it has been approved—directly or by implication—by a superior rank.

The Organization of Knowledge

The question is how to create and use knowledge without undermining the organization. Some knowledge is formulated and applied in strictly private situations. In the traditional professions, medicine and law, much work is carried out in non-organizational contexts—in face-to-face interaction with clients. But as the need for costly resources and auxiliary staff has grown, even the traditional professions face mounting pressures to transfer their work to organizational structures such as the hospital and the law firm. Similarly, while most artistic work is still conducted in private contexts, often in specially segregated sectors of society in which an individual's autonomy is particularly high, much of the cognitive creativity, particularly in scientific research, has become embedded in organizational structures for reasons similar to those in medicine and law.

In addition there are several professions in which the amount of knowledge (as measured in years of training) and the degree of personal responsibility (as measured in the degree to which privileged communications—which the recipient is bound not to divulge—or questions of life and death are involved) are lower than in the older or highly creative, cognitive professions. Engineering and nursing are cases in point. These professions can be more easily integrated into organizational structures than can medicine or law, for example. Most professional work at this level is carried out within organizations rather than in private practice, and it is more given to supervision by persons higher in rank (who have more administrative authority but no more, or even less, professional competence) than the work of the professions discussed above.

To some degree, organizations circumvent the problem of knowledge by "buying" it from the outside, as when a corporation contracts for a market study from a research organization; i.e., it specifies the type of knowledge it needs and it agrees with the research group on price, but then it largely withdraws from control over the professional work. There are, however, sharp limitations on the extent to which knowledge can be recruited in this way, particularly since organizations consume such large amounts of knowledge and they tend to need more reliable control on its nature and flow. There are three basic ways in which knowledge is handled within organizations:

1. Knowledge is produced, applied, preserved, or communicated in organizations especially established for these purposes. These are *professional organizations,* which are characterized not only by the goals they pursue but also by the high proportion of professionals on their staff (at least 50 per cent) and by the authority relations between professionals and non-professionals which are so structured that professionals have superior authority over the major goal activities of the organization, a point which is explored below. Professional organizations include universities, colleges, most schools, research organizations, therapeutic mental hospitals, the larger general hospitals, and social-work agencies. For certain purposes it is useful to distinguish between those organizations employing professionals whose professional training is long (5 years or more), and those employing professionals whose training is shorter (less than 5 years). The former we call *full-fledged professional* organizations; the latter, *semi-professional* organizations. Generally associated with differences in training of the professionals in these two types of organizations are differences in goals, in privileges, and in concern with matters of life and death. "Pure" professional organizations are primarily devoted to the creation and application of knowledge; their professionals are usually protected in their work by the guarantee of privileged communication, and they are often concerned with matters of life and death. Semi-professional organizations are more concerned with the communication and, to a lesser extent, the application of knowledge, their professionals are less likely to be guaranteed the right of privileged communications, and they are rarely directly concerned with matters of life and death.

2. There are *service organizations* in which professionals are provided with the instruments, facilities, and auxiliary staff required for their work. The professionals however are not employed by the organization nor subordinated to its administrators.

3. Professionals may be employed by organizations whose goals are *non-professional,* such as industrial and military establishments. Here professionals are often assigned to special divisions or positions, which to one degree or another take into account their special needs.

We shall first discuss the relation between the two authority principles—that of knowledge and that of administration—in non-professional organizations, then in "full-fledged" professional organizations, in semiprofessional organizations, and finally in service organizations.

Professional Authority in Non-professional Organizations

Superiority of Administrative Authority

By far the largest and most common non-professional organizations are the production organizations which are privately owned and managed. The organizational goal of private business is to make profits. The major means are production and exchange. While professionals deal with various aspects of the production and exchange process—that is, with means such as engineering, quality control, and marketing—the manager (the corporation's equivalent of the administrator) is expected to coordinate the various activities in such a way that the major organizational goal—profit-making—will be maximized. This seems to be one of the reasons why modern corporations prefer to have as top executives people with administrative experience rather than professionals. (In a study of the occupational backgrounds of the chief executives of American industry in 1950, administration was found to have been the principal occupation of 43.1 per cent; 11.8 per cent were defined as entrepreneurs; finance had been the field of 12.4 per cent; and only 12.6 per cent had been engineers.[2] People with scientific backgrounds such as research workers are even less likely to become heads of private business. Only about 4 per cent of the presidents of American corporations had such a background.[3]) In general, the goals of private business are consistent with administrative orientations. The economic orientation of the organization and the bureaucratic orientation of the administrative role share an orientation toward rational combination of means and development of rational procedures to maximize goals which are considered as given. The social and cultural conditions that support modern economic activities also support modern administration. Professional and economic orientations are less compatible.

When people with strong professional orientations take over managerial roles, a conflict between the organizational goals and the professional orientation usually occurs. Homans reports an interesting case in which the influence of professionally oriented participants was greater than in most corporations.[4] He discusses an electrical equipment company which was owned, managed, and staffed by engineers. Management, which was in the hands of administration-oriented engineers, suffered from pressure to pursue uneconomic goals by the professionally oriented design engineers. The design engineers were charged with being indifferent to the "general welfare of the company"—that is, to profit-making—as "shown by their lack of concern with finance, sales, and the practical needs of the consumer and by their habit of spending months on an aspect of design that had only theoretical importance." This caused considerable tension between the managerial and professionally oriented groups, tension to which this company was especially sensitive because of its high dependence on professional work and the special structure of ownership. A power struggle resulted which ended with a clearer subordination of the design engineers (staff) to the managerial engineers (line). This was mandatory "if the company was to survive and increase its sales," as Homans put it. The treasurer (a non-professional in this context) became the most influential member of the new management. In short, in a corporation where the professionals exerted a strong influence, the existence of the organization was threatened, considerable internal tension was generated, and finally the organizational power structure was changed toward a more usual structure, with the professionally minded more clearly subordinated. In other words, the organizational authority structure was made more compatible with the goals of the organization. The orientations of the managers and the goals of private business seem to match. When a professional orientation dominates, this tends to "displace" the profit goal of privately owned economic organizations.

Staff and Line

The way the two kinds of authority are combined in corporations and other non-professional organizations is often referred to as "staff and line." The managers, whose authority is administrative, direct the major goal activities; the professionals deal with knowledge as a means, and with the knowledge aspect of other means. They are in a subordinate position to the managers. Thus, in cases of conflict between the two criteria for decision-making, the organizational power structure is slanted in favor of the administrative authority. However, professional subordinates are treated differently from regular subordinates; they are not treated as are lower ranks in a line structure, but as "staff," a term which designates positions outside the regular chain of command or "line" and implies a certain amount of autonomy.

There are two interpretations of the relationship between staff and line. According to one approach, the staff has no administrative authority whatsoever. It advises the administrators (line authority) on what action to take. The staff does not issue orders to those lower in rank; if it desires any action or correction, this must be achieved through those in the line rank. According to the second approach, the staff, while advising the line on various issues, also takes responsibility for limited areas of activity.[5] That is, on some matters the staff directly issues orders to the lower participants.

Both combinations of the two authority principles generate considerable strain. In the first, where the line alone issues orders, the line tends to be overloaded by demands for decisions, and tends to repel at least some of the professional advice and requests for action of the staff. Line personnel have a large number of other functional requirements they must look after. They rarely comprehend fully the bases of actions requested by the staff, and they tend to neglect or at least to under-represent the staff demands. In the second approach the lower line is subordinated to two authorities at a time. There is a functional division of control between the two authorities, in the sense that professional matters are assigned to staff control and all the others to line control. In practice, while there are some matters that fall clearly into one category or the other, many issues can be viewed as either professional or administrative matters or both. This leads to the issuance of conflicting orders and gives the lower in rank the opportunity to play one authority against the other.

Dalton called attention to the tendencies of the higher- and lower-ranking line personnel to form a coalition against the staff personnel. He found the reason in the sociological differences that unite the line against the staff. The staff is generally younger and much more likely to be college-educated than the line, although the latter have greater organizational experience and hence resent advice and suggestions from the relatively inexperienced staff. Furthermore, the two groups are divided by differences in patterns of speech and dress, recreational preferences, etc.[6] In these areas, the higher-ranking line is often closer to the lower-ranking line than to the staff. Thus the tensions between staff and line derive not only from the organizational conflicts resulting from overloading or lack of clear division of authority, but also from differences in sociological background. (These differences might decline as more and more higher line officials gain college education, or a new division might emerge between the A.B. and B.S. on the one hand, and the Ph.D.'s on the other.)

In spite of important differences between the two approaches, staff authority in both is subordinate to line authority and the line is identified with administrative authority and the staff with professional authority. While it is obvious that there are some staff functions which are not carried out by professionals, and that there are some professionals among the line personnel, there is a high correlation between staff and professionals, and between line and non-professionals.

In organizations whose goal is non-professional (e.g., profit-making), it is considered desirable for administrators to have the major (line) authority because they direct the major goal activity. Professionals deal only with means, with secondary activities. Therefore it is functional for the organization that they have no, or only limited (staff), authority, and they be ultimately subordinated to administrators. This generally is the case in corporations and armies.

Professionals in Professional Organizations

In full-fledged professional organizations the staff-professional line-administrator correlation, insofar as such distinctions apply at all, is reversed. Although administrative authority is suitable for the major goal activities in private business, in professional organizations administrators are in charge of secondary activities; they administer *means* to the major activity carried out by professionals. In other words, to the extent that there is a staff-line relationship at all, professionals should hold the major authority and administrators the secondary staff authority. Administrators offer advice about the economic and organizational implications of various activities planned by the professionals. The final decision is, functionally speaking, in the hands of the various professionals and their decision-making bodies, such as committees and boards. The professor decides what research he is going to undertake and to a large degree what he is going to teach; the physician determines the treatment to be given to the patient.

Administrators may raise objections. They may point out that a certain drug is too expensive or that a certain teaching policy will decrease the number of students in a way that endangers the financing of a university. But functionally the professional is the one to decide on his discretion to what degree these administrative considerations should be taken into account. It is interesting to note that some of the complaints usually made against professionals in nonprofessional organizations are made against administrators in professional organizations: They are said to lose sight of the major goal of the organization in pursuit of their specific limited responsibilities. Professionals in private business are sometimes criticized as being too committed to science, craftsmanship, and abstract ideas; administrators in professional organizations are deprecated because they are too committed to their specialties—"efficiency" and economy.

Many of the sociological differences between professionals and managers in private business are reversed in professional organizations. Professionals enter professional organizations younger and at lower positions (i.e., as students, research assistants, or interns) than managers do. The range of mobility of administrators is usually relatively limited, and a professional is more likely to reach the top position of institutional head.

In private business, overinfluence by professionals threatens the realization of organizational goals and sometimes even the organization's existence. In professional organizations overinfluence by the administration, which takes the form of ritualization of means, undermines the goals for which the organization has been established and endangers the conditions under which knowledge can be created and institutionalized (as, for instance, academic freedom).

Who Is Superior?

Heading a professional organization constitutes a special dilemma. It is a typical case of institution-alized role conflict.[7] On the one hand, the role should be in the hands of a professional in order to ensure that the commitments of the head will match organizational goals. A professional at the head of the authority structure will mean that professional activity is recognized as the major goal activity, and that the needs of professionals will be more likely to receive understanding attention. On the other hand, organizations have needs that are unrelated to their specific goal activity. Organizations have to obtain funds to finance their activities, recruit personnel to staff the various functions, and allocate the funds and personnel which have been recruited. Organizational heads must know how to keep the system integrated by giving the right amount of attention and funds to the various organizational needs, including secondary needs. A professional may endanger the integration of the professional organization by over-emphasizing the major goal activity and neglecting second-ary functions. He may lack skill in human relations. In short, the role of head of professional organizations requires two incompatible sets of orientations, personal characteristics, and aptitudes. If the role is performed by either a lay administrator or a typical professional, one set of considerations is likely to be emphasized to the neglect of the other.

The severity of the dilemma is increased because of the motivational pattern of typical profession-als. Most successful professionals are not motivated to become administrators. Some would refuse any administrative role, including the top one of university president or hospital chief, because of their commitment to professional values and ties to professional groups, and because they feel that they would not be capable of performing the administrative role successfully. Even those profession-als who would not reject the distinguished and powerful role of organizational head avoid the admin-istrative roles that are training grounds for and channels of mobility to these top positions. Thus many academicians refuse to become deans, not to mention associate or assistant deans, and try to avoid if possible the role of department chairman. Those who are willing to accept administrative roles are often less committed to professional values than their colleagues,[8] or view it as a transitional status, not a career. The same can be said about administrative appointments in hospitals. For instance, in the mental hospital studied by Stanton and Schwartz, the role of administrative psychiatrist is fulfilled at the beginning of the training period.[9] It is considered an undesirable chore that must be endured be-fore turning to the real job. Psychiatrists who complete their training tend to withdraw to private prac-tice. From other studies, especially those of state mental hospitals, it appears that those who stay are often less competent and less committed to professional values than those who leave.

The Professionally Oriented Administrator

There are various solutions to this dilemma. By far the most widespread one is the rule of the pro-fessionally oriented administrator. Such an administrator is one who combines a professional edu-cation with a managerial personality and practice. Goal as well as means activities seem to be handled best when such a person is the institutional head. Because of his training, he is more likely to understand the special needs of a professional organization and its staff than a lay administrator, and, because of his personal characteristics, he is more likely to be skilled in handling the needs and requests of his professional colleagues as well as those of the administrative staff.

There are two major sources of professionally oriented administrators. One is the professionals themselves. Some feel that they have little chance of becoming outstanding professionals in their field. Often the same people find that they are relatively more skilled in administrative activities. Thus they gravitate toward administrative jobs by serving on committees and by assuming minor administrative roles; some eventually become top administrators. Contrary to the popular belief, most university presidents are former professors. Wilson found that out of the 30 universities he studied, 28 had presidents who had been professors, albeit none a very eminent scholar.[10] It seems that academicians who are inclined to take administrative jobs, or who are organization-oriented, not only publish less in quantity and quality after they have entered administrative positions but also tended to publish less before they accepted such jobs.

Of the heads of mental hospitals studied, 74.2 per cent are physicians.[11] Although there is no study on their professional eminence as compared to that of private practitioners, it seems that the heads of mental hospitals do not include the most successful psychiatrists. Only about 22 per cent of the heads of general hospitals are physicians. Where these are full-time jobs, the statement made about the heads of mental hospitals seems to apply here also.

The second source of professionally-oriented administrators is special training. In recent years there has been a movement toward developing training programs for specialized administration, such as hospital administration and research administration. A considerable number of teachers, for example, return to universities to take courses in administrative education before they become school principals.

The advantages of specialized administrators over lay administrators are obvious. They are trained for their particular role and have considerable understanding of the organization in which they are about to function before they enter it. They are sensitized to the special tensions of working with professionals, and they share some of their professional values. On the other hand, they are less prepared for their role than the professionally oriented administrators from the first source who have a deeper commitment to professional values, command more professional respect, and have a greater number of social ties with professionals.

Although most professional organizations are controlled by professional or professionally oriented administrators, some are controlled by lay administrators. By lay administrators we mean, administrators who have no training in serving the major goal activities of the organization. This holds for 2 out of the 30 universities studied by Wilson, for fewer than 10 per cent of the schools, for 20.5 per cent of the mental hospitals, and for about 38 per cent of the general hospitals. (Wilson's study is small, the other data is based on large populations).

The strain created by lay administrators in professional organizations leads to goal displacement. When the hierarchy of authority is in inverse relation to the hierarchy of goals and means, there is considerable danger that the goals will be subverted. Of course there are many other factors which may have such a distorting influence; but lay administrators are more likely to cause displacement than are other administrators.

References

1. Max Weber (Talcott Parsons, ed.; A. M. Henderson and Talcott Parsons, trans.), *The Theory of Social and Economic Organization* (New York: Oxford University Press, 1947), p. 339.
2. M. Newcomer, *The Big Business Executive* (New York: Columbia University Press, 1955), p. 92.
3. See G. H. Copeman, *Leaders of British Industry* (London: Gee and Co., 1955).
4. George C. Homans, *The Human Group* (New York: Harcourt, Brace, 1950), pp. 369–414.
5. On the two approaches, see H. A. Simon, D. W. Smithburg, and V. A. Thompson, *Public Administration* (New York: Knopf, 1956), pp. 280–295; and A. W. Gouldner, *Patterns of Industrial Bureaucracy* (Glencoe, Ill.: The Free Press, 1954), PP. 224–228.
6. Melville Dalton, "Conflicts Between Staff and Line Managerial Officers," *American Sociological Review* 15: (1950): 342–351.
7. By role we mean the behavior expected from a person in the particular position. Seeman, "Role Conflict and Ambivalent Leadership," *American Sociological Review* 18 (1953), 373–380.
8. A. W. Gouldner, "Cosmopolitans and Locals: Toward an Analysis of Latent Social Roles," *Administrative Science Quarterly* (1957), 2:281–306. For a more recent study, see Barney C. Glaser, "Attraction, Autonomy, and Reciprocity in the Scientist-Supervisor Relations," *Administrative Science Quarterly* (1963), 8–379–398.
9. A. H. Stanton and M. S. Schwartz, *The Mental Hospital* (New York: Basic Books, 1954).
10. L. Wilson, *The Academic Man* (New York: Oxford University Press, 1942), p. 85.
11. L. Block, "Ready Reference Of Hospital Facts," *Hospital Topics* (1956), 34:23.

Evolution of University Organization

E. D. Duryea

It has become customary in histories of American higher education to begin with a description of medieval origins. In general, there is good basis for looking back to those distant and turbulent days. The idea of a university itself as a formal, organized institution is a medieval innovation, which contrasts to the Greek schools and to the rudimentary organizational precedents in ancient Alexandria and in the Byzantine and Arabian cultures. The medieval universities instituted the use of many contemporary titles such as *dean, provost, rector,* and *proctor.* They initiated the idea of formal courses and of the curriculum leading to the baccalaureate and the master's and doctor's degrees. Our commencements are graced annually by the color and distinction of medieval garb. Fascinating anecdotes confirm that student violence has early precedents.

The point is, of course, that complex institutions such as universities do not appear full-blown at a particular point in time. They evolve through that complicated process by which men and cultures mingle over a history fraught with traditions and happenstance. Contemporary Western culture itself originated in the centuries that followed the "dark ages," and the university has served as one of the major institutions by which this culture has been transmitted over the years.

Within this context, certain aspects of the university's organization do have some important medieval precedents. Other aspects of its organization reflect the more direct influence of the English colleges of the sixteenth and seventeenth centuries. A history of American colleges and universities must be written also with due recognition of that educational revolution which took place in this country during the four decades following the Civil War. As Laurence R. Veysey (1965, p. 2) comments in his detailed interpretation of that era, "The American university of 1900 was all but unrecognizable in comparison to the colleges of 1860." The contemporary system of higher education dominated by the large, multifunctional university stands as a heritage of those years. Organizationally as well as educationally, its form and function were set by the time of the First World War. Its history during this century is primarily a chronicle of expansion and consolidation.

Reflecting these major historical influences, the following analysis examines the evolution of university organization from three major perspectives. The first deals with (1) the origins and use of the corporate form by which authority was granted to lay governing boards and (2) how their legal control has been modified by alumni and faculty influences that go back well into the nineteenth century. The second views the origins and expansion of the organizational structure of universities, an evolution epitomized by the comment that the old-time college president has all but disappeared behind a bureaucracy of academic and administrative offices and councils. In this sense the transition from the small, struggling colleges of the past to the large multiversity with its complex administration is first of all the history of the presidency. The third views the twentieth-century period of organizational expansion and consolidation. A concluding section identifies very briefly the evidences of dysfunction that have emerged in recent years.

Corporate Origins

By the twelfth century in Europe the church not only reigned supreme as a ruler of man's conscience but also exercised great temporal power over his mundane affairs. Rare were the individuals who would, when threatened with excommunication, choose to face an uncertain future in the hereafter. As the arbitrator of an ultimate destiny which included the possibility so vividly described in Dante's *Inferno* and as the only effective organization for all Europe, the church entered into the total life of the culture. But early in the thirteenth century, the more astute popes began to feel the rumblings of a shift of temporal power to political states and kings. The remote threat of hell began to give way to the more tangible thrust of the sword. As a result, the church hierarchy moved to bring its scattered organizations—religious orders, cathedral chapters, and universities—under more effective papal control. To this end, canon lawyers looked back to Roman law and its concept of corporations as fictitious legal entities. Their learned investigations led to a number of papal statements in the first decades of the thirteenth century and in 1243 to the famous bull or proclamation of Pope Innocent IV. The central idea in the Innocentean doctrine was that each cathedral chapter, collegiate church, religious fraternity, and university constituted a *Universitas*, i.e., a free corporation. Its corporate personality, however, was not something natural in the sense of a social reality but rather "an artificial notion invented by the sovereign for convenience of legal reasoning," existent only in the contemplation of law. This was a theoretical conception but nonetheless a very real one, since the corporation thereby derived its right to exist from an external authority and not from the intrinsic fact of its being (Brody, 1935, pp. 3–4).

The efforts of the papacy, the need of universities for protection against the immediate threats to their freedom from local bishops and townspeople, and the fact that the kings also intruded on their sovereignty—all these supported the corporate idea. The theory of corporate existence meant ultimately the end of the guild system and, for universities, of the idea of an independent association of scholars. The history of this development is complex and detailed, certainly beyond the scope of this particular analysis. It is sufficient to note that Emperor Frederick II rivaled Pope Gregory IX during the later years of the thirteenth century in the issuance of grants of authorization to universities, which in turn did not hesitate to strengthen their own hand by playing off pope against king (Rashdall, 1936, vol. 1, pp. 8–9). As national states gained dominance, however, universities ultimately had to look solely to kings for their charters and what the king gave the king could take away.

The concept of corporations which served as precedent for the early colleges in this country matured in England during the fifteenth and sixteenth centuries. It provided an effective legal means by which the king and later parliament would delegate in an orderly way authority for designated activities, not only to universities but to municipalities, trading companies, charitable establishments, and various other institutions. Charters provided for perpetual succession and the freedom for corporate bodies to set up and maintain the rules and regulations which in effect constituted internal or private governments. They also carried the right of supervision and visitation by representatives of the state. They established, in addition, legal protections associated with the rights of individuals in the sense that the corporation existed as an artificial or juristic individual. This conception of governmental grant of authority served also as the basis for the charters and statutes of the colleges of the English universities, which in general included provisions for external visitors or overseers, a head elected by the teaching staff or fellows, and a formal body constituted of these fellows which "exercised the legislative powers" (Davis, 1961, pp. 303–305).

The influence of this English college model was evident in the founding of the first two colonial colleges, Harvard (1636) and William and Mary (1693). For example, the language of the 1650 charter for Harvard is very similar to that of the royal charters for the colleges of Oxford and Cambridge (Morison, 1935, p. 10). Both these institutions were formed with governing councils composed of internal members (the presidents and teaching fellows) in tandem with external supervising boards that held final approval powers and the right of visitation.[1]

Another medieval precedent, however, came to the colonies with the early settlers and caused a significant modification of the English practice. In place of immediate control of the colleges by the teachers or professors, the practice evolved of granting complete corporate power to governing boards composed of external members. The origins of the use of external control lie in the medieval universities of northern Italy. Initially guilds of students who hired their professors, universities proved good for local business. The Italian towns competed for their presence in part by subsidizing salaries of outstanding teachers. The inexorable result was a blunting of student economic power and the establishment of municipal committees, in effect the first lay governing boards, to guard their financial interests (Rashdall, 1936, vol. 2, p. 59). Again, the detailing of the history of this tradition goes beyond the scope of this chapter. The lay board of control proved an appropriate mechanism for the direction of advanced education under the Calvinists at Geneva in the early sixteenth century, at the Dutch University of Leyden a few years later, at the Scottish universities of that same era, and finally at the Protestant Trinity College in Dublin. It was in part from these Dutch, Scottish, and Irish sources that the concept of lay boards came to the colonies (Cowley, 1964; 1971).

The English pattern of internal control by academics which was followed by Harvard and William and Mary did not set the precedent for university government in this country. That distinction fell to Yale College, established in 1701. Whether because of direct influences from the European Calvinistic practices noted above or simply because of parallel sectarian desires to maintain religious orthodoxy, the founders of Yale petitioned for a single nonacademic board of control. As a consequence, the colonial legislature of Connecticut granted authority to a board of "Trustees, Partners, or Undertakers" to "erect a collegiate school." Renamed in the revised 1745 charters as the "President and Fellows of Yale College," it continued as an external board with the right of self-perpetuation and with final control of the affairs of the institution (*The Yale Corporation*, 1952; see also Brody, 1935, Ch. 1).

Meanwhile, yet another deviation from English precedents also had begun to emerge. The right of the king and parliament to grant a charter carried with it an equal right to withdraw this charter. In fact, during the times of religious conflict in England this did occur, as first a Protestant and then a Catholic sovereign reconstituted the organization of the English universities in terms of religious biases. In the eighteenth century a new philosophy, that formalized by John Locke, gained acceptance, especially in the American colonies so strongly committed to a separation of church and state. This view stressed the nature of government as a compact among individuals, with sovereignty held by the people. In these terms of reference, having legal status as a person in law, although a fictitious or juridical person, corporations gained protection from legislative intrusions associated with the rights of individuals. Early in the nineteenth century court decisions began to interpret charters as contracts equally as binding upon the state as upon their recipients. The first intimation of this position regarding corporate autonomy appeared in the 1763 statement of President Clap of Yale to the colonial legislature. He was protesting a threatened legislative visitation of the college on the grounds that such action would be contrary to the nature of the charter and the private legal nature of the institution.[2] Clap's position was novel in his day, but after the turn of the eighteenth century support of a judicial theory which interpreted charters to private corporations as contracts or compacts between the state and the founders began to appear. This point of view received its legal judicial confirmation in the famous Dartmouth College case decision of the Supreme Court under Chief Justice Marshall. In that decision, the Court viewed the college as a private institution and interpreted its charter as a contract binding upon the state of New Hampshire as well as the trustees, "a contract, the obligation of which cannot be impaired without violating the constitution of the United States" (Wright, 1938, p. 45).

The Dartmouth College decision led to a reexamination of the state-college relationship. Faced with a loss of control, legislators understandably questioned the award of public funds to private corporations. As a result there emerged in subsequent decades a number of public or state colleges, but not as agencies of state government under ministers of education in the continental tradition. Rather, the early public colleges took the form of public corporations parallel in their general organization to the private colleges. In the nineteenth century, it became common practice for legislatures to delegate governing power over state institutions to boards of control established as public corporations.[3] These boards received authority to control property, contracts, finances, forms of internal governance, and relationships with internal personnel—students, faculty members, and administrative employees (Brody, 1935, Ch. 6).[4]

Modification of Board Control: Faculty and Alumni Participation

Whatever the legal authority inherent in lay governing boards, continuing modification of their actual power is documented by a history of university organization. Early in the nineteenth century, accounts of the administration of Jeremiah Day at Yale College attest to the influence of faculty members with whom Day conferred regularly on policy decisions. Students, while rarely a direct component of government until recent years, have traditionally participated as alumni.

Earlier precedents than Yale exist. Professor W. H. Cowley (1964, Ch. 7) has uncovered a number of such instances. Overall, it is clear from his analysis and from histories of the leading universities that faculties greatly expanded their influence over academic affairs during the nineteenth century. The period from 1869 to 1900 illustrates the gradual but decisive involvement of professors in academic policies (Morison, 1930, p. xxxiv). The trustees at Cornell in 1889, for example, established a University Senate of the president and full professors (Kingsbury, 1962, pp. 263–264). Similar arrangements existed at Michigan, Illinois, Wisconsin, and other Midwestern institutions. At Johns Hopkins and Chicago, professors were accepted as the guiding force for all matters concerned with education and research. Faculty influence reached the point that, by the 1890s, President Jacob G. Schurman of Cornell saw his influence in educational affairs limited to final approval of appointments and his role as "the only man in the University who is a member of all boards, councils and organizations" (Kingsbury, 1962, p. 323).

By the turn of the century the trend to faculty participation was definite in the larger universities and major colleges. The decades that followed have chronicled the extension of faculty control over academic affairs, a development influenced by the policies and pressures of the American Association of University Professors subsequent to its founding in 1915.[5]

During the nineteenth century, alumni also entered actively into the government of colleges and universities. In doing this, they had well-established precedents in both England and Scotland, though little evidence exists to support a causal relationship. It is probably more accurate to explain alumni participation as the result of a unique commitment epitomized by the spirit of alma mater and reinforced by recollections of campus camaraderie. The college class has constituted a primary social as well as academic unit which, early in the history of the colleges, led to campus reunions and thus served regularly to reinforce the loyalty of graduates. In turn, it was natural for the members of governing boards and leaders of state governments to look to graduates of colleges for service on these boards when openings occurred. "From the very beginnings," Professor Cowley (1964, Ch. 10, p. 10) has written, "alumni have contributed to the support of private colleges and universities; and as legislators, lobbyists, and moulders of public opinion they have strategically influenced the subsidizing of civil institutions." Formal representation by means of elected members to governing boards first appeared at Harvard in 1865, a pattern that was followed by many other institutions in the subsequent decades.[6]

In summary, university government had coalesced into the pattern we know today by shortly after the turn of the century. It reflected a continuation of medieval and English precedents whereby institutional autonomy received a high degree of protection, modified perhaps in American higher education by a more overt sense of commitment to societal needs. Private colleges and universities had the protection afforded them by their status as corporations under law.[7] In practice, public institutions obtained much of this same autonomy through their status as public corporations under the control of boards established by state constitution or legislative law. But even before the end of the nineteenth century, evidences of growing restrictions upon the actual power of governing boards had begun to emerge.

Over and above any incipient faculty militance, the practical result of growing size and complexity necessitated the delegation of some policy-making and managerial responsibilities to presidents and faculties. Finally, the unique role and influence of presidents during this era require recognition. In contrast to earlier periods when presidents served more as principals responsible for campus conduct and morality—of professor and student alike—and trustees sat importantly at commencements to examine graduating seniors, by 1900 presidents had become a positive force. Every university to rise to major status did so under the almost dominating influence of such presidential leaders as

Charles W. Eliot at Harvard, Andrew D. White at Cornell, Daniel Coit Gilman at Johns Hopkins, Charles R. Van Hise at Wisconsin, William Rainey Harper at Chicago, David S. Jordan at Stanford, and Benjamin Ide Wheeler at California. The office of president emerged as the central force that has given United States higher education a distinctive character among systems of higher education in the world. Whether one viewed the president as the alter ego of boards or as a discrete unit in institutional government had little bearing on practice. Whatever faculty voices may have been raised to the contrary, university government by the twentieth century centered upon the office of the president.

Administrative Structure

In his history of Williams College, *Mark Hopkins and the Log* (1956), Frederick Rudolph vividly portrays a typical college from 1836 to 1872. President Hopkins presides as the paternal head of a small and personal college family, responsible for the character of its children, the students. The curriculum was fixed and limited. In any event, what the students studied was secondary to the quality of personal moral life. In contrast, the "new education" of the last half of the nineteenth century reflected the new morality of the times, a turning away from Christian theology as the basis for life's judgments and toward values oriented far more to the marketplace and material success. In the words of Veysey (1965, Ch. 2), "discipline and piety" gave way to "utility" as the hallmark of a college education. Specialized knowledge replaced the "disciplining of the mind and character" as the raison d'être for higher education. Adherents of reform rallied to elective ideas which supported, to a degree at least, the rights of students to choose their subjects and thus to open the universities to the new studies of science and technology and of specialization in the humanities, all of which stressed the advancement of knowledge and a utilitarian commitment. By 1900 graduate studies, professional schools, and professors whose careers rested upon their published research rather than upon their role as teachers were moving to positions of the highest status in the academic hierarchy. Harvard University offered good evidence of the impact of this influence upon the curriculum. The 1850 catalog described the entire four years of undergraduate study on four pages; in 1920, 30 times that number of pages were required to list the courses offered at the university.

Two shifts in organizational structure inevitably followed. On the one hand, by the turn of the century departments and professional schools had become the basic units for academic affairs. The academic structure of the university coincided with the structure of knowledge. On the other hand, the impact of this "new education" fitted the times. In contrast to the declining enrollment of the 1840s and 1850s, the latter half of the nineteenth century marked the beginning of what has become a constantly increasing rate of college attendance. More students meant more professors, more buildings, more facilities and equipment, and, above all, more money from private and public sources. As chief executive, the president inherited the responsibility both for securing this support and for coordinating and managing the inevitable internal complexities that resulted. Initially, a vice-president and a few professors who served as part-time registrars, bursars, and librarians assisted him. By 1900, however, such staffs proved insufficient; the managerial burden of the president had begun to necessitate what has become a burgeoning administrative bureaucracy.

Academic Organization

Some imitations of the specialized departments and professional schools which have become the basic organizational units of universities do appear in the early colleges. The University of Virginia, for example, opened in 1825 with eight schools, each headed by a professor and each offering a program of studies. In that same year, the statutes reorganizing Harvard College established nine "departments" for instruction, each of which (in the pattern already set for medicine, law, and divinity) would be "governed by a board of its full professors" (Cowley, 1964, Ch. 7, p. 4). The use of departments appeared also in 1826 at the University of Vermont, a decade later at Wisconsin, and at Michigan in 1841. But these departments served only as progenitors of the disciplinary and professional units that fashioned the academic organization of universities later in the century.

The appearance of departments as organizational entities accompanied the expansion of knowledge—particularly scientific and technological—and the elective system, by means of which the adherents of specialized study forced their point of view into institutions with traditions of a fixed, classical curriculum. But the reason for the association of departments of scholars in this country (in contrast to the chair held by one professor in foreign universities) has not been documented historically. That they had become the established structural units by 1900 is evident nonetheless in the histories of all major universities.[8]

A similar development occurred in the various professional studies, which appeared with few exceptions first as departments and later as schools, which in turn procreated their own departments. Certainly by 1900 professional specializations in more than a dozen areas were well established, ranging from the traditional trinity of medicine, law, and theology to such new areas as business administration, veterinary medicine, journalism, librarianship, and architecture.

The departmental structure that followed in the wake of specialized knowledge was accompanied by other evidence of disciplinary and professional segmentation, such as journals and national societies. Professors, as the authorities for their respective specializations, assumed more and more control over academic affairs. This revolutionary change from the earlier colleges had evolved by 1910 to the extent that a study of physics departments complains about their having "too much autonomy." The report describes the department as "usually practically self-governing" in control of its own affairs—that is, its students, staff, and curriculum (Cooke, 1910).

Administrative Organization

Responding to the pressures of office work, travel, supervising new construction, employing new faculty, and initiating educational programs, in 1878 President Andrew Dickson White of the new Cornell University appointed a professor of modern languages and history, William C. Russel, as vice-president. Russel functioned as a kind of executive associate—hiring and dismissing junior faculty members, answering correspondence, and carrying out routine responsibilities as well as acting as institutional head in White's absence. The same year, a presidential colleague at Harvard, Charles W. Eliot, appointed Professor Ephriam W. Gurney as dean of the college faculty. In contrast to Russel's initial tasks, Dean Gurney's primary responsibility was to relieve the president of the burden of contacts with students.

These appointments at two major universities signaled the beginning of a trend. For the college growing into a large and complex university, the office of the president quickly ceased to be a one-man job. Those part-time assistants, usually professors, who served as librarian, bursar, or registrar had by 1900 turned into full-time administrative officers, and by the 1930s they were supervising large staffs. A 1936 study by Earl J. McGrath documents the trend. The author charts the growth from a median of three or four administrative officers in the 1880s to a median of nearly sixty for the larger universities by 1930. As noted previously in this chapter, the decades from 1890 to 1910 proved to be the turning point. The lines on McGrath's chart after 1890 turn upward abruptly, showing a doubling of these officers from an average of about 12 in that year to 30 in 1910.

What brought about this transformation of American universities into complex administrative systems, especially in contrast to the much simpler organization of European universities? Many determinants exerted influence, of course. In large part, administrative expansion responded to the need to coordinate and, to a degree, control the expansion of the academic structure. In part, it grew out of a relationship with the general society, unique to this country, which imposed on the university the task of securing financial support from both public and private sources and concurrently of attending to public relations. In part, the enlarged administration implemented an intricate credit system for student admissions and educational accounting.

Fundamentally, however, the administrative organization of universities resulted from the managerial role of the American college president, the coincidental result of the fact that early founders looked to the colleges of the English universities for their patterns. In doing this they carried over the concept of a permanent headship, designated in the English colleges as *warden*, *master*, *provost*, *president*, or *rector* (Cowley, 1971, Ch. 11, p. 10; Davis, 1961, p. 304).[9] In contrast to the English custom of election by the fellows of the college, the presidents in this country from the very beginning have been appointed by governing boards. Thus, the presidents of the early colleges had responsibilities as executives for boards. For the first two centuries this constituted a relatively simple and personal, almost paternal, relationship with student and teachers. When, after the Civil War, colleges ceased to be small and universities appeared with expanded enrollments, academic fragmentation, and diversified relationships with the external society, presidents found their responsibility elaborated and their need for staff assistance imperative.

By 1900 it could be said that the general administration had developed something like its full measure of force in American higher education. In 1902, President Nicholas Murray Butler assumed the presidency of Columbia complete with clerical staff, abetted by well-established offices for the registrar and bursar (Veysey, 1965, p. 307). Probably typical of its times, the University of North Carolina administration included a registrar, bursar, librarian, and part-time secretary for the university. The office of alumni secretary was not unknown by 1900 (McGrath, 1936). Although largely a product of this century, business officers commonly served as bursars or collectors of fees. By the turn of the century, librarians had established themselves on a full-time basis and had begun to employ assistants—in contrast with the rudimentary condition of these services 40 years previously. The first press bureau appeared at the University of Wisconsin in 1904 (Seller, 1963, p. 3). The office of registrar was nearly universal. The office of vice-president, usually assigned to handle specific functions such as university relations, academic affairs, medical affairs, or similar constellations of administrative services, had appeared in some numbers by the First World War.

Concurrently, presidents turned to the title of *dean* to further delegate their academic responsibilities. By 1900 this title was used for the heads of professional schools, especially medicine and law, and of schools or divisions of arts and sciences. The office of dean served in smaller colleges to designate the "second in command." In an 1896 reorganization at Cornell, for example, President Schurman appointed deans of academic affairs and of graduate studies. All the universities and two-thirds of the colleges included in the McGrath study had academic deans by 1900. The designation of the title of dean for student affairs also has precedent in the late nineteenth century. At Harvard, Eliot's appointment of Dean Gurney, as noted above, was a response to the pressures of his responsibilities for students. Similar appointments were made at Swarthmore, Oberlin, and Chicago in the 1890s. The same forces that had fragmented the unitary curriculum of the early colleges in support of specialized knowledge made the orientation of faculty members more intellectual and pushed into secondary or tertiary importance their concern with students. Into this void came the forerunners of contemporary student personnel services. Deans of women began to meet annually in 1903; directors of student unions appeared in 1914; the National Association of Deans of Men was organized in 1917.

In summary, then, the organizational structure of American universities was etched clearly enough by the first decade of this century. Its two mainstreams flowed to and from the offices of presidents: one an academic route to deans and thence to departmental chairmen; the other a managerial hierarchy. Whatever the organizational charts designated, as early as 1910 it had become apparent that initiative on the academic side had begun to rest heavily at the departmental level.

Twentieth-Century Expansion

If the late nineteenth century constitutes the formative years of American higher education, the present century has been an era of growth and consolidation. During the decades following the Civil War, colleges began their search for a personality appropriate to the times and to their position in society. As the years of maturity approached, each found its particular role in what has become a spectrum from small, unitary schools to large, complex universities which set the pace and pattern for the whole system. Diversity became the pervasive quality of the new era—diversity among institutions and within the major universities.

Expansion in this century has led to colleges and universities that number faculty members in the hundreds and thousands and students in the thousands and tens of thousands. Society's commitment to send youth to college as a major preparation for adult roles is evident in the steady increase from 52,000 students in 1869 to 2,650,000 in 1949 to more than double this by the 1970s. The less than 2 percent of the age group who attended college at the close of the Civil War has grown to more than 40 percent and approaches 50 percent. This expansion in numbers has carried with it a similar expansion in functions. By the early 1960s Clark Kerr, then president of the University of California, could comment that his university employed more people "than IBM . . . in over a hundred locations, counting campuses, experiment stations, agricultural and urban extension centers, and projects abroad involving more than fifty countries." He pointed to "nearly 10,000 courses in its catalogues; some form of contact with nearly every industry, nearly every level of government, nearly every person in its region" (Kerr, 1966, pp. 7–8). The "multiversity" has proved to be the ultimate outcome for the "new university" of 70 years ago.

Since 1900 no radical departures have altered the form of university organization or changed in any substantial way its function. In the retrospect of the last 60 years, the major thrusts that have characterized this era are the following: first, the expansion in numbers of both personnel and of units of the administrative structure, both academic and managerial; second, the consolidation of departmental control over academic matters; and, third, the diffusion of participation in government with a concurrent lessening of the influence of boards and presidents.

Administrative Expansion

Aside from the study by McGrath (1936) and a recent article by David R. Witmer (1966), little documentation exists to delineate the specifics of administrative expansion in this century. But the outward manifestations are obvious. What university of any size today lacks that imposing administration building located near the center of the campus? Within its walls dozens and even hundreds of clerks, typists, secretaries, bookkeepers, accountants, staff assistants, and a variety of administrative officers labor diligently over correspondence and reports, accounts and records, and a variety of managerial services—frequently in a high degree of efficient isolation from the classroom, laboratory, and library across the campus. In addition, one finds a plethora of service positions ranging from dietitians and delivery men to personnel for institutional research.

Paralleling the managerial services, the academic organization has had its own expansion of new functions and offices appended to departments and professional schools. It takes only a quick glance at the telephone directory of a major university to spot such activities as the animal facilities, athletic publicity and promotion, black studies program, carbon research, program in comparative literature, council for international studies, continuing education division, cooperative urban extension center, and creative art center at the top of the alphabet through to technical research services, theater program, upward bound project, urology studies, and urban studies council at the bottom. Each of these activities has its director or head who reports to a chairman, a dean, or a vice-president. Each has a professional staff of one to a dozen individuals aided by secretaries and research assistants. The totality presents a bewildering complex of functions requiring administrative coordination and control.

As one looks over charts for the period, what stands out clearly is the steady, inexorable increase in administrative personnel and services paralleling the increase in numbers of students and faculty members.

Departmental Influence

Specialization of knowledge has its counterpart in specialization of departments. But more than this it has led to what amounts to a monopoly of the expert. This specialization has left the university-wide administrators, and at times deans as well, unable to do more than respond to initiative on matters of personnel facilities, teaching, curriculum, and research. Authors Paul L. Dressel and Donald J. Reichard (1970, p. 387)[10] observed in their historical overview that the department "has become a potent force, both in determining the stature of the university and in hampering the attempts of the university to improve its effectiveness and adapt to changing social and economic requirements." As early as 1929 a study of departments in small colleges demonstrated that they exercised a major influence in matters related to teaching, curriculum, schedule, and promotion

(Reeves & Russell, 1929). More recent studies confirm the trend toward departmental autonomy and control over its own affairs (Caplow & McGee, 1958), evidenced by what David Riesman (1958) has called an academic procession in which the less prestigious institutions have followed the leadership of the major, prestigious universities.

This departmental autonomy has come as a logical outgrowth of size and specialization and of the pressing necessity to delegate and decentralize if major administrators were not to find themselves overwhelmed. A new kind of professor, the specialist and expert and man of consequence in society, has replaced the teacher and has augmented his (the specialist's) influence with a national system of professional and disciplinary societies. Together they have set the standards and the values, both oriented to productive scholarship, that dominate the universities.

Diffusion of Government

Following hard on the downward shift of academic power, governing boards have withdrawn extensively from active involvement in university affairs. This condition was incipient in 1905, as noted by James B. Munroe, industrialist and trustee at Massachusetts Institute of Technology. The trustees, he observed then, "find less and less opportunity for usefulness in a machine so elaborate that any incursion into it by those unfamiliar may do infinite harm—(Munroe, 1913). Fifty years later, in the same vein, the 1957 report on The Role of Trustees of Columbia University, (Columbia University, 1957) stated flatly that, while governing boards may hold final legal authority, their actual role in government leaves them removed from the ongoing affairs of their institutions. And as Trustee Ora L. Wildermuth, secretary of the Association of Governing Boards of State Universities, commented in 1949: "If a governing board contents itself with the selection of the best president available and with him develops and determines the broad general principles . . . and then leaves the administration and academic processes to the administrative officers and the Faculty, it will have done its work well." It serves best to select a president, hold title to property, and act as a court of last appeal, he summarized (Wildermuth, 1949, p. 238).

Pressing up from a departmental base, faculty members have moved into governmental affairs via the formalization of a structure of senates, councils, and associated committees. Evidence supports the contention that by 1910 professors were not hesitant to refer to their "rightfully sovereign power" (Veysey, 1965, p. 392). President Harper of Chicago formally stated in his decennial report that it was a "firmly established policy of the Trustees that the responsibility for the settlement of educational questions rests with the Faculties" (Bogert, 1945, p. 81). During the first half of this century the precedent of the major universities slowly carried over to other institutions. In 1941 a survey of 228 colleges and universities by the AAUP (American Association of University Professors) Committee T on College and University Government led to the comment that "in the typical institution the board of trustees appointed the president, the president appointed deans, and the deans in turn designated executives. . . . Consultation concerning personnel and budget . . . took place between administrative and teacher personnel through departmental executives—("The Role of Faculties . . ." 1948). A decade later, however, the same committee reported an increase in faculty communication with trustees, participation in personnel decisions, influence on personnel policies, consultation about budgetary matters, and control of academic programs ("The Place and Function . . ." 1953). By the late 1960s the basic position of the AAUP had the strength of general tradition; in the eyes of a new breed of faculty radicals it had become a conservative force. In essence, the AAUP's position was based upon five principles: (1) that faculties have primary responsibility over educational policies; (2) that they concur through established committees and procedures in academic personnel matters; (3) that they participate actively in the selection of presidents, deans, and chairmen; (4) that they are consulted on budgetary decisions; and (5) that appropriate agencies for this participation have official standing.

Precedents for student involvement in university and college government (distinct from extracurricular campus activities) have gained a new force, although their roots lie deep in the history of higher education. Professor Cowley (1964, Ch. 11, p. 16) has described the abortive two-year "House of Students" at Amherst in 1828 as a legislative body concerned with security on campus, study hours, and similar matters. In this century, something of the same spirit has appeared sporadically. At Barnard during the academic year 1921–22, students carried out a sophisticated analysis of the curriculum. At Dartmouth in 1924, a committee of 12 seniors submitted a critical review of the education program. At Harvard in 1946, following the publication of the faculty report General Education in a Free Society (Harvard Committee, 1946), students published an equally formidable document. Overall, as Cowley (1964, Ch. 11, p. 47) observes, "American students have continuously and sometimes potently affected the thinking and actions of professors, presidents, and trustees." Historically their influence has been an informal one. Their drive for direct participation on the governing councils and boards of colleges and universities generated real potency only during the late 1960s.[11] Its effectiveness remains conjectural, although the evidence suggests that the student drive for participation will tend to dissipate further the influence of boards and presidents.

Alumni have maintained their traditional voice in government, although one can perceive an undermining of the spirit of alma mater and the significance of financial contributions so long associated with their institutional commitments. This participation was substantiated by a 1966 survey of 82 public and private universities and colleges which reported that 31 of the institutions have elected alumni trustees and an additional 24 have trustees nominated by alumni. Nearly all had alumni on their boards, however.[12] Cornell University's situation is typical of private institutions. In a 1966 letter the president of the Alumni Association noted that "a trustee is not required to be an alumnus of the University unless he is elected by the alumni. At present, however, of the 40 members, 35 are alumni." In retrospect, then, higher education is moving into the final decades of the twentieth century with a pattern of organization similar in its major dimensions to that with which it entered the century. The question readily comes to mind whether this form will continue to prove effective.

Conclusion

That the American university, the hallmark of the American system of higher education, has flourished as an institution uniquely fitted to its times stands without question. Its commitment to the expansion of knowledge and its application are emulated throughout the world. Similarly, its organizational arrangements have grown out of and suited well its particular kind of educational enterprise. Inevitably governing boards and presidents had to delegate as institutions expanded. That they did so in a manner that enhanced the effectiveness of the academic endeavor has proved to be no minor achievement. Departments, in turn, have served well by translating the essence of specialized knowledge into workable organizational forms. Student personnel administrators, in their turn, have filled that void between individual and organization left by the impersonalism inherent in a faculty pre-eminently concerned with the extension of knowledge. A faculty governing structure has given an organizational channel to the exercise of professorial influence, in turn an academically essential counterbalance to the authority of governing boards and external constituencies. In sum, universities have proved an effective organizational means by which scholarship and learning could flourish within the confines of large, complex organizations.

Yet, as the decade of the 1970s unfolds, a sense of uncertainty about just how well universities do perform has begun to settle over the campuses of the nation. Students in large universities, and even to a degree in smaller institutions, find themselves caught in a complex of increasingly impersonal relationships and an educational endeavor which enhances advanced study and research more than student learning. Both influences tend to dull any sense of intellectual awakening or of personal meaning for life on the part of students. Most faculty cling hard to the traditional fields of knowledge and to specialization despite a societal need for synthesis and application of what is known. As, historically, cultures and nations in their greatest flowering have begun to show their inherent weaknesses, so the university in the last few decades has provided evidence of its limitations. The changing nature of the social order, as it too reaches a pinnacle of scientific-technological achievement, amplifies these weaknesses.

A historical survey such as this would be inadequate indeed if it did not at least suggest some clues to the future. In conclusion, therefore, we note three pervasive organizational inadequacies.

One can be attributed to size and complexity, a second to specialization and departmentalization, and the third to the shifting pattern of institutional government. All were incipient but generally underway as higher education emerged from the First World War.

The size and complexity of United States universities seem to dictate that they have become large bureaucracies. Actually, however, one finds two bureaucracies. On the one hand, over the past 50 years faculties have created a hierarchy of departments, schools, and senates or executive councils well larded with a variety of permanent and temporary committees. This bureaucracy claims rights of control over the totality of the academic function. On the other hand, administrators have formed a separate hierarchy to grapple with the immense tasks of management of essential yet supportive services which maintain the university, not the least of which are budget and finance. The lines of relationship between the two bureaucracies have become tenuous. The different attitudes and values associated with each have driven a psychological wedge between faculty members and administrators. Faculty remain committed to a traditional ideal of the university as an integrated community, at the same time giving constant evidence that they fail to grasp its real operational nature and managerial complications. Administrators find their managerial tasks so consuming that they become forgetful of the nature of the academic enterprise.

The second evidence of dysfunction stems from the nature of the department as the organizational unit for disciplinary and professional specialization. The commitment to specialization energizes centrifugal forces that tend to push faculty loyalties out from the universities. Thus the university is often merely a base, temporary or permanent, from which the scholar pursues his primary concern with research activities. Specialization has produced a similar tendency toward fragmentation of the academic organization. While exercising a dominant influence on instruction, curriculum, research, and other academic matters, schools and departments show a low regard for university values and a high concern for disciplinary and professional values. Despite many evidences to the contrary during the student disruptions of the last few years, this condition is reinforced by academic condescension toward administrators, who are viewed as servants rather than leaders of the professorate. It reflects what one might call a faculty schizophrenia which categorizes administrators as minions while condemning them for failure to stand firmly as defenders of the academic faith in times of crisis.

At times this divergency threatens an atrophy in leadership for large universities in an era when leadership is of utmost importance. The remedy, however, inevitably must lie beyond the bounds of organizational factors. Forms of government serve only as well as they are supported in the general values and commitments of those affected by them. Any rectification of this condition, therefore, must stem from deep within the higher education enterprise. In particular, there must be some resolution of the conflict between the clear and direct rewards that accompany achievement in scholarship and research and the nominal recognition, despite societal expectation, accorded to the education of students. From this base line one moves into explorations of reward systems that conform to stated purposes. One also has to reflect upon organizational systems that prove responsive to changing conditions as against those that support existing arrangements.

The third problem—the shifting power in institutional government—was anticipated in 1903 by President Schurman of Cornell when he characterized his role as that of a mediator. Sixty years later Clark Kerr made the same observation with greater force. Presidential deference to faculty expertise in academic affairs is only one facet of the situation, however. The history of university organization in the twentieth century has been an account of the disintegration of the traditional form of government conceived in terms of formal authority granted to governing boards, which have exercised it through the president as executive officer.

The diffusion of government by means of dissipation of boards and presidential influence and dispersion of operating control to departments, administrative offices, and faculty governing bodies has been accompanied by the intrusion of external forces. Professional and disciplinary associations, accrediting agencies, agencies of the federal government for all institutions and state executive offices for public ones—all have tended to bypass presidents and boards. It appears that higher education has experienced one of those historic circles. Governing boards today serve much the way the original visitors or overseers did. What is lacking is a new corporation in the sense of a controlling or managerial council to fill the vacuum. As one English observer phrased it, organizationally American universities have tended to become "confederations of largely autonomous departments." It adds up to what he has characterized as "the hole in the centre" (Shils, 1970).

As universities enter the decade of the 1970s, the pressures on the established organization are evidenced in student dissent and the public reaction to it. The movement toward decentralization of control over educational and administrative functions has begun to come up against external demands for more forceful central authority to the end not only of "law and order" but of a "more efficient use of resources." Mass higher education and the possibility of almost universal higher education exacerbate the problems. More fundamentally, one finds growing evidences of academic inadequacies in the face of the need for new kinds of education and scholarship. These must relate to the role of the university in a society pressed by ecological and social dislocation stemming from scientific and technological achievement. One readily suspects that the organizational forms effective in 1900 may serve but poorly for the year 2000.

Notes

1. These arrangements for the College of William and Mary were stated in a manner that led to conflicts between the two boards during its early years, although essentially they remained in effect until it became a state institution shortly after 1900. At Harvard, however, practice nullified the apparent intent of the 1650 charter, so that by the eighteenth century the immediate governing council (the Corporation) had passed into the hands of external members. The practice was disputed from time to time by tutors until an 1825 vote of the Overseers finally and formally stated that "the resident instructors of Harvard University" did not have any exclusive right to be chosen members of the Corporation (Quincy, 1860, vol. 2, 324).

2. Yale historians apparently have tended to credit Clap with a successful defense. Recent investigation of this incident by Professor W. H. Cowley, however, discloses that a visitation was made the following year, about which one of the visitors later observed that "we touch'd them so gently, that till after ye Assembly, they never saw they were taken in, that we had made ourselves Visitors, & subjected them to an Annual Visitation" (a point made in correspondence with this author).

3. This precedent has undergone modification in more recent decades as state budget bureaus, civil service commissions, and coordinating boards have intruded directly into the internal affairs of public institutions.

4. Exceptions to these rights do exist, particularly in connection with the control of property and the borrowing of monies. Frequently special corporations are set up within the control of state universities to handle private funds. Actual practice varies among the states, some of which limited the powers of boards in the founding legislation.

5. In recent decades the growth in academic status and influence of the disciplines and professional departments and schools has further strengthened faculty power within institutions. The status associated with productive scholarship and research has given faculty members a greatly improved position vis-á-vis administration in internal affairs, a condition documented by Theodore Caplow and Reece J. McGee in their classic study, *The Academic Marketplace*, 1958.

6. Amherst in 1874, Dartmouth in 1875, Rutgers in 1881, Princeton in 1900, Columbia in 1908, Brown in 1914. (In the 1865 modification of its charter, Harvard adopted a plan whereby alumni gained the right to elect all new members to the Board of Overseers, the body with ultimate responsibility for that institution.)

7. Little attention is given, unfortunately, to the uniquely significant role of the governing board in this country as the agency that both has protected internal autonomy and intellectual freedom and has served as a force to keep institutions relevant to the general society. This history badly needs doing. Despite occasional intrusions into internal affairs and matters related to academic freedom, the governing board has served as a point of balance for that essential dualism between institutional and academic autonomy and public accountability which has characterized American higher education. Current forces pressing for greater internal participation on the one hand and increased public control on the other need tempering by the experience of the past in this connection.

8. For example, Harvard established 12 divisions, each including one or more departments, in 1891; Chicago had 26 departments in three faculties in 1893; Cornell, Yale, Princeton, Johns Hopkins, and Syracuse, among others, all reveal the trend toward departmentalization during the decade of the 1890s (Forsberg & Pearce, 1966).

9. Actually, the first head of Harvard had the title of master and that of Yale, rector. The Harvard custom lasted two years, that at Yale about forty. Both colleges shifted to the title of president.

10. This report anticipated a more complete study by Dressel, Marcus, and Johnson entitled The *Confidence Crisis*, Jossey-Bass, Inc., San Francisco, 1970.

11. In his 1970 book, *Should Students Share the Power?* Earl J. McGrath reports a survey of existing practice, noting that more than 80 percent of 875 institutions admit some students to membership in at least one policy-making body. In the same year the University of Tennessee admitted students to its trustee committees. A House bill submitted in 1969 in the Massachusetts legislature proposed an elected student member of each of the governing boards of public universities.

12. Conducted by Howard University with the sponsorship of the American Alumni Council. The questionnaire was mailed to 112 institutions, from which 82 usable responses were received.

THE ORGANIZATIONAL CONCEPTION

BURTON R. CLARK

An organizational perspective on higher education commonly takes analysts inside the system. It sends researchers in search of what academics actually do. With a little imagination it allows observers to see the system from the bottom up, looking out from the positions and perspectives of faculty, students, and local administrators, as well as from the top down, where analysis flows toward the problems and orientations of central officials, national legislators, and those who advise and influence them. In either event, this approach allows us to see the world through the eyes of the main actors and hence to portray the relations of the system to the environment from the inside out. When this perspective is at the top of its form, it becomes a way to give the system its due. The higher education system is taken seriously when observers focus on how it initiates and responds, how it maintains stability and induces change, as well as how it follows paths that are determined by others.

When we take an internal approach to the shaping of action and policy we are able to resist the temptation to say that "society" or "social forces" determine higher education. By emphasizing immediate contexts, we start close in; then, as need be, analysis moves outward to larger settings. This tactic is parsimonious, since we take up proximate causes first and clarify the local contexts that mediate the effects of larger ones. It is also increasingly necessary. As in other major spheres of society, sectorial hegemony develops when bureaucrats and professionals occupy key internal sites in ever more complicated webs of work and authority. Modern systems of higher education develop massive structures and elaborate procedures that strengthen internal control over operations and provide defense in depth against environmental turbulence. Analysts of diverse conviction have argued the need to go inside "the black box" of organized higher education. The organizational approach does so, joined increasingly by investigators converging on internal features as they pursue specific historical developments, political dimensions of the system, the economic behavior of universities, the determinants of access and achievement—in short, those applying other perspectives presented in this volume. A focus on organizational dimensions assists these other ways of viewing higher education by helping to establish which internal characteristics are important, pulling together in integrative frameworks the crucial features of organizations that otherwise would be treated in a fragmented fashion.

The view from the inside also emphasizes institutional response. Identifying such external "demands" as more consumers or more available jobs is only the beginning of analysis. We need further to ask: What is the response to a particular change in external conditions? Or, as a "demand" flows into the system, who supports it, who resists it, and how is it organizationally implemented and thereby shaped? How much did the system determine the demand in the first place, as, for example, when decades of enforcing high standards in the educational system convince the overwhelming majority of young people that higher education is not for them?

An internalist perspective leads researchers to search for the ways in which the higher education system, moving by its own internal logics and its forms of response, will shape other institutions and society in general. This point hardly needs any further initial support than to emphasize the obvious effects of scientific research being carried out in academic systems, particularly in the international centers of learning, but also flowing out from them to other systems to make them dynamic too. We are near the end of a half century in which academic physicists have harnessed atomic energy, academic biologists have made revolutionary advances in genetic engineering, and academic mathematicians and engineers have helped develop the computer. And since academics prepare nearly all the professional cadres of society, as well as those persons who engage in research and development elsewhere, it is appropriate to view the academic system as the home of the key profession, the one that trains all the others.[1] With so many major avenues of influence there is growing reason to pursue the question of how higher education shapes society.

After the comparative research of the past decade, it is possible to offer a major first cut in what can be seen when we approach higher education as an organized system. First, knowledge is the common substance involved in the activities of the system: research creates it; scholarship preserves, refines, and modifies it; teaching and service disseminate it.[2] The handling of advanced bodies of knowledge has been central to higher education since its beginning and remains common ground across varied national systems. When we look to "the factory floor" of higher education, what we see are clusters of professionals tending various bundles of knowledge. They are the "subjects" or "subject matters," and it is around them that organization takes place. Hence, the concentration on knowledge is what academics have most in common. But what they have least in common is common knowledge, since the bundles they tend are specialized and separated one from another.

To start with subjects as substance is to steer analysis toward actual operations and away from the stated goals and purposes of higher education. For several decades, organizational analysts have been conscious of the distinction between nominal and operative ends. Sophisticated administrators in higher education, as well as elsewhere in society, surely have long been aware of the difference. The analysis of proclaimed ends of universities and higher education soon degenerates into a largely empty exercise of determining who proclaims which clichés, focusing on the broad statements that tell little about what is being done or what will occur. The "purposes" of any major sector of society are increasingly stated in general terms, as activities within the sector become more numerous, complex, and ambiguous. Stated purposes then become wide philosophies that leave the determination of action and policy largely to interest-group struggles and operational mandates. It matters not whether we study small or large systems, in the West or in the Communist bloc. Swedish statements of purpose in higher education, for example, "democracy, personality development, social change," tell us no more than American statements, such as research, teaching, and service. Official declarations in Communist nations, such as those in Poland—"education for self-fulfillment" and "instruction of qualified personnel for all jobs in the economy, culture, and all sectors of social life requiring credentials of higher education"—are hardly an improvement.[3] In contrast, to pick up on the many bundles of knowledge which are the substances of the system is to steer attention to the operating levels where specific groups have specific operative goals: the improvement of research in physics; the teaching of history to undergraduates; the provision of outpatient medical services in an urban neighborhood.

The organization of the system around subjects has its first important dimension in a structure of work.[4] It is inescapable that research, teaching, and other academic activities are heavily conditioned by how tasks are apportioned to academic groups within and among academic enterprises. There is a highly structured division of labor, a finely tuned specialization, and the specific location of academics in that structure becomes the prime determinant of their more material interests. For example, physicists behave like physicists, not like professors of Greek literature. Further, physicists in community colleges, or in other short-cycle units where they teach introductory materials many hours a week to large numbers of first-year students, and do virtually only that, cannot possibly think and act like physicists in research universities.

The higher education system as a whole portions its personnel along at least four different horizontal and vertical dimensions: sectors, hierarchies, sections, and tiers. The sectors are different types of universities and colleges, including those that many countries prefer to categorize as further, or postsecondary, rather than higher education. Academics also find places in an institutional hierarchy, since the sectors, and enterprises within them, become arranged everywhere to some degree in functional and status ranks. Attached to positions in the hierarchy are different sets of tasks and duties, privileges and punishments. Then, within the individual academic enterprise, similar horizontal and vertical assignments take place: to sections, that is, departments, chairs, and institutes; and to tiers, essentially to a graduate or professional specialized higher tier or to the less specialized work of the undergraduate segment. In all its many divisions, the structure of work everywhere becomes a primary element.[5]

It is also inescapable that activities and outcomes, indeed the nature of knowledge itself, are conditioned by the orientations that academics absorb from their disciplines, universities and colleges, the academic profession overall, and even their national system at large.[6] There are "thought styles" rooted in "thought collectives";[7] there is a symbolic side of academic life, a "culture" as well as a social structure. In a section of society which traffics in ideas, many types of symbols, with related meanings, loom large. Quiet fanaticism may even be characteristic, since academics seem inclined to view their own disciplines and subspecialties as superior to all others. Academic subcultures are frequently in conflict: among students, for example, and between them and the faculty; or between those of the faculty and those of the administrators grouped in institutional and national offices. Notable is the ascendance of disciplinary cultures and subcultures, now catching the attention of researchers internationally, as reported by Tony Becher on the cultural view and suggested by Simon Schwartzman on scientific activity.[8] In all its many divisions, the belief or cultural side of academic organization everywhere becomes a second primary element.

Third, as elsewhere, organization is authority, a way of concentrating and diffusing legitimate power.[9] As work and belief are joined together in amalgams of material and subjective interest around particular subjects—the location of some physicists in a university department together with the beliefs they have absorbed from the culture of physics—then the many academic groups thereby solidified in the understructure seek influence that will aid their efforts and protect their positions. They particularly develop professional or guild forms of authority at the local level—some personal, some collegial—and try to extend them upward to control or influence action at the higher levels, including the national center. At the institutional level there are independent bases of influence in many countries in the form of trustee control and institutional bureaucracy. At the system level we often find an administrative class of civil servants occupying roles in which they are responsible for systemwide allocation and order. There, legitimately, they are joined by some legislators, some other public executives, and, increasingly, by judges. Outside interest groups seek and often gain systematic representation, leading toward corporatist or semicorporatist patterns of influence. Again, the divisions are many and the picture is increasingly complex. But the structure of authority is without doubt a primary component. From the bottom to the top, the many groups that wish to steer the course of events will seek to lay hands on some levers of control.[10]

To focus on these three broad elements is to see the higher education system itself as a principal determinant of the behavior of academics, even of the behavior of the flow-through clientele we call students. The participants take up shared positions, or roles, in the system, which come equipped with duties and responsibilities, incentives and sanctions. They learn from vicarious and personal experiences in the system, experiences of those who have gone before and of their contemporary peers as well as their own, what they can and cannot accomplish, what is worth doing, what effort and achievement will cost. From the broadest roles of administrator, faculty, and student and the more specific ones, such as registrar, professor of chemistry, or art student, come conceptions of necessity and possibility. Differentially integrated in the set of roles are three faces of power: power to prevail in overt conflict over explicit issues, power to keep issues off the agendas of action, and power to shape conceptions of what can and ought to be done.

Considerable advance has been made during the 1960s and 1970s in grasping these elements and understanding how they vary within and among systems. We have learned how to compare universities and colleges, within and across countries, in the horizontal arrangements of academic tasks and groups. For example, cross-national research has isolated the chair, the department, and the interdisciplinary college or program as the three primary ways of organizing at the operating level and has provided some footing for estimating the advantages and disadvantages of each. As the rigidities of the chair in the systems of continental Europe, as well as the excesses of personal influence it permits, have become more apparent, they have generated reforms that move toward broader operating units as supports for fields of study growing in size and complexity. We have also observed that national systems vary significantly in how they vertically organize elementary and advanced work, with related rungs of certification and exit, and again can point to broad effects. As an example, the two-tier structure of undergraduate and graduate levels in the American university clearly separates and supports the most advanced research and training in a way not possible in universities of many other countries where specialization became rooted in the first tier, with less deliberate structure above that level. Those universities then have to contend with the access and selection problems of the lower rungs of mass higher education.

In the pursuit of beliefs, we are now more aware than we were two decades ago about how national systems vary in supporting disciplinary cultures and institutional identities. Some turn the disciplines loose to fragment as they please, as in the United States; others rein them in, as in Italy. Some leave institutions to form character individually, as in Great Britain; others try to render them interchangeable parts of a larger collectivity, as in France traditionally. And we clearly have learned much about the exercise of legitimate academic power at several levels, with many possible combinations of such basic forms as the personal, collegial, bureaucratic, and political thinning down empirically into several modes. We can specify a traditional European mode that combined central bureaucracy with local and national academic oligarchy, and compare it with a traditional American mode of weak central staff, trustee and bureaucratic strength at the institutional level, and faculty influence at the local level which has not become, to the same extent as in Europe, a basis for national control. On all these topics, cross-national comparison has broadened research horizons and widened conceptions of the possible, including many unanticipated ways of lessening the effectiveness of higher education.

Perhaps the most significant awareness that has come from cross-national organizational analysis is the sense that modern national systems contain an ever expanding, inordinate complexity of tasks and relationships. We find Islamic poetry and biometeorology, forestry and international studies, French literature and econometrics—and on and on, virtually without end. We are not very surprised when the proliferation of subjects moves on to auto repairing, hair styling, and belly dancing. If the core faculty of the university will not permit certain subjects, then the Extension Division or evening college will. If the university as a whole will not, then other colleges take up the new subjects. General nomenclature shifts to widen the boundaries, from "higher education" to "postsecondary." The boundaries are stretched, even under strongly centralized and concentrated rule; some Communist nations, such as Poland, count colleges of sport and tourism as part of postsecondary education.[11] In short, the modern university is in itself a relatively open system. When various nonuniversity sectors and specific specialized schools develop, the openness is greatly extended and boundaries become virtually impossible to define. In their willingness and capacity to take on new subjects as additional tasks, we are increasingly confronted by systems of ever expanding scope. Modern higher education becomes an almost limitless system.

To seek the more important joints of this complex system, we may pursue three questions: What is central in the way that so many fields of study coexist and relate? What then follows for the operation of the system as a system? What follows for changes the system undergoes? In short, we may pursue composition, coordination, and change. Composition has pride of place, since it comes first in the logic of the system.

The Master Matrix

Academics have a host of memberships that bring them under various influences. They often belong to a specific subspecialty within a discipline while belonging to the discipline as a whole. They often belong to a discipline and a multidisciplinary unit: an undergraduate college such as a residential college at Oxford or Cambridge; a multidisciplinary professional school such as medicine or education; an area studies program such as Latin American or African studies; a problem-centered unit such as urban or environmental studies. Academics belong to a discipline and to the academic profession at large. They belong to a particular university or college and to the entire national system, the latter turned into a potent membership in nationalized systems by means of civil service rank and salary and other systemwide categories. Academics are caught up in various matrices,[12] with multiple memberships that shape their work, call upon their loyalties, and apportion their authority. Central among the matrices is the most common fact of academic work: the academic belongs simultaneously to a discipline, a field of study, and an enterprise, a specific university or college.

These two primary modes of organization crisscross each other. The individual university or college collects in one place some members of the disciplines, putting some physicists, economists, and historians together. It thereby links together small segments of the separate disciplines but also fragments each discipline, scattering physicists, for example, among a host of sites and thereby turning them all into local operators. The enterprise mode of organization clearly cuts sharply across the lines of the disciplines. In turn, the discipline is a point of common commitment and identification along precise lines of specialization. But it is also comprehensive in that it pulls together a craftlike community of interest which reaches across large territories, nationally and, usually, internationally. We may see its members as specialists who are "assigned" to the enterprises. The discipline links parts of one enterprise with similar parts in others but it also thereby fragments each institution. As has been widely noted, locals are made into cosmopolitans, reducing local identification while orienting academics to the far-flung norms and interests of national and international cohorts of colleagues. As a result, a national system of higher education may be and often is as much a set of disciplines and professions as it is a set of universities and colleges.

The crossing of these two lines of membership provides the master matrix of the higher education system. Therein lies much of the underlying uniqueness of higher education, since the discipline-enterprise matrix is not found elsewhere in anything like the same scope and intensity. Nearest to it is the independent research institute and the research and development (R&D) laboratory in business and industry, each of which is staffed with university-trained experts concentrating on their specific subjects. In this regard higher education diverges sharply from elementary and secondary education. The lower levels lack the disciplinary commitments, and related rewards, which in higher education so strongly slash across institutions and national systems. They are more bounded by local structure and national culture.

This master matrix of higher education is not the same everywhere. The relative weight of the discipline and the enterprise varies across and within national systems. The primary source of variation is the importance given to research rather than teaching. The dominance of research in the German system since the early part of the nineteenth century means that modern German universities "emphasize disciplinary criteria almost to the exclusion of collegiate ones."[13] In partial contrast, British universities, influenced by the Oxford-Cambridge pattern of primary membership in interdisciplinary colleges and the concentration on teaching undergraduates, ensnare their academic staff in a stronger set of institutional commitments and values. In sharp contrast with the German model, universities in many developing countries, for example, Nigeria,[14] with little money for research, have weak rewards for disciplinary competence and strong incentives for pleasing those who control the institution from within and without.

Within the American system the research university gives substantial weight to the specialty and to recognized performance in it. It becomes discipline-centered and relatively professor-driven. In contrast, the community college emphasizes teaching to the exclusion of research and weakens the bonds of specialty. The instructor may teach all of sociology rather than a segment of it and then also teach anthropology and psychology. The enterprise becomes more administrator-driven and student-driven.

At bottom, higher education needs disciplines to concentrate on research and scholarship and it needs universities and colleges to concentrate on teaching and dissemination. If teaching were not necessary higher education could and probably would dismantle its enterprises and concentrate each discipline in a lesser number of major clusters, as happens in part whenever research is divorced from the university and given over to a set of institutes, as in the French structure of research academies. It is teaching that insists on wider dispersal of specialists, moving the disciplinarians to where the students are. If research were not necessary, higher education could and probably would have fewer disciplines, and more general major ones, as happens in part in the teaching-centered sectors in differentiated systems.

Another source of variation is the importance given to general or liberal education compared with specialized education. For example, the independent liberal arts college in the United States, in comparison with the university, reduces the weight of the discipline and makes professors more enterprise-centered. Within the American research university, the undergraduate level is more enterprise-centered than the graduate level. Notably, selection of undergraduate students is carried out by offices and committees of the whole, whereas selection at the graduate level is primarily made by the individual departments and professional schools. The packaging of larger bundles of knowledge pulls specialized personnel together, thereby changing their mix of commitments toward a more holistic view at the local level.

But amid such differences we discern a basic trend: as bundles of high knowledge multiply and knowledge-bearing groups proliferate, the higher levels of education take the form of this master matrix. Disciplines ascend, as they have been doing in the leading systems for a century and a half, with disciplines and enterprises then crosscutting one another in ever more complicated arrangements. To analyze matrix organization is then to cut analytically at the joints of the confusing complicated structures of modern higher education. And to emphasize the matrix concept is to insist that analysis pursues the disciplines as concerns that have their own peculiar nature, individually and collectively. As Norton Long wrote some thirty years ago,[15] "The organization of a science is interesting for a student of administration because it suggests a basis of cooperation in which the problem and the subject matter . . . control the behavior of those embarked in the enterprise. Thus physics and chemistry are disciplines, but they are not organized to carry out the will of legitimate superiors. They are going concerns with problems and procedures that have taken form through generations of effort and have emerged into highly conscious goal-oriented activities." These going concerns go far in determining the nature of academic work. We may even view them as institutional instruments of fundamental importance in efficiently serving certain values and achieving certain outcomes. R. Steven Turner has noted "that universal characteristic of the modern professoriate which underlies its unparalleled efficiency as an instrument of science and scholarship: appointive procedures which subordinate institutional to disciplinary values."[16]

Since the discipline and the enterprise converge and commingle in the operating units of universities and colleges, a department or a chair is simultaneously an arm of a discipline and a part of an enterprise and draws strength from the combination. Thus there is an organic base for the impressive primacy of these units which has been widely noted in the research literature.[17] Bottom-heavy organization, we may call it, with each disciplinary (or interdisciplinary) unit within the enterprise having self-evident and acclaimed primacy in a front-line task. Special status accrues to each unit as it becomes authoritative, within the organization, in its "own" field of learning. The degree of authoritativeness naturally varies: across national systems, higher in the more advanced; across sectors within differentiated systems, higher in those concentrating on higher levels of expertise; and across subjects within the university or college, higher where knowledge is the most plentiful, structured, and arcane. But overall it is in the individual and combined strength of these authoritative units that we find the first reason that universities and colleges are something other than unitary organizations, that the considerable exercise of personal and collegial forms of authority is not a mere historical survival, and that an unusual vocabulary of craft and guild, federation and conglomerate, is required to tease out the realities of academic organization which remain hidden when approached by the standard terminologies of organizational life.

Bureaucracy and Its Alternatives

How are disciplines and enterprises and their many members concerted, linked together in larger systems of state, region, and nation? Clearly not in neat patterns, not anywhere. The master matrix ensures confusing complexity, for if a larger system is a set of disciplines as well as a set of enterprises, operating on different axes, then who can be clearly in charge? The concept of loose coupling which has been creatively applied to higher education at the institutional level[18] has to be applied in the large, so broadly, in fact, that we shift from organizational imagery as normally understood. Here analysis is aided by the body of thought developed in political economy which centers on politics and markets,[19] a literature that explores the pros and cons of state authority and market linkages in coordinating the efforts of large numbers of people.

As elsewhere, state authority in higher education divides into political and bureaucratic forms. In turn, the market form is found everywhere in national systems of higher education but in varying strength in such subtypes as the consumer market, the internal labor market, and the institutional market in which institutions voluntarily compete, cooperate, and imitate more on the basis of reputation than of monetary exchange.[20] It is then also necessary to add professional oligarchy as a basic form of national integration, since research has revealed in one country after another, from Italy to Sweden, from Mexico to Japan, that professors are a major and often dominant force at national as well as local levels, using mechanisms of influence they have constructed over a long period of time.[21] Coordination can now be seen as vastly more complicated than depicted when the eyes of coordinators and planners fix only on the formal channels of state allocation and supervision. The concerting of action proceeds along varied, intermingled channels. The four general types of coordination labeled as political, bureaucratic, professional, and market offer only the beginning of a useful analytical grasp.

All these major means of linking actors and actions seem to have expanded in recent decades. The bureaucratic tools are clearly more noticeable than those of a quarter century ago, in small as well as in large systems. Bureaucratic staffs have been strengthened; the jurisdictions of educational bureaus have been enlarged; administrative layers have been added, at national, regional, and local levels; bureaucratic rules have become far more numerous; administrators have specialized more and have become more professional in many matters of allocation and supervision. Bureaucracy becomes more assertive and seemingly more dominant. Yet, at the same time, the political modes of coordination have been strengthened. The use of higher education as a political issue has expanded considerably, first increased by the dramatic events of student discontent in the 1960s but held to a higher level of attention over the long run by the much higher cost of expanded and enriched systems and the stronger popular concern and interest that are entailed in more accessible higher education. The regular political channels of legislative committees, top officials in the executive branch, the courts, and the political parties are now more involved in higher education than they were earlier. Internal interest groups have multiplied and hardened their own organizations and representation, as when faculty move into collective bargaining or establish lobbying consortia. External interest groups pay more attention, given the higher stakes and more numerous payoffs, moving toward corporatist patterns of formal participation in governmental decision making in higher education.

Then, too, professors are not pushed aside in national coordination or in local control. Subject expertise everywhere pushes for home rule on the part of the many local groups. These groups carry their influence up the dual lines of discipline and enterprise, and thus a basic source of influence grows in importance. With it, there is a long-run expansion of collegial, if oligarchical, bodies of academics which have jurisdictions at higher levels: research councils are the most obvious, moving along disciplinary lines; national bodies of rectors, vice-chancellors, and presidents develop as representatives of the local enterprises; the headquarters of the associations of the individual disciplines shift from amateur operation toward professional and bureaucratic expertise in representation. Although senior professors visibly lost power in many countries during the 1960s and 1970s, the professoriat as a whole continued to deepen and widen its involvement in the integration of national systems. The increased influence of the bureaucratic and political channels steadily stimulates a reaction by professors and related staff, with the always powerful leverage of expertise. Knowledge is power, more here than elsewhere.

Finally, analysis has begun to grasp the many ways that marketlike exchanges concert national systems, whether small or large, centralized or decentralized, expanding their role as members increase and tasks multiply. Consumer markets are everywhere at work: there is some consumer choice, some voting with one's feet, in even the most state-driven systems, and of course there are many such choices, among courses, departments, disciplines, enterprises, and even national systems, when state constraints are light. And everywhere there is a powerful latent consumer market in the basing of budgets on enrollments. This common practice institutionalizes an enrollment economy that sharply limits the discretion of politicians, administrators, and professors. The budgeting problem then becomes "one of finding a set of allocations that produces an educational program that attracts enough enrollment to provide the allocations."[22] This latent dependence on customers becomes sharply manifest when institutions, individually or collectively, face a dwindling number of students. Then everything may be up for grabs, including academic tenure, as changes in the enrollment base produce "financial exigencies" that change some of the fundamental rules of the game. In any event, consumer markets, in various forms, coorder academic structures and practices, shuffling allocations, changing personnel assignments, and altering the respective places of whole enterprises.

Internal labor markets are also everywhere at work, ever more sharply differentiated by discipline and even by precise specialties within disciplines and professional fields; universities go looking not for an academic person but for a physicist or a historian and then for a particular kind of physicist or historian who may even serve locally as one of a kind. And from the side of labor there is always some choice, for nowhere is the state allocation of persons to academic posts so complete as to eliminate choice by faculty and administrators. But there are very large differences in degree and range of choice, and hence in the contribution of the labor market itself to coordination. This market form of linkage may be steered or strongly constrained by a host of conditions: primarily firm regime control (e.g., in the Soviet Union), but also including strong inhibition on the flow of academic labor by uniform national rules and norms (e.g., France), strong control by senior academics over junior staff and advanced students (e.g., Italy), and cultural traditions of lifelong employment in particular institutions (e.g., Japan). A modest amount of mobility is found in such systems as those of the United Kingdom, Canada, and Australia in which institutions hire personnel on their own and stress individual achievement as the basis for the aggregate prestige of the whole. Among the national systems that have mostly full-time personnel, the United States remains the extreme example of academic labor mobility, even when economic depression and/or an "oversupply" of academics seriously dampens the job market for young recruits.

Such functions as high-quality research may heavily depend on the way this type of market operates. The most powerful hypothesis in the comparative sociology of science remains the one advanced by Joseph Ben-David and Abraham Zloczower in 1962: major national systems that are decentralized and competitive are more conducive to scientific progress than are centralized and noncompetitive ones, in large part because of the opportunities thereby given to talented academics, especially younger ones, to move from less to more attractive settings for the development of their ideas.[23]

Institutional markets consist of the interactions of whole enterprises with one another. Reputation seems to be the main commodity of exchange; relative prestige not only affects the judgments of consumers and workers but also guides the actions of institutions. Highly valued institutions may sit astride the whole structure. As they do so, they commonly generate strong tides of academic drift, with other enterprises imitating and attempting to converge upon their ways. In the more competitive systems institutions also try to carve out a protected niche in the consumer market, against others, to ensure a favorable enrollment economy.

Notably, we may now observe whole sectors of institutions emerging and developing in response to "market failure" or "state failure." State-financed sectors have often been encouraged by the "failures" of private sectors to provide sufficient access, low-cost education, and secular education. In turn, private sectors are encouraged by the "failures" of public sectors to provide high-quality education or better access or religious education. Latin America is now a laboratory of public-private experiments, with important private sectors emerging as academically superior in some instances, as mass service in others, as religious, and often as escape from politicization.[24] The idea occurs that as national systems continue to come under pressure for "more and better" higher education, a differentiation is likely to occur in the simply structured state systems in which there will be a major residual market, of tasks, for private sectors. If public institutions are providing "the better," they become stubborn about the more, and much of the expansion is likely to go into that residual market. If public enterprises carry "the more," the residual institutional market echoes with demands for the better. And when the public sector is providing neither the more nor the better, government officials as well as multitudes of consumers and workers are likely to tilt toward those institutions, new and old, which compete in that residual market. The interplay among sectors as well as among particular institutions, actions constituting an institutional market, is then an important dynamic driving the interior differentiation of modern systems.

These several major forms of market coordination express a bias that is fundamentally different from political and bureaucratic forms. When an activity is transferred from market contexts to state control, it comes under a bias for aggregation.[25] Things are to be added up. The expectation grows within and outside the government that someone will deliberately pull things together and otherwise systematize. When an activity remains under market conditions or creeps away from state regulation to a more marketlike context, it comes under a bias for disaggregation. Things are not to be added up in one heap, in one place: they are to be in a piecemeal state. "System" is then a different matter, but it is still a system.

* * * * *

The coordination and integration of national systems become ever more entangled. The nearest to a root cause within the system is the growing complexity of tasks and related groups. Central to that complexity is the matrix of disciplines and enterprises. As disciplines subdivide and proliferate, they stretch one axis of complexity. As additional institutions emerge, they stretch the second dimension. Since the two intersect, parts and relationships are created at a rapid rate. Five disciplines in five institutions produce twenty-five intersects. The addition of five of each—making ten disciplines in ten institutions—produces a hundred intersects. Even allowing for a partial allocation of disciplines among types of institutions, the master matrix leads toward exponential expansion in the structures of work, belief, and authority which support the tasks and technologies of higher education.

Change: The Moving Matrix

Change remains the most recalcitrant subject in the social sciences. The term is used to refer to alterations that vary from simple reproduction, more units of the same kind, to revolution and radical transformation. Those who seek the causes of changes in different institutions bog down in the complexities of history, perplexed by unique conditions and trends that seemingly converge and part in accidental and hence unpredictable ways. As Harold Perkin points out, historical analysis is weak in "covering laws," weak in systematically grasping linkages. Yet historians, like other social scientists, want to go beyond facts and particulars to explanations. All are interested in some degree of determinism, some lawlike statements. If to understand the past is to help us understand the present, and the past and present give us some guide to the future, then we mean there are regularities, recurrent phenomena, and constraints at time one that delimit, even decide, events at time two. In one sense, organizational analysts are deeply involved in such searches, fixing on the more, firmly built structures that we call organizations with the strong belief that these structures make a difference, over time as well as in contemporary events. Yet organizational analysis has been history poor, rarely engaged in systematic study of development over an extended period of time.

In considering how the analysis of change might be positioned and strengthened within the organizational analysis of higher education, it helps to distinguish between the emergence of a system of higher education as an obviously major form of change and the alteration of a system already in place and structured.[26] In the first, the system itself has little or no structure and culture, generic to it, to guide interaction and change. Bits and pieces are brought in, even impressed upon it, from other segments of society. But as the system develops it builds its own sources of continuity and change.[27] It usually grows larger and definitely becomes much more complex. It acquires the structures, discussed above, of work, belief, and authority. Institutions and subsectors thereby become rooted, turned into centers of interest and influence which have their own traditions and rationales. Budgets become entrenched, personnel remain fixed in categories, and costly physical plants turn into sunk costs. Sectorial hegemony develops, as pointed out at the beginning of this chapter, as inside professionals and bureaucrats occupy key sites and expand their influence.

Thus we progress in studying change in systems of higher education by pursuing the question as to how their structures and beliefs—their many parts individually and collectively—constrain and induce changes. As simply put by Margaret Archer, "once a given form of education exists it exerts an influence on future educational change."[28] This internalist logic has thus far divided into two analytical approaches: (1) to seek historical explanation of contemporary forms and (2) to try to link change to existing properties of the system.

To explain contemporary forms it is possible simply to walk back through time in search of critical periods and conditions. Thus, one study of the character of three leading liberal arts colleges in the United States at the end of the 1950s placed the crucial period of character definition, in one instance, as occurring in the earliest years, and hence effected under the conditions of new organization so many innovators desire, but in the other two instances as taking place much later in the life of the college, when transforming leaders worked under different sets of evolutionary and revolutionary conditions.[29] The accounts were historically specific in considerable detail, but the analyst used them to identify common and unique developments and outcomes, highlighting their commonality in having sturdy self-belief, a self-love worked up over time which amounted to an "organizational saga." Ethnographic in nature, this approach is heavily inductive.

Another analysis has shown that the development of a large institutional sector in higher education may be explained by deducing from theory what could happen and then determining what actually took place and what institutional responses did not occur. Studying the expansion of California higher education in the 1950s and 1960s, Neil Smelser hypothesized six types of structural adaptation which could have been made, noting that several occurred while others did not, and then used certain "missing" responses as explanations of discontent and conflict.[30] This systematic approach to change is particularly beneficial in its emphasis on institutional responses. Even though the context was severely constraining, the analyst posed alternatives that were to some degree open for consideration.

For analysis over a long time span, a powerful argument is presented by Arthur L. Stinchcombe on the persistence of types of organization.[31] Why does a particular mosaic of organizational types exist in a sector of society at the present time, with the parts "deposited" into the present out of different periods in the past? Persistence may come from effectiveness, from doing better than competing alternatives; or from location in a niche that protects against competition; or from the phenomena of institutionalization which turn a form into an end in itself and a center of group interest and legitimating ideology. The third possibility may readily dominate the other two, particularly in public sectors and especially in such normative organizations as schools and colleges. In academic systems, forms are in perpetuity as they become centers of vested interest located in protective noncompetitive niches.

As we pursue the persistence of organizational types and forms from the past to the present we are led on to probe how forms established early conditioned those that came later, as seen in the overwhelming influence of Oxford and Cambridge, with a six-hundred-year head start, on the styles of all the other sectors that have emerged in Britain since the mid-nineteenth century, or in the similarly strong influence of the University of Tokyo on everything else that was to follow in the modernization of Japanese higher education. In the American system, one can find in the successive emergence of major sectors the transference of beliefs and forms from the earlier to the later. The tradition of the liberal arts college, two hundred years old before the birth of the American university, in effect dictated that the university would have an undergraduate level of somewhat general or liberal education, with European-style specialization then added on in a second, graduate tier; the trustee form of control flowed from the college to the university and from the private market-oriented sectors into the public state-budget-oriented ones. Explaining types of institutions, their practices and beliefs, by referring to their predecessors is a fairly precise way of engaging in historical analysis within an organizational perspective.

The above approaches to the development of contemporary forms have centered almost entirely on institutions and sectors. Another angle of vision applies particularly well to the emergence and institutionalization of disciplines. This is the sociological approach to the ever expanding division of labor and the dynamics that drive it. Emile Durkheim placed high among the causes of social differentiation the mutual interests that existing and emerging groups have in protecting themselves.[32] Specialization pulls apart groups that otherwise may have to fight it out or share meager resources. This peace-from-conflict perspective may readily be applied to higher education. Sociologists and anthropologists did not have to fight over common turf when they gave up joint departments and went their separate ways, one to "structure" and the other to "culture." Historians of science and medicine reduce conflict with historians and those who populate medical schools, and gain in claims on resources, as they pull away in new departments. Cell splitting occurs within academic departments as subgroups use their specialization to protect themselves against domination by others and to reduce conflict over unified courses of action. Important dynamics of academic differentiation are thus to be found in interest-group struggles. The motor power is found in the interests of specific academic groups and their resulting interactions.

The second major stream of thought in pursuing the organizational determination of change is less historical, concentrating instead on linking current change or lack thereof, in a general or specific way, to current properties of the system. Various recent analysts have concluded their studies of innovation and change on the theme of the importance of the system's own composition and dynamics. After an extensive review of the literature on innovation in United States higher education, and intensive analysis of a major reform effort at the Buffalo campus of the State University of New York, Arthur Levine pointed to "the centrality of organizational facts of life in shaping change."[33] After conducting a systematic study of the entire British system, Tony Becher and Maurice Kogan concluded that "the main constraints on change are social, not psychological: they depend more on the way the system operates than on the particular stand that its individual members choose to take."[34] The broad dictum of the approach that builds on such findings is to put change in context by linking it to immediate structures and procedures, then, as need be, working out from there to increase the power and fullness of explanation. The existing forms have predispositions, we might say, tendencies that when identified inform us not only about systematic resistance to change but also about imperatives for change, as in the huge commitment to the production of new knowledge, hence to innovation, found in the research imperatives of most fields of knowledge in the advanced national systems. We may look for the way change is conditioned by "the way the system operates"—at many levels, in many ways.

Finally, if we sum up my earlier discussion about the matrix composition of higher education, we are confronted by a system of concerted activity which tends to have the following characteristics: it is relatively bottom-heavy, since large numbers of thought groups take up authoritative location at the operating level; it is multicoordinated, as the many groups found at administrative as well as operating levels use different forms of authority and as integrating actions range from political dictates to market involvements; the system is ambiguously bounded and virtually limitless in absorption of knowledge tasks; and the backbone of the structure is a grand matrix of disciplines and enterprises. Such properties encourage changes of the following types.

Grass-roots innovation.—Invention and diffusion of thought styles and specific ideas, with related practices, are institutionalized in the work of departments and schools that embody the disciplines and professions. Academic enterprises move ahead in a somewhat self-propelled, or at least internally guided, fashion in the areas of new thought which academics perceive to be acceptable within general conceptions of academic knowledge: biochemistry becomes more readily established than ethnic studies, computer science than urban affairs. This basic form of change is widely overlooked. It is typically not announced in ministerial bulletins or master plans as an item of reform. It is not introduced on a global scale and it is not taken as changing a structural feature of the whole system. But in a bottom-heavy matrix of disciplines and enterprises, grass-roots innovation is a crucial form of change.

Innovation by persuasion.—More than elsewhere, changes initiated at the top commonly need the support of interests residing at lower levels. With the characteristic diffusion of types and amounts of authority, and the lower placement of authoritativeness, those at the top generally have to "carry the field" rather than command it, negotiating with equals and building internal coalitions in order to implement their own desires, even their own "orders." The thought groups located at the grassroots level become key participants in implementing policies and reforms.

Incremental change.—Since tasks and powers are so extensively divided, global changes are ordinarily very difficult to effect. The more advanced the system, the more true it is that "anything that requires a coordinated effort of the organization in order to start is unlikely to be started. Anything that requires a coordinated effort of the organization in order to be stopped is unlikely to be stopped,"[35] despite the growth of managerial tools and theories. The leading false expectation in academic reform, especially in democracies, is that large results can be obtained by systemwide plan and central edict. Such major reforms are occasionally initiated and a few even succeed, but the more characteristic flow of change is that small alterations in small parts follow from a mélange of confusing actions. There are diverse and contradictory efforts at the top, in the middle, and especially at the bottom which entail false starts, wrong experiments, and zigzag adjustments, as in the "reform" of the history curriculum, for example, in most nations over a period of several decades. And, as indicated at the outset, dramatic examples of such change are to be found in the evolutionary buildup of knowledge in the twentieth century in the physical and biological sciences, flows that have been accompanied by increased dominance of those fields within universities and national systems. Of course, in systems under authoritarian or totalitarian rule, the centralization of authority and the central concentration of administration allow more manipulation from above and on a large scale. But even in the more top-influenced systems, with such controls as those found in the Soviet Union, observers report that adaptation characteristically takes place "by small steps instead of far-reaching reform."[36] Small steps come with the territory. Incremental adjustment is the pervasive form of change.

We may suggest that inertia increases with scale. A university is more difficult to change than a department. A national system is more difficult to change than a university. We face then a central dilemma of planning. In the name of change, planners make systems. They thereby produce more inertia, large batches of rigidities that reduce the capacity for flexible response by institutions and departments.

Boundary-leaking change.—The master matrix ensures that boundary-spanning roles are diffused throughout the operating levels of the individual university or college. Boundary roles in organizations are normally viewed as limited to offices that specialize in contact with the environment, such as the admissions office, the public relations bureau, and the grants and contracts office in the university. But boundary roles spread through the operating structure as those in the basic disciplines and the professional schools reach to their counterparts within and outside the larger system. Professors scan and monitor events in their own fields which are external to their local enterprise; they engage in information gatekeeping; they transact with other groups; they link and coordinate between the inside and the outside.[37] Thus the bridges to the outside are numerous, structurally dispersed, and unsupervised by hierarchical superiors. Changes creep across those bridges quietly and with little notice.

Invisible change.—Knowledge is relatively invisible as a material, a product, and especially as a process. Developing thoughts, as in research; transmitting thoughts, as in teaching; absorbing thoughts, as in learning—all are difficult to see and evaluate directly at the time they occur. Of course professors and administrators track these activities or give them external markers as best they can: reports on research show what came out of research activities; textbooks, examinations, and course grades, even certificates, represent tangibly what is happening in teaching and learning. But much is intangible or beyond measurable touch. Then, too, since the basic academic operations are diverse, arcane, and increasingly shielded by layers of organization, they are particularly opaque. It is difficult to perceive from on high or from the outside, or indeed from within, what is constant and especially what is changing. The relative invisibility of the main substance of work may be at the core of the difficulty in sensing what occurs in academic systems.

And thus the matrix moves: with much grass-roots initiative; with persuasion and voluntary initiative rather than command; incrementally rather than grandly; with changes flowing quietly over institutional boundaries; and often in highly intangible ways. These tendencies are rooted in the received, enduring structures of work, belief, and authority, in the basic composing of the system around disciplines and institutions, and the coordinating of the systems by multifarious means. To the extent they differ from patterns of change in other sectors of society, these tendencies testify to and help illuminate the underlying unique features of higher education. When the underlying internal structure is well explicated, then what we see largely determines what we get and reveals much about how altered states come about.

The Necessity of an Organizational Approach

A robust organizational perspective leaps over the fences of the social sciences. It is no accident that organizational theory is written by sociologists, political scientists, economists, psychologists, and anthropologists, as well as by analysts in business management and public administration, and that even historians pursue the development of specific organizations and sectors thereof. All are looking at the major tools of modern social action, the key collective actors who bind and divide. As a general approach, the organizational perspective is thus in luck, at once particular and even idiosyncratic but also flowing readily into wider streams of thought. There is some arcane language and even an emerging subculture, but its carriers penetrate a number of disciplines and therein have to make their peace. The particular organizational approaches to higher education emphasized here flow naturally toward the other perspectives presented in this volume, which center on historical, political, economic, status, scientific, cultural, and policy dimensions. There is also often the touchstone of application to practical affairs, in the service of improvement, and thereby the need to interact with common sense.

Organizational analysis of postsecondary education cuts a large cloth. It needs to cover levels of activity from "the factory floor" of classroom and laboratory to the national ministry and legislature, relating parts, suggesting causes, and indicating effects. It needs to span large sectors of universities and colleges which together stretch across nearly all advanced knowledge and, increasingly, do not know where to stop. It must track disciplines as well as enterprises, thereby following lines of functional connection which leap across institutional, regional, and national boundaries and turn pursuit into an international chase. Included in the tapestry of analysis is the flow of academic forms and ideas from one country to another, making central the problems of the new hosts accepting transplants voluntarily or under imposition and, in either event, adapting them to fit different contexts.

From an organizational perspective we may claim that higher education has an essential nature. That nature begins with high knowledge cast in the form of specialized bundles that have been awarded legitimacy by academic groups and are carried by them over time and space. Around those bundles there develop characteristic compounds of forms of work, belief, and authority, with each of these elements having its own peculiar configuration. To be organized around multifarious subjects is to have a particular structure of work which is found in only a weak degree in other sectors of society. The discipline is the touchstone. In turn, to emphasize disciplinary points of view and such doctrines of the academic profession as freedom of research and freedom of teaching is to have a configuration of core beliefs which is characteristic of the system and reflected only lightly elsewhere. Group autonomy and individual choice are magnified. To put much authority on a personal and collegial footing, combining the two in a guild or craft type of authority, and then to interweave that type with bureaucratic and political forms of control is to produce unique configurations of authority which occur elsewhere only to the extent that "noneducational" sectors engage in high-level educational work and behave, in part, like universities and colleges. Much guild organization in the understructure is characteristic.

As these three elements, with local and national variation, combine in national systems, all else about those systems is heavily conditioned. If it is not to be out of phase with the underlying organic reality, the superstructure of higher echelons must adjust to and extensively reflect the organization of work around subjects, the cultural life of the disciplines and the professional fields, and the legitimated powers of individuals and groups in many specialties. Changes are strongly guided by the underlying internal features and the beliefs of internal groups which help mold responses to external pressures. The streams of diverse incremental changes that follow at the operating level from the internal logics of the individual disciplines are missed or poorly grasped by those who fix their sights on higher levels in the search for holistic change. But many flows of change are brought within our analytical imagination when we pursue the underlying structures of work, belief, and authority and seek the actions that thereby follow.

At the organizational heart of higher education is the crisscrossing matrix of disciplines and enterprises which turns larger systems into thousands of linked intersects occupied by autonomy-seeking groups of thinkers upholding specific styles of thought. It is at those intersects that the work gets done; within them the productive powers of disciplines and enterprises converge. It is upon them that we may fruitfully center much future research.

At the end of the twentieth century, the need to grasp the central place of organizational elements is no different from the same need eight centuries ago at the beginning of the Western university. Then, too, in simpler ways, sustained intellectual commitment required appropriate organization. A. B. Cobban has brilliantly analyzed the earliest efforts to construct universities in medieval Europe, facing the central question of why Bologna and its imitators in northern Italy survived to become a strong influence on higher education in the Western world, while an earlier promising effort in Salerno died out. "The central weakness of Salerno," he notes, "was its failure to develop a protective and cohesive organization to sustain its intellectual advance." Cobban concludes from the fate of Salerno and the history of medieval universities in the large that "institutional response must follow quickly upon academic achievement if the intellectual moment is not to be dissipated. The absence of regular organization may initially provide a fillup for free-ranging inquiry, but perpetuation and controlled development can only be gained through an institutional framework."[38] Then and now, it is regular organization that supports and perpetuates intellectual advance and indeed helps to create the intellectual moment.

Notes

1. Perkin, *Key Profession*.
2. Clark, *Higher Education System*, chap. 1, "Knowledge."
3. Kerr et al., *12 Systems of Higher Education*.
4. Clark, *Higher Education System*, chap. 2, "Work."
5. For some of the better descriptive materials on the structure of higher education in various countries, see Ben-David, *Centers of Learning*; Blau, *Organization of Academic Work*; Clark, *Academic Power in Italy*; Halsey and Trow, *British Academics*; Van de Graaff et al., *Academic Power*; Becher and Kogan, *Process and Structure in Higher Education*; Premfors, *Politics of Higher Education*; Geiger, *Private Sectors in Higher Education*; Levy, *The State and Higher Education in Latin America*.
6. Clark, *Higher Education System*, chap. 3, "Belief."
7. Fleck, *Genesis and Development of a Scientific Fact*, passim.
8. See also Becher, "Towards a Definition of Disciplinary Cultures"; Dill, "Management of Academic Culture."
9. Clark, *Higher Education System*, chap. 4, "Authority."
10. In addition to the references specified in note 5 above, most of which deal with power and politics, see Moodie and Eustace, *Power and Authority in British Universities*; Levy, *University and Government in Mexico*; Clark and Youn, *Academic Power in the United States*; van den Berghe, *Power and Privilege at an African University*; Epstein, *Governing the University*; Berdahl, *British Universities and the State*.
11. Szczepanski, *Systems of Higher Education: Poland*; Matejko, "Planning and Tradition."
12. On the concept of matrix in organizational thought, see Sayles, "Matrix Organization"; Mintzberg, *Structuring of Organizations*, pp. 168–175.
13. Turner, "Growth of Professorial Research in Prussia," p. 159.
14. Van den Berghe, *Power and Privilege at an African University*.
15. Long, "Power and Administration," p. 262.
16. Turner, "Growth of Professorial Research in Prussia," p. 159.
17. See Moodie and Eustace, *Power and Authority in British Universities*, p. 61; Berg and Östergren, *Innovations and Innovation Processes in Higher Education*, p. 102; Becher and Kogan, *Process and Stricture in Higher Education*, chap. 6, "Basic Units."
18. See Cohen and March, *Leadership and Ambiguity*; March and Olsen, *Ambiguity and Choice in Organizations*; Baldridge et al., Policy Making and Effective Leadership.
19. Lindblom, *Politics and Markets*.
20. Clark, *Higher Education System*, chap. 5, "Integration."
21. Clark, *Academic Power in Italy*; Premfors and Östergren, *Systems of Higher Education: Sweden*; Levy, *University and Government in Mexico*; Cummings et al., *Changes in the Japanese University*; Van de Graaff et al., *Academic Power*.

22. Cohen and March, *Leadership and Ambiguity*, p. 102. On the concept of the enrollment economy, see Clark, *Adult Education in Transition*, pp. 61–63.
23. Ben-David and Zloczower, "Universities and Academic Systems in Modern Societies."
24. Levy, *The State and Higher Education*. On the interaction of private and public sectors in western Europe, the United States, Japan, and the Philippines, see Geiger, *Private Sectors in Higher Education*.
25. Windham, *Economic Dimensions of Education*.
26. This is the primary distinction in Margaret Archer's mammoth historical and comparative analysis of change in educational systems, reflected in the division of her volume into a first part devoted to the "emergence of state education systems" and a second part centered on "educational systems in action" (Archer, *Social Origins of Educational Systems*).
27. Clark, *Higher Education System*, chap. 6, "Change."
28. Archer, *Social Origins of Educational Systems*, p. 3.
29. Clark, *Distinctive College*.
30. Smelser, "Growth, Structural Change, and Conflict."
31. Stinchcombe, "Social Structure and Organizations."
32. Durkheim, *Division of Labor in Society*.
33. Levine, *Why Innovation Fails*, p. 43.
34. Becher and Kogan, *Process and Structure in Higher Education*, p. 147.
35. Cohen and March, *Leadership and Ambiguity*, p. 206.
36. Glowka, "Soviet Higher Education between Government Policy and Self-Determination," p. 182.
37. For criteria used in the definition of boundary roles, see Miles, *Macro Organizational Behavior*, chap. 11.
38. Cobban, *Medieval Universities*, pp. 47, 38.

References

Determination: A German View. In *Higher Education in a Changing World*. World Year Book of Education 1971–72, pp. 175–185. London: Evans Brothers, 1971.

Halsey, A. H., and M. A. Trow. *The British Academics*. Cambridge: Harvard University Press, 1971.

Kerr, Clark, John Millett, Burton R. Clark, Brian MacArthur, and Howard Bowen. *12 Systems of Higher Education: 6 Decisive Issues*. New York: International Council for Educational Development, 1978.

Levine, Arthur. *Why Innovation Fails*. Albany: State University of New York Press, 1980.

Levy, Daniel C. *University and Government in Mexico: Autonomy in an Authoritarian System*. New York: Praeger, 1980.

———. *The State and Higher Education in Latin America: Private-Public Patterns*. Forthcoming.

Lindblom, Charles E. *Politics and Markets: The World's Political-Economic Systems*. New York: Basic Books, 1977.

Long, Norton E. "Power and Administration." *Public Administration Review* 9 (1949):257–264.

March, James G., and Johan P. Olsen. *Ambiguity and Choice in Organizations*. Bergen, Norway: Universitetsforlaget, 1976.

Matejko, Alexsander. "Planning and Tradition in Polish Higher Education." *Minerva* 7 (1969):621–648.

Miles, Robert H. *Macro Organizational Behavior*. Santa Monica, California: Goodyear, 1980.

Mintzberg, Henry. *The Structuring of Organizations*. Englewood Cliffs, N.J.: Prentice-Hall, 1979.

Moodie, Graeme C., and Rowland Eustace. *Power and Authority in British Universities*. Montreal: McGill-Queens University Press, 1974.

Perkin, Harold. *Key Profession: The History of the Association of University Teachers*. London: Routledge and Kegan Paul, 1969.

Premfors, Rune *The Politics of Higher Education in a Comparative Perspective: France, Sweden, United Kingdom*. Studies in Politics, 15. Stockholm: University of Stockholm, 1980.

Premfors, Rune, and Bertil Östergren. *Systems of Higher Education: Sweden*. New York: International Council for Educational Development, 1978.

Sayles, L. R. "Matrix Organization: The Structure with a Future." *Organizational Dynamics* (Autumn 1976):2–17.

Smelser, Neil. "Growth, Structural Change, and Conflict in California Public Higher Education, 1950–1970." In *Public Higher Education in California*, ed. Neil Smelser and Gabriel Almond. Berkeley, Los Angeles, London: University of California Press, 1974.

Stinchcombe, Arthur L. "Social Structure and Organizations." In *Handbook of Organizations*, ed. James G. March. Chicago: Rand McNally, 1965.

Szczepanski, Jan. *Systems of Higher Education: Poland.* New York: International Council for Educational Development, 1978.

Turner, R. Steven. "The Growth of Professorial Research in Prussia, 1818 to 1848: Causes and Context." In *Historical Studies in the Physical Sciences*, ed. Russell McCormmach. Philadelphia: University of Pennsylvania Press, 1971. Vol. 3, pp. 137–182.

Van de Graaff, John H., Burton R. Clark, Dorotea Furth, Dietrich Goldschmidt, and Donald F. Wheeler. *Academic Power: Patterns of Authority in Seven National Systems of Higher Education.* New York: Praeger, 1978.

Van den Berghe, Pierre L. *Power and Privilege at an African University.* Cambridge, Mass.: Schenkman, 1973.

Windham, Douglas M. *Economic Dimensions of Education.* Washington, D.C.: National Academy of Education, 1979.

Emerging Developments in Postsecondary Organization Theory and Research: Fragmentation or Integration

Marvin W. Peterson

Abstract. Developments in theory and research on postsecondary institutions as organizations are proceeding in many different directions, threatening to fragment this critical area of research. This article examines the major developments and identifies dilemmas in theory development research methods, organizational behavior context, relating theory to practice, and identifying professional colleagues. These areas need to be understood and addressed to assure the continued, integrated development of postsecondary organization theory and research.

Reflecting on the emerging developments in organization theory and research in postsecondary education over the past decade suggests a major concern: There is a substantial tension between the current tendency to fragment and proliferate knowledge about organizational behavior in postsecondary education and the need to integrate it. Opening this topic brings to mind a few past warnings by some astute observers of colleges and universities.

In commenting on universities, Alfred North Whitehead (1928) said, "the heart of the matter is beyond all regulation" (p. 638).

Frederick Rudolph (1962) concludes his history of the *American College and University* with the observation that change in higher education is best typified as "drift, reluctant accommodation, and belated recognition that, while no one was looking, change had in fact taken place" (p. 491).

In a more current practical observation, Kingman Brewster (1965) suggests "the real trouble with attempting to devise a strategy, let alone a plan, for a university is that basically we (faculty) are all anarchists—significant thought, art, and action must have creativity. Creativity by definition defies predictions plan" (p. 45).

For those of us who think our work in postsecondary organizational behavior can make a difference, these observations should give reason to pause. Yet it is precisely these complexities and the variety of students, learning and research styles, faculty and administrative behavior, academic and administrative structures, external demands and pressures, and institutional roles, missions, structures, processes, and characteristics that challenge us to understand the patterns of organizational behavior in these institutions with their strong fragmenting tendencies. The organizing challenge is to preserve the positive aspects of that variety and richness while assuring that we accomplish our mutual educational and academic purposes and to make each college or university more effective. The dilemma is not whether to organize, but how to organize, to what degree, and for what purpose. The challenge of postsecondary organizational theory and research is to try to understand what holds together these fascinating institutions as organizations and what makes them more effective.

An Image of Adolescence

Before examining some of the recent developments and the dilemmas they raise, it is useful to recall that this is still an emerging scholarly arena. For example, the larger field of organizational behavior is almost entirely a post World War II phenomenon. It has grown rapidly as an interdisciplinary arena of study and has spawned graduate degree programs, departments, schools, and professional associations of scholars and practitioners. It has also produced an extensive literature and some highly sophisticated journals on organizational theory, research, and application. Indeed, Pfeffer (1982) describes it as a "thicket."

Although not yet of thicket proportions, the literature on organizational theory and research in postsecondary education is also growing rapidly. Using a human "developmental" rather than a "thicket" image, one might mark 1963 as the beginning of "infancy" of our interest in postsecondary organizational theory and research. In separate articles, McConnell (1963) of Berkeley and Henderson (1963) of Michigan decried the paucity of literature and research about the organization and administration of higher education. In the decade following, numerous practical and conceptual writings and some serious research efforts emerged.

By 1974, one might describe the area as past "early childhood" and entering "preadolescence." In that year, a comprehensive review of the research literature on "Organization and Administration in Higher Education" for Volume II of *Review of Research in Education* highlighted some of the theoretical and conceptual bases of the research, assessed the sophistication of the research, and attempted to identify major gaps (Peterson, 1974). An initial list of 500 publications was quickly reduced to less than 200, which were research based. That review noted that the quantity of research had increased substantially after 1970, that it was attracting researchers from several social science fields who were doing some excellent work, and that most major issues of the late 1960s and early 1970s were receiving attention. However, major concerns were noted and recommendations focused on the following:

1. The limited development or use of theoretical models or concepts from related disciplines and the need for greater emphasis in this area.

2. Studies were too often exploratory case studies or descriptive surveys. Longitudinal, before and after, field experiments, and comparative studies were almost nonexistent. Studies used exploratory as a rationale for avoiding conceptualization and/or quantification. Even quantitative surveys seldom used bivariate statistical analyses and ignored multivariate or causal path approaches, even when data might have allowed. There was a need for greater sophistication in research strategy, design, and methodology.

3. Replication studies and use of reliably constructed instruments on different populations to extend generalizability of any findings had seldom occurred and was needed.

4. Since the most sophisticated theoretical formulations and sophisticated designs came from scholars with disciplinary backgrounds, a professional network for involving them was needed.

The most recent decade has been one of substantial progress. Research that examines the organizational behavior of colleges and universities at the individual, group or process, organization, and interorganization of organization environment level has expanded both in quantity and sophistication. A formal review such as the one 10 years ago would be extensive. This paper only examines the high points and scans the major theoretical, methodological, and application developments and dilemmas that face us today. The current stage seems to be one of "advanced adolescence"—maturing rapidly, capable of extremes of sophistication and foolishness, and alternately confident and uncertain. The current high level of productivity is generating a wide array of theoretical, methodological, and application activities that create a tension that can either lead to proliferation and fragmentation or a new synthesis and integration.

As an "adolescent," the research area is struggling with problems of identity and commitment—what is the field? Where are developments in postsecondary organizational theory and research methods going and do we want to go there? It is struggling with the issue of relevance—are we dealing with important issues and relating theory to practice (or vice-versa) in constructive ways? Also, it is struggling with the issue of legitimacy—what professional peer group provides intellectual criticism and guidance to direct these efforts? An overview of developments in five areas—theory, research, content, relation to practice, and peers—poses some interesting images and dilemmas to stimulate discussion about where we should go.

Because organizational behavior has few bounds, these comments focus primarily on organizational level phenomenon, that is, where the entire college or university or major segment of it is dealt with as an organization. Also, because the literature is growing rapidly, the attempt is not to summarize what we have learned but rather to ask: How is the area developing?

On Theory Development

Since the 1974 review that found limited use of theoretical concepts and models in higher education, the area has exploded. At that time there were three basic models of organization (six, if one includes their derivatives): bureaucracy or formal-rational and goal models; collegial and professional community models; and political and public bureaucracy models. These were basically internally oriented and used to analyze the pervading governance issues. In the intervening decade, conceptual discussions and research in postsecondary education now includes open systems, environmental contingency, organizational life cycle, and strategic models that reflect the increased concern for external developments and forces. Task-technology and information or resource models reflect our growing concern with the impact those changes have on us. The list now includes a variety of emergent social system models. Temporary adaptive, loosely coupled, organized anarchy, and social network models reflect primarily internal models that attempt to account for some of the postsecondary education special characteristics. The cultural model, which Peters and Waterman (1982) have popularized, has also reemerged in higher education. Clark's (1970) *Distinctive Colleges* and Riesman, Gusfeld, and Gamson's (1970) study of *Academic Values and Mass Education* introduced us to the concern for culture 15 years ago. More recently, Dill (1982) has examined our changing institutional value systems at professional meetings, and researchers like Bess have been challenging us at professional meetings to examine the larger values that postsecondary institutions and educators should address. Closely related to the study of organizational cultures and values are proponents of the natural study of organizational phenomenon—an antimodel perspective. Finally, there are interorganizational models: Systems of organizations, organizational networks, organizational ecology, and industry models are being used to examine broader patterns of relationships among postsecondary organizations. (See Table 1.)

The list is not comprehensive and includes only organizational level models. The intent is not to examine each model; rather, the character of the list itself prompts some observations and raises issues about where we are going in the expansion of models and frameworks.

First, and perhaps most important, the pre-1974 models are what Pfeffer (1982) classified as "internal, purposive" models; they focus on a managed set of activities that impact on the organizations' performance—they see organizations as self directed. The recent models give more credence to technology, the environment, or the emergent social structure as the major determinants of action. (The distinction between "internal, purposive" and "emergent and social structure" will be discussed later.)

Second, as it did a decade ago, the list consists primarily of "borrowed" models. Admittedly, many have been distorted or modified to fit our postsecondary context, but only two—Cohen and March's (1974) model of organized anarchy and Weick's (1976) loosely coupled notion—were generated primarily to reflect the postsecondary context. Even those, however, have roots in other settings because neither are new concepts. It is ironic that in postsecondary education, which many

TABLE 1

Some Organizational Models in Postsecondary Education

Internal Purposive:	Formal-rational/goal
	Collegial/professional community
	Political/public bureaucracy
Environmental:	Open systems
	Contingency
	Strategic
	Life cycle
Technology:	Task/techno-structure
	Information system/resource models
Emergent Social Systems:	Temporary adaptive
	Organized anarchy
	Loosely coupled
	Social networks
	Organizational culture/values
	Organizational learning
	Natural/anti-models
Interorganizational:	Systems of organizations
	Organizational networks
	Ecology models
	Industry model

argue is unique, so little attention is given to theory generation and so much reliance is placed on borrowing models from institutional settings. Clearly, theory generation deserves greater attention.

A third observation on the list of models has to do with the fragmented nature of the models themselves and with how one deductively builds theory.[1] Borrowing models has led to a multitude of models that focus on different phenomena. The models also vary in normative, analytic, or predictive purpose and often have different assumptions about explanatory forces (e.g., internal or external, guided or emergent). The concern is that little attention has been given either to *mapping* the organizational territory covered by these borrowed theories or to *examining* comparatively the nature of each model. The need to relate our theoretical models to organizational phenomena (the territory) to identify gaps is noted by Bess (1983) in his edited volume of *Review of Higher Education*.

The direct comparison of models dealing with a similar phenomenon is also useful to highlight their differing perspectives and content. Baldridge's (1971) comparison of bureaucratic, collegial, and political models over a decade ago covered the organizational and governance models in vogue at the time. More recently, we have many limited comparisons of models (or submodels) or concepts that focus on only one level or type of organizational phenomenon—for example, Cameron's (1984) comparison of four models of organizational adaption (population ecology, life cycles, strategic choice, and symbolic action) in the *Journal of Higher Education*. But many questions remain. For example, how does the loose-coupling model compare with a social network model? Is a coupling element the same as or different from a linkage element? Mapping our theories in relation to organizational phenomena and analytic comparison of models offers useful ways of reducing fragmentation and/or discovering overlaps; however, a comprehensive scheme for comparing all our models still needs considerable conceptual thought and effort.

The final observation is our failure to examine the "appropriateness" or "adequacy" of each of our borrowed models or constructs, evidently because they appear to be intuitively logical or seem to make sense. In much of the conceptual literature and research, writers have a tendency to become advocates of the model they are discussing. They seldom ask critical analytic questions. Is the model an analytic framework, a normative theory, or an explanatory or predictive theory? Does the model satisfy simple criteria for a good theory? Five come to mind (Pfeffer, 1982, p. 38). First, is there "clarity" in the phenomenon being examined and definition of key concepts and variables? Are conceptual and operational definitions of variables clear? For example, one still sees influence defined and measured in different ways, yet discussed without recognizing the differences. Second, is the model "parsimonious" in the number of variables it contains (or loaded with inexplicable contingencies)? Third, does the theory have a "logical coherence"? For example, Weick (1976) proposed "loose-coupling" as an idea and an analytic perspective that was yet to be defined, evaluated, and developed. However, several researchers have discussed it as if it were already an explanatory theory rather than challenging it (Lutz, 1982). Fourth, do we ask if the model exhibited "consistency" with real data and whether the conditions or "contingencies" are present? For example, organizational anarchy is a popular way of explaining some of our less predictable behavior but others have questioned its usefulness when "organizational slack," one of its key assumptions, is declining or not present. In a recent analysis of the review and reorganization of the biological sciences at Berkeley, Trow (1984) suggests it is not as useful as a more rational paradigm.

A fifth criterion for theory is "refutability." Do we attempt to refute or disconfirm our models? It prompts comments at two levels. First, as research has accumulated using some of these models or their key concepts, there has not been an inductive, balanced, and systematic examination of the convergent or divergent evidence for or against a particular model. Because so much organizational research in higher education is problem oriented, the research reviews have focused on categorizing the research around issues addressed, patterns of descriptive findings, types of institutions studied, methods used, and so forth—not on evidence converging with or diverging with a model or its prediction. There are few scholarly outlets for reviews of this nature, and it also appears that critical, comparative analysis of research findings is not a high priority that postsecondary organizational researchers have emphasized. Many review articles and even entire books report only findings and insights supporting their argument for their model and do not systematically weigh the counter evidence. An exemplary exception is the research on attrition in which several careful research scholars have examined quantitative studies in a systematic and balanced fashion around theoretical frameworks (Pascarella & Terenzini, 1979; Tinto, 1982). But even this group has not used meta-analysis to statistically test the convergence of predictions and theory across studies.

The second concern about refuting or disconfirming the research models is that although organizational research is now more likely to be theoretically or conceptually oriented and to develop a hypothesis, it is often based on one model. The studies are designed either to support or not support the theory. Seldom do we use what Platt (1964) referred to in *Science* as "strong inference"—testing different models or competing hypotheses in the same study. Although she did not use statistical tests, Chaffee's (1984) recent study comparing adaptive vs. interpretive strategies in institutions that had suffered decline is one example of this approach.

This abbreviated overview of the organizational theories and models portrays it as a *muddled* arena and highlights one of our developmental dilemmas. Should postsecondary organizational research focus on theory *generation* that can more adequately reflect the uniqueness of higher education? Should it focus on *systematic synthesis* of the many theoretical models and extensive research to establish if there is more convergence or less fragmentation than appears? Should it focus on systematic model *testing*, which is the most convincing way to establish results but which is time consuming, expensive, and of limited practical interest? I shall return to the dilemmas later.

On Research Developments

In 1974, postsecondary organizational research was characterized as primarily descriptive surveys or exploratory case studies. Although these are still present, research strategies, methods, and techniques have also expanded and become more sophisticated. Before noting some of the changes, it is useful to note what has not changed. There is still little or no use of experimental research strategies and primary emphasis remains on field research. Few longitudinal, prepost, or quasi-experimental designs are noted. Some simulation strategies have been tried, but mostly in quantitative computer simulations. Cohen, March, and Olsen's (1972) test of their organized anarchy model and the many resource flow and forecasting simulations developed in the mid-1970s are most notable. Interestingly, behavioral simulations that have been used to model organizational behavior in other professional settings have received little use. The changes, on the other hand, are most instructive and are a product of our changing models, the conditions affecting higher education, and our increasing research sophistication.

First, comparative case studies that combine both structured qualitative and quantitative methods appear to be used more often. This enhances the opportunity to validate variables and causal patterns, enhances generalizability, and in some instances allows sophisticated statistical comparisons and even multivariate analysis. Mortimer's (1979) studies of resource decline processes emphasize content analysis of documents and interviews from several institutions, whereas Baldridge's (1979) study of the impact of management systems in several liberal arts colleges uses both qualitative and quantitative approaches for making comparisons.

Second, more large survey studies now incorporate institutional characteristics along with individual survey results and have led to enriched analysis examining the effects of individual and organizational variables. Baldridge's (1978) extensive study of governance in the mid to late 1970s, which produced numerous studies of different governance issues, is an example. Both the comparative case studies and large-scale surveys have on occasion used complex index building and even causal path modeling.

Third, there has been some increase in the use of standardized data bases of institutional characteristics for secondary analysis in large-scale studies. Birnbaum's (1983) study of changing patterns of institutional diversity and Zammuto's (1984) study of shifting patterns of liberal arts colleges and their enrollment are examples that draw on the Higher Education General Information Survey (HEGIS) data base for an ecological analysis of our institutions.

Fourth, out of the renewed emphasis on organizational culture and the models reflecting less formal, more emergent phenomena (loose-coupling, organized anarchy, natural models, etc.) has come a substantial interest in less structured qualitative methods. Strategies such as content analysis of documents and interviews, use of unobtrusive measures, and ethnographic and phenomenological approaches appear to be used more frequently.

Large-scale studies that combine a thorough synthesis of research, carefully develop models and variables, employ institutional surveys with comparative case studies, and use both quantitative and qualitative methods are still rare. Cameron's (1983) current series of studies of effectiveness, Chaffee's (1984) studies of strategic management, and Peterson's (1978) study of the impact of black students on predominantly white colleges are examples. Such studies are expensive, time consuming, and require long-term commitments. Unfortunately, funding for such large-scale research has declined and is seldom available.

These observations on research strategies and methods highlight the fact that organizational research in higher education is becoming a complex "methodological maze" that is increasingly sophisticated and raises the second dilemma: Do we emphasize larger scale *quantitative* studies that yield greater generalizability and potential for statistical modeling but are expensive and uncertain, or *intensive qualitative* studies that may be more helpful in generating new theory and new ideas?

Organizational Behavior: The Contextual Debate

The previous theoretical and methodological dilemmas are a reflection of a debate that has been raging in the larger realm of organizational behavior for the past 5 years. Since the advances in postsecondary education have both been borrowed from and lag the developments in organizational behavior, it can be useful to examine that debate briefly. In an exaggerated form, it can be posed as a dialectic between two extreme positions or paradigms, as an argument about basic philosophical and metaphysical assumptions: What constitutes reality in organizations (the ontological issue)? How do we gain knowledge about them (the epistemological issue)? What are our assumptions about causation (the teleological dimension)? (See Table 2.)

TABLE 2

Two Cultures of Organizational Theory and Research

Paradigm:	Traditional, conservative or social fact	Cultural, radical, or social definition
Elements of Reality:	Objective	Subjective
View of Knowledge:	Positivism	Interpretive
Causation:	Predictive	Diagnostic, final cause
Content Focus:	Structures, patterns	Emergent processes, dynamics
Use of Theory:	Variance testing	Process or developmental
Research Design:	Planned	Audit
Methodology:	Reductionist	Wholistic
Measurement:	Quantitative	Qualitative

Stated simply: The first is variously called the "Traditional," "Conservative," or "Social Fact" paradigm (Cummings, 1981; March, 1982; Meryl, 1981). It views organizational elements as objective, accepts them as positive facts, and is concerned with predicting events. The major focus is on structures, observable behaviors and organizational elements, and respondents' attitudes and self reports. Theories are posed in terms of how one set of variables varies with others, and the concern is to test them. The methodologies are primarily reductionist and quantitative in nature.

The second, the "Cultural," "Radical," or "Social Definition" paradigm views organizational elements as those that are subjective and must be interpreted, primarily by the organizational actors themselves. It is more concerned with diagnosis or final causes. The major focus is on emergent processes and dynamics. Theories are process theories, and the concern is mostly with development of theory. However, some supporters of this view reject the notion of any theoretical models and recommend describing or auditing the phenomenon under study. The methodologies tend to be more wholistic, viewing the entire context of organizational behavior and making more extensive use of qualitative research methods.

Setting aside the externally oriented and technological organizational models noted earlier, the distinction, although not as clear or sharp, has emerged in our postsecondary models. For example, prior to 1974 the formal-rational, political, and collegial models more closely fit the traditional paradigm. They all suggest that objective phenomena can be used to explain events and that institutions can be managed or intentionally directed if one understands the formal, political, or collegial patterns. All have been the basis of research using primarily statistical or other forms of objective analysis based on survey data of attitude and perceptions, on measures of individual and institutional characteristics, and on content of documents and structured interviews.

On the other hand, the more recent models such as social networks, loose-coupling, organizational learning, and examining institutions as cultures reject the more intentional and rational assumptions of the traditional models, and they often criticize their failure to account for much of what happens in higher education. These models choose to focus on understanding how people in higher education interpret events, how they are influenced by the setting and the content of events, and how they ascribe meaning to them. The focus is on the examination and diagnosis of behavior and how processes emerge or are shaped. Their methodologies tend to rely more on ethnography (intensive, anthropological case studies), in-depth interviews and participant observations, and phenomenological investigation.

Naturally, these two positions are extremes, and many of the discussions of theory, research, and methodology in postsecondary education either incorporate or acknowledge both perspectives. Nonetheless, the intensity of the debate that mirrors the two previous dilemmas does suggest a potential third one for the development of organizational theory and research in postsecondary education: Will these *dialectical views* continue as two potentially *divisive paradigms* or will there be an *accommodation?*

Theory to Practice

The second topic on our developmental agenda is the "relevance" issue, the relationship of theory and research to practice. Because organizational research on postsecondary education has often been heavily practice oriented, the topic is important. However, several changes appear to be reshaping this interface.

First, the tendency to be responsive to current practical issues continues and often leads to extremely descriptive research. Fortunately, the recent research on retrenchment or decline and on effectiveness (e.g., Cameron, 1983; Mortimer, 1979) have resisted this criticism by examining issues that are not ephemeral and by placing the problem in a sound conceptual framework. Given postsecondary education's current pressures, researchers need to weigh the temptation for visible, descriptive studies and give equal attention to research on important longer-term issues.

Second, there is an increasing administrative research capacity and sophistication in higher educational institutions. This can reduce the pressure on scholars for immediate useful studies. It can also provide faculty members interested in postsecondary organizational and administrative issues with greater opportunity to synthesize research and to translate it to knowledgeable administrators. This is a potentially useful development and is reflected in the increasing array of monograph series such as the *ASHE/ERIC Research Reports,* the *New Directions* series from Jossey-Bass, and other association publications that provide opportunities for synthesis around current and practical issues.

Third, the increased emphasis on conceptual models and more complicated array of research strategies and methods previously noted may tend to make postsecondary organizational research either less useful or more difficult for administrators to comprehend. This makes the translation and dissemination of research results to practitioners more critical than it has been in the past. It is my observation that the issue of research utilization is getting less emphasis by postsecondary organizational researchers than in the past just when the need may be increasing. This issue, which has become a central concern to institutional researchers, is the topic of a recent *New Directions for Institutional Research* volume (Lindquist, 1981).

Fourth, closely related to the previous points is the tendency of current organizational research efforts to adopt an approach in which the researcher is viewed as neutral or noninvolved. In courses and literature on higher and postsecondary research design that I have reviewed, applied research techniques related to the practice of institutional research, policy analysis, and evaluation are approached largely from the perspective of a neutral researcher. Little attention is given to strategies of action research or organizational development where the researcher participates with the actors. Almost no attention is given to advocacy research. Yet many graduate students in postsecondary education enter administrative careers requiring such skills. However, scholars have recently made such contributions. For example, Gamson's (1984) *Varieties of Liberal Education* was based on her experience as a Fund for the Improvement of Postsecondary Education (FIPSE) project coordinator in which she assisted project institutions in designing and carrying out evaluations. Victor Baldridge has recently directed a project to design, implement, and evaluate attrition reduction programs in several schools in which he adopted a more active research role. Clifton Conrad, Robert Blackburn, and Robert Berdahl among others have participated in advocacy research roles for U.S. Department of Justice Investigations of desegregation in Louisiana. The point is that strategies of research involvement as well as dissemination may be called for in this theory to practice interface.

These observations suggest the fourth dilemma: Are researchers to become more isolated or more involved? The key issue is not so much, the interest in theoretical versus practical problems, but whether the postsecondary organizational researcher should emphasize roles as neutral or uninvolved experts who conceptualize and design, as intermediaries who translate and disseminate, or as involved research-practitioners or advocates.

Professional Peers

The final developmental topic is concerned with defining the legitimate professional colleagues and mentors in postsecondary organizational theory and research to whom one looks for criticism and guidance. Individuals who have done the conceptual writing and research are identifiable. However, there are still few programmatic efforts or organizations concentrating primarily on postsecondary organizational studies. Associations like AERA and ASHE do not have a formal special interest group devoted to this area alone. There is not a single postsecondary journal or monograph series with this focus, although all give it attention in special sections or special publications. In light of the fragmenting tendencies of the theory and research and absence of professional foci, a few brief comments on professional peers are appropriate.

First, the previous theory to practice discussion suggests a dilemma in the identification of peers. Are they other scholars or administrators? Clearly, other scholars should be a source of critical scholarly interchange. But what of administrators? Are we allies or increasingly aliens as our previous theory-practice dilemma hints? Off campus, a few postsecondary organizational researchers have found colleagues and rewards in institutional membership associations (e.g., AGB, ACE, etc.) and the other administrative associations (e.g., AIR, AAUA, etc.). On campus, administrators can be a source of stimulation in problem identification and provide access to applied projects, data, local resources, opportunities for dissemination, and even influence. One increasingly finds senior administrators with some organizational theory or research expertise. Many institutions have an expanded institutional research and planning staff who have applied research assignments. Unfortunately budget pressures often make administrators reluctant to have their own faculty probing sensitive and often conflicting events and issues.

Second, among scholarly colleagues one also has some peer choices. In the field of education, the network of postsecondary researchers as noted is still embryonic or loosely coupled. On campus, other education school faculty are accessible, but the numbers interested in organizational concepts and research issues are limited and often have a heavy practitioner orientation. Educational statistics and research faculty often focus on or emphasize individual and small group level phenomena rather than organizations as the unit of analysis.

Outside of education, more faculty are involved in organization behavior, both on and off campus, they are but not as interested in postsecondary education. As in any interdisciplinary field, one has the choice of an association-based disciplinary group (e.g., ASA's Organization Section), another professional school unit (e.g., a department of organization behavior in a business school), or a less clearly defined interdisciplinary network. As an example of the network, an "organizational behavior seminar" at the University of Michigan involves about 25 faculty from Law, Business, Education, Social Work, Engineering, Public Policy, Sociology, Psychology, Public Health, Political Science, and so on, and meets occasionally to share someone's research or to interact with an invited outside scholar. Interestingly, while many of the members have known each other for years, it did not become organized until a visiting scholar who had met us individually invited us all to lunch.

The point is that the sources of professional peers are numerous, but they are still ill defined as a resource for the criticism, guidance, and collaboration that are so useful in furthering this area of study. Stimulating such a network is probably a valuable activity, but involves basic choices about orientation and membership: practitioners or scholars; education lists, professionals, or disciplinarians. Resolving this dilemma may influence the direction on many of the previous dilemmas.

Dilemmas Revisited

This overview suggests there is a great deal of potential fragmentation in the rapidly developing area of postsecondary organizational theory and research highlighted by these five dilemmas. Further development may involve answering all five of them with a resounding, "Yes."

There is a *muddled array of models.* Yet we need to emphasize further theory "development" to find better ways to understand postsecondary education's uniqueness. The newer emergent models offer useful examples. But there is also a need to encourage theory and research "synthesis" to clarify the theories and constructs, to examine more critically the applicability of the borrowed models, and to see what has been learned conceptually as well as about practice. And there is a need to pursue more rigorous "testing" of individual models and the comparative testing of competing explanations to confirm or refute them, rather than continuing to advocate them.

The *methodological maze* that is necessary to understand the complexity of organizational behavior in any setting will continue to be many faceted. There is a need to continue the emphasis on large-scale comparative and survey research strategies and to utilize "quantitative" techniques and multivariate or causal analysis to enhance the generalizability of our findings and to test our competing theories. But there is also a need to expand efforts in using the more intensive, "qualitative" strategies and methods to give construct validity to the quantitative variables, to examine the causal assumptions in the theories, and to generate new insights or models for more extensive examination.

It is useful not only to emphasize both paradigms but also to seek an integration to avoid becoming embroiled in an extended and exaggerated *philosophical dialectic.* The different models and theories and different research strategies and methods each need to be examined in relation to criteria for sound theory and methodology and to be used as appropriate to the purpose, problem, and setting of the research project. Sensitive manipulation and open-minded interpretation of quantitative approaches and causal models can lead to the refutation of existing models and the suggestion of questions for intensive qualitative exploration. Examples that merge the two paradigms are the combined use of survey and comparative case studies employing both qualitative and quantitative approaches in large studies such as the NCHEMS research on effectiveness and decline and the use of grounded theory in more focused studies such as Richardson, Fisk, and Okun's (1983) study of literacy.

Clearly, the theory-practice or relevance dilemma is a product of the conflict between our expanded efforts in research and theory development and the urgent demands of postsecondary education today. There is a need for good "conceptualizers and designers" to place the practical findings in a broader context and to guide the development of explanatory frameworks. We need "translators" who can effectively disseminate the extensive array of theoretical and research literature. We also need "practitioner researchers" who can involve subjects in the research process and not just do research on practical problems. More importantly, we need more balanced attention to the range of methods from theory development and critique, to strategies of dissemination and utilization of research, and to research approaches that stress research involvement.

Rogers and Gamson (1982) have a recent article on "Evaluation as a Developmental Process." In a chapter of *Black Students on White Campuses* (Blackburn, Gamson, & Peterson, 1978), the authors discuss the use of an interracial team in the study of a sensitive social issue. There is a need to analyze and share our insights into how to do organizational research in postsecondary education. In these examples and in the theory to practice and professional roles discussion, the thesis is that, in the establishment of a "peer" group of colleagues and mentors, form follows function—it may be timely to bring colleagues together around some of the developmental issues in postsecondary organization theory and research.

Such efforts may determine whether postsecondary organizational theory and research survives its adolescent dilemmas and grows to wholesome, integrated maturity or becomes more fragmented and stifles its development.

Note

1. For an excellent discussion of theory development in organizations, see Larry Mohr's *Explaining Organizational Behavior* (Jossey-Bass, 1982) and Jeffrey Pfeffer's *Organizations and Organization Theory* (Pitman, 1982).

References

Baldridge, J. V. *Power and Conflict in the University*. San Francisco: Jossey-Bass, 1971.

_____. *Policy Making and Effective Leadership*. San Francisco: Jossey-Bass, 1978.

Baldridge, J. V. & Tierney, M. *New Approaches to Management*. San Francisco: Jossey-Bass, 1979.

Bess, J. "Maps and Gaps in the Study of College and University Organization." *Review of Higher Education*, 1983, 6; 239–251.

Birnbaum, R. *Maintaining Diversity in American Higher Education*. San Francisco: Jossey–Bass, 1983.

Blackburn, R., Gamson, Z., & Peterson, M. "Chronology of the Study and First Steps." In M. Peterson, et al. (Eds.), *Black Students on White Campuses*. Ann Arbor: Institute for Social Research, University of Michigan, 1978.

Brewster, K., Jr. "Future Strategy of the Private University." *Princeton Alumni Weekly*, 1965; 45–46.

Cameron, K. *A Study of Organizational Effectiveness and its Predictors*. Unpublished manuscript, 1983.

_____. "Organizational Adaptation and Higher Education." *Journal of Higher Education*, 1984, 55, (2); 122–144.

Chaffee, E. "Successful Strategic Management in Small Private Colleges." *Journal of Higher Education*, 1984, 55, (2); 212–241.

Clark, B. *The Distinctive Colleges*. Chicago: Aldine, 1970.

Cohen, M., & March, J. *Leadership and Ambiguity*. New York: McGraw-Hill, 1974.

Cohen, M., March, J., & Olsen, J. "A Garbage Can Model of Organizational Choice." *Administrative Science Quarterly*, 1972, 17, 1–25.

Conrad, C. "Grounded Theory: An Alternative Approach to Research in Higher Education." *Review of Higher Education*, 1982, 5 (4); 239–249.

Cummings, L. L. "Organizational Behavior in the 1980's." *Decision Sciences*, 1981,12; 265–377.

Dill, D. "The Structure of the Academic Profession: Toward a Definition of Ethical Issues." *Journal of Higher Education*, 1982, 3; 255–267.

Gamson, Z. *Varieties of Liberal Educational*. San Francisco: Jossey-Bass, 1984.

Henderson, A. "Improving Decision-Making Through Research." In G. Smith (Ed.), *Current Issues in Higher Education*. Washington, DC: AAHE, 1963.

Kuhns, E., & Martorana, S.V. (Eds.). "Qualitative Methods in Institutional Research." In *New Directions for Institutional Research*. San Francisco: Jossey-Bass, 1982.

Lindquist, J. (Ed.). "Increasing the Use of Institutional Research." In *New Directions for Institutional Research*. San Francisco: Jossey-Bass, 1981.

Lutz, F. "Tightening up Loose Coupling in Organizations of Higher Education." *Administration Science Quarterly*, 1982, 27; 653–669.

March, J. *Handbook of Organizations*. Chicago: Rand McNally, 1965.

_____. "Emerging Developments in the Study of Organizations." *Review of Higher Education*, 1982, 6; 1–18.

McConnell, T. R. "Needed: Research in College and University Organization and Administration." In T. Lunsford (Ed.), *Study of Academic Organizations*. Boulder, CO: Western Institute Commission on Higher Education, 1963.

Meryl, L. "A Cultural Perspective on Organizations: The Need for and Consequences of Viewing Organizations as Culture-Bearing Milieux." *Human Systems Management*, 1981, 2; 246–258.

Mohr, L. *Exploring Organizational Behavior*. San Francisco: Jossey-Bass, 1982.

Mortimer, K. *The Three R's of the Eighties: Reduction, Reallocation, and Retrenchment* (ERIC/AAHE Research Reports, No. 4). Washington, DC: AAHE, 1979.

Pascarella, E. T., & Terenzini, P. "Interaction Effects in Spady's and Tinto's Conceptual Models of College Dropout." *Sociology of Education*, 1979, 52; 197–210.

Peters, T., & Waterman, R. In *Search of Excellence*. New York: Harper and Row, 1982.

Peterson, M., et al. *Black Students on White Campuses*. Ann Arbor: Institute for Social Research, University of Michigan, 1978.

_____. "Organization and Administration in Higher Education: Sociological and Social-Psychological Perspectives." In F. Kerlinger (Ed.), *Review of Research in Education*, Vol. II. Itasca, IL: Peacock, 1974.

Pfeffer, J. *Organizations and organization theory*. Marshfield, MA: Pitman, 1982.

Platt, J. R. Strong inference. *Science*, 1964, 146 (3642); 347–353.

Richardson, R., Fisk, E., & Okun, M. *Literacy in the Open Access College*. San Francisco: Jossey-Bass, 1983.

Riesman, D., Gusfeld, J., & Gamson, Z. *Academic Values and Mass Education*. Garden City, NY: Doubleday, 1970.

Rogers, T., & Gamson, Z. "Evaluation as a Developmental Process." *Review of Higher Education*, 1982, 5, 225–238.

Rudolph, F. *The American College and University: A History*. New York: Knopf, 1962.

Tinto, V. "Limits of Theory and Practice in Student Attrition." *Journal of Higher Education*, 1982, 6; 687–700.

Trow M. "Reorganizing the Biological Sciences at Berkeley." *Change*, 1984, 28; 44–53.

Weick, K. "Educational Organizations as Loosely Coupled Systems." *Administrative Science Quarterly*, 1976, 21 (1); 1–19.

Whitehead, A. M. "Universities and Their Functions." *Atlantic Monthly*, 1928, 141 (5); 638–644.

Zammuto, R. "Are the Liberal Arts an Endangered Species?" *Journal of Higher Education*, 1984, 55 (2); 184–211.

ORGANIZATIONAL CONCEPTS UNDERLYING GOVERNANCE AND ADMINISTRATION

ELLEN EARLE CHAFFEE

Higher education executives and policymakers are in the business of leading organizations. Their colleges and universities are organizations, like and unlike other kinds of organizations, similar to and different from each other. The fundamental properties and dynamics that can explain those similarities and differences are the focus of organizational theory and research. Organizational studies are multidisciplinary, involving such academic fields as psychology, sociology, political science, anthropology, and history, as well as the professional fields of business management, public administration, and higher education administration.

Those who study organizations share with administrators and members of governing boards the search for behaviors that will make organizations more effective. Organizational theory and research provide the basic science that undergirds the practice of organizational leadership. They offer insights into the fundamental dynamics of the complex situations with which administrators and policymakers must deal.

Practical applications often are not immediately evident in basic sciences, and this is also the case with organizational studies. Applied works that are well grounded in research results have not yet appeared in significant number. However, the administrator or policymaker who turns to the literature on organizations for help with a given situation often finds insights that can be applied to practical ends. The more important an administrative problem is, the less likely it is to respond to "how-to" recipes and the more likely it is that understanding organizational studies will guide effective administrative action.

This chapter deals with the two levels of organizational analysis that are most critical for top executives and policymakers—those of the organization as a whole and of organization-environment interactions. Other levels exist, such as individual and group action within organizational contexts, but this review includes only one such entry. David Dill's review of research on administrator behavior (no. 455) is included because it directly addresses issues that concern top executives.

This chapter provides a perspective on the way decision making works in organizations, what organizations need from their leaders, and what happens in organizations when resources become scarce or crises occur. It focuses on strategic matters, those which by definition arrive at the president's desk or the boardroom table. The pervasive theme is organizational change, recognizing both the refusal of organizations to stand still and the unremitting efforts of organizational leaders to change them for the better.

Development of the Literature

Organizational research and theory began to develop in the 1950s and grew through the 1960s, but only since 1970 have scholars begun to produce a coherent field of organizational studies. One of the most common tools in the field is the model, which allows researchers to communicate efficiently with one another and with those who seek practical benefit from organizational studies. A model is a metaphor or analogy. For example, a common model depicts organizations as biological entities, complete with processes of evolution and natural selection. Models cannot capture the full complexity of an organization, but they do provide useful lenses through which both theorists and working administrators can attempt to bring a particular situation into focus.

As organizational studies evolved, they followed the pattern of a model Boulding (1956) proposed to help understand any kind of system. The validity of Boulding's general systems theory is evident in the fact that it describes not only the evolution of the body of knowledge about organizations (Peterson, no. 137, and Pfeffer, 1982) but also the properties of organizations themselves (Chaffee, 1985).

Briefly, Boulding identified nine levels of systems that may be clustered into three groups, ranging from the simplest to the most complex: linear, adaptive, and interpretive. Linear systems are mechanical, having direct cause-effect relationships and definable parts that interact in stable, predictable ways. For example, colleges typically follow a linear model when they plan capital construction projects. Adaptive systems, by contrast, are biological. They respond to their environments, reproduce themselves, and can organize their awareness of the environment into a knowledge structure. When the number of eighteen-year-olds began to decline, colleges followed the adaptive model by increasing their recruiting efforts and courting adults as students. Interpretive systems, finally, are cultural. They are conscious of themselves and develop elaborate shared systems of meaning. A president typically follows the interpretive model in offering the annual "state of the university" address.

Each system level incorporates those that are less complex. Adaptive systems have machinelike properties, and interpretive systems exhibit both linear and adaptive characteristics. For example, the president's address has structure in its ideas and sequencing, and the president adapts the speech to the nature of the audience and often to audience responses during the speech. Human beings and organizations are interpretive systems. Understanding and working with them requires attention to their characteristics on all three levels.

The earliest literature on organizations typically viewed them as linear entities. Authors sought to identify key organizational parts and their interrelationships—organizational size, structure, control, design, and technology—as a way to make sense of unfamiliar territory. They dealt primarily with hierarchical organizations such as businesses, which lent themselves relatively well to linear analysis because of their structured management forms and clear technologies. They looked for answers to such issues as the best way to organize work groups or the optimum size for an organization with a certain kind of goal. The business management literature began to define key tasks of managers, such as planning, organizing, and controlling.

When they began attempting to refine the linear approach, authors encountered ever greater difficulty in making that model fit reality. In the language of quantitative researchers, the model did not explain much of the variance in organizational performance because of the impact of powerful, rapidly changing environments. In the late 1960s and throughout the 1970s, authors no longer treated organizations as tightly structured, monolithic agencies, but rather as systems that are open to their surroundings.

This new view corresponded to Boulding's biological, adaptive model. Authors suggested that organizations have life cycles. They defined the entities and forces that constituted an organization's environment, recommending that leaders monitor external events, shape them, and position their organizations effectively within them. Decline in organizational markets and resource scarcity came into focus and was often attributed to adaptive failures. Flexibility became recognized as a primary necessity to keep an organization from going the way of the dinosaur. Population ecologists took the metaphor further, suggesting that like a population of animals, a population of organizations inevitably contains weaker members that cannot survive the natural selection process. Political concepts such as power, interest groups, conflict, and coalition building arose as mechanisms for both intraorganizational responsiveness and organization-environment negotiations.

In the late 1970s and early 1980s, the literature turned toward understanding organizations not just as biological entities but as human ones. It focused on the distinctive human capacities for thought, language, communication, and culture building. This latest trend brought back an interest in people, both those who comprise the organization and those who deal with it. The change corresponds to Boulding's interpretive level.

Interpretive organizational literature dealt with perceptions, organizational stories and sagas, socialization into an organization, loyalty, and, most popularly, organizational cultures. It treated organizations as collections of people who agree to cooperate, more or less, to serve diverse purposes. It assumed that organizational success was due both to the effectiveness of that cooperation and to the perceptions of outsiders about the desirability of associating themselves with the organization as consumers, employees, board members, students, investors, or in other ways.

Recent exhortations for better leadership of organizations fit especially well with the interpretive model. People are looking for leaders who can, like Winston Churchill, put into words their thoughts and feelings, giving them a vision of what they can achieve. Organizational authors are becoming increasingly interested in understanding how leaders manage meaning through various forms of communication.

Framework for Organizing the Literature

The annotations in this chapter, like the development of the literature, follow Boulding's hierarchy of systems. Despite the chronological development of the field through linear, adaptive, and interpretive phases, authors continue to produce valuable works that fit each model.

The annotations move through the three models twice, first with works that focus attention on intraorganizational dynamics and then with works that deal with organization-environment relations. This structure permits an examination of materials that deal with all three levels of organizational complexity and both of the levels of analysis that concern chief executives and policymakers.

Organization Focus—Linear entries in this chapter deal with the structure of organizations, rational decision making, and responding to decline.

Organization Focus—Adaptive entries deal with loosely coupled organizational structure, political decision making, power in higher education organizations, and organizational life cycles.

Organization Focus—Interpretive entries deal with interpretations of educational organizations, collegiate sagas, the nature of administrative work, and organizational socialization.

Organization/Environment Focus—Linear entries include coordination of interorganizational relations and strategy in higher education organizations.

Organization/Environment Focus—Adaptive entries extend the concepts of strategy and responding to decline and crisis in higher education. One entry reviews the literature on organization-environment relations, and another discusses the importance of organizational flexibility.

Organization/Environment Focus—Interpretive entries include two discussions of organizations as language-laden cultures as well as extensions of strategy and leadership to the interpretive level.

Commentary on the Literature

Organizational literature has attracted researchers from a wide variety of fields. It has grown relatively fast and has also moved rapidly to highly sophisticated, complex models. However, several liabilities counterbalance these assets.

The study of organizations encompasses numerous and diverse subtopics. At this point, few subtopics are well developed. Each subtopic typically attracts a few interested authors, but it could benefit from the scrutiny of many investigators with different perspectives. Comprehensive organizational models that integrate these subtopics and approximate complex organizational realities probably will not appear for a long time. The field would benefit greatly from more works that synthesize existing knowledge by subtopics, by theories, and by types of organizations.

In the short term, research and theory need to investigate interpretive aspects of organizations more extensively and also to examine how the three models interact. Just because the linear model came first does not mean it is obsolete. Administrators facing the challenges likely to be presented to higher education in the 1980s and 1990s would benefit from understanding model interactions. Definition and differentiation of institutional missions is an increasingly important interpretive issue. Leaders need thoughtful assistance in deciding how to focus and communicate their mission (interpretive), how far to let the mission stray from its historical definition in order to respond to new environments (adaptive), and how to organize the institution in order to implement the mission (linear).

The organizational studies field is young and is still oriented toward basic science rather than practical applications. Therefore, many of its best works do not attract the attention of those who might benefit most from their insights. Most books for practitioners continue to present personal opinion, expert experience, or case histories, buttressed when convenient with theory and research. A few exceptions, books that are well-grounded in research and theory but written for policymakers, are beginning to appear and should be encouraged.

References

Boulding, K. E. "General Systems Theory—The Skeleton of Science." *Management Science*, 1956, 2, 197–208.

Chaffee, E. E. "The Concept of Strategy: From Business to Higher Education." In J. C. Smart (ed.), *Higher Education: Handbook of Theory and Research*. Vol. 1. New York: Agathon, 1985.

Pfeffer, J. *Organizations and Organization Theory*. Boston: Pitman, 1982.

A Comparison of Private and Public Educational Organizations

Daniel C. Levy

Bases of Comparison

In education, as in many other fields where there is significant nonprofit activity, to compare private and public organizations is to grapple with complex material. Yet the challenges are compelling. Within and beyond the United States, disenchantment with the performance of public educational organizations has added a sense of urgency to the often substantial interest in examining alternatives. Thus private-public issues are crucial to many of the important educational debates of our time, as a growing policy literature illustrates (James & Levin 1983; Gaffney 1981; Everhart 1982; Breneman & Finn 1978; Levy 1986b). Instead of joining the policy debate, however, I step back in this chapter and try to identify and understand salient empirical differences between the two types of organizations.

The chapter concentrates on the potency of one basic concept—that of scope—and analyzes how well essential private-public differences can be appreciated by reference to it. To use terminology from organizational sociology, a limited scope (or "niche") characterizes "specialist" institutions; at the other end of a continuum, greater scope characterizes "generalist" institutions (Hannan & Freeman 1978, 152–53). Related to specialism are narrowness, selectivity, focus, and coherence; related to generalism are breadth, openness, looseness, and ambiguity.[1] The principal hypothesis here is that we can associate private more than public educational organizations with limited scope. Private *sectors* may often rival public sectors in breadth, but they tend to do so by adding narrow organization upon narrow organization.

The complexity of the private-public terrain in education ensures that no one hypothesis will prove accurate in nearly all cases. Observers have searched in vain for behavioral characteristics that consistently distinguish educational organizations labeled private from those labeled public: thus, many scholars, as well as partisans of one sector or the other, have belittled the private-public distinction (Levy 1986b, 170–92). I therefore define *private* and *public* only according to legal nomenclature, not scope or any other hypothesized criterion.[2] Notwithstanding the conceptual concern to discover private-public patterns, this then is an inductive approach, taking private and public organizations as labeled and proceeding to identify certain characteristics with them.

The private organizations analyzed here are private *non-profit* ones. I restrict my comments about for profits to capsule footnotes suggesting general contrasts to the other two sectors. I do so largely because for-profits have been far less important than the other two types. As a corollary, my private nonprofit versus public comparison naturally excludes single-sector educational systems. Although there are no fully private systems, many fully public ones exist, particularly in communist nations and in higher education (as in much of Western Europe and Africa).

Consequently, the thematic concern with private-public comparisons helps in the selection of this chapter's three principal geographical and educational contexts. These are (1) Latin American higher education, (2) U.S. schools, and (3) U.S. higher education, though I add footnoted comparisons to other settings, mostly Western European. The choice of U.S. contexts is obvious, given both readership interest and literature availability. I use Latin American higher education partly because it is my own area of expertise, and I can simplify the complex findings of my twenty-nation study without incurring an author's wrath.[3] More objective scholarly rationales for this choice relate to identified private-public characteristics in Latin American higher education.[4] In any case, conclusions from my own book become hypotheses for more general comparisons in most of the discussion below.

The analysis of private-public differences in our three principal contexts employs four categories: finance, governance, mission, and effectiveness.[5] The use of these categories could facilitate comparisons between education and other major fields where private-public differences may be usefully considered in terms of specialism and generalism. Beyond this, the main reason for the four-part approach is to draw private-public educational comparisons over wider criteria than often considered. I believe that too much of the recent U.S. policy debate on private versus public in education has turned on an assessment of quality, as gauged by achievement test scores. Certainly the most discussed study comparing private and public educational organizations concerns these scores (Coleman, Hoffer, & Kilgore 1982b), dealing with matters like governance only as they may influence differential achievement. Yet even fuller measures of academic stature and pedagogical success would cover part of our effectiveness category only. Quality is merely one basis on which to compare private and public, either for our purposes of understanding differences between the two sectors or for making policy decisions based on those differences. And these other bases appear often to mark larger differences, offering greater alternatives for individuals and policymakers, alternatives relating to values such as equity, accountability, autonomy, pluralism, and contrasting notions of democracy.[6]

Finally, before proceeding to the heart of the chapter, a quick overview of the sectoral sizes in question is needed. Our three cases illustrate the rule that private educational sectors are typically smaller than public ones. The relationship holds in sixteen of the eighteen dual-sector systems studied in Latin America. The private enrollment share varies widely, from 6 percent or less in a few small nations, to nearly 60 percent in Colombia and roughly 70 percent in Brazil, with 10 to 15 percent fairly common. These figures represent startling private growth, largely a reaction to extraordinary growth and transformation in the public sector. Compared to only 3 percent in 1930 and 14 percent in 1955, the private share of the region's now roughly 5 million enrollments has reached 34 percent. In contrast, U.S. private school percentages dropped dramatically from the late nineteenth century through the first few decades of this century, mostly because of the growth of public high schools (Kraushaar 1972, 13–14). Recently, after a small decline between the mid-1960s and mid-1970s, the private share has been fairly stable, its more than 5 million students holding something over 10 percent of enrollments, slightly higher at the elementary level and slightly lower at the high school level (Erickson 1986; Williams et al. 1983, 4–8), though there is reason to suppose that the overall percentage could be a little higher (Cooper, McLaughlin, & Manno 1983, 95–97). By comparison, the private share is much higher, but has declined substantially, in U.S. higher education. Although it was still one-half in 1950, it dropped in the ensuing three decades to just over one-fifth (22 percent) of the now more than 11 million enrollments (Geiger 1986a).

Our three principal cases also illustrate the tendency for the private share of institutions to exceed the private enrollment share.[7] In the United States, the over 10 percent private enrollment share is spread over approximately 18 percent of the institutions (Erickson 1986), whereas the private sector's one-fifth share of higher education enrollments is spread over roughly one-half the institutions (Geiger 1986a). I have no reliable aggregate figure for Latin American institutions, but I have enough evidence to know that the private sector's institutional share exceeds its enrollment share in *each* of the eighteen dual-sector systems studied. In sum, private educational institutions are usually smaller than public ones.[8]

Finance: Depth versus Breadth

A crucial issue in comparing private and public educational organizations is who shoulders the financial burden. We can associate specialism with policies whereby individuals pay their own way directly to the institutions that serve them, and broader scope with policies whereby institutions are funded through general tax revenues. In the former, there is a much tighter, well-identified relationship between paying for and receiving services than is the case in the latter.

Higher education finance in Latin America displays something approaching complete distinctiveness between the sectors. The public sector usually receives around 95 percent of its income from the national government. A basic rationale is that all education is a public good benefiting society at large, not just individual members. From Brazil to Venezuela to Mexico, students have blocked attempts to impose tuition, attempts based on notions of equity and the weakness of the public financial base.

In comparison, Latin American private higher education is funded overwhelmingly through private funds. Contributions widen the financial scope some, but are usually specific to particular universities; financial scope widens significantly in the private sector only when we add together the individually narrow but different bases of given institutions. Catholic universities receive funds and donated services from their religious communities, and elite secular universities draw support from domestic businesses as well as international businesses and foundations. Yet *tuition* remains the major source at all types of the region's private higher education organizations, and it is nearly the exclusive source at nonelite ones. Government subsidies are rare (although tax exemptions are available on the basis of the nonprofit status that virtually all the private institutions enjoy, nominally if not always in fact). The major exceptions regarding subsidies are found for some high-quality Catholic universities, as in Ecuador and Peru; they are based on the rationale that their missions tend to be the widest, or most publicly oriented, that the private sector undertakes. Nonelite institutions have cited their broadening socioeconomic status (SES) base in soliciting aid, but so far to little avail. The fundamental private-public difference remains that private institutions are privately funded, and public institutions are publicly funded.

How well can these private-public findings from Latin America be generalized? They can be rather strikingly extended to the United States, at least at the school level. Again there is great private-public distinctiveness, with the private sector relying mostly on tuition and adding other private funding, and the public sector relying even more exclusively on government funding. Although noteworthy, corporate donations to certain public schools, and the establishment of local private foundations to subsidize public school districts hit hard by government cutbacks, are still marginal in most states. Public financial responsibility for public elementary schools has long been seen as essential to the "public school tradition," and a similar responsibility was subsequently established for the high school level. The prime financial responsibility, however, has never been lodged with the national government, thus in some sense limiting the breadth of public-sector finance. Even the major shift away from local responsibility in recent decades has been toward the state level, not the national level, so that localities and the states now each contribute roughly 45 percent of public school income (Wirt & Kirst 1982, 237).

Private schools depend much less on support from any government level. Instead, they rely heavily on individual payments for individual benefits. As Erickson (1986) aptly puts it, fees are exacted "at the schoolhouse door," whereas public income depends on "sources far removed from the individual's pocketbook." Given that big endowments are a rarity, private secular schools usually receive more than 80 percent of their income through tuition, though the figure may drop below 50 percent in some Catholic schools, where expenditures are subsidized by parishes and donated services (Kraushaar 1972, 203–08). Recent figures, however, show that, overall, Catholic schools depend on tuition for roughly three-fourths of their income and on government for but 1 percent (Greeley 1981, 13). Turning back to non-Catholic private schools, there is substantial variation among the southern segregationist academies between tuition and donated services, often tied to fundamentalist congregations (Nevin & Bills 1976, 71–80, 118–19). Tuition more clearly dominates, running as high as $6,000 per year at the secular and some academically prestigious Protestant schools (Vitullo-Martin 1981, 39–40), thus narrowing the pools of potential applicants (Baird 1977, 36). In sum, notwithstanding the role of Catholic and certain other churches, most individual private schools are funded "narrowly and deeply" by their users and committed supporters. As with Latin American private higher education, only the addition of separately narrow bases makes the sector's financial base appear wide, though still not as wide as the tax-sustained public base.

Government aid has broadened the financial profile of U.S. private schools. Even the federal government has assumed an important role since 1965. The two major obstacles to government funding of private schools have been the broad commitment to public schooling and the idea that general funding for specialized private aims, especially religious ones, is inappropriate. Counterarguments emphasize the public benefits of private choice, the social or public character of private schooling, and the sometimes exclusive practices of *public* schooling.

Seeking compromises among such competing notions, government ties most of its private school aid to particular purposes deemed socially important. Federal aid goes largely to economically and physically disadvantaged students and is mostly handled by state and local authorities (Kutner, Sherman & Williams 1986). State aid goes largely for similar purposes, though also for public transportation, health services, textbooks, and other activities (Hirschoff 1986; Kraushaar 1972, 289–90). Especially important is the child-benefit theory whereby courts allow aid targeted directly for students but not for broad institutional support. Additionally, like other U.S. nonprofit organizations, more than 95 percent of private schools receive tax exemptions, notably on property, and perhaps as much as one-fourth of total private school expenses are covered by government assistance (Encarnation 1983, 177, 187; Sullivan 1974, 92–95).

Even if we were to go beyond the U.S. school and Latin American higher education contexts and add Western Europe and much of the rest of the world, at both the school and university levels, U.S. *higher* education would stand nearly alone in having a public sector that draws significantly on private funds. Tuitions are higher than in any other public sector in the world, and no other nation has matched the U.S. corporate, foundation, and individual traditions of giving to public universities (Geiger 1986a). The public sector does depend on government over private sources by roughly a 4:1 ratio, but, as at the K–12 level, even most of the government funds do not come from as wide a base as found in the dominant worldwide tendency, where centralized national ministries are the key actors (Levy 1982). Indeed, only state governments provide annual institutional subsidies for U.S. public universities; even more local responsibility is the rule for public community colleges. Federal funding is mostly restricted to two concerns—one is student aid, the other, research (Carnegie . . . 1975b).

And these two federal concerns actually favor the private sector, where tuition is higher and a proportionally greater share of expensive research is conducted (Shils 1973; Geiger 1986a). Federal aid has also been sustained by the argument, upheld in *Tilton* v. *Richardson* (1971), that even church-related colleges are eligible, since higher education students are presumed to be "less impressionable" than grade school students. On the other hand, compared to federal aid, state aid for the private sector has been less important. Although most states provide such aid, it rarely equals 5 percent of either the state's higher education budget or the private sector's total income (Berdahl 1978, 349). Student aid is common, and support for the private institutions is most often targeted for service contracts or plants or is based on enrollment or degree formulas (Carnegie . . . 1976b, 80; Breneman & Finn 1978, 46). State aid tends to be greatest where private sectors are largest (Nelson 1978, 68; McCoy & Halstead 1979, 21); New York leads in this respect. This suggests a correlation between enrollment scope and financial scope. As at the school level, so at the higher education level, tax exemptions and deductions are important.

Thus, government finance further complicates a private-sector picture also characterized by a myriad of private financial contributors; but sectoral complexity can be simplified if we concentrate on subsectors (Geiger 1986a; Minter & Bowen 1978; Jellama 1973; E. James 1986a). The great majority of private colleges are not tied into a wide financial network, either governmental or private. Most rely greatly on tuition, perhaps adding the voluntary support of some local church or loyal alumni or other supporters (Bartell 1980; Jencks & Riesman 1968, 345). To be sure, the Harvards and Yales have wide national ties to private donors across the land; still, they represent the exceptions. Thus, intersectoral tuition gaps are frequently on the statewide order of 4:1 or 5:1, with major policy debates raging in state after state over the desirability of cutting that ratio, whether through more state aid to privates or higher tuition at publics; in fact, however, major policy changes have not occurred (Rusk & Leslie 1978; Carnegie . . . 1976b, 80; Breneman & Finn 1978, 12–13, 27). Justification for public tuitions rests partly on the belief that there is less government responsibility for higher education than for school education, in part because there is less need to foster widely shared beliefs at the higher level.

To sum up, U.S. finance proves to be much less intersectorally distinctive at the higher than at the school level.[9] The public sector draws considerably off private sources and the private sector has a much wider private (beyond tuition) and even government base in higher education. Nonetheless, even within U.S. higher education, private institutions tend to rely on much narrower bases than public ones. Most have a very narrow financial base tied to tuition. So even as we add U.S. higher education to the cases considered above, it is clear that public institutions typically rely overwhelmingly on the broad coverage of government, whereas private institutions rely much more on direct tuition payments, with other private contributions often tied by specific actors to specific institutions, and even government money, where available, often tied to specific rather than general institutional purposes.[10]

Governance: Close versus Overarching and Complex Authority

There are important parallels, some causal, in the financing and governing of educational organizations. Again private activity tends to concentrate rather closely in and around private institutions, whereas public institutions tend to be treated as parts of wider systems. Government is generally far more critical to the running of public institutions. And, notwithstanding the socially stratified basis on which it tends to function, government usually represents a wider array of groups and interests than individual private actors do. Consequently, differences in the scope of governance often relate to vital private-public contrasts in matters such as autonomy and accountability.

Latin American private and public universities are substantially distinct in governance, resembling the situation in finance except that the distinctiveness is not as great. Many public universities, though almost fully dependent on government funds, achieve considerable autonomy from government. Still, government is the overarching actor, playing an important role in virtually every public institution. On the other hand, governance within the public universities of many nations is characterized by a dispersion of power among administrators, faculty, students, and even office and physical plant workers (as in Mexico).

Most of Latin America's private universities, elite and nonelite alike, enjoy substantial autonomy from government, sometimes even under authoritarian regimes. This does not mean that they are more autonomous than public counterparts, however, for there is often a special, close, accountability to key financial and other authorities. These authorities, mostly businesses and churches, vary from institution to institution, making the private sector notably decentralized. But individual institutions have tightly packed, concentrated power structures, with the business or religious authorities appointing governing boards directly responsible to them. Nor is the power shared within institutions nearly as widely as it is in the public sector. Most private universities are centralized and hierarchical institutions, allowing little room for dissent. Indeed, academic freedoms are not allowed to threaten the chosen, often specialized or restricted orientation of the organization. The private power structure is comparatively coherent, headed by authorities whose influence does not extend nearly as widely across institutions as the government's does, but instead penetrates more selectively and deeply.

Turning to U.S. schools, the private sector once had to struggle (though not as wrenchingly as in Latin American higher education) for the right to exist, until the *Pierce* case of 1925 provided legal security.[11] Since then there has been a near consensus that states should maintain some governance role but a far more limited one than in public schools (Erickson 1969; Campbell et al. 1980, 425). Within these bounds, and while the role has generally expanded over time, interstate variations has been enormous. This variation is found in all areas of state supervision—from safety codes to zoning, truth in advertising, admissions policy, and personnel credentials (Encarnation 1983, 187–93). Curriculum is another good example: control varies from slight in some states to formidable equivalency requirements in others. Then too, regulations are often vague (Coons & Sugarman 1978, 168) and courts vary in what they uphold (although they rarely strike down regulations as unconstitutional). Moreover, just as in Latin America, some private institutions welcome government regulations (for example, in curriculum standardization) because they do not want to appear "too different" (Kraushaar 1972, 323) or illegitimate. For one thing, they may want to be distinctive in only one way, but to attract clients to that distinctive orientation, they have to assure them there will not be sacrifices along other lines. Such reasoning has been common among Catholic institutions, concerned to maintain decent and acceptable academic credentials, from the first private Catholic university in Latin America (Chile 1888) to some U.S. Catholic schools earlier in this century. In any case, the overriding rule in the United States is still that private schools are much freer than public schools from government commands tied to constitutional requirements and financial subsidies (Elson 1969, 104, 122–23; Hirschoff 1986; Kraushaar 1972, 316); this holds for the policies just cited, as well as for control over administrative boards, hiring, dismissal, programs for non-English speakers, and so forth. If approved, tuition tax credits could erode some of these private-public differences, as government money has already done (Glazer 1983, 196; Hirschoff 1986).

In accordance with the analysis of finance, however, we see again that there are both shorter and longer arms of government. A distinguishing characteristic of U.S. schooling has traditionally been local control (Ramírez & Robinson 1979; Meyer et al. 1977). By concentrating power closer to individual institutions than is the case in a nationally centralized system, local control limits public-private differences in governance scope.[12] But the trend in intergovernmental relations in the postwar period has been toward the higher levels, state and federal. This wider governance network has limited local authority to follow the distinctive desires of local constituencies. Even though at least the federal role often remains tied to specific concerns, and the impact of funding on governance varies (Meyer 1983, 187–88; Scott & Meyer 1983, 145–48; Kutner, Sherman, & Williams 1986), a broadened concept of publicness is reflected in court decisions, student rights, racial integration, mainstreaming of the handicapped, restrictions on prayer, and so forth (T. James 1983, 68; Hirschoff 1986; Coleman, Hoffer, & Kilgore 1982b, 163). This broadened publicness often promotes exits to private schools.

In contrast, the locus of private power remains much more tightly wrapped in and around individual schools. Boards of trustees, however they may be selected (Nevin & Bills 1976, 123), typically hold the fundamental authority to set policy directions and delegate power to a principal who becomes "the captain of the ship," whereas the public school is more tied to the "uniformity, standardization and spelled-out procedures" of a comparatively distant central administration (Kraushaar 1972, 161, 144, 12, 173; Meyer 1983). Some Catholic schools collectively come under an overarching authority, but that varies, and real power often remains at the school level. Protestant, evangelical, and elite secular schools tend to be even more individually administered (Campbell et al. 1980, 430–32; McCready 1977, 74; Kraushaar 1972, 9, 144, 266–67). Therefore, the private sector's changing composition (Cooper, McLaughlin, & Manno 1983; Catterall 1984; Erickson 1986) makes the concentration of power around the school itself an increasingly salient private characteristic.

As in Latin American higher education, the issue is less the degree than the contours of institutional autonomy versus external control. And these differing ties to the environment relate to the distribution of power *within* organizations. Again the privates tend to be more autocratic, though perhaps decreasingly so (Kraushaar 1972, 174, 267–68). Again shared assumptions, which are ensured by the school's authority to select its personnel and to dismiss them quickly if disputes arise, play a crucial role (Nevin & Bills 1976, 41–43; Kraushaar 1972, 163–64). Most participants, notably parents, exercise power through choice, and retain voice essentially through the implicit exit option (Hirschman 1970). Thus, while they may have little formal ongoing power within institutions, this power may be less cumbersome than that found in the public sector (Kraushaar 1972, 265, 102), a point sometimes cited in calling for public-sector reform (Coons & Sugarman 1978, 162–64, 177).

Several of these private-public contrasts in governance scope can be reinforced and elaborated by reference to some of the extensive work by Scott and Meyer (1984), including some empirical findings from a recent Bay Area sample. These authors argue that private decision making is much more likely than public decision making to occur within the school (where there is a higher administrator/student ratio) that is less constrained by external inspection and authorities over it (district, regional, or otherwise) (Scott & Meyer 1984, 25–38). Moreover, recent trends have enormously increased the complexity and reduced the clarity of public governance. Centralization has pushed decision making further from individual schools without, however, producing a clear top-down command structure. Instead, we see a mix of competing authorities at various levels, higher levels layered upon rather than replacing lower ones, thus producing a "fragmented centralization" with lots of "autonomous lateral relationships" (Meyer 1983, 181, 185) and a "much more elaborate organizational structure," with "a considerable cost in internal organizational consistency"; in sum, compared to private schools, public schools exist in a "complex and inconsistent controlling environment," as less "bounded and internally coherent organizations" (Scott & Meyer 1984, 32, 39).

Without probing the historical reasons, it is clear that U.S. higher education has been characterized by less private-public distinction in terms of the breadth and complexity of governance than has been found in our other two educational contexts. Yet many similar patterns hold, even though in more blurred form.

The scope of government control is much wider in the public than the private sector. Granted, as at the U.S. school level, the federal role is limited even in the public sector (though not nearly so much as it was a few decades ago). But, outside the community college network, local control is hardly a factor; rather, state capitals tend to wield power across the breadth of their states' public institutions. Two more similarities to the school level further qualify the private-public contrasts in scope tied to the government role. One is that the government role varies greatly by state. Some state departments of education require teacher education programs to develop curricula leading to teacher certification, and others require the use of particular budget formulas and program-planning systems; certain state legislatures (as in Florida and New York) have even gone so far as to stipulate minimum numbers of classroom hours (Mortimer & McConnell 1978, 3–4, 207). A second qualification to the private-public tendencies I am emphasizing is that the government role has expanded even for the *private* sector. For example, some states have required or banned new course offerings, and there have been increased pressures with regard to such concerns as minority representation and rights. Nonetheless, the lengthening arm of government—the rule in state after state—shapes the public much more than the private sector.

Evidence on differing government roles according to sector accumulates from several related spheres of action. As at the school level, regulations (state and federal) have multiplied to hold especially the public institutions responsible for a host of wide social concerns (Bok 1980; Mortimer & McConnell 1978, 190). Newly active state legislatures (with vastly beefed-up staffs) turn their energies toward public more than private institutions. Similarly, most statewide coordinating boards have gone much further in trying to mold public than private institutions into their systemwide planning (Berdahl 1975; Odell & Thelin 1981). Along these lines, the role of the courts has increased over both sectors but differentially. In the most extensive study related to our interests, Kaplin (1978, 1–3, 19–21, 31, 97, 232) finds that the courts have recognized and reinforced the authority of private organizations to pursue distinctive ends. Private higher education, unlike its public counterpart, is not bound to the doctrine of religious neutrality (at least unless it seeks government funding). Additionally, private institutions are left much freer to bargain with their employees and to set and enforce disciplinary standards for students because the courts are inclined to view such matters as related to contractual relations between private institutions and the individuals associated with them by choice. Private institutions are also less bound than public ones by federal policy regarding discrimination. In many particulars, the degree of government imposition over private organizations depends largely on criteria concerning privateness; for example, universities receiving substantial government subsidization are less free than others from constitutional constraints and from the authority of coordinating boards (Mortimer & McConnell 1978, 220).

Largely because of the contrasting sweeps of government authority, the locus of the private policy-making process, much more than the public one, is centered around individual institutions themselves. This private-public contrast echoes what we found at the school level. An important difference in higher education, however, is that even many public institutions have considerable autonomy compared to public schools. They are much less tied to overarching authorities, thereby allowing much more interinstitutional differentiation, with the policy-making process more particularized by institution. Nevertheless, compared to private higher education institutions, public ones do not concentrate their power as tightly around individual institutions (Shils 1973).

Boards of trustees provide good illustrations of basic private-public differences. Even public universities have these bodies (normally more associated with private organizations), but with different tendencies. Public boards typically allow for a major government role, through the appointment of most trustees, and are accountable to the states as broad representatives of the public interest. Private boards, on the other hand, tend to be appointed by, and remain more directly accountable to, particular constituencies, variable by institution but specific in most individual cases (Mortimer & McConnell 1978, 152–153; Millett 1973, 51; Epstein 1974, 37). Moreover, the close authority of individual boards over individual private organizations is not diluted by the formidable multiuniversity coverage found in the public sector, and, of course, it is less diluted by broad governmental authority. Consequently, the private organizations are generally less tied to standardized practices, whether in affirmative action plans, salary scales, tenure plans, or so many other concerns (Carnegie . . . 1975a, 61–65; Commission . . . 1973, 161, 180).

Finally, U.S. private higher education follows the patterns found for Latin American higher education and U.S. grade school education (though less sharply than either), not only by enjoying more autonomy from centralized government authority and less autonomy from closer private authorities, but also by tending to centralize *intra*institutional power more than public counterparts do.[13] Such intrainstitutional centralization and lesser internal voice (for example, in student representation; Mortimer & McConnell 1978, 148) help sustain the private organization's clear and direct accountability to its board and specific external constituencies.[14]

Mission: Selectivity versus Coverage

This section compares the missions of organizations that are financed and governed differently, exploring whether these missions differ, especially in scope.

In several important ways, the missions carved out by Latin America's private universities provide distinctiveness. There is distinctiveness across institutions, reflecting the heterogeneity in governance discussed earlier. And there is distinctiveness between sectors, despite some overlapping missions. A major concern related to the thematic private-public contrasts highlighted in this chapter is that the private missions tend to be narrower than the public ones.

One manifestation of the different breadth of private and public missions concerns student clienteles. Although Latin America's public sector rarely draws off more than a fifth of the age-relevant population, and although many unprestigious private institutions are no more elite than many public ones, the strong tendency is toward greater selectivity (in both academic and SES terms) within the private sector. This is especially true for the prestigious secular universities, but also for many Catholic ones. Among the latter, restrictive religious missions have become less common in recent decades yet still make for a marked distinction from public openness. Moreover, many Catholic and especially most other private universities can reasonably be described as narrower than public counterparts in their political orientations. The private universities are often identified with the political ideology and even the policies of the privileged, whereas the public ones are usually identified with calls for a much wider distribution of power and wealth. Beyond this contrast, the private universities, more than the public ones, can be accurately identified with some particular ideology. Based largely on the disciplined private governance structure and selection process, there is less likelihood of ambiguity, incoherence, or widely heterogeneous ideologies.

These points apply well to another mission, an easily quantifiable one. Latin America's private sectors, in nation after nation, tend to be much more specialized in the academic areas of concentrations or fields of study (such as law) they offer to their students. The most striking private-public differences come when we compare organizations rather than sectors. In Venezuela, for example, where eight fields of study are offered, each of the four private universities holds a minimum of 64 percent of its enrollment in just one field of study, such as engineering, and none offers more than five different fields. By comparison, three of the four public-autonomous universities offer all eight fields, and none concentrates more than 36 percent of its students in any single field. Even when we aggregate data from the organizational to the sectoral level and across fifteen nations (those in which at least 90 percent of the enrollments could be categorized into fourteen identified fields), another powerful private-public difference related to scope is found: the private sector has proportionally more of its students in each of seven fields, with rough private-public parity in another, and every one of these seven fields is less expensive to offer than every one of the six fields where the public sector has the proportional lead. To illustrate, the private proportional edge is two to one in business fields, the public edge better than two to one in medicine.[15]

Important similarities to these private-public comparisons emerge for U.S. schools. Many have noted the extraordinary diversity among private schools compared to public schools. There are a multitude of different kinds of religious schools, segregationist academies, ghetto schools, progressive-experimental schools, boarding schools, and so forth (Cooper 1984; Erickson 1986; Esty 1974, 1–20). Even within most of these individual categories, there is great variation among institutions, as Baird (1977, 1–2) and Nevin and Bills (1976, 103) have shown for elite secular schools and segregationist academies, respectively.[16] The religious dimension is especially important; seven of eight private enrollments are in religiously affiliated institutions (Catterall 1984, 8). The Catholic subsector alone, despite strong proportional declines from the mid-1960s until the early 1980s, accounts for well over half the private enrollments (Cooper, McLaughlin, & Manno 1983, 94). Many Catholic institutions have lost some religious flavor over time (as the clientele they have served have become more integrated into the rest of society) but, as in Latin America, still preserve some distinctiveness from other institutions, both public and private. Other religious schools, such as the "new Christian," or fundamentalist schools, tend to be at once more specialized and more intensive in their individual missions, insisting, for example, on particular prayers, theories of creation, and born-again fervor (Nevin & Bills 1976, 37–39; Skerry 1980, 21); examples of common curriculum notwithstanding, such schools tend to reinforce the interinstitutional distinctiveness characteristic of private sector missions.

While this interinstitutional diversity is often recognized, the intrainstitutional *lack* of diversity is perhaps equally noteworthy. Choice is ensured across private institutions much more than within them. As Nevin and Bills (1976, 2) observe for the segregationist academies that are so different from one another, "Perhaps the single most important point about these schools is their sameness . . . once you are inside you are in a fixed and unchanging world." The public dynamic is significantly different. As one would guess from its financial and governance profiles, the common school, at the elementary level, or the comprehensive high school is simultaneously intended to serve a considerable range of purposes and to be fairly similar one institution to the next. Clark (1984) laments that "a substantial overload of conflicting expectations" drives out the "advantages of specialization," distinctiveness, and clarity as the "huge hope of the system at large is thereby recapitulated in each of some sixteen thousand small worlds," the worlds of the "unfocused" comprehensive high school.

Beyond this, Erickson (1986) emphasizes how, by handling the bulk of the market, the public sector pushes the private sector to concentrate on a few special tasks. Similarly, Scott and Meyer's Bay Area sample (1984, 33, 38) shows public schools under many pressures to address a full range of needs, whereas private schools, receiving neither the pressure nor resources to do the same, instead seek discrete niches—thereby achieving greater goal coherence. Levin (1983, 28) and others have noted the ramifications for disenchantment with the public schools and for the growth of private alternatives.

The narrowness and depth of private missions clearly applies to self-consciously moral orientations, where there usually is a more rigidly defined sense of right and wrong than in public schools. Even in curriculum and the range of subjects offered, however, narrowness is often characteristic. Boarding and other elite schools are the most striking exceptions (Baird 1977, 4) and Catholic schools probably fit this generalization less than other private schools (Kraushaar 1972, 55). At the other extreme, some private schools portray their limited curriculum as relevant only for certain racial (Nevin & Bills 1976, 85, 13) or religious groups. For all the variation, a fair generalization might parallel my findings on Latin American universities (though in a diluted form) that private schools have a comparatively narrow focus. They offer a more restricted and specialized range of courses (vocational, for example) and other activities, even if we control for size (Salganik & Karweit 1982, 155, 159; Coleman, Hoffer, & Kilgore 1982b, 72–84) or the percentage of minority students (Scott & Meyer 1984, 34–36). Beyond just the curriculum, private school offerings are often limited, though again one would have to distinguish the elite schools with their huge libraries, art galleries, and media and other special programs (Baird 1977, 4) from, say, the segregationist academies that "offer bare bones education" in terms of libraries, physical plants, health facilities, and so forth (Nevin & Bills 1976, p. 74). As James and Levin (1983, 8) point out, few private schools provide expensive services unless public finance and regulation alter the private profile, as with education for the handicapped (Weintraub 1981, 49–51; Kutner, Sherman, & Williams 1986). More generally, there is reason to doubt how well private choices can meet the broad challenges of a modern democratic society (Levin 1983; Hirschoff 1986).

Crucial to narrowly and coherently defined missions is the selection process. Here I consider students, as I did for Latin American higher education, though the selection of teachers and administrators is also important and follows a similar logic. Private schools tend to tap constituencies that fit in comfortably with the organization's complexion, that want a good deal of what in fact is offered in depth—and that are relatively unconcerned about (or even zealously do not want) what is not offered. Granted, there is controversy over how broadly representative the typical public school is (or ever was) and over whether its SES base has widened or narrowed.[17] Clearly we have some highly selective public schools, notably in New York City (Doyle & Cooper 1983), but these are still the exceptions.

One key generalization is that private schools tend to be aimed much more to privileged groups. Roughly 5 percent of families earning under $15,000 a year send their children to private schools versus roughly five times that percentage for families earning over $50,000 a year (Williams et al. 1983, 15). Second, beyond economic factors, private schools have been more oriented to preserving particular identities and beliefs than have public schools. Race has been a crucial example, though one must note that Catholic schools are attracting an increasing share of their students for non-religious reasons, even attracting an increasing share of non-Catholics, including blacks. The black private enrollment proportion is still less than half that for whites, with Hispanics in between (Williams et al. 1983, 11; Catterall 1984, 18).

Turning to mission in U.S. higher education, one again finds, as in finance and governance, that private-public distinctiveness is less marked than at the U.S. school level, certainly less than in Latin American higher education. A major factor is the interorganizational diversity characterizing even the public sector, where colleges and universities are not as bound as public schools to accommodate the range of interests found in given local geographical areas, nor as bound as Latin American public universities to nationwide standards set by ministries.

Nevertheless, even in U.S. higher education, organizational distinctiveness and specialized niches are especially associated with the private sector (Geiger 1986a). As Jencks and Riesman note (1968, 287–88), it is more difficult for public than private institutions to hold to unusual missions; this helps explain why there are "no public Amhersts, Oberlins, or Reeds." Herein lies one of the major reasons for the large U.S. support for the private sector, which performs "a function in our society that we cannot afford to lose" (Jellama 1973, x). An extensive array of Carnegie Commission and Council studies attests to this concern. The Carnegie classification finds private institutions extremely overrepresented among those types of institutions that tend to be most-differentiated; 96 percent of all liberal arts and 67 percent of all specialized institution enrollments are in a private sector that includes one-half the institutions and fewer than one-fourth of overall enrollments (Carnegie . . . 1976a, xii, 36–40; El-Khawas 1976, 4).

Prominent examples of restrictive scope have involved race, gender, and (to a lesser extent) ethnicity, but also progressive experimentation and conservatism (Jencks & Riesman 1968, 346). Religion has been most important, though less than at the school level. Even if a sizable proportion of the private higher education institutions are religiously affiliated, that affiliation is often marginal and many Protestant institutions are very small. The contribution to diversity is nonetheless significant, as there is marked differentiation even among Catholic (Greeley 1967, 1–3) and especially among Protestant colleges (Pace 1974; Jencks & Riesman 1968, 312–14). Interinstitutional diversity has also been strong within other categories, such as women's colleges (Kendall 1975, 30).

Consequently, it is to the private sector that Burton Clark turns (1972, 178) to explore the "distinctive college" and the "organizational saga," that "collective understanding of a unique accomplishment in a formally established group," all beginning with a strong sense of mission. The ability to choose distinctive missions is often related to private governance and therefore freedom, leaving public institutions, tied to the state, at a relative disadvantage (Keeton 1971, 17–18; El-Khawas 1976, 43, 51). It is also often related to the much smaller average size of private than public institutions (Pace 1974; Kershaw 1976) mentioned above; and privates tend to be smaller within each category, such as doctorate-granting institutions (El-Khawas 1976, 13).

Some observers, however, have questioned whether the private sector is so characterized by interorganizational diversity. Perhaps conformity is the dominant tendency in U.S. higher education, public or private, with institutions prostituting themselves to extrauniversity financial interests (Goodman 1962, 169–71; Nisbet 1971). Perhaps private universities have betrayed their distinct corporate identities in favor of a bland academic pluralism (Buckley 1977). Or perhaps almost all institutions really perform "public" missions (Silber 1975). For one additional example, it has been argued that, contrary to conventional wisdom, privates more often lapse into "institutional imitation," whereas public institutional missions can be anchored by law (Baldridge et al. 1978, 55–56). In any case, there is abundant evidence that many once highly distinctive private colleges have moved toward the mainstream, whether by mixing clienteles (by religion, race, gender, income), by pursuing academic quality, or by a controversial strategy of adapting to a changing environment through greater comprehensiveness (Pfnister & Finkelstein 1984).

Possibly the principal basis for downplaying private-public differences, however, is that other organizational categorizations can be more decisive. For example, a private doctorate-granting university is likely to have more in common with a public doctorate-granting university than with a private liberal arts college. Also, private research universities do not fit many of the indicators of narrow scope, and in forty-nine states the private sector attracts the higher out-of-state percentage (Carnegie . . . 1977, 50). Thus, even more than at the school level, prestigious private institutions reach out over a wide geographical scope.[18]

Nevertheless, ample grounds exist for associating privateness with an institution's ability to focus on a comparatively narrow clientele. We have already noted that some very strong correlations exist between private-public and other organizational categorizations. Additionally, private-public differences may hold in areas such as "public service" (McCoy & Halstead 1979, 39). Another example, applicable to the Latin American context as well, is regional distribution. Public institutions are more widely spread out across the nation and more responsible for meeting varied regional missions, whereas private institutions are freer to choose their own specialized missions (Carnegie . . . 1976a, 1–126; El-Khawas 1976, 11–13). In some sense, then, public institutions go to the clients, whereas the private institutions draw their clients. Finally, one of this century's most important transformations in the missions of U.S. private institutions has involved their increasing selectiveness (Grant & Riesman 1978, 291).

In considering clientele or any other factor related to mission, the distinction between sector and individual organization again proves crucial. For example, the private sector matches the public sector's black-to-total-student ratio as well as its female ratio largely by relying on distinctively black, and women's, colleges (El-Khawas 1976, 25). Similarly, individual private institutions are much more likely than public ones to cover only a narrow range of academic statures (whether high or low), curricula, religious or normative orientations, SES backgrounds, and so forth.[19] Even relatively homogeneous organizations, if different from one another, can build sectoral diversity, but we must appreciate how this diversity differs significantly from that based on institutions of broader scope.[20]

Effectiveness: Conventional Indicators

In this section I will deviate from the analysis by region and educational level used to this point. Instead, drawing on evidence about those regions and levels, I discuss effectiveness in terms of two dimensions frequently invoked in making private-public comparisons, often invidious ones. The first is academic quality. Although usage varies in the literature as well as in popular discourse, I emphasize here the academic level, in terms of knowledge bases and skills, especially of students. A common measure is the achievement score. The second dimension of effectiveness considered below—client satisfaction—obviously addresses perceptions of effectiveness.

Accumulated, if scattered, evidence often suggests an average edge in the academic level of private over public educational institutions. Powerful qualifications are warranted, but first a bit of the evidence should be sketched. The private edge is possibly strongest where private-public distinctiveness has been most evident—in Latin American higher education. As many as fourteen of eighteen Latin American countries with dual sectors show a private advantage, often a strong one; a public edge is evident in no more than two. For U.S. schools the Coleman, Hoffer, and Kilgore study (1982b; also Greeley 1982) offers the most publicized evidence; debate has turned mostly on whether private school policies produce higher achievement, not on the reality of a higher private standing. Even in U.S. higher education, where we have seen less private-public distinctiveness, most evidence again suggests an average private edge, based on surveys (since 1925), peer rankings, admissions to graduate schools, graduate training, research, and awards received (Cyert 1975, 48; Shils 1973, 8–9; Cartter 1966; Keeton 1971, 7–41; Jencks & Riesman 1968, 288; Carnegie . . . 1976b, 9, 79).

The qualifications should follow closely upon the sort of evidence just sketched, however. First, we often must fall back on prestige as a substitute concept for quality, as quantitative indicators of educational performance are frequently unavailable or questionable in terms of what they really measure; for example, seemingly impressive ratios of teachers, administrators, and expenditures per pupil may have as much to do with inefficiency as with quality, and achievement tests may be culturally or otherwise biased. A second qualification is that the private edge is usually an average edge, with considerable overlap between sectors and often greater gaps within each sector than between the average of each. This includes Latin American higher education, where the average private edge appears so large, for most observers base their private-public comparisons on the best-known institutions, and that is where the private edge tends to be clearest.[21] So it sometimes is in the United States, where people think more readily of the Harvards and Chicagos than of the lesser known colleges sometimes labeled "invisible" or "liberal arts II" (Astin & Lee 1972; Carnegie . . . 1976a; Roose & Anderson 1971), but many public institutions are superior to many private ones (Baldridge et al. 1978, 103). Similarly for U.S. schools, it makes a world of difference whether we focus on the elite boarding and prep schools (Baird 1977; Campbell et al. 1980, 435) or on the segregationist schools (Nevin and Bills 1976, 111). So great is the overlap that a few scholars reject the private claim to quality (Campbell et al. 1980, 448).

Even where private-public differences in quality remain notable in the face of institutional overlap, however, further qualifications are necessary. Crucially, are institutions academically superior because they provide more value added or simply because they start with an edge, as with better prepared or motivated students? This, most researchers agree, is a more important question than the popular one of which sector boasts higher average achievement scores or other measures of knowledge. There is by now important work relating client selection to achievement scores, much of it explaining variation in the latter largely in terms of the former, thereby casting doubt on whether private schools really bring about the superior scores often associated with them (Williams 1984; Murnane 1986a, 1986b; McPartland & McDill 1982). One key certainly lies in the admission of students, typically more selective, as we have seen, in the private sector. Where selection is more restrictive in the public sector, as in Brazilian, Japanese, and Philippine higher education, the average quality tends to be higher in the public sector (Geiger 1986b). Jencks and Riesman (1968, 270, 284), while emphasizing the growing similarity of private and public missions, identify differences in "raw material" as the determinant of still significantly different results; publics must constantly "play the numbers game," going "wide rather than deep," but privates "normally seek a small group" of "enthusiastic" followers. Thus, just as in Latin America, even the best public institutions usually have a comparatively heterogeneous clientele, more than the best private ones.[22]

In any event, quality is not the only component of effectiveness. In fact, not all educational organizations make quality their highest priority; most combine it with other goals, and some clearly subordinate it. Therefore, effectiveness can be thought of as fulfilling chosen missions, among which quality may be only one among several. As there are few longitudinal studies that measure the comparative success of educational organizations in producing the types of graduates they strive for, observers have often relied on client satisfaction.[23] Clients may cite effectiveness or success on any of many factors important to them, ranging from enforcing discipline to transmitting religious faith to instilling an interest in learning.

Concentrating here only on U.S. schools, there is substantial evidence of a private advantage. True, negative feelings about the public schools are easily and often exaggerated. Catterall (1984, 9–11) points out that there has in fact been no major shift from the public to the private sector and the School Finance Project (Williams et al. 1983, 56) finds that only 14 percent of parents are dissatisfied with their child's public school. Nonetheless, other observers see reasons to underscore a shift to the private sector, anticipating its acceleration (Cooper, McLaughlin, & Manno 1983), and the School Finance Project finds that only 3 percent of parents are dissatisfied with their child's private school. Kraushaar (1972, 127, 130, 133, 107) finds the level of satisfaction for private students to be "extraordinarily high," despite complaints about competitiveness, limited "voice," and the "relative uniformity or lack of wide variation" within institutions. And parental satisfaction may run even higher. Baird (1977, 112–19) finds that students, teachers, and administrators believe that their elite schools fulfill proclaimed goals, and he attributes this to both the academic stature and the intensity of the environment. Intensity alone appears sufficient at the segregationist academies, where many students and parents readily express love for their schools, feel comfortable with the internal homogeneity, and even see many of the educational limitations in a positive light (Nevin & Bills 1976, 3, 39, 81, 143).

Effectiveness: Comparing Apples and Oranges?

If the private sector often surpasses the public sector on commonly utilized indicators, however, these indicators may be biased toward the former. We have already seen that higher achievement scores, for example, do not show that private schools necessarily educate more effectively. A broader point about the difficulty of comparing effectiveness between two sectors typically so different in scope can be forwarded by considering (1) the different meaning of client satisfaction between sectors and then (2) the more specialized nature of private-than public-sector endeavors.

The Different Meaning of Client Satisfaction

Without reference to our thematic contrast between private depth and public breadth, the data on client satisfaction cited above may be misleading. Most surveys gauge the support of the users of each sector; if the private schools please only a small group a good deal while the public schools please a larger group but only moderately, the former score higher. A different yet not necessarily more biased approach would gauge the satisfaction of the *general* public with each sector.[24] Relatedly, the widespread stability, high survival rate, and even historically striking expansion of public educational institutions (certainly including both the school and the university levels most closely considered in this chapter) probably reflect considerable popular support and an extraordinary effectiveness in garnering resources.[25]

Clearly, the demonstrable patron satisfaction with private schools is based heavily on the choice—reciprocal choice—characteristic of that sector. Individuals choose, and pay for, organizations that suit them (Esty 1974), and organizations try to choose individuals who will fit comfortably. There is a tight linkage here that is uncharacteristic of the public sector, where organizations tend to be more heterogeneous and less able or disposed to choose narrowly, and individuals link up with organizations more for reasons of physical than normative proximity and cannot count on encountering like-minded individuals; notably greater knowledge, care, and purpose appear to surround the choice of private than public schools in the United States and Canada (Kutner, Sherman, & Williams 1986; Erickson 1986).

The ways in which mutual matching between clientele and private institutions lead to either effectiveness or at least the perception of effectiveness have been explored by several authors (Kraushaar 1972, 106; Salganik & Karweit 1982, 152–54; Murnane 1986a, 1986b; Clark 1972, 182).

Some evidence suggests that private teachers may give up $2,000 to $9,000 a year to teach in the private rather than the public sector (Chambers 1984, 39). Sizer (1984) argues that private curricula—though narrower and offering less choice than public curricula—are more effectively tailored to students. Coons and Sugarman (1978, 116–19) refer to a "stable integration," with some empirical evidence to support the notion that this is more likely to lead to effectiveness than is imposed heterogeneity, which often produces tensions. The correlation between focused choice and satisfaction, which both *tend* to be greater in the private than public sector, is also underscored by El-Khawas's findings (1976, 41) that the most specialized institutions in U.S. higher education, whether private or public, enjoy the highest satisfaction rates. Not surprisingly, then, some analysts are exploring ways in which more heterogeneous public institutions, for example, at the U.S. school level, could match people, structures, and programs more closely (Coleman 1984; Clark 1984).

More Specialized Endeavors

Connected with reciprocal choice are other considerations that help simultaneously to explain and qualify the perception and even the reality of private effectiveness as gauged by common indicators. One is that private organizations frequently select less difficult missions. We have already seen how private missions tend to be more specialized; the point here is that it is easier to be successful when one undertakes simpler tasks. It is more difficult to attend to a heterogeneous constituency. It is especially challenging to try to produce high test grades or secure enviable future educational and job placements for students who are from lower SES backgrounds and are often less educationally prepared. The same could be said of trying to achieve success in a wide range of curricula options, including expensive ones, as opposed to focusing on a few inexpensive ones. If society demands that an educational task be attempted, the private sector may have an option, the public sector a responsibility. The public sector more often tackles the difficult tasks, even the dirty work. In short, private-sector effectiveness often depends on public-sector coverage.

Choice must be seen in this context. Although private sectors are continually hailed for providing choice, it is unclear which sector generally provides more.[26] There is a pronounced tendency to take for granted the public sector and the choices it offers; the private sector is then regarded as the welcome addition. In truth, it is less the amount than the *contours of choice* that differ in characteristic ways between the sectors. Individual public organizations usually offer *more* choice than individual private ones, whereas interorganizational distinctiveness among the latter produces choice within the sector. Therefore, although certain efforts to explain the creation of nonprofit private organizations postulate that these organizations offer something over the average that the public as a whole supports or receives, and there is evidence for that proposition in education (for example, in providing elite quality), there is also a strong sense in which private organizations provide *less* than the mean. This, of course, relates to the often heard normative reservations (for example, on elitism or racism) about the chosen exclusiveness of private organizational pursuits. Moreover, expanded choice for some in the private sector can lessen choice for others in the public sector. Where, for example, private institutions are socially or academically elite, they may in effect limit the options of public students regarding social interaction, further educational opportunities, and job selection.[27]

The Finance-Governance-Mission-Effectiveness Nexus

In wrapping up this exploration into the roots of private-public contrasts in *effectiveness*, we can logically bring together prior points about our other major categories—finance, governance, and mission.[28] Strong bases of private effectiveness lie in the specialism we have found repeatedly in restrictively but deeply based finance, in narrowly concentrated governance, and in selectively limited mission. And a powerfully reinforcing basis lies in the comparatively coherent, tight connection among the three in the mutually reinforcing interactions among income sources, power holders, and chosen missions. In all this, we usually find the most persuasive explanations, both unflattering (elitism) and flattering (choice and commitment) for private effectiveness.

Private organizations are more likely than public ones to have identifiably chosen missions, backed by a centralized power structure, itself integrally tied to (if not largely overlapping) the key financial actors.[29] There is less propensity for conflict or countervailing tendencies as one comes closer (than in public organizations) to choosing the characteristics he desires, whether as student, parent, teacher, administrator, or donor. Fundamentally contradictory demands are therefore relatively rare—and can be dealt with convincingly—as organizational legitimacy rests less on voice and debate than on faithfulness to known and chosen orientations. In this connection, even the very narrow conceptions of morality that dominate in many private organizations—whether Mexico's socially very conservative Autonomous University of Guadalajara or a segregationist academy in the United States—are preserved, indeed, nurtured, more than coercively imposed (Skerry 1980, 24; Nevin & Bills 1976, 18). Furthermore, paying customers, and donors, expect a level of dedication to chosen missions and usually retain the governance reigns to secure the type of personnel who fit and promote these (Kraushaar 1972, 155–56, 182, 267; El-Khawas 1976, 38; Nevin & Bills 1976, 129; Erickson 1986), to ensure what Salganik and Karweit (1982, 155) call a "coherent set of attributes." Even in U.S. higher education, where the private-public differences tend to be less than in our other educational settings, Geiger (1986a) emphasizes the tight links between the financial services private institutions must seek and the distinctive purposes and intimate environment they must champion, in contrast to public counterparts, which are more loosely connected to majoritarian pursuits. Shils (1973, 15) points out that the private research universities (in many ways the broadest institutions in the private sector and the ones most tied to government) "tend to have their centres of initiative and decision within themselves to a greater extent than is the case among the state universities, even the most eminent."

Although there are also linkages among finance, governance, and mission in public organizations, they are characteristically looser than in their private counterparts. The "state" and the "public" tend to be nebulous concepts, as ill-defined as they are wide ranging. Commitment is comparatively broad and thin. And so, frequently, is accountability. Private accountability is usually more defined, focused, direct; based on some understanding of mutual choice, it diminishes the importance of autonomy and the legitimacy of conflicting voices among various actors within the sector.[30] Consequently, generalizations concerning the relative ambiguity of educational (especially university) organizations, as opposed to other organizations (Weick 1976; Clark 1983, 18–26), apply better to public than private ones. Similarly, I read Meyer's work (1983, 182–83, 190–92) on the "loose coupling" within educational organizations, involving structures and activities, means and ends, policies and outcomes, as much more characteristic of the public than the private institutions I have considered, a contrast consistent with Meyer's belief that decoupling is often an adaptive strategy to cope with the complex layerings of governance associated earlier with the public sector.

Conclusion

Thematic attention to salient private-public comparisons leaves us with the question of how much characteristics normally associated with one sector can thrive in the other. For example, as Levin (1983, 31–34) points out, there already are a greater number of options available within the public school sector than most people think. One illustration cited above concerned New York City's special public high schools—with noteworthy specializations (like music or science) in mission and with selection procedures that diverge from the public school norm, creating a comparatively narrow environment with deep commitment and often achieving great effectiveness (Doyle & Cooper 1983). Other alternative public schools are also relevant (Campbell et al. 1980, 423–48), including magnet schools, which attract students from different neighborhoods to something distinctive. Yet nearly all tendencies found within a complex real world yield important exceptions, and one is struck by the absence of more such public schools around the nation. Additionally, evidence from Latin American higher education suggests, amid such great disenchantment with public institutions, that the implantation into public institutions of many characteristics (like tuition) associated with private ones has usually produced disappointing results, though sometimes mixed ones. It appears that public policy cannot easily alter the private-public distinctions examined here by experimenting in the public sector with certain characteristics more associated with the private sector.[31]

In practice, private-public differences have diminished, or blurred, less as a result of the public sector emulating the private one than the private one "becoming more public." And public policy, especially through increased funding and regulation, has provided much of the thrust. The relevant evidence in this chapter comes mostly from U.S. education at all levels, though Western European education, especially primary and secondary (Neave 1983; Rust 1982; Mason 1983) would provide even more potent corroboration, sustained by higher education transformations in nations such as Belgium and the Netherlands (Geiger 1986b). Latin American higher education has provided much less evidence, at least partly because most private universities are still comparatively new.

Future transformations and relevant policy issues notwithstanding, this chapter has emphasized empirically contrasting private-public patterns, trying to identify and understand them. Most important, it has found private-public differences to be substantial, despite intrasectoral variation, intersectoral similarities, and intersectoral blurring over time. These differences hold for all three educational contexts explored, especially for Latin American higher education and U.S. schools. The parallels found across disparate educational, social, economic, and political contexts suggest that the identified patterns are not random ones but are logically (though by no means inevitably) associated with privateness and publicness, a conclusion that apparently would be strongly promoted by the inclusion of additional geographic regions.[32] Private-public distinctions do make—or at least mark—crucial differences at both the institutional and the sectoral levels.[33]

Naturally, it is easier to identify than to conceptualize the private-public tendencies discussed here. Nonetheless, scope (as well as related concepts) seems to advance our understanding. Where private and public educational sectors differ, which is not always but often, those differences can be conceived of largely in terms of the scope found in finance, governance, mission, and effectiveness. The core in each of these categories tends to be more specialized and concentrated in the individual private than public organization, with private breadth and diversity attainable at the sectoral level through the aggregation of differentiated organizations. All this points to contrasting bases on which private and public should be understood in education.

Notes

1. Obviously, different terms can connote praise (for example, coherence, breadth) or criticism (narrowness, ambiguity), but I try to use them straightforwardly.

2. The literature on for-profits is comparatively small and scattered in isolated institutional and policy reports rather than concentrated in scholarly works (Wine 1980; Trivett 1974, 48–54; Hartle 1976, 52–54; Levy 1986b, Introduction). Among other limitations not elaborated on in the text are the following: I deal only with formal teaching institutions, excluding the growing networks (often nonprofit) of nonformal, research, and interest group organizations in education. I do not compare the reasons for private and public growth nearly as much as the relevance of that comparison to scope could warrant; relatedly. I devote little attention to historically dominant private-public patterns. Additionally, I often group religious with other private institutions, not analyzing their special characteristics (Greeley 1969, 1982; Greeley, McCready, & McCourt 1976; McCluskey 1969, 1970; Bartell 1980), even though most or a very sizable minority of private enrollments are usually found in religiously affiliated institutions; U.S. schools and higher education provide respective examples. Finally, even though this chapter only selectively reviews the education literature with an eye toward private-public comparisons in scope, and even though it concentrates on only certain geographical areas, it still ranges so widely (for example, including schools and higher education cross-nationally) that its major limitations are that it suggests more than it proves and that it underplays intrasectoral variation and intersectoral similarity.

3. All information on Latin American higher education is based on Levy (1986a), so I do not include the citation repetitively. The best book I know on Latin American private schools deals with Chile (Brahm, Cariola, & Silva 1971). I have analyzed Latin America's Jewish schools as a subset of private schools that illustrate many of the private-public contrasts found in this chapter (Levy, forthcoming).

4. As the text shortly shows, private universities throughout much of Latin America have grown greatly in importance in numerical and other terms. Yet the twenty nations are varied, providing many different political, economic, and social contexts for private-public comparisons; all these contexts are

markedly different from U.S. ones, upon which most of the literature's private-public comparisons have been based. Additionally, important qualifications notwithstanding, "private" and "public" in Latin American higher education turn out to be extremely distinctive; the separate sectors are respectively characterized by striking privateness and publicness on most criteria employed to assess such qualities. More than any other major educational context I know of, this one provides fairly clear dual-sector categories from which to start.

5. These represent four of five concerns sometimes set forth as critical to Yale's Program on Non-Profit Organizations (Simon 1980, 5–11). Deleted is the power dilemma—how much nonprofits can or shall have power over decision making in the public and for-profit sectors.

6. While it is important to point out (Murnane 1986a) that Coleman's recent work contrasts with his influential earlier work that cast doubt on the impacts that schools make (Coleman 1966; also Jencks et al. 1973), contrasts in achievement scores would be far from the most crucial ways in which schools "make a difference." It is interesting that Coleman himself (as expressed in panel discussion comments at the Conference Comparing Public and Private Schools, Institute for Research on Educational Finance and Governance, Stanford University, October 25–26, 1984) regards the greatest contribution of his recent work as showing—contrary to some popular notions, often about private inferiority—that there is *not* a terribly decisive private versus public effect on achievement scores, thus allowing us to explore other explanations of differential achievement and, I take it, other bases of private-public comparisons. The 1984 conference just cited provides the basis for a volume (James and Levin, forthcoming) that will be a major addition to the literature comparing public and private schools.

7. It is difficult to generalize about private shares of Western European schooling, as there is variation by nation, primary-secondary within nation, and definition of private, though private can usually be read nonprofit (Mason 1983, 1, 19). Nevertheless, we can provide a loosely aggregated sketch here. Sweden and Norway have tiny private sectors, and Denmark, Great Britain, Greece, Italy, Luxembourg, and West Germany are less than 10 percent private, France and Spain go higher, and Belgium, the Netherlands, and Ireland go over one-half private (Neave 1983, 7; Rust 1982, 30; Mason 1983, 40). Private shares are generally smaller in Western Europe *higher* education. According to most assessments, the private sector is nonexistent or under 10 percent in almost all nations; the two striking exceptions are the Netherlands 23 percent and Belgium's 69 percent (Geiger 1986b; Levy 1982). Beyond Western Europe, percentages vary widely at all educational levels. Both Asia and Africa have many school systems with private sectors under 10 percent, over 30 percent, and in between (Cooper & Doyle, forthcoming). In Latin America, the private sector has a much longer tradition at the school than at the university level; but private percentages are now lower (roughly 16 percent; 13 percent primary, 28 percent secondary) at the school level. Even outside the communist world, *higher* education varies from insignificance in most nations to 80 percent in Japan and higher in the Philippines (Geiger 1986b; Levy 1982).

8. Private-public contrasts in average institutional size would be even greater if for-profits were included, certainly in U.S. schools and higher education (Katz 1978, 9) as well as English schools (Robinson 1971, 130). Private-public contrasts in sectoral size would sharpen especially at the higher level, though much depends on how strictly we define both "higher" and "nonprofit." Higher can include multitudinous commercial schools, and nonprofit can include (as in Brazil) many small institutions that are behaviorally for-profit yet manage to retain nonprofit legal status. Clearly, in the United States and beyond, the for-profit sector is much more important at higher than at school levels. Whether U.S. corporations will be tempted to make a major effort at establishing for-profit schools (Levy 1986b, Introduction) remains to be seen.

9. To bring for-profits into the financial analysis would be to make our private-public comparisons even starker. At both school and higher education levels, this sector is the most dependent on direct client payments; government aid is minimal, especially as for-profits do not get the exemptions and tax-deductible contributions that nonprofits do (Hirschoff 1986; Encarnation 1983, 177), though they can benefit from some money given to college students. On the other hand, our private-public comparisons would blur if either tuition tax credits or vouchers were implemented (James & Levin 1983; LaNoue 1972; Levy 1986b).

10. Compared to U.S. practice, school finance in Western Europe tends to show fewer private-public differences, as most nations now give substantial aid to private schools (especially where the private enrollment percentage is high), often through direct institutional subsidization, sometimes through vouchers (Neave 1983, 1–8; Rust 1982, 17–18, 25; E. James 1986b). Nonetheless, many private schools rely heavily on tuition and some receive no government support, whereas public schools are fully funded by the government (Mason 1983, 3; Halsey, Heath, & Ridge 1980, 39; Neave 1983, 1; Rust 1982, 23). In higher

education, there is basically public funding of private institutions in the two nations where these institutions hold substantial enrollments, whereas private sectors with under 10 percent of enrollments typically rely on private funding; private-public distinctiveness is promoted, as almost all public sectors (even beyond Western Europe) are funded almost fully by government, usually through a widely standardized national role (Geiger 1986b; Levy 1982).

11. The Supreme Court struck down an Oregon law under which compulsory schooling (ages eight to sixteen) had meant public schooling only (Tyack 1968).

12. Of course, local control can mean different things in the two sectors. Much of the literature has explored how democratic the public sector is; Dahl's classic work (1961) found notable participation, but most subsequent research has emphasized how limited public participation is compared to the role of professionals and elites (Zeigler & Jennings 1974).

13. As U.S. government regulation frequently accompanies its finance for nonprofits, so for-profits may operate with the relative absence of both. Coordinating boards, accrediting agencies, and courts have advanced the government role in for-profit higher education, but still minimally compared to what nonprofits face (Trivett 1974, 1–3, 38–42; Katz 1978, 7), though see Zumeta and Mock (1985). Another way in which for-profits add to the private-public contrasts in governance concerns their direct accountability to their owners, and their internal centralization, even authoritarian hierarchy, with little internal distribution of power (Katz 1978, 13); the principal of a for-profit school is less likely than his nonprofit counterpart to share power even with a governing board. In higher education, at least, these basic contrasts can be extended beyond the United States, where legally (for example, the Philippines; Geiger 1986b), and behaviorally (Brazil) for-profit institutions exist.

14. Private-public governance differences in Western Europe are limited by governments' extensive regulations over most of the private sectors it heavily subsidizes, usually the ones with the widest enrollment breadth (Neave 1983, 5–11; Rust 1982, 16, 19). However, this leaves considerable power with some private schools and their headmasters, and many nations free private schools from the public school stipulation of religious neutrality; moreover, on the Continent more than in Great Britain, the public sector is very widely controlled by standardized national government policy (Neave 1983, 3, 12–13; Mason 1983, 1–2). In higher education as well, we see some correlation between government finance and regulation of private sectors (though the relationship is by no means uniform), while also seeing (especially if we add some Asian cases) authority vested in boards or trustees orienting their institutions to specific constituencies (Geiger 1986b). Once again private-public contrasts are sustained in part because the public sector is typically so much more standardized to national government authority than in the United States (Clark 1983).

15. There are also striking private-public contrasts, beyond fields of study, concerning job markets. Private graduates are much more likely to seek employment in private enterprises, whereas public graduates have long depended heavily on government bureaucracies.

16. On Canadian counterparts to the kind of elite schools Baird (1977) discusses, see Gossage (1977); Gossage notes the limited enrollments, "independent" self-designation, nonprofit status, high tuition, absence of government subsidies, autonomous power through a private board, old-boy connections, and attractiveness as an alternative to decreasingly satisfying public schools.

17. The view more cited in this essay is that the public sector has opened up (contributing to an exit by previously more satisfied groups). Another view, whose proponents have included Milton Friedman and James Coleman, holds that increased economic segregation by neighborhoods has increased the exclusiveness of individual public schools.

18. Furthermore, clientele differences are greater within than across sectors (El-Khawas 1976, 23; Monroe 1977, 1–13; Jonsen 1978, 9) and have been diminished by government regulation.

19. For-profit higher education weakens the private-public tendencies established here insofar as its students include a comparatively high percentage of minority and of less academically oriented students (Trivett 1974, 27–31). With its vocational orientations, for-profit institutions worldwide probably often attract a relatively low SES profile within the higher education context. On the other hand, the SES scope of individual institutions may still be narrow. More generally, most missions undertaken by for-profits are notable for their specificity and narrowness. They typically offer a limited curriculum, perhaps only one or a few disciplinary specializations, little general education, and "very limited services" (Katz 1978, 5, 8–9). Preparing students quickly for jobs is a major and measurable goal well suited to the profit motive (Trivett 1974, 16–17). The specific focus on job preparation to the exclusion of so many other missions pursued by nonprofits and especially public institutions, appears to characterize for-profit higher and school education outside the United States as well as in England (Robinson 1971, 129).

20. Although Western European public upper-secondary schools sometimes specialize more than comprehensive U.S. high schools (Clark 1984), most Western European private schools can choose more defined and narrow tasks than public schools. Religion has been critical, but political orientations, SES, and gender have also been factors (E. James 1986b; Mason 1983, 12; Halsey, Heath, & Ridge 1980). Also in higher education, alongside intersectoral similarities in missions where there is substantial government finance and regulation of private institutions that have relatively broad missions, peripheral private institutions generally choose niches with explicitly limited purposes (for example, preparation for business employment). As in finance and governance, a major factor producing private-public distinctiveness along lines related to scope concerns the role of national ministries in the public sector—the preoccupation, mostly alien to U.S. policy, for standardization (for example, in degrees granted and in civil service procedures) across public institutions.

21. In Colombia, for example, the private Los Andes and Javeriana universities could easily rank at the top, but Colombia also has many private universities of abysmal quality, offering its poorly prepared students few facilities or opportunities for learning; although many public universities share the low ground, others are above it.

22. I have no idea about the effectiveness of for-profit educational organizations, except in regard to academic stature for higher education. As one would expect from their SES compositions, they tend to achieve little academic prestige. Indeed, both in the United States (Trivett 1974, 4) and beyond, the question more often concerns academic legitimacy. Clearly, however, this does not mean that they are failing in their chosen missions.

23. Contrary to a widespread feeling that Catholic educational organizations have not been contributing to Catholic values, research has produced mixed to encouraging results (Greeley 1969; Greeley, McCready, & McCourt 1976).

24. I thank John Meyer (personal correspondence, November 1984) for highlighting this difference between private and public support. In fact, Meyer goes further when he argues that we should see school success at least partly as it is truly gauged and rewarded in the political process—by work or output less than by social and ritualistic functions; from this perspective, U.S. schools have generally been quite successful (Meyer & Rowan 1983a, 73, 92; Meyer 1983, 182). I would guess that this insight is applicable more to the public than the private sector, with the latter more likely to set and be measured by explicit work and performance standards.

25. On the other hand, to regard greater public than private survival rates as showing greater effectiveness is to use an indicator biased against the private sector, as specialist organizations assume the risks that often go with "putting all eggs in one basket."

26. Before we control for its greater size, the public sector would usually have a substantial edge. An argument that has been made for both Latin American and U.S. higher education (Shils 1973, 29) is that the private sector's effective pursuit of certain specific goals helps preserve the public sector's ability to pursue broader functions.

27. Probing the quality/effectiveness issue, Halsey, Heath, and Ridge (1980, 210–13) find that British students in private schools do better, even controlling for material aspects of the home environment, but they believe that "*unmeasured*" (their italics) attitudes at home shape propensities (at least of primary school students) in an intersectorally significant way, as seen by sibling comparisons between the two sectors. In a follow-up article, the authors (forthcoming) conclude that "private education conferred some, albeit small, educational advantage" for a privileged cohort group, but they could not tell how much selectivity and home effects, as opposed to school effects, were responsible. Also see E. James (1986b) and Mason (1983, 3) on the roots of perceived private effectiveness in the Dutch and other Western European cases, respectively. In higher education, Geiger's eight-nation study, with four Western European cases, (1986a) concludes that neither the private nor the public sector has a consistent edge in quality, but that private institutions do tend to innovate and respond to environmental stimuli more readily and that public action is more contingent on government action.

28. The varied and complex interrelationships in the nexus suggest to me that caution is warranted in tracing the roots of specialism or generalism to any one aspect. For example, we could say that certain institutions start with narrow missions and that this has implications for their financial base and governance structure. But others may see the process starting more on the governance side, as the state preempts most of the space for its public institutions, leaving private institutions as the leftovers that face the problems/opportunities of specialists with narrow niches. A particular danger in this second approach, however, is that it *may* assume a sequence and causality that does not operate, as when private institutions arise simultaneously or even before public ones. More generally, the partial validity of each of several such approaches argues for restraint in identifying just one as central.

29. Corollaries to such tendencies help explain the substantial association of privateness and small size. Thus, while small size relates to limited scope, that is a private-public factor. Additionally, much of our evidence links privateness with comparatively limited scope even when we control for size.

30. Where one dimension widens in scope it is likely that others will as well. Thus, among Latin American private universities, Catholic ones most often receive government money—and most often have the widest participatory governance base and offer the widest variety of fields of study. And of the three educational contexts considered here, U.S. higher education offers the most evidence of how a broadening in one category is likely to be accompanied by a broadening in others and by some loosening in the finance-governance-mission nexus; yet even the U.S. higher education context would be a weak example alongside Western European schooling.

31. Such general observations cast doubt on how much the private sector truly innovates in ways that serve as models for the public sector, but they also leave substantially open the vital questions of the *degree* to which valued private characteristics could be extended through public policy decisions, or how the public sector is affected by the private sector's presence. See, for example, how Coleman, Hoffer, and Kilgore (1981, 538–45; 1982b, 162–64) respond to those who dismiss the implications they derive regarding policies that affect achievement. At an extreme, Kraushaar (1972, 317) concludes: "In short, if there were no private schools, people would have to create them." Paradoxically, this could be true if publics really do learn from privates *or* if they do not and only privates can achieve certain goals.

32. For example, five or six (depending on how one assesses Belgium) of Geiger's seven non-U.S. higher education cases show considerable private-public differentiation (1986b).

33. Moreover, private-public differences would have been even more substantial had the for-profit sector been integrally included with the nonprofit sector in this analysis.

References

Astin, Alexander W., and Calvin B. T. Lee. 1972. *The Invisible Colleges: A Profile of Small Liberal Arts Colleges with Limited Resources.* New York: Carnegie Foundation for the Advancement of Teaching.

Baird, Leonard L. 1977. *The Elite Schools: A Profile of Prestigious Independent Schools.* Lexington, Mass.: D. C. Heath.

Baldridge, Victor J., David V. Curtis, George Ecker, and Gary Riley. 1978. *Policy Making and Effective Leadership: A National Study of Academic Management.* San Francisco: Jossey-Bass.

Bartell, Rev. Ernest, C.S.C. 1980. *Enrollment, Finances, and Student Aid at Catholic Colleges and Universities.* Washington, D.C.: Association of Catholic Colleges and Universities.

Berdahl, Robert O. 1975. *Evaluating Statewide Boards: New Directions for Educational Research.* San Francisco: Jossey-Bass.

———. 1978. "The Politics of State Aid." In D. W. Breneman and C. E. Finn, Jr., eds. *Public Policy and Private Higher Education,* 321–52. Washington, D.C.: Brookings Institution.

Bok, Derek. 1980. "The Federal Government and the University." *Public Interest* 58:80–101.

Brahm, Luis A., Patricia Cariola, and Juan José Silva, eds. 1971. *Educación Particular en Chile.* Santiago: Centro de Investigación y Desarrollo de la Educación.

Breneman, David W., and Chester E. Finn, Jr., eds. 1978. *Public Policy and Private Higher Education.* Washington, D.C.: Brookings Institution.

Buckley, William F. 1977. Introduction to *God and Man at Yale.* South Bend, Ind.: Gateway Editions, 1951.

Campbell, Ronald F., Luvern L. Cunningham, Raphael O. Nystrand, and Michael D. Usdan. 1980. "Alternative Schools." In *The Organization and Control of American Schools,* 423–48. Columbus: Charles E. Merrill Co.

Carnegie Council on Policy Studies in Higher Education. 1975a. *Making Affirmative Action Work in Higher Education.* San Francisco: Jossey-Bass.

———. 1975b. *The Federal Role in Postsecondary Education.* San Francisco: Jossey-Bass.

———. 1976a. *A Classification of Institutions of Higher Education.* Berkeley, Calif.: Carnegie Foundation for the Advancement of Teaching.

———. 1976b. *The States and Higher Education.* San Francisco: Jossey-Bass.

———. 1977. *The States and Private Higher Education.* San Francisco: Jossey-Bass.

Cartter, Allan. 1966: *An Assessment of Quality in Graduate Education.* Washington, D.C.: American Council on Education.

Catterall, James S. 1984. "Private School Participation and Public Policy." Paper presented at the Conference on Public and Private Schools and Educational Policy, Stanford University, October 25–26.

Chambers, Jay G. 1984. "Patterns of Compensation of Public and Private School Teachers." Stanford University, Project Report no. 84–A18 of the Institute for Research on Educational Finance and Governance.

Clark, Burton R. 1972. "The Organizational Saga in Higher Education." *Administrative Science Quarterly* 17:178–83.

———. 1983. *The Higher Education System: Academic Organization in Cross-National Perspective.* Berkeley: University of California Press.

———. 1984. "The School and the University: What Went Wrong in America." Paper presented at the Rockefeller Institute of Government Policy Forum, Albany, N.Y.

Coleman, James S. 1966. *Report on Equality of Educational Opportunity.* Washington, D.C.: U.S. Government Printing Office.

———. 1984. "Public and Private Schools beyond Achievement." Paper presented at the 140th anniversary of the SUNY at Albany School of Education, September 21, Albany, N.Y.

Coleman, James S., Thomas Hoffer, and Sally Kilgore. 1981. "Questions and Answers: Our Response." *Harvard Educational Review* 51:526–45.

———. 1982a. "Achievement and Segregation in Secondary Schools: A Further Look at Public and Private School Differences." *Sociology of Education* 55:162–82.

———. 1982b. *High School Achievement: Public, Catholic and Private Schools Compared.* New York: Basic Books.

Commission on Academic Tenure in Higher Education. 1973. *Faculty Tenure.* San Francisco: Jossey-Bass.

Coons, John E., and Stephen D. Sugarman. 1978. *Education by Choice: The Case For Family Control.* Berkeley: University of California Press.

Cooper, Bruce S. 1984. "The Changing Demography of Private Schools: Trends and Implications." *Education and Urban Society* 16:429–42.

Cooper, Bruce S., and Denis P. Doyle. Forthcoming. "Private Schools, Worldwide." In *International Encyclopedia of Education.* London: Pergamon Press.

Cooper, Bruce S., Donald H. McLaughlin, and Bruno V. Manno. 1983. "The Latest Word on Private-School Growth." *Teacher College Record* 85:88–98.

Cyert, Richard M., ed. 1975. "Public and Private Higher Education." In *The Management of Nonprofit Organizations,* 45–52. Lexington, Mass.: D. C. Heath.

Dahl, Robert A. 1961. *Who Governs?* New Haven: Yale University Press.

Doyle, Denis, and Bruce S. Cooper, 1983. "Is Excellence Possible in Urban Public Schools?" *American Education* 19, no. 9:16–26.

El-Khawas, Elaine H. 1976. *Public and Private Higher Education: Differences in Role, Character, and Clientele.* Washington, D.C.: American Council on Education.

Elson, John. 1969. "State Regulation of Nonpublic Schools: The Legal Framework." Pp. 103–34 In D. A. Erickson, ed., *Public Controls for Nonpublic Schools,* 103–34, Chicago: University of Chicago Press.

Encarnation, Dennis J. 1983. "Public Financing and Regulation of Nonpublic Education: Retrospect and Prospect." In T. James and H. M. Levin, eds., *Public Dollars for Private Schools,* 175–95. Philadelphia: Temple University Press.

Epstein, Leon D. 1974. *Governing the University.* San Francisco: Jossey-Bass.

Erickson, Donald A. 1986. "Choice and Private Schools: Dynamics of Supply and Demand." In D. C. Levy, ed., *Private Education: Studies in Choice and Public Policy.* New York: Oxford University Press.

Erickson, Donald A., ed. 1969. *Public Controls for Nonpublic Schools.* Chicago: University of Chicago Press.

Esty, John C. 1974. *Choosing a Private School.* New York: Dodd, Mead.

Everhart, Robert B., ed. *The Public School Monopoly: A Critical Analysis of Education and the State in American Society.* Cambridge, Mass.: Ballinger.

Gaffney, Edward McGlynn, Jr., ed. 1981. *Private Schools and the Public Good.* Notre Dame: University of Notre Dame Press.

Geiger, Roger L. 1986a. "Finance and Function: Voluntary Support and Diversity in American Private Higher Education." In Daniel C. Levy, ed., *Private Education: Studies in Choice and Public Policy.* New York: Oxford University Press.

———. 1986b. *Private Sectors in Higher Education: Structure, Function, and Change in Eight Countries.* Ann Arbor: University of Michigan Press.

Glazer, Nathan. 1983. "The Future under Tuition Tax Credits." In T. James and H. M. Levin, eds., *Public Dollars for Private Schools*, 87–100. Philadelphia: Temple University Press.

Goodman, Paul. 1962. *Compulsory Mis-education and the Community of Scholars.* New York: Vintage Books.

Gossage, Carolyn. 1977. *A Question of Privilege: Canada's Independent Schools.* Toronto: Peter Martin Associates.

Grant, Gerald, and David Riesman. 1978. *The Perpetual Dream: Reform and Experiment in American Education.* Chicago: University of Chicago Press.

Greeley, Andrew M. 1967. *The Changing Catholic College.* Chicago: Aldine Publishing Co.

———. 1969. *From Backwater to Mainstream: A Profile of Catholic Education.* New York: McGraw Hill.

———. 1981. "Catholic High Schools and Minority Students." In E. M. Gaffney, Jr., ed., *Private Schools and the Public Good*, 3–16. Notre Dame: University of Notre Dame Press.

———. 1982. *Catholic High Schools and Minority Students.* New Brunswick, N.J.: Transaction Books.

Greeley, Andrew M., William C. McCready, and Kathleen McCourt. 1976. *Catholic Schools in a Declining Church.* Kansas City: Sheed & Ward.

Halsey, A. H., A. F. Heath, and J. M. Ridge. 1980. *Origins and Destinations: Family, Class, and Education in Modern Britain.* Oxford: Oxford University Press.

———. Forthcoming. "The Political Arithmetic of Public Schools." In G. Waltford, ed., *The British Public Schools.* London: Falmer Press.

Hannan, Michael T., and John H. Freeman. 1978. "The Population Ecology of Organizations." In Marshall W. Meyer and associates, *Environment and Organizations*, 131–71. San Francisco: Jossey-Bass.

Hartle, Terry. 1976. *Recent Research on Private Higher Education.* Washington, D.C.: American Council on Education.

Hirschman, Albert O. 1970. *Exit, Voice, and Loyalty: Responses to Decline in Firms, Organizations, and States.* Cambridge, Mass.: Harvard University Press.

Hirschoff, Mary-Michelle Upson. 1986. "Public Policy toward Private Schools: A Focus on Parental Choice." In D. C. Levy, ed., *Private Education: Studies in Choice and Public Policy.* New York: Oxford University Press.

James, Estelle, 1986a. "Cross-Subsidization in Higher Education: Does it Pervert Private Choice and Public Policy?" In D. C. Levy, ed., *Private Education: Studies in Choice and Public Policy.* New York: Oxford University Press.

———. 1986b. "Public Subsidies for Private and Public Education: The Dutch Case." In Levy, ed., *Private Education.*

James, Thomas. 1983. "Questions about Educational Choice: An Argument from History." In T. James and H. M. Levin, eds., *Public Dollars for Private Schools*, 55–70. Philadelphia: Temple University Press.

James, Thomas, and Henry M. Levin, eds. 1983. *Public Dollars for Private Schools.* Philadelphia: Temple University Press.

———. Forthcoming. *Comparing Public and Private Schools.* London: Falmer Press.

Jellama, William. 1973. *From Red to Black? The Financial Status of Private Colleges and Universities.* San Francisco: Jossey-Bass.

Jencks, Christopher, et al. 1973. *Inequality: A Reassessment of the Effect of Family and Schooling in America.* London: Allen Lane.

Jencks, Christopher, and David Riesman. 1968. *The Academic Revolution.* Garden City, N.Y.: Doubleday.

Jonsen, Richard W. 1978. *Small Liberal Arts Colleges: Diversity at the Crossroads?* AAHE–ERIC/Higher Education Research Report no. 4. Washington, D.C.: American Association of Higher Education.

Kaplin, William A. 1978. *The Law of Higher Education.* San Francisco: Jossey-Bass.

Katz, Neil. 1978. "A Review of the Literature on Non-Profit Organizations in Higher Education." Unpublished manuscript, SUNY at Stony Brook.

Keeton, Morris T. 1971. *Models and Mavericks.* New York: McGraw Hill.

Kendall, Elaine. 1975. *Peculiar Institutions.* New York: G. P. Putnam's Sons.

Kershaw, Joseph. 1976. *The Very Small College.* New York: Ford Foundation.

Kraushaar, Otto F. 1972. *American Non-Public Schools: Patterns of Diversity.* Baltimore: Johns Hopkins University Press.

Kutner, Mark, Joel D. Sherman, and Mary Williams. 1986. "Federal Policies for Private Schools." In D. C. Levy, ed., *Private Education: Studies in Choice and Public Policy.* New York: Oxford University Press.

LaNoue, George R., ed. 1972. *Educational Vouchers: Concepts and Controversies.* New York: Teachers College Press.

Levin, Henry M. 1983. "Educational Choice and the Pains of Democracy." In T. James and H. M. Levin, eds., *Public Dollars for Private Schools,* 17–38. Philadelphia: Temple University Press.

Levy, Daniel C. 1982. "Private versus Public Financing of Higher Education: U.S. Policy in Comparative Perspective." *Higher Education* 11:607–28.

———. Forthcoming. "Jewish Education in Latin America: Challenges to Autonomy and Group Identity." In J. Elkin and G. Merkx, eds., *The Jewish Presence in Latin America.* Winchester, Mass.: Allen & Unwin.

———. 1986a. *Higher Education and the State in Latin America: Private Challenges to Public Dominance.* Chicago: University of Chicago Press.

Levy, Daniel C., ed. 1986b. *Private Education: Studies in Choice and Public Policy.* New York: Oxford University Press.

McCluskey, Neil. 1969. *Catholic Education Faces Its Future.* Garden City, N.Y.: Doubleday.

McCluskey, Neil G., ed. 1970. *The Catholic University: A Modern Appraisal.* Notre Dame: University of Notre Dame Press.

McCoy, Marilyn, and D. Kent Halstead. 1979. *Higher Education Financing in the Fifty States: Interstate Comparisons Fiscal Year 1976.* Washington, D.C.: National Institute of Education.

McCready, William C. 1977. "Parochial Schools: The 'Free Choice' Alternative." In James S. Coleman et al., *Parents, Teachers, and Children: Prospects for Choice in American Education,* 67–75. San Francisco: Institute for Contemporary Studies.

McPartland, James M., and Edward L. McDill. 1982. "Control and Differentiation in the Structure of American Education." *Sociology of Education* 55:77–88.

Mason, Peter. 1983. *Private Education in the EEC.* London: National Independent and Schools Information Service.

Meyer, John W. 1983. "Centralization of Funding and Control in Educational Governance." In J. W. Meyer and W. R. Scott, eds., *Organizational Environments: Ritual and Rationality,* 179–98. Berkeley, Calif.: Sage.

Meyer, John W., Francisco Ramírez, Richard Robinson, and John Boli-Bennett. 1977. "The World Educational Revolution, 1950–1970." *Sociology of Education* 50:242–58.

Meyer, John W., and W. Richard Scott, eds. 1983. *Organizational Environments: Ritual and Rationality.* Berkeley, Calif.: Sage.

Meyer, John W., and Brian Rowan. 1983a. "Institutionalized Organizations: Formal Structure as Myth and Ceremony." In Meyer and Scott, eds., *Organizational Environments,* 21–44.

———. 1983b. "The Structure of Educational Organizations." In Meyer and Scott, eds., *Organizational Environments,* 71–98.

Millett, John D. 1973. "Similarities and Differences among Universities of the United States." In James A. Perkins, ed., *The University as an Organization,* 39–56. New York: McGraw Hill.

Minter, W. John, and Howard R. Bowen. 1978. *Independent Higher Education.* Washington, D.C.: American Association of American Colleges.

Monroe, Charles. 1977. *Profile of the Community College.* San Francisco: Jossey-Bass.

Mortimer, Kenneth P., and T. R. McConnell, 1978. *Sharing Authority Effectively.* San Francisco: Jossey-Bass.

Murnane, Richard J. 1986a. "Comparisons of Private and Public Schools: The Critical Role of Regulations." In D. C. Levy, ed., *Private Education: Studies in Choice and Public Policy.* New York: Oxford University Press.

———. 1986b. "Comparisons of Private and Public Schools: What Can We Learn?" In Levy, ed., *Private Education.*

Neave, Guy. 1983. "The Non-State Sector in the Education Provision of Member States of the European Community." Internal memo to the Educational Services of the Commission of the European Communities, Brussels.

Nelson, Susan C. 1978. "Financial Trends and Issues." In D. W. Breneman and C. E. Finn, Jr., eds., *Public Policy and Private Higher Education,* 63–142. Washington, D.C.: Brookings Institution.

Nevin, David, and Robert E. Bills. 1976. *The Schools that Fear Built: Segregationist Academies in the South.* Washington, D.C.: Acropolis Books.

Nisbet, Robert A. 1971. *The Degradation of the Academic Dogma.* New York: Basic Books.

Odell, Morgan, and John Thelin. 1981. "Bringing the Independent Sector into Statewide Higher Education Planning." *Policy Studies Journal* 10:59–70.

Pace, Robert C. 1974. *The Demise of Diversity? A Comparison of Eight Types of Institutions.* New York: McGraw Hill.

Pfnister, Allan O., and Martin J. Finkelstein. 1984. "Introduction." *Journal of Higher Education* 55:117–21.

Ramírez, Francisco O., and Richard Robinson. 1979. "Creating Members: The Political Incorporation and Expansion of Public Education." In John W. Meyer and Michael Hannan, eds., *National Development and the World System.* Chicago: University of Chicago Press.

Robinson, Gordon. 1971. *Private Schools and Public Policy.* Loughborough, England: Loughborough University of Technology.

Roose, Kenneth D., and Charles J. Anderson. 1971. *A Rating of Graduate Programs.* Washington, D.C.: American Council on Education.

Rusk, James, and Larry Leslie. 1978. "The Setting of Tuition in Public Higher Education." *Journal of Higher Education* 49:531–47.

Rust, Val D. 1982. "Public Funding of Private Schooling: European Perspectives." *Private School Quarterly*, Winter, pp. 11–34.

Salganik, Laura Hersh, and Nancy Karweit. 1982. "Voluntarism and Governance in Education." *Sociology of Education* 55:152–61.

Scott, Richard W., and John W. Meyer. 1983. "The Organization of Societal Sectors." In Meyer and Scott, eds., *Organizational Environments: Ritual and Rationality*, 129–54. Berkeley, Calif.: Sage.

———. 1984. "Environmental Linkages and Organizational Complexity: Public and Private Schools." Stanford University, Project Report 84–A16 of the Institute for Research on Educational Finance and Governance.

Shils, Edward. 1973. "The American Private University." *Minerva* 11:6–29.

Silber, John. 1975. "Paying the Bill for College: The Private Sector and the Public Interest." *Atlantic Monthly* 235:33–40.

Simon, John G. 1980. *Research on Philanthropy.* An Independent Sector Research Report. Washington, D.C.: Independent Sector.

Sizer, Theodore R. 1984. *Horace's Compromise: The Dilemma of the American High School.* Boston: Houghton Mifflin.

Skerry, Peter. 1980. "Christian Schools versus the I.R.S." *Public Interest* 61:18–41.

Sullivan, Daniel J. 1974. *Public Aid to Nonpublic Schools.* Lexington, Mass.: D. C. Heath.

Trivett, David A. 1974. *Proprietary Schools and Postsecondary Education.* Washington, D.C.: ERIC Clearing House on Higher Education Research Report.

Tyack, David B. 1968. "The Perils of Pluralism: The Background of the Pierce Case." *American Historical Review* 74:74–98.

Vitullo-Martin, Thomas. 1981. "How Federal Policies Discourage the Racial and Economic Integration of Private Schools." In E. M. Gaffney, ed., *Private Schools and the Public Good*, 25–43. Notre Dame: University of Notre Dame Press.

Weick, Karl E. 1976. "Educational Organizations as Loosely Coupled Systems." *Administrative Science Quarterly* 21:1–19.

Weintraub, Frederick J. 1981. "Nonpublic Schools and the Education of the Handicapped." In E. M. Gaffney, ed., *Private Schools and the Public Good*, 49–55. Notre Dame: University of Notre Dame Press.

Williams, Mary Frase, Linda Addison, Kimberly Small Hancher, Amy Hutner, Mark A. Kutner, Joel D. Sherman, and Esther O. Tron. 1983. "Private Elementary and Secondary Education." Vol. 2 of a final report to Congress of the Congressionally Mandated Study of School Finance, July.

Williams, J. Douglas. 1984. "Public and Private School Outcomes: Results from the High School and Beyond Follow-up Study." Stanford University, Program no. 84–B4 of the Institute for Research on Educational Finance and Governance.

Wine, Mary B. 1980. *Bibliography on Proprietary Postsecondary Education.* Washington, D.C.: Association of Independent Colleges and Schools.

Wirt, Frederick M., and Michael W. Kirst. 1982. *Schools in Conflict.* Berkeley, Calif.: McCutchan.

Zeigler, Harmon, and M. Kent Jennings. 1974. *Governing American Schools: Political Interaction in Local Districts.* North Scituate, Mass.: Duxbury.

Zumeta, William, and Carol Mock. 1985. "State Policy and Private Higher Education: A Preliminary Research Report." Paper presented at the Association for the Study of Higher Education meetings, March 16, Chicago.

Part III

Administrative and Governance Models

STATEMENT ON GOVERNMENT OF COLLEGES AND UNIVERSITIES

AMERICAN ASSOCIATION OF UNIVERSITY PROFESSORS, AMERICAN COUNCIL ON EDUCATION, ASSOCIATION OF GOVERNING BOARDS OF UNIVERSITIES AND COLLEGES

Editorial Note. The Statement which follows is directed to governing board members, administrators, faculty members, students and other persons in the belief that the colleges and universities of the United States have reached a stage calling for appropriately shared responsibility and cooperative action among the components of the academic institution. The Statement is intended to foster constructive joint thought and action, both within the institutional structure and in protection of its integrity against improper intrusions.

It is not intended that the Statement serve as a blueprint for government on a specific campus or as a manual for the regulation of controversy among the components of an academic institution, although it is to be hoped that the principles asserted will lead to the correction of existing weaknesses and assist in the establishment of sound structure and procedures. The Statement does not attempt to cover relations with those outside agencies which increasingly are controlling the resources and influencing the patterns of education in other institutions of higher learning, e.g., the United States Government, the state legislatures, state commissions, interstate associations or compacts and other interinstitutional arrangements. However it is hoped that the Statement will be helpful to these agencies in their consideration of educational matters.

Students are referred to in this Statement as an institutional component coordinate in importance with trustees, administrators and faculty. There is, however, no main section on students. The omission has two causes: (1) the changes now occurring in the status of American students have plainly outdistanced the analysis by the educational community, and an attempt to define the situation without thorough study might prove unfair to student interests,[1] and (2) students do not in fact presently have a significant voice in the government of colleges and universities; it would be unseemly to obscure, by superficial equality of length of statement, what may be a serious lag entitled to separate and full confrontation. The concern for student status felt by the organizations issuing this Statement is embodied in a note "On Student Status" intended to stimulate the educational community to turn its attention to an important need.

This Statement, in preparation since 1964, is jointly formulated by the American Association of University Professors, the American Council on Education, and the Association of Governing Boards of Universities and Colleges. On October 12, 1966, the Board of Directors of the ACE took action by which the Council "recognizes the Statement as a significant step forward in the clarification of the respective roles of governing boards, faculties, and administrations," and "commends it to the institutions which are members of the Council." On October 29, 1966, the Council of the AAUP approved the Statement, recommended approval by the Fifty-Third Annual Meeting in April, 1967, and recognized

"Statement on Government of Colleges and Universities," by AAUP/ACE/AGB, reprinted with permission from *Academe*, Vol. 52, No. 4, December 1966.

that "continuing joint effort is desirable, in view of the areas left open in the jointly formulated Statement, and the dynamic changes occurring in higher education." On November 18, 1966, the Executive Committee of the AGB took action by which that organization also "recognizes the Statement as a significant step forward in the clarification of the respective roles of governing boards, faculties and administrations," and "commends it to the governing boards which are members of the Association."

I. Introduction

This Statement is a call to mutual understanding regarding the government of colleges and universities. Understanding, based on community of interest, and producing joint effort, is essential for at least three reasons. First, the academic institution, public or private, often has become less autonomous; buildings, research, and student tuition are supported by funds over which the college or university exercises a diminishing control. Legislative and executive governmental authority, at all levels, plays a part in the making of important decisions in academic policy. If these voices and forces are to be successfully heard and integrated, the academic institution must be in a position to meet them with its own generally unified view. Second, regard for the welfare of the institution remains important despite the mobility and interchange of scholars. Third, a college or university in which all the components are aware of their interdependence, of the usefulness of communication among themselves, and of the force of joint action will enjoy increased capacity to solve educational problems.

II. The Academic Institution: Joint Effort

A. Preliminary Considerations

The variety and complexity of the tasks performed by institutions of higher education produce an inescapable interdependence among governing board, administration, faculty, students and others. The relationship calls for adequate communication among these components, and full opportunity for appropriate joint planning and effort.

Joint effort in an academic institution will take a variety of forms appropriate to the kinds of situations encountered. In some instances, an initial exploration or recommendation will be made by the president with consideration by the faculty at a later stage; in other instances, a first and essentially definitive recommendation will be made by the faculty, subject to the endorsement of the president and the governing board. In still others, a substantive contribution can be made when student leaders are responsibly involved in the process. Although the variety of such approaches may be wide, at least two general conclusions regarding joint effort seem clearly warranted: (1) important areas of action involve at one time or another the initiating capacity and decision-making participation of all the institutional components, and (2) differences in the weight of each voice, from one point to the next, should be determined by reference to the responsibility of each component for the particular matter at hand, as developed hereinafter.

B. Determination of General Educational Policy

The general educational policy, i.e., the objectives of an institution and the nature, range, and pace of its efforts, is shaped by the institutional charter or by law, by tradition and historical development, by the present needs of the community of the institution, and by the professional aspirations and standards of those directly involved in its work. Every board will wish to go beyond its formal trustee obligation to conserve the accomplishment of the past and to engage seriously with the future; every faculty will seek to conduct an operation worthy of scholarly standards of learning; every administrative officer will strive to meet his charge and to attain the goals of the institution. The interests of all are coordinate and related, and unilateral effort can lead to confusion or conflict. Essential to a solution is a reasonably explicit statement on general educational policy. Operating responsibility and authority, and procedures for continuing review, should be clearly defined in regulations.

When an educational goal has been established, it becomes the responsibility primarily of the faculty to determine appropriate curriculum and procedures of student instruction.

Special considerations may require particular accommodations: (1) a publicly supported institution may be regulated by statutory provisions, and (2) a church-controlled institution may be limited by its charter or bylaws. When such external requirements influence course content and manner of instruction or research, they impair the educational effectiveness of the institution.

Such matters as major changes in the size or composition of the student body and the relative emphasis to be given to the various elements of the educational and research program should involve participation of governing board, administration and faculty prior to final decision.

C. Internal Operations of the Institution

The framing and execution of long-range plans, one of the most important aspects of institutional responsibility, should be a central and continuing concern in the academic community.

Effective planning demands that the broadest possible exchange of information and opinion should be the rule for communication among the components of a college or university. The channels of communication should be established and maintained by joint endeavor. Distinction should be observed between the institutional system of communication and the system of responsibility for the making of decisions.

A second area calling for joint effort in internal operations is that of decisions regarding existing or prospective physical resources. The board, president and faculty should all seek agreement on basic decisions regarding buildings and other facilities to be used in the educational work of the institution.

A third area is budgeting. The allocation of resources among competing demands is central in the formal responsibility of the governing board, in the administrative authority of the president, and in the educational function of the faculty. Each component should therefore have a voice in the determination of short and long-range priorities, and each should receive appropriate analyses of past budgetary experience, reports on current budgets and expenditures, and short and long-range budgetary projections. The function of each component in budgetary matters should be understood by all; the allocation of authority will determine the flow of information and the scope of participation in decisions.

Joint effort of a most critical kind must be taken when an institution chooses a new president. The selection of a chief administrative officer should follow upon cooperative search by the governing board and the faculty, taking into consideration the opinions of others who are appropriately interested. The president should be equally qualified to serve both as the executive officer of the governing board and as the chief academic officer of the institution and the faculty. His dual role requires that he be able to interpret to board and faculty the educational views and concepts of institutional government of the other. He should have the confidence of the board and the faculty.

The selection of academic deans and other chief academic officers should be the responsibility of the president with the advice of and in consultation with the appropriate faculty.

Determinations of faculty status, normally based on the recommendations of the faculty groups involved, are discussed in Part V of this Statement; but it should here be noted that the building of a strong faculty requires careful joint effort in such actions as staff selection and promotion and the granting of tenure. Joint action should also govern dismissals; the applicable principles and procedures in these matters are well established.[2]

D. External Relations of the Institution

Anyone—a member of the governing board, the president or other member of the administration, a member of the faculty, or a member of the student body or the alumni—affects the institution when he speaks of it in public. An individual who speaks unofficially should so indicate. An official spokesman for the institution, the board, the administration, the faculty, or the student body should be guided by established policy.

It should be noted that only the board speaks legally for the whole institution, although it may delegate responsibility to an agent.

The right of a board member, an administrative officer, a faculty member, or a student to speak on general educational questions or about the administration and operations of his own institution is a part of his right as a citizen and should not be abridged by the institution.[3] There exist, of course, legal bounds relating to defamation of character, and there are questions of propriety.

III. The Academic Institution: The Governing Board

The governing board has a special obligation to assure that the history of the college or university shall serve as a prelude and inspiration to the future. The board helps relate the institution to its chief community: e.g., the community college to serve the educational needs of a defined population area or group, the church-controlled college to be cognizant of the announced position of its denomination, and the comprehensive university to discharge the many duties and to accept the appropriate new challenges which are its concern at the several levels of higher education.

The governing board of an institution of higher education in the United States operates, with few exceptions, as the final institutional authority. Private institutions are established by charters; public institutions are established by constitutional or statutory provisions. In private institutions the board is frequently self-perpetuating; in public colleges and universities the present membership of a board may be asked to suggest candidates for appointment. As a whole and individually when the governing board confronts the problem of succession, serious attention should be given to obtaining properly qualified persons. Where public law calls for election of governing board members, means should be found to insure the nomination of fully suited persons, and the electorate should be informed of the relevant criteria for board membership.

Since the membership of the board may embrace both individual and collective competence of recognized weight, its advice or help may be sought through established channels by other components of the academic community. The governing board of an institution of higher education, while maintaining a general overview, entrusts the conduct of administration to the administrative officers, the president and the deans, and the conduct of teaching and research to the faculty. The board should undertake appropriate self-limitation.

One of the governing board's important tasks is to ensure the publication of codified statements that define the over-all policies and procedures of the institution under its jurisdiction.

The board plays a central role in relating the likely needs of the future to predictable resources; it has the responsibility for husbanding the endowment; it is responsible for obtaining needed capital and operating funds; and in the broadest sense of the term it should pay attention to personnel policy. In order to fulfill these duties, the board should be aided by, and may insist upon, the development of long-range planning by the administration and faculty.

When ignorance or ill-will threatens the institution or any part of it, the governing board must be available for support. In grave crises it will be expected to serve as a champion. Although the action to be taken by it will usually be on behalf of the president, the faculty, or the student body, the board should make clear that the protection it offers to an individual or a group is, in fact, a fundamental defense of the vested interests of society in the educational institution.

IV. The Academic Institution: The President

The president, as the chief executive officer of an institution of higher education, is measured largely by his capacity for institutional leadership. He shares responsibility for the definition and attainment of goals, for administrative action, and for operating the communications system which links the components of the academic community. He represents his institution to its many publics. His leadership role is supported by delegated authority from the board and faculty.

As the chief planning officer of an institution, the president has a special obligation to innovate and initiate. The degree to which a president can envision new horizons for his institution, and can persuade others to see them and to work toward them, will often constitute the chief measure of his administration.

The president must at times, with or without support, infuse new life into a department; relatedly, he may at times be required, working within the concept of tenure, to solve problems of obsolescence. The president will necessarily utilize the judgments of the faculty, but in the interest of academic standards he may also seek outside evaluations by scholars of acknowledged competence.

It is the duty of the president to see to it that the standards and procedures in operational use within the college or university conform to the policy established by the governing board and to the standards of sound academic practice. It is also incumbent on the president to insure that faculty views, including dissenting views, are presented to the board in those areas and on those issues where responsibilities are shared. Similarly the faculty should be informed of the views of the board and the administration on like issues.

The president is largely responsible for the maintenance of existing institutional resources and the creation of new resources: he has intimate managerial responsibility for a large area of nonacademic activities, he is responsible for public understanding, and by the nature of his office is the chief spokesman of his institution. In these and other areas his work is to plan, to organize, to direct, and to represent. The presidential function should receive the general support of board and faculty.

V. The Academic Institution: The Faculty

The faculty has primary responsibility for such fundamental areas as curriculum, subject matter and methods of instruction, research, faculty status, and those aspects of student life which relate to the educational process. On these matters the power of review or final decision lodged in the governing board or delegated by it to the president should be exercised adversely only in exceptional circumstances, and for reasons communicated to the faculty. It is desirable that the faculty should, following such communication, have opportunity for further consideration and further transmittal of its views to the president or board. Budgets, manpower limitations, the time element and the policies of other groups, bodies and agencies having jurisdiction over the institution may set limits to realization of faculty advice.

The faculty sets the requirements for the degrees offered in course, determines when the requirements have been met, and authorizes the president and board to grant the degrees thus achieved.

Faculty status and related matters are primarily a faculty responsibility; this area includes appointments, reappointments, decisions not to reappoint, promotions, the granting of tenure, and dismissal. The primary responsibility of the faculty for such matters is based upon the fact that its judgment is central to general educational policy. Furthermore, scholars in a particular field or activity have the chief competence for judging the work of their colleagues; in such competence it is implicit that responsibility exists for both adverse and favorable judgments. Likewise there is the more general competence of experienced faculty personnel committees having broader charge. Determinations in these matters should first be by faculty action through established procedures, reviewed by the chief academic officers with the concurrence of the board. The governing board and president should, on questions of faculty status, as in other matters where the faculty has primary responsibility, concur with the faculty judgment except in rare instances and for compelling reasons which should be stated in detail.

The faculty should actively participate in the determination of policies and procedures governing salary increases.

The chairman or head of a department, who serves as the chief representative of his department within an institution, should be selected either by departmental election or by appointment following consultation with members of the department and of related departments: appointments should normally be in conformity with department members' judgment. The chairman or department head should not have tenure in his office; his tenure as a faculty member is a matter of separate right. He should serve for a stated term but without prejudice to re-election or to reappointment by procedures which involve appropriate faculty consultation. Board, administration, and faculty should all bear in mind that the department chairman has a special obligation to build a department strong in scholarship and teaching capacity.

Agencies for faculty participation in the government of the college or university should be established at each level where faculty responsibility is present. An agency should exist for the presentation of the views of the whole faculty. The structure and procedures for faculty participation should be designed, approved and established by joint action of the components of the institution. Faculty representatives should be selected by the faculty according to procedures determined by the faculty.

The agencies may consist of meetings of all faculty members of a department, school, college, division or university system, or may take the form of faculty-elected executive committees in departments and schools and a faculty-elected senate or council for larger divisions or the institution as a whole.

Among the means of communication among the faculty, administration, and governing board now in use are: (1) circulation of memoranda and reports by board committees, the administration, and faculty committees, (2) joint *ad hoc* committees, (3) standing liaison committees, (4) membership of faculty members on administrative bodies, and (5) membership of faculty members on governing boards. Whatever the channels of communication, they should be clearly understood and observed.

On Student Status

When students in American colleges and universities desire to participate responsibly in the government of the institution they attend, their wish should be recognized as a claim to opportunity both for educational experience and for involvement in the affairs of their college or university. Ways should be found to permit significant student participation within the limits of attainable effectiveness. The obstacles to such participation are large and should not be minimized: inexperience, untested capacity, a transitory status which means that present action does not carry with it subsequent responsibility, and the inescapable fact that the other components of the institution are in a position of judgment over the students. It is important to recognize that student needs are strongly related to educational experience, both formal and informal. Students expect, and have a right to expect, that the educational process will be structured, that they will be stimulated by it to become independent adults, and that they will have effectively transmitted to them the cultural heritage of the larger society. If institutional support is to have its fullest possible meaning it should incorporate the strength, freshness of view and idealism of the student body.

The respect of students for their college or university can be enhanced if they are given at least these opportunities: (1) to be listened to in the classroom without fear of institutional reprisal for the substance of their views, (2) freedom to discuss questions of institutional policy and operation, (3) the right to academic due process when charged with serious violations of institutional regulations, and (4) the same right to hear speakers of their own choice as is enjoyed by other components of the institution.

Notes

1. Note: 1950, the formulation of the Student Bill of Rights by the United States National Student Association: 1956, the first appearance of *Academic Freedom and Civil Liberties of Students*, published by the American Civil Liberties Union: 1961, the decision in *Dixon v. Alabama State Board of Education* currently the leading case on due process for students: 1965, the publication of a tentative Statement on the Academic Freedom of Students, by the American Association of University Professors.
2. See the 1940 *Statement of Principles on Academic Freedom and Tenure* and the *1958 Statement on Procedural Standards in Faculty Dismissal Proceedings*. These statements have been jointly approved or adopted by the Association of American Colleges and the American Association of University Professors; the 1940 Statement has been endorsed by numerous learned and scientific societies and educational associations.

3. With respect to faculty members, the 1940 *Statement of Principles on Academic Freedom and Tenure* reads: "The college or university teacher is a citizen, a member of a learned profession, and an officer of an educational institution. When he speaks or writes as a citizen, he should be free from institutional censorship or discipline, but his special position in the community imposes special obligations. As a man of learning and an educational officer, he should remember that the public may judge his profession and his institution by his utterances. Hence he should at all times be accurate, should exercise appropriate restraint, should show respect for the opinion of others, and should make every effort to indicate that he is not an institutional spokesman."

Alternative Models of Governance in Higher Education

J. Victor Baldridge, David V. Curtis, George P. Ecker, and Gary L. Riley

Organizations vary in a number of important ways: they have different types of clients, they work with different technologies, they employ workers with different skills, they develop different structures and coordinating styles, and they have different relationships to their external environments. Of course, there are elements common to the operation of colleges and universities, hospitals, prisons, business firms, government bureaus, and so on, but no two organizations are the same. Any adequate model of decision making and governance in an organization must take its distinctive characteristics into account.

This chapter deals with the organizational characteristics and decision processes of colleges and universities. Colleges and universities are unique organizations, differing in major respects from industrial organizations, government bureaus, and business firms.

Distinguishing Characteristics of Academic Organizations

Colleges and universities are complex organizations. Like other organizations they have goals, hierarchical systems and structures, officials who carry out specified duties, decision-making processes that set institutional policy, and a bureaucratic administration that handles routine business. But they also exhibit some critical distinguishing characteristics that affect their decision processes.

Goal Ambiguity

Most organizations are goal-oriented, and as a consequence they can build decision structures to reach their objectives. Business firms want to make a profit, government bureaus have tasks specified by law, hospitals are trying to cure sick people, prisons are in the business of "rehabilitation."

By contrast, colleges and universities have vague, ambiguous goals and they must build decision processes to grapple with a higher degree of uncertainty and conflict. What is the goal of a university? This is a difficult question, for the list of possible answers is long: teaching, research, service to the local community, administration of scientific installations, support of the arts, solutions to social problems. In their book *Leadership and Ambiguity*, Cohen and March comment:

> Almost any educated person could deliver a lecture entitled "The Goals of the University." Almost no one will listen to the lecture voluntarily. For the most part, such lectures and their companion essays are well-intentioned exercises in social rhetoric, with little operational content. Efforts to generate normative statements of the goals of the university tend to produce goals that are either meaningless or dubious [Cohen and March, 1974, page 195].

Goal ambiguity, then, is one of the chief characteristics of academic organizations. They rarely have a single mission. On the contrary, they often try to be all things to all people. Because their existing goals are unclear, they also find it hard to reject new goals. Edward Gross (1968) analyzed the goals of faculty and administrators in a large number of American universities and obtained some remarkable results. To be sure, some goals were ranked higher than others, with academic freedom consistently near the top. But both administrators and faculty marked as important almost every one of forty-seven goals listed by Gross!

Not only are academic goals unclear, they are also highly contested. As long as goals are left ambiguous and abstract, they are readily agreed on. As soon as they are concretely specified and put into operation, conflict erupts. The link between clarity and conflict may help explain the prevalence of meaningless rhetoric in academic policy statements and speeches. It is tempting to resort to rhetoric when serious content produces conflict.

Client Service

Like schools, hospitals, and welfare agencies, academic organizations are "people-processing" institutions. Clients with specific needs are fed into the institution from the environment, the institution acts upon them, and the clients are returned to the larger society. This is an extremely important characteristic, for the clients demand and often obtain significant input into institutional decision-making processes. Even powerless clients such as schoolchildren usually have protectors, such as parents, who demand a voice in the operation of the organization. In higher education, of course, the clients are quite capable of speaking for themselves—and they often do.

Problematic Technology

Because they serve clients with disparate, complicated needs, client-serving organizations frequently have problematic technologies. A manufacturing organization develops a specific technology that can be segmented and routinized. Unskilled, semiskilled, and white collar workers can be productively used without relying heavily on professional expertise. But it is hard to construct a simple technology for an organization dealing with people. Serving clients is difficult to accomplish, and the results are difficult to evaluate, especially on a short-term basis. The entire person must be considered; people cannot be separated easily into small, routine, and technical segments. If at times colleges and universities do not know clearly *what* they are trying to do, they often do not know *how* to do it either.

Professionalism

How does an organization work when its goals are unclear, its service is directed to clients, and its technology is problematic? Most organizations attempt to deal with these problems by hiring expertly trained professionals. Hospitals require doctors and nurses, social welfare agencies hire social workers, public schools hire teachers, and colleges and universities hire faculty members. These professionals use a broad repertoire of skills to deal with the complex and often unpredictable problems of clients. Instead of subdividing a complicated task into a routine set of procedures, professional work requires that a broad range of tasks be performed by a single employee.

Sociologists have made a number of important general observations about professional employees, wherever they may work:

1. Professionals demand *autonomy* in their work. Having acquired considerable skill and expertise in their field, they demand freedom from supervision in applying them.

2. Professionals have *divided loyalties*. They have "cosmopolitan" tendencies and loyalty to their peers at the national level may sometimes interfere with loyalty to their local organization.

3. There are strong tensions between *professional values* and *bureaucratic expectations* in an organization. This can intensify conflict between professional employees and organizational managers.

4. Professionals demand *peer evaluation* of their work. They believe that only their colleagues can judge their performance, and they reject the evaluations of others, even those who are technically their superiors in the organizational hierarchy.

All of these characteristics undercut the traditional norms of a bureaucracy, rejecting its hierarchy, control structure, and management procedures. As a consequence, we can expect a distinct management style in a professional organization.

Finally, colleges and universities tend to have *fragmented* professional staffs. In some organizations there is one dominant professional group. For example, doctors are the dominant group in hospitals. In other organizations the professional staff is fragmented into subgroups, none of which predominates. The faculty in a university provides a clear example. Burton R. Clark comments on the fragmented professionalism in academic organizations:

> The internal controls of the medical profession are strong and are substituted for those of the organization. But in the college or university this situation does not obtain; there are twelve, twenty-five, or fifty clusters of experts. The experts are prone to identify with their own disciplines, and the "academic profession" overall comes off a poor second. We have wheels within wheels, many professions within a profession. No one of the disciplines on a campus is likely to dominate the others ... The campus is not a closely knit group of professionals who see the world from one perspective. As a collection of professionals, it is decentralized, loose, and flabby.

> The principle is this: where professional influence is high and there is one dominant professional group, the organization will be integrated by the imposition of professional standards. Where professional influence is high and there are a number of professional groups, the organization will be split by professionalism. The university and the large college are fractured by expertness, not unified by it. The sheer variety supports the tendency for authority to diffuse toward quasi-autonomous clusters [Clark, 1963, pages 37, 51].

Environmental Vulnerability

Another characteristic that sets colleges and universities apart from many other complex organizations is environmental vulnerability. Almost all organizations interact with their social environment to some extent. But though no organization is completely autonomous, some have considerably greater freedom of action than others. The degree of autonomy an organization has vis-à-vis its environment is one of the critical determinants of how it will be managed.

For example, in a free market economy, business firms and industries have a substantial degree of autonomy. Although they are regulated by countless government agencies and constrained by their customers, essentially they are free agents responsive to market demands rather than to government control. At the other extreme, a number of organizations are virtually "captured" by their environments. Public school districts, for example, are constantly scrutinized and pressured by the communities they serve.

Colleges and universities are somewhere in the middle on a continuum from "independent" to "captured." In many respects they are insulated from their environment. Recently, however, powerful external forces have been applied to academic institutions. Interest groups holding conflicting values have made their wishes, demands, and threats well known to the administrations and faculties of academic organizations in the 1970s.

What impact does environmental pressure have on the governance of colleges and universities? When professional organizations are well insulated from the pressures of the outside environment, then professional values, norms, and work definitions play a dominant role in shaping the character of the organization. On the other hand, when strong external pressure is applied to colleges and universities, the operating autonomy of the academic professionals is seriously reduced. The faculty and administrators lose some control over the curriculum, the goals, and the daily operation of the institution. Under these circumstances, the academic professionals are frequently reduced to the role of hired employees doing the bidding of bureaucratic managers.

Although colleges and universities are not entirely captured by their environments, they are steadily losing ground. As their vulnerability increases, their governance patterns change significantly.

"Organized Anarchy"

To summarize, academic organizations have several unique organizational characteristics. They have ambiguous goals that are often strongly contested. They serve clients who demand a voice in the decision-making process. They have a problematic technology, for in order to serve clients their technology must be holistic and adaptable to individual needs. They are professionalized organizations in which employees demand a large measure of control over institutional decision processes. Finally, they are becoming more and more vulnerable to their environments.

The character of such a complex organizational system is not satisfactorily conveyed by the standard term "bureaucracy." Bureaucracy carries the connotation of stability or even rigidity; academic organizations seem more fluid. Bureaucracy implies distinct lines of authority and strict hierarchical command; academic organizations have blurred lines of authority and professional employees who demand autonomy in their work. Bureaucracy suggests a cohesive organization with clear goals; academic organizations are characteristically fragmented with ambiguous and contested goals. Bureaucracy does adequately describe certain aspects of colleges and universities, such as business administration, plant management, capital outlay, and auxiliary services. But the processes at the heart of an academic organization—academic policy making, professional teaching, and research—do not resemble the processes one finds in a bureaucracy. Table 1 summarizes the differences between the two types of organizations.

Perhaps a better term for academic organizations has been suggested by Cohen and March. They describe the academic organization as an "organized anarchy"—a system with little central coordination or control:

> In a university anarchy each individual in the university is seen as making autonomous decisions. Teachers decide if, when, and what to teach. Students decide if, when, and what to learn. Legislators and donors decide if, when, and what to support. Neither coordination . . . nor control [is] practiced. Resources are allocated by whatever process emerges but without explicit accommodation and without explicit reference to some superordinate goal. The "decisions" of the system are a consequence produced by the system but intended by no one and decisively controlled by no one [Cohen and March, 1974, pages 33–34].

The organized anarchy differs radically from the well-organized bureaucracy or the consensus-bound collegium. It is an organization in which generous resources allow people to go in different directions without coordination by a central authority. Leaders are relatively weak and decisions are made by individual action. Since the organization's goals are ambiguous, decisions are often by-products of unintended and unplanned activity. In such fluid circumstances, presidents and other institutional leaders serve primarily as catalysts or facilitators of an ongoing process. They do not so much lead the institution as channel its activities in subtle ways. They do not command, but negotiate. They do not plan comprehensively, but try to apply preexisting solutions to problems.

TABLE 1

Organizational Characteristics of Academic Organizations and More Traditional Bureaucracies

	Academic Organizations (Colleges and Universities)	Traditional Bureaucracies (Government Agency, Industry)
Goals	Ambiguous, contested, inconsistent	Clearer goals, less disagreement
Client service	Client-serving	Material-processing, commercial
Technology	Unclear, nonroutine, holistic	Clearer, routinized, segmented
Staffing	Predominantly professional	Predominantly nonprofessional
Environmental relations	Very vulnerable	Less vulnerable
Summary image	"Organized anarchy"	"Bureaucracy"

Decisions are not so much "made" as they "happen." Problems, choices, and decision makers happen to come together in temporary solutions. Cohen and March have described decision processes in an organized anarchy as

> sets of procedures through which organizational participants arrive at an interpretation of what they are doing and what they have done while they are doing it. From this point of view an organization is a collection of choices looking for problems, issues and feelings looking for decision situations in which they might be aired, solutions looking for issues for which they might be the answer, and decision makers looking for work [Cohen and March, 1974, page 81].

The imagery of organized anarchy helps capture the spirit of the confused organizational dynamics in academic institutions: unclear goals, unclear technologies, and environmental vulnerability.

Some may regard "organized anarchy" as an exaggerated term, suggesting more confusion and conflict than really exist in academic organizations. This is probably a legitimate criticism. The term may also carry negative connotations to those unaware that it applies to specific organizational characteristics rather than to the entire campus community. Nevertheless, "organized anarchy" has some strong points in its favor. It breaks through the traditional formality that often surrounds discussions of decision making, challenges our existing conceptions, and suggests a looser, more fluid kind of organization. For these reasons we will join Cohen and March in using "organized anarchy" to summarize some of the unique organizational characteristics of colleges and universities: (1) unclear goals, (2) client service, (3) unclear technology, (4) professionalism, and (5) environmental vulnerability.[1]

Models of Academic Governance

Administrators and organization theorists concerned with academic governance have often developed images to summarize the complex decision process: collegial system, bureaucratic network, political activity, or participatory democracy. Such models organize the way we perceive the process, determine how we analyze it, and help determine our actions. For example, if we regard a system as political, then we form coalitions to pressure decision makers. If we regard it as collegial, then we seek to persuade people by appealing to reason. If we regard it as bureaucratic, then we use legalistic maneuvers to gain our ends.

In the past few years, as research on higher education has increased, models for academic governance have also proliferated. Three models have received widespread attention, more or less dominating the thinking of people who study academic governance. We will examine briefly each of these models in turn: (1) the bureaucracy, (2) the collegium, and (3) the political system. Each of these models has certain points in its favor. They can be used jointly to examine different aspects of the governance process.

The Academic Bureaucracy

One of the most influential descriptions of complex organizations is Max Weber's (1947) monumental work on bureaucracies. Weber discussed the characteristics of bureaucracies that distinguish them from less formal work organizations. In skeleton form he suggested that bureaucracies are networks of social groups dedicated to limited goals and organized for maximum efficiency. Moreover, the regulation of a bureaucratic system is based on the principle of "legal rationality," as contrasted with informal regulation based on friendship, loyalty to family, or personal allegiance to a charismatic leader. The hierarchical structure is held together by formal chains of command and systems of communication. The bureaucracy as Weber described it includes such elements as tenure, appointment to office, salaries as a rational form of payment, and competency as the basis of promotion.

Bureaucratic Characteristics of Colleges and Universities

Several authors have suggested that university governance may be more fully understood by applying the bureaucratic model. For example, Herbert Stroup (1966) has pointed out some characteristics of colleges and universities that fit Weber's original description of a bureaucracy.

They include the following:

1. Competence is the criterion used for appointment.
2. Officials are appointed, not elected.
3. Salaries are fixed and paid directly by the organization, rather than determined in "free-fee" style.
4. Rank is recognized and respected.
5. The career is exclusive; no other work is done.
6. The style of life of the organization's members centers on the organization.
7. Security is present in a tenure system.
8. Personal and organizational property are separated.

Stroup is undoubtedly correct in believing that Weber's paradigm can be applied to universities, and most observers are well aware of the bureaucratic factors involved in university administration. Among the more prominent are the following.

1. The university is a complex organization under *state charter*, like most other bureaucracies. This seemingly innocent fact, has major consequences, especially as states increasingly seek to exercise control.
2. The university has a *formal hierarchy*, with offices and a set of bylaws that specify the relations between those offices. Professors, instructors, and research assistants may be considered bureaucratic officers in the same sense as deans, chancellors, and presidents.
3. There are *formal channels of communication* that must be respected.
4. There are definite *bureaucratic authority relations*, with certain officials exercising authority over others. In a university the authority relations are often vague and shifting, but no one would deny that they exist.
5. There are *formal policies and rules* that govern much of the institution's work, such as library regulations, budgetary guidelines, and procedures of the university senate.
6. The bureaucratic elements of the university are most vividly apparent in its *"people-processing" aspects:* record keeping, registration, graduation requirements, and a multitude of other routine, day-to-day activities designed to help the modern university handle its masses of students.
7. *Bureaucratic decision-making processes* are used, most often by officials assigned the responsibility for making routine decisions by the formal administrative structure. Examples are admissions procedures, handled by the dean of admissions; procedures for graduation, routinely administered by designated officials; research policies, supervised by specified officials; and financial matters, usually handled in a bureaucratic manner by the finance office.

Weaknesses in the Bureaucratic Model

In many ways the bureaucratic model falls short of encompassing university governance, especially if one is primarily concerned with decision-making processes. First, the bureaucratic model tells us much about authority—that is, legitimate, formalized power—but not much about informal types of power and influence, which may take the form of mass movements or appeals to emotion and sentiment. Second, it explains much about the organization's formal *structure* but little about the dynamic *processes* that characterize the organization in action. Third, it describes the formal structure at one particular time, but it does not explain changes over time. Fourth, it explains how policies may be carried out most efficiently, but it says little about the critical process by which policy is established in the first place. Finally, it also ignores political issues, such as the struggles of various interest groups within the university.

The University Collegium

Many writers have rejected the bureaucratic model of the university. They seek to replace it with the model of the "collegium" or "community of scholars." When this literature is closely examined, there seem to be at least three different threads running through it.

A Description of Collegial Decision Making

This approach argues that academic decision making should not be like the hierarchical process in a bureaucracy. Instead there should be full participation of the academic community, especially the faculty. Under this concept the community of scholars would administer its own affairs, and bureaucratic officials would have little influence (see Goodman, 1962). John Millett, one of the foremost proponents of this model, has succinctly stated his view:

> I do not believe that the concept of hierarchy is a realistic representation of the interpersonal relationships which exist within a college or university. Nor do I believe that a structure of hierarchy is a desirable prescription for the organization of a college or university . . .

> I would argue that there is another concept of organization just as valuable as a tool of analysis and even more useful as a generalized observation of group and interpersonal behavior. This is the concept of community . . .

> The concept of community presupposes an organization in which functions are differentiated and in which specialization must be brought together, or coordination, if you will, is achieved not through a structure of superordination and subordination of persons and groups but through a *dynamic of consensus* [Millett, 1962, pages 234–235].

A Discussion of the Faculty's Professional Authority

Talcott Parsons (1947) was one of the first to call attention to the difference between "official competence," derived from one's office in a bureaucracy, and "technical competence," derived from one's ability to perform a given task. Parsons concentrated on the technical competence of the physician, but others have extended this logic to other professionals whose authority is based on what they *know* and can *do*, rather than on their official position. Some examples are the scientist in industry, the military adviser, the expert in government, the physician in the hospital, and the professor in the university.

The literature on professionalism strongly supports the argument for collegial organization. It emphasizes the professional's ability to make his own decisions and his need for freedom from organizational restraints. Consequently, the collegium is seen as the most reasonable method of organizing the university. Parsons, for example, notes (page 60) that when professionals are organized in a bureaucracy, "there are strong tendencies for them to develop a different sort of structure from that characteristic of the administrative hierarchy . . . of bureaucracy. Instead of a rigid hierarchy of status and authority there tends to be what is roughly, in formal status, a company of equals."

A Utopian Prescription for Operating the Educational System

There is a third strand in the collegial image. In recent years there has been a growing discontent with our impersonal contemporary society. The multiversity, with its thousands of students and its huge bureaucracy, is a case in point. The student revolts of the 1960s and perhaps even the widespread apathy of the 1970s are symptoms of deeply felt alienation between students and massive educational establishments. The discontent and anxiety this alienation has produced are aptly expressed in the now-famous sign worn by a Berkeley student: "I am a human being—do not fold, spindle, or mutilate."

As an alternative to this impersonal, bureaucratized educational system, many critics are calling for a return to the "academic community." In their conception such a community would offer personal attention, humane education, and "relevant confrontation with life." Paul Goodman's *The Community of Scholars* (1962) still appeals to many who seek to reform the university. Goodman cites the need for more personal interaction between faculty and students, for more relevant courses, and for educational innovations to bring the student into existential dialogue with the subject matter of his discipline. The number of articles on this subject, in both the mass media and the professional journals, is astonishingly large. Indeed, this concept of the collegial academic community is now widely proposed as one answer to the impersonality and meaninglessness of today's large multiversity. Thus conceived, the collegial model functions more as a revolutionary ideology and a utopian projection than a description of actual governance processes at any university.

Weaknesses in the Collegial Model

Three themes are incorporated in the collegial model: (1) decision making by consensus, (2) the professional authority of faculty members, and (3) the call for more humane education. These are all legitimate and appealing. Few would deny that our universities would be better centers of learning if we could somehow implement these objectives. There is a misleading simplicity about the collegial model, however, that glosses over many realities.

For one thing, the *descriptive* and *normative* visions are often confused. In the literature dealing with the collegial model it is often difficult to tell whether a writer is saying that the university is a collegium or that it ought to be a collegium. Discussions of the collegium are frequently more a lament for paradise lost than a description of reality. Indeed, the collegial image of round-table decision making is not an accurate description of the processes in most institutions.

Although at the department level there are many examples of collegial decision making, at higher levels it usually exists only in some aspects of the committee system. Of course, the proponents may be advocating a collegial model as a desirable goal or reform strategy. This is helpful, but it does not allow us to understand the actual workings of universities.

In addition, the collegial model fails to deal adequately with the problem of *conflict*. When Millett emphasizes the "dynamic of consensus," he neglects the prolonged battles that precede consensus, as well as decisions that actually represent the victory of one group over another. Proponents of the collegial model are correct in declaring that simple bureaucratic rule making is not the essence of decision making. But in making this point they take the equally indefensible position that major decisions are reached primarily by consensus. Neither extreme is correct, for decisions are rarely made by either bureaucratic fiat or simple consensus.

The University as a Political System

In *Power and Conflict in the University* (1971), Baldridge proposed a "political" model of university governance. Although the other major models of governance—the collegial and the bureaucratic—have valuable insights to offer, we believe that further insights can be gained from this model. It grapples with the power plays, conflicts, and rough-and-tumble politics to be found in many academic institutions.

Basic Assumptions of a Political Model

The political model assumes that complex organizations can be studied as miniature political systems. There are interest group dynamics and conflicts similar to those in cities, states, or other political entities. The political model focuses on policy-forming processes, because major policies commit an organization to definite goals and set the strategies for reaching those goals. Policy decisions are critical decisions. They have a major impact on an organization's future. Of course, in any practical situation it may be difficult to separate the routine from the critical, for issues that seem minor at one point may later be decisive, or vice versa. In general, however, policy decisions bind an organization to important courses of action.

Since policies are so important, people throughout an organization try to influence them to reflect their own interests and values. Policy making becomes a vital target of interest group activity that permeates the organization. Owing to its central importance, then, the organization theorist may select policy formation as the key for studying organizational conflict and change, just as the political scientist often selects legislative acts as the focal point for his analysis of a state's political processes. With policy formation as its key issue, the political model operates on a series of assumptions about the political process.

1. To say that policy making is a political process is not to say that everyone is involved. On the contrary, *inactivity* prevails. Most people most of the time find the policy-making process an uninteresting, unrewarding activity. Policy making is therefore left to the administrators. This is characteristic not only of policy making in universities but of political processes in society at large. Voters do not vote; citizens do not attend city council meetings; parents often permit school boards to do what they please. By and large, decisions that may have a profound effect on our society are made by small groups of elites.

2. Even people who are active engage in *fluid participation.* They move in and out of the decision-making process. Rarely do people spend much time on any given issue. Decisions, therefore, are usually made by those who persist. This normally means that small groups of political elites govern most major decisions, for they invest the necessary time in the process.

3. Colleges and universities, like most other social organizations, are characterized by fragmentation into *interest groups* with different goals and values. When resources are plentiful and the organization is prospering, these interest groups engage in only minimal conflict. But they are likely to mobilize and try to influence decisions when resources are tight, outside pressure groups attack, or internal groups try to assume command.

4. In a fragmented, dynamic social system *conflict* is natural. It is not necessarily a symptom of breakdown in the academic community. In fact, conflict is a significant factor in promoting healthy organizational change.

5. The pressure that groups can exert places severe *limitations on formal authority* in the bureaucratic sense. Decisions are not simply bureaucratic orders but are often negotiated compromises between competing groups. Officials are not free simply to issue a decision. Instead they must attempt to find a viable course acceptable to several powerful blocs.

6. *External interest groups* exert a strong influence over the policy-making process. External pressures and formal control by outside agencies—especially in public institutions—are powerful shapers of internal governance processes.

The Political Decision Model versus the Rational Decision Model

The bureaucratic model of organizational structure is accompanied by a rational model of decision making. It is usually assumed that in a bureaucracy the structure is hierarchical and well organized, and that decisions are made through clear-cut, predetermined steps. Moreover, a definite, rational approach is expected to lead to the optimal decision. Graham T. Allison has summarized the rational decision-making process as follows:

1. *Goals and objectives.* The goals and objectives of the agent are translated into a "payoff" or "utility" or "preference" function, which represents the "value" or "utility" of alternative sets of consequences. At the outset of the decision problem the agent has a payoff function which ranks all possible sets of consequences in terms of his values and objectives. Each bundle of consequences will contain a number of side effects. Nevertheless, at a minimum, the agent must be able to rank in order of preference each possible set of consequences that might result from a particular action.

2. *Alternatives.* The rational agent must choose among a set of alternatives displayed before him in a particular situation. In decision theory these alternatives are represented as a decision tree. The alternative courses of action may include more than a simple act, but the specification of a course of action must be sufficiently precise to differentiate it from other alternatives.

3. *Consequences.* To each alternative is attached a set of consequences or outcomes of choice that will ensue if that particular alternative is chosen. Variations are generated at this point by making different assumptions about the accuracy of the decision maker's knowledge of the consequences that follow from the choice of each alternative.

4. *Choice.* Rational choice consists simply of selecting that alternative whose consequences rank highest in the decision maker's payoff function [Allison, 1971, pages 29–30].

The rational model appeals to those who regard their actions as essentially goal-directed and rational. Realistically, however, we should realize that the rational model is more an ideal than an actual description of how people act. In fact, in the confused organizational setting of the university, political constraints often undermine the force of rationality. A political model of decision making requires us to answer some new questions about the decision process:

The first new question posed by the political model is *why* a given decision is made at all. The formalists have already indicated that "recognition of the problem" is one element in the process, but too little attention has been paid to the activities that bring a particular issue to the forefront. Why is *this* decision being considered at *this* particular time? The political model insists that interest groups, powerful individuals, and bureaucratic processes are critical in drawing attention to some decisions rather than to others. A study of "attention cues" by which issues are called to the community's attention is a vital part of any analysis.

Second, a question must be raised about the right of any person or group to make the decisions. Previously the *who* question was seldom raised, chiefly because the decision literature was developed for hierarchical organizations in which the focus of authority could be easily defined. In a more loosely coordinated system however, we must ask a prior question: Why was the legitimacy to make the decision vested in a particular person or group? Why is Dean Smith making the decision instead of Dean Jones or why is the University Senate dealing with the problem instead of the central administration? Establishing the right of authority over a decision is a political question, subject to conflict, power manipulation, and struggles between interest groups. Thus the political model always asks tough questions: Who has the right to make the decision? What are the conflict-ridden processes by which the decision was located at this point rather than at another? The crucial point is that often the issue of *who* makes the decision has already limited, structured, and pre-formed *how* it will be made.

The third new issue raised by a political interpretation concerns the development of complex decision networks. As a result of the fragmentation of the university, decision making is rarely located in one official; instead it is dependent on the advice and authority of numerous people. Again the importance of the committee system is evident. It is necessary to understand that the committee network is the legitimate reflection of the need for professional influence to intermingle with bureaucratic influence. The decision process, then, is taken out of the hands of individuals (although there are still many who are powerful) and placed into a network that allows a *cumulative buildup* of expertise and advice. When the very life of the organization clusters around expertise, *decision making is likely to be diffused, segmentalized, and decentralized.* A complex network of committees, councils, and advisory bodies grows to handle the task of assembling the expertise necessary for reasonable decisions. Decision making by the individual bureaucrat is replaced with decision making by committee, council, and cabinet. Centralized decision making is replaced with diffuse decision making. The process becomes a far-flung network for gathering expertise from every corner of the organization and translating it into policy [Baldridge, 1971, page 190].

The fourth new question raised by the political model concerns alternative solutions to the problem at hand. The rational decision model suggests that all possible options are open and within easy reach of the decision maker. A realistic appraisal of decision dynamics in most organizations, however, suggests that by no means are all options open. The political dynamics of interest groups, the force of external power blocs, and the opposition of powerful professional constituencies may leave only a handful of viable options. The range of alternatives is often sharply limited by political considerations. Just as important, there is often little time and energy available for seeking new solutions. Although all possible solutions should be identified under the rational model, in the real world administrators have little time to grope for solutions before their deadlines.

In *Power and Conflict in the University*, Baldridge summed up the political model of decision making as follows:

First, powerful political forces—interest groups, bureaucratic officials, influential individuals, organizational subunits—cause a given issue to emerge from the limbo of on-going problems and certain "attention cues" force the political community to consider the problem. Second, there is a struggle over locating the decision with a particular person or group, for the location of the right to make the decision often determines the outcome. Third, decisions are usually "preformed" to a great extent by the time one person or group is given the legitimacy to make the decision; not all options are open and the choices have been severely limited by the previous conflicts. Fourth, such political struggles are more likely to occur in reference to "critical" decisions than to "routine" decisions. Fifth, a complex decision network is developed to gather the necessary information and supply the critical expertise. Sixth, during the process of making the decision political controversy is likely to continue and compromises, deals, and plain head cracking are often necessary to get any decision made. Finally, the controversy is not likely to end easily. In fact, it is difficult even to know when a decision is made, for the political processes have a habit of unmaking, confusing, and muddling whatever agreements are hammered out.

This may be a better way of grappling with the complexity that surrounds decision processes within a loosely coordinated, fragmented political system. The formal decision models seem to have been asking very limited questions about the decision process and more insight can be gained by asking a new set of political questions. Thus the decision model that emerges from the university's political dynamics is more open, more dependent on conflict and political action. It is not so systematic or formalistic as most decision theory, but it is probably closer to the truth. Decision making, then, is not an isolated technique but another critical process that must be integrated into a larger political image [Baldridge, 1971, pages 191–192].

It is clear that a political analysis emphasizes certain factors over others. First, it is concerned primarily with problems of goal setting and conflicts over values, rather than with efficiency in achieving goals. Second, analysis of the organization's change processes and adaptation to its environment is critically important. The political dynamics of a university are constantly changing, pressuring the university in many directions, and forcing change throughout the academic system. Third, the analysis of conflict is an essential component. Fourth, there is the role of interest groups in pressuring decision makers to formulate policy. Finally, much attention is given to the legislative and decision-making phases—the processes by which pressures and power are transformed into policy. Taken together these points constitute the bare outline for a political analysis of academic governance.

The revised political model: an environmental and structuralist approach. Since the political model of academic governance originally appeared in *Power and Conflict in the University*, we have become aware that it has several shortcomings. For this reason we offer a few observations about some changes in emphasis, a few corrections in focus.

First, the original political model probably underestimated the impact of routine bureaucratic processes. Many, perhaps most, decisions are made not in the heat of political controversy but according to standard operating procedures. The political description in *Power and Conflict in the University* was based on a study of New York University. The research occurred at a time of extremely high conflict when the university was confronted with two crises, a student revolution and a financial disaster. The political model developed from that study probably overstresses the role of conflict and negotiation as elements in standard decision making, since those were the processes apparent at the time. Now we would stress that it is important to consider routine procedures of the governance process.

Second, the original political model, based on a single case study, did not do justice to the broad range of political activity that occurs in different kinds of institutions. For example, NYU is quite different from Oberlin College, and both are distinctive institutions compared to local community colleges. Many of the intense political dynamics observed in the NYU study may have been exaggerated in a troubled institution such as NYU, particularly during the heated conflicts of the late 1960s.

Third, we want to stress even more strongly the central role of environmental factors. The NYU analysis showed that conflict and political processes within the university were linked to environmental factors. But even more stress on the environmental context is needed.

Finally, as developed in *Power and Conflict in the University,* the political model suffered from an "episodic" character. That is, the model did not give enough emphasis to long-term decision-making patterns, and it failed to consider the way institutional structure may shape and channel political efforts. Centralization of power, the development of decision councils, long-term patterns of professional autonomy, the dynamics of departmental power, and the growth of unionization were all slighted by the original model. There are other important questions concerning long-term patterns: What groups tend to dominate decision making over long periods of time? Do some groups seem to be systematically excluded from the decision-making process? Do different kinds of institutions have different political patterns? Do institutional characteristics affect the morale of participants in such a way that they engage in particular decision-influencing activities? Do different kinds of institutions have systematic patterns of faculty participation in decision making? Are decision processes highly centralized in certain kinds of institutions?

Finally, we are not substituting the political model for the bureaucratic or collegial model of academic decision making. In a sense, they each address a separate set of problems and, taken together, they often yield complementary interpretations. We believe, however, that the political model has many strengths, and we offer it as a useful tool for understanding academic governance. See Table 2 for a comparison of the three decision-making models.

Images of Leadership and Management Strategies

Thus far we have made two basic arguments: (1) colleges and universities are unique in many of their organizational characteristics and, as a consequence, it is necessary to create new models to help explain organizational structure, governance, and decision making; and (2) a political model of

TABLE 2

Three Models of Decision Making and Governance

	Bureaucratic	Collegial	Political
Assumptions about structure	Hierarchical bureaucracy	Community of peers	Fragmented, complex professional federation
Social	Unitary: integrated by formal system	Unitary: integrated by peer consensus	Pluralistic: encompasses different interest groups with divergent values
Basic theoretical foundations	Weberian bureaucracy, classic studies of formal systems	Professionalism literature, human-relations approach to organization	Conflict analysis, interest group theory, community power literature
View of decision-making process	"Rational" decision making; standard operating procedures	Shared collegial decision: consensus, community participation	Negotiation, bargaining, political brokerage, external influence
Cycle of decision making	Problem definition; search for alternatives; evaluation of alternatives; calculus; choice; implementation	As in bureaucratic model, but in addition stresses the involvement of professional peers in the process	Emergency of issue out of social context; interest articulation; conflict; legislative process; implementation of policy; feedback

academic governance offers useful insights in addition to those offered by the bureaucratic and collegial models. In this section we will suggest that some alternative images of leadership and management style are needed to accommodate the unique characteristics of academic organizations.

Leadership Under the Bureaucratic Model

Under the bureaucratic model the leader is seen as a hero who stands at the top of a complex pyramid of power. The hero's job is to assess problems, propose alternatives, and make rational choices. Much of the organization's power is held by the hero. Great expectations are raised because people trust the hero to solve their problems and to fend off threats from the environment. The image of the authoritarian hero is deeply ingrained in most societies and in the philosophy of most organization theorists.

We expect leaders to possess a unique set of skills with emphasis on problem-solving ability and technical knowledge about the organization. The principles of "scientific management," such as Planning, Programming, Budgeting Systems (PPBS) and Management by Objectives, are often proposed as the methods for rational problem solving. Generally, schools of management, business, and educational administration teach such courses to develop the technical skills that the hero-planner will need in leading the organization.

The hero image is deeply imbedded in our cultural beliefs about leadership. But in organizations such as colleges and universities it is out of place. Power is more diffuse in those organizations; it is lodged with professional experts and fragmented into many departments and subdivisions. Under these circumstances, high expectations about leadership performance often cannot be met. The leader has neither the power nor the information necessary to consistently make heroic decisions. Moreover, the scientific management procedures prescribed for organizational leaders quickly break down under conditions of goal ambiguity, professional dominance, and environmental vulnerability—precisely the organizational characteristics of colleges and universities. Scientific management theories make several basic assumptions: (1) the organization's goals are clear; (2) the organization is a closed system insulated from environmental penetration; and (3) the planners have the power to execute their decisions. These assumptions seem unrealistic in the confused and fluid world of the organized anarchy.

Leadership Under the Collegial Model

The collegial leader presents a stark contrast to the heroic bureaucratic leader. The collegial leader is above all the "first among equals" in an organization run by professional experts. Essentially, the collegial model proposes what John Millett calls the "dynamic of consensus in a community of scholars." The basic role of the collegial leader is not so much to command as to listen, not so much to lead as to gather expert judgments, not so much to manage as to facilitate, not so much to order but to persuade and negotiate.

Obviously, the skills of a collegial leader differ from those required by the scientific management principles employed by the heroic bureaucrat. Instead of technical problem-solving skills, the collegial leader needs professional expertise to ensure that he is held in high esteem by his colleagues. Talent in interpersonal dynamics is also needed to achieve consensus in organizational decision making. The collegial leader's role is more modest and more realistic. He does not stand alone since other professionals share the burden of decision making with him. Negotiation and compromise are the bywords of the collegial leader; authoritarian strategies are clearly inappropriate.

Leadership Under the Political Model

Under the political model the leader is a mediator or negotiator between power blocs. Unlike the autocratic academic president of the past, who ruled with an iron hand, the contemporary president must play a political role by pulling coalitions together to fight for desired changes. The academic monarch of yesteryear has almost vanished. In his place is not the academic hero but the academic statesman. Robert Dahl has painted an amusing picture of the political maneuvers of Mayor Richard Lee of New Haven, and the same description applies to academic political leaders:

> The mayor was not at the peak of a pyramid but rather at the center of intersecting circles. He rarely commanded. He negotiated, cajoled, exhorted, beguiled, charmed, pressed, appealed, reasoned, promised, insisted, demanded, even threatened, but he most needed support and acquiescence from other leaders who simply could not be commanded. Because the mayor could not command, he had to bargain [Dahl, 1961, page 204].

The political interpretation of leadership can be pressed even further, for the governance of the university more and more comes to look like a "cabinet" form of administration. The key figure today is not the president, the solitary giant, but the political leader surrounded by his staff, the prime minister who gathers the information and expertise to construct policy. It is the "staff," the network of key administrators, that makes most of the critical decisions. The university has become much too complicated for any one man, regardless of his stature. Cadres of vice-presidents, research men, budget officials, public relations men, and experts of various stripes surround the president, sit on the cabinet, and help reach collective decisions. Expertise becomes more critical than ever and leadership becomes even more the ability to assemble, lead, and facilitate the activities of knowledgeable experts.

Therefore, the president must be seen as a "statesman" as well as a "hero-bureaucrat." The bureaucratic image might be appropriate for the man who assembles data to churn out routine decisions with a computer's help. In fact, this image is fitting for many middle-echelon officials in the university. The statesman's image is much more accurate for the top administrators, for here the influx of data and information gives real power and possibilities for creative action. The statesman is the innovative actor who uses information, expertise, and the combined wisdom of the cabinet to plan the institution's future; the bureaucrat may only be a number manipulator, a user of routine information for routine ends. The use of the cabinet, the assembly of expertise, and the exercise of political judgment in the service of institutional goals—all this is part of the new image of the statesman leader which must complement both the hero leader and the collegial leader.

Table 3 presents a summary and comparison of the three basic images of leadership and management we have just described.

TABLE 3

Images of Leadership and Management Under Three Models of Governance

	Bureaucratic	Collegial	Political
Basic leadership image Leadership skills	Hero Technical problem-solving skills	"First among equals" Interpersonal dynamics	Statesman Political strategy, interpersonal dynamics, coalition management
Management Expectation	"Scientific management" Very high: people believe that hero-leader can solve problems and he tries to play the role	Management by consensus Modest: leader is developer of consensus among professionals	Strategic decision making Modest: leader marshalls political action, but is constrained by the counter efforts of other groups

Summary

Colleges and universities are different from most other kinds of complex organizations. Their goals are more ambiguous and contested, they serve clients instead of seeking to make a profit, their technologies are unclear and problematic, and professionals dominate the work force and decision-making process. Thus colleges and universities are not standard bureaucracies, but can best be described as "organized anarchies" (see Cohen and March, 1947).

What decision and governance processes are to be found in an organized anarchy? Does the decision process resemble a bureaucratic system, with rational problem solving and standard operating procedures? Does it resemble a collegial system in which the professional faculty participate as members of a "community of scholars"? Or does it appear to be a political process with various interest groups struggling for influence over organizational policy? Each image is valid in some sense; each image helps complete the picture. Finally, we question the standard image of leadership and management. Classic leadership theory, based on a bureaucratic model, suggests the image of the organizational leader as a hero who uses principles of scientific management as the basis for his decisions. We have suggested that the leader's image should be that of the academic statesman, and that management should be considered a process of strategic decision making.

The research reported in this paper was supported by the Stanford Center for Research and Development in Teaching, by funds from the National Institute of Education (contract no. NE-C-00-3-0062).

Note

1. Our list of characteristics of an organized anarchy extends Cohen and March's, which contains (1) and (3), plus a characteristic called "fluid participation."

References

Allison, Graham T. *Essence of Decision.* Boston: Little, Brown, 1971.

Baldridge, J. Victor. *Power and Conflict in the University.* New York: John Wiley, 1971.

Clark, Burton R. "Faculty Organization and Authority." *The Study of Academic Administration,* edited by Terry Lunsford. Boulder, Colo.: Western Interstate Commission for Higher Education, 1963. Reprinted as chapter 4 in this volume.

Cohen, Michael D., and March, James G. *Leadership and Ambiguity: The American College President.* New York: McGraw-Hill, 1974.

Dahl, Robert. *Who Governs?* New Haven, Conn.: Yale University Press, 1961.

Goodman, Paul. *The Community of Scholars.* New York: Random House, 1962.

Gross, Edward, and Grambsch, Paul V. *Changes in University Organization, 1964–1971.* New York: McGraw-Hill, 1974.

Gross, Edward. *University Goals and Academic Power.* Washington, D.C.: Office of Education, 1968.

Millett, John. *The Academic Community.* New York: McGraw-Hill, 1962.

Parsons, Talcott. "Introduction." *The Theory of Social and Economic Organization,* by Max Weber. New York: Free Press, 1947.

Stroup, Herbert. *Bureaucracy in Higher Education.* New York: Free Press, 1966.

Weber, Max. *The Theory of Social and Economic Organization.* New York: Free Press, 1947.

The Academic Life
Small Worlds, Different Worlds

Burton R. Clark

The American professoriate is enormously differentiated by discipline and type of institution on such primary dimensions of professionalism as patterns of work, identification, authority, career, and association. Integration across the professoriate no longer comes primarily from similarity of function and common socialization, but from the overlap of subcommunities and the mediating linkages provided by the ties of discipline and institution.

Educational Researcher, Vol. 18, No. 5, pp. 4–8

Today, near the end of the 20th century, the American system of higher education is highly diversified, steadily dividing along the two basic lines of discipline and type of institution. As the system goes, so does the academic profession reap, evolving into a multisided occupation composed of many different professions, semiprofessions, and nonprofessional fields. I want to explore the nature of this extreme differentiation, particularly its self-amplifying tendency, and then suggest some largely hidden links that may yet connect academics one to another even as common values and experiences recede.

The Growing Division of Labor

The modern differentiation of the American professoriate means straightaway that we deceive ourselves, and others, every time we speak in simplistic terms of *the* professor in *the* university, or *the* college professor. Disciplinary differences alone demand a more exacting approach in which the field of competence and study is front and center. In the leading universities, for example, the clinical professor of medicine is as much a part of the basic work force as is the professor of English. The medical academic can be found in a cancer ward, interacting intensively with other doctors, nurses, orderlies, laboratory assistants, a few students perhaps, and many patients in a round of tightly scheduled activities that may begin at seven in the morning and extend into various evenings and weekends. Such academics are often under considerable pressure to generate income from patient-care revenues: They frequently negotiate with third-party medical plans and need a sizable administrative staff to handle patient billing. Salary may well depend on group income that fluctuates from year to year and that is directly affected by changes in the health-care industry and by the competitive position of a particular medical school–hospital complex. Hence salary may not be guaranteed, even in a tenured post. Sizable research grants must also be actively and repetitively pursued, and those who do not raise funds from research grants will find themselves loaded up with more clinical duties.[1]

The humanities professor operates in a totally different environment: Teaching "loads" are in the range of four to six hours a week. Office hours are at one's discretion; administrative assignments vary considerably with one's willingness to cooperate. The humanities academic typically interacts with large numbers of beginning students in lecture halls, in an occasional turn in introductory classes; with smaller numbers of juniors and seniors, in specialized upper division courses; and then with a few graduate students in seminars and dissertation consultation, around such highly specialized topics as Elizabethan lyric and Icelandic legend. Much valuable work time can be spent at home, away from the "distractions" of the university office.

About what is one thinking and writing? Attention may center on a biography of Eugene O'Neill, an interpretation of what Jane Austen really meant, an effort to trace Lillian Hellman's political passions, or a critique of Derrida and deconstructionism. Professors seek to master a highly specialized segment of literature and to maximize individual interpretation. The interests of humanities professors are reflected not only in the many sections and byways of such omnibus associations as the Modern Language Association, but also in the specificities of the Shakespeare Association of America, the Dickens Society, the D. H. Lawrence Society of North America, the Speech Association of America, the Thomas Hardy Society of America, and the Vladimir Nabokov Society. Tocqueville's famous comment on the propensity of Americans to form voluntary associations is nowhere more true than in the academic world.

Disciplinary differences are of course not limited to the sharp contrast between life in a medical school and in a department of English. The work of Tony Becher and others on the cultures of individual disciplines has shown that bodies of knowledge variously determine the behavior of individuals and departments (see especially Becher, 1987). Disciplines exhibit discernible differences in individual behavior and group action, notably between "hard" and "soft" subjects and "pure" and "applied" fields; in a simple fourfold classification, between hard-pure (physics), hard-applied (engineering), soft-pure (history), and soft-applied (social work). Across the many fields of the physical sciences, the biological sciences, the social sciences, the humanities, and the arts, fieldwork reveals varied work assignments, symbols of identity, modes of authority, career lines, and associational linkages.[2] More broadly, great differences in the academic life often appear between the letters and science departments and the many professional school domains in which a concern for the ways and needs of an outside profession must necessarily be combined with the pursuit of science and truth for its own sake. Far from the popular images of Mr. Chips chatting up undergraduates and of Einsteinian, white-haired, remote scholars dreaming up esoteric mathematical equations are the realities of academic work that helps prepare school teachers, librarians, social workers, engineers, computer experts, architects, nurses, pharmacists, business managers, lawyers, and doctors—and, in some academic locales, also morticians, military personnel, auto mechanics, airport technicians, secretaries, lathe operators, and cosmetologists. As Robert Wiebe (1967) and Walter Metzger (1987) have noted in historical detail, American higher education has been generous to a fault in admitting former outside fields into the academy, thereby administering a dose of legitimacy.

Because research is the first priority of the leading universities, the disciplinary differentiation of every modern system of higher education is self-amplifying. The American system is currently the extreme case of this self-amplification: Its great size, decentralization, diversity, and competitiveness magnify the pursuit of new knowledge. The reward system for this self-amplification began to emerge a century ago, when Johns Hopkins and other new upstart universities competitively prompted Eliot at Harvard and others in the old colleges of the day to speed up the nascent evolution from the age of the college to the age of the university. This evolution turned professors loose to pursue specialized research and to teach specialized subjects at the newly created graduate level, even as students were turned loose to pick and choose in an array of undergraduate courses that was to become ever more bewildering. The reward system of promoting academics on the grounds of research and published scholarship has become more deeply rooted in the universities, and would-be universities and leading 4-year colleges, with every passing decade. The many proliferating specialties of the disciplines are like tributaries flowing into this mammoth river of the research imperative.

The most serious operational obstacles to this research-driven amplification are the limitations of funding and the institutional need to teach undergraduates and beginning graduate students with packages of introductory materials that they can understand. Then, too, there remains in the American system the long-standing belief in the importance of undergraduate liberal or general education. The saving remnant of academics who uphold the banners of liberal and general education are able to sally forth in full cry periodically—the 1920s, the late 1940s, the 1980s—to group some specialties into more general course offerings, narrow the options in distribution requirements from, say, 400 to 100 courses, insist that teaching take priority over research, and in general raise a ruckus about the dangers of the specialized mind. Meanwhile, however, campus promotion committees continue their steady scrutiny of the record of research and scholarship. Central administrators work actively to build an institutional culture of academic first-rateness as that is defined competitively across the nation and even internationally on the basis of the reputation of noted scholars. Sophisticated general educators and liberal arts proponents in the universities recognize the primacy of the substantive impulse and learn how to work incrementally within its limits.

Institutional Differentiation

As powerful as are the self-amplifying disciplinary differences in dividing the professoriate, institutional differentiation now plays an even more important role. Useful classifications of the 3,400 accredited institutions in American higher education now run to 20 categories of major types—and still leave unidentified such important subtypes as historically black colleges, women's colleges, and Catholic colleges (Carnegie Foundation for the Advancement of Teaching, 1987). The creation of individual niches within the types has become a high art, especially among private universities and colleges but not limited to them—a self-amplifying tendency propelled by competition for resources, clientele, and reputation. The extensive differentiation places most academics in settings other than that of the research university. We find a third of them in public and private 4-year colleges and "comprehensive colleges," numbering together about 1,200, that offer degree work as far as the master's. Another fourth to a third are to be found in the nearly 1,400 community colleges.

These major locales exhibit vast differences in the very basis of the academic life, namely, the balance of effort between teaching and research. Teaching loads in the leading universities come in at around 4 to 6 hours a week, tailing down to 2 to 3 hours—a class a week, a seminar a week—more often than rising above 6. The reciprocal is that faculty commonly expect to spend at least half their time in research, alone or in the company of a few advanced graduate students. We need not stray very far, however, before we encounter teaching loads that are 50%, 100%, and 200% higher. What are called "doctorate-granting universities," rather than "research universities," exact teaching loads of 9 to 12 hours. So too for liberal arts colleges, especially outside the top 50. In comprehensive colleges, loads of 12 hours a week in the classroom are common. In turn, in the community colleges, the standard climbs to 15 hours, and loads of 18 and 21 hours are not unknown. And as we move from the top of the institutional hierarchy to the bottom, faculty involvement shifts from advanced students to beginning students; from highly selective students to open-door clientele; from young students in the traditional college age group to a mix of students of all ages in short-term vocational programs as well as in course work leading toward a bachelor's degree. In the community colleges, students in the college-transfer track are now numerically overshadowed by students in terminal vocational programs, and both are frequently outnumbered by nonmatriculated adults who turn "college" into "community center."

The burdens of remedial education are also much heavier as we descend the hierarchy. The open-door approach, standard in 2-year colleges and also operational in 4-year colleges that take virtually all comers, confronts college teachers with students in the classroom who are still operating at a secondary-school, and even an elementary-school, level. Then, to add insult to injury, as we descend the hierarchy, we encounter more part-time academic work. During the last two decades, the ranks of the part-timers have swollen to 200,000 or so, a third of the total academic workforce, with heavy concentrations in the less prestigious colleges and especially in community colleges, where a half or more of the faculty commonly operate on a part-time schedule.

At the extreme opposite end of the institutional hierarchy from those who serve primarily in the graduate schools and graduate-level professional schools in the major universities are the full-time and part-time teachers in English or mathematics in downtown community colleges who teach introductory and subintroductory courses over and over again—the rudiments of English composition, the first course in mathematics—to high school graduates who need remediation and to adults struggling with basic literacy. As faculty pointed out in interviews, "scholars" are then transformed into "mere teachers," serving in a fashion more similar to high school teaching than to university work.

With the very nature of academic work varying enormously across the many types of institutions that make up American postsecondary education, other dimensions of the academic life run on a parallel course. If we examine the cultures of the institutions by discussing with faculty members their basic academic beliefs, we find different worlds. Among the leading research universities, the discipline is front and center, the institution is prized for its reputation of scholarship and research, and peers are the primary reference group. A professor of physics will say: "What I value the most is the presence of the large number and diverse collection of scientists who are constantly doing things that I find stimulating." A professor of biology tells us that his university "has a lot of extremely good departments . . . there are a lot of fascinating, interesting people here." A political scientist adds that what he values most "is the intellectual level of the faculty and the graduate students. . . . Good graduate students are very important to me personally and always have been, and having colleagues that are smart is important." And a professor of English told us that his institution "is a first-rate university . . . we have a fine library, and we have excellent teachers here, and we have first-rate scholars." Academics in this favored site have much with which to identify. They are proud of the quality they believe surrounds them, experiencing it directly in their own and neighboring departments and inferring it indirectly from institutional reputation. The strong symbolic thrust of the institution incorporates the combined strengths of the departments that in turn represent the disciplines. Thus, for faculty, disciplinary and institutional cultures converge, a happy state indeed.

The leading private liberal arts colleges provide a second favored site. Here, professors often waxed lyrical in interviews about the small college environment tailored to undergraduate teaching: "It is a very enjoyable setting. The students are—the students we get in physics—a delight to work with"; "I can't put it in a word, but I think that it is one of the least constraining environments I know of"; "it is a better form of life"; or, "My colleagues are fantastic. The people in this department are sane, which in an English department is not always the case." These institutions retain the capacity to appear as academic communities, not bureaucracies, in their overall integration and symbolic unity.

But soon we encounter sites where faculty members are troubled by inchoate institutional character and worry about the quality of their environment. In the lesser universities, and especially in the comprehensive colleges that have evolved out of a teachers-college background, at the second, third, and fourth levels of the institutional hierarchy, the setting was often summed as follows:

> I think the most difficult thing about being at an institution like [this one] is that it has a difficult time coming to terms with itself. I think the more established institutions with strong academic backgrounds don't have the problem that an institution that pretty much is in the middle range of higher educational institutions around the country does. I'm not saying that [this institution] is a bad institution, but it certainly doesn't have the quality students, the quality faculty, the quality programs of the University of Chicago, Harvard, Yale. . . . When it talks about standards, what sort of standards? When it talks about practicality, how practical does it have to be? . . . It doesn't have a strong sense of tradition.

Compared to the research universities, the overall institutional culture is weaker and less satisfying for many faculty members, at the same time that disciplinary identifications are weakened as heavy teaching loads suppress research and its rewards.

In these middle-level institutions, professors often spoke of their relationship with students as the thing they value most. Students begin to replace peers as the audience of first resort. That shift is completed in the community colleges, with the identifications of faculty reaching a high point of student-centeredness. In a setting that is distinctly opposed to disciplinary definitions of quality and excellence, pleasures and rewards have to lie in the task of working with poorly prepared students who pour in through the open door, for example: "We are a practical teaching college. We serve our community and we serve . . . the students in our community, and given them a good, basic, strong education. . . . We are not sitting here on our high horses looking to publish"; and "I really do like to teach, and this place allows me to teach. It doesn't bog me down with having to turn out papers." In the community colleges, the equity values of open door and open access have some payoff as anchoring points in the faculty culture. But in the overall institutional hierarchy, where the dominant values emphasize quality, selection, and advanced work, the community college ideology can play only a subsidiary role. The limitations cannot be missed: "It would be nice to be able to teach upper division classes."

As for work and culture, so go authority, careers, and associational life. To sum the story on authority, at the top of the institutional hierarchy faculty influence is well and strong. Many individuals have strong personal bargaining power; departments and professional schools are strong, semiautonomous units; and all-campus faculty bodies have dominant influence in personnel and curricular decisions. University presidents speak lovingly of the faculty as the core of the institution and walk gently around entrenched faculty prerogatives. But as we descend the hierarchy, faculty authority weakens and managerialism increases. Top-down command is noticeably stronger in the public comprehensive colleges, especially when their genetic imprint is that of a teachers college. The 2-year colleges, having evolved mainly out of secondary systems and operating, like schools, under local trustees, are quite managerial. Faculty then feel powerless, even severely put upon. Their answer has been unionization. The further down the hierarchy of prestige we go, the more widespread do unions become, especially among public-sector institutions.

To sum the associational life of faculty: In the leading universities, faculty interact with one another across institutional boundaries in a bewildering network of disciplinary linkages: formal and informal; large and small; visible and invisible; local, regional, national, and international. When university specialists find "monster meetings" not to their liking, they go to participate in a smaller division or section that best represents their specific interests, or, as of late, they find kindred souls in small, autonomous meetings of several dozen people. The jet set is everywhere, from physicists pursuing high-energy physics to professors of English off to a conference in Paris on structuralism. As we move down the hierarchy, however, there is less reason to be involved, less to learn that is relevant to one's everyday life, and the travel money is gone from the institutional budget. Then, academics do not go to national meetings, or they go only if the national association comes to their part of the country and develops special sessions on teaching—or they break away to form associations appropriate to their sector. Community college teachers have been developing associations in such broad areas as the social sciences and the humanities and in such special areas of teaching as mathematics and biology, and doing so on a home-city or home-region as well as national basis.

Different worlds, small worlds. The institutional differentiation interacts with the disciplinary differentiation in a self-amplifying fashion that steadily widens and deepens the matrix of differences.

What Integrates?

If academic life in America is so divided, and the future promises even greater fragmentation, does any integration obtain? I mentioned at the outset that common values and experiences recede. When we searched in faculty interviews for common beliefs, we found some possible cultural linkages in widely used expressions. As faculty members attempted to formulate what professors have in common, they turned often to expressions about serving knowledge, searching for answers, and striving for new understanding. We frequently encountered norms of academic honesty in which plagiarism—the stealing of someone else's intellectual property—is the worst crime of all. The ideology of academic freedom was often raised, with personal freedom portrayed as an extremely attractive aspect of academic life that, like recognition, sometimes serves in lieu of material rewards.

But we had to scrap to find values that might still be widely shared, sensing that so often the same words had different meanings. Academic freedom means in one context primarily the right to pursue research and publish as you please; in another, the right to give failing grades and the right not to punch in and out on a time clock for so many hours on campus each day. The concern about plagiarism drops off sharply among those in all-teaching settings; the norms of academic honesty then more often refer to fair grading and fair treatment of students. In short, the ongoing differentiation not only erodes common values but also gives stated common values different meanings in different contexts.

Because this is the case, a search for common values is not now the best way to identify linkages among professors. The claim that academics must and should find their way back to agreement on core values becomes more unrealistic with each passing year. Instead, as commonness recedes, we have to determine how "unity in diversity" comes about. One path to such unity is normative systems that hook self-interest to larger institutional chariots. In the normal course of their work, biologists or political scientists or literature professors can serve simultaneously their own achievement, the progress of their department and discipline, and the education of the young, the advancement of scholarship, and other ideals that give meaning to the academic world. The bright side of modern professionalism, especially its academic version, is that self-regarding, other-regarding, and ideal-regarding interests can be blended and simultaneously served. (These three forms of interest have been brilliantly conceptualized in Mansbridge, 1983.) In an age of specialization, academic callings are constructed primarily in the many cultural homes of the individual disciplines. Tunnel by tunnel, the disciplines qua professions serve as critical centers of meaning and as primary devices for linkage into the larger world.

Further, the disciplines do not exist simply as isolated tunnels, linking individuals in parallel chains that never meet. Both in their coverage of empirical domains and as modes of reasoning, they overlap. Michael Polanyi (1967) has acutely observed that modern science consists of "chains of overlapping neighborhoods" (p. 72). Donald T. Campbell (1969) has stressed that a comprehensive social science, or any other large domain of academic knowledge, is "a continuous texture of narrow specialties" (p. 328). Multiple specialties overlap much like the scales on the back of a fish. That overlap produces "a collective communication, a collective competence and breadth" (Campbell, p. 330). In attempting to figure out how cultural integration may coexist with diversity in a highly differentiated society, Diana Crane (1982) has observed that the social system of science is an appropriate model: "Contemporary science comprises hundreds of distinct specialities, but each speciality has connections, both intellectual and social, with other specialities. . . . Cultural integration occurs because of overlapping memberships among cultural communities that lead to the dissemination of ideas and values" (p. 239). What we find, in science and in academia, are "interlocking cultural communities" (p. 241).

In the subcultures of academe, it is a long way from physics and chemistry to political science and sociology, let alone history and literature. As cultural communities, however, physics and chemistry overlap with mathematics, which connects to statistics, both of which in turn link importantly to the "hard" social sciences of economics and psychology. They in turn shade into the softer disciplines of political science, sociology, and anthropology, fields that readily shade into the perspectives of history and then further on into the humanities. Also, more broadly, the letters and science disciplines serve as academic links to professional fields. They contribute substantive materials; and, as the "basic" disciplines, they continue to define what is scholarly.

Our imagery of cultural overlap is also heightened when we see the academic world stretching from center to periphery in the form of institutional as well as disciplinary chains. Institutionally, the hard core of academic values in the American professoriate is found in the leading research universities and top liberal arts colleges. The first exemplifies modern science and advanced scholarship; the second upholds the much-respected tradition of liberal education for undergraduates. These locales are centers whose cultural influence radiates first to adjacent types of institutions and then in weakening rays to institutional sectors more divorced in character. The top 10 universities are a powerful cultural magnet to the second 10, the top 20 to the top 50, the recognized universities to the many comprehensive colleges that so dearly want to be recognized as universities. The many different types of institutions do not operate as watertight compartments—witness the high transferability of course credit—but rather overlap to the point of heavily confusing the efforts of classifiers to draw lines between them.

The analytical handle is the idea of integration through overlap. Then we no longer need to think, as observers or participants, that integration can come about only by means of some combination of identical socialization, similarity of task, commonly held values, and united membership in a grand corps or a single association. Academics need not think that they must somehow pull themselves together around a top-down pronouncement of a fixed set of values and a universal core curriculum, swimming agains the tides of history and seeking a return to a golden age that never was. As we probe the nature of the modern academic life, especially in America, it is much more fruitful to grasp that integration can come from the bit-by-bit overlap of narrow memberships and specific identities. Specialties and disciplines, and whole colleges and universities, may serve as mediating institutions that tie individuals and small groups into the whole of the system.

For a profession that is so naturally pluralistic, and for which the future promises an ever-widening complexity of task and structure, a large dollop of pluralist theory is not a bad idea. The many dualities of commitment to discipline and institution, and the many linkages among units on these primary lines of affiliation, provide an academic version of the great federal motto: *E pluribus unum.* Whatever the future unities of the academic life in America, they will have to be rooted in the developmental differences that inhere in the ways of modern academe.

Notes

1. Unless otherwise indicated, all empirical materials reported in this paper come from a 1973–75 study that centered on 170 intensive faculty interviews in the six fields of physics, biology, political science, English, business, and medicine, in 16 universities and colleges, chosen nationally to represent six types of institutions, from leading research universities to community colleges. The interviews, taped and transcribed, led to lengthy protocols that could be variously grouped and analyzed by discipline and institutional type. Some quantitative data from the 1984 Carnegie faculty survey were also available and used. Fuller description of the research study can be found in *The Academic Life* (1987), Introduction and Appendix A.
2. These five categories of work, culture, authority, career, and association, defined as primary dimensions of academic professionalism, are developed as central chapters in *The Academic Life* (1987) to group and analyze the rich materials obtained in the 1983–85 field interviews.

References

Becher, T. (1987). The disciplinary shaping of the profession. In B. R. Clark (Ed.), *The academic profession: National, disciplinary, and institutional settings* (pp. 271–303). Berkeley and Los Angeles: University of California Press.

Campbell, D. T. (1969). Ethnocentrism of disciplines and the fish-scale model of omniscience. In M. Sherif & C. Sherif (Eds.), *Interdisciplinary relationships in the social sciences* (pp. 328–348). Chicago: Aldine.

Carnegie Foundation for the Advancement of Teaching (1987). *A classification of institutions of higher education.* Princeton, NJ: Author.

Clark, B. R. (1987). *The academic life: Small worlds, different worlds.* Princeton, NJ: Carnegie Foundation for the Advancement of Teaching and Princeton University Press.

Crane, D. (1982). Cultural differentiation, cultural integration, and social control. In J. P. Gibbs (Ed.), *Social control: Views from the social sciences* (pp. 229–244). Beverly Hills, CA: Sage.

Mansbridge, J. J. (1983). *Beyond adversary democracy.* Chicago: University of Chicago Press.

Metzger, W. P. (1987). The academic profession in the United States. In B. R. Clark (Ed.), *The academic profession: National, disciplinary, and institutional settings* (pp. 123–208). Berkeley and Los Angeles: University of California Press.

Polanyi, M. (1967). *The tacit dimension.* Garden City, NJ: Doubleday.

Wiebe, R. H. (1967). *The search for order, 1877–1920,* New York: Hill and Wang.

THE LATENT ORGANIZATIONAL FUNCTIONS
OF THE ACADEMIC SENATE

ROBERT BIRNBAUM

Academic senates[1] are generally considered to be the normative organizational structure through which faculty exercise their role in college and university governance at the institutional level [1]. Although no complete census is available, analysis of data in past studies [23, 25] suggest that senates may exist in one or another form on between 60 to 80 percent of all campuses.

With the advent of faculty collective bargaining in the late 1960s, concern was expressed that senates, unable to compete with the more adversarial and aggressive union, might disappear on many campuses [351]. Not only has this prediction proven to be false [5, 6], but there is evidence that the proportion of institutions with senates has increased over the past decades [3].

This growth is somewhat perplexing in view of the stream of criticisms that increasingly has been directed against the senate structure. It has been called weak, ineffective, an empty forum, vestigial, unrepresentative, and inept [2, 12, 24, 33, 35, 38]. Its detractors have referred to it as "slowly collapsing and becoming dormant" [24, p. 61] and "purely ceremonial" [7]. In a 1969 national study, 60 percent of faculty respondents rated the performance of their campus senate or faculty council as only "fair" or "poor" [11]. A more recent consideration of faculty governance has stated that "traditional structures do not appear to be working very well. Faculty participation has declined, and we discovered a curious mismatch between the agenda of faculty councils and the crisis now confronted by many institutions" [12, p. 12.].

These negative evaluations of faculty governance structures are not new. A trenchant observer in 1918 [47, p. 186] noted the administrative use of faculty "committees-for-the-sifting-of-the-sawdust" to give the appearance, but not the reality, of participation, and called them "a nice problem in self-deception, chiefly notable for an endless proliferation" (p. 206).

There is not complete agreement that the senate has no real instrumental value. Blau's [9] finding of a negative correlation between senate participation and educational centralization at over one hundred colleges and universities, for example, led him to state that "an institutionalized faculty government is not mere window dressing but an effective mechanism for restricting centralized control over educational programs, in accordance with the professional demands of the faculty. Formal institutionalization of faculty authority fortifies it" (p. 164). Another supporter of the senate [21], after reviewing the literature, reported that the senate continued to be "a useful mechanism for campus-wide faculty participation" (p. 26) at certain types of research universities and elite liberal arts colleges in some governance areas, although it was less useful in others. But despite the support of a small number of observers, the clear weight of evidence and authoritative opinion suggests that, except perhaps in a small number of institutions with particular characteristics, the academic senate does not work. Indeed, it has been suggested that it has never worked [2]. Yet it survives and, in many respects, thrives.

After citing a litany of major criticisms of the senate and proposing reasons for its deficiencies, Lieberman [30, p. 65] added, "what is needed is not so much a critique of their inherent weaknesses, but an explanation of their persistence in spite thereof." Similarly, Hobbs [22], in looking at the functions of university committees, suggested that rather than focusing attention on recommending ways in which these committees might be made more effective, greater attention should be given to examining their roles in university organization. This article will conduct such an examination by considering the roles that senates are presumed to play—and the roles they actually play—within four alternative organizational models that consider the senate as part of bureaucratic, collegial, political, or symbolic organizational systems.

Manifest and Latent Functions

The manifest functions of an organizational structure, policy, or practice can be thought of as those for which behavior leads to some specified and related achievement. Institutional processes that usually lead to expected and desired outcomes should be expected to persist. Often, however, organizations engage in behavior that persists over time even though the manifest function is clearly not achieved. Indeed, such behavior may persist even when there is significant evidence that the ostensible function *cannot* be achieved. There is a tendency to label such organizational behavior as irrational or superstitious and to identify an institution's inability to alter such apparently ineffectual behavior as due to "inertia" or "lack of leadership."

Merton's [36] concept of functional analysis suggests an alternative explanation. Some practices that do not appear to be fulfilling their formally intended functions may persist because they are fulfilling unintended and unrecognized latent functions that are important to the organization. As Merton describes it, functional analysis examines social practices to determine both the planned and intended (manifest) outcomes and the unplanned and unintended (latent) outcomes. This is particularly useful for the study of otherwise puzzling organizational behavior because it "clarifies the analysis of seemingly irrational social patterns . . . , directs attention to theoretically fruitful fields of inquiry . . . , and precludes the substitution of naive moral judgments for sociological analysis" (p. 64–66, 70). In particular, it points towards the close examination of persistent yet apparently ineffective institutional processes or structures to explore the possibility that they are meeting less obvious, but still important, organizational needs. "We should ordinarily (not invariably) expect persistent social patterns and social structures to perform positive functions which are at the time not adequately fulfilled by other existing patterns and structures" [36, p. 72]. The senate may do more than many of its critics believe, and "only when we attend to all the functions and their social contexts can we fully appreciate what it is that the senate does" [42, p. 174].

This article shall examine two major questions. First, and briefly, what are the manifest functions of the academic senate that its critics claim appear not to be fulfilled, and what organizational models do they imply? Second, and at greater depth, what may be the latent functions of the academic senate that may explain its growth and persistence despite its failure to meet its avowed purposes, and how do these functions relate to organizational models?

The Manifest Functions of the Academic Senate

In general, those who criticize the senate have not clearly articulated the criteria they have employed, and their analyses tend to be narrative and anecdotal with no explicit conceptual orientation. Their comments and conclusions, however, suggest that they evaluate the senate implicitly using the three traditional models of the university as a bureaucracy, as a collegium, and as a political system.

Probably the most prevalent implicit model is that of the university as bureaucracy. In his study of the effectiveness of senates (which is one of the few studies to specify desired outcomes) Millett established eight criteria that "would provide some reasonable conclusions about the contributions and the effectiveness of campus-wide governance to the process of institutional decision making" [38, p. xiv]. These included the extent to which senates clarified institutional purpose, specified program objectives, reallocated income resources, and developed new income sources, as well as the extent to which they were involved in issues such as the management of operations, degree requirements, academic behavior, and program evaluation. The identification of the senate's role in decision making and the emphasis upon goal-setting, resource allocation, and evaluation suggest an implicit view of the senate as an integral part of a hierarchical, rational organization. This bureaucratic orientation is also seen in one of the two "modal" university committee types identified by Hobbs [22]. This type, among other characteristics, meets often, has a decision-making function, records minutes, prepares written reports for administrative officers, and has a clear sense of task. Other analysts have also used language that either explicitly or metaphorically identifies the senate in bureaucratic terms. Senates are needed to deal with "the full range of academic and administrative matters" [12, p. 13], their purpose "approximates that of the college's management" [24, p. 126], and they assist "the discovery and employment of techniques to deal with deficit spending, with increasing enrollments, with healing the wounds resulting from student dissent, with curriculum expansion, with faculty salary increases in a tight budget, with parking, and so forth" [41, p. 40].

A second model implicitly views the senate as part of a political system. In this model the senate is seen as a forum for the articulation of interests and as the setting in which decisions on institutional policies and goals are reached through compromise, negotiation, and the forming of coalitions. Senates serve as a place for campus politicians to exercise their trade, which in its worst sense may identify them as "poorly attended oratorical bodies" [24, p. 127] and in the best sense means that they can "provide a forum for the resolution of a wide range of issues involving the mission and operation of the institution" [1, p. 57]. Given the significant differences that typify the interest groups that make up its constituencies, the senate enables participants to deal with inevitable conflict as they "engage one another civilly in dispute" [22, p. 242].

The model of the university as collegium is less explicitly identified in analyses of the senate than the other two models, but it appears to be recognized through constant references in the literature to the concept of collegiality. The senate in this view would be a forum for achieving Millett's [37] goal of a dynamic of consensus.

Depending upon the organizational assumptions used, an observer might consider the senate to be effective in governance either (a) to the extent that it efficiently considered institutional problems and, through rational processes, developed rules, regulations, and procedures that resolved them, or (b) to the extent that, perceived as fully representative of its constituencies, it formulated and clarified goals and policies, or (c) to the extent that, through interaction in the senate forum, it developed shared values leading to consensus. But senates often appear to do none of these things well. From the bureaucratic perspective they are slow and inefficient, from a political position they are oligarchical and not representative, and from a collegial viewpoint faculty interactions may be as likely to expose latent conflict as to increase feelings of community [39].

These alternative organizational models suggest a range of activities, processes, and outcomes as the manifest functions of the senate. Because these functions do not appear to be performed adequately, the senate has been judged to be ineffective. In many ways the senate appears to be a solution looking for problems. Millett, for example, provides a list of eight specific problems and questions raised by student activism in the 1960s (such as the role of higher education in defense research, or the role of higher education in providing community service to the disadvantaged) to which appropriately comprised senates were presumably an answer. He found that there was "very little evidence that organs of campus-wide governance, after they were established, were particularly effective in resolving these issues" [38, p. 200]. Because its manifest functions are not being fulfilled, the persistence of the senate suggests that it is filling important latent functions. What might some of these be?

The Latent Functions of the Academic Senate

The Senate as Symbol

In addition to whatever effects they may have upon outcomes, organizational structures and processes also often have symbolic importance to participants [20]. Academic senates may fill a number of important symbolic purposes. We will consider three: the senate may symbolize institutional membership in the higher education system, collective and individual faculty commitment to professional values, and joint faculty-administration acceptance of existing authority relationships.

Faculty participation in governance is generally accepted as an essential characteristic of "mainstream" colleges and universities. Since 1950 there has been a significant increase in the types and kinds of institutions that many consider only marginally identified with higher education. These include, for example, community colleges with strong administrative hierarchies, unselective state colleges with traditions rooted in teacher education and the paternalistic practices of school systems, and small and unselective independent institutions with authoritarian presidents. By establishing an academic senate structure that was more typical of the system to which they aspired than it was of the one from which they developed, an institution could suggest the existence of faculty authority even when it did not exist. This structural symbol of a faculty voice could support a claim to being a "real" college.

The development of a senate can also symbolize a general faculty commitment to substantive values. The most visible and public matters of faculty concern at some institutions have been related to faculty collective bargaining, which has tended to focus upon employee issues that in many ways were similar to those of other workers. Particularly in the public sector, but sometimes in the private sector as well, faculty emphasis upon salary, working conditions and other mundane matters has eroded in the minds of the public their claim to professional status. Creating a senate may be a response to that erosion, symbolizing a commitment to professional values and faculty concern for more purely academic matters. This helps to legitimate the institution's desire to be treated differently than other organizations and the faculty's claim to be treated differently than other groups of workers. Through a senate, the faculty can symbolically endorse such desirable attributes or outcomes as increased quality, standards, and integrity even though (or perhaps because) they cannot define either the problems or their solutions in operational terms. The senate may thus serve as a forum through which, individually and collectively, faculty may symbolically embrace values in lieu of actual behavior. Within the senate, academics who have never had controversial new ideas can publicly defend academic freedom, and those without scholarly interests can argue for reduced teaching loads to encourage research. In this way even faculty who cannot do so through the publication of scholarship or research, can publicly display their academic *bona fides*.

Senates may also serve as symbols of campus authority relationships. A major criticism directed against the senate is that it exists at the pleasure of the administration and board of trustees [3, 30]. Because of this, its authority has been described as "tenuous" [39, p. 26]. However, the fact is that although trustees have rejected senate recommendations, they have not abolished senates (except in rare circumstances involving the introduction of faculty collective bargaining). Indeed, administrations support senates and believe them to be even more "effective" than do faculty members [23]. Why should both the faculty and the administration continue to support the senate structure? It is obvious that faculty would wish to maintain senates because they are a symbol of administrative acceptance of the idea of faculty participation in governance. Administrators may support senates because voluntary faculty participation in such bodies is a tacit acknowledgement by the faculty that they recognize and accept the ultimate legal authority of the administration and board. The senate is thus a symbol of cooperation between faculty and administration. As in other organizational settings, parties may cooperate in perpetuating an already established structure even when the objective utility of the structure is agreed by the parties to be of little value [17]. The continued existence of the senate therefore is not only a visible manifestation of the ability of the parties to cooperate but also reflects an intent to further increase cooperative activities.

The symbolic value of the senate is so strong that even those like Millett [38] who after study have concluded that the senate is ineffective when evaluated against specific criteria, continue to support it. Even if it doesn't work in terms of its ostensible aims, it may be preferable that an institution have a nonfunctioning senate than that it have no senate at all.

The Senate as Status Provider

Cohen and March [13] have suggested that "most people in a college are most of the time less concerned with the content of a decision than they are with eliciting an acknowledgment of their importance within the community. . . . Faculty members are more insistent on their right to participate in faculty deliberations than they are on exercising that right" (pp. 201–2). In an analogous vein, the existence of a senate certifies the status of faculty members by acknowledging their right to participate in governance, while at the same time not obligating them to do so. The vigorous support of faculty for a strong and active voice in campus governance, coupled with their reluctance to give the time that such participation would require [16, 18], should therefore not be surprising.

The senate also offers a route of social mobility for older and less prestigious faculty locals whose concern for status based on traditional norms is frustrated by a lack of scholarly achievement [27]. Participation in committee affairs and opportunities it brings to work with higher status administrators provides a local means for enhancing their own importance.

In addition to certifying the status of participants in general, providing an opportunity for individuals to serve as senator is a means of conferring status that protects the institution from two quite different, but potentially disruptive, elements: informal leaders and organizational deviants.

Universities are normative organizations that rely upon the manipulation of symbols to control the behavior of their members [19]. Unlike organizations characterized by control through coercive or utilitarian power, normative organizations tend to have more "formal leaders" (those who influence others both through their personal power and through the organizational positions they hold) and fewer informal leaders (personal power only) or officials (positional power only). Formal leadership provides a relatively effective means of exercising power in a decentralized and loosely coupled system. By the same token, the development of informal leaders can be dysfunctional by facilitating the development of semiautonomous subgroups that can diminish the formal leader's influence.

Formal leaders cannot prevent the development of informal leaders, but in normative organizations "to the degree that informal leaders arise . . ., the tendency is to recruit them and gain their loyalty and cooperation by giving them part-time organizational positions. . . . The tendency is for the informal leaders to lose this status within the given organization and for control to remain largely in the hands of the formal leaders" [19, p. 64]. Membership in a prestigious body such as a senate with presumed quasi-administrative responsibilities can be used towards the same end "of providing alternative channels of social mobility for those otherwise excluded from the more conventional avenues for 'social advancement'" [36, p. 76]. Senate membership provides legitimate organizational roles in which informal leaders can participate and have their status confirmed while at the same time preventing them from disrupting ongoing organizational structures and processes.

There is a second group of campus participants whose activities, if not channelled through a legitimate structure such as a senate, might prove disruptive to the organization. They are the institutional deviants, often highly vocal persons with a single-minded devotion to one or another cause. Senates offer these deviant faculty a legitimized opportunity to vent their grievances and solicit potential support. Election of such persons may sometimes lead administrators to discount the senate as "nonrepresentative" and may be seen by them as yet another example of senate weakness. On the other hand, the need for even deviants to allocate attention means that time spent acting in the relatively stable environment of the senate is time they do not have available for participating in relatively more vulnerable settings, such as the department. The senate may thus serve as a system for absorbing the energies of potentially disruptive faculty members. Because the senate, like the administration, is subject to overload, it can attend to only a small number of items at any one time. The difficulty of convincing senate colleagues of the justice of their position is more likely to reduce aspirations of deviants than would be constant rebuffs by administrators or departmental colleagues; if a faculty member cannot convince his or her colleagues, how can the administration possibly be convinced?

The Senate as Garbage Can and Deep Freeze

Sometimes a college or university can use rational processes to make choices and solve problems when it is called upon to make a decision. However, this becomes difficult when unexpectedly other people become involved in the decision process, new problems are introduced, and new solutions are proposed. These independent streams of participants, problems, and solutions may somehow become attached to each other, often by chance, just as if they were all dumped into a large container, leading to what has been referred to as "garbage can decision making" [15]. Choices become more difficult as they become increasingly connected with "garbage" (that is, with problems, potential solutions, or new participants who, at least to the decision maker, appear irrelevant). Choices become easier if they can be made either before these irrelevant matters become attached to them (decision making by oversight), or after these irrelevant matters can be made to leave the choice (decision making by flight). Because of the essential ambiguity of the college and university processes, any choice point can become a garbage can. One of the latent functions of the senate may be to function as a structural garbage can, and the inability of the senate to make speedy decisions may increase its effectiveness in this role by putting some problems into an organizational "deep freeze."

An administrator who wishes to make a decision but finds it difficult to do so because irrelevant problems have become associated with it, can refer those irrelevant problems to the senate. The decision can then be made by flight while the attention of participants is directed elsewhere.

The deliberate speed of the senate makes it possible for many problems that are referred to it to resolve themselves over time with no need for any specific action. This kind of outcome is shown by the disparaging statement of one faculty member: "The committees [of the senate] report, but usually it has taken so long to 'study the issue' that the matter is long since past" [3, p. 80].

Other issues, particularly those that deal with goals and values and thus might be divisive if an attempt were made to resolve them, may be referred to the senate with the justifiable expectation that they will absorb a significant amount of energy and then will not be heard of again. Still, the senate debate has an important outcome even if it does not lead to taking action. Through the presentation of alternative positions and arguments, participants come to realize that an issue whose resolution initially appeared to be self-evident and therefore enjoying wide support is in fact complex and contentious. As the attractiveness of simplistic solutions is reduced, aspirations are modified and potential conflict is therefore managed.

The Senate as Attention Cue

The number of problems available in a university searching for decision opportunities and forums in which they can be resolved, although perhaps finite in number, is at any specific time far greater than can be acted upon. Administrative attention is in comparatively short supply, and as administrators "look for work" they must decide to which of many different potential attention cues they should pay attention. This is a nontrivial issue, because the ability of problems, solutions, decision makers, and choice opportunities to become coupled through temporal rather than through logical relationships makes it exceptionally difficult for an administrator to know on an *a priori* basis what is most important. In the absence of a calculus or an algorithm that permits administrators to predict how important any specific problem may prove to be, they must rely on heuristics (such as "oil the squeaky wheel") to indicate when an item may have reached a level of concern sufficient to require administrative attention. There are many sources of such cues: a telephone call from a state legislator or an editorial in the local paper or student press are examples. So too is discussion and action (potential or actual) by the senate. As Mason [33] and others have commented, senate agendas "tend to be exceedingly crowded . . . [and] even if a senator has succeeded in placing a policy-question in the agenda 'it will not be reached until the meeting has gone on so long that the member's one overwhelming desire is to go home'" [p. 75]. As a result, not every item that is proposed for the senate agenda actually gets on it, and not every item that gets on it is attended to. The presence of a specific item on an agenda that becomes the subject of extended discussion and possible action therefore signifies that it is of unusual importance and worth an investment of administrative time. By the same token, a matter proposed to the senate but not considered by it can be used as a justification for administrative indifference. The senate thus operates in the university in a manner similar to that of a public agency before a budget subcommittee. When there are no more than the usual level of complaints, no action need be taken. But when "an agency shouts more loudly than usual, subcommittee members have a pretty good idea that something is wrong" [46, p. 154].

Because most items which someone wants discussed by the senate are never acted upon, the use of the senate as an attention cue is an efficient way of allocating attention. It relieves the administration of responsibility for dealing with every problem, establishes a rationale for a system of priorities, provides a justification for inattention to some items, and maintains the symbolic relationship of administration responsiveness to faculty concerns.

The Senate as Personnel Screening Device

Universities constantly have to fill administrative positions, and it is often less disruptive institutionally as well as desirable financially to do so with faculty members. However, not every faculty member is acceptable, and at least two characteristics not often found in combination are desirable: a person should have the confidence of faculty colleagues and should also be sympathetic to the administrative point of view. The senate provides a forum in which such persons can be more easily identified and evaluated.

Election to the senate itself provides strong (although not absolutely reliable) evidence of acceptability to faculty colleagues, and working with administrators in preparing reports or other committee assignments allows senators to demonstrate through the equivalent of on-the-job participation their commitment to administrative values.

Anecdotal evidence indicates that administrators are often selected from among faculty "committeemen," [27, p. 83], and case study material [34] has shown how the intimate involvement of faculty committee members with administrative officers in policy formulation has meant that "many senate committee members have moved easily and naturally into regular administrative positions" [34, p. 103]. Of course, persons selected for administrative positions because they perform well in the kinds of ideological and noninstrumental debates of the senate may turn out not to be the most effective institutional leaders [13].

The Senate as Organizational Conservator

More attention has traditionally been given to the presumed negative consequences of the university's acknowledged resistance to change than to the potentially positive aspects of maintaining the ongoing system. From a functional perspective, ongoing organizational processes and structures exist in an equilibrium that is a response to and a resultant of a number of forces operating upon and within the institution. As with any open system, the university is homeostatic in nature and tends to react to the instability caused by change by responding in a manner that returns it to its former state. The senate, by inhibiting the propensity to change that increasingly characterizes the administration, serves as a major element in this homeostatic process of organizational conservation.

Administrators in general, and presidents in particular, usually do not wish to change the university in dramatic ways, and the processes through which they are selected and socialized tend to make their roles conservative [13]. Yet they occupy boundary positions in the organization and find themselves exposed, as faculty members are not, to the demands of the external environment as well as those of the organization. In that external environment there are a number of factors that implicitly or explicitly pressure university administrators to become more intrusive in organizational life [see, for example, 24]. Administrators may attempt to introduce new institutional policies in response to regulations enacted or proposed by state agencies, calls for accountability by external study groups, or potential fiscal emergencies based on worse-case scenarios. These policies almost always seek to increase administrative authority. Faculty are less likely to be directly influenced by such pressures and therefore less likely to be persuaded that dramatic action is required. By opposing such administrative initiatives, senates act not only as "an effective mechanism for restricting centralized control over academic programs" [9, p. 164], but also serve as a constraint upon an ambitious administration [18].

In addition to external pressures, there are powerful, if less obvious, reasons for increased administrative activism, and these reasons are related to the increased availability of institutional information. The movement toward the "management" of higher education has, among other things, led to complex systems for the collection and analysis by administrators of previously inaccessible institutional data. These data illuminate anomalies, inequities, and nonstandard practices that must then be justified or abolished and therefore provoke administrative intervention. But as Trow [43] has pointed out, it is precisely the obscurity caused by bad data collection that may permit the diversity and innovation upon which institutional quality is based. The senate's ability to resist administrative initiatives can therefore be seen, at least in some cases, as protecting the institution from making changes based upon measurable but ultimately unimportant factors and thus preserving those enduring organizational and institutional qualities that are beyond routine measurement.

In addition to the increased quantity of data, there are also changes in the processes through which data reach administrators in executive positions, as well as in the speed with which they move through the organization. In the past, data might eventually have come to administrative attention after having first been passed through and manipulated by a series of committees and long after corrective administrative measures could be applied. Today these same data may be transmitted directly to the president from a state coordinating board, often with a time lag measured in weeks rather than years. The effect on a university can be similar to that in other social systems characterized by "symptoms of communication failures based on a superabundance of information, inadequately assimilated, rather than its scarcity" [Douglas Cater, cited in 31, p. 1]. Today administrators may face an endless and often real-time stream of data calling for corrective action before there is time to plan, consult, or fully consider.

The existence of a senate reduces administrative aspirations for change and increases the caution with which the administration acts. This not only protects much of value within the organization but also prevents the unwitting disruption of ongoing but latent systems through which the university keeps the behavior of organizational participants within acceptable bounds. The senate thus is the structure through which, in Clark Kerr's [26] terms, the faculty serve as the institution's balance wheel, "resisting some things that should be resisted, insisting on more thorough discussion of some things that should be more thoroughly discussed, delaying some developments where delay gives time to adjust more gracefully to the inevitable. All this yields a greater sense of order and stability" (p. 100).

The Senate as Ritual and as Pastime

Senates usually meet on a regular schedule, follow a standard agenda format, involve the same core of participants, and engage in their activities under stipulated rules of order. In an organization typified by ambiguity, it is often comforting to engage in scheduled and structured activities in which the behaviors of others can be generally predicted. The senate thus serves as a ritual, a "formality of procedure or action that either is not directed towards a pragmatic end, or if so directed, will fail to achieve the intended aim" [10, cited in 32, p. 164]. The identification of the senate as "theatrical and debate-oriented" [24, p. 127] underscores its ritualistic qualities.

The rituals of senates serve a number of important organizational functions. Among other things, it helps stabilize and order the organization, it provides assurances that mutually expected interactions will occur, and it reduces anxiety [32]. Senates also provide organizational participants with opportunities for engaging in acceptable behavior when faced with ambiguous or uncertain stimuli. When one doesn't know what else to do, participating in senate debate can appear to be a contribution towards solutions and can enable faculty members to "pretend that they are doing something significant" [3, p. 80].

Ritual provides participants with a sense of membership and integration into an organization and into a profession. For others, however, the senate may be enjoyed purely as a pastime. It is a place where one can meet friends, engage in political intrigues, gossip about the administration, and complain about parking—all common forms of faculty recreation. It is also a place where speeches can be made, power can be displayed, nits can be picked, and the intricacies of Robert's Rules of Order can be explored at infinite depth. Those faculty who do enjoy such things have a vested interest in perpetuating the senate, for without it a forum for their involvement would be lost.

The Senate as Scapegoat

The best-laid plans of institutions often go awry. To some extent, this may be due to cognitive limits to rationality that suggest that only a small proportion of potentially important variables may be attended to at any given time. Equally as important may be the organizational characteristics of colleges and universities as decentralized and loosely coupled systems [44]. In such systems it is often difficult to predict events, and intentions, actions, and outcomes may be only modestly related. Even the power of the president, usually considered the single most influential person in the institution, is severely circumscribed.

When plans are not enacted or goals not achieved, organizational constituents search for reasons. In order to meet psychological needs, these reasons must of course blame others and not oneself; and in order to meet political needs, these reasons must be specific rather than conceptual. A president is unlikely to blame an institutional failure on weak presidential performance, and a board of trustees is not likely to accept a president's argument that a certain task cannot be performed because it is beyond the capabilities of a loosely coupled system. On the other hand, Boards can understand a president's assertion that a specific act was made difficult or impossible because of opposition by the senate and may even entertain a claim that it would be impossible to implement a program because of the likelihood of future senate opposition. In the same way, faculty members at the department or school level can argue against considering a new policy on the grounds that the senate would not approve it and can blame the senate when a program supported by the senate breaks down when implemented at lower organizational levels.

Cause and effect relationships are extremely difficult to assess in the equivocal environment of the college or university. The actions (or lack thereof) of a structure such as the senate, which has high visibility and an ambiguous charge, can plausibly be blamed for deficiencies of all kinds in institutional operation. An academic department can use the senate as a scapegoat for its own unwillingness to make the difficult choices necessary to strengthen its departmental curriculum as easily as a politically incompetent president can accuse it of scuttling a major policy initiative. In these and in similar cases, the senate helps the participants "make sense" of an exceptionally complex system while at the same time preserving their self-images of acumen and professional competence.

Academic Senates in Symbolic Organizational Systems

This article began by discussing the perceived shortcomings of senates when traditional organizational models of the bureaucracy, collegium, and political system are used to assess their effectiveness. It then suggested a number of important latent functions that senates may play. Let us now consider these latent functions in the context of newer models that view organizations as symbolic or cultural systems.

Our world is too complex, equivocal, and confusing to be understood completely, and people must find ways of simplifying and interpreting it if they are to function effectively. There are many ways in which the world can be interpreted, and organizations can be seen as groups of people who interact regularly in an attempt to construct and understand reality, to make sense of ambiguous events, and to share meanings in distinctive ways. Through their regular interactions they develop a culture, which may be defined as "the values or social ideals and the beliefs that organizational members come to share. These values or beliefs are manifested by symbolic devices such as myths, rituals, stories, legends, and specialized language" [40, p. 344].

Within the context of these cultural inventions, people decide what is important, take indeterminate relationships and develop them into coherent beliefs about cause and effect, and retrospectively make sense of events that were too equivocal to be understood as they occurred. A major organizational model built upon these ideas is that of the "organized anarchy," an institution characterized by problematic goals, unclear technology and fluid participation. "The American college or university is a prototypical organized anarchy. It does not know what it is doing. Its goals are either vague or in dispute. Its technology is familiar but not understood. Its major participants wander in and out of the organization. These factors do not make the university a bad organization, or a disorganized one; but they do make it a problem to describe, understand, and lead" [13, p. 3].

An organized anarchy is a loosely coupled system in which individuals and subunits within the organization make essentially autonomous decisions. Institutional outcomes are a resultant of these only modestly interdependent activities and are often neither planned nor predictable. It is difficult in such an environment to make inferences about cause and effect, to determine how successful one is, or even to be certain in advance whether certain environmental changes or evolving issues will turn out to be important or trivial. In this situation of great ambiguity, people spend more time in sense making than in decision making [45] and in engaging in activities that verify their status. The decoupling of choices and outcomes makes symbolic behavior particularly important, and particular choices, problems, solutions, and participants often become associated with one another because of their temporal, rather than their logical relationships.

Organized anarchies need structures and processes that symbolically reinforce their espoused values, that provide opportunities for individuals to assert and confirm their status, and that allow people to understand to which of many competing claims on their attention they should respond. They require a means through which irrelevant problems and participants can be encouraged to seek alternative ways of expressing themselves so that decision makers can do their jobs. They should also be able to "keep people busy, occasionally entertain them, give them a variety of experiences, keep them off the streets, provide pretexts for storytelling, and allow socializing" [45, p. 264].

Given these requirements, the issue of the "success" of the academic senate can be seen from a completely different perspective. Questions concerning its rationality, efficiency, ability to resolve important issues, representatives, and community-building effectiveness, which may be important under other models, are of less consequence here. If one uses notions of symbolic or cultural systems to consider a college or university as an organized anarchy, academic senates may be effective indeed. This may be the reason they have survived and prospered even though they have not fulfilled the manifest purposes that their charters claim. If senates did not exist, we would have to invent them.

It's time to say something nice about senates. The concept of organized anarchy appears to capture a significant aspect of the role of the senate on many campuses but certainly not of all senates on all campuses at all times. There are many examples of senates that have taken responsibility for resolving a specific problem and have done so in a timely and efficient manner. There are senates in which important institutional policy has been determined and through whose processes of interaction faculty have developed shared values and increased feelings of community. Given the comments of observers of the senate, however, these appear to be exceptional rather than common occurrences.

Those who observe the workings of senates and find them deficient should be particularly careful in making recommendations for change, because these changes might affect not only performance of manifest functions but their important latent functions as well. This is particularly true when making recommendations based upon normative and ultimately moral concepts such as "shared authority" or "representativeness." Merton [36, p. 71] warned that "since moral evaluations in a society tend to be largely in terms of the manifest consequences of a practice or code, we should be prepared to find that analysis in terms of latent functions at times runs counter to prevailing moral evaluations. For it does not follow that the latent functions will operate in the same fashion as the manifest consequences which are ordinarily the basis of these judgments."

Anyone who recommends that senates change or be eliminated in favor of some other organizational structure should carefully consider their latent functions. As a general principle, "any attempt to eliminate an existing social structure without providing adequate alternative structures for fulfilling the functions previously fulfilled by the abolished organization is doomed to failure [and] is to indulge in social ritual rather than social engineering" [36, p. 81]. Functional analysis also enables us to evaluate more clearly warnings such as that senates are "ineffective because faculty [are] not active participants. If faculty do not become involved in . . . senate . . . affairs, the ominous predictions about the demise of faculty governance may come true" [4, p. 345–46]. To the extent that the organized anarchy model is an appropriate one, the future of the senate in governance is unlikely to be related to increased faculty involvement.

Notes

1. The term "academic senate" is used in this article to identify a formal, representative governance structure at the institutional level that may include only faculty (a "pure" senate), or one that, in addition to a faculty majority, may also include representatives of other campus constituencies, such as administrators, academic staff members, and/or students (a "mixed" senate), as defined by the Report of the AAHE Task Force on Faculty Representation and Academic Negotiations [1, p. 34].

References

American Association for Higher Education. *Faculty Participation in Academic Governance.* Washington, D.C.: American Association for Higher Education, 1967.

Baldridge, J. V. "Shared Governance: a Fable about the Lost Magic Kingdom." *Academe,* 1982, 68; 12–15.

Baldridge, J. V., D. V. Curtis, G. Ecker, and G. L. Riley. *Policy Making and Effective Leadership.* San Francisco: Jossey-Bass, 1978.

Baldridge, J. V., and F. R. Kemerer. "Academic Senates and Faculty Collective Bargaining." *Journal of Higher Education,* July/August 1976, 47; 391–411.

Baldridge, J. V., F. R. Kemerer, and Associates. *Assessing The Impact of Faculty Collective Bargaining.* Washington, D.C.: American Association for Higher Education, 1981.

Begin, J. P. "Faculty Collective Bargaining and Faculty Reward Systems." In *Academic Rewards in Higher Education,* edited by L. Becker. Cambridge: Ballinger, 1979.

Ben-David, J. *American Higher Education: Directions Old and New.* New York: McGraw-Hill, 1972.

Berry, M. F. "Faculty Governance." In *Leadership for Higher Education,* edited by R. W. Heyns. Washington, D.C.: American Council on Education, 1977.

Blau, P. M. *The Organization of Academic Work.* New York: John Wiley and Sons, 1973.

Burnett, J. H. "Ceremony, Rites, and Economy in the Student System of an American High School." *Human Organization,* 1969, 28; 1–10.

Carnegie Commission on Higher Education. *Governance of Higher Education: Six Priority Problems.* New York: McGraw-Hill, 1973.

Carnegie Foundation for the Advancement of Teaching. "A Governance Framework for Higher Education." *Educational Record,* 1983, 64; 12–18.

Cohen, M. D. and J. G. March. *Leadership and Ambiguity: The American College President.* New York: McGraw-Hill, 1974.

_____. "Decisions, Presidents, and Status." In J. G. March and J. P. Olsen, *Ambiguity and Choice in Organizations,* 2d ed., Bergen: Universitetsforlaget, 1979.

Cohen, M. D., J. G. March, and J. P. Olsen. "A Garbage Can Model of Organizational Choice." *Administrative Science Quarterly,* 1972, 17; 1–25.

Corson, J. J. *Governance of Colleges and Universities.* New York: McGraw-Hill, 1960.

Deutsch, M. *The Resolution of Conflict: Constructive and Destructive Forces.* New Haven: Yale University Press, 1973.

Dykes, A. R. *Faculty Participation in Academic Decision Making.* Washington, D.C.: American Council on Education, 1968.

Etzioni, A. *Modern Organizations.* Englewood Cliffs, N.J.: Prentice-Hall, 1964.

Feldman M. S. and J. G. March. "Information in Organizations as Signal and Symbol." *Administrative Science Quarterly,* 1981, 26; 171–86.

Floyd, C. E. *Faculty Participation in Decision Making: Necessity or Luxury?* Washington, D.C.: Association for the Study of Higher Education, 1985.

Hobbs, W. C. "Organizational Roles of University Committees." *Research in Higher Education,* 1975, 3; 233–42.

Hodgkinson, H. L. *The Campus Senate: Experiment in Democracy.* Berkeley: Center for Research and Development in Higher Education, 1974.

Keller, G. *Academic Strategy: The Management Revolution in American Higher Education.* Baltimore: The Johns Hopkins University Press, 1983.

Kemerer, F. R., and J. V. Baldridge. *Unions on Campus.* San Francisco: Jossey-Bass, 1975.

Kerr, C. *The Uses of the University.* Cambridge, Mass.: Harvard University Press, 1964.

Ladd, E. C., Jr., and S. M. Lipset. *Professors, Unions, and American Higher Education.* Washington, D.C.: American Enterprise Institute for Public Policy Research, 1973.

Lee, B. A. *Collective Bargaining in Four-Year Colleges.* Washington, D.C.: American Association for Higher Education, 1978.

_____. "Contractually Protected Governance Systems at Unionized Colleges." *Review of Higher Education,* 1982,5; 69–85.

Liberman, M. "Representational Systems in Higher Education." In *Employment Relations in Higher Education,* edited by S. Elam and M. H. Moskow. Washington, D.C.: Phi Delta Kappa, 1969.

Magarrell, J. "The Social Repercussions of an 'Information Society'." *Chronicle of Higher Education,* 1980, 20; 1, 10.

Masland, A. T. "Simulators, Myth, and Ritual in Higher Education." *Research in Higher Education,* 1983, 18; 161–77.

Mason, H. L. *College and University Government: A Handbook of Principle and Practice.* New Orleans: Tulane University, 1972.

McConnell, T. R. "Faculty Government." In *Power and Authority,* edited by H. L. Hodgkinson and L. R. Meeth. San Francisco: Jossey-Bass, 1971.

McConnell, T. R., and K. P. Mortimer. *The Faculty in University Governance.* Berkeley: Center for Research and Development in Higher Education, 1971.

Merton, R. K. *Social Theory and Social Structure,* rev. ed. Glencoe, Ill.: The Free Press, 1957.

Millett, J. D. *The Academic Community.* New York: McGraw-Hill, 1962.

_____. *New Structures of Campus Power.* San Francisco: Jossey-Bass, 1978.

Mortimer, K. P., and T. R. McConnell. *Sharing Authority Effectively: Participation, Interaction and Discretion.* San Francisco: Jossey-Bass, 1978.

Smircich, L. "Concepts of Cultural and Organizational Analysis." *Administrative Science Quarterly,* 1983, 28; 339–58.

Stone, J. N., Jr. "Achieving Broad-Based Leadership." In *Leadership for Higher Education,* edited by R. W. Heyns. Washington, D.C.: American Council on Education, 1977.

Tierney, W. G. "Governance by Conversation: An Essay on the Structure, Function, and Communicative Codes of a Faculty Senate." *Human Organization,* 1983, 42; 172–77.

Trow, M. "The Public and Private Lives of Higher Education." *Daedalus,* 1975, 104; 113–27.

Weick, K. E. "Educational Organizations as Loosely Coupled Systems." *Administrative Science Quarterly,* 1976, 21; 1–19.

_____. *The Social Psychology of Organizing,* 2nd ed. Reading, Mass.: Addison-Wesley, 1979.

Wildavsky, A. *The Politics of the Budgetary Process,* 2nd ed. Boston: Little, Brown, 1974.

Veblen, T. *The Higher Learning in America.* New York: Sagamore Press, 1957. (Originally published in 1918.)

Presented at the Annual Meeting of the Association for the Study of Higher Education, San Diego, California, 14–17 February 1987.

The project presented or reported herein was prepared pursuant to a grant from the Office of Educational Research and Improvement/Department of Education (OERI/ED). However, the opinions expressed herein do not necessarily reflect the position or policy of the OERI/ED, and no official endorsement by the OERI/ED should be inferred.

Robert Birnbaum was professor of higher education at Teachers College, Columbia University, when this article was written. He is currently professor of higher education at the University of Maryland, College Park, and project director at the National Center for Postsecondary Governance and Finance.

STATEMENT ON BOARD RESPONSIBILITY FOR INSTITUTIONAL GOVERNANCE

ASSOCIATION OF GOVERNING BOARDS OF UNIVERSITIES AND COLLEGES

Foreword

The enormous diversity among American colleges and universities is reflected in their disparate governance structures and functions. Although the culture and process of governance varies widely among institutions, the presence of lay citizen governing boards distinguishes American higher education from most of the rest of the world, where universities ultimately are dependencies of the state. America's public and private institutions also depend on government, but they historically have been accorded autonomy in carrying out their educational functions through the medium of independent governing boards, working collaboratively with presidents, senior administrators and faculty leaders. These boards usually are appointed by governors (and less frequently elected), in the case of public institutions, and are generally self-perpetuating (selected by current board members), in the case of private institutions.

The "AGB Statement on Board Responsibility for Institutional Governance" encourages all governing boards and presidents to examine the clarity, coherence, and appropriateness of their institutions' governance structures, policies, and practices, and recommends a number of principles of good practice related to institutional governance. Moreover, it reflects a governing board perspective, taking into consideration the many changes that have occurred in American higher education during the four decades since the American Association of University Professors promulgated its "Statement on Government of Colleges and Universities" (1966), a document that AGB commended to its members.

AGB's original Statement on Institutional Governance was inspired by the work of the Commission on the Academic Presidency, whose report and recommendations AGB published in 1996. After gathering insights from college and university chief executives, trustees, administrators, and faculty from across higher education and considering hundreds of public comments in response to a draft of the statement, the AGB Board of Directors approved it in November 1998. Much has happened in the succeeding decade to suggest the need for a revision of the original statement.

In 2006, AGB's Task Force on the State of the Presidency in American Higher Education completed a year-long study of the contemporary presidency that recognized a series of new demands on and expectations of academic presidents. As a result, the task force urged presidents and governing boards to embrace "integral leadership" in which the president "exerts a presence that is purposeful and consultative, deliberative yet decisive, and capable of course corrections as new challenges emerge." In addition, the group recommended that presidents focus more on the larger higher education community in order to "sustain the public trust and serve the nation's needs." Finally, signaling the need for a new collaborative spirit in governance, the task force called on presidents and governing boards to partner in leadership, with the support and involvement of the faculty: "Leadership of this sort links the president, the faculty, and the board together in a well-functioning partnership purposefully devoted to a well-defined, broadly affirmed institutional vision."

http://www.agb.org/news/2010-03/statenet-board-responsibility-institutional-governance.

Shortly thereafter, AGB's Board of Directors offered further guidance to boards and presidents in their "Statement on Board Accountability" (2007). They challenged boards to remember that they are accountable for institutional mission and heritage, for the transcendent values of American higher education (self-regulation and autonomy, academic freedom and due process, shared governance, transparency, and educational quality and fiscal integrity), to the public interest and public trust, and to the legitimate interests of various constituencies.

Like the original statement, this revision is not intended to be prescriptive. Rather, it is intended to serve as a template and resource for discussion of good governance policies, principles, and practices. Influenced by the current environment for higher education and its governance and informed by the association's work in the last decade, it also strives to be true to the academic traditions of board responsibility and accountability, shared governance, and faculty professionalism while still confronting the rapidly changing and oftentimes threatening political, social and economic environment in which higher education works to serve the nation and students.

Changing Environment and Perspectives

American higher education is increasingly important today to individuals, the country, and the world. For higher education and those responsible for governance, continuous and accelerating change—social, political, economic and technological—presents many challenges, including:

- Students: College-going students are older and more racially and ethnically diverse; nearly 40 percent are over 25 and 32 percent are racial and ethnic minorities (2008 Digest of Education Statistics, US DOE). More than ever before, students attend part-time, start their education in a two-year institution, enroll in more than one institution before completing a degree, and take more than four years to complete an undergraduate degree.

- Faculty: The proportion of full-time tenured and tenure-track faculty has declined to about one-third, nationally, and the number of full-time non-tenure track, part-time, and contingent faculty has increased, especially in two-year colleges. In most institutions, only full-time tenured or tenure-track faculty participate in faculty senates and other governance bodies. There is a widespread perception that faculty members, especially in research universities, are more loyal to their academic disciplines than to the welfare of their own institutions, eschewing, therefore, a commitment to institutional citizenship. In addition, participation in institutional governance is not always recognized or rewarded on par with other faculty work.

- Insufficient Resources: Persistent national and global financial difficulties have intensified the already challenging economic circumstances of all segments of American higher education. State appropriations for higher education have not kept pace with the funding needs of institutions and systems. The long-term economic outlook is challenging for all and desperate for some.

- Higher Education's Highly Competitive Marketplace: While American higher education's prominence and stature in the world remain high, other nations' investment in postsecondary education has challenged that standing. Intense competition for students, faculty, and resources from both within and outside the enterprise is a diversion from higher education's attention to the educational mission. Colleges and universities are challenged to demonstrate and defend their value and to reassert the public purposes they serve.

- Accountability and Scrutiny: The public demands greater accountability—particularly regarding student learning outcomes and escalating tuition and fees—and elected officials at both state and national levels have intensified their scrutiny of higher education.

- Effectiveness of Institutional Governance: Higher expectations for effectiveness and a growing need to be responsive to changes outside of higher education have increased the importance of good communication among the president, administration, governing board, and faculty. Many presidents, governing boards, and faculty members believe that institutional governance is so cumbersome that timely and effective decision making is imperiled; factionalism, distrust and miscommunication, and lack of engagement among the parties can impede the decision-making process.

- Focus on Jobs and the Economy: Higher education officials are increasingly sensitive at the undergraduate level to changing student interests, continuing pressure for career preparation, shifting demands of the job market, and the desire of governments to have higher education serve as the economic engine of states and regions.

- Pace of Change: Scholars, institutes, and a variety of commissions continue to anticipate a major transformation of higher education as a result of a revolution in information technology, the reorientation of the focus of education from teaching to learning, and increased competition from corporate, for-profit and online enterprises in the higher education market. Evidence of such change is abundant, but transformation hardly describes the nature of the change that is occurring. Indeed, many observers and critics of higher education see the changes as inadequate and too slow to meet current societal and market needs and economic realities.

Higher education and its governance structures need to work well to ensure the success of colleges and universities and their responsiveness to a changing environment. In this context, AGB's Board of Directors examined, revised and approved this statement on board responsibility for institutional governance.

Richard D. Legon
President
Association of Governing Boards of Universities and Colleges

AGB Statement on Board Responsibility for Institutional Governance

This statement was approved on January 22, 2010, by the Board of Directors of the Association of Governing Boards of Universities and Colleges. The following principles are intended to guide boards in the governance of colleges, universities, and systems, inform them of their roles and responsibilities, and clarify their relationships with presidents, administration, faculty, and others involved in the governance process.

Principles

1. **The ultimate responsibility for governance of the institution (or system) rests in its governing board.** Boards are accountable for the mission and heritage of their institutions and the transcendent values that guide and shape higher education; they are equally accountable to the public and to their institutions' legitimate constituents. The governing board should retain ultimate responsibility and full authority to determine the mission of the institution (within the constraints of state policies and with regard for the state's higher education needs in the case of public institutions or multi-campus systems), in consultation with and on the advice of the president, who should consult with the faculty and other constituents. The board is also responsible for the strategic direction of the institution or system through its insistence on and participation in comprehensive, integrated institutional planning. As with many other issues, the board should collaborate with the president, senior leadership team, and faculty leaders to arrive at an understanding concerning strategic direction, then to ensure that the institution has or can raise the resources necessary to sustain the mission, compete in the educational marketplace, and accomplish these strategic goals.

   While they cannot delegate their ultimate fiduciary responsibility for the academic quality and fiscal integrity of the institution, boards depend upon the president for institutional leadership, vision, and strategic planning, and they delegate to the president abundant authority to manage the operations of the institution. The board partners with the president and senior leadership to achieve the mission, sustain core operations, and attain the strategic priorities of the institution. A board must clearly convey the responsibilities it expects the president to fulfill and hold the president accountable, but it also must establish conditions that generate success for the president.

2. **The board should establish effective ways to govern while respecting the culture of decision making in the academy.** Colleges and universities have many of the characteristics of business enterprises, and their boards are accountable for ensuring that their institutions are managed in accordance with commonly accepted business standards. At the same time, colleges and universities differ from businesses in many respects. They do not operate with a profit motive, and the "bottom line" of a college or university has more to do with human development and the creation and sharing of knowledge—as measured in student learning outcomes, persistence to graduation, degrees conferred, quality of campus life, and the level of excellence attained by faculty in teaching and scholarly pursuits—than with simply balancing the budget, as important as that annual goal is. Moreover, by virtue of their special mission and purpose in a pluralistic society, colleges and universities have a tradition of both academic freedom and constituent participation—commonly called "shared governance"—that is strikingly different from that of business and more akin to that of other peer-review professions, such as law and medicine. The meaningful involvement of faculty and other campus constituencies in deliberations contributes to effective institutional governance.

Perhaps the most striking attribute of American higher education—sometimes explicit, sometimes implicit—is that faculty are accorded significant responsibility for and control of curriculum and pedagogy. This delegation of authority has historically resulted in continuous innovation and the concomitant effect that American college curricula and pedagogy define the leading edge of knowledge, its production, and its transmission. Board members are responsible for being well informed about and for monitoring the quality of educational programs and pedagogy. Defining the respective roles of boards, administrators, and faculty in regard to academic programs and preserving and protecting academic freedom are essential board responsibilities.

In concert with presidents, senior administrators, and faculty leaders, boards should make a conscious effort to minimize the ambiguous or overlapping areas in which more than one governance participant or campus constituency has authority. Governance documents should state who has the authority for specific decisions—that is, to which persons or bodies authority has been delegated and whether that which has been delegated is subject to board review. Boards should recognize that academic tradition, especially the status accorded faculty because of their central role in teaching and generating new knowledge, creates the need for deliberation and participation of faculty and other key constituents in decision making. The board, however, should reserve the right to review, challenge, and occasionally override decisions or proposals it judges to be inconsistent with mission, educational quality, or fiscal integrity. For example, the delegation of authority to the administration and faculty for adding, reducing, or discontinuing academic programs is made with the understanding that the board retains the ultimate responsibility for approving such actions.

The respective roles of the administration, faculty, and governing board in faculty promotions and tenure illustrate the principle of collaboration, a principle best achieved when responsibilities and expectations are clearly articulated. For example, although in most institutions the board will exercise its ultimate responsibility by approving individual tenure and promotion decisions, it might choose to delegate other kinds of actions to the president and senior leadership team, which might, in turn, delegate some authority for specific decisions to an appropriate faculty body.

Boards and presidents should plan reasonable time for consultative and decision-making processes and establish deadlines for their conclusion with the clear understanding that failure to act in accordance with these deadlines will mean that the next highest level in the governance process will have to proceed with decision making. Even in the context of academic governance, with its sometimes lengthy processes, a single individual or group should not be allowed to impede decisions through inaction.

Clarity does not preclude overlapping areas of responsibility, but each group should understand whether its purview, as well as that of others in the governance process, is determinative, consultative or informational. Moreover, the board and the president or chancellor should ensure the systematic, periodic review of all institutional policies, including those affecting institutional governance. "Communication," "consultation," and "decision making" should be defined and differentiated in board and institutional policies. For example, governing boards should communicate their investment and endowment spending policies, but they may choose not to invite consultation on these matters. Student financial-aid policies and broad financial-planning assumptions call for both communication and meaningful consultation with campus constituents.

3. **The board should approve a budget and establish guidelines for resource allocation using a process that reflects strategic priorities.** Budgets are usually developed by the administration, with input from and communication with interested constituents. The board should not, however, delegate the final determination of the overall resources available for strategic investment directed to achieving mission, sustaining core operations, and assuring attainment of priorities. Once the board makes these overarching decisions, it should delegate resource-allocation decisions to the president who may, in turn, delegate them to others.

   In those instances in which the board believes resources will need to be reallocated in ways that will lead to reducing or eliminating some programs, faculty, or staff, the board should charge the president and senior leadership team to create a process for decision making that includes consultation, clear and explicit criteria, and communication with constituent groups. The board should recognize that effective institutional action is more likely when all parties have some joint responsibility for and have collaborated on the process and criteria. For example, if the board decides the institution is in such financial jeopardy that faculty and staff reductions and reallocations are necessary, it first should consult, through the president, with constituent groups, then share appropriate information and describe the analysis that led it to such a determination.

4. **Boards should ensure open communication with campus constituencies.** Faculty, staff, and students have a vital stake in the institution and should be given opportunities to be heard on various issues and participate in the governance process. Historically, higher education governance has included three principal internal participants: governing boards, senior administrators, and the full-time tenured and tenure-track faculty. In fact, other campus constituents exist, and in increasing numbers. For example, the nonacademic staff substantially outnumbers the faculty, but this group rarely has a formal voice in governance. The same is true of the non-tenure-eligible, part-time, and adjunct or contingent faculty. These latter groups now predominate in community colleges and are an ever-larger component of the faculty in four-year colleges and universities, particularly in the public sector.

   It is AGB's view that faculty, staff, and students ordinarily should not serve as voting members of their own institution's governing board because such involvement runs counter to the principle of independence of judgment required of board members. Particularly in the case of faculty or staff members, board membership can place them in conflict with their employment status. Even when constituent groups are represented on the board, the board should be mindful that the presence of one or more students, faculty, or staff as members of the board or its committees or institutional task forces neither constitutes nor substitutes for communication and consultation with these constituent groups.

   The involvement of these diverse internal constituent groups will vary according to the issue or topic under consideration and the culture of the institution—for instance, full-time faculty will have a primary role in decisions concerning academic programs and faculty personnel matters—but the board is responsible for establishing the rules by which these voices are heard and their perspectives considered. Moreover, boards should strive to ensure opportunities for participation in governance, while recognizing that the subject matter in question will determine which constituent groups have predominant or secondary interests and voice.

Although the board is an independent policy-making body, it routinely relies upon the president as its major window on the institution; the board should expect candor, frequent communication, and sufficient information from the administration and its leaders. In turn, the board should support the president, while maintaining a healthy degree of independence, and ensure that the voices of other campus constituents are heard.

In institutions with faculty or staff collective bargaining agreements, it is important to ensure strong institutional governance and to clarify its relationship to the agreement. For example, academic senates and unions coexist effectively in many settings, but their effectiveness is contingent on the clarity of the respective responsibilities of the senate, other traditional academic governance structures, and the bargaining unit. The board should consider a formal policy regarding the role of union officials in institutional governance and articulate any limitations on their participation.

5. **The governing board should manifest a commitment to accountability and transparency and should exemplify the behavior it expects of other participants in the governance process.** From time to time, boards should examine their membership, structure, policies, and performance. Boards and their individual members should engage in periodic evaluations of their effectiveness and commitment to the institution or public system that they serve. In the spirit of transparency and accountability, the board should be prepared to set forth the reasons for its decisions.

Just as administrators and boards should respect the need for individual faculty members to exercise both academic freedom and responsible professionalism in their instruction, research, and scholarly activities, boards should exercise restraint in matters of administration. And just as responsible faculty participation in governance places good institutional citizenship ahead of disciplinary, departmental, or personal interest, so should individual board members avoid even the perception of any personal agendas or special interests. Board members and governing boards should not be seen as advocates for their appointing authorities or for certain segments among their constituents or the electorate; regardless of how they were selected or elected as board members, their commitment should clearly be to the welfare of the institution or system as a whole. Board members as well as faculty members and staff should strive to collaborate with, and avoid undermining, their presidents and senior leadership teams.

6. **Governing boards have the ultimate responsibility to appoint and assess the performance of the president.** Indeed, the selection, assessment, and support of the president are the most important exercises of strategic responsibility by the board. The process for selecting a new president should provide for participation of constituents, particularly faculty; however, the decision on appointment should be made by the board. Boards should assess the president's performance on an annual basis for progress toward attainment of goals and objectives, as well as for compensation review purposes, and more comprehensively every several years in consultation with other constituent groups. In assessing the president's performance, boards should bear in mind that board and presidential effectiveness are interdependent.

7. **System governing boards should clarify the authority and responsibilities of the system head, campus heads, and any institutional quasi-governing or advisory boards.** Most public colleges and universities are part of multi-campus systems that accord the system board the legal authority and responsibility for governing a set of institutions or campuses. The system board should ensure that governance documents address the relationships and respective responsibilities among system and institutional boards and administrators, including, for example, boards and administrative officers of the professional schools of law, medicine, health sciences, and business, and of intercollegiate athletics. Governing boards of multi-campus systems should lean strongly in the direction of maximum possible autonomy for individual campuses or schools, operating within the framework of an overall system-wide plan and public agenda.

8. **Boards of both public and independent colleges and universities should play an important role in relating their institutions to the communities they serve.** The preceding principles primarily address the internal governance of institutions or multi-campus systems. Governance should also be informed by and relate to external stakeholders. Governing boards can facilitate appropriate and reciprocal influence between the institution and external parties in many ways.

Public institutions receive a significant percentage of their financial resources through state governments, statewide coordinating bodies (in some cases), and increasingly through foundations affiliated with the institution or system; governing boards are accountable for these funds. The responsibilities of these officials and bodies vary widely among the states, but governing boards should serve as important buffers between the college or university and the political structures, partisan politics, and pressures of state government. Boards should also serve as bridges to state government leaders whose views and perspectives concerning the conduct of public higher education, as it relates to state needs and priorities, should be heard and considered. Together with the president, the board should also serve as a bridge between the institution or system and its affiliated asset management and fund-raising organization. These board responsibilities require a skillful balancing of effective communication and sensitive advocacy in articulating and defending the mission, core programs and operations, and strategic priorities of the institution and in conveying to institutional constituents the concerns of external stakeholders.

The relationships among the institution or system and the various external political and regulatory oversight groups should reflect an understanding by which the institution or system is held accountable for results in relation to agreed-upon objectives. This arrangement preserves the essential autonomy of the institution or system, which differentiates it from other state entities, and makes it clear that it is accountable for results.

Governing boards of independent colleges and universities also play an important role in connecting the institution to the community and representing the broader public interest in higher education. In their deliberations, in addition to advocating for the mission of the institution, board members should advocate for fulfillment of the public purposes of higher education, such as an educated citizenry, prepared workforce, and equal opportunity, to which colleges and universities with widely varying missions contribute. In coordination with the administration, board members should also advocate on behalf of their institution and higher education in their communication and relationships with political, community, philanthropic and economic leaders, and other constituents.

All boards, public and private, should exercise caution in adopting the policies and procedures promulgated by any outside organizations. With the possible exception of those institutions owned by or closely affiliated with sponsoring organizations that contribute to their finances or otherwise hold title to their property and assets, the board should not feel obligated to adopt the policies and prescriptions of other bodies.

Conclusion

College and university governing board membership is one of the most serious and consequential exercises of voluntary leadership in our society. It calls for balancing and sometimes buffering the often-conflicting claims of multiple internal and external constituents. It requires good judgment in avoiding micromanagement while being sufficiently informed to assess professional performance and institutional effectiveness. It calls for listening and questioning more than pronouncing and demanding. Most of all, it requires a commitment to the institution as a whole rather than to any of its parts. Governing board membership is both challenging and enormously rewarding in the service of the current and future generations of students and, ultimately, the nation's well-being.

Questions to Consider

The following questions should help boards assess whether policies and practices concerning the participation of board members, administrators, faculty, staff, and students in institutional governance are reasonably clear, coherent, and consistent. Answers to these questions will help boards and presidents determine whether to establish a process, to revise policies and procedures or to improve how they are implemented.

1. Do board members, the president, administrators, faculty, staff, and students understand those areas for which the board has ultimate responsibility, in consultation with appropriate constituent groups or bodies?

2. What information does the board receive and monitor to fulfill its fiduciary responsibilities and oversee the quality of academic programs? How rigorous is this oversight?

3. In what areas has the board's authority been delegated and in what documents can this be found? How does the board hold accountable those who have received this delegation of authority?

4. How do board orientation and education support board understanding of the institution's governance structure, procedures, faculty participation in institutional governance, and the tradition of academic freedom? How do faculty orientation and professional development support faculty understanding of the institution's governance structure and procedures and encourage participation in institutional governance?

5. If the board governs a multi-campus system, is the authority of the system head, campus heads, and institution-based advisory or quasi-governing boards reasonably clear and effective? How is this authority communicated to the various parties/constituents? How does the board monitor the effectiveness of various parties/constituencies in exercising their authority?

6. How does the board stay informed about collective bargaining at its institution or in its system, and how does it assess the effect of collective bargaining on institutional governance?

7. Does the board conduct its affairs in a manner that exemplifies the behavior it expects from other governance participants and campus constituents in the course of institutional decision making? How does the board demonstrate a commitment to the quality of its own performance?

8. Has the board, in concert with the president and in consultation with appropriate constituent groups, assessed the participation of constituents in institutional decision making and their collaboration in policy implementation? Has it clearly distinguished among information gathering, consultation, and decision making in its communication with campus constituents? What initiatives might be undertaken to clarify and strengthen communication, participation, and collaboration in institutional governance?

9. Does the board allow reasonable time for meaningful deliberation and establish clear deadlines for the conclusion of consultative and decision-making processes? What does the board do to ensure timely information and decisions from campus constituents? How effective is this?

10. When were the key institutional policies and procedures governing institutional decision making (for example, board bylaws, administrative policy manuals, and faculty handbooks) last reviewed?

HIGHER EDUCATION BOARDS OF TRUSTEES

BENJAMIN E. HERMALIN

Universities and colleges in the United States are overseen by boards of trustees, regents, overseers, or similarly titled entities. With respect to their place in the hierarchical structure, such boards are similar to boards of directors in corporations. Indeed, for nonstate institutions of higher education, their legal status is effectively the same. Although similar in structure to corporate boards, they—and in fact nonprofit boards more generally—have not received much scrutiny from economists. The purpose of this chapter is to suggest ways in which economists could go about making amends and trying to anticipate some of the difficulties they may face. In addition, this essay attempts to point out how our understanding of for-profit corporate boards may provide insight into boards of trustees and suggest questions to investigate.

As Kerr and Gade (1989) observe, within the United States, boards of trustees and boards of directors come from the same legal tradition.[1] Indeed, institutions such as Harvard and Yale are among the oldest corporations (in the legal sense) within the English legal tradition. And almost as long as there have been corporations, there has been criticism of the boards that oversee them.[2] Yet, in the for-profit arena, corporations are the dominant form of business organization. Similarly, in the United States the "corporate" model is the dominant model in higher education. Moreover, there are two separate pieces of evidence to suggest that it is a pretty good model: First, state colleges and universities have almost invariably copied this model even though there is no legal requirement for them to do so. That is, for instance, a state university could easily be overseen by civil-service bureaucrats in some state agency of higher education, similar to the way many states oversee grade K through 12 education. To be sure, the corporate model could simply be some historical accident; but if it were a truly poor form of organization, one might have expected to see some alternatives arise in American higher education (for instance, because of emulation of alternative models observed in Europe or utilized by the service academies, such as West Point).

The second piece of evidence is that there are alternative models employed elsewhere in the world (a point also made by Kerr and Gade [1989]). In particular, there are models in which universities are controlled by ministries of education (e.g., as in France). There are models in which they are controlled by faculty guilds (as were Oxford and Cambridge until nineteenth-century reforms). There are even models in which they are controlled by student guilds (as was Bologna University, the oldest in the Western world).[3] Yet all these models seem to yield universities that are generally perceived as inferior to American universities organized along the corporate model. Although neither of these pieces of evidence is conclusive proof that the corporate model is the best or even a superior model, they at least make clear that it can't be a particularly terrible model, at least vis-à-vis alternatives.

But the historical durability of the corporate model and its apparent success relative to alternative models only begs further questions. What, in fact, do boards of trustees do? How do they affect what happens in colleges and universities? What can we reasonably expect of them? Why if it's a successful model has it generated so much criticism?[4] Moreover, the possible fact that the corporate model is the best available model is merely a relative comparison, and doesn't deal with whether boards satisfy some absolute objective (i.e., achieve some *un*constrained optimum) or are just the least bad of the available evils (i.e., achieve some constrained optimum). In the context of for-profit corporations, these questions and issues have recently received considerable attention, primarily in the form of empirical analyses, but also in terms of some theoretical treatments.

The next section of this chapter explores what lessons from empirical work on boards of directors might apply to boards of trustees. It also considers to what extent this empirical work can serve as a road map for future work focused directly on boards of trustees. The section following it turns to theoretical issues concerning directors and governance.

What We Know about Corporate Boards and How It Might Apply to Trustees

In a recent survey of the literature on corporate boards, Michael Weisbach and I (Hermalin and Weisbach 2003) made the following observations. First, formal theory on boards of directors has been quite limited. Most of the work has instead been empirical, seeking to answer one or more of the following three questions:

1. How do board characteristics such as composition or size affect the achievement of firm objectives?

2. How do board characteristics affect the observable actions of the board?

3. What factors affect the makeup of boards and how they evolve over time?

Research thus far has established a number of empirical regularities. First, board composition, as measured by the ratio of inside directors (e.g., executives of the firm) to outside directors (e.g., executives of outside organizations),[5] is not correlated with firm performance.[6] However, the number of directors on a firm's board is negatively related to its financial performance. Second, board actions *do* appear to be related to board characteristics. Firms with higher proportions of outside directors and smaller boards tend to make arguably better—or at least different—decisions concerning acquisitions, poison pills, executive compensation, and CEO replacement, ceteris paribus. Finally, boards appear to evolve over time depending on the bargaining position of the CEO relative to that of the existing directors. Firm performance, CEO turnover, and changes in ownership structure appear to be important factors affecting changes to boards.

To what extent should we expect a similar picture to hold for boards of trustees? Anecdotal evidence (e.g., Bowen 1994) suggests that large boards are no more effective in higher education than in the corporate world, although I am unaware of any formal statistical analyses for boards of trustees demonstrating that size is negatively related to performance.[7] Other results, such as those pertaining to acquisitions, poison pills, and changes in ownership, are clearly less applicable to higher education.

One problem with replicating these studies using data for boards of trustees is deciding how to define—to say nothing of measuring—"firm objectives" in the higher education context. When it comes to boards of trustees, there is no unambiguous dimension along which to measure performance—does one measure research, teaching effectiveness, fundraising success, or what? Moreover, even if we let researchers decide to concentrate on one dimension,[8] there is no unambiguous yardstick to employ for most dimensions—is research, for instance, measured by articles in scholarly journals, citations, grants received, faculty memberships in prestigious scholarly societies, or what?

The definition-of-objectives problem is not the only problem facing a would-be researcher addressing question 1 as it relates to boards of trustees (i.e., how do board characteristics affect objective attainment?). Other problems face the researcher as well. First, many of the board characteristics that have been hypothesized to matter in the corporate context are either not meaningful or difficult to define in the higher education context. For instance, given that typically the only director from management is the university or college president, one might conclude that there is not much scope for an empirical analysis of the impact of insiders versus outsiders. On the other hand, one might object that even the definition of "insider" is unclear: There are boards of trustees, for instance, that include student representatives or faculty representatives. Are they insiders, outsiders, or something that has no real analog in the corporate world?

Of course, even if there weren't issues measuring performance or the factors that we hypothesize could determine performance, there is no reason to suspect that an attempt to answer question 1 would reveal anything.[9] As reviewed in Hermalin and Weisbach 2003, almost all such attempts in the corporate context are inconclusive; that is, researchers typically find no evidence that corporate board characteristics affect firm performance.[10] The one exception, in fact, has been the relation between board size and corporate performance (Yermack 1996; Eisenberg, Sundgren, and Wells 1998), where it has been found that larger board size is associated with worse performance. However, as I discuss later, there are reasons to wonder whether those results indicate a causal relation; that is, this association need not mean that larger boards *cause* worse performance.

In retrospect, there are two reasons why we should perhaps not be surprised by the lack of clear results when looking empirically at whether board characteristics affect firm performance. First, firm performance is relatively volatile and buffeted by many forces. Moreover, it is not clear whether board characteristics have an immediate or more delayed effect on performance. Given the difficulties in measuring performance clearly and not knowing whether the effects of board characteristics show up in the short term or the long term, it is not surprising that detecting a relationship between characteristics and performance would be difficult, at least as a statistical matter. Although some measures of university or college performance are no doubt less volatile over time than financial performance measures, they are likely harder to assess accurately, so the "noise" problem—the difficulty of differentiating a true relation, from random variation—would likely be equally severe were one to attempt to explain university or college performance on the basis of trustee characteristics.

The second reason not to be surprised is that presumably organizations want to perform well. If there is some way in which board characteristics affect performance, organizations should ensure that their boards exhibit those characteristics that yield optimal performance. That is, if there is an optimal set of characteristics, we should expect, all else equal, for organizations to adopt these characteristics. In steady state (equilibrium), then, there should be no meaningful differences in board characteristics with respect to performance, which means—unless there are a number of firms in the sample still in the process of adjusting toward these optimal characteristics—there isn't the variation in the explanatory variables necessary to detect the relation between board characteristics and performance. Put another way, recall that to detect that a characteristic affects performance, we need to see that institutions that set the characteristic one way systematically perform differently from institutions that set it another way; but if it is optimal for all institutions to set the characteristic a single way, and they do, then it is impossible to see how *variation* in that characteristic, given that it doesn't exist, is systematically related to variations in performance.

This notion of optimality in steady state or equilibrium also raises questions of how one would interpret any apparently conclusive results from addressing question 1 empirically (see Hermalin and Weisbach 2003 for a complete discussion). In particular, one can imagine that the set of board characteristics that would be optimal in terms of performance under a given set of circumstances differs from the set that would be optimal under a different set of circumstances. If, in fact, all organizations adopt the board structure that is optimal for them given their circumstances, then any relation found between board structure and performance would necessarily be meaningless—the correlation is simply the consequence of both structure and performance being correlated with the underlying circumstances. For instance, suppose that the more complex an organization is, the more difficult it is to manage well. Because of the difficulty in managing such a complex organization, it might be optimal to have a large board. A large board would, perhaps, allow for a range of expertise on the many problems confronting a complex organization. At the same time, because it is difficult to manage, a complex organization's performance would be worse ceteris paribus than a simpler organization's. Given my premises, one would readily find institutions with smaller boards outperforming those with larger boards, but this relationship would *not* indicate that small boards *cause* better performance. In particular, it would be an erroneous policy prescription to encourage an organization with a large board to shrink it—the organization would end up with a board that was *less* well suited to its specific purposes, and its performance would be even worse than before.

This "equilibrium" caveat could, however, be less pronounced for boards of trustees than boards of directors. For-profit firms are subject to the forces of economic Darwinism—in the long run, competition from more efficient firms either induces improvement in inefficient firms or drives them out of business. It is, thus, difficult for a for-profit firm to maintain a board structure that grossly departs from optimality for an extended period of time. Universities and colleges, while not wholly immune to Darwinian forces, are not, as a rule, hit with them as strongly (a point also made by Bowen [1994, 9–13]). This is especially true of well-endowed and state institutions. Moreover universities and colleges are much more affected by other, noneconomic forces, such as political pressures and a greater need to respect tradition, which could yield and perpetuate boards that are nonoptimal in structure (this would seem especially true of state institutions, where there is little reason to imagine that the political process will yield an optimal board).[11] Consequently, we can expect much greater variation in the characteristics and structures of boards of trustees than boards of directors, which, in turn, means there could be hope of having sufficient variation in the independent variables to detect their impact on performance.

Table 1 "confirms" the hypothesis of great variation. It summarizes some of the characteristics of the trustees of four universities. Although the table reflects the considerable heterogeneity in boards of trustees, it also raises doubts about finding any relation between institutional performance and the structure of the board and its characteristics. While admittedly four is a rather small sample, it is worth noting that all four of these universities are widely considered to be among the very top universities in the United States. Looking at the variation in Table 1 and the uniform excellence of these schools, the hypothesis that the structure of its board of trustees has no effect on a university or college's performance would seem the more logical hypothesis than that it does have an effect. Hence, while higher education offers greater variability in boards than does the corporate world, there still seems no reason to expect to find that these boards matter for institutional performance, at least in an empirically detectable way.

A potentially more profitable issue to tackle is question 2—how do board characteristics affect the observable actions of the board? In the corporate board arena, this question has been a more fruitful line of research than question 1. Specifically, evidence indicates that both board composition and size are systematically related with the board's decisions regarding CEO replacement, acquisitions, poison pills, and executive compensation. Because the first and last of these have greater relevance in the higher education context, I will limit my review to these two sets of findings.

The most commonly discussed responsibility of the board of directors is to choose and to monitor the firm's CEO (see, e.g., Mace 1986). Indeed, rather than make day-to-day decisions, boards appear to play a crucial role in picking the firm's CEO and to view their primary responsibility as monitoring and potentially replacing him. One way, therefore, to evaluate the board's effectiveness is by looking at the quality of these decisions.

A large number of articles have documented that there is a positive relation between CEO turnover and poor performance in large corporations, as well as in other types of organizations.[12] The standard interpretation of this relation is that it measures the board's monitoring; when performance is worse, the board is more likely to find the current CEO unacceptable and to make a change.

Simply documenting a relation between poor performance and an increased probability of CEO turnover, although suggestive of board monitoring, is nonetheless far from conclusive. After all, a sense of failure or pressure from shareholders could explain this relationship. To better identify the role played by the board, Weisbach (1988) tested whether the effect of firm performance on CEO turnover varies systematically with board composition. His results indicate that when boards are dominated by outside directors, CEO turnover is more sensitive to firm performance than it is in firms with insider-dominated boards. This result is consistent with the view that outsider-dominated boards—those a priori likely to be independent of management—are responding to corporate performance when they make CEO-retention decisions. In contrast, turnover in insider-dominated boards is not performance-driven, suggesting that insider-dominated boards make turnover decisions for reasons unrelated to corporate performance. This is not surprising: Inside directors' careers

TABLE 1

Four Universities and Their Trustee Characteristics

University	Method of Selection (Composition)	Number of Trustees	Frequency of Regular Meeting
University of California[a]	18 regents appointed by governor for 12-year terms 1 regent (a student) appointed by the regents for a 1-year term 4 state officials: governor, lieutenant governor, speaker of the assembly, and superintendent of public instruction 2 alumni officials: president and vice president of the alumni associations President of the university	26	6 times annually
University of Michigan[b]	8 regents elected in biennial statewide elections President of the university	9	12 times annually
Harvard University	Two boards: Corporation (7 members) self-perpetuating with consent of board of overseers (includes president of the university); members appointed for life Board of overseers elected by alumni at large	NA	Corporation meets 15 times annually[c]
Princeton University	13 alumni trustees (elected by alumni for 4-year terms), one of whom, at least, must be an alumnus/a of the graduate school 4–8 term trustees, elected by the board for 4-year terms Governor of New Jersey President of the university Unspecified number of charter trustees, elected by the board for 10-year terms	23–40 (currently 39)	5 times annually

Sources: Except where noted, sources are the respective Web sites of the universities.
[a] Nine-campus system.
[b] One main campus and two secondary campuses.
[c] Kerr and Gade 1989, 60.

tend to be tied to the CEO's, which gives them incentives to advance the CEO's career regardless of the stock price. Consistent with this tied-career explanation is evidence from Borokhovich, Parrino, and Trapani (1996) and Huson, Parrino, and Starks (2000), who find outsider-dominated boards are more likely than insider-dominated boards to replace a CEO with someone from *outside* the firm.

Yermack (1996) and Wu (2000) performed a similar analysis of CEO turnover, measuring the impact of board size on the relation between CEO turnover and firm performance. These researchers estimated similar equations to those of Weisbach 1988, except that they considered how board size changes the relation between firm performance and CEO turnover. Yermack and Wu found that firms with smaller boards have a stronger relation between firm performance and CEO turnover than do firms with larger boards. This finding is consistent with the view that smaller boards are more effective overseers of the CEO than are larger boards. In particular, in response to poor performance, they may not be paralyzed by free-riding or otherwise plagued with inertia the way larger boards are.

To interpret these studies, the key issue is whether the relations they uncover are causal. In other words, do the particular attributes of the board, such as composition or size, directly affect the boards monitoring? Alternatively, it could be that boards are independent for some other reason (as suggested, e.g., by the bargaining-game model of Hermalin and Weisbach [1998], which I discuss later). Although observationally difficult to distinguish, it is hard to imagine that it is the board characteristics per se that matter; rather what is at issue is whether the board is dominated by a CEO. A dominated board will not monitor regardless of its visible characteristics; however, visible characteristics tend, on average, to be correlated with independence from the CEO. Conversely, a board made up of directors who wish to be independent of management will arrange themselves, in term of size and composition, in a way that best facilitates oversight of management.

Another role of the board is to set and to oversee the firm's compensation policies. A view, prevalent since at least the time of Berle and Means (1932), is that CEOs can exert control over their boards and use this control to extract "excessive" levels of compensation. For example, Michael Eisner, the longtime CEO of Disney, was able to have his personal attorney appointed to the Disney board, and even got him a seat on the compensation committee (see *Wall Street Journal*, 2 February 1997). Not surprisingly, Eisner has been one of the most highly compensated CEOs in recent years.

Core, Holthausen, and Larcker (1999) studied the relations among board composition, ownership structure, and CEO pay. Their results suggest that firms with weaker governance structures tend to pay their CEOs more. In particular, they found that a CEO's pay rises with the number of outside directors appointed during his tenure, the number of directors over age sixty-nine, board size, and the number of busy directors, where "busy" is defined in terms of the number of additional directorships held by a director.[13] In addition, both Core, Holthausen, and Larcker (1999) and Hallock (1997) found that CEO pay increases when a board contains interlocking directors (e.g., when the CEO of firm A sits on firm B's board and the CEO of firm B sits on firm A's board). Finally, Yermack (1996) found that the pay-performance relation for CEOs decreases with board size, suggesting that small boards give CEOs larger incentives and force them to bear risk more so than do large boards. This evidence suggests that CEOs' influence over their boards does result in higher pay for them.

It seems plausible that similar studies investigating how trustees make decisions about replacing college and university presidents and setting their compensation could be undertaken, although to the best of my knowledge such studies have not yet been conducted.[14] Of course, to some extent, any such studies would face many of the same empirical problems raised earlier (e.g., defining trustee types, measuring performance, etc.). In addition, the data collection could be more daunting than it is in the corporate setting: Although the *Chronicle of Higher Education* does, for instance, collect and report salary information for university and college presidents (see Ehrenberg, Cheslock, and Epifantseva 2001), collecting data on trustee characteristics and certain measures of performance (e.g., research output) could be more difficult.

Replicating studies of how different types of boards of trustees respond to performance in their decisions to retain or remove their institutions' presidents would be fascinating. One potential pitfall would be the noise that exists because not every change in president is due to the removal of the incumbent. Although presumably exogenous causes of change, such as death, can be dealt with, it is still the case that some separations are voluntary (e.g., the president retires) while others are involuntary (e.g., the president announces she is retiring, but would have preferred to stay on if the trustees had permitted her to do so). Weisbach (1988) discusses some of the ways in which voluntary separations might be distinguished from involuntary, but, as he notes, the consequences of failing to identify correctly the two types of separation need not be fatal: Leaving voluntary separations in the sample adds noise to the regression analysis but should not bias the results; the only consequence, therefore, would be that statistical tests would not be as strong as ideal.

In addition to replicating the analyses conducted for corporate boards, research on boards of trustees could consider the effect of boards on decisions that are unique to higher education. One example of this type of work is Lowry 2001b, which examines how differences in trustee selection across different public universities affect the setting of tuition and other fees. Lowry found that tuition and other fees are lower, ceteris paribus, the greater the representation on the board of trustees of "external" trustees, defined as state officials serving ex officio or trustees selected by the governor, state legislature, or popular election.

The third type of empirical analysis has been to answer the questions, What factors affect the makeup of boards and How do they evolve over time? These studies typically measure the impact of *changes* in a firm's characteristics on subsequent *changes* in board composition. Looking at changes minimizes the potential joint endogeneity problem that would arise if one considered levels (i.e., distinguishing the effect of firm characteristics on board characteristics from the effect of board characteristics on firm characteristics).

Hermalin and Weisbach (1988) took this approach and estimated the factors that lead to changes in corporate boards. They found three sets of factors that predict changes in the board. First, poor firm performance increases the likelihood that inside directors leave and that outside directors join the board. Second, the CEO succession process appears to be intertwined with the board selection process. When a CEO nears retirement, firms tend to add inside directors, who are potential candidates to be the next CEO. Just after a CEO change, inside directors tend to leave the board, consistent with the hypothesis that these directors are losing candidates to be CEO. Finally, after a firm leaves a product market, inside directors tend to depart and outside directors tend to join the board. Denis and Sarin (1999) confirmed these findings on a much larger sample of firms from a nonoverlapping time period. They found that large changes in board composition tend to occur after abnormally poor performance and around the time of a CEO change.

Replication of studies of this third type using trustee data could be difficult for a number of reasons. First, whereas corporate directors serve relatively short terms,[15] many trustees serve far longer terms (e.g., the ten- to twelve-year terms of trustees or regents of Princeton and the University of California—see Table 1). This suggests fewer turnovers in trustees,[16] which makes detecting sensitivity of changes in board composition to institutional performance more difficult. A second difficulty could be the now familiar difficulty of measuring performance, or more precisely focusing on the relevant measures of performance. A third difficulty is defining different types of trustees, an issue raised earlier.

One strategy would be simply to avoid the third difficulty by just looking at what increases turnover rates, regardless of type of trustee. In particular, a reasonable prediction is that events that increase "headaches" for trustees, such as scandals or financial problems, also increase turnover. Another possible line of research would be the "flip side" of the question Lowry (2001b) asked: He hypothesizes that political pressures cause "external" trustees to hold down fee increases. Is there evidence for such pressures? Do, for instance, fee increases lessen reelection rates for elected trustees? Do they influence state elections more generally?[17]

In this section, I have reviewed the empirical literature on corporate boards to see the extent to which it can serve as a road map for similar work on boards of trustees in higher education. At an abstract level, much of the work on corporate boards could be replicated for boards of trustees, but, as I've indicated, there are reasons to suspect that in a number of instances such work is unlikely to yield interesting results. This is particularly true of attempts to determine how the characteristics of the board of trustees affect the achievement of institutional objectives (i.e., question 1). Measuring both the variables to be explained and the explanatory variables could prove messy. Moreover, there are fundamental theoretical reasons to question whether any significant relationship should exist and what, if one were found, it would mean. The one line of inquiry on this dimension of which I would be less negative would be to determine whether a *statistical* relation between board size and performance, which has been established in the corporate setting (Yermack 1996; Eisenberg, Sundgren, and Wells 1998) and hypothesized by Bowen (1994) for higher education, indeed exists for higher education. But should such a relation be uncovered, I would caution against necessarily accepting the "obvious" causal interpretation.

As noted earlier, more fruitful lines of research would be to address questions 2 and 3 in the board of trustees context. With respect to question 2—how do characteristics of the board affect its observable actions?—there are a number of interesting analyses to be conducted. For instance, one could extend the analysis of Ehrenberg, Cheslock, and Epifantseva (2001) to see whether board characteristics affect how the various determinants they studied influence presidential pay or even whether board characteristics *directly* affect presidential pay. In particular, based on the work of Main, O'Reilly, and their coauthors (O'Reilly, Main, and Crystal 1988; Main, O'Reilly, and Wade 1995), one would hypothesize that the socioeconomic status of trustees will have a significant effect on presidential compensation. One could also seek to do a similar study to that by Ehrenberg and colleagues, but seek to explain the change in the president rather than her compensation, and then add in board features as Weisbach (1988) did in the corporate board context. Finally, more work like Lowry's (2001b), which looked at the role of board of trustee characteristics on important higher education decisions (e.g., fee setting), would be most welcome.[18]

For question 3, a sensible focus would be on the determinants of trustee turnover. Basic facts need to be uncovered, such as the underlying rate of turnover. Beyond that it would be good to know what the determinants of turnover are. Of particular importance would be to see what actions affected the tenure of elected regents of state schools and, more generally, the extent to which political issues affect trustee tenure.

Governance Theory and Its Application to Boards of Trustees

The prototypical view of hierarchy is that those who hold higher positions in the hierarchy control those beneath them. Under this view, the board of trustees should have all the power with regard to the running of universities and colleges.[19] Reality, of course, is clearly different, and there are a number of reasons why.

One reason that boards cannot possess all the power is that they don't possess the necessary knowledge, incentive, and time. Most boards of trustees consist primarily of *lay* trustees, that is, trustees who are not academics and whose primary employment is not in higher education. They, thus, haven't the time to make all the decisions and must rationally delegate much of the decision making to the officers of the college or university.[20] Such delegation necessarily implies the ceding of power. In the same line, the lack of necessary knowledge and experience makes the trustees reliant on the officers for background and briefings, which again shifts power to the officers. Finally, as with any group effort, there is the usual "teams problem," whereby each individual trustee under-provides effort because he feels that he can leave the work to his fellow trustees (i.e., an individual trustee will "free-ride" on the efforts of the other trustees).[21] This means less attention overall to the institution and, in particular, less oversight of the administration and a power vacuum that administrators (and others) will seek to fill.

Organization scholars sometimes refer to such shifts of power as the board retaining the right to *govern* (oversee) while management is granted the right to *manage* (take action).[22] But even the board's right to govern is not absolute. A second reason, then, that the board cannot possess all the power is that it must also make concessions on the right to govern, at least in a de facto sense. These concessions are part of the bargaining—implicit or explicit—between the president and the board over the latter's ability to govern. This bargaining model, set forth in Hermalin and Weisbach 1998, runs as follows: At any point in time, the board can fire the current president and draw a new one from the relevant population of new presidents. Such a decision is rational only if the board concludes the current president is less able than a president randomly drawn from this population is likely to be.[23] Conversely, if the board doesn't wish to replace the current president, then that means the trustees see her as better, in expectation, than any available replacement. But this makes her a "rare commodity," which in turn bestows on her bargaining power vis-à-vis the board. She can, of course, use this bargaining power to extract more compensation and perks from the board. But, as Michael Weisbach and I showed, she will also use it to gain looser governance and less oversight.

Although written in the context of corporate boards, the Hermalin and Weisbach model carries over straightforwardly to higher education.[24] Indeed, it may be even more powerful in that latter context than the former. Observation suggests that changing a university or college president is a more costly undertaking, particularly for board members, than is changing a corporate CEO. It's rare to have an internal successor, who's been groomed for the job, just sitting there at a college or university, whereas succession planning is an ongoing process at most corporations (see, e.g., Vancil 1987 for a study). Moreover, even when a corporation goes outside for a new CEO, the process can be done more quickly and less publicly than it can in most college or university settings. Raising the cost of replacing the president increases her bargaining power and, thus, results in less oversight in equilibrium.

The president may also gain bargaining power to the extent that faculty and students are effectively her allies. A large proportion of a college or university's assets are in human capital—moreover, in human capital that is exceedingly mobile (at least in comparison to most corporate alternatives). Particularly on academic issues of importance to the faculty, the president can utilize that mobility to strengthen her bargaining power vis-à-vis the board of trustees. Similarly, to the extent that conflict between board and president adversely affects applications or yield, the president can capture bargaining power. Ironically, though, this bargaining-power story also means that a president who loses the support of faculty or students may lose a tremendous amount of bargaining power vis-à-vis the board, even if she has otherwise proved to be a strong administrator. Ultimately, then, there is a greater devolution of power from the board and top management to the employees (faculty) and customers (students) in higher education than there is in the typical corporation.

In the Hermalin and Weisbach model (1998), the manner in which the president secures less oversight is by having trustees appointed who are less "independent" of the president. Operationally, less independence means the trustee finds oversight more costly personally, enjoys reduced personal benefit from oversight, or both, ceteris paribus. Comparing the higher education and corporate contexts, it seems reasonable to imagine that the personal benefits of oversight are lower in the former than in the latter. Trustees do not have the financial incentives (stock, stock options, fear of being sued) that corporate directors have. In addition, to the extent trustees see their positions as honorific, they may enter the board expecting not to work hard, which could lead them to act as if they have a high disutility of effort.[25] In contrast, corporate directors presumably understand that they are making a serious commitment. So, all else equal, we could expect boards of trustees to be less effective monitors of management than corporate boards. Moreover, in the Hermalin and Weisbach model, the bargaining between boards and presidents never results in the boards becoming *more* effective monitors—either effectiveness is unchanged, if the president has insufficient bargaining power, or it is reduced.[26] Hence, one can see the Hermalin and Weisbach model as predicting that boards of trustees should be less powerful overseers of presidents than corporate boards are over CEOs, a prediction that is consistent with anecdotal comparisons, such as Bowen's (1994).

Another model that could be applied, a variant of the ideas in Hermalin and Weisbach 1998, would be to imagine that the board of trustees needs to be sensitive to many objectives. In this sense, the board is analogous to a consumer who may wish to buy many different goods. One of these is oversight of the president and other administrators. If, however, the president appears able and capable, then the benefit of monitoring relative to other objectives is lower. A lower relative benefit is analogous to a higher cost; hence, the situation is similar to a consumer who sees the price of one good rise—he consumes less of that good and more of the other goods. Similarly, the board will "purchase" more of its other objectives. For instance, it may add "honorific" trustees to reward large donors (or potential donors); it may expand to allow for greater diversity on the board to mollify critics; or it may expand to have a greater range of expertise. But whatever the motive, the board may rationally respond to capable management by pursuing courses of action that lessen its effectiveness as a monitor. Moreover, although rational, many of these actions are in some ways irreversible—large donors cannot readily be dropped; it is hard to shrink a board, particularly at the expense of diversity. Although it is admittedly a sample of one, it is nonetheless consistent with this view that Princeton's board is currently just one trustee shy of its permitted maximum (see Table 1).

A diverse board, while desirable for many reasons, can also result in a weaker board with regard to oversight. Unlike a corporation, which ostensibly has a single objective—to make money—a university or college has multiple objectives. If these different objectives acquire different champions on the board, or even if there is simply considerable disagreement about their relative importance, then the board can become dysfunctional.[27] A power vacuum at the top means more power devolves to the president and others in the institution.

To summarize, there are a number of reasons to expect the governance and management exercised by a board of trustees to be relatively weak:

1. Lack of expertise on the part of lay trustees, which increases reliance on the president and other administrators for information and guidance.
2. Lack of time to devote to the job, which increases the amount of delegation to the president and other administrators. This also means less effort expended on monitoring.
3. Free-riding (teams problem), which reduces the amount of oversight.
4. Bargaining power of a successful president, which leads to less monitoring.
5. Bargaining power of faculty and students, which reduces board power in general, but can also bolster the president's bargaining power vis-à-vis the board to the extent she can mobilize the bargaining power of these other stakeholders.
6. The temptation to use the board for nonoversight purposes, such as to reward large donors or increase diversity.
7. Divisiveness among the directors, which results in a power vacuum at the top.

Although there are all these reasons to imagine that boards of trustees will be "weak," it is worth remembering that not *all* institutions are, necessarily, governed by weak trustees. For instance, political or other pressures could make trustees attentive and focused. Restrictions imposed by charters and by-laws on board size or selection could limit the amount of power a board can bargain away. Finally, in some instances, the board will consist of "strong" trustees, who, by dint of their personality, political clout (e.g., a state governor), or financial clout (e.g., a large donor), are able to "recapture" some amount of power from administrators.[28] On net, however, given that the majority of complaints about boards, corporate or collegiate, is that they are insufficiently vigilant (see, e.g., Berle and Means 1932; Chait and Taylor 1989; Lipton and Lorsch 1992; Jensen 1993; Bowen 1994), the seven reasons for weakness just given would, in whole or in part, seem to apply to most boards.[29]

In contrast to their critics, at least two members of the board, its chair and the president, typically view the board as functioning well according to survey results presented in Kerr and Gade 1989. Chairs give their boards passing marks on all issues except the issue of raising and securing adequate funding (see Kerr and Gade 1989, Table 3, 89). Of particular interest, is that 80 percent or more of the chairs describe their boards' review of the president, its delegation of authority to the president, and its level of commitment and involvement as "good" or "excellent" (Kerr and Gade 1989, Table 3). Presidents are somewhat tougher graders, but nonetheless tend to assign good marks as well. Interestingly, the presidents' views vary from the chairs' on the questions of authority, where they give lower marks.[30]

How can one reconcile the good marks assigned by presidents and board chairs with the criticism leveled by observers (including faculty—Kerr and Gade [1989] report considerable faculty dissatisfaction with their institutions' boards, see their Table B–11)? Part of the answer is simply that people typically assign themselves higher marks than outside observers do—a fact made abundantly clear to me first as a professor and, more recently, as an academic administrator. Another part, though, and one consistent with the Hermalin and Weisbach bargaining model, is that chairs and presidents are reasonably satisfied with the, perhaps implicit, agreement they've reached concerning the degree of oversight and involvement of the board. Outside parties, who may not understand this bargaining or who wish or believe that one side or the other could have been more effective bargainers, are more inclined to express dissatisfaction with the outcome. (An analogy would be the not uncommon occurrence of the rank and file expressing dissatisfaction with the contracts that union leaders achieve with management.)

Personally, my sympathies lie more with the chairs and the presidents than with the outside critics. Within the reality that trustees face—the trade-offs, the true incentives, the allocation of bargaining power, and so on—they achieve the best solution possible in terms of oversight and control.

To be sure, we can conceive of better oversight and better control. But we can also conceive of two-hour flights from New York to Tokyo—something that, in the world we currently live in, is not going to happen. To be sure, there are board failures: Occasionally, trustees shirk duties that can be reasonably expected of them; sometimes they could reasonably be tougher bargainers; sometimes they accept actions that we would rightly expect them to reject; and so forth. But one must be careful not to make idiosyncratic mistakes the basis of a condemnation of a system. To do so would be analogous to asking that the rules of football be rewritten because occasionally receivers drop passes and quarterbacks throw interceptions.

Although much of the existing theory of governance, derived in the context of considering for-profit firms, can be exported to nonprofits, such as colleges and universities, there are certainly differences between for-profit and nonprofit firms that could call for the development of new models. In particular, the fact that some nonprofits, like institutions of higher education, have multiple objectives pushed by multiple stakeholders means that there are governance issues that are absent or less pressing in the for-profit realm, where presumably making money is essentially the only objective. For instance, an argument could be made that while the purpose of governance in a for-profit is to ensure effective achievement of the one objective, to make money, the purpose of governance in a college or university is to keep the various stakeholders content to continue with the school and to engage with each other.

To give a concrete example, students want a greater variety of courses. With a finite faculty, more variety means more teaching by the faculty. The faculty, in contrast, want less teaching because they have other uses for that time, such as conducting research. The administration's task is, therefore, to achieve a compromise that keeps each group sufficiently satisfied. The role of governance is, thus, to ensure that the administration properly affects a compromise solution, a role made difficult by the lack of clear performance metrics and uncertainty over objectives on the part of the governors. Although the basic toolkit of the modern economic theorist, including agency theory, game theory, and information economics, can be employed, the model that will be constructed from this toolkit could easily be far different from any model built in the for-profit context.

As these new models are built, they will start to shape how we perceive the role of the board of trustees and will give further guidance toward models and theories of its functioning. This is not to say that the seven points made previously will be shown not to apply or that insights from corporate boards will be shown to be nonapplicable to higher education. Rather, these new models and theories will add additional points to those made previously and will help us think about the relative importance of all these points in understanding the functioning of boards of trustees. Because, however, mapping out a research agenda for looking at higher education governance more generally is beyond the scope of this chapter, it is not feasible to say more on this point at this time.

Conclusion

This chapter has considered boards of trustees of institutions of higher education. The aim has been to consider how the insights that have been gained over the years concerning corporate boards of directors, whether empirical or theoretical, could be applied to boards of trustees. To a large extent, the focus has been on the degree to which this earlier research on corporate boards can serve to guide future research on boards of trustees.

For the most part, the theory of boards should apply to both directors and trustees. The principal differences are in degree. The basic insights concerning lack of expertise, lack of time, free-riding among board members, and the Hermalin-Weisbach bargaining model (1998) apply to both directors and trustees, although, as discussed, they could loom larger in the trustee context. The dependence on highly mobile human capital creates problems for higher education governance that are less pronounced in most corporate settings. Higher education also suffers from two other issues not generally present in the corporate world: first, a temptation to use the board for purposes other than governance; and second, a susceptibility to divisiveness on the board that comes from less focused objectives as compared to the essentially single objective of corporations. Although there is every reason to believe that theoretical insights about boards derived from the for-profit corporate context apply to boards of trustees of colleges and universities, with some modification, it is also true that colleges and universities face governance issues unlike those typically seen in the for-profit context. As some of these issues enjoy greater study, a consequence will be that our perception of the role and functioning of the board of trustees will be adjusted. That is, the corporate model provides a good picture of boards of trustees, but a more complete picture awaits advances in the theory of collegiate and university governance.

With respect to empirical analyses of boards of trustees, analyses of corporate boards are generally good guides concerning what to study and what can be found. In particular, it is unlikely that any analysis will find a relation between characteristics of boards of trustees and the overall performances of the institutions in question.[31] More promising lines of inquiry are with respect to whether trustee characteristics help explain specific board actions (e.g., presidential compensation and replacement, setting of fees, specific types of expansion, etc.) and with respect to what causes turnover in trustees.

When I began to formulate this chapter, I started with two beliefs: first, that boards of trustees are very much like corporate boards of directors; and second, that boards are a reasonably good solution to a set of governance problems affecting any complex organization, whether for-profit or nonprofit. Basically, I still hold to both beliefs. As discussed, there are differences between the two types of boards, and these differences will have an impact on both empirical and theoretical analyses. Nonetheless, these differences are primarily ones of degree and not of substance. Both directors and trustees are, for instance, imperfect agents with respect to oversight of management, but institutional aspects of colleges and universities suggest that trustees could be the more imperfect agents, at least in some dimensions. Moreover, despite the criticisms that both types of boards engender, I still maintain that they are a reasonably good solution within the constraints within which they operate. Corporate boards, for instance, do in the end replace incompetent management, and there is every reason to believe that so too do boards of trustees. The real evidence is that despite numerous critics, alternative organizational forms have generally not functioned better. This is true in the for-profit context, where the corporate form with directors is the dominant form of organizing a large company. And it is true in the college and university context, where American universities, with their boards of trustees, dominate higher education and have outperformed, along any reasonable metric, non-American universities organized along different lines.[32]

Notes

1. As a shorthand, I use "board of trustees" to refer to governing bodies of college and universities and "board of directors" to refer to the governing bodies of for-profit corporations. Similarly, a "trustee" is an overseer of a college or university, while a "director" is an overseer of a for-profit corporation.

2. Adam Smith (1776, 700), commenting on director-overseen companies, complained that "negligence and profusion . . . must always prevail, more or less, in the management of the affairs of such a company."

3. For modern-day faculty who complain of the tyranny students exercise through course evaluations, school rankings, etc., it may be worth noting that in Bologna the tyranny was quite real: Professors could not leave the campus without the permission of the students and had to make a monetary deposit against their return if permission was granted. Professors were also subject to fines for "poor" lectures (Kerr and Gade 1989, 11).

4. A short list of critics, of varying degrees of vehemence, includes Chait and Taylor (1989), Kerr and Gade (1989), Bowen (1994), and Taylor, Chait, and Holland (1996). Many of their criticisms of nonprofits' boards echo complaints leveled at for-profits' boards by Smith (1776), Berle and Means (1932), and more modern critics (some of whom are discussed in the text—see, too, Hermalin and Weisbach 2003, for a more complete survey of boards and their critics).

5. Most corporate directors can be classified as inside directors or outside directors. Inside directors are employees or former employees of the firm. They generally are not thought to be independent of the CEO, because the success of their careers is often tied to the CEO's. Outside directors are not employees of the firm and usually do not have any business ties to the firm aside from their directorship. Outside

directors are typically CEOs from other firms or prominent individuals in other fields. Finally, a small minority of directors fall into neither category; often these are attorneys or businesspeople who have a longstanding relationship with the firm. These directors are usually referred to as "affiliated" or "gray" directors.

6. In the literature, "firm performance" is a convenient phrase meant to capture various possible measures of a firm's success (e.g., return to investors, profitability, and successful execution of the firm's strategy). In many of the empirical studies, firm performance is operationalized in a precise way (e.g., stock return or performance on some accounting measure). In the more limited theoretical literature, firm performance has typically meant economic profits in static models or firm value (the present discounted value of economic profits) in dynamic models.

7. In the corporate setting, Jensen (1993) and Lipton and Lorsch (1992) were among the first to suggest a negative relation should hold between board size and corporate performance. Yermack (1996) was the first to provide compelling statistical evidence in support of this view. Eisenberg, Sundgren, and Wells (1998) provide additional statistical support.

8. As is, to some extent, done in the corporate context—see note 6.

9. One can think of question 1 as the regression, $p_{t+s} = \phi c_t + \varepsilon_t$, where p is a performance measure (e.g., profits in the corporate context), c is a measure(s) of board characteristics (e.g., insider-outsider ratio), ϕ is the coefficient(s) to be estimated, ε is an error term (including, possibly, other controls), t is a time index, and $s > 0$ to reduce joint endogeneity problems.

10. The one study of which I'm aware in the nonprofit—but *not* higher education—context (Herman and Renz 1998) suggests some relation between the prestige of board members and organizational effectiveness. Given, however, that this study lacks controls for joint endogeneity—do, for instance, effective organizations attract high-prestige board members or do high-prestige board members make organizations effective?—it is impossible to view the results as indicative of any causal relationship *from* board characteristics *to* institutional performance. Furthermore, the subjective manner in which the variables are measured also raises questions about how one might interpret the results.

11. Although, interestingly, a survey of presidents and board chairs finds that they generally feel their board structure, at least in terms of size, is good (see Table 3 of Kerr and Gade [1989, 89]).

12. Among them, Coughlan and Schmidt (1985), Warner, Watts, and Wruck (1988), Weisbach (1988), Barro and Barro (1990), Jensen and Murphy (1990), Blackwell, Brickley, and Weisbach (1994), Kaplan (1994), and Huson, Parrino, and Starks (2000).

13. "Busy" could also be a proxy for professional directors. Such people may have motives to develop reputations for *not* rocking the boat and for being supportive of the CEO in order to increase the number of directorships they're offered.

14. Ehrenberg, Cheslock, and Epifantseva (2001) consider some of the determinants of college and university presidents' pay, but composition of the board of trustees or other characteristics of the trustees are not among the determinants considered. It would appear from Ehrenberg and colleagues that there are not many other studies of presidential pay.

15. The norm was one-year terms in the Hermalin and Weisbach 1988 data, but these days, in response to the takeover wave of the late 1980s, the norm is three-year staggered terms.

16. Whether turnover rates on university and college boards are in fact lower than those for corporate boards is ultimately an empirical question. One possible study would, therefore, be to compare these rates.

17. That elected officials believe fee increases influence state elections is evidenced by the current governor of California, Gray Davis, who has steadily resisted fee increases at the University of California as part of his attempt to establish his "bona fides" as an "education governor."

18. Chait and Taylor (1989) offer a list of possible decisions, including the decision to begin offering graduate education, discontinue church affiliation, establish new academic departments, and set investment policies. An interesting historical decision would be the decision to go coeducational. A topical set of decisions to analyze would be those connected with affirmative action and minority outreach.

19. In state schools, this view could be questioned on the grounds that the legislature and governor, through their control of the purse strings, might be the ultimate authorities. In California, for example, the immense power the governor has over the state budget makes him essentially a "super-regent" with respect to many University of California decisions, particularly when it comes to fees. This view could also be questioned for a school that is owned by a religious organization, in which case important authority may reside with church officials who are not directly connected to the school.

20. This isn't to say that boards of trustees do not, from time to time, involve themselves in decisions that are inappropriate uses of their time. See Chait and Taylor 1989 or Bowen 1994 for anecdotes. Kerr and Gade (1989) offer some survey data on the prevalence of "inappropriate" decision making (see, e.g., their Tables B-9, B-10, and B-17).

21. Free-riding is an externality problem long recognized by economists. For a formal analysis of it in the context of a team, see Holmstrom 1982.

22. Recently, economists have begun to model such shifting of power (see, e.g., Aghion and Tirole 1997 or Levitt and Snyder 1997), but such analyses are quite abstract and do not deal with board-management issues per se.

23. Alternatively, if there is a cost to replacing a president (e.g., search costs, costs of disruption, etc.), then the rational decision is to fire only if the incumbent is worse than the expected ability of a randomly drawn replacement minus the replacement costs.

24. The only possible problem would be with interpreting the single dimensional performance variable in the Hermalin and Weisbach model in the higher education context. This is not a critical problem because the model can be readily extended to have *the* performance variable be some statistic over multi-dimensional performance measures.

25. See Chait and Taylor 1989, Bowen 1994, and Taylor, Chait, and Holland 1996 for discussions of the problem of trustees who see their positions as largely honorific.

26. The reason for this is as follows. The incumbent board has an ideal level of monitoring given the preferences of the existing members. The president/CEO always prefers as little monitoring as possible. So by agreeing to less monitoring than their ideal (e.g., by adding even less vigilant members to the board), the incumbent members suffer only a second-order loss—they're moving from their optimum—while the president/CEO enjoys a first-order gain; hence the bargaining must always lead to less monitoring than that which the incumbent board would otherwise have done. (This prediction of a steady decline or "entropy" in board effectiveness could be seen as a weakness of the Hermalin and Weisbach model. There are, however, radical breaks in corporate governance, such as from takeovers, that could periodically "reset" board effectiveness—see Hermalin and Weisbach 1998, p. 106, for a discussion. Interestingly, many of these "reset" mechanisms don't operate in higher education, which further bolsters the view that boards of trustees may be less effective monitors than corporate boards.)

27. Bowen (1994), among others, warns of this danger in nonprofit boards.

28. It is worth noting that this powerful trustee "solution" is not always desirable, at least from some perspectives. Bowen (1994) warns against institutional capture by a large donor, urging nonprofits to diversify their donor base. Governor Gray Davis's refusal to increase fees despite funding problems at the University of California is almost surely not the best course of action from the university's perspective.

29. This view is echoed by a significant number of faculty, who, among other criticisms, believe the board cedes too much authority to the president (40 percent hold this view according to survey results reported in Kerr and Gade 1989, Table B-11).

30. To the item, "understands and observes the line between policy and administration," 86 percent of public institution chairs rated the board's performance as good or excellent, while only 69 percent of the presidents of these institutions did (the numbers are 94 percent and 88 percent, respectively, for private institutions)—see Table B-9 of Kerr and Gade 1989. To the item, "effectively reviews the performance of the president," 80 percent of chairs rated the board's performance as good or excellent, while only 68 percent of presidents did (see Table B-8).

31. As discussed earlier, one possible exception would be between board size and performance. Measuring performance in the higher education context is, however, difficult, and moreover, it is not clear that any relation uncovered is causal.

32. A point also made by Kerr and Gade (1989).

References

Adelman, C. 2000. *A Parallel Postsecondary Universe: The Certification System in Information Technology.* Washington, D.C.: U.S. Government Printing Office.

Adler, D. 1977. *Governance and Collective Bargaining.* Washington, D.C.: American Association of University Professors.

Aghion, P., and J. Tirole. 1997. "Formal and Real Authority in Organizations." *Journal of Political Economy* 105:1–29.

American Association of University Professors. 1915. *Report of the Committee on Academic Freedom and Tenure.* Washington, D.C.: American Association of University Professors.

———. 1971. "Report of the Subcommittee of Committee T." *AAUP Bulletin* 57 (Spring): 68–124.

———. 1995. *Policy Documents and Reports.* Washington, D.C.: American Association of University Professors.

Ashraf, J. 1997. "The Effect of Unions on Professors' Salaries: The Evidence over Twenty Years." *Journal of Labor Research* 18 (Summer): 439–50.

Association of Higher Education Facilities Officers. 1999. *1997–98 Comparative Costs and Staffing Report for Educational Facilities.* Alexandria, Va.: Association of Higher Education Facilities Officers.

Baldridge, J. V. 1971. *Power and Conflict in the University.* New York: Wiley.

Baldwin, R. G., and J. L. Chronister. 2001. *Teaching without Tenure: Policies and Practices for a New Era.* Baltimore: Johns Hopkins University Press.

Barbezat, D. 1989. "The Effect of Collective Bargaining on Salaries in Higher Education." *Industrial and Labor Relations Review* 42 (April): 443–55.

Barro, J., and R. Barro. 1990. "Pay, Performance, and Turnover of Bank CEOs." *Journal of Labor Economics* 8:448–81.

Bendor, J., T. M. Moe, and K. W. Shotts. 2001. "Recycling the Garbage Can: An Assessment of the Research Program." *American Political Science Review* 95:169–90.

Benjamin, R. 1993. *The Redesign of Governance in Higher Education.* Santa Monica: Rand.

Berger, J. B., and J. F. Milem. 2000. "Organizational Behavior in Higher Education and Student Outcomes." In *Higher Education: Handbook of Theory and Research*, edited by J. C. Smart. Vol. 15, 268–338. New York: Agathon Press.

Berger, M. C., and T. Kostal. 2002. "Financial Resources, Regulation, and Enrollment in U.S. Public Higher Education." *Economics of Education Review* 21:101–10.

Berle, A., and G. Means. 1932. *The Modern Corporation and Private Property.* New York: Macmillan.

Bernheim, B. D., and M. D. Whinston. 1986a. "Common Agency." *Econometrica* 54:923–42.

———. 1986b. "Menu Auctions, Resource Allocation, and Economic Influence." *Quarterly Journal of Economics* 101:1–31.

Biemer, P. P., and R. S. Fesco. 1995. "Evaluating and Controlling Measurement Error in Business Surveys." In *Business Survey Methods*, edited by B. G. Cox, D. A. Binder, and B. Nanjamma Chinnappa. New York: Wiley.

Birnbaum, R. 1988. *How Colleges Work: The Cybernetics of Academic Organization and Leadership.* San Francisco: Jossey-Bass.

Blackwell, D., J. Brickley, and M. Weisbach, 1994. "Accounting Information and Internal Performance Evaluation: Evidence from Texas Banks." *Journal of Accounting and Economics* 17:331–58.

Blau, P. 1973. *The Organization of Academic Work.* New York: Wiley.

Blum, D. 1995. "All Part of the Game." *Chronicle of Higher Education* (24 February): A39–40.

Borokhovich, K., R. Parrino, and T. Trapani. 1996. "Outside Directors and CEO Selection." *Journal of Financial and Quantitative Analysis* 31:337–55.

Boulding, K. 1964. "A Pure Theory of Conflict Applied to Organizations." In *The Frontiers of Management Psychology*, edited by George Fisk, 41–49. New York: Harper and Row.

Bowen, H. 1977. *Investment in Learning: The Individual and Social Value of American Higher Education.* San Francisco: Jossey-Bass.

Bowen, W. G. 1994. *Inside the Boardroom: Governance by Directors and Trustees.* New York: Wiley.

Bowen, W. G., T. I. Nygren, S. E. Turner, and E. A. Duffy. 1994. *The Charitable Nonprofits.* San Francisco: Jossey-Bass.

Brenneman, D. 1994. *Liberal Arts Colleges: Thriving, Surviving, or Endangered?* Washington, D.C.: Brookings Institution.

Brown, M. C. 2000. *Organization and Governance in Higher Education.* 5th ed. Boston: Pearson Custom Publishing.

Brubacher, J. S., and W. Rudy. 1976. *Higher Education in Transition: A History of American Colleges and Universities, 1636–1976.* 3d ed. New York: Harper and Row.

Bucovetsky, S. 1991. "Asymmetric Tax Competition." *Journal of Urban Economics* 30:67–181.

Burke, J. C., and Associates. 2002. *Funding Public Colleges and Universities for Performance: Popularity, Problems and Prospects.* Albany: Rockefeller Institute Press.

Burke, J. C., and H. Minassians, 2001. *Linking State Resources to Campus Results: From Fad to Trend—The Fifth Annual Report*. Albany: Rockefeller Institute Press.

Burke, J. C., and S. Modarresi. 1999. *Performance Funding and Budgeting: Popularity and Volatility—The Third Annual Survey*. Albany: Nelson A. Rockefeller Institute of Government, State University of New York.

Burt, R. S. 1983. *Corporate Profits and Cooptation: Networks of Market Constraints and Directorate Ties in the American Economy*. New York: Academic Press.

Burton, R. M., and B. Obel. 1984. *Designing Efficient Organizations: Modelling and Experimentation*. Amsterdam: North-Holland.

Carnegie Foundation for the Advancement of Teaching, 1994. *A Classification of Institutions of Higher Education*. Princeton, N.J.: Carnegie Foundation for the Advancement of Teaching.

Carpenter, D. P. 2001. *The Forging of Bureaucratic Autonomy: Reputations, Networks, and Policy Innovation in Executive Agencies, 1862–1928*. Princeton, N.J.: Princeton University Press.

Cerych, L., and P. Sabatier. 1986. *Great Expectations and Mixed Performance: The Implementation of European Higher Education Reforms*. Stoke-on-Trent, U.K.: Trenton Books.

Chaffee, E. E. 1984. *After Decline, What? Survival Strategies at Eight Private Colleges*. Boulder, Colo.: National Center for Higher Education Management Systems.

———. 1985. "Three Models of Strategy." *Academy of Management Review* 10:89–98.

Chait, R., and B. Taylor. 1989. "Charting the Territory of Nonprofit Boards." *Harvard Business Review* 67:44–54.

Chambers, M. M. 1941–1976. *The Colleges and the Courts: Recent Judicial Decisions regarding Higher Education in the United States*. New York: Carnegie Foundation.

Chandler, A. D., Jr. 1962. *Strategy and Structure: Chapters in the History of Industrial Enterprise*. Cambridge: MIT Press.

Clark, B. R., and T. I. K. Youn. 1976. *Academic Power in the United States: Comparative Historic and Structural Perspectives*. Washington, D.C.: American Association for Higher Education.

Cohen, M. D., and J. G. March. 1974. *Leadership and Ambiguity: The American College President*. New York: McGraw-Hill.

———. 1986. *Leadership and Ambiguity: The American College Presidency*. 2d ed. Boston: Harvard Business School Press.

Cohen, M. D., J. G. March, and J. P. Olsen. 1972. "A Garbage Can Model of Organizational Choice." *Administrative Science Quarterly* 17:1–25.

College Board. 2001. *Trends in Student Aid*. Washington, D.C.: College Board. Available at http://www.collegeboard.com/press/cost01/html/TrendsSA01.pdf.

Conway, J. K. 2001. *A Woman's Education*. New York: Knopf.

Core, J., R. Holthausen, and D. Larcker. 1999. "Corporate Governance, Chief Executive Officer Compensation, and Firm Performance." *Journal of Financial Economics* 51:371–406.

Cornell Higher Education Research Institute. 2001 (Spring). "Survey of Tuition Reciprocity Agreements." Available at www.ilr.cornell.edu/cheri/survey2001/summary.

Corry, D. J. 2000. *Negotiations: The Art of Mutual Gains Bargaining*. Aurora, Ont.: Canada Law Book.

Coughlan, A., and R. Schmidt. 1985. "Executive Compensation, Managerial Turnover, and Firm Performance: An Empirical Investigation." *Journal of Accounting and Economics* 7:43–66.

Courant, P. N., and M. Knepp. 2001. "Budgeting with the UB Model at the University of Michigan." Unpublished manuscript, University of Michigan.

Crawford, V. P., and J. Sobel. 1982. "Strategic Information Transmission. *Econometrica* 50:1431–51.

Cross, J. G. 1996. "A Brief Review of 'Responsibility Center Management.' " Unpublished manuscript, University of Michigan.

Dahl, R. A. 1957. "The Concept of Power." *Behavioral Science* 2:201–15.

Debande, O., and J. L. Demeulemeester, 2000. "Quality and Variety Competition Between Higher Education Institutions." Unpublished manuscript, European Investment Bank, Luxembourg.

Denis, D., and A. Sarin. 1999. "Ownership and Board Structures in Publicly Traded Corporations." *Journal of Financial Economics* 52:187–224.

Dillman, D. A. 2000. *Mail and Internet Surveys: The Tailored Design Method*. 2d ed. New York: Wiley.

DiMaggio, P., and W. Powell. 1983. "The Iron Cage Revisited: Institutional Isomorphism and Collective Rationality in Organizational Fields." *American Sociological Review* 48 (April): 147–60.

Dogan, M., and R. Pahre. 1989. "Fragmentation and Recombination of the Social Sciences." *Studies in Comparative International Development* 24:1–18.

Donaldson, L. 2001. *The Contingency Theory of Organizations.* Thousand Oaks, Calif.: Sage Publications.

Duderstadt, J. 2000. *A University for the 21st Century.* Ann Arbor: University of Michigan Press.

Duryea, E. D. 1973. "Evolution of University Organization." In *The University as an Organization,* edited by J. A. Perkins, 15–37. New York: McGraw-Hill.

Education Commission of the States. 1974. *Collective Bargaining in Postsecondary Educational Institutions.* Denver: Education Commission of the States.

———. 2002. *Postsecondary Governance Structures Database.* Denver: Education Commission of the States.

Ehrenberg, R. G. 2000a. *Tuition Rising: Why College Costs So Much.* Cambridge: Harvard University Press.

———. 2000b. "Internal Transfer Prices." In *Tuition Rising: Why College Costs So Much,* edited by R. G. Ehrenberg, 157–70. Cambridge: Harvard University Press.

———. 2000c. "Financial Forecasts for the Next Decade." *Presidency* 3 (April): 30–35.

Ehrenberg, R. G., and G. S. Goldstein. 1975. "A Model of Public Sector Wage Determination." *Journal of Urban Economics* 1 (June): 223–45.

Ehrenberg, R. G., and P. G. Mavros. 1995. "Do Doctoral Student Financial Support Patterns Affect Their Times to Degree and Completion Rates?" *Journal of Human Resources* 30 (July): 581–609.

Ehrenberg, R., J. Cheslock, and J. Epifantseva. 2001. "Paying Our Presidents: What Do Trustees Value?" *Review of Higher Education* 25:15–37.

Eisenberg, T., S. Sundgren, and M. Wells. 1998. "Larger Board Size and Decreasing Firm Value in Small Firms." *Journal of Financial Economics* 48:35–54.

Elliott, E. C., and M. M. Chambers. 1936. *The Colleges and the Courts: Judicial Decisions regarding institutions of Higher Education in the United States.* New York: Carnegie Foundation.

Emerson, R. M. 1962. "Power-Dependence Relations." *American Sociological Review* 27 (April): 31–41.

Ende, H., E. Anderson, and S. Crego. 1997. "Liability Insurance: A Primer for College and University Counsel." *Journal of College and University Law* 23:609–753.

Epple, D., R. Romano, and H. Sieg. 2000. "Peer Effects, Financial Aid, and Selection of Students into Colleges and Universities: An Empirical Analysis." Unpublished manuscript, Carnegie Mellon University.

Fama, E., and M. C. Jensen. 1983a. "Separation of Ownership and Control" *Journal of Law and Economics* 26 (June): 301–26.

———. 1983b. "Agency Problems and Residual Claims." *Journal of Law and Economics* 26 (June): 327–48.

Finkin, M. W. 1994. "The Unfolding Tendency in the Federal Relationship to Private Accreditation in Higher Education." *Law and Contemporary Problems* 57:89–120.

Firestone, D., with M. L. Wald. 2002. "Flight Schools See Downside to Crackdown." *New York Times,* 27 May, 1A.

Flawn, P. T. 1990. *A Primer for University Presidents.* Austin: University of Texas Press.

Flexner, A. 1910. *Medical Education in the United States and Canada: A Report to the Carnegie Foundation for the Advancement of Teaching.* Carnegie Foundation for the Advancement of Teaching Bulletin No. 4. New York: Carnegie Foundation for the Advancement of Teaching.

Flores, M. 2002. "Regents Sack Veteran UTSA Prof." *San Antonio Express-News,* 15 February, 1B.

Fogg, P. 2002. "Bill in Washington State Would Allow Professors to Bargain Collectively, If. . . ." *Chronicle of Higher Education* (29 March): A12.

Freedman, J. O. 1987. "A Common Wealth of Liberal Learning: Inaugural Address of James O. Freedman Delivered at His Installation as Fifteenth President of Dartmouth College." Hanover, N.H.: Dartmouth College.

———. 1996. *Idealism and Liberal Education.* Arm Arbor: University of Michigan Press.

French, J. R. P., Jr., and B. Raven. 1968. "The Bases of Social Power." In *Group Dynamics.* 3d ed. Edited by D. Cartwright and A. Zander, 259–69. New York: Harper and Row.

Furner, M. O. 1975. *Advocacy and Objectivity: A Crisis in the Professionalization of American Social Science.* Lexington: University of Kentucky Press.

Garvin, D. 1980. *The Economics of University Behavior.* New York: Academic Press.

Gibbard, A. 1973. "Manipulation of Voting Schemes: A General Result." *Econometrica* 41:587–601.

Glaeser, E. 2002. "The Governance of Not-for-Profit Firms." NBER Working Paper No. w8921. Cambridge, Mass.: National Bureau of Economic Research.

Goldin, C., and L. Katz. 1999. "The Shaping of Higher Education: The Formative Years in the United States, 1890 to 1940." *Journal of Economic Perspectives* 13 (Winter): 37–62.

Graham, H. D., and N. Diamond. 1997. *The Rise of American Research Universities: Elites and Challengers in the Postwar Era.* Baltimore: Johns Hopkins University Press.

Green, M., P. Eckel, and A. Barblan. 2002. *The Brave New (and Smaller) World of Higher Education: A Transatlantic View.* Changing Enterprise Series. Washington, D.C.: American Council on Education.

Groen, J., and M. J. White. 2000 (June). "In-State versus Out-of-Stare Students: The Divergence of Interests between Public Universities and State Governments." CHERI Working Paper No. 25. Ithaca, N.Y.: Cornell Higher Education Research Institute. Available at http://www.ilr.cornell.edu/cheri.

Grossman, G. M., and E. Helpman. 2001. *Special Interest Politics.* Cambridge: MIT Press.

Gulick, L. 1937. "Notes on the Theory of Organization." In *Papers on the Science of Administration*, edited by L. Gulick and L. Urwick, 1–45. New York Institute of Public Administration, Columbia University.

Gumport, P., and B. Pusser. 1997. "Restructuring the Academic Environment." In *Planning and Management for a Changing Environment*, edited by M. D. Peterson, D. D. Dill, and L. Mets, 453–78. San Francisco: Jossey-Bass.

Hall, P. D. 1997. *A History of Nonprofit Boards in the United States.* Washington, D.C.: National Center for Nonprofit Boards.

Hallock, K. 1997. "Reciprocally Interlocking Boards of Directors and Executive Compensation." *Journal of Financial and Quantitative Analysis* 32:331–34.

Halpern, S. A. 1987. "Professional Schools in the American University." In *The Academic Profession: National, Disciplinary, and Institutional Settings*, edited by Burton R. Clark, 304–30. Berkeley: University of California Press.

Hammond, T. H. 1986. "Agenda Control, Organizational Structure, and Bureaucratic Politics." *American Journal of Political Science* 30:379–420.

———. 1990. "In Defense of Luther Gulick's 'Notes on the Theory of Organization.'" *Public Administration* 68:143–73.

———. 1993. "Toward a General Theory of Hierarchy: Books, Bureaucrats, Basketball Tournaments, and the Administrative Structure of the Nation-State." *Journal of Public Administration Research and Theory* 3:120–45.

———. 1994. "Structure, Strategy, and the Agenda of the Firm." In *Fundamental Issues in Strategy: A Research Agenda*, edited by R. P. Rumelt, D. E. Schendel, and D. J. Teece, 97–154. Boston: Harvard Business School Press.

Hammond, T. H., and J. H. Horn. 1984. "Clones, Coalitions, and Sophisticated Choice in Hierarchies." Paper presented at the annual meeting of the Public Choice Society, Phoenix, Ariz.

———. 1985. " 'Putting One over on the Boss': The Political Economy of Strategic Behavior in Organizations." *Public Choice* 45:49–71.

Hammond, T. H., and G. J. Miller. 1985. "A Social Choice Perspective on Authority and Expertise in Bureaucracy." *American Journal of Political Science* 29:611–38.

Hammond, T. H., and P. A. Thomas. 1989. "The Impossibility of a Neutral Hierarchy." *Journal of Law, Economics, and Organization* 5:155–84.

———. 1990. "Invisible Decisive Coalitions in Large Hierarchies." *Public Choice* 66:101–16.

Hansmann, H. 1980. "The Role of the Nonprofit Enterprise." *Yale Law Journal* 89:835–901.

———. 1996. *The Ownership of Enterprise.* Cambridge: Harvard University Press.

Haskell, T. 1976. *The Emergence of Professional Social Science: The American Social Science Association and the Nineteenth Century Crisis in Authority.* Urbana: University of Illinois Press.

Haunschild, P. R., and C. M. Beckman. 1998. "When Do Interlocks Matter? Alternate Sources of Information and Interlock Influence." *Administrative Science Quarterly* 43(4): 815–44.

Hearn, J. C., and C. P. Griswold. 1994. "State-Level Centralization and Policy Innovation in U.S. Postsecondary Education." *Educational Evaluation and Policy Analysis* 16(2): 161–90.

Heckman, J. J. 1979. "Sample Selection Bias as a Specification Error." *Econometrica* 47 (January): 153–61.

Heller, D. E., ed. 2001. *The States and Public Higher Education Policy: Affordability, Access, and Accountability.* Baltimore: Johns Hopkins University Press.

———. 2002. "The Policy Shift in State Financial Aid Programs." In *Higher Education: Handbook of Theory and Research*, edited by J. C. Smart. Vol. 17, 221–61. New York: Agathon Press.

Hermalin, B., and M. Weisbach. 1988. "The Determinants of Board Composition." *RAND Journal of Economics* 19:589–606.

——. 1998. "Endogenously Chosen Boards of Directors and Their Monitoring of the CEO." *American Economic Review* 88:96–118.

——. 2003. "Boards of Directors as an Endogenously Determined Institution: A Survey of the Economic Literature." *Economic Policy Review* 9:7–26.

Herman, R., and D. Renz. 1998. "Nonprofit Organizational Effectiveness: Contrasts between Especially Effective and Less Effective Organizations." *Nonprofit Management and Leadership* 9:23–38.

Hines, E. R. 2000. "The Governance of Higher Education." In *Higher Education: Handbook of Theory and Research*, edited by J. C. Smart. Vol. 15, 105–56. New York: Agathon Press.

Hirsch, W. Z., and L. Weber, eds. 2001. *Governance in Higher Education: The University in a State of Flux.* London: Economica; distributed by Brookings Institution.

Hirschman, A. O. 1970. *Exit, Voice and Loyalty: Responses to Decline in Firms, Organizations, and States.* Cambridge: Harvard University Press.

Holmstrom, B. 1982. "Moral Hazard in Teams." *Bell Journal of Economics* 13:324–40.

Hosios, A., and A. Siow. 2001 (November). "Unions without Rents: The Curious Economics of Faculty Unions." Mimeograph, University of Toronto.

Huson, M., R. Parrino, and L. Starks. 2000. "Internal Monitoring and CEO Turnover: A Long-Term Perspective." Working paper, University of Texas, Austin.

Ingram, R. T. 1996. "New Tensions in the Academic Boardroom." *Educational Record* 77 (Spring–Summer): 49–55.

Institute for Higher Education Policy. 1998. *Reaping the Benefits: Defining the Public and Private Value of Going to College.* Washington, D.C.: Institute for Higher Education Policy.

Iseminger, J. 1999. "Study. Bargaining Doesn't Inhibit Grad Education." *Wisconsin Week*, 20 October. Available at http://www.news.wisc.edu/wisweek/

James, E. 1998. "Commercialism among Nonprofits: Objectives, Opportunities, and Constraints." In *To Profit or Not to Profit. The Commercial Transformation of the Nonprofit Sector*, edited by B. A. Weisbrod, 271–86. Cambridge: Cambridge University Press.

Jencks, C., and D. Riesman. 1968. *The Academic Revolution.* 1st ed. Garden City, N.Y.: Doubleday.

——. 1977. *The Academic Revolution.* With a new foreword by Martin Trow. Chicago: University of Chicago Press.

Jensen, M. 1993. "The Modern Industrial Revolution, Exit, and the Failure of Internal Control Systems." *Journal of Finance* 48:831–80.

Jensen, M., and K. Murphy. 1990. "Performance Pay and Top-Management Incentives." *Journal of Political Economy* 98:225–64.

Jones, G. A., and M. L. Skolnik. 1997. "Governing Boards in Canadian Universities." *Review of Higher Education* 20(3): 277–95.

Kaplan, S. 1994. "Top Executive Rewards and Firm Performance: A Comparison of Japan and the U.S." *Journal of Political Economy* 102:510–46.

Kaplan, W. A., and B. A. Lee. 1995. *The Law of Higher Education.* 3d ed. San Francisco: Jossey-Bass.

——. 2000. *The Law of Higher Education.* Supplement to 3d ed. Washington, D.C.: National Association of Colleges and University Attorneys.

Keller, M., and P. Keller. 2001. *Making Harvard Modern: The Rise of America's University.* New York: Oxford University Press.

Kerr, C., and M. Gade, 1989. *The Guardians: Boards of Trustees of American Colleges and Universities.* Washington, D.C.: Association of Governing Boards of Universities and Colleges.

Kesselring, R. 1991. "The Economic Effects of Faculty Unions." *Journal of Labor Research* 12 (Winter): 61–72.

Klaff, D. B., and R. G. Ehrenberg. 2002. "Collective Bargaining and Staff Salaries in American Colleges and Universities." CHERI Working Paper No. 21. Ithaca, N.Y.: Cornell Higher Education Research Institute. Available at http://www.ilr.cornell.edu/cheri.

Knoke, D., P. V. Marsden, and A. L. Kalleberg. 2002. "Survey Research Methods." In *The Blackwell Companion to Organizations*, edited by Joel A. C. Baum, 781–804. Malden, Mass.: Blackwell.

Krause, G., and J. D. Wilson. 2000. "Responsibility Center Budgeting within a University." Unpublished manuscript, Michigan State University.

Ladd, E. C., and S. M. Lipset. 1973. *Professors, Unions, and American Higher Education.* Washington, D.C.: American Enterprise Institute for Public Policy Research.

——. 1975. *The Divided Academy: Professors and Politics.* New York: McGraw-Hill.

Lafer, G. 2001. "Graduate Students Fight the Corporate University." *Dissent* 48 (Fall): 63–71.

LaNone, G., and B. A. Lee. 1987. *Academics in Court: The Consequences of Faculty Discrimination Litigation.* Ann Arbor: University of Michigan Press.

Leatherman, C. 2000. "Union Movement at Private Colleges Awakens after a 20-Year Slumber." *Chronicle of Higher Education* (21 January): A16.

Lee, L. 1978. "Unionism and Wage Rates: A Simultaneous Equations Model with Qualitative and Limited Dependent Variables." *International Economic Review* 19 (June): 415–33.

Levin, J. S. 2001. *Globalizing the Community College: Strategies for Change in the Twenty-First Century.* New York: Palgrave Press.

Levitt, S., and C. Snyder. 1997. "Is No News Bad News? Information Transmission and the Role of 'Early Warning' in the Principal-Agent Model." *RAND Journal of Economics* 28:641–61.

Light, R.J., J. D. Singer, and J. B. Willett. 1990. *By Design: Planning Research in Higher Education.* Cambridge: Harvard University Press.

Lillydahl, J. H., and L. D. Singell. 1993. "Job Satisfaction, Salaries and Unions: The Determination of Faculty Compensation." *Economics of Education Review* 12 (September): 233–45.

Liptak, A. 2002. "Religion and the Law, Insurance Companies Often Dictate Legal Strategies Used by Dioceses." *New York Times*, 14 April.

Lipton, M., and J. Lorsch. 1992. "A Modest Proposal for Improved Corporate Governance." *Business Lawyer* 48:59–77.

Lobbyist Watch. 2001. "University of Phoenix Parent Company Names Former GOP Congressman to Board." *Chronicle of Higher Education* (2 February): A21.

Lodge, D. 1984. *Small World: An Academic Romance.* London: Seeker and Warburg.

Lohmann, S. 2003. "How Universities Think." Manuscript. University of California, Los Angeles.

Lorsch, J. 1989. *Pawns or Potentates: The Reality of America's Corporate Boards.* Boston: Harvard Business School Press.

Lowen, R. S. 1997. *Creating the Cold War University.* Berkeley: University of California Press.

Lowry, R. C. 2001a. "The Effects of State Political Interests and Campus Outputs on Public University Revenues." *Economics of Education Review* 20:105–19.

———. 2001b. "Governmental Structure, Trustee Selection, and Public University Prices and Spending: Multiple Means to Similar Ends." *American Journal of Political Science* 45(4): 845–61.

Mace, M. 1986. *Directors: Myth and Reality.* Boston: Harvard Business School Press.

MacTaggart, T. J. 1996. *Restructuring Higher Education: What Works and What Doesn't in Reorganizing Governing Systems.* San Francisco: Jossey-Bass.

———. 1998. *Seeking Excellence through Independence: Liberating Colleges and Universities from Excessive Regulation.* San Francisco: Jossey-Bass.

Main, B., C. O'Reilly III, and J. Wade. 1995. "The CEO, the Board of Directors, and Executive Compensation: Economic and Psychological Perspectives." *Industrial and Corporate Change* 4:293–332.

Manning, R. 2000. *Credit Card Nation.* New York: Basic Books.

March, J. G., and H. A. Simon. 1958. *Organizations.* New York: Wiley.

Marchese, T. 1998. "Not-so Distant-Competitors: How New Providers Are Remaking the Post-secondary Marketplace." *AAHE Bulletin* 50 (May–June): 3–11.

Marginson, S., and M. Considine. 2000. *The Enterprise University.* Cambridge: Cambridge University Press.

Martin, J. C. 1994. "Recent Developments concerning Accrediting Agencies in Postsecondary Education" *Law and Contemporary Problems* 57:121–49.

Masten, S. E. 2000. "Commitment and Political Governance: Why Universities, Like Legislatures, Are Not Organized as Firms." Unpublished manuscript, University of Michigan Business School.

McLendon, M. K. 2003. "State Governance Reform of Higher Education: Patterns, Trends, and Theories of the Public Policy Process." In *Higher Education: Handbook of Theory and Research*, edited by J. C. Smart. Vol. 18. Dordrecht, Netherlands: Kluwer.

McLendon, M. K., D. E. Heller, and S. P. Young. 2001 (April). "State Postsecondary Policy Innovation: Politics, Competition, and the Interstate Migration of Policy Ideas." Paper presented at the annual meeting of the Midwest Political Science Association, Chicago.

McNamee, M. 2002a. "Insuring Ourselves." *NACUBO Business Officer* 35 (March): 35–37.

——. 2002b. "Coping with Today's Hard Insurance Market." *NACUBO Business Officer* 35 (May): 24–25.

Meador, M., and S. J. K. Walters. 1994. "Unions and Productivity: Evidence from Academe." *Journal of Labor Research* 15 (Fall): 373–86.

Means, H. B., and P. W. Semas, eds. 1976. *Faculty Collective Bargaining.* Washington, D.C.: Educational Project for Educators.

Miller, G. J. 1992. *Managerial Dilemmas: The Political Economy of Hierarchy.* New York: Cambridge University Press.

Mingle, J. R. 2000. "Higher Education's Future in a 'Corporatized' Economy." Occasional Paper No. 44. Washington, D.C.: Association of Governing Boards of Universities and Colleges.

Mizruchi, M. S. 1996. "What Do Interlocks Do: An Analysis, Critique, and Assessment of Research on Interlocking Directorates." *Annual Review of Sociology* 22:271–98.

Monks, J. 2000. "Unionization and Faculty Salaries: New Evidence from the 1990s." *Journal of Labor Research* 21 (Spring): 305–14.

National Center for Education Statistics. 1994. *Digest of Education Statistics, 1994.* NCES publication no. 94–115. Washington, D.C.: National Center for Education Statistics.

——. 1999. *Postsecondary Institutions in the United States: 1997–98.* Washington, D.C.: U.S. Department of Education. Available at http://nces.ed.gov/pubs99/1999174.pdf.

——. 2001a. *Digest of Education Statistics, 2000.* NCES publication no. 2001–034. Washington, D.C.: U.S. Department of Education.

——. 2001b. *Fall Enrollment in Title IV Degree-Granting Postsecondary Institutions: 1998,* by Frank B. Morgan. NCES publication no. 2002–162. Washington, D.C.: U.S. Department of Education.

——. 2002. *Tenure Status of Postsecondary Instructional Faculty and Staff: 1992–98,* by Basmat Parsad and Denise Glover. NCES publication no. 2002–210. Washington, D.C.: U.S. Department of Education.

National Center for the Study of Collective Bargaining in Higher Education and the Professions. 1995. *Directory of Staff Bargaining Agents in Institutions of Higher Education.* New York: National Center for the Study of Collective Bargaining in Higher Education and the Professions.

——. 1997. *Directory of Faculty Contracts and Bargaining Agents in Institutions of Higher Education.* New York: National Center for the Study of Collective Bargaining in Higher Education and the Professions.

National Research Council. 1995. *Research-Doctorate Programs in the United States: Continuity and Change.* Washington, D.C.: National Academy Press.

——. 1998. *Trends in the Early Careers of Life Scientists.* Washington, D.C.: National Academy Press.

Nelson, C. 1999. "The War against the Faculty." *Chronicle of Higher Education* (16 April): B4.

Nesse, R. M., and G. C. Williams. 1994. *Why We Get Sick: The New Science of Darwinian Medicine.* New York: Vintage Books.

Newman, F., and L. Couterier. 2001. "The New Competitive Arena: Market Forces Invade the Academy." *Change* 33 (September–October): 10–17.

Olivas, M. A. 1992. "The Political Economy of Immigration, Intellectual Property, and Racial Harassment." *Journal of Higher Education* 63 (September–October): 570–98.

——. 1997. *The Law and Higher Education: Cases and Materials on Colleges in Court.* 2d ed. Durham: Carolina Academic Press.

——. 2000. "Ideological Balance in Immigration Law Teaching and Scholarship." *University of Illinois Law Review* 102–26.

O'Reilly, C., III, B. Main, and G. Crystal. 1988. "CEO Salaries as Tournaments and Social Comparisons: A Tale of Two Theories." *Administrative Science Quarterly* 33:257–74.

Pahre, R. 1995. "Positivist Discourse and Social Scientific Communities: Towards an Epistemological Sociology of Science." *Social Epistemology* 9:233–55.

Palmer, D. 1983. "Broken Ties: Interlocking Directorates and Inter-corporate Coordination." *Administrative Science Quarterly* 28:40–55.

Parsons, T., and G. Platt. 1973. *The American University.* Cambridge: Harvard University Press.

Paxson, M. C., D. A. Dillman, and J. Tarnai. 1995. "Improving Response to Business Mail Surveys." In *Business Survey Methods,* edited by B. G. Cox, D. A. Binder, and B. Nanjamma Chinnappa, 303–15. New York: Wiley.

Pfeffer, J., and G. R. Salancik. 1974. "Organizational Decision-Making as a Political Process: The Case of the University Budget." *Administrative Science Quarterly* 19(1): 135–51.

——. 1978. *The External Control of Organizations: A Resource Dependence Perspective.* New York: Harper and Row.

Pulley, J. L. 2002. "Money Talks; More So When It Walks." *Chronicle of Higher Education* (25 October): A29.

Pusser, B. 2002. "Higher Education, the Emerging Market, and the Public Good." In *The Knowledge Economy and Post-secondary Education,* edited by P. A. Graham and N. Stacey, 105–26. Washington, D.C.: National Academy Press.

——. 2003. "Beyond Baldridge: Extending the Political Model of Higher Education Governance." *Educational Policy* 17 (January): 121–40.

——. Forthcoming. *Burning Down the House: Politics, Governance, and Affirmative Action at the University of California.* Albany: SUNY Press.

Pusser, B., and D. J. Doane. 2001. "Public Purpose and Private Enterprise: The Contemporary Organization of Post-secondary Education." *Change* 33 (September–October): 18–22.

Rabban, D. M. 1990. "A Functional Analysis of 'Individual' and 'Institutional' Academic Freedom under the First Amendment." *Law and Contemporary Problems* 53:227–302.

Rees, D. I. 1993. "The Effects of Unionization on Faculty Salaries and Compensation: Estimates from the 1980s." *Journal of Labor Research* 14 (Fall): 399–422.

——. 1994. "Does Unionization Increase Faculty Retention?" *Industrial Relations* 33 (July): 297–321.

Rey, E. D. 2001. "Teaching versus Research: A Model of State University Competition." *Journal of Urban Economics* 49:356–73.

Rhoades, G. 1998. *Managed Professionals: Unionized Faculty and Restructuring Academic Labor.* Albany: SUNY Press.

——. 2001. "Whose Property Is It? Negotiating with the University." *Academe* 87 (October–November): 38–43.

Rhodes, F. H. T. 2001. *The Creation of the Future: The Role of the American University.* Ithaca, N.Y.: Cornell University Press.

Richardson, R. C., Jr., K. Reeves Bracco, P. M. Callan, and J. E. Finney. 1999. *Designing State Higher Education Systems for a New Century.* Phoenix: Oryx Press.

Rosenzweig, R. M. 1998. *The Political University.* Baltimore: Johns Hopkins University Press.

Rosovsky, H. 1990. *The University: An Owner's Manual.* New York: Norton.

Rothschild, M., and L. J. White. 1905. "The Analytics of the Pricing of Higher Education and Other Services in Which the Customers Are Inputs." *Journal of Political Economy* 103:573–86.

Ruch, R. S. 2001. *Higher Education, Inc.: The Rise of the For-Profit University.* Baltimore: Johns Hopkins University Press.

Rudolph, F. 1990. *The American College and University: A History.* Athens: University of Georgia Press.

Sabatier, P. 1987. "Knowledge, Policy-Oriented Learning, and Policy Change: An Advocacy Coalition Framework." *Knowledge Creation, Diffusion, Utilization* 8:649–692.

Sanderson, A., et al. 1999. *Doctorates Received from U.S. Universities: Summary Report 1998.* Chicago: National Opinion Research Council.

Satterthwaite, M. A. 1975. "Strategy-Proofness and Arrow's Conditions: Existence and Correspondence Theorems for Voting Procedures and Social Welfare Functions." *Journal of Economic Theory* 10:187–217.

Schmidt, P. 1996. "More States Tie Spending on Colleges to Meeting Specific Goals." *Chronicle of Higher Education* (24 May): A26.

——.1997. "Rancor and Confusion Greet Change in South Carolina Budgeting." *Chronicle of Higher Education* (4 April): A26.

Schuster, J. H., D. G. Smith, K. C. Sund, and M. M. Yamada. 1994. *Strategic Governance: How to Make Big Decisions Better.* Phoenix: Oryx Press.

Seftor, N., and S. Turner. 2002. "Financial Aid and the College Enrollment of Non-traditional Students: Evidence from the Pell Program." *Journal of Human Resources* 37(2): 336–52.

Selingo, J. 1999. "For-Profit Colleges Aim to Take a Share of State Financial Aid Funds." *Chronicle of Higher Education* (24 September): A41.

——. 2001. "Aiming for a New Audience, University of Phoenix Tries Again in New. Jersey." *Chronicle of Higher Education* (21 September): A23–24.

Shepherd, G. B. 2003. "No African-American Lawyers Allowed: The Inefficient Racism of the ABA's Accreditation of Law Schools." *Journal of Legal Education* 53(1): 103–156.

Simon, H. A. 1946. "The Proverbs of Administration." *Public Administration Review* 6:53–67.

Slaughter, S. 2001. "Professional Values and the Allure of the Market." *Academe* 87 (October–November): 22–26.

Slaughter, S., and L. L. Leslie, 1997. *Academic Capitalism.* Baltimore: Johns Hopkins University Press.

Smallwood, S. 2001. "A Big Breakthrough for T.A. Unions." *Chronicle of Higher Education* (16 March): A10.

———. 2002a. "NYU and Its TA Union Reach a Pact on a Contract." *Chronicle of Higher Education* (15 February): A18.

———. 2002b. "U. of Michigan Strikes Deal with TA Unions." *Chronicle of Higher Education* (19 March). Available http://chronicle.com.

———. 2002c "UAW Wins Union Election to Represent Part-Time Faculty Members at New York U." *Chronicle of Higher Education* (10 July). Available at http://chronicle.com.

Smith, A. 1776. *An Inquiry into the Nature and Cases of the Wealth of Nations.* New York: Modern Library.

South Carolina Legislative Audit Council. 2001. *A Review of the Higher Education Performance Funding Process.* Columbia: South Caroline Legislative Audit Council.

Taylor, B., R. Chait, and T. Holland. 1996. "The New Work of the Nonprofit Board." *Harvard Business Review* 74:36–46.

Thomas, S. L., S. Slaughter, and B. Pusser. 2002. "Playing the Board Game: An Empirical Analysis of University Trustee and Corporate Board Interlocks." Working paper, Institute of Higher Education, University of Georgia, Athens.

Tiebout, C. M. 1956. "A Pure Theory of Local Public Goods." *Journal of Political Economy* 64:416–24.

Toma, E. F. 1986. "State University Boards of Trustees: A Principal-Agent Perspective." *Public Choice* 49:155–63.

———. 1990. "Boards of Trustees, Agency Problems, and University Output," *Public Choice* 67:1–9.

Trow, M. A. 1977. *Aspects of American Higher Education, 1969–1975.* Berkeley: Carnegie Council on Policy Studies in Higher Education.

———. Forthcoming. "Biology at Berkeley." In *Fostering Scientific Discovery: Organizations, Institutions, and Major Breakthroughs in Biomedical Science,* edited by J. R. Hollingsworth, J. Hage, and E. J. Hollingsworth: New York: Cambridge University Press.

Useem, M. 1984. *The Inner Circle.* Cambridge: Oxford University Press.

Van Alstyne, W. W. 1990. "Academic Freedom and the First Amendment in the Supreme Court of the United States: An Unhurried Historical Review." *Law and Contemporary Problems* 53(3): 79–154.

Vancil, R. 1987. *Passing the Baton: Managing the Process of CEO Succession.* Boston: Harvard Business School Press.

Van Der Werf, M. 2001. "How Much Should Colleges Pay Their Janitors? Student Protests Force Administrators to Consider Issues of Social Justice and Practicality." *Chronicle of Higher Education* (3 August): A27.

Volkwein, J. F., and S. M. Malik. 1997. "State Regulation and Administrative Flexibility at Public Universities." *Research in Higher Education* 38(1): 17–42.

Volkwein, J. F., S. M. Malik, and M. Napierski-Pranci. 1998. "Administrative Satisfaction and the Regulatory Climate at Public Universities." *Research in Higher Education* 39(1): 43–63.

Warner, J., R. Watts, and K. Wruck. 1988. "Stock Prices and Top-Management Changes." *Journal of Financial Economics* 20:461–92.

Ways and Means Committee. 2001. "Senate Confirms Former Congressional Aide as Top Higher Education Policy Maker." *Chronicle of Higher Education* (29 March): A23.

Webster, D. 1819. "The Dartmouth College Case: Peroration of Daniel Webster." Available at http://www.constitution.org/dwebster/peroration.htm.

Weeks, K. M., and D. Davis, eds. 1982. *Legal Deskbook for Administrators of Independent Colleges and Universities.* 2d. ed. Washington, D.C.: National Association of College and University Attorneys and Center for Constitutional Study, Baylor University.

Weisbach, M. 1988. "Outside Directors and CEO Turnover." *Journal of Financial Economics* 20:431–60.

Weisbrod, B. A. 1988. *The Nonprofit Economy.* Cambridge: Harvard University Press.

Whalen, E. L. 1991. *Responsibility Center Budgeting: An Approach to Decentralized Management for Institutions of Higher Education.* Indianapolis: Indiana University Press.

Williams, A. Y. 2002. "Colleges Scramble for Insurance as Premiums Rise to New Levels." *Chronicle of Higher Education* (3 May): A27–28.

Williamson, O. E. 1985. *The Economic Institutions of Capitalism.* New York: Free Press.

Wilson, J. D. 1991. "Tax Competition with Interregional Differences in Factor Endowment." *Regional Science and Urban Economics* 21:423–52.

———. 2002. "The Efficiency Implications of Responsibility Center Management within State Universities." In *Incentive-Based Budgeting Systems in Public Universities*, edited by D. M. Priest, W. E. Becker, D. Hossler, and E. P. St. John, 25–54. Northampton, Mass.: Edward Elgar.

Wilson, R. 2001. "Proportion of Part-Time Faculty Members Leveled off from 1992 to 1998, Data Shows." *Chronicle of Higher Education* (4 May): A17.

Winston, G. 1998. "Why Can't a College Be More Like a Firm?" In *New Thinking on Higher Education: Creating a Context for Change*, edited by J. Meyerson, 1–14. Bolton, Mass.: Anker.

———. 1999. "Subsidies, Hierarchy, and Peers: The Awkward Economics of Higher Education." *Journal of Economic Perspectives* 13 (Winter): 13–36.

Wu, Y. 2000. "Honey, I Shrunk the Board." Working paper, University of Chicago.

Yermack, D. 1996. "Higher Valuation of Companies with a Small Board of Directors." *Journal of Financial Economics* 40:185–212.

Zellner, A. 1962. "An Efficient Method of Estimating Seemingly Unrelated Regressions and Testing for Aggregation Bias." *Journal of the American Statistical Association* 67 (June): 348–65.

Zimbalist, A. 1999. *Unpaid Professionals: Commercialism and Conflict in Big-Time College Sports.* Princeton, N.J.: Princeton University Press.

Zumeta, W. 1996. "Meeting the Demand for Higher Education without Breaking the Bank: A Framework for the Design of State Higher Education Policies for an Era of Increasing Demand." *Journal of Higher Education* 67(4): 367–425.

———. 2001. "Public Policy and Accountability in Higher Education: Lessons from the Past and Present for the New Millennium." In *The States and Public Higher Education Policy: Affordability, Access, and Accountability*, edited by Donald E. Heller, 155–97. Baltimore: Johns Hopkins University Press.

PART IV

UNDERSTANDING CAMPUS CLIMATES AND CULTURES

THE ORGANIZATIONAL SAGA IN HIGHER EDUCATION

BURTON R. CLARK

An organizational saga is a collective understanding of a unique accomplishment based on historical exploits of a formal organization, offering strong normative bonds within and outside the organization. Believers give loyalty to the organization and take pride and identity from it. A saga begins as strong purpose, introduced by a man (or small group) with a mission, and is fulfilled as it is embodied in organizational practices and the values of dominant organizational cadres, usually taking decades to develop. Examples of the initiation and fulfillment of sagas in academic organizations are presented from research on Antioch, Reed, and Swarthmore.[1]

Saga, originally referring to a medieval Icelandic or Norse account of achievements and events in the history of a person or group, has come to mean a narrative of heroic exploits, a unique development that has deeply stirred the emotions of participants and descendants. Thus a saga is not simply a story but a story that at some time has had a particular base of believers. The term often refers also to the actual history itself, thereby including a stream of events, the participants, and the written or spoken interpretation. The element of belief is crucial, for without the credible story, the events and persons become history; with the development of belief, a particular bit of history becomes a definition full of pride and identity for the group.

Introduction

An *organizational saga* is a collective understanding of unique accomplishment in a formally established group. The group's definition of the accomplishment, intrinsically historical but embellished through retelling and rewriting, links stages of organizational development. The participants have added affect, an emotional loading, which places their conception between the coolness of rational purpose and the warmth of sentiment found in religion and magic. An organizational saga presents some rational explanation of how certain means led to certain ends, but it also includes affect that turns a formal place into a beloved institution, to which participants may be passionately devoted. Encountering such devotion, the observer may become unsure of his own analytical detachment as he tests the overtones of the institutional spirit or spirit of place.

The study of organizational sagas highlights nonstructural and nonrational dimensions of organizational life and achievement. Macroorganizational theory has concentrated on the role of structure and technology in organizational effectiveness (Gross, 1964; Litterer, 1965; March, 1965; Thompson, 1967; Price, 1968; Perrow, 1970). A needed corrective is more research on the cultural and expressive aspects of organizations, particularly on the role of belief and sentiment at broad levels of organization. The human-relations approach in organizational analysis, centered largely on group interaction, showed some awareness of the role of organization symbols (Whyte, 1948: ch. 23), but this conceptual

"The Organizational Saga in Higher Education," by Burton R. Clark, reprinted with permission from *Administrative Science Quarterly*, Vol. 17, No. 2, June 1972.

lead has not been taken as a serious basis for research. Also, in the literature on organizations and purposive communities, "ideology" refers to unified and shared belief (Selznick, 1949; Bendix, 1956; Price, 1968: 104–110; Carden, 1969); but the concept of ideology has lost denotative power, having been stretched by varying uses. For the phenomenon discussed in this paper, "saga" seems to provide the appropriate denotation. With a general emphasis on normative bonds, organizational saga refers to a unified set of publicly expressed beliefs about the formal group that (a) is rooted in history, (b) claims unique accomplishment, and (c) is held with sentiment by the group.

To develop the concept in this paper, extreme cases and exaggerations of the ideal type are used; but the concept will be close to reality and widely applicable when the phenomenon is examined in weak as well as strong expression. In many organizations, even some highly utilitarian ones, some segment of their personnel probably develop in time at least a weak saga. Those who have persisted for some years in one place will have had at minimum, a thin stream of shared experience, which they elaborate into a plausible account of group uniqueness. Whether developed primarily by management or by employees, the story helps rationalize for the individual his commitment of time and energy for years, perhaps for a lifetime, to a particular enterprise. Even when weak, the belief can compensate in part for the loss of meaning in modern work, giving some drama and some cultural identity to one's otherwise entirely instrumental efforts. At the other end of the continuum, a saga engages one so intensely as to make his immediate place overwhelmingly valuable. It can even produce a striking distortion, with the organization becoming the only reality, the outside world becoming illusion. Generally the almost complete capture of affect and perception is associated with only a few utopian communities, fanatical political factions, and religious sects. But some formal rationalized organizations, as for example business and education, can also become utopian, fanatical, or sectarian.

Organizational sagas vary in durability. They can arise quickly in relatively unstructured social settings, as in professional sports organizations that operate in the volatile context of contact with large spectator audiences through the mass media. A professional baseball or football team may create a rags-to-riches legend in a few months' time that excites millions of people. But such a saga is also very fragile as an ongoing definition of the organization. The story can be removed quickly from the collective understanding of the present and future, for successful performance is often unstable, and the events that set the direction of belief can be readily reversed, with the great winners quickly becoming habitual losers. In such cases, there seems to be an unstable structural connection between the organization and the base of believers. The base of belief is not anchored within the organization nor in personal ties between insiders and outsiders, but is mediated by mass media, away from the control of the organization. Such sagas continue only as the organization keeps repeating its earlier success and also keeps the detached followers from straying to other sources of excitement and identification.

In contrast, organizational sagas show high durability when built slowly in structured social contexts; for example, the educational system, specifically for the purposes of this paper, three liberal arts colleges in the United States. In the many small private colleges, the story of special performance emerges not in a few months but over a decade or two. When the saga is firmly developed, it is embodied in many components of the organization, affecting the definition and performance of the organization and finding protection in the webbing of the institutional parts. It is not volatile and can be relegated to the past only by years of attenuation or organizational decline.

Since the concept of organizational saga was developed from research on Reed, Antioch, and Swarthmore, three distinctive and highly regarded colleges (Clark, 1970), material and categories from their developmental histories are used to illustrate the development of a saga, and its positive effects on organizational participation and effectiveness are then considered.[2]

Development of Saga

Two stages can be distinguished in the development of an organizational saga, initiation and fulfillment. Initiation takes place under varying conditions and occurs within a relatively short period of time: fulfillment is related to features of the organization that are enduring and more predictable.

Initiation

Strong sagas do not develop in passive organizations tuned to adaptive servicing of demand or to the fulfilling of roles dictated by higher authorities (Clark, 1956, 1960). The saga is initially a strong purpose, conceived and enunciated by a single man or a small cadre (Selznick, 1957) whose first task is to find a setting that is open, or can be opened, to a special effort. The, most obvious setting is the autonomous new organization, where there is no established structure, no rigid custom, especially if a deliberate effort has been made to establish initial autonomy and bordering outsiders are preoccupied. There a leader may also have the advantage of building from the top down, appointing lieutenants and picking up recruits in accord with his ideas.

Reed College is strongly characterized by a saga, and its story of hard-won excellence and nonconformity began as strong purpose in a new organization. Its first president, William T. Foster, a thirty-year-old, high-minded reformer, from the sophisticated East of Harvard and Bowdoin went to the untutored Northwest, to an unbuilt campus in suburban Portland in 1910, precisely because he did not want to be limited by established institutions, all of which were, to his mind, corrupt in practice. The projected college in Oregon was clear ground, intellectually as well as physically, and he could there assemble the people and devise the practices that would finally give the United States an academically pure college, a Balliol for America.

The second setting for initiation is the established organization in a crisis of decay. Those in charge, after years of attempting incremental adjustments (Lindblom, 1959), realize finally that they must either give up established ways or have the organization fail. Preferring that it survive, they may relinquish the leadership to one proposing a plan that promises revival and later strength, or they may even accept a man of utopian intent. Deep crisis in the established organization thus creates some of the conditions of a new organization. It suspends past practice, forces some bordering groups to stand back or even to turn their backs on failure of the organization, and it tends to catch the attention of the reformer looking for an opportunity.

Antioch College is a dramatic example of such a setting. Started in the 1860s, its first sixty years were characterized by little money, weak staff, few students, and obscurity. Conditions worsened in the 1910s under the inflation and other strains of World War I. In 1919 a charismatic utopian reformer, Arthur E. Morgan, decided it was more advantageous to take over an old college with buildings and a charter than to start a new one. First as trustee and then as president, he began in the early 1920s an institutional renovation that overturned everything: as president he found it easy to push aside old, weak organizational structures and usages. He elaborated a plan of general education involving an unusual combination of work, study, and community participation; and he set about to devise the implementing tool. Crisis and charisma made possible a radical transformation out of which came a second Antioch, a college soon characterized by a sense of exciting history, unique practice, and exceptional performance.

The third context for initiation is the established organization that is not in crisis, not collapsing from long decline, yet ready for evolutionary change. This is the most difficult situation to predict, having to do with degree of rigidity. In both ideology and structure, institutionalized colleges vary in openness to change. In those under church control, for example, the colleges of the more liberal Protestant denominations have been more hospitable than Catholic colleges, at least until recently, to educational experimentation. A college with a tradition of presidential power is more open to change than one where the trustees and the professors exert control over the president. Particularly promising is the college with a self-defined need for educational leadership. This is the opening for which some reformers watch, the sound place that has some ambition to increase its academic stature, as for example, Swarthmore College.

Swarthmore began in the 1860s, and had become by 1920 a secure and stable college, prudently managed by Quaker trustees and administrators and solidly based on traditional support from nearby Quaker families in Pennsylvania, New Jersey, and Maryland. Such an organization would not usually be thought promising for reform, but Frank Aydelotte, who became its president in 1920, judged it ready for change. Magnetic in personality, highly placed within the élite circle of former Rhodes scholars, personally liked by important foundation officials, and recommended as a scholarly leader, he was offered other college presidencies, but he chose Swarthmore as a place open to change through a combination of financial health, liberal Quaker ethos, and some institutional ambition. His judgment proved correct, although the tolerance for his changes in the 1920s and 1930s was narrow at times. He began the gradual introduction of a modified Oxford honors program and related changes, which resulted in noteworthy achievements that supporters were to identify later as "the Swarthmore saga" (Swarthmore College Faculty, 1941).

Fulfillment

Although the conditions of initiation of a saga vary, the means of fulfillment are more predictable. There are many ways in which a unified sense of a special history is expressed; for example, even a patch of sidewalk or a coffee room may evoke emotion among the believers; but one can delimit the components at the center of the development of a saga. These may center, in colleges, on the personnel, the program, the external social base, the student subculture, and the imagery of the saga.

Personnel

In a college, the key group of believers is the senior faculty. When they are hostile to a new idea, its attenuation is likely; when they are passive, its success is weak; and when they are devoted to it, a saga is probable. A single leader, a college president, can initiate the change, but the organizational idea will not be expanded over the years and expressed in performance unless ranking and powerful members of the faculty become committed to it and remain committed even after the initiator is gone. In committing themselves deeply, taking some credit for the change and seeking to ensure its perpetuation, they routinize the charisma of the leader in collegial authority. The faculty cadre of believers helps to effect the legend, then to protect it against later leaders and other new participants who, less pure in belief, might turn the organization in some other direction.

Such faculty cadres were well developed at Reed by 1925, after the time of its first two presidents; at Antioch, by the early 1930s, after Morgan, disappointed with his followers, left for the board of directors of the new TVA; and at Swarthmore, by the 1930s, and particularly, by 1940, after Aydelotte's twenty years of persistent effort. In all three colleges, after the departure of the change agent(s), the senior faculty with the succeeding president, a man appropriate for consolidation, undertook the full working out of the experiment. The faculty believers also replaced themselves through socialization and selective recruitment and retention in the 1940s and 1950s. Meanwhile, new potential innovators had sometimes to be stopped. In such instances, the faculty was able to exert influence to shield the distinctive effort from erosion or deflection. At Reed, for example, major clashes between president and faculty in the late 1930s and the early 1950s were precipitated by a new change-oriented president, coming in from the outside, disagreeing with a faculty proud of what had been done, attached deeply to what the college had become, and determined to maintain what was for them the distinctive Reed style. From the standpoint of constructing a regional and national model of purity and severity in undergraduate education, the Reed faculty did on those occasions act to create while acting to conserve.

Programs

For a college to transform purpose into a credible story of unique accomplishment, there must be visible practices with which claims of distinctiveness can be supported; that is, unusual courses, noteworthy requirements, or special methods of teaching. On the basis of seemingly unique practices, the program becomes a set of communal symbols and rituals, invested with meaning. Not reporting grades to the students becomes a symbol, as at Reed, that the college cares about learning for learning's sake; thus mere technique becomes part of a saga.

In all the three colleges, the program was seen as distinctive by both insiders and outsiders. At Swarthmore it was the special seminars and other practices of the honors program, capped by written and oral examination by teams of visiting outsiders in the last days of the senior year. At Antioch it was the work-study cycle, the special set of general education requirements, community government, and community involvement. At Reed it was the required freshman lecture-and-seminar courses, the junior qualifying examination, and the thesis in the senior year. Such practices became central to a belief that things had been done so differently, and so much against the mainstream, and often against imposing odds, that the group had generated a saga.

Social Base

The saga also becomes fixed in the minds of outside believers devoted to the organization, usually the alumni. The alumni are the best located to hold beliefs enduringly pure, since they can be as strongly identified with a special organizational history as the older faculty and administrators and yet do not have to face directly the new problems generated by a changing environment or students. Their thoughts can remain centered on the past, rooted in the days when, as students, they participated intimately in the unique ways and accomplishments of the campus.

Liberal alumni as those of Reed, Antioch, and Swarthmore here, seek to conserve what they believe to be a unique liberal institution and to protect it from the conservative forces of society that might change it—that is, to make it like other colleges. At Reed, for example, dropouts as well as graduates were struck by the intellectual excellence of their small college, convinced that college life there had been unlike college life anywhere else, and they were ready to conserve the practices that seemed to sustain that excellence. Here too, conserving acts can be seen for a time as contributing to an innovation, protecting the full working out of a distinctive effort.

Student Subculture

The student body is the third group of believers, not overwhelmingly important but still a necessary support for the saga. To become and remain a saga, a change must be supported by the student subculture over decades, and the ideology of the subculture must integrate with the central ideas of the believing administrators and faculty. When the students define themselves as personally responsible for upholding the image of the college, then a design or plan has become an organizational saga.

At Antioch, Reed, and Swarthmore, the student subcultures were powerful mechanisms for carrying a developing saga from one generation to another. Reed students, almost from the beginning and extending at least to the early 1960s, were great believers in the uniqueness of their college, constantly on the alert for any action that would alter it, ever fearful that administration or faculty might succumb to pressures that would make Reed just like other colleges. Students at Antioch and Swarthmore also offered unstinting support for the ideology of their institution. All three student bodies steadily and dependably transferred the ideology from one generation to another. Often socializing deeply, they helped produce the graduate who never quite rid himself of the wish to go back to the campus.

Imagery of Saga

Upheld by faculty, alumni, and students, expressed in teaching practices, the saga is even more widely expressed as a generalized tradition in statues and ceremonies, written histories and current catalogues, even in an "air about the place" felt by participants and some outsiders. The more unique the history and the more forceful the claim to a place in history, the more intensely cultivated the ways of sharing memory and symbolizing the institution. The saga is a strong self-fulfilling belief; working through institutional self-image and public image, it is indeed a switchman (Weber, 1946), helping to determine the tracks along which action is pushed by men's self-defined interests. The early belief of one stage brings about the actions that warrant a stronger version of the same belief in a later period. As the account develops, believers come to sense its many constituent symbols as inextricably bound together, and the part takes its meaning from the whole. For example, at Antioch a deep attachment developed in the 1930s and 1940s to Morgan's philosophy of the whole man and to its expression in a unique combination of work, study, community participation, and many practices thought to embody freedom and nonconformity. Some of the faculty of those years who remained in the 1940s and 1950s had many memories and impressions that seemed to form a symbolic whole: personnel counselors, folk dancing in Red Square, Morgan's towering physique, the battles of community government, the pacifism of the late 1930s, the frequent dash of students to offcampus jobs, the dedicated deans who personified central values. Public image also grew strong and sharp, directing liberals and radicals to the college and conservatives to other places. The symbolic expressions themselves were a strong perpetuating force.

Conclusion

An organizational saga is a powerful means of unity in the formal place. It makes links across internal divisions and organizational boundaries as internal and external groups share their common belief. With deep emotional commitment, believers define themselves by their organizational affiliation, and in their bond to other believers they share an intense sense of the unique. In an organization defined by a strong saga, there is a feeling that there is the small world of the lucky few and the large routine one of the rest of the world. Such an emotional bond turns the membership into a community, even a cult.

An organizational saga is thus a valuable resource, created over a number of years out of the social components of the formal enterprise. As participants become ideologues, their common definition becomes a foundation for trust and for extreme loyalty. Such bonds give the organization a competitive edge in recruiting and maintaining personnel and helps it to avoid the vicious circle in which some actual or anticipated erosion of organizational strength leads to the loss of some personnel, which leads to further decline and loss. Loyalty causes individuals to stay with a system, to save and improve it rather than to leave to serve their self-interest elsewhere (Hirschman, 1970). The genesis and persistence of loyalty is a key organizational and analytical problem. Enduring loyalty follows from a collective belief of participants that their organization is distinctive. Such a belief comes from a credible story of uncommon effort, achievement, and form.

Pride in the organized group and pride in one's identity as taken from the group are personal returns that are uncommon in modern social involvement. The development of sagas is one way in which men in organizations increase such returns, reducing their sense of isolation and increasing their personal pride and pleasure in organizational life. Studying the evocative narratives and devotional ties of formal systems leads to a better understanding of the fundamental capacities of organizations to enhance or diminish the lives of participants. The organization possessing a saga is a place in which participants for a time at least happily accept their bond.

Notes

1. Revised version of paper presented at the 65th Annual Meeting of the American Sociological Association, September, 1970, Washington, D.C. I wish to thank Wendell Bell, Maren L. Carden, Kai Erikson, and Stanley Udy for discussion and comment. Parts of an early draft of this paper have been used to connect organizational belief to problems of governance in colleges and universities (Clark, 1971).
2. For some discussion of the risks and tensions associated with organizational sagas, particularly that of success in one period leading to later rigidity and stagnation, see Clark (1970: 258–261). Hale (1970) gives an illuminating discussion of various effects of a persistent saga in a theological seminary.

References

Bendix, R., *Work and Authority in Industry*. New York: John Wiley, 1956.

Carden, M. L., *Oneida: Utopian Community to Modern Corporation*. Baltimore: The Johns Hopkins Press, 1969.

Clark, B. R., *Adult Education in Transition: A Study of Institutional Insecurity*. Berkeley: University of California Press, 1956.

_____. *The Open Door College. A Case Study*. New York: McGraw-Hill, 1960.

_____. *The Distinctive College: Antioch, Reed, and Swarthmore.* Chicago: Aldine, 1970.

_____. "Belief and loyalty in college organization," *Journal of Higher Education,* 1971, XLII, 6: 499–515.

Gross, B. M., *The Managing of Organizations.* (2 vols.) New York: Free Press, 1964.

Hale, J. R. *The Making and Testing of an Organizational Saga: A Case-Study of the Lutheran Theological Seminary at Gettysburg, Pennsylvania, with Special Reference to the Problem of Merger, 1959–1960.* Unpublished Ed.D. dissertation, Columbia University, 1970.

Hirschman, A. O., *Exit, Voice, and Loyalty.* Cambridge, Mass.: Harvard University Press, 1970.

Lindblom, C. E. "The science of 'muddling through.'" *Public Administration Review,* 1959, 19:79–88.

Litterer, J. A. *The Analysis of Organizations.* New York: John Wiley, 1965.

March, J. G. (ed.), *Handbook of Organizations:* Chicago: Rand McNally, 1965.

Perrow, C. *Organizational Analysis.* Belmont, California: Wadsworth, 1970.

Price, J. L. *Organizational Effectiveness: An Inventory of Propositions.* Homewood, Illinois: Richard D. Irwin, 1968.

Selznick, P. *TVA and the Grass Roots.* Berkeley: University of California Press, 1949.

_____. *Leadership in Administration.* New York: Harper & Row, 1957.

Swarthmore College Faculty. *An Adventure in Education: Swarthmore College Under Frank Aydelotte.* New York: Macmillan, 1941.

Thompson, J. D. *Organizations in Action.* New York: McGraw-Hill, 1967.

Weber, M. *From Max Weber: Essays in Sociology.* Translated and edited by H. H. Gerth and C. Wright Mills. New York: Oxford, 1946.

Whyte, W. F. *Human Relations in the Restaurant Industry.* New York: McGraw-Hill, 1948.

Burton R. Clark is a professor of sociology at Yale University.

The Effect of Institutional Culture on Change Strategies in Higher Education
Universal Principles or Culturally Responsive Concepts?

ADRIANNA KEZAR AND PETER D. ECKEL

The array of challenges that higher education faces today is virtually unparalleled when compared to any other point in U.S. history. The litany of changes is familiar to those in the field of higher education: financial pressure, growth in technology, changing faculty roles, public scrutiny, changing demographics, competing values, and the rapid rate of change in the world both within and beyond our national borders. The changes many institutions face have accelerated beyond tinkering; more campuses each year attempt to create comprehensive (or transformational) change. Yet, change strategies have not been exceedingly helpful in their capacity to guide institutions, and we know even less about how to facilitate major, institutionwide change.

The current change literature in higher education provides mostly generalized strategies about what is effective: a willing president or strong leadership, a collaborative process, or providing rewards (Roberts, Wergin, & Adam, 1993). This broad writing may mask information helpful to advance institutional change on a specific campus. "Achieving buy-in" or "communicating effectively" can seem very empty to institutional leaders and higher education scholars. Can this strategy be used at every institution and in the same way? The assumptions behind this approach are that each strategy is enacted similarly on each campus and that nuance and context do not much matter. Broad change strategies are presented as uniform, universal, and applicable.

As an alternative, some scholars of organizations suggest that meaningful insight to understand the change process comes from context-based (micro-level) data (Bergquist, 1992). Context-based data help the change agent to understand why and under what circumstances strategies work at a particular institution at a particular time. The difficulty of working at the micro-level is becoming too specific and idiosyncratic to be of much help to others. As Hearn noted, the first and fundamental proposition we can stress about change is so simple as to seem banal or deflating, "it depends" (Hearn, 1996). Idiosyncratic observations are often of little use to practitioners. The challenge is to chart a middle ground and identify findings informative at a level that can be used to guide change processes. This task is challenging, because markers that one might use to determine the level of detail or the appropriate level of abstraction are not readily apparent.

One solution to charting meaningful middle ground is through a cultural perspective. Organizational research in the 1980s illustrated the impact of culture on many aspects of organizational life (Peterson & Spencer, 1991). Yet, there have been few empirical studies examining how institutional culture affects change processes and strategies. The assumption from the organizational literature is that culture will be related to the change process; specifically, change processes can be thwarted by violating cultural norms or enhanced by culturally sensitive strategies (Bergquist, 1992). This study attempts to fill the gap in the literature, moving beyond generalized principles of change, by adopting a two-tiered cultural framework to examine the effect of institutional culture on change strategies across six institutions. The two research questions addressed are: (1) is the institutional culture related to the change process, and how is it related? and (2) are change processes thwarted by violating cultural norms or enhanced by culturally sensitive strategies? The two theories adopted for exploring the relationship of culture and change are Bergquist's (1992) four academic cultures and Tierney's (1991) individual institutional culture framework. The dual level of analysis offers a multiple-lens perspective that is better suited to understand complex organizational phenomena (Birnbaum, 1988; Bolman & Deal, 1991).

Analyses of the six institutions (three are presented as detailed case examples) engaged in change processes over a four-year period through case study methodology (interviews, document analysis, and observation) are presented, examining five core change strategies: senior administrative support, collaborative leadership, robust design (vision), staff development, and visible actions. In addition to demonstrating a relationship between institutional culture and change, the results support several assumptions from cultural theory, including the significance of culturally appropriate strategies, the importance of examining multiple layers of culture (enterprise, institutional, group), and the possibility of predicting which strategies will be more important. This study challenges conventional notions about change processes; namely, that one can follow a general principle or approach and not be aware of how distinct organizational cultures impact the process. Its findings suggest the need for practitioners to become cultural outsiders in order to observe their institutional patterns. The Bergquist and Tierney cultural frameworks provide initial templates for this analysis.

Understanding Organizational Culture and Change: A Review

Six main categories of change theories[1] exist throughout a multidisciplinary literature, including biological, teleological, political, life cycle, social cognition, and cultural. (For detailed descriptions of these various models please see: Burns, 1996; Collins, 1998; Levy & Murray, 1986; Morgan, 1986; Sporn, 1999; Van de Ven & Poole, 1995). Biological (unplanned change) and teleological models (planned change) have received the most attention in higher education and have the longest histories; most recently biological models were used in a major study by Sporn (1999) and teleological models in a study by Eckel, Hill, and Green (1998). Biological and teleological models tend to produce the generalized change strategies noted in the introduction as problematic (Burns, 1996; Collins, 1998). Political models also have a long history but have been critiqued for their inability to provide solutions for organizational participants in facilitating or reacting to the change process (Burns, 1996; Collins, 1998; Van de Ven & Poole, 1995). Researchers have recently touted cultural and social cognitive theories for their sophistication in illustrating complexity in showing the ambiguity, context based nature, and human aspects of the change process (Collins, 1998). This study attempted to examine the promise of cultural theories to understand change within the higher education context, because they are mostly unexplored, yet show great potential. The researchers also assumed that comprehensive change, the type focused on in this study, might best be examined through a framework in which values and beliefs are a focus because major alterations to an organization usually impact underlying belief systems (Schein, 1985).

This next section provides the context for the study by briefly reviewing the evolution of cultural approaches to studying organizations and the implications of the culture literature for this study. Next, a review of the extant literature on institutional culture and change in higher education is presented. Lastly, the theoretical frameworks guiding this study of culture (Tierney and Bergquist) and change (Lindquist) are reviewed.

Organizational Culture

In the 1980s, organizational researchers across various disciplines began examining the role of culture within organizational life (Morgan, 1986; Schein, 1985; Smirich & Calas, 1982) and then connected it to effectiveness (Tichy, 1983) and central processes (i.e., leadership, governance) of the organization (Schein, 1985). Culture shifted from being used as a descriptive device to becoming linked with improvement and success. Higher education followed that pattern. Early research used culture to illustrate that campuses had unique cultures from other types of institutions, describing the myths and rituals of colleges, and student and faculty subcultures (see Clark 1970; Lunsford, 1963; Riesman, Gusfield, & Gamson, 1970). Several later studies on higher education linked institutional culture with organizational success (Chaffee & Tierney, 1988; Peterson, Cameron, Jones, Mets, & Ettington, 1986). Further studies demonstrated the way that different cultures shaped various institutional functions including governance (Chaffee & Tierney, 1988), leadership (Birnbaum, 1988), and planning (Hearn, Clugston, & Heydinger, 1993; Leslie & Fretwell, 1996).

Two links between culture and change have been made in the higher education literature. The first set of literature suggests that institutions need to have a "culture" that encourages change (Curry, 1992). The goal of this body of research is to determine the aspects of culture or type of culture that need to be fostered to promote institutional change (Schein, 1985). The second set of ideas suggests that culture or key institutional elements that shape culture, i.e., vision or mission, are modified as a result of the change process (Chaffee & Tierney, 1988; Eckel, Hill, & Green, 1998; Guskin, 1996). In other words, the outcome of change is a modified culture (Schein, 1985). The research presented here pursues a third path, investigating the ways in which culture shapes an institution's change processes or strategies. It is the modifying element rather than the subject of the modification.

Conceptual Frameworks for Studying the Effect of Culture on Change Strategies

Within this study, we define culture as "the deeply embedded patterns of organizational behavior and the shared values, assumptions, beliefs, or ideologies that members have about their organization or its work" (Peterson & Spencer, 1991, p. 142). Culture provides meaning and context for a specific set of people (Bergquist, 1992; Schein, 1985). Other scholars suggest nuances to this broad definition. For example, some view it as a variable (such as corporate culture), while others see it as a fundamental metaphor for a specific type of organization (see Morgan, 1986). Some researchers conceptualize culture as strong and congruent, or weak and incongruent (see Tierney, 1988); others merely note that cultures vary, without assigning a value to different cultures (see Bergquist, 1992; Martin, 1992). With these nuances in mind, culture is conceptualized within this study as a fundamental metaphor, emerging as a composite of many different levels—the enterprise, the institution, the subgroup (faculty, administrators), and the individual levels (Martin, 1992). The researchers assumed that cultures differ and that they are not necessarily negative or positive; nor are multiple cultures or fragmented cultures necessarily to be avoided.

This study adopts two conceptual frameworks of culture: (1) Bergquist's institutional archetypes of culture and (2) Tierney's unique institutional culture. First, the inquiry builds on Bergquist's (1992) work on institutional culture. Bergquist focuses on archetypes by which numerous institutions might be categorized and described.[2] He hypothesized (yet never empirically tested) that different change strategies would be needed and appropriate within the four different academic culture archetypes that reflect any higher education institution—collegial culture, managerial culture, developmental culture, and negotiating culture.[3] The *collegial culture* arises primarily from the disciplines of the faculty. It values scholarly engagement, shared governance and decision making, and rationality, whereas the *managerial culture* focuses on the goals and purposes of the institution and values efficiency, effective supervisory skills, and fiscal responsibility. This contrasts with the *developmental culture*, which is based on the personal and professional growth of all members of the collegiate environment. Lastly, the *negotiating culture* values the establishment of equitable and egalitarian policies and procedures, valuing confrontation, interest groups, mediation, and power. Bergquist illustrated how the managerial culture, for example, might hinder an institution's ability to change structures, whereas a collegial culture was better equipped to modify institutional structures because there was greater trust.

Although Bergquist's framework provides one lens for examining the effect of institutional culture on change strategies, these institutional cultural archetypes can mask many of the complexities of individual institutional cultures. This study adopts a second conceptual framework to explore the ways in which culture affects change processes within unique institutions. The Tierney framework includes the following six categories: environment, mission, socialization, information, strategy, and leadership. Analysis consists of examining each category in depth, asking such questions as, how is the mission defined and articulated? Is it used as a basis for decisions? What constitutes information and who has it? Or how are decisions arrived at and who makes them? This approach assumes that the values, beliefs, and assumptions of an institution are reflected in its processes and artifacts. By examining the key elements suggested by Tierney (1991), the researcher develops a clearer picture of the institutional culture.

When using both frameworks together, they provide a more powerful lens than when using only one in helping to interpret and understand culture. The archetypes provide a ready framework for institutions unfamiliar with cultural analysis; the framework establishes patterns for them to identify. The Tierney lens provides a sophisticated tool for understanding the complexities of unique institutions. Although Tierney's framework is an important framework, it may be more difficult for practitioners to use readily. Thus, both frameworks were used in this study; the dual level of analysis offers a multiple-lens perspective better suited to understand complex organizational phenomena (Birnbaum, 1988; Bolman & Deal, 1991).

Framework for Studying Change

The change under investigation in this study is comprehensive change; it is defined as change that is pervasive, affecting numerous offices and units across the institution; deep, touching upon values, beliefs and structures, is intentional, and occurs over time (Eckel et al., 1998). To study the effect of culture on the change process, it is important to focus on a type of institutional change that was neither isolated in a particular unit nor affected only the surface of the institution. Lindquist's (1978) work on change, one of the most comprehensive sets of change strategies found in the higher education literature, was used as a change strategy framework for the study. Bergquist also used Lindquist's framework in his speculation of the impact of culture on change. The applicability of Lindquist's approach was recently tested on a broader set of institutions undertaking change (he only examined liberal arts institutions), and the following core change strategies emerged (Kezar & Eckel, in press):

1. *Senior administrative support*, refers to individuals in positional leadership providing support in terms of value statements, resources, or new administrative structures.

2. *Collaborative leadership*, defined as a process where the positional and nonpositional individuals throughout the campus are involved in the change initiative from conception to implementation.

3. *Robust design*, a more complex and less well known term than vision; it is adopted from the work of Eccles and Nohria (1992). Leaders develop a "desirable" and flexible picture of the future that is clear and understandable and includes set goals and objectives related to the implementation of that picture. The picture of the future and the means to get there are flexible and do not foreclose possible opportunities.

4. *Staff development*, a set of programmatic efforts to offer opportunities for individuals to learn certain skills or knowledge related to issues associated with the change effort.

5. *Visible actions*, refers to advances in the change process that are noticeable. Activities must be visible and promoted so that individuals can see that the change is still important and is continuing. This is an important strategy for building momentum within the institution.

These five core strategies contain sets of substrategies; for example senior administrative support is related to incentives, change in governance structures, and providing support structures. Because it is not the intent of this article to investigate the specific strategies for change, please see Kezar and Eckel (in press) for a detailed discussion of the core strategies and substrategies. These strategies are identified here to provide a framework through which the investigation of culture and its relationship to the strategies for change can proceed.

In summary, the following diagram illustrates the relationships among the various concepts reviewed and used to frame the study:

Bergquist's cultural + archetypes	Tierney's individual → institutional culture	Change strategies
Collegial culture	Environment	Senior administrative support
Managerial culture	Mission	Collaborative leadership
Developmental culture	Socialization	Robust design
Negotiating culture	Information	Staff development
	Strategy	Visible actions
	Leadership	

Each institution in the study will be examined using the four elements of Bergquist's cultural archetype in addition to Tierney's six characteristics that define unique individual institutional culture. These two cultural frameworks will then be explored in relation to the way the change process occurred at all six institutions along the five core strategies.

Research Design and Methodology

Case Selection Criteria

This study is based on six institutions participating in the ACE Project on Leadership and Institutional Transformation; the project included 23 institutions. The project focused on understanding the process of institutional transformation. A subset of six institutions was identified through purposeful sampling utilizing four criteria: (1) they made the most progress on their identified change agendas; (2) they had the capacity and willingness to collect detailed data on change strategies and institutional culture; (3) they represented different institutional types; and (4) they had similar change initiatives. The six institutions in the study included one research university, three doctoral-granting universities, a liberal arts college, and a community college. Because institutional type has been related to Bergquist's cultural archetypes (Bergquist, 1992; Birnbaum, 1988), various institutional types were purposefully examined. As noted previously, all of the institutions were engaged in intentional comprehensive change. But to ensure additional consistency across cases, institutions were selected that had similar change initiatives; i.e., they were all working to transform teaching and learning. Thus, differences in strategies would be associated with cultural differences, rather than related to diffuse change agendas.

Data Collection and Analysis

In order to examine the effect of organizational culture on change and to move beyond the broad generalizations in the literature, an ethnographic approach was adopted. The project was a five-and-a-half year initiative on institutional transformation; the reported data were collected in years one through four. Participant-observers from each institution provided data on a semesterly basis in response to open-ended questionnaires and at biannual project meetings. Outside researchers visited each campus twice a year for the first three years and once during the fourth year. Researchers additionally collected and analyzed internal institutional documents.

Data analysis was conducted through three different approaches. First, theme analysis of the change strategies was conducted, using Lindquist's framework, examining ways each strategy was enacted on that campus. Categorical analysis was used to search for micro and macro themes (Miles & Huberman, 1994). Second, researchers developed institutional culture profiles of all six institutions based on the Bergquist and Tierney frameworks for examining institutional culture.[4] This analysis resulted in the example profiles provided in the results section. Third, Bergquist's and Tierney's frameworks were applied to the data to identify whether institutional culture patterns could be identified in the change strategies. Variations from the cultural lens were also noted. Emergent themes were identified and negotiated between the two reviewers. After the analysis was completed, the profiles of institutional culture, change strategies, and the relationship between the two conditions were sent to the site visit researchers (other than the lead researchers) to confirm interpretations of institutional culture and to have outsiders check the themes that emerged.

Due to space constraints, profiles of three sample institutions are presented to illustrate the relationship of institutional culture and change strategies common to all six institutions. These three were selected because they represent three different types of institutions (a research university, a doctoral university, and a community college), they illustrate three different Bergquist cultural archetypes (developmental, managerial, and collegial), and they had the most and the richest data to best capture their culture and change strategies.

Limitations

First, because institutions self-selected to be part of the project from which this subsample was taken, they may not represent the range of institutions undergoing comprehensive change. Second, although we attempted to identify institutions with similar change initiatives, there were small variations in their agendas. Finding institutions engaging in identical change efforts is almost impossible. Third, since much of the data are self-reported they may be biased to reflect success.

Results

This section is organized as follows: (1) descriptions of the three highlighted institutions, introducing the institutions, their change initiatives, and their cultures; and (2) presentations of the way the cultures have a bearing on institutional change strategies. Because the intent of this study is to understand the effect of culture on specific change strategies, the results are organized by each of the five core change strategies. Space limitations prevent a detailed description of the institutions and all the ways that institutional culture manifests itself across all five core change strategies. It is hoped that the summary tables and results section provide some of the key data to make these institutions real for the reader. Each of the five tables focuses on one change strategy, describing the way the strategy emerged at all three institutions. The notation "B" or "T" next to each theme reflects the way it related to the Bergquist or Tierney frameworks.

Institutional Profiles

Informal Trusting University (ITU) is a public doctoral university located in a small Midwestern town. It enrolls approximately 18,000 students, of whom over half are women. Close to 90% of its students come from within its state, and 1% are international; approximately 40% live on campus. The university has seven academic colleges and a graduate school with over 870 full-time faculty. Included among the colleges are architecture, business, fine arts, communications, and applied sciences and technology. Its 100-year history is that of a teacher's college developing into a doctoral university. It is endeavoring to integrate technology into the core of the teaching and learning process. This initiative had the ambitious goal of having the entire faculty involved in rethinking their courses and curricula around infusing technology to enrich the undergraduate student experience.

At ITU, both the organizational culture and change strategies used reflect the developmental culture in Bergquist's typology. The mission and faculty socialization strongly supported the importance of learning; at one time the institution defined itself as a "premier teaching university." Bergquist noted that many developmental cultures tend to have a strong focus on teaching. The leadership process on developmental campuses tends to be facilitative and strongly collaborative, as was the case at ITU. Developmental campuses like ITU also tend to share information widely, because it is critical to growth.

From a Tierney perspective, ITU's institutional culture is best characterized by the terms informal and trusting. Although a sense of trust is likely to develop within the developmental culture, it is stronger than described in Bergquist's framework. Trust at ITU appears to result from the long and stable leadership created by having the same president and provost for over 15 years, the large number of long-term dedicated employees (over 60% have only worked under the current president and provost), and the strong connection between the campus and its community. The institution also is run exceedingly informally. For example, the institution does not have a strategic planning process, and institutional direction is set informally and communicated through a series of conversations between the president, the provost, and various key stakeholders. ITU's policies and practices were developed locally in departments and colleges, were modified frequently, and lacked uniformity. Although some campus decision-making structures are in place, such as a faculty senate, there appears to be little reliance on them as the primary decision-making venues. Much of the business of the campus happens around a lunch table, in the hallways, or through various different meetings. People who work at ITU are likely to know each other well, for many interact both within the workplace and outside of it in the local community.

Responsible and Self-Reflective Community College (RSCC) is a multi-campus community college of approximately 54,000 students, located outside a major Southern metropolitan area. It serves two of the fastest growing counties in the state. Founded in the late 1960s, close to 70% of RSCC students enroll in credit courses, and over 60% of its students are enrolled in at least one developmental course. The average age of its credit students is 25. The college ranks fourth in the nation in the number of A.A. and A.S. degrees it awards. It has 326 full-time faculty and approximately 1,100 part-time instructors. Last year, it generated over $8 million in federal and state grants. It is attempting to shift from a teaching- or faculty-centered institution to a more learning-centered one, a process that the institution views as a major transformation in the ways it conducts its business. If successful, institutional leaders note that the structures, processes, pedagogies, and beliefs will change dramatically.

The culture at RSCC is best classified as managerial, using Bergquist's framework. It is characterized by strong senior administrative directive, driven by goals, plans, and assessment, is cognizant of outside forces pressing the institution, strives to meet customer needs, and frequently experiences clashes in values between faculty and administrators.

However, there are many ways that this campus is different from the managerial archetype. RSCC has a strong commitment to student learning, which pervades this large and complex four-campus college, and we therefore label it "responsible." RSCC's responsible culture is not simply driven by managerial accountability, but a deeply human desire to help. RSCC also is strongly introspective. Central administrators force introspection by the types of questions they ask faculty and the heads of the four campuses. Faculty and administrators also spend significant time discussing "the way we do things around here" and how to improve those practices. Institutional leaders note that the environment is changing and seek to effect change on campus that will align it with these external shifts. Information and data are collected not only to assess college goals, but also to understand institutional identity. There was a strong desire across the campus to understand RSCC students and their needs and, additionally, to understand who RSCC is and how it works. Staff development through workshops such as managing personal transformations (based on personal introspection) provide additional self-reflective mechanisms.

Autonomous Insecure University (AIU) is a private research university, located in a major urban area on the Eastern seaboard. It has seven academic colleges, including a law school, and a school for continuing education. It has approximately 13,000 undergraduate and 6,000 graduate students, and close to 750 full-time faculty. Close to 85% of new students live on campus, and 55% come from out of state. Its expected tuition and fees for new students is approximately $20,000. It is attempting to re-craft its general education program. Its agenda for change will lead to a profound shift in the campus' thinking about the purposes and structures of general education and in the strategies to actualize the new general education objectives, disseminating to all faculty responsibility for the goals of general education.

AIU manifests Bergquist's collegial culture. Colleges and schools are highly independent; the institution is focused on research and the disciplines. One of AIU's main goals is striving to move up in the traditional academic rankings. Academic affairs issues and priorities dominate governance, and decision making occurs at the department and school levels.

Through the Tierney lens, the autonomous nature of AIU far exceeds that described within the collegial archetype. The change initiative itself—to reexamine the general education curriculum, its structure and its purposes, as well as its modes of delivery—results from a history of high fragmentation across the extremely autonomous schools and colleges and a poor accreditation review. The institution is private, which may contribute to the high level of autonomy, as it is neither part of a system nor dependent on state funds, but is responsible for its own resources in a continually shrinking fiscal environment. Central administrators, in the past, have had a high turnover rate, leaving colleges and schools responsible for their own continuity of purposes and for providing their own direction. Many people in the highly academic city where it is located view it as a low-status institution. New faculty are quickly socialized to learn that they work at a less prestigious institution. AIU has recently gone through a downturn in enrollment, creating significant financial distress at the university, which included laying off academic staff. Its insecurity was additionally reinforced and heightened by the poor accreditation review.

Change Strategies

Having briefly described the cultures of the three institutions through both the Bergquist and Tierney frameworks, the following discussion is framed around the five core change strategies. The intent of this organization is to present examples that highlight the different ways each distinct culture appears to shape the application of each change strategy.

Senior administrative support. Senior administrative support concerns itself with the way senior administrators can facilitate change through resources, structures, and so on. This strategy varied across the three campuses discussed here. A summary of the variations in senior administrative support across the three institutions is found in Table 1.

At ITU senior administrative support appeared in the background of the change efforts and consisted primarily of providing needed resources and facilities regarding technology. Senior administrators also continually reminded the campus of the importance of technology and computer competency, but they were laissez faire in the direction of the initiatives. At managerial oriented RSCC, the senior administration provided very visible project leadership: developing the plan and a conceptual model to drive campus transformation, coordinating the leadership team, facilitating and coordinating communication among the four campuses, and securing external resources and reallocating internal ones. RSCC also created a new position, vice president for transformation, to help facilitate the campus' efforts. At collegial AIU, the provost and his administrative staff designed the overall process and oversaw it from a distance but moved much of the key decision making to the faculty of each college. Senior administrative support took the role of launching the efforts and then providing resources and creating accountability mechanisms. They were fairly absent from shaping decisions directly and worked intentionally to stay out of the way. All decisions were pushed down to the college.

Although Bergquist's archetypes were partially helpful in explaining the way senior administrative support emerged, the Tierney individual-level cultural analysis, provided additional insight. ITU differed from the developmental culture in the way senior administrative support emerged; for example, no governance structures were altered or support mechanisms established. Within the developmental culture Bergquist predicted that leaders would establish many support mechanisms to facilitate change; governance structures were typically altered to assure inclusiveness and formal communication vehicles were typically established. Yet, within this informal environment, people, not processes or structures were the core support. Furthermore, the informal communication around lunch tables and in hallways with senior leaders was the ideal process rather than the more deliberate communication mechanisms established within typical developmental cultures. The insecure culture of AIU seemed linked to the reliance on incentives as a major strategy for change. It appeared that incentives became the primary way that senior administrators could develop a sense of efficacy among insecure faculty. Thus, the unique culture of AIU seemed to alter the central processes needed for change from those offered in Lindquist's framework. Incentives became more important than senior administrative support, which was the general pattern on other campuses. Table 1 presents the different manifestations of senior administrative support.

Collaborative leadership. Lindquist's change framework suggests that leadership at the top alone is insufficient and that change requires collaborative leadership from throughout the institution, particularly from the faculty. Collaborative leadership was a natural element of the developmental culture of ITU, where decisions and much of the action was pushed out to individual academics and departments. Mechanisms for collaborative leadership were already established through informal information networks and cross-departmental groups that met on a regular basis to discuss improvements. Developing people's leadership capacities and tapping their creativity had been a long-term philosophy for the current administration.

This manifestation was quite a contrast from RSCC, where the managerial culture had not historically created mechanisms for collaborative leadership. Cross-campus input was foreign to RSCC, thus several different committees were established by central administrators to tap leadership across the college. One of the first big steps in sharing leadership was to help people understand that they could now shape institutional direction and that their leadership was welcome. To promote shared leadership, twelve collegewide forums and campus structured dialogues were held in order to capture the good ideas from the faculty and staff. To demonstrate their willingness to share leadership, central administrators started writing "draft" on all documents and encouraged written and electronic comments throughout the change process.

AIU reflected the collegial culture in its approach to collaborative leadership by tapping its decentralized bureaucracy. Deans and chairs were expected to take leadership within their various units. The senior administrators delegated leadership to them and encouraged them to get faculty involvement and ownership in key unit decisions. Many key decisions and valuable solutions to institutional problems were made in cross-functional task forces that brought together faculty and staff from different units. AIU also learned that the term "draft" needed to be placed on documents until there was official approval from each college. On a few occasions a document was sent out without one or two schools' official approval, which led to great disruption.

TABLE 1

Senior Administrative Support Strategies by Institution

Informal, Trusting University (Developmental)	Responsive, Self-Reflective Community College (Managerial)	Autonomous, Insecure University (Collegial)
Provide resources[B]	Formal communication[B]	Top-down plan, turned over to units[B]
In the background[B]	Sr. admin. actively involved and center of communication[B]	College-level focus[B]
Provide opportunities and support[B]	Securing funding[B]	Respected faculty promoted to VP to oversee related change area[B]
Informal communication[T]	Coordinate leadership team[B]	Develop mechanisms to work with colleges[B]
Few changes to governance or structures[T]	Developed new structures to facilitate communication and decision making[B]	College-level incentives as key support[B]
Facilitate indirectly[T]	VP for Transformation hired from outside[B]	Saw outside influences as interference, not help[B]
External forces encourage and coalesce community[T]	Provide incentives through central structure[B]	Outside influence important to facilitate change[T]
Remind campus of importance[T]	Frame external forces to motivate (threat)[B]	Colleges involved in grant-writing process, money as central[T]
	Develop conceptual framework[T]	Few changes to governance or structures[T]
		Cross-functional teams[T]
		Public deadlines and discussions[T]

Note: [B]refers to Bergquist Framework; [T]refers to Tierney Framework

Examining these institutions through the lens of their individual cultures, collaborative leadership was enacted in distinctive ways. The trusting and informal environment of ITU shaped involvement; campus leaders did not need to invite participation or develop channels for communication, and there was no need to work through troubled relations on campus. Within most managerial cultures, the level of participation that RSCC obtained at their dialogues, forums, and voluntary action teams would be unheard of. The reason so many people attended the meetings was their commitment to students. This sense of responsibility made them attend meetings where they were not sure if they would be heard, events that might simply be a waste of time. Also, RSCC's focus on self-reflection seemed to make communication a core strategy; the forums and dialogues took on a distinctive form with people expressing feelings, beliefs, and interpretations. Collaboration on this campus meant people needed to understand each other and themselves. Another helpful insight through the Tierney framework is the way in which AIU's autonomous culture related to collaborative leadership. Few institutions would "truly" delegate responsibility solely to the colleges and schools for the change initiative. But, at AIU, this was the only way to successfully achieve faculty ownership and participation. Many other initiatives had failed because they had not been attuned to this aspect of the culture on AIU's campus. Several faculty noted that this respect for the nature of collaborative leadership is what made this particular initiative succeed.

Robust design. This concept is an extension of Lindquist's ideas modified with the work of Eccles and Nohria (1992). It suggests that a flexible vision is needed, one that does not foreclose future opportunities. ITU, with its developmental culture, epitomizes the flexibility inherent in the concept of robust design. Institutional leaders had no overall grand scheme for change; instead they established

TABLE 2

Collaborative Leadership Strategies by Institution

Informal, Trusting University (Developmental)	Responsive, Self-Reflective Community College (Managerial)	Autonomous, Insecure University (Collegial)
Individual initiative, no central initiation[B]	Collaboration foreign to the campus; needed outreach and invited participation[B]	Faculty ownership of initiative key to success[B]
Individual unit-level invitation[B]	Cross-site planning team representing all groups[B]	Campuswide committee to gain involvement across campus[B]
Part of the long-time philosophy[B]	Invited to comment on notes; action teams asked for volunteers[B]	Formal newsletter; Faculty Center for communication[B]
Trust; positive working relations[B]	Realized importance of communication—12 structured dialogues[B]	Draft until colleges were able to provide feedback[B]
No formal structure[T]	"Draft" on everything sent out from central source[B]	Forum to discuss relationships among different colleges—historically tension between some disciplines[B]
All individuals realize process involved authentic opportunity for communication[T]	Forums to discuss relationships between groups[B]	Cross-unit interest groups to assure all of faculty voice included; older students involved as well[T]
Decentralized efforts[T]	Had to provide stipends to get participation[B]	Delegation of all key decisions[T]
No new collaborative mechanisms[T]	Consensus of collegewide vision based on responsibility to student[T]	Used fear of being behind competition as motivator for involvement[T]
Loose cross-unit teams[T]	Public reflection of college purposes[T]	
	Comprehensive leadership development program for self-reflection[T]	

Note: [B]refers to Bergquist Framework; [T]refers to Tierney Framework

a process that launched a series of uncoordinated, yet broadly linked change efforts. Decisions and ideas emerged at the local, departmental level, often informally. The few planning documents evolved at the local level (within programs and departments) were for local use. The vision and "real" plan for the future regarding technology and the educational experience was in each individual's head or within the strategy of each department. Even new promotion and tenure criteria that reflected the institution's technology goals were left to the design of each unit to best fit their specific intellectual contexts.

The managerial culture of RSCC, which gravitated toward having a mandated vision and clear plan, at first had difficulty in creating a strategy characterized by robust design. After a slow start, the change leaders developed mechanisms by which they could be more flexible and yet stay visionary. The message behind labeling every document with the word "draft" was an artifact of a new flexible mindset. The leadership team also incorporated the comments and feedback from the various campus dialogues and feedback sessions in ways that continued to leave future options open. Outside pressures, in particular concerning performance indicators, also helped to promote the change design.

AIU's collegial culture was evident in its strategies to create robust design. Members of the campus immediately rejected the initial plan developed by the president as too restrictive and unwarranted. The responsibility for designing and implementing the change then shifted to the college/school level. The design was created to allow for flexibility at the departmental level. For example, the central administrators created a master document tracking aspects of the plan that had been delegated to the colleges and departments, yet central administrators allowed each unit to create the specifics to meet institutional goals. Careful communication, always in writing, existed between the various levels of the organization related to the design of the change process. Central administrators also moderated the pace of change based on faculty feedback about the implementa-

TABLE 3

Robust Design Strategies by Institution

Informal, Trusting University (Developmental)	Responsive, Self-Reflective Community College (Managerial)	Autonomous, Insecure University (Collegial)
Local planning; they know best[B]	Centralized communication, design at administrative level[B]	Goals and implementation plan designed at local level[B]
Accountability was connected to ideal of being a better teacher[B]	Setting expectations for accountability and gather baseline data and asses core processes over time[B]	Strong planning documents top-down design of project created tension[B]
Long-term orientation: visionary, future perspective part of leadership culture[B]	Long-term orientation: Data-driven planning[B]	Accreditation team provides support for initiative[B]
Celebrated accomplishments[B]	Outside perspective: Performance indicators in state heavily influenced planning[B]	Used externally generated legitimacy[B]
Informal communication facilitates momentum[T]	Reports written up and shared; esp. meeting-targeted goals[T]	Highly coordinated, intentional, structured communication[T]
Few planning documents[T]	Establishing plan by describing other campuses with similar plans[T]	Master document[T]
Uncoordinated, but loosely linked strategies[T]	Type of data collection, organizational index[T]	Tapped campus insecurity for action[T]
Outside perspective did not play a role[T]		Moderated pace of change through setting range of goals and obtaining feedback from faculty to change rate[T]
Did not put change in larger context[T]		Publicity of high achieving faculty[T]
		Putting change in broader context; trends among peer institutions[T]

Note: [B]refers to Bergquist Framework; [T]refers to Tierney Framework

tion scheduling. Finally, because faculty did not want to have responsibility to be accountable for each other, also a familiar aspect of the collegial culture, they gravitated toward an outside, legitimate source, an accreditation team.

The archetypes were not a powerful enough explanatory lens to understand some of the unique ways that the robust design efforts were shaped on these campuses. For example, RSCC attempted to develop a robust design through a whole series of data collection efforts. Data collection seemed to be such a strong element of robust design because it reflected the campuses' drive to be responsible and to become more self-aware. Some of the types of data collection mechanisms are extremely self-analytic, including an organizational character index and a collective vision index. These different assessments focused on learning about the nature of the organization and working to develop a more functional culture and vision, if needed. Data collection that focused on students was also seen as important to better respond to their needs and to improve the learning environment. On most campuses with a developmental culture similar to ITU, a detailed and clear robust plan would be critical for moving forward with change. Yet, within ITU's family-type environment, it appears that there was little need for this type of documentation, which was unique to their distinctive culture. At AIU, the central administration built the plan around areas of insecurity and used faculty and staff insecurity as a lever to coalesce the campus around the robust design. They also used outreach to help gain momentum for the plan; for example, externally publicizing faculty's new ideas about general education. In the past, designs for change were thwarted at AIU; leaders knew it would be difficult to coalesce people without some strategy or crisis. Building on faculty insecurity was identified after months of searching for a motivational technique that would reach faculty, in particular. No generalized cultural archetypes would have been helpful in discovering these nuanced aspects of developing a robust design.

Visible actions. People need to see that their hard work is leading toward progress, thus visible actions are an important change process strategy. Table 4 reflects the following discussion. There were very distinct ways in which the three institutions used visible actions to facilitate change. The developmental culture at ITU, heavily tied to the growth of people on campus, appeared to necessitate a change in the people and their attitudes as a means to maintain momentum. This was achieved through the award of developmental grants for staff development and through a change in hiring policies aimed at bringing in new faculty. At managerial RSCC, goals needed to be met to maintain the momentum for change. A short-term action team was established and initially documented a 20% increase in graduation rates. This strategy created a surge of energy, bringing many holdouts to the change initiative. The collegial culture at AIU focused on resources as a motivation. The acquisition of several grants provided the needed incentive to build the change initiative. Although each institution obtained grants for their initiatives, they seemed to be valued most at AIU. Allocating grant money to faculty within departments at AIU developed a sense of ownership and enthusiasm.

Two examples will help illustrate the ways that their unique cultures emerge within the visible-action-taking strategy. The informal culture at ITU appeared to result in numerous activities throughout the campus, falling under visible actions. This differed from most developmental campuses, where centralized staff development was the core feature. Activities ranged from a faculty group that wrote one of the guiding documents that created a new language on campus to centrally administered developmental grants to a regular newspaper column that described efforts to incorporate technology into classrooms. All these efforts helped to build momentum throughout this informal environment. However, at AIU, bringing in outside money seemed to provide the incentive that made the campus feel that they were becoming more prestigious, and therefore successful, in their change process. The insecure culture at this campus seemed to link outside recognition through money as a validation of its robust design and change initiative. Although the collegial culture would have predicted that money would be important to taking action, the consuming nature of this strategy would not have been predicted or understood purely through the cultural archetypes.

Staff development. Staff development, a set of programmatic efforts to build new capacities within faculty and staff, was extremely important to the change processes at all three institutions. Yet, it was enacted in very different ways, based on the culture of the institution. ITU utilized a local departmental model for technology staff development. Leaders within different schools or colleges led the efforts to develop the needed support for their colleagues. The training programs were focused on the individual and their needs. At RSCC, however, most of the staff development was produced by outside consultants or outside speakers. The decision to create the formal staff development program emerged from the president and vice president for transformation's office. There was little if any input from individuals on campus about the content or approach for staff development. The focus of the learning was how to develop staff to better serve the college, an objective that is closely aligned with a managerial culture rather than personal development for the individual, as was stressed at ITU within a developmental culture. In AIU's collegial culture, several different models emerged. Many faculty were sent off campus to observe how their peers were working to transform general education. In addition, speakers were often brought to specific colleges and schools to describe new approaches to general education, particularly in disciplines such as engineering. Experts within each college were also called upon to describe innovative ideas and ways to facilitate the change process. The focus of the development was at the departmental level; the outcome was that the faculty member could serve his or her department more effectively.

What is the relationship between the individual cultures and the ways these strategies emerged? The developmental culture of ITU would have predicted staff development as the most important strategy for change. Yet, it was not emphasized heavily on this campus. The culture of this unique campus also seemed to affect the way staff development was enacted. The informal and trusting nature of ITU appeared to shape the staff development initiative, which was much more unstructured than that on any of the other campuses in this study or within the entire project. This institution drew exclusively on internal staff for development because of the deep trust they held, knowing they would be the best guides for assisting each other's growth. At RSCC, staff development was the dominant strategy in the change process, which appears to be related to their unique culture of self-reflection. This fact also counters the cultural archetypes, because robust design and senior administrative support would have been predicted to be the most important of the core strategies within a managerial culture. It appears that their great interest in self-reflection and personal transformation made this area a high priority and a successful strategy. The unique culture at AIU can also be seen in the way staff development emerged. The autonomy of AIU appeared to have resulted in multiple levels of staff development by various colleges/schools and throughout levels within the college—department, program, and other levels. Their insecure culture seemed to

TABLE 4

Visible Action Strategies by Institution

Informal, Trusting University (Developmental)	Responsive, Self-Reflective Community College (Managerial)	Autonomous, Insecure University (Collegial)
Needed people change; hiring criteria[B]	Meet goals. Short term action—20% increase in graduation rates[B]	Secured new resources and prestigious grants[B]
Faculty development[B]	Developed new policies and procedures[B]	Allocated money to departments for related initiatives[B]
Focused on personal growth[B]	Incentives: small grants and monies provided for any initiative related to the change initiative[B]	Support structures: cross unit interest groups[T]
Local, informal multilevel action: guiding document written by faculty, institutionally grants, faculty-led workshops[T]	Gave national presentations and received national recognition[T]	Faculty ownership, immediate change in curriculum and department culture[T]
Make individual responsible[T]	New leadership development program[T]	Getting funding to support projects[T]
	Measure progress of student learning via data[T]	Prestigious publicity and recognition[T]

Note: [B]refers to Bergquist Framework; [T]refers to Tierney Framework

make them seek outside expertise, not trusting their own knowledge for various aspects of the staff development. Table 5 compares the variety of ways staff development played itself out across the three institutions.

Discussion

The results of this study illuminate several new insights into higher education organizational change processes. In addressing the first research question, whether there appears to be a relationship between institutional culture and change, the results suggest that at all institutions and among every strategy there was a relationship. In examining the nature of this relationship (the second part of the first research question), several patterns were identifiable. First, exploring the strategies used by institutions to effect change through a cultural approach appears to provide a richer description of the often empty strategies, such as collaborative leadership or senior administrative support. Each campus enacted strategies in different ways. The distinctions are important, because the approach to senior administrative support taken at RSCC most likely would not have been acceptable on the two other campuses, and vice versa. The findings about how institutional culture and change are related also sheds light on the second research question, whether ignoring institutional culture can thwart change processes. Where strategies for change violate cultural norms, change most likely will not occur (Eckel et al., 1998; Schein, 1985). The three case studies illustrate the weakness of and the challenge to presenting change strategies as universal principles. Future research might be more insightful if it were more sensitive to the relationship of culture to strategies for change.

A second finding about how institutional culture and change are related is the recognition that Bergquist's four cultural archetypes are a helpful lens for understanding the ways in which culture is related to the change process. The findings note a relationship between institutional cultural archetypes and the way the change process was enacted. For example, IAU, a collegial campus, followed the predicted pattern of engaging in a change process where faculty and traditional academic governance structures and bodies were central to the change process, where motivation was derived from prestige, where collaborative leadership utilized the traditional academic leaders, and where key planning and decision making occurred at the college and departmental level.

A third result is the discovery that each campus' change process could not be explained by the archetypes alone. The distinct nature of the campus cultures cannot be overlooked in trying to understand how change processes unfold and which strategies institutional leaders should emphasize. The self-reflective tendency of RSCC would have been overlooked if that institution had only been examined through Bergquist's managerial lens. A structured change process, as predicted by

TABLE 5

Staff Development Strategies by Institution

Informal, Trusting University (Developmental)	Responsive, Self-Reflective Community College (Managerial)	Autonomous, Insecure University (Collegial)
Focus on individual needs[B]	Outside expertise and administratively decided[B]	Faculty sent to off campus conferences by school, see what other faculty are doing[B]
Faculty development program[B]	Centrally coordinated leadership development program[B]	Department level, serve department[B]
Internal grants program[B]	Efforts were coordinated and purposeful[B]	Outside experts[T]
Decentralized by school or department[T]	Focused on serving college[B]	Different models across units[T]
Technical support developed at local level[T]	Central focus of the change process[T]	Cross-departmental teams[T]
Not well developed[T]	Transformation series[T]	
Unstructured[T]		
Tapped internal experts[T]		

Note: [B] refers to Bergquist Framework; [T] refers to Tierney Framework the developmental culture, most likely would have derailed the change effort at ITU. Furthermore, the lack of structure to support change at ITU could not have been predicted by the developmental culture. Examining institutional culture in depth, beyond the four archetypes, provides a deeper and richer understanding of the change process and appears to facilitate change.

A fourth finding in this vein is the understanding that cultural archetypes and unique institutional cultures may help to determine which strategies might take prominence in the change process. For example, at RSCC staff development appeared to be the most important core strategy based on the self-reflective culture of the campus. At ITU, collaborative leadership seemed to play a prominent role based on the family atmosphere on the campus. Also, certain substrategies emerged as core strategies based on the culture of the institution in the same way as incentives did at AIU or communication at RSCC. Understanding the strengths and relative contributions of different strategies may help leaders determine where to focus their efforts.

These results clearly reaffirm what we assumed was the answer to our second research question— that change strategies seem to be successful if they are culturally coherent or aligned with the culture. In this study, institutions that violated their institutional culture during the change process experienced difficulty. Because of the culture's collegial nature, AIU's process was almost immediately halted when the president tried to initiate change. Not writing the word "draft" on documents hurt the process at RSCC, because it showed insensitivity to the feelings of faculty, who did not see themselves as the natural allies of administrators. These examples reinforce the idea that missteps in the change process are often cultural misunderstandings. Leaders might be more successful in facilitating change if they understood the cultures in which they were working.

These results have several implications for campus change agents. First, they need to attempt to become cultural outsiders, or as Heifetz (1994) suggests, they need to be able to "get on the balcony" to see the patterns on the dance floor below. Reading institutional culture in order to develop and match the strategies for change are fundamental to an effective change process. Change agents' strategies for achieving this outside perspective on campuses include working with a network of institutions, using outside consultants, presenting at and attending conferences where they publicly explore their assumptions, bringing in new leadership, and participating in exchange programs to broaden the horizons of personnel. Second, individuals or campuses interested in change need to be aware of the four cultures of the academy and how these are reflected within their campus. Bergquist's (1992) typology can be a useful tool for leaders undertaking comprehensive change.

Finally, future research is needed regarding culture and institutional change. Drawing on this analysis, there is evidence that working within the culture facilitates change. If change strategies violate the institution's cultural norms and standards, they might be viewed as inappropriate and stifle the change process. Yet, this study was not designed specifically to address this question. Are there certain instances (for example during a crisis) that cultural norms can be violated to affect change? Further research should examine, in what situations, it might be necessary or important to challenge institutional culture, rather than work within it. As noted in the literature review, some studies have identified how certain cultures facilitate and hinder change; these various lines of culture research need to be examined together (Curry, 1992). We want to emphasize that this study did not attempt to ascertain the efficacy of various change strategies, rather it sought to understand the relationship between institutional culture and strategies. Although working within the culture of the institutions appeared to assist institutions in moving forward, this relationship and its complexities need further study. Additionally, the archetypes were examined as exemplifying the institutional culture. Bergquist (1992) notes how campuses will have different subcultures that operate within a specific archetypal culture. These nuances and effects of subcultural archetypes need further investigation.

The intent of this study is to urge researchers and practitioners to reflect on change as a cultural process. As Bergquist notes, "one of the best ways to begin to prepare for (change) and to cope with challenges is to examine our own institutions in order to appreciate and engage diverse and often conflicting cultures that reside in them" (1992, p. 230). This article provides a framework for ways that institutions can begin to engage in this type of examination and reflection.

Notes

1. Model and theory are not necessarily interchangeable, although many scholars use them this way. Instead, "theory" is a broader term suggestive of contemplation of reality or insight, whereas "model" delineates a set of plans or procedures. Certain disciplines tend to develop models of change, such as business or psychology, whereas other fields tend to discuss theories. We use the term "theory" generically within this article.

2. Although he did not focus specifically on the change process, instead focusing more on general issues of administration and leadership and how these processes are influenced by the four cultures, a small component of his work did speculate on change and culture.

3. Birnbaum also examined different institutional types as representing different cultural archetypes (1988).

4. The researchers acknowledge that even more detailed data could reveal interesting subcultures within the institution that would also assist in our understanding of comprehensive change. These two frameworks are illustrative of the levels of culture but do not examine the department- or program-specific level of culture, for example. This is an area for future research.

References

Bergquist, W. (1992). *The four cultures of the academy.* San Francisco: Jossey Bass.

Birnbaum, R. (1988). *How college works.* San Francisco: Jossey Bass.

Bolman, L., & Deal, T. (1991). *Reframing organizations.* San Francisco: Jossey Bass.

Burns, B. (1996). *Managing change: A strategic approach to organizational dynamics.* London: Pitman Publishing.

Chaffee, E., & Tierney. W. (1988). *Collegiate culture and leadership strategies.* New York: ACE/ORYX.

Clark, B. (1970). *The distinctive college: Antioch, Reed, Swarthmore.* Chicago: Aldine.

Collins, D. (1998). *Organizational change: Sociological perspectives.* London: Routledge.

Curry, B. (1992). *Instituting enduring innovations: Achieving Continuity of change in higher education.* Washington, DC: ASHE-ERIC Higher Education Report No. 7.

Eccles, R. G., & Nohria, N. (1992). *Beyond the hype: Rediscovering the essence of management.* Cambridge, MA: Harvard Business School Press.

Eckel, P., Hill, B., & Green, M. (1998). *On change: En route to transformation.* Occasional Paper, No. 1. Washington DC: American Council on Education.

Guskin, A. E. (1996). Facing the future: The change process in restructuring universities. *Change, 28*(4), 27–37.

Hearn, J. C. (1996). Transforming U.S. higher education: An organizational perspective. *Innovative Higher Education, 21,* 141–151.

Hearn, J. C., Clugston, R., & Heydinger, R. (1993). Five years of strategic environmental assessment efforts at a research university: A case study of an organizational innovation. *Innovative Higher Education, 18,* 7–36.

Heifetz, R. (1994). *Leadership without easy answers.* Boston: Harvard University Press.

Kezar, A., & Eckel, P. (in press). Examining the institutional transformation process: The importance of sense-making and inter-related strategies. *Research in Higher Education.*

Leslie, D., & Fretwell, L. (1996). *Wise move in hard times.* San Francisco: Jossey Bass.

Levy, A., & Merry, U. (1986). *Organizational transformation: Approaches, strategies, theories.* New York: Praeger.

Lindquist, J. (1978). *Strategies for change.* Washington, DC: Council for Independent Colleges.

Lunsford, I. (1963). *The study of campus cultures.* Boulder, CO: WICHE.

Martin, J. (1992). *Cultures in organizations: Three perspectives.* New York: Oxford University.

Miles, M. B., & Huberman, A. M. (1994). *Qualitative data analysis* (2nd ed.). Thousand Oaks, CA: Sage.

Morgan, G. (1986). *Images of organization.* Thousand Oaks, CA: Sage.

Peterson, M., & Spencer, M. (1991). Understanding academic culture and climate. In M. Peterson (Ed.), *ASHE reader on organization and governance* (pp. 140–155). Needham Heights, MA: Simon & Schuster.

Peterson, M., Cameron, K., Jones, P., Mets, L., & Ettington D. (1986). *The organizational context for teaching and learning: A review of the research literature.* Ann Arbor: National Center for Research to Improve Postsecondary Teaching and Learning, University of Michigan.

Reisman, D., Gusfield, J., & Gamson, Z. (1970). *Academic values and mass education: The early years of Oakland and Monteith.* New York: Doubleday.

Roberts, A. O., Wergin, J. F., & Adam, B. E. (1993). Institutional approaches to the issues of reward and scholarship. *New Directions for Higher Education*, No. 81, pp. 63–86.

Schein, E. (1985). *Organizational culture and leadership: A dynamic view.* San Francisco: Jossey Bass.

Smirich, L., & Calas, M. (1982). Organizational culture: A critical assessment. In M. Peterson (Ed.), *ASHE reader on organization and governance* (pp. 139–151), Needham Heights, MA: Ginn Press.

Sporn, B. (1999). *Adaptive university structures: An analysis of adaptation to socioeconomic environments of US and European universities.* Philadelphia: Francis and Taylor, Higher Education Policy Series 54.

Tichy, N, (1983). *Managing strategic change: Technical, political, and cultural dynamics.* New York: Wiley.

Tierney, W. (1988). Organizational culture in higher education. *Journal of Higher Education, 59,* 2–21.

Tierney, W. (1991). Organizational culture in higher education: Defining the essentials. In M. Peterson (Ed.), *ASHE reader on organization and governance* (pp. 126–139), Needham Heights, MA: Ginn Press.

Van de Ven, A. H., & Poole, M. S. (1995). Explaining development and change in organizations. *Academy of Management Review, 20,* 510–540.

ENHANCING CAMPUS CLIMATES
FOR RACIAL/ETHNIC DIVERSITY:
EDUCATIONAL POLICY AND PRACTICE

SYLVIA HURTADO, JEFFREY F. MILEM,
ALMA R. CLAYTON-PEDERSEN, AND WALTER R. ALLEN

Probably few policy areas of higher education have received more recent attention than the issue of race on campus. Evidence appears in policies and programs related to college admissions, financial aid, affirmative action, discrimination and harassment, and desegregation. Yet, at the same time, probably no area of campus life has been so devoid of policy initiatives as the racial climate at individual institutions. Until recently, there has been no common framework for understanding the campus racial climate in a way that helps develop policies and practices that can be used to enhance the campus climate.

We pose four possible explanations for this phenomenon. First, higher education leaders and higher education institutions have taken the *laissez-faire* approach that people will (should) work things out interactively and that it is wrong to intervene too closely in student interactions (Horowitz, 1987). The second explanation involves ambiguity in the role that colleges and universities perform as agents of socialization. Administrators and faculty recognize that students bring with them to college a sense of identity and purpose shaped by their parents, their communities, their religions, etc., and that these influences are critically important to students' growth and development. The quandary lies in just how much of a resocializing agent higher education institutions wish to be. Higher education has not decided whether it should merely reflect our society or whether it should try to consciously shape the society. Third, while research findings document the important role that faculty serve as the "designated socializing agents" in higher education (Feldman & Newcomb, 1969, p. 227), policy initiatives that address faculty attitudes and behaviors have been implemented only with great hesitation and caution. Until now, it seems that only the most problematic discriminatory behaviors of faculty have been addressed. Finally, the situation has been exacerbated by neglect. A rich history of research on issues that affect the campus racial climate has existed for some time. However, this research has not always been valued by the higher education community. A study analyzing the major paradigms used in manuscripts published in "major" higher education journals found that fewer than 2% used paradigms that addressed issues of race from a critical perspective with the goal of producing meaningful change (Milam, 1989).

Attorneys, policy-makers, and institutional leaders across the country are searching for research evidence that demonstrates the benefits of diversity and documents persistent discrimination and inequality in higher education. Perhaps at no other time in our history have higher education scholars had the opportunity to provide evidence of the educational outcomes of diversity in a way that puts the benefits of diversity at the center of the educational enterprise. The purpose of this paper is to illustrate how research on issues related to campus racial climate can be used to enhance educational policy and practice. Both classic and contemporary research can inform national policy and debates surrounding affirmative action and other policies to create diverse learning environments

(Hurtado, Milem, Clayton-Pedersen, & Allen, in press). What is needed are vehicles that translate higher education research into thoughtful policies incorporating the goal of educating diverse students. While such vehicles, or "translation documents," can be written in any number of higher education policy arenas, this paper focuses on the critical need for sustaining progress in educating diverse students.

We conducted an extensive multidisciplinary analysis of the research literature on the sources and outcomes of campus racial climate and developed a framework for understanding and describing the campus climate. It is our hope that policy-makers, institutional leaders, and scholars of higher education will find this framework useful as they seek to create comfortable, diverse environments for learning and socializing that facilitate the intellectual and social development of all students.

A Framework for Understanding Campus Climate

Considerable research on various racial/ethnic students in higher education addresses an array of cognitive and affective outcomes and group differences in educational attainments (Durán, 1983; Pascarella & Terenzini, 1991; Sedlacek, 1987). While these earlier research syntheses represent scholarly work on the achievement of various racial/ethnic groups, they contain almost no specific references to the institutional climate's potential influence on diversity. Some literature refers to the climate as important but "intangible." Recently, both qualitative and quantitative researchers have provided greater definition for this "intangible" quality by examining how students, faculty, and administrators perceive the institutional climate for racial/ethnic diversity, their experiences with campus diversity, and their own attitudes and interactions with different racial/ethnic groups. Multi-institutional studies have also shown, using a variety of measures, that the climate for diversity varies substantially from one institutional context to another (El-Khawas, 1989; Gilliard, 1996; Hurtado, 1992; Peterson, Blackburn, Gamson, Arce, Davenport, & Mingle, 1978).

This manuscript provides a framework for understanding four dimensions of the campus climate and a conceptual handle for understanding elements of the environment that were once thought too complex to comprehend. This framework was first introduced in a study of the climate for Latino students (Hurtado, 1994) and further developed in a synthesis of research done for practitioners (Hurtado, Milem, Clayton-Pedersen, & Allen, in press). It makes concrete observations of institutions and individuals. It also defines areas where research has been conducted and, more importantly, where practical or programmatic solutions can be targeted.

Most institutions, when considering diversity on campus, tend to focus on increasing the numbers of racial/ethnic students. While this area of institutional effort is important, the four-part framework underscores other elements that require also attention, defining key areas upon which to focus diversity efforts. The studies we reviewed contain specific references to these various dimensions of the climate, describe the climate's impact on students from different racial/ethnic groups, and capture the experiences or unique perspectives of racial/ethnic groups that have historically been underrepresented in higher education.

Central to the conceptualization of a campus climate for diversity is the concept that students are educated in distinct racial contexts. These contexts in higher education are shaped by external and internal (institutional) forces. We represent the external components of climate as two domains: (a) the impact of governmental policy, programs, and initiatives and (b) the impact of sociohistorical forces on campus racial climate. Examples of the first include financial aid policies and programs, state and federal policy on affirmative action, court decisions on the desegregation of higher education, and the manner in which states provide for institutional differentiation within their state system of higher education. Sociohistoric forces influencing the climate for diversity on campus are events or issues in the larger society, nearly always originating outside the campus, that influence how people view racial diversity in society. They stimulate discussion or other activity within the campus. Obviously, these two domains influence each other. Tierney (1997) points out, "No policy can be isolated from the social arena in which it is enacted" (p. 177). While research literature documents the effect of governmental policy, programs, and initiatives (particularly in financial aid), there are fewer studies of the influence of sociohistorical forces on the campus racial climate.

The institutional context contains four dimensions resulting from educational programs and practices. They include an institution's historical legacy of inclusion or exclusion of various racial/ethnic groups, its structural diversity in terms of numerical representation of various racial/ethnic groups, the psychological climate of perceptions and attitudes between and among groups, and the behavioral climate dimension, characterized by intergroup relations on campus. We conceive the institutional climate as a product of these various elements.

It is important to note that these dimensions are connected, not discrete. For example, the historical vestiges of segregation have an impact on an institution's ability to improve its racial/ethnic student enrollments, and the underrepresentation of specific groups contributes to stereotypical attitudes among individuals within the learning and work environment that affect the psychological and behavioral climate. In short, while some institutions are now trying to take a "multi-layered" approach toward assessing diversity on their campuses and are developing programs to address the climate on campus, very few recognize the importance of the dynamics of these interrelated elements of the climate.

The Institutional Context Historical Legacy of Inclusion or Exclusion

In many ways, the historical vestiges of segregated schools and colleges continue to affect the climate for racial/ethnic diversity on college campuses. The best example is resistance to desegregation in communities and specific campus settings, the maintenance of old campus policies at predominantly White institutions that best serve a homogeneous population, and attitudes and behaviors that prevent interaction across race and ethnicity. Because they are embedded in the culture of a historically segregated environment, many campuses sustain long-standing, often unrecognized, benefits for particular student groups (Duster, 1993).

Desegregation policies in schools and colleges were designed to alter their racial/ethnic composition, improve educational opportunity, and ultimately, change the environments of our educational institutions. Research on the outcomes of desegregation suggests that individuals who attend desegregated schools and colleges accept desegregation as adults in other educational settings, occupations, and social situations. Moreover, White adults who attended desegregated schools have fewer racial stereotypes and less fear of hostile reactions in interracial settings (Braddock, 1980, 1985; Braddock, Crain, & McPartland, 1984; Braddock & Dawkins, 1981; Braddock & McPartland, 1982, 1989; Green, 1982; Scott & McPartland, 1982).

While some campuses have a history of admitting and graduating students of color since their founding days, most predominantly White institutions (PWIs) have a history of limited access and exclusion (Thelin, 1985). A college's historical legacy of exclusion can determine the prevailing climate and influence current practices (Hurtado, 1992). Various institutional case studies document the impact of the historical context on the climate for diversity and on attempts to create a supportive climate for students of color (Peterson et al., 1978; Richardson & Skinner, 1991). Researchers found that success in creating supportive campus environments often depends on an institution's initial response to the entrance of students of color. Among important factors were the institutional philosophy of education for students of color, commitment to affirmative action, institutional intent for minority-specific programs, and attention to the psychological climate and intergroup relations on campus (Peterson et al., 1978). Higher education has had a long history of resistance to desegregation. The need for legal pressures and extended litigation to require institutions to accept their obligation to serve equitably a more diverse group of students has conveyed not only the message of institutional resistance but, in some cases, outright hostility toward people of diverse backgrounds.

Historically Black colleges and universities (HBCUs) and American Indian colleges (AICs) have historic commitments to serve populations previously excluded from higher education. These students continue to face seemingly intractable problems at PWIs. In recent years, due to dramatic changes in Latino enrollment, Hispanic-serving institutions (HSIs) have also begun to emphasize their commitment to educating Latino students. Today, as before, HBCUs, AICs, and HSIs not only represent alternative choices for students but also include attention to the cultural and academic development of these students and their communities as part of their mission.

Research that has examined differences in outcomes for African American students who have attended HBCUs as compared to students who have attended PWIs suggest that HBCUs provide more social and psychological support, higher levels of satisfaction and sense of community, and a greater likelihood that students will persist and complete their degrees (Allen, 1992; Allen, Epps, & Haniff, 1991; R. Davis, 1991; Jackson & Swan, 1991; Pascarella, Smart, Ethington, & Nettles, 1987). Recent findings from the National Study of Student Learning indicate that HBCUs also provide educational environments that support their students' intellectual development (Pascarella, Whitt, Nora, Edison, Hagedorn, Terenzini, 1996).

However, most racially and ethnically diverse students are educated in predominantly White environments (Carter & Wilson, 1993); therefore, PWIs's responses to desegregation are key in defining the campus racial climate. A positive response requires a clear definition of desegregation and strategic planning by the institution (Stewart, 1991). Further, the goals of desegregation plans must be precisely articulated with the objective of increasing overall representation of the historically excluded group.

Implications for Policy and Practice

Colleges and universities cannot change their past histories of exclusion nor should they deny that they exist. However, they can take steps to insure that diversity becomes a central value of their educational enterprise. Campus leaders should not assume that members of their community (particularly incoming students) know these histories, nor should they assume that teaching about these histories will lead to dissatisfaction. By being clear about an institution's past history of exclusion and the detrimental impact that this history has had on the campus, colleges and universities may garner broader support for their efforts to become more diverse through affirmative action programs and other programs and services designed to improve the climate for diversity. Moreover, acknowledging a past history of exclusion implies an institutional willingness to actively shed its exclusionary past. Such efforts may be even more effective if they are coupled with a clearly articulated vision for a more inclusive future.

In assessing the influence of the campus's history, leaders must consider whether "embedded benefits" may still exist on their campus. Institutions with a history of exclusion are likely to have evolved in ways that disproportionately benefit some group. For example, at many PWIs, fraternities and sororities have been a part of campus life much longer than people of color. Predominantly White fraternities and sororities frequently have houses that provide members with a place to meet or to live that are centrally located on campus or directly adjacent to the campus while the Greek system is deeply involved in daily campus activities, politics, socials, etc. In contrast, African American fraternities and sororities at these institutions seldom have been able to accumulate similar benefits for their members. The likelihood of finding the same quality of houses in equally convenient locations is quite low. In fact, students in these organizations may struggle to find places that they can meet on or near some campuses. Research shows that these organizations are critically important to the students who join them, but African American fraternities and sororities frequently seem less central than their White counterparts in daily campus activities, politics, and socials. As campus leaders thoughtfully consider their histories of exclusion, they are likely to find many more examples.

The success of legislation and litigation regarding desegregation in higher education has been mixed at best (Williams, 1988). In the prevailing climate, the federal government is taking a somewhat passive role and deferring to states. Even where the willingness to pursue desegregation exists, the capacity for most states to regulate their colleges and universities (particularly their flagship institutions) has been limited (Williams, 1988). Hence, efforts to maintain a commitment to desegregation and equality of opportunity in higher education are most likely to succeed at the campus level with provisions for support at the state level. Desegregating predominantly White institutions is particularly important in states and communities where high-school segregation has continued; as a result, college may be the first chance for many students to encounter and interact with someone of different race or ethnicity.

According to the Southern Education Foundation (1995), HBCUs and PWIs are the result of "purposeful, state-imposed segregation," hence "no set of institutions has any more right than another to survive. The burden of desegregation should not fall exclusively or disproportionately on HBCUs" (p. xix). To require this effort would be unfair and unwise. E. B. Davis (1993) explains: "Institutions that retain a specifically black identity will not easily be able to reach the level of integration which reflects the population. They are being challenged to change their very character, while historically White schools are being asked only to broaden access" (p. 523). HBCUs serve an essential role in the higher education system by providing educational environments that facilitate positive social, psychological, and intellectual outcomes for students who attend them. Hence, they must be maintained. Moreover, PWIs can learn much from HBCUs, AICs, and HSIs about enhancing their environments to insure the success of students of color on campus.

Structural Diversity and Its Impact on Students

Given recent assaults on affirmative action in states like California and judicial rulings like that in *Hopwood*, it is critically important to understand how changes in the enrollment of racial/ethnic students (or the lack thereof) transform into educational benefits for students. Research supports the concept that increasing the structural diversity of an institution is an important initial step toward improving the climate. First, environments with highly skewed distributions of students shape the dynamics of social interaction (Kanter, 1977). Campuses with high proportions of White students provide limited opportunities for interaction across race/ethnicity barriers and limit student learning experiences with socially and culturally diverse groups (Hurtado, Dey, & Treviño, 1994). Second, in environments that lack diverse populations, underrepresented groups are viewed as tokens. Tokenism contributes to the heightened visibility of the underrepresented group, exaggeration of group differences, and the distortion of images to fit existing stereotypes (Kanter, 1977). The sheer fact that racial and ethnic students remain minorities in majority White environments contributes to their social stigma (Steele, 1992) and can produce minority status stress (Prillerman, Myers, & Smedley, 1989; Smedley, Myers, & Harrell, 1993). Third, an institution's stance on increasing the representation of diverse racial/ethnic groups communicates whether maintaining a multicultural environment is a high institutional priority. For example, African American, Chicano, and White students tended to report that commitment to diversity was a high institutional priority on campuses with relatively high percentages of African American and Latino students (Hurtado, 1990).

Loo and Rolison (1986) conclude that sufficient racial/ethnic enrollments can give potential recruits the impression that the campus is hospitable: "No matter how outstanding the academic institution, ethnic minority students can feel alienated if their ethnic representation on campus is small" (p. 72). However, increasing the numbers of students of color on campus is not free from problems. The racial/ethnic restructuring of student enrollments can trigger conflict and resistance among groups. It can also create a need for institutional changes more substantial than first envisioned. Resulting changes affect both the academic and social life of the institution, resulting in, for example, the development of ethnic studies programs, diverse student organizations, specific academic support programs, and multicultural programming (Muñoz, 1989; Peterson et al., 1978; Treviño, 1992).

Increases in diverse student enrollment, however, have also become problematic for the White majority and racial/ethnic minority groups. Race relations theorists hypothesize that the larger the relative size of the minority group, the more likely it is that there will be minority/majority conflict over limited resources (Blalock, 1967). On campuses where Asian American enrollments have increased substantially, Asian American students have reported more personal experiences of discrimination than any other group (Asian Pacific, 1990). White students tend to perceive racial tension on predominantly White campuses with relatively high African American enrollments (Hurtado, 1992). However, results from this study also show that, when students feel that they are valued and that faculty and administrators are devoted to their development, they are less likely to report racial/ethnic tension on campus. This finding suggests that campuses can minimize racial tension and competition among groups by creating more "student-centered" environments.

Chang (1996) found that maximizing cross-racial interaction and encouraging ongoing discussions about race are educational practices that benefit all students. However, when minority enrollments increased without implementing these activities, students of color reported less overall satisfaction with their college experience (Chang, 1996). Thus, increasing only the structural diversity of an institution without considering the influence of each of the other dimensions of the campus racial climate is likely to produce problems for students at these institutions.

Implications for Policy and Practice

Clearly, one important step toward improving the campus climate for diversity is to increase the representation of people of color on campus. Hence, institutional and government policy must insure that access to college is available to all members of our society. Admissions practices and financial aid policies are two areas in which changes can be made that will have prompt, positive effects.

Some critics have suggested that college and graduate/professional admissions policies and practices place too much emphasis on standardized test scores and not enough on evidence of previous achievement such as high school or college grade point averages and a student's drive to achieve (Frierson, 1991; Guanier, 1997). Guanier (1997) has suggested that college and graduate/professional school admission committees decide on a minimum acceptable score, then hold a lottery to draw the entering class from the pool of candidates meeting that criterion. Students who offer qualities considered valuable to the institution would have their names entered more than once to increase the likelihood that they would be selected. "These could be students who have overcome adversity, who have particular skills and credentials, who have outstanding academic records, or who have special and worthy career aspirations" (Guanier, 1997, p. 60).

Another approach to college admissions can be found in a proposal offered in response to the *Bakke* decision (Astin, 1985; Astin, Fuller, & Green, 1978). The authors reported that standardized tests presented a significant obstacle for students from historically disadvantaged backgrounds and that the negative impact of these tests increases dramatically as the selection ratio (number of applicants compared to the number of students admitted) increases at institutions. They suggested the use of a "disadvantagement index" derived from parental income, father's educational level, and mother's educational level. This index assumes that affluent parents are more likely to provide their children with greater access to educational opportunities and are more likely to live in communities where local schools are better funded and have more educational resources.

Neither proposal is likely to provide a single best answer about reforming the college admissions process to insure that diverse people are appropriately represented. Indeed, in the case of the disadvantagement index, critics might argue that class is an insufficient proxy for race (Tierney, 1997). However, in discussing the relative merits of such approaches, a discussion might begin on how college admissions policies and programs can be reformed to insure appropriate levels of structural diversity.

Without a doubt, state and federal financial aid policies have increased the diversity of college enrollments. Researchers of student financial aid have found that financial aid generally does what it was designed to do: It increases access to higher education by increasing the probability that students will attend college (St. John 1991a; Stampen & Fenske, 1988). While all forms of aid are positively associated with the decision to attend college when *all* students are considered, not all forms of aid are equally effective for students from historically disadvantaged backgrounds. Aid packages with loans are less consistently significant in facilitating access for minority applicants than for White applicants (St. John, 1991a), and Black, Latino, and American Indian students borrow considerably less than White or Asian students (Stampen, 1985).

Maintaining appropriate forms of financial aid at the state, federal, and institutional levels is critical in increasing the diversity of student enrollments. However, federal funding has not kept pace with increases in tuition in recent years (Orfield, 1992). Recent federal policies related to financial aid still disadvantage poor families from various racial/ethnic groups, thus reducing equity and college access for them (Olivas, 1986; Orfield, 1992). The expanded availability of and extended eligibility for loan dollars (and the decreased availability of grant and work study funds) has increased access for students from middle-income families while restricting access for students from low-income backgrounds. A key component of any long-term and short-term response to these trends should involve substantial increases in federal student grant funding, rather than an increased emphasis on loans (Astin, 1982; St. John, 1991b). Moreover, additional investment in financial aid programs makes good fiscal sense. Funding federal financial aid programs provides a substantial return on investment of public funds (St. John & Masten, 1990).

Recent research on the impact of financial aid provides an example of how external factors (governmental policy, programs, and initiatives) influence the campus climate for diversity. Campuses must find ways to counteract the negative consequences of changes in financial aid programs for students from historically disadvantaged backgrounds. If schools are sincere in their effort to attract more diverse students, they should change institutional aid policies so that they offer as much aid as possible in grants. Moreover, institutional leaders should work with state and federal policy-makers for appropriate levels of funding for financial aid and put this money into the aid programs that are most helpful to students from historically disadvantaged backgrounds— i.e., grants and work study programs.

Campus leaders and policy-makers should not expect to substantively improve the campus racial climate by increasing only the structural diversity of institutions. In fact, problems are likely to arise without improvements in other aspects of campus climate. Increased structural diversity will likely fail in achieving its goals unless accompanied by efforts to make institutions more "student-centered" in approaches to teaching and learning (Hurtado, 1992) and by regular and on-going opportunities for students to communicate and interact cross-racially (Chang, 1996).

The Psychological Dimension of Climate and Its Impact on Students

The psychological dimension of the campus racial climate involves individuals' views of group relations, institutional responses to diversity, perceptions of discrimination or racial conflict, and attitudes toward those from other racial/ethnic backgrounds than one's own. It is important to note that more recent studies show that racially and ethnically diverse administrators, students, and faculty tend to view the campus climate differently. Thus, an individual's position and power within the organization and his or her status as "insider" or "outsider" strongly influence attitudes (Collins, 1986). In other words, who you are and where you are positioned in an institution will affect how you experience and view the institution. For example, Loo and Rolison (1986) found that 68 percent of White students thought their university was generally supportive of minority students; only 28 percent of the African American and Chicano students expressed the same opinion. Cabrera and Nora (1994) found that students of color were more sensitive to different forms of prejudice and discrimination; White students were less likely to perceive nuances. Variations within ethnic groups also occur, depending on the student's background and sense of ethnic identity. For example, one study found that American Indian students who closely held to American Indian values were likely to report more negative racial encounters in college than other students (Huffman, 1991). These perceptual differences of the college experience are significant, for perception is both a product of the environment and potential determinant of future interactions and outcomes (Astin, 1968; Tierney, 1997). As past and contemporary research reveals, these differing perceptions and experiences have real consequences for individuals.

General student perceptions of discrimination have a significant and negative effect on African American students' grades (Nettles, 1988; Prillerman et al., 1989; Smedley et al., 1993). First-year students who felt that they were singled out or treated differently in the classroom reported a higher sense of alienation at the end of their freshman year (Cabrera & Nora, 1994). While significant for all racial/ethnic groups, this form of discrimination was particularly detrimental to African Americans. A longitudinal study of highly talented Latino students found that perceptions of racial tension between groups on campus in the first year had a consistently negative effect on academic and psychological adjustment in subsequent college years (Hurtado, Carter, & Spuler, 1996). The study also found that while reports of overt instances of personal harassment/discrimination did not significantly affect academic and personal-emotional adjustment, they diminished Latino students' feelings of attachment to the institution. Another study of freshman minority students found that perceptions of discrimination affected their academic and social experiences but not their persistence in college (Nora & Cabrera, 1996). It may be that, although academically confident students of color continue to feel marginalized, they learn how to deal with discrimination (Tracey & Sedlacek, 1985).

However, even students of color who persist through graduation may feel high levels of alienation: one study found less satisfaction and more social alienation among African American and Asian American students who stayed at the institution as compared to those who left the university, presumably for better environments (Bennett & Okinaka, 1990). Introducing ways for students to report and seek redress for negative experiences is important, but campuses must also be aware that many psychological aspects of the college climate go unreported. A study of California State institutions revealed that Asian Pacific Americans often do not use formal grievance procedures when they experience discrimination or harassment (Asian Pacific, 1994). Native American students confirmed that perceptions of racial hostility were strongly associated with feelings of isolation, but the effect on their attitudes toward college or grade point average was not decisively significant (Lin, LaCounte, & Eder, 1988).

In a multi-campus study, Gilliard (1996) found that the most significant climate measure for Black students was their perceptions of racial discrimination by college administrators. She also found that White students' sense of belonging was negatively affected by a poor racial climate but was positively tied to having non-White friends and to perceptions that the campus accepted and respected African American students. Similarly, Nora and Cabrera (1996) found that White students' persistence in college was both directly and indirectly affected by perceptions of discrimination. These studies show that White students are also affected by the climate for racial/ethnic diversity.

Research on the impact of peer groups and other reference groups is helpful in understanding another important aspect of the psychological dimension of climate on campus. Peer groups influence students' attitudes and behavior through the norms that they communicate to their members. While faculty play an important role in the educational development of students, most researchers believe that student peer groups are principally responsible for socialization (Chickering, 1969; Feldman & Newcomb, 1969). This finding does not minimize the role of faculty; rather, it suggests that their normative influence will be amplified or attenuated by the interactions students have with their peers. While peer groups clearly have the greatest impact in the undergraduate socialization process, recent research on the impact of college on students' racial attitudes, cultural awareness/acceptance, and social/political attitudes suggests that faculty may have a larger, more important role than traditionally believed (Hurtado, 1990, 1992; Milem, 1992, 1994, 1998).

Implications for Policy and Practice

Institutional leaders can significantly strengthen the psychological climate on their campuses by purposefully becoming deliberate agents of socialization. They can begin by designing and implementing systematic and comprehensive educational programs to help all members of the campus community to identify and confront the stereotypes and myths that people have about those who are different from them. While much of what is known about the development and reduction of prejudice and bias comes from the research of college and university faculty, many businesses and organizations in the private sector have shown a greater willingness to apply these findings in the hope of strengthening their organizational effectiveness. If these activities provide opportunities for cross-racial interaction, the magnitude of difference in perceptions of the racial climate between White students and students of color on campus is likely to be dramatically reduced (Pascarella et al., 1996).

Because perceptions of discrimination have consequences for all students, institutions should do all that they can to insure that students perceive the institutional climate as fair and just. Hence, institutions must have clearly stated policies and procedures to help the campus community confront and resolve incidents of harassment and discrimination. These policies and procedures should include formal processes for resolving conflicts or disputes that involve representatives from all members of the campus community (students, faculty, staff).

As we discussed earlier, there will almost certainly be significant differences in perceptions of the climate based on the experience and position of the person being asked. Campus leaders should insure that the perspectives of all members of the campus community be considered in decision-making processes. Hence, institutions must implement regular and on-going assessments of the campus climate for diversity.

Research findings clearly document the important role of ethnic student organizations and other student support services for students of color on predominantly White campuses. Hence, campuses must insure that these services and organizations have enough staff, funding, and resources to serve students successfully.

An emerging body of research on mentoring suggests that academe poorly socializes graduate students of color into the culture of academic departments. Students of color who pursue research on issues relevant to their cultural/ethnic background frequently report difficulty in finding faculty who encourage and support their work. This faculty indifference probably influences negatively student perceptions of the climate of the institution and may have a detrimental effect on their graduate student experience (Nealy, 1996; Turner & Thompson, 1993; Willie, Grady, & Hope, 1991). Institutional leaders can address these concerns by providing formal mentoring programs where students are matched with faculty who will support them and their work as emerging scholars.

The research in social psychology and higher education has suggested for some time that peer groups are critical in students' educational experience. However, institutions of higher education have not done all that they can to incorporate these groups into the formal educational process. Rather than leaving cross-racial interactions among students to chance, educators should make peer groups a deliberate and positive part of the educational process in colleges and universities.

Recent research also suggests that faculty serve a more important role in influencing students' attitudes and values than had been previously thought. It is time to shift the debate from whether faculty can (or should) be "objective" to how to give faculty support and guidance in becoming aware of their biases and the effect of these biases on their students.

The Behavioral Dimension of Climate and Its Impact on Students

The behavioral dimension of the institutional climate consists of (a) actual reports of general social interaction, (b) interaction between and among individuals from different racial/ethnic backgrounds, and (c) the nature of intergroup relations on campus. Student involvement plays a central role in undergraduates' successful educational experience; it enhances cognitive and affective student outcomes (Astin 1988, 1991, 1993; Kuh, Schuh, Whitt, Andreas, Lyons, Strange, Krehbiel, & MacKay, 1991; Pascarella & Terenzini, 1991) and retention (Tinto 1987, 1993). "Involving colleges" foster high expectations for student performance, minimize status distinctions, and have an unwavering commitment to multiculturalism (Kuh et al., 1991).

The prevailing contemporary view is that campus race relations are poor, social interaction is low, and students from different racial/ethnic groups are segregating themselves from other groups (Altbach & Lomotey, 1991; Bunzel, 1992). To be sure, incidents of overt racism and harassment occurred with greater frequency at the end of the 1980s and received much press coverage (Farrell & Jones, 1988). However, several research studies based on students' interactions and relations on campus paint a different picture. White students interpreted ethnic group clustering as racial segregation, while minority students viewed this behavior as cultural support within a larger unsupportive environment (Loo & Rolison, 1986). Chicano, Asian American, and African American students reported widespread and frequent interaction across race/ethnicity in various informal situations (i.e., dining, roommates, dating, socializing), but White students were least likely to report any of these activities as interracial (Hurtado, Dey, & Treviño, 1994). Although African Americans and Asian Americans reported more frequent racial/ethnic harassment (32% and 30% respectively), such experiences did not significantly diminish interaction across race/ethnicity for these groups.

The absence of interracial contact clearly influences students' views toward others, support for campus initiatives, and educational outcomes. White students who had the least social interaction with someone of a different background were less likely to hold positive attitudes toward multiculturalism on campus (Globetti, Globetti, Brown, & Smith, 1993). Conversely, White students who had socialized with someone of another race, had discussed racial/ethnic issues with other students, or had attended racial/cultural awareness workshops were more likely to value the goal of promoting racial understanding (Milem, 1992, 1994, 1998). Another study revealed that socializing across race and discussing racial/ethnic issues have a positive effect on students' retention, overall satisfaction with college, intellectual self-concept, and social self-concept (Chang, 1996). After studying the complex dynamics of interaction on the U.C. Berkeley campus, where dramatic changes in racial/ethnic enrollments have occurred, Duster (1993) suggested continued support for strong ethnic identities and affiliations as well as institutional encouragement for multiracial contacts.

Although some suggest that racial/ethnic student organizations and minority programs contribute to campus segregation, a series of studies refutes this perspective. These studies have empirically demonstrated that students join racial/student organizations because they are identity enhancing and that such increased identity comfort may lead to a greater interest in both cultural and cross-cultural activities (Treviño, 1992; Mitchell & Dell, 1992). Treviño (1992) found that members of racial/ethnic student organizations were more likely to participate in racial/cultural awareness workshops. Students in such organizations also report more frequent informal interactions across race/ethnicity (Hurtado, Dey, & Treviño, 1994). In addition, Gilliard (1996) found that participation in racially focused cultural activities and support programs (e.g., Black Student Union, minority peer support services) was correlated with African Americans' higher social involvement, informal social interactions with faculty, and higher use of general support services.

Implications for Policy and Practice

Research on the behavioral dimension of racial climate suggests a wide range of beneficial practices for students. While institutions cannot change their pasts, they can clearly articulate to all members of the community the expectation that interracial dialogue and interaction are highly valued on campus. They should try to provide students with opportunities for cross-racial interaction whenever possible—both in and out of the classroom. This interaction should be structured so that it will be positive for participants. The contact should be regular, on-going, and viewed as equal in status by all participants. Finally, the contact should occur in an environment characterized by cooperation and not competition (Allport, 1954).

Faculty can facilitate positive interaction in the classroom by insuring that racial/ethnic diversity is part of the course content. Moreover, faculty can promote interaction across racial/ethnic groups and student achievement. Cooperative learning activities, inside and outside of the classroom, increase interaction across race/ethnicity and lead to intergroup friendships (Slavin, 1985). When students work cooperatively on course content, they learn more about one another as well as about the specific content areas. Faculty members should also consider how to modify their classroom practices to reduce competition in the classroom. Finally, given the important role of faculty contact (in and out of the classroom), institutions should provide abundant opportunities for all faculty-student contact in and out of the classroom. Given the academic reward structure at many institutions, institutional leaders may need to provide incentives to encourage faculty to engage students in this way.

Cross-race interactions can be also enhanced by the programs and activities of multicultural centers. These centers frequently house the ethnic student organizations that are critical to the educational success of the students they represent. Given the importance of these organizations in affirming a sense of identity for students and in their role of encouraging students to become involved in other aspects of campus life, campus leaders should vigorously support these organizations for all students, communicating their importance as essential educational resources. Such an approach should help overcome the problem that, while multicultural centers are frequently the center of activity and support for students of color, White students are less likely to be involved in these centers' programs and activities.

Finally, research in race relations indicates that increased structural diversity is usually accompanied by increased levels of conflict. However, conflict should not be viewed as a destabilizing force in higher education institutions. Parker Palmer (1987) suggests that conflict is an essential component of meaningful communities, which he defines "as a capacity for relatedness within individuals—relatedness not only to people but to events in history, to nature, to world of ideas, and yes, to things of the spirit" (p. 24). In communities that are not perceived as supportive, conflict is likely viewed as a threat to be avoided. Hence, it is essential that institutions provide ways for members of the campus community to successfully understand and resolve conflict. Then conflict can become a stimulus for creativity and community-building. Dialogue groups can provide both a structure and process for addressing the intergroup dynamics of multiculturalism within the learning environment. Activities for the learning process include the opportunity to break down barriers, challenge the ignorance inside and outside oneself, create new insights, forge new connections and identities, and finally, build coalitions to work toward a common goal (Zúñiga & Nagda, 1992). The issue of group conflict and social attitudes surrounding communities of difference addressed in dialogue groups are "not easily resolvable as long as the lack of adequate structures and processes for intergroup interactions in the college community maintains the invisible, but psychologically real walls that separate different groups" (Zúñiga and Nagda, 1992, p. 251).

From Research to Policy and Practice: Strategies for Improving Campus Diversity

Recent research on the campus climate for diversity has enabled campuses to better understand institutions and their impact on students, student responses to climate issues, and relationships that develop among diverse students and faculty. While many institutions are still contending with issues of diversifying their campus enrollments, more campuses need information to help them address the psychological and behavioral dimensions of the climate. At national higher education conferences, more individuals are talking about improving the climate and are sharing practices that work. The empirical evidence and policy recommendations provided here will help institutional administrators and program planners use a wealth of research, about both specific institutions and national samples of students and institutions. In addition, many institutions are undertaking assessments of their climate for diversity to understand better their own institutional contexts. While a wealth of knowledge is now available and institutions are better informed as they begin self-examinations, designing an action plan that will significantly improve the quality of experiences for undergraduates is perhaps the next important challenge in the process.

Campuses are complex social systems defined by the relationships between the people, bureaucratic procedures, structural arrangements, institutional goals and values, traditions, and larger socio-historical environments. Therefore, any effort to redesign campuses with the goal of improving the climate for racial and cultural diversity must be comprehensive and long term. Institutions change slowly. It is the nature of a stable system of higher education. Therefore, the success of efforts to achieve institutional change will rely on leadership, firm commitment, adequate resources, collaboration, monitoring, and long-range planning.

Institutional change can be implemented at several levels. Most important is the structural level. An institution should increase at all levels the number of previously excluded and underrepresented racial/ethnic minorities (i.e., students, faculty, staff, administrators). Ideally minorities should be represented on the campus in proportionate numbers. While efforts to increase the representation of minorities on campus and to remove barriers to their participation are crucial, these steps alone are not sufficient to achieve the goal of improving the climate for diversity.

Beyond the observable make-up of the students and faculty are the attitudinal and behavioral characteristics of how particular groups of individuals "feel" about and relate to one another. How does the campus "feel" to minority individuals (e.g., Do they feel welcome? Do they sense hostility? Do they feel valued?). How does the campus respond to racially and culturally different groups (e.g., Does the campus strive to change to incorporate these students or does the campus communicate that adaptation is the job of only the minority students? Does the campus genuinely value diversity?).

In short, two sets of issues are important when considering the success of efforts to improve the campus racial climate: (a) How diverse does the campus look in its representation of different cultural groups? and (b) To what extent do campus operations demonstrate that racial and ethnic diversity is an essential value?

References

Allen, W. R. (1992). The color of success: African-American college student outcomes at predominantly white and historically black public colleges and universities. *Harvard Educational Review, 62*(1), 26–44.

Allen, W. R., Epps, E. G., & Haniff, N. Z. (Eds). (1991). *College in Black and White: African American students in predominantly White and in historically Black public universities.* Albany: State University of New York Press.

Allport, G. W. (1954). *The nature of prejudice.* Reading, MA: Addison-Wesley.

Altbach, P. G., & Lomotey, K. (Eds.). (1991). *The racial crisis in American higher education.* Albany: State University of New York Press.

Asian Pacific American Education Advisory Committee. (1990). *Enriching California's future: Asian Pacific Americans in the CSU.* Long Beach, CA: Office of the Chancellor, The California State University.

Asian Pacific American Education Advisory Committee. (1994). *Asian Pacific Americans in the California State University: A follow-up report.* Long Beach, CA: Office of the Chancellor, The California State University.

Astin, A. W. (1968). *The college environment.* Washington, DC: American Council on Education.

Astin, A. W. (1982). *Minorities in American higher education.* San Francisco: Jossey-Bass.

Astin, A. W. (1985). *Achieving educational excellence.* San Francisco: Jossey-Bass.

Astin, A. W. (1988). Student involvement: A developmental theory for higher education. *Journal of College Student Personnel, 25*(4), 297–308.

Astin, A. W. (1991). *Assessment for excellence: The philosophy and practice of assessment and evaluation in higher education.* New York: Macmillan.

Astin, A. W. (1993). *What matters in college: Four critical years revisited.* San Francisco: Jossey-Bass.

Astin, A. W., Fuller, B., & Green, K. C. (1978). *Admitting and assisting students after Bakke.* New Directions for Higher Education, No. 23. San Francisco: Jossey-Bass.

Bennett, C., & Okinaka, A. M. (1990, March). Factors related to persistence among Asian, Black, Hispanic, and White undergraduates at a predominantly White university: Comparison between first and fourth year cohorts. *Urban Review, 22*(1), 33–60 .

Blalock, J. M. (1967). *Toward a theory of minority-group relations.* New York: Wiley.

Braddock, J. H. (1980). The perpetuation of segregation across levels of education: A behavioral assessment of the contact hypothesis. *Sociology of Education, 53,* 178–186.

Braddock, J. H. (1985). School desegregation and Black assimilation. *Journal of Social Issues, 41*(3), 9–22.

Braddock, J. H., Crain, R. L., & McPartland, J. M. (1984, December). A long-term view of school desegregation: Some recent studies of graduates as adults. *Phi Delta Kappan,* 259–264.

Braddock, J. H., & Dawkins, M. (1981). Predicting achievement in higher education. *Journal of Negro Education, 50,* 319–327.

Braddock, J. H., & McPartland, J. M. (1982). Assessing school desegregation effects: New directions in research. In A. C. Kerckhoff (Ed.) & R. C. Corwin (Guest Ed.), *Research in Sociology of Education and Socialization, Vol. 3* (pp. 259–292) . Greenwich, CT: JAI.

Braddock, J. H., & McPartland, J. M. (1989). Social-psychological processes that perpetuate racial segregation: The relationship between school and employment desegregation. *Journal of Black Studies, 19*(3), 267–289.

Bunzel, J. H. (1992). *Race Relations on Campus: Stanford Students Speak.* Stanford, CA: Stanford Alumni Association.

Cabrera, A. F., & Nora, A. (1994). College student perceptions of prejudice and discrimination and their feelings of alienation: A construct validation approach. *Review of Education/Pedagogy/Cultural Studies, 16*(3-4), 387–409.

Carter, D. J., & Wilson, R. (1993). *Minorities in higher education: Eleventh annual status report.* Washington DC: American Council on Education.

Chang, M. J. (1996). *Racial diversity in higher education: Does a racially mixed student population affect educational outcomes?* Unpublished doctoral dissertation, University of California, Los Angeles.

Chickering, A. W. (1969). *Education and identity.* San Francisco: Jossey-Bass.

Collins, P. H. (1986). Learning from the outsider within: The sociological significance of Black feminist thought. *Social Problems, 33*(6), 514–532.

Davis, E. B. (1993). Desegregation in higher education: Twenty-five years of controversy from Geier to Ayers. *Journal of Law and Education, 22*(4), 519–524.

Davis, R. (1991). Social support networks and undergraduate student academic-success-related outcomes: A comparison of Black students on Black and White campuses. In W. R. Allen, E. G. Epps, & N. Z. Haniff (Eds.), *College in Black and White: African American students in predominantly White and in historically Black public universities* (pp. 143–57). Albany: SUNY Press.

Durán, R. P. (1983). *Hispanics' education and background: Predictors of college achievement.* New York: College Board Publications.

Duster, T. (1993). The diversity of California at Berkeley: An emerging reformulation of "competence" in an increasingly multicultural world. In B. W. Thompson and Sangeeta Tyagi (Eds.), *Beyond a dream deferred: Multicultural education and the politics of excellence* (pp. 231–255). Minneapolis, MN: University of Minnesota Press.

El-Khawas, E. (1989). *Campus Trends, 1989.* Higher Education Panel Reports, No. 78. Washington, DC: American Council on Education.

Farrell, W. C., Jr., & Jones, C. K. (1988). Recent racial incidents in higher education: A preliminary perspective. *Urban Review, 20*(3), 211–233.

Feldman, K. A., & Newcomb, T. M. (1969). *The impact of college on students, Vol. 1.* San Francisco: Jossey-Bass.

Frierson, H. T. (1991). Intervention can make a difference: The impact on standardized tests and classroom performance. In W. R. Allen, E. G. Epps, & N. Z. Haniff (Eds.), *College in Black and White: African American Students in predominantly White and in historically Black public universities* (pp. 225–238). Albany: SUNY Press.

Gilliard, M. D. (1996). *Racial climate and institutional support factors affecting success in predominantly White Institutions: An examination of African American and White student experiences.* Unpublished doctoral dissertation, University of Michigan.

Globetti, E. C., Globetti, G., Brown, C. L., & Smith, R. E. (1993). Social interaction and multiculturalism. *NASPA Journal, 30*(3), 209–218.

Green, K. C. (1982). *The impact of neighborhood and secondary school integration on educational achievement and occupational attainment of college-bound Blacks.* Unpublished doctoral dissertation, University of California, Los Angeles.

Guanier, L. (1997, August 7). The real bias in higher education. *Black Issues in Higher Education,* p. 60.

Horowitz, H. L. (1987). *Campus life: Undergraduate cultures from the end of the eighteenth century to the present.* Chicago: University of Chicago.

Huffman, T. E. (1991). The experiences, perceptions, and consequences of campus racism among Northern Plains Indians. *Journal of American Indian Education, 30*(2), 25–34.

Hurtado, S. (1990). *Campus racial climates and educational outcomes.* Unpublished doctoral dissertation, University of California, Los Angeles. Ann Arbor: University Microfilms International, No. 9111328.

Hurtado, S. (1992). The campus racial climate: Contexts for conflict. *The Journal of Higher Education, 63*(5), 539–569.

Hurtado, S. (1994). The institutional climate for talented Latino students. *Research in Higher Education, 35*(1), 21–41.

Hurtado, S., Carter, D. F., & Spuler, A. (1996). Latino student transition to college. *Research in Higher Education, 37*(2), 135–157.

Hurtado, S., Dey, E., & Treviño, J. (1994). *Exclusion or self-segregation? Interaction across racial/ethnic groups on college campuses.* Paper presented at the American Educational Research Association conference, New Orleans.

Hurtado, S., Milem, J. F., Clayton-Pedersen, A. R., & Allen, W. R. (in press). *Enacting diverse learning environments: Improving the campus climate for racial/ethnic diversity.* ASHE/ERIC Higher Education Report Series.

Jackson, K. W., & Swan, L. A. (1991). Institutional and individual factors affecting Black undergraduate student performance: Campus race and student gender. In W. R. Allen, E. G. Epps, & N. Z. Haniff (Eds.), *College in Black and White: African American students in predominantly White and in historically Black public universities* (pp. 127–141). Albany: SUNY Press.

Kanter, R. M. (1977). Some effects of proportions on group life: Skewed sex ratios and responses to token women. *American Journal of Sociology, 82,* 965–989.

Kuh, G., Schuh, J. S., Whitt, E. J., Andreas, R. E., Lyons, J. W., Strange, C. C., Krehbiel, L. E., & MacKay, K. A. (1991). *Involving colleges: Successful approaches to fostering student learning and personal development outside the classroom.* San Francisco: Jossey-Bass.

Lin, R., LaCounte, D., and Eder, J. (1988). A study of Native American students in a predominantly White college. *Journal of American Indian Education, 27*(3), 8–15.

Loo, C. M., & Rolison, G. (1986). Alienation of ethnic minority students at a predominately White university. *Journal of Higher Education, 57*, 58–77.

Milam, J. H. (1989). The presence of paradigms in the core higher education journal literature. *Research in Higher Education, 32*(6), 651–668.

Milem, J. F. (1992). *The impact of college on students' racial attitudes and levels of racial awareness.* Unpublished doctoral dissertation, UCLA. Ann Arbor: University Microforms International (UMI), No. 9301968.

Milem, J. F. (1994). College, students, and racial understanding. *Thought and Action, 9*(2), 51–92.

Milem, J. F. (1998). Attitude change in college students: Examining the effect of college peer groups and faculty normative groups. *Journal of Higher Education, 69*(2), 117–140.

Mitchell, S. L., & Dell, D. M. (1992). The relationship between Black students' racial identity attitude and participation in campus organizations. *Journal of College Student Development, 33*, 39–43.

Muñoz, C. (1989). *Youth, identity, and power in the Chicano movement.* New York: Verso.

Nealy, C. (1996). *The musing of an at-risk student.* Paper presented at the annual meeting of the American Educational Research Association, New York.

Nettles, M. (Ed.). (1988). *Toward Black undergraduate student equality in American higher education.* Westport, CT: Greenwood Press.

Nora, A., & Cabrera, A. F. (1996). The role of perceptions of prejudice and discrimination on the adjustment of minority students to college. *Journal of Higher Education, 67*(2), 119–148.

Olivas, M. A. (1986). The retreat from access. *Academe, 72*(6), 16–18.

Orfield, G. (1992). Money, equity, and college access. *Harvard Educational Review, 62*(3), 337–372.

Palmer, P. J. (1987). Community, conflict, and ways of knowing. *Change, 19*(5), 20–25.

Pascarella, E. T., & Terenzini, P. T. (1991). *How college affects students: Findings and insights from twenty years of research.* San Francisco: Jossey-Bass.

Pascarella, E. T., Smart, J. C., Ethington, C., & Nettles, M. (1987). The influence of college on self-concept: A consideration of race and gender differences. *American Educational Research Journal, 24*, 49–77.

Pascarella, E. T., Whitt, E. J., Nora, A., Edison, M., Hagedorn, L. S., & Terenzini, P. T. (1996). What have we learned from the first year of the national study of student learning? *Journal of College Student Development, 37*(2), 182–192.

Peterson, M. W., Blackburn, R. T., Gamson, Z. F., Arce, C. H., Davenport, R. W., & Mingle, J. R. (1978). *Black students on White campuses: The impacts of increased Blacks enrollments.* Ann Arbor: Institute for Social Research, University of Michigan.

Prillerman, S. L., Myers, H. F., & Smedley, B. D. (1989). Stress, well-being, and academic achievement in college. In G. L. Berry and J. K. Asamen (Eds.), *Black students: Psychosocial issues and academic achievement* (pp. 198–217). Newbury Park, CA: Sage.

Richardson, R., & Skinner, E. (1991). *Achieving diversity.* Washington, DC: ACE/Macmillan.

Scott, R. R., & McPartland, J. M. (1982). Desegregation as national policy: Correlates of racial attitudes. *American Educational Research Journal, 19*(3), 397–414.

Sedlacek, W. (1987). Black students on White campuses: 20 years of research. *Journal of College Student Personnel, 28*(6) 484–95.

Slavin, R. E. (1985). Cooperative learning: Applying contact theory in desegregated schools. *Journal of Social Issues, 41*(1), 45–62.

Smedley, B. D., Myers, H. F., & Harrell, S. P. (1993). Minority-status stresses and the college adjustment of ethnic minority freshmen. *Journal of Higher Education, 64*(4), 434–452.

Southern Education Foundation. (1995). *Redeeming the American promise: Report of the panel on educational opportunity and postsecondary desegregation.* Atlanta: Southern Education Foundation.

St. John, E. P. (1991a). The impact of student financial aid: A review of recent research. *Journal of Student Financial Aid, 21*(1), 18–32.

St. John, E. P. (1991b). What really influences minority attendance? Sequential analyses of the high school and beyond sophomore cohort. *Research in Higher Education, 32*(2), 141–158.

St. John, E. P., & Masten, C. L. (1990). Return on investment in student financial aid: An assessment for the high school class of 1972. *Journal of Student Financial Aid, 20*(3), 4–23.

Stampen, J. O. (1985). *Student aid and public higher education: Recent changes.* Washington, DC: American Association of State Colleges and Universities.

Stampen, J. O., & Fenske, R. H. (1988). The impact of financial aid on ethnic minorities. *Review of Higher Education, 11*(4), 337–353.

Steele, C. M. (1992, April). Race and the schooling of Black Americans. *Atlantic Monthly,* 68–78.

Stewart, J. B. (1991). Planning for cultural diversity: A case study. In H. E. Cheatham (Ed.), *Cultural Pluralism on Campus* (pp. 161–191). N.p.: American College Personnel Association.

Thelin, J. (1985). Beyond the background music: Historical research on admissions and access in higher education. In John C. Smart (Ed.), *Higher Education Handbook of Theory and Research, Vol. 1.* (pp. 349–380). New York: Agathon.

Tierney, W. G. (1997). The parameters of affirmative action: Equity and excellence in the academy. *Review of Educational Research, 67*(2), 165–196.

Tinto, V. (1987). *Leaving college: Rethinking the causes and cures of student attrition* (1st ed.) Chicago: University of Chicago Press.

Tinto, V. (1993). *Leaving college: Rethinking the causes and cures of student attrition* (2nd ed.). Chicago: University of Chicago Press.

Tracey, T. J., & Sedlacek, W. E. (1985). The relationship of noncognitive variables to academic success: A longitudinal comparison by race. *Journal of College Student Personnel, 26,* 405–410.

Treviño, J. G. (1992). *Participating in ethnic/racial student organizations.* Unpublished doctoral dissertation, University of California, Los Angeles.

Turner, C., & Thompson, J. (1993). Socializing women doctoral students: Minority and majority experiences. *The Review of Higher Education, 16,* 355–370.

Williams, John B., III. (1988). Title VI regulation of higher education. In J. B. Williams (Ed.), *Desegregating America's Colleges and Universities* (pp. 3–53). New York: Teachers College Press.

Willie, C., Grady, M., & Hope, R. (1991). *African-Americans and the doctoral experience: Implications for policy.* New York: Teachers College.

Zúñiga, X., & Nagda, B. A. (1992). Dialogue groups: An innovative approach to multicultural learning. In David Schoem (Ed.), *Multicultural teaching at the university* (pp. 233–248). New York: Praeger.

Sylvia Hurtado, Associate Professor at the University of Michigan's Center for the Study of Higher and Postsecondary Education, has a PhD in higher education from UCLA, and currently researches diverse college students and the impact of campus racial climates on their transition and development in college. *Jeffrey F. Milem,* Assistant Professor at Peabody College of Vanderbilt University, received his PhD in higher education from UCLA, and currently focuses in his research on the socialization processes of college students and faculty and the ways in which issues of race, class, and gender affect the experience of students and faculty members in institutions of higher education. *Alma R. Clayton-Pedersen,* Associate Dean for Undergraduate Academic Affairs and Assistant Professor of the Practice of Education and Public Policy at Peabody College of Vanderbilt University, received her PhD in Education and Human Development with an emphasis on policy development and program evaluation from Vanderbilt University. She studies the process of coordination between two or more organizational entities, particularly human service organizations. *Walter Allen,* Professor of Sociology at the University of California, Los Angeles, received his PhD from the University of Chicago. His research and teaching concentrate on family patterns, socialization, and personality development, race and ethnic relations, social inequality, and higher education.

An Integrative Model of Organizational Trust

Roger C. Mayer

James H. Davis
University of Notre Dame

F. David Schoorman
Purdue University

Scholars in various disciplines have considered the causes, nature, and effects of trust. Prior approaches to studying trust are considered, including characteristics of the trustor, the trustee, and the role of risk. A definition of trust and a model of its antecedents and outcomes are presented, which integrate research from multiple disciplines and differentiate trust from similar constructs. Several research propositions based on the model are presented.

The topic of trust is generating increased interest in organizational studies. Gambetta (1988) noted that "scholars tend to mention [trust] in passing, to allude to it as a fundamental ingredient or lubricant, an unavoidable dimension of social interaction, only to move on to deal with less intractable matters" (unnumbered foreword). The importance of trust has been cited in such areas as communication (Giffin, 1967), leadership (Atwater, 1988), management by objectives (Scott, D., 1980), negotiation (Bazerman, 1984), game theory (Milgrom & Roberts, 1992), performance appraisal (Cummings, 1983), labor-management relations (Taylor, 1989), and implementation of self-managed work teams (Lawler, 1992).

Although a great deal of interest in trust has been expressed by scholars, its study in organizations has remained problematic for several reasons: problems with the definition of trust itself; lack of clarity in the relationship between risk and trust; confusion between trust and its antecedents and outcomes; lack of specificity of trust referents leading to confusion in levels of analysis; and a failure to consider both the trusting party and the party to be trusted. The purpose of this article is to illuminate and resolve these problems in the presentation of a model of trust of one individual for another. Through this model we propose that this level of trust and the level of perceived risk in the situation will lead to risk taking in the relationship.

Need for Trust

Working together often involves interdependence, and people must therefore depend on others in various ways to accomplish their personal and organizational goals. Several theories have emerged that describe mechanisms for minimizing the risk inherent in working relationships. These theories are designed to regulate, to enforce, and/or to encourage compliance to avoid the consequences of broken trust. In order to avoid self-serving behaviors as well as potential litigation, many firms utilize control mechanisms and contracts, and they alter their decision-making processes, internal processes, reward systems, and structures (Jensen & Meckling, 1976; Meyer, 1983; Sitkin & Bies, 1994; Williamson, 1975). Legalistic remedies have been described as weak, impersonal substitutes for trust (Sitkin & Roth, 1993), which may bring organizational legitimacy, yet often are ineffective (Argyris, 1994; Donaldson & Davis, 1991; Granovetter, 1985; Sitkin & Roth, 1993).

Current trends in both workforce composition and the organization of the workplace in the United States suggest that the importance of trust is likely to increase during the coming years. One important trend in workforce composition is the increase in diversity. Jamieson and O'Mara (1991) projected that the minority share of the workforce will grow from 17 percent in the late 1980s to over 25 percent by the year 2000. Jackson and Alvarez (1992) pointed out that increases in workforce diversity necessitate that people with very different backgrounds come into contact and deal closely with one another. A diverse workforce is less able to rely on interpersonal similarity and common background and experience to contribute to mutual attraction and enhance the willingness to work together (Berscheid & Walster, 1978; Newcomb, 1956). In this context, the development of mutual trust provides one mechanism for enabling employees to work together more effectively.

Another trend related to changes in the organization of work also will lead to an increased interest in the study of trust. Lawler (1992) cited continuing changes in the workplace in the direction of more participative management styles and the implementation of work teams. A recent survey indicates that 27 percent of American companies are implementing self-directed work teams in some part of the organization (Wellins, Byham, & Wilson, 1991). The emergence of self-directed teams and a reliance on empowered workers greatly increase the importance of the concept of trust (Golembiewski & McConkie, 1975; Larson & LaFasto, 1989) as control mechanisms are reduced or removed and interaction increases.

The trends just cited suggest that the development of a model of trust in organizations is both timely and practical. In the use of self-directed teams, trust must take the place of supervision because direct observation of employees becomes impractical. Further, a clear understanding of trust and its causes can facilitate cohesion and collaboration between people by building trust through means other than interpersonal similarity. In spite of the growing importance of trust, a number of institutions that measure trust have witnessed diminishing trust among employees (Farnham, 1989).

One of the difficulties that has hindered previous research on trust has been a lack of clear differentiation among factors that contribute to trust, trust itself, and outcomes of trust (Cook & Wall, 1980; Kee & Knox, 1970). Without this clear distinction, the difference between trust and similar constructs is blurred. For example, many researchers have agreed with Deutsch (1958) that risk, or having something invested, is requisite to trust. The need for trust only arises in a risky situation. Although numerous authors have recognized the importance of risk to understanding trust (Coleman, 1990; Giffin, 1967; Good, 1988; Lewis & Weigert, 1985; Luhmann, 1988; March & Shapira, 1987; Riker, 1974; Schlenker, Helm, & Tedeschi, 1973), no consensus on its relationship with trust exists. It is unclear whether risk is an antecedent to trust, is trust, or is an outcome of trust. This key issue of how risk fits with trust must be resolved, and it is dealt with later in this article. The model developed in this article complements the risk literature by clarifying the role of interpersonal trust in risk taking. A parsimonious model (James, Mulaik, & Brett, 1982; Runkel & McGrath, 1972) with a manageable number of factors should provide a solid foundation for the empirical study of trust for another party.

Each of the essential trust issues that have just been described will be explored as a model of dyadic trust is developed. Although there is a growing body of literature in social psychology that examines trust in dating and other such relationships (e.g., Larzelere & Huston, 1980), the nature and bases of such relationships may be different from those in organizations. Thus, the model developed here is designed to focus on trust in an organizational setting involving two specific parties: a trusting party (trustor) and a party to be trusted (trustee) (Driscoll, 1978; Scott, C. L., 1980). The model explicitly encompasses factors about both the trustor and the trustee, which previous models have neglected. This relationship-specific boundary condition of our approach is important, because a number of authors have dealt with trust for generalized others (e.g., Rotter, 1967) and trust as a social phenomenon (e.g., Lewis & Weigert, 1985). Even though such approaches help provide a general sense of the considerations involved in trust, they do not clarify the relationship between two specific individuals and the reasons why a trustor would trust a trustee. Further, the failure to clearly specify the trustor and the trustee encourages the tendency to change referents and even levels of analysis, which obfuscates the nature of the trust relationship.

In the following sections, the definition of trust developed from our research is presented, and it is differentiated from similar constructs. Next, characteristics of both the trustor and the trustee, which affect the amount of trust the trustor has for the trustee, are considered. Following that, the relationship of trust and risk is considered. Finally, the effects of context as well as the long-term development of trust are considered.

Definition of Trust

Johnson-George and Swap (1982: 1306) asserted that "willingness to take risks may be one of the few characteristics common to all trust situations." Kee and Knox (1970) argued that to appropriately study trust there must be some meaningful incentives at stake and that the trustor must be cognizant of the risk involved. The definition of *trust* proposed in this research is *the willingness of a party to be vulnerable to the actions of another party based on the expectation that the other will perform a particular action important to the trustor, irrespective of the ability to monitor or control that other party.* This definition of trust is applicable to a relationship with another identifiable party who is perceived to act and react with volition toward the trustor. This definition parallels that of Gambetta (1988), with the critical addition of vulnerability. Being vulnerable (Boss, 1978; Zand, 1972) implies that there is something of importance to be lost. Making oneself vulnerable is taking risk. Trust is not taking risk *per se*, but rather it is a *willingness* to take risk. This distinction will be further explored in a later section.

Several terms have been used synonymously with trust, and this has obfuscated the nature of trust. Among these are *cooperation*, *confidence*, and *predictability*. The sections that follow differentiate trust from these constructs.

Cooperation

One conceptual difficulty with studying trust is that it has often been confused with cooperation (Bateson, 1988). For instance, Gambetta (1988: 217) asserted that trusting someone means "the probability that he will perform an action that is beneficial or at least not detrimental to us is high enough for us to consider engaging in some form of cooperation with him." The distinction of trust from cooperation is unclear.

Although trust can frequently lead to cooperative behavior, trust is not a necessary condition for cooperation to occur, because *cooperation does not necessarily put a party at risk*. An employee could cooperate with and, indeed, even appear to act like he or she trusts another employee who he or she does not trust. However, the reason for the cooperation may be due to a powerful manager who is clearly expected to punish the other employee for any act that damages the focal employee's interests. The focal employee may cooperate with and appear to trust the other employee, but his or her actions are due to a lack of perceived risk. Such means as control mechanisms and lack of available alternatives may lead a party to cooperate, even in the absence of trust. As Gambetta stated, "As the high incidence of paranoid behaviour among dictators suggests, coercion can be *self-defeating*, for while it may enforce 'cooperation' in specific acts, it also increases the probability of treacherous ones: betrayal, defection, and the classic stab in the back" (1988: 220).

Kee and Knox (1970) also concluded that there were a number of reasons why individuals may be observed to act in cooperative or competitive fashions that are not reflective of the level of trust in the relationship. For example, a person may not be able to avoid a situation structured like the prisoner's dilemma. His or her behavior may appear to be trusting, but it is based on other motives or rationales.

Even though trust and cooperation have at times been treated as synonymous, it is important to distinguish between them. You can cooperate with someone who you don't really trust. If there are external control mechanisms that will punish the trustee for deceitful behavior, if the issue at hand doesn't involve vulnerability to the trustor over issues that matter, or if it's clear that the trustee's motives will lead him or her to behave in a way that coincides with the trustor's desires, then there can be cooperation without trust. In each of these cases, vulnerability is minimal or absent.

Confidence

The relationship between confidence and trust is amorphous in the literature on trust. For example, Deutsch (1960) considered the reasons why one person would trust another person to produce some beneficial events. The "individual must have *confidence* that the other individual has the ability and intention to produce it" (Deutsch, 1960: 125). Cook and Wall (1980: 39) defined *trust* as "the extent to which one is willing to ascribe good intentions to and have *confidence* in the words and actions of other people." A number of other authors have not clearly distinguished between the two (e.g., Coleman, 1990; Frost, Stimpson, & Maughan, 1978; Jones, James, & Bruni, 1975).

Luhmann (1988) proposed a distinction that helps to differentiate trust from confidence. He asserted that both concepts refer to expectations that may lead to disappointment. Luhmann argued that trust differs from confidence because it requires a previous engagement on a person's part, recognizing and accepting that risk exists. Although Luhmann suggested that both confidence and trust may become routine, the distinction "depends on perception and attribution. If you do not consider alternatives (every morning you leave the house without a weapon!), you are in a situation of confidence. If you choose one action in preference to others in spite of the possibility of being disappointed by the action of others, you define the situation as one of trust" (1988: 102).

Luhmann's differentiation between trust and confidence recognizes that in the former risk must be recognized and assumed, and such is not the case with confidence. The trustor's explicit recognition of risk within our model precludes the conceptual ambiguity present in the research just cited.

Predictability

There is clearly a relationship between predictability and trust, but, again, the association is ambiguous. Both prediction and trust are means of uncertainty reduction (Lewis & Weigert, 1985). However, much of the literature tends to equate predictability with trust. For example, Gabarro (1978: 294) cited several definitions of trust, including "the extent to which one person can expect predictability in the other's behavior in terms of what is 'normally' expected of a person acting in good faith." Several other theorists have defined trust in ways that also appear to overlap substantially with predictability (Dasgupta, 1988; Gambetta, 1988; Good, 1988; Rotter, 1967).

To be meaningful, trust must go beyond predictability (Deutsch, 1958). To equate the two is to suggest that a party who can be expected to consistently ignore the needs of others and act in a self-interested fashion is therefore trusted, because the party is predictable. What is missing from such an approach is the willingness to take a risk in the relationship and to be vulnerable. One can believe such a trustee to be predictable in a situation in which the trustee influences resource distribution between the trustee and the trustor but also be unwilling to be vulnerable to that trustee.

Another party's predictability is insufficient to make a person willing to take a risk. If a person's superior always "shoots the messenger" when bad news is delivered, the superior is predictable. However, this predictability will not increase the likelihood that the individual will take a risk and deliver bad news. On the contrary, predictability can reduce the likelihood that the individual will trust and therefore take actions that allow vulnerability to the superior.

Predictability might best be thought of as influencing cooperation. If one expects that a party will predictably behave positively, one will be disposed to cooperate with the party. However, the reason for that predictability may be external to the party, such as strong control mechanisms (Friedland, 1990). Without those mechanisms, a person may be unwilling to be vulnerable to the party. Thus, predictability is insufficient to trust.

The previous section dealt with the nature of trust itself, differentiating it from similar constructs. The following sections of this paper deal first with factors concerning the trustor and then the trustee that lead to trust. These components of the model can be seen in Figure 1.

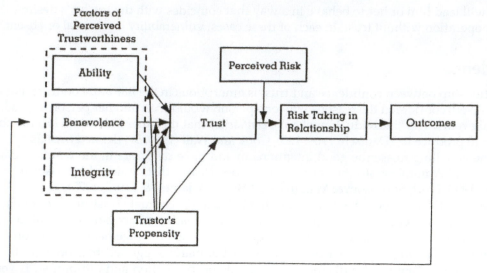

Figure 1   Proposed model of trust.

Characteristics of the Trustor

One factor that will affect the trust one party has for another involves traits of the trustor. Some parties are more likely to trust than are others. As discussed in this section, several authors have considered trust from the perspective of a person's general willingness to trust others.

Among the early trust theorists was Rotter (1967: 651), who defined *interpersonal trust* "as an expectancy held by an individual or a group that the word, promise, verbal or written statement of another individual or group can be relied upon." Although his definition appears to suggest the author is speaking of trust for a specific referent, Rotter's widely used measure focuses on a generalized trust of others—something akin to a personality trait that a person would presumably carry from one situation to another. For example, typical items in his scale are "In dealing with strangers one is better off to be cautious until they have provided evidence that they are trustworthy" and "Parents usually can be relied upon to keep their promises."

Several other authors have discussed trust in similar ways. For example. Dasgupta's treatment of trust includes generalized expectations of others; for example, "Can I trust *people* to come to my rescue if I am about to drown?" (1988: 53; emphasis added). Similarly, Farris, Senner, and Butterfield (1973: 145) defined trust as "a personality trait of people interacting with peripheral environment of an organization." In this approach trust is viewed as a trait that leads to a generalized expectation about the trustworthiness of others. In the proposed model this trait is referred to as the *propensity to trust*.

Propensity to trust is proposed to be a stable within-party factor that will affect the likelihood the party will trust. People differ in their inherent propensity to trust. Propensity might be thought of as the *general willingness to trust others*. Propensity will influence how much trust one has for a trustee prior to data on that particular party being available. People with different developmental experiences, personality types, and cultural backgrounds vary in their propensity to trust (e.g., Hofstede, 1980). An example of an extreme case of this is what is commonly called blind trust. Some individuals can be observed to repeatedly trust in situations that most people would agree do not warrant trust. Conversely, others are unwilling to trust in most situations, regardless of circumstances that would support doing so.

Some evidence exists that this dispositional approach is worth pursuing. For example, using Rotter's (1967) measure, Conlon and Mayer (1994) found the willingness to trust others was significantly related to the behavior and performance of persons working in an agency simulation. Other researchers also have found this dispositional trust factor to be related to behaviors of interest in organizational research (e.g., Moore, Shaffer, Pollak, & Taylor-Lemcke, 1987; Sabatelli, Buck, & Dreyer,

1983). Propensity should contribute to the explanation of variance in trust if used as a part of a more complete set of variables.

Propensity to trust is similar to Sitkin and Pablo's (1992) definition of propensity in their model of the determinants of risk behavior. They define *risk propensity* as "the tendency of a decision maker either to take or avoid risks" (1992:12). However, our approach differs in that propensity to trust others is viewed as a trait that is stable across situations, whereas according to Sitkin and Pablo's approach, risk propensity is more situation specific, affected both by personality characteristics (i.e., risk preference) and situational factors (i.e., inertia and outcome history).

> Proposition 1. The higher the trustor's propensity to trust, the higher the trust far a trustee prior to availability of information about the trustee.

Even though an understanding of trust necessitates consideration of the trust propensity of the trustor, a given trustor has varied levels of trust for various trustees. Thus, propensity is by itself insufficient. To address this variance, in the next section we examine the characteristics of the trustee.

Characteristics of the Trustee: The Concept of Trustworthiness

One approach to understanding why a given party will have a greater or lesser amount of trust for another party is to consider attributes of the trustee. Ring and Van de Ven (1992) argued that because of the risk in transactions, managers must concern themselves with the trustworthiness of the other party. A number of authors have considered why a party will be judged as trustworthy.

Some of the earliest research on characteristics of the trustee was conducted by Hovland, Janis, and Kelley (1953) in the famous Yale studies on communication and attitude change. According to these researchers, credibility was affected by two factors: expertise and trustworthiness. Trustworthiness was assessed as the motivation (or lack thereof) to lie. For example, if the trustee had something to gain by lying, he or she would be seen as less trustworthy.

In more recent work, Good (1988) suggested that trust is based on expectations of how another person will behave, based on that person's current and previous implicit and explicit claims. Similarly, Lieberman (1981) stated that trust in fiduciary relationships is based on a belief in the professional's competence and integrity. Examination of the items in Johnson-George and Swap's (1982) measure of trust reveals that they reflect inferences about the trustee.

All of these authors have suggested that characteristics and actions of the trustee will lead that person to be more or less trusted. These characteristics are important if researchers are to understand why some parties are more trusted than others. In the remainder of this section, three characteristics of the trustee that determine trustworthiness are examined. Although they are not trust per se, these variables help build the foundation for the development of trust.

The Factors of Trustworthiness

Conditions that lead to trust have been considered repeatedly in the literature. Some authors identify a single trustee characteristic that is responsible for trust (e.g., Strickland, 1958), whereas other authors delineate as many as 10 characteristics (e.g., Butler, 1991). A review of factors that lead to trust is summarized in Table 1. Even though a number of factors have been proposed, three characteristics of a trustee appear often in the literature: ability, benevolence, and integrity. As a set, these three appear to explain a major portion of trustworthiness.[1] Each contributes a unique perceptual perspective from which to consider the trustee, while the set provides a solid and parsimonious foundation for the empirical study of trust for another party.

Ability

Ability is that group of skills, competencies, and characteristics that enable a party to have influence within some specific domain. The domain of the ability is specific because the trustee may be highly competent in some technical area, affording that person trust on tasks related to that area. However,

TABLE 1

Trust Antecedents

Authors	Antecedent Factors
Boyle & Bonacich (1970)	Past interactions, index of caution based on prisoners' dilemma outcomes
Butler (1991)	Availability, competence, consistency, discreetness, fairness, integrity, loyalty, openness, promise fulfillment, receptivity
Cook & Wall (1980)	Trustworthy intentions, ability
Dasgupta (1988)	Credible threat of punishment, credibility of promises
Deutsch (1960)	Ability, intention to produce
Farris, Senner & Butterfield (1973)	Openness, ownership of feelings, experimentation with new behavior, group norms
Frost, Stimpson, & Maugham (1978)	Dependence on trustee, altruism
Gabarro (1978)	Openness, previous outcomes
Giffin (1967)	Expertness, reliability as information source, intentions, dynamism, personal attraction, reputation
Good (1968)	Ability, intention, trustees' claims about how (they) will behave
Hart, Capps, Cangemi & Caillouet (1986)	Openness/congruity, shared values, autonomy/feedback
Hovland, Jamis & Keiley (1953)	Expertise, motivation to lie
Johnson-George & Swap (1982)	Reliability
Jones, James, & Bruni (1975)	Ability, behavior is relevant to the individual's needs and desires
Kee & Knox (1970)	Competence, motives
Larzelere & Huston (1980)	Benevolence, honesty
Liberman (1981)	Competence, integrity
Mishra (In press)	Competence, openness, caring, reliability
Ring & Van de Ven (1992)	Moral integrity, goodwill
Rosen & Jerdee (1977)	Judgment or competence, group goals
Sitkin & Roth (1993)	Ability, value congruence
Solomon (1960)	Benevolence
Strickland (1958)	Benevolence

the trustee may have little aptitude, training, or experience in another area, for instance, in interpersonal communication. Although such an individual may be trusted to do analytic tasks related to his or her technical area, the individual may not be trusted to initiate contact with an important customer. Thus, trust is domain specific (Zand, 1972).

A number of theorists have discussed similar constructs as affecting trust, using several synonyms. Cook and Wall (1980), Deutsch (1960), Jones, James, and Brunt (1975), and Sitkin and Roth (1993) all considered *ability* an essential element of trust. Others (e.g., Butler, 1991; Butler & Cantrell, 1984; Kee & Knox, 1970; Lieberman, 1981; Mishra, In press; Rosen & Jerdee, 1977) used the word *competence* to define a similar construct. In the Yale studies described previously, *perceived expertise* was identified as a critical characteristic of the trustee. Similarly, Giffin (1967) suggested expertness as a factor that leads to trust. Finally, Gabarro (1978) identified nine bases of trust, including functional/specific competence, interpersonal competence, business sense, and judgment. All of these are similar to *ability* in the current conceptualization. Whereas such terms as *expertise* and *competence* connote a set of skills applicable to a single, fixed domain (e.g., Gabarro's interpersonal competence), *ability* highlights the task- and situation-specific nature of the construct in the current model.

Benevolence

Benevolence is the extent to which a trustee is believed to want to do good *to the trustor*, aside from an egocentric profit motive. Benevolence suggests that the trustee has some specific attachment to the trustor. An example of this attachment is the relationship between a mentor (trustee) and a protégé (trustor). The mentor wants to help the protégé, even though the mentor is not required to be helpful, and there is no extrinsic reward for the mentor. Benevolence is the perception of a positive orientation of the trustee toward the trustor.

A number of researchers have included characteristics similar to benevolence as a basis for trust. Hovland and colleagues (1953) described trustworthiness in terms of the trustee's motivation to lie. This idea is clearly consistent with the view that perceived benevolence plays an important role in the assessment of trustworthiness, in that high benevolence in a relationship would be inversely related to motivation to lie. Several authors have used the term *benevolence* in their analyses of trust, focusing on the specific relationship with the trustor (Larzelere & Huston, 1980; Solomon, 1960; Strickland, 1958). Others have considered intentions or motives as important to trust (e.g., Cook & Wall, 1980; Deutsch, 1960; Giffin, 1967; Kee & Knox, 1970; Mishra, In press). Although these authors reflect a belief that the trustee's orientation toward the trustor is important, the terms *intentions* and *motives* can include wider implications than the orientation toward the trustor (e.g., the trustee's profit motives). Benevolence connotes a personal orientation that is integral to the proposed model. Also, in a similar vein, Frost, Stimpson, and Maughan (1978) suggested that altruism contributes to the level of trust. Butler and Cantrell (1984) identified loyalty among their determinants of dyadic trust, Jones, James, and Bruni (1975) suggested that confidence and trust in a leader are influenced in part by the extent to which the leader's behavior is relevant to the individual's needs and desires. Rosen and Jerdee (1977) considered the likelihood that the trustee would put organizational goals ahead of individual goals. Thus, all of these researchers used some construct similar to benevolence, as defined in our model.

Integrity

The relationship between integrity and trust involves the trustor's perception that the trustee adheres to a set of principles that the trustor finds acceptable. McFall (1987) illustrated why both the adherence to and acceptability of the principles are important. She suggested that following some set of principles defines *personal integrity*. However, if that set of principles is not deemed acceptable by the trustor, the trustee would not be considered to have integrity for our purposes (McFall called this *moral integrity*). The issue of acceptability precludes the argument that a party who is committed solely to the principle of *profit seeking at all costs* would be judged high in integrity (unless this principle is acceptable to the trustor). Such issues as the consistency of the party's past actions, credible communications about the trustee from other parties, belief that the trustee has a strong sense of justice, and the extent to which the party's actions are congruent with his or her words all affect the degree to which the party is judged to have integrity. Even though a case could be made that there are differentiable reasons why the integrity of a trustee could be perceived as higher or lower (e.g., lack of consistency is different from acceptability of principles), in the evaluation of trustworthiness it is the perceived level of integrity that is important rather than the reasons why the perception is formed.

Integrity or very similar constructs have been discussed as antecedent to trust by a number of theorists. Lieberman (1981) included integrity per se as an important trust factor. Sitkin and Roth's (1993: 368) approach utilizes a similar but more constrained construct of *value congruence*, which they defined as "the compatibility of an employee's beliefs and values with the organization's cultural values." Their approach compares the trustee's values with those of an organizational referent, rather than a judgment of the acceptability of the trustee's values to the trustor. Integrity and consistency were trust determinants in Butler and Cantrell's (1984) model. Likewise, Butler (1991) included consistency, integrity, and fairness as conditions of trust. Although a lack of consistency would cause one to question what values a trustee holds, being consistent is insufficient to integrity, as the trustee may consistently act in a self-serving manner. Gabarro (1978) suggested that three bases of trust were commonly mentioned by their interviewees, one of which was *character*. He contended that character includes integrity. Hart, Capps, Cangemi, and Caillouet's (1986) analysis of 24 survey items revealed three factors, one of which was openness/congruity (i.e., the integrity, fairness, and openness of management). Inclusion of integrity in the proposed model is well grounded in previous approaches to trust.

It is apparent from the previous discussion that the three factors of ability, benevolence, and integrity are common to much of the previous work on trust. Earlier models of trust antecedents either have not used the three factors together or have expanded into much larger sets of antecedents (e.g., Butler, 1991; Gabarro, 1978). These three factors appear to explain concisely the within-trustor variation in trust for others.

> Proposition 2. Trust for a trustee will be a function of the trustee's perceived ability, benevolence, and integrity and of the trustor's propensity to trust.

Interrelationship of the Three Factors

Ability, benevolence, and integrity are important to trust, and each may vary independently of the others. This statement does not imply that the three are unrelated to one another, but only that they are separable.

Consider the case of an individual and would-be mentor. Ideally, the individual would want the mentor to be able to have the maximum positive impact on the protégé's career and to help and guide the protégé in any way possible. To what extent would the protégé trust the mentor? The mentor would need to be knowledgeable about the profession, have a thorough knowledge of the company, be interpersonally and politically astute, and so on. All of these attributes would contribute to the protégé's perception that the mentor has the ability to be helpful. This perception, alone, would not assure that the mentor *would* be helpful; it would mean only that the possibility exists.

Previous positively viewed actions of the mentor in his or her relationships with others, compatibility of the mentor's statements and actions, and credible communications from others about honorable actions by the mentor would build the assessment of the mentor's integrity. However, even if the individual is deemed to have high integrity, he or she may or may not have the knowledge and capabilities to be a helpful mentor. Thus, integrity by itself will not make the individual a trusted mentor.

But what about the person whose integrity is well known and whose abilities are stellar? Would this potential mentor be trusted? Perhaps not—this individual may have no particular attachment to the focal employee. Would the focal employee trust this person enough to divulge sensitive information about mistakes or shortcomings? If the manager also were benevolent toward the employee, he or she may try to protect the employee from the possible ramifications of mistakes. A manager who is less benevolent to the focal employee may be more disposed to use the information in a way that helps the company most, even at the possible expense of the employee. However, benevolence by itself is insufficient to cause trust. A well-intentioned person who lacks ability may not know who in the organization should be made aware of what. Aside from not being helpful, the person could actually do significant harm to the employee's career. Thus, it is possible for a perceived lack of any of the three factors to undermine trust.

If ability, benevolence, and integrity were all perceived to be high, the trustee would be deemed quite trustworthy. However, trustworthiness should be thought of as a continuum, rather than the trustee being either trustworthy or not trustworthy. Each of the three factors can vary along a continuum. Although the simplest case of high trust presumes a high level of all three factors, there may be situations in which a meaningful amount of trust can develop with lesser degrees of the three. Consider the case in which a highly able manager does not demonstrate high integrity (e.g., in dealings with others) but forms an attachment to a particular employee. The manager repeatedly demonstrates strong benevolence toward the employee, providing resources even at others' expense. Will the employee trust the manager? On one hand, it can be argued that if the employee strongly believes in the benevolence of the manager, the employee has no reason to doubt how the manager will behave in the future. On the other hand, if the manager's integrity is questionable, can the employee help but wonder how long it will be until the manager betrays her or him as well? Whether or not the employee will trust the manager depends in part upon the employee's propensity to trust. In addition to propensity affecting trust when there are no data on characteristics of the trustee, propensity can enhance the effect of these factors, thereby producing a moderating effect on trust. The point is that the employee may or may not trust the manager in such a scenario. Clearly, if all three factors were high, the employee would trust, but how low can some of the three factors be before the employee would not trust the manager? In what situations is each of the three factors most sensitive or critical? These questions clearly deserve investigation.

The proposed model can explain trust (based on propensity) before any relationship between two parties has developed. As a relationship begins to develop, the trustor may be able to obtain data on the trustee's integrity through third-party sources and observation, with little direct interaction. Because there is little information about the trustee's benevolence toward the trustor, we suggest that integrity will be important to the formation of trust early in the relationship. As the relationship develops, interactions with the trustee allow the trustor to gain insights about the trustee's benevolence, and the relative impact of benevolence on trust will grow. Thus, the development of the relationship is likely to alter the relative importance of the factors of trustworthiness.

> Proposition 3. The effect of integrity on trust will be most salient early in the relationship prior to the development of meaningful benevolence data.

> Proposition 4. The effect of perceived benevolence on trust will increase over time as the relationship between the parties develops.

Each of these three factors captures some unique elements of trustworthiness. Previously we suggested that as a set, ability, benevolence, and integrity appear to explain a major portion of trustworthiness while maintaining parsimony. Each element contributes a unique perceptual perspective from which the trustor considers the trustee. If a trustee is perceived as high on all three factors, it is argued here that the trustee will be perceived as quite trustworthy.

Even though there are many conceptualizations of which factors of trustworthiness are important, ability, benevolence, and integrity appear to encompass the major issues. Using three of the most current models available, Table 2 illustrates that factors of trustworthiness from earlier models are subsumed within the perceptions of these three factors. For example, Mishra's (In press) conceptualization includes competence, openness, caring, and reliability. Competence and ability are clearly similar, whereas caring parallels benevolence. A lack of trustee reliability as Mishra conceptualizes it would clearly damage the perception of integrity in the current model. Mishra's openness is measured through questions about both the trustee's general openness with others and openness with the trustor, which could be expected to be related to either integrity or benevolence, respectively, Likewise, if a trustor perceived that a trustee were low on any one of Butler's (1991) 10 factors of trustworthiness, that perceived deficiency would also lower the perception of one of three factors in our current model. Specifically, if a trustor perceived a trustee to be deficient on any of Butler's loyalty, openness, receptivity, or availability factors, it would also lower the perception of the trustee's benevolence in the current model. Butler's factors of consistency, discreetness, fairness, integrity, and promise fulfillment are encompassed within the current conceptualization of integrity.

TABLE 2

Apparent Overlap of Recent Models

Authors	No. of Factors	Similar Factors Included			
		Propensity	Ability	Benevolence	Integrity
Butler (1991)	10	No	Competence	Loyalty openness, receptivity, availability	Consistency, discreetness, fairness, integrity, promise fulfillment
Mishra (In press)	4	No	Competence	Caring openness	Reliability, openness
Sitkin & Roth (1993)	2	No	Ability	No	Value congruence

If a trustor were concerned with a trustee's competence in Butler's model, those concerns would be reflected in the perception of ability in our model. Like the current model, Sitkin and Roth's (1993) model includes ability. Their definition of value congruence parallels the considerations encompassed in integrity. Thus, the factors of trustworthiness described in earlier, more complex models are accounted for in the current approach while gaining the advantage of parsimony (James, Mulaik, & Brett, 1982; Runkel & McGrath, 1972).

In the preceding sections, characteristics of a trustor and a trustee that lead to trust were examined. The distinction between a trustor's characteristics and trustee's characteristics is important. Perceptions of ability, benevolence, and integrity of another party leave a considerable amount of variance in trust unexplained, because they neglect between-trustor differences in propensity to trust. Likewise, understanding the propensity to trust does not include the trustworthiness of a given trustee. In sum, to understand the extent to which a person is willing to trust another person, both the trustor's propensity to trust and the trustor's perceptions of the trustee's ability, benevolence, and integrity must be discerned.

The above presentation dealt with characteristics of the trustor and trustee that lead to trust. What follows is a consideration of risk and its relationship with engaging in trusting actions.

Risk Taking in Relationship

It was argued previously that risk is an essential component of a model of trust. It is important for researchers to understand the role of risk. There is no risk taken in the *willingness* to be vulnerable (i.e., to trust), but risk is inherent in the *behavioral manifestation* of the willingness to be vulnerable. One does not need to risk anything in order to trust; however, one must take a risk in order to engage in trusting action. The fundamental difference between trust and trusting behaviors is between a "willingness" to assume risk and actually "assuming" risk. Trust is the willingness to assume risk; behavioral trust is the *assuming* of risk. This differentiation parallels Sitkin and Pablo's (1992) distinction in the risk-taking literature between the *tendency* to take risks and risk *behavior*. This critical differentiation highlights the importance of clearly distinguishing between trust and its outcomes.

Trust will lead to risk taking in a relationship, and the form of the risk taking depends on the situation. For example, a supervisor may take a risk by allowing an employee to handle an important account rather than handling it personally. The supervisor risks repercussions if the employee mishandles the account. Likewise, an employee may trust a manager to compensate for exceptional contributions that are beyond the scope of the employee's job. If the employee allows performance on some aspects of his or her formal job description to suffer in order to attend to a project that is important to the supervisor, the employee is clearly taking a risk. If the supervisor fails to account for the work on the project, the employee's performance appraisal will suffer. In both examples, the level of trust will affect the amount of risk the trustor is willing to take in the relationship. In the former case, trust will affect the extent to which the supervisor will empower the employee; in the latter case, trust will affect the extent to which the employee will engage in organizational citizenship behavior. Even though the form of the risk taking depends on the situation, in both cases the amount of trust for the other party will affect how much risk a party will take.

Thus, the outcome of trust proposed in this article is risk taking in relationship (RTR). RTR differentiates the outcomes of trust from general risk-taking behaviors because it can occur only in the context of a specific, identifiable relationship with another party. Further, RTR suggests that trust will increase the likelihood that a trustor will not only form some affective link with a trustee, but also that the trustor will allow personal vulnerability. The separation of trust from RTR is illustrated in Figure 1 by the inclusion of a box representing each construct.

Trust is not involved in all risk-taking behavior. For example, when a farmer invests time and resources into planting crops, the farmer is taking a risk that sufficient rain will fall during the critical times of the growing season so that there will be a profitable crop to harvest. Although this behavior involves risk, it does not involve trust as defined in this theory, because there is no relationship with an identifiable "other party" to which the farmer would make himself or herself vulnerable. Even though proponents of a sociological approach might argue that this is an example of trust because there is a system that produces meteorological forecasts, it is important to remember that the meteorologists do not control the weather—they merely provide data about the likelihood of various weather scenarios. Perceptions of meteorologists' accuracy would affect risk perception (Sitkin & Pablo, 1992). Thus, the farmer does not trust the weather but takes a risk on what the weather will do (Deutsch, 1958).

Assessing the risk in a situation involves consideration of the context, such as weighing the likelihood of both positive and negative outcomes that might occur (Bierman, Bonini, & Hausman, 1969; Coleman, 1990). If a decision involves the possibility of a negative outcome coupled with a positive outcome, the aggregate level of risk is different than if only the possibility of the negative outcome exists. Thus, the stakes in the situation (i.e., both the possible gains and the potential losses) will affect the interpretation of the risk involved. In an integrative review of risk behavior, Sitkin and Pablo (1992) identified a number of other factors that influence the perception of risk, such as familiarity of the domain of the problem, organizational control systems, and social influences.

It is important that we clarify what is meant by the perception of risk in this model, because it extends the risk literature in its meaning. In our model, the perception of risk involves the trustor's belief about likelihoods of gains or losses *outside of considerations that involve the relationship with the particular trustee*. Current approaches to perceived risk implicitly incorporate knowledge of the relationship with the trustee with nonrelational reasons for assessments of risk, and, therefore, they do not clarify how trust for a given trustee is related to risk behavior. For example, Sitkin and Pablo (1992: 10) defined risk as "a characteristic of decisions that is defined here as the extent to which there is uncertainty about whether potentially significant and/or disappointing outcomes of decisions will be realized." In our model of trust, the decision to which Sitkin and Pablo refer is the RTR, wherein the trustor takes action. Two categories of factors influence the assessment of the likelihood of significant and/or disappointing outcomes: the relationship with the trustee (i.e., trust) and factors outside the relationship that make the decision significant and uncertain. In sum, to understand how trust actually affects a person's taking a risk, one must separate trust from other situational factors that *necessitate* trust (i.e., perceived risk in the current model).

We propose that the *level* of trust is compared to the *level* of perceived risk in a situation. If the level of trust surpasses the threshold of perceived risk, then the trustor will engage in the RTR. If the level of perceived risk is greater than the level of trust, the trustor will not engage in the RTR.

In sum, trust is a willingness to be vulnerable to another party, but there is no risk involved with holding such an attitude. Trust will increase the likelihood of RTR, which is the behavioral manifestation of trust. Whether or not a specific risk will be taken by the trustor is influenced both by the amount of trust for the trustee and by the perception of risk inherent in the behavior.

> Proposition 5. RTR is a function of trust and the perceived risk of the trusting behavior (e.g., empowerment of a subordinate).

Early in this article it was argued the placement of risk in a model of trust was important, and this section clarifies that issue. Two other issues warrant exposition: the effects of context and the evolution of trust.

The Role of Context

The preceding discussion of risk-taking behavior makes a clear argument for the importance of the context in which the risk is to be taken. Even though the level of trust (as determined by ability, benevolence, integrity and propensity to trust) may be constant, the specific consequences of trust will be determined by contextual factors such as the stakes involved, the balance of power in the relationship, the perception of the level of risk, and the alternatives available to the trustor.

Similarly, the assessment of the antecedents of trust (ability, benevolence, and integrity) are affected by the context. For example, in the previous discussion of ability we noted that ability was domain specific—high ability at one task does not necessarily imply high ability at another task. Furthermore, perceived ability will change as the dynamics of the situation in which the task is to be performed change. For example, a protégé may believe that the mentor is able to advance his or her career, but a change in top management's philosophy may change the situation. Although the mentor's skills are constant, the context in which those skills will be utilized has changed. The net result of the change in context (i.e., politics) has decreased the protégé's perception of the mentor's ability.

Perceived levels of benevolence also are influenced by context. For example, if an employee perceives that a new supervisor has attitudes and preferences similar to his or her own, the employee will perceive higher levels of benevolence from that supervisor (Berscheid & Walster, 1978; Newcomb, 1956). The context of the situation (i.e., perceived similarity) helps to determine the perceived level of benevolence that the supervisor has for the employee.

The context of a party's actions affects the perception of integrity as well. A middle manager may make a decision that appears to be inconsistent with earlier decisions. Knowing nothing else about the situation, employees may question the manager's integrity. However, if the employees learn that the manager's actions were in response to orders from those higher in the organization, the manager's integrity will no longer be questioned. The manager's actions are seen as unavoidable given the context, and they are not deemed to be his or her fault. Thus, the perception of integrity can be influenced by the context of the actions.

In sum, the trustor perception and interpretation of the context of the relationship will affect both the need for trust and the evaluation of trustworthiness. Changes in such factors as the political climate and the perceived volition of the trustee in the situation can cause a reevaluation of trustworthiness. A strong organizational control system could inhibit the development of trust, because a trustee's actions may be interpreted as responses to that control rather than signs of trustworthiness. A clear understanding of trust for a trustee necessitates understanding how the context affects perceptions of trustworthiness.

Long-Term Effects

Up to this point, in the proposed model we have described trust at a given point in time. A more complete understanding of trust would come from consideration of its evolution within a relationship (Boyle & Bonacich, 1970; Kee & Knox, 1970). The level of trust will evolve as the parties interact. Several factors that affect the process by which trust evolves have been explored in the literature and are discussed next.

Strickland's (1958) analysis of monitoring and employee locus of motivation provides an interesting insight into the evolution of trust. He suggested that low trust will lead to a greater amount of surveillance or monitoring of work progress. Kruglanski (1970: 215) suggested that a frequently monitored employee might interpret the supervisor's surveillance as illustrating distrust for the employee. The employee may react in retaliation by "double-crossing the supervisor whenever the opportunity arises. The supervisor's anticipation of such an effect might lead him to continue his surveillance of the subordinate."

A number of researchers have suggested that the emergence of trust can be demonstrated in game theory as a reputation evolves from patterns of previous behavior. For example, Solomon (1960) described effects of reputation on trust utilizing a prisoner's dilemma. He asserted that an individual who receives cooperation from another develops a liking for that individual, increasing the likelihood of the person's behaving in a trustworthy fashion. Boyle and Bonacich described the dynamic interplay between experiences and trust. They argued that "a Cooperative move by Opponent will increase Player's trust in him, while a Noncooperative move will decrease Player's trust" (1970: 130). Other researchers have used a repeated decision game to show how trust emerges in a transaction between two parties (e.g., Butler, 1983; Dasgupta, 1988; Davis, Helms, & Henkin, 1989; Milgrom & Roberts, 1992).

Our proposed model incorporates the dynamic nature of trust. This is represented in Figure 1 by the feedback loop from the "Outcomes" of RTR to the perceived characteristics of the trustee. When a trustor takes a risk in a trustee that leads to a positive outcome, the trustor's perceptions of the trustee are enhanced. Likewise, perceptions of the trustee will decline when trust leads to unfavorable conclusions. Boyle and Bonacich (1970) have suggested that the outcomes of engaging in a trusting behavior will affect trust directly. We propose that the outcome of the trusting behavior (favorable or unfavorable) will influence trust indirectly through the perceptions of ability, benevolence, and integrity at the next interaction. For example, a manager empowers an employee to deal with a task that is critical to the manager's performance. If the employee's performance of the task is very good, the manager's perception of the employee's trustworthiness will be enhanced. Conversely, if the employee performs poorly and damages the manager's reputation, the manager's perception of the employee's trustworthiness is diminished. The manager may attribute the employee's high or low performance to ability, benevolence, and/or integrity, depending upon the situation.

> Proposition 6. Outcomes of trusting behaviors (i.e., RTR) will lead to updating of prior perceptions of the ability, benevolence, and integrity of the trustee.

Conclusions and Future Directions

This article raises a number of issues for the study of trust in organizations. Each is considered and dealt with in the development of a model of dyadic trust in an organizational context. The model proposed in this article is the first that explicitly considers both characteristics of the trustee as well as the trustor. The model clearly differentiates trust from factors that contribute to it, and it also differentiates trust from its outcome of risk taking in the relationship. The current approach defines trust in a way that distinguishes trust from other similar constructs (cooperation, confidence, predictability), which often have been confused with trust in the literature. Likewise, the critical role of risk is clearly specified in this model. This article develops a versatile definition of trust and a parsimonious set of determinants.

The differentiations between factors that cause trust, trust itself, and outcomes of trust are critical to the validation of this model. All three must be measured in order to fully test the model. Measures of the perceptions of a trustee's ability, benevolence, and integrity must be developed that are consistent with the definitions provided. Behaviors that are characterized by vulnerability and the lack of ability to monitor or control can be assessed to operationalize RTR. RTR must be measured in terms of actual behavior, not willingness to engage in behavior. Such behaviors as monitoring are examples of a lack of risk taking in relationship. Dealing with these behaviors from a measurement perspective requires a reverse scoring of the measure of their occurrence. The extent of perceived risk involved in engaging in the trusting behavior should be assessed either directly (e.g., through survey items) or controlled for, such as structuring a simulation wherein the subjects have a limited number of possible responses that clearly vary in the amount of risk they involve. The most problematic component of the model from the standpoint of measurement is trust itself. Because trust is a willingness to be vulnerable, a measure that assesses that willingness is needed. Even though trust is conceptually easy to differentiate from perceived ability, benevolence, and integrity of the trustee, separating the *willingness* to be vulnerable from *actually* being vulnerable constitutes a finer distinction. To measure trust itself, a survey or other similar methodology that taps into the person's *willingness* to be vulnerable to the trustee is needed, because this is distinct from observable RTR.

The question "Do you trust them?" must be qualified: "trust them to do what?" The issue on which you trust them depends not only on the assessment of integrity and benevolence, but also on the ability to accomplish it. Thus, if a party is trusted on one task, will that increase the trust on another unrelated task, even in the absence of data on the party's ability on the new task? Consistent with the arguments of Sitkin and Roth (1993), this model suggests that assessments of ability may not generalize across dissimilar tasks or situations.

Several limitations of the proposed theory should be recognized. First, its focus is limited to trust of a specific trustor for a specific trustee. Thus, its contribution to understanding trust in a social system (e.g., Barber, 1983; Lewis & Weigert, 1985) is beyond the scope of this model. Second, trust as considered in this model is unidirectional: from a given trustor to a given trustee. In its present form it is not designed to examine the development of mutual trust between two parties. Third, this model is focused on trust in an organizational relationship, and its propositions may not generalize to relationships in other contexts. Finally, the labels for the constructs in this model were selected from several options used earlier in the trust literature. To us, these labels most clearly reflected the constructs as defined in the proposed model; however, in some cases this necessitated that the definitions vary somewhat from some of the prior uses of the same terms.

In addition to model-specific hypotheses, a number of other avenues of research should be pursued. For example, the process by which trust develops needs further exploration. We propose that the need for trusting behavior often arises while there is still a lack of data regarding some of the three factors. For instance, an employee may not have had enough interaction with a given manager to be able to assess the manager's benevolence toward him or her. In order to gather such data, the employee first may have to be vulnerable (i.e., to trust the manager) to see how the manager deals with the vulnerability. In this instance, the employee may have to display a type of trust similar to blind faith. Depending on how the manager responds to the vulnerability, the employee will develop more or less trust.

A number of theorists have suggested that trust evolves over time based on a series of observations and interactions. A critical issue is the process by which trust evolves, given the framework of our model. Further research should investigate the relationship between trust and cooperation. Game theorists tend to equate cooperation and trust, suggesting that over time a pattern of cooperative behavior develops trust (Axelrod, 1984). To what extent does cooperation that can be attributed to external motivations develop trust? This idea also suggests the need to test the feedback loop in the proposed model.

There are many areas in organizational studies in which trust has been cited as playing a key role. Further development and operationalization of the model proposed in this article would benefit the study of organizations through an increased understanding of such topics as employee-organization linkages, negotiation, and the implementation of self-managed teams.

Note

1. It is interesting to note that Aristotle's *Rhetoric* suggests that a speaker's ethos (Greek root for ethics) is based on the listener's perception of three things: intelligence; character (reliability, honesty); and goodwill (favorable intentions toward the listener). These bases provide an interesting parallel with the factors of ability, integrity, and benevolence, respectively.

References

Argyris, C. A. 1994. Litigation mentality and organizational learning. In S. B. Sitkin & R. J. Bies (Eds.), *The legalistic organization*. Thousand Oaks, CA: Sage.

Atwater, L. E. 1988. The relative importance of situational and individual variables in predicting leader behavior. *Group and Organization Studies*, 13: 290–310.

Axelrod, R. 1984. *The evolution of cooperation*. New York: Basic Books.

Barber, B. 1983. *The logic and limits of trust*, New Brunswick, NJ: Rutgers University Press.

Bateson, P. 1988. The biological evolution of cooperation and trust. In D. G. Gambetta (Ed.), *Trust:* 14–30. New York: Basil Blackwell.

Bazerman, M. H. 1994. *Judgment in managerial decision making*. New York: Wiley.

Berscheid, E., & Walster, E. H. 1978. *Interpersonal attraction* (2nd ed.). Reading, MA: Addison-Wesley.

Bierman, H., Jr., Bonini, C. P., & Hausman, W. H. 1969. *Quantitative analysis for business decisions* (3rd ed.). Homewood, IL.: Irwin.

Boss, R. W. 1978. Trust and managerial problem solving revisited. *Group and Organization Studies*, 3: 331–342.

Boyle, R., & Bonacich, P. 1970. The development of trust and mistrust in mixed-motive games. *Sociometry*, 33: 123–139.

Butler, J. K. 1983. Reciprocity of trust between professionals and their secretaries. *Psychological Reports*, 53: 411–416.

Butler, J. K. 1991. Toward understanding and measuring conditions of trust: Evolution of a conditions of trust inventory. *Journal of Management*, 17: 643–663.

Butler, J. K., & Cantrell, R. S. 1984. A behavioral decision theory approach to modeling dyadic trust in superiors and subordinates. *Psychological Reports*, 55: 19–28.

Coleman, J. S. 1990. *Foundations of social theory*. Cambridge, MA. Harvard University Press.

Conlon, E. J., & Mayor, R. C. 1994. *The effect of trust on principal-agent dyads: An empirical investigation of stewardship and agency*. Paper presented at the annual meeting of the Academy of Management, Dallas, TX.

Cook, J., & Wall, T. 1980. New work attitude measures of trust, organizational commitment, and personal need nonfulfillment. *Journal of Occupational Psychology*, 53: 39–52.

Cummings, L. L. 1983. Performance-evaluation systems in context of individual trust and commitment. In F. J. Landy, S. Zedrick, & J. Cleveland (Eds.), *Performance measurement and theory*: 89–93. Hillsdale, N.J: Earlbaum.

Dasgupta, P. 1988. Trust as a commodity. In D. G. Gambetta (Ed.), *Trust*: 49–72. New York: Basil Blackwell.

Davis, J., Helms, L., & Henkin, A. B. 1989. Strategic conventions in organizational decision making: Applications from game theory. *International Review of Modern Sociology*, 19: 71–85.

Deutsch, M. 1958. Trust and suspicion. *Journal of Conflict Resolution*, 2: 265–279.

Deutsch, M. 1960. The effect of motivational orientation upon trust and suspicion. *Human Relations*, 13: 123–140.

Donaldson, L., & Davis, J. H. 1991. Stewardship theory or agency theory: CEO governance and shareholder returns. *Australian Journal of Management*, 16(1): 49–64.

Driscoll, J. W. 1978. Trust and participation in organizational decision making as predictors of satisfaction. *Academy of Management Journal*, 21: 44–56.

Farnham, A. 1989. The trust gap. *Fortune*, Dec. 4: 56–78.

Farris, G., Senner, E., & Butterfield, D. 1973. Trust, culture, and organizational behavior. *Industrial Relations*, 12: 144–157.

Friedland, N. 1990. Attribution of control as a determinant of cooperation in exchange interactions. *Journal of Applied Social Psychology*, 20: 303–320.

Frost, T., Stimpson, D. V., & Maughan, M. R. C. 1978. Some correlates of trust. *Journal of Psychology*, 99: 103–108.

Gabarro, J. 1978. The development of trust, influence, and expectations. In A. G. Athos & J. J. Gabarro (Eds.), *Interpersonal behavior: Communication and understanding in relationships*: 290–303. Englewood Cliffs, NJ: Prentice Hall.

Gambetta, D. G. (Ed.). 1988. Can we trust trust? In D. G. Gambetta (Ed.), *Trust*: 213–237. New York: Basil Blackwell.

Giffin, K. 1967. The contribution of studies of source credibility to a theory of interpersonal trust in the communication department. *Psychological Bulletin*, 68: 104–120.

Golembiewski, R. T., & McConkie, M. 1975. The centrality of interpersonal trust in group processes. In C. L. Cooper (Ed.), *Theories of group processes*. New York: Wiley.

Good, D. 1988. Individuals, interpersonal relations, and trust. In D. G. Gambetta (Ed.), *Trust*: 131–185. New York: Basil Blackwell.

Granovetter, M. 1985. Economic action and social structure: The problem of embeddedness. *American Journal of Sociology*, 91: 481–510.

Hart, K. M., Capps, H. R., Cangemi, J. P., & Caillouet, L. M. 1986. Exploring organizational trust and its multiple dimensions: A case study of General Motors. *Organization Development Journal*, 4(2): 31–39.

Hofstede, G. 1980. Motivation, leadership, and organization: Do American theories apply abroad? *Organizational Dynamics*, 9(1): 42–63.

Hovland, C. I., Janis, I. L., & Kelley, H. H. 1953. *Communication and persuasion*. New Haven, CT: Yale University Press.

Jackson, S. E., & Alvarez, E. B. 1992. Working through diversity as a strategic imperative. In S. Jackson (Ed.), *Diversity in the workplace*: 13–29. New York: Guilford Press.

James, L. R., Mulaik, S. S., & Brett, J. M. 1982. *Causal analysis: Models, assumptions, and data*. Beverly Hills, CA: Sage.

Jamieson, D., & O'Mara, J. 1991. *Managing workforce 2000: Gaining the diversity advantage*. San Francisco: Jossey-Bass.

Jensen, M. C., & Meckling, W. H. 1976. Theory of the firm: Managerial behavior, agency costs and ownership structure. *Journal of Financial Economics*, 3: 305–360.

Johnson-George, C., & Swap, W. 1982. Measurement of specific interpersonal trust: Construction and validation of a scale to assess trust in a specific other. *Journal of Personality and Social Psychology*, 43: 1306–1317.

Jones, A. P., James, L. R., & Bruni, J. R. 1975. Perceived leadership behavior and employee confidence in the leader as moderated by job involvement. *Journal of Applied Psychology*, 60: 146–149.

Kee, H. W., & Knox, R. E. 1970. Conceptual and methodological considerations in the study of trust. *Journal of Conflict Resolution*, 14: 357–366.

Kruglanski, A. W. 1970. Attributing trustworthiness in supervisor-worker relations. *Journal of Experimental Psychology*, 6: 214–232.

Larson, C. E., & LaFasto, F. M. J. 1989. *Teamwork: What must go right/what can go wrong*. Newbury Park. CA: Sage.

Larzelere, R., & Huston, T. 1980. The dyadic trust scale: Toward understanding interpersonal trust in close relationships. *Journal of Marriage and the Family*, 42: 595–604.

Lawler, E. 1992. *The ultimate advantage: Creating the high-involvement organization*. San Francisco: Jossey-Bass.

Lewis, J., & Weigert, A. 1985. Trust as a social reality. *Social Forces*, 63: 967–985.

Lieberman, J. K. 1981. *The litigious society*. New York: Basic Books.

Luhmann, N. 1988. Familiarity, confidence, trust: Problems and alternatives. In D. G. Gambetta (Ed.), *Trust*: 94–107. New York: Basil Blackwell.

March, J. G., & Shapira, Z. 1987. Managerial perspectives on risk and risk taking. *Management Science*, 33: 1404–1418.

McFall, L. 1987. Integrity. *Ethics*, 98: 5–20.

Meyer, J. W. 1983. Organizational factors affecting legalization in education. In J. W. Meyer & W. R. Scott (Eds.), *Organizational environments: Ritual and rationality*: 217–232. San Francisco: Jossey-Bass.

Milgrom, P., & Roberts, J. 1992. *Economics, organization and management*. Englewood Cliffs. NJ: Prentice Hall.

Mishra, A. K. In press. Organizational responses to crisis: The centrality of trust. In R. M. Kramer & T. Tyler (Eds.). *Trust in organizations*. Newbury Park. CA: Sage.

Moore, S. F., Shatter, L. S., Pollak, E. L., & Taylor-Lemcke, P. 1987. The effects of interpersonal trust and prior common problem experience on common management. *Journal of Social Psychology*, 127: 19–29.

Newcomb, T. M. 1956. The prediction of interpersonal attraction. *American Psychologist*. 11: 575–586.

Riker, W. H. 1974. The nature of trust. In J. T. Tedeschi (Ed.), *Perspectives on social power*: 63–81. Chicago: Aldine.

Ring, S. M., & Van de Ven, A. 1992. Structuring cooperative relationships between organizations. *Strategic Management Journal*, 13: 483–498.

Rosen, B., & Jerdee, T. H. 1977. Influence of subordinate characteristics on trust and use of participative decision strategies in a management simulation. *Journal of Applied Psychology*, 62: 628–631.

Rotter, J. B. 1967. A new scale for the measurement of interpersonal trust. *Journal of Personality*, 35: 651–665.

Runkel, P. J., & McGrath, J. E. 1972. *Research on human behavior: A systematic guide to method*. New York: Holt, Rinehart, & Winston.

Sabatelli, R. M., Buck, R., & Dreyer, A. 1983. Locus of control, interpersonal trust, and nonverbal communication accuracy. *Journal of Personality and Social Psychology*, 44: 399–409.

Schlenker, B., Helm, B., & Tedeschi, J. 1973. The effects of personality and situational variables on behavioral trust. *Journal of Personality and Social Psychology*, 25: 419–427.

Scott, C. L., III. 1980. Interpersonal trust: A comparison of attitudinal and situational factors. *Human Relations*, 33: 805–812.

Scott, D. 1980. The causal relationship between trust and the assessed value of management by objectives. *Journal of Management*, 6: 157–175.

Sitkin, S. B. & Bias, R. J. 1994. The legalization of organizations: A multitheoretical perspective. In S. B. Sitkin & R. J. Bies (Eds.), *The legalistic organization*: 19–49. Thousand Oaks, CA: Sage.

Sitkin, S. B. & Pablo, A. L. 1992. Reconceptualizing the determinants of risk behavior. *Academy of Management Review*, 17: 9–38.

Sitkin, S. B. & Roth, N. L. 1993. Explaining the limited effectiveness of legalistic "remedies" for trust/distrust. *Organization Science*, 4: 367–392.

Solomon, L. 1960. The influence of some types of power relationships and game strategies upon the development of interpersonal trust. *Journal of Abnormal and Social Psychology,* 61: 223–230.

Strickland, L. H. 1958. Surveillance and trust. *Journal of Personality,* 26: 200–215.

Taylor, R. G. 1989. The role of trust in labor-management relations. *Organization Development Journal,* 7: 85–89.

Wellins, R. S., Byham, W. C., & Wilson, J. M. 1991. *Empowered teams: Creating self-directed work groups that improve quality, productivity, and participation.* San Francisco: Jossey-Bass.

Williamson, O. E. 1975. *Markets and hierarchies: Analysis and antitrust implications.* New York: Free Press.

Zand, D. E. 1972. Trust and managerial problem solving. *Administrative Science Quarterly,* 17: 229–239.

Roger C. Mayer is an assistant professor of management at the University of Notre Dame. He received his Ph.D. in organizational behavior and human resource management from the Krannert Graduate School of Management, Purdue University. His research interests include trust, motivation, employee attitudes, and decision making.

James H. Davis is an assistant professor of strategic management at the University of Notre Dame. He received his Ph.D. from the University of Iowa. His research interests include corporate governance, stewardship theory, and trust.

F. David Schoorman is an associate professor of organizational behavior and human resource management at Purdue University. He received his Ph.D. in industrial administration from Carnegie Mellon University. His interests include decision making, work teams, and organizational effectiveness.

ORGANIZATIONAL CULTURE IN HIGHER EDUCATION

Defining the Essentials

WILLIAM G. TIERNEY

Within the business community in the last ten years, organizational culture has emerged as a topic of central concern to those who study organizations. Books such as Peters and Waterman's *In Search of Excellence* [37], Ouchi's *Theory Z* [33], Deal and Kennedy's *Corporate Cultures* [20], and Schein's *Organizational Culture and Leadership* [44] have emerged as major works in the study of managerial and organizational performance.

However, growing popular interest and research activity in organizational culture comes as something of a mixed blessing. Heightened awareness has brought with it increasingly broad and divergent concepts of culture. Researchers and practitioners alike often view culture as a new management approach that will not only cure a variety of organizational ills but will serve to explain virtually every event that occurs within an organization. Moreover, widely varying definitions, research methods, and standards for understanding culture create confusion as often as they provide insight.

The intent for this article is neither to suggest that an understanding of organizational culture is an antidote for all administrative folly, nor to imply that the surfeit of definitions of organizational culture makes its study meaningless for higher education administrators and researchers. Rather, the design of this article is to provide a working framework to diagnose culture in colleges and universities so that distinct problems can be overcome. The concepts for the framework come from a year-long investigation of organizational culture in American higher education.

First, I provide a rationale for why organizational culture is a useful concept for understanding management and performance in higher education. In so doing, I point out how administrators might utilize the concept of culture to help solve specific administrative problems. The second part of the article considers previous attempts to define culture in organizations in general, and specifically, in colleges and universities. Third, a case study of a public state college highlights essential elements of academic culture. The conclusion explores possible avenues researchers might examine in order to enhance a usable framework of organizational culture for managers and researchers in higher education.

The Role of Culture in Management and Performance

Even the most seasoned college and university administrators often ask themselves, "What holds this place together? Is it mission, values, bureaucratic procedures, or strong personalities? How does this place run and what does it expect from its leaders?" These questions usually are asked in moments of frustration, when seemingly rational, well-laid plans have failed or have met with unexpected resistance. Similar questions are also asked frequently by members new to the organization, persons who want to know "how things are done around here." Questions like these seem difficult to answer because there is no one-to-one correspondence between actions and results. The same leadership style can easily produce widely divergent results in two ostensibly similar institutions. Likewise, institutions with very similar missions and curricula can perform quite differently because of the way their identities are communicated to internal and external constituents and because of the varying perceptions these groups may hold.

Institutions certainly are influenced by powerful, external factors such as demographic, economic, and political conditions, yet they are also shaped by strong forces that emanate from within. This internal dynamic has its roots in the history of the organization and derives its force from the values, processes, and goals held by those most intimately involved in the organization's workings. An organization's culture is reflected in what is done, how it is done, and who is involved in doing it. It concerns decisions, actions, and communication both on an instrumental and a symbolic level.

The anthropologist, Clifford Geertz, writes that traditional culture, "denotes a historically transmitted pattern of meanings embodied in symbols, a system of inherited conceptions expressed in symbolic forms by means of which [people] communicate, perpetuate, and develop their knowledge about and attitudes toward life" [25, p. 89]. Organizational culture exists, then, in part through the actors' interpretation of historical and symbolic forms. The culture of an organization is grounded in the shared assumptions of individuals participating in the organization. Often taken for granted by the actors themselves, these assumptions can be identified through stories, special language, norms, institutional ideology, and attitudes that emerge from individual and organizational behavior.

Geertz defines culture by writing, "Man is an animal suspended in webs of significance he himself has spun. I take culture to be those webs, and the analysis of it to be therefore not an experimental science in search of law, but an interpretive one in search of meaning" [25, p. 5]. Thus, an analysis of organizational culture of a college or university occurs as if the institution were an interconnected web that cannot be understood unless one looks not only at the structure and natural laws of that web, but also at the actors' interpretations of the web itself. Organizational culture, then, is the study of particular webs of significance within an organizational setting. That is, we look at an organization as a traditional anthropologist would study a particular village or clan.

However, not unlike traditional villagers, administrators often have only an intuitive grasp of the cultural conditions and influences that enter into their daily decision making. In this respect they are not unlike most of us who have a dim, passive awareness of cultural codes, symbols, and conventions that are at work in society at large. Only when we break these codes and conventions are we forcibly reminded of their presence and considerable power. Likewise, administrators tend to recognize their organization's culture only when they have transgressed its bounds and severe conflicts or adverse relationships ensue. As a result, we frequently find ourselves dealing with organizational culture in an atmosphere of crisis management, instead of reasoned reflection and consensual change.

Our lack of understanding about the role of organizational culture in improving management and institutional performance inhibits our ability to address the challenges that face higher education. As these challenges mount, our need to understand organizational culture only intensifies. Like many American institutions in the 1980s, colleges and universities face increasing complexity and fragmentation.

As decision-making contexts grow more obscure, costs increase, and resources become more difficult to allocate, leaders in higher education can benefit from understanding their institutions as cultural entities. As before, these leaders continue to make difficult decisions. These decisions, however, need not engender the degree of conflict that they usually have prompted. Indeed, properly informed by an awareness of culture, tough decisions may contribute to an institution's sense of purpose and identity. Moreover, to implement decisions, leaders must have a full, nuanced understanding of the organization's culture. Only then can they articulate decisions in a way that will speak to the needs of various constituencies and marshal their support.

Cultural influences occur at many levels, within the department and the institution, as well as at the system and state level. Because these cultures can vary dramatically, a central goal of understanding organizational culture is to minimize the occurrence and consequences of cultural conflict and help foster the development of shared goals. Studying the cultural dynamics of educational institutions and systems equips us to understand and, hopefully, reduce adversarial relationships.

Equally important, it will enable us to recognize how those actions and shared goals are most likely to succeed and how they can best be implemented. One assumption of this article is that more often than not more than one choice exists for the decision-maker; one simple answer most often does not occur. No matter how much information we gather, we can often choose from several viable alternatives. Culture influences the decision.

Effective administrators are well aware that they can take a given action in some institutions but not in others. They are less aware of why this is true. Bringing the dimensions and dynamics of culture to consciousness will help leaders assess the reasons for such differences in institutional responsiveness and performance. This will allow them to evaluate likely consequences before, not after they act.

It is important to reiterate that an understanding of organizational culture is not a panacea to all administrative problems. An understanding of culture, for example, will not automatically increase enrollments or increase fund raising. However, an administrator's correct interpretation of the organization's culture can provide critical insight about which of the many possible avenues to choose in reaching a decision about how to increase enrollment or undertake a particular approach to a fund-raising campaign. Indeed, the most persuasive case for studying organizational culture is quite simply that we no longer need to tolerate the consequences of our ignorance, nor, for that matter, will a rapidly changing environment permit us to do so.

By advocating a broad perspective, organizational culture encourages practitioners to:

- consider real or potential conflicts not in isolation but on the broad canvas of organizational life;

- recognize structural or operational contradictions that suggest tensions in the organization;

- implement and evaluate everyday decisions with a keen awareness of their role in and influence upon organizational culture;

- understand the symbolic dimensions of ostensibly instrumental decisions and actions; and

- consider why different groups in the organization hold varying perceptions about institutional performance.

Many administrators intuitively understand that organizational culture is important; their actions sometimes reflect the points mentioned above. A framework for organizational culture will provide administrators with the capability to better articulate and address this crucial foundation for improving performance.

Thus far, however, a usable definition of organizational culture appropriate to higher education has remained elusive. If we are to enable administrators and policy makers to implement effective strategies within their own cultures, then we must first understand a culture's structure and components. A provisional framework will lend the concept of culture definitional rigor so that practitioners can analyze their own cultures and ultimately improve the performance of their organizations and systems. The understanding of culture will thus aid administrators in spotting and resolving potential conflicts and in managing change more effectively and efficiently. However, if we are to enable administrators and researchers to implement effective strategies within their own cultures, then we first must make explicit the essential elements of culture.

Cultural Research: Where Have We Been

Organizations as Cultures

Ouchi and Wilkins note: "Few readers would disagree that the study of organizational culture has become one of the major domains of organizational research, and some might even argue that it has become the single most active arena, eclipsing studies of formal structure, of organization-environment research and of bureaucracy" [34, pp. 457–58].

Researchers have examined institutions, organizations, and subunits of organization as distinct and separate cultures with unique sets of ceremonies, rites, and traditions [30, 32, 38, 49]. Initial attempts have been made to analyze leadership from a cultural perspective [3, 39, 43, 45]. The role of cultural communication has been examined by March [28], Feldman and March [22], and Putnam and Pacanowsky [41], Trujillo [50], Tierney [46], and Pondy [40]. Organizational stories and symbols have also been investigated [17, 18, 29, 47].

Recent findings indicate that strong, congruent cultures supportive of organizational structures and strategies are more effective than weak, incongruent, or disconnected cultures [7, 27]. Moreover, the work of numerous theorists [5, 26, 31, 42] suggests that there is an identifiable deep structure and set of core assumptions that may be used to examine and understand culture.

Colleges and Universities as Cultures

Numerous writers [11, 21] have noted the lack of cultural research in higher education. Dill has commented: "Ironically the organizations in Western society which most approximate the essential characteristics of Japanese firms are academic institutions. They are characterized by lifetime employment, collective decision making, individual responsibility, infrequent promotion, and implicit, informal evaluation" [21, p. 307]. Research in higher education, however, has moved toward defining managerial techniques based on strategic planning, marketing and management control.

Higher education researchers have made some attempts to study campus cultures. Initially, in the early 1960s the study of culture primarily concerned student cultures [2, 6, 12, 19, 35, 36]. Since the early 1970s Burton Clark has pioneered work on distinctive colleges as cultures [13], the role of belief and loyalty in college organizations [14], and organizational sagas as tools for institutional identity [15]. Recent work has included the study of academic cultures [1, 23, 24], leadership [8, 10, 48], and the system of higher education as a culture [4, 16]. Thus, a foundation has been prepared on which we can build a framework for studying culture in higher education.

A Cultural Framework: Where We Might Go

Anthropologists enter the field with an understanding of such cultural terms as "kinship" or "lineage." Likewise, productive research depends on our being able to enter the field armed with equally well defined concepts. These terms provide clues for uncovering aspects of organizational culture as they also define elements of a usable framework. Necessarily then, we need to consider what cultural concepts can be utilized by cultural researchers when they study a college or university. This article provides an initial attempt to identify the operative cultural concepts and terms in collegiate institutions.

The identification of the concepts were developed through the analysis of a case study of one institution. By delineating and describing key dimensions of culture, I do not presume to imply that all institutions are culturally alike. The intense analysis of one institution provides a more specific understanding of organizational culture than we presently have and presumably will enable researchers to expand upon the framework presented here.

Of the many possible avenues that exist for the cultural researcher to investigate, Table 1 outlines essential concepts to be studied at a college or university. That is, if an anthropologist conducted an in-depth ethnography at a college or university and omitted any mention of institutional mission we would note that the anthropologist had overlooked an important cultural term.

Each cultural term occurs in organizational settings, yet the way they occur, the forms they take, and the importance they have, differs dramatically. One college, for example, might have a history of formal, autocratic leadership, whereas another institution might operate with an informal, consensually oriented leader. In order to illustrate the meaning of each term I provide examples drawn from a case study of a public institution identified here as "Family State College." The data are drawn from site visits conducted during the academic year 1984–85. Participant

TABLE 1

A Framework of Organizational Culture

Environment:	How does the organization define its environment?
	What is the attitude toward the environment?
	(Hostility? Friendship?)
Mission:	How is it defined?
	How is it articulated?
	Is it used as a basis for decisions?
	How much agreement is there?
Socialization:	How do new members become socialized?
	How is it articulated?
	What do we need to know to survive/excel in this organization?
Information:	What constitutes information?
	Who has it?
	How is it disseminated?
Strategy:	How are decisions arrived at?
	Which strategy is used?
	Who makes decisions?
	What is the penalty for bad decisions?
Leadership:	What does the organization expect from its leaders?
	Who are the leaders?
	Are there formal and informal leaders?

observation and interviews with a random sample of the entire college community lend "thick description" [25] to the analysis. Each example highlights representative findings of the college community.

Family State College

"The intensity of an academic culture," writes David Dill, "is determined not only by the richness and relevance of its symbolism for the maintenance of the professional craft, but by the bonds of social organization. For this mechanism to operate, the institution needs to take specific steps to socialize the individual to the belief system of the organization. . . . The management of academic culture therefore involves both the management of meaning and the management of social integration" [21, p. 317]. Family State College offers insight into a strong organizational culture and exemplifies how administrators at this campus utilize the "management of meaning" to foster understanding of the institution and motivate support for its mission.

In dealing with its environment Family State College has imbued in its constituents a strong feeling that the institution has a distinctive purpose and that the programs reflect its mission. By invigorating old roots and values with new meaning and purpose, the president of Family State has largely succeeded in reconstructing tradition and encouraging a more effective organizational culture. As with all executive action, however, the utilization, strengths, and weaknesses of a particular approach are circumscribed by institutional context.

Environment

Founded in 1894, Family State College exists in a fading industrial town. The institution has always been a career-oriented college for the working class in nearby towns and throughout the state. "I came here," related one student, "because I couldn't afford going to another school, and it was real close by." Fifty percent of the students remain in the local area after graduation, and an even higher percentage (80 percent) reside in the state. In many respects the city of Family and the surrounding area have remained a relatively stable environment for the state college due to the unchanging nature of the working-class neighborhoods. An industrial arts professor explained the town-gown relationship: "The college has always been for the people here. This is the type of place that was the last stop for a lot of kids. They are generally the first generation to go to college and college for them has always meant getting a job."

When Family State's president arrived in 1976, he inherited an institution in equilibrium yet with a clear potential to become stagnant. The institution had low visibility in the area and next to no political clout in the state capital. Family State was not a turbulent campus in the late 1970s; rather, it was a complacent institution without a clear direction. In the past decade the institutional climate has changed from complacency to excitement, and constituents share a desire to improve the college.

The college environment provided rationales for change. Dwindling demand for teachers required that the college restructure its teacher-education program. A statewide tax that eliminated "nonessential" programs in high schools reduced the demand for industrial arts at Family State. New requirements by state hospitals brought about a restructured medical-technology program. The college's relationship to its environment fostered a close identification with its working-class constituency and prompted change based on the needs of a particular clientele.

Mission

Individuals spoke of the mission of the college from one of two angles: the mission referred either to the balance between career-oriented and liberal arts programs or to the audience for whom the college had been founded—the working class. Although people spoke about the mission of the college in terms of both program and clientele, the college's adaptations concerned programmatic change, not a shift in audience. That is, in 1965 the college created a nursing program that easily fit into the mission of the college as a course of study for working-class students. An industrial-technology major is another example of a program that responded to the needs of the surrounding environment and catered to the specified mission of the institution. Rather than alter or broaden the traditional constituency of the institution, the college tried to create new curricular models that would continue to attract the working-class student to Family State.

As a consequence, the college continues to orient itself to its traditional clientele—the working people of the area. The city and the surrounding area have remained a working-class region throughout the college's history; the town has neither prospered and become middle class nor has it faded into oblivion. Continuing education programs and the courtship of adult learners have broadened the clientele of the college while maintaining its traditional, working-class constituency.

The president frequently articulates his vision of the institutional mission in his speeches and writing. One individual commented: "When I first came here and the president said that 'we're number one' I just thought it was something he said, like every college president says. But after [you're here] awhile you watch the guy and you see he really believes it. So I believe it too." "We are number one in a lot of programs," said the president. "We'll go head to head with a lot of other institutions. Our programs in nursing, communication, and industrial technology can stack up against any other state college here. I'd say we're the best institution of this kind in the state."

Presidential pronouncements of excellence and the clear articulation of institutional mission have a two-fold import. First, institutional mission provides the rationale and criteria for the development of a cohesive curricular program. Second, the president and the other organizational participants have a standard for self-criticism and performance. All too often words such as "excellence" can be so vague that they have no measurable meaning. Family State however, can "stack up against any other state college." That is, rather than criterion-referenced performance measures such as standardized tests and achievement levels of incoming students, Family State College has standards of excellence that are consistent with the historic mission of state colleges.

Socialization

One individual who had recently begun working at the college noted: "People smiled and said hello here. It was a friendly introduction. People said to me, 'Oh, you'll really love it here.' It was that wonderful personal touch. When they hire someone here they don't want only someone who can do the job, but someone who will also fit in with the personality of the place." One individual also noted that, soon after he arrived, the president commented on how well he did his work but was worried that he wasn't "fitting in" with the rest of the staff. What makes these comments interesting is that they are about a public state college. Such institutions often have the reputation of being impersonal and bureaucratic, as opposed to having the "personal touch" of private colleges.

A student commented: "If a student hasn't gotten to know the president in a year then it's the student's damn fault. Everybody sees him walking around here. He's got those Monday meetings. He comes to all the events. I mean, he's really easy to see if you've got something you want to talk to him about. That's what's special about Family. How many places can a student get to know the president? We all call him 'Danny' (not to his face) because he's so familiar to us." The student's comment is particularly telling in an era of declining enrollments. One reason students come to the school, and one reason they stay at Family, is because the entire institution reflects concern and care for students as personified by the president's open door and the easy accessibility of all administrators.

Information

People mentioned that all segments of the institution were available to one another to help solve problems. Every Monday afternoon the president held an open house where any member of the college community could enter his office and talk to him. All segments of the community used the vehicle. As one administrator reported: "That's sacred time. The president wants to know the problems of the different constituencies. People seem to use it. He reflects through the open house that he really cares."

The president also believes in the power of the written word, especially with respect to external constituencies. It is not uncommon to read about Family State or the president in the local press. A survey done by the college discovered that the local citizenry had a positive, working knowledge of the president and the college. The president attends a multitude of local functions, such as the chamber of commerce and United Way meetings, and civic activities. He also invites the community onto the college campus.

Although mailings and written information are important vehicles for sharing information with external constituencies, oral discourse predominates among members of the institution. Internal constituencies appear well informed of decisions and ideas through an almost constant verbal exchange of information through both formal and informal means. Formal means of oral communication include task forces, executive council meetings, and all-college activities. At these gatherings individuals not only share information but also discuss possible solutions to problems or alternatives to a particular dilemma.

The president's communicative style percolates throughout the institution. Information from top administrators is communicated to particular audiences through weekly meetings of individual departments. One vice president described the process: "The president's executive staff meets once a week and we, in turn, meet with our own people. There's lots of give and take. The key around here is that we're involved in a process to better serve students. Open communication facilitates the process. God help the administrator or faculty member who doesn't work for students."

Informal channels of communication at Family State are an equally, if not more important means for sharing and discussing ideas as well as developing an esprit de corps. The president hosts several functions each year at his house near campus. He brings together disparate segments of the college community, such as different faculty departments, for a casual get-together over supper, brunch, or cocktails. "This is like a family," explained the president. "Too often people don't have the time to get together and share with one another food and drink in a pleasant setting."

It is not uncommon to see many different segments of the institution gathered together in public meeting places such as the cafeteria or a lounge. In discussions with faculty, staff, and administrators, many people showed a working knowledge of one another's tasks and duties and, most strikingly, the student body.

Throughout the interviews individuals consistently mentioned the "family atmosphere" that had developed at the college. As one individual noted: "Everything used to be fragmented here. Now there's a closeness."

Strategy

Family State's decision-making process followed a formal sequence that nevertheless accommodated informal activity. Initiatives often began at the individual or departmental level, as with proposals to create a new program. Eventually the new program or concept ended up in the College Senate—composed of faculty, students, and administration. A subcommittee of the senate decided what action should be taken and recommended that the idea be accepted or defeated. The senate then voted on the issue. Once it had taken action, the next step was presidential—accept the proposal, veto it, or send it back to the senate for more analysis. The final step was approval by the Board.

Formalized structures notwithstanding, a strictly linear map of decision analysis would be misleading. Most often the administration made decisions by widespread discussion and dialogue. "It's participative decision making," commented one individual. The president's decisions existed in concrete, but individuals saw those decisions as building blocks upon which further, more participative decisions were made. "The key around here," observed one administrator, "is that we're involved in a process to better serve students. Open communication facilitates the process."

Although, as noted, the college has adapted to its environment, the college did not rely solely on adaptive strategy. The president noted: "I don't believe that an institution serves its culture well if it simply adapts. The marketplace is narrow and changes quickly." Instead, the administration, particularly the president, has brought about change through an interpretive strategy based on the strategic use of symbols in the college and surrounding environment.

Chaffee defines interpretive strategy as ways that organizational representatives "convey meanings that are intended to motivate stakeholders" [9, p. 94]. Interpretive strategy orients metaphors or frames of reference that allow the organization and its environment to be understood by its constituents. Unlike strategic models that enable the organization to achieve goals or adapt to the environment, interpretive strategy proceeds from the understanding that the organization can play a role in creating its environment. Family State's president accentuates process, concern for the individual as a person, and the central orientation of serving students. He does so through several vehicles, foremost among them being communication with constituencies and the strategic use of space and time.

The president's use of space is an important element in his leadership style and implementation of strategy. He frequently extends his spatial domain beyond the confines of the college campus and into the city and surrounding towns. Conversely, invitations to the community to attend events at the college and utilize the library and other facilities have reduced spatial barriers with a city that otherwise might feel excluded. Informal gatherings, such as suppers at the president's house, or luncheons at the college, have brought together diverse constituencies that otherwise have little reason to interact with one another. Moreover, the president has attended to the physical appearance of the institution, making it an effective symbol to his constituencies that even the grounds demand excellence and care.

The president's symbolic use of space sets an example emulated by others. His open-door policy, for example, permeates the institution. Administrators either work in open space areas in full view of one another or the doors to their offices are physically open, inviting visits with colleagues, guests, or more importantly, students. The openness of the president's and other administrators' doors creates an informality throughout the college that fosters a widespread sharing of information and an awareness of decisions and current activities.

The president is also a visible presence on the campus. He spends part of every day walking throughout the institution for a casual inspection of the grounds and facilities. These walks provide a way for people to talk with him about matters of general concern and enable him to note something that he may not have seen if he had not walked around the campus. Administrators, too, interact with one another and with students not only in their offices but on the other's "turf." "The atmosphere here is to get to know students," said one administrator, "see them where they are, and not have a host of blockades so students feel as if they are not listened to."

The discussion of communication and space has made reference to time. The president continually integrates formal and informal interactions with his constituencies. According to his secretary and a study of the presidential calendar, about one and one-half hours per day are scheduled as "free time" that he uses as he sees fit—for reading, writing, or perhaps walking around the campus.

The president regularly schedules meetings with his executive circle or individuals such as the treasurer. The meetings revolve around both a mixture of formal agenda-like items and ideas or problems that either the president or his lieutenants feel they have. Although his schedule is generally very busy, it is not difficult to see the president. His secretary makes his appointments. She notes that if a faculty member or administrator asked to see the president, she would schedule an appointment when he was available in the very near future. Students, too, can see the president, but his secretary generally tries to act as a gatekeeper to insure that the students really need to see the president and not someone else.

Leadership

The president's awareness of patterns and styles of communication and his conscious use of time and place are perhaps best illustrated by a meeting we had during one of our site visits to Family State. We waited in the president's outer office with the director of institutional research.

The door swung open and the president walked out to greet us. He said: "I'm sorry for being late. I knew about your appointment and had planned to be back here on time, but I was walking around the campus for forty-five minutes, and just at the last minute I made a detour to check out the cafeteria, to see how things were going. I met a guy down there who works in the kitchen and he and I have always said we should play cribbage some time (he's a cribbage player) and wouldn't you know he had a board with him today and he asked me to play. So I did. He beat me too. So I wasn't doing anything very presidential in being late for you. I was just walking around the campus on this beautiful day, and playing cribbage in the kitchen with a friend."

The president's disclaimer notwithstanding, his actions are presidential in that they develop and reinforce an institutional culture. His effective use of symbols and frames of reference, both formally and informally, articulates the college's values and goals and helps garner support from faculty, students, staff, and the community. This should not imply, however, that presidents should necessarily spend their time walking around campus or playing cribbage with the kitchen help. What is effective at one institution is unlikely to work at another. Nevertheless, the role of symbolic communication that we witness on this campus, buttressed by tangible, constructive change, provides valuable clues about effectiveness and organizational culture.

Tying the Framework Together

People come to believe in their institution by the ways they interact and communicate with one another. The ongoing cultural norms of Family State foster an implicit belief in the mission of the college as providing a public good. In this sense, staff, faculty members, and administrators all feel they contribute to a common good—the education of working-class students. When individuals apply for work at Family State, they are considered not only on the basis of skill and qualifications but also on how they will fit into the cultural milieu. Socialization occurs rapidly through symbols such as open doors, the constant informal flow of communication punctuated by good-natured kidding, access throughout the organization, dedication to hard work, and above all, commitment to excellence for students. When people speak of their mission, they speak of helping people. Members of the college community work from the assumption that an individual's actions do matter, can turn around a college, and can help alter society.

Belief in the institution emerges as all the more important, given an unstable economic and political environment. The district in which the college resides has little political clout, and consequently the institution is not politically secure. Rapidly shifting employment patterns necessarily demand that the institution have program flexibility. Although the college has created programs such as medical technology and communication/media, it has not made widespread use of adaptive strategy.

"The strength of academic culture," states David Dill, "is particularly important when academic institutions face declining resources. During these periods the social fabric of the community is under great strain. If the common academic culture has not been carefully nurtured during periods of prosperity, the result can be destructive conflicts between faculties, loss of professional morale, and personal alienation" [21, p. 304]. Family State College exemplifies a strong organizational culture. Further, the academic culture nurtures academic excellence and effectiveness.

It is important to reiterate, however, that all effective and efficient institutions will not have similar cultures. The leadership exhibited by the president at Family State, for example, would fail miserably at an institution with a different culture. Similarly, the role of mission at Family State would be inappropriate for different kinds of colleges and universities. The rationale for a cultural framework is not to presume that all organizations should function similarly, but rather to provide managers and researchers with a schema to diagnose their own organizations.

In providing a provisional framework for the reader, I have neither intended that we assume the different components of the cultural framework are static and mutually exclusive, nor that an understanding of organizational culture will solve all institutional dilemmas. If we return to the Geertzian notion of culture as an interconnected web of relationships, we observe that the components of culture will overlap and connect with one another. In the case study, for example, the way the leader articulated organizational mission spoke both to the saga of the institution as well as its leadership.

How actors interpret the organizational "web" will not provide the right answers to simplistic choices. Rather, a cultural analysis empowers managers with information previously unavailable or implicit about their organization which in turn can help solve critical organizational dilemmas. As with any decision-making strategy, all problems cannot be solved simply because an individual utilizes a particular focus to an issue. For example, a specific answer to whether or not tuition should be raised by a particular percentage obviously will not find a solution by understanding culture. On the other hand, what kind of clientele the institution should have, or what its mission should be as it adapts to environmental change are critical issues that speak to the costs of tuition and demand cultural analysis.

Conclusion: Where Do We Go from Here?

Many possible avenues await the investigation of organizational culture. This article has provided merely the essential terms for the study of academic culture. A comprehensive study of organizational culture in academic settings will demand increased awareness of determinants such as individual and organizational use of time, space, and communication. In this case study, we observed the president's formal and informal uses of different cultural concepts. Individuals noted, for example, how they were well-informed of administrative decisions and plans primarily through informal processes. Evidence such as the president's casual conversations with administrators or walking around the campus were effective examples of the informal use of time. Further work needs to be done concerning the meaning and effective use of formality and informality with regard to time, space, and communication.

I have used the term "organizational culture" but have made no mention of its subsets: subculture, anticulture, or disciplinary culture. An investigation of these cultural subsets will provide administrators with useful information about how to increase performance and decrease conflict in particular groups. We also must investigate the system of higher education in order to understand its impact on individual institutions. For example, state systems undoubtedly influence the culture of a public state college in ways other than budgetary. A study of the influence of states on institutional culture appears warranted.

Each term noted in Table 1 also demands further explication and analysis. Indeed, the concepts presented here are an initial attempt to establish a framework for describing and evaluating various dimensions of organizational culture. Developing such a framework is an iterative process that should benefit from the insights of further research endeavors. An important research activity for the future will be the refinement and extension of this framework. The methodological tools and skills for such cultural studies also need elaboration.

By developing this framework and improving ways of assessing organizational culture, administrators will be in a better position to change elements in the institution that are at variance with the culture. This research will permit them to effect orderly change in the organization without creating unnecessary conflict. Moreover, the continued refinement of this framework will permit research to become more cumulative and will help foster further collaborative efforts among researchers.

References

1. Becher, T. "Towards a Definition of Disciplinary Cultures." *Studies in Higher Education,* 6 (1981), 109–22.
2. Becker, H. S. "Student Culture." In *The Study of Campus Cultures,* edited by Terry F. Lunsford, pp. 11–26. Boulder, Col.: Western Interstate Commission for Higher Education, 1963.
3. Bennis, W. "Transformative Power and Leadership." In *Leadership and Organizational Culture,* edited by T. J. Sergiovanni and J. E. Corbally, pp. 64–71. Urbana, Ill.: University of Illinois Press, 1984.
4. Bourdieu, P. "Systems of Education and Systems of Thought." *International Social Science Journal,* 19 (1977), 338–58.
5. Burrell, G., and G. Morgan. *Sociological Paradigms and Organizational Analysis.* London: Heinemann, 1979.
6. Bushnell, J. "Student Values: A Summary of Research and Future Problems." In *The Larger Learning,* edited by M. Carpenter, pp. 45–61. Dubuque, Iowa: Brown, 1960.
7. Cameron, K. S. "Measuring Organizational Effectiveness in Institutions of Higher Education." *Administrative Science Quarterly,* 23 (1987), 604–32.
8. Chaffee, E. E. *After Decline, What? Survival Strategies at Eight Private Colleges.* Boulder, Col.: National Center for Higher Education Management Systems, 1984.
9. _____. "Three Models of Strategy." *Academy of Management Review,* 10 (1985), 89–98.
10. Chaffee, E. E., and W. G. Tierney. *Collegiate Culture and Leadership Strategy.* New York: Macmillan, forthcoming.
11. Chait, R. P. "Look Who Invented Japanese Management!" *AGB Quarterly,* 17 (1982), 3–7.
12. Clark, B. R. "Faculty Culture." In *The Study of Campus Cultures,* edited by Terry F. Lunsford, pp. 39–54. Boulder, Col.: Western Interstate Commission for Higher Education, 1963.
13. Clark, B. R. *The Distinctive College,* Chicago, Ill.: Aldine, 1970.
14. _____. "Belief and Loyalty in College Organization." *Journal of Higher Education,* 42 (June 1971), 499–520.
15. _____. "The Organizational Saga in Higher Education." In *Readings in Managerial Psychology,* edited by H. Leavitt. Chicago, Ill.: University of Chicago Press, 1980.
16. Clark B. R. (ed.) *Perspectives in Higher Education.* Berkeley, Calif.: University of California Press, 1984.
17. Dandridge, T. C. "The Life Stages of a Symbol: When Symbols Work and When They Can't." In *Organizational Culture,* edited by P. J. Frost, L. F. Moore, M. R. Louis, C. C. Lundberg, and J. Martin, pp. 141–54. Beverly Hills, Calif.: Sage, 1985.
18. Dandridge, T. C., I. Mitroff, and W. F. Joyce. "Organizational Symbolism: A Topic to Expand Organizational Analysis." *Academy of Management Review,* 5 (1980), 77–82.
19. Davie, J. S., and A. P. Hare. "Button-Down Collar Culture." *Human Organization,* 14 (1956), 13–20.
20. Deal, T. E., and A. A. Kennedy. *Corporate Cultures: The Rites and Rituals of Corporate Life.* Reading, Mass.: Addison-Wesley, 1982.
21. Dill, D. D. "The Management of Academic Culture: Notes on the Management of Meaning and Social Integration." *Higher Education,* 11 (1982), 303–20.
22. Feldman, M. S., and J. G. March. "Information in Organizations as Signal and Symbol." *Administrative Science Quarterly,* 26 (1981), 171–86.

23. Freedman, M. *Academic Culture and Faculty Development*. Berkeley, Calif.: University of California Press, 1979.

24. Gaff, J. G., and R. C. Wilson. "Faculty Cultures and Interdisciplinary Studies." *Journal of Higher Education*, 42 (March 1971), 186–201.

25. Geertz, C. *The Interpretation of Cultures*. New York: Basic Books, 1973.

26. Koprowski, E. J. "Cultural Myths: Clues to Effective Management." *Organizational Dynamics*, (1983), 39–51.

27. Krakower, J. Y. *Assessing Organizational Effectiveness: Considerations and Procedures*. Boulder, Col.: National Center for Higher Education Management Systems, 1985.

28. March, J. G. "How We Talk and How We Act: Administrative Theory and Administrative Life." In *Leadership and Organizational Culture*, edited by T. J. Sergiovanni and J. E. Corbally, pp. 18–35. Urbana, Ill.: University of Illinois Press, 1984.

29. Mitroff, I. I., and R. H. Kilmann. "Stories Managers Tell: A New Tool for Organizational Problem Solving." *Management Review*, 64 (1975), 18–28.

30. _____. "On Organizational Stories: An Approach to the Design and Analysis of Organizations through Myths and Stories." In *The Management of Organization Design*, edited by R. H. Kilmann, L. R. Pondy, and D. P. Slevin, pp. 189–207. New York: North Holland, 1976.

31. Mitroff, I. I., and R. Mason. "Business Policy and Metaphysics: Some Philosophical Considerations." *Academy of Management Review*, 7 (1982), 361–70.

32. Morgan, G., P. J. Frost, and L. R. Pondy. "Organizational Symbolism." In *Organizational Symbolism*, edited by L. R. Pondy, P. J. Frost, and T. C. Dandridge. Greenwich, Conn.: JAI Press, 1983.

33. Ouchi, W. G. "Theory Z: An Elaboration of Methodology and Findings." *Journal of Contemporary Business*, 11 (1983), 27–41.

34. Ouchi, W. G., and A. L. Wilkins. "Organizational Culture." *Annual Review of Sociology*, 11 (1985), 457–83.

35. Pace, C. R. "Five College Environments." *College Board Review*, 41 (1960), 24–28.

36. _____. "Methods of Describing College Cultures." *Teachers College Record*, 63 (1962), 267–77.

37. Peters, T. J., and R. H. Waterman. *In Search of Excellence*. New York: Harper and Row, 1982.

38. Pettigrew, A. M. "On Studying Organizational Cultures." *Administrative Science Quarterly*, 24 (1979), 570–81.

39. Pfeffer, J. "Management as Symbolic Action: The Creation and Maintenance of Organizational Paradigms." *Research in Organizational Behavior*, 3 (1981), 1–52.

40. Pondy, L. R. "Leadership is a Language Game." In *Leadership: Where Else Can We Go*, edited by M. McCall and M. Lombardo, pp. 87–99. Durham, N.C.: Duke University Press, 1978.

41. Putnam, L. L., and M. E. Pacanowsky (eds.) *Communication and Organizations: An Interpretive Approach*. Beverly Hills, Calif.: Sage, 1983.

42. Quinn, R. E., and J. Rohrbaugh. "A Competing Values Approach to Organizational Effectiveness." *Public Productivity Review*, 5 (1981), 122–40.

43. Schein, E. H. "The Role of the Founder in Creating Organizational Culture." *Organizational Dynamics*, 12 (1983), 13–28.

44. _____. *Organizational Culture and Leadership*. San Francisco: Jossey-Bass, 1985.

45. Smircich, L., and G. Morgan. "Leadership: The Management of Meaning." *Journal of Applied Behavioral Science*, 18 (1982), 257–73.

46. Tierney, W. G. "The Communication of Leadership." Working paper. Boulder, Col.: National Center for Higher Education Management Systems, 1985.

47. _____. "The Symbolic Aspects of Leadership: An Ethnographic Perspective." *American Journal of Semiotics*, in press.

48. _____. *The Web of Leadership*. Greenwich, Conn.: JAI Press, forthcoming.

49. Trice, H. M., and J. M. Beyer. "Studying Organizational Cultures through Rites and Ceremonials." *Academy of Management Review*, 9 (1984), 653–69. Trujillo, N. " 'Performing' Mintzberg's Roles: The Nature of Managerial Communication." In *Communication and Organizations: An Interpretive Approach*, edited by L. L. Putnam and M. E. Pacanowsky. Beverly Hills, Calif.: Sage, 1983.

THE IMPORTANCE OF ACKNOWLEDGING CONTEXT IN INSTITUTIONAL RESEARCH

JASON E. LANE AND M. CHRISTOPHER BROWN II

Institutions of higher learning increasingly face the need to respond to accountability mandates. These mandates originate from various entities, including the federal government, state government, accreditation agencies, students, parents, and the public at large. According to the National Center for Education Statistics (NCES), there existed in 2001–2002 almost forty-two hundred public and private, two- and four-year institutions within the complex typology of institutional diversity in U.S. higher education (http://nces.ed.gov). Although a number of methodological measures have been developed to differentiate among these institutions, there remain a number of unique segments of this population of which very little is known.

Because of the complexity of America's higher education system and the constituents it serves, institutional researchers, policymakers, and scholars face considerable methodological challenges to paint a holistic picture of the rich diversity. Moreover, prospective students who seek access to the different types of higher education institutions with differing cultural, environmental, and community norms and values face numerous choices. As a result, the higher education system serves an increasingly diverse student population with respect to age, experience, racial or ethnic background, and level of expectation (Brown and Lane, 2003). Therefore, the fabric of America's higher education institutions is becoming more complex as students take advantage of specialized educational environments. Both centuries-old debates about the purpose of education and the continual emergence of new educational contexts create increased challenges in conducting meaningful and relevant research.

Expanding the Meaning of Institutional Research

If one were to take a swath of the population of American institutions of higher learning, a cursory look would reveal a number of variations in institutional characteristics. These differences emanate from the type of students served, educational programs offered, institutional missions pursued, and ideas generated. Research on higher education institutions tends to assume similar cultural and physical contexts while focusing analyses and assessment on more tangible variables, such as retention and graduation rates. Yet the characteristics of any institution derive primarily from an institution's contextual components and should be interpreted within the contextual framework. The organizations and programs that are the focus of this volume were selected because of their contextual uniqueness as compared to more traditional entities, such as comprehensive or research institutions.

In an earlier issue of the New Directions for Institutional Research series, *Studying Diverse Institutions: Contexts, Challenges, and Considerations* (Brown and Lane, 2003), we concluded by observing that "institutional mission, student diversity, and history" (p. 105) are among the primary threads that help create a diversified educational system and calling for additional research on institutional diversity. The authors of this volume have responded to that call in interesting and meaningful ways. To the original list of factors institutional researchers need to consider in their work, we now add physical and cultural context.

Most institutions possess a unique campus culture. Some cultures manifest themselves through intense school spirit or athletic rivalries. On other campuses, aged traditions and folklore bind together generations of students and alumni. Still others use physical symbols such as statues, unique buildings, or aesthetic landscaping to create a special sense of the campus. (For more information on myths and the symbolic nature of organizations, see Bolman and Deal, 1997; Manning, 2000; Ortner, 1973.) This symbolism is often so ingrained in an institution's belief structure that its importance is taken for granted by actors within the institution, leaving external reviewers or analysts in the dark and having to interpret data out of context.

The Importance of the Institutional Context: The Impact of Culture and Location

Within the research setting, context tends to be the great unknown. Rarely accounted for within quantitative research because of its ambiguous and often unquantifiable nature, context typically comprises many of the most important variables involved in constructing institutional meaning and sense making. Because of the relative lack of research attention that institutional context tends to receive in the profession's literature, this chapter highlights important components of context and reviews the distinct contexts included in this volume. For this discussion, *context* is used to capture both the location of the organization and the cultural components of the organizational life of educational institutions.

As observed in the preceding chapters, context can have a large impact on institutional performance and decision making. Whether an organization resides on a traditional college campus or, for example, as part of a corporate retreat site affects the extent to which traditional academic values and norms influence decision making and governance. Furthermore, being geographically dispersed creates a whole different set of issues, from ensuring efficient communication to maintaining effective governance procedures. If campuses exist within different political boundaries such as states or nations, they may become subject to different sets of regulatory or accountability measures and influenced by different external cultures. Thus, the physical location of the entity under study needs to be accounted for within research measures.

Institutional culture is a much more difficult concept to define than location. Schein (1985), in one of the initial attempts to define the idea of culture within the study of organizational theory, used the following definition: "A pattern of shared basic assumptions that the group learned as it solved its problems of external adaptation and internal integration, that has worked well enough to be considered valid and, therefore, to be taught to new members as the correct way to perceive, think, and feel in relation to those problems" (p. 12).

Culture, according to this definition, infiltrates all components of the institutions under study. It drives the way participants think and feel and interpret their surroundings. So inherent are these beliefs that they are not readily identified. The lack of acknowledgment of culture is easily permissible when the same culture influences all actors; it becomes problematic, however, when actors not aware of or influenced by the inherent culture attempt to understand organizational dynamics or characteristics.

The three main components of context we discuss may aid institutional researchers in identifying and incorporating context into their work. The first two items, artifacts and basic underlying assumptions, come from the work of organizational theorists such as Schein (1992) and Ott (1989). The third component, location, is added based on the work of this volume's chapter authors. The evidence provided in the preceding chapters illustrates how location can have an impact on the creation and evolution of organizational culture.

Artifacts

The most visible component of organizational culture, artifacts derive from the physical and social environment (Schein, 1985) and "intentionally or unintentionally communicate information about the organization's technology, beliefs, values, assumptions, and ways of doing things" (Ott, 1989, p. 24). This level of culture includes a variety of overt and conspicuous variables, such as physical surroundings, language, ceremonies, and technology. For example, in a comparison of corporate and comprehensive universities, the difference in artifacts becomes readily apparent. The most obvious difference may be the type of language used by the actors involved. It is very likely that both topics and word choice at a faculty senate meeting and a staff meeting of corporate faculty would vary. Allen and McGee allude to this difference when they point out that the term *institutional research* has not been incorporated into the jargon of corporate universities. What those in more traditional academic organizations refer to as "institutional research," analysts at corporate universities refer to as "measurement and evaluation." Furthermore, the ceremonies incorporated within each organization's culture differ. Traditionally, universities use symbols such as commencement ceremonies, presidential inaugurations, athletic symbols, or ivy-covered brick buildings to construct their contexts, whereas corporate universities may use mission statements, corporate imagery, and clothing choice to communicate culture.

While artifacts are the most apparent components of organizational culture, the significance behind the artifacts is much more important and much more difficult to determine (Schein, 1992), particularly for those on the outside of the organization looking in. Artifacts construct meaning, determine status, and convey organizational beliefs and norms. Commencements, inaugurations, graduate seminars, and large lecture classes represent artifacts readily prevalent on college campuses. In many cases, actors within the organization do not know the reasons that some of these artifacts exist, even if there are very practical reasons, such as not having the physical space or requisite number of faculty to take one three-hundred-person class and split it into ten thirty-person classes. One extreme example of how those external to the organization could misinterpret an organizational artifact came in a set of articles collectively labeled, "What's Wrong with the American University?" Using the corporate theme, Finn and Manno (1996) attempt to pull back the curtain on higher education and reveal the true nature of the beast, at least through the lens of corporate culture. For example, they claim that institutions have "pandered to some of the worst impulses of students, encouraging (and sometimes requiring) them to take 'courses' that indulge the contemporary trend of self-absorption" (p. 47). The authors go on to describe what those in higher education know as the freshman seminar. The first problem with this criticism emanates from the idea that these courses were developed because students wanted them. Those who have taught such courses know that students often require faculty to justify the existence of the course. Second, research suggests that freshman seminars increase retention rates of students (Fidler and Moore, 1996; Strumpf and Hunt, 1993). Such a course should be valued from a business perspective as increased retention of students both improves the educational experience of students (product) and increases the revenues of an institution. Both are outcomes highly valued within corporate culture.

If a common and very practical artifact such as the freshman seminar can be misconstrued as a waste of institutional resources, is it any wonder that more esoteric components receive a high level of scrutiny? Certainly the idea of basing an entire grade on a final exam, as is often done in law school, may seem foreign to those used to a number of graded assignments throughout the semester. Moreover, many components of seminary training may seem unusual or even backward to external observers. Those who chronicle the activities of corporate universities may wonder whether the entity deserves to be called a *university*.

Conveying context to those who read reports from the institutional research office is critical for ensuring an accurate interpretation of the relevant data. Reporting an increase in the number of students enrolled in freshman seminars may be perceived as universities responding to self-indulgence rather than an indicator of success in the area of retention without the appropriate context being provided.

Basic Underlying Assumptions

Basic underlying assumptions manifest after credibility of certain values and beliefs have been repeatedly proven. Such "implicit assumptions . . . guide behavior [and] . . . tell group members how to perceive, think about, and feel about things" (Schein, 1985, citing Argyris, 1976; Argyris and Schön, 1974). Often the actors involved in an organization do not even realize the reason for which they engage in certain activities, so inherent and embedded are the implicit assumptions. Few people probably know why most degrees are based on a four-year course of study or why a standard bachelor degree requires the completion of approximately 120 credit hours. Why is the college semester fifteen weeks on some campuses and seventeen weeks on others? Why is the department chair elected by the faculty rather than appointed by the dean? Why are students in one degree program required to take a course from another department that appears to bear no relevance to the subject? When a new faculty member asks such questions, a senior colleague may regale the junior faculty member with a tale of how this arrangement resulted from a compromise of a grand debate more than twenty years ago. Often, though, many individuals (students, faculty, and staff) do not even know why certain courses are required, which can result in many outdated courses and programs that remain on the books for no apparent reason. Not all departments or institutions are so resistant to change, but one would be hard pressed to find an institution that fully understands the justifications for all that it does.

With change coming relatively slowly and few individuals truly knowing or understanding the reasons behind certain institutional artifacts or assumptions, is it any wonder that critics of higher education have a difficult time understanding how the enterprise operates? In the vacuum of meaning, critics often use their own beliefs and values to understand higher education. One extreme example comes from a speech given by James Carlin, the former chair of the Massachusetts Board of Higher Education, to the Greater Boston Chamber of Commerce in 1997 in which he stated, "I have never seen any business, institution, public agency . . . anything . . .as managerially dysfunctional . . . as misfocused . . . as lacking in goals and objectives, as devoid of accountability . . . as ineffective and inefficient . . . as America's colleges and universities."

There are many aspects of higher education that seem inefficient and illogical when viewed through the lens of business; among them are small class sizes, independent studies, service projects for the region, economic studies of the local economy, and limited number of teaching hours. Each of these initiatives "increases" costs rather than contains them. These aspects of higher education, however, are necessities in terms of providing quality education, quality research, and quality service to the community. While educational researchers discuss the merits of class size and the reasons that numerous studies indicate smaller classes contribute to greater learning potential of students (for example, Korostoff, 1998), business executives try to figure out how to produce more products or services for a lower cost. If these same executives used business principles to lead higher education institutions, initiatives would include bigger classrooms and the hiring of more part-time faculty and teaching assistants. Why pay a full-time faculty member a salary of $60,000 when an institution can hire a teaching assistant for $10,000 a year to teach the same classes? Yet how many of these critics would want their children taught by graduate students instead of full-time faculty members? The problem boils down to the fact that the public and the state legislators are being influenced by those outside the organization who know very little about the culture of higher education, yet these critics claim to know how to fix its problems.

Location

Organizational context should not be interpreted without consideration for the location in which the organization under study resides. While corporations may transcend geographical and political boundaries with ease, institutions of higher learning do not. Boorstin (1965), in discussing colonial colleges in America, referred to them as neither public nor private, but rather as community institutions. Through this organizational conceptualization, he conveys the premise that the institution belonged to the community and was heavily affected by community norms and values. While the idea of institutional ownership has progressed beyond the simplistic community model into an elaborate system of governance and accountability procedures, institutions still remain heavily influenced by the communities in which they reside.

At the subinstitution level, the culture of colleges and schools reflects where the school is located in relation to other institutional components. A medical school may have a different culture if it is located on the main campus or isolated in a distant town across the state. The same may be true for a theological seminary. Its culture depends on whether it evolved isolated from other academic entities or as part of a wider educational system. Corporate universities serve as one of the best examples of how location can have an impact on cultural development. In addition to developing different jargon, the corporate university culture is geared toward different outcomes from those of a traditional college or university. Most corporate universities were created with a specific purpose in mind: to assist in the professional development of their employees and thus the success of the organization. A college or university rarely benefits directly from the investment it puts into the development of a student, with the possible exceptions of alumni donations or improved institutional reputations.

The development of transnational education further highlights the importance of incorporating contextual issues into institutional research (Knight, 2003; Organization for Economic Cooperation and Development, 2003). Institutions with campuses located in two or more nations must be able to adapt to multiple external cultures, suggesting that institutional researchers need to be able to assess, interpret, and understand multiple cultures within their own institutions. In fact, it may be the emergence of transnational campuses that demonstrates the need for institutional researchers to understand and incorporate culture into their analyses. As institutions begin to incorporate multiple distinct cultures within their organization, the importance of culture will become increasingly apparent. "It is important to remember that behind the norms lies this deeper taken-for-granted set of assumptions that most members of a culture never question or examine. The members of a culture are not even aware of their own culture until they encounter a different one" (Schein, 1996, p. 234). This becomes particularly evident when administrators on one campus with its own set of embedded and basic underlying assumptions attempt to interpret data from another campus with its own set of embedded and basic underlying assumptions. If the two institutional cultures are distinct enough from each other, there exists a high likelihood that interpretation of data without appropriate contextual considerations will lead to misleading evaluations or judgments.

Incorporating Campus *Fahrvergnügen* into Institutional Research

Several years ago, the Volkswagen Corporation launched a new series of advertisements that centered on proclaiming their vehicles were different because they possessed *fahrvergnügen*. Few individuals who watched these ads knew exactly what that word meant. Some thought it meant stylish, others thought fun, and still others simply thought it meant new. The overall impression, however, was that *fahrvergnügen* conveyed that special, indefinable characteristic of the Volkswagen that set it apart from other vehicles on the market.

Similarly, the institutional types selected as the focus of this volume distinguish themselves from other higher education entities based on their unique contexts—their *fahrvergnügen*. These institutions evolved with different motivations, are located in disparate locations, or simply stand out from the other administrative components on their respective campuses. Institutional researchers sometimes overlook these unique organizational aspects because they do not recognize the importance of the setting or fail to differentiate the unique traits from the norm.

All campuses possess their own *fahrvergnügen*—a distinct culture that is often difficult to define. The other chapters in this book highlight some of the most acute contexts. As illustrated in the discussion here, culture permeates all aspects of the organization yet is rarely considered or incorporated into research models. Schein (1996), often considered the father of the study of organizational culture, wrote: "Even though I have worked on culture as a variable for over 10 years, I keep being surprised by how little I understand its profound influence in situation after situation. I believe our failure to take culture seriously enough stems from our methods of inquiry, which put a greater premium on abstractions that can be measured than on careful ethnographic or clinical observation of organizational phenomena" (p. 229).

The lack of incorporating context into research is not limited to institutional research, but probably has the most practical import for this area of work. The following are a few summary research considerations for incorporating context into institutional research.

Question Everything; Assume Nothing

Before sending a report to an external group, attempt to interpret the data presented as if you were an outsider, or ask a colleague unfamiliar with the project to do the same, instructing them to be overly critical. Being too close to data can cause one to lose focus, but being too close and a part of the organization under study can be problematic as one may not even be aware of the assumptions driving decisions or interpretations. As Donald Rumsfeld has stated in reference to the war on terrorism, "There are things we know we don't know, and there are things we don't know that we don't know." It is this latter condition that institutional researchers need to be the most wary of.

Location, Location, Location

When dealing with a service, such as education, that is so closely tied to cultural and environmental influences, it is imperative to recognize the importance location can play on institutional research. Even within a single state, institutional missions may vary based on geography. Urban campuses differ from rural campuses. Commuter campuses differ from residential. Even the northern half of a state may differ from the southern half. Astute administrators know that the characteristics of a service region and the nature of the town-gown relationships greatly influence the effectiveness of an institution, but such differences may not be readily apparent to legislators in the state capital who have never visited the campus. Thus, it is important to communicate not just the nature of the institution but also the unique characteristics of the region being served.

Identify and Explain Artifacts

Artifacts both create and communicate cultures. Due to their size and internal diversity, educational enterprises, particularly within the postsecondary sector, tend to possess many artifacts. While the meaning or purpose of such items may be easily understood by those within the culture, the same may not be true from those who do not understand the culture of academia or choose to interpret them through their own cultural lens. Furthermore, although acknowledging context may not alleviate all comparisons with corporate environs, context may aid in creating a large appreciation and understanding for the unique aspects of the academic environment.

Culture Is Difficult to Change

One possible outcome of contextual inclusion is the desire for administrators and policymakers to want to change culture. If this occurs, institutional researchers need to be aware that while changing culture is possible, it is often a long and difficult process. Morgan (1997), in his best-selling book *Image of Organizations*, writes:

> Corporate culture rests in distinctive capacities and incapacities which, as a result of the evolution of the culture, have become defining features of the way the organization works by being built into the attitudes and approaches of its employees. Managers can influence the evolution of culture by being aware of the symbolic consequences of their actions and by attempting to foster desired values, but they can never control culture.... The holographic diffusion of culture means that it pervades activity in a way not amenable to direct control by a single group of individuals [p. 139].

Morgan is obviously writing about business corporations. Simply replace *corporation* with *academic* and *manager* with *administrator* and *employee* with *faculty and staff*, however, and he could just as easily be describing the culture on any college or university campus. In fact, the culture of academic universities presents additional challenges to attempts at controlling or changing. Where most corporations use hierarchical control mechanisms that empower management, the use of collegial and shared governance empowers the employees, who are then better able to resist changes suggested by the administration.

One of the reasons many laypeople have difficulty understanding higher education operations is that they attempt to interpret data using different cultural paradigms. Whether through a business class in high school or a microeconomics course in college, most students learn about basic business culture: hierarchical reporting, profit motivations, and the need for efficiency, among others. When these remedial business lenses are employed to interpret higher education outcomes and data, the enterprise may look like a failure. The problem, again, is that contexts of business and academic organizations are different.

Conclusion

This volume concentrates on exposing some of the epistemological and conceptual issues associated with research development. In addition to providing knowledge about unique and changing aspects of the higher education system, the intent of this volume is to challenge existing beliefs and assumptions about higher education. If a researcher continues to base research methods, constructs, and interpretations on beliefs forged five years ago or more, outcomes and analysis may be faulty or misleading.

As researchers, we must constantly ask ourselves how we know what we know. Is the information that we base our assumptions and beliefs on still accurate? Or have the constructs on which our assumptions are based changed? The academic world appears to be evolving much faster than many individuals in academia realize or want to know. In many ways, the traditional constructs are dissipating. The creation of corporate universities blurs the line of demarcation between education and corporation. The advent of the General Agreement of Trade in Services deconstructs national borders, creating a global system of education that must accommodate diversity in language, culture, and economic principles.

The immediate impact of these changes remains unknown; no crystal ball exists that will allow us to foretell the future. The important element is that change is occurring and will propel the postsecondary education system in directions as yet unseen and possibly unfathomable. Ten years ago, barely anyone used e-mail or the Internet; now it is difficult to imagine academia existing without it. Whether attempting to assess unique campus contexts or to be able to understand, account for, and appreciate change and its impact, researchers need to be able to recognize and comprehend the motivating factors.

References

Argyris, C. *Increasing Leadership Effectiveness.* New York: Wiley-Interscience, 1976.

Argyris, C., and Schön, D. A. *Theory in Practice: Increasing Professional Effectiveness.* San Francisco: Jossey-Bass, 1974.

Bolman, L. G., and Deal, T. E. *Reframing Organizations.* (2nd ed.) San Francisco: Jossey-Bass, 1997.

Boorstin, D. J. *The Americans: The National Experience.* New York: Random House, 1965.

Brown, M. C., and Lane, J. E. (eds.). *Studying Diverse Institutions: Contexts, Challenges, and Considerations.* New Directions for Institutional Research, no. 118. San Francisco: Jossey-Bass, 2003.

Carlin, J. *I Know My Campus Is Broken, But If I Try to Fix It I'll Lose My Job.* Speech presented to the Greater Boston Chamber of Commerce, Nov. 1997.

Fidler, P. P., and Moore, P. S. "A Comparison of Effects of Campus Residence and Freshman Seminar Attendance on Freshman Dropout Rates." *Journal of the Freshman Year Experience,* 1996, *8*(2), 7–16.

Finn Jr., C., and Manno, B. "Behind the Curtain." *Wilson Quarterly,* Winter 1996, pp. 44–53.

Knight, J. *GATS, Trade and Higher Education: Perspectives 2003: Where Are We?* London: Observatory on Borderless Higher Education, 2003.

Korostoff, S. "Tackling California's Class Size Reduction Policy Initiative: An Up-Close and Personal Account of How Teachers and Learners Responded." *International Journal of Educational Research,* 1998, *29,* 797–807.

Manning, K. *Rituals, Ceremonies, and Cultural Meaning in Higher Education.* Westport, Conn.: Bergin and Garvey, 2000.

Morgan, G. *Images of Organization.* (2nd ed.) Thousand Oaks, Calif.: Sage, 1997.

Organization for Economic Cooperation and Development. *Enhancing Consumer Protection in Cross-Border Higher Education: Key Issues Related to Quality Assurance, Accreditation and Recognition of Qualifications.* Trondlheim, Norway: Organization for Economic Cooperation and Development/Center for Educational Research and Innovation, Nov. 2003.

Ortner, S. B. "On Key Symbols." *American Anthropologist,* 1973, 75(5), 1338–1346.

Ott, J. S. *The Organizational Cultural Perspective.* Chicago: Dorsey Press, 1989.

Schein, E. H. *Organizational Culture and Leadership.* (1st ed.) San Francisco: Jossey-Bass, 1985.

Schein, E. H. *Organizational Culture and Leadership.* (2nd ed.) San Francisco: Jossey-Bass, 1992.

Schein, E. H. "Culture: The Missing Concept in Organization Studies." *Administrative Studies Quarterly,* 1996, 41(2), 229–241.

Strumpf, G., and Hunt, P. "The Effects of an Orientation Course on the Retention and Academic Standing of Entering Freshmen, Controlling for the Volunteer Effect." *Journal of the Freshman Year Experience,* 1993, 5(1), 7–14.

PART V

EXPLORATIONS OF LEADERSHIP

LEADERSHIP IN AN ORGANIZED ANARCHY

MICHAEL D. COHEN AND JAMES G. MARCH

The Ambiguities of Anarchy

The college president faces four fundamental ambiguities. The first is the ambiguity of *purpose*. In what terms can action be justified? What are the goals of the organization? The second is the ambiguity of *power*. How powerful is the president? What can he accomplish? The third is the ambiguity of *experience*. What is to be learned from the events of the presidency? How does the president make inferences about his experience? The fourth is the ambiguity of *success*. When is a president successful? How does he assess his pleasures?

These ambiguities are fundamental to college presidents because they strike at the heart of the usual interpretations of leadership. When purpose is ambiguous, ordinary theories of decision making and intelligence become problematic. When power is ambiguous, ordinary theories of social order and control become problematic. When experience is ambiguous, ordinary theories of learning and adaptation become problematic. When success is ambiguous, ordinary theories of motivation and personal pleasure become problematic.

The Ambiguity of Purpose

Almost any educated person can deliver a lecture entitled "The Goals of the University." Almost no one will listen to the lecture voluntarily. For the most part, such lectures and their companion essays are well-intentioned exercises in social rhetoric, with little operational content.

Efforts to generate normative statements of the goals of a university tend to produce goals that are either meaningless or dubious. They fail one or more of the following reasonable tests. First, is the goal clear? Can one define some specific procedure for measuring the degree of goal achievement? Second, is it problematic? Is there some possibility that the organization will accomplish the goal? Is there some chance that it will fail? Third, is it accepted? Do most significant groups in the university agree on the goal statement? For the most part, the level of generality that facilitates acceptance destroys the problematic nature or clarity of the goal. The level of specificity that permits measurement destroys acceptance.

Recent discussions of educational audits, of cost-benefit analysis in education, and of accountability and evaluation in higher education have not been spectacularly successful in resolving this normative ambiguity, even in those cases where such techniques have been accepted as relatively fruitful. In our judgment, the major contributions (and they are important ones) of operational analysis in higher education to date have been to expose the inconsistencies of current policies and to make marginal improvements in those domains in which clear objectives are widely shared.

Similarly, efforts to infer the "real" objectives of a university by observing university behavior tend to be unsuccessful. They fail one or more of the following reasonable tests. First, is the goal uniquely consistent with behavior? Does the imputed goal produce the observed behavior and is it the only goal that does? Second, is it stable? Does the goal imputed from past behavior reliably predict future behavior? Although it is often possible to devise a statement of the goals of a university by some form of revealed preference test of past actions, such goal statements have poor predictive power.

The difficulties in imputing goals from behavior are not unique to universities. Experience with the complications is shared by revealed preference theorists in economics and psychology, radical critics of society, and functionalist students of social institutions. The search for a consistent explanation of human social behavior through a model of rational intent and an imputation of intent from action has had some successes. But there is no sign that the university is one of the successes, or very likely to become one.

Efforts to specify a set of consciously shared, consistent objectives within a university or to infer such a set of objectives from the activities or actions of the university have regularly revealed signs of inconsistency. To expose inconsistencies is not to resolve them, however. There are only modest signs that universities or other organized anarchies respond to a revelation of ambiguity of purpose by reducing the ambiguity. These are organizational systems without clear objectives, and the processes by which their objectives are established and legitimized are not extraordinarily sensitive to inconsistency. In fact, for many purposes the ambiguity of purpose is produced by our insistence on treating purpose as a necessary property of a good university. The strains arise from trying to impose a model of action as flowing from intent on organizations that act in another way.

College presidents live within a normative context that presumes purpose and within an organizational context that denies it. They serve on commissions to define and redefine the objectives of higher education. They organize convocations to examine the goals of the college. They write introductory statements to the college catalog. They accept the presumption that intelligent leadership presupposes the rational pursuit of goals. Simultaneously, they are aware that the process of choice in the college depends little on statements of shared direction. They recognize the flow of actions as an ecology of games (Long, 1958), each with its own rules. They accept the observation that the world is not like the model.

The Ambiguity of Power

Power is a simple idea, pervasive in its appeal to observers of social events. Like *intelligence* or *motivation* or *utility*, however, it tends to be misleadingly simple and prone to tautology. A person has power if he gets things done, if he has power, he can get things done.

As students of social power have long observed, such a view of power has limited usefulness.[1] Two of the things the simple view produces are an endless and largely fruitless search for the person who has "the real power" in the university, and an equally futile pursuit of the organizational locale "where the decision is *really* made." So profound is the acceptance of the power model that students of organizations who suggest the model is wrong are sometimes viewed as part of the plot to conceal "the real power" and "the true locus of decision." In that particular logic the reality of the simple power model is demonstrated by its inadequacy.

As a shorthand casual expression for variations in the potential of different positions in the organization, *power* has some utility. The college president has more potential for moving the college than most people, probably more potential than any one other person. Nevertheless, presidents discover that they have less power than is believed, that their power to accomplish things depends heavily on what they want to accomplish, that the use of formal authority is limited by other formal authority, that the acceptance of authority is not automatic, that the necessary details of organizational life confuse power, (which is somewhat different from diffusing it), and that their colleagues seem to delight in complaining simultaneously about presidential weakness and presidential willfulness.

The ambiguity of power, like the ambiguity of purpose, is focused on the president. Presidents share in and contribute to the confusion. They enjoy the perquisites and prestige of the office. They enjoy its excitement, at least when things go well. They announce important events. They appear at important symbolic functions. They report to the people. They accept and thrive on their own importance. It would be remarkable if they did not. Presidents even occasionally recite that "the buck stops here" with a finality that suggests the cliché is an observation about power and authority rather than a proclamation of administrative style and ideology.

At the same time, presidents solicit an understanding of the limits to their control. They regret the tendency of students, legislators, and community leaders to assume that a president has the power to do whatever he chooses simply because he is president. They plead the countervailing power of other groups in the college or the notable complexities of causality in large organizations.

The combination is likely to lead to popular impressions of strong presidents during good times and weak presidents during bad times. Persons who are primarily exposed to the symbolic presidency (e.g., outsiders) will tend to exaggerate the power of the president. Those people who have tried to accomplish something in the institution with presidential support (e.g., educational reformers) will tend to underestimate presidential power or presidential will.

The confusion disturbs the president, but it also serves him. Ambiguity of power leads to a parallel ambiguity of responsibility. The allocation of credit and blame for the events of organizational life becomes—as it often does in political and social systems—a matter for argument. The "facts" of responsibility are badly confounded by the confusions of anarchy; and the conventional myth of hierarchical executive responsibility is undermined by the countermyth of the nonhierarchical nature of colleges and universities. Presidents negotiate with their audiences on the interpretations of their power. As a result, during the recent years of campus troubles, many college presidents sought to emphasize the limitations of presidential control. During the more glorious days of conspicuous success, they solicited a recognition of their responsibility for events.

The process does not involve presidents alone, of course. The social validation of responsibility involves all the participants: faculty, trustees, students, parents, community leaders, government. Presidents seek to write their histories in the use of power as part of a chorus of history writers, each with his own reasons for preferring a somewhat different interpretation of "Who has the Power?"

The Ambiguity of Experience

College presidents attempt to learn from their experience. They observe the consequences of actions and infer the structure of the world from those observations. They use the resulting inferences in attempts to improve their future actions.

Consider the following very simple learning paradigm:

1. At a certain point in time a president is presented with a set of well-defined, discrete action alternatives.

2. At any point in time he has a certain probability of choosing any particular alternative (and a certainty of choosing one of them).

3. The president observes the outcome that apparently follows his choice and assesses the outcome in terms of his goals.

4. If the outcome is consistent with his goals, the president increases his probability of choosing that alternative in the future; if not, he decreases the probability.

Although actual presidential learning certainly involves more complicated inferences, such a paradigm captures much of the ordinary adaptation of an intelligent man to the information gained from experience.

The process produces considerable learning. The subjective experience is one of adapting from experience and improving behavior on the basis of feedback. If the world with which the president is dealing is relatively simple and relatively stable, and if his experience is relatively frequent, he can expect to improve over time (assuming he has some appropriate criterion for testing the consistency of outcomes with goals). As we have suggested earlier, however, the world in which the president lives has two conspicuous properties that make experience ambiguous even where goals are clear. First, the world is relatively complex. Outcomes depend heavily on factors other than the president's action. These factors are uncontrolled and, in large part, unobserved. Second, relative to the rate at which the president gathers experimental data, the world changes rapidly. These properties produce considerable potential for false learning.

We can illustrate the phenomenon by taking a familiar instance of learning in the realm of personnel policies. Suppose that a manager reviews his subordinates annually and considers what to do with those who are doing poorly. He has two choices: he can replace an employee whose performance is low, or he can keep him in the job and try to work with him to obtain improvement. He chooses which employees to replace and which to keep in the job on the basis of his judgment about their capacities to respond to different treatments. Now suppose that, in fact, there are no differences among the employees. Observed variations in performance are due entirely to random fluctuations. What would the manager "learn" in such a situation?

He would learn how smart he was. He would discover that his judgments about whom to keep and whom to replace were quite good. Replacements will generally perform better than the men they replaced; those men who are kept in the job will generally improve in their performance. If for some reason he starts out being relatively "humane" and refuses to replace anyone, he will discover that the best managerial strategy is to work to improve existing employees. If he starts out with a heavy hand and replaces everyone, he will learn that being tough is a good idea. If he replaces some and works with others, he will learn that the essence of personnel management is judgment about the worker.

Although we know that in this hypothetical situation it makes no difference what a manager does, he will experience some subjective learning that is direct and compelling. He will come to believe that he understands the situation and has mastered it. If we were to suggest to the manager that he might be a victim of superstitious learning, he would find it difficult to believe. Everything in his environment tells him that he understands the world, even though his understanding is spurious.

It is not necessary to assume that the world is strictly random to produce substantially the same effect. Whenever the rate of experience is modest relative to the complexity of the phenomena and the rate of change in the phenomena, the interpretation made of experience will tend to be more persuasive subjectively than it should be. In such a world, experience is not a good teacher. Although the outcomes stemming from the various learned strategies in the personnel management example will be no worse because of a belief in the reality of the learning, the degree of confidence a manager comes to have in his theory of the world is erroneously high.

College presidents probably have greater confidence in their interpretations of college life, college administration, and their general environment than is warranted. The inferences they have made from experience are likely to be wrong. Their confidence in their learning is likely to have been reinforced by the social support they receive from the people around them and by social expectations about the presidential role. As a result, they tend to be unaware of the extent to which the ambiguities they feel with respect to purpose and power are matched by similar ambiguities with respect to the meaning of the ordinary events of presidential life.

The Ambiguity of Success

Administrative success is generally recognized in one of two ways. First, by promotion: An administrator knows that he has been successful by virtue of a promotion to a better job. He assesses his success on the current job by the opportunities he has or expects to have to leave it. Second, by widely accepted, operational measures of organizational output: a business executive values his own performance in terms of a profit-and-loss statement of his operations.

Problems with these indicators of success are generic to high-level administrative positions. Offers of promotion become less likely as the job improves and the administrator's age advances. The criteria by which success is judged become less precise in measurement, less stable over time, and less widely shared. The administrator discovers that a wide assortment of factors outside his control are capable of overwhelming the impact of any actions he may take.

In the case of the college president all three problems are accentuated. As we have seen earlier, few college presidents are promoted out of the presidency. There are job offers, and most presidents ultimately accept one; but the best opportunity the typical president can expect is an invitation to accept a decent version of administrative semiretirement. The criteria of success in academic administration are sometimes moderately clear (e.g., growth, quiet on campus, improvement in the quality of students and faculty), but the relatively precise measures of college health tend neither to be stable over time nor to be critically sensitive to presidential action. For example, during the post–World War II years in American colleges, it was conventional to value growth and to attribute growth to the creative activities of administrative leaders. In the retrospective skepticism about the uncritical acceptance of a growth ethic, we have begun to reinterpret a simple history that attributed college growth to the conscious prior decision of a wise (or stupid) president or board. The rapid expansion of higher education, the postwar complex of student and faculty relations and attitudes, and the massive extension of governmental subsidies to the research activities of colleges and universities were not the simple consequences of decisions by Clark Kerr or John Hanna. Nor, retrospectively, does it seem plausible to attribute major control over those events to college administrators.

An argument can be made, of course, that the college president should be accustomed to the ambiguity of success. His new position is not, in this respect, so strikingly, different from the positions he has held previously. His probable perspective is different, however. Success has not previously been subjectively ambiguous to him. He has been a success. He has been promoted relatively rapidly. He and his associates are inclined to attribute his past successes to a combination of administrative savoir-faire, interpersonal style, and political sagacity. He has experienced those successes as the lawful consequence of his actions. Honest modesty on the part of a president does not conceal a certain awareness of his own ability. A president comes to his office having learned that he is successful and that he enjoys success.

The momentum of promotion will not sustain him in the presidency. Although, as we have seen, a fair number of presidents anticipate moving from their present job to another, better presidency, the prospects are not nearly as good as the hopes. The ambiguities of purpose, power, and experience conspire to render success and failure equally obscure. The validation of success is unreliable. Not only can a president not assure himself that he will be able to lead the college in the directions in which others might believe, he also has no assurance that the same criteria will be applied tomorrow. What happens today will tend to be rationalized tomorrow as what was desired. What happens today will have some relation to what was desired yesterday. Outcomes do flow in part from goals. But goals flow from outcomes as well, and both goals and outcomes also move independently.

The result is that the president is a bit like the driver of a skidding automobile. The marginal judgments he makes, his skill, and his luck may possibly make some difference to the survival prospects for his riders. As a result, his responsibilities are heavy. But whether he is convicted of manslaughter or receives a medal for heroism is largely outside his control.

One basic response to the ambiguities of success is to find pleasure in the process of presidential life. A reasonable man will seek reminders of his relevance and success. Where those reminders are hard to find in terms of socially validated outcomes unambiguously due to one's actions, they may be sought in the interactions of organizational life. George Reedy (1970) made a similar observation about a different presidency: "Those who seek to lighten the burdens of the presidency by easing the workload do no occupant of that office a favor. The workload—especially the ceremonial work load—are the only events of a president's day which make life endurable."

Leader Response to Anarchy

The ambiguities that college presidents face describe the life of any formal leader of any organized anarchy. The metaphors of leadership and our traditions of personalizing history (even the minor histories of collegiate institutions) confuse the issues of leadership by ignoring the basic ambiguity of leadership life. We require a plausible basic perspective for the leader of a loosely coupled, ambiguous organization.

Such a perspective begins with humility. It is probably a mistake for a college president to imagine that what he does in office affects significantly either the long-run position of the institution or his reputation as a president. So long as he does not violate some rather obvious restrictions on his behavior, his reputation and his term of office are more likely to be affected by broad social events or by the unpredictable vicissitudes of official responsibility than by his actions. Although the college library or administration building will doubtless record his presidency by appropriate portraiture or plaque, few presidents achieve even a modest claim to attention 20 years after their departure from the presidency; and those who are remembered best are probably most distinguished by their good fortune in coming to office during a period of collegiate good times and growth, or their bad fortune in being there when the floods came.

In this respect the president's life does not differ markedly from that of most of us. A leadership role, however, is distinguished by the numerous temptations to self-importance that it provides. Presidents easily come to believe that they can continue in office forever if they are only clever or perceptive or responsive enough. They easily come to exaggerate the significance of their daily actions for the college as well as for themselves. They easily come to see each day as an opportunity to build support in their constituencies for the next "election."

It is an old story. Human action is frequently corrupted by an exaggeration of its consequences. Parents are intimidated by an exaggerated belief in their importance to the process of child-rearing. Teachers are intimidated by an exaggerated belief in their importance to the process of learning. Lovers are intimidated by an exaggerated belief in their importance to the process of loving. Counselors are intimidated by an exaggerated belief in their importance to the process of self-discovery.

The major consequence of a heroic conception of the consequences of action is a distrust of judgment. When college presidents imagine that their actions have great consequences for the world, they are inclined to fear an error. When they fear an error, they are inclined to seek social support for their judgment, to confuse voting with virtue and bureaucratic rules with equity. Such a conception of the importance of their every choice makes presidents vulnerable to the same deficiencies of performance that afflict the parents of first children and inexperienced teachers, lovers, or counselors.

A lesser, but important, result of a heroic conception of the consequences of action is the abandonment of pleasure. By acceding to his own importance, the college president is driven to sobriety of manner. For reasons we have detailed earlier, he has difficulty in establishing the correctness of his actions by exhibiting their consequences. He is left with the necessity of communicating moral intent through facial intensity. At the same time, he experiences the substantial gap between his aspirations and his possibilities. Both by the requirements of their public face and by their own intolerant expectations, college presidents often find the public enjoyment of their job denied to them.

The ambiguities of leadership in an organized anarchy require a leadership posture that is somewhat different from that implicit in most discussions of the college presidency. In particular, we believe that a college president is, on the whole, better advised to think of himself as trying to do good than as trying to satisfy a political or bureaucratic audience; better advised to define his role in terms of the modest part he can play in making the college slightly better in the long run than in terms of satisfying current residents or solving current problems. He requires an enthusiasm for a Tolstoyan view of history and for the freedom of individual action that such a view entails. Since the world is absurd, the president's primary responsibility is to virtue.

Presidents occupy a minor part in the lives of a small number of people. They have some power, but little magic. They can act with a fair degree of confidence that if they make a mistake, it will not matter much. They can be allowed the heresy of believing that pleasure is consistent with virtue.

The Elementary Tactics of Administrative Action

The tactics of administrative action in an organized anarchy are somewhat different from the tactics of action in a situation characterized by clearer goals, better specified technology, and more persistent participation. Nevertheless, we can examine how a leader with a purpose can operate within an organization that is without one.

Necessarily, any presentation of practical strategies suggests a minor Machiavellianism with attendant complications and concerns. There is an argument that strategies based upon knowledge contribute to administrative manipulation. There is a fear that practical strategies may be misused for evil ends. There is a feeling that the effectiveness of the strategies may be undermined by their public recitation.

We are aware of these concerns, but not persuaded by them. First, we do not believe that any major new cleverness that would conspicuously alter the prevailing limits on our ability to change the course of history will be discovered. The idea that there are some spectacularly effective strategies waiting to be discovered by some modern Machiavelli seems implausible. Second, we believe that the problem of evil is little eased by know-nothingness. The concern about malevolent manipulation is a real one (as well as a cliché), but it often becomes a simple defense of the status quo. We hope that good people interested in accomplishing things will find a list of tactics marginally helpful. Third, we can see nothing in the recitation of strategic recommendations that changes systematically the relative positions of members of the organization. If the strategies are effective, it is because the analysis of organization is correct. The features of the organization that are involved are not likely to change quickly. As a result, we would not anticipate that public discussion of the strategies would change their effectiveness much or distinctly change the relative positions of those (e.g., students, presidents) who presumably stand to profit from the advice if it is useful.

As we will indicate later in this chapter, a conception of leadership that merely assumes that the college president should act to accomplish what he wants to accomplish is too narrow. A major part of his responsibility is to lead the organization to a changing and more complex view of itself by treating goals as only partly knowable. Nevertheless, the problems of inducing a college to do what one wants it to do are clearly worthy of attention. If presidents and others are to function effectively within the college, they need to recognize the ways in which the character of the college as a system for exercising problems, making decisions, and certifying status conditions their attempts to influence the outcome of any decision.

We can identify five major properties of decision making in organized anarchies that are of substantial importance to the tactics of accomplishing things in colleges and universities:

1. Most issues most of the time have *low salience* for most people. The decisions to be made within the organization secure only partial and erratic attention from participants in the organization. A major share of the attention devoted to a particular issue is tied less to the content of the issue than to its symbolic significance for individual and group esteem.

2. The total system has *high inertia.* Anything that requires a coordinated effort of the organization in order to start is unlikely to be started. Anything that requires a coordinated effort of the organization in order to be stopped is unlikely to be stopped.

3. Any decision can become a *garbage can* for almost any problem. The issues discussed in the context of any particular decision depend less on the decision or problems involved than on the timing of their joint arrivals and the existence of alternative arenas for exercising problems.

4. The processes of choice are easily subject to *overload.* When the load on the system builds up relative to its capabilities for exercising and resolving problems, the decision outcomes in the organization tend to become increasingly separated from the formal process of decision.

5. The organization has a *weak information base.* Information about past events or past decisions is often not retained. When retained, it is often difficult to retrieve. Information about current activities is scant.

These properties are conspicuous and ubiquitous. They represent some important ways in which all organizations sometimes, and an organization like a university often, present opportunities for tactical action that in a modest way strengthen the hand of the participant who attends to them. We suggest eight basic tactical rules for use by those who seek to influence the course of decisions in universities or colleges.

Rule 1: Spend Time

The kinds of decision-making situations and organizations we have described suffer from a shortage of decision-making energy. Energy is a scarce resource. If one is in a position to devote time to the decision-making activities within the organization, he has a considerable claim on the system. Most organizations develop ways of absorbing the decision-making energy provided by sharply deviant participants; but within moderate boundaries, a person who is willing to spend time finds himself in a strong position for at least three significant reasons:

- By providing a scarce resource (energy), he lays the basis for a claim. If he is willing to spend time, he can expect more tolerant consideration of the problems he considers important. One of the most common organizational responses to a proposal from a participant is the request that he head a committee to do something about it. This behavior is an acknowledgment both of the energy-poor situation and of the price the organization pays for participation. That price is often that the organization must allow the participant some significant control over the definition of problems to be considered relevant.[2]

- By spending time on the homework for a decision, he becomes a major information source in an information-poor world. At the limit, the information provided need have no particular evidential validity. Consider, for example, the common assertions in college decision-making processes about what some constituency (e.g., board of trustees, legislature, student body, ethnic group) is "thinking." The assertions are rarely based on defensible evidence, but they tend to become organizational facts by virtue of the shortage of serious information. More generally, reality for a decision is specified by those willing to spend the time required to collect the small amounts of information available, to review the factual assertions of others, and to disseminate their findings.

- By investing more of his time in organizational concerns, he increases his chance of being present when something important to him is considered. A participant who wishes to pursue other matters (e.g., study, research, family, the problems of the outside world) reduces the number of occasions for decision making to which he can afford to attend. A participant who can spend time can be involved in more arenas. Since it is often difficult to anticipate when and where a particular issue will be involved (and thus to limit one's attention to key times and domains), the simple frequency of availability is relatively important.

Rule 2: Persist

It is a mistake to assume that if a particular proposal has been rejected by an organization today, it will be rejected tomorrow. Different sets of people and concerns will be reflected each time a problem is considered or a proposal discussed. We noted earlier the ways in which the flow of participants leads to a flow of organizational concerns.[3] The specific combination of sentiments and people that is associated with a specific choice opportunity is partly fortuitous, and Fortune may be more considerate another day.

For the same reason, it is a mistake to assume that today's victory will be implemented automatically tomorrow. The distinction between decision making and decision implementation is usually a false one. Decisions are not "made" once and for all. Rather they happen as a result of a series of episodes involving different people in different settings, and they may be unmade or modified by subsequent episodes. The participant who spends much time celebrating his victory ordinarily can expect to find the victory short-lived. The loser who spends his time weeping rather than reintroducing his ideas will persistently have something to weep about. The loser who persists in a variety of contexts is frequently rewarded.

Rule 3: Exchange Status for Substance

As we have indicated, the specific substantive issues in a college, or similar organization, typically have low salience for participants. A quite typical situation is one in which significant numbers of participants and groups of participants care less about the specific substantive outcome than they do about the implications of that outcome for their own sense of self-esteem and the social recognition of their importance. Such an ordering of things is neither surprising nor normatively unattractive. It would be a strange world indeed if the mostly minor issues of university governance, for example, became more important to most people than personal and group esteem.

A college president, too, is likely to become substantially concerned with the formal acknowledgment of office. Since it is awkward for him to establish definitively that he is substantively important, the president tends to join other participants in seeking symbolic confirmation of his significance.

The esteem trap is understandable but unfortunate. College presidents who can forgo at least some of the pleasures of self-importance in order to trade status for substance are in a strong position. Since leaders receive credit for many things over which they have little control and to which they contribute little, they should find it possible to accomplish some of the things they want by allowing others to savor the victories, enjoy the pleasures of involvement, and receive the profits of public importance.

Rule 4: Facilitate Opposition Participation

The high inertia of organizations and the heavy dependence of organizational events on processes outside of the control of the organization make organizational power ambiguous. Presidents sense their lack of control despite their position of authority, status, and concern. Most people who participate in university decision making sense a disappointment with the limited control their position provides.

Persons outside the formal ranks of authority tend to see authority as providing more control. Their aspirations for change tend to be substantially greater than the aspirations for change held by persons with formal authority. One obvious solution is to facilitate participation in decision making. Genuine authoritative participation will reduce the aspirations of oppositional leaders. In an organization characterized by high inertia and low salience it is unwise to allow beliefs about the feasibility of planned action to outrun reality. From this point of view, public accountability, participant observation, and other techniques for extending the range of legitimate participation in the decision-making processes of the organization are essential means of keeping the aspirations of occasional actors within bounds. Since most people most of the time do not participate much, their aspirations for what can be done have a tendency to drift away from reality. On the whole, the direct involvement of dissident groups in the decision-making process is a more effective depressant of exaggerated aspirations than is a lecture by the president.

Rule 5: Overload the System

As we have suggested, the style of decision making changes when the load exceeds the capabilities of the system. Since we are talking about energy-poor organizations, accomplishing overload is not hard. In practical terms, this means having a large repertoire of projects for organizational action; it means making substantial claims on resources for the analysis of problems, discussion of issues, and political negotiation.

Within an organized anarchy it is a mistake to become absolutely committed to any one project. There are innumerable ways in which the processes we have described will confound the cleverest behavior with respect to any single proposal, however imaginative or subjectively important. What such processes cannot do is cope with large numbers of projects. Someone with the habit of producing many proposals, without absolute commitment to any one, may lose any one of them (and it is hard to predict a priori which one), but cannot be stopped on everything.

The tactic is not unlike the recommendation in some treatments of bargaining that one should introduce new dimensions of bargains in order to facilitate more favorable trades.[4] It is grounded in the observation that the press of proposals so loads the organization that a large number of actions are taken without attending to problems. Where decisions are made through oversight or flight, considerable control over the course of decision making lies in the hands of two groups: the initiators of the proposals, who get their way in oversight, and the full-time administrator, who is left to make the decision in cases of flight. The college president with a program is in the enviable position of being both a proposal initiator and a full-time administrator. Overload is almost certainly helpful to his program. Other groups within a college or university are probably also advantaged by overload if they have a positive program for action, but their advantage is less certain. In particular, groups in opposition to the administration that are unable to participate full time (either directly or through representatives) may wish to be selective in the use of overload as a tactic.

Rule 6: Provide Garbage Cans

One of the complications in accomplishing something in a garbage can decision-making process is the tendency for any particular project to become intertwined with a variety of other issues simply because those issues exist at the time the project is before the organization. A proposal for curricular reform becomes an arena for a concern for social justice. A proposal for construction of a building becomes an arena for concerns about environmental quality. A proposal for bicycle paths becomes an arena for discussion of sexual inequality.

It is pointless to try to react to such problems by attempting to enforce rules of relevance. Such rules are, in any event, highly arbitrary. Even if they were not, it would still be difficult to persuade a person that his problem (however important) could not be discussed because it is not relevant to the current agenda. The appropriate tactical response is to provide garbage cans into which wide varieties of problems can be dumped. The more conspicuous the can, the more garbage it will attract away from other projects.

The prime procedure for making a garbage can attractive is to give it precedence and conspicuousness. On a grand scale, discussions of overall organizational objectives or overall organizational long-term plans are classic first-quality cans. They are general enough to accommodate anything. They are socially defined as being important. They attract enough different kinds of issues to reinforce their importance. An activist will push for discussions of grand plans (in part) in order to draw the garbage away from the concrete day-to-day arenas of his concrete objectives.

On a smaller scale, the first item on a meeting agenda is an obvious garbage can. It receives much of the status allocation concerns that are a part of meetings. It is possible that any item on an agenda will attract an assortment of things currently concerning individuals in the group, but the first item is more vulnerable than others. As a result, projects of serious substantive concern should normally be placed somewhat later, after the important matters of individual and group esteem have been settled, most of the individual performances have been completed, and most of the enthusiasm for abstract argument has waned.

The garbage can tactic has long-term effects that may be important. Although in the short run the major consequence is to remove problems from the arena of short-term concrete proposals, the separation of problem discussion from decision making means that general organizational attitudes develop outside the context of immediate decisions. The exercise of problems and the discussion of plans contribute to a building of the climate within which the organization will operate in the future. A president who uses the garbage can tactic should be aware of the ways in which currently irrelevant conversations produce future ideological constraints. The same tactic also provides a (partly misleading) device for the training and selection of future leaders of the organization. Those who perform well in garbage can debates are not necessarily good leaders, though they may frequently be identified as potential leaders. Finally, the tactic offers a practical buffer for the organization from the instabilities introduced by the entry and exit of problems that drift from one organization to another. In recent years universities have become an arena for an assortment of problems that might have found expression in other social institutions. Universities and colleges were available and accessible to people with the concerns. Although the resulting strain on university processes was considerable, the full impact was cushioned by the tendency of such problems to move to decision-irrelevant garbage cans, to be held there until they could move on to another arena in another institution.

Rule 7: Manage Unobtrusively

If you put a man in a boat and tell him to plot a course, he can take one of three views of his task. He can float with the currents and winds, letting them take him wherever they wish; he can select a destination and try to use full power to go directly to it regardless of the current or winds; or he can select a destination and use his rudder and sails to let the currents and wind eventually take him where he wants to go. On the whole, we think conscious university leadership is properly seen in third light.

A central tactic in high-inertia systems is to use high-leverage minor actions to produce major effects—to let the system go where it wants to go with only the minor interventions that make it go where it should. From a tactical point of view, the main objection to central direction and control is that it requires an impossible amount of attention and energy. The kinds of organizations with which we have been concerned are unable to be driven where we want them to go without making considerable use of the "natural" organizational processes. The appropriate tactics of management are unobtrusive and indirect.

Unobtrusive management uses interventions of greater impact than visibility. Such actions generally have two key attributes: (1) They affect many parts of the system slightly rather than a few parts in a major way. The effect on any one part of the system is small enough so that either no one really notices or no one finds it sensible to organize significantly against the intervention. (2) Once activated, they stay activated without further organizational attention. Their deactivation requires positive organizational action.

Given all the enthusiasm for elaborating a variety of models of organizations that bemoan bureaucracy and the conventional managerial tools associated with bureaucratic life, it is somewhat surprising to realize that the major instruments of unobstrusive management are bureaucratic. Consider the simple act of committing the organization by signing a piece of paper. By the formal statutes of many organizations, some people within the organization are conceded authority to sign pieces of paper. College presidents tend, in our judgment, to be timid about exercising such authority. By signing a piece of paper the president is able to reverse the burden of organizing the decision-making processes in the system. Many people have commented on the difficulty of organizing the various groups and offices in a college or university in order to do something. What has been less frequently noted is that the same problems of organization face anyone who wants to overturn an action. For example, the official charter of an institution usually has some kind of regulation that permits a desired action, as well as some kind of regulation that might be interpreted as prohibiting it. The president who solicits general organizational approval for action is more likely to obtain it if the burdens of overcoming organizational inertia are on his opposition. He reverses the burden of organization by taking the action.

Major bureaucratic interventions lie in the ordinary systems of accounting and managerial controls. Such devices are often condemned in academic circles as both dreary and inhibiting. Their beauty lies in the way in which they extend throughout the system and in the high degree of arbitrariness they exhibit. For example, students of business have observed that many important aspects of business life are driven by accounting rules. What are costs? What are profits? How are costs and profits allocated among activities and subunits? Answers to such questions are far from arbitrary. But they have enough elements of arbitrariness that no reasonable business manager would ignore the potential contribution of accounting rules to profitability. The flow of investments, the utilization of labor, and the structure of organization all respond to the organization of accounts.

The same thing is true in a college or university, although the process works in a somewhat different way because the convenient single index of business accounting, profit, is denied the university executive. Universities and colleges have official facts (accounting facts) with respect to student activities, faculty activities, and space utilization. In recent years such accounting facts have increased in importance as colleges and universities struggled first with the baby boom and now with fiscal adversity. These official facts enter into reports and filter into decisions made throughout the system. As a typical simple example, consider the impact of changing the accounting for faculty teaching load from number of courses to student credit hours taught. Or, consider the impact of separating in accounting reports the teaching of language (number of students, cost of faculty) from the teaching of literature in that language at a typical American university. Or, consider the impact of making each major subunit in a university purchase services (e.g., duplication services, computer services, library services) at prices somewhat different from the current largely arbitrary prices. Or, consider the consequences of allowing transfer of funds from one major budget line to another within a subunit at various possible discount rates depending on the lines and the point in the budget year. Or, consider the effect of having students pay as part of their fees an amount determined by the department offering the instruction, with the amount thus paid returning to the department.

Rule 8: Interpret History

In an organization in which most issues have low salience, and information about events in the system is poorly maintained, definitions of what is happening and what has happened become important tactical instruments. If people in the organization cared more about what happened (or is happening), the constraints on the tactic would be great. Histories would be challenged and carefully monitored. If people in the organization accepted more openly the idea that much of the decision-making process is a status-certifying rather than a choice-making system, there would be less dependence on historical interpretation. The actual situation, however, provides a tactically optimal situation. On the one hand, the genuine interest in keeping a good record of what happened (in substantive rather than status terms) is minimal. On the other hand, the belief in the relevance of history, or the legitimacy of history as a basis for current action, is fairly strong.

Minutes should be written long enough after the event as to legitimize the reality of forgetfulness. They should be written in such a way as to lay the basis for subsequent independent action—in the name of the collective action. In general, participants in the organization should be assisted in their desire to have unambiguous actions taken today derived from the ambiguous decisions of yesterday with a minimum of pain to their images of organizational rationality and a minimum of claims on their time. The model of consistency is maintained by a creative resolution of uncertainty about the past.

Presidents and Tactics

As we observed at the outset, practical tactics, if they are genuine, will inevitably be viewed as somewhat cynical. We will, however, record our own sentiments that the cynicism lies in the eye of the beholder. Our sympathies and enthusiasm are mostly for the invisible members of an organized anarchy who make such tactics possible. We refer, of course, to the majority of participants in colleges and universities who have the good sense to see that what can be achieved through tactical manipulation of the university is only occasionally worth their time and effort. The validity of the tactics is a tribute to their reluctance to clutter the important elements of life with organizational matters. The tactics are available for anyone who wants to use them. Most of us most of the time have more interesting things to do.

But presidents, as full-time actors generally occupying the best job of their lives, are less likely to have more interesting things to do. In addition, these tactics, with their low visibility and their emphasis on the trading of credit and recognition for accomplishment, will not serve the interests of a president out to glorify himself or increase his chances to be one of the very few who move up to a second and "better" presidency. Instead, they provide an opportunity chiefly for those who have some conception of what might make their institution better, more interesting, more complex, or more educational, and are satisfied to end their tenures believing that they helped to steer their institutions slightly closer to those remote destinations.

The Technology of Foolishness

The tactics for moving an organization when objectives are clear represent important parts of the repertoire of an organizational leader.[5] Standard prescriptions properly honor intention, choice, and action; and college presidents often have things they want to accomplish. Nevertheless, a college president may sometimes want to confront the realities of ambiguity more directly and reconsider the standard dicta of leadership. He may want to examine particularly the place of purpose in intelligent behavior and the role of foolishness in leadership.

Choice and Rationality

The concept of choice as a focus for interpreting and guiding human behavior has rarely had an easy time in the realm of ideas. It is beset by theological disputations over free will, by the dilemmas of absurdism, by the doubts of psychological behaviorism, and by the claims of historical, economic, social, and demographic determinism. Nevertheless, the idea that humans make choices has proved robust enough to become a matter of faith in important segments of contemporary Western civilization. It is a faith that is professed by virtually all theories of social policy making.

The major tenents of this faith run something like this:

> Human beings make choices. Choices are properly made by evaluating alternatives in terms of goals and on the basis of information currently available. The alternative that is most attractive in terms of the goals is chosen. By using the technology of choice, we can improve the quality of the search for alternatives, the quality of information, and the quality of the analysis used to evaluate alternatives. Although actual choice may fall short of this ideal in various ways, it is an attractive model of how choices should be made by individuals, organizations, and social systems.

These articles of faith have been built upon and have stimulated some scripture. It is the scripture of the theories of decision making. The scripture is partly a codification of received doctrine and partly a source for that doctrine. As a result, our cultural ideas of intelligence and our theories of choice display a substantial resemblance. In particular, they share three conspicuous interrelated ideas:

The first idea is the *preexistence of purpose*. We find it natural to base an interpretation of human-choice behavior on a presumption of human purpose. We have, in fact, invented one of the most elaborate terminologies in the professional literature: "values," "needs," "wants," "goods," "tastes," "preferences," "utility," "objectives," "goals," "aspirations," "drives." All of these reflect a strong tendency to believe that a useful interpretation of human behavior involves defining a set of objectives that (1) are prior attributes of the system, and (2) make the observed behavior in some sense intelligent vis-à-vis those objectives.

Whether we are talking about individuals or about organizations, purpose is an obvious presumption of the discussion. An organization is often defined in terms of its purpose. It is seen by some as the largest collectivity directed by a purpose. Action within an organization is justified or criticized in terms of purpose. Individuals explain their own behavior, as well as the behavior of others, in terms of a set of value premises that are presumed to be antecedent to the behavior. Normative theories of choice begin with an assumption of a preexistent preference ordering defined over the possible outcomes of a choice.

The second idea is the *necessity of consistency*. We have come to recognize consistency both as an important property of human behavior and as a prerequisite for normative models of choice. Dissonance theory, balance theory, theories of congruency in attitudes, statuses, and performances have all served to remind us of the possibilities for interpreting human behavior in terms of the consistency requirements of a limited-capacity, information-processing system.

At the same time, consistency is a cultural and theoretical virtue. Action should be consistent with belief. Actions taken by different parts of an organization should be consistent with each other. Individual and organizational activities are seen as connected with each other in terms of their consequences for some consistent set of purposes. In an organization, the structural manifestation of consistency is the hierarchy with its obligations of coordination and control. In the individual, the structural manifestation is a set of values that generates a consistent preference ordering.

The third idea is the *primacy of rationality*. By rationality we mean a procedure for deciding what is correct behavior by relating consequences systematically to objectives. By placing primary emphasis on rational techniques, we have implicitly rejected—or seriously impaired—two other procedures for choice: (1) the processes of intuition, through which people do things without fully understanding why; and (2) the processes of tradition and faith, through which people do things because that is the way they are done.

Both within the theory and within the culture we insist on the ethic of rationality. We justify individual and organizational action in terms of an analysis of means and ends. Impulse, intuition, faith, and tradition are outside that system and viewed as antithetical to it. Faith may be seen as a possible source of values. Intuition may be seen as a possible source of ideas about alternatives. But the analysis and justification of action lie within the context of reason.

These ideas are obviously deeply embedded in the culture. Their roots extend into ideas that have conditioned much of modern Western history and interpretations of that history. Their general acceptance is probably highly correlated with the permeation of rationalism and individualism into the style of thinking within the culture. The ideas are even more obviously embedded in modern theories of choice. It is fundamental to those theories that thinking should precede action: that action should serve a purpose; that purpose should be defined in terms of a consistent set of preexistent goals; and that choice should be based on a consistent theory of the relation between action and its consequences.

Every tool of management decision making that is currently a part of management science, operations research, or decision-making theory, assumes the prior existence of a set of consistent goals. Almost the entire structure of microeconomic theory builds on the assumption that there exists a well-defined, stable, and consistent preference ordering. Most theories of individual or organizational choice accept the idea that goals exist and that (in some sense) an individual or organization acts on those goals, choosing from among some alternatives on the basis of available information. Discussions of educational policy with their emphasis on goal setting, evaluation, and accountability, are in this tradition.

From the perspective of all of man's history, the ideas of purpose, consistency, and rationality are relatively new. Much of the technology currently available to implement them is extremely new. Over the past few centuries, and conspicuously over the past few decades, we have substantially improved man's capability for acting purposively, consistently, and rationally. We have substantially increased his propensity to think of himself as doing so. It is an impressive victory, won—where it has been won—by a happy combination of timing, performance, ideology, and persistence. It is a battle yet to be concluded, or even engaged, in many cultures of the world; but within most of the Western world individuals and organizations see themselves as making choices.

The Problem of Goals

The tools of intelligence as they are fashioned in modern theories of choice are necessary to any reasonable behavior in contemporary society. It is inconceivable that we would fail to continue their development, refinement, and extension. As might be expected, however, a theory and ideology of choice built on the ideas outlined above is deficient in some obvious, elementary ways, most conspicuously in the treatment of human goals.

Goals are thrust upon the intelligent man. We ask that he act in the name of goals. We ask that he keep his goals consistent. We ask that his actions be oriented to his goals. We ask that a social system amalgamate individual goals into a collective goal. But we do not concern ourselves with the origin of goals. Theories of individual, organizational, and social choice assume actors with preexistent values.

Since it is obvious that goals change over time and that the character of those changes affects both the richness of personal and social development and the outcome of choice behavior, a theory of choice must somehow justify ignoring the phenomena. Although it is unreasonable to ask a theory of choice to solve all the problems of man and his development, it is reasonable to ask how such conspicuous elements as the fluidity and ambiguity of objectives can plausibly be ignored in a theory that is offered as a guide to human choice behavior.

There are three classic justifications. The first is that goal development and choice are independent processes, conceptually and behaviorally. The second is that the model of choice is never satisfied in fact and that deviations from the model accommodate the problems of introducing change. The third is that the idea of changing goals is so intractable in a normative theory of choice that nothing can be said about it. Since we are unpersuaded of the first and second justifications, our optimism with respect to the third is somewhat greater than that of most of our fellows.

The argument that goal development and choice are independent behaviorally seems clearly false. It seems to us obvious that a description that assumes that goals come first and action comes later is frequently radically wrong. Human choice behavior is at least as much a process for discovering goals as for acting on them. Although it is true enough that goals and decisions are "conceptually" distinct, that is simply a statement of the theory, not a defense of it. They are conceptually distinct if we choose to make them so.

The argument that the model is incomplete is more persuasive. There do appear to be some critical "holes" in the system of intelligence as described by standard theories of choice. Incomplete information, incomplete goal consistency, and a variety of external processes facilitate goal development. What is somewhat disconcerting about the argument, however, is that it makes the efficacy of the concepts of intelligent choice dependent on their inadequacy. As we become more competent in the techniques of the model and more committed to it, the "holes" become smaller. As the model becomes more accepted, our obligation to modify it increases.

The final argument seems to us sensible as a general principle, but misleading here. Why are we more reluctant to ask how human beings might find "good" goals than we are to ask how they might make "good" decisions? The second question appears to be a more technical problem. The first seems more pretentious. It claims to say something about alternative virtues. The appearance of pretense, however, stems directly from the prevailing theory of choice and the ideology associated with it.

In fact, the conscious introduction of goal discovery for consideration in theories of human choice is not unknown to modern man. For example, we have two kinds of theories of choice behavior in human beings. One is a theory of children. The other is a theory of adults. In the theory of children, we emphasize choices as leading to experiences that develop the child's scope, his complexity, his awareness of the world. As parents, teachers, or psychologists, we try to lead the child to do things that are inconsistent with his present goals because we know (or believe) that he can develop into an interesting person only by coming to appreciate aspects of experience that he initially rejects.

In the theory of adults, we emphasize choices as a consequence of our intentions. As adults, educational decision makers, or economists, we try to take actions that (within the limits of scarce resources) come as close as possible to achieving our goals. We try to find improved ways of making decisions consistent with our perceptions of what is valuable in the world.

The asymmetry in these models is conspicuous. Adults have constructed a model world in which adults know what is good for themselves, but children do not. It is hard to react positively to the conceit. The asymmetry has, in fact, stimulated a large number of ideologies and reforms designed to allow children the same moral prerogative granted to adults—the right to imagine that they know what they want. The efforts have cut deeply into traditional childrearing, traditional educational policies, traditional politics, and traditional consumer economics.

In our judgment, the asymmetry between models of choice for adults and for children is awkward; but the solution we have adopted is precisely wrong-headed. Instead of trying to adapt the model of adults to children, we might better adapt the model of children to adults. For many purposes, our model of children is better. Of course, children know what they want. Everyone does. The critical question is whether they are encouraged to develop more interesting "wants." Values change. People become more interesting as those values and the interconnections made among them change.

One of the most obvious things in the world turns out to be hard for us to accommodate in our theory of choice: A child of two will almost always have a less interesting set of values (indeed, a worse set of values) than a child of 12. The same is true of adults. Values develop through experience. Although one of the main natural arenas for the modification of human values is the arena of choice, our theories of adult and organizational decision making ignore the phenomenon entirely.

Introducing ambiguity and fluidity to the interpretation of individual, organizational, and societal goals obviously has implications for behavioral theories of decision making. We have tried to identify and respond to some of those difficulties in the preceding chapters. The main point here, however, is not to consider how we might describe the behavior of systems that are discovering goals as they act. Rather it is to examine how we might improve the quality of that behavior, how we might aid the development of interesting goals.

We know how to advise a society, an organization, or an individual if we are first given a consistent set of preferences. Under some conditions, we can suggest how to make decisions if the preferences are consistent only up to the point of specifying a series of independent constraints on the choice. But what about a normative theory of goal-finding behavior? What do we say when our client tells us that he is not sure his present set of values is the set of values in terms of which he wants to act?

It is a question familiar to many aspects of ordinary life. It is a question that friends, associates, students, college presidents, business managers, voters, and children ask at least as frequently as they ask how they should act within a set of consistent and stable values.

Within the context of normative theory of choice as it exists, the answer we gave is: First determine the values, then act. The advice is frequently useful. Moreover, we have developed ways in which we can use conventional techniques for decision analysis to help discover value premises and to expose value inconsistencies. These techniques involve testing the decision implications of some successive approximations to a set of preferences. The object is to find a consistent set of preferences with implications that are acceptable to the person or organization making the decisions. Variations on such techniques are used routinely in operations research, as well as in personal counseling and analysis.

The utility of such techniques, however, apparently depends on the assumption that a primary problem is the amalgamation or excavation of preexistent values. The metaphors—"finding oneself," "goal clarification," "self-discovery," "social welfare function," "revealed preference"—are metaphors of search. If our value premises are to be "constructed" rather than "discovered," our standard procedures may be useful: but we have no *a priori* reason for assuming they will.

Perhaps we should explore a somewhat different approach to the normative question of how we ought to behave when our value premises are not yet (and never will be) fully determined. Suppose we treat action as a way of creating interesting goals at the same time as we treat goals as a way of justifying action. It is an intuitively plausible and simple idea, but one that is not immediately within the domain of standard normative theories of intelligent choice.

Interesting people and interesting organizations construct complicated theories of themselves. To do this, they need to supplement the technology of reason with a technology of foolishness. Individuals and organizations sometimes need ways of doing things for which they have no good reason. They need to act before they think.

Sensible Foolishness

To use intelligent choice as a planned occasion for discovering new goals, we require some idea of sensible foolishness. Which of the many foolish things that we might do now will lead to attractive value consequences? The question is almost inconceivable. Not only does it ask us to predict the value consequences of action, it asks us to evaluate them. In what terms can we talk about "good" changes in goals?

In effect, we are asked either to specify a set of supergoals in terms of which alternative goals are evaluated, or to choose among alternatives *now* in terms of the unknown set of values we will have at some future time (or the distribution over time of that unknown set of future values). The former alternative moves us back to the original situation of a fixed set of values—now called "supergoals"—and hardly seems an important step in the direction of inventing procedures for discovering new goals. The latter alternative seems fundamental enough, but it violates severely our sense of temporal order. To say that we make decisions now in terms of goals that will be knowable only later is nonsensical—as long as we accept the basic framework of the theory of choice and its presumptions of preexistent goals.

As we challenge the dogma of preexistent goals, we will be forced to reexamine some of our most precious prejudices: the strictures against imitation, coercion, and rationalization. Each of those honorable prohibitions depends on the view of man and human choice imposed on us by conventional theories of choice.

Imitation is not necessarily a sign of moral weakness. It is a prediction. It is a prediction that if we duplicate the behavior or attitudes of someone else, not only will we fare well in terms of current goals but the chances of our discovering attractive new goals for ourselves are relatively high. If imitation is to be normatively attractive, we need a better theory of who should be imitated. Such a theory seems to be eminently feasible. For example, what are the conditions for effectiveness of a rule that one should imitate another person whose values are close to one's own? How do the chances of discovering interesting goals through imitation change as the number of people exhibiting the behavior to be imitated increases? In the case of the college president we might ask what the goal discovery consequences are of imitating the choices of those at institutions more prestigious than one's own, and whether there are other more desirable patterns of imitation.

Coercion is not necessarily an assault on individual autonomy. It can be a device for stimulating individuality. We recognize this when we talk about education or about parents and children. What has been difficult with coercion is the possibility for perversion, not its obvious capability for stimulating change. We need a theory of the circumstances under which entry into a coercive relationship produces behavior that leads to the discovery of interesting goals. We are all familiar with the tactic. College presidents use it in imposing deadlines, entering contracts, making commitments. What are the conditions for its effective use? In particular, what are the conditions for goal-fostering coercion in social systems?

Rationalization is not necessarily a way of evading morality. It can be a test for the feasibility of a goal change. When deciding among alternative actions for which we have no good reason, it may be sensible to develop some definition of how "near" to intelligence alternative "unintelligent" actions lie. Effective rationalization permits this kind of incremental approach to changes in values. To use it effectively, however, we require a better idea of the metrics that might be possible in measuring value distances. At the same time, rationalization is the major procedure for integrating newly discovered goals into an existing structure of values. It provides the organization of complexity without which complexity itself becomes indistinguishable from randomness.

The dangers in imitation, coercion, and rationalization are too familiar to elaborate. We should, indeed, be able to develop better techniques. Whatever those techniques may be, however, they will almost certainly undermine the superstructure of biases erected on purpose, consistency, and rationality. They will involve some way of thinking about action now as occurring in terms of a set of future values different from those that the actor currently holds.

Play and Reason

A second requirement for a technology of foolishness is some strategy for suspending rational imperatives toward consistency. Even if we know which of several foolish things we want to do, we still need a mechanism for allowing us to do it. How do we escape the logic of our reason?

Here we are closer to understanding what we need. It is playfulness. Playfulness is the deliberate, temporary relaxation of rules in order to explore the possibilities of alternative rules. When we are playful, we challenge the necessity of consistency. In effect, we announce—in advance—our rejection of the usual objections to behavior that does not fit the standard model of intelligence.

Playfulness allows experimentation at the same time that it acknowledges reason. It accepts an obligation that at some point either the playful behavior will be stopped or it will be integrated into the structure of intelligence in some way that makes sense. The suspension of the rules is temporary.

The idea of play may suggest three things that are, in our minds, quite erroneous in the present context. First, play may be seen as a kind of "holiday" for reason, a release of the emotional tensions of virtue. Although it is possible that play performs some such function, that is not the function with which we are concerned. Second, play may be seen as part of some mystical balance of spiritual principles: fire and water, hot and cold, weak and strong. The intention here is much narrower than a general mystique of balance. Third, play may be seen as an antithesis of intelligence, so that the emphasis on the importance of play becomes a support for simple self-indulgence. Our present intent is to propose play as an instrument of intelligence, not a substitute.

Playfulness is a natural outgrowth of our standard view of reason. A strict insistence on purpose, consistency, and rationality limits our ability to find new purposes. Play relaxes that insistence to allow us to act "unintelligently" or "irrationally" or "foolishly" to explore alternative ideas of purposes and alternative concepts of behavioral consistency. And it does this while maintaining our basic commitment to intelligence.

Although play and reason are in this way functional complements, they are often behavioral competitors. They are alternative styles and alternative orientations to the same situation. There is no guarantee that the styles will be equally well developed, that all individuals, organizations, or societies will be equally adept in both styles; or that all cultures will be sufficiently encouraging to both.

Our design problem is either to specify the best mix of styles or, failing that, to assure that most people and most organizations most of the time use an alternation of strategies rather than persevering in either one. It is a difficult problem. The optimization problem looks extremely complex on the face of it, and the learning situations that will produce alternation in behavior appear to be somewhat less common than those that produce perseverance.

Consider, for example, the difficulty of sustaining playfulness as a style within contemporary American society. Individuals who are good at consistent rationality are rewarded early and heavily. We define consistent rationality as intelligence, and the educational rewards of society are associated strongly with it. Social norms press in the same direction, particularly for men. "Changing one's mind" is viewed as feminine and undesirable. Politicians and other leaders will go to enormous lengths to avoid admitting an inconsistency. Many demands of modern organizational life reinforce the same rational abilities and preferences for a style of unchanging purposes.

The result is that many of the most influential and best-educated citizens have experienced a powerful overlearning with respect to rationality. They are exceptionally good at maintaining consistent pictures of themselves, of relating action to purposes. They are exceptionally poor at a playful attitude toward their own beliefs, toward the logic of consistency, or toward the way they see things as being connected in the world. The dictates of manliness, forcefulness, independence, and intelligence are intolerant of playful urges if they arise. The playful urges that arise are weak ones, scarcely discernible in the behavior of most businessmen, mayors, or college presidents.

The picture is probably overdrawn, but we believe that the implications are not. Reason and intelligence have had the unnecessary consequence of inhibiting the development of purpose into more complicated forms of consistency. To move away from that position, we need to find some ways of helping individuals and organizations to experiment with doing things for which they have no good reason, to be playful with their conceptions of themselves. We suggest five things as a small beginning:

First, we can treat *goals as hypotheses*. Conventional theories of decision making allow us to entertain doubts about almost everything except the thing about which we frequently have the greatest doubt—our objectives. Suppose we define the decision-making process as a time for the sequential testing of hypotheses about goals. If we can experiment with alternative goals, we stand some chance of discovering complicated and interesting combinations of good values that none of us previously imagined.

Second, we can treat *intuition as real*. We do not know what intuition is or even if it is any one thing. Perhaps it is simply an excuse for doing something we cannot justify in terms of present values or for refusing to follow the logic of our own beliefs. Perhaps it is an inexplicable way of consulting that part of our intelligence and knowledge of the world that is not organized in a way anticipated by standard theories of choice. In either case, intuition permits us to see some possible actions that are outside our present scheme for justifying behavior.

Third, we can treat *hypocrisy as a transition*. Hypocrisy is an inconsistency between expressed values and behavior. Negative attitudes about hypocrisy stem mainly from a general onus against inconsistency and from a sentiment against combining the pleasures of vice with the appearance of virtue. It seems to us that a bad man with good intentions may be a man experimenting with the possibility of becoming good. Somehow it seems more sensible to encourage the experimentation than to insult it.

Fourth, we can treat *memory as an enemy*. The rules of consistency and rationality require a technology of memory. For most purposes, good memories make good choices. But the ability to forget or overlook is also useful. If you do not know what you did yesterday or what other people in the organization are doing today, you can act within the system of reason and still do things that are foolish.

Fifth, we can treat *experience as a theory*. Learning can be viewed as a series of conclusions based on concepts of action and consequences that we have invented. Experience can be changed retrospectively. By changing our interpretive concepts now, we modify what we learned earlier. Thus we expose the possibility of experimenting with alternative histories. The usual strictures against "self-deception" in experience need occasionally to be tempered with an awareness of the extent to which all experience is an interpretation subject to conscious revision. Personal histories and national histories need to be rewritten continuously as a base for the retrospective learning of new self-conceptions.

If we knew more about the normative theory of acting before thinking, we could say more intelligent things about the functions of management and leadership when organizations or societies do not know what they are doing. Consider, for example, the following general implications.

First, we need to reexamine the functions of management decision making. One of the primary ways in which the goals of an organization are developed is by interpreting the decisions it makes, and one feature of good managerial decisions is that they lead to the development of more interesting value premises for the organization. As a result, decisions should not be seen as flowing directly or strictly from a preexistent set of objectives. College presidents who make decisions might well view that function somewhat less as a process of deduction or a process of political negotiation, and somewhat more as a process of gently upsetting preconceptions of what the organization is doing.

Second, we need a modified view of planning. Planning can often be more effective as an interpretation of past decisions than as a program for future ones. It can be used as a part of the efforts of the organization to develop a new consistent theory of itself that incorporates the mix of recent actions into a moderately comprehensive structure of goals. Procedures for interpreting the meaning of most past events are familiar to the memoirs of retired generals, prime ministers, business leaders, and movie stars. They suffer from the company they keep. In an organization that wants to continue to develop new objectives, a manager needs to be tolerant of the idea that he will discover the meaning of yesterday's action in the experiences and interpretations of today.

Third, we need to reconsider evaluation. As nearly as we can determine, there is nothing in a formal theory of evaluation that requires that criteria be specified in advance. In particular, the evaluation of social experiments need not be in terms of the degree to which they have fulfilled our prior expectations. Rather we can examine what they did in terms of what we now believe to be important. The prior specification of criteria and the prior specification of evaluational procedures that depend on such criteria are common presumptions in contemporary social policy making. They are presumptions that inhibit the serendipitous discovery of new criteria. Experience should be used explicitly as an occasion for evaluating our values as well as our actions.

Fourth, we need a reconsideration of social accountability. Individual preferences and social action need to be consistent in some way. But the process of pursuing consistency is one in which both the preferences and the actions change over time. Imagination in social policy formation involves systematically adapting to and influencing preference. It would be unfortunate if our theories of social action encouraged leaders to ignore their responsibilities for anticipating public preferences through action and for providing social experiences that modify individual expectations.

Fifth, we need to accept playfulness in social organizations. The design of organizations should attend to the problems of maintaining both playfulness and reason as aspects of intelligent choice.

Since much of the literature on social design is concerned with strengthening the rationality of decision making managers are likely to overlook the importance of play. This is partly a matter of making the individuals within an organization more playful by encouraging the attitudes and skills of inconsistency. It is also a matter of making organizational structure and organizational procedures more playful. Organizations can be playful even when the participants in them are not. The managerial devices for maintaining consistency can be varied. We encourage organizational play by insisting on some temporary relief from control, coordination, and communication.

Presidents and Foolishness

Contemporary theories of decision making and the technology of reason have considerably strengthened our capabilities for effective social action. The conversion of the simple ideas of choice into an extensive technology is a major achievement. It is, however, an achievement that has reinforced some biases in the underlying models of choice in individuals and groups. In particular, it has reinforced the uncritical acceptance of a static interpretation of human goals.

There is little magic in the world, and foolishness in people and organizations is one of the many things that fail to produce miracles. Under certain conditions, it is one of several ways in which some of the problems of our current theories of intelligence can be overcome. It may be a good way, for it preserves the virtues of consistency while stimulating change. If we had a good technology of foolishness, it might (in combination with the technology of reason) help in a small way to develop the unusual combinations of attitudes and behaviors that describe the interesting people, interesting organizations, and interesting societies of the world. The contribution of a college president may often be measured by his capability for sustaining that creative interaction of foolishness and rationality.

Notes

1. For anyone who wishes to enter the literature, see by way of introduction Raymond Wolfinger (1971a, 1971b), and Frederick W. Frey (1971).
2. For a discussion of this point in the context of public school decision making, see Stephen Weiner (1972).
3. For a discussion of the same phenomenon in a business setting, see R. M. Cyert and J. G. March (1963).
4. See, for example, Iklé (1964) and Walton and McKersie (1965).
5. These ideas have been the basis for extended conversation with a number of friends. We want to acknowledge particularly the help of Lance Bennett, Patricia Nelson Bennett, Michael Butler, Soren Christensen, Michel Crozier, Claude Faucheux, James R. Glenn, Jr., Gudmund Hernes, Heiga Hernes, Jean Carter Lave, Harold J. Leavitt, Henry M. Levin, Leslie Lincoln, André Massart, John Miller, Johan Olsen, Richard C. Snyder, Alexander Szalai, Eugene J. Webb, and Gail Whitacre.

The Ambiguity of Leadership[1]

Jeffrey Pfeffer

Problems with the concept of leadership are addressed: (a) the ambiguity of its definition and measurement, (b) the issue of whether leadership affects organizational performance, and (c) the process of selecting leaders, which frequently emphasizes organizationally-irrelevant criteria. Leadership is a process of attributing causation to individual social actors. Study of leaders as symbols and of the process of attributing leadership might be productive.

Leadership has for some time been a major topic in social and organizational psychology. Underlying much of this research has been the assumption that leadership is causally related to organizational performance. Through an analysis of leadership styles, behaviors, or characteristics (depending on the theoretical perspective chosen), the argument has been made that more effective leaders can be selected or trained or, alternatively, the situation can be configured to provide for enhanced leader and organizational effectiveness.

Three problems with emphasis on leadership as a concept can be posed: (a) ambiguity in definition and measurement of the concept itself; (b) the question of whether leadership has discernible effects on organizational outcomes; and (c) the selection process in succession to leadership positions, which frequently uses organizationally irrelevant criteria and which has implications for normative theories of leadership. The argument here is that leadership is of interest primarily as a phenomenological construct. Leaders serve as symbols for representing personal causation of social events. How and why are such attributions of personal effects made? Instead of focusing on leadership and its effects, how do people make inferences about and react to phenomena labelled as leadership (5)?

The Ambiguity of the Concept

While there have been many studies of leadership, the dimensions and definition of the concept remain unclear. To treat leadership as a separate concept, it must be distinguished from other social influence phenomena. Hollander and Julian (24) and Bavelas (2) did not draw distinctions between leadership and other processes of social influence. A major point of the Hollander and Julian review was that leadership research might develop more rapidly if more general theories of social influence were incorporated. Calder (5) also argued that there is no unique content to the construct of leadership that is not subsumed under other, more general models of behavior.

Kochan, Schmidt, and DeCotiis (33) attempted to distinguish leadership from related concepts of authority and social power. In leadership, influence rights are voluntarily conferred. Power does not require goal compatability—merely dependence—but leadership implies some congruence between the objectives of the leader and the led. These distinctions depend on the ability to distinguish voluntary from involuntary compliance and to assess goal compatibility. Goal statements may be retrospective inferences from action (46, 53) and problems of distinguishing voluntary from

"The Ambiguity of Leadership," by Jeffrey Pfeffer, reprinted with permission from *Academy of Management Review*, Vol. 12, No. 1, January 1977.

involuntary compliance also exist (32). Apparently there are few meaningful distinctions between leadership and other concepts of social influence. Thus, an understanding of the phenomena subsumed under the rubric of leadership may not require the construct of leadership (5).

While there is some agreement that leadership is related to social influence, more disagreement concerns the basic dimensions of leader behavior. Some have argued that there are two tasks to be accomplished in groups—maintenance of the group and performance of some task or activity—and thus leader behavior might be described along these two dimensions (1, 6, 8, 25). The dimensions emerging from the Ohio State leadership studies—consideration and initiating structure—may be seen as similar to the two components of group maintenance and task accomplishment (18).

Other dimensions of leadership behavior have also been proposed (4). Day and Hamblin (10) analyzed leadership in terms of the closeness and punitiveness of the supervision. Several authors have conceptualized leadership behavior in terms of the authority and discretion subordinates are permitted (23, 36, 51). Fiedler (14) analyzed leadership in terms of the least-preferred-co-worker scale (LPC), but the meaning and behavioral attributes of this dimension of leadership behavior remain controversial.

The proliferation of dimensions is partly a function of research strategies frequently employed. Factor analysis on a large number of items describing behavior has frequently been used. This procedure tends to produce as many factors as the analyst decides to find, and permits the development of a large number of possible factor structures. The resultant factors must be named and further imprecision is introduced. Deciding on a summative concept to represent a factor is inevitably a partly subjective process.

Literature assessing the effects of leadership tends to be equivocal. Sales (45) summarized leadership literature employing the authoritarian-democratic typology and concluded that effects on performance were small and inconsistent. Reviewing the literature on consideration and initiating structure dimensions, Korman (34) reported relatively small and inconsistent results, and Kerr and Schriesheim (30) reported more consistent effects of the two dimensions. Better results apparently emerge when moderating factors are taken into account, including subordinate personalities (50), and situational characteristics (23, 51). Kerr, et al. (31) list many moderating effects grouped under the headings of subordinate considerations, supervisor considerations, and task considerations. Even if each set of considerations consisted of only one factor (which it does not), an attempt to account for the effects of leader behavior would necessitate considering four-way interactions. While social reality is complex and contingent, it seems desirable to attempt to find more parsimonious explanations for the phenomena under study.

The Effects of Leaders

Hall asked a basic question about leadership: is there any evidence on the magnitude of the effects of leadership (17, p. 248)? Surprisingly, he could find little evidence. Given the resources that have been spent studying, selecting, and training leaders, one might expect that the question of whether or not leaders matter would have been addressed earlier (12).

There are at least three reasons why it might be argued that the observed effects of leaders on organizational outcomes would be small. First, those obtaining leadership positions are selected, and perhaps only certain, limited styles of behavior may be chosen. Second, once in the leadership position, the discretion and behavior of the leader are constrained. And third, leaders can typically affect only a few of the variables that may impact organizational performance.

Homogeneity of Leaders

Persons are selected to leadership positions. As a consequence of this selection process, the range of behaviors or characteristics exhibited by leaders is reduced, making it more problematic to empirically discover an effect of leadership. There are many types of constraints on the selection process. The attraction literature suggests that there is a tendency for persons to like those they perceive as similar (3). In critical decisions such as the selections of persons for leadership positions, compatible styles of behavior probably will be chosen.

Selection of persons is also constrained by the internal system of influence in the organization. As Zald (56) noted, succession is a critical decision, affected by political influence and by environmental contingencies faced by the organization. As Thompson (49) noted, leaders may be selected for their capacity to deal with various organizational contingencies. In a study of characteristics of hospital administrators, Salancik (42) found a relationship between the hospital's context and the characteristics and tenure of the administrators. To the extent that the contingencies and power distribution within the organization remain stable, the abilities and behaviors of those selected into leadership positions will also remain stable.

Finally, the selection of persons to leadership positions is affected by a self-selection process. Organizations and roles have images, providing information about their character. Persons are likely to select themselves into organizations and roles based upon their preferences for the dimensions of the organizational and role characteristics as perceived through these images. The self-selection of persons would tend to work along with organizational selection to limit the range of abilities and behaviors in a given organizational role.

Such selection processes would tend to increase homogeneity more within a single organization than across organizations. Yet many studies of leadership effect at the work group level have compared groups within a single organization. If there comes to be a widely shared, socially constructed definition of leadership behaviors or characteristics which guides the selection process, then leadership activity may come to be defined similarly in various organizations, leading to the selection of only those who match the constructed image of a leader.

Constraints on Leader Behavior

Analyses of leadership have frequently presumed that leadership style or leader behavior was an independent variable that could be selected or trained at will to conform to what research would find to be optimal. Even theorists who took a more contingent view of appropriate leadership behavior generally assumed that with proper training, appropriate behavior could be produced (51). Fiedler (13), noting how hard it was to change behavior, suggested changing the situational characteristics rather than the person, but this was an unusual suggestion in the context of prevailing literature which suggested that leadership style was something to be strategically selected according to the variables of the particular leadership theory.

But the leader is embedded in a social system, which constrains behavior. The leader has a role set (27), in which members have expectations for appropriate behavior and persons make efforts to modify the leader's behavior. Pressures to conform to the expectations of peers, subordinates, and superiors are all relevant in determining actual behavior.

Leaders, even in high-level positions, have unilateral control over fewer resources and fewer policies than might be expected. Investment decisions may require approval of others, while hiring and promotion decisions may be accomplished by committees. Leader behavior is constrained by both the demands of others in the role set and by organizationally prescribed limitations on the sphere of activity and influence.

External Factors

Many factors that may affect organizational performance are outside a leader's control, even if he or she were to have complete discretion over major areas of organizational decisions. For example, consider the executive in a construction firm. Costs are largely determined by operation of commodities and labor markets; and demand is largely affected by interest rates, availability of mortgage money, and economic conditions which are affected by governmental policies over which the executive has little control. School superintendents have little control over birth rates and community economic development, both of which profoundly affect school system budgets. While the leader may react to contingencies as they arise, or may be a better or worse forecaster, in accounting for variation in organizational outcomes, he or she may account for relatively little compared to external factors.

Second, the leader's success or failure may be partly due to circumstances unique to the organization but still outside his or her control. Leader positions in organizations vary in terms of the strength and position of the organization. The choice of a new executive does not fundamentally alter a market and financial position that has developed over years and affects the leader's ability to make strategic changes and the likelihood that the organization will do well or poorly. Organizations have relatively enduring strengths and weaknesses. The choice of a particular leader for a particular position has limited impact on these capabilities.

Empirical Evidence

Two studies have assessed the effects of leadership changes in major positions in organizations. Lieberson and O'Connor (35) examined 167 business firms in 13 industries over a 20 year period, allocating variance in sales, profits, and profit margins to one of four sources: year (general economic conditions), industry, company effects, and effects of changes in the top executive position. They concluded that compared to other factors, administration had a limited effect on organizational outcomes.

Using a similar analytical procedure, Salancik and Pfeffer (44) examined the effects of mayors on city budgets for 30 U.S. cities. Data on expenditures by budget category were collected for 1951–1968. Variance in amount and proportion of expenditures was apportioned to the year, the city, or the mayor. The mayoral effect was relatively small, with the city accounting for most of the variance, although the mayor effect was larger for expenditure categories that were not as directly connected to important interest groups. Salancik and Pfeffer argued that the effects of the mayor were limited both by absence of power to control many of the expenditures and tax sources, and by construction of policies in response to demands from interests in the environment.

If leadership is defined as a strictly interpersonal phenomenon, the relevance of these two studies for the issue of leadership effects becomes problematic. But such a conceptualization seems unduly restrictive, and is certainly inconsistent with Selznick's (47) conceptualization of leadership as strategic management and decision making. If one cannot observe differences when leaders change, then what does it matter who occupies the positions or how they behave?

Pfeffer and Salancik (41) investigated the extent to which behaviors selected by first-line supervisors were constrained by expectations of others in their role set. Variance in task and social behaviors could be accounted for by role-set expectations, with adherence to various demands made by role-set participants a function of similarity and relative power. Lowin and Craig (37) experimentally demonstrated that leader behavior was determined by the subordinate's own behavior. Both studies illustrate that leader behaviors are responses to the demands of the social context.

The effect of leadership may vary depending upon level in the organizational hierarchy, while the appropriate activities and behaviors may also vary with organizational level (26, 40). For the most part, empirical studies of leadership have dealt with first line supervisors or leaders with relatively low organizational status (17). If leadership has any impact, it should be more evident at higher organizational levels or where there is more discretion in decisions and activities.

The Process of Selecting Leaders

Along with the suggestion that leadership may not account for much variance in organizational outcomes, it can be argued that merit or ability may not account for much variation in hiring and advancement of organizational personnel. These two ideas are related. If competence is hard to judge, or if leadership competence does not greatly affect organizational outcomes, then other, person-dependent criteria may be sufficient. Effective leadership styles may not predict career success when other variables such as social background are controlled.

Belief in the importance of leadership is frequently accompanied by belief that persons occupying leadership positions are selected and trained according to how well they can enhance the organization's performance. Belief in a leadership effect leads to development of a set of activities oriented toward enhancing leadership effectiveness. Simultaneously, persons managing their own careers are likely to place emphasis on activities and developing behaviors that will enhance their own leadership skills, assuming that such a strategy will facilitate advancement.

Research on the bases for hiring and promotion has been concentrated in examination of academic positions (e.g., 7, 19, 20). This is possibly the result of availability of relatively precise and unambiguous measures of performance, such as number of publications or citations. Evidence on criteria used in selecting and advancing personnel in industry is more indirect.

Studies have attempted to predict either the compensation or the attainment of general management positions of MBA students, using personality and other background information (21, 22, 54). There is some evidence that managerial success can be predicted by indicators of ability and motivation such as test scores and grades, but the amount of variance explained is typically quite small.

A second line of research has investigated characteristics and backgrounds of persons attaining leadership positions in major organizations in society. Domhoff (11), Mills (38), and Warner and Abbeglin (52) found a strong preponderance of persons with upper-class backgrounds occupying leadership positions. The implication of these findings is that studies of graduate success, including the success of MBA's, would explain more variance if the family background of the person were included.

A third line of inquiry uses a tracking model. The dynamic model developed is one in which access to elite universities is affected by social status (28) and, in turn, social status and attendance at elite universities affect later career outcomes (9, 43, 48, 55).

Unless one is willing to make the argument that attendance at elite universities or coming from an upper class background is perfectly correlated with merit, the evidence suggests that succession to leadership positions is not strictly based on meritocratic criteria. Such a conclusion is consistent with the inability of studies attempting to predict the success of MBA graduates to account for much variance, even when a variety of personality and ability factors are used.

Beliefs about the bases for social mobility are important for social stability. As long as persons believe that positions are allocated on meritocratic grounds, they are more likely to be satisfied with the social order and with their position in it. This satisfaction derives from the belief that occupational position results from application of fair and reasonable criteria, and that the opportunity exists for mobility if the person improves skills and performance.

If succession to leadership positions is determined by person-based criteria such as social origins or social connections (16), then efforts to enhance managerial effectiveness with the expectation that this will lead to career success divert attention from the processes of stratification actually operating within organizations. Leadership literature has been implicitly aimed at two audiences. Organizations were told how to become more effective, and persons were told what behaviors to acquire in order to become effective, and hence, advance in their careers. The possibility that neither organizational outcomes nor career success are related to leadership behaviors leaves leadership research facing issues of relevance and importance.

The Attribution of Leadership

Kelley conceptualized the layman as:

> an applied scientist, that is, as a person concerned about applying his knowledge of causal relationships in order to exercise control of his world (29, p. 2).

Reviewing a series of studies dealing with the attributional process, he concluded that persons were not only interested in understanding their world correctly, but also in controlling it.

> The view here proposed is that attribution processes are to be understood not only as a means of providing the individual with a veridical view of his world, but as a means of encouraging and maintaining his effective exercise of control in that world (29, p. 22).

Controllable factors will have high salience as candidates for causal explanation, while a bias toward the more important causes may shift the attributional emphasis toward causes that are not controllable (29, p. 23). The study of attribution is a study of naive psychology—an examination of how persons make sense out of the events taking place around them.

If Kelley is correct that individuals will tend to develop attributions that give them a feeling of control, then emphasis on leadership may derive partially from a desire to believe in the effectiveness and importance of individual action, since individual action is more controllable than contextual variables. Lieberson and O'Connor (35) made essentially the same point in introducing their paper on the effects of top management changes on organizational performance. Given the desire for control and a feeling of personal effectiveness, organizational outcomes are more likely to be attributed to individual actions, regardless of their actual causes.

Leadership is attributed by observers. Social action has meaning only through a phenomenological process (46). The identification of certain organizational roles as leadership positions guides the construction of meaning in the direction of attributing effects to the actions of those positions. While Bavelas (2) argued that the functions of leadership, such as task accomplishment and group maintenance, are shared throughout the group, this fact provides no simple and potentially controllable focus for attributing causality. Rather, the identification of leadership positions provides a simpler and more readily changeable model of reality. When causality is lodged in one or a few persons rather than being a function of a complex set of interactions among all group members, changes can be made by replacing or influencing the occupant of the leadership position. Causes of organizational actions are readily identified in this simple causal structure.

Even if, empirically, leadership has little effect, and even if succession to leadership positions is not predicated on ability or performance, the belief in leadership effects and meritocratic succession provides a simple causal framework and a justification for the structure of the social collectivity. More importantly, the beliefs interpret social actions in terms that indicate potential for effective individual intervention or control. The personification of social causality serves too many uses to be easily overcome. Whether or not leader behavior actually influences performance or effectiveness, it is important because people believe it does.

One consequence of the attribution of causality to leaders and leadership is that leaders come to be symbols. Mintzberg (39), in his discussion of the roles of managers, wrote of the symbolic role, but more in terms of attendance at formal events and formally representing the organization. The symbolic role of leadership is more important than implied in such a description. The leader as a symbol provides a target for action when difficulties occur, serving as a scapegoat when things go wrong. Gamson and Scotch (15) noted that in baseball, the firing of the manager served a scapegoating purpose. One cannot fire the whole team, yet when performance is poor, something must be done. The firing of the manager conveys to the world and to the actors involved that success is the result of personal actions, and that steps can and will be taken to enhance organizational performance.

The attribution of causality to leadership may be reinforced by organizational actions, such as the inauguration process, the choice process, and providing the leader with symbols and ceremony. If leaders are chosen by using a random number table, persons are less likely to believe in their effects than if there is an elaborate search or selection process followed by an elaborate ceremony signifying the changing of control, and if the leader then has a variety of perquisites and symbols that distinguish him or her from the rest of the organization. Construction of the importance of leadership in a given social context is the outcome of various social processes, which can be empirically examined.

Since belief in the leadership effect provides a feeling of personal control, one might argue that efforts to increase the attribution of causality to leaders would occur more when it is more necessary and more problematic to attribute causality to controllable factors. Such an argument would lead to the hypothesis that the more the *context* actually effects organizational outcomes, the more efforts will be made to ensure attribution to *leadership*. When leaders really do have effects, it is less necessary to engage in rituals indicating their effects. Such rituals are more likely when there is uncertainty and unpredictability associated with the organization's operations. This results both from the desire to feel control in uncertain situations and from the fact that in ambiguous contexts, it is easier to attribute consequences to leadership without facing possible disconfirmation.

The leader is, in part, an actor. Through statements and actions, the leader attempts to reinforce the operation of an attribution process which tends to vest causality in that position in the social structure. Successful leaders, as perceived by members of the social system, are those who can separate themselves from organizational failures and associate themselves with organizational successes. Since the meaning of action is socially constructed, this involves manipulation of symbols to reinforce the desired process of attribution. For instance, if a manager knows that business in his or her division is about to improve because of the economic cycle, the leader may, nevertheless, write recommendations and undertake actions and changes that are highly visible and that will tend to identify his or her behavior closely with the division. A manager who perceives impending failure will attempt to associate the division and its policies and decisions with others, particularly persons in higher organizational positions, and to disassociate himself or herself from the division's performance, occasionally even transferring or moving to another organization.

Conclusion

The theme of this article has been that analysis of leadership and leadership processes must be contingent on the intent of the researcher. If the interest is in understanding the causality of social phenomena as reliably and accurately as possible, then the concept of leadership may be a poor place to begin. The issue of the effects of leadership is open to question. But examination of situational variables that accompany more or less leadership effect is a worthwhile task.

The more phenomenological analysis of leadership directs attention to the process by which social causality is attributed, and focuses on the distinction between causality as perceived by group members and causality as assessed by an outside observer. Leadership is associated with a set of myths reinforcing a social construction of meaning which legitimates leadership role occupants, provides belief in potential mobility for those not in leadership roles, and attributes social causality to leadership roles, thereby providing a belief in the effectiveness of individual control. In analyzing leadership, this mythology and the process by which such mythology is created and supported should be separated from analysis of leadership as a social influence process, operating within constraints.

Note

1. An earlier version of this paper was presented at the conference, Leadership: Where Else Can We Go?, Center for Creative Leadership, Greensboro, North Carolina, June 30–July 1, 1975.

References

Bales, R. F. *Interaction Process Analysis: A Method for the Study of Small Groups,* Reading, Mass.: Addison-Wesley, 1950.

Bavelas, Alex. "Leadership: Man and Function," *Administrative Science Quarterly,* 1960, 4; 491–498.

Berscheid, Ellen, and Elaine Walster. *Interpersonal Attraction,* Reading, Mass.: Addison-Wesley, 1969.

Bowers, David G., and Stanley E. Seashore. "Predicting Organizational Effectiveness with a Four-Factor Theory of Leadership," *Administrative Science Quarterly,* 1966, 11; 238–263.

Calder, Bobby J. "An Attribution Theory of Leadership," in B. Slaw and G. Salancik (Eds.), *New Directions in Organizational Behavior,* Chicago: St. Clair Press, 1976, in press.

Cartwright, Dorwin C., and Alvin Zander. *Group Dynamics: Research and Theory,* 3rd ed., Evanston, Ill.: Row, Peterson, 1960.

Cole, Jonathan R., and Stephen Cole. *Social Stratification in Science,* Chicago: University of Chicago Press, 1973.

Collins, Barry E., and Harold Guetzkow. *A Social Psychology of Group Processes for Decision-Making,* New York: Wiley, 1964.

Collins, Randall. "Functional and Conflict Theories of Stratification," *American Sociological Review,* 1971, 36; 1002–1019.

Day, R. C., and R. L. Hamblin. "Some Effects of Close and Punitive Styles of Supervision," *American Journal of Sociology,* 1964, 69; 499–510.

Domhoff, G. William. *Who Rules America?* Englewood Cliffs, N.J.: Prentice-Hall, 1967.

Dubin, Robert. "Supervision and Productivity: Empirical Findings and Theoretical Considerations," in R. Dubin, G. C. Homans, F. C. Mann, and D. C. Miller (Eds.), *Leadership and Productivity*, San Francisco: Chandler Publishing Co., 1965; 1–50.

Fiedler, Fred E. "Engineering the Job to Fit the Manager," *Harvard Business Review*, 1965, 43; 115–122.

Fiedler, Fred E. *A Theory of Leadership Effectiveness*, New York: McGraw-Hill, 1967.

Gamson, William A., and Norman A. Scotch. "Scapegoating in Baseball," *American Journal of Sociology*, 1964, 70; 69–72.

Granovetter, Mark. *Getting a Job*, Cambridge, Mass.: Harvard University Press, 1974.

Hall, Richard H. *Organizations: Structure and Process*, Englewood Cliffs, N.J.: Prentice-Hall, 1972.

Halpin, A. W., and J. Winer. "A Factorial Study of the Leader Behavior Description Questionnaire," in R. M. Stogdill and A. E. Coons (Eds.), *Leader Behavior: Its Description and Measurement*, Columbus, Ohio: Bureau of Business Research, Ohio State University, 1957; 39–51.

Hargens L. L. "Patterns of Mobility of New Ph.D.'s Among American Academic Institutions," *Sociology of Education*, 1969, 42; 18–37.

Hargens, L. L., and W. O. Hagstrom. "Sponsored and Contest Mobility of American Academic Scientists," *Sociology of Education*, 1967, 40; 24–38.

Harrell, Thomas W. "High Earning MBA's," *Personnel Psychology*, 1972, 25; 523–530.

Harrell, Thomas W., and Margaret S. Harrell. "Predictors of Management Success." *Stanford University Graduate School of Business, Technical Report No. 3 to the Office of Naval Research*.

Heller, Frank, and Yukl, Gary. "Participation, Managerial Decision-Making and Situational Variables," *Organizational Behavior and Human Performance*, 1969, 4; 227–241.

Hollander, Edwin P., and James W. Julian. "Contemporary Trends in the Analysis of Leadership Processes," *Psychological Bulletin*, 1969, 71; 387–397.

House, Robert J. "A Path Goal Theory of Leader Effectiveness," *Administrative Science Quarterly*, 1971, 16; 321–338.

Hunt, J. G. "Leadership-Style Effects at Two Managerial Levels in a Simulated Organization," *Administrative Science Quarterly*, 1971, 16; 476–485.

Kahn, R. L., D. M. Wolfe, R. P. Quinn, and J. D. Snoek. *Organizational Stress: Studies in Role Conflict and Ambiguity*, New York: Wiley, 1964.

Karabel, J., and A. W. Astin. "Social Class, Academic Ability, and College 'Quality'," *Social Forces*, 1975, 53; 381–398.

Kelley, Harold H. *Attribution in Social Interaction*, Morristown, N.J.: General Learning Press, 1971.

Kerr, Steven, and Chester Schriesheim. "Consideration, Initiating Structure and Organizational Criteria—An Update of Korman's 1966 Review," *Personnel Psychology*, 1974, 27; 555–568.

Kerr, S., C. Schriesheim, C. J. Murphy, and R. M. Stogdill, "Toward A Contingency Theory of Leadership Based Upon the Consideration and Initiating Structure Literature," *Organizational Behavior and Human Performance*, 1974, 12; 62–82.

Kiesler, C., and S. Kiesler. *Conformity*, Reading, Mass.: Addison-Wesley, 1969.

Kochan, T. A., S. M. Schmidt, and T. A. DeCotiis. "Superior-Subordinate Relations: Leadership and Headship," *Human Relations*, 1975, 28; 279–294.

Korman, A. K. "Consideration, Initiating Structure, and Organizational Criteria—A Review," *Personnel Psychology*, 1966, 19; 349–362.

Lieberson, Stanley, and James F. O'Connor. "Leadership and Organizational Performance: A Study of Large Corporations," *American Sociological Review*, 1972, 37; 117–130.

Lippitt, Ronald. "An Experimental Study of the Effect of Democratic and Authoritarian Group Atmospheres," *University of Iowa Studies in Child Welfare*, 1940, 16; 43–195.

Lowin, A., and J. R. Craig. "The Influence of Level of Performance on Managerial Style: An Experimental Object-Lesson in the Ambiguity of Correlational Data," *Organizational Behavior and Human Performance*, 1968, 3; 440–458.

Mills, C. Wright. "The American Business Elite: A Collective Portrait," in C. W. Mills, *Power, Politics, and People*, New York: Oxford University Press, 1963; 110–139.

Mintzberg, Henry. *The Nature of Managerial Work*. New York: Harper and Row, 1973.

Nealey, Stanley M., and Milton R. Blood. "Leadership Performance of Nursing Supervisors at Two Organizational Levels," *Journal of Applied Psychology*, 1968, 52; 414–442.

Pfeffer, Jeffrey, and Gerald R. Salancik. "Determinants of Supervisory Behavior: A Role Set Analysis, *Human Relations,* 1975, 28; 139–154.

Pfeffer, Jeffrey, and Gerald R. Salancik. "Organizational Context and the Characteristics and Tenure of Hospital Administrators," *Academy of Management Journal,* 1977, 20, in press.

Reed, R. H., and H. P. Miller. "Some Determinants of the Variation in Earnings for College Men," *Journal of Human Resources,* 1970, 5; 117–190.

Salancik, Gerald R., and Jeffrey Pfeffer. "Constraints on Administrator Discretion: The Limited Influence of Mayors on City Budgets," *Urban Affairs Quarterly,* in press.

Sales, Stephen M. "Supervisory Style and Productivity: Review and Theory," *Personnel Psychology,* 1966,19; 275–286.

Schutz, Alfred. *The Phenomenology of the Social World,* Evanston, Ill.: Northwestern University Press, 1967.

Selznick, P. *Leadership in Administration,* Evanston, Ill.: Row, Peterson, 1957.

Spaeth, J. L., and A. M. Greeley. *Recent Alumni and Higher Education,* New York: McGraw-Hill, 1970.

Thompson, James D. *Organizations in Action,* New York: McGraw-Hill, 1967.

Vroom, Victor H. "Some Personality Determinants of the Effects of Participation," *Journal of Abnormal and Social Psychology,* 1959, 59; 322–327.

Vroom, Victor H., and Phillip W. Yetton. *Leadership and Decision-Making,* Pittsburgh: University of Pittsburgh Press, 1973.

Warner, W. L., and J. C. Abbeglin. *Big Business Leaders in America,* New York: Harper and Brothers, 1955.

Weick, Karl E. *The Social Psychology of Organizing,* Reading, Mass.: Addison-Wesley, 1969.

Weinstein, Alan G., and V. Srinivasan. "Predicting Managerial Success of Master of Business Administration (MBA) Graduates," *Journal of Applied Psychology,* 1974, 59; 207–212.

Wolfle, Dael. *The Uses of Talent,* Princeton: Princeton University Press, 1971.

Zald, Mayer N. "Who Shall Rule? A Political Analysis of Succession in a Large Welfare Organization," *Pacific Sociological Review,* 1965, 1; 52–60.

Jeffrey Pfeffer (Ph.D.—Stanford University) is Associate Professor in the School of Business Administration and Associate Research Sociologist in the Institute of Industrial Relations at the University of California, Berkeley.

SYMBOLISM AND PRESIDENTIAL PERCEPTIONS OF LEADERSHIP

WILLIAM G. TIERNEY

In the last decade, organizational researchers have shown considerable interest in the interpretive aspects of organizational life. Rather than viewing an organization as rational and objective, theorists have used the perspective that organizations are socially constructed and subjective entities. Symbolism has emerged as a critical theme. For example, Birnbaum (in press) has investigated the symbolic aspects of the academic senate, Pfeffer (1981) has considered management as symbolic action; and Tierney has undertaken a semiotic analysis of a private, liberal arts college (1987).

Researchers have also noted the significance of a leader's use of symbols. "The only thing of real importance that leaders do is to create and manage culture," asserts Edgar Schein. "The unique talent of leaders is their ability to work with culture" (1985, 2). Birnbaum has commented, "To emphasize the importance of leadership as myth and symbol is not to denigrate the role of leaders, but rather to identify a particularly critical function that they play" (1988, 208). If a central task of leadership is managing the symbolic aspects of the organization, then obviously it is helpful to investigate what leaders perceive leadership to be and what activities leaders perceive they have used to realize those perceptions.

This paper seeks to shed light on the discussion of leadership in higher education from the perspective of its symbolic dimensions. By investigating presidential perceptions of leadership using the National Center of Postsecondary Governance and Finance's Institutional Leadership Project, I developed a schema of symbolic categories leaders use to accomplish their goals. First, I consider leadership and symbolism from an interpretive perspective. Second, I discuss the methodology and how I developed the symbolic categories; I then incorporate the data used from the Institutional Leadership Project to examine the symbolic aspects of presidential perceptions of leadership. I conclude by discussing the implications for administrators of understanding the symbolism of their leadership.

Leadership and Symbolism

First, how does one think about a symbol? Second, how does symbolism enhance and help define leadership? Third, what constraints does the organization impose on a leader's use of symbols?

The Nature of Symbols

Organizational theorists (Dandridge, Mitroff, and Joyce 1980; Peters and Waterman 1982; Pettigrew 1979; Trice and Beyer 1984) have tended to view symbols either as objects or as reified objects that serve as vehicles for conveying meaning. I assume, however, that symbols connote more than objectivized meaning, and they are not simply vehicles in which meaning resides—tabernacles which hold institutional beliefs.

Symbols exist within an organization whether or not the organization's participants are aware of these symbols. To speak of organizations is to speak of interpretation and symbols. An organization void of symbolism is an organization bereft of human activity. Given that symbols exist wherever human activity occurs, a central question for researchers is how to define and uncover symbols in organizations. Particularly germane for this paper is how to interpret symbols of leadership.

Symbols reside in a wide variety of discursive and nondiscursive message units: an act, event, language, dress, structural roles, ceremonies, or even spatial positions in an organization. Hence, we must understand the context in which symbols function and how leaders communicate symbols to create and interpret their organizational reality.

Symbols and Leadership

As with any act of communication, the audience that receives a message must necessarily interpret what the message means. A manager who walks around a building, casually talking with subordinates, for example, may be considered a symbol of management's respect for everyone in the organization. Conversely, organizational participants may feel that the leader is "checking up" on everyone and that such symbolic behavior is intrusive.

Similarly, leaders who remain in their offices, and never converse informally with subordinates may symbolize in their business-oriented approach the message that formalized tasks, rules, and procedures are what the organization values. The point is not that a leader must use this or that trait to be an effective leader. Rather, I suggest that "management by walking around," as well as any other management strategy, is a symbolic act, open to interpretation. Indeed, a manager's informal style can symbolize any number of messages to different constituencies—friendship, accessibility, intrusiveness, or harassment, to name but a few possible interpretations.

As conscious or unconscious forms for participant understanding of the organization, symbols change and evolve due to historical ruptures, responses to the exterior environment, and individual influence. Individuals attach significance to any number of phenomena, and it is in the context of the organization itself that symbols acquire shared meaning. Thus, the key to understanding organizational symbols lies in delineating the symbolic forms whereby the participants communicate, perpetuate, and develop their knowledge about and attitudes toward life (Geertz 1973).

Conversely, symbolism enhances and helps define leadership. Clifford Geertz observes that leaders

> . . . justify their existence and order their actions in terms of a collection of stories, ceremonies, insignia, formalities, and appurtenances that they have either inherited . . . or invented. It is these—crowns and coronations, limousines and conferences—that mark the center as center and give what goes on there its aura of being not merely important but in some odd fashion connected with the way the world is built (1983, 124).

Symbolism is intertwined with participants' expectation and understanding of leadership. The symbolic role of a college or university president allows an individual to try to communicate a vision of the institution that other individuals are incapable of communicating. We understand leadership through such symbols as the president's yearly speech at convocation or, as will be shown, by a host of activities that "mark the center as center."

Organizational Constraints

Yet leaders are not entirely free to define what is or is not symbolic. Organizations channel activity and interpretation, constraining a leader's use of symbols. Merely because a college president intends for an open door to signify open communication does not assure that the faculty will so interpret it. Almost all leaders in higher education inherit organizations with a history; thus, the parameters of the organization's culture and ideology help fix not only what is or is not symbolic but also what that symbol signifies.

Organizational participants need to feel that they comprehend what is going on in the organization. To do so, they interpret abstractions, often following suggestions made by their leaders. Bailey notes, "We focus on some things and ignore others; we impose a pattern on the flow of events, and thus 'falsify' them if only by simplifying the diversity and the complexity . . . and so make the real world comprehensible" (1983, 18).

College presidents highlight some activities and ignore others; they employ a wide variety of symbolic forms to communicate their messages to different constituencies. To adequately understand how leaders make sense of the organizational universe for their followers, it is important to deconstruct the underlying conceptual orientations that presidents bring to their leadership roles and contexts. It is these concepts and ideologies that shape presidents' perceptions of their organizations and presidential actions within those organizations. Symbolism both defines leadership and is defined by the organization in which the leader resides.

Methodology and Data

Research teams collected data through on-site, semi-structured interviews with the presidents of thirty-two colleges and universities participating in the Institutional Leadership Project (ILP), a five-year longitudinal study conducted by the National Center for Postsecondary Governance and Finance. (For the purposes of the ILP and its purposive stratified sampling procedure, see Birnbaum, Bensimon, and Neumann 1989.)

Data for this paper comes from the presidents' responses to three analytical questions.

1. What is the meaning of "good" presidential leadership?
2. What have you done as a presidential leader?
3. What are you like as a presidential leader?

I reviewed the transcripts of presidential responses, looking especially for comments that were symbolic in nature. Building on previous discussions of what defines a symbol (Deal and Kennedy 1982; Eco 1979; Trice and Beyer 1984), 1 then disaggregated the data into six categories: metaphorical, physical, communicative, structural, personification, and ideational. These categories are not always mutually exclusive; a symbol may fall within more than one category or reinforce another symbolic category. Nor do these six categories necessarily cover all organizational symbols. This is an "essay" in the root sense of the word—a trial of some ideas.

It is also important to point out that I built the categories from previous work on symbolism. The presidents did not devise them. Needless to say, when presidents act they do not generally think, "I am now using a structural symbol." Indeed, one intent of this paper is to provide a provisional framework which presidents might use in reflecting on their leadership acts and thinking about the use of symbols.

In reviewing the data I neither found differences due to institutional type in how presidents symbolically perceived leadership nor did I find substantial differences between presidents appointed within the last three years and "old" presidents. Instead, I found similarities across type and between new and old presidents, as well as differences within type and among the same presidential generation. However, as we will see, what is particularly important when we analyze symbols in an organization is the manner and intention with which presidents use symbols. That is, two presidents may use the same symbolic form with the same frequency, but their purposes will be quite different.

The limitations of this study have already been referred to in the Introduction to these articles. We have analyzed presidents' responses but not the context surrounding those responses. That is, the data of this paper comes from the mouths of presidents. Analyzing the data of faculty and other constituents about their perceptions of presidential symbols is yet to come. It also was not my purpose to count or gradate the frequency of symbolic categories. Prior to such a task we will first need a clearer understanding of symbolic categories. What follows is a discussion of each category that highlights how presidents act symbolically.

Metaphorical Symbols

Metaphors are figures of speech. Presidents provide figures of speech for themselves, their organization, environment, and activities as if something were that particular other. The metaphors an individual uses provide participants with a portrait of how the organization functions. One president noted:

> My philosophy of leadership is to have a team approach to managing the university. The executive committee is a group that shares certain values and expectations, and we push each other hard for the good of the college. What is essential is that we have an effective team, and that we portray that to the board and the community.

Another individual consistently mentioned how it was important "to provide the glue" so that the organization "sticks together." And still another president spoke of organizational participants as "troops" that needed to be rallied.

Presidents also use different metaphors to describe themselves. "I am militaristic . . . like a football coach," observed one. "I am their counselor," commented another. And a third individual was a maestro: "Being president is like an orchestra conductor."

Metaphors give participants a way of seeing and, hence, of acting in the organizational universe. The organization where the participants see themselves as a team presumably interacts differently than the organization led by a general who commands troops. Similarly, an organization that needs glue is different from an organization where it is unimportant to stick together but where a prime metaphorical value concerns "everyone pulling his or her own weight."

Presidents perceive themselves as leaders in a multitude of ways. By focusing on particular metaphors, a president simplifies the organizational universe by providing an image of leadership and the organization. However, the success or failure of a metaphor as a strategy may depend on how the metaphor fits with the organization's culture. That is, a faculty that sees itself as an academy of scholars may rebel at the idea that they are troops being led by a general.

Physical Symbols

Physical symbols refer to objects that are meant to mean something other than what they really are and are perhaps the most common symbols. Artifacts are tangible examples of a particular message. However, as with all symbols, physical symbols may not signify what the leader intends. For example, one president said that getting personal computers for each faculty member made "a statement about the distinctiveness of the learning experience here. The purpose of this action was not to give PC's to the faculty but to set forth a philosophy, to make a statement that we are changing teaching here."

As the president notes, the intention was to make a statement with physical symbols. Clearly, on some campuses, alternative interpretations may exist. A humanities faculty might interpret the uninvited appearance of computers in their offices as the sciences' encroachment on their turf. A science faculty who already owned personal computers but worked in a building that needed renovation could interpret computers as a sign that the president was pandering to the liberal arts. The point is not that one interpretation is right and the other wrong, but rather that physical objects need to be seen within the context of the organization and its constituencies.

New libraries, attention to the grounds, a faculty club, school ties and scarves, and a host of other physical artifacts are designed as symbolic representations to various constituencies by presidents. Another president observed that the university had remained open when students took over the administration building. The president noted how the campus "carried on." By the president's symbolic use of space the president intended for the community to understand that the college was more than buildings and that, even under duress, the institution would continue.

Communicative Symbols

Communication entails not only symbolic acts of oral discourse but also written communicative acts and nonverbal activities that convey particular meanings from a president to a constituency. "I try to rub elbows with students and faculty on a regular basis," related one president. "I spend evenings in the student center. I try to make faculty council meetings, and I talk to faculty on campus." Another individual reported, "I call each of the faculty by their first name. During the year, all of them will be entertained in my home. I send birthday cards to all full-time faculty," noted a third leader. And a fourth commented:

> During a normal workday I will walk over to some other person's office maybe seven or eight times. It is really time consuming to be doing that, and I could save time by just picking up the phone. But I get mileage out of doing that, however, that is immeasurable . . . I am visible.

Given the popularity of such texts as *In Search of Excellence* and *Corporate Cultures,* it is commonplace to hear leaders refer to their style as "management by walking around." And, indeed, many leaders do "walk around." As American organizations struggle to emulate what they perceive to be Japanese models of effectiveness and efficiency, communicative symbols serve as functional vehicles for organizational success.

Talking with students "on their turf," entertaining faculty, strolling around campus, or walking into offices are all presidential perceptions of symbolic communication. Most often, the symbol is meant to communicate presidential concern; presidents think of themselves as caring individuals when they talk with students about student concerns. To use yet another symbolic metaphor, presidents perceive themselves as understanding their constituencies when they know everyone's first name or send someone a birthday card.

Structural Symbols

Symbolic structures refer to institutional structures and processes that signify more than who reports to whom. Of the six symbolic forms mentioned in this paper, the structural form most often differentiates new presidents from old. New presidents, those in office three years or less, often feel the need to alter the organizational structure to signify change. Birnbaum has noted, "New presidents . . . may talk off the record to colleagues . . . and complain (but with a certain degree of pride), 'You wouldn't believe the mess I found when I got here, but I've finally begun to get it turned around'" (1986, 392). Although I have not uncovered any aggregated differences between new and old presidents' symbolic perceptions—including the structural form—within the structural form, I have found Birnbaum's comment correct. That is, the intent of new presidents differs from that of old presidents when they use the structural form.

New presidents tend to embrace decision-making structures as symbols of change more than individuals who have served in their positions longer. Although older presidents use structures as symbols, structures do not necessarily connote change. Instead they may imply any number of significations. Commented one new president: "I did not create the faculty council. It was here when I arrived. But under my predecessor, people on that council were selected by the president and it was an at large position. I have changed that so that there is one faculty representative per division and they are elected by the faculty."

Another new president set up a task force primarily composed of senior faculty who helped the president create fundamental changes in the university. An older president said, "When I came in, I developed the traditional vice presidential offices. The first thing I did was to create a traditional administrative structure, an administrative team."

One new college president spoke indirectly about the symbolic implications of structural changes:

> I created two vice president positions—one for academic affairs and the other for public relations; I upgraded the dean of research to vice president. More reorganization took place at the deans' level too. I had to change the football coach and the athletic director. This situation enabled me to establish the fact that the president would be running the university, not the athletic director.

None of these examples, indeed, no examples of symbols in general, serve a singular purpose. When a president takes office, it is certainly conceivable that an administrative structure may be unsuitable to the president's style or needs. Changing such a structure may achieve particular goals. At the same time, by changing a structure the president also signals to the college community that life as it previously existed will change. From this perspective, the president's action accounts not only for structural change but also for the perception of change.

Borrowing from Merton (1957), Birnbaum (in press) has termed symbols such as those noted here as functionally "latent." Although structural change may produce needed outcomes, Birnbaum contends that some latent functions "are meeting less obvious, but still important, organizational needs." The findings from the data tend to suggest that new presidents use structural change in large part because of its latent function; they draw heavily on structural symbols to place their imprimatur on the institution.

Task forces may provide someone with good ideas and a different electoral system may be an improvement upon a previous system; but in essence, the president uses these devices to symbolize change. An older president commented, "During my time, we have elaborated the administrative style of the university. [My predecessor] was more of a one-person operator." Again, the administrative structure had come into play as a presidential perception of structural change or evolution.

Personification Symbols

Symbolic personification refers to a leader's intent to represent a message with an individual or group. For example, on a national level, we often find political appointees who symbolize an elected leader's commitment to a particular constituency. President Reagan's appointing a woman to the Supreme Court was intended to symbolize his concern for women.

College presidents also perceive that particular groups or individuals symbolize particular messages to different communities. One president noted, "When we changed the governance structure, we put the president of the student government on [it]; and he or she is involved in everything we discuss. The individual is a full member of the administrative structure." Thus, the president perceived not only that the administrative structure symbolized a message but also that who sat on the governing body symbolized, in this case, concern for student ideas.

Another president commented about the rising quality of the student body and noted, "We have finally started getting the recognition we deserve to have." This recognition was that the Big Eight accounting firms had been recruiting on campus. The presence of major marketing companies symbolized a rise in the institution's quality.

One college president felt the need to emphasize "excellent teaching." A potent symbol was appointing "three campus deans and a VP who have all had teaching experience and have had department chair experience. And I told the deans that they were required to teach also." Thus, this president's perception of leadership was to use personal symbols as a means of reorienting the culture of the organization.

Presidents also see themselves as symbols of the institution. One president spoke for many: "I had to get out in the community because no one had been out there before. I wanted people to think of the college as entering a new era." The presidents' willingness to meet the public was perhaps the most tangible example of symbolic personification. Presidents are the university; or, at least, they perceive themselves to be.

Ideational Symbols

Ideas as symbols refer to images leaders convey about the mission and purpose of the institution. Presidents generate ideas that serve as symbolic ideologies about their institutions. Clark's (1980) concept of an institutional saga is a cogent example of an ideational symbol by which leaders attempt to seize a unique role for their institution. A president perceives that leadership is often inextricably bound up with the symbolic generation of an institutional mission or ideology.

Ideational symbols are often the most difficult symbols for constituents to interpret if the symbol is divorced from tangible contexts. That is, particular ideas that presidents perceive as important may appear to be no more than presidential rhetoric to a constituency if the symbol cannot be palpably interpreted to them.

"I wanted a new image, a comprehensive quality," commented one leader. A second downgraded the importance of football at the institution:

The first statement I would make as president would be about athletics, and I knew that it would be heard throughout all the towns and cities. I wanted it to be a statement not about athletics but about what the institution would be and do in the future. I want us to be known for great education and not great athletics. I wanted it to be a statement about the kind of students we want.

The images that presidents struggle to convey to their constituencies are symbolic representations of institutional values. What a president perceives to be the value of the institution is oftentimes what the institution will struggle to achieve. By definition, an institution with a unique identity cannot be all things to all people. The symbolic idea serves as the unifying principle for the organization. Many colleges and universities are committed to distinctive ideas. College presidents who emphasize one idea over another impart to constituents what they believe to be the primary goal of the institution.

Discussion

I offer organizational leaders three suggestions about the symbolic aspects of leadership. Rather than formulaic prescriptions of how to function in the organizational universe, I tender three proposals for understanding one's own perceptions and the culture in which one operates. The suggestions are components of a diagnostic frame of reference, a way of interpreting one's organization. I propose ways for leaders to identify what they must do to comprehend the symbolic dimensions of their leadership.

1. Symbols Demand Corroboration

As noted, the research team queried the presidents about how they defined good leadership and what they had done as leaders. The interviews revealed several contradictions between what the individuals used as a symbol and how they acted. That is, on occasion discrepancies existed between what leaders perceive as good leadership and how they actually act.

One president who believes in visibility, for example, meets formally with the faculty only once a year. Another president's ideational symbol was "excellence" and to be known as a top-rate institution yet later in the interview spoke of institutional survival as the top priority. A third president cited the faculty council as a structural-personal symbol to communicate the critical importance of the faculty, yet no formal vehicles existed whereby the president actually met with them. Still another president tried to communicate symbolically that open, frank discussion was extremely important yet simultaneously demanded "extraordinary loyalty" to the president.

The point is not that individuals seek to deceive their constituencies. Instead, leaders should be aware of how symbolic forms may contradict one another. Walking around a campus or stressing "teamwork" does not necessarily confirm that collegiality exists. Leaders need to contextualize their perceptions and search for contradictions. We all have discrepancies between what we say and what we do. For an organizational leader, greater consistency between words and deeds allows followers a clearer understanding of a leader's intention.

2. Use Symbols Consistent with the Organization's Culture

The culture of an organization is a social construction, dependent not only on the perceptions of a leader but also on the unique history of the organization, the individual orientations and perceptions of followers, and larger environmental influences. The cultural paradigm assumes that an organization does not consist of rational, "real" entities (Tierney 1988).

Everyday existence is a constant matter of interpretation among organizational participants. Rather than assume a functional view of symbols and a passive view of individuals, we need to reconceptualize culture as an interpretive dynamic whereby a leader's symbols may or may not be interpreted the way he or she intended. Thus, dissonance will occur even when a president's symbols corroborate each other if he or she has used symbols that are inconsistent with the organization's culture.

A new president, for example, may want to symbolize care and concern for the faculty and structurally reorganize the decision-making process, adding councils and committees to make it more participative. The president's perception and symbolic intent is to highlight a structural symbol. The strategy may fail, however, if the culture has relied for a generation on presidential informality and one-on-one conversations with faculty.

The challenge for the president is not only to search for contradictions in symbolic forms but also to understand how those symbolic forms exist within the organization's culture. If symbols are neither reified nor functional, then we must necessarily investigate their contextual surroundings to understand them.

3. Use All Symbolic Forms

Leaders, not unlike most individuals, are intuitively aware that particular objects or activities are highly imbued with symbolism. This essay has reported on the use of new buildings or new computers to convey a message. Similarly, the well-read manager today believes that management tips about communication hold symbolic value.

Yet as we have seen, leaders may employ a wide array of symbolic forms. Within each category exist a potential multitude of symbols. Further, an abundance of activities, acts, and the like also exist within a symbolic form. Rather than rely on the symbolic content of a single convocation speech every year, a president might benefit from employing a wide array of consistent symbolic forms. We tend to compartmentalize activities to simplify them, yet that is not how organizational participants experience reality.

All acts within an organization are open to interpretation. Virtually everything a leader does or says (or does not do or say) is capable of symbolic intent or interpretation. To acknowledge the pervasiveness of symbols in an organization does not imply that a leader is in charge of an anarchic organization that interprets messages any way it wants. Instead, a central challenge for the leader is to interpret the culture of the organization and to draw upon all of the symbolic forms effectively so that organizational participants can make sense of organizational activities.

Conclusion

A symbolic view of leadership and organizations needs to move beyond functionalist definitions of organizational symbolism. We need to pay attention to the processes whereby organizational members interpret the symbolic activities of leaders, rather than assume that all individuals march to the same organizational beat. We need to investigate why a particular symbol may be potent in one organization at one particular time and relatively useless in another organization.

The assumption at work in this paper has been that, although both the structure and expressions of colleges and universities change, the inner necessities that drive them do not. "Thrones may be out of fashion," states Geertz, "and pageantry too; but authority still requires a cultural frame in which to define itself and advance its claims" (1983, 143). If symbolism helps define authority, then we should continue the quest to understand the symbolic manifestations of organizational life and leadership.

References

Bailey, Frederick George. *The Tactical Uses of Passion*. Ithaca, NY: Cornell University Press, 1983.

Birnbaum, Robert. *How Colleges Work: The Cybernetics of Academic Organization and Leadership*. San Francisco: Jossey-Bass Publishers, 1988.

_____. "Leadership and Learning." *Review of Higher Education* 9, no. 4 (1986): 381–95.

_____. "The Latent Organizational Functions of the Academic Senate." *Journal of Higher Education* in press.

Birnbaum, Robert, Estela M. Bensimon, and Anna Neumann. "Leadership in Higher Education: A Multidimensional Approach to Research." *Review of Higher Education* 12, no. 2 (Winter 1989): 101–105.

Clark, Burton R. "The Making of an Organizational Saga." In *Readings in Managerial Psychology*, edited by Harold J. Leavitt and Louis R. Pondy. Chicago: University of Chicago Press, 1980.

Dandridge, Thomas C., Ian Mitroff, and William F. Joyce. "Organizational Symbolism: A Topic to Expand Organizational Analysis." *Academy of Management Review* 5, no. 1 (1980): 77–82.

Deal, Terrence, and Allan A. Kennedy. *Corporate Cultures: The Rites and Rituals of Corporate Life.* Reading, Mass.: Addison-Wesley, 1982.

Eco, Umberto. *A Theory of Semiotics.* Bloomington: Indiana University Press, 1979.

Geertz, Clifford. *The Interpretation of Cultures.* New York City: Basic Books, 1973.

_____. "Reflections on the Symbolics of Power." In *Local Knowledge,* edited by Clifford Geertz. New York City: Basic Books, 1983.

Merton, Robert K. *Social Theory of Social Structure.* Glencoe, Ill.: Free Press, 1957.

Peters, Thomas J., and Robert H. Waterman, Jr. *In Search of Excellence.* New York: Harper and Row, 1982.

Pettigrew, Andrew M. "On Studying Organizational Cultures." *Administrative Science Quarterly* 24 (1979): 570–81.

Pfeffer, Jeffrey. "Management as Symbolic Action." In *Research in Organizational Behavior,* edited by Larry L. Cummings & Barry Staw. Greenwich, Conn.: JAI Press, 1981.

Schein, Edgar H. *Organizational Culture and Leadership.* San Francisco: Jossey-Bass Publishers, 1985.

Tierney, William G. "The Semiotic Aspects of Leadership: An Ethnographic Perspective." *The American Journal of Semiotics* 5, no. 1 (1987): 223–50. In press-a.

_____. "Organizational Culture in Higher Education: Defining the Essentials." *Journal of Higher Education* 59, no. 1 (1988): 2–21. In press-b.

Trice, Harrison M., and Janice M. Beyer. "Studying Organizational Cultures through Rites and Ceremonials." *Academy of Management Review* 9 (1984): 653–69.

William G. Tierney is assistant professor and research associate, Center for the Study of Higher Education, Pennsylvania State University.

This document was prepared with financial support from the Office of Educational Research and Improvement/Department of Education (OERI/ED). However, the opinions expressed herein do not necessarily reflect the position, policy, or official endorsement of the OERI/ED.

Organizational Learning and Communities-of-Practice: Toward a Unified View of Working, Learning, and Innovation

JOHN SEELY BROWN AND PAUL DUGUID

XEROX PALO ALTO RESEARCH CENTER
AND INSTITUTE FOR RESEARCH ON LEARNING,
PALO ALTO, CALIFORNIA

Recent ethnographic studies of workplace practices indicate that the ways people actually work usually differ fundamentally from the ways organizations describe that work in manuals, training programs, organizational charts, and job descriptions. Nevertheless, organizations tend to rely on the latter in their attempts to understand and improve work practice. We examine one such study. We then relate its conclusions to compatible investigations of learning and of innovation to argue that conventional descriptions of jobs mask not only the ways people work, but also significant learning and innovation generated in the informal communities-of-practice in which they work. By reassessing work, learning, and innovation in the context of actual communities and actual practices, we suggest that the connections between these three become apparent. With a unified view of working, learning, and innovating, it should be possible to reconceive of and redesign organizations to improve all three.
Keywords: Learning; Innovation; Groups; Downskilling; Organizational Cultures; Noncanonical Practice

Introduction

Working, learning, and innovating are closely related forms of human activity that are conventionally thought to conflict with each other. Work practice is generally viewed as conservative and resistant to change; learning is generally viewed as distinct from working and problematic in the face of change; and innovation is generally viewed as the disruptive but necessary imposition of change on the other two. To see that working, learning, and innovating are interrelated and compatible and thus potentially complementary, not conflicting forces requires a distinct conceptual shift. By bringing together recent research into working, learning, and innovating, we attempt to indicate the nature and explore the significance of such a shift.

The source of the oppositions perceived between working, learning, and innovating lies primarily in the gulf between precepts and practice. Formal descriptions of work (e.g., "office procedures") and of learning (e.g., "subject matter") are abstracted from actual practice. They inevitably and intentionally omit the details. In a society that attaches particular value to "abstract knowledge," the details of practice have come to be seen as nonessential, unimportant, and easily developed once the relevant abstractions have been grasped. Thus education, training, and technology design generally focus on abstract representations to the detriment, if not exclusion of actual practice. We, by contrast, suggest that practice is central to understanding work. Abstractions *detached from practice* distort or obscure intricacies of that practice. Without a clear understanding of those intricacies and the role they play, the practice itself cannot be well understood, engendered (through training), or enhanced (through innovation).

We begin by looking at the variance between a major organization's formal descriptions of work both in its training programs and manuals and the actual work practices performed by its members. Orr's (1990a, 1990b, 1987a, 1987b) detailed ethnographic studies of service technicians illustrate how an organization's view of work can overlook and even oppose what and who it takes to get a job done. Based on Orr's specific insights, we make the more general claim that reliance on espoused practice (which we refer to as *canonical practice*) can blind an organization's core to the actual, and usually valuable practices of its members (including *noncanonical practices*, such as "work arounds"). It is the actual practices, however, that determine the success or failure of organizations.

Next, we turn to learning and, in particular, to Lave and Wenger's (1990) practice-based theory of learning as "legitimate peripheral participation" in "communities-of-practice." Much conventional learning theory, including that implicit in most training courses, tends to endorse the valuation of abstract knowledge over actual practice and as a result to separate learning from working and, more significantly, learners from workers. Together Lave and Wenger's analysis and Orr's empirical investigation indicate that this knowledge–practice separation is unsound, both in theory and in practice. We argue that the composite concept of "learning-in-working" best represents the fluid evolution of learning through practice.

From this practice-based standpoint, we view learning as the bridge between working and innovating. We use Daft and Weick's (1984) interpretive account of "enacting" organizations to place innovation in the context of changes in a community's "way of seeing" or interpretive view. Both Orr's and Lave and Wenger's research emphasize that to understand working and learning, it is necessary to focus on the formation and change of the communities in which work takes place. Taking all three theories together, we argue that, through their constant adapting to changing membership and changing circumstances, evolving communities-of-practice are significant sites of innovating.

Working

Canonical Practice

Orr's (1990a, 1990b, 1987a, 1987b) ethnography of service technicians (reps) in training and at work in a large corporation paints a clear picture of the divergence between espoused practice and actual practice, of the ways this divergence develops, and of the trouble it can cause. His work provides a "thick" (see Geertz 1973), detailed description of the way work actually progresses. Orr contrasts his findings with the way the same work is thinly described in the corporation's manuals, training courses, and job descriptions.[1]

The importance of such an approach to work in progress is emphasized by Bourdieu (1973), who distinguishes the *modus operandi* from the *opus operatum*—that is, the way a task, as it unfolds over time, looks to someone at work on it, while many of the options and dilemmas remain unresolved, as opposed to the way it looks with hindsight as a finished task. (Ryle (1954) makes a similar point.) The *opus operatum*, the finished view, tends to see the action in terms of the task alone and cannot see the way in which the process of doing the task is actually structured by the constantly changing conditions of work and the world. Bourdieu makes a useful analogy with reference to a journey as actually carried out on the ground and as seen on a map ("an abstract space, devoid of any landmarks or any privileged centre" (p. 2)). The latter, like the *opus operatum*, inevitably smooths over the myriad decisions made with regard to changing conditions: road works, diversions, Memorial Day parades, earthquakes, personal fatigue, conflicting opinions, wrong-headed instructions, relations of authority, inaccuracies on the map, and the like. The map, though potentially useful, *by itself* provides little insight into how *ad hoc* decisions presented by changing conditions can be resolved (and, of course, each resolved decision changes the conditions once more). As a journey becomes more complex, the map increasingly conceals what is actually needed to make the journey. Thick description, by contrast, ascends from the abstraction to the concrete circumstances of actual practice, reconnecting the map and the mapped.

Orr's study shows how an organization's maps can dramatically distort its view of the routes its members take. This "misrecognition," as Bourdieu calls it, can be traced to many places, including pedagogic theory and practice. Often it has its more immediate cause in the strategy to downskill positions. Many organizations are willing to assume that complex tasks can be successfully mapped onto a set of simple, Tayloristic, canonical steps that can be followed without need of significant understanding or insight (and thus without need of significant investment in training or skilled technicians). But as Bourdieu, Suchman (1987a), and Orr show, actual practice inevitably involves tricky interpolations between abstract accounts and situated demands. Orr's reps' skills, for instance, are most evident in the improvised strategies they deploy to cope with the clash between prescriptive documentation and the sophisticated, yet unpredictable machines they work with. Nonetheless, in the corporation's eyes practices that deviate from the canonical are, by definition, deviant practices. Through a reliance on canonical descriptions (to the extent of overlooking even their own noncanonical improvisations), managers develop a conceptual outlook that cannot comprehend the importance of noncanonical practices. People are typically viewed as performing their jobs according to formal job descriptions, despite the fact that daily evidence points to the contrary (Suchman 1987b). They are held accountable to the map, not to road conditions.[2]

In Orr's case, the canonical map comes in the form of "directive" documentation aimed at "single point failures" of machines. Indeed, the documentation is less like a map than a single predetermined route with no alternatives: it provides a decision tree for diagnosis and repair that assumes both predictable machines and an unproblematic process of making diagnoses and repairs through blindly following diagnostic instructions. Both assumptions are mistaken. Abstractions of repair work fall short of the complexity of the actual practices from which they were abstracted. The account of actual practice we describe below is anything but the blind following of instructions.

The inadequacies of this corporation's directive approach actually make a rep's work more difficult to accomplish and thus perversely demands more, not fewer, improvisational skills. An ostensible downskilling and actual upskilling therefore proceed simultaneously. Although the documentation becomes more prescriptive and ostensibly more simple, in actuality the task becomes more improvisational and more complex. The reps develop sophisticated noncanonical practices to bridge the gulf between their corporation's canonical approach and successful work practices, laden with the dilemmas, inconsistencies, and unpredictability of everyday life. The directive documentation does not "deprive the workers of the skills they have;" rather, "it merely reduces the amount of information given them" (Orr 1990a, 26). The burden of making up the difference between what is provided and what is needed then rests with the reps, who in bridging the gap actually protect the organization from its own shortsightedness. If the reps adhered to the canonical approach, their corporation's services would be in chaos.

Because this corporation's training programs follow a similar downskilling approach, the reps regard them as generally unhelpful. As a result, a wedge is driven between the corporation and its reps: the corporation assumes the reps are untrainable, uncooperative, and unskilled; whereas the reps view the overly simplistic training programs as a reflection of the corporation's low estimation of their worth and skills. In fact, their valuation is a testament to the depth of the rep's insight. They recognize the superficiality of the training because they are conscious of the full complexity of the technology and what it takes to keep it running. The corporation, on the other hand, blinkered by its implicit faith in formal training and canonical practice and its misinterpretation of the rep's behavior, is unable to appreciate either aspect of their insight.

In essence, Orr shows that in order to do their job the reps must—and do—learn to make better sense of the machines they work with than their employer either expects or allows. Thus they develop their understanding of the machine not in the training programs, but in the very conditions from which the programs separate them—the authentic activity of their daily work. For the reps (and for the corporation, though it is unaware of it), learning-in-working is an occupational necessity.

Noncanonical Practice

Orr's analyses of actual practice provide various examples of how the reps diverge from canonical descriptions. For example, on one service call (Orr 1990b, 1987b) a rep confronted a machine that produced copious raw information in the form of error codes and obligingly crashed when tested. But the error codes and the nature of the crashes did not tally. Such a case immediately fell outside the directive training and documentation provided by the organization, which tie errors to error codes. Unfortunately, the problem also fell outside the rep's accumulated, improvised experience. He summoned his technical specialist, whose job combines "trouble-shooting consultant, supervisor, and occasional instructor." The specialist was equally baffled. Yet, though the canonical approach to repair was exhausted, with their combined range of noncanonical practices, the rep and technical specialist still had options to pursue.

One option—indeed the only option left by canonical practice now that its strategies for repair had been quickly exhausted—was to abandon repair altogether and to replace the malfunctioning machine. But both the rep and the specialist realized that the resulting loss of face for the company, loss of the customer's faith in the reps, loss of their own credit within their organization, and loss of money to the corporation made this their last resort. Loss of face or faith has considerable ramifications beyond mere embarrassment. A rep's ability to enlist the future support of customers and colleagues is jeopardized. There is evidently strong social pressure from a variety of sources to solve problems without exchanging machines. The reps' work is not simply about maintaining machines; it is also and equally importantly, about maintaining social relations: "A large part of service work might better be described as repair and maintenance of the social setting" (Orr 1990b, 169). The training and documentation, of course, are about maintaining machines.

Solving the problem *in situ* required constructing a coherent account of the malfunction out of the incoherence of the data and documentation. To do this, the rep and the specialist embarked on a long story-telling procedure. The machine, with its erratic behavior, mixed with information from the user and memories from the technicians, provided essential ingredients that the two aimed to account for in a composite story. The process of forming a story was, centrally, one of diagnosis. This process, it should be noted, *begins* as well as ends in a communal understanding of the machine that is wholly unavailable from the canonical documents.

While they explored the machine or waited for it to crash, the rep and specialist (with contributions from the ethnographer) recalled and discussed other occasions on which they had encountered some of the present symptoms. Each story presented an exchangeable account that could be examined and reflected upon to provoke old memories and new insights. Yet more tests and more stories were thereby generated.

> The key element of diagnosis is the situated production of understanding through narration, in that the integration of the various facts of the situation is accomplished through a verbal consideration of those facts with a primary criterion of coherence. The process is situated, in Suchman's terms, in that both the damaged machine and the social context of the user site are essential resources for both the definition of the problem and its resolution.... They are faced with a failing machine displaying diagnostic information which has previously proved worthless and in which no one has any particular confidence this time. They do not know where they are going to find the information they need to understand and solve this problem. In their search for inspiration, they tell stories (Orr 1990b. 178–179).

The story-telling process continued throughout the morning, over lunch, and back in front of the machine, throughout the afternoon, forming a long but purposeful progression from incoherence to coherence: "The final trouble-shooting session was a five hour effort.... This session yielded a dozen anecdotes told during the trouble shooting, taking a variety of forms and serving a variety of purposes" (Orr 1990b, 10).

Ultimately, these stories generated sufficient interplay among memories, tests, the machine's responses, and the ensuing insights to lead to diagnosis and repair. The final diagnosis developed from what Orr calls an "antiphonal recitation" in which the two told different versions of the same story: "They are talking about personal encounters with the same problem, but the two versions are significantly different" (Orr 1987b 177). Through story-telling, these separate experiences converged, leading to a shared diagnosis of certain previously encountered but unresolved symptoms. The two (and the ethnographer) had constructed a communal interpretation of hitherto uninterpretable data and individual experience. Rep and specialist were now in a position to modify previous stories and build a more insightful one. They both increased their own understanding and added to their community's collective knowledge. Such stories are passed around, becoming part of the repertoire available to all reps. Orr reports hearing a concise, assimilated version of this particular false error code passed among reps over a game of cribbage in the lunch room three months later (Orr 1990b, 181ff.). A story, once in the possession of the community, can then be used—and further modified—in similar diagnostic sessions.

Central Features of Work Practice

In this section, we analyze Orr's thick description of the rep's practice through the overlapping categories, "narration," "collaboration," and "social construction"—categories that get to the heart of what the reps do and yet which, significantly, have no place in the organization's abstracted, canonical accounts of their work.

Narration

The first aspect of the reps' practice worth highlighting is the extensive narration used. This way of working is quite distinct from following the branches of decision tree. Stories and their telling can reflect the complex social web within which work takes place and the relationship of the narrative, narrator, and audience to the specific events of practice. The stories have a flexible generality that makes them both adaptable and particular. They function, rather like the common law, as a usefully underconstrained means to interpret each new situation in the light of accumulated wisdom and constantly changing circumstances.

The practice of creating and exchanging of stories has two important aspects. First of all, telling stories helps to diagnose the state of a troublesome machine. Reps begin by extracting a history from the users of the machine, the users' story, and with this and the machine as their starting point, they construct their own account. If they cannot tell an adequate story on their own, then they seek help—either by summoning a specialist, as in the case above, or by discussing the problem with colleagues over coffee or lunch. If necessary, they work together at the machine, articulating hunches, insights, misconceptions, and the like, to dissect and augment their developing understanding. Story telling allows them to keep track of the sequences of behavior and of their theories, and thereby to work towards a coherent account of the current state of the machine. The reps try to impose coherence on an apparently random sequence of events in order that they can decide what to do next. Unlike the documentation, which tells reps *what* to do but not *why*, the reps' stories help them develop causal accounts of machines, which are essential when documentation breaks down. (As we have suggested, documentation, like machines, will always break down, however well it is designed.) What the reps do in their story telling is develop a causal map out of their experience to replace the impoverished directive route that they have been furnished by the corporation. In the absence of such support, the reps Orr studied cater to their own needs as well as they can. Their narratives yield a story of the machine fundamentally different from the prescriptive account provided by the documentation, a story that is built in response to the particulars of breakdown.

Despite the assumptions behind the downskilling process, to do their job in any significant sense, reps need these complex causal stories and they produce and circulate them as part of their regular noncanonical work practice. An important part of the reps' skill, though not recognized by the corporation, comprises the ability to create, to trade, and to understand highly elliptical, highly referential, and to the initiated, highly informative war stories. Zuboff (1988) in her analysis of the skills people develop working on complex systems describes similar cases of story telling and argues that it is a necessary practice for dealing with "smart" but unpredictable machines. The irony, as Orr points out, is that for purposes of diagnosis the reps have no smart machines, just inadequate documentation and "their own very traditional skills."

It is worth stressing at this point that we are not arguing that communities simply can and thus should work without assistance from trainers and the corporation in general. Indeed, we suggest in our conclusion that situations inevitably occur when group improvisation simply cannot bridge the gap between what the corporation supplies and what a particular community actually needs. What we are claiming is that corporations must provide support that corresponds to the real needs of the community rather than just to the abstract expectations of the corporation. And what those needs are can only be understood by understanding the details and sophistications of actual practice. In Orr's account, what the reps needed was the means to understand the machine causally and to relate this causal map to the inevitable intricacies of practice. To discern such needs, however, will require that corporations develop a less formal and more practice-based approach to communities and their work.

The second characteristic of story telling is that the stories also act as repositories of accumulated wisdom. In particular, community narratives protect the reps' ability to work from the ravages of modern idealizations of work and related downskilling practices. In Orr's example, the canonical decision trees, privileging the decontextualized over the situated, effectively sweep away the clutter of practice. But it is in the face of just this clutter that the reps' skills are needed. Improvisational skills that allow the reps to circumvent the inadequacies of both the machines and the documentation are not only developed but also preserved in community story telling.

Jordan's (1989) work similarly draws attention to the central, dual role of informal stories. She studied the clash between midwifery as it is prescribed by officials from Mexico City and as it is practiced in rural Yucatan. The officials ignore important details and realities of practice. For instance, the officials instruct the midwives in practices that demand sterile instruments though the midwives work in villages that lack adequate means for sterilization. The midwives' noncanonical practices, however, circumvent the possibility of surgical operations being carried out with unsterile instruments. These effective practices survive, despite the government's worryingly decontextualized attempts to replace them with canonical practices, through story telling. Jordan notes that the two aspects of story telling, diagnosis and preservation, are inseparable. Orr also suggests that "The use of story-telling both to preserve knowledge and to consider it in subsequent diagnoses coincides with the narrative character of diagnosis" (Orr 1990b, 178). We have pulled them apart for the purpose of analysis only.

Collaboration

Based as it is on shared narratives, a second important aspect of the reps' work is that it is obviously communal and thereby *collaborative*. In Orr's example, the rep and specialist went through a collective, not individual process. Not only is the learning in this case inseparable from working, but also individual learning is inseparable from collective learning. The insight accumulated is not a private substance, but socially constructed and distributed. Thus, faced with a difficult problem reps like to work together and to discuss problems in groups. In the case of this particular problem, the individual rep tried what he knew, failed, and there met his limits. With the specialist he was able to trade stories, develop insights, and construct new options. Each had a story about the condition of the machine, but it was in telling it antiphonally that the significance emerged.

While it might seem trivial, it is important to emphasize the collaborative work within the reps' community, for in the corporation's eyes their work is viewed individually. Their documentation and training implicitly maintain that the work is individual and the central relationship of the rep is that between an individual and the corporation:

> The activities defined by management are those which one worker will do, and work as the relationship of employment is discussed in terms of a single worker's relationship to the corporation. I suspect the incidence of workers alone in relations of employment is quite low, and the existence of coworkers must contribute to those activities done in the name of work. . . . The fact that work is commonly done by a group of workers together is only sometimes acknowledged in the literature, and the usual presence of such a community has not entered into the definition of work (Orr 1990a, 15).

In fact, as Orr's studies show, not only do reps work with specialists, as in the example given here, but throughout the day they meet for coffee or for meals and trade stories back and forth.

Social Construction

A third important aspect of Orr's account of practice, and one which is interfused with the previous two and separated here only to help in clarification, involves *social construction*. This has two parts. First and most evident in Orr's example, the reps constructed a shared understanding out of bountiful conflicting and confusing data. This constructed understanding reflects the reps' view of the world. They developed a *rep's* model of the machine, not a trainer's, which had already proved unsatisfactory, nor even an engineer's, which was not available to them (and might well have been unhelpful, though Orr interestingly points out that reps cultivate connections throughout the corporation to help them circumvent the barriers to understanding built by their documentation and training). The reps' view, evident in their stories, interweaves generalities about "this model" with particularities about "this site" and "this machine."

Such an approach is highly situated and highly improvisational. Reps respond to whatever the situation itself—both social and physical—throws at them, a process very similar to Levi-Strauss's (1966) concept of *bricolage*: the ability to "make do with 'whatever is to hand'" (p. 17). What reps need for *bricolage* are not the partial, rigid models of the sort directive documentation provides, but help to build, *ad hoc* and collaboratively, robust models that do justice to particular difficulties in which they find themselves. Hutchins, in his analysis of navigation teams in the U.S. Navy (in press, 19911, similarly notes the way in which understanding is constructed within and distributed throughout teams.

The second feature of social construction, as important but less evident than the first, is that in telling these stories an individual rep contributes to the construction and development of his or her own identity as a rep and reciprocally to the construction and development of the community of reps in which he or she works. Individually, in telling stories the rep is becoming a member. Orr notes, "this construction of their identity as technicians occurs both in doing the work and in their stories, and their stories of themselves fixing machines show their world in what they consider the appropriate perspective" (Orr 1990b, 187). Simultaneously and interdependently, the reps are contributing to the construction and evolution of the community that they are joining— what we might call a "community of interpretation," for it is through the continual development of these communities that the shared means for interpreting complex activity get formed, transformed, and transmitted.

The significance of both these points should become apparent in the following sections, first, as we turn to a theory of learning (Lave and Wenger's) that, like Orr's analysis of work, takes formation of identity and community membership as central units of analysis; and second as we argue that innovation can be seen as at base a function of changes in community values and views.

Learning

The theories of learning implicated in the documentation and training view learning from the abstract stance of pedagogy. Training is thought of as the *transmission* of explicit, abstract knowledge from the head of someone who knows to the head of someone who does not in surroundings that specifically exclude the complexities of practice and the communities of practitioners. The setting for learning is simply assumed not to matter.

Concepts of knowledge or information transfer, however, have been under increasing attack in recent years from a variety of sources (e.g., Reddy 1979). In particular, learning theorists (e.g. Lave 1988; Lave and Wenger 1990) have rejected transfer models, which isolate knowledge from practice, and developed a view of learning as social construction, putting knowledge back into the contexts in which it has meaning (see also Brown, Collins, and Duguid 1989; Brown and Duguid, in press; Pea 1990). From this perspective, learners can in one way or another be seen to construct their understanding out of a wide range of materials that include ambient social and physical circumstances and the histories and social relations of the people involved. Like a magpie with a nest, learning is built out of the materials to hand and in relation to the structuring resources of local conditions. (For the importance of including the structuring resources in any account of learning, see Lave 1988.) What is learned is profoundly connected to the conditions in which it is learned.

Lave and Wenger (1990), with their concept of *legitimate peripheral participation* (LPP), provide one of the most versatile accounts of this constructive view of learning. LPP, it must quickly be asserted, is *not* a method of education. It is an analytical category or tool for understanding learning across different methods, different historical periods, and different social and physical environments. It attempts to account for learning, not teaching or instruction. Thus this approach escapes problems that arise through examinations of learning from pedagogy's viewpoint. It makes the conditions of learning, rather than just abstract subject matter, central to understanding what is learned.

Learning, from the viewpoint of LPP, essentially involves becoming an "insider." Learners do not receive or even construct abstract, "objective," individual knowledge; rather, they learn to function in a community—be it a community of nuclear physicists, cabinet makers, high school classmates, street-corner society, or, as in the case under study, service technicians. They acquire that particular community's subjective viewpoint and learn to speak its language. In short, they are enculturated (Brown, Collins, and Duguid 1989). Learners are acquiring not explicit, formal "expert knowledge," but the embodied ability to behave as community members. For example, learners learn to tell and appreciate community-appropriate stories, discovering in doing so, all the narrative-based resources we outlined above. As Jordan (1989) argues in her analysis of midwifery, "To acquire a store of appropriate stories and, even more importantly, to know what are appropriate occasions for telling them, is then part of what it means to become a midwife" (p. 935).

Workplace learning is best understood, then, in terms of the communities being formed or joined and personal identities being changed. The central issue in learning is *becoming* a practitioner not learning *about* practice. This approach draws attention away from abstract knowledge and cranial processes and situates it in the practices and communities in which knowledge takes on significance. Learning about new devices, such as the machines Orr's technicians worked with, is best understood (and best achieved) in the context of the community in which the devices are used and that community's particular interpretive conventions. Lave and Wenger argue that learning, understanding, and interpretation involve a great deal that is not explicit or explicable, developed and framed in a crucially *communal* context.

Orr's study reveals this sort of learning going on in the process of and inseparable from work. The rep was not just an observer of the technical specialist. He was also an important participant in this process of diagnosis and story telling, whose participation could legitimately grow in from the periphery as a function of his developing understanding not of some extrinsically structured training. His legitimacy here is an important function of the social relations between the different levels of service technician, which are surprisingly egalitarian, perhaps as a result of the inherent incoherence of the problems this sort of technology presents: a specialist cannot hope to exert hierarchical control over knowledge that he or she must first construct cooperatively. "Occupational communities . . . have little hierarchy; the only real status is that of member" (Orr 1990a, 33).

Groups and Communities

Having characterized both working and learning in terms of communities, it is worth pausing to establish relations between our own account and recent work on groups in the workplace. Much important work has been done in this area (see, for example, the collections by Hackman (1990) and Goodman and Associates (1988)) and many of the findings support our own view of work activity. There is, however, a significant distinction between our views and this work. Group theory in general focuses on groups as canonical, bounded entities that lie within an organization and that are organized or at least sanctioned by that organization and its view of tasks. (See Hackman 1990, pp. 4–5.). The communities that we discern are, by contrast, often noncanonical and not recognized by the organization. They are more fluid and interpenetrative than bounded, often crossing the restrictive boundaries of the organization to incorporate people from outside. (Orr's reps can in an important sense be said to work in a community that includes both suppliers and customers.) Indeed, the canonical organization becomes a questionable unit of analysis from this perspective. And significantly, communities are emergent. That is to say their shape and membership emerges in the process of activity, as opposed to being created to carry out a task. (Note, by contrast, how much of the literature refers to the *design* or *creation* of new groups (e.g. Goodman and Associates 1988). From our viewpoint, the central questions more involve the *detection* and *support* of emergent or existing communities.)

If this distinction is correct then it has two particularly important corollaries. First, work practice and learning need to be understood not in terms of the groups that are ordained (e.g. "task forces" or "trainees"), but in terms of the communities that emerge. The latter are likely to be non-canonical (though not necessarily so) while the former are likely to be canonical. Looking only at canonical groups, whose configuration often conceals extremely influential interstitial communities, will not provide a clear picture of how work or learning is actually organized and accomplished. It will only reflect the dominant assumptions of the organizational core.

Second, attempts to introduce "teams" and "work groups" into the workplace to enhance learning or work practice are often based on an assumption that without impetus from above, an organization's members configure themselves as individuals. In fact, as we suggest, people work and learn collaboratively and vital interstitial communities are continually being formed and reformed. The reorganization of the workplace into canonical groups can wittingly or unwittingly disrupt these highly functional noncanonical—and therefore often invisible—communities. Orr argues:

> The process of working and learning together creates a work situation which the workers value, and they resist having it disrupted by their employers through events such as a reorganization of the work. This resistance can surprise employers who think of labor as a commodity to arrange to suit their ends. The problem for the workers is that this community which they have created was not part of the series of discrete employment agreements by which the employer populated the work place, nor is the role of the community in doing the work acknowledged. *The work can only continue free of disruption if the employer can be persuaded to see the community as necessary to accomplishing work* (Orr 1990, 48, emphasis added).

Fostering Learning

Given a community-based analysis of learning so congruent with Orr's analysis of working, the question arises, how is it possible to foster learning-in-working? The answer is inevitably complex, not least because all the intricacies of context, which the pedagogic approach has always assumed could be stripped away, now have to be taken back into consideration. On the other hand, the ability of people to learn *in situ*, suggests that as a fundamental principle for supporting learning, attempts to strip away context should be examined with caution. If learners need access to practitioners at work, it is essential to question didactic approaches, with their tendency to separate learners from the target community and the authentic work practices. Learning is fostered by fostering access to and membership of the target community-of-practice, not by explicating abstractions of individual practice. Thus central to the process are the recognition and legitimation of community practices.

Reliance on formal descriptions of work, explicit syllabuses for learning about it, and canonical groups to carry it out immediately set organizations at a disadvantage. This approach, as we have noted, can simply blind management to the practices and communities that actually make things happen. In particular, it can lead to the isolation of learners, who will then be unable to acquire the implicit practices required for work. Marshall (in Lave and Wenger 1990) describes a case of apprenticeship for butchers in which learning was extremely restricted because, among other things, "apprentices . . . could not watch journeymen cut and saw meat" (p. 19). Formal training in cutting and sawing is quite different from the understanding of practice gleaned through informal observation that copresence makes possible and absence obviously excludes. These trainees were simply denied the chance to become legitimate peripheral participants. If training is designed so that learners cannot observe the activity of practitioners, learning is inevitably impoverished.

Legitimacy and peripherality are intertwined in a complex way. Occasionally, learners (like the apprentice butchers) are granted legitimacy but are denied peripherality. Conversely, they can be granted peripherality but denied legitimacy. Martin (1982) gives examples of organizations in which legitimacy is explicitly denied in instances of "open door" management, where members come to realize that, though the door is open, it is wiser not to cross the threshold. If either legitimacy or peripherality is denied, learning will be significantly more difficult.

For learners, then, a position on the periphery of practice is important. It is also easily overlooked and increasingly risks being "designed out," leaving people physically or socially isolated and justifiably uncertain whether, for instance, their errors are inevitable or the result of personal inadequacies. It is a significant challenge for design to ensure that new collaborative technologies, designed as they so often are around formal descriptions of work, do not exclude this sort of implicit, extendable, informal periphery. Learners need legitimate access to the periphery of communication—to computer mail, to formal and informal meetings, to telephone conversations, etc., and, of course, to war stories. They pick up invaluable "know how"—not just information but also manner and technique—from being on the periphery of competent practitioners going about their business. Furthermore, it is important to consider the periphery not only because it is an important site of learning, but also because, as the next section proposes, it can be an important site for innovation.

Innovating

One of the central benefits of these small, self-constituting communities we have been describing is that they evade the ossifying tendencies of large organizations. Canonical accounts of work are not only hard to apply and hard to learn. They are also hard to change. Yet the actual behaviors of communities-of-practice are constantly changing both as newcomers replace old timers and as the demands of practice force the community to revise its relationship to its environment. Communities-of-practice like the reps' continue to develop a rich, fluid, noncanonical world view to bridge the gap between their organization's static canonical view and the challenge of changing practice. This process of development is inherently innovative. "Maverick" communities of this sort offer the core of a large organization a means and a model to examine the potential of alternative views of organizational activity through spontaneously occurring experiments that are simultaneously informed and checked by experience. These, it has been argued (Hedberg, Nystrom and Starbuck 1976; Schein 1990), drive innovation by allowing the parts of an organization to step outside the organization's inevitably limited core world view and simply try something new. Unfortunately, people in the core of large organizations too often regard these noncanonical practices (if they see them at all) as counterproductive.

For a theoretical account of this sort of innovation, we turn to Daft and Weick's (1984) discussion of interpretive innovation. They propose a matrix of four different kinds of organization, each characterized by its relationship to its environment. They name these relationships "undirected viewing," "conditioned viewing," "discovering," and "enacting." Only the last two concern us here. It is important to note that Daft and Weick too see the community and not the individual "inventor" as the central unit of analysis in understanding innovating practice.

The *discovering organization* is the archetype of the conventional innovative organization, one which responds—often with great efficiency—to changes it detects in its environment. The organization presupposes an essentially prestructured environment and implicitly assumes that there is a correct response to any condition it discovers there. By contrast, the *enacting organization* is proactive and highly interpretive. Not only does it respond to its environment, but also, in a fundamental way, it creates many of the conditions to which it must respond. Daft and Weick describe enacting organizations as follows:

> These organizations construct their own environments. They gather information by trying new behaviors and seeing what happens. They experiment, test, and stimulate, and they ignore precedent, rules, and traditional expectations (Daft and Weick 1984, p. 288).

Innovation, in this view, is not simply a response to empirical observations of the environment. The source of innovation lies on the interface between an organization and its environment. And the process of innovating involves actively constructing a conceptual framework, imposing it on the environment, and reflecting on their interaction. With few changes, this could be a description of the activity of inventive, noncanonical groups, such as Orr's reps, who similarly "ignore precedent, rules, and traditional expectations" and break conventional boundaries. Like story telling, enacting is a process of interpretive sense making and controlled change.

A brief example of enacting can be seen in the introduction of the IBM Mag-I memory typewriter "as a new way of organizing office work" (Pava cited in Barley 1988). In order to make sense and full use of the power of this typewriter, the conditions in which it was to be used had to be reconceived. In the old conception of office work, the potential of the machine could not be realized. In a newly conceived understanding of office practice, however, the machine could prove highly innovative. Though this new conception could not be achieved without the new machine, the new machine could not be fully realized without the conception. The two changes went along together. Neither is wholly either cause or effect. Enacting organizations differ from discovering ones in that in this reciprocal way, instead of waiting for changed practices to emerge and responding, they enable them to emerge and anticipate their effects.

Reregistering the environment is widely recognized as a powerful source of innovation that moves organizations beyond the paradigms in which they begin their analysis and within which, without such a reformation, they must inevitably end it. This is the problem which Deetz and Kersten (1983) describe as closure: "Many organizations fail because . . . closure prohibits adaptation to current social conditions" (p. 166). Putnam (1983) argues that closure-generating structures appear to be "fixtures that exist independent of the processes that create and transform them" (p. 36). Interpretive or enacting organizations, aware as they are that their environment is not a given, can potentially adopt new viewpoints that allow them to see beyond the closure-imposing boundary of a single world view.

The question remains, however, how is this reregistering brought about by organizations that seem inescapably trapped within their own world view? We are claiming that the actual noncanonical practices of interstitial communities are continually developing new interpretations of the world because they have a practical rather than formal connection to that world. (For a theoretical account of the way practice drives change in world view, see Bloch 1977.) To pursue our connection with the work of the reps, closure is the likely result of rigid adherence to the reps' training and documentation and the formal account of work that they encompass. In order to get on with their work, reps overcome closure by reregistering their interpretation of the machine and its ever changing milieu. Rejection of a canonical, predetermined view and the construction through narration of an alternative view, such as Orr describes, involve, at heart, the complex intuitive process of bringing the communicative, community schema into harmony with the environment by reformulating both. The potential of such innovation is, however, lost to an organization that remains blind to noncanonical practice.

An enacting organization must also be capable of reconceiving not only its environment but also its own identity, for in a significant sense the two are mutually constitutive. Again, this reconceptualization is something that people who develop noncanonical practices are continuously doing, forging their own and their community's identity in their own terms so that they can break out of the restrictive hold of the formal descriptions of practice. Enacting organizations similarly regard both their environment and themselves as in some sense unanalyzed and therefore malleable. They do not assume that there is an ineluctable structure, a "right" answer, or a universal view to be discovered; rather, they continually look for innovative ways to impose new structure, ask new questions, develop a new view, become a new organization. By asking different questions, by seeking different *sorts* of explanations, and by looking from different points of view, different answers emerge—indeed different environments and different organizations mutually reconstitute each other dialectically or reciprocally. Daft and Weick (1984) argue, the interpretation can "shape the environment more than the environment shapes the interpretation" (p. 287).

Carlson's attempts to interest people in the idea of dry photocopying—xerography—provide an example of organizational tendencies to resist enacting innovation. Carlson and the Batelle Institute, which backed his research, approached most of the major innovative corporations of the time—RCA, IBM, A. B. Dick, Kodak. All turned down the idea of a dry copier. They did not reject a flawed machine. Indeed, they all agreed that it worked. But they rejected the *concept* of an office copier. They could see no use for it. Even when Haloid bought the patent, the marketing firms they hired consistently reported that the new device had no role in office practice (Dessauer 1971). In some sense it was necessary both for Haloid to reconceive itself (as Xerox) and for Xerox's machine to help bring about a reconceptualization of an area of office practice for the new machine to be put into manufacture and use.

What the evaluations saw was that an expensive machine was not needed to make a record copy of original documents. For the most part, carbon paper already did that admirably and cheaply. What they failed to see was that a copier allowed the proliferation of copies and of copies of copies. The quantitative leap in copies and their importance independent of the original then produced a qualitative leap in the way they were used. They no longer served merely as records of an original. Instead, they participated in the productive interactions of organizations' members in a unprecedented way. (See Latour's (1986) description of the organizational role of "immutable mobiles.") Only in use in the office, enabling and enhancing new forms of work, did the copier forge the conceptual lenses under which its value became inescapable.

It is this process of seeing the world anew that allows organizations reciprocally to see themselves anew and to overcome discontinuities in their environment and their structure. As von Hippel (1988), Barley (1988), and others point out, innovating is not always radical. Incremental improvements occur throughout an innovative organization. Enacting and innovating can be conceived of as at root sense-making, congruence-seeking, identity-building activities of the sort engaged in by the reps. Innovating and learning in daily activity lie at one end of a continuum of innovating practices that stretches to radical innovation cultivated in research laboratories at the far end.

Alternative world views, then, do not lie in the laboratory or strategic planning office alone, condemning everyone else in the organization to submit to a unitary culture. Alternatives are inevitably distributed throughout all the different communities that make up the organization. For it is the organization's communities, at all levels, who are in contact with the environment and involved in interpretive sense making, congruence finding, and adapting. It is from any site of such interactions that new insights can be coproduced. If an organizational core overlooks or curtails the enacting in its midst by ignoring or disrupting its communities-of-practice, it threatens its own survival in two ways. It will not only threaten to destroy the very working and learning practices by which it, knowingly or unknowingly, survives. It will also cut itself off from a major source of potential innovation that inevitably arises in the course of that working and learning.

Conclusion: Organizations as Communities-of-Communities

The complex of contradictory forces that put an organization's assumptions and core beliefs in direct conflict with members' working, learning, and innovating arises from a thorough misunderstanding of what working, learning, and innovating are. As a result of such misunderstandings, many modern processes and technologies, particularly those designed to downskill, threaten the robust working, learning, and innovating communities and practice of the workplace. Between Braverman's (1974) pessimistic view and Adler's (1987) optimistic one, lies Barley's (1988) complex argument, pointing out that the intent to downskill does not *necessarily* lead to downskilling (as Orr's reps show). But the intent to downskill may first drive noncanonical practice and communities yet further underground so that the insights gained through work are more completely hidden from the organization as a whole. Then later changes or reorganizations, whether or not intended to downskill, may disrupt what they do not notice. The gap between espoused and actual practice may become too large for noncanonical practices to bridge.

To foster working, learning, and innovating, an organization must close that gap. To do so, it needs to reconceive of itself as a community-of-communities, acknowledging in the process the many noncanonical communities in its midst. It must see beyond its canonical abstractions of practice to the rich, full-blooded activities themselves. And it must legitimize and support the myriad enacting activities perpetrated by its different members. This support cannot be intrusive, or it risks merely bringing potential innovators under the restrictive influence of the existing canonical view. Rather, as others have argued (Nystrom and Starbuck 1984; Hedberg 1981; Schein 1990) communities-of-practice must be allowed some latitude to shake themselves free of received wisdom.

A major entailment of this argument may be quite surprising. Conventional wisdom tends to hold that large organizations are particularly poor at innovating and adapting. Tushman and Anderson (1988), for example, argue justifiably that the *typical*, large organization is unlikely to produce discontinuous innovation. But size may not be the single determining feature here. Large, *atypical*, enacting organizations have the potential to be highly innovative and adaptive. Within an organization perceived as a collective of communities, not simply of individuals, in which enacting experiments are legitimate, separate community perspectives can be amplified by interchanges among communities. Out of this friction of competing ideas can come the sort of improvisational sparks necessary for igniting organizational innovation. Thus large organizations, *reflectively structured*, are perhaps particularly well positioned to be highly innovative and to deal with discontinuities. If their internal communities have a reasonable degree of autonomy and independence from the dominant world view, large organizations might actually accelerate innovation. Such organizations are uniquely positioned to generate innovative discontinuities incrementally, thereby diminishing the disruptiveness of the periodic radical reorganization that Nadler calls "frame breaking" (Nadler 1988). This occurs when conventional organizations swing wholesale from one paradigm to another (see also Bartunek 1984). An organization whose core is aware that it is the synergistic aggregate of agile, semiautonomous, self-constituting communities and not a brittle monolith is likely to be capable of extensible "frame bending" well beyond conventional breaking point.

The important interplay of separate communities with independent (though interrelated) world views may in part account for von Hippel's (1988) account of the sources of innovation and other descriptions of the innovative nature of business alliances. Von Hippel argues that sources of innovation can lie outside an organization among its customers and suppliers. Emergent communities of the sort we have outlined that span the boundaries of an organization would then seem a likely conduit of external and innovative views into an organization. Similarly, the alliances Powell describes bring together different organizations with different interpretive schemes so that the composite group they make up has several enacting options to choose from. Because the separate communities enter as independent members of an alliance rather than as members of a rigid hierarchy, the alternative conceptual viewpoints are presumably legitimate and do not get hidden from the core. There is no concealed noncanonical practice where there is no concealing canonical practice.

The means to harness innovative energy in any enacting organization or alliance must ultimately be considered in the design of organizational architecture and the ways communities are linked to each other. This architecture should preserve and enhance the healthy autonomy of communities, while simultaneously building an interconnectedness through which to disseminate the results of separate communities' experiments. In some form or another the stories that support learning-in-working and innovation should be allowed to circulate. The technological potential to support this distribution—e-mail, bulletin boards, and other devices that are capable of supporting narrative exchanges—is available. But narratives, as we have argued, are embedded in the social system in which they arise and are used. They cannot simply be uprooted and repackaged for circulation without becoming prey to exactly those problems that beset the old abstracted canonical accounts. Moreover, information cannot be assumed to circulate freely just because technology to support circulation is available (Feldman and March 1981). Eckert (1989), for instance, argues that information travels differently within different socio-economic groups. Organizational assumptions that given the "right" medium people will exchange information freely overlook the way in which certain socio-economic groups, organizations, and in particular, corporations, implicitly treat information as a commodity to be hoarded and exchanged. Working-class groups, Eckert contends, do pass information freely and Orr (1990a) notes that the reps are remarkably open with each other about what they know. *Within* these communities, news travels fast; community knowledge is readily available to community members. But these communities must function within corporations that treat information as a commodity and that have superior bargaining power in negotiating the terms of exchange. In such unequal conditions, internal communities cannot reasonably be expected to surrender their knowledge freely.

As we have been arguing throughout, to understand the way information is constructed and travels within an organization, it is first necessary to understand the different communities that are formed within it and the distribution of power among them. Conceptual reorganization to accommodate learning-in-working and innovation, then, must stretch from the level of individual communities-of-practice and the technology and practices used there to the level of the overarching organizational architecture, the community-of-communities.

It has been our unstated assumption that a unified understanding of working, learning, and innovating is potentially highly beneficial, allowing, it seems likely, a synergistic collaboration rather than a conflicting separation among workers, learners, and innovators. But similarly, we have left unstated the companion assumption that attempts to foster such synergy through a conceptual reorganization will produce enormous difficulties from the perspective of the conventional workplace. Work and learning are set out in formal descriptions so that people (and organizations) can be held accountable; groups are organized to define responsibility; organizations are bounded to enhance concepts of competition; peripheries are closed off to maintain secrecy and privacy. Changing the way these things are arranged will produce problems as well as benefits. An examination of both problems and benefits has been left out of this paper, whose single purpose has been to show where constraints and resources lie, rather than the rewards and costs of deploying them. Our argument is simply that for working, learning, and innovating to thrive collectively depends on linking these three, in theory and in practice, more closely, more realistically, and more reflectively than is generally the case at present.

Acknowledgments

This paper was written at the Institute for Research on Learning with the invaluable help of many of our colleagues, in particular Jean Lave, Julian Orr, and Etienne Wenger, whose work, with that of Daft and Weick, provides the canonical texts on which we based our commentary.

Notes

1. For a historical overview of anthropology of the workplace, see Burawoy (1979).
2. Not all the blame should be laid on the managers' desk. As several anthropologists, including Suchman (1987a) and Bourdieu (1977) point out, "informants" often describe their jobs in canonical terms though they carry them out in noncanonical ways. Lave (1988) argues that informants, like most people in our society, tend to privilege abstract knowledge. Thus they describe their actions in its terms.

References

Adler, P. S. (1987), "Automation and Skill: New Directions," *International Journal of Technology Management* 2 [5/6], 761–771.

Barley, S. R. (1988), "Technology, Power, and the Social Organization of Work: Towards a Pragmatic Theory of Skilling and Deskilling," *Research in the Sociology of Organizations*, 6, 33–80.

Bartunek, J. M. (1984), "Changing Interpretive Schemes and Organizational Restructuring: The Example of a Religious Order," *Administrative Science Quarterly*, 29, 355–372.

Bloch, M. (1977), "The Past and the Present in the Present," *Man*[NS], 12, 278–292.

Bourdieu, P. (1977), *Outline of a Theory of Practice*, trans R. Nice. Cambridge: Cambridge University Press. (First published in French, 1973.)

Braverman H. (1974), *Labor and Monopoly Capitalism: The Degradation of Work in the Twentieth Century*, New York: Monthly Review Press.

Brown, J. S. and P. Duguid, (in press), "Enacting Design," in P. Adler (Ed.), *Designing Automation for Usability*, New York: Oxford University Press.

Brown, J. S., A. Collins and P. Duguid (1989), "Situated Cognition and the Culture of Learning," *Education Researcher*, 18, 1, 32–42. (Also available in a fuller version as IRL Report 88-0008, Palo Alto, CA: Institute for Research on Learning.)

Burawoy, M. (19791, "The Anthropology of Industrial Work," *Annual Review of Anthropology*, 8, 231–266.

Daft, R. L. and K. E. Weick (1984), "Toward a Model of Organizations as Interpretation Systems," *Academy of Management Review*, 9, 2, 284–295.

Deetz, S. A. and A. Kersten (1983), "Critical Models of Interpretive Research," in L. L. Putnam and M. E. Pacanowsky (Eds.), *Communication and Organizations: An Interpretive Approach*, Beverly Hills, CA: Sage Publications.

Dessauer, J. H. (19711, *My Years with Xerox: The Billions Nobody Wanted*, Garden City, Doubleday.

Eckert, P. (19891, *Jocks and Burnouts*, New York: Teachers College Press.

Feldman, M. S. and J. G. March (1981), "Information in Organizations as Signal and Symbol," *Administrative Science Quarterly*, 26, 171–186.

Geertz, C. (1973), *Interpretation of Cultures: Selected Essays*, New York: Basic Books.

Goodman, P. and Associates (1988), *Designing Effective Work Groups*, San Francisco: Jossey-Bass.

Hackman, J. R. (Ed.) (1990), *Groups that Work (and Those that Don't)*, San Francisco: Jossey-Bass.

Hedberg, B. (1981), "How Organizations Learn and Unlearn," in P. C. Nystrom and W. H. Starbuck, *Handbook of Organizational Design*, Vol. I: Adapting Organizations to their Environments, New York: Oxford University Press.

_____, P. C. Nystrom and W. H. Starbuck (1976), "Designing Organizations to Match Tomorrow," in P. C. Nystrom and W. H. Starbuck (Eds.), *Prescriptive Models of Organizations*, Amsterdam, Netherlands: North-Holland Publishing Company.

Hutchins, E. (19911, "Organizing Work by Adaptation," *Organization Science*, 2, 1, 14–39.

_____ (in press), "Learning to Navigate," in S. Chalkin and J. Lave (Eds.), *Situated Learning*, Cambridge: Cambridge University Press.

Jordan, B. (1989), "Cosmopolitical Obstetrics: Some Insights from the Training of Traditional Midwives," *Social Science and Medicine*, 28, 9, 925–944. (Also available in slightly different form as *Modes of Teaching and Learning: Questions Raised by the Training of Traditional Birth Attendants*, IRL report 88-0004, Palo Alto, CA: Institute for Research on Learning.)

Latour, B. (1986), "Visualization and Cognition: Thinking with Eyes and Hands," *Knowledge and Society*, 6, 1–40.

Lave J. (1988), *Cognition in Practice: Mind, Mathematics, and Culture in Everyday Life*, New York: Cambridge University Press.

_____ and E. Wenger (1990), *Situated Learning: Legitimate Peripheral Participation*, IRL report 90-0013, Palo Alto, CA.: Institute for Research on Learning. (Also forthcoming (1990) in a revised version, from Cambridge University Press.)

Levi-Strauss, C. (1966), *The Savage Mind*, Chicago: Chicago University Press.

Martin, J. (1982), "Stories and Scripts in Organizational Settings," in A. H. Hastorf and A. M. Isen (Eds.), *Cognitive and Social Psychology*, Amsterdam: Elsevier.

Nadler, D. (1988), "Organizational Frame Bending: Types of Change in the Complex Organization," in R. H. Kilman, T. J. Covin, and associates (Eds.), *Corporate Transformation: Revitalizing Organizations for a Competitive World*, San Francisco: Jossey-Bass.

Nystrom, P. C. and W. H. Starbuck (1984), "To Avoid Organizational Crises, Unlearn," *Organizational Dynamics*, Spring, 53–65.

Orr, J. (1990a), "Talking about Machines: An Ethnography of a Modern Job," Ph.D. Thesis, Cornell University.

_____ (1990b), "Sharing Knowledge, Celebrating Identity: War Stories and Community Memory in a Service Culture," in D. S. Middleton and D. Edwards (Eds.), *Collective Remembering: Memory in Society*, Beverley Hills, CA: Sage Publications.

_____ (1987a), "Narratives at Work: Story Telling as Cooperative Diagnostic Activity," *Field Service Manager*, June, 47–60.

_____ (1987b), *Talking about Machines: Social Aspects of Expertise*, Report for the Intelligent Systems Laboratory, Xerox Palo Alto Research Center, Palo Alto, CA.

Pea, R. D. (1990), *Distributed Cognition*, IRL Report 90-0015, Palo Alto, CA: Institute for Research on Learning.

Putnam, L. L. (1983), "The Interpretive Perspective: An Alternative to Functionalism," in L. L. Putnam and M. E. Pacanowsky (Eds), *Communication and Organizations: An Interpretive Approach*, Beverley Hills, CA: Sage Publications.

Reddy, M. J. (1979), "The Conduit Metaphor," in Andrew Ortony (Ed.), *Metaphor and Thought*, Cambridge: Cambridge University Press, 284–324.

Ryle, G. (1954), *Dilemmas: The Tarner Lectures*, Cambridge: Cambridge University Press.

Schein, E. H. (1990), "Organizational Culture," *American Psychologist*, 45, 2, 109–119.

Schön, D. A. (1971), *Beyond the Stable State*, New York: Norton.

_____ (1984), *The Reflective Practitioner*, New York: Basic Books.

_____ (1987), *Educating the Reflective Practitioner*, San Francisco: Jossey-Bass.

Scribner, S. (1984), "Studying Working Intelligence," in B. Rogoff and J. Lave (Eds). *Everyday Cognition: Its Development in Social Context*, Cambridge, MA: Harvard University Press.

Suchman, L. (1987a), *Plans and Situated Actions: The Problem of Human–Machine Communication*, New York: Cambridge University Press.

_____ (1987b), "Common Sense in Interface Design," *Techné*, 1, 1, 38–40.

Tushman, M. L. and P. Anderson (1988), "Technological Discontinuities and Organization Environments," in A. M. Pettigrew (Ed.), *The Management of Strategic Change*, Oxford: Basil Blackwell.

Van Maanen, J. and S. Barley (1984), "Occupational Communities: Culture and Control in Organizations," in B. Straw and L. Cummings (Eds), *Research in Organizational Behaviour*, London: JAI Press.

von Hippel, E. (1988), *The Sources of Innovation*, New York: Oxford University Press.

Zuboff, S. (1988), *In the Age of the Smart Machine: The Future of Work and Power*, New York: Basic Books.

Academic Leaders as Thermostats

Jouni Kekäle

Abstract. University of Joensuu launched a two-year development and training project on academic management and leadership in the beginning of 2002. Open seminars were arranged for heads for departments, deans and administrative managers. In addition, personnel administration started pilot projects with two departments in co-operation with the Finnish Institute of Occupational Health. The idea was to develop both (a) leadership and management and (b) division of work, work ability and workplace health. The author's book Academic Leadership (Nova Science Publishers, New York) provides a background for this practical development project. The article deals with academic leadership, leadership philosophy and the system of personnel management at the University of Joensuu, the development projects, and lessons learned from them so far.

Introduction

The explicit reference to managers in universities is a relatively new phenomenon, which has developed in the western world in the 80s (Miller 1995: 167). Middlehurst (1995) has identified several trends (such as political and economic pressures, increasing size and scope of university business, and increased demand for accountability), which have underlined the fact that "management and leadership have become necessary" in the current academic context (see also Prichard 2000).

The increasing demand on academic leadership is reflected in growing volumes of leadership and management literature. Tight (2000) estimates that at least one hundred books on the broad topic were published in the UK in 1999; the number of journals on leadership and management in universities has also increased rapidly. Many of these books and texts deal with the management of practical tasks and challenges as faced by academic leaders. Indeed, the power and the responsibilities of individual leaders such as heads of departments have also considerably increased—at least officially, formally and in principle. [My case studies have shown that different departments may develop rather persistent leadership cultures and patterns of management which tend to continue to work in the traditional manner regardless of the external changes in legislation, formal power relations and university regulations (Kekäle 2001).] At the University of Joensuu, for example, the heads are now practically responsible for the efficiency of their departments and for the decisions to be taken in their departments. The demanding role has inevitably implications for training and development projects dealing with leadership and management in academia.

In this article I shall deal with academic leadership and describe the ongoing development project on academic management and leadership at the University of Joensuu and the experiences gained from the project so far. I shall first provide the reader with some background by describing the University of Joensuu and its management structure, and by shedding light on the system of personnel leadership and leadership philosophy related to this system. The discussion will be connected to official policies at the University of Joensuu, but will reflect my own viewpoints also.

The discussion will inevitably remain on a rather general level in relation to different view-points and opinions on leadership and management matters. The potential controversy starts with the concepts of *leadership* and *management* which are open to numerous definitions and interpretations

(Birnbaum 1989: 22; Middlehurst 1993: 7; Bush 1995). Leadership and management can be seen as two complementary aspects or systems of action (Middlehurst 1993). A loose conceptual distinction is often made between them: *Management* refers to orientation towards results and goals, organising tasks and systems, while *leadership* alludes to orientation towards human relations and organising people. Studies have demonstrated that persons in charge often have a tendency to stress either leadership or management functions and behaviour in their work; different organisational or leadership cultures may also maintain this kind of emphases (e.g. Kekäle 2001). However, in practice both these functional aspects need to be taken into account if a leader/manager wishes to be effective (Blake & Mouton 1964). Middlehurst (1993: 129) notes that leadership and management functions have been closely integrated at the departmental level.

When the university started the general education/development programme for administrators and academic leaders in the beginning of the year 2002, the emphasis was initially on management issues such as administrative regulations. The university had previously arranged leadership training with the help of some external experts. This time it was felt that after the renewal of certain service regulations and the university strategy, it is of a crucial importance to discuss these issues with newly appointed leaders who had just started their four-year periods as head of departments or deans. However, the new leaders stressed leadership and personnel policy issues so much that leadership training became a more substantial part of the development programme. As a result, the development programme has emphasised both the aspects of leadership and management—as will this paper. In this article, I shall deal mainly with the management and leadership of academic units. However, before starting a more detailed discussion of the development project let us look at the relevant background of the institution itself, the University of Joensuu and its management structure.

The University of Joensuu and Its Management Structure

The University of Joensuu was founded in 1969. The institution is a multidisciplinary university with six Faculties: Education, Forestry, Humanities, Science, Social Sciences and Theology. In addition to the main campus in Joensuu, the university has a second campus in Savonlinna, a city known for its medieval castle and world-famous opera festival. The university has currently over 7,000 students, approximately 1,000 of whom study at the Savonlinna campus. The staff comprises about 1,300 people, of whom 180 work in Savonlinna. The university participates in several international networks, including ECIU (European Consortium of Innovative Universities, see www.eciu.org).

The university's particular strengths and areas of expertise are:

1. Multi-disciplinary teacher training programme, which trains teachers for all levels of the education system

2. Teaching and research related to forests, other renewable resources and the environment

3. Proficiency in the development and application of high technology

4. Teaching and research relating to the social and cultural development of the European peripheral areas and border regions.

The highest decision-making body at the university is the senate. It is responsible for the general development of the university's operations; it also, among other things, appoints professors and approves the university's main official documents such as the accounts and annual report. The rector directs the activities of the university and deals with and resolves matters relating to its general administration, unless otherwise provided in acts, decrees or university regulations. The university has one vice-rector who is responsible for personnel matters. The director of administration leads the administration office, and, among other things, decides on major acquisitions of equipment and property and on study leave applications by members of staff.

The faculties (with the exception of the faculty of forestry which does not have separate departments) are divided into eighteen departments. In addition, there are two practice schools and nine separate institutes and centres, such as the computer centre, the university library and the educational technology centre, to mention only a few. The faculties are led by deans and faculty councils; the departments, institutes and centres have heads of departments and—in the case of rather independent institutes and centres—directors as their leaders. As noted, the heads of departments are responsible to deans and to the rector for the effectiveness (in terms of degree production) of their departments. The degree targets aimed at are set by the university after negotiations with the Ministry of Education (for the background of the negotiation system, see Rekilä 1995).

Over the years, there have been discussions in Finland on the issue whether or not academic leaders and managers should be professionals who are appointed to their leadership posts on a permanent basis. Today, the senate, faculty councils and deans are still elected by their peers for a period of four years (student members of the collegial bodies for two years) at a time. The deans appoint heads of departments for four years after taking advice from the department in question. Rectors are elected for five years at the time. As the key leaders may change—and the new ones may not be experienced in leadership and management—the development of leadership/management training and the development of support structures for personnel management and leadership have become crucial issues.

The System of Personnel Management and Leadership

The delegation of the functions of personnel management and leadership to local leaders is a typical feature in personnel strategies of many Finnish universities, including the strategy of the University of Joensuu. A post-modern and multi-disciplinary university is too complex an organisation to be managed and run completely from the top down. The dynamics and development within the various disciplinary fields tend to be much too complicated to be controlled even by the academics, let alone by the university management (Clark 1997). The many cultures within academia are too diverse to be led by using a single, uniform pattern of leadership (Becher 1989; Becher & Trowler 2001; Kekäle 2001).

At the University of Joensuu, managerial solutions in such an original and complex leadership environment has been sought from Birnbaum's (1989) ideas on cybernetics and self-regulation as well as from Clark's (1983) seminal work (Hölttä & Pulliainen 1996). A university is an *open system* in constant interaction with its environments. A university is also a *loosely coupled* system in the sense that the organisational units of a university are only partially connected to each other. The administrative action connects the basic units with certain rules and regulations, which normally do not strictly direct the core issues of academic work, namely research and teaching. The basic academic tasks largely belong to the realm of academic freedom and are, therefore, directed mainly by academic professionals. Consequently, a university should rely on self-regulating control loops and monitor only a limited number of variables and strategic issues (Hölttä & Pulliainen 1996).

There are other grounds for the delegation of leadership and management functions to local managers such as heads of departments: The basic academic tasks are carried out in the departments, which may differ from each other on the basis of culture, disciplinary basis, economical resources and expectations of the personnel (Kekäle 2001). At the level of the basic unit, there is (or should be) the best understanding for the operational (local and academic) environment and the best prerequisites for leadership, and for smooth self-regulative actions when needed. In both good and bad times, the key professors can have power and influence over the kind of research conducted within their department, the expectations concerning that research, and the tempo or the manner of work. Although researchers may often be rather independent, academic leaders can hinder or help the pursuit of the scholarly activities of the researchers in many ways (Moses 1985: 338). In particular, the academic's contribution to research constitutes a very strong source of personal power, influence and respect in his/her own department and field (Tucker 1993: 44–46; Kekäle 2001).

This does not imply that the university cannot direct the basic academic tasks at a certain level, or to some degree, on the basis of its strategical, policy-driven and economic considerations. After hearing the faculties, the rector of the University of Joensuu decides annually which teaching and research posts or offices will be established, declared vacant or done away with. The document, which is called "the strategic personnel plan" has proved to be an important tool in implementing the strategy and in keeping overall expenditures in control. Another mechanism for implementing strategy is the process of internal target negotiations in which the basic funding of the departments is the issue, and in which other questions can also be discussed before the rector decides on the internal allocation of funds (on the basis of key results of the department in comparison with the results of other departments in the same disciplinary field in Finnish higher education).

The central management also has other ways to make an impact. The use of the university's reward systems (which, however, mainly monitor the quantity and quality of the work being done) and the allocation of economic resources to certain preferred projects, for example. In addition, a new, more rewarding salary system is under negotiation in Finnish higher education. The university of Joensuu has taken an active and a pioneering role in this major reform. [The author has acted as a chairman of a national working group dealing with the new salary system, and also participates in the ongoing central negotiations with trade unions.]

In the issues of personnel management and leadership the division of labour between different administrative levels is as follows: The central decision-makers (the senate, rectors and director of administration) decide on the common and general guidelines and principles which can be evaluated, corrected and rethought on the basis of the feedback gained. Within these broad outlines, the departments will develop their own policies and practices.

Academic Leaders as Thermostats

Leadership is not an action with an inherent value. Rather, the aim is to support the basic tasks and excellent performance, to maintain a good working atmosphere, personnel policy and well-functioning internal cooperation. On a broad scale, leadership is perhaps best assessed on the basis of how well the basic work is carried out by the group in question, and on the basis of the evaluations of the "subordinates" (Hogan, Curphy & Hogan 1994).

It has often been argued that the idea of strong management and heroic leadership is inappropriate in the context of academic institutions (e.g. Becher 1989; Birnbaum 1989; Middlehurst & Kennie 1995). As Dearlove (1995: 13) stresses:

> Precisely because fundamental research involves going beyond the frontiers of established understanding, good researchers can hardly be told what to do.

Academic leaders act as thermostats: he/she does not have to control or direct everything, but instead concentrates on promoting the most important strategic issues. In "normal times", when everything is running smoothly and well, the leader supports basic conditions of work, maintains a creative working atmosphere and tries to keep things in a proper balance and within the range of normal operational conditions. The responsibility of the leaders and managers is to keep things going and keep the organisation working. One good way to achieve this is to make the followers more independent, to facilitate commitment and reflective *self-management* (Hersey & Blanchard 1982; Sims & Lorenzi 1992). The reward structures and salary systems of the organisation should support and reward work which is done well and according to the strategic preferences of the university.

However, when serious problems arise, the limits of acceptable operation are exceeded, or the self-management skills of the members of staff are tottering, leaders may have to contribute more actively to the process by providing support, advice or a more direct leadership (Hersey & Blanchard 1982; also Birnbaum 1989). The thermostat reacts by trying to resolve the tension between different contradictions and pressures. If the problems cannot be solved at local departmental level, the leader can contact the dean or central administration which will act as further thermostats, by resolving the tensions and by seeking solutions to the problems at hand.

This structure works especially in relation to social tensions and administrative problems. In extreme cases the rector has the power to take stronger actions if needed (e.g. by giving warnings). The departments have also been encouraged to establish a body consisting of respected members of senior staff, which would support the head of a department in his/her leadership role during the times of crises. The university has also established other similar buffer-structures,

-organs and -groups, which will initially deal with (potential) problems related to conflicts between staff or, among other things (suspicions of) sexual harassment or discrimination.

A general starting point is that leadership and management do not take place in a social vacuum. Currently, influential trends in leadership theories have taken fully into account the impact of power and cultural influence, subjectivist perspectives, and they emphasise the idea of leadership as a process. Contingency (and cultural) theories, which have remained influential from the late 1960s to the present, have discarded the notion of One Best Way of Leadership (Smith & Petterson 1988). These theories are based on at least three assumptions: (1) different circumstances require different qualities or patterns of behaviour for a leader to be effective; (2) leadership is not unidimensional, but the dynamic interaction between leader and context will inevitably shape the nature of leadership; (3) context and circumstances place different demands and constraints on leaders (Middlehurst 1993: 20).

The pressures and possibilities a leader will have to deal with—as well as, to a great extent, the "limits of acceptable operation" according to which the "thermostat" will have to react—may arise from legislation, (sub)cultural norms and values, economic resources, power issues or the (mis)fit of human competence in relation to the needs of the work (Kekäle 1998). An academic leader inevitably operates in a complex, changing and historically developing *field of possibilities* loosely framed by features, pressures and possibilities arising from the simultaneous interaction of the contextual spheres (legislation, economic resources, human competence and resources, the cultural sphere and the sphere of power and interests). In principle, any action can be fostered or hindered by the different spheres. In the negative case: the action can be illegal, against cultural values, impossible to carry out in financial terms or because of the lack of the competence needed. The relationship between the act and the contextual sphere may be ambiguous or neutral, or legislation, culture, etc. may also support certain acts or behavioural patterns.

The contextual spheres change in time and place, but the diverse contextual aspects—the field of possibilities—largely determine what is good and appropriate in terms of leadership, and what is not. Previous leaders may have contributed to the current field of possibilities; and an academic leader may also broaden the field of possibilities by applying funding, by negotiating with the staff in order to bring about cultural change, by starting training/development programmes which provide the personnel with new competencies, etc. (for further discussion on the heuristic model of the field of possibilities, see Kekäle 1998). Since the local and disciplinary contexts vary, different basic units may develop their own leadership cultures and ways of working within the broad frames set by the university (Kekäle 2001).

Blau (1974) has maintained that the dilemma of leadership is that it requires both power over others, and their legitimating approval of that power. The collective approval of a leadership position must be earned. This is a challenge faced by each and every academic leader. It has to be dealt with mainly on the basis of his/her own competence and merits. Holding a managerial position alone cannot guarantee the approval of a leadership position by the staff. Management training and development projects cannot guarantee this either, but at least they can provide the leaders with some solutions, contextual and theoretical knowledge and information needed in their demanding task.

The Development Project on Leadership and Management

The project developing management and leadership consisted of two parts: (1) General training for all managers and academic leaders (heads of departments, deans and leading administrators), and (2) pilot projects for two departments in cooperation with the Finnish Institute of Occupational Health. The initial idea in the latter has been to develop both (a) leadership and management and (b) working ability and health at the workplace. The basic aim has been to find good practices and, especially, simple and working structures for management training.

A rather unique feature in Finland is that the systems of occupational healthcare and occupational safety are strong and both of them have an active, preventive orientation and connections to legislation. To my knowledge, there have been no development projects combining workplace health and leadership training in the university sector so far, but there is one such project going on in the Finnish communal sector. However, the State Treasury has launched a special programme providing funding for development projects with this kind of orientation. At the university of Joensuu, the project derived its basic orientation from the personnel strategy of the university, in which the aim is to develop simultaneously both (a) leadership, efficiency and quality of work, and (b) health at the workplace, and to find a balance between these broad aims.

The project is basically a practical one. The author was responsible for organising the development project. The considerations in the previous section provided a theoretical background for the project. In particular, the idea of the field of possibilities of academic leaders (Kekäle 1998) was crucial. In order to act as thermostat, an academic leader has to know the operational context she/he finds her/himself in. This concerns, among other things, the partly overlapping spheres of the field of possibilities mentioned in the previous section: (1) Economic resources (funding possibilities and regulations), (2) legislation, (3) leadership in the cultural context and leadership of culture, (4) power and authority issues in connection with the leadership position, and (5) human resource management (HRM, including recruitment and management of human competence). The broad aim was to provide the audience with training that would help them to better understand their leadership context and to foster their ability to manage their role: To promote strategic aims and to keep things going and the organisation working by acting as "thermostats" and by working with concrete and symbolic, established and ambiguous aspects of the field of possibilities open to them (Kekäle 1998).

The General Training

The general management/leadership training started in February 2002. All key administrators and the new elected leaders were invited to participate in the training programme. The idea in this first meeting was to screen the hopes and expectations of the participants in relation to the seminars to be arranged. This was done in order to facilitate commitment among academic leaders. As different contexts and circumstances involve different demands, constraints and choices on leaders, the idea was also to bring the local pressures the participants are facing into open discussion.

The first meeting started with a task which provided a background for open discussion. The participants were first asked to consider and to define themselves their core (key) tasks as leaders/managers. Then each was asked to list three criteria for successful leadership/management on the basis of their previous understandings. They completed the task in 15 minutes.

The next task dealt with the actual leadership/management training: each participant was asked to list three to five (3–5) most important topics for the forthcoming training programme when considering the basic leadership/management tasks they have just listed. The proposals were written on large memo-stickers which were then collected by the organisers. The organisers classified the proposals on the basis of the themes or leadership functions they represented. A large circle divided into seven segments, each named after the pre-selected leadership functions (Mäntyranta et al. 1999) was set on the wall of the lecture hall. The proposals (stickers) were then set on their corresponding segments. These leadership functions and the number of corresponding proposals for leadership/management training topics were those listed in Table 1.

Obviously, there are overlaps between the categories and leadership functions. It is always possible to argue for different kinds of distinctions and categorisations of leadership functions. The classification of leadership functions was used solely as a heuristic tool and as an illustrator of different potential training topics and the wishes by the participants. According to my observation it served well for this purpose. The Universities of Oulu and Helsinki have used it (in a somewhat different manner) for this purpose too. The demonstration allowed the participants to have a concrete picture of the emphases in their proposals for topics in leadership training, and provided the seminar a good starting point for further discussion of the forthcoming training programme.

Two striking issues arose on the basis of this demonstration: (1) No direct and concrete proposals were made in relation to transformational leadership (Birnbaum 1989; Middlehurst 1993) and (2) personnel management and, especially, leadership received most of the votes. The absence of direct proposals for transformational leadership as a theme for common leadership training might

TABLE 1

Leadership/Management Functions by Mäntyranta et al. (1999) and the Number of Corresponding Proposals for Training Topics

Function or Theme	Number of Proposals for Training Topics
1. Strategic management	12
2. Financial management	23
3. Operative leadership/management	25
4. PR-issues	19
5. Self-management	14
6. Personnel management and leadership	42
7. Transformational leadership and development work	–

have to do with the categorisation and classification of the proposals, but in hindsight and when viewed from another angle, the interpretation remains that this particular perspective was not directly stressed in the short proposals. However, transformational leadership was stressed in an indirect manner. It can be interpreted that at least part of the proposals which dealt with personnel leadership had to do with leading towards change and new values—in other words, transformational leadership. This is, of course, an issue of great importance at the University of Joensuu and in other institutions of higher education also. As noted, personnel management and leadership issues have become more important with the increased accountability and delegation of decision-making powers to local leaders. The heads of departments may indeed find themselves in the role of a mediator—or a thermostat—between the academic departmental culture and the current managerial demands, set in the spirit of management by objectives.

A thorough general discussion followed the classification of proposals for training topics made at the first meetings. This discussion lasted for a couple of hours; the author continued as a chairman and consultant responsible for the seminar. The participants gave more feedback, clarifications and ideas within the basic framework of their previous proposals. It was agreed that the proposals would be taken fully into consideration in the training programme, but also the strategic needs and considerations of the University would be taken into account during the forthcoming seminars. By following this principle, the personnel administration then classified the proposals on a new basis, namely according to the areas of competence and responsibility of the administrative professionals at the university. The general training programme was to be run mainly by internal experts—with the help of some external consultants, when needed.

After some initial discussions within a central management team of the University the following outline for the seminars was agreed (compare to Walker 1998):

1. Internal and external communications at the university

2. Legal grounds for action and leadership roles; supporting database management systems

3. The university's strategy. The management of—and the support services for—core tasks: research and instruction (including funding possibilities)

4. Financial management (including relevant regulations)

5. Personnel management and leadership (including HRM issues and leadership in the contexts of disciplinary and departmental cultures; Kekäle 2001)

It was ensured that the seminars, as a whole, covered key contextual aspects of leadership (Kekäle 1998), emphasised both the aspects of leadership and management, and also dealt with general issues and tasks of the managers. The logic in this schedule was basically to move from general aspects of the leadership environment towards more specific and practical regulations and tools—in the following manner: The director of communications started, as the area represented a current emphasis of the University and he had materials for the seminar ready. After this, the participants were provided with an overview of the underlying legislation (by the vice-rector) and the means for finding more information from the university information systems. Then the University's own strategies and priorities were discussed by the rector; the support services from the central administration provided their contributions in financial and personnel management. Each organiser paid special attention to the original proposals from the first meeting. The seminars typically lasted for one working day each.

The seminars were mainly organised around lectures and open discussions. All the seminars were held by the end of April. Some of the participants gave written feedback after the seminars. The feedback was mainly positive: the structure and the organisation of the general training were considered as good. The main complaint was that some of the leaders found it difficult to find time for participation in the seminars. It was proposed that the training should be arranged over a period of a few days outside the university. Leadership and personnel management were still the most frequently mentioned themes for further seminars, but also financial and legal matters were considered as areas worth further personnel training. More training was expected in the future. Consequently, the university started a series of seminars during the autumn 2002. This time the training was open for the whole staff. The broader scope in training is based on the educational plan of the University of Joensuu and on the demands by the staff. However, also direct leadership training will be continued as a part of the educational plan.

The Pilot Projects

After the general leadership/management training, two pilot development projects with volunteer departments were started in cooperation with Finnish Institute of Occupational Health (see also Pirttilä 2002). As noted, the initial idea in these pilots has been to dig deeper and to develop both (1) leadership and management and (2) division of work, work ability and workplace health. This idea is in line with the personnel strategy of the University of Joensuu, which emphasises both quality and efficiency of working teams and the well-being of the employees.

Two departments—which I shall not name here for the sake of potentially confidential information—volunteered to participate in the project. It was agreed that the participating departments would be able to bring their own priorities to the development work and that the development work would be carried out in the manner—and on the conditions—that suit the departments. The ongoing projects started in the beginning of June 2002. They were considered as processes (see Walker 1998). The consultants have acted in the spirit of process consultation, mainly in the roles of trainers and facilitators.

The project started in the first department (*department A*) with a light version of the method called "future workshop" (Zukunftwerkstätten; Jungk & Müllert 1989). First, the participants were asked to list problems in the functioning of the department. The participants wrote down the problems they considered as important and attached the papers to the wall (the participants were allowed to write only one problem per paper). No further discussion was allowed at this point, just the brief listings by each individual (one person tried to give the audience a lecture on the problems he considered as crucial). The idea was to facilitate democratic assessment of the situation in the department so that no individual voices would be emphasised nor silenced. After the papers indicating the problems experienced by the staff were attached on the wall, the participants were provided with a list of the problems identified, and they were asked to vote for the (eight) most important problems.

The results were then announced. The problems considered as the most important dealt with issues which are generally considered as problematic in many organisations, such as (insufficient) flow of information, (insufficient) induction of new members of the staff, temporary contracts of employment, and imbalances in division of labour. It was also felt that it would be useful to strengthen the spirit of community among the staff.

The participants were then divided into groups which gathered brainstorming solutions for the problems identified. Each group presented their ideas about the development programme needed, while others commented on the development ideas. After this, a working group (which was to develop the programme further) was established. The working group consisted of representatives of the department's management, members of the staff and personnel administration. The members of the working group from department A have met several times. Concrete actions have been agreed and taken and most of the problems identified in the 'future workshop' have now been resolved.

However, some contrasting views among certain central members of staff were still remaining (this is not a new phenomenon in the department). The contrasting viewpoints have been basically connected to a "sufficient" degree of openness in certain decisions that are, according to the university's internal regulations, currently for the departmental head to decide. Meetings have been arranged in order to solve these disagreements. It was apparent that the knowledge of internal regulations was still not deep enough among some members of staff, but there also seem to be different ideals about good ways of taking decisions. Central administration has clarified the issues and has provided consultancy for the departmental leaders. Key members of the staff participated in an open seminar which was arranged by the organisers. At this point, the disagreements seem to have resolved to some extent, but not completely.

The project has started in *department B* in a different way. In June 2002 the department had an internal meeting in which the staff discussed departmental strategies. The workshop started with a short lecture on strategic management. During the workshop, two exercises were carried out: First, the participants were divided into groups which were asked to consider the (internal) strengths and weaknesses and (external) opportunities and threats (the so-called SWOT method). The analyses by different groups were then discussed together so that different viewpoints could be taken into consideration.

The general discussion was followed by another short lecture, this time dealing with social-psychological dynamics within organisations, especially in relation to decision-making precesses and the development of a shared vision for the future. The second group-task dealt with different scenarios for the future. The participants were encouraged to consider potential changes in the relevant working environment of the department. The groups would then have to come up with strategies that would work in every context and that would provide the department with some guidelines in achieving their goals in the uncertain future. It was stressed that these exercises are a part of an ongoing development project and that the work will be continued and made more specific during the later sessions and "future workshop".

The "future workshop" was carried out in the department B in a similar manner to that in the other department. The analysis brought in the forefront problems such as temporary contracts of employment, too little time for research, and generally, the need for direction for the recently established unit. It was rather commonly held that the department is going to have to continue its strategic work in order to gain a respected place and a niche within its operational environment and in order to secure its future. Once the common direction becomes clearer there is less potential for confusion and conflict, and more energy left for finding solutions to problems in division of labour and similar practical issues. The work has been carried out over several internal sessions later on. The project has organised seminars and meetings for the department. In the discussions many issues become clearer for the participants. The relatively recently established unit has grown rapidly, but it seems that the public funding of the unit will decrease somewhat during the year 2003. Therefore, strategic choices will indeed become necessary in the near future and the process of strategic development of the department will have to be continued.

Along these seminars and workshops, different seminars and occasions dealing directly with workplace health have been arranged for the pilot departments. The aim has been to facilitate both physical and psychological well-being in the workplace. The meetings have been organised around exercises and short lectures as a part of health services provided by the University of Joensuu. The project also aims at providing better conditions for workplace health by improving internal cooperation, division of labour and leadership, and by solving practical problems which otherwise cause an unnecessarily heavy drain on energy and human resources.

Concluding Remarks

So far the development processes described have shown rather good results. They have been run at relatively low cost. During the general leadership training, the participant generally seemed to prefer local experts as lecturers. The impression remains that the training made it possible to deal with several problematic issues which would have had to be dealt with sooner or later in any case—in some cases maybe too late and perhaps with severe consequences. The knowledge of where to find help in managerial and leadership problems has also increased.

The pilot projects are estimated to last for two years (2002–2004). The Finnish Institute of Occupational Health will carry out a follow-up on the pilot projects by interviewing staff in each department in the beginning and at the end of the project. Therefore, it is not possible to draw too far-reaching conclusions at this point. Still, the methods of consultancy (used for deciding on the areas to be developed) seem to work rather well. The general impression has been that it is fruitful to start the development project with strategy work, as it helps to focus the process towards the most important issues from the department's point of view. The strength of the "future workshop" is that it gives each person a right to affect the process, therefore potentially increasing the commitment of the staff. The process can also help to maintain a certain realism, in the sense that it keeps the otherwise dominating persons in line with others. In this kind of development processes much depends on the activity of the participating departments and departmental leaders. Lack of time and various other commitments seem to limit the possibilities of the staff to participate fully in the development work. Central administration and external consultants can only provide support and help in the demanding development tasks of the departments.

In this article my assumption has been that in universities—and other organizations dealing so much with creativity—it is only reasonable to construct leadership and management systems and structures in order to support the continuous flow of basic functions and in order to avoid severe problems in these. If the scope of leadership and management is extended too far, the results can prove to be counter-productive. In practice, a great many leadership problems remain to be solved when they appear—and sometimes they have to be tolerated as a suitable solution is not at hand. Each academic leader has to find his/her way to gain competence and respect in supporting his/her unit's basic operations within the current and potentially changing field of possibilities (Kekäle 1998). However, positive development can be supported by the means of leadership training.

On a whole, the idea of academic leaders as thermostats and the basic leadership philosophy seem to be fruitful. As noted, leadership is perhaps best assessed on the basis of how well the basic work is carried out and on the basis of evaluations by the staff (Hogan, Curphy & Hogan 1994). While these are complex issues to assess, it can be noted that the university has continuously reached higher outcomes in terms of annual degree production. According to an annual questionnaire, which is a part of the annual personnel report of the university, and which has been responded to by a large part of the staff at the University of Joensuu, the staff has expressed positive development three years in succession in the vast majority of the sections of the study, including working atmosphere, leadership, flow of information and internal cooperation. Knowledge gained from the personnel reports and the surveys is taken fully into account when future priorities in development work and leadership training are considered.

References

Becher, T. (1989). *Academic Tribes and Territories. Intellectual Enquiry and the Cultures of Disciplines.* Suffolk: Society for Research into Higher Education & Open University Press.

Becher & Trowler (2001). *Academic Tribes and Territories* (2nd edn.). Suffolk: Society for Research into Higher Education & Open University Press.

Birnbaum, R. (1989). *How Colleges Work. The Cybernetics of Academic Organization and Leadership.* San Francisco: Jossey-Bass.

Blake, R.R. & Mouton, J.S. (1964). *The Managerial Grid.* Houston, Texas: Gulf Publishing Co.

Blau, P.M. (1974). *Exchange Theory*. (First published in 1964.) In O. Grusky & G.A. Miller (eds), *The Sociology of Organizations*. New York: Basic Studies. The Free Press.

Bush, T. (1995). *Theories of Educational Management*. Gateshead: Paul Chapman Publishing.

Clark, B.R. (1983). *The Higher Education System*. Berkeley: University of California Press.

Clark, B.R. (1997). Common Problems and Adaptive Responses in the Universities of the World: Organizing for Change, *Higher Education Policy* 10(3/4), 291–295.

Dearlove, J. (1995). *The Deadly Dull Issue of University 'Administration'? Good Governance, Managerialism, and Organising Academic Work*. A Paper Presented at SRHE Conference, 12–14 December. Edinburgh.

Hersey, P. & Blanchard, K.H. (1982). *Management of Organizational Behaviour. Utilizing Human Resources*. New Jersey: Prentice Hall.

Hogan, R., Curphy, G.J. & Hogan, J. (1994). What We Know About Leadership. Effectiveness and Personality, *American Psychologist* 49(6), 493–504.

Höltta, S. & Pulliainen, K. (1996). The Changing Regional Role of Universities, *Tertiary Education and Management* 2(2), 119–126.

Kekäle, J. (1998). Academic Leaders and the Field of Possibilities, *International Journal of Leadership in Education* 1(1), 237–255.

Kekäle, J. (2001). *Academic Leadership*. New York: Nova Science Publishers.

Jungk, R. & Müllert, R. *Tulevaisuusverstaat [Future Workshops]*. Kerava: Helsingin Yliopiston Ylioppilaskunta, Kansan Sivistystyön Liitto ja Ruohonjuuri Oy.

Mäntyranta, T., Tuulonen, A., Rantamäki, J., Tähtinen, J., Halonen, K., Martikainen, A., Rajamäki, J. & Aaltonen, M. (1999). *Portfolio johtamisen välineenä [Portfolios as a Management Tool]*. Raportti työpajatyöskentelystä opetuksen meritoinnin talvipäiviltä 26–27.11.1998.

Middlehurst, R. (1993). *Leading Academics*. Suffolk: SRHE & Open University Press.

Middlehurst, R. (1995). Changing Leadership in Universities. In T. Schuller (ed.), *The Changing University?* Suffolk: SRHE & Open University Press.

Middlehurst, R. & Kennie, T. (1995). Leadership and Professionals: Comparative Frameworks, *Tertiary Education and Management (TEAM)* 1(2), 120–130.

Miller, H.D.R. (1995). *The Management of Change in Universities. Universities, State and Economy in Australia, Canada and the United Kingdom*. Suffolk: SRHE & Open University Press.

Moses, I. (1985). The Role of Head of Department in the Pursuit of Excellence, *Higher Education* 14(4), 337–354.

Pirttilä, I. (2002). *The Enhancing of Well Being in Academic Work: A Case Study 2002–2004*. A Poster Presentation at 24th Annual EAIR Forum, 8–11 September. Prague.

Prichard, C. (2000). *Making Managers in Universities and Colleges*. Suffolk: SRHE & Open University Press.

Rekilä, E. (1995). Contracts as a Management Instrument: New Policies in Relationships between the Universities and the Ministry of Education, *Tertiary Education and Management* 1(1).

Sims, H.P. & Lorenzi, P. (1992). *The New Leadership Paradigm. Social Learning and Cognition in Organizations*. Newbury Park: Sage Publications.

Smith, P.B. & Peterson, M.F. (1988). *Leadership, Organizations and Culture*. London: Sage Publications.

Tight, M. (2000). *The Higher Education Management Literature: An Analysis and Critique*. A Paper Presented at EAIR Forum, 6–9 September. Berlin.

Tucker, A. (1993). *Chairing the Academic Department. Leadership among Peers*. American Council on Education. Series on Higher Education. Phoenix, AZ: Oryx Press.

Walker, E. (1998). Developing Managers. In D. Warner & E. Crosthwaite (eds), *Human Resource Management in Higher Education*. Suffolk: SRHE & Open University Press.

JAZZ AS A PROCESS
OF ORGANIZATIONAL INNOVATION

DAVID T. BASTIEN
TODD J. HOSTAGER

Jazz is an art form that is inventive and social. It enables individual musicians to create new musical ideas in a collective context and, thereby, to achieve an inventive and integrated performance. Here we present a case study of the process through which four jazz musicians were able to coordinate an inventive performance without the benefit of a rehearsal or the use of sheet music. A videotape of the performance and participant observations provided the data for our analysis. We identify two levels of information—musical and social structures—that constrain invention and enable integration. We then adapt Poole's Multiple Sequence Model (1983) as a device for tracking cognitive and behavioral components of the jazz process in, and across, time. Our analysis highlights the crucial roles of shared information, communication, and attention in this process and identifies a basic strategy that enabled the musicians to invent and coordinate increasingly complex musical ideas. We conclude with implications of our findings for the study and management of organizational innovation in contexts beyond those of group jazz.

Jazz is more than just a style of music that is captured in our collections of records, tapes, and compact discs. It is a celebration of the process of creating music, a form for musical innovation that engages performers as active composers in the collective invention, adoption, and implementation of new musical ideas. As a process of organizational innovation, jazz addresses some central concerns of organizations and their managers. First, jazz is self-consciously spontaneous, creative, and expressive. It is fundamentally concerned with *inventiveness* as an expected mode of thought and behavior. Second, jazz is most typically a social process, involving a group of inventive musicians. Jazz enables individual musicians to coordinate the innovation process so that they achieve a credible and aesthetically pleasing *collective* outcome. The jazz process is built on the assumption that each individual musician is simultaneously and consciously adapting to the whole, supporting the other players, and mutually influencing the outcome. Jazz is thus a truly collective approach to the entire process of innovation, for it requires that the invention, adoption, and implementation of new musical ideas by individual musicians occurs within the context of a shared awareness of the group performance as it unfolds over time.

Jazz is produced through a theory of music and a set of known social practices, both of which enable inventive and integrated performances. As with all of the arts, jazz is also an industry and a profession. Those practitioners who work at jazz as a full-time profession learn the theories and practices more fluently than practitioners who work at it on a part-time basis. Studying how adroit jazz professionals successfully manage the coordination of an inventive performance ought to provide insight into at least one way of managing the process of organizational innovation.

In this article, we examine the jazz process by analyzing a concert in which four musicians accomplished a group performance without the benefit of rehearsal or the guidance of sheet music. By focusing on the process involved in this type of performance, our study differs from prior social scientific investigations of jazz in two important regards. First, previous studies (e.g., Bougon, Weick, & Binkhorst, 1977; Voyer & Faulkner, 1986a, 1986b) focused on a different type of group jazz performance, in which (a) rehearsal is a means for working out an authoritative version of a musical innovation prior to group performance, (b) sheet music is a mechanism of constraint on innovation during performance, and (c) group performance largely consists of the reproduction of previously innovated musical ideas for an audience. Our study instead examines a group performance in which musical invention, adoption, and implementation are collectively determined directly in front of an audience without rehearsal or sheet music.

The second difference between our study and previous investigations is in our use of a "process research" perspective as opposed to a "variance research" perspective (Rogers, 1983, p. 194). Previous studies advanced our understanding of group jazz performance by establishing a map of the perceived causal relationships between such variables as (a) satisfaction with the rehearsal, (b) time spent rehearsing, and (c) the quality of the performance. Our study, however, seeks to advance understanding of group jazz performance by establishing a basic understanding of the "time-ordered sequence of a set of events" (Rogers, 1983, p. 194) in the musical performance.

We begin with an overview of the methods used to generate data in our study, which include a videotape of the performance and observations made by participants in the performance. We then briefly describe the known structural conventions through which the jazz process occurs. Next, we use these structural conventions to interpret the case study data and to identify two basic patterns for organizational innovation in the jazz process. We probe further into the first pattern by adopting Poole's Multiple Sequence Model (1983) as an analytic device for tracking cognitive and behavioral components of the jazz process in, and across, time. This analysis highlights the crucial roles of shared information, communication, and attention in the jazz process. Next, we examine the second pattern in greater detail and identify a basic strategy that enables musicians to invent and coordinate increasingly complex musical ideas. Finally, we close with implications of our findings for organizational innovation in contexts beyond those of group jazz.

Methods

Our case study consists of a jazz concert that was produced by Bob DeFlores and Maytime Productions and performed on June 29, 1985, in Saint Paul, Minnesota. The data for the present study reside in three sources: (a) a videotape of the concert, (b) our written notes of one participant's observations during a review of the videotape, and (c) written observations made by the other participants, based on their review of the videotape and their reading of a case study report that we wrote about the jazz concert.

Arranging and Videotaping the Concert

As students of organizational innovation, we were fortunate to happen upon the videotaped record of a jazz performance that embodied a process of collective musical innovation. The advent of a relatively inexpensive and unobtrusive videotaping technology allows researchers such as ourselves to obtain a fairly complete record of complex behavioral events as they unfold across time in particular organizational contexts. Videotaped data facilitate process research by enabling us to better track events in, and across, time.

The conditions for the jazz concert and the production of the videotape were established by Bob DeFlores and Maytime Productions. Four musicians were selected by the procedures, each according to his general level of professional competence and, in particular, to his ability to play traditional jazz songs (i.e., "standards"). Four participants were invited and received monetary compensation for playing the concert: Bud Freeman on tenor saxophone, Art Hodes on piano, Biddy Bastien (the father of one of the authors) on bass, and Hal Smith on drums. As a group, they represented over 200 years of individual professional experience, although they had no professional experience in playing together as a quartet. Because they had not played together as a quartet, they constituted a "zero-history" group (Bormann, 1975), a group that attempts to accomplish a task collectively without the benefits bestowed by a history of working together.

Although the producers did not conceive of their actions as those of social scientists, the conditions they established for the concert can be viewed as a set of controls for a collective musical innovation task: zero-history, no rehearsal, and no sheet music. In bringing such a group together under these circumstances, DeFlores and Maytime Productions planned a performance in which the entire process of musical invention and integration took place in front of an audience. Arrangements were made with K-TWIN, a video production company, to videotape the entire performance.

Participant Observations on the Videotape and the Written Case

Upon obtaining a copy of the videotape, we arranged to have one of the participants (Biddy Bastien) view the videotape and make observations about the performance for us. We instructed Bastien to point out and explain the important organizing and communicative behaviors displayed by all four participants as the performance unfolded. On the basis of his observations, we then drafted a written case of the jazz concert, which we provided with the videotape to the other three participants for their observations. The participant observation data were a valuable source of insight for us. Many understandings of the jazz process discussed herein were either explicitly contained in, or directly stimulated by the participant observations. This data source was especially valuable for our description of the structural conventions in jazz.

Structural Conventions in the Jazz Process

Jazz is a process of musical innovation in which a group of performers collectively invents new musical ideas, adopts some of these ideas, and implements the adopted ideas by incorporating them into their performance and by using them as bases for further musical invention. As a collective approach to the process of innovation, jazz specifies a turbulent (Emery & Trist, 1975) task environment for individual musicians, a complex field for interaction in which individuals are simultaneously required to invent new musical ideas and to adapt their playing to that of the collectivity. Turbulence in this environment not only results from the dynamic process of individual invention; turbulence also arises from the dynamic process of coordinating invention. Moreover, these dynamic processes are not independent of one another: The invention of musical ideas affects and is affected by the adoption and implementation of musical ideas. The inherent turbulence in this jazz process produces uncertainty for performers insofar as each musician cannot fully predict the behavior of the other musicians or, for that matter, the behavior of the collectivity.

How is it possible for musicians to manage these dynamic processes and produce an inventive and integrated musical outcome? The answer lies in two sets of structural conventions contained in the jazz profession: musical structures and social practices. These structures serve to constrain the turbulence of the jazz process by specifying particular ways of inventing and coordinating musical ideas. By imposing particular limitations on the range of potential musical and behavioral choices available to performers, these structural conventions also serve as "information" that reduces individual uncertainty (Rogers, 1983, p. 6). Paradoxically, these structures enable collective musical innovation by constraining the range of musical and behavioral choices available to the players (see Appendix).

Musical Structures

The structural conventions specified by jazz music *theory* consist of the cognitively held rules for generating, selecting, and building upon new musical ideas, including rules for proper chords, chordal relationships, and chordal progressions. Musical innovation in jazz is thus neither entirely random nor entirely determined; new musical ideas are invented, adopted, and implemented through rules for musical grammar, much as our everyday discourse is generated through grammatical conversational rules (see Clark, Escholz, & Rosa, 1981). A second type of musical structure—a *song*—is often employed in group performance. As with music theory, songs can be viewed as cognitively held rules for musical innovation. Songs are more concrete and limiting musical structures than jazz theory in that they embody particular patterns of chords and chordal progressions. However, songs allow for inventive variations on such core musical patterns as (a) time, (b) chords and chordal progressions, (c) phrasing, (d) chorus length, and (e) levels of embellishment (complexity). When a particular song is called in a group jazz performance, musicians who know the song have immediate information concerning these and other musical patterns. This information reduces their uncertainty about the collective task and enables them to focus on producing the coordinating inventive variations on musical themes contained in the song. Group jazz based on chordal theory is a type of group jazz performance that does not rely on songs to facilitate invention and coordination. Most group jazz does rely on the musical structures contained in both music theory and songs. Both of these structures were used in the concert that we examined (our appendix contains a more technical and detailed discussion of musical structures).

Social Practices

Social practices, including both *behavioral norms* and *communicative codes*, are a second source of constraint on the jazz process. These unwritten structural conventions are contained in the profession of jazz and are passed on through various socialization practices. *Behavioral norms* are shared expectations about appropriate behavior (Mitchell, 1978). Behavioral norms facilitate integration among the musicians. Examples of behavioral norms in jazz are the following:

1. The nominal leader of the group decides and communicates each song and the key in which it is to be played.

2. The soloist determines the style (time, level of complexity, etc.), and the other musicians are expected to support this determination.

3. At one point or another during the performance, each musician gets an opportunity to be the soloist (i.e., the dominant voice that is supported by the others).

4. The chorus is the basic unit of soloist control, unless otherwise specified by the nominal leader (see Appendix).

Each of these norms specifies a particular qualification to the collective or consensual character of group jazz. The first norm indicates an authoritarian function of the nominal leader in determining a particular musical/task structure—a song—through which individual musicians produce an inventive and coordinated performance. The second, third, and fourth norms indicate an authoritarian function that is sequentially shared among all performers; every musician gets to play the role of a leader at some point in the jazz process.

A second type of social practice structure, *communicative codes*, consists of behaviors that are intended to be communicative and that rely on the arbitrary assignment of meaning to behavior, with the arbitrary assignment agreed upon by a community of code users. These codes include (a) lexical items, or words and phrases of distinct meaning in the profession, and (b) nonverbal codes that have become a tradition in the profession (e.g., turning to an individual, eye contact at particular points in the performance, hand signals, changing the volume of one's playing). Codes are vehicles through which musicians communicate about their performance while it is occurring. They are designed to enable clear communication among the performers while remaining relatively unobtrusive to the viewing audience.

Taken together, jazz music theory, songs, and social practices impose structural constraints on the process of collective innovation, constraints that enable inventive and integrated group jazz performances. Next we interpret the case study data in terms of these structural conventions and identify basic patterns in the jazz process of organizational innovation.

Basic Patterns of Events in the Group Jazz Performance

Prior to the actual performance, the four musicians had very little time to discuss what would happen. In the discussion that did occur backstage, the following agreements were reached:

1. Freeman (the nominal leader) would call the songs and their keys.

2. The songs called by Freeman would be standards, songs presumably known to most jazz players.

3. Each song would begin with a piano introduction by Hodes, after which Freeman would play the melody and then a few choruses of inventive solo on tenor sax. Next, Hodes would take a chorus or two of inventive solo. Following Hodes, either Freeman would pick up the lead again or Bastien on bass and Smith on drums would alternate on four- or eight-bar "breaks" (i.e., inventive solos in four- or eight-bar lengths).

4. There would be no dragging (i.e., no gradual slowing of tempo).

All four of these agreements reduced the uncertainty of the musicians by providing them with information regarding what to expect and how to behave during the concert. The first agreement cemented a shared understanding that this behavioral norm would be in effect during the performance and reinforced the use of cognitively held information on the level of social practice structures. The information reduced some of the uncertainty for the players, who now knew that Freeman would call the songs and that they should pay attention to him at particular times during the concert. The second agreement also reduced the uncertainty of the musicians by informing them that Freeman would invoke shared musical/task structures—songs known by all four players—on which they would inventively vary, using jazz music theory generative rules. Like the first agreement, the third agreement added to the shared information contained on the level of social practice structures. This agreement reduced at least two sources of uncertainty by providing musicians with information that (a) they would all get a chance to solo during the performance, and (b) they could expect to solo only at particular times during the performance. Like the second agreement, the fourth agreement also added information about musical structures. The musicians now shared an understanding that, regardless of the tempo specified by a particular song, they were not to gradually slow this tempo over the course of the song.

When the players reached their places on stage, Freeman called the first song, "Sunday." This rather simple song has a musical/task structure that specified a relatively limited range of musical choices for the performers. As agreed, the song began with a piano introduction by Hodes. Freeman followed Hodes with a solo on tenor sax. Each musician knew that Freeman would follow Hodes and would play the melody and a few choruses of inventive solo. Toward the end of Freeman's solo, we observed two forms of communicative behavior by Freeman, behavior that signaled to the rest of the musicians that he was relinquishing the lead to Hodes. One such behavior was the music theoretical cue of "winding down" the solo; Freeman signaled the end of his solo by directing his musical invention toward the full resolution of the current chord (see Appendix).

The other communicative behavior was a nonverbal visual cue that Freeman directed at Hodes; shortly (a beat or two) before the end of his solo, Freeman looked at Hodes in order to signal the end of his solo. Both behaviors accessed shared, cognitively held information on the social practice level by signaling that Freeman was indeed giving up the lead according to group expectations. Toward the end of Hodes's solo, Freeman became more active physically, and this activity appeared to focus the attention of the entire group on the change that was forthcoming. At the end of Hodes's solo, Freeman directed a nonverbal communicative behavior—a questioning look—to Bastien and Smith. This behavior accessed information on the social practice level and, congruent with the preconcert agreement, provided Bastien and Smith with an opportunity to take the lead. Both Bastien and Smith responded to Freeman by nodding in the affirmative. The end of the song was verbally cued by Freeman's use of the code "going out."

Following a long bit of banter with the audience, Freeman called the second song, "You Took Advantage of Me." This song had more potential for inventive variation than did "Sunday." As in the first song, the musicians paid a great deal of attention to the soloist. During his solo, Hodes introduced a bass line that was unexpected by Bastien, but because of the heightened attention among group members to the soloist, Bastien readily picked up the change and followed it. Freeman continued to use visual cues to underscore changes in the soloist, looking at the coming soloist and nodding at him. Freeman also used verbal cues to heighten attention at change points and to cue particular behavior patterns. For example, Freeman looked at Smith and called a chorus of "fours." At the end of Smith's chorus, Freeman said "again," indicating to Smith and the rest of the group that Smith would play a second chorus.

The third song, "Misty," allowed for a great deal of inventive variation, particularly in the use of embellished, complex chordal progressions. Despite this opportunity to extend the group's musical inventiveness radically in the direction of greater complexity, Freeman and Hodes chose to stick with simple variations during their solos. This behavior cemented an understanding among the performers on the level of musical structure, an understanding that, from a music theory standpoint, the group would constrain their musical invention to relatively unembellished, simple ideas, regardless of the level of potential embellishment in a particular song.

The first set was finished by a fourth and fifth song, a Hodes solo piece and an early thirties standard. During the fourth song, Hodes used a hand sign—two fingers—to signal a change from 4/4 to 2/4 time. Hodes had used 2/4 time in a previous solo, and his use of the hand sign reinforced an understanding among the other musicians that he preferred to play in this meter during his solos, despite a preference among the others for 4/4 time during their solos. The fifth song was characterized by patterns established in the earlier songs, including unembellished musical invention and Freeman's use of verbal codes to signal his approval of their playing.

The second set began in a less uncertain and turbulent social task environment than did the first set, because musicians could rely on their knowledge of the precedents and preferences worked out in the first set. Because everything was relatively new and unpredictable during the first set, constant visual attention was required of the musicians. During the second set, there was a marked shift from the constant visual attention of the first set to a more selective attention. In the second set, attention was high around the points of potential change by the soloist, but dropped off noticeably between these points. Because they could rely on a greater pool of shared information, musicians could better predict upcoming changes in soloists as well as the preferred patterns of musical invention for each soloist. Due to this phenomenon, Freeman was able to extend his solo by an additional chorus on one song in the second set. He recognized that the attention of the others was focused on him in anticipation of a potential change while they waited for his signals. When Freeman did not cue a change, the others simply followed him into a third chorus of his solo.

The third and final set began in an even less uncertain and turbulent social task environment for the performers. Having two sets of shared performance history to rely on, the group became increasingly adventurous in their invention from the standpoint of musical theory. For the final part of the concert, the group dropped its use of song structures and relied solely on music theory and shared performance history to invent an entirely new song, "Twin Cities Blues."

In terms of cognition and behavior, we found at least two basic patterns of events in this case study of collective musical innovation:

1. During the first set, musicians displayed a great deal of attention to each other, with particular emphasis on the soloist and the nominal leader (Freeman), who actively solicited the attention of the musicians during points of potential change in soloists. Freeman's communicative behavior at these points helped to coordinate the group during actual changes by managing attention (Van de Ven, 1986) and by invoking cognitively held norms for behavior. As the concert progressed, this cycle of cognition and behavior became ingrained as shared information among the group members. Attention clearly became more selective among the musicians, for now they could better predict when and to whom they should pay attention. In the latter part of the concert, heightened attention occurred only around points of potential change in the soloist. Freeman found that he no longer had to work at soliciting attention during these points of change and could instead focus on communicating his preferences to the

group. Throughout the performance, points of potential change were specified as shared information on two cognitive levels—musical and social practice structures—and were invoked through nonverbal and verbal behavior. As the jazz performance proceeded and a shared social task history was established, information was added on these cognitive levels. This information reduced the uncertainty and turbulence of the jazz process and allowed the musicians to become more selective in their attention.

2. The performance began with Freeman calling songs of limited potential for musical complexity/embellishment and with players inventing simple/unembellished musical ideas. As the concert progressed, Freeman called songs with greater potential for musical complexity, and the jazz players, building on the musical ideas invented during earlier songs, invented more complex musical ideas. Importantly, however, the group did not radically increase the complexity of the ideas it invented from song to song, despite the fact that such increases were allowed by the song structures. Instead, the group established a shared understanding that musical invention would be constrained to simple variations on core musical patterns contained in each song structure (that is, simple relative to the complexity allowed by this structure). By using this strategy for musical invention, the group relied on its history of collectively invented musical ideas to explore a new song and creatively extend its repertoire of invented idea in the direction of greater complexity. Indeed, the concert culminated in a social task with a great deal of potential for musical complexity: the invention of an entirely new song.

Tracking Cognition and Behavior in the Group Jazz Performance

Poole (1983) developed a multiple sequence model to relate different aspects of social task processes. This model suggests portraying group processes as a set of parallel strands or tracks of activity as they emerge over time. Each track represents a different aspect of the process and concerns a different level of data. One of the strengths of this approach is that it allows the analysis of relationships within and across levels. We adapted Poole's approach to our present purposes by designating three tracks to represent the cognitive and behavioral components of change events in the jazz concert: (a) *musical structure*, including cognitively held structural conventions as specified by music theory and by songs, (b) *social structure*, involving cognitively held norms for behavior and communicative codes, and (c) *communicative behavior*, consisting of nonverbal and verbal signs.

In his multiple sequence model, Poole (1983) introduced the concept of breakpoints—points in time when changes occur across all tracks—and found that the direction and basic nature of group activity changed at these points. The breakpoint concept is important to the present study, in that it provides means of analyzing changes in group activity in terms of their cognitive and behavioral components. Figure 1 portrays the multiple sequence tracking for the first three songs of the jazz concert. As shown by the musical structure track, from a music theory standpoint changes in group activity (e.g., changes in soloists) could occur at almost any point during the song on a note-by-note basis, but would most likely occur at the beginnings of bars and phrases.

The level of social structure is shown in the second track that portrays the change event potentials specified by behavioral norms and by the preconcert agreements. Information at this level is more specific as to when the musicians can expect changes to occur; according to the norms of the profession, changes will occur at the ends of choruses. Moreover, the preconcert agreements provided the four musicians with an even greater level of detailed information by specifying who would solo at what point in time and for how many choruses. The social structure imposes even greater constraints on individual and group behavior than does the musical structure.

The level of communicative behavior, shown in the third track, indicates that actual changes in the group task were invoked less frequently than allowed by the change event potentials contained in the musical and social structure. What the three tracks reveal is a basic pattern of increasing constraints on individual and group behavior. As we descend from the level of musical structure to the level of social structure to the level of actual communicative behavior, each level further limits the

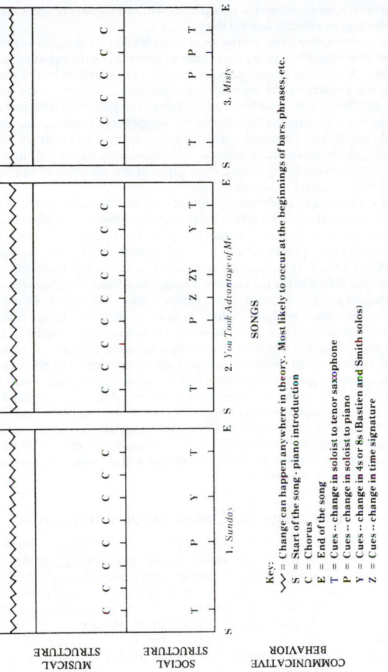

Figure 1 Multiple sequence tracking of musical structure, social structure, and communicative behavior for the first three songs in the concert.

range of behavioral choices available to the jazz performers and thereby enables coordinated musical invention by reducing uncertainty among the players.

Perhaps more important, however, are the revelations (a) that all changes in group activity that occurred during the song were invoked by some form of communicative behavior and (b) that these changes occurred only at the times of change potential that were specified by the musical and social structures. The multiple sequence tracking of a song shows that the potential for change must exist on the levels of musical and social structure before change can be considered and acted on by the players. Moreover, in order for an actual breakpoint or change event to occur, change potentials contained in the shared knowledge of musical and social structure must be explicitly invoked by coded communication among the individual performers. This redundancy across cognitive and behavioral components of the change event is important, for it captures the attention of individual musicians and enables them to enact changes in unison.

Over the course of the concert, preferred patterns of change became ingrained as shared information on both musical and social structure levels. Relying on this information, the musicians could better predict when and to whom they should pay attention. For example, at one point of potential change during the third song, Hodes looked at the drummer and bassist and communicated a change in time from 4/4 to 2/4. These players were able to pick up and enact this change because, based on the pattern established in the previous two songs, they knew that they should pay attention to Hodes at this particular point in the song. When Hodes again switched to 2/4 time in a subsequent solo, this pattern was reinforced as shared information on musical and social structure levels, enabling the other musicians to better predict what was going to happen during Hodes's solos.

One important implication flowing from the multiple sequence tracking concerns a relationship between individual knowledge of music theory and social practices and the overall knowledge level of the group. Because the group jazz process relies on *shared* musical and social knowledge, the total knowledge that is usable by the entire group can only equal or slightly exceed the knowledge of the least informed (i.e., the least competent) member of the group. In the concert of study, all four musicians were highly competent in music theory and social practices and shared a knowledge of standard jazz songs. We predict that groups that include musicians of very different knowledge bases will either produce jazz that is not well integrated or will perform at a level roughly equivalent to that of the least competent member.

Centering as a Basic Strategy for Organizational Innovation

The second pattern we identify in the case study is a particular strategy for achieving even greater constraint on musical invention (and hence easier coordination) through choice of repertoire or songs. Freeman began the concert by calling a relatively simple song that contained a limited potential for musical variation. By choosing such a song at the outset, Freeman specified a relatively placid environment for musical invention, a territory in which the musicians tested simple variations on simple core musical patterns in a relatively predictable and certain social task setting. These variations were either rejected or adopted. If adopted, they were implemented through repetition and were used as bases for further variation. One way of conceiving this collective process of inventing, adopting, and implementing musical ideas is as a "centering strategy." As represented in Figure 2a, the jazz musicians began with a center that consisted of shared information regarding jazz music theory, song structures, behavioral norms, and communicative codes. This center of shared information specified potential paths of musical invention for the musicians, who then selectively invented ideas along some of these paths. The group, in turn, then selectively adopted some of these ideas/paths and implemented them into organizational practice as shared bases for further musical invention. As represented in Figure 2b, the center of shared knowledge was extended outward by incorporating all of the ideas/paths implemented in the previous songs and the group became capable of inventing and coordinating more complex musical variations.

This phenomenon allowed Freeman confidently to lead the group in the direction of greater inventive complexity as the jazz concert progressed. With each successive song, the group relied on its

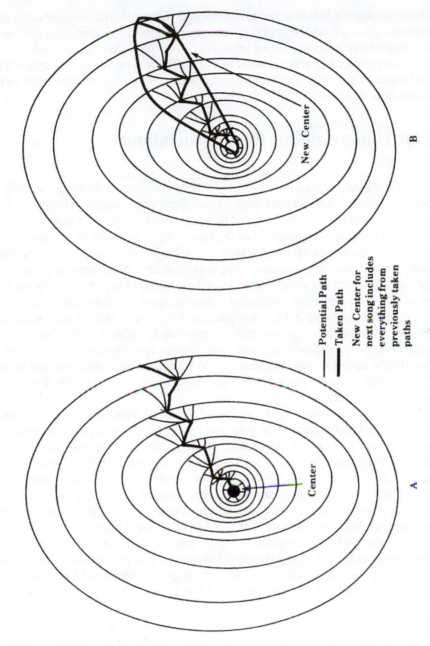

Figure 2 The centering strategy for organizational innovation.

Potential Path
Taken Path

New Center for next song includes everything from previously taken paths

Center

New Center

A

B

ever-increasing center of shared information to invent and integrate increasingly complex musical ideas. Indeed, this strategy allowed the group to extend its center of shared information to the extent that it could successfully accomplish an immensely complex task: Unguided by an existing song structure, the group invented and coordinated an entirely new song. The centering strategy can be a successful method for incrementally moving a group or organization into new and unknown social task environments.

Implications for Understanding the Organizational Innovation Process

As in group jazz, the social task environment for many modern organizations is basically turbulent and only marginally predictable; situations such as mergers, acquisitions, divestitures, joint ventures, entries into new markets, and development of new industries entail considerable turbulence and uncertainty for organization members (Van de Ven, Angle, & Poole, in press). Individuals in these organizational circumstances face uncertainty similar to that experienced by jazz players during a collectively improvised performance. We saw that jazz musicians rely on two types of structural conventions to constrain their behavior, reduce uncertainty, and diminish turbulence. The level of musical structure specifies particular limitations on the musical choices available to the players. Similarly, task structures in business (such as formally specified and coded constraints like legislation, industry regulation, governmental mandates, technical theories, organizational mission statements, strategic plans, policies, and procedures) specify particular limitations on behavioral choices available to organization members. In both jazz and business, the social level of structural constraint on behavior involves relatively informal norms and codes that concern interpersonal relations and communication.

In the present case study information on the level of social structure mediates between task structure and behavior. Social structure is, in jazz and business, essential for innovation in organizations. This level informs the players of potential changes in the nature of the innovation activity and the probability that changes will occur. Moreover, we found that social task processes in general are critically reliant on shared knowledge. This evidence implies that social tasks involving individuals of different knowledge bases will be problematic. Lastly, we identified a successful strategy for moving an organization into new, unknown territory. This case study shows that a centering strategy can be effective in accomplishing this goal, for it allows organization members to accommodate a new and unknown social task environment gradually and transform it into an old, known environment. Indeed, Bastien (in press) observed this phenomenon in a corporate acquisition, where centering was effectively used as a strategy for managing the disjunctive change felt by the organization. Kanter (1985) also discussed the strategy of centering as a technique for managing change.

Consistent with these findings, we anticipate that communication and management researchers will be able (a) to isolate certain of the operative task and social structures in cases of organizational innovation, (b) to track these structures and communicative behavior across time, (c) to identify breakpoints in the process of innovation, and (d) to generate additional data concerning the shared knowledge hypothesis and centering strategy. We believe that this line of research holds promise for increasing our knowledge of organizational innovation, knowledge that can be used to critique instances of socially improvised task activity, instruct individual players in task and social structures, and to train players in necessary attention and communication skills.

The history of jazz has been recorded in such a way that we primarily remember great individual musicians and we think of their contributions as solely owned. A more complete review of the history of jazz would reveal that the great contributions to the art form (and indeed the great individuals) were realized in a social and professional context. Lester Young's contribution, for example, would not have been realized outside of a contest in which he *and* his supporting players were all thoroughly competent in the structural knowledge and processual skills of the jazz profession. An overemphasis on individual expression and creativity occurred during the past 25 years or so in the jazz profession, an emphasis that leads us to forget the extent to which jazz is inherently and fundamentally a collective activity. The present study emphasizes a more balanced approach to understanding and managing organizational innovation, one in which individual invention is embedded in a collective context and is inseparable from the inventive and integrative activity of the entire group. Great jazz and great advances in the art have not been achieved by stars against a placid background. Rather, greatness in jazz resulted from a constellation of cooperatively improvising artists, each of whom has a chance to shine as a star.

Appendix

A Technical Overview of Musical Structures in Jazz

Jazz is a variant of Western music theory that is concerned with various arithmetic relationships and sequences. Jazz theory enables the production of inventive and coordinated musical outcomes through the spontaneous and creative use of generative rules that specify particular ways of inventing and coordinating musical ideas. Although this approach to music theory is unique in Western music, there are similar approaches to music theory in Eastern music (notably, the raga music of India). The technical overview that follows is an extremely simplified representation of musical structures in jazz, intended as an introductory illustration of these structures.

In the jazz theory of music generation, an octave is divided into 12 evenly spaced intervals, each of which is given a letter name: C, D flat, D, E flat, E, F, G flat, G, A flat, A, B flat, and B. This array of 12 notes is called a *chromatic scale*. Major and minor scales, however, are the compositional basis of most jazz. These are specific sequences of an uneven division of the octave into 8 intervals. For instance, a C Major scale contains only the following intervals: C D E F G A B C. In other words, in a major scale, the second, fourth, seventh, and eleventh intervals are skipped. In minor scales, a different pattern of skipping chromatic tones is used to achieve the scale. Jazz has traditionally relied on four scales, although others are sometimes employed: major scales, minor scales, dominant seventh scales, and minor seventh scales. All four employ the same logic of selecting 8 unequal intervals from a 12-tone chromatic scale, but the sequences are different in each of the scales.

A chord is a specific sequence of tones within a major or minor scale, further eliminating some notes. For instance, a C Major chord (called a *triad*, in this case) includes only the first, third, and fifth interval in a C Major scale (C E G). Chords in each of the scale families can be embellished through the addition of further tones from the scale. For example, a C6 chord is the major triad (C E G) plus the sixth interval of the C Major scale (A).

Either embellishments resolve to a specific following chord, or they do not resolve at all (i.e., they are terminal, signaling the end of a phrase). This characteristic of chordal embellishment allows musicians to take many different theoretical paths within the same basic chord.

In jazz theory, a song is principally a sequence or progression of chords. Often these are repeating short sequences, with AABA sequences being the most common. Here a sequence of chords is established (the A sequence), played through a second time (AA), followed by a different sequence of equal length (AAB), and finally repeated (AABA). The AABA sequence is called a *chorus*. In general, songs prescribe only basic chord families and not specific embellishments, leaving embellishment choices up to the musicians.

The melody of a song is composed of notes contained within the chords of the progression, as are all of the notes played by the musicians who provide the background that supports the melody. For example, if a saxophonist is playing the melody and is backed up by a bassist, pianist, and drummer, all four will be playing notes that are different and yet congruent with the chordal structure of the song. The relationship between melody and accompaniment is complicated by the concept of embellishment, however, and when one musician plays notes from a specific embellished chord, the others must pick up that embellishment if the performance is to sound good or integrated. Finally, the dominant or lead voice is called the soloist, despite the fact that often the other musicians are still playing and providing background support to the soloist.

Authors' Note: We gratefully acknowledge the assistance of Bob DeFlores, Maytime Productions (Dr. Sheldon Pinsky and Arlene Fried), and K-TWIN in securing access to the videotaped data for the present study. Maytime Productions is a nonprofit corporation created to promote and preserve the enjoyment and understanding of jazz as a living American art form. We are especially indebted to the four musicians—Bud Freeman, Art Hodes, Biddy Bastien, and Hal Smith—for their performance and for their willingness to be studied. Without the generous contributions of all of these individuals, the present study could not have been carried out. We acknowledge the assistance and encouragement of Dr. Reginald T. Buckner, who organized the conference at which an earlier version of this article was presented. We also extend our appreciation to Dr. Mary L. Nichols for including an earlier version of this article in the discussion paper series of the Strategic Management Research Center (University of Minnesota). This article benefited from the helpful comments and suggestions of Everett M. Rogers, Andrew H. Van de Ven, and an anonymous reviewer.

References

Bastien, D. T. (in press). Communication, conflict, and learning in mergers and acquisitions. In A. H. Van de Ven, H. L. Angle, & M. S. Poole (Eds.), *Research on the management of innovation* (Vol. 1, chap. 11). Cambridge, MA: Ballinger.

Bormann, E. G. (1975). *Discussion and group methods* (2nd ed.). New York: Harper & Row.

Bougon, M., Weick, K., & Binkhorst, D. (1977). Cognition in organizations: An analysis of the Utrecht Jazz Orchestra. *Administrative Science Quarterly, 22,* 606–639.

Clark, V. P., Escholz, P. A., & Rosa, A. F. (1981). *Language: Introductory readings* (3rd ed.). New York: St. Martin's.

Emery, F. E., & Trist, E. L. (1975). *Towards a social ecology: Contextual appreciations of the future in the present.* London: Plenum.

Kanter, R. M. (1985). *The change masters: Innovations for productivity in the American work place.* New York: Simon & Schuster.

Mitchell, T. R. (1978). *People in organizations: Understanding their behavior.* New York: McGraw-Hill.

Poole, M. S. (1983). Decision development in small groups: III. A multiple sequence model of group decision development. *Communication Monographs, 50,* 321–341.

Rogers, E. M. (1983). *Diffusion of innovations* (3rd ed.). New York: Free Press.

Van de Ven, A. H. (1986). Central problems in the management of innovation. *Management Science, 32,* 590–607.

Van de Ven, A. H., Angle, H. L., & Poole, M. S. (Eds.). (in press). *Research on the management of innovation* (Vols. 1 & 2). Cambridge, MA: Ballinger.

Voyer, J. J., & Faulkner, R. R. (1986a). Cognition and leadership in an artistic organization. *Proceedings of the National Academy of Management* (pp. 160–164). Chicago: Darby Press.

Voyer, J. J., & Faulkner, R. R. (1986b). *Strategy and organizational cognition in a simple professional bureaucracy.* Unpublished manuscript, Rutgers University, Newark, NJ.

PART VI

PRINCIPLES FOR STRATEGIC MANAGEMENT

THREE MODELS OF STRATEGY[1]

ELLEN EARLE CHAFFEE
NATIONAL CENTER FOR HIGHER EDUCATION MANAGEMENT SYSTEMS

Three models of strategy that are implicit in the literature are described—linear, adaptive, and interpretive. Their similarity to Boulding's (1956) hierarchical levels of system complexity is noted. The strategy construct is multifaceted, and it has evolved to a level of complexity almost matching that of organizations themselves.

Researchers and practitioners have used the term strategy freely—researchers have even measured it—for over two decades. Those who refer to strategy generally believe that they are all working with the same mental model. No controversy surrounds the question of its existence; no debate has arisen regarding the nature of its anchoring concept.

Yet virtually everyone writing on strategy agrees that no consensus on its definition exists (Bourgeois, 1980; Gluck, Kaufman, & Walleck, 1982; Glueck, 1980; Hatten, 1979; Hofer & Schendel, 1978; Lenz, 1980b; Rumelt, 1979; Spender, 1979; Steiner, 1979). Hambrick (1983) suggested that this lack of consistency is due to two factors. First, he pointed out, strategy is multidimensional. Second, strategy must be situational and, accordingly, it will vary by industry.

The literature affirms Hambrick's assessment that strategy is not only multidimensional and situational but that such characteristics are likely to make any consensus on definition difficult. Strategy also suffers from another, more fundamental problem; that is, the term strategy has been referring to three distinguishable mental models, rather than the single model that most discussions assume. Beyond reflecting various authors' semantic preferences, the multiple definitions reflect three distinct, and in some ways conflicting, views on strategy. This paper seeks to analyze the ways strategy has been defined and operationalized in previous treatises and studies. It highlights those aspects of strategy on which authors in the field appear to agree and suggests three strategy models that are implicit in the literature.

Strategy: Areas of Agreement

A basic premise of thinking about strategy concerns the inseparability of organization and environment (Biggadike, 1981; Lenz, 1980a). The organization uses strategy to deal with changing environments. Because change brings novel combinations of circumstances to the organization, the substance of strategy remains unstructured, unprogrammed, nonroutine, and nonrepetitive (Mason & Mitroff, 1981; Mazzolini, 1981; Miles & Cameron, 1982; Narayanan & Fahey, 1982; Van Cauwenbergh & Cool, 1982). Not only are strategic decisions related to the environment and nonroutine, but they also are considered to be important enough to affect the overall welfare of the organization (Hambrick, 1980).

Theorists who segment the strategy construct implicitly agree that the study of strategy includes both the actions taken, or the content of strategy, and the processes by which actions are decided and implemented. They agree that intended, emergent, and realized strategies may differ from one another. Moreover, they agree that firms may have both corporate strategy ("What businesses shall we be in?") and business strategy ("How shall we compete in each business?"). Finally, they concur that the making of strategy involves conceptual as well as analytical exercises. Some authors stress the analytical dimension more than others, but most affirm that the heart of strategy making is the conceptual work done by leaders of the organization.

Beyond these general factors, agreement breaks down. Yet the differences in point of view are rarely analyzed. Only the existence of multiple definitions of strategy is noted and, as in Mintzberg (1973), definitions are sometimes grouped by type. Analysis reveals that the strategy definitions in the literature cluster into three distinct groups.

Three Models of Strategy

The name assigned to each model of strategy represents its primary focus. Although these descriptions represent a collective version of similar views, each model also includes many variations of its central theme. Moreover, as will be shown later, the three models are not independent. However, for present purposes, the three models will be treated according to their independent descriptions in the literature.

Model I: Linear Strategy

The first model to be widely adopted is linear and focuses on planning. The term linear was chosen because it connotes the methodical, directed, sequential action involved in planning. This model is inherent in Chandler's definition of strategy.

> Strategy is the determination of the basic long-term goals of an enterprise, and the adoption of courses of action and the allocation of resources necessary for carrying out these goals (1962, p. 13).

According to the linear view, strategy consists of integrated decisions, actions, or plans that will set and achieve viable organizational goals. Both goals and the means of achieving them are results of strategic decision. To reach these goals, organizations vary their links with the environment by changing their products or markets or by performing other entrepreneurial actions. Terms associated with the linear model include strategic planning, strategy formulation, and strategy implementation.

The linear model portrays top managers as having considerable capacity to change the organization. The environment is, implicitly, a necessary nuisance "out there" that is composed mainly of competitors. Top managers go through a prototypical rational decision making process. They identify their goals, generate alternative methods of achieving them, weigh the likelihood that alternative methods will succeed, and then decide which ones to implement. In the course of this process, managers capitalize on those future trends and events that are favorable and avoid or counteract those that are not. Because this model was developed primarily for profit-seeking businesses, two of its important measures of results are profit and productivity.

Several assumptions that underlie the linear model are not made explicit in most discussions, but they nonetheless follow from the authors' tendency to emphasize planning and forecasting. For example:

> Conceptually, the process [of strategic planning] is simple: managers at every level of a hierarchy must ultimately agree on a detailed, integrated plan of action for the coming year; they [start] with the delineation of corporate objectives and [conclude] with the preparation of a one- or two-year profit plan (Lorange & Vancil, 1976, p. 75).

If a sequential planning process is to succeed, the organization needs to be tightly coupled, so that all decisions made at the top can be implemented throughout the organization. This tight coupling assumption enables intentions to become actions. A second assumption arises from the time-consuming and forward-looking nature of planning. In other words, though decisions made today are based on beliefs about future conditions, they may not be implemented until months, even years, from now. In order to believe that making such decisions is not a waste of time, one

TABLE 1

Summary of Linear Strategy

Variable	Linear Strategy
Sample definition	". . . determination of the basic long-term goals of an enterprise, and the adoption of courses of action and the allocation of resources necessary for carrying out these goals" (Chandler, 1962, p. 13, italics added).
Nature of strategy	Decisions, actions, plans Integrated
Focus for strategy	Means, ends
Aim of strategy	Goal achievement
Strategic behaviors	Change markets, products
Associated terms	Strategic planning, strategy formulation and implementation
Associated measures	Formal planning, new products, configuration of products or businesses, market segmentation and focus, market share, merger/acquisition, product diversity
Associated authors[a]	Chandler, 1962
	Cannon, 1968
	Learned, Christensen, Andrews, & Guth, 1969
	Gilmore, 1970
	Andrews, 1971
	Child, 1972
	Drucker, 1974
	Paine & Naumes, 1974
	Glueck, 1976
	Lorange & Vancil, 1976
	Steiner & Miner, 1977

[a]Classified by their *definitions* of strategy. Classification is not intended to imply that authors omit discussion of topics relevant to other models.

must assume either that the environment is relatively predictable or else that the organization is well-insulated from the environment. Also, most authors explicitly assume that organizations have goals and that accomplishing goals is the most important outcome of strategy.

Major characteristics of the linear model and the names of several authors whose definitions of strategy are consistent with this model are listed in Table 1. Note that though the authors' definitions of strategy constitute grounds for classifying them in the model, nearly all authors extend their discussions of strategy into areas that are relevant to more than one model.

As the dates in these citations suggest, interest in the linear model waned in the mid-1970s. Ansoff and Hayes (1976) suggested that the emphasis moved away from the linear model as the strategic problem came to be seen as much more complex. Not only does it involve several dimensions of the managerial problem and the process, but also technical, economic, informational, psychological, and political variables as well. The model that arose next is labeled here the adaptive model of strategy.

Model II: Adaptive Strategy

Hofer's definition typifies the adaptive model of strategy, characterizing it as

> concerned with the development of a viable match between the opportunities and risks present in the external environment and the organization's capabilities and resources for exploiting these opportunities (1973, p. 3).

The organization is expected continually to assess external and internal conditions. Assessment then leads to adjustments in the organization or in its relevant environment that will create "satisfactory alignments of environmental opportunities and risks, on the one hand, and organizational capabilities and resources, on the other" (Miles & Cameron, 1982, p. 14).

The adaptive model differs from the linear model in several ways. First, monitoring the environment and making changes are simultaneous and continuous functions in the adaptive model. The time lag for planning that is implicit in the linear model is not present. For example, Miles and Snow (1978) portray strategic adaptation as recurring and overlapping cycles with three phases: the entrepreneurial phase (choice of domain), the engineering phase (choice of technology), and the administrative phase (rationalizing structure and process, and identifying areas for future innovation).

Second, the adaptive model does not deal as emphatically as the linear model with decisions about goals. Instead, it tends to focus the manager's attention on means, and the "goal" is represented by coalignment of the organization with its environment. Third, the adaptive model's definition of strategic behaviors goes beyond that of the linear model to incorporate not only major changes in products and markets, but also subtle changes in style, marketing, quality, and other nuances (Hofer, 1976a; Shirley, 1982).

A fourth difference follows from the relative unimportance of advance planning in the adaptive model. Thus, as might be expected, strategy is less centralized in top management, more multifaceted, and generally less integrated than in the linear model. However, top managers in the adaptive model still assume overall responsibility for guiding strategy development.

Finally, in the adaptive model the environment is considered to be a complex organizational life support system, consisting of trends, events, competitors, and stakeholders. The boundary between the organization and its environment is highly permeable, and the environment is a major focus of attention in determining organizational action. Whether taken proactively or reactively, action is responsive to the nature and magnitude of perceived or anticipated environmental pressures.

In sum, the adaptive model relies heavily on an evolutionary biological model of organizations. The analogy is made explicit in the following passage:

> As a descriptive tool, strategy is the analog of the biologist's method of "explaining" the structure and the behavior of organisms by pointing out the functionality of each attribute in a total system (or strategy) designed to cope with or inhabit a particular niche. The normative use of strategy has no counterpart in biology (as yet!), but might be thought of as the problem of designing a living creature . . . to exist within some environment . . . (Rumelt, 1979, pp. 197–198).

As interest in strategy as adaptation increased so, too, did attention to the processes by which strategy arises and is carried out. Beginning with Mintzberg's (1973) modes of strategy making, a number of discussions have been presented to deal with the social, political, and interactive components of strategy (Fahey, 1981; Ginter & White, 1982; Greenwood & Thomas, 1981; Guth, 1976; Hofer, 1976b; E. Murray, 1978; J. Murray, 1978–79; Narayanan & Fahey, 1982; Tabatoni & Jarniou, 1976). Each of the authors dealt with organizational processes in the adaptive strategy model.

Adaptive strategy rests on several assumptions. The organization and its environment are assumed to be more open to each other than is implied in the linear model. The environment is more dynamic and less susceptible to prediction in the adaptive model. It consists of competitors, trends, and—of increasing importance—stake-holders. Rather than assuming that the organization must *deal with* the environment, the adaptive model assumes that the organization must *change with* the environment.

The adaptive model attempts to take more variables and more propensity for change into account than does the linear model. Table 2 lists terms that reflect this complexity, along with those authors whose strategy definitions fit the adaptive model. It also outlines the characteristics of the model. A number of authors using the adaptive model suggest that it can successfully handle greater complexity and more variables than the linear model. However, opinion is mounting that the situation is complex in other ways. To meet this need, a third model of strategy is emerging.

TABLE 2

Summary of Adaptive Strategy

Variable	Adaptive Strategy
Sample definition	". . . concerned with the development of a viable match between the opportunities and risks present in the external environment and the organization's capabilities and resources for exploiting those opportunities" (Hofer, 1973, p. 3).
Nature of strategy	Achieving a "match" Multifaceted
Focus for strategy	Means
Aim of strategy	Coalignment with the environment
Strategic behaviors	Change style, marketing, quality
Associated terms	Strategic management, strategic choice, strategic predisposition, strategic design, strategic fit, strategic thrust, niche
Associated measures	Price, distribution policy, marketing expenditure and intensity, product differentiation, authority changes, proactiveness, risk taking, multiplexity, integration, futurity, adaptiveness, uniqueness
Associated authors[a]	Hofer, 1973
	Guth, 1976
	Hofer & Schendel, 1978
	Litschert & Bonham, 1978
	Miles, Snow, Meyer, & Coleman, 1978
	Miller & Friesen, 1978
	Mintzberg, 1978
	Dill, 1979
	Steiner, 1979
	Rumelt, 1979
	Hambrick, 1980
	Bourgeois, 1980
	Snow & Hambrick, 1980
	Quinn, 1980
	Jemison, 1981
	Kotler & Murphy, 1981
	Green & Jones, 1981
	Hayman, 1981
	Jauch & Osborn, 1981
	Gluck et al., 1982
	Chakravarthy, 1982
	Hatten, 1982
	Shirley, 1982
	Camillus, 1982
	Miles & Cameron, 1982
	Galbraith & Schendel, 1983

[a]Classified by their *definitions* of strategy. Classification is not intended to imply that authors omit discussion of topics relevant to other models.

Model III: Interpretive Strategy

Development of interpretive strategy parallels recent interest in corporate culture and symbolic management outside the strategy literature (Dandridge, Mitroff, & Joyce, 1980; Deal & Kennedy, 1982; Feldman & March, 1981; Meyer & Rowan, 1977; Peters, 1978 Peters & Waterman, 1982; Pfeffer, 1981; Smircich & Morgan, 1982; Weick & Daft, 1983). The parameters of the emerging interpretive model of strategy are still unclear. However, a recurring theme suggests that the model is based on a social contract, rather than an organismic or biological view of the organization (Keeley, 1980) that fits well with the adaptive model. The social contract view portrays the organization as a collection of cooperative agreements entered into by individuals with free will. The organization's existence relies on its ability to attract enough individuals to cooperate in mutually beneficial exchange.

The interpretive model of strategy further assumes that reality is socially constructed (Berger & Luckmann, 1966). That is, reality is not something objective or external to the perceiver that can be apprehended correctly or incorrectly. Rather, reality is defined through a process of social interchange in which perceptions are affirmed, modified, or replaced according to their apparent congruence with the perceptions of others.

Strategy in the interpretive model might be defined as orienting metaphors or frames of reference that allow the organization and its environment to be understood by organizational stakeholders. On this basis, stakeholders are motivated to believe and to act in ways that are expected to produce favorable results for the organization. "Metaphors" is plural in this definition because the maintenance of social ties in the organization precludes enforcing agreement on a single interpretation (Weick & Daft, 1983).

Pettigrew (1977) provided an early example of the interpretive model by defining strategy as the emerging product of the partial resolution of environmental and intraorganizational dilemmas. Although his emphasis on the political and processual nature of strategy might be considered compatible with the adaptive model, he offered several innovative contributions. Among them are: (1) his interest in the management of meaning and symbol construction as central components of strategy and (2) his emphasis on legitimacy, rather than profit, productivity, or other typical goals of strategy.

Van Cauwenbergh and Cool (1982) defined strategy broadly as calculated behavior in nonprogrammed situations. They went on to posit middle management's central position in the strategy formulation process, as well as to point out that managing the organizational culture is a powerful tool in the hands of top management. The authors concluded by suggesting that their views differed from the traditional strategy literature in three ways: (1) organizational reality is incoherent in nature, not coherent; (2) strategy is an organization-wide activity, not just a top management concern; and (3) motivation, not information, is the critical factor in achieving adequate strategic behavior. Congruent with these authors' interest in organizational culture, Dirsmith and Covaleski dealt with what they called strategic norms, or

> institutional level action postures . . . that serve to guide acceptable behavior. [S]trategic norms involve the establishment of maps of reality or images held of organizations and environments (1983, p. 137).

The new themes in these writings suggest a strategy model that depends heavily on symbols and norms. Hatten (1979) saw this change as moving from the goal orientation of the linear model to a focus on desired relationships, such as those involving sources of inputs or customers. He envisaged a new theory of strategy that was oriented toward managerial perceptions, conflict and consensus, as well as the importance of language. The relatively few entries in Table 3 indicate that the model is too new to have become well-developed.

Rather than emphasizing *changing with* the environment, as is true of the adaptive model, interpretive strategy mimics linear strategy in its emphasis on *dealing with* the environment. There is, however, an important difference. The linear strategist deals with the environment by means of organizational actions that are intended to affect relations instrumentally, but the interpretive strategist deals with the environment through symbolic actions and communication.

Interpretive strategy, like adaptive strategy, assumes that the organization and its environment constitute an open system. But in interpretive strategy the organization's leaders shape the attitudes of participants and potential participants toward the organization and its outputs; they do not make physical changes in the outputs. This attitude change seeks to increase credibility for the organization or its output. In this regard, interpretive strategy overlaps with the adaptive model. For example, when an adaptive strategist focuses on marketing to enhance product credibility, the strategist's behavior could be classified as interpretive. Because strategy is multifaceted, however, examining

TABLE 3

Summary of Interpretive Strategy

Variable	Interpretive Strategy
Sample definition	Orienting metaphors constructed for the purpose of conceptualizing and guiding individual attitudes of organizational participants
Nature of strategy	Metaphor Interpretive
Focus for strategy	Participants and potential participants in the organization
Aim of strategy	Legitimacy
Strategic behaviors	Develop symbols, improve interactions and relationships
Associated terms	Strategic norms
Associated measures	Measures must be derived from context, may require qualitative assessment
Associated authors[a]	Pettigrew, 1977 Van Cauwenbergh & Cool, 1982 Dirsmith & Covaleski, 1983 Chaffee, 1984

[a]Classified by their *definitions* of strategy. Classification is not intended to imply that authors omit discussion of topics relevant to other models.

marketing in combination with other strategic moves permits surer classification into either the adaptive or interpretive model.

A final noteworthy distinction between the adaptive and interpretive models relates to the ways in which each conceptualizes complexity. Adaptive strategy arose from and attempts to deal with structural complexity, notably conflicting and changing demands for organizational output. Interpretive strategy emphasizes attitudinal and cognitive complexity among diverse stakeholders in the organization.

Each of the three models may be summarized briefly. In linear strategy, leaders of the organization plan how they will deal with competitors to achieve their organization's goals. In adaptive strategy, the organization and its parts change, proactively or reactively, in order to be aligned with consumer preferences. In interpretive strategy, organizational representatives convey meanings that are intended to motivate stakeholders in ways that favor the organization. Each model provides a way of describing a certain aspect of organizational functioning to which the term *strategy* has been applied. By analogy, one would have three descriptions of a single phenomenon if a geologist, a climatologist, and a poet were to model the Grand Canyon.

One value of diverse models, whether they relate to strategy or the Grand Canyon, is that they provide options. In future development of strategy, one might delineate the circumstances under which one model of strategy is more appropriate than the others. However, before such delineation is warranted, the models and their interrelationships require further theoretical attention.

As noted earlier, the three strategy models may not be independent of one another, although so far they have been treated separately in both the literature cited and this discussion. The basis for suggesting that the models are interrelated is that they show some similarity to a well-known hierarchy of systems in which each level incorporates the less complex levels that precede it (Boulding, 1956). If the strategy models were analogous to the systems hierarchy, the relationships among the models would also be hierarchical. The systems hierarchy has certain similarities to the three strategy models. Certain characteristics at each set of system levels match those of one of the strategy models. Furthermore, similarities between each level of systems and one of the strategy models suggest that an organization that functions at a given level in the systems hierarchy will benefit from using the corresponding model of strategy.

Therefore, relating the strategy models to the systems hierarchy makes three contributions toward elaborating on the strategy construct. First, it suggests a means of ordering and interrelating the disparate, more narrowly focused definitions of strategy in the existing literature. Second, discrepancies between system levels and strategy models suggest areas in which the models could profitably be developed. Third, the analogy provides a bridge for moving from a survey of theoretical literature to its implications for practice.

The Hierarchy of Strategy Models

Boulding (1956) developed a nine-level hierarchical framework that was keyed to all classes of systems, including human systems. At the most basic level were three classes that Pondy and Mitroff (1979) grouped together under the metaphor of a machine. In the highest of the three machine classes, a control mechanism regulates system behavior according to an externally prescribed target or criterion. Information flows between the regulator and the system operator. Linear strategy shows similar properties in that the executive is expected to control the organization according to predetermined goals and to change the goals when circumstances warrant.

The three intermediate classes constitute the biological set, the highest of which is the internal image system. At this level, because the system has differentiated receptors, it is imbued with detailed awareness of its environment. Awareness is organized into an image, but the system is not self-conscious. Other characteristics of the biological set include its having the same internal differentiation as the environment, as well as its having a generating mechanism that produces behavior. Adaptive strategy corresponds to the biological level, in that the model calls for the organization to scan, anticipate, and respond to various elements in its environment.

Boulding's most complex set of system levels is the cultural set. It consists of the symbol processing level, in which the system is a self-conscious user of language, and the multicephalous level, a collection of individuals acting in concert and using elaborate systems of shared meaning. Boulding's third level in the cultural set is transcendental, not fully specified. The cultural set is analogous to interpretive strategy. Weick and Daft (1983) place interpretation at level 6, the highest biological level, but they identify interpretation as a cultural phenomenon. Wherever it is placed, interpretive strategy, like the cultural level of systems, emphasizes the importance of symbol manipulation, shared meaning, and cooperative actions of individuals. Although the emphases are the same, interpretive strategy is not as fully developed as its correspondence to the cultural level might imply.

Each level in Boulding's hierarchy subsumes those that preceded it. If the same were true of the strategy models, then adaptive strategy would incorporate linear strategy, and interpretive strategy would incorporate both adaptive and linear strategies. Although the evolution of the strategy construct proceeded sequentially through the hierarchy, beginning at the machine level and recently reaching the cultural level, the shift from each level to the next abandoned, rather than incorporated, the preceding level(s). Boulding's cultural level is more complex than his biological level precisely because it builds on the base of the machine and biological levels. Interpretive strategy ignores linear and adaptive strategy. Dealing with stakeholder attitudes is not inherently more complex than dealing with consumer preferences, nor is conveying productive interpretations necessarily more complex than achieving coalignment with the environment. No interpretive strategist has evaluated the extent to which linear and adaptive strategy are subsumed in the "higher" model. Moreover, the adaptive strategists have largely ignored the linear model.

Some hints at relating the three models have appeared in the literature. For example, Weick and Daft (1983) suggested that one criterion of effective interpretation is detailed knowledge of the particulars of the environment (adaptive model) so that the phenomenon to be interpreted may be seen in context. Another paper implied that the models constitute a series of stages through which the organization itself moves over time as it becomes more sophisticated and adept at strategic management (Gluck et al., 1982). The authors stated that organizations start with financial and forecast-based planning (linear model), then shift to strategic analysis (adaptive model), and finally achieve strategic management (interpretive model). Cummings (1983) outlined two major themes in the literature: management by information (linear/adaptive) and management by ideology (interpretive). Cummings argued that both themes must be integrated to achieve an instrumental organization that serves the purposes of its participants. But he did not explain in operational terms how integration occurs. In the only empirical study that relates directly to the strategy models, Chaffee (1984) found that organizations recovering from decline used adaptive strategy, but it was their use of interpretive strategy that differentiated them from organizations unable to recover. However, like Cummings and like Gluck and his colleagues, Chaffee did not deal with how or why the two models were integrated in organizational functioning.

It is important to integrate each lower level model with models that represent more complex systems because organizations exhibit properties of all levels of system complexity. Adaptive and interpretive strategies that ignore less complex strategy models ignore the foundations on which they must be built if they are to reflect organizational reality. Furthermore, a comprehensive interpretive strategy probably requires some planning as would fit with a linear strategy and some organizational change as would fit with an adaptive strategy; and a viable adaptive strategy may well require some linear planning. But rather than building toward a sophisticated construct that equals the complexities for which it is intended, strategists have selected three key themes and treated them separately. Each may have value as far as it goes, but none integrates all levels of complexity and options for action that are inherent in an organization.

Finding three models of strategy holds implications for organizations, for managers, and for future development of the strategy construct. Even at this point, without deepening the adaptive and interpretive models to include lower levels of complexity, the analysis specifies three diverse ways of viewing the organizational problem and three classes of potential solutions. The models may be used conceptually to examine an organizational situation and consider alternatives for coping with it. For example, a manager might consider whether predictions about the declining demand for a product are: (a) based on firm evidence that will provide sufficient lead time for a planning task force to convene and generate alternatives to deal with the decline, (b) fundamental shifts in consumer preferences that could be addressed by modifying the product or replacing it with another, or (c) symptomatic of a loss of confidence among the buying public that could be remedied by better marketing to build legitimacy.

Futhermore, strategic decision making may profit from an analysis of a given situation's level of complexity. If an organization or a problem exhibits characteristics that are predominantly mechanistic, a linear strategy is called for. Adaptive strategies can be applied when issues of supply and demand are especially salient. Complex interpretive strategies may be reserved for situations in which modifying the attitudes of organizational stakeholders is the primary key to success.

The full value of strategy cannot be realized in practical terms, however, until theorists expand the construct to reflect the real complexities of organizations. Each successive level of strategy should incorporate those that are less complex. Then researchers can examine the ways this construct behaves in real organizations. Ultimately, the construct may emerge as a unitary merger of the three models, such as an interpretive model that incorporates adaptive and linear strategy. Or it may emerge as a hierarchy of three models: a mechanistic linear model; a biological adaptive model incorporating linear strategy; and a cultural interpretive model, incorporating both linear and adaptive strategy. Theoreticians also may find value in still greater model differentiation. Perhaps this can be done by specifying a hierarchy that contains a model of strategy for each of Boulding's nine levels of system complexity.

Whatever the end products may be—and whether or not they finally relate to Boulding's hierarchy—it is time for strategy theoreticians and researchers to begin putting the pieces together. During the past 20 years, the strategy literature has greatly evolved. Today, in fact, it has almost arrived at the point at which it is capable of reflecting the actual level of complexity at which organizations operate. The way is now open to capitalize, both theoretically and empirically, on the richness of that complexity.

Note

1. The research reported here was supported by a contract (#400-83-0009) from the National Institute of Education. An abbreviated version was presented at the annual meeting of the Academy of Management, Boston, 1984, and appears in the *Proceedings* of the meeting. The author is grateful to Jane Dutton for several excellent suggestions.

References

Andrews, K. R. *The concept of corporate strategy.* Homewood, IL: Irwin, 1971.

Ansoff, H. I., & Hayes, R. L. Introduction. In H. I. Ansoff, R. P. Declerck, & R. L. Hayes (Eds.), *From strategic planning to strategic management.* New York: Wiley, 1976, 1–12.

Berger, P., & Luckmann, T. *The social construction of reality.* New York: Doubleday, 1966.

Biggadike, E. R. The contributions of marketing to strategic management. *Academy of Management Review,* 1981, 6, 621–632.

Boulding, K. E. General systems theory—The skeleton of science. *Management Science,* 1956, 2, 197–208.

Bourgeois, L. J., III. Strategy and environment: A conceptual integration. *Academy of Management Review,* 1980, 5, 25–39.

Camillus, J. C. Reconciling logical incrementalism and synoptic formalism—An integrated approach to designing strategy planning processes. *Strategic Management Journal,* 1982, 3, 227–283.

Cannon, J. T. *Business strategy and policy.* New York: Harcourt Brace Jovanovich, 1968.

Chaffee, E. E. Successful strategic management in small private colleges. *Journal of Higher Education,* 1984, 55, 212–241.

Chakravarthy, B. S. Adaptation: A promising metaphor for strategic management. *Academy of Management Review,* 1982, 7, 35–44.

Chandler, A. D., Jr. *Strategy and structure.* Cambridge, MA: MIT Press, 1962.

Child, J. Organizational structure, environment, and performance: The role of strategic choice. *Sociology,* 1972, 6, 1–22.

Cummings, L. L. The logics of management. *Academy of Management Review,* 1983, 8, 532–538.

Dandridge, T. C., Mitroff, I., & Joyce, W. F. Organizational symbolism: A topic to expand organizational analysis. *Academy of Management Review,* 1980, 5, 77–82.

Deal, T. E., & Kennedy, A. A. Corporate cultures: *The rites and rituals of corporate life.* Reading, MA: Addison-Wesley, 1982.

Dill, W. R. Commentary. In D. E. Schendel & C. W. Hofer (Eds.), *Strategic management: A new view of business policy and planning.* Boston: Little, Brown, 1979, 47–51.

Dirsmith, M. W., & Covaleski, M. A. Strategy, external communication and environment context. *Strategic Management Journal,* 1983, 4, 137–151.

Drucker, P. F. *Management: Tasks, responsibilities, practices.* New York: Harper & Row, 1974.

Fahey, L. On strategic management decision processes. *Strategic Management Journal,* 1981, 2, 43–60.

Feldman, M., & March, J. G. Information in organizations as signal and symbol. *Administrative Science Quarterly,* 1981, 26, 171–186.

Galbraith, C., & Schendel, D. An empirical analysis of strategy types. *Strategic Management Journal,* 1983, 4, 153–173.

Gilmore, F. F. Formulating strategy in smaller companies. *Harvard Business Review,* 1970, 49(5), 71–81.

Ginter, P. M., & White, D. D. A social learning approach to strategic management: Toward a theoretical foundation. *Academy of Management Review,* 1982, 7, 253–261.

Gluck, F., Kaufman, S., & Walleck, A. S. The four phases of strategic management. *Journal of Business Strategy,* 1982, 2(3), 9–21.

Glueck, W. F. *Business policy: Strategy formation and management action.* New York: McGraw-Hill, 1976.

Glueck, W. F. *Strategic management and business policy.* New York: McGraw-Hill, 1980.

Green, J., & Jones, T. Strategic development as a means of organizational change: Four case histories. *Long Range Planning,* 1981, 14(3), 58–67.

Greenwood, P., & Thomas, H. A review of analytical models in strategic planning. *Omega,* 1981, 9(4), 397–417.

Guth, W. D. Toward a social system theory of corporate strategy, *Journal of Business,* 1976, 49, 374–388.

Hambrick, D. C. Operationalizing the concept of business-level strategy in research. *Academy of Management Review,* 1980, 5, 567–575.

Hambrick, D. C. Some tests of the effectiveness and functional attributes of Miles and Snow's strategic types. *Academy of Management Journal,* 1983, 26, 5–25.

Hatten, K. J. Quantitative research methods in strategic management. In D. E. Schendel & C. W. Hofer (Eds.), *Strategic management: A new view of business policy and planning.* Boston: Little, Brown, 1979, 448–467.

Hatten, M. L. Strategic management in not-for-profit organizations. *Strategic Management Journal*, 1982, 3, 89–104.

Hayman, J. *Relationship of strategic planning and future methodologies.* Paper presented at the 1981 Annual Convention of the AERA, Los Angeles, 1981.

Hofer, C. W. Some preliminary research on patterns of strategic behavior. *Academy of Management Proceedings*, 1973, 46–59.

Hofer, C. W. *Conceptual scheme for formulating a total business strategy.* Boston: HBS Case Services, 1976a.

Hofer, C. W. Research on strategic planning: A survey of past studies and suggestions for future efforts. *Journal of Economics and Business*, 1976b, 28, 261–286.

Hofer, C. W., & Schendel, D. *Strategy formulation: Analytical concepts.* St. Paul, MN: West, 1978.

Jauch, L. R., & Osborn, R. N. Toward an integrated theory of strategy. *Academy of Management Review*, 1981, 6, 491–498.

Jemison, D. B. The contributions of administrative behavior to strategic management. *Academy of Management Review*, 1981, 6, 633–642.

Keeley, M. Organizational analogy: A comparison of organismic and social contract models. *Administrative Science Quarterly*, 1980, 25, 337–362.

Kotler, P., & Murphy, P. E. Strategic planning for higher education. *Journal of Higher Education*, 1981, 52, 470–489.

Learned, E. P., Christensen, C. R., Andrews, K. R., & Guth, W. R. *Business policy.* Homewood, IL: Irwin, 1969.

Lenz, R. T. Strategic capability: A concept and framework for analysis. *Academy of Management Review*, 1980a, 5, 225–234.

Lenz, R. T. Environment, strategy, organization structure and performance: Patterns in one industry. *Strategic Management Journal*, 1980b, 1, 209–226.

Litschert, R. J., & Bonham, T. W. Conceptual models of strategy formulation. *Academy of Management Review*, 1978, 3, 211–219.

Lorange, P., & Vancil, R. F. How to design a strategic planning system. *Harvard Business Review*, 1976, 54(5), 75–81.

Mason, R. O., & Mitroff, I. I. *Challenging strategic planning assumptions.* New York: 1981.

Mazzolini, R. How strategic decisions are made. *Long Range Planning*, 1981, 14(3), 85–96.

Meyer, J. W., & Rowan, B. Institutionalized organizations: Formal structure as myth and ceremony. *American Journal of Sociology*, 1977, 83, 340–363.

Miles, R. E., & Snow, C. C. *Organizational strategy, structure, and process.* New York: McGraw-Hill, 1978.

Miles, R. E., Snow, C. C., Meyer, A. D., & Coleman, H. J., Jr. Organizational strategy, structure, and process. *Academy of Management Review*, 1978, 3, 546–563.

Miles, R. H., & Cameron, K. S. *Coffin nails and corporate strategies.* Englewood Cliffs, NJ: Prentice-Hall, 1982.

Miller, D., & Friesen, P. Archetypes of strategy formulation. *Management Science*, 1978, 24, 253–280.

Mintzberg, H. Strategy-making in three modes. *California Management Review*, 1973, 16(2), 44–53.

Mintzberg, H. Patterns in strategy formation. *Management Science*, 1978, 24, 934–948.

Murray, E. A. Strategic change as a negotiated outcome. *Management Science*, 1978, 24, 960–972.

Murray, J. A. Toward a contingency model of strategic decision. *International Studies of Management and Organization*, 1978–79, 8, 7–34.

Narayanan, V. K., & Fahey, L. The micro-politics of strategy formulation. *Academy of Management Review*, 1982, 7, 25–34.

Paine, F. T., & Naumes, W. *Strategy and policy formation: An integrative approach.* Philadelphia: Saunders, 1974.

Peters, T. J. Symbols, patterns, and settings: An optimistic case for getting things done. *Organizational Dynamics*, 1978, 7(2), 3–23.

Peters, T. J., & Waterman, R. H., Jr. *In search of excellence: Lessons from America's best-run companies.* New York: Harper & Row, 1982.

Pettigrew, A. M. Strategy formulation as a political process. *International Studies of Management and Organization*, 1977, 7, 78–87.

Pfeffer, J. Management as symbolic action: The creation and maintenance of organizational paradigms. In L. L. Cummings & B. M. Staw (Eds.), *Research in organizational behavior.* Greenwood, CT: JAI Press, 1981, 1–52.

Pondy, L. R., & Mitroff, I. I. Beyond open system models of organization. In B. M. Staw (Ed.), *Research in organizational behavior.* Greenwood, CT: JAI Press. 1979, 3–39.

Quinn, J. B. *Strategies for change: Logical incrementalism.* Homewood, IL: Irwin, 1980.

Rumelt, R. P. Evaluation of strategy: Theory and models. In D. E. Schendel & C. W. Hofer (Eds.), *Strategic management: A new view of business policy and planning.* Boston: Little, Brown, 1979, 196–212.

Shirley, R. C. Limiting the scope of strategy. A decision based approach. *Academy of Management Review,* 1982, 7, 262–268.

Smircich, L., & Morgan, G. Leadership: The management of meaning. *Journal of Applied Behavioral Science,* 1982, 18(3), 257–273.

Snow, C. C., & Hambrick, D C. Measuring organizational strategies: Some theoretical and methodological problems. *Academy of Management Review,* 1980, 5, 527–538.

Spender, J. C. Commentary. In D. E. Schendel & C. W. Hofer (Eds.), *Strategic management: A new view of business policy and planning.* Boston: Little, Brown, 1979, 383–404.

Steiner, G. A. *Strategic planning.* New York: Free Press, 1979.

Steiner, G. A., & Miner, J. B. *Management policy and strategy.* New York: Macmillan, 1977.

Tabatoni, P., & Jarniou, P. The dynamics of norms in strategic management. In H. I. Ansoff, R. P. Declerck, & R. L. Hayes (Eds.), *From strategic planning to strategic management.* London: Wiley, 1976, 29–36.

Van Cauwenbergh, A., & Cool, K. Strategic management in a new framework. *Strategic Management Journal,* 1982, 3, 245–265.

Weick, K. E., & Daft, R. L. The effectiveness of interpretation systems. In K. S. Cameron & D. A. Whetten (Eds.), *Organizational effectiveness: A comparison of multiple models.* New York: Academic Press, 1983, 71–93.

THE FALL AND RISE OF STRATEGIC PLANNING

HENRY MINTZBERG

When strategic planning arrived on the scene in the mid-1960s, corporate leaders embraced it as "the one best way" to devise and implement strategies that would enhance the competitiveness of each business unit. True to the scientific management pioneered by Frederick Taylor, this one best way involved separating thinking from doing and creating a new function staffed by specialists: strategic planners. Planning systems were expected to produce the best strategies as well as step-by-step instructions for carrying out those strategies so that the doers, the managers of businesses, could not get them wrong. As we now know, planning has not exactly worked out that way.

While certainly not dead, strategic planning has long since fallen from its pedestal. But even now, few people fully understand the reason: *strategic planning* is not *strategic thinking*. Indeed, strategic planning often spoils strategic thinking, causing managers to confuse real vision with the manipulation of numbers. And this confusion lies at the heart of the issue: the most successful strategies are visions, not plans.

Strategic planning, as it has been practiced, has really been *strategic programming*, the articulation and elaboration of strategies, or visions, that already exist. When companies understand the difference between planning and strategic thinking, they can get back to what the strategy-making process should be: capturing what the manager learns from all sources (both the soft insights from his or her personal experiences and the experiences of others throughout the organization and the hard data from market research and the like) and then synthesizing that learning into a vision of the direction that the business should pursue.

Organizations disenchanted with strategic planning should not get rid of their planners or conclude that there is no need for programming. Rather, organizations should transform the conventional planning job. Planners should make their contribution *around* the strategy-making process rather than *inside* it. They should supply the formal analyses or hard data that strategic thinking requires, as long as they do it to broaden the consideration of issues rather than to discover the one right answer. They should act as catalysts who support strategy making by aiding and encouraging managers to think strategically. And, finally, they can be programmers of a strategy, helping to specify the series of concrete steps needed to carry out the vision.

By redefining the planner's job, companies will acknowledge the difference between planning and strategic thinking. Planning has always been about *analysis*—about breaking down a goal or set of intentions into steps, formalizing those steps so that they can be implemented almost automatically, and articulating the anticipated consequences or results of each step. "I favour a set of analytical techniques for developing strategy," Michael Porter, probably the most widely read writer on strategy, wrote in the *Economist*.[1]

The label "strategic planning" has been applied to all kinds of activities, such as going off to an informal retreat in the mountains to talk about strategy. But call that activity "planning," let conventional

Henry Mintzberg is professor of management at McGill University in Montreal, Quebec, and visiting professor at INSEAD in Fontainebleau, France. This article, his fifth contribution to HBR, is adapted from his latest book, *The Rise and Fall of Strategic Planning* (Free Press and Prentice Hall International, 1994).

planners organize it, and watch how quickly the event becomes formalized (mission statements in the morning, assessment of corporate strengths and weaknesses in the afternoon, strategies carefully articulated by 5 P.M.).

Strategic thinking, in contrast, is about *synthesis*. It involves intuition and creativity. The outcome of strategic thinking is an integrated perspective of the enterprise, a not-too-precisely articulated vision of direction, such as the vision of Jim Clark, the founder of Silicon Graphics, that three-dimensional visual computing is the way to make computers easier to use.

Such strategies often cannot be developed on schedule and immaculately conceived. They must be free to appear at any time and at any place in the organization, typically through messy processes of informal learning that must necessarily be carried out by people at various levels who are deeply involved with the specific issues at hand.

Formal planning, by its very analytical nature, has been and always will be dependent on the preservation and rearrangement of established categories—the existing levels of strategy (corporate, business, functional), the established types of products (defined as "strategic business units"), overlaid on the current units of structure (divisions, departments, etc.). But real strategic change requires not merely rearranging the established categories, but inventing new ones.

Search all those strategic planning diagrams, all those interconnected boxes that supposedly give you strategies, and nowhere will you find a single one that explains the creative act of synthesizing experiences into a novel strategy. Take the example of the Polaroid camera. One day in 1943, Edwin Land's three-year-old daughter asked why she could not immediately see the picture he had just taken of her. Within an hour, this scientist conceived the camera that would transform his company. In other words, Land's vision was the synthesis of the insight evoked by his daughter's question and his vast technical knowledge.

Strategy making needs to function beyond the boxes, to encourage the informal learning that produces new perspectives and new combinations. As the saying goes, life is larger than our categories. Planning's failure to transcend the categories explains why it has discouraged serious organizational change. This failure is why formal planning has promoted strategies that are extrapolated from the past or copied from others. Strategic planning has not only never amounted to strategic thinking but has, in fact, often impeded it. Once managers understand this, they can avoid other costly misadventures caused by applying formal technique, without judgment and intuition, to problem solving.

The Pitfalls of Planning

If you ask conventional planners what went wrong, they will inevitably point to a series of pitfalls for which they, of course, are not responsible. Planners would have people believe that planning fails when it does not receive the support it deserves from top management or when it encounters resistance to change in the organization. But surely no technique ever received more top management support than strategic planning did in its heyday. Strategic planning itself has discouraged the commitment of top managers and has tended to create the very climates its proponents have found so uncongenial to its practice.

The problem is that planning represents a *calculating* style of management, not a *committing* style. Managers with a committing style engage people in a journey. They lead in such a way that everyone on the journey helps shape its course. As a result, enthusiasm inevitably builds along the way. Those with a calculating style fix on a destination and calculate what the group must do to get there, with no concern for the members' preferences. But calculated strategies have no value in and of themselves; to paraphrase the words of sociologist Philip Selznick, strategies take on value only as committed people infuse them with energy.[2]

No matter how much lip service has been paid to the contrary, the very purpose of those who promote conventional strategic planning is to reduce the power of management over strategy making. George Steiner declared, "If an organization is managed by intuitive geniuses there is no need for formal strategic planning. But how many organizations are so blessed? And, if they are, how many times are intuitives correct in their judgments?"[3] Peter Lorange, who is equally prominent in the field, stated, "The CEO should typically not be . . . deeply involved" in the process, but rather be "the designer of [it] in a general sense."[4] How can we expect top managers to be committed to a process that depicts them in this way, especially when its failures to deliver on its promises have become so evident?

At lower levels in the hierarchy, the problem becomes more severe because planning has often been used to exercise blatant control over business managers. No wonder so many middle managers have welcomed the overthrow of strategic planning. All they wanted was a commitment to their own business strategies without having to fight the planners to get it!

The Fallacies of Strategic Planning

An expert has been defined as someone who avoids the many pitfalls on his or her way to the grand fallacy. For strategic planning, the grand fallacy is this: because analysis encompasses synthesis, strategic planning is strategy making. This fallacy itself rests on three fallacious assumptions: that prediction is possible, that strategists can be detached from the subjects of their strategies, and, above all, that the strategy-making process can be formalized.

The Fallacy of Prediction

According to the premises of strategic planning, the world is supposed to hold still while a plan is being developed and then stay on the predicted course while that plan is being implemented. How else to explain those lockstep schedules that have strategies appearing on the first of June, to be approved by the board of directors on the fifteenth? One can just picture competitors waiting for the board's approval, especially if they are Japanese and don't believe in such planning to begin with.

In 1965, Igor Ansoff wrote in his influential book *Corporate Strategy*, "We shall refer to the period for which the firm is able to construct forecasts with an accuracy of, say, plus or minus 20 percent as the *planning horizon* of the firm."[5] What an extraordinary statement! How in the world can any company know the period for which it can forecast with a given accuracy?

The evidence, in fact, points to the contrary. While certain repetitive patterns, such as seasons, may be predictable, the forecasting of discontinuities, such as a technological innovation or a price increase, is virtually impossible. Of course, some people sometimes "see" such things coming. That is why we call them "visionaries." But they create their strategies in much more personalized and intuitive ways.

The Fallacy of Detachment

In her book *Institutionalizing Innovation*, Mariann Jelinek developed the interesting point that strategic planning is to the executive suite what Taylor's work-study methods were to the factory floor—a way to circumvent human idiosyncrasies in order to systematize behavior. "It is through administrative systems that planning and policy are made possible, because the systems capture knowledge *about* the task." Thus "true management by exception, and true policy direction are now possible, solely because management is no longer wholly immersed in the details of the task itself."[6]

According to this viewpoint, if the system does the thinking, then strategies must be detached from operations (or "tactics"), formulation from implementation, thinkers from doers, and so strategists from the objects of their strategies.

The trick, of course, is to get the relevant information up there, so that senior managers on high can be informed about the details down below without having to immerse themselves in them. Planners' favored solution has been "hard data," quantitative aggregates of the detailed "facts" about the organization and its context, neatly packaged and regularly delivered. With such information, senior managers need never leave their executive suites or planners their staff offices. Together they can formulate—work with their heads—so that the hands can get on with implementation.

All of this is dangerously fallacious. Innovation has never been institutionalized. Systems have never been able to reproduce the synthesis created by the genius entrepreneur or even the ordinary competent strategist, and they likely never will.

Ironically, strategic planning has missed one of Taylor's most important messages: work processes must be fully understood before they can be formally programmed. But where in the planning literature is there a shred of evidence that anyone has ever bothered to find out how it is that managers really do make strategies? Instead many practitioners and theorists have wrongly assumed that strategic planning, strategic thinking, and strategy making are all synonymous, at least in best practice.

The problem with the hard data that are supposed to inform the senior manager is they can have a decidedly soft underbelly. Such data take time to harden, which often makes them late. They tend to lack richness; for example, they often exclude the qualitative. And they tend to be overly aggregated, missing important nuances. These are the reasons managers who rely on formalized information, such as market-research reports or accounting statements in business and opinion polls in government, tend to be detached in more ways than one. Study after study has shown that the most effective managers rely on some of the softest forms of information, including gossip, hearsay, and various other intangible scraps of information.

My research and that of many others demonstrates that strategy making is an immensely complex process, which involves the most sophisticated, subtle, and, at times, subconscious elements of human thinking.

A strategy can be deliberate. It can realize the specific intentions of senior management, for example, to attack and conquer a new market. But a strategy can also be emergent, meaning that a convergent pattern has formed among the different actions taken by the organization one at a time.

In other words, strategies can develop inadvertently, without the conscious intention of senior management, often through a process of learning. A salesperson convinces a different kind of customer to try a product. Other salespeople follow up with their customers, and the next thing management knows, its products have penetrated a new market. When it takes the form of fits and starts, discoveries based on serendipitous events, and the recognition of unexpected patterns, learning inevitably plays *a*, if not *the*, crucial role in the development of novel strategies.

Contrary to what traditional planning would have us believe, deliberate strategies are not necessarily good, nor are emergent strategies necessarily bad. I believe that all viable strategies have emergent and deliberate qualities, since all must combine some degree of flexible learning with some degree of cerebral control.

Vision is unavailable to those who cannot "see" with their own eyes. Real strategists get their hands dirty digging for ideas, and real strategies are built from the occasional nuggets they uncover. These are not people who abstract themselves from the daily details; they are the ones who immerse themselves in them while being able to abstract the strategic messages from them. The big picture is painted with little strokes.

The Fallacy of Formalization

The failure of strategic planning is the failure of systems to do better than, or even nearly as well as, human beings. Formal systems, mechanical or otherwise, have offered no improved means of dealing with the information overload of human brains; indeed, they have often made matters worse. All the promises about artificial intelligence, expert systems, and the like improving if not replacing human intuition never materialized at the strategy level. Formal systems could certainly process more information, at least hard information. But they could never *internalize* it, *comprehend* it, *synthesize* it. In a literal sense, planning could not learn.

Formalization implies a rational sequence, from analysis through administrative procedure to eventual action. But strategy making as a learning process can proceed in the other direction too. We think in order to act, to be sure, but we also act in order to think. We try things, and those experiments that work converge gradually into viable patterns that become strategies. This is the very essence of strategy making as a learning process.

Formal procedures will never be able to forecast discontinuities, inform detached managers, or create novel strategies. Far from providing strategies, planning could not proceed without their prior existence. All this time, therefore, strategic planning has been misnamed. It should have been called strategic programming, distinguished from other useful things that planners can do, and promoted as a process to formalize, when necessary, the consequences of strategies that have already been developed. In short, we should drop the label "strategic planning" altogether.

Planning, Plans, and Planners

Two important messages have been conveyed through all the difficulties encountered by strategic planning. But only one of them has been widely accepted in the planning community: business-unit managers must take full and effective charge of the strategy-making process. The lesson that has still not been accepted is that managers will never be able to take charge through a formalized process. What then can be the roles for planning, for plans, and for planners in organizations?

Planners and managers have different advantages. Planners lack managers' authority to make commitments, and, more important, managers' access to soft information critical to strategy making. But because of their time pressures, managers tend to favor action over reflection and the oral over the written, which can cause them to overlook important analytical information. Strategies cannot be created by analysis, but their development can be helped by it.

Planners, on the other hand, have the time and, most important, the inclination to analyze. They have critical roles to play alongside line managers, but not as conventionally conceived. They should work in the spirit of what I like to call a "soft analyst," whose intent is to pose the right questions rather than to find the right answers. That way, complex issues get opened up to thoughtful consideration instead of being closed down prematurely by snap decisions.

Planning as Strategic Programming

Planning cannot generate strategies. But given viable strategies, it can program them; it can make them operational. For one supermarket chain that a colleague and I studied, planning was the articulation, justification, and elaboration of the strategic vision that the company's leader already had. Planning was not deciding to expand into shopping centers, but explicating to what extent and when, with how many stores, and on what schedule.

An appropriate image for the planner might be that person left behind in a meeting, together with the chief executive, after everyone else has departed. All of the strategic decisions that were made are symbolically strewn about the table. The CEO turns to the planner and says, "There they all are; clean them up. Package them neatly so that we can tell everyone about them and get things going." In more formal language, strategic programming involves three steps: codification, elaboration, and conversion of strategies.

Codification means clarifying and expressing the strategies in terms sufficiently clear to render them formally operational, so that their consequences can be worked out in detail. This requires a good deal of interpretation and careful attention to what might be lost in articulation: nuance, subtlety, qualification. A broad vision, like capturing the market for a new technology, is one thing, but a specific plan—35% market share, focusing on the high end—is quite another.

Elaboration means breaking down the codified strategies into substrategies and ad hoc programs as well as overall action plans specifying what must be done to realize each strategy: build four new factories and hire 200 new workers, for example.

And conversion means considering the effects of the changes on the organization's operations—effects on budgets and performance controls, for example. Here a kind of great divide must be crossed from the nonroutine world of strategies and programs to the routine world of budgets and objectives. Objectives have to be restated and budgets reworked, and policies and standard operating procedures reconsidered, to take into account the consequences of the specific changes.

One point must be emphasized. Strategic programming is not "the one best way" or even necessarily a good way. Managers don't always need to program their strategies formally. Sometimes they must leave their strategies flexible, as broad visions, to adapt to a changing environment. Only when an organization is sure of the relative stability of its environment and is in need of the tight coordination of a myriad of intricate operations (as is typically the case of airlines with their needs for complicated scheduling), does such strategic programming make sense.

Plans as Tools to Communicate and Control

Why program strategy? The most obvious reason is for coordination, to ensure that everyone in the organization pulls in the same direction. Plans in the form of programs—schedules, budgets, and so on—can be prime media to communicate strategic intentions and to control the individual pursuit of them, in so far, of course, as common direction is considered to be more important than individual discretion.

Plans can also be used to gain the tangible as well as moral support of influential outsiders. Written plans inform financiers, suppliers, government agencies, and others about the intentions of the organization so that these groups can help it achieve its plans.

Planners as Strategy Finders

As noted, some of the most important strategies in organizations emerge without the intention or sometimes even the awareness of top managers. Fully exploiting these strategies, though, often requires that they be recognized and then broadened in their impact, like taking a new use for a product accidentally discovered by a salesperson and turning it into a major new business. It is obviously the responsibility of managers to discover and anoint these strategies. But planners can assist managers in finding these fledgling strategies in their organizations' activities or in those of competing organizations.

Planners can snoop around places they might not normally visit to find patterns amid the noise of failed experiments, seemingly random activities, and messy learning. They can discover new ways of doing or perceiving things, for example, spotting newly uncovered markets and understanding their implied new products.

Planners as Analysts

In-depth examinations of what planners actually do suggests that the effective ones spend a good deal of time not so much doing or even encouraging planning as carrying out analyses of specific issues. Planners are obvious candidates for the job of studying the hard data and ensuring that managers consider the results in the strategy-making process.

Much of this analysis will necessarily be quick and dirty, that is, in the time frame and on the ad hoc basis required by managers. It may include industry or competitive analyses as well as internal studies, including the use of computer models to analyze trends in the organization.

But some of the best models that planners can offer managers are simply alternative conceptual interpretations of their world, such as a new way to view the organization's distribution system. As Arie de Geus, the one-time head of planning at Royal Dutch/Shell, wrote in his HBR article "Planning as Learning" (March-April 1988), "The real purpose of effective planning is not to make plans but to change the . . . mental models that . . . decision makers carry in their heads."

Planners as Catalysts

The planning literature has long promoted the role of catalyst for the planner, but not as I will describe it here. It is not planning that planners should be urging on their organizations so much as any form of behavior that can lead to effective performance in a given situation. Sometimes that may even mean criticizing formal planning itself.

When they act as catalysts, planners do not enter the black box of strategy making; they ensure that the box is occupied with active line managers. In other words, they encourage managers to think about the future in creative ways.

Such planners see their job as getting others to question conventional wisdom and especially helping people out of conceptual ruts (which managers with long experience in stable strategies are apt to dig themselves into). To do their jobs, they may have to use provocation or shock tactics like raising difficult questions and challenging conventional assumptions.

Left- and Right-Handed Planners

Two very different kinds of people populate the planning function. One is an analytic thinker, who is closer to the conventional image of the planner. He or she is dedicated to bringing order to the organization. Above all, this person programs intended strategies and sees to it that they are communicated clearly. He or she also carries out analytic studies to ensure consideration of the necessary hard data and carefully scrutinizes strategies intended for implementation. We might label him or her the *right-handed planner.*

The second is less conventional but present nonetheless in many organizations. This planner is a creative thinker who seeks to open up the strategy-making process. As a "soft analyst," this planner is prepared to conduct more quick and dirty studies. He or she likes to find strategies in strange places and to encourage others to think strategically. This person is somewhat more inclined toward the intuitive processes identified with the brain's right hemisphere. We might call him or her the *left-handed planner.*

Many organizations need both types, and it is top management's job to ensure that it has them in appropriate proportions. Organizations need people to bring order to the messy world of management as well as challenge the conventions that managers and especially their organizations develop. Some organizations (those big, machine-like bureaucracies concerned with mass production) may favor the right-handed planners, while others (the loose, flexible "adhocracies," or project organizations) may favor the left-handed ones. But both kinds of organization need both types of planners, if only to offset their natural tendencies. And, of course, some organizations, like those highly professionalized hospitals and educational systems that have been forced to waste so much time doing ill-conceived strategic planning, may prefer to have very few of either!

The Formalization Edge

We human beings seem predisposed to formalize our behavior. But we must be careful not to go over the formalization edge. No doubt we must formalize to do many of the things we wish to in modern society. That is why we have organizations. But the experiences of what has been labeled strategic planning teach us that there are limits. These limits must be understood, especially for complex and creative activities like strategy making.

Strategy making is not an isolated process. It does not happen just because a meeting is held with that label. To the contrary, strategy making is a process interwoven with all that it takes to manage an organization. Systems do not think, and when they are used for more than the facilitation of human thinking, they can prevent thinking.

Three decades of experience with strategic planning have taught us about the need to loosen up the process of strategy making rather than trying to seal it off by arbitrary formalization. Through all the false starts and excessive rhetoric, we have learned what planning is not and what it cannot do. But we have also learned what planning is and what it can do, and perhaps of greater use, what planners themselves can do beyond planning. We have also learned how the literature of management can get carried away and, more important, about the appropriate place for analysis in organizations.

The story of strategic planning, in other words, has taught us not only about formal technique itself but also about how organizations function and how managers do and don't cope with that functioning. Most significant, it has told us something about how we think as human beings, and that we sometimes stop thinking.

References

1. Michael Porter, "The State of Strategic Thinking," *Economist*, May 23, 1987, p. 21.
2. Philip Selznick, *Leadership in Administration: A Sociological Interpretation* (New York: Harper & Row, 1957).
3. George Steiner, *Strategic Planning: What Every Manager* Must *Know* (New York: Free Press, 1979), p. 9.
4. Peter Lorange, "Roles of the CEO in Strategic Planning and Control Processes," in a seminar on The Role of General Management in Strategy Formulation and Evaluation, cosponsored by E.S.S.E.C., E.I.A.S.M., and I.A.E. (Cergy, France: April 28–30, 1980), p. 2.
5. H. Igor Ansoff, *Corporate Strategy: An Analytic Approach to Business Policy for Growth and Expansion* (New York: McGraw-Hill, 1965), p. 44.
6. Mariann Jelinek, *Institutionalizing Innovation: A Study of Organizational Learning Systems* (New York: Praeger, 1979), p. 139.

A MEMO FROM MACHIAVELLI

DANIEL J. JULIUS, J. VICTOR BALDRIDGE, AND JEFFREY PFEFFER

To: Presidents, Senior Administrators, and Faculty Leaders Who Would Seek Change
From: Niccolo Machiavelli, Former Assistant to Presidents, University of the Medici

Permit me to take a brief moment of your valuable time to introduce myself. I served for years as special assistant to kings, dukes, generals, several popes and, as well, numerous presidents, senior executives and faculty at the University of the Medici. I have significant domestic and international experience—for in this capacity I have also worked with governors, state and national legislators, wealthy donors, foundations, public relations firms, religious societies, city and county officials, law enforcement agencies, and community activists. I have also coordinated activities with ministers of education throughout Europe.

I had the distinct pleasure of hearing your recent address to the Faculty Senate. You spoke of a bold tomorrow, the need for change in your institution, including the manner in which work is accomplished and evaluated. You discussed technology, distance learning, diversity, student services, the need for alternative criteria to evaluate faculty, new relationships with unions, funding, and student and alumni constituencies. You discussed how the role of the university, with the state, the city, and the federal government will change. You cited emerging relationships with the business community and argued persuasively, in my opinion, that unless the academic establishment begins to refocus its priorities, the university, as it once existed, will lose the autonomy and freedom to offer sound educational programs.

I am in no position to quarrel with your premises. (I am unemployed at the moment.) I was impressed with your grasp of fundamental issues facing higher education. I am, however, curious as to how you will implement these new ideas. Because I have advised over one hundred senior executives and faculty on change and implementation strategies, I thought you might appreciate my observations. My comments are based on real experiences. They are offered to you as a gift, yours to keep or discard at your pleasure.

Parenthetically, I do not mean to be presumptuous or overbearing in this letter. University executives and faculty leaders are (on occasion) startled at my directness and characterization of the uses of power and influence. I understand you are a gifted individual and would not hold your position and title unless you possessed exemplary traits. Like most intelligent people with whom I have worked, they appreciate candor. (Please ignore my biases though!) I do not want to sound as though I were sending you into an armed battle. Neither should we pretend, if you are serious about your ideals and goals, that people will simply adopt "your" new vision.

Decision Processes in Professional Organizations: Contemporary Realities

The key to being effective and the ability to make change begins first with an accurate assessment of the type of organization in which you work. Secondly, you must appreciate how decisions are made and who, if anyone, implements them.

451

Universities and colleges have a number of unique characteristics. Fundamentally, they are people-processing organizations, and, in order to handle that complex and delicate task, they usually have large staffs of highly trained professionals. Because people cannot be divided into segmentalized tasks in the same way that physical products can, professionals with a high level of expertise are needed to deal holistically with clients' needs. Thus it is that the first characteristic of academic organizations is that they are highly professionalized, client-serving systems.

Second, "people-processing" organizations have extremely ambiguous goals, and a list of legitimate activities for a university is extremely long. Because goals are often unclear, almost any activity that serves a "client" may be considered legitimate. Though many activities can be considered legitimate, many are also questioned. This is important for understanding change processes. If a college or university does not know its specific objectives, then an individual with an idea (and the energy) can often bend the institution in his direction. Ambiguity and contest over goals pave the way for the skillful politician.

Finally, colleges and universities are extremely vulnerable to outside pressures. Because the clients themselves—students—are relatively powerless, society generally demands accountability from the organization. As a consequence, outsiders demand the right to influence internal decisions. Be assured, however, that the public's success varies considerably: in school systems outside voices are often influential; in hospitals or legal firms, the organization has generally listened with deaf ears.

Characteristics of the Decision-Making Process

You operate in an unusual kind of organization. It is one that serves clients, has a highly professionalized staff, has unclear and contested goals, and is subject to much external pressure. The decision-making process can be characterized by the following:

Decision is by committee. Because expertise, not hierarchical office, is the organizing principle, then committees of experts decide many of the critical issues.

Fluid participation. Many of the decision makers are amateurs, engaged in pursuing their professions, not in making decisions. As a consequence, they wander in and out of the decision process, and power belongs to those who stay long enough to exercise it.

An issue carousel. Issues have a way of always coming around again. Decisions do not last long because pressure from outside groups, from clients, and from other professionals push the same or similar issues full circle. Decisions are not made as much as they are pinned down temporarily.

A "subsidiary" process. The longer it takes to make a decision, the greater the number of issues that are piled onto the original subject. People, hoping to accomplish several things at one time, burden simple decisions with countless subsidiary ones.

Conflict is common. Professional groups, clients, and outsiders support divergent interests in setting the ambiguous goals of academic organizations. As a consequence, conflict over goals is common as decision makers cope with the pressures from diverse interest groups.

How can I summarize? The image that captures the spirit of the decision process in an academic organization does not resemble a normal bureaucracy; nor does it look like the "community of peers" that is often associated with the medieval guild. Several images capture the spirit of the decision-making process. First, the structure of the organization is fluid, can be challenged and is highly political. Second, the decision-making process reflects competing groups and who often conflict. Finally, the unsettled character of the decision-making process can be captured by using the term *decision flowing* instead of decision making. Decision making has a finality to it; decision flowing sounds like a never-ending process that must be continued in order to make outcomes really work.

Change and the Ability to Make It

In the academic organization, seeking change, or accommodation to new trends, ideas, contexts, political or fiscal realities, is not for the faint-hearted. This is so particularly in your school. At least in your case, you will have some formal authority over internal constituents—but it is not formal authority in the real sense. As one ascends the organizational hierarchy in academic organizations, one has less and less real authority over anyone needed to get the job accomplished. Put another way, if you ever have to "invoke" your authority, you have, in effect, lost it. Success depends on managerial savvy coupled with moral and political persuasiveness.

Most in higher education believe "change" is laudable, but it remains difficult to manage. Said another way, we are busy reacting to change instead of being proactive. We even ask our search consultants to bring us candidates who can implement "change." In my experience, however, our colleagues in academe do not readily adopt new definitions of what is or is not important, or how work is accomplished or evaluated. (I suspect this may be attributable to the notion that professionals believe that what is good for them is also good for the student.) Everyone will sign on to the platitudes—the real work remains in the details of implementation: persuading; cajoling and, in reality, making it impossible for others not to follow you; exercising power and influence in non-hierarchical and informal settings. Implementation is the realm where the truly successful and effective administrators flourish.

The truth of the matter is that anyone who seeks to transcend the status quo will be met with opposition. Those who can neutralize or overcome opposing constituencies (or individuals) will succeed. Most senior executives and faculty, however, cannot and, for that reason, do not succeed in changing the organization in a positive way (and so they relegate their efforts around the margins of the institution, ignoring or shying away from the difficult structural issues). Of course the worst case scenario results when change is effectuated without accommodating careers and egos of others. There are numerous examples of "negative" or destructive changes.

Rules and Tactics for the "Change-Oriented"

Rule No. 1: Integrity, Wisdom, Selflessness

A new vision cannot be successfully implemented unless the individual (you) motivating others to change is perceived to have the highest of values; e.g., integrity, sensitivity, selflessness, striving for the good of the organization: Creative organizational evolution will not occur unless your constituency perceives you to be sincere, honest, fair; one who understands the university, scholarship and, as well, the role of other core constituents.[1] The one absolute I can offer is this: if the perception exists that you do not have integrity, wisdom, or selflessness, or if this issue is effectively presented or manipulated in a negative way by an opposing constituency, you will lose your influence and ability to manage change in the organization. There are presidents, for example, who are president in title only. This is fine as long as the organizational goal does not entail implementation of a new vision. Within the context of this first rule, I would offer a word about your personal relationships and the importance of managing external constituencies.

Personal Relationships

Protect those individuals and allies who risk their professional standing and administrative careers for you. Many good efforts flounder because senior executives or faculty (who desire institutional transition and convince others to implement it) do not support these individuals when conflict emerges. If those who articulated change (on your behalf) are abandoned, few will trust you again. Professional administrators and colleagues are a pretty smart lot. They can make or break you! You must guard those individuals (and honor formal lines of authority; e.g., those who report to them). Reward the constituents who give you their support. However, while engaging in this action be very wary of your "open door" policy! Few messengers are without a personal agenda. Reward those who are. Never expel the messenger though! Utilize their services wisely. Cultivate informal channels of communication without undermining the reporting or political relationships of others. Moderate your "reaction" to information gained through informal networks. If those around you feel you overreact to "negative" information, they will funnel only "good" news and, like most leaders who encourage or tolerate only good news, your authority and influence will eventually fracture and vanish, probably while you are busily engaged in what you consider important (and others consider trivial); e.g. designing the alumni magazine or visiting facilities off-site.

External Constituencies

As I noted earlier, colleges and universities usually have strong external constituents who apply pressure to the decision-making process. The wise strategist uses support from these external constituencies to influence the internal process. In building coalitions, it is useful to associate with outside groups as well as inside groups, particularly because major decision makers themselves are often tied to outside groups. Insiders, with their limited view of the outsiders' role, naively overlook the political strategy of cultivating external allies. Legislators, trustees, parents, alumni, and foundations can help change universities. The potential power of external constituencies must never be neglected.

Rule No. 2: Build a Team

You will need one. In this respect do not underestimate the value of loyalty as well as competency. New appointments will be important ones, particularly senior nonacademic appointments. Nonacademic administrators are crucial, because without them you cannot maintain your influence and run the institution effectively. Some academic types do not understand this. However, loss of confidence in your regime will come when your primary constituents (faculty, trustees, students, the public, academic administrators) feel they (a) cannot trust university data; (b) think that student services or student-related issues are out of control; (c) perceive that a crisis (usually fiscal) exists on campus with personnel, auxiliary services, etc.; (d) believe "funding" or "political" problems exist; (e) suspect that some senior advisors are out of control or incompetent.

Your agenda cannot be accomplished in the academic division alone. Good politicians know that much of their job is not influencing decisions as much as it is building a political base for influencing decisions. This means that a dedicated cadre of change agents must be formed, a committed group that exchanges ideas and reinforces each other's efforts. In addition, a strong change group needs equally strong links to those in viable political coalitions. In this respect, I should discuss the mechanics of building a team. This may entail making new appointments. Here is where many inexperienced administrators and faculty make fatal mistakes!

I advise that you break out of traditional recruitment and appointment processes. Be wary of a search committee's propensity to find the right people. Search committees often recommend those who are acceptable to the group (or those who may offend the fewest)! Assembling a team requires you to resist strong pressures to appoint "traditional" individuals. Traditionalists are not often comfortable with nor do they usually understand how to manage "change" or "conflict." Go outside of the traditional realm. The appointment of excellent and supportive academic administrators will be a task to which you should devote attention. Do not assume a search committee will simply do what you ask. Check the details of "who" serves on the committee, the charge of the committee, read the position description before the position is advertised. I would offer a word here about the concept of accountability.

Accountability

You must demand it. Unless there are consequences for "behavior" you cannot realize your objectives. Many in academe are not held accountable because much of what we do is not readily measurable (so it is difficult to determine success or failure!). People who care more about popularity than being strong managers (or effectuating change) do not hold others accountable. (I have rarely witnessed a situation where a well-liked individual could (a) remain on excellent terms with faculty and staff and (b) initiate change in the school, division or college.) Nor can you succeed with administrators who are vindictive, territorial, jealous, too lax (classic symptoms of "powerlessness"), or those who sanction inappropriate behavior, for example, when the "wrong" people are promoted. Unfortunately, many in academe often do a less than stellar job of evaluating managerial and academic effectiveness. It is not realistic to believe that senior faculty or administrators can be held accountable in an environment where there is little or no agreement on performance objectives. Appoint self-motivated people, set goals, ask for benchmark measures of success, demand more than "acquiescence."

In summary, your senior team must be provided with a positive emotional atmosphere: reward and encourage them in visible and immediate ways, express confidence, let them do their jobs, promote independence, initiative, and responsibility.

Rule No. 3: Concentrate Your Efforts

A basic mistake made by people interested in change is that they frequently squander their efforts by chasing too many rainbows. An effective political change agent, realizing that change is really difficult, concentrates efforts on only the important issues. Remember that in academe, most people do not care about all the issues. If you care enough to concentrate, you have enormous power to be effective. The frustration caused by the resistance offered by an immovable system is usually the result of scattered and dispersed efforts. Remember, if "fluid participation" is the rule, then most people wander in and out of the issue. If you stick with one or two critical issues, you are more likely to be effective. Make a list of priorities. Select the top three or four. Force yourself to ask the following questions in regard to these priorities:

- Who else is or will be influential as you endeavor to accomplish this priority?
- Whose cooperation and support will be needed?
- Whose opposition could delay or derail this action?
- In regard to those whose support is necessary or those who will oppose you, analyze:

    What are the sources of their influence and authority?

    Who will be more influential in the decision-making process?

    Under what circumstances will (the) opposition coalesce?

    Who will be affected by what you are trying to accomplish; e.g., effect on "their" power or status?

- Ask which strategies and tactics will be the most appropriate given faculty and administrative support (or opposition) for the idea or action.
- Ask who will determine success or failure.

In this context, may I offer advice on the notion of timing?

Timing

You must get a core constituency to (a) agree upon priority objectives early in the game and (b) agree on measurable criteria for success. Following this you should ensure that (someone) evaluates the effectiveness of actions against these measures. The sooner the process starts, the better. Academic organizations are tolerant of new presidents for short periods of time. They are, in a real sense, skeptical of anyone in a position of authority. The honeymoon will end quickly. Afterwards, a bureaucracy (and your opponents) can destroy creativity. Do not, however, take on the whole community at once! Choose your priorities (your allies and your adversaries) carefully.

Remember also, after one year, your predecessor's problems (largely through "nonaction") become your problems. Be a visionary and a missionary to constituents who object to your goals or who have power to block new initiatives. Understand where those constituencies derive their status and support.

Rule No. 4: Know When to Engage Conflict

To concentrate is to choose a few issues, and a tactical genius knows which ones to choose. Most of the time, it makes sense to support issues when you know you can be effective. If it is obvious that you will lose, wait. Remember, with the "issue carousel," the situation will probably return, allowing you time to master your resources for the next battle. There are exceptions to the "fight to win" rule. Sometimes it is wise to engage confrontation because the moral issue is great, or because it is possible to make future martyrs. We do not always fight to win today; sometimes we fight today so that we can win tomorrow. Most of the time, however, the rule is to choose issues with high payoff.

The sophisticated and astute observer can usually tell the difference between who is effective and who is not. A word here about conflict in the academic environment. Don't avoid it, manage it. Many presidents and senior executives fail to grasp this. Redirecting the priorities, possibilities and, if you will, the mission of a university requires organizational tension. Very simply put, you must convince your core constituencies to support (and buy into) new ways of conceiving and evaluating work and, perhaps, new educational or process outcomes, e.g., new relationships with unions or other core constituencies. This will require those who are "secure" with the current mission or comfortable with present priorities and outcomes, to change. Change can evolve peacefully to be sure. However, when it is necessary to "redirect" institutional priorities, change is more often associated with conflict primarily because folks have a vested interest in the way work is accomplished now.

Remember that your institution is a place wedded to its "traditions." This cultural trait will manifest itself, cloaked in the argument that "we never did it that way here" or, those who oppose you will hear in your words, "he (or she) doesn't value my (our) work." Managing this kind of conflict successfully requires that you:

- Encourage opposing constituencies to choose a course of action early in the game.
- Offer real alternatives for those who oppose you.
- Advance the notion of "mutual interests" rather than focusing on the positions of those who disagree.
- Act decisively, act soon, act in a determined manner.
- If you feel senior administrators will not be supportive, find another place for them soon. You are probably not going to win them over and you will not succeed as long as they hold their positions.
- Have a strategic plan, stay to it. Pay attention to detail. Develop measurable criteria for success. Remember that most academic folks are trained to make a critical analysis but are not trained to implement decisions. People need guidance and supervision.
- You must love the academic soul. But remember, faculty, as a group, will complain. Offer them some cheese with their whine.
- Find the right incentives. Do not assume others will follow you simply because you are right. People will embrace your vision when your ideas provide them with (intrinsic/extrinsic) rewards.
- How you go about managing conflicting interests and personalities may be almost as important as what you actually do. Be very humane and civil.
- Once a constituency (or an individual) is neutralized or won over, allow for face saving, but do not be obsequious to those who opposed you.
- Declare your program a success; find small successes to celebrate along the way.
- Utilize (rely) on external pressures to encourage internal change. Redirect and manage those pressures. Force convergence of internal and external policy.
- Be wary of showing weakness. Do not readily admit you do not know something. Few are sanguine about following a person who has never "been there" before.
- Colleges and universities are organizations with low tolerance for conflict. Use this resource wisely.

Rule No. 5: Learn the History

Every issue has roots deep in the past. The issue carousel has trotted it past several times before. Consequently, the wise tactician searches for the historical bases of an issue. When was it around before? Who took what position? Who won? Who lost? Knowing the history can reveal what coalitions fight together and what tactics prove useful—information that helps in planning strategy. Under most circumstances, the person who is historically naive about the issue is not effective.

A word here about two issues related to "history." The first concerns the use of data and research and the second involves policy convergence.

Data/Research

Many ideas go awry because the data and/or research underpinning these issues can be criticized or, worse, is faulty. Just as there is nothing so good as good theory, there is no substitute for well-conceived and adequately presented institutional research. Be sure your opinions and ideas are based on solid assumptions and that they are defensible. Once anyone demolishes the basis of your (informational or research) objectives, you will lose your influence. In the academic milieu, if people cannot trust your data, they will not trust you.

Policy Convergence

Unless institutional policies and procedures reflect new visions and priorities, you cannot succeed. Policies and procedures form the basis upon which others act and, through implementation of policy, how others are evaluated. Once you articulate a new direction, institutional policies must conform to them. A "vision" cannot overcome policy which in itself may serve as a disincentive. Take the example of "fiscal prudence." A seemingly harmless policy that requires returning unused funds to a central account, may undermine this idea. Policies such as these sometimes work as an incentive for an administrator or faculty member to spend funds unwisely or "hide" accounts in an effort to circumvent the policy. (Of course, those who hide moneys will do so for the best of academic reasons!)

The policy criteria upon which people are evaluated will determine, to a large extent, their behavior and priorities. For example, you must endeavor to modify standards for promotion and tenure if you want to redirect the academic priorities of faculty. (No mean feat!) Making even small changes in this realm will require agreement and assistance of deans and department chairpersons. Redirection will come, ultimately, only if new criteria are related to outcomes that the "academic establishment" can support. In this respect, new priorities can be engineered if they are not seen as "imposed" but come as a product of mutual agreement. I am not suggesting this be done in all disciplines, but it must be attempted for some, as I understood your goals.

Rule No. 6: Strategic Planning

Your goals cannot be realized without a strategic plan. Everyone knows this. However, what many do not do is demand answers to the "right questions" in the plan. Review key priorities and concomitant strategic planning issues with your senior team. Next, force the team to address the following:

- Have you defined short-term and long-term objectives?
- Is a strategy adequately developed?

    Identify the key assumptions underlying your strategy. What evidence are you relying on to ensure assumptions are valid?

    Is the action plan feasible given the constraints and opportunities inherent in the situation?

    Is the action plan realistic given your sources of power?

- Has the impact of the action plan been assessed? (Is the plan ethical, will it benefit the institution?)

    Are you cognizant of trade-offs, or who will be directly and indirectly affected by your plan?

    Were the risks of the plan analyzed?

- Were all contingencies planned for?
- Are mechanisms in place to ensure the plan is periodically evaluated?

    Can the plan be modified?

- Have you assessed the timing and sequence of decisions?

    Differentiate between urgent and less important matters.

    Does the plan contain incremental steps?

    Do early steps preclude future alternatives?

- Will you be able to reflect on and communicate successes or failures with overarching plan objectives?

I have known of administrators who manage the development of elaborate plans (or "mission" statements) but fail to understand that unless these statements revolutionize the nature in which work is accomplished or the actual behavior of individuals responsible for merging fiscal and academic priorities, these documents will remain abstract concepts. Implementing a strategic plan requires closure on the following issues and actions (basic, yet essential):

- Assuming the identification of participants, accountability matters, institutional goals and objectives, and the timing and sequence of implementation;

    How will new initiatives or programs be introduced in different functional units?

    How will you approach the management of organizational resistance?

    What resources will be required?

    Who will coordinate the plan?

    How will everyone know when the plan becomes an integral part of the values and mission of the organization?

    What steps must be taken in each organizational unit to reflect integration in the way decisions are made, relationships are maintained, and services are provided?

    How will the organization (you) respond to any decrease in the will to sustain implementation of the plan? What is the appropriate response to loss of motivation and support? What is the minimum support needed in order to proceed?

- Assuming the plan will enhance the function, efficiency, and productivity of others;

    What actions need to be taken to inform the organization of the plan and its purpose?

    What will be the actual impact of the plan on people, functions, etc.? How will you know when everyone has possessed requisite knowledge and skills?

    How will the consequences of the plan be identified and assessed?

    What behavioral and process changes are expected of employees?

- Assuming the plan will result in development of new standards of productivity, compensation, performance, or evaluation (to reflect desired changes or mitigate unacceptable actions or reactions);

    How will the organization demonstrate the value of the plan?

    Will it connect to performance and productivity?

    At what point in the process are individuals and units expected to adopt new behaviors?

    What behaviors and achievements should be acknowledged and rewarded?

How will formal and informal rewards be managed? Care should be taken to prevent the process of acknowledging and rewarding from being misinterpreted by others in the organization. (Always one of the challenges posed by compensation systems that purport to reward—competence and merit.)

- Assuming the plan will measure the quality and quantity of change;

What information is needed? How will this information be acquired to determine the quality of changes?

How will "change" be reviewed and quantified to insure continual movement toward desired goals?

What are the agreed upon elements, functions, and services considered most important to the success of the plan? How will they be measured?

Will it be known that benchmarks have been met?

Will alternate strategies or assessments of benchmarks be developed?

As you can see, simply writing a plan is only a small first step. Small wonder then that most plans are eventually relegated to a store room in the library.

Rule No. 7: Use Committees Effectively

Most major decisions in academic organizations are made by committees of experts who combine their specialized knowledge to solve organizational problems. Therefore, organizational politics often center around committee politics. Having influence on a committee is frequently equal to having influence over the decision.

How can a committee be used to effect organizational change? First, appoint the right people to the right committee or get appointed by simply asking for an appointment from an incumbent official. If the organization has a "committee on committees," it is wise either to know someone on it or to be on it yourself. Such rule-making appointive committees wield power in all academic organizations, and this can be exploited to the best advantage. In addition, after acquiring membership, it is critical simply to *be there*. Remember, fluid participation is a characteristic of colleges and universities. The first tactic, then, is to get on the committee, be there with great regularity, stick it out even when others drop off.

The second tactic of committee success is to do your homework. Expertise is vital in a professional organization. If you observe the earlier rule of concentrating your efforts, you have more time to accumulate the knowledge that will put you ahead of others. In addition, it is always useful to make part of your homework the job of being secretary or chairperson of a group. The chairperson can set the agenda and often has the power to call committee meetings, while the secretary controls the memory of the committee. Committees are blessed with short memories, because most members do not recall or care what is recorded in the minutes. Controlling the memory of a committee means reiterating the issues that you consider important, a definite advantage for political bargaining. Doing your homework—whether it is gathering knowledge, learning the history, being the chairperson, or doing the secretarial chores—puts you in a strategically advantageous position.

A third tactical procedure in effective committee management is to keep ideas flowing. Because decision issues, like garbage dumps, attract various irrelevant material, they can be used to the change agent's advantage. Dump new ideas into the discussion and then compromise readily on the unimportant issues. Helping to load the garbage can leaves plenty to bargain over when the deadlines are close and allows you the chance to insist stubbornly about retaining key issues.

A fourth tactical consideration concerns structuring the decision-making process. Decisions do not, in themselves, result in action. More often, we spend a negligible amount of time making a decision and a great deal of time (sometimes a lifetime) managing the consequences of our decisions! Decisions are effectuated through people. It is a well-known premise that more efficient and concrete outcomes of the decision-making process will result if the human processes used to implement decisions are structured; e.g., committees are appointed, tasks are defined, priorities are set, deadlines are met, and, perhaps most importantly, as decisions are prioritized and legitimized, core constituencies (who are represented on committees) are given a vested interest in decisional outcomes. Task forces, committees, group consultation, all are essential components of governance in higher education. I advocate a decision-making structure that blends ad hoc and permanent constituent members, legitimized through formal appointment. However, unless the consultative process is directed with a firm hand, endless debate may result.

A formalized approach permits administrators to effectuate decisions, when they lack the "status" of president. Used correctly it precludes the "end run" and it mandates that everyone in the room, after discussion, "agree." As decisions are legitimized by sources (groups) holding increased status, it becomes difficult for your opponents to undermine, ridicule, or sabotage (through inaction) decisions arrived at using this model. The structure is especially effective when implementation, discussion, review, and analysis must cross jurisdictional divisions. It will permit input from the best minds in the organization. Too often do we preclude ourselves from obtaining the benefit of the brightest and most intelligent in the organization because (a) there is no formal mechanism to accommodate their views in decision-making processes and (b) academic and administrative leaders rarely reach out beyond their division or school (or their trusted friends) when studying a critical issue. It remains your job to insure that the best opinions, even those voiced by organizational pariahs, are resourced. This normally does not occur in informal consultative systems or when institutional concerns cross organizational lines of authority.

Rule No. 8: Use the Formal System

Colleges and universities, like other bureaucracies, have complex formal systems to carry out their activities. Often naive change agents are not aware that they can achieve a desired outcome simply by asking the appropriate official for it. This requires savvy. It requires experience within the organization. It requires knowing where the levers are, and which ones to push.

Inexperienced change agents may fail to realize that most organization officials are eager to please. Success is difficult to judge in most professional organizations because the tasks are too ambiguous to be assessed. As a consequence, most officials depend upon "social validation" for judgments of success. That is, they are successful if people are pleased and think they have done a good job. The ambiguity of the task, the lack of hard evaluation criteria, and the psychological need of most faculty and administrators for approval gives tremendous advantage to partisans who want to get something done. Do not forget a basic idea: ask for what you want and you will be surprised how many times you get it.

Rule No. 9: Follow Through to Push the Decision Flow

I have said that the concept of "decision making" is a delusion. Decisions are not really made; instead, they come unstuck, are reversed, get unmade during the execution, or lose their impact as powerful political groups fight them. In real life, decisions go round and round in circles, and the best one can hope for in the political battle is a temporary win.

As a consequence, the effective individual knows that he must follow important decisions even after they have supposedly been made. What do most people do after the committee has reached its decision? They evaporate. The person who traces the decision flow on through to execution and who fights when issues are distorted is the person who really has power. The truly dedicated partisan who wants to implement change is a tenacious watchdog, monitoring the steps of the decision and calling public attention to lapses in implementation.

Permit a final word on tactics associated with this rule. Set deadlines in the process of making decisions. Delay is the enemy of change; deadlines are flags that help call attention to stalling. Second, give ideas "sheltered starts." If placed back into the regular routine of the organization, a new change will be smothered by powerful old routines. As a consequence, the shrewd individual builds a shelter around the change in its infancy. This often means giving the program or idea a home under the wing of a strong, hospitable executive or faculty member in the college. Only later, after the new idea has established roots, should it be placed into the regular structure of the organization.

Several follow-through techniques involve managing people. It is always useful to place your allies in the vanguard of those responsible for executing the decision. If allies embodying your ideas are influential, the change is more likely to succeed. Reward systems are also very important. Do you want things to change? Then reward people whose behavior helps promote the change. Rewards can be straightforward in the form of money, or they can take the equally valuable form of prestige, status, and public acclaim.

Rule No. 10: Glance Backward

Let us assume you have followed my advice and have been effective. The last admonition is the hardest to make: be skeptical about your own accomplishments. Few good changes have eternal lives. A deep ego-investment can be made in a project that does not work. In this sense, following through means evaluating, judging, and deciding whether performance lives up to expectations. If it does not, you must start again. Evaluating your own idea as objectively as possible and listening carefully to the evaluations of others are valuable and necessary skills for true change agents.

Any organization's vitality and creativity depend heavily on the constant influx of new ideas and people. Even the new idea that you worked so hard to establish will, in time, be dull and old. The conservatives of the present area championed ideas that, at one time, were considered radical. The last step, then, is the most ruthless of all: kill your own project when it has outlived its usefulness. This is where most fail. After building their investments they fight like Phoenicians to hang on to ideas long since grown old. Cycles must continue, and the change agent must once more struggle to infuse creativity and excitement into the academic organization.

A Final Word to Academic Leaders

A final word to would-be leaders. There are many books that concern themselves with leadership and mountains of articles. Much of what is written is valuable but it is written, by and large, by those who study the topic. As you are no doubt aware, there is a big difference. My concept of leadership is simple and direct—leaders identify an issue that is perceived by a larger community as an important dilemma or a critical problem. The true leader offers (and implements) a solution. For example, Moses conceived of freedom and a vision of the promised land—and led a group of former slaves through the desert. (And even Moses was allowed only to see Israel, never to set foot there!) Leaders are those who identify and articulate a vision and successfully manage a solution. Implementation demands a "buy-in" and sacrifice from key constituents/community members.

It is my hope you will find a few valuable ideas hidden within my rhetoric. Were it your pleasure, I would be honored to follow up and discuss your reactions to the enclosed. I am, at the moment, planting tomatoes in my garden and would welcome a return to the challenges of advising esteemed individuals such as yourself.

Note

1. In the case of nontraditional executives or presidents you will be judged on a different (higher) standard than would a more "traditional" person.

Bibliography

Adams, H. (1976). *The academic tribes.* New York: Liveright.

Alinsky, S. (1969). *Reveille for radicals.* New York: Random House.

Argyris, C. (1957). *Personality and organization: The conflict between system and the individual.* New York: Harper & Row.

Baker, W. E. (1994). *Networking smart: How to build relationships for personal and organizational success.* New York: McGraw Hill.

Barry, J. M. (1989). *The ambition and the power: The fall of Jim Wright: A true story of Washington.* New York: Viking.

Baldridge, J. V. (1971). *Academic governance in the university.* Berkeley, CA: McCutchan.

Baldridge, J. V. (1983). Rules for a Machiavellian change agent: Transforming the entrenched organization. In J. V. Baldridge & T. Deal (Eds.), *Managing change in educational organizations.* Berkeley, CA: McCutchan.

Bazerman, M. H., & Lewicki, R. J. (1983). *Negotiating in organizations.* Beverly Hills, CA: Sage.

Ben-David, J. (1972). *American higher education.* New York: McGraw-Hill.

Bennis, W. G., & Nanus, B. (1985). *Leaders: The strategies for taking charge.* New York: Harper and Row.

Bennis, W. G. (1989). *Why leaders can't lead: The unconscious conspiracy continues.* San Francisco: Jossey-Bass.

Bergquist, W. H. (1992). *The four cultures of the academy.* San Francisco: Jossey-Bass.

Bergquist, W. H., & Armstrong, J. L. (1986). *Planning effectively for educational quality: An outcomes-based approach for colleges committed to excellence.* San Francisco: Jossey-Bass.

Birnbaum, R. (1988). *How colleges work: The cybernetics of academic organization and leadership.* San Francisco: Jossey-Bass.

Blake, R., Mouton, J. S., & Williams, M. S. (1981). *The academic administrator grid.* San Francisco: Jossey-Bass.

Blau, P. M. (1964). *Exchange and power in social life.* New York: John Wiley & Sons.

Bolman, L. G., & Deal, T. E. (1991). *Reframing organizations: Artistry, choice, and leadership.* San Francisco: Jossey-Bass.

Brubacher, J. S., & Rudy, W. (1958). *Higher education in transition.* New York: Harper Collins.

Caro, R. A. (1974). *The power broker: Robert Moses and the fall of New York.* New York: Alfred A. Knopf.

Caro, R. A. (1982). *The years of Lyndon Johnson: The path to power.* New York: Alfred A. Knopf.

Charan, R. (1991, September-October). How networks reshape organizations for results. *Harvard Business Review,* 104–115.

Cohen, A. R., & Bradford, D. L. (1990). *Influence without authority.* New York: John Wiley and Sons.

Conger, J. A. (1989). Leadership: The art of empowering others. *Academy of Management Executive,* 45–53.

Davis-Blake, A., Pfeffer, J., & Julius, D. J. (1995, January). The effect of affirmative action officer salary on changes in managerial diversity: Efficiency wages or power. *Industrial Relations, 34*(1), 73–95.

Deal, T. E., & Kennedy, A. A. (1982). *Corporate cultures: The rites and rituals of corporate life.* Reading, MA: Addison-Wesley.

Drucker, P. F. (1988, January-February). The coming of the new organization. *Harvard Business Review,* 45–53.

Fulbright, J. W. (1966). *The arrogance of power.* New York: Vintage Books.

Gabarro, J. J. (1986). The development of working relationships. In J. Lorsch (Ed.), *Handbook of organizational behavior* (pp. 172–189). Englewood Cliffs, NJ: Prentice Hall.

Gabarro, J. J. (1987). *The dynamics of taking charge.* Boston: Harvard Business School Press.

Gabarro, J. J., & Kotter, J. P. (1980, January-February). Managing your boss. *Harvard Business Review,* 92–100.

Gillam, R. (1971). *Power in postwar America: Interdisciplinary perspectives on a historical problem.* Boston: Little, Brown and Company.

Halberstam, D. (1979). *The powers that be.* New York: Alfred A. Knopf.

Heifetz, R. A. (1994). *Leadership without easy answers.* Cambridge, MA: The Belknap Press of Harvard University Press.

Hill, L. (1992). *Becoming a manager: Mastery of a new identity.* Boston: Harvard Business School Press.

Hirschhorn, L., & Gilmore, T. (1992, May-June). The new boundaries of the boundaryless company. *Harvard Business Review,* 108–115.

Jencks, C., & Riesman, D. (1968). *The academic revolution.* Chicago: University of Chicago Press.

Julius, D. J. (1995). *Managing the industrial labor relations process in higher education.* Washington, DC: College and University Personnel Association.

Julius, D. J. (1998, Spring). Applying Machiavellian principles to university management. *University Manager, 6*(2), 33–34.

Kanter, R. M. (1977). *Men and women of the corporation.* New York: Basic Books.

Kanter, R. M. (1979, July-August). Power failure in management circuits. *Harvard Business Review,* 65–75.

Kanter, R. M. (1983). *The change masters: Innovation for productivity in the American corporation.* New York: Simon and Schuster.

Kanter, R. M. (1989, November-December). The new managerial work. *Harvard Business Review,* 85–92.

Kaplan, R. E. (1994, Spring). Trade routes: The manager's network of relationships. *Organizational Dynamics,* 37–52.

Katz, R. L. (1974, September-October). Skills of an effective administrator. *Harvard Business Review,* 90–102.

Kemerer, F. R., & Baldridge, J. V. (1975). *Unions on campus.* San Francisco: Jossey-Bass.

Kerr, C. (1963). *The uses of the university.* Cambridge, MA: Harvard University Press.

Keys, B., & Case, T. (1990). How to become an influential manager. *Academy of Management Executive, 4,* 38–49.

Kotter, J. P. (1977, July-August). Power, dependence, and effective management. *Harvard Business Review,* 125–136.

Kotter, J. P. (1982). *The general managers.* New York: Free Press.

Kotter, J. P. (1985). *Power and influence: Beyond formal authority.* New York: Free Press.

Kotter, J. P. (1988). *The leadership factor.* New York: Free Press.

Krackhardt, D., & Hanson, J. R. (1993, July-August). Informal networks: The company behind the chart. *Harvard Business Review,* 104–111.

Lawler, E. E., III. (1986). *High-involvement management: Participative strategies for improving organizational performance.* San Francisco: Jossey-Bass.

Lawler, E. E., III. (1992). *The ultimate advantage: Creating the high-involvement organization.* San Francisco: Jossey-Bass.

Lax, D. A., & Sebenius, J. K. (1986). *The manager as negotiator: Bargaining for cooperation and competitive gain.* New York: Free Press.

Lenski, G. E. (1966). *Power and privilege: A theory of social stratification.* New York: McGraw-Hill.

Lewicki, R. J., & Litterer, J. A. (1985). *Negotiation.* Boston: Irwin.

Luthans, F. (1988, May). Successful versus effective real managers. *Academy of Management Executive,* 127–132.

Luthans, F., Hogdetts, R.M., & Rosenkrantz, S. A. (1988). *Real managers.* Cambridge, MA: Ballinger.

Maccoby, M. (1981). *The leader: A new face for American management.* New York: Simon and Schuster.

Manz, C. C., & Sims, H. P. (1989). *Superleadership: Leading others to lead themselves.* Englewood Cliffs, NJ: Prentice Hall.

McCall, M., Lombardo, M., & Morrison, A. (1988). *The lessons of experience.* Lexington, MA: Lexington Books.

Mills, C. W. (1959). *The power elite.* New York: Oxford University Press.

Mintzberg, H. (1973). *The nature of managerial work.* New York: Harper & Row.

Mintzberg, H. (1975, July-August). The manager's job: Folklore and fact. *Harvard Business Review,* 49–71.

Mintzberg, H. (1983). *Power in and around organizations.* Englewood Cliffs, NJ: Prentice Hall.

Pfeffer, J. (1981). *Power in organizations.* Marshfield, MA: Pitman Publishing.

Pfeffer, J. (1992). *Managing with power: Politics and influence in organizations.* Boston: Harvard Business School Press.

Pfeffer, J. (1994). *Competitive advantage through people.* Boston: Harvard Business School Press.

Pfeffer, J., & Davis-Blake, A. (1987). Understanding organizational wage structures: A resource dependence approach. *Academy of Management Journal, 30,* 437–455.

Pfeffer, J., & Konrad, A. (1991). The effects of individual power on earnings. *Work and Occupations.*

Pfeffer, J., & Moore, W. L. (1980). Average tenure of academic department heads: The effects of paradigm, size, and departmental demography. *Administrative Science Quarterly, 25,* 387–406.

Pfeffer, J., & Moore, W. L. (1980). Power in university budgeting: A replication and extension. *Administrative Science Quarterly, 25,* 637–653.

Pfeffer, J., & Salancik, G. R. (1974). Organizational decision making as a political process: The case of a university budget. *Administrative Science Quarterly, 19,* 135–151.

Pfeffer, J., & Salancik, G. R. (1977). Administrator effectiveness: The effects of advocacy and information on resource allocations. *Human Relations, 30,* 641–656.

Pfeffer, J., & Salancik, G. R. (1978). *The external control of organizations: A resource dependence perspective.* New York: Harper and Row.

Posner, B. Z., & Kouzes, J. R. (1993). *Credibility: How leaders gain and lose it, why people demand it.* San Francisco: Jossey Bass.

Raymond, J. (1964). *Power at the Pentagon.* New York: Harper & Row.

Reynolds, M. O. (1984). *Power and privilege: Labor unions in America.* New York: Universe Books.

Russell, B. (1938). *Power: A new social analysis.* New York: W. W. Norton & Company.

Sayles, L. R. (1980). *Managerial behavior: Administration in complex organizations.* Huntington, NY: Robert E. Krieger.

Schien, E. J. (1981, Winter). Improving face-to-face relationships. *Sloan Management Review,* 43–52.

Smith, H. (1988). *The power game: How Washington works.* New York: Random House.

Snow, C. C., Miles, R. E., & Coleman, J. J., Jr. (1992, Winter). Managing 21st-century network organizations. *Organizational Dynamics,* 5–20.

Summerfield, H. L. (1974). *Power and process: The formulation and limits of federal educational policy.* Berkeley, CA: McCutchan.

Tuchman, B. W. (1984). *The march of folly: From Troy to Vietnam.* New York: Alfred A. Knopf.

Ury, W. (1993). *Getting past no: Negotiating your way from confrontation to cooperation.* New York: Bantam Books.

Walton, R. E. (1985, March-April). From control to commitment in the workplace. *Harvard Business Review,* 76–84.

Whetten, D. A., & Cameron, K. S. (1993). *Developing Management Skills: Gaining power and influence.* New York: Harper Collins College.

Zaleznik, A. (1970, May-June). Power and politics in organizational life. *Harvard Business Review,* 47–48.

AN ORGANIZATIONAL LEARNING FRAMEWORK: FROM INTUITION TO INSTITUTION

MARY M. CROSSAN, HENRY W. LANE, AND RODERICK E. WHITE
RICHARD IVEY SCHOOL OF BUSINESS

Although interest in organizational learning has grown dramatically in recent years, a general theory of organizational learning has remained elusive. We identify renewal of the overall enterprise as the underlying phenomenon of interest and organizational learning as a principal means to this end. With this perspective we develop a framework for the process of organizational learning, presenting organizational learning as four processes—intuiting, interpreting, integrating, and institutionalizing—linking the individual, group, and organizational levels.

Organizational learning has existed in our lexicon at least since Cangelosi and Dill (1965) discussed the topic over 30 years ago. Lately, its popularity has grown dramatically (Crossan & Guatto, 1996), yet little convergence or consensus on what is meant by the term, or its basic nature, has emerged (Huber, 1991; Kim, 1993).

In large part, convergence has not occurred because different researchers have applied the concept of organizational learning, or at least the terminology, to different domains. For example, Huber (1991) takes an information-processing perspective of organizational learning, whereas Nonaka and Takeuchi (1995) are concerned with product innovation, and March and Olsen (1975) are interested in exploring how the cognitive limitations of managers affect learning. These works share some common threads, but the domains differ significantly. They concern different phenomena: information processing, product innovation, or bounded rationality. Although the phenomenological domains of various researchers do sometimes overlap, the differences in domains do much to explain the lack of convergence among organizational learning frameworks.

In this article we identify strategic renewal as the underlying phenomenon of interest. Renewal harmonizes continuity and change at the level of the enterprise (Hurst, 1995; Hurst, Rush, & White, 1989). Organizational learning can be conceived of as a principal means of achieving the strategic renewal of an enterprise. As we argue in this article, strategic renewal places additional demands on a theory of organizational learning. Renewal requires that organizations explore and learn new ways while concurrently exploiting what they have already learned (March, 1991). In contrast, learning applied to the domain of new product development, for example, tends to focus on the exploration side of the exploration-exploitation tension identified by March. Recognizing and managing the tension between exploration and exploitation are two of the critical challenges of renewal and, hence, become a central requirement in a theory of organizational learning.

For renewal to be strategic it should encompass the entire enterprise—not simply the individual or group—and it should recognize that the organization operates in an open system, rather than having a solely internal focus (Duncan & Weiss, 1979). Although theorists have recognized the strategic importance of organizational learning as a means of providing a sustainable competitive advantage (DeGeus, 1988; Stata, 1989), few organizational learning frameworks have illustrated the tension between exploration and exploitation that is at the heart of strategic renewal (see Table 1).

Here we develop an organizational learning framework to address the phenomenon of renewal. A framework defines the territory and takes us a step closer to a theory. A good framework has several requirements. First, it should identify the phenomenon of interest in this case strategic renewal. Second, the key premises or assumptions underlying the framework need to be stated (Bacharach, 1989). Third, the relationship among the elements of the framework needs to be described (Sutton & Staw, 1995; Weick 1995a, Whetton 1989). As Sutton and Staw state. "Theory is about connections among phenomena, a story about why acts, events, structure and thoughts occur" (1995: 378). Our framework makes high-level connections. Further theory development will expand and deepen these connections and will enable development of testable hypotheses.

Four key premises or assumptions form the underpinnings of this framework and support one central proposition:

Premise 1:   Organizational learning involves a tension between assimilating new learning (exploration) and using what has been learned (exploitation).

Premise 2:   Organizational learning is multilevel: individual, group, and organization.

Premise 3:   The three levels of organizational learning are linked by social and psychological processes: intuiting, interpreting, integrating, and institutionalizing (4I's).

Premise 4:   Cognition affects action (and vice versa).

Proposition: The 4I's are related in feed-forward and feedback processes across the levels.

TABLE 1

Propositions Applied to Established Organizational Learning Frameworks

Source	Strategic Renewal Tension	Multilevel Framework	One Level Affects the Others	Process Linking Levels	Cognition/ Action Link
March & Olsen (1975)	Not considered	No group level	Not considered	Not considered	Yes
Daft & Weick (1984)	Not considered	Not considered	Not considered	Processes described but not a levels perspective	Learning is a change in behavior
Senge (1990)	Not considered	No organizational level	Not considered	Processes focus on individual and group—not a levels-related model	Yes
Huber (1991)	Not considered	Yes	Not considered	Processes within level but no model or processes to link levels	Cognition affects behaviors
March (1991)	Yes	No group level	Not considered	Not considered	Yes
Watkins & Marsick (1993)	Not considered	Yes	Not considered	Six action imperatives of the learning organization	Consistent with Senge's perspective
Nonaka & Takeuchi (1995)	Not considered	Recognized, but not a substantial part of the model	Some discussion of the link between individual and group	Focuses on processes that link individual and group—weak on link between group and organization	Knowledge focus

As stated in Premise 1, organizational learning reveals a tension between exploration and exploitation (March, 1991). March focuses more on the balance rather than the tension, but he recognizes its fundamental role in strategic renewal: "Maintaining an appropriate balance between exploration and exploitation is a primary factor in system survival and prosperity. . . . Both exploration and exploitation are essential for organizations, but they compete for scarce resources" (1991: 71).

This competition for resources creates a tension. As we discuss in subsequent sections, this tension is seen in the feed-forward and feedback processes of learning across the individual, group, and organization levels. Feed forward relates to exploration. It is the transference of learning from individuals and groups through to the learning that becomes embedded—or institutionalized—in the form of systems, structures, strategies, and procedures (Hedberg, 1981; Shrivastava, 1983). Feedback relates to exploitation and to the way in which institutionalized learning affects individuals and groups.

As noted in Premise 2, organizational learning is multilevel. A basic assumption is that insight and innovative ideas occur to individuals—not organizations (Nonaka & Takeuchi, 1995; Simon, 1991). However, knowledge generated by the individual does not come to bear on the organization independently. Ideas are shared, actions taken, and common meaning developed (Argyris & Schon, 1978, 1996; Daft & Weick, 1984; Huber, 1991; Stata, 1989). Complex organizations are more than ad hoc communities or collections of individuals. Relationships become structured, and some of the individual learning and shared understandings developed by groups become institutionalized as organization artifacts (Hedberg, 1981; Shrivastava, 1983). There is a reasonable degree of consensus that a theory of organizational learning needs to consider the individual, group, and organizational levels (Crossan, Lane, White, & Djurfeldt, 1995).

The 4I processes introduced in Premise 3 are described in detail in the next section. Throughout the feed-forward and feedback processes, the interactive relationship between cognition and action (Premise 4) is critical—one cannot be divorced from the other (Neisser, 1976). Understanding guides action, but action also informs understanding (Seely-Brown & Duguid, 1991; Weick, 1979). Organizational learning links cognition and action. This differentiates it from the related fields of knowledge management and intellectual capital. In spite of arguments to the contrary (Nonaka & Takeuchi, 1995), the fields of knowledge management (Conner & Prahalad, 1996; Davenport & Prusak, 1997; Foss, 1996; Grant, 1996; Kogut & Zander, 1992) and intellectual capital (Edvinsson & Malone, 1997; Stewart, 1997) remain largely focused on cognition. However, these fields share common ground with organizational learning in recognizing the importance of knowledge to the success of the enterprise. Quinn suggests that "looking beyond mere product lines to a strategy built around core intellectual or service competencies provides both a rigorously maintainable strategic focus and long-term flexibility" (1992: 216). Research in knowledge management and intellectual capital informs organizational learning, but it does not capture the ongoing cycle of action taking and knowledge acquisition found in learning theories.

There have been several reviews of the organizational learning literature (Fiol & Lyles, 1985; Huber, 1991; Levitt & March, 1988), but scholars have not recognized the importance of understanding organizational learning from the perspective of strategic renewal. As noted in Table 1, few of the well-known organizational learning frameworks (Daft & Weick, 1984; Huber, 1991; March, 1991; March & Olsen, 1975; Nonaka & Takeuchi, 1995; Senge, 1990; Watkins & Marsick, 1993) recognize the tension of strategic renewal. Further, the frameworks vary in the degree they address the other key premises.

In the following section we expand these key premises by describing the 4I processes of organizational learning that link the levels, using the well-known story of Apple Computer to illustrate these processes. We then discuss the dynamic nature of the 4I processes as they relate to the feed-forward and feedback processes of learning. Finally, we present implications for research and management.

The 4I Framework of Organizational Learning

The 4I framework of organizational learning contains four related (sub)processes—intuiting, interpreting, integrating, and institutionalizing—that occur over three levels: individual, group,

TABLE 2

Learning/Renewal in Organizations: Four Processes Through Three Levels

Level	Process	Inputs/Outcomes
Individual	Intuiting	Experiences, Images Metaphors
	Interpreting	Language, Cognitive map Conversation/dialogue
Group	Integrating	Shared understandings, Mutual adjustment Interactive systems
Organization	Institutionalizing	Routines, Diagnostic systems Rules and procedures

and organization. The three learning levels define the structure through which organizational learning takes place. The processes form the glue that binds the structure together; they are, therefore, a key facet of the framework. Intuiting and interpreting occur at the individual level, interpreting and integrating occur at the group level, and integrating and institutionalizing occur at the organizational level (see Table 2). There are a sequence and progression to these processes through the different levels, and while there is some "spillover" from level to level, not every process occurs at every level.

For example, intuition is a uniquely individual process. It may happen within a group or organizational context, but the recognition of a pattern or possibility comes from within an individual. Organizations do not intuit. This is a uniquely human attribute that organizations do not possess. Similarly, organizations do not interpret. Interpreting has to do with refining and developing intuitive insights. The development of language, principally through an interactive conversational process, is a basic interpretive process. The proverbial person on a deserted island could have an intuitive insight and begin to make sense of it through an internal conversational process (i.e., talking to one's self), but the interpretive process is likely to be much richer and more robust if the conversations and interactions are with others. This process spans the individual and group levels, but it does not extend to the organizational level.

When actions take place in concert with other members of a workgroup, the interpreting process quite naturally blends into the integrating process. Integrating entails the development of shared understanding and the taking of coordinated action by members of a workgroup. Actions that are deemed to be effective will be repeated. Initially, the workgroup informally makes this judgment about what actions should be replicated. Eventually, the workgroup may establish formal rules and procedures, and routines become embedded. The process of institutionalizing occurs.

The process of institutionalizing is an organization-level phenomenon. Organizations, like other social institutions, are socially constructed (Berger & Luckmann, 1966). The routines and rules that make up an enduring organization exist independently of any one individual (although individuals and their actions are affected by these rules and routines).

The 4I's Defined and Developed

We define the learning processes as follows: *Intuiting* is the preconscious recognition of the pattern and/or possibilities inherent in a personal stream of experience (Weick, 1995b: 25). This process can affect the intuitive individual's actions, but it only affects others when they attempt to (inter)act with that individual. *Interpreting* is the explaining, through words and/or actions, of an insight or idea to one's self and to others. This process goes from the preverbal to the verbal, resulting in the development of language. *Integrating* is the process of developing shared understanding among individuals and of taking coordinated action through mutual adjustment. Dialogue and joint action are crucial to the development of shared understanding. This process will initially be ad hoc and informal, but if the coordinated action taking is recurring and significant, it will be institutionalized. *Institutionalizing* is the process of ensuring that routinized actions occur. Tasks are defined, actions specified, and organizational mechanisms put in place to ensure that certain actions occur. Institutionalizing is the process of embedding learning that has occurred by individuals and groups into the organization, and it includes systems, structures, procedures, and strategy.

The four learning processes operate over the three levels. Because the processes naturally flow from one into another, it is difficult to define precisely where one ends and the next begins. Quite clearly, intuiting occurs at the individual level and institutionalizing at the organizational level; however, interpreting bridges the individual and group levels, while integrating links the group and organizational levels. Insights, the seeds of adaptiveness and exploration, begin with the individual but, if "successful," eventually become embedded in the formal organization.

We describe the framework in a sequential way, although there are necessarily many feedback loops among the levels, given the recursive nature of the phenomenon (as we discuss in subsequent sections). In the following discussion we develop each of the 4I learning processes in greater conceptual detail.

Intuiting

Scholars often assume that learning, whether it be at the individual, group, or organization level, is a conscious, analytical process. However, Underwood (1982) suggests that the links between experience, knowledge, and consciousness are more complex than generally assumed. The subconscious is critical to understanding how people come to discern and comprehend something new, for which there was no prior explanation. A theory of learning needs to be able to address how this occurs. Accordingly, the process of intuiting—a largely subconscious process—is an important part of the framework presented here.

At its most basic level, individual learning involves perceiving similarities and differences—patterns and possibilities. Although there are many definitions of intuition, most involve some sort of pattern recognition (Behling & Eckel, 1991). The expert and entrepreneurial views of intuition are most closely aligned with the framework presented here.

The expert view of intuiting is a process of (past) pattern recognition. A highly sophisticated and complex map enables the expert to perceive patterns that novices cannot (Neisser, 1976). Prietula and Simon (1989) suggest that becoming an expert takes 10 years and requires the acquisition of 50,000 chunks of knowledge. Neisser (1976) has used the example of chess masters to explain expert intuition. One must play a lot of chess, reflect on past experiences, and learn about great plays; all this and much more are required to become a grandmaster. But an interesting thing seems to happen on the way to expertise. What once required conscious, deliberate, and explicit thought no longer does. What once would have taken much deliberation and planning becomes the obvious thing to do. What has been learnt becomes tacit knowledge (Polanyi, 1967).

The expert no longer has to think consciously about action. Having been in the same, or similar, situations and recognizing the pattern, the expert knows, almost spontaneously, what to do. Indeed, if asked to explain their actions, experts may be unable to do so. While the pattern (and associated actions) is familiar, the underlying justification has receded from conscious memory. In a simple way expertise can be thought of as unconscious recollection. This helps explain why expertise is so hard to transfer from one person to another. It is highly subjective; deeply rooted in individual experiences; and very difficult to surface, examine, and explain.

Whereas expert intuition provides insight into the important process of pattern recognition, entrepreneurial intuition has more to do with innovation and change. No two situations are the same, and patterns, while similar, are never identical. The ability to make novel connections and to discern possibilities is also key to intuiting. "Entrepreneurs" are able to make these novel connections, perceive new or emergent relationships, and discern possibilities that have not been identified previously. Whereas expert intuition may be past pattern oriented, entrepreneurial intuition is future possibility oriented.

Expert intuition supports exploitation; entrepreneurial intuition supports exploration. Entrepreneurial intuiting generates new insights. Koestler (1976) suggests that in the natural sciences such insights, when they occur, happen after the individual has had a long period of immersion in the problem, followed by a brief period of disassociation from the specifics of the problem. Although this may be true for breakthrough insights, more mundane acts of innovation may have more humble beginnings (Anderson, 1992). Imagery and metaphor also seem to be important in this process.

For entrepreneurs in a business situation, there is always the question of whether these individuals are intuitive or just lucky. However, this question is difficult to answer because novel, intuitive insights cannot be judged right or wrong ex ante. They are simply possibilities. It is rare to see a business entrepreneur able to convert intuitive insight into business reality on a consistent basis. Fred Smith perceived the potential of reliable, overnight, small package delivery, and Federal Express emerged as a very successful business (Maister & Wyckoff, 1974). He was unable to replicate this success with Zapmail—an electronic mail service. There are exceptions, however. Howard Head, the entrepreneurial genius behind the Head metal ski, was also the inventor of the Prince oversized tennis racket.

The connection between quality of intuition and commercial success is difficult to make. Intuition is the beginning of new learning. Eventual commercial success is dependent upon effective learning at all levels—not simply the original intuitive insights of the entrepreneur.

Intuiting, especially of the entrepreneurial type, appears to be a largely subconscious process. In fact, trying to force it to a conscious level too soon may prevent it from happening (Watson, 1969). The outcome of individual intuiting is an inexplicable sense of the possible, of what might be done. Entrepreneurial intuitions are preverbal, and expert intuitions may be nonverbal as well. No language exists to describe the insight or to explain the intended action. Consequently, intuition may guide the actions of the individual, but this intuition is difficult to share with others (Nonaka & Takeuchi, 1995). Imagery, sometimes called "visions," and metaphors aid the individual in his or her interpretation of the insight and in communicating it to others.

Scholars have recognized metaphors as a critical link in the evolution from individual intuitive insight to shared interpretation. Individuals use metaphors to help explain their intuition to themselves and to share it with others. As Tsoukas explains, "Metaphors involve the transfer of information from a relatively familiar domain . . . to a new and relatively unknown domain" (1991: 568)—that is, from the known to the unknown, from that for which we share literal language to that emerging insight for which language does not yet exist. As such, metaphors mark the beginning of the interpreting process. Srivastava and Barrett provide the example of a child trying to describe for the first time to his mother that his foot is asleep. The child has no literal language to relay this strange sensation:

> In frustration, he says to his mother: "It feels like there are stars hitting my foot." Having no available literal terms, the child associates a new unfamiliar experience with one he understands. He has a sparkling, glittering, tingling sensation that seems to impact his foot from somewhere outside his body. At the age of four he is unable to say. "Mother, there is a certain numbness in my foot which is a result of an inadequate supply of blood which I have inadvertently seemed to circumvent" (1991: 568).

In this example the child perceives something he has no words to describe, although the words do exist, and no doubt his mother would explain that the word "numbness" can be used to describe the sensation.

True innovators have a problem akin to the child. They have a sensation—an insight into a possibility—but they have no literal language to describe it. Unfortunately, they do not have a "parent" to provide that language: indeed, none exists if the insight is truly novel. Individuals employ metaphors to bound and describe the insight. As Tsoukas elaborates.

> In lay discourse, metaphors constitute an economical way of relaying primarily experiential information in a vivid manner, and they can be used as variety reduction mechanism in situations where experience cannot be segmented and imparted through literal language (1991: 567).

Indeed, for entrepreneurial insights, metaphors may be the only language available for one to communicate with another.

Early in the evolution of the personal computer. Steve Jobs of Apple employed the "appliance" metaphor. This metaphor evokes a whole set of subsidiary images: easy to use, small, affordable. Subsequently, more literal language was used to name more precisely many of the attributes associated with the original metaphor (e.g., graphical user interface). This example also points to the reciprocity between thinking and acting that is inherent in the development of language.

> Naming also directs actions towards the object (or image) you have named because it promotes activity consistent with the related attribution (i.e., the name or the metaphor) it carries. To change the name of an object connotes changing your relationship to it because when we name something, we direct anticipations, expectations, and evaluations toward it (Srivastava & Barrett, 1988: 34–35).

Using this reasoning, if Jobs had used a different metaphor to describe his initial insight, perhaps the personal computer as "business assistant," it would have led to very different actions, and Apple would have become a very different company. Early in a company's development, when it is far from equilibrium, small differences in the metaphors employed and the ways in which conversations unfold and language develops may ultimately result in great differences in where the company ends up.

Interpreting

Whereas intuiting focuses on the subconscious process of developing insights, interpreting begins picking up on the conscious elements of the individual learning process. Through the process of interpreting, individuals develop cognitive maps about the various domains in which they operate (Huff, 1990). Language plays a pivotal role in the development of these maps, since it enables individuals to name and begin to explain what were once simply feelings, hunches, or sensations. Further, once things are named, individuals can make more explicit connections among them.

Interpreting takes place in relation to a domain or an environment. The nature or texture of the domain within which individuals and organizations operate, and from which they extract data, is crucial to understanding the interpretive process. The precision of the language that evolves will reflect the texture of the domain, given the tasks being attempted. The well-known example of the Inuit having over a dozen different words for (various types of) snow illustrates the rich interaction between the task domain and the sophistication of language. Moreover, a person with very rich and complex cognitive maps of a domain, like the chess master, will be able to see things and act in ways that others cannot.

The cognitive map is affected by the domain or environment, but it also guides what is interpreted from that domain. As Weick (1979) suggests, people are more likely to "see something when they believe it" rather than "believe it when they see it." As a result, individuals will interpret the same stimulus differently, based on their established cognitive maps. The same stimulus can evoke a different or equivocal meaning for different people (Hambrick & Mason, 1984; Walsh, 1988). This difference is not a result of uncertainty about the stimulus. Uncertainty is related to the quality of information. But for any group of people, even high-quality information may be equivocal: it may hold multiple, and often conflicting, meanings (Daft & Huber, 1987). Although equivocality is an issue in the development of both individual understanding and shared understanding within a group, equivocal situations are often resolved through a group interpretive process (Weick & Van Orden, 1990).

Just as language plays a pivotal role in enabling individuals to develop their cognitive maps, it is also pivotal in enabling individuals to develop a sense of shared understanding. Interpreting is a social activity that creates and refines common language, clarifies images, and creates shared meaning and understanding. Equivocality is reduced through interpreting by "shared observations and discussion until a common grammar and course of action can be agreed upon" (Daft & Weick, 1984: 291). Groups will have an interpretive capacity related to the makeup of the group and to the group dynamics (Hurst et al., 1989). As the interpretive process moves beyond the individual and becomes embedded within the workgroup, it becomes integrative. Individual interpretive processes come together around a shared understanding of what is possible, and individuals interact and attempt to enact that possibility.

Integrating

Whereas the focus of interpreting is change in the individual's understanding and actions, the focus of integrating is coherent, collective action. For coherence to evolve, shared understanding by members of the group is required. It is through the continuing conversation among members of the community and through shared practice (Seely-Brown & Duguid, 1991) that shared understanding or collective mind (Weick & Roberts, 1993) develops and mutual adjustment and negotiated action (Simons, 1991) take place.

The evolution of language extends the process of interpreting to interactions among individuals: the realm of workgroups, organizations, communities, and even societies. Language developed through conversation and dialogue allows the evolution of shared meaning for the group. As Daft and Weick explain:

> The distinctive feature . . . is sharing. A piece of data, a perception, a cognitive map is shared among managers. . . . Passing a startling observation among members, or discussing a puzzling development enables managers to converge on an approximate interpretation (1984: 285).

Language not only helps us learn—it preserves, for better and for worse, what has been learned. For an organization to learn and renew, its language must evolve. Conversation can be used not only to convey established meaning but also to evolve new meaning.

Not all conversational styles are equally effective, however, for developing shared meaning. Isaacs suggests that "dialogue is a discipline of collective thinking and inquiry, a process for transforming the quality of conversation and, in particular the thinking that lies beneath it" (1993: 25). Through dialogue the group can evolve new and deeper shared understandings. This shared meaning can cause those who have participated to more or less spontaneously make mutual adjustments to their actions. As Isaacs goes on to explain,

> Dialogue proposes that . . . some of the most powerful forms of coordination may come through participation in unfolding meaning, which might even be perceived differently by different people. A flock of birds suddenly taking flight from a tree reveals the potential coordination of dialogue: this movement all at once, a wholeness and listening together that permits individual differentiation but is still highly interconnected (1993: 25).

The dialogue process attempts to convey both the message and a deep interconnected meaning. A consensual approach that attempts to get agreement on the message without delving into the underlying meaning(s) risks a groupthink outcome (Janis, 1982).

As with the process of interpreting, the context surrounding the integrating process is critical. Seely-Brown and Duguid's (1991) notion of "communities of practice" captures the importance of the integrative context. These authors and their colleagues have been involved in ethnographic research on workplace practices and suggest that understanding and impacting learning and innovation require one to study and understand the situation in which practice occurs. Neither occurs ex situ:

> Practice is essential to understanding work. Abstractions detached from practice distort or obscure intricacies of that practice. Without a clear understanding of those intricacies and the role they play, the practice itself cannot be well understood, engendered (through training) or enhanced (through innovation) (1991: 40).

Observations from these ethnographic studies reveal that actual practice is not what is specified in manuals or necessarily what is taught in classrooms. Rather, it is captured and promulgated by stories told by community members. Storytelling is a significant part of the learning process. Stories reflect the complexity of actual practice rather than the abstractions taught in classrooms. As stories evolve, richer understanding of the phenomenon is developed, and new integrated approaches to solving problems are created. Stories themselves become the repository of wisdom—part of the collective mind/memory (Weick & Roberts, 1993).

Institutionalizing

The process of institutionalizing sets organizational learning apart from individual or ad hoc group learning. The underlying assumption is that organizations are more than simply a collection of individuals; organizational learning is different from the simple sum of the learning of its members. Although individuals may come and go, what they have learned as individuals or in groups does not necessarily leave with them. Some learning is embedded in the systems, structures, strategy, routines, prescribed practices of the organization, and investments in information systems and infrastructure.

For new organizations there are few established routines or structures: there is no organizational memory. Often by the nature of their small size, their open communication, and their formation based on common interest and dreams, individual and group learning dominate in young organizations. As organizations mature, however, individuals begin to fall into patterns of interaction and communication, and the organizations attempt to capture the patterns of interaction by formalizing them.

This institutionalization is a means for organizations to leverage the learning of the individual members. Structures, systems, and procedures provide a context for interactions. Over time, spontaneous individual and group learning become less prevalent, as the prior learning becomes embedded in the organization and begins to guide the actions and learning of organizational members.

Organizations naturally outgrow their ability to exclusively use spontaneous interactions to interpret, integrate, and take coherent action. Relationships become formalized. Coherent action is achieved with the help of plans and other formal systems. If the plan produces favorable outcomes, then the actions deemed to be consistent with the plan become routines. There is a need to ensure that the routines continue to be carried out and that the organization produces and performs. This is the role for what Simons calls "diagnostic systems" (1991, 1994). An organization uses these systems to regulate the day-to-day routines of the business—to exploit the current understanding of the business. Simons also identifies another type of formal system he calls "interactive." Organizations use interactive systems to consider how the future can or may be different from the past.

As one moves from the individual level of intuiting/interpreting through group integrating to organizational institutionalizing, the process of learning is less fluid and incremental and becomes more staccato and disjointed. Generally, that which becomes institutionalized in organizations has received, at some point, a certain degree of consensus or shared understanding among the influential members of the organization. Before a formal organizational system or structure is established or changed, the modification generally undergoes some process of consideration. Once something is institutionalized, it usually endures for a period of time.

Changes in systems, structures, and routines occur relatively infrequently in organizations; as a result, although the underlying processes of intuiting, interpreting, and integrating are more fluid and continual, significant changes in the institutionalized organization typically are punctuated. For this reason much organizational change is interpreted as being radical or transformational, rather than incremental, in nature. However, even though the institutional changes may appear disjointed, the underlying learning processes of intuiting and interpreting at the individual and group levels that result in these changes may be more continuous.

Institutionalized learning cannot capture all the ongoing learning at the individual and group levels. It takes time to transfer learning from individuals to groups and from groups to the organization. As the environment changes, the learning that has been institutionalized may no longer fit the context; there may be a gap between what the organization needs to do and what it has learned to do. As the gap widens, the organization places more reliance on individual learning and initiative. For example, Seely-Brown (1993) reports on studies that examined the informal routines of experienced order clerks in comparison with the formal institutionalized system. Although the product of their day's work gave the appearance that the clerks had followed the formal routine, they had, in fact, improvised in ways that proved more efficient and effective.

Given that the environment is constantly changing, the challenge for organizations is to manage the tension between the embedded institutionalized learning from the past, which enables it to exploit learning, and the new learning that must be allowed to feed forward through the processes of intuiting, interpreting, and integrating. Although the 4I's have been presented in a linear fashion for ease of explanation, appreciating the iterative nature of the processes is critical, as we will discuss in a subsequent section.

In the following section we present the Apple story in a linear fashion to illustrate the 4I processes. The focus of the story is on the exploration side of strategic renewal. We then broaden the discussion to examine the dynamic nature of organizational learning.

Understanding the Learning Processes: The Apple Story

The relationship between each of the levels and processes perhaps can best be illustrated by way of a story—that of Apple Computer.[1] By all accounts, Steve Jobs, through an **intuitive process**, had the insights upon which Apple was founded. Jobs perceived patterns and evolved certain *images*[2] about possibilities, which developed into a *metaphor* (e.g., the personal computer as an appliance—one in every home) that guided Apple during its early years. These images were based, at least in part, upon his unique *experiences* and cognitive orientation. He provided much of the insight and energy that were the genesis of Apple.

But these initial images were necessarily vague when it came to specific actions. At the intuitive stage actions are improvised, rooted more in feeling than thinking (Hurst et al., 1989). The language used to explain improvised action is necessarily underdeveloped, vague, and imprecise. On the basis of Jobs' own experiences and his perceptions of the events, along with Wozniak's technical expertise, these men improvised actions as they went along.

Language plays a pivotal role as insights become more sophisticated and concrete through the **interpretive process.** In part, it was through the group process of *dialogue* and *conversation* that Jobs' own understanding and individual cognitive complexity were enhanced. Talking and acting with others, developing words to describe what had been vague insights, and enacting these insights enabled a deeper meaning to evolve (Bruner, 1990).

Many researchers talk about this evolution of meaning in terms of cognitive complexity and *cognitive maps* (Huff, 1990). Although one must be careful with this metaphor, it is helpful to think of Jobs initially navigating his chosen territory more or less mapless, guided only by some vague vision of what lay over the next hill. As he, with others, experimented and explored the territory, a mental picture or map slowly emerged, with finer and finer levels of detail. (This metaphor is only helpful to a point. Jobs was not just exploring the territory—through his actions he was helping to create or enact the territory.)

As insightful as Jobs was, he could not accomplish his vision alone. He needed to involve others. The conversation and dialogue, which served to develop his understanding, also helped to **integrate** the cognitive maps of the group—to develop a *shared understanding.* Language, which plays a critical role in the development of individual maps, is essential as a means of integrating ideas and negotiating actions with others. Through conversation, workgroups identify areas of difference and agreement, gain language precision, and develop a shared understanding of their task domain. They quite naturally, as a part of this process, use their common language and the conversational process to negotiate *mutual adjustments* to their actions. These adjustments are an integral part of the learning process. The assumption is that a certain coherence of actions should emerge from a shared understanding of the business situation—that is, the emergent strategy (Mintzberg, 1994).

But what is the context within which shared understandings and mutual adjustments occur? Early in an organization's life, as was the case with Apple, these processes are largely informal and spontaneous. As organizations grow larger and more people are involved, informal interactions do not suffice. What had happened more or less spontaneously must now be arranged; what had been an informal conversation over coffee about the future of the company becomes a formal planning process with *interactive systems* (Simons, 1991, 1994).

The organization naturally outgrows its ability to exclusively use spontaneous interactions to interpret, integrate, and take concerted action. Relationships become formalized and *routines* develop. There is a need to ensure that the routines continue to be carried out and that the organization produces and performs. This is the role of *diagnostic systems* (Simons, 1991, 1994).

In the Apple situation John Sculley was brought in, at least in part, to provide needed systems, structures, and other formal mechanisms. Individual and communal learning became **institutionalized** in the hope that the learning could be more systematically exploited. Institutionalization contributes to more efficient operations, enabling the organization to better deliver on the founder's original vision. With Apple, however, it also may have hindered the organization's ability to renew itself by intuiting, interpreting, and integrating emerging patterns and new possibilities. Unable to realize his new vision within Apple, Steve Jobs left to start a new enterprise, appropriately called NeXT.

Essentially, the process of institutionalizing embeds learned behaviors that have worked in the past into the routines of the organization. Diagnostic systems develop *rules and procedures* to facilitate the repetition of routines. But the process of institutionalizing also feeds back by creating a context through which subsequent events and experiences are interpreted. This context may facilitate and/or impede the organization's ability to (re)interpret and respond to its environment. The Apple example, while useful, is a simplification. In entrepreneurial startup situations like Apple, there is originally little or no past learning embedded in the formal organization. Indeed, there is no formal organization. Established organizations do have past learning embedded within them. As such, learning and renewal in these situations must deal with this difference in context and its associated challenges.

Organizational Learning As a Dynamic Process

Organizational learning is a dynamic process. Not only does learning occur over time and across levels, but it also creates a tension between assimilating new learning (feed forward) and exploiting or using what has already been learned (feedback). Through feed-forward processes, new ideas and actions flow from the individual to the group to the organization levels. At the same time, what has already been learned feeds back from the organization to group and individual levels, affecting how people act and think. The concurrent nature of the feed-forward and feedback processes creates a tension, which can be understood by arraying the levels against one another, as shown in Figure 1. Doing so illustrates that, in addition to the processes that feed forward learning from the individual and groups to the organization, learning that has been institutionalized feeds back and impacts individual and group learning. The importance of these interactions can be highlighted by two relationships that are especially problematic: interpreting-integrating (feed forward) and institutionalizing-intuiting (feedback).

Moving from interpreting to integrating (feed forward) requires a shift from individual learning to learning among individuals or groups. It entails taking personally constructed cognitive maps

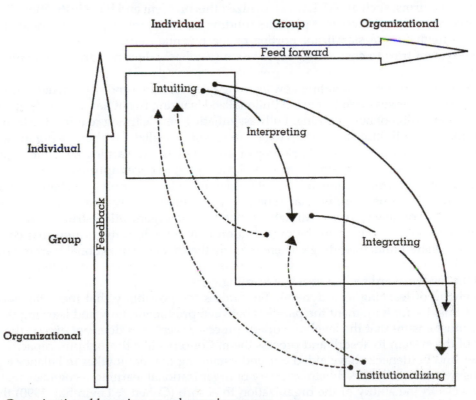

Figure 1   Organizational learning as a dynamic process.

and integrating them in a way that develops a shared understanding among the group members. There are many challenges in changing an existing shared reality. The first is that individuals need to be able to communicate, through words and actions, their own cognitive map. Since many aspects of cognitive maps are tacit, communicating them requires a process of surfacing and articulating ideas and concepts. This process makes tacit knowledge explicit (Polanyi, 1967).

Assuming individuals can surface and articulate their maps, a second challenge arises from the collective interpretation of the maps. Making something explicit does not necessarily mean the understanding is shared. Imprecision of language is complicated by cognitive maps that act as unique filters on the communication; we tend to "see/hear what we believe" rather than "believe what we see." The real test of shared understanding is coherent action. Yet, for novel ideas, shared understanding may not evolve unless shared action or experimentation is attempted. The learning perspective suggests that leading with action, rather than bluntly focusing on cognition, may provide a different migration path to shared understanding. As in experiential learning (Crossan et al., 1995), action provides the opportunity to share a common experience, which may aid in the development of shared understanding.

The second problematic interaction is between institutionalizing and intuiting (feedback). Institutionalization can easily drive out intuition. Intuiting within established organizations with a high degree of institutionalized learning requires what Schumpeter (1959) refers to as "creative destruction"—destroying, or at least setting aside, the institutional order to enact variations that allow intuitive insights and actions to surface and be pursued. This is extremely difficult because the language and logic that form the collective mindset of the organization and the resulting investment in assets present a formidable fortress of physical and cognitive barriers to change. Further, members of the organization must step back from proven, objective successes and allow unproven, subjectively based experimentation.

One example of the tension and the potential for resolution is in the resource allocation process (institutionalized learning). Many resource allocation processes inhibit the development of new insights, given their emphasis on track record and proven success (Bower, 1970; Burgelman, 1983). However, some firms, such as 3M, have recognized this problem and have institutionalized a different resource allocation process that provides funding for new projects, and also holds the business accountable for having a significant portion of the revenue derived from new products (Hurst, 1995). The system tries to ensure that exploitation (feedback) does not drive out exploration (feed forward).

The tension between assimilating new learning (feed forward) and using what has already been learned (feedback) arises because the institutionalized learning (what has already been learned) impedes the assimilation of new learning. Fully assimilating new learning requires the feed forward of learning from the individual and group to become institutionalized within the organization. Utilizing what has been learned is a feedback loop of institutionalized learning from the organization to groups and individuals. For example, rules and routines that once captured the logic and learning of how to facilitate learning at the individual level may no longer apply in a changed circumstance, yet the systems still focus an individual's energy and attention in ways that impede the assimilation and feed forward of new learning (Mintzberg, 1994). Or an organization structure that has a strong impact on who talks to whom in the organization may impede conversation that could develop valuable new shared understandings. Therefore, any theory of organizational learning needs to recognize the levels, processes, and dynamic nature of the learning process itself that create a tension between the feed forward and feedback of learning.

Conceiving of learning as a dynamic flow raises the possibility that these flows can be constrained. Consider for a moment the parallels between production flow and learning flow. Production flow must ensure that the level of work-in-process inventories does not exceed the capacity of any part of the system to absorb and process them. Concepts like throughput, capacity utilization, cycle time, and bottlenecks have aided our understanding of what it takes to balance a production line to ensure smooth flow. A dynamic theory of organizational learning recognizes that there may be bottlenecks in the ability of the organization to absorb (Cohen & Levinthal, 1990) the feed forward of learning from the individual to the group and organization. Investment in individual learning and pressures for new product innovation may become stockpiled if the organization has limited capacity to absorb the learning. However, in the production process, work-in-process inventory does not "care" whether it is stockpiled, whereas in the learning process individuals (and their ideas) do. As a result, individuals may become frustrated and disenchanted, and may even leave the organization.

A dynamic theory of organizational learning provides a means of understanding the fundamental tensions of strategic renewal: the tension between exploration (feed forward) and exploitation (feedback). Although one may be tempted to equate organizational learning solely with the innovative feed-forward process, in doing so one fails to recognize that the feedback process provides the means to exploit what has been learned (Crossan & Sorrenti, 1987). However, because learning that has become institutionalized at the organization level is often difficult to change, it runs the risk of becoming irrelevant and may even obstruct feed-forward learning flows. This has led to the call to liberate organizations and destroy bureaucracy (Pinchot & Pinchot, 1993), yet bureaucracy (or institutionalization) is not necessarily negative. Institutionalizing learning is necessary to reap the ongoing benefits of what has already been learned.

With the 4I framework we identify the flow of learning between levels and the tension between feed-forward (exploration) and feed-back (exploitation) processes as fundamental challenges of strategic renewal. There are many factors that could facilitate and inhibit this process, some of which are part of the institutionalized learning itself (e.g., reward systems, information systems, resource allocation systems, strategic planning systems, and structure). However, in the 4I model we recognize that ideas occur to individuals and that individuals ultimately share those ideas through an integrating process. It is the individuals, and the social processes and group dynamics through which they interact, that may facilitate or inhibit organizational learning. One promising area for further research is to examine the role of leadership and management of the 4I learning process.

Implications for Research and Management

The central contribution of this work is the 4I's and the related feed-forward and feed-back processes. Further, the interplay between the levels and the processes reveals the tensions associated with strategic renewal. It is our hope that this framework will stir a reaction in the organizational learning community and help scholars research the links among the levels and the tensions inherent in organizational learning.

The same questions that we as researchers seek to answer form the basis of inquiry for managers. Is there a satisfactory level of intuitive, innovative insights in the organization? Do individuals have the motivation, understanding, capability, and opportunity to interpret their environment? How do individual and group experiences help to develop shared understanding? How well do individual insights become shared, integrated, and institutionalized in the organization? What impediments are there to integrating individual perspectives? How much of the organization's intellectual capital resides in individual heads? Is there enough institutionalized learning? How does institutionalized learning facilitate or impede intuiting, interpreting, and integrating? What is the nature of the interplay between the feed-forward and feedback processes?

The responses to these questions need to take into account the dynamic nature of organizational learning as it relates to strategic renewal. Compartmentalization of the issues will lead to a simplification that disguises the many essential challenges of the phenomenon. For example, in the case of the first question, a simple focus on intuiting may yield a better understanding of the individual processes of innovation. However, such a focus will miss the tension and, hence, challenge of feeding forward intuitive insights with the hope of interpreting, integrating, and institutionalizing them, while concurrently working within a setting where institutionalized learning continues to positively impact upon the performance of the enterprise.

The question of whether individuals have the motivation, understanding, capability, and opportunity to interpret their environment suggests the need to examine more than just individuals. It requires an examination of the link between interpreting and institutionalizing. Individuals may be motivated and capable, but if they turn their attention toward interpreting things that have little impact, the organization will reap few benefits from that learning. Furthermore, even if individuals are interpreting things of relevance, their learning needs to be integrated and institutionalized to realize its future value. This theory suggests it is not simply a matter of transferring data, information, or knowledge—it is a matter of organizational learning.

The role of experience in the development of shared understanding reinforces the learning premise that cognition (knowledge, understanding, and beliefs) and action (behaviors) are tightly intertwined, and changes in knowledge do not necessarily lead to changes in action. In contrast to knowledge management and intellectual capital, which focus management and research attention on cognition, this view of organizational learning acknowledges the rich interrelationship between cognition and action.

The foregoing examples emphasize the need to pursue questions of organizational learning with a dynamic perspective. We encourage researchers and managers to extend their thinking to consider how different parts of the organizational learning system impact one another. This framework should serve as a map to help researchers and managers expand their horizons.

While this framework should encourage and assist the pursuit of a more holistic understanding of organizational learning, there are two particular areas of research that will help advance theory. The first is understanding the mechanisms that enhance or restrict the stocks and flows of learning. Here we have suggested that learning processes can be compared to production processes. This point should generate substantial dialogue, because it begins to question some of the traditional leverage points for organizational learning. For example, continued investment in individual and even group learning may be counterproductive if the organization does not have the capacity to absorb or utilize it. If this is the case, future research in organizational learning needs to move from the reasonably well-developed understanding of individual- and group-level learning to understanding the flows of learning (feed forward and feedback) between the levels.

Yet, all intuitive insights should not, and cannot, be immediately interpreted, integrated, and institutionalized. What enables the organization to "separate the wheat from the chaff"—the good from the bad—as ideas and practices develop and are refined over time? We have suggested that the strategic context helps to frame things that are more or less relevant, but the decision rules, criteria, and processes are not so clear. For example, if 3M had framed the discovery of a glue that does not stick in a narrow strategic context, we would not have reaped the benefits of Post-It® Notes.

A second area that will advance theory is an understanding of how to reconcile the tension between exploitation and exploration—between continuity and change. The 4I model directs our attention to the interplay of these processes, but it does not specifically address how organizations deal with this tension. Although a few management scholars have considered this problem (Hurst, 1995; Miller, 1990; Pascale, 1990), answers have proven elusive. This important question merits further consideration and investigation.

This dynamic framework of organizational learning will place significant demands on both researchers and managers. It requires capability for cross-level examination with a critical eye for the tensions inherent in the feed-forward and feedback processes. It requires the capability to link human resource management, strategic management, and the management of information technology and systems as a means to facilitate the flow of learning. Although such research poses challenges, the potential benefits are significant. Strategic renewal is one of the central challenges of every organization. This dynamic process of organizational learning could yield important insights into strategic renewal.

In summary, in this article we have pushed in the direction of advancing a theory of organizational learning by describing an organizational learning framework that incorporates the dynamic multilevel nature of the phenomenon and captures the rich interplay between process and level. This framework should provide clarity, promote dialogue, foster convergence (Pfeffer, 1993), and encourage new directions in research that begin to examine organizational learning flows that enable strategic renewal.

Notes

1. This description is not represented as an accurate case history. Rather, it is a story we use to help illustrate the conceptual model, we do not employ it as empirical support for the model.
2. The italicized words represent the key words used to describe the inputs and outcomes of the processes as shown in Table 2.

References

Anderson, I. V. 1992. Weirder than fiction: The reality and myths of creativity. *Academy of Management Executive*, 6(4): 40–47.

Argyris, C., & Schon, D. A. 1978. *Organizational learning: A theory of action perspective.* Reading. MA: Addison-Wesley.

Argyris, C., & Schon, D. A. 1996. *Organizational learning II: Theory, method, and practice.* Reading, MA: Addison-Wesley.

Bacharach, S. 1989. Organizational theories: Some criteria for evaluation. *Academy of Management Review*, 14: 496–515.

Behling, O., & Eckel, H. 1991. Making sense out of intuition. *Academy of Management Executive*, 5(1): 46–54.

Berger, P., & Luckmann, T. 1966. *The social construction of reality: A treatise in the sociology of knowledge.* Garden City, NY: Anchor Books.

Bower, J. L. 1970. *Managing the resource allocation process,* Boston: Harvard Business School Press.

Bruner, J. 1990. *Acts of meaning.* Cambridge, MA: Harvard University Press.

Burgelman, R. A. 1983. A model of the interaction of strategic behavior, corporate context and the concept of strategy. *Academy of Management Review*, 8: 61–70.

Cangelosi, V. E., & Dill, W. R. 1965. Organizational learning observations: Toward a theory. *Administrative Science Quarterly*, 10: 175–203.

Cohen, W. M., & Levinthal, D. A. 1990. Absorptive capacity: A new perspective on learning and innovation. *Administrative Science Quarterly*, 35: 128–152.

Conner, K., & Prahalad, C. 1996. A resource-based theory of the firm: Knowledge versus opportunism. *Organization Science*, 7: 469.

Crossan, M., & Guatto, T. 1996. Organizational learning research profile. *Journal of Organizational Change Management*, 9(1): 107–112.

Crossan, M., Lane, H., White, R. E., Djurfeldt, L. 1995. Organizational learning: Dimensions for a theory. *International Journal of Organizational Analysis*, 3: 337–360.

Crossan, M., & Sorrenti, M. 1997. Making sense of improvisation. In A. Huff & J. Walsh (Eds.), *Advances in strategic management*, vol. 14: 155–180. Stamford, CT: JAI Press.

Daft, R. L., & Huber, G. 1987. How organizations learn: A communication framework. *Research in the Sociology of Organizations*, 5(2): 1–36.

Daft, R. L., & Weick, K. E. 1984. Toward a model of organizations as interpretation systems. *Academy of Management Review*, 9: 284–295.

Davenport, T., & Prusak, L. 1997. *Information ecology: Mastering the information and knowledge environment,* New York: Oxford University Press.

DeGeus, A. 1988. Planning as learning. *Harvard Business Review*, 66 (March–April): 70–74.

Duncan, R. B., & Weiss, A. 1979. Organizational learning: Implications for organizational design. *Research in Organizational Behavior*, 1(4): 75–124.

Edvinsson, L., & Malone, M. 1997. *Intellectual capital.* New York: Harper Business.

Fiol, C. M., & Lyles, M. A. 1985. Organizational learning. *Academy of Management Review*, 10: 803–813.

Foss, N. 1996. Knowledge-based approaches to the theory of the firm: Some critical comments. *Organization Science.* 7: 470–476.

Grant, R. M. 1996. Toward a knowledge-based theory of the firm, *Strategic Management Journal*, 17: 109–122.

Hambrick, D., & Mason, P. A. 1984. Upper echelons: The organization as a reflection of its top managers. *Academy of Management Review,* 9: 193–206.

Hedberg, B. 1981. How organizations learn and unlearn. In P. C. Nystrom & W. H. Starbuck (Eds.), *Handbook of organizational design:* 3–27. New York: Oxford University Press.

Huber, G. P. 1991. Organizational learning: The contributing processes and the literatures. *Organization Science,* 2: 88–115.

Huff, A. S. 1990. *Mapping strategic thought.* New York: Wiley.

Hurst, D. K. 1995. *Crisis and renewal.* Boston: Harvard Business School Press.

Hurst, D. K., Rush, J. C., & White, R. E. 1989. Top management teams and organizational renewal. *Strategic Management Journal,* 10: 87–105.

Isaacs, W. H. 1993. Dialogue, collective thinking, and organizational learning. *Organizational Dynamics,* 22(2): 24–39.

Janis, I. 1982. *Groupthink: Psychological studies of policy decisions and fiascoes.* Boston: Houghton Mifflin.

Kim, D. H. 1993. The link between individual and organizational learning. *Sloan Management Review,* 33(1): 37–50.

Koestler, A. 1976. *The act of creation.* London: Hutchinson.

Kogut, B., & Zander, U. 1992. Knowledge of the firm, combinative capabilities, and the replication of technology. *Organization Science,* 3: 383–397.

Levitt, B., & March, J. G. 1988. Organizational learning. *Annual Review of Sociology,* 14: 319–340.

Maister, D., & Wyckoff, D. 1974. *Federal Express (A) & (B).* Case No. 9-674-093-094. Boston: Harvard Business School Case Services.

March, J. G. 1991. Exploration and exploitation in organization learning. *Organization Science,* 2: 71–87.

March, J. G., & Olsen, J. P. 1975. Organizational learning under ambiguity. *European Journal of Policy Review,* 3(2): 147–171.

Miller, D. 1990. *The Icarus paradox: How exceptional companies bring about their own downfall.* New York: Harper Business.

Mintzberg, H. 1994. *The rise and fall of strategic planning.* New York: Free Press.

Neisser, U. 1976. *Cognition and reality.* San Francisco: Freeman.

Nonaka. I., & Takeuchi, H. 1995. *The knowledge creating company.* Oxford, England: Oxford University Press.

Pascale, R. T. 1990. *Managing on the edge: How the smartest companies use conflict to stay ahead.* New York: Simon and Schuster.

Pfeffer, I. 1993. Barrier to the advance of organizational science: Paradigm development as a dependent variable. *Academy of Management Review,* 18(4): 599–620.

Pinchot, G., & Pinchot, E. 1993. *The end of bureaucracy and the rise of the intelligent organization.* San Francisco: Berrett-Koehler.

Polanyi, M. 1967. *The tacit dimension.* London: Routledge.

Prietula, M. J., & Simon, H. A. 1989. The experts in your midst. *Harvard Business Review,* 61(January–February): 120–124.

Quinn, J. B. 1992. *Intelligent enterprise: A knowledge and service based paradigm for industry.* New York: Free Press.

Schumpeter, I. A. 1959. *The theory of economic development.* Cambridge, MA: Harvard University Press.

Seely-Brown, I. 1993. Thinking, working, and learning. In M. M. Crossan, H. W. Lane, J. Rush, & R. E. White (Eds.), *Learning in organizations monograph:* 81–99. London, Ontario: Western Business School.

Seely-Brown, I., & Duguid, P. 1991. Organizational learning and communities of practice: Toward a unified view of working, learning and innovation. *Organization Science,* 2: 40–57.

Senge, P. 1990. *The fifth discipline: The art and practice of the learning organization.* New York: Doubleday/Currency.

Shrivastava, P. 1983. A typology of organizational learning systems. *Journal of Management Studies.* 20(1): 7–28.

Simon, H. A. 1991. Bounded rationality and organizational learning. *Organization Science,* 2: 125–134.

Simons, R. 1991. Strategic orientation and top management attention to control systems. *Strategic Management Journal,* 12: 49–62.

Simons, R. 1994. How new top managers use control systems as levers of strategic renewal. *Strategic Management Journal,* 15: 169–189.

Srivastava, S., & Barrett, F. J. 1988. The transforming nature of metaphors in group development: A study in group theory. *Human Relations*, 41: 31–64.

Stata, R. 1989. Organizational learning: The key to management innovation. *Sloan Management Review*, 30(3): 63–74.

Stewart, T. A. 1997. *Intellectual capital: The wealth of nations.* New York: Doubleday/Currency.

Sutton, R., & Staw, B. M. 1995. What theory is not. *Administrative Science Quarterly*, 40: 371–384.

Tsoukas, H. 1991. The missing link: A transformational view of metaphors in organizational science. *Academy of Management Review*, 16: 566–585.

Underwood, B. J. 1982. *Studies in learning and memory: Selected papers.* New York: Praeger.

Watkins, K. E., & Marsick, W. J. 1993. *Sculpting the learning organization.* San Francisco: Jossey-Bass.

Walsh, J. P. 1988. Selectivity and selective perception. An investigation of managers' belief structures and information processing. *Academy of Management Journal*, 31: 873–896.

Watson, I. D. 1969. *The double helix.* New York: Mentor Books.

Weick, K. 1979. *The social psychology of organizing.* Reading, MA.: Addison-Wesley.

Weick, K. 1995a. What theory is not, theorizing is. *Administrative Science Quarterly*, 40: 385–390.

Weick, K. E. 1995b. *Sensemaking in organizations.* Thousand Oaks, CA: Sage.

Weick, K., & Roberts, K. 1993. Collective mind and organizational reliability: The case of flight operations in an aircraft carrier deck. *Administrative Science Quarterly*, 38: 357–381.

Weick, K., & Van Orden, P. W. 1990. Organizing on a global scale: A research and teaching agenda. *Human Resource Management*, 29: 49–61.

Whetton, D. A. 1989. What constitutes a theoretical contribution? *Academy of Management Review*, 14: 490–495.

THE LIFE CYCLE OF ACADEMIC MANAGEMENT FADS

ROBERT BIRNBAUM

Institutions of higher education are always under pressure to become more efficient and effective. In response, many have attempted (either voluntarily or under mandate) to adopt new management systems and processes that were originally designed to meet the needs of (presumably) more efficient business or governmental organizations. One contemporary observer, referring to "the hum of corporate buzzwords" in the academy, has commented that "a person would be hard pressed these days to find a college that doesn't claim to be evaluating or reshaping itself through one of these approaches" (Nicklin, 1995, p. A33). This "hum" is not new; it has been a feature of the higher education landscape for at least the past forty years.

Among the first of these processes was the Planning, Programming, and Budgeting System (PPBS), initially developed by Rand for use by the Defense Department and adopted by many higher education institutions in the early 1960s. Among the most recent are Business Process Reengineering (BPR), and Benchmarking. In between, business management scholars have documented over two dozen management innovations that were proposed between 1950 and 1990 (Pascale, 1990), some of which were adopted by institutions of higher education. The development and advocacy of new management approaches in both nonacademic and academic management continues, and at an increasing pace.

In the business sector these new ideas are often "presented as universally applicable quick-fix solutions—along with the obligatory and explicit caution that their recommendations are *not* quick fixes and will require substantial management understanding and commitment. As many managers will attest, the result has been a dazzling array of what are often perceived as management fads—fads that frequently become discredited soon after they have been widely propagated" (Eccles & Nohria, 1992, p. 7).

Many of these management innovations, when adopted by higher education, also exhibit the characteristics that led Allen and Chaffee (1981) to define them as fads; they are usually borrowed from other settings, applied without full consideration of their limitations, presented either as complex or deceptively simple, rely on jargon, and emphasize rational decision making. Following Allen and Chaffee, I use the term "fads" to refer collectively and non-pejoratively to certain higher education management innovations enjoying brief popularity, a use consistent with the definition in *Webster's Ninth New Collegiate Dictionary* (p. 444) of a fad as "a practice or interest followed for a time with exaggerated zeal." Not all management innovations are fads. Some (for example, fund accounting) may diffuse and be adopted rapidly through institutional networks to become an accepted part of the system. On the other hand, fads, by definition, are ultimately not widely adopted throughout an organizational system.

This study is grounded in two basic propositions: first, that it is possible to use the literature to trace the evolution of a management fad from the time of its creation to its eventual abandonment and second, that management fads may diffuse between nonacademic and academic systems. These are not novel notions. Informal observations of one or both of them have been noted previously by higher education scholars. For example, commenting on the movement of management innovations between the nonacademic and academic sectors, Baldridge and Okimi (1982) said "Every six months, it seems, a new fad sweeps through management circles. First it strikes the business community, then government, and finally education. Think back a few years and the mind stumbles on the carcasses of fads once touted as the newest 'scientific' way to manage an organization." These fads may "arrive at higher education's doorstep five years after their trial in business, often just as corporations are discarding them" (Marchese, 1991, p. 7). Once the fad has been introduced into higher education, a standard sequence is suggested: "First, the system will be widely acclaimed in the higher education literature; institutions will eagerly ask how best to implement it. Next, the publication of a number of case studies will appear, coupled with testimonials to the system's effectiveness. Finally, both the term and the system will gradually disappear from view" (Chaffee, 1985, p. 133). Management fads in higher education thus appear to follow the cycle of educational innovations in general: "Early enthusiasm, widespread dissemination, subsequent disappointment, and eventual decline" (Slavin, 1989, p. 752). The movement of fads has been noted not only between different sectors in the same country, but also between the same sectors in different countries, and America may be the world leader in such management exports. Neave (1997, p. 278) has commented, "Never in the recent history of higher education in Europe have we seen such a frenzy of model exportation, from North America to Western Europe and from thence eastwards. We have a dangerous faith in management models, often developed in organisational settings other than the university, and no less in their capacity to act as a 'quick fix'."

The comments of these previous observers have for the most part been anecdotal and casual. In contrast, this study takes a more systematic approach to understanding the management fad phenomenon. It analyzes the literature of academic management fads to seek patterns permitting the construction of a Weberian ideal type, a conceptualization "based on observations of reality that are designed to make comparisons possible" (Rogers, 1995, p. 263). This ideal type allows us retrospectively to consider the "life cycle" of academic management fads from the time of their diffusion into higher education until the time of their eventual abandonment, re-invention, or partial incorporation. Analysis of this life cycle may improve our understanding of the effects of management innovations of the past and give both institutional and political policymakers a context in which to understand the possible trajectories of academic management techniques that may be introduced in the future.

The life cycle developed here is based on data from seven case studies in which the cases were not institutions but the natural histories of specific management techniques. Each case study[1] was based on an analysis of a selected sample of periodical, monograph, and technical literature for the period 1960 to the present, describing and analyzing seven widely discussed management techniques which were advocated for use in higher education. The management innovations considered were Planning, Programming, and Budgeting System (PPBS), Zero-Based Budgeting (ZBB), Management by Objectives (MBO), Strategic Planning, Total Quality Management/Continuous Quality Improvement (TQM/CQI), Business Process Reengineering (BPR) and Benchmarking. The literature sampled was selected to include foundational works for each technique both in and outside higher education, repeatedly cited journal articles, conference presentations and fugitive materials identified through the ERIC data base (*ERIC on CD-ROM, 1966–1979, 1980–September 1996*, 1995), and a snowball sample of other references cited in these materials. Each case interrogated the literature database to ask the following questions:

- What were the essential characteristics of the management innovation?
- When, in what setting, and under what circumstances did the innovation originally appear?
- How did the innovation diffuse into higher education?
- What were the outcomes of the innovation in its original and higher education settings?
- When, and for what reasons, was the management technique abandoned?

The cases were then reviewed iteratively using a process of explanation building (Yin, 1984) to develop the cross case analysis presented in this article. The analysis proposes the stages in the life cycle of management fads within organizational sectors, suggests the lagged phases through which fads are diffused between the nonacademic and the academic sectors, and discusses some similarities and differences in the fad adoption process in both academic and nonacademic systems.

The Life Cycle Stages of the Fads Process

The cross-case analysis found a consistent and predictable five-stage cycle which describes the trajectory of management fads: creation, narrative evolution, time lag, narrative devolution, and dissonance resolution. The stage process is depicted in Figure 1. This section describes the fad trajectory as it appears *within* either the non-academic or academic organizational sectors. The following section considers how the innovation moves *between* organizational sectors.

Stage 1: Creation

A crisis is claimed to exist in an organizational sector, usually related to an enacted environment (Weick, 1979) of the larger social system (for example, the Cold War, recession) or an organizational subsystem within it (for example, lack of international competitiveness in business, or lack of attention to customer needs in higher education). Present modes of operation are alleged to be inadequate to address the crisis, and the adoption of a new management technique is proposed to solve the problem. The new technique is supported by advocates (often, paid consultants whose livelihood depends on creating and disseminating this new management technique), by dramatic but unverified narratives by external champions, and by enthusiastic statements of early institutional adopters. The stories, or narratives (Roe, 1994) developed in this creation stage include claims of unusual success.

As a consequence of these claims, additional institutions participating in common interorganizational networks (Rogers, 1995) and accepting the claims of crisis, are encouraged to adopt the new technique. The technique is initially presented in simplified terms, which appear to be so consistent with common sense and with rationalized organizational myths related to efficiency and effectiveness (Meyer & Rowan, 1992) as to make counterarguments difficult. Advocates state that, unlike previous techniques (which may be explicitly denigrated as fads), the technique now being promoted will significantly improve core organizational processes and functions. Promises of extraordinary outcomes are made, and resistors are painted as traditionalists unwilling or unable to respond to change. The technique is often presented as both necessary and sufficient to transform the organizational sector; true believers may present their views with messianic zeal and suggest that the success, perhaps even the survival, of the sector depends on adopting this innovation. Adoption of the technique may be supported, or in some cases driven, by the availability of a new technology that appears to make its implementation feasible. In retrospect, the new technology being promoted may be seen by some as an example of a solution seeking out a problem to which it might be the answer (Cohen & March, 1974).

Stage 2: The Narrative Evolution

Narratives begun in the Creation Stage become elaborated and more widely disseminated. Stories of successful implementation are increasingly distributed and the innovation hailed. The narrative focuses on claimed benefits; little attention is given to potential costs. There are few counternarratives, and those who attempt to relate traditional counternarratives are labeled as apologists out of touch with contemporary needs. It is asserted that the new technique has been widely adopted, if not throughout the system then at least by the higher status members of the system. The allegations of widespread adoption persuade even more institutions to adopt through imitation or to maintain legitimacy (Meyer & Rowan, 1992). Consultants, champions, purveyors of the technology, and adopters increasingly circulate within the organizational system, making presentations at professional meetings and writing articles for professional journals that contribute to the diffusion of the innovation. These presentations serve to certify and reinforce the status of the person making them,

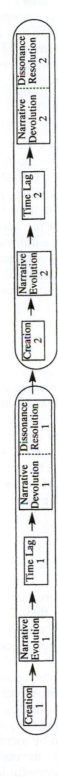

Figure 1 The life cycle stages of the fads process.

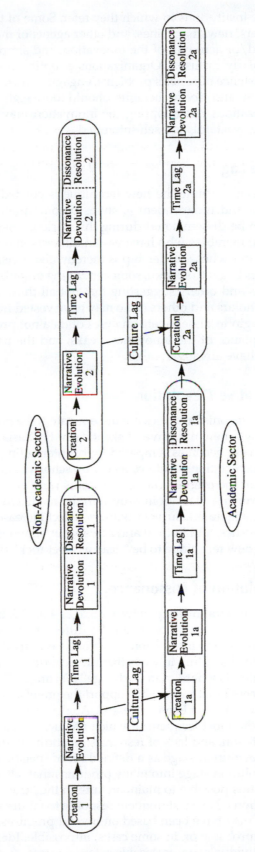

Figure 2 The movement of fads between sectors.

as well as that of the institutions to which they refer. Some of the stories of success prove to be attractive to newspapers, newsmagazines, and other agents of mass media eager to spot new trends, so that the name and/or acronym of the innovation, and simplistic statements of its foundational ideas, become popularly diffused. Organizations adopting the innovation are applauded for acknowledging the existence of serious problems, engaging in efforts to improve and reform, and recognizing that system and social benefits should outweigh selfish interests of organizational participants. Organizations not adopting the innovation may be criticized for being resistant to change, conservative, wasteful, and self-interested.

Stage 3: The Time Lag

There is a lag between the time the new technique is created and disseminated and the time at which user reactions and independent analyses become publicly available. Stories of successful adoption continue to be disseminated during this period. These stories are usually written by, or about, organizational members who have vested interests in being seen as being associated with a successful program and whose leadership is thereby given visibility. At the same time, revisionist and cautionary stories begin to surface, some reminding organizations of the unfulfilled promises of previous innovations and others suggesting that not all those adopting the innovation have been successful with it. Scholars and others (who may have vested interests different from the promoters of the innovation) begin to disseminate analyses of data not previously available. During this time lag period, the acceptance of the innovation peaks, and the pace of new adopters slows as those most likely to adopt have already done so.

Stage 4: The Narrative Devolution

As the more recent revisionist analyses are disseminated, the power of the original narrative of creation is challenged by a new narrative of skepticism. Enthusiasm for the new technique based on initial reports of success becomes tempered by countervailing reports of failure as outcomes fall short of unrealistic expectations. Data collected by scholars and other observers studying the new technique suggest that the original claims of success were either overstated or were not sustained, organizational performance was not improved in the predicted manner, and claims of the extent of adoption had been exaggerated. Surveys of users reflect increased dissatisfaction. Acceptance of the new technique diminishes, and journal and newspaper commentaries report on the reversal of fortune and declare the new technique to be "dead as a pet rock" (Byrne, 1997, p. 47).

Stage 5: The Resolution of Dissonance

There is significant temporal overlap between Stages 4 and 5, but they are separated here for purposes of analyses because they appear to have different dynamic properties. As champions and adopters see the demise of the innovation which only recently they had vigorously advocated, there is a need to account for its failure in ways that protect both their status and their ideological views. "A man with conviction is a hard man to change" (Festinger, Riecken, & Schachter, 1956), so that it should not be unexpected that those who support the premises of a fad are not dissuaded from their views merely because it has not been successful. Analyses of these seven fads reveal many of the rationalizations used, the most frequent of which are lack of leadership, intransigence of followers, improper implementation, and lack of resources. In addition, the innovation, which was described during its narrative evolution stage as a defined set of specific ideas and practices, had developed by the narrative devolution stage into many programs that, although sharing the same name, were quite different. It is thus possible to maintain faith in the "true" innovation by ascribing failures to the flaws of its mutations. The least frequent response to failure is to consider the possibility that the new technique itself may have been based on invalid premises, so that successful implementation was either highly improbable or, in some cases, impossible. Identifying failure as due to the weaknesses of specific individuals, unforeseeable external forces, or correctable flaws in implementation sets the stage for either reinventing the innovation and recycling it with minor modifications and a major change of name (Rogers, 1995) or for proposing a better innovation (clearly labeled as "not a fad") which is claimed as both necessary and sufficient for organizational improvement and in which the unfortunate problems leading to the abandonment of the earlier innovation have been corrected. The Creation Stage begins anew, and the stages of the cycle are repeated.

The Movement of Fads Between Sectors

Each of the management fads considered in this study was initially implemented in either business or governmental organizations before being diffused into higher education. There is relatively little overlap between the interorganizational networks of the innovation source groups and the higher education systems in which they were later applied. Members of both academic and nonacademic organizations have more association and communication with those inside their own sector than with those outside. Most people in different sectors read different journals, attend different meetings, share different values and perspectives, and live in different organizational cultures. This discontinuity leads to a culture lag so that events that are disseminated and generally known in one sector may not be immediately available to another.

As the apparently successful implementation of a management innovation in the original sector becomes conventional wisdom as part of its Narrative Evolution Stage, groups or individuals concerned with issues of organizational efficiency and effectiveness suggest the innovation may be suitable for adoption in new settings, such as higher education. Exactly how the transition between sectors is accomplished is unclear. It may be related to the increasing availability of stories in the popular press, but research on the adoption of innovation (Rogers, 1995) suggests that interpersonal communications are more effective than mass communications in disseminating innovations. Moreover, interpersonal communications about innovations are more effective when they occur between individuals who are similar or, as Rogers (p. 286) calls them, homophilous, than between members of different sectors, who are more likely to be dissimilar (or heterophilous). This suggests that a major vector of management innovation in higher education may be boundary spanning individuals with homophilous identities in both the nonacademic and academic sectors. These might include business leaders or legislators serving on higher education boards of trustees, college presidents and other academics appointed to business boards of directors, members of professional associations formed at least in part to maintain linkages between higher education and external groups, academics who read journals in multidisciplinary areas, such as business or human resource management, and consultants who solicit clients in both the education and non-education sectors.

As a consequence of the culture lag, champions in academic institutions become familiar with innovations in the nonacademic sector at about that time in the nonacademic sector's Narrative Evolution Stage in which expectations are high and increased levels of adoption are claimed. Unaware of the revisionist analyses taking place during the latter part of the Time Lag and early part of the Narrative Devolution Stages in the nonacademic sector, but persuaded by the enthusiastic reports developed during the earlier Narrative Evolution Stage, champions in higher education begin the Creation Stage in their sector. The higher education sector then recapitulates the cycle of the nonacademic sector, but in Academic Procession-like fashion, always one to two stages behind. This relationship is depicted in Figure 2.

Similarities and Differences Between Sectors

Innovations are ideas or practices perceived as new by the adopting organization (Rogers, 1995), regardless of whether they are objectively new, so it is not surprising that the process of fad adoption seen in academic settings is similar to that followed by the same innovation in nonacademic settings. In both sectors, initial decisions to adopt management innovations appear to be based on subjective judgments disseminated by homophilous peers, rather than analyses of empirical data, and in both sectors the momentum of innovators and early adopters is accelerated during the Narrative Evolution Stage. When 10–20% of a population has adopted an innovation, it has reached the "take-off" point (Rogers, 1995, p. 259). At this time the fate of an innovation is in the hands of a group that Rogers refers to as the "Early Majority." Compared with innovators and early adopters, the Early Majority is more deliberative and has a longer decision time. Acceptance by the Early Majority sets the stage for further acceleration and possible adoption of the innovation by all members of the social system, thus embracing it as part of standard practice. Rejection by the Early Majority leads to a drop in adoption rates and eventual discontinuance within the system, thus identifying the innovation as a fad.

It is during the Time Lag of Stage 3 that a major difference between fads in the academic and nonacademic sectors appears as they move toward Narrative Devolution. In the nonacademic sector, it is a period during which data of various kinds are collected, analyzed, and distributed within the sector. These data may come from surveys of the extent of adoption within the sector, scholarly comparisons of differences in outcomes between adopters and non-adopters, or surveys of users that assess their satisfaction with the new procedures. Results are likely to be presented quantitatively. In contrast, in the academic sector, information collected during the Time Lag of Stage 3, with infrequent exceptions, is limited to nonquantitative claims of the extent of adoption. These are usually presented as generalizations with no supporting documentation and commonly based on subjective judgments of outcomes by champions or adopters. There are few published examples in the academic sector of attempts to assess the institutional consequences of a management fad through data that provide evidence either of organizational outcomes or of the satisfaction of users. I can suggest two possibilities to account for the differences in how fads are assessed in the two sectors.

The first, and most obvious, is that the two sectors respond to different kinds of data and in different ways. An innovation's meaning in either sector is not self-evident, but instead is "gradually worked out through a process of social construction" (Rogers, 1995, p. xvii). It is stereotypical, but perhaps not without some justification, to think of business as being data-driven and bottom-line oriented; quantitative data are sought after and considered of great consequence when produced. Results can be measured in profit and loss statements, numbers are important, and decisions to retain or abandon an innovation can be made rapidly. In the more loosely coupled academic sector, quantitative measures are suspect. Interpretations develop slowly, and it takes longer for the meaning of an innovation to be shared by organizational participants. The data to which the business sector responds may move quickly up the system, whereas in the academic sector it may move more slowly, as counternarratives of shared authority and other myths begin to respond to the original narrative of efficiency. The Narrative Devolution Stage may be initiated by quantitative data in the nonacademic sector and by interpretive data in the academic sector.

The second, and less obvious possibility, is that the meaning of "adoption" may differ between the sectors. In both the academic and nonacademic sectors, organizations may claim to have adopted an innovation without truly having done so. However, the hierarchical structures and legal authority systems of the nonacademic sector make it more likely that senior management can impose management innovations on the institution's technical core. In contrast, the unique dual governance structure and loosely coupled processes of academic institutions buffer educational from administrative procedures and permit subgroups to operate with significant autonomy. This makes it easier in higher education for an innovation to be publicly "adopted," but not actually implemented in a way that affects core institutional processes. In this way, academic institutions may have greater opportunities than others to engage in what I call the "virtual adoption" of fads. For example, TQM/CQI, which entered higher education through the business sector, was said by senior academic administrators to be used by 70% of all colleges and universities by 1994 (El-Khawas, 1994). But by 1997 even TQM/CQI's strongest advocates acknowledged that only several hundred institutions had actually experimented with it in any meaningful way, and no more than a dozen had implemented it as a central component of their program (Marchese, 1997). Similar discrepancies between early claims of adoption and later analyses of actual use exist for each of the fads in this study. Academic institutions may have the ability to respond to fads as they respond to educational reforms—they may adopt them as policy, but never implement them (Cuban, 1990). Because business and government can impose fad processes that influence what people actually do, they may be more sensitive to data that may confirm or deny the validity of the fad practice. In contrast, because the "adoption" of fads at academic institutions may be primarily symbolic and have little effect on what most people do, there may be less emphasis on collecting and analyzing quantitative data to validate or invalidate the innovation and more emphasis on collecting impressionistic data that can justify the original adoption decision. Virtual adoption of fads allows an institution to have its cake and eat it too. Public claims of adopting an externally hailed innovation certify an institution's progressive attitude and concern for efficiency and improved management; private isolation of the fad protects the institution from the disruptive effects it would have if it were really implemented.

Virtual adoption is essentially superficial, although at some institutions where adoption initiatives of senior administrators have been particularly intense it may lead to some localized and undue disruption and discomfort. However, for the most part it is unlikely to have significant impact on the institutional core. Virtual adoption means that academic institutions may find it easier than other organizations both to "adopt" management fads and to abandon them. Because the fad has been embraced only by the senior administration, and not the technical core, neither adoption or abandonment requires significant attention or effort from most of the organization's members or has a major impact on their daily lives. In this way, the adoption of academic management fads is similar to the academic propensity regularly to form societies for the purpose of making silk purses out of sows' ears. As Cornford put it ninety years ago, "This tendency is not as dangerous as it may seem; for it may be observed that the sows, after taking their washing with a grunt or two, trundle back to the wallow; and the purse-market is quoted as firm" (1964/1908, p. 13).

Discussion

Suggestions by previous analysts of the existence of regularities in the management fad adoption process in higher education are confirmed by patterns in this cross-case analysis of data describing the life cycle of seven management innovations. On a small number of campuses, a fad may take hold and be maintained over an extended period, long after most institutions have rejected it. Occasionally, the fad may be integrated into an institution's culture and become a means by which the institution differentiates itself from others. These exceptional successes provide the evidence true believers may use to argue that the innovation is sound and that its generalized failure is due to faulty implementation rather than an inadequate conceptual base. But perhaps a more realistic lesson to be learned is that in the context of the great diversity of colleges and universities in the United States, an idea may find fertile soil in some microclimates, even as it proves to be sterile in most others. If the success of management fads over the past 40 years is measured by the extent to which they have been adopted and maintained in recognizable form in a reasonable number of institutions of higher education, it can it be said with confidence that these innovations have uniformly failed.

Still, management fads in the academic sector continue to be created or reinvented despite the absence of data suggesting that they have been successful and in the face of the failure of most of them to be widely adopted by the sector. Why does this happen? Those who develop the fads, as well as those who support them, appear to view academic organizations through the lens of an organizational paradigm that emphasizes the importance of goals, rationality, and causality. The acceptance of this paradigm leads those who believe it to choose problems "that while the paradigm is taken for granted, can be assumed to have solutions" Kuhn (1970, p. 37). Fads therefore are proposed solutions to puzzles seen as problems because of the paradigm being used. Management fads, even though they may sometimes be explicitly claimed by their creators to reflect a new paradigm, in reality reflect the old paradigms expected as part of "ordinary science."

Although fads fail, the paradigm supporting them remains. As Kuhn pointed out, failure of a paradigm to solve problems does not by itself negate the paradigm; it merely suggests to its adherents that the puzzle has not yet been solved and that further work is necessary. For example, after acknowledging that TQM/CQI has been ignored or rejected by most potential users, advocates still point to a small number of limited but presumably successful programs to claim that the system does work; it just isn't being implemented properly (Marchese, 1997). It is typical to deny the failure of fads by arguing that others have used it successfully, that it takes time to overcome past practices, and that results will be achieved in the future (Nohria & Berkley, 1994). Because of these arguments, there are no data that can convince a true believer that a fad is not effective, and claims that a fad "works" therefore cannot be disproved. Just as failure cannot negate a paradigm, the failure of a narrative to assist in solving policy dilemmas does not necessarily negate the narrative. Narratives cannot be overturned by countervailing evidence, but only by a different paradigm or "an equally straightforward narrative that tells a better story" (Roe, 1994, p. 40). Unless and until higher education is able to tell its story with a narrative more compelling than market-oriented economic utility, it is safe to assume that another fad, similar in many ways to those we have seen over the past 40 years is around the corner, and it will go through the stages within sectors and the phases between sectors described here.

Fads develop outside higher education and then are imported. I can think of no example in which a management innovation developed in higher education has been explicitly exported to business. Why is business in the lead? Some may say it's because business is more concerned with management than is education. A more cynical suggestion is that business has more consultants who make money by proposing and marketing fads than does higher education. Why do consultants give priority to marketing fads to business over education? As Willie Sutton said about why he robbed banks, "because that's where the money is."

Although management fads in higher education have not had the positive outcomes promised by their proponents, it is also true that the loose coupling of academic organizations has prevented the dire consequences predicted by some fad opponents. However, it would be a mistake to believe that fads have no consequences at all for the organizations or systems that adopt them. Some of these consequences may be negative, as people become cynical and resistant to new ideas, the judgment of leaders is questioned, and funds and energy are seen as being diverted from important institutional activities. But there may be positive consequences as well if fads "are kept in the proper perspective and incorporated into the collective wisdom of a company" (Rifkin, 1994, p. 11). Fads contain a "kernel of truth" that can help institutions reconsider familiar processes. Fads may have important latent functions in cuing attention, promoting action, and increasing the variety necessary for organizational evolution (Birnbaum, 2000). Fads may improve some nonacademic support activities at some institutions. And even after the fad itself has faded from view, its residual legacy, like the smile of the Cheshire Cat, may remain and indirectly influence institutional structure and values (Bohl & Luthans, 1996). Even when fads fail, they are important; the more we understand them, the greater the opportunity to increase their potential for institutional improvement and decrease their potential for institutional disruption.

Note

1. These case studies, and the citations to the literature on which each is based, are presented in chapters two through four of R. Birnbaum, *Management Fads in Higher Education,* San Francisco: Jossey-Bass, 2000.

References

Allen, R., & Chaffee, E. (1981, May 17–20). Management fads in higher education. Annual Forum of the Association for Institutional Research. Minneapolis, MN.

Baldridge, J. V., & Okimi, P. H. (1982, October). Strategic planning in higher education: New tool—or new gimmick? *AAHE Bulletin, 35*(6), 15–18.

Birnbaum, R. (2000). *Management fads in higher education.* San Francisco: Jossey-Bass.

Bohl, D. L., & Luthans, F. (1996, Winter). To our readers. *Organizational Dynamics,* pp. 2–3.

Byrne, J. A. (1997, June 23). Management theory—or fad of the month? *Business Week,* p. 47.

Chaffee, E. E. (1985). The concept of strategy: From business to higher education. In J. C. Smart (Ed.), *Higher education: Handbook of theory and research* (pp. 133–172). New York: Agathon Press.

Cohen, M. D., & March, J. G. (1974). *Leadership and ambiguity: The American college president.* New York: McGraw-Hill.

Cornford, F. M. (1964/1908). *Microcosmographia academica: Being a guide for the young academic politician.* New York: Halcyon-Commonwealth Foundation.

Cuban, L. (1990, January). Reforming again, again, and again. *Educational Researcher*, pp. 3–13.

Eccles, R. G., & Nohria, N. (1992). *Beyond the hype: Rediscovering the essence of management.* Cambridge, MA: Harvard Business School Press.

El-Khawas, E. (1994). *Campus trends 1994.* Washington, DC: American Council on Education.

ERIC on CD-ROM, 1966–1979, 1980–September 1996. (1995). Baltimore, MD: National Information Services Corporation.

Festinger, L., Riecken, H. W., & Schachter, S. (1956). *When prophecy fails.* New York: Harper and Row.

Kuhn, T. S. (1970). *The structure of scientific revolutions.* (2d ed., enlarged). Chicago, IL: University of Chicago Press.

Marchese, T. (1991, November). TQM reaches the academy. *AAHE Bulletin*, pp. 3–9.

Marchese, T. J. (1997). Sustaining quality enhancement in academic and managerial life. In M. W. Peterson, D. Dill, L. A. Mets, & Associates (Eds.), *Planning and management for a changing environment: A handbook on redesigning postsecondary institutions* (pp. 502–521). San Francisco: Jossey-Bass.

Meyer, J. W., & Rowan, B. (1992). Institutionalized organizations: Formal structure as myth and ceremony. In J. W. Meyer & R. W. Scott (Eds.), *Organizational environments: Ritual and rationality* (pp. 21–44). Newbury Park, CA: Sage.

Neave, G. (1997). Back to the future: Or, a view on likely brain teasers with which university management is likely to be faced in a Fin de Siècle world. *Tertiary Education and Management, 3,* 275–283.

Nicklin, J. L. (1995, January 27). The hum of corporate buzzwords. *Chronicle of Higher Education,* pp. A33–A34.

Nohria, N., & Berkley, J. D. (1994, January-February). Whatever happened to the take-charge manager? *Harvard Business Review, 128–137.*

Pascale, R. (1990). *Managing on the edge: How the smartest companies use conflict to stay ahead.* New York: Simon & Schuster.

Rifkin, G. (1994, September/October). When is a fad not a fad? *Harvard Business Review, 11.*

Roe, E. (1994). *Narrative policy analysis: Theory and practice.* Durham, NC: Duke University Press.

Rogers, E. M. (1995). *Diffusion of innovations.* (4th ed.). New York: Free Press.

Slavin, R. E. (1989, June). PET and the pendulum: Faddism in education and how to stop it. *Phi Delta Kappan, 20,* 752–758.

Weick, K. E. (1979). *The social psychology of organizing.* (2nd ed.). Reading, MA: Addison-Wesley.

Yin, R. K. (1984). *Case study research: Design and methods.* Beverly Hills, CA: Sage.

THE APPLICABILITY OF INSTITUTIONAL GOALS TO THE UNIVERSITY ORGANISATION

GLENYS PATTERSON, MASSEY UNIVERSITY, NEW ZEALAND

Abstract. Demands for greater accountability have emphasised the need for universities to clarify systematically their institutional goals. This article explores the issue of whether goal statements provide the essential framework and direction for the university's operation, or whether they are little more than idealistic rhetoric. Advocates for the use of goal strategy in universities have tended to adopt simplistic assumptions derived from business management models and overlook the considerable complexities and ambiguities of the university's operational reality: the fragmented professional structure, multiple goals, widely dispersed decision making, complex work, the rewards for extreme non-uniformity. Various problems and consequences of goal selection are outlined: problematic assumptions of a direct relationship between establishing qualitative statements of goals and achieving quantitative objectives, difficulties of goal valuation and measurement, goal interdependence, political processes that emphasise particular goals and de-emphasise others, and the goal diversity of stakeholder constituencies and interest groups. The article counsels universities against accepting unquestioningly an imposed system of goal setting, but rather to determine the minimum level of specificity needed to satisfy external demands and internal policy planning needs, while maintaining the university's essential character and purpose.

Introduction

'Almost any educated person could deliver a lecture entitled "The Goals of the University." Almost no one will listen to the lecture voluntarily. For the most part, such lectures and their companion essays are well-intentioned exercises in social rhetoric, with little operational content. Efforts to generate normative statements of the goals of the university tend to produce goals that are either meaningless or dubious' (Cohen & March, 1974, p. 195). The purpose of this discussion is to explore the issue of whether statements of university mission, goals and objectives are indeed little more than rhetorical idealism, as Cohen and March intimate, or whether, on the contrary, they provide the essential framework and direction for the university's operation. It is the normative statement of goals which is commonly perceived and intended as the crucial determinant of institutional purpose, policy and practice. 'To define the goals of an organisation is to clarify the very nature of its essence' (McKelvie, 1986, p. 151). Attention will therefore be focused primarily on goals, the intermediate level between the more general institutional philosophy of the mission, and the more specific objectives.

Why Goals Are Deemed to Be—or Not to Be—Important

Most organisation theorists agree on one thing—the importance of defining and studying goals. 'The entire subject of organizational analysis cannot be understood apart from goals' (Hall, 1999, p. 29). The setting of goals and goal achievement are seen as the critical task of any organisation, having priority over all other problems. 'No aspect of an organization's strategy, structure, or operating policies can be intelligently discussed or rationalized without a firm understanding and analysis of the unit's goals' (Hambrick, 1976, pp. 45–46). Goals provide the framework for planning, for deciding where the organisation is going and how it is going to get there. Goals, it is claimed, also enable progress to be evaluated, give a feeling of belonging and motivation, and provide a means of justifying the institution to its various publics. In recent years increasing demands that universities be more accountable for their activities and their use of limited resources have highlighted their need to examine and question what their goals are now, and to clarify and articulate what they should be.

Yet the concept of organisations as rational instruments of articulated goals has been challenged. Traditional organisation theory emphasises goals as being central, and sees deviations from goals as being due to such things as poor motivation, misperceived goals, poor management, inadequate resourcing—pathology that must be corrected. Perrow's (1978) alternative position suggests that announced goals are one of the least important constraints on organisational behaviour, that goals are peripheral rather than central, and that they serve largely as legitimating devices for a variety of participant group interests. Workers, including academics, use organisations primarily for their own ends, and are not concerned about the goals of the organisation or efficiency. Griffiths (1979) concurs that, in his experience, goals may be important to top executives and board members of educational institutions, but they are of little consequence to the teachers or professors. This is reflected in a common finding in strategic university research projects—that 'organizational units, particularly academic departments, are only marginally driven by the strategic goals and priorities of the University as a whole' (Cabrera et al., 2000, p. 11). Organisational theories, says Griffiths, tend to be based on the perceptions of top executives, rather than the lower participants; whereas the concept of informal organisation builds upon ways in which the lower participants seek to achieve their own goals, which are generally not the goals of top management. In any organisation there are clearly many things that go on that are not institutional-goal-related activities. Seeking similarly to 'explode the myth of organizational rationality', Morgan (1986, p. 195) agrees that organisations may pursue goals and stress the importance of rational, efficient and effective management, but he asks, 'Rational, efficient, and effective for whom? Whose goals are being pursued? What interests are being served? . . . Organizational goals may be rational for some people's interests but not for others . . . Rationality is always interest-based and thus changes according to the perspective from which it is viewed.' He asserts that managers, like others, use the organisation as a legitimising umbrella under which to pursue a variety of interests.

Other analysts have expressed considerable reservations about the applicability of goal theory to the university organisation. Fenske (1980, p. 177), for example, registered strong doubts about 'the efficacy of many present goal studies and the validity of models borrowed from business management to measure academic efficiency in higher education'. He goes on to state his particular concern 'that the misapplication of techniques will become legitimate by default and through continued usage may ultimately change the nature of higher education—the genius and characteristics of which have taken centuries to build'. Etzioni warned in 1964 of the distorting effects of frequent measurement, which encourages overproduction of highly measurable items and neglect of the less measurable ones. Certainly the current emphasis on performance measurement against goals ensures that Etzioni's warning remains highly pertinent. Davies (1985) also notes the instability created by repeated requests to justify the existence of certain goals and their fulfilment, as does Mintzberg (1994). Stressing the point that many of the goals most important for professional organisations such as universities simply do not lend themselves to measurement, Mintzberg is highly critical of what he sees as the damage and wastage of time caused by trying to fit the square pegs of conventional planning into the round holes of university organisations—organisations that, he says, are driven by highly complex operating work, are notoriously loosely coupled in their operating core, and have a strategy-making process quite different to that of the 'conventional wisdom' as reflected in machine-type organisations.

One of the notably unique features of universities is their complexity of mission and multiplicity of goals. Universities, says Perkins (1973, p. 247), 'have a bad case of organizational indigestion because they have swallowed multiple and conflicting missions'. The business corporation, in contrast, has a clear unity of mission—the making of profits; and the amount or rate of profit gives a straightforward, quantifiable measure of performance. The business corporation has well-defined lines of authority, to maintain a unity of action in order to achieve its unity of purpose. Authority for the management of a university is, in comparison, fragmentary and diffused, with many major facets of academic activity (for example, the teaching itself) under little direct control. Decision making is more widely dispersed. As Fenske (1980) points out, models of goal setting that work with other complex organisations cannot be directly applied to the university, because all such models assume a clear line of authority and a consensual set of goals, neither of which exists in the university organisation.

The Complexity of the University Goals Issue

Attempts to derive a clearly articulated and meaningful statement of institutional goals for the university are invariably complicated by a number of factors.

The Existence of Covert as Well as Overt Organisation Goals

There are likely to be informal and covert goals at all levels of the organisation, and these may be more significant for staff than are the formal overt goals, even where there is apparent consensus for the latter. An example would be where ostensible commitment to research is at variance with staff actually spending as much non-teaching time as possible in private consultancy work; or an institution's allocation of resources may not be in line with its stated priority of goals. Goal displacement can occur where an emphasis on routines and procedures, the means to an end, becomes more important than the end goal itself. For example, a head of department may become so involved in administrative procedures that departmental research goals are displaced. A study by Gross (1969) discovered that many activities went on in universities which became goals of the organisation but which were not actually perceived as 'goals'. In analysing the goals issue, Gross maintained that two kinds of evidence are required before a goal can be deemed to be present: intentions and activities. 'Intentions' are what the people in the organisation believe the goals of the organisation to be; 'activities' are what people in the organisations are actually doing. Gross described as 'utopian' a goal that ranks high as an intention but is only minimally evident in activities (for example where there is high support for research goals, but where people spend most of their time in teaching activities). An 'unstated' goal is one ranked low as an intention but much in evidence in activities (for example, where substantial academic time is spent on professional services for private clients). 'Outputs', what the organisation produces, are the third dimension. Gross claims that although there must be some degree of correspondence between intentions and activities for a goal to exist, there is no necessary correspondence between these measures and outputs. An organisation can produce unintended outputs that may not be related to its intentions.

Different Kinds of Organisational Goals

Ball and Halwachi (1987) distinguish between 'outcome' goals (goals relating to how the institution meets the needs of society—for example, vocational preparation); and 'process' goals (goals relating to the internal functioning of the organisation—for example, staff development). Livingstone (1974) distinguished 'end product' or 'output' goals, and 'system' or 'system maintenance' goals; and he also added a third goal type, the 'quality/characteristics' goal. This goal distinguished between different types of product—different types of graduate or knowledge (for example, a 'pure researcher' or 'graduates oriented towards human relations skills'). Gross (1969) believed that the study of organisations had suffered from a too simple view of goals. He made a similar differentiation between universities' 'output goals' and 'support goals', but also divided support goals into four categories: adaptation goals (those which reflect the need for the organisation to come to terms with its environment); management goals (those which reflect decisions on who should run the university and the establishment of output goal priorities); motivation goals (those which seek staff and student satisfaction and loyalty); and positional goals (those which serve to maintain the comparative position of the university). Gross argued that the ability of the organisation to attain its output goals is dependent on its ability to grapple successfully with these non-output goals.

A Diversity of Insider and Outsider Goals

As already noted, universities have a complexity and multiplicity of goals compared with a profit-oriented organisation. Their various constituencies and interest groups—academic staff, students, administrators, councils, government, the Ministry, the public, funding bodies, professional groups—hold divergent, even opposing views on university goals and goal priorities, both within and between the groups. Most academics pursue both teaching and research, but have different strengths of commitment to each, and research rather than teaching tends to be rewarded. Students may be interested primarily in gaining vocational certification, or in learning for its own sake. Administrators seek an efficient use of resources, but academic staff largely determine the expenditure. The Education Ministry pursues policy for the whole education sector, which by no means necessarily accommodates to specific university goals. Government may emphasise equity goals while at the same time encouraging maximisation of full fee courses and privately funded research. Governments are also subject to change, and with a change of government come new priorities—for example, labour force planning policies may take precedence over purely market demand. Councils have formal powers and responsibilities, but delegate most real authority. Research funding bodies are concerned about standards, excellence, and the ownership of research. Professional bodies may favour elitism rather than universalism in university education. And the overall public has widely divergent views, values and expectations for university directions. Higher education is indeed many things to many people: 'a mosaic of conflicting values' (Fenske, 1980).

Difficulties of Goal Valuation and Measurement

The diversity of goal and goal type raises problems for goal assessment. University goals may relate to the general mission of the advancement and dissemination of knowledge, but there is no systematised way of valuing the wide range of 'knowledge' involved. Nor is there an easy way to derive comparative values for goals pertaining to breadth versus those pertaining to depth of study; comprehensiveness versus subject selectiveness; vocational versus general education; pure versus applied research; the value of community service goals; or goal interdependencies. It may be difficult to define whether a goal is an 'aspired to' goal or an actual goal. It is difficult to weigh the comparative value of goals held to be significant by one university group (e.g. academics) over those deemed important by another university group (e.g. students). And should there be any value difference between process goals and outcome goals? The prioritising of university goals is highly problematic, inevitably a political process. Immense difficulties also arise over the measurement of institutional outcomes and impacts. This is particularly the case for the more abstruse goals, such as, for example, 'To develop in students inquisitiveness, and a willingness to question orthodoxy and to consider new ideas'. Is the outcome the student, the course taken, the qualification achieved, or the learning experience, asks Peeke (1994). There is the problem of time, i.e. short-term versus long-term effects. And should the effect of covert goals also be accounted for? Hambrick (1976, p. 48) concluded that 'the nature of university goals makes them quite unmeasurable. To attempt to measure the goals, is to probably mis-measure them.' But 'the principle of verifiability is not a reality test,' argues Davies (1986, p. 101), 'so we must not assume that if something cannot be verified, it does not exist'; nor can we assume that the unverifiable has no value.

Particular Characteristics of the University Institution Which Further Inhibit Goal Clarification

Clark (1983a) makes the point that although academics may share in common the fact that they work with and upon knowledge, they do not share common knowledge; indeed, they are rewarded primarily for going off in opposite directions. Disciplinary fields continue to become ever more specialised, and tend to function as separate cell groups. There is as a consequence a high degree of professional autonomy and authoritativeness at the operating level of the university. Furthermore, the most crucial links for the specialist groups are from identification with others working in the same specialised fields, either within or outside the academic system; with loyalty to the employing university institution frequently of a second order. The university is therefore both discipline based and discipline diversified. It can be viewed as a loose confederation of knowledge-bearing groups, continually cell splitting and mutating, disunited by their disparate loyalties, interests, ideas and approaches to knowledge, each with a high degree of self-control. Attempts to impose uniformity through specific goal-directed activity will always lie uneasily alongside this structure of segmented professionalism, and be inconsistent with the essential character and purpose of the institution—the challenging, reworking, maintaining, disseminating, expanding, defending, and evolving of knowledge generated by the commitment to research.

In addition to professional fragmentation, there is a wide diversity in leadership style and status found at the faculty departmental level. Heads of department, selected for their positions largely on the basis of originality in research, are far from comprising a managerial level that will uniformly interpret, adopt and reflect upper-echelon philosophy. Many, in the interests of research achievement, will place a higher priority on their own and departmental goals than on overall organisational goals. The perception by heads of department of their departmental role also varies considerably, with different emphases placed on the relative importance of research leadership, teaching leadership, and administrative functions. Some may perceive their role as leaning more towards the organisational hierarchy, whereas others see it as primarily representing their departmental colleagues. Such leadership divergence is not conducive to either clarification or implementation of a uniform set of institutional goals.

With individual, group and institutional goals disparate and even conflicting, it is likely to be extremely difficult to formulate a statement of meaningful goals for the university which will elicit any real commitment from its constituent members. 'It is not irrational, self interested academics who stand in the first instance against the wishes of planners who seek greater uniformity and coherence,' argues Clark (1983a, p. 23). 'It is the very nature of the enterprise . . . The variation in subject matter that is part and parcel of the system produces a need for extreme non-uniformity: in structure and procedure, in policy and governance.' So the concept of a university mission statement and its application can be seen as somewhat fragile in this organisational context of complex and multiple goal and personal interests, and fragmentation. The establishment of a statement of goals assumes that it will be used as the basis for action, that organisation members will identify with and subscribe to it. But the significance of individual interests and goal diversity means that this is by no means certain or indeed likely. Peeke (1994, p. 126), in a substantial study of mission statements in higher and further education, concluded that institutional mission is thus a rather illusory concept, and that the more the nature of mission is explored, the more it appears that an overall institutional mission can be little more than a veneer. Recent reviews of higher education institutional mission statement use in the UK lend support to this notion of veneer, albeit a useful formulaic veneer to satisfy expectations and requirements. A study of the mission statements of 118 higher education institutions (Mackay et al., 1995, p. 203) described the statements as imprecise instruments, conveying an impression of sameness. 'Their vacuous, even vapid language, suggests they are devised to a formula, rather than emerging as the result of careful deliberation of institutional priorities.' The Davies and Glaister (1996) investigation of mission statement use at 68 universities had a 'strong impression' of statements being produced for the requirements of an external stakeholder or because it was seen as 'the thing to do'.

In extending the idea of the university as a loosely coupled system, Clark (1983b) presents a model in which the overall structure of the academic system has three main segments: the understructure, consisting of the operating units and departments; the middlestructure, which is the institution itself; and the superstructure, which is the wider system and its inter-institutional links. Clark argues that there is a considerable tension between the different levels. The understructure segment is made up of a disunited aggregation of disciplines and professional fields, a loosely coupled system. The superstructure comprises the state-constructed administrative pyramid, which, in contrast to the understructure, seeks to impose order, to coordinate, to systematise, to make more uniform the otherwise fragmented segments, enterprises and sectors. It stresses hierarchy and formal links. Requiring the formulation of goals and their articulation in institutional charters and formal statements of mission, and the measurement of performance through goal achievement are methods by which the superstructure can achieve order and impose its priorities on the system. As the superstructure grows larger and more dominant, many external trends and demands (for example, demands by business leaders for a greater element of private enterprise) are interpreted by the superstructure political and administrative personnel, and processed into the system. 'The vehicle for change is thus political and bureaucratic coordination, as against the vehicle of professional influence that is primary in the understructure' (Clark, 1983b, p. 107). In the middlestructure, the university heads are placed in a mediating role, acting between the demands and pressures from the superstructure above, and those from the understructure below. In centralised economies, such as the former USSR, the university heads have been the arms of the superstructure administration; whereas in systems where universities have had a greater measure of autonomy, the university heads have acted as the arms of their academic colleagues. For many universities in the latter category, recent 'reforms' in their academic systems, the imposition of greater accountability measures, and the emphasis on goal-directed activity are forcing heads into adopting a role closer to the arms of the superstructure and away from a role as the collegial arms of the operating level understructure.

Goal Selection

Notwithstanding the complexity of the goals issue for universities, and the characteristics of the university institution which inhibit goal clarification, and similarly as in other higher education systems (e.g. UK, Australia), from 1990 New Zealand universities have been obliged by law to clarify their goals. Determining the goals of the institution is usually perceived as the first and most important stage of an organisation's planning procedure. Allen (1988) presents three planning models: the autonomous model, in which planning is participative and operates from the bottom up; the centralised model, operating from the top down, in which decisions are made at the national level; and a compromise model, which sits somewhere between the other two. In the autonomous model, decisions on the goals of the university take into account the views of the main constituent and interest groups, but are made by the academic staff, or representatives of the academic staff. The model assumes that agreement on goals can be attained through open rational discussion. In practice, decisions may be made on a political basis, or there may be such serious dissension within the institution or group that agreement is impossible. Nevertheless, this model can satisfy both external demands for accountability mechanisms and internal demands for participative decision-making on goals. In the centralised model, the goals are essentially those of the state, rather than the institution, and are likely to be closely linked with labour force planning and the economy in general. This model was found in the centrally controlled economies of the former communist bloc countries. The model assumes that adequate data are available on which decisions can be made, and that plans can be modified in response to changing requirements. However, it is unlikely that any state really has the capacity to collect all the necessary data and to make sufficiently rapid adjustments to its plans and goals to avoid imbalances occurring.

The New Zealand, British and Australian systems are examples of the compromise model, in which goal determination takes place both at the national level and within the institutions—a mixture of centralised and autonomous procedures. In all three countries there has been a recently accelerating trend towards more influence by the central authority. Governments are exerting pressure and imposing legal requirements to ensure that universities respond to national needs and adopt specified policy goals and objectives. (In New Zealand, the imposed charter framework states, for example, that there must be a proactive statement on socioeconomic, gender and ethnic equity.) The individual universities make their own decisions on internal goal setting and resource allocation. In practice, however, there is little room for significant manoeuvre. The high degree of differentiation and segmentation in the university creates a large number of independent units, which actively compete for power and resources. The realisation that goals are competing, rather than compatible and complementary, that resources put into one area must be taken away from another, is the real crux of the issue of internal goal setting. The choice of goals is essentially a value judgement, and universities engage in a great deal of political action concerning which goals are going to be emphasised.

Political models of the university (e.g. Baldridge et al., 1978) assume there is no consensus on the organisation's goals and purposes, and that the management process consists of engaging or mediating in conflict, bargaining, power and exchange. Decisions on goals may emerge as negotiated compromises. The focus here is primarily on the problems involved in goal setting and values, rather than on problems of maximising efficiency in achieving the goals. The political model argues that goals are not selected rationally, on the basis of a carefully assessed hierarchy of goals, but are selected through the university's internal political processes, which emphasise particular goals and de-emphasise others. In this way, power blocs and small groups of political elites are able to shape goal selection and structure to their benefit. The model supports Morgan's (1986) self-interest theory, discussed earlier, in which managers and others use the idea of rationality as a resource for pursuing political agendas. Baldridge et al. (1978) contend that when resources are plentiful, interest groups engage in only minimal conflict. However, when resources are tight, groups mobilise and fight to influence decisions, other groups try to take over their goals, and they become more subject to attack from outside pressure groups.

Fenske (1980), noting the large political element in goal setting, has emphasised the importance of institution-wide involvement in goal setting. The Davies and Glaister (1996) study in the UK found a poor level of participation during the goal formulation stage. In New Zealand, it is a legislative requirement that before submission of an institution's charter of its goals and purposes, the university council must consult with staff, students, and appropriate community groups, and consider the views expressed. But the Act does not stipulate that these views must be incorporated into the university's goal statement.

Consequences of Goal Selection

Although a goal statement may be accepted and supported by the various university constituencies, it may actually be incompatible with the ability of the institution to deliver, i.e. the gap between intent and achievement may be too great. In addition, a tendency to regard goals as fixed can preclude the consideration of alternative or additional ways of achieving the institution's purpose. Simpson (1985) has drawn attention to the interdependence of goals: where there is competition for resources, the opportunity cost of one goal activity may be the reduction of an activity that serves another goal; the pursuit of one goal may be in conflict with another, even where there are no resource constraints; a prioritising of goal activities may be simplistic, in that beyond a certain point the marginal value of adding to one activity may be less than putting resources into a lower-ranked goal; or the achievement of one goal may be dependent on the extent to which another goal is achieved.

The concept of goal interdependence raises the issue of suboptimisation. In the goals context, suboptimisation arises from the tendency for a unit to exaggerate the importance of its own contribution, to the extent that organisation goals are perceived in terms of the activities of the unit. The unit tries to make its particular contribution perfect, disregarding the effect of this on the rest of the organisation. Perfect optimisation of a subsystem usually means that the system as a whole is functioning less well than it might. Where two subsystems have competing goals, there is a clear potential for suboptimisation, and where all or most subsystems are striving to be optimal, the result will be extensive suboptimisation. As an example, suboptimisation would occur where a chemistry department, in striving to become a 'centre of excellence', concentrates on its advanced graduate and doctoral students, undertakes extensive research, including contract research projects, allocates funds to obtain the most up-to-date journals and technical equipment in highly specialised areas of study, and employs only the most eminent scientists. Yet in optimising its high-level academic excellence, the department neglects basic first-year service courses for various other applied science areas, with the consequence that many students are inadequately prepared for their subsequent study in those areas. Or a university's resources may be channelled into setting up a prestigious law school, while the English Department operates virtually as a service centre, teaching written expression skills to large classes of undergraduate law students, leaving the department little time to pursue scholarly research. An optimal system, that is, a system operating with overall optimum performance, is one in which no subsystem is operating with perfect optimality. However, the problem is that system optimisation is only possible where it is known what a state of total optimisation would be; but because of the complexity and diffusion of university goal systems, this is extremely difficult to ascertain. Any exercise in optimisation will invariably be a political process, in which the achievement of optimal goal selection and system integration will prove highly elusive.

Conclusion

In their current political and financial contexts universities are required to identify their institutional goals and purpose. If universities are not to function purely reactively, that is, responding disjointedly to these environmental pressures imposed on the one hand and to their internal political pressures on the other, then they must clarify their essential purpose, and select a set of goals to serve as guides to decision making. A university without a sense of its goals has been likened to a rudderless ship. Indeed, the setting of goals and goal achievement are widely held to be the most crucial task in any organisation. A set of goals can provide a sense of direction and a means for institutional performance to be assessed and controlled. Goal clarification forces a university to decide what it wants to do in the future, and to consider and prioritise the various options open to it. Only then can policy planning strategies be determined which will enable it to achieve its goals.

Yet goals are not simple concepts, and the university is a highly complex organisation. Advocates for the use of goal formulation strategies in universities have tended to adopt a simplistic and idealistic approach to the goals issue, using assumptions derived from business management models, and overlooking the considerable complexities and ambiguities of the university's operational reality. Universities have a multiplicity of goals, compared with a profit-oriented organisation, and decision making is widely dispersed. The diversity of goal and goal type raises considerable difficulties for goal assessment and selection, for there is no easy way of deriving comparative goal values. The imposition of uniformity through specific goal-directed activity does not fit easily alongside the fragmented professional structure. The essential character and purpose of the university support extreme non-uniformity, with staff rewarded for originality and difference. The existence of a statement of goals does not, in itself, mean that organisation members will subscribe to it. In a situation where institutional goal setting is demanded by the superstructure (which seeks to impose order through increased bureaucratic controls), is led and imposed by the middlestructure hierarchy (in an attempt to mediate between the superstructure and understructure), but gets little or no real support or professional influence from the understructure (which tends to pursue autonomy, fragmentation and differentiation, and has primary allegiance to specialised fields of study, rather than to the institution), it is not difficult to understand why Cohen and March (1974) should have found that 'efforts to generate normative statements of the goals of the university tend to produce goals that are either meaningless or dubious'; or to concur with Peeke (1994) that the closer one moves towards the concept of institutional mission, the more blurred it becomes.

In New Zealand and elsewhere governments are exerting pressure and imposing legal requirements to ensure that universities clarify their goals, including the adoption of specified policy goals and objectives—a mixture of imposed goals and internal goal setting. Universities may engage in a great deal of political activity concerning which goals are going to be emphasised. But the achievement of optimal goal selection and system integration is highly elusive, an extremely difficult task. Where this is not achieved (and given the many problems with the university goals issue it would not be surprising if this is in the majority of cases), then statements of university mission, goals and objectives may indeed remain little more than idealistic rhetoric. Where this position is achieved, then such statements can provide meaningful operational directives. But the recognition and acceptance of goal statement directives do not automatically ensure the effectiveness and efficiency of the organisation, nor that good decision making will ensue. The assumption of a direct relationship between establishing qualitative statements of goals and achieving quantitative objectives is problematic; goal applications often simply fail to translate directly into practical management processes.

It is clear that as universities continue to be inextricably caught up in the general environmental turbulence and change, the demands for their greater explicitness, overtness and accountability will not diminish. In such an environment, the traditional acceptance of the university as a loosely coupled system, the belief that the flexibility of loose coupling is analogous to academic freedom and therefore an essential feature of the university organisation, must be questioned. Lutz's (1982) view is that 'organised anarchy' is a convenient term that means no one is accountable, and that loose coupling may be merely an empirical description of some things that could in fact be changed without doing damage to academe. Certainly the application of mission, goals and objectives, and their follow-on imply tight rather than loose coupling. Anarchy is not a necessary characteristic of the university organisation, and the university can undoubtedly survive a measure of tighter coupling, more public scrutiny, and greater accountability. However, what is imperative is that universities do not embark with unquestioning acceptance into a superstructurally imposed system of institutional goal setting. Rather, they must seek to determine what level of specificity is needed to satisfy the environmental requirements, while maintaining the university's essential character and purpose.

Correspondance: Glenys Patterson, Department of Management, Massey University, Hamilton, New Zealand.

References

Allen, M. (1988) *The Goals of Universities*. Milton Keynes: SRHE and Open University Press.

Baldridge, J. V., Curtis, D. V., Ecker, G. & Riley, G. L. (1978) *Policy Making and Effective Leadership*. San Francisco, CA: Jossey-Bass.

Ball, R. & Halwachi, J. (1987) Performance indicators in higher education, *Higher Education*, 16, pp. 393–405.

Cabrera, A., Ratcliff, J. & de Vries, W. (2000) Of institutional strategic decisions and performance indicators: a strategy to improve institutional effectiveness. Paper presented at EAIR 22nd Annual Forum, Berlin, September.

Clark, B. R. (1983a) Governing the higher education system, in: M. Shattock (Ed.) *The Structure and Governance of Higher Education*. Guildford: Society for Research into Higher Education.

Clark, B. R. (1983b) The contradictions of change in academic systems, *Higher Education*, 12, pp. 101–116.

Cohen, M. D. & March, J. G. (1974) *Leadership and Ambiguity: the American college president*. New York: McGraw-Hill.

Davies, G. K. (1986) The importance of being general: philosophy, politics, and institutional mission statements, in: J. C. Smart (Ed.) *Higher Education: handbook of theory and research*, Vol. 11, pp. 85–102. New York: Agathon Press.

Davies, J. (1985) Institutional mission and purpose, in: G. Lockwood & J. Davies, *Universities: the management challenge*, pp. 80–101. Windsor: NFER-NELSON.

Davies, S. W. & Glaister, K. W. (1996) Spurs to higher things? Mission statements of UK universities, *Higher Education Quarterly*, 50(4), pp. 261–294.

Etzioni, A. (1964) *Modern Organizations*. Englewood Cliffs, NJ: Prentice-Hall.

Fenske, R. H. (1980) Setting institutional goals and objectives, in P. Jedamus, M. W. Peterson et al., *Improving Academic Management: a handbook of planning and institutional research*, pp. 177–199. San Francisco, CA: Jossey-Bass.

Griffiths, D. E. (1979) Intellectual turmoil in educational administration, *Educational Administration Quarterly*, 15(3), pp. 43–65.

Gross, E. (1969) The definition of organizational goals, *British Journal of Sociology*, 20, pp. 277–294.

Hall, R. H. (1999) *Organizations: structures, processes, and outcomes*, 7th edn. New Jersey: Prentice-Hall.

Hambrick, D. C. (1976) The university as an organisation. How is it different from a business?, in: G. L. Anderson (Ed.) *Reflections on University Values and the American Scholar*, pp. 41–58. College Park, PA: Pennsylvania State University.

Livingstone, H. (1974) *The University: an organizational analysis.* Glasgow: Blackie.

Lutz, F. W. (1982) Tightening up loose coupling in organizations of higher education, *Administrative Science Quarterly*, 27(4), pp. 653–669.

Mackay, L., Scott, P. & Smith, D. (1995) Restructured and differentiated? Institutional responses to the changing environment of UK higher education, *Higher Education Management*, 7(2), pp. 193–205.

McKelvie, B. D. (1986) The university's statement of goals: an idea whose time has arrived, *Higher Education*, 15, pp. 151–163.

Mintzberg, H. (1994) *The Rise and Fall of Strategic Planning.* New York: Free Press.

Morgan, G. (1986) *Images of Organization.* Beverly Hills: Sage.

Peeke, G. (1994) *Mission and Change: institutional mission and its application to the management of further and higher education.* Buckingham: SRHE and Open University Press.

Perkins, J. A. (1973) Missions and organization: a redefinition, in: J. A. Perkins (Ed.) *The University as an Organization*, pp. 247–260. New York: McGraw-Hill.

Perrow, C. (1978) Demystifying organizations, in R. C. Sarri & Y. Hasenfeld (Eds.) *The Management of Human Services*, pp. 105–120. New York: Columbia University Press.

Simpson, W. B. (1985) Revitalizing the role of values and objectives in institutions of higher education: difficulties encountered and the possible contribution of external evaluation, *Higher Education*, 14, pp. 535–551.

PART VII

THE PRACTICE OF MAKING AND ASSESSING CHANGE

PERFORMANCE AND PARALYSIS

THE ORGANIZATIONAL CONTEXT OF THE AMERICAN RESEARCH UNIVERSITY

DANIEL ALPERT

Introduction: Universities in Transition

> Organizationally the university is, in fact, one of the most complex structures in modern society; it is also increasingly archaic. It is complex because its formal structure does not describe either actual power or responsibilities; it is archaic because the functions it must perform are not and cannot be discharged through the formal structure provided in its charter.
>
> James A. Perkins [35, p. 3]

> [Organizational] learning cannot proceed effectively without maps which can be used to relate errors to features within the organization. Maps . . . are organized pictures which show how the features of the system have been placed in some sort of pattern which illuminates the interdependence among the parts of the system.
>
> Chris Argyris and Donald A. Schön [2, p. 159]

Despite a record of remarkable performance since World War II, American universities have been facing increasingly hard times in the 1970s and 1980s. The current period of economic retrenchment has called into sharp focus the question of the nation's commitment to its institutions of higher education and equally serious questions regarding the responsibilities of universities to society. Retrenchment has also revealed within the academy serious problems relating to management and governance, on the one hand, and identity and purpose on the other. The symptoms of trouble include loss of confidence in the future, decline in faculty morale, and a slowdown of the infusion of talented young recruits into graduate study. Paradoxically, these problems have intensified at the same time that corporations declare their entry into the "knowledge business" as a new growth industry, and technological revolutions in computers and telecommunications herald the arrival of the "information age."

In the early 1970s, a study by Lanier and Anderson [28, p. 77] for the American Council on Education found "massive evidence of widespread retrenchment in higher education." Since then, universities have experienced continuing financial restraints but have dealt with each subsequent cutback as a short-term crisis. In 1981, Robert Barak [5, p. 213] observed that "little has changed since 1976. Higher education still desperately needs an ongoing and continuous strategic approach to management."

This article was stimulated by the author's participation in an ongoing series of seminar-workshops on organizational responses to retrenchment, sponsored by the Center for Advanced Study at the University of Illinois at Urbana–Champaign. Resource persons for specific issues in the series included an interesting diversity of administrators, faculty members, legislators, and other stakeholders in the academic enterprise from this campus and elsewhere. The continuing inquiry was carried out by an informal, self-selected network of faculty members from various departments, including Stuart Albert, Richard Boland, Clark Bullard, Fred Coombs, Hugh Petrie, Sue Schneider, James Votruba, and David Whetten, to whom I am indebted for an introduction into the literature of organizational behavior and for many illuminating and provocative discussions.

And Herman Neibuhr, Jr. of Temple University concurs: "Retrenchment may be a short range solution to avoid deficits, but it is hardly a strategy to pursue until the year 2000" [33, p. 16]. But the perceived need for long-range strategies is in marked contrast to the short-term, belt-tightening tactics that have dominated academic responses to retrenchment for more than a decade.

Any organization confronting a period of retrenchment is faced with a central dilemma: should it respond by increasing organizational efficiency or should it embark on innovative efforts to improve effectiveness? As these terms are defined by Pfeffer and Salancik [38, p. 11], "organizational efficiency is an *internal* standard of performance. . . . The question whether what is being done should be done is not posed, but only how well it is being done. Efficiency is measured by the ratio of resources utilized to output produced." In contrast, "the effectiveness of an organization is its ability to create acceptable outcomes and actions . . . [it] is an *external* standard of how well an organization is meeting the demands of the various groups and organizations that are concerned with its activities." The efficiency-effectiveness dilemma has been phrased in terms of organizational learning by Argyris and Schön [2, pp. 18–26] as follows: Does the situation call for "single-loop" organizational learning, that is, retaining the existing norms, goals, and structures and doing better the things we are now doing? Or does it call for "double-loop" learning, that is, reformulating the norms, goals, and structures and embarking in innovative directions to create acceptable outcomes? Petrie and Alpert [37] define the central problem of retrenchment in higher education as the necessity to choose sensibly between these alternatives. Whetten [58] argues persuasively that the single-loop search for greater efficiency has dominated academic responses to retrenchment because of our greater ability to measure efficiency and the difficulty of conclusively settling debates over goals and priorities. Argyris and Schön [2] assert that the tendency to limit organizational learning to single-loop learning is so strong that new organizational maps and new theories that govern organizational actions—what they call "theories-in-use"—are required even to postulate alternative strategies.

Not surprisingly, the difficulties associated with retrenchment have most often been framed in financial terms, and in some ways, this approach to defining the problems makes them simpler to handle: financial problems cannot indefinitely be deferred or ignored, and the language is widely understood. Furthermore, budget shortages do not suggest failures of leadership and do not of themselves call for major modification of internal goals or ways of doing things; if money could somehow be found, the organization could go about its business as usual. In short, financial difficulties are attributable to changes in the external economic environment, an arena in which universities are presumed to have little control. But to many observers (e.g., Boyer and Hechinger [11], Mingle and Associates [31], Richman and Farmer [41]) the cutbacks associated with recent retrenchment are coincident with significant, longer term structural and attitudinal changes in the society, which themselves constitute demands for changes in higher education. In this view, the financial crunch of the past fifteen years is a symptom as well as a problem—a symptom of difficulties that reside not in the financial environment but in the way universities respond. To these thoughtful observers, retrenchment is partly an indication that our universities are not sufficiently adaptive or responsive to the needs of society.

Faced with retrenchment, the dominant tendency within academic institutions has been to deal with each budget reduction as though it were unique to the institution in question, to contend among departments in a zero-sum game for the limited available resources, and to seek to maintain the status quo. In the absence of clear lines of authority or consensus among equals, even a minimal cutback (a few percent) can reduce a highly regarded campus to a state of sharp confrontation, low morale, and serious discontent. The resulting impasse constitutes what Yarmolinsky calls "institutional paralysis:" "One of the more remarkable things about universities . . . is that, with a few honorable exceptions, they have managed to survive, and even to prosper, without developing any conscious process for making institutional choices" [59, p. 61]. Institutional paralysis is a result, Yarmolinsky argues, of "four major disjunctions within the body politic . . . no one group in the university has all the factors necessary for institutional change: the concern, the status, the authority, and the equipment to achieve institutional change" [59, p. 61]. In his view, the system of governance is hopelessly inadequate, and he proposes some significant organizational changes. In the opinion of Eric Ashby, another astute observer of the academic scene, institutional paralysis is also attributable to serious differences among academics regarding the purposes of the enterprise. More than a decade ago, he warned that "the gravest single problem facing American higher education is [the] alarming disintegration of consensus about purpose . . . [This grave threat] requires a reevaluation of the relation between universities and American society" [4, p. 104]. To deal with this problem, he proposed an internal "restoration of consensus within the academic community about the rights and responsibilities of universities in society . . ." [4, p. 105].

Despite the cogency of these observations, little attention has been given to these and similar exhortations for change—either in the governance of universities or in the formulation of their purposes. That such powerfully stated concerns have been largely ignored in academic deliberations of the past decade may be a symptom in itself—perhaps a symptom that Yarmolinsky is correct in his assertion that none of the constituencies has the capacity to effect change. Perhaps their admonitions have been disregarded because Yarmolinsky and Ashby did not place the problems in an organizational context that would suggest a workable process for corrective action. In any event, exhortations to the academic community-at-large must necessarily go unheeded if each of the individual constituencies believes they are addressed to someone else.

These circumstances add weight to the need for appropriate organizational models, which are needed in any complex organization to aid in the framing of institutional problems and in identifying the system domain in which they should be addressed. In the case of the university, the problems are obfuscated and made even more intractable because the formal organizational chart of the university is such a poor representation of reality. Hence, students of academic organizational behavior have for some time found it necessary to develop alternative models as a framework for investigation. Among the models that have been described in the organizational literature are the collegial model, the bureaucratic model, the political model, and the organized anarchy model, each emphasizing different aspects of the university, as suggested metaphorically by their names (for a survey, see Garvin [22] or Richman and Farmer [41]). However, as Garvin points out, most of them share a key drawback: "they focus exclusively on internal decision-making rules and procedures, while paying little attention to the environment in which universities operate" [22, p. 4]. Garvin [22, p. 21] has proposed a utility maximizing model, using an economic approach that pays special attention to the motivation and goals of the key actors. Richman and Farmer [41] describe the university in terms of an open-systems approach [25], which takes into account the external environment. Each of these models has merit and, in many ways, they are complementary. But because they are typically process models, focusing on different actors in the academic community, the relationships among the models is unclear. They provide little insight into the structural relationships within the university and do not clearly define the interdependence among the parts of the overall system.

This article presents a new descriptive model, a matrix model, that was developed in an attempt to portray the organizational structure and practices of the university and to locate organizational problems in a problem-solving space. The motivation for creating a new map arose from an ongoing study of universities' responses to retrenchment (for other reports of this inquiry, see Whetten [57] and Petrie and Alpert [37]) that identified many paradoxes, incongruities, and inconsistencies not only in the rhetoric used to describe the problem issues but in the underlying structures and theories-in-use. The matrix model is intended to portray in concise and visual terms some key features of the organization, mission, and inner workings of the university while also describing its relationships with the external environment. This model is not based on new theories of organizational behavior or on new data relating to the operational characteristics of the institutions. Rather, it is intended to portray and make sense of various features of organizational behavior that have been observed by others; it incorporates or is compatible with many key features of the models mentioned above. The matrix model takes as its reality the modern comprehensive research university as described by such authorities as Kerr [26], Perkins [35], Jencks and Riesman [24], and Cohen and March [15]. Although it could be modified to include most of the 240 institutions offering the Ph.D., the model is specifically focused on the 100 or so leading universities that confer more than 95 percent of these degrees and are identified as "research universities" in *A Classification of Institutions of Higher Education (Revised Edition 1976)* issued by the Carnegie Foundation for the Advancement of Teaching.

This presentation starts with a simple linear model of the university, as proposed by Alpert [37], and then the matrix model is developed. Initially generated as an organizational map of a given campus, the matrix model has also evolved as a descriptive model of the American university system as an interdependent whole. Next, the matrix model is utilized to provide a context for some major dissonances and incongruities in the academic enterprise that have been highlighted by retrenchment and to suggest directions for organizational learning. Special attention is given to changing expectations and demands and the need for addressing the different and often conflicting purposes of the overall university system. Finally, the need for new maps for the future university is discussed and some observations about settings for creating them are offered.

A Linear Model of the University

It is generally agreed that institutions of higher learning are best understood as collections of fundamentally autonomous units rather than in terms of a central authority, or conception of a whole, to which they are subordinate. Departments were . . . designed to avoid curricular chaos and to shift power from the president to the faculty.

Elizabeth Coleman [16, p. 48]

The idea of a matrix model of the modern research university started with a "linear model" used by Petrie and Alpert [37, p. 107] to describe the university's structure, its internally perceived mission, and many aspects of its organizational behavior under conditions of budgetary restraint. As shown in Figure 1, the linear model embodies Coleman's description. It portrays the university as a set of autonomous academic departments and professional schools, each represented by a separate rectangle and tied together by its institutional identity, geographic location, administration, support services, and board of trustees. It is a classic example of a "loosely coupled" organization as described by Weick [56]; in its basic structure, the whole is identical to the sum of its departmental parts.

The linear model goes beyond the portrayal of organizational structure; it symbolizes the perceived institutional mission as well. The basic departmental mission is considered to be "the pursuit of excellence," interpreted by most faculty members and administrators as the successful, self-directed search for new knowledge in the many areas of specialization of the comprehensive research university. The assessment of academic quality is identified with the quality of the research in the various disciplines and professional fields and is carried out through the process of peer group evaluation. The most prevalent measure of departmental quality has come to be its prestige among peer groups, that is, its comparative standing in a national ordering assembled by colleagues in the discipline [12, 18, 43]. For many academics, the improvement of prestige has become the departmental mission itself [22]. Given these perceptions, the mission of the university is seen as the sum of its departmental missions and the quality of the institution is seen as the separately measured quality of its departments. In both structure and mission, therefore, the whole of the university has come to be viewed as the sum of its individual departmental parts. As a result, the proposed responses to external crises are largely restricted to those which can be handled with the available resources, personnel, and motivation of the individual units.

Structure
$$U = \boxed{d_1} + \boxed{d_2} + \boxed{d_3} + \boxed{d_4} + \boxed{d_5} + \cdots + \boxed{d_n}$$

Quality
$$Q = \boxed{q_1} + \boxed{q_2} + \boxed{q_3} + \boxed{q_4} + \boxed{q_5} + \cdots + \boxed{q_n}$$

Mission
$$M = \boxed{m_1} + \boxed{m_2} + \boxed{m_3} + \boxed{m_4} + \boxed{m_5} + \cdots + \boxed{m_n}$$

Figure 1   Linear model of the university.

The next section identifies the connections that relate the departments to external stakeholders, giving added insights about institutional behavior. However, even in the absence of a description of the external environment, the linear model serves to portray many of the characteristics of the modern research university, some of which are:

1. The department has become the key unit of academic life; it is virtually autonomous in such important functions as appointments and selection of areas of research emphasis, setting standards for individual faculty performance, and establishing curricular and degree requirements for students.

2. The decentralized organizational structure and the project system for the support of research are well-suited to the scientific research activities of the university; they have helped to make American academic scientists the world-leaders in almost every discipline.

3. Due to the autonomy of departments and the lack of shared goals, retrenchment has been accompanied by an increase in competition for scarce resources among departments and a resulting loss of faculty morale.

4. The faculty senate has lost status and effectiveness as a factor in campus governance.

The linear model helps to explain the very different organizational responses of the university under conditions of growth and of retrenchment. During the growth period of the 1950s and 1960s, the increasingly decentralized system of governance was highly adaptive. Change took place by enlarging the institution, keeping the old structure intact and adding new academic units under the stimulus of readily available federal research funds and the rapid growth in student enrollments. Academic units were added to accommodate new research activities, developed by outstanding faculty members with entrepreneurial instincts; at the same time, many existing departments also grew substantially. New programs, departments, and institutes were seen as contributors to the prestige of the institution, and there was relatively little opposition to their formation, provided they did not directly compete with existing units. Proposals to add units were often based on the availability of new sources of external funding and did not call on existing units to give up their claims on resources. The period of growth was accompanied by greatly increased responsibilities for the individual professor, especially the successful scientific researcher. Faculty members became entrepreneurs, assuming responsibilities for proposal-writing and project management, recruiting graduate assistants, completing annual reports, consulting in Washington, and sitting on peer review panels—all in addition to previous commitments to teaching undergraduates and guiding graduate students. Given the academic reward system, recognition of research by one's peers in the discipline had a much higher priority than concerns about the internal governance of the campus. In any event, the successful professor felt much too busy to sit through tedious faculty senate meetings on issues of minor import. Thus, for individual as well as institutional reasons, the system of faculty participation in the governance of the overall university atrophied.

In times of retrenchment, slack is reduced and competition among units increases; maintaining support for one department implies reducing support for others. In the absence of consensus on priorities or of effective mechanisms for making institutional choices, there are few alternatives for the various departments but to dig in and protect their political turf. Thus, the decentralization that was highly adaptive during a period of expansion becomes maladaptive in times of retrenchment. To reduce or eliminate programs in times of retrenchment is far more difficult than to add them in times of growth.

The linear model of the university helps to clarify some of the dilemmas of current university life, providing insights into such issues as:

1. why faculty members define the overall mission of the university solely in terms of their individual departmental missions and consider adaptation to change possible only in the same terms;

2. why proposed changes, budgetary or otherwise, justified in the larger campus interest, are perceived primarily in terms of departmental interests;

3. why the accepted mechanisms for assessing departmental performance severely limit modification of structure or change in institutional priorities;

4. why the expectations of external stakeholders, to whom the university is presented (by the administration) as a single organization with clearly defined institutional structure and goals, are often at odds with the expectations of faculty members.

At the same time, the linear model has inherent limitations. It says little about the relationship of the university to the external environment; the linear model does not illuminate the external mechanisms for the evaluation of internal performance nor does it differentiate between sources of financial support and how these affect the mission and governance of the university. By looking inward to the university campus, the linear model suffers from one of the limitations experienced by the universities themselves; that is, it highlights internal barriers to change without providing insights into external constraints. The next section expands the linear model to include the roles of institutions and actors external to the local campus and their effects on its administration, governance, and mission.

The Matrix Model

> To understand the behavior of an organization you must understand the context of that behavior—that is, the ecology of the organization. . . . No organization is completely self-contained or in complete control of the conditions of its own existence.
>
> Jeffrey Pfeffer and Gerald R. Salancik [38, p. 1; 19]

A matrix is constructed by presenting in one diagram the linear models for the n leading universities in the nation (U_1, U_2, U_3, . . . U_n). As shown in Figure 2, each linear representation is placed above the other, and the departments at the various universities are aligned one above the other, so that all anthropology departments, for example, are in the same column. Thus any given department, d_{ij}, is located on a row corresponding to a specified university (U_i) and in a column corresponding to a specified discipline (D_j). It is immediately apparent that each department has special relationships with the other departments in its own row, which represents the campus community, and with the other departments in its own column, which represents the disciplinary community. Each of these, the horizontal and the vertical communities, may be viewed as a loosely coupled system, with significantly different forms of coupling in the horizontal and vertical directions. The departments in a given row (campus) share the same institutional name, geographic location, board of trustees, and overall organizational identity, while the departments in a given column are coupled in other significant ways, for example, professional missions, research activities, and reward and recognition systems.

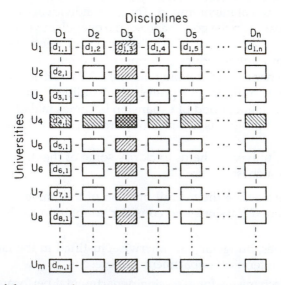

Figure 2   Matrix model of the research university.

Historically, the increase in the relative influence of the disciplinary communities has been continuous since the turn of the century, as the mission of universities has shifted from the dissemination of known truths to the search for new knowledge [47, 54]. As Perkins has observed, "Before the nineteenth century, a primary rationale for scholarship or research was its impact on teaching. . . . Today teaching and research are missions with distinctive styles and different, often contradictory, requirements for organizational structure. The differences are important" [35, pp. 6–7]. The shift in emphasis from teaching to research as the primary institutional goal was accompanied by a related but different organizational change—a change which Jencks and Riesman [24] refer to as "the academic revolution"—the transfer of authority in academic matters from the president to the faculty. The emergence of the disciplinary communities as the arbiters of institutional life corresponds to the takeover by the professoriate of the dominant role in the governance of the university. This shift was accelerated by the entry of the federal government as a major source of funds allocated directly to individual researchers and handled by their departments. A principal consequence of the enlargement of the federal role was to hasten the decentralization of the individual university; the various departments became more independent of the internal administration and more dependent on the support of external constituencies.

The roles of the campus and disciplinary communities in the life of the typical department can readily be identified with the academic functions that the departmental staff is called on to carry out. Table 1 lists those functions and responsibilities that are primarily associated with one or the other of the two communities. By and large, the horizontal (campus) community addresses itself to the undergraduate teaching mission of the university, whereas the vertical (disciplinary) community addresses itself primarily to graduate education, research, and faculty selection and performance. The campus community was originally shaped and its structure defined by the teaching mission of the university. For alumni, for state legislators, and for many of its friends and benefactors, the teaching mission still represents the principal goal of the university as an educational institution. It is the campus community that relates and is meaningful to undergraduate students, student organizations, and student life. In the university of today, the disciplinary communities have assumed the central responsibilities not only for graduate and professional education, but also for setting the goals, justifying and selling research agendas to federal sponsors, allocating academic research grants, and implementing the peer review process for the rating of individual and departmental quality. To department heads, the disciplinary community establishes standards for faculty and departmental performance, manages the professional societies and refereed journals, and staffs the advisory panels controlling the dispersal of federal research funding. The sister departments in the disciplinary community constitute the sources of talent for graduate students and faculty recruits. To individual faculty members at comprehensive research universities, the national disciplinary community is typically more meaningful to their professional careers and more familiar in terms of culture and day-to-day contacts than are faculty members in the other departments on their own campus.

TABLE 1

Community Responsibilities and Activities

Campus Community	Disciplinary Community
Undergraduate education	Graduate education and research
Student life	
Shared facilities: library, physical plant	Professional journals, meetings
Faculty appointments	Peer review system
Faculty security: tenure	Faculty mobility
Campus governance	Accreditation boards
Campus administration	Professional societies
Allocation of institutional funds	Allocation of research grants and contracts

If every university in the nation had the same number and identity of departments and professional schools, the representation of all universities in Figure 2 would be the same and the matrix would be completely symmetrical. Obviously, there are differences in the departmental make-up of comprehensive universities; in fact, the number of departments among research universities varies substantially, ranging from about fifty to more than a hundred. In the matrix diagram, the absence of a given department or professional school is indicated by a vacancy in the regular structure; if a given university does not have a department of astronomy or a school of agriculture, these units do not appear on the corresponding row of the matrix. The greatest variance among institutions lies in the number and identity of their professional schools, a factor which makes for differences in campus ambiance and stated mission. But the professional colleges themselves are aligned in national "disciplinary communities" that, like the departments of arts and sciences, are characterized more by their similarities than their differences. By and large, the basic linear array of departments fits sensibly into a matrix. As is evidenced by the various comparative assessments of graduate and professional programs, there are few among the major research universities that do not organize and identify their disciplines and professional departments in similar ways.

The similarity of departmental organization and goals is itself an indicator of the power exercised by the national disciplinary communities in setting the standards and scholarly goals of American universities. In a few recently established campuses, for example, the University of California at Santa Cruz and the University of Illinois at Chicago, there were at the outset significant departures from the norm, with unorthodox organizational structures intended to support a distinctive campus mission. After the first few years of operation, however, the pressures (both internal and external) to adopt more conventional structure and mission were inexorable; except for a few departures from standard nomenclature, both campuses today fit comfortably on the matrix diagram.

The significant influence of the disciplinary communities in the mission and composition of universities is enhanced by the activities of a number of professional, economic, and political institutions external to any given campus. Providing services and support to the academic community, they obviously belong in the matrix diagrams as extensions of the vertical (disciplinary) columns as shown schematically in Figure 3; they include: (1) federal agencies and private research foundations, (2) accrediting agencies, (3) national professional associations (e.g., American Psychological Association), (4) associations of practicing professionals (e.g., American Medical Association), (5) client organizations (e.g., the American Farm Bureau), and (6) national laboratories (e.g., the Fermilab high energy physics facility).

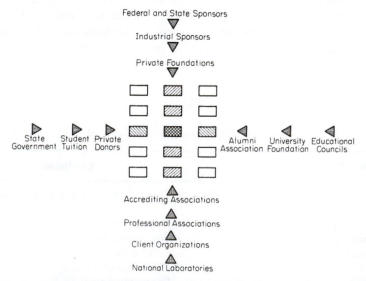

Figure 3   External support agencies and associations. Disciplinary support in the vertical column; institutional support in the horizontal row.

Since World War II, the federal sponsorship of academic research has played a crucial role in the strengthening of the disciplinary communities. In fact, the sponsoring agencies can be considered integral parts of the disciplinary communities. And the sponsors' contributions to academic research are reciprocated by the key roles that the disciplinary communities play in the management of the agencies. Academic researchers sit on advisory committees, carry out the peer review of grant proposals, and help to recruit the disciplinary colleagues who make up the agency staffs. Channeled through the vertical columns of the matrix, federal research support is allocated directly to individual principal investigators in the form of grants and contracts. Although the institution is allotted a share of the funding in the form of indirect costs, the central university administration is typically bypassed or plays only a minor role in a process that cumulatively defines the priorities, the staffing, and the research mission of the institution. In Washington, the allocation of federal funds among the many agencies and subdivisions is carried out in a complex political process involving the executive and legislative branches of government, the agencies themselves, and the intellectual leaders of the disciplines. With few exceptions, the central administrators of universities play a minor role in determining federal research policy or the allocating of federal funds to the various disciplines.

The supportive relationship of powerful external organizations to the disciplinary communities has its counterpart in a similar array of organizations that relate directly to the campus communities. As shown schematically in the horizontal communities of Figure 3, these external campus-related organizations include: (1) state governments, (2) students (tuition) and private donors, (3) alumni associations, (4) university foundations, and (5) councils of American educators and universities. Both the sources and uses of institutional funding are identified strongly with the undergraduate educational mission, especially at private universities, where student tuition and alumni giving comprise major portions of the overall budget. In public (state-supported) universities, the institutional funding from the state government is also identified with the undergraduate teaching function, though it may include support for graduate education and research as well. Institutional funds are not allocated directly to departments or individual faculty members but go to the campus and are dispensed through the office of the president or chancellor.

Figure 4 includes in the matrix both the horizontal and vertical groups of external organizations. The differences in the character of these external stake-holders are matched by the wide differences in the purposes of the academic activities with which they identify.

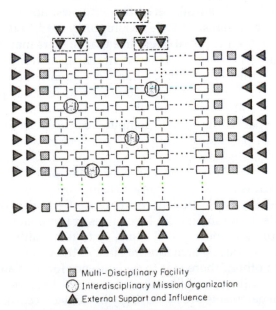

■ Multi-Disciplinary Facility
◯ Interdisciplinary Mission Organization
▲ External Support and Influence

Figure 4   Matrix model including external agencies and internal cross-disciplinary research units.

The Rating of Disciplinary Communities: Role of Intellectual Leaders

I have previously referred to the quality rating of academic departments and have commented on the importance of these ratings in the lives of the institutions. Carried out by the disciplinary communities, the comparative ratings of departments reflect their reputations for research excellence and have had an enormous effect on the internal organizational behavior of the universities [22, 37]. A department with a rating substantially above others on campus has great leverage in the internal competition for resources, appointments to key committees, and faculty perquisites such as lower teaching loads and higher salaries. Taken together, the various departmental ratings comprise an informal institutional rating, which represents the university's comparative standing among institutions.

In a matrix diagram such as Figure 4, it is possible, at least in principle, to identify each major university in the nation and, based on the published ratings of its departments, to arrange the universities in descending order of institutional excellence from top to bottom. Thus, the matrix diagram could be used as a convenient way of recording both the departmental and institutional ratings for every research university in the nation. The chart could also be used to identify the departments on a given campus that are well above or below the rating of the institution as a whole. That institutional ratings have not been formally published is due to certain ambiguities in the relation of institutional ratings to departmental ratings. If all departments were equally valued, the institutional rating would logically be derived by taking the average of the departmental ratings. In fact, however, the disciplines are not considered to be of equal importance to the status of a research university; a physics department rated twentieth in the nation typically has more status and power on its campus than a Spanish department rated tenth. That is to say, the disciplinary communities themselves vary in status and size just as do the campus communities. Although no comparable ranking among disciplines has been published or widely acknowledged, a survey of the nation's research campuses today would quickly reveal commonly held opinions of the relative status of corresponding departments.

In principle, then, just as the campus communities could be ordered along the vertical axis of the matrix in terms of prestige or quality, the disciplinary communities could be arranged along the horizontal axis in terms of status, affluence, and political power. An appraisal of the status of the disciplines reveals a number of features of the organizational behavior of universities and their leadership. Because it is the disciplinary communities that rate the campuses in terms of their contributions to the disciplines, it might be anticipated that it would be the campus communities who rate the disciplines on the basis of their perceived contributions to the campuses. In some measure, this is indeed the case; in setting curricular requirements, for example, the campus faculty identifies those disciplines considered most central. On some campuses, however, special circumstances of tradition or of intellectual or administrative leadership may lead to disparities between local departmental status and that of their national discipline: that is, there may be high status departments in disciplines that are weak or vice versa. To the extent that such variations exist, the campus communities can be said to affect the ratings of disciplinary communities on the "micro" level. But since internal and external factors are strongly coupled, there is a widespread pattern of similarity among the nation's campuses in the status accorded to the disciplines on the "macro" level. Currently, for example, the high status departments include computer science, electrical engineering, chemistry, business administration, and psychology—quite independent of whether the university is fifth or fiftieth in the institutional pecking order.

Although campus faculty preferences are significant, disciplinary status is even more strongly affected by such external factors as the level of research support available from federal agencies, the job market for Ph.D.s in the field, and "student consumerism"—undergraduate student preferences for degree programs (see David Riesman [42]). Disciplines or professions considered essential to the nation's defense posture, to its economic well-being, or to the health of its citizens are clearly favored for gaining access to federal research funding. Just as the values of the most prestigious campuses influence the goals of others, there is a strong tendency for the values of the most prestigious disciplines to be imposed on other disciplines; even for professional fields in which scholarly journals play a minimal role, departments are increasingly evaluated according to norms of scientific or scholarly publication.

The consideration of disciplinary status highlights the multiple roles of the intellectual leaders on the nation's campuses. They carry out political activities in Washington in addition to their primary roles as disciplinary leaders: (a) directing the research activities in their own laboratories, which set the standards of disciplinary research achievement in their fields, (b) writing proposals for grants and contracts for this research, and (c) implementing the peer review system, which determines which papers are published and which researchers will receive grants (and promotions). Because they play important roles on government advisory boards and on the boards of professional organizations that affect the federal allocation of funds to the various disciplines, the charisma and persuasiveness of the disciplinary intellectual leaders, as well as their connections to other powerful organizations, are critical to disciplinary status. As the various fields of research have expanded, these demands have increased accordingly; to put it mildly, the intellectual leaders of the nation are overloaded. In recognition of these realities, the outstanding intellectual leaders in many prestigious departments are spared—indeed protected from—the chores on the home campus (committee work and day-to-day participation in the campus governance process). It isn't that they are spared from chores as such; rather, they carry out these duties in the service of the disciplinary rather than the campus community. And because their contributions as researchers are greatly valued by the department, both in terms of internal leadership and maintaining external visibility, the leading researchers often receive special treatment in departmental assignments and perquisites. In fact, the intellectual leaders on the nation's campuses rarely have time enough to become involved in problems of curricular reform or institutional reorganization and are dragooned into campus budget administration only at times of crisis. Indeed, except during crises, there is a distinct separation of the preoccupations and concerns of intellectual leadership and administrative leadership. The intellectual leaders are primarily involved professionally with the activities of their disciplinary communities, while the administrators (presidents, deans, and faculty committee persons) are aligned with their responsibilities in the local campus community.

In partial summary, the matrix model describes the overall institutional complex that influences the policies and practices of a typical research university. The research universities include some 10,000 departments that are arrayed rather symmetrically in about 100 disciplinary communities on about 100 major research campuses and tied together in an interdependent national system.

By recognizing the importance and nationwide character of the disciplinary communities, the model calls attention to the fact that no American university is fully autonomous, able to set a course independent of the other universities in the nation. Many of the persons and institutions that determine the goals and assess the performance of a given university do not live on its campus or report to its board of trustees. In fact, the matrix diagram is simultaneously a portrayal of the entire assembly of institutions of higher education and a portrayal of any one of them. In other words, all of the universities in the nation comprise a single interconnected organism for higher education and research. Despite differences in the number or composition of departments and other academic units, the regularities and national dimensions of the matrix serve to explain the similarity of aspirations among research universities, whether they are public or private, whether they are in the top decile or the bottom. Because quality is defined primarily in terms of a single measure of research "excellence," the pressures for conformity to the disciplinary conventions and fashions are often greater for less distinguished universities than for those at the top. This pressure for conformity is in turn imposed on the individual faculty member. Because mobility and rewards are associated with climbing the departmental status ladder, individuals can be visible to disciplinary leaders only if they are turning out papers that are readily published and recognized as being in the mainstream of the discipline. In specifying the orthogonal roles of intellectual and administrative leaders on the nation's campuses, the matrix formulation calls attention to the complex issues of leadership and responsibility in the comprehensive university, the key features of which are hidden from view by formal organizational charts. (I will return to these issues in the discussion of the role of university presidents in the matrix model.)

As with any attempt to portray this highly complex organizational system, the matrix model has limitations. Because the model is intended to identify problems and to locate them in an organizational problem-solving space, it tends to highlight certain problematic situations, such as the fragmentation of the university community. The model is also biased toward emphasizing the forces encouraging conformity among universities; it does not adequately portray the ways in which universities differ in cultural traditions and ambiance, in disciplinary emphasis, or in functional emphasis. Furthermore, the model undoubtedly reflects my greater familiarity with state-supported, land-grant universities than with private universities, and some of the inferences or conclusions may not be generalizable for all categories of research universities. Despite these limitations, many features of the matrix model are applicable, not only to most research universities but to a wide variety of other universities and colleges. Even small liberal arts colleges, primarily oriented to undergraduate education, exhibit strong loyalties to the values of the research universities, particularly in their dependence on the disciplinary communities for measuring professorial performance, for providing faculty mobility, and for strengthening professional identity.

Relating Research to Other Campus Activities: Multidisciplinary Facilities and Interdisciplinary Mission Organizations

For the sake of clarity, I have postponed a brief discussion of academic organizational units that do not fit into the standard departmental matrix array, in particular, units involving faculty members from several departments in organized collaborative enterprises. I am not referring to the hierarchical groupings of departments into schools and colleges, typically headed by a dean or director. In some of the professional colleges strongly identified with a single profession (e.g., law, medicine, education), these officers play the same roles as department heads and their colleges are symbolized in the matrix model accordingly. In colleges made up of a number of quite different departments, the dean typically plays an intermediary role between the departments and the central administration. It does not detract from the importance of such deans in the university to say that they play a staff rather than a line role, providing administrative services to departments and acting as spokespersons for their faculties and departments in the president's office. Rather, I attend to those special academic units whose activities involve faculty members from a number of departments and start with a brief discussion of interdepartmental organizations, mostly oriented to research activities, though some such organizations are devoted to instruction, applied research, and/or public service.

Although the organizational literature often refers to all such units as "organizational research units" (ORUs), it is useful to distinguish between two classes of interdepartmental research units [1, 21]. The first, directed to serving the disciplinary research needs of faculty members in many departments, I refer to as "multidisciplinary facilities" (MDFs). The second, directed to addressing problems transcending the know-how and knowledge of any one discipline, I refer to as "interdisciplinary mission organizations" (IMOs). The management of MDFs is well understood in the academic community. One such facility, the central library, has been successfully managed in universities for centuries. Other examples are the various language and area centers, computer service organizations, electron microscope laboratories, and other major instrument facilities. Operated under guidelines and priorities established by an interdepartmental advisory committee, the MDF is so commonplace on the campus that some academics take it for granted that all interdepartmental activities can and should be governed in the same way. Because a prime goal of the MDF is to provide access to shared facilities by the participating faculty, administration of the MDF is typically assigned to a director, operating under guidelines specified by a representative committee made up of the various departmental clients. The MDF may be staffed by nonfaculty professionals to provide sophisticated services to its faculty clients. In some cases, the MDF includes a common building, offering contiguous offices or laboratories to encourage collaboration between individuals in different disciplines. However, the research goals are set, not by the organizational unit, but by the faculty investigators—acting individually or at most with a few colleagues working on related research problems. The problems under investigation are typically disciplinary in character, occasionally applying techniques developed in one discipline to the problems posed by another. In Figure 4, the MDFs are shown as shaded squares; they are part of the (horizontal) campus community and governed accordingly. Interestingly, some of the most prominent MDFs (e.g., libraries, computer service organizations) are common to most campuses; like their departmental counterparts, they have formed national organizations and may also be represented as vertical communities on the matrix chart.

Contrasting with MDFs, the successful management of interdisciplinary mission organizations runs contrary to traditional ways of doing things in academia. If the operating metaphor for managing the MDF is the faculty advisory committee, the corresponding metaphor for the management of IMO activities is the participating network or team. Since the IMO is typically utilitarian, problem-focused, and accountable to mission-oriented sponsors, success depends critically on the commitment, inventiveness, and breadth of problem-related experience of the participants rather than their expertise in specialized fields. It follows that the personnel composition of each IMO is unique to the campus on which it is located even when committed to the same goals as those on other campuses. Hence the IMOs are symbolically represented in Figure 4 as stippled circles and are randomly located among overlapping departments to reflect the variability in staffing and administration. Examples are the Center for Policy Alternatives at MIT, the Computer-based Education Research Laboratory at the University of Illinois at Urbana-Champaign, and the Center for Energy and Environmental Studies at Princeton University.

In a university setting focusing on individual faculty publication and relying on external peer group evaluation as the dominant means for assessing performance, it is not surprising that IMOs constitute anomalies in the scheme of things. In the first place, a central requirement for success is that the individual leaders of the interdisciplinary team must themselves be interdisciplinary persons. This requirement means that academic today is not a likely source of such leaders; when they do emerge, they may not be acknowledged as legitimate scholars by the disciplinary communities or promotion committees. Because project success depends on collaboration, invention, and concern with the solution of problems while promotion depends on individual scholarly (scientific) achievement and publication in refereed journals, interdisciplinary, problem-focused activity is dangerous territory for untenured faculty members. Hence, the staffing of IMOs is largely made up of non-tenured professionals who do not aspire to professorial status. Furthermore, successful policy- or problem-oriented research must meet deadlines and serve real clients, which calls for a form of corporate accountability to the sponsor or client. These performance requirements are not well served by conventional procedures on such administrative matters as selection of leadership or personnel, tenure, performance evaluation, and so on.

Because the IMO does not figure prominently in the overall research university, academic innovation takes place largely within the boundaries of the existing departments. The department (or integrated professional school) is the largest organizational unit having the capacity to encourage collaboration or new directions among its faculty; it provides research facilities, financial and moral support, graduate students, and perhaps most significantly, the authority to select the new faculty recruits. On occasion, research problems of one discipline are attacked with instruments or methodologies that have been developed in other disciplines; in such cases, innovation depends on the individual faculty member who has the capacity and style for reaching across departmental lines. But the departmental structure is seen to be so "natural" that cross-disciplinary fields (such as biochemistry, geophysics, and bioengineering) that originate at the boundaries soon become formalized as new departments. As soon as this is accomplished, collaboration across departmental lines again depends on individuals' initiative.

In the research university, the research, educational, and public service missions are integrated at the level of the individual department and, most often, at the level of the individual professor. In the matrix model, the individual department is at the intersection between the disciplinary (research-oriented) community and the campus (undergraduate-oriented) community. Thus, the department is the nominal organizational structure for relating the research and educational missions. However, as Bess points out, "There are many who argue that the integrity of the university is preserved by interplay among the (research, education and public service) missions. What in fact takes place, however, is that instead of integration of the missions through organizational structure, the 'multiple-function' professional faculty member is expected personally to make the necessary connections" [6, p. 209]. The individual faculty member is also the principal source of initiatives for problems that do not fall within the perceived mission of any department.

That cross-disciplinary programs have been initiated even during the years of retrenchment is a tribute to a small number of unorthodox academics whose personal dedication has overcome the general low level of institutional recognition or support. The typical organizational form in which such programs evolve is the informal network made up of self-selected individual faculty members with overlapping interests. Such recently developed interdepartmental programs as "Science, Technology, and Society" and "Women's Studies" are widely dispersed on the nation's campuses, but they face a double-bind situation making their long-term survival uncertain. Departmental status seems essential if they are to achieve program continuity, financial support, and a voice in the appointment and promotion of qualified faculty participants. On the other hand, departmental status is a hazard because the objectives of such programs call for collaborating with other departments rather than competing with them. Thus, program success may be antithetical to the coordinative role; in the development of initiatives transcending departmental lines, the research university depends on dedicated (and often unconventional) individual faculty members rather than organizational structure or administrative leadership.

Role of the President's Office in the Matrix Model

Even the astute Daniel Moynihan exhibits serious confusion about the nature of academic leadership and the role of administrators in the modern university. In his widely quoted article, "State vs. Academe: Nationalizing the Universities" [32], he spells out some of the negative consequences of federal involvement in sponsoring of academic research. Moynihan bemoans the growth of federal influence on the academic mission and makes the significant point that "no money was made available for the universities to do with as they thought best." In particular, he has some scorching things to say about the failure of university presidents a decade or two ago to foresee this predicament: "It was at least possible [between 1957 and 1972] for the universities to have negotiated a distinctive relationship between themselves and the national government. . . . That this was not done involved a profound failure of leadership" [32, p. 33].

Moynihan has leveled valid and serious criticism at the federal contract with universities, but by assuming that the presidents of American universities had the power suggested by their position at the top of the formal organization chart, Moynihan ignores the reality of the circumstances. If the university presidents of the 1950s and early 1960s had followed Moynihan's prescription and demanded from the federal government direct institutional support for their campuses, they would have come into direct confrontation with faculties who were well along in the process of relegating the administrators to secondary roles in the research enterprise and making use of the project support system to do so. As indicated previously, the principal effect of the exponential growth of federal support was not to centralize the management of the university in Washington, as Moynihan avers, but to further remove the president from a significant role in the management of the campus. The new contract with the federal agencies transferred power from the campus communities to the disciplinary communities, who did not seek and did not assume responsibility for the university as an institutional whole. By the late 1960s and early 1970s, many of the universities, led by the National Association of State Universities and Land-Grant Colleges, had become sufficiently concerned to lobby strongly in Congress for implementation of institutional grants to universities [3]. However, under the impetus of the Nixon administration, Congress chose in 1972 to enhance the federal subsidy to higher education, not in the form of direct institutional support but through scholarship aid and loans to students.

Moynihan's view of academic administration is consistent with the "great man" theory of academic administration—a view unusually prevalent among faculty members today [42]. Faced with unresolvable dilemmas of competing priorities and overly busy schedules, many faculty members acknowledge their own feeling of powerlessness and look upward in the organizational chart for institutional salvation. They take seriously the possibility of calling upon an all-knowing and all-powerful "great man" in the presidency who will "make the right decisions" and lead the university out of its troubles. More often than not, the goal they would have the president pursue is to persuade donors or legislators to new levels of financial commitment that would permit them to carry on as before and so remove by sheer charisma the baffling constraints exposed by retrenchment. Failing that, the "strong" departments would ask the "great man" to make the hard decisions (to eliminate the "weaker" programs) and the "weak" departments would have him maintain the integrity of the university by resisting the pressures of passing scholastic fads. The limited record of success has not perceptibly lessened the attractiveness of "great man" solutions to the university's problems.

Most of the university presidents in office today are able, perceptive, and articulate. They assume responsibility for a broad variety of tasks, they work painfully long hours, and they are concerned for the university and the integrity of its relationship to society. But as Cohen and March have observed, their influence on the activities of the campus is limited: "Compared to the heroic expectations he and others might have, the president has modest control over the events of college life. The contributions he makes can easily be swamped by outside events or the diffuse qualities of university decision making" [15, p. 2]. The matrix model reveals the basic dilemma of university presidents: they are expected to carry the burden of leadership for institutions that are separately accountable to individual legislatures and boards of trustees but governed as part of an inseparable and interdependent nationwide system of institutions. The ambiguities associated with this situation are exacerbated by the differences in accountability to sponsors and clients of the president and of the intellectual leaders of the campus. The president feels directly accountable not only to federal sponsors but also to the state legislature, students, parents, donors, and all other constituencies who provide institutional support for the campus. In contrast, faculty members generally tend to view their prime responsibilities in terms of national goals, contributing to the body of published scientific and scholarly knowledge, and educating future scientists and scholars.

The dilemmas of the president's role of accountability to external sponsors are matched by the dilemmas of his or her responsibilities within the university. As chief spokesperson for their universities, presidents are prominent in searching for funds; as chief budgetary officers, they are responsible for keeping the books balanced. The president is also expected to provide the necessary coordination between departmental and institutional goals and to balance the educational, public service, and research functions of the campus. But the discretionary funds and resources at the disposal of the president of a typical university are remarkably limited. Thus, lacking authority and legitimacy in matters of educational policy and divorced from initiatives in the research enterprise, the president's capacity for providing coordination among academic units and for revitalizing the institutional mission is, to say the least, limited. It is a "Catch-22" situation: the president lacks enough understanding of departmental problems to justify the extension of his or her power and also lacks the power to justify the expansion of his or her understanding.

Given these discordant views of the president's role, how should the president's office be symbolized in the matrix model? Two alternatives seem plausible:

1. the president as mediator and spokesperson for an array of semiautonomous academic units, providing administrative services to the campus as a whole under guidelines and legitimizing influence of the faculty senate and a variety of related faculty committees (note the similarity to the role of director of an MDF);

2. the president as leader of an interdisciplinary mission organization of faculty and staff from all colleges and departments and charged with the responsibility for making decisions—on his or her own, if necessary—regarding the overall campus mission (note the corresponding similarity to the role of leader of an IMO; undergraduate education was the original interdisciplinary mission).

Both of these representations of the president's office in the matrix model appropriately suggest responsibilities far exceeding authority and suggest accountability to internal as well as to external constituencies of the university. Which of these descriptions is most appropriate? It seems fair to say that in Kerr's comprehensive "multiversity" of the 1950s and early 1960s, the president was primarily a mediator/spokesperson, a provider of administrative services to the campus at large [26]. On occasion, however, even in those days, the president was called on to act as initiator and leader. Thus, it may be more appropriate to assert that the president is called on to play both roles, the mix depending on the size of the campus, the reputation and national stature of the faculty, and the makeup of institutional and disciplinary sources of funding. The president's role also depends on the economic environment. When retrenchment became a fact of life on the nation's campuses, the mediator/spokesperson role was inadequate for rapid-response cutback management, if only because the process was too time-consuming and revealed irreconcilable conflicts of purpose. Retrenchment thus provides opportunities, as well as demands, for the president to go beyond the symbolic role of leadership and, in concert with intellectual leaders and administrative leaders at other universities, to set the stage for organizational learning for the local campus as well as for the larger academic community.

Directions for Organizational Learning

There is much urgent educational work to be done in the United States and the years ahead are no time for retreat or retrenchment.

Howard R. Bowen [10, p. 154]

The status quo is the only solution that cannot be vetoed.

Clark Kerr [27, p. 30]

The major dissonances in governance and purpose forcefully articulated by Yarmolinsky and Ashby suggest the need for double-loop organizational learning, that is, reformulating the organizational structure as well as the norms of institutional behavior. Some further dissonances are here identified that are highlighted by the matrix model as characteristics of the national system of universities and suggest the need for organizational learning at the level of the overall enterprise as well as at the individual institution.

A first set of dissonances is associated with the growing awareness of the inadequacies of undergraduate education, in the preparation of students for life in a complex society. Perhaps these inadequacies are most apparent to university and college presidents. F. W. Wallin, president of Earlham College, is persuaded that "Our inherited concepts about education need significant revision, when information itself becomes a pivotal resource in society. . . . It is clear that in the future we and our universities will have to be more interdisciplinary, interprofessional and more interdepartmental [55, pp. 7–8]. Boyer and Hechinger advocate major new priorities for higher education: "The nation's schools, colleges, and universities have a special obligation to combat growing illiteracy about public issues. . . . [America's colleges and universities] must perform for society an *integrative* function, seeking appropriate responses to life's most enduring questions, concerning themselves not just with information, but with wisdom" [11, pp. 48, 60]. Another former university president, Harlan Cleveland, wants us to educate students who can "put it all together" and "who can relate 'hard' technologies to their soft impacts and implications" [14]. Still others want universities to deal with growing scientific and technological illiteracy; Rustum Roy, editor of the *Bulletin of Science, Technology, and Society,* offers the following statement: "In a world with increasing technological and scientific complexity, science literacy must be more than the understanding of a few basic principles in the biological or physical sciences. Rather, it must encompass the ability to apply an understanding of science principles, methodology, capabilities, and limitations to the wide range of decisions students will face both as citizens and as professionals" [46, p. 290].

But such exhortations, directed to the academic world at large, seldom address the organizational mechanisms through which reforms in instructional programs could be implemented. And they tend to beg the question about whether the faculties—including those in our most prestigious universities—are qualified to combat illiteracy about public policy or the role of science and technology in society. By the above criteria for science literacy, the large majority of science and engineering faculties (as well, of course, as humanities faculties) are scientifically illiterate. Education for citizenship is discussed as though all that were necessary would be a change in the curricular requirements imposed on students. But in an increasingly complex and interconnected world, literacy concerning public issues—and cultural literacy more broadly defined—calls for extensive learning by professors beyond their specializations. Most research-oriented professors are too busy to get involved, even if they recognize the need for it. On most campuses, there are a few dedicated individuals who have aspirations for redirecting educational programs across departmental boundaries, but they typically are denied sufficient organizational, financial, or moral support to translate these intentions into functional programs. In times of retrenchment, even less support is available. On occasion, the financial stimulus for new educational programs is provided by external foundations. All too often, however, a few faculty participants may embark on such a new interdisciplinary program only to see the system revert to "normal" soon after the external support dries up. In the absence of viable organizational mechanisms for supporting and maintaining the quality of interdisciplinary instruction, faculty initiatives that cross departmental lines frequently accomplish the exact opposite of what was intended. As I. I. Rabi once remarked about the efforts to promote general undergraduate education in the 1960s, "We are developing still another breed of specialists, called generalists."

The performance of the university as an educational institution is also limited by a lack of institutional commitment to research and development in the educational process itself. This paradoxical situation has been sharply criticized by Professor F. Reif, a member of the Group in Science and Mathematics Education at the University of California at Berkeley:

> ... the educational mode of the functioning of the university today is basically not very different from what it was 50 years ago, all the talk of an impending educational revolution notwithstanding. Educational innovations are few in number and often marginal in their impact. Nor is this situation surprising, since the university, unlike any progressive industry, is not in the habit of improving its own performance by systematic investment in innovative research and development. Indeed, the resources allocated by the university to educational innovation are usually miniscule or nonexistent. . . . there is a tendency to view education narrowly as mere classroom teaching and thus to ignore important issues. . . . Is it too farfetched to suggest that the university should take education at least as seriously as the Bell Telephone Company takes communication? [40, p. 538]

In contrast, there has been a growing tendency for industrial corporations to take education seriously, not only as a profit-making venture but as an essential process in the development of their own management and personnel. In fact, Guzetta describes a "quiet revolution," embodied in the movement of traditionally nonteaching organizations into the arena of education, fulfilling demands to which "traditional educational institutions have been reticent in responding" [23, p. 10]. Thus, universities have not maintained their share of the market for advanced education. In certain fields, such as computer science and engineering, some industrial corporations are hiring recruits at the baccalaureate level and providing advanced professional training themselves.

A second major dissonance in the nation's universities is their adherence to an institutional rating game based on a single measure of departmental performance—peer assessment of disciplinary research achievement. Although the concept of an appropriate institutional mission unique to the individual campus is a popular rhetorical notion among educational administrators, the matrix model suggests that adherence to a standard departmental structure and a national system of evaluating university quality department-by-department enforces a remarkable conformity. Under conditions of retrenchment, this system tends to discourage diversity even further. On many of the campuses subjected to major cutbacks in the past few years, the departments threatened with serious reduction or discontinuance were often much the same. The "smaller but better university" is one that focuses a greater fraction of its resources on research in the high status disciplines and, as a result, resembles its sister institutions even more [50]. A university that depends entirely on external peer evaluation of its departments as the measure of its quality is not likely to modify its structure, merge departments, or establish new academic units. Nor is it likely to shift priorities from disciplinary research to other institutional functions.

An important consequence of the lack of diversity is a related dissonance involving the overall magnitude of the academic commitment to disciplinary research, both on an absolute basis and relative to educational activities, applied research, and public service. If the sole justification and function of the academic enterprise were the production of new knowledge in the existing disciplines, its current size is too large by at least an order of magnitude; most of the important advances in research are made by a small fraction of the faculty members associated with a small fraction of the nation's universities. Ernest Lynton, Commonwealth Professor at the Center for Studies in Policies and the Public Interest, University of Massachusetts, points out:

> With a quarter million full-time faculty members in institutions called universities, it is very difficult to maintain the position that all of them are scholars capable of significant original research. . . .
>
> There are tens of thousands of scholarly journals which each year carry literally hundreds of thousands of articles. Much of what is published is second rate and trivial. . . . Even in the more prestigious institutions, a substantial number of faculty in fact carries out little or no research. . . . Yet throughout that vast and heterogeneous array of institutions . . . there is but one accepted, valued and rewarded scholarly goal: To conduct original research and to publish it in scholarly refereed journals. [29, pp. 20–21]

The use of a single measure of institutional excellence assures that lesser institutions refusing to accept mediocrity as a permanent station in life will fight to enlarge the disciplinary research commitment of their faculty and thus to increase the size of each of the disciplinary research communities. This tendency exacerbates competition for limited research funds and offers little incentive to embark in new areas of basic or applied research or to develop new approaches to instruction.

A third major dissonance results from the operating premise within universities that successful professors, having achieved tenure as young scholars in their thirties, should be engaged in the same academic pursuits throughout their careers. The tenure system evolved in an academic enterprise geared for undergraduate education; it is distinctly at odds with the goals of the disciplinary communities oriented to maximizing the quality of the basic research enterprise. The disciplinary communities do not offer tenure or security. The peer review system rewards researchers on the basis of promise or past performance, but it makes no long-term commitment to the support of old warhorses. In times of retrenchment, the tenure system results in serious barriers to the hiring of younger faculty and places those who are appointed in competition with established scholars. We have noted the pressures on untenured faculty members to stay within the mainstream of their disciplines; similar pressures are placed on older faculty to run harder to maintain their departmental status. Because there are few avenues for tenured faculty to change careers, the resultant situation, observed by Bess, is that those faculty members who do not excel in research and are not rewarded for performance in other academic roles often lapse into self-serving, "satisficing" behavior [6, p. 28].

Administrators, keenly aware of the "deadwood" problem, seek to ease out unproductive older faculty—through early retirement and other means—and thus to maintain quality. But the process is fraught with ethical as well as practical problems associated with dismissing tenured faculty. By adhering to a single measure of performance, universities do not encourage older faculty members to develop competence and commitments in directions other than basic disciplinary research: for example, educating for citizenship, carrying out and managing applied research, or codifying and disseminating knowledge. By contrast, industrial laboratories have long recognized the value of career changes. Young industrial scientists may excel in basic research, but as they mature, they are often encouraged to address their knowledge and skills to applied problems and management, making greater contributions to the corporate mission and being rewarded accordingly. In the university, the single measure of academic performance limits the diversity of individual, as well as institutional, objectives.

At the heart of these dissonances is an unexamined assumption held by many academics, a widespread belief in the automatic benevolence of science and scholarly research. That is to say, the search for new knowledge is viewed as a good in itself, from which benefits to society flow automatically or as byproducts, including better education, technological innovation, greater industrial productivity, national well-being, and military supremacy. A corollary of this belief is another premise, identified by Churchman as equally untenable: "In the main, basic science is a separable part of the total system of humanity" [13, p. 109]. This assumed separability, he goes on to explain, "is why basic research is deemed to be value free and apart from politics, and why we have to call on the researcher's peers to judge his excellence." These notions of separability and accountability only to one's peers are slowly being brought into explicit scrutiny by the academy under the impetus of the continuing inadequacies of federal funding and retrenchment imposed by state governments.

In response to the new realities, virtually every university in the nation has embarked on a search for added support from industrial corporations. Although this search has been largely motivated by the desire to maintain the status quo and to augment federal support for ongoing programs, the industrial connection at some universities is being reconsidered in the larger context of the relationships of universities to other institutions in society. The new realities of the past few years include the emergence of Japan as a leading industrial nation despite a secondary role in basic science. In a recent article [8], Harvard president Derek Bok presents the thesis that universities should assume a responsibility for the uses of science, for the "transfer" of science to society in the complex process of innovation. Bok is keenly aware of the potential conflicts of interest that may be inherent in the university-industry connection and the potential harm to institutional integrity. But he is also sensitive to the need for a transfer of knowledge between academic researchers and industry; he recognizes that research is not a separable enterprise. Bok's justification for university involvement in industrial development is presented in simple terms: ". . . Every institution that depends on public support should recognize a responsibility to serve society's legitimate needs" [8, p. 25]. This renewed commitment to public service, articulated in the language of the land-grant universities, comes from the president of one of the most independent of the nation's private universities.

A change in university-industry relationships is exemplified by the appearance on some of the nation's leading campuses of major research and development facilities dedicated to the encouragement of high-technology industry. These new facilities are not dedicated solely to a search for new knowledge but to developing an infrastructure for relating scientific advance and technological innovation. Recently organized examples are the Center for Integrated Systems at Stanford University, the Robotics Laboratory at Carnegie-Mellon University, and the Whitehead Institute for Biomedical Research associated with MIT. It remains to be seen whether the new laboratories will be successful in relating basic academic research to new technological initiatives. Roy [45] has his doubts; he proposes that the laboratories be managed directly by industrial corporations. And there is reason for concern; the recent record of universities in managing mission- or policy-oriented research is uninspired [44, 53] if not downright irresponsible, as Coleman concludes:

> The history of faculty-directed research on problems posed by government and foundations is one of deception and disappointment; deception by the university academic in transforming the client's problem to a problem that interested him (i.e., one that could gain him status in his discipline) and disappointment on the client's part when he received a research report which failed to address his problem or which, addressing it, failed to solve it. . . . The very structure which made these intellectual skills available—the autonomy of university faculty members, the absence of an organized chain of command—also incapacitates the faculty member for systematic and organized attack on the problems . . . [17, p. 376]

The poor record is due, as previously indicated, to a worrisome lack of appreciation of the organizational and support mechanisms required for effectively carrying out problem-oriented research. Coleman attributes the difficulties to a serious "structural fault" of the university [17, pp. 375–85].

Potentially, IMOs for research and education could perform important "impedance matching" functions between the basic research activities of the academic community and the needs of a mission-oriented society. That is to say, IMOs could be structured as parallel organizations with authority comparable to that of departments—providing faculty participants with opportunities to serve both the disciplinary missions of their departments and the interdisciplinary missions (either education, public service, or research) of the special units and rewarding the individual faculty participant for successful performance in either. In practice, with a few notable exceptions such as the agricultural experiment stations, the interdisciplinary organizations have neither the prestige nor the authority to carry out a coordinating function among the various academic missions.

The matrix model highlights the inadequacy of organizational structures for relating the basic research mission to the other missions of the university. We have called attention to the fact that the responsibilities for coordinating and integrating the multiple functions and missions are typically assigned to individual faculty members. And because they are selected and rewarded for their attributes as specialized researchers, it is not surprising that some dimensions of the university's objectives are not adequately addressed. Bess points out that "since faculty are trained in graduate schools largely to perform research in their disciplines, they have little cross-disciplinary background, inclination, and understanding; little training in the pedagogical nuances needed in teaching; and inadequate awareness of skills in the organizational and administrative techniques" [6, p. 209]. Furthermore, faculty members are under increasing time pressures. The pressures on the individual affect morale; the focus on narrowly defined activities threatens the integrity of the collective mission.

It is interesting to contrast the organizational structures of universities with those widely adopted in other research and development and policy research organizations in the public or the private sector. At such organizations as A. D. Little, the Rand Corporation, or many innovative industrial laboratories, technical research personnel may be organized in departments corresponding to disciplinary backgrounds or areas of research activity. However, when the corporation is called on to carry out a novel development task or policy study, it creates a flexible and often temporary infrastructure designed to encourage collaboration and to assign accountability among a team of experts of differing backgrounds and skills. Such infrastructures are sometimes referred to in organizational literature [20] as "matrix organizations," but aside from the use of the term, there is no direct relationship to the matrix model presented here. In the "matrix organization," a set of systems managers (e.g., research and development project leaders) share or contend for resources controlled by a set of functional managers. As Sayles explains, "Organizational goals are, at once, multiple and conflicting and changing—and they need to reuse the same technical talent and technology for a multiplicity of end results. . . . [Matrix management introduces] structural imperatives that serve to maintain fluidity in the balance of power among the major subdivisions of the organization . . . and discourage the formation of rigid, exclusionary norms and suboptimal, vested-interest groups" [48, p. 16].

In their best-selling book, *In Search of Excellence* [36], Peters and Waterman express a strong aversion to the term "matrix organization" but advocate similar organizations with quite different labels, such as temporary structures, ad hoc groups, fluid organizations, shadow organizations, or skunk works. Such parallel organizations are not oriented to enhance organizational efficiency—to do better the things now being done—but to encourage innovation and collaboration toward novel goals. Whatever the nomenclature, such temporary groupings of key personnel and resources constitute organizational mechanisms aimed at achieving organizational effectiveness, defined previously as the ability to create acceptable outcomes and actions. We have noted that interdisciplinary mission (or "matrix") organizations are not altogether foreign to the campus. On some campuses, successful IMOs have been built around the personalities of unique individuals [44]. But these activities are idiosyncratic; by and large, universities have not acknowledged the need for mission-oriented organizations that transcend departmental lines, nor have they developed the leadership required to manage such activities. This lack severely limits their capacity to coordinate the efforts of faculty members on complex tasks, to effect changes in mission, and to integrate the various missions of the university.

Where Do We Wish to Go?

> There are three kinds of maps needed to help organizations learn for action. The first is a map of where the organization is; the second is a map of where it wishes to go; the third is a map of how to get there from here.
>
> Chris Argyris and Donald A. Schön [2, p. 160]

> No matter how much pressure is put on a person or social system to change through disconfirmation and the induction of guilt-anxiety, no change will occur unless members of the system feel it is safe to give up the old responses and learn something new.
>
> Edgar H. Schein [49, p. 77]

During the past decade, pervasive environmental changes have confronted all of the major institutions of American life. On the industrial scene, these changes have been so traumatic for many major industries—automobiles, steel, heavy industry, consumer electronics—that "double-loop" organizational learning has become a condition for survival. In universities, the changes in environment have been manifested as an extended period of retrenchment, imposing stresses on every dimension of the academic enterprise. Universities have responded primarily by single-loop organizational learning—making every effort to maintain the existing norms, goals, and structures—and doing with less support today the things that were being done yesterday. This article has presented an organizational map of the comprehensive research university as it is, and it has addressed the growing evidence that the norms, theories-in-use, and structures of the university may no longer be adequate to the missions they are intended to serve. The matrix model reveals that the problems facing universities are exacerbated by the divergent goals of the disciplinary and campus communities. As has been indicated, the intellectual leaders are predominantly oriented to basic research and to the goals and directives of federal agencies that sponsor it; they properly justify their activities in terms of contributions to national welfare. The administrative leaders play only a limited role in developing research initiatives on the home campus; they are, however, necessarily involved in the instructional programs and public service activities and accountable to the local and regional sponsors who represent the major sources of financial support for research universities. In fact, the federal government allocates for academic research and development only about $5 billion annually (for fiscal year 1983), providing less than 20 percent of the operating costs of the overall system of research universities. This support is clearly inadequate if the current priorities of research universities are to continue. That is to say, the major burden of financial support for research universities is assumed by stakeholders other than research agencies of the federal government, and much of the institutional support (including student tuition, state subsidies, and federal aid to students) is oriented to undergraduate education and public service rather than basic research. This offers a major dilemma that has not been confronted directly in the academic enterprise: science cannot be well served by inadequately funded universities, but given the current support mechanisms, universities will not be adequately funded if they default on their education and service missions.

The matrix model offers a starting point for universities wishing to redefine their roles in either the local or the national context. It reveals some of the features of both the internal and external environments that have constrained efforts to redefine organizational goals. Under pressures of retrenchment, many universities have been induced to reexamine their priorities on a campus-wide basis and to try to provide a rationale for the support of their individual campuses. By and large, however, they have proceeded as though the crisis were unique to their own campuses—as though the rest of the system would continue to function in a business-as-usual fashion. There have been relatively few efforts to reexamine the educational and research needs of the nation or the purposes of the national university system as a whole.

This article has suggested a particular need to reconsider the evaluation of institutional performance. Although inspired by the worthy motive of defining and achieving "excellence," the research universities of the nation have been led into a rating game that places far greater rewards on conformity than diversity, measuring performance primarily in terms of original research published in scholarly journals. This situation has served to impose the values and the mission of the outstanding research institutions on most of the other colleges and universities without providing, even in principle, for the justification or support of the overall research enterprise. A narrow definition of excellence has also served to impose the values of the most powerful disciplines on many of the less prestigious disciplines and professional schools and, in the process, has denigrated their intended purposes. At the same time, the national needs for undergraduate education and for advanced continuing education are not being adequately addressed, and little attention has been given to the local and regional needs for applied research and public service. Because it is highly unlikely that a single model of an educational institution can adequately serve the diversity of the educational and research needs, it seems necessary to develop alternative measures of excellence that will emphasize the individuality of the various campuses and, at the same time, will develop an image of the system of universities as complementary centers of learning. In reconceiving measures of excellence, a special responsibility falls on the leaders of the most prestigious universities, who educate the faculties and set the cultural climate for the enterprise as a whole.

Developing a new sense of purpose or a new approach to the evaluation of performance will call for new maps of the future university, either for the individual campus or for the nation's universities viewed as differentiated parts of an interconnected enterprise. How could the academic community go about designing maps of the future university? The matrix model has illuminated two significant barriers to addressing organizational problems of the university community in a systematic way. One barrier is the commitment to suboptimization along both of the axes of the matrix; some academic leaders do not even acknowledge the existence of problems except as they impinge directly on their own communities. A second barrier is a resulting lack of candor in discussing such problems: the presidents of our universities are subject to criticisms from so many constituencies, internal as well as external, that they find it difficult to discuss publicly substantive inadequacies in any dimension of performance. Similar vulnerabilities are experienced by faculty members, who are typically held accountable to their immediate departmental colleagues in formal deliberations regarding larger academic issues. Under these circumstances, a first step in organizational learning, either at the local or the national level, is the creation of a "safe place" for the candid discussion of matters that have been heretofore undiscussable. Some form of informal organization seems essential, transcending the governance structures of individual institutions and transcending the professional disciplinary and professional communities. In "The Management of Decline," Boulding suggested: "It may be indeed that a prime institutional need is the development of 'invisible colleges,' that is, small groups of people with similar tasks who are in close, constant communication and operate as a 'discipline'. . . . The invisible college indeed is the social invention that gave rise to science" [9, p. 64].

Though informal networks rarely control access to major financial resources, they do provide access to a critical human resource—independent actors who think for themselves. Following World War II, an informal national network of academic scientists utilized their prominence in the war effort to establish a powerful national commitment to the support of basic scientific research. In the recent past, such interinstitutional networks have been created to deal with problems experienced by many campuses on such issues as codes of professional ethics in university-industry relations and modification of government regulations on accounting operations [19, 34, 51]. It is interesting to note that the public pronouncements of outcomes are often identified by the "safe place" (Pajaro Dunes, Asilomar) where the meetings of such networks were convened. The leading academic scholars and administrators in the nation are remarkably gifted; many of them have the stamina as well as the talent to perform multiple tasks in superlative fashion. They already participate in informal networks that transcend their campuses, and with the rapid development of computer-communications technologies, they will be in day-to-day contact on a world-wide scale. This article has argued the need for new maps for the future university, the design of which would call for interdisciplinary and interinstitutional networks, made up of self-selected participants on the nations' campuses and elsewhere, and the creation of "safe places" for contemplating and discussing these issues.

References

1. Alpert, D. "The Role and Structure of Interdisciplinary and Multidisciplinary Research Centers." Paper presented at Conference of Graduate Schools meeting, Washington, D.C., 1969.
2. Argyris, C., and D. Schön. *Organizational Learning: A Theory of Action Perspective.* Reading: Addison-Wesley, 1978.
3. Arnold, C. K. "The Federal Role in Funding Education." *Change,* 14 (September 1982), 39–43.
4. Ashby, E. *Any Person, Any Study: An Essay on Higher Education in the United States.* New York: McGraw-Hill, 1971.
5. Barak, R. J. "Program Evaluation as a Tool for Retrenchment." In *Challenges of Retrenchment,* edited by J. R. Mingle and Associates, pp. 212–25. San Francisco: Jossey-Bass, 1981.
6. Bess, J. L. *University Organization: A Matrix Analysis of the Academic Professions.* New York: Human Sciences Press, 1982.
7. Birnbaum, P. H. "Assessment of Alternative Management Forms in Academic Interdisciplinary Research Projects." *Management Science,* 24 (November 1977), 272–84.
8. Bok, D. "Balancing Responsibility and Innovation." *Change,* 14 (September 1982), 16–25.
9. Boulding, K. E. "The Management of Decline." *Change,* 7 (June 1975), 8–9, 64.
10. Bowen, H. R. *The State of the Nation and the Agenda for Higher Education.* San Francisco: Jossey-Bass, 1982.

11. Boyer, E. L., and F. M. Hechinger. *Higher Education in the Nation's Service.* Washington, D.C.: Carnegie Foundation for the Advancement of Teaching, 1981.

12. Cartter, A. M. *An Assessment of Quality in Graduate Education.* Washington, D.C.: American Council on Education, 1966.

13. Churchman, C. W. "An Interdisciplinary Look at Science Policy in an Age of Decreased Funding." In *Research in the Age of the Steady-State University,* edited by D. I. Phillips and S. P. Shen, pp. 109–13. Boulder: Westview Press, 1982.

14. Cleveland, H. "What's Higher about Higher Education?" Paper presented at National Conference of the American Association for Higher Education, mimeographed, Washington, D.C., March 1981.

15. Cohen, M. D., and J. G. March. *Leadership and Ambiguity: The American College President.* New York: McGraw-Hill, 1974.

16. Coleman, E. " 'More' Has Not Meant 'Better' in the Organization of Academe." *Chronicle of Higher Education,* 1 (June 1981), 48.

17. Coleman, J. S. "The University and Society's New Demands Upon It." In *Content and Context: Essays on College Education,* edited by C. Kaysen, pp. 359–400. New York: McGraw-Hill, 1973.

18. Conference Board of Associated Research Councils. *An Assessment of Research Doctorate Programs in the United States.* 5 vols. Washington, D.C.: National Academy Press, 1982.

19. Culliton, B. J. "Pajaro Dunes: The Search for Consensus." *Science,* 216 (9 April 1982), 155–58.

20. Davis, S. M., and P. R. Lawrence. *Matrix.* Reading: Addison-Wesley, 1977.

21. Friedman, R. C., and R. S. Friedman. "The Role of Organized Research Units in Academic Science." Research report, Pennsylvania State University, June 1982.

22. Garvin, D. A. *The Economics of University Behavior.* New York: Academic Press, 1980.

23. Guzzetta, D. J. "Education's Quiet Revolution—Changes and Challenges." *Change,* 14 (September 1982), 10–11, 60.

24. Jencks, C., and D. Riesman. *The Academic Revolution.* Garden City: Doubleday, 1968.

25. Katz, D., and R. L. Kahn. *The Social Psychology of Organizations.* 2nd ed. New York: Wiley and Sons, 1978.

26. Kerr, C. *The Uses of the University.* Cambridge: Harvard University Press, 1963.

27. ——— . "Postscript 1982." *Change,* 14 (October 1982), 23–31.

28. Lanier, L. H., and C. J. Anderson. *A Study of the Financial Condition of Colleges and Universities: 1972–75.* Washington, D.C.: American Council on Education, 1975.

29. Lynton, E. A. "A Crisis of Purpose: Reexamining the Role of the University." *Change,* 15 (October 1983), 18–23, 53.

30. Mingle, J. R., R. O. Berdahl, and M. W. Peterson. "Political Realities of Statewide Reorganization, Merger, and Closure." In *Challenges of Retrenchment,* edited by J. R. Mingle and Associates, pp. 273–97. San Francisco: Jossey-Bass, 1981.

31. Mingle, J. R., and Associates. *Challenges of Retrenchment.* San Francisco: Jossey-Bass, 1981.

32. Moynihan, D. P. "State vs. Academe: Nationalizing the Universities." *Harper's,* 261 (December 1980), 31–40.

33. Niebuhr, H., Jr. "Strengthening the Human Learning System." *Change,* 14 (November/December 1982), 16–21.

34. Norman, C. "Faculty v. OMB: One More Time." *Science,* 215 (5 February 1982), 642.

35. Perkins, J. A. *The University as an Organization.* New York: McGraw-Hill, 1973.

36. Peters, T. J., and R. H. Waterman, Jr. *In Search of Excellence.* New York: Harper and Row, 1983.

37. Petrie, H. G., and D. Alpert. "What is the Problem of Retrenchment in Higher Education?" *Journal of Management Studies,* 20 (January 1983), 97–119.

38. Pfeffer, J., and G. R. Salancik. *The External Control of Organizations: A Resource Dependence Perspective.* New York: Harper and Row, 1978.

39. Phillips, D. I., and S. P. Shen. *Research in the Age of the Steady-State University.* Boulder: Westview Press, 1982.

40. Reif, F. "Educational Challenges for the University." *Science,* 184 (3 May 1974), 537–42.

41. Richman, B. M., and R. N. Farmer. *Leadership, Goals, and Power in Higher Education.* San Francisco: Jossey-Bass, 1974.

42. Riesman, D. *On Higher Education.* San Francisco: Jossey-Bass, 1980.

43. Roose, K. D., and C. J. Anderson. *A Rating of Graduate Programs.* Washington, D.C.: American Council on Education, 1970.

44. Rossini, F. A., and A. L. Porter. "Frameworks for Integrating Interdisciplinary Research." *Research Policy,* 8 (1979), 70–79.

45. Roy, R. "Graduate Universities—A New Model." *Science,* 214 (December 1981), 1297.

46. ———— . "STS: Core of Technological Literacy." *Bulletin of Science, Technology, & Society,* 2 (1982), 289–90.
47. Rudolph, F. *The American College and University: A History.* New York: Alfred A. Knopf, 1962.
48. Sayles, L. R. "Matrix Management: The Structure with a Future." *Organizational Dynamics,* 5 (Autumn 1976), 2–17.
49. Schein, E. H. *Professional Education.* New York: McGraw-Hill, 1972.
50. Shapiro, H. T. "What Does 'Smaller But Better' Mean?" *University Record* (University of Michigan), 1 (April 1981), 1–3.
51. Shapiro, H. T., and R. Heller. "Circular A-21 Negotiations." *Science,* 216 (9 April 1982), 126.
52. Smith, B. L. R., and J. J. Karlesky. *The Universities in the Nation's Research Effort.* New Rochelle: Change Magazine Press, 1977.
53. Teich, A. H. "Research Centers and Non-Faculty Researchers: A New Academic Role." In *Research in the Age of the Steady-State University,* edited by D. I. Phillips and S. P. Shen, pp. 91–108. Boulder: Westview Press, 1982.
54. Veysey, L. R. *The Emergence of the American University.* Chicago: University of Chicago Press, 1965.
55. Wallin, F. W. "Universities for a Small Planet—A Time to Reconceptualize Our Role." *Change,* 15 (March 1983), 7–9.
56. Weick, K. E. "Educational Organizations as Loosely Coupled Systems." *Administrative Science Quarterly,* 21 (March 1976), 1–19.
57. Whetten, D. A. "Sources, Responses, and Effects of Organizational Decline." In *The Organizational Life Cycle,* edited by J. R. Kimberley and R. H. Miles, pp. 342–74. San Francisco: Jossey-Bass, 1980.
58. ———— . "Organizational Responses to Scarcity: Exploring the Obstacles to Innovative Responses to Retrenchment in Education." *Education Administrative Quarterly,* 17 (Summer 1981), 80–97.
59. Yarmolinsky, A. "Institutional Paralysis." *Daedalus,* 2 (Winter 1975), 61–67.

THE ROLE OF SHARED GOVERNANCE IN INSTITUTIONAL HARD DECISIONS: ENABLER OR ANTAGONIST?

PETER D. ECKEL

Many colleges and universities are straining to respond to changing environments that include increased economic pressure, new technology, nontraditional competitors, and increased public discontent and criticism that higher education is unresponsive. The required and difficult solutions tend to be the "re" words so prevalent in organizational life throughout the 1990s—restructuring, reducing, reallocating, and refocusing—all of them strategies with which higher education struggles.

Many suggest that higher education's difficulties with change are due to shared governance (Association of Governing Boards, 1996; Benjamin, Carroll, Jacobi, Krop, & Shires, 1993; Kennedy, 1994; Schuster, Smith, Corak, & Yamada, 1994). Cole (1994), as provost at Columbia University, articulated the difficulties:

> It is no longer possible for research universities to afford excellence in all areas of knowledge. . . . Nonetheless, there has been far more talk about the need to make critical choices than a willingness to engage directly the problems associated with choice. . . . The fundamental problem . . . has more to do with basic ambiguity over governance than with the ability to articulate alternatives. Who has the authority . . . to make such choices? What are the processes by which the choices of the decision makers are legitimated within the university community? What is the role of faculty, students, administrative leaders, trustees, and alumni in making such choices? (pp. 5–6)

One group renders a harsher judgment—that the current "governance system virtually makes inevitable the inability of institutions and systems to set priorities, focus missions, and implement choice among academic programs" (Benjamin et al., 1993, p. 28).

All do not criticize shared governance. Some argue that it involves many people, thus increasing the likelihood that a change will be institutionalized and have greater impact (Curry, 1992). It creates arenas for dissent and debate (Walker, 1979), allows for policy and program modifications, and guarantees accountability and faculty involvement (Rosovsky, 1990). Changes also are more likely to be implemented when discussed thoroughly and altered to fit the local situation (Levine, 1980). Without faculty support and acceptance, a change most likely will not last, nor will it have significant impact (Birnbaum, 1992; Walker, 1979).

As environments continue to change and institutions face more complicated and intense challenges, the demands on shared governance to act and to act quickly and in ways beneficial to the institution will increase (Benjamin et al., 1993; Kennedy, 1994). Dill and Helm (1988) noted even 10 years ago that "the substance of governance has changed" (p. 323) as "maintenance" decisions like the allocation of incremental budgets, modifications to the curriculum, and issues of faculty life are replaced with "strategic-policy making" like tackling high-stakes challenges related to the changing nature of scholarship and prioritizing among programs. This shift places an even heavier burden on governance.

The preponderance of literature on shared governance and institutional change mostly consists of opinions, typically by those interested in carving out a stronger role for senior administrators and trustees or for faculty. The purpose of this study is to provide a deeper understanding of the ability (or inability) of shared governance to facilitate tough institutional choices. For this study, "shared governance" is defined as the system, composed of structures and processes, through which faculty, administrators, and other campus constituents make collective institutional decisions (Association of Governing Boards, 1996; IMHE/OECD, 1999).

Much of the current thinking on shared governance is shaped by the 1966 *Statement on Government of Colleges and Universities* (AAUP, 1995), jointly formulated by the American Association of University Professors (AAUP), the American Council on Education (ACE), and the Association of Governing Boards of Universities and Colleges (AGB). The *Statement*, although not intended to serve as a blueprint for institutional decision making, outlines roles for faculty, administrators, and trustees in governance decisions. For example, it suggests that issues such as managing the endowment be assigned to the trustees, maintaining and creating new resources to the president, and developing the curriculum to the faculty. Not all decisions fall neatly into the domain of one of the three groups. It notes that, therefore, much of institutional governance is (or should be) conducted jointly. Decisions about general education policy, the framing and execution of long-range plans, budgeting, and presidential selection should be made jointly.

The *Statement* may cause as much confusion as clarity. Because of its broad categories of responsibilities, different groups can easily make a case that a specific decision falls in their domain. For example, how can an institution determine if a change like offering a new continuing education program is the responsibility of the president (who, according to the *Statement*, is responsible for maintaining and creating new resources), the faculty (who are responsible for the curriculum), or the trustees (who are the conduit between the public with its needs and the institution)? Or is this new initiative part of long-range planning, which the *Statement* identifies as a joint effort? If so, is participation equal? Answers to questions about who takes the lead on institutional decisions most likely depend on where one sits and the case each party can make for ownership. When high stakes are involved, the probability of conflict over who decides most likely rises.

The High Stakes Challenges of Academic Program Discontinuance

The institutional "hard decision" in this study was academic program discontinuance. This decision can be extremely difficult as outcomes can be emotionally charged (Dill & Sporn, 1995), faculty can lose their jobs and have their life's work interrupted (American Association of University Professors, 1995), and the cuts can potentially threaten institutions' core values and alter institutional identities (Melchiori, 1982). Program discontinuance also tends to occur during times of fiscal constraints (Gumport & Prusser, 1997; Levine, 1997; Slaughter, 1993).

On most campuses, discontinuing academic programs is a last resort (Breneman, 1993; Yezer, 1992) and one which is painful and emotional for those involved (Hardy, 1993). Its outcomes are likely to have an adverse impact on some; people may believe that the institution should engage in it; and leaders are inexperienced at making that type of decision (Cameron, 1983; Dougherty, 1979; Levine, Rubin, & Wolohojian, 1981). Combine these negative aspects with the fact that the academy is highly participative and grounded in a history of collegiality, shared governance, and professional prerogative (Bess, 1988; Birnbaum, 1988; Hardy, 1990), and the stresses of program discontinuance on shared governance come into focus.

The difficulty of program termination is intensified when, through shared-governance mechanisms, faculty must make decisions to close their colleagues' departments and, potentially, their own. Program discontinuance, because it involves curricular decisions, institutional financial well-being, and institutional strategy, falls into the gray area of shared governance and cannot simply be decided independently by faculty, administrators, or trustees (Gumport, 1993). It is not a decision simply about the curriculum for the faculty, about institutional strategy for trustees, or about the institution's financial well-being for administrators. (For a further discussion of program discontinuance, please see Eckel, 1998).

Conceptual Framework

Because institutional "governance concerns power: who is in charge; who makes decisions; who has a voice, and how loud that voice is" (Rosovsky, 1990, p. 261), this study adopted a framework concerned with interest-group struggle to reach a specific set of outcomes—in this study, discontinuing academic programs, or for some, preventing programs from being terminated. Interest-group struggle is about power and who has it. These are central components when no single group has the ability to dictate decisions (Baldridge, 1971; Bolman & Deal, 1992), such as in university decision-making about academic retrenchment. These core decisions typically cannot be made and implemented without the consent of multiple interest groups (Association of Governing Boards, 1996; Gumport, 1993; Schuster et al., 1994). "If there is an issue at hand that the faculty cares deeply about and you can't persuade them," as Walker puts it, "you certainly can't bulldoze them" (1979, p. 10).

The fundamental assumption in this framework is that organizations are comprised of coalitions of interest groups in which decisions are made based upon power and conflict, not for optimizing objectives (Baldridge, 1971; Pfeffer & Salancik, 1980). Subgroups must negotiate with one another to build coalitions and pool their respective influence to generate desired outcomes (Bolman & Deal, 1992; Pfeffer, 1981). Focusing on the subgroups involved in the process and on the ways in which they interact helps answer the questions about who has a voice and how loud is that voice. As for how decisions are made, shared governance becomes the arena in which different subgroups gather to make institutional choices (Birnbaum, 1988).

The purpose of this study is to provide a deeper understanding of the ability (or inability) of shared governance to facilitate tough institutional choices. Following the lead of the *Statement on Government of Colleges and Universities* (AAUP, 1995), and because many discussions of governance do so as well, this study viewed faculty, administrators and trustees as the interest groups involved in program-closure decisions. Therefore, this study sought to understand the extent to which shared governance can make hard decisions and facilitate institutional change. In difficult institutional decisions, what role does shared governance play? To what extent is decision making shared? Which decisions are made separately by faculty, administrators, and trustees, and which are made collectively?

The Study

This study investigated shared governance processes at four research universities. The intent was to identify themes and patterns across institutional decision-making processes; thus, in the hope of building explanations, I adopted a multiple case study method (Herriott & Firestone, 1983; Yin, 1994). An institution, to be eligible for this study, had to have discontinued at least one academic program within the last seven years that had not been reinstated, must be classified as a research I or II university, and must be accessible. I sought to identify institutions that had similar structures, cultures (i.e., research faculty culture as compared to teaching faculty culture), and purposes, because retrenchment decisions may vary by institutional type (El-Khawas, 1994). I used the Carnegie classification system as a tool to identify institutions that were more similar than different. From searches of *The Chronicle of Higher Education, Academe, Trusteeship,* I generated a list of universities that had discontinued programs recently. I selected the study institutions—the University of Maryland at College Park, Oregon State University, the University of Rochester (in New York), and Kent State University (in Ohio)[1]—from this list.

I interviewed between 11 and 16 individuals from each institution using structured, open-ended question protocols. Participants included individuals involved in the discontinuance process—for example, key central administrators or members of involved governance committees and individuals from the terminated units who were still on campus. In addition to interviews, I reviewed meeting minutes, institutional reports, speeches, other relevant campus documents and on- and off-campus newspaper accounts (Merriam, 1988). I obtained these documents from informants, through meetings with campus archivists, and from searches of electronic data bases.

From the collected data, I drafted case reports that included all of the potentially relevant collected material (Yin, 1994). Out of the larger case reports, I crafted each case study, telling the story of the discontinuance process. I then used two three-step data analysis processes: pattern coding, memoing, and proposition writing (Miles & Huberman, 1994)—first within each case and then across the four cases.

Findings

This section provides brief synopses that describe the governance processes used to close academic programs at each of the four research universities. It also explores the shared governance processes involved in bringing about and impeding program closures. These four cases show that shared governance can play a facilitative role in institutional change, particularly in such difficult changes as program closure. Of the two colleges and 25 programs/departments closed among the four institutions, only one was overturned because of faculty resistance.

University of Maryland at College Park

On April 24, 1992, the College Park Senate of the University of Maryland at College Park approved recommendations to eliminate seven academic departments and one college; for all intents and purposes, this action concluded the discontinuance process begun at the start of the 1990–1991 academic year.

The governance and academic decision-making apparatus at Maryland–College Park included (a) the Academic Planning Advisory Committee (APAC)—a joint faculty-administration committee, advisory to the provost; it had been created 10 years earlier to review financial implications of changes in academic programs; (b) the College Park Senate—the campus governance body comprised predominantly of elected faculty but also including students and staff; (c) the Programs, Curricular, and Courses Committee (PCC)—a standing committee of the senate that deals with curricular changes; and (d) the president and the provost—long-time campus citizens who believed in the value of shared decision making and saw the senate as important to institutional decision making.

In the fall of 1990, the provost persuaded campus executives that reducing the number of academic units and departments was a wise move while continuing across-the-board reductions to compensate for its share of the $24.5 million—10% of the university's state budget—that had been rescinded by the legislature. In the previous academic year, the campus had faced a cut of $20.5 million, bringing the two-year total reductions to $45 million in public funds. The provost saw the financial recession as a bona fide crisis but one that could be used as a lever to improve the institution.

The provost asked the senate's executive committee (acting in lieu of the senate because of deadlines set by the provost) to develop a set of criteria and principles for discontinuance, which it did in a document called *Criteria for Planning*. Concurrently, the provost requested a report from each college dean identifying programs to close. He strongly suggested that each college form its own "mini-APAC" to make recommendations. Upon submission of the deans' reports, the Academic Planning Advisory Committee conducted its own reviews, starting with the deans' reports and including available internal or external program reviews and meetings with deans, faculty, and department chairs from all of the colleges. From this work, the provost and the Academic Planning Advisory Committee identified nine departments and two colleges for potential elimination. Most of the recommendations closely followed those of the deans; deviations occurred in only three cases, two of which were the proposed elimination of the two colleges. Based upon the work of the Academic Planning Advisory Committee, the provost drafted *Preserving Enhancement,* the first preliminary report, which he said was open to debate and codification, and submitted it to the president seven months after the Labor Day recision.

The provost, his staff, and the Academic Planning Advisory Committee then organized a series of campus-wide subcommittees that were asked, not to address the validity of the recommendations, but rather to investigate the *implications* of closing the unit on the campus and the state. Each subcommittee was comprised of faculty from various departments within and outside of the college and at least one faculty member from the targeted unit. Approximately 120 faculty became involved in the discontinuance process through these subcommittees, equivalent to 10% of Maryland–College Park's total full-time, tenure-track faculty. At the conclusion of the subcommittee work, the Academic Planning Advisory Committee held a series of open hearings for department supporters to make their cases and influence the decisions.

Based upon the information gathered through the summer subcommittees and the open hearings, the provost, with guidance from the Academic Planning Advisory Committee, produced a second report, *Hard Choices: The Next Step in Preserving Enhancement* at the end of January 1992. This report identified seven departments (agriculture and extension education; housing and design; radio, television, and film; urban studies and planning; industrial, technological, and occupational education; recreation; and textiles and consumer economics) and one college (human ecology) for elimination. *Hard Choices* not only identified programs to be cut, but removed three units previously slated for closure from the list—the Hearing and Speech and Nuclear Engineering Departments, and the College of Library and Information Sciences.

The provost sent the recommendations in *Hard Choices* to the College Park Senate at the end of January 1992 for action by the close of the academic year. The senate's decisions would then be forwarded to the president and, ultimately, to the board of trustees. By chance, in the year the cuts were to occur, all of the senate committee chairs became vacant, which allowed the senate chair-elect to deliberately fill the PCC chair vacancy with a respected faculty leader. Senators were deliberately appointed to the Programs, Curricular, and Courses Committee who also were well respected by their peers. The Programs, Curricular, and Courses Committee reviewed the information assembled by the Academic Planning Advisory Committee and collected on its own, conducted interviews, and held a second set of open hearings. The Programs, Curricular, and Courses Committee then drafted a report that unanimously accepted the Academic Planning Advisory Committee's recommendations. This report went to the senate for a vote. The senate executive committee scheduled three meetings to consider the Programs, Curricular, and Courses Committee's recommendations, but they were not needed, as all of the decisions were made the first day. At the conclusion of the voting, the senate had overwhelmingly supported the recommendations.

Oregon State University

On Thursday, February 7, 1991, the president of Oregon State University informed faculty that he would recommend closing one college and 13 academic departments to the Chancellor, who, in turn, would submit his recommendations to the Board of Higher Education. Action by the board would be forwarded to and made official by an act of the state legislature.

Strong deans in autonomous colleges mark Oregon State's governance history. Faculty involvement varied. In some colleges the dean and associate deans made most of the decisions. Other colleges operated through a council of department chairs or similar structure, and still others filled college committees through faculty elections.

At the institutional level, the Faculty Senate was advisory to the president and provost. The Faculty Consultative Group (FCG), an emergency group of the senate, is constituted when program cuts are imminent, as required by the institution's policy for discontinuing programs. The 12-person Faculty Consultative Group is composed of members of the Faculty Senate executive committee and the chairs of three senate subcommittees. According to the procedural document, this group should "confidentially offer constructive suggestions and comment" to the president and the provost. The president was a long-time faculty member who had become president in 1984 after a stint in the Reagan White House. An administrative restructuring created the position of provost; and this provost, a newcomer to Oregon State in 1985, was the first to serve in it. Much of the institutional decision making occurred through personal communications between the president and/or the provost, and college administrators, mid-level university administrators, or key faculty members. The final actors in the governance process resided off-campus: the chancellor, the Board of Higher Education, and the State Legislative Assembly. These bodies make decisions on major institutional changes following campus recommendations. Decisions are not final until acted upon by the state legislature.

At the time of the president's announcement to close programs, the university expected a mandated reduction of $13.4 million each year in its 1991–1993 bi-annium budget resulting from Ballot Measure Five, a voter-initiated tax cut. The chancellor gave all public institutions three months to craft their recommendations so he could forward a system-wide plan to the board. The three-month deadline, according to the president, drastically reduced consultation and deliberation.

As a result of a state revenue shortfall three years earlier, during which Oregon State merged two departments, the president and the provost assigned three deans to draft two documents that were accepted with slight modification by the senate and ultimately by the president. The first document, *Guidelines for Program Redirection,* laid out the process and guiding philosophies; its companion document, *Criteria for Program Reduction, Termination, and Reorganization,* spelled out the criteria.

During the 1990–1991 discontinuance process, the campus followed its *Guidelines for Program Redirection:* The president and provost charged the dean of each college with developing a plan specifying which programs would be discontinued. Each dean had a "budget hearing" before the provost, after which the cabinet began outlining its recommendations for the Faculty Consultative Group to review. The senate convened the Faculty Consultative Group to respond to the president's recommendations and to explore and articulate potential implications of the recommendations. At this point, the confidentiality clause from the Oregon State policy created problems as the members of the Faculty Consultative Group had difficulty obtaining information. They could not go to deans, department heads, or faculty in the targeted units to collect information or to explore hunches because they had to treat the procedures and the identity of the targeted programs with a high level of confidentiality.

The Faculty Consultative Group strongly recommended that certain programs slated for closure be taken off the list because of potentially damaging spillover effects. After discussions with the Faculty Consultative Group, the president and the provost, with the help of the rest of the cabinet, began developing the final recommendations. They had to balance a number of competing priorities: First, they made sure that no recommendation would create significant adverse effects in other units or institutions outside the university. Second, the president and the provost had to coordinate their efforts with the chancellor's office and other public institutions to prevent the system from eliminating similar programs across the state. To many faculty and college administrators, these constraints created a feeling that important campus decisions were being made in a black box. Many interviewees said that they did not know how the final decisions actually came about. Once the coordination among other institutions was complete, the president and provost readied the list for public announcement identifying the units to be closed and made the announcement.

University of Rochester

On November 16, 1995, the dean of the College at the University of Rochester,[2] with the president and provost present, announced at an emergency meeting of the Council of Department Chairs that, as part of a larger effort intended to return the institution to more solid financial ground, which they labeled the Renaissance Plan, four Ph.D. programs would be "suspended."[3] These four programs—chemical engineering, mathematics, linguistics, and comparative literature—would not be allowed to accept graduate students, thus in effect terminating those doctoral programs. Four additional doctoral programs would be "refocused," meaning that the department's focus would be narrowed and the number of its graduate students reduced. The hope was that the institution would reduce faculty size and departmental expenditures by an estimated $3 million. Rochester, a private tuition-dependent institution, fell on hard financial times in the early 1990s—the results of enhancing research and graduate programs that brought in little tuition money, a costly period of endowment mismanagement, a rapidly increasing tuition discount ratio (35% to 50% in ten years), and an unsustainable 12% draw on its endowment.

The primary body for faculty governance in the College is the Council of Department Chairs (CDC), a formal group chaired by the dean that meets at least monthly and includes all of the department chairs and directors. Decisions not made in the Council of Department Chairs usually are made through extensive consultation among the president, provost, and dean who formed a leadership triumvirate. The president was newly hired (July 1994) and charged with solving the financial problems. He intentionally selected an institutional insider as the new provost. The dean, a long-time faculty member, had resigned in visible protest against actions taken by the previous administration; but the new president asked him to stay on to lead the change effort. Two other campus governance bodies are the Faculty Council and Faculty Senate. Neither is influential, nor did they play substantive roles in the discontinuance process.

In one of his first campus-wide communiqués, the president articulated his view of the financial problem and the idea of targeted closures. The letter sent "a very important signal to the faculty" about the problem and "set the stage for the subsequent detailed process," said the dean. The dean and the provost also engaged the Council of Department Chairs, the Faculty Council, and the Faculty Senate in conversations about the problems and the proposed solutions to get their feedback. Beyond formal governance, administrative leaders talked about the problems incessantly and convened informal groups of faculty opinion leaders. The idea of targeted reductions, when broached on campus, received favorable agreement.

The dean and the provost held a series of individual meetings with faculty and chairs from each department to collect data and hear faculty opinions first-hand. They interviewed three people from each department: the chair, a department representative identified by the chair, and a representative selected by the department as a whole, totaling 75 meetings in all. Administrators believed that this approach was more feasible than meeting with each of the approximately 340 faculty. Prior to the meetings, the dean sent the interview questions to the college's entire faculty and asked for comments either in writing or by e-mail. He received fewer than a dozen responses. After the 75 interviews, the dean, provost, and president sent another letter to all college faculty recapping the process and outlining the next steps: reducing faculty size, targeting budget cuts, and closing Ph.D. programs.

At this point in the process, senior administrators believed that they would have to make the ultimate decisions. If they did not, the dean said, there might be too much "wiggle room" and the closure process might be "undone before it is actually completed." This approach was a hard sell to the faculty, especially to those who thought that the decisions should be made in open hearings or by a committee. The dean, provost, and president sent a memo in mid-September to the college's faculty outlining their plan to make the decision themselves and asking once again for comments on the process and the dates. The dean also met with the Faculty Council to review the process to date and discuss how the decisions were ultimately going to be made.

With the assistance of the dean and provost, the president drafted a plan to attend to the institution's financial problems. Prior to unveiling the Renaissance Plan, the president, provost, and dean convened a group of informal campus faculty leaders to get their feedback. This discussion, held in complete confidence, allowed administrators to see initial reactions, to articulate their rationale and their expected outcomes, and to prepare responses to the expected naysayers.

The administrators also believed that it was imperative to get full board support before proceeding. The trustees would provide the needed funds; but more important, once signed on, they would not override the administrators' plan. The president scheduled a special weekend retreat for the board in mid-November to gain their support. The board chair, to show his personal commitment, gave the institution $10 million to implement the Renaissance Plan.

A few days after the board retreat, the dean gave 24-hour notice for an emergency meeting of the Council of Department Chairs. The morning of the meeting, he telephoned each of the affected chairs and told them about the announcement that would be made that afternoon. At the later meeting, the dean then announced the decisions to close four Ph.D. programs and refocus four others.

Five months later the dean announced that the administration and the Department of Mathematics had reached an agreement to reinstate its Ph.D. program. This department, upon the announcement of its Ph.D. program's discontinuance, had raised a national call to arms. The department was able to get negative press in the Sunday *New York Times* and the *Chronicle of Higher Education*. The American Mathematical Society (AMS) joined the fight because it believed that, if Rochester could do away with its mathematics Ph.D. program, others would follow. Together the AMS and the department organized an extensive publicity campaign to reverse the decision. The Rochester president received over 200 letters, including several from Nobel laureates, criticizing the proposed action.

Mathematics was the only department able to negotiate successfully with the administration to save its Ph.D. program. As part of the deal to reinstate the doctoral program, mathematics faculty agreed to improve their teaching and to develop specific courses for nonmathematics majors. They also formed new linkages with other units.

Kent State University

In the early spring of 1996, the dean of the College of Education at Kent State University, the program coordinator of the counseling psychology program, and the chair of the department housing the program, following a series of conversations, announced their joint decision to discontinue the Ph.D. program in counseling psychology. This decision was approved smoothly by the departmental faculty, the campus's Educational Policies Council, the Faculty Senate, and the institution's Board of Trustees. On September 19, 1996, the Ohio Board of Regents unanimously authorized the discontinuance.

Kent State is a unionized institution with a strong history of faculty governance. Within the College of Education, most decisions are made collectively by faculty and the dean. The dean, a long-time and well-trusted administrator and faculty member, tended to begin college-wide decisions through small targeted conversations, and then brought all interested faculty into the decision processes. Sometimes decisions are made informally; at other times, they become part of a formal decision-making process in the College Advisory Council (CAC). The College of Education's CAC is composed of three faculty elected from each of the three academic departments. CAC decisions are then passed to the Educational Policies Council (EPC), a campus-wide body whose membership is divided evenly between administrators and faculty. Kent State's faculty union is affiliated with the AAUP and concerns itself primarily with issues of process and violations of faculty contracts.

In 1995–1996, the College of Education was hit with its second budget reduction in four years. At the same time, it was trying to cope with the loss of more than half its faculty because of an early retirement program (40 of 90 faculty) and through normal attrition (an additional 15 faculty). As a result, the college could not replace departing faculty on a one-to-one basis. One small program lost all of its four faculty. The school psychology program went from five faculty to one. Counseling psychology had one faculty member left from five. That program had to cope simultaneously with two deaths, a third faculty member who retired early, and a fourth who was denied tenure. The low number of faculty threatened the two psychology programs' accreditation. The decision to discontinue programs was not intentional or strategic; rather, it emerged from the circumstances at that time.

To decide which program should receive scarce resources and which should be closed, college administrators held many formal and informal discussions and challenged college faculty to come up with alternatives. Over the course of the many conversations that the dean initiated, it became increasingly clear that the counseling psychology program was not going to receive needed resources or new faculty. The program coordinator, who was the only remaining faculty member in the program, eventually agreed that it would be better to discontinue the program than have it stagger along. This admission allowed the dean to take action. The College Advisory Council discussed the situation and gave the dean its support. Because of continued widespread discussion by the college's faculty, department chairs, and the dean, the decision to close the counseling psychology program was no surprise. The announcement to discontinue the program was made to the students by letter. They were also invited to a special meeting organized by the program coordinator and the chair to discuss the decision and transition for the students.

The decision to close the Ph.D. program in counseling psychology met with little resistance from the faculty and was swiftly approved by the college's College Advisory Council, by the Educational Policies Council and the Faculty Senate at the campus level, and at the university and system levels by the board of trustees and the Ohio Board of Regents. Neither the Faculty Senate nor the union became involved because these decisions had been made with the approval of the faculty in the affected departments; according to a senator, "If the faculty in the departments are willing to go along with the cuts, then there is not much basis for the Faculty Senate to overturn the decision."

Analysis

This study sought to explore questions about shared governance's ability to faciliate institutional "hard decisions" and the roles of key campus interest groups in the process. This analysis first explores the roles that the three key interest groups played in the processes and the extent to which decisions were made jointly. The second part outlines the roles played by shared governance in academic program discontinuance.

Who Did What and How

This section explores the questions: What are the roles of faculty, administrators, and trustees in institutional hard decisions? What is done independently and collectively? How "shared" is shared governance when institutions close programs?

Administrators. In all of the cases, central administrators initiated and led the process. At Maryland–College Park, administrators decided to undertake program termination, and they chose to use the Academic Planning Advisory Committee as the first decision-making body. The provost and the associate provost were the leaders of the process—designing it, determining how to involve people, and shepherding it through the institution. They became partners with faculty in key decisions, but administrators wrote the two primary reports—*Preserving Enhancement* and *Hard Choices*—the second of which was forwarded to the senate for response.

At Oregon State, administrators played a much more independent role than at Maryland–College Park. Prior to Ballot Measure Five, a committee of deans drafted the procedures that the campus later followed. The president and provost held budget hearings with the deans to craft the initial proposal; the president and the provost made the final decision.

The president, provost, and dean at Rochester crafted and led the process. They sold the process to the faculty, conducted the individual interviews, interpreted the data they collected, garnered board support, and, in the end, made and announced the final decisions. They also intentionally did not create a faculty appeals process, as a "definitive decision" was their goal.

At Kent State, the dean of the college and the department chair that housed counseling psychology framed the challenge to the college. They facilitated conversations within the department and college to create understanding of the factors driving the decision. They met with the remaining faculty member and, in the end, facilitated his move to a new department.

Faculty Decision Makers. Some faculty were active participants in determining which programs to close and others tried to dissuade decision makers from closing specific units. Both sets of faculty were involved in the discontinuance process both through formal governance structures and outside of them. At Maryland–College Park faculty were active partners with administrators and frequently the leaders of the process. Faculty were involved formally through the Academic Planning Advisory Committee, the Programs, Curricular, and Courses Committee, and the senate. They were asked by the provost to develop criteria and principles for the process to follow. The process began through a joint faculty-administrative standing body (APAC), which was instrumental in designing the process and developing the first two sets of recommendations. Faculty were additionally involved through the summer subcommittees in which 120 faculty investigated the implications of recommended closures. Faculty commented during the APAC's open hearings, were involved in the PCC's investigation (running and participating in their open hearings), and were responsible for taking the final vote in the College Park Senate.

At Oregon State, faculty involvement was limited to the Faculty Consultive Group and, depending upon the college, to helping the dean craft his initial recommendations. The role of faculty at Oregon State was consultative. Rather than making the actual decisions, like the faculty at Maryland–College Park, faculty at Oregon State provided advice. They helped the administration think through implications and encouraged them to remove some programs on the list. The confidentiality clause and the short time-frame may have limited Oregon State faculty involvement. In the end, some faculty felt frustrated because confidentiality limited their ability to widen the conversation and collect more information.

Although not the key decision makers, faculty at Rochester were nevertheless highly involved in the process. Through the Council of Department Chairs, faculty provided needed information (chairs are thought of as the faculty), helped the administration think through issues of quality and productivity, and helped shape the process. Informal faculty leaders were the first to see the Renaissance Plan, helping to polish it and test reactions. One-third of all faculty (75 in all) were involved in the individual interviews and faculty had other opportunities to participate, although only a few availed themselves of these invitations. Faculty were kept abreast of and discussed the closure process in the Faculty Senate and the Faculty Council.

Two sets of faculty were involved at Kent State: faculty within and outside the college. Within the college, faculty were involved informally in the discussions surrounding the inevitable closure. They were also involved in the more formal discussions in the College Advisory Council. Outside the college, faculty were involved through the formal decision-making processes to approve closure in the Educational Policies Council and the senate. They also might have become involved through the union if a grievance had been filed.

Faculty resistors also worked to prevent closures from occurring. At Maryland–College Park, leaders of some departments, such as recreation and radio, and television and film, tried to develop support for their departments and curtail the closure efforts. They spoke out at the two sets of open hearings, and some participated in protests on the steps of the administration building.

Kent State and Oregon State saw little faculty resistance. The closing program at Kent State had only one program faculty member, and he had agreed to the closure. At Oregon State, possibly because of the short time frame and because the long history of financial downturns, faculty resistance did not organize. Said one faculty member, "If Ballot Measure Five is fully implemented we would not exist. There really was a feeling of futility."

The most active and successful faculty resistors were the mathematics faculty at Rochester. They played the political game effectively, building coalitions both on- and off-campus to mobilize support. They generated negative attention through major news outlets at a time when the institution was trying to ratchet up its perceived academic value and recruit more talented students. Finally, the faculty leaders were able to negotiate with university administrators and find a middle ground. They did build support from other faculty through shared governing bodies, but their outside activities were what led to the administrative recision.

Trustees. The final group involved in the discontinuance process was the board of trustees. At none of the campuses did the decision become contentious at the board level. In three of the cases, the exception being Rochester, boards played peripheral roles, merely approving decisions that the institutions forwarded. At Rochester, the board had to both approve the idea and make the required funding available. Board members attended a retreat prior to the announcement and provided requested support. Additionally, the board chair gave the institution $10 million for implementation.

The Sharing of Governance. To what extent was governance and decision making shared? The answer to that question varied across institutions. At Maryland–College Park, faculty and administrators made many decisions together, literally sitting in the same room, participating on the same committees, reviewing data together, and attending the same open hearings. The same was true at Kent State, where it was through joint conversations that the dean, department chair, and the sole faculty member in counseling psychology agreed to discontinue the program. In contrast, the decision-making processes were different at Oregon State and Rochester. At these institutions, although faculty were "involved" they tended not to be sitting around the table making decisions with administrators. The surprising factor about the variations in the degree to which the processes were shared was that at none of the institutions did faculty complain that they had not been involved enough or in legitimate roles, nor did administrators complain that faculty were involved too much or in the wrong ways. Even though the processes varied, all met a satisfying threshold of collaboration, which tended to be determined as much by the history, norms, and expectations of the campus than by any other factor (such as national standards proposed by the AAUP or AGB).

Although the amount and types of involvement of the various groups depended on the process used, all of these institutions had an "adequate" amount of sharing in the decision-making process. For example, at Maryland–College Park, faculty and administrators made most decisions jointly through the Academic Planning Advisory Committee, or the faculty made decisions independently through the Programs, Curricular, and Courses Committee or the senate. At Oregon State decisions were made sequentially—administrators passed their recommendations to the Faculty Consultive Group, which returned its modifications to administrators for the final decision. It is unlikely that either of these processes would be acceptable if attempted at any of the other institutions, but here they were acceptable because they were expected.

The Role of Governance

The processes used at the four institutions varied greatly. They occurred in different time-frames, with a different number of steps, in opportunities for appeal, and in the number and types of people involved. Nevertheless, they all included, at some level, a commingling of faculty and administrators working together. They all were *shared* processes.

Shared governance facilitated the discontinuance process in three ways. First, governance provided the stage from which administrators could gain a commitment and persuade the campus of the seriousness of the problems. Leaders evoked symbols such as the enhancement plan at Maryland–College Park, and at Rochester the dean and provost gave presentations on the dangers of endowment drain and high tuition discounts. At Oregon State, the president and provost, by simply requesting the formation of the Faculty Consultive Group, symbolically articulated the severity of the task created by Ballot Measure Five. Governance bodies—places where faculty and administrators come together to make decisions—became the platform where problems were articulated, the situation's seriousness conveyed, and direction set.

Second, shared governance brought the various interest groups together in legitimate ways to accomplish a high-stakes task. Shared governance became the place to create supportive coalitions. These processes played themselves out in established governance bodies (Academic Planning Advisory Committee and the Programs, Curricular, and Courses Committee at Maryland–College Park, the Faculty Consultive Group at Oregon State, the Council of Department Chairs at Rochester, and College Advisory Council and the Educational Policies Council at Kent State) that had campus legitimacy, rather than in newly created (and never tried) ad hoc structures. Attention to process is important because procedural violations can quickly become a rallying call for opposing interest groups. Academic leaders benefited from utilizing decision-making bodies and processes already viewed as legitimate rather than trying to develop ad hoc committees that would have had to overcome suspicion or that would needed to have spent their limited time and energy gaining acceptance. By building on established legitimacy, academic leaders avoided debates over representation, authority, decision-making turf, and inclusion. The history of the institution already has determined those answers. Outside a legitimate and time-tested arena, the efforts to close programs may have fallen under suspicion.

Third, shared governance provided a mechanism to correct potential errors. Administrators recognized that they did not have all the information required to make the best decisions for the university. Thus, they involved faculty, who have different perspectives and experiences, to help them understand the implications of closing certain programs. At Maryland–College Park, Oregon State, and Rochester programs were removed because of insights provided by faculty, and faculty at Kent State through its Educational Policies Council and the senate, approved the decision. Administrators asked faculty groups (summer subcommittees at Maryland–College Park, the Faculty Consultive Group at Oregon State, the Council of Department Chairs and individual faculty at Rochester, and the Educational Policies Council and senate at Kent State) to help them understand the effects of closures and prevent missteps. Because shared governance provided a mutual veto, poor decisions were avoided.

Implications

The findings refute two commonly held myths of shared governance: first, that faculty won't participate constructively in institutional decision making, particularly in decisions that may have a negative effect on colleagues; and second, that faculty are responsible for the effectiveness of shared governance. The findings also point to legitimacy in the process as a centerpiece of shared governance. Finally, they suggest modifications to AAUP program-termination procedures.

Shared Governance and Hard Choices

Discontinuing academic programs—making hard choices—is possible in an environment of shared decision making. The processes described here suggest that, under some conditions, faculty are willing and able to participate in making potentially adverse decisions, and that their involvement adds value.

Critics suggest that shared governance weakens presidential leadership and makes it difficult, if not impossible, for institutions to be responsive and adaptive (e.g., Association of Governing Boards, 1996). Other higher education commentators call for rethinking governance structures and processes, claiming that they are outdated models, ill suited for today's world. The findings of this study do not support these views. When hard decisions needed to be made, faculty and administrators (and, in one case, the board) worked together to get the job done. This study challenges frequently articulated beliefs that faculty cannot and will not make hard decisions, are more concerned with preserving the status quo than with making institutionally beneficial decisions, and work to prolong rather than expedite campus decision-making. It additionally refutes the belief that more authority for administrators will lead to better institutional decision making. Precisely because of their different understanding of the institution, faculty made important contributions that administrators were unable to provide. For example, faculty at Maryland–College Park investigated the implications and collected information to inform the process through APAC subcommittees and PCC open hearings. Shared governance does not have to be a bottleneck; it can add value to campus decision making.

At the same time, this study does not suggest that governance always works well and cannot be improved or that the structures on most campuses are always effective. Nor does it deny the possibility that administrators invoke shared governance to insulate themselves from criticism and accountability. By sharing decision making, the burden and responsibility become those of all involved. This study also does not suggest that all types of governance structures at all types of institutions (e.g., liberal arts colleges) work well.

Some faculty did resist program discontinuance, but those successful at overturning decisions (the mathematics faculty at Rochester) did so outside of formal governance structures. It was not the fiery protest on the faculty senate floor that led to the changes, but rather the coalition building with strong external groups that prevented the change.

Administrative Responsibility for Sharing Governance

The experiences of these four institutions challenge the notion of who is responsible for "good" shared governance. Faculty frequently are identified as the weak link in shared governance (Association of Governing Boards, 1996; Benjamin et al., 1993; Kennedy, 1994). They typically are criticized as protecting the status quo, as slowing (or halting) campus decision-making, and as being parochial and not concerned or well informed about institutional matters. Critics may unduly place the burden for governance's problems on faculty. The faculty at these four institutions understood the challenges facing the institution, recognized the importance of crafting a good process, and helped determine beneficial outcomes.

The faculty's recognition and acceptance of the challenge were the result, in large part, of effective administrators who translated environmental pressures, framed the challenge in meaningful ways, and designed a process that allowed faculty to contribute. Administrators at Maryland–College Park brought faculty into the immediate discussions through the Academic Planning Advisory Committee. Oregon State had a faculty-approved discontinuance procedure already in place that outlined meaningful faculty roles.

How administrators treat faculty shapes the ways in which faculty react within the governance arena. When administrators act in ways consistent with trusting faculty and appreciating their special knowledge and perspectives, these cases suggest that faculty will play active and complementary roles in governance. Administrators must acknowledge their own roles as participants in the shared governance process.

The experiences of these four campuses suggest that the responsibility for creating good shared governance is itself shared between faculty and administrators. Faculty are responsible for making institutional issues a priority, for coming to the table prepared and informed, and for acknowledging the time frame within which decisions must be reached. Administrators are responsible for creating the climate in which good governance can operate. Where administrators do not frame the challenges in ways meaningful to faculty, are unable to validate the importance of the tasks at hand, do not draw upon legitimate avenues of faculty involvement, and do not tap faculty strengths such as exploring implications and acting as systems of checks and balances, shared governance cannot be expected to work well.

Additionally, formal structures are only part of the acceptable and effective shared governance processes. Important faculty-administrative decision making occurred outside formal governance structures, such as at Maryland–College Park through the summer subcommittees, at Rochester through the individual interviews, or informal "kitchen cabinet" structures at Maryland–College Park and Rochester. Administrators may go outside the system but only if they are careful to do so in legitimate ways, leaving the formal structures to play regulatory roles. Nevertheless, at some point the decisions made outside formal governance must be intentionally brought inside the system, such as into the Programs, Curricular, and Courses Committee and senate at Maryland–College Park and the College Advisory Council and Educational Policies Council at Kent State.

Legitimacy as the Coin of the Governance Realm

One governance system does not fit all. Each of the four institutions followed different processes and involved faculty and administrators (and trustees) through different structures, at different times, and for different purposes. What aspects of these different processes were essential for shared governance to allow and enhance difficult decision making?

These four cases demonstrate that leaders must create decision-making processes that meet institutionally defined expectations for legitimacy. As the provost from Columbia asks in the quotation at the beginning of this article, Who has the authority to make decisions and what are the processes by which they are legitimated? Legitimacy is important to program discontinuance because leaders who develop processes that are perceived as illegitimate must face the prospect that opposing interest groups may try to derail their process. Illegitimacy creates opportunities for "work avoidance" (Heifetz, 1994), which are distractions that "divert attention from the issues on the table and diminish a sense of shared responsibility" (p. 38). By creating legitimate processes that are procedurally defensible, leaders focus attention on making hard decisions.

Legitimacy is grounded in campus expectations, histories, and norms. For example, faculty at the four institutions were all "involved," but the type and extent of involvement varied, from consultation at Rochester to making the final decisions at Maryland–College Park, and from periodic at Oregon State to constant at Maryland–College Park. "Good governance depends on acceptance, and to be acceptable, it must conform to the expectations of the participants" (Birnbaum, 1992, p. 179). Solutions to questions, such as who should be involved and in what ways, are not transferable. What is important to shared governance is not the specific elements of each process but the fact that each is defensible in terms of the expectations of various groups.

Recommendations for AAUP Guidelines

The AAUP (1995) proposes four guidelines for discontinuing academic programs. Three of the four recommendations are consistent with this study's findings: (a) faculty should be involved early on and in meaningful ways; (b) faculty should provide "considerable advice" on the long- and short-term effects of the closures; and (c) tenure should be protected.[4] (The fourth is discussed below.) Without these three elements the processes at the four institutions might not have been successes. Faculty easily could have formed opposing coalitions around key procedural points, halting the process if they were not involved in meaningful ways early on in the process, if they (or their representatives through governance) did not have opportunities to explore the implications and provide advice, or if tenured faculty had been terminated. Additionally, because faculty gave "considerable advice," administrators at Oregon State, Rochester, and Maryland–College Park revised some of their original recommendations. The outcomes may have been damaging had faculty not articulated potential negative unintended consequences.

The fourth AAUP recommendation not followed was that faculty should have "primary responsibility" for determining where closures occur. At none of the four institutions did faculty have the primary responsibility. Administrators made most of the decisions. Only at Maryland–College Park were faculty partners in crafting the recommendations, and only there did faculty make the final recommendations (through the senate). Nonetheless, at Rochester, Oregon State, and Kent State, faculty played meaningful roles, providing information and counsel, and helping to explore the potential implications of closures.

These findings suggest recommendations that the AAUP might make to its policy. First, the AAUP might recommend that program closures occur in conjunction with other steps to save money (something that happened at all four institutions) because, either alone or as first steps, they may be less likely to succeed. It might specify using faculty governance groups to explore the potential implications of proposed closures, which might be done through open deliberations (as at Maryland–College Park) or in confidence (as at Oregon State or Rochester). The AAUP might also include language acknowledging that the processes used to close programs most likely will differ across institutions because of variations in institutional cultures and norms in decision making. A process that might be acceptable to faculty at one campus where they play consultative roles (Oregon State) might not be acceptable at another where faculty are equal partners in decision making (Maryland–College Park). The AAUP should recognize the important role administrators play and the direction they provide in program discontinuance. In none of these four cases did faculty carry the process alone. Finally, the AAUP might note that retaining tenured faculty is important to keeping the institution focused and the process on track. At the same time, keeping tenured faculty may create a trade-off in terms of generating significant savings.

Beyond specific discontinuance guidelines, the findings suggest that AAUP should reconsider its stance on the broader topic of shared governance. The concept of shared governance in practice is fairly broad: It includes faculty-administrator collaboration that occurs both inside and outside the formal governance structure; it varies by institution as one size clearly does not fit all; it may include decisions where parties act sequentially (e.g., at Oregon State, administrators passed decisions to the Faculty Consultive Group, who in turn passed its decisions back to administrators) and jointly (e.g., at Maryland–College Park, where both faculty and administrators sit on the Academic Planning Advisory Committee); and it is based on institutionally defined norms, not on a schema adopted from the outside. Last, and possibly most important, shared governance that is successful (a structure and process that allows many constituencies to make mutually acceptable decisions) depends on expectations that the various parties find agreeable.

Notes

1. Campus leaders at all four institutions declined offers of institutional anonymity.
2. The college was the largest of six colleges at the University of Rochester and the only one facing program closures. It was created in a 1994 merger between the College of Arts and Sciences and the School

of Engineering and Applied Sciences and is responsible for the bulk of undergraduate education and much of the nonprofessional graduate education. It holds a separate endowment.

3. Programs were not officially terminated, but rather suspended, a technical term in New York that does not require state permission and which leaves open the door for reinstatement.

4. See Eckel (1998) for further discussion of tenure and academic program discontinuance.

References

American Association of University Professors. (1995). *Policy documents and reports* (8th ed.). Washington DC: American Association of University Professors.

Association of Governing Boards of Universities and Colleges. (1996). *Renewing the academic presidency: Stronger leadership for tougher times.* Washington DC: Association of Governing Boards.

Baldridge, V. J. (1971). *Power and conflict in the university.* New York: Wiley, 1971.

Benjamin, R., Carroll, S., Jacobi, M., Krop, C., & Shires, M. (1993). *The redesign of governance in higher education.* Santa Monica, CA: RAND.

Bess, J. L. (1988). *Collegiality and bureaucracy in the modern university: The influence of information and power on decision-making structures.* New York: Teachers College Press.

Birnbaum, R. (1992). *How academic leadership works: Understanding success and failure in the college presidency.* San Francisco: Jossey-Bass.

Birnbaum, R. (1988). *How colleges work: The cybernetics of academic organization and leadership.* San Francisco: Jossey-Bass.

Bolman, L. G., & Deal, T. E. (1992). *Reframing organizations: Artistry, choice, and leadership.* San Francisco: Jossey-Bass.

Breneman, D. W. (1993). *Higher education: On a collision course with new realities.* AGB Occasional Paper No. 22. Washington DC: Association of Governing Boards.

Cameron, K. S. (1983). Strategic responses to conditions of decline: Higher education and the private sector. *Journal of Higher Education, 54*(4), 359–380.

Cole, J. R. (1994). Balancing acts: Dilemmas of choice facing research universities. In J. R. Cole, E. G. Barber, & S. R. Graubard (Eds.), *The research university in a time of discontent* (pp. 1–36). Baltimore, MD: Johns Hopkins University Press.

Curry, B. K. (1992). *Instituting enduring innovations: Achieving continuity of change in higher education.* ASHE-ERIC Higher Education Report No. 7. Washington DC: George Washington University, School of Education and Human Development.

Dill, D. D., & Helm, K. P. (1988). Faculty participation in strategic policy making. In J. Smart (Ed.), *Higher Education: Handbook of Theory and Research* (Vol. 4, pp. 319–354). New York: Agathon Press.

Dill, D. D., & Sporn, B. (1995). Implications of a postindustrial environment for the university: An introduction. In D. D. Dill & B. Sporn (Eds.), *Emerging patterns of social demand and university reform: Through a glass darkly* (pp. 119). Tarrytown, NY: IAU Press.

Dougherty, E. A. (1979, April). *What is the most effective way to handle program discontinuance? Case studies from 10 campuses.* Paper presented at the National Conference of the American Association of Higher Education. Washington, DC.

Eckel, P. D. (1988). *How institutions discontinue academic programs: Making potentially adverse decisions in an environment of shared decision making.* Unpublished dissertation. University of Maryland, College Park.

El-Khawas, E. (1994). *Restructuring initiatives in public higher education: Institutional response to financial constraints.* Research Briefs, Report No. 5, Vol. 8. Washington DC: American Council on Education.

Gumport, P. J. (1993). The contested terrain of academic program reduction. *Journal of Higher Education, 64*(3), 283–311.

Gumport, P. J., & Prusser, B. (1997). Restructuring the academic environment. In M. W. Peterson, D. D. Dill, & L. A. Mets (Eds.), *Planning and management for a changing environment: A handbook on redesigning postsecondary institutions* (pp. 452–478). San Francisco: Jossey-Bass.

Hardy, C. (1990). Strategy and context: Retrenchment in Canadian universities. *Organization Studies, 11*(2), 207–237.

Hardy, C. (1993). The cultural politics of retrenchment. *Planning for Higher Education, 21*(4), 16–20.

Heifetz, R. A. (1995). *Leadership without easy answers.* Cambridge, MA: Harvard University Press.

Herriott, R. E., & Firestone, W. A. (1983). Multi-site qualitative policy research: Optimizing description and generalizability. *Educational Researcher, 12,* 14–19.

IMHE/OECD. (1999, March). *Governance in higher education.* Discussion Paper. Paris: IMHE.

Kennedy, D. (1994). Making choices in the research university. In J. R. Cole, E. G. Barber, & S. R. Graubard (Eds.), *The research university in a time of discontent* (pp. 85–114). Baltimore, MD: Johns Hopkins University Press.

Levine, A. (1980). *Why innovation fails.* Albany, NY: SUNY.

Levine, A. (1997, January 31). Higher education's net status as a mature industry. *Chronicle of Higher Education,* A48.

Levine, C. H., Rubin, I. S., & Wolohojian, G. G. (1981). *The politics of retrenchment.* Beverly Hills, CA: Sage.

Melchiori, G. S. (1982). *Planning for program discontinuance: From default to design.* AAHE-ERIC Higher Education Report No. 5. Washington DC: AAHE.

Merriam S. B. (1988). *Case study research in education: A qualitative approach.* San Francisco: Jossey-Bass.

Miles, M. B., & Huberman, A. M. (1994). *Qualitative data analysis* (2nd ed.). Thousand Oaks, CA: Sage.

Pfeffer, J. (1981). *Power in organizations.* Marshfield, MA: Pitman.

Pfeffer, J., & Salancik, G. R. (1980). Organizational decision making as a political process: The case of a university budget. In D. Katz, R. L. Kahn, & J. S. Adams (Eds.), *The study of organizations* (pp. 397–413). San Francisco: Jossey-Bass.

Rosovsky, H. (1990). *The university: An owner's manual.* New York: W. W. Norton.

Schuster, J. H., Smith, D. G., Corak, K. A., & Yamada, M. M. (1994). *Strategic governance: How to make big decisions better.* Washington DC: American Council on Education/Oryx Press.

Slaughter, S. (1993). Retrenchment in the 1980s: The politics of prestige and gender. *Journal of Higher Education, 64,* 250–282.

Walker, D. E. (1979). *The effective administrator.* San Francisco: Jossey-Bass.

Yezer, A. M. (1992). Do procedures that succeed in a growing institution fail in a period of decline? *Journal of Higher Education Management, 7*(2), 15–21.

Yin, R. K. (1994). *Case study research: Design and methods.* Thousand Oaks, CA: Sage.

ACADEMIC RESTRUCTURING: ORGANIZATIONAL CHANGE AND INSTITUTIONAL IMPERATIVES

PATRICIA J. GUMPORT
STANFORD UNIVERSITY

Abstract. A perennial challenge for universities and colleges is to keep pace with knowledge change by reconsidering their structural and resource commitments to various knowledge areas. Reflecting upon changes in the academic landscape of public higher education in the United States over the past quarter of a century, the author diagnoses a macro-trend whereby the dominant legitimating idea of public higher education has changed from higher education as a social institution to higher education as an industry. Three interrelated mechanisms are identified as having advanced this process: academic management, academic consumerism, and academic stratification.

This pattern of academic restructuring reflects multiple institutional pressures. While public universities and colleges have increasingly come to rely on market discourse and managerial approaches in order to demonstrate responsiveness to economic exigencies, they may end up losing legitimacy as they move away from their historical character, functions, and accumulated heritage as educational institutions. Thus, responsiveness to compelling economic pressures that dominate contemporary organizational imperatives in an attempt to gain legitimacy in one dimension may result in loss for another. Wholesale adaptation to market pressures and managerial rationales could thereby subsume the discourse about the future of colleges and universities within a logic of economic rationality at a detriment to the longer-term educational legacies and democratic interests that have long characterized American public education.

Introduction

A perennial challenge for higher education institutions is to keep pace with knowledge change. In addition to investing in new faculty positions and launching targeted fund-raising activities, a prominent set of responses at the local campus level is to alter the academic structure by adding, or conversely by deleting, courses, degree programs, and departments. While the prevailing image of knowledge change in higher education has tended to be either inertia or expansion, those who have made their professional lives within higher education settings during the recent past also know otherwise—that is, they understand the threat, if not the reality, of selective consolidation and program elimination, particularly for those academic areas that are deemed of insufficient centrality, quality, or cost-effectiveness (Gumport 1993).

No doubt these are difficult times for those who manage higher education institutions. In addition to a difficult political climate with diminished public confidence, financial realities loom large alongside pressure to consider alternative structural and resource commitments to various knowledge areas. For the most part, administrators and faculty do not have the option of widespread additive solutions that their predecessors enjoyed. Deliberations over academic restructuring and resource reallocation seem endless—often bogged down by process without adequate attention to the substance and likely consequences of proposed changes. Unprecedented public scrutiny of the academic enterprise exacerbates tensions on campus between proponents of different academic areas, between those responsible for planning as opposed to those responsible for safeguarding faculty governance, and between those who advocate compliance with external demands for demonstrated accountability versus those who argue for resistance.

The intermingling of academic considerations with wider economic and political concerns suggests that deliberations over whether or not and how to reorganize academic units are likely to be ongoing. At the same time though, little is known about the consequences of structural and material resource shifts across academic areas, for either the students or the broader society. Moreover, we do not know whether there will remain any shared sense of institutional purpose and a basis for interdependence on campuses, and whether core academic activities of knowledge creation, preservation, and transmission will remain viable either as a complementary set or as separate functions.

Against this backdrop of concerns, the primary objective for this article is to sketch out a thesis about a set of neglected yet critical issues for public higher education organizations as they consider their commitments to various knowledge areas and possibly reshape their landscape of academic offerings.[1] In order to draw some parameters and to make manageable ensuing empirical research, the thesis focuses on a macro trend that depicts changes in the last quarter of the twentieth century in public colleges and universities in the United States.

This thesis has three parts, each putting forward important conceptual distinctions.

1. Over the past 25 years, academic knowledge in U.S. public colleges and universities has been reorganized along a utilitarian trajectory such that, at the macro level, the dominant legitimating idea of public higher education has changed from higher education as a social institution to higher education as an industry.

2. Three interrelated mechanisms have converged to advance this process: a) the rise of academic management in colleges and universities, drawing upon discourse from management science and organizational research for its professional ideology and position descriptions; b) the rise of academic consumerism, moving beyond the post–World War II decades of massification and its attendant democratic gains to elevating as paramount economic-consumer interests; and c) the re-stratification of academic subjects and academic personnel, based upon the increased use-value and exchange-value of particular knowledges in the wider society.

3. One consequence of these converging forces is that the management of public higher education institutions faces formidable legitimacy challenges, where reconciling competing institutional logics is difficult. The inherent tensions are evident in academic restructuring dynamics on a range of campuses.

Before presenting the thesis, identifying my assumptions at the outset may be helpful. When considering the nature and direction of change in higher education, there seems to be consensus that the locus of academic reform, if not control, extends to a range of factors beyond local campus settings. Not only have economic and political demands proliferated, but satisfying them all is ultimately elusive—due either to the prohibitive cost or to the irreconcilability of conflicting mandates. For higher education in the United States, particularly public colleges and universities, there are formidable expectations to improve access, enhance quality, and cut costs, even as campuses are expected to embrace new information and communications technologies that are in themselves costly and unproven. Moreover, the contemporary accountability climate has in effect squeezed public higher education into a vise, even as various legislative and state actors have taken it upon themselves to dissect the enterprise, inspecting slices of academic life/work/teaching/learning under a microscope. The assessment paradigm has an apparently unlimited reach, imposing an organizational and individual performance metric on every aspect of higher education with profound consequences for the academic workplace (Gumport 1997). This trend is also evident in Europe (Neave and Van Vught 1991; Dill and Sporn 1995).

In an effort to demonstrate responsiveness, the organizational willingness to embrace efficiency and flexibility as priorities is both impressive and, unfortunately very troubling. It is "impressive" because such adaptive responses just may help public higher education survive an era of unprecedented competition and public scrutiny, and "troubling" because of the potential damage to public higher education as an intellectual enterprise, the further erosion of knowledge as an end in itself and the narrowing of academic offerings for different segments of student populations.

Within the study of higher education as well as the management of colleges and universities, I am concerned that the ways in which we talk and think about higher education have increasingly relied upon a production metaphor, borrowing imperatives from corporate settings. I am concerned that technical, market imperatives run wild, urging colleges and universities to adapt to short-term market demands, to re-deploy resources (which include people, e.g., faculty), in an effort to reposition themselves within an increasingly competitive context. I am concerned that a premium has been placed upon adaptation without careful scrutiny of the gradual institutional change underway in the character of public higher education. I am concerned that the educational and societal consequences emerging from changed academic commitments will be far-reaching, as very different academic programs become available to different segments of student populations, further stratifying the inequality of life chances across socioeconomic groups. Furthermore, and somewhat selfishly I suppose, I fear that the things I care most about will be deemed inefficient, inflexible, and thus no longer affordable. I disclose these concerns to make explicit the normative underpinnings of the thesis as well as to foreshadow my criticism of attempts to reduce higher education institutions to organizations *per se*, my concern over adapting public higher education to short-term economic exigencies at a detriment to longer-term educational legacies and democratic interests, and my hope for further deliberation about the legacy of higher education as a social institution within which knowledge has to some extent been considered a public good.

The Legitimating Idea of Public Higher Education

The macro trend is in essence an historical proposition that the dominant legitimating idea of public higher education has been moving away from the idea of higher education as a social institution, and moving toward the idea of higher education as an industry.

A legitimating idea at the macro societal level suggests that there are taken-for-granted understandings that constitute parameters for what is legitimate—that is, what is expected, appropriate, and sacred, as well as the converse. In the realm of higher education, both of the aforementioned legitimating ideas have distinct premises regarding what is valued, what is problematic, and what is in need of improvement in public higher education. Simply stated, from the perspective of higher education as an industry, public colleges and universities are seen increasingly as a sector of the economy; as with firms or businesses, the root metaphor is a corporate model of production—to produce and sell goods and services, train some of the workforce, advance economic development, and perform research. Harsh economic challenges and competitive market pressures warrant better management, which includes swift programmatic adjustment, maximum flexibility, and improved efficiency in the direction of greater accountability and thus customer satisfaction. In contrast, from the perspective of higher education as a social institution, public colleges and universities by definition must preserve a broader range of social functions that include such essential educational legacies as the cultivation of citizenship, the preservation of cultural heritage(s), and the formation of individual character and habits of mind.

The tension between the two legitimating ideas is profound. The former perspective is dominated by a concern that higher education's inability or unwillingness to adapt will result in a loss of centrality and perhaps ultimately a loss of viability. Evidence is found in widely-cited proclamations that higher education has already lost the ability to judge itself in the United States (Pew 1993a, b, c, 1994; Zemsky and Massy 1990; Gumport and Pusser 1999) and in Europe (Neave and Van Vught 1991). In contrast, the latter perspective is dominated by a concern that adaptation to market forces gives primacy to short-term economic demands at the neglect of a wider range of societal responsibilities, thereby jeopardizing the long-term public interest including the notion of knowledge as a public good. Further explication of the contrast may be instructive, in order to show that public colleges and universities may change how they try to link up with wider institutional logics.

Higher Education as an Industry

The perception of higher education as an industry primarily views public colleges and universities as quasi-corporate entities producing a wide range of goods and services in a competitive marketplace. A research university may be thought of as offering a very diverse product line, especially in the post–World War II era of Kerr's (1995, orig. 1963) "multiversity." Alternatively, an entire state's public system of higher education may be seen as offering an even more diverse range of goods and services: community colleges offer degrees or one course at a time, in many fields, to people of all ages, while the flagship university offers many courses and levels of degrees across hundreds of fields of study, professes to serve national, state, local economic needs, and sells entertainment in sporting and cultural events to the local community.

Ideally, according to microeconomic theory, organizations are managed based upon values of economic rationality. The main services of teaching and research are variously supplied and priced to correspond to laws of supply and demand. Students, parents, state legislatures, employers, and research funders are seen as customers. Particular customers have different tastes and preferences. Other people, such as faculty employed by the organization, are presumed to participate out of calculative involvement. As such, they can be motivated to be more productive through the use of incentives and sanctions. Major obstacles to maintaining the organization's viability include: fixed costs and inefficiencies; competition and oversupply; uncertainty and imperfect information. Guiding principles for the organization's managers are to know its liabilities and assets, to anticipate costs and benefits, to enhance efficiency and flexibility, and—as realized in the contemporary quality movement—to increase customer satisfaction (e.g., Seymour 1992).

The insights of this perspective focus on the harsh realities of market forces and the urgency of doing something to stay competitive, be it planning strategically, scanning environments, attempting to contain or cut costs, correct inefficiencies, or doing whatever it takes to maximize flexibility. Adjustments include changing product lines, substituting technology for labor, and reducing fixed costs through such means as outsourcing and privatizing as well as increasing the proportion of part-time and temporary personnel. Doing nothing is not an option. Such imperatives have been popularized in the reengineering movement in the 1990s, catapulted by variations on Hammer and Champy (1993).

Within this conceptualization, it is valuable to view higher education as having not just one major marketplace, as determined by type of student served, or geographic location, or degrees granted. Instead, we can see several types of markets at work simultaneously—not only for obtaining students, but for placing graduates, hiring and retaining faculty, obtaining research funding, establishing collaboration with industry, maintaining endowments, sustaining and extending alumni giving and other fundraising sources, and so on.

A contemporary feature of higher education markets is the increased presence of non-traditional providers in several markets, the most prominent being the emergence of virtual higher education aided by new telecommunications technologies and altering the competitive playing field by attracting students (Marchese 1998). The major barometer for managers is to read the market for constraints and opportunities relevant to the viability of their niche; if done well, a higher education organization can capitalize on untapped demand, allowing it to supply the educational product at a higher price. The decision to add an academic program could be seen as a strategy to position the college or university to attract new customers and thereby increase revenue. Similarly, an increase in tuition can be explained as appropriate due to increased demand or decreased supply of a particular educational product (for example, a professional degree in engineering, business, or law). Hence, programmatic changes can be seen as prudent market corrections.

All of this should sound quite familiar to observers of contemporary higher education management. The corporate metaphors of production in a competitive marketplace are omnipresent. Knowing one's resources, comparative advantage, and strategy has become standard in the U.S. and increasingly in Europe (Keller 1983; Chaffee 1985; Hearn 1988; Hardy 1990; Cameron and Tschirhart 1992; Massy 1996; Peterson et al. 1997; Clark 1998). Of course, one might argue that these principles are rendered irrelevant for public higher education, given that the market is heavily regulated by state and federal government through several types of public subsidies, restrictions in pricing, regulated degree offerings and admissions standards. Yet the industry perspective and its dominant corporate metaphor have nonetheless acquired a certain resilience, due in part to their parsimony, to today's uncritical acceptance of business and economic rhetoric, and to the very real complexity of today's campus operations. (For example, see Duderstadt's (1995) characterization of "the University of Michigan, Inc.," which with an annual budget of over $2.5 billion would rank roughly 200th on the list of Fortune 500 companies.) In many ways, adopting business rationales with strategic management principles has become *de rigueur* for repositioning higher education organizations to compete within new economic realities.

There are several consequences, of course, to this conception of higher education coming to dominate as the legitimating idea that is used to make sense of, and ultimately to redefine the parameters of, public higher education. It is worth noting that leaders of public colleges and universities today are expected to demonstrate some willingness, if not enthusiasm, to consider market forces and demands for relevance, or else risk losing some legitimacy. However, in this conception, there is no attention to what is at stake in shortsighted adaptation to market forces; nor is there a provision for public good that may exceed the market's reach.

Higher Education as a Social Institution

I turn now to the legitimating idea of higher education as a social institution, which I argue has been gradually displaced. A social institution may be seen as an organized activity that maintains, reproduces, or adapts itself to implement values that have been widely held and firmly structured by the society. According to Turner (1997), human history is characterized by the evolution of social institutions, relatively stable and conservative in norms, structures, and general standards of good/bad, appropriate/inappropriate, worthy/unworthy, and other evaluative criteria for behavior. Over time, as institutions change, they do so in relation to one another. Turner is among those who argue that social institutions have been in a process of ongoing differentiation with far-reaching consequences due to their interdependence with one another.

Thus, when one uses the lens of "social institution" to examine the institutional imperatives for public higher educations, one sees educational organizations devoted to a wide array of social functions that have been expanded over time: the development of individual learning and human capital, the socialization and cultivation of citizens and political loyalties, the preservation of knowledge, and the fostering of other legitimate pursuits for the nation-state. It is commonly acknowledged that the decades following World War II entailed not only an expansion of higher education, but also a dramatic diversification of the activities regarded as the legitimate province of public higher education. These include educating the masses, advancing knowledge through research, contributing to economic development by employing and producing workers, and developing industrial applications. In this sense, shifts in societal imperatives reshaped expectations for higher education and redefined what activities are or are not recognized as "higher education." Of course, such expectations and definitions continue to be reconstituted over time, at times signalling a major shift akin to the remaking of a social contract.

An additional dimension of the historical proposition warrants our consideration. As a social institution, public higher education exists in an enduring interdependence with other social institutions—not only with other levels of education, but also with the family, government, industry, religion, and popular culture. Social institutions evolve in their interchanges with one another. As Turner argues, over time, societal expectations for education in part stem from broadened expectations that it take on human capital functions, political legitimation functions, and socialization functions (1997, pp. 258–259): "Today, political leaders in industrial societies often view education as the key to economic development and political stability, since it performs such critical functions for political legitimation and for developing human capital. As education has differentiated and elaborated, many of the socialization and social-placement functions from kinship have been assumed by schools; and it has come to have increasingly far-reaching consequences for the economy (as a source of human capital and technology) and polity (as a source of political legitimation)." The relevance of this proposition for higher education, particularly for contemporary public higher education, warrants further exploration. It is entirely possible that, with the decline of public trust in social (and particularly public) institutions, there is a corresponding redefinition of expectations for public higher education as a social institution; as a result, the expected Parsonian pattern-maintenance and socialization functions may be receding, while economic functions may come to dominate the foreground.

From this perspective, it is essential to acknowledge that the terms "institution" and "organization" do not have the same meaning, even though they are often used interchangeably. While colleges and universities are frequently referred to as organizations, the use of the term "institution" is more common, often intended as a synonym, refering to organization-wide constructs such as institutional leadership, decisions, or policies. Bellah et al. (1991, p. 11) have observed that this tendency has profound consequences in that it reflects reductionist thinking, where focusing on the organization reduces complexity to the point of oversimplifying what is problematic and at the neglect of historical patterns of rights and responsibilities that shape our lives. (Another possibility is that speakers are basically unaware of the sociological distinction and its import.)

In short, the language used to talk about higher education is important, for it not only reflects our thinking but it contributes to a construction of reality. While this observation has been noted by philosophers, linguists, and sociologists alike, Bellah et al. (1991, p. 15) state it powerfully: "Institutions are very much dependent upon language: what we cannot imagine and express in language has little chance of becoming a sociological reality." This observation carries with it even more weight when one considers the moral import. As Bellah et al. (1991, p. 11) explain, in our thinking we often neglect "the power of institutions as well as their great possibilities for good and evil;" the process of creating and recreating institutions "is never neutral, but always ethical and political." For example, speaking of alternatives in a language of tradeoffs (such as tradeoffs between health care, prisons, higher education or other public goods) ". . . is inadequate for it suggests that the problems are merely technical, when we need a richer moral discourse with which to conduct public discussion . . ." (p. 26). Heeding Bellah et al.'s admonishment, conceptualizing higher education as subject to a logic of "social institution" invokes normative considerations. Thus, in addition to the ways that contemporary public universities and colleges are being reshaped by their environments, the very discourse about those changes and challenges itself plays a significant role in such reshaping.

It is critical to identify a distinction regarding what may have changed: Is it that the social functions of higher education may have changed, or is it that our talk and ideals about higher education have changed? That is, has public higher education taken on principally economic functions, abandoning the more comprehensive institutional mandate of performing not only educational but also socialization and political functions? Or has it become commonplace to speak of higher education in industry terms, in common parlance expecting of public colleges and universities a set of objectives that are economic (e.g., human capital, workforce training, and economic development)? Or is it both? The distinction between the two is critical as we consider the recent past and future prospects. While changes in the social functions may signal a *de facto* shifting of the charter for public colleges and universities, the industry discourse that has come to dominate contemporary organizations reduces the scope and legitimacy of a wider range of organizations and individual academic commitments within public higher education. For example, the logic of managerial production renders irrelevant or unvalued the notion of higher education as a place for dissent and unpopular ideas, for creativity and the life of the mind, for caring and relationships, except as inefficiencies that will likely be deemed wasteful or unaffordable.

Converging Mechanisms

Three interrelated mechanisms are proposed as advancing this process whereby the legitimating idea of public higher education that has come to dominate is that of an industry (rather than that of a social institution). They are: 1) academic management, 2) academic consumerism, and 3) academic stratification.

Academic Management

The expansion in size, authority, and professionalization, of academic managers in public colleges and universities has drawn upon discourse from management science and organizational research for its ideology and position descriptions. The core premises of these literatures position campus leaders and key administrators as managers who diagnose and prescribe organizational well-being. The rationale is simple: Organizations can and do adapt, and organizational survival is dependent upon the ability of the organization to respond to its environment, which is characterized as dynamic and thus uncertain and potentially threatening. Thus, among other responsibilities, managers are expected to monitor the organization-environment interface, determine appropriate strategies, and develop effective bridging and buffering mechanisms.

When applied to the academic enterprise, campus leaders attend to both resources as well as resource relationships. The management of resources—their acquisition, maintenance and internal allocation—and the management of resource relationships between the organization and its environment—in itself becomes a major organizational practice to position their organizations for survival. (See Gumport and Sporn (1999) for discussion of this adaptation dynamic.) Prominent examples include: monitoring vulnerabilities that arise from resource dependence, trying to reduce existing dependencies, and meeting expectations for compliance. In the arena of public higher education, all three of these concepts have gained currency and are reflected in campus discourse and academic management rationales.

First, with regard to monitoring vulnerabilities that come from environmental turbulence, campus managers give ongoing attention to forecasting enrollment changes, shifts in state appropriations, and how such changes are handled by their peer institutions. It is essential to note that attention must be paid to multiple environments (e.g., local, state, regional, national), especially when considering those resources on which the organization has had the greatest dependence.

Second, and extremely visible in the contemporary era, is the cultivation of new resources to reduce existing dependencies. For public universities and colleges, this primarily takes the form of adopting strategies that will generate revenue for the organization—whether it be seeking to improve public relations with the state legislature, seeking out new student markets, finding new sources for research funding, stepping up efforts for alumni giving, or cultivating new sources of private revenue. The cultivation of a plurality of resources to reduce existing dependencies has long been seen as a prudent course for organizations, but has gained greater currency for public higher education in the contemporary era where dependence on funding from state appropriations has created financial challenges.

A third ongoing function of managers is to ensure compliance with demands. Various mechanisms are established to ensure and then demonstrate that an academic organization is in compliance with demands from a number of different sources, some of which are expensive for the organization. Health and safety regulations abound, for example, as both public and private universities well know. With the most recent wave of accountability extending from operations to educational functions, mandates for satisfactory compliance are often tied to state and national funding (e.g., national funds for student financial aid, state general fund appropriations for institutions, etc.)—funding that is essential to organizational survival. These initiatives range from asking public colleges and universities to demonstrate faculty productivity as well as student learning outcomes. One study documented that approximately half of the states in the U.S. have already instituted some type of performance-based funding, with twenty additional states anticipating it in the near future (Burke and Serban 1998).

The need to manage these challenges positions higher education administrators in the central mediating role of determining the potential costs and benefits of any course of action (or non-action). In so doing, administrators who occupy the most visible leadership roles in public universities and colleges function as interpreters for the rest of the organization. They address such key concerns as: Who are the constituencies from whom the organization is seeking legitimacy and what do they want? What are successful peer institutions doing to manage contradictory demands? Can some demands be responded to symbolically, superficially, or minimally, as in a "satisficing" mode? Attending to these concerns, administrators can symbolically present the organization as responsive to a variety of external stakeholders as well as to organizational members internally. While a dissonance-free organization is unlikely to result, such efforts by managers can have powerful results in terms of securing a sense of stability as the organization navigates through times of environmental uncertainty and turbulence.

The above discussion characterized higher education managers as positioned in an expanded role, with authority over a broad domain of organizational decision-making as well as representing the organization's purposes and priorities to the environment. This characterization contains a key premise that warrants careful scrutiny—that they are appropriately and effectively positioned to act for the organization. This premise is of course questionable. Who should speak for the organization? Under what conditions and to what extent is it appropriate to reposition the organization to meet the demands of its changing environments? While the need to manage resources and resource relationships and the need to reduce resource dependence provide a compelling post-hoc rationale for an expanded managerial domain, the role of faculty within academic governance should not be overlooked, particularly when restructuring the academic landscape of programs offered.

This critical concern falls under the general category of "the politics of professional work." It is compatible with related critical analyses of "managerialism" (Enteman 1993) and "the emergence of technocracy" (Heydebrand 1990), a term that is intended to replace the simple bureaucracy-professionalism dualism that has previously been used to characterize academic organizations. Building on the historical argument that research universities have become more entrepreneurial through increased academic capitalism, scholars have proposed that research universities have become more managerial in their governance and the division of labor (Rhoades and Slaughter 1997). In particular, as Rhoades (1998) has proposed, faculty have become "managed professionals," while middle-level administrators have become "managerial professionals." While changes in the power dynamics remain for empirical study, the trend toward increased formalization and evaluation of faculty work is clear. Management has assumed more organizational space and visibility in running the enterprise.

This notion has obvious relevance for the full range of U.S. public colleges and universities as well. A key rationale for this shift in authority to academic managers has been the need for flexibility to adapt swiftly and a concomitant need for discretion over resource reallocation and programmatic investment. However, the consequences for the organization are, of course, profound, as such centralized decisions determine where and how the organization will invest its academic resources and ultimately possible change in the very character of the enterprise. This includes such defining practices as selecting among academic priorities, eliminating or making the case to eliminate or downsize academic programs, and determining the academic workforce and its characteristics (e.g., full-time vs. part-time, course load, etc.). Critics of this expansion in managerial authority and its ensuing consequences have suggested that environmental conditions should not predetermine such academic restructuring. For example, in questioning the presumption that managerialism is a natural academic adaptation, Rhoades and Slaughter (1997, p. 33) argue: "The structural patterns we describe are not just inexorable external developments to which colleges and universities are subject and doomed. . . . The academy itself daily enacts and expresses social relations of capitalism and heightened managerial control grounded in a neo-conservative discourse." Thus, they make explicit a mechanism that has contributed to displacing organizational practices that advocated for preserving educational legacies where human development and citizenship were central imperatives alongside a full range of knowledge areas that were supported for reasons other than their anticipated human capital or market value.

Academic Consumerism

A second mechanism that has contributed to the legitimating idea of public higher education as an industry is the sovereignty of the consumer. The rise of academic consumerism can be seen as a phenomenon that has emerged after the post-World War II decades of massification and its attendant democratic gains. The conceptual shift elevates consumer interests as paramount considerations in the restructuring of academic programs and the reengineering of academic services.

The needs and interests of several types of consumers (e.g., taxpayers, employers, research funders, students) come to mind, when considering who public universities and colleges serve. However, it is most commonly the student-as-consumer of public higher education, and particularly the student as potential or current employee who seeks workforce training or economic security.

The rise of academic consumerism in the contemporary era has been accelerated by four essential presumptions, although each is problematic in its own way.

First, the student-consumer is presumed to be capable of informed choice, with the ability to pay (Readings 1996). To view prospective students as prospective buyers conjures up the image of the smartest shoppers among them perusing *Consumer Reports,* as one would when considering the purchase of an automobile or major household appliance. The premise is that the intelligent consumer will select that which has the best value for the money. While in itself the spirit of this premise is not unsound, in practice the U.S. higher education system has no such organizational performance data available; in fact, campuses themselves have been resistant to such attempts, even as they are vocal in their criticism of the widely-cited *US News and World Report* rankings.

A second and related presumption is that the enrolled student-consumer is assumed to have chosen to attend that particular college or university. This would be consistent with the economic theory of revealed preferences whereby behaviors are seen as matching desires. Thus, a student who has enrolled at a community college wanted to go there because it maximized his or her utility, rather than as a result of socialization, truncated aspirations, socioeconomic barriers, or a discriminatory culture.

Third, enrolled students-consumers are ". . . encouraged to think of themselves as consumers of services rather than as members of a community," as Readings (1996, p. 11) insightfully observed. Campus administrators and faculty may even be encouraged to think of students as consumers too. The basis for exchange is the delivery of an academic service (e.g., lecture, course, piece of advice). This conception of students drastically reduces the potential richness of teaching and learning relationships, inclinations toward mentoring and sponsorship, and students forging meaningful bonds with their peers. In effect, it would place an emphasis on the campus as a business of academic transactions rather than as a community of inquirers, teachers and learners.

Fourth, consumer taste and satisfaction can become elevated to new heights in the minds of those responsible for designing academic services and programs. The translation of this presumption into practice can be seen in the vocationalization of academic programs that seem to be altered as easily as changing the time that courses are offered or rushing to establish them on-line. It is also evident in the academic quality movement, which places a premium on customer satisfaction. While attention to student needs and preferences is not by any means inherently misguided, it is the *reduction* of students to consumers in this way and the supremacy of presumed consumer interests in academic restructuring that may cumulatively do the educational enterprise a disservice.

In this way, consumer taste rather than professional expertise may become the basis for legitimate change in public higher education. As such academic consumerism would increasingly dictate the character of the academic enterprise, as public colleges and universities cater to the desires of the individual (short-sighted though they may be), thereby further displacing faculty authority and perhaps ultimately the collective force of diverse educational legacies.

Academic Stratification

The third mechanism entails a re-stratification of academic subjects and academic personnel, based upon the increased use-value of particular knowledges in the wider society and exchange-value in certain markets. The increased use-value of knowledge is evident in both the culture of ideas and the commerce of ideas, defining features at the heart of postindustrial society (Bartley 1990; Drucker 1993; Gibbons et al. 1994; Slaughter and Leslie 1997). The culture of ideas acknowledges an accumulated heritage of knowledge accepted by society, sometimes seen as a storehouse or stock of knowledge with shared understandings and values. From this perspective, public colleges and universities may be seen as social organizations of knowledge that contribute to society in the Durkheimian sense of integration. Similarly, the commerce of ideas casts a spotlight on the creation and distribution of ideas in the knowledge industry as well as on the growing exchange-value of knowledges in specific markets. From this perspective, public colleges and universities—particularly research universities—may also be seen as competitors in the commercial activities of publications and copyrights, patents and licenses, positioning themselves and the nation for global competitiveness. Such knowledge activities have, on some campuses, come to be seen as essential—even increasingly, as core—pursuits of public colleges and universities. (And, in addition, this is quite compatible with the revenue-generating aspirations of academic managers, as discussed above.)

In order to grasp the full import of this idea, higher education needs to be understood primarily as a knowledge-processing system. This stands in contrast to the conventional view that characterizes higher education as a people-processing system in which goals, structures, and outcomes support students undergoing personality development, learning skills, and acquiring credentials that may enable upward mobility. In posing the alternative—that higher education has central knowledge functions—knowledge is then seen as the defining core of academic work and academic workers. As Clark (1983) insightfully explains, knowledge is "the prime material around which activity is organized . . . Knowledge materials, and advanced ones at that, are at the core of any higher education system's purposes and essence. This holds true throughout history and across societies as well" (1983, p. 13). Following Meyer (1977), Clark suggests that knowledge is processed so as to have a wide array of intellectual, professional, economic and social consequences: "As educational institutions in general evolve, they develop categories of knowledge and thereby determine that certain types of knowledge exist and are authoritative. They also define categories of persons privileged to possess the bodies of knowledge and to exercise the authority that comes from knowledge. Educational structures, in effect, are a theory of knowledge, in that they help define what currently counts as knowledge" (1983, p. 26). Clark (1996, pp. 429–430) has since developed the conception even further by prescribing that universities, as "knowledge-based institutions," should be more conscious of possibilities for risk-taking investment in new fields along with recombinations of old fields; with optimism regarding as-of-yet unrealized potential, he proposes that "certain ways of organizing knowledge offer the possibility of sustained insight, even to the point of a systematic claim on wisdom." Although gains in insight and wisdom have indisputable significance for society, neither one has yet made it onto the report card of organizational performance indicators. Nonetheless, we continue to see self-described strategic efforts to reorganize academic areas in public universities and colleges.

An instrumental orientation toward academic knowledge also seems widespread in the contemporary era. The notions of knowledge as a public good and academic knowledge as a free market of ideas seem increasingly unsustainable in a context where academic subjects and knowledge workers are not buffered from market forces. Given the realities of complex organizations, where resource acquisition and status considerations abound, these developments also have consequences for the stratified social order on campuses. In the contemporary era, academic knowledge areas require capital for fuel and the promise of future resources for sustained legitimacy. The resource requirements of knowledge areas and the likelihood of generating revenue have a salience that cannot be overstated, so much so, that today's knowledge creation and management may be interpreted as increasingly dominated by a proprietary ethic in the spirit of advanced capitalism. This characterization may be problematic for some, in that it uses predominately the managerial metaphor to talk about higher education in terms of entrepreneurial dynamics that can help a campus sustain its inventory and pursue its core competencies (Prahalad and Hamel 1990). However, in the present era, the resource requirements of creating, sustaining and extending knowledge activities figure prominently in campus deliberations over what academically is worthy of support.

Selection processes are at work to determine what knowledge is considered most valuable and hence worthy of support. As an illustration, consider the ways in which state governments conceptualize public higher education as services to procure. Particularly in the past fifteen years, we see evidence of a willingness to support (i.e. allocate financial resources to) public universities to procure teaching (and where applicable, research) services. This procurement orientation suggests an underlying production function approach, where higher education is valued for its instrumental contributions vis-à-vis the preparation and retraining of individuals for work and the application of useful knowledge to social and economic needs, rather than one in which all fields of study have inherent worth. In this sense, the context quite directly shapes what knowledge is considered to have value for instruction, research or service. Conversely, the context neglects—or perhaps actively dismantles—those areas not valued. In this way, the context alters the academic landscape and its knowledge areas, and public universities themselves come to internalize this conception (see, e.g., NASULGC 1997).[2]

Selection processes are also at work given external demands for managers to reshape the structure of the academic landscape. Evidence suggests that academic re-organization in times of resource constraint differs from the differentiation that accompanies expansion along with stratification of academic subjects and personnel (Blau 1970, 1973; Clark 1983, 1993; Gumport 1993; Metzger 1987; Rhoades and Slaughter 1997). Thus, what has come to count as knowledge has not simply unfolded or evolved out of existing areas, but has resulted in part from the differential valuing and resourcing of academic units competing for epistemological, organizational, and physical space. When additive solutions have not been possible, priorities are identified; particular units are constructed as failing to pull their weight, and are targeted for downsizing and elimination. For example, small humanities programs (such as foreign languages) have been losing resources and status.

In the contemporary era, the rhetoric of selective reinvestment has gained ascendancy, while comprehensive field coverage is increasingly considered not viable for every campus, something that not every university can afford or aspire to—due to budget and management considerations. The discourse of restructuring for selective reinvestment on campuses is a marked departure from comprehensive field coverage, and it directly parallels the discussions to maximize one's comparative advantage that dominates corporate approaches. In contrast, the histories of many of this country's public colleges and universities suggest that they were established with the ideal of openness to all knowledge, regardless of immediate applications and relevance. Thus, it used to be assumed that access to the full range of knowledge is desirable, and that higher education is the appropriate gateway to that reservoir. However, in the contemporary era, an era in which comprehensiveness is not a widespread option, academic reorganization is cast as a set of budget issues and a management problem, albeit with educational implications. Such restructuring limits the scope of academic knowledge that students are offered on any given campus, with the longer range potential of further stratifying who learns what. (An interesting irony of course is seen in the ascendancy of the Internet which promises access to everything.)

At the same time, new forms of collaboration have been proposed as a partial antidote to the narrowing of subject matter. In one historical case study of academic planning in a state university system (Gumport 1994), an official from the university's systemwide office explained the need to depart from the ideal of comprehensiveness in order to facilitate consolidation and urged the campuses to share resources with one another in an unprecedented cooperation:

> Despite the great need for economies in [our academic programs] and for directed applications of knowledge, the University and its publics should reaffirm the principle of the pursuit of knowledge irrespective of its immediate applications. Intrinsic to the idea of the university is that, in principle, no corner of knowledge should remain unexplored. It is equally clear, however, that this ideal, while remaining a principle for our University as a whole, is not viable as a principle for each campus. The idea of a general campus implies the capacity to cover those subjects necessary for a liberal arts education and to sustain subjects (such as mathematics and computer science) that are necessary to sustain different kinds of research. But it cannot imply that every campus develop every research and teaching program that the pursuit of knowledge and the impetus to excellence might suggest. Given that constraint, it is evident that each campus of the University should specialize in some ways, and that such specialization should be coordinated. Coordination would permit and encourage innovative and cutting-edge programs to develop, but would also control excess provision and unnecessary duplication in the interests of economy. Furthermore, access of students and faculty to highly specialized programs could be augmented by designing them on an intercampus or regional basis, by permitting students to move more freely through programs of campus interchange and by other institutional and technological inventions.

It remains to be seen whether campuses that comprise a public system can be prodded into cooperation by such top-down pleas for "one system thinking." At the very least, it runs directly counter to the competitive dynamic that is ingrained in the academic socialization of some faculty.

It also remains to be seen whether campuses will become increasingly divided by contemporary initiatives, such as responsibility-centered budgeting and the pursuit of selective excellence where the paramount consideration is the revenue-generating capability of discrete academic units and their proximity to thriving industries, such as software and microelectronics. The longer-range consequences, of course, are not just organizational but institutional, as the dominant institutional logic is reconstituted. As knowledge is seen as a source of wealth, it is increasingly constructed as a private good rather than a public good. The commodification of knowledge proceeds alongside negotiations over the ownership of knowledge and is refined in policies for intellectual property rights and responsibilities. Market-consciousness of knowledge outputs and property rights is bound to constrain teaching and research, and perhaps even thinking, in public higher education.

Managing for Legitimacy

One consequence of these converging forces is that the management of public higher education institutions faces formidable legitimacy challenges, where reconciling competing institutional logics is difficult. The tensions are evident in academic restructuring dynamics on different types of campuses.

The central balancing act in contemporary academic restructuring is that of adequately responding to seemingly irreconcilable expectations, when to make gains in one dimension may mean loss in another. For example, achieving strategic positioning in new knowledge markets may yield immediate gains for a campus in generating resources but a loss of moral legitimacy, core purposes and values such that it is no longer recognizable and identified as the entity that it was expected to be. Alternatively, a campus could have all the legitimacy it can muster and no revenue, and thereby go out of business. Thus, organizational repositioning is a complex matter, not reducible to strategic prescriptions or technical manipulation. Particularly for public colleges and universities, repositioning with respect to contemporary environmental demands is difficult—not only in terms of determining how to reconcile conflicting demands, but also in terms of determining the extent to which the organization can respond to demands that threaten its survival. The question of whether or not the organization *can* respond should be preceded by the question of whether or not it *should* respond to whatever is demanded by the resource relationships on which it depends, for an entirely different kind of organization may result.

For example, consider a situation in which both a local community college and a liberal arts college are facing demands to offer more vocationally-oriented programs, including electronic access through expanded distance learning programs. It is prudent for the community college to do so, given that those community colleges nationwide which are perceived to be cutting edge are offering such programs and advertising through relevant media that they can enthusiastically and swiftly accommodate these demands. For the liberal arts college, however, the path is not clear. While some liberal arts colleges may come to add professional or vocationally-oriented programs, the bulk of the academic program cannot shift too far afield from its institutional charter to provide liberal education. In fact, the institutional unwillingness to offer such programs may earn it greater legitimacy within a smaller, selective, elite niche for holding steadfast to its commitment to distinctive core values. In this situation, it would be prudent to see what its peer institutions are doing, in particular its most successful peers. One organizational study has documented both the trend and the peer effect: the proportion of professional and vocational majors graduating from non-selective liberal arts colleges has skyrocketed (Zammuto 1984). However, another study documented the trend in vocationalization, but no peer effect, suggesting that the colleges in the study did not mimic their peers and suffered no loss of legitimacy (Kraatz and Zajac 1996). Perhaps the major implication to draw from these studies is that predictions about ensuing legitimacy must take into account the history as well as present context along with its stock of legitimacy. With this in mind, one can predict whether a campus is particularly vulnerable and in need of repairing its legitimacy or is riding high and likely to be resilient. (For discussion of legitimacy, see Suchman 1995.)

However, managing legitimacy challenges cannot be reduced to a simple calculation or weighing discrete tradeoffs. Acknowledging public higher education's institutional legacies, the full range of expectations must be considered along with their moral import. Consider for example, the commonly-cited array of demands on public higher education: to reduce or contain costs, to improve teaching and learning, to remain technologically cutting edge, and to expand access. The demand to reduce or cut costs can be achieved in several ways—by streamlining, budget discipline, elimination of programs that are not cost-effective, not investing in expensive ventures, or trying to achieve economies of scale. Improvement of teaching and learning may be achieved by reducing class size, providing more faculty attention to individual students, obtaining more state-of-the-art equipment, or enhancing the learning environments. Similarly, upgrading technology may entail major overhauls of the organizational infrastructure and access to information systems in addition to providing students and faculty with the training to use it. Finally, expanding access may involve admitting students who are academically under-prepared and in need of expanded and extensive remedial programs across subject matters. Accomplishing any one of these four would be an outstanding feat, while achieving two or more in a resource-constrained environment is unlikely. The demands in themselves are not at cross-purposes, but the strategies for responding to them simultaneously may be costly and in conflict. Thus, challenge for public higher education's leaders in the U.S. is to invite collective deliberation over appropriate responses—not only at the campus level, but at state and national levels as well. And the challenge for the rest of us is to participate actively and critically in these determinations. Given the decentralized structure of U.S. higher education, few forums exist for such purposeful discussion of the cumulative impact of local academic restructuring.

In the absence of such collective deliberations, I see an ongoing struggle, where public higher education is increasingly using market discourse and managerial approaches to restructure in an attempt to gain legitimacy; yet, in so doing, they may end up *losing* legitimacy by changing their business practices to such a degree that they move away from their historical character, functions, and accumulated heritage as educational institutions. In this sense, it may be argued that adapting to short-term economic exigencies may be harmful for public higher education, as it subsumes the campus-by-campus discourse about prospective futures within a logic of economic rationality.

It is entirely possible that no loss of legitimacy will result, if the multiple institutional logics can be made compatible through superficial conformity, loose coupling or buffering. Empirical research needs to examine the conditions in which these dynamics are played out, as well as how institutional logics are reconstituted, including whether organizational actors can participate as purposive challengers or only as passive carriers of institutional scripts.

Conclusion

Those who grapple with contemporary reform dilemmas in the public higher education system must necessarily reflect upon histories as well as futures, what Kerr (1987, p. 183) has called "accumulated heritage versus modern imperatives." As Kerr (p. 184) has asserted, the "confrontation" between the past and the future results in a tension that is so profound that the current era is "*the* greatest critical age" for higher education in industrialized nations. This confrontation is characterized by a simultaneous call for protection and for redefinition. On the one hand, there is a call to protect: How can higher education protect its legacy, including decades of public investment in an enterprise whose strengths must not be diluted or deteriorated for short-term market demands? On the other hand, there is a call to respond: How can higher education redefine itself to attend to the signals of those it is supposed to serve? Several observers of contemporary calls for change share Kerr's observation that this historical moment is a defining moment for higher education, perhaps as significant as the late 19th century transformations (Clark 1998; Marchese 1998; Noll 1998).

In the process of rapidly assimilating concepts from managerial approaches and bolstered by concepts from management science, contemporary public colleges and universities are at risk for losing sight of the historical record that they are more to society than organizations *per se*, and that prescriptions for their management must not be reduced to technical organizational imperatives. There are those who believe that this discourse is merely the fashion of the moment. I however suggest that the discourse has a deeper significance—just as the ebb of poetry, manners, and Truth signal important changes at the societal level. Unfettered organizational imperatives have the potential to run wild in public colleges and universities—free of content, history and values, without regard to their accumulated heritage as particular types of social institutions, within yet not entirely of society, with educational legacies grounded in the centrality of knowledge and democratic values. To guard against this, I suggest that contemporary academic restructuring be viewed not only as organizational change but also as institutional change. And as such, we need to pause and reflect on the cumulative record of the recent past.

We are witnessing a reshaping of the institutional purposes of public higher education: in its people-processing activities as well as its knowledge-processing. The change entails not only what knowledges are deemed worthy but also who has access to and ownership of them. The converse must be considered as well. Furthermore, as is the case when there is a deviation from accumulated heritage, questions of moral import arise that warrant explicit deliberation. For example, should public colleges and universities primarily serve the needs of the economy, and in so doing see its customers as students/employees? If so, will core educational and socialization functions be redistributed among other social institutions—such as the family, religion, or the media—that already serve in part to fulfill some of these functions? Can public universities sustain knowledge transmission, production and creation as compatible activities? Or will each set of activities in their own way become privatized? Who will judge the academic worth of specific subjects—faculty, students, state legislators, employers? I raise these issues in the spirit of considering unintended consequences in a Mertonian sense as well as reflecting upon the cumulative impact of the ways we talk and the ways we think about the settings in which we study and work.

Notes

1. The development of this thesis has an empirical counterpart in my case study research on public colleges and universities in the U.S. (Gumport 1993, 1994, 1997, 1998; Gumport and Pusser 1999). This article puts forward some key conceptual distinctions. They are stated as propositional, even though I believe evidence abounds that may serve as descriptive substantiation; and I restrict them to the domain of public higher education in the U.S., which is the focus of my empirical work-in-progress, even though they may have relevance for higher education in other settings.

2. Examples of such state-level restructuring initiatives were seen in several states in the 1990s: over 80 academic programs were eliminated in Virginia; over 70 were eliminated or consolidated in Massachusetts (Gumport and Pusser 1999). Significant cost savings can result, as seen in Illinois public universities where 300 programs were eliminated, reduced or consolidated, for a savings of $181 million, and in Illinois community colleges where the same occurred 335 programs and a savings of $209 million; in each case, the savings were reallocated to salaries or new programs (IBHE 1998).

References

Bartley, W.W. (1990). *Unfathomed Knowledge, Unmeasured Wealth: On Universities and the Wealth of Nations*. La Salle, IL: Open Court Press.

Bellah, R.N., Madsen, R., Sullivan, W.M., Swidler, A. and Tipton, S.M. (1991). *The Good Society*. New York, NY: Random House Books.

Blau, P. (1970). 'A formal theory of differentiation in organizations', *American Sociological Review* 35, 201–218.

Blau, P. (1973). *The Organization of Academic Work*. New York, NY: John Wiley.

Burke, J.C. and Serban, A. (eds.) (1998). 'Performance funding for public higher education', in *New Directions for Institutional Research*, Number 97 (Spring). San Francisco, CA: Jossey-Bass.

Cameron, K.S. and Tschirhart, M. (1992). 'Postindustrial environments and organizational effectiveness in colleges and universities', *Journal of Higher Education* 63, 87–108.

Chaffee, E.E. (1985). 'The concept of strategy: From business to higher education', in Smart, J. (ed.), *Higher Education: Handbook of Theory and Research*, Volume I. New York: Agathon.

Clark, B.R. (1983). *The Higher Education System: Academic Organization in Cross-National Perspective*. Berkeley, CA: University of California Press.

Clark, B.R. (1993). 'The problem of complexity in modern higher education', in Rothblatt, S. and Wittrock, B. (eds.), *The European and American University Since 1800*. Cambridge: Cambridge University Press.

Clark, B.R. (1996). 'Substantive growth and innovative organization', *Higher Education* 32(4), 417–430.

Clark, B.R. (1998). *Creating Entrepreneurial Universities: Organizational Pathways of Transformation*. Surrey, UK: Pergamon Press.

Dill, D. and Sporn, B. (eds.) (1995). *Emerging Patterns of Social Demand and University Reform: Through a Glass Darkly*. Oxford: Pergamon Press.

Drucker, P.F. (1993). *Post-Capitalist Society*. New York, NY: Harper Collins Books.

Duderstadt, J. (1995). 'Academic renewal at Michigan', in Meyerson, J. and Massy, W. (eds.), *Revitalizing Higher Education*. Princeton, NJ: Peterson's.

Durkheim, E. (1933). *The Division of Labor in Society*. New York: The Free Press.

Enteman, W.F. (1993). *Managerialism: The Emergence of a New Ideology*. Madison, WI: The University of Wisconsin Press.

Gibbons, M., Limoges, C., Nowotny, H., Schwartzman, S., Scott, P. and Trow, M. (1994). *The New Production of Knowledge: The Dynamic of Science and Research in Contemporary Societies*. Thousand Oaks, CA: Sage Publications.

Gumport, P.J. (1993). 'The contested terrain of academic program reduction', *The Journal of Higher Education* 64, 283–311.

Gumport, P.J. (1994). 'Academic Restructuring in Historical Perspective: Shifting Priorities in the University of California'. *Presented at Association for the Study of Higher Education Annual Meeting* (November). Tucson, AZ.

Gumport, P.J. (1997). 'Public universities as academic workplaces', *Daedalus (Journal of the American Academy of Arts and Sciences)* (Fall) 126(4), 113–136.

Gumport, P.J. (1998). 'Academic restructuring in public higher education: A framework and research agenda', *Technical Report Number NCPI-1130 for the U.S. Department of Education*. Grant #R309A60001. Stanford, CA: National Center for Postsecondary Improvement.

Gumport, P.J. and Pusser, B. (1999). 'University restructuring: The role of economic and political contexts', in Smart, J. (ed.), *Higher Education: Handbook of Theory and Research*, Volume XIV. Bronx, NY: Agathon Press, pp. 146–200.

Gumport, P.J. and Sporn, B. (1999). 'Institutional adaptation: Demands for management reform and university administration', in Smart, J. (ed.), *Higher Education: Handbook of Theory and Research*, Volume XIV. Bronx, NY: Agathon Press, pp. 103–145.

Hammer, M. and Champy, J. (1993). *Reengineering the Corporation: A Manifesto for Business Revolution*. New York: Harper Collins.

Hardy, C. (1990). ' "Hard" decisions and "tough" choices: The business approach to university decline', *Higher Education* 20, 301–321.

Hearn, J.C. (1988). 'Strategy and resources: Economic issues in strategic planning and management in higher education', in Smart, J. (ed.), *Higher Education: Handbook of Theory and Research*, Volume IV. New York: Agathon.

Heydebrand, W. (1990). 'The technocratic organization of academic work', in Calhoun, C., Meyer, M.W. and Scott, W.R. (eds.), *Structures of Power and Constraint: Papers in Honor of Peter M. Blau*. Cambridge, MA: Cambridge University Press.

IBHE (Illinois Board of Higher Education) (1998). 'Results and benefits of PQP', in *Progress report* (March) IL: Springfield.

Keller, G. (1983). *Academic Strategy: The Management Revolution in American Higher Education*. Baltimore: The Johns Hopkins University Press.

Kerr, C. (1987). 'A critical age in the university world: Accumulated heritage versus modern imperatives', *European Journal of Education* 22(2), 183–193.

Kerr, C. (1995 [Orig. 1963]). *The Uses of the University*, 4th Edn. Cambridge, MA: Harvard University Press.

Kraatz, M. and Zajac, E. (1996). 'Exploring the limits of the new institutionalism: The causes and consequences of illegitimate organizational change', *American Sociological Review* 61 (October), 812–836.

Marchese, T. (1998). 'Not-so-distant competitors: How new providers are remaking the postsecondary marketplace', *AAHE Bulletin* 50(9) (May).

Massy, W.F. (1996). 'Productivity in higher education', in Massy, W.F. (ed.), *Resource Allocation in Higher Education*. Ann Arbor, MI: University of Michigan Press.

Metzger, W.P. (1987). 'The academic profession in the United States', in Clark, B. (ed.), *The Academic Profession: National, Disciplinary, and Institutional Settings*. Berkeley, CA: The University of California Press.

Meyer, J.W. (1977). 'The effects of education as an institution', *American Journal of Sociology* 83, 55–77.

NASULGC (1997). *Value Added—The Economic Impact of Public Universities*. Washington, DC: National Association of State Universities and Land-Grant Colleges (December).

Neave, G. and van Vught, F. (eds.) (1991). *Prometheus Bound: The Changing Relationship between Government and Higher Education in Western Europe*. Oxford: Pergamon Press.

Noll, R.G. (ed.) (1998). *Challenges to Research Universities*. Washington, DC: The Brookings Institution Press.

Peterson, M.W., Dill, D. and Mets, L.A. (eds.) (1997). *Planning and Management for a Changing Environment*. San Francisco, CA: Jossey-Bass.

Pew (1993a). 'A call to meeting', in *Policy Perspectives*. Institute for Research on Higher Education, University of Pennsylvania.

Pew (1993b). 'A transatlantic dialogue', in *Policy Perspectives*. Institute for Research on Higher Education, University of Pennsylvania.

Pew (1993c). 'An uncertain terrain', in *Policy Perspectives*. Institute for Research on Higher Education, University of Pennsylvania.

Pew (1994). 'To Dance with Change', in *Policy Perspectives*. Institute for Research on Higher Education, University of Pennsylvania.

Prahalad, C.K. and Hamel, G. (1990). 'The core competence of the corporation', *Harvard Business Review* 68, 79–91.

Readings, B. (1996). *The University in Ruins*. Cambridge, MA: Harvard University Press.

Rhoades, G.L. (1998). *Managed Professionals: Unionized Faculty and Restructuring Academic Labor*. Albany, NY: SUNY Press.

Rhoades, G.L. and Slaughter, S. (1997). 'Academic capitalism, managed professionals, and supply-side higher education', *Social Text* 15(2), 11–38.

Seymour, D.T. (1992). *On Q: Causing Quality in Higher Education*. New York, NY: American Council on Education, Macmillan Publishing Company.

Slaughter, S. and Leslie, L.L. (1997). *Academic Capitalism: Politics, Policies, and the Entrepreneurial University*. Baltimore, MD: Johns Hopkins Press.

Suchman, M. (1995). 'Managing legitimacy', *Academy of Management Review* 20(3), 571–610.

Turner, J.H. (1997). *The Institutional Order: Economy, Kinship, Religion, Polity, Law, and Education in Evolutionary and Comparative Perspective*. Menlo Park, CA: Addison Wesley Longman, Inc.

Zammuto, R.F. (1984). 'Are the liberal arts an endangered species?', *Journal of Higher Education* 55(2), 184–211.

Zemsky, R. and Massy, W.F. (1990). 'Cost containment: Committing to a new economic reality', *Change* 22(6), 16–22.

EXPERIENCES OF ACADEMIC UNIT REORGANIZATION: ORGANIZATIONAL IDENTITY AND IDENTIFICATION IN ORGANIZATIONAL CHANGE

MICHAEL MILLS, PAMELA BETTIS, JANICE W. MILLER, AND ROBERT NOLAN

The academic unit, whether called a department, school, or division, is the primary work venue for college and university faculty members. Since departments are relatively small, make some policies for themselves, and have relatively homogeneous memberships due to the similarity of discipline and socialization, they readily lend themselves to developing sets of shared norms, beliefs, and values enacted within the unit. In this sense, an academic department establishes its own culture and becomes the locus for how its members define their roles and identify with their institution and academic discipline.

However, departments have also been criticized because, some suggest, they promote balkanization of the faculty by separating and maintaining barriers to cross-discipline cooperation. Further, they pursue narrowly conceived and organizationally misplaced goals while protecting outmoded practices and inefficient work patterns from reform (Massey, Wilger, & Colbeck, 1994). Many calls for changing higher education include restructuring departmental units to overcome some of these negative traits, often creating new and more inclusive units that bring more faculty members into intradepartmental interaction (Wergin, 1994). Such restructuring is also consistent with broader recommendations to promote more dynamic interactions across specializations within organizations in order to create more innovation and organizational adaptability. However, the intentional disruption of old work groups may not facilitate patterns of work that overcome the perceived problems of academic units.

This study examines one case of a reorganization of academic departments and reports the events and interactions that followed from the creation of a new, more inclusive academic unit. In particular, this study focuses on the experiences and perspectives of five faculty members during the first year of the reorganization.

Context for the Study

The reorganization under study began in 1997–1998 when the six academic departments of the College of Education at Plains State University (pseudonym) were collapsed into three departments. The three departments were of roughly equal size. One department housed programs leading to teacher and other certifications; another combined educational psychology and counseling programs with physical education; and the third, the Department of Educational Studies (DES), is the focus of this study.

DES included some foundational areas of education (sociology of education, instructional technology) and noncertificate programs, housed nine programs, and had 31 faculty members drawn from five of the six previous departments of the college. The Administrative Council (the dean and

561

department chairs) developed and promoted the reorganization plan, and the dean selected one of the previous chairs as interim head of each of the new departments for the first year.

With the change in primary work unit and a new set of colleagues, the new department's faculty had to create a new culture and establish some identification with the new unit. To work effectively as an academic unit, the faculty needed to create enough agreement on a set of work norms, values, and behaviors to let the faculty members locate themselves vis-à-vis the orientations and expectations of the new unit as part of their conception of themselves as faculty members. Thus, the identity of the new unit was important if faculty members were to see it and its culture as a guide for how they should carry out their tasks as faculty members. This study examines the conditions, both conducive and detrimental, to identity construction and organizational identification as faculty members from different academic programs came together in this new academic unit.

Literature

As the social and organizational sciences have turned to constructionist perspectives, issues of meaning, sense-making, culture, and identity construction have become central concepts. For example, the notion of organizational culture has become a common concept in organizational analysis, although there are different schools of thought about how it is defined and analyzed (Martin, 1992). However, organizational culture has been conceived and analyzed primarily as an internal phenomenon, emphasizing the group's norms, beliefs, and values developed through interactions among members of the organization. To study and understand the role of external influences on social construction in organizations, analysts have turned to the notion of organizational identity. (See Gioia, 1998, for a review of the literature.) As Mary Jo Hatch and Majken Schultz (1997) described their approach, "We view organizational identity as grounded in local meanings and organizational symbols and thus embedded in organizational culture, which we see as the internal symbolic context for the development and maintenance of organizational identity" (p. 358). In this literature, organizational identity is seen as something formed by the interaction and construction of meaning between internal and external audiences of the organization. The external image and reputation of an organization affect organizational identity in some ways. In other words, those outside the organization are a party to the identity construction process, and some analysts go so far as to suggest that the internal construction of culture can be affected by the image of the organization communicated in the interaction of internal and external stakeholders (Gioia & Thomas, 1996).

Organizational culture and identity, in turn, become prime considerations in organizational identification. In effect, the affiliations that we use to define ourselves are often the organizations in which we participate (Pratt, 1998). Organizational culture sets the context for organizational identity, which, in turn, says a lot about who organization members are and how they like to think about themselves. Michael Pratt (1998) presents identification as a process of either affinity (believing that the organization has values similar to one's own) or emulation (adjusting your own values to match those of the organization). Through organizational identification, organization members fulfill such psychological needs as safety, affiliation, self-enhancement, and self-actualization, while the organization gets members who are more likely to act in ways congruent with organizational goals and needs.

The process of identification is complicated because neither the individual nor the organization has a single identity or even consistency among identities. Just as more nuanced views of organizational culture go beyond an integrationist perspective to allow for multiplicity of meanings in differentiation and fragmentation perspectives (Martin, 1992, 2002), the conception of organizational identity has moved beyond something that people take to be central, distinctive, and enduring about an organization (Albert & Whetten, 1985) to thinking about identity as a social construction susceptible to variation and change (Gioia, 1998; Humphreys & Brown, 2002; Wenger, 2000). According to Pratt (1998):

> Ascertaining whether or not one is "congruent" with an organization is likely to involve retrospective interpretations on [sic] one's own values as well as those of the organization. This process, in addition, is likely to involve more than a simple "matching process" considering that individuals and organizations have multiple and sometimes conflicting identities. (p. 180)

However, moving beyond this insight often proves difficult. As Mats Alvesson and Hugh Willmont (2002) explain:

> Those working in interpretive and critical traditions of organizational analysis, in contrast, have paid attention to the negotiated and problematical status of allegedly shared meanings, values, beliefs, ideas and symbols as targets of, as well as productive elements within, normative organizational control. . . . But these studies have not focused directly upon the discursive and reflexive processes of identity constitution and regulation within work organizations. (p. 621)

Alvesson and Willmont then attempt to address that shortcoming in the interpretive literature. They provide an overview of nine ways individuals' identities are influenced and changed in organizations (pp. 629–632), which they then group into four modes that address: (a) the employee by directly defining characteristics, (b) action orientations by defining appropriate work through motives, morals, and abilities, (c) social relations by defining belongingness and differentiation, and (d) fit with the social, organizational, and economic terrain. After naming these identity-defining mechanisms, however, Alvesson and Willmont admit: "In practice, these forms of identity regulation occur simultaneously, and may contradict as well as reinforce each other" (p. 632); and they rely on context-laden case studies to demonstrate the application of these modes.

Another substantial body of literature, particularly related to Alvesson and Willmont's third category, attempts to analyze the processes of and influences on identity formation and identification in organizations. In effect, researchers seek to extend to organizations the insights of Social Identity Theory (SIT) and Self-categorization Theory (SCT) (Ashforth & Mael, 1989; Gioia, 1998). These theories posit that we construct our identities based on memberships and affiliations and that we accept the characterizations of these groups based on others' expectations and definitions of them (Hogg, Terry, & White, 1995). Pratt (1998) applies these theories to the process of identification within organizations. In SIT, social groups provide systems of categorizations to define one's identity, and members conform to the norms and stereotypes of their social groups. SCT suggests a similar group-definition mechanism but ascribes it to the creation of group prototypes by which people compare their own and others' membership in social groups. Working from these theories, researchers hypothesize that clear and distinct differences between groups, a high salience for organizational categories in accounting for differences between groups, and membership in an attractive or prestigious group will enhance identification with a social group (Hogg & Terry, 2001; Pratt, 1998). Conversely, identification with an organization is likely to be more difficult if members are highly heterogeneous or too much like members of other organizations. Thus, organizations seeking to promote organizational identification should seek to maximize and emphasize internal similarities and external differences with other organizations (Pratt, 2001) and to maintain in-group/out-group comparisons that favor the organization (Ashforth & Johnson, 2001; Elsbach & Kramer, 1996).

Combining sense-making with the insights from applying SCT, Pratt (2000) sketches an emulative process of organizational identification that begins with (a) sense-breaking, a disruption of the sense of self, followed by (b) sense-giving, in which one searches for and is provided with alternative meanings and affiliations for one's self based on characteristics of an organization, and finally to (c) identification with the organization. Pratt found, however, alternative outcomes for sense-giving, including disidentification and ambivalent identification, which indicated that the effort to steer or manage the identification process often was not successful because people had other affiliations to provide meaning and identity for them.

Of particular interest for this study, the application of formal identification theories to organizational contexts has also included specific discussions of mergers in organizations. (For reviews of this literature, see Gaertner et al., 2001; Terry, 2001; van Knippenberg & van Leeuwen, 2001.) Mergers are problematic because

> conflict between groups in merged organizations is generally more intractable than conflict between individuals because disputants arrive with a network of social support for their respective positions. Ironically, in an atmosphere of distrust and propensity for conflict, members of merging groups are expected to identify with the merged entity and to become committed to its well-being, with the hopes of possibly living together "happily ever after." (Gaertner et al., 2002, p. 266)

Instead, "employees of merged organizations tend to act on the basis of their premerger identity . . . rather than on the basis of the identity implied by the merger" (van Knippenberg & van Leeuwen, 2002, p. 251). The literature recommends emphasizing the identity of the new, larger organization over the identity of the prior groups. If one of the former organizations is dominant in the merger, issues of in-group and out-group membership and status differentials will cause problems for organizational identification among members of the "out" or lower-status organization. Success in organizational mergers has been connected to "conditions of contact such as equal status, cooperative intergroup interaction, opportunities for personal acquaintance, and egalitarian norms" (van Knippenberg & van Leeuwen, 2002, p. 252), which they summarize as the permeability of groups within the merged organization.

While the use of social identity and categorization theories has allowed some hypotheses testing and the formal development of a theory of organizational identification, progress toward understanding such complicated phenomena remains limited. As discussed above, the list of modes for influencing identity presented by Alvesson and Willmont (2002) suggests that the theories based on mechanisms of belonging and differentiation account for only a few of the identification processes that may be operating in organizations. Furthermore, too much of that literature assumes an integrationist view of a dominant organizational culture and identity. Thus, Pratt (1998) urges more research to clarify the role that multiple identifications play in disidentification (p. 186), how individuals choose the level and "targets" of comparison (p. 191), and how particular identities become salient for individuals in particular contexts (p. 191). Alvesson and Willmont's list of identification modes presented earlier suggests some of the value, developmental, environmental, and contextual dimensions that are part of the process. Our analysis of the case of the reorganization and merger that produced DES reinforces these recommendations.

Method

The focus of this study is the experiences of five faculty members as they lived through the development of their new department. Keeping journals that serve as fieldnotes describing one's own activities, thoughts, and feelings is one method for collecting and making this type of information available for analysis (Clandinin & Connelly, 1994; Janesick, 1999; Rhodes, 2000; Smith, 1994). When the College of Education was reorganized, the lead author invited the other participants based on representation along several dimensions. As a result, the journalers included (a) one person from each of the former departments included in the new unit, (b) a mix of tenured (three) and untenured (two) faculty, (c) both men (three) and women (two), (d) a range of one to 20 years of experience at the institution, and (e) generally speaking, proponents (three) and opponents (two) of the initial reorganization proposal.

We individually recorded our thoughts and reactions concerning our experiences of DES's activities and development in journal entries. We did not seek to standardize our approach to keeping and organizing our individual journals, and we ended up employing different journaling styles. The main element of standardization in the journal entries was that, at five points during the year, one of us asked the group to respond to specific question(s) in our journals. The questions were meant to prompt some reflection and create some common subject matters in the entries, including such topics as changes in professional identity, perceived influence over one's academic program, and the continued role of the former departmental affiliations.

We also maintained a collection of documents produced as part of the reorganization and the operation of the new department. These included reports, position papers, memoranda, college- and department-wide emails, and minutes of meetings. These documents helped specify the contexts presented by the reorganization activities and provided verification of, as well as additional information and perspectives on, the events reported in our journals.

We analyzed the journal entries by establishing a set of forty-eight codes to be applied to all the journal entries. After our journaling concluded, each of us read our own and one other complete set of entries. Then we discussed and agreed upon a set of descriptors that would reflect the journals' content as fully as possible. The coding facilitated collecting journal passages by topical convergences into twelve large groupings; codes could be part of more than one grouping. Four of us (one person did not continue with the project beyond this point) reviewed, interpreted, and analyzed each set of text passages and related documents in weekly meetings. We also noted when our interpretations converged with themes in the different academic literatures we were individually familiar with or were reviewing for this project. We pursued those connections to larger concepts and theories to explain or test our interpretations and to extend the implications of the data analysis.

Findings and Interpretations

Preliminaries

The dean of the college announced in January 1997 that the departments would be reorganized, effective the following academic year. She then invited the faculty to discuss and present proposals for the form of the new departments and how the academic programs of the college would be aligned. Naturally, there were contrasting views about the need for a reorganization, the process by which it was carried out, and the final alignment of programs. In the structure the dean finally approved, it seemed that the unit later named the Department of Education Studies was a collection of programs that did not fit logically into the other two departments formed in the reorganization. As one of us wrote:

> In many ways we are the catch-all department, including such diverse programs as social foundations to aviation to statistics to higher ed. The other departments are more coherent in nature just because of their composition. Although I like several of my new colleagues, the ones with whom I have spent some time, I don't feel that I have much in common in terms of intellectual endeavors with most of them.

In addition to the four programs listed above, DES included programs in educational technology, adult education, human resource development, educational administration, and college student personnel.

The goals for the reorganization remained vague. While some motives for the move were publicly stated, many faculty, including those who wrote for this study, were skeptical that the expressed motives constituted the full set of reasons, and we speculated in our journals about implicit motives for the structural changes. For example, one of us wrote:

> At this meeting, [a recently hired full professor] questioned the need for a promotion and tenure document in the first place, and said he had talked to people who came up for P&T and submitted their stuff without ever referring to the document. This really shows, in my mind, how low the standards for P&T were in some of the old departments. This is a perfect example, I think, of why we have the reorganization of the college in the first place. The cultures of the departments were hugely variable, and there were some in which there were few recognizable academic standards applied. Unfortunately, I don't think the dean or admin. council ever stated in a direct way that changing this was part of the rationale behind the reorg. It was implied in some subtle ways, but many folks never picked up on it, so they don't know what are going to be problematic preferences and activities in the new organization of the college.

As a result, the goals and direction of the changes remained unclear, and we did not have a shared framework for directing our attentions and efforts. The college administration did not effectively communicate what about the previous departments prompted the changes (the problems) and what should shape the new departments' cultures and identities (the solutions).

An early interaction between the department chair and a recently tenured faculty member also became a critical incident that affected at least a few of us. As one of us described the event:

> This is our first meeting, and I don't think that it goes very well. Much of the group time is spent listening to a diatribe by one young and naive tenured male faculty member who thinks that [the chair] is unethical and academically dishonest. He asks for [the chair's] resignation. This is the focal point for me of this meeting.

A second person in the same meeting wrote:

> The first faculty meeting of the year left me unsettled. The dominant interaction was between [an associate professor] and [the department chair]. [The faculty member] clearly feels that [the chair] is on the side of administration rather than faculty and that he has acted in inappropriate ways. He was very aggressive and challenging, mostly to [the chair] but also to others who tried to comment on his comments or ask him a question.

This dispute was waged in very personal terms. Subsequent confrontations and threats of lawsuits between these two people meant that their interactions continued to be a factor in departmental dynamics during the first year of operation. The five of us mostly stayed out of any direct involvement in the conflict and preferred not to be identified with one side or the other. However, the incidents established a brittle backdrop for the department's meetings and work.

Each of us felt some initial defensiveness and reservation in our interactions. Part of these feelings was the normal result of working with new people and becoming part of a unit still under formation. One early entry read:

> We are just not alike in DES. . . . It may be that we are just too disparate a group. In general, I like the people I've gotten to know, but I get the feeling that everyone has an agenda, based on old-department ties. I'm actually glad to be working with some new people, but I feel like I have to prove myself all over again—to be taken seriously.

There were also demonstrations of lack of trust and "us/them" thinking in our journal entries:

> I also heard some horror stories about other (old) departments—such as senior faculty out to "get" more junior members, and department chairs unequally enforcing policy. No wonder people are nervous. Although we didn't have anything like that in my old dept, I still feel paranoid. . . . I still can't shake the feeling that I need to protect myself, and I'd prefer not to feel this way.

Key Tasks in Creating Organizational Culture and Identity

Much of the journaling recorded work on a key set of tasks that dominated the faculty experiences of the new department that first year. These were our involvements in and reactions to (a) the individual faculty performance appraisal meetings with the department chair, (b) meetings of the instructors of the quantitative and qualitative research courses, (c) the development of the department's policies and guidelines for promotion and tenure decisions, (d) curricular integration discussions between programs, and (e) the process for selecting the department's permanent chair. Each of these topics and the interactions around them created opportunities for the faculty of the new unit to establish the goals and values we would share and the work expectations we had for each other, as well as what we wanted to be characteristic of our new unit and the conditions of our individual involvement with it.

For this paper, we focus on two tasks: (a) drafting guidelines for promotion and tenure, and (b) considering ways to cooperate across, and perhaps even integrate, programs. Both had the potential to connect with our professional identities and play a primary role in defining an important component of our new unit and expressing the values and beliefs of DES.

Developing Policies for Promotion and Tenure

Under institutional policy, the academic units prepared their criteria and rules for promotion and tenure (P&T) before getting the document approved at higher levels within the institution. Establishing the departmental policy for the P&T process was arguably the primary piece of work for the faculty of the new unit, as well as an early test of faculty governance under the new structure. Its focus was producing a statement of how faculty roles would be valued in DES as well as laying out the rules for acquiring the status and rewards of membership. In effect, the policy development process became a signal case of the dysfunctions of faculty governance in the new unit in which scant knowledge about each other, suspicions, little foundation for working together, and a lack of leadership hindered the process.

A journal passage quoted earlier suggested the wide differences in how departments handled promotion and tenure cases prior to the reorganization. These differences made it very difficult to write a P&T policy document for DES. One of us summed up the major issue the faculty faced:

> It seems to me that the core disagreement of the P&T document is between those who want to delineate concrete standards for all members of the department that reflect what we as a research university are about and those who want to leave the document vague so that program areas can determine what works for them and so that each individual can negotiate their way through the process. [A senior colleague] kept on haranguing the group about being more specific, that the vague terminology and language that was going into the document did not help matters.

Another member of the research group had an exchange that illustrated the point:

> I was discussing the whole matter with [a faculty member], who was tenured some years ago as an assistant professor without a doctorate or publications. I was talking about the president's push for Research I designation and requirement for refereed publications, and [this colleague] claimed that he was proof that you don't have to do research to be tenured. I think he and [the other people in his program] really believe that if they can keep an explicit research requirement out of the department document, they can continue to operate as before and get people tenured who do only teaching and service.

In effect, disagreement over the degree of specificity and the use of external reviewers became the bases for dispute, with one group arguing for creating explicit standards for promotion and tenure and another group claiming that programs should have autonomy on the issue. Even faculty members and programs with relatively high claims to prestige due to research output joined in the autonomy argument. Perhaps wanting to maintain program viability in the new unit, they held that collegiality and egalitarianism, which are values also highly regarded among academics, suggested that vague P&T guidelines would give appropriate flexibility for programs to decide on these matters. Thus, proponents citing three basic tenets of academic culture (autonomy, egalitarianism, and collegiality) justified the right of each program to stand apart and not require that the faculty seek other norms and values to guide the P&T process.

Two of the journalers were on the committee drafting the P&T document. That committee had a difficult time resolving the differences of opinion of its members. As one noted, "Since the P&T committee has met for four or five times on this topic already, I would have expected us to have a draft of the entire document by this date. Instead, we are still talking in circles." The other committee member wrote, "The first four weeks were spent in whining and bringing up past nefarious practices" and added several months later, "What amazes me still about our P&T group is that we rarely have had what I consider to be truly substantive discussions about important issues."

The draft document the committee sent to the full faculty for consideration contained very few specifics about the criteria for promotions or awarding tenure. In faculty meetings, the defenders of the committee document and those who wanted more specific language staked out their positions. Both sides refused to move. One of us, working with another colleague, made some specific suggestions for language the committee and department could consider. However, the attempt at input was never accepted:

> We even found out during this meeting that some specific language on criteria for the different ranks and for external review that [a colleague] and I drafted apparently was not reviewed or discussed by the committee in any manner. Needless to say, having my effort at a contribution so summarily dismissed soured me even further on this whole process and how it is being conducted.

It eventually became clear that repeated meetings to discuss the issues were not going to produce any consensus or compromise. As this same journaler later characterized the meetings on P&T guidelines:

> It is clear to me that there is simply no willingness to compromise or even to consider alternative possibilities on the part of some faculty, and no stomach on the part of various others to force some compromise or decision on the contentious issues.

Someone else reported on a faculty meeting in which,

> the same few just took over as usual. It is my opinion that these "few" aren't challenged because they hold very strong opinions, and as one that doesn't want to argue every point, it's just easier to go along. I'm glad we have votes on the issues, because then everyone's side will be represented.

But another journaler took a dimmer view of the voting procedure and the effects it had on faculty consideration of P&T issues:

> The P&T committee members kept quiet unless prompted by the faculty to discuss a topic. Even then, they seemed reluctant to speak and did not say much to help the conversation. Predictably, we spent a lot of time on the first few items and the later items got little attention at the meeting. The result is that we sometimes voted on questions that we may not have fully understood or appreciated the complexity of, and we did not always have the benefit of a full discussion to inform our vote. Thus, this exercise in pseudo-democracy really turned out to limit our ability to have full and informed input into some important decisions. The result is that I feel, and I have heard others express, that we still have not had sufficient time to discuss and deal with the issues that the P&T document raises.

This same person reported equal dissatisfaction about a later meeting of the same committee:

> We kind of plodded along, one section at a time, while people could ask questions and raise issues. Most of the time, if someone brought up a serious issue, it was quickly referred back to the committee without a full discussion to see how other people felt about it.

By the end of the year, attendance at meetings to discuss the P&T policy was sparse. Concerning the last faculty meeting of the year, one of us wrote:

> [The convener of the meeting wanted] to discuss why the turnout for the meeting was so low. That's easy! Because our discussions of P&T issues have always been so excruciating, conflictive, and unproductive, people have just begun to stay away. At least that's how I interpret it, and the remaining discussion was a case in point. We spent most of the time going section by section through the document discussing little edits and nit-picks. Again, every effort was made to avoid talking about the issues that we have disagreements about—and really, what would be the point?

> Finally, [the department chair] tried to force us to take up the issues of specific statements of standards and external reviewers, and we agreed that we did not have enough people present today to decide the issues and that we would never come to agreement, so we just decided to hold a vote of the full faculty by secret ballot to decide what the P&T document should contain.

The new department's first year passed without the faculty approving an P&T document. Because early debates were left unresolved, subsequent discussions tended to avoid difficult or controversial issues. The meetings were, therefore, unproductive and never created a forum in which faculty engaged in the types of discussion that would allow airing of values, recognition of the bases for similarities and differences among them, and some discovery or creation of mutual ground. These foundations of a group culture that might encourage a group identity and ability to work together seldom occurred in DES.

Discussing Curricular Integration

One goal of the reorganization that the dean endorsed was that duplication between programs would be reduced, program resources would be shared, and perhaps programs could even be consolidated. Larger, inclusive departments would allow faculty members to work and forge bonds with people whom they had not known well. Integration and more efficient use of program resources required that the faculty explore each others' programs to find commonalities and arrive at some sense of (a) what the programs could do for each other and (b) how people's efforts could be redirected. Decisions about these issues would affect a faculty member's course content and which students he or she would teach. Therefore, these topics, at least potentially, had a direct bearing on how faculty would think of themselves as part of the new department. As some of our journal entries make clear, faculty saw these issues as important and threatening. About one of these exchanges, one of us wrote:

I've got to admit that just engaging in that type of discussion puts you on edge and gets your blood rushing. It is tough opening up what you teach for scrutiny and allowing people to suggest what you should do in your classes, especially when you already have the courses set up like you like them, and you may have to change them based on someone else's view of the world and the field that you don't fully agree with (and that makes more work for you).

In these curriculum discussions, we saw potential threats to the autonomy of our programs:

One concern I do have with the restructuring is that top-down control will somehow muddle up our program. We have worked hard over a number of years to get the course sequence appropriate to the needs of our students. We have worked to recruit students and build a quality doctoral program. If we become totally service-oriented, as I believe some would like, then our program will suffer. I am concerned that our chair doesn't value our area and that we will somehow be cannibalized for the benefit of others.

Another member of the group reported:

After the meeting I was walking away with [a colleague] and she said something like, "Can you assure me that this is not just some effort to get us all working for the educational administration program?" It struck me as a strange thing to say, but it also reflects some of the suspicion and lack of clarity about this meeting.

Thus, the desire for curricular integration was not shared by all concerned, so progress on these efforts seemed slow and blocked. The suspicions never flared up into explicit turf wars. Rather, faculty seemed to use stalling techniques to block progress on this agenda of the reorganization. For example, a group called together to discuss doctoral curricula made little progress:

We had another meeting of the "curriculum integration" group. This one, like the last, was marked by very general talk, especially about the differences between the Ed.D. and Ph.D. degrees. There was little specific to focus on and push us forward, which is unfortunate given the progress we had made in the meeting just before Christmas break. [The convener] is clearly getting frustrated with the drift of the group.

As with the P&T considerations, the parties to the curricular discussions avoided any tough decision making in the first year. As one of us saw it:

All the work I have seen so far has clearly been tinkering around the edges, and I have not seen any real threatening talk about duplication between programs. When I tried to bring up these issues, what we see is people avoiding the issue in any way they can.

When the faculty of two different areas met to discuss courses and turned up a pair of courses that might be considered duplicative, one of us observed:

This is an obvious place to look for the possibility of some working together and perhaps a consolidation of course offerings. What is really interesting is that it was hinted at, but no one ever expressed it directly and put on the table for consideration. We were all being very careful not to ruffle each other's feathers.

Faculty meetings avoided key issues, with the result that there was no full exploration of practices, beliefs, and values. By the end of the academic year, we had made no progress toward identifying course duplication or consolidating program offerings.

Helen Swartzman (1987) points out that "meetings are sense makers" (p. 288) in which people exchange views and perceptions and negotiate beliefs and meanings to come to mutual understandings. Karl Weick (1995, pp. 99–100) suggests that the fact that people can talk face-to-face is important when the value dimensions, multiple meanings, and ambiguity surrounding issues mean that people need many clues to ascertain others' meanings and to determine when they are approaching agreement. He refers to "rich personal media" such as meetings as just the sort of circumstances for sense-making to take place and, therefore, for shared culture and identity to develop. In DES, however, "rich-media" discussions about promotion and tenure guidelines and curricular integration were curtailed, and potentially significant interactions that would have allowed for the shared understanding it takes to build a common culture were lost.

Withdrawal

These two work processes within the faculty of DES and their meager accomplishments were repeated in several other incidents of faculty decision making within the department during its first year. The conflict and lack of progress made it hard to determine what beliefs and values the department would ultimately embody. As a result, faculty had a hard time feeling much identification with the new unit. As the year progressed, we began to disengage and pull away from the department and its governance processes. As one of us commented,

> When you get right down to it, I'm not at all feeling like I can have much influence on this document drafting process anyway, so why alienate people in the process? On the other hand, it would be nice if someone on the faculty stepped forward and offered some leadership on the P&T process.

Tentative efforts at providing leadership were also unsatisfactory. One of the journaling group tried to stir the department into taking a stance on the appointment of a permanent department chair. She wrote:

> Tomorrow we're having our DES meeting where we will discuss our selection of new chair. The process doesn't seem very fair to me—basically the dean is just going to make our current chair permanent. It seems faculty don't have a say. [A colleague] and I, as CFC [College Faculty Council] representatives, asked that the Friday agenda include time for those seeking the chair position to make a statement, followed by a question and answer period. We plan on taking a vote of the faculty for new department chair. We want this to be confidential and very, very fair. We plan to give this to the dean in the hope that it will influence her.

Another member of the journaling team wrote about that same meeting:

> After a few quick items of business, the meeting was handed over to [the CFC representatives] to moderate the discussion. They raised the issue of ground rules, a public vote, and a commitment to abide by the will of the majority. This quickly became a matter of dispute, with [some faculty] arguing for the vote and [two senior full professors] being the most vocal against it. They did not want to hold a vote because they saw it as tying the dean's hands. One of them also made a comment that, at the time, went unexplained, about being concerned that the vote push seemed to be part of a "hidden agenda" that we shouldn't be part of. After some further discussion, we seemed stalled and I and others were getting frustrated with the non-productive "process" discussion, so I suggested we go on and have the session with candidates, and we could get back to the process issue. All agreed, so the presentations and Q&A session began. . . .

> During this whole discussion, people were drifting away. At the designated stopping time we didn't have enough people left to have a vote about the candidates to establish who was acceptable to the department. [The FGC representatives] were clearly disappointed and a bit crestfallen.

The person who initiated the effort at faculty input later noted, "The dean has done what she wants with respect to department chairs, so we basically have very little input in my opinion. The bureaucracy continues to develop into a top-down structure, and it seems like it's every person for themselves. Too depressing to think about."

Another journaler discussed the effect of a different but equally unsatisfactory faculty work group:

> The first four or five meetings were a complete bust for me; I am beginning to intellectually and emotionally withdraw from my belonging to the group. When I commit to something, I try to take the task seriously and contribute to the group. This wasn't working for me with this group. . . . and perhaps it's not working for me with this department anymore. I have begun to develop a somewhat cynical attitude towards much of my faculty committee work. . . . I don't give it my heart, body, and soul anymore, and I really try not to get too excited when it doesn't work very well.

By the end of the year, the consensus among the journalers were that we were operating like a collection of autonomous units rather than an academic department in any traditional sense. By maintaining the relationships from our old units, we could still get work done and still have some basis of group identity and social support within the institution, something the new department was not providing.

[My former department] faculty, which is now split between two departments, has agreed to begin meeting regularly to attend to program issues common to the group, to take care of administrative issues (admissions, comps, scholarships) that still apply to all segments of the old department and to do a better job of keeping each other informed about the activities in the two departments. In effect, I continue to have monthly meetings of my old department as well as the monthly meetings of the new department.

Another person observed:

My old area moved as a unit to DES. We were a very cohesive group and that has not changed. The only time I really feel comfortable is when this group gets together—which we do on a regular basis. Even though we're split up across two floors, we still maintain close contact—particularly in spirit. So my old dept is still very important to my work life.

Later in the spring term, this person added, "I've been in closer contact with my old work group. I wonder if others revert to old associations when things get stirred up?"

As initial efforts to work on problems in the new department went unrewarded by much movement toward shared agreements, we began to disengage from DES. As the year went on, our journals reflected our discouragement. Our participation and engagement in department issues waned. We and, it seemed, the rest of the faculty reduced our efforts to construct a new identity for the full department as an organizational unit and instead retreated to the programmatic units with already established identities. Rather than develop a new culture for DES and establish a professional identification within it, we instead maintained our previous connections and identifications with our separate academic programs.

Conclusions and Implications

John Bean (1998) suggests that "if faculty members can talk of their work in a new way, they can work in a new way" (p. 496). Indeed, language has been identified in the literature as a vital component to producing change within organizations (Ford & Ford, 1995; Weick, 1995). Our journal narratives illustrate the ineffective use of language and communication to build a social identity during the reorganization that created DES. We, as faculty colleagues, did not interact effectively to construct some level of agreement about a set of beliefs, norms, and values that would have allowed us to establish a new culture and a related organizational identity.

The new unit did not create conditions for fruitful discourse. Therefore, individual faculty felt they had no ability to influence its path. We could not find agreement on what things could be like or how to move toward such an agreement. This confusion is reflected in our journals by the realization that "we don't have a shared value system" and our concern about having "holes in our common understanding of what we think we should be doing." Thus, rather than reaching toward the new and as yet undefined collective of the new department, we seemed to cling to what we knew and understood from the past. In effect, it became even less likely as the year went on that we would get beyond our past affiliations and program associations.

The case and analysis highlights implications for the merger of academic units. It particularly expresses dubiousness about combining diverse units for administrative convenience rather than for an academic or curricular rationale. As the literature cited previously suggests, mergers encourage the airing of differences and separation within the new unit because they increase attention to the differences and tensions between subgroups. As this case shows, simply creating the larger organizational structure does not assure that the interactions within it will foster identification at that level, at least not in the short term. The larger unit may produce administrative savings, but it may not be a source of cross-fertilization, revitalization, and synergy, effects which are sometimes cited as potential benefits and justifications for new organizational arrangements. In fact, the interactions in DES had the opposite effect. Trying to establish an operating foundation for the new unit deflected attention onto organizational and administrative matters. The necessity of finding new ways of working in the new unit led to reduced efficiency and effectiveness in group processes and often turned attention away from the substantive issues of academic and curricular issues.

It is easy to conclude that there was a failure of leadership in this case and that the college dean and department chair did not present a coherent vision, steer a proper course, or promote faculty participation in the unit's development. Further, it is too tempting to end an analysis of leadership at this point. Such a conclusion, however, posits too much authority for the formal leaders of the organization and absolves the other members of the unit from their share of responsibility. Insofar as organizational culture and identity are co-constructed by all involved, they cannot be formulated by a leader and simply bestowed upon the members (Humphreys & Brown, 2002). Instead, a new organizational identity must emerge from the interactions of those involved in the organization. Perhaps Barbara Czarniawska's (1997, 2000) metaphor expresses the status of constructed identity most vividly. She likens the process to the quest of medieval lore, in which the end is not known and in which, in fact, attaining the end is secondary. Instead, undertaking the journey and defining the self through the challenges faced are the source of value and the true goal.

From this perspective, the faculty in the new department, including those of us keeping journals, could have exercised leadership in establishing dialogue and crossing discipline and programmatic boundaries to build a sense of culture and identity for the new unit. However, faculty members did very little to create understandings, to exercise their governance prerogatives, and to move constructively toward decision making. When the faculty came together to discuss common issues of goals, directions, and policy, they reacted with diversions, delays, and avoidance of substantive discussions. Occasional efforts from within the faculty to encourage productive first steps were not successful in overcoming the group's paralysis.

As Bean (1998) suggests, it is through language that we create legitimacy for chosen images. A positive environment for dialogue and interaction must be promoted, which means that both commonalities and differences must be explored for the value of each, and that interactions and communications must be open and respectful. Open communication could have facilitated sense-making, and identifying shared values and orientations could have allowed us to establish agreement on the important issues the department's faculty faced. If a common language had been presented or developed as an early step in the reorganization, we might have had a baseline from which to build new culture and identity. But it was on this issue that the leaders of the new organization failed to prepare for a successful synthesis of the former units and that the members of the new department failed to generate their own sense of mutual trust and a foundation for developing a new culture and identity.

For formal theorizing based on Social Identity Theory and Self-categorization Theory, the DES case supports the conclusion that mergers promote conflict between the self-identified sub-groups that are joined together. In addition, our findings also support the general connection between the permeability of sub-groups and the success of mergers, since, in this unsuccessful merger, the unit quickly became characterized as a collection of separate programs rather than a coherent department.

However, the role of prestige factors in this case is more complicated than the SIT/SCT literature might suggest. For example, the literature says that low-prestige groups would emphasize alternative characteristics related to their identity that would deemphasize characteristics on which they were relatively weaker. For DES, research orientation and productivity—obvious elements of academic prestige—were central issues in the conflict over promotion and tenure standards. However, *both* high- and low-prestige programs in the new department opposed stricter standards in the criteria language, opting instead to emphasize values of autonomy, collegiality, and egalitarianism—also highly prized among academics. As a consequence, prestige was less of a factor in members' orientation to and identification with the new unit than previous research suggests, and egalitarianism became an argument for subgroup autonomy rather than group "permeability."

The case also highlights a second shortcoming of discussions and models of identification based on SIT and SCT as exhibited, for example, in Pratt's (1998) categorization of identification processes into affinity or emulation. Neither process accounts for identification promoted by making organizational values and beliefs more congruent with the individual's. However, in the case of the new academic unit, such a movement was clearly part of the dynamic. Faculty members wanted to influence the decisions about the P&T document so that they could shape DES toward their beliefs and values. While this effort to establish identification is easier to see in a new and developing organization, it nevertheless should be part of any theory of organizational identification based on social construction.

Even in organizations with established cultures and identities, sense-making is a continuous and reiterative process that sustains the possibility for organizational flexibility and change (Weick, 1995).

Pratt notes that among the topics needing further research is "what role might multiple identifications play in the process of disidentification" (1998, p. 186). In this study of five individuals, we cannot give a comprehensive answer to that question, but we can say that, for us, the identification provided by affiliations other than the department served at least two roles. First, for some of us, other identities provided support in defining beliefs and values during the process of negotiating the new organization's culture and policies. They helped us define meanings and identifications that we wanted to bring to the new unit. Second, when the identity of DES became one with which we did not want to be affiliated, there were other sources of identification readily available.

Ultimately, the DES case urges us to think beyond the models and hypotheses of SIT/SCT approaches to organizational identity. Those approaches emphasize the cognitive process of recognizing characteristics that promote belongingness in or difference from the organization. While acknowledging the multiplicity and variability of identity in both people and organizations, SIT/SCT conceptions still focus identification on the primacy of defining or prototypical characteristics. Further, this approach focuses too much on the instrumentalities of organizational identification for fostering members' self-definitions consistent with an organization's interest. While admitting that over-identification could be problematic—contributing to inflexibility and restricting adaptability in new situations (Dukerich, Kramer, & Parks, 1998)—the predominant approach is still to conceive of multiple, variable, and inconsistent characteristics as problematic, leading to an ambiguity of identity and even disidentification.

However, a broader and more comprehensive view of identity suggests that there are inescapable multiplicities, complications, and even contradictions in identity. Complications arise in part because of multiple organizational cultures and identities and various interpretations of those identities. Likewise, individuals have multiple sources of identity and different aspects of themselves that they apply with different salience in the contexts of each of their affiliations. DES had a mix of organizational values, goals, and behaviors as well as individual values, professional identities, and external group memberships that affected identification within the unit.

These complexities, however, should not be considered a problem to be overcome. As Etienne Wenger (2000) reminds us, membership and identity are "at once one and multiple." Mere multiplicity and mere singularity are both oversimplifications. Rather, various forms of identity "conflict with, influence, complement and enrich each other" and we "combine, confront, or reconcile various aspects" of identity to produce both cohesion and growth. "The work of identity constantly reshapes boundaries and reweaves the social fabric of our learning communities" (p. 242). For individuals and organizations, identity includes both the cohesion of integration and the richness of variation. Complexity means more opportunities for diversity, inclusiveness, and adaptability as well as more opportunities for individuals to find conditions for identification.

In the end, the problems of identification in DES do not stem from too many alternatives for identification or from any ambiguity in the identity of the department. Instead, they can be traced to the group's inability to launch substantive interactions that would have allowed the members to build a rich culture with which to connect. The faculty members were not part of any iterative process of meaning construction and, thus, were unable to co-create and influence the identity or to identify with what resulted. In the end, DES did not accomplish a rich and meaningful combination, but the multiplicity of identities allowed for a co-existence of affiliations and a way for the faculty to continue to fulfill their basic roles in the institution. DES was not an organizational home in which the faculty built new, entwined identities from and for themselves.

References

Albert, S., & Whetten, D. (1985). Organizational identity. In L. L. Cummings & B. Staw (Eds.), *Research in organizational behavior* (Vol. 7, pp. 263–295). Greenwich, CT: JAI Press.

Alvesson, M., & Willmott, H. (2002). Identity regulation as organizational control: Producing the appropriate individual. *Journal of Management Studies, 39,* 619–644.

Ashforth, B., & Johnson, S. (2001). Which hat to wear? The relative salience of multiple identities in organizational contexts. In M. Hogg & D. Terry (Eds.), *Social identity processes in organizational contexts* (pp. 31–48). Philadelphia: Psychology Press.

Ashforth, B. E., & Mael, F. A. (1989). Social identity theory and the organization. *Academy of Management Review, 14,* 20–39.

Bean, J. P. (1998). Alternative models of professional roles. *Journal of Higher Education, 69,* 496–512.

Clandinin, D. J., & Connelly, F. M. (1994). Personal experience methods. In N. Denzin & Y. Lincoln (Eds.), *Handbook of qualitative research* (pp. 413–427). San Francisco: Sage Publications.

Czarniawska, B. (1997). *Narrating the organization: Dramas of institutional identity.* Chicago: University of Chicago Press.

Czarniawska, B. (2000). Identity lost or identity found? Celebration and lamentation over the postmodern view of identity in social science and fiction. In M. Shutz, M. J. Larsen, & M. Holten (Eds.), *The expressive organization: Linking identity, reputation and the corporate brand* (pp. 271–283). Oxford, Eng.: Oxford University Press.

Dukerich, J., Kramer, R., & Parks, J. (1998). The dark side of organizational identification. In D. Whetten & P. Godfrey (Eds.). *Identity in organizations: Building theory through conversations* (pp. 245–256). Thousand Oaks, CA: Sage Publications.

Elsbach, K., & Kramer, R. (1996). Members' responses to organizational identity threats: Encountering and countering the Business Week rankings. *Administrative Science Quarterly, 41,* 442–476.

Ford, J., & Ford, L. (1995). The role of conversations in producing intentional change in organizations. *Academy of Management Review, 20,* 541–570.

Gaertner, S., Bachman, B., Dovidio, J., & Banker, B. (2001). Corporate mergers and stepfamily marriages: Identity, harmony, and commitment. In M. Hogg & D. Terry (Eds.), *Social identity processes in organizational contexts* (pp. 265–282). Philadelphia: Psychology Press.

Gioia, D. (1998). From individual to organizational identity. In D. Whetten & P. Godfrey (Eds.), *Identity in organizations: Building theory through conversations* (pp. 17–31). Thousand Oaks, CA: Sage Publications.

Gioia, D., & Thomas, J. (1996). Identity, image, and issue interpretation: Sensemaking during strategic change in academia. *Administrative Science Quarterly, 41,* 370–403.

Hatch, M., & Schultz, M. (1997). Relations between organizational culture, identity and image. *European Journal of Marketing, 31,* 356–365.

Hogg, M., & Terry, D. (2001). Social identity theory and organizational processes. In M. Hogg & D. Terry (Eds.), *Social identity processes in organizational contexts* (pp. 1–12). Philadelphia: Psychology Press.

Hogg, M., Terry, D., & White, K. (1995). A tale of two theories: A critical comparison of identity theory with social identity theory. *Social Psychology Quarterly, 17,* 255–269.

Humphreys, M., & Brown, A. (2002). Narratives of organizational identity and identification: A case study of hegemony and resistances. *Organization Studies, 23,* 421–447.

Janesick, V. (1999). A journal about journal writing as a qualitative research technique: History, issues, and reflections. *Qualitative Inquiry, 5,* 505–524.

Martin, J. (1992.) *Cultures in organizations: Three perspectives.* New York: Oxford University Press.

Martin, J. (2002). *Organizational culture: Mapping the terrain.* Thousand Oaks, CA: Sage Publications.

Massey, W., Wilger, A. & Colbeck, C. (1994). Department cultures and teaching quality: Overcoming "hallowed" collegiality. *Change, 26,* 11–20.

Pratt, M. (1998). To be or not to be? Central questions in organizational identification. In D. Whetten & P. Godfrey (Eds.), *Identity in organizations: Building theory through conversations* (pp. 17–31). Thousand Oaks, CA: Sage.

Pratt, M. (2000). The good, the bad, and the ambivalent: Managing identification among Amway distributors. *Administrative Science Quarterly, 45,* 456–493.

Pratt, M. (2001). Social identity dynamics in modern organizations: An organizational psychology/organizational behavior perspective. In M. Hogg & D. Terry (Eds.), *Social identity processes in organizational contexts* (pp. 13–30). Philadelphia: Psychology Press.

Rhodes, C. (2000). Reading and writing organizational lives. *Organization, 7,* 7–29.

Schwartzman, H. B. (1987). The significance of meeting in an American mental health center. *American Ethnologist, 14,* 271–294.

Smith, L. (1994). Biographical method. In N. Denzin & Y. Lincoln (Eds.), *Handbook of qualitative research* (pp. 286–305). San Francisco: Sage Publications.

Terry, D. (2001). Intergroup relations and organizational mergers. In M. Hogg & D. Terry (Eds.), *Social identity processes in organizational contexts* (pp. 229–249). Philadelphia: Psychology Press.

van Knippenberg, D., & van Leeuven, E. (2001). Organizational identity after a merger: Sense of continuity as the key to postmerger identification. In M. Hogg & D. Terry (Eds.), *Social identity processes in organizational contexts* (pp. 249–264). Philadelphia: Psychology Press.

Weick, K. E. (1995). *Sensemaking in organizations.* Thousand Oaks, CA: Sage Publications.

Wenger, E. (2000). Communities of practice and social learning systems. *Organization, 7,* 225–246.

Wergin, J. (1994). *The collaborative department: How five campuses are inching toward cultures of collective responsibility.* Washington, DC: American Association for Higher Education.

Managing Productivity in an Academic Institution: Rethinking the Whom, Which, What, and Whose of Productivity

Gary Rhoades

Drawing on a review of scholarly literature, this article suggests rethinking productivity in academic institutions along four dimensions: the productivity of whom, productivity for which unit of analysis, productivity according to what functions, and productivity in whose interests. It offers principles for promoting enlightened discussion and pursuit of productivity at all levels of the organization. In contrast to the dominant discourse, which emphasizes focus, centralized standard measures, and accountability, the bias in my principles is toward balance, decentralized diversity, and recalibration. I suggest the ideal is not for employees and units to produce to centrally managed objectives but for all individuals and units to manage individually and collectively to design their work to improve their productivity along multiple dimensions.

In this article I draw on scholarship to reframe how we think about managing productivity in academic institutions. My aim is to affect practitioners' conceptualization of productivity in four regards. First, who is focused on in efforts to increase productivity? Second, which unit of analysis or organizational level is addressed? Third, what functions or organizational roles are considered? Fourth, whose interests are invoked and served in designing productivity initiatives?

The research literature has much to tell practitioners but not by way of formulas that practitioners can easily follow. Scholarly literature is not well suited to that task.

> The strength of scholars is that . . . they know that they must not be distracted by irrelevant details if they are to develop basic principles. The strength of policy makers is that . . . they know that only those embedded in the daily chaos of seemingly irrelevant details can make sound judgments in a dynamic environment. (Birnbaum, 2000, p. 126)

I offer general principles to inform the perception of "the problem," leaving it to practitioners to apply those principles to develop policies and practices appropriate to their context.

There has long been a certain perspective and storyline in the research that has influenced the way practitioners think about the whom, which, what, and whose of productivity. The focus has been on full-time faculty's activities. The unit of analysis has largely been the individual faculty member. The functions considered have been narrow, short-term inputs and outputs in teaching and research. The interests invoked have been general categories of stakeholders.

Recent research alerts us to limitations of the prevailing perspective. I draw on this work to sensitize practitioners to alternative conceptualizations of productivity in academic institutions. I focus on data regarding faculty activities and productivity, and on the growing importance of support professionals in production processes. I address research findings regarding different organizational levels of analysis in regards to productivity. I consider studies regarding the interactive, long-term features of the various functions that colleges and universities perform. I invoke studies regarding stratification within and beyond higher education, pointing to whose interests in particular higher education emphasizes. Based on this literature review and inspired by Birnbaum's (2000) Laws of Policy Scholarship (BLOPS), I pose questions and generate Rhoades' Principles of Managing Productivity (RPMPs).

The Productivity of Whom?

In discussing the productivity of whom, I start where the prevailing perspective begins and ends—with faculty. Scholarly literature and policy discussion about productivity in academic institutions focus primarily on faculty activities. Most studies conceive of teaching and research as discrete, competitive activities; most concentrate almost exclusively on faculty and teaching.

Recent research findings suggest a broader view. Research on individual faculty yields counter-intuitive findings about instructional activities and productive educational and research outcomes. Scholarship points to the interactive aspects of faculty work, underscoring the significance of joint production. Finally, studies point to the increasing presence of nonfaculty professionals and to their involvement in production activities.

Contrary to prevailing views, recent national data show that faculty's class time and time with undergraduates have increased (Rhoades, 2000). Milem, Berger, and Dey (2000) found statistically significant increases from 1972 to 1992 in faculty time in teaching for liberal arts colleges and for comprehensive and doctoral granting universities; for research universities there was a statistically insignificant (2%) decrease. Leslie, Rhoades, and Oaxaca (2000) found an increase in average teaching loads in public research universities. Although faculty prefer research (Finkelstein, 1995) and rewards favor research (Fairweather, 1996), faculty have not been able to "ratchet" (Massy and Zemsky, 1994) down their involvement in classroom teaching.

Recent research has also examined faculty's advising time, an instructional activity that unlike teaching load or time in the classroom has been found to impact student outcomes. A large literature attests to the significance of such informal contact on student satisfaction, development, and persistence (Astin, 1993; Kuh, Schuh, Whit, and Associates, 1991; Pascarella and Terenzini, 1991). Milem, Berger, and Dey (2000) find a decline from 1972–1992 in faculty time on advising in all institutional types. Massy and Zemsky (1999) found that more time in the classroom may be correlated with less time with students outside the classroom. In short, emphasizing one indicator (teaching load) of the "input side . . . of the productivity function" (Layzell, 1996, p. 277) may be counterproductive in terms of another key indicator (out-of-class contact) that significantly affects student outcomes.

In the area of faculty research, studies have addressed productivity as well as activity. The focus has been on publications (e.g., Bellas and Toutkoushian, 1999). Publication productivity has increased significantly in all institutional types (Dey, Milem, and Berger, 1997).

The prevailing view about faculty's research activity is that it dominates their time to the detriment of instruction. Yet the strength of the claims about a trade-off is not matched by the strength of the evidence. In literature reviews, Feldman (1987) finds that research is weakly and positively related to teaching performance, and Braxton (1996) and Hattie and Marsh (1996) find no relationship between research and teaching time. For practitioners, it is important to keep in mind that with the exception of *private* research universities, faculty spend the largest amount of their time on instructional activities and no more than a third on research (Rhoades, 2000).

Moreover, several recent studies point to a "symbiotic relationship" between teaching and research (Middaugh, 1999). Clark (1987), Colbeck (1998), and Leslie, Rhoades, and Oaxaca (2000) find evidence of "joint production" that accounts for between 10 to 20% of faculty's time. Faculty, like any employee with multiple roles, can realize efficiencies by jointly producing two of them (Brinkman, 1990). By incorporating students into their research activity as assistants, faculty jointly produce contact with students (productive instructional activity) and research.

Finally, data from recent studies point to growing numbers of nonfaculty professionals who represent major labor costs and are often involved in producing teaching, research, service, and revenue. Most campus employees (over 70% in the 1990s) are not faculty. Faculty account for slightly more than half of professional employees, versus nearly two thirds in the 1970s (Rhoades, 1998a).

The ratio of administrators to faculty and of administrative to instructional costs has risen (Clotfelter, 1993; Gumport and Pusser, 1995; Leslie and Rhoades, 1995), yet the largest growth in personnel has been in support professionals, who are neither administrators nor faculty. From 1975 to 1985 their ranks grew 10 times faster than faculty (and three times faster than administrators), and their numbers continued to grow (by over 10%) in the early 1990s (when faculty numbers did not grow). Support professionals are increasingly involved in production. Multimedia, teaching center, and other professionals contribute to instructional productivity in traditional and distance delivery systems. Technology transfer professionals contribute to research productivity. Development professionals generate revenue. Support professionals are part of the matrix of production (Rhoades, 1998a). In short, to understand productivity in academic institutions one has to go beyond faculty.

Given the recent literature, I offer general principles and corollaries for practitioners to consider regarding "the productivity of whom."

> *RPMP #1:* The focus on production principle: The focus of initiatives should be more on encouraging productive (and quality) outcomes than on controlling employees' activities.

Controlling how faculty spend their time is one thing; fostering increased productivity in how that time is spent is another. In instructional activity, too much effort is being focused on directing faculty's teaching load; too little is focused on enhancing productive outcomes such as student credit hour generation, timely graduation, and student growth and satisfaction, as well as on activities such as out-of-class contact with students that enhance these outcomes.

> *RPMP #2:* The joint production principle: Productivity measures should promote and factor in efficiencies in teaching and research obtained through joint production.

There are interactions among faculty activities. For instance, encouraging greater student engagement with faculty's research activities can enhance various educational outcomes. Such involvement should be part of the calculus of faculty's instructional performance.

> *RPMP #3:* The counterproductive principle: Every effort to promote productivity has the potential to trigger counterproductive responses and outcomes.
>
> *The calibration corollary:* Every effort to promote productivity should assess its effects after successive intervals of 1 year, up to 7 years.

Faculty not only may resist change they may respond to incentives/directives in ways that lead to unintended and undesirable outcomes. Not all activities translate equally into productivity (e.g., in versus out-of-class student contact). The effects of productivity initiatives should be evaluated.

> *RPMP #4:* The factors of production principle: Efforts to promote productivity must include key nonfaculty factors and costs of production.

Nonfaculty technical and professional employees are part of instructional, research, service, and revenue production. Their activities and work should be part of any calculus of productivity.

Productivity for Which Unit of Analysis?

In discussing productivity for which unit of analysis, I look beyond individual faculty and standardized models of production, which typifies the focus of the prevailing perspective. Recent research points to the importance of looking laterally and vertically in the organization. Laterally, production takes place in departments and colleges, which have different production functions. In addition, studies indicate that distinctive divisions of labor (of tasks, individuals, and functions) within and among units make for joint production efficiencies that again vary by unit. Finally, looking vertically, production takes place at various institutional levels. Increased productivity at one level does not necessarily translate into increased productivity at another level.

Individual faculty's productivity is partly a function of their fields of work. Course loads and the nature of production vary by discipline. There are disciplinary differences in how faculty conceive of and organize their research (Becher, 1989; Clark, 1987). Intellectual products also vary. Faculty in experimental sciences often coauthor articles of less than 10 pages with as many as 10 or more colleagues; faculty in social sciences generally write fewer articles of longer length and books. There is similar variation within science and engineering (Baird, 1991). The relationship between research productivity and teaching effectiveness varies as well in the social versus natural sciences (Hoyt and Spangler, 1976; Michalak and Friedrich, 1981).

Departmental patterns of production, processes, and outcomes also vary by field (Braxton and Hargens, 1996). Different fields (and departments, colleges, and institutions) have different "production functions." That affects time to degree (Stricker, 1994). Doctoral students in science are supported by external and internal research monies; in humanities they are supported by teaching assistantships that slow their time to completion. In engineering and physical sciences a high ratio of graduate students to faculty is positively related to research productivity; in social and behavioral sciences the relationship is negative (Dundar and Lewis, 1998). What Middaugh (1999, p. 131) says about institutions and systems is true of colleges within large universities: "[P]roductivity . . . and costs at an institution or in a system are shaped by the mix of academic disciplines." In short, a common productivity algorithm, such as is developed for responsibility center management (RCM), makes no sense. The espoused aim of RCM and similar mechanisms to increase efficiency by decentralizing responsibility to the production units is undermined by the centrally established standardized algorithms that fail to recognize, reward, and encourage efficiencies particular to the distinctive productive functions of various units.

Relatedly, departments, like faculty, have joint production efficiencies. It is cheaper to produce undergraduate instruction with graduate education, and to produce the latter with research, than to produce them separately (Dundar and Lewis, 1995). Contrary to popular perception, a department's student credit hour production is not negatively affected by its research spending per faculty member (Ward, 1997). In addition, balance in a department is key to student learning: Volkwein and Carbone (1994) find that student growth outcomes are greatest in departments with strong research and teaching environments, and are greater in exclusively research- as opposed to exclusively teaching-oriented departments. Educational productivity is enhanced by a "research-teaching nexus" (Clark, 1997). At the same time, research productivity is enhanced by having some centers and organized research units that enable institutions to tap into external research markets (Geiger, 1990; Stahler and Tash, 1994).

There is limited data on support units' organization and productivity. Yet, existing studies suggest that organizational choices—for example, whether to centralize development offices—are not driven by productivity concerns and outcomes (e.g., Grunig, 1995; Tolbert, 1985).

Looking vertically within universities, scholars and practitioners are coming to recognize an ecological fallacy in efforts to increase productivity by increasing faculty teaching load.

> What must be resolved is the potentially dysfunctional aspect of a . . . policy that focuses on individual productivity rather than institutional productivity. An institution could . . . have all its faculty teach the standard load, but reduce the total amount of teaching provided. (Presley and Engelbride, 1998, p. 36)

Increased activity at one organizational level may not increase productivity at another. Incentive structures designed to increase educational productivity by rewarding departmental and college credit hour generation can have counterproductive effects (Rhoades, 2000a). Units may pursue strategies that increase student numbers and credit hours in some units at the expense of others (and of educational quality) without impacting the institution's student numbers.

Given the recent literature, I offer general principles and corollaries for practitioners to consider regarding "productivity for which unit of analysis."

> *RPMP #5:* The fair measurement principle (b): It seems most "objective," to apply uniform productivity measures across units, but is unfair and counterproductive to do so.

> *The decentralization corollary:* Productivity measures should be specified to local production units, not standardized across the institution.

The nature and factors of production vary systematically by field. So, too, should the measures by which we gauge and hold units accountable for their productivity vary.

RPMP #6: The production function principle: Productivity initiatives should be tailored to units' (including support units') distinctive production functions, and to maximizing efficiencies obtained by a distinctive balance among its various activities.

As with individual faculty (RPMP #2), academic and support units can realize joint production efficiencies. The nature of these efficiencies varies by units. In general, a balanced division of labor in departments is optimal, although some specialization (e.g., in research) can be effective.

RPMP #7: The ecological fallacy principle: Initiatives to promote productivity of academic units largely overlook support units and have the counterproductive potential to promote undesirable behaviors that do not increase productivity at the institutional level.

The calibration corollary (b): Every initiative to promote productivity of and among units should assess its effects on units' behaviors and institutional productivity after successive intervals of 1 year, up to 7 years.

What is productive for a department/college may not be for the institution. Productivity is increasingly a function of cooperation among academic and support units. In this context, initiatives that focus on academic units and pit them against each other can be counterproductive.

Productivity According to What Functions?

In discussing productivity according to what functions are considered, I begin with the functions most commonly identified with colleges and universities—teaching and research. Most state-based systems of accountability focus on faculty and institutional performance in instruction, with far less emphasis on research. In most cases, such outputs are measured and presented in annual reports. Typical of the general policy discourse, framed by concerns about bottom lines and revenue generation, the emphasis is on increasing efficiency. Yet, recent research calls into question the effectiveness of a narrow focus on and conceptualization of teaching and research, which overlooks key educational, social, and economic functions, and units of higher education.

State-based accountability efforts focus on instructional inputs and outputs, premised on the assumption that there is a trade-off between teaching and research. Yet econometric analysis of national data on institutional expenditures challenges the view that there is a "substitution effect," that the more an institution attends to research the less it attends to instruction. Instead, there is an "income effect": as institutions gain income from research some of that additional revenue is used for instruction (Hasbrouck, 1997). Along the same lines, another (regression) analysis found a positive relationship between institutional prestige, research activity, and graduation rates (Kim, Rhoades, and Woodard, 2000).

In short, balance is important. In the case of research and teaching, comparing the U.S. to Europe, Clark (1993, 1995) found that what sets us apart, and what other systems seek to imitate, is the "research-teaching nexus" in departments and institutions. Balance is also important in nonresearch settings. In a national study of community colleges, Smart and Hamm (1993) found that performing multiple missions is associated with effectiveness. Thus, we must go beyond one-dimensional conceptions of production to incorporate institutions' full range of functions, with the aim of optimizing the relationship among them.

Indeed, focusing on short-term efficiencies can be counterproductive. For example, some performance-based models focus on administrative size and/or expenditures. Yet, student affairs expenditures are positively related to affective and cognitive outcomes for students (Astin, 1993). As the latter measures are longer term and more complex than simple measures of administrative cost (or student graduation rates), they remain relatively unconsidered. By emphasizing short-term efficiency, as state-level performance-based systems do (Burke and Modarresi, 2000; Lovell, 2000), we run the risk of sacrificing long-term quality.

An efficiency focus can be self-defeating in another regard. Burke and Modarresi (2000) find that performance funding systems that have been most effective and have been more likely to survive are those that stress quality more than efficiency. Those systems that have been abandoned tend to have focused more on efficiency and on a long list of performance indicators.

Further, the goal of optimizing efficiency and the pattern of increasingly restricted state support for higher education can lead institutions away from their basic functions of instruction and access. They are not diverted so much by research as they are by pursuing new sources of revenue. Slaughter and Leslie (1997) explore patterns of "academic capitalism" in which faculty and institutions invest in efforts to generate external revenues, pursuing new monies at the margins at the expense of instructional activities. Along similar lines, there is a pattern in student services of expanding and increasing the range and cost of various student fees (Woodard, 1995). If this is efficient in terms of one bottom line, it can be costly in terms of another bottom line for not-for-profit institutions, expanding access to lower income students.

Given the recent literature, I offer general principles and corollaries for practitioners to consider regarding "productivity according to what functions."

> *RPMP #8:* The optimization principle: The goal should be less to maximize any goal or function than to optimize the performance of various goals and functions, grounded in a data-based understanding of interactions and cross-subsidies across units and functions.

As with individuals and intermediary production units, institutions have interrelated functions and units. Efficiencies attach to the performance of various functions and units (including support) in combination. Inefficiencies result from overemphasis on one at the expense of others.

> *RPMP #9:* The misplaced efficiency principle: The tendency is for isolated, short-term, simple efficiency and revenue-focused measures of outputs to take preeminence over interactive, longer-term, complex quality considerations, to the detriment of fundamental educational, social, and economic functions of the institution.
>
> *The substantive function corollary:* Productivity initiatives should address qualitative issues as to the particular content and value of what is being produced.

Current initiatives can be pennywise and pound foolish in concentrating on short-term costs, revenues, and measurables. Academic institutions are nonprofit organizations that serve multiple constituencies. They must perform a healthy mix of functions. Currently, efforts concentrate too much on productivity and too little on the substance of what is being produced.

Productivity in Whose Interests?

In discussing productivity in whose interests, I begin with two categories that are invoked in discussions of stakeholders—faculty and students. As the story goes, institutions are now organized to serve the interests of faculty; they should be reorganized to serve the interests of students. Recent research points to competing interests within these two categories. Much the same holds true with respect to the commonly invoked external stakeholder, employers. There are competing categories of employers, and we focus on some more than on others. Using universalistic categories blinds us to the differential and stratifying effects of higher education.

Policies aimed at increasing efficiency in instruction differentially impact different student populations. Efforts to enhance institutions' revenues and student populations have corresponded to reduced access for underserved populations. Shifts in federal and state financial aid policy to high tuition and not enough aid (Griswold and Marine, 1996), and from grants to loans (both of which disadvantage lower middle and working class students) are also found at the institutional level, where the greatest growth is in nonneed-based aid, and where leveraging and tuition discounting focus monies on high scoring students, disproportionately of upper middle to upper class backgrounds. The result is, in relative terms, increased access for students from the highest family income quartile and reduced access for those from the other quartiles (Mortenson, 1995).

So, too, with the faculty. Reorganizing to enhance productivity has meant retrenching some faculty and units while reallocating new monies and faculty lines to others (Gumport, 1993; Slaughter, 1993). Recent decades have seen a supply side higher education: resources flow to already well-resourced units, which are seen as close to the market and potentially productive (of external monies), they flow away from under resourced units, which are seen as far from the corporate market, and as subsidized (Rhoades and Slaughter, 1997). That pattern is related to increasingly stratified salaries for faculty (Bellas, 1997; Rhoades, 1998b), administrators, and support professionals (Rhoades, 1995). The pattern favors fields connected to the private sector over those linked to public and human services sectors; it disadvantages fields with higher percentages of students from underserved populations.

The need to disaggregate also applies to external stakeholders, such as employers. That term is generally equated with private sector employers. Indeed, academic capitalism (Slaughter and Leslie, 1997) has involved academic institutions linking academics more closely to a particular type of private capital—global corporations. The interests of these companies are not the same as those of smaller, local enterprises. Moreover, the public sector is a major employer. The interests of this sector, in terms of curriculum and outreach/service activity, are different than those of the private sector. To invoke "employers" generally is to ignore the particular interests being served.

Given the recent literature, I offer general principles and corollaries for practitioners to consider regarding "productivity in whose interests."

RPMP #10: The disaggregated stakeholder principle: Definitions of the stakeholders who may be consulted about and affected by productivity efforts should go beyond general categories such as "students" to include important subgroups within larger populations.

Current definitions of stakeholders gloss over important differences within them. In order to get meaningful input and to meaningfully assess the impact of productivity initiatives, we must move to more specific definitions that capture the real political interests involved.

RPMP #11: The stratification principle: In developing productivity initiatives, their affect on social stratification within and outside of the institution should be considered.

The social justice corollary: Productivity initiatives should be assessed, each year for at least a decade, as to their impact on social stratification within the institution and in society, and external interest groups should participate in the assessment.

As not-for-profit institutions, higher education should focus on the public interest, as defined in part by increasing access. As institutions that are central to the American dream of achieving upward mobility, and to social justice, they should consider the extent to which they serve and provide real opportunities to segments of American society to move up the economic ladder versus providing a mechanism by which the already advantaged maintain and gain position.

Closing Thoughts

In sum, what can be said about productivity in higher education? Recent research leads to the conclusion that the prevailing perspective regarding productivity should be laid to rest. Too often initiatives focus on the activities of individual faculty, as the only production workers, and on a linear, standardized process of mass production. Yet, we know that work in higher education involves teamwork and collectivities at various levels, overlap and interaction among faculty and other professionals, and multidimensional production processes that vary by unit.

As a result, instead of revving up an institution's engines of productivity by trying to gear everyone to central management's measures, I suggest promoting an enlightened discussion and pursuit of productivity by adhering to RPMPs. In contrast to the dominant discourse, which emphasizes focus, centralized standard measures, and accountability, the bias in my principles is toward balance, decentralized diversity, and recalibration. Each institutional context may yield varying responses in rethinking the productivity of whom, for which unit of analysis, according to what function, and in whose interests. At their best, discussions and initiatives will raise the consciousness not only of employees but of employers and managers, challenging them to think and work creatively and strategically to improve productivity. The key is not for employees and units to produce to centrally managed uniform objectives, but for them to manage individually and collectively to strategically design their work to improve productivity along multiple dimensions.

References

Allen, Henry L. (1996). Faculty workload and productivity in the 1990s: preliminary findings. In *The NEA 1996 Almanac of Higher Education*, pp. 21–34. Washington, DC: National Education Association.

Astin, Alexander W. (1993). *What Matters in College?: Four Critical Years Revisited*. San Francisco: Jossey-Bass.

Baird, Leonard L. (1986). What characterizes a productive research department? *Research in Higher Education* 25(3): 211–225.

Baird, Leonard L. (1991). Publication productivity in doctoral research departments: interdisciplinary and intradisciplinary factors. *Research in Higher Education* 32(3): 303–318.

Becher, Tony. (1989). *Academic Tribes and Territories: Intellectual Enquiry and the Cultures of Disciplines*. Milton Keynes, England: The Society for Research into Higher Education & Open University Press.

Bellas, Marcia L. (1997). Disciplinary differences in faculty salaries: does gender bias play a role? *The Journal of Higher Education* 68(3): 299–321.

Bellas, Marcia L., and Toutkoushian, Robert K. (1999). Faculty time allocations and research productivity: gender, race, and family effects. *The Review of Higher Education* 22(4): 367–390.

Birnbaum, Robert. (2000). Policy scholars are from Venus; policy makers are from Mars. *The Review of Higher Education* 23(2): 119–132.

Braxton, John M. (1996). Contrasting perspectives on the relationship between teaching and research. In John M. Braxton (ed.), *Faculty Teaching and Research: Is There a Conflict? New Directions for Institutional Research*, No. 90, pp. 5–14. San Francisco: Jossey-Bass.

Braxton, John M., and Hargens, Lowell L. (1996). Variations among academic disciplines: analytic frameworks and research. In John C. Smart (ed.), *Higher Education: Handbook of Theory and Research*, pp. 1–46. New York: Agathon.

Brinkman, Paul. (1990). Higher education cost functions. In Stephen Hoenack and Eileen Collins (Eds.), *The Economics of American Universities*, pp. 107–128. Albany: State University of New York Press.

Burke, Joseph C., and Modarresi, Shahpar. (2000). To keep or not to keep performance funding: signals from shareholders. *The Journal of Higher Education* 71(4): 454–475.

Clark, Burton R. (1987). *The Academic Life: Small Worlds, Different Worlds*. Princeton, NJ: Carnegie Foundation for the Advancement of Teaching.

Clark, Burton R. (Ed.) (1993). *The Research Foundations of Graduate Education: Germany, Britain, France, United States, Japan*. Los Angeles: University of California Press.

Clark, Burton R. (1995). *Places of Inquiry: Research and Advanced Education in Modern Universities*. Los Angeles: University of California Press.

Clark, Burton R. (1997). The modern integration of research activities with teaching and learning. *The Journal of Higher Education* 68(3): 241–255.

Clotfelter, C. T. (1993). *Economic Challenges in Higher Education*. Chicago: University of Chicago Press.

Colbeck, Carol L. (1998). Merging in a seamless blend: how faculty integrate teaching and research. *The Journal of Higher Education* 69(6): 647–671.

Dey, Eric L., Milem, Jeffrey F., and Berger, Joseph B. (1997). Changing patterns of publication productivity: accumulative advantage or institutional isomorphism? *Sociology of Education* 70(4): 308–323.

Dundar, Halil, and Lewis, Darrell R. (1995). Departmental productivity in American universities: economies of scale and scope. *Economics of Education Review* 14(2): 119–144.

Dundar, Halil, and Lewis, Darrell R. (1998). Determinants of research productivity in higher education. *Research in Higher Education* 39(6): 607–632.

Fairweather, James. (1996). *Faculty Work and the Public Trust: Restoring the Value of Teaching and Public Service in American Academic Life*. Boston: Allyn and Bacon.

Feldman, Kenneth A. (1987). Research productivity and scholarly accomplishments of college teachers as related to their instructional effectiveness. *Research in Higher Education* 26(3): 227–298.

Finkelstein, Martin J. (1995). College faculty as teacher. In *The NEA 1995 Almanac of Higher Education*, pp. 33–48. Washington, DC: National Education Association.

Geiger, Roger L. (1990). Organized research units—their role in the development of university research. *The Journal of Higher Education* 61(1): 1–19.

Griswold, Carolyn P., and Marine, Ginger Minton. (1996). Political influences on state policy: higher tuition, higher aid, and the real world. *The Review of Higher Education* 19(4): 361–390.

Grunig, Stephen D. (1995). The impact of development office structure on fund-raising efficiency for research and doctoral institutions. *The Journal of Higher Education* 66(6): 686–699.

Gumport, Patricia J. (1993). The contested terrain of academic program reduction. *The Journal of Higher Education* 64(3): 283–311.

Gumport, Patricia J., and Pusser, Brian. (1995). A case of bureaucratic accretion: context and consequences. *The Journal of Higher Education* 66(5): 493–520.

Hasbrouck, Norma Sue. (1997). *Implications of the changing funding base of public universities.* Doctoral Dissertation, Center for the Study of Higher Education, University of Arizona.

Hattie, John, and Marsh, H. W. (1996). The relationship between research and teaching: a meta-analysis. *Review of Educational Research* 66(4): 507–542.

Hoyt, D. P., and Spangler, R. K. (1974). Interrelationships among instructional effectiveness, publication record, and monetary reward. *Research in Higher Education* 2(1): 81–88.

Kim, Mikyong, Rhoades, Gary, and Woodard Jr., Dudley B. (2000). *Sponsored research versus graduating students?: public research universities.* Unpublished manuscript, under review.

Kuh, George, Schuh, J., Whitt, Elizabeth, and Associates. (1991). *Involving Colleges.* San Francisco: Jossey-Bass.

Layzell, Daniel T. (1996). Faculty workload and productivity: recurrent issues with new imperatives. *The Review of Higher Education* 19(3): 267–282.

Leslie, David W. (1996). "Strategic Governance:" The Wrong Questions? *The Review of Higher Education* 20(1): 101–112.

Leslie, Larry L., and Rhoades, Gary. (1995). Rising administrative costs: on seeking explanations. *The Journal of Higher Education* 66(2): 187–212.

Leslie, Larry L., Rhoades, Gary, and Oaxaca, Ron. (2000). *The effects of changing revenue patterns on public research universities.* NSF Report for NSF Grant #9628325.

Lovell, Cheryl D. (2000). Past and future pressures and issues of higher education: state perspectives. In Joseph Losco and Brian L. Fife (eds.), *Higher Education in Transition: The Challenges of the New Millennium,* pp. 109–133. Westport, CT: Bergin and Garvey.

Massy, William F., and Zemsky, Robert. (1994). Faculty discretionary time: departments and the "Academic Ratchet." *The Journal of Higher Education* 65(1): 1–22.

Michalak, S. J., and Freidrich, R. J. (1981). Research productivity and teaching effectiveness at a small liberal arts college. *The Journal of Higher Education* 52(6): 578–597.

Middaugh, Michael F. (1999). Instructional productivity of systems. In Gerald H. Gaither (ed.), *The Multicampus System: Perspectives on Practice and Prospects,* pp. 122–142. Sterling, VA: Stylus.

Milem, Jeffrey F., Berger, Joseph B., and Dey, Eric L. (2000). Faculty time allocation: a study of change over time. *The Journal of Higher Education* 71(4): 454–475.

Mintzberg, H. (1994). *The Rise and Fall of Strategic Planning: Reconceiving Roles for Planning, Plans, Planners.* New York: Free Press.

Mortenson, T. (1995). Educational attainment by family income, 1970–1994. *Postsecondary Education OPPORTUNITY* 41: 1–8.

Pascarella, Ernest T., and Terenzini, Patrick T. (1991). *How College Affects Students: Findings and Insights from Over Twenty Years of Research.* San Francisco: Jossey-Bass.

Presley, Jennifer B., and Engelbride, Edward. (1998). Accounting for faculty productivity in the research university. *The Review of Higher Education* 22(1): 17–38.

Rhoades, Gary. (1995). Rising, stratified administrative costs: student services' place. In Dudley B. Woodard Jr. (ed.), *Budgeting as a Tool for Policy in Student Affairs. New Directions for Student Services,* No. 70, pp. 25–38. San Francisco: Jossey-Bass.

Rhoades, Gary. (1998a). Reviewing and rethinking administrative costs. In John C. Smart (ed.), *Higher Education: Handbook of Theory and Practice,* pp. 11–47. New York: Agathon Press.

Rhoades, Gary. (1998b). *Managed Professionals: Unionized Faculty and Restructuring Academic Labor.* Albany: State University of New York Press.

Rhoades, Gary. (2000a). Who's doing it right: strategic activity in public research universities. *The Review of Higher Education* 24(1): 41–66.

Rhoades, Gary. (2000b). The changing role of faculty. In Joseph Losco and Brian L. Fife (eds.), *Higher Education in Transition: The Challenges of the New Millennium,* pp. 29–50. Westport, CT: Bergin and Garvey.

Rhoades, Gary, and Slaughter, Sheila. (1997). Academic capitalism, managed professionals, and supply side higher education. *Social Text 51* 15(2): 9–38.

Slaughter, Sheila, and Leslie, Larry L. (1997). *Academic Capitalism: Politics, Policies, and the Entrepreneurial University.* Baltimore: The Johns Hopkins University Press.

Smart, John C., and Hamm, Russell E. (1993). Organizational effectiveness and mission orientation of two-year colleges. *Research in Higher Education* 34(4): 489–502.

Stahler, Gerald J., and Tash, William R. (1994). Centers and Institutes in the research university: issues, problems, and prospects. *The Journal of Higher Education* 65(5): 540–554.

Stricker, Lawrence J. (1994). Institutional factors in time to the doctorate. *Research in Higher Education* 35(5): 569–588.

Tolbert, Pamela. (1985). Institutional environments and resource dependence: administrative structure in institutions of higher education. *Administrative Science Quarterly* 30: 1–13.

Volkwein, J. Fredericks, and Carbone, David A. (1994). The impact of departmental research and teaching climates on undergraduate growth and satisfaction. *The Journal of Higher Education* 65(2): 147–167.

Ward, Gary Tripp. (1997). *The effects of separately budgeted research expenditures on faculty instructional productivity in undergraduate education.* Doctoral Dissertation, Center for the Study of Higher Education, University of Arizona.

Woodard, Dudley B. Jr. (Ed.) (1995). *Budgeting as a Tool for Policy in Student Affairs. New Directions for Student Services,* No. 70. San Francisco: Jossey-Bass.

Zemsky, Robert, and Massy, William F. (1999). Telling time: comparing faculty instructional practices at three types of institutions. *Change* (March/April): 55–58.

Who's Doing It Right? Strategic Activity in Public Research Universities

Gary Rhoades

"So who's doing it right?" That is what a department head in physical sciences at a public research university asked me at the end of an interview about departmental activities and central administrative initiatives affecting research and instruction. In the 45 minutes he had spent detailing his department's efforts over the past five years to survive in the difficult fiscal environment of public higher education, this head had also detailed the ineffective strategic initiatives of his university's central administration. Hence, his question.

As part of a larger study (see Leslie, Rhoades, & Oaxaca, 1999) of public research universities, I had completed similar interviews with 40 department heads at four public research universities in engineering, life science, physical science, math and computer science, and social science.[1] What follows is my reply, as much to presidents, provosts, deans, and scholars as to department heads and faculty.

I replied that "Who's doing it right?" is the wrong question. It assumes too much and specifies too little. It assumes that there is one best way, that exemplary practices can be copied and implemented in other universities, and that the answer lies in central managerial initiatives. Further, the question fails to specify what "right" is, how strategic goals connect to institutions' educational and political economic contexts, and how to assess strategic activities. My reply was grounded partly in the prevailing scholarship on strategic leadership and partly in a critique of central beliefs embedded in that literature regarding change, focused vision, and rationality. I do not offer a standard review of the literature but rather speak more directly to the department head's question and to practitioners in general, of which I am one, as are many other scholars of higher education who are serving as center directors, department heads, program heads, associate deans, central administrators, and on committees at all levels. I address the higher education literature in the course of discussing the beliefs that we confront and promulgate both as scholars and practitioners of higher education.

Before answering the department head's question, I rephrase it: "What are some *principles* for doing it right?" By "doing it right," I mean contributing to thoughtful growth in public research universities by facilitating, supporting, and encouraging constructive strategic thinking and activity in academic units toward multiple goals. I emphasize the plural, goals, for public research universities must necessarily pursue progress toward multiple and often competing goals.

Myths of Management

My principles for doing it right address key myths in the current received wisdom about public research universities. I first briefly discuss these myths, grounding them in the literature and in the managerial dilemmas with which they confront presidents, provosts, and deans. Then I debunk the myths with the cases of four public research universities, using my interviews with department heads. The three myths are that: (a) no change occurs without managerial initiative, (b) managers focus fragmented academic units and loyalties, and (c) they rationalize budgeting and planning.

Each of the myths centers managers as leaders—as the answer to organizational problems. That positioning is a key feature of our society's mythology about organizations, not only where colleges and universities are concerned (e.g., Keller, 1983; Leslie & Fretwell, 1996), but for all sorts of organizations and enterprises (Meindl, Ehrlich, & Dukerich, 1985). It is a central feature of the language by which we explain change in business and government, as well as in higher education (Birnbaum, 1992). It is a central feature of the way we name programs and courses (leadership) and define our purpose—developing higher education leaders, focusing on those in formal positions of power. As a lower-level "manager" myself and as a faculty member, I explore and challenge these myths because they set managers up for frustration and set faculty up for disillusionment and resistance.

In my conclusions, I offer some principles for "doing it right" that correspond to the myths. Because of my belief that part of "doing it right" involves having a conversation about assumptions, purposes, and possibilities, I eschew the conventional form of a research paper in favor of an essay that is no less serious for the informality of its style. I believe that in our scholarship we should not dismiss the informal and even occasionally playful tones of discourse in the world of our professional practice. My essay is grounded in the findings of a NSF-supported research project and weaves in relevant literature. However, it analyzes and challenges myths about strategic activity that emerge from the evocative voices and experiences of the department heads I interviewed. And in discussing principles for doing it right, my paper draws on and offers alternatives to the sometimes colorful metaphors we use in public research universities.

First Myth: No Change Without Managerial Initiative

The received wisdom is that research universities, particularly public ones, are slow to change. Faculty and their departments are mired in tradition, resistant to change. Managerial initiative is essential to moving the institution forward. These beliefs are so common that they are often taken as unstated premises, as Birnbaum clearly articulates: "To strengthen academic leadership, we are told, we must reform structures, adopt more rationalized management systems, and increase the power of executive leadership to make faster, more efficient, and more effective decisions" (1999, p. 14).

In higher education literature, leaders, generally at the top and in the center of the organization, are seen as the key change agents on campus (Bennis & Nanus, 1985; Bensimon & Neumann, 1993; Clark, 1998; Julius, Baldridge, & Pfeffer, 1999; Keller, 1983; Leslie & Fretwell, 1996)—hence the title of Bennis and Nanus's book, *Leaders: The Strategies for Taking Charge*. In it they explain:

> This book was written in the belief that leadership is the pivotal force behind successful organizations and that to create vital and viable organizations leadership is necessary to help organizations develop a new vision of what they can be, then mobilize the organization to change toward the new vision. (1985, pp. 2–3)

Although Bensimon and Neumann focus on leadership "teams," they study presidents and "their" teams. Clark conceptualizes entrepreneurship as characteristic of an institution rather than of individuals, and his "steering core" is a centrally located group (including senior faculty) that is the source of coordinated initiatives. Julius et al. (1999) address "presidents, senior administrators, and faculty leaders who would seek change," but their focus (like Machiavelli's) is on central leaders who, in seeking to "transcend the status quo will be met with opposition" (1999, p. 116). Keller indicates that university management "is in shackles" due in part to the "buildup of strong faculty power" (1983, p. 27). Invoking the great university presidents of the late 19th century, he maintains that change is contingent on "a single authority . . . authorized to initiate, plan, decide, manage, monitor, and punish its members" (p. 35). Similarly, Leslie and Fretwell note a "vigorous resistance to change" among faculty, who sometimes "are focused on preserving their autonomy as an end in itself" and who "may resist efforts to strategize" (1996, pp. 78–79). In short, change is contingent on central management.

The myth presents a *managerial dilemma:* how to overcome resistance to change in academic units when the constraints on changing academics and their units are so considerable. At the institutional level, the most readily available pressure point that managers have is in the budget process—reallocating resources and restructuring activities, units, and faculty work to address new realities.

(At the state and national levels, the policy response is to attack tenure as a legal obstacle to change, which, in fact, it is not. See Rhoades, 1993, 1998.) Working out of this model of central stimulus and departmental response, presidents and provosts at each of the four public research universities I studied had established institution-wide initiatives promoting change in the academic colleges and departments. Although they varied, all the institutions set up review and incentive structures uniformly targeting academic units and aimed at focusing state monies and unit activities in common directions. The strategy was to provide clear, competitive monetary incentives for changing the behaviors of resistant academics and their departments.

In the eyes of department heads, such incentives were the most prominent and problematic central initiatives, affecting annual allocations of state monies from central administration to academic colleges and departments. At East Coast University (all schools are identified by pseudonyms), heads emphasized the significance of a recent review. All graduate departments had been reviewed by a faculty committee and rated on a five-point scale. The review's purpose was to identify centers of excellence to be targeted for a systematic, yearly reallocation of state monies. Each year, all academic units returned 1% of their budgets to a central pool and submitted proposals requesting a reallocation of monies for purposes consistent with the institution's strategic plan. These second-wave allocations centered on excellence, focusing increments of resources on the top 15–20% of academic departments. The physical science department head commented:

> One of the hottest topics on this campus is the [review process], a blue ribbon internal committee. There were five categories. Top level was "distinguished," next was "very good." That was us. But each year we are being asked to give back a percentage of our budget, and then plead for the money in a reallocation.

Southwest University had experienced somewhat the same strategic push for excellence. It, too, had undertaken a quality review of academic programs by faculty committees, with reviews aimed at identifying the institution's programmatic strengths. However, there was no systematic follow-through in reallocating resources based on the reviews. At best, the institution had experienced sporadic pushes—fits and starts related to turnover in managerial personnel. The head of Southwest's computer science department complained:

> There is no connection between—or very little—doing the right things in a quality way, and being rewarded for that. . . . I guess that we have been burned, and we react accordingly. Promises have been made to grow our department to undertake new initiatives. We do the initiative, but we get no support.

When I asked heads about the budgetary process, they indicated that there was no public discussion of allocations. They referred to private negotiations among heads, deans, and the provost. As one physical science head said, "Well, the department heads go to the dean and beg for money, and the deans go to the provost and beg for money." Heads and deans politically position themselves to gain more resources, rather than working according to a public strategic plan (Rhoades, 1995).

In contrast, Midwest and Northwest universities had a strong, public, strategic emphasis on instructional productivity, about which virtually all the heads spoke. In mechanisms evocative of a responsibility center management approach, the institutions had set student credit hour and course load targets for colleges and departments; allocations were connected to those targets. Northwest's physical science department head described:

> There is tremendous pressure from the provost to increase student credit hours. The pressure from the dean is to maintain or increase student credit hours. The main emphasis is, not to turn away students. Don't turn away students who want classes. . . . The idea was that faculty numbers would stay about the same, but we would increase numbers of students and thereby increase productivity.

In consequence, a public incentive structure encourages units to attract and retain more students.

If this premise—that central initiative and incentives are required to generate departmental response and change—is accurate, then we would expect a close correlation between the strength of central initiatives and the extent and focus of strategic, innovative activity in the units. That is *not* what I found. At Southwest University, which lacked systematic follow-through in its strategic efforts, units showed much innovative activity. More than half had at least these strategic initiatives underway: (a) curricular revisions of the undergraduate program to make it more relevant, marketable, and technology intensive, (b) new "professional" master's degree programs to more closely link the unit to private sector employers, (c) connecting with employers to provide in-kind and monetary support to departments, and (d) enhancing the private support of commercially relevant research. Southwest's level of innovative activity surpassed that of two of the other three universities. Only one unit yielded no evidence of strategic departmental initiatives in recent years, the same as that found at the three other universities.

Moreover, at each of the other universities, departmental strategic initiatives existed that were not responses to the central incentive structure. At East Coast, some departments were undertaking master's level curricular and program initiatives that ran directly counter to the university's emphasis on research performance and doctoral program reputation that it hoped would increase the school's national prestige. At Midwest and Northwest, units were undertaking initiatives in commercial research and fund raising that had nothing to do with the major central focus on student credit hours.

Innovation in academic units is not merely or even primarily a function of central strategic initiatives. Academics and their departments may resist central administration's change efforts. At the same time, they may be undertaking strategic initiatives of their own, partly in response to the general fiscal condition of the university (Slaughter & Leslie, 1997). Each of the universities I studied had experienced substantial fiscal distress over the past 5 to 10 years. Departmental initiatives may also be a response to challenges and changing conditions in the external environment. Some of these are financial, as in changing patterns of federal research funding. For example, department heads in mathematics and physics spoke of the impact that the end of Star Wars and the Cold War had had on federal funding for research in these fields. The head of Northwest's math/computer science department summarized:

> Grants and contracts are way down. When the evil empire died, we came upon hard times. Weapons are down. The Department of Defense and Department of Energy are way down. The focus of NSF, at least in [the field], is on education, and on interdisciplinary studies.

Other external challenges are professional. For example, some engineering department heads referred to initiatives they were undertaking in undergraduate education due to the new emphasis on student outcomes by the Accrediting Board for Engineering and Technology (ABET). As the engineering department head at Southwest put it:

> Part of it is the engineering accreditation, ABET. It used to be the requirements were very specific—150 pages of requirements about lab time, faculty, and so on. . . . Now ABET has become more flexible, focused on outcomes. . . . And it is more outcomes-based assessment. So we can experiment now.

In focusing on internal resistance to change, the prevailing myth overlooks the effects of external changes and conditions that affect not only the university as a whole, but units within the institution, to different degrees and in different ways. Such external factors are a stimulus for change, to which units respond. All strategic initiative does not lie in the central administration.

Second Myth: Managers Focus Fragmented Academic Units and Loyalties

A second piece of received wisdom is that universities need to be focused and that the problem in focusing them lies in their diverse array of academic units and in the faculty's fragmented loyalties. Large public research universities often have over 100 academic departments, centers, and institutes. Centrifugal forces are powerful. Each of these units is committed to its own purposes. Its faculty are oriented more to the interests and goals of these units and subunits and of themselves than they are to those of the institution (Massy & Zemsky, 1994). Literature on faculty loyalties and the culture of universities substantiates this view (Clark, 1987, 1998).

The solution to the problem, according to the received wisdom, again lies in central management. The belief is that focus must come from central managers who will articulate a coherent vision for the institution. That belief is evident in our metaphors and scholarship. Strong leadership and authority are needed to establish a vision. As Bennis says, "The president should be a conceptualist. . . . [That] means being a leader with entrepreneurial vision" (1989, p. 17). Consider the often-used nautical terminology in higher education that suggests the need for "steering instead of drifting" (Clark, 1998, p. 5). For Julius et al., "Leaders are those who identify and articulate a vision and successfully manage a solution" (1999, p. 129). In relating examples of successful "strategy making" at several institutions, Keller (1983) offers stories about dynamic leaders who articulate a vision that transforms the institution. For Leslie and Fretwell, one of the necessary "wise moves" in "hard times" is "developing a vision"; and in their conclusions, they entitle their discussion of this challenge: "Whose Vision? The Presidential Burden" (1996, p. 221). In short, focus is contingent on central management, and part of these managers' job description.

From the perspective of managers, the *managerial dilemma* is how to establish a common direction and coordinate common activity in the face of extraordinary academic diversity and among extremely independent, even isolated academic units and faculty members.

Embedded in the answer to the problem of fragmentation is an un(der)considered premise, the presumption that the center itself (administration) is focused. So much attention is devoted to academic diversity that diversity within administration tends to be overlooked. Public research universities have an enormously complex array of units and academic functions that may indeed be relatively fragmented. Yet they also have enormously complex and variegated administrative and support infrastructures, and large numbers of academic deans who champion the separate interests of their academic units (Rhoades, 1995, 1998). Scholars and central academic managers devote too little attention to balkanization within administration, with different vice-presidents and deans establishing incentive structures and allocating resources in ways that may compete with the public, strategic, central efforts to focus the institution's energies. Moreover, too little attention is devoted to central office(r)s and deans' lack of focus. Instead, in the mythology about managers focusing fragmented academics, managerial focus is in some sense taken for granted.

My cases call this premise into question. At each university, central managers had tried to establish a public commitment to certain strategic directions. Heads' comments centered on these efforts. But they also pointed to incentive structures and allocations that ran counter to the central initiatives. Sometimes these themes attached to central administrators other than the provost; sometimes they attached to the provost. To some extent, the themes spoke to public research universities' multiple missions. To some extent, the themes spoke to private negotiations that are a part of personnel management and resource allocation in large organizations.

For example, interviewees at each university reported clear exhortations from the central administration for faculty and units to develop closer research ties with private enterprise. This push to generate new revenues through entrepreneurial science is a national pattern (Etzkowitz, 1983; Slaughter & Leslie, 1997). Heads referred to central managers' efforts to encourage faculty to connect more with private enterprise in their research. Research parks had been established. Yet nowhere were entrepreneurial goals linked to the institution's central strategic initiatives. Indeed, they often competed with those initiatives (Fairweather, 1996).

Similarly, each of the universities had incentives related to overhead monies from external grants and contracts. Indirect cost recovery policies varied across and within institutions. In no case was it evident how policies were related to the central managers' strategic efforts.

The situations described in the preceding paragraphs speak to public research universities' multiple missions and complex, multi-layered administrative structures. Multiple vice-presidents are responsible for the institution's distinct missions. The incentive structures that each of them establishes may not be consistent with one another. Factor in another administrative layer of academic deans, whose colleges likewise have multiple and distinct missions, and who themselves articulate diverse incentive structures and resource allocation patterns, and one begins to get a sense of the difficulty of establishing managerial focus.

Of course, multiple and competing managerial messages may stem from the actions of a single administrative office(r). For example, provosts deal with various political and professional pressures and may change their message in response to shifting conditions. The literature focuses on new responsibilities and roles for chief academic officers but overlooks the extent to which external pressures and internal roles are in constant flux (Martin & Samels, 1997; Mech, 1997). Moreover, central managers may exercise discretionary judgments that run counter to the institution's publicly proclaimed strategic efforts. Similarly, deans may exercise discretion in ways that run counter to the publicly proclaimed strategic efforts of the central administration (and of their colleges). Finally, personnel turnover may lead to shifts in signals, or to recruitment offers that run against the publicly identified criteria for resource allocation to academic units.

Provosts in the four universities I studied were not only trying to move the institutions in particular strategic directions but were also trying to respond to multiple external pressures related to faculty workload and other matters. Part of that response involved developing accountability practices that impacted departmental and faculty activity. East Coast University was dealing with much legislative pressure to increase teaching load and credit-hour production. That pressure translated into accountability measures on campus and, on occasion, state audits of some departments. Such pressures in some sense diverted attention and focus away from the institution's strategic push toward excellence in the research rankings of graduate departments.

In each institution, deals had been made between provosts and some deans that were inconsistent with public strategic efforts. At East Coast University, although the strategic focus was on rewarding excellence, the College of Life Sciences, which had several departments that got poor reviews, received a large reallocation of monies.

At each of the universities, deans had invested in departments in ways that diverged from publicly proclaimed strategic plans. For example, East Coast, Midwest, and Northwest each had physical science departments with declining enrollments but increasing financial support. The head of East Coast's physical science department commented:

> The proposals of the [review] are good for us. . . . We have had a significant drop in undergraduate majors. . . . We want to keep the resources, and we've been successful in that. . . . Starting experimentalists is very expensive, and we will use the extra monies for that.

At Southwest University, some department heads expressed concern that the only outcomes they could see of an institution-wide quality assessment of programs was that some deans invested in lower-quality units to "beef them up" at the expense of higher quality units. This university's social science department head bitterly commented:

> The [program] was a whole lot of effort, and it made absolutely no difference whatsoever. We put thousands of hours of people's time into that, and it was a total waste. . . . There were loads of units that were identified as not meeting requirements. There lots that were low rated. But zero happened. And when it looked like one might finally get cut, they would form a coalition to fight it, and they won. . . . They would get resources to bail them out, taking dollars away from good units that had been rated well. It was crazy.

Such patterns contributed to cynicism about and resistance to the central strategic initiatives.

Finally, each of the institutions experienced turnover in key administrative positions, a common situation given the limited average tenure of most top managers. Such a change often meant a change in policy. Department heads at each of the institutions pointed to the link between such personnel and policy changes. More than just an immediate change in policy, such turnover often stalls administrative activities and reduces heads' (and faculty's) commitment to strategic initiatives. New administrators often need a semester or two to learn about the institution and get to know the players. Department heads and others often adopt a wait-and-see attitude about the new administrators' policy pronouncements, reserving judgement, as much as academics can, until they had been through the new person's first budget cycle. The life science department head at East Coast expressed this typical attitude:

> We have a new provost. He says he will reallocate. But it is hard to know. Strategic plans come and go. I've been through four or five of them. The university goes on. And remember, the new provost is not the author of the strategic plan. . . . It's hard to know what will happen.

Turnover can also undermine central strategic initiatives in a more indirect way. The four universities provide examples of new deans negotiating a resource commitment for their colleges that ran counter to resource allocation criteria embedded in the institution's strategic effort. Often the negotiations focused on a college that was not performing well by the terms of the central strategic initiative. To turn these units around, central administrators often had to invest new resources in the unit to get the dean candidate they wanted.

In short, the cases suggest that fragmentation is due not only to the number of faculty and departments but also to the very nature of central administrators and deans who are subject to multiple pressures and who send multiple messages to departments and faculty. As one head noted:

> There is no one in the institution who has a sense of the priorities in the university. . . . I asked the dean of the Graduate School for priorities—for which one of the tasks was more important. He can't tell me. He had no answer. . . . One of my colleagues in the math department . . . gives the best description of our situation. Formerly our role was to produce top-quality research and graduate education and to do a reasonable job of teaching. Now he's told to return undergraduates at a certain rate, to be diverse, to use technology in teaching, to be innovative in teaching, to do outreach in the community, and to keep doing research and graduate education. All with no new resources.

For all the talk from managers about "hard choices," it is far from clear to department heads that managers are making such choices—encouraging more of one activity and less of another and thereby acknowledging the hard reality that something has to give. To the heads, the central message appears to be "do more of everything," with no sense of priorities.

In focusing on academic fragmentation, the prevailing myth overlooks the need for focus and coordination among managers. It is not only academic units that are diverse and widespread. The support/administrative side of the institution is also varied and far reaching in its location and activities. All divergence and push for (sub)divisional autonomy does not lie in academic units.

Third Myth: Managers Rationalize Planning and Budgeting

A third piece of received wisdom is that institutional decision making is irrational and politicized. Again, a major cause of the problem is seen as the powerful centrifugal forces in the institution in the form of self-interested academics and their units (Massy & Zemsky, 1994). Too often, the story goes, institutions, units, and faculty are not simply mired in tradition but are stuck in a morass of irrational and self-serving practices.

However, the literature offers somewhat different signposts and paths for practitioners. On the one hand, some scholars argue that the solution lies in managers taking the lead in a relatively linear process: developing a program of implementation that links (and subordinates) budgetary decisions to the overall plan. Leaders must establish incentive systems that will move the institution forward, providing clear-cut processes, goals, and measures (Bennis, 1989). Structures must be created at the center of the organization to coordinate and manage planning and budgeting. Resource allocations must follow a clear strategic plan, ensuring that academics and their units will orient their activities toward the institution's priorities. In the process, leaders must instill an entrepreneurial culture (Clark, 1988), transforming the institution.

Such a perspective fits with a major push among practitioners to rationalize resource allocation. What provost or dean has not tried to take the politics out of internal resource allocation? As a colleague of mine, Sheila Slaughter, observes, they are searching for the "algorithm of absolution." By reducing allocations to a formula, they seek to make them more "objective" and logical. In setting up strategic planning committees, undertaking strategic planning exercises, and publicly establishing criteria for allocating monies or faculty lines to units, and salary monies to faculty, most managers seek to rationalize planning and budgeting.

Yet the scholarly literature in higher education offers another signpost, pointing to the inherent uncertainty and ambiguity of goals and technology in universities. Such literature promotes not linear but interactive processes. Based on a different conception of "how colleges work" (Birnbaum, 1988), some studies suggest a more flexible pursuit of strategic objectives. For example, Julius et al. say that leaders should "glance backward": "Be skeptical about your own accomplishments. Few good changes have eternal lives. . . . In this sense, following through means evaluating, judging, and deciding whether performance lives up to expectations" (1999, p. 129). Similarly,

Leslie and Fretwell (1996) suggest a process of "enlightened strategic planning" that involves continuous experimentation and continuous learning. The metaphors suggest incremental innovation rather than transformation.

Despite their differences, each of the two paths described above leads to an objective of more rational planning and budgeting. One offers a more linear route; the other offers a more interactive, spiraling one. But both suggest that rationalization is contingent on central managers. Thus, in Keller's words:

> A university president . . . must also be a manager of change, a navigator who steers his or her institution through the treacherous channels of constant transformation. . . . The president must give direction to the college and devise the strategies, make the hard decisions, and allocate the resources that will support movement in that direction. (1983, pp. 123–124)

Leslie and Fretwell suggest a far less heavy-handed, top-down model, yet it still depicts central players initiating, coordinating, and converging on solutions:

> Someone has to synthesize what is going on and communicate what is being learned to the community as a whole. . . . Simultaneous tracking requires leadership of a particular kind. It requires a great deal of confidence in people and an ability to stimulate, monitor, and shape learning. . . . Instead of imposing solutions, a leader . . . would attempt to stimulate convergence around ideas that are consistent with the values of the institution. (1996, pp. 235–236)

Finally, despite the language of vision, the particular destination toward which rationalization is supposed to steer the university remains relatively vague in both cases. Rationalization becomes the end.

Managerial Dilemmas

Whatever the particular path that is adopted, from the perspective of managers the *managerial dilemma* is how to establish clear, fair, and rational criteria for allocating monies to prioritized activities in a highly variable and politicized environment. In each of the universities I studied, provosts and some deans had pursued a path that was much more linear than interactive, establishing incentive structures that would objectively and systematically move academic units and faculty toward a particular focus in their work. Such structures were uniformly applied. Unfortunately, I saw little evidence of the feedback loops and continuous learning processes promoted in the more interactive path to rationality. Such mechanisms are difficult to establish and even more difficult to maintain, particularly in settings characterized by considerable turnover in managerial personnel. In such a context, the "continuous learning" that is taking place is less a learning curve for the organization than a pattern of individual administrators learning the ropes over and over again, and of faculty and department heads waiting to learn over time what the actions of these administrators will reveal.

For all the efforts to rationalize planning and budgeting, my cases suggest that there are very real limits to managerial rationality. In each university, there were unintended and undesirable effects that attached to the rational incentive structures—irrationalities embedded in the rational efforts. In their efforts to focus institutions with central incentive structures, central managers sacrificed an important dimension of clear-sightedness—broad-scoped and peripheral vision. Administrators tended to be blind to the ill effects of the incentives they had established, not looking around and behind to see and evaluate the outcomes of the incentive structures (Julius et al., 1999). They also tended to be blind to alternatives and to realities that fell outside their immediate focus, overlooking important strategic opportunities. They devoted far more time to the technical processes of reallocation—the algorithm and the decision-making structures (the means)—than to a discussion about the desirable goals (the ends). In short, the managerial search for rationality was marked by various types of managerial myopia.

Managerial Myopia: Irrational Effects of Misplaced Rational Emphases

In setting up incentive structures, many presidents and provosts nationally are now focusing on increasing contact hours and credit-hour production at the undergraduate and lower division level. It is not hard to understand why. Public research universities have been criticized for not paying enough attention to undergraduate instruction. Thus, managerial initiatives have been shaped by framing the problem in the prevailing policy terms of teaching productivity vs. research standing. Yet the experience of Midwest and Northwest universities, and stories told by department heads, suggest at least two irrational effects of such an incentive structure.

One ironic, irrational effect of the incentives at Midwest and Northwest is that they failed to increase the universities' overall credit-hour production or their enrollments. In retrospect, this is not surprising. Academic departments do not admit undergraduates; university admissions offices do. As a result, academic departments sought to increase credit-hour production by competing with other departments for a finite pool of existing undergraduates, mostly for general education students. "Productivity" here is often a function of changes in general education rules, not in the strategic initiatives of academic units. Thus, geology was taking students from chemistry, which was taking students away from astronomy, and so on—all without increasing student numbers for arts and sciences or for the university as a whole. As the incentive structure focused on each unit's student credit-hour productivity, it did not encourage units to work cooperatively or creatively to increase instructional productivity for the institution.

Herein lies a second irrational effect of incentives based on credit-hour production. The structure set up a cannibalistic, counterproductive competition for general education students. To generate more credit hours, academic units engaged in practices that no provost would publicly support, practices that could be called not cut-throat, but cut-quality. For example, department heads in the colleges of arts and sciences at Midwest and Northwest noted that some professional schools had dropped math requirements to attract undergraduates. Others had hired part-time faculty to teach language, programming, and other service courses to capture credit hours previously generated in other colleges. If the professional schools had increased their credit-hour production and enrollments, the numbers for the institution overall had not increased.

The two other institutions I studied had implemented a different incentive structure. To advance the research position of their institutions in the context of increasingly restricted revenues from the state, central managers adopted a "centers of excellence" strategy that is fairly common nationally. The thinking was that you cannot excel at everything, or even do everything. Rather than whittle departments down to a common level of mediocrity, they focused resources on centers of excellence—at East Coast University on twelve of seventy departments.

Although the centers-of-excellence strategy seems rational, it has built-in irrationalities. One has to do with the units that are not "chosen." As a department head at East Coast University said, drawing an analogy between rewarding units and rewarding faculty: "If I give even only 25% of my 80 faculty merit monies, that means I'm giving 60 faculty nothing, which destroys their morale and commitment. Yet I need those 60 faculty to be productive. And in fact, more than 25% of the faculty *are* meritorious."

This comment came from a department head whose unit had received a reallocation. His point about declining morale and productivity—and about the implied punishment of many who actually merited rewards—takes on added meaning when applied to academic units. He explained that another department had received a mediocre rating; its head had pointed out that there are some really good faculty in that department. Not only are they not being rewarded, they are likely to leave, further detracting from the quality of the unit and the institution. The idea of the centers of excellence model is to encourage competition that will raise quality. But faculty can be mobile and may respond to such a system by leaving when their unit is not targeted as excellent.

The strategic efforts to focus resources on centers of excellence follow the maxim, coined by Robert Merton and then Martin Trow from the gospel of Matthew (Trow, 1984), "To them that have shall be given" (Matt. 25:29). Without debating this reading of the gospel (we might also cite the line: "So the last will be first"), I would point out that this strategy—which could also be called supply-side higher education (Rhoades & Slaughter, 1997)—assumes that strong communities can be built around a few centers of excellence. There is good reason to doubt this assumption in universities that are increasingly interdisciplinary and interdependent. As a department head in science at Northwest University indicated in discussing the effects of responsibility-centered management:

> I favor responsibility-center management, with the caveat that we should cancel the idea of taking away from others to fund a few. You don't want to be a strong branch of a weak tree. A high-quality academic community should be funded for success. . . . We are dependent on cross-disciplinary research, so we need others to be strong. We cooperate with other departments. . . . If departments around us are not strong, it is unlikely that we will be strong, because more and more research is interdisciplinary.

A centers-of-excellence strategy can easily translate into feeding (or planting) a few isolated sites, simultaneously starving the surrounding environment. In the complex academic ecosystem, this approach can be both short sighted and self defeating.

Finally, both the instructional-productivity and centers-of-excellence incentive structures had the effect of punishing small, interdisciplinary units. When the emphasis is on productivity, big is seen as better. When the emphasis is on research funding and standing, big is better. Small, innovative units may have relatively few undergraduates and few national peers to whom they can be compared. Yet it may make little sense for them to increase student numbers or to merge with a larger, more conventional unit so that they can be more easily compared with established departments. As one interdisciplinary unit head said, "We are not going to serve society by creating a large number of hydrologists." In each of the universities, many small, productive, high-quality interdisciplinary units did not fare well in the incentive systems. From the standpoint of the colleges in which they were located, they were not "central. "Again, the incentive structures run counter to the changing ecology of higher education, in which increasingly diverse, small interdisciplinary units are seen as having been a key to universities' past success and critical to their future (Geiger, 1993).

Managerial Myopia: Missed Opportunities

The linear pursuit of rationality and the conventional categories by which we discuss productivity constrain managers in another important respect. Policy discourse counterposes and dichotomizes undergraduate and graduate education. Classes are either one or the other, with little attention directed to curricula and programs that cut across those boundaries or to internal divisions within those categories. Through such lenses, central administrators limit their ability to see important new developments and growth areas in university degree programs. As a result, the initiatives and incentive structures established in the universities that I studied neither focused on nor supported key opportunities involving a closer linking of university curricula to external employment.

Most engineering schools nationally, like those I studied, are moving toward five-year joint bachelor's/master's degree programs. Such professional master's degrees are designed to be better articulated with students' and employers' needs. Yet nothing in either the instructional-productivity or centers-of-excellence incentive structures encourages such efforts. One stresses undergraduate instruction, the other research and doctoral work. As one engineering head said:

> Undergraduates must get master's degrees to get jobs. In some years, engineering has more master's degrees than the total university. It is always number two or three. We have relatively few Ph.D. students. The opposite is true in other engineering departments. And the pressure in the college is to be more like them.

At Southwest, another engineering head noted that they are working on a nonthesis master's to attract more students from business, but the dean is pushing for an increase in undergraduate numbers. This same head noted that, ironically, small-class size had attracted students in the past: "We're small. So freshmen and seniors get to know each other and are often working side by side. It's a really good atmosphere. And that attracts students. They like the treatment they get. It's very personalized."

The central incentive structures are not aligned with professional and market realities in engineering. The pull of the workplace and the push of market competitors in engineering is to develop professional, nonthesis master's degrees. Yet the university incentive structure emphasizes increased undergraduate student credit hours and/or doctoral work and research.

What is counterproductive in engineering schools is also counterproductive in social science and science departments. At East Coast and Southwest universities, I came across departments that were quite productive in their master's work, in credit hours, quality, and service to the community.

Yet these departments were not being rewarded. Indeed, the pressure was on them to move away from this work. As one social science head at East Coast University lamented:

> We offer a master's degree. I think it is more efficient than the doctorate. There is discussion about master's degrees at the university. But they don't have standing. Everyone knows that they're efficient. But they're not in the strategic plan. We have a 90% employment rate. But there are no resources for it. No teaching assistants. No fellowships. No thanks from anyone. . . . The university wants to be raised in the National Academy rankings. To do that you have to have a doctoral program.

Similarly, in talking about master's level and continuing professional education, a science head at East Coast said, "This is something the university has tried to do on the cheap, to respond to political pressure. So there is no real administrative support for it." Likewise, at Southwest University, a department head in science noted his department's considerable success in its clinical work—forming partnerships with the community and placing students at a high rate. However, there is no incentive in his college or in the university to expand this successful program.

> Sure, there's less reward for such students than for doctoral students. We get less student aid. . . . We could fill our master's program four times over and not compromise quality in terms of the students. But we cannot get even one faculty line from our dean. He said, "If you got two clinical supervisors, could you double the number of master's students? And they would pay full tuition." They want us to double our student numbers with no increase in regular faculty, in a unit that is already understaffed.

The reward structure at both the university and college levels favors doctoral over masters' programs, for they are the route to enhanced national prestige.

At Midwest and Northwest universities, the situation was slightly different but equally problematic. There, due to an incentive structure focused on undergraduates and to competition over general education students, most of the curricular action was focused on undergraduates. If a few departments were developing applied masters' programs, it had nothing to do with central strategic initiatives. Central managers were largely bound by traditional categories (graduate versus undergraduate), blinding them to new opportunities.

Managerial Myopia: Means Displacing Ends

The extent of the missed opportunities in the universities that I studied reflects the narrowly and conventionally defined goals targeted by central managers and deans. What is striking at each of the universities is the undistinguished and unstrategic nature of the ends that were identified in central initiatives. It appeared from the interviews with department heads that the lion's share of campus deliberations involved debating and developing the means, not the ends. The ends were in some sense givens—increased student credit-hour production and national research standing—imposed by such external constituencies as state legislatures, boards, or the national academic marketplace. Hardly novel goals.

The goals embedded in the incentive structures do not offer any distinctive future for the institutions. Nor do they build on the distinctive positions of the institutions. Incentive structures at Midwest and Northwest emphasizing credit hour production were not particular in any way to the futures or pasts of those institutions and regions. So, too, with East Coast and Southwest's research standing focus. It is as if these settings were interchangeable, as if there was nothing distinctive about their settings or pasts. Are the opportunities available to an east coast institution the same as those available to an institution in the northwest or the southwest border? Are the opportunities of institutions in large urban settings no different than those in rural or small city settings?

The incentive structures of the four universities that I studied had no specific content embedded within them. Producing more credit hours in political science was apparently no more or less desirable than producing more credit hours in computer science. Increasing the national standing of geology was apparently no more or less desirable than increasing the standing of psychology. These one-size-fits-all incentive systems avoided context and content, the distinctive configuration of historical strengths, and future opportunities in the university's academic work as it related to the physical, cultural, and economic regions in which it operated.

Not only are the central initiatives at the institutions I studied undistinguished, they are also unstrategic. The emphasis on student credit-hour production mistakes the critical strategic issue, which is enrollments and graduation rates, not credit hours. The key point is to increase an institution's market share of students and to enhance the efficiency with which these students move through to graduation, not to redistribute college/departmental shares of credit hours within the institution. Productivity in the latter sense would not address legislators' and regents' efficiency concerns about graduation rates and time to completion, or their accountability concerns about faculty workload and contact with undergraduates. Similarly, the strategy of picking a few winners in research mistakes the key strategic issue, which is to create a critical mass of units that can, as a collectivity, advance the scholarly work and reputation of a wide range of units and thus of the university. Identifying and supporting a few existing winners, and relegating most units to the status of losers, with no attention directed to the interactive effects among units, would likely not enhance the overall research standing of the university. The top universities are not prestigious in only a few fields. Highly ranked universities are known for being strong in various related areas.

The central initiatives are also unstrategic in terms of positioning the institution for future changes in their environments. Midwest and Northwest universities, like many public research universities, face significant competitive challenges for students at the undergraduate, master's, and doctoral levels. Different challenges confront the institutions at the different degree levels. At the undergraduate level, it may be liberal arts colleges and community colleges. At the master's level, it may be proprietary institutions that are taking away continuing professional education students in education, nursing, and business. At the doctoral level, it may be other Research I's competing for the top students. A strategic initiative would differentiate among these educational levels and challenges. It would build on the university's strengths in some particular fields and target future areas of growth to establish a market niche in which it has a competitive advantage.

Much the same criticism attends the efforts of East Coast and Southwest universities in the area of research. The research economy of higher education is changing. In an increasingly interdisciplinary professional world, reputational rankings in a few relatively traditional, discipline-based fields is likely to be less important than before. In a world increasingly emphasizing revenue generation and interaction with the private sector, such rankings are even less meaningful. A strategic initiative would build on the university's historic strengths, targeting areas of opportunity and working to establish a market niche in which it has competitive advantage.

In sum, by focusing on the irrational, politicized nature of planning and budgeting, the prevailing mythology encourages managers to rationalize planning and budgeting according to a linear process. Such a path has its own embedded irrationalities. One of the most ironic irrationalities is the displacement of means by ends. In the rush to rationality, too little time has been devoted to rationale. What are the distinctive purposes and goals of the university, given its current locale and historical context? Not all myopia is academic.

What Are Some Principles for Doing It Right?

In concluding, I answer my rephrasing of the department head's question. Given the problematic myths of no change without managerial initiative, managers focus fragmented academic units and loyalties, and managers rationalizing planning and budgeting, what are some principles for doing it right? How can central managers help contribute to growth in their universities by facilitating, supporting, and encouraging constructive strategic activity in academic units toward key institutional goals? In this section, I also develop implications for higher education scholars, for the myths are central not only to professional practitioners but also to higher education scholarship. In challenging them, I am suggesting that we should rethink the language, analytical focus, and questions that drive our studies of strategic activity in public research universities.

In regard to the first myth—that change does not occur without managerial initiative—managers must resist the external pressure and internal temptation to act as "white knights." Higher education is often portrayed as a feudal institution that is resistant to change; the solution is conceptualized in feudal and business language—"white knights," heroic individuals who turn the enterprise around and get it moving. We expect too much of new presidents, provosts, and deans. In turn, they take too much on themselves. Managers are expected to take the lead, to set the course. To a considerable extent, that is how they are evaluated, especially in "hard times." This image can blind managers to the fact that the organization may already be experiencing ongoing change and adaptation.

I would suggest the following principle: *Managers should not try to be knightly crusaders but rather insightful observers, facilitators, and persuaders.* The primary task at hand is not to convert or conquer the infidels; it is to recognize the initiatives already being undertaken by many units, to support them, and to seed strategic efforts elsewhere through selective and gentle persuasion. The key is to recognize and build on the ability of others to get it right. Much is written about how managers must earn the trust of the faculty. Such discourse still centers the managers. I think instead that the key is for managers to trust the faculty, to see them as a resource more than as a problem and obstacle to change, and to recognize that, in complex and multi-varied ways, units are changing to address new political, economic, cultural, and professional realities.

Such a perspective suggests that, as scholars, we need to rethink our language, analytical focus, and questions about initiative in strategic activity. That means reconceptualizing what we mean by "leaders," who we think of as "leaders," and where we look for them. Leaders are not simply those who are "in charge" and who "take charge," and "manage" change. Given what we know about the limits of managerial control in higher education, research needs to focus more on how practitioners observe, facilitate, and persuade. Moreover, research needs to concentrate on leaders at various organizational levels and on informal leaders. Further, initiative and leadership comes not only from individuals but from groups and social movements, on and off campus.

The alternative perspective I suggest means building on an organizational understanding that units within the institution are connected to various external constituencies and environments without the mediation or intervention of central institutional managers. We know that, in business, different divisions of an enterprise face different environments and adapt independently. So, too, do colleges and universities. Different departments face different challenges that higher education scholars need to systematically explore. To what extent do changes in accreditation impact curricular initiatives? What strategic efforts do academic units pursue in relation to changing funding patterns? Rather than bemoaning the academy's feudal character, scholars need to recognize that capitalism has arrived in the academy. We need language, analyses, and questions that are relevant and sensitive to the current political and economic context of higher education.

In regard to the myth that managers must focus fragmented academic units and loyalties, I suggest instead that managers must reorient their thinking about the structure of influence and resistance in the university and widen their focus to include administration. Confronted with myriad faculty and departments, central managers orient themselves based on an oversight about where the threats to focus lie. Seeing the university as a collection of fragmented fiefdoms overseen by individual faculty and by departments, central managers try to bring coherence to these units, ensuring that they are working in a common, direction. Yet central managers do too little by way of ensuring *managerial* focus. Focused on academic fragmentation, they overlook managerial fragmentation.

I would suggest the following principle: *remember the Magna Carta.* My invocation of a feudal negotiation between the central monarch and the barons reflects again the prevalence of metaphors drawn from this period in identifying the problem. Academics are portrayed as "barons" working to protect their "fiefdoms." But our operationalization of the feudal hierarchy to higher education is wrong. Faculty are not barons with extensive castles, lands, wealth, and armies. Rather, they are the artisans who work in various academic "guilds" in the cities. It is the deans who are the barons. The Magna Carta is also known as the Article of the Barons. Under threat of revolt from the barons (due in part to increased taxation related to the previous king's crusade), King John granted a charter of liberties significantly curtailing the monarch's powers. The lesson? Presidents and provosts must work toward coherence among various branches and levels of administrators. Buy-in must come not only from academic guilds (faculty), but from barons (deans), as well as the administration's court(iers), and titled leaders (vice-presidents). The key to successful strategic activity lies partly in recognizing the realities of managerial diversity, influence, resistance, and balance of power.

Such a perspective on practice suggests that as scholars we need to rethink our language, analytical focus, and questions about focus in strategic activity. That means directing attention to management, not just to individual managers, to the administration of academic colleges, not just to central administration. Studies of administrative teams (Bensimon & Neuman, 1993) offer one example of how to analyze interactions among central administrators. Scholarship needs to concentrate as much on the actual behaviors and connections among administrators as on a formal delineation of their roles as individuals. In addition, given the investment of universities in support/administrative tasks and activities (nearly half of all professional employees), and the increasing involvement of such units and individuals in processing and producing teaching and research (e.g., through distance education and other uses of instructional technology, and through nonfaculty personnel in labs and technology transfer), we need studies of nonacademic units' organization and productivity. And the analysis needs to extend beyond central administrators to academic deans as members of a class of middle administrators that as a collectivity (e.g., in deans' councils) profoundly shape universities' ability to shift and pursue strategic priorities.

The existing literature is too grounded in an industrial model of managers and employers. Presuming an ongoing feud and struggle between faculty and administration, it decries the control of universities by academic barons who have little interest in the common good. Based on a model that separates managers' supervisory activities from workers' production activities, existing literature largely overlooks administrators in favor of a focus on production workers (the faculty). We have much research on the preferences and productivity of academics, and very few studies of the behaviors and productivity of administrative/support employees. An industrial model of controlling and focusing faculty is inadequate and inappropriate for professional, postindustrial universities—organizations in which most employees are not academics and in which boundaries between production and support are not as clear as they are in industrial enterprises. Our language needs to fit the current professional and political economic context of higher education.

In regard to the third myth—that managers rationalize planning and budgeting—managers must avoid trying to objectively rationalize and standardize what is a complex, interdependent system. What is truly *ir*rational in a large university is to believe that central managers know enough to construct and apply criteria that will apply uniformly across the board to all units.

> A university with many colleges and other program units probably does not have enough centralized intelligence (or information) to impose some standardized strategy on, say, an engineering school, a school of nursing, and a department of Slavic languages simultaneously. (Leslie, 1996, p. 105)

What is also *ir*rational is to focus the institution's academic units in such a way that they are all following the same path. Finally, what is *ir*rational in an institution focused on knowledge creation is to sacrifice the individual pursuit and interpretation of meaning and purpose on the altar of a monolithic incentive structure that is insensitive to the particular substantive content and historical/social context of the institution's academic work.

I would suggest the following principle: *remember the Renaissance*. The Renaissance unleashed the enormous creative potential of human beings, dismantling monopolies on what can be studied, on what is right or valuable, encouraging the pursuit of knowledge through experimentation and reevaluation. The Renaissance saw a pursuit not only of scientific knowledge but also of art. Managers must recognize that the richness of their universities, like the richness of the Renaissance, lies in the future unfolding of knowledge and possibilities in ways that they (and we) cannot understand.

The current threat to universities is not diversity but homogeneity. Rather than seeking to routinize faculty and units on a single path, driven by a standardized incentive structure, managers should search for ways to encourage and reward experimentation, creativity, and excellence of various forms along various paths. Current right-sizing is enforcing narrow conceptions of higher education's work and purpose—quantitative productivity, revenue generation, and contributing to business and industry's economic growth (not necessarily to communities' economic health). Too often, deliberations about means—how to enhance flexibility—displace full discussion of the ends. The key to successful strategic activity is not to rationalize according to measures of short-term productivity but to ensure ongoing consideration of new opportunities, to reevaluate present strategies and activities, and to promote thoughtful elaboration and clarification of organizational purposes and of the gap between them and organizational practices (Birnbaum, 1999).

Such a perspective on practice suggests that as scholars we need to rethink our language, analytical focus, and questions about rationalizing strategic activity. That means directing attention to the diverse arenas that affect how we conceptualize strategic activity. Where do our rationales for reengineering come from? (Birnbaum, 2000) To answer this question, we need to study leaders as groups, and in terms of their connections to external groups of leaders, such as business. Presidents, provosts, and deans meet with other academic managers and with business leaders in various settings. Higher education scholars need to explore the social construction of the beliefs that drive efforts to rationalize and restructure universities.

In addition, we need to attend to strategic activity at various organizational levels. My interviews with heads revealed a remarkable range in terms of strategic activity. Some heads were quite astute in working with colleagues to position their units for the future; others were pining for the good old days; and some, like deer in headlights, saw the oncoming challenges but were paralyzed. It is at this level that much adaptation takes place. In this context, it is more rational to have many units experimenting with many strategies than to try to move the institution in a particular direction. Over-rationalizing is futile. There is a need to foster consciousness-raising, so that all may act strategically. Again, this is a postindustrial model of community vs. an industrial, corporate model of changing the culture from the center.

As we move into a new millennium, it may seem odd to look back to medieval metaphors and to the renaissance. Yet the university is a combination of feudal and renaissance forms. And there are enduring truths about universities, change without crusades, internal divisions within seemingly centralized structures, and the limits of rationalizing a dynamic, creative enterprise. I am not promoting a hands-off return to the power of the academic guilds. However, to do it right involves not only engineering metaphors of design and *how* to do it, but social metaphors of community and consciousness-raising about *what* to do. The goal should not be developing a strategic plan and reengineering the university with algorithms and rational incentive structures to ensure that everyone works to the same design; rather, it should be to encourage and contribute to an ongoing conversation that raises faculty's consciousness about what they are (and are not) doing and what possibilities exist. Such a dynamic creates a community in which strategic thinking and activity take the institution in various and unanticipated directions.

In closing, I want to offer a metaphor to capture and encapsulize the points I am making. My example stems from an exchange in a central strategic planning committee that is advisory to the provost. At one early morning meeting, the provost was presenting some thoughts about why it was necessary to sweep resources into central administration, which would then coordinate reinvestments in units based on various strategic criteria, thereby ensuring a more rational allocation that would enable the institution to move in a more focused direction, despite the narrow interests of intransigent academic units. Normally given to military metaphors, in this case the provost invoked an example from music: "It's like a symphony. The conductor has to call the shots, ensure that everybody is on the same page, playing the right notes. Otherwise it sounds horrible." I replied, "You have a curious notion of classical music, not one that resonates with the creativity and individuality of solos and interpretation. More than that though, you've got the wrong metaphor. A university is more a jam session of jazz musicians." I invoked jazz because of its taste for independence, autonomy, and improvisation.

The university is not a symphony (except in its demographics). It is not playing one piece of music at a time. It does not perform in one building. It does not only (re)interpret scripted scores. And presidents or provosts are not like conductors. They do not start the music—it is already playing when they arrive and continues after they depart. They do not know all the instruments and how they are played. More than that, they should not want to script the pieces even if that were possible. The creativity and dynamism of a university derives from the energy and independence of its players. Universities should promote independent creativity and jamming more than scripting and adherence to central managers' score and interpretations. We need more leaders who: (a) appreciate the music of different units and understand the ongoing changes of and movements within that music, (b) facilitate and support units in getting together, and (c) help persuade musicians to play to existing strengths and to develop new ones. That is how to do it right: rethink the myths and the language of strategic activity.

Note

1. The larger study randomly sampled physical science, life science, math and computer science, social science, and engineering departments at 11 public research universities that had most consistently reported objective data on three factors (student credit hours, sponsored project revenues, and allocations of state monies) to the American Association of Universities Data Exchange. Within the randomly sampled units, we interviewed the department head and three randomly sampled track faculty. We focused on public research universities (because they have received most of the public criticism about teaching and research) and on science and engineering units (because of the funding agency's particular interest). The interviews with 133 department heads focused on entrepreneurial activities and initiatives within the department, changes in teaching load, factors in promotion and tenure, and central administrative initiatives and incentive structures. The interviews with 414 faculty addressed many of these questions and analyzed faculty time allocation.

References

Bennis, W. G. (1989). *Why leaders can't lead: The unconscious conspiracy continues.* San Francisco: Jossey-Bass.

Bennis, W. G., & Nanus, B. (1985). *Leaders: The strategies for taking charge.* New York: Harper and Row.

Bensimon, E. M., & Neumann, A. (1993). *Redesigning collegiate leadership: Teams and teamwork in higher education.* Baltimore. MD: Johns Hopkins University Press.

Birnbaum, R. (1988). *How colleges work: The cybernetics of academic organization and leadership.* San Francisco: Jossey-Bass.

Birnbaum, R. (1992). Will you love me in December as you do in May?: Why experienced college presidents lose faculty support. *Journal of Higher Education, 63*(1), 1–25.

Birnbaum, R. (1999). Academic leadership at the millennium: Politics or porcelain? *Academe, 85*(3), 14–19.

Birnbaum, R. (2000). The life cycle of academic management fads. *Journal of Higher Education, 71*(1), 1–17.

Clark, B. R. (1987). *Academic life: Small worlds, different worlds.* Princeton, NJ: Carnegie Foundation for the Advancement of Teaching.

Clark, B. R. (1998). *Creating entrepreneurial universities: Organizational pathways of transformation.* Oxford: Pergamon Press, for the International Association of Universities Press.

Etzkowitz, H. (1983). Entrepreneurial scientists and entrepreneurial universities in American academic science. *Minerva, 21,* 198–233.

Fairweather, J. (1996). *Faculty work and the public trust.* Boston: Allyn and Bacon.

Geiger, R. (1993). *Research and relevant knowledge: American research universities since World War II.* New York: Oxford University Press.

Julius, D. J., Baldridge, J. V., & Pfeffer, J. (1999). A memo from Machiavelli. *Journal of Higher Education, 70*(2), 113–133.

Keller, G. (1983). *Academic strategy: The management revolution in higher education.* Baltimore, MD: Johns Hopkins University Press.

Leslie, D.W. (1996). "Strategic governance": The wrong question? *Review of Higher Education, 20*(1), 101–112.

Leslie, D. W., & Fretwell, E. K., Jr. (1996). *Wise moves in hard times: Creating and managing resilient colleges and universities.* San Francisco: Jossey-Bass.

Leslie, L. L., Rhoades, G., & Oaxaca, R. (1999). *Effects of changing revenue patterns on public research universities.* A Report to the National Science Foundation, Grant Number 9628325.

Martin, J., & J. E. Samels. (1997). *First among equals: The role of the chief academic officer.* Baltimore, MD: Johns Hopkins University Press.

Massy, W. F., & Zemsky, R. (1994). Faculty discretionary time: Departments and the academic "ratchet." *Journal of Higher Education, 65*(1), 1–22.

Mech, T. (1997). The managerial roles of chief academic officers. *Journal of Higher Education, 68*(3), 282–298.

Meindl, J. R., Ehrlich, S. B., & Dukerich, J. M. The romance of leadership. *Administrative Science Quarterly, 30*(1), 78–102.

Rhoades, G. (1993). Retrenchment clauses in faculty union contracts: Faculty rights and administrative discretion. *Journal of Higher Education, 64*(3), 312–347.

Rhoades, G. (1995). Rising administrative costs in instructional units. *Thought and Action, 11*(1), 7–24.

Rhoades, G. (1998). Reviewing and rethinking administrative costs. In J. C. Smart (Ed.), *Higher education: Handbook of theory and research* (Vol. 13, pp. 111–147). New York: Agathon Press.

Rhoades, G., & Slaughter, S. (1997). Academic capitalism, managed professionals, and supply-side higher education. *Social Text, 51 15*(2), 9–38.

Slaughter, S., & Leslie, L. (1997). *Academic capitalism: Politics, policies, and the entrepreneurial university.* Baltimore, MD: Johns Hopkins University Press.

Trow, M. (1984). The analysis of status. In Burton R. Clark (Ed.), *Perspectives on higher education* (pp. 132–164). Los Angeles: University of California Press.

Part VIII

Bureaucracies and Behavior

THE NATURE OF ADMINISTRATIVE BEHAVIOR IN HIGHER EDUCATION[1]

DAVID D. DILL

The rapid growth of American higher education after World War II produced several outputs in large measure. In addition to the largest number of faculty members and students in the world, a significant volume of research and a vast and growing literature on the enterprise itself resulted. A sizable portion of the literature on higher education has addressed a still amorphous area usually referred to as higher education administration. The intent of this review is to focus on a particular slice of that literature: the research on administrative behavior.

The focus of the review was prompted by three important publications that appeared over a two-year period. In 1974, Peterson published the only extant review of the research literature on the organization and administration of higher education.[2] As his review made clear, the large volume of research as of 1974 addressed colleges and universities as organizations—their goals and purposes, organizational climate, institutional decision making, governance structures, patterns of influence, and processes of conflict, innovation, participation, and change. Peterson also identified and reviewed a growing literature on planning and management techniques in higher education. In contrast, empirical studies on administrative behavior or on what administrators in these settings actually did were rare, and Peterson identified this as a particular weakness of the literature at the time.

In the same year, March presented a classic but generally unknown address on educational administration.[3] In it, March argued that the training of higher education administrators should be based on knowledge of the context of education. This knowledge should ideally include the nature of educational organizations as well as what educational managers actually do. As March pointed out, a persistent difficulty with attempts to improve administrative effectiveness has been that efforts in that direction are often unrelated to the ordinary organization and conduct of administrative life. Unless one begins with some appreciation of what administrators do and why they organize their lives the way they do, such efforts are unlikely to improve administrative performance.

In the prior year, Mintzberg's landmark book, *The Nature of Managerial Work*, was published.[4] Mintzberg's original investigations as well as his codification of existing research revealed consistent patterns in managerial work. These patterns were at variance with existing models of administrative behavior that tended to emphasize the rational processes of planning, organizing, and controlling. Subsequent research by Kurke and Aldrich,[5] Kotter,[6] and Lau and his associates[7] has generally supported Mintzberg's findings. Taken as a whole, this research raised the question of whether or not the successful implementation of technologies and processes advocated for contemporary managers was seriously compromised by a failure to understand the nature of managerial work itself.

Following the lead of these three publications, this review will focus on the state of knowledge on administrative behavior in institutions of higher education.

Method

A review of research represents a fundamental activity in the behavioral sciences, but the methods, techniques, and procedures for conducting such reviews are sometimes ambiguous or unstated.[8] As a result, it is quite likely that two people conducting a similar review may arrive at substantially different conclusions. This variation may be due to the questions asked, the methods of selecting material, the form the analysis takes, and/or to unstated biases that shape each of the above. In sum, reviews of research are subject to the same sources of error as traditional research studies.

The review that follows is an integrative review, that is, a review "inferring generalizations about substantive issues from a set of studies directly bearing on those issues."[9] To increase the potential value of the review, several strategies were employed. First, the basic organization of the review was derived from a framework that is reliably grounded in the nature of managerial work. Second, some care was taken in selecting the material for the review. A computerized search was conducted of both the *Social Sciences Citation Index* and *ERIC*. The key words utilized were: "administrative behavior," "management," "leadership," "higher education," "college," and "university." Citations were collected for the period of 1974 (i.e., the date of the last such review by Peterson) through September 1983. This yielded 345 references. In addition, a separate review was made of the best known research journals in the field. These journals were: the *Educational Administration Quarterly, Higher Education, Journal of Higher Education, Research in Higher Education*, and *The Review of Higher Education*. This resulted in an additional 50 references. Each of these was reviewed to determine those articles that presented the results of empirical research, and 30 more references were identified. To these were added a number of articles and book chapters reporting research that was known to be relevant by the author but that had not been uncovered in the keyword search.

It is at this point that substantial bias can enter into a review. Therefore, one important control is for the author to state his or her own bias(es). The writer's own views of management and academic organizations have been heavily influenced by the writings of Clark,[10] March,[11] and Mintzberg.[12] As a result, personal knowledge of references in the field was likely to over-represent literature on subjects such as "ambiguity," "culture," "influence," and "political models," as well as research pertinent to the categories of Mintzberg's framework. In contrast, literature addressing "rational" analyses and techniques were apt to be underrepresented. Furthermore, although the techniques of decision analysis, cost-benefit analysis, and MBO may, if implemented, lead to improvements in academic management, the empirical research supporting the utility of such models for managerial work is scant in the writer's judgment. Finally, the author's knowledge of material relating to research universities is greater than for other types of institutions. Having stated these biases, it is incumbent on the writer to attend to contradictory research evidence in the articles reviewed.

An additional control employed in this review was the means of presenting and analyzing the results of the primary materials.[13] Because the variety of research methodologies and approaches employed in the field of higher education administration and management compromise the additive results of different studies, the present review will attend principally to general trends in research results as well as to issues related to methodology.

Finally, this discussion of method must conclude with an important *caveat*. The plan for selecting material for the review has limitations which may affect the results. In addition to the title keyword search, subject key words or key words reflecting the organizing or analytical framework employed in the review could have been pursued. Furthermore, dissertations and books could have been included along with journal articles. The decision to restrict the search and material considered was mandated by limitations of time and funds. One implication of the procedure used is that the review over-represents research published in traditional research journals. As such, the research results may under-represent new directions in inquiry not yet evident in published sources. However, it can be assumed that the review is representative of the accrued knowledge in the field to date.

Analytical Framework

The concept of "administrative behavior" refers to the behavior of those within the boundaries of organizations who occupy administrative positions.[14] Traditionally the research in this area has focused on leadership traits and patterns of individual or group decision making. The literature has also included normative prescriptions for the managerial activities of planning, coordinating, and controlling that have been based on little if any research. Because classical perspectives on administrative behavior have been supplanted by more recent observational approaches, the general managerial skill framework of Katz[15] will be linked with the empirically derived categories of Mintzberg[16] as a means of organizing and presenting the research analyzed in this review. Katz has argued that successful managers exhibit three categories of skills: human relations skills, conceptual skills, and technical skills. Anderson[17] has suggested that linking these categories with the behavior exhibited by the executives observed by Mintzberg provides greater insight to the understanding of managerial behavior (see Figure 1).

By human relations skills, Katz means those interpersonal skills that are applied when a manager relates to superiors, peers, and subordinates. They are thereby relevant to every managerial level. In terms of Mintzberg's research, human relations skills include: (1) peer-related behavior such as developing contacts in the organization, maintaining information networks, and negotiating and communicating with peers; (2) leadership behavior that relates to dealing effectively with subordinates; and (3) conflict resolution behavior.

Conceptual skills relate to the manager's ability to think through the coordination and integration of the organization's diverse activities, what in contemporary terms is thought of as "strategic thinking." Mintzberg discovered five types of behavior that may be categorized as conceptual skills: (1) information processing behavior or the monitoring of one's networks for obtaining information, extracting and assimilating information, and communicating the "pictures" the manager develops; (2) decision making in unstructured and ambiguous situations; (3) resource allocation behavior or the allocation of the organization's critical assets (i.e., time, money, and skill) among competing demands; (4) entrepreneurial behavior that relates to discovering problems and opportunities for which "improvement projects" will be initiated; and (5) introspective behavior that relates to the manager's understanding of the job, sensitivity to his or her personal impact, and learning from these insights.

By technical skill Katz means two things: first, the technique or expertise of "management" (e.g., knowledge of budgeting and accounting), and second, the professional expertise or skill that the individual practiced prior to becoming a manager. In the case of the academic manager, professional

Katz	Mintzberg
Human Relations Skills	Peer-related Behavior Leadership Behavior Conflict-resolution Behavior
Conceptual Skills	Information-related Behavior Decision-making Behavior Resource Allocation Behavior Entrepreneurial Behavior Introspective Behavior
Technical Skills	Profession-related Behavior

Source: Adapted from K. Anderson, *Management: Skills, Functions, and Organizational Performance* (Dubuque, IA: W.C. Brown, 1984).

Figure 1   Framework for administrative behavior based upon Katz and Mintzberg (1973, 1974).

expertise is equivalent to academic expertise, that is, knowledge of a disciplinary field as well as acknowledged capabilities in teaching and research. Because several of Mintzberg's categories of observed management behavior (e.g., conflict resolution behavior, decision-making behavior, and resource allocation behavior) are relevant to Katz's first meaning of technical skill, technical skill in this review will be limited to a discussion of the relevance of the aspect of this skill area referred to as professional expertise. Both Katz and Mintzberg argue that professional expertise becomes less relevant as one moves up the managerial hierarchy and assumes responsibility for a broader range of activities. However, a distinctive aspect of academic management is the attempts of faculty members to sustain their professional expertise by teaching and conducting research while occupying administrative positions. Thus, the relationship of technical academic skills to managerial behavior is of special interest in higher education administration.

There is no assumption here that the research on administrative behavior in higher education will be evenly distributed among these various categories or that the results within each category will be unequivocal. Some categories will probably contain no research at all, and further, some material may well logically be placed in more than one of the classification categories. Nevertheless, by organizing the review in this fashion, the state of knowledge regarding what administrators in higher education do can be codified and implications for practice and research can be more effectively drawn.

Knowledge concerning the allocation of administrative time and patterns of communication is an important contribution of the research of Mintzberg and others who study managerial work. This review will begin with the related research on academic administrators as an introduction. In the sections of the review that follow, the published research will be reviewed in terms of the above categorization of administrative behavior. Put another way, what little is known about how administrators in higher education distribute their time will be discussed first. Then the skills and behavior associated with the categories of human relations skills, conceptual skills, and professional technical skills will be explored in turn.

Managerial Time in Academia

Mintzberg's study of five managers of large organizations concluded that the managers performed a great deal of work at an unrelenting pace; that managerial work was characterized by variety, fragmentation, and brevity; and that managerial work was conducted essentially in a verbal medium. Related analyses of the time allocations of college presidents and deans or department heads have reached similar conclusions about academic managerial work.

Cohen and March in a national survey of college presidents discovered that these executives worked an average of 60 hours a week.[18] This compared with 55 hours of weekly work for the average dean or department head in Lewis and Dahl's small sample study done at the University of Minnesota.[19] As Cohen and March have pointed out, such an average work week is consistent with reported work schedules of academics generally, and it is at the high end of the scales in terms of studies of managers in other fields.

Cohen and March's data on university presidents were comparable in other ways to those on general managers. For example, the presidents spent proportionally similar amounts of time around their office (approximately 30%), in the vicinity of the university (approximately 60%), and out of town (approximately 22%) as did the executives in Mintzberg's study. University presidents were also similar to the executives in terms of their distribution of contact time with other parties. Approximately one-third of their contact time was with those outside the organization, less than 10% was with trustees, and over 50% was with subordinates (i.e., students, faculty, and administrators). Although the university presidents came in contact with a wide variety of people, more time was spent by them with fellow administrators than with any other single group.

University presidents, department heads or deans, and managers from other fields are also alike in that they spend approximately 25% of their time alone, but over 40% of their time in meetings, usually with two or more people. Similarly, management in all settings is a reactive job. Further, the majority of meetings that all these managers attend is initiated by others.

The studies of academic managers reveal some interesting variations and similarities in role both by institution and administrative level. For example, presidents of large universities are more likely to be alone, in town, and spending time with "academic" administrators and dealing with people in groups. In contrast, deans and department heads reported only 45% of their time in administrative work. (The sample in the Lewis and Dahl study contained more department heads than deans.) Approximately 9% of their time was reported in the area of research, 16% in teaching, and over 20% in university service. Lewis and Dahl also reported that the administrators indicated greatest stress came from their administrative duties and that the greatest stress reducer would be increasing the number of hours each week voluntarily devoted to management. This is consistent with the survey results of Weisbord, Lawrence, and Chains of academics in a large medical complex who perceived the functions of research, teaching, patient care, and departmental administration as essentially conflicting functions.[20]

In summary, academic administrators lead a busy, reactive life in which they heavily utilize their verbal skills, particularly in meetings. Observed variations exist as a result of differences in role between full-time administrators (e.g., presidents) and part-time administrators (e.g., department heads). How academic managers apportion their time and contacts is of interest, but what do they actually do? That is, what are their characteristic administrative behaviors? In the following sections, the available research will be discussed according to the framework established for this review.

Human Relations Skill

There is high level of agreement in the literature on administrative behavior that human relations or interpersonal skills are critical to the role of manager, particularly as one moves up the hierarchy of an organization. Mintzberg clarified those skills by focusing on peer-related behavior that deals with the manager's behavior in entering into and effectively maintaining peer or horizontal relationships. Leadership behavior, on the other hand, was conceived by Mintzberg (and many others as well) as the vertical relationships between managers and their subordinates. In this sense, leadership addresses the interpersonal processes of motivation, training, helping, and dealing with issues of authority and dependence. Conflict resolution behavior was described as attempting to mediate between conflicting individuals and decisions or handling disturbances.

Peer-Related Behavior

Cohen and March reported that the amount of time spent by university presidents on peer-related behavior was substantial. Over a third of their time was spent with outsiders and nearly 30% was spent with constituents (trustees, students, and faculty members) who were not direct subordinates. (Cohen and March also quoted very comparable data from a study conducted in New York State that included community college presidents.)

The large amount of external contact suggests that high level administrators become more distinct and isolated. Lunsford has argued: "The growth in size and importance of universities, together with increasing specialization, has sharpened the separation of administrators from the rest of university life. Their authority is consequently mixed and precarious."[21] In his ethnographic study at the University of California at Berkeley, Lunsford observed that certain core values or beliefs reinforced this isolation and made it a more significant problem for academic managers than for their industrial counterparts. These core values were beliefs in the esoteric quality of specialized research, in academic freedom, in "collegial" decision making, and in the separation of powers between academic and non-academic decisions. Whitson and Hubert in a national study of department chairmen in large public universities confirmed that decision-making authority was perceived to reflect a separation of powers.[22] Department heads reported primary influence or greater influence than all other groups or individuals in personnel decisions, faculty selection and evaluation, salary decisions, dismissal and nonreappointment of faculty, and administration of the budget. Faculty were reported as having had primary influence in student admissions' policy, departmental academic standards, and the selection and recruitment of graduate students. Department heads and faculty had equal influence in tenure and promotion issues. Lunsford further suggested that academic beliefs in conjunction with the impacts of institutional growth and increased administrative accountability have led to the isolation of high-level administrators. The specialization of administrative tasks, the nature of associations (less with faculty and students, and more with trustees, alumni, and legislators), the visibility and prestige of executive status, and the unwelcome burden of conveying bad news have led in Lunsford's analysis to a separate administrative culture, one distinct and alien.

As a consequence of this separation, Lunsford observes that managers must spend time building channels of communication and support. This involves seeking opportunities for frequent, informal communication with internal constituents such as faculty and students (for example, through teaching a class as a means of staying in touch or using task forces composed of faculty members to address administratively defined problems). Another such possible means is through the use of special assistants drawn from the faculty at large. Stringer, in a study within a large public university, found these "colleague" special assistants to be the most influential of all "assistant-to" types.[23] The relationships of these assistants to executives was what Stringer termed, "collegial": that is, they participated in all major policy discussions and had frequent informal contacts with the executives. As Stringer pointed out, this type of staff role is unique to higher education.

The earlier analysis of administrator time devoted to peer contacts and this modest research suggests that peer-related behavior is both a significant part of an academic manager's job and, given the potential for isolation, a potentially critical component of behavior. However, little work has been done on the means managers use to develop and maintain their networks of contacts. Also lacking is knowledge about how academic managers negotiate with peers for needed resources or how they consult effectively with the many colleagues and experts that they must utilize.

Leadership Behavior

Cohen and March reported that contact with direct subordinates, such as members of the president's staff as well as academic and non-academic administrators, occupied the largest single block of the university president's time. There is also some evidence that this time is perceived as important to administrative success and satisfaction. Peterson asked four-year college presidents in public midwestern colleges to identify incidents critical to their success.[24] Staffing problems and subordinate ineffectiveness (i.e., subordinate incompetence in decision making or handling a problem that still necessitated presidential intervention) were mentioned by both new and experienced presidents as the major constraint on their productivity. Solmon and Tierney in a national study of administrative job satisfaction in higher education discovered that a great emphasis on authority relationships between leaders and subordinates was negatively correlated with satisfaction.[25] In contrast, when interpersonal behaviors were emphasized, satisfaction increased. Given the apparent importance of leadership behavior, how do higher education managers act in these kinds of situations?

A number of studies have been conducted with department chairpersons. Hoyt and Spangler, using a sample drawn from four diverse universities, studied the relationship between department chairperson management emphases and rated performance of the chair by the faculty.[26] Personnel management—faculty recruitment; allocating faculty responsibilities; stimulating research scholarship and teaching; maintaining faculty morale; and fostering faculty development—represented six of the nine positive relationships in this regard. Coltrin and Glueck,[27] and Glueck and Thorp[28] reported analyses of data collected from research-oriented departments at the University of Missouri. These studies revealed that a leadership style emphasizing ethical behavior, helpfulness in research projects, accurate and complete communication, frequency of communication, and a willingness to represent the interests of the staff was positively associated with faculty satisfaction with the department head in all departments. There was also some evidence that keeping track of research activities in progress through discussion rather than formal report was also positively related to faculty satisfaction. In contrast, attempts to restrict the selection of projects by researchers was negatively associated with faculty satisfaction. When given a choice of leader roles, faculty members consistently preferred the leader as a "resource person/coordinator." That is, they ideally saw the administrator as a "facilitator" or one who smoothed out problems and sought to provide the resources necessary for the research activities of faculty members. Researchers' perceptions of department heads' attempts to reward them were also positively associated with both satisfaction and effort (i.e., reported hours worked). However, there was no observed direct relationship between leader style and faculty publications, although a later reanalysis led Coltrin and Glueck to question whether an "ideal style" was or was not department independent.

This issue has also been raised in a number of related studies. Neumann and Boris found support that highly ranked paradigmatic departments (e.g., physics and chemistry) were characterized by task-oriented leaders, while lesser ranked paradigmatic departments and highly ranked preparadigmatic departments (e.g., sociology and political science) were both characterized by task and people-oriented department heads.[29] Similarly, Groner used the Group Atmosphere Scale of Fiedler to measure the quality of leader-member relations.[30] He found that the quality of department head-faculty member relations was positively associated with feelings of control over the destiny of the department. But, in both the community college and the university settings, leader-member relations also correlated positively with the amount of task clarity in the department (i.e., extent to which the department was paradigmatic). More specifically, in the university setting there was a strong negative relationship between the heterogeneity of faculty research interests and department head-faculty member relationships.

One traditional argument about the role of department chair is that it is a marginal position in which the chairperson is presented with conflicting demands from above to be a manager and from below to be an academic colleague. Carroll[31] applied the Kahn et al. model for studying role conflict with a sample of department heads from Florida universities.[32] He reported that intersender conflict, a situation in which the focal person perceives incompatible expectations from individuals having influence on his or her position, was most commonly reported and was negatively associated with chairperson satisfaction. As Carroll noted, intersender conflict appears to stem primarily from hierarchical relationships of superiors and subordinates.

Two studies, one within a single university and the other a survey of physical education departments, utilized the Leadership Behavior Description Questionnaire to study department heads. Madron, Craig, and Mendel found that high consideration by the department head was related to departmental morale.[33] They also found a negative relationship between morale and department size suggesting that departmental size may serve as a constraint on leadership style. Milner, King, and Pizzini discovered no significant difference between male and female department heads in their perceptions of ideal leadership qualities or in their rating of their actual qualities.[34] In contrast, faculty members in the departments reacted differently to the department head depending on their sex. Faculty members of both sexes tended to perceive heads of the same sex as more considerate.

When viewed from the perspective of research on leadership generally, the studies reported above offer at best modest insights. However, within this review, leadership behavior has been defined consistent with Mintzberg's emphasis as relational behavior between leaders and subordinates. Viewed from this perspective, the studies indicate the potential contribution that the quality of leader-subordinate relationships has for the morale and satisfaction of *both* parties. As well, the research gives some indication that the nature of leader-subordinate relations may vary by department size, type of department, and the sex match of leaders and followers. Nonetheless, it is unclear whether the findings about the leadership behavior of department chairpersons is generalizable to other levels of the academic hierarchy. What is clear from such studies, given their limitations, is that there is a need to investigate leadership behavior in the higher education context and to study the leadership of administrators at all levels of the organizational hierarchy. Uniquenesses and potentially substantial complexities argue for the need for carefully conducted studies that account for a variety of variables and control for known sources of variation. Conversely, the tendency to continue to rely on correlational research methods in leadership studies can be questioned in terms of the insights they will yield into the practice of leadership.

Conflict Resolution Behavior

Only two studies were found that directly addressed managerial mediation and disturbance-handling behavior. Hobbs focused on the management of academic disputes utilizing a critical incident methodology.[35] The disputes studied included those involving academic administrators, faculty, nonfaculty professionals, and ancillary personnel as well as community versus institutional personnel. In all categories, disputes were held sub rosa; they were avoided or muted whenever possible. The nature of disputes varied, however, among the constituencies. Non-professional personnel tended to have conflicts of interest, and faculty and administrators more often engaged in value conflicts. Administrative disputes were generally settled through compromise or resignation after due consideration of the tactical or sometimes strategic value of compromise. Compromising behavior was less characteristic of conflict resolution involving the other groups. Hobbs inferred that compromise was more endemic to the role of administrators—it was seen as more familiar and legitimate. Administrators also often assumed the third party role in disturbances involving other parties. They seldom served in the role of the mediator but, rather, as the intervenor—intruding into events after crises, adjudicating issues in question, and establishing parameters for future interactions. Intervention was most typical in disputes among ancillary personnel. In these cases, administrators imposed new arrangements in order to terminate controversy. With non-faculty professionals, administrators attempted to optimize the needs of both parties while observing institutional priorities. From the sides of the disputants, however, such interventions were usually perceived as one more aspect of the conflict. The specific tactics of administrative intervention employed depended on astute timing and the use of the substance of the administrator's own participation. "I learned from watching (another third party administrator) when to act and when not to. At times he'd listen, at times he'd cajole and at times he'd question. But sometimes he'd say, 'stop; that's it; go no further.' And things would stop."[36] In contrast to this prevalent use of a personal style of intervention, Hobbs found little evidence of the use of quasi-legal practices such as grievance committees.

Some support for Hobbs' research comes from Weisbord, Lawrence, and Chains' study of conflict management practices in academic medical centers.[37] They found that bargaining or splitting differences in an attempt to maximize one's own interest was the preferred mode for resolving conflicts between departments as well as between faculty and administrators. Smoothing or letting people discuss issues in which differences existed without dealing with substantive issues was the second most preferred method of resolving conflict. Weisbord, Lawrence, and Chains suggested that these results contrasted dramatically with the industrial setting where confronting and forcing or where using power plays were identified as the major means of conflict management.

The research on conflict-resolution behavior is quite modest. Available research on peer-related behavior, leadership behavior, and conflict-resolution behavior in higher education partially confirms Mintzberg's research. Such behaviors are part of the managerial repertoire, and they are important components of overall managerial skill. The nature of behavior in this skill area is partially obscured by the researchers' tendencies to ignore it and by the tendency of some to fragment it through methodological reductionism. This problem was graphically revealed in the contrast of the rich insights on disturbance-handling behavior in Hobbs' research with the more limited observations on administrative behavior provided in other reported studies.

Conceptual Skills

Conceptual skills include the manager's capacity to collect and use different types of information for decision making in ambiguous situations. These decisions often entail allocating resources (e.g., money, space, and the manager's time). Mintzberg has provided additional insight into this area by his discovery that conceptual skills also involve the manager's capacity for identifying opportunities for change and gaining insight into the managerial role itself. Essentially these are the cognitive and creative behaviors of managers.

Information-Related Behavior

Fenker developed a questionnaire for evaluating administrators that he distributed among the faculty and staff of a single university[38] A factor analysis of the responses yielded four factors, one of which was an information/communication factor. Components of this factor included the accumulation of pertinent information before acting and communicating important information. Although information is important, Lunsford observed that it often comes from unconventional sources.[39] The hierarchical separation of academic administrators means they have restricted associations. Therefore, they place a premium on "political" information and informal knowledge of constituent attitudes as well as their academic knowledge based on past faculty experience. In contrast, the everyday knowledge of operating information for administrators is variable. Astin and Christian studied the variance between administrators' everyday knowledge of basic institutional information and the "actual" data.[40] The study, which was conducted in liberal arts colleges, resulted in the finding that there was an average error of between 6 and 8% among all administrators on data about student enrollment, faculty size, and finances or budgets. Directors of development had the greatest error and academic administrators the least. Presidents were most accurate on student-related data, least accurate on faculty data, and consistently overestimated revenues—what Astin and Christian characterized as "wishful thinking." Administrators use their political information and experience, Lunsford has argued, to explain and define the institution with "socially integrating myths."[41] These broad abstractions help to hold a loosely coordinated institution together and provide members a sense of mission. Patrick and Caruthers in a national survey of college and university presidents provided some support for Lunsford's ethnographic insights.[42] The presidents perceived communicating institutional strengths to internal constituencies, trustees, and the public as a major current focus. There was almost universal agreement among the presidents, however, that data and analytical reports were of low priority. Adams, Kellogg, and Schroeder discovered that when administrators provided information to guide operational decision making, it was often limited.[43] That is, at most it included a due date, guidelines for a report format, and individual or group responsibilities. Rarely were administrators precise about the types of final output needed or about assumptions, constraints, or implementation issues. In sum, while information is deemed critical to administrators, the sources and uses of information appear somewhat unconventional when viewed in the light of the recommendations of traditional management texts.

Administrative behavior in relationship to management, especially computer-based, information systems, has received particular attention in the research literature. Wyatt and Zeckhauser conducted in-depth interviews at six different sized institutions including both public and private universities.[44] The attitudes of administrators toward quantitative data and management reports appeared to be a function of individual background, discipline, and prior experience. Size of institution[45] also seemed positively related to the use of such data. Some individuals with a non-quantitative background tended to hold a "technological mystique" and were unrealistic about the kind of improvements that were possible with improved management information. Management information systems that were in use were often manual, idiosyncratic, and ad hoc—the information was in an individual's head and the procedures were unwritten. Centralized information systems were criticized for being too late, being too hard to decipher, or lacking critical data. Baldridge in a comparable study of liberal arts colleges observed that reports contained too much "junk" (or unfocused data).[46] If administrators had to stop and translate raw data, it was perceived as slowing down the decision-making process. Baldridge also discovered that, to the extent data were used, their major value was in facilitating "hot spot" analyses—the data highlighted or made more obvious those issues previously neglected. Wyatt and Zeckhauser concluded that the difficulties with using existing information systems led to three typical administrative responses.[47] The first was to use data that were available on the spur of the moment, the second was to use interpreters who understood and could translate existing information, and the third was to create parochial or local level information systems.

Research on particular types of quantitative information has resulted in similar conclusions.[48] Large amounts of data are often available, but they are used principally for operating purposes and for outside reporting. The management applications of the information (e.g., for establishing recruitment costs per student admitted) are minimal, and relevant management analytical techniques (e.g., long-term cash budgeting) are rarely utilized. In concluding, Adams, Kellogg, and Schroeder argued that these results were due overwhelmingly to utilization rather than to availability factors.[49]

Feldman and March have provided insight into the information-related behavior of academic managers.[50] Consistent with the research just reviewed they observed that academic administrators appear to value information that has no great decision relevance—they gather information and do not use it, they ask for reports and do not read them, and they act first and ask for information later. Feldman and March suggested that this behavior can be understood as a function of belief, that is, a general academic commitment to reason and rational discourse as well as to a decision theory perspective on the nature of life. As a result, displaying the use of information symbolizes a commitment to rational choice and signals personal and organizational competence. This dichotomy between the symbolic and the real may be attributed to the background and training of academic managers as well as to the organizational characteristics of academic institutions. It can also be attributed, as Mintzberg discovered in business organizations, to a general ignorance about the true nature of managerial work among those who design and develop information systems.

Decision-Making Behavior

Research on decision-making behavior falls into three general arenas: the locus or location of decision making, the sources of influence on decision making, and actual decision-making behavior.

In a survey of Canadian community colleges, Heron and Friesen discovered a parallel between structuring and decentralization of decision making.[51] That is, as institutions grew and aged, the size of the administrative component and the use of formal documents in administration increased. But decentralization of decision making also increased in these institutions. This was particularly true when institutional growth was accompanied (as it usually was) by increasing academic specialization. Similarly, Ross, using a national data set found that organizational complexity and certain aspects of administrative apparatus, such as administrative use of the computer and presence of an institutional research office, were positively associated with decentralized decision making.[52] Ross concluded that culture—local traditions, beliefs, and values as influenced by an institution's history—may be a better predictor of the locus of decision making than are structural variables. Studies such as these are helpful in indicating the pitfalls of simplistic or dichotomous thinking about the location of decision making. Put another way, a large administrative structure or a high degree of structuring activity is not necessarily incompatible with decentralization of authority.

In studies of influences on managerial decision making, the type of decision influenced appears to vary with administrative positions.[53] Faculties, department heads, deans, and central level administrators in public universities were perceived as having primary influence on different clusters of decisions although they partially influence one another on many decisions. Demographic factors such as the region of the country, type of field, size, and existence of collective bargaining also affected the pattern of influence within an institution. McLaughlin, Montgomery, and Sullins suggested that the pattern of influence was associated with the decisions made by the chairmen.[54] When faculty were most influential, the chairman's goals were faculty oriented. In contrast, chair-dominated departments were characterized by goals less orientated to faculty development. There has also been limited research on the influence of individual differences on decision making. In a survey of public university administrators in California, Walker and Lawler discovered an association between political orientation, expectations regarding the impact of collective bargaining, and support for implementation of collective bargaining.[55] Strong opposition to collective bargaining was, therefore, partially explained by unfavorable perceptions and political attitudes. Two studies that investigated sex differences, however, suggested that the decision-making behavior of male and female academic administrators was more similar than dissimilar.[56] In sum, level in the hierarchy, distribution of influence, and personal perceptions and attitudes have all been found to relate to decision-making behavior.

In a study of administrators in community colleges, four-year colleges, and one university, Taylor provided one of the few direct studies of decision-making behavior.[57] Utilizing the well known Vroom-Yetton model of decision styles, in the study administrators chose a style of encouraging faculty participation over two-thirds of the time. They also preferred decision styles which protected the "quality" of a decision rather than those that ensured decision acceptance or implementation. Nonetheless, a closer analysis by Taylor revealed little relationship between the nature of the problem and the preferred style of decision making. For example, in those situations where more information was required, where commitment to the decision was critical to success, where non-acceptance could generate high conflict, or where fairness was at issue, the administrators often selected autocratic styles. Taylor's evidence also indicated support for faculty participation was an ideological response among department heads as opposed to an explicitly considered decision-making style. As Lunsford argued, administrators seemed to assume that universities are united by strongly shared and well understood values that provide guidelines for tough decisions.[58] The administrator, therefore, can make decisions as a benevolent representative of the institution. The interests of the institution, like the public interest, are assumed to be equivalent to the interests of all participants and thereby become a basis for choice. As a consequence, academic administrators rely strongly on the myth of consultation as a legitimizing force for their decisions. Taylor's research, when combined with Lunsford's analysis, suggests a potential dichotomy between what is espoused and what is practiced in academic decision making. The gap is likely to vary by institution depending both on institutional history and on the prior socialization of faculty.

Several studies examined decision-making behavior related to substantive areas such as budgeting and program evaluation. Moyer and Kretlow in a national study of vice-presidents of finance in colleges and universities found little use of commonly employed business techniques in program evaluation decisions or in capital investment decisions.[59] Instead of capital evaluation techniques, current demand—usually expressed as demonstrated academic need—was not only the primary, but usually also the exclusive criterion. Adams, Kellogg, and Schroeder in an in-depth study of decision making and information systems at small colleges came to similar conclusions.[60] In faculty position allocations, institutional goal setting, and budgeting, decision making was responsive rather than anticipatory and was characterized by reacting to requests for expansion and setting goals only when demand was great. Again, the technical apparatus which might have been appropriate or supportive of these decision processes was not in evidence. At least well through the 1970s, therefore, decision making continued to be present oriented and subject to both influence and negotiation.

The research on decision-making behavior is not inconsistent with, and to some extent supports, the well known "garbage can" model of decision making developed by Cohen, March, and Olsen.[61] In this model, university decision making frequently does not resolve problems. Choices are more likely to be made in these settings by flight or oversight, and the decisions made are apt to be among those of intermediate importance rather than of most or least importance. The matching of problems, choices, and decision makers is partly determined by problem content, problem relevance, and the competence of the decision maker. However, decision choices are sensitive to timing, the current catalog of problems, and the overall load on the system. For example, Cohen and March suggested that decision-making style was apt to vary by institutional size and wealth as well as by changes in organizational slack or the relative availability of financial resources.[62] The research on decision making just reviewed, provides detailed insight into the dynamics of the garbage can model. The possible effects of demographic factors, influence, personality, beliefs, and technology are suggested, and the tendency toward decision making by flight and oversight is quite apparent.

Resource-Allocation Behavior

Mintzberg characterized resource allocation behavior as involving the allocation of all resources—the manager's time, the delegation of responsibility, and the allocation of financial resources. As discussed previously in the section on time-related behavior, academic administrators are similar to managers generally in the amount of their time that they allocate to different constituencies, activities, and media. That is, academic administrators allocate their largest block of work time to other administrators (peers and subordinates), to meetings and committee work, and to the verbal medium, particularly telephone conversations and informal discussions. Contact with faculty and students, and solitary work (and, by inference, reading and analytical activity) receive less time. Of particular importance is the fact that academic managers are largely responsive to the demands of others in allocating their time. The most distinctive characteristic of time allocation, particularly at the departmental level, is the high allocation of time to academic work (averaging between 45–50%) as contrasted to managerial or administrative work. Although this behavior undoubtedly diminishes as one moves up the administrative hierarchy, the continued allocation of time to academic work helps to explain much of the dissatisfaction and stress in academic administration as well as the frequent observation that academic institutions are undermanaged.[63] It also seems to influence the behavior of subordinates. Glueck and Thorp reported a negative relationship between perceived amount of time department heads spend on their own research and faculty satisfaction with the administrator.[64]

There was no direct research evidence on delegation behavior, although the previously discussed research on the decentralization of decision making and the use or non-use of participative decision making by department heads could be viewed from this perspective. There has, however, been substantial research on the allocation of financial resources. In a national sample of college presidents, Patrick and Caruthers discovered that fiscal resource allocation and reallocation were among the two highest current priorities for change.[65] Moyer and Kretlow reported that facilities allocations were usually based on presidential "wish lists." Although institutional standards for space needs had been developed, no institution in their study had assigned facilities costs to programs or used discounting methods of cost/revenue matching techniques.[66] Similarly, Adams, Kellogg, and Schroeder found little use of class size and teaching load standards or unit costs in the allocation of faculty positions and discretionary budgets.[67]

A series of related studies have suggested that administrators base their resource allocations on perceptions of influence and power. The results of the studies, all conducted in major research universities, reveal that universalistic criteria such as workload or numbers of students are less powerful predictors of the allocation of faculty slots and discretionary funds than are various measures of subunit power.[68] In the most recent test of this model, it was discovered that the state of paradigm development of a unit increases its power since high paradigm units are more likely to receive outside funds.[69] High paradigm departments also possess greater consensus and, therefore, act as a stronger coalition in fights for internal resources.[70] Power, operationalized as the ability to attract grants and contracts as well as student enrollments, was thus inferred to be a de facto administrative criterion for the allocation of scarce resources. Finally, power was a more important criterion during periods of resource scarcity, suggesting that attempts to develop more universalistic criteria for allocation decisions during retrenchment may run counter to normal managerial behavior.[71]

Of particular interest in the research on resource allocation behavior is the tendency toward present-oriented responsiveness to other's demands, the relative lack of independent criteria or values on which to base resource allocation decisions, and the avoidance by administrators of management technology or expertise as inputs to resource allocation decision processes.

Entrepreneurial Behavior

Mintzberg's concept of entrepreneurial behavior is metaphorically similar to the process of project management. Managers search their organizations for problems or opportunities for change and then initiate improvement projects to address them. Some of these projects are supervised personally, such as a study of the age distribution of faculty, and others are delegated by the manager to staff members while retaining responsibility for review and quality control. Implicit in Mintzberg's analysis are two critical assumptions: (1) that the manager is constantly involved in developing and implementing improvement projects and is juggling a number of such projects at any one time; and (2) that, like R and D projects, many improvement projects fail or lead to no implementable result. These insights derived from the observation of managers at work have a face validity for those who have been involved in academic management. Patrick and Caruthers in their national survey reported that college presidents identified with certain managerial change priorities and placed greater importance on developing procedures for managerial change than on reports and data analysis of results.[72] However, the research analyzed for this review does not directly address entrepreneurial behavior. In part, this may be due to a methodological or conceptual bias in which organizational change has been interpreted as a response to changes in the external environment.[73] For example, Manns and March discovered a measurable relationship between changes in resource availability and departmental curricula change at Stanford University, but because of the methods and variables selected, no insight was provided about how this process was managed at the departmental level.[74] Similarly, Salancik, Staw, and Pondy studied the relationship between external change and department chair turnover, and they concluded that the largest amount of turnover was explained by factors associated with organization and context, and was not directly affected by the individual capacities or characteristics of administrators (although these characteristics and capacities were not measured and, therefore, could not be controlled in the study).[75] Mintzberg's interpretation of the manager as a change agent also conflicts with the prevailing model of organizational development which advocates an external change agent.[76] A possible result of such methodological and theoretical biases, therefore, is a relative lack of knowledge about the means by which academic managers act in an entrepreneurial manner to bring about change in their organizations. The implications of this will be explored below.

Introspective Behavior

Mintzberg suggested that managers need the capacity to thoroughly understand their jobs, that they should be sensitive to their own impact on their organizations, and that they should have the ability to learn by introspection. Argyris developed a model of organizational learning, based in part on research with academic administrators, that takes a similar position to that taken by Mintzberg.[77] Argyris advocates that academic professionals need the capacity to take technical actions and, simultaneously, to reflect on their practice. This in effect double-loop learning will become even more critical in the future, Argyris believes, because the management dilemmas that will be encountered will require examination of both current values and underlying policies. Argyris therefore advocates double loop learning as a theoretical basis for professional and executive education.

Academic managers, of course, are not by and large professionally trained in management. Further, research continually suggests that professionals learn little from seminars and continuing professional education opportunities; instead, they are most influenced by learning that takes place in conjunction with the job itself. What would be of most value for the higher education setting would be research on effective patterns of learning and introspective behavior of academic managers in the context of their work. Regrettably, such research does not appear to have been conducted. Lewis and Dahl's research suggested that academic administrators at the department head and dean levels either deny, resist, or do not fully comprehend the obligations of their administrative duties.[78] The greatest amount of stress was induced for these administrators because they appeared to resist allocating sufficient time to administrative demands. This suggests that accurate knowledge of the job, of the current demands of the job, and of their own preferences was inadequate. McLaughlin, Montgomery, and Sullins discovered a relationship between a chairperson's perception of who has influence and his or her own professional goals.[79] If these administrators perceived themselves in control or as making the major decisions, they characteristically spent more time in guiding the growth and development of the department as well as its personnel and programs, and had a greater desire to continue in administration. In contrast, if they perceived control to be above them, they typically spent more time in working with students, in doing liaison work, and in activities with expected return to the faculty. Similarly, Solmon and Tierney found that institutional reward systems that were perceived to foster acceptance of authority created less job satisfaction for administrators because they created a sense that the job was not challenging, that the administrator had little autonomy in decision making, and that the job had little variety.[80] Although this research can be related to the issue of introspective behavior, it is insufficiently illuminating because it does not provide any insight into the nature of the behavior itself.

Technical Skills: Profession-Related Behavior

Mintzberg suggested that managerial behavior can be separated from profession-related behavior in that the manager makes the transition from technical activity such as teaching and research to managerial activity. However, in the academic environment, this transition is rarely completed. Most academic administrators, in fact, continue to engage in academic responsibilities. The allocation of time between profession-related and administrative activities and its relationship to administrative stress and satisfaction has already been addressed. A more fundamental question involves the relationship between academic skill or background and interpersonal behavior, conceptual behavior, and overall management success. For example, research in a related setting—R and D organizations—suggests that scientific expertise is an important predictor of managerial effectiveness.[81] The results from anecdotal evidence in recent publications on computer modelling provide an indication that the disciplinary background of senior academic administrators can be of primary importance in influencing the successful implementation of contemporary planning and management techniques.[82] It is worth noting that, although a number of the research studies reported here identify discipline or field as a variable with implications for faculty behavior, departmental leadership style, and centralized allocation behavior, no study directly examined the relationship between the technical and professional skills of administrators and administrative behavior.[83] This seems odd, because there is well validated research on substantive differences in behavior among faculty members from different disciplines.[84] Such studies suggest that the relationship between technical skill or background and administrative behavior could be a fruitful and particularly important component of research in higher education administration and would have practical implications for management selection, training, and development.

Discussion

In the sections above, the available research over the last ten years on administrative behavior in higher education has been analyzed utilizing the combined conceptual frameworks of Katz and Mintzberg. In this section some broader issues will be explored including the author's possible bias, methodological issues of research in this area, and implications for future research.

The available research on higher education suggests that the use and allocation of time among academic administrators is not untypical of managers generally. Academic managers: (1) perform a great quantity of work at a continual pace; (2) carry out activities characterized by variety, fragmentation, and brevity; (3) prefer issues that are current, specific, and ad hoc; (4) demonstrate a preference for verbal media (telephone calls, meetings, and brief discussions); and (5) develop informal information systems. Unlike their management counterparts in other organizations, academic managers are apt to sustain substantial academic technical activity while in their managerial roles. They are also, particularly department heads and deans, less likely to be comfortable with full-time administrative responsibilities. Both interpersonal skill and what Katz terms conceptual skill play an important part in academic managerial work. Research on interpersonal skills has been addressed somewhat in terms of leadership skills. Given the organizational structure and belief systems of academic organizations, the development of horizontal peer networks for information and influence could, however, be more important to academic administrators than to other managers. Unfortunately, there has been little definitive research on this topic. Similarly, conflict negotiation and dispute settlement deserve more attention, and Hobbs has suggested some fruitful leads in this regard.[85] In the category of conceptual behavior, substantial attention has been given to information-processing, decision-making, and resource allocation behavior, but relatively little is known about the entrepreneurial and introspective behavior of academic managers. Since the management of change is routinely advocated as the role of the administrator, the apparent paucity of research on how academic administrators *actually manage* change is somewhat surprising.

The writer began this review effort with a certain bias—that is, that academic management is an ambiguous process highly dependent on flows of influence and power, and subject to the beliefs and values of the academic culture. If anything, this bias has been strengthened by the analysis of available research. First, it is apparent that informal influence, negotiations, and networks of contacts are important aspects of academic administration as it is currently practiced. Second, the results of research on information-related behavior, decision making, and resource allocation provide some indication that academic management is still highly intuitive, tends to avoid the use of quantitative data or available management technology, and is subject to the political influence of various powerful groups and interests. Third, the traditions, beliefs, and values of individuals, disciplines, and institutions appear to play a more substantial role than is generally acknowledged in the extant prescriptive literature on management. In short, the garbage can model of decision making and the institutional context of organized anarchy as articulated by March and his colleagues receives much support from the available research on administrative behavior.

Nevertheless, it is wise to be cautious about these generalizations. Although the models of ambiguity and influence may better fit the available data than do the highly rational models, current understandings are based on historical evidence. Furthermore, the contextual environment which obviously influences the development of current patterns of administrative behavior is currently changing, perhaps dramatically. Those studies that have sampled administrative behavior over time provide evidence of differing patterns of managerial behavior under various environmental circumstances. For example, Cohen, March, and Olsen's simulation of the garbage can model predicted modification of administrative decision-making behavior (i.e., organizational learning) over time and as organizational slack was reduced.[86] In other words, it is important to maintain a constant willingness to test models and biases against current empirical data.

In sum, available research, not surprisingly, prompts the notion that a better understanding of administrative behavior is critical to improved management: (1) for example, sophisticated information systems that are planned without sufficient attention to the needs and working habits of academic administrators appear to make little (immediate) impact; (2) further, since human beings need and seek meaning, an important part of academic administration involves the creation and maintenance of academic beliefs;[87] and finally, (3) interpersonal relationships and skills are an important part of management in organizations that depend for their effectiveness on the talent of autonomous, creative, and often "spikey" individuals. It is reasonable to assume that managerial behavior in academic organizations may change in response to new conditions. However, the understanding of that process is most apt to occur through research on the relationships between administrative behavior, technology, and structure.

The methodologies of studies reviewed deserve special attention. In the first place, sampling strategies vary substantially. Some studies are focused on single institutions and the elite, research institutions are over-represented in this respect. Other studies have surveyed particular clusters of institutions such as private liberal arts colleges, public universities, or community colleges. Overall, research seems to be heavily focused on larger research universities and published studies of administrative behavior in small or community colleges are far less common. While available information on the focus and source of data for each study was included in the analysis above, specificity in this regard was often difficult to ascertain. One of the consistently reliable findings of research in this area is that institutions of higher education vary in organization and management by type and level of institution.[88] The research reviewed here confirms that institutional type, level, region, size, and culture can all contribute to variance in administrative behavior. It is reasonable, of course, to argue that the study of a single case can provide a model suitable for testing in later studies. March and Pfeffer, and their colleagues, have demonstrated the value of this approach. However, among the research studies reviewed for this article, more than half seem to be unaware of the obvious weaknesses in terms of their focus and sampling procedures, or of the relevant research on institutional types. Future research on administrative behavior in higher education needs to give significantly greater attention to measuring and controlling for variance between types of institutions.

A second major issue relates to the conceptual frameworks employed in some of the studies. Studies tend to employ a psychological model that reduces behavior to the study of relationships between variables relevant to the psychological models used, or they employ a sociological unit of analysis which tends to bypass individual behavior altogether. There are, of course, fundamentally important reasons for such selectivity. The psychological approach places emphasis on precision of measurement and the potential for prediction, often with some penalty in overall understanding. The sociological logic has been well expressed by March.[89] Throughout his work, March has evolved a Tolstoyan perspective on academic administrators that argues that great leadership is unlikely, particularly in organizations of this type. Academic administration, in this view, is an art of small adjustments in which larger and, by inference, slow-moving forces determine the evolution of events. But each of these two perspectives, the psychological and the sociological, limits the understanding of administrative behavior. The framework and precision of the psychological view causes researchers to overlook key interpersonal processes. For example, the means by which administrators build and maintain networks for information and influence were ignored by traditional management researchers until they were emphasized in the observational work of Mintzberg and his followers. Even today, there has been little informative research that suggests the relationships of importance in this domain. Although the sociological point of view provides an appropriate sense of humility toward administrative accomplishment, its results are similarly impoverished in terms of advancing knowledge. If the contribution of management is at the margin through small adjustments and improvements, then how is this accomplished? As the results of research on managers continually indicate, it is a profession of action. Therefore, illuminating the nature of administrative action and its consequences in different settings is apt to be of substantial value to theory and to practice. With the exception of a few of the studies reviewed, there is little insight into administrative behavior in action. This criticism is not a plea for a particular type of methodology but, rather, for a more creative application and interchange between the disciplines and methodologies available to inquirers.

Conclusion

The research on administrative behavior in higher education over the last ten years has helped to fill an important gap that Peterson observed in his 1974 review of the field. While the research is modest in amount and limited in approach, it provides some insight into the nature of managerial work in higher education as well as suggestions for promising directions in both research and practice.

The nature of academic organizations and of administration in these settings highlights the centrality of human behavior, beliefs, and values. Although organizational structure and management technology are very important, studies of those mechanisms and processes in the absence of an understanding of administrative behavior at best make a limited contribution to theory or to practice. Ironically, while the best known research on academic organizations provides a rich understanding of the role of human behavior, culture, and meaning in the development of these institutions (see, for example, the many writings of Burton Clark, James March, David Riesman, and Lawrence Veysey), it is currently the students of business organizations who argue most strongly for an emphasis on entrepreneurship, organizational culture, the development of human assets, and the importance of interpersonal skills.[90]

The intent of this review was to provide an integrative understanding of the current knowledge concerning administrative behavior in higher education. Taking stock at certain periods is a necessary and important part of the ongoing attempts to advance both practice and research. To paraphrase A. N. Whitehead, the scientist does not inquire in order to know, the scientist knows in order to inquire.

David D. Dill is Associate Professor of Education and Assistant to the Chancellor at the University of North Carolina at Chapel Hill.

References

1. The writer would like to acknowledge the help of Peter Cistone, Ralph Kimbrough, James Lemons, Sandra Reed, Jay Smout, John Walker, and two anonymous reviewers in the preparation of this article.
2. M. W. Peterson, "Organization and Administration in Higher Education: Sociological and Socio-Psychological Perspectives," in *Review of Research in Education*, Volume 2, F. N. Kerlinger and J. B. Carroll, eds. (Itasca, Ill.: F. E. Peacock, 1974).

3. J. G. March, "Analytical Skills and University Training of Educational Administrators," *Education and Urban Society* (6,4 (August 1974): 382–427.

4. H. Mintzberg, *The Nature of Managerial Work* (New York: Harper and Row, 1973).

5. L. B. Kurke and H. E. Aldrich, "Mintzberg Was Right!: A Replication and Extension of *The Nature of Managerial Work*" (Paper presented at the Annual Meeting of The Academy of Management, Atlanta, Ga., 1979).

6. J. P. Kotter, *The General Managers* (Glenco, Ill.: The Free Press, 1982).

7. C. M. Pavett and A. W. Lau, "Managerial Roles, Skills, And Effective Performance," *Proceedings of the Forty-Second Annual Meeting of The Academy of Management* (New York: The Academy, 1982).

8. G. B. Jackson, "Methods for Integrative Reviews," *Review of Educational Research* 50, 3 (Fall 1980): 438–460.

9. Ibid., p. 438.

10. Burton Clark's collective work on academic organizations has had a substantial impact on the field. For a useful synthesis of his findings, see B. R. Clark, *The Higher Education System* (Berkeley, Calif.: University of California Press, 1983).

11. M. D. Cohen and J. G. March, *Leadership and Ambiguity: The American College President* (New York: McGraw-Hill, 1973); M. O. Cohen, J. G. March, and J. P. Olsen, "A Garbage Can Model of Organizational Choice," *Administrative Science Quarterly* 17 (March 1972): 1–25; M. S. Feldman and J. G. March, "Information in Organizations as Signal and Symbol," *Administrative Science Quarterly* 26 (1981): 171–186; C. L. Manns and J. C. March, "Financial Adversity, Internal Competition and Curriculum Change in a University," *Administrative Science Quarterly* 23, 4 (1978): 541–552; and J. G. March, "How We Talk and How We Act: Administrative Theory and Administrative Life" (Seventh David D. Henry Lecture in Higher Education, University of Illinois, September, 1980).

12. Mintzberg, *Nature of Managerial Work*.

13. Jackson, "Methods for Integrative Reviews."

14. H. R. Bobbitt and O. C. Behling, "Organizational Behavior: A Review of the Literature," *Journal of Higher Education* 52, 1 (January/February 1981): 29–44.

15. R. L. Katz, "Skills of an Effective Administrator," *Harvard Business Review* (September/October 1974): 90–102.

16. Mintzberg, Nature of Managerial Work.

17. K. Anderson, *Management: Skills, Functions, and Organizational Performance* (Dubuque, Iowa: W. C. Brown Company, 1984).

18. Cohen and March, *Leadership and Ambiguity*.

19. D. R. Lewis and T. Dahl, "Time Management in Higher Education Administration: A Case Study," *Higher Education* 5 (1976): 49–66.

20. M. R. Weisbord, P. R. Lawrence, and M. P. Chains, "Three Dilemmas of Academic Medical Centers," *Journal of Applied Behavioral Sciences* 14, 3 (1978): 284–304.

21. T. F. Lunsford, "Authority and Ideology in the Administered University," in *The State of the University: Authority and Change*, C. E. Kruytbosch and S. L. Messinger, eds. (Beverly Hills, Calif.: Sage Publications, 1970).

22. L. J. Whitson and F. W. R. Hubert, "Interest Groups and The Department Chairperson: The Exertion of Influence in the Large Public University," *Journal of Higher Education* 53, 2 (1982): 163–176.

23. J. Stringer, "The Role of the 'Assistant To' in Higher Education," *Journal of Higher Education* 48, 2 (March/April): 193–201.

24. W. O. Peterson, "Critical Incidents for New and Experienced College and University Presidents," *Research in Higher Education* 3 (1975): 45–50.

25. L. C. Solmon and M. L. Tierney, "Determinants of Job Satisfaction among College Administrators," *Journal of Higher Education* 48, 4 (July/August 1977): 412–431.

26. D. P. Hoyt and R. K. Spangler, "The Measurement of Administrative Effectiveness of the Academic Department Head," *Research in Higher Education* 10, 4 (1979): 291–303.

27. S. Coltrin and W. Glueck, "Effect of Leadership Roles on Satisfaction and Productivity of University-Research Professors," *Academy of Management Journal* 20, 1 (1977): 101–116.

28. W. F. Glueck and C. D. Thorp, "The Role of the Academic Administrator in Research Professors' Satisfaction and Productivity," *Educational Administration Quarterly* 10, 1 (Winter 1974): 72–90.

29. Y. Neumann and S. B. Boris, "Paradigm Development and Leadership Style of University Department Chairmen," *Research in Higher Education* 9 (1978): 291–302.

30. N. E. Groner, "Leadership Situations in Academic Departments: Relations among Measures of Situational Favorableness and Control," *Research in Higher Education* 8 (1978): 125–143.

31. A. B. Carroll, "Role Conflict in Academic Organizations: An Exploratory Examination of the Department Chairman's Experience," *Educational Administration Quarterly* 10, 2 (Spring 1974): 51–64.

32. R. L. Kahn, D. M. Wolfe, R. P. Quinn, J. O. Snoek, and R. A. Rosenthal, *Organizational Stress: Studies in Role Conflict and Ambiguity* (New York: John Wiley, 1964).

33. T. M. Madron, J. R. Craig, and R. M. Mendel, "Departmental Morale as a Function of the Perceived Performance of Department Heads," *Research in Higher Education* 5 (1976): 83–94.

34. E. K. Miner, H. A. King, and E. L. Pizzini, "Relationship Between Sex and Leadership Behavior of Department Heads in Physical Education," *Research in Higher Education* 10, 2 (1979): 113–121.

35. W. C. Hobbs, "The 'Defective Pressure-Cooker' Syndrome," *Journal of Higher Education* 45, 8 (1974): 569–581.

36. Ibid, p. 578.

37. Weisbord, Lawrence and Charns, "Three Dilemmas."

38. R. M. Fenker, "The Evaluation of University Faculty and Administrators: A Case Study," *Journal of Higher Education* 56, 6 (November/December 1975): 665–686.

39. Lunsford, "Authority and Ideology."

40. A. W. Astin and C. E. Christian, "What do Administrators Know about Their Institutions?" *Journal of Higher Education* 49, 4 (July/August 1977): 389–400.

41. Lunsford, "Authority and Ideology."

42. C. Patrick and J. K. Caruthers, "Management Priorities of College Presidents," *Research in Higher Education* 12, 3 (1980): 195–214.

43. C. R. Adams, T. E. Kellogg, and R. C. Schroeder, "Decision-Making and Information Systems in Colleges," *Journal of Higher Education* 47, 1 (January/February 1976): 33–49.

44. J. B. Wyatt and S. Zeckhauser, "University Executives and Management Information: A Tenuous Relationship," *Educational Record* 56, 3 (Summer 1975): 175–189.

45. R. C. Moyer and W. J. Kretlow, "The Resource Allocation Decision in U.S. Colleges and Universities: Practice, Problems and Recommendations," *Higher Education* 7 (1978): 35–46.

46. J. V. Baldridge, "Impact on College Administration: Management Information Systems and Management by Objectives Systems," *Research in Higher Education* 10, 3 (1979): 263–282.

47. Wyatt and Zeckhauser, "University Executives and Management Information."

48. Adams, Kellogg, and Schroeder, "Decision-Making and Information Systems"; and Moyer and Kretlow, "The Resource Allocation Decision."

49. Adams, Kellogg, and Schroeder, "Decision-Making and Information Systems."

50. Feldman and March, "Information Organizations."

51. R. P. Heron and D. Friesen, "Growth and Development of College Administrative Structures," *Research in Higher Education*, Vol. 1 (1973): 333–346.

52. R. D. Ross, "Decentralization of Authority in Colleges and Universities," *Research in Higher Education* 6, 2 (1977): 97–123.

53. G. W. McLaughlin, J. R. Montgomery, and W. R. Sullins, "Roles and Characteristics of Department Chairmen in State Universities as Related to Level of Decision Making," *Research in Higher Education* 6 (1977): 327–341; Whitson and Hubert, "Interest Groups and the Department Chairperson."

54. McLaughlin, Montgomery, and Sullins, "Roles and Characteristics."

55. J. M. Walker and J. D. Lawler, "University Administrators and Faculty Bargaining," *Research in Higher Education* 16, 4 (1982): 353–372.

56. O. Andruskin and N. J. Howes, "Dispelling a Myth: That Stereotypic Attitudes Influence Evaluations of Women as Administrators in Higher Education," *Journal of Higher Education* 51, 5 (1980): 475–496; and Mimer, King, and Pizzini, "Relationship between Sex and Leadership Behavior."

57. A. L. Taylor, "Decision-Process Behaviors of Academic Managers," *Research in Higher Education* 16, 2 (1982): 155–173.

58. Lunsford, "Authority and Ideology."

59. Moyer and Kretlow, "The Resource Allocation Decision."

60. Adams, Kellogg, and Schroeder, "Decision-Making and Information Systems."

61. Cohen, March, and Olsen, "A Garbage Can Model."

62. Cohen and March, *Leadership and Ambiguity*.

63. Adams, Kellogg, and Schroeder, "Decision-Making and Information Systems"; Lewis and Dahl, "Time Management"; and C. W. McLaughlin, J. R. Montgomery, and L. F. Malpass, "Selected Characteristics, Roles, Goals, and Satisfactions of Department Chairmen in State and Land-Grant Institutions," *Research in Higher Education* 3 (1975): 243–259.

64. Glueck and Thorp, "The Role of the Academic Administrator."

65. Patrick and Caruthers, "Management Priorities."
66. Moyer and Kretlow, "The Resource Allocation Decision."
67. Adams, Kellogg, and Schroeder, "Decision-Making and Information Systems."
68. F. S. Hills and T. A. Mahoney, "University Budgets and Organizational Decision Making," *Administrative Science Quarterly* 23, 3 (1978): 454–465; J. Pfeffer and G. R. Salancik, "Organizational Decision Making as a Political Process: The Case of a University Budget," *Administrative Science Quarterly* 19, 2 (1974): 135–151; G. R. Salancik and Jeffrey Pfeffer, "The Bases and Use of Power in Organizational Decision Making: The Case of a University," *Administrative Science Quarterly* 19, 4 (1974): 453–473; and Manns and March, "Financial Adversity."
69. J. Pfeffer and W. L. Moore, "Power in University Budgeting: A Replication and Extension," *Administrative Science Quarterly* 25, 4 (1994): 637–653.
70. Groner, "Leadership Situations"; and Pfeffer and Moore, "Power in University Budgeting."
71. Hills and Mahoney, "University Budgets"; and Pfeffer and Moore, "Power in University Budgeting."
72. Patrick and Caruthers, "Management Priorities."
73. D. Katz and R. L. Kahn, *Social Psychology of Organizations*, 2nd Edition (New York: John Wiley, 1978).
74. Manns and March, "Financial Adversity."
75. G. Salancik, B. Staw, and L. Pondy, "Administrative Turnover as a Response to Unmanaged Organizational Interdependence." *Academy of Management Journal* 23, 3 (1980): 422–437.
76. Bobbitt and Behling, "Organizational Behavior."
77. C. Argyris, "Educating Administrators and Professionals," in *Leadership in the '80s*, C. Argyris and R. M. Cyert (Cambridge, Mass.: Institute for Educational Management/Harvard University, 1980).
78. Lewis and Dahl, "Time Management."
79. McLaughlin, Montgomery, and Sullins, "Roles and Characteristics."
80. Solmon and Tierney, "Determinants of Job Satisfaction."
81. N. Rosen, R. Billings, J. Turney, "The Emergence and Allocation of Leadership Resources Over Time in a Technical Organization," *Academy of Management Journal* 20 (1976): 165–183.
82. D. S. P. Hopkins and W. F. Massey, *Planning Models for Colleges and Universities* (Stanford, Calif.: Stanford University Press, 1981).
83. Coltrin and Glueck, "Effect of Leadership Roles"; Groner, "Leadership Situations"; Neumann and Boris, "Paradigm Development"; Pfeffer and Moore, "Power in University Budgeting"; Salancik, Straw, and Pondy, "Administrative Turnover."
84. J. M. Beyer and T. M. Lodahl, "A Comparative Study of Patterns of Influence," *Administrative Science Quarterly* 21 (1976): 104–129; and A. Biglan, "Relationships Between Subject Matter Characteristics and the Structure and Output of University Departments," *Journal of Applied Psychology* 57, 3 (1973): 204–213.
85. Hobbs, "The Syndrome."
86. Cohen, March, and Olsen, "A Garbage Can Model."
87. D. Dill, "The Management of Academic Culture," *Higher Education* 11, 3 (1982): 303–320.
88. J. V. Baldridge, D. V. Curtis, G. Ecker, and G. L. Riley, *Policy Making and Effective Leadership* (San Francisco: Jossey-Bass, 1978).
89. March, "How We Talk."
90. See, for example, T. E. Deal and A. A. Kennedy, *Corporate Cultures* (Reading, Mass.: Addison-Wesley, 1982); W. G. Ouchi, *Theory Z* (Reading, Mass.: Addison-Wesley, 1981); and T. J. Peters and R. H. Waterman, Jr., *In Search of Excellence* (New York: Harper and Row, 1982).

THE BUREAUCRATISATION OF UNIVERSITIES

ÅSE GORNITZKA, SVEIN KYVIK
AND INGVILD MARHEIM LARSEN

Teaching, research and the dissemination of knowledge are the primary tasks of universities. These activities also have to be administered, both by a professional apparatus and by faculty members themselves. Because large resources are used for administration, it is of substantial interest to examine how these resources are used. Universities themselves, as well as the external society, have questioned whether the administrative component of universities has now become too large. Administrative positions tend to grow faster than others at universities, and faculty spend an increasing part of their time on administrative matters. We refer to these tendencies respectively as administrative and academic bureaucratisation.

First, there is some empirical evidence for the contention that an increasing share of university resources is used for administration, and the number of administrative staff increases relatively more than the number of teaching and research staff. In the United States, administrative costs in universities have risen dramatically in the past two decades, disproportionately more than the costs of instruction and research. For example, at the University of California at Los Angeles, the number of faculty members declined by 7 per cent from 1977 to 1987, while administrative employees increased by 36 per cent. At the Massachusetts Institute of Technology, faculty members increased by 8 per cent from 1981 to 1989, whereas administrative personnel increased by 37 per cent.[1] At the University of California, the estimated increase in expenditure on instruction during a 25-year period was over 175 per cent, while expenditure on administration increased by more than 400 per cent.[2] This development has caused concern—three quarters of institutions in the Association of American Universities report having recently attempted to reduce administrative costs.[3] A relatively larger increase in numbers of administrative staff than in faculty numbers has also been reported in Sweden,[4] Norway[5] and Finland.[6]

Second, it is frequently argued that administrative work takes too much time away from research. A recent international survey conducted by the Carnegie Foundation reports that considerable time is spent on such activities. On average, 15–20 per cent of faculty working hours is spent on administration.[7] A Norwegian study found that 38 per cent of academic staff members assessed administrative work as causing great problems for their opportunities to do research—far fewer complained about a lack of research funding or any other condition that might hamper their research.[8] A Danish study corroborates the latter finding.[9] There is, however, not much empirical evidence that the administrative load for faculty has been increasing. An exception is Great Britain, where survey data show that the proportion of working time spent on administration and management by academic staff increased from 19 to 24 per cent between 1976 and 1989.[10]

Although surveys do not necessarily reveal significant increases in individual time spent on administrative work in the last decade, the large growth in faculty numbers could have led to a decrease in average time per staff member. It might be expected that increased administrative capacity would reduce such work by faculty members because administrative staff to a certain extent can substitute these duties for academics.

Empirical Data from Norwegian Universities

In trying to explain why administrative and academic bureaucratisation take place, we drew on empirical data from Norwegian universities.[11] Although an analysis based on developments in one country cannot be transferred directly to others, the global tendencies in this field seem to be parallel, and we believe the results are to a great extent relevant to other countries.

Statistical data are drawn from the sources for the years 1987 to 1995. The Norwegian civil servants' data register and the research personnel register provide statistics on manpower at universities. The Norwegian civil servants' data register contains salary statistics which give a survey of the number of person-years in higher administrative and office positions of persons who are paid through the basic appropriations of an educational institution. The research personnel register contains data on the number of person-years performed by all academic staff in full-time posts at higher education institutions, including those with stipends and those who are externally funded. Norwegian educational statistics contain data on all students registered at higher education institutions. Data which illuminate academic bureaucratisation are mainly from surveys among all staff members with the rank of assistant professor and higher at Norway's four universities: Bergen, Oslo, Trondheim and Tromsø. These surveys were undertaken by the Norwegian Institute for Studies in Research and Higher Education in 1966, 1970, 1981 and 1991. Staff members were asked to estimate the percentage of time used for various tasks—such as university administration—in the year prior to the questionnaire.

In addition, we interviewed nearly 50 senior administrative and academic staff at the universities of Bergen and Oslo in 1995 and 1996, both faculty in elected leadership positions and administrators at selected university departments from different fields of learning at the two universities. Interviews were also conducted at faculty and central level.

A Conceptual Clarification

Administrative Bureaucratisation

The concept of bureaucratisation usually takes on three different meanings. First, a Weberian bureaucracy, which entails a formal organisation where work is conducted according to formal rules within a hierarchy based on rational-legal authority, and individuals are recruited to fill roles in the organisation based on their formal competence and educational qualifications. This type of rational administration replaces other, usually more traditional, ways of organising work. Second, the everyday use of the term has strong derogatory connotations and bureaucratisation is thought of as "red tape taking over." In many ways the term denotes a situation where the classical virtues of a Weberian bureaucracy have become perverted: rule-following becomes a purpose in its own right, predictability and equal treatment are turned into rigidity, and so on. The third treatment of bureaucratisation depicts the growth of the part of the organisation that does not directly carry out the work but which regulates, supervises and supports those who do. Administrative positions and activities increase more than productive activities and the number of staff involved directly in productive activities.

This third meaning of bureaucratisation is our point of departure. As far as universities are concerned, bureaucratisation in this sense occurs when administration increases more than teaching and research within the institution.[12] There are at least two ways in which this can be measured. Looking at the share of expenses devoted to administrative activities as opposed to "production" activities is one possibility. Our approach, however, is to investigate the number of administrative positions and person-years within universities, as opposed to the number of academic positions and person-years. What then constitutes an administrative position within a university?

Categorising university positions is not easy. The most clear-cut distinction can be drawn between academic positions and "non-academic" staff, but this categorisation is too coarse for our purposes. Types of non-academic positions have to be differentiated so as to single out those whose primary task is university administration. We have excluded technical auxiliary staff, such as laboratory assistants, engineers and university librarians. Likewise, we do not consider maintenance personnel, such as janitors, gardeners and cleaning staff, to be part of university administration. This leaves two basic groups of nonacademic positions: clerical staff and higher administrative staff, the latter being the core administrators at universities ranging from consultants, middle and senior managers. Whether clerical workers should be considered part of the administrative staff is more open for discussion. Blau has argued that they are part of the administrative apparatus at universities: "Whereas clerks in government agencies cannot be considered part of the administrative apparatus, since many of them are line personnel (not staff) and provide basic services such as unemployment services, clerks in universities and colleges are part of the administrative apparatus, furnishing support for and not being themselves engaged in academic work."[13]

Granted that in many instances clerical functions do in fact verge on being administrative activities, we include clerks in the total administrative staff at universities. Nevertheless, we regard administrative officers as the prime constituents of university bureaucracy, and give special attention to how these positions develop at the universities. When these positions grow faster than academic positions, this will be taken as an indication of administrative bureaucratisation of universities.

The Concept of Academic Bureaucratisation

University administration entails many different types of activities for academic staff.[14] Finding a generally valid definition of the concept is not easy. There is, for example, no clear boundary between performing primary work, such as teaching and research, and administering it. Nonetheless, some forms of activity clearly lie within what may be called internal university administration, such as participation in meetings and preparing meetings for university management agencies. The Norwegian Institute for Studies in Research and Higher Education survey used the following definition of administration: "Comprises administrative work, meetings, etc., at the university. Include all administrative work at the university which has not been included in the categories above (i.e. teaching, supervision and research). For example, the time spent on evaluating applications for positions at your own university, evaluating students for admission, replying to minor inquiries, etc."

The questionnaire also contained quite detailed information on the activities that should be regarded as teaching and research: for example, planning of the curriculum and research projects both contain an element of administration. However, it is more appropriate here to include them under teaching and research.

Evaluation of applications for positions at the home institution can be very time-consuming for individuals, and some might consider it as academic work. It is, nonetheless, difficult to include it in categories other than university administration. This is one example of an activity which is neither teaching nor research but which nevertheless cannot be delegated to administrators. A certain administrative load does belong to academic positions at universities. Thus, we regard academic bureaucratisation as an increase in administrative work, as defined above, done by faculty members.

Administrative Bureaucratisation of Norwegian Universities: Main Results

From 1987 to 1995 the number of total administrative positions increased considerably. There were differences in the relative growth rate between total administrative staff and academic staff at the four Norwegian universities (Figure 1). Total administrative staff—i.e., clerical positions and administrative officers and managers—increased by 58 per cent, whereas academic positions increased by 48 per cent. More than anything this period marks the entry of a significant corps of administrative officers and managers. In 1987, 584 person-years were performed by administrative officers and managers at the four universities: eight years later the number had grown to 1,469 person-years. In this respect, the universities undoubtedly underwent a process of bureaucratisation in the

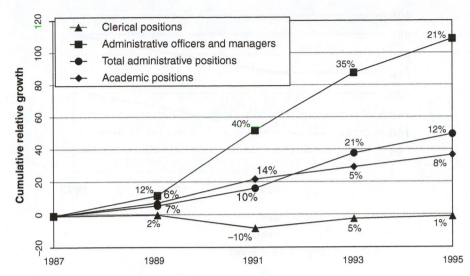

Figure 1   Biannual and cumulative growth in administrative and academic positions, 1987–1995 (percentages).

late 1980s and first half of the 1990s. The extent of growth in the number of administrative officers and managers is unprecedented in the history of Norwegian universities; although such positions have steadily increased since the 1970s,[15] they were hardly known before their introduction in that decade.

A significant shift within the total administrative staff at universities occurred over the same period. The number of clerical positions remained virtually unchanged while at the same time administrative officers and managers increased considerably. In 1991 administrative officers and managers outnumbered clerical positions at the universities. Consequently, university administration no longer consists primarily of secretaries and auxiliary office services, but of professional administrators.

In 1993 half of administrative officers and managers had a university degree. Furthermore, about 15 per cent of the administrative officers and managers had held an academic university position. To some extent there is mobility between the two types of positions. Thus, the bureaucratisation of Norwegian universities also shows the tendency reported in other countries that senior academics become university administrators.[16]

Parallel to the disproportionate growth in the managerial stratum and number of administrative officers, signs of an emerging profession of university administrator have appeared. At an institutional, national and international level there are now associations for university managers and officers with a significant constituency. The replacement of clerks in university administration by administrative officers and managers indicates a "silent managerial revolution" at Norwegian universities.

Within the group of administrative officers and managers, there is a pattern of growth that further underlines the development of a professionalised university administration. Middle management has experienced the highest relative increase during this period, together with senior executive officers. Both groups increased by more than 200 per cent from 1987 to 1995, whereas the number of top managers increased by about 180 per cent. The relative increase in junior executive officers, on the other hand, is the lowest compared to the growth of other administrative officers and managers.

University departments have absorbed the bulk of the new administrative officers and managers (Figure 2). The increase has been considerable at faculty and central levels as well, albeit not as steep as at departmental level.

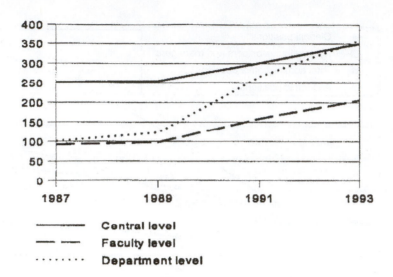

Figure 2 Number of administrative positions at the Universities of Bergen and Oslo by level, 1987–1993.

Academic Bureaucratisation of Norwegian Universities: Main Results

On average, faculty members used 17 per cent of their total working day on university administration in 1991. This is about the same percentage as in 1981 and in 1970, compared to 14 per cent in 1966. Most staff used 10 per cent of their working time for such activities—the same amount of time as the norm set by universities in Norway—but the substantial number with leading administrative positions such as department head, course administrator, head of permanent committees, etc., raises the average figures.

Even though there has been no increase in average time used for administration by tenured faculty during the last 20 years, the total number of person-years used for such activities has increased substantially with the growth of universities. On the basis of the survey data, we estimate that tenured academic staff used 575 person-years for university administration in 1993: 82 more than in 1981. This indicates that although there was a large increase in faculty members, and equally many teachers and researchers to share administrative duties, the contribution to university administration by each academic staff member has not decreased.

Other data support this picture. The proportion of tenured academic staff who were members of boards, councils and committees at their universities (about 75 per cent), and the proportion having leading administrative positions (about 40 per cent) were about the same in 1991 as in 1981.

Three Theoretical Perspectives of Bureaucratisation

Administrative and academic bureaucratisation have occurred in a period of more or less constant growth in the size of universities, and when the social contract between society and universities is being renegotiated. In addition to maintaining their classical role as educational and cultural institutions, universities are required to be more actively concerned with the social and economic needs of society.

These changes are the background for our theoretical approach. With a basis in organisation theory we shall distinguish between three perspectives on bureaucratisation processes. The first is the question of diseconomies of scale: whether the size and growth of institutions have effects on such processes. Within this structural perspective, the size of the administrative component is regarded as a technical question determined by the overall size and complexity of the organisation. Second are external demands and pressure: administrative and academic bureaucratisation are results of state regulations and demands from society. The third question is posed from the perspective of internal processes: this regards administrative growth as a result of internal processes at universities, where both administrative and academic staff support the introduction of new administrative routines and more administrative staff which might relieve them from administrative work.

While the question of whether there are economies or diseconomies of scale in higher education has been investigated in several empirical studies, the relationship between internal and external processes and bureaucratisation of universities has been examined much less. Theories and explanations of such a relationship flourish,[17] but few studies have actually tried to specify the mechanisms that link internal and external factors to growth in university bureaucracy.

These differences in knowledge status between the three perspectives on the bureaucratisation of universities are therefore reflected in the analysis. With regard to the question of economies or diseconomies of scale, we have found it important and fruitful to give an account of former findings before the analysis of the Norwegian data. The lack of solid empirical research within the two other perspectives has, however, made it necessary to go directly from theory to analysis.

Economies or Diseconomies of Scale?

A key question in our analysis of possible bureaucratic tendencies in the universities is whether institutional size is important for the relative extent of administrative costs. This issue has concerned researchers as well as those responsible for forming and changing different kinds of organisations. Two contradictory viewpoints of the matter both build upon theoretical considerations.

The theory of administrative economies of scale states that in large organisations administrative costs will be relatively lower than in small organisations, because size in itself enables the administrative apparatus to be used more efficiently. Another hypothesis states that the larger an organisation is, the more complex it will be, and thus the higher its administrative costs, since complexity itself demands administrative resources. We call this the theory of administrative diseconomies of scale.

Administrative Economies of Scale

The theory of administrative economies of scale has its roots in theories on economies of scale in manufacturing companies. A common assumption is that the unit costs of producing a commodity will sink to an optimal level with increasing quantity; after this level, unit costs of production will increase again. Economic theory of production can be a useful way of looking at other sectors, i.e., higher education, although higher education is publicly financed, does not sell its products, and is not concerned with economic utility or competitiveness.[18]

According to this theory, a large university needs relatively fewer employees in administrative positions than a smaller one because administrative personnel can be used more efficiently in two ways: first, by applying the principle of the division of labour and specialisation to reduce the different types of task that an individual administrator performs. Second, computing systems permit a relatively small number of specialists to handle a large amount of data, so it is now easier to adjust the number of administrative personnel to the structure of the tasks and the volume of work—examples are salary, budgeting and accounting systems. Small universities need special personnel to take care of different special functions, although in consequence their competence will not be fully utilised because the number of similar tasks are too few.

Universities are exceptional organisations due to the great influence the academic staff have in governing and managing the institution. As academic and administrative staff can substitute for each other to some extent in performing administrative tasks, no strong conclusion can be drawn from looking at each separately. The theory of administrative economies of scale can, however, also be applied to analysing academic staff's participation in administrative work. The premise is that the average amount of time used for administration by faculty will decrease with an increase in the size of a university, because more faculty members will be able to share such work and relatively fewer will need to participate in boards, committees, councils and panels.

Administrative Diseconomies of Scale

Large organisations are more complex than smaller ones, and an assumption is that they need relatively more administrative resources than smaller, less complex institutions. Complexity here can mean at least three things: first, horizontal distribution of different special functions. In a university system this will mean a distribution in many departments and centres as well as many administrative units. Second, complexity includes a vertical distribution over different management levels. At universities this includes three or four levels: central administration, faculties, departments and sometimes sections within departments. In addition, research groups often function at an informal level under departments or sections. Third, complex organisations are often spread out geographically, with different units in different places within a particular city.

According to this theory, horizontal, vertical and geographical differentiation will mean that large organisations, in this case universities, need extra administrative resources to keep the institution together. An organisation's different activities must be coordinated and controlled, and the larger the organisation, the more emphasis will be put on these tasks.[19] The need for horizontal and vertical communication in the organisation will increase, which makes demands on both time and resources. The more units an organisation has, the more relationships there will be, and the more time needed to maintain them, e.g., through planning, collecting, preparing and disseminating information, conversations, reporting and meetings. Special personnel will be needed in many of the basic units of an organisation.

Faculty participation in administrative work will, according to the theory of administrative diseconomies of scale, be more extensive in large than in small universities. Increased institutional size with a more complex organisational structure increases the need for the participation of faculty in administering universities, e.g., in boards, councils, committees and panels.

Size and Complexity

According to the theory of administrative economies of scale, costs for administration will decrease relatively in relation to production costs when an organisation becomes larger. This assumption is in sharp contrast to the hypothesis that large, complex institutions need relatively more administrative resources to hold them together.

Size thus has two contradictory effects on the relative extent of the administrative component. Economies of scale will tend to reduce this, while complexity increases it because of the greater need to coordinate activities. These contradictory processes have led to the hypothesis that administrative economies of scale decrease with increasing institutional size.[20] After a certain point, the positive effects of size in a large organisation will gradually vanish. However, as these processes can be concurrent, the net effect could be small.

Blau and Schonherr, and Hall, conclude from their own studies and reviews of previous research that in general the administrative component decreases in size as organisational size increases, but, in very large organisations, the relative size of the administrative component again increases—although not to the level it assumes in small organisations.[21] On the other hand, Pfeffer and Scott maintain that the research literature does not yield such a clear relation between organisational size and administrative costs.[22]

Methodological objections have been raised about some of this literature. Pfeffer points out that it is problematic to draw general conclusions about the relation between organisational size and administrative costs without considering whether the organisation's staff has increased or decreased.[23] Similarly, Brinkman and Leslie report that the time of measuring the possible effects of economies of scale can be decisive for the conclusions reached.[24] If an organisation grows quickly, it can take time to adjust the size of its administration to the new production capacity. Positive effects of administrative economies of scale can gradually lessen or vanish.

Some studies show that administrative economies or diseconomies of scale depend on how the administrative component is made operational. Rushing points out that different groups can be viewed as administrative personnel—for example, senior managers, clerks, office personnel and technical personnel—and that the numbers in the various groups can be influenced by the size of an organisation in different ways.[25] Scott refers to several studies which conclude that the number of administrative leaders declines relatively in relation to increasing size, while the opposite is the case for technical and office personnel.[26]

The relation between size and administrative costs has also been studied within higher education, but here only the relation between the size of the administrative apparatus and expenditure on teaching and research was investigated. These studies lack a crucial element: the time that faculty actually spend on administration. They cannot therefore give a complete picture of the administrative expenditure in large and small institutions.

Blau compared 115 American universities and colleges and concluded that economies of scale are larger than diseconomies of scale.[27] However, he also found that although the relative share of purely administrative positions decreased with the increasing size of institutions, the relative share of office personnel increased. This result, which has also been reported in other earlier studies,[28] raises the question about the extent to which older studies are relevant today. Over the last ten to 20 years, the use of computer technology has reduced the number of traditional office posts. Nevertheless, the need for administrators at universities has increased, partly because the state and society have placed new demands on universities to undertake new tasks, improve documentation of their activities, etc.

Blau's study has been the basis for much of the subsequent research in this field, but more recent studies only partially confirm his findings. A search of the literature covering 60 years of research on possible economies of scale within American higher education concludes that there is a positive relation between institutional size and institutional complexity and administrative costs.[29] A similar study at the University of California both supports and contradicts Blau's conclusions. On the one hand there have been fewer administrators per faculty member at the largest campuses than at the smaller ones at a given period. On the other hand, during the course of a 25-year period, administrative employees have increased relatively more than academic staff at the two largest campuses.

Lane used both time-series data and cross-sectional data to test the theory of administrative economies of scale in Swedish higher education.[30] Between 1969 and 1985 the number of administrative employees, including office personnel, increased at Swedish universities and colleges relatively more than the number of faculty members, while at the same time numbers of students and of employees grew strongly. A comparison of 34 higher education institutions in 1984 indicated a curvilinear relation between size and the number of administrative positions. The relative size of the administrative component was lower the larger the institutions were, but only until an institutional size of approximately 5,000 students. At larger colleges and universities, the relation between administrative and academic personnel was fairly similar, regardless of the number of students.

A more recent Swedish survey documents that expenditure on administration at universities and colleges continues to increase more than resources devoted to research and teaching, and that large institutions have relatively lower administrative costs than small ones, although the ratio is becoming smaller.[31] The Norwegian data were collected from 1987 to 1995: a period when the universities grew dramatically and student numbers almost doubled, and there was also strong growth in academic and administrative personnel. The number of universities is too small to test the theories of economies and diseconomies of scale, but the results corroborate the findings from similar studies in other countries. Large institutions have had lower administrative costs than small institutions, but all universities have over time become more expensive to administer. This result remains valid when controls are done for student numbers.[32]

To what extent does the participation of faculty in administrative work affect these tendencies? At universities with a relatively large share of administrative employees, academic staff might on average reduce their time spent on administration compared with those at universities where support services are less adequate—in other words, where faculty might have to do a larger proportion of administrative work themselves. However, no significant differences were found between universities in our survey of faculty use of time in 1991.

To conclude, most studies indicate that small institutions are relatively more expensive to run than large ones, but also that when universities and colleges get more students and employees, administrative expenditure increases relatively more than expenditure on teaching and research.

How can these apparently contradictory tendencies be explained? One explanation is the different methodological approaches to the problem of size. While analyses of cross-sectional data find that large organisations use relatively fewer resources for administration, time-series analyses show that when organisations grow, administrative costs increase relatively more than expenditure on teaching and research. This tendency is also found in studies of other types of organisations.[33]

On the basis of these results it is reasonable to conclude that growth in itself does not result in higher administrative costs, and that these are generated by other conditions. Clearly, the external and internal processes which might have led to increased administrative costs need analysis.

External Demands and Pressures

Norms of university self-governance run deep in the Norwegian university system. However, universities are constantly interacting with the world beyond and over the last few decades they have been under stronger pressure to satisfy external expectations. The label of "multiversity"[34] is a fitting description of how Norwegian universities have evolved in recent years. A "multiversity" faces increasingly complex and diverse demands and expectations from outside interests. In order to investigate the assumption that changes in universities' relations to their environments cause administrative changes and an ensuing bureaucratisation, it is necessary to discover which parts of the environment induce internal bureaucratisation, and how external pressures and demands are linked to changes in university administration.

Theoretical perspectives drawn from the study of organisations are a helpful way of ordering environmental actors and relations. Research on how organisations are linked and interact with their environment draws on two theoretical traditions: a resource-dependence perspective and an institutional perspective. Both see organisational actions and choices as limited by various external pressures, and responses to such pressures as essential to an organisation's survival and wellbeing.[35] The two traditions highlight different aspects of the organisational environments and mechanisms that link environments to organisations.

Resource-dependence theory emphasises that external actors provide the resources which sustain and develop organisations' activities, and, to secure a flow of resources, organisations meet the needs and demands of those providing the resources.[36] From this perspective, the basic mechanism is exchange: organisations trade their output for external resources, and the focus is on the technical features of organisational environments, i.e., their tasks. When external actors control vital resources they also have power over an organisation. Organisations will and should respond to the parts of their environment that control critical resources because they depend on them. But, in addition, resource-dependence theory attends to how organisations act strategically to manage their dependency.

While resource-dependence theory stresses economic dependency, institutional theory highlights the rules and requirements to which organisations must conform in order to receive legitimacy and support. In general, this perspective has been less concerned with how organisations use strategies to manage their environment.[37] Institutional theory is by no means homogenous. Among the different versions particularly relevant to the study of bureaucratisation are those which focus on regulatory and normative aspects of organisational environments.[38] Some institutionalists see the essence of institutions as residing in the formal rules and regulations that govern interorganisational relations. Their primary focus is on laws and regulations, and the accompanying monitoring and sanctioning that exist between organisations.[39] The basic mechanism is coercion through legal sanctions. The pressures ensuing from state regulations and laws are of special interest in such an approach.

Focusing on the normative aspect of environments draws attention to organisational adaptation, not as a result of either resource dependency or hierarchical pressure, but rather because organisations influence each other when values and definitions of what is appropriate disseminate between them. Meyer and Rowan emphasise the survival value of conformity to institutionalised myths about how organisations should act and look.[40] Conformity can be a way for organisations to obtain legitimacy and support from their surroundings; organisations adopt pre-rationalised structures because they are symbolically efficient. Such myths can take the form of fads and fashions, and here organisations are open to relatively short-term swings in the collective beliefs that communicate improvements to their audience.[41] Organisations often find themselves in uncertain and ambiguous situations and one way to handle them is to conform to current fashions.

A primary mechanism of change under such circumstances is imitation. In particular, organisations with similar goals tend to react in similar ways.[42] Of special interest here is the way they imitate each other in how they are organised and in what they do. Imitation is a factor in university bureaucratisation if universities adopt organisational structures and procedures of leading universities.[43] An example is the attempt to copy offices of technology transfer at successful institutions like the Massachusetts Institute of Technology, Stanford University and the University of Cambridge.

These theoretical perspectives lead to the question of whether internal administrative growth at universities is the consequence of state regulations, the result of normative pressures, or the effect of dependence on external resources.

Administrative Consequences of Changes in State Regulations

From an institutional perspective, administrative growth would be an expected result of adaptation to changes in university policy, and in reforms and regulations that apply to universities as state institutions.

Universities may be viewed as administrative agencies in a state hierarchical structure. Despite strong traditions of self-governance, they cannot ignore the signals and demands of public authorities. The relationship is governed by law, and it is the duty of universities to follow state regulations. Universities must relate to two types of governmental changes: in regulations and expectations of research and higher education, and in regulations pertaining to public activities generally. How have these changes influenced administrative structure and procedures within Norwegian universities?

In state directives which are specific to educational and research institutions, the growth in student numbers is particularly important. The number of persons applying for higher education has been high over the last decade, and government has put pressure on universities to increase student numbers. From 1987 to 1995 there was an almost twofold increase in students registered at Norwegian universities. Our interviewees emphasised the increase in student numbers as a key factor in explaining administrative growth. Nevertheless, our data show that the relative growth in higher administrative person-years is stronger than the growth in student numbers. Other factors must be present.

The increase in formal postgraduate education (PhD level) is another element stressed by state directives. A doctoral degree was not traditionally viewed as a part of the educational system, but a new formal doctoral training system is placing stronger demands on universities to organise courses, take care of legal rights of students, etc. Priority is also given to the internationalisation of research and education. This has administrative consequences at the institutions, particularly with respect to participation in the European Union's student exchange programmes and the various programmes for research.

Some administrative changes apply to all state organisations. From the mid-1980s there has been much emphasis on the modernisation of the public sector. The Norwegian government's 1987 renewal programme for administrative activities was significant. The period was characterised by reform within public administration, including the universities. The introduction of result-oriented planning and cash-limit budgeting is the result of greater focus on the governance of the public sector, and both these reforms have been introduced at the universities. Authorities have also demanded more evaluation, including continuous reporting and thorough evaluations of units.

This set of state reforms is the Norwegian version of more general European trends in how governments relate to higher education institutions—a new way of steering higher education—emphasising self-control, deregulation and institutional accountability.[44] Our study shows that these new tools of governance and institutional management have contributed to both academic and administrative bureaucratisation, and are an important element in the rise of professional university administration, irrespectively of whether state policy has served to secure more autonomous universities.

Of the other changes in state regulations for public activities in general, it is significant that universities face new expectations and obligations as employers, with regard to employees and working environment. New policy here appears to have considerable consequences for units dealing with personnel issues and organisational development at a central level within universities. Government authorities have for the past ten years encouraged delegation in personnel administration. One effect is that more attention is given to the professionalism of personnel administrators—which corresponds to the general pattern of increase in qualified administrative officers.

This type of internal organisational change may thus be considered the result of conformity to new state regulations within both university policy and state administrative policy. Here internal bureaucratisation is a result of state coercion, not in the sense of a specific demand, but as the by-product of laws and regulations to which universities as public organisations must automatically adapt. In our context this is an apt description of the administrative growth which is said to accompany increases in student numbers. The continual rise in applicants for university education, and the fact that the Norwegian national assembly sets the framework for how many students universities should accept, are factors outside the control of the universities. Nonetheless, there are internal administrative consequences because there is an administrative price-tag for every student who is accepted. This also applies to the increase in the number of employees in the wake of growth in student numbers. Thus, there are elements of coercion and natural adaptation in the relationship between authorities and universities which have internal administrative growth as a consequence. This is also evident within legally regulated changes in personnel and administrative policy.

We do not argue that state regulations aim at increasing the size of university administration, but rather that the universities' adaptation to changes in laws and regulations has had significant administrative side-effects—an aspect that has been largely overlooked in public policy-making.

Political decisions and changes in state laws and regulations clearly bring about internal administrative change, but there are variations and internal adjustments in universities' responses; they have latitude in how to implement reforms and handle changes in law. Laws and regulations vary in specificity and allow scope for local adjustment and implementation.[45] Our study clearly demonstrates this leeway: during interviews it became apparent that individual administrators have "favourite children," and their use of time owes more to their own priorities than to external directives. Internal administrative change thus contains a strong element of local adaptation to external demands and regulations.

Furthermore, different sections of a university have different relations and interests in regard to external actors. The administrative system and elected leaders may emphasise external signals in a different way from the academic staff. Staff may use external conditions as a basis for legitimating their own activities in relation to other groups within the university. This is especially evident when administrators use state regulations to legitimate new activities, when faced with academic staff who are reluctant to accept new administrative procedures or to spend university funds on administrative activities.

Administrative Consequences of Normative Pressure

Imitation between universities and between public organisations generally is also a mechanism whereby external expectations are coupled to internal change. Several studies show that Norwegian universities are influenced by the public definition of how organisations should look.[46] The issue here is that what is regarded as a good and well-run university is subject to a common definition among universities themselves and other interested actors. A professional identity has gradually formed among university administrators, which clearly affects what is regarded as good university administration, and sets standards for how external expectations are put into effect locally and what the standards for the latter should be. For example, administrative personnel participate in national and international networks which disseminate ideas and norms about administrative practice. This has resulted in the expansion of different job categories such as office managers, student counsellors and research officers at a departmental level, but also in special administrative units such as research administration departments and departments for international affairs. It is difficult to discern whether this is a response to external or internal needs, or whether it arises from general changes in the norms for good administration.

We have seen this expansion in the inter-university dissemination of types of administrative positions, special types of administrative units and departments, and types of administrative/managerial activities such as newly established courses for administrative and academic leaders. A related mechanism is coupled to the development of a professional administration at universities, as documented in our study. Once administrative structures and routines are defined as the norm in the relevant profession, they are adopted throughout the network of university administrators, nationally and internationally. In Norway, professional degree-holding administrators clearly hold different views and expectations of their own role from those of the clerical workers who traditionally made up the hulk of university administration. The professionals to some extent seem to have developed a common definition of the "state-of-the-art" in university administration.

A key aspect of this process is that it represents the unanticipated consequences of ordinary action in response to environmental change. "Local" sub-units have reacted to environmental and in-house expectations in the same way, i.e., by appointing more professional administrators. This seems to be the standard response to such changes, and can be regarded as the explanation for the bureaucratisation of Norwegian universities.

The process affected the development of a professional identity for university administrative staff, related to their level and qualifications. During the period studied, the four universities arrived at a common understanding of the type of administrative support system associated with good modern universities. The largest university, Oslo, set the standard—for instance, for what departmental administrative staff should consist of—and the others followed suit.

The case studies demonstrate how this common understanding of the size and shape of university administration developed; as such imitation is part of the explanation of bureaucratisation. The changes in administrative norms must be viewed as long-lasting shifts, rather than short-lived managerial fads. However the latter were important because they indirectly occasioned the pattern of administrative growth found in Norwegian universities. Many of the external demands facing universities in the 1980s and 1990s can be seen as management fashions[47] that were particular to institutions in higher education: how these were handled within universities contributed to their bureaucratisation.

Administrative Consequences of Resource Dependency

As complex organisations universities are not only concerned with government policy. Although the basic appropriation through the state budget is the primary source of income for Norwegian universities, it is far from the only one. It is now more common for universities to supplement their resources with external research funding. From a resource-dependence perspective, we would expect them to develop administrative structures and procedures to complement the structures of resource providers[48]—i.e., we would anticipate administrative growth in the parts of the university engaged in extracting and cultivating external funding.

From 1983 to 1993, external funds for university research and development increased by an average of 15 per cent per year. In 1993 external research funds amounted to between 30 and 40 per cent of the total research and development activities at the universities.[49] External funding comes from different sources such as the Research Council of Norway, ministries, local authorities, industry, private foundations and foreign donors. Information about new funding systems has to be collected and disseminated within the system, applications have to be written and contracts drawn up. The demands for reporting and feedback are much higher than previously, and both faculty and administrators need more time to administer externally funded activities. In addition, the search for and maintenance of external funding has led to new administrative units at central and faculty level and special positions at departmental level.

Thus, the change in the universities' quest for external resources has had consequences for both faculty and administrators. Interaction with external actors involves drawing up written contracts, filling out forms and writing reports. Research is increasingly an object for administrative treatment. It also appears that, for the last ten to 15 years, university faculty have increasingly been engaged in administrative work which occurs in external collegial committees. In 1991, 51 per cent of the faculty were members of external boards, councils or committees related to their work at the university, compared to 36 per cent in 1981.[50] It appears that this happened mainly because university researchers have to finance a higher proportion of their work externally, and because this form of funding has a different administrative "portfolio" than research performed via a university's own funds.

We have made a distinction between a resource-dependence theory and institutional theory. The perspectives are not mutually exclusive, but they highlight different aspects of environments. It is difficult to maintain a sharp distinction between the effects of resource dependency and rule-following; universities relate to external actors that are both resource providers and formally superior agencies. Norwegian universities are highly dependent upon public funding and failing to comply with government regulations might result in budget cuts. In this respect, rule-following and adaptation to external resources reinforce each other. However, the administrative consequences of increased external funding can be seen mainly as a result of managing resource dependency by seeking diverse providers.

Internal Factors as Explanations for Administrative Growth

Bearing in mind how groups at a university relate in different ways to external actors, how can administrative growth be generated internally? We may assume that universities consist of different groups of employees with differing roles and interests in administrative questions and tasks.

Common-sense explanations about internal sources of administrative growth usually fall into three categories. Growth is created by the administrative staff itself, or by faculty staff, or is generated at other levels than the one to which an individual belongs. Common to the three categories is that it is "the others" who are responsible for growth in administration. In a sense, these three myths have theoretical parallels. In theories on the growth of public expenditure, it is usual to distinguish between supply-driven versus demand-driven growth.[51] To some extent this distinction can apply when considering university administrative growth and whether it is internally generated. However, administrative growth may also occur at the intersection between the "producers and consumers" of university administration.

Demand-Driven Growth?

Students and faculty generally demand administrative services at universities—so the demand for administrative services naturally increases in relation to student and faculty numbers. Technological changes have also altered demands for administrative services. This applies particularly to the introduction of computer technology, an important background to understanding the transition from secretarial help to professional administration. Another example is the increase in contract work and the internationalisation of research and teaching, especially in relation to various European Union programmes.

If the pattern of bureaucratisation we found is to be explained as "demand-driven," we must look at how faculty relate to administration. Spending time on administrative activities is a poor investment for academics, if both career rewards and personal satisfaction are primarily associated with research performance. It is in the interest of faculty that others perform administrative work, that it is done by competent people, and not by academics who are often administrative amateurs. Herein lies an assumption that more professionally performed administrative and support services will ease the burden of administration for faculty. But there is also a dilemma in that administrative resources and positions do not directly benefit teaching and research.

Furthermore, we can expect a germ of administrative growth to lie in faculty's need for administrative relief balanced against their wish for influence and control. There is "power in administration," but it is not a career path—and it creates a dilemma for academic staff.[52] The division of labour for administrative work includes a distribution of influence on how a university is governed. From this vantage point, it can be assumed that faculty oppose delegating administrative work to full-time administrators as this might mean that influence is also "delegated." Faculty traditions and the desire for influence can thus contribute to the growth of total administration at universities.

Our study indicates that this is not significant at a horizontal level. Duplication of administrative work, arising because individuals do not want to lose control and influence in administrative matters, is more prevalent in the relations between levels. University departments are in general more transparent and there is considerable interaction and cooperation between administrative staff and appointed heads of department and faculty leaders. Sufficient control over administrative matters, faculty claim, is secured informally, and particularly by department administrators who are sensitive to issues of faculty control over academic policy. A remaining concern, however, is that strengthening the professional administrative apparatus at this level may channel resources to administrative positions and not directly to academic activities.

Faculty to a larger extent than before appear to value efficiency in university governance more than representation and democracy, and are more tolerant of transferring work and influence to administrative staff at departmental level. However, according to our study this shift in attitudes has not meant less participation in boards and committees, or in the time spent on administration. The total picture is thus consistent with the assumption that demand contributes to growth in the administrative apparatus because faculty seek relief from administrative tasks, while still engaging in administrative activities because in practice it is difficult to leave this to others. Ambivalence results in both administrative and academic bureaucratisation.

Perhaps this pattern of administrative growth belongs to a transition period in the sense that the new possibilities for professional relief have not yet resulted in reduced administrative loads for academics. However, faculty have themselves taken on tasks such as externally financed activities which produce new administrative work which they have to do themselves.

Our study shows that academics largely delegate administrative tasks to administrative support staff at departmental level, and the trend towards a professional administration for each department has enabled academics to entrust new administrative tasks to local administrators. Academic staff appreciate and use the new opportunities to shed such tasks. Clearly this has increased the administrators' workload and in turn has led them to push for additional colleagues.

Supply-Driven Growth?

Theories about producer-driven growth in expenditure rest on three main assumptions. A political understanding of supply-driven growth states that administrators will maximise growth for their own activities; the second states that administrative costs are the unintended consequences of the logics of administration and management; while the third gives weight to ideological changes among the producers of administrative services.

A widely publicised theory on the growth of public expenditure is that of budget-maximising bureaucrats.[53] Briefly the theory states that government bureaucrats use their monopoly over information on the true cost of supply of public services in securing budgetary output levels that are higher than the socially optimal. This gives a strategic advantage to the "bureau," and the allocation of public resources is inefficient given the preferences of the "sponsor." The theory echoes the popular sentiment that bureaucracy is inefficient and growing out of control.

Despite the criticism of the theory,[54] this perspective might have some relevance for the analysis of higher education and administrative growth.[55] In the context of a university, it means that administration will grow because senior administrators direct appropriations to their own activities. Senior administrators have a self-interest in doing this—not just because their organisational units will have more at their disposal, but because more resources increase the prestige of their own work, and employ more fellow professionals.[56] This could explain why higher administrative posts increase more than others at universities. However, the assumption is that administrators are in a position within organisations which allows them to maximise budgets for their activities, i.e., they have a strategic advantage because of "information asymmetry." An empirical study of university budgetary allocations would be necessary to test this hypothesis. Nonetheless, our interviews with both faculty and administrators indicate that the growth seen at departmental level in particular is hard to explain as the result of bureaucrats maximising appropriations for their own activities. At this level budgetary decisions are collective decisions involving both academics and administrators, and the latter have little opportunity to exercise a monopoly on information.

This illustrates the problematic aspect of applying such a theory in a Norwegian university context. Bureaucratic behaviour which might maximise administrative budgets is subject to formal constraints, stemming from the fact that faculty and elected academic leaders hold central positions in budgetary allocations within universities. Consequently, the relationship between administrators and faculty is more symmetrical than is assumed in a budget maximisation model. Furthermore, it is hard to determine what the optimal size of the administrative component of universities is and what constitutes an "over-supply" of bureaucracy, since faculty preferences are not unequivocal and faculty is not the only relevant group in determining an optimal level of administration.

Another explanation is that bureaucratisation is a consequence of a built-in logic in administrative work and the management system under which administrators work; they create work for themselves and other administrators and, in our context, also for faculty and collegiate committees. This is not to say bureaucratisation is the result of action motivated by self-interest, but rather that it is the by-product of internal processes. Most persons in such a system will agree that administrators do what they are employed to do, but ". . . managers typically respond to the pressures by putting demands on others, sharing the work and sharing the risk and hiring help . . . And the situation becomes exacerbated."[57]

Many of our interviewees mentioned the self-perpetuating growth of university administration. Some said that when administration grows it needs a continuous increase in resources to administer itself; administrators are needed to administer other administrators. So do administrators themselves contribute to establishing new administrative routines which increase administrative costs, not only in the need for more professionals, but also in the form of faculty staff time needed for administration?

The demand for higher quality in administration from its producers, new doctrines and knowledge, can contribute to administrative change. Studies of the growth of public expenditure show that the producers of public services are often at the forefront in pressing for new services and higher quality.[58] We have shown that such effects occur when bonds exist between university administrators at different universities, but they also happen within a university. It is quite usual for administrators in similar positions to meet regularly, arrive at a common definition of what different sections should be doing, and diffuse routines and standards within the university. It seems plausible to assume that such processes are at work, but they are hard to measure empirically, and it is difficult to find an empirical basis to support this explanation for the growth in the professional administrative apparatus.

Organisational Structure and Administrative Growth

Administrative growth cannot be completely explained on the basis of "supply and demand." The distinction between supply-driven and demand-driven growth is especially difficult to maintain because faculty can also be seen as producers of university administration. A major assumption is that internally driven administrative growth arises from unintended processes which result from a mixture of different management and decision-making principles at universities—and that this condition is the key to understanding both administrative and academic bureaucratisation, as well as the relationship between the two forms of administrative growth at universities.

Theories about governance and management at universities often state that such organisations have an in-built unique dualism: a conventional administrative bureaucracy existing side by side with a collegial governing system, and the division of labour between these two systems is not obvious.[59] We suggest a third factor: university democracy, the system which not only includes faculty representation in collegiate agencies, but also students and other employees. The democratic aspect in university administration receives little attention in international literature—nevertheless, it is important for understanding administration and governance at Norwegian universities.

Norwegian universities attempt to achieve a balance between "meritocracy," "democracy" and "bureaucracy," and the values these carry. How the balance is tilted at a particular time affects the relationship between academics and administrators and the understanding of administrative change. It is not only significant for the roles and positions of university administrators, it is essential for understanding the participation of academic staff in administrative matters. An assumption is that the connection between different management principles is at the kernel of administrative growth. But how does this connection take place? Legitimacy in university administration is a consideration here. In university management the results of decisions are important, but their legitimacy is strongly connected with how the decisions have been made. An administrative boomerang effect can occur if the matters generated and dealt with in the "bureaucracy" need to be handled by collegiate/democratic agencies to be regarded as legitimate. Nonetheless, the democratic organs of a university need support from administrative staff.

In this perspective administrative growth can be regarded as an unintended consequence of the duplication of work resulting from internal processes. Different decision-making principles operating side by side encourage administrative growth, but it also appears that a large kernel of this growth lies in duplication along a vertical dimension in the university structure.

Although faculty staff clearly express the need for reducing the complexity of the democratic governance structure, very little in our data leads us to conclude that growth in the number of professional administrators has entailed a reduction of either the number of democratic bodies or their significance. Furthermore, the fragmented university decision-making system has in itself clearly been a factor in the pattern of administrative growth. Judging from our data, this growth has not been part of a strategy for administrative development at an institutional level, but rather the result of many independent local decisions and actions. Moreover, as far as academic bureaucratisation is concerned, using time on administration is not the object of collective decision-making: it is largely a by-product of the decision to establish committees, boards, etc., and as such it does not show on any university budgets or demand direct budgetary allocations. The cost of academic bureaucratisation is invisible in the short run.

Vertical Forces

The modernisation of the public sector as a means of solving financial problems is a trend in most Western countries,[60] as it is in Norway. The delegation of tasks from a superior to a subordinate level has been a central part of a general policy of autonomy and accountability in higher education. Delegation is meant to increase efficiency; it is assumed that the use of resources will improve if the distance between those who make decisions, those who implement and those who are affected is minimalised.[61] But organisational studies disagree on whether delegation improves efficiency: if it is to do so, the premise is that administrative resources are transferred from a superior level to local units. If delegation of tasks is not followed by delegation of resources, including personnel, duplication rather than efficiency could result. Furthermore, studies show that vertical delegation means individuals are less exposed and sensitive to superior political signals.[62] In the subsequent round this increases the need for control and coordination of activities and formalisation of such processes.[63]

Delegation from central authorities has been a key element in some of the changes in state regulations affecting universities, and it has been accepted within universities. Tasks, responsibility and authority have been transferred from central administration to faculties and then to departments, as is reflected in the fact that growth in senior administrative positions is greatest in the basic units. Delegation is given as the main explanation for the growth of departmental administration and student numbers. However, it has not been followed by reduction in staff numbers at other levels. At a central and faculty level there has also been considerable growth in administrative positions. The picture is one of duplication rather than efficiency. According to our data, there is little reason to doubt that the vertical complexity of universities fosters administrative growth.

Conclusion

We conclude that a bureaucratisation of Norwegian universities has taken place in the sense that relatively more resources than before are used for administration than for research and teaching.

What are the forces behind the growth in administrative positions? Our analysis does not give grounds for selecting any one reason. External expectations and demands have had important internal consequences for both the administrative support apparatus and the administrative work of faculty. The immense increase in student numbers has contributed significantly to administrative growth. Other changes in state university policy, such as formalising postgraduate education and developing strategies for the internationalisation of research and education are examples of state regulations and expectations to which an administrative price-tag is attached. The same applies to both university adaptation to general state reform programmes and regulations and university involvement in the external funding of research. These changes are not individually of great importance, but cumulatively they contribute to the pattern of academic and administrative bureaucratisation we have documented. These are incremental changes in administration of universities that have not been the object of coherent decision-making, either at the policy-making level or at universities.

What is the role of internal processes in administrative growth at universities? There is still a dilemma: faculty demand administrative support but they need to retain control and influence, and this contributes to academic and administrative bureaucratisation. At the same time, the influx of professional administrators has contributed to changing expectations about what university administration should be. Another important internal cause for administrative growth lies in the relationship between levels.

It is reasonable to view the bureaucratisation of universities not as a process planned and regulated at a high level in institutions, but as the result of many small decisions taken at different levels and in various forums at the universities. In a decentralised and fragmented decision-making system as found within universities, there are few centres of strong and unitary leadership that might be able to curb administrative growth.

The most noticeable characteristic of the 1980s and 1990s is the change within university administration. While the number of office workers has not altered in the last decade, there has been strong and disproportionate growth in the number of administrative officers and managers. Therefore it is reasonable to conclude that despite a bureaucratisation of the universities, there are signs of an even stronger professionalisation of university administration. University administrators have diverse educational backgrounds and experience. University administration is not a profession in the sense of clear links between a particular educational background and formal gateways to a career as a university bureaucrat. However, the character of university administration has been changed significantly by the introduction of a corps of administrators, consisting largely of degree-holding officers and managers with their own professional associations and standards of administrative practice.

Administrative growth and professionalisation have been possible because Norwegian universities are in a period of general growth and internal differentiation. A concurrence of different forces has thus meant that the 1980s and 1990s are the epoch of university administration.

Notes

1. Leslie, L. and Rhoades, G., "Rising Administrative Costs. Seeking Explanations," *Journal of Higher Education*, LXVI (March–April 1995), pp. 187–212.
2. Gumport, P. and Pusser, B., "A Case of Bureaucratic Accretion. Context and Consequences," *Journal of Higher Education*, LXVI (September–October 1995), pp. 493–520.
3. Leslie, L. and Rhoades, G., "Rising Administrative Costs," *op. cit.*
4. Lane, J.E., *Institutional Reform: A Public Policy Perspective* (Aldershot: Dartmouth Publishing, 1990); Statskontoret, *Högskolan: Administrasjon i förändring?* (Stockholm: Statskontoret, 1992), p. 8.
5. Gornitzka, Å. and Schwach, V., *Forskere og forvaltere* (Oslo: Institute for Studies in Research and Higher Education, 1990).

6. Visakorpi, J.K., "Academic and Administrative Interface: Application to National Circumstances," *Higher Education Management*, VIII, 2 (1996), pp. 37–40.

7. Teichler, U., "The Conditions of the Academic Profession," in Maassen, P.A.M. and van Vught, F.A. (eds.), *Inside Academia: New Challenges for the Academic Profession* (Utrecht: De Tijdstroom, 1996).

8. Kyvik, S., *Universitetspersonalets syn på sine forskningsmuligheter* (Oslo: Institute for Studies in Research and Higher Education, 1983).

9. Jacobsen, B., "Universitetsforsker i Danmark," *Nyt fra Samfundsvidenskabeme* (1990).

10. Halsey, A.H., *Decline of Donnish Dominion: The British Academic Professions in the Twentieth Century* (Oxford: Clarendon Press, 1992).

11. This article is based on a larger report to the Norwegian Ministry of Education, Research and Church Affairs: Gornitzka, Å., Kyvik, S. and Larsen, I.M., *Byråkratisering av universitetene? Dokumentasjon og analyse av administrativ endring* (Oslo: Norwegian Institute for Studies in Research and Higher Education, 1996), Report 3/96.

12. Maurice Kogan points out that, in higher education institutions, bureaucratisation is also used in two other ways: the move from individual and academic power to the system or institution, and the growth of power of administrators. See his "Academics and Administrators in Higher Education," paper for the CHER conference, Turku, June 1996.

13. Blau, P.M., *The Organization of Academic Work* (New York: John Wiley, 1973), p. 71.

14. On faculty participation in administrative work, see Dill, D.D., "Administration: Academic," in *The Encyclopedia of Higher Education* (Oxford: Pergamon Press, 1992).

15. Gornitzka, Å. and Schwach, V., *Forskere og forvaltere, op. cit.*

16. Kogan, M., *Academics and Administrators, op. cit.*

17. See, e.g., Leslie, L. and Rhoades, G., "Rising Administrative Costs," *op. cit.*

18. Sear, K., "Economies of Scale in Higher Education," in Goodlad, S. (ed.), *Economies of Scale in Higher Education* (Guildford: Society for Research into Higher Education, 1983).

19. Mintzberg, H., *Structures in Fives: Designing Effective Organizations* (New Jersey: Prentice-Hall, 1983).

20. Blau, P.M., *The Organization of Academic Work, op. cit.*, p. 15; and *On the Nature of Organizations* (New York: John Wiley, 1974).

21. Blau, P.M. and Schonherr, R.A., *The Structure of Organizations* (New York: Basic Books, 1971); Hall, R.H., *Organizations: Structure and Process* (London: Prentice Hall, 1991).

22. Pfeffer, J., *Organizations and Organization Theory* (Boston: Pitman, 1982); Scott, W. R., *Organizations: Rational, Natural and Open Systems* (Englewood Cliffs: Prentice Hall, 1992).

23. Pfeffer, J., *Organizations and Organization Theory, op. cit.*

24. Brinkman, P. and Leslie, L., "Economies of Scale in Higher Education," *Review of Higher Education*, X (Fall 1986), pp. 1–28.

25. Rushing, W.A., "Organizational Size and Administration: The Problems of Causal Homogeneity and a Heterogeneous Category," *Pacific Sociological Review*, IX (1966), pp. 100–108.

26. Scott, W.R., *Organizations, op. cit.*

27. Blau, P.M., *The Organization of Academic Work, op. cit.*

28. Scott, W.R., *Organizations, op. cit.*

29. Brinkman, P. and Leslie, L., "Economies of scale," *op. cit.*

30. Lane, J.E., *Institutional Reform, op. cit.*

31. Statskontoret, *Högskolan, op. cit.*

32. Gornitzka, Å., Kyvik, S. and Larsen, I.M., *Byråkratisering av universitetene?, op. cit.*

33. Scott, W.R., *Organizations, op. cit.*

34. Kerr, C., *The Uses of the University* (Cambridge, Mass.: Harvard University Press, 1963).

35. Oliver, C., "Strategic Responses to Institutional Processes," *Academy of Management Review*, XVI, 1 (1991), pp. 145–179.

36. Pfeffer, J. and Salancik, G.R., *The External Control of Organizations: A Resource Dependence Perspective* (New York: Harper & Row, 1978); Pfeffer, J., *Organizations and Organization Theory, op. cit.*

37. Oliver, C., "Strategic Responses," *op. cit.*

38. Scott, W.R., *Institutions and Organizations* (Thousand Oaks: Sage, 1995).

39. North, D., *Institutions, Institutional Change and Economic Performance* (Cambridge: Cambridge University Press, 1990).

40. Meyer, J.W. and Rowan, B., "Institutionalised Organisations: Formal Structure as Myth and Ceremony," *American Journal of Sociology*, LXXXIII (1977), pp. 734–749.

41. Abrahamson, E., "Management Fashion," *Academy of Management Review*, XXI, 1 (1996), pp. 254–285.

42. Abrahamson, E., "Managerial Fads and Fashions: The Diffusion and Rejection of Innovation," *Academy of Management Review*, XVI, 3 (1991), pp. 586–612.

43. DiMagggio, P. and Powell, W., "The Iron Cage Revisited: Institutional Isomorphism and Collective Rationality in Organizational Fields," *American Sociological Review*, XLVIII (April 1983), pp. 147–160.

44. Van Vught, F., "A New Autonomy in European Higher Education? An Exploration and Analysis of the Strategy of Self-regulation in Higher Education Governance," *Institutional Management in Higher Education*, XII, 1 (1988), pp. 16–25.

45. Edelmann, L.B., "Legal Ambiguity and Symbolic Structures: Organisational Mediation of Civil Rights Law," *American Journal of Sociology*, VI (May 1992), pp. 1531–1576.

46. Christensen, T., *Virksomhetsplanlegging i forsknings- og utdanningsinstitusjoner—myteskaping eller instrumentell problemløsning?* (Oslo: Tano, 1991); Gornitzka, Å., *Organisasjonsreformer ved Universitetet i Oslo 1980–årene* (Oslo: Universitetet i Oslo, Institutt for statsvitenskap, 1989); Larsen, I.M. and Gornitzka, Å., "New Management Systems in Norwegian Universities: The Interface between Reform and Institutional Understanding," *European Journal of Education*, XXX, 3 (1995), pp. 347–361.

47. Larsen, I.M. and Gornitzka, Å., "New Management Systems," *op. cit.*

48. Leslie, L. and Rhoades, G., "Rising Administrative Costs," *op. cit.*

49. *R&D Statistics and Science and Technology Indicators* (Oslo: Institute for Studies in Research and Higher Education, 1995).

50. Kyvik, S. and Enoksen, J.A., *Universitetspersonalets tidsbruk* (Oslo: Institute for Studies in Research and Higher Education, 1992), Report 10/92.

51. Tarschys, D., "The Growth of Public Expenditures: Nine Modes of Explanation," *Scandinavian Political Studies*, X (1975), pp. 9–31.

52. Mintzberg, H., *Structures in Fives, op. cit.*

53. Niskanen, W.N., *Bureaucracy and Representative Government* (Chicago: Rand McNally, 1971).

54. Miller, G.J. and Moe, T.M., "Bureaucrats, Legislators, and the Size of Government," *American Political Science Review*, LXXVII (1983), pp. 297–322; Meyer, M., *Limits to Bureaucratic Growth* (Berlin: Walter de Gruyther, 1985).

55. Gumport, P. and Pusser, B., *A Case of Bureaucratic Accretion, op. cit.*

56. Hannaway, J., "Supply Creates Demands: An Organizational Process View of Administrative Expansion," *Journal of Policy Analysis and Management*, VII, 1 (1987), pp. 118–134.

57. *Ibid.*, p. 121.

58. Hernes, G. and Martinussen, W., *Demokrati og politiske ressurser* (Oslo: Universitetsforlagct, 1980), p. 7.

59. Bensimon, E.M., Neumann, A. and Birnbaum, R., *Making Sense of Administrative Leadership: The "L" Word in Higher Education*, ASHE-ERIC Higher Education Report No.1. (Washington, DC: George Washington University, 1989); Birnbaum, R., *How Colleges Work: The Cybernetics of Academic Organisation and Leadership* (San Francisco: Jossey-Bass, 1990).

60. Metcalfe, L. and Richards, S., "Evolving Public Management Cultures," in Kooiman, J. and Eliassen, K.A. (eds.), *Managing Public Organisations* (London: Sage, 1987).

61. Selle, P., *Desentralisering: Troll med minst to hovud* (Bergen: LOS-senteret, 1990). Report 90/28.

62. Egeberg, M. (ed.) *Institusjonspolitikk og forvaltningsutvikling: Bidrag til en anvendt statsvitenskap* (Oslo: Tano, 1989).

63. Scott, W.R., *Institutions and Organizations, op. cit.*; Hall, R.H., *Organizations, op. cit.*

TRUST, MARKETS AND ACCOUNTABILITY IN HIGHER EDUCATION: A COMPARATIVE PERSPECTIVE[1]

MARTIN TROW
GRADUATE SCHOOL OF PUBLIC POLICY
UNIVERSITY OF CALIFORNIA, BERKELEY

Introduction

In recent years problems have emerged around the American system of accrediting colleges and universities—a peculiar system involving voluntary regional associations of colleges and universities, public and private, which appoint committees of academics to make visits to their member institutions and report first on whether they are reasonably decent institutions of higher education, and secondly, on how they might improve themselves. In 1994 the immediate issue in the US was the danger that new federal legislation threatened to give federal or state governments a larger role in this process; public discussions were heated but shallow and ill-informed. At that point the Mellon Foundation of New York and Princeton commissioned a three person committee, of which I was a member, to write a report which might put our problems of accountability into a broader and more illuminating perspective.[2] Over the next six months the three of us talked to college and university presidents, people in government and the higher education associations in Washington, leaders of the regional accrediting bodies, and so forth—at the end of which we produced a report which was widely distributed in the US and which included detailed recommendations on the reform of accreditation. Incidentally, the immediate problems that gave rise to our study disappeared with the election of a new Congress, but the deeper issues remain.

This paper is an effort to explore the same issues in comparative perspective. Many of these comparative observations arise out of my study and direct experience, both in Washington and in college and university governance in America and Europe. My justification for making this comparison is first that there is already a very large European literature on accountability, which mostly takes the form of discussions of quality assessment. But there are two other reasons for starting from the American experience: first because as European institutions gain greater autonomy (as they are doing outside the UK) they find themselves, like American colleges and universities, more deeply involved with market forces—we begin to see that in connection with the commercialization of university research. But more broadly, the sharply contrasting situation in American higher education may allow us to see more clearly the underlying nature of accountability as one of three fundamental ways in which colleges and universities are linked to their surrounding and supporting societies: the others are trust and the market. Every institution is linked to its surrounding society, to its support community, through some combination of these kinds of links—and of course that combination will vary greatly depending on the kind of institution we speak of. Each institution has a kind of social contract with its society, and its support community in that society, defining the relative weight and combination of these three kinds of links, but a) these contracts are as diverse as the institutions themselves, and b) they are almost everywhere currently in the process of change. Let's look briefly at each of these in turn, and then come back to their relationships. And at the end I would like to say something about the relation of teaching to external accountability.

Accountability is the obligation to report to others, to explain, to justify, to answer questions about how resources have been used, and to what effect. Accountability to others takes many different forms in different societies, with respect to different actions and different kinds of support. The fundamental questions with respect to accountability are: who is to be held accountable, for what, to whom, through what means, and with what consequences.

The link of higher education to society through the market is visible when support is provided to a college or university in return for the immediate provision of goods or services—in the case of higher education these are almost always services—in a situation where buyers of those services face multiple sellers (who really want to sell!) and where the sellers face multiple buyers. The clearest examples are the proprietary schools in the US which depend wholly on student tuition fees, and provide in return technical and vocational skills, and help in getting started in a job or career. But an element of market links can be found in most American institutions, though often concealed or obscured by other kinds of linkages. Markets are still a relatively minor factor in Europe, which on the whole does not provide a market for higher education, and whose governments rather dislike the idea of a market for higher education and its potential effects on quality and status. Government in the UK employs the rhetoric of the market in connection with higher education, but since government controls the price universities can place on their services, and the amount and variety of services they can sell, universities currently operate not in a market but in something more like a command economy.[3]

The third of the fundamental links between higher education and society is trust—that is, the provision of support, by either public or private bodies, without the requirement that the institution either provide specific goods and services in return for that support, or account specifically and in detail for the use of those funds. To a high degree the provision of the block grant to the universities by the British Treasury (and then the DES) through the University Grants Committee before its demise (and really before the Thatcher revolution) was an example of the provision of support on trust; largely trust that the universities would continue to do and be what they had been and done for the previous century or so. Trust is also the central element in the very significant contributions by private organizations and individuals to American colleges and universities both public and private, for which no accountability is demanded. Trust, indeed, is the basis of the very large measure of autonomy of colleges and universities anywhere which are able to raise substantial sums of private money, or which are funded by governments which voluntarily delegate much of their power over the institutions, and thus give to the institutions a large measure of autonomy in the use of the funds they provide.

With respect to its basic functions: first, accountability is a constraint on arbitrary power, and on the corruptions of power, including fraud, manipulation, malfeasance and the like. In serving these functions, accountability strengthens the legitimacy of institutions, including colleges and universities, which meet its obligations to report on their activities to the appropriate groups or authorities. In addition, it is claimed that accountability sustains or raises the quality of performance of institutions by forcing them to examine their own operations critically, and by subjecting them to critical review from outside. And beyond those functions of constraining power and raising standards, accountability can be (and is) used as a regulatory device, through the kinds of reports it requires, and the explicit or implicit criteria it requires the reporting institutions to meet. While in principle accountability operates through reports on past actions, the anticipation of having to be accountable throws its shadow forward over future action. It thus is a force for external influence on institutional behavior, an influence which can vary from a broad steer, leaving to the institution a measure of autonomy over the implementation of policy, to the direct commands of an external regulatory agency which uses accountability to ensure compliance with specific policies and directives, and designs its system of reports to ensure that conformity.[4]

But that note reminds us that accountability is a double-edged sword. While it generally gets a good press in a populist society, we have to keep in mind that accountability is exercised at a price to the institutions under its obligations, and not least to colleges and universities. For one thing, accountability is an alternative to trust; and efforts to strengthen it usually involve parallel efforts to weaken trust. Accountability and cynicism about human behavior go hand in hand. But trust has much to recommend it in the relation of institutions to their supporting societies, and not least for colleges and universities, even though it is sometimes violated and exploited.[5]

Related to this, and of special interest to educators: accountability to outsiders weakens the autonomy of institutions. Obligations to report are usually disguised obligations to conform to external expectations. And there is, or at least has been, a special case to be made for a high measure of autonomy for institutions of higher education.

Accountability to outsiders, depending on the nature of the obligation, can also be at odds with the confidentiality of sensitive issues within colleges and universities, of which personnel decisions, and preliminary discussions about the treatment of departments and units at times of financial stringency are only the most obvious. It can thus be the enemy of effective governance, and also of plain truth-telling within the institution, as aspects of accountability to outsiders tend toward the character of public relations. External accountability can also be a threat to the freedom of professionals to manage their own time and define their own work. And external accountability, when it applies common standards and criteria to many institutions, can work against diversity among them.

But whatever our ambivalence, the obligations inherent in accountability are central to democratic societies, and have become increasingly so over the long secular trend toward the fundamental democratization of life that Max Weber spoke of. Where traditional authority is weakened and trust in traditional elites undermined, more formal and open accounts and justifications have to be made to the variety of bodies which claim the right to judge the performance of institutions. Accountability, as I have noted, is a major constraint on the exercise of power; the constraint lies in what people and institutions to whom reports are owed might do if they do not like what they hear.

In Europe, higher education's links to society through market mechanisms and trust relations are less commonly debated than are accountability procedures—the market because it has not been a major factor in European higher education, and is only now coming to be a factor in the commercial support for university-based research. And trust is not much discussed because its role in university life is not recognized, or because it is not seen as directly responsible to policy and action, either by the state or by the institution. In the US, where trust is still a central element in the life and autonomy of our institutions, an enormous amount of time, thought and effort goes into creating and sustaining the element of trust in support communities. And nothing frightens American educators so much as the charge that American society is losing its trust and confidence in its institutions of higher education. This charge is frequently made—often by those urging greater measures of formal accountability to take up the slack allegedly left by declining trust. The claim that higher education is losing the trust of the larger society is a convenient one for those who have an interest in increasing the accountability of higher education to the state, and thus of its power over those institutions.

In the UK my sense is that the withdrawal of trust from the universities over the past decade and a half may have been more an aspect of government policy than of changes in attitudes in the broader society. Even if that were so, the British universities never developed political mechanisms that would allow it to convert trust in the society into direct political support when it came under attack by government. That is perhaps the price Britain paid for seventy years or more of elite university politics, involving informal discussions at the Athenaeum between the great and good on one side and civil servants and ministers on the other, many of whom on both sides had gone to school and university together. But however satisfactory that arrangement, the universities did not quite know what to do when they got a Prime Minister who was no gentleman; or put differently, they did not know how to develop and then translate support in the society at large into political support so as to be able to defend themselves through the ordinary devices of real politics in democratic societies. (My British friends will remind me that the universities did not have all that much support in the larger society when they enrolled five percent of the age grade, and did not see public service as a major part of their mission.) Nevertheless, there is everywhere a potential connection between trust and support among groups in the civil society, and political influence through them. The effectiveness of the old elite politics for so long made it seem unnecessary for British universities to convert that potential into a political reality.

We tend to think of trust in connection with the support by private individuals and foundations for higher education and science, but we can also see trust in the relations of states to higher education. While trust in universities is ultimately rooted in the attitudes and sentiments that define the ordinary use of the word, it can also be institutionalized in law and funding arrangements, and thereby gain a measure of independence from underlying attitudes in the broader society.[6] I have already mentioned the role of the UGC in the UK as a symptom and instrument of a trust relationship, though the UK also reminds us that trust can be deinstitutionalized as well. But trust on the part of governments is much more widespread, showing itself in a variety of ways. Many states have observed various self-denying ordinances, voluntarily surrendering some of their power to universities through the endowments of institutions and chairs, through formula funding which links funding directly to enrollments, through block grants and multi-year grants, through the radical dispersion of public research support (as in the US) where the lack of coordination among government agencies in providing research support to the universities insulates them from central government policy. We see levels of trust by governments rising, for example, in the granting of greater autonomy by the Swedish state to the Swedish universities and the endowment by the state of two as private universities, and a similar very marked tendency toward the decentralization of authority to the institutions where we might least expect it, in France, where the old stereotype of a highly centralized Napoleonic university system is no longer tenable. Indeed, a measure of trust is visible in all those cases where states reduce their discretionary powers over the universities, or even delay substantially their exercise of it. The significance of this leaps out at us in the British case, where the government's leash is very short indeed. Again, the UK is exceptional in that on the Continent governments are easing traditional forms of state management of the universities, whereas in the UK government has greatly strengthened its control over universities which formerly were much freer than their Continental counterparts.

Ironically, the more severe and detailed are accountability obligations, the less can they reveal the underlying realities for which the universities are being held accountable. And here my views have been shaped by ongoing research by Oliver Fulton and myself on the ways British universities, old and new, have been coping with the severe but frequently changing requirements for reports and information placed on them by the HEFC. On the research side, of course, we know how cleverly academic departments manage their reports to the HEFC: the care with which they sort out the sheep from the goats on their staffs (with what effect on the morale of the goats?); the intense interest that has arisen around gaining certified publication before closing date—an interest that in some cases has involved the withdrawal of scholarly papers from one journal to place them with another solely on the ground of publication date; the recruitment of stars trailing clouds of publications and glory in their train. And on the teaching side, the anxious rehearsals for a forthcoming site visit, whole days given to walking through the visit, with every moment and conversation choreographed and planned for fullest effect; the even more anxious employment of consultants on how best to present themselves to those review committees—often consultants who themselves mirror the composition of the visiting committees, so that old and distinguished universities can learn how reviewers from new universities are likely to view their teaching methods. And behind the scenes registrars and finance officers and planning officers match wits with the HEFC bureaucracy in arcane manipulations of (for example) the numbers of part-time students who are almost full-time; indeed, looked at from one point of view they are full-timers; of the maths students, who in the right light are very like physicists, at least until their degrees are awarded. And so on and on; I am not about to reveal our respondents' most successful scams. Some of the best university administrators in the country devote a very large amount of time and energy to the creation and manipulation of information that goes into their assessment or directly up to the HEFC, information on which their funding and rankings depend. Many little scams aggregate to real money; they are part of the armamentarium of the skillful university administrator; but they take precious time and intelligence from the challenging administrative and financial problems of the universities which employ them to do creative and not just adversarial planning.

Whatever we might call all this, it is accountability in name only. It much more resembles the reports by a civil service in a defeated country to an occupying power, or by state-owned industrial plants and farms to central government in a command economy. In all such cases, the habits of truth-telling erode, and reports flowing up from the field come to have less and less relation to the facts on the ground that they purportedly represent. When information flowing up the line powerfully affects the reputation and resources flowing down from the center, then we know that those reports become less and less exercises in discovery or truth telling, and more and more public relations documents which are, shall we say, parsimonious with the truth, especially of awkward truths that reveal problems or shortcomings in the reporting institution. But accountability depends on truth-telling. So a central problem is how to create a system of accountability that does not punish truth-telling and reward the appearance of achievement.

Varying Forms of Accountability

The forms of accountability vary with circumstances. In the United States, where the federal government is not the major player in the system, formal accountability to "society" has largely been through "accreditation." Our national report recommended considerable reforms of this system.

In the UK, as we know, by contrast, formal accountability is strong and direct, and discharged in part through quality assessments of research linked directly to funding, but also through external reviews of teaching quality, together with many other instruments of reporting and accountability mandated by a government which has largely withdrawn its trust and precludes an active role for the market.

In many Continental countries, funded largely by the state which maintains control over expenditures, accountability is discharged chiefly through financial and (increasingly) academic audits, rather than through direct assessments of the work of the institutions linked to funding. As John Brennan has observed, "Quality assessment rarely exists as the sole form of external regulation. The role it plays in achieving accountability is likely to be influenced by the other forms of external control which exist. These are principally state regulation by funding and legislation and the operation of the market. Where either of these is strong (the former traditionally in many parts of continental Europe, the latter in the USA), it might be hypothesized that the role for quality assessment is weaker. Where these are both weak (e.g. in the UK) then it may be hypothesized that the accountability role for quality assessment will be stronger."[7]

But some forms of support are mixtures of all three kinds of links: for example, student tuition payments in many American colleges and universities are partly based on their (and their parents') trust in the institution, partly as a market transaction. But this kind of support also calls forth intense efforts at accounting through publications to both students and parents for their support by the colleges, which go to great lengths to keep in touch with parents about what the college is doing with their resources. Alumni also contribute very substantially to American institutions, both public and private: that support is largely based on trust in the institution, partly in the expectation of another kind of accountability which the institution discharges through publications of all kinds. What we see in higher education, in Europe as in the US, are complex and variable combinations of formal measures of accountability, trust and market mechanisms. The combinations of these ways of linking colleges and universities to their support communities vary enormously among different kinds of institutions, different departments, different activities, different stakeholders. To understand the problems facing universities and university systems anywhere, it would be helpful to see the nature of the balance among these three links to their support communities. For example, formal accountability in higher education can be seen as a substitute for trust in situations where market forces are weak—a situation that currently characterizes the UK. And it will also be helpful to understand the effects of changes in the balance of these forces—changes in the ways universities are linked to their societies. That might even be useful in informing institutional and government policy.

Aspects of Accountability

Before going any further it may be helpful to point to two dimensions or aspects of accountability in higher education: the first comprising the distinction between *external* and *internal* accountability; the second the distinction between *legal and financial* accountability, on one side, and *academic* (moral and scholarly)[8] accountability on the other.

On the first distinction: *external accountability* is the obligation of colleges and universities to their supporters, and ultimately to society at large, to provide assurance that they are pursuing their missions faithfully, that they are using their resources honestly and responsibly, and that they are meeting legitimate expectations. *Internal accountability* is the accountability of those within a college or university to one another on how its several parts are carrying out their missions, how well they are performing, whether they are trying to learn where improvement is needed, and what they are doing to make those improvements. External accountability is something like an audit, giving grounds for confidence and continued support, while internal accountability is a kind of research: inquiry and analysis by the institution into its own operations, aimed primarily at improvement through investigation and action. And our published report[9] was particularly concerned with how the forms and practices of external accountability can be made to reinforce rather than undermine good internal accountability.

The second distinction, between legal/financial accountability and academic accountability cuts across the first. *Legal and financial accountability* is the obligation to report how resources are used: is the institution doing what it is supposed to be doing by law, are its resources being used for the purposes for which they were given? Accountability for the use of resources has its own traditions and norms, and the financial audit by both internal and external independent bodies is a well-developed mechanism for discharging it. *Academic accountability* is the obligation to tell others, both inside and outside the institution, what has been done with those resources to further teaching, learning and public service, and to what effect. There is usually a good deal more controversy over academic accountability than about legal/financial accountability: the rules governing inputs are generally clearer than our ability to assess and evaluate the outcomes of teaching and research. We can see the contrast also in the forms by which these two kinds of obligations are discharged or enforced: in one case through financial reports, audits and law suits; in the other by the myriad of ways that academics and academic administrators talk to one another and to outsiders about what they are doing.

In America efforts to provide accountability to outsiders for the academic quality of whole institutions through accreditation are currently the most contentious of these various forms of accountability. To a considerable extent, external academic accountability in the United States, mainly in the form of accreditation, has been irrelevant to the improvement of higher education; in some cases it has acted more to shield institutions from effective monitoring of their own educational performance than to provide it; in still other cases it distinctly hampers the efforts of institutions to improve themselves. It encourages institutions to report their strengths rather than their weaknesses, their successes rather than their failures—and even to conceal their weaknesses and failures from view. As long as accreditation is seen as *the* means by which higher education polices itself, alternative and better means suffer from inattention. Moreover, this is where much dispute has occurred, and where our national report[10] made one of its central recommendations: that we transform accreditation from external reviews of institutional quality into searching audits of each institution's own scheme for critical self-examination, its own internal quality control procedures. This is a familiar recommendation to Europeans: it is a central theme in the writings of the leading European scholars on this subject.[11]

A stress on trust as a key element in the relation of society to higher education in no way implies turning a blind eye on the shortcomings of academics and their institutions; it does center our attention on the question of who is responsible to whom for what. There are of course in every country many pathologies of academic life. Indeed, some academics and whole departments transform Laurie Taylor from a satiric humorist into a sober and restrained anthropologist. One of the most common of these pathologies—found everywhere—are academics in research universities who do little or no research. Academics in research universities usually have light teaching loads to allow them to do their research and scholarship; if they don't they turn a privileged tenured post into a sinecure. But this is a problem for a department or a university to deal with, monitored by external audits of its internal reviews; it is not one that can be reached effectively by central government funding formulas. Trying to reach it from outside may cause more problems than it cures. The UK is the only country I know of that assesses whole departments for funding purposes. Research is done by individuals and research teams (increasingly interdisciplinary), not by departments. Britain's funding arrangements, in my view, confuse an administrative unit with a research unit, and introduces new pathologies into the life of the department—for example, by discouraging interdisciplinary research.

I have stressed that these three forces—accountability, trust and markets—are often interrelated in any particular situation. Accountability and trust particularly are in a peculiar relation of tension, sometimes mutually supportive, sometimes at odds. For example, trust by adults in people and their institutions is not ordinarily blind, but assumes the operation of different kinds of informal accountability, kinds that formal accountability procedures do not recognize.

One of these is the accountability demanded of their members by the academic guilds—their departments and the disciplines. We hear about that kind of accountability when professional and scholarly norms are violated, as in recurrent scandals about academic plagiarism or the falsification of research findings. The fact that they *are* scandals attests to the power of the norms that are violated, and the structure of sanctions still in place to enforce the norms.

There is in addition the personal accountability to which one is held by one's conscience, accountability to values that are internalized. Some people in academic life still think in terms of what they conceive to be their duty, who do it without external constraint or coercion, but see it as meeting the dictates of honor, or of loyalty, or of what is required to be a good citizen of the university. All of these forms of inner direction, as David Riesman called them many years ago, stand apart from, and indeed are opposed by, the formal requirements of accountability. That is because formal requirements for accountability are inherently suspicious of claims to professional and personal responsibility, claims which were in fact the basis on which academics in elite colleges and universities in all countries formerly escaped most formal external accountability for their work as teachers and scholars.

In Britain, as I have suggested, we are currently seeing the loss by academics of the persuasive power of their claims to personal and professional responsibility, claims which when honored underlay the extraordinary trust that British and American society have placed in their colleges and universities.[12] Academics in British universities were assumed to be "gentlemen," men and women who governed their own behavior according to the dictates of conscience, or considerations of honor, or professional norms, depending on their social origins.[13] And that is why, in transforming that elite system of higher education into a system of mass higher education, the British government in the past decade has gone to such lengths to deny the relevance of such claims to trust, and to subject the whole of the system and its members to what can only be seen as a kind of mass degradation ceremony, involving the transformation of academic staff—scholars and scientists, lecturers and professors alike—into employees, mere organizational personnel. And like other employees, they are expected to respond to penalties and incentives devised by the funding agency, required like any other employee of the state to account for themselves and their behavior to a bureaucracy that knows little of honor, conscience or trust. In such a world, claims to personal responsibility in academic life are met with derision or cynicism, as a transparent device to justify the old privileges of university life, and incompatible with state policies for higher education. (Which, of course, they mostly are).[14] References by academics to their personal responsibilities for their work, or to professional standards and obligations are often totally incomprehensible to people to whom the very vocabulary of personal responsibility is foreign. Unfortunately, when these claims to personal responsibility or professional status have to be made explicit, they are already weak. Trust cannot be demanded but must be freely given. In Trollope's novels, a gentleman who demands to be treated as a gentleman is almost certainly no gentleman.

But the decline in trust as one of the three basic forces in the support of higher education, where it has occurred, is not wholly the result of policies aimed at reshaping higher education in the image of private enterprise while increasing the regulatory power of central government, though the British case might lead us to believe so. A case can be made that in European countries a decline in trust is inherent in the growth of mass higher education since WWII, in the tremendous increase in its costs, especially to the public purse, and in the increasing diversity of forms that higher education takes, many of which cannot claim the academic authority of elite forms of higher education.[15] In Europe more than in the United States, the enormous growth of enrollments over the past four decades has not only made higher education into a competitor for support with other elements of the welfare state, but has also raised questions about the quality and standards of those institutions. That anxiety about "quality" has been exacerbated by tendencies in all European countries to cut the budgets for higher education, at least on a per capita basis. And that in turn has generated what can only be called an evaluation industry engaged in writing and consulting about problems in the assessment of teaching and research in postsecondary education, and the possible linkage of assessment to state funding. In all this the UK is exceptional chiefly in its greater anxiety about "economic decline," and the political weakness of its universities in the face of a hostile government which, under both Margaret Thatcher and John Major, has shown mistrust of all the old institutions of the establishment, and most particularly the universities, as agents of decline.

But while these pressures linking accountability to mass higher education are present everywhere, in many countries on the Continent there are countervailing forces arising out of the same movement toward mass higher education. The growing and increasingly diversified systems of higher education in many countries simply cannot be managed effectively from the center, and in countries as different as Sweden, Austria, France and the Netherlands universities have in recent years been granted greater autonomy. As Brennan notes, "In continental Europe, there is a general movement away from state authority."[16] I do not know of any other country, except perhaps Australia, which has shown the same pattern of management of higher education as in the UK: growth, the reduction of formal institutional diversity, and tighter administrative controls by an agency of central government.

There is a temptation to exaggerate the role of Britain's peculiar and highly intrusive forms of accountability that have been imposed on its colleges and universities over the past decade or more. But they are a symptom or response to other more fundamental forces that have transformed British higher education over the past 15 years: the very great increase in the proportion of the age grade enrolled in higher education, the dramatic decline in the unit of resource,[17] and the casual merger of the two big segments into a single system have been the forces behind the very rapid creation of mass higher education in the UK. The new forms of management and accountability are aspects of that transformation, though with significant consequences of their own independent of the other forces. But a growth of student numbers under circumstances of financial constraint did not require the merger of the segments, and the three together did not require the creation of the HEFC and the elaboration of the instruments of central management and control. There were and are unconsidered alternatives.

If there is less anxiety about the "quality" of higher education in the United States it is both because our system is so variable in that regard, and because we never made (or could make) any commitment as a nation to the maintenance of common standards across our thousands of colleges and universities. We also are less embarrassed by the role of the market in cultural affairs. As Louis Hartz reminded us, in America, by contrast with Europe, the market preceded the society.[18] That has not relieved our colleges and institutions from the problem of defining and defending a distinctive character or mission not wholly defined by market forces. But it has greatly reduced the pressures in America for strong systems of accountability to external bodies.

On the Measurement and Assessment of Teaching

I have suggested that the pressure for greater accountability in the UK, and especially the pressures for the direct assessment of the quality of teaching, arise chiefly out of the emergence of mass higher education and its effects on both teachers and students. On the latter score, the institutions of mass higher education recruit a more diversified body of students with respect to class origins, age, interests and talents. These institutions also recruit different kinds of people to the academic profession, more diverse in their origins, and increasingly from less privileged origins. The increasing diversity of both students and teachers forces a fundamental change in the curriculum and in pedagogy. Even when the new students are academically able, their interests and motivations will differ. Teachers and lecturers in the mass system can no longer assume that students will learn on their own; it comes to be doctrine that students can only be expected to learn what they are taught. That leads to a greater emphasis on teaching as a distinct skill that itself can be taught (and assessed), and places the student and the process of learning, rather than the subject, at the center of the educational enterprise, a Copernican revolution. The differences between secondary and higher education, in this as in other respects, narrow.

The growth and diversification of higher education, along with associated changes in pedagogy will require that a society and its systems of higher education surrender any idea of broad common standards of academic performance between institutions, and even between subjects within a single university—ministerial assertions to the contrary notwithstanding. But if students gain their degrees or credentials with widely varying levels of proficiency and at different levels of difficulty, then the meaning of the degree itself must change; higher education leaves the gold standard, and degrees are increasingly assessed by the name (and reputation) of the institution where it was earned and the department in which the student took the degree. But for many products of mass higher education who are not going on to the civil service, teaching, the higher professions or postgraduate study, the degree is less important except as a generalized statement that the student has a certain kind of cultural sophistication, has learned how to learn, can probably learn more, and has shown the self-discipline necessary to pass courses and earn a degree.

In the UK, as elsewhere, the growth in the size of departments makes it impossible for a professor to stand as a guarantor of the quality of work of everyone in his department. And appointment procedures to lower ranks become more various. So governments and institutions develop more rationalized assessments and quality assurance procedures, in part because the old quality assurance mechanism are not trusted under the new circumstances, in part because the system is now very expensive and becoming more so, in part because government is anxious about how the universities are performing in the face of the growing globalization of economic competition. So what to American eyes seems to be a manic concern for quality assurance arises in part from the withdrawal of trust in the institutions, now seen as full of less able students and teachers; and in part from anxiety about what these less distinguished students and teachers are doing, especially in the new non-elite sector as per capita support declines drastically.

Nevertheless, even if the pressures in this direction in the United States are still modest by comparison with the UK and some other European nations, public colleges and universities in some American states are the object of demands by their state governments for more evidence, preferably quantitative, bearing on their efficiency or effectiveness. This approach to the assessment of the quality of an education is to try to measure the effects of that education on individual students by testing their performance on various tasks, and then aggregating individual student performance on these tests into "performance indicators." But such measures of academic "outputs" capture only a fraction, and indeed a small fraction, of the contributions of higher education to the life of students, and the life of the society.

But why, we may ask, need we confine the assessment of the outcomes of higher education to those that can be captured on objective tests of student performance? There are other ways to assess the impact of higher education, not only on students but on institutions and society as a whole. What large effects do we hope our systems of higher education will have on society? How do we weigh the effects of higher education, for example, in reducing levels of racial and ethnic prejudice; or of enabling people to change their jobs, their skills and their professions as the economy changes; or of motivating people to enroll in continuing education throughout life; or of enabling people to raise children who want and get more schooling than their parents?

Should we use the school achievement rates of children twenty-five years after the graduation of their parents as performance indicators of the colleges and universities of 1970? How do we weigh the value to the society of the organizations created to protect the environment, defend battered wives, reform the criminal justice system, or help new immigrants, or the emotionally disturbed—all the voluntary institutions outside of government that make life more civilized and compassionate, and all of them disproportionately led and staffed by college and university graduates? Are leadership or participation rates in those institutions to be used as performance indicators as well?

Education is a process pretending to have a measurable outcome. That is what makes all measures of educational outcomes spurious. We may need to measure something to justify awarding degrees and certificates; but we need not share the illusion that our examinations measure the effects of education. Our impact on our students can never be fully known; it emerges over their whole lifetimes and takes various forms at different points in their lives. Those effects are mixed up with many other forces and factors over which we in higher education have no control—and among these are the student's character and life circumstances. Moreover, our influence on their lives takes many different forms, the most important of which are unmeasurable. One of the major functions of higher education which evades all measurement is our ability to raise the horizons of our students, to encourage them to set their ambitions higher than if they had not come under our influence. Colleges and universities at their best teach students that they can actually have new ideas, ideas of their own rather than merely the manipulation of ideas produced by others. That is not a conception of self very often gained in secondary school, and yet it lies at the heart of most of what people who gain a post-secondary education achieve in their lives. No formal assessment measures this increased self-confidence and belief in one's capacity to think originally and effectively, yet can we doubt that it is one of the great goods that attaches to a university education? And it is wrong and snobbish of us to think that it is only people like ourselves, professional academics and intellectuals, who possess this capacity. More and more we see the importance of initiative, originality, and the capacity to think in bold and fresh ways as a central element in success in the professions and in business enterprise. We do, at our best, teach people how to think and how to think more effectively, but whether they do so is a function of how well we communicate the novel idea that they can have novel ideas. How successfully they can put that idea into effect is a function not only how they think, but of other qualities of character, mind, habit, and life circumstance. The real and substantial effects of the experience of higher education extend over the whole lifetime of graduates, and are inextricably entwined with other forces and experiences beyond our walls and reach.

We can see the process of education, we can get a sense of the intelligence and energy that goes into it, but we cannot see very clearly what contributions universities are making to the life of the society, any more than we can measure the enduring influences of particular teachers on their students. But our inability to measure the outcomes of teaching does not preclude our learning about what the institution is doing well and what it is doing badly. And that is the work of internal accountability through internal reviews. *If internal reviews and assessments are to be more valid and fruitful than those done by outside accreditors, it is necessary that the institution subject itself and its units to serious and recurrent internal review, with real teeth and real consequences.* The loss of institutional autonomy is both cause and consequence of the abdication of responsibility by colleges and universities for managing their own affairs. And preeminent among those affairs is the maintenance of the quality of their teaching and research. But the creation and operation of serious, tough internal reviews of quality can be monitored through external audits, not of teaching quality or outcomes, but of the procedures in place for self-study and self-criticism , and of the effects those internal review have on practice. That is the way to link external and internal reviews, and make them mutually supporting.

On the Effects of the Revolution in Communications and Information

In all of the above I have been talking about colleges and universities of a kind which have existed in the West in recognizable form for 800 years, in North America for over 350 years, and in wholly familiar form in the United States for about a hundred years. I have left to last any consideration of the implications of the information revolution currently underway for colleges and universities and for their accountability. The authors of the essay on Accountability reflected on this question, and commissioned an informative report by a specialist on the impact to date of new forms of instructional technology on higher education.[19] But we declined to address the issue in our report chiefly because that revolution is in its earliest stages, and the nature of its future impact on higher education is still quite unclear. However unclear its lineaments, I believe that impact will be very large. I believe it will make learning at a distance much more common, and raise questions for many institutions of how they might best teach various parts of their curriculum, or revise their curriculum to accord with the new modes of instruction.

One clear effect of the new forms of instruction made possible by new technologies is that in some subjects they reduce the importance of teachers and students being in the same place at the same time, as increasing amounts of teaching are carried electronically. This could either complicate or facilitate the efforts institutions make to monitor and maintain the quality of teaching and learning. It certainly will make more difficult the tasks of accrediting institutions which provide instruction to students thousands of miles away, many of whom are interested in gaining skills and knowledge rather than grades or additional academic credentials. Accountability in higher education assumes a distinguishable institution with recognizable boundaries, employing an academic staff with identifiable qualifications to instruct a defined population of students enrolled for some kind of credential. But the new technologies threaten many of those assumptions, and begin to blur the distinction between "higher education" and "lifelong learning." The latter, however much to be welcomed, will be more difficult to assess and accredit or hold accountable to anyone.

Over twenty years ago I published an analysis of the movement of educational systems and institutions in all advanced societies from elite to mass forms, and pointed to a variety of strains and difficulties that would attend this major transformation.[20] That analysis in 1974 also included a discussion of a further movement toward universal access to higher education that I believed would follow naturally and inevitably from the move to mass higher education.

The best examples of universal access at the time were the Open University in Great Britain and the American community colleges, both genuinely open door colleges which also either granted a recognized degree, as did the Open University, or provided credits toward such a degree through transfer, as did the community colleges. But both were limited in their outreach, though wider than anything else at the time. I then thought that the move toward universal access, like the move toward mass access, would happen more rapidly in Europe than it did. I underestimated just how difficult these transformations would be, how great would be the social and political constraints on fundamental change in this key area of social life. And it really is only in the past five or ten years, and even more recently in the UK, that we see real transformations in the old system, rather than merely an expansion and dilution of the elite system.

But now, quite suddenly, universal access is not a secondary or marginal or future phenomenon, but threatens (or promises) to transform the relations between teachers and learners, between employers and education, between work and learning, between higher education and the rest of society. The communications revolution is upon us, symbolized by the Internet and the World Wide Web. Many, in this country and elsewhere, are learning to exploit the new capacities that technology gives us. More slowly, because more difficult, is the job of finding out what is going on in the world of higher education as a result of these developments. More energy is being put into the creation of new educational possibilities—for example, highly sophisticated courseware—than in analyzing their long and short term effects. I believe these new forms of teaching and learning will have large effects on the character of our colleges and universities, as well as on the capacity of those institutions to account for what they are doing to their support communities.

I have the impression that there is less discussion of these issues in Europe than in the US, though many of the technical advances have been made in European universities and industries. That may be in part because these developments threaten to develop outside of governmental control; it may be also that European social scientists are a bit shy of dealing with problems that are so heavily based on technological developments. Whatever the reasons, the issues that European and American higher education are currently struggling with, issues of expansion, cost, organization and management, quality, internal and external accountability and the survival or decline of trust, all will be profoundly affected in the immediate future by developments in interactive communications and distance learning currently under way.

Notes

1. Paper prepared for a seminar organized by the Society for Research into Higher Education, Oxford, June 12, 1996. Published as "Trust, markets and accountability in higher education: a comparative perspective," *Higher Education Policy*, Vol. 9, No. 4, 1996, pp. 309–324. My thanks to Oliver Fulton for his critical reading of a draft of this paper.

2. Patricia Graham, Richard Lyman and Martin Trow, *Accountability of Colleges and Universities: An Essay*, The Accountability Study, Columbia University, October 1995. For a fuller discussion of the American scene, see Martin Trow, "On the Accountability of Higher Education in the United States," in William G. Bowen and Harold K. Shapiro, eds, *Universities and their Leadership*, Princeton, Princeton University Press, 1998, pp. 15–63.

3. The UK has introduced the rhetoric and vocabulary of the market into higher education—much talk about customers, efficiency gains, marketing and the like—but without allowing the emergence of real markets. Not long ago some universities were responding to a quaesi-market situation by buying some active researchers along with their bibliographies (or perhaps the other way around) to improve their standing in the next round of research assessments. This was perfectly rational market-oriented behavior; but on hearing about it the then Director of the Higher Education Funding Council(E) was quite irritated, made clear that is not what he had in mind, and suggested that he would be looking for some way to stop that kind of behavior. It is difficult to explain to Americans that the UK has the ideology of market relations in higher education without markets.

4. The nature and detail of required reports can and often do have effects on institutions quite apart from the policies which they are designed to implement. The heavy burden of the many and lengthy reports which marks the current system of central government funding of British universities has effects on them over and above the problems for British universities generated by central government policies and cost cutting.

5. The two most successful federal programs in higher education in American history—the Morrill Land Grant Act of 1863 and the GI Bill after WWII—were both marked by relatively light oversight and little accountability for the large sums expended. Both were attended by a measure of corruption in the administration of the programs. But most people would see the gains to American society from both these programs as far outweighing the costs, both the legitimate costs and those of corruption. I believe that this was true in both cases less as a result of considered policy than of the small size of the federal bureaucracy at both times available for oversight. Nevertheless, the examples do raise questions about the bearing of accountability, of its nature and detail, on the effectiveness of public policy, perhaps especially in higher education.

6. Though these sentiments remain the underpinning for both law and institutionalized forms of funding.

7. John Brennan, "Authority, Legitimacy and Change: the rise of quality assessment in higher education," Quality Support Center, The Open University, n.d., 1996, p. 7.

8. I include "moral" as an aspect of accountability to stress the obligations of higher education to groups and individuals who are part of a support community but who are not in the narrow sense "stake holders." One example might be foreign scholars; another might be secondary school teachers.

9. *Accountability of Colleges and Universities, op. cit.*

10. *ibid.*

11. See, for example, Guy Neave, *The Core Functions of Government: Six European perspectives on a shifting educational landscape*, National Advisory Council (the Netherlands), June 1995; M. Trow, "Reflections on Higher Education Reform in the 1990s: The Case of Sweden," in Thorsten Nybom, ed., *Studies in Higher Education and Research*, The Council for Studies in Higher Education, Stockholm, 1993:94; Guy Neave and Frans Van Vught, eds.., *Prometheus Bound: The Changing Relationship Between Government and Higher Education in Western Europe*, Oxford: Pergammon Press, 1991; Guy Neave, "The Politics of Quality: developments in higher education in Western Europe 1992–1994, *European Journal of Education*, vol. 29, no. 2, 1994, pp. 115–134; and Frans Van Vught and Don Westerheuden, "Towards a general model of quality assessment in higher education," *Higher Education*, 28, 1994, pp. 355–371.

12. On the Continent, academics have had something of the status of civil servants, and with obvious exceptions in dictatorships, were by virtue of their special work accorded a considerable measure of academic freedom in universities which were not as autonomous as in the U.S. and Britain.

13. Of course these concerns for personal and group responsibility for behavior were and are not confined to "gentlemen." For a recent discussion of these issues in Victorian England, see Gertrude Himmelfarb, *The De-moralization of Society*, New York, Vintage Books, 1995, pp. 143–169.

14. For a fuller discussion of the motivations and consequences of central government policy toward higher education in the UK see my "Managerialism and the Academic Profession: The Case of England," *Higher Education Policy*, vol. 7, no. 2, 1994, pp. 11–18. These issues are currently the object of study by Oliver Fulton and myself.

15. I am skeptical about widespread claims of a deep decline of trust in higher education in America, since that is a convenient, and indeed almost a necessary condition for introducing greater regulation by way of more formal accountability. There is considerable evidence in various measures of tangible confidence and support that trust in American colleges and universities has not declined in recent years as is widely assumed, though there is no doubt that it occupies a different position in the public mind than it did before, say, 1966. Over the decade 1981–1991, total enrollments continued to grow (by 14%) despite the fact that colleges and universities were raising their tuition rates much more rapidly (by 54% in constant dollars) than the Consumer Price Index; during that decade the differential in income between college and high school graduates grew very sharply, by 88%; private giving to colleges and universities increased by 66% in constant dollars; federal support for academic research increased by 53% in real terms between 1981 and 1991; the number of foreign students in American colleges and universities grew by 31%; and measures of "satisfaction" in surveys of students and recent graduates have not declined in recent years. (Source: Ross Gotler, "Indicators of Confidence," memorandum prepared for the Accountability Project, Columbia University, March 2, 1995.) On the other hand, between 1981 and 1995 the proportion of people who expressed "a great deal of confidence" in "major educational institutions such as colleges and universities" fell from 37% to 27% on a national poll, though it has been rising slightly in recent years. (The Harris Poll 1995 #17, March 6, 1995.) In this poll higher education "rank[ed] third on the list of institutions in which the public has the most confidence . . . the public's loss of faith in higher education lags behind its loss of faith in institutions on the whole." *ibid*. There is certainly room for debate on this issue and its implications. See *Accountability, op. cit.*, pp. 3–5.

16. Brennan, *op. cit.*, p. 3.

17. Lord Dainton, using official figures, calculates that the average unit of resource—that is, "the average amount of recurrent income per student from government directly and also from fees in respect of British and European Union students," declined between 1972/3 and 1995/6 by two-thirds, with worse to come. (Hansard, the House of Lords Official Report, 570, no. 56, 6 March 1996, 310).

18. Louis Hartz, *The Liberal Tradition in America*, New York, Harcourt Brace, 1955.

19. Pamela H. Atkinson, "Distance Education in Institutions of Higher Learning in the United States: A background paper for the *Study on Accountability of Colleges and Universities*," October 1995, *op. cit.*

20. "Problems in the Transition from Elite to Mass Higher Education." In *Policies for Higher Education*, from the General Report on the Conference on Future Structures of Post-Secondary Education, 55–101. Paris: Organisation for Economic Co-operation and Development, 1974.

A CASE OF BUREAUCRATIC ACCRETION
CONTEXT AND CONSEQUENCES

PATRICIA J. GUMPORT AND BRIAN PUSSER

> It is not the business of the botanist to eradicate the weeds. Enough for him if he can tell us just how fast they grow.
>
> C. Northcote Parkinson

The dramatic expansion of the higher education enterprise in the United States over the past half-century is a well-documented phenomenon [7, 17]. It has also been observed that administrative structures have grown with this expansion [25, 27]. However, whether the administration of higher education organizations has grown in proportion with the increased demands on the enterprise is unclear. Although popular perceptions of administrative growth in public research universities have reflected widespread concern over the nature of that growth [20, 26, 34], there has been little empirical research that directly documents administrative growth, its context, and its consequences [25]. To shed light on this issue, we examine a twenty-five-year period of sustained financial and systemic growth in the University of California through an analysis of budget data and relevant archival documents.[1]

Using classical Weberian concepts of bureaucratization as well as more recent literature on adaptation and economies of scale, we analyze the data from a number of perspectives. Primary among them is the proposition that adaptation to environmental complexity has demanded an increase and differentiation of university functions and hence the need for a more complex administrative component. We also consider some unexplored functions of complexity, primarily that under a broad university mission the process of adaptation to complexity may have served as de facto university policy-making. In addition to applying these concepts to the case of the University of California, we examine challenges that have emerged in the transition from an era of rising resources to a subsequent period of retrenchment.

The Case, the Concepts, and the Methods

The University of California

The University of California provides an ideal case study opportunity for examination of administrative growth. Founded in 1868, the University of California was created as a public land-grant university and is administered under the authority of an independent board of regents. At present, the university consists of nine campuses: Berkeley, Davis, Irvine, Los Angeles, Riverside, San Diego, San Francisco, Santa Barbara, and Santa Cruz. Eight campuses provide undergraduate, graduate, and professional education; a ninth, San Francisco, focuses on the health sciences. Throughout the state the university has established teaching hospitals and clinics, as well as over one hundred fifty university institutes, centers, and research laboratories, including contract laboratories for the De-

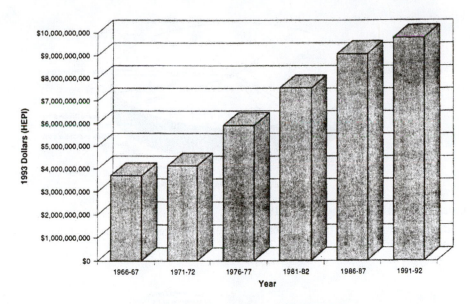

Total = $9,803,070,000 (1993 Dollars/HEPI)

Figure 1   Current fund expenditures by the UC system 1966/67–1991/92.

Source: Data adapted from University of California Office of the President Campus Financial Schedules and Annual Financial Reports 1966–92.

partment of Energy.[2] National Science Foundation data reflect that five University of California campuses (Berkeley, Los Angeles, San Francisco, San Diego, and Davis) ranked in the top twenty-two universities nationally in 1992 for R&D expenditures.[3] Annually, the university awards over twenty-seven thousand bachelor's degrees, and over eleven thousand advanced degrees. Since its founding the university has awarded over a million degrees. Current enrollment is over one hundred fifty thousand students.

In the twenty-five-year period under examination for this study, a defining characteristic of the University of California (hereafter also referred to as UC) has been growth. The nine campuses, systemwide administration, and auxiliary enterprises taken together had total fund expenditures just over $3,700,000,000 (1993 HEPI) in 1966–67.[4] For 1991–92 these UC entities accounted for expenditures of just over $9,800,000,000.[5] This is an increase of 164 percent in constant dollars[6] (see figure 1). Student FTEs rose from 79,293 for 1966–67 to 156,371 for 1991–92, an increase of just over 97 percent.[7] The number of employees also shows marked growth. The permanently budgeted system staff in 1966–67 of 33,305 can be compared to the permanently budgeted system staff in 1991–92 of 68,024.[8] This is an increase of 104 percent. The total UC staff grew over this period at a rate nearly double the rate of population growth for the state of California, which at the time was one of the fastest growing states in the nation.[9]

From its origins as the state of California's land-grant university with a focus on teaching and public service, UC has grown into a massive, diversified economic enterprise with total expenditures of just under ten billion dollars a year. One quarter of total system expenditures goes to Department of Energy Laboratories, just over 20 percent to teaching hospitals and clinics, and just under 15 percent to research. Less than 20 percent of the annual expenditures for the system fall in the category Instruction (see figure 5).[10]

In the twenty-five-year period under examination for this study, our analysis of expenditure data shows disproportionate growth in expenditures on administrative functions relative to expenditures for instruction. The ratio of spending on instruction to spending on administration shows a

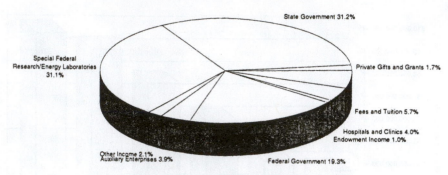

Figure 2   Current fund income by source 1966–67.

Source: Data adapted from University of California Office of the President Campus Financial Schedules and University of California Financial Report 1966–67.

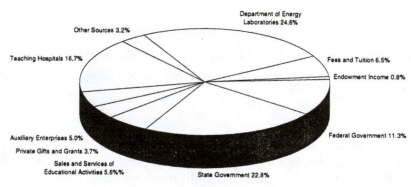

Figure 3   Current fund income by source 1991–92.

Source: Data adapted from University of California Office of the President Campus Financial Schedules and Financial Report 1991–92.

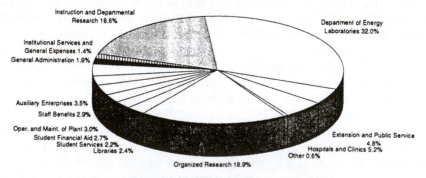

Figure 4   Current fund expenditures by UCC 1966–67.

Source: Data adapted from University of California Office of the President Campus Financial Schedules and Financial Report 1966–67.

Note: For figures 2–5 percentages may not add up to 100 due to rounding.

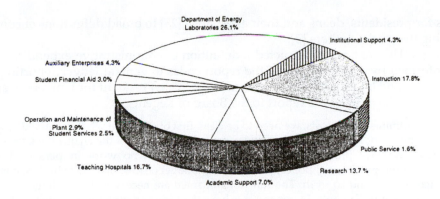

Total = $9,803,070,000 (1993 Dollars/HEPI)

Figure 5   Current fund expenditures by UCC 1991–92.

Source: Data adapted from University of California Office of the President Campus Financial Schedules and Financial Report 1991–92.

shift from roughly six dollars of instructional spending for each dollar spent on administration in 1966–67 to a ratio of about three dollars spent on instruction for each dollar spent on administration in 1991–92 (see figure 7).

Concepts and Working Definitions

Before delving into the data for the case of UC, it is essential to clarify the concept "administration" and to state the rationale for our working definitions.

Both conceptually and empirically, the issue of what constitutes administration has been an enduring interest of sociologists of organization and, secondarily, of interest to sociologists of knowledge. Originating in Weber's classic work on bureaucracy, the research agenda has evolved into descriptions and explanations of the increase in size and elaboration of administrative structures in large-scale organizations, and in these approaches scholars have sought to delineate the consequences for coordination and control of diverse segments of work [2, 3, 6, 43].

Despite numerous thoughtful contributions by a wide range of scholars of administrative growth, a number of unresolved issues persist as core concerns for researchers in higher education. Most prominent among these is an effort to describe and explain the linkages between administrative growth, the organization of academic work, and the authority underlying resource allocation decisions [2, 3, 7, 10, 16, 18, 21, 38, 44, 45, 46]. Much attention is directed to fundamental questions about structure: What counts as administration? What is the ideal size of the administration?[11] What constitute the parameters of administrative authority? [2, 3, 10, 39, 48].

Such scholarly and practical concerns about administration dovetail with ongoing inquiries by sociologists of knowledge directed at understanding how boundaries and categories of systems of knowledge are constituted and how patterns of authority located in organizations influence both the content and structure of knowledge [18, 47].[12] Another powerful influence on the shaping of these boundaries and categories has been the remarkable growth in resources to higher education since World War II [17]. One of our central concerns in this study addresses what happens to the ostensible necessity for differentiation and the adaptive potential of campuses when resources become finite or are diminished.

Much of the literature [4, 25, 27] directly relevant to administrative growth in universities takes for granted organizationally derived categories (for example, from NACUBO); however, there is no uniform definition in higher education research of what constitutes administration or administrative functions. Definitions of administrative functions range from such quite specific delineations as "expenditures for presidents, deans and their assistants" [25] to broad definitions encompassing all those organizing the work of others [2].

For the case of UC we have constructed a definition of administrative expenditures and positions that is informed by close analysis of the report codes in general ledger reporting categories, personnel manuals, and by a definition presented by UC Vice-President for University and External Relations William B. Baker in a 1993 report to the Board of Regents:

> With respect to administrative costs, we need to be clear, first of all, about what is defined as administration in the University. Administration includes not only the offices of the chancellors, vice chancellors, president and vice presidents, but also all the people who work in personnel services, accounting, auditing, purchasing, police, planning and budget offices, mail distribution, community relations, legal counsel and so forth. The functions I named are necessary to any large organization that employs thousands of people. In our case, we have the added administrative complexities related to students, federal contracts and grants, hospitals, agricultural field stations, and oversight of the DOE laboratories [49].

Vice-President Baker's definition corresponds closely to the functions incorporated within the reporting category Institutional Support from the system's Uniform Accounting Structure (UAS).[13] However, reliance on the Institutional Support category does not incorporate a number of expenditures and positions that can appropriately be considered administrative functions and that are located within other reporting categories. For example, the administration of instructional functions at the level of department chairs, administration incorporated in the UAS reporting category Research, and administrative functions reported in the categories Operation and Maintenance, Student Services, and Teaching Hospitals are not incorporated under Institutional Support.

In literature that examines higher education accounting, administrative costs have been defined as either the uniform classification category of Institutional Support, or the combination of Institutional Support, Academic Support (minus libraries) and Student Services [25, 27]. In defining administration for this article, we have deliberately taken a cautious approach of using data from only two of the University of California uniform reporting categories.

We analyze Institutional Support and the subcategory of Academic Support known as Academic Administration separately, prior to combining them as one measure of administration, in order to draw comparisons with the growth over time of instructional expenditures. (The distinction is evident in figure 6 and figure 7.) The subcategory Academic Administration contains expenditures which are

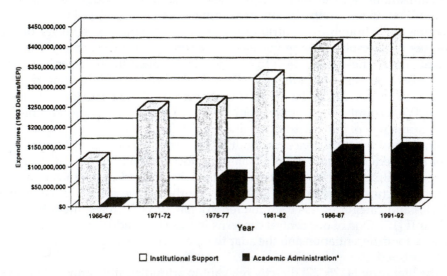

Figure 6   Expenditures for institutional support and academic administration.

Source: Data adapted from University of California Office of the President Campus Financial Schedules and Financial Reports 1966–92

*The UAS subcategory Academic Administration was first captioned in 1974.

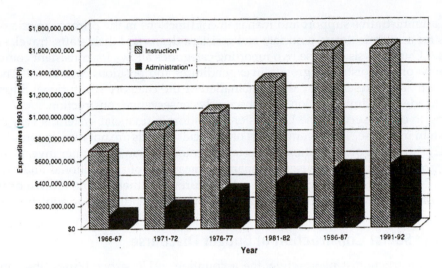

Figure 7 Expenditures for instruction and "administration."

Source: Data adapted from University of California Office of the President Campus Financial Schedules and Financial Reports 1966–92.

*Instruction consists of UAS category 40 (Instruction) minus expenditures for UAS subcategory Extension.

**"Administration" combines UAS category 72 (Institutional Support) and subcategory (Academic Administration).

Legend to Figure 7

Uniform Accounting Structure, Report Codes, Reporting Categories and Selected Subcategories for Expenditure Data.

40—Instruction: General Academic, Summer Session, University Extension

42—Teaching Hospital: Davis, Irvine, Los Angeles, San Diego, San Francisco. This category includes all expenditures associated with hospital patient care operations, general, fiscal and administrative, physical plant and institutional support.

43—Academic Support: Libraries, Museums and Galleries, Audio Visual, Computing Support, Ancillary Support (demonstration schools, clinics, labs), Academic Administration (Deans and their immediate offices)

44—Research: Institutes and Research Centers, Individual or Project Research

62—Public Service: Arts and Lectures, Cooperative Extension, Community Service

64—Maintenance and Operation of Plant: Administration, Maintenance and Repairs, Janitorial, Grounds Maintenance.

68—Student Services: Office of Financial Aid, Admissions, Registrar, Counseling, Career Guidance.

72—Institutional Support: Executive Management (Regents, President and Vice President, Chancellor, General Counsel); Fiscal Operations (Accounting, Auditing, Insurance, Cashiers); General Administration Services (Environmental Health, Information Systems, Personnel, Computer Centers); Logistical Services (Business Management, Construction Management, Duplicating, Materiel Management, Police); Public Relations/Development (Development, Public Information, Relations with Schools, Publications).

76—Auxiliary Enterprises: Bookstores, Housing, Food Service, Intercollegiate Athletics, Residence Halls, Parking

78—Student Financial Aid: Expenditures for scholarships and fellowships

Expenditures for Instruction and "Administration" presented in figure 7:

Instruction—UAS reporting category Instruction (40) minus expenditures in the subcategory Extension (400900).

"Administration"—UAS reporting category Institutional Support (72) plus the subcategory Academic Administration (430801) within UAS reporting category Academic Support.

Source: UC *Accounting Manual*—Uniform Accounting Structure (Second revision 11/1/83, Bill Chan and Don Alter), and *Campus Financial Schedules*, various years. University of California Office of the President.

identified as administrative support and management functions in the primary missions. It includes expenditures for academic deans, associate and assistant deans and their staffs, travel, supplies, and expenditures.[14] Our analysis of these two reporting categories allows for consistent comparisons of a significant arena of administrative growth in expenditures and positions over time.[15] The analysis of "Administration" as represented by the combination of the category Institutional Support and the subcategory Academic Administration is a consciously conservative construction.

According to one observer, "the University of California financial system is very complex and its record system immense. The several layers of financial records are not readily found or easily understood" [42].[16] Because our intention is to establish a foundation for further investigation into administrative growth, we have devised comparable measures of instructional and administrative expenditures. Moreover, our designation of expenditures as either administrative or instructional has the effect of consistently underestimating the amount of spending on administration.

A Note on the Social Construction of Budget Discourse

From a social constructionist perspective, the accounting of UC expenditures, the construction of budget categories, and the accompanying narrative represent a symbolic ideology for the system and its campuses [35, 44]. The annual University of California *Financial Report*, 1991–92 compresses nearly one thousand pages of allocation and expenditure data into two dozen summary pages. The section "Facts In Brief" presents nearly ten billion dollars of expenditures in a dozen line items. One of those line items, the category Other, accounts for over one and a quarter billion dollars of expenditure.[17]

University accounting and reporting procedures have changed over time, as have the captions over general ledger accounts. A useful example follows the evolution of the uniform accounting category now known as Institutional Support. Prominent in the summary document of current fund expenditures, the University of California *Financial Report* for 1966–67, is a category captioned General Administration, with expenditures 60 percent greater than a related category captioned Institutional Services and General. For the year 1991–92, in two summary accounting reports produced by the UC Office of the President, neither the *Budget for Current Operations* nor the University of California *Financial Report* uses the word "administration" to caption expenditure categories. General Administration is now a subcategory. It has been subsumed into a more recently established category, Institutional Support.[18]

Public universities depend on popular support, and the UC system itself has been active in shaping public perceptions of the University's operations.[19] State funding and private gifts provide a quarter of the total system income. The construction of categories in the University of California financial summaries and the specific subsuming of the caption General Administration deserve further consideration. It can be seen as a standard accounting shift, and it may also suggest institutional sensitivity to the change over time in connotation of certain words, particularly "administration." The recent decline in state general fund allocations to UC[20] may reflect in part a growing perception that the university's administration is too large.[21] California State Senator Hayden expressed that point of view, referring to UC in *The New York Times:* "The administrative bureaucracy is bloated" [37].

The change over time in UC accounting nomenclature is consistent with historical examples of the construction of public discourse in other contexts.[22] While some of the shifts in nomenclature were in keeping with changes in NACUBO policy, others such as the ordering and naming of categories in the summary documents appear to be independently constructed. Shedding light on this practice of captioning budget categories, Mullard has developed a concept, the politics of discourse, drawing upon a definition of discourse provided by Laclau and Mouffe [24, 35].[23] In an exemplary analysis of the "linguistic structuring" utilized to shape perceptions of public expenditure, Mullard reveals how the practice of organizing and captioning financial categories in public summaries may be interpreted as an effort to establish signification for types of expenditures. Mullard's work also extends Foucault's conceptualization of the construction of discourse as a political practice [9, 15].

The politics of discourse can be applied to our analysis of UC expenditure categories and captioning practices. For example, the caption General Administration may be seen as a signifier. As political economic contexts change over time, what has come to be signified by the word administration may be something akin to bureaucracy or similar concepts with increasingly negative connotations [3]. An application of the politics of discourse of public expenditure would predict a new signifier in response. Although the linkage is not definitive, in 1974, General Administration did become a subcategory and was subsumed into a new category captioned Institutional Support. The signifier Institutional Support presumably generates more positive images. It is noteworthy that even Institutional Support is placed in the category captioned Other in the annual summary section, "Facts in Brief."[24]

There is little in the signifier Other to bring to mind such signifieds as administration or bureaucracy. In the context of the discourse of public expenditure, within the current UC system accounting summaries, administration has become a missing signifier and bureaucratic accretion a missing signified.

Methods and Data Analysis

Quantitative data used in this study come from the official income, allocation and expenditure schedules prepared by the University of California Office of the President. All financial data are stated in constant 1993 dollars using the Higher Education Price Index (HEPI), unless otherwise indicated.

The primary analytical focus for this study is the change over time in expenditures and in positions. The reason for extending the data analysis to both expenditures and positions is to address the issue of rising administrative costs [10, 25, 27]. By analyzing data on the growth in positions, we are able to include an indicator of relative growth that is less dependent on rising costs.

Expenditures

The financial data that show the increase over time in total expenditures for UC are presented in figures 1, 4, and 5.

Figure 6 shows the growth over time of the Uniform Accounting Structure reporting category Institutional Support and the UAS subcategory designated Academic Administration. In figure 7 the total of those two categories is combined and captioned "Administration."[25] Our calculation of instructional spending shown in figure 7 presents the entire UAS reporting category Instruction,[26] minus expenditures in the subcategory Extension.[27]

As figure 7 shows, the expenditure in our category "Administration" has increased more rapidly than the expenditure in Instruction. The expenditure in the UAS category Instruction increased during the twenty-five-year period over 175 percent. The expenditure in "Administration" increased for the same period by over 400 percent.[28] These figures can be compared to a total system expenditure increase of 164 percent. Another way to consider this change over time is to note that for the entire UC system in 1966–67 approximately six dollars were spent on Instruction for each dollar spent on "Administration." By the year 1991–92, approximately three dollars were spent on Instruction for each dollar spent on "Administration."

Positions

The percentage growth in instructional and administrative positions over twenty-five years is shown in figures 8 and 9. As detailed in these figures and the accompanying legend, our category "Administration" consists of the total of the permanently budgeted staff positions in the categories General Administration and Institutional Support.[29] Our accounting for the growth of instructional positions utilizes the total of the permanently budgeted positions in the category Instruction.[30] Instruction includes academic positions, instructional staff and nonadministrative instructional support positions.

As figure 8 shows, over the twenty-five years the number of positions in "Administration" has increased nearly two and a half times faster than positions in the category Instruction.[31] In the five-year period of 1986/87–1991/92, shown in figure 9, a period marked by state recession, the number of positions in the category "Administration" grew twice as fast as the number of positions in Instruction.

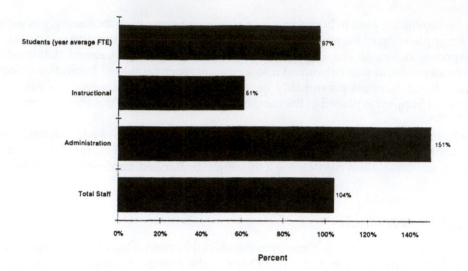

Figure 8   Percentage growth in permanently budgeted UC staff and students (FTE) 1966/67–1991/92.

Source: Data adapted from University of California Office of the President Campus Financial Schedules and Financial Reports 1966–92.

Note: Administration = categories 66 (General Administration) and 72 (Institutional Support) from Departmental Allocations; Instructional = category 40 from Departmental Allocations.

Legend to Figure 8

Reporting Categories Utilized for FTE Staff Positions

40—Instruction: Academic departments and instructional support
41—Summer Session
42—Teaching Hospital: Davis, Irvine, Los Angeles, San Diego, San Francisco
43—Academic Support
44—Research: Institutes and Research Centers, Individual or Project Research
60—Libraries
61—University Extension
62—Public Service: Arts and Lectures, Cooperative Extension
64—Maintenance and Operation of Plant
66—General Administration: President's Office, Chancellors Offices, Personnel, Campus Planning, Regents Office and Counsel
68—Student Services: Office of Financial Aid, Admissions, Recreation
72—Institutional Support: Corporate Services, Public Information, Police, Development Office
76—Auxiliary Enterprises: Bookstores, Housing, Food Service, Intercollegiate Athletics, Residence Halls, Parking
78—Student Financial Aid

Categories for Instruction and "Administration" FTE positions presented in figure 8:

Instruction—(40)

"Administration"—General Administration (66), Institutional Support (72)

Source: *Departmental Allocations—University of California Budget for Current Operations*, various years.

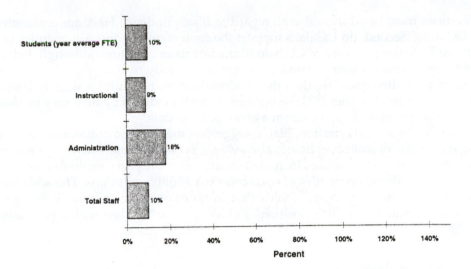

Figure 9   Percentage growth in permanently budgeted UC staff and students (FTE) 1986/87–1991/92.

Source: Data adapted from University of California Office of the President Annual Financial Report and Departmental Budgetary Allocations 1986/87 and 1991/92.

Bureaucratic Accretion

Our data suggest the existence of a disproportionate amount of administrative growth relative to growth in instruction. We refer to this as bureaucratic accretion.

Based on our analysis of expenditures in the UC system the data show that over the past twenty-five years the rate of growth in expenditures for administration has significantly exceeded the rate of growth in expenditures for instruction and the rate of growth of student FTE. This growth is above and beyond the increase in administrative expenditures embedded in categories other than our category of "Administration." Based on our analysis of the data, we consider this as evidence of bureaucratic accretion with respect to expenditures in the University of California.

Similarly, the rate of growth in permanently budgeted FTE for administrative positions has significantly exceeded the rate of growth in either permanently budgeted instructional positions or student FTE over the past twenty-five years. These disproportionate increases are above and beyond the increase in administrative positions embedded in categories other than our category "Administration." We consider this as evidence of bureaucratic accretion with respect to positions in the University of California.[32]

Interpreting Administrative Growth

The data depicted in figures 1–9 present remarkable growth in the UC system, particularly for expenditures and positions within our category of "Administration." We now turn our attention to prevailing propositions about administrative growth, its context and consequences, to shed light on the UC data.

Economies of Scale

Blau [2] applied a regression analysis developed in his study of the differentiation and growth of administration in employment security agencies to large universities. He pointed out that larger universities have lower ratios of administrators to faculty than smaller universities. On that basis he suggested that there is the possibility for economies of scale in large academic institutions, with proportionately fewer administrators needed for larger organizations. He also found that economies of scale occurred at a declining rate over time in larger organizations.[33]

Two questions must be addressed with regard to Blau's findings. First, are economies of scale evident in UC data? Second, do UC data support the contention that those economies of scale decline over time? Data from the case of UC help illuminate these questions, although definitive resolution would require investigation beyond the scope of this study.

With regard to the first question, the ratio of administrators to faculty is slightly lower at larger UC campuses than at smaller ones.[34] The economies of scale predicted by Blau may be shown when contrasting UC campuses of different size at a given point in time.

With regard to the second question, Blau's suggestion that larger institutional size may lead to diminishing economies of scale over time is also evident in the UC data. The ratio of administrators to faculty on the two largest campuses increased steadily over the past twenty-five years.[35] One explanation of these declining economies of scale concerns additive solutions. The additive explanation, following Durkheimian precepts, holds that in times of rising revenue intraorganizational conflicts may be mediated by adding positions and resources rather than making exclusive choices [14, 18, 40, 45].

Adaptation to Complexity

Another prominent explanation of growth in higher education is that university structures expand and diversify, becoming ever more complex over time, making a number of systemic accommodations in response to environmental demands for the university to perform more and more tasks [7, 8, 23]. Little empirical research has been done to determine to what degree administrative functions grow in response to those demands [25]; nor is it clear in the literature whether the complexity proposition is contingent upon a resource-rich context, or whether it might still apply in conditions of steady-state or financial scarcity.

The application of the complexity proposition to the phenomenon of administrative growth would suggest that with expansion over time universities require more administrative personnel and expenditures. Few empirical studies have tested the correlation between increased complexity in environmental demands and increased expenditures, and even fewer have tested the role of complexity as a causal factor in administrative growth. In one landmark study, Brinkman and Leslie [4] suggest that greater complexity is associated with higher administrative costs. Whether disproportionate growth in administration may be a consequence of adaptation to complexity has not yet been addressed. In that spirit our UC data may offer some preliminary insights, even though this study was not designed to test the complexity proposition.

Accounting for Complexity

As academic departments and administrative units are added, expanded, and differentiated in response to greater and more specialized environmental demands, it would seem to follow that expenditures and positions devoted to administrative functions would also expand. In the case of UC, given the countervailing force of labor-saving technology and possible economies of scale, it is difficult to predict whether the corresponding rate of administrative growth should be proportionate to university expansion.

As we suggested, UC expenditures and positions have shown enormous growth over time (see figures 1 and 8). Indeed, administrative expenditures and positions have grown significantly and disproportionately with regard to instructional expenditures and positions. While expansion of functions at lower levels would predict some centralized administrative growth for coordination, economies of scale may also come into play. The question of the reasonable proportion of growth in administrative expenditures that should be attributed to complexity warrants further analysis.[36] For example, the UC administration has recently cited the necessity to adapt to an increase in externally mandated regulations as a stimulus for administrative growth. Given that these regulations and the changing environment they represent influence the conduct of university affairs at many levels, our data indicate that expenditures for such often-cited complexors as Affirmative Action, Environmental Health and Safety, and Collective Bargaining contribute a relatively small percentage to total expenditures in our category "Administration."[37]

This finding is supported by Meyer et al. [31] and Parkinson [40]. They propose that quantitative increases in task demands do not appear to be the principal cause of administrative growth. An alternative proposition is that bureaucracies are called upon to cultivate stability of present functions as well as innovations. One consequence is consistent bureaucratic growth.

Adaptation to Institutional Forces for Legitimacy

A third proposition addresses the source of universities' legitimacy. This approach moves beyond adaptation to technical demands in the environment and focuses on adaptation to such wider institutional forces as commonly accepted beliefs and socially defined rules about desirable organizational forms and practices [29]. From this point of view technical demands exist, but their relative emphasis is dramatically downplayed. An interrelated conceptualization suggests that in the pursuit of legitimacy a university will emulate structural forms of successful organizations in its organizational field, leading to similar structures across universities [13, 41, 48].[38]

An empirical examination of isomorphism is beyond the scope of this exploratory inquiry; however, it is worthwhile to pursue the question of what forms and practices a leading institution in its field (like UC) attempts to emulate. The significant growth over time of such UC operations as auxiliary enterprises and hospital services may suggest that UC increasingly looks to private sector enterprises [19]. As evidence in support of this observation, at an October 1993 UC Regents meeting the Regents passed an amendment to the salary schedules, enabling UC hospital administrators to earn as much as $230,000 per year, a salary significantly higher than that of the campus chancellors. The primary rationale was that the increases were necessary to compete with private sector salaries for hospital management.

It is also important to acknowledge that the institutional forces in an organization's wider environment may yield ambiguous signals. In the quest for legitimacy, an organization may respond to multiple and conflicting pressures for adaptation, with subsequent increases in expenditures and personnel.

Tactical Administrative Growth

A fourth explanatory proposition for disproportionate administrative growth refers to administrative responses to perceived political economic pressures for short-run excellence. For public research universities in particular, resource dependence creates political economic dependence. In the case of UC, one perspective suggests that the University may have increasingly directed resources to managing perceptions of quality and utility at some cost to core quality processes. From this perspective the UC has discovered that the return (measured, for example, in terms of keeping donors and legislators happy in the short run) is considerably higher from expenditures on administrative functions than from expenditures on instructional functions. In this scenario, reputation and resource acquisition respond more to administrative interventions than to instructional interventions. As a result, resource-dependent public organizations increasingly respond to their competitive environment by allocating resources to the periphery, image management, and bridges with funding sources. Hence, over time, not only does spending on administration increase disproportionately relative to instructional expenditures, the effects of these expenditures on quality may not become apparent for quite some time.[39]

Mission as Policy

Another proposition that may account for disproportionate administrative growth is that, under certain circumstances, the university mission may stand in for explicit university policy. The university mission provides few clear institutional mechanisms for selecting among priorities or making resource allocation decisions in accord with those priorities; more specifically, it provides little guidance for limiting adaptation and directing selective differentiation. The use of mission as de facto policy is particularly problematic in times of resource abundance and in periods of fiscal constraint. Mission as policy in a time of abundant resources may lead to unanticipated, capital-intensive consequences [1, 8]. In times of fiscal constraint, mission as policy may lead to ad hoc approaches to retrenchment, with significant institutional and professional consequences [18, 45].

Administrative Maximizers

Another perspective that may shed light on our data comes from research on the growth of public-sector bureaucracies [31, 39]. In this conceptualization, bureaucracy exists in a political economic environment defined by three groups: the collective organizations that provide appropriations and grants, the suppliers of labor and factors of production, and the customers. The line of inquiry that grows out of this perspective proposes that budget maximization is an essential pursuit and that those who do not maximize will not persist. The literature also predicts rewards in legitimacy and increased authority for budget maximizers [31, 39, 40]. The effective constraint on bureaucratic budget maximization is that a bureau must deliver output which meets the reasonable expectation of the sponsoring agency. This notion is elaborated by Niskanen, who argues that the relationship between budget and output is generally unclear, and sometimes purposively so; consequently it is a dysfunction in the balance between the sponsoring agencies and the institutional bureaucracy that leads to unrealistic growth [39].

This line of inquiry has been further advanced and made useful for the analysis of public higher education through a specific focus on the joint decision-making processes of legislative sponsors and bureaucratic recipients. While shifting focus and responsibility toward legislatures and funding sources, such studies affirm the possibility that an ambiguous relationship between a collective organization responsible for oversight and the administrative bureaucracy may be a significant source of bureaucratic budget maximization and accretion [5, 31, 32]. In a study of conflict between the UC Board of Regents and the California legislature, Zusman [51] found limited evidence of legislative authority over the Regents. Although the legislature presently provides some two billion dollars in annual appropriations to the system, the university's autonomous charter status limits legislative control over policy.

The account of bureaucratic growth developed by Meyer et al. suggests that revisions of neo-classical theory are too limited: "Concepts of rational administration themselves generate complexity beyond that imposed by task demands" [31, p. 191]. Thus, the organization itself begins to pose the same challenge to bounded rationality that the environment does. We arrive at a paradoxical situation in which organizations charged with managing problems are unable to implement solutions in part because they do not sufficiently limit their internal processes. From this perspective, in a time of increasing resources, growth becomes less a possibility than an inevitability of inertia.

Bureaucratic Accretion and Changing Contexts

In looking at administrative growth as a historical phenomenon, it appears that administrators have gained prominence. Clark Kerr, a former president of the University of California, addressed the concept of the emerging "multiversity" [22]. Kerr traced three general evolutionary stages in higher education, from Newman's "Idea of a University" through Flexner's "Idea of a Modern University" into Kerr's own "multiversity." Kerr's assessment of the chief supporters of each of the mutations provides an avenue into discussion of the multiversity today and the consequence of bureaucratic accretion. Kerr cited humanists, generalists, and undergraduates as the primary devotees of the "University," with scientists, specialists, and graduate students as the supporters of the "modern university." Of the multiversity he wrote that "the Idea of a multiversity has its practitioners— chiefly the administrators, who now number many faculty among them, and the leadership groups in society at large" [22, p. 9].

That the chief supporters of the multiversity would be administrators is not surprising, if we consider a few of the unique attributes of the multiversity cited by Kerr. He noted specifically that, "the multiversity has demonstrated how adaptive it can be to new opportunities for creativity; how responsive to money; how eagerly it can play a new and useful role; how fast it can change while pretending that nothing has happened at all; how fast it can neglect some of its ancient virtues" [22, p. 45].

The adaptation to new opportunities can be seen in the university's expansion and differentiation. The ability to change while pretending not to change may be facilitated by an ambiguous relationship between the university administration and the board of regents. The neglect of some ancient virtues can be seen as a de facto change in the university's stated mission. Taken together, they set a context for bureaucratic accretion.

In the contemporary era the social construction of scarcity drives a reassessment of university priorities. The state of California's general fund contribution to the UC has declined from 2.83 billion dollars for 1986/87 to 2.07 billion dollars for 1991/92 [19]. In response UC has implemented new policies and proposed new strategies for responding to this revenue shift. The initial policies have been to raise student fees, which were increased over one hundred-twenty percent between 1989/90 and 1993/94,[40] and to reduce university payrolls through early retirement incentive programs. The Office of the President has also presented proposals for retrenching the size of campus and systemwide administration, consolidating academic programs, and increasing revenue-generating partnerships.[41] These policies and proposals have raised serious concerns about the possible differential valuing of disciplines and trends towards privatization of the university.[42]

In this context, as demands for retrenchment figure prominently in policy discussions, the perception of bureaucratic accretion takes on increased symbolic importance. Various actors have expressed the opinion that the initial policies and proposals presented by the Office of the President have affected students and faculty more significantly than they have the administration [12, 20, 33, 34]. Controversy over the growth of administrative expenditures and positions has been widely reported in major media [cf. 1, 26, 34], and the state's largest newspaper questioned whether UC needs a systemwide administration at all [26]. The situation has been exacerbated by a number of recent controversies over executive compensation and allegations of administrative malfeasance.[43]

Given the importance to UC of continued popular support and state general fund contributions, an important area of future research will address the influence of the perception of bureaucratic accretion on the future political and economic climate for the university.

Conclusion

The University of California data examined in this article document a twenty-five-year period of growth in expenditures and positions for administration and instruction. We use the data to discuss bureaucratic accretion and its changing contexts and consequences. We have considered whether, in the aftermath of an era of rising resources and elaborating structures, contemporary retrenchment initiatives have intensified underlying political economic strain over the appropriate size of administration.

One intention of this article has been to inspire further case studies of public research universities in order to document and explain the growth of administration relative to instruction. The correlations and causes for disproportionate growth warrant further systematic study. In pursuing this line of inquiry, we think it is essential to consider whether administrative expenditures and positions have grown beyond predictions derived from the complexity proposition. Further research could also consider a number of possible implications of growth beyond complexity. For example, has administrative growth been accompanied by concomitant changes in administrative roles within university authority structures and decision-making processes? Research along these lines can inform our understanding of shifting patterns of governance.

Providing another context in which to examine organizational adaptation, the contemporary period of retrenchment reflects environmental demands for dedifferentiation and consolidation. In this context emerging restructuring initiatives extend longitudinal data to determine whether adaptation to complexity has relevance across historical eras. Given perceptions of scarcity and demands for efficiency, it is increasingly apparent that expanded administrative units will compete alongside instructional and other units for limited resources. Thus, as the context has changed, one unanticipated consequence of administrative growth may be that administrative units have become, not only managers and coordinators of the educational enterprise, but consumers of significant core resources as well.

Our analysis of administrative growth also suggests that it is worthwhile to look historically at expenditure and personnel data as well as data on the social construction of discourse. Categories of resource allocation need to be analyzed for what they may reveal or obscure about the changing nature of organizational practices.

Finally, while our data on expenditures and positions for administration and instruction describe these two areas of systemic growth in the University of California, similar data on the change over time in such areas as funded research, teaching hospitals and auxiliary enterprises may supplement our effort to illuminate the changing nature of the public research university enterprise.

Notes

1. The period under analysis begins at the close of fiscal year 1966–67 and covers a twenty-five-year interval ending at the close of fiscal year 1991–92. References to expenditures in a given year (for example, 1966–67) refer to expenditures reported at the close of that fiscal year. We have examined prior years to guard against any anomalies in the data for either expenditures or positions that would impact on the period of analysis.
2. *Budget for Current Operations 1991–92,* University of California, Office of the President.
3. National Science Foundation, Academic R & D Expenditures, 1994 [36].
4. The precise figure in 1966–67 dollars was $749,247,668, and $3,710,907,000 in 1993 (HEPI) dollars. It includes expenditures for atomic energy laboratories (*Financial Report 1966–67,* University of California, Office of the President). See figure 4. For related income data, see figure 2.
5. The precise figure was $9,803,070,484, and it includes expenditures for Department of Energy Laboratories (University of California *Financial Report, 1991–92,* Office of the President). See figure 5. For related income data, see figure 3.
6. Adjusted to 1993 dollars based on Higher Education Price Index.
7. Student FTE data were obtained from *Financial Report* and *Budget for Current Operations,* various years, University of California, Office of the President.
8. The total of UC system staff FTEs (including positions not permanently budgeted) in 1991–92 was 92,758 (*Financial Report, 1991–92,* University of California, Office of the President).
9. The population of California in 1967 was 19,175,000. The population in 1991 was 30,646,000. This is an increase of 59.8 percent (*Statistical Abstracts 1992,* California Department of Finance).
10. This percentage is arrived at by taking the percentage of total system expenditures represented by the Uniform Accounting category of Instruction, excluding expenditures within that category for University Extension (*Campus Financial Schedules, 1991–92,* University of California, Office of the President).
11. Size of the administrative component relative to actual production positions ("the A/P ratio") has been characterized by sociologists as the most common single measure of bureaucratization; observers note a growth trend during the twentieth century: the A/P ratio went from 1:10 in 1900, to 2:10 in 1950 to 4.5:10 in the 1980s in manufacturing as well as in other industries [Bendix quoted in 3]. Such increases in this administrative ratio have paralleled increases in organizational size, making it difficult to separate out whether increased size causes administrative growth [3, p. 102]. The overarching concern is whether the administrative component reflects an excessive bureaucratization that creates inefficiencies and/or heightens the public's skepticism.
12. As Gumport [18] has argued elsewhere, a careful examination of university resource allocation practices can enhance our understanding of the subsequent change over time in what constitutes legitimate categories (for example, categories of personnel, categories of academic units/curriculum); and it can delineate implications of those incremental resource shifts for more broad-scale changes in the nature of university knowledge transmission and knowledge production activities.
13. The UC system's Uniform Accounting Structure (UAS) has been developed in accord with standard procedures outlined in *College and University Business Administration* [11]. When making reference to specific UAS captions for either categories (for example, Instruction) or subcategories (for example, Academic Administration) we capitalize the titles. When combining the categories Institutional Support and Academic Administration for comparison purposes, we capitalize the new caption "Administration" within quotation marks. For example, in figure 7 we combine the category Institutional Support with a portion of the category Academic Support (that portion subcategorized as Academic Administration) in order to create a category we call "Administration," as a reference point for comparison of growth in instructional and administrative expenditures. Our references to instructional expenditures refer to the total of the UAS expenditure category Instruction, minus that subcategory of Instruction which is captioned Extension, where noted. UC data are presented somewhat differently for appropriation and expenditure accounting and for FTE positions. For that reason we use two primary documents compiled by the UC Office of the President (*Campus Financial Schedules* and *Departmental Allocations-University of California Budget for Current Operations*) to analyze expenditures and positions, respectively. See also legend accompanying figure 7.

14. Academic Administration includes, "expenditures that provide administrative support and management direction for the three primary missions. This sub-category is intended to identify separately the expenditures for the management function in the primary missions" (*UC Accounting Manual—Uniform Accounting Structure*, Office of the President, 11/1/83).

15. In the *UC Financial Report 1973–74* changes in nomenclature and accounting categories were implemented to create an additional level of detail in accord with changes prescribed in the 1973 edition of CUBA. Changes included placing Extension as a subdivision of Instruction. The title Instruction and Departmental Research was changed to Instruction, though Departmental Research remained in this category. The title Organized Research was changed to Research. The reporting category Academic Support was created to incorporate a number of activities which support integral parts of the mission. The expenditures for deans' offices which are now listed as Academic Administration within Academic Support were removed from Instructional and Departmental Research. The categories General Administration and Institutional Services and General were combined under the new caption Institutional Support. Our basic classification of administrative expenditures for the period 1966–67 through 1971–72 is the combination of categories General Administration and Institutional Services and General, and for the subsequent years the sum of the category Institutional Support and Academic Administration (See also note 25). We have also made small adjustments to the data to account for the categorical relocation of certain expenditures, such as Police Services, over time.

16. As an example, allocating transfers, or "recharges," is particularly problematic. For this study we have chosen not to include any transfers in our accounting of UC expenditures. This decision has the effect of understating the total expenditures on administration in the UC.

17. The caption Other in this case consists of Institutional Support, Student Services, Operation and Maintenance, and Auxiliary Enterprises (*Financial Report, 1991–92*).

18. Institutional Services and General and General Administration were combined in 1973–74 and subsequently reported in the University of California *Financial Report* as Institutional Support (see also note 15 above).

19. The University spent over $60,000,000 on Community Relations (Development, Public Information, Publications, for example) (*Campus Financial Schedules, 1991–92*).

20. The state of California's general fund contribution to the UC has declined from 2.83 billion dollars in 1986/87 to 2.07 billion dollars in 1991/92 [19].

21. An editorial in the state's largest daily newspaper, *The Los Angeles Times* (26 November 1992), addressed the size of the administrative cohort on UC campuses and in the President's Office [26].

22. For example, Maurice Mullard studied the shaping of public expenditure discourse in Great Britain during the decade of the 1970s [35].

23. Their definition focuses on articulation: "Articulation is any practice establishing a relation among elements such that their identity is modified as a result of the articulatory practice. The structured totality resulting from this articulatory practice we will call discourse" [24, p. 103].

24. Additional shifts in captioning over the twenty-five years include elimination of the word "organized" from two categories and as noted "administration." Two new words appeared in the captions: "teaching" and "academic support." The seven expenditure categories listed in "Facts in Brief" for 1991–92 are, in order of appearance: Instruction, Research, Public Service, Student Financial Aid, Teaching Hospitals, Academic Support, and Other. Ranked by level of expenditure they would appear this way: Instruction, Teaching Hospitals, Other, Research, Academic Support, Student Financial Aid, and Public Service.

25. As stated in note 15 above, the category now captioned Institutional Support was represented in 1966–67 by two categories: Institutional Services and General, and General Administration. At that time, the portions of academic administrative expenditures that became the UAS subcategory Academic Administration in 1974 were accounted as portions of Institutional services and General and Instruction and Departmental Research. We consider the overall effect of this shift to be minimal (*Financial Report, 1973–74*).

26. In the period 1966–67 through 1971–72 the category currently known as Instruction was designated Instruction and Departmental Research. In 1973–74 the caption Instructional and Departmental Research was changed to Instruction (*Financial Report, 1966–67 to 1973–74*).

27. Until 1973–74 the subcategory Extension was included under the caption Extension and Public Service. We have chosen not to include Extension in our accounting of instructional expenditures over the period of analysis, primarily because the majority of Extension classes do not provide UC academic credits, do not tend to use UC ladder faculty, and do not use typical university fee schedules or salary schedules.

28. The precise figure is 407 percent.

29. The budgetary allocation categories captioned Institutional Support (72) and General Administration (66) need to be distinguished from the UAS expenditure category Institutional Support and subcategory General Administration (*Departmental Allocations, University of California Budget for Current Operations*, selected years).

30. In accounting for positions, we use data from *Departmental Allocations—University of California Budget for Current Operations*. Those data are disaggregated so that there is no need to factor out University Extension, a separate allocation category. It should be noted again that our category of "Administrative" positions does not include administrative staff at the level of academic departments or research units reported in the categories of Instruction and Research, respectively. Neither General Administration nor Institutional Support include the administration of Libraries, Operation and Maintenance of Plant, Student Services, or Auxiliary Enterprises. The dean of students, registrar, chief admissions officer, and director of housing, for example, are not included in this definition of administrative positions. Our decisions have the effect of understating the growth of administrative positions over time.

31. Administrative positions increased from 10 percent of total permanently budgeted FTE staff for 1966–67 to 12 percent of the total for 1991–92. Instructional positions made up 40 percent of permanently budgeted FTE positions in 1966–67 and only 31 percent of those positions by 1991–92.

32. We have chosen to present the accretion of positions as well as expenditures in order to present a measure of relative growth that is more independent of increased administrative costs (refer to this article, under the heading *Methods and Data Analysis*).

33. Broomal et al. (1978) cited in Brinkman and Leslie [4] produced similar findings, although in the case of large public research universities they found less evidence of economies of scale.

34. The ratio of administrative to academic FTE (permanently budgeted) at UC Berkeley in 1991–92 was 0.417 to 1. For UC Riverside, a campus with a student population less than one third of Berkeley's, the 1991–92 ratio was 0.441 to 1. This observation holds for similar comparisons within the system; however, it should be noted that comparisons between the individual campuses are problematic, because campus characteristics vary.

35. In 1966–67 the ratio of permanently budgeted FTE administrators to academic positions at UC Berkeley was 0.1990 to 1. In 1971–72 it was 0.2803 to 1; in 1981–82, 0.4002 to 1; in 1991–92, 0.4170 to 1. For UCLA: 1966–67: 0.2696 to 1; 1971–72: 0.3390 to 1; for 1981–82: 0.3610 to 1; 1991–92: 0.4690 to 1 (*Departmental Allocations, University of California Budget for Current Operations*, various years).

36. In a report to the regents on 2/18/93, Vice President Baker noted that "administrative expenditures, as a proportion of total expenditures have remained relatively constant over twenty years, 1971–1992" [49]. Our preliminary investigations show considerable variation between campuses and over time with regard to "administrative expenditures" on Institutional Support as a percentage of total UC expenditures. Additionally, the political economic effect of proportional growth needs to be carefully considered.

37. For example, Schwartz [42] found that for FY 1992 UC expenditures for Affirmative Action, Environmental Health and Safety, and Collective Bargaining within the categories Institutional Support and Academic Administration comprised less than 10 percent of the total expenditures in those categories. Similarly, his analysis found that the number of FTE positions devoted in FY 1992 to Affirmative Action, Environmental Health and Safety, and Collective Bargaining within the categories Institutional Support and General Administration accounted for less than 10 percent of the total FTE positions in those categories.

38. Tolbert [48] considered both isomorphism and resource dependence explanations.

39. We are grateful to Professor James G. March for his assistance in formulating this proposition.

40. The resident undergraduate fee average increased from $1,634 to $3,727 (*Budget for Current Operations*, various years).

41. The extent to which these proposals will be implemented is an area of some controversy. For example, between 1989/90 and 1993/94, spending for Institutional Support actually increased according to one analysis [42].

42. See Minutes from the Academic Senate, University of California [33]. For further discussion see Gumport and Pusser [18, 19].

43. See for example, "UC Patents Director May Have Violated State Law." *San Francisco Examiner*, 12 September 1993; "UC's Secret Stock Deals." *San Francisco Chronicle*, 20 June 1993; "Who Killed Cal?" *SF Weekly*, 25 August 1993; "UC Hot Line Lights Up with Tales of Waste," *San Jose Mercury News*, 29 May 1993. See also [1, 12, 20, 34, 42].

References

1. Bergmann, B. "Bloated Administration, Blighted Campuses." *Academe*, 77 (Nov.-Dec. 1991), 12–16.
2. Blau, P. M. *The Organization of Academic Work.* New York: John Wiley, 1973.
3. Blau, P. M., and M. Meyer. *Bureaucracy in Modern Society.* 3rd ed. New York: McGraw-Hill, orig. 1956, 1987.
4. Brinkman, P., and L. L. Leslie. "Economies of Scale in Higher Education: Sixty Years of Research." *Review of Higher Education*, 10 (Fall 1986).
5. Brunson, N. "Ideas and Action: Justification and Hypocrisy as Alternatives to Control." *Accounting, Organizations, and Society*, 18 (1993), 489–506.
6. Calhoun, C., M. Meyer, and W. R. Scott (eds.) *Structures of Power and Constraint.* Cambridge: Cambridge University Press, 1990.
7. Clark, B. R. *The Higher Education System.* Los Angeles: University of California Press, 1983.
8. ———. "The Problem of Complexity in Modern Higher Education." In *The European and American University since 1800*, edited by Sheldon Rothblatt and Bjorn Wittrock. Cambridge: Cambridge University Press, 1993.
9. Clegg, S. "Weber and Foucault: Social Theory for the Study of Organizations." *Organization*, 1 (1994), 149–78.
10. Clotfelter, C. T. *Economic Challenges in Higher Education.* Chicago: University of Chicago Press, 1993.
11. *College and University Business Administration.* 5th ed. Washington, D.C.: NACUBO, 1992.
12. *Daily Californian*, 19 January 1993, pp. 1 and 5.
13. DiMaggio, P., and W. Powell. "The Iron Cage Revisited." *American Sociological Review*, 48 (1983), 147–60.
14. Durkheim, E. *Division of Labor in Society.* New York: Macmillan, 1933.
15. Foucault, M. "The Order of Discourse." In *Language and Politics*, edited by M. Shapiro. Oxford: Basil Blackwell, 1984.
16. Geiger, R. L. *To Advance Knowledge: The Growth of American Research Universities, 1900–1940.* Oxford: Oxford University Press, 1986.
17. ———. *Research and Relevant Knowledge.* Oxford: Oxford University Press, 1993.
18. Gumport, P. J. "The Contested Terrain of Academic Program Reduction." *Journal of Higher Education*, 64 (May/June 1993), 283–311.
19. Gumport, P. J., and B. Pusser. "Higher Education Funding Shifts: Privatization and the Case of UC." Paper presented at the American Educational Research Association Annual Meeting, New Orleans, April 1994.
20. Hayden, T. "Why College Doors Are Closing," *The New York Times*, 19 March 1993.
21. Heydebrand, W. "The Technocratic Organization of Academic Work." In *Structures of Power and Constraint*, edited by Craig Calhoun, Marshall Meyer, and W. Richard Scott, pp. 271–320. Cambridge: Cambridge University Press, 1990.
22. Kerr, C. *The Uses of the University.* 3rd. ed. Cambridge, Mass.: Harvard University Press, 1982.
23. Kogan, M. "The Political View." In *Perspectives on Higher Education: Eight Disciplinary and Comparative Views*, edited by Burton Clark. Los Angeles: University of California Press, 1984.
24. Laclau, E., and C. Mouffe. *Hegemony and Socialist Strategy.* London: Verso, 1985.
25. Leslie, L. L., and G. Rhoades. "Rising Administrative Costs: On Seeking Explanations." *Journal of Higher Education*, 66 (March/April 1995), 187–212.
26. *Los Angeles Times.* "Putting The UC System under the Microscope," 26 November 1992, p. B4.
27. Massy, W., and T. Warner. "Causes and Cures of Cost Escalation in College and University Administrative and Support Services." Unpublished manuscript, 1991 (available from first author upon request).
28. Massy, W., and A. Wilger. "Productivity in Postsecondary Education: A New Approach." *Educational Evaluation and Policy Analysis*, 14 (Winter 1992), 361–76.
29. Meyer, J. W., and B. Rowan. "Institutionalized Organizations: Formal Structure as Myth and Ceremony." *American Journal of Sociology*, 83 (1977), 340–63.
30. Meyer, M. "The Weberian Tradition in Organizational Research." In *Structures of Power and Constraint*, edited by Craig Calhoun, Marshall Meyer, and W. Richard Scott, pp. 191–216. Cambridge: Cambridge University Press, 1990.
31. Meyer, M., W. Stevenson, and S. Webster. *Limits to Bureaucratic Growth.* Berlin: Walter de Gruyther, 1985.
32. Miller, G., and T. Moe. "Bureaucrats, Legislators, and the Size of Government." *American Political Science Review*, 77 (1983), 297–322.
33. Minutes from the Academic Senate, University of California Berkeley, 8 March 1993.
34. Muchnick, I. "Who Killed Cal?" *SF Weekly*, 25 August 1993.

35. Mullard, M. *The Politics of Public Expenditure.* London: Croom Helm, 1987.

36. National Science Foundation Data, Academic R & D Expenditures. *CHE Almanac,* 1 September 1994.

37. *The New York Times,* 19 March 1993.

38. Niskanen, W. A., Jr. *Bureaucracy and Representative Government.* Chicago: Aldine-Atherton, 1971.

39. Nobel, D. *America by Design.* New York: Alfred Knopf, 1977.

40. Parkinson, C. N. *Parkinson's Law.* Cambridge, Mass.: Houghton Mifflin, 1957.

41. Powell, W., and P. DiMaggio (eds.). *The New Institutionalism in Organizational Analysis.* Chicago: University of Chicago Press, 1991.

42. Schwartz, C. "Looking into the UC Budget." Unpublished manuscripts, 1993–95 (available from the author upon request).

43. Scott, W. R. *Organizations: Rational, Natural, and Open Systems.* 3rd ed. Englewood Cliffs, N.J.: Prentice Hall, 1992.

44. Slaughter, S. *The Higher Learning and High Technology: Dynamics of Higher Education Policy Formation.* Albany, N.Y.: SUNY Press, 1991.

45. ———. "Retrenchment in the 1980s: The Politics of Prestige and Gender." *Journal of Higher Education,* 64 (May/June 1993), 250–82, 1993.

46. Slaughter, S., and G. Rhoades. "Renorming the Social Relations of Academic Science: Technology Transfer." *Educational Policy,* 4 (1990), 341–61.

47. Swidler, A., and J. Arditi. "The New Sociology of Knowledge." *Annual Review of Sociology,* 20 (1994), 305–29.

48. Tolbert, P. "Institutional Environments and Resource Dependence: Administrative Structure in Institutions of Higher Education." *Administrative Science Quarterly,* 30 (1985), 1–13.

49. University of California, Report to the Board of Regents on 18 February 1993, by William Baker, Vice-President for University and External Relations, from the amended text provided by the Office of the President, 22 February 1993. In C. Schwartz, "Report #2B." Unpublished manuscript, 1993 (available from the author upon request).

50. Weber, M. "Bureaucracy." In *From Max Weber,* edited by H. Gerth and C. Wright Mills, chap. 8. New York: Oxford University Press, 1946.

51. Zusman, A. "Legislature and University Conflict: The Case of California." *Review of Higher Education,* 9 (1986), 397–418.

A GAME-THEORETIC EXPLANATION
OF THE ADMINISTRATIVE LATTICE
IN INSTITUTIONS OF HIGHER LEARNING

ANDREAS ORTMANN[1] AND RICHARD SQUIRE

Abstract. We provide a game-theoretic model of academic organizations, focusing on the strategic interaction of prototypical overseers, administrators, and professors. By identifying key principal-agent games routinely played in colleges and universities, we begin to unpack the black box typically used to conceptualize these institutions. Our approach suggests an explanation for the seemingly inevitable drift of institutions of higher education into such well-documented phenomena as academic ratchet and administrative lattice and builds an understanding of the organizational conditions in which drift would be restrained. © 2000 Elsevier Science B.V. All rights reserved.

JEL classification: C72; D23; D82; I21

Introduction

Many, if not most, institutions of higher education have fallen on fiscal hard times. Costs continue their dramatic rise which began in the early 1980s and which, interestingly, has been more pronounced for private than public colleges and universities. The sticker price for a 4-year college education at selective private liberal arts colleges crossed several years ago the US\$ 100,000 barrier (Honan, 1994) and continues to outpace inflation by a wide margin (Larson, 1997; Bronner, 1998; Mabry, 1999). Costs per student are even higher (Winston and Yen, 1995), with administrative accretion being a major driver of this development (Zemsky and Massy, 1990; Leslie and Rhoades, 1995; National Commission, 1998; Chronister, 1999).

That administrative accretion is a problem is widely acknowledged;[2] it is not well understood, however, *why* administrative costs have grown so dramatically. Massy has identified the increased use of information technology as an important cost driver 'at the present time' (National Commission, 1998, p. 89), the qualification expressing the hope that higher education will ultimately reap rich rewards for its investment in IT and overcome the 'cost disease' that allegedly afflicts labor-intensive industries (Baumol and Bowen, 1966). Several authors have suggested 'what is perhaps the most commonly identified source of administrative cost increases, government regulation' (Leslie and Rhoades, 1995, p. 190; see also National Commission, 1998, pp. 11/12 and p. 88). Indeed, the 7000 regulations reportedly governing the award of student grants and loans alone (Ritter, 1996) seem to be a reasonable indication of an important cost driver, and that is not counting more complex accounting rules and increasing regulatory requirements (OSHA, EEOC). Clotfelter (1996) has suggested the perceived need to provide new services and 'amenities' as the culprit. Leslie and Rhoades have argued that external demands, such as increased regulatory and information requests or 'mission creep' increase organizational complexity, which, in turn, fuels administrative accretion.

Massy and collaborators have identified the 'academic ratchet' and the 'administrative lattice' as important cost drivers. The academic ratchet describes the tendency for faculty to shift effort over time toward research and personal income opportunities and away from teaching, student advising and counseling, governance tasks, etc. (Massy and Wilger, 1992; Zemsky et al., 1993; Massy and Zemsky, 1994; see also James, 1990; Clotfelter, 1996, Figs. 7.3–7.6). The administrative lattice describes the tendency for college administrative staffs to grow relative to the faculty over time, partially in reaction to the academic ratchet, but also as the result of 'consensus management' and the self-perpetuating growth of administration (Massy and Warner, 1991; see also James and Clotfelter).

With the notable exception of Massy and Zemsky's conceptualization of the academic ratchet, the internal workings of educational institutions were, until recently, regarded as a black box not accessible to analysis. A key reason was the assumption that the preferences of constituencies in such organizations were inconsistent, ill-defined, and in any case hopelessly multi-layered. To wit, 'the goals of some members of the university community (faculty and students) are perhaps not too difficult to model, but the motivations of others (in particular, senior administrators, regents, and trustees) resist easy characterization' (Rothschild and White, 1991, p. 14; see also Cohen et al., 1972; Massy, 1981; Hoenack, 1990; Hopkins, 1990; James, 1990).

Here, we provide such a characterization. Specifically, we first identify what we believe to be the relevant goals and motivations of prototypical professors, administrators, and overseers. We then provide a game-theoretic model of the principal-agent games in which these players routinely engage and identify the conditions under which incentives can become misaligned and, ultimately, become an important determinant of cost structure.

We assume that being a member of a constituency shapes one's incentives. Thus, we identify preferences of constituencies as representative of the goals of the individuals therein. Although individuals surely are heterogeneous, we assume that membership in a constituency prevails over individual idiosyncracies as a predictor of behavior. Obviously, this is not an innocent assumption. [3] To emphasize the representative-agent aspects of our modeling, we identify these constituencies as Overseer, Administrator, and Professor.

By identifying the degree to which incentives faced by agents are not aligned with the goals of the corresponding principals, we provide an explanation of the forces underlying the organizational drift toward administrative lattice and academic ratchet. In particular, we suggest how these two phenomena are causally related. By focusing on the strategic interaction among Overseer, Administrator, and Professor, we also build an understanding of the organizational conditions in which administrative accretion, to the extent that it is driven by misaligned incentives, would be restrained.

The balance of the paper is organized as follows. Section 2 describes the players and enumerates their respective objectives. Section 3 analyzes the principal-agent game between Administrator and Professor and the drift of professors out of 'sharable management duties' such as student advising, counseling, and a variety of governance tasks. Section 4 analyzes the principal-agent game between Overseer and Administrator and the emergence of the administrative lattice. Section 5 concludes.

Players and Objectives

In Ortmann and Squire, 1996, we have suggested that institutions of higher learning can be conceptualized as a cascade of principal-agent games. Specifically, we explicated four levels of such a cascade, representing the key college constituencies of the students and alumni, the overseers, the administrators, and the professors. Through this approach, we explored the degree to which the formal modeling of strategic interaction among prototypical players with representative objectives and institutional constraints can explain observations about the conduct and performance of real world institutions of higher learning. In the present article, we demonstrate how academic ratchet and administrative lattice are predictable results of principal-agent interactions among overseers, administrators, and professors. In this section, we lay the groundwork for our model by briefly introducing the relevant players, their goals, and their institutional constraints.

Our prototypical Professor has three related objectives: job security, freedom to spend his time on activities he prefers, and maximization of professional reputation and income. To achieve these goals, the Professor engages in some mixture of the traditional professorial roles of teaching, research and publishing, advising and counseling students, and college governance tasks, such as committee work, fund raising, recruiting, and other forms of 'public relations' work. For our purposes, we categorize advising, counseling, and the various governance tasks as 'sharable management' duties, because they are tasks that to some extent can also be performed by college administrators and their support staff. Finally, our Professor may also be tempted by lucrative opportunities, such as consulting or speaking engagements.

The most common means for the Professor to achieve his objective of job security is through the institution of tenure. At many colleges and universities, tenure is a reward for success in research and publishing, with less emphasis placed on teaching quality and virtually no emphasis on performance of sharable management duties. Massy and Zemsky suggest as one explanation for the de-emphasis of teaching and sharable management duties the relative difficulty in measuring performance in these areas. Although individual professors differ in their proclivity to teach and perform sharable management duties, all experience the strong incentive to disengage from them due to their high opportunity cost relative to the goal of achieving job security through tenure.

Tenure also enables the Professor to achieve his objective of freedom of activity. Although a tenured Professor may choose to allocate greater effort to teaching and sharable management duties, he also faces the heightened allure of consulting and public speaking, which, like research, allow him to earn outside income and enhance his professional reputation. [4] In contrast, teaching and sharable management duties offer, at best, intangible rewards, because most colleges base salaries almost exclusively on seniority and research, and few professors can build a meaningful external reputation based on teaching and performance of sharable management duties. Even if the Professor prefers to teach and spend time advising, counseling, and/or recruiting students, opportunity costs provide disincentive to do so. Thus, the academic ratchet is the predictable outcome of the incentives experienced by most college faculty members (Massy and Zemsky, 1994).

The Professor's principal, the Administrator, has objectives that are similar to his agent's. The Administrator seeks to keep his job, build his reputation, and to free his own time for outside income opportunities (Zemsky, 1992). Furthermore, the Administrator also shares the goals that Williamson (1970) identified as common to all managers, such as desire for status and power manifested in a large office and support staff. In fact, such rewards may be especially meaningful for college administrators, who do not have access to the performance-based financial incentives, such as stock options, available to their private-sector counterparts.

To keep his job the Administrator must ultimately please his own principal, the Overseer, on an ongoing basis, because the overseers of a college are not bound to its administration, as they are to its faculty, by tenure. As discussed below, the Overseer is primarily concerned with enhancing the college's reputation for educational quality, and will reward the Administrator accordingly. In addition, the Administrator has personal incentives to enhance his college's reputation, because this bears directly on the prestige of his administrative post and, thus, on his personal marketability.

Because he shares the Professor's goal of freeing his time for external opportunities, the Administrator has incentive to delegate sharable management duties. One option is to try to get the Professor to do them, although, especially when the Professor has tenure, the Administrator may lack the leverage to bring this about. More attractive is delegation to administrative support staff members, who are more controllable as direct reports, and who, as they increase in number, bring the Administrator the intangible rewards described by Williamson. Thus, in order to both avoid conflict with the Professor and achieve intangible managerial rewards, the Administrator has incentive to increase his support staff.

Here, we see how the academic ratchet drives the administrative lattice and serves the interests of both Professor and Administrator. The ratchet allows the Professor to devote his time to activities that are more rewarding financially and professionally; in its wake it creates a series of neglected duties that the Administrator can use to justify the administrative lattice. The lattice, in turn, further relieves the pressure on the Professor to perform sharable management duties.

We ascribe one goal to the Administrator's principal, the Overseer. The Overseer, who can be conceptualized as the agent of the students and alumni, and who is himself probably a diploma-holder of the college he oversees, has the objective of enhancing the college's reputation for educational quality. Like his counterpart in the private sector, i.e. a director, the Overseer seeks to select a senior management team that will spend resources to maximize shareholder (or diploma-holder) value. However, the Overseer does not have access to the equivalent of quarterly earning reports and must rely upon more attenuated and time-delayed measures of college performance, such as student selectivity statistics. Because academic quality is difficult to measure directly, the Overseer is especially dependent upon the Administrator for budget recommendations and hiring and firing decisions, and is disadvantaged in quickly recognizing poor Administrator performance. As we will explore in Section 3, this problem of asymmetric information in the Overseer/Administrator interaction clears the structural pathway for the accretive momentum created by the Administrator/Professor interaction.

Sharable Management Duties: Administrator versus Professor

The Administrator and Professor that meet here are the same in terms of goals and demands as the two so-named players we constructed in the previous section. To formalize the structure within which the players interact, we make the following additional assumptions:

1. The Professor has tenure.
2. Shirking by the Professor on the performance of sharable management duties to pursue consulting opportunities, additional research, or leisure, has a cost to the quality of education at the college.
3. Monitoring the Professor in his performance of sharable management duties has a cost to the Administrator in terms of diverted time and resources, as well as possible backlash from intracollege political conflict.
4. Monitoring the Professor creates a cost to the quality of education at the college as a whole, in that it causes administrative resources to be diverted from other uses.

The Administrator/Professor game is similar to a standard commitment game (Aron, 1990), in that the principal, here the Administrator, may choose either a Monitor or Not Monitor strategy, and the Professor, as agent, may choose either Work or Shirk. The game has four possible outcomes.

To assess which outcomes each player will prefer, and how the game will actually turn out, we must construct its payoffs. For this game we define the following primitives:

W_a, W_p the one-period wages of the Administrator and the Professor, respectively

U_p the benefit that the Professor receives when he shirks on his sharable management duties. Another way to understand this primitive is to see—(U_p) as the Professor's opportunity cost of participating in sharable management duties.

X_a the cost to the Administrator caused by the Professor's shirking. This primitive combines two costs: direct hassles, because administrative work is left undone, and indirect reputational costs resulting from damaged quality of education at the college. Recall that we assume that the Administrator's personal reputation is associated with the reputation of the college where he works.

C_a the cost to the Administrator of his choice to monitor the Professor. Again, this primitive combines several costs, including extra work and diverted resources, political conflict, and reputation costs resulting from a change in educational quality.

P_p the contractual penalty that the Professor incurs if he is monitored while shirking.

X_p the reputational cost to the Professor of his own shirking that results from damaged educational quality.

C_p the reputational cost to the Professor of the Administrator's choice to monitor, again as a result of damaged educational quality.

These primitives allow us to construct our payoff matrix generically without specifying dollar values:

Professor (Agent)	Administrator (Principal)	
	Not Monitor	Monitor
Work	$(W_p;\ W_a)$	$(W_p - C_p;\ Wa - Ca)$
Shirk	$(W_p + U_p - X_p;\ W_a - X_a)$	$(W_p + U_p - X_p - C_p - P_p;\ W_a - X_a - C_a)$

From this model, a specific college could be studied by determining the value of its primitives and then plugging them into the matrix to discover which outcome is predicted. For our purposes, we will choose values for primitives that we believe are indicative of colleges in general. Although we aim for realism in our choices, the absolute values of the primitives are not strictly important to the outcome of our model. As will become clear, the important consideration is the relative magnitude of the primitives.

W_p and W_a are present in every payoff, so that, although they are likely to be the largest in magnitude of the primitives, they can be normalized out of the matrix. Of the rest, U_p is probably the largest primitive. The Professor can make a considerable amount of money as a professional consultant, say US$ 5000, instead of spending his efforts on sharable management duties. P_p we will make the smallest primitive, because at many institutions of higher learning pay is not based on performance. For now, let $P_p = 0$.

This leaves X_a, C_a, X_p, and C_p. Each of these primitives is based, at least in part, on the impact of player actions on the reputation of the college. We would not expect this impact to be realized instantaneously. The actions must first have a noticeable effect on educational quality, which in turn must cause a reduction in the college's reputation, and then must damage individual reputations and salaries. In addition to delaying the impact of actions, this cause-and-effect chain would also create negative externalities, because the damage would be spread relatively evenly across all members of the college community and not be focused exclusively on the perpetrator. From these considerations we assume that X_p and C_p are small: US$ 100 each. X_a and C_a would also be only US$ 100, save that they also contain, in addition to reputational costs, immediate productivity and political costs to the Administrator. These costs are usually irksome, but seldom ruinous; let them be US$ 250 each. Thus, X_a and C_a have a total value of US$ 350.

With these values plugged in our payoff matrix now looks like this:

Professor (Agent)	Administrator (Principal)	
	Not Monitor (US$)	Monitor (US$)
Work	(0, 0)	(−100, −350)
Shirk	(4900, −350)	(4800, −700)

Given these payoffs, the Administrator has no incentive to monitor; the monitoring cost makes Not Monitor a dominant strategy. In addition, the Professor is always better off playing Shirk and cashing in on the benefits represented by U_p. (Shirk, Not Monitor) will be this game's outcome. Of course, this outcome is not optimal for the Administrator, nor does it maximize value to the college due to the negative externalities created by the Professor's shirking. X_a and X_p, at US$ 100 each, may be small to any single individual, but would be much larger if we were to add up the similar costs experienced by every student, employee, and diploma-holder of the college. Here, we see a game-theoretic explanation of the academic ratchet, and an outcome that will lead to the administrative lattice.

While the model predicts that a sub-optimal outcome will result, it also indicates how someone (such as the Overseer) might try to engineer a preferable result. (Work, Not Monitor) is the optimal outcome from the college's perspective. For this outcome to come about, the Professor must be penalized for getting caught shirking, and the Administrator must not mind trying to catch him. Because the sub-optimal strategies for both players are dominant, both players' incentives would need to be changed; P_p would need to be made greater than US\$ 4800. In addition, a reward that would make monitoring worthwhile to the Administrator, call it R_a, would need to be inserted into his contract. In this model, that reward would only need to be around US\$ 700. This would be a bargain to the Overseer, surely less than the wages of administrative staff hired to perform the duties that the Professor is neglecting.

We see that the relative magnitudes of the primitives is the important consideration. The greater the value of U_p relative to P_p, the greater the tendency for the Professor to neglect sharable management duties. Meanwhile, the greater the value of C_a relative to R_a, the greater the tendency for the Administrator to seek other ways to get the work done. We know that at most colleges neither R_a nor P_p exist. The Administrator/Professor model shows the consequences of this fact for the performance of sharable management duties. Our next model shows the consequences for the size of the college's budget.

Sharable Management Duties: Overseer versus Administrator

As we have seen, shirking by the Professor places pressure upon the Administrator to take care of sharable management duties by other means. One option is to increase the administrative support staff. As we stated earlier, this option has benefits for the Administrator. An increase in the number of subordinates brings about an increase in prestige, power, and salary negotiation leverage.

Typically, college administrators cannot increase budgets autonomously; such measures need the approval of the board of overseers. The Administrator and Overseer who meet in this game are the same in terms of goals and incentives as the two so-named players we constructed in Section 2. To formalize the structure within which the players interact, we make the following additional assumptions:

1. Once per year, the Overseer requests a recommendation from the Administrator about the optimal size of the following year's administrative budget. Here, an optimal budget is one that would maximize diploma-holder value and achieve the ideal trade-off between expenditures and educational quality. See Figure 1.

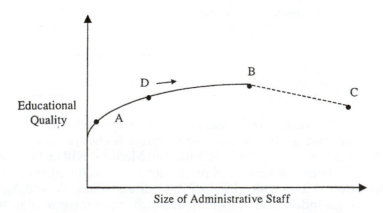

Figure 1   The costs and benefits of transferring sharable management duties from professors to administrative support staff.

2. The Administrator can make one of two recommendations. One, he can recommend that the administrative budget remain the same size (the small budget), signifying that he believes that the level of administrative expenditures is near the ideal point. Two, he can recommend that the budget grow (the Big Budget), signifying that he believes that more staff must be added in order for the ideal point to be achieved.

3. The Overseer does not know with certainty which budget is actually optimal. However, he does know the *probability*, represented by the variable r, that the Big Budget is optimal.

4. Like the Overseer, the Administrator knows the value of r. However, unlike the Overseer, he also knows with certainty which budget is actually optimal. To put it another way, he knows the college's true position on the graph in Figure 1, and the distance (if any) to the ideal point. [5]

5. After the Administrator makes his recommendation, the Overseer chooses which budget to actually implement.

In our previous game, the agent had a choice about how much effort to expend. Now, the agent's choice is about honesty (e.g. Pitchik and Schotter, 1987). The Administrator knows which budget is optimal, but he is not compelled to recommend it. The principal's options are also different from before. Short of employing a lie-detector machine, the 'monitor' choice is no longer available. The Overseer's only choice is to either accept or reject the Administrator's recommendation.

We can identify four primitives for each player. Instead of specifying dollar values for these primitives, we will simply assign them the value of their ordinal rank. In other words, the primitive with the greatest value to a player will have the value 4, the next-best the value 3, and so on. Again, our contention is that, in terms of primitives, relative magnitudes are more important than absolute values. First, we provide the Administrator's primitives:

Primitive	Definition	Rank	Reason for Rank
$B_a s_a$	The Administrator's payoff from implementation of the Big Budget, given that the small budget is optimal.	4	The administration has more money than it needs to carry out its normal duties. The Administrator can expand his staff, and shift to them a greater share of the sharable management duties.
$B_a B_a$	The payoff from the Big Budget, given that the Big Budget is optimal.	3	On the positive side, the staff is bigger. On the negative side, the budget has no 'fat', and sharable management duty conflict may still pose a problem.
$s_a s_a$	The payoff from the small budget, given that the small budget is optimal.	2	The administration does not expand, but at least it has enough resources to accomplish its normal set of tasks.
$s_a B_a$	The payoff from the small budget, given that the Big Budget is optimal.	1	Worst-case scenario for the Administrator. The staff is insufficient to accomplish all of its normal duties.

From these primitives, we can derive the strategies that the Administrator might play. One available strategy we will call Always Truth. Under this strategy, the Administrator always recommends the optimal budget. Alternately, the Administrator can play Always Big, in which, regardless of what is actually optimal, he always recommends the Big Budget. Always Truth and Always Big are the strategies we will include in our model. Conceivably, the strategies Always False and Always Small also exist. But the ranking of the Administrator's payoffs tells us that he has no reason to ever recommend the small budget when the Big Budget is optimal. Thus, the Administrator will never play Always False or Always Small, and we can exclude these strategies from our model. Here, we see how the phenomenon of the academic ratchet serves the Administrator's interest in that it gives him a potential defense if the Overseer questions his recommendation of the Big Budget.

The Overseer's primitives are as follows:

Primitive	Definition	Rank	Reason for Rank
s_os_o	The Overseer's payoff from implementation of the small budget, given that the small budget is optimal.	4	The Overseer can implement the optimal budget without raising expenditures by increasing tuition, dipping into the endowment, or running a budget deficit.
B_oB_o	The payoff from the Big Budget, given that the Big Budget is optimal.	3	Although expenditures must increase, the money is well spent. The level of educational quality is optimized.
B_os_o	The payoff from the Big Budget, given that the small budget is optimal.	2	Although money is spent unnecessarily, at least all required administrative duties can be carried out.
s_oB_o	The payoff from the small budget, given that the Big Budget is optimal.	1	Worst-case scenario for the Overseer. A slip in educational quality is likely because the administration will have insufficient resources.

From these primitives, we can derive the strategies that the Overseer might play. Again, we find that there are four possible strategies, but only two that would be rational to play. The Overseer might play Always Approve, in which he always implements the budget that the Administrator recommends. Alternately, he might play Always Small, in which, regardless of the Administrator's recommendation, he always implements the small budget. The strategies Always Reject and Always Big are available but irrational, because the Overseer has no reason to ever reject a recommendation for the small budget given that the Administrator would only recommend the small budget if it were optimal.

The payoff matrix for this game is as follows. In this matrix, the payoffs of the Overseer are listed above the payoffs to the Administrator.

		Overseer (Principal)	
		Always Accept	**Always Small**
Administrator (Agent)	Always Truth	$r(B_oB_o) + (1 - r)(s_os_o)$ $r(B_aB_a) + (1 - r)(s_as_a)$	$r(s_oB_o) + (1 - r)(s_os_o)$ $r(s_aB_a) + (1 - r)(s_as_a)$
	Always Big	$r(B_oB_o) + (1 - r)(B_os_o)$ $r(B_aB_a) + (1 - r)(B_as_a)$	$r(s_oB_o) + (1 - r)(s_os_o)$ $r(s_aB_a) + (1 - r)(s_as_a)$

When the Overseer plays Always Small, the outcome is the same regardless of the Administrator's strategy. If the Overseer has already decided upon the small budget, the Administrator's recommendation is irrelevant.

With the values plugged in for the primitives, the payoff matrix looks like this

Administrator (Agent)	Overseer (Principal)	
	Always Accept	**Always Small**
Always Truth	$4 - r$ [from $3r + 4(1 - r)$, etc.] $2 + r$	$4 - 3r$ $2 - r$
Always Big	$2 + r$ $4 - r$	$4 - 3r$ $2 - r$

Against Always Small, the Administrator's payoffs are identical. Against Always Accept, the Administrator is better off playing Always Big, as shown by the equation:

$$4 - r \geq 2 + r$$

We know that this equation is always true because r, as a probability variable, is always 1. Thus, Always Big is the Administrator's dominant strategy.

Knowing that the Administrator will surely play Always Big, the Overseer can choose between his two strategies. He will choose Always Accept when the following equation is true:

$$2 + r > 4 - 3r$$

This equation will be true whenever r is greater than 0.5. If the probability that the Big Budget is actually optimal is greater than 50%, the Overseer will choose Always Accept. If r is less than 50%, he will choose Always Small. Interestingly, we see that the Administrator's choice is irrelevant. The Overseer simply gauges the more probable outcome and picks the corresponding strategy. The opinion of the player who actually knows which budget is better for the college has no bearing on the outcome of the game.

Of course, this exact 50/50 split is dependent on the values we chose. The game's outcome, however, is not arbitrary. As long as the relative rank of the primitives remains, variances in their values will not change the prediction that the optimal outcome cannot be achieved. (Always Truth, Always Accept), the outcome that would optimize educational value, is not a possibility given our player's goals and the structure in which they interact.

In order to change the outcome, either player goals or the structure would need to change. If we inspect the payoff matrix, we see that the Overseer's highest payoff is at the outcome (Always Truth, Always Accept). To make the Administrator prefer this outcome, we would need to make $s_a s_a$ more valuable than $B_a s_a$. In other words, we would need to provide the Administrator with structural incentives to keep the budget small, in order to counterbalance his personal incentives to make it bigger. Possible remedies are numerous. For example, we could base a component of the Administrator's salary on the leanness of his administrative budget relative to those at comparable colleges. The advantage of the model is that it provides a framework for testing which remedies would be most effective at restraining this form of drift.

In both the Administrator/Professor and Overseer/Administrator games, we have suggested explanations for the emergence of academic ratchet and administrative lattice. We accomplished this using the minimal assumptions of game theory: that our players act in their self-interest, and that they respond rationally to the incentives presented to them by the organizations in which they work. In addition, we have shown how game theory, by elucidating the forces that underlie suboptimal outcomes, indicates how better outcomes might be achieved.

Conclusion

We have provided a simple game-theoretic model of academic organizations. By identifying key principal-agent games routinely played between overseers, administrators, and professors, we have suggested an explanation of the well-documented administrative accretion in institutions of higher learning. To the extent that we focus on sharable management duties, such as advising and counseling students, and college governance tasks, such as committee work, fund raising, recruiting and other forms of 'public relations' work, the scope of our model is bounded. Professors, for example, can shirk also on teaching and/or scholarship margins, especially if they are tenured. Or, less opportunistically, they may trade better teaching and/or scholarship for less participation in governance tasks. Casual empiricism suggests indeed that faculty members have different propensities and abilities to shirk on each margin, and that administrators have different incentives and abilities to monitor each component of production. Further research that introduces such heterogeneity would provide a useful description of resource allocation in academic departments and could investigate the degree to which apparent shirking by individuals may be complementary and enable efficient specialization. In addition, research that explores the potentially different conceptions of what constitutes the components of educational quality, with the students and alumni perhaps focusing on teaching and the overseers focusing on faculty publishing, may provide further explanation of the accretive tendencies of higher education institutions.

A referee for this journal pointed out that increased division of labor is another explanation for administrative accretion: 'non-faculty academic advisors and career counselors may prove to be better than faculty members at providing these services. Staffs of professional fund raisers and admission counselors may be more effective achieving these goals. Modern computing and database skills may have made the philosopher/registrar obsolete. The growth of state and federal government financial aid programs, more complex accounting rules, and increasing regulatory requirements (OSHA, EEOC) have no doubt led to the need for individuals with specialized skills to handle many of the tasks previously completed by faculty members.' While we agree that some division of labor may be beneficial for the reasons the referee suggests, we believe that misaligned incentives ensure that it will go too far. Unfortunately, direct measures of the relative merits of our and other explanations must await wider availability of relevant empirical data (Leslie and Rhoades, 1995; see also Massy, 1998, p. 88).

This said, we are convinced that understanding the relative merits of our and other explanations of administrative accretion empirically is an important question. One interesting strategy could be a comparison of types of traditional, and often ossified, non-profit educational institutions with exemplars of the new breed of for-profit institutions of higher learning whose incentives are not saddled with institutional and curricular inertia (Siegfried et al., 1995; see also Ortmann, 1997, 1999) and that seemingly inevitable 'way of life in colleges and universities': cross-subsidization (Massy, 1998, p. 87).

Notes

1. Program on Non-Profit Organizations, Yale University, New Haven, CT 06520-8236, USA.

2. Using data from the National Center for Education Statistics of the US Department of Education, Chronister finds that the number of faculty and staff in higher education institutions grew as follows: those with executive and faculty status by 46% and 47%, respectively, those classified as 'other professional' (i.e. administrative staff) by 152% and other staff by 16%. These numbers are likely to underestimate the true growth of administrative accretion since they do not account for outsourcing of auxiliary and other services, such as payroll, dining services, bookstores, etc. In any case, there seems to be consensus that administrative costs grew dramatically, i.e. not just in absolute but in relative terms, for much of the 1980s. Since the end of the 1980s the share of administrative costs seems to have leveled off. However, that is not necessarily good news as during the same time other manufacturing and service industries have managed to reduce their bureaucracies (McKinsey, 1992, 1993; Brynjolfson et al., 1994; Zenger and Hesterly, 1997). These reductions seem to have been the result of productivity gains from advanced information technologies and of outsourcing.

3. Birnbaum (1992, p. 17) demonstrated that individual idiosyncracies, such as 'cognitive complexity' and 'concern for people and process' determines whether a college presidency moves toward success or failure. Faculty, in turn, may choose voice (vocal opposition) or exit (retreat from governance). Clearly, a faculty's response is conditioned on the characteristics of the president, the history of the institution and its traditions and organizational culture. In addition, whatever action the faculty takes at any point in time will have to work its way through a loosely coupled system that admits typically several possible outcomes. We, therefore, readily admit the possibility of multiple equilibria. However, Birnbaum also showed that most presidencies are modal in that they follow a typical path (to failure) that is characterized by presidents 'maintaining trustee and administration support even as they become increasingly distant from the faculty'. Furthermore, such phenomena as academic ratchet and administrative lattice are, by any account, wide-spread phenomena across various institutional forms.

4. James reports that the research/teaching mix of time inputs at universities has grown substantially during the post-World War II period, and is now about 2/1. Bodenhorn (1997) and Hartley and Robinson (1997) show that a similar trend exists at (selective) liberal arts colleges.

5. Figure 1 shows how educational quality changes as the burden of sharable management duties is shifted from professors to administrative (support) staff. At point A, the administration is very small, and professors essentially run the college and perform almost all administrative duties. This was the status of

many US liberal arts colleges before 1960, when even the president was a professor. Scholarship, as measured by research and publishing, was minimal, and one could make a strong case that educational quality suffered. From this point, increased administrative expenditures enabling productivity gains from specialization likely would improve educational quality, here maximized at point B. At point C, all sharable management duties are performed by the administration, and professors teach and do research only. The shape of the curve between B and C is arguable. It might be flat, or it might even fall, as the administrative bureaucracy becomes so cumbersome and the faculty so distanced from the students that educational quality suffers. Of course, a particular college's exact position on the curve is difficult to pinpoint, opening the door for budget battles. We show in this paper that both administrators and professors have incentive to claim that their college is to the left of point B, say at point D, and to advocate the further shifting of sharable management duties to administrative staff.

References

Aron, D.J., 1990. Firm organization and the economic approach to personnel management. *American Economic Review* 80, 23–27.

Baumol, W.J., Bowen, W.G., 1966. *Performing Arts—The Economic Dilemma*, Twentieth Century Fund, Cambridge, MA.

Birnbaum, R., 1992. Will you love me in December as you do in May? Why experienced college presidents lose faculty support. *Journal of Higher Education* 63, 1–25.

Bodenhorn, H., 1997. Teachers, and scholars too: economic scholarship at elite liberal arts colleges. *Journal of Economic Education* 28, 323–336.

Bronner, E., 1998. College tuition rises 4%, outpacing inflation. *New York Times*, 8 October.

Brynjolfson, E., Malone, T.W., Gurbaxani, V., Kambil, A., 1994. Does information technology lead to smaller firms? *Management Science* 40.12, 1628–1644.

Chronister, J. 1999. *Personal communication*.

Clotfelter, C.T., 1996. *Buying the Best: Cost Escalation in Elite Higher Education*. Princeton University Press, Princeton.

Cohen, M., March, J.G., Olsen, J.P., 1972. A garbage can model of organizational choice. *Administrative Science Quarterly* 17, 1–25.

Hartley, J.E., Robinson, M., 1997. Economic research at national liberal arts colleges. *Journal of Economic Education* 28, 337–349.

Hoenack, S.A., 1990. Introduction. In: Hoenack, S.A., Collins, E.L. (Eds.), The economics of American universities. *Management, Operations and Fiscal Environment*. State University of New York, Albany, NY, pp. 1–10.

Honan, W.H., 1994. Cost of 4-year degree passes $100,000 mark. *New York Times*, 4 May.

Hopkins, D.S.P., 1990. The higher education production function: theoretical foundations and empirical findings. In: Hoenack, S.A., Collins, E.L. (Eds.), The economics of American universities. *Management, Operations and Fiscal Environment*. State University of New York, Albany, NY, pp. 11–32.

James, E., 1990. Decision processes and priorities in higher education. In: Hoenack, S.A., Collins, E.L. (Eds.), The economics of American universities. *Management, Operations and Fiscal Environment*. State University of New York, Albany, NY, pp. 77–106.

Larson, E., 1997. Why colleges cost too much. *Time*, 17 March.

Leslie, L.L., Rhoades, G., 1995. Rising administrative costs: on seeking explanations. *Journal of Higher Education* 66, 197–212.

Mabry, T., 1999. College tuition outpaces inflation again. *The Wall Street Journal*, 12 March.

Massy, W.F., 1981. In: Hopkins, D.S.P., Massy, W.R., (Eds.), *A microeconomic theory of colleges and universities*, pp. 73–130.

Massy, W.F., 1998. In: *National Commission on the Cost of Higher Education 1998*. Remarks on restructuring higher education, pp. 84–91.

Massy, W.F., Warner, T.R., 1991. Causes and cures of cost escalation in college and university administrative support services. In: *Proceedings of the National Symposium on Strategic Higher Education Finance and Management Issues*, National Association of College and University Business Officers, Washington, DC.

Massy, W.F., Wilger, A.K., 1992. Productivity in postsecondary education: a new approach. *Educational Evaluation and Policy Analysis* 14, 361–376.

Massy, W.F., Zemsky, R., 1994. Faculty discretionary time. Departments and the 'academic ratchet'. *Journal of Higher Education* 65, 1–22.

McKinsey, Global Institute. 1992. *Service Sector Productivity*. McKinsey and Company, Washington, DC.

McKinsey, Global Institute. 1993. *Manufacturing Productivity*. McKinsey and Company, Washington, DC.

National Commission on the Cost of Higher Education. 1998. *Straight talk about college costs and prices: The report of the National Commission on the Cost of Higher Education*. Oryx Press, Phoenix, AZ.

Ortmann, A., 1997. How to survive in post industrial environments: Adam Smith's advice for to day's colleges and universities. *Journal of Higher Education* 68, 483–501.

Ortmann, A., 1999. The nature and causes of corporate negligence, sham lectures, and ecclesiastical indolence: Adam Smith on joint-stock companies, teachers, and preachers. *History of Political Economy* 31, 297–315.

Ortmann, A., Squire, R.C., 1996. The internal organization of colleges and universities: a game-theoretic approach. Discussion paper #232, Program on Non-profit Organizations, Yale University.

Pitchik, C., Schotter, A., 1987. Honesty in a model of strategic information transmission. *American Economic Review* 77, 1032–1036.

Ritter, J., 1996. School puts its principles first. *USA Today*, 9 December.

Rothschild, M., White, L.J., 1991. The university in the marketplace: some insights and some puzzles. Working Paper No. 3853, National Bureau of Economic Research, Cambridge, MA.

Siegfried, J.J., Getz, M., Anderson, K.H., 1995. The snail's pace of innovation in higher education. *The Chronicle of Higher Education*, 19 May, p. A56.

Williamson, O.E., 1970. Managerial discretion and business behavior. *American Economic Review* 60, 1032–1056.

Winston, G.C., Yen, I., 1995. Costs, prices, subsidies, and aid in US higher education. Discussion Paper DP-32, William's Project on the Economics of Higher Education.

Zemsky, R.E., 1992. Testimony from the belly of the whale. *Policy Perspectives*, September, p. 1A–8A.

Zemsky, R.E., Massy, W., 1990. Cost containment: committing to a new economic reality. *Change* 226, 16–22.

Zemsky, R., Massy, W.F., Oedel, P., 1993. On reversing the ratchet. *Change* 25.3, 56–62.

Zenger, T.R., Hesterly, W.S., 1997. The disaggregation of corporations: selective intervention, high-powered incentives, and molecular units. *Organization Science* 8.3, 209–222.

ADAM SMITH GOES TO COLLEGE: AN ECONOMIST BECOMES AN ACADEMIC ADMINISTRATOR

RONALD G. EHRENBERG

I have conducted research and taught classes on the economics of higher education for almost 20 years. I spent the last three years as a senior central administrator and executive officer of Cornell University. A description of my administrative responsibilities as Vice President for Academic Programs, Planning and Budgeting at Cornell University can be found at my web page at (www.ipr.cornell.edu/RGEsPage/Ronshome.html). My experiences in this position opened my eyes to the use and uselessness of economic analysis in trying to help guide a major university and what I have learned is the focus of this essay.

I begin by asking whether it is useful to view universities in a utility-maximizing framework, as I and others have done in the past. I show that the way universities are organized often guarantees that the utility-maximizing model is unlikely to be the correct approach. I then proceed to discuss a number of resource allocation issues that we faced at Cornell and reflect upon how concepts that are obvious to economists, and that we teach in principles of economics courses, helped or hindered decision-making at the university. The message that I hope comes through is not that economic concepts are irrelevant in operating a university, but rather that it takes a long time to explain to all the actors in the system why they should matter and even longer to make them actually matter.

Most of the discussion draws from my experiences at Cornell University. Cornell is an institution that I love and that I have devoted most of my professional life to trying to help prosper. Hence, nothing that follows should be interpreted as a slap at that institution. Discussions with colleagues around the country, the wonderful essay by John Siegfried (1997) on academic economists as presidents and provosts, and Henry Rosovsky's (1990) discussion of professors and governance at Harvard, suggest that my experiences at Cornell are very typical.

Should Universities Be Viewed as Utility-Maximizing Entities?

Starting with the work of David Garvin (1980), academic economists have used utility-maximizing models of behavior to try to explain the behavior of academic institutions. In Garvin's original work, utility functions for individual departments were aggregated to obtain a utility function for an institution as a whole. Departments, and hence the institution, were assumed to maximize prestige and from this could be derived a whole set of implications for behavior. Garvin used such a model to explain changing patterns of graduate program prestige, the growth of new graduate programs, and resource allocation across departments.

I have used utility-maximizing models myself to explain how institutions should allocate scarce undergraduate financial aid dollars across different categories of students, and in doing so provided an early justification for what has become known as "preferential packaging" in the financial aid literature (Ehrenberg and Sherman, 1984), to explain why cutbacks in federal funding for one type of graduate student (for example, physical sciences) will result in changes in institutional support

687

given to all categories of graduate students (Ehrenberg, Rees and Brewer, 1993) and more recently to talk about the likely future of research universities (Ehrenberg, 1997; see also James, 1990).

While such models are useful both in a normative sense and as analytical devices, they provide little guidance as to how many decisions are actually made at complex universities that have multiple colleges. To see this, consider the institutional structure of a typical university. The central administrative offices of the university include the president, provost, and all the administrative and support services: admissions, registrar, bursar, athletics, housing, dining, utilities, student services, grant administration, the campus store, information technology, telecommunications, libraries, and so on. Some of these services may be enterprises, which charge prices for their services and must at least break even. The rest of the university is made up of the individual undergraduate colleges, professional schools and graduate colleges of the university. In some universities, the graduate school, in which Ph.D. study is undertaken, is formally a separate college. In others, graduate study formally takes place in the other colleges.

The financial relations between the center and the colleges go a long way towards determining if the utility-maximizing model is relevant. Revenue comes into the university from sources such as tuition, government appropriations, endowment income, annual giving, enterprise income, research funding, continuing and executive education programs, and distance learning. At one extreme, all revenue flows to the center, which covers all of the central costs and then allocates the remaining revenue out to the colleges. At the other extreme, the university operates as a set of "tubs," with each college keeping all the revenue it produces and remitting to the center only a sum sufficient to cover its share of the costs of the central administrative and support services. The latter approach is often called a "Responsibility Center Management" (RCM) approach to budgeting (Strauss, Curry and Whalen, 1996). Sometimes under a RCM model, the colleges remit to the center more than the funds necessary to cover their share of the administrative costs. The subsidy, or "franchise fee," that they send to the center can then be reallocated by the central administration across the colleges on a one-time or continuing basis to further institution-wide objectives.

Fund raising for current operating funds, building support, and endowment is often an activity that each college pursues, although access to major donors may be rationed by the center which tries both to match the donors' interests with the colleges' needs and to stress institutional priorities. In some universities, there is a "tax" placed on external gifts that come into the university, either in the form of a share of the gift, a share of the first year income that it provides or a share of its endowment return. Development officers hate such taxes, which they believe discourage donors from giving. Central administrators find them useful to further the objectives of the university, which may differ from the objectives of the donors, and to cover costs that gifts impose on the university as a whole. Similarly, while the university would like the annual giving and endowment it raises to be unrestricted in purpose, donors often have specific objectives in mind. To the extent that a donor's objective coincides with an institutional priority, the donation in practice proves to be unrestricted even though it goes to fund a very specific item; that is, it may simply free up internal funds that the institution would have used otherwise to be used elsewhere.

While the above paragraphs cannot do justice to the complexity of university budget-making, they should make clear that a utility-maximizing model of university behavior is most likely to be a useful way to derive predictions about university behavior in those cases in which the central administration makes unilateral decisions about behavior, such as undergraduate financial aid policies, and in situations in which the central university controls all of the revenue, or at least obtains a "franchise fee" from all of the tubs, and/or "captures" some fraction of the extra income/wealth that comes to the colleges from external donations. The utility-maximizing model also describes fairly well the behavior of small liberal arts colleges, which typically lack separate centers of power.

At my own university, the provost directly controls the budgets of only three of the ten colleges on the Ithaca campus. These three are the Colleges of Arts and Sciences, Engineering and Art, Architecture and Planning, and they are referred to as the "general purpose" colleges. The other seven colleges are tubs, either by statute (the four state-assisted statutory units at Cornell, the School of Industrial and Labor Relations and the Colleges of Agriculture and Life Sciences, Human Ecology, and Veterinary Medicine) or by trustee designation (the Schools of Law, Management, and Hotel

Administration). Through a complicated cost-accounting scheme, the tubs are billed only for the average costs of the central and support services provided to them, as well as for the "net" credit hours that their students take in the three general purpose colleges that the provost directly funds (net of the credit hours that the students from the general purpose colleges take in each of the tubs). The center also does not "tax" the annual giving and endowments that the tub-like colleges obtain. Not surprisingly, given these rules Cornell has operated historically like a system of fiefdoms, rather than one university.

This problem is exacerbated by the method by which deans are selected. At Cornell, and many other universities, searches for college deans are conducted by committees that consist primarily of the faculty, and sometimes students and alumni, from the college in question. Although typically a few faculty and administrators from outside the college in question are on the committee and the president or provost nominally picks the dean from a small group of finalists recommended by the committee; in the main, it is the views of the search committee members that carry the day because the president and provost know from discussions of each candidate's strengths and weaknesses who the committee really favors.

Once in office, a primary role for many deans is external relations, including fund-raising, and they build up strong external constituent support. Hence, it is unlikely that a dean would be censured or fired for focusing on the goals of the particular college and not worrying about the overall goals of the institution. Indeed, in many cases, once a dean is appointed, in the absence of discontent from the faculty and/or alumni of a college, the president and provost substantially lose the ability to influence a dean's behavior. For example, during the summer of 1997, the president of Columbia University bowed to strong criticism from alumni and reappointed a college dean only a few days after dismissing him (Schneider, 1997). Similarly, in April 1998, the president of Georgetown bowed to alumni criticism, which included resignations from advisory boards and the threat of withholding large contributions, and reversed a decision not to reappoint a popular law school dean. It is believed that the dean's unwillingness to share the law school's revenue with the university precipitated the initial decision, although this was never confirmed by the university (Mangan, 1998).

Former Secretary of Labor Robert Reich (1997, pp. 150–51) had a passage in his recent book in which he described his reaction to attending a Cabinet meeting.

> . . . Cabinet officers have nothing in common except the first word in our titles . . . even the formal titles belie reality. Each of us has a special responsibility for one slice of America. . . . I make a list of the real Cabinet . . .
>
> Secretary of the Interior—Secretary of the West
>
> Secretary of the Treasury—Secretary of Wall Street
>
> Secretary of HUD—Secretary of Big Cities
>
> Secretary of Agriculture—Secretary of Small Towns
>
> Secretary of Commerce—Secretary of Corporate America
>
> Secretary of Labor—Secretary of Blue-Collar America
>
> And so forth . . . No wonder we rarely meet.

If one substitutes the words "Dean of . . ." or "Vice President of . . ." for Reich's words "Secretary of . . ." and a college or administrative unit name for a cabinet department name, my sense is that his description also often applies to Cornell and to many other large universities.[1] Hence, the notion that we can treat these institutions as if they are seeking to maximize a well-defined objective function seems farfetched in many cases.

Indeed, inasmuch as university decision-making often consists of negotiations between various units, each motivated by its own self-interests, it may well be productive to apply formal bargaining models to the internal behavior of universities, just as these models have been applied with some success to the internal workings of families.[2] An alternative approach to understanding the behavior of universities that may prove useful is to think of them in the context of models of organizations and address how they seek to solve principal-agent problems between faculty and department chairs, department chairs and deans, and deans and central administrators, as Masten (1997, 1998) does. In future research I hope to use such models to provide a theory of how universities choose where to locate in the spectrum of centralized financial control and responsibility center management and to analyze whether the choice of organizational form influences a university's "performance."

I naïvely assumed when I agreed to help lead my university that my major contributions would come through my skills as an economist. While my skills as an economist were important, in truth, most of my major contributions depended upon my skills as a negotiator and mediator. Because multilateral negotiations take time and are likely to succeed only if, with the help of the parties, one can identify "win-win" situations, the number of major initiatives that an administrator can undertake is actually quite limited. The most frustrating lesson that I had to learn, which should have been obvious to an economist, was that constraints on my time limited what I could achieve as an administrator.

The Uses or Uselessness of Economics in University Decision-Making

Relative Prices Should Matter

Cornell has long been an institution that is known for its strengths in the physical sciences and engineering. The cost of conducting research in these areas has increased substantially as researchers have come to rely more on high technology laboratories, as the federal government has cut back on permissible indirect cost recoveries and exerted increased pressure for matching funds as part of grant proposals, and as the start-up funds needed to attract young physical scientists and engineers have increased dramatically.[3]

One of the first things that economists teach undergraduate students is that relative prices matter and that as the relative price of something increases, one should substitute away from that commodity. Hence, it appeared quite obvious to me that, to the extent that the increased relative cost of the physical sciences and engineering is permanent, unless the marginal importance to the university of being preeminent in the physical sciences and engineering had also risen relative to the marginal importance of our being strong in other areas, we should seriously consider reducing our investments in engineering and the physical sciences and redirecting these saved resources to other areas.[4]

To even suggest this in the presence of faculty from these fields would have marked me as a very dangerous person in the administrative hierarchy. The notion of a university backing away from the areas in which it had been traditionally strong was not something that any physical scientist or engineer would rationally be willing to entertain. In fact, all of Cornell's six Nobel Prize-winning faculty during the last 30 years had come from physics and chemistry. By an ironic twist favoring our physical scientists and engineers, Cornell's president and provost are both humanists and, given the complaints by our physical scientists and engineers that they were not represented at the highest levels of Cornell's central administration, I suspect that neither is likely to want to bear the heat of suggesting that we should contemplate whether maintaining Cornell's relative investments in these areas made sense. Just as it took a Republican, Richard Nixon, to move the United States towards diplomatic relations with China and a Democrat, Bill Clinton, to end welfare as we knew it, it is my conjecture that Cornell will have to wait for a president who comes from the physical sciences or engineering before serious thoughts are given to reducing our emphasis on these areas.[5]

Buildings, Buildings, Buildings

To remain preeminent in the physical sciences and engineering requires state-of-the-art facilities. These facilities are very expensive to construct, operate and maintain. When our engineering dean presented a proposal to develop a new facility to do research on advanced materials, we stressed to scientists around the university that we probably would build only one new science building during the next decade, and that they had better be sure that this was the one that would be of most use to them. We involved scientists from around the university in extensive discussions and everyone concluded that this indeed was the investment in science infrastructure that Cornell should be undertaking.

There is, of course, the matter of having to raise the money to put up the building. Furthermore, our trustees have long been aware that new buildings add to the operating and maintenance cost of the university. A rough estimate is that if the building was expected to have a total project cost of a given amount, it would take an equivalent endowment to provide the funds for utilities, custodial services, and routine and planned maintenance over the useful life of the building. This estimate derives from these costs averaging roughly 4 percent of the project costs and 4 percent is what Cornell "targets" as the annual payout, after investment expenses, on its endowment funds. To the extent that indirect cost recoveries could be used to defray some of these costs, the necessary endowment would be lower. However, our best estimate was that indirect cost recoveries could contribute at most one-third of the necessary operating and maintenance funds for the proposed building. This was an optimistic projection based on current indirect cost recovery rates, the assumption that all research space in the building would always be filled with funded research and that none of this research would be research that would have otherwise been conducted in other existing facilities.

Cornell's trustees have long required that a plan for meeting operating and maintenance costs be present before construction of a building can begin. Realistically, however, once a major donor has committed to funding half the cost of a building and it has been publicly announced that the building will be named after that donor, the idea that construction on the building would be held up because an endowment for maintenance had not been raised is a non sequitur. Furthermore, our ability to raise the additional construction costs, let alone the endowment for operations and maintenance, was somewhat uncertain and based upon forecasts of our development staff. So, while the university hoped that funds to endow a maintenance fund for the building will be raised, we instead planned to pay for the needed operating and maintenance funds that will not come out of indirect cost recoveries from our annual operating budgets.

Inevitably then, this new building will compete for funds with faculty positions, graduate student support and faculty salaries. The very same faculty members who vehemently argued that the institution needed the new facilities to remain competitive in the physical sciences and engineering are likely to turn around and chastise the administration for spending too much on buildings and not enough on faculty salaries, new faculty positions, and graduate student support. Proposals for a moratorium on new construction will be put forth. Many faculty members understand the tradeoff between buildings and other costs, but apparently only *after* their unit's new building is finished.

This highlights a general point that will also be evident in several of the "vignettes" that follow. The university is an institution that is dedicated to rational discussion and intellectual exploration. However, often faculty members' self-interests prevent or delay them from recognizing obvious truths. This tension between the expressed values of the university and the internal political maneuvering that takes place within the institution is often present.

Faculty Salaries

I take it as a fundamental proposition of faculty life that no matter what university one is at, the faculty believe that faculty salaries are too low. The Cornell administration actually happens to believe that this is true at Cornell and is making a determined effort to improve this situation. We reached this conclusion by tracking how our faculty salaries have changed relative to our competitors' faculty salaries over a number of years. In judging the "appropriate level" of our faculty salaries, we are cognizant of the fact that housing prices are low in Ithaca relative to those in our nation's largest cities in which many of the nation's premier institutions of higher education are located. Hence, we periodically hire a firm that specializes in computing how executives' salaries should be changed when their firms relocate them to different areas to compute cost of living indices for Cornell and our competitors.[6] Not surprisingly, a large fraction of the difference between our faculty members' salaries and those of faculty at competitor institutions can be explained by cost of living differences.

Faculty on our faculty budget committee, who tend not to be economists, view attempts to control for the cost of living as an administrative ploy to avoid raising their salaries sufficiently. One faculty member in a leadership position also insisted on comparing the faculty salaries of Cornell's endowed faculty (faculty employed in the private colleges at Cornell) only to the faculty salaries of faculty at other private universities. I patiently tried to explain to him that it is well-known that over the last decade the salaries of faculty at private research universities have risen relative to the salaries of faculty at public research universities, as states have run into fiscal problems and public higher education has faced competing demands for state funds from other public priorities like health care, welfare, and prisons (Bell, 1997). Moreover, in virtually all of the fields in which we employ faculty in the private part of Cornell, 40 to 60 percent of the leading competitor departments are located in public institutions. I presented him with data showing that faculty members who have left Cornell usually have gone to public institutions rather than private institutions and that at the new assistant professor level the public schools are often our competitors as well. Hence, I argued that his comparisons overstated the amount that our faculty salaries have fallen relative to our competitors' because his comparisons neglected all of public higher education. These analyses fell on deaf ears, either because I was wrong, because since I was temporarily an administrator I was perceived as being the enemy, or because the faculty member was up for re-election to his leadership position and had to appear to be a militant leader to be reelected.[7]

We and our faculty observed that Cornell's faculty salaries are most competitive at the assistant professor and associate professor ranks and lag behind the competition the most at the full professor rank. This relationship is not surprising because it is at the former two ranks that we are competing most strenuously to attract and retain new and existing faculty and we have to meet the market in these circumstances. I dared not show the faculty committee my own research of some years ago that showed that the sensitivity of faculty turnover to relative salaries is higher for assistant professors than it is for associate professors and higher for associate professors than it is for full professors (Ehrenberg, Kasper and Rees, 1991). In fact, our deans who allocate salary funds are behaving perfectly rationally when they pay our assistant and associate professors relatively more than they pay our full professors vis-á-vis faculty at other institutions. In effect, they are exploiting the monopsony power that they have over their least mobile faculty. When they face the possibility of losing a desired senior faculty member, the deans have the flexibility to respond with a salary adjustment. As such, our overall turnover rate for tenured faculty members (excluding retirements) has been less than 1.5 percent a year for over a decade.

The vast majority of our faculty are full professors. The vast majority of faculty on our faculty budget committee are full professors. It is therefore not surprising that the faculty committee recommended that the salary pool that we deliver to them be heavily weighted towards full professors. Because of the fallout that we are experiencing from the end of mandatory retirement, I did not have the heart to tell them that such a policy may not be in the institution's best interest.

The End of Mandatory Retirement

Effective January 1, 1994, faculty at American colleges and universities are no longer subject to mandatory retirement. Studies conducted prior to that time by Hammond and Morgan (1991) and by Rees and Smith (1991) had suggested that abolition of mandatory retirement would affect primarily major research universities, where faculty members are often so tied to their work that they can not conceive of leaving their jobs if they are not compelled to do so. In the private part of Cornell, prior to the abolition of mandatory retirement, two-thirds of our faculty retired prior to age 70 and the other one-third retired when compelled to do so at age 70. Since January 1, 1994, the behavior of the former group has not changed, but the behavior of the latter group has. In particular, members of this group have tended to stay on well past age 70.

Many of the faculty staying on beyond age 70 are among Cornell's best and brightest faculty and we are delighted to have them continually associated with the university. When they continue to draw a salary, however, the flow of new faculty into the university is slowed down and there is less money available to increase the salaries of other continuing faculty members each year. When a senior faculty member retires and is replaced by a lower paid assistant professor, the difference between the two salaries can be redistributed to other faculty in the form of salary increases. My calculations indicated that before the end of mandatory retirement, we were generating the equivalent of over a 1 percent salary increase for all continuing faculty each year due to retirements. An increase in the age at which faculty retire will reduce the size of this "self-financing" annual salary increase pool.

Because of these concerns, a joint faculty-administrative committee was appointed with me as chair to look into how the university should respond to the elimination of mandatory retirement. Our preliminary recommendations included that: the university should encourage faculty to use tax-sheltered retirement savings vehicles starting early in their life-cycle so that faculty who wanted to retire would have the resources to do so; the university should provide for a phased retirement option in which faculty members could work for up to five years half-time but receive full health and retirement benefits; and the university should drastically enhance the status of emeritus professors to help that position be seen as a desirable stage of a faculty member's career. We explicitly ruled out expensive buy out plans because evidence from a number of campuses suggests that those plans are not usually cost effective.[8] Finally, we suggested that if people were staying in faculty positions longer than had been expected, the university should consider capping its contributions into the faculty defined contribution retirement system, either after a specified number of years or, as Yale and Chicago have done, after the university's contributions, invested in some predetermined conservative manner, generate an annuity at least equal to a specified percentage of the faculty member's final salary.[9]

Faculty response to our report was that the "carrots" we had proposed were too small; Congress had made tenure truly indefinite and we had to "buy out" their property rights if we wanted them to retire. Congress had given them enhanced rights; however, the notion that the university in its role as an employer could take actions to try to offset the effects of the change in the law was foreign to many of them. While economists who evaluate the effects of changes in federal policies such as the minimum wage often argue about what the magnitudes of employer responses actually are, no economist questions the right of employers to respond. In general, faculty do not think like economists and some faculty even asserted that if we tried to pursue policies to encourage voluntary retirement we would be violating the intent of the federal law. In fact, a provision in the bill passed by Congress in November 1998 to extend the Higher Education Act explicitly permits such policies for tenured faculty.

The faculty response to the one "stick" in the interim report, limitations on retirement contributions, is instructive. Many saw it as an attempt to cut total faculty compensation, even though it was explicit that any money saved would be used to provide benefits for emeritus faculty. Most could not comprehend that the contribution rates chosen by universities to make to their faculty members' retirement accounts were based on a number of assumptions including the expected age of retirement. To the extent that faculty are retiring later, a smaller contribution rate would be required to fund any desired level of annuity because the annuity would be paid out over a smaller number of years and because savings in the account would experience compound earnings tax-free over a longer number of years. Rather, faculty saw the contribution rate, rather than the implied annual pension benefit, as something that was due to them. Ultimately, given faculty perceptions that their salaries were too low (see above), we backed off this proposal in our final report.[10]

Although economists use several different models to conceptualize the existence of tenure—as McPherson and Schapiro indicate in their companion paper in this symposium—one that I often find useful is based on Lazear's (1979) model of mandatory retirement. To think about this in the simplest of terms, suppose a faculty member's productivity is constant over the life cycle (to avoid questions of the relationship between productivity and age) and that the faculty member is paid a salary that starts below the productivity level and then rises continually with experience. Suppose also that the present value of a faculty member's salary is higher with this increasing salary profile than it would be if the faculty member received a salary equal to the constant productivity— assuming that the faculty member retires at, say, age 70. In such a world, the faculty member has an incentive to exert extra effort to earn tenure and get to the point on the salary profile at which salary exceeds productivity. After that point, the faculty member still has an incentive to work hard because tenure does not guarantee any real salary and, if the faculty member reneges on effort, the university has the freedom to reduce salary, at least by the rate of inflation. In such a world, both the university and the faculty member are better off than they would be in a world in which salary always equaled productivity, because the faculty member's present value of salary is higher under such a scheme and the university gets a greater output from the faculty member because of the induced extra effort.

Of course, for this model to make sense, mandatory retirement is needed so that the faculty member does not receive a salary greater than productivity indefinitely. Put another way, for this to be an equilibrium, the present value of the faculty member's marginal productivity over the life cycle must just equal the present value of salary over the life cycle. If the retirement age goes up, then to maintain the optimality of the model, either the number of faculty must fall or the level or the slope of the faculty salary profile must diminish. You can imagine what the response of our senior faculty who already felt that they are underpaid would have been if I suggested to them that, because of the abolition of mandatory retirement, perhaps our goal should be to reduce senior faculty salary increases rather than increasing them.[11]

Space Planning, Deferred Maintenance and Imperfect Information

Early on in my term as an administrator, I inherited the "Sage shuffle." Sage Hall is a historic building on the Cornell campus that unfortunately needed about $3.5 million in deferred maintenance expenditures to maintain it in usable, but outdated, condition. Such funds are not easily found in university annual operating budgets. (As one trustee said to me, students want low tuition, faculty want high salaries, and neither pushes for higher maintenance expenditures). Thus, at Cornell we have tended to fund deferred maintenance expenditures, such as the replacement of mechanical systems, as part of major renovations that modernize and improve the space within a building.[12] Given the historic nature of Sage Hall, historic preservation organizations had made sure that we did not have the option of totally tearing the building down and replacing it with a new one.

Cornell's Johnson Graduate School of Management, which had outgrown its space, was the only college on campus thought to have the donor base needed to fund a major renovation of the building. Ultimately, a $38 million project was undertaken which has now been completed. To renovate the building, we first had to move all of its current inhabitants (including the graduate school and a number of miscellaneous offices) out of the building and into other locations. A series of moves were set into place, which became known as "Sage shuffle" because other offices had to be vacated in turn to make room for those displaced from Sage Hall. When finished, these moves involved 26 different units and over 390 faculty and staff, as well as a roughly equivalent number of graduate students. Ultimately, this series of moves cost Cornell's current operating budget almost $5.7 million, which far exceeded what the cost of simply making the deferred maintenance expenditures would have been. Of course, if Cornell had opted to make the deferred maintenance expenditures, rather than renovating the building, the university would have incurred some additional costs associated with temporarily housing residents of the building in other locations and would not have gained the benefits associated with a renovated facility.

As we neared the end of the series of moves, one important scheduled move was canceled because at the last minute a unit realized that it did not make sense for it to locate far from the dean who financed it. This cancellation caused us to scramble for other options. One proposal was to take a building that had been promised to a second unit and to move a third unit into that building as well. There was excess space in the building and the third unit could have been accommodated with some squeezing.

The director of the second unit came to my office and pounded his fist on my table, informing me that if he did not get all the space that he had been promised, he would resign. Because the provost told me that one of my roles was to solve, not create, problems for him, I swallowed hard, told the director that he could have the whole building and moved the third unit elsewhere. To do so generated much controversy, and in the process I had to "dump" on a nonacademic support unit that reported to me by moving them away from the center of campus. Two months later the director of the second unit was not reappointed by the vice president to whom he reported. In fact, the decision not to reappoint him had been made well in advance of the director's discussion with me, although he had not yet been informed.

Information does not always flow smoothly between university administrators who work for the same institution because there are too many things going on for them to be continually filling each other in on everything that each is doing. Imperfect information leads to less than optimal decisions. Conversely, information flows very quickly around the university whenever an administrator says anything, even in confidence, to any faculty member. This leads prudent administrators to "tell the same story" to everyone. However, since information flows are often less than perfect, multiple views on what the administrator said often arise even in this case. Thus, the optimal policy for an administrator is often to say nothing, even when the administrator has no desire to withhold information.

The Cost of Space

Many observers of Cornell's financial situation have pointed to the costs associated with all of the buildings that Cornell has constructed and must maintain as limiting the university's ability to hold down tuition costs and raise faculty salaries. Using measures such as building space per student or faculty, Cornell does have more space than most of its competitors. Of course, it is difficult to hold all other relevant factors equal when comparing building space across universities. Some universities house all their students in university-owned buildings while others house few. The mix of undergraduate and graduate teaching and research varies across universities. The science intensity of different universities differs. Finally, some universities are located in urban areas where land is expensive and others, such as Cornell, are located in more rural surroundings, in which land for research facilities is less expensive. If Cornell has "too much space," part of the reason undoubtedly is that many users of space are totally unaware of the costs of the space that they occupy and bear none of the costs of the space directly.[13]

It seemed quite reasonable to me that we should attempt to compute the actual operating costs of the space each unit occupies. These costs would include the actual costs for routine and preventive maintenance, utilities and custodial services. Our building and grounds people tell us that to properly maintain buildings, approximately 1.5 percent of the replacement value of the building should be set aside each year for planned maintenance, and this too would be included in the cost. Certain overhead costs of buildings, including insurance and police and fire protection, would also have to be included.

Such estimates would have a number of uses. At the college level, such information would allow deans to identify the space costs associated with each of their departments just as they identify the number of faculty, teaching assistants, support personnel and other direct allocations. Deans, at least implicitly, base their allocation of faculty and other operating resources on the activity levels of their departments, such as students taught and external research funding, and having this information would allow them to do the same things with space.

To take another example, when I was discussing moving one unit into a building that had far more space than they currently occupied, the unit was not very anxious to share the building with a second unit, even though it still would be better off in the new location than in the current location. To encourage them to accept a shared arrangement, I suggested to them that I could compute the cost of the space that I wanted the second unit to occupy and reduce the operating budget of the college in which the first unit was located by an equivalent amount. That is, I would "bill" their college for the space that they were refusing to give up in the new location and leave it to the college to decide whether the reduction in their budget would affect only the department. I had no authority to do this; however, faculty sometimes believe that administrators have more power than they actually do and my "threat" provided a strong incentive for the first unit to negotiate a compromise with the second, which was done. To have the ability to think systematically about trading off operating and space budgets in this manner should be very important to universities.

At the provost and deans' levels, such estimates are important to help the university understand the extent that cross-subsidies are occurring. Resource allocation decisions at universities should always be based on the academic values of the different activities; however, the monetary benefits and costs of the activities provide the context in which such decisions should be made. The systematic failure to include space costs in the calculations will cause a university to spend too much on activities that are space-intensive and that have high operating and maintenance costs per unit of space.

Finally, knowledge of space costs can be used to help ration space and curb people's appetites for space. Placing "prices" on space and permitting units to trade off spaces for operating budgets is likely to be an efficient way of carving out space and minimizing the need for new space.[14] While the argument is often made that freeing up only one or two contiguous offices does not always do the institution much good, in a world in which universities must worry about providing office space for emeritus faculty to encourage faculty retirement, even small contractions of space use would be very valuable to universities.

However, after two years of effort, I gave up trying to implement a space cost model for Cornell. Too many objections were raised to the details of the calculations that we were proposing to assure that the approach would have significant support to be adopted. One major set of criticisms revolved around our inability to distinguish whether "high cost" space was high cost because it was "high quality" or whether it was high cost because it was inefficiently designed. The problem could be addressed in theory, but was difficult to handle in practice.[15]

I met with the business officers for each college and they encouraged me to write a statement for the weekly faculty newspaper that would educate faculty about the costs of space. (Given the importance of getting faculty to think about this issue, I still intend to do this.) They indicated, however, they would not use space cost estimates on a regular basis, preferring instead to negotiate with departments over space, using a set of space standards that the university had developed long ago. So, for example, as a full professor I am "entitled" to an office of a certain size and as a vice president to an office of another size. If departments have more space than the standards indicate they "deserve," the college business officers can then negotiate with the departments for reductions.

I took pride during my term as a central administrator that my office was 40 percent smaller than the space standards indicated that my position entitled me to have. One of my responsibilities was to supervise Cornell's office of space planning. Whenever people came to me complaining that they did not have enough space, I simply shrugged my shoulders and complained to them about my own allocation of space. I also never told the business officers that imposing fixed space to faculty ratios that do not change as either relative costs change, or as the budget constraint facing the university shifts, does not make a lot of sense from the perspective of an economist. Instead, I followed the dictum of the provost, who while a musicologist often thought more like an economist than I did, that if information is not going to be used, don't bother to incur the costs of collecting it. The marginal cost of developing space cost information for Cornell currently far exceed the marginal benefits the institution will get from collecting the information.

Concluding Remarks

The examples I have discussed above are only a few of the many issues that confront university decisionmakers in which economic models and methods can usefully contribute to decisions. Some of the other issues that I confronted during my term as a Cornell vice president in which my skills as an economist were most relevant included endowment spending policies; choosing among alternative ways to air-condition a campus in the face of changing environmental regulations; using internal transfer pricing mechanisms to facilitate academic objectives; deciding how library resources should be allocated; designing financial aid policies to enhance student quality and diversity; studying the extent to which compensation policies are gender neutral; pricing parking; designing employee benefit programs; and using hedonic models to understand graduate program rankings and to help decide where to allocate resources. I will elaborate on my discussions above and discuss all of these other topics and much more in a forthcoming Harvard University Press book.

I loved the time I spent as a senior central administrator at Cornell. Although one might not sense it from the tone of some of my remarks above, I accomplished an enormous amount during my administrative term. For example, I helped to integrate the many economics departments across the campus and improved the quality of their senior faculty hires, helped to create a new university-wide department of statistics, worked with the faculty senate to create Cornell's first university-wide faculty tenure review committee, helped to establish our response to the end of mandatory retirement, and helped to evaluate and redesign some of our financial aid policies.[16]

To paraphrase the words of James Freedman (1996, p. 20), the best part of my job was that I was able to raise very fundamental issues with my colleagues in the administration, on the faculty, and on Cornell's Board of Trustees and to force them to think about these issues. They did not always respond to these issues in the way that I personally would have preferred, but I had the satisfaction of knowing that the university was thinking seriously about the situation. I enjoyed trying to explain simple economic concepts to my faculty and administrative colleagues and to push them to think about these concepts when major issues were debated. This is perhaps the major and unique contribution that economists can make when they serve as senior central administrators.

Notes

1. Rojas (1998) presents case studies of resource allocation at six unidentified private research universities that reinforce this sense.

2. See, for example, McElroy (1990) and Lundberg and Pollak (1996). A key application of such models is in explaining household formation and divorce. Only rarely do individual colleges within a university contemplate separating from the larger university and only slightly more frequently do we see mergers of independent colleges.

3. Indirect, or overhead, costs are the expenses incurred by the university as a result of the sponsored research on campus that cannot be easily attributed to any specific project. These include, but are not limited to, research administration, depreciation, operation and maintenance of facilities and equipment, university computing and libraries. Cordes (1998) shows that the average indirect cost recovery rate at leading private research universities fell by 1.2 percentage points between fiscal years 1991 and 1997. At Cornell's private colleges (those other than the four statutory colleges) in Ithaca, the rate actually fell 13.9 percentage points. In contrast, on average, rates at public institutions rose during the period.

4. It is often much harder to improve relatively weak departments than it is to maintain the strength of a top-rated department. A university's reputation also depends heavily on the reputation of its top departments. Hence, a case can be made that it would be prudent for Cornell to reduce its investment in the physical sciences and engineering areas only gradually. An observant reader might note that I have said nothing above about the implications of the rapidly rising costs of biological research. This is because perceptions of the relative benefits of being strong in biology have also increased due to the growing importance of biomedical research and the intellectual excitement caused by recent advances in biology.

5. See Cukierman and Tommasi (1998) for a formal treatment of why substantial policy changes may be implemented by "unlikely" parties.

6. The index they developed is a fixed weight index, which has well-known problems, but I have judged it to be about as good as can be done. See Ehrenberg and Smith (1997, p. 33), for a discussion of the problems inherent in fixed weight price indices.

7. There is a useful analogy here to Ashenfelter and Johnson's (1969) model of union behavior in which the objectives of union leaders and union members are assumed to diverge. The union members care about their salaries, while the leaders also care about the survival of the union and their personal political survival. Suppose that the union leader, after negotiating with management, realizes the "best" settlement likely to be obtained is below the union members' expectations. The leader can either try to "sell" this settlement to the members or take a militant stance and lead them out on a strike. Since the former strategy leaves union leaders open to the charge of "being in bed" with management, the latter is often the preferred strategy for leaders who want to remain in office. This model is described in detail in Ehrenberg and Smith (1997). Substitute the words "professor" for "union member," "faculty leader" for "union leader," and "university administration" for "management" and the analogy is clear.

8. A recent retirement incentive plan at the University of California did induce substantial faculty retirements (Pencavel, 1998). However, the U.C. faculty were covered by a defined benefit plan and the cost of "sweetening" their benefits was borne by the state retirement system, not the university. For a discussion of why it is more difficult to "encourage" retirement when faculty are covered by a defined contribution retirement system rather than a defined benefit system, see Appendix B of our committee's preliminary report, available on the web at (http://www.ipr.cornell.edu).

9. The complete text of our April 1997 preliminary report is available on the web at (http://www.ipr.cornell.edu).

10. Our November 1997 final report is also available at (http://www.ipr.cornell.edu). In May 1998, Cornell's provost announced the adoption of the recommendations contained in the final report as formal university policy. A more complete discussion of our analyses and recommendations is found in Ehrenberg, Matier and Fontanella (1998).

11. See Appendix C of our preliminary report for a more complete discussion of the economics of the professorial employment relationship, available on the web at (http://www.ipr.cornell.edu).

12. Cornell's trustees have taken it upon themselves to mandate that we spend more on planned maintenance than we would otherwise have done. Thus, relative to many other universities our buildings are now in relatively good shape. Of course, the extra funds we spend maintaining the buildings could have gone to faculty salaries or other current operating needs.

13. As with most general statements about Cornell, this statement must be qualified. The designated colleges are billed directly for the operating and maintenance costs of their space (although planned maintenance is at their discretion). Statutory college costs are paid by state appropriations which to date have risen automatically when new construction or renovations are undertaken. Hence, the statement applies primarily to the endowed general purpose colleges and to individual departments and faculty members within each of the colleges. Faculty members with external research grants that provide for indirect cost recoveries are also implicitly billed for their space costs and the College of Agriculture and Life Sciences explicitly bills faculty for using some specialized facilities like greenhouses.

14. In this journal, Boyes and Happel (1989) describe how one economics department allocated faculty offices through an auction mechanism rather than by seniority or other means. The amount that faculty as a group have been willing to pay for offices has been used to support graduate students.

15. One way an economist might get around this problem would be to develop a hedonic model of space costs that would enable one to "price" various characteristics—wet lab, air-conditioning, double pane windows, and so on—and then compute and assign the implied price of each specific space. Such an effort was far beyond the capabilities of Cornell's data systems.

16. Much of my success as an administrator derived from faculty members' perceptions that I was one of them and would eventually return to my faculty position. However, if faculty members believe an administrator's return is imminent, they will try to outlast the administrator. Hence, to maintain my effectiveness, I regularly had to claim that my expected term in office was longer than I actually planned. Even administrators with the utmost integrity must sometimes withhold information.

References

Ashenfelter, Orley and George Johnson. 1969. "Bargaining Theory, Trade Unions and Industrial Strike Activity." *American Economic Review.* March, 59, pp. 35–49.

Bell, Linda. 1997. "Not So Good: The Annual Report on the Economic Status of the Professor, 1996–97." *Academe.* May, 83, pp. 12–20.

Boyes, William J. and Stephen K. Happel. 1989. "Auctions As An Allocation Mechanism in Academia: The Case of Faculty Offices." *Journal of Economic Perspectives.* Summer, 3, pp. 37–40.

Cordes, Colleen. 1998. "Overhead Rates for Federal Research Are As High As Every Survey Finds." *Chronicle of Higher Education.* Jan. 23, A30.

Cukierman, Alex and Mariano Tommasi. 1998. "When Does It Take a Nixon to Go to China?" *American Economic Review.* March, 88, pp. 180–97.

Ehrenberg, Ronald G. 1997. "The American University: Dilemmas and Directions," in *The American University: National Treasure or Endangered Species.* Ronald G. Ehrenberg, ed. Ithaca, NY: Cornell University Press.

Ehrenberg, Ronald G., Hirschel Kasper and Daniel Rees. 1991. "Faculty Turnover at American Colleges and Universities." *Economics of Education Review.* 10, pp. 99–110.

Ehrenberg, Ronald G., Michael W. Matier and David Fontanella. 1998. "Cornell University Confronts the End of Mandatory Retirement." Paper presented at the conference on *Examining Life After the End of Mandatory Retirement*. Washington, DC, May 18.

Ehrenberg, Ronald G., Daniel Rees and Dominic Brewer. 1993. "Institutional Responses to External Support for Graduate Students." *Review of Economics and Statistics*. November, 75, pp. 671–82.

Ehrenberg, Ronald G. and Daniel S. Sherman. 1984. "Optimal Financial Aid Policies for a Selective University." *Journal of Human Resources*. Spring, 19, pp. 202–30.

Ehrenberg, Ronald G. and Robert S. Smith. 1997. *Modern Labor Economics: Theory and Public Policy*, 6th ed. Reading, MA: Addison-Wesley.

Freedman, James O. 1996. *Idealism and Liberal Education*. Ann Arbor, MI: University of Michigan Press.

Garvin, David. 1980. *The Economics of University Behavior*. New York, NY: Academic Press.

Hammond, P. Brett and Harriet P. Morgan, eds. 1991. *Ending Mandatory Retirement for Tenured Faculty*. Washington, DC: National Academy Press.

James, Estelle. "Decision Processes and Priorities in Higher Education," in *The Economics of American Universities*. Stephen A. Hoenack and Eileen L. Collins, eds. Albany, NY: State University of New York Press, pp. 77–107.

Lazear, Edward. 1979. "Why is There Mandatory Retirement?" *Journal of Political Economy*. December, 87, pp. 1261–1284.

Lederman, Douglas. 1998. "Senior Citizens Group and Colleges Compromise on Early Retirement Measure." *Chronicle of Higher Education* (internet version, April 29).

Lundberg, Shelly and Robert A. Pollak. 1996. "Bargaining and Distribution in Marriage." *Journal of Economic Perspectives*. Fall, 10, pp. 139–58.

Mangan, Katherine. 1998. "An Unfair Tax? Law and Business Schools Object to Bailing Out Medical Centers." *Chronicle of Higher Education*. May 5, pp. A43–44.

Masten, Scott E. 1997. "The Internal Organization of Higher Education; or Why Universities, Like Legislatures, Are Not Organized as Markets." University of Michigan Business School Working Paper, April.

Masten, Scott E. 1998. "Old School Ties: Financial Aid Coordination and the Governance of Higher Education." *Journal of Economic Behavior and Organizations*. September 28, pp. 23–47.

McElroy, Marjorie B. 1990. "The Empirical Content of Nash-Bargained Household Behavior." *Journal of Human Resources*. Fall, 25, pp. 559–83.

Pencavel, John. 1998. "The Response of Employees to Severance Incentives: The University of California's Faculty, 1991–94." Stanford University Economics Department Working Paper, April.

Rees, Albert and Sharon Smith. 1991. *Faculty Retirement in the Arts and Sciences*. Princeton, NJ: University Press.

Reich, Robert B. 1997. *Locked in the Cabinet*. New York, NY: Knopf.

Rojas, Daniel J. 1998. *Resource Allocation in Private Research Universities*. Stanford, CA: Stanford University School of Education Unpublished Doctoral Dissertation.

Rosovsky, Henry. 1990. *The University: An Owner's Manual*. New York, NY: W. W. Norton and Co.

Schneider, Alison. 1997, "Columbia U. President Hires Back a Dean He Forced Out." *Chronicles of Higher Education*. July 18, A38.

Siegfried, John J. 1997. "Should Economists Be Kicked Upstairs?" *Southern Economic Journal*. April, 63, pp. 853–87.

Strauss, John, John Curry and Edward Whalen. 1996. "Revenue Responsibility Budgeting," in *Resource Allocation in Higher Education*. William F. Massy, ed. Ann Arbor, MI: University of Michigan Press. Pp. 163–90.

Part IX

Political and Market Contexts in Higher Education

AFTER GLOBALIZATION: EMERGING POLITICS OF EDUCATION

SIMON MARGINSON

Globalization refers to the formation of world systems, as distinct from internationalization which presupposes nations as the essential unit. Globalization includes finance and trade; communications and information technologies; migration and tourism; global societies; linguistic, cultural and ideological convergence; and world systems of signs and images. While it does not negate the nation-state, it changes its circumstances and potentials. In the global era, government continues to be largely national in form, and education is, if anything, more central to government, while issues of identity and difference become more important in the politics of education.

Elements of Globalization

Globalization is irreversibly changing the politics of the nation-state and its regional sectors, domestic classes and nationally-defined interest groups. It is creating new potentials and limits in the politics of education. Its effects in the politics of education are complex. Though modern education systems are creatures of the nation-building project, a project which, in its high modern post–1945 form, is rendered increasingly problematic in a global order, education itself also operates as one of the subject-objects of globalization. Increasingly shaped as it is by globalization—both directly and via the effects of globalization in national government—education at the same time has become a primary medium of globalization, and an incubator of its agents. As well as inhibiting or transforming older kinds of education, globalization creates new kinds. If the nation-state is in a "mutually constitutive relationship" with global systems and practices (Lingard and Rizvi forthcoming), even as that same nation-state is buffeted and re-worked by global pressures, then education is implicated in both sides of the global/national relationship.

"Globalization" here refers to more than internationalization of goods and services, money, people and ideas. Internationalization is about bi-lateral or multi-lateral relations between individual nations: it presupposes the nation-state as the essential unit (Taylor et al. 1997: 56). The notion that globalization is about linkages and inter-connections between states is moving closer. Another aspect is its supra-national dynamic of perpetual transition and what often seems to be irresistible change, in which the processes of modernization are no longer the singular property of the nation-state. Put simply, globalization is about *world systems* which have a life of their own that is distinct from local and national life, even while these world systems tend to determine the local and national. This does not mean that the global determines the national and local in a total or one-directional fashion—but it has the potential to affect every part of the world, including educational institutions and programmes, and the subjectivities formed in education. There is no longer any part of the world that is immune from global systems.

As such, globalization is complex and multiple, embracing practices which are conventionally described as "economic," "political," "sociological," "cultural," "linguistic," "semiotic" and so on. It is argued elsewhere (Marginson 1997b) that real phenomena are irreducibly complex and cannot be wholly reduced to thought; and still less can a single intellectual discipline or school of thought capture all that can be known about these phenomena. Any school of thought, no matter how "holistic" its claims, tends to focus on certain phenomena while excluding other phenomena from its horizon. The real-world phenomena falling under the broad heading of "globalization" are too complex to be captured by any one single branch of social theory, though the literature on globalization is replete with studies based on one branch of social theory and the contending claims of one branch against another, for example "cultural" versus "economic" accounts of globalization (for some discussion of the various analyses of globalization see Waters 1995).

This leaves two possible courses for analysis. One is to use a single branch of social theory for analytical purposes and acknowledge the limitations of such an analysis—though it must be noted that in practice such admissions are rarely made, probably more because they are seen to detract from force of argument than from any deep-seated essentialism. The other is to use more than one branch of social theory, drawing the different insights together into an accumulating lattice of explanation. "This mode of thought involves approaching any issue from a variety of starting points, using a range of partial analyses in order to build up a picture." In this approach "the axioms of one chain of reasoning may be the conclusions of another . . . more weight is attached to the conclusion of any one chain of reasoning if it is confirmed by the conclusions of other chains of reasoning" (Dow 1990: 146–147). The approach is akin to Bohr's "complementarity" principle in physics (Hobsbawm 1995: 539). Thus, for example, cultural insights into globalization might be useful in the study of its economic relationships, and theorizations of its economic dynamics provide one way into its political and cultural potentials.

The problem then becomes how to bind the different elements together. This is determined by the purpose of the inquiry. In discussing the politics of education, in the context of globalization, the (temporary!) "master discipline" is political analysis and power relations. In this article the understanding of politics is constituted by a junction between Foucauldian power-knowledge and Marxist and post-Keynesian political economy (Marginson 1997b: 7–26). Normatively, the argument developed here is sympathetic to both social democratic and liberationist political positions: that is, it is normatively plural and this is consistent with its theoretical plurality.

The article begins by touching on six aspects of globalization, each of which is dealt with briefly, though worth an extended discussion in its own right. Note that the importance given to these elements is by no means universally agreed. In addition to the "mono-disciplinarity" already discussed, which leads to emphasis on some factors to the exclusion of others, there are tendencies to over-play or under-play the importance of globalization. At one extreme, in market liberal accounts, globalization is seen in terms of a universal world market that operates as an irresistible meta-historic force. In essence there are no politics, national or inter-national (except as an obstacle), there are only global market forces. At the opposite extreme, there is nothing happening at all. The phenomena tagged as "globalization" are seen as nothing but the continuation of older trends. From this viewpoint, statements about globalization become seen as claims designed to justify the failures of national economic strategy and the shift to more market liberal and corporate-aligned policies. These contrasting positions on globalization are explored below.

The six aspects of globalization are:

Finance and trade;
Communications and information technologies;
International movements of peoples;
The formation of global societies;
Linguistic, cultural and ideological convergence; and
World systems of signs and images.

Finance and Trade

Nations have been economically inter-dependent for a long time. The new element is an increase in the weight of global corporate power, particularly financial power. This constitutes not a single world financial and trading system as such (a "world market"), but "triadization": a process of intensified system exchange within a financial market based on the three main economic blocs of North America, Europe, and Japan in concert with the Asian NIC's and Eastern China. "The ownership of capital still matters and it still remains the dominant factor of economic and socio-political power in the world" (Petrella 1996: 68). The picture is dominated by huge flows of money. In 1983, when the Australian foreign exchange was deregulated, the total world trade in commodities and services was about US $3 trillion. In 1995, foreign exchange transactions in which one currency is traded against another were running at US $1 trillion *a day*. Between 1983 and 1989, world GDP rose by 7.8% a year, total world exports rose by 9.4% a year, and total world foreign direct investment rose by 28.9% a year (Petrella 1996: 73).[1] The principal carrier of economic globalization is the business firm, an organizational form that has proven to be especially flexible across national boundaries. Global agencies such as the IMF/World Bank have also played a key role in securing the policies of economic deregulation that have progressively meshed the triad together and opened an increasing part of the rest of the world to triad-dominated flows of capital.

Communications and Information Technologies

The last decade has seen major growth in the use of information technologies and the rise of the internet and other global communications. These technologies facilitate the growth of global market exchange—especially trade in money in all its forms—and speed the translation of knowledge into transmittable information so that knowledge is more readily turned into saleable commodities, and more widely and rapidly available, often at lower cost. Like the telephone before it, the internet enables instantaneous relationships to be conducted at a distance: unlike the telephone it facilitates text and document transfer as well as personal intimacy. Many industries are undergoing transformation, especially those with international dimensions. The OECD refers to the resulting cycle of skill displacement as "creative destruction" (OECD 1996b: I.7). In education, communications and information technologies have enabled new and diversified methods of teaching, learning, information retrieval and service delivery, and greatly expanded the potential for international distance education, not to mention cross-border communication among academics. There is longer term potential for the convergence of educational systems with media, financial and retail industries via common telecommunications and satellite networks (for a recent discussion see Cunningham et al. 1997).

International Movements of Peoples

International transfers for the purposes of tourism, work and migration are now easier than at any other period in history. Between 1995 and 2005, travel and tourism within Europe are expected to increase by 78% (OECD 1996a: 30). Significantly—and in contrast with earlier times—after transferring location, people are able to maintain instantaneous links with their point of origin through media and communications systems, strengthening the capacity of migrants to manage their own diasporic identities while resisting full assimilation into the new nation. In *Modernity at Large* Appadurai (1996) argues that media and migration provide resources for experiments with self-making. Together with the generalization of the skills of forming and maintaining identity and relationships—through education, media and consumption—this enables a broader range of subjectivities to form. Even the OECD, which has traditionally focused on the economic aspects of globalization, identifies such cultural aspects. "As cultures mix, some of the traditional norms, values and cultural "maps" of communities and families no longer apply." Some communities have created "multimedia houses of culture and learning where different traditions can meet" (OECD 1996a: 30). One result is that the notion of culturally homogenous nations is difficult to sustain, and the exclusion of would-be immigrants is arbitrary (Hirst and Thompson 1996: 182). Another is the potential for what Appadurai (1996) calls "diasporic public spheres":

> Electronic mass mediation and transnational mobilization have broken the monopoly of autonomous nation states over the project of modernization. The transformation of everyday subjectivities,

through electronic mediation and the work of the imagination, is not only a cultural fact. It is deeply connected to politics, through the new ways in which individual attachments, interests, and aspirations increasingly crosscut those of the nation state (Appadurai 1996: 10).

The Formation of Global Societies

Communications systems, transport, linked banking and finance systems and common global media such as CNN enable the formation of cross-national societies based on people sharing interests and associations in specific fields such as business, education or the arts. The cheapening of conversation at a distance, its speed and the multiplicity of its modes increases the potential density of these relationships. To a lesser extent there is also the formation of specific communities of genuinely extra-national people detached from both their country of origin and their country of residence. Migration, cross-national education and business activities can all establish pre-conditions for extra-national society.

Linguistic, Cultural and Ideological Convergence

On one hand, globalization in its contemporary forms is colonialism writ large, in that it is associated with the further and more complete spread of Western specific and especially Anglo-American specific language, economic practices, cultural forms and social relations. Ideologically it is often associated with market liberal power-knowledge systems (Marginson 1997a, b), and the movement of the English language—which is increasingly a common global language for doing business—into hitherto other linguistic spaces. On the other hand, global relationships call up potential for multilingualism and multi-culturalism, and, by bringing languages into more frequent collision and contact and creating larger and more active cosmopolitan zones between them, are associated with new potential for hybridity. There is also longer term potential for the plurality of global horizons, in that global linguistic-cultural sets other than English can develop, for example Mandarin Chinese.

Convergence of Signs and Images

Globalization is also carried by key symbols, associated with world products and especially images of physical activity and totem-persons imagined as properties of the self: the Coke bottle, McDonald's hamburger, Nike's Michael Johnson, Princess Diana and so on. These are markers for the spread of commodity relations and key English language words and concepts, and the reach of newly universalized desires. Again, globalization forms new consumer subjectivities and hybrid identities in which the world products undergo local referencing and reconstruction.

How new is globalization? Though the internet and CNN are recent phenomena, the telephone and telegraph have been around longer. Banking systems, worldwide markets, the universalization of logics of consumption and desire, the spread of mono-cultural European language and cultural systems are at least as old as 19th century imperialism, and have much earlier roots. The 19th century imperial projects were global in intent (and their obverse, the First International's call of "Workers of the World Unite," was another attempt to construct a particular global identity). In this context, political claims that are premised on the notion of a global market liberal order, powered by market forces driven by a quantitative logic and a material necessity "beyond" states or politics or human agency—claims prevalent in neo-classical economic literature and in the public discourse associated with it, and used to underpin a politics in continuity with the older Anglo-American imperial mission—should be treated with some scepticism.

There is no doubt that globalization has provided a conjunctural fillip for the market liberal paradigm in government. After the failure of monetarism and supply side strategies in the mid 1980s, market liberalism might have faltered: by appearing to confirm the image of the imagined universal market that lay at the core of market liberal theory, the real world trends to globalization and the collapse of communism underwrote continuing market liberal policies of fiscal restraint, deregulation, marketization and welfare denial. The material trends to globalization and the market liberal knowledge claims about globalization have been drawn together so as to reinforce each other. Claims about globalization have underpinned the successive national deregulations of international capital movements and the weakening of distinctive national social policies, such as the Swedish welfare state. In response to this, in *Globalisation in question* (Hirst and Thompson 1996: 2–6) the authors deplore the manner in which descriptions of globalization have encouraged "a pathology of diminished expectations" about democracy, political practices and the role of the nation-state. They are right about the political effects, but Hirst and Thompson go too far, dismissing the notion of anything novel in contemporary globalization. In order to establish this assumption/conclusion they occlude those aspects which are new, such as intensive communications and media, and downplay the increased world-wide penetration of transport, trade and totem commodities.[2]

Nor is globalization reducible simply to colonialism writ large. That is, to neglect its potential for forming cultural differences, as well as erasing them. Appadurai (1996) is at pains to emphasize that it does *not* necessarily lead to universal Americanization. If anything, identities are becoming more multiple and complex, as "individuals and groups seek to annex the global into their own practices of the modern"; and media and communications do *not* necessarily function as a mass narcotic. They also call up resistance, irony, local adaptation. Their local appropriation is selective. In the complex exchange between setting and self, the media regulate agency, and also enhance agency by providing resources with which people remake themselves. Even "the harshest of lived inequalities are now open to the play of the imagination" using global resources (Appadurai 1996: 4, 11, 17, 54).

It is important to maintain an empirical fix on trends to globalization, so that the momentum to universalism that seems inherent in the concept is retarded, and counter-universal denials of the Hirst-Thompson type are rendered unnecessary. When the heterogeneity of globalization is recognized—as argued above—its partial nature also becomes more apparent. Empirically, globalization is radically incomplete. Even the globalization of financial markets really only extends to the nations in the "Triad," and a fully integrated world economy—let alone a fully integrated world polity or society—is a long way off. Global societies are tiny, and global citizenship is an idea that has not yet come into governmental form, although the new subjectivities infused by global relations have a much wider spread. Market liberal claims that the nation-state and the politics of the nation-state are on their last legs should also be treated with scepticism, as will now be discussed.

Globalization and the Politics of the Nation-State

Globalization is not the only process that is affecting the nation-state and the politics of the nation-state. There have been at least three other changes of equivalent order—changes not in themselves determined by globalization, but changes that provide part of the context in which its effects are played out.

First, there is the trend to the universalization of national citizenship and participation in governance, civil affairs, education, labour markets and consumption, including the participation of formerly excluded minorities. The trend to civic universality (which has helped to open the way for global economy and global media and communications, signs and images) has long been associated with state-driven modernization, industrialization, mass markets and democratic political forms. It sustains the politics of multi-culturalism, and strategies of equity in social programmes. From a liberationist standpoint its implications are ambiguous. On one hand, it continues the old imperial project, resting as it does on a universalizing liberal humanism with its notion of a singular human nature, and as such tends to suppress difference and local identities. On the other, this liberal humanism can be turned around so as to enhance the capacity for difference and local self-determination, within a framework of universal rights. The key move is to break with the notion of one human nature and to understand identity—and universal rights—as variable and constructed. As Said (1994: 69) argues, an "effective intervention" in the public realm rests on an "unbudgeable conviction in a concept of justice and fairness that allows for differences between nations and individuals, without at the same time assigning them to hidden hierarchies, preferences, evaluations."

Second, there has been an increase in governmental sophistication, so that state effects are secured not so much by the volume of fiscal outlays and of direct production in the public sector, as through civil institutions and through the shaping of individual behaviour. Increasingly governments use the techniques of steering from a distance—systems of regulation, incentive and sanctions in which autonomous individuals and autonomous quasi-governmental and non-government institutions such as universities are in Foucault's words, "caused to behave" in ways consistent with the objectives of government. This has partly dissolved the old political boundaries between public and private sectors. The key figure in late modern systems of government is the self-regulating, choice-making, self-reliant individual. Education and social programmes are increasingly directed towards producing such an individual and shaping her/his "independent" behaviour. More directly authoritarian methods of government are in decline (Rose 1993, Marginson 1997b). The techniques of government and of capitalist marketing and consumption are moving closer together, in education as in other sectors. This change is consistent with the rise of market liberal government, but it is not solely a function of market liberalism. The trend to self-regulating individualism is apparent also in social democratic regimes.

Third, in the rise of market liberal forms of government, including the partial deregulation of global finance and consequent constraints on national fiscal policies, universal welfare provision has eroded and unemployment and income disparities have increased. Welfare states are under pressure everywhere, though entitlements in much of Western Europe continue to be more generous than those in the Anglo-American countries and in East Asia.

In the light of globalization plus these changes, what then has been the impact of globalization on the nation-state? Globalization has not replaced the nation-state, but it has undermined the old nation-state in certain respects, forcing it to change. Globalization means that, in contrast with the Keynesian era and all previous eras in government, the nation-state is no longer able to sustain indefinitely a zone of economic and cultural isolation. It means the end of the national market as the primary theatre of economic activity, because in the last analysis the nation-state no longer controls capital markets and the larger patterns of investment within its territorial borders. The regulatory protection afforded to the national labour force is weakened, so that unionism declines, unless it takes an international dimension of its own. National economic management is abbreviated. The nation-state, once the principal agent of modernization, is now partner to global economic players.

If it is to remain viable in the global era, each nation-state must become embedded in the larger network of global regulation, bilateral and multi-lateral links, supranational bodies and multinational companies. Those governments that seek to choose their global links at will, such as Indonesia, face increasing difficulties. As Hirst and Thompson (1996: 183) note, "politics is becoming more polycentric, with states as merely one level in a complex system of overlapping and often competing agencies of governance."

Nevertheless, the nation-state remains the key site of law, governance and politics, and democratic organization. It commands an impressive range of portfolios, such as national economic restructuring, taxation, industrial relations, transport, police and security, social programmes, health, children's services, aged care, much of research and development, education and training, environmental regulation, often utilities such as power and water; not to mention cultural policy, the arts and other portfolios affecting national and global identities. The nation-state continues to manage national populations, and it remains an agent of national economic competition, though national economic statistics are diminishing in importance as descriptors of economic welfare. The nation-state still provides legal and social conditions for the operation of economic markets. At the same time it guarantees the provision of certain goods and services which tend to be under-provided in markets, for example those with long or uncertain investment horizons such as research and development, transport infrastructure, and education and training.

It is proving difficult to reconcile the shape of the global market and global cultures with the shape of politics, which remain overwhelmingly national in character. There is a lack of fit. Thus, it is easier for national government to pursue a programme of deregulation and reforms that free the workings of global markets and enhance their efficiency in their own terms—reforms that tend to diminish this problem of fit between global and national—than to create activities which distort the internal logic of economic markets, reforms that exacerbate the problem of fit. Despite this, national electorates remain subject to a "democracy illusion" in which politics lags behind globalization. National politics continue to be defined so as to suggest that when people exercise the rights of citizens *within the nation-state*, somehow they can gain a purchase on global markets and cultural flows. At the same time, people often resist social protection by supra-national or potential supra-national bodies, such as the European Union, on the grounds that such bodies erode national sovereignty. The result is political-ideological instability. Voters and politicians swing between refusal to recognize the determining effects of external factors, and the tendency to blame everything on those factors. In the new conditions of complex *international inter-dependence*, populist politics oscillates between independence and despair. Political leaders stage performances designed to demonstrate they are still in control—especially in areas that have been abandoned to the market, such as bank interest rates or international currency movements.

For social democratic and liberationist political activism globalization implies new limits and new opportunities. The role of political knowledge and skills dependent on a sealed national environment has been diminished, while those aspects of government and politics affected by global and international relations, and difference and multiple identity, have become more important. Here the nation-state is the chief battleground of identity politics. It is the place where "culturalism" (the formal fashioning of identities) takes place; while political reactions against globalization are mostly expressed against those state programmes in education or migration that are seen to have fostered multiple identity and extra-national influence; and against the media, seen as fused with a political establishment whose loyalties to singular national identity are in question. Appadurai (1996: 156–157) remarks that even "as states lose their monopoly over the idea of the nation" because of pluralization, hybridization and diasporation, "all sorts of groups will use the logic of the nation to capture some or all of the state." The politics of identity are played out in "the contradiction between the idea that each nation-state can truly represent only one ethos and the reality that all nation-states historically invoke the amalgamation of many identities."

The nation-state remains the location of social cohesion, and the place where the politics of class and socio-economic distribution are fought out. In the wake of globalization, with its new tensions between diversity and the two kinds of homogenization (global and national), and its differential impacts on social groups, the politics of social equity are, if anything, rendered more volatile. Some socio-economic issues retain their pungency by appearing also as issues of difference and identity, for example the struggles of indigenous people for land. Global politics of post-colonialism and indigenous rights allows indigenous people to draw on external networks to sustain struggles conducted within the boundaries of particular nation-states. To the extent that traditional property-ownership in those nation-states is weakened, these indigenous struggles can provide indirect support for class-based struggles.

With inter-connected national and global dimensions that tend to feed each other, liberationist politics of difference are more readily carried from the national to the global era, than are the social democratic politics that often dominated the high time of modern nation-building. Despite Marx's call of "Workers of the World Unite," a conscious international class struggle scarcely exists. This is not to argue that globalization lacks a socio-economic dimension: it is associated with the dramatic creation of new power elites as well as the sharpening of material inequalities. In *The global trap* (1997) Martin and Schumann argue that globalization leads to a 20/80 percentile binary division between a globally-connected elite (20), and a subordinated social layer (80) whose control is the responsibility of national governments, and connected to the global dimension mostly through passive consumption (Martin and Schumann 1997). This binary world creates pre-conditions for conflict around access to the primary global networks of money, power, and knowledge-information, not to mention educational institutions.

Politics of Education

In the 1960s and 1970s in all industrialized countries, national education became an important site of struggle over class formation and social distribution within the national framework. In the expansion of education—which was attended by intense political contests over education spending, facilities and structural barriers in system organization—the state-driven modernization of national populations via the extension of education was fed also by pressures for the democratization of educational access (and later education contents and pedagogies) from below. It was difficult to tell where the state's human capital building stopped and the expansion of popular opportunities began (Marginson 1997a: 11–45). These struggles continued into the 1980s and 1990s, but globalization and the market liberal fiscal imperative have rendered the earlier project of socio-economic equalization through education increasingly problematic. There is less scope for using education to compensate for the effects of class or as a surrogate for income redistribution: the education of elites tends to cross national borders, the material base of the wealthy is increasingly sustained by global activities, and the old Keynesian consensus on national taxation and universal services has collapsed. Further, in a more global setting, the function of public education systems as a crucible of national democratic relations—a project pursued with varying vigour by governments in the US, Canada and Australia for most of the century—has diminished importance. If it is to regain centrality in the politics of education, this democratic mission will need to be recast and reasserted.

The old politics of equality of opportunity is fading. In the high modern governmental project of equality of opportunity, it was believed that publicly regulated education systems could and should constitute a scientific form of social competition, ensuring the merit-based selection of future social leaders. It was believed that the link between social origin and social destination could be broken, so that education would distribute social rewards entirely on the basis of educational merit, which was defined as "ability" plus effort. The corollary was that to enable a singular system of educational competition, that competition was necessarily framed by curricula, pedagogy and methods of assessment that were mono-cultural in process and culturally homogenizing in effect. Although the culturally homogenizing instruments of educational selection survive, the long policy-driven effort to secure genuine equality of opportunity seems to have petered out. First, that policy effort has been attended by an increasing individualization of teacher-student relations (the corollary of ever-more intensive attempts to create equality of opportunity) and the growing valorization of cultural difference. Secondly, decades of egalitarian educational reform have led to much higher participation, but little equalization of the socio-economic composition of the leading universities. It is no longer widely expected that educational competition can be rendered socially neutral through government action. The prevailing welfare ethic of self-responsibility has taken root also in education: increasingly, an individual's success or failure in education is once again seen as a function of the "character" of student and family, to the exclusion of social structures and government provision. Struggles around education funding, or organization (for example the roles of private and public schools) continue, but they have lost something of their previous urgency and their power to displace elected governments.

In contrast, in the global era, the politics of difference in education becomes more important than before—though, as noted, this does not in itself imply the disappearance of a class-based political dynamic, for the politics of difference often intersects with class relations. Education has a growing national governmental role in the management of difference, or "the challenge of valuing diversity" as the OECD puts it (1996a: 30). There will be more debates between possible readings of each nation's past, reflecting the pluralization of views and of the means of interpretation. Most important, questions of access and exclusion remain crucially important because of the power of education in allocating life chances, and these questions are now more likely to focus on cultural groups and on concerns about the cultural character of curricula and assessment. Countering this trend is the growing dominance of a singular global model of good education, especially university education, centred on the American models that carry increasing weight in policy circles and are enforced by international bench-marking.

Given the politics of difference, and the key role of education in identity formation, there are already increased demands by different social groups for their own schools and school systems, demands mediated by electoral politics. At best this debate will move beyond the stand-off between a monocultural mainstream and diversity as separateness, to build newly inclusive structures with more provision for self-determination than in the old public education system. Here it is necessary to talk about cultures as both separated from each other, and overlapping with and resembling each other, without *starting* from the assumption that they are necessarily separated. Because contemporary government routinely recognizes choice and self-determination, the relation between particular cultural needs and common rights is now very sensitive, and issues of this kind always have the potential to move to centre stage.

This new importance of education in the management of national diversity is matched by the recurrence of its central role in national economic strategies. As in the 1960s, education is again central to governmental programmes designed to maximize economic competitiveness, as confirmed in the advice of global agencies such as the World Bank and the OECD on the knowledge-intensive industries and the diffusion of technological competences. Indeed, all the talk about an emerging knowledge economy renders educational practices even more important in political symbolism, than in the manufacturing and construction-centred 1960s. The OECD argues in *Technology, Productivity and Job Creation*: "Human capital and technology are two faces of the same coin, two inseparable aspects of knowledge accumulation" (OECD 1996b: I.13). Again:

> In the long run, knowledge, especially technological knowledge, is the main source of economic growth and improvement in the quality of life. Nations which develop and manage effectively their knowledge assets perform better. . . . This strategic role of knowledge underlies increasing investments in research and development, education and training and other intangible investments, which are growing more rapidly than physical investments (OECD 1996b: I.9).

For national governments, following the well-known arguments expressed by President Clinton's former adviser Robert Reich, Harvard's Michael Porter and others, education is seen as perhaps the principal policy lever whereby national economic competitiveness is increased. Capital is mobile, but labour is more fixed. The augmentation of skills and knowledge (including management capacity) are means of coupling units of "footloose capital" to particular populations in particular nations. Further, education retains its core role in the formation of the skills of personal self-management, including the skills required to operate in the global environment itself, including the practices of codified lifelong learning, and reflexive consumption and media use. No doubt education will become the primary means of generalizing the skills of globalization, but the hopes of national governments that education will usher in a new wave of economic prosperity and success are bound to be disappointed, just as the hopes of 1960s human capital reformers were disappointed. Education cannot in itself generate capital movements or create wealth, except to the extent that it becomes a fully-fledged market commodity in its own right. The inevitable economic "failure" of education, associated with credentialism and the demands of educators for more resources to fulfil their multiplying tasks, sustains the recurring policy cycle of illusion/disillusion, and its partner cycle of spending/cuts, that has dominated educational politics since the 1950s. The difference between the cycle in the high modernization period and in the global era is that while governmental illusions about education are as large as they ever were, government capacity to pay is not.

Thus education institutions are more politically central than ever, yet they also seem to be weakened, fallen from a former high estate, hostage to the diminishing of the nation-state's room to move and its growing fiscal constraints. The globalization of certain education institutions themselves provides one avenue whereby national fiscal limits can be overcome, through fee-based international education, the conduct of research and consultancy for global companies, and the growth of virtual delivery and interactive modes. Only some institutions—mostly universities, and specialist colleges involved in business education—are able to assume a primary role in the emerging global education markets. A binary division is emerging between the global education players that, like their corporate counterparts, are partly free of the constraints of national regulation, and the remaining domestic institutions. This binary division among producers has its counterpart in the 20/80 world of the users of education: the emerging global elite (particularly in business training) is already using the global institutions, while the large majority remain mired in the more impoverished and more regulated nation-specific institutions. How the national 80 will secure the political levers to challenge the structure of privilege enjoyed by the global 20 is not yet clear.

However, it is clear that access to technology is one of the emerging political battlegrounds. There are not only the issues of who uses information and communications technologies, but also who shapes the cyber-systems, and who decides the dominant cyber-languages? How can cultural differences be expressed at the level of language and system organization? Is there market failure in the universalization of these networks? Is there a public interest to be expressed, for example the distribution of free or low cost access to screens, data bases and multi-media production skills? What about the consequences of global Anglo-American content for local cultures? Is universal access to global information and consumption a boon or a burden? Education programmes are becoming the site of new kinds of political contention.

Notes

1. These data do not constitute a complete picture of material economic production in the larger sense—including subsistence farming in the third world, and home-based production and non-market services such as education in the industrialized world—but represent that part of economic activity which calls up value in the capitalist sense (Marginson 1997b: 28, 100) and is liable to organization within modern national economic systems. Given that economic globalization rests on the terrain established by nation-building, the growth of the GDP economy represents the growth of the terrain on which economic globalization is taking place.

2. Unfortunately, the method of argument used by Thompson and Hirst is to seize on the most exaggerated claims about globalization, and proceed to demolish the straw figure. They note that more moderate notions of globalization exist but do not address these notions, arguing simply that the term "globalization" should not be associated with them. They also acknowledge the existence of some of the global phenomena described above; but rather than acknowledging the novelty of these phenomena, they describe them as the continuation of previous trends, or tend to diminish their importance. Hirst and Thompson's book is insightful in certain respects, especially in its political economic data, yet it is also Eurocentric and Anglo-centric in character (Hirst and Thompson 1996: 2–6).

References

Appadurai, A. (1996) *Modernity at Large: Cultural dimensions of globalisation* (Minneapolis: University of Minnesota Press).

Cunningham, S., Tapsall, S., Ryan, Y., Stedman, L., Bagdon, K. and Flew, T. (1997), *New media and borderless education: A review of the convergence between global media networks and higher education provision*, Department of Employment, Education, Training and Youth Affairs (Canberra: Australian Government Publishing Service).

Dow, S. (1990) Beyond dualism, *Cambridge Journal of Economics*, 14, 143–157.

Hirst, P. and Thompson, G. (1996) *Globalisation in question* (Cambridge: Polity Press).

Hobsbawm, E. (1995) *Age of extremes: The short twentieth century 1914–1991* (London: Abacus).

Lingard, R. and Rizvi, F. (forthcoming) Globalisation, the OECD and Australian higher education, in J. Currie and J. Newson (eds), *Globalisation and the University: Critical Perspectives* (California: Sage).

Marginson, S. (1997a) *Educating Australia: Government, economy and citizen since 1960* (Cambridge and Melbourne: Cambridge University Press).

Marginson, S. (1997b) *Markets in Education* (Sydney: Allen and Unwin).

Martin, H.-P. and Schumann, H. (1997) *The global trap: Globalisation and the assault on prosperity and democracy*, translated by Patrick Camiller (Sydney: Pluto Press).

Organisation for Economic Co-operation and Development, OECD (1996a) *Lifelong learning for all* (Paris: OECD).

Organisation for Economic Co-operation and Development, OECD (1996b) *Technology, Productivity and Job creation*, Volumes I and II (Paris: OECD).

Petrella, R. (1996) Globalisation and internationalisation: the dynamics of the emerging world order, in R. Boyer and D. Drache (eds), *States against Markets: The limits of globalisation* (London: Routledge), 62–83.

Rose, N. (1993) Government, authority and expertise in advanced liberalism, *Economy and Society*, 22(3), 283–300.

Said, E. (1994) *Representations of the intellectual: the 1993 Reith lectures* (London: Vintage).

Taylor, S., Rizvi, F., Lingard, B. and Henry, M. (1997) *Educational Policy and the Politics of Change* (London: Routledge).

Waters, M. (1995) *Globalisation* (London: Routledge).

THE POLITICAL CONTEXT
OF HIGHER EDUCATION

MARILYN GITTELL AND NEIL SCOTT KLEIMAN
CITY UNIVERSITY OF NEW YORK

This is a comparative study of the impact of state politics and culture on higher education policy in three states: California, North Carolina, and Texas. By comparing higher education systems in these states, the study describes the degree of influence state government actors and culture have on higher education. This article explores the key policy areas of access and economic development to determine the effect of higher education regimes and state political culture on policy outcomes. The article evaluates access by evaluating who is not attaining higher education degrees and analyzing the current battles over affirmative action. With regard to economic development, the article determines the extent of actual economic development and the influence of state actors on that activity. The study's primary conclusion is that politics matter. Higher education systems and policy directions varied widely in each state, but state politics always proved to have a significant impact on major policy decisions.

Little has been written about the effects of politics on higher education policy. Since the publication of V. O. Key's (1949) *Southern Politics* and Daniel Elazar's (1966) *American Federalism: A View From the States*, few comprehensive volumes have been published on states, and there are few books available on the comparative political culture of states. Most of the contemporary higher education literature focuses on management and internal (whether institutional or systemwide) decision-making processes rather than determining how systems operate externally—in relation to state government processes or with one another. One exception is *Designing State Higher Education Systems for a New Century*. This book by Patrick Callan and his colleagues (Richardson, Callan, Finney, & Bracco, 1999) describes politics and governance structures in seven study states, providing an invaluable foundation for examining politics and policy decisions in those states. This study takes a similar approach, describing political structures and drawing conclusions about policy outcomes in relation to those political structures.

Each state's political culture is a combination of political history and lasting social factors and state values. Higher education regimes consist of key formally and informally empowered political actors. Primary and secondary sources were assessed to determine the types of political processes present in each state. Also, more than 100 interviews of state-level higher education officials were conducted over an 8-month period between 1998 and 1999. The political importance of state culture and regimes was then tested through an analysis of access and economic development policies at the state and local levels.

Political Culture and Higher Education Regimes

Each state's political culture—a combination of history and social factors—is distinct, and it shapes all state policies, including its system of higher education. For example, Texas individualism has contributed to the sprawling and decentralized nature of its college systems just as the populist traditions of California are seen in the state's enshrinement of universal access in its 1960 Master Plan. The higher education regimes, consisting of the key formally and informally empowered political actors of the states under study, tend to be similar. They are composed of only a few of the state's legislators, higher education officials, and the governor, who has a major influence over higher education policy. Regimes were also affected by the underlying presence of private sector leaders on the governing boards involved in statewide policy-making decisions, and the features of each regime critically influenced policy.

State Political Culture

Elazar (1966) noted that "the states are well-integrated parts of the American society and also separate civil societies in their own right with their own political system" (p. 1). This is also true for state systems of higher education. The strong connection between political culture and higher education systems was noted often by interviewees, who discussed typical policy outcomes by saying, "That's the way our state operates." We found that North Carolina's centralized system reflects a state governed by elites. The political culture of Texas, which values individualism and local authority, can be seen in its decentralized system. And the populist tradition in California has created a system of open access and large investment in higher education. Culture can also be an obstacle to reform. In the 1970s, North Carolina resisted the introduction of affirmative action policies at Chapel Hill, the "crown jewel" in the system. Texas resisted dozens of proposals to more logically coordinate and centralize its disparate systems of higher education. Adherence to the ideal of access in California's Master Plan has prevented a serious discussion of how the state has actually drifted away from those ideals. Given that political culture sets the tone of policy debates in each state, an examination of it is essential to this analysis of higher education regimes and policy outcomes. What follows is a brief synopsis of each state's political culture and the connection of that culture to its system of higher education.

North Carolina politics is defined by an intimate co-mingling of business and politics. Regardless of political ideologies, virtually all elected leaders are marked by a strong connection to private sector interests (Luebke, 1998). As Key (1949) noted,

> An economic oligarchy has held sway and consequently a sympathetic respect for the problems of corporate capital and large employers permeates the state's government. [But] it would be inaccurate to portray a direct line of authority from the skyscraper offices of industrial magnates to the state capital. The effectiveness of the oligarchy's control has been achieved through the elevation to office of persons fundamentally in harmony with its viewpoint. Its interests, which are often the interests of the state, are served without prompting. (p. 211)

The "progressive plutocracy" that Key described is still found in North Carolina. Its political culture is sharply divided between what General Assembly Representative and Greensboro sociology professor Paul Luebke (1998) terms modernist and traditionalist political leanings. The modernist and traditionalist categories are not easily associated with typical notions of conservatives and liberals or Democrats and Republicans. Instead, both political types are fiercely pro-business, with the modernists distinguished by their advocacy of highly skilled economic sectors of high technology and finance in the state's urban regions and a practice of racial tolerance, whereas the traditionalists defend the traditional economic sectors of manufacturing and rural county agriculture and harbor deep suspicions of racial integration. Politicians like modernist Governor James Hunt, who pioneered microelectronics growth and heavy investments in higher education, and traditionalist Senator Jesse Helms, who defends the entrenched tobacco industry and reactionary race politics, are excellent examples.

Progressive plutocracy is evident in the highly segmented and elite system of higher education in North Carolina. The flagship university at Chapel Hill educates most of the state's future business and political leaders.[1] This group is commonly referred to as the "old well network."[2] Those who attended Chapel Hill in the 1930s, 1940s, and 1950s developed a sense of camaraderie, and when they graduated, they stayed connected and moved on to governing the state. Even as late as the 1950s, there was little interest in expanding access of what remained a small, male institution of fewer than 350 students. The indelible effects of this system are visible today in such areas as underfunded public schools, poor quality at traditionally Black colleges and nonflagship institutions, and a community college system focused almost exclusively on private sector interests.

California's political culture is based on a long tradition of populist reforms and an electorate that has readily accepted these reforms. Since 1911, citizens of California have enjoyed the direct democracy tools of initiative, referendum, and recall that are part of the state constitution. The will of the electorate figures strongly in the state's political thinking. California was one of the first states to establish 2-year colleges that were locally based and operated, and the state has led the nation in such schools and the number of people enrolled in them (Brint & Karabel, 1989; Gollattscheck, Suppiger, Wattenbarger, & Witt, 1994). The populist tradition also influenced the creation of a large network of 4-year colleges in the 1950s and 1960s (Schrag, 1998). The Master Plan, California's much-lauded strategic plan for higher education, promises complete access and affordability to all residents and is a reflection of popular will.

In recent years, the state has had a surge of voter initiatives. Voters, rather than elected leaders, have assumed the role of policy makers, beginning with the passage of Proposition 13 in 1978, which capped local property tax assessments at 1975 levels and required a two-thirds majority vote by local governments to impose any future tax levies (Purdum, 1998; Schrag, 1998). Subsequent voter-approved initiatives have banned bilingual education, excluded illegal alien children from public schools, and imposed three-strike penalties for felony crimes. Critical decisions in the area of higher education are also being made by voter initiative. The most important piece of legislation that affects access to higher education in California was Proposition 209, which eliminated affirmative action at the college level. Proposition 98, another voter-approved measure that passed in 1988, ensures that 40% of annual state appropriations are earmarked for community colleges and the public school system. This proposition has radically altered how education money is allocated in Sacramento, each year placing K–14 schools in competition with the California State University (CSU) and the University of California (UC) systems for budget appropriations. In addition to the concrete effect of ballot measures on education and other policy, "government by plebiscite" has fostered an atmosphere at the state's various higher education institutions that is more dependent on public approval than ever before.

Elazar's (1966) original characterization of Texas describes voter acceptance of individualism in politics. The state's political culture values personal freedom and decentralized control above all else. Individualism is also fostered by the lack of a unifying force in Texas politics. There are few strong district or statewide organizations such as unions or political parties. Consequently, power in Texas politics is dependent on business interests and on the personality and ideology of the individual candidate rather than on party or organizational affiliations.

Political culture in Texas translates into one of the country's largest and most decentralized systems of public higher education. There are 105 public colleges in the state in six separate systems, 4 free-standing universities, and 50 college districts, all with their own boards of regents and governing structures. The system has been perennially scattered and impervious to retrenchment due to the fierce protection that all schools receive from locally elected officials. Virtually all interviewees agreed that politicians view the individual colleges as public pork for their districts. There is a university in every state senatorial district, and where an institution or system does not exist, state legislators will often fight vociferously to establish one.

All three states demonstrate the close connection between political culture and the structure of higher education systems (see Table 1). Identifying and understanding the political culture and the connection to the state's higher education culture is a major factor in understanding the context of current higher education debates. But culture is not the only factor affecting policy decisions. In fact, the state higher education culture is more helpful in outlining the parameters within which policy decisions are made than in understanding how they are made. An understanding of exactly how and who makes the decisions affecting higher education demands an examination of higher education regimes.

TABLE 1

Political Culture and Its Reflection in the Study States' Systems of Higher Education

	Cultural Trait	Reflection in Higher Education System
North Carolina	Progressive plutocracy	Centralized and stratified university system; 2-year colleges focused on business needs
California	Direct democracy	Volatile system subject to sudden changes from initiative process
Texas	Individual and decentralized	Sprawling, uncoordinated, and pork-barrel-driven system

TABLE 2

Common Traits in States' Higher Education Regimes

Few members
Stability of members
Supremacy of elected leaders
Lack of communication among members
Mobilization only in times of crisis

Higher Education Regimes

In locating and defining higher education regime members, this study did not seek out specific groupings of policy actors. Instead, it looked at the influence of campus presidents, business leaders, public officials, bureaucrats, and faculty and the role of private institutions in each state and found many similarities. In contrast to the distinct culture of each state higher education system, the three regimes were fairly uniform. Salient features of each study state's regime included small size, stable composition of regime members, and the supremacy of elected leaders over institutional representatives (see Table 2).

The higher education regime in each state is small. The three states have large and diverse populations and a large number of postsecondary institutions, but the number of individuals who set the terms of the debate and determine policy outcomes are few.[3] Regime actors typically consist of the governor (the lieutenant governor in Texas), key state legislative leaders, and the system heads of the major 4-year college systems. Although not influential on the state level, campus presidents were autonomous in their ability to implement policy. There was notably weak participation in statewide regimes from private and community colleges, faculty members, and community groups.

Regime members have rarely changed since the major expansion and restructuring of the postwar growth era in higher education, yet the working relationships between regime actors in the states are not close. In California, the governor has significant influence over higher education institutions but rarely meets with other regime members. It took the 1990 recession for the UC and the CSU systems to create the Governor's Compact. The compact was a funding guarantee in the form of a budget agreement between Governor Pete Wilson and UC and CSU. Under the agreement, which lasted from 1995 until 1998, the governor promised to increase the UC and CSU budgets by 2% during the first year and 4% each of the following three years. The Governor's Compact was spurred on by UC and CSU looking to find their own budget guarantees after the passage of Proposition 98, but the compact was an executive commitment. Governor Wilson honored the compact and supplied more funding than the promised 4% during the boom years that came during his last budgets.

Because regime members were such a small collection of actors and rarely met, formally or informally, we found that when members agreed easily on an issue, they acted decisively, but inaction could create a policy vacuum that stymied needed reform. Despite the many similarities in the study states' higher education regimes, there were a few sharp differences that affected policy outcomes. For example, greater legislative involvement in education in Texas and weak legislative involvement in California profoundly shaped affirmative action policies, creating different outcomes in each state.

A commonly held perception is that public higher education institutions are above state politics and able to make their own policies. In all our study states, the decisions of elected leaders, not public education leaders, had the greatest influence on policy outcomes. Although each state's higher education institutions are more insulated than other state service-delivery systems, they are still governed and affected by state politics of regimes. Each state has officials in government, often no more than four, who are members of the higher education regime. These actors are directly responsible for policy decisions and are gatekeepers of policy reform or inaction. Typically, they include the governor and the top elected leaders of both houses of the legislature. One interviewee in Texas said, "If the governor, lieutenant governor and heads of both houses agree, the policy will pass. If one of them does not agree, it will stall." Chairs of legislative education committees also play a significant role in initiating new policy, but decision-making authority often rests with the top three or four elected officials.

The Governor

The most noticeable feature of each state's regime is the extent to which the governor or lieutenant governor imposes himself or herself. The top executive's power originates in different ways: through formal power, as in California; through strong interest, as in North Carolina; and through influence over the legislature, as in Texas. All governors also benefit from appointment power and effective use of the bully pulpit. The top executive in each study state was often cited as the single most important regime actor, although in reality, the governors in Texas and North Carolina have wielded little influence, and despite the fact that California's governors have power over the higher education system, the past four governors have shown little interest in it.

In California, the governor's strong formal powers stem from wide appointment power,[4] strong tenure potential,[5] a streamlined executive bureaucracy,[6] and the most potent tool, the budget line-item veto. Governor Edmund "Pat" Brown used all of these powers to double the size of the higher education systems during his 8-year tenure in the 1960s. The power of the California governor is even in evidence when governors have not been interested in higher education. Recently, Governor George Deukmejian, never captivated by higher education issues, tilted expenditures toward the CSU and UC systems, which drastically destabilized the community colleges (Chavez, 1998; Schrag, 1998). Three months into his tenure, current Governor Gray Davis exerted his power with the passage of the Four Percent Plan, which admits the top 4% of all graduating high school seniors into UC. Analysts say the Four Percent Plan would not have been possible without the governor's support (Terry, 1999).

North Carolina's governor is one of the most limited in formal power of all U.S. governors (Mueller, 1985). The governor lacks the most potent force enjoyed by all other American executives—the power to veto legislation—and prior to 1978, governors were limited to one term in office.[7] In spite of this, successive postwar governors have shaped and created entire systems of higher education.

Although past North Carolina governors each had only one term in office, they all tried to outdo their predecessors by leaving an education legacy through proposed legislation. In the late 1950s, Governor Luther Hodges was instrumental in erecting Research Triangle Park (RTP), the nation's first public research park. Governor Terry Sanford enacted a politically risky sales tax to create the state's community college system, and Governor Bob Scott devoted considerable time to merging various public colleges into the University of North Carolina (UNC) system in 1973. Often, the governors' policies also reflected their ties to business interests, as they would describe policies as contributing to economic development.

In Texas, a top executive holds a disproportionate share of influence over higher education policy, but unlike other states, this regime actor is not the governor but the lieutenant governor. In a recent index of gubernatorial power, Texas's governor tied with South Carolina's for the least amount (Mueller, 1985, p. 427). There have been few reforms in the past decade to increase gubernatorial authority, and the governor has little appointment power or authority to reform or restructure governmental agencies. Most limiting is the governor's lack of input into the state budget, which is written by the nonpartisan Legislative Budget Board. Thus, gubernatorial influence in Texas is limited to the bully pulpit and the power to make some appointments. Only Governor John Connally of the 1960s was seen as exerting significant influence on higher education policy. He has been widely credited with transforming the University of Texas (UT) system into one of the country's leading public universities in the 1960s (Peirce & Hagstrom, 1984).

In marked contrast, the lieutenant governor holds the greatest formal power in Texas. As the head of the state senate, the lieutenant governor appoints senate committee chairs, including chairs of the powerful fiscal committee. The inherent powers of this office are buttressed by long terms—there have been only two lieutenant governors in the past 25 years. The lieutenant governor sets the tone and pace of day-to-day operations in the legislature. This is one of the few structural features that has allowed the state government any implementation power. The past two lieutenant governors have been ardent supporters of enhanced funding for higher education. Lieutenant Governor William Hobby (1973–1991) championed a series of new higher education initiatives during his tenure and won protracted public brawls with then-Governor Bill Clements over increasing college funding during the late-1980s oil recession (Burka, 1997).

Regardless of power or personal interest, the top executive in each of the study states is widely viewed as the most important higher education actor. He or she, more than any member of the legislature, has the power to move the system forward, to create new institutions, or to stymie reform proposals. In their political role, governors are directly involved with key businesses in the state, and their higher education policies reflect this relationship.

State Legislatures

Apart from gubernatorial power, there exist key members of a state's legislature who affect higher education policy. These key actors are often a combination of majority and minority party leaders and sometimes appropriations committee chairs and higher education or education committee chairs. One interviewee stated, "Anything that has approval of the leaders of both houses of the legislature passes and if one of them is opposed it doesn't pass—it's that simple." Other than these key legislative regime actors, state legislatures as a body tend to limit their role in higher education policy discussions to the patronage to be gained by creating institutions in their districts or securing funds for special projects.

In California, the Master Plan successfully removed legislative politics from higher education decisions (Kerr, 1992). In North Carolina, the elite role of the UNC system and its revered position in the public's eye relegated most general assembly votes to a rubber stamp of the priorities of the governor and UNC officials. There has been a movement for increased legislative input in both North Carolina and Texas. The Texas legislature, which has always had more input into policy making than other state legislatures, has had its role significantly increased. Both states' legislatures have become more active in higher education policy discussions because of growth in the number of minority legislators. However, in California, the legislature has actually lost power in recent years due to the implementation of term limits.

The traditional reserve of the North Carolina General Assembly on higher education policy and governance has broken in recent years as the legislature has begun to intervene in the issue of equitable representation at UNC. This newfound policy muscle arrived with the influx of Republicans, African Americans, and women into the general assembly. From 1971 to 1997, the percentage of

African American general assembly members jumped from 1 to 14, and Dan Blue (Wake County) became the first African American chair of the house in 1991.[8] The percentage of women elected climbed from 1 to 17 between 1971 and 1997. The number of Republicans has more than doubled; they currently hold a majority in the house. These new members have questioned high appropriations to the state's flagship institutions and injected themselves into higher education governance. Blue has held numerous hearings on the lack of attention to historically Black institutions, and two major outside audits on this issue have been commissioned by the general assembly in the past 15 years.[9] Another notable contribution to diversity is the increased GOP presence, which has directly led to a non-UNC insider being chosen as president of the system. Interviewees attribute the strong influence of Republican general assembly members on the UNC search committee to the decision to choose Molly Corbett Broad to be the first female UNC president in history, as well as the first from outside of the state.

For a time in California, there were signs that the state legislature would become more active in higher education policy making. It had increased power and professionalism under the leadership of Speaker Jesse Unruh, who transformed a part-time legislature that had little leverage against the governor into a full-time body backed by a large professional staff (Schrag, 1998, p. 49). The increasing autonomy of the state legislature was rolled back with the passage of Proposition 104 in 1990. Proposition 104's effects were almost immediate, establishing the strictest term limits for elected state officials in the country and cutting the number of professional legislative staff by 40%. In addition to displacing all of the career politicians, it threw the entire legislature into a paralyzing state of confusion (Schrag, 1998, p. 245).

The Texas State Legislature has long been involved in higher education decision making. Unlike other states, lawmakers in Texas are very comfortable weighing in on higher education debates, particularly if the debates concern site selection for a new institution or system. The majority of higher education reforms are still controlled by a small group of regime leaders, but Texas lawmakers are more willing and able to participate in these debates because of the individually driven, pork barrel politics that revolve around postsecondary institutions. Public colleges are one of the few substantial state-funded enterprises in the home districts of legislative leaders, and they are fiercely protected. Because the state has no corporate or personal income tax, there is little for individual lawmakers to defend other than higher education institutions in their districts. Financial support for higher education institutions, which are situated in every legislative district, is often the only pork that an official can bring home. All lawmakers want "to [get] their slice of the higher education pie," says Bernard Weinstein, an economist at the University of North Texas.

Texas has also begun to see diversity, as recent legislatures have expressed greater interest in higher education. The number of African Americans in the state legislature increased by 2% to 8% from 1971 to 1997, the number of Mexican American representatives increased from 5% to 21%, and the number of Republicans increased from 7% to 50% (Brown, Ericson, Langengger, Jones, & Trotter, 1998). The increased minority presence was directly responsible for the establishment of graduate programs and improved funding in the South Texas region.

Business Community

One hypothesis of this study was that key business leaders play an active role in state higher education regimes and influence policy directions. After all, the private sector depends on quality graduates for employees, on workforce training, and on research and development by postsecondary institutions. Generally, the effect of the private sector is more indirect, and in the three study states, it is conveyed through a number of outlets. The most noticeable influence of business is governing board membership. In a detailed analysis of governing board composition, this report found that private sector representatives dominate. At each of the state's 4-year institutions, representatives from the private sector made up more than 70% of governing board membership systemwide and came from the state's major banking, law, and corporate firms.[10] In addition to the private sector presence on governing boards, each state had prominent business leaders who had a significant impact on statewide higher education policy. The most notable example is former Texas Lieutenant Governor William Hobby. Hobby does not represent a unified business lobby but has made the importance of the private sector felt on higher education in his state for more than 25 years (Bryce, 1998; Burka, 1997). Hobby comes from one of the wealthiest Houston families and is himself a newspaper magnate. He was the state's lieutenant governor for 18 years and the president of the University of Houston, and he has chaired numerous commissions, including the recent Texas Commission on a Representative Student Body, which was established to develop alternative affirmative action policies in the wake of the Texas *Hopwood* ruling. In an interview for this study, Hobby made clear his view of the importance of the relationship between higher education and the private sector, suggesting, "All higher education is economic development."

The influence of the private sector also surfaced in each state's education policy emphasis on economic development and responsiveness to business needs. This was also evident in North Carolina, which has continually used its 2-year and 4-year college systems to focus its economic growth strategies, creating a local labor force in each county trained specifically to meet the needs of local businesses. In all three states, interviewees cited the need for higher education systems to "listen to the needs of business." This responsiveness to business has become increasingly important in each of the states as justification for state budget allocations. A review of education system publications and government relations documents reveals an increasing tendency to include economic justifications for continued and increased government support (see Gittell & Sedgley, 2000 [this issue]).

Higher Education Officials

Although not always as influential as top state elected leaders, the administrators of public postsecondary institutions in the three states are active players in higher education regimes. In North Carolina, a highly centralized system only allows for the president of the UNC system and the powerful UNC Board of Governors to exert influence. In California, the heads of the three public college systems are always at the table in major statewide policy discussions, but faculty bodies actually have the most influence in policy implementation. The chancellors of Texas's two flagship campuses at Austin and College Station exert almost as much power as the system leaders and the commissioner of the nonpartisan Texas Higher Education Coordinating Board (THECB). This study found that in each state only a small number of system officials were active in statewide policy decisions. One reason that power is so concentrated is in the reaction to the desire of state government to negotiate with a limited number of representatives.

For example, when the UNC system was formed in North Carolina, immense power was given to the president of the system as a way of avoiding individual lobbying by each campus for additional funds or flagship status (Link, 1995). In California, faculty members and individual campus presidents have the most governing power in the UC and the CSU systems, but state government tends to negotiate with the system heads. And in Texas, the THECB was specifically created to avoid the rampant lobbying of the many separate systems and institutions within them.

The exact governance structure in each state varies, but the heads of the 4-year systems tended to have the greatest role in government relations and statewide policy discussions. Despite popular impressions to the contrary, governing boards in Texas and California do not typically hold much sway over major policy areas. Power in the UNC system rests squarely with the system president, who is based at Chapel Hill. Even after the UNC system was expanded in 1972 from 3 to 16 schools, it retained centralized leadership. The president's power includes oversight of all budget requests, and individual campuses are not allowed to lobby independently, only through the system president.

The president's power is linked to a tradition of co-mingling business and political interests in the governance of UNC Chapel Hill. William Friday, president of UNC from 1956 to 1986, embodied all of the qualities of elite public education in North Carolina. Friday was educated at Chapel Hill and North Carolina State University at Raleigh, forming friendships with the state's power elite, including future Governor Terry Sanford. When Friday assumed the reigns of the unified system in the early 1970s, his political acumen fostered tremendous faith in UNC from state business and political leaders who essentially allowed him free reign with policy and budget priorities. The dominance of the centralized system office in Chapel Hill also emanates from its high-profile board of governors, which is packed with the state's top political and business leaders. Next to the board governing the Transportation Administration, the board of governors is the most coveted appointment in the state. The university president works directly with the board of governors, ensuring the precedence of system-wide goals over individual campus needs.

California has weak leadership heading its 4-year systems. The president of the UC system has limited governing powers. Unlike former UNC President William Friday, who built in a strong central role for his office during the mass consolidation and expansion in North Carolina, such powers were not instituted by President Clark Kerr during the implementation of the California Master Plan in 1960. Subsequently, during the growth of UC, the president has had to engage in a constant tug-of-war for power with the individual campuses. The UC president's role has more to do with coordination than actual governance. The president is responsible for the annual negotiation of the budget with the legislature and the governor, and all high-profile policy matters such as budget cuts, tuition increases, and affirmative action are left to the president to discuss with state leaders and the media.

Despite the national attention UC Regent Ward Connerly has attracted for his position on affirmative action, the UC Board of Regents has very little formal power when compared with other higher education governing boards. It does not formally evaluate the president, the campus chancellors, curriculums, or the budget. It is given little information by the administration about ongoing operations and is made to feel as though its intrusion in substantive concerns is unwanted. In the past, individual regents have typically been disengaged and rubber-stamped most UC requests (Richardson et al., 1999). The regents' current influence is due to the Wilson administration, which appointed younger, more partisan members from outside of academia (Healy, 1999).

The CSU system functions much the same way as UC, with campus presidents functioning autonomously. In this system, the independence of individual campuses has been attributed to each school's specific history, as CSU colleges are older and more entrenched than those in the UC system. San Jose State University, the first public higher education institution in the state, was founded in 1857, a full 11 years before the founding of UC Berkeley. By 1938, there were eight CSU schools to UC's two.

In Texas, there are two primary players in higher education politics: UT and Texas A&M. The two systems overshadow the half dozen other Texas state systems in size and scope and are the two 4-year systems on which this study is focused. Both systems are unique in this comparative study because the campus president at the flagship holds power almost equivalent to that of the system leader in most aspects of governance, including government relations and dispersion of funds, while the influence of nonflagship presidents is minimal.

The dominance of UT, and particularly of Texas A&M, is far greater than even that of Chapel Hill in North Carolina. The UT flagship at Austin houses its law school, policy school, most of the professional degree programs, a research foundation, and all central administrative offices. The Texas A&M flagship at College Station houses a research foundation, most of the major research facilities, and the central administrative offices. One interviewee, referring to the dominance of College Station, said the Texas A&M system was long called "Snow White and the Seven Dwarfs."

Faculty

Traditionally, higher education was thought to hold special status as a statewide service area that protected faculty control over academic policy. This study found that in the three study states, higher education is not the ivory tower commonly believed, and the increasingly diminished role of academic faculty is one of the clearest signals of this. Academic faculty in Texas and North Carolina have virtually no influence over systemwide policy. There is a systemwide faculty body at both UT and Texas A&M, but it is powerless to effect change and consequently attracts little participation by the faculty leaders. Both states are right-to-work states and have been vociferously antiunion. This antilabor ethos is directly linked to the weak roles given to faculty input on policy and budget.

In sharp contrast, faculty in California have substantial power. The UC system has the most influential faculty of any 4-year public system in the country (Richardson et al., 1999). Faculty power and input in decision making date back to the founding of the university. Beginning in 1883, the regents called on faculty to assist in matters they felt were outside their purview (Stadtman, 1970, p. 504). Throughout UC's history, most presidents have followed the regents' lead and relied on faculty to help govern the increasingly expanding universities.

Today, faculty power rests largely in a representative body called the Academic Senate. Its powers include mandated consultations on all academic appointments, promotions, tenure, and changes to curriculum. Consultation has come to mean actual governance, as the Academic Senate typically makes requests that are then rubber-stamped by the regents and the president. Campus-based faculty are also the primary force behind the selection of new chancellors and presidents at each of the eight campuses. Consequently, many of those selected for leading positions are from within the system and favorable to the Academic Senate's views.

Even more than at UC, community colleges in California are increasingly controlled by powerful faculty unions. As with other public schools, community college governance and funding underwent a sea change with the passage of Proposition 13. Prior to the proposition, more than 60% of funding for 2-year colleges was raised through local property taxes, but after the tax initiative passed in 1978, state funding came to dominate the budget. The system is still administered and planned at the district level, but it is now centrally funded. With all funding (including local property taxes) dispensed through state government, turnout for both school board and community college board elections has suffered a massive decline. Faculty unions have stepped into the vacuum and spent considerable amounts of money on these relatively unmonitored campaigns, buying off locally elected trustees who now pass sweetheart deals for faculty members and employees (Hill-Holtzman, 1998; Richardson et al., 1999; Schrag, 1998; Trombley, 1996). There is little in the way of board accountability or local checks on faculty control; local chancellors and presidents are not unionized and have little power to govern independently of faculty-controlled boards of trustees.

With faculty unions dominating governance, corruption and mismanagement have become the norm in many districts, particularly those in urban areas like Los Angeles and San Francisco. The Los Angeles Community College district is the worst example, as the system has been on the verge of bankruptcy for more than 2 years, with little improvement in sight (Hill-Holtzman, 1998).[11]

The strength of faculty members in California creates a unique dynamic because the faculty hold much of the power to implement and steer policy. System presidents and chancellors have less power to steer policy and instead act as statewide spokespeople and negotiators.

Coordinating Boards

Over the years, many states have created nonpartisan, statewide boards to monitor systems of higher education. As higher education continued to grow in size and complexity, state governments relied on these boards to report to them and advise lawmakers on needed reforms. The state boards themselves have always straddled a fine line between professional responsiveness to the educational systems and political responsiveness to the elected officials. In our study, only Texas has a strong coordinating board. North Carolina never created one, and California's is extremely weak. In North Carolina, centralized leadership obviates the need for a coordinating board, and in California, the sharp distinctions of the three systems instill a sense of order. But in Texas, with so many higher education systems trying to lobby the legislature, it became necessary to create an empowered coordinating entity.

In 1965, the THECB was created as an independent voice in a highly politicized system. Its objective was to instill logic by eliminating duplicative programs, make efficient use of resources, and develop statewide goals through periodic master plans. Overall, most interviewees conclude that the numerous systems of public higher education in Texas are more manageable with the THECB's presence. But interviewees were also quick to note that the THECB has few teeth when it comes to its broad mission of reigning in the systems and that it at best coordinates disorganization. Richard Murray, a political scientist at the University of Houston, said, "On the whole I would say they are a plus. Without them, things would be even more chaotic and there would be even more duplication, but it is such a struggle to maintain any rationality in the system." This study's overall assessment is that despite some of the criticism, the THECB is viewed by all state policy makers as a valuable source of nonpartisan information and is looked to for key advice on difficult policy issues.

The California Postsecondary Education Commission (CPEC) was created in 1974 to better oversee the three systems, but it does not govern or have direct influence over them. CPEC's duties consist primarily of data collection and budgetary projections. Periodically, proposals surface that call for a strengthened coordinating agency in California, as when the California Citizens Commission on Higher Education proposed that CPEC play a direct role in budget making and offer independent proposals and critiques of all three systems. (California Citizens Commission on Higher Education, 1998). But the strong and independent systems in California seem secure in their current roles, and such proposals often remain just that.

Private Institutions

Private colleges play a small but growing role in higher education regimes in California, North Carolina, and Texas. Unlike the tradition in northeastern states, private colleges have not been active in each state's development of postsecondary systems. The tradition of public universities and the sheer enormity of in-state public institutions have made it difficult for private institutions to engage in state politics on higher education policy. What's more, interviewees said that independent universities and colleges are often uninterested in pursuing government relations. Prominent schools are more concerned with national recruitment than with state budget lobbying. In California, private schools enroll 22% of all resident undergraduate 4-year students, but they are rarely recognized by government policies. The complete absence of a mention of private schools in the 1960 Master Plan is emblematic of the state's neglect of them in higher education planning. Recent revisions of the Master Plan have discussed the role of the independent sector, but even these mentions are more an afterthought than a planning effort. Moreover, the California state constitution prevents public money from being directly allocated to private schools. State aid is distributed to individual students in the form of Cal Grants, but private institutions are unable to lobby state government for aid.

In North Carolina and Texas, most of the private colleges are small, enrolling no more than 1,000 students each. The schools are often religious and focus primarily on teacher education. For many years, these colleges did not organize to gain access to funds because of their insular nature. "These are religious schools that tend to keep to themselves. Baylor just started dancing a few years ago, and I mean literally just started dancing," said Texas higher education author Gerald Gaither. In addition to being outnumbered, the preeminent private institutions in Texas and North Carolina have not advocated for state funds because they are primarily concerned with pursuing a national reputation. The prominent schools like Southern Methodist University, Wake Forest, and Rice have all been successful in attracting quality out-of-state students who pay enough tuition to contribute to their endowments. This success has allowed the schools to forgo lobbying for state dollars. In Texas, Trinity College is marketed as the "Carleton College of the South" and attracts high-caliber students from across the country. Rice University has an endowment that ranks in the top 25 in size in the country. In North Carolina, Duke University is known as the "Southern Ivy." And both Duke and Wake Forest are well endowed through the largesse of local tobacco money, as the Duke and Reynolds families, respectively, founded the schools and have foundations that continually donate large sums to them.

In Texas, private schools have become more active through the Texas Independent Colleges and University Association and have successfully lobbied for state need-based grant funds essential to their low- to moderate-income student bodies. The Tuition Equalization Grant (TEG) program received a boost of $20 million during the 1998–1999 legislative session and now receives $94.4 million per biennium. Currently, more than 30,000 students receive TEG grants of up to $2,500 a year. Despite the private schools' success in winning increased funding for the TEG, interviewees believe that they have few goals beyond maintenance of the TEG program and that they would never attempt to take on the public college's secure lock on most state monies.

Recently, private institutions in Texas and California have been increasingly figuring into higher education discussions. Surprisingly, it is state government that is reaching out to the institutions, rather than the other way around. State governments are beginning to reach out to private institutions to become more involved in access issues. In California, there is an increasingly desperate need to find classroom space for the predicted tidal wave of new students entering the system in the next 20 years. In Texas, private schools are seen as an alternative to public institutions for keeping qualified minority candidates in state after the recent *Hopwood* decision that legally ended affirmative action at all state colleges.

Community Colleges

All three states are similar in governance of and policy toward the 2-year community colleges. All have strong, independent community colleges based locally, with weak chancellors in North Carolina and California and no system head in Texas. The lack of strong or centralized power at the top has proven to be a major obstacle to accessing statewide influence. Consequently, community colleges are rarely at the negotiating table during statewide policy decisions.

When the community colleges have been able to affect policy debates it has occurred as a result of allegiances with other systems. In California, the community colleges successfully aligned with the K–12 system and passed Proposition 98, which guaranteed K–14 funding, and in Texas, the community colleges joined a coalition with the 4-year systems to pass major funding increases in the 1997 budget biennium.

Interest Groups

Higher education is unique among policy areas because many of the stakeholders are not organized to participate in the policy process or in state decision regimes. Students organize selectively around tuition issues and have also participated in advocacy of school programs and curriculum issues. Faculty protest for control of curriculum offerings and graduation requirements in their colleges, and if they are well organized, they bargain collectively regarding salaries and benefits. However, there are few higher education advocacy groups in any of the states that promote general support for higher education. In every study state, there was not one example of student input on any major policy areas being debated statewide. Minority groups exhibited weak influence on higher education policy making.

We think the lack of information regarding higher education policy that is available to the public and interest groups explains the lack of any participatory process in the existence of advocacy groups. But a more important explanation is the impact of the specialness and economic development arguments used by higher education elites that limit the role of outsiders.

The Effect of Higher Education Regimes on Access and Economic Development

Access and economic development are fundamental to higher education policy. We found that California, North Carolina, and Texas provide very rich settings to explore higher education policy debates. Both access and economic development policy are in flux. Affirmative action policies are under attack or being rolled back through lawsuits in a number of states. Other policy areas that determine access are heavily debated across the nation, including remedial education, standards, articulation agreements between 2- and 4-year institutions, and the degree of linkage between K–12 and higher education systems. In the area of economic development, states are increasingly looking to, if not relying on, their systems of higher education to fuel what Peter Eisinger (1988) calls the "rise of the entrepreneurial state."

What role do state and political culture play in these critical educational policy debates? Does an understanding of state politics allow predictions of how states will resolve these issues? And are systems of higher education working with state governments to pursue answers to these difficult policy areas? Clearly, many factors affect the policy outcome of access and economic development decisions. Whether a governor is running for higher office or whether a state has been struck by a deep recession are factors in determining statewide higher education policy or legislation. Our purpose is to determine how higher education politics and culture play a part in affecting these debates and their outcomes.

Affirmative Action Policies

Access can be defined in many different ways. This study defines it as equal representation of a state's ethnic and racial population in its public higher education institutions. The policy areas of affirmative action and the K–16 educational pipeline were used to measure access in each state and the influence of political culture and higher education regimes on access.

Each of the three states is in the midst of rolling back or reevaluating longstanding affirmative action policies at its public universities. Affirmative action, unlike educational policies such as student financial aid or academic standards, is not an area that directly affects all students. Instead, it is a tool targeted specifically at racial and ethnic minorities that seeks to secure their fair representation at the state's most selective institutions. The origin of the retreat from affirmative action has been different in each state: in California, it was grounded in politics; in Texas in a legal battle; and in North Carolina in the UNC system itself. The response in each state has also varied. These variations highlight the role and importance of the political culture of each state's higher education regimes. In California, there has been public debate and discussion; in Texas, significant legislative intervention; and in North Carolina, a process of low-key reevaluation of race-specific policies at each campus. California's culture of direct democracy set the stage for a plebiscite-sanctioned proposition to repeal affirmative action policies, with the governor—the primary regime actor—as the champion of the measure. Texas's legislatively active higher education regime responded with a string of initiatives to ameliorate the effects of its loss. In North Carolina, affirmative action is being reexamined by the powerful UNC president, who is the locus of change for the whole UNC system, but the debate has not captured the public's attention.

Texas and California warrant a thorough comparison because in 1996 they became the first states to completely eliminate affirmative action.[12] Despite the high level of attention in both states, however, their responses have differed significantly. Interviewees in both Texas and California stated that they believed that the elimination of affirmative action can and should lead to a positive reevaluation of the educational pipeline as well as the degree of support provided for minorities to assist them with completion of higher education degrees. Both the debate and the response in Texas has focused on issues of financial support and improved articulation. California, lagging far behind, has enacted little to ameliorate the affects of the loss of affirmative action. The following discussion will assess the influence of higher education regimes to determine why Texas, a state thought of as politically conservative, is proactively addressing access issues, while the Democratic legislature in California has remained relatively silent throughout the recent implementation of Proposition 209.

California's elimination of affirmative action began at the governing board level. First, UC Regent Ward Connerly, originally appointed by Republican Governor Pete Wilson in 1995, mustered regent support to end the use of race as a selection criteria for admission to UC. The UC ban on affirmative action evolved into the California Civil Rights Initiative (CCRI), Proposition 209, which eliminated affirmative action at all public sector agencies, including UC. Connerly became the campaign chair of CCRI, backed by Governor Wilson, who championed the rollback of affirmative action as the centerpiece of his failed 1996 presidential bid. The governor's role as the most influential higher education regime actor allowed Wilson to enact the ban despite opposition by the UC president and all nine campus chancellors. The governor lent visible support to UC ban of affirmative action,[13] and Proposition 209 passed with 55% of the vote, based on Wilson's strong political and monetary support. In short, Wilson, more than any other regime actor, was able to implement his higher education agenda.

Since Proposition 209's passage, there has been little discussion of the issue or legislative action by the state's Democratic legislature. The legislature has been hobbled by term limits and its historical lack of a role in the state's higher education regime. The body has shown little to no re-solve in efforts to ease the impact of affirmative action's loss.

In the absence of a legislative response, the full effects of Proposition 209 were immediately felt. In the fall of 1998, in the first freshman class admitted to Berkeley since the ban, the number of Black freshman totaled 3%, a drop of more than 50% and the lowest level since the university began keep-ing figures in 1981. The number of Hispanics enrolled dropped by 43% to 7% of the total freshman class, and White student enrollment increased 7%. Recent numbers just released for the fall 1999 term indicate a rise in the number of minority students admitted to UC (although numbers are still low for Berkeley), but the jump is credited entirely to campus-by-campus efforts to recruit and broaden admissions criteria to attract minorities.

The affirmative action issue remained static until the 1998 election of Democratic Governor Gray Davis. In March of 1999, just 2½ months after Davis's inauguration, the Board of Regents passed the Four Percent Plan, which will automatically admit the top 4% of the state's high school students. The measure originated in a lobbying campaign by UC faculty members and was sup-ported by Governor Davis, who included the proposal in his inaugural address (Healy, 1999; Terry, 1999).

The repeal of affirmative action in Texas was enacted by a legal decision in 1996. The first in the country, it occurred when the U.S. Supreme Court let a lower court ruling stand in *Hopwood v. Texas*, which found race-based admissions policies at UT Law School unconstitutional. The case, com-monly referred to as *Hopwood*, was then interpreted by State Attorney General Dan Morales to apply not only to UT Law School but to every public college in Texas.

In sharp contrast with California, Texas has been aggressive in dealing with the impact of the loss of affirmative action. Political culture was a strong factor in the state legislature's proactive re-sponse. Interviewees noted that Texas's fierce independent tradition does not easily tolerate deci-sions made by those on the outside, be it the federal government or the courts. An analyst at the THECB said, "This is Texas and by God, outsiders do not tell us what to do."

The Texas higher education regime was also well prepared to respond. Governor George W. Bush chose to bow out of the debate, but the legislature, which was used to playing an active role in higher education policy, responded quickly to the sudden loss of affirmative action (a tool seen as useful in the effort to attract minority students to UT and Texas A&M). The passion and determina-tion that Texas lawmakers brought to bear has been noted by many commentators. There was a con-sensus among both White and newly elected minority representatives that something had to be done to deal with the impact of the termination of affirmative action. Expressing an urgent need for answers, Henry Cuellar, a state representative from Laredo, stated, "I'm satisfied with the efforts (of UT admission officers), but not the results. They're doing the best with what they have, but we want higher numbers and we want them now. We have to diversify as soon as possible," (quoted in Lum, 1998). Texas lawmakers commissioned a number of high-profile commissions and panels to assess the impact of *Hopwood* and propose legislative responses. Several proposals for reform were enacted during the 1997 legislative session, and implementation is under way.

The most far reaching measure was the Ten Percent Plan, which guarantees admission to the top 10% of all public high school applicants to UT and Texas A&M. Also, the legislature passed measures to increase the affordability of college by increasing the budget of the Texas Tuition As-sistance Grant program for low-income students, from $150,000 to $5 million. They authorized an increase of $20 million (on a base of $74 million) in the Texas Tuition Equalization Grant for in-state students attending private colleges. To improve articulation, the legislature passed a bill that calls for the development of a core curriculum for freshman and sophomores in public 4-year institu-tions. The most symbolic and revealing action of the Texas legislature in 1997 was the reendorse-ment of Access and Equity 2000, the state's latest equal opportunity plan for higher education. It is essentially a list of goals for increasing minority representation of both students and faculty at flag-ship institutions.

In the 1999 legislative session, new measures aimed at increasing opportunity and access for mi-norities are slotted for review and possible passage. These include eliminating the requirement of standardized test scores for admissions to 4-year institutions, mandating annual systemwide strategies to identify and attract students that reflect the population of the state, and the abolition of all remedial testing in the state.

Texas's higher education system representatives have also responded to the repeal of affirmative action. Under the umbrella of the Texas Higher Education Coalition, major system heads and community college presidents[14] came together to work on an agenda for access. During the 1997 legislative session, the coalition organized around the *Hopwood* ruling to call for increased funding not just for higher education but for all systems and levels of education from K–12 to the flagships. The unique decentralized structure allowed the systems to unite and collectively lobby in a way that interviewees say is impossible in highly segmented systems in states like North Carolina and California. For the 1999 legislative session, the coalition has organized again around access issues and calls their efforts "Access and Affordability."

State-level activity in Texas has led to some very tangible results in the wake of *Hopwood*. The greatest success is most evident at UT Austin, the state's premiere flagship. The last freshman class that entered UT Austin before *Hopwood* took effect was 4.1% Black and 14.7% Hispanic. Following the ruling, the numbers in 1997 slipped to 2.7% and 12.6% for Blacks and Hispanics, respectively. Preliminary numbers for fall 1999 enrollments show a bounce back to 3.9% for Blacks and 13.5% for Hispanics.

Beginning in 1974, UNC underwent a tumultuous period of litigation with the NAACP Legal Defense Fund and of ongoing battles with the federal government's Office of Civil Rights. These battles did not end until a consent degree was agreed upon in 1981 between UNC and the U.S. Department of Education (Link, 1995, pp. 249–338). The ongoing litigation fostered a substantive rise in African American enrollment at traditionally White UNC campuses—the numbers of African American students more than doubled during the litigation years, 1972 to 1980. But since the consent decree of 1981, African American enrollment has only nudged up 2 more points to 9.8% in 1997. The number of African Americans actually dropped at 4 of the 10 historically White universities between 1980 and 1997.[15] In other words, only during litigation and pressure by the federal government did diversity at UNC improve, but even after formal agreements with the federal government were established, their effects were minimal.

Like Texas and California, North Carolina's affirmative action changes highlight the role of regime actors in policy decisions and outcomes (see Table 3). The state has quietly been reexamining and eliminating affirmative action policies throughout the UNC system at the initiative of the system's president, Molly Corbett Broad. Whereas the Texas and California affirmative action battles were systemwide, North Carolina's President Broad has called for a full reevaluation of race-specific programs on a campus-by-campus basis. The influential role of the UNC president office has allowed Broad to call for the first ever review of all affirmative action policies at each UNC campus, including the traditionally Black institutions (TBIs). She has not issued a mandate but is instead calling this review process preventive maintenance to avoid litigation similar to that which occurred in Texas and California. Some within the system have interpreted the review as pressure to open up to all applicants and students scholarship and support programs exclusively for Black students. Gerald Horne, UNC Chapel Hill's director of African American Research, has gone as far as to say that the review "might herald a return to slavery" (quoted in Lederman, 1997).

TABLE 3

Redrawing Affirmative Action in the States: Origins, Response, and Link to Culture or Higher Education Regime

	Regime Origin	Regime Response	Link to Regime
California	Regent vote/initiative	Weak	Strong governor and weak legislature
Texas	Courts	Active	Active legislature
North Carolina	University of North Carolina president	Moderate	Strong and centralized leadership at University of North Carolina

Most schools have yet to determine a course of action based on the call for the review, but a few have already altered or eliminated race-specific policies, including Chapel Hill (Southern Education Foundation, 1998). The general assembly has not responded to Broad's calls to reassess affirmative action but has instead focused on issues of growing student enrollment and equity at TBIs. Interviewees felt that Broad displayed sharp political acumen by avoiding legislative interference in her review of affirmative action. Ferrel Guillory, a communications professor at Chapel Hill, said that Broad's review "did not generate much controversy. If she proposed repealing affirmative action that would have stirred up controversy and if she proposed expanding it, that would have stirred up controversy. But she did neither."

Instead of affirmative action, the issue of parity for the state's TBIs has consumed the North Carolina General Assembly in recent years. There are a large number of public and private TBIs in the state, but none are highly successful or prominent.[16] None of them are research universities, and out of the 11 public and private TBIs, only 2 (North Carolina Agriculture & Technical and Fayetteville State University) offer Ph.D.s. Most have low enrollment, averaging about 2,000 at the public schools and about 1,000 at the private schools.

Although the lack of diversity has been a source of frustration for the general assembly's Black Caucus, more troubling has been the perceived fiscal inequities within the system. Three reviews of the UNC system have occurred since desegregation began, two ordered by the general assembly.[17] All equity studies conducted by the UNC Board of Governors concluded that indeed a few schools were victim to inequitable funding, but only one, Fayetteville State University, was a TBI. The findings have not quelled the anger of many in the state, particularly African American Representatives Mickey Beshaw and Dan Blue. Champions of the TBIs argue that even if the schools are receiving more per full-time equivalent, they are still far behind, given the history of inequity. George Esser, the president of the North Carolina Community Development Initiative said, "It's like filling a chasm with a rock. They still have a long way to go." Currently, the general assembly's Black Caucus is determined to issue another review of UNC and focus on physical, not fiscal, conditions at all 16 campuses.

Educational Pipeline

The educational pipeline measures a state's ability to move residents up the educational ladder from public K–12 schools to research universities. It is a concept also referred to as K–16. Indicators of the educational pipeline include high school graduation rates, the rate of transfer from 2-year to 4-year colleges, minority representation at each level, and the level of connection among all levels of education in the state. The two most important components of a strong educational pipeline are affordability and educational preparedness. Unlike affirmative action, policies surrounding the educational pipeline affect all state residents aiming to receive postsecondary degrees.

Cross-state indicator analyses reveal that the three study states each have leaky educational pipelines. At each juncture in the pipeline, many students, particularly minority students, do not progress to the next level. Also, funding for and performance in K–12 education in each state was significantly below the national average, the number of high school graduates progressing to higher education institutions was below the national average, and only a small percentage of minorities enrolled in flagships and traditionally White institutions. Responding to the fundamental problems of a poor pipeline, many interviewees say that the best outcome that could and should result from the retreat from affirmative action would be greater attention to the issues of retention and progress up the educational ladder.

In the wake of affirmative action debates, each of the three states has begun to seriously look at these issues and the K–16 connection with public systems of education. Again, Texas has been the most active of the study states and California the least. Texas's proactive approach to educational pipeline issues as compared to California's inaction are similar to those discussed in the section on affirmative action. Texas's legislature is active and not reluctant to debate and become involved in issues of access and opportunity. In California, the lack of legislative involvement, coupled with a lack of gubernatorial interest in general, has suspended much discussion of improving articulation in the school systems. The highly segmented and rigid structure of California's separate college systems has also slowed progress. North Carolina has made progress because of an increasingly active legislature concerned about equal access and a governor who has staked his administration on improving performance in lower education.

Increasingly, states are asserting control over the educational pipeline issue through standardized tests. Texas demonstrates the most control over lower education in this regard. All Texas public school students take the Texas Assessment of Academic Skills (TAAS) in Grades 3 through 8 and must pass the Grade 10 test to graduate. Schools become accredited when they meet required percentages of passing students. In this way, higher education admissions are determined by tests in the lower grades. Furthermore, all higher education institutions administer a standardized Texas Academic Skills Program test, more difficult than the TAAS, to identify students who need remediation. These tests have been used to hold students accountable, rather than schools or teachers, and the high drop-out rate in Texas reflects that fact. California has only recently begun statewide testing for basic skills in lower grades. In 1998, it developed a complete set of academic standards that are voluntary guidelines for districts. It does not have a test for graduation that is used by higher education. North Carolina began a new accountability system, called the ABCs of Public Education, in September 1997. Schools must meet testing goals, or they will receive special assistance. Bonuses are awarded to teachers and staff of successful schools.

Besides standardized testing, some states are finding additional ways to link public primary and secondary schools to in-state colleges. Such connections can come in many different forms, including regional boards and articulation agreements. The movement to forge K–16 connections in the three study states is limited but increasingly active since affirmative action's loss has been felt. The Texas legislature passed an articulation agreement that calls for the development of a core curriculum for first- and second-year college and university students. The various systems conduct more of the outreach to the K–12 schools, a situation that is a vestige of desegregation agreements with the Office of Civil Rights in the 1970s. For example, UT San Antonio has an academic program, TexPREP, for high school juniors and seniors. Thus far, 81% of participants in the program have been from racial minority groups. Other campuses have similar programs.

In North Carolina, the general assembly has taken a significant step toward uniting the historically unconnected UNC and community college systems. North Carolina ranks at the bottom of the study states in transfer rates and is 27% below the national average. After 10 years of discussion and debate, the general assembly passed a landmark articulation agreement in 1997. For years, community college students were forced to retake their entire first 2 years of college if they were accepted to a UNC college. A higher education analyst for the general assembly, said,

> It started with [general assembly] representatives hearing too many of these horror stories. One or two of these stories you can pass off, but there were far too many. Their constituents felt robbed, half of their work at the community college didn't count towards a degree.

An increasingly empowered general assembly spent 10 years leaning on the UNC system to improve transfer rates before the assembly passed the articulation agreement. Another state effort to encourage articulation is aimed at campus outreach to public K–12 schools. Under a new racial diversity program, universities work with specific schools in which they conduct outreach and planning efforts to increase K–12 achievement and enrollment in college. Each UNC campus receives $50,000 for these activities. These programs often take the form of regional partnerships between the universities and low-income districts nearby.

The most important sign of an improved educational pipeline in North Carolina is Governor James Hunt's increased funding and attention to K–12 public schools. Governor Hunt has staked his administration's performance on improving primary and secondary schools. In 1997, he passed the Excellent Schools Act, which, among other measures, dictates that the state budget must bring teacher salaries above the national average by the year 2000 (a significant jump for a state whose salary compensations were near the bottom nationwide). Gubernatorial focus has begun to show results: Math scores for fourth- and eighth-graders improved 8% between 1992 and 1996 on the National Assessment of Education Progress exams (*Education Week*, 2000).

California has seen little pipeline improvement or innovation. It was once widely emulated because of the access guaranteed under the 1960 Master Plan, but over the past 25 years, the state's higher education regime actors have drifted from the plan's mandate of making low-cost higher education widely accessible to all residents (McCurdy, 1994). The Master Plan promises that any student who works hard and meets necessary requirements can easily traverse from K–12 to community college to the prestigious UC campuses.

The initial retreats from the Master Plan began in the early 1980s when Governor George Deukmejian capped funding of statewide community college enrollment growth and when state support for all systems fell below per student costs (Benjamin & Carrol, 1998, p. 16; McCurdy, 1994). State budget reductions and tuition increases accelerated during the 1989–1994 recession. Over the course of the most recent recession, tuition increased 134% at UC, 103% at CSU, and 290% at the community colleges (James Irvine Foundation, 1998). This resulted in 200,000 fewer students served; many were unable to enroll because of the increased cost of education (McCurdy, 1994).

In addition to the increased costs of education, the state is in the midst of a major population boom referred to as Tidal Wave II.[18] It is this population boom and the increased demand for education that interviewees identified as equally harmful to California's educational pipeline and to the ideals of the Master Plan, as are budget cuts and tuition increases. The fact of dropping enrollments during a population boom proves a significant retreat from the fundamental promise of access and educational fluidity to California's residents in the 1960s.

California has emerged from its recession and is replenishing funding for all public higher education systems, which are now funded above prerecession levels. However, tuition is still as high as it was in the depths of the recession, and enrollment has not climbed back to prerecession levels despite the need for education. Enrollment declines have been particularly severe at the two main entry points of the system: CSU and the community colleges (James Irvine Foundation, 1998).

At least at the individual campus level, the universities sponsor programs aimed at reaching out to local public schools. The university now has about 800 outreach and intervention programs around the state, which include tutorials, workshops, test preparation courses, and campus visit programs, often established to replace affirmative action.

Disinterest in higher education policies, particularly by the governor, was evident in the lack of a response in California to this situation. The state was caught in a "policy vacuum" (Trombley, 1996). Patick Callan of the National Center for Public Policy and Higher Education describes the effects of this policy vacuum by saying, "The governor and the legislature neither gave encouragement nor exerted pressure for more creative responses. Rather, they cut higher education budgets and distanced themselves from such unpopular consequences as fee increases and enrollment reductions." Thus, California's access policies and educational pipeline fell victim to the lack of influence of legislators in the higher education regime and the lack of attention from the most influential regime actor, the governor.

Withdrawal from the open access ideals of the Master Plan is also linked to faculty dominance of the systems. As student tuition soared, the cutbacks had little effect on full-time faculty salaries or amenities. UC faculty even benefited from a faculty buyout that was so generous it is commonly referred to as the Golden Handshake.

Each study state's experience with educational pipeline issues highlights the importance of state regime actors (see Table 4). Addressing fundamental and far-reaching issues of how to better link students between education systems is a policy issue that cannot be solved entirely at the local level and that demands state attention. It is not surprising that Texas has addressed pipeline issues, particularly in the wake of the *Hopwood* decision. In California, there has been virtually no substantive discussion of the educational pipeline, even after Proposition 209's passage. North Carolina has benefited from a more active state legislature, particularly from the strength of minority representatives who are demanding increased accountability from postsecondary systems.

Economic Development

Public colleges have long made an argument for their support by claiming that they are an integral part of statewide economic development strategies (Gittell & Sedgley, 2000). Public colleges provide

TABLE 4

**The Policy Response to the States' Educational Pipelines
and the Influence of Higher Education Regimes**

	Status	Link to Higher Education Regime	Policy Movement
Texas	Active	Active state legislature	Standards, articulation
North Carolina	Increasingly active	More active legislature and strong education governor	Articulation, increased funding of lower education
California	Inactive	Weak legislature and lack of interest from governor	Falling enrollment, increased tuition

a skilled workforce and academic experts available for consultation on numerous economic matters, and they generate revenue for the state through matching federal and foundation grants.

Originally, this study had planned to assess the general links between public colleges and economic development, but through the cross-state indicators, it was revealed that no linear connection exists. Analysis showed that a state policy of investing in higher education does not necessarily lead to improved economic conditions (see Gittell & Sedgley, 2000).

North Carolina has supported major statewide programs for the past 50 years, but both California and Texas have little in the way of economic development programs. What programs California and Texas do have are either small in scale or recent additions at the state level. In Texas and California, there is no state-centered development strategy. Eisinger's (1988) *The Rise of the Entrepreneurial State* provides one of the first comparative surveys of state-sponsored university-business partnerships. Although Eisinger's account of increasing state activity was accurate, and this study did uncover a few programs recently implemented, neither Texas nor California could claim that its efforts comprise a focused or comprehensive plan. The state programs were not entrepreneurial as much as a response to a specific need (i.e., job training assistance or coordination of existing programs) that had previously gone unmet. Taken together, the two states' programs formed a disparate assemblage of helpful funds that did more to support than pioneer or encourage local planning efforts.

Within the limits of our study, it is difficult to assess whether North Carolina is an anomaly in its success in incorporating all levels of postsecondary education into a statewide economic development strategy. The shortage of substantive state programs, even in two of the states in this study—California and Texas—proves that unlike issues of access, economic development can be driven successfully at the local or campus level just as much as at the state level. However, because of limited access, the effects of North Carolina policies did not reach the lowest strata or Blacks.

Higher education regimes and culture are reflected in each state's approach to economic development efforts, whether at the local or state level. The progressive plutocracy culture of North Carolina business and political partnerships is responsible for the state's pioneering models of community college training programs and state-sponsored university parks. With Texas, cultural aversion to marketplace intervention, coupled with a decentralized structure of the state's higher education regime, has fostered a wealth of innovation at the campus level. And in California, stronger faculty participation in the state's higher education regime has fostered a research and development focus at the university level. Each state's higher education efforts to link to the private sector were also closely tied to its overall economic development efforts. North Carolina has historically focused more on economic development and statewide planning efforts than have other states.[19] In Texas, state-supported economic development has been shunned and only in recent years has the notion of public sector involvement in economic development concerns gained currency in political discussions. California maintains a wide array of scattered programs.

Building on the nexus of business, politics, and higher education traditionally at the core of North Carolina's culture, the state has gotten publicity for developing model postsecondary economic development programs. The most famous partnership program is Research Triangle Park (RTP), the first state-sponsored research park in the nation. Using state funding and visible support from two successive governors, RTP connected UNC Chapel Hill and NSCU with Duke University to create a joint university research center focused on assisting private sector companies that moved into the park. RTP is now home to the largest concentration of Ph.D.s, scientists, and engineers in the country (RTP, 1997) and has spurred one of the greatest high-technology and bio-technology boom areas in the country (Labio, 1993; Nance-Nash & Smith, 1993).[20] Building on the RTP model, there are also now more than 200 such public university–sponsored university parks across North America.

In 1958, North Carolina was also the first to create a community college model for economic development—subsidized customized job training. Now virtually every state has some type of customized job training program; in North Carolina, job training has become the basis of the community college curriculum. A director of economic development for the state's community colleges, explains the state's competitive edge by saying,

> North Carolina is unique [because of the] ongoing training we provide. The vast majority of [North Carolina Community College System] programs are for existing firms, so where some states throw a lot of cash and a quick job training offer, we have a training infrastructure and a long [vocational education] culture to back it up.

What North Carolina lacks, however, is a strong liberal arts component to the programs, which would offer flexibility in career development.

California's postsecondary economic development successes at the public university level grew directly out of the strong influence of faculty in the UC system. Since the turn of the century, strong faculty control at UC has favored a research-oriented approach to learning. Faculty-influenced governance led to research-friendly policies such as light teaching loads, subsidized research travel, and seed money for new experiments. Good faculty are also attracted to UC because the system gives so much power to instructors. Immense faculty and research prowess developed in the 1960s, and UC President Clark Kerr used the faculty amenities and a large budget from then-Governor Pat Brown to travel the country hunting for the most talented researchers. By the end of the decade, he had amassed 32 current and future Nobel Prize winners (one third of the total in the entire country and far more than at any other public institution) and 20% of the members of the National Academy of Science (Gladwell, 1998; Schrag, 1998, p. 37). Research funds also ballooned to support new talent in UC, with the overall research budget increasing more than tenfold between 1950 and 1970, even faster than UC's general budget (Smelser, 1974, pp. 54–55).

The net effect of this research focus and funding has been to make UC one of the preeminent research systems in the world. UC ranks first in the United States in patent revenue, generating more than $65 million in 1997 (New York Academy of Sciences, 1999). UC researchers attract one tenth of all research funds awarded to colleges and universities in the United States and receive virtually all of the U.S. Department of Energy's and Department of Defense's research dollars.[21]

At the community college level, California has created programs in economic development at the local campuses. California's community colleges pioneered vocational education (Brint & Karabel, 1989, p. 43; Gollattscheck et al., 1994, p. 49). California's first community college at Fresno specialized in practical and terminal courses in dairy farming and peach growing. The state legislation that created junior colleges stated that courses should be "designed to prepare persons for agriculture, industry, commerce, home-making and other vocations" (Gollattscheck et al., 1994, p. 40).

In 1992, the state legislature created EDNet, the first substantive assistance program for economic development at the community colleges. The program is coordinated through the central chancellor's office, with the goal of linking community colleges within the system and with businesses to respond to workforce needs in a particular region of the state. The state legislature has increasingly invested in the EDNet program, augmenting funds from an initial base of $4.9 million to a projected budget of $40 million in 1999. However, the program is scheduled to sunset by the year 2000.

In Texas, there has never been much support for economic development efforts at the state level. Any substantive state efforts are administered at the local level and consequently vary widely by re-

TABLE 5

**State Economic Development Programs and the Influence
of Culture and Higher Education Regimes**

	Cultural/Higher Education Regime Influence	Locus of Program Activity	Type of Program
North Carolina	Progressive plutocracy	State	University/business partnerships
California	Faculty dominance	Local	Research dominance
Texas	Decentralized systems	Local	Programs scattered but entrepreneurial

gion and county. Most of these programs are administered with little or no state support. Explaining the entrepreneurial drive needed to maintain a successful college-based economic development effort in Texas, Gary Sera, director of the Technology and Economic Development Center at Texas A&M said, "It's like the government says, 'Go help, but we won't help you help.' So you have to hustle and be entrepreneurial. If I don't hustle to keep [my program] going, it will crumble."

One example of a campus-based economic development program is the Bill J. Priest Institute for Economic Development, a unique community college campus in the Dallas County Community College District dedicated entirely to serving the local business community and disenfranchised workers. The institute runs one of the largest small-business incubators in Dallas and pulls down federal Job Training Partnership Act money through the institute's Job Training Center to offer employer-directed short-term intensive vocational education.

Recently, the Texas state government has become more proactive. Looking to address the lack of state support for research efforts at Texas schools, Lieutenant Governor William Hobby helped create the Advanced Technology Program (ATP) in 1987. ATP is one of the largest competitive funding streams in the country;[22] it is awarded to researchers in applied fields that offer promise of near-term commercialization.

Looking to establish a North Carolina–type customized job training program, Texas established the Skills Development Fund in 1995. With the goal of assisting businesses to work with community colleges, the Texas Workforce Commission hired North Carolina economic development organization MDC, Inc., to draft plans for specific programs for the Skills Development Fund. The fund has filled a gap at the local level for many community colleges that were previously providing business assistance with no state support. The primary complaint against the Skills Development Fund is its underfunding. At $25 million per biennium,[23] it is far too small to make a significant impact or meet need, and demand for these programs outstrips funding by a margin of three to one.

In sum, all three states have visible economic development activity in all their systems of higher education, but only North Carolina claims to incorporate this activity into statewide economic development planning. Whether local or state sponsored, economic development programs in each of the states are framed by the state's unique culture and higher education regime (see Table 5). California's faculty prominence in governance allowed for strong research efforts, and Texas's decentralized system fostered on-the-ground entrepreneurial experimentation.

Conclusion

The most important conclusion is the influence of politics on statewide higher education policies. Public universities are not above and apart from politics, as is commonly thought to be the case. Political leaders, particularly the governor and top elected legislative representatives, play a significant role, often dominating design and implementation and sometimes frustrating policy reforms. It is important for higher education systems to understand the vital role of elected leaders in policy formation and to work with those leaders to craft the most sensible policy outcomes.

Equally important is the positive contribution that an active state legislature can make to higher education policy. In California, the state legislature has been virtually silent on postsecondary issues for nearly 40 years, resulting in a system neglected and without needed reforms. As a body, the Texas legislature is much more comfortable participating in higher education debates and in recent years has enacted a flurry of reforms to address shortcomings in the areas of access and economic development. And in North Carolina, not until the legislature increased its role were unaddressed issues of equity and articulation broached.

Another conclusion is that poor communication exists between higher education policy makers within the states. Virtually all members of higher education regimes, from the governor to the heads of the different systems, to faculty leaders, rarely, if ever, conferred on future policy directions. Only in times of crisis did system and political leaders act in concert. This poor communication had the noticeable effect of weak and often long overdue policy responses to issues of rising tuition, weak connection to the K–12 system, and inequity among the campuses.

The importance of state politics combined with poor communication among policy makers creates a precarious policy environment for most public postsecondary institutions. These public institutions and systems need to better relate to their natural constituencies of students, alumni, taxpayers, and K–12 schools to build a successful coalition and political argument for continued funding and public support.

Notes

1. State leaders still graduate from the flagships. The last seven governors (1954 to 1998) all received their bachelor's degrees in state: three from the University of North Carolina (UNC), Chapel Hill; two from North Carolina State University; and two from Davidson College. Four received law degrees from UNC Chapel Hill, and virtually all general assembly members attended school within the UNC system.
2. The reference is to a well at the center of the UNC Chapel Hill campus that is the oldest structure in the UNC system.
3. California, Texas, and North Carolina are the Number 1, 2, and 10 most populated states in the country, respectively, and each has a higher-than-average growth rate.
4. The governor selects all of the trustees of the California State University system and of the statewide Board of Governors of the community college system. The governor also appoints 16 of 22 members of the Board of Regents, the body that governs the University of California.
5. California's executive is ranked in the top 10 in the country in likelihood of incumbent reelection. Indeed, every post–World War II governor has been reelected. This is primarily attributable to low voter turnout and the state's large size (Mueller, 1985; Purdum, 1998).
6. Although the number of local jurisdictions is immense, under Governor Reagan, the executive agencies were narrowed to four superagencies.
7. Curbs on executive power are a remnant of the strong tradition of Jacksonian democracy in 19th-century North Carolina. Another feature is a fractionalized executive branch with nine other executive officials elected on a statewide ballot. The governor's power, like that of most governors, has increased over the years and includes wide appointment power and more control over the state budget (Fleer, 1994, p. 119).
8. Blue lost the chair in 1994 when Republicans became the majority party in the house.
9. Both of these audits did not find the degree of inequity on a per student basis that the general assembly members expected. The inequitable formulas that were found were quickly corrected through general assembly appropriations.
10. The 70% figure of private sector representation on postsecondary governing boards was compiled through an assessment of governing boards at the major 4-year systems in the study states in 1998. The systems assessed were the University of Texas, Texas A&M, University of North Carolina, the California State University, and the University of California.
11. The bankruptcy is a result of a $13 million deficit, a botched real estate deal that cost the system more than $20 million, and a state-imposed $2.8 million fine because the system lost track of the number of full-time teachers it employed. Chancellors in the system have publicly blamed the board and faculty for the mismanagement but have been unable to make a dent in the financial problems. Recent Chancellor Bill Segura, one of the system's most severe internal critics, resigned in December 1997, just

16 months into a 4-year contract. The new chancellor, the fourth in 5 years, would sign only a 14-month contract.

12. The legal ban on affirmative action in Texas is presently being argued in state courts in Washington and Michigan, and a similar initiative to California's that banned affirmative action was passed in Washington in 1998.

13. The governor is the official president of the Board of Regents but rarely attends meetings. In a visible display of support, Wilson attended the July 1995 meeting where affirmative action was banned and stood his ground against Jesse Jackson and scores of other protesters also in attendance (Chavez, 1998).

14. Coalition members include systems heads from the community colleges; University of Texas, North Texas University, and Texas A&M University; Texas State University; Texas Tech University; and the University of Houston.

15. The number of Whites attending public traditionally Black institutions faired better, but only slightly, increasing from 11% in 1980 to 15% in 1997.

16. North Carolina has an African American population of 22% (1990 census) and ranks sixth in the nation in its proportion of African American residents. It has the second highest number of historically Black colleges and universities in the nation, with 11 institutions, 6 of which are private (7,400 students in fall 1997) and 5 public (22,000 students).

17. The first was in 1974, and the last two ordered by the general assembly were conducted in 1989 and 1995.

18. Since the Master Plan was implemented, enrollment has increased ninefold. It is predicted to double in the next 15 years from 1.3 million to 2.0 million students (Benjamin & Carrol, 1998).

19. North Carolina established the first statewide economic development bureau in 1925.

20. The development of targeted economic sectors through state universities continues today. Governor Sanford supported the first state institution dedicated to the arts in Winston-Salem at the UNC School of the Arts. This institution has helped spark an arts and cultural revival in the area. More recently, the state has invested millions into Global Trans Park, a partnership between Chapel-Hill, local community colleges, and the transportation industry.

21. After World War II, UC took over the Los Alamos laboratory, which was used to develop the atomic bomb. This lab is still run by UC as one of three national labs UC runs for the Department of Energy. The three labs receive $2.8 billion a year in federal funds.

22. In 1997, Texas overtook California in state support of research and development and is now ranked 23rd nationally (New York Academy of Sciences, 1999).

23. By comparison, the North Carolina program is "as of right" available to any company that qualifies.

References

Benjamin, R., & Carrol, S. J. (1998). *Breaking the social contract: The fiscal crisis in California higher education.* New York: Council for Aid to Education.

Brint, S., & Karabel, J. (1989). *The diverted dream.* New York: Oxford University Press.

Brown, L. C., Ericson, J. E., Langengger, J. A., Jones, E. W., & Trotter, R. S. Jr. (1998). *Practicing Texas politics.* New York: Houghton Mifflin.

Bryce, R. (1998, September 10). Do not go gentle: Former Lieutenant Governor Bill Hobby fights on for better, more diverse education. *Houston Press.Com* [Online]. Available: www.houstonpress.com/1998/091098/feature2-1.html

Burka, P. (1997, September). Bill Hobby. *Texas Monthly.*

California Citizens Commission on Higher Education. (1998, June). *A state of learning: California higher education in the twenty-first century.* Los Angeles: Author.

Chavez, L. (1998). *The color bind: California's battle to end affirmative action.* Berkeley: University of California Press.

Education Week. (2000). Quality counts 2000 [Online]. Available: www.edweek.org/sreports/qc0...es/state_data.cfm?slug=nc_data.htm

Eisinger, P. K. (1988). *The rise of the entrepreneurial state: State and local economic development policy in the United States.* Madison: University of Wisconsin Press.

Elazar, D. J. (1966). *American federalism: A view from the states.* New York: Harper & Row.

Fleer, J. D. (1994). *North Carolina government and politics.* Philadelphia: Temple University Press.

Gittell, R., & Sedgley, N. (2000). High technology and state higher education policy: Myths and realities. *American Behavioral Scientist, 43*, 1092–1120.

Gladwell, M. (1998, February 23). Brain trust. *The New Yorker*, pp. 120–121.

Gollattscheck, J. F., Suppiger, J. E., Wattenbarger, J. L., & Witt, A. A. (1994). *America's community colleges: The first century.* Washington, DC: American Association of Community Colleges.

Healy, P. (1999, April 2). U. of California to admit top 4% from every high school. *Chronicle of Higher Education*, p. A37.

Hill-Holtzman, N. (1998, August 2). Los Angles' community colleges under siege. *Los Angeles Times*, p. A1.

James Irvine Foundation. (1998, March). *The California Higher Education Policy Center: An assessment.* San Francisco: Author.

Kerr, C. (1992). The California Master Plan of 1960 for higher education. In S. Rothblatt (Ed.), *The OCED, the master plan and the California dream.* Berkeley, CA: Center for Studies in Higher Education.

Key, V. O. (1949). *Southern politics.* Knoxville: University of Tennessee Press.

Labio, K. (1993, November 15). The best cities for knowledge workers. *Fortune.*

Lederman, D. (1997, December 5). U. of North Carolina reviews policies based on race. *Chronicle of Higher Education*, p. A45.

Link, W. A. (1995). *William Friday.* Chapel Hill: University of North Carolina Press.

Luebke, P. (1998). *Tar Heel politics.* Chapel Hill: University of North Carolina Press.

Lum, L. (1998, October 5). Proposals seek more minorities at UT, Texas A&M. *Houston Chronicle*, p. A1.

McCurdy, J. (1994, November). *Broken promises: The impact of budget cuts and fee increases on California community college.* San Jose: California Higher Education Policy Center.

Mueller, K. J. (1985, September). Explaining variation and change in gubernatorial powers. *Western Political Science Quarterly, 38*, 424–431.

Nance-Nash, S., & Smith, M. Y. (1993). The top place. *Money Magazine.*

New York Academy of Sciences. (1999, February/March). *Tri-state trends: Research and development.* New York: Author.

Peirce, N. A., & Hagstrom, J. (1984). *The book of America: Inside 50 states today.* New York: Norton.

Purdum, T. S. (1998, March 31). When lawmakers waffle, and sometimes before, voters turn to the ballot measure. *New York Times*, p. A1.

Research Triangle Foundation (RTF). (1997). *Where the minds of the world meet.* Research Triangle Park, NC: Author.

Richardson, R. C., Callan, P. M., Finney, J. E., & Bracco, K. R. (1999). *Designing state higher education systems for a new century.* Phoenix: Oryx.

Schrag, P. (1998). *Paradise lost: California's experience, America's future.* New York: New Press.

Smelser, N. J. (1974). Growth, structural change, and conflict in California higher education, 1950–1970. In G. Almond, & N. J. Smelser (Eds.), *Public higher education in California.* Berkeley: University of California Press.

Southern Education Foundation. (1998). *Miles to go: Report on Black students and postsecondary education in the South.* Atlanta: Author.

Stadtman, V. A. (1970). *The University of California 1868–1968.* New York: McGraw-Hill.

Terry, D. (1999, March 20). California guaranteeing some a place in universities. *New York Times*, p. A24.

Trombley, W. (1996, May). *Shared responsibility.* San Jose: California Higher Education Policy Center.

UNIVERSITIES AND MARKETS

ROGER L. GEIGER

The four spheres of activity of contemporary American universities—finances, undergraduates, research, and relations with industry—do not encompass the full range of university responsibilities and operations, but all are important and each has changed substantially in the current era. Potent market forces have been central to the nature and direction of these changes. Hence the recurring metaphor of the marketplace. This chapter aims to provide some deeper understanding of these processes by considering the advantages that market relationships have brought, which are for the most part more immediate and apparent, and the real or potential costs, which may be longer term and less direct.

The "age of privatization" has been accompanied by an apotheosis of free-market ideology.[1] The extension of the market economy around the globe has been paralleled by a kind of functional extension, actual or advocated, of market relationships beyond the for-profit realm of the economy. However, the operation of markets depends on contextual factors that regulate, constrain, or otherwise influence the economic forces of capitalism. Such factors play an even larger role in sectors that lie outside the for-profit sector, notably education. Economist Charles E. Lindblom has offered such an encompassing view in *The Market System*. Although he does not discuss higher education specifically, his critical perspective on markets offers insight into these issues.[2]

Markets in essence perform the task of social coordination. Market coordination is the antithesis of central or government coordination. It has the virtue of being noncoercive since it proceeds largely through processes of mutual adaptation. But it is far from being the only form of social coordination. Considering just higher education, the distribution of opportunities for postsecondary instruction is a ubiquitous concern in modern societies and hence invites a large degree of central coordination. Everywhere, the coordination of educational opportunity is heavily influenced by government decisions about the availability of places and the terms of attendance. In the same way, one might consider the coordination of the multiple social roles of universities. Market coordination certainly plays an important role here, but so do the actions of government, philanthropy, and voluntary associations of universities themselves. From this perspective, the question becomes, what is the role of market coordination in the social coordination of universities, and how has it changed during the current era?

A second set of considerations requires closer scrutiny of the supposed benefits of market coordination. Market coordination ought to move social coordination in the direction of greater efficiency, but such movement occurs within a constraining structure. The domain of market coordination is limited by prior conditions and numerous contextual factors. In particular, in areas where large spillovers exist (that is, where benefits or costs are not reflected in prices) prices are relatively arbitrary. It has already been seen that this was true for the price of undergraduate education. Other factors also constrict the domain of market coordination, and "its limited domain is a limit on its capacity to achieve efficient allocations."[3]

Governments have a large influence on market systems, affecting social coordination in three ways: they make significant purchases of goods and services; they penalize some activities through taxation; and they encourage behaviors they favor through subsidization. The result is not a free market, but rather an administered market system—one, moreover, in which the values of the polity play a large role in affecting approved and disapproved activities. It is chimerical, Lindblom argues, to believe that unalloyed market coordination can achieve economic efficiency. Rather, a mix of factors, including values and legal systems, determines at any moment the balance between market coordination and other forms of social coordination.

In the current era, for example, the United States made numerous choices that affected that balance. Policies were enacted at both the state and federal levels that channeled public funds to students rather than institutions in order to help pay the costs of higher education. The federal government brought legal action to prevent universities from cooperating instead of competing in the award of institutional student financial aid. The 1980 Bayh-Dole Act was the most conspicuous of several pieces of legislation that encouraged the commercialization of the results of academic research. And in the 1990s, the federal government decreed that the special facilities and treatments offered by university health care centers would no longer be exempted from the pricing system for managed health care. Each of these actions introduced an element of market coordination in areas that had, in Lindblom's words, very limited "capacity to achieve efficient allocations."[4] Yet they also represented values that favored voluntary choice and distrusted institutional determinations of the social good.

The discussion that follows invokes some of the fundamental properties of markets suggested by Lindblom. Most basic is the opposition between market and other forms of social coordination. Next is the role of pricing and the choices it effects. Finally, there is the realm of incentives—the stimulation of motivation for participants to seek benefits, or avoid harm, in the market system. This perspective highlights the paradoxes of market aggrandizement—the real gains achieved versus the actual and potential costs.

Private Universities

Although the system of independent colleges and universities in the United States may appear to possess many of the characteristics of a free market, the institutions have often eschewed competitive behavior and sought the shelter of voluntary coordination. The industry is itself highly segmented, and participants have formed associations for purposes ranging from sharing information to outright collusion. The College Board was an early effort by top schools to coordinate admissions. The Consortium for Financing Higher Education (COFHE, founded in 1975) later facilitated a kind of mutual coordination among many of the same institutions. And the formation of the Ivy League permitted the coordination of athletics. Coordination in these instances allowed private schools to control with whom they would compete and on what terms.

Voluntary coordination, in particular, achieved a crucial consensus over student financial aid. Beginning with the establishment of the College Scholarship Service in 1954, the leading universities sought to promote the understanding that student aid would be awarded solely on the basis of financial need. It probably took two decades, but after the federal government fashioned a need-based system of aid in 1972, this principle was firmly accepted across the selective sector.

The following quarter-century appears in retrospect as the "student aid era."[5] Highly selective universities and colleges agreed in principle that price should be eliminated insofar as possible as a factor in student choice. They specifically accepted a common formula for determining the expected family contribution and an implicit obligation by the institution to cover a student's "unmet need." Of course, a single price system inherently favored the top institutions since, given equal prices, the most highly sought-after students would naturally prefer schools with the greatest resources and highest prestige. But less-affluent institutions nevertheless benefited by being associated with the academic elite. The process of queue and overflow assured them of highly qualified students as well.

The incipient decline of the Student Aid Era was signaled by the Department of Justice challenge of the Overlap Group in 1991. When the leading institutions could no longer cooperate on setting financial aid awards, overt voluntary coordination had to be abandoned. Actual practice was slow to change, no doubt because of the advantage of these arrangements for participants. However, the consensus of the student aid era, which had been formalized in the Overlap Group, merely served to suppress for a time powerful forces being generated in the admissions market.[6]

The market conditions of the 1980s encouraged private universities to raise quality by spending more and to raise their prices as well. The secular trend toward an increasingly integrated national market advanced markedly in these years, and with it the competition for high-ability students.[7] Universities that were able to enhance their quality were also able to increase their selectivity and prestige. They increased income as well, through escalating tuition (list and net) and the generosity of their benefactors. This form of qualitative competition was the most important economic consequence of the student aid era, although it was obscured somewhat by the veneer of voluntary coordination. Moreover, it persisted and intensified as the student aid consensus began to crumble. Perhaps its most striking characteristic was the inherent advantage possessed by institutions that already enjoyed high quality and wealth. The phenomenon of the rich getting richer was the natural result of qualitative competition. These competitive forces also produced increasing market coordination in the selective sector, and as this occurred market power migrated from universities to prospective students.

During the student aid era, the renunciation of price competition accorded leading universities a form of "rent" (or unearned profit); they matriculated high-ability students without paying the full market value for those students' contribution to educational quality through peer effects. But even before federal intervention, market forces were eroding this form of market power. Less selective colleges offered merit aid in lieu of qualitative competition, and even the less wealthy cartel members bent the rules for financial aid.[8] By the late 1990s, such rents were disappearing: a competitive market began forcing even the most highly selective institutions to pay additional "wages" for talented students. The taboo against merit aid persisted among the most prestigious institutions, but they found other ways to bid for students.

The system of qualitative competition with voluntary coordination was roundly criticized for boosting tuition prices, but in retrospect it may have been preferable to the form of market coordination that succeeded it. With respect to prices, net tuition rose far less than list tuition, and as universities increased general subsidies, quality in theory rose faster than net tuition. More fundamentally, this system created conditions in which institutions were motivated to enrich educational opportunities for highly able students, and those students obtained greater choice of institutions to attend. This process produced greater segregation of students by ability level through the hierarchy of institutions, a pattern that also likely produced a more efficient distribution of students for purposes of optimizing educational benefits. Still, market coordination has had problematic consequences for (1) social stratification, (2) price competition, (3) institutional trust, and (4) what economists call the arms race.

Qualitative competition, combined with increasing returns to selective college graduates, attracted more potential students to these institutions. This high-stakes competition for places naturally favored those students with the cumulative advantages of high social background and privileged schooling. More precisely, the more competitive admission to high-quality colleges becomes, the greater the effect of social attributes, acquired from privileged social backgrounds, and the less the effect of innate intelligence (however defined).[9]

Elite universities are not only aware of this situation; they ostensibly work to counteract it in the name of diversity and democracy. The recruitment of underrepresented minorities and financial aid mitigate these forces to some extent, and assuage institutional consciences far more; but the dominant effect can scarcely be reversed. The places at highly selective universities, and the presumed subsequent earnings advantage, have increasingly been filled by high-achieving, wealthy students.[10] Furthermore, the system would be unsustainable if this were not the case, since tuition income has provided the principal fuel for spending growth.

Market coordination has brought a subtle yet profound alteration in the role of pricing. High-tuition/high aid was originally intended to generate revenue without impeding access for those who could not afford to pay high prices—in other words, to achieve price neutrality for the prospective student. In the new market for selective private universities, the mix of tuition and aid reflects the "wage" that highly desirable students can command, irrespective of need.[11] Of course, need-based financial aid remains a large part of the mix; but universities now often pay an additional wage for sought-after students.[12] This situation—and the specter of "ruinous competition"—is precisely what universities originally sought to avoid through voluntary coordination. Perhaps no private research university is likely to be ruined in this way, but the cost of such wages still must be borne. These wages purchase the input that is now most highly valued: high-ability students and the peer effects attributed to them. For all but the wealthiest universities, however, these expenditures must substitute for other inputs to the learning process.

Market coordination has produced another troubling consequence in differential pricing. During the student aid era differential prices were determined by the single criterion of financial need. Now the price a student pays reflects a combination of financial need, merit wages, and how well or poorly she games the system. Prevailing notions of strategic aid or enrollment management justify institutional practices for maximizing the revenue derived from each student.[13] Yet the classic justification for the nonprofit status of educational institutions is asymmetry of information between buyers and sellers. Because consumers cannot adequately monitor the quality of educational services, they prefer dealing with institutions they can trust not to take advantage of them to realize a profit.[14] But maximizing revenue now looks a good deal like making a profit. Private universities now engage in such deceptive practices as awarding less aid to early-admission students or front-loading the first year of aid packages.[15] Students in the aggregate may gain greater wages through these arrangements, but each student must fend for herself. Trust in this relationship can no longer be assumed.

The final negative feature of market coordination has been termed the arms race among selective schools, meaning the tendency to spend ever greater sums ostensibly for educational quality, but more accurately to avoid losing position in the steep institutional hierarchy.[16] This phenomenon has affected the entire selective sector, but for the wealthiest institutions spending has reached seemingly ridiculous levels. For them, surely, the point of diminishing returns to university costs was passed some time ago.

The arms race makes sense for the actors involved, though. For consumers, particularly devoted parents who seek the best possible education for their children, a college cannot offer too much. They are motivated by the prestige of the institution, which depends in turn on its exclusivity. Prestige is presumably enhanced as the bundle of services becomes larger and more lavish. For universities, the admissions process has assumed a higher priority than classroom instruction. The foremost challenge is to enroll the prodigies of those devoted parents in order to sustain and bolster peer effects and status. Hence the imperative to meet or exceed the service bundles offered by their most immediate competitors.

But from a social perspective, the arms race is inefficient or downright wasteful. Educational opportunities for society would be more optimal if high-cost institutions would offer a superior educational experience to far more students. Would not two students being educated for $25,000 per year yield a greater social benefit than one being schooled for $50,000? The question is obviously moot, since the incentives for universities and consumers under market coordination are otherwise—so much so that any institution attempting such a course would be severely penalized by the market.[17]

In sum, the extraordinary expansion of resources for private universities has undoubtedly bolstered quality across the sector, but has especially favored the leaders since the 1990s. Moreover, this growing affluence has been accompanied by greater dependence on wealthy students, erosion of trust as nonprofit fiduciaries, predatory pricing practices, and seemingly unbounded spending to bolster selectivity.

Public Universities

The flagship universities of most states have historically been centrally coordinated. Before the current era almost all their income came from their respective legislatures, and with this support often came directives on how funds were to be spent. Many of these universities operated with considerable autonomy, but their purview extended little beyond their state borders. Their horizons widened with the rise of federally sponsored research after World War II. Large performers of research were less beholden to the state capitol, at least for some departments. Soon, a different form of coordination emerged. Statewide coordination became widespread in the 1970s, in part through federal urging. The major state universities now had to balance various state controls with the open competition of the national research system. These institutions also sought voluntary cooperation among their peers, but central coordination far outweighed the impact of such links. Since 1980, market coordination has increasingly intruded into this mix. For state universities in the twenty-first century, perhaps the biggest challenge has become balancing the forces of central and market coordination.

States support universities in the belief, explicit or implicit, that these institutions generate positive externalities—that they provide social benefits in addition to the private benefits for students, and that in the absence of public support fewer such benefits would be produced.

This premise has engendered a distinctive form of production. State universities are large enough to accommodate substantial numbers of resident students, access must be provided on an equitable basis, and the institution is expected to serve the state economy in ways that go beyond training educated workers. On the whole, universities are remarkably free to determine the academic details. But states are vigilant about enforcing their specific interests. They monitor and sometimes dictate tuition prices, and they frequently insist that sufficient places be reserved for state residents. They typically feel strongly about equity, among students and institutions, sometimes to the point of failing to recognize the special needs of research universities. And, invoking their budgetary authority over appropriations, state legislatures occasionally intervene directly in university operations. For states the basic questions to be addressed are: How much state support should be given? How much should students pay? What level of quality is desirable or affordable, and at which institutions? Remarkably, there are fifty sets of answers.

For state universities the perennial challenge has been to acquire the resources to support a high level of academic quality. Their research roles are coordinated to a large extent by the national research economy, which distributes research funds on a competitive basis. But the academic competitiveness of universities reflects the quality of the personnel and infrastructure at individual institutions, and the willingness of states to make such investments varies enormously. In the 1990s, many states hesitated to support academic quality and occasionally criticized the research role. With the erosion of state support, universities were left to their own devices to augment their spending base. Their alternatives were tuition increases and voluntary support.[18]

A high-tuition strategy became increasingly attractive to public universities as state support faltered during the 1990s, and especially after the recession of 2001. But unlike privates, they could not leverage high tuition with extensive institutional financial aid. Since tuition covered only a portion of cost, education at public universities was substantially underpriced. For most schools, higher prices would have little impact on demand.

State policies nevertheless varied widely. In most states the impulse toward higher in-state tuition collided with state coordination. Where state boards set tuition, as in Arizona, tuition hikes were sometimes rejected in the name of protecting students from "greedy" universities. Some legislatures froze tuition outright, and others imposed deals that linked tuition with appropriations. In all these cases, universities were precluded from charging more nearly what the market would bear.[19] Perhaps one-quarter of public research universities can be placed in the high-tuition category, which for the 2001 academic year meant charges of more than $4,800 for in-state students.[20] These prices represent only one leg of a successful high-tuition strategy.

In order to boost tuition revenues significantly, public universities also need to attract higher-paying out-of-state students. To do this they must enter the national market for undergraduates where, as described for private universities, market power has shifted from universities to students. How can they compete against more affluent private institutions? They start with a price advantage. Tuition for out-of-state students in 2001 was about $10,000 less than at private universities: $12,000 to $15,000 in most cases, with some as low as $10,000 and only Michigan and Colorado approaching private levels. Thus state universities are able to compete in the middle band of tuition pricing. Moreover, most offer some wage or subsidy from their state appropriation. And they have a great deal to offer in terms of quality—but it is configured differently from their more exclusive and homogeneous private competitors.

Market coordination in the private sector was seen to produce vertical differentiation, through selectivity and spending, and horizontal differentiation through special offerings.[21] The typical large state university accomplishes these same effects through internal differentiation. That is, students sort themselves out by college and major to produce more homogeneous groupings of peers. But state universities can no longer assume that high-ability students will matriculate close to home. Traditionally, flagship campuses in most parts of the country laid claim to a large portion of high-achieving students in their states. Now, the advent of student market power has plunged them into qualitative competition in the national marketplace.

The increasing emphasis on capital campaigns and voluntary support plays a crucial role for public universities in this competition. Building endowment for private universities is fundamental to the financing of the institution; but in public universities endowment income tends to be ear-marked for specific qualitative improvements. The income per FTE may be paltry, but it is targeted to produce maximum effects.[22] Capital campaigns typically have focused on attracting better students and better scholars through scholarships (wages), endowed professorships, and new facilities.

Public universities participate to varying degrees in the national market dominated by student power and qualitative competition. In this respect they have become more like private institutions, maximizing tuition revenues through strategic use of financial aid and seeking gifts and endowment to bolster quality. At the same time, they preserve as a base of operations the services traditionally offered to their respective states. The former orientation reflects market coordination, and the latter central coordination, although these forces are weighted differently for each institution.

These divergent tendencies represent an incipient paradox for public universities. Those institutions with sufficient autonomy from state coordination are best able to adapt to the national market by enhancing their quality and competitiveness. Responding to these incentives, however, may detract from their direct service to state citizens. Universities that are hindered from adapting to the national market by state controls may remain focused on their state roles, but will perform them less effectively.

Internal Coordination

The coordination of activities within universities is balanced between the top-down activities of fiscal and administrative control and the bottom-up academic authority of the faculty over teaching, learning, and activities stemming from the university's knowledge base. University administrators, in theory, face the challenge of optimizing three activities: (1) the flow of revenues to the university; (2) the distribution of those revenues among units to accomplish the multiple missions of the institution; and (3) the efficient utilization of those resources by the constituent units. In practice, these tasks are performed serially and incrementally, starting from the existing annual budget and organizational structure.

On the other side, the operating units exemplify the revenue theory of costs. They receive annual allocations of funds that largely define what they can, and often must, spend. External income, such as research grants, is usually designated for specific purposes, and hence by definition must be spent. For units, then, the challenge is to increase revenues, if possible, but particularly to optimize the mix of activities given the income available. The growing influence of the marketplace in the current era has had an impact on both administrative and academic coordination.

By any measure, the capacity of universities for administrative coordination has been extended greatly in the modern era. Management information systems, institutional research, and permanent planning units have all provided administrators with an avalanche of quantitative data about every facet of their institutions. This capacity together with an abundance of organizational theories for improving university performance falls under the rubric of managerialism. A long-standing trend, the growth of managerialism in the current era should have provided academic managers with the tools to rationalize and lead universities into the new century.

Contemporary universities are undoubtedly run more tightly than those of preceding generations, yet managerialism probably deserves little of the credit. Despite inflated claims, universities largely persist in their accustomed state of internal incoherence. That is, managers coordinate the fiscal and administrative structure—chiefly task 2 above. But the real work of the university remains with the knowledge workers and is not easily coordinated by managers (task 3). Moreover, with respect to task 1, the thrust of managerialism has not always been consistent with the market forces that affect university revenues.

Many of the management schemes transposed from business to universities were predicated on the need for cost containment and efficiency, given limited or shrinking revenues.[23] Strategic planning was enthusiastically adopted as a panacea for the fiscal woes of the early 1980s; responsibility-centered management (RCM) was intended to introduce resource-conscious decision-making by operating units; and performance measures promised to introduce greater efficiency. However, these approaches were all implemented at a time when the marketplace was rewarding colleges and universities for spending more, not less, on their students and professors. Of course, universities were not blind to this reality. Private universities especially, and many publics as well, enthusiastically sought to expand revenues; and some fiscal discipline had to be imposed on units through administrative coordination no matter how affluent the institution. But managerialism tended to work at cross purposes with this trend.

Responsibility-centered management provides perhaps the best example of the confusion of managerialsim and markets. Inspired by the ascendancy of market ideology, RCM sought to introduce marketlike incentives at the level of operating units, chiefly by having them earn income through student credit hours. Making academic units responsible for their own income and instituting a system of real prices would create an incentive structure for adaptive behavior, thus encouraging efficiency. By creating an internal market, RCM claimed to shift the locus of coordination from the central administration to the academic units.

Predictably, the first complaint about RCM was the loss of capacity for central leadership. RCM in practice was nothing like a free market where units could control their revenues and expenditures. Rather, it was an administered system with set prices more closely resembling the planned economy of the Soviet Union. Units, as rational actors, tended to engage in strategic behavior. While units had an incentive to reduce costs, this could best be accomplished by minimizing the purchase of university services or ducking university taxes. The greater incentive, however, was to increase revenues. Larger course enrollments were achieved more readily through coercion (required courses) than through qualitative competition. Beyond the administered system, external revenue might also be gained through entrepreneurship.

In either case, results were likely to be different from original expectations. RCM exacerbated internal inequality, facilitated greater spending by affluent units, weakened central leadership, and did nothing to promote quality.[24] It provided a workable framework, one especially congenial to powerful autonomous professional schools, but results scarcely justified the large informational and managerial efforts it demanded.

The idea of using market coordination within universities had several laudable objectives. It sought to decentralize decision-making to the operating units and provide them with incentives for greater effectiveness (in this case defined as raising demand for their services) and efficiency (reducing costs). In any university the effectiveness and efficiency of academic units should be a paramount concern, and one that virtually mandates a substantial degree of local control. However, internal markets take this form of coordination away from academics and concede it to students. Academic coordination, through control of the curriculum, is supposed to structure student learning. In a market based on student demand, student choices will coordinate the curriculum. For example, in any university students may choose to take "gut" courses, but departments do not have an incentive to offer them.[25] Consequently, schemes like RCM probably work best in situations where little competition exists between units (and thus are least marketlike), as has always been true for the Harvard tubs.

More generally, the increasing immersion of universities in external markets tends to work counter to managerial efforts to assert greater control. As market coordination assumes greater importance for institutions, the scope of administrative coordination is likely to diminish.

Enrollment management provides one example. What first appeared to be a managerial technique actually ceded decision-making power to market forces. Enrollment management is intended to manipulate the admissions process in order to optimize financial outcomes. The goal is to enroll the best possible class that will meet a given revenue target. Although a university with surplus applicants would have a certain amount of leeway, at some point in the admissions process the potential income from an admitted student becomes the deciding factor. When this occurs, the market coordinates the admissions process.[26]

The consequences of artificially induced internal market coordination are more perverse than paradoxical. The supposed benefit of greater efficiency is illusory, but far worse is the intent to encourage departments to optimize expenditures rather than academic tasks. Such systems provide little incentive for quality, and even less for cooperation. They promote unwelcome forms of internal competition, as well as encourage the trend toward student consumerism.[27]

Undergraduate Education

Undergraduate education remains the most conspicuous and consequential activity of universities. It was seen that no fewer than four powerful sets of forces contend in this arena: (1) the national admissions market for high-ability and (mostly) affluent entering students; (2) the ascendancy of student consumerism; (3) the critique of teaching at research universities and the attendant advocacy for pedagogical alternatives; and (4) the fundamental values, practices, and dynamics of the academic fields. Each is a complex and perhaps not entirely consistent phenomenon. Each can also be represented at least in part as resulting from market coordination. And largely for that reason, each exerts a vector of influence over developments in undergraduate education.

The national market of prospective students exerts a huge influence on institutions in the selective sector. The financial implications have already been reviewed, but market coordination extends much further. The operation of this market has been described as a queue-and-overflow process.

The most preferred institutions would thus appear to be in enviable positions—and they are. Yet they still have to compete among themselves for the most coveted students. Beyond the top twenty institutions, the pecking order becomes more muddled and the competition more diffuse. Degrees of prestige among these very good institutions depend heavily on the quality of each entering class, which in turn affects the well-being of the university. Under these conditions, the admissions process assumes paramount priority. Of course, only after students matriculate does the real work of the university begin. However, the priority of admission means that certain aspects of that work, such as fashionable academic programs, will be tailored to enhance the admissions profile. Certainly the pressure is great for universities to avoid any actions that might detract from factors that matter in undergraduate admissions.

The influence of the national market has been so pervasive among private universities that the behaviors it has molded might be taken for granted. Its effects stand out more clearly for universities that are closer to the borders of the selective sector. Syracuse University had to invest more heavily in student quality and was rewarded for its sacrifice. A similar investment in students occurred among the private universities of the South as they sought a more diversified, national clientele. The impact of this form of coordination has become increasingly visible among some leading state universities. To attract lucrative out-of-state students from the national market, and to avoid losing home-state talent, they were compelled to compete on similar terms.

Student consumerism and the national market are mutually reinforcing, which can produce disquieting consequences. Consumers, Lindblom points out, "swim in an ocean of information and misinformation." Yet the efficiency of this market depends on the intelligence of their choice.[28] Students begin choosing a college by narrowing the multitude of choices down to some semblance of a manageable list. Prospective students may include schools for bizarre reasons at this stage. Most important for institutions is the cultivation of a "brand name" to increase the likelihood that students will give them serious consideration. At the next stage, prospective students exhibit considerable rational behavior in identifying and matching their own goals with institutional capabilities; and they are sensitive to whether an institution is a likely route to postgraduate educational or career aspirations.

Students also manifest price sensitivity, especially when personal loans are at stake. The proclivity of students to seek the most selective college that would have them is economically rational according to the Hoxby model.[29] And most high-ability students choose a research university; but many institutions can usually fulfill such criteria. When it comes to choosing among these worthy alternatives, other consumer desires may intrude. Here amenities and activities become significant factors in quality competition. And since they play a salient role in all-important final decisions, they become part of the arms race as well. However, consumerism may play a more dubious role in the curriculum.

Critics and reformers sometimes promote the idea that students are the customers of colleges and universities and ought to be treated accordingly. Traditionalists try to deflect this notion by pointing out that students should be regarded as clients. What is the difference?

In retail trades the well-worn motto holds that "the customer is always right"; but clients seek professional services in the belief that professionals are "right" and provide valuable services with their expertise. Universities have traditionally accorded control over the curriculum to the faculty with the understanding that it knew best what students ought to learn. Scarcely a hard-and-fast principle, this matter has been negotiated ever since the elective system displaced the classical course at the end of the nineteenth century. In the current era, however, the market power of students has consistently shifted the balance in the direction of "customers."

In the period preceding the current era, student power and administrative appeasement loosened the curriculum by eliminating required courses, attenuating the threat of failure, and permitting courses demanded by student activists. The beginning of the current era actually witnessed curricular stiffening as some past excesses were rectified and as universities, in keeping with their growing selectivity, sought to project images of academic excellence.

But the pervasive market power of students continued to transform the curriculum from within. As student satisfaction became a more highly valued goal, the assumed forms of student expression became more consequential. Student course evaluations, for example, which can provide useful feedback to instructors, were incorporated into assessments of faculty job performance. Factors such as student retention became performance indicators that might have budgetary impacts. RCM, as mentioned, allowed students to vote for school budgets with their course elections. When students objected to actual course content, as in the protests against Western heritage and material written by "dead European white males," they often had their way.

Perhaps the most pervasive changes were least visible: universities became increasingly averse to the traditional negative sanctions of college—not just bad grades and the threat of failure, but everyday matters like mandatory attendance, pop quizzes, and comprehensive final examinations. Grade inflation, whatever else its cause, is consistent with this reluctance to coerce, as opposed to cajole, effort from students. Academic traditionalists have long and loudly deplored such trends. The highly selective schools, in contrast, find these concerns to be minor or irrelevant to their model for undergraduate education.

The ideal in the selective sector is to assemble a relatively homogeneous (but demographically diverse!) class of bright, well-prepared, energetic, and highly motivated achievers. Such students may be trusted to respond enthusiastically to the rich educational opportunities arrayed before them. The positive pull of intellectual interests, stimulated by teachers, fellow students, and structured activities, will guide their learning. Negative sanctions? A gentle prod perhaps for those temporarily disoriented (all these schools offer extensive psychological services); but this is a model of positive inducements for students who are ready and eager to learn. And it is not caricature.

At the most selective colleges and universities, students who are carefully chosen to behave in this way by and large seem to do so.[30] However, the distribution of ideal students is a market phenomenon. As one descends the pecking order for universities (and the rest of higher education) student bodies on the whole possess relatively less brightness, preparation, energy, and motivation. As these qualities attenuate at the margins, the impact of student consumerism becomes incrementally more pernicious. Student consumerism, on balance, detracts from student learning even as universities seek formal measures to bolster it.

The critique of undergraduate education emanated from self-appointed spokesmen rather than market forces, but over time its effects became assimilated with student consumerism. The original impact of the critique brought pressure for outcomes assessment and performance measures—in essence, forms of administrative coordination. In the main, such metrics were influenced more strongly by the quality of the students than by how they were being educated, as the critics implied.

Universities nevertheless undertook a corrective process to address alleged weaknesses. These steps probably improved student satisfaction, if not academic performance. When it came to enhancement, however, public universities in particular were compelled by the market to bolster their tarnished images and compete more effectively for talented undergraduates. The reforms that ensued—honors programs, living-learning arrangements, undergraduate research—all held promise of appealing to high-ability students and specifically enriching *their* learning. The consequence of such programs was seldom acknowledged: greater internal differentiation in the treatment of students.

Despite a disparity in resources, it should probably not be assumed that the benefits conferred on this talented minority detract from the educational experience of the majority. Still, in the age of student consumerism it has become monumentally difficult to impose any requirement on the entire student body. Curricular initiatives are presented instead as choices. These developments suggest that even pedagogical reform tends to find the path of least resistance—a form of market coordination resulting from individual adaptation.

This last pattern appeared in somewhat different form in the experiences of "student-centered research universities." The market forces to be contended with in these cases were those that confer faculty distinction and academic standing. Proponents of student-centeredness attacked the value of research and advocated changing faculty reward structures, as if an individual institution could defy the forces that coordinated the systemic distribution of academic prestige. Thus from the outset, student-centered universities experienced deep contradictions.

At Syracuse University, research and academic standing were consciously sacrificed to the new image and its fiscal demands. Unable to compete in the markets for both students and research, it opted to invest in students. After the university was restructured, however, it became apparent that academic distinction would have to be rebuilt for the institution to attain the prestige it sought among its peers.

At Arizona the initial fiscal situation was not so dire, and the university sought to become student-centered without eroding its reputation for research. Walking this tightrope was nevertheless a trying experience. Arizona at best sustained its position in the markets for both students and research, without advancing in either. And it failed to mollify its external detractors.

Market coordination of undergraduate education has probably risen as precipitously as tuition, but with paradoxical results. The increasing segregation of undergraduates by ability level has largely worked in favor of research universities. Some universities have appreciably raised the quality of undergraduate entrants in the current era, and all have probably made marginal improvements. This matching of better students with richer educational settings should work to the advantage of both. At the same time, the admissions market and powerful accompanying cultural trends have accentuated student consumerism throughout American higher education. The consequence is diminished influence of institutions over student learning and an underlying anti-intellectual drift. Ironically, this situation has frustrated attempts to force improvements in student learning through administrative coordination.

Markets for Research

Academic research constitutes an administered market with unique characteristics. When viewed as a part of national R&D, it dominates the subsector for basic research. In this market, university scientists are the sellers of research; outside funders are the purchasers. The service for sale—research—is priced at cost, direct costs in this case being defined by conventions, with a mark-up allowed for indirect costs. The crucial element in these transactions is the quality of the research proffered. Purchasers seek to maximize the quality of the investigations they support; scientists compete for this support chiefly on the basis of the quality of the research they propose.

The research market is beautifully efficient. It is nationally integrated, with units of the federal government independently purchasing 60 percent of research. At the same time it is highly decentralized, with no unit buying more than a small portion (2 percent) of the total. Buyers and sellers know one another extremely well, exchanging visits, attending the same meetings, and cooperating in evaluations. There is considerable latitude for negotiations between the parties over the terms of work. Forms of contracting are flexible as well.

Agencies that wish to advance a scientific field typically invite investigator-initiated proposals. Those with predilections for the direction research should follow issue "requests for proposals" that specify those interests. Funders seeking research on particular topics can draft appropriate contracts with university scientists. Each arrangement represents a different combination of buyer interests and seller interests. By mutual adjustment these complementary goals are fulfilled. At the end of the day (or fiscal year) the market clears. The highest quality and most apposite academic research is supported by the funds available for these purposes.

Academic scientists who endure the tribulations of grantsmanship may regard this process as neither beautiful nor efficient (although many would). The continual preparation and evaluation of proposals represents a kind of friction consuming (although not entirely wasting) scientific energy. Other kinds of difficulties arise. The 1990s witnessed occasional examples of fraud; problems of secrecy or vested interest; a congressional penchant for pork-barrel funding; and as always, criticism of peer review.[31] However, the indignation with which these matters are aired is testimony that the system rests on a solid foundation of strongly held normative values. The market for academic research has not only effectively coordinated the distribution of academic research over half a century; it has also shaped American universities.

University accommodations to the research market go much further than the offices that report to the vice president for research. Basic operations have been adapted to the requirements of sponsored research. Teaching schedules, for example, are malleable enough to permit professors receiving grants to buy out courses, in effect privileging externally supported research over instruction. More fundamental is the development of the autonomous research role, most conspicuous in organized research units (ORUs), but generated by the demand for more or different research than can be provided through joint production. The current era brought significant alterations in the relationship of the university to the academic research market.

Research in this set of universities more than doubled in the 1980s and 1990s while the academic core grew by barely 10 percent. This change in the balance of university activity was brought about by a significant expansion of autonomous research, but also by enhanced productivity from the academic core. Specifically, a significant number of middle- and lower-rated universities advanced toward optimal levels of research activity. Intuitively, one can envision such a change, but the notion of optimum begs a more precise definition.

In a 1972 paper on tuition pricing, economist Marc Nerlove incidentally proposed a model of possible trade-offs between research and graduate education on one hand and undergraduate instruction on the other. He hypothesized that at the extremes (nearly all teaching or all research) the alternate activity could be obtained cost-free as a by-product of the primary activity. In between those extremes, teaching and research were substitutes, although at varying price ratios. And at some point the marginal cost of the two activities would be equal:

> Thus, if society subsidizes the higher education sector to produce research in a socially optimal way, the sector will always operate at a point . . . where teaching and research are substitutes in the sense

that for a given level of resources devoted to higher education more research [and graduate education] can only be obtained by providing fewer undergraduate educational services, and conversely.[32]

Nerlove was not referring to anything as tangible as faculty time. Rather, he posited research and undergraduate education measured in "quality-adjusted units," so that the amount of either represented some combination of quality and quantity. Although he envisioned an optimum for society, the same principle might be applied to a university, a department, or a single faculty member. In fact, universities routinely and intuitively make such adjustments, and they apparently have done so to adjust the balance of activities in the current era.[33]

This process presupposes certain conditions. Research subsidies and also research students are scarce goods, rationed according to academic quality. The ability to perform valuable research is in scarce supply as well. It is doubtful that the average faculty member operates at a point where greater value could be had by substituting research for teaching.

However, after 1980 conditions in this research market changed. Universities for the most part were able to enlarge their core costs, placing more resources at their disposal. The abundance of well-qualified Ph.D.s made faculty appointments opportunities for improvement. And social subsidies for research were rapidly rising. Universities were able to displace less-productive faculty researchers with more-productive ones; and funds were available to support their research. These universities had the capacity and the opportunity to move toward a mix of activities with relatively greater research. This movement was evident in the dispersion of academic research as well as in the average improvement in academic ratings. But what happens when an institution approaches its optimal balance, where the marginal value of each activity is the same?

An optimal mix for a high-quality institution would imply that units of undergraduate education were also quite valuable. At this point, research should not be increased in relative terms because it would then be more costly than instruction. Research might still be increased by expanding the academic core, but doing that would require adding similarly valued units of undergraduate education. Given the inelasticity of that market, universities were loath to increase enrollments.[34] Most were content to maintain a stable academic core. Optimality in this sense is a wonderful condition, but it discourages further development. These considerations, however, do not affect autonomous research.

Centers and institutes, and medical schools too, have important links with the academic core. They exist to some extent because external patrons wish to connect with university scientists. And their volume of research depends more on external than on internal factors. Thus MIT saw its research share shrink as large defense research projects were phased out; and the University of Colorado gained research share as its federal centers were enlarged.

In general, state universities feel a greater obligation than privates to provide the kinds of services that much of this research entails. Outside of medicine, the largest performers of research are public universities with numerous autonomous ORUs. For private universities, medical research has provided the chief form of autonomous research, which could be expanded without affecting optimal conditions in the academic core. Hence the observed pattern of stable academic cores and burgeoning expenditures for medical research. Universities faced variable inducements to participate in the research market, and these had consequences for supply, demand, and costs.

When academic research was under siege by its critics in the early 1990s, it was sometimes alleged that sponsored research actually cost universities more than the revenues brought in. Never mind that research was a mission of these universities; if it could be shown (or not disproved) that student fees were subsidizing research for sponsors, the institutions would indeed be embarrassed.

This issue prompted evaluation specialist Lawrence Mohr to attempt to determine all of the impacts of sponsored research on universities using available empirical data, and thus to simulate issues that universities face in deciding to pursue such support.[35] The study was significant for what it did not find. No discernible effects from federal grants were detected on student tuition or expenditures for instruction. Nor was any impact found on endowment growth, voluntary support, or the quality of incoming undergraduates. Data indicated that research grants did have a positive influence where it might be most expected: faculty quality and working conditions, professional standing (National Research Council ratings), and quality of incoming graduate students.

More speculatively, Mohr concluded that the impact would be positive on the content of undergraduate learning and graduate teaching. In sum, the spillovers from sponsored research were all positive: better faculty, greater prestige, stronger graduate education, and possibly more effective undergraduate teaching as well. Other factors, most importantly costs, appeared unaffected. Mohr thus provided a rational explanation for the observed behavior of universities in the current era: important incentives existed, especially for suboptimal producers, to increase participation in sponsored research. This factor has likely affected the balance of supply and demand in the market for academic research.

In light of the robust growth in the social consumption of academic research, one might on first impression conclude that social demand was the dominant factor in this market. In addition, as just seen, private universities have had good reason to resist or moderate any expansion of research capacity in their academic cores. But given the attractiveness of research for universities, it seems more likely that supply has on the whole exceeded demand.

Judging by effects, market forces appear to have worked to the advantage of consumers. In the case of industry, proactive policies by universities increased their share of industry-sponsored research beginning in the mid-1980s.[36] Liberal government subsidies also encouraged industrial consumption of academic research. In the case of federal grants, marginal decreases occurred during the 1990s in the price paid for research. Some agencies, particularly the National Science Foundation, asked universities to assume greater matching and cost-sharing obligations; and all paid lower indirect cost rates after 1991.[37] Most important, ample research capacity among universities stimulated greater competition.

One effect of increased competition should be to raise prices of key inputs. There is naturally a reciprocal relationship between spending power and the ability to bid up inputs, but most universities seem to have devoted greater resources (paid higher prices) to secure additional research funds. Most telling, the funds that universities themselves devote to separately budgeted research have been the most rapidly rising expenditure category in the current era. The proportion of these funds rose by about one-third, with most of the jump coming in the 1980s.[38]

Competition for faculty who bring in abundant grant support has been keen, but difficult to quantify. Some professorial "stars" are hired more for celebrity and brand-name enhancement than for prowess in research. Still, there can be little doubt that the price of hiring or keeping prolific researchers has risen disproportionately. Typically, private universities have led in the salary wars, while public universities have allocated far more of their own funds to sponsored research.

The competition for faculty spills over into a demand for facilities. Start-up costs for new faculty in the sciences have far outpaced salary costs and now routinely reach seven figures. Facilities may well be the most costly university input factor for maintaining competitiveness. The construction and renovation of research space is an ongoing process. Such spending peaked at the end of the 1980s, and that level was surpassed by another surge at the end of the 1990s.[39]

Research has become more expensive for universities in the current era, but more valuable too. Universities, on balance, have expanded the quantity of research they perform, its salience in their mix of activities, and its value to society. This could not have occurred if research were solely a joint product with teaching; more than ever it has become an autonomous role and a separate output. As such, research interacts at times in awkward ways with other university roles. Universities nevertheless face strong incentives to make substantial investments in their research role, above all because the payoffs are greatest to those who do it best.

Economic Development

No one can doubt that universities make substantial contributions to the economy. First and foremost, they create human capital through the transfer of knowledge and skills to students. Human capital makes graduates more productive in their occupations, and the returns to society are greater than the returns to individuals themselves. The second great contribution of universities is the creation of new knowledge through research. A third contribution, grown prominent in the current era, is technology development: specifically, the mobilization of university expertise to advance or create new technology. Fourth, one could cite the many services that universities offer, including direct technical assistance, agricultural extension, and continuing education.[40]

Each university produces a unique combination of these benefits. Although these benefits accrue to government, nonprofit organizations, and private industry, university assistance to industry has been most explicitly linked with economic growth. In the age of privatization, the litmus test for university involvement with the economy has been developing technology for the private sector.

Academic research and industrial R&D are two enormous subsystems of the national research economy with a fairly small area of overlap. For that reason the economic forces governing their interaction have been difficult to specify. Industry largely draws on academic expertise to enhance the efficacy of its own internal R&D. Knowledge gained in this way constitutes an intermediate good, without intrinsic value, that the firm hopes will contribute to the development of marketable products. Consumption of such an uncertain commodity is naturally highly variable. It depends on the universities' eagerness to sell, industry's preference for vendors, and especially the nature of the industry. All these factors favored a growing volume of research after 1980.

The knowledge supplied in this enhancement role represents a positive spillover from the production of academic knowledge.[41] Firms pay for access to this knowledge through grants and contracts, but these transactions are priced at marginal cost. The direct costs calculated in university research agreements are literally marginal costs, and ICR represents only a small additional increment. Because the actual (or average) costs of creating and sustaining academic knowledge are far greater, industry benefits from this spillover.

Universities, for their part, have been eager to sell more research at these prices in order to enhance their knowledge-creating activity and cover a portion of their sunk costs. As universities sought greater collaboration, industry found it advantageous to purchase more research, particularly at favorable prices. Moreover, the appearance of new research technologies enlarged areas of interaction between the two subsystems.

This latter development, in particular, stimulated a second source of spillover. Academic research increasingly made discoveries of tangible value, sufficiently developed to foreshadow an ultimate product. Discoveries of this sort had always emerged from university research, but infrequently and unexpectedly. The new involvement with research technologies increased the odds. Biotechnology is the famous example. And the presence or likelihood of valuable inventions prompted universities to make accommodations that would continue to capture and enhance these spillovers.

Adopting this opportunistic strategy could have been expected. Spillovers, Lindblom notes, "represent gains that could be enlarged by parties to the transaction." Failure to do so constitutes "opportunities wasted?"[42]

The technology transfer architecture erected (largely) in the 1980s was specifically intended to seize these opportunities. Several kinds of outcomes were foreseen. Universities hoped that the establishment of research parks, as well as other encouragement of research for industry, would enlarge research relations with industry, primarily for enhancement. Their explicit strategies were often vague, with propinquity perhaps being most prominent; and some expected that greater interaction with firms would somehow stimulate a second objective of technology development. To accomplish this on more than an occasional basis, however, required dedicated internal organizations—ORUs.

Universities were greatly assisted in this respect by the common interest of the states and federal government in technology development. The subsidies they provided created cooperative university-industry research centers focused on technology development in a targeted area. The outputs were somewhere in between enhancement of industrial R&D and the creation of new products, but the subsidized price made participation attractive for industry.

A third source of spillover to universities was the expectation of technology transfer itself. This process encompassed two related challenges: moving innovations from the academic laboratory to the marketplace and appropriating some portion of the value created. The organization of technology transfer offices (TTOs), business incubators, and in-house venture capital funds each addressed different pieces of this puzzle. These units aid the transformation of discoveries made in universities into intellectual property and eventual products. At most universities their operations begin with and rely heavily on the uncertain procedure of invention disclosures. The efficiency and efficacy of this triad of TTOs, incubators, and venture capitalists determine to a large extent how much of the potential value spillover can be captured by the institution. The role of the TTO in garnering disclosures and evaluating them for patenting and licensing is the key, but the proper capitalizing and nurturing of start-ups is also critical for inventions following that route.[43]

The rationalizing of university-industry research relationships has thus been a distinctive feature of the current era, and these formal arrangements have largely succeeded in capturing some degree of spillover. Universities have greatly enlarged the volume of the traditional research performed for industry to the benefit of both parties; and universities are now well prepared to take advantage of the decreasingly serendipitous occurrence of inventions in their laboratories. However, in the spirit of Lindblom's injunction, why should universities stop there? Why not seize more opportunities and realize greater gains? In effect, at least some universities have been doing precisely that, following this logic toward increasing commercialization. There are two paths toward this destination, one that emphasizes technology development, and another, in biotechnology, that focuses on patenting. Each would seem to have different implications for American universities.

The logic of commitment to economic development has drawn universities toward the role of technology innovation or development. Sustained technology development requires more than single grants or stand-alone centers. Rather, it presupposes the kind of dense networks that exist in agglomerations and that include participants at all levels of the creative process. Efficient mechanisms are also needed for moving innovations through the pipeline from discovery to patenting to commercialization. Such arrangements seem to demand a separate organization, or set of organizations, to accomplish these specialized tasks. These requirements pose a fundamental question for universities. When universities were induced to perform research above and beyond the scope of their teaching infrastructure, they responded by creating an autonomous research role. Is it possible for universities similarly to develop an autonomous role for technology development and transfer—a kind of enterprise zone within the university?

Georgia's Yamacraw Project, particularly at Georgia Tech, may represent the best model of such a development. An examination of its structure reveals the exacting requirements of such an undertaking. Financially, the project was launched by an enormous commitment of state funds specifically linked with job creation. Public subsidies would seem to be indispensable for supporting technology development, even though the ultimate objective may be a self-sustaining unit. Industry, which pays the full cost of its internal technology development, tends to contribute nominal amounts to participate in consortia. Organizationally, Yamacraw is embedded in a superstructure of state and Georgia Tech units. This complex structure is actually an asset, guaranteeing its autonomous status within the university. The structure also provides for the effective disposition of intellectual property through the channels already developed by Georgia Tech. Academically, by funding and appointing Yamacraw professors, the project created faculty who were committed from the outset to the role of technology development. Elsewhere, it might prove difficult to persuade professors already overburdened with teaching and research to dedicate time for technology as well. The essence of an autonomous technology role is the network interaction of university and industry scientists, which, however fruitful, still demands faculty time.

The Centennial Campus at NC State has approximated an autonomous technology role with a somewhat different formula. Although assisted by the state, the campus has not been financed by direct subsidies. Instead, it has pursued networking through design and organization. In this respect, the organizational superstructure has played a crucial role in facilitating collaboration and technology transfer. The faculty culture at NC State has apparently reinforced the commitment of significant time and effort to working with industry, at least among the faculty on the new campus.

Powerful trends are impelling universities toward commitments to autonomous technology development, but relatively few campuses are yet in a position to embrace this role. Superficially, it may appear that the potential revenues from commercialization are the foremost inducement, but that is not true. The big money from patent licenses, and probably start-ups too, is in biotechnology; and there a different dynamic is at work. Outside of the life sciences the principal incentive for universities comes from economic development rather than, commercialization per se. Public funds to subsidize economic development, and to leverage private contributions, are far more valuable for building university resources than licensing revenues or equity in start-ups. Economic development represents a social contribution that is consistent with—in fact one facet of—the university's larger economic role. Commercialization is inherently connected with this role, but the cash nexus is more muted and more in line with normal patterns of small business entrepreneurship.

The path from academic research to technology development to commercialization follows a different route in biotechnology. First, universities are largely assured of aggregate research funding. The massive investment from the NIH and other supporters of biomedical research guarantees that the seedbeds of future technology will be assiduously cultivated. Second, patenting tends to precede rather than follow technology development. This is a subtle distinction, but one that fundamentally affects the life sciences.

In engineering and the physical sciences, patentable inventions tend to emerge from intensive research in laboratories that were created and designed for technology development. Inventions are in fact the expected outcomes, and the labs proceed from that point to licensing them and then developing practical applications. Patents in biotechnology are more likely to result from basic academic research. In the spirit of DNA pioneers Cohen and Boyer, biologists have a powerful incentive to patent the most basic processes, as soon as possible. This phenomenon amounts to *jackpot patenting:* the most lucrative biotech patents assert ownership over processes that have become essential to subsequent technologies. There is no relationship between the time and intellectual effort expended or the capital invested and the blockbuster earnings generated by a few lucky patents. As a consequence of jackpot patenting, the crucial stage of technology development follows the establishment of a patent, usually outside the university.

So the third major difference in biotechnology is that discoveries in academic laboratories tend to be developed in start-up firms or licensed to corporate laboratories. Thus the university has little role to play in technology development, and certainly no need to establish special university centers and an autonomous technology role. However, universities and their TTOs must act deftly to capture some of this value.

Again in contrast to other technologies, commercialization in biotechnology will occur whether or not the university claims its share or assists in the process. But the university is scarcely irrelevant. Life scientists depend on their universities to make continuing investments in the research technologies that propel these advancements. Genomics institutes and similar installations have received the highest priorities for facilities construction. But these scientific facilities are aimed at maintaining cutting-edge research and are not specifically dedicated to technology development.

The commercialization of university research at the dawn of the twenty-first century would seem to possess an inexorable momentum. Under the guise of economic development it carries the cachet of rendering public service. The form it has assumed in the life sciences is hitched to biocapitalism and beyond academic control. Those who fear the potential threat to disinterested inquiry must contend with the depressing spectacle of universities selling all manner of goods and services—their brand names, athletics, entertainment, real estate developments, executive MBAs—not to mention academic disdain for the very notion of disinterestedness. Clearly this is squishy ground on which to oppose the commercialization of research.[44] But are there more solid reasons for concern?

From the perspective of spillover benefits, as just presented, a case can be made for some degree of commercialization. If universities are producing knowledge with tangible value, who should reap the benefits? Surely universities should be entitled to some portion of that value. In a dynamic perspective, this argument becomes far more compelling. By making valuable knowledge more widely available, universities perform a public service, but one that consumes resources and requires compensation. A flow of commercial revenues then both enhances the amount of pubic service and enlarges the university's knowledge resources.[45] Moreover, the university's research role would seem to demand an extension into emerging research technologies that straddle the academic and commercial realms. University leadership in basic research depends on such growth, which can only be sustained through links with commercial users. Continued involvement with commercial markets, including the generation of revenue, will likely be a permanent facet of research universities, but caveats remain.

Critics have good reason to sense an incompatibility between the basic missions of instruction and research and the commercialization of knowledge. But these concerns for the reasons just stated, are unlikely to impede this phenomenon. More likely they represent normative standards that have constrained commercialization and will probably continue to do so.

The first caveat is the incongruity of nonprofit universities making profits. It is not a matter of profit per se—nonprofits are only barred from distributing profits. They must, and do, plow any surpluses back into the enterprise. Rather, a murky area surrounds the private individuals and companies that reap benefits from commercialization. What is economic development for a social scientist is profit for an entrepreneur. But private profits are derived in this case from publicly subsidized activities. Public universities in particular (because of the use of public funds) would prefer to obscure the fact that commercialization of technology brings wealth to a few. They risk the appearance of conflict of interest, and possibly the real thing.

The second caveat derives from the limitations of the academic core. As remarked throughout this study, nonacademic activities have grown out of all proportion to the academic core, and commercialization promises to increase this lopsidedness. The question has already been raised whether faculty would accept technology transfer as an additional mission. Striking an optimal balance between teaching and research has been an academic conundrum; adding technology transfer as another responsibility would compound these difficulties. As a case in point, one factor that plagued the ill-fated ventures to create on-line universities was the problem of defining the role of faculty and compensating them. The additional duties associated with such endeavors do not easily fit into the existing structure of faculty work.[46] Of course, pundits have prophesied the reinvention of the university to make it more compatible with these "inevitable" realities. Until that happens, the nature and coherence of the academic core will remain a constraint on unbridled commercialization.

And third, much the same could be said of the basic university mission of advancing and disseminating knowledge. The preeminence of the American university, as well as the synergistic activities that threaten to engulf it, all stem from the primacy of this commitment. This mission is lodged above all in the faculty, their expertise, behavior, and roles. In order for learning to be primary in the university, it must also be foremost in the motivation of the faculty. This mainspring requires a degree of insulation from commercialism. It also requires a continuous investment by universities in the learning of their faculty.

University patrons also play an important role in supporting and validating the commitment to disinterested knowledge, providing a very heavy counterweight, in effect, to the pull of commercial markets. Ultimately, the unique qualities of the American university as a center of learning generate the knowledge and expertise sought by the commercial realm. Commercial relations, should they become too dominant, would tend to corrode the very qualities responsible for producing those results. At the beginning of the twenty-first century an appropriate balance still held. But for universities that have shown themselves to be increasingly influenced by market forces, how long is this balance likely to endure?

The Paradox of the Marketplace

Time was when American universities were valued chiefly for the public good they engendered. Support from governments and philanthropy reflected an appreciation of those social benefits and was not intended to "coordinate" university behavior. Rather, institutions were accorded considerable freedom to determine how best to fulfill their role. Students were presumed to have earned the right to attend through merit and hard work. Universities tended to occupy well-understood niches in the system of higher education. Competition was relegated to the playing fields. Markets were an alien realm. But that was not the Golden Age of universities: the Golden Age is now.

Conditions have changed in higher education, and changed decisively in the current era. For universities in the twenty-first century none of those former traits prevail. The intangible social returns to higher education have been overshadowed by the private benefits attained by students and other consumers.

With private benefits predominating, the costs of universities have steadily shifted from public to private sources. Privatization has not merely been fiscal; it has also meant that revenue streams are now more closely linked with university functions, limiting the discretion of university leaders.

Competition has also become keener, driven by the increased reliance on private revenues and, more fundamentally, by the national integration of the university system. The competition for students has bred consumerism—a reversal of attitude from students as clients, fortunate to attend, to students as customers who must be pleased. In all these areas, coordination of behavior has migrated from within universities to the markets governing these activities.

Prosperity has not come without a price. The intent of this study has been to gauge the dimensions of these developments, understand the forces at work, and fathom the consequences.

The current era has brought a revolution in the financing of universities. Private universities, capitalizing on federal and institutional financial aid, established a system of differential tuition that allowed them to escalate prices with minimal resistance. Public universities compensated for the slow growth in state funding by following their lead, nearly doubling the proportion of their costs derived from students. As these trends accelerated, competition intensified for the students who were best prepared for university study and best able to pay for it.

Growing market coordination in this case produced three social consequences. First, the total resources garnered by universities grew impressively. Per-student spending rose by 62 percent at public universities and more than double that at privates. It is difficult to imagine another scenario that might have brought universities a similar augmentation of resources.

Second, market forces brought greater inequality among universities. Most notably, private universities dramatically outpaced their public counterparts. But within the private sector, disparities grew as well, as the top institutions enjoyed unparalleled prosperity. Inequality in the public sector actually declined in the 1980s, but the cause was greater state appropriations for laggard institutions, not the market. When privatization became more pronounced in the 1990s, inequality among public universities increased as well.

Third, the development of a more pronounced institutional hierarchy was accompanied by greater social stratification among students. This too is a market phenomenon. A policy of high-tuition/high-aid requires large numbers of students who can afford high tuition. However, this trend was exacerbated by the selectivity sweepstakes. The differential returns to selective schools were both a social fact and a self-fulfilling prophecy. That is, graduates of selective schools on average appear to achieve higher career earnings, but as this datum was publicized it increased both the attractiveness of these universities to students and their use as a screening device by employers. Highly competitive admissions placed a premium on preparation, favoring students from more privileged backgrounds and the cumulative advantage they possess. Merit in American higher education has a pronounced social gradient.

That said, American higher education in the current era has become more stratified by academic ability than ever before. The market forces that produced this result acted with particular power on both students and institutions. The emergence of a single national market for selective higher education has largely been responsible for the fine gradations of merit among students at selective institutions.

For institutions, each additional increment of selectivity has meant greater prestige and affluence. For that reason, the battle for high-ability students intensifies each year, not only with growing amounts of merit aid but also in conflicts over the rules of engagement.[47] Universities, ironically, have endeavored mightily to exempt some portion of entering classes from their own ruthless standards with special criteria based on race, ethnicity, or hardship. Social implications aside, the meritocratic stratification of American higher education has brought universities the most highly qualified students they have ever had. Moreover, matching the students best equipped to learn with institutions having the greatest learning resources is an efficient social outcome in itself.

Market coordination through the seeming irrationality of the selectivity sweepstakes has yielded a rational and efficient result. Another consequence is perhaps less welcome. Competition in the admissions market has contributed substantially to the ascendancy of student consumerism. Universities may have attracted the most capable students in their history, but in the process they have ceded some control over their learning.

An entirely different form of market coordination prevails in the research system. This administered market rigorously enforces standards of academic excellence through the predominance of peer-reviewed research grants. As a greater number of universities participated more actively in the research system in the current era, academic standards tended to rise. Universities faced strong inducements to participate because research contributed to enhancing prestige, enlarging resources, improving graduate education, and multiplying benefits to society.

But the resources needed to engage in research were by their nature in scarce supply. The competitive market for talented researchers and state-of-the-art research facilities determined which universities acquired how much research funding from the administered market. Most universities were able to expand their capacity for research during the current era.

The expansiveness of their actions in this market contrasted markedly with the strategy of increasing the selectivity rather than the size of undergraduate programs. This discrepancy meant that much of the growth in academic research occurred outside of core departments as part of an autonomous research role. Although the increasing ratio of researchers to faculty is a disconcerting trend, their separation from departmental structures may have been an important ingredient for success. Academic research proved quite effective at accommodating and incorporating the evolving demands for new knowledge. In doing so, academic research became more integrated with the economy and a more productive contributor to economic growth. That development brought a new set of market relationships.

The economic contributions of academic research have been a notable achievement of universities in the current era. Moreover, the coordinating effects of this portion of the research market, despite fears, have done little to destabilize the larger research enterprise. One reason is the predominance of the academic standards enforced by the administered research market. Another is the prominence of research technologies, which allow university scientists to pursue basic research that has a high probability of subsequent economic relevance.

A thicket of commercial activities has grown downstream from these research activities, as universities have responded to incentives to transfer technology to industry and to take their cut in the process. But on balance these activities have had a relatively minor impact on the research process itself. The weight of evidence about the nature of university-industry research relationships suggests that commercialization and its temptations continue to be largely compartmentalized. The risk here seems manageable, especially in relation to the benefits. Involvement with industry and with commercially relevant technologies has brought substantial additional resources to universities and has resulted in substantial returns to society in the form of new technologies.

Market relationships have the capacity to produce great wealth and to promote efficiency through the combination of incentives and free choice. The accentuation of market relationships among American universities since 1980 has done all of these things. Market relationships also generate negative outcomes or externalities, and this has been true in higher education as well.

Just as capitalist markets generate wealth inequality in the economy, the working of market forces in higher education has exaggerated wealth inequalities among universities. The wealth of some private universities is devoted both to wise, knowledge-enhancing investments and to wasteful competition. Other universities lack the resources to realize their potential. Consumer sovereignty exacerbates this situation, creating a kind of winner-take-all phenomenon typical of mass markets. Greater social stratification, furthermore, is the ineluctable result of colleges competing for preferred students and students competing for preferred colleges.

Markets, when unimpeded, have a tendency to exploit all the inherent possibilities—to drive good fortune to excess and thereby jeopardize the accomplishment itself. The differential pricing system for private higher education seems to have done just that. By exploiting federal and institutional aid to maximize net tuition income, private institutions pushed nominal prices to stratospheric levels. The greater the overpricing, the more precarious these arrangements become. Specifically, these artificial prices are vulnerable to the depredations of merit aid, increased competition from public institutions, fluctuations in the prosperity of the upper middle class, or changes in their taste in colleges. The same constellation of forces now motivates state universities to rectify their relative underpricing by raising tuition. Here a different set of externalities arises, as quality higher education for state residents becomes more expensive and exclusive. The worries about commercialization reflect a similar process. If universities were to exploit commercial possibilities to their fullest, the nature of the institution would indeed be altered and its contribution to society impaired.

The results of coordination through market systems are also affected by imperfections. Most of the markets in higher education discussed here may be decentralized and fairly competitive, but embedded in each is the heavy hand of government. The federal government chiefly administers the markets for research, and the states still provide three of every five dollars of general funds at state universities. Moreover, governments provide the bulk of the funds for student financial aid. And wherever economic development is invoked, public funds are sure to be found. In these latter cases, public funding has been supplied in ways that encouraged or incorporated market mechanisms. But forms of coordination shaped by artificial prices will always be sensitive to fluctuations in the levels and conditions of subsidization.

Hence the paradox of the marketplace for American universities: the marketplace has, on balance, brought universities greater resources, better students, a far larger capacity for advancing knowledge, and a more productive role in the U.S. economy. At the same time, it has diminished the sovereignty of universities over their own activities, weakened their mission of serving the public, and created through growing commercial entanglements at least the potential for undermining their privileged role as disinterested arbiters of knowledge.

The gains have been for the most part material, quantified, and valuable; the losses intangible, unmeasured, and at some level invaluable. The consequences of the university's immersion in the marketplace are thus incommensurate. In the near term, no doubt, the tangible payoffs from these markets will prove greater than the intangible dangers. Nevertheless, increasing market coordination of universities should not be construed as a prescription for unceasing material gains. The markets that have shaped American universities were contrived by human rather than invisible hands. And what succeeded in one era, if left unchanged, has a strong likelihood of failing in the next.

The health of these national treasures will depend in the future, as it has in the past, on continual adjustment to changing conditions. Adaptation demands constant attention to the signals of the marketplace. But it also requires wise and deliberate coordination by the numerous actors who shape and lead these dynamic and enduring institutions.

Notes

1. Robert Kuttner, *Everything for Sale* (New York: Knopf, 1997).
2. Charles E. Lindblom, *The Market System* (New Haven, Conn.: Yale University Press, 2001).
3. Ibid., p. 175.
4. Ibid.
5. Michael S. McPherson and Morton Owen Schapiro, "The End of the Student Aid Era? Higher Education Finance in the United States," in Michael C. Johanek, ed., *A Faithful Mirror: Reflections on the College Board and Education in America* (New York: College Entrance Examination Board, 2001), pp. 335–78.
6. Caroline M. Hoxby, "Benevolent Colluders? The Effects of Antitrust Action on College Financial Aid and Tuition" (Harvard University, Department of Economics, n.d.).
7. The microeconomic consequences of this development are explained in Caroline M. Hoxby, "Tax Incentives for Higher Education," in James M. Poterba, ed., *Tax Policy and the Economy*, vol. 12 (Cambridge, Mass.: MIT Press/NBER, 1998), pp. 49–81. Much of the argument that follows is indebted to Hoxby's analysis summarized here (pp. 60–64) and documented in other papers.
8. As described in Michael S. McPherson and Morton Owen Schapiro, *The Student Aid Game* (Princeton, N.J.: Princeton University Press, 1998).
9. Roger L. Geiger, "High Tuition—High Aid: A Road Paved with Good Intentions" (paper presented at the meeting of the Association for the Study of Higher Education, Sacramento, Calif., Nov. 2002).
10. Two independent data sets show lower-income students increasing their presence at high-tuition/highly selective institutions, but wealthy students increasing far more; see Caroline M. Hoxby, "Testimony Prepared for United States Senate, Committee on Governmental Affairs, Hearing on "The Rising Cost of College Tuition and the Effectiveness of Government Financial Aid" (Feb. 9, 2000), pp. 7–8 (comparing 1972 with 1992); McPherson and Schapiro, "End of the Student Aid Era," pp. 374–76 (comparing 1981 with 1999).
11. Hoxby, "Tax Incentives," pp. 62–63. Lest the concept of a student "wage" be considered an abstraction, DePauw University (among many others) provides this information to prospective students on its website: an SAT score of 1,020 and a 3.25 GPA earned a tuition discount of $3,000; 1,200 SAT and 3.75 GPA earned $10,000: June Kronholz, "On Sale Now: College Tuition," *Wall Street Journal*, May 16, 2002, pp. D1, 6.

12. Note that Princeton has, in effect, preserved the old student aid philosophy while also paying very high wages to students. Recent changes created more generous financial aid packages for all qualifying students, while Princeton's subsidy to all students is the highest. The combination represents an enormous "wage" for all Princeton students without violating the student aid ethos. Only the wealthiest universities have been able to execute this strategy.

13. Price discrimination and rationing interact in complex ways. Some possibilities are modeled by Richard Steinberg and Burton A. Weisbrod, "Give It Away or Make Them Pay? Price Discrimination and Rationing by Nonprofit Organizations with Distributional Objectives," Indiana University, draft, June 17, 2002.

14. Described by Henry Hansmann as contract failure: "Economic Theories of the Nonprofit Sector," in Walter W. Powell, ed., *The Nonprofit Sector: A Research Handbook* (New Haven, Conn.: Yale University Press, 1987), pp. 27–42.

15. See McPherson and Schapiro, *Student Aid Game.* As in other things, the wealthier the institution, the less the incentive for sharp practices.

16. Gordon C. Winston, "The Positional Arms Race in Higher Education," Discussion Paper 54, Williams Project on the Economics of Higher Education, Williams College, Apr. 2000.

17. To opt out of the arms race, according to Gordon Winston, would border on "fiduciary irresponsibility": "In a positional market there's never too much of a good thing—or even much stomach for asking that question—and in the hierarchy, wealth is quite fundamentally a good thing": "Subsidies, Hierarchies, and Peers: the Awkward Economics of Higher Education," *Journal of Economic Perspectives* (Winter 1999); 13–36, quotation on p. 31.

18. These universities have sought to raise revenue through commercial channels, including setting logos and licensing inventions. To date, though, such sources have added little to general funds.

19. In a few states, elasticity of demand was a significant consideration. Local markers were such that increased prices at state universities would bring about enrollment losses. Quality must be factored into such situations: either the clientele is uninterested in paying for higher quality, or the quality differential does not match the price differential.

20. *Chronicle of Higher Education,* "Facts & Figures" for ninety-seven public universities offering the doctoral degree (http://chronicle.com/stats/tuition/2001/). The median tuition and fees were $4,000, and the lowest quartile charged $3,000 or less.

21. Hoxby, "Tax Incentives."

22. Endowment income per FTE student in sixty-six public universities rose from an average of $176 in 1980; to $195 in 1990, and to $448 in 2000; fox thirty-three private universities the figures were: $2,536, $3837, $8124 (all in $1996).

23. Robert Birnbaum, *Management Fads in Higher Education: Where They Come from, What They Do, and Why They Fail* (San Francisco: Jossey-Bass, 2000).

24. Daniel Rodas, *Resource Allocation in Private Research Universities* (New York: Routledge Falmer, 2001), p. 15.

25. The argument is often made that tying resources to enrollments promotes quality teaching. But one need not be a cynic to concede that students may choose courses in order to maximize learning, entertainment, convenience, or leisure time—with corresponding incentives for course offerings.

26. The spread of enrollment management has been studied as a kind of organizational anomaly precisely because it is "so deeply problematic" for academic values; see Matthew S. Kraatz and Marc Ventresca, "Toward the Market Driven University: Pragmatic Institutionalism and the Spread of Enrollment Management" (paper presented at the conference "Universities and the Production of Knowledge," SCANCOR, Stanford University, Apr. 2003), quotation on p. 37.

27. "Every tub on its own bottom" promotes autonomy among noncompeting units, and possibly quality; however, this system does not induce internal market coordination or promote efficiency.

28. Lindblom, *Market System,* p. 160. For college choice models, see Don Hossler, Jack Schmit, and Nick Vesper, *Going to College: How Social, Economic, and Educational Factors Influence the Decisions Students Make* (Baltimore: Johns Hopkins University Press, 1999), pp. 141–56.

29. Caroline M. Hoxby, "The Return to Attending a More Selective College: 1960 to the Present" (Department of Economics, Harvard University, n.d., photocopy).

30. David Brooks has dubbed such students "Organization Kids": "at the top of the meritocratic ladder we have a generation of students who are extraordinarily bright, morally earnest, and incredibly industrious. They like to study and socialize in groups. They create and join organizations with great enthusiasm." "The Organization Kid," *Atlantic Monthly* (Apr. 2001): 40–54, quotation on p. 42.

31. James D. Savage, *Funding Science in America: Congress, Universities, and the Politics of the Academic Pork Barrel* (New York: Cambridge University Press, 1999); Daryl E. Chubin and Edward J. Hackett, *Peerless Science: Peer Review and U.S. Science Policy* (Albany: SUNY Press, 1990).

32. Marc Nerlove, "On Tuition and the Costs of Higher Education: Prolegomena to a Conceptual Framework," *Journal of Political Economy*, pt. 2 (May 1972): S178–S218, quotation on p. S206.

33. A study by Carlo S. Salerno found that universities on the whole allocate faculty efficiently so that the marginal value of their research is equal to the marginal productivity of teaching; see Carlo S. Salerno, "On the Technical and Allocative Efficiency of Research-Intensive Higher Education Institutions" (Ph.D. diss., Pennsylvania State University, 2002).

34. Princeton is the exception that proves the rule. Recall that Princeton justified its decision to expand undergraduate enrollment by 500 by arguing that it expected to *increase* average student quality. Having in effect already expanded its academic core (including graduate education), it resolved to add undergraduate education to restore an optimal balance. For nearly all other universities, however, expanding undergraduate education would tend to dilute what Nerlove calls its "quality-adjusted" value.

35. Lawrence B. Mohr, "The Impact Profile Approach to Policy Merit: The Case of Research Grants and the University," *Evaluation Review* (Apr. 1999): 212–49.

36. Roger L. Geiger, "The Ambiguous Link: Private Industry and University Research," in William E. Becker and Darryl R. Lewis, eds., *The Economics of American Higher Education* (Boston: Kluwer, 1992), pp. 265–98.

37. Irwin Feller, "Social Contracts and the Impact of Matching Fund Requirements on American Research Universities," *Educational Evaluation and Policy Analysis* 22, no. 1 (2000): 91–98; Ronald G. Ehrenberg and Jaroslava K. Mykula, "Do Indirect Cost Rates Matter?" Working Paper 6976, National Bureau of Economic Research, Cambridge, Mass., Feb. 1999. Universities typically utilize indirect cost reimbursements to fund cost-sharing obligations.

38. In 2000, institutional support for research constituted 24 percent of research expenditures at public universities and 10 percent at privates. As an accounting category, this figure contains many different items, including matching funds, seed grants, and salary attributable to research. Earnings from research (licensing revenues and part of ICR) are typically devoted to such purposes. Nevertheless, the trend has been in the direction of greater university contributions. Geiger and Feller found that universities devoting more of their own funds to research tended to gain in research share; see "Dispersion of Academic Research," pp. 344–45.

39. Leslie Christovich, "Top 100 R&D-Performing Academic Institutions Continue Increased Facilities Construction," *Data Brief* (Washington, D.C., National Science Foundation, Division of Science Resources Studies, June 22, 2000). The boom in construction of academic research space has no doubt accelerated into the new decade.

40. Universities are also large economic actors in themselves—major employers in their regions and important sources of capital investment, which is significant for economic impact rather than economic development. See Michael I. Luger and Harvey A. Goldstein, "What Is the Role of Public Universities in Regional Economic Development?" in Richard D. Bingham and Robert Mier, eds., *Dilemmas of Urban Economic Development*, Urban Affairs Annual Reviews 47 (London: Sage, 1997), pp. 104–34, esp. 106–15. For social returns see Larry L. Leslie and Paul T. Brinkman, *The Economic Value of Higher Education* (New York: Macmillan, 1988), pp. 70–80; for returns to research see Edwin Mansfield et al., "Academic Research and Industrial Innovation," *Research Policy* 20 (1991): 1–12.

41. Ammon J. Salter and Ben R. Martin, "The Economic Benefits of Publicly Funded Basic Research: A Critical Review," *Research Policy* 30 (2001): 509–32, esp. 517–20.

42. Lindblom, *Market System*, p. 153.

43. See the study by Jason Owen-Smith. Performance pressure in technology transfer has clearly intensified: Goldie Blumenstyk, "How Colleges Get More Bang (or Less) from Technology Transfer," *Chronicle of Higher Education* (July 17, 2002): A24–A26.

44. Derek Bok offers just such a case in *The University in the Marketplace: The Commercialization of Higher Education* (Princeton, N.J.: Princeton University Press, 2003).

45. Some universities have stretched this argument quite far; see Goldie Blumenstyk, "Knowledge Is 'a Form of Venture Capital' for a Top Columbia Administrator: Michael Crow Seeks Our Business Projects Designed to Exploit the University's Academic Prowess," *Chronicle of Higher Education* (Feb. 9, 2001): A29.

46. This is not to deny a role for the Internet in higher education, but rather to highlight one persistent obstacle. See Diane Harley et al., eds., *University Teaching as E-Business? Research and Policy Agendas* (University of California, Berkeley, Center for Studies in Higher Education, 2002).

47. The chief skirmish in the 2002 campaign occurred over early admissions, a practice that protects less-selective schools from more-selective rivals. Harvard threatened to ignore early-admission commitments, which would have made this market more efficient—and more relentlessly meritocratic.

Interests, Information, and Incentives in Higher Education: Principal-Agent Theory and Its Potential Applications to the Study of Higher Education Governance

Jason E. Lane and Jussi A. Kivisto

Abstract. In recent years, a handful of scholars have begun to focus on the role of individual and organizational interests, information flows, and incentives in higher education administration and governance, particularly in the realm of public institutions. These scholars ground their work on assumptions derived from the principal-agent framework, a theoretical perspective that views relationships from a contractual paradigm wherein a principal actor or organization contracts with an agent to carry out certain functions. The framework allows for analysis of how structures impact the agent's willingness and/or ability to fulfill the contracted obligations. This chapter explores the economic and political assumptions of the principal-agent framework and introduces scholars to its utility for understanding how governance and policy making operates in the postsecondary setting. Further, the chapter provides insights as to how the principal-agent framework can help reframe and extend current practical and scholarly conceptions of postsecondary governance and policy decisions.

How do governance structures impact university actions? Why does it matter if a governance structure is centralized or decentralized? How does an institution respond to a governor and legislature with differing higher education agendas? Why are some campus activities politically significant while others go unnoticed? Is a university more responsive to a government that provides annual appropriations or students who are paying an increasing portion of university expenses? While some scholars (e.g., Lowry, 2001; Nicholson-Crotty & Meier, 2003; Payne & Roberts, 2004; Toma, 1986, 1990) have provided evidence that suggests the way in which governance structures are organized can impact policy outputs, theoretical explanations for this finding have been modest.

Indeed, the study of the relationship between higher education institutions and governments has long lacked a systematic and theoretical foundation (McLendon, 2003).[1] In part, scholarship of higher education politics has given little attention to understanding how the external political bureaucracy that governs colleges and universities actually operates and how that operation influences institutional activity.[2] Of late, however, a small set of researchers have been integrating principal-agent theory (aka agency theory, principal-agency theory) into the study of higher education governance, accountability, and oversight (e.g. Kivisto, 2005, 2007; Lane, 2003, 2005, 2007; Nicholson-Crotty & Meier, 2003; McLendon, 2003; McLendon et al., 2006; Payne, 2003; Payne & Roberts, 2004). Principal-agent theory (PAT) provides common assumptions for investigating the role of individual and organizational interests, information flows, and incentives in higher education administration and governance. This chapter provides higher education scholars with an introduction to PAT, explores the divergent currents in its emerging use in the higher education field, and suggests new questions to further understanding of the governance process and policy implementation.

PAT focuses on the relationship between entities, either individuals or organizations, and can be used to understand motivations behind the activities of actors within hierarchical and contractual relationships. Among other areas of inquiry, the PAT can be useful for investigating and explaining why universities respond to legislative action in different ways, the impact of competing demands from different government officials on the decision making of institutional officials, and how bureaucratic governance arrangements can alter policy effectiveness and institutional autonomy.

Governments have long valued the societal contributions of colleges and universities and have used their resources to support these hallowed centers of learning. Those institutions that operate in the public sector, whether begotten through constitution, statute, or charter, were made in order to fulfill the educational needs of the citizenry. As such, these institutions often fall subject to oversight and regulation by the government. The structures that govern these institutions, particularly in how the institution relates to its sponsoring government, vary between states and nations; however, in every case there exists an underlying assumption that the institution, in some way, is responsible to the government. Edwin Duryea (2000), a historian of higher education governance, has noted that in the US, "Public boards have a direct responsibility to authorities of the state government that supports them and are subject to its executive and legislative governments—although governors and legislators traditionally have acceded to them substantial independence and, as a rule, have not meddled directly into internal affairs" (p. 3). In Europe, the relationship between the institution and the government has been even closer. National, federal and local governments in various European countries have traditionally had a dominant and direct role in governing and funding the public universities. Within the context of the US higher education system, Dunn (2003) discusses the tensions between increasing calls for accountability by external stakeholders and the ever-present expectation for autonomy and professional deference by internal stakeholders. He suggests that, "The conceptual problem centers on the necessity that non-elected public sector personnel, including . . . administrators and faculty, be simultaneously empowered (by the definition of their responsibility, both objectively and subjectively) and constrained (through mechanisms of accountability that then feed into definitions of responsibility)" (p. 73). This tension is one of the classic dilemmas at the heart of the principal-agent framework: how does one empower an agent to fulfill the needs of the principal, while at the same time constraining the agent from shirking on their responsibilities?

Public colleges and universities operate as public bureaucracies, at least in part responsible to the governments that fund them and endow them with the power to grant degrees. In many nations there is a shift away from government spending on higher education, but a continued interest in ensuring those institutions remain accountable to the government. Specifically in the US, even though states now fund smaller proportions of institutional budgets than in the past, state governments continue to exert substantial influence over post-secondary policy development, institutional decision-making, and governance organization. Literature focusing on the external politics of higher education (e.g., Doyle, 2006; Doyle et al., 2005; Hearn & Griswold, 1994; Hicklin & Meier, 2004; McLendon et al., 2007; McLendon et al., 2006; McLendon et al., 2005; Knott & Payne, 2004; Lowry, 2001; Nicholson-Crotty & Meier, 2003; Payne & Roberts, 2004; Toma, 1990) suggests that the structure of higher education governance impacts policy outputs and institutional decision making. Such findings resonate with the growing political science literature that utilizes "new institutionalism" perspectives founded upon rational theories of politics that "deemphasize the dependence of the polity on society in favor of an interdependence between relatively autonomous social and political institutions" (March & Olsen, 1984, p. 738). Evidencing the interactive role of external actors in higher education governance, Gittell and Kleiman (2000) concluded in their study of higher education political contexts:

> Public universities are not above and apart from politics. . . . Political leaders, particularly the governor and top elected legislative representatives, play a significant role, often dominating design and implementation and sometimes frustrating policy reforms. (p. 1088)

Political theories derived from neo-institutionalism provide a theoretical foundation from which to study how government structures allow or inhibit actors such as political leaders to influence public bureaucracies like universities.

Similar to other public bureaucracies, public colleges and universities operate in an environment of hierarchical control and information asymmetry. Created, or at least funded, by governments to perform particular functions, colleges and universities serve as agents of the state (or nation). These agents have historically been allowed a high degree of autonomy and freedom from direct legislative control (Duryea, 2000). This freedom derives partially from the highly professionalized nature of academia, with faculty and administrators viewed as experts (see Mintzberg, 1979 for a more in-depth discussion of the characteristics of a professional bureaucracy).[3] This expertise creates a knowledge imbalance, as it is usually not possible for politicians or other actors in the governing structure to monitor and assess whether faculty and administrators operate in the best interest of the government, the institution, or the individual (assuming that these interests differ). Further exasperating the issue, the highly specialized nature of academic work and the complexities in the organizational structure (e.g. Clark, 1983; Birnbaum, 1988; Holtta, 1995) and production technology (e.g. Bowen, 1977; Johnes & Taylor, 1990; Cave et al., 1997) often create favorable conditions for high levels of information asymmetry.

In light of these dynamics, a handful of scholars have used the PAT to model, study, and understand the functions of higher education governance systems. In general, PAT describes the relationship between two or more parties, in which one party, designated as the principal, engages another party, designated as the agent, to perform some task or service on the behalf of the principal (e.g. Ross, 1973; Moe, 1984). PAT has been considered relevant in different kinds of agency relationships where there exists goal conflict between the parties of a relationship and informational asymmetries favoring the agent. These two conditions activate the possibility of a moral hazard problem known as "shirking".[4] One of the main purposes of PAT is to solve this shirking problem (i.e., to find instruments that will motivate the agent to behave in the principal's interests). Although the traditional forms of PAT have focused on the relations between individuals, the applicability of the PAT has proved to be relevant at the group and organizational level as well (e.g. Ferris, 1991; Braun, 1993; Lassar & Kerr, 1996; Moe, 1990, 2005). Both theoretically- and empirically-oriented research conducted by scholars of different disciplines can be found in increasing numbers. PAT is not and has never been the exclusive property of a certain scientific paradigm; rather, it has been and could be a useful theoretical framework for many different disciplines and approaches (Kivisto, 2007).

As public bureaucracies, public colleges and universities are replete with principal-agent relationships, both internal and external to the institutions. This chapter examines how the principal-agent framework applies to the higher education setting (primarily external to the institution) and possibly reframe how both scholars and practitioners assess governance operations. In particular, the chapter begins with an overview of the economic and political science origins of PAT, focusing on the importance for scholars to be aware of how differing assumptions of the two disciplines impact adaptation of the model to different organizational settings. The chapter then reviews existing work that incorporates PAT in higher education studies, discusses application of the theory to higher education, and explores potential applications for future work.

Overview of the Principal-Agent Relationship

Originating in the study of economics, the principal-agent framework is based upon a basic contractual relationship in that a principal contracts with an agent to engage in certain functions that will improve the status of the principal relative to the status quo (Alchian & Demsetz, 1972; Jensen & Meckling, 1976). Examples of such a relationship include: patient-doctor, investor-broker, client-lawyer, and employee-employer. In such relationships, the premise is that the principal does not have enough time, knowledge, and/or energy to fulfill all of its own needs in an adequate fashion. As such, the principal contracts with an agent, usually one with the necessary time and specialized skills, to act on behalf of the principal. In its most basic form, this model suggests the concept of a market where decisions concerning the allocation of resources are made by a delegate or representative of the resource owner (Whynes, 1993). The agent is trusted to make decisions that are in the best interest of the principal. However, agent preferences derived from self-interest and self-preservation do not always ally with the preferences of the principal. The potential, and likely, difference in principal and agent preferences calls for the principal to provide incentives and monitor agent behavior to ensure compliance with "the contract."

According to Moe (1984), "The logic of the principal-agent model . . . immediately leads us to the theoretical issues at the heart of the contractual paradigm: issues of hierarchical control in the context of information asymmetry and conflict of interest" (p. 787). The model is based upon the rational assumption that an individual prefers to pursue self-interest before the interests of others. Therefore, the contractual paradigm requires the principal to ensure the agent acts in the best interest of the principal, particularly given the fact that the agent's specialized abilities and knowledge advantage the agent in using the principal's resources to pursue ends that benefit the agent (Shepsle & Boncheck, 1997; Ortmann & Squire, 2000). The principal must utilize an array of oversight, compensatory, and punitive initiatives to ensure the agent acts in the principal's best interest. Provision of compensation to the agent, should mean the principal has the right to expect a minimum level of utility from the agent in exchange for the compensation (Sobel, 1993). Yet, there is still no guarantee that the agent will not shirk on its responsibilities to the principal.

In a rational world, "[a]gents relentlessly exploit every opportunity to ease their work burden, as long as the principals do not react and punish them so severely that their net utility from shirking is decreased" (Frey, 1993, p. 663). Given this expectation, it is assumed that the principal does not only need to consider instituting various oversight mechanisms, but also must have the means to alter the actions of the agent when shirking exists. When shirking is reported to the principal and verified, the principal takes action either by limiting or eliminating compensation or initiating some sort of punitive action to entice or force the agent to alter its actions. An important part of the relationship is that fear of the corrective actions of the principal may be enough of a motivation to prevent or decrease the agent's shirking. So, while one may not witness the agent altering its actions in response to the principal's demands, this lack of action does not mean that the relationship is absent of oversight mechanisms or that methods of control do not exist (LaFollette, 1994). It may, in fact, represent an almost perfectly balanced principal-agent model, where there is just enough incentive to limit agent shirking to a level of non-concern to the principal.

To ensure that the principal receives the appropriate return on its investment from the agent, the principal establishes oversight mechanisms. However, political science and economics portray these oversight mechanisms in different ways. From the vantage of political science, governments employ a range of oversight tools to ensure that the bureaucratic agents pursue legislated goals. McCubbins and Schwartz (1984) famously suggested that government oversight can be divided between "police patrols" and "fire alarms." Police patrols are direct and centralized and tend to be in operation regardless of whether an agent is believed to be shirking or not. In higher education, police patrols include annual reports, purchase approvals, performance audits, and other forms of required reporting (Lane, in press). Comparatively, a fire alarm is ". . . less centralized and involves less active and direct intervention than police-patrol oversight; . . . [a legislature] establishes a system of rules, procedures, and informal practices that enable individual citizens and organized interest groups to examine administrative decisions (sometimes in progress), to charge executive agencies with violating [legislative] goals, and to seek remedies from agencies, courts, and [the legislature] itself" (McCubbins & Scwartz, 1984, p. 166). In essence, these fire alarms rely largely on non-governmental actors to oversee the activities of bureaucratic agents and sound an alarm should shirking believe to be observed. Lane (in press) found state governments to monitor university behavior through a web of oversight that, in addition to typical direct mechanisms (e.g., purchase approvals, program reviews, budget reviews, etc.), also includes such indirect mechanisms as investigative reports by the press, communiqué from constituents, and legislative hearings where individuals can raise concerns about an institution's activities. Upon learning about a potential shirking activity, the legislature may engage in a more formal investigation.

In terms of oversight, the economics PAT focuses more on the type of behavior to be overseen rather than the mechanisms used to oversee the behavior. In particular, economists make a distinction between "behavior-based contracts" and "outcome-based contracts" (Eisenhardt, 1989). When choosing behavior-based contracts the principal chooses to monitor agent's behaviors (actions) and then reward those behaviors. The basic idea behind monitoring behavior is to decrease the information asymmetry between the principal and the agent. In some situations, the monitoring procedures may be too expensive or difficult to be worthwhile or violates some agents' expectation of professional autonomy. In these situations, the other option, namely outcome-based contracts, could be a more logical choice for the principal. As the name implies, outcome-based contracts compensate agents for achieving certain outcomes. As a concrete example, reward schemes such as performance-based (or merit-based) salary structure can be considered as forms of outcome-based contract. Outcome-based contracts are considered to be effective in curbing the possibility of an agent acting in an opportunistic way. The rationale is that such contracts are likely to reduce goal conflict because they motivate the agent to pursue outcomes that are incentive compatible with the principal's goals (Eisenhardt, 1989; Bergen et al., 1992).

No matter how it is constructed or codified, oversight is the lynch pin of the PA relationship; for without it the agent has little incentive to pursue the goals of the principal and the principal has no means to ensure that its goals are being pursued by the agent.

The Emergence of Principal-Agent Theory[5]

PAT derives from the development of neo-institutionalism, which emerged in reaction to shortcomings identified in both neo-classical and behavioral approaches to studying organizations (Moe, 1984; Powell & DiMaggio, 1991). The neo-classical (or "old institutionalism") view of organizations centered around the "entrepreneur, a hypothetical individual who, by assumption, makes all decisions for the firm and is endowed with a range of idealized properties defining his knowledge, goals, and computational skills and transaction costs" (Moe, 1984, p. 740). As such, aspects of individual choice, environmental contexts, and goal conflict are assumed away. In response to the neo-classical school of thought, behaviorists centered on individual choices and often viewed organizations as a collection of individual processes. One major criticism of behavioral models is that they neglected the fact that "social, political, and economic institutions have become larger, considerably more complex and resourceful, and prima facie more important to collective life" (March & Olsen, 1984, p. 734).

New institutionalism developed as a way to incorporate theories about the power of institutional structures with theories about the power of individuals. Humans purposefully designed social institutions to help structure the world in which they operate. These institutions subsequently both constrain and structure individual behavior. For example, colleges and universities evolved as a way for society to preserve and transmit knowledge. Now, the structures within universities clearly impact individual and collective behavior of faculty, staff, students, and administrators (see e.g., Cohen et al., 1972; Ortmann & Squire, 2000). The focus of new institutionalism, as applied to higher education, includes understanding the influence of organizational structure on individual action and decision making behavior.[6] Further, institutions structure the nature of the relationship between individuals and organizations, empowering and subordinating various actors and groups. Moe (1984) describes this amalgamation of the power of the organization and the power of the individual as two-way authority. While bureaucratic structures purposefully create power imbalance between actors, the extent of one actors' authority over another actor is limited by a " 'zone of acceptance', within which [the subordinate actor] willingly allows the [other actor] to direct his behavior" (p. 745).

One theoretical strand to emerge from neo-institutionalism was PAT, which accounts for both actor motivation (e.g., self-interest) and the role of organizational structures in constraining that behavior. After its birth, the development of the mainstream principal-agent research in economics has developed along two lines, which are usually referred to as "positive theory of agency" and "principal-agent" (Jensen, 1983; Eisenhardt, 1989). The two streams share a common unit of analysis, the contract between the principal and the agent, as well as some of the common assumptions of the theory. Nevertheless, the two streams also differ in many respects. The principal-agent literature is generally more abstract, mathematical and non-empirically oriented. Characteristic of formal theory, the principal-agent stream involves careful specification of assumptions, which are followed by logical deduction and mathematical proof. The main focus is on determining the optimal form of the contract. The other stream, the positivist literature, is generally non-mathematical and more empirically oriented. Positive researchers have focused more on identifying situations in which the principal and the agent are likely to have conflicting goals and then describing governance mechanisms that limit the agent's self-serving behavior. Positive researchers have also focused more exclusively on the intra-organizational principal-agent relationships, especially shareholder-manager relationships (Jensen, 1983; Eisenhardt, 1989). Although the differences between the two streams are notable, the streams can also be seen as complementary to each other: whereas positive theory may identify the behavior of the agent and various contract alternatives available, the principal-agent stream may indicate which contract is the most efficient in a given situation (Eisenhardt, 1989).[7] The higher education literature applying economics PAT has not made analytical distinction between the two streams. This is because the majority of previous studies have treated the PAT primarily as conceptual framework to be used for illustrative purposes, not as a theory which should be modelled mathematically or tested empirically.

The economics PAT has been considered especially valuable in re-establishing the importance of incentives, interests and information in organizational thinking. It assumes that, whether we like it or not, much of organizational life is based, at least partly, on people's self-interest, opportunism and goal conflicts. In addition, the theory has drawn attention to the issues related to information, and especially the asymmetries of information (Eisenhardt, 1989; Petersen, 1993).

Application of PAT to public bureaucracies and other political entities follows the basic tenets of the economic model discussed above; however, due to differences in the administrative and governance structures of private firms/corporations and government bureaucracies, aspects of the model need modification and further elucidation in order to be useful in the political context. As Miller (2005) observed in his review of the use of PAT in political science, "principal-agency has been substantially challenged, modified, and even turned upside down in order to accommodate the distinctly political aspects of several key Weberian asymmetries" (p. 203). Usage of PAT in the public realm aids in identifying and understanding the complex relationship among the various actors involved in public bureaucracies—structures filled with a vast array of oversight, purposeful and de facto autonomy, and intertwined lines of hierarchical structures not found in most private sector companies and thus largely excluded from economic models. The theory has most frequently been used to model legislative (e.g., McCubbins & Schwartz, 1984; McCubbins, 1985; McCubbins et al., 1987; Wood, 1988; Wood & Waterman, 1991) and executive (e.g., Moe, 1985) oversight of the bureaucracy; but it has also been used in the study of the President's relationship with voters (Downs & Rocke, 1994) oversight of police officers (Brehm & Gates, 1993), congruence between Supreme Court decisions and the subsequent rulings of lower courts (Songer et al., 1994), and the relationship between a regulatory agency and the non-governmental entities that it regulates (Scholz, 1991).

Mitnick (1980) first recognized the value of using the PAT to study public bureaucracies; however the theory did not begin its move toward the mainstream until about four years later when several articles sought to apply the PAT to the study of political institutions. Weingast and Moran (1983), Weingast (1984), and McCubbins and Scwartz (1984) used the principal-agent assumptions of information asymmetry and agent outcomes to reinvent the study of Congressional oversight. They posited that even though Congress did not constantly monitor the activities of bureaucracies, this did not mean that Congress was shirking on their regulatory responsibility (which is what many scholars of the time were concluding). Instead, Congress employed a combination of direct and indirect oversight, along with different forms of incentives, to retain control over bureaucratic outputs.

Moe (1984) and March and Olsen (1984) provided a broader discussion of the theories application to political sciences. These articles discussed how the behavior within political structures may not simply be studied as an accumulation of individual preferences and choices, but also a result of organizational structures. Moe's (1984) classic overview, "The New Economics of Organization" elucidated the application of the PAT to political models through an extensive comparison of political and economic organizations. Moe suggested that the entire governmental enterprise is based on the contractual paradigm (e.g., voters contract with elected officials, elected officials contract with bureaucrats, public governing boards contract with CEOs, etc.), thus postulating (and in some cases illustrating) the ubiquitous existence of agency problems throughout public bureaucracies. Noting the contractual foundation, Moe went on to observe that PAT can be used to explain various aspects of government bureaucracies: policy products, bureaucratic influence, oversight, control, shirking, and information asymmetry.

Almost immediately, a new field of research was "sparked" in political science. As Miller (2005) concludes:

> For the first time, the field of public bureaucracy had a research agenda that was based on deductive theory and demanded the highest level of methodological competence. At the same time, the empirical results suggested a more complicated story—one that led to challenges to the canonical model and opened the door to reformulations of PAT that better fit this important political relationship. (p. 209)

In much the same way that PAT prompted political scientists to take a different look at oversight and accountability, the theory has the potential to further and reframe current understanding of the governance and policy making of public higher education.

Comparison of Perspectives: Economics vs. Political Science

Due to the divergent development of PAT in different disciplines, application of the theory to higher education governance and policy has been somewhat disjointed as scholars using the same "theory" utilize different assumptions based on disciplinary perspective. To help scholars better understand the use of PAT in higher education research, this section provides a comparison of the differing assumptions used by political scientists and economists.

Political and economic PAT both developed as part of the growth of new-institutionalism and attempt to predict how actors and organizational structures behave in hierarchical and quasi-hierarchical situations. Much like the economic applications, PAT in political science investigates the role of incentives, interests and information in organizational thinking. Certain assumptions regarding agent desires to shirk on responsibilities and the need for the principal to provide oversight and incentives to reduce agent shirking remain fairly constant between applications. However, a number of key differences do exist. Moe (1990) argues that the two primary differences between economic and political models can be found in the construction of the principal and the type of output produced by the agent. Political principals tend to be comprised of collective entities that produce a single contract (e.g. voters collectively electing a representative or the members of Congress creating and funding a bureaucracy) and multiple entities that create multiple contracts (e.g., the legislature and the governor placing different demands on higher education). Likewise agents can be comprised of: (1) collective entities that work together to produce an output, which typically resembles a public good (rather than a more easily measurable output such as a private consumable or corporate profit); or (2) multiple entities responding to the same principal such as when several institutions are governed by a single board.

Comparing the two disciplinary perspectives reveals a number of other critical theoretical differences in how economists and political scientists apply PAT in their respective fields. (Table 1 provides an overview of these differences.)

TABLE 1

Differences Between PAT Assumptions in Economics and Political Science

	Economics	Political science
Contract	Explicit	Implicit
Unit of Analysis	Principal	Principal/agent
Actor Motivation	Economic utility	Economic utility and political power
Principal-Agent Relationships	Bilateral	Multilateral
Principal's Primary Mode of Control	Economic contract	Social/political contract
Output	Private good	Public good
Source of Shirking	Individual	Individual or structural

Contract

Traditionally, economics PAT has considered PA relationships primarily as codified contractual relationships. For this reason, economics PAT usually understands contracts as more formal and explicit instruments for enabling the economic co-operation between the principal and the agent.[8] According to Perrow (1986), PAT "assumes that social life is a series of contracts . . . specifying what the agent should do and what the principal must pay in return" (p. 224). Political science also views the relationship as a contractual one, but that contract can also be a vaguely defined agreement between two autonomous or semi-autonomous entities with varying levels of expertise. In fact, while the economic contract typically stipulates what is to be produced, leaving the "how" of production to the expertise of the agent; public bureaucracies often retain an information asymmetry in both how best to produce a policy output and what that policy output should look like. For example, a public university operates under the auspices of a contract with the state in that the state appropriates money to the institution with the expectation that the institution contributes to the public good through teaching, research, and service. In some cases, the state even provides some guidelines about the expected output (e.g., establishing performance measures or funding specific types of research activity); however, how those outputs are achieved are usually left up to relevant administrators or faculty members because of their expertise. This expertise "gives bureaus (agents) strategic opportunities" (Bendor et al., 1987, p. 1041) not typically observed in relationships regulated by economic contracts.

Unit of Analysis

Economics PAT gives conceptual priority to economic aspects of the principal-agent relationship by investigating and analyzing the agent's shirking behavior and the principal's means to overcome it. In this sense, the economics PAT is primarily "principal's theory" since it takes the perspective of securing the principal's welfare against potential or actual agent shirking. While shirking and oversight are central to political science PAT as well, political scientists investigate the welfare of both the principal and the agent. Given that it is much more difficult to exchange political agents, recognizing and understanding the impact of a PA relationship on the agent (e.g., politician or a public bureaucracy) is much more important in political science than economics.

Principal-Agent Relationships

Economics PAT understands and examines relationships as bilateral relationships between one principal and one or more agents. Influenced by the assumptions common to rational choice and methodological individualism, it assumes a homogenous incentive structure from the principal. In political science, two significant departures from economics are generally acknowledged: (1) political PA relationships often involve multiple and collective principals (Bendor & Meirowitz, 2004; Moe, 1990; Lyne & Tierney, 2003); and (2) there can exist intermediary principals/agents between a primary principal and agent. In the first distinction, multiple principals act independently of each other and can create heterogeneous incentive structures, sometimes forcing the agent into scenarios not noted in economics, such as the agent having to choose between competing contracts. Also, studies of collective principals (e.g., governing boards) investigate sources of real power. For example, what is the functional difference between boards with unanimous or split votes? Does the power of the Board chair impact the operation of the principal? In the second deviation from economics, political scientists recognize that hierarchical structures can create long chains of principals and agents. These PA chains can create different agency problems than exist in a bilateral relationship.

Actor Motivation

Both economics and political science PAT considers the principal and the agent as self-interested utility maximizers. Therefore, given the choice between two alternatives, the rational principal or agent is always assumed to choose the option that increases its individual utility (Davis et al., 1997).[9] However, as Waterman and Meier (1998) observe, "In the marketplace, principals and agents clearly have different goals and/or preferences. Obviously agents want to make as much money as possible while principal's want to pay as little as possible for services . . . in the bureaucratic setting, with a focus on policy and process instead of profit, goal conflict may not always exist between principals and agents. Principals and agents may disagree over policy, or they may not" (p. 185). Yet, it is possible for principal and agent to agree on policy while also disagreeing over how to implement the policy.

Principal's Primary Mode of Control

For economics PAT, 'contract' is understood to be an instrument enabling economic co-operation between the principal and the agent. The main purpose of the contract is to explicitly set the task for the agent, and introduce the detailed means through which the agent will be compensated for performing the task. The nature of political arrangements leads to a mode of control that is often less explicit than witnessed in relationships assessed by economic PAT. As such, while the contracts may govern economic relationships, political PA relationships can often be governed through elections, appointment of intermediary principals, power brokering, and signaling from political elites. For example, political scientists have raised questions such as whether the electorate uses elections as a type of game to select the best representative of the voters (Fearon, 1999) or a moral hazard game designed to punish politicians who fail to fulfill the desires of the polity (Ferejohn, 1986). Similar questions could be raised about how legislators use state appropriations to either reward or sanction bureaucratic behavior or governors use their power of appointment to influence board decisions.

Output

For economics PAT the output of the PA relationship is a private rather than public good.[10] This means that the output is usually somehow observable to both the agent and the principal, and it could also have many facets, such as quality and quantity. It can be, for example, the number of shoes produced by a factory worker, the volume of sales generated by a department store salesperson, the success of a surgical procedure, and so forth. Governments, however, are often in the business of producing public goods, making it much more difficult, although not impossible, in political science PAT to measure agent outputs (Moe, 1990).[11]

Source of Shirking

Economic PAT assumes that it is the self-interested utility maximization which drives the agents to act opportunistically towards their principals (i.e. to shirk). The existence of information asymmetries further encourage the shirking activity. Indeed, the assumption and existence of agent self-interest is crucial for economics PAT. If the utility functions of self-serving principals and agents coincide, there would be no possibility for shirking to appear (Davis et al., 1997). Similarly, if the information available to both the principal and the agent were to be the same, self-interest would not matter since the principal could immediately detect any shirking behavior on the part of the agent (Ricketts, 2002). Many studies in political science also focus on shirking as defined by economists; however, some recent work has attempted to identify various gradients of shirking. For example, shirking could occur due to "slippage"—unintentional shirking. In principal-agent relationships, particularly those with long principal-agent chains, information may not be fully or accurately communicated between the primary principal and the primary agent. As such, an agent's actions may be perceived as "shirking" when the agent actually thought it was pursuing the principal's goals. Thus, the source of the agents behavior would be information slippage rather then self-interested shirking.

Principal-Agent Theory in Higher Education in Governance and Policy Research

As a field of study, higher education scholars often draw on the theories of other disciplines to analyze postsecondary institutions. Usually a scholar or set of scholars adapt a theory to higher education research and then others build upon and further refine the application of that theory. However, the writing using PAT in higher education suggests a somewhat spontaneous interest in PAT by scholars working on different governance questions in varying governmental contexts (e.g. a decentralized federal system such as in the US vs. a centralized system such as in Finland).

Despite its strong research tradition in economics and political science, until recently the PAT was only sparingly the study of higher education.[12] Wider application of PAT was seemingly ignored not only by mainstream higher education researchers, but also economists and political scientists working in the higher education field. Nevertheless, a change has seemingly taken place during the last few years; authors such as Lowry (2001), Lane (2003), Liefner (2003), McLendon (2003), Nicholson-Crotty and Meier (2003), Payne (2003), Gornitzka et al. (2004), and Kivisto (2005) have now more thoroughly introduced PAT to the field of higher education governance and policy studies. The rapidly growing usage is a testament to the theory's utility and flexibility. However, it also means that there has been no systematic evolution of the theory in higher education.

A review of the recent work using PAT reveals two distinct tracks of analysis with about half of the authors adhering more to economic assumptions and the other half aligning more with the assumptions derived from political science. For example, Liefner (2003), Gornitzka et al. (2004), and Kivisto (2005, 2007) align with the economic origins of PAT, which Miller (2005) refers to as the "canonical" PAT as it relies on the traditional assumptions of the theory. Knott and Payne (2004), Lane (2003, 2005, 2007), Lowry (2001), McLendon (2003), McLendon et al. (2006), and Nicholson-Crotty and Meier (2003) approach PAT from a political science perspective, which tends to slacken some of the canonical assumptions as to better fit the model to the operations of a public bureaucracy. Interestingly, due to the quasi-private, quasi-public nature of most colleges and universities, both approaches further our understanding of the academic enterprise.

The use of PAT to study higher education governance began with a mostly canonical approach by a set of papers by economist Eugenia Toma (1986, 1990), who first introduced PAT to higher education politics through a study of public university governing boards. In her first analysis, Toma asked a very simple question: what factors lead to politicians' selecting a certain type of governing board structure over competing structures? Toma's (1986) analysis suggested that states in which there were minimal barriers to taxpayers' ability to influence legislative decision making tend to have less centralized boards than those states in which citizens had to overcome high barriers to political involvement. The second analysis (Toma, 1990) investigated how board type impacts the operations of public universities. She found that:

> The structure of the boards is important because it helps to define the constraints on the board members and on the internal agents of the universities. An implication of this study is that public universities can be made to function more like private ones by placing them under separate governing boards. (p. 7)

Toma's initial inquiry demonstrated the utility of using PAT to study higher education governance; but the work also raised a number of important questions that only recently have scholars begun to address: (1) What factors influence the structural design of university governance? (2) How does the design of a governance structure influence policy outputs and the operations of a university?

The general conclusion that board structure impacts the operation of colleges and universities has been supported by subsequent studies. Following the work of Toma in higher education and building on the work of Horn and Shepsle (1989), McCubbins et al. (1987, 1989) and Moe (1989, 1990) in political science, several authors began investigating how governance structures impacted institutional characteristics. In particular, scholars were interested in how the organization of governance structures impacted funding—specifically, the cost of a college education to a student. The work of Bowen et al. (1997) and Lowry (2001) found evidence suggesting that centralization of state governance leads to lower costs for students. Moving beyond the extent of centralization, Lowry's study also suggested that how board members are selected can also influence costs (i.e., elected, as opposed to appointed, boards lead to lower tuition).[13]

Essentially, these studies indicate that the way in which a board is organized and its members are selected can impact the interests of the board and the effectiveness of various incentives to prevent the board from shirking. This supports the suggestion of McLendon et al. (2006) that we should view, "governance arrangements as serving to institutionalize the preferences of different sets of stakeholders, which seek to shape policy consistent with their premises" (p. 19). For example, Lowry (2001) explained that his findings of centralized governance structures leading to lower costs demonstrated the board's responsiveness to a certain set of stakeholders. In his view, coordinating boards, which are generally appointed by either the governor or legislature, are likely to pursue the interests of elected officials and the general public (i.e., keeping tuition low and having higher levels of spending on student service). Whereas, non-consolidated boards were more responsive to internal academic stakeholders (i.e., faculty and administrators) and would have higher tuition costs and lower levels of spending on student services as to free up money for academic expenditures. Lowry's is a speculative explanation as the data did not directly assess board responsiveness, but it does demonstrate the feasibility of how a structure can impact the principal-agent relationship and, thus, board priorities and actions.

In a more recent study of American governance structures, Nicholson-Crotty and Meier (2003) investigated how the composition of a principal may impact the output of an agent. The study examines how consolidated governing boards (i.e., boards that governing more than one institution; often serving as the sole board for all institutions in one state) either mitigate or enhance the external political influences on the operations of universities. Using an array of structural and political variables, the authors ran a series of multiple regressions to determine the impacts of politics on different economic variables (i.e., cost of higher education per student; tuition per student, need-based scholarships and financial aid per student, and state/local appropriations per student). While there was not a clear set of themes across the states, the study did determine that the type of structure did significantly impact the influence of politics. The authors attempt to explain the complexities of their findings:

> The widely varying pattern of coefficients as politics interacts with structure suggests that the relationships are highly complex. Providing an explanation for the patterns and how those patterns should appear will require additional theoretical work. One possibility is that the relationships are even more complex than the current regressions reveal them to be. For example, the direction of effect of legislative professionalism might be a function of both the structure of higher education and the ideology or partisanship of the legislature. This notion suggests a three-way or perhaps even a four-way interaction of these terms. (p. 93)

Such interaction should not be surprising as higher education governance structures contain an array of principals and agents. In an empirical study of European tertiary governance structures, Liefner (2003) attempted to identify the possible principals and agents in the context of higher education.

> In higher education the principal can be a ministry of science and education, the management board of a university, a president, dean, or department chair. The agents are those actors in higher education, who receive assignments, funds, and salaries from the principals. Therefore, a number of higher education managers, for example, heads of departments, are simultaneously principals and agents, whereas most of the professors, researchers, and lecturers can be viewed primarily as agents. (p. 477)

The findings of the Nicholson-Crotty and Meier (2003) and Liefner (2003) studies support Toma's (1990) and Lowry's (2001) premise that any theory of higher education governance cannot merely account for the existence of principals, but rather must also account for the composition of those principals.

The complexity, however, is not limited to the operation of multiple principals, but is in part due to the operation of different types of principals. Building on the work of Moe (1990) and Lyne and Tierney (2003), Lane (2005) argued that the impact of a governance structure is difficult to explain because such structures are not standard hierarchies, but contain up to three different types of principals: single, multiple, and collective. A single principal is that typically described in the PAT and often the focus of economic analysis. A multiple principal relationship involves more than one single principal, each of which having separate, independent contracts with the agent. A collective principal is where there are multiple members of a single principal, such as a governing board. The governing board acts as a single entity, but is actually comprised of multiple members. The existence of more than one principal can create competing goals, confusing the agent and leading to inconsistent outcomes. Failure to recognize the existence and operation of complex principals could lead to a misinterpretation of actor motivation and behavior.

Lane (2003, 2007) also found that the governance arrangements can impact the type of oversight used by principals. Drawing on the political science literature (e.g., Moe, 1984; Ogul & Rockman, 1990), he employed the PAT as a conceptual framework for investigating how states engage in oversight of public higher education. Using a comparative case study approach, the study uncovered that universities operate in a "spider-web" of oversight that uses multiple latent and manifest forms of oversight to keep legislators informed of the activities of postsecondary institutions. While further study is needed, the data suggested that systems with fewer direct forms of oversight compensate with indirect forms.

Scholars outside of the US have also used PAT to analyze higher education governance, but view the relationship from more a canonical perspective. While American studies of PAT tend to focus on the structure of governance systems, Liefner (2003) analyzed forms of resource allocation in higher education systems and their effects on the performance of universities. Liefner recognized that the assumptions concerning goal conflicts and information asymmetries are especially relevant in the higher education context. Because of the specialized knowledge of the faculty, the production of higher education is very difficult to monitor, particularly at the level of research groups and individual scholars, but also at the institutional level. In order to avoid a situation where some agents take advantage of the fact that their efforts are hard to control, Liefner suggested that the principal should use outcome-based contracts in a form of performance-based funding procedures. Based on this analysis, Liefner formulated two hypotheses:

1. Agents that have been rather inactive before the introduction of performance-based resource allocation will have to work harder.

2. With performance-based resource allocation agents will tend to avoid projects with a high chance of failure. Departments and individuals will concentrate on activities where success can be expected because they will have to meet a formula's criteria or market demand. (pp. 478–479)

Liefner 'tested' these hypotheses with empirical (qualitative) data that consisted of interviews with 53 professors at six universities in the US, Switzerland, the Netherlands, and Great Britain. On the basis of his empirical analysis, Liefner found that the instruments of performance-based budgeting worked largely as predicted in theory. However, although the hypotheses concerning the changes in individual behavior were correct, Liefner found that universities with a large number of highly motivated and qualified faculty were successful regardless of the form of resource allocation. Despite the result that a form of resource allocation could not directly influence the long-term success of universities, Liefner explained that it still could (1) force universities and individuals to pay attention to the needs of governments and taxpayers, (2) help to adjust the organizational structures of universities more quickly to the emerging needs and opportunities, and (3) be used to re-allocate funds to those groups and scholars that have proved to be successful and to reduce the budgets of those who are not performing in an acceptable way.

Seeking to find additional empirical evidence of the PAT applicability to higher education, Gornitzka et al. (2004) attempted to integrate the perspective of PAT into the sphere of contract arrangements between state and higher education institutions. Gornitzka et al. analyzed the strengths and weaknesses of established contract arrangements in Finland, Sweden, and Denmark. The authors made several tentative and incidental observations through the PAT constructs like adverse section, moral hazard, and information asymmetry. After their analysis, they concluded that a closer integration of the external quality evaluation system with other instruments of regulation is likely to decrease informational asymmetries and thus provide greater accountability; however, it is not possible to reduce this information asymmetry to zero, because the institutions will always know more about their functioning, efficiency, and quality than the state authorities.

Kivisto (2005), also focusing on the European context, examined some of the key perceptions and insights that PAT could offer for higher education researchers. He applied PAT concepts to the context of government-university relationships and concluded that PAT could provide a useful and applicable framework for analyzing this relationship since it is able to offer explanation for certain government behaviors (e.g. why governments acquire information before making funding decisions, why governments are creating quality assurance mechanisms and performance-based funding procedures instead of input-based funding procedures). Kivisto's other work (2007) continued this discussion by focusing more deeply on the concept of moral hazard opportunism in the context of Finnish higher education system and program implementation. He also examined the potential strengths and weaknesses of PAT more systematically. As a result of his analysis, Kivisto argued that the strengths of PAT lie mostly in its capability of offering theoretical understanding and solutions for the phenomenon of inefficiency and cost growth. Through exploring the weaknesses of PAT, Kivisto identified its limited perspective on human nature and behavior, and the theory's simplicity with regards to its capability of providing accurate descriptions of a complex reality. As a conclusion to his analysis, Kivisto suggested that PAT should be understood as an incomplete, partial, but still justified perspective for examining government-university relationships.

If anything, these recent works show the rapidly growing interest towards PAT and its applicability in studying higher education governance. Reasons for this development are various, but the general emphasis on topics like accountability (economic/political), governance, funding, and performance measurement have guided different researchers to examine PAT in the higher education context. What is interesting is that because of the unique nature of public higher education as both a public bureaucracy and a revenue producing corporation both the economic and political traditions of PAT traditions are represented in these contributions.

Economic PAT Applications to the Study of Higher Education Governance and Policy

The most central issue in economics PAT is contract effectiveness, which focuses on agent shirking and the principal's choice of options available to neutralize it. Logically, different aspects of shirking in universities could be illustrated using approaches that model the economic behavior of universities. Probably two of the best known models are referred to as the 'revenue theory of cost' (Bowen, 1980) and the utility maximizing models of (Garvin, 1980) and James (1986, 1990). In short, Bowen's revenue theory of cost assumes that universities raise as much money as they can, and then spend it all. Utility maximizing models assume that the main goal of the universities is to maximize utility, usually in a form of prestige. Prestige is important to universities for both non-pecuniary and pecuniary reasons. It is highly associated with good quality and good quality is associated with effective and expensive educational and research services. Further, possessing a good reputation enhances a university's social standing in the larger academic community. Prestige is also important because it contributes to the financial survival of the university. By developing a reputation as a prestigious institution, the market area of a university is likely to be expanded (Garvin, 1980).

Prestige maximization usually includes intra-organizational cross-subsidization. From an economic perspective, cross-subsidization can be understood as activity, where an organization carries out a set of profitable activities that do not yield utility per se to derive revenues it can then spend on utility maximizing activities that do not cover their own costs (James, 1990). Probably the most usual form of cross-subsidization takes place between undergraduate education and research. There, resources of low-prestige undergraduate education are transferred to subsidize high-prestige graduate studies or research (see, e.g. James, 1990; Mora & Vila, 2003). Although research excellence can improve teaching and learning experiences, it often competes directly with undergraduate instruction for the monetary resources and the time and attention of the faculty (Goldman et al., 2001). In fact, undergraduate instruction can be seen as a disutility-making activity preventing faculty from concentrating on prestige generating graduate training and research (Holtta, 1995).

Revenue theory of cost and utility maximizing models indicate the possibility of various types of shirking behavior, which may appear at both the individual and organizational level. Recognizing both levels of shirking is important as governing principals often do not discern the difference between the two, construing most shirking activity as coming from the institution. At the individual level, shirking is likely to come in the form of occasional and uncoordinated activity by individuals. For instance, faculty members could increase their discretionary time largely at the expense of meeting their institutional responsibilities due the increased revenues. This would represent shirking in the full meaning of the word (i.e. faculty divert those working hours not already taken up by teaching, grading, or conducting research to private activities such as accepting speaking engagements or private consulting). Simultaneously, the shirker may benefit from the prestige generated by the collective output of other faculty in his or her department or even elsewhere at the university (James, 1990; Massy & Zemsky, 1994; Ortmann & Squire, 2000).[14] At the institutional level, shirking could mean opportunistic cross-subsidization. The government can provide the same level of resources per undergraduate and graduate student, but the university may actually spend more on prestige-generating graduate students against the will of the government. The latter tend to be taught by expensive expert scholars in small classes, compared with undergraduates who are taught in large classes by less-expensive, relatively inexperienced teaching assistants. Similarly, university administration may base its allocations to departments on enrollments, but departments may assign low teaching loads, thereby transferring much of their resources to more prestige-generating research activities (James & Neuberger, 1981; James, 1990; Vedder, 2004).

The main problem of shirking from the government's perspective is that it decreases the productivity of universities as assessed by the efficiency and effectiveness of government provided funds. A university behaves opportunistically when it deliberately produces less or less effective outputs with the same inputs or consumes more inputs with same output.[15] Any form of shirking—whether individual or organizational—will have lowering effects on a university's efficiency since it deploys productive resources to other, non-productive purposes. It can also have a negative impact on effectiveness, including the quality of teaching and research. For instance, the shirking activity of the faculty members leading to a constant absence from the scheduled instructional tasks may lead to lower learning outcomes and unnecessary prolonging of students' time to graduation. Effectiveness is also lost when funds intended to be spent on undergraduate education are opportunistically transferred to subsidize research or other more prestige generating activities. Bigger class and group sizes or easier pass-rates in exams may produce "savings" that lower the quality of undergraduate instruction. As a result of this, lower learning outcomes of under-resourced undergraduates also result in ineffectiveness (Kivisto, 2007).

In addition to analyzing shirking behavior of universities, economics PAT offers insights to categorize the alternative government oversight mechanisms (behavior-based contracts vs. outcome-based contracts). Governments perform numerous oversight procedures in their relationships with universities, and many of these procedures have a logical analogy with behavior-based contracts. These include reporting requests, site visits, reviews and evaluations that focus on monitoring the productive activities, with the primary purpose of informing the government about how universities are behaving in economic and operational terms. As in behavior-based contracts, the amount of government funding has a connection with the observed behavior. Different forms of input-based funding arrangements (line-item budgeting/input-based formula funding) applied by the governments represent one type of behavior-based governance procedure (Kivisto, 2007).

The other option for the government to prevent shirking is to offer output/outcome-related incentives to universities. Similarly with outcome-based contracts, the general objective of output-based governance[16] is to reduce goal conflicts by aligning the goals of universities with the ones of the government. It is usually organized through performance-based funding practices which are constructed on some output-based funding formula. Because of the intangible nature of teaching and research outputs, governments have been forced to create surrogate measures and proxies, indicators, to describe and represent the outputs (Cave et al., 1997). Output indicators derived from teaching activities can include the number of study credits obtained, the number of exams passed, the number of undergraduate and graduate degrees granted and graduates' employment rates.

Output indicators derived from research activities can include the number of research publications, research income, the number of patents and licenses received, the number of doctoral students, and the number of doctoral degrees granted (e.g. Jongbloed & Vossensteyn, 2001). In addition, the government may also use more complex output-based performance indicators, like 'value-added', 'graduation rate', 'graduation time', and various output-connected average cost measures (Cave et al., 1997; Kivisto, 2007).

The central challenge for governments is to make a choice between behavior-based and output-based governance. For this challenge, PAT presents the two inter-related concepts of 'agency variables' (Eisenhardt, 1989) and 'agency costs' (Jensen & Meckling, 1976). Agency variables describe the levels of different internal and external conditions connected to the agency relationship that may have implications for the choice of oversight methods. In other words, agency variables are believed to be able to predict the most efficient governance choice for a given situation.[17] When choosing between different behavior-based and output-based governance procedures, the government can analyze and make predictions about the applicability and cost of each procedure in light of the agency variables. In addition to their predictive capabilities, the use of these variables offers help both for conceptualizing and analyzing many of the strengths and weaknesses that are inherent in using particular behavior- and output-based governance procedures. The other concept, agency costs, can be defined as the total sum of the costs resulting from governing universities plus the costs incurred because of the shirking behavior of the universities. The total governance costs include the direct costs associated with the governing procedures, but also the indirect costs that are incurred because of the dysfunctional effects they cause. The government faces a trade-off between two costly options: either it attempts to decrease informational asymmetries and pay the costs related to behavior-based governance, or, it reduces goal conflict by choosing the output-based form of governing and pays the agency costs related to output-based governance (Kivisto, 2007).[18]

Political Science PAT Applications to the Study of Higher Education Governance and Policy

As noted above, there exists a strong if quite varied relationship between public universities and the government of their state and/or nation. This relationship, however, cannot always be construed as one of a standard hierarchical PAT relationship. Universities, as government agents, operate, in part, as public bureaucracies. This type of operation gives need for incorporating aspects of the political PAT to the study of public colleges and universities.

First, like most public bureaucracies, the relationship between the governing principal(s) and universities does not cease to exist should one entity dislike or no longer value the relationship. As previously discussed, the use of performance and behavior-based contracts to guide university behavior are increasingly common. The contracts act as sub-contracts to the more fundamental contract that link the university with the government. While the government can use the subcontracts to regulate specific behaviors, it cannot altogether end its relationship with the university.[19] As Moe (2005) has noted, once created public bureaucracies assume a life of their own and their survival is protected by democratic rules which greatly inhibit governments' ability to eliminate existing parts of the bureaucracy. Thus, while the subcontracts can be renegotiated, the university does not operate under the assumption that its funding will completely disappear nor that its survival could be totally threatened.

Universities were formed and funded by the government to fulfill the need of society to create, preserve, and transmit knowledge. In order to empower the university to be able to fulfill its mission for the public, the government typically appropriates money to the institution. This is the basis of the implied PAT contract: the government pays for services provided by the university (an agent often created and protected by government rules). However, as noted earlier in the paper, agents (both individual and collective) are self-interested entities and prefer to pursue their own goals in the lieu of those of the principal. Not being able to completely leave or void the contract inhibits the government's ability to enforce the contract and, thus, must create new and vast incentive-based sub-contracts to guide university behavior.

Second, some of the products produced by a university are a public good. Universities engage in ever increasing array of activities, including teaching, research, social criticism, and most recently economic development (Fischer, 2006). These public goods are difficult to measure and it is even more difficult to assess how they are most effectively achieved (Trow, 1996). Above we discussed differences in teaching and research, where a faculty member could be viewed to be shirking teaching responsibilities to focus on graduate education or research. However, one could also argue that the research engaged in by the faculty member makes her a better teacher. Such linkages, realized by some faculty, are not easily measurable or demonstrable. Assuming that research aids in fulfilling the teaching function, it is not always evident at what point does time spent on research begin to negatively impact teaching. This point may vary based on institution, discipline, and faculty member. However, although research excellence can improve teaching, in all disciplines it usually competes directly with undergraduate instruction for the monetary resources and the time and attention of the faculty (Goldman et al., 2001). As such, no performance contract issued by the government can fully cover all aspects of a university's behavior. Thus, while the government may use such subcontracts to guide university behavior, there is no way to completely eradicate the moral hazard problem as it is impossible to fully measure or observe all of the functions of the university without drastically reorganizing the university structure and diminishing the professional and academic autonomy of the enterprise (e.g. Berdahl, 1990; Gornitzka et al., 2004; Kivisto, 2007).

Third, the government does not operate as a single principal. While there exists some rare occasions when a university can turn to a subcontract that clearly defines the goals of the government, universities usually operate under multiple explicit and implicit contracts (most of which declare a relationship between the university and a specific principal, but the terms of the contract are in constant flux depending on who holds a specific office or title). Universities operate in an environment of multiple, complex principals that created numerous agency problems (Lane, 2005). Shirking can be avoided when the agent's utility from fulfilling the goals of the principal is higher than the utility achieved in pursuing other goals (Frey, 1993). Thus, in order to alleviate shirking, the principal(s) that oversee the university must be identified.

The standard PAT is based on a single-principal relationship, in which the agent assesses and pursues the goals of one principal. The problem with public bureaucracies like universities, however, is that they operate in an environment filled with a range of multiple and collective principals. A multiple principal is when there exists more than one single principal relationship. For example, in the US, Congress and the President operate as multiple principals in that neither is subjugated to the other, but both can monitor and sanction a bureaucracy without consent of the other (Lyne & Tierney, 2003; see also Calvert et al., 1989; Hammond & Knott, 1996). Assessing shirking in such relationships becomes increasingly difficult, particularly if the multiple principals draft competing contracts with the agent. In such cases, the agent may need to pursue the goals of principal in lieu of the goals of another principal. Is this shirking? More importantly, it raises a set of question not directly addressed by economic models—how does an agent decide to which principal to subjugate? How does the other principal respond? Or, what happens when one principal benefits from the actions of a different principal? Space limitations inhibit our ability to fully explore all of these issues, but we will briefly discuss some of these implications in order to illuminate the implications of politics on the development of this model.

Like economists, political scientists suggest that agents choose which principal to follow based on utility maximization. The problem is how one assesses utility maximization in a political environment. It has already been suggested that survivability is not a concern as democratic rules provide extensive protections. In the corporate realm, the situation would be assessed based on which option would provide the most monetary profit for the agent. However, in politics, strings are usually attached to money, but money is not always the principal motivator. Universities are sometimes principled entities and choose to forego monetary rewards in order to do what they believe is right and proper. Thus, a university may find autonomy more important than increased appropriations.

Further, in the political realm actors constantly change. Thus, the university may choose a less profitable contract from an actor with the chance of reelection over that of a lame duck.

Collective principals present particularly interesting agency concerns not witnessed in the other PA relationships because of issues pertaining to collective action (Kiewiet & McCubbins, 1991). While collective principals can be viewed as single agents (e.g., a governing board) their differentiation from a single actor is that multiple individuals must agree on the nature of the contract with the agent. One potential problem with the collective principal is the possibility of underperformance in achieving goals because of the need to appease multiple entities. As such policy proposals may be weakened in order to achieve necessary votes for passage. Or, because of the delegation of power to an agent (e.g., president), the possibility arises for a subset of the collective to influence the agent for their benefit. "In this case, the de facto principal is distinct from the de jure principal, and thus the delegation must be analyzed in this light" (Lyne & Tierney, 2003, p., 12). Understanding the differences between de facto and de jure principal is critical for understanding such relationships as that between a governing board and a president. If a board chair rules with nearly absolute authority over the board, the chair becomes the de facto principal, even though by law all members of the board comprise the de jure principal. In this case, the president is likely to spend most of her time educating and responding to the board president. Time spent on the other members may be viewed as wasted time as they have little impact on the contract. Further, in this example, the board chair may be able to unilaterally influence agent behavior. If the president knows the Chair has the support of the other Board members, requests from the Chair may be perceived as contract changes, even though no formal vote of the de jure principal was taken.

The basic tenets of the contractual paradigm, including the existence of information, incentives, and oversight, hold constant in all PAT models. However, the existence of multiple and collective principals and an output that is difficult to measure make it difficult to clearly define the nature of the contract and the parties to that contract. As such, shirking, which continues to exist, becomes difficult to measure and thus more difficult address.

PAT's Application to Higher Education and Directions for Future Research

Like any other theory, PAT has confronted criticism (see, e.g. Perrow, 1986; Donaldson, 1990, 1995; Davis et al., 1997; Ghosal, 2005) and part of this criticism can also be considered relevant in higher education context. PAT has been criticized mostly because of the behavioral assumptions it makes concerning human motivation and behavior. The critics of PAT argue that the theory presents too narrow a model of human motivation and that it makes unnecessary negative and cynical moral evaluations about people. According to critics, focusing on self-interested and opportunistic behavior makes it possible to ignore a wider range of human motives, including altruism, trust, respect and intrinsic motivation of an inherently satisfying task. This criticism has validity also when PAT is utilized for analyzing government-university relationships. If universities are considered only as aggregates of self-interested shirkers, a high level of realism, objectivity and tactfulness will undoubtedly be lost.

Also, the fact that PAT examines agency relationships without questioning the legitimacy or justification of a principal's goals or the task to be accomplished can be considered as a limitation of the theory. In the free market environment, this framework is more understandable because of the free exit option the agents have. Because of the freedom of entry and exit to contracts, those agents that can accept the terms of a principal's contract are assumed to be willing to engage in principal-agent relationships. On the other hand, those agents who do not agree with the terms of a contract are not assumed to be engaged in a principal-agent relationship in the first place. The situation is usually somewhat different in the relationships between the government and public universities, in where universities' exit option is more limited or even denied by legislation. Therefore, one could justly ask the following questions: Should universities accept all the goals of the government without questioning their effects on freedom of speech, academic freedom or other aspects of institutional autonomy? Or, what happens if universities understand better than the government which higher education goals the government should be promoting (Kivisto, 2007)?

While certain objections about the model's assumptions may exist, PAT offers a range of heuristic and theoretical benefits for the study of higher education governance. In particular, the development of the theory in both economics and political science makes it particularly useful and versatile. Universities are driven by both economic and political motives (as well as philosophical beliefs about the role of the academy). As such both the economic and political derivatives of PAT help explain the behaviors of the various actors involved in the government-university relationship. Yet, as noted throughout this chapter, they neither fully explain the motives of the university; and in some cases the balance of power between the principal and agent leans toward the agent—more so than is typically seen in either economic or political models.

As discussed, economics PAT gives conceptual priority to economic aspects of the principal-agent relationship by investigating and analyzing the agent's shirking behavior and the principal's means to overcome it. In this sense, the economics PAT is "principal's theory" since it takes the perspective of securing the principal's welfare against potential or actual agent opportunism. In the context of higher education, this approach manifests itself in the focus on economic issues like costs, university productivity, and the efficiency and effectiveness of government's control and governance procedures. Moreover, economics PAT understands and examines government-university relationships as bilateral relationships between one principal (government) and one or more agents (universities). Influenced by the assumptions common to rational choice and methodological individualism, it assumes a homogenous incentive structure from the government. Since the concepts and problematizations are derived from markets and private sector settings, special emphasis is put on the explicit nature of explicit governance mechanisms and contracts. Therefore, the funding relationships between government and universities are considered in essence contractual, and they come close to the standard economic form with specific economic agreements distributing the exact responsibilities and rights of contracting parties. For this reason, although teaching, research, and service outputs and outcomes can be considered totally or partially as public goods, they are characterized by the contractual exchange process which is more typical for the transmission of private goods.

From the vantage of political science, universities cannot be viewed merely as contractual agents of the government. While they were originally created by the government to fulfill the needs of citizens, universities possess a level of autonomy that provides some protection from external interference. As such, the university may behave somewhat differently than an agent in a relationship in which a principal can readily end a contract and stop payment should the agent shirk on its responsibilities. Further, political PAT suggests that the government cannot often be viewed as a single entity, rather one that is comprised of multiple principals. When these separate principals act in concert, then the government may be assumed to be acting as a single principal. However, when these principals act in contradictory ways, it is important to recognize the existence of these multiple entities as it has a significant impact on how the university operates. At times, it is assumed that the university may have to select between competing goals—thus it becomes important to know why the university behaved in the way it did.

Finally, in adapting the model to the study of political governance in higher education, we must be vigilant in not just acknowledging what assumptions the different PA models bring to the table; but also how those assumptions impact perceptions of the operation under study. In fact, understanding the assumptions driving decisions may also help us in understanding certain patterns of institutional behavior. For example, does it make a difference to view the output of the university as a public or private good? To what extent can the output be construed as a private good? However, if we begin to view all of the work of the university in such a light, it may be easy to want to convert all of its work to easily measurable outputs. For example, it is much easier to measure the wages of recent graduates rather than how cultured that student may be. As such, a state may tend to focus on a graduate's employability instead of the quality of his liberal arts education, thus leading government agencies with oversight responsibilities to seek to replace humanities classes with more focused career education.

The vast majority of previous higher education studies applying PAT has utilized the theory primarily as conceptual framework, heuristic tool, or as an organizing concept with a purpose to offer new insights related to government oversight of universities.[20] These studies have been able to offer many definitions and operationalizations which can be considered as groundwork for further applications of the theory.[21] However, the number of empirical studies applying PAT, especially, the studies utilizing quantitative methods, have remained relatively low. For many of the PAT studies containing empirical data, the role of PAT has been treated as being of secondary importance, with priority given to the subject of the study. There may be various reasons for this, but the outcome has probably been influenced by the general lack of familiarity social scientists working in the field of higher education have had with the theory. In addition, suspicions about economic theories and some of their negative behavioral assumptions (e.g. self-interest, opportunism) also have presumably reduced empirical applications of PAT. On the other hand, other studies have given priority to theoretical development of PAT in higher education context without corresponding empirical analysis. Such developments occur, in part, due to the desire to develop more theoretically robust explanations for the operation of higher education governance; and, in part, related to the general problems of testing the PAT's explanatory and predictive potential as a theory.[22]

Regardless of the difficulties associated with the competing economic and political assumptions unique to higher education, or the difficulties with testing PAT-based hypothesis, which transcends disciplines and organizational types, PAT does provide much potential for furthering our understanding of complexities of higher education governance. There exists a fertile field for those interested in incorporating PAT into their work and the following section overviews the practical and theoretical areas ripe for further empirical exploration.

(1) *How can PAT improve understanding of policy and policy making?*

While most of this chapter has explored the theoretical and conceptual issues related to importing PAT into the study of higher education governance, it is important to note the practical benefits of using PAT to study, understand, and improve policy and policy making. Tuition setting, government funding programs (e.g., performance-based funding), governing board restructuring and performance, presidential appointments and decision making, and the implementation of almost any policy (e.g., affirmative action, aid programs, access issues, etc.) could benefit from the use of PAT. For example, by introducing the concept of shirking, PAT offers alternative explanations for lower levels of performance by universities. Shirking behavior may also explain why governments are so willing to invest time, effort and monetary resources in the governing and monitoring of universities. Important questions such as faculty productivity, higher education cost growth, tuition setting, and the quality of undergraduate education can all be analyzed in the light of the shirking concept. PAT is also able to offer insights for policymakers by analyzing the efficacy of alternative oversight mechanisms, such as legislative committee hearings, program reviews, budget reviews, selection of funding mechanisms, performance measurement, or simply allowing students, parents or the press to trigger "fire-alarms". Indeed, it is important for policy makers to ensure that various oversight mechanisms intended to verify university accountability are both valid, and theoretically and empirically sound, and that they have been developed within a conceptual framework coherent with the ideas and purposes for which they will be used (Cave et al., 1997).

Further, studying the role of information, interests, and incentives could provide a much more rich understanding of the complex dynamics between governors and boards, boards and presidents, legislators and presidents, and so forth. Why is it possible for governor, against the will of the legislature, to influence board behavior? If boards are intended as political buffers, why do politicians often circumvent the board when trying to influence policy? These same factors can help with studying policy decisions made by presidents and how presidents interact with boards. Why could a president be successful by only communicating with the board chair at one institution but lose favor of a board at a different institution with the same behavior? It could simply be because the organization of the board is different and the president failed to appropriately adjust for the differences. Turning to policy implementation, why do institutions embrace some policies while adamantly fight others (or simple ignore their implementation)? Could the explanation be based on philosophical (dis)agreement or the amount of money (incentive) attached to the policy implementation? All of these very practical situations are filled with principal-agent variables that, when acknowledged, could greatly aid in unpacking issues of administration, governance, and policy.

(2) *Does shirking exist in postsecondary governance structures? What might such shirking look like? How does it manifest itself?*

Even though PAT does not suggest that self-interest and opportunism are the only motivators of human beings or organizations, part of the problem is that the theory partly fails to explain the principal's utility losses by any other factor than agent opportunism. This problem is especially severe in government-university relationships. Given the ulterior nature of university opportunism, it can possibly be detected mainly from the low productivity levels of universities. With the exception of identifying some issues related to output uncertainty, economics PAT has not attempted to provide any analytical apparatus (except the agency variable of outcome uncertainty) by which the principal could distinguish an agent's non-opportunistic performance failures from the opportunistic ones.[23] Political science, however, has identified an issue of slippage—the concept that shirking may be due to information lost in communication, particularly when there are extended principal-agent chains.

More specifically, as noted previously, shirking can assume both aggressive and passive forms. This is a particularly critical issue in studying the behavior of educational institutions, which must deal with multiple and complex principal-agent relationships in addition to both economic and political motivations. If a government demands change that violates the fundamental tenets of the academy, does the academy shirk if it does not comply with the will of the government? For example, if a legislature demands the university not allow an event with a controversial subject matter (e.g., sex, drugs, offensive art) to occur on campus and the university refuses to comply citing freedom of speech principles, is the university shirking? Further, if the enabling statute suggests that the purpose of the university is "serve the state," who has the right to determine how the university serves the state?[24] Should it be the legislature or should it be the faculty? What if the faculty and the legislature have competing conceptions of appropriate university service? Is it shirking for the university to align itself with the conceptions of the faculty rather than the legislature? If a university refuses to admit an unqualified student that a specific legislator demands be admitted, is the university shirking on its contract with the government? These examples all relate directly to government relations, but similar questions could be raised about relationships with other actors such as students and donors. In an environment with multiple lines of authority, multiple sources of funding, and multiple sets of priorities, the concept of shirking exists but is exceedingly more complicated than that of a simple principal-agent hierarchy.

(3) *How do governments oversee university activities? What are the costs and impacts of different oversight mechanisms? To what extent do oversight mechanisms differ between systems/structures?*

Institutional arrangements differentially impact decision making and decision making processes. As Moe (2005) notes, governments create specific governance structures as a way to enact and institutionalize their agendas and empower specific groups. Therefore, understanding the impact of the arrangement of governance structures can help explain political processes and institutional behavior. A centralized governing board may provide political actors with greater influence over a state's system of higher education by consolidating power at one point of influence; paradoxically, it could increase institutional autonomy as the span of control increases as that one board is charged with overseeing the operations of multiple agents. The existence of multiple agents could make it more difficult for a board to hold institutions accountable. On the other hand, in a decentralized system with a separate board for each institution, the board may be better able to oversee the actions of an institution; but it does make it more difficult for a politician to control or influence a state's higher education system. Other arrangements that PAT could help us understand include the locus of power (constitutional vs. statutory), formation of board membership (elected vs. appointed), identification of board membership (body politic vs. special interest), or construction of reward structures (behavior-based vs. output-based). This topic could include at least the following research questions: Do governments use different types of oversight for constitutionally versus statutorily created institutions? To what extent can the utilization of different governance mechanisms be explained by perceived or real information asymmetries and conflicts of interests between government and universities? What are the impacts of governance mechanisms on the assumed or perceived shirking behavior of universities? What counter-incentives and dysfunctional effects may oversight mechanisms create? How does the selection of board members impact policy outputs (e.g., tuition setting or access)?

(4) *What is the differential impact of single, collective, and multiple principals?*
The existence of multiple and complex principals presents a number of complicating issues for institutions and the recognition of such is fundamental for understanding how a university interacts with different types of powerbrokers and decision makers. This line of research overlaps with the first two points on shirking and the organization of governance structures, but is significant enough to warrant separate mention. Above, we discussed the fact that higher education governance is more complex than the standard single-principal, single-agent relationship at the foundation of most PAT discussions. In reality, universities are responsible to an array of multiple and collective principals. In many cases, principals such as a governor and a legislature have the authority to oversee the activities of a university, but neither need the consent of the other to deal with the agent (Calvert et al., 1989; Hammond & Knott, 1996; Lyne & Tierney, 2003). If the governor and the legislature have two competing plans for higher education, one's interpretation of an institution's activities may differ whether one uses a single-principal or multiple-principal lens. An action that may be interpreted as shirking in a single-agent model, may be determined to be a strategic political decision when analyzed from a multiple-principal perspective. Both are shirking, but interpretations about institutional intentions may differ. Further research is needed to determine which principal an institution chooses to follow when competing contracts exist. In addition, research needs to explore how competing principals interact with each other, how competition among principals impacts the autonomy of an institution, and the extent to which collective principals operate cohesively or allow individual members to influence the agent. For example, if the members of a coordinating board are caught in a scandal that attracts the ire of the legislature, what is the impact on the institution? Political fighting between the board and the legislature could allow a university to freely engage in activity that might otherwise be questioned or investigated or the event could bring additional attention upon a university causing rather ordinary activities to receive additional scrutiny. In the case of collective principals, many interesting research questions exist that could significantly redefine how boards are studied. As Lane (2005) has noted:

> If a board chair rules with nearly absolute authority over the board, the chair becomes the *de facto* principal, even though by law all members of the board comprise the *de jure* principal. In this case, the institution's president is likely to spend must of her time educating and responding to the board president. Time spent on the other members may be viewed as wasted time as they have little impact on the contract between the board the president. Further, in this example, the board chair may be able to unilaterally influence agent behavior. If the president knows the Chair has the support of the other Board members, requests from the Chair may be perceived as contract changes, even though no formal vote of the *de jure* principal was taken. (p. 22)

Such research areas are not easily pursued as data can be difficult to obtain as such activities usually occur around the edges of sunshine laws, yet a framework such as PAT can aid in understanding the actions of presidents and boards.

(5) *How do interests, information, and incentives motivate institutional behavior?*
Finally, there is need for further exploration of the different motivations for university behavior and the creation of a model to predict when a university will behave more like an economically-motivated firm or more like a politically-motivated public bureaucracy. The evidence suggests that both types of motivations drive the university and that both economic and political models can partially explain its behavior. Yet, neither model can provide a full exploration and the two models actually contain competing assumptions of organizational and actor behavior. Both models can continue to be used independently, so long as researchers make clear the model which they are employing. However, in order to improve the robustness of the PATs explanatory ability, work needs

to be done to identify the conditions under which each model is most appropriate and how the interactions of economic and political motivations impact agent behavior. For instance, more information is needed on the behaviors, motivations and attitudes of the faculty and administrators. The extent in which extrinsic incentives (e.g. salary, positions, promotions, power) and intrinsic incentives (e.g. self-esteem, self-actualization, pleasure from helping others) are motivating the faculty and administrators needs to be assessed both from the economical and political perspectives.

These areas of inquiry demonstrate the need for deepening the dialogue between theoretical assumptions and empirical reality. The final solution of a PAT model for higher education must be context-bound and flexible in a way that some assumptions can be relaxed and some applied from both the economic and political PATs when empirical changing contexts require different approaches and assumptions.[25] Rather than viewing this final solution as a simple merger of two incomplete models; it must be built on the most basic assumptions of PAT, but also driven by observations of higher education governance. It cannot be completely driven by the two existing models as they are built on assumptions about organizations that do not fully mirror the nature of tertiary educational institutions. As such, we must move forward in determining commonalties among tertiary educational institutions as well as determining in what ways they compare and differ from corporations and public bureaucracies.

Conclusions

One of the great strengths of PAT has been in its generic nature. Nevertheless, PAT as a framework also evidences various tensions between economics and political science. Therefore, simply applying PAT to the study of higher education without appropriately recognizing the differences between the economic and political versions of PAT may lead to incorrect or misleading conclusions. In adapting PAT from economics to political science, contractual relationships often become implicit rather than explicit, some agents possess various levels of protected autonomy from principal control, principals are not always concerned about agent behavior, and agent performance is not always easily or immediately measurable (such as the case with the profit produced by a business). Both perspectives are useful in attempting to understand and explain the interrelationship of government bureaucracies, the structure and impact of governmental oversight, and the vast information asymmetries that exist within the government. However, failure to realize or acknowledge the specific perspectives guiding a study can result in inaccurate or incomplete explanations of the behavior/actions being examined.

While possessing great benefit, adapting PAT to higher education governance must account for these conflicting assumptions. For instance, university behavior that seem to be shirking from the perspective of economics PAT may be only legitimate political survival strategy from the perspective of political science PAT. Making the merger even more difficult, in most cases it is not simply determining which assumption is correct or the better fit for the model. Indeed, the best fitting assumption may be dictated by the confines of a given situation. As such, we cannot pick one or the other; we must determine the conditions under which a given assumption applies. Acknowledgement of the conditional requirements of an assumption is critical for further development of the model as misapplication of an assumption may lead to misdiagnosis of a particular behavior or an ineffective solution to the defined agency problem.

It should not be construed that a theory of higher education governance can not be achieved through the application of PAT. Rather, PAT holds great benefit for scholars of tertiary governance systems. Indeed, contracts, both implicit and explicit, are ubiquitous throughout the university and government relationship. Because the university operates as both a firm and a public bureaucracy, assumptions from both the economic and political PAT are applicable; however, neither is consistently in play and universities may switch between the two depending on the context. As illustrated through this paper, the difficulty is that higher education institutions operate under both economic and political assumptions; thus, understanding their behavior is not as easy as understanding that of a traditional firm or a pure public bureaucracy.

Notes

1. Readers should note that our discussion relates primarily to the general relationship between governments and public higher education institutions. Throughout the chapter, we use such terms as university, college, and higher education institution interchangeably to represent all public postsecondary institutions. In addition, while our examples are primarily drawn from the US and Europe, as that is the focus of current work in the field, the PAT can be applied to many government-higher education governance arrangements.

2. Notable exceptions include the work of Ferris (1991), Gourdrian and DeGroot (1990), and Toma (1986, 1990) who were among the first to introduce a neo-institutional perspective to the study of higher education governance; however, their work was largely unnoticed by mainstream higher education governance scholars.

3. Even though trust in the academia has decreased in the last several years, the information asymmetry caused by faculty expertise still exists. External stakeholders may use indicators such as graduation rates to determine compliance with principal goals, but this does not mean they have ability to assess such things as faculty use of time (e.g., to what extent does writing a book impact student learning?).

4. Shirking in the principal-agent literature is defined as the action of evading one's work or pursuing one's own goals in lieu of the principal's (Fiorina, 1982). Shirking in this context may be either passive or aggressive. It may mean that the agent advertently fails to pursue the goals of the principal or purposefully engages in actions not in line with the goals of the principal.

5. This section provides only a brief overview of the major aspects of the evolutionary pattern of new institutionalism, primarily in the context of economics and political science research. New institutionalism has had significant impacts on the study of organizations in other fields such as sociology, organizational theory, and history. While basic concepts remain the same, each field has developed various sets of assumptions and goals associated with new institutionalism. See Powell and DiMaggio (1991) for a comparative discussion of new institutionalism in political science, economics, and sociology.

6. One of the classic applications of new institutionalism to higher education is Cohen et al.'s (1972) "garbage can model" explanation of university decision making.

7. The positive theory of agency seems to have connected to a broader body of theoretical work known as 'Organizational Economics' (see, e.g. Barney & Ouchi, 1986; Donaldson, 1990; Barney & Hesterly, 1996). Organizational Economics (OE) is composed of transaction cost economics (see Coase, 1937; Williamson, 1975, 1985) and property rights literature (Alchian & Demsetz, 1972). Although some other contributions of OE exist (see Barney & Hesterly, 1996), PAT and transaction cost economics are clearly its best known components. As the name implies, OE basically applies different economic models and assumptions to the field of organization studies (Kivisto, 2007).

8. The contract was the central concept for the early PAT theorists because it distinguished PAT from classical and neoclassical economics, in which market forces act as a disciplining mechanism on the owner/entrepreneurs who actively manage firms (Tosi et al., 1997). However, inside the various approaches of economics PAT there exist different ways to understand the nature of the contract. Some scholars including Eisenhardt (1989) and Bergen et al. (1992) have seemingly interpreted the contract to be more like a "metaphor" of a PA relationship, not as a specific and detailed construct that should be rigorously operationalized.

9. The utility maximization assumption is especially important for mathematically oriented principal-agent researchers, because it allows different situations to be modeled and predicted mathematically in a way that would not be otherwise possible (Hendry, 2005).

10. In the traditional sense, a 'private good' is a good consumed by one person which cannot be consumed by another person (i.e. exclusion feasible, private use). A 'public good' is a good that, even if it is consumed by one person, is still available for consumption by others (exclusion infeasible, collective use) (see e.g. Begg et al., 1994).

11. This is not to ignore attempts to measure university outputs though such indicators as graduation rates, exam scores, and graduate school acceptance; but there remains debate about the appropriateness of these indicators to measure institutional productivity.

12. Previous higher education governance studies using PAT include Toma (1986, 1990) and Gourdrian and DeGroot (1990) as well as a few occasional references and some short analyses that took place in 1990s (e.g. Ferris, 1991; Braun, 1993; Williams, 1995; Massy, 1996; Geuna, 1999).

13. One possible explanation for this finding is that the way in which a member is selected can impact that member's ability to shirk. Let us assume that the board member is an agent of those who enable their

membership on the board. Let us also assume that the electorate is generally highly concerned about the cost of a higher education to the student. If a board member is elected by the public, they should be responsive to the desires of the public (the public's ability to prevent shirking is in their ability to remove or choose not to re-elect a board member with whom they are displeased). However, appointment of members removes the public's ability to directly punish shirking. In appointment situations, the board member's principal become the government official making the appointment (likely the governor). The new principal's priorities may be freeing up state funds by shifting the costs to the individual. Even though the public still prefers lower costs, it is unlikely that they would unseat a politician simply because they refused or were unable to reign in a university board. Because there is little punishment for not following the priorities of the public, there is little incentive to keep costs low.

14. The phenomenon of benefiting from the group while not contributing is also referred to as "free riding."

15. For this general discussion, we are not considering inflationary increases.

16. PAT usually utilizes the term 'outcome' in the traditional meaning of 'output', and therefore, these terms are considered here as synonymous.

17. Although the exact number of agency variables has varied in different research settings, at least five variables known as 'outcome measurability', 'outcome uncertainty', 'task programmability', 'goal conflict', and 'length of agency relationship', can be identified.

18. The monetary costs of governance in a given concrete situation are practically impossible to calculate. It is unlikely that government cost calculation systems would be able to count all the costs that are related to the use of a certain type of governance procedures. Nevertheless, these costs can be indirectly estimated and perceived in other than monetary terms. For instance, the cost of governance procedures could be evaluated indirectly as the amount of planning they require to be established and to operate, the number of new employment positions required, or new hierarchies their application creates and the observable or estimated dysfunctions they inflict on the production behavior of the universities. Due to the invisible and unperceivable nature of shirking behavior, the costs of detected and undetected shirking, 'opportunism costs', are even more difficult to calculate, although analytically they are possible to distinguish (see Vining & Globerman, 1999). Nevertheless, as a theoretical concept, they could offer interesting perspectives in speculating on the meaningfulness and effects of the government governance of universities (Kivisto, 2007).

19. In a standard corporate model, the principal could fire the agent should the agent expend the principal's money in a manner with which the principal does not agree. Further, should the agent not like the terms of the agreement (i.e., expending the money to support undergraduate education), it could choose not to enter into a relationship with the principal or seek to cancel its contract. (Or they could both complete the contract and simply choose not to work together in the future.) However, when dealing with public bureaucracies, such actions are not typically possible. Indeed, the government could try to dissolve the university by revoking its charter or deleting the enabling statutes. While such an action is theoretically possible, the practicality is near impossible as it is very difficult to eliminate a public bureaucracy. Structures created through political means often assume a life of their own and thus work to sustain their survivability. In particular, while it is often easy to garner votes to create an entity, it is much more difficult to garner votes to eliminate a public entity, particularly one that provides a public service (Moe, 2005). This inherent sustainability of public bureaucracies allows them a level of power agents in other PAT relationships may not exist. If one realizes that a principal cannot threaten your survival, one may be less likely to fully abide by or pursue the goals of the principal. However, the government does possess options than can threaten the stability or thrivability of an institution. For example, governments can choose to reduce or eliminate funding, can influence personnel actions against those supporting insubordinate action, or use their public presence to influence public opinion (possibly resulting in decreases in student quality or private donations).

20. A very few scholars (e.g. Gomez-Mejia & Balkin 1992; Wiseman, 1999; Ortmann & Squire, 2000) have used PAT to examine the internal workings of universities, but such analysis is beyond the scope of this discussion. Nevertheless, it seems that also focusing on intra-university agency relationships and their role and influence on government-university relationships still need further empirical clarification and modeling.

21. See Kivisto (2007) for more in-depth discussion of the theoretical strengths and weaknesses of the economic theory, particularly in relation to European settings where there tend to be a strong and unitary government organization acting as the principal.

22. For a general discussion of empirical testing of PAT from an economic perspective, see, e.g. Perrow (1986), Eisenhardt (1989), Barney (1990), Donaldson (1990), Petersen (1993) and Ghoshal (2005).

23. For recent discussion of organizational performance failures, see, e.g. Meier & Bohte (2003), Mellahi & Wilkinson (2004), Andrews et al. (2006), and Murray & Dollery (2006).
24. Dunn (2003) provides an excellent discussion of the applicability of the classic Friedrich-Finer debates about the appropriate relationship between elected and non-elected officials to the study of higher education governance.
25. Of course, the types of assumptions may also be dictated by the focus of the research question.

References

Alchian, A. A., & Demsetz, H. (1972). Production, information costs, and economic organization. *The American Economic Review, 62*(5), 777–795.

Andrews, R., Boyne, G. A., & Enticott, G. (2006). Performance failure in the public sector. Misfortune or mismanagement? *Public Management Review, 8*(2), 273–296.

Barney, J. B. (1990). The debate between traditional management theory and organizational economics: Substantive differences or intergroup conflict? *Academy of Management Review, 15*(3), 382–393.

Barney, J. B., & Hesterly, W. (1996). Organizational economics: Understanding the relationship between organizations and economic analysis. In Glegg, S. R., Hardy, C., & Nord, W. R. (eds.), *Handbook of organization studies* (pp. 115–147). London: Sage.

Barney, J. B., & Ouchi, W. G. (eds.) (1986). *Organizational economics* (3rd printing). San Francisco, CA: Jossey-Bass.

Begg, D., Fischer, S., & Dornbusch, R. (1994). *Economics* (4th ed.). London: McGraw-Hill.

Bendor, J., & Meirowitz, A. (2004). Spatial models of delegation. *American Political Science Review, 98*(2), 293–310.

Bendor, J., Taylor, S., & Van Gaalen, R. (1987). Politicians, bureaucrats, and asymmetric information. *American Journal of Political Science, 31*, 796–828.

Berdahl, R. O. (1990). Academic freedom, autonomy and accountability in British universities. *Studies in Higher Education, 15*(2), 169–180.

Bergen, M., Dutta, S., & Walker, O. C. Jr. (1992). Agency relationships in marketing: A review of the implications and applications of agency and related theories. *Journal of Marketing, 56*, 1–24.

Birnbaum, R. (1988). *How colleges work. The cybernetics of academic organization and leadership*, San Francisco, CA: Jossey-Bass.

Bowen, H. R. (1977). *Investment in learning. The individual and social value of American higher education.* San Francisco, CA: Jossey-Bass.

Bowen, H. R. (1980). *The costs of higher education. How much do colleges and universities spend per student and how much should they spend?* San Francisco, CA: Jossey-Bass.

Bowen, F.M., Bracco, K.R., Callan, P.M., Finney, J.E., Richardson, Jr., R.C., Trombley, W. (1997). *State Structures for Governance of Higher Education: A comparative study.* San Jose, CA: The California Higher Education Policy Center.

Braun, D. (1993). Who governs intermediary agencies? Principal-agent relations in research policy-making. *Journal of Public Policy, 13*(2), 135–162.

Brehm, J., & Gates, S. (1993). Doughnut shops and speed traps. *American Journal of Political Science, 37*(2), 555–581.

Calvert, R., McCubbins, M., & Weingast, B. (1989). A theory of political control and agency discretion. *American Journal of Political Science, 33*(3), 588–611.

Cave, M., Hanney, S., Henkel, M., & Kogan, M. (1997). *The use of performance indicators in higher education. The challenge of the quality movement* (3rd ed.). London: Jessica Kingsley Publishers.

Clark, B. R. (1983). *The higher education system. Academic organization in cross-national perspective.* Berkeley, CA: University of California Press.

Coase, R. H. (1937). The nature of the firm. *Economica, 4*(16), 386–405.

Cohen, M. D., March, J. G., & Olsen, J. P. (1972). A garbage can model of organizational choice. *Administrative Science Quarterly, 17*(1), 1–25.

Davis, J. H., Schoorman, F. D., & Donaldson, L. (1997). Toward a stewardship theory of management. *Academy of Management Review, 22*(1), 20–47.

Donaldson, L. (1990). The ethereal hand: Organizational economics and management theory. *Academy of Management Review, 15*(3), 369–381.

Donaldson, L. (1995). *American anti-management theories of organization. A critique of paradigm proliferation.* New York: Cambridge University Press.

Downs, G. W., & Rocke, D. M. (1994). Conflict, agency, and gambling for resurrection: The principal-agent problem goes to war. *American Journal of Political Science, 38*(2), 362–380.

Doyle, W. R. (2006). Adoption of merit-based student grant programs: An event history analysis. *Educational Evaluation and Policy Analysis, 28*(3), 259–285.

Doyle, W. R., McLendon, M. K., & Hearn, J. C. (2005). *The adoption of prepaid tuition and savings plans in the American states: An event history analysis.* Paper presented at the annual meeting of the Association for the Study of Higher Education, Philadelphia, PA.

Dunn, D. (2003). Accountability, democratic theory, and higher education. *Educational Policy, 17*(1), 60–79.

Duryea, E. D. (2000). *The Academic corporation: A history of college and university governing boards.* New York: Falmer.

Eisenhardt, K. (1989). Agency theory: An assessment and review. *Academy of Management Review, 14*(1), 57–74.

Fearon, J. D. (1999). Electoral accountability and the control of politicians: Selecting good types versus sanctioning poor performance. In Przeworski, A., Stokes, S. C., & Manin, B. (eds.), *Democracy, Accountability, and Representation.* Cambridge: Cambridge University Press.

Ferejohn, J. (1986). Incumbent performance and electoral control. *Public Choice, 50,* 5–25.

Ferris, J. M. (1991). Contracting and higher education. *The Journal of Higher Education, 62*(1), 1–24.

Fiorina, M. P. (1982). Legislative choice of regulatory reforms: Legal process or administrative process? *Public Choice, 39,* 33–61.

Fischer, K. (2006). The university as economic savior. *The Chronicle of Higher Education, 52*(45), A18.

Frey, B. S. (1993). Does monitoring increase work effort? The rivalry with trust and loyalty. *Economic Inquiry, 31*(4), 663–670.

Garvin, D. A. (1980). *The economics of university behavior.* New York: Academic.

Geuna, A. (1999). *The economics of knowledge production. Funding and structure of university research.* Cheltenham, England: Edward Elgar.

Ghoshal, S. (2005). Bad management theories are destroying good management practices. *Academy of Management Learning & Education, 4*(1), 75–91.

Gittell, M., & Kleiman, N. S. (2000). The political context of higher education. *American Behavioral Scientist, 43*(7), 1058–1091.

Goldman, C. A., Gates, S. M., & Brewer, D. J. (2001). Prestige or reputation: Which is a sound investment? *Chronicle of Higher Education, 48*(6), B13–B15.

Gomez-Mejia, L. R., & Balkin, D. B. (1992). Determinants of faculty pay: An agency theory perspective. *Academy of Management Journal, 35*(5), 921–955.

Gornitzka, Å., Stensaker, B., Smeby, J-C., & de Boer, H. (2004). Contract arrangements in the Nordic countries. Solving the efficiency/effectiveness dilemma? *Higher Education in Europe, 29*(1), 87–101.

Gourdrian, R., & DeGroot, H. (1990). A principal-agent model of regulation applied to the case of American universities. In Prud'homme, R. (ed.), *Public finance with several levels of government* (pp. 181–194). The Hague, The Netherlands: Foundation Journal Public Finance.

Hammond, T. H., & Knott, J. H. (1996). Who controls the bureaucracy? Presidential power, Congressional dominance, legal constraints and bureaucratic autonomy in a model of multi-institutional policy-making. *Journal of Law, Economics and Organization, 12*(1), 119–166.

Hearn, J. C., & Griswold, C. P. (1994). State-level centralization and policy innovation in U.S. postsecondary education. *Educational Evaluation and Policy Analysis, 16*(2), 161–190.

Hendry, J. (2005). Beyond self-interest: Agency theory and the board in a satisfying world. *British Journal of Management, 16*(1), S55–S63.

Hicklin, A., & Meier, K. (2004). *Race, structure, and state governments: The politics of higher education diversity.* Paper presented at the annual meeting of the Midwest Political Science Association, Chicago, IL.

Holtta, S. (1995). *Towards the self-regulative university.* Publications Joensuu: University of Joensuu.

Horn, M. J., & Shepsle, K. A. (1989). Commentary on "administrative arrangements and the political control of agencies": Administrative process and organizational form as legislative responses to agency costs. *Virginia Law Review, 75*(2), 499–508.

James, E. (1986). Cross-subsidization in higher education: Does it pervert private choice and public policy? In Levy, D. C. (ed.), *Private education. Studies in choice and public policy* (pp. 237–257). New York: Oxford University Press.

James, E. (1990). Decision processes and priorities in higher education. In Hoenack, S. A. & Collins, E. L. (eds.), *The economics of American universities. Management, operations, and fiscal environment* (pp. 77–106). Albany, NY: State University of New York Press.

James, E., & Neuberger, E. (1981). The university department as a non-profit labor cooperative. In Bowman, M. J. (ed.), *Collective choice in education* (pp. 207–234). Boston, MA: Kluwer/Nijhoff.

Jensen, M. C. (1983). Organization theory and methodology. *The Accounting Review, 58*(2), 319–339.

Jensen, M. C., & Meckling, W. H. (1976). Theory of the firm: Managerial behavior, agency costs and ownership structure. *Journal of Financial Economics, 3*(4), 305–360.

Johnes, J., & Taylor, J. (1990). *Performance indicators in higher education. UK universities.* Buckingham: SRHE/Open University Press.

Jongbloed, B., & Vossensteyn, H. (2001). Keeping up performances: an international survey of performance-based funding in higher education. *Journal of Higher Education Policy and Management, 23*(2), 127–145.

Kiewiet, D. R., & McCubbins, M. (1991). *The logic of delegation: Congressional parties and the appropriations process.* Chicago, IL: University of Chicago Press.

Kivisto, J. A. (2005). The government-higher education institution relationship: Theoretical considerations from the perspective of agency theory. *Tertiary Education and Management, 11*(1), 1–17.

Kivisto, J. A. (2007). *Agency theory as a framework for the government-university relationship.* Tampere: Higher Education Group/Tampere University Press.

Knott, J. H., & Payne, A. A. (2004). The impact of state governance structures on management and performance of public organizations: A study of higher education institutions. *Journal of Policy Analysis and Management, 23*(1), 13–30.

LaFollette, M. C. (1994). The politics of research misconduct: Congressional oversight, universities, and science. *The Journal of Higher Education, 65*(3), 261–285.

Lane, J. E. (2003). *State government oversight of public higher education: Police patrols and fire alarms.* Paper presented at the annual meeting of the Association for the Study of Higher Education, Portland, OR.

Lane, J. E. (2005). *State oversight of higher education: A theoretical review of agency problems with complex principals.* Paper presented at 2005 Annual Conference of the Association for the Study of Higher Education, Philadelphia, PA.

Lane, J. E. (2007). Spider Web of Oversight: Latent and Manifest Regulatory Controls in Higher Education. *Journal of Higher Education, 78*(6), 1–30.

Lassar W. M., & Kerr, J. L. (1996). Strategy and control in supplier-distributor relationships: An agency perspective. *Strategic Management Journal, 17*(8), 613–632.

Liefner, I. (2003). Funding, resource allocation, and performance in higher educations systems. *Higher Education, 46,* 469–489.

Lowry, R. C. (2001). Governmental structure, trustee selection, and public university prices and spending. *American Journal of Political Science, 45*(4), 845–861.

Lyne, M., & Tierney, M. (2003) *The politics of common agency: Unitary, multiple and collective principals.* Paper presented at the annual meeting of The American Political Science Association, Philadelphia, PA.

March, J. G., & Olsen, J. P. (1984). The New Institutionalism: Organizational factors in political life. *The American Political Science Review, 78*(3), 734–749.

Massy, W. F. (1996). Reengineering resource allocation systems. In Massy, W. F. (ed.), *Resource allocation in higher education* (pp. 15–47). Ann Arbor, MI: The University of Michigan Press.

Massy, W. F., & Zemsky, R. (1994). Faculty discretionary time. Departments and the "academic ratchet". *Journal of Higher Education, 65*(1), 1–22.

McCubbins, M. D. (1985). Legislative design of regulatory structure. *American Journal of Political Science, 29*(4), 721–748.

McCubbins, M. D., & Schwartz, T. (1984). Congressional oversight overlooked: Police patrols versus fire alarms. *American Journal of Political Science, 28*(1), 165–179.

McCubbins, M. D., Noll, R. G., & Weingast, B. R. (1987). Administrative procedures as instruments of political control. *Journal of Law, Economics, and Organization, 3*(2), 243–277.

McCubbins, M. D., Noll, R. G., & Weingast, B. R. (1989). Structure and process, politics and policy: Administrative arrangements and the political control of agencies. *Virginia Law Review, 75,* 431–482.

McLendon, M. K. (2003). The politics of higher education: Toward an expanded research agenda. *Educational Policy, 17*(1), 165–191.

McLendon, M. K., Deaton, R., & Hearn, J. C. (2007). The enactment of state governance reforms in higher education. *The Journal of Higher Education, 78*(6), 645–675.

McLendon, M. K., Hearn, J. C. & Deaton, R. (2006). Called to account: Analyzing the origins and spread of state performance-accountability policies for higher education. *Educational Evaluation and Policy Analysis, 28*(1), 1–24.

McLendon, M. K., Heller, D. E., & Young, S. (2005). State postsecondary education policy innovation: Politics, competition, and the interstate migration of policy ideas. *The Journal of Higher Education, 76*(4), 363–400.

Meier, K. J., & Bohte, J. (2003). Not with a bang, but a whimper. Explaining organizational failures. *Administration & Society, 35*(1), 104–121.

Mellahi, K., & Wilkinson, A. (2004). Organizational failure: A critique of recent research and a proposed integrative framework. *International Journal of Management Reviews, 5/6*(1), 21–41.

Miller, G. J. (2005). The political evolution of principal-agent models. *Annual Review of Political Science, 8*, 203–225.

Mintzberg, H. (1979). *The structuring of organizations: A synthesis of the research.* Englewood Cliffs, NJ: Prentice-Hall.

Mitnick, B. M. (1980). *The political economy of regulation.* New York: Columbia University Press.

Moe, T. M. (1984). The new economics of organization. *American Journal of Political Science, 28*(4), 739–777.

Moe, T. M. (1985). Control and feedback in economic regulation: The case of the NLRB. *American Political Science Review, 79*(4), 1094–1116.

Moe, T. M. (1989). "The Politics of Bureaucratic Structure." In J. E. Chubb and P. E. Peterson, (eds). *Can Government Govern?* Washington, D.C.: Brookings, 267–324.

Moe, T. M. (1990). Political institutions: The neglected side of the story. *Journal of Law, Economics and Organization, 6*, 213–253.

Moe, T. M. (2005). Power and political institutions. *Perspectives on Politics, 3*(2), 215–234.

Mora, J.-G., & Vila, L. E. (2003). The economics of higher education. In Begg, R. (ed.), *The dialogue between higher education research and practice* (pp. 121–134). Dordrecht, The Netherlands: Kluwer.

Murray, D., & Dollery, B. (2006). Institutional breakdown? An explanatory taxonomy of Australian universities. *Higher Education Policy, 19*, 479–494.

Nicholson-Crotty, J., & Meier, K. J. (2003). Politics, structure, and public policy: The case of higher education. *Educational Policy, 17*(1), 80–97.

Ogul, M.S. & Rockman, B. (1990). Overseeing Oversight: New Departures and Old Problems. *Legislative Studies Quarterly, 15*(1), 5–24.

Ortmann, A., & Squire, R. (2000). A game-theoretic explanation of the administrative lattice in institutions of higher learning. *Journal of Economic Behavior & Organization, 43*, 377–391.

Payne, A. A. (2003). The effects of Congressional appropriation committee membership on the distribution of federal research funding to Universities. *Economic Inquiry, 41*(2), 325–345.

Payne, A. A., & Roberts, J. (2004). *Government oversight of organizations engaged in multiple activities: Does centralized governance encourage quantity or quality?* Unpublished manuscript, McMaster University.

Petersen, T. (1993). The economics of organization: The principal-agent relationship. *Acta Sociologica, 36*, 277–293.

Perrow, C. (1986). *Complex organizations. A critical essay* (3rd ed.). New York: Random House.

Powell, W. W., & DiMaggio, D. J. (eds.) (1991). *The New Institutionalism in organizational analysis.* Chicago, IL: University of Chicago Press.

Ricketts, M. (2002). *The economics of business enterprise. An introduction to economic organization and the theory of firm* (3rd ed.). Cheltenham, England: Edward Elgar.

Ross, S. A. (1973). The economic theory of agency: The principal's problem. *American Economic Review, 63*(2), 134–139.

Scholz, J. T. (1991). Cooperative regulatory enforcement and the politics of administrative effectiveness. *American Political Science Review, 85*(1), 115–136.

Shepsle, K. A., & Boncheck, M. S. (1997) *Analyzing politics: Rationality, behavior, and institutions.* New York: W. W. Norton.

Sobel, J. (1993). Information control in the principal-agent problem. *International Economic Review, 34*(2), 259–269.

Songer, D., Segal, J. A., & Cameron, C. M. (1994). The hierarchy of justice: Testing a principal-agent model of supreme court-circuit court interactions. *American Journal of Political Science, 38*(3), 673–696.

Toma, E. F. (1986). State university boards of trustees: A principal-agent perspective. *Public Choice, 49*, 155–163.

Toma, E. F. (1990). Boards of trustees, agency problems, and university output. *Public Choice, 67*, 1–9.

Tosi, H. L. Jr., Katz, J. P., & Gomez-Mejia, L. R. (1997). Disaggregating the agency contract: The effects of monitoring, incentive alignment, and term in office on agent decision making. *Academy of Management Journal, 40*(3), 584–602.

Trow, M. A. (1996). Trust, markets and accountability in higher education: A comparative perspective. *Higher Education Policy, 9*(4), 309–324.

Vedder, R. (2004). *Going broke by degree. Why college costs too much?* Washington, DC: AEI.

Vining, A. and Globerman, S. (1999), "A Conceptual Framework for Understanding the Outsourcing Decision," *European Management Journal, 17*(6), 645–54.

Waterman, R. W., & Meier, K. J. (1998). Principal-agent models: An expansion? *Journal of Public Administration Research and Theory, 8*, 173–202.

Weingast, B. R. (1984). The Congressional bureaucratic system: A principal-agent perspective (with application to the SEC). *Public Choice, 44*(1), 147–191.

Weingast, B. R., & Moran, M. J. (1983). Bureaucratic discretion or congressional control: Regulatory policymaking by the federal trade commission. *Journal of Political Economy, 91*(5), 765–800.

Whynes, D. K. (1993). Can performance monitoring solve the public services' principal-agent problem? *Scottish Journal of Political Economy, 40*, 434–446.

Williams, G. (1995). The "marketization" of higher education: Reforms and potential reforms in higher education finance. In Dill, D. D. & Sporn, B. (eds.), *Emerging patterns of social demand and university reform: Through a glass darkly.* Oxford: IAU/Pergamon.

Williamson, O. E. (1975). *Markets and hierarchies: Analysis and antitrust implications. A study in the economics of internal organization.* New York: Free Press.

Williamson, O. E. (1985). *The economic institutions of capitalism. Firms, markets, relational contracting.* New York: Free Press.

Wiseman, M. S. (1999). *Faculty performance: Evaluation and principal-agent concerns at Texas state-supported universities.* Unpublished dissertation, Texas Tech University.

Wood, B. D. (1988). Principals, bureaucrats, and responsiveness in clean air enforcements. *The American Political Science Review, 82*(1), 213–234.

Wood, B. D. & Waterman, R. W. (1991). The dynamics of political control of the bureaucracy. *American Political Science: Review, 85*(3), 801–828.

How to Survive in Postindustrial Environments

Adam Smith's Advice for Today's Colleges and Universities

Andreas Ortmann

> In every profession, the exertion of the greater part of those who exercise it, is always in proportion to the necessity they are under of making that exertion.
>
> Adam Smith

Introduction

Many, if not most, institutions of higher education have fallen on fiscal hard times. Because revenue-enhancing strategies have for the most part been exhausted, administrators in such institutions increasingly "restructure" or "reengineer" their institutions to balance budgets.[1] Unfortunately, reengineering and similar "quality practices" have failed to deliver on their promises in one out of every two cases in manufacturing and other service industries (Hammer & Champy, 1994, pp. 217–218). Keidel (1994) has suggested that this high failure rate is the result of a lack of theorizing. Specifically, he proposes to "rethink" organizational design while keeping in mind that organizational outcomes are a function of cognitive patterns of managers. Abrahamson and Park (1994), Cameron (1983), Cameron and Tschirhart (1992), Zammuto and O'Connor (1992), and Ostroff and Schmidt (1994) have provided empirical support for this proposition. With many colleges and universities embarking on "restructuring" and "reengineering" experiments, Keidel's proposition seems relevant.

For higher education, the analysis is complicated by the fact that most colleges and universities are nonprofit organizations. Hence, their optimization criteria are less clearly defined (Cohen, March, & Olsen, 1972; March & Simon, 1993; Oster, 1995; Young, 1983; Rothschild & White, 1991; Steinberg, 1993; Young & Steinberg, 1995). Complicating matters is the high degree of autonomy that faculty is often granted and its nonhierarchical organization (Massy & Zemsky, 1994). Organizational outcomes are thus also functions of cognitive patterns of faculty.

Drawing on his own quite diverse experiences, Adam Smith reflected extensively on educational institutions. In doing so, Smith also made the connection between organizational patterns and cognitive patterns. In addition, he linked the origin and evolution of cognitive patterns to teachers' and administrators' preferences and incentives. I propose that his disinterested advice from yesterday can be helpful in analyzing incentive problems that currently afflict higher education and in understanding emerging trends that seem to address them.

This article is organized as follows: First, I summarize Smith's analysis of the incentive problems that afflicted higher education at his time. I then discuss incentive problems that plague higher education today and emerging trends that signify attempts to deal with them. After a review of related literature I conclude with a discussion of the relevance and implications of Adam Smith's insights for our understanding of postindustrial environments.

Incentive Problems That Afflicted Higher Education in Smith's Day

Smith discusses education in Book V, Part III, Article II of *The Wealth of Nations* (Smith 1776). In that Book, Smith reviews the duties of the sovereign, which he identifies as defense, justice, infrastructure, and the provision of educational and ecclesiastical institutions. Throughout his discussion, a central concern of Smith is whether the necessary expenses can be repaid by those that benefit from the good or service to be provided. Smith argues that

> the institutions for the education of the youth may . . . furnish a revenue sufficient for defraying their own expense. The fee or honorary which the scholar pays to the master naturally constitutes a revenue of this kind (p. 716).

Having postulated that she or he who benefits ought to pay,[2] Smith notes that most schools and colleges in Europe have significant endowments, which tend to translate into guaranteed salaries for teachers, and he asks,

> Have those public endowments contributed in general to promote the end of their institution? Have they contributed to encourage the diligence, and to improve the abilities of the teachers? Have they directed the course of education towards objects more useful, both to the individual and to the public, than those to which it would naturally have gone of its own accord? (p. 716).

In answering these three questions Smith identifies the main components of modern agency theory: (1) the problem of adjustable quality and effort, which, when combined with asymmetric information, generates what is generally known as the principal-agent problem;[3] (2) the disadvantages of third-party enforcement; and (3) the advantages of reputational enforcement (Klein & Leffler, 1981).

The key to his analysis is the insight that education is an experience good, i.e., a service whose quality cannot be ascertained easily upon inspection (Nelson, 1970; Darby & Karni, 1973; Tirole, 1988). Education, like organic bananas, car repairs, and secretarial, child, or old age care services, is therefore subject to moral hazard and quality assessment problems.[4]

Smith's argument unfolds as follows: He first establishes what it takes for teachers to exert the effort that makes for a quality education. It is the "necessity they are under of making that exertion" (p. 717). Smith next links that necessity to the payment mode of teachers. Those whose income is based on fees or honoraria experience more necessity than those whose income draws—in the form of guaranteed salaries—on endowments. Those who can count on salaries, he argues, will have no incentive to worry about their reputations and their teaching, especially if their salaries are "altogether independent of their success and reputation in their particular professions" (p. 717). Smith knew what he was talking about. At Glasgow College he drew more than half of his salary from fees (Rae, 1895, pp. 48–49); he also observed the impact of less incentive-compatible payment modes during stays at Oxford and in France.

Smith next ponders the question of curricular innovation (pp. 720, 722–727), where he sees the same misalignment of incentives at work. His argument regarding curricular innovation is a straightforward extension of his argument regarding the quality of teaching. Once again, Smith ties the lack of curricular innovation to public endowments, which he thinks, erode teachers' incentives to exert effort. To wit:

> The improvements which, in modern times, have been made in several branches of philosophy, have not the greater part of them, been made in universities; though some no doubt have. The greater part of universities have not even been very forward to adopt those improvements, after they were made; and several of those learned societies have chosen to remain, for a long time, the sanctuaries in which exploded systems and obsolete prejudices found shelter and protection, after they had been hunted out of every corner of the world. In general, the richest and best endowed universities have been the slowest in adopting those improvements, and the most averse to permit any considerable change in the established plan of education. Those improvements were more easily introduced into some of the poorer universities, in which the teachers, depending upon their reputation for the greater part of their subsistence, were obliged to pay more attention to the current opinions of the world (p. 727).

At this point, someone might be tempted to argue that peer pressure and administrative supervision should be sufficient to keep teachers from shirking on their duties. Surely there must be ways for faculty to police itself; if not, persons extraneous to the faculty, say a bishop, governor, minister of state, or their agent(s), ought to be able to intervene and take care of professorial slackers.

Not so, says Smith, once more demonstrating his insights in the applicability of the two major competing enforcement mechanisms, third-party and reputational enforcement. He notes that a faculty member will allow other faculty members to neglect their duty, "provided he himself is allowed to neglect his own," and in regard to bishops, governors, ministers of state, or their agents he observes,

> All that such superiors . . . can force him to do, is to attend upon his pupils a certain number of hours, that is, to give a certain number of lectures in the week or in the year. What those lectures shall be, must still depend upon the diligence of the teacher; and that diligence is likely to be proportioned to the motives which he has for exerting it. An extraneous jurisdiction of this kind, besides, is liable to be exercised both ignorantly and capriciously (p. 718).

In sum, Smith anticipates the reasoning that underlies today's reputational theories of quality, efficiency wages, firms, and other organizations (Klein & Leffler, 1981; Weiss, 1990; Holmstroem & Tirole, 1989; Tirole, 1994, 1996). He comes to the same conclusion and policy prescription: The provision of the experience good education is not easily enforceable by way of contracting or third parties. Good teaching and curricular innovation have to rely on agents' recognition and appreciation of the power of reputation. In fact, Smith goes beyond that. He stresses that third-party enforcement is likely to produce additional problems, such as that of administrators making decisions that they are not qualified to make. As Smith points out, the shift of decision-making power will lead to obsequiousness on the part of those potentially exposed to administrators' ignorance and capriciousness, which results in influence costs (Milgrom & Roberts, 1990) and distracts from both the ability and the diligence of teachers. Third-party enforcement is likely to attenuate existing problems and to create new ones.

Incentive Problems That Afflict Higher Education in Our Day

Many, if not most, colleges and universities have fallen on fiscal hard times. A key concern of the interested public is that the costs of higher education, which until approximately 1980 had remained roughly constant in real terms, have since gone up dramatically, significantly more so for private than for public institutions (Clotfelter, 1996; Honan, 1994). The standard rationalization for this is the Bowen-Baumol hypothesis, which states that labor-intensive service industries carry a systematic productivity handicap because they cannot substitute labor. Hence, the argument often goes, increases in sticker prices and costs in excess of the inflation rate ought to be expected (and tolerated.) The argument explains neither why until 1980 the costs of higher education were level, nor why private and public institutions report differential cost increases; it also contrasts with the experience of other service industries that have reported cost decreases (McKinsey, 1992).

Administrative and academic productivity have been identified as likely drivers of the cost increases.[5] Because the administrative lattice has been explained elsewhere (Gumport & Pusser, 1995; Massy & Warner, 1991; Massy & Wilger, 1992; Williamson 1970), and because, in addition, it may be the consequence of the academic ratchet, I focus here on issues of faculty productivity. Massy and Zemsky (1994) trace the academic ratchet back to departments' having the central role in conferring membership and tenure to individual faculty members, to deciding what ought to be taught and how, and to insisting that "all members be treated not just fairly but nearly identically" (p. 3). The authors suggest how the resulting perception of ever expanding property rights leads in myriad ways to increases in discretionary time. Roughly, faculty discretionary time results from spending less time on teaching—either as a function of fewer courses, or as a function of reduced effort. Massy and Zemsky argue that rewards and penalties at colleges and universities are such that good teaching and curricular innovation will fall by the wayside, because investments in research and scholarship (for example in the form of consulting) pay personally and financially higher returns. In addition, investments in research and scholarship are alleged to provide more professional prestige and more mobility. The authors support their argument with first results from a "case study" of four liberal arts colleges and two universities. Their argument mirrors Smith's suggestion that faculty will collude if allowed to do so and if emoluments are not paid in proportion to the exertion that individual faculty members expend. Massy, Wilger, and Colbeck (1994) come to the convincing and somewhat disturbing conclusion that the misalignment of incentives makes for an unproductive departmental environment.

Massy and Zemsky also note that "there has been an incipient destructuring—or deconstructing—of the undergraduate curriculum over the last two decades" (p. 2), which has fueled questions of the "value added" at colleges and universities (Applebome, 1995; Manegold, 1994; SCANS, 1992). Massy and Zemsky trace the destructuring of the undergraduate curriculum to the misaligned incentives that faculty face. Their observation mirrors Smith's suggestion that the mode by which teachers are paid ultimately affects curricular content.

Ortmann and Squire (1996) employ rudimentary game theory and model colleges and universities as a cascade of principal-agent games. By explicitly defining the objective function of a college and enumerating the aligned and unaligned goals of four classes of players—alumni/students, overseers, administrators, tenured and untenured professors—the authors demonstrate that the common denominator underlying both administrative lattice and academic ratchet is a lack of monitoring technology and accountability. Their analysis suggests that to the extent that faculty members manage to shirk on such "sharable management duties" as advising and governance, the administrative lattice is partially driven by the academic ratchet. By modeling educational institutions as a cascade of principal-agent games, the authors explain organizational outcomes as a result of the cognitive patterns and incentives of the major constituencies of a college.

There is scant evidence that colleges and universities address the problems in the same dramatic manner that has been forced on firms in manufacturing and other service industries (McKinsey Global Institute, 1992, 1993). Higher education's continued fiscal crisis, reflecting a cost structure out of line with revenues, is a strong indicator. Equally indicative are recent results by Siegfried, Getz, and Anderson (1995). Based on a survey conducted at more than 200 institutions, these authors investigated the adoption of 30 specific innovations. They find that it takes higher education twice the time it takes industry to adopt innovations. They furthermore find that technological innovations are adopted faster than academic ones. Pondering the results of their survey, they conjecture that colleges and universities are insulated from many competitive pressures and that the lack of accountability and ready performance measures is responsible for higher education's inertia.

Emerging Trends in Response to Incentive Problems

In the meantime, a number of intriguing, only seemingly disjointed phenomena have emerged in higher education. These trends parallel trends in other service industries; keeping Smith's analysis in mind helps to make sense of them. The phenomena are: The initial public offering (IPO) of the Apollo Group, Inc., the case of (overwhelmingly private) proprietary schools, the reorientation of many colleges and universities toward vocationalism, and the dramatic increase of instructors with limited-time and piece-rate contracts.

Apollo Group, Inc. This company is the first institution of higher education to go public (Smith Barney, 1994, 1996). It provides education programs through its subsidiaries, the University of Phoenix (UOP) and the Institute for Professional Development (IPD). IPD is a consulting division that helps other schools implement and manage education programs tested at UOP. UOP itself offers bachelor's and master's degree programs in business, management, computer information systems, education, and health care and targets working adults and their employers as its customers. This strategy is promising for the simple reason that continuing education has, in the light of the dramatic labor market changes of the past decade, become an indispensable requirement. (The U.S. Department of Education National Center for Education Statistics estimated that in 1992 about 45% of the students enrolled in higher education programs were adults over 24 years of age (Smith Barney, 1994, p. 19). This insight has reached the Pew Higher Education Roundtable (1995a), which acknowledged that "colleges and universities must . . . become more nearly interchangeable nodes on an expanding educational network" (p. 5A). Empirically, the Apollo Group's successful IPO in December 1994, subsequent stock splits, and its stock price trajectory are signs that private colleges and universities can be viable for-profits.

While UOP currently targets a specific market segment, it pursues a number of interesting strategies, all of which seem transferable to other market segments in higher education. The following three are of particular importance. First, its curricula draw on input from faculty, students, and student employers. Second, faculty are teacher-practitioners and are contracted on a course-by-course basis. Third, for some of its programs the company uses computerized educational delivery systems that make student participation less dependent on the constraints imposed by classroom instruction.

Proprietary schools. Drawing on two surveys dated 1986 and 1988, Apling (1993) has provided a survey of this segment of the education industry. Offering training in business, cosmetology, health, and technical occupations, the more than 6,000 proprietary schools provide significant portions of postsecondary occupational training; 3 out of every 5 proprietary schools also offer academic programs of sorts. It is noteworthy that "cosmetology schools, which make up 40 percent of all proprietary schools, enrolled only 14 percent of students attending proprietary schools in the fall of 1986. Business and marketing programs and technology programs, which together account for less than one-third of the schools, enrolled nearly two-thirds of all students in the fall of 1986" (p. 386) Overall, proprietary schools seem very responsive to labor market needs.

Students of those proprietary schools are more likely to be women, minority students, and poor as compared to their peers attending other postsecondary educational institutions, such as community colleges (Apling, 1993, p. 391). They receive sizable portions (about 30%) of federal student financial aid under Title IV of the Higher Education Act. (They receive about one-quarter of all Pell grants and one-third of all Stafford loans.) The costs of attending proprietary schools (tuition and fees plus other costs such as room and board) are fairly high and in 1986–87 amounted to $8,000 (as compared to $ 5,000 for community colleges). In the current context, it is noteworthy that among the reasons students choose proprietary schools are "the school's reputation, availability of desired courses, financial aid, and job placement rates." (Apling, 1993, p. 397) It appears that students at proprietary schools are rational consumers concerned with school quality as well as job prospects. They do vote with their feet, although increasingly their choice is constrained by reductions in funds (Burd, Healy, Lively, & Shea, 1996; McPherson and Shapiro, 1996).

Although proprietary schools aim at a specific market segment, they pursue two strategies that are of general interest in the current context. First, their curricula are informed by market demands. Second, faculty are contracted on a course-by-course basis.

Reorientation toward vocationalism. The orientation toward marketable skills is not restricted to institutions such as UOP or proprietary schools. Not surprisingly, one finds adoption of market-oriented curricula at business schools and specialty colleges like Babson. More important is that the orientation toward marketable skills has already changed the majority of liberal arts colleges in fundamental ways. Breneman (1994, appendix A) analyzes curricular changes over time by way of degree data from 1972 through 1988 at all Liberal Arts I and Liberal Arts II colleges. He concludes that liberal arts colleges are rapidly becoming professional schools—schools that offer increasingly professional degrees in areas such as business, education, nursing, engineering, computer science, agriculture, and health sciences. The changes have been truly radical: "According to a liberal definition that calls any school awarding less than 60 percent of its degrees in professional fields a liberal arts college, there are only about 200 of them left in the country" (p. 139).

Limited-time, piece-rate contracts. The practice of hiring teachers on limited-time, piece-rate contracts is widespread and can increasingly be found at colleges and universities. More than 40% of college faculty members today are estimated to be on such contracts, up from 20% two decades ago (Mydans, 1995; Wilson, 1996).

One could argue that the emergence of the Apollo Group and the existence of proprietary schools are a function of the closeness of curricular content to market demands—an argument not easily applicable to Bennington College, a small private liberal arts college in Vermont. The Bennington experiment was necessitated by persistent budget deficits brought about by dramatically declining enrollments, which some of its participant observers linked to the kind of problems that could well have been the object of Smith's drastic description of the reality of higher education in his time (Edmundson, 1994). To address the problem, the college's new president closed departments, fired tenured teachers, dissolved the institution of tenure as such, and more generally forced Bennington into a process of radical redefinition, as a part of which it has hired teacher-practitioners on limited-time contracts. Since then two other high-profile cases, the University of Rhode Island and the University of Minnesota, have initiated similarly radical reinventions (Roush 1995; Chandler 1996; Magner, 1996; Wilson, 1996). With some officials estimating that more than one out of every four educational institutions currently in existence will be out of business within a decade (Healy et al., 1996, p. A15), dramatic changes like the ones at Bennington, URI, and UM are guaranteed to be only the beginning.

Summary. The following pervasive trends in higher education can thus be identified: First is an emphasis on (and reorientation of curricula toward) skills that are marketable. This reorientation of curricula is more and more influenced by demand-side considerations, and the curricula themselves are increasingly taught by teacher-practitioners. A second pervasive trend is the rising number of teachers on limited-time, piece-rate contracts. A third trend is the increasing use of computerized delivery programs (Blumenstyk, 1996; Noam, 1995). These developments address issues of a desirable quality of teaching and curricular innovation and, ultimately, questions of accountability, the misalignment of incentives, and influence costs by way of market pressures. An interesting and important feature of these developments is that they solve the ossification of institutions of higher education not through reform from within the institutions but through the discipline of the market. (Of course, to some extent the results force even ossified institutions to reconsider their internal organization.)

Discussion of Related Literature

Sherwin Rosen (1987), in a review and assessment of Smith's discussion of higher education, dismisses the idea that Smith's analysis of the impact of payment modes could enlighten today's discourse on how higher education operates. He appeals to the Survival Principle, which asserts that "the salary system was 'fittest' because the fee system withered away" (p. 566). Rosen identifies several "scale factors" (p. 564) as having contributed to the demise of the fee system. As a result of the specialization of knowledge, students will have to learn from a number of teachers. By agglomerating teachers in one place, colleges and universities reduce transportation costs; furthermore, they capture the scale economies alleged to be inherent to using fixed resources such as libraries and classrooms and promote interaction among and between students and faculty. Finally, they develop brand names of their own, which reduces information costs, because it is easier to keep track of the reputation and qualities of educational institutions than of the teachers and students that populate them. To the extent that transportation, communication, and information scale factors are not easily priced, they work against the fee system and in favor of the salary system. So does, Rosen argues, the difficult relationship between teaching and research. To the extent that their characters and interaction are not easily identifiable, the salary system seems once again to offer an easy way out. "An education represents a complicated bundling . . . and is seldom closely tied to a specific teacher compared with the collectivity of a school's faculty, student body, and administration. The reputation of a school rests far more on this collectivity than on the specific identities of its individual members" (p. 567).

Intriguing as it is, (and though it makes sense of historic accounts of the origin and evolution of colleges and universities, and the salary system, for that matter), I propose here that modern information technologies, and the competitive market of ideas that they support, invalidate Rosen's arguments and give renewed explanatory power to Smith's ideas.

Understanding of parallel developments in other service industries is instructive. The emphasis on (and orientation of curricula toward) marketable skills has its analogue in other industries' orientation toward quality customer service. The increasing number of teachers on limited-time, piece-rate contracts can be compared to the widespread outsourcing of services—value-added partnerships of sorts. The increasing use of computerized delivery programs has its analogue in the extensive use of new information technologies, which are the technological foundation that made outsourcing possible. That these trends emerge now can be attributed to the postindustrial environment that higher education, like other service industries, finds itself in.

Postindustrial environments are characterized by scarcer resources, increasing competitiveness, and a more turbulent, less predictable environment. In a series of articles with different coauthors, Thomas Malone (Malone & Smith, 1987; Brynjolfson, Malone, Gurbaxani, & Kambil, 1994) has suggested that postindustrial environments are the product of modern information technologies. By dramatically reducing the costs of coordination—between, as well as within firms—the new information technologies systematically affect the institutional choice between firm and market allocation. Specifically, Malone and Smith demonstrate that relative changes in coordination costs force the substitution of one organizational form for another in a predictable manner, from decentralized and centralized markets, via product and functional hierarchies all the way back to decentralized markets. Malone and Smith predict the outsourcing and flattening of hierarchies—the two key phenomena of organizational changes observed over the past few years—as consequences of reduced coordination costs. Brynjolfson, Malone, Gurbaxani, and Kambil verify empirically one of the key predictions to come from this earlier line of work: firms have grown smaller. "The implication of our findings is that the current downsizing of firms, the popularity of outsourcing, and the rise of value-adding partnerships is not simply a management fad, but rather may have a technological and theoretical basis" (Brynjolfson et al., 1994, p. 1642). Indeed, it is now widely accepted that the new information technologies drove outsourcing and flattening of hierarchies (Daft & Lewin, 1993).

In a recent article Eli Noam points out the implication of modern technologies for (higher) education and scholarly activities (Noam, 1995). The old direction of information flows implied scholars coming to the information that was centrally stored in libraries. Students, in turn, would come to those places where scholars could be found—colleges and universities built around information depositories. This model justifies the physical existence of colleges and universities as the result of (agglomeration) economies of scale.

The modern information technologies are about to destroy this model. Instead of scholars coming to information depositories, information is increasingly coming to scholars and their students. (See also, Blumenstyk, 1996; Bongiorno, 1995; Weiner, 1996.) This new direction of information flows makes scholars and their students increasingly independent of physical structures, such as the physical plant that many colleges and universities maintain. The new direction of information flows undermines the basis of colleges and universities—(agglomeration) economies of scale. It thus undermines the basic rationale that Rosen described.

With information increasingly at one's fingertips, informational economies of scale become similarly less and less important.[6] A comparison with developments in financial and health-care markets is instructive. Take mutual funds: consumers now do comparative shopping among literally thousands of such funds, relying on a plethora of rankings, all-star teams, and so on. Likewise, medical report cards and *U.S. News and World Report* rankings unbundle health-care organizations. Analogously, umbrella branding in higher education is in the process of being unbundled. Over the past decade graduate school rankings for most disciplines and specialties have been published yearly in *U.S. News and World Report*. Increasingly, such rankings are based on hard data (Tracy & Waldfogel, 1994). Likewise, rankings of undergraduate programs are well established in such publications as *U.S. News and World Report* and *Money Guide*). In fact, recent entries by *Time* and *Newsweek* have made the rankings game into a rather competitive one. The added competition is likely to increase the quality of the provided assessments.

The rankings are a sign of the times. Though they are full of dubious data and should be taken as a screening device only, their very existence and undoubtable impact on decision making at colleges and universities lays the foundation for widespread reputational enforcement.

The same economic rationale drives the developments in mutual funds and higher education ratings. First, necessary data are becoming more easily available. Second, higher education has become more expensive and risky, making it imperative for those interested in such an investment to ensure the likelihood of reasonable returns. Third, indications are that these ratings are profitable enterprises that will not go away—much as many in higher education, health-care, or financial markets hope they would.

Other service industries had to acknowledge the arrival of postindustrial environments long ago; in contrast, higher education in parts has been able to avoid addressing these developments. As the previous section's discussion of emerging trends suggests, such avoidance strategies may not work much longer. Acknowledging that higher education is bound to follow similar developments is important, because postindustrial environments tend to lead to Pavlovian reflexes by administrators. Cameron and Tschirhart (1992) show that these reflexes are systematic and have a negative effect on institutional effectiveness. Specifically, the authors find that conditions of postindustrial environments elicit "a constricted capacity to process information, a reduction in the search for new information, consideration of fewer alternatives, and an over-emphasis on familiar, self-conforming information. . . . [Others] . . . found that a mechanistic shift in control also can occur, resulting in more centralized, formalized, and rigid procedures. Loss of institutional adaptability and flexibility result . . ." (p. 100). Administrators become self-protective and resist truly participative decision making, which is essential to accommodate the need for multiple sources of information and multiple perspectives.

What to Learn from Smith's Analysis and Policy Prescriptions

Adam Smith's study of higher education in his day was guided by the insight that education is an experience good not unlike organic bananas, car repairs, and secretarial, child care, or old age services. This is a key insight for three reasons. It deflates the notion that education is a unique good. It highlights the temptation for teachers whose remuneration is not incentive compatible to neglect teaching and curricular innovation. It highlights the temptation for administrators to employ third-party enforcement instead of reputational enforcement. These insights are as relevant today as they were more than two hundred years ago.

Specifically, Smith suggested that, due to the nature of higher education at his time, neither a desirable quality of teaching nor innovative curricula would be forthcoming if emoluments would be drawn from public endowments without concern for performance. Being rather skeptical of third party enforcement through administrators, Smith favored reputational enforcement through market forces. His underlying conceptualization of the academic was that of the intellectual entrepreneur—with books and publications possibly as loss leaders.

While Smith was concerned about the incentive problems created by endowments and in this respect continues to offer guidance to our understanding of a puzzling problem (Hansmann, 1990), his arguments apply to all institutional arrangements that reduce the necessity of exerting effort. Tenure is a case in point. Historically, it was meant to create conditions for academic freedom. As such, it essentially constituted a job guarantee. These days, tenure is often coupled with automatic pay increases that are not linked to research productivity, quality of teaching, curricular innovation, advising, or participation in governance, thus creating the free-rider problems that can be shown to drive the academic ratchet (Massy & Zemsky, 1994; Ortmann & Squire, 1996). It seems easy to infer from his analysis of the debilitating effects of endowments that Smith would not have been in favor of such coupling of job guarantees and pay increases based on seniority or similar incentive-incompatible schemes. More difficult to answer is the question of whether he would have been in favor of tenure itself. The possibility cannot be excluded that Smith, as a second-best solution, would favor tenure as a protection device against incompetence and capriciousness of administrators. That said, his work also suggests that his preference would be for a solution that would sort out incompetent administrators and not give them the opportunity to act capriciously in the first place. It is important then to keep in mind that colleges and universities in Smith's days were very different from those of today, particularly when considering the pervasiveness of the administrative lattice in the here and now. Smith's analysis of administrators seems to apply with force to today's colleges and universities.

Reforms in higher education seem particularly prone to the impact of vested interests (Cameron & Tschirhart, 1992; Bergmann 1991). It is no coincidence that much of the current debate is being conducted, and many of the policy prescriptions are provided, by administrators and professional researchers (Pew, 1993a, 1993b, 1994, 1995a, 1995b). On the other hand, notwithstanding the fact that total quality management, customer orientation, and reengineering are the buzzwords *du jour* in much of higher education, faculty and students seem marginalized in the current discourse—a curious aspect in light of the key tenets of the total quality movement.

One of the more disconcerting aspects for the reader of this journal is likely to be the fact that Smith's reasoning seems to assume that market forces would automatically direct the course of education toward objects that are useful both to the individual and to the public. The question thus has to be asked whether higher education can live with curricular innovations driven by market forces. It seems worthwhile to note that the current reorientations of curricula do not necessarily conform to traditional notions of vocationalism. With environments becoming more and more uncertain, human capital assets need to become increasingly more flexible and portable (Nussbaum, 1991a, 1991b; SCANS, 1992). These requirements encourage the acquisition of a portfolio of foundational skills. The more turbulent or postindustrial the environment becomes, the less industry-specific the acquisition of skills ought to be. The set of necessary skills can thus be conceptualized as a portfolio of skills that is a more sophisticated version of the basic "3R" paradigm (reading, writing, arithmetic). There is little in the foundation skills listed in the SCANS report (basic skills like reading, writing, arithmetic, mathematics, listening, speaking; thinking skills like creative thinking, decision making, problem solving, mental visualization, knowing how to learn and reason; and personal qualities like responsibility, self-esteem, sociability, self-management, and integrity/honesty) that seems irreconcilable even with notions of a liberal arts undergraduate curriculum (SCANS, 1992, appendix B).

The current developments in higher education—the arrival of the Apollo Group, the increasing vocationalism of curricula, the increasing practice of hiring teachers on limited, piece-rate contracts, not to mention the widespread experimentation with management fads have mostly been met with apprehension by the faculty. This apprehension parallels the apprehension of labor in manufacturing and other service industries where parallel developments have taken place. Not surprisingly, the developments have often been framed as threats rather than opportunities. Given the marginalization of faculty and students in much of the current discourse, there are good reasons for such perceptions.

However, I have argued that certain trends are pervasive and irreversible. It is hence important to understand the forces that drive them and the opportunities that they offer. Because the current discourse is as yet mostly untheorized and, in any case, muddled by the utterances of vested interests, it may be worthwhile to listen to a disinterested voice from the past for guidance in the process of rethinking higher education.

Notes

1. See Pew Higher Education Roundtable (1993a, 1993b, 1994, 1995). The Pew Higher Education Roundtable started as an informal gathering of selected chief officers of institutions of higher education committed to "restructuring." In February 1983 they extended an invitation to chief officers of all two-year and four-year institutions to join in a formative session of the so-called Pew Collaborative (Pew, 1993a). Pew (1993b) is based on discussions that took place at a meeting in November 1993, which brought together leaders of over 400 colleges and universities.

2. Although Smith (1776) favors the application of the benefit principle as a basic rule, he stresses that "the laboring poor, that is the great body of the people" (p. 735) may not have the means to become literate and numerate. "For a very small expense the public can facilitate, and can even impose upon almost the whole body of the people, the necessity of acquiring those most essential parts of the education" (p. 737). Such state intervention, Smith argues, is desirable because of the detrimental consequences of the division of labor on the human mind and ultimately the social fabric (pp. 734–735).

3. An agent (a seller of bananas, car repairs, secretarial, or day care services) can provide different levels of quality. For ease of exposition, assume that she can provide either high or low quality. Typically, the principal (the buyer of the good or service) will not be able to ascertain whether he bought high or low quality without inspecting the good. The implied asymmetric information can be overcome only by way of

inspection. Unfortunately, inspection typically entails costs. Buyers thus face a "dilemma of trust"—not to inspect and thus gamble that the agent will provide what she promised, or to inspect and incur the corresponding cost. Agent (seller) and principal (buyer) are caught in a game of strategic interaction that has four possible outcomes—{high quality, not inspect}, {low quality, not inspect}, {high quality, inspect}, and {low quality, inspect}. For examples like the one given above, agent and principal are likely to have conflicting individual rankings over the outcomes. Whereas the principal might prefer the outcome {high quality, not inspect}, the agent might prefer {low quality, not inspect}. On the other hand, whereas the agent might prefer {low quality, not inspect}, the principal might prefer {low quality, inspect}. A similar problem is pervasive in labor markets where the agent would be the seller of her labor (say, secretarial or child care services) and the buyer would have the choice to either monitor those services (proof-read, drop by the childcare center frequently) or trust that the expected effort is provided. The literature on so-called efficiency wages (Weiss 1990) collects the relevant insights, which, though they are couched in slightly different terminology, are identical to those regarding product markets.

4. Klein and Leffler, whose path-breaking 1981 article on the role of markets in enforcing contractual arrangements has inspired much of the modern literature on moral hazard and quality assessment problems, give credit where due: in their footnote 5 they point out that Smith's discussion of what is nowadays called efficiency wages (Smith 1776, Book 1, chap. 10) lays out the essence of their argument.

5. See, for example, Massy and Warner (1991), and Massy and Zemsky (1994), and more recently, Leslie and Rhoades (1995) and Gumport and Pusser (1995).

6. Empirically Getz et al. (1991) have made an impressive theoretical and empirical case for their claim that past analyses of economies of scale in higher education in general were flawed, because they averaged the seemingly increasing returns to scale of growing institutions and the decreasing returns to scale of institutions in decline. Their study suggests that the minimum efficient scale lies significantly lower than heretofore assumed and that, for all practical purposes, economies of scale in higher education do not exist.

References

Abrahamson, E., & Park, C. (1994). Concealment of negative organizational outcomes: An agency theory perspective. *Academy of Management Journal, 37*(5), 1302–1334.

Apling, R. N. (1993, July/August). Proprietary schools and their students. *Journal of Higher Education, 64*, 379–416.

Applebome, P. (1995, February). Employers wary of school system. *The New York Times*, p. 1.

Bergmann, B. R. (1991, November-December). Bloated administration, blighted campuses. *Academe*, 12–16.

Blumenstyk, G. (1996, May 31). Learning from afar: Students and professors have mixed reactions to the education network of Maine. *Chronicle of Higher Education*, pp. A15–A17.

Bongiorno, L. (1995, October 23). Virtual B-Schools. *Business Week*, 64–74.

Breneman, D. W. (1994). *Liberal arts colleges: Thriving, surviving, or endangered?* Washington, DC: The Brookings Institution.

Brynjolfson, E., Malone, T. W., Gurbaxani, V., & Kambil, A. (1994, December). Does information technology lead to smaller firms? *Management Science, 40*(12), 1628–1644.

Burd, S., Healy P., Lively, K., & Shea, C. (1996, June 14). Low income students say college options are limited by the actions of lawmakers and campus officials. *Chronicle of Higher Education, 42*(40), pp. A10–A12.

Cameron, K. S. (1983, July/August). Strategic responses to conditions of decline: Higher education and the private sector. *Journal of Higher Education, 54*, 359–380.

Cameron K. S., & Tschirhart, M. (1992, January/February). Postindustrial environments and organizational effectiveness in colleges and universities. *Journal of Higher Education, 63*, 87–108.

Chandler, S. (1996, June 10). Poisoned ivy? Academe is closely watching Minnesota attack on tenure. *Business Week*, p. 40.

Clotfelder, C. T. (1996). *Buying the best: Cost escalation in elite higher education*. Princeton: Princeton University Press.

Cohen, M. D., March, J. G., & Olsen, J. P. (1972). A garbage can model of organizational choice. *Administrative Science Quarterly, 17*, 1–25.

Daft, R. L., & Lewin, A. Y. (1993). Where are the theories of the "new" organizational forms? An editorial essay. *Organization Science, 4*(4).

Darby, M. R., & Karni, E. (1973). Free competition and the optimal amount of fraud. *Journal of Law and Economics, 16*(1), 67–88.

Edmundson, M. (1994, October 23). Bennington means business. *The New York Times Magazine*, pp. 43–47, 60, 62, 70, 74.

Getz, M., Siegfried, J. J., & Zhang, H. (1991). Estimating economies of scale in higher education. *Economics Letters, 37*, 203–208.

Gumport, P. J., & Pusser, B. (1995, September/October). A case of bureaucratic accretion: Context and consequences. *Journal of Higher Education, 66*, 493–520.

Hansmann, H. (1990). Why do universities hold endowments? *Journal of Legal Studies, 19*, 3–42.

Hammer, M., & Champy, J. (1994). *Reengineering the corporation.* New York: Harper Collins.

Healy, P., Lively, K., Mercer, J., Nicklin, J., & Schmidt, P. (1996, June 14). Private colleges fight for financial health: Public institutions find state support unreliable. *Chronicle of Higher Education*, pp. A15–A16.

Holmstroem, B., & Tirole, J. (1989). The theory of the firm. In R. Schmalensee & R. D. Wittig (Eds.), *Handbook of industrial organization* (pp. 61–133). New York: Elsevier.

Honan, W. H. (1994, May 4). Cost of 4-year degree passes $100,000 mark. *The New York Times.*

Keidel, R. W. (1994). Rethinking organizational design. *Academy of Management Executive, 8*(4), 12–30.

Klein, B., & Leffler, K. B. (1981, August). The role of market forces in assuring contract compliance. *Journal of Political Economy, 89*, 615–641.

Leslie, L. L., & Rhoades, G. (1995, March/April). Rising administrative costs: Seeking explanations. *Journal of Higher Education, 66*, 187–212.

Malone, T., & Smith, S. A. (1987, May-June). Modeling the performance of organizational structures. *Operations Research, 36*, 421–436.

Magner, D. K. (1996, May 17). A parlous time for tenure: Minnesota professors are furious over plans they say would erode job security. *Chronicle of Higher Education*, pp. A21–A23.

Manegold, C. S. (1994, September 23). Study says schools must stress academics. *The New York Times*, p. 22.

March, J. G., & Simon, H. A. (1993). *Organizations* (2nd ed.). Cambridge, MA: Blackwell.

Massy, W. F., & Warner, T. K. (1991). Causes and cures of cost escalation in college and university administrative and support services. In *National symposium on strategic higher education finance and management issues: Proceedings.* Washington, DC: National Association of College and University Business Officers.

Massy, W. F., & Wilger, A. K. (1992, Winter). Productivity in postsecondary education: A new approach. *Educational Evaluation and Policy Analysis, 14*(4), 361–376.

Massy, W. F., Wilger, A. K., & Colbeck, C. (1994, July/August). Overcoming "hollowed" collegiality. *Change, 26*, 11–20.

Massy, W. F., & Zemsky, R. (1994, January/February). Faculty discretionary time: Departments and the "academic ratchet." *Journal of Higher Education, 65*, 1–22.

McKinsey Global Institute. (1992). *Service sector productivity.* Washington, DC: McKinsey & Company.

McKinsey Global Institute. (1993). *Manufacturing productivity.* Washington, DC: McKinsey & Company.

McPherson, M. S., & Schapiro, M. O. (1996, January). *Are we keeping college affordable? Student aid, access, and choice in American higher education.* Williams College Project on the Economics of Higher Education, Discussion Paper No. 34.

Milgrom, P., & Roberts J. (1990). The Efficiency of equity in organizational decision processes. *American Economic Review, 80*(2), 154–159.

Mydans, S. (1995, January 4). Part-time teaching rises, as do worries. *The New York Times*, p. 17.

Nelson, P. (1970). Information and consumer behavior. *Journal of Political Economy, 78*(2), 311–329.

Noam, E. M. (1995, October 13). Electronics and the dim future of the university. *Science, 270*, 247–249.

Nussbaum, B. (1991a, October 7). I'm worried about my job! *Business Week*, pp. 94–97.

Nussbaum, B. (1991b, October 7). A career survival kit. *Business Week*, pp. 98–101.

Ortmann, A., & Squire, R. (1996). *The organization of the liberal arts college: A game-theoretic analysis.* New Haven, CT: Program on Non-profit Organizations, Yale University.

Oster, S. (1995). *Strategic management of nonprofit organizations.* Oxford: Oxford University Press.

Ostroff, C., & Schmidt, N. (1994, December). Configurations of organizational effectiveness and efficiency. *Academy of Management Journal, 36*(6), 1345–1362.

Pew Higher Education Roundtable. (1993a, February). A call to meeting. *Policy Perspectives, 4,* 1A–9A.

Pew Higher Education Roundtable. (1993b, February). Toward restructuring: Assessing the impact of budgetary constraints on college and university operations. *Policy Perspectives, 4,* 7B–16B.

Pew Higher Education Roundtable. (1994, April). To dance with change. *Policy Perspectives, 5,* 1A–12A.

Pew Higher Education Roundtable. (1995a, April). Twice imagined. *Policy Perspectives, 6,* pp. 1A–12A.

Pew Higher Education Roundtable. (1995b, July). A calling to account. *Policy Perspectives, 6,* pp. 1A–12A.

Rae, J. (1895). *The Life of Adam Smith.* London: Macmillan & Co.

Rosen, S. (1987). Some economics of teaching. *Journal of Labor Economics, 5*(4), Pt. 1, 561–575.

Rothschild, M., & White, L. J. (1991). *The university in the marketplace: Some insights and some puzzles.* Working Paper No. 3853. National Bureau of Economic Research, 1050 Massachusetts Avenue, Cambridge, MA 02138.

Roush, W. (1995, April 19). URI tries downsizing by formula. *Science, 272,* 342–344.

(SCANS) Secretary's Commission on Achieving Necessary Skills. (1992, April). *Learning a living: A blueprint for high performance. A SCANS Report for America 2000.* Washington, DC: U.S. Department of Labor.

Siegfried, J. J., Getz, M., & Anderson, K. H. (1995, May 19). The snail's pace of innovation in higher education. *Chronicle of Higher Education,* p. A56.

Smith, A. (1776). *An inquiry into the nature and causes of the wealth of nations.* New York: The Modern Library (Cannan ed.).

Smith Barney. (1994). *Prospectus: Apollo Group, Inc.* New York: author.

Smith Barney. (1996, January 24). Research report. New York: author.

Steinberg, R. (1993, Spring). Public policy and the performance of nonprofit organizations: A general framework. *Nonprofit and Voluntary Sector Quarterly, 22*(1), 13–31.

Tirole, J. (1988). *The theory of industrial organization.* Cambridge, MA: MIT Press.

Tirole, J. (1994). The internal organization of government. *Oxford Economic Papers, 46*(1), 1–19.

Tirole, J. (1996). A theory of collective reputations (with applications to the persistence of corruption and to firm quality). *Review of Economic Studies, 63,* 1–22.

Tracy, J., & Waldfogel, J. (1994). The best business schools: A market-based approach. *Journal of Business, 70*(1), 1–31.

Weiner, E. (1996, August 4). Reflections of an on-line graduate: Cyberspace is convenient, but what happens to the teacher-student relationship? *The New York Times* (Education Life), p. 42.

Weiss, A. (1990). *Efficiency wages: Models of unemployment, layoffs, and wage dispersion.* Princeton: Princeton University Press.

Williamson, O. E. (1970). Managerial discretion and business behavior. *American Economic Review, 80,* 1032–1056.

Wilson, R. (1996, June 14). Scholars off the tenure track wonder if they'll ever get on. *Chronicle of Higher Education, 42*(40), pp. A12–A13.

Young, D. (1983). *If not for profit, for what?* Lexington, MA: Heath.

Young, D. R., & Steinberg, R. (1995). *Economics for nonprofit managers.* New York: The Foundation Center.

Zammuto, R. F., & O'Connor, E. J. (1992). Gaining advanced manufacturing technologies' benefits: The roles of organization design and culture. *Academy of Management Review, 17*(4), 701–728.

BEYOND BALDRIDGE: EXTENDING THE POLITICAL MODEL OF HIGHER EDUCATION ORGANIZATION AND GOVERNANCE

BRIAN PUSSER

This article presents a case study of organizational decision making in higher education through an analysis of the contest over affirmative action at the University of California. It presents an overview of the development of the prevailing model of the politics of higher education, J. Victor Baldridge's interest-articulation framework, and discusses the evolution of the study of the politics of higher education organizations. The findings from this case suggest that contemporary models for understanding the political dynamics of postsecondary governance and decision making will be more effective if they extend the interest-articulation framework to include positive theories of institutions and State theoretical perspectives.

Consider the following case of organizational decision making for a public university system of nine campuses: A proposal is put before the system's governing board to end a long-standing policy. Accept for the moment that the policy is widely considered to be mandated by the state constitution, that it is seen as a key component of organizational culture throughout the university system, central to the system's mission, and an important symbol of institutional progress. The policy is publicly supported by the system president, each of the nine campus chancellors, each of the nine campus academic senates, each of the nine campus student associations, the systemwide alumni association, and all of the system's major staff and labor organizations. Given the prevailing understandings of organizational decision making in higher education, what are the prospects for terminating this policy at the governing board level?

The answer is, quite good. The policy contest was the struggle over affirmative action; the system is the University of California (UC); and affirmative action was eliminated in admissions, contracting, and hiring by vote of the Regents of the UC in July 1995. Given the context, it is not surprising that the decision came as a shock to many participants and observers.[1] One of the more enduring challenges in higher education research has been the effort to understand the politics of postsecondary organizational behavior. Although research on other types of organizations has benefited for nearly three decades from emerging models of institutional behavior based in political science (Weingast & Marshall, 1988; Wilson, 1973) and economics (Arrow, 1974; Stigler, 1971; Williamson, 1985), until quite recently, efforts to understand university organization and governance have relied on multidimensional models (MDMs) that have little grounding in political or economic theory (Berger & Milem, 2000; Pusser, 2001).

This gap in the research agenda can be traced to a number of causes. Foremost, universities are complex systems with myriad interests that do not lend themselves to the rational modeling found in the new economics of organizations. Furthermore, given collegial traditions favoring shared governance and consensus, it has been difficult to establish the individual preferences fundamental to modeling in political science.

However, just as Graham Allison's landmark case study of the Cuban missile crisis led to new understandings of organizational decision making under crisis, the bitter and divisive contests over public university policy that marked the end of the 20th century present an opportunity to revise our existing models for understanding these issues in higher education (Pusser, 2001). This research reconsiders the utility of the political frame of MDMs of organizational behavior in higher education on the basis of a longitudinal case study of one of the more prolonged and contentious policy disputes in higher education in the United States, the struggle over affirmative action at the UC.

The findings from this case suggest that the political frame of MDMs is insufficient to explain contested decision-making processes. The political frame is lacking on five basic grounds: (a) Decision making and organizational processes are seen as fundamentally endogenous processes, (b) there is little attention to the role of public institutions as both sites of contest and instruments in broader political economic struggles, (c) there is little attention to the dynamics of external interest articulation or the structural politics of higher education governance and decision making, (d) there is little attention to the role of the administrative hierarchy as an interest group in its own right, and (e) the political frame assumes an essentially pluralist[2] decision-making context.

The Prevailing Model of Organizational Behavior in Higher Education

The MDM of organizational behavior is one of the fundamental analytical frameworks in higher education research (Bensimon, 1989; Berger & Milem, 2000). The model varies somewhat in the number of dimensions incorporated, ranging from Baldridge's (1971) original three dimensions (bureaucratic, collegial, and political) through Bolman and Deal's (1984, 1997) four-cornered frame (structural, human resource, political, and symbolic) to Birnbaum's (1988) five dimensions (bureaucratic, collegial, political, anarchical, and cybernetic). What these models have in common is that each iteration has incorporated the political dimension developed by J. Victor Baldridge. The political dimension has been cited as both the most useful element of MDMs for contemporary research (Berger & Milem, 2000) and as the framework most in need of revision (Pusser & Ordorika, 2001). To understand the influence of the political dimension, it is useful to briefly review the other prominent elements of the models.

The Bureaucratic Dimension

The bureaucratic dimension is essentially the rational, goal-driven model developed in the work of Max Weber (1947). The central elements of the Weberian bureaucratic frame are an efficient organizational process; formal, hierarchical administrative structures; well-delineated institutional rules; and a similarly well-defined division of labor. The bureaucratic frame relies on a clear distinction between personal and institutional property rights, the centrality of credentials and expertise in determining institutional hierarchies, and a focus on merit as a source of organizational legitimacy (Bush, 1995; Weber, 1947). Organizational decision making is characterized as a process of top-down, rational deliberation that leads to stability and legitimate administrative control (Mintzberg, 1991; Scott, 1992).

The Collegial Dimension

Within the collegial dimension, organizations are viewed as entities based on collective action and widely shared values. Decision making is seen as a participatory, pluralist, and democratic process within a collegium or community of scholars (Bush, 1995; Millet, 1962). Here goals are shaped by collective deliberation, action is guided by consensus, and power and decision making are shared throughout the organization (Bensimon, 1989). In the collegial frame, conflict is a form of collegial dysfunction, and Baldridge (1971) incorporated a number of elements of the collegial dimension in his depiction of interest articulation in higher education.

The Symbolic Dimension

The symbolic dimension stresses informal authority, with shared networks of norms, beliefs, meanings, and cultural understandings key to shaping organizational structures and processes (Clark, 1972; Cohen & March, 1974; Meyer & Rowan, 1977). Here organizational decisions emerge in response to social and cultural demands for conformity to prevailing values and sources of legitimacy, as under conditions of considerable uncertainty, organizational actors rely on symbolic action to increase institutional confidence and stability (Bensimon, 1989). What people believe is legitimate organizational behavior binds the institution, in this perspective, as surely as any rational decisions handed down through a hierarchical structure (Meyer & Rowan, 1977).

The Political Frame

The political dimension of the MDMs has its origin in the work of the sociologist J. Victor Baldridge (1971; see also Baldridge, Curtis, Ecker, & Riley, 1978). In *Power and Conflict in the University*, a case study of organizational conflict at New York University in the late 1960s, he suggested that complex organizations could be considered political systems. His interest-articulation model, drawing on the work of the sociologist Talcott Parsons (1960), was based in conflict theory (Dahrendorf, 1959) and community action studies (Dahl, 1966). Baldridge depicted the organizational decision-making process as one driven by "authorities" who make decisions for the whole, and "partisans" within the organization who are affected by the decisions (p. 136).

Although Pfeffer and Salancik (1978) would later suggest that organizational decisions emerged from organizational structure, Baldridge (1971) emphasized organizational process, the activities of institutional subgroups, internal interests, coalition building, and bargaining. These activities take place in a pluralistic decision-making context, where administrative leaders serve as *boundary spanners*, key actors who mediate, or articulate, between internal and external constituencies.

In subsequent work (Baldridge et al., 1978; Riley & Baldridge, 1977), Baldridge presented what he termed a "revised political model: an environmental and structuralist approach" (Baldridge et al., 1978, p. 41). The revised model turned more attention to external context, internal agenda control, interest groups, and legitimate authority in the higher education decision-making process. In this subsequent work, higher education organizational decision making under the political frame was still seen as a largely endogenous process. That is, although environmental factors shape decision context, and interest groups weigh in, the articulation and mediation of demands remains an internal, administrative process (Baldridge, 1971; Baldridge et al., 1978; Bolman & Deal, 1997).

Bolman and Deal (1984, 1997) further revised the political aspect of their MDM over time to more fully incorporate exogenous actors and conflicts. Although limited considerations of power and resource dependence (Hardy, 1990; Millet, 1984; Pfeffer & Salancik, 1978) have been added to the political dimension over time, it retains Baldridge's (1971) original conceptualization of interest articulation, mediation, and internal interest group action as the essential variables in political behavior in postsecondary organizations. As a result, there is little that a contemporary political theorist would recognize in the political model for research on higher education organizations. This paradox can be traced to the evolution of the study of organizations.

The Division of Political Theory and the Study of Organizations

For nearly half a century, organizations and politics have been separate arenas in the study of public institutions. Research on administration, organization, and leadership emerged as the central concern of public administration, whereas political scientists focused on electoral politics and bureaucracy (Moe, 1991).

During the past two decades, work in political science and economics has led to the development of positive theories of institutions (PTI) that have been widely used to study public organizations as sites of contest in the wider political economy (Dixit, 1996; McCubbins, Noll, & Weingast, 1987; Moe, 1991, 1996). From initial research on legislatures, regulatory agencies, and the nature of the bureaucracy, this work has been applied to elementary-secondary education (Chubb & Moe, 1990) and, more recently, to postsecondary institutions (Masten, 1995; McLendon, in press; Pusser, 2001; Youn & Arnold, 1997).

Unlike Baldridge's (1971) early work and the subsequent application of the political dimension of MDMs in higher education research, PTI moves beyond the analysis of organizational decision making as an endogenous process, as it suggests that external influences and interests benefit from, and endeavor to influence, organizational structures and policies. The central elements of efforts to gain influence over political institutions include efforts to control the agenda for organizational activity (Kingdon, 1984), ex ante design of institutional governance structures (Hammond & Hill, 1993; Weingast & Marshall, 1988), personal and formal relationships between institutional governors and external interests (M. D. Parsons, 1997), and efforts to control the allocation of institutional costs and benefits (Wilson, 1989).

Initial applications of PTI to postsecondary organization and governance have relied primarily on aspects of PTI drawn from economics, including the role of contracting and transactions costs in shaping organizational structures. This research has focused on efforts to build institutional structures, such as the tenure system, that help privilege gains and enforce bargains (Masten, 1995; McCormick & Meiners, 1988; Toma, 1986). Efforts to extend the political model in higher education will rely more directly on political theoretical elements of PTI, and other political theories, to conceptualize postsecondary organizations as political institutions and as sites of broader political economic contest (Pusser & Ordorika, 2001).

Public Higher Education Institutions as Political Institutions

Political institutions are those entities that control significant public resources; that have the authority to allocate public costs and benefits; that implement policies with significant political salience, such as conditions of labor or standards of credentialing; and that stand as particularly visible sites of public contest. A number of researchers have argued that these conditions describe public higher education institutions in the United States (Pusser, 2000; Rhoades, 1992; Slaughter, 1990). Ordorika (in press) has argued that higher education is a fundamental public good and that the structuring of institutions and the institutional policy-formation process should be seen as part of a larger contest for the utility of that good. A primary goal of this research is to evaluate the degree to which contemporary public universities can be seen as political institutions.[3]

Another significant attribute of PTI models is that positive theories are grounded in pluralist perspectives on the governance of public institutions (Moe, 1991; Weingast & Marshall, 1988). A pluralist political framework assumes that a political system enables legitimate, representative expression of minority and majority preferences. PTI and interest-articulation models both depend on pluralist decision processes, and it is a significant limitation on their ultimate utility. There are many constituencies in higher education and other public institutions that do not necessarily have what they perceive as meaningful access to a given decision process. How their interests are expressed and how they influence policy contests cannot be entirely understood within a positive theoretical or interest-articulation framework. Contest and resistance beyond the pluralist decision-making process has been the subject of considerable research on the state and education, although little of that work has addressed higher education.

Theories of the State and Higher Education Research

A significant challenge to understanding the politics of higher education organization and governance is that the state is virtually absent from research on postsecondary institutions. Wirt and Kirst (1972) pointed three decades ago to the separation of the study of the state and the study of education, and little has changed since then. Research in higher education has generally conceptualized the university as distinct from the state and the state as a set of forces operating independent of higher education institutions (Rhoades, 1992). This view of the role of higher education in a state context has traditionally limited the range of understandings available to researchers in higher education.

More recently, Sheila Slaughter (1988) has examined the interdependence of higher education and the state during the past five decades. Slaughter built on Carnoy and Levin's (1985) contention that the educational system is a complex and contradictory site of contest, capable of reducing inequality or of increasing social stratification.

The analysis of this case brings to bear state theoretical perspectives, with its attention to the ways in which actions and interests beyond the institution and outside of the pluralist framework shape the organization and governance of universities, in an effort to extend the reach of MDMs and the PTI perspective on public institutions.

The Contest over Affirmative Action at the University of California

In July 1995, after a year of intensely public organizational contest, the Regents of the UC voted 14 to 10 to end the use of "race, religion, sex, color, ethnicity or national origin as a criterion for admission to the University"[4] and 15 to 10 to eliminate those criteria for university hiring and contracting. Their votes were cast at the conclusion of a 14-hour meeting attended by more than 1,000 people, after being twice interrupted by bomb threats.

The regents' votes constituted an unprecedented repudiation of three decades of affirmative action policy at the UC and created a new historical legacy for the UC, as the first prominent public university to eliminate the use of affirmative action in admission and employment practices. The decision was given extra symbolic force as it dramatically reshaped a UC legacy that had been defined by its role as a defender of affirmative action in the 1978 United States Supreme Court ruling in *U.C. Regents v. Bakke*. It was also a decision with political dynamics that could not easily be explained using an interest-articulation framework.

The UC's struggle over affirmative action policy provides a particularly useful case for research on contemporary organizational decision making for three primary reasons: (a) In the contemporary era, the UC has been one of the nation's most visible and contested arenas of public higher education policy; (b) the national debate on race, in which affirmative action policies play a central role, has become increasingly critical in national electoral and interest group contests (Tolbert & Hero, 1996); and (c) the bitter divide between factions contesting this policy led to a public declaration of individual regents' preferences rarely seen in postsecondary education.

Research Design and Data

Two fundamental strands of data collection were used in this research. The first consisted of building a historical record of the contest over affirmative action at the UC, using more than 2,000 pages of documents from individual campuses, the UC Office of the President and the UC Office of the Secretary of the Regents. These documents included minutes of regents meetings; public correspondence; personal letters, notes, and memoranda obtained from individual regents; and UC Office of the President briefing materials. These data were supplemented by historical documents including public records, analyses, and policy papers addressing the development of access and affirmative action policies at the university since its founding and such state-level data as budget documents and gubernatorial reports and legislative committee transcripts.

The second phase of data collection centered on semistructured interviews with actors central to the contest. These included regents, UC system and campus leaders, state political leaders, student and staff representatives, alumni representatives to the Board of Regents, faculty senate representatives, community activists, and state coordinating board authorities.[5]

Research Propositions

A series of propositions was constructed prior to data collection to examine the utility of a broader political framework for understanding this case. Three are presented here as particularly useful for reconsidering the political model of higher education organization and governance.

Proposition 1: The instrumental political value of the university. Efforts at interest articulation by the administrative leadership will have limited effectiveness if the policy contest has utility in broader state and national political contests. If there is an instrumental political value in the outcome of the policy contest, external political actors, interest groups, and coalitions will resist administrative efforts to mediate the contest.

Proposition 2: Exogenous efforts to structure the university decision process. Where there is instrumental political value in contests over public university policy, the outcome of the policy contest will be significantly shaped by the long-term exogenous political dynamic of structuring the decision-making board.

Proposition 3: The limits of pluralism and the role of the state. The efforts of interest groups and actors, who do not perceive that they have direct or significant representation in the governance process, or who feel their representation is not legitimate, will shape the policy contest. If the university is situated as a political institution in a broader contest over state efforts to redress inequality, the issue of higher education as a site of contest over the appropriate redress for inequity will emerge as central to the decision process.

Analysis and Findings

The data collected for this case were coded for a number of key elements from Baldridge's (1971) interest-articulation framework, positive theoretical approaches to institutional structure and process, and state theoretical propositions. Documents and interview data were examined for evidence of the efficacy of institutional efforts to articulate and mediate disparate interests, the perception of the use of the university as an instrument in a broader political struggle, and for signs of sustained partisan efforts to structure the decision-making board. Data were further analyzed for evidence of a contest between internal and external interests for control of the decision-making agenda, indications of limits on the efficacy of bureaucratic expertise, efforts by actors or interests who did not see themselves as represented in a pluralist process, and for the perception of the university as a site for the redress of historical inequality. The analysis of these data point to a number of key factors that shaped the regents' decision and that offer insights into the original propositions.

Proposition 1: The Instrumental Political Value of the University

In its earliest stages, the contest unfolded in ways that were in keeping with an interest-articulation model. The process began with a request by Regent Ward Connerly for the university to reevaluate its admissions and hiring procedures. UC President Jack Peltason responded by committing the Office of the President to a major review of existing policy and to preparing recommendations for policy revisions, where appropriate.

As the institutional deliberation proceeded, the dynamic shifted from an internal review to a far more extensive and public challenge. It was the belief of many of those interviewed for this research that some of the regents calling for a review of affirmative action had a broader agenda. In that view, the challenge to affirmative action at the institutional level was part of an effort to use the university as an instrument in a broader state and national political effort. The broader effort was intended to help place an initiative to end affirmative action in California on the state ballot (the eventual Proposition 209) and to assist in efforts to secure the Republican presidential nomination in 1996 for Governor Wilson.[6] That broader struggle would ultimately overwhelm the Office of the President's efforts at interest articulation. The following two quotes from UC regents, both members of the state Republican leadership, point to the broader contest in which the University was enmeshed.[7]

> Had Pete [Wilson] not been involved, had the governor not been involved, we would have never passed the resolution. The governor got involved because he was running for president. The governor used my university as a forum to run for president. (William T. Bagley, personal communication, June 1, 1998)

Regent Ward Connerly presented a different rationale for the governor's role, as he acknowledged the governor's larger goals:

> You know, so, it helped his presidential campaign, but Pete Wilson is the kind who says, "The reason I'm running for office is to lay my values on the line and if you agree with them, fine. If you don't agree with them, well, that's okay, too, but the role of my running for president is to put my positions to the test." That's how you make public policy. So he never had any apology for getting involved and using this to further his own presidential ambitions and when people say, "Oh, you made it a political issue," he says, "What the hell is politics? It's the art of shaping public policy." (Connerly, personal communication, March 27, 1998)

Karl Pister, the Chancellor of UC Santa Cruz at the time of the contest, expressed his belief that the use of the university in broader political contests was increasingly difficult to resist:

> My first reaction would be that it's a consequence of a much broader societal phenomenon because if I look beyond higher education and just look at the public education in California, K–12, the degree of political intervention in K through 12 is just astounding today. Witness the State Board of Education's behavior on the math standards, and God knows what's going to happen on the science standards when they come up before the state board. Education, indeed, is part of the larger issue. Our society is often being driven by political design, by which issues make people identify either with left or right, or whatever camps you want to use to explain it. (Pister, personal communication, June 10, 1998)

These and other data from the case demonstrate the difficulty in presuming that an administrative cohort has the authority to effectively mediate a conflict that includes powerful external actors. Nor is it clear that the institutional leadership is even aware of some external challenges to the university. Documents released recently under court order revealed efforts in the early 1960s by the Federal Bureau of Investigation, with the assistance of then–California Governor Ronald Reagan, to influence UC regents' deliberations over the presidency of Clark Kerr. President Kerr himself was unaware of the extent of external political efforts in that case until the full documentation of the episode was released (Rosenfeld, 2002).

Proposition 2: Exogenous Efforts to Structure the University Decision Process

The long-term structuring of the membership of the decision-making board, through gubernatorial appointment and legislative confirmation, emerges as a key element of the policy outcome.[8] At the time of the regents' votes, all but 1 of the 18 appointed members of the board were Republicans, appointed by Republican governors.[9] These regents generally had close ties to the state and national Republican parties and were significant contributors to the governor.[10]

In light of prevailing models of confirmation dynamics (Hammond & Hill, 1993; Pusser, 2001), the unwillingness of Democrats on the Senate Rules Committee to contest gubernatorial appointments to the Board of Regents in the period between 1974 and 1994 raises questions about our understanding of the political constituency of selective public higher education. Despite holding the senate majority for all but a few months of the period from 1972 to 1994, the Democrats neither rejected, nor even particularly contested, the appointments made by Republican governors. Shortly after the regents' votes, the Democrats began a concerted effort to intervene in the composition of the Regents by opposing nominations put forward by Governor Wilson (see Table 1).

Then–Senate Rules Committee Chair Bill Lockyer described the Democrats' stance this way in explaining Democratic opposition to the reappointment of Regent Tirso del Junco, a leading opponent of UC's affirmative action policies:

> Dr. del Junco was a Regent when he chose to be Chair of the California Republican Party, when he chose to sign a lot of questionable attack mail pieces sent against my colleagues. Now, that wasn't somebody who had much regard for the non-political role of Regents. You know, I've had colleagues say to me in the Senate, "I've never met this guy. I don't know him. The only thing I know about him is that when I was running for the Senate, mail landed in my district, attacking me personally that was inaccurate, and it was signed by him as Chair of the Republican Party." (Senate Rules Committee, State of California, 1997, p. 85)[11]

TABLE 1

Confirmation Dynamics for University of California Regents (1972–2002)

| Governor | Governor's Party | Senate Majority | Nominees | Party of Nominees | | Confirmation Outcome | | |
				Democrats	Republicans	Yes	No	Pending
R. Reagan (1967–1974)[a]	Republican	Democrat	2	0	2	2	0	0
J. Brown (1975–1982)	Democrat	Democrat	13	13	0	13	0	0
G. Deukmejian (1983–1990)	Republican	Democrat	18	1	17	18	0	0
P. Wilson (1991–1998)	Republican	Democrat	15	0	15	9	6	0
G. Davis (1999 to present)	Democrat	Democrat	9	9	0	7	0	2
Total			57	23	34	49	6	2

Source. Senate Rules Committee, State of California, 1997.

Note. Nominees include nominations and renominations.

a. Only Reagan nominations made after passage of Measure 5 are tabulated.

Given the election in 1998 of Governor Gray Davis, a Democrat, both the appointment and confirmation of regents is now controlled by the governor's party. However, given the heightened awareness of the political utility of board votes, it is likely that gubernatorial appointments to the board will again be contested if the state returns to divided governance.

Proposition 3: The Limits of Pluralism and the Role of the State

The analysis of the data from this case also supports the contention that significant contest takes place outside of the pluralist frame. As student coalitions organized to preserve affirmative action, they expressed an increasing disenfranchisement from the board and the administration. Students also questioned their own lack of direct representation under a decision-making structure that gave students 1 of the 26 votes on the board. UC staff organizations, although prominent in public demonstrations and institutional forums, had no voting representative on the Board of Regents.

The Reverend Jesse Jackson's speech to the regents on the day of their votes and his association with the civil rights and voting rights movements of the 1960s raised significant challenges to the legitimacy of the regents' decision-making process. In his remarks, Jackson directly challenged the composition of the board, at one point reading from a list of campaign contributions made by individual regents to Governor Wilson. He likened the process to earlier eras of African American disenfranchisement from predominantly White institutions.

> We now can vote, but we couldn't always vote. And now, know that you can have the right to vote, but if the lines are drawn funny, gerrymandering, annexation, your vote can be diminished. (University of California Office of the Secretary of the Regents, 1995b)

Although student protest over the legitimacy of the decision-making process was seen as a significant force by many actors in the contest, it is not clear that it produced votes to preserve affirmative action. Resistance efforts attributed to student demonstrators, such as disrupting meetings and, in particular, a protest outside of Regent Connerly's home, solidified support for Regent Connerly and Governor Wilson with some conservative regents. Furthermore, Student Regent Ed Gomez argued that it was students' perception of their lack of representation and support that compelled them to invite Reverend Jackson to come before the board to speak on the students' behalf. According to UC Academic Council Co-Chair Daniel Simmons, that invitation proved to be a turning point in the contest.

> I felt during the year, all during the year, that we had enough votes on the Board to put it off. And we did, I think, until the day Jesse Jackson announced he was coming to California. It was Jesse Jackson who lost the issue! Because his announcement put the thing at a much higher level in terms of national politics. Now you had the opportunity for debate over the issue between two people ostensibly running for president of the United States. (Simmons, personal communication, April 21, 1998)

There was agreement from a number of students that protest and resistance did increase student linkages and connections across campuses. Increased student activism was further seen as an important factor in resistance to gubernatorial appointments in the months after the regents' votes on affirmative action (Pusser, 2001).

The data from this case also support the utility of a state theoretical standpoint that conceptualizes public higher education institutions as sites of contest over the redress of historical inequities. The issue of redress was raised throughout the contest by supporters and opponents of affirmative action. The feeling of many of those in support of affirmative action was forcefully stated by a UC Irvine student, Nancy Barreda, in testimony before the Board on the day of the votes:

> We don't want to pick your fruit, to be your maids, to be your busboys, to do your laundry and tend your gardens. Unfortunately, some of our parents have taken those jobs to give us a better chance. We too are Americans, and it is a shame that we have to fight constantly to remind those in power who seem to ignore that fact. Affirmative action was the first time we were provided access into these institutions. We will not forget those who sacrificed in the past so that we could have a chance today. We will not stand by while you take away affirmative action, we will not stand by and watch you destroy our right to access. (University of California Office of the Secretary of the Regents, 1995b)

Cheryl Hagen, the chair of the university's largest labor organization, also pointed to the need to address historical inequality in her remarks to the board:

> The reasons for racism and sexism are rooted in issues of economics, political power, social order and psychological factors. The question has never been whether or not minorities and women should be accepted and treated as equals; it has been a question of whether or not power is to be shared, and on what basis. The issue of power seeps through and permeates all thought when it comes to any movement within our society. There is nothing inherently wrong in the good-old-boy methodology. It works. It is only problematic because for faculty positions and senior staff positions within the University of California, women and minorities have not had the same access. (University of California Office of the Secretary of the Regents, 1995b)

Extending the Political Framework for Research in Higher Education

The contest over affirmative action at the UC offers a significant opportunity to extend our frameworks for understanding the politics of university decision making. The case affirms the utility of aspects of MDMs for understanding postsecondary organizational behavior. The efforts of the bureaucratic hierarchy in the unfolding contest, the collegial approach taken by the university faculty, and the symbolic power of the UC's historical commitment to affirmative action all shaped the outcome to some degree. Yet in this most political of contests, the interest-articulation model at the center of the political dimension of MDMs does little to increase our understanding of the outcome in this case.

The contest over affirmative action at the UC also brought to the fore a paradox in the university's mission: The university faces demands to be both an elite institution and a public institution. Understanding the role of public higher education in broader state efforts to promote equity, and the political dynamics that shape the role of the state, will be central to understanding the future allocation of access, costs, and benefits of higher education.

In Ernest Hemingway's *The Sun Also Rises*, the character Mike Campbell is asked how he went bankrupt. He explains that there are two ways one goes bankrupt: slowly, and then all of a sudden. It is a useful construct for thinking about contested decision making in higher education and for extending the political model of higher education governance. The contest over affirmative action at the UC was decided slowly, through nearly 20 years of political action on gubernatorial appointments to the Board of Regents and legislative confirmation of those appointments and, all of a sudden, by votes of the regents. It was also decided near at hand by the unsuccessful efforts of the UC administration to articulate the various interests weighing in on the contest and at some distance by the efforts of a powerful governor in the state capitol and his political allies across the country.

To the extent that Baldridge's (1971) "authorities" and "partisans" contended over UC policy, the definition of both groups needs to be revisited. The set of authorities that shape binding decisions for public institutions should be expanded beyond the borders of the institution to include a broad array of leaders and interest groups in the democratic political system. It also needs to include community leaders and public figures like Reverend Jackson, who can mobilize individuals and bring resources to bear on a public policy contest. The definition of partisans—those who are bound by decisions shaping the institution—also needs to be extended beyond the institution itself to include the state and national constituency for higher education.

As one example, for nearly 20 years, the Democratic majority in the state senate did not contest the appointments of Republican nominees to the Board of Regents, a group of nominees that included political contributors, activists, and party leaders. Those regents were subsequently positioned to vote on policies with significant consequences for a number of traditionally Democratic constituencies such as the labor unions at the UC and on contested issues such as the nature of university medical research. Further research is needed on legislators' perceptions of the constituency for higher education and on legislative deference in appointments to postsecondary governing boards to more fully understand institutional organization and governance.

Policy transformation in higher education also seems to happen slowly and all of a sudden. Although there are a number of revelations that emerge from case studies of decision making under crisis, crisis offers a unique window into organizational process. It may be a window that best reveals how policies change all of a sudden. A continuing challenge for researchers in higher education is to address the slow change process, the long-term political economic dynamics that structure public institutions and their decision-making procedures.

The findings from this case support the contention that a public university can be seen as a political institution and that public university policies have great salience, visibility, and political value. The political dimension of MDMs of university behavior can be significantly advanced with propositions developed from positive theories of institutions and state theoretical standpoints. Taken together, these theoretical approaches offer a pathway beyond Baldridge's (1971) interest-articulation model to a more complete understanding of the political dynamics of contemporary higher education.

Notes

1. The director of admissions of one of the system's largest campuses expressed the view of many observers when he commented on the day after the votes, "I never thought it would pass" (William J. Villa in Santa Barbara *News Press*, July 22, 1995).
2. *Pluralist* here refers to a system of interest representation in which many groups have access to authority and rights to access and participation in the decision-making process (Carnoy & Levin, 1985).
3. A case can be made that private universities are political institutions as well (Pusser, in press), although here the discussion is confined to public universities.
4. From the text of Regents proposal SP-1, July 20, 1995 (University of California Office of the Secretary of the Regents, 1995a).
5. All interview responses were analyzed and coded according to an index linked to the core analytical categories in the research framework (Strauss & Corbin, 1994).
6. Efforts to place Proposition 209 on the California ballot are detailed in Chavez (1998).
7. These interviews are presented in greater detail in Pusser (2001, in press).

8. The importance of the confirmation dynamic is demonstrated by the voting record in this case. On SP-1, the motion to end affirmative action in University of California admissions, regents appointed by Republican governors voted 13 to 5 to eliminate affirmative action; ex-officio regents voted 5 to 1 in favor of preserving affirmative action (Pusser, 2001).

9. Although trustee political affiliation has not generally been seen as a predictor of trustee voting behavior (cf. Kerr & Gade, 1989), in this case it appears that such variables as political ties, party affiliation, and financial contributions to political causes were good predictors of trustee voting patterns (Pusser, 2001).

10. The appointed regents who voted to end affirmative action included a former state chair of the Republican party, a national fund-raising chair of the Republican party, two former Republican state legislators, a former Republican congressman, and one of the governor's college roommates.

11. This confirmation hearing is related in greater detail in Pusser (2001, and also in press).

References

Arrow, K. J. (1974). *The limits of organization.* New York: Norton.

Baldridge, J. V. (1971). *Power and conflict in the university: Research in the sociology of complex organizations.* New York: John Wiley.

Baldridge, J. V., Curtis, D. V., Ecker, G., & Riley, G. L. (1978). *Policy making and effective leadership.* San Francisco: Jossey-Bass.

Bensimon, E. M. (1989). The meaning of good presidential leadership: A frame analysis. *Review of Higher Education, 12,* 107–123.

Berger, J. B., & Milem, J. F. (2000). Organizational behavior in higher education and student outcomes. In J. C. Smart (Ed.), *Higher education: Handbook of theory and research* (Vol. 15, pp. 268–338). New York: Agathon.

Birnbaum, R. (1988). *How colleges work: The cybernetics of academic organization and leadership.* San Francisco: Jossey-Bass.

Bolman, L. G., & Deal, T. E. (1984). *Modern approaches to understanding and managing organizations.* San Francisco: Jossey-Bass.

Bolman, L. G., & Deal, T. E. (1997). *Reframing organizations: Artistry, choice, and leadership* (2nd ed.). San Francisco: Jossey-Bass.

Bush, T. (1995). *Theories of educational management.* London: Paul Chapman.

Carnoy, M., & Levin, H. M. (1985). *Schooling and work in the democratic state.* Stanford, CA: Stanford University Press.

Chavez, L. (1998). *The color bind: California's battle to end affirmative action.* Berkeley: University of California Press.

Chubb, J. E., & Moe, T. (1990). *Politics, markets and America's schools.* Washington, DC: Brookings Institution.

Clark, B. R. (1972). The organizational saga in higher education. *Administrative Science Quarterly, 17,* 178–184.

Cohen, M. D., & March, J. G. (1974). *Leadership and ambiguity: The American college president.* New York: McGraw-Hill.

Dahl, R. A. (1966). *Who governs? Democracy and power in an American city.* New Haven, CT: Yale University Press.

Dahrendorf, R. (1959). *Class and class conflict in industrial society.* Stanford, CA: Stanford University Press.

Dixit, A. (1996). *The making of economic policy: A transaction costs politics perspective.* Cambridge, MA: MIT Press.

Hammond, T. H., & Hill, J. S. (1993). Deference or preference? Explaining Senate confirmation of presidential nominees. *Journal of Theoretical Politics, 5,* 23–59.

Hardy, C. (1990). Putting power into university governance. In J. C. Smart (Ed.), *Higher education: Handbook of theory and research* (pp. 393–426). New York: Agathon.

Kerr, C., & Gade, M. L. (1989). *The guardians: Boards of trustees of American colleges and universities.* Washington, DC: AGB Press.

Kingdon, J. W. (1984). *Agendas, alternatives, and public policies.* Boston: Little, Brown.

Masten, S. E. (1995). Old school ties: Financial aid coordination and governance of higher education. *Journal of Economic Behavior and Organizations, 28,* 23–47.

McCormick, R. E., & Meiners, R. E. (1988). University governance: A property rights perspective. *Journal of Law, Economics and Organization, 31,* 423–442.

McCubbins, M. D., Noll, R. G., & Weingast, B. R. (1987). Administrative procedures as instruments of political control. *Journal of Law, Economics and Organization, 3,* 243–277.

McLendon, M. K. (in press). State governance reform of higher education: Patterns, trends, and theories of the public policy process. In J. C. Smart (Ed.), *Higher education: Handbook of theory and research* (Vol. 18). New York: Agathon.

Meyer, J. W., & Rowan, B. (1977). Institutionalized organizations: Formal structure as myth and ceremony. *American Journal of Sociology, 83,* 340–363.

Millett, J. D. (1962). *The academic community: An essay on organization.* New York: McGraw-Hill.

Millett, J. D. (1984). *Conflict in higher education: State government coordination versus institutional independence.* San Francisco: Jossey-Bass.

Mintzberg, H. (1991). The professional bureaucracy. In M. W. Peterson (Ed.), *Organization and governance in higher education* (pp. 53–75). Lexington, MA: Ginn Press.

Moe, T. M. (1991). Politics and the theory of organization. *Journal of Law, Economics and Organization, 8,* 237–254.

Moe, T. M. (1996). *The positive theory of public bureaucracy.* New York: Cambridge University Press.

Olsen, M. (1965). *The logic of collective action: Public goods and the theory of groups.* Cambridge, MA: Harvard University Press.

Ordorika, I. (in press). *Power and politics in university governance: Organization and change at the National Autonomous University of Mexico.* Boston: Routledge Kegan Paul.

Parsons, M. D. (1997). *Power and politics: Federal higher education policymaking in the 1990s.* Albany: State University of New York Press.

Parsons, T. (1960). *Structure and process in modern societies.* Glencoe, IL: Free Press.

Pfeffer, J., & Salancik, G. (1978). *The external control of organizations: A resource dependence perspective.* New York: Harper & Row.

Pusser, B. (2000). The role of the state in the provision of higher education in the United States. *Australian Universities Review, 43*(1), 24–35.

Pusser, B. (2001). The contemporary politics of access policy: California after Proposition 209. In D. E. Heller (Ed.), *The states and public higher education: Affordability, access, and accountability* (pp. 121–152). Baltimore: Johns Hopkins University Press.

Pusser, B. (2002). Higher education, the emerging market, and the public good. In P. A. Graham & N. G. Stacey (Eds.), *The knowledge economy and postsecondary education* (pp. 105–125). Washington, DC: National Academy Press.

Pusser, B. (in press). *Burning down the house: The contest over affirmative action at the University of California.* Albany: State University of New York Press.

Pusser, B., & Ordorika, I. (2001). Bringing political theory to university governance: A comparative case study of the University of California and the Universidad Nacional Autónoma de Mèxico. In N. P. Stromquist (Ed.), *Higher education: Handbook of theory and research* (Vol. 16, pp. 147–194). New York: Agathon.

Rhoades, G. (1992). Beyond "the state": Interorganizational relations and state apparatus in post-secondary education. In J. C. Smart (Ed.), *Higher education: Handbook of theory and research* (pp. 84–142). New York: Agathon.

Riley, G. L., & Baldridge, J. V. (1977). *Governing academic organizations.* Berkeley, CA: McCutchan.

Rosenfeld, S. (2002, June 9). Secret FBI files reveal covert activities at UC. *San Francisco Chronicle, special report: The campus files,* p. A1.

Scott, W. R. (1992). *Organizations: Rational, natural, and open systems* (3rd ed.). Englewood Cliffs, NJ: Prentice Hall.

Senate Rules Committee, State of California. (1997). *Archives of Senate rules committee transcripts.* Sacramento, CA: Senate Publications.

Senate Rules Committee, State of California. (1997, June 23). *Transcript of Senate rules committee hearing.* Sacramento, CA: Senate Publications.

Slaughter, S. (1988). Academic freedom and the state. *Journal of Higher Education, 59,* 241–265.

Slaughter, S. (1990). *The higher learning and high technology: Dynamics of higher education policy formation.* Albany: State University of New York Press.

Stigler, G. (1971). The theory of economic regulation. *Bell Journal of Economics, 2,* 114–141.

Strauss, A. L., & Corbin, J. (1994). Grounded theory methodology: An overview. In N. K. Denzin & Y. S. Lincoln (Eds.), *Handbook of Qualitative Research*. Thousand Oaks, CA: Sage.

Tolbert, C. J., & Hero, R. E. (1996). Race/ethnicity and direct democracy: An analysis of California's illegal immigration initiative. *Journal of Politics, 58*, 806–818.

Toma, E. F. (1986). State university boards of trustees: A principal-agent perspective. *Public Choice, 49*, 155–163.

University of California Office of the Secretary of the Regents. (1995a, July 12). *Regents SP-1*. Oakland, CA: Author.

University of California Office of the Secretary of the Regents. (1995b, July 20). Transcripts of audiotapes of the Regents meeting, unpublished.

Villa, W. J. (1995, July 22). *Santa Barbara News-Press*.

Weber, M. (1947). *The theory of social and economic organization*. Glencoe, IL: Free Press.

Weingast, B. R., & Marshall, W. J. (1988). The industrial organization of Congress: Or, why legislatures, like firms, are not organized as markets. *Journal of Political Economy, 96*, 132–163.

Williamson, O. E. (1985). *Economic organization: Firms, markets, and policy control*. New York: New York University Press.

Wilson, J. Q. (1973). *Political organizations*. New York: Basic Books.

Wilson, J. Q. (1989). *Bureaucracy: What government agencies do and why they do it*. Cambridge, MA: Basic Books.

Wirt, F. M., & Kirst, M. W. (1972). *Political and social foundations of education*. Berkeley, CA: McCutchan.

Youn, T. I. K., & Arnold, G. B. (1997, November). *What does the reform of undergraduate curriculum tell us about the political order in academia?* Paper presented at the meeting of the Association for the Study of Higher Education, Albuquerque, NM.

PART X

DIVERSITY MATTERS IN INSTITUTIONS

Tribal Colleges and Universities in an Era of Dynamic Development

D. Michael Pavel (Skokomish), Ella Inglebret,
and Susan Rae Banks (Arapaho)
Washington State University

In this article, we discuss the development of a new higher education phenomena within the United States—tribal colleges and universities (TCUs). The article highlights how these institutions have dramatically changed the higher education realm for American Indians and Alaska Natives in just the short time span of 30 years. A historical overview of TCUs portrays the growth of the TCU movement from previous externally imposed Indian education efforts that failed to meet the needs of students. Selected institutional portraits demonstrate the intersections between culture and community as tribal communities create and control their own institutions of higher education. These intersections are further illuminated through examination of broad TCU curricular functions. Successes and challenges experienced by Native teacher preparation programs nationally, as well as a case study of curriculum development for a specific Native teacher preparation program, provide further insight into how community members identify their own educational needs and develop programs that are specifically tailored to meet those needs. The article concludes that TCUs are promoting a new mindset that is leading to renewed economic, social, political, cultural, and spiritual vitality through education. As a consequence, American Indian people are hopeful about regaining their greatness in America with TCUs leading the way.

We live in an era when dramatic changes are impacting the access and achievement of American Indians and Alaska Natives (AI and AN)[1] in higher education. Today there are 31 tribally controlled colleges and universities (TCUs) that enroll approximately 8% of the estimated 130,000 Native students attending 3,600 postsecondary institutions across the United States (U.S. Department of Education, 1998). This is a remarkable achievement, given that the TCU movement just started in 1968 with Diné Community College (formerly Navajo Community College) and that AI and AN students have historically been enrolled in higher education at rates far below the national average (Pavel, Swisher, & Ward, 1995; Stein, 1992).

It is clear that TCUs have a profound influence on the presence of Native people in American higher education.

> Research, site visits, accreditation reports, and government audits all confirm their effectiveness. Tribal colleges have proven their ability to enroll students who were not served by higher education, to graduate students who have dropped out from other institutions, and to sponsor successful community development programs. (Boyer, 1997, p. 2)

However, the higher education community is largely unaware of TCUs, their unique attributes, and their similarities to other institutions of higher education (IHE). Considering the dismal track record of many IHEs at recruiting and retaining AI and AN students (Pavel & Padilla, 1993), postsecondary educators, researchers, and policymakers may benefit from an examination of the modern TCU (Pavel, 1999a).

This article begins with a historical overview of Indian education and TCUs, followed by portraits of selected institutions. Together, these two sections attempt to provide the reader with a basic understanding of the motivation for creating TCUs. The third section examines the curricular functions of TCUs and curriculum development efforts in Native teacher preparation programs. An overview of curricular functions describes what TCUs provide to their communities. The focus on teacher preparation shows a way in which education is a top priority for tribal communities. In conclusion, we openly advocate that the higher education community and society embrace the developments that bring prosperity to AI and AN peoples so that these communities continue to make significant and long-lasting contributions to American society.

Historical Overview

We believe that Indian education dates back to a time when all AI and AN children were gifted and talented. Everyone in the community was expected and trained to be teachers. Elders were entrusted with administering and governing the process of sharing knowledge. With ever-growing sophistication, Native people built remarkable civilizations (Crum, 1991). Native systems of education functioned smoothly until newcomers from a foreign land came to the Old World of the Indian people. For at least 350 years, the higher education of AI and AN people has been a preoccupation of the non-Indian. Several of America's oldest and most established universities had as part of their original charter a provision to educate the infidels who inhabited the land the newcomers coveted (Wright, 1988). However, the opportunity for a foreign education did not always bring joy to the hearts of Indian leaders (Franklin, 1794). "The concepts of rights and truths that were self-evident to early American leaders were equally self-evident to the Native occupants of the land. The difference [was] in the freedom to practice and enjoy such principles" (Pavel, Inglebret, & Van Den Hende, 1999, p. 115). From the time that European newcomers began arriving to American shores in droves, AI and AN peoples experienced little or no freedom to continue their time-honored systems of education (Wright & Tierney, 1991).

The early opportunists who acted under the banner of missionary zeal represented the first offense launched to civilize the Native people. When this failed, the next order of business was to practice genocide and implement removal policies such as the British declared Proclamation Line of 1763 (which was to push back the Iroquois Confederacy) and later United States's efforts to address what was called the "Indian problem." When it became obvious that simply killing or removing Native people from their aboriginal territory were not going to solve the Indian problem, an era of federal governmental control emerged in the form of treaties. This control was founded by belief that "The Indian under no circumstances should be permitted . . . to lose confidence in public authorities; for if they do, all efforts to civilize them or to improve their condition must be unavailing" (Nicholson, 1854, p. 9).

The United States then turned to an era of management, characterized by viewing the Indian nations as wards of the federal government (Conlin, 1987). This period spawned the Dawes Severalty Act of 1887 that changed communally held land into private land ownership by individual Indians. The effect was devastating; by 1932, Indian people had lost an estimated 82,800,000 acres of land (Haymond, 1982; Hodge, 1981). A progressive period of federal administration of Indian affairs laced with paternalism arose as the effects of genocide and forced assimilation. People found it difficult to accept any rationale of actions resulting in the almost complete decimation of Indian people and their traditional ways of life. Public sentiment and policy toward Native people wavered back and forth from the Meriam Report of 1928 that provided documentation of outrageous treatment of the Indian people (Miller, 1971), to the treaty termination policies of the 1950s that again destroyed AIs and ANs ties to the land and traditional culture, and back to the Kennedy Report of 1969 that sought funding and assistance for social, economic, and education purposes.

In many ways, the modern tribal college movement emerged from the centuries-long struggles culminating in civil rights efforts spanning the 1950s and 1960s (Crum, 1989; Oppelt, 1990). Starting with Navajo (Diné) Community College in 1968, 15 tribal colleges were chartered by tribal governments within the next 10 years (Stein, 1992). Presently, of the 31 IHEs chartered by Native governments, 5 offer 4-year degrees and 2 offer Master's degrees. This period of development clearly establish the present TCU movement. In the following section, we analyze more revealing data on the origin of individual TCUs.

Selected Institutional Portraits

Introduction

Although general patterns common to the operation of all TCUs can be discerned, each institution molds its educational process to the community in which it exists. Therefore, this discussion begins by providing individual portraits of selected TCUs to depict the unique history that exists within each institution.[2] Particular attention is given to origin, mission, and purpose of each institution. In this manner, the reader gains an understanding of how each institution blended with specific community values. A sense of the modest beginnings of each institution as well as growing institutional breadth and depth is conveyed. The route that individual institutions have taken to build viable educational systems using available cultural, natural, economic, social, and technological resources becomes apparent. Moreover, the multiple ways in which TCUs have cultivated these resources to respond to community needs is exemplified.

Bay Mills Community College (BMCC)

Currently enrolling about 100 students, BMCC in Michigan was chartered in 1984 by the Bay Mills Indian Community. BMCC grew out of a small vocational training program funded by the federal government in 1981 to prepare students for tribal employment. Steady growth over the years necessitated expansion of the physical facilities to include science and computer laboratories, a learning center, a library, and student housing. Today, the library also houses a cultural heritage center, which serves an educational function in the college's Great Lakes Native American studies program. The BMCC (1994) catalog stated, "The curriculum is designed to integrate traditional Native American values with vocational training and general education as a way of preparing students to assume responsible roles in their respective communities" (p. 2). Further recognizing its role in community service, BMCC has provided extension courses for every reservation in Michigan and for neighboring communities. It has become a major participant in an interactive television cooperative that serves students in regional universities and in several local K–12 school districts.

College of the Menominee Nation (CMN)

The CMN in Wisconsin was chartered in 1993 by the Menominee Tribal Legislature to serve the Menominee Indian people and their neighbors. Demonstrating tremendous growth in just its first 2 years of existence, the college expanded from initially offering four classes to offering coursework leading to a wide array of academic and technical specializations, including such areas as natural resources, hospitality and gaming, and human services. To facilitate transfer of credits to 4-year institutions, CMN has entered into partnerships with selected Wisconsin universities. One aspect of CMN's three-part mission to provide the student with a quality educational environment centered in Menominee culture, community research, and development projects, and to implement curriculum designed around the tribal concepts of learning by doing and community service (College of the Menominee Nation, 1995).

Ilisagvik College

Ilisagvik College is located in the North Slope Borough of Alaska. The North Slope Borough, a local governmental entity, was established in 1972 just after the Alaska Native Claims Settlement Act was passed during the previous year. The borough structure allowed the Inupiat people of the North Slope to engage in self-governance and to obtain revenues from oil production to promote economic development. Implementing the Inupiat vision of locally controlled education, the

North Slope Borough and the University of Alaska-Fairbanks jointly created the North Slope Higher Education Center in 1986. With the evolution of the institution into a community college, its name was changed to Arctic Sivunmun Ilisagvik College in 1991. Growth in vocational education opportunities was further supported in 1994 when the college merged with the Mayor's Workforce Development Program. The following year, the North Slope Borough passed an ordinance creating the Ilisagvik College Corporation with full governance power given to the board of trustees. The Northwest Association of Schools and Colleges recently named Ilisagvik College a candidate for accreditation. The mission of Ilisagvik College is to serve "the residents of North Slope Borough by providing quality post-secondary academic, vocational and technical education in a learning environment that perpetuates and strengthens Inupiat culture, language, values and traditions" (Ilisagvik College, 1998, p. 7).

Little Big Horn College (LBHC)

LBHC in Montana enrolls approximately 300 students (90% Indian). The Crow Tribe of Indians chartered the college in 1980, and initial coursework was offered in affiliation with the Montana University System. Although programs of study were primarily vocational at the college's onset, their emphasis became more academic and evolved into serving as a transfer function. The purposes of the college include "establishing, maintaining and operating educational institutions at the post-secondary level on the Crow Indian Reservation, with educational, vocational and technical programs and curricula leading to degrees and certificates that may be granted by the college" (LBHC, 1994, p. 5). LBHC fulfills this purpose with a commitment to preserve, perpetuate, and protect Crow culture and language while vitalizing Crow and American Indian scholarship.

Little Priest Tribal College (LPTC)

LPTC was chartered in 1996 by the Winnebago Tribe of Nebraska and received its name from Little Priest, the last war chief of the Ho-Chunk (Winnebago) people. LPTC is seeking accreditation from the North Central Association of Schools and Colleges. Its current offerings are sponsored by Wayne State College. LPTC's mission is to implement 2-year associate degree programs, certificate programs, and community education programs that provide students with Winnebago language and culture, personal and social development, and

> The ability to integrate culture, academics, physical, psychological, and spiritual behavior so that students can interface within a diverse world. Little Priest Tribal College recognizes that the quest for knowledge is on-going, and attempts to achieve a balance between educational advancement and cultural preservation. (LPTC, 1997, p. 6)

Medicine Creek Tribal College (MCTC)

The Puyallup Tribe of Indians in Washington established MCTC in 1993. The name was derived from the Medicine Creek Treaty that had given federal recognition to a number of South Puget Sound tribes. The Puyallup Tribe began its educational endeavors in 1975 with the creation of Chief Leschi School to serve students from preschool to Grade 12. The success of Chief Leschi School led to expansion of educational pursuits into the higher education level. In association with its urban location, MCTC enrolls students from tribes across the United States, as well as almost 40% non-Native students. As a 2-year institution, MCTC grants Associate of Arts degrees and professional certifications in partnership with Pierce College. Coursework is offered in liberal arts, tribal management systems, tribal mental health, and criminal justice. MCTC endorses environmental concerns through an Indian Country Environmental Science curriculum and the development of an Environmental Research Center. MCTC's mission is to provide quality education for Native peoples that promotes skill development necessary to be competitive in a rapidly changing world (MCTC, 1998).

Northwest Indian College (NWIC)

NWIC in Washington evolved from the Lummi Indian School of Aquaculture established in 1971. With a decline in demand for fisheries technicians, the Lummi Tribe concurrently desired to address Native American educational needs. As a consequence, the Lummi Indian Business Council chartered Lummi Community College in 1983. Because the college intended to serve Native American communities in Northwest Washington, in 1989 the institution's name was changed to NWIC to better reflect its mission. NWIC consists of a main campus on the Lummi Indian Reservation and 17 instructional centers located in various tribal communities in the Pacific Northwest. NWIC's educational philosophy is based on the belief that postsecondary education must be provided within the Native American community and that a program must include a study of Native American culture, values, and history. An essential part of the NWIC's mission is "to provide opportunities for individuals to gain self-sufficiency in a rapidly changing, technological world while recognizing and nurturing their cultural identity" (NWIC, 1998, p. 6).

Sisseton Wahpeton Community College (SWCC)

SWCC in South Dakota was chartered in 1979 by the Sisseton Wahpeton Sioux Tribe to serve the Lake Traverse Reservation. Since its inception, the college has developed five divisions, including the academic departments, a vocational and technical education department, a nursing center, the Joseph Robbie Adult and Community Education Center, and the Institute of Dakota Studies. Students and staff from the college's vocational and technical department built a tribal resource center, library, and tribal archives. SWCC initiated the accreditation process with the North Central Association of Schools and Colleges in 1983. Accredited in 1990, SWCC's guiding philosophy follows:

> With the belief that education should be responsive to the social, political and economic needs of the tribal community, the glacial lakes region, and the world, [therefore] students are prepared to assume productive and responsible roles in society, to participate with competence in both the Indian and the non-Indian worlds, and to appreciate the merits of both. (SWCC, 1994, p. 2)

Turtle Mountain Community College (TMCC)

Chartered by the Turtle Mountain Chippewa Tribe in 1972, TMCC in North Dakota was founded to prepare tribal members to serve their reservation. In association with North Dakota State University–Bottineau Branch, initial funding was obtained through a Higher Education Act grant to administer the college. Affiliation was maintained with this branch campus as well as with Mayville State College from 1973 to 1979. TMCC was granted candidate status for accreditation by the North Central Association of Colleges and Schools in 1978 and received full accreditation in 1984. Its expressed philosophy recognizes its "obligations of direct community service to the Turtle Mountain Chippewa Tribe. Under this unifying principle, the college seeks to maintain, seek out, and provide comprehensive higher education services in fields needed for true Indian self determination" (TMCC, 1995, p. 3).

Summary

A common characteristic of TCUs is the high level of commitment to culture and community, both locally and globally. It is embodied in the shared vision of drawing on ancient insights when people invoke their ancestors in name, image, and story to address contemporary issues. Today, the campuses, buildings, halls, and offices are adorned with heroes from the past, respected elders, and other people who made tremendous sacrifices. Clearly, these people are still recognized and valued for their cultural symbolism. People find strength in the promise of TCUs; for many tribal members, they know how difficult it was to get a college education before there was a TCU in their community. Another aspect of the institutional portraits reveals the importance of partnerships with state colleges and universities that extended expertise and established relations with accreditation agencies. The following section provides an examination of curricular functions provided by TCUs and of a curriculum development effort in the area of teacher preparation that meets the education needs of tribal communities.

Curricular Functions and Curriculum Development

TCUs are in a position to provide strong leadership in curriculum planning and development for AIs and ANs in higher education (Inglebret & Pavel, 2000). TCU curricula are viewed broadly as encompassing all aspects of the educational process. Curricula are inclusive of institutional climate, philosophy, and mission; student advising, recruitment, and retention; and professional development and mentoring for faculty. Curricula cross the boundaries of 2- and 4-year degree time frames to engage graduates in the long-term continuation of their intellectual, emotional, physical, and spiritual growth. Perhaps most important, curricula extend beyond the institution to become intertwined with all aspects of community functioning. Some of the unique and stable curricular functions of TCUs are to (a) respond to community needs, (b) empower communities, (c) preserve and revitalize Native culture and language, and (d) facilitate community healing. The subsequent discussion explores these functions and adds preliminary insights gained from a case study in progress on developing curriculum for a Native teacher preparation program.

Curriculum Responds to Community Needs

TCUs are inextricably linked to the communities in which they exist. At the very heart of the TCU's operation lies the culture of the local community (Boyer, 1989–1990; Willeto, 1997). Community values, beliefs, traditions, and language serve as the foundation from which curricula is derived. All of these sources of knowledge enable TCUs to be familiar, comfortable, and comprehensible to community members. A result of their connection with tribal communities, TCUs are highly responsive to community needs (Burke, 1997). TCUs contribute to essentially every aspect of community life by providing curricula that address both the needs of people and land use practices to enhance quality of life (Ambler, 1999a; Cunningham, 1998–1999; Davis & Jerome, 1992; DeLong, 1998; Dolberry, 1992; NICC Staff, 1998–1999).

Recognizing that the sustainability of tribal well-being lies in its future generations, TCU curricula focus on meeting the needs of young people in the community. For example, Cankdeska Cikana Community College in North Dakota trains Head Start instructors while providing an Early Head Start program for 88 infants representing 75 families (Yellow Bird, 1998). Twenty-four TCUs have collaboratively developed culturally relevant science and mathematics curricula for school-age Indian students as part of the All Nations Alliance for Minority Participation (Colomeda, 1998). Through the Circle of Learning project in Minnesota, Indian educators are being trained to prepare at-risk learners for higher education. This project represents a collaborative venture between the Fond du Lac Tribal and Community College, the University of Minnesota, and the Fond du Lac Band of Chippewa Indians (Ness, 1998).

Although these efforts focus on meeting the needs of people in specific communities, other educational endeavors emphasize caring for the land base (Boyer, 1998; Cordero, 1992; Semken, 1992). For AIs and ANs, this represents a particularly important focus, as sense of identity is often closely aligned with the land that Indian people and their ancestors have inhabited (Marker, 2000). TCUs address land-related issues through a variety of curricular pursuits. Through Oglala Lakota College's (OLC) Model Institutions of Excellence program, students at five TCUs in North Dakota and South Dakota gain scientific expertise necessary for environmental preservation (Allen, 1998). Diné College, which serves an interstate land base crossing Arizona and New Mexico, provides an example of curriculum designed to deal with the consequences of uranium mining (Ambler, 1998b). Salish Kootenai College in Montana approaches environmental concerns by integrating related ethical, cultural, political, and scientific issues across the curriculum (Ambler, 1998a). These interactive forces are considered central to preservation of the land for future generations.

Curriculum Empowers Communities

Lomawaima (1995) portrayed Indian education as "a 500-year-old battle for power" (p. 331). During the past half century, the power to define education, to develop educational policies and curricula, and to decide what constitutes knowledge has predominantly resided outside of Indian communities. As we have seen in the historical overview, this imbalance in power has perpetuated racism and discriminatory practices that have kept the voices of AIs and ANs out of the forefront in higher education dialogue. TCUs have turned the balance of power around by placing control of their programs and curricula in the hands of AIs and ANs themselves. Native people now create educational curricula that simultaneously allow them to build their community infrastructures and to promote participation in the larger democratic society of the United States. In this manner, AI and AN people empower themselves.

Native people see the need for a range of postsecondary educational opportunities to provide them with knowledge and skills necessary to reconstruct community infrastructures essential to renewed prosperity and community well-being (Boyer, 1992). A key element of empowerment involves Indian people in identifying their own needs. The community-based nature of TCUs makes them optimally suited to serve as resources for data collection and dissemination pertaining to areas such as economic growth, production, and trends (Ambler, 1992). As economic needs are identified, Native people can respond by developing their own business ventures. The majority of TCUs promote entrepreneurship or small business development using at least one of a variety of program types (Robinson & Hogan, 1992). Some offer single courses specific to entrepreneurship, others provide more comprehensive educational programs, and others provide consultation and technical assistance (Ambler, 1999b; Lansdowne, 1992; Red Eagle, 1998). The Sicangu Enterprise Center in conjunction with Sinte Gleska University, for example, even offers loans for aspiring entrepreneurs (Haase,1992). These programs share a common concern with the generation of strategies that will prove sustainable over the long term.

TCUs recognize that a key aspect of empowerment involves building leadership from within the communities where they exist (Ambler, 1997a; Bad Wound, 1991; Pavel & Colby, 1993; Stein & Eagleeye, 1993; Yellow Bird, 1998–1999). Many TCUs have begun by placing Native people in administrative positions within their institutions (Krumm, 1997–1998; Shanley & Ryan, 1993). This practice carries multifaceted implications. For instance, Janine Pease-Windy Boy (1995), who serves as President of LBHC in Montana, advocates local control of curricula. Through participatory program development and decision making, Pease-Windy Boy weaves the expertise of scholars educated through traditional Native means into curriculum development. This process legitimizes the Native educational leadership that already exists in the community and provides a highly visible role model of Native leadership. As another example, Salish Kootenai College in Montana directly capitalizes on the knowledge and skills of traditionally educated elders to educate future cultural leaders (Finley, 1997). Control over curriculum development efforts empowers tribal members to envision and determine their own futures, while attracting more youth to TCUs.

Curriculum Preserves and Revitalizes Native Culture and Language

Native language and cultural survival is a primary concern of tribal communities. Many Native languages have been lost or are only spoken by a few elders. The extent of overall indigenous cultural survival varies immensely from reservation to reservation. However, a renewed focus on Indian self-determination and tribal self-governance has resulted in a resurgence of efforts to preserve and renew traditional Native ways of living and communicating (Pavel, 1992).

Words serve as a key purveyor of cultural information for generations to come. Recognizing the critical role of language in cultural continuity, TCUs have assumed responsibility for renewing Native language through curriculum development and implementation efforts (Haase, 1993; Knowles, Gill, Beauvais, & Medearis, 1992; Littlebear, 1997; Slate, 1993). As specific examples, TMCC in North Dakota has developed a written Chippewa–Cree dictionary, whereas Sinte Gleska University in South Dakota recently produced a textbook to accompany its Lakota language coursework (Ambler & Crazy Bull, 1997). Fort Peck Community College immerses preschoolers in Dakota and Nakota instruction, while their parents are simultaneously trained to facilitate Dakota and Nakota language acquisition in the home environment (Campbell, 1998). This program blends language immersion with traditional spiritual practices, legends, games, art activities, music, and foods. In this manner the language is integrated back into the traditional culture out of which it has grown.

Looking more broadly at cultural transmission, elders play a central role in shaping the cultural ethos of TCUs. As culture bearers, elders pass on traditional skills, knowledge, values, and beliefs through various forms of involvement in colleges (Barnhardt, 1991; Hornby & Dana, 1992; Srivastava, 1997; Willeto, 1997). Some TCUs, such as Dull Knife Memorial College in Montana, involve elders in forums and advisory committees. Others, such as Lac Courte Oreilles Ojibwa College in Wisconsin, provide a cultural foundation by involving students in talking circles with elders (Rosado & Teuber, 1992). Salish Kootenai College's Cultural Leadership Program in Montana brings students and elders together full time to pass on traditional knowledge and practices in natural sites (Finley, 1997).

Traditional culture takes center stage in both educational content and process at TCUs, because education historically has revolved around a caring attitude. Reflecting a humanistic orientation, caring has been identified as a key element underlying educational access for AI and AN students at TCUs. Pavel (1997) described caring relationships among TCU faculty, staff, and students that were distinguished by honesty and sincerity as well as by interactions of an encouraging and comforting nature. Underlying a caring context for learning was the faculty members' belief in Indian students' capacity to learn and direct action taken by teaching staff to integrate traditional concepts and ways of knowing into the educational process (Inglebret & Pavel, 2000). For example, at LBHC, a cultural emphasis on approaching life holistically and cooperatively has been expressed through an interdisciplinary curricular orientation and cooperative learning strategies (Pease-Windy Boy, 1995). These traditional educational orientations have been recognized as assets for preparing students to develop solutions in response to the multidimensional problems confronted in today's world.

Curriculum Facilitates Healing

TCUs serve as a symbol of hope to many AI and AN communities. With unemployment, poverty, and other acts of oppression running rampant across Indian communities, TCU students often enter the educational arena with decreased self-esteem and concomitant problems linked to effects of poverty and oppression (Ambler, 1997b). Although TCU curricula recognize the need to address these specific symptoms of unwellness, they also frame their efforts more systemically toward cultural healing and recovery at a community level (McDonald, McDonald, & Thomkins, 1992; Rosado & Teuber, 1992; Silverthorn, 1992).

Butterfield, Boyer, and Reddish (1992) contended that as AI and AN communities regain a sense of pride in their identities, an environment will be created in which sobriety and wellness can flourish. To promote healing at the individual and family level, TCUs directly confront outward symptoms of ill health by training community members as human service providers. Collective well-being is targeted through multifaceted efforts, such as the community outreach program run by Sinte Gleska University. This program enhances community awareness of alcohol-related issues, supports community members in the recovery process, and develops alternative activities open to all community members.

OLC has embarked on a collaborative effort with four other community organizations, including the Lakota Nation Wellness Team, to bring multiple forces together to develop healthy communities. This community-wide approach incorporates a belief that to achieve and sustain wellness, each community must create its own definition of health and its own vision of itself as a healthy community. To carry this vision forward, it is necessary to address the interplay among various forces, including those of a "political, economic, environmental, spiritual, mental, and physical" nature (Demarest, 1999, p. 27). By addressing these interconnected forces holistically, harmony and balance can be achieved.

Curriculum Development in Native Teacher Preparation

National Movement

Severe underrepresentation of AI and AN people in the teaching profession nationally translates into a need for Native teachers in many of the local communities served by TCUs (Banks, 1999; Boone & Ruhl, 1995; Pavel, 1995, 1999b; U.S. Department of Education, 1995, 1997; Wald, 1996). As a consequence, several TCUs are currently taking on the task of developing curriculum for teacher preparation. This is occurring through individual institutional efforts and partnerships between existing 4-year teacher education programs and TCUs. In either case, the TCUs base their service delivery on "a firm understanding of local control and equal access to education" (Pease-Windy Boy, 1995, p. 400). State colleges and universities (SCUs) that choose to partner with TCUs have unique opportunities to build bridges of understanding and to work collaboratively on educational reform to pave the way for more culturally responsive education across all levels. The TCU–SCU partnership programs are relatively new with a developmental continuum ranging from infancy (1–3 years old) to adolescence (4–8 years old).

It is a complex undertaking to develop Native teacher preparation programs that meet the diverse cultural and educational needs of students. Like painting community murals, decisions must be made collaboratively with regard to design, medium, colors, brushes, and size to reflect the spirit of each community. To address these complexities, personnel from TCU and TCU–SCU teacher preparation programs across the country have begun meeting and networking to facilitate efforts to achieve systemic change. Attendees at a recent Native Teacher Preparation Conference shared successes that have occurred and the challenges each confronted. Success was experienced in the graduation of students, in the integration of Native language and culture across the curriculum, and development of effective mentoring programs.

Challenges revolved around accreditation and certification issues, funding, infusion of Native culture and language when students represent diverse tribal backgrounds, student services, recruitment and retention of Native faculty, and credit transfer across institutions. Some factors were identified as representing both successes achieved and challenges posed for differing institutions. These included program scheduling to match community needs, use of technology, and partnerships with mainstream institutions. Although the challenges are many, tribal voices in education are focusing on their successes in volume and intensity by uniting with others to effect systemic change. Education is a sociopolitical endeavor that can provide the means for people to empower themselves. For TCUs and tribal schools this requires working together as agents of change to address the pressing needs of Indian children, families, and communities.

Case Study in Progress

As part of a larger Native American Higher Education Initiative, the W. K. Kellogg Foundation (undated) funded a partnership between Washington State University (WSU) and NWIC to develop a Native Teacher Preparation Program. This "case study in progress" of the WSU–NWIC partnership provides a focused look into a collaborative project that was formed for the purpose of developing and implementing a culturally sensitive and responsive teacher preparation program for Indian people (NWIC–WSU Curriculum Planning Committee, 1999). A brief historical context will be provided to facilitate understanding of the project at its present state of adolescence.

The WSU–NWIC project began in the fall semester of 1997. The design of the grant required immediate start-up of a teacher education program with 12 students initially enrolled. Major and frequent changes in personnel within both institutions have posed challenges to the continuity of the project and have impacted its developmental pace. Total enrollment of Native students in WSU's teacher preparation program during the project period of 1997 to 2002 is four times that of any 5-year period prior to the NWIC–WSU partnership. Graduation rates are expected to be six times as high by 2002, when 16 Native students are scheduled to receive their degrees and teaching certificates.

Strengthening the partnership remains the high leverage point to ensure program success. Regular communication across institutional leadership and program personnel through meetings held at each institution provides opportunities for joint dialogue, decision making, and problem solving. Face-to-face meetings are supplemented by regular communication via e-mail, phone, or fax. Consistent, active, committed personnel in leadership positions within each institution can facilitate timely progress across all areas of program development. The partnership is strengthened as leaders convey the willingness to sit beside each other as equals with openness to the possibility of knowing in a different way. A major insight is that building partnerships (mutually respectful, caring relationships built on trust and equity) is a fragile process that is strengthened by memorandums of understanding, parting agreements, and contracts.

Conceptualization of a curriculum revision effort to add Native content to WSU teacher education curriculum began in February 1998. Following a review of literature and extensive inquiries, a committee of seven core members was formed and numerous cultural resource consultants were identified. Committee members were representative of WSU, NWIC, the local tribal community, local Indian educators in schools and the tribal college, and state and national Indian education consultants. Initial core committee meetings focused on establishing a context for the curriculum development process. Each committee member shared personal experiences, and group reflection served to inform the past, present, and future impacts of those histories. Members of the committee also discussed various community needs that directly impact Indian people such as passing on traditional languages, culture, and critical values for empowering young people to succeed in contemporary society.

Members' stories and ideas gave rise to a synthesis of members' voices regarding essential threads that need to be woven throughout the teacher preparation courses (e.g., sovereignty, U.S. Indian policies, intertribal languages and culture, health and wellness). The committee reached consensus on the need for preservice teachers to complete course work in conjunction with practicum. Immersion in the educational culture of schools and communities would enable preservice teachers to (a) construct knowledge about learning and learners, (b) develop observational and self-reflective skills by integrating experiential learning with theoretical constructs found in traditional texts, and (c) construct knowledge about the social–political contexts of education. In addition, students would gain insights into effectiveness of specific practices and professional skills.

The committee agreed that a narrow definition of curriculum encompassing syllabi, materials, and instructional methods is insufficient. Currently, the inclusive view of curriculum consists of four phases (see Table 1). Phase 1 delineates student involvement prior to enrollment in the program, and Phase 2 encompasses factors influencing student involvement, while participating in coursework. Phase 3–In Schools refers to practicums and student teaching. Phase 4–Returning will occur when students return to mentor new students, share their experiences and insights, assist in guiding ongoing program development, and so on. The multiphase vision of becoming a teacher was conceptualized as a continual circular path in which lifelong learning and community giving is modeled. Traditional education is a community responsibility, and all members are teachers and learners in keeping with their gifts. The essential phases (i.e., the curriculum components) of this evolving Native teacher preparation program are interrelated and interdependent.

The process of this holistic curriculum development effort reflects the desire to achieve consensus decision making involving voices of multiple communities engaged in respective, reflective communicative interactions. Goddard and Shields (1997) pointed out, "The more students are steeped in their own language and culture, the better they achieve academically and economically" (p. 42). National and global impacts of an educational system that facilitated such achievement for all its citizens would, indeed, be exemplary of equity in education and reflective of community health and wellness. The focus on community involvement and the process of becoming a teacher rather than a product are thought to result in a flexible, dynamic, and durable program that encourages lifelong learning. "In its programs, Native education must excite and challenge students, teachers, and the community . . . " (Charleston, 1994, p. 36). The visions shared and synthesized, thus far, indicate that an evolving philosophy is taking shape to ground, guide, and inspire all participants.

U.S. educational systems and Indian education are in the midst of educational reform efforts. The spirit of educational reform in Indian education lies in grassroots efforts; that is, parents, com-

TABLE 1

Phases 1 and 2 of Developing a Native Teacher Preparation Program

Phase 1–Before Program Phase	Phase 2–In Program Phase
Hospitality (care and concern)	Retention
Advising	Financial aid
Sites, placement testing	Childcare, housing
Student services personnel need to be	Transportation services
aware of program requirements	Collaborative agreements
Recruiting	Distance learning = 2 + 2
Brochures, orientation, visitations	Quality experience
High school: GED, tutoring, mentoring	Professional development
Academic preparation	Assessment
Financial aid, scholarships	Cultural immersion and sensitivity
Self-reflection–actualization	Hospitality–orientation
Entering the teaching profession	Academic freedom (limited and respectful)
Interview	Trust
Coping skills	Institutional review board
People skills	Collaborative agreements
Health and wellness	Syllabi
Link preteacher preparation with teacher	Faculty
preparation—transition plan	Faculty retention
	Endowed faculty

Note. GED = general equivalence degree.

munity members, active local school personnel, and professional organizations advocate change together. "Whatever information is obtained in higher education must, in the Indian context, have some direct bearing with human individual and communal experience" (Deloria, 1991, p. 20). The unique sovereign relation that exists between Indian Nations and the U.S. Government spans public schools, tribal schools, and IHEs (mainstream colleges and universities as well as TCUs). Native teacher preparation programs reflect reform efforts aimed at changing systems to meet the needs of children, families, and communities as opposed to changing children, families, and communities to meet the needs of systems. As such, Native teacher education programs facilitate systemic change by empowering Native peoples to embrace traditional lifestyles that promote cultural sensitivity and success in life.

Summary

TCUs offer tribal communities a means to rebuild the greatness of their past as they respond to immediate community needs, promote collective empowerment, revitalize culture and language, and facilitate community healing. By closely interlinking curricula with community, TCUs create environments that promote sustainable economic, social, political, cultural, and spiritual vitality through education. Taken together, these curricular functions comprise a substantial social force that can serve as a catalyst for rejuvenated prosperity and well-being in Native communities. As we have seen in the case study in progress on developing curriculum for a Native teacher preparation program, this is generally not achieved by overlaying existing curriculum from other IHEs on to the TCU educational framework. Rather, TCU curricular construction involves community members in identifying their own educational needs and in developing programs and policies that are specifically tailored to meet these needs.

Conclusion

TCUs are an important development in American higher education. Although the true history of TCUs is ancient, the modern movement of institutions of higher education charted by tribal governments started in 1968. Remarkable that in a short period of institutional history, tribal sovereignty and self-governance has led to Indian nations developing higher education curricular that touches every facet of tribal life. People who work with, for, or benefit from TCUs share a desire for institutional and community change; they want to make a difference and positively influence the future.

TCUs are not alone in serving as community vanguards. National initiatives are recognizing the need to support institutions that further the aims of underrepresented groups throughout American higher education (Kee & Mahoney, 1995). The Ford Foundation, W. K. Kellogg Foundation, Gates Foundation, National Science Foundation, and U.S. Department of Education all have initiatives to assist TCUs, historically black colleges and universities, predominately Hispanic serving institutions, and institutions serving the needs of low-income Whites. Still, it is not enough to meet the financial needs of these communities. On a positive side, funding does help to develop the capacity of minority-serving institutions of higher education; however, it is not the greatest strength. These institutions are by nature community oriented. There is a prevailing love of family, culture, and land that typify institutions successful at increasing postsecondary access and improving economic development.

The alignment of strengths is an important step to sustain initiatives, and the accumulated strengths in alignment will correspond to likelihood of success. Team building and partnerships are no longer choices. The poor economic condition of reservations and rural America already makes it difficult to develop the infrastructure necessary to be part of the global economy. Collaboration is necessary to share resources to address common problems (Scholtes, Joiner, & Streibel, 1996).

If given the proper support and opportunity to evolve, the TCUs will continue to serve as catalysts to improve the quality of life for AI and AN peoples. The movement of federal Indian policy and public sentiment should be to further self-determination and self-governance while presenting equitable ways to enter into partnerships with state governments. Without an authentic role in decision making, it is doubtful that Indian people will have a real say in the mission, scope, and influence of developing an education system—and it is easy to tell when you do not have a real contribution. The TCUs play an authentic role in tribal communities and in higher education.

Notes

1. The following terms are used interchangeably throughout this article: *American Indian, Alaska Native, Native American, Indian,* and *Native.*
2. Space and organizational constraints prevent the presentation of all tribal colleges and universities (TCUs). However, as with the TCUs not listed, all share common characteristics in terms of their inception. For more information on TCUs, please contact the American Indian Higher Education Consortium, 121 Oronoco Street, Alexandria, VA 22314 or the American Indian College Fund, 21 West 68th Street, 1F, New York, NY 10023.

References

Allen, M. (1998). Oglala MIE program responds to budding scientists' prayers. *Tribal College, 10*(1), 9–12.

Ambler, M. (1992). The wealth of (Indian) nations: Tribes are creating a new model of economic development by building on old strengths. *Tribal College, 4*(2), 8–12.

Ambler, M. (1997a). Native scholarship: Explorations in the new frontier. *Tribal College, 9*(1), 8–10.

Ambler, M. (1997b). Re-envisioning American Indian education. *Tribal College, 9*(2), 8–10.

Ambler, M. (1998a). Land-based colleges offer science students a sense of place. *Tribal College, 10*(1), 6–8.

Ambler, M. (1998b). Tribal colleges reach out to future students, pre-K through 12. *Tribal College, 9*(4), 6–9.

Ambler, M. (1999a). Diné College students research diabetes for their people. *Tribal College, 11*(1), 18–20.

Ambler, M. (1999b). For Native people, art is not optional. *Tribal College, 10*(4), 6–9.

Ambler, M., & Crazy Bull, C. (1997). Survey: Tribal colleges deeply involved in research. *Tribal College, 9*(1), 12–15.

Bad Wound, E. (1991). Teaching to empower: Tribal colleges must promote leadership and self-determination in their reservations. *Tribal College, 3*(1), 15–19.

Banks, J. (1999). *An introduction to multicultural education* (2nd ed.). Boston: Allyn & Bacon.

Barnhardt, R. (1991). Higher education in the fourth world. *Tribal College, 3*(2), 11–13, 21–26.

Bay Mills Community College. (1994). *Bay Mills community college 1994–1996 catalog.* Brimley, MI: Bay Mills Indian Community.

Boone, R. S., & Ruhl, K. L. (1995). Controllable factors in recruitment of minority and nonminority individuals for doctoral study in special education. *Multiple Voices, 1*(1), 23–37.

Boyer, P. (1989–1990). The tribal college: Teaching self-determination. *Community, Technical, and Junior College Journal, 60*(3), 24–29.

Boyer, P. (1992). Education for economic development. *Tribal College, 4*(2), 4–5.

Boyer, P. (1997). *Native American colleges: Progress and prospects.* San Francisco: Jossey-Bass.

Boyer, P. (1998). SKC protecting Native plants. *Tribal College, 9*(4), 40–41.

Burke, G. (1997). Crownpoint building veterinary hospital. *Tribal College, 9*(1), 36–38.

Butterfield, N., Boyer, P., & Reddish, J. G. (1992). Cultures in recovery: A powerful sobriety movement is transforming Indian societies from Alaska to Florida. *Tribal College, 4*(1), 8–11.

Campbell, M. H. (1998). Fort Peck combines language immersion with Montessori methods. *Tribal College, 9*(4), 15.

Charleston, M. G. (1994). Toward true Native education: A treaty of 1992. *Journal of American Indian Education, 33*(2), 1–55.

College of the Menominee Nation. (1995). *College of the Menominee Nation catalog 1995–1996.* Keshena, WI: Menominee Nation.

Colomeda, L. (1998). A literature guide: Resources for teaching math and science to American Indian students. *Tribal College, 10*(1), 18–22.

Conlin, J. R. (1987). *The America past* (2nd ed.). New York: Harcourt Brace Jovanovich.

Cordero, C. (1992). Healing the earth. *Tribal College, 3*(3), 8–10.

Crum, S. (1989). The idea of an Indian college or university in twentieth century America before the formation of the Navajo Community College in 1968. *Tribal College, 1*(1), 20–23.

Crum, S. (1991). Colleges before Columbus. *Tribal College, 3*(2), 14–17.

Cunningham, A. F. (1998–1999). Survey reports tribal colleges' response to welfare reform. *Tribal College, 10*(2), 36.

Davis, S. A., & Jerome, D. (1992). Turtle Mountain's college for kids. *Tribal College, 3*(3), 14–15.

DeLong, L. (1998). Indian controlled schools—The unrealized potential. *Tribal College, 9*(4), 13–14.

Deloria, V., Jr. (1991). Higher education and self-determination. *A Magazine for American Indians, 6*(1), 18–25.

Demarest, D. (1999). Healthy tribal colleges create healthy communities. *Tribal College, 11*(1), 26–27.

Dolberry, J. (1992). Nursing education in Indian country. *Tribal College, 3*(3), 20–21.

Finley, V. (1997). Designing a cultural leadership program. *Tribal College, 9*(2), 19–22.

Franklin, B. (1794). *Two tracks: Information to those who would remove to America, and remarks concerning the savages of North America* (2nd ed.). London: Stockdale.

Goddard, J. T., & Shields, C. M. (1997). An ethnocultural comparison of empowerment in two districts: Learning from an American Indian and a Canadian First Nations school district. *Journal of American Indian Education, 36*(2), 19–45.

Haase, E. (1992). Joining the circle: Circle banking on the Rosebud Reservation. *Tribal College, 4*(2), 16–18.

Haase, E. (1993). Healing the generations. *Tribal College, 4*(4), 20–23.

Haymond, J. H. (1982). *The American Indian in higher education: From the college for children of the infidels (1619) to Navajo Community College (1969).* Unpublished doctoral dissertation, Washington State University, Pullman.

Hodge, W. H. (1981). *The first Americans.* New York: Holt, Rinehart & Winston.

Hornby, R., & Dana, R. H. (1992). Human service training in tribal colleges. *Tribal College, 3*(3), 24–27.

Ilisagvik College. (1998). *Ilisagvik College 1998–99 catalog.* Barrow, AK: Author.

Inglebret, E., & Pavel, D. M. (2000). Curriculum planning and development for American Indians and Alaska Natives in higher education. In F. W. Parkey & G. Hass (Eds.), *Curriculum planning: A contemporary approach* (7th ed., pp. 493–502). Boston: Allyn & Bacon.

Kee, A. M., & Mahoney, J. R. (1995). *Multicultural strategies for community colleges.* Washington, DC: American Association of Community Colleges.

Knowles, T., Gill, J., Beauvais, A., & Medearis, C. (1992). Teacher education and the Rosebud tribal education code. *Tribal College, 4*(2), 21–23.

Krumm, B. L. (1997–1998). Leadership reflections: Women tribal college presidents. *Tribal College, 9*(3), 24–28.

Lansdowne, M. (1992). Entrepreneurs with the power of a tribe behind them. *Tribal College, 4*(2), 19–20.

Little Big Horn College. (1994). *Little Big Horn College catalog 1994–1997.* Crow Agency, MT: Crow Tribe.

Little Priest Tribal College. (1997). *Little Priest Tribal College 1997–98 general catalog.* Winnebago, NE: Winnebago Tribe of Nebraska.

Littlebear, R. (1997). Montana adopts landmark language certification process. *Tribal College, 9*(2), 26–29.

Lomawaima, K. T. (1995). Educating Native Americans. In J. A. Banks & C. A. McGee Banks (Eds.), *Handbook of research on multicultural education* (pp. 331–347). New York: Macmillan.

Marker, M. (2000). Ethno-history of Indigenous education: A moment of uncertainty. *History of Education, 29*(1), 79–85.

McDonald, A., McDonald, D., & Thomkins, D. (1992). Healthy body, healthy mind. *Tribal College, 4*(1), 20–21.

Medicine Creek Tribal College. (1998). *Medicine Creek Tribal College 1998–1999 catalog.* Tacoma, WA: Author.

Miller, F. C. (1971). *The problem of Indian administration. An unaltered reprint of the work originally published by Lewis Meriam in 1928.* New York: Johnson Reprint Corporation.

Ness, J. E. (1998). Completing the circle: Training Indian educators to prepare "at risk" students for college. *Tribal College, 9*(4), 26–27.

NICC Staff. (1998–1999). NICC builds team to address welfare reform. *Tribal College, 10*(2), 32–33.

Nicholson, A. (1854). *Commissioner of Indian Affairs annual report, 1854.* Washington, DC: Indian Affairs Documents.

Northwest Indian College. (1998). *Northwest Indian College 1999–2000 catalog.* Bellingham, WA: Author.

Northwest Indian College–Washington State University Curriculum Planning Committee. (1999). *Oksale teacher education program: Curriculum planning documents.* Pullman: Washington State University, Department of Teaching and Learning.

Oppelt, N. T. (1990). *The tribally controlled Indian college: The beginning of self determination in American Indian education.* Tsaile, AZ: Diné Community College Press.

Pavel, D. M. (1992). *The emerging role of tribal college libraries in Indian education.* Charleston, WV: ERIC Clearinghouse on Rural Education and Small School.

Pavel, D. M. (1995). Comparing BIA and tribal schools with public schools: A look at the year 1990–91. *Journal of American Indian Education, 35*(5), 10–15.

Pavel, D. M. (1997). *Promoting postsecondary access through tribal colleges.* Washington, DC: American Association of Community Colleges and the Ford Foundation.

Pavel, D. M. (1999a). American Indians and Alaska Natives in higher education: Promoting access and achievement. In K. G. Swisher & J. W. Tippeconnic III (Eds.), *Next steps: Research and practice to advance Indian education* (pp. 271–296). Charleston, WV: ERIC Clearing House on Rural and Small Schools.

Pavel, D. M. (1999b). *Schools, principals, and teachers serving American Indian and Alaska Native students.* Charleston, WV: ERIC Clearinghouse on Rural Education and Small Schools.

Pavel, D. M., & Colby, A. (1993). *American Indians in higher education: The community college experience.* Los Angeles, CA: ERIC Clearinghouse on Junior and Community Colleges.

Pavel, D. M., Inglebret, E., & Van Den Hende, M. (1999). Tribal colleges. In B. Townsend (Ed.), *Community colleges for women and minorities: Enabling access to the baccalaureate* (pp. 113–150). New York: Garland.

Pavel, D. M., & Padilla, R. V. (1993). American Indian and Alaska Native postsecondary departure: An example of assessing a mainstream model using national longitudinal data. *Journal of American Indian Education, 32*(2), 1–23.

Pavel, D. M., Swisher, K., & Ward, M. (1995). Special focus: American Indian and Alaska Native demographic and educational trends. In D. J. Carter & R. Wilson (Eds.), *Thirteenth annual status report: Minorities in higher education* (pp. 33–59). Washington, DC: American Council on Education.

Pease-Windy Boy, J. (1995). Cultural diversity in higher education: An American Indian perspective. In C. E. Sleeter & P. L. McLaren (Eds.), *Multicultural education, critical pedagogy, and the politics of difference* (pp. 399–413). Albany: State University of New York Press.

Red Eagle, C. (1998). Sitting Bull College celebrates 25 years of vision. *Tribal College, 9*(4), 48–50.

Robinson, S., & Hogan, S. (1992). Tribal college entrepreneurship programs: The family emphasis. *Tribal College, 3*(4), 27–30.

Rosado, J., & Teuber, H. (1992). Looking inward: Lac Courte Oreilles Ojibwa college helps students challenge alcohol and drugs. *Tribal College, 4*(1), 19.

Scholtes, P. R., Joiner, B. L., & Streibel, B. J. (1996). *The TEAM handbook* (2nd ed.). Madison, WI: Oriel Incorporated.

Semken, S. C. (1992). Looking after the land. *Tribal College, 3*(3), 11–12.

Shanley, J., & Ryan, K. (1993). Wise men and elegant speakers: Reflecting on traditional Assiniboine leadership. *Tribal College, 5*(2), 12–15.

Silverthorn, J. (1992). Salish Kootenai College produces programs on children, families, and substance abuse. *Tribal College, 4*(1), 30.

Sisseton Wahpeton Community College. (1994). *Sisseton Wahpeton community college catalog 1994–96.* Sisseton, SD: Sisseton Wahpeton Sioux Tribe.

Slate, C. (1993). Finding a place for Navajo. *Tribal College, 4*(4), 10–14.

Srivastava, R. (1997). A report from the trenches: Cultural integration in science and math. *Tribal College, 9*(2), 17–18.

Stein, W. J. (1992). *Tribally controlled colleges: Making good medicine.* New York: Lang.

Stein, W. J., & Eagleeye, D. (1993). Learned leadership: Preparing the next generation of tribal college administrators. *Tribal College, 5*(2), 33–36.

Turtle Mountain Community College. (1995). *Turtle Mountain community college 1995–96 catalog.* Belcourt, ND: Turtle Mountain Band of Chippewa.

U. S. Department of Education, National Center for Education Statistics. (1995). *Characteristics of American Indian and Alaska Native education: Results from the 1990–91 schools and staffing survey* (NCES No. 95–735). Washington, DC: Author.

U.S. Department of Education, National Center for Education Statistics. (1997). *Characteristics of American Indian and Alaska Native education: Results from the 1993–94 and 1990–91 schools and staffing survey* (NCES No. 97–451). Washington, DC: Author.

U.S. Department of Education, National Center for Education Statistics. (1998). *American Indians and Alaska Natives in postsecondary education* (NCES No. 98–291). Washington, DC: Author.

Wald, J. L. (1996). *Culturally and linguistically diverse professionals in special education: A demographic analysis.* Reston, VA: National Clearinghouse for Professions in Special Education.

Willeto, P. (1997). Diné College struggles to synthesize Navajo and Western knowledge. *Tribal College, 9*(2), 11–15.

W. K. Kellogg Foundation. (Undated). *Journeying on: The W. K. Kellogg Foundation's Native American higher education initiative.* Battle Creek, MI: Author.

Wright, B. (1988). For the children of the infidels?: American Indian education in the colonial colleges. *American Indian Culture and Research Journal, 12*(3), 1–14.

Wright, B., & Tierney, W. G. (1991). American Indians in higher education: A history of cultural conflict. *Change, 23*(2), 11–18.

Yellow Bird, D. (1998). Spirit Lake Sioux children start school at 6 weeks. *Tribal College, 9*(4), 10–12.

Yellow Bird, D. (1998–1999). Turtle Mountain faculty helps build model assessment tool. *Tribal College, 10*(2), 10–13.

The Historically Black College as Social Contract, Social Capital, and Social Equalizer

M. Christopher Brown II
Educational Organization and Leadership
University of Illinois at Urbana–Champaign

James Earl Davis
Department of Higher Education
Temple University

Historically Black colleges and universities (HBCUs) have a unique educational history in comparison to other postsecondary institutions in the United States. HBCUs are institutions founded prior to 1964 for the purpose of providing collegiate education to African Americans. There are 103 public, private, 4-year, and 2-year HBCUs. In addition to the 103 HBCUs, there are approximately 50 predominantly Black institutions. Predominantly Black colleges and universities are institutions with greater than 50% Black student enrollment, which were not founded primarily for the education of African American students, and may or may not have been founded prior to 1964.

Comparable to other American postsecondary institutions, HBCUs vary widely in size, curriculum specializations, and a host of other characteristics. The one commonality across HBCUs is their historic responsibility as the primary providers of postsecondary education for African Americans in a social environment of racial discrimination. Given the historic focus of HBCUs on the education of Black students, Walter Allen (1992) identified six specific goals endemic to these institutions. The six goals of HBCUs include (a) the maintenance of the Black historical and cultural tradition (and cultural influences emanating from the Black community); (b) the provision of key leadership for the Black community given the important social role of college administrators, scholars, and students in community affairs (i.e., the HBCU functions as a paragon of social organization); (c) the provision of an economic function in the Black community (e.g., HBCUs often have the largest institutional budget within the Black community); (d) the provision of Black role models to interpret the way in which social, political, and economic dynamics impact Black people; (e) the provision of college graduates with a unique competence to address the issues between the minority and majority population groups; and (f) the production of Black agents for specialized research, institutional training, and information dissemination in dealing with the life environment of Black and other minority communities.

According to the U.S. Department of Education (1996), the 103 HBCUs enroll approximately 300,000 students and employ approximately 60,000 persons. HBCUs award 28% of the Black bachelors degrees, 16% of the Black first-professional degrees, 15% of the Black masters degrees, and 9% of the Black doctoral degrees. Notwithstanding, Vernon Jordan stated that the historically Black college remains the undergraduate home of "75 percent of all Black Ph.D.s, 75 percent of all Black army officers, 80 percent of all Black federal judges, and 85 percent of all Black doctors" (cited in Roebuck & Murty, 1993, p. 13). Predominantly Black colleges have experienced similar educational gains.

Understanding the fundamental characteristics that shape historically Black colleges serves as a framework of analysis for meaningful equity and access. These fundamental characteristics shape how all colleges play out their role in society. There are simultaneous and competing roles of knowledge construction, information transmission, and status allocation. On one hand, historically Black colleges serve to develop, create, and teach advanced knowledge to society. In this fashion, they serve to transmit and transform a society's culture while educating its citizens. On the other, these institutions make critical gains in ensuring that growing numbers of African Americans will be competent to serve as leaders or knowledge workers in society. These roles call on historically Black colleges to aid all who enter their doors to gain knowledge.

Given the historical and present circumstances of HBCUs, the purpose of this article is threefold. First, we posit that Black colleges enjoy a unique social contract in the national history. HBCUs act as "social agencies" for society by fulfilling the need to provide an equal educational opportunity and attainment, not only for African Americans, but for all students. Second, this social contract that Black colleges broker between the nation and African Americans is realized through social capital or the distribution and reproduction of social networks and resources that HBCUs provide for their students and graduates. Finally, we argue that Black colleges act as a "social equalizer" for individuals historically denied access to higher educational opportunity and excluded from full participation in society.

Black Colleges as Participants in a Social Contract

HBCUs are participants in a social contract with postbellum American society. Prior to the Civil War, the combination of slavery and segregation restricted educational access and opportunity for African Americans. Although there were a few Northern exceptions (e.g., Amherst College, Oberlin College), African American students were summarily denied entry to institutions of higher learning. Speaking broadly, Reginald Wilson (1988) wrote,

> The historically Black colleges and universities have a history unique to American higher education. That history is a consequence of the presence of slavery in the American colonies, beginning with the importation of the first Blacks in 1619. Slavery precluded Blacks from participating in the general institutional life of the colonies even after the Declaration of Independence in 1776 declared that slaves would be counted as "three-fifths of a man" in those states where slavery was permitted. Although the first college for Blacks (now called Cheyney [State] University) was established in Pennsylvania in 1837, the major history of historically Black universities and colleges did not begin until after the Civil War. (p. 121)

The aftermath of the War Between the States led to a proliferation of HBCUs. More than 200 HBCUs were founded prior to 1890. As previously mentioned, philanthropic associations, churches, local communities, missionaries, and private donors founded many. However, the end of the Civil War brought a new founder and funder of HBCUs—state governments. Southern states were required by law to respond to the Thirteenth, Fourteenth, and Fifteenth Amendments by providing public education for the former slaves and other Black Americans. Supplementary public support came with the passage of the Second Morrill Act of 1890. The first Morrill Act of 1862 provided federal support for state education, particularly in agriculture, education, and military sciences. The Morrill Act of 1890 mandated that those funds be extended to institutions that enrolled African Americans. Because of the stronghold of segregation in the South, many states established separate public HBCUs for the sole purpose of having a legal beneficiary for the federal support. These public HBCUs are often referred to as the "1890 schools."

The post-war era of reconstruction formed a unique social contract with the American citizenry. In *The Social Contract and Discourses*, Rousseau (1762/1947) argued that humanity must regain their freedom within society. The social contract, according to Rousseau, seeks to reconcile conflicts by fulfilling the good of society. Rousseau's social contract theory sees general will as the will of all—a unanimous expression of public sentiment (Gutek, 1997); such is the case in post-Civil War America. In response to the racial inequities and conflicts of antebellum society, three things emerge—constitutional amendments (i.e., XIII, XIV, XV), other federal legislation (i.e., Emancipation Proclamation, Freedmen's Bureau, and Morrill Acts), and historically Black colleges (e.g., Howard University). All of these primarily government initiated, post-war activities focus on reconciling the tattered relation between America and the descendants of Africa.

Without question, the historically Black college is the tangible manifestation of America's social contract with free African Americans immediately following the Civil War. According to political philosophy, a social contract results from any combination of persons who agree to some aim for mutual benefit. This thesis argues that, although no major federal legislation was enacted solely for the development of Black colleges (as with land-grant institutions), the combination of amendments, legislation, creation of Howard University, and financial support from the Freedmen's Bureau establishes a commutative social contract by implication. Robert Solomon (1977) wrote that a social contract is

> An agreement, tacit or explicit, that all members of society shall abide by the laws of the state in order to maximize the public interest and insure cooperation among themselves. It is important that such a contract need never have been signed in history; what is important is that every member of a society, by choosing to remain in that society, implicitly makes such an agreement. (p. 579)

The founding, development, and maintenance of 103 Black colleges for over 100 years evinces this implicit agreement (see Charles Mills's [1997] *The Racial Contract*).

Although the official conclusion of the Civil War does not occur until 1865, it is clear that the national conscious began to rethink the state and place of the enslaved Africans[1] (Nash & Jeffrey, 1986). In 1862, the first Morrill Act was passed providing federal support for colleges offering agricultural and mechanical studies. These provisions were to be made without respect to racial categorization. The assumption was that all students would benefit. This is important given that at least seven Black colleges were already in operation—Cheyney State University (PA), Harris-Stowe State College (MO), LeMoyne-Owen College (TN), Lincoln University (PA), University of the District of Columbia (DC), Wilberforce University (OH), and Winston-Salem State University (NC). In 1863, the Emancipation Proclamation was enacted granting freedom to the slaves in confederate states. In January 1865, Congress passed the Thirteenth Amendment prohibiting slavery in the United States. In March of that same year, Congress approved the Freedmen's Bureau to aid White refugees and former slaves. The Freedmen's Bureau provided financial support for the maintenance and establishment of a substantial number of Black "day schools, night schools, industrial schools, institutes and colleges" (Bennett, 1984, p. 218).

Immediately following the Civil War, Congress passed the Fourteenth Amendment declaring the equality of the entire national citizenry without respect to race in 1866. The amendment stated that all persons born in the United States are entitled to equal protection under the law. In 1867, Congress passed legislation creating Howard Normal and Theological Institute for the Education of Teachers and Preachers (now Howard University[2]). The Congress named General Oliver Otis Howard, the commissioner of the Freedmen's Bureau, as the institution's first president. According to the President's Board of Advisors on Historically Black Colleges and Universities (1996), General Howard was selected because of his "unyielding desire to establish an institution of higher learning for the descendants of former slaves" (p. iv).

In 1869, Congress passed the Fifteenth Amendment prohibiting the denial of the right to vote based on race, color, or prior condition of servitude. As a result of the national ideological shift and the aforementioned legislative changes, numerous Black colleges began to take shape across the country. This propagation was bolstered by the passage of the Morrill Act of 1890. The Second Morrill Act provided for regular annuities for land-grant colleges. Moreover, Brown (1999) stated,

> The act specifically prohibited payments of federal funds to states that discriminated against Blacks in the admission to tax-supported colleges or who refused to provide "separate but equal" facilities for the two races. It was this latter clause that led to the immediate establishment of [Black] public land-grant institutions in seventeen of the nineteen southern states. (p. 3)

Although unintentional, the Second Morrill Act of 1890 cemented the prevailing doctrine of segregation. It formalized the manifestation of separate but unequal in higher education. The vestiges of this disparate treatment remain evident in most Black colleges to this day. Despite over 100 years of development, Black college conditions remain incongruent with their predominantly White counterparts. There are 103 HBCUs, all of which remain clustered in 19 southern and border states (Alabama, Arkansas, Delaware, Florida, Georgia, Kentucky, Louisiana, Maryland, Mississippi, Missouri, North Carolina, Ohio, Oklahoma, Pennsylvania, South Carolina, Tennessee, Texas, Virginia, and West Virginia), plus Michigan and the District of Columbia.[3] Table 1 is a list of historically Black colleges by state, character, type, and date of founding.

TABLE 1

Historically Black Colleges and Universities by State

Alabama
1. Alabama A & M University (public, 4 year, 1875)
2. Alabama State University (public, 4 year, 1874)
3. Bishop State Community College (public, 2 year, 1927)
4. C. A. Fredd State Technical College (public, 2 year, 1965)
5. Concordia College (private, 2 year, 1922)
6. J. F. Drake Technical College (public, 2 year, 1961)
7. Lawson State Community College (public, 2 year, 1965)
8. Miles College (private, 4 year, 1905)
9. Oakwood College (private, 4 year, 1896)
10. Selma University (private, 4 year, 1878)
11. Stillman College (private, 4 year, 1876)
12. Talladega College (private, 4 year, 1867)
13. Trenholm State Technical College (public, 2 year, 1963)
14. Tuskegee University (private, 4 year, 1881)

Arkansas
15. Arkansas Baptist College (private, 4 year, 1884)
16. Philander Smith College (private, 4 year, 1877)
17. Shorter College (private, 2 year, 1886)
18. University of Arkansas at Pine Bluff (public, 4 year, 1873)

Delaware
19. Delaware State University (public, 4 year, 1891)

District of Columbia
20. Howard University (mixed, 4 year, 1867)
21. University of the District of Columbia (private, 4 year, 1851)

Florida
22. Bethune-Cookman College (private, 4 year, 1904)
23. Edward Waters College (private, 4 year, 1866)
24. Florida A & M University (public, 4 year, 1877)
25. Florida Memorial College (private, 4 year, 1879)

Georgia
26. Albany State College (public, 4 year, 1903)
27. Clark Atlanta University (private, 4 year, 1989)
28. Fort Valley State College (public, 4 year, 1895)
29. Interdenominational Theological Center (private, 4 year, 1958)
30. Morehouse College (private, 4 year, 1867)
31. Morehouse School of Medicine (private, 4 year, 1975)
32. Morris Brown College (private, 4 year, 1881)
33. Paine College (private, 4 year, 1882)

(continued)

TABLE 1 (cont.)

34. Savannah State College (public, 4 year, 1890)
35. Spelman College (private, 4 year, 1881)

Kentucky

36. Kentucky State University (public, 4 year, 1886)

Louisiana

37. Dillard University (private, 4 year, 1869)
38. Grambling State University (public, 4 year, 1901)
39. Southern University A & M College-Baton Rouge (public, 4 year, 1880)
40. Southern University at New Orleans (public, 4 year, 1959)
41. Southern University at Shreveport-Bossier City (public, 2 year, 1964)
42. Xavier University of Louisiana (private, 4 year, 1915)

Maryland

43. Bowie State University (public, 4 year, 1865)
44. Coppin State College (public, 4 year, 1900)
45. Morgan State University (public, 4 year, 1867)
46. University of Maryland-Eastern Shore (public, 4 year, 1886)

Michigan

47. Lewis College of Business (private, 2 year, 1874)

Mississippi

48. Alcorn State University (public, 4 year, 1871)
49. Coahoma Community College (public, 2 year, 1949)
50. Hinds Community College (public, 2 year, 1954)
51. Jackson State University (public, 4 year, 1877)
52. Mary Holmes College (private, 2 year, 1892)
53. Mississippi Valley State University (public, 4 year, 1946)
54. Rust College (private, 4 year, 1866)
55. Tougaloo College (private, 4 year, 1869)

Missouri

56. Harris-Stowe State College (public, 4 year, 1857)
57. Lincoln University (public, 4 year, 1866)

North Carolina

58. Barber-Scotia College (private, 4 year, 1867)
59. Bennett College (private, 4 year, 1873)
60. Elizabeth City State University (public, 4 year, 1891)
61. Fayetteville State University (public, 4 year, 1877)
62. Johnson C. Smith University (private, 4 year, 1867)
63. Livingstone College (private, 4 year, 1879)
64. North Carolina A & T State University (public, 4 year, 1891)
65. North Carolina Central University (public, 4 year, 1910)
66. St. Augustine's College (private, 4 year, 1867)
67. Shaw University (private, 4 year, 1865)
68. Winston-Salem State University (public, 4 year, 1862)

Ohio

69. Central State University (public, 4 year, 1887)
70. Wilberforce University (private, 4 year, 1856)

Oklahoma

71. Langston University (public, 4 year, 1897)

Pennsylvania

72. Cheyney State University (public, 4 year, 1837)
73. Lincoln University (public, 4 year, 1854)

South Carolina

74. Allen University (private, 4 year, 1870)
75. Benedict College (private, 4 year, 1870)
76. Claflin College (private, 4 year, 1869)
77. Clinton Junior College (private, 2 year, 1894)

(continued)

TABLE 1 (cont.)

78. Denmark Technical College (public, 2 year, 1948)
79. Morris College (private, 4 year, 1908)
80. South Carolina State University (public, 4 year, 1896)
81. Voorhees College (private, 4 year, 1897)

Tennessee

82. Fisk University (private, 4 year, 1867)
83. Knoxville College (private, 4 year, 1875)
84. Lane College (private, 4 year, 1882)
85. LeMoyne-Owen College (private, 4 year, 1862)
86. Meharry Medical College (private, 4 year, 1876)
87. Tennessee State University (public, 4 year, 1912)

Texas

88. Huston-Tillotson College (private, 4 year, 1876)
89. Jarvis Christian College (private, 4 year, 1912)
90. Paul Quinn College (private, 4 year, 1872)
91. Prairie View A & M University (public, 4 year, 1876)
92. Saint Phillip's College (public, 2 year, 1927)
93. Southwestern Christian College (private, 4 year, 1949)
94. Texas College (private, 4 year, 1894)
95. Texas Southern University (public, 4 year, 1947)
96. Wiley College (private, 4 year, 1873)

Virginia

97. Hampton University (private, 4 year, 1868)
98. Norfolk State University (public, 4 year, 1935)
99. Saint Paul's College (private, 4 year, 1888)
100. Virginia State University (public, 4 year, 1882)
101. Virginia Union University (private, 4 year, 1865)

West Virginia

102. Bluefield State College (public, 4 year, 1895)
103. West Virginia State University (public, 4 year, 1891)

The early history of descendants of Africa in American higher education, especially the period of slavery through Jim Crow, is chronicled as a period of almost categorical exclusion from postsecondary education. In American society, formal education at any level for African Americans prior to 1862 was not considered necessary. In fact, the legal and social institutions in the pre-Civil War period were designed to maintain the separation of the races and perpetuate White control. One particular mechanism of maintaining White control was enshrined in the so-called "Black Codes." As Bond (1934) stated,

> The "Black Codes" of 1865–1868 in South Carolina, Georgia, Mississippi, and other states were reflected in similar enactments of county and municipal bodies. These acts, preliminary to a final adjustment, were invalidated by the passage of the thirteenth, fourteenth, and fifteenth amendments, but their transient popularity at this time helps us to understand the prevailing opinion of the men who dictated the course of the newly reconstituted political bodies. (p. 16)

It is interesting to note that much of the early legislation in the South affecting African American education was influenced by the Black Codes. For example, in every southern state prior to the conclusion of the Civil War, Black Codes found themselves in statutes explicitly restricting the schooling of enslaved Africans (Anderson, 1988; Morgan, 1995).

Historians have presented three primary reasons as to why African descendants were excluded from formal public education in the United States. First, most White Americans, not solely in the South, believed that the "Black race" was inferior to the "White race" in terms of intelligence and consequently were not viewed as capable beneficiaries of formal education (Bullock, 1967; Morgan,

1995). Second, public formal education would greatly minimize the usefulness of African Americans as workers in a caste-like workplace environment (Ogbu, 1978). Third, public formal education for African Americans was seen as a viable threat to the American social order because the belief among White Americans was that it would encourage violence and insurgence (Aptheker, 1969). Some African Americans received formal education; however, it was often a disparate and subordinate form of education compared to White Americans of the period. Only 28 African Americans had received baccalaureate degrees from American colleges or universities prior to the Civil War (Roebuck & Murty, 1993).

At the conclusion of the Civil War, less than 5% of the approximately 4.5 million African descendants in the United States were literate (Anderson, 1988). The era of reconstruction created a social contract that began three endeavors in African American education: (a) a substantial investment by the nation in equalizing education, (b) financial support and academic guidance from the Freedmen's Bureau for developing schooling opportunities for African Americans, and (c) state-level initiation of (primarily segregated) public school systems for the general citizenry (Brown, 1999; Ogbu, 1978; Roebuck & Murty, 1993). Consequently, the historically Black college becomes the primary channel to social mobility and equality for African Americans.

Black Colleges as Purveyors of Social Capital

Historically Black colleges are products of America's social contract with African Americans. Of the various social institutions in Black communities, historically Black colleges occupy a unique place as a source of social capital for African Americans. Black colleges founded prior to emancipation and during the reconstruction era came into existence during the age of legal segregation (McPherson, 1970). Hence, the educational structure at all levels was polarized—one system for White Americans and another for African Americans. The historical conditions in which HBCUs emerged reflect a dynamic social order, as well as the ambivalent attitudes toward the education of African Americans and their role in the national infrastructure (Anderson, 1988; Brown, 1999; Bullock, 1967; Cohen, 1998; Rudolph, 1965). It was this initial developmental context that provided the fertile ground that cultivated HBCUs into institutions focused on rearranging the American hierarchy with African Americans scattered within every echelon.

The imparting of specific sociocultural resources and networks are often cited as important justifications for the existence, maintenance, and continuation of historically Black colleges. In short, a primary role of the Black college is that of social capital purveyor. Due to the social contract that underpins the development and maintenance of HBCUs, social capital frames a way to think about how these institutions have used their particular social and legal position in the higher education landscape to advance the interest of African Americans. In other words, the relations and networks that Black colleges construct into tangible and meaningful resources are known as social capital (Bourdieu, 1973, 1977; Bourdieu & Passeron, 1977).

The concept is drawn in part from Bourdieu's (1977) theory of social reproduction, where he argued that social capital, like economic capital, can be accumulated and has the capacity to reproduce itself over time. The idea of social reproduction has currency in its explanation of how social properties are generated, given value, and reified among individuals in social institutions. In general, social capital is a type of resource that is socially reproduced, such as the possession of knowledge, accomplishments, or formal and informal relations and networks. Through these means an individual may gain entry and secure social rewards, such as status, privilege, and position in particular socials circles, professions, or organizations (Bourdieu, 1973). Social capital marks and reinforces differing kinds of relative advantage and disadvantage within African American communities and in the general society. Therefore, social capital is particularly useful in understanding the historic and contemporary role of HBCUs. Because of their unique constellation of Black intellectuals and professionals among institutional staff and alumni, HBCUs serve as conduits for the production and transmission of social capital to African American students. Furthermore, Black colleges offer institutional agents and agencies (e.g., committed faculty, compensatory curricula, alumni leaders in the professions and society; Stanton-Salazar, 1997). These institutional agents constitute an array of channels that identify, negotiate, and transmit resources, particularly formal and informal relations, that purchase opportunities for the accomplishment of HBCUs' collective agenda—the educational development and attainment of African Americans.

The decoding and transmission of social capital is seen generally as the providence of families and their networks, rather than schools; higher education often implicitly demands these qualities of their students (Bourdieu & Passeron, 1977). Traditionally, this reality established the role of HBCUs as primary sources of social capital and as vehicles for the provision of techniques useful for receiving and decoding African American social and cultural knowledge. In addition, social class and family background often determine the sources of networking and relation that particularly advantages individuals for better employment opportunities, connections to politically influential people, and access to services and resources that improve life chances. Therefore, Black colleges have produced a "privileged class" of African Americans who use their college and community ties that lead to differential advantages in the post-college marketplace (J. E. Davis, 1998). This class of students and graduates have at their disposal a much larger reservoir of social capital because of the relations formed within the context of HBCUs that offer access to specific knowledge of the Black experience in America. This cultural knowledge and dispensation positioned many Black colleges traditionally as finishing schools for students from disadvantaged economic class backgrounds (Thompson, 1986). In many ways, these institutions originally were considered "cultural starting" schools or places where students began the accumulation of social connections and support that would not only ease their transition and progression through college, but also increase their social market value and employment opportunities after graduation. Various strategies, such as explicit, direct instruction of socially appropriate behaviors, career-related information, and opportunities for internships and mentoring, have been typical experiences of students at HBCUs (Freeman, 1998). Such opportunities provided students with personal views of how social ties, specifically among Black professionals, secure important social and economic resources.

Social relationships and networks refer to the extensiveness of connected personal ties through which information about jobs and other opportunities can be diffused or allocated. These networks are based on the characteristics of the contact person who has the potential to influence access to opportunity and outcomes of these and other privileges. Although the term *social capital* is used in the job search context to signify the personal or social networks that can provide information or influence, Lee and Brinton (1996) argued that it is important to delineate the social structural origin of this form of social capital. Although educational institutions can generate social capital for their students, social resources or ties can only be acquired through an individual's attendance at a particular college or university. Institutional social capital is used to distinguish it from the social ties represented by nonuniversity friends, family members, and other resources that provide private social capital. Clearly, Black colleges disseminate particular social resources to their students and graduates. Consequently, HBCUs transpose Bourdieu's (1973) notion of social capital from one of precollege structures (e.g., families, communities, and previous schooling) to one of that generates new cultural resources (e.g., networks, attitudes, behaviors, and expectations) within the environment and experience.

Given the wide range of options for African Americans in higher education, the relevance of the social capital thesis is contested among researchers, policy analysts, and activists. However, the continued preference of many African American students for HBCU environments provides important evidence, specifically the increases in undergraduate enrollment at the 103 HBCUs. About one fifth of all African Americans enrolled in institutions of higher education make their collegiate home at one of these institutions. Although 83% of all students attending these schools are African Americans, there is tremendous variation in the racial makeup of student populations at these schools—the enrollment of non-Black students ranges from zero to over 20% (U.S. Department of Education, 1996). Historically Black colleges not only occupy significant space in diversifying the nation's higher educational landscape but also play a critical role in the lives of their students and within African American communities that benefit culturally and economically from their presence.

Recent studies offer new evidence of the unique ability of historically Black colleges to distribute social capital and effectively structure environments that lead to greater achievement outcomes for their students. For instance, attending an HBCU equalizes future wages relative to non-HBCU graduates (Constantine, 1994). This finding is very significant when compared to previous expectations that students attending HBCUs would have lower future wages (Ehrenberg & Rothstein, 1993). Moreover, research using the National Post-Secondary Aid Study of 1990 found that African American students enrolled in Black colleges are more likely to pursue postgraduate education and become professionals than African American students at predominantly White enrolled institutions (Wenglinsky, 1996). There are three primary facets of the historically Black colleges' ecological psychology (Brown, 1998) that contribute to their ability to generate and transmit social capital—compensation, climate, and condition. James Earl Davis (1998) wrote,

> The compensatory and remediation model focuses on the role of HBCUs' effectiveness with African American students who have relatively poor high school backgrounds and college preparation. Here, much evidence exists to show that early in students' college careers, HBCUs are able to provide effective remedial instruction that enables students to persist in college, obtain degrees, and eventually form attachment to the labor market. . . . Second, environmental support models argue that these schools provide support so that students will become more confident, are more involved in campus activities, and are more engaged with faculty. . . . Another framework for explaining the role of HBCUs lies not in what actually occurs in college per se. Instead, outcomes are determined by what students bring to the college experience. These dispositions and demographics, such as whether students are inclined to concentrate in a particular field or certain study habits, academic behaviors, and characteristics related to gender and other demographics of HBCU enrollments, are primarily responsible for student outcomes in these settings. . . . Although these conceptual frames are useful in explaining some of the variation in the outcomes of students enrolled at Black colleges, they fail to explicitly focus on the cultural content and context of HBCUs and how the cultural milieu of these institutions affects students. (pp. 147–148)

These three facets of the Black college character are central to their historic and continuing ability to proffer social capital to their students.

We have clearly detailed the role of HBCUs as a source and generation of social capital. One of the functions of HBCUs is to be repositories of Diaspora history and the history of social hostility. Although it is possible for African American students to attend any institution without prohibition based on race, this legal access to the institution does not guarantee authentic participation to the informal social networks within the institution. In fact, the college-going experiences of African American students on predominantly White campuses remain fraught with social isolation and cultural estrangement. HBCUs, on the other hand, have historically assumed a greater responsibility for educating African American students (Gurin & Epps, 1975) for participation in a broader society that has been exclusive, indifferent, and hostile. Also, HBCUs continue to provide the experience for African American students to become beneficiaries of their unique social capital. This ability is endemic to the functions of providing academic remediation, environmental support, and cultural relevance that appear to minimize the effects of differential precollege preparation. The transferal of the social information, achievement, and credentials needed for African Americans to enjoy full participation in the larger society remain a primary role of the Black college. This purveyance of social capital sustains the equalization of African Americans in the nation and world. Indeed, Black colleges are important mediators in the pursuit of African Americans for both equality of opportunity and equity in outcomes.

Black Colleges as Agents of Social Equality

Historically Black universities are the premier agency of African American educational attainment (Allen, Epps, & Haniff, 1991; Brown, 1999; Brown, in press; Fleming, 1984; Freeman, 1998; Garibaldi, 1984; Merisotis & O'Brien, 1998; Thomas, 1981; U.S. Department of Education, 1996; Willie, Reed, & Garibaldi, 1991). The historically Black college has among its myriad missions an egalitarian component. According to Roebuck and Murty (1993), "HBCUs continue to function as institutions necessary for the education of many students who otherwise would not obtain college degrees" (p. 202). Black colleges facilitate the preparation and participation of African Americans in the corpus of national and global life.

African American students, more than any other group, face incalculable barriers to higher education participation and attainment. These barriers include social backgrounds that are incongruous with Eurocentric campus climates, limited financial resources, and trepidation of school failure. Even at the dawn of a new millennium, many African American students are their families first-generation to attend a 4-year institution. The combined effect of these extant barriers with the consternation related to postsecondary matriculation produce an elongated and formidable college adjustment. Fortunately, African American students at the historically Black college are unshackled from the fetters of this deleterious encounter. In 1965, Congress passed a law that included the following language: "Historically Black colleges and universities have contributed significantly to the effort to attain equal opportunity through postsecondary education for Black, low income, and educationally disadvantaged Americans" (Strengthening Historically Black Colleges and Universities, 1965, p. 1062).

The strength of the historically Black college does not release higher education of its duty to create multiple institutional communities that support the educational attainment of African American students. Researchers have documented the failure of the broader academic community to respond to the particular educational needs of African American students (Stikes, 1984; Taylor, 1970). Stikes, in particular, argued that African Americans "need something to relate to their experiences and culture that gives them legitimacy" (p. 126). The historically Black college provides such an experience.

The negative experiences that many African American students encounter on campuses with predominantly White enrollments can potentially have injurious effects. J. A. Davis and Borders-Patterson (1973) posited that growing mistrust and alienation cause many students to take refuge in institutions reflective of their experiences (e.g., for the African American student the HBCU). Chickering and Associates (1981) and Weathersby (1981) likewise suggested that the college experience has the potential to facilitate and stimulate the development of the student. Any sudden changes in the environment may mean a change in the individual. Sanford (1967) stated,

> If the development of the individual as a whole is the primary aim, then colleges should organize all their resources in efforts to achieve it. Such planning of a total educational environment must be guided by a theory of personality—a theory in the terms of which it is possible to state specific goals for the individual, describe the interrelations of his various psychological processes, and understand the ways in which he changes under the impact of environmental influences. (p. xv)

This holistically focused education is a central theme in the educational mission of the Black college.

In a discussion of the mission and goals of historically Black institutions, Roebuck and Murty (1993) said,

> HBCUs, unlike other colleges, are united in a mission to meet the educational and emotional needs of Black students. They remain the significant academic home for Black faculty members and many Black students. The goals described in Black college catalogs, unlike those of White schools, stress preparation for student leadership and service roles in the community. (p. 10)

Lamont (1979) went on to say that for many African American students the historically Black institution is "culturally more congenial" (p. 32) than the traditionally mainstream university. Finally, the literature concludes that "there is also a general level of satisfaction and camaraderie among Black students at Black schools that is not found among Black students on White campuses" (Roebuck & Murty, 1993, p. 15). The increasing numbers of African American students attending historically Black colleges indicate that these institutions provide an appropriate environment for their postsecondary studies.

Historically Black institutions have made their most prominent educational contribution through their profound commitment to and encouragement of their students (Halpern, 1992). It is important, however, to also regard the commentary by Antoine Garibaldi (1984), which declared

> Black colleges are not monolithic. Although they are similar to predominantly White institutions in many ways, their historical traditions and their levels and types of support make them distinct. Like many other institutions of higher learning, Black colleges reflect the diversity that is so characteristic of the United States' postsecondary education system. This diversity should always be remembered when considering their past, their current conditions, and their future roles in higher education. (p. 6)

Although HBCUs, both public and private, do not constitute one "academic monolith" because they differ in many characteristics, HBCUs share one uniform characteristic. Black colleges are distinctly unique from other American postsecondary institutions because they were founded and developed in an environment marked by hostile legal segregation. Therefore, any dialogue pertaining to the contemporary situation and function of HBCUs necessitates a historical understanding of the context in which they were developed.

Conclusion

HBCUs participate in a social contract, purvey social capital, and promote social equality. In addition, Black colleges enrich the academy, add to the national scholarship, and create atmospheres that epitomize the best of society. Kenneth Redd (1998) wrote,

> Historically Black colleges and universities (HBCUs) have made great strides in providing educational opportunities for African Americans. From their humble beginning in the early 1800s, these institutions have grown to make significant contributions to American society and to provide educational opportunities for low-income and academically disadvantaged students who would have otherwise been denied a higher education. HBCUs have achieved this success despite discrimination from state and federal governments, severely inadequate funding, economic and enrollment downturns, and lack of support from most political leaders and the general public. (p. 33)

Without question, historically Black colleges are firmly rooted in America's higher education landscape. HBCUs provide a unique educational function that cannot be replaced.

> There exists sound educational justification for maintaining historically Black colleges. (*United States v. Fordice*, 1992)

Notes

1. The shift in national conscious is partially the result of the military victory at Antietam, Maryland in September 1862.
2. Howard University enjoys the same legal designation as other federal institutions of higher education (e.g., West Point, U.S. Naval Academy). Howard University is a standing line item in the federal budget.
3. The nation's predominantly Black colleges have a wider geographic spread.

References

Allen, W. R. (1992). The color of success: African American college student outcomes at predominately White and historically Black college and universities. *Harvard Educational Review, 62*, 26–44.

Allen, W. R., Epps, E., & Haniff, N. Z. (Eds.). (1991). *College in black and white: African American students in predominately White and in historically Black public universities.* Albany: State University of New York Press.

Anderson, J. D. (1988). *The education of Blacks in the South, 1860–1935.* Chapel Hill: University of North Carolina Press.

Aptheker, H. (Ed.). (1969). *A documentary history of the Negro people in the United States.* New York: The Citadel.

Bennett, L. (1984). *Before the Mayflower: A history of Black America; the classic account of the struggles and triumphs of Black Americans.* New York: Penguin.

Bond, H. M. (1934). *The education of the Negro in the American social order.* New York: Octagon.

Bourdieu, P. (1973). Cultural reproduction and social reproduction. In R. Brown (Ed.), *Knowledge, education, and cultural change* (pp. 71–112). London: Tavistock.

Bourdieu, P. (1977). Cultural reproduction and social reproduction. In J. Karabel & A. H. Halsey (Eds.), *Power and ideology in education* (pp. 487–511). New York: Oxford University Press.

Bourdieu, P., & Passeron, J. C. (1977). *Reproduction in education, society, and culture.* London: Sage.

Brown, M. C. (1998). African American college student retention and the ecological psychology of historically black colleges. *National Association of Student Affairs Professionals Journal, 1*, 50–66.

Brown, M. C. (1999). *The quest to define collegiate desegregation: Black colleges, Title VI compliance, and post-Adams litigation.* Westport, CT: Bergin & Garvey.

Brown, M. C. (in press). *Black colleges at the millennium: Perspectives on policy and practice.* Stamford, CT: Ablex.

Bullock, H. A. (1967). *A history of Negro education in the South: From 1619 to the present.* Cambridge, MA: Harvard University Press.

Chickering, A. W., & Associates. (1981). *The modern American college: Responding to the new realities of diverse students and a changing society.* San Francisco: Jossey-Bass.

Cohen, A. M. (1998). *The shaping of American higher education: Emergence and growth of the contemporary system.* San Francisco: Jossey-Bass.

Constantine, J. M. (1994). *Measuring the effect of attending historically Black colleges and universities on future labor market wages on Black students.* Paper presented at the Institute for Labor Market Policies Conference, Cornell University, Ithaca, NY.

Davis, J. A., & Borders-Patterson, A. (1973). *Black students in predominantly White North Carolina colleges and universities* (College Board Rep. No. 2). New York: College Entrance Examination Board.

Davis, J. E. (1998). Cultural capital and the role of historically black colleges and universities in educational reproduction. In K. Freeman (Ed.), *African American culture and heritage in higher education research and practice* (pp. 143–153). Westport, CT: Praeger.

Ehrenberg, R. G., & Rothstein, D. S. (1993, June). *Do historically Black institutions of higher education confer unique advantages on Black students? An initial analysis* (NBER Working Paper No. 4356). Ithaca, NY: Cornell University.

Fleming, J. (1984). *Blacks in college: A comparative study of students' success in Black and White institutions.* San Francisco: Jossey-Bass.

Freeman, K. (Ed.). (1998). *African American culture and heritage in higher education research and practice.* Westport, CT: Praeger.

Garibaldi, A. (1984). *Black colleges and universities: Challenges for the future.* New York: Praeger.

Gurin, P., & Epps, E. (1975). *Black consciousness, identity, and achievement.* New York: Wiley.

Gutek, G. L. (1997). *Philosophical and ideological perspectives on education* (2nd ed.). Boston: Allyn & Bacon.

Halpern, S. (1992). Black college would be closed in Mississippi's plan to comply with court's ruling on desegregation. *Chronicle of Higher Education, 39*(10), A29.

Lamont, L. (1979). *Campus shock: A firsthand report on college life today.* New York: Dutton.

Lee, S., & Brinton, M. C. (1996). Elite education and social capital: The case of South Korea. *Sociology of Education, 69*, 177–192.

McPherson, J. M. (1970). White liberals and Black power in Negro education. *American Historical Review, 75*, 1357–1386.

Merisotis, J. P., & O'Brien, C. T. (Eds.). (1998). *Minority-serving institution, distinct purposes, common goals.* San Francisco: Jossey-Bass.

Mills, C. W. (1997). *The racial contract.* Ithaca, NY: Cornell University Press.

Morgan, H. (1995). *Historical perspectives on the education of Black children.* Westport, CT: Praeger.

Nash, G. B., & Jeffrey, J. R. (1986). *The American people: Creating a nation and a society.* Cambridge, England: Harper & Row.

Ogbu, J. (1978). *Minority education and caste: The American system in cross-cultural perspective.* New York: Academic.

President's Board of Advisors on Historically Black Colleges and Universities. (1996). *A century of success: Historically black colleges and universities—America's national treasure (1995–96 Annual Report).* Washington, DC: Government Printing Office.

Redd, K. E. (1998). Historically black colleges and universities. In J. P. Merisotis & C. T. O'Brien (Eds.), *Minority-serving institution, distinct purposes, common goals* (pp. 33–42). San Francisco: Jossey-Bass.

Roebuck, J. B., & Murty, K. S. (1993). *Historically black colleges and universities: Their place in American higher education.* Westport, CT: Praeger.

Rousseau, J. J. (1947). *The social contract and discourses* (G. D. H. Cole, Trans.). New York: Dutton. (Original work published 1762)

Rudolph, F. (1965). *The American college and university: A history.* New York: Vintage.

Sanford, N. (1967). *Where colleges fail: A study of the student as a person.* San Francisco: Jossey-Bass.

Solomon, R. C. (1977). *Introducing philosophy: Problems and perspectives.* New York: Harcourt Brace Jovanovich.

Stanton-Salazar, R. D. (1997). A social capital framework for understanding the socialization of racial minority children and youth. *Harvard Education Review, 67*, 1–40.

Stikes, C. S. (1984). *Black students in higher education.* Carbondale: Southern Illinois University Press.

Strengthening Historically Black Colleges and Universities, 20 U.S.C. 1060 (1965).

Taylor, O. L. (1970). New directions for American education: A Black perspective. *Journal of Black Studies, 1,* 101–112.

Thomas, G. E. (Ed.). (1981). *Black students in higher education: Conditions and experiences in the 1970s.* Westport, CT: Greenwood.

Thompson, D. C. (1986). *A Black elite: A profile of graduate of UNCF colleges.* Westport, CT: Greenwood.

United States v. Fordice, 505 U.S. 717 (1992).

U.S. Department of Education, National Center for Education Statistics. (1996). *Historically Black colleges and universities, 1976–1994.* Washington, DC: Government Printing Office.

Weathersby, R. P. (1981). *The modern American college: Responding to the new realities of diverse students and a changing society.* San Francisco: Jossey-Bass.

Wenglinsky, H. H. (1996). The educational justification of historically Black colleges and universities: A policy response to the U.S. Supreme Court. *Educational Evaluation and Policy Analysis, 18,* 91–103.

Willie, C. V., Reed, W. L., & Garibaldi, A. M. (Eds.). (1991). *The education of African-Americans.* New York: Auburn House.

Wilson, R. (1988). Historically Black colleges. In George T. Kurian (Ed.), *Yearbook of American universities and colleges: Academic year, 1986–1987* (pp. 121–125). New York: Garland.

HISPANIC-SERVING INSTITUTIONS: MYTHS AND REALITIES

BERTA VIGIL LADEN
EDUCATIONAL LEADERSHIP AND POLICY STUDIES
UNIVERSITY OF WASHINGTON

We recognize the contributions that these institutions make for Latino students, for many of our largest cities, and for the nation as a whole. (Richard W. Riley, 2000)

Hispanic-serving institutions (HSIs) play a key but still largely unrecognized role in the higher educational attainment of Hispanics. Despite this lack of national recognition among educators, researchers, and decision makers, HSIs are finally emerging from the shadows as institutions of success for Hispanics seeking college degrees. Defined by the reauthorization of the Higher Education Act, as amended in 1992, HSIs are those 2-and 4-year colleges and universities with 25% or more total undergraduate Hispanic full-time equivalent (FTE) enrollments. HSIs account for nearly 6% of all postsecondary institutions and enroll more than 1.4 million Hispanic students. More specifically, HSIs educate nearly 50% of all Hispanic college students in the United States and another 20% of students from other ethnic backgrounds (The White House Initiative, 2001). In a sense, they might also be called minority-serving institutions in light of the diverse student populations they routinely educate (Merisotis & O'Brien, 1998). In sum, as noted by former Secretary of Education Richard W. Riley (2000), it is not an overstatement to assert that HSIs' presence and role in educating Hispanics—and other minority groups—can neither be underestimated nor ignored any longer as vital players in higher education.

More to the point, as a young population with an average age of 29 and an even distribution between men and women, Hispanics currently constitute 12.5% of the U.S. population and are projected to rise to 22% by the year 2015. That is, the Hispanic population will nearly double in number in less than 15 years (U.S. Census Bureau, 2000). Already the fastest growing minority group in the nation, Hispanics have migrated to urban areas in record numbers in search of jobs and a better life. Metropolitan areas, such as San Antonio, Los Angeles, Houston, San Jose, New York, Dallas, San Diego, Phoenix, Chicago, San Francisco, Philadelphia, Detroit, and Miami, are magnets that continue to attract Hispanics. But even less-populated states like Idaho, Wyoming, Nebraska, Nevada, Utah, and Iowa have become attractive meccas as Hispanics follow employment and housing opportunities (U.S. Census Bureau). Regardless of where they live, however, at present most Hispanics fill a demand from certain sectors of the U.S. economy for cheap, unskilled, and often temporary labor (Benítez, 1998; Carnevale, 1999). Consequently, Hispanics pose educational and economic challenges that will not go away in light of their current and projected numbers.

The next section focuses on the historical perspective of HSIs, followed by an examination of access to college for Hispanic students. Next, some myths about Hispanic students and HSIs are explored. Finally, the article ends with a brief discussion of the future prospects of HSIs.

Historical Perspective

The majority of HSIs were not created to serve this specific population; rather, they evolved over the last 30 years due primarily to their geographic proximity to Hispanic populations. Hence, with a few exceptions, such as Hostos Community Colleges, Boricua College, or National Hispanic University, they do not have charters or missions that address distinctive purposes and goals for Hispanics (Laden, 1999b). On the other hand, institutions classified as Historically Black Colleges and Universities (HBCUs), begun in the mid-1800s, and Tribal Colleges, founded in the last 30 years, very intentionally serve their special student populations (O'Brien & Zudak, 1998). However, the rising presence of Hispanic students in certain colleges and universities since the mid-1960s has conferred on them ad hoc missions to better address the educational needs of this population.

The rapid growth of HSIs stems primarily from four significant factors. One factor is due to the Civil Rights Movement in the 1960s and varied outreach efforts that opened up college campuses to less traditional college-going populations, including individuals from diverse racial and ethnic backgrounds. This movement was accompanied by the development of federal and state student grants and loans that made it possible for more students to go to college (Justiz, Wilson, & Björk, 1994). A second, rather significant factor is due to increased Hispanic immigration to the United States in the past 3 decades. A third factor is twofold: the ongoing Hispanic demographic shifts occurring nationally, especially in large urban cities (Benítez, 1998; Justiz et al.) and Hispanic movement more recently into less-populated areas in the central United States where they have not resided before (U.S. Census Bureau, 2000). The fourth factor is that HSIs are located in geographic areas where large numbers of Hispanic populations reside (Laden, 1999b).

The recognition HSIs enjoy thus far is due primarily to the efforts of the Hispanic Association of Colleges and Universities (HACU), an advocacy membership association that was formed in 1986 to call national attention to higher education institutions serving large numbers of Hispanics. Supported by predominantly Hispanic educational and business leaders, HACU successfully united 2-year and 4-year colleges and universities serving high proportions of Hispanics into a professional association. Its professed mission was to improve educational access and raise the quality of college opportunities for Hispanics. Therefore, it established two offices with headquarters in San Antonio, Texas, and an office in Washington, DC, for ready access to national political and educational policymakers. In 1992, HACU succeeded in getting HSIs recognized as part of the reauthorization of the Higher Education Act, Title III, which also allowed them to apply for federal funds. The most recent reauthorization of the Higher Education Act, amended in 1998, led to the inclusion of HSIs under Title V, alongside HBCUs and Tribal Colleges, and eligible for a larger allocation of federal funds by Congress (Basinger, 2000).

Since its founding, HACU has accomplished its goals by making significant inroads nationally. This association has done so by gaining national recognition and resources and serving as an advocate for federal and state public policies and initiatives that support HSIs (Laden, 1999b). More recently, it has begun a series of collaborative projects with organizations such as the Educational Testing Service, the W. K. Kellogg Foundation, and other higher education professional associations dedicated to improving educational access for minorities (Flores, 1999a, 1999c).

It should be noted, however, that HSIs do not have the same status within Title V that HBCUs and Tribal Colleges have, because HSIs do not have a declared, specific mission to serve Hispanics as these other more focused population-specific institutions do (The White House Initiative, 2001). Rather, as mentioned earlier, the institutional mission of serving Hispanics is ad hoc due to their increasing presence in certain 2-and 4-year colleges and universities. It should be further noted that HACU recognizes members as any higher education institution with at least 25% head count Hispanic enrollment, whereas the Department of Education identifies Hispanic institutions as those with at least 25% Hispanic full-time equivalent enrollment and also have 50% or more low-income students. HACU admits associate members who have at least 1,000 Hispanic students enrolled, but the Department of Education now recognizes developing HCIs as those that are clearly rapidly moving toward meeting Title V criteria (HACU, 2000; The White House Initiative, 2001).

Another outgrowth of HACU's efforts is the President's Advisory Commission on Educational Excellence for Hispanic Americans. Established by President Clinton's Executive Order 12900 in

1994, it calls on the nation to improve education for Hispanic Americans. Among its recommendations, the executive order makes a collective call to each executive agency to

> Increase Hispanic American participation in Federal education programs where Hispanic Americans currently are under served . . . and to improve educational outcomes for Hispanic Americans participating in Federal education programs . . . and emphasize the facilitation of technical, planning, and development advice to Hispanic-serving school districts and institutions of higher education. (President's Advisory Commission, 1996, p. 85)

The President's Advisory Commission consists of 25 members appointed by the President to 5-year terms, who report directly to the Secretary of Education. Its directive is to provide advice to both the President and the Secretary of Education on the progress of Hispanics' educational achievement and accomplishments; the development of federal efforts to promote quality education for Hispanics; and to explore ways to increase state, private, and community involvement in education (President's Advisory Commission, 1996).

The White House Initiative for Educational Excellence for Hispanic Americans is an interagency working group coordinated by the Department of Education to provide the staff, resources, and assistance to the President's Advisory Commission (1996). The White House Initiative seeks to further increase an awareness of the role HSIs play in serving the community and by educating federal agencies and others about HSIs' vital assets in the areas of research, development, and other services (The White House Initiative, 2000). As a liaison between HSIs and federal agencies, The White House Initiative facilitates access to federal resources and enhances these agencies' utilization of HSIs' assets. The White House Initiative also collects and disseminates information of HSIs in an effort to educate agencies, policymakers, and the nation about the role of HSIs and its efforts to raise the educational attainment rates of Hispanics and to increase their economic prosperity (The White House Initiative, 2000).

Because identification of HSIs began under the auspices of The White House Initiative, their numbers have been increasing annually. As of 2001, using the Higher Education Act Title V definition (of 25% Hispanic FTE enrollment), there are 203 HSIs located in 12 states and in the Commonwealth of Puerto Rico (see Table 1). In particular, HSIs are located primarily around the periphery of the United States—more specifically, in the Pacific Northwest, the Southwest, the Southern Tip, the

TABLE 1

Location and Number of Hispanic-Serving Institutions

Location	Number of HSIs	Percentage of FTE Hispanic Students	Percentage Hispanic of State Population
Arizona	9	31.1	42.1
California	57	36.9	32.4
Colorado	5	30.6	17.1
Florida	9	52.2	16.8
Illinois	7	41.0	12.3
Kansas	1	25.3	7.0
Massachusetts	1	33.2	6.8
New Jersey	5	37.7	13.3
New Mexico	17	40.6	42.1
New York	12	40.6	15.1
Texas	32	59.3	32.0
Washington	1	32.1	7.5
Puerto Rico	47	99.9	98.8
Total	203	51.9	

Note. HSIs = Hispanic-serving institutions; FTE = full-time equivalent enrollment. Sources of data are The White House Initiative (2001) and U.S. Census Bureau (2000).

TABLE 2

Type and Sector of Hispanic-Serving Institutions

Type and Sector	Number of HSIs	Percentage of Total
Public, 4 year	44	21.7
Private, 4 year	52	25.6
Public, 2 year	94	46.3
Private, 2 year	13	6.4
Total	203	100.0

Note. HSIs = Hispanic-serving institutions. Source for data is The White House Initiative (2001).

Northeast, and with some inroads into the Midwest. The 12 states are Arizona, California, Colorado, Florida, Illinois, Kansas, Massachusetts, New Jersey, New Mexico, New York, Texas, and Washington. In the continental United States, California leads the way with 57 of all HSIs, followed by Texas (32) and New Mexico (17). Kansas, Massachusetts, and Washington emerged recently as states with 1 identified HSI each. Puerto Rico has 47 HSIs (The White House Initiative, 2001).

In terms of type and control (see Table 2), there are 96 four-year HSIs, of which 44 are public and 52 are private. Among the 107 two-year HSIs, 94 are public compared to 13 private institutions (The White House Initiative, 2001).

Access for Hispanic Students in HSIs

Despite the presence of HSIs, overall college-going rates for Hispanics continue to be lower compared to other student populations. Nevertheless, the good news is that these rates have nearly doubled since 1990 (Wilds, 2000). As of 1997, of the 14.5 million students enrolled in postsecondary institutions, 1.4 million or approximately 10% are Hispanics (The White House Initiative, 2001). Moreover, of all college-going Hispanics, 46% (full-time equivalent) are enrolled in HSIs (The White House Initiative, 2001), offering strong evidence that these small number of HSIs are educating almost one half of all Hispanic college students.

In examining access to college for Hispanics, it must be remembered that 57% of these students are enrolled in community colleges (Wilds, 2000); therefore, Hispanic transfer rates to 4-year institutions further affect their educational attainment rates. Although it is difficult to get a clear picture of national transfer data, *The Condition of Education* (National Center for Education Statistics [NCES], 1998) reports that Hispanics represented 22.5% of all students who began in community colleges in 1989 through 1990 had transferred to 4-year institutions by 1994. No national data are available for 2-year HSIs regarding transfer rates. Notwithstanding this, a study by Laden (2000) showed that of the 109 California community colleges, those institutions with the highest transfer rates for Hispanics are HSIs. Research by Solorzano (1993, 1995) revealed that the origins of Hispanic doctoral recipients occurs largely through the pipeline from 2- to 4-year HSIs into doctoral-granting institutions, many of which are also HSIs. Some of the biggest transfer producers are HSI urban community colleges in California, Texas, New Mexico, Arizona, Florida, and New York ("Top 50 Community," 2000; "Top 100 Colleges," 2000).

Furthermore, a review of all degrees granted in 1997 by postsecondary institutions to Hispanics compared to degrees granted by HSIs presents a strikingly different picture of completion rates (see Table 3). In that year, Hispanics earned only 7.6% of all associate degrees, 5.3% of all bachelor's degrees, 3.7% of all master's degrees, 4.6% of all first-professional degrees, and 3.7% of all doctoral degrees awarded in the United States. In contrast, Hispanics enrolled in HSIs earned 46% of all associate degrees, 23% of all bachelor's degrees, 19.5% of all master's degrees, 4.4% of all first professional degrees, and 6.1% of all doctorates awarded in the United States (Wilds, 2000). HSIs also represent approximately 30% of the top 25 institutions where Hispanics earning doctoral degrees re-

TABLE 3

College Completion Rates for Hispanic Students in 1997

Degrees Awarded	Percentage of All Institutions	Percentage of HSI
Associate degree	7.6	45.9
Bachelor's degree	5.3	22.9
Master's degree	3.7	19.5
First-professional degree	4.6	4.4
Doctoral degree	3.7	6.1

Note. HSI = Hispanic-serving institution. Source for data is Wilds (2000).

ceived their undergraduate education and approximately one half of Hispanics who earned doctoral degrees in physical science, social science, and psychology (The White House Initiative, 1999).

Although HSIs clearly produce remarkable outcomes, as evidenced here, one must consider what it is that HSIs actually do for Hispanic students that lead to these higher outcomes. Put another way, is it the already high numbers of Hispanics enrolled in these institutions that obviously produce a higher number of completers in comparison to their lower numbers in non-HSIs? Certainly, some research (Laden, 1999a, 2000) suggests that many HSIs do indeed offer a variety of academic and student support programs and holistic approaches that are specifically designed to raise Hispanic student aspirations and enhance their retention and completion rates. Moreover, the recent availability of Title V funds and the corporate and business involvement due to efforts by HACU are infusing more fiscal and human resources into HSIs to create infrastructures that facilitate these outcomes.

Myths About Hispanic Students and HSIs

Myths—beliefs mingled with facts—abound about the educational and economic prospects of Hispanics. As highlighted already, it cannot be denied that Hispanics' educational attainment rates and economic prospects have improved slowly since the 1960s. The low Hispanic educational attainment rates, from high school through college and into graduate school, still reveal a bleak outlook for their potential social, economic, and educational gains unless a number of dramatic changes occur. One such dramatic and profound catalysis with the potential for promoting substantive changes for Hispanics' socioeconomic well-being stems from the increasing presence of HSIs. However, with increasingly lower state resources for education in general coupled with still increasing numbers of students and a serious teacher shortage, even HSIs must deal with these grim realities. They clearly cannot address all the social ills that have plagued Hispanics and other minorities. They can, however, offer models of what is possible. Next is an examination of some prevailing myths and critical realities about Hispanics and HSIs that also offer some positive examples.

Myth 1: Hispanics Have Little Interest in Going to College

A prevailing societal perception appears to be that Hispanics have very little interest in going to college. Certainly, Hispanics are not finishing high school or going to college in proportion to their numbers in the United States. Their high school completion rates continue to be among the lowest of all groups, and they continue to be underrepresented in higher education in general. Nonetheless, because the Civil Rights movement forced open the ivory tower doors to all nontraditional college-going populations, Hispanics have been going to college in increasingly larger numbers. More than one half of these students continue to choose community colleges as their starting point due to these institutions' close proximity to students' homes. In addition, these institutions typically offer more welcoming environments, easier admissions requirements, less restrictive "second chance" academic policies, and lower tuition and fees. Other offerings that appeal to students are part-time attendance options, smaller classes, wider selection of evening and weekend courses, and numerous instructional and student support programs (Cohen & Brawer, 1996; Laden, 1999a).

This is not to say, however, that Hispanics do not prefer to attend 4-year institutions if given the opportunity. Rather, their college choices highlight the fact that community colleges typically offer greater access and opportunity for these students who are frequently from low-income socioeconomic backgrounds, who are often the first in their families to attend college, and who may be less prepared academically to undertake college level work due to little or no academic guidance in course selections, ongoing academic assistance and mentoring, or tutoring while in middle and senior high school.

As a younger population, the education of young Hispanics is critical to their overall economic success. The good news is that Hispanic youths have improved their high school completion rate by more than nine percentage points since 1990, after a sharp decline in the previous decade. The rise continues according to the most recent data, with 62% of Hispanics completing high school in 1997 (Wilds, 2000). Nonetheless, much work still needs to be done to narrow the dropout rate and retain Hispanics in high school through graduation. Additional good news is that Hispanics from ages 18 to 24 are going to college in increasingly greater numbers. Since 1990, the Hispanic college participation rate has increased by 8%, with 36% of this age group enrolling in college in 1997. It cannot be denied, however, that critical work still needs to be done to raise the college-going rates for this age group.

During the past 10 years, Hispanics have recorded gains in all degree categories, particularly doubling their completion of bachelor's degrees. Upward gains in all categories were recorded in 1997, from 11.7% gain in associate degrees to 2.2% gain in first-time professional degrees. Moreover, Hispanic men exceeded Hispanic women in earning associate degrees (reflecting a 12% gain), whereas Hispanic women achieved higher gains in all other degree categories (Wilds, 2000).

Myth 2: Hispanic Parents Do Not Encourage Their Children to Go to College

Embedded within the mythology of why Hispanics have low educational attainment rates is the oft repeated refrain that Hispanic parents neither encourage their children to go to college nor support their going if they choose to do so. According to an analysis of U.S. Census Bureau data, projections by The White House Initiative (1999) indicate that in 2005, 20% of all Hispanic children will be under 5 years of age, 17% will be in the 5-to 17-year-old school-age population, and 15% will be in the 18-to 29-year-old college-age population. In other words, more than 50% of Hispanics will be under 30 years of age in 2005 and in need of an education and occupational skills. Will Hispanic parents deny their children the opportunity to be educated and to be better off economically? If current findings are any indicator, no they will not. Rather, parents themselves will continue to seek educational opportunities for their children as well as for themselves.

It is indisputable that a key determinant that influences the educational attainment of students is their parents' educational levels. On the one hand, about 11% of Latinos today have parents with college degrees (Carnevale, 1999); therefore, some Latino students are from socioeconomically advantaged homes and have a greater chance for achieving academic success. On the other hand, at least 37% of working Hispanic adults do not have a high school diploma and are typically employed in low-paying, low-skilled service jobs (The White House Initiative, 1999). Another 40% who are service workers in low-level jobs have attended some college and could increase their employment opportunities and career mobility with additional education, technical training, and higher level skills (Carnevale, 1999).

Certainly, with little formal education or limited English skills, some Latino parents neither understand what higher education is and entails nor do they fully realize the effects a college degree has on increasing their children's social and economic opportunities. However, it is not surprising that when bilingual–bicultural counselors and faculty, outreach recruiters, and other program specialists work closely and sensitively with Hispanic parents to help them understand what a college education is and how it can increase their children's economic mobility, parents become willing supporters who motivate their children to go to college and help them stay in college. Programs for first-generation college-going students, such as the Puente Project in California high schools and community colleges, involve Hispanic parents in a variety of activities. These include workshops to understand financial aid, the college admissions process, and the transfer and graduation processes. Along with their children, parents also visit college campuses and attend college and career fairs. All of these activities help to demystify the concept of college and to involve the parents more fully in their children's educational experiences. Moreover, a plethora of HSI programs in metropolitan areas with high concentrations of Hispanics, such as Los Angeles, San Antonio, Miami, and New York City, have special outreach and community programs to assist parents. These include improving their literacy skills, participating in reading programs with their young children, preparing for the general equivalency diploma and citizenship tests, and upgrading their technical skills (Laden, 1999b).

Another example of a collaborative approach to working with Hispanic students and parents is the Community College of Denver La Familia Scholars. Designed to help erase the fear of college as an alien environment, La Familia Scholars program acts as a surrogate family away from the home but also strives for getting parental support and including them in special activities. The program assists students with financial aid, academic and personal counseling, tutoring, mentoring, and other support services including special topic workshops. La Familia Scholars also offers its students a place to go before and after classes where they can study quietly. More important, the program's involvement with the parents has been shown to increase the students' retention and graduation rates. The program gets parents familiar with the college, the goals of the program, and introduces faculty as critical partners in their children's education ("This Is HACU," 1999).

Results show that when educators reach out to parents, inform them, and involve them with their children's education, parental support and encouragement increases for their children to attend and persist in college. Exemplar HSI programs bear this out in their efforts to work with students' parents.

Myth 3: Hispanic Students Do Not Seek Financial Assistance

Hispanic students and their parents often do not apply for Pell grants and other financial assistance because of a reluctance to answer intrusive personal and family financial questions, financial aid forms that are difficult to understand, and suspicion about "free money" or loans to go to college. Workshops for parents conducted in both English and Spanish, however, are quite helpful in dispelling some of the angst about financial aid and its purpose. Other forms of financial assistance also have sprung up in the past 30 years to encourage Hispanics to go to college and to aid with expenses. Most of these programs link financial aid with other forms of assistance, such as academic counseling, mentoring, and peer tutoring. Often these students are first generation college going and benefit from close guidance and understanding of what they experience as first-time college students. Two exemplar programs are offered here.

A unique and still ongoing program is the College Assistance Migrant Program (CAMP) inaugurated by the federal government in 1972. CAMP offers educational and financial support to children of migrant workers with the express goal of lifting them out of the cycle of poverty they have known all their lives. Now in 12 colleges, CAMP pays for college tuition, books, room and board, and provides a monthly stipend. These programs also offer personal attention to help these Hispanic students prepare for college, with special precollege classes such as note taking, study skills, library research, tutors and study partners, and special counseling assistance with academic, personal, or cultural problems (Stern, 2000).

Another form of aid comes from the Hispanic Scholarship Fund (HSF), the largest scholarship organization for Hispanic students nationally. Begun by the founders of *Hispanic Magazine* over 25 years ago, HSF is now partnered with major business and industry firms, such as AT&T, Anheuser-Busch, Coca Cola, General Motors, Merrill Lynch, and Hewlett-Packard (HSF, 2000). HSF differs from other financial programs in that it grants awards to Hispanic students who have demonstrated an academic commitment to college by completing at least 15 college credit units, have maintained at least a 2.7 grade point average, and are enrolled fulltime. Students must apply for the HSF assistance annually, but they may receive these scholarships through graduate and professional schools. Other merit scholarships are available based on individual donor guidelines that may include majoring in select fields of study or being from specific geographical areas (Simmons, 2000). A distinct feature of HSF is a recent program funded by the Lily Foundation that assists community college students in their transition to 4-year institutions. Unlike many other aid programs for Hispanics, the HSF itself offers only financial assistance and some general mentoring through their Web site. Any personal guidance and mentoring occurs through auspices of the individual partners involved with HSF.

Myth 4: Hispanic Students Have Few Educational Role Models

In general, Hispanic students are exposed to few faculty from their own cultural backgrounds. In 1996, for instance, although Hispanics represented 10.3% of all undergraduate and 4.9% of all graduate students (although clearly not high figures in themselves), Hispanic faculty constituted a tiny 2.6% of all higher education faculty (NCES, 1999). Given these data, it is fair to state that Hispanic students find few culturally sensitive role models in their college classrooms.

A very different picture emerges, however, when one examines the presence of Hispanic faculty in HSIs. Among the top 50 two-year HSIs that confer the most associate degrees to Hispanic students, the range of Hispanic faculty is from 67.4% at Laredo Community College to 5.1% at City Colleges of Chicago-Wilbur Wright college and Valencia Community College ("Top 50 Community," 2000). Among the top 25 four-year HSIs that confer the most baccalaureate degrees to Hispanics, the range of Hispanic faculty is from 31.6% at the University of Texas-Pan American to 7.1% at CUNY-City College ("Top 100 Colleges," 2000). Finally, at the top five doctoral HSIs, the range of Hispanic faculty is from 22% at the University of Texas at El Paso to 9% each at the University of New Mexico-Main Campus and the New Mexico State University-Main Campus ("Top 100 Colleges," 2000).

Overall, Hispanic administrators are better represented than Hispanic faculty in most higher education institutions, particularly in the area of student affairs. This notwithstanding, according to 1998 data from the NCES (cited in "Top 100 Colleges," 2000), Hispanic administrators at HSIs have a much higher profile than at non-HSIs. For example, the University of Texas at El Paso leads the way with Hispanics representing 40% of their administrators, followed by the University of Miami with 31%, and Florida International University with 26%.

The higher presence of Hispanic faculty and administrators in HSIs suggests several things. It suggests not only that there are many more role models in the classrooms, in faculty offices, and in administrative posts who look like the students themselves, but also that these are faculty and administrators who are more likely to have a much greater understanding about and commitment to meeting Hispanic students' academic, cultural, and personal needs. Research reveals that Hispanic and other faculty of color also are much more likely to offer emotional support and encouragement, raise Hispanic and other racial and ethnic students' aspirations, and be willing to serve as formal and informal advisors, mentors, and sponsors (Laden, 1999a; Laden & Hagedorn, 2000; Turner & Myers, 2000). Moreover, with more Hispanic faculty present, there are more faculty available to share the advising and mentoring than is typical in more mainstream, majority institutions where there are fewer Hispanic faculty who are in greater demand by Hispanics and other students of color.

On the other hand, the fact cannot be ignored that Hispanic faculty and administrators have greater demands placed on their time by not only Hispanic students in need of guidance and support but by other students interested in their cross-cultural comparative research and their greater sensitivity to student needs. This cultural taxation (Padilla, 1994), however, places them at a disadvantage in trying to attend to their own research that affects tenure and promotion considerations. Notwithstanding these considerations, the stark fact remains that Hispanic students have very few educational role models in general. Many more are needed in HSIs as well as in all other K–20 settings.

Myth 5: HSIs Siphon off Resources From Other Special Focus Institutions

As HSIs expand in number, a more recent myth to emerge is that because HSIs were not founded with the expressly stated mission of educating Hispanics, they are not entitled to federal funds that rightfully and historically belong to institutions with specific charters and missions, such as HBCUs and Tribal Colleges. This myth took root during the period leading to the 1998 reauthorization of the Higher Education Act. In that period, media reported on higher education and public policy discussions that centered on the impact of anticipated changes in Title III. These changes were reported as potentially impacting HBCUs severely if HSIs and Tribal Colleges were granted their claim for full inclusion and received guaranteed annual federal assistance as HBCUs do (Dervarics, 1997; Mealer, 1998). The anticipated fear was that if HSIs and Tribal Colleges were fully included, funds would be siphoned off from the HBCUs' anticipated increase, thereby creating a loss they could not supplement from other sources in an era of shrinking resources for all of higher education.

In reality, the latest reauthorization of the Higher Education Act ultimately included Tribal Colleges as a Title III category, but it also created a new category, Title V, to include HSIs. Moreover, neither change reduced the HBCUs' allocation as more federal funds were allocated to cover the additions. Under the new Title V category, HSIs were authorized to receive as much as $80 million per year (Mealer, 1998).

Public policies are critical to expanding educational and economic opportunities for Hispanics, African Americans, American Indians, and Asian Pacific American groups. The overall national population of these groups is expected to grow from 28% in the year 2000 to a minimum of 36% by the year 2020, according to the recently formed Alliance for Equity in Higher Education (2000). This is all the more important when one remembers that minority-serving institutions—the HBCUs, Tribal Colleges, HSIs, and predominantly Black and Hispanic postsecondary institutions—also serve large concentrations of other minorities from more than one ethnic group (Merisotis & O'Brien, 1998). The cooperation and collaboration among these institutions are thus vital to the continued improvement of the educational attainment of all minority groups.

The Alliance for Equity in Higher Education was formed after the 1998 reauthorization of the Higher Education Act. It includes members from HBCUs, HSIs, Tribal Colleges, and predominantly Black and Hispanic institutions. The Alliance for Equity in Higher Education promotes greater collaboration and cooperation among postsecondary institutions that serve large numbers of students of color (Alliance for Equity, 2000). Their overall collective goal is to "play a central role in supporting cultural values and traditions, reinforcing community and civic responsibility, and producing citizens who are more attuned to the diverse nation in which we live" (p. 1).

The HACU still remains critical to promoting HSIs and their role in providing educational opportunity to Hispanics. Through a series of initiatives it has developed since its founding, HACU offers a variety of opportunities to promote HSIs and educational enhancements for students. Forming collaborative partnerships with corporate sponsors, HACU facilitates scholarships, fellowships, and summer internships for undergraduate and graduate students. It also offers an array of institutional services to increase HSI resources and raise skill levels of administrators, faculty, and staff (HACU, 2000). Special outreach and community partnership programs extend into neighborhoods. These reach into Hispanic homes and K–12 schools with large concentrations of Hispanics to raise parents' literacy rates, motivate youth to stay in school, offer tutoring and mentoring for students, and improve Hispanics' overall high school completion, college going, and college completion rates (Laden, 1999b).

Myth 6: HSIs Do Not Figure Prominently in the Community

There are those who might assume that HSIs do not figure prominently—that is, play a significant role—within their communities because there are still dismally low high school and college completion rates of Hispanics and their high employment rates in low-skilled, low-paying service jobs. The reality is that if it were not for the presence of the local HSIs in many Hispanic communities, these communities would be intellectually and culturally underserved. In many instances, HSIs serve as the primary cultural centers within their communities by featuring performance arts programs and other free or low-cost public speaker events ("Top 50 Community," 2000).

In providing educational access to more than one half of all Hispanic college students, HSIs also fill the gap by aiding more Hispanics and other minority groups with innovative after school, weekend, and summer programs in a number of areas, including some literacy and English classes for parents (Laden, 1999b). HSIs are working also to reverse the historic shortages of Hispanics in science, mathematics, engineering, and advanced technological professions. HSI and HACU partnerships with national entities such as the National Science Foundation, NASA, AT&T, Abbott Laboratories, and Union Carbide are a few examples of collaborative K–20 programs that aid Hispanics (Flores, 1999b). These programs not only assist Hispanic college students to be a part of innovative programs, they also receive highly personalized mentoring from working professionals. Students, in turn, work with middle and high school Hispanic students as tutors and mentors to raise educational aspirations, increase skill levels, and encourage earlier interest in math and science. Antonio Flores (1999b), current president of HACU, cited the example of NASA and its support of Proyecto Access, a national collaborative program for middle and high school students who have an interest in pursuing mathematics, engineering, and science careers.

New approaches to offering courses that better fit rapidly changing work force needs are becoming a part of many HSIs. St. Philip's College in Texas, for instance, expanded its weekend college program to offer more courses for students who work full time during the regular school week. Passaic County Community College now offers "by special request" courses in fast-growing areas such as allied health fields and computer science ("This Is HACU," 1999).

All in all, HSIs and its partners are making significant contributions by offering a powerful combination of fiscal and human resources to HSIs and within the Hispanic communities. These sources of support within communities and across the nation for Hispanics are often open to other minority groups as well, thereby attending to raising the educational and economic aspirations and attainment rates for the more marginalized among the nation's population.

Future Prospects and Conclusions

The last third of the 20th century saw the emergence of HSIs, in most cases the result of demographic default rather than conscious design. The organizational and advocacy efforts of HACU since its advent in 1986 have created a national awareness of HSIs and procured critical political, federal, and corporate support for HSIs. In sum, by linking together all colleges and universities serving high proportions of Hispanics to gain national recognition and resources, HACU literally forced the federal government to include HSIs in the 1992 reauthorization of the Higher Education Act; its leadership led to further inclusion of HSIs under the latest reauthorization. Moreover, HACU's persistent efforts helped lead to the establishment of the President's Advisory Commission on Educational Excellence for Hispanic Americans in 1996 and its supportive arm, The White House Initiative on Educational Excellence for Hispanic Americans. The debt by HSIs to HBCUs for enjoying the national attention it has thus far is obvious. This is notwithstanding the little actual acknowledgment HSIs have received thus far in the larger higher education picture, as stated at the beginning of this article. Nonetheless, much remains to be done for and by these institutions.

The future of HSIs is clearly one of continued growth. In light of the projected rise of the Hispanic population in the United States, more culturally sensitive teachers in K–12 schools, and 2- and 4-year colleges will be needed to educate this particular group. As more Hispanics enroll in college, more of these institutions will become institutions that approach or exceed 25% or more of the total full-time equivalent population; hence, they too will become HSIs.

Greater rather than less attention and sensitivity will have to be paid to the curricular, social, economic, and cultural expectations of these students and those from other ethnic groups as the role of HSIs is not limited to educating only Hispanics. It must be remembered that HSIs serve large concentrations of ethnic minorities from other ethnic groups. This rather large phenomenal influx is expected to continue for the foreseeable future in light of the immigrant and minority demographic projections for the 21st century (U.S. Census Bureau, 2000). Also, it cannot be forgotten that non-Hispanic White students also attend HSIs. Therefore, the dynamics of cultural and social diversity will continue to be played out in a variety of dimensions within HSIs. Hispanic and other ethnic administrators and faculty will be in greater demand. These individuals bring to the classroom and campus a personal sensitivity, cultural awareness and orientation, and curricular valuing of who

Hispanics are and Hispanic cultural and experiential knowledge. These faculty and administrators often make the difference in improving Hispanics' overall undergraduate and graduate college enrollment, retention, and completion rates.

There is a shadow side to the success of HSIs that must also be acknowledged. Predominantly White institutions should look at HSIs to learn from them how to increase Hispanic educational attainment rates; instead, predominantly White institutions may assume they are no longer responsible for attending to the needs of these students, especially as state and other resources shrink. Another concern is that HSIs themselves need to consider creating more partnerships with selective and more elite public and private non-HSIs to increase Hispanics' presence in these institutions. One example of the possibilities is articulation and transfer partnerships, such as Miami-Dade Community College and Santa Monica College have with Smith College and other such selective institutions (Wolf-Wendel, Morphew, & Twombly, 2001).

In closing, it cannot be forgotten that a spate of antiaffirmation institutional policies and state legislation emerged as the 20th century drew to a close. The large and small steps taken to improve the educational attainment of Hispanics must not now be undone by a flurry of antirace sensitive policies. One of the ways to respond to critics who fear changes to the known and traditional ways of doing things is to debunk the stereotypic myths that perpetuate inequities and limit access for those who do not fit the traditional, known student profiles and contexts of the past century. The 21st century brings a new era of multicultural diversity and equity for all. HSIs, along with HBCUs and Tribal Colleges, will continue to offer greater educational access and opportunities for Hispanics and other students who attend these institutions. The social and economic well-being of these individuals, hence of the nation, depends on the educational benefits accrued by them. The interplay of a college education coupled with career and occupational preparation, and expected economic benefits can only lead to improved lifestyles for Hispanics, to a healthier economy for the nation, and to greater social and cultural integration of the United States as a whole. Therefore, the vital role of HSIs in contributing to these individual and national outcomes cannot be ignored, but rather should be highlighted as exemplars.

References

Alliance for Equity in Higher Education. (2000). *Key trends and issues.* Washington, DC: Institute for Higher Education Policy. Retrieved April 25, 2000 from the World Wide Web: http://www.ihep.com/alliance

Basinger, J. (2000). A new way of classifying colleges elates some and perturbs others. *The Chronicle of Higher Education, XLVI*(49), 31–42.

Benítez, M. (1998). Hispanic-serving institutions: Challenges and opportunities. In J. P. Merisotis & C. T. O'Brien (Eds.), *Minority-serving institutions: Distinct purposes, common goals* (pp. 57–68). San Francisco: Jossey-Bass.

Carnevale, A. P. (1999). *Education = success: Empowering Hispanic youth and adults.* Princeton, NJ: Educational Testing Service.

Cohen, A. R., & Brawer, F. B. (1996). *The American community college* (3rd ed.). San Francisco: Jossey-Bass.

Dervarics, C. (1997). Can a rift be avoided? *Black Issues in Higher Education, 14*(19), 20–28.

Flores, A. R. (1999a). Message from the president: Annual conference a great success. *The Voice of Hispanic Higher Education, 8*(12), 4.

Flores, A. R. (1999b). Message from the president: Community colleges and the next millennium. *The Voice of Hispanic Higher Education, 8*(5), 4.

Flores, A. R. (1999c). Message from the president: Reaping the rewards. *The Voice of Hispanic Higher Education, 8*(10), 4.

Hispanic Association of Colleges and Universities. (2000). *Hispanic association of colleges and universities 2000 membership directory.* San Antonio, TX: Author. Retrieved April 25, 2001 from the World Wide Web: http://www.hacu.net

Hispanic Scholarship Fund. (2000). *About the Hispanic scholarship fund.* San Francisco, CA: Author. Retrieved April 25, 2001 from the World Wide Web: http://www.hsf.net

Justiz, M. J., Wilson, R., & Björk, L. G. (1994). *Minorities in higher education.* Phoenix, AZ: American Council on Education.

Laden, B. V. (1999a). Celebratory socialization of culturally diverse students through academic programs and services. In K. M. Shaw, J. R. Valadez, & R. A. Rhoads (Eds.), *Community colleges as cultural texts* (pp. 173–194). New York: State University of New York.

Laden, B. V. (1999b). Two-year Hispanic-serving colleges. In B. Townsend (Ed.), *Two-year colleges for women and minorities: Enabling access to the baccalaureate* (pp. 151–194). New York: Falmer.

Laden, B. V. (2000, November). *Hispanic serving two-year institutions: What account for their high transfer rates?* Paper presented at the annual meeting of the Association for the Study of Higher Education, Sacramento, CA.

Laden, B. V., & Hagedorn, L. S. (2000). Job satisfaction among faculty of color in academe: Individual survivors or institutional transformers. In L. S. Hagedorn (Ed.), *What contributes to job satisfaction among faculty and staff* (pp. 57–66). San Francisco: Jossey Bass.

Mealer, B. (1998, January 16). Hispanic-serving institutions seek more federal funds, angering black colleges. *The Chronicle of Higher Education: Academe Today,* p. A31. Retrieved April 25, 2001 from the World Wide Web: http://www.chronicle.com.data/articles/eguid-44.dir/19eguide

Merisotis, J. P., & O'Brien, C. T. (1998). Editors' notes. In J. P. Merisotis & C. T. O'Brien (Eds.), *Minority-serving institutions: Distinct purposes, common goals* (pp. 1–3). San Francisco: Jossey-Bass.

National Center for Education Statistics. (1998). *The condition of education 1998.* Washington, DC: Author. Retrieved April 25, 2001 from the World Wide Web: http://nces.ed.gov/pubs98/condition98

National Center for Education Statistics. (1999). *Digest of education statistics 1998.* Washington, DC: U.S. Department of Education.

O'Brien, C. T., & Zudak, C. (1998). Minority-serving institutions: An overview. In J. P. Merisotis & C. T. O'Brien (Eds.), *Minority-serving institutions: Distinct purposes, common goals* (pp. 5–16). San Francisco: Jossey-Bass.

Padilla, A. M. (1994). Ethnic minority scholars, research, and mentoring: Current and future issues. *Educational Researcher, 23*(4), 24–27.

President's Advisory Commission on Educational Excellence for Hispanic Americans. (1996). *Our nation on the fault line: Hispanic American education.* Washington, DC: Author.

Riley, R. W. (2000, March 15). *HSIs: Serving the community, serving the nation* [Press release]. Washington, DC: U.S. Department of Education.

Simmons, J. (2000). Coca-Cola investing in education and bottlers support community projects nationwide. *The Hispanic Outlook in Higher Education, 10*(20), 6–8.

Solorzano, D. C. (1993). *The road to the doctorate for California's Chicanas and Chicanos: A study of Ford Foundation minority fellows.* Berkeley: California Policy Seminar.

Solorzano, D. G. (1995). The baccalaureate origins of Chicana and Chicano doctorates in the social sciences. *Hispanic Journal of Behavioral Sciences, 17*(1), 3–32.

Stern, G. M. (2000). Prospects poor for immigrant children. *The Hispanic Outlook in Higher Education, 10*(17), 12–13.

This is HACU: At the community college of Denver "la familia" helps first-generation students. (1999). *The Voice of Hispanic Higher Education, 8*(5), 5.

Top 50 Community and Junior Colleges for Hispanics. (2000). *The Hispanic Outlook in Higher Education, 10*(13), 10–12.

Top 100 Colleges for Hispanics. (2000). *The Hispanic Outlook in Higher Education, 10*(16), 7–23.

Turner, C. S. V., & Myers, S. L., Jr. (2000). *Faculty of color in academe: Bittersweet success.* Boston: Allyn & Bacon.

U.S. Census Bureau. (2000). *Resident population estimates of the United States by sex, race, and Hispanic origin: April 1 to July 1, 1999, with short-term projection to June 1, 2000.* Washington, DC: Author. Retrieved April 25, 2001 from the World Wide Web: www.ed.gov/offices/census

The White House Initiative on Educational Excellence for Hispanic Americans. (1999). *What are Hispanic-serving institutions?* Washington, DC: Author. Retrieved April 25, 2001 from the World Wide Web: http://www.ed.gov/offices/OIIA/Hispanic

The White House Initiative on Educational Excellence for Hispanic Americans. (2000). *What are Hispanic-serving institutions?* Washington, DC: Author. Retrieved April 25, 2001 from the World Wide Web: http://www.ed.gov/offices/OIIA/Hispanic

The White House Initiative on Educational Excellence for Hispanic Americans. (2001). *Hispanic serving institutions.* Washington, DC: Author. Retrieved April 25, 2001 from the World Wide Web: http://www.ed.gov/offices/OIIA/Hispanic

Wilds, D. J. (2000). *Minorities in higher education 1999–2000. Seventeenth annual status report.* Washington, DC: American Council on Education.

Wolf-Wendel, L., Morphew, C., & Twombly, S. (2001, April). *A second change story: Qualitative analysis of innovative transfer agreements.* Paper presented at the annual meeting of the American Educational Research Association, Seattle, WA.

The Confluence of Race, Gender, and Class Among Community College Students: Assessing Attitudes Toward Affirmative Action in College Admissions

Eboni M. Zamani-Gallaher

This article examines the attitudes of baccalaureate aspiring community college students with regard to affirmative action in college admissions. Using data from UCLA's Cooperative Institutional Research Program (CIRP) Annual Freshman Year Survey, the study assessed determinants of approval or disapproval of affirmative action for 20,339 community college students. Because students in traditionally disadvantaged groups (e.g., first-generation, racial/ethnic minorities, female, and low-income) are overrepresented at the community college, critical theoretical perspectives concerning social mobility and self-interest were utilized to guide the study. The findings indicate that race/ethnicity and political views were significant predictors of affirmative action attitudes for males and females. The impact of family income and transfer intent significantly contributed to male support for abolishing affirmative action. Age yielded a significant association for support of affirmative action as reported by older African American and white students.

Community colleges[1] often go unnoticed in much of the public policy literature, particularly as it pertains to issues of social justice. However, nearly half of all undergraduates attending public colleges and universities are at two-year institutions. Community colleges serve over 6.5 million credit earning and roughly 5 million non-credit enrolled students (Phillippe & Sullivan, 2005). Within the 11+ million students attending community colleges lie interesting demographic realities that mirror the population shifts occurring in society.

At present, one in three Americans is a person of color (U.S. Bureau of the Census, 2005). Demographic shifts illustrate population growth among racial/ethnic minorities collectively. The expansion of communities of color has primarily been due to immigration and swelling birth rates among Hispanics over the last 25 years that have consistently outpaced other racial/ethnic groups (Lindsay & Singer, 2003). By 2050, white non-Hispanic persons are projected to account for less than half of U.S. citizens (U.S. Bureau of the Census, 2002). The marked increased of racial/ethnic groups has been coined the "new majority" (Rendon & Hope, 1996).

Correspondingly, institutions of higher learning are becoming increasingly heterogeneous. However, in contrast to their four-year counterparts, community colleges have provided the primary vehicle for postsecondary access and inclusion for growing numbers of underrepresented and disenfranchised college aspirants (Cohen & Brawer, 2003; Dougherty, 1987). Hence, the aims of this article are three-fold: (1) to highlight the student demographics of community college attendees, (2) to review the literature on affirmative action as it relates to admissions to four-year colleges for two-year colleges students, and (3) to explore the responses to UCLA's Cooperative

Institutional Research Program (CIRP) Annual Freshman Year Survey as well as the educational plans of those students with regard to their affirmative action attitudes.

Community College Students: A Profile

Previously referred to as the "people's college" or "democracy's doors," a central aim of community colleges is the open door mission to offer postsecondary study to diverse members of the community with a host of educational interests (Cohen & Brawer, 2003). Similar to the demography of the general population, community colleges have experienced growth in student numbers, particularly among those from underrepresented and/or disenfranchised groups. According to the American Association of Community Colleges (AACC; 2006), 47% of African American and Asian/Pacific Islander undergraduates, 55% of Hispanic, and 57% of Native American college students attend two-year institutions. Parallel to four-year institutions, the majority of undergraduate students at community colleges are women (59%).

The vast pool of students at two-year institutions are enrolled part-time, are first-generation collegians, and are frequently from low-income backgrounds; unlike four-year institutions where the majority of collegians are of traditional college age (18–24), the mean student age at community colleges is 29 years old (AACC, 2006). Central to their mission to serve diverse learners, community colleges have commonly engaged older students through emeritus college programs for seniors (e.g., elder learner classes and OPALs—Older People with Active Lifestyles offerings) illustrating how two-year institutions have been proficient in augmenting services and instructional support consistent with societal needs and population shifts (Darden, Cloud, & Illich, 2003; Olson, 2006).

As community college students range in age, gender, race/ethnicity, and ability, there is an assortment of educational goals (e.g., continuing education, receiving a certificate of completion, pursing an associate's degree, and transferring to a four-year college or university) among student constituents. Some of the literature suggests that over three-quarters of community college students desire baccalaureate degrees and intend to transfer to a four-year institution (Keener, 1994; Laanan, 2001). Recent findings from the Community College Survey of Student Engagement (2005) indicate that 48% of students responding indicated that their primary goal was transferring to a four-year institution of higher education.

Community colleges provide routes to baccalaureate degrees by filling existing gaps in educational access for those who may not have other options for postsecondary attendance. Nonetheless, community colleges are often criticized for further disadvantaging the subsequent educational attainment of students desiring four-year degrees (Brint & Karabel, 1989; Dougherty, 1992, 1994; Pascarella, Edison, Nora, Hagedorn, & Terenzini, 1998). Additionally, the figures for community college students transferring directly into four-year baccalaureate programs are dismal in contrast to the numbers who aspire to obtain academic credentials beyond the tier of higher education where they are enrolled (National Center for Education Statistics, 1997, 2003). Given the notable educational plans and demographics of community college students, many two-year students are in social identity groups (e.g., first-generation, low-income, minority students, reentry women, students with disabilities) that have been underserved and underrepresented in higher education. Hence, many community college students could potentially benefit from affirmative action initiatives in college admissions.

Access, Affirmative Action, and Community College Contexts

Affirmative action evolved from the social justice agenda of the Kennedy and Johnson administrations. Affirmative action was initially forwarded by President John F. Kennedy as Executive Order 10925, and later enacted by President Lyndon B. Johnson on September 24, 1965 (Executive Order 11246). Affirmative action can be defined as policies and programs that seek to eliminate disparate treatment, disparate impact, and institutionalized hurdles to access for minorities and women (Crosby, 2006; Fleming, Gill, & Swinton, 1978; Rubio, 2001; Spann, 2000). In part, affirmative action seeks to reinforce the basic doctrine of the 14th Amendment to the U.S. Constitution and to extend the 1964 Civil Rights Act. The 1964 Civil Rights Act's Title VI made discrimination against persons due to their race, color, religion, sex, or national origin illegal; Title VII introduced equal employment opportunities. Despite the legacy of de jure bigotry and inequity prior to the passage of the Civil Rights Act of 1964, de facto discrimination followed, making policies affirm that access to equal opportunities in education and employment necessary (Fleming, Gill, & Swinton, 1978; Howard, 1997).

Although issues regarding affirmative action in higher education largely occur in relatively selective four-year institutions, the debate around affirmative action has extended to community colleges as well (DeMitchell, 2004; Johnson, 1997). Unlike four-year institutions of higher learning, concerns surrounding affirmative action at community colleges have traditionally pertained to employment (i.e., hiring, promotion, salary/benefits, and/or dismissal). The number of racial/ethnic minorities among the faculties at two-year institutions is not proportional to the student population. Hence, the diversity of faculty is important in shaping an instructional climate and institutional culture that places value on the educational experiences of students of color. Students are more apt to feel affirmed and to persist to degree completion when there are faculty and staff that culturally mirror them with regard to race/ethnicity and gender (Zamani, 2006). Therefore, cultural congruence between the student and institution are significant to the retention and subsequent educational outcomes of students of color (Zamani, 2000).

Student Access and Affirmative Action

The literature addressing student affirmative action at community colleges is scant due to the nature of the open system of admissions. However, an open door does not necessarily equate to open access. According to Dougherty and Kienzl (2006), "There is growing policy interest in community colleges as gateways to the baccalaureate degree" (p. 452). The case of *Camarena v. San Bernardino Community College District* (1995) is one example of how issues of access and perceptions of equitable opportunities are parceled out in the two-year college context. The suit, filed in a Sacramento U.S. District Court, alleged that the California community college operated segregationist programs and challenged it on the basis of the *Brown v. the Board of Education* (1954) decision. Camarena charged that she was not given access to a section of English 101 that had been earmarked for the Bridge Transition Program. The plaintiff took issue with the program's practice of targeting students of color, providing mentors and additional support services in seeking to increase the transfer rates of students who are of African or Mexican descent. The Camarena case was settled out of court (Caso & Corry, 1996); however, this suit exhibits that within the open door environment of community colleges lies scrutiny over the right of entry in courses earmarked for special populations and admittance to competitive technical programs (e.g., nursing, pre-engineering, etc.).

While Camarena challenged San Bernardino Valley Community College with limiting access relative to course enrollment practices, one barrier for many students across race/ethnic and gender lines is the cost associated with college attendance. For many community college students, financial support, such as Pell grants and subsidized loans, is needed to assist with their education. Therefore, financial aid in the form of grants and scholarships for disadvantaged and underrepresented students is a means of affirming access particularly for first-generation, low-income students.

Affirmative action in the form of financial aid designated for special populations has been found objectionable as the promotion of race-based scholarships has been disputed at the two-year college level. A race-based merit award at Northern Virginia Community Colleges (NVCC) resulted in a civil rights lawsuit regarding the race-conscious, privately funded $500.00 Leslie V. Forte Scholarship, which is earmarked for students of color (Barnes, 1996; Wright, 1997). A complaint filed by Christopher Thompson with the Office of Civil Rights argued reverse discrimination, stating that NVCC's awarding scholarships that are race-targeted was unconstitutional and discriminatory against white students (Wright, 1997). The complaint was settled out of court.

The Pendulum Swings: An Era of Retrenchment

The growing interest in various forms of affirmative action (i.e., employment, admissions, and financial aid) raises questions over fairness, illustrates conflicts with access policies, and highlights disagreements over who is afforded opportunities for advancement in an attempt to levelize the playing field. In 1996, California's Proposition 209 was the first ballot measure forwarded to abolish affirmative action in publicly funded institutions in the areas of hiring/employment, admissions, and financial aid. Following its passage, the governor (Pete Wilson) requested that the court invalidate the California law[2] allowing race and gender-targeted affirmative action in community colleges (Schmidt, 1998). The initial ruling in December 1998 challenged that the statute was not out of alignment with Proposition 209, which banned the consideration of race and gender in employment decisions at all publicly controlled state institutions. The ruling that preference was not being afforded to applicants on the basis of race/ethnicity or gender allowed California community colleges some leeway in affirming diversity. However, in 2001 a California court struck down the statute that allowed two-year institutions to use race- and gender-conscious policies in hiring practices. The judge held that the two-year institutions violated the tenets of Proposition 209 in addition to the 14th Amendment relative to specifying diversity goals and timelines for hiring minority and female candidates (Schmidt, 2001).

The matter of affirmative action and how individuals resolve the consideration of race/ethnicity, gender, and so forth in business, education, and government has far-reaching consequences. How Americans perceive fairness in relation to affirmative action runs from laws promoting equity to reversed racial and gender-based discrimination. The Proposition 209 initiative to abolish affirmative action in California gained momentum with the passage of Initiative 200, a similar proposal to ban affirmative action in Washington State in 1998 (Trick, 2004). While Florida and Texas have retrenched affirmative action efforts in recent years, neither did so via referendum. In 2006, Michigan became the third state to vote to amend its constitution to prohibit the use of affirmative action by public institutions (O'Brien, 2006). Ironically, however, this followed the 2003 *Grutter v. Bollinger* case involving the University of Michigan's law school admissions procedures in which the U.S. Supreme Court ruled in favor of the institution stating that diversity is a compelling state interest and that race as one of a myriad of factors may be used in admissions decisions (Eckes, 2004).

Rationale for Study and Research Questions

It is quite possible, similar to the California post-Prop 209 era, that the universities in Michigan will experience a steep decrease in the proportion of African American and Hispanic students after the passage of Michigan's Proposal 2, which banned affirmative action.[3] This decline will most notably occur at the state's elite research institutions: University of Michigan-Ann Arbor, Michigan State University, and Wayne State University. As such, states without affirmative action policies have started to pay increased attention to the community college transfer function as an alternate means of achieving diversity (Hebel, 2000). For instance, institutions, such as the University of California and the University of Washington, have collaborated to draw diverse student populations through dual enrollment initiatives, transfer alliance programs, honors program partnerships, and cooperative admissions programs in specialized technical areas in this anti-affirmative action period to circumvent the elimination of affirmative action in their states (Burdman, 2003; Chiang, 1998; Gallego, 1998; Hugo, 2001).

Since community college students are often members of culturally diverse groups (e.g., racial/ethnic minorities, reentry women, first-generation, and/or low-income collegians) that could potentially seek to benefit from the new collaborations during the backlash against affirmative action policies in admissions, research is necessary to examine their opinions regarding the policy. Yet research assessing attitudinal responses to affirmative action policies and programs in college admissions has primarily focused on favor or disfavor of four-year college students and to a lesser degree investigated graduate and professional students (Sax & Arredondo, 1999; Smith, 1998, 2006;

Zamani-Gallaher, 2006). The omission of community college students is relevant to the discourse on collegiate attitudes toward affirmative action as the discussion has largely been framed from an institutionally elitist perspective. Given the lack of inquiry with community college students on affirmative action in admissions as a means of achieving social justice, the main objective of this study is to examine attitudes toward affirmative action in conjunction with the educational plans of students attending community colleges. In particular, the study examined the relationship between levels of support or resistance toward affirmative action in college admissions among two-year collegians in association with student demographics, educational plans, self-interest, and racial ideologies. The two overarching research questions were as follows:

1. How do the racial/ethnic demographics of community college students relate to their attitudes toward affirmative action in admissions?

2. To what extent do gender, educational plans, self-interest, and racial ideologies predict affirmative action attitudes in college admissions?

Theoretical Perspectives and Conceptual Underpinnings

There are disparities in educational and occupational attainment in the U.S. due to differential access across groups due to social background (Dougherty & Kienzl, 2006). As applied to this study, student demographic variables (i.e., race/ethnicity, gender, age, parent's highest level of education, and annual family income) illustrate the parameters that are thought to contribute to differentiation in social structure and have an effect on social mobility and ultimate attainment (Lin, 1990). Social mobility refers to the degree to which individuals can or are impeded from upward movement in a given social order and whether one's status can be less stratified educationally, occupationally, and economically throughout one's lifetime (Strauss, 2005).

Researchers contend that the application of social mobility theory is appropriate in consideration of individual characteristics as educational plans or experiences and social psychological characteristics as reflected in measures of self-interest and racial ideologies (Dovidio, Mann, & Gaertner, 1989; Sax & Arredondo, 1999; Smith, 1998, 2006). Embedded in the conceptual framework of this study are: educational plans (i.e., highest degree planned, chances of getting a bachelor's degree, and transfer intent); self-interest (i.e., high school grade point average, college choice, and concern about financing education); and racial ideology variables (i.e., cross-race socialization, view of racial discrimination, promoting racial understanding). These variables are used as a means of operationalizing the educational and psychosocial characteristics of interest. Thus, social mobility theory is adapted to determine whether two-year students desiring a bachelor's degree feel affirmative action should be retained in college admissions.

In addition to social mobility theory, the concepts of self-interest and racial ideology were applied in this study as individual/group interest in addition to beliefs regarding how racial equality or race relations bear influence on policy opinions of various parties. This in turn could assist in explaining attitudes people hold toward affirmative action. The ways in which people view their status individually and collectively entail important considerations of social justice and policy issues such as affirmative action in college admissions. Jackman (1996) states:

> Self-interested individuals tend to evolve attitudinal strategies that promote the interests of their group, since their long-term fate is linked to those other members of society who share similar life chances and who are subject to the same general constraints as themselves. (p. 764)

Arguably race- and gender-targeted initiatives are favored less by the dominant group in preference to class-based, income-targeted programming efforts due to competitive individual and group self-interest (Bobo & Kluegel, 1993; Bobo & Smith, 1994). Hence, self-interest coupled with social mobility theory serve as useful theoretical frameworks for examining the relationship between attitudes toward affirmative in correspondence with racial ideologies and educational plans of community college students.

Data Sources and Methods

The data for the study come from the 1996 Cooperative Institutional Research Program (CIRP) provided from the University of California at Los Angeles (UCLA) Higher Education Research Institute. The CIRP freshman year survey is designed to evaluate the importance of college to students (Sax, Astin, Korn, & Mahoney, 1996). The sample for this study consists of a subsample of first-time entering college students at community colleges who participated in the 1996 CIRP annual freshmen survey.

For the purposes of this study, race/ethnicity was restricted to the three largest racial/ethnic groups attending community colleges, thereby including a sample comprised of individuals enrolled as community college students in 1996 who self-identified as African American, Caucasian/white, or Hispanic. The net sample for this study consisted of first-time, full-time, two-year college respondents from a total of 73 community colleges across the U.S. Over three-fourths of the student sample was white ($n = 15,614$), while 11.3% was Hispanic ($n = 2,300$) and approximately 12% ($n = 2,425$) was African American, comprising the total sample of 20,339.

Variables of Interest

The current study examined the relationship between the dependent variable (attitudes toward affirmative action in college admissions) and five sets of independent variables. The dependent variable, "Affirmative action in college admissions should be abolished," was coded as $0 =$ disagree and $1 =$ agree to conduct logistic regression analysis. The independent variables were organized into four categories: student demographics, educational plans, self-interest, and racial ideologies.

It was of primary interest to assess community college student intentions to obtain the baccalaureate or beyond in correspondence with views on affirmative action in college admissions. For this investigation, student demographics reflect race/ethnicity, gender, age, parents' highest level of education, annual family income, enrollment status, and political ideologies. The self-interest construct referred to academic preparedness (i.e., GPA), college choice and ability to finance education. Educational plans consisted of three independent variables that pertain to chances of getting a bachelor's degree, transferring to another college, and highest degree intentions. Students identifying "other" as their highest degree planned were retained for multivariate analyses to curb the total number of cases rejected due to missing data under the assumption that a degree was desired that may not be equivalent to the response options provided. Finally, racial ideologies included student responses regarding cross-race socializing, the degree to which racial discrimination is still considered a problem, and opinions on promoting racial understanding.

Data Analysis and Limitations

Cross tabulations/Chi-Square were utilized for descriptive analysis. Logistic regression methods were used to examine the relationship between the dichotomous dependent variable and the independent variables. As in any study there are limitations, and it was not possible within the confines of this secondary analysis to investigate the myriad factors that may influence community college students' attitudes toward affirmative action in college admissions. Due to the variables of interest being limited to the CIRP data set, it is possible that the factors used for this investigation are not an exhaustive representation of the total possible determinants of affirmative action policy beliefs.

Though this study is robust in sample size, it would be inappropriate to consider the findings representative of how all community college students feel about affirmative action in admissions. This study is limited to the use of the 1996 CIRP data set. It is the only[4] normative sample of community college students drawn from the first year CIRP collected data from community college freshmen.

Findings

Descriptive Analysis of the Sample[5]

In the sample of 20,339, three-fourths of the student sample was white, while 11.3% was Hispanic, and approximately 12% was African American, Overall, females represented the majority of the total sample, comprising 55.4% of the students. With regard to students' age, 2% of students were under 18 years of age with roughly 80% of students being of traditional college age (between 18–24 years old) and 17% of students reported being 25 years old or older. Self-reported measures of family income revealed 34.7% of students were from families with an annual income of $30,000 to $59,999. Twenty percent indicated annual family incomes from $15,000 to $29,999. However, parents earning under $15,000 and those with incomes of $60,000 or more each accounted for 17% of the sample.

In addressing the highest educational attainment of their parents, 27.5% of students had one or both parents who were high school graduates, but roughly 13% of students' parents had educational attainment less than high school. About 23% of parents had completed some college whereas 23.6% were college graduates and 11.5% of students reported parents' highest educational level as a graduate degree. In terms of their own enrollment in community colleges, 85% of the participants indicated being full-time students.

For the overall sample, 54% of students indicated being bipartisan in that they were in the "middle of the road" in reference to their political views. However, 20.5% reported being conservative, while 19.7% said they were liberal. Less than 2% of students stated their political ideologies as being far right and around 4% referred to themselves as far left.

In conjunction with educational plans, over 50% of students stated there was a very good chance they would get bachelor's degrees, with another 30.3% reporting some chance they would earn a bachelor's degree. In the CIRP Freshman Survey, students were asked if they intended to transfer to another college. Roughly 33% stated there was no chance that they would transfer and almost 20% reported very little chance of transferring. Accordingly, 47% of students indicated there was some to a very good chance they would transfer to another institution. One-third of students indicated they had no intentions to transfer, which may be attributed to over two-thirds of the sample attending their first choice college.

Over half of students reported having high school grade point averages (GPAs) in the B range, and over 67% reported academic preparedness of B- or better. Reinforcing findings regarding their chances of earning a bachelor's degree, the vast majority of students aspired to attain degrees beyond the two-year level. About one-third of respondents aspired to the baccalaureate as the highest degree planned, while another one-third aspired to attain master's degrees, and almost 14% desired doctoral or professional degrees.

Nearly one-quarter of the students expressed a major concern about their ability to finance their education. While 45% had some concerns over financing their education, 30.7% did not have any concerns regarding college costs. The overwhelming majority of students (97%) were enrolled at historically white two-year institutions of higher learning, and 85% was enrolled in public colleges. A little over half reported attendance at colleges with high enrollments, with about one-quarter at medium-sized and 21.9% and .7% of students at colleges with small or very small enrollments, respectively.

With respect to racial attitudes, only 27% of the students felt it was not important to promote racial understanding. Thirty-nine percent thought promoting racial understanding was somewhat important, and roughly 34% of the students indicated that it was very important or essential. Fifty-five percent of the students frequently engaged in socializing with members of different racial/ethnic groups. Nevertheless, approximately 18% of the students agreed somewhat or strongly that racial discrimination was no longer a problem in society.

In a cross tabulation, it was found that students of color favored the role of affirmative action in college admissions more than white students. Overall, fewer males in each racial/ethnic group supported retaining affirmative action in college admissions than women.

Multivariate Analysis

The second research question asked to what extent gender, educational plans, self-interest, and racial ideologies predict affirmative action attitudes in college admissions. Logistic regression analysis was conducted with the dichotomous dependent variable being agreement or disagreement with abolishing affirmative action in college admissions. The independent variables were characterized in blocks with student demographics as block 1, block 2 as educational plans; block 3 as self-interest, and racial ideologies as block 4. Separate logistic regression analyses were conducted for males and females to determine the impact of the independent variables on the likelihood of support for abolishing affirmative action in college admissions for each sex. Below I highlight only the relationships among the variables that showed statistical significance.

Logistic Regression Results: Males[6]

The first model of logistic regression found that the likelihood of male students of color favoring dismantling affirmative action were lower than the likelihood of their white counterparts. Higher annual family income was a predictor of higher likelihood of favoring abolishing affirmative action in college admissions. Men espousing more liberal political views had a lower likelihood of agreeing with abolishing affirmative action in college admissions, illustrating the significant effect of political views on affirmative action attitudes.

In the second model, block 1 and 2 variables were entered in the second logistic regression model, revealing five independent variables associated with attitudes toward affirmative action at a statistically significant level. In examining the exponentiation of B, the findings suggest that African American and Hispanic male students had lower likelihood of disfavoring affirmative action in college admissions than their white male counterparts. Higher income for males was associated with a slightly higher likelihood of rejecting affirmative action.

The likelihood of being an opponent of affirmative action in college admissions decreased as male students held more liberal views. Also in model 2, the addition of transfer intent helped in the ability to predict support for affirmative action abolition in college admissions, suggesting that males indicating higher chances of transfer had greater likelihood for supporting abolishing affirmative action.

Chi-square analysis yielded a significant improvement in fit for males from model 1 ($\chi^2 = 168.071$, df = 7, $p = .000$) to model 2 ($\chi^2 = 15.315$, df = 3, $p = .002$). In comparison to model 1 that classified 58.08% of males favored dismantling affirmative action; the introduction of block 2 educational aspiration variables resulted in a model of best fit classification that was slightly higher at 58.24%.

In the third model, the overall percentage classified correctly rose marginally for males to 58.56% with the addition of the self-interest variables. Chi-square was conducted in an attempt to examine the intersections and relationship if any, of independent variables with the dependent variable. The Chi-square yielded a significant fit for males in model 3 ($\chi^2 = 11.359$, df = 3, $p = .01$). In this model, race/ethnicity, annual family income, and political views continued to significantly impact the likelihood of males supporting abolishing affirmative action in college admissions. Specifically, white males with higher family incomes and more conservative political views had higher likelihood of supporting abolishing affirmative action.

Stronger intent to transfer continued to be significantly associated with increased likelihood of support for abolishing affirmative action for male students. In addition, the better grades male students earned, the more likely they were to agree with removing affirmative action in college admissions. Thus, in model 3, the likelihood increased about 20% for each one-point increase in the GPA scale, as coded. College choice and concern about ability to finance education were not statistically significant in predicting the likelihood of affirmative action resistance for two-year male students.

In the full model, adding the block of variables representing racial ideologies yielded a significant chi-square improvement in model fit for males ($\chi^2 = 49.265$, df = 3, $p = .000$). The overall percentage classified correctly for the final equation was 58.84% for male students. Therefore with the addition of block 4 variables, the percentage of male students classified correctly varied little from the previous model. Considering the final equation for males, students of color, students from lower income families, and those espousing more liberal political views were more favorable to maintaining affirmative action in college admissions in the final equation.

Higher high school GPAs and greater chances of transfer increased the likelihood of disfavoring affirmative action in college admissions among male students with the addition of the racial ideology variables. Also with regard to the racial ideologies variables, for each one-point increase in the variable "racial discrimination no longer being a major problem in America," there was a 26% increase in the likelihood of males opposing affirmative action in college admissions. However, neither cross-race socializing nor promoting racial understanding had an impact on the likelihood of male support for abolishing affirmative action.

Logistic Regression Results: Females

In the first model for female students, significant effects were found for race/ethnicity and political views. The likelihood of female students of color favoring affirmative action dismantling was lower than the likelihood of their white female counterparts. Those espousing more liberal political views had lower likelihood of agreeing with doing away with affirmative action in college admissions. The overall percentage classified correctly in the first model including student demographics was 61.50% for females resulting in significant model fit ($\chi^2 = 117.517$, df $= 7$, $p = .000$).

The overall percentage classified correctly in model 2 rose slightly to 61.81% for females. The fit of the model was still better than chance (model $2\chi^2 = 124.340$, df $= 10$, $p = .000$), but illustrated no improvement in fit over the first model ($\chi^2 = 6.823$, df $= 3$, $p = .078$). Therefore, educational aspiration variables did not add to the ability of student demographics to predict attitudes of women toward affirmative action in college admissions.

While none of the block 2 variables were significant in impacting likelihood of support for abolishing affirmative action in college admissions for female students, race/ethnicity and political views continued to produce significant effects in the second model. In examining the Exp(B) or exponentiation of B in model 2, the findings suggest that African American and Hispanic female students had lower likelihood of disfavoring affirmative action in college admissions in comparison to white females. No significant impact of age on the likelihood of support for abolishing affirmative action for female students was found. Higher annual family income was not significantly associated with higher likelihood of rejecting affirmative action for females. In addition, the likelihood of being an opponent of affirmative action in college admissions decreased as female students held more liberal views.

The overall percentage classified correctly fell slightly for females (61.70%) with the addition of self-interest variables in model 3 (i.e., GPA, college choice, and concern regarding ability to finance education), but the block of variables representing self-interest produced a significant increase in model fit ($\chi^2 = 12.108$, df $= 3$, $p = .007$). The effect of race/ethnicity and political views continued to be significant on female attitudes toward affirmative action in college admissions in this third model.

Of the self-interest measures, college choice was statistically significant in predicting the likelihood of affirmative action disapproval among female two-year students. More specifically, the likelihood of resisting affirmative action increased 1.1109 times among female students entering a second choice institution as compared to their first choice, and this increase occurred for each lower choice institution beyond that for this predictor variable. The block of variables representing racial ideologies was added to the full model yielding a significant chi-square for improvement in model fit for females ($\chi^2 = 61.745$, df $= 3$, $p = .000$). The overall percentage classified correctly for the final equation was 62.88% for female students. Considering the final equation for female students, African American and Hispanic students remained more supportive of retaining affirmative action than white females. Female students with more liberal political views were more favorable to maintaining affirmative action in college admissions. Being enrolled at an institution that was a lower choice college appeared to increase female opposition toward affirmative action. With regard to the racial ideology variables, for each one-point increase in the variable of "racial discrimination no longer being a major problem in America," there was a 33% increase in the likelihood of female students being opposed to affirmative action in college admissions.

Conclusion

Overall, the findings of this study illustrate that relative to student demographics, race/ethnicity was a significant predictor of attitudes toward affirmative action in college admissions for both male and female community college students in each logistic regression. Males were less favorable toward affirmative action than females. Overall, white males largely accounted for those most opposed to affirmative action in college admissions.

Similar to prior research, the results of this study reveal that African Americans and Hispanics approve of affirmative action at higher rates than do their white counterparts (Meader, 1998; Smith, 1998, 2006; Zamani, 2002; Zamani-Gallaher, 2006). However, in contrast to Sax and Arredondo's study (1999), which utilized 1995 CIRP data with four-year collegians, the authors found no statistically significant effect of annual family income on Hispanic or African American community college students' support for affirmative action in college admissions. Furthermore, previous research noted African American support for affirmative action is more consistent, while Hispanic support is less cohesive and more complex (Smith, 1998, 2006). Perhaps differences between African Americans and Hispanics in supporting affirmative action stem from the history behind today's affirmative action and the unique experiences of each group (i.e., the legacy of slavery endured by African Americans and more recent disenfranchisement of voluntary Hispanic immigrants).

Annual family income and political views were the only additional background characteristics shown statistically significant in predicting affirmative action attitudes regarding college admissions for male students in each model with the addition of other independent variables. Additionally, political views were always significant for males. As for females, annual family income as indicative of socioeconomic status was never significantly related to affirmative action attitudes. With student demographics controlled, there was no effect of educational plans on affirmative action attitudes for female students. Still transfer intent as a measure of educational plans was found to be a predictor of the likelihood of male support for abolishing affirmative action in college admissions. In particular, opposition of male students toward affirmative action in college admissions increased as intent to transfer rose.

With the addition of self-interest variables, GPA was found to affect the likelihood of male support for abolishing affirmative action while controlling for student demographics and education aspiration variables. Among male students, the higher their GPA, there was greater likelihood to support abolishing affirmative action in college admissions. Unlike males, college choice was the self-interest variable found to significantly impact the likelihood of female support for abolishing affirmative action. As female students attended lower choice institutions, the greater were the likelihood of their favor for abolishing affirmative action in college admissions. Having controlled for the effects of student demographics, educational plans, and self-interest, views on racial discrimination was the only racial ideology variable in the final equation that significantly predicted the likelihood support of affirmative action abolishment in college admissions for both male and female students.

While little research has examined student attitudes toward affirmative action in college admissions (Amirkhan, Betancourt, Graham, Lopez, & Weiner 1995; Bowen & Bok, 1998; Sax & Arredondo, 1999), even less is known about community college student affirmative action attitudes, particularly those seeking transfer in pursuit of bachelor's degrees. This study illustrates race/ethnicity, gender, annual family income, political views, GPA, and views on racial discrimination influenced the likelihood of agreeing with abolishing affirmative action in college admissions among community college baccalaureate aspirants.

In sum, the community college makes sense for a growing number of students because it is often the most academically, geographically, and financially accessible to women and students of color (Townsend, 1999). It seems particularly relevant to consider baccalaureate aspiring, two-year student affirmative action attitudes in college admissions, given the inequities by social background (i.e., along racial, gender, and class lines) faced by many of its attendants (Dougherty & Kienzl, 2006). More specifically, understanding both two-and four-year student views of affirmative action in college admissions may assist educational leaders in establishing or revising policies and programming efforts as tools for enhancing campus diversity such as: (1) to take a clear stance on diversity, (2) to articulate a clear message to campus constituents, (3) to communicate with the press by educating the media on your diversity initiatives, (4) to foster ongoing dialogues within the campus community, and (5) to use a leadership team approach in revising and/or correcting failed diversity practices (Zamani-Gallaher, Green, Brown, & Stovall, forthcoming).

The opinions of community college students on social policies as well as their knowledge regarding a wide range of political issues are often neglected in the larger discourse. The findings of this study have implications for how community colleges and four-year institutions promote access via the transfer track. It is unclear whether support among two-year students for affirmative action in college admissions in this study was based on it being generalized, that is, not framed as race-, gender- or class-targeted. Research by Roska, Grodsky, and Horn (2006) found that in the ten years since Proposition 209 passed in California, racial/ethnic minority students did not increase their reliance on utilizing the transfer function as a pathway to the baccalaureate. The researchers found that transfer among African American and Hispanic students has declined post-Proposition 209 (particularly to the elite University of California system in contrast to California State Universities). Thus, additional attention should be paid to articulation initiatives and collaborative programs between two- and four-year institutions that seek to invigorate the transfer function as a means of increasing educational opportunities and outcomes for underserved and underrepresented students of color.

Perhaps future studies could seek to further examine community college student attitudes toward affirmative action in admissions as well as to gauge support based on the type of affirmative action effort (e.g., gender-specific, race-based, or need-targeted). In addition, research utilizing qualitative methods of inquiry may be useful in more fully exploring the degree to which students have been exposed to affirmative action, the extent to which they consider themselves potential beneficiaries, or their awareness of the ongoing debate surrounding its use in college admissions.

Notes

1. The terms "community college" and "two-year institution" are used interchangeably in this article.
2. California State Education Code P.M.3.02 Equal Employment Opportunity and Affirmative Action.
3. Michigan's Proposal 2 prohibits public institutions from using affirmative action programs that give consideration to groups or individuals based on their race, gender, color, ethnicity, or national origin relative to employment, education, or contracting purposes. The public institutions affected by the proposal include state government, local governments, public colleges and universities, community colleges, and school districts.
4. There had been a virtual end to data collection from two-year respondents in 2003 due to consistent low participation in the administration of the survey during 1997–2003. The 1996 data is the most robust, representative sample as there was a significant decline in community colleges participating in the years that followed. Therefore, in spite of the limitations, the data reported in this article coincide with the retrenchment trend toward of affirmative action of the last decade; and is the best available data-to-date for quantitatively exploring the attitudes of community college student attitudes toward affirmative action (W. Korn, Associate Director for Operations, personal communication, August 16, 2006). Due to space limitations, readers are invited to contact me directly for a copy of the analysis tables.
5. Due to limitations of space here, please contact the author for the table of demographic data.
6. Please contact the author for the regression tables.

References

American Association of Community Colleges. (2006). *Community college fact sheet.* Retrieved April 10, 2007, from http://www.aacc.nche.edu/Content/NavigationMenu/AboutCommunityColleges/Fast_Facts1/Fast_Facts.htm

Amirkhan, J., Betancourt, H., Graham, S., Lopez, S. R., & Weiner, B. (1995). Reflection on affirmative action goals in psychology admissions. *Psychological Science, 6*(3), 140–148.

Barnes, E. (1996). Community college becomes battleground for complaint about privately funded scholarship. *Black Issues in Higher Education, 13*(16), 8–10.

Bobo, L., & Kluegel J. R. (1993). Opposition to race-targeting: Self-interest, stratification ideology, or racial attitudes? *American Sociological Review, 58*(4), 443–464.

Bobo, L., & Smith, R. A. (1994). Antipoverty policy, affirmative action, and racial attitudes. In S. Danziger, G. Sandefur, & D. Weinberg (Eds.), *Confronting poverty: Prescriptions for change* (pp. 365–395). New York: Russell Sage.

Bowen, W. G., & Bok, D. (1998). *The shape of the river: Long-term consequences of considering race in college and university admissions.* Princeton, NJ: Princeton University.

Brint, S., & Karabel, J. (1989). American education, meritocratic ideology, and the legitimization of inequality: The community college and the problem of American exceptionalism. *Higher Education, 18*(6), 725–735.

Brown v. the Board of Education, Topeka, Kansas. (1954). 347 U.S. 483, 98 L.Ed. 873, 74 S.Ct. 686.

Burdman, P. (2003). Taking an alternative route. *Black Issues in Higher Education, 20*(14), 32–35.

Camarena v. San Bernardino Community College District (1995). No. CIV-S-95-589

Caso, A. T., & Corry, R. J. (1996). Whites need not apply: The conservative Pacific Legal Foundation challenges college classes designed exclusively for minorities. *California Lawyer, 16*(9), 42–45.

Chiang, S. (1998). UCLA feeder program takes sting out of anti-affirmative action policies. *Black Issues in Higher Education, 15*(16), 12–13.

Civil Rights Act of 1964. (1964). Pub. L. 88–352, 78 Stat. 252, 42 U.S.C. §2000d. Cohen, A. M., & Brawer, F. B. (2003). *The American community college* (4th ed.). San Francisco: Jossey-Bass.

Community College Survey of Student Engagement. (2005). *Final report.* Retrieved November 22, 2006, from http://www.ccsse.org/publications/CCSSE_reportfinal2005.pdf

Crosby, F. J. (2006). Understanding affirmative action. *Annual Review of Psychology, 57,* 585–611.

Darden, M. L., Cloud, R.C., & Illich, P. (2003, April). *What senior citizens want from the community college.* Paper presented at the annual meeting of the Council for the Study of Community Colleges, Dallas, TX.

DeMitchell, T. A. (2004). Employment issues in the community college. *New Directions for Community Colleges No. 125* (pp. 29–39). San Francisco: Jossey-Bass.

Dougherty, K. (1987). The effects of community colleges: Aid or hindrance to socioeconomic attainment? *Sociology of Education, 60*(2), 86–103.

Dougherty, K. J. (1992). Community colleges and baccalaureate attainment. *The Journal of Higher Education, 63*(2), 188–214.

Dougherty, K. J. (1994). *The contradictory college: The conflicting origins, impacts, and future of the community college.* Albany: State University of New York.

Dougherty, K. J., & Kienzl, G. S. (2006). It's not enough to get through the open door: Inequalities by social background in transfer from community colleges to four-year colleges. *Teachers College Record, 108*(3),452–487.

Dovidio, J. F., Mann, J. A., & Gaertner, S. L. (1989). Resistance to affirmative action: The implication of aversive racism. In F. A. Blanchard & F. J. Crosby (Eds.), *Affirmative action in perspective* (pp. 83–102). New York: Springer-Verlag.

Eckes, S. E. (2004). Race-conscious admissions programs: Where do universities go from Gratz and Grutter? 33 *Journal of Law & Education* 21.

Fleming, J. E., Gill, G. R., & Swinton, D. H. (1978). *The case for affirmative action for blacks in higher education.* Washington, DC: Howard University Press.

Gallego, A. P. (1998). Proposition 209 and Hopwood make transfer education crucial. *Community College Journal, 68*(6), 4.

Grutter v. Bollinger. (2003). 539 US 306.

Hebel, S. (2000, May 26). States without affirmative action focus on community-college transfers. *The Chronicle of Higher Education,* pp. A35–A37.

Howard, J. R. (1997). Affirmative action in historical perspective. In M. Garcia (Ed.), *Affirmative action's testament of hope: Strategies for a new era in higher education* (pp. 19–45). Albany: State University of New York Press.

Hugo, E. B. (2001). Dual enrollment for underrepresented student populations. *New Directions for Community Colleges No. 113* (pp. 67–72). San Francisco: Jossey-Bass.

Jackman, M. R. (1996). Individualism, self-interest, and white racism. *Social Science Quarterly, 77*(4), 760–767.

Johnston, G. H. (1997). *Piecing together the "mosaic called diversity": One community college's experience with hiring a more diverse faculty.* Unpublished dissertation. University of Illinois at Urbana-Champaign.

Keener, B. J. (1994). Capturing the community college market. *Currents, 20*(5), 38–43.

Laanan, F. S. (2001). Transfer students adjustment. *New Directions for Community Colleges No. 114* (pp. 5–13). San Francisco: Jossey-Bass.

Lin, N. (1990). Social resources and social mobility: A structural theory of status attainment. In R. L. Breiger (Ed.), *Social mobility and social structure* (pp. 247–271). New York: Cambridge University.

Lindsay, J. M., & Singer, A. (2003). *Changing faces: Immigrants and diversity in the twenty-first century.* Retrieved October 13, 2006, from http://www.brookings.edu/views/papers/lindsay/20030601.pdf

Meader, E. W. (1998, November). *College student attitudes toward diversity and race based policies.* Paper presented at the annual meeting of the Association for the Study of Higher Education, Miami, FL.

National Center for Education Statistics. (1997). *Transfer behavior among beginning postsecondary students: 1989–94.* Washington, DC: U.S. Department of Education, Office of Educational Research and Improvement.

National Center for Education Statistics. (2003). *Community college students: Goals, academic preparation and outcomes.* Retrieved April 12, 2007, from http://nces.ed.gov/pubs2003/2003164.pdf

O'Brien, M. (2006, June 14). Preferences preferred: Michigan Republicans line up to oppose the MCRI. *National Review Online,* Retrieved August 22, 2006, from http//:article.nationalreview.com/print/?=NWNjMDM0ZmFmMzYyYjk3ZjBiOGZ1Y

Olson, E. (2006, October 24). Community colleges want you. *The New York Times,* p. G2.

Pascarella, E. T., Edison, M., Nora, A., Hagedorn, L. S., & Terenzini, P. T. (1998). Does community college attendance versus four-year college attendance influence students' educational plans? *Journal of College Student Development, 39* (2), 179–193.

Phillippe, K., & Sullivan, M. (2005). *National profile of community colleges: Trends and statistics* (4th ed.). Washington, DC: Community College Press.

Rendon, L. I., & Hope, R. O. (1996). *Educating a new majority: Transforming American's educational system for diversity.* San Francisco: Jossey-Bass.

Roska, J., Grodsky, E., & Hom, W. (2006, October). *The role of community colleges in promoting student diversity in California.* Paper presented for the Equal Opportunity in Higher Education: Proposition 209–Past and Future Conference, University of California, Berkeley, CA.

Rubio, P. F. (2001). *A history of affirmative action 1619–2000.* Jackson, MI: University Press of Mississippi.

Sax, L. J., & Arredondo, M. (1999). Student attitudes toward affirmative action in college admissions. *Research in Higher Education, 40*(4), 439–459.

Sax, L. J., Astin, A. W., Korn, W. S., & Mahoney, K. (1996). *The American freshman: National norms for Fall 1996.* Los Angeles: Higher Education Research Institute, University of California, Los Angeles.

Schmidt, P. (1998, December 11). California judge upholds law allowing 2-year colleges to use hiring preferences. *The Chronicle of Higher Education,* p. A52.

Schmidt, P. (2001, September 14). California court strikes down minority-hiring gorals for community colleges. *The Chronicle of Higher Education,* p. A29.

Smith, W. A. (1998). Gender and racial/ethnic differences in the affirmative action attitudes of U.S. college students. *Journal of Negro Education, 67*(2), 127–141.

Smith, W. A. (2006). Racial ideology and affirmative action support in a diverse college student population. *Journal of Negro Education, 75*(4), 589–605.

Spann, G. A. (2000). *The law of affirmative action: Twenty-five years of Supreme Court decisions on race and remedies.* New York: New York University Press.

Strauss, A. L. (2005). *The contexts of social mobility, ideology and theory.* New York: Aldine De Gruyter.

Townsend, B. (1999). *Two-year colleges for women and minorities: Enabling access to the baccalaureate.* New York: Falmer.

Trick, R. (2004, February 6). Race bill unlikely to see action. *The UW Daily Online.* Retrieved May 6, 2006, from http://www.adversity.net/washington/i200_news.htm

U.S. Bureau of the Census. (2002). *Population division, population projections branch. Retrieved September 12, 2005, from* http://www.census.gov/population/www/projections/natsum-T5.html

U.S. Bureau of the Census. (2005). *American community survey: Population and housing narrative profile.* Retrieved November 22, 2006, from http://factfinder.census.gov/servlet/NPTable?_bm=y&-geo_id=01000US&-qr_name=ACS_2005_EST_G00_NP01&-ds_name =&-redoLog = false

Wright, S. W. (1997). Private scholarships for minorities challenged. *Black Issues in Higher Education, 14*(5), 14–16.

Zamani, E. M. (2000). Sources and information regarding effective retention strategies for students of color. *New Directions for Community Colleges, No. 112* (pp. 95–104). San Francisco: Jossey-Bass.

Zamani, E. M. (2002). Exploring racial policy views of college-age white Americans: Implications for campus climate. In R. Moore (Ed.), *The quality and quantity of contact between black and white collegians* (pp. 160–185). New York: Mellen.

Zamani, E. M. (2006). African American student affairs professionals in community college settings: A commentary for future research (reprint). In B. K. Townsend, D. D. Bragg, K. Dougherty, F. S. Laanan, & B. V. Laden (Eds.), *ASHE reader on community colleges* (3rd ed., pp. 173–180). Boston, MA: Pearson.

Zamani-Gallaher, E. M. (2006, November). *Cultural competency and affirmative action attitudes of graduate/professional students.* Paper presented at the annual meeting of the Association for the Study of Higher Education, Anaheim, CA.

Zamani-Gallaher, E. M., Green, D. O., Brown, M. C., & Stovall, D. O. (forthcoming). *The case for affirmative action on campus: Concepts of equity, considerations for practice.* Sterling, VA: Stylus.

Achieving Equitable Educational Outcomes with All Students: The Institution's Roles and Responsibilities

Georgia L. Bauman, Leticia Tomas Bustillos,
and Estela Mara Bensimon
Center for Urban Education
Rossier School of Education, University of Southern California

M. Christopher Brown II and RoSusan D. Bartee
Frederick D. Patterson Research Institute

Introduction

In a stirring speech delivered at Howard University shortly after the passage of the 1964 Civil Rights Act, President Lyndon B. Johnson proclaimed, "We seek not just freedom, but opportunity. We seek not just legal equality but human ability. Not just equality as a right and a theory, but equality as a fact and equality as a result" (Johnson 1965). For the intended beneficiaries of the act, "equality as a fact and equality as a result" remains mostly unrealized. On virtually every indicator of economic and social well-being, students historically underrepresented in higher education—by which we mean African American, Latino/a, and Native American students[1]—lag well behind white students and also some Asian American students.[2] In spite of encouraging headlines about record numbers of African Americans and Latino/as enrolling in college, the reality is that, in terms of access as well as degree completion, the gap is now larger than it was at the time of Johnson's famous declaration (Renner 2003). Evidence of these inequities has been revealed in numerous research studies that report bleak outcomes in higher education as well as bleak future prospects for African Americans and Latino/as in the United States (Barton 2003; Carnevale and Fry 2000; Fry 2002).

For those of us who witnessed the birth of the civil rights movement and viewed education as the prime engine for social as well as economic mobility in the United States, these trends are both appalling and frustrating. One is moved to ask, how is it that forty years later, in spite of initiatives of all kinds, progress toward equality in higher education participation and completion has been so slow and so small? How is it that institutions take pride in the racial and ethnic diversity of their student bodies yet are incapable of producing equitable results for some of the very students who make diversity possible?

In this paper, we regard the challenge of narrowing the college education gap and achieving equitable educational outcomes for historically underrepresented students as a problem of institutional responsibility and performance rather than as a problem that is exclusively related to student accountability, motivation, and academic preparation. We have chosen to emphasize inequality as a question of institutional responsibility because the majority of studies on college student success take the opposite perspective. These studies focus on characteristics such as students' social and academic integration (Braxton and Lein 2000; Tinto 1987), student involvement (Astin 1999), intensity of their high school curriculum (Adelman 1999), lack of cultural capital (Bourdieu 1985), and other risk factors associated with poor performance. Because of this, we tend to accept the findings at face value without considering the possibility of deficits at the *institutional* level. While we agree that students must accept responsibility for their own success or failure, we also believe that institutional actors, particularly faculty members, also bear individual and collective responsibility for student outcomes.[3]

This paper describes:

- key national indicators of a race/ethnicity-based achievement gap;
- one tool to help college and university leaders assess and rectify race/ethnicity-based achievement gaps on their campuses.

Our premise is that gathering evidence of student outcomes disaggregated by race/ethnicity can be an effective and powerful means of raising awareness of a problem and motivating institutional actors to seek a solution. To illustrate the connection between evidence and such institutional motivation, we provide a case study of Loyola Marymount University (LMU), a Jesuit institution located in Los Angeles, California. LMU is one of fourteen initial partner campuses in an action research project on equitable educational outcomes. The project is supported by a grant from The James Irvine Foundation and directed by the Center for Urban Education[4] at the University of Southern California.

The Achievement Gap: *What Is It?*

The achievement gap is a phenomenon that occurs early in childhood and persists through adulthood. In *The Black-White Test Score Gap*, Jencks and Phillips (1998) point out that the achievement gap between African American and white students is evident prior to entering kindergarten and continues through secondary and postsecondary educational levels. Second- and third-grade test scores and grades reveal that African American and Latino/a students trail behind white and Asian students (College Board 1999). The most recent National Assessment of Educational Progress test (NAEP 2003), which is given to fourth and eighth graders nationwide, indicates that African Americans and Latino/as continue to lag behind their white and Asian peers in both reading and mathematics. As Derek Bok notes, "the [achievement] gap is nationwide, it is substantial, and it has not diminished in the last 15 years" (2003, 20).

In fact, the American Council on Education's *Minorities in Higher Education 2002–2003: 20th Annual Status Report* (Harvey 2003) clearly illustrates a *growing* achievement gap between minority and white students in higher education. Some of the key findings indicate that while the total college enrollment of minority students has increased by 122 percent in the past twenty years, the gap in college participation between white students and particular groups of minority students has widened. In 1978–1980, among white, Latino/a, and African American 18–24 year old high school graduates, the college participation rate for each group was approximately 30 percent. By 1998–2000, the college participation rate for white high school graduates in this age bracket had risen to 46 percent, compared to 40 percent for African Americans and 34 percent for Latino/as in this same age bracket (Harvey 2003). In a press release for the report, author William B. Harvey, vice president of the American Council on Education (ACE) and director of the Center for Advancement of Racial and Ethnic Equity (formerly the ACE Office of Minorities in Higher Education), notes, "The 20th anniversary *Status Report* challenges us to recognize the demographic, political, and social realities of the 21st century. The data tell us how far we have come in our quest for educational excellence for all students, but also caution us that equity in education for all Americans remains a goal that we must strive to reach" (American Council on Education 2003).

Figure 1 shows the percentages of students enrolled in college the October following their high school graduation in the years 1972–2001. The figure shows a much more erratic pattern of college enrollment for African American and Latino/a students than for white students. For example, in 1993 and 1997, the gap in enrollment between white and Latino/a students nearly closed, but significant drops in enrollment occurred for Latino/as following each of these years. In 2000, Latino/as had an approximate 10 percent increase in enrollment, but they nonetheless remained below the percentages of white students enrolled.

In 1987, the enrollment gap between African American and white students was similar to the gap that existed in 1980, but in the intervening years, the gap was significantly wider—at a time

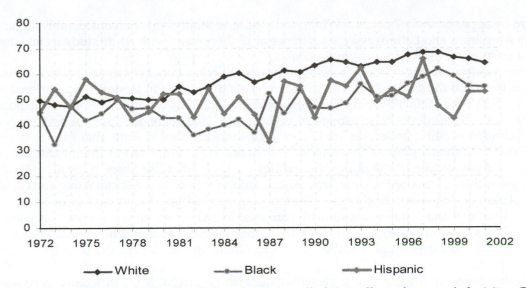

Figure 1   Percentage of high school completers enrolled in college, by race/ethnicity: October 1972–2001.

Source: U.S. Department of Commerce, Bureau of the Census, October Current Population Surveys, 1972–2001, in NCES 2003. *The Condition of Education*, 127. Available at http://nces.ed.gov/pubs2003/2003067.pdf.

when white student enrollment stayed above 50 percent and, in many years, increased. By 2001, the gap between African Americans and whites was approximately 9 percent. Overall, although Latino/as and African Americans have demonstrated gains in enrollment at various points in the last thirty years, the gains have not been sustained. Throughout this period, there were no major drops in the enrollment rates for whites.

Figure 2 shows the bachelor's degree completion of African Americans and Latino/as lagging appreciably behind whites. Overall, in the last thirty years, the number of degrees conferred to African Americans went up by approximately 8 percent and the number conferred to Latino/as

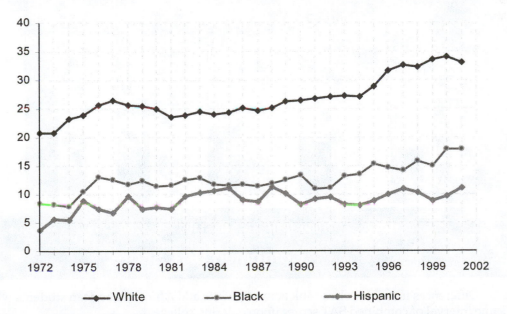

Figure 2   Percentage of the 25- to 29-year-old population with a Bachelor's degree or higher, by race/ethnicity: March 1971–2000.

Source: U.S. Department of Commerce, Bureau of the Census, March Current Population Surveys, 1971–2001, in NCES 2002. *The Condition of Education*, 174. Available at http://nces.ed.gov/pubs2002/2002025.pdf.

went up by approximately 7 percent. White student degree attainment was considerably larger than African Americans and Latino/as by a difference of 15–20 percent, with white students making significant gains in the last eight years in particular.

When confronted with data that show differences in educational outcomes by race, a visceral reaction, based on the assumption that the gaps reflect differences in students' educational backgrounds, is to ask whether "input" measures were considered. Although we do not dispute the fact that minority students concentrated in underfunded and segregated school districts have a high likelihood of being underprepared for college, there are data to show that gaps may persist regardless of academic preparation. One of the clearest representations of the magnitude of the achievement gap can be found in Bowen and Bok's widely cited *The Shape of the River* (1998), in which the authors compare the class graduation ranks of whites and African Americans who entered college with the same SAT scores. The bar graph reproduced below as Figure 3 shows that African American and white students with comparable SAT scores ended up with very unequal class rankings. Bowen and Bok's most discouraging finding was that white students with SAT scores below 1000 earned higher GPAs on average than African Americans with SAT scores of 1300 and higher.

Another aspect of the gap that is becoming increasingly critical is the difference in college enrollment between females and males. Almost 8 million women participate in higher education at all levels annually, compared to only 6.3 million men (King 2000). African American students are particularly affected by this growing trend in enrollment. Table 1 shows the enrollment increases of African American and white students according to gender. Since 1976, African American women have demonstrated significant gains in undergraduate, graduate, and professional enrollments. Comparatively, African American males have demonstrated only nominal increases over the last twenty-five years.

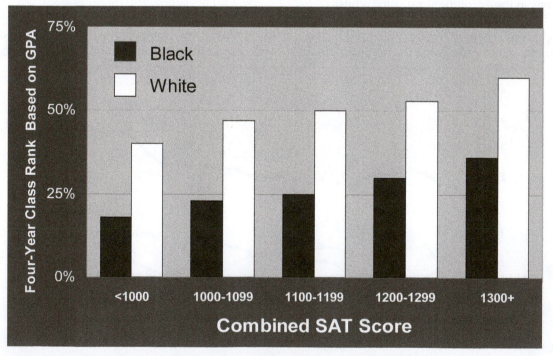

Figure 3   Differences in college class rank between white and African American students who were in the same interval of combined SAT scores upon entering college.

Source: Bowen, W. G., and D. Bok. 1998. *The shape of the river: Long-term consequences of considering race in college and university admissions.* Princeton, NJ: Princeton University Press.

TABLE 1

Higher Education Enrollment Increases by Race, Gender, and Level of Study, 1976–2000

Degree Level	African American Women	African American Men	White Women	White Men
Undergraduate	+94%	+36%	+38%	-1%
Graduate	+69%	+21%	+16%	-24%
Professional	+236%	+36%	+58%	-25%

Source: Frederick D. Patterson Research Institute analysis of IPEDS data, 2002. www.patterson-uncf.org/home.htm

TABLE 2

Enrollment of African American College Students at All Institutions and at Historically Black Colleges and Universities and College Fund Institutions, by Gender: Fall 1990, 1995, and 2000

African Americans Attending:	1990		1995		2000	
	Men	Women	Men	Women	Men	Women
All Institutions						
Number	484,700	762,300	555,911	917,761	640,354	1,099,934
Percent	39%	61%	38%	62%	37%	63%
Historically Black Colleges and Universities						
Number	82,897	125,785	90,130	136,391	86,410	134,958
Percent	40%	60%	40%	60%	39%	61%
College Fund Institutions						
Number	20,484	29,375	20,143	31,069	23,066	35,121
Percent	41%	59%	39%	61%	40%	60%

Source: *United Negro College Fund 2001 Statistical Report,* Frederick D. Patterson Research Institute, 2002.

In recent years, as table 2 indicates, women consistently represented approximately 60 percent of the total African American student population at all institutions, including historically black colleges and universities (Hurst 2002). In 2000, African American women attending all institutions represented 63 percent of the total African American student enrollment, while they represented 61 and 60 percent of the total African American enrollment at historically black colleges and universities and United Negro College Fund member institutions, respectively.

One explanation for the continuing gender gap is that African American women are more likely to be financially independent with dependents of their own, and therefore more eligible for (and in need of) financial assistance than are African American men. Cohen and Nee (2000) found that African American women are more likely to receive financial aid from most types of institutions. Trent (1991) notes that funding policies that constrict educational access overall are clearly more restrictive for African Americans, and they are most severe for African American males at the early degree levels. Thus, there is some evidence that, for African American men considering a college education, the cost may outweigh the perceived benefits.

Yet earnings research demonstrates the economic benefits to be derived from postsecondary degree attainment. African Americans, whites, and Latino/as—both male and female—had higher median earnings with higher levels of educational attainment. In 2000, for example, the difference between median earnings for African American males with a high school diploma and no college and those for African American males with a bachelor's degree or higher was $17,000 (NCES 2003).

In the same year, the difference between median earning for African American females with a high school diploma and no college and those for African American females with a bachelor's degree or higher was $20,000 (National Center for Education Statistics 2003).[5]

Diversity and the Gap in Achievement

The civil rights movement and particular changes in national policies in the 1960s ushered in an era in which the greater inclusion of minorities in mainstream society was paramount (Massey et al. 2003). The passage of the Civil Rights Act of 1964 and the call for "affirmative action" in federal contracts led to the dismantlement of "de jure and de facto mechanisms" (Massey et al. 2003, 1) that excluded minority groups from fully participating within the public sphere. As more efforts were focused on increasing opportunities for African Americans and Latinos/as in society, institutions of higher education began to recruit students from minority populations more aggressively (Massey et al. 2003). Then, over time, recruitment practices initially designed to rectify racial discrimination and exclusion changed to encompass a more diversity-oriented approach. As Massey and others (2003) suggest, "as immigration from Asia and Latin America transformed the United States, the rationale [for recruitment] shifted from righting past wrongs to representing racial and ethnic 'diversity' for its own sake" (1). Bowen and Bok (1998, 7) identify two reasons that motivated colleges and universities to diversify:

> To begin with, [colleges and universities] sought to enrich the education of all their students by including race as another element in assembling a diverse student body of varying talents, backgrounds, and perspectives. In addition, perceiving a widely recognized need for more members of minority groups in business, government, and the professions, [colleges and universities] acted on the conviction that minority students would have a special opportunity to become leaders in all walks of life.

Efforts to increase the diversity of the student body, coupled with the proliferation of community colleges in the 1960s,[6] produced a tremendous increase in the number of African Americans, Latino/as, Native Americans, and Asian Americans going to college over the last four decades. Yet as noted earlier in this paper, in spite of greater emphasis on campus diversity and launching myriad programs to make formerly all-white campuses more inclusive, the gaps in college participation and completion between whites and African Americans and between whites and Latino/as grew larger. As Massey and others (2003, 2) point out

> Despite a variety of retention efforts—increased financial aid, remedial education, special tutoring, peer advising, culturally sensitive dorms, and ethnically supportive student unions—once admitted to institutions of higher education, African Americans and Latino/as continually under perform relative to their white and Asian counterparts, earning lower grades, progressing at a slower pace, and dropping out at higher rates.

This achievement gap will continue to widen unless campus leaders recognize that diversity and equity are different goals requiring different strategies. Unlike public elementary and secondary schools, most colleges and universities are not subject to comprehensive accountability systems that require the reporting of student outcomes data disaggregated by race/ethnicity, gender, special education, and so on. Consequently, even though stratification based on race/ethnicity is a reality within the majority of institutions of higher education—whether they are highly selective and predominantly white or open-access or classified as Hispanic-serving—the details of this stratification are largely invisible to institutional actors.

Indeed, equity in educational outcomes is not a measure of postsecondary institutional performance that is tracked continuously at the national, state, or local levels. With respect to historically underrepresented student populations in the K–12 public schools, the central concern of educators and scholars has been the academic achievement gap, particularly in mathematics, reading, and writing. In contrast, the central concern in higher education, at least since the 1980s, has been diversity and affirmative action. While most campuses today have diversity statements, programs, and staff positions, the monitoring of equity in student outcomes is rarely an integral component of diversity efforts. Yet, it is our belief that a campus with a diversity agenda that does not incorporate equity into its educational outcomes as a measurable goal cannot truly be inclusive. Moreover, an institution that does not produce equitable educational outcomes and has not made equity a priority cannot truly be educationally excellent.

Equity and Inclusive Excellence

Disparity in academic achievement across racial/ethnic groups is a major dilemma facing higher education today and one of four that fueled the Association of American Colleges and Universities (AAC&U) call for institutions to make excellence inclusive.[7] AAC&U's conception of inclusive excellence—found in the introduction to this series of papers—differs from ours. It points to more expansive notions of inclusion and excellence than are generally embraced in the academy today.

Our conception of inclusion focuses on specific groups who comprise "involuntary" minorities (Ogbu 1978), that is, groups whose historical connection to the United States is a consequence of enslavement, colonization, or the forced annexation of territory. These groups are historically underrepresented in higher education and include African Americans, Latino/as, and Native Americans. We stress the need for attention to these groups because of our concern over the persistent achievement gap that we see evidenced in our research and work with campuses. AAC&U's notion of inclusion also recognizes the fundamental need to redress inequities, but it then also challenges campuses to help *all* students examine and understand differences—their own and others—and actively engage these differences for learning.

From our perspective, "inclusive excellence" is achieved when these historically underrepresented students exhibit traditional academic characteristics of high achievers, such as high grade point averages, honors, high class rankings, and so on. We emphasize traditional measures of academic excellence because for too long, institutions of higher education have approached the college participation of historically underrepresented students as a matter of producing "survivors,"—students who persist and graduate—largely disregarding the institution's responsibility and effectiveness in producing "leaders" (Gándara 1999). To illustrate our point: if the presidents or provosts of Ivy League colleges or universities were asked, "Of your most recent bachelor's degree recipients ranked in the top 10 percent, what percentage are African American or Latino/a?", they probably would not know the answer. Most institutions evaluate their effectiveness in serving historically underrepresented students in terms of access, to a lesser extent in terms of persistence and completion, and rarely ever in terms of high achievement among specific groups.

While recognizing that traditional measures of educational excellence currently serve as the academy's most common proxy for educational quality and student learning, AAC&U contends that these measures are inadequate to assess the new levels of learning espoused in its report, *Greater Expectations: A New Vision for Learning as a Nation Goes to College* (2002). Still, we all agree that however indirect or incomplete many of these traditional measures may be, disparities in these measures along racial/ethnic lines point to a major breakdown in our quest to serve all students currently entering higher education.

Fundamentally, we and AAC&U both seek to provide mechanisms for *institutional* action to address the achievement gap. They agree with our contention that to truly make excellence inclusive, institutions must be committed to identifying and monitoring indicators of excellence disaggregated by race/ethnicity. Paraphrasing John Dewey, to form relevant and effective ideals, we must first be acquainted with and take notice of actual conditions; otherwise our ideals become vacuous or else filled with Utopian content. Unless colleges and universities create structures to monitor educational achievement among *all* students—African American, Latino/a, Native American, Asian American, white—the ideal of inclusive excellence will be meaningless.

We believe that an institution takes inclusive excellence seriously if it (1) accepts the responsibility for producing equitable educational outcomes for students from historically underrepresented groups and (2) monitors the development of high achievement among students from these groups. Furthermore, institutional personnel, such as faculty, deans, and counselors, must demonstrate personal responsibility for the educational outcomes of students from historically underrepresented groups.

Rather than attributing underperformance among historically underrepresented students to "dysfunctional" backgrounds, "not knowing how to be a student," or lack of motivation, faculty members who take inclusive excellence seriously must internalize the responsibility for equitable educational outcomes.

For example, a dean must recognize that, even though the student body may be as "diverse as the United Nations," diversity in and of itself does not guarantee that all students are equally well served by the institution. Indeed, as we mentioned earlier, race/ethnicity-based disparity in educational outcomes is the norm at virtually every institution of higher education that is not a historically black college or university, a tribal college, or one that is located in Puerto Rico.

For the most part, these disparities are not noticed because equity is missing from external and internal accountability structures. Accrediting associations proclaim the merits of evidence-based cultures but fail to require evidence of equitable outcomes broken down by race/ethnicity or other dimensions, such as gender. The majority of states have some type of accountability system for higher education (Burke and Minassians 2003), but very few hold institutions accountable for the outcomes of historically underrepresented students, in either the aggregate or disaggregate (Bensimon et al. forthcoming). Significantly, the biennial national report card, *Measuring Up* (National Center for Public Policy in Higher Education 2000, 2002), which grades states on several education indicators, does not include a student enrollment indicator based on race and ethnicity. Commenting on this absence, Burke and Minassians (2003, 106) observe, "in an age when ethnic groups have already attained—or will soon attain—majority status in the population, an indicator comparing the racial composition of the state population and student enrollment seems desirable as a performance measure in the category of participation."

Recognizing Inequities

A plethora of data is currently available at most institutions of higher education. College and university leaders have made considerable investments in technology and training to develop the capacity for collecting all sorts of information about their institution and their students—from incoming grade point averages (GPAs), to every course taken, to graduating GPAs. The Knight Higher Education Collaborative (2000, 5), made up of educational leaders and researchers, notes

> Today, universities and colleges expend more time, effort, and money than ever before in gathering data . . . [Yet] for all that, higher education institutions still have not learned to organize and use data effectively for internal decisions or public accountability . . . most institutions have yet to learn how to use data strategically.

Many questions can be answered through the use of data. Who starts but does not finish, and why? What is being learned, and for what purpose? Answers to such questions, found in part through the examination of institutional data, provide new knowledge about institutional effectiveness and performance and promote organizational learning. Too often, individuals make decisions and judgments on the basis of their own experiences and what they believe to be true of their institution and its students. They feel that the students they have encountered could benefit from a particular program, and therefore they implement that program without examining institutional data or other sources of information in their own contexts. For example, if students are not doing well in mathematics, this must mean that an institution needs a tutoring program; if engineering students are changing to other majors, it must mean that the campus needs a summer bridge program. The issue is not that tutoring or bridge programs are bad ideas, but rather that there is a tendency to assume a problem is understood and to come up with solutions that may do nothing to address it.

In sum, institutional actors may claim that inclusiveness and diversity are important goals but fail to notice that the ideals of "equality in fact and equality in results"—which gave rise to affirmative action and later to diversity efforts—are far from being attained on their own campuses. In 2000, concerned about the chasm between what the higher education community espouses and how we act, researchers at the Center for Urban Education, supported by grants from the James Irvine Foundation and in partnership with fourteen campuses in the Los Angeles metropolitan area, developed and began field testing a tool—called the Diversity Scorecard[8]—designed to help campuses increase institutional capacity to produce equality in results for African American and Latino/a students.[9] Work with the fourteen initial partner campuses continues, and the project is expanding to include additional colleges and universities from around the country.

The Diversity Scorecard

The Diversity Scorecard is a mechanism to help campuses put existing institutional data to good use by using them to identify inequities in educational outcomes for African American and Latino/a students in postsecondary education. The goal of the Scorecard is for campus leaders to establish indicators and scales that will enable them to assess their institution's effectiveness in improving access, retention, institutional receptivity, and excellence for these historically underrepresented students.

The Diversity Scorecard is theory-based, practical, and cost-effective and allows institutions of higher education to hold themselves accountable for race/ethnicity-based equitable educational outcomes. One of the tool's important aspects is that it was designed to be adaptable to particular institutional circumstances and to build internal capacity to address the problem of unequal results. Neither a best practice nor a packaged intervention, the Scorecard is a *process*—built upon theories of organizational and individual learning—that is intended to bring about institutional and individual ownership of the problem of race/ethnicity-based inequality. Key to this approach is the core principle that individual practitioners are far more likely to examine their practices, attitudes, and beliefs to find the causes of and remedies for unequal results if they are in charge of defining the problem.

Institutional Accountability for Student Outcomes

The Diversity Scorecard is based on two premises. First, the prevalence of inequitable educational outcomes for African American, Latino/a, and other historically underrepresented students needs to be viewed as a problem in institutional performance. Typically, higher education leaders have sought ways to change or influence "at-risk" students so that these students can succeed at institutions that remain relatively static. In contrast, we believe that both students and institutions need to be held accountable for educational outcomes and be open to examining, and possibly changing, their practices. While there is an extensive literature on what historically underrepresented students lack and how they can change to better meet the rigors of college, in this paper we introduce an approach that focuses on change on the part of the institution.

Second, individuals' awareness of the importance of equity in student outcomes is a necessary prerequisite for institutional change. In this sense, the Diversity Scorecard is based on the principles of organizational learning. Individuals can develop a new or deeper awareness of equity in educational outcomes by engaging in and learning from routine data analysis.

Turning Data into Knowledge

We maintain that in order to bring about change in an institution, individuals must see for themselves, and as clearly as possible, the magnitude of the inequities affecting students from historically underrepresented groups. With the Diversity Scorecard project, the opportunity for learning is cultivated by involving campus teams in the examination of data that is disaggregated by race/ethnicity[10] and that reflects educational outcomes at their respective institutions. For example, at most institutions in the project, Latinas tend to be overrepresented in education majors and severely underrepresented in science, mathematics, engineering, and technology majors. However, many faculty members, counselors, and deans were not fully aware of the unbalanced distribution of Latinas across majors because such data are not typically disaggregated or routinely reported. When individuals examine data together and discuss what they notice and what it might mean, they construct new knowledge. Through their conversation, they translate tables of raw numbers into knowledge that can then be acted upon to bring about positive changes for students. Becoming aware that Latinas are underrepresented in certain fields can motivate a deeper inquiry into why this is so.

> **The Diversity Scorecard's Conceptualization of Institutional Change**
>
> In order to bring about institutional change, individuals have to see for themselves, as clearly as possible, the magnitude of inequities (awareness); and they have to integrate the meaning of these inequities (interpretation), so that they are moved to act upon them (action).

It is through this learning experience that an individual's consciousness is raised, and this is how change—beginning at the individual level—can spread throughout an institution. Here, this process of learning and change is illustrated through the experience of one of the project's partner institutions, Loyola Marymount University (LMU).

Loyola Marymount University

Founded in 1911 and located in Los Angeles, LMU is one of twenty-eight Jesuit universities in the United States. The student body consists of 5,465 undergraduates; 1,639 graduate students, largely majoring in education; and 1,377 law students. Among the undergraduates, Latino/as constitute the largest minority group (19 percent), followed by Asian/Pacific Americans (11 percent), African Americans (6 percent), and American Indians (less than 1 percent), while European Americans[11] account for 50 percent of the student population. There are also 534 students (11 percent) who declined to report their racial/ethnic background. Interestingly, the lattermost group is twice as large as it was in 1997, reflecting a curious trend that has occurred in other private institutions.

LMU is organized into four colleges—Liberal Arts, Business Administration, Communication and Fine Arts, and Science and Engineering—and two schools—the School of Education and the School of Film and Television. Its mission statement reads

> Loyola Marymount University understands and declares its purpose to be: the encouragement of learning, the education of the whole person, the service of faith and the promotion of justice.

LMU's Evidence Team

In 2000, the presidents of the fourteen initial partner campuses were asked to each appoint a group of people to work with the USC researchers, with one person in each group coming from the office of institutional research. The composition of the fourteen teams differs, but collectively they include deans, vice presidents, assistants to the president, counselors, and faculty members in various disciplines, including English, philosophy, psychology, ethnic studies, and mathematics. The USC researchers call these groups "evidence teams" because their role in the project is to hold up a mirror to their respective institutions and reflect the status of underrepresented students on basic educational outcomes.

On most campuses, data are collected and organized into reports by an office of institutional research. Very few individuals see these reports, and even fewer actually discuss them. To raise the teams' awareness of inequities, the USC researchers asked them to take on the role of researcher—team members would become responsible for developing equity indicators and actively analyzing data. In a change from customary practice, the USC researchers did not undertake the data gathering or analysis but rather served as facilitators of the process and as resource people for the teams.

The evidence team at LMU included team leader Dr. Abbie Robinson-Armstrong, special assistant to the president for intercultural affairs; Dr. Brian Hu, director of institutional research; Dr. David Killoran, professor of English and department chair; and Mr. Marshall Sauceda, associate dean of ethnic and intercultural services. In terms of diversity, LMU's evidence team included an African American female, an Asian American male, a Latino male, and a white male.

At the start, some of the LMU team members were skeptical about the value of the Diversity Scorecard project. Their skepticism seemed to originate primarily from previous experiences with assessment-related, data-driven initiatives that never made any difference. Several months after the project started, Dr. Killoran admitted his initial dubiousness. "I don't know whether I was ever a disbeliever in assessment," he said, "[but] you would do it, then they would throw it away and things would go on; and when changes occurred, it was because somebody intuited that change was needed, not because they had a lot of evidence for it."

Dr. Robinson-Armstrong came to LMU from the University of Illinois at Champaign-Urbana a few months after the project started. Hired as a special assistant to the president for intercultural affairs, she immediately became the leader of the evidence team. Before she joined the group, the other members felt they did not have the power or influence to set equity goals for their institution. The consensus was that "everything we do, we have to ask them before we do it."

After Dr. Robinson-Armstrong joined the team, the sense of powerlessness diminished considerably. As one of the members observed, "now that people know that she [Robinson-Armstrong] has the ear of the president, she's permanent, and she has a lot of guts, people stand up and take notice." The combination of her title, her collegial leadership style, and her confidence seemed to empower the group. Undoubtedly, she was critical to this team's success because she provided the space and opportunity for each member to be the expert in his or her area of specialization. As the project proceeded and the team members became more and more involved in data analysis, we saw them overcome their initial reticence and passive detachment to form a highly effective team.

Vital Signs and Disaggregating Data

To start their work, the teams from the fourteen initial partner campuses were directed to collect what are called "vital signs" data. Like blood pressure and temperature, these are particular indicators that every institution uses and reports as baseline measures of institutional "health" and/or status. The most critical aspect of this exercise was that the data were disaggregated by race/ethnicity and, in many cases, gender. The purpose of this was for each team to look for potential differences in outcomes between groups. In many instances, the teams looked at data from more than one year in order to detect trends.

The indicators used at LMU included enrollment by race/ethnicity, enrollment in major or college by race/ethnicity, retention from freshman to sophomore year by race/ethnicity, retention to graduation by race/ethnicity, and the number of tenured and tenure-track faculty by race/ethnicity. From studying these data, the evidence team at LMU was able to formulate follow-up questions and to request new data from Dr. Hu, the director of institutional research.

TABLE 3

Undergraduate Student Enrollment by Race/Ethnicity, 1997 and 2001

	1997		2001		
	N	% of total	N	% of total	
African American	321	7.8%	317	6.4%	⇓
American Indian	38	0.9%	39	0.8%	⇓
Asian/Pacific American	575	14.0%	545	11.0%	⇓
European American	**1946**	**47.3%**	**2516**	**50.7%**	⇑
Latino/a	847	20.6%	918	18.5%	⇓
International	155	3.8%	90	1.8%	⇓
Decline to State	**231**	**5.6%**	**534**	**10.8%**	⇑
Total	4113	100.0%	4959	100.0%	⇑

In reviewing LMU's vital signs data, the team members became aware that the percentages of African American and Latino/a students had decreased over the preceding five years (see table 3), even though the undergraduate population had increased by 21 percent, from 4,113 students in 1997 to 4,959 students in 2001. Between 1997 and 2001, the African American population decreased from 7.8 to 6.4 percent, and the Latino/a population decreased from 20.6 to 18.5 percent. European American students represented 67 percent of the increase in undergraduate students.

Once they learned about the declining enrollment of African Americans and Latino/as, the LMU team generated new questions. For example, a team member wondered whether the proportion of male versus female minority students had changed over time. This led the team to examine the gender composition for each group (see table 4). By examining the data presented in table 4, the team learned that more than 60 percent of the African American and Latino/a students on campus were women, while the gender distribution was more balanced in other groups.

Next, the team decided to examine the distribution of students across the four academic colleges. Their findings are shown in table 5.

The data presented in table 5 led to additional questions. For example, how do minority students end up being concentrated in particular colleges? Are they migrating out of their original majors or applying to particular majors? Questions such as these led to the collection of additional data, which in turn provided the foundation for LMU's Diversity Scorecard. The disaggregated data turned out to be "eye-opening" for most LMU team members—even the skeptics.

TABLE 4

Undergraduate Student Enrollment by Race/Ethnicity and Gender, Fall 1997

	Male		Female		Total
	N	%	N	%	N
African American	**107**	**33.3%**	**214**	**66.7%**	**321**
American Indian	23	60.5%	15	39.5%	38
Asian/Pacific American	245	42.6%	330	57.4%	575
European American	867	44.6%	1079	55.4%	1946
Latino/a	**311**	**36.7%**	**536**	**63.3%**	**847**
International	88	56.8%	67	43.2%	155
Decline to state	108	46.8%	123	53.2%	231
Total	1749	42.5%	2364	57.5%	4113

TABLE 5

Undergraduate Degrees Conferred by College and Race/Ethnicity, 2000/2001

College	European American #	%	Asian/Pacific American #	%	African American #	%	Latino/a #	%	American Indian #	%	Non-Res. #	%	Decline to State #	%	Total #	%
Business Adm.	135	39.7	65	19.1	22	6.5	58	17.1	2	0.6	36	10.6	22	6.5	340	31.4%
Comm. & Fine Arts	146	55.7	29	11.1	21	8.0	32	12.2	6	2.3	8	3.1	20	7.6	262	24.2%
Liberal Arts	192	52.3	37	10.1	15	4.1	89	24.3	3	0.8	11	3.0	20	5.4	367	33.9%
Sci. & Eng.	42	36.5	28	24.3	7	6.1	27	23.5	1	0.9	3	2.6	7	6.1	115	10.6%
Total	515	47.5	159	14.7	65	6.0	206	19.0	12	1.1	58	5.4	69	6.4	1084	100.0%

The Diversity Scorecard's Four Perspectives on Equity

Each evidence team in the project examines institutional data concurrently from four perspectives on equity in educational outcomes: access, retention, excellence, and institutional receptivity. These four perspectives form the Scorecard's framework.[12] While each team interprets the four perspectives differently to reflect the needs and priorities of their respective institutions, the following general definitions were used.

Access perspective. Access refers to programs and resources that can significantly improve life opportunities for historically underrepresented students. Indicators in the access perspective are concerned with questions such as the following:

- To what programs/majors do underrepresented students have access?
- Do the programs/majors to which underrepresented students have access lead to high-demand, high-paying career opportunities?
- Do underrepresented students have access to select academic and socialization programs, such as special internships or fellowships?
- What access do underrepresented students have to financial support?
- What access do community college students have to four-year colleges?
- What access do community college students have to "hot" programs, for example, programs leading to fields with the highest starting salaries?
- What access do underrepresented students have to graduate and professional schools?

Retention. Retention refers to continued attendance from one year to the next and/or to degree completion. Retention can also refer to continued progress toward degrees in competitive majors. Equity indicators within the retention perspective provide answers to questions such as the following:

- What are the retention rates for underrepresented students according to program types?
- What are the drop-out patterns for underrepresented students from particular "hot" programs, for example, engineering and computer sciences?
- What are the completion rates for underrepresented students in basic skills courses?
- What are completion rates for associate's degrees, bachelor's degrees, and credential/certificate programs?

Excellence. Within these four perspectives, excellence refers to measurements of achievement for historically underrepresented students. Such indicators help answer questions such as the following:

- Might different majors or courses function as "gatekeepers" for some students and "gateways" for others? (For example, is there racial/ethnic bias in physics and mathematics? Is there a Western culture bias in the humanities?)
- Are historically underrepresented students concentrated in particular majors?
- What are the underrepresented student completion rates in highly competitive programs?
- What percentage of historically underrepresented students graduate with a GPA of 3.5 or higher?
- What is the size of the pool of high-achieving, underrepresented students who are eligible for graduate study in the full range of academic disciplines?
- What percentage of underrepresented students graduate in the top 10 percent of their class?

Institutional receptivity. Institutional receptivity refers to goals and measures of institutional support that have been found to be influential in the creation of affirming campus environments for historically underrepresented students. Receptivity indicators provide information to answer questions such as the following:

- Do new appointments enhance the racial and ethnic diversity of faculty, administrators, and staff?

- Does the racial and ethnic composition of the faculty reflect that of the student body?

Every four to six weeks, each team from the fourteen initial partner campuses met with two USC researchers for two hours to examine data from these four perspectives. As the data examination progressed, teams learned new things about educational outcomes and the equity gap, and many preconceived notions based on anecdote and experience were dispelled. The LMU team met with USC researchers sixteen times between January 1, 2001, and January 28, 2003.

Fine-grained Measures of Educational Outcomes

As the fourteen evidence teams delved deeper into the data, they continually asked new questions and developed new measures of equity in educational outcomes. The USC researchers refer to these as fine-grained measures. Such measures go beyond traditional indicators used by institutions and enables teams to identify problem areas more specifically. The LMU team, in particular, embarked on a second-order level of inquiry and began to examine educational *processes* as well as educational outcomes. For example, after examining the vital signs, the team became interested in access to different majors and wanted to know whether African American and Latino/a students were proportionately represented in those that lead to careers in high-demand fields, such as engineering and computer science. They also wanted to know whether these students were overrepresented in particular majors.

Initially, the LMU team looked at graduation rates by major, disaggregated by race/ethnicity. From these data, they learned that African Americans and Latino/as were underrepresented in certain majors. However, this did not help them understand the reasons for this underrepresentation. When the team decided to track cohorts of students from their original major to the major in which they graduated, Dr. Hu proposed the following:

> We can track from entry major to graduating major. This might show if students intended on majoring in one major, then changed their mind later on. If many students sign up for more economically advantageous majors, like engineering, but then graduate with majors in the humanities, this might give us an idea about access to certain majors for African American and Latino/a students.

By doing this, the evidence team found that 42 percent of the 1997 cohort of African American students who had enrolled in the College of Science and Engineering had left that college and the African American enrollment in the College of Liberal Arts had increased by 31 percent (see table 6).

By tracking the transfer of African American and Latino/a students from engineering to other majors, such as communications, the team identified courses and prerequisites that create barriers for these students. Their learning was increased through intensive investigation of the fine-grained measures of educational outcomes. This approach revealed the point at which African American and Latino/a students frequently left particular majors, a finding that will enable the faculty and counselors to intervene in a timely and more proactive manner.[13]

Keeping the Measures Simple and Manageable

The USC researches recommended that each of the fourteen evidence teams limit the number of measures to twenty—no more than five per perspective. At first, some of the teams felt this was too limiting, but the rationale was that if there were too many measures, the scorecard would devolve into a laundry list of metrics rather than a list of actionable items. In the end, many teams used between four and twelve measures—no more than three per perspective.

In developing their Diversity Scorecard, the LMU team chose measures that complemented the university's mission, their Intercultural Vision Statement and Principles, and their new ten-year strategic plan. The following measures comprised LMU's final Diversity Scorecard:

TABLE 6

Student Migration from Entering Major to Degree Major by Ethnicity

European American					**Asian/Pacific American**			
College	**Entering**	**Degree**	**Difference**		**College**	**Entering**	**Degree**	**Difference**
BA	647	650	0%		BA	258	311	**21%**
LA	763	955	**25%**		LA	169	180	7%
CF	521	478	–8%		CF	79	82	4%
SE	517	365	–29%		SE	272	205	–25%
Total	2448	2448			Total	778	778	

African American					**American Indian**			
College	**Entering**	**Degree**	**Difference**		**College**	**Entering**	**Degree**	**Difference**
BA	71	67	–6%		BA	8	7	–13%
LA	71	93	**31%**		LA	7	7	0%
CF	49	**49**	0%		CF	2	4	100%
SE	43	25	–42%		SE	10	9	–10%
Total	234	234			Total	27	27	

Latino/a					**Decline to State**			
College	**Entering**	**Degree**	**Difference**		**College**	**Entering**	**Degree**	**Difference**
BA	256	269	5%		BA	18	20	11%
LA	323	387	20%		LA	30	34	13%
CF	103	94	–9%		CF	18	21	17%
SE	208	140	–33%		SE	22	13	–41%
Total	890	890			Total	88	88	

BA-Business Administration; **LA**-Liberal Arts; **CF**-Communication and Fine Arts; **SE**-Science and Engineering

Access.

- Undergraduate enrollment by race/ethnicity and gender, 1997 vs. 2001 cohorts
- Transfer students by race/ethnicity, 1999 vs. 2001 cohorts
- Financial aid recipients by race/ethnicity and by aid type, 2000–2001
- Student migration from entering major to degree major by school and by race/ethnicity

Retention.

- Year-by-year retention rate for first year cohorts by race/ethnicity, fall 1997 vs. fall 2001
- Graduation in 4, 5, 6, and 7+ years by race/ethnicity, 1997 vs. 2001 cohorts
- Undergraduate degrees conferred by college and by race/ethnicity, 1997 vs. 2001 cohorts

Excellence.

- Student representation in GPA intervals (i.e., those students who achieved 3.0–3.49 vs. those who achieved 2.0–2.49, etc.) by race/ethnicity, 1995–2000

Loyola Marymount University

Diversity Scorecard Framework

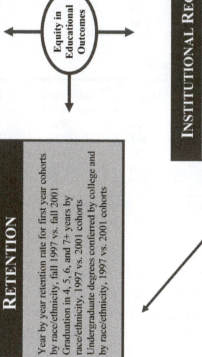

ACCESS

- Undergraduate enrollment by race/ethnicity and gender, 1997 vs. 2001 cohorts
- Transfer students by race/ethnicity, 1999 vs. 2001 cohorts
- Financial aid recipients by race/ethnicity and by aid type, 2000–2001
- Student migration from entering major to degree major by school and by race/ethnicity

EXCELLENCE

- Student representation in GPA intervals by race/ethnicity, 1995–2000
- Students on the Dean's list by race/ethnicity, 1996, 1998, and 2001
- Honors students by race/ethnicity, 1995, 1998, and 2001

RETENTION

- Year by year retention rate for first year cohorts by race/ethnicity, fall 1997 vs. fall 2001
- Graduation in 4, 5, 6, and 7+ years by race/ethnicity, 1997 vs. 2001 cohorts
- Undergraduate degrees conferred by college and by race/ethnicity, 1997 vs. 2001 cohorts

INSTITUTIONAL RECEPTIVITY

- Gender and race/ethnicity of faculty, 2001–2003
- Student–faculty ration by race/ethnicity, 2001
- Faculty and administrative staff by rank, gender, and race/ethnicity, 2000
- Board of trustees composition vs. student composition by race/ethnicity, 2001

Equity in Educational Outcomes

- Students on the Dean's list by race/ethnicity, 1996, 1998, and 2001
- Honors students by race/ethnicity, 1995, 1998, and 2001

Institutional Receptivity

- Gender and race/ethnicity of faculty, 2001–2003
- Student-faculty ratio by race/ethnicity, 2001
- Faculty and administrative staff by rank, gender, and race/ethnicity, 2000
- Board of trustees composition vs. student composition by race/ethnicity, 2001

Benchmarking—Equity and Improvement Targets

In the Diversity Scorecard project, the ultimate benchmark is equity—the point at which proportional representation is reached.[14] For example, if 25 percent of the student body is Latino/a, equity would be reached when 25 percent of the graduates in engineering are also Latino/a. Improvement targets are annual, mid-range goals for the institutions to accomplish while striving to reach equity. For example, a team may determine that, to reach equity for Latino/as in engineering, the institution will need to increase Latino/a enrollment in calculus by 5 percent each year for five years. The LMU team explained the benchmarking in their final report to the president:

> Equity is defined as the point at which the share of students of a given ethnic group with a particular academic feature is equal to that same group's share of the total student population. For example, at LMU, Latino/a students comprised 14.7 percent of the total number of students on the Dean's list in fall 2001. We then compared this number to their share of the overall student population—18.5 percent in 2001—in order to determine whether there was an equity gap. In this case the equity gap was 3.8 percent; Latino/a students are underrepresented on the Dean's list. Our data analysis helped us to determine whether we had equity of educational outcomes.

As indicated in table 7, African American, American Indian, Asian Pacific American, and Latino/a students at LMU are all underrepresented among students who have earned GPAs in the top 10 percent (red numbers indicate underrepresentation). African Americans account for 6.8 percent of the student population, but only 4.1 percent of these students have GPAs in the top category.

TABLE 7

Top 10 Percent Students by Race/Ethnicity

	Number	Percent in the Top 10 Percent	Percent in the Student Population
African American	19	4.1%	6.8%
Latino/a	60	12.9%	19.9%
American Indian	2	0.4%	0.9%
Asian/Pacific American	52	11.2%	14.9%
European American	292	62.7%	49.5%
Decline to state	41	8.8%	8.8%
TOTAL	466	100%	100%

In contrast, 62.7 percent of European Americans ranked in the top category, which is considerably higher than this group's representation in the undergraduate student population (49.5 percent). The purpose of the Diversity Scorecard is to call attention to proportional disparities such as these.

Report to the President and Campus Community

As mentioned earlier, the fourteen teams were appointed by the presidents of their institutions. Once teams identified the types of data they wanted to examine and performed their analyses, they submitted reports back to their presidents describing their findings on the state of equity in educational outcomes for African American and Latino/a students on their campuses.

The process of developing these reports was critical for the project. In writing the report, the teams had to make several commitments. First, the team members had to reach a consensus on which of the many equity indicators they had examined would be included in the final Scorecard and report. What were the most important indicators of inequity in educational outcomes? Which were aligned with institutional priorities? What were the advantages and disadvantages of presenting certain indicators? Who might react defensively?

The teams understood that they had to choose the indicators and data carefully in order for the report to gain acceptance and to prompt others to take action. Their role was to present the evidence in such a way that it would motivate faculty members and administrators to eliminate the inequities that were now apparent to all team members. However, as a member of one of the teams acknowledged, the statistics could lead to political problems.

The teams also had made a commitment to share their findings with their campus communities as well as their presidents. Documenting and describing the magnitude of the inequities in educational outcomes on campus is an unenviable task, and in almost every case, the teams were the bearers of bad news. At the ends of their reports, each team made recommendations for action, such as volunteering to continue their data analysis as a group, seeking involvement from other departments, and encouraging the use of institutional resources (e.g., employee time and/or budgetary allocations) to eradicate the existing inequities. In addition, the teams had to review and summarize all they had learned in months of data analysis and reflection.

After receiving the report and the request for a meeting with the LMU evidence team, Father Robert Lawton, the president of LMU, convened a "town hall" meeting to which everyone on campus was invited. Faculty, deans, and staff attended. Copies of the report were provided for everyone in attendance, and it was available on the institution's internal Web site as well.[15] The meeting was opened by the provost, who described it as "an important gathering," praised the team's work, and reiterated the importance of disaggregating institutional data by race/ethnicity and gender. Each team member presented a section of the report, using a PowerPoint presentation to display the data and indicators so that the audience could easily see the inequities they had discovered. At the conclusion of the presentation, the team leader told the audience that "everyone has to commit to being evidence monitors" and reminded them that "equal access does not guarantee equity in success."

In the introduction to the report, the LMU team recalled their early reactions to the project. "The LMU Scorecard team initially believed that the project would be quick and easy. We had data to demonstrate that LMU could improve the opportunities and academic achievement for underrepresented students. We simply needed to bring the problem to the attention of the appropriate administrators, and offer solutions." It did not take long for the team to realize that this strategy would not work. They could present the evidence and offer solutions, but they could not develop programs to meet demonstrated needs and establish assessment measures for the various units of the university. Therefore, the team stated that "if we wanted the best results, we needed to rely on the experts who worked in these areas. We further realized we needed their commitment. The Diversity Scorecard had to be their project. They needed to be part of the team, and we had to work to facilitate their efforts on behalf of LMU's underrepresented students."

In the section on recommendations, the team wrote, "we assumed responsibility for raising awareness of the current situation at LMU by providing statistical evidence. We saw ourselves as both 'evidence monitors' and a group that could provide resources and facilitate continuing work in this area. Now it is time for broader campus involvement in the work of being 'evidence monitors.' " Accordingly, at the town hall meeting, the LMU team recommended that each college within the university and several other programs and departments, such as admissions and the Honors program, create their own Diversity Scorecards. The president accepted this recommendation and asked the deans and program heads to build on the report and develop Diversity Scorecards.

There were a number of important findings in the LMU team's report to the president:

- Latino/as had the highest final graduation rate, with 81 percent graduating in seven or more years. The comparable figures for African Americans and European Americans were 54.5 percent and 75.4 percent, respectively.

- In fall 2001, out of 105 students in the honors program, seven were Latino/as and two were African Americans. Almost three-fourths of the honors students were European Americans.

- Both Latino/as and African Americans were underrepresented among the students who earned GPAs of 3.7 and above at the end of their first year.

- Between 1997 and 2002, forty-two new, full-time faculty members were hired, of whom eight were African Americans, nine were Latino/as, nine were Asian/Pacific Islanders, and two were American Indians. Overall, faculty of color constitute 67 percent of the new faculty.

Organizational Learning at LMU

The Diversity Scorecard approach is based on theories of organizational learning. Like "evidence-based cultures," "organizational learning" is currently a popular term on college campuses. However, what these terms mean in real action or behaviors is not always understood or specified. Because the words "organization" and "learning" are assumed to be self-explanatory, there is a tendency to oversimplify organizational learning by regarding it simply as a data collection method. Indeed, empirical studies of organizational learning in general are very scarce, and those that deal specifically with higher education are even rarer (Bauman 2002).

The USC researchers were keenly aware that many projects said to be guided by the principles of organizational learning often pay no heed to the importance of empirical documentation. Consequently, an important goal of this project was to observe and document organizational learning in real time from start to finish. In particular, the USC researchers wanted to have sound empirical evidence for their claims to successful (or unsuccessful) organizational learning. Therefore, they observed the meetings of the evidence teams over two years and documented their conversations in order to capture learning as it occurred.[16]

Four major strands of learning took place among most of the teams. First and foremost, the teams in the project identified inequities in educational outcomes. The LMU team, specifically, learned that African American women were the most "at risk" student population in terms of retention; that females accounted for two-thirds of the growth in African American and Latino/a student enrollment; that minority students tended to leave science and engineering at higher rates than any of the other colleges; and how the size of the gap in faculty diversity compared to that of the gap in student diversity in particular colleges.

Second, the project teams learned what it means to develop a culture of evidence as well as the importance of data in terms of shaping one's work and making institutional decisions. At one of the team meetings, LMU's Dr. Killoran, who had been skeptical of the project at first, said

> We have a chance to look at where we are. We can make arguments supported with the numbers. Maybe we could even ask some new questions. For instance, I never knew to ask the institutional research department to disaggregate the data for the English department. I didn't have a reason. I had mentioned in meetings that our students were really, really white, but now I have proof that the department is white. It has been obvious to me, but I haven't been able to get some of my white colleagues to acknowledge this.

Third, the members of the teams in the project became empowered and developed agency at the individual level. After learning so much from analyzing the data with colleagues, many felt sufficiently well "armed" with information to advocate institutional change in ways that they would not have attempted before. Dr. Hu, the director of institutional research at LMU, felt that, as a member of a minority group, he could not have brought up these issues previously. Now the Diversity Scorecard project has given him the "permission" to do so. "Doing the Diversity Scorecard gives us a good opportunity to have dialogues. Now we can raise issues. I, myself, am a minority. I could not generate this profile on my own. People might have asked why or would have been suspicious of my data. Now I can say, look at this report I did for the Diversity Scorecard project."

Finally, team members across the project developed a sense of institutional responsibility for the inequities that occurred on their campuses and communicated this responsibility to others in the institution. Dr. Robinson-Armstrong, LMU's team leader, said that "if we have a problem, we have to own up to it, 'fess up to it.' " She went on to say that she will engage in "other kinds of ways that will tell them [the campus community] that this is not going to go away." Marshall Sauceda, associate dean of ethnic and intercultural services at LMU, said that, between foundation grants aimed at diversity and accreditation efforts, "the university is making diversity a campus-wide priority. The timing is right for LMU to change. Before, it's been a program here and a program there, but not with universal buy-in."

Sustaining and Spreading the Diversity Scorecard

Among the biggest challenges faced by the project's campuses is how to sustain the Scorecard's impact and broaden its reach. For LMU, it was important that awareness about inequities in educational outcomes be spread to others on campus; otherwise, it would not be possible to bring about systematic change. The LMU team recommended that each school and program develop its own Diversity Scorecard. The LMU evidence team members coached these units on how to construct their own Scorecards. In total, LMU created ten new teams. Using the original report to the president as their point of departure, each of the new teams identified one measure to investigate more thoroughly in their own college.

For example, in response to the findings reported in table 5, the College of Science and Engineering set out to review grades in what might be considered "gateway" courses—courses, such as calculus, required to advance in the major. The director of the University Honors Program developed a Scorecard to address the problem of underrepresentation among Latino/as, African Americans, and Asian Pacific Americans. As a result, she discovered that underrepresentation among these groups was a function of the process used to recruit students, and that there were more students who qualified than had been selected for the program. Each new Diversity Scorecard evidence team at LMU presented its findings and recommendations to the president at another town hall meeting, thirteen months after the original report was issued.[17]

Most campuses tend to treat diversity efforts in an ad hoc manner, and these efforts rarely become a central part of institutional decision making. Provosts bring deans together to consider questions of enrollments, retention, program review, student assessment, and so on, but even though diversity and equity are integral to each of these topics, they are rarely taken into account. Furthermore, academic decision makers do not typically assess the impact of new initiatives *from the perspective of equity.*

Given the ad hoc status of equity efforts on most college campuses, the second town hall meeting at LMU—convened by the president to discuss the scorecards developed by each academic unit—was impressive. Upon entering the room in which the meeting was held, one's attention was immediately drawn to the large stack of three-ring binders labeled "DIVERSITY SCORECARD REPORTS." Deans, directors, and faculty members made brief individual presentations of their findings. In most cases, the recommendations for addressing inequities involved changing internal practices, rather than creating new programs or other initiatives that would require additional funding. For example, the Beyond LMU international study program found some interesting new information about the applicants to the Fulbright program. The person spearheading the scorecard effort for this program noted

> The Diversity Scorecard [DS] got me to look at the small number of students [with whom] I work, which represents a "micro sample," but still interesting. People who apply to the Fulbright program

tend to be in the top 10 percent of their class, but really they only need a 3.0 or better GPA to qualify. In response to my DS, I am going to create a network of mentoring groups for regions and for areas of study.[18] Students would join in their junior year. There's a whole raft of other things they could apply for as well. There are bigger implications . . . the 5,000 students [nationally] who apply have a great experience just in the application process. They have a "running start" in terms of applying to graduate school and other stuff.

After all of the deans and program heads presented their Scorecard findings, one of the deans gave the president three recommendations, concerning the areas of budgeting, collaborating, and reporting. In terms of budgeting, the dean recommended that budgetary decisions be based on information such as the data the teams analyzed for their reports. Financial support ought to be provided in response to *evidence* of need and to maintain successful programs. In terms of collaborating, it was pointed out that certain deficiencies identified in the Diversity Scorecard reports could only be addressed by collaborative efforts across units. In the words of the dean, "We need to collaborate across campus with those who can have an impact." Finally, in terms of reporting, the dean noted that the institution and these teams needed to continue monitoring and reporting in this manner on a regular basis.

All of the individual Diversity Scorecard reports provided evidence of unequal results, and several of the presenters acknowledged that they were delivering bad news by saying that the experience was "like going to confession." Following this line of thought, Father Lawton closed the meeting by saying

> I want to talk about temptations. First, there is the temptation to be overwhelmed by data. I am very happy to see that you have avoided it. Second, is the temptation to relish knowledge but not allow it to lead to action. Here you're all taking action, which is great. Third, is the temptation to do too much and therefore make your efforts too diffuse. I am happy that you are taking manageable actions. I applaud you and your commitment.

Institutional Factors to Help Achieve Equity

Several of the elements in place at LMU are critical for success in working toward equity of educational outcomes for all students and, thus, for the larger project of Inclusive Excellence. These elements are: (1) committed leadership at both the institutional and the team level; (2) team member expertise; (3) openness to self-criticism; (4) motivation; (5) credibility; and (6) resources.

Committed Leadership

Presidential. To a great extent, the success of the Diversity Scorecard project at LMU can be attributed to the president. Father Lawton, as one might say colloquially, "walks the walk" and "talks the talk." His genuine commitment to inclusive excellence is demonstrated through the appointment of Dr. Robinson-Armstrong as his special assistant and through his willingness to examine data that had the potential for creating discomfort within the university.

With regard to the appointment of Dr. Robinson-Armstrong, what is important is not that a position for a special assistant for intercultural affairs exists at LMU. Such positions are now commonplace. Unfortunately, individuals who hold positions that are specifically associated with diversity and minority affairs can often be marginalized. At LMU, the president has made it clear that the position, the individual who fills it, and the work the position represents, must be taken seriously. For example, the president has spoken about the Diversity Scorecard project in his annual convocation address; he has regularly scheduled meetings with Dr. Robinson-Armstrong; and he supported the first Diversity Scorecard's recommendation that all academic units be asked to participate in the process. When the deans and directors presented their own Diversity Scorecard findings in the second town hall meeting, Father Lawton listened attentively throughout the two-hour gathering. He also showed his commitment by giving his full attention to the implications of the Scorecards' findings for the institution.

In a post-affirmative action environment, particularly in California, there is heightened sensitivity about the examination of data disaggregated by race/ethnicity. We have found that, on the campuses where the project has been least successful, there is a general reluctance to talk about race/ethnicity and/or an institutional culture that encourages sharing of only positive information in order to reinforce a desirable image. In such institutions, the revelation of inequities in educational outcomes violates an important cultural norm. Organization learning theorists have observed that an unwillingness to look at information that challenges leaders' images of themselves as well as of their organizations is the biggest obstacle to institutional learning and change (see, for example, Argyris 1977). LMU was unusual in that no one—not the members of the team, the president, or anyone else—questioned the usefulness or appropriateness of disaggregating data by race/ethnicity. Even more unusual is the fact that campus leaders decided to post all of the Diversity Scorecards on the LMU Web site, thereby making them available to the public. The willingness to admit vulnerability is a characteristic of highly effective leaders, and Father Lawton did so without hesitation. In his most recent convocation address, Father Lawton told the LMU community that "modern corporations emphasize data. Decisions need to be, if not data-driven, then at the very least data-sensitive and data-informed. And we are becoming more data conscious as evidenced by the Diversity Scorecard."

Team-based. Dr. Robinson-Armstrong was a driving force behind the success of the LMU project. It was evident from the start that she was committed to the notion of equity in educational outcomes and did not need to be convinced. However, she was well aware that others on the campus would resist the concept and would have to be convinced of its importance. The fact that she was able to persuade the deans and directors of ten units—some of whom may have been less than enthusiastic—to develop their own Scorecards attests to the potency of her interpersonal and political skills.

Team Member Expertise

The Diversity Scorecard consists of fine-grained measures (e.g., class rankings by race/ethnicity) that are not typically part of routine institutional reports. The ability of a team to carry out the work thus depends greatly on having an institutional researcher who is not only competent, but also willing to prepare the data in formats different from those to which he or she is accustomed. LMU's director of institutional research, Dr. Hu, was a critical asset to the team because he had the expertise and ability to produce analyses quickly. Moreover, because he was committed to the goals of the project, he did not feel overburdened or put upon by its demands.

The evidence team also had other important forms of expertise. Dr. Killoran, a long-time professor of English and chair of the department, gave the group a high degree of legitimacy with the faculty and served as a very effective ambassador for the project. He was particularly effective in representing the project because he admitted his initial skepticism and explained why he eventually changed his mind. His speaking about the value of the Scorecard to faculty members at LMU and other institutions made the project more appealing. The fourth member of the team, Marshall Sauceda, associate dean for ethnic and intercultural services, brought a strong understanding of the academic and social experiences of minority students at LMU.

Openness to Self-criticism

The willingness of institutional actors to examine themselves and their institutions critically is a prerequisite for addressing the problem of inequities based on race/ethnicity. One of the greatest obstacles to learning and change at the institutional level is a natural tendency to look past ourselves for the source of problems or to avoid examining them at all. At LMU, with the president setting the standard, there was never any question that holding up a mirror to the institution was the right thing to do.

Motivation

The members of the original LMU evidence team found the Diversity Scorecard to be a promising tool from the very start of the project. Each team member had been involved in diversity-related initiatives on campus prior to their participation in the project, and they were at the forefront of many of the institution's efforts to increase the enrollment of minority students. They were also aware that not all of their colleagues were conscious of the pressing issues facing minority students or committed to the goals of diversity. In the Diversity Scorecard, the team found a non-threatening means for calling attention to the status of African American and Latino/a students at LMU and, in turn, motivating others to redress inequities. The LMU team members were highly motivated to complete the Scorecard because they saw it as an opportunity to connect diversity to core institutional goals, and thus, to make diversity more central to the institution's work.

The LMU team's motivation was also shown in their task orientation and enthusiasm. The team met regularly and completed individual tasks on schedule. Team members focused their discussions on the data and on the development of new questions and rarely wasted time. They were eager to share their work with the campus and at conferences. Indeed, the team members' belief in the aims of the Scorecard provided them with the energy and will to engage in a process that was new and time-consuming, and where the data results could not be known in advance.

Credibility

In appointing the evidence team, Father Lawton, the LMU president, selected individuals who enjoyed the respect of the campus community. The choice of individuals was important because it was a way of signaling to the campus at large that this was an important and serious undertaking. There were additional ways in which the credibility of the project was established. The president convened the aforementioned town hall meeting at which the evidence team presented the Scorecard results to the campus community, and he mentioned the Scorecard in his speeches. As noted, the Scorecard reports were posted on the LMU Web site, and the reports were referenced in materials for accreditation, conference proposals, and grant applications.

Resources

Two types of resources were especially valuable to the project: team members' investment of time—without additional remuneration or release time from other responsibilities—and the office of institutional research. With regard to the latter, because the Scorecard relies on data that are disaggregated by race and ethnicity (and in the case of LMU, by gender as well) and is based on fine-grained measures (e.g., the migration of students from their chosen majors), LMU's capacity to complete the project depended greatly on the willingness of their director of institutional research to run data in a variety of ways and present it in formats that were easily decipherable.

Conclusion

We have approached the persistent college achievement gap for African American and Latino/a students as a problem of institutional responsibility and performance. Within this approach, campus community members—particularly faculty—share the responsibility of rectifying inequities and striving for parity in educational outcomes for all students. Based on the USC researchers' experience with the fourteen initial partner campuses in the Scorecard project, we believe that gathering evidence about outcomes—disaggregated by race/ethnicity—is an effective and powerful means of first *raising awareness* of institutional problems and then *motivating* faculty and staff to seek solutions.

When the USC researchers began the Scorecard project in 2000, they did not fully realize how important leadership, motivation, credibility, and resources were with regard to the successful implementation of the Scorecard. The LMU team has shown us that these elements are critical. As the project expands to other institutions in California and beyond, these elements will be woven into criteria for participation.

Recent scholarship has also identified these elements as vital for change-oriented interventions to be successful in educational organizations (Coburn 2003; McLaughlin and Mitra 2001). For other campuses looking to undertake such a process of institutional transformation, there are several action items that can be derived from the observations we have made at LMU and elsewhere.

To raise *commitment*, campuses looking to undertake such a data examination process should consider

- making diversity and excellence central concepts in the hiring process of senior leaders and requiring that candidates demonstrate sustained work and commitment in these areas;
- identifying a team leader who can create a cohesive group that draws on the strengths of its members;
- selecting a team leader with sufficient campus clout who is experienced in navigating the politics of change efforts, particularly those related to diversity.

To ensure *motivation*, campuses looking to undertake such a data examination process should consider

- recruiting team members who are experienced in campus diversity work and able to introduce such work to inexperienced, and possibly skeptical, audiences;
- identifying team members who can move from discussion to action and meet deadlines;
- estimating the time commitment needed for project participation, reaching out to potential team members who can commit the necessary time, and exploring ways to free up time for participants—through mini-grants, course release time, student assistance, etc.;
- providing and supporting opportunities for team members to present their work on and off campus.

To increase *credibility*, campuses looking to undertake such a data examination process should consider

- identifying team members who have clout across campus;
- providing numerous venues, over time, for raising the visibility of Scorecard findings, formulating action plans to redress inequities that are discovered, and receiving updates and progress reports;
- incorporating results from this work into accreditation self-studies, conference proposals, and grant applications.

To ensure adequate *resources*, campuses looking to undertake such a data examination process should consider

- discovering creative ways to reward the efforts of the team(s), particularly if the service to the campus comes without additional remuneration or release time;
- exploring ways to provide release time, mini-grants, graduate assistantships, or other fiscal resources toward the project;
- identifying people from the institutional research office who can translate data into materials that are relevant, focused, and easily understood by a diverse readership.

The USC researchers have also learned that the very characteristics that make the Diversity Scorecard appealing could also defeat its purposes. Readers of this brief case study may become interested in developing a Scorecard for their campus, and the USC researchers welcome their participation. At the same time, it would be irresponsible not to acknowledge some of the potential pitfalls.

As was discussed earlier, the Scorecard has many characteristics that make it appealing. It is simple and easy to understand. Its logic is self-evident. It is manageable. It provides a roadmap. It results in tangible evidence. However, these qualities can also cause potential users to ignore the principles of institutional change that underlie it. The Scorecard is a theory-based intervention. It is grounded in principles of organizational change, and specifically on those related to organizational learning theory and situated inquiry.

The USC researchers view the group process of constructing a Scorecard—selecting the measures, gathering and analyzing the data—as consisting of an intervention aimed at developing "equity-minded" individuals who are in positions of influence and power. Simply put, the purpose is to encourage institutions—through the beliefs, values, and actions of its members—to be equity-driven. The Scorecard is important as a means of creating a context for change, and it represents the first phase toward building equity-based academic cultures. However, the Scorecard itself—even if campuses faithfully complete it year after year—will not alter inequities in educational outcomes. One of the pitfalls of the Scorecard is the very high risk that the process will become mechanical or perfunctory. In the USC researchers' experience, this typically occurs when campus leaders are not fully cognizant of the Scorecard's underlying principles, or when they fail to integrate these principles into their everyday work.

The way in which most people make sense of problems such as those revealed by the Scorecard is one of the most intractable challenges to creating equitable institutions. The typical response that the Scorecard elicits from campuses is a search for a program or practice that can be applied to the students in question to make educational disparities disappear. But one of the core principles underlying the Scorecard is that the solution to the problem lies *within the institution*—in its culture and in the beliefs and values that influence the expectations and practices of individuals. The USC researchers view the process of creating the Scorecard as an *intervention* that heightens a campus community's awareness of inequities and, hopefully, motivates the members to want to know more about how they can reduce them in a systematic and comprehensive fashion. An institution that discovers overwhelming GPA disparities between white students and African American students in certain majors, for example, may want to assess whether such disparities are at least partially based on the use of a narrow set of pedagogical techniques, lowered faculty expectations of African American students, or lack of African American representation on the faculty or in the curriculum, to name just a few factors.

Attaining Inclusive Excellence is a very ambitious undertaking. It demands that those in higher education shift their thinking about diversity. Rather than simply referring to the increased presence of racial and ethnic minority students on campus, diversity must have equity in educational outcomes for all students at its conceptual core. The experiences of Loyola Marymount University and the several other initial partner campuses in the project illustrate the positive shifts that can occur when academic communities are motivated to become more equity-minded and to help all students move toward high academic achievement and success.

Notes

1. Generally, we use the term "historically underrepresented students" to describe these three groups. In places, we focus on the status of African American and Latino/a students in particular to parallel an action research project we describe later in the paper.
2. We use the terms "African American," "Latino/a," "Native American," "white," and "Asian American" throughout the paper, except where source materials use alternative terms.
3. The concept of collective responsibility for student learning is derived from Lee and Loeb's (1996) construct.
4. The Center for Urban Education is an action research center located at the Rossier School of Education in the University of Southern California. The mission of the center is to create educational environments that produce equitable educational outcomes for children, youth, and adults from historically disenfranchised communities.
5. This research highlights some persistent equity issues as well. In 2000, median earnings for African American and Latino males were lower than those of white males at all education levels (NCES 2003). However, no statistically significant differences were detected between the median incomes of African American and white females at any educational level. African American males had higher median earnings than African American females at every education level, as did males in all groups in relation to their female peers.
6. See "Community Colleges Past to Present," available at www.aacc.nche.edu.
7. The four dilemmas, described in the introduction to this series of papers, are: (1) islands of innovations with too little influence on institutional structures, (2) the disconnect between diversity and educational excellence, (3) disparities in academic success across groups, and (4) the "post-Michigan" environment. For more on AAC&U's Making Excellence Inclusive initiative, see www.aacu.org/inclusive_excellence/index.cfm.

8. The tool has been renamed the Equity Scorecard, but we retain the original name in this paper for clarity. For more detailed information about the project, including a listing of the participating institutions, see www.usc.edu/dept/education/CUE. For a discussion of the theory behind the project, see "Research that Makes a Difference" in the *Journal of Higher Education* (Bensimon et al. 2004), and for a description of the implementation steps, see "A Learning Approach to Institutional Change" in *Change* (Bensimon 2004).

9. The project focuses on African American and Latino/a students because it is being field tested at institutions that have a very high representation of students from each of these groups. However, the methods of this project can be applied to any population that has a history of inequality.

10. Many of the campuses also disaggregated their data by gender to investigate possible differences in outcomes within particular racial/ethnic groups.

11. These are the terms used by LMU to describe the racial/ethnic identities of students.

12. This framework was adapted from Kaplan and Norton's (1992) "balanced scorecard" for use in institutions of higher education by O'Neil et al. (1999) as the "academic scorecard." Bensimon then adapted the framework for the Diversity Scorecard.

13. While individual students may choose new majors that better suit their interests, it is in cases where disproportionate or large numbers of underrepresented students are migrating that institutional barriers may be revealed.

14. We remind readers that this benchmarking framework was developed specifically for the Diversity Scorecard project and does not reflect any official position of AAC&U.

15. LMU's report is available online at www.lmu.edu/pages/6546.asp.

16. Several research-oriented publications that address various aspects of organizational learning are forthcoming, and they will be accessible via the Center for Urban Education's Web site, www.usc.edu/dept/education/CUE.

17. The reports from each of these teams are available on LMU's Web site, www.lmu.edu.

18. Also noteworthy, there are no planned costs attached to the development of the mentoring network. The director of the international study program intends to ask for volunteers from the faculty and students who have studied abroad to help new applicants with the process.

References

Adelman, C. 1999. *Answers in the tool box: Academic intensity, attendance patterns, and a bachelor's degree attainment.* Jessup, MD: U.S. Department of Education Office of Educational Research and Improvement.

American Council on Education. 2003, October 8. Minority college enrollment surges over the past two decades; Students of color still lag behind whites in college participation. Press release. Available at: http://www.acenet.edu/AM/Template.cfm?Section=20032&CONTENTID=3719&TEMPLATE=/CM/ContentDisplay.cfm.

Argyris, C. 1977. Double loop learning in organizations. *Harvard Business Review* 55 (5): 115–25.

Association of American Colleges and Universities. 2002. *Greater expectations: A new vision for learning as a nation goes to college.* Washington, DC: Association of American Colleges and Universities.

Astin, A. 1999. Involvement in learning revisited: Lessons we have learned. *Journal of College Student Development* 40 (5): 587–98

Barton, P. E. 2003. Parsing the achievement gap: Baselines for tracking progress. Princeton, NJ: Educational Testing Service.

Bauman, G. L. 2002. *Developing a culture of evidence: Using institutional data to identify inequitable educational outcomes.* Unpublished dissertation, University of Southern California, Los Angeles, California.

Bensimon, E. M. 2004. The diversity scorecard: A learning approach to institutional change. *Change* 36 (1): 45–52.

Bensimon, E. M., L. Hao, and L. T. Bustillos, in press. Measuring the state of equity in higher education. Harvard Civil Rights Project.

Bensimon, E. M., D. E. Polkinghorne, G. L. Bauman, and E. Vallejo. 2004. Research that makes a difference. *The Journal of Higher Education* 75 (1): 104–26.

Bok, D. 2003. Closing the nagging gap in minority achievement. *The Chronicle of Higher Education* 50 (9): 20.

Bourdieu, P. 1985. The forms of capital. In *Handbook of theory and research for the sociology of education*, ed. J. G. Richardson, 241–58. New York: Greenwood Press.

Bowen, W. G., and D. Bok. 1998. *The shape of the river.* Princeton, NJ: Princeton University Press.

Braxton, J.M., and L. A. Lein 2000. The viability of academic integration as the central construction in Tinto's interactionalist theory of college student departure. In *Reworking the student departure puzzle*, ed. J. M. Braxton, 11–28. Nashville, TN: Vanderbilt University Press.

Burke, J.C., and H. P. Minassians, ed. 2003. *Reporting higher education results: Missing links in the performance chain. New directions for institutional research*, no. 116. San Francisco: Jossey-Bass.

Carnevale, A. P., and R. A. Fry. 2000. *Crossing the great divide: Can we achieve equity when generation Y goes to college?* Princeton, NJ: Educational Testing Service.

Coburn, C. E. 2003. Rethinking scale: Moving beyond numbers to deep and lasting change. *Educational Researcher* 32 (6): 3–12.

Cohen, C. J., and C. E. Nee. 2000. Educational attainment and sex differentials in African American communities. *American Behavioral Scientist* 43 (7): 1159–1206.

College Board, The. 1999. *Reaching the top: A report of the national task force on minority high achievement*. New York: author.

Fry, R. 2002. *Latino/as in higher education: Many enroll, too few graduate*. Washington, DC: Pew Hispanic Center.

Gándara, P. (with J. Maxwell-Jolly). 1999. *Priming the pump: Strategies for increasing the achievement of underrepresented minority undergraduates*. Princeton, NJ: The College Board.

Harvey, W. B. 2003. *Minorities in higher education 2002–2003: 20th* Annual status report. Washington, DC: American Council on Education.

Hurst, T. 2002. *United Negro College Fund 2001 statistical report*. Fairfax, VA: Frederick D. Patterson Research Institute.

Johnson, L. B. 1965. To fulfill these rights. Commencement address at Howard University, June 14. Available at: http://www.lbjlib.utexas.edu/johnson/archives.hom/speeches.hom/650604.asp.

Jencks, C., and M. Phillips. 1998. *The black-white test score gap*. Washington, DC: The Brookings Institution.

Kaplan, R., and D. Norton. 1992. The balanced scorecard: Measures that drive performance. *Harvard Business Review* 70 (1): 71–9.

King, J. E. 2000. *Gender equity in higher education: Are male students at a disadvantage?* Washington, DC: American Council on Education Center for Policy Analysis.

Knight Higher Education Collaborative, The. 2000. The data made me do it. *Policy Perspectives* 9 (2): 1–12.

Lee, V. E., and J. B. Loeb. 1996. Collective responsibility for learning and its effects on gains in achievement for early secondary school students. *American Journal of Education* 104: 103–47.

Massey, D. S., C. Z. Charles, G. F. Lundy, and M. J. Fisher. 2003. *The source of the river: The social origins of freshmen at America's selective colleges and universities*. Princeton, NJ: Princeton University Press.

McLaughglin, M.W., and D. Mitra. 2001. Theory-based change and change-based theory: Going deeper, going broader. *Journal of Educational Change* 2: 301–23.

National Center for Public Policy and Higher Education. 2000. *Measuring up 2000: The state-by-state report card for higher education*. Washington, DC: The National Center for Public Policy and Higher Education.

National Center for Public Policy and Higher Education. 2002. *Measuring up 2002: The state-by-state report card for higher education*. Washington, DC: The National Center for Public Policy and Higher Education.

National Assessment of Educational Progress. 2003. *The nation's report card: 2003*. Mathematics and reading assessments results. Available at: http://nces.ed.gov/nationsreportcard/mathematics/results2003/ and http://nces.ed.gov/nationsreportcard/reading/results2003/.

National Center for Education Statistics. 2003. *Status and trends in the education of Blacks* (NCES 203–034). Washington, DC: U.S. Department of Education.

Ogbu, J. U. 1978. *Minority education and caste: The American system in cross-cultural perspective*. New York: Academic Press.

O'Neil, H. F., Jr., E. M. Bensimon, M. A. Diamond, and M. R. Moore. 1999. Designing and implementing an academic scorecard. *Change* 31 (6): 32–41.

Renner, K. E. 2003. Racial equity and higher education. *Academe* 89 (1): 38–43.

Tinto, V. 1987. *Leaving college: Rethinking the causes and cures of student attrition*. Chicago, IL: University of Chicago Press.

Trent, W. T. 1991. Focus on equity: Race & gender differences in degree attainment 1975–76; 1980–81. In *College in black and white: African American students in historically black and predominantly white public universities*, ed. W. Allen and E. Epps, 41–59. Albany, NY: SUNY Press.

WHEN AND WHERE INTERESTS COLLIDE: POLICY, RESEARCH, AND THE CASE FOR MANAGING CAMPUS DIVERSITY

T. ELON DANCY II

America is changing at a rapid pace. America is increasingly pluralistic in race, gender, ethnicity, class as well as the ways in which people express behavior, faith, love, and creed. Social issues of the day are consistently levied against human rights doctrine. Pressure is increasing for individuals to develop competencies for a global citizenry. To meet social transformation and change, American colleges and universities are rethinking the characteristics that make them distinct and that contribute to higher education and society writ large (Kuh et al., 1991). Perhaps nowhere is this rethinking more readily located than in institutional mission statements. As more than 3,000 American institutions of higher education define and redefine their beliefs about student potential, teaching and learning, one certainty remains—American college graduates are charged to become culturally sensitive and culturally competent to meet the needs of the 21st century. In response, institutional mission statements affirm the role diversity plays in preparing students for social, civic, and professional futures.

Diversity in higher education is a topic about which scholars agree is troubling to collegiate work and policy (M. J. Chang & Kiang, 2002; Hurtado, 2007; Hurtado, Milem, Clayton-Pedersen, & Allen, 1999). College administrators are often in a quandary when personnel, students, or others argue that disparities exist between diversity-focused institutional programming and institutional core values and mission (Milem, 2003). Another way to envision diversity conflicts is that institutional priorities around diversity are often politically wedged between law and sociohistorical forces (Milem, Chang, & antonio, 2005). In addition, scholars have argued that this tension exists given that traditional institutional strategies fail to adequately centralize diversity and potentially assume the following: (1) diverse individuals must change, (2) diverse student, faculty, staff, and administrators are responsible for socializing each other, (3) individuals from underprivileged cultures must adapt to privileged culture, (4) only "identifiably" diverse students need aid, (5) equitable educational opportunities to all students or professional opportunities to personnel are not needed (6) educating the dominant culture about diverse colleagues is not needed (Mayhew, Grunwald, & Dey, 2006; Stage & Manning, 1992).

In developing this chapter, I conducted a multidisciplinary analysis of the scholarly and research literature toward understanding how effective management of diversity benefits the work of colleges and potentially works to relieve tensions that exist. A three-pronged framework is used in this effort. First, the sociohistorical and legal history is interrogated as its shape colliding interests in diversity for higher education. Second, this chapter discusses how diversity benefits students and institutions. Student benefits are discussed in light of learning outcomes enhanced by the presence or work of diversity on campus, while institutional benefits refer to how diversity enhances organizational effectiveness nationally and internationally. Third, I propose methods for managing diversity, synthesizing discussion from empirical and scholarly literature.

Early Diversity Movements, Collegiate Desegregation, and Transdemography

Early Diversity Movements

Prior to the Civil War, higher education remained primarily the province of white men (Cohen, 1998; Thelin, 2004). Following the Civil War, the demise of slavery promoted other social revisions and reforms including educational exclusion. Women and formerly enslaved African Americans used this time to fight for educational access and equal rights. Responding to these new demands, higher education took action. Colleges and universities began to open admissions to both women and minorities during the mid-19th century albeit the process of equalization of educational opportunity occurred gradually.

Efforts to create a place for women and minorities generally derived from a need to protect the social, political, and economic dominance of White men. However, in 1837, Oberlin College became the first institution to admit women (Cohen, 1998; Rudolph, 1962; Thelin, 2004). However, between 1861 and 1875, Matthew Vassar, Henry Wells, Sophia Smith, and Henry Durant created colleges exclusively for women (Geiger, 1999). These institutions allowed women to fully participate in higher education at institutions where they were the focus of both the curriculum and the administration. Yet, the purpose was to educate them to succeed at the tasks assigned to them in an industrializing society, which largely included rearing educated children to continue the progress of the nation (Geiger, 1999).

Systemic privilege emerged where predominantly White colleges and universities began to accept students who were not White Anglo-Saxon, Protestant (WASP) and men. When White women integrated predominantly White colleges, the conventions of then Victorian culture insisted upon separation of the sexes (Gordon, 1997). More specifically, men were viewed as natural leaders in public, political and economic venues while women were relegated to uneducated lives in which they tended to the household and children (Gordon, 1997). White women, particularly those who lived in the antebellum North, gained access to higher education given arguments that secondary education equipped women with tools needed to be better wives and mothers. Unmarried women largely used higher education to prepare themselves for teaching professions (Gordon, 1997). Southern women were expected to view higher education as preparation for roles as wives and mothers. During this period, restrictive admissions policies to maintain White Anglo-Saxon Protestant (WASP) tradition became strategic plan and policy.

In the early 1900s, colleges were still seeking to preserve higher education for the sons of WASP businessmen or professionals (Levine, 1997). In doing so, "elite" predominantly White colleges of the 1920s and 1930s were replete with ethnic and class prejudice. Critical numbers of liberal arts colleges chose to limit the size of their classes and seek national and upper-middle class students at the expense of local and more diverse students after WWI. With little accountability, restrictive admissions policies justified the exclusion of Jewish students, who were discriminated against when they applied to elite colleges in the Northeast. This "Jewish problem," as it is described in the literature, was further shaped by no formal admissions procedures, modest attempts to attract regionally diverse students, widespread anti-semitism, and an increase of Jewish applicants (Dancy & Brown, in press; Levine, 1997). Institutions adhering to quotas included Dartmouth, Harvard, and the New England colleges. Forthcoming litigation would work to dismantle such quotas and discrimination.

Collegiate Desegregation

Between the late 1930s and the early 1950s, colleges made minimal progress in racially desegregating. Legal challenges during this period resulted in decisions that sanctioned specific institutions for practicing race-based discrimination rather than addressing desegregation writ large. Defining cases of this period included *Sipuel v. Board of Regents of the University of Oklahoma* (1948), *McLaurin v. Oklahoma State Regents* (1950), and *Sweatt v. Painter* (1950). Although the Supreme Court stopped short of overturning the *Plessy* decision, they did make sufficient use and application of the Fourteenth Amendment in each of these cases (Brown & Lane, 2003). By aggressively applying the Equal Protection Clause of the Fourteenth Amendment in *Sipuel, McLaurin,* and *Sweatt,* the Supreme Court altered and limited the ability of states to discriminate in higher education. These rulings forced states to commit to segregation by providing equal facilities for different student groups or integrate. Although there was considerable impact on state policy in Texas and Oklahoma, change was not widespread nationally (Brown & Lane, 2003).

From the mid-1950s to the late 1970s, federal legislation and court cases impacted colleges and universities in all states. *Brown v. Board of Education* (1954) is largely regarded as a watershed case in impacting national policy on collegiate desegregation although the case primarily considered elementary and secondary schools (Bowen & Bok, 1998; Brown, 1999; Brown & Lane, 2003). In this case, parents of four black children sued the Board of Education in Topeka, Kansas for denying their children access to the school district's all-white public schools solely because of their race. Although the Board of Education provided schools specifically designated to educate African American children, these schools could not provide an equal education due to poor facilities, a lack of materials, weak curricula, and inadequately trained and compensated teachers. In the *Brown* decision, the Supreme Court finally reversed and overturned its earlier ruling in *Plessy v. Ferguson* (1896). Under *Plessy,* states had been given the legal right to operate race-based, dual educational systems. The U.S. Supreme Court now repealed its earlier ruling, forcing all states to provide the same education to all public school students. The Civil Rights Act of 1964 followed the *Brown* decision, shaping the arguments of this ruling into a legal reality. In addition, the *Brown* decision was also supported and specifically applied to higher education through *Florida ex rel. Hawkins v. Board of Control* (1954/1956), *Tureaud v. Louisiana State University* (1954), and *Adams v. Richardson* (1973).

Similar to the *Sipuel, McLaurin* and *Sweatt* cases, the case of *Florida ex rel. Hawkins v. Board of Control* involved a black student suing to gain access to a graduate/professional degree program. Scholars suggest that the Florida and U.S. Supreme Court's reluctance to apply the *Brown* decision to higher education contexts is reflected in this case (Brown & Lane, 2003). First, the court ordered that *Florida ex rel. Hawkins* be remanded for further review under the new legal standard (*Florida ex rel. Hawkins v. Board of Control of Florida,* 347 U.S. 971 [1954]). Oddly, the court did not issue a final decision in *Florida ex rel. Hawkins* until 1958. Eventually, the court ruled that the Board of Control could not deny admissions to University of Florida's graduate and professional schools on the basis of race but upheld Hawkins' denial from the University of Florida Law School (*Hawkins v. Board of Control,* 162 F.Supp. 851 [N. D. Fl. 1958]). Brown and Lane (2003) note a key difference between K-12 schools and collegiate contexts in the *Florida ex rel. Hawkins* decision. They observe that states are obligated by law to provide an equal elementary and secondary education to all students but not required to provide a college education to anyone. Brown and Lane further point out that, as demonstrated in the *Florida ex rel. Hawkins* case, the courts were reluctant to become involved in collegiate admissions decisions, making large-scale higher education desegregation difficult. Another case regarding higher education is also similar.

In the case, *Tureaud v. Louisiana State University* (1954), Black students wanted the State of Louisiana to allow them to enroll in a combined six-year arts and sciences and law program at Louisiana State University. The plaintiffs in the case argued that a similar state-sponsored program at Southern University was not equal to the program at Louisiana State University. The state attempted a failed compromise in light of precedents set forth in *Brown. Tureaud* extended the reach of *Brown* and *Florida ex rel. Hawkins* to all collegiate levels given that the six-year program involved in the case concerned both undergraduate and professional study (Brown & Lane, 2003). Notwithstanding, the win for collegiate desegregation in the *Tureaud* case still did not lead to desegregation policy across states.

In 1964, however, President Lyndon B. Johnson signed the Civil Rights Act of 1964, which led to many states' attempts to end segregation. Scholars argue that the Civil Rights Act of 1964 enhanced the implementation of *Brown v. Board of Education* (Brown and Lane, 2003; Williams, 1988). Specifically, Title VI of the Civil Rights Act provided previously nonexistent sanctions which punished institutions that failed to abide by anti-discrimination legislation. Title VI of the Civil Rights Act of 1964 prohibited segregated schools and colleges from receiving federal funds to ensure compliance.

The Civil Rights Act of 1964 also led to the development of diversity programs in addition to providing sanctions for noncompliance. Historically, diversity programs called for special consideration in employment, education, and contracting decisions for minorities and women. Title VI's premise was to end the practice of the "separate but equal" doctrine and to allow greater participation in higher education among American citizens. According to scholars, Title VI thus became the basis for diversity programs in higher education (Brown & Lane, 2003). In June of 1965, President Johnson issued Executive Order #11246 at the Historically Black Howard University in Washington D.C. Executive Order #11246 required equal opportunity employment. More specifically, federal contractors or federally assisted construction contractors were prohibited from discriminating based on race, color, religion, sex, or national origin. President Johnson observes,

> You do not wipe away the scars of centuries by saying: Now you are free to go where you want, and do as you desire, and choose the leaders you please. You do not take a person who, for years, had been hobbled by chains and liberate him, bring him up to the starting line of a race and then say, 'you are free to compete with all the others,' and still justly believe that you have been completely fair (Brunner, 2001, p. 4).

Brown and Lane (2003) argue that, in issuing Executive Order #11246, President Johnson effectively adopted one of the first diversity programs to be supported by the Civil Rights Act of 1964. The U.S. Department of Education also developed a variety of programs and initiatives designed to increase participation in higher education among women and students of color at previously segregated institutions. First, the department awarded fellowships to interested researchers from traditionally underrepresented groups. Second, the department gave priority in awarding grants for new facilities to institutions serving a significant number of economically disadvantaged students and students of color. Other federal agencies created set-aside programs for universities engaged in increasing participation among people of color. Colleges and universities followed this pattern.

Many colleges and universities also developed their own diversity programs, crafting goals, timetables, and incentives for recruiting persons of color. Notwithstanding, Office of Civil Rights (OCR) investigations found many Southern colleges and universities refused to comply with the Civil Rights Act of 1964. More specifically, nineteen southern and border states continued to operate dual higher education systems albeit that Title VI sanctioned this behavior.

Reversing this trend was the goal of *Adams v. Richardson* (1973). In this case, plaintiffs brought a lawsuit against Elliot Richardson, Secretary of Health, Education, and Welfare (HEW) who, the plaintiffs alleged, failed to enforce Title VI of the Civil Rights Act of 1964. The District of Columbia Circuit Court of Appeals ruled in favor of the plaintiffs. In addition, this court implemented mechanisms (i.e., less state control) to force HEW to uphold Title VI. Like cases before it, however, *Adams* did not define strategies for attaining desegregation or any related issues of applying and enforcing policy (Brown & Lane, 2003). The following era, though, would be one in which desegregation efforts were heavily debated.

Post-1970s collegiate desegregation legislation continues to largely affect diversity programs today (Brown, 1999). Much dissension and debate have emerged in the wake of changing public priorities and divergent court decisions. Namely, *Regents of University of California v. Bakke* (1978) is one case which has complicated how colleges develop diversity programs and initiatives. In this case, Alan Bakke, a White male seeking admission to the University of California-Davis Medical School, charged the institution with practicing reverse discrimination after he was twice rejected. At the time, the UC-Davis Medical School operated a special admissions program in which disadvantaged members of underrepresented minority groups were chosen to fill 16 out of the 100 places allotted to each year's entering class. The Supreme Court upheld the California Supreme Court's earlier decision which found the admissions program to use a quota system and thus violating the Equal Protection Clause of the Fourteenth Amendment. However, the Supreme Court also reversed part of the California Supreme court's decision finding unacceptable considerations of race in the admissions process. Ambiguity emerged from the very justices who brought judgment. Justice Lewis Powell, who casted a swing-vote in the ruling, argued against race as a factor in the admissions process while simultaneously arguing an ethnically diverse student body carries educational benefits. (Brown, 1999; Justiz, Wilson, & Bjork, 1994). This ruling thus added little direction to higher education regarding the place and function of diversity programs. Subsequently, challenges to diversity programs and civil rights legislation emerged after judgment in *Bakke*.

In fact, a variety of legal challenges have sought more lucid judgment of collegiate diversity programs. Though neither considered collegiate contexts specifically, *Wygant v. Jackson Board of Education* (1986) and *Richmond v. Croson* (1989) impacted debate over diversity programs. In both cases, people of color received protections or differential treatments via quota systems which were later deemed violations of the Equal Protection Clause in the Fourteenth Amendment. Adding to the *Bakke* ruling, the Supreme Court argued that diversity programs must support a compelling interest of the state. The Court also established the "strict scrutiny" test to provide additional clarity regarding how diversity programs may be shaped. This ruling eliminated the general use of historical discrimination to justify the existence of diversity programs. The strict scrutiny test is referenced in significant legal disputes emergent in collegiate contexts. *Kirwan v. Podberesky* (1992), for example, led to the repeal of the Benjamin Banneker Scholarship Program at the University of Maryland (which served African American students) the Fourth Circuit Court eventually found that the university scholarship program did not satisfy the strict scrutiny test. The final resolution not only ended the Benjamin Banneker Scholarship but highlighted the difficulties institutions face in legally shaping diversity programs even within institutions with the worst histories of segregation (Brown, 1999).

Like *Podberesky*, *Hopwood v. State of Texas* (1994) also involved the *strict scrutiny* test. In this case, Cheryl Hopwood and three other White students filed suit against the State of Texas, the University of Texas Board of Regents, the University of Texas School of Law, and other affiliated defendants, Hopwood and her co-plaintiffs alleged that the defendants violated both the Equal Protection Clause of the Fourteenth Amendment and Title VI of the Civil Rights Act of 1964 by operating a quota system that gave preferential treatment to African American and Mexican American law school applicants. Eventually, the Fifth Circuit Court decided that University of Texas School of Law violated both the Fourteenth Amendment and the Civil Rights Act of 1964. In addition, the Fifth Circuit also ruled that the School of Law must eliminate race from its admissions decisions. Since the *Hopwood* decision, few states have successfully eliminated the use of diversity programs altogether and thus made the future of diversity programs and initiatives more uncertain (Brown, 1999).

Nationally, the use of diversity programs to achieve collegiate desegregation remains unresolved (Brown & Lane, 2003). State university systems in California and Texas, for example, have adopted various methods to maintain enrollments among students of color in certain universities. Given statewide elections, diversity programs and college systems were forced to think about attaining diversity in different ways. Subsequently, new priorities for college systems included reconsidering how qualifying exams are assessed or guaranteeing acceptances for students who graduate in the top 10 percent of their high school classes. However, attempts to enact legislation ending diversity programs in Michigan failed (Brown & Lane, 2003).

Diversity programs remain controversial in Michigan. In both *Gratz v. Bollinger* (2001) and *Grutter v. Bollinger* (2001), plaintiffs contended that University of Michigan admissions programs violated both the Equal Protection Clause of the Fourteenth Amendment and Title VI of the Civil Rights Act of 1964. Respectively, White undergraduates were rejected by the University of Michigan College of Literature, Science, and the Arts (LSA) and the University of Michigan Law School. In the *Gratz* ruling issued on February 26, 2001, the Southern Division of the Eastern District Court of Michigan found unconstitutional use of race in admissions by the University of Michigan College of LSA. This same court provided a similar decision a month later in the *Grutter* case, ruling that the University of Michigan Law School's admissions program violated both the Fourteenth Amendment and Title VI of the Civil Rights Act. In addition, the court also issued an injunction barring the Law School from considering race in its admissions process. Although the University is appealing the *Grutter* case, diversity programs at the University of Michigan appear likely to end (Brown & Lane, 2003). Today, transdemographic enrollments represent ways in which colleges may work to attain diverse enrollments.

Transdemography

Colleges, among other societal institutions, inherited the challenge of righting the effects of past wrongs. The perennial discourses on collegiate desegregation highlight this challenge. Notwithstanding, state coordinating boards and institutional boards of trustees are moving forward with implementing collegiate desegregation compliance initiatives (Brown, 1999; Brown, 2001; Brown & Freeman, 2004). The result is a collection of ad hoc policies and practices which promote changing the statistical composition of the student population within the corresponding institutions based solely on race—transdemography (Brown, 2002).

Transdemography offers colleges dominated by both Black and/or White enrollments an opportunity to enrich the student campus context and to encourage intercultural communication within the academic environment (Brown, 1999). However, transdemography simultaneously threatens to eradicate the rich campus culture for which colleges with population focus (i.e., HBCUs) are lauded, with scant implications for campuses populated primarily by White constituents (Brown & Freeman, 2004; Fleming, 1984; Garibaldi, 1984; Hytche, 1989; Roebuck & Murty, 1993). Current collegiate desegregation initiatives have as their primary aim attracting White students to Historically Black Colleges and Universities (HBCUs) (Brown, 1999; Brown & Freeman, 2004). As an interesting turn, existing compliance plans proffer limited resources or support for targeting significant increases in African American student attendance at Historically White Institutions (HWIs) within the respective states. Collegiate desegregation has morphed into a transdemographic enrollment initiative. It is important for scholars and administrators to attend to the unintended consequences that have and continue to emerge from these shifting enrollments, terrains, and possibly paradigms.

One way of attending to these consequences is through effectively managing diversity on college campuses. This requires thinking about diversity management differently from a diversity program as discussed above in the review of turbulently evolving legal policy. Thinking about diversity management as affirmative action programs likely leads to the debates which shaped the court cases in this section. Notwithstanding, colleges campuses benefit when personnel and policy pay close attention to inclusion of diverse individuals and work to manage diversity effectively. It is the research on these topics that the following section considers.

The Benefits of Diversity

> Change is difficult in higher education, and if judged by past performance, change to enact diverse learning and professional environments is particularly hard. The values and organizational dynamics of higher education are unique and especially problematic for making foundational and cultural change. At their core, higher education institutions do function like corporations, hospitals, or any other type of for-profit or nonprofit organization. Irrational systems, nebulous and multiples goals structures, complex and differentiated campus functions, conflicts between espoused and enacted values, and loosely coupled systems of organization and governance are just some of the dynamics that make organizational change in higher education so hard. Such change requires frameworks and tools that are able to respond to these complex campus dynamics as well as to the external environment (Williams, Berger, & McClendon, 2005, p. 2).

In the above quote, Williams, Berger, and McClendon (2005) describe how diversity-focused change in higher education is complicated by the divergent interests of colleges to provide high-quality education while also holding true to national policy and core values shared across organizations. In this section, this chapter considers the ways in which diversity benefits colleges and universities in their capacities as organizations as well as spaces in which students are educated. First, research is explored that finds diversity as an educational benefit to students, demanding interventions that potentially conflict with organizational values and dynamics. Second, this chapter turns to the limited empirical work that considers how diversity influences colleges and universities organizationally. Research on how diversity influences organizational effectiveness in the private sector is more aptly located. Much of this work indicates that racial, cultural, and ethnic diversity advantages organizations and presents strategies for effectively managing diversity.

Educational Benefit for Students

Research describing the ways in which individuals benefit from diversity on campus undergirds sustained attention to diversity on college campuses and universities. Educational benefit refers to the ways in which educational experiences and outcomes of individual students are enhanced by the presence of diversity on campus (Milem, 2003). The research on the educational benefits of diversity for students clusters around three types: (1) structural diversity or the numerical representation of diverse groups on a campus; (2) informal interactional diversity or the actual experience students have with diverse peers; and (3) classroom diversity or the exposure to knowledge about race and ethnicity in formal classrooms (Gurin, Dey, Gurin, & Hurtado, 2003). In this framework, structural diversity represents a fundamental level of diverse interactions (Gurin et al., 2003). As benefits evokes diversity outcomes, three major types of outcomes are outlined in the literature.

First, learning outcomes describe students' active learning processes including campus engagement and academic learning as well as student motivation to engage and students' reflection on the value of the college experience after graduation (Gurin et al., 2003). Second, democracy outcomes refer to how higher education prepares students to become involved as active participants in an increasingly diverse society. In their work, Gurin and colleagues suggest three levels of democracy outcomes: citizenship-engagement, racial/cultural engagement, and compatibility of differences. Citizenship engagement describes students' interest and motivation in influencing society and the political structure, in participating in the community and volunteer service. Racial/cultural engagement refers to students' levels of cultural awareness and appreciation and their commitment to participate in activities that promote racial understanding. Compatibility of differences describes students' comprehension of common values across racial/ethnic groups and constructive ways in which to dissolve conflict. Milem (2003) expounds on Gurin et al.'s concepts with two types of diversity outcomes. Process outcomes reflect the ways in which students perceive diversity as shaping their college experiences. Material benefits describe students' material outcomes (i.e., higher salary) associated with attendance at diverse colleges. Much of the research on the relationship between diversity and student outcomes is conducted within these conceptual parameters.

Hurtado (2003) studied how colleges prepare students to live and work in a diverse democracy and the ways in which students learn from their interaction with diverse peers in college. Hurtado surveyed chief academic officers at four-year institutions, entering freshman classes at ten public universities, classroom-based studies, focus groups, document analysis and administrator interviews. Regarding the benefits of diversity on college campuses, Hurtado found that students who report frequent contact with diverse peers experience greater cognitive complexity, self-confidence in being culturally aware and see conflict as natural in the democratic process. More specifically, positive and meaningful interactions were found to predict cognitive, social and democratic outcomes. Additionally, diversity courses or diversity-related programming had a consistently positive effect on most educational outcomes. This research joins with other widely cited research findings which emphasize the significant impact diversity-focused courses have on cultural understanding and overall satisfaction in college (Astin, 1993). Additional studies have also sought to understand the link between diversity and learning on college campuses.

Chang (1996) studied racial diversity in higher education with the understanding that little consensus exists regarding the essentiality of racially diverse campus to college student educational gains. He found that White students largely benefit in developing cultural competency from engaging racially diverse others and, in particular, discussing topics of race. Findings also indicated institutions with greater institutional diversity among collegiate personnel tend to have greater faculty diversity emphasis, diverse student bodies, and enhanced opportunities to promote learning around diversity (i.e., attending cultural awareness workshops, enrolling in ethnic studies courses).

Studying informal interactions with diversity, antonio (1998) examines the development of leadership skills, cultural knowledge, and understanding among college students. According to the author, findings suggest that casual interracial interaction is particularly beneficial among students with more racially homogeneous friendship circles, especially in developing leadership skills. In addition, findings indicate that frequent interracial interaction among students may be more important in developing cultural knowledge than involvement in formal activities such as cultural awareness workshops. antonio argues that the positive effects of interracial interaction on leadership ability and cultural knowledge support claims that a diverse student body matters in preparing students for multicultural citizenship.

Later, antonio (2001) studied diversity in the context of friendship groups at the University of California, Los Angeles (UCLA). More specifically, he was interested in the influence of friendship groups on students' development of racial understanding, cultural awareness, and interracial interaction. antonio observes that structural diversity in the student body increases opportunity for students to develop friendships with people of different cultures and ethnicities. He found that students identified racial diversity to be the most positive of their interpersonal experiences on campus. In addition, he argues that developing interracial relationships shapes a sense of courage in students to socialize across races. This finding brings to mind widely cited research findings which showed that students who reported frequent interactions with diverse peers were more open to diverse perspectives and willing to challenge their own beliefs (Pascarella, Edison, Nora, Hagedorn, & Terenzini, 1996). Additional study explores factors that predict these and similar cross-racial interactions among college students.

Saenz, Ngai, and Hurtado (2007) explore factors that promoted positive interactions across race for African American, Asian American, Latino, and White college students. Drawing upon survey data from incoming students at nine public institutions, the authors found that exposure to a predominantly White pre-college environment significantly predicted for interracial interactions. More specifically, diverse neighborhood, school, and peer group environments helped students become more comfortable in interactions across race. For Latino students, high SAT scores and gender (being female) was a high predictor for cross-race interaction. In a similar vein as research presented in this review, White students became more comfortable with cross-racial interactions after interacting with diverse peers.

Based on the review of research above, overwhelming evidence shows important relationships between diversity and student gains. Specifically, cross-racial interactions as well as campus and classroom opportunities to engage issues of racial/ethnic/cultural difference positively impact student outcomes. Considerable evidence also shows that students develop confidence in engaging topics of difference and competence for assuming roles in a diversified, global citizenry. In the next section, research is considered on how organizations engage topics of diversity to enhance effectiveness.

Managing Diversity as Organizational Benefit

Taylor Cox (1994) defines managing diversity as planning and implementing organizational systems and practices to maximize the potential advantages of diversity while minimizing the potential disadvantages of diversity. He notes that three types of organizational goals are achieved by managing diversity. Largely, these goals involve moral, ethical, and social responsibility, legal obligations of organizations, and economic performance goals. In a review of arguments on how diversity creates competitive advantage in organizations, Cox and Blake (1991) surmise that effectively managing diversity leads to the following constructive outcomes for organizations: (1) social responsibility goals are met; (2) cost advantage is created; (3) resource acquisition is increased; (4) marketing efforts are improved; (5) creativity is increased (6) better problem solving and decision making is promoted; and (7) system flexibility to better react to environmental changes is created. In this, and additional work (Cox, 1994) argues that properly managing diversity leads to lower turnover rates, greater time-on-task flexibility, and greater organizational productivity.

It is important that the concept of diversity management not be confused with affirmative action. Organizations more readily perceive affirmative action with legal obligation to diversify a workforce (Cox, 1994). Research evidence in the private sector casts doubt on the simple assertion that a diverse workforce inevitably improves organizational performance (Jayne & Dipboye, 2004). Diversity management, rather, involves strategies that recognize connectedness between inclusiveness and overall organizational goals and does not attempt to advantage a specific group as affirmative action does (Gilbert, Stead, & Invancevich, 1999). Though research shows affirmative action programs have made organizations more equitable, little research connects affirmative action programs to an organization's achievement of its goals (Reskin, 1998). However, research does show that inclusion of minority perspectives stimulates alternative ways to achieve goals (Cox, 1994). In addition, these groups are found in the research literature to be more creative in ways that move organizations effectively toward their goals.

However, Cox (1994) also identifies problems associated with organizations that seek to diversify. First, he observes that heterogeneity in groups may lead to lower levels of cohesiveness. Cox argues that cohesiveness is more attainable in groups that are homogeneous. Yet communication among diverse groups may negatively impact cohesiveness. Cox writes that communication among heterogeneous groups is less effective. Communication difficulty, Cox argues, is linked with discomfort in participating in groups, increased anxieties among organization members, and increased conflict and potential for conflict. Cox's observations lend support to arguments that mere diversification of individuals is not always positive.

Notwithstanding, research among colleges and universities does find the simple inclusion of women or faculty of color as important factors in enriching the primary missions of universities (Milem, 2003). In a recent study of diverse faculty impact on university work, Milem found race and gender to serve as significant predictors of the use of active learning methods in the classroom. These, in turn, positively impacted the learning process for students. In his recent review of research, Milem (2003) cited a study conducted by Statham, Richardson, and Cook (1991) which found that assistant professors were more likely to adopt participatory teaching practices than full professors. In this same research review, he notes other studies he conducted in which he found strong correlations between faculty members race and gender and student-centered approaches which positively impact student learning. The majority of research that considers issues of hiring or inclusion of collegiate personnel largely implicates faculty (Milem et al., 2005). However, a study is located that identifies factors for creating a positive climate for diversity and factor predictability regarding positive campus climate for diversity.

In their work, Mayhew, Grunwald, and Dey (2006) studied factors that influenced staff perceptions of their campus community as positive climates for diversity. Based on their empirical evidence, the researchers argue that an institution's ability to achieve a positive climate for diversity reflects not only the personal characteristics of staff members but also their perceptions of the work environment. Additional empirical work is needed to investigate how diversity impacts collegiate personnel and how diversity is managed in collegiate contexts.

This chapter has reviewed a range of policy and research that shapes higher education's understanding of how diversity matters to the work of colleges and universities. The research reviewed provides evidence that diversity not only matters in colleges but must be effectively managed in order to sustain positive outcomes for student learning. Therefore, it is important that institutional structures and practices that present barriers to diversity are identified, examined, challenged, and removed. It is additionally important to understand practical strategies that enhance colleges' and universities' abilities to manage diversity. These ideas are presented in the following section.

Managing Diversity in Colleges and Universities

As the research evidence shows, structural diversity alone does not guarantee that students will benefit from positive learning outcomes. Along these lines, Liu (1998) writes, "often neglected in the debate about diversity is the fact that achieving a racially diverse study body by itself is not sufficient to bring about desired educational outcomes. How that diversity is managed matters greatly" (p. 438). The chapter joins with additional writing that warns colleges and universities against thinking about challenges of diversity as concerning only affirmative action or admissions (Liu, 1998; Milem, 2003). Liu argues,

To establish a "compelling interest" in educational diversity, a university must

demonstrate clear, consistent internal policies and practices designed to facilitate interracial contact, dialogue, and understanding on campus. (Liu, 1998, p. 439)

With this in mind, this chapter offers ideas and strategic questions to campuses to help them in their efforts to effectively manage diversity. Ability to implement these strategies may vary depending on a number of institutional factors.

1. *Colleges and universities should thread diversity-focused questions through all aspects of planning and implementation.* Questions include: What policies, practices, and ways of thinking within colleges and universities (and their divisions and units) have differential impact on different groups? What organizational changes should be made to meet the needs of a diverse workforce we employ as well as the one we plan to graduate? Do these changes maximize the potential of all workers, positioning colleges to meet the demands of a global citizenry? These questions may be posed within academic affairs, within student affairs, and in conversations about collaboration between the two divisions. Collegiate personnel and students must be encouraged to challenge institutional barriers that present cultural barriers without fear of retaliation. This notion should be expressed in policy and among the senior leadership of the institution.

2. *College offices, divisions, and units should make every attempt to diversify personnel on multiple dimensions.* First, colleges must continue to evolve their understanding of diversity. Dimensions of diversity include but are not limited to: age, ethnicity, ancestry, gender, affect, endeavor, physical abilities/qualities, race, sexual orientation, educational background, geographic location, income, marital status, military experience, religious beliefs, parental status, and work experience. Second, colleges should remember that, in organizations, heterogeneity is found to promote creativity, to produce thoughtful solutions to problems, and a higher level of critical analysis. Third, when diversifying personnel hires, college units should do the following: (1) specify in job announcements that skills to work effectively in a diverse environment are required; (2) recognize that diverse efforts may be required to recruit a diverse applicant pool, particularly underutilized minorities and women. A key question emerges: On what e-mail list-servs and websites or in what publications that center diverse issues might we advertise? (3) consider transferable skills (i.e., communication, coordination) alongside other desired skills; (4) use a panel interview format comprised of committees in which individuals represent various dimensions of diversity to represent different perspectives and to eliminate bias from the selection process. Soliciting feedback may also eliminate potential bias; (5) ensure disabled applicants have appropriate accommodations.

3. *Colleges and universities should mine opportunities where collegiate personnel and students may openly discuss racial, ethnic, and cultural issues.* Cultural awareness workshops involving college and university faculty and staff should be mandated. Colleges are also encouraged to recognize connectedness to atypical individuals or groups (i.e., board of trustee members, parents, community organizations, professional associations) in building committees, panels, groups, and teams who participate in cultural awareness and intercultural communications. Individuals or groups who facilitate these efforts should attempt to introduce knowledge of diverse cultures and oppressed groups to provide all with a language of awareness, pushing against language of assumption and bias. Such can engage simple but important questions: What does respect look like across cultures? How is it shown across cultures? What are the politics of greeting each other, holding conversation, and eye contact? How do we know what various cultures need?

4. *Individual and team assessment must be developed.* Colleges and universities must recognize the importance of assessment given the accountability to students as shaped by national policy and large-scale research. College personnel must assess their own values, skills, understanding of norms and truth. They must also be able to recognize that these may not be shared by others and to envision difference as potential learning opportunities. Assessment teams, staff, or staff members must continue to monitor personnel work climate and student learning and engagement climate. Technology-based assessments conveniently lend themselves to these efforts. However, more in-depth assessments are conducted in focus group contexts. All staff must recognize the ways in which assessment benefits their offices and the ways in which they can act as assessors.

5. *Faculty may manage diversity in class.* Faculty are in position to shape classroom environments that clarify, tease out, and eradicate the presence of cultural stereotypes where they reside in-class and out-of-class. In complement, faculty who seek to shape an equity pedagogy must develop knowledge about different cultures as well as embrace communication patterns, norms, teaching that are culturally sensitive. Additionally, faculty should be creative in shaping in-class and out-of-class group projects that may hold potential for students to develop cross-cultural competencies.

6. *College units must envision connectedness where it is not readily apparent.* Colleges units (i.e., academic affairs, student affairs, fiscal affairs) and sub-units of these must not balkanize themselves. Rather, they are challenged to re-think means that achieve ends and, where possible, establish connections across campus in the interests of student learning and success. Academic affairs and student affairs collaborations are perhaps the most cutting-edge examples. Establishing student-centered communities or practicum opportunities, for example, where student affairs staff and faculty may participate to engage topics of diversity, ethnicity, or multiculturalism show tremendous promise to enhance learning for all students.

7. *Colleges and universities must be inclusive in their recruitment strategies.* Colleges and universities that actively recruit students are required to be inclusive when inviting area, regional, or national high schools to send their students for recruitment weekends or visits. Colleges and universities should make efforts to diversify pools of alumni who may also formally and informally recruit on their behalf.

Given extant policy and research, the ideas presented above represent effective ways in which colleges and universities may potentially manage diversity. Colleges and universities should recall that they are reflections of the broader society, often mimicking society's thinking and actions (Bowman & Smith, 2002). When students arrive on campus, they should discover open institutional climates where difference is envisioned as important for learning, collaboration, and conflict resolution.

Conclusion

Like other organizations, managing diversity on college campuses focuses on maximizing the ability of all employees to contribute to college and university goals. Colleges and universities must intentionally divorce the concept of managing diversity from affirmative action. As described in this chapter, affirmative action focuses on specific groups who have experienced historical discrimination (i.e., people of color, women). Managing diversity, conversely, pushes beyond merely rectifying underrepresentation to envision ways in which racial, ethnic, and cultural diversity enhances college and university missions of teaching, research, and service. In policy and practice, these differences can be clear. Institutional commitment and conditions are necessary to transform practical ideas to reality.

References

antonio, a. l. (1998). *Student interaction across race and outcomes in college.* Paper presented at the American Educational Research Association.

antonio, a. l. (2001). Diversity and the influence of friendship groups in college. *The Review of Higher Education, 25*(1), 63–89.

Astin, A. W. (1993). *What matters in college?: Four critical years revisited.* San Francisco, CA: Jossey-Bass.

Bowen, W., & Bok, D. (1998). *The shape of the river: Long-term consequences of considering race in college and university admissions.* Princeton, NJ: Princeton University Press.

Bowman, P., & Smith, W. A. (2002). Racial ideology in the campus community: Emerging cross-ethnic differences and challenges. In W. A. Smith, P. G. Altbach & K. Lomotey (Eds.), *The racial crisis in American higher education: Continuing challenges for the twenty-first century.* New York: SUNY Press.

Brown, M. C. (1999). *The quest to define collegiate desegregation: Black Colleges, Title VI compliance, and post-Adams litigation.* Westport, CT: Bergin & Garvey.

Brown, M. C. (2001). Collegiate desegregation and the public black college: A new policy mandate. *Journal of Higher Education, 72,* 46–62.

Brown, M. C. (2002). Good intentions: Collegiate desegregation and transdemographic enrollments. *The Review of Higher Education, 25,* 263–280.

Brown, M. C., & Lane, J. (2003). Studying diverse institutions: Contexts, challenges, and considerations, *New directions for institutional research.* San Francisco: Jossey-Bass.

Brown, M.C., & Freeman, K. (Eds.). (2004). *Black colleges: New perspectives on policy and practice.* Westport, CT: Praeger.

Brunner, B. (2001). *Timeline of affirmative action milestones.* Retrieved March 6, 2002, from http://www.factmonster.com/spot/affirmativetimeline1.html#1965.

Chang, M. (1996). Racial diversity in higher education: Does a racially mixed student population affect educational outcomes? Unpublished doctoral dissertation. University of California, Los Angeles.

Chang, M. J., & Kiang, P. N. (2002). New challenges of representing Asian American students in U.S. higher education. In W. A. Smith, P. G. Altbach & K. Lomotey (Eds.), *The racial crisis in American higher education: Continuing challenges for the twenty-first century.* Albany: SUNY Press.

Cohn, A. M. (1998). *The shaping of American higher education: emergence and growth of the contemporary system.* San Francisco: Jossey Bass.

Cox, T. H. (1994). *Managing cultural diversity in organizations: Theory, research, and practice.* San Francisco: Berrett-Koehler.

Cox, T. H., & Blake, S. (1991). Managing cultural diversity: Implications for organizational competitiveness. *The Executive, 5*(3), 45–56.

Dancy, T. E., & Brown, M. C. (in press). Predominantly white colleges and universities. In K. Lomotey (Ed.), *The encyclopedia of African American education.* Thousand Oaks, CA: Sage.

Fleming, J. (1984). Blacks in college: A comparative study of students' success in black and in white institutions. San Francisco: Jossey-Bass.

Garibaldi, A. (Ed.). (1984). *Black colleges and universities: Challenges for the future.* New York: Praeger.

Geiger, R. (1999). The ten generations of American higher education. In P. Altbach, R. Berdahl & P. Gumport (Eds.), *American higher education in the twenty-first century: Social, political, and economic challenges.* Baltimore: Johns Hopkins University Press.

Gilbert, J., Stead, B., & Invancevich, J. (1999). Diversity management: A new organizational paradigm. *Journal of Business Ethics, 21*(1), 61–76.

Gordon, L. A. (1997). From seminary to university: An overview of women's higher education, 1870–1920. In L. F. Goodchild & H. S. Wechsler (Eds.), *The history of higher education.* Boston, MA: Pearson.

Gurin, P. Y., Dey, E. L., Gurin, G., & Hurtado, S. (2003). How does racial/ethnic diversity promote education? *The Western Journal of Black Studies, 27*(1), 20–29.

Hurtado, S. (2003). *Preparing college students for a diverse democracy: Final report to the U.S. Department of Education. OERI. Field Initiated Studies Program.* Ann Arbor, MI: Center for the Study of Higher and Postsecondary Education.

Hurtado, S. (2007). Linking diversity with the educational and civic missions of higher education. *The Review of Higher Education, 30*(2), 185–196.

Hurtado, S., Milem, J. F., Clayton-Pedersen, A. R., & Allen, W. (1999). *Enacting diverse learning environments: Improving the climate for racial/ethnic diversity in higher education.* ASHE-ERIC Higher Education Report. Washington, DC: George Washington University.

Hytche, W. P. (1989). *A national resource—A national challenge: The 1890 land-grant colleges and universities.* Washington, D.C.: United States Department of Agriculture.

Jayne, M., & Dipboye, R. (2004). Leveraging diversity to improve business performance: Research findings and recommendations for organizations. *Human Resource Management, 43*(4), 409–424.

Justiz, M. J., Wilson, R., & Björk, L. G. (1994). *Minorities in higher education.* Phoenix, AZ: American Council on Education.

Kuh, G. D., Schuh, J. H., Whitt, E. J., Andreas, R. E., Lyons, J. W., Strange, C. C., et al. (1991). *Involving colleges: Successful approaches to fostering student learning and personal development outside the classroom.* San Francisco: Jossey-Bass.

Levine, D. O. (1997). Discrimination in college admissions. In L. F. Goodchild & H. S. Wechsler (Eds.), *The history of higher education*. Boston, MA: Pearson.

Liu, G. (1998). Affirmative action in higher education: The diversity rationale and the compelling interest test. *Harvard Civil Rights-Civil Liberties Law Review, 33*, 381–442.

Mayhew, M., Grunwald, H., & Dey, E. L. (2006). Breaking the silence: Achieving a positive campus climate for diversity from the staff perspective. *Research in Higher Education, 47*(1), 63–88.

Milem, J. F. (2003). The educational benefits of diversity: Evidence from multiple sectors. In M. J. Chang, D. Witt, J. James & K. Hakuta (Eds.), *Compelling interest: Examining racial dynamics in colleges and universities*. Palo Alto, CA: Stanford University Press.

Milem, J. F., Chang, M. J., & antonio, a. 1. (2005). *Making diversity work on campus: A research based perspective*: Making Excellence Inclusive Initiative, Association of American Colleges and Universities.

Pascarella, E., Edison, M., Nora, A., Hagedorn, L., & Terenzini, P. (1996). Influences on students' openness to diversity and challenge in the first year of college. *Journal of Higher Education, 67*(2), 174–195.

Reskin, B. F. (1998). *The realities of affirmative action in employment*. Washington, D.C.: American Sociological Association.

Roebuck, J. B., & Murty, K. S. (1993). *Historically black colleges and universities: Their place in American higher education*. Westport, Connecticut: Praeger Publishers.

Rudolph, F. (1962). *The American college and university*. New York: Random House.

Saenz, V. B., Ngai, H. N., & Hurtado, S. (2007). Factors influencing positive interactions across race for African American, Asian American, Latino, and White college students. *Research in Higher Education, 48*(1).

Stage, F. K., & Manning, K. (1992). Enhancing the multicultural campus environment: A cultural brokering approach, *New directions for student services*. San Francisco: Jossey-Bass.

Statham, A., Richardson, L., & Cook, J. (1991). *Gender and university teaching: A negotiated difference*. Albany, NY: SUNY.

Thelin, J. R. (2004). *A history of American higher education*. Baltimore, MA: JHU Press.

Williams, D., Berger, J., & McClendon, S. (2005). *Toward a model of inclusive excellence and change in postsecondary institutions: Making Excellence Inclusive Initiative*. Association of American Colleges and Universities.

Williams, J. (Ed.). (1988). *Desegregating America's colleges and universities: Title VI regulation of higher education*. New York: Teachers College Press.

Part XI

Examining Race and Gender in the Academy

PART XI

EXAMINING RACE AND GENDER IN THE ACADEMY

THE CAMPUS RACIAL CLIMATE: CONTEXTS OF CONFLICT

SYLVIA HURTADO

Racial conflict was becoming commonplace on American college campuses throughout the 1980s, with more than one hundred college campuses reporting incidents of racial/ethnic harassment and violence in each of the last two years of the decade [40]. The most highly publicized racial incidents, ranging from verbal harassment to violent beatings, occurred at some of the most elite institutions in the country [25, 56]. In many cases students organized protests as a direct response to these problems, or to express solidarity with students facing similar problems at other institutions [60]. Although these events have provided the impetus for examining the quality of race relations on individual college campuses, researchers have not explored at any great length the nature of campus race relations across a variety of institutional contexts.

The research on minorities in higher education is extensive, yet a surprisingly small number of empirical studies have focused specifically on campus racial climates. Only a few studies include measures of campus race relations in their models of student persistence [54, 57, 58], academic achievement [2, 41, 42, 46], and social involvement [1]. Although this is an important step toward developing appropriate models that describe the college experiences of minority students, these studies have revealed a conflicting pattern of relations between hostile racial climates and student outcomes [29]. Part of the problem is that we need a better understanding of what constitutes a racially tense interpersonal environment before considering how these climates are related to student development.

Drawing upon previous work on race relations, inequality, and campus diversity, the goal of this study is to examine comparative institutional data that may help identify contexts for racial conflict. This study offers a unique opportunity to examine racial tension on campus because it focuses on the experiences of a student cohort that attended predominantly white colleges from 1985 to 1989, a period when racial incidents occurred on many campuses. A central premise of the study is that such incidents are part of a wide range of climate issues on college campuses that require our attention. Much of what we observe on campus is undoubtedly influenced by the general social context, yet we can learn a great deal about the nature of our campuses by examining black, Chicano, and white student perceptions in institutional contexts associated with campus racial tension.

The Social Context

The civil rights movement, the elimination of *de jure* segregation in the public sector *(Brown v. the Board of Education* [16]), litigation in areas related to the Civil Rights Law (Title VI), and a surge in minority enrollments up until the mid-1970s raised the level of public consciousness regarding inequalities in the education of minority groups. These events represented tremendous strides in progress toward eliminating overt aspects of discrimination in educational institutions, making such practices illegal and unethical in the public mind. However, scholars concede that institutional compliance with legal injunctions for increased minority participation in higher education continues to be problematic [59, 61, 65], the system of higher education remains racially stratified [62], and vestiges of discrimination exist in everyday administrative practices [50]. Thus, important progress has yet to be made in removing some of the more intractable forms of racial inequality and discrimination at both the institutional and individual level.

The research literature suggests that instances of overt racial conflict can no longer be viewed as aberrations or isolated incidents, but rather are indicators of a more general problem of unresolved racial issues in college environments and in society at large. Researchers investigating racial climates in the mid-1970s found that though college campuses exerted considerable energy in initiating programs and services in response to the initial entrance of black students, institutions did not attend to minority-majority relations or the psychological climate [49]. Recent studies have shown that even on relatively calm campuses there are differences in students' racial attitudes and considerable social distance among students of different racial or ethnic backgrounds [37, 38]. Alienation from the mainstream of campus life is also reported to be particularly acute among minority students on predominantly white campuses [2, 46, 53]. The 1989 American Council on Education (ACE) survey of academic administrators revealed that only one in four felt their campus provided an "excellent" to "very good" climate for black students, and only 21 percent felt they provided a supportive climate for Hispanics [23]. If these issues have been left unattended since the influx of minorities into higher education in the 1960s, it is no wonder that campuses continue to deal with racial tensions.

External forces and the events of the past decade have helped to make these unresolved issues more salient. The resurgence of overt hostilities on campuses, reported as early as 1979 [54], accompanied events that signaled the questioning of affirmative action practices (for example, *Bakke*), declining federal commitment to issues that affect minorities, renewed Ku Klux Klan activity, and increasing racial discord in urban communities [25, 33, 59]. At the same time, college campuses reflected a political shift toward conservatism in the country during the 1980s. Students who identified with the far right and political conservatives became more vocal, while their classmates shied away from the liberal label and increasingly characterized their political views as middle-of-the road [22]. Moreover, significant policy trends that are connected with issues of inequality directly affected institutions of higher education. For example, reductions in federal aid programs during the Reagan years resulted in changes in financial aid packaging policy at the institutional level, which many contend have disproportionately affected blacks and Hispanics in their decisions to attend or remain in college [8, 19, 43, 44. 56]. Diminishing federal support for Pell grants and minority-targeted fellowships promises to complicate institutional efforts to stem the decline of college participation rates for low-income and minority groups [17, 18, 30, 45].

Institutional Contexts

Although the general social context influences all institutions, researchers have found considerable institutional variability in reports of racial conflict and responses to improve the racial climate. Early studies found that institutional selectivity and size were both positively associated with student unrest involving campus racial policies [5]. Researchers offered two alternative interpretations: (a) selective institutions and large campuses are environments that are more likely to attract protest-prone students, and (b) large institutions are characterized by an impersonal atmosphere and lack of concern for the individual student, thereby promoting student discontent. The first interpretation suggests that conflict on campus is largely due to the types of students an institution recruits. Studies support the notion that elite institutions tend to attract students with strong ideological commitments and foster political liberalism [7, 28]. The second interpretation states that institutional size may be a proxy for attention to students, suggesting that the extent to which institutions are supportive of students helps maintain a conflict-free environment. Recent research shows that higher rates of institutional spending (per student) in the areas of student services and student aid (non-repayable grants and fellowships) are correlated with student perceptions of relatively low racial tension on campuses [29]. Although there is research support for both interpretations, one focuses on the individual as the source of conflict, while the other suggests that institutional contexts are largely responsible for setting the stage for conflict. These interpretations were tested in the current study, along with others which suggest that both size and selectivity are proxies for other phenomena that include changes in minority enrollment and institutional priorities that help shape the climate.

One of the most comprehensive studies of the racial climate, initiated on the campuses of thirteen four-year institutions, systematically documented the historical and environmental forces that accompanied substantial increases in black student enrollment from 1968 to 1975 [49]. In addition to campus site visits, extensive surveys of administrators, faculty, and students at four of the large institutions explored three broad areas of institutional responsiveness to the entrance of black students: institutional commitment, program responses, and the attitudinal or perceptual climate. Although the large institutions had invested a fair amount of time and funds in minority programs and services, researchers found that these institutions differed substantially in ratings of relative priorities placed on the recruitment of black students, provision for nonacademic support, and commitment to affirmative action. They also observed that campuses paid little attention to the interpersonal aspects of race relations, which were characterized by "voluntary segregation or by indifference thinly covering interracial conflicts and feelings of mistrust" [49, p. 319]. They concluded that a failure to deal with any of the issues at the institutional, programmatic, or individual level was "likely to become a source of difficulty at some point in these institutions' relationships with minorities" [49, p. 316]. Although researchers anticipated problems with minority students, they did not foresee the extent to which an institution's relationship with majority students would become equally problematic in matters such as admissions (for example, *Bakke*), student organizations (fraternities), and student publications (for example, *Dartmouth Review*). Still, these early findings hold important implications for the examination of contemporary racial tension with regard to the role of institutional priorities and the impact of changing enrollments.

The 1989 ACE survey of academic administrators at 456 institutions revealed distinct differences by institution type in priorities for cultural diversity, programmatic activity, and the amount of racial tension reported on campus [23]. Administrators at doctoral institutions reported the most programmatic activity to improve minority participation at all levels of the university, including efforts to increase the number of minority faculty and increase the enrollment of minority students at the undergraduate level. Comprehensive universities were the next most active in this regard. At the same time, however, racial tensions were reported more often at comprehensive and doctoral institutions than at other types of institutions. In direct contrast, administrators from private baccalaureate institutions reported the least racial tension among the four-year institutions; but also gave their institutions the lowest ratings in their ability to attract black and Hispanic students. These ratings, from one of the top academic administrators at each campus, indicate distinct differences among four-year institutions that include both a public/private dichotomy and contradictions in campus racial climates.

Conducted some fourteen years apart, both studies suggest that despite visible programmatic activity, institutions continue to vary considerably in their commitment to diversity and in the amount of racial conflict on campus. These findings run counter to the commonly held assumption that the introduction of a few programs would essentially lead to better racial climates. Apparently, a shift in institutional priorities for diversity is more difficult to achieve and may involve resolving a more complex set of institutional priorities or problems. Richardson and Skinner's [51] model of institutional adaptation to diversity proposes that goals for quality and diversity may be seen as sources of conflict within institutions. Scholars have raised questions regarding this issue, stating that the assumptions underlying these concepts may inappropriately place the two goals in conflict [53]. Though there has been substantial attention to the debate regarding the relationship between the two priorities, there has been little concern about whether the quest for institutional quality or a shift in priorities of institutional commitment to diversity may be related to racial tension on campus.

The adaptation model has several underlying premises that are reexamined here in relation to the campus climate. The model equates quality with individual achievement, suggesting that the focus of selective institutions is high on achievement and low on diversity, whereas the reverse is true for open-access institutions. The problem with this logic is that all educational institutions have a concern for individual achievement; the difference between these types of institutions is that student achievement must be proven *prior* to admission with selective institutions, whereas open-access institutions are willing to allow students to prove achievement *during* college. Therefore, selective institutions may have less to do with improving individual achievement than with maintaining institutional status and reputation [6]. This forces us to reexamine the conflict in priorities: the source of conflict is not between diversity and achievement but originates from differences in institutional priorities that work to preserve inequalities. For example, although campus race relations is not an aspect of the adaptation model, researchers acknowledge that "our society has historically treated minority populations as inferior" [51] and report that the social environment of the large predominantly white universities has been problematic, even for minority students with strong academic preparation [52, p. 487]. Traditional notions of quality are often linked to both selectivity and an institutional preoccupation with resource accumulation and reputation enhancement [6]. It may be that minority students are generally undervalued (regardless of their achievement characteristics), whereas high achieving white students are viewed as resources. Therefore, priorities that guide an institution and its members may have underlying ideological assumptions that are linked with racial issues.

A theoretical tradition supports the view that our institutions, particularly our schools, have embedded ideologies that work to preserve inequality [14, 27]. Research on racial inequality and attitudes has adopted a similar notion of dominant ideological interests. Arce [4] introduced the concept of "academic colonialism" when referring to Chicano participation in academe. Academic colonialism refers to the imposition of dominant ideologies (for example, intellectual premises, concepts, practices) and/or the uncritical acceptance of these ideologies by subordinate groups. Similarly, others assert that dominant group interests are served in maintaining a status quo that justifies unequal social relations and achieves some level of consensus about such arrangements among subordinate groups [31, 32, 38]. Viewed from this perspective, the conflict between quality and diversity appears contrived and arguments for "quality" may be used as a way to uniformly exclude minorities (faculty and students) and their perspectives.

When "harmonious inequality" is challenged by subordinates, dominant groups are forced to defend their privilege [32]. This perspective suggests that mean-spirited acts of racial harassment on the part of white students may represent a reassertion of group dominance in an era when prevailing dominant group ideologies are in question. However, the defense of dominant group privilege is less often characterized by such acts of "traditional" racism on campus and more often takes on a sophisticated guise as an expressed concern for the individual that is consistent with prevailing democratic values—so long as one chooses to ignore *both* the historical and continuous disadvantages under which subordinate groups operate. As researchers point out, this concern for individual privilege is at the heart of the meritocratic ethic in higher education [38]. It is also at the center of contention with regard to virtually every institutional response to eliminate inequalities and discriminatory practices for various groups, including affirmative action, the development of disciplinary codes to prohibit harassment, and the practice of providing minority-targeted scholarships.[1] Although this view suggests dominant group opposition to institutional commitment to diversity, we have yet to obtain evidence which shows that diversity priorities are related to racial tension on predominantly white campuses.

Race relations theorists propose that racial conflict arises out of a sense of threat to group position, when the dominant group perceives the risk of losing power, resources, or other advantages [12, 63]. Work in the area of relative numbers of underrepresented groups suggests that the proportions of socially and culturally different people in a group are critical in shaping the dynamics of social interaction [35]. Blalock hypothesized that "as the minority percentage increases, we would expect to find increasing discriminatory behavior" [11, p. 148] because more members of the minority group will be in direct competition with someone from the dominant group. Recent research on racial attitudes shows decreases in white support for integration and increases in perceived threat from blacks as the relative size of the black population increased in communities [26]. Thus, differences in minority enrollment may account for variations in racial tension and contradictions observed in studies of institution type and the racial climate. Faced with impending changes in the ethnic composition of the college-age population [24], such effects may have important implications for college campuses.

Student Perceptions and Ethnic Group Differences

Researchers have found that student perceptions vary by race in college environments, yet only a handful of studies have compared perceptions of the racial climate among black, Chicano, and white college students [64]. A study at one predominantly white university showed that although a higher percentage of blacks than Chicanos reported that they have personally experienced discrimination, these reports were positively correlated with feelings of alienation only among Chicano students [46]. Loo and Rolison [37] also found that the majority of white students (68 percent) thought that the university was generally supportive of minority students, while only 28 percent of the black and Chicano students expressed the same opinion. In the same study, certain behaviors (for example, ethnic group clustering) were interpreted by white students as racial segregation, whereas minority students tended to view them as modes of cultural support within a larger unsupportive environment. In a comparative study of two institutions [48], researchers found black students were most likely to perceive a hostile racial climate on campus, but Hispanics were also more likely than white students to perceive such hostility. Perceptions of the racial climate also differed by institution, although it appears that dimensions of location and ethnic composition of the campus were confounded with group differences. These studies show that ethnic groups differ in their view of the racial climate, highlighting the need to conduct comparative group analyses across institutions to understand environments with considerable racial tension.

Method

Conceptual Framework

The structural properties of the environment are central to shaping social interaction and the individual's attitude and behavior within it [36]. These structural properties are often assessed with measures that social psychologists refer to as "contextual variables" [36] or distal characteristics [34]. In higher education research these measures are often institutional characteristics such as size, type, control, selectivity, and racial composition of the college. In Jessor's [34] view, there are a multiplicity of environments in which human interaction takes place. These multiple environments can be ordered along a continuum according to proximity to the individual. Demographic and structural attributes of environments are considered distal, whereas the perceived environment is considered the most proximal and is of immediate significance to the actor. Studies have begun to validate the notion that proximal measures are more important than distal characteristics in relation to student outcomes [47, 55]. Research in social psychology also suggests that proximal measures mediate the effect of these distal characteristics on other outcomes [34, 39]. In this particular study the distal environmental dimensions include size, selectivity, ethnic enrollments, and campus expenditures. The proximal environment is represented by student perceptions of institutional priorities that reflect institutional commitment to cultural diversity, a resource/reputation orientation, and a student-centered orientation. Within this framework, the proximal measures (student perceptions of the environment) are hypothesized to have a greater influence than the distal measures of the environment on student perceptions of racial tension.

Data Sources

This study draws upon several major data sources. The primary source of student data came from responses to a four-year longitudinal survey, the 1989 Follow-up Survey (FUS) to the 1985 Freshman Survey, a project of the Cooperative Institutional Research Program (CIRP) and the Higher Education Research Institute at UCLA. The 1985 Freshman Survey was administered during freshman orientation and the FUS was sent to the student's home address in the summer and fall of 1989, four years after college entry. The FUS was administered according to two different sampling techniques to address the need for national normative data and to facilitate separate group analyses. The first sample was drawn from the population of first-time, full-time freshmen (192,453) responding to the 1985 Survey. A stratified, random procedure was used to ensure representation of students based on sex within the different types of institutions in higher education. (Stratification involved 23 cells reflecting institutional selectivity, control, race, sex, and the type of institution). Based on patterns of response observed in earlier FUS studies, a random sample (20,317) was selected to yield a minimal number (175) of respondents in each stratification cell. This yielded data on 4,672 respondents (23 percent response rate), which were statistically adjusted for nonresponse and weighted to approximate the national population of students. (The statistical weighting methodology used in HERI Follow-up surveys can be found in all FUS reports [30]).

Although this sampling procedure is well suited for analyses of national normative data, the numbers of minority students drawn randomly across institutions remains extremely small for the purposes of separate group analyses. A second procedure was necessary to yield a sample more conducive to analyses on ethnic groups. Four-year institutions were selected to maximize variability according to student academic programs and minority enrollment in addition to institutional type, control, and selectivity. Full cohorts of students (34,323) were surveyed, yielding 10,640 respondents (31 percent response rate). A secondary data sampling procedure was employed to select only those students representing three ethnic groups (black, Chicano, and white students) from among respondents at 116 predominantly white institutions. Each institution was considered a separate stratum with stratified, random sampling conducted on a 3:1 white/minority ratio. The purpose of this procedure was to yield a sample of white students that was distributed across institutions in a manner similar to the distribution of minority students. Most institutions had both black and Chicano students but in some institutions, due to distinct patterns of college attendance among minorities, white students were matched with only one of these ethnic groups. This final selection criteria yielded a sample of 1,825 white students, 328 black, and 340 Chicano students. The major part of the study utilized the data from this selected sample for separate group analyses.

Institutional characteristics and undergraduate ethnic enrollments were obtained from the data files of the U.S. Department of Education's Integrated Postsecondary Data System (IPEDS, formerly HEGIS).[2] Black, Hispanic, and total enrollment data for 1982, 1986, and 1988 at each institution were obtained from this national source. These years were used to create enrollment change variables for the ethnic groups in each institution. Financial data on 1985 expenditures (per student) for student services and grants/fellowships were similarly obtained, and all institutional data were merged with student survey data for analyses.

Measures

A total of 21 independent variables were selected for the analyses. Variable definitions are shown on table A1, along with coding schemes and scales. The dependent variable consisted of a factorially confirmed scale representing student perceptions of racial tension among students, faculty, and campus administrators [29]. Items constructing all scales are shown on table A2. The rationale for including specific measures in analyses is described below.

Because the distribution of students across different college environments is never random, one of the basic features of any research design is to control for student characteristics at the point of initial exposure to the environment. For example, selective institutions tend to attract students who are more critical of their environments (for example, liberal and protest "prone"), come from families with higher incomes, and have higher academic ability [5, 7]. Parental income and student academic performance (high-school grade point average) served as control variables, along with a number of student self-rating and value measures on the 1985 Freshman Survey. Measures that controlled for predispositions in student perceptions included student self-ratings of political view, estimated chances of becoming involved in campus protest, and the importance attributed to the goal of helping to promote racial understanding. Aside from the need for statistical control, additional student background characteristics were included in analyses because they are established correlates of racial attitudes and perceptions. For example, females are generally more supportive of affirmative action and racial integration [13]; the well-educated tend to be more supportive of principles of racial integration (but not decidedly more willing to support specific equity policies) [31, 32]; and age is negatively associated with racial integration [26]. Previous research has also suggested that a sense of interpersonal accomplishment or social self-confidence may be an important precursor to social involvement among minorities [2] and perceptions of racial tension on campus among white students [29]. Therefore, additional student background variables included gender, mother's and father's level of education, age, and a social self-confidence scale.

Factor scales constructed from student perceptions of their environment included institutional priorities that reflect a commitment to diversity, a reputation/resource orientation, and a student-centered orientation. Parallel measures, obtained independent of student observation, for an institution's student-centered priorities included campus expenditures (per student) in the areas of student services and student aid (non-repayable grants and fellowships). High expenditures in these areas reflect student-centered priorities, particularly in an era of budget constraint and shrinking governmental resources. Measures reflecting the college composition, the proportion of black and Hispanic undergraduate enrollment in 1986 and ethnic enrollment changes over a six-year period (1982–88), served to test race relations theories based on relative numbers. They also controlled for institutional differences that were observed in previous studies of the racial climate [23], and as parallel measures of institutional commitment to diversity. The enrollment change measures were designed to capture changes in student diversity at each institution prior to and during the enrollment of the 1985–89 cohort. Two additional college composition variables, institutional size and selectivity, served to test alternative interpretations regarding campus conflict [5].

Five factors derived from previous climate studies [20, 29] were used in the regression analyses of campus racial tension on student and institutional characteristics. Because items were on similar scales (table A2), new variables were created by summing responses on each item to construct a factor scale. Table 1 shows that all the scales have fairly high reliabilities that are similar across groups. The range on reliabilities across groups for a socioeconomic status factor was too wide to be considered a generalizable construct in analyses across groups, therefore, multiple indicators (parental income and the level of mother's and father's education) were entered in the equation with full recognition that this might underestimate the effects of each indicator. The effects of these variables and other complex relationships among the independent variables were carefully monitored prior to and after entry into the equation using a computer software program, *Betaview*, designed for this purpose [21].

TABLE 1

Factor Scales: Estimates of Internal Consistencies (Alpha) by Student Sample

Factor Scale	Number of Items	Black	Chicano	White
Campus racial tension	3	0.66	0.66	0.64
Social self-confidence	3	0.76	0.75	0.73
Institutional commitment to diversity	4	0.88	0.86	0.80
Student-centered orientation	5	0.75	0.80	0.83
Resource/reputation orientation	5	0.77	0.79	0.76

Note: Confirmatory and exploratory procedures used to develop factors are reported in Hurtado [29] and Dey [20]. Items constituting each scale are reported in table A2.

Analyses

Student perceptions of racial climate issues at all types of four-year institutions were examined using bivariate analyses of national normative data. Ethnic group differences on all variables were assessed using two-tailed tests of significance on the selected sample of black, Chicano, and white students. Because ethnic groups differed significantly in their perceptions of the environment, separate group analyses were conducted using multiple regression techniques to assess the relationship between perceptions of campus racial tension and student and institutional characteristics. Variables were entered in three stages to observe changes in regression coefficients. The first stage explored the extent to which perceptions of racial tension were a function of the cultural and psychological baggage that students bring with them to college, including demographic attributes and tendencies that might suggest a precollege bias in their views regarding the climate. Institutional priorities, hypothesized to be the primary explanatory variables that would diminish the impact of college composition variables (size and selectivity), were entered in the next stage. College composition variables were entered in the final stage to determine if these structural aspects of the environment remain central to shaping perceptions of the climate. Interaction terms representing (1) high resource/reputation priorities and institutional commitment to diversity and (2) high resource/reputation and student-centered priorities were forward entered in a second regression model for each group to determine if these combinations could account for a significant addition in the proportion of variance in the dependent variable.

Results

National normative data are presented in table 2 to provide an overview of student perceptions of the racial climate, highlighting differences among four-year colleges and universities. Student views on the existence of racial discrimination show the least variation across all institution types. Only about 12 percent of all students at four-year institutions agreed with the statement that "racial discrimination is no longer a problem in America," indicating that most undergraduates feel that this form of discrimination is still an issue to contend with in our society. At the same time, items measuring student perceptions of campus race relations reflect a much wider range of responses between institution types. This suggests that though most students acknowledge the existence of racial discrimination, their perceptions of race relations on campus vary according to their experiences in different institutional contexts.

Data show that approximately one in four students at all four-year institutions perceive considerable racial conflict; however, this proportion is higher in university settings (approximately one in three students). It is also important to note that most students agree that "students of different ethnic origins communicate well with one another" on their campus, with the lowest proportion of students agreeing with this statement at private (59 percent) and public universities (61 percent). When compared with other institution types, students at both public and private universities were also more likely to report a lack of trust between minority student groups and administrators (36 and 39 percent, respectively). These results support accounts of racial incidents and related protests occurring primarily at public and private universities from 1985 to 1989 [25].

Private four-year colleges fared better than universities and public four-year colleges on most racial climate measures. Students at Catholic institutions are least likely to report racial conflict (12 percent) or mistrust between minority groups and administrators (16 percent); and are most likely to report good communication among ethnic groups (82 percent). While over two-thirds of all students report that most faculty are sensitive to the issues of minorities, a higher proportion of students at Protestant (81 percent) and nonsectarian four-year colleges (76 percent) perceive this to be the case. In addition, a general measure of curriculum integration shows that the highest proportion of undergraduates (50 percent) report that many courses include minority perspectives at nonsectarian four-year colleges.

Two general observations are made regarding student perceptions of specific institutional priorities for cultural diversity. First, there is a somewhat smaller institutional range of student views on

TABLE 2

Student Perceptions of Racial Issues at Four-Year Colleges and Universities, 1989 Follow-up Survey of Fall 1985 Freshmen

	All Institutions	Universities		Four-Year Colleges				Institutional Range (high to low)
		Public	Private	Public	Private Nonsectarian	Catholic	Protestant	
Agreement with the Statement:[1]								
Racial discrimination is no longer a problem in America	12	11	9	15	11	8	12	7
Statements about the Institution:[1]								
There is a lot of campus racial conflict here	25	34	34	21	17	12	16	22
Many courses include minority perspectives	47	46	41	49	50	43	47	9
Students of different ethnic origins communicate well with one another	68	61	59	69	77	82	76	23
There is little trust between minority student groups and administrators	31	36	3	34	21	16	19	23
Most faculty here are sensitive to the issues of minorities	67	61	65	65	76	70	81	20
Institutional Priorities:[2]								
Create a diverse multicultural environment on campus	42	43	40	42	42	45	37	8
Develop among faculty and students an appreciation for a multicultural society	31	36	40	42	46	45	45	10
Increase minority representation in the faculty and administration	29	30	25	32	27	23	22	10
Recruit more minority students	41	40	40	47	36	29	33	18

Source: National normative data, Higher Education Research Institute, UCLA. Responses are statistically adjusted to correct for non-response and weighted to approximate the national population of 1985 first-time, full-time freshmen. (For weighting procedures see Higher Education Research Institute, 1991).

1. Percent who "agree strongly" or "agree somewhat."

2. Percent rating priority is "high" or "highest."

diversity priorities compared with views on campus race relations, indicating diversity priorities may be more consistent across institutions. Institutions differed most on priorities to diversify the student body, faculty, and the administration. Students at public four-year colleges (47 percent) and universities (40 percent) are more likely than students at private four-year colleges to report minority student recruitment was a "high" or the "highest priority" at their institution. Students at public institutions were also more likely than students at private institutions to report that increasing the representation of minorities in the faculty and administration was a high priority (30–32 percent).

Although these differences in priorities for diversity may be cause for concern, perhaps a more general concern is related to the second observation: less than a third of the students perceive specific goals to change the racial composition of the institution, and less than half perceive general goals for fostering cultural or racial diversity to be a high institutional priority. Given public statements regarding the importance of diversity and the general nature of items reflecting priorities to "create a diverse multicultural environment on campus" and "develop an appreciation for a multicultural society among faculty and students," one wonders why more students do not perceive these to be a high priority on campuses. To what extent are students' perception of racial tension on campus related to their view of institutional priorities for cultural diversity? What can explain the institutional contradictions between priorities and race relations observed here and in previous studies [49, 23]? While institutional type and control are helpful in locating the problems within the higher education system, they are of limited practical significance to administrators in addressing problems within institutional settings. Subsequent analyses focused on the relationship between institutional priorities and campus racial tension, with appropriate controls for student and institutional characteristics, to provide insights into contexts for conflict and contradiction.

Table 3 shows means, standard deviations, and tests of significance on all measures used in analyses of the selected sample of black, Chicano, and white students. This table describes the sample and shows that significant group differences were detected on most freshmen characteristics and perceptions of the environment. The Chicano students came from families with significantly lower levels of educational attainment and lower incomes ($\overline{X} \approx \$27,850$) than either their black or white classmates. Upon college entry in 1985, Chicanos were also less likely to characterize themselves as politically liberal. Black students entered college with significantly higher social self-confidence. They were more likely than other students in the sample to become involved in campus protest, characterize their views as politically liberal, and place a high value on helping to promote racial understanding. In contrast, white students had significantly higher GPAs, college-educated parents, higher family incomes ($\overline{X} \approx \$42,100$), and were less likely to place a high value on promoting racial understanding than the minority students. These results suggest that these are important student background characteristics to take into account in assessing institutional contexts that inform perceptions of campus racial tension.

Given these freshmen differences in relative status and social views, we would expect their perceptions of the environment to vary considerably four years after college entry. Black students were more critical of their environments than the other student groups: they perceive relatively higher levels of racial tension and lower levels of institutional commitment to diversity at their institutions. Chicanos were least likely to perceive that their institution had student-centered priorities. However, there appeared to be consensus across all groups on institutional priorities for resource and reputation enhancement, as there were no significant differences among groups. Significant group differences were also detected among college composition variables (size, selectivity, ethnic enrollment). This is due primarily to the distinct distribution of Chicano and black students among institution types: Chicanos were concentrated in larger, less selective institutions with a higher proportion of Hispanic enrollment.

Table 4 shows the regression results for the three ethnic groups. Beta coefficients are shown at two steps: β^1 is the value of each regression coefficient at the step where all student characteristics are controlled, and β^2 represents the value of the coefficient at the final step of the equation. The β^1 coefficient represents the effect of a variable, net of student characteristics and prior to competing with other environmental variables in the equation. These coefficients are shown to (1) consider alternative interpretations that can be derived from other models that may exclude some of the environmental

TABLE 3

Means, Standard Deviations, and Tests of Significance on Variables by Group

Variables	White (n = 1821) Mean	S.D.	Black (n = 325) Mean	S.D.	Chicano (n = 340) Mean	S.D.	Significant Differences
1985 Student Characteristics							
Sex (female)	1.58	0.49	1.61	0.49	1.64	0.48	C*
Age	3.12	0.47	3.03	0.48	3.19	0.53	A** B** C*
High-school GPA	6.36	1.39	5.59	1.60	5.95	1.41	A** B** C**
Mother's education	5.36	1.78	5.07	1.95	3.50	2.10	A** B** C**
Father's education	6.10	1.90	4.87	2.11	3.89	2.37	A** B** C**
Income	9.19	2.97	6.73	3.18	6.54	3.12	A** B** C**
Social self-confidence	10.78	1.95	10.99	2.17	10.55	2.03	B**
Expect to protest	2.35	0.83	2.44	0.83	2.24	0.87	B** C**
Political view (liberal)	3.06	0.78	3.32	0.64	3.02	0.71	A** B**
Promote racial understanding	2.27	0.83	3.14	0.79	2.55	0.83	A** B** C**
Institutional Characteristics							
Institutional Priorities							
Expenditures:							
Student services	865.32	701.54	899.54	618.67	842.93	764.22	
Non-repayable aid	1345.88	939.09	1576.17	1008.69	1124.31	730.68	A** B** C**
Student Perceptions:							
Student-oriented	12.45	2.98	12.39	2.66	11.78	3.11	A** B** C**
Resource/reputation-oriented	14.33	3.23	14.35	3.30	14.61	3.47	
Commitment to diversity	9.51	2.73	8.94	3.38	9.57	3.08	A** B**
College composition:							
Selectivity (Average SAT)	105.38	14.27	108.16	15.72	98.42	13.64	A** B** C**
Enrollment:							
Size (total FTE)	6.28	2.16	5.72	1.95	6.39	2.38	A** B**
Black percent in 1986	4.68	3.10	5.53	3.35	4.21	2.45	A** B** C**
Hispanic percent in 1986	5.60	6.84	3.30	5.33	14.29	16.27	A** B** C**
Black increase (1982–89)	1.64	0.48	1.57	0.50	1.70	0.46	A* B** C*
Hispanic increase (1982–88)	2.55	0.83	2.48	0.87	2.69	0.73	B** C**
Dependent Variable							
Campus Racial Tension	6.70	1.90	7.85	2.07	6.73	2.03	A** B**

Note: Variable scales are reported in table A1. Significant group differences, *p ≤ 0.05. ** p ≤ 0.01 (two-tailed probability): A = white/black difference, B = black/Chicano difference, C = Chicano/white difference.

TABLE 4

Regression of Campus Racial Tension on Student and Institutional Characteristics by Group

| | Standardized Regression Coefficients and T Ratios for: | | | | | | | | |
| | White ($n = 1821$) | | | Black ($n = 325$) | | | Chicano ($n = 340$) | | |
	β^1	β^2	t	β^1	β^2	t	β^1	β^2	t
1985 Student Characteristics									
Sex (female)	0.02	0.06	2.65	0.02	0.05	0.86	−0.05	0.03	0.64
Age	−0.03	−0.01	−0.56	−0.03	−0.01	0.23	−0.02	0.06	1.11
High-school GPA	0.10**	0.01	0.53	0.01	−0.06	−1.10	0.04	−0.04	−0.86
Mother's education	0.04*	0.04	1.64	−0.03	−0.02	−0.32	−0.02	−0.00	−0.04
Father's education	0.02	−0.01	−0.35	−0.01	−0.00	−0.05	−0.10	−0.13	−1.88
Income	0.05*	0.01	0.48	0.05	−0.03	−0.47	0.08	0.01	0.22
Social self-confidence	0.06*	0.03	1.55	0.01	0.05	1.00	0.03	−0.01	−0.21
Expect to protest in college	0.15**	0.12	5.20	0.06	0.04	0.70	0.18**	0.10	1.89
Political view (liberal)	0.02	0.02	0.85	0.23**	0.18	3.41	0.09	0.04	0.88
Goal: helping to promote racial understanding	0.00	0.02	0.68	0.02	0.04	0.70	0.06	0.09	1.70
Institutional Characteristics									
Institutional Priorities									
Expenditures (per student):									
Student services	−0.09**	0.01	0.48	−0.15**	−0.08	−1.17	−0.07	−0.04	−0.60
Non-repayable student aid	−0.09**	−0.00	−0.05	−0.11	−0.12	−1.32	−0.19**	0.01	0.14
Student Perceptions of Priorities:									
Student-centered	−0.28**	−0.20	−7.48	−0.29**	−0.22	−3.58	−0.38**	−0.18	−3.06
Resource/reputation	0.17**	0.06	2.64	0.20**	0.12	2.15	0.22**	0.08	1.57
Commitment to diversity	−0.05*	−0.03	−1.28	−0.28**	−0.18	−3.14	−0.23**	−0.20	−4.03
College composition:									
Selectivity (Average SAT)	0.16**	0.19	5.56	0.09	0.17	2.13	0.31**	0.29	3.17
Enrollment:									
Size (total FTE)	0.23**	0.14	3.48	0.14**	−0.12	−1.42	0.36**	0.10	0.97
Black percent in 1986	0.07**	0.11	5.09	−0.05	0.00	−0.01	−0.13*	0.05	0.68
Hispanic percent in 1986	−0.08**	−0.05	−2.15	−0.03	0.02	0.42	−0.31**	−0.07	−0.64
Black increase (1982–88)	0.13**	0.06	2.08	−0.06	0.01	0.14	0.28**	0.13	1.94
Hispanic increase (1982–88)	0.07**	−0.02	−0.66	−0.12*	−0.10	−1.65	0.12*	0.04	0.62
R^2	0.19			0.24			0.36		

Note: β^1 is reported at the step where all student characteristics were controlled. (* $p \leq 0.05$. ** $p \leq 0.01$); β^2 is reported at the final step of the evaluation. T ratios (reported at final step) of approximately 1.96 or greater are significant at the 0.05 level, and 2.59 or greater are significant at the 0.01 level.

measures and (2) evaluate the performance of some of the data obtained independent of student observation (expenditures and enrollments) in comparison to student perceptions. T-ratios represent the magnitude of the coefficient, taking into account its standard error of estimate; these values are presented in lieu of unstandardized coefficients to compare effects across groups at the final step of the equation. Overall, the regression models account for 36 percent of the variance in campus racial tension in the Chicano, 24 percent in the black, and 19 percent in the white student samples.

Student Characteristics

Results show that white students who entered college expecting to become involved in campus protest, white females, and black students who characterized their views as politically liberal are inclined to perceive racial tension on campus. It may be that these types of students are predisposed to view the climate critically and are sensitive to issues of racial and social inequality. In the wake of harassment incidents on campus, these students may have also found themselves in the forefront of protests to pressure institutions into formulating a response. Prior to the entry of institutional characteristics in the equations, the significant betas (β^1) of other student variables show that perceptions of racial tension are also prevalent among Chicanos who expected to become involved in campus protest. Additional characteristics of white students who perceive racial tension include those with a higher level of social self-confidence, parental income, mother's education, and a higher GPA. These latter student characteristics do not maintain significant coefficients in the final steps of the regression equations due to their association with institutional characteristics that have relatively strong effects (for example, selectivity). Thus, perceptions of racial tension are not created solely in the minds of specific individuals, but rather are rooted in a shared institutional reality.

Institutional Characteristics

Across all groups, students perceive low racial tension at institutions with high student-centered priorities. This relationship remains significant after controlling for institution size, college composition variables, and other institutional priorities. Betas at the step where all student characteristics are controlled (β^1) also indicate that institutional spending priorities may play an indirect role in relation to campus racial tension. Campus expenditures for student aid (among Chicano and white students) and student services (among black and white students) are negatively associated with perceptions of racial tension. The changes in the coefficients for these expenditure measures were monitored throughout the equations, revealing that perceptions of student-centered priorities account for much of their effect on perceptions of racial tension. These institutional spending priorities are associated with perceptions of an overall environment of student support that, in turn, are associated with perceptions of lower racial tension. Results on these parallel measures of student support extend earlier findings that were derived from a model of campus racial tension that included only expenditure measures (distal measures) [29].

Data support the notion that an institutional commitment to diversity can substantially improve minority and, to some extent, white student perceptions of race relations on campus. Perceptions of institutional commitment to diversity maintained a strong negative association with perceptions of racial tension among black and Chicano students. Similarly, white students' perceptions of institutional commitment to diversity were associated with a small negative effect on racial tension prior to controlling for other environmental characteristics (β^1). However, the effect for white students became non-significant when measures of student-centered priorities were controlled (β^2). This difference between white and minority groups will be discussed in the latter part of this article. It is important to note here, however, that perceptions of institutional commitment to diversity do not significantly contribute to white student perceptions of racial tension.

Although college selectivity and priorities for resource/reputation enhancement are often associated with traditional notions of quality, they maintain unique effects on racial tension in the black and white student samples and are more closely linked in the Chicano sample. Black and white students who perceive that their institutions have high resource and reputation priorities perceive high racial tension. In addition, institutional selectivity was a positive indicator of perceptions of racial tension across all ethnic groups. The unique effects of selectivity on perceptions of racial tension are maintained over and above student characteristics and campus priorities for resource and reputation enhancement. This suggests that selectivity is not merely a proxy for the type of student an institution recruits, nor can priorities for resource/reputation enhancement fully explain why we observe racial conflict in selective institutions.

Interaction terms that represent (1) high resource/reputation and institutional commitment to diversity and (2) high resource/reputation and student-centered orientation were introduced in subsequent models (not shown) to test whether these combinations of priorities were significantly related to racial tension. The interaction terms did not contribute significantly to the proportion of variance explained in the dependent measure. Therefore, these dimensions of institutional priorities appear to work independently and are not likely to have an additive effect on perceptions of racial tension.

Differences among the ethnic groups are evident in the relationship between enrollments and perceptions of racial tension. The effect of institutional size on perceptions of racial tension was diminished substantially by other institutional measures in all student groups, yet it maintains a positive association with perceptions of racial tension among white students. Similarly, the various effects of the ethnic enrollment measures on minority student perceptions of racial tension were diminished when other institutional characteristics were taken into account (β^2). In contrast, white students' perceptions of racial tension were significantly influenced by minority enrollments. The proportion of black students and increases in black enrollment are positively associated and Hispanic enrollment is negatively associated with white students' perception of racial tension on campus. There are at least two possible explanations for this difference between white and minority students and the contradictory effect of Hispanic enrollment: (1) as some race relations theories propose, white students may feel threatened by the presence of an increasing number of black students [11] or (2) ethnic enrollment differences in the institutional sample may indicate that the effects of the minority composition of a college on racial tension may be nonlinear.

To investigate nonlinear effects, the quadratic and cubic terms of the proportion of black students were added hierarchically to the regression models for each group. Although the cubic term was significant in the white student sample, when compared with the base model, there was no change in the direction of effects and the additional proportion of variance accounted for was too small to determine a nonlinear trend in the data. Still, the different distribution of black and Hispanic enrollments at the institutions in this sample may be indicative of nonlinear effects. None of the institutions had a black student population higher than 26 percent, and two institutions in the sample were Hispanic-serving institutions (HSIs)[3] with Hispanic enrollments approaching 30 and 50 percent respectively. Moreover, these institutions were located in cities with predominantly Hispanic populations. It may be that white students' perceptions of racial tension are lower in these institutional contexts not so much because of the ethnicity of the changing population, but because of the higher proportion of culturally diverse students and the general multicultural context of community in which they are located.

Summary and Discussion

National data show that approximately one in four students perceived considerable racial conflict at four-year institutions in the late 1980s. Considering the substantial media attention devoted to racial issues on campus in recent years, some may think this proportion is small. However, the proportion of students reporting racial conflict was higher in university settings (approximately one-third). This proportion is significant given that racial tension escalated to the point of creating serious disruptions at several campuses [25, 60]. At the same time that institutions were experiencing racial conflict, students were critical of institutional priorities to improve the racial climate. Less than a third of the students reported priorities to increase the representation of minorities through student and administrator/faculty recruitment, and less than half reported that general goals for fostering a multicultural environment were a high priority at their institution.

Although there are slight differences in reporting categories, results from the 1989 Follow-up of students replicate several general findings of the 1989 ACE survey of academic administrators [23]. Perceptions of campus race relations and various diversity priorities are not uniform across different institutional contexts. A higher proportion of universities and public four-year colleges have initiated efforts to diversify their environments, yet these institutions also have relatively higher racial tension than private four-year colleges. There also appears to be a public/private institutional dichotomy among four-year colleges in the quality of race relations and priorities for diversity: students at private four-year colleges perceive better overall campus race relations than public four-year institutions. At the same time, a smaller proportion of students perceive that the recruitment of minority students and administrators/faculty is a high priority at private four-year institutions. Ethnic group analyses revealed that these contradictory patterns may be due to differences in college composition and distinct institutional priorities that shape the general campus climate.

Institutions may foster racial tension when they support priorities that work against promoting a better climate. Specifically, traditional notions of quality based on selectivity and resource/reputation priorities are associated with perceptions of high racial tension. Selective institutions are unique environments, they are not simply contexts of individual achievement as proposed in the adaptation model for diversity [51]. They represent an extreme in American wealth and privilege, are staunch promoters of tradition, and are the rungs to powerful positions in society. Although resistance to change may be greatest at these institutions, they are also birthplaces for progressive thought. Racial tension may be highest in these contradictory environments because institutional commitment to diversity is often ambivalent, mitigated by other institutional actions that systematically exclude minorities and their perspectives.

In retrospect, the narrow focus on the enhancement of reputation and resources and moves to increase the selectivity of institutions may have more to do with maintaining inequalities than with actually improving the overall quality of college environments. Our definition of quality and its implementations are laden with assumptions that carry implicit messages to members of the campus community. Narrow conceptions of "quality" often favor elitism rather than egalitarianism, homogeneity rather than diversity, and the unequal distribution of resources. Institutions have opposed diversification of the curriculum, student body, and faculty; concentrated resources in a few individuals (for example, "faculty stars"); and often excluded minorities—all in the name of "quality." This justification is constructed to maintain" harmonious inequality" and may heighten racial tension when groups challenge these actions and their underlying assumptions. The apparent link between racial tension and traditional notions of quality should serve as the impetus for reframing our conceptions of quality to focus on improving the overall condition of life on campus. The quality of life on campus includes both the campus racial climate and the environment of support for students.

Along these lines, black and Chicano student perceptions of institutional commitment to diversity are associated with perceptions of relatively low racial tension. Among white students, this relationship is weaker and appears to be indirect: institutional commitment to diversity is tied to how an institution treats students (student-centered priorities), which in turn, affects perceptions of racial tension on campus. The difference between groups may be partially explained by results that show white students are less likely to perceive racial tension. Minorities are more aware of racial tension both for historical reasons and because they, unlike white students who are a numerical majority, must depend on constant interracial contact in social, learning, and work spheres on predominantly white campuses.

History reflects that substantial barriers delayed minority progress to attain full participation in American life, and removal of these barriers for racial integration and participation in education required both collective action and institutional change [15]. This progress is still in evolution in our society, as minorities continue to enter college from substantially different social backgrounds (income and parental education) compared to white classmates. Black and Chicano students may feel that institutional initiatives can improve the condition of a racial climate that affects daily interactions, whereas white students may feel the same way about more general climate issues. Thus, institutions that increase their commitment to diversity may significantly improve minority student perceptions of the racial climate. Results also indicate that institutional commitment to diversity does not fuel perceptions of racial tension among the majority of white students. A small proportion (12 percent) of students believe that racial discrimination is no longer a problem in our society, suggesting that only a small (sometimes vocal) group may oppose measures designed to improve the climate for diversity.

A central finding of this study is that racial tension may arise in environments where there is a lack of concern for individual students. Across all groups, perceptions of student-centered priorities were important predictors of perceptions of low racial tension. These results provide empirical support for the importance of "setting a 'tone' that is congenial to all students" [47, p. 645) on college campuses. It may be that racial tensions are higher in environments where students believe that particular groups have special privileges or receive more attention when, in fact, all groups are experiencing a decline in the quality of support for students. Expenditures in the areas of student services and student grant/scholarship aid secure the environment of support for student development, resulting in a more favorable climate. Institutions should stand firm on issues that maintain support for students, particularly in light of declining federal commitment to issues that affect minority and low-income students. Campuses should seek opportunities to reconfigure resources and rewards to create student-centered priorities that will benefit all students. For example, institutions may devote more attention to student-centered approaches that involve faculty in both the personal and academic development of students. This approach may both reduce racial tension and improve social and academic outcomes for students.

Researchers have proposed that the effect of institutional size on campus conflict and racial policies was due to the impersonal environment of large campuses and their ability to attract more liberal or protest "prone" students [5]. Controls for student characteristics and student-centered priorities in the analyses show that these conclusions are only partially supported. While certain types of students may be more critical of the racial climate and an environment of student support was found to be essential, institutional size remains a significant predictor of perceptions of racial tension among white students. This suggests that there is more to large campus environments and their differential impact on racial/ethnic groups than we understand. Minority student perceptions of racial tension may be mediated by other institutional characteristics (for example, ethnic enrollments) and perhaps their ability to develop their own niche in large institutional settings [10]. Although all students may use this adaptive strategy, white students may view the prevalence of "niches" developed along mutual interests and ethnicity as increasing racial tension on large campuses. This area requires further research to understand how minority and white students make sense of large environments and whether their approaches may be conducive to relations across ethnic groups.

Results from assessing the effect of ethnic composition of a college, or the "compositional hypothesis" [26], are mixed. Increases in black enrollment over the last six years and the proportion of black enrollment are associated with white students' perception of high racial tension; however, the proportion of Hispanic enrollment had the opposite effect. It is difficult to determine whether different effects of relative size of the two ethnic groups may be due to substantially different relations with white students or may be explained by institutional sampling variability. Institutions with a broad range of ethnic enrollments should be added to the sample in the future to settle the question of whether there is a population "threshold" point that determines differences in relations among various ethnic groups on college campuses.

In any case, predominantly white campuses may be relatively unprepared for some of the problems accompanying change in their student bodies—particularly in the wake of impending demographic changes [24]. These findings indicate, and reports of racial incidents confirm [25], that black-white relations are generally in need of improvement on college campuses where enrollment shifts are occurring. Race relations theorists would conclude that, due to competition for resources, white students view black students as a threat to their group position [11]. The fact that student-centered priorities are associated with lower racial tension suggests that some campuses may have minimized feelings of competition among groups. The relative status differences among students of different racial/ethnic groups (social background and relative size of the groups) suggest structural conditions that may inform a sense of group position; however, it is not clear whether white students feel they are in competition with black students for limited institutional resources. The actual motivations for racial tension require further research to conclusively determine how different ethnic groups perceive one another in relation to their environments.

Conclusion

This study has shown that perhaps no single element of the environment may work to produce racial tension on college campuses. It is a configuration of external influences (historical and contemporary), structural characteristics of institutions and group relations, and institutionalized ideologies. Each of these areas requires our attention in efforts to promote civility and foster values in students that will serve them in an increasingly multicultural society. These efforts should be guided by a willingness to question our assumptions, consideration of the experiences of different ethnic groups, and an overriding concern for a quality of life on campus that will be conducive to student development. Further research on the experiences of different ethnic groups may help determine elements of our environments that uniquely contribute to the development of each group.

Notes

1. In the case of minority-targeted scholarships, the defense of individual privilege ran counter to group norms. As the Bush Administration questioned the legality of minority-targeted scholarships, the 1990 General Social Survey showed that the majority of the American public (69 percent of the white and 95 percent of the black population) supported special college scholarships for black students who maintain good grades [13]. Shaky legal rationale was used to defend individual privilege [45], even while there was widespread public support for minority-targeted scholarships.

2. The U.S. Department of Education still collects and reports data on Chicanos under the umbrella category of "Hispanic" even though census data and educational data show dramatic differences among Latino groups [24]. Chicanos represent the majority of the Hispanic enrollment in this sample of institutions.

3. According to the Hispanic Association of Colleges and Universities (HACU), a Hispanic-serving institution is one that meets a Hispanic enrollment minimum of 25 percent.

References

1. Allen, W. R. "Black Student, White Campus: Structural, Interpersonal, and Psychological Correlates of Success." *Journal of Negro Education*, 54 (1985), 134–37.
2. _____. "Black Students in U.S. Higher Education: Toward Improved Access, Adjustment, and Achievement," *The Urban Review*, 20 (1988), 165–87.
3. American Council on Education. "Bush's Plan Would Reduce Pell Grants." *Higher Education and National Affairs*, 40 (11 March 1991).
4. Arce, C. H. "Chicano Participation in Academe: A Case of Academic Colonialism," *Grito del Sol: Chicano Quarterly*, 3 (1978), 75–104.
5. Astin, A. W. "New Evidence on Campus Unrest, 1969–70." *Educational Record*, (Winter 1971), 41–46.
6. _____. *Achieving Educational Excellence*. San Francisco: Jossey-Bass, 1985.
7. _____. *Four Critical Years*. San Francisco: Jossey-Bass. 1977.
8. _____. *The Black Undergraduate: Current Status and Trends in the Characteristics of Freshmen*. Los Angeles: Higher Education Research Institute, 1990.
9. Astin, A. W., and J. W. Henson. "New Measures of College Selectivity." *Research in Higher Education*, 7 (1977), 1–9.
10. Attinasi, L. C., Jr. "Getting In: Mexican Americans' Perceptions of University Attendance and the Implications for Freshman Year Persistence." *Journal of Higher Education*, (May/June 1989), 247–77.
11. Blalock, J. M., Jr. *Toward a Theory of Minority-Group Relations*. New York: Wiley, 1967.
12. Blumer, H. "Race Prejudice as a Sense of Group Position." *Pacific Sociological Review*, 1 (1958), 3–7.
13. Bobo, L., and J. R. Kluegel. "Opposition to Race-Targeting: Self-interest, Stratification Ideology, or Prejudice?" A paper delivered at the American Association of Public Opinion Research, Phoenix, Arizona, May 1991.

14. Bowles, S., and H. Gintis. *Schooling in Capitalist America*. London: Routledge and Kegan Paul, 1977.
15. Branch, T. *Parting the Waters: America in the King Years, 1954–63*. New York: Simon and Schuster. 1989.
16. Brown v. Board of Education, 347 US 483 (1954).
17. Carter, D. J., and R. Wilson. *Minorities in Higher Education: Eighth Annual Status Report*. Washington, D.C.: American Council on Education, 1990.
18. _____. *Minorities in Higher Education: Ninth Annual Status Report*. Washington, D.C.: American Council on Education, 1991.
19. Carter-Williams, M. "The Eroding Status of Blacks in Higher Education: An Issue of Financial Aid." In *Black Education: A Quest for Equity and Excellence*, edited by W. D. Smith and E. W. Chunn. New Brunswick, N.J.: Transaction Publishers, 1989.
20. Dey, E. L. *Perceptions of the College Environment: An Analysis of Organizational, Interpersonal, and Behavioral Influences*. Ph.D. dissertation, University of California, Los Angeles, 1991. Ann Arbor: University Microfilms International. No: 9119161.
21. _____. *Beta View*. [Computer program]. Los Angeles: Higher Education Research Institute, 1990.
22. Dey, E. L., A. W. Astin, and W. S. Korn. *The American Freshman: Twenty-Five Year Trends*. Los Angeles: Higher Education Research Institute, 1991.
23. El-Khawas, E. *Campus Trends, 1989*. Higher education panel reports, no. 78. Washington, D.C.: American Council on Education, 1989.
24. Estrada, L. F. "Anticipating the Demographic Future." *Change*, 20 (1988), 14–19.
25. Farrell, W. C. Jr., and C. K. Jones. "Recent Racial Incidents in Higher Education: A Preliminary Perspective." *The Urban Review*, 20 (1988). 211–33.
26. Fossett, M. A., and K. J. Kiecolt. "The Relative Size of Minority Populations and White Racial Attitudes." *Social Science Quarterly*, 70 (1989), 820–35.
27. Giroux, H. A. "Theories of Reproduction and Resistance in the New Sociology of Education: A Critical Analysis." *Harvard Educational Review*, 53 (1983). 257–93.
28. Gurin, P., and E. Epps. *Black Consciousness, Identity, and Achievement: A Study of Students in Historically Black Colleges*. New York: Wiley, 1975.
29. Hurtado, S. *Campus Racial Climates and Educational Outcomes*. Ph.D. dissertation, University of California. Los Angeles, 1990. Ann Arbor: University Microfilms International, No: 9111328.
30. Higher Education Research Institute. *The American College Student, 1989: National Norms for 1985 and 1987 College Freshmen*. Los Angeles: Higher Education Research Institute, 1991.
31. Jackman, M. R. "Prejudice, Tolerance, and Attitudes Toward Ethnic Groups." *Social Science Research*, 6 (1977), 145–69.
32. Jackman, M. R., and M. J. Muha. "Education and Intergroup Attitudes: Moral Enlightenment. Superficial Democratic Commitment, or Ideological Refinement?" *American Sociological Review*, 49 (1984), 751–69.
33. Jacob, J. E. "Black America 1987: An Overview." In *The State of Black America*, 1988, edited by J. Dewart. New York: National Urban League, 1988.
34. Jessor, R. "The Perceived Environment in Psychological Theory and Research." In *Toward a Psychology of Situations: An Interactional Perspective*, edited by D. Magnusson. Hillsdale, N.J.: Lawrence Erlbaum Associates, 1981, 297–317.
35. Kanter, R. M. "Some Effects of Proportions on Group Life: Skewed Sex Ratios and Responses to Token Women." *American Journal of Sociology*, 82 (1977), 965–89.
36. Kiecolt, K. J. "Recent Developments in Attitudes and Social Structure." *Annual Review of Sociology*, 14 (1988), 381–403.
37. Loo, C. M., and G. Rolison. "Alienation of Ethnic Minority Students at a Predominantly White University." *Journal of Higher Education*, 57 (1986), 58–77.
38. McClelland, K. E., and C. J. Auster. "Public Platitudes and Hidden Tensions: Racial Climates at Predominantly White Liberal Arts Colleges." *Journal of Higher Education*, 61 (November/December 1990), 607–42.
39. Moos, R. H. *Evaluating Educational Environments*. San Francisco: Jossey-Bass, 1979.
40. National Institute against Prejudice and Violence, "Conflict Continues on U.S. Campuses." *Forum*, 5 (November 1990), 1–2.
41. Nettles, M. T. "Black and White Students' Academic Performance in Majority White and Majority Black College Settings." In *Desegregating America's Colleges and Universities*, edited by J. B. Williams III. New York: Teachers College Press, 1988.

42. Nettles, M. T., A. R. Thoeny, and E. J. Gosman. "Comparative and Predictive Analyses of Black and White Students' College Achievement and Experiences." *Journal of Higher Education,* 57 (1986), 289–318.

43. Olivas, M. A. "Research and Theory on Hispanic Education: Students, Finance, and Governance." *Atzlan, International Journal of Chicano Studies Research,* 14 (1983), 111–46.

44. _____. "Research on Latino College Students: A Theoretical Framework for Inquiry." In *Latino College Students,* edited by M. A. Olivas. New York: Teachers College Press, 1986.

45. _____. "Federal Law and Scholarship Policy: An Essay on the Office for Civil Rights, Title VI, and Racial Restrictions." *Journal of College and University Law,* 18 (1991), 21–28.

46. Oliver, M. L., C. J. Rodriguez, and R. A. Mickelson. "Brown and Black in White: The Social Adjustment and Academic Performance of Chicano and Black Students in a Predominantly White University." *The Urban Review: Issues and Ideas in Public Education,* 17 (1985), 3–24.

47. Pascarella, E. T., and P. T. Terenzini. *How College Affects Students.* San Francisco: Jossey-Bass, 1991.

48. Patterson, A. M., W. E. Sedlacek, and F. W. Perry. "Perceptions of Blacks and Hispanics in Two Campus Environments." *Journal of College Student Personnel,* 25 (1984), 513–18.

49. Peterson, M. W., et al. *Black Students on White Campuses: The Impacts of Increased Black Enrollments.* Ann Arbor: Institute for Social Research, 1978.

50. Reyes, M. D., and J. J. Halcón. "Racism in Academia: The Old Wolf Revisited." *Harvard Educational Review,* 58 (1988), 299–314.

51. Richardson, R. C., Jr., and E. F. Skinner. "Adapting to Diversity: Organizational Influences on Student Achievement." *Journal of Higher Education,* 61 (September/October 1990), 485–511.

52. Skinner, E. F., and R. C. Richardson, Jr. "Making It in a Majority University." *Change,* 20 (May/June 1988), 34–42.

53. Smith, D. G. "The Challenge of Diversity: Involvement or Alienation in the Academy?" *ASHE-ERIC Higher Education Report* 5, 1989. Washington: George Washington University.

54. Smith, D. H. "Social and Academic Environments of Black Students on White Campuses." *Journal of Negro Education,* 50 (1981), 299–306.

55. Stoecker, J., E. T. Pascarella, and L. M. Wolfle. "Persistence in Higher Education: A 9-year Test of a Theoretical Model." *Journal of College Student Personnel,* 29 (1988), 196–209.

56. Sudarkasa, N. "Black Enrollment in Higher Education: The Unfulfilled Promise of Equality." In *The State of Black America,* edited by J. Dewart. New York: National Urban League, 1988.

57. Tracey, T. J., and W. E. Sedlacek. "A Comparison of White and Black Student Academic Success Using Noncognitive Variables: A LISREL Analysis." *Research in Higher Education,* 27 (1987), 333–48.

58. Tracey, T. J., and W. E. Sedlacek. "Noncognitive Variables in Predicting Academic Success by Race." *Measurement and Evaluation in Guidance,* 16 (1984), 171–78.

59. Trent, W. T. "Student Affirmative Action in Higher Education: Addressing Underrepresentation." In *The Racial Crisis in American Higher Education,* edited by P. G. Altbach and K. Lomotey. Albany: State University of New York Press, 1991.

60. Vellela, T. *New Voices: Student Activism in the '80s and '90s.* Boston: South End Press, 1988.

61. Vera, R. *Texas' Response to the Office of Civil Rights: Progress Made Under the Texas Equal Educational Opportunity Plan for Higher Education.* Claremont: Tomas Rivera Policy Center, 1989.

62. Verdugo, R. R. "Educational Stratification and Hispanics." In *Latino College Students,* edited by M. A. Olivas. New York: Teachers College Press, 1986.

63. Wellman, D. T. *Portraits of Whim Racism.* New York: Cambridge University Press, 1977.

64. White, T. J., and W. E. Sedlacek. "White Student Attitudes Toward Blacks and Hispanics: Programming Implications." *Journal of Multicultural Counseling and Development,* 15 (October 1987), 171–83.

65. Williams, J. B., III. "Title VI Regulation of Higher Education." In *Desegregating America's Colleges and Universities,* edited by J. B. Williams Ill. New York: Teachers College Press, 1988.

The Exxon Education Foundation provided generous support for the administration of surveys at selected institutions, thereby facilitating analyses by ethnic group. This funding was provided as part of a project on the outcomes of general education conducted at the Higher Education Research Institute, UCLA. Research was conducted in UCLA's Department of Sociology and the Graduate School of Education with the support of the University of California President's Postdoctoral Fellowship. The author extends her appreciation for Walter R. Allen's and Michael A. Olivas's helpful comments on an earlier draft of this article.

TABLE A1

Variable Definition and Coding Scheme

Dependent Variable

Campus Racial Tension	Four-item factor scale, (see table A2 for items).

1985 Student Characteristics

Sex	Dichotomous: 1 = "male"; 2 = "female."
Age	Ten-point scale: 1 = "16 or younger," to 10 = "55 or older."
High-school GPA (self-report)	Eight-point scale: 1 = "D," to 8 = "A or A+."
Mother's education	Eight-point scale: 1 = "grammar school or less," to 8 = "graduate degree."
Father's education	Eight-point scale: 1 = "grammar school or less," to 8 = "graduate degree."
Parental Income	Fourteen-point scale: 1 = "less than $6000," to 14 "$150,000 or more."
Social self-confidence (see Table A2).	Three-item factor scale based on student self ratings
Expect to protest in college	Four-point scale: 1 = "very little chance," to 4 = "very good chance."
Political view (self-rating)	Five-point scale: 1 = "far right," to 5 = "far left."
Helping to promote racial understanding	Four-point scale: 1 = "not important," to 4 = "essential."

Institutional Characteristics

Institutional Priorities
Expenditures per student:

Student services	Expenditures for admissions and all activities designed to contribute to the emotional, physical, intellectual, cultural, and social development of students outside the formal educational program
Non-repayable aid	Monies given in the form of grants and scholarships to students enrolled in formal coursework. Excludes college work study and Pell grants.

Student Perceptions of Priorities:

Student-centered	Five-item factor scale. (see table A2 for item scales).
Resource/reputation	Five-item factor scale. (see table A2 for item scales).
Commitment to diversity	Four-item factor scale. (see table A2 for item scales).

College composition:

Selectivity	Average SAT of entering freshmen divided by 10 (ACT converted to SAT equivalents using Astin & Henson, 1977).

Enrollment:

Size (total FTE)[1]	Total graduate and undergraduate FTE.
Black percent in 1986	Black undergraduate FTE divided by total undergraduate FTE.
Hispanic percent in 1986 FTE	Hispanic undergraduate FTE divided by total undergraduate.
Black increase (1982–88)[2]	Dichotomous: 1 = "decrease," 2 = "increase" (absolute numbers of undergraduate FTE).
Hispanic increase (1982–88)	Three-point scale: 1 = "decrease," 2 = "no change." 3 = "increase" (absolute numbers of undergraduate FTE).

1. Three part-time students are equivalent to one FTE.

2. All institutions in the sample experienced change in black undergraduate enrollment over six years.

TABLE A2

Items Constituting Factor Scales

Social Self-Confidence Factor
(Student self-rating compared to the average person his/her age)
  Leadership ability[1]
  Popularity[1]
  Self-Confidence (social)[1]

Campus Racial Tension Factor
(Statements about the freshman college)
  There is a lot of campus racial conflict here[2]
  Students of different racial/ethnic origins communicate well with one another[3]
  There is little trust between minority student groups and campus administrators[2]

Institutional Priority: Commitment to Diversity Factor
(Priorities of the freshman college)
  Increase the representation of minorities in the faculty and administration[4]
  Develop among students and faculty an appreciation for a multicultural society[4]
  Recruit more minority students[4]
  Create a diverse multicultural environment on campus[4]

Institutional Priority: Resource/Reputation Factor
(Priorities of the freshman college)
  Increase or maintain institutional prestige[4]
  Enhance the institution's national image[4]
  Hire faculty "stars"[4]
  Raise money for the institution[4]
  Conduct basic and applied research[4]

Institutional Priority: Student-centered Factor
(Statements about the freshman college)
  It is easy to see faculty outside of office hours[5]
  Most students are treated like "numbers in a book"[6]
  Faculty here are interested in students' personal problems[2]
  Faculty here are strongly interested in the academic problems of undergraduates[2]

NOTE: Full details of the exploratory and confirmatory procedures used to develop factors are reported in Hurtado (1990) and Dey (1991).

1. Five-point scale: 1 = "bottom 10%" to 5 = "highest 10%."

2. Four-point scale: 1 = "Disagree strongly" to 4 = "Agree strongly."

3. Four-point scale: 1 = "Agree strongly" to 4 = "Disagree strongly" (reversed for analyses).

4. Four-point scale: 1 = "Low Priority" to 4 = "Highest priority."

5. Three-point scale: 1 = "Not descriptive" to 3 "Very descriptive."

6. Three-point scale: 1 = "Very descriptive" to 3 "Not descriptive" (reversed for analyses).

AN ORGANIZATIONAL ANALYSIS OF RACISM IN HIGHER EDUCATION[1]

MARK A. CHESLER AND JAMES CROWFOOT

The Program in Conflict Management Alternatives: The Program in Conflict Management Alternatives was established in January, 1986, by a grant from the William and Flora Hewlett Foundation, and additional funds from the University of Michigan. These basic grants were renewed in July, 1988. The Program supports an agenda of research, application, and theory development. PCMA also establishes links among other University research and teaching efforts relevant to conflict management alternatives, and maintains liaison and collaboration with similar efforts in other Universities and Practitioner agencies. The Program staff's own work focuses explicitly on the relationship between social justice and social conflict, specifically: (a) the use of innovative settlement procedures and roles for disputants and third parties; (b) the institutionalization of innovative mechanisms and the adoption of organizational and community structures that permanently alter the way conflicts are managed; and (c) the fundamental differences and inequalities between parties that often create conflict and threaten its stable resolution.

We examine these issues primarily in United States' settings, in conflicts arising within and between families, organizations and communities, and between different racial, gender, and economic constituencies. These specific efforts are supported by a variety of research and action grants/contracts with governmental agencies, foundations, and private and public organizations/agencies.

I. Introduction

Complexity, contradiction and confusion are paramount in American race relations. Our national history is fraught with contradictory messages about "equal rights" and "slavery," about "equality of opportunity" and the "reproduction of poverty," about "affirmative action" and "reverse discrimination." Overriding this confusion, our history of racial injustice is maintained through contemporary policies and practices, and is reflected in the dramatic differentials in life expectancy, opportunity and other outcomes that still exist between people of color and white persons. In addition, in order to defend and sustain the moral imperative of democracy and equality, we have created ideologies that legitimate and justify these racial differentials as reflections of minority inadequacy or as aberrations from the otherwise fair workings of an open and meritorious political and economic system. As a result, even people who perceive obvious racial inequalities often find it difficult to recognize the injustice embedded in these inequalities. It is hard to act with fairness when we do not understand the basis upon which fairness applies, or what it even means when applied to people of color and to situations involving racial inequality.

"Racism in Higher Education: An Organizational Analysis," CRSO Center for Research on Social Organization, *The Working Paper Series*, by Mark A. Chesler and James Crowfoot, PCMA Working CRSO Work, Paper #21 Paper #412, November 1989

If individuals' moral choices regarding racial relations and racial injustice are generally difficult, they are even more difficult when set within an organizational context. Here there are collective as well as individual choices to make, and actors must act amidst diffuse (and often impersonal)
organizational criteria and competing claims. Moreover, the organizational imperative often requires individual claims (moral, economic and otherwise) to be subordinated to collective priorities.
Sometimes organizational rules and cultures are so pervasive that there is an inability to perceive realities other than those posed or promulgated by the organization, or if choices are perceived people
are unable to act on them. Nevertheless, organizational actors must make decisions, allocate resources and adjudicate competing claims. To the extent that organizations play powerful roles in
providing their members and customers with access to vital life resources and opportunities, these
decisions are profoundly moral and have crucial and lasting consequences.

Organizations propagate (implicitly or explicitly) frameworks within which individuals operating in the name or context of the organization make choices and engage in formal and informal behavior. Most organizations go further; they provide quite specific rewards and sanctions for
behavior that is deemed to be appropriate or inappropriate (e.g., with regard to white collar crime,
pursuit of prudent decisions in the interest of stockholders, sexual harassment on the job, stealing
competitors' secrets, bribery that serves the organization's welfare, whistle blowing that surfaces
malfeasance, etc.). Some organizations, moreover, have an explicitly moral agenda: school systems,
particularly, have a goal of preparing the young to recognize moral issues and to make choices consistent with the values of prior generations. Colleges and universities are at the apex of educational
systems, and as the secularization of society has progressed, they have increasingly replaced
churches and synagogues as purveyors of core values and standards. The public often expects organizations of higher education to embody and articulate traditional moral values and to prepare
students for exemplary lives.

When the complex realities of organizational life are joined with the confusing and often contradictory nature of race relations in American life, we enter very difficult territory. Clear understanding of relevant racial issues, let alone a capacity for wise and appropriate behavior, is difficult. The
sheer invisibility of racism to white people makes it difficult to perceive (and correctly interpret) the
reality of organizational life as it exists for people of color. Since this invisibility is historic as well as
contemporary, white people also often are blind to their enmeshment in well established patterns of
racial advantage and disadvantage, and to the privileges they and their ancestors have gained
thereby. Without such clarity, or pressures to be clear, it is hard to own and take personal or organizational responsibility for injustice, or for the need to strive for justice. Thus, patterns of institutional racism often operate without white people being aware of them and without their conscious
intent. Nevertheless, these patterns of racism reproduce themselves: they are aided by the ways in
which people with power and advantage in the society, white people and people with wealth, cannot see racism clearly, deny responsibility for action to remove it, and thus passively if not actively
contribute to the maintenance of the status quo.

One essential component of morally appropriate behavior is an ability to see the issues clearly:
in the context of organizational racism that means clarity about the organization's impact on peoples' options, the existence and operation of racism in the organization, and the role and impact of
racism in the lives of people of color and white people. As noted, what is hard to perceive at a personal level is even harder to see clearly at an organizational level, where individual capacities for
clarity and responsibility often are obscured by organizational rules and norms. Without such clarity and responsibility, the potential for sound organizational decision making and implementation
of decisions—including those necessary to achieve change—is virtually non-existent.

Our purpose in this paper is to contribute to an understanding of race relations and racism, and
actions to combat racism, in institutions of higher education. We do so by conducting a conceptually
based diagnosis and analysis of the operations of racism in typical colleges and universities. This
analysis grows out of our work as white male faculty members and administrators at a major university. These background and role characteristics shape our perspectives in certain ways, and undoubtedly in ways that differ from those of people of a different race, status, gender, etc. Our hope
in this paper is to move beyond a discussion of white peoples' individual attitudes and behaviors,

or guilt and responsibility, or choice and non-choice; we focus on racism occurring at an organizational level—institutional racism. Moreover, we place organizational/institutional racism in the context of the specific activities and operations of colleges and universities, relatively unique kinds of organizations. The potential for organizational change to reduce racism also is described briefly.

II. From Individual Incidents to Institutional Racism

Numerous scholars and activists have drawn attention to the historic state of race relations and racial injustice in American higher education (Astin, 1982; Blauner, 1972; Clark and Plotkin, 1963; Fleming et al, 1978; Peterson et al, 1978; Thomas, 1981; Vetter et al, 1982). Many of these early efforts were spurred by the turbulence of the late 1960s and early 1970s. As relative "peace" returned to the campus, however, concern with these issues gradually receded. Fiscal crises, debates about appropriate public-sector private-sector relationships, potential declines in student applications and other issues became more important. Recent events have spurred new empirical and political analyses of institutional racism in our colleges and universities (Allen, 1986; Steele, 1989; Sudarkasa, 1988; Wilson and Carter, 1988).

Recent attention to racism on campus has been galvanized by a series of noteworthy public "incidents." Included among these incidents reported at 174 different colleges (Bayh, 1989) have been the following:

Citadel—A group of white students dressed in white sheets and hoods threatened a Black cadet with racial obscenities and a burnt cross.

Dartmouth—White students destroyed shanties erected in protest of corporate investment in South Africa.

Macalester College—The room of five Asian women was vandalized with the letters KKK written on the door.

Michigan State University—Threatening phone calls and written messages were received by students of color.

University of Massachusetts—Physical attacks were made on Black students by a mob of white students.

The University of Michigan—Black women were harassed in dormitories with flyers announcing an intention to "get them" and suggesting they go back to Africa.

University of Mississippi—Arson destroyed a Black fraternity house.

University of Wisconsin—A group of fraternity men held a mock auction of Black slaves with white pledges wearing blackface and Afro wigs.

Yale University—A swastika and racist comments were written on the Afro-American cultural center.

When first noted by administrators and faculty, many of these incidents were described as accidents, as departures from norms of civility and justice, or at least tolerance, prevailing on our campuses; indeed, they often were analyzed as not being "racial incidents" at all, but as instances of drunkenness, playfulness or political protest (e.g., Hurst, 1987). Moreover, they were seen as evidence of problems residing in the student community, reflecting ill on the state of mind of American college youth. And finally, they often were analyzed as individual actions, as the behaviors of one or a small group of individuals who were presumed to be ignorant, prejudiced, filled with hate or perhaps partially deranged.

It is of course true that growing up in America predisposes most white people to ignorance, indifference and fear or antipathy toward people of color. For some, this is learned through deliberate instruction at home and in school, instruction explicitly designed to maintain racial distance and to pass on accumulated social lessons regarding the inferiority of people of color. For others, this is incidental learning, messages gathered as a result of seeing how people of color are treated as systematically inferior and undeserving of the privileges and advantages of an affluent society.

For our society to maintain the illusion that it is democratic and just, the young must perceive the oppressed position of people of color as their own due, as the deserved result of their own inadequacies. In an uncertain world, these lessons have great psychic and social import, protecting us from our own insecurities as well as from the intrusion of others and discomforting ideas. Thus, the workings of institutional racism are deeply embedded in the psyches of white people, as well as in the structure of social, political, and economic relationships. They also impact on these psychic and social structures in ways that maintain and reproduce inequality over generations.

We suggest, however, that those analytic frames that focus primarily on prejudice, or that depend primarily on individual or incidental explanations of racism, are inadequate and thereby erroneous. More than that, they serve to distract attention from the true nature of racism on the university campus. What is real is neither incidental nor accidental; what is real is not located merely in the minds and actions of a few students; what is real is not solely individual ignorance or prejudice. What is real is institutional racism on campus, just as institutional racism is real throughout the warp and woof of the American society.

The path to a reanalysis of these phenomena, from explanations of individual incidents to explanations of institutional structure and process, often is provided in the extended nature of the incidents themselves, and in campus responses to them. For instance, in response to incidents occurring at the University of Michigan in early 1987, groups of students of color presented the University administration with the series of proposals/demands illustrated in Figure 1. Examination of the demands makes it obvious that these students have discerned some of the organizational roots of the incidents of individual racism practiced by white students. Indeed, the proposals focus on changes in the programs and structures of the University, and not solely on the behavior of students. In follow-up conversations and confrontations, these students have identified the behaviors (and non-behaviors) of faculty and administrators that encourage, permit or tolerate (even unconsciously) continued harassment and discrimination against students of color.

This list is in many ways quite similar to the list of demands presented to the University of Michigan administration by the original Black Action Movement, in 1970 (see Figure 2). The similarity of concerns, and therefore demands, is not surprising, since the character of racism at most colleges and universities has remained quite similar to the situation in 1970. Responses made at that

UCAR Anti-Racist Proposals

1. Submit a specific plan to guarantee a substantial increase in black student enrollment.
2. Establish an Office of Minority Affairs with an autonomous supervisory commission elected by the minority campus community.
3. Create a Financial Aid Appeals Board to make sure no student is forced out of the University because of economic discrimination.
4. Establish a mandatory workshop on racism and diversity for all incoming students.
5. Set up a program of orientation for minority students to meet and talk with already enrolled minority students and faculty to minimize feelings of isolation.
6. Institute a program of tuition waivers for all under-represented and economically disadvantaged minority students until the goals for minority enrollment are realized.
7. Create a Minority Student Lounge and Office in the Michigan Union where minority students can meet in a comfortable and supportive atmosphere on a regular basis.
8. Establish a required course on diversity and bigotry to be taken by all matriculated students before graduation from the University, with input from the Center for Afroamerican and African studies.
9. Full observance of the Dr. Martin Luther King holiday including cancellation of classes and the closing of offices.
10. Honorary degree for S. African leader Nelson Mandela at May commencement.
11. Full, public and immediate investigation of all reported incidents of racial harassment, and a mechanism set up, to facilitate the on-going reporting and documentation of such incidents.

Figure 1   Selected student proposals/demands to counter racism at the University of Michigan.[2]

1. Ten percent black enrollment by Fall, 1973;
2. Nine hundred new black students by Fall, 1971—450 freshmen, 250 transfers, 300 graduate students;
3. An adequate supportive services program including financial aid to finance black students' education;
4. Graduate and undergraduate recruiters (9) to recruit black students;
5. A referendum on the March Student Government Council ballot to have students vote on assessing themselves $3.00 for one year for the Martin Luther King Scholarship Fund;
6. Tuition waivers for minority group students who are also residents of the state of Michigan;
7. The establishment of a Community-located Black Student Center;
8. All work of a permanent nature on the Black Studies program is to be halted until an effective input is fully developed by a Community-University forum;
9. The creation of a University-wide appeal board to rule on the adequacy of financial aid grants to students;
10. A revamping of the Parent's Confidential Statement;
11. There should be one recruiter for Chicano students to assure 50 Chicano students by Fall, 1970;
12. Black students are to be referred to as Black and not as Negro or anything else

Figure 2   Summary of the original BAM demands (1970).[3]

time focused on new services, but not on changing the institutional basis of racism. The result has been a continuation of the conditions of disadvantage and discrimination that have led again to overt conflict and protest in the late 1980s.

For instance, when incidents of racial harassment surfaced at the University of Michigan, and when students of color voiced their concerns and grievances, most academic Deans and senior officials of the University expressed shock and surprise at the level and consistency of humiliation and discrimination these students reported. For so many well-meaning officials to be so poorly-informed about the experiences of this constituency is in itself revealing. It suggests, of course, that academic administrators (and often much of the faculty as well) are out of touch with and ignorant about student life in general, and of the conditions faced by students of color in particular. This lack of information is neither accidental nor individual. It is socially constructed ignorance, and is created by the separate cultures, life experiences and responsibilities of whites and of people of color—in the society, in the neighborhood and in the University. Moreover, it is ignorance that was permitted to exist because most individuals did not inquire proactively into the conditions of life of students of color: there was no payoff for such concern and no sanctions for such ignorance.

The situation at the University of Michigan is instructive, but not, we think, unique.[4] The institutional racism existing at·the University of Michigan is quite probably no greater or lesser than that which exists at many other major institutions of higher education. What may be different at Michigan, however, is the University's tradition of student activism, and of student leadership in highlighting and protesting various campus and societal problems. Thus, these challenges to racism, and learning about it as well as changing it, are more publically and vigorously debated, advocated, and resisted.

In an analysis of the 1960–1970 state of race relations and race conflict on campus, Blauner drew attention to the differing analytic frames often used then by (even liberal) white academics and students of color (1972, p 276–278).

> ... (For) the liberal professor ... racism connotes conscious acts, where there is an intent to hurt or degrade or disadvantage others because of their color or ethnicity ... He does not consider the all-white or predominantly white character of an occupation or an institution in itself to be racism. He does not understand the notion of covert racism, that white people maintain a system of racial oppression by acts of omission, indifference, and failure to change the status quo. The Third World definition of racism ... focuses on the society as a whole and on structured relations between people rather than on individual personalities and actions. From this standpoint, the university is racist because people of color are and have been systematically excluded from full and equal participation and power— as students, professors, administrators, and, particularly, in the historic definition of the character of the institution and its curriculum.

These different perspectives still exist. What is this concept of institutional racism?

Individual Racism and Institutional Racism

It is not new to argue, as have a number of scholars of race relations, that individual racial attitudes or behaviors must be analyzed in the context of organizational and societal parameters and frames of reference (Alvarez and Lutterman, 1979; Carmichael and Hamilton, 1976; Jones, 1970; Knowles and Prewitt, 1969; Schwartz and Disch, 1970; Omi and Winant, 1986; USCCR, 1981). Much like other forms of human behavior, racism would not persist as an individual attitude or behavior were there not organizational and societal norms teaching, supporting, and rewarding such activity.

The establishment and maintenance of racial difference, and the political, economic and cultural dominance of white people and groups, is part of the history of our nation. No serious student need be reminded by an examination of the history of colonization and its impact on Native Americans and Latinos, or by a re-reading of the Constitution and other founding documents of the Republic, of the ways in which support for white superiority and domination, slavery and a non-citizen class of people of color is part of our birthright as a nation. Nor do the facts of subsequent generations of white people's political and economic privilege and dominance, and the deprivation and oppression of people of color need retelling.

But it often is more difficult to see how this racially discriminatory history is sustained in the present, and how large-scale institutional structures currently operate to "pass on" and reinforce historic patterns of privilege and disadvantage and dominance. In Figure 3, Feagin and Feagin emphasize the especially potent roles of Direct Institutionalized Discrimination and Indirect Institutionalized Discrimination in this process (1986, p. 28).

"Direct Institutionalized Discrimination refers to organizationally-prescribed or community-prescribed actions which have an intentionally differential and negative impact on members of subordinate groups . . . carried out . . . routinely by a large number of individuals guided by the rules of a large scale organization" (1986, p. 30). Examples include deliberate efforts to track (or counsel) minority students into certain colleges and universities and into certain career paths, or to exclude minority content from the curriculum or social life of an institution.

Of even greater subtlety, and therefore interest to those of us working within manifestly "liberal" and "non-discriminatory" organizations, is Indirect Institutionalized Discrimination. This category "refers to practices having a negative and differential impact on minorities and women even though the organizationally prescribed or community-prescribed norms or regulations guiding these actions were established, and are carried out, with no prejudice or no intent to harm laying immediately behind them. On their face and in their intent, the norms and resulting practices appear fair or at least neutral" (p. 31). It is important to emphasize the minimal role that conscious intent or personal prejudice plays in Indirect Institutionalized Discrimination, since many people (white people, especially, and certainly much of the white judiciary) continue to think of racism as

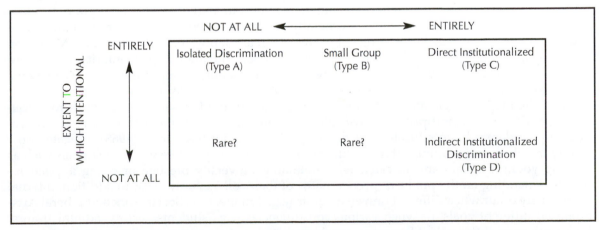

Figure 3 Types of discriminatory behavior extent of imbeddedness in larger organizations.

involving conscious discriminatory purposes. The very point of institutional racism is that organizational procedures can have discriminatory impact even if individual actors are unaware of such impacts or are non-discriminatory in their personal beliefs, and even if their behavior appears to be a fair-minded application of "race-neutral" or "colorblind" rules and norms. Examples of such subtle racism in organizational operations include denying minority scholars access to faculty positions because of their lack of "appropriate" or traditional credentials (which credentials were denied them because of prior discrimination), or because they lack some attributes of white males that are assumed to be relevant for certain positions but which, on examination, may not be. It also would include acts of omission, such as the failure to vigorously recruit minority students/scholars, the failure to generate hiring criteria more appropriate to the pool of minority scholars, or the failure to confront racism when it occurs; such failures subtly reinforce the continuation of discrimination. Given our legacy of racial oppression and disadvantage, apparently fair and racially neutral or color-blind policies and practices continue to have discriminatory impact. In order to overcome racism, self-conscious anti-discriminatory actions are required; and they in turn will require changes in current organizational structures and processes.

III. Organizational Factors Promoting Institutional Racism in Universities

Understanding institutional racism in universities requires attention to the general nature of these organizations and their operations. Moreover, a thorough and coherent diagnosis should not only identify the institutional nature of racism in these organizations, but should also point the way for change. Drawing from a framework first generated by Terry (1981), we suggest that five elements of all organizations' operations influence universities' policies and practices, including those that affect members of different racial groups. These elements are: mission, culture (not identified as a separate element by Terry), power, structure and resources. This certainly is not the only model or typology of complex organizations that could direct diagnostic and change planning. Tichy reviews a series of useful examples on the way to creating his own emphasis on the technical, political and cultural sub-systems in complex organizations (1983, especially Chapter 2). Baldridge and Deal's analysis of change processes in higher educational institutions uses a taxonomy which has several points of overlap with Terry's (1975, taken from Udy): it includes goals, environment, technology, formal structure and group-individual factors. Our preference for Terry's model (with modifications) is based on its heuristic value in noting specific elements which could be the basis of local college/university or unit diagnoses and change efforts. The model, and specific elements of the five-part taxonomy, is presented in Figure 4.

Mission refers to the official and unofficial vision and purposes of the organization, as these purposes or goals are reflected both in written policy statements and informal understandings and priorities. The emphasis on strategic planning, with regard to market concerns, program development and human resource management, generally flows from or creates clarification of an organization's mission, as it may be challenged by current circumstances and future options. Moreover, most organizations have several different sub-missions, and the complementarity or balance among them becomes quite critical, as in the ways in which different universities seek to satisfy the tri-partite commitment to research, teaching, and public service. Mission may become a focus of conflict when vigorous debates center on the relative priorities of these three standards for excellence, or when public and private universities differentially commit themselves to research productivity, undergraduate education or public service as priorities. Gross (1968) indicates how faculty members and administrators in different institutions may differentially rank goals such as training young scholars and researchers, maintaining university prestige or doing applied research, depending on the public or private status of their college/university. In addition, internal conflict may occur when different university units (e.g., Engineering, Social Work and Liberal Arts) espoused different goals, or when various constituencies (e.g., students, faculty, administrators) rank goals very differently. Mission-centered conflict also can result from divergent public pres-

MISSION
    Statement of goals and purposes
    Vision of the future
    Source of legitimacy for status quo or for change
    Relates organizational goals to broader society's goals
    Includes multiple or conflicting goals or subunits
    Relatively not open to debate
    Official (manifest) or unofficial (latent) purposes

CULTURE
    Dominant belief systems reflected in values, rituals, technology, styles and customs
    Norms for "proper" behavior and criteria for success
    Degree of monoculturalism or pluralism of the approved culture
    Standard for the allocation of rewards and sanctions
    Includes alternative (complementary or conflicting) cultures based on age, gender, race, class, etc.
    May include procedures for negotiating dominant and alternative cultures
    "Rules of the game"
    Belief system justifying basic organizational tasks and procedures

POWER
    Formal decision-making hierarchies and procedures
    Degree to which access to power hierarchy is closed or open
    Degree to which power hierarchy is open to people of different race, gender, class, internal status, age, etc.
    Constituencies that influence power-holders
    Degree of grass roots participation in key decisions
    Procedures for dealing with alternative power bases, formal (unions) and informal
    Decentralized unit control

STRUCTURE
    Division of labor among units and subunits, and related roles
    Technology for achieving organizational goals (pedagogy)
    Networks of social interaction and communication
    Planned activities that help accomplish basic tasks
    Boundary systems mediating organization's relationship with the external social and physical world
    Procedures used to achieve goals

RESOURCES
    Materials required to accomplish organization's goals
    People
    Money
    Plant and facilities
    Raw materials and markets
    Information

Figure 4   Universal organizational elements.

sures, as when white and Black or Latino people (or other people of color) and their political representatives seek different racial compositions for the student body, faculty and administration of the university, or promote different instructional, service and research programs.

    All organizations also develop a culture that permeates institutional functioning (Deal and Kennedy, 1982; Peters and Waterman, 1982; Van Maanen and Barley, 1984). The organizational culture consists of those core values which are reflected in the common understandings, assumptions or preferences regarding how people are expected to behave in the organization—from dress to deportment, whether competitively or cooperatively, whether caringly or sneeringly (Tichy, 1983). These preferences may, of course, differ at different status levels and for different task assignments within the organization. College and university cultures help define the unique styles of different educational institutions, as Clark points out in his research with small innovative, liberal arts colleges (Clark, 1970). Organizational cultures are deeply rooted in the history of each college or university, and serve to give special meaning to life at a particular institution (Dill, 1982; Masland, 1985). As many other organizations, a large university generally exists with several different subcultures simultaneously operative and potentially in conflict: at least a dominant culture and a counter-culture, in which the latter often serves as "a safe haven for the development of innovative ideas (Martin and Siehl, 1983, p. 52)"; a faculty culture and a student culture; a scientific culture and a humanities culture; an academic culture and an athletic culture, etc.

The power element in an organization is manifest in its decision-making structures and processes. The typical hierarchial and centralized organization concentrates formal power at the top, in the hands of a relatively small number of persons—usually white men. Other actors in the system also exercise formal power, generally as the agents of senior stakeholders. Just how much latitude middle level managers and administrators have, as well as whether their power is formal or informal, is a clue to the level of participatory or decentralized decision-making in the system. Regardless of how tightly controlled the organizational power system is, lower level employees (frontline services providers) always have some discretionary power, and can implement or not implement higher level decisions, can engage in compliance or sabotage, etc. (March and Simon, 1958). In the modern university, administrative power typically is located in central offices ruled by a white patriarchy of Presidents and Vice-Presidents, but these decision-makers often are dependent upon Collegiate Deans or Department Heads for the implementation of new policies and procedures. Faculty members have minimal opportunity for decisional input in university policies, and only are able to exert formal institutional influence at the sub-unit level. Their decisional roles generally are limited to the curriculum and their own research programs. Especially in the classroom, however, they have unilateral and often exclusive power to decide what to teach, and how to do it. Students, the nominal clients of the institution, have little power to affect major decisions. So, too, are lower level staff members (some of whom have very significant impact on students) generally excluded from decisions.

Organizational structure refers to those procedures, technologies and activities that define the ways in which the organization acts to meet its goals. The definition of the functions and roles of specific units, through which decisions are implemented, constitute the core of organizational structures. The social network of units and subunits, and their lines of communication and social interaction, represent the threads by which various units and activities are integrated. Reflecting the power system, university structures often are highly decentralized, and multiple activities organize the life of faculty, students, and staff members. The dominant instructional pedagogy, an activity explicitly focused on realizing the organization's educational goals, typically involves high faculty autonomy and one-way transmission of knowledge to students in isolated classrooms.

Resources are those goods, people and funds (capital) that constitute the raw materials that organizations transform into finished products or services. The degree to which an organization is a material-processing or people-processing system helps determine just what resources are crucial to its activities (Katz & Kahn, 1978). For universities, people (students, faculty and staffs), and funds (private and public), are among the most crucial tangible resources, with the development and renewal of plant and equipment also occupying a lot of administrative energy.

Most organizational theorists and researchers would agree that these five elements are basic to all organizations, although many would use different labels and names (Baldridge and Deal, 1975; Katz and Kahn, 1978). Scholars disagree, however, on which of these elements is most likely to be dominant; i.e., which most influences the others. As a theologian and social ethicist, Terry himself emphasizes the primacy of mission and culture (1981); the structural-functional school of social thought emphasizes the role of structure and culture; and power elite theorists emphasize the vital driving force of power in organizations. In addition, some observers would argue that the university primarily reflects the organization of wealth and power in the society at large, and that an elite capitalist structure lies at the root of contemporary and historic patterns of institutional racism. While we are quite sympathetic to the latter point of view, and to the powerful role of external influences, in this paper we elect to focus attention on the internal organizational system of the university and/or college.

These five elements can be examined separately, but they are interdependent with and generally reinforce one another. In terms of our specific concerns, they fit together to create what Katz has called a "web" of organizational discrimination (1978, p. 75). Thus, for instance, the mission of a university influences its culture and vice versa. Moreover, if the resource base changes dramatically the mission might change (as in the search for a "smaller but better" university in the wake of fiscal crises of the early 1980s), and then the structure itself might follow suit. If the culture promotes inadequate respect for or unfair treatment of people of color, it is unlikely that the mission will articulate (explicitly) a concern for racial justice. If the mission and culture do not express a concern for reducing racial injustice or ignorance, it is unlikely that resources will be allocated to such an agenda on any other than a temporary and crash basis. Without specifically allocated resources, structures and power systems are not likely to operate in ways that pursue anti-racist goals and practices.

At the same time that this set of interdependent elements operates in an integrated fashion, there is also constant internal contradiction and conflict in diverse, complex organizations. Multiple missions and cultures exist, and subsidiary ones constantly struggle overtly or covertly with the dominant tradition. For instance, universities seek to pass on the history and traditions of their society as well as to prepare students to make new history and create or at least adapt a new social order. The culture of the young student and the culture of the middle-aged professional strive to co-exist. Although formal power structures represent and extend the prevailing culture, the organization is populated with myriad informal influence arrangements. Interest groups of all kinds curry favor and wheedle special deals that depart from and may even sabotage the decisions and policies of the formal system.

Such contradictions and conflicts in the organization's dominant patterns of operation are essential points of access and opportunity for people committed to change, for here is where the greatest potential for innovation and reform lies. Thus, as we discuss the pervasive and powerful character of institutional racism in universities, we constantly seek to identify the sources of contradiction and deviance from this dominant pattern. These inconsistencies, whether or not they are manifest in overt conflict, present us with the hope, the opportunity and perhaps the resources (including conflict) for change.

In Terry's own language, racism is evident when a group intentionally or unintentionally (1981, p. 124):

perpetuates an unclear and/or dehumanizing mission (M)

refuses to share power (P)

denies appropriate support and challenge, and maintains inflexible and unresponsive structures(S)

inequitably distributes resources to another racial/ethnic group for either group's supposed benefit (R)

rationalizes (any of) the(se) process(es) by blaming or ignoring the other group.

To which we add:

promulgates a monocultural or exclusionary set of values/styles (C)

With this overview in mind, we now discuss the operations of and evidence for institutional racism within each of these organizational elements of organization of colleges and universities. Figure 5 provides examples of institutional racism present within each element.

Mission

The mission statements of colleges and universities are expressions of the vision of why the organization exists and what it seeks to achieve. They are likely to be highly abstract and sometimes vague statements of generally agreed upon principles and goals. Most statements of mission advocate transmitting Western cultural traditions, advancing knowledge, providing an education to the young, and performing public service. In general, they speak more to the conservation of tradition than to the creation of change.

MISSION
    Lack of explicit attention to justice and racial equity as a goal
    Lack of recognition of plural goals
    Commitment to the status quo . . . of the society and the institution
    Creators are limited to whites

CULTURE
    Monocultural norms for success are promulgated
    No explicit rewards for anti-racist behavior of the faculty, staff
    Diversity and excellence are seen as competitive/contradictory/played off
    Alternative cultures are not explicitly recognized or promoted
    Stance toward "racial incidents" is reactive
    Rituals and technology reflect white and Eurocentric dominance/exclusivity (graduation ceremonies,
        athletic mascots, pedagogy, etc.

POWER
    Power holders in senior positions are overwhelmingly white
    Informal access to the power hierarchy is limited to the "white male club"
    Constituencies of people of color have no formal access to power holders
    Protests by students of color are seen as trivial and disruptive and are dealt with via short term resolutions
    Sub units are not required to deal with racism proactively

STRUCTURE
    Opportunities do not exist for (re)training the white faculty to deal with students of color
    Social networks of the faculty generally exclude people of color
    Traditional pedagogies for classroom instruction are unaltered
    Social relations among students of different races are not seen as a university-wide concern. If they are so
        seen, they are seen as a curriculum concern
    Curriculum does not explicitly address issues of racism
    No coherent policy of response to racial harassment exists
    An Office of Minority Affairs exists but is not a central part of the university structure

RESOURCES
    Funds generally not available to support new anti-racist practices
    Community and physical settings usually include pervasive racism
    Active recruitment of students and faculty of color does not exist
    Post-recruitment support for students and faculty of color is minimal

Figure 5   Institutional racism in higher education organizations.

The emphasis on preserving and passing on the traditions of Western (Eurocentric and Anglo-Christian) civilization reflects higher education's origins in service by and for privileged white males. Although recent history has extended college to more people of color and to women, little systematic attention in general education requirements is given to Asian, African and Southern American civilizations, although some concern for international and global problems may be expressed. Likewise, Hispanic, Black and Native American civilizations and traditions seldom are mentioned specifically as vital elements of the U.S.'s cultural tradition.

Mission statements rarely are debated or discussed vigorously, except in times of major change, major reallocations of external resource bases, dramatic alterations in relations with state or federal governments, or presidential transitions. Yet, daily matters of what and how knowledge and wisdom is sought (e.g., which cultural traditions and epistemologies), who is to be educated (which regional, racial, gender and socioeconomic groups), what public services are to be performed (e.g., for which interest groups or stakeholders) and what leadership should be committed to doing (e.g., what characteristics and commitments they should reflect), are precisely the cornerstone issues and conflictual choices that underlie a university's mission. For the most part these crucial issues are dealt with by default, typically via omission rather than specific commission, and thus the stage is set for the promotion and continuation of established traditions, including racism promulgated in the larger society of which the university is a part.

Jackson and Holvino (1988) emphasize the importance of establishing a clear mission or a concrete vision for the direction of change in institutions, especially when the changes involve matters as complex as anti-racism or multiculturalism. They also provide several competing images and definitions of organizations that are monocultural (committed to enhancing the dominance, privilege and access to those in power who are white and male, etc.), non-discriminating (committed to bringing people of different cultures together without changing the way things operate) and multicultural (committed to diverse and equitable distributions of power and influence that actively support the elimination of oppression).

Although some institutions of higher education include in their mission statements a deliberate and conscious policy to fight injustice, a commitment to go beyond non-discrimination to a multicultural, anti-discrimination or pro-social justice stance is rare in other than a few religious, private and small colleges. In large universities, this oversight may create conflict with subunits that do explicitly state an emphasis on service to traditionally oppressed or excluded constituencies (most notably Schools of Social Work, Education, Public Health or Community Service). The inclusion of a deliberate and articulate commitment to reduce institutional racism appears to be a high risk act for a contemporary public and secular university. It often appears to be a partisan agenda, anathema to the university's desire for a non-controversial stance and the maintenance of an illusion of value-free research and learning. It often appears as a change-oriented agenda, anathema to an institution devoted to conserving and transmitting the cultural and intellectual heritage of a nation. And it often appears to be an ideological agenda, anathema to an institution committed to transmitting information and factual knowledge in a "non-ideological" way (yet within the prevailing societal value system and organizational culture).

Culture

The culture of contemporary colleges and universities reflects, for the most part, the core values of the society/community with which they operate. Indeed, one basic mission of a university, at the apex of an extensive system of public and semi-public education, is to prepare the young for (at least partial) acceptance of and participation in the dominant culture—with individual freedom, democratic governance, etc. The socialization of the young into conformity with adult values does not occur without conflict, however, and the intergenerational tensions that mark the university reflect both the cultural distance between these age groups as well as their differential access to organizational power and autonomy.

Generally the ruling values and modes of operation in the university are those of white, Western and Eurocentric civilization. They are not necessarily seen as such; people who are not aware of the existence and shape of white culture may see these as universal moral principles or behavioral norms. Nonetheless, as Katz points out (1988, p. 10):

> The white culture that exists is the synthesis of ideas, values and beliefs coalesced from descendents of white European ethnic groups in the United States. White culture is the dominant cultural norm in the United States and acts as the foundation of our institutions. The truth is that the white cultural system is one system and yet many people believe it is the only system.

A particular (positivist) version of the scientific method has also come to dominate university life and the scientific curriculum—physical, biological and social. In the search for the authority and expertise of universal principles grounded in empirically established facts, whole systems and their elements are subjected to positivist and reductionist methods, whereby phenomena are taken apart into their constituent elements and then reconstructed. Distance and detachment is maintained between the knower and the (to be) known. Emotion or intuition and preference (now seen as bias), rather than being seen as potentially rich and productive forces in human inquiry, generally are shunned and depreciated (Keller, 1985). They ultimately are seen as biases or vices to be controlled, perhaps only of central importance to the arts.

The social organization of science, based upon this rationalist and formal culture and its associated procedures, carries innumerable conflicts and tensions as well. Individual scientific knowledge-seekers compete with one another to test, confirm and/or disconfirm one another's theories. They typically work in isolation or in small cadres, with substantial conflict among competing departments, universities or schools of thought. Hierarchies of seniority and prestige, themselves often a focus of conflict, dominate the professions, the scientific disciplines and the university. As Ernst Benjamin, general secretary of the AAUP, argues (1989, p. 64):

> Our participation in institutional policies fostering individual entrepreneurship rather than collective responsibility has contributed to lower median salaries as well as to the uncertainty inherent in academic careers. Our pursuit of institutional prestige has fostered a campus climate that subordinates teaching, mentoring, collegial responsibility and mutual tolerance to the disciplinary market and institutional status.

When such disciplinary prestige is taken as primary evidence of merit, scholars outside of one another's specialized tradition may no longer understand (or care) what others are doing, and no one may care for the life of the local institution or community.

As these modes of inquiry and social relations dominate the culture of the university, they accompany the instructor into the college classroom. Zorn argues that the culture of the university is passed on by faculty members as they act on and interact with students in the classroom (1986, p. 8):

> . . . most of what students learn about the faculty's values comes from observing the examples set by individual faculty functioning in the teacher/scholar role. The structure of courses and curricula, the use of language, the priorities on use of time and the mode of student-faculty interaction all convey faculty values in an implicit and sustained way that can be understood by every student.

The culture of the lone and specialized expert and the moral commitment to maintain adult control of the young, is transferred into the authority of the teacher as the font of wisdom in and out of class. This wisdom is transmitted to students, or "banked" into them in the language of Friere (1970). Seldom are students seen as reliable resources for co-instruction of their peers and the instructor, let alone as having expertise or wisdom based upon their own life experiences. The teacher as dispassionate expert, with specialized and empirically verified information, is center stage and the primary focus of attention and control in the classroom. Moreover, the organization's support for the cultural values of academic freedom and freedom of speech are generally interpreted as meaning that faculty members can do and say almost anything in the classroom. These same principles often are invoked to resist evaluation, or even comment upon, instructors' choices of classroom substance or procedure.

Students and faculty members of different races, with different cultural values and styles, often make new and different demands on this traditional system and culture. As Kochman (1981) points out, most Black people and members of white ethnic groups are embedded in different cultures than are most white-anglos. As such, these groups often have different ways of talking, relating, fighting, learning—and undoubtedly teaching and administering as well. Although anyone discussing such differences must be cautious about overgeneralizations and stereotypes, substantial additional evidence suggests that white people (students and faculty) and people of color perceive and experience university environments quite differently. For instance, in the Stanford University self-study, most of the white faculty agreed that the University administration was "genuinely committed (to) promoting multiracial understanding and cooperation," but only a minority of the Black and Asian and Hispanic faculty agreed with this statement (Stanford University Committee on Minority Issues, 1989, p. 24). There is a long history of social scientific studies, from many different public and institutional arenas, indicating that whites and people of color often disagree on whether people of different races are being treated equally, whether policy-makers or administrators are acting fairly with regard to racial issues, and whether the nation (or community or organization, etc.) is making progress on eliminating or reducing racism (see, for example, Alderfer et al., 1980; Campbell and Schuman, 1968; Schuman et al., 1985).

Since most contemporary universities are enmeshed in the white-anglo culture, the entrance of substantial numbers of people of color (or of lower class origins) inevitably escalates perceptual contrasts and cultural conflict, and creates extraordinary pressures on these newer populations. These added pressures and realities in the lives of people of color (such as racial and cultural differences and experiences of racism) typically are seen as extra-classroom or extra-professional issues, and typically go unrecognized and unchecked in the classroom. At best, they are seen as matters appropriately dealt with by "student services" units, and not germane to the disciplinary or classroom agenda. Whereas alternative pedagogies and epistemologies might allow room for the expression and satisfaction of different styles of learning and relating (to knowledge and to one another), the maintenance of traditional cultures and classroom procedures creates deviance out of non-normative preferences, inadequacy out of different adequacies, and continues to disadvantage students and colleagues with different cultural styles and preferences.

Several scholars have indicated how difficult it is for students of color to negotiate the alien and often hostile culture of predominantly white colleges and universities. Allen argues, for instance, that in addition to the individual background and talent characteristics of Black students, their collegiate outcomes are influenced strongly by the organizational environment, by (1988, p. 412):

> . . . situational and interpersonal characteristics: the quality of life at the institution, the level of academic competition, university rules/procedures/resources, relationships with faculty, and friend support networks.

These aspects of the organizational culture also are reported as crucial to the success of Hispanic students. Fiske (1988) emphasizes the problems encountered by Hispanic students who have to find their way "in institutions built around an alien (Anglo) culture (p. 29)," and Richardson et al. (1987) note that successful programs for minority students "rely on the student culture to establish an environment conducive to involvement and achievement (p. 23)."

In some institutions Ethnic and Gender Studies' Departments have begun to challenge the dominant culture of the (white and male) scientific establishment, to suggest the need for alternative research espistemologies and methodologies, and alternative classroom pedagogies. To the extent such Programs or Departments accept the dominant culture, but serve special interest groups, they can be maintained on the fringe of the established system. But if and when they challenge the assumptions underlying the dominant tradition they potentially create change, and thereby encounter conflict. Then they typically are characterized as ideological rather than scholarly in character, and as social service centers for (marginal) faculty of color, rather than as meaningful loci for intellectual discourse. Debates about the intellectual viability and vitality of these Programs often reflect underlying assumptions of the superiority of white (and male) cultures and norms for scholarly pursuits. For instance, the argument that women/feminist and Black or Hispanic scholars might engage in a legitimately different kind of science by virtue of their gender and racial experiences, per se, and that these alternatives might contribute positively to the broader body of scientific methods and knowledge, is generally dismissed. Epps (1989) argues that the dominant culture of the university determines what the faculty will support as appropriate intellectual (research and teaching) priorities. As a result, "the minority scholar is constrained by the culture of the major research university to select research paradigms, research topics and publication outlets that conform to the traditionals of institutions that have historically excluded minorities (1989, p. 24)." Thus, he notes, "African-American, Hispanic and Native-American students and faculty encounter a culture that rejects them as legitimate participants in the life of the academy (p. 25)."

The dominance of a monocultural orientation in colleges and universities thus encourages unidimensional standards of evaluation. Students and faculty are sorted by these limited, and often quite skewed, expectations. Departments and programs, as well as students and faculty, are ranked, like baseball teams and their players. The "star system" seldom questions the definition of star qualities, and unidimensional criteria for academic excellence are raised to a level of abstraction that is seen as transcending considerations of race or gender. Thus, race and gender diversity can be ignored or discounted as having no relevance to defining or achieving excellence. They may be seen as necessary parts of a diverse environment, but not as necessary for the enrichment or modification of monocultural settings and standards. People who do not do well by the star metric are labelled as inferior—not as different or as valued—and generally they are perceived as being responsible for their own mediocre or otherwise flawed and deviant status and performance to boot.

The reward metric, focused predominantly on research, and research as it is determined and evaluated by a specific (usually white and male) peer group, seldom identifies combating racism as an essential area of performance for the faculty or administration in higher education. To the contrary, serious efforts to reduce racism require new forms of research and service in the university and in the community, in K-12 education, in student services, in campus and community housing and law enforcement, etc. If service as an arena of activity is little valued it is unlikely that anti-racist service activities that extend work beyond the boundary of the university will occur, even in publicly supported systems (Checkoway, 1989). Moreover, combating racism in the classroom requires substantial new designs for teaching and learning. If teaching and service are of minor importance compared to research activity, it is quite unlikely that this challenge can be met in the system "as is."

All too often, efforts to achieve racial diversity are seen as undermining the cultural commitment to academic excellence. At the University of Michigan, for instance, over the course of two years, various Presidents first articulated the need for "Excellence," then for "Achieving Diversity without Compromising Excellence," then for "Balancing Excellence with Diversity," then for "Diversity as part of Excellence," and finally for "Diversity as a Necessary Component of Excellence." At each step of the way, of course, there was conflict and pressure to maintain the status quo (in language and in practice).

In a recent welcoming address to students in Yale University's Graduate and Professional Schools, Dean Rosenberg suggested that the prevailing culture of many universities could be challenged by an increased public and private "commitment to decency and civility for minorities (1988, p. 47)." He illustrated this alternative cultural commitment with a code of conduct that students and faculty had prepared for Yale's School of Medicine (ibid.):

> Teaching, learning, research, and the delivery of medical care are best carried out in an atmosphere of civil relationships. Such relationships are possible only where there is mutual respect, decency, and sensitivity one to another—students, faculty, staff, and patients. Overt racism is not only morally wrong. It interferes with the quality of care received by patients, is debilitating to the victims, and compromises the integrity and stature of the offender. Less obvious forms of racism such as disparaging comments, inappropriate labels, or subtle innuendoes which unfairly classify or criticize others on the basis of race are equally unacceptable. Wherever and whenever racist or insensitive remarks are heard or inappropriate actions witnessed, it should be the duty of every one of us to protest and to inform the offender about the reasons for our disapproval. Furthermore, it is our responsibility to help those who have been wronged to obtain satisfactory redress.

Such affirmations of positive and proactive anti-racist behaviors are rare, and more often applauded in rhetoric than followed in practice. They do, however, provide us with alternative visions of our options.

The culture of the university usually is not perceived or analyzed clearly, and it operates as part of the "givens" or general and unquestioned assumptions by which we go about our daily business. Only when open challenges are made, or when different cultures come into contact with one another, do we readily identify and critically evaluate the domains of the dominant culture. This is but one more reason it is so difficult to diagnose, as well as to alter, the monocultural basis of institutional racism in universities.

Power

The public trust of public and private universities generally is established and protected by appointed or elected boards of trustees made up of individuals from outside the academic organization. In practice, these trustees represent only a part of the general public, that part that is most white, most male and most upper middle class in origin and orientation (Ridgeway, 1968). Quite naturally, they establish policies and govern in ways that reflect the prevailing values and perspectives of these dominant constituencies. As in the political and economic spheres of the society in general, the dominant perspectives of these trustees, and the constituencies they represent, generally do not include the quest to increase racial justice as a high priority.

Where people in authority are predominantly white and male, and where authority is silent on the unfairness of this pattern and does not include explicit and concerted means of changing it, racism and sexism are present and maintained. Established authorities in higher education claim to be operating in the interest of everyone in the college and university. Again and again, however, faculty, students and staff of color assert that their needs are not met and that they are not treated as favorably as are their white counterparts. Individual and institutional racism prevents authorities from fully perceiving and meeting the needs of people of color who are part of the organization.

Without representation in centers of institutional power and authority, and often having different needs and cultural styles, students of color often are alienated and regularly experience discrimination. In an extraordinarily honest self-study, MIT reports minority students' perspectives on the collegiate environment as follows (McBay, 1986, p. 5):

Feelings of isolation;

Insecurity about their admission because of the perception that others at the Institute believe lower standards are used when admitting minority students;

Belief that others consider all minority students as high risks;

Anxiety about their families' ability to provide the financial assistance expected by the Institute;

Perceived contempt from non-minority students, faculty, administrators, and staff;

Feelings of non-acceptance by faculty; and

The existence of a generally non-supportive environment in which minorities must constantly prove they are equal, both intellectually and socially.

The message of isolation and rejection is obvious.

Institutional racism also helps authorities rationalize why they are not meeting the needs students or faculty members of color. It typically is asserted that their special needs are inappropriate, their problems a result of their own inadequacies, their demands a call for unfair favoritism, etc. Without access to institutional power, people who are mistreated seldom can gain attention to their concerns, let alone redress. One stunning example of the kinds of demeaning and discriminatory treatment experienced by Black scholars is provided in reports of Harvard University Law Professor and constitutional scholar Derrick Bell's encounter with the Stanford Law School. While he was a visiting lecturer at Stanford in 1986, "white students and professors, dissatisfied with his performance as a teacher, surreptitiously created a series of lectures to supplement his course on constitutional law (Kennedy, 1989, p. 1767; Bell, 1986)." The Dean and faculty of the Stanford Law School have long since formally apologized to Bell, but that this should occur (both the level of expressed dissatisfaction and the collusion of white faculty and students in creating a covert substitute) to such a prominent Black scholar, only emphasizes the regularity with which other faculty of color must also encounter subtle and not so subtle forms of disdain and disregard.

From chief executives to faculty, students and staff members at all levels, the organizational power arrangements of universities are subject to hierarchical administrative control. As a result, Birnbaum (1988) argues, it is crucial for university presidents to go out of their way to demonstrate their commitment to a social justice and anti-racist agenda if it is to be acted on by administrative staff and faculty. Generally, he notes, presidents act vigorously only when things go wrong; it is important to counter this trend by engaging in proactive and preventive leadership. This same theme is echoed in a report from the University of California system (Justus et al., 1987). Regardless of the style (management or leadership) of the President and senior administrators (1987, p. 59):

Available research on effective faculty affirmative action, however, does stress the importance of leadership at all levels within the university—from the chief executives to deans to department chairs . . . Significantly, at the most successful institutions we were told that CEOs, whether called Chancellors or Presidents, do make a difference; that the commitment of an institution can be measured by the relative weight the chief executive places on affirmative action success, and his/her ability to translate commitment into action.

Commitment, in this arena, includes the visible exercise of both formal authority and responsibility and informal power and influence.

The senior administration of a college or university, and its key deans, set the tone and context for dealing with racism and race relations on campus. Whether they do so actively or passively, overtly or covertly, by example of courageous acts or of acts of omission and ignorance, they set the stage. Administrative pronouncements and actions (especially actions, because policies are often not believed unless followed by explicit actions) can help create climates of fear or of hope, of concern or of disregard, of open discussion or of secretive conversation, of positive change or of negative retreat. They create the context and the conditions within which faculty, staff and students must deal with one another and, unfortunately, often play out their concerns and antagonisms upon one another.

The authority that Presidents and Vice-Presidents have can be exercised in a variety of forms, but it often is implemented most effectively and practically via a series of budgetary and financial policies, supplemented by centrally controlled personnel policies. Although these policies and practices can have major impact on subunit programs and priorities, they also have their limits—especially in our most elite research universities. Efforts to alter the prevailing power structure of the university, such as required in challenges to racism, can be resisted readily by the decentralized academic control of specialized units (Schools and Departments). Principles of unit autonomy and academic freedom permit each major unit of a university to retain decision making control over its own curricula, personnel and financial policies; thus they can resist innovations generated by the central administration on "a legitimate 'non-racist' basis (Exum, 1983, p. 390)." This delicate balance of centralized and decentralized power makes it very difficult for centrally mandated programs of change to be effective or for institution-wide changes to be implemented. At the same time, of course, it invests considerable room for innovation in local units, should they take the lead in generating programs to reduce racial injustice.

It is especially difficult to mobilize a broad consensus on reducing racism in predominantly white and monocultural systems of higher education where narrowly specialized areas of expertise and departmental loyalties are the basis of individual legitimacy and influence. Thus, we seldom see progressive initiatives developing from the white faculty at large or from faculty-led units of the system. When all the responsibility for initiating and implementing anti-racism programs remains with the central administration, the problems of unit and faculty resistance loom large.

In most large universities, the faculty as a group has little power to affect institutional priorities directly. Their role generally is limited to advice and debate on administrative decisions, and to passive (and covert) resistance to dicta with which they disagree individually or collectively. Traditions of collaborative decision-making, or multi-level involvement in participatory decision-making, are not readily represented in systems of higher education. This tradition constantly places the power of the faculty in an institutionally reactive mode. Just as the culture of the university supports the exercise of authoritative (and often authoritarian) power in the classroom, it reproduces that style in administrative-faculty relations at the departmental and central unit level.

Students, a subordinate group in the power structure of higher educational systems, typically are perceived by faculty and administrators as marginal and temporary members of the community. The experience of marginality, in turn, often gives students an impetus and opportunity (even a freedom) to organize and exert influence through extraordinary and even illegitimate channels. Students of color are doubly marginalized and disempowered, both on grounds of their racial as well as student status. As a result, their only path to the expression of their unique needs and desires for change may be through public protest, disruption and demonstration. The history of minority protest and challenge to racism throughout our society lends support and legitimacy to this tradition in the exercise of power in institutions of higher education (a large body of literature on student protest movements, and on oppressed social movements generally, supports this view).

Indeed, in the aftermath of the current spate of "racial incidents" occurring across campuses, it is the students of color who have taken the lead in demanding institutional change. More than faculties of color, more than white staff members or faculty or administrators, students of color have correctly noted that such incidents of harassment are not incidental or unique, that they represent the overt manifestations of deeply entrenched cultural and structural racism within our institutions. When their concerns and demands have gone unheeded and unmet, as so often has been the case when white faculty and administrators have been "caught by surprise" or have resisted change, these students have generated the initial thrust for change. The power of these students of color, stemming from their historic experience and contemporary need, has been the major energizer of change in racism in many universities.

In turn, many university faculty and administrations have been prone to see these expressions of student and minority power as illegitimate and ill-conceived, possibly dangerous to the welfare of the university as well as to their sense of students' more appropriate priority on classroom learning. Since the culture of the university promotes a view of itself as a non-partisan, objective and non-political system, it (administrators and faculty and students in the dominant cultural group) normally is shocked and outraged at a moral level by political protest of any sort, and especially from students—the most temporary and non-expert members of the system. When the students are people of color the emotional reaction often is even stronger.

Structure

The organizational structures of most colleges and universities create a large number of decentralized units defined by particular academic specializations. These specialized units, and the behavior of faculty members associated with them, are heavily influenced by external forces, especially their national scientific and/or professional societies. To the extent that prestige and merit are based upon evaluation standards rooted in these disciplinary and professional associations, faculty members are more likely to invest in these "cosmopolitan" reference groups than in "provincial" arenas within the local university. The trend for the most prestigious faculty to invest externally heightens the degree to which local units and departments become "feudal estates"; they often are seen as the concern only of those faculty who have been "left behind," and as such faculty influence is once more trivialized. This dynamic also reduces faculty commitment to their unit, particularly as it involves changes requiring greater time and energy for "local" or "provincial" pursuits.

However, these semi-autonomous local units, buttressed by concerns for faculty autonomy and academic freedom, remain the arena for most of the faculty's exercise of decisional authority. Some prestigious senior faculty always have private access to key decision-makers, and their "invisible influence" can be very effective. To alter racism in the curriculum, research programs and teaching pedagogies of local units generally requires challenges not only to the intellectual bases of the professions and disciplines, but also to the senior and influential faculty in these units.

To the extent that the structure and technology of instruction (pedagogy) relies on teacher dominance and student obedience, lone teacher and massed students, teacher expertise and student ignorance, it establishes a structure of social relations between the faculty and students that is pernicious and destructive of mutual respect and maximum learning opportunities. This sort of limited pedagogy is systematically insensitive to many students' needs: it falls especially hard on students of color. Authoritarian control of the classroom is most destructive to students with the least power to resist such dominance; cultural insensitivity in the classroom is most destructive to students whose cultures are most divergent from the mainstream; difficulty in gaining personal contact with the faculty is most disadvantageous to students with a minimal history of positive contact with white faculty; and so on. Any form of oppression and insensitivity falls hardest on the most vulnerable members of the system; thus the "normal" workings of the institutional structure of the classroom and the university organization most severely disadvantage students of color.

Crenshaw (1989) details several ways in which white faculty (Law School faculty, in her experience and examples, but we think the implications are nearly universal) may place students of color in a "difficult situation." She argues that problems of objectification, subjectification and alienation of minority students occur when white faculty fail to understand that what they consider to be "objective or neutral is often the embodiment of a white middle-class world view (p. 3)." Crenshaw labels this unawareness (or disregard) of the race or class basis of one's approach to the world or to academic subject matter "perspectivelessness." Objectification occurs when discussions are framed as simple exercises in the application of general rules, and when students are required to keep their comments within that system of rules. Since most legal, social and academic rules predominately reflect white persons' consciousness and rule-making power, and often are unfair to people of color, such exercises often require a student to "abstract herself from her identity as African-American" (ibid, p. 5) and to deny or ignore much of her own experience in the world. Subjectification occurs when students of color "are unexpectedly dragged into the classroom by an instructor to illustrate a point or to provide a basis for a command performance of 'show and tell' (ibid, p. 6)." Such "testifying" not only focuses substantial (and often undesired) attention on the student, and implies that any student of color can be an expert on her culture, it also suggest limits to other areas of probable expertise attributable to that student. Alienation occurs when "discussions focus on problems, interests and values that either minorities do not share or that obscure or overlook issues that are particularly relevant to minorities (ibid, p. 9)." Certainly not every student will be "touched" by every topic in the collegiate curriculum, but when problems of taxation, savings, family life, natural resources depletion, psychotherapy, congressional decision-making, illness, etc., are discussed in apparently race-neutral or race-irrelevant ways, they subtly suggest that white and middle-class ways of experiencing and coping with these issues are the only experiences and perspectives that are relevant.

Partly as a result of prior discrimination in educational organizations, and partly as a result of the attitudes and behaviors of the white professoriat, students of color are generally expected to know less and perform less well than their white counterparts. People of color in a class of mostly whites often are less frequently called on to offer their ideas and questions in discussions, laboratories and studios. Not surprisingly, then, people of color generally volunteer less often to participate in classroom discussions than do their white counterparts. College and university faculty rarely receive preparatory training of any kind for teaching; they subsequently are not taught ways of creating more anti-racist or equitable approaches to classroom instruction. Only recently, for instance, have the following criteria for what constitutes equitable or multicultural or anti-racist science instruction appeared in sources like the *American Biology Teacher* (Gardner, Mason & Matyas, 1989, p. 73):

Criteria for Equitable Science Activities

- Teacher is enthusiastic and has equal expectations for all students.
- Written materials and verbal instructions use gender-free language.
- Relevance of activity to students' lives is stressed.
- "Hands-on" experience is required for all students.
- Small group work is used.
- Activity develops science process skills.
- Exercise does not demand one "right" answer.
- Activities do not utilize materials and/or resources exclusively familiar to white, male students.
- Career information relevant to the activity is presented.
- Examples of female and minority role models are included in the follow-up.

The MIT self-study highlights the cost of such inexperience, indicating that while most minority students positively evaluated the quality of their education at the institution, they felt that faculty members' behaviors often created and escalated problems (McBay, 1986, p. 11–12).

The majority of the respondents (55%) communicated generally negative perceptions of the personal and academic support provided by MIT faculty members (of the remainder, 26% indicated positive perceptions, 12% were mixed, and 7% had minimal interactions); 31% voluntarily said that faculty members expected failure or a lack of ability in Blacks; many (32%) voluntarily said that they developed negative attitudes about going for help; and some (15%) voluntarily mentioned specific racial incidents involving MIT faculty members.

Comments on low expectations and incidents:

The main effect of being Black was the teachers' expectations—they think that you automatically won't make it in the class. I was very frustrated. You had to be in the absolute top to overcome that.

One professor had a hang-up about Black people. I went to talk to him about a grade, and he said that "maybe you people should go somewhere and do things you people can do." This was not uncommon. Many of my friends had this happen. Some departments were worse than others.

Blacks were discriminated against in some departments. I had a professor who talked about reverse discrimination and how unfair it was for Blacks to be given the opportunity when they did not deserve it. He said the Institute should not help Black students through various programs like interphase because things were not like that in the real world. He said we were given an unfair advantage. I went to him after I graduated and he apologized to me and said I was an exception.

One classmate had a professor tell her that Blacks don't do well in math because they lack spatial sense and math sense. She was a straight "A" student and this blew her mind—and mine.

These experiences certainly are not unique to MIT.

In addition to the necessity of dealing with racism in the classroom, it is important to deal with racism (or anti-racism) as part of the formal curriculum. Teaching about racism has not been a required part of the curriculum in most institutions, nor has the topic of reducing institutional and individual racism been a popular concern (Takaki, 1989). Faculties in several major universities currently are debating whether or not to have a curriculum requirement focused on racism and ethnic studies. In the Spring of 1989 faculty at the University of Michigan voted against such a requirement, while faculty at the University of Wisconsin and the University of California (Berkeley) voted for it. In 1987, "Stanford University expanded its required Western Culture Program to include the study of minorities, women, other cultures and class issues (Maclay, 1988, p. 15)." Stanford's recent experience with incidents of racial harassment might have had an impact on this decision. For instance, the report of the Stanford University Committee on Minority Issues notes that (1989, p. 5):

> Many students who participated in these incidents said they simply did not understand why their actions offended minority students or how their actions could be interpreted by others on campus as derogatory racial stereotyping.

Such "widespread ignorance about the history and culture of American racial minorities" (ibid, p. 5) may be shocking, but it is by no means rare. Nor is it limited to students. Widespread ignorance is a product of the culture and structure of invisibility which surrounds people of color in a white-dominated society or organization. While it may not constitute intentional or purposive discrimination it certainly is part of the passive racism and "indirect institutionalized discrimination" that pervades life in our colleges and universities.

Public ignorance of the culture and life-experience of people of color deprives and diminishes us all. People of color suffer because their culture is not represented in the institution of which they ostensibly are a part; dominant groups suffer because they fail to see or hear the full richness of the human experience. Racism mutes and sometimes obliterates the voices of people of color in two ways; directly, by denying them access to the institution or to institutional platforms for self expression; and, indirectly, by having white "experts" on people of color speak for them. To counter both problems it is important for the voices of people of color to be heard in direct and powerful ways, in the curriculum, in admissions/hiring, in discussions of public policies and issues, etc.

Many faculty members, themselves socialized in predominantly or exclusively white environs, educated in predominantly or exclusively white undergraduate and graduate schools, teaching in predominantly white universities, and living in predominantly white communities do not have the knowledge and skills required to live in, no less teach in, a multicultural environment. Thus, for much of the faculty, problems arise with regard to recognition and management of the following race-related issues:

How to recruit a multiracial student body into a class.

Whether and how to deal with racially self-segregated seating patterns in a class.

How to counsel students of color.

How to deal with culturally different learning styles.

How to facilitate students of different racial groups working together in learning teams.

How to respond to students of color who find traditional presentations of course material alienating or "offensive."

How to explain the lack of senior scholars of color in a given field.

How to deal with a "racial incident" that occurs in class.

Whether and how to respond in class to a "racial incident" that occurred elsewhere on campus.

How to counsel whites who feel threatened by students of color.

How to critically review course content and design in order to identify changes that could reduce racism and move toward multicultural understandings and relationships.

The day-to-day acts of teaching and research occur within individual classrooms, laboratories, studios, etc., where there are deeply entrenched traditions of faculty autonomy and freedom. This emphasis on the academic freedom and autonomy of the individual faculty makes it quite difficult to challenge and change customary ideas and procedures. In the case of racism, a poorly understood, self-interest based, deeply ingrained phenomenon, it is especially difficult. For instance, consider the dilemma of a faculty member who overhears (or is told about) a colleague making a prejudicial remark to or about a student of color (or engaging in sexual harassment of a student). General norms of civility and racially appropriate behavior suggest that such remarks or actions should be confronted: gently perhaps, in an educational frame perhaps, but confronted. But what if the colleague who has engaged in such behavior is senior, and holds informal or implicit review and reward power over the would-be-confrontor? How do we deal with a lack of consensus on the meaning of racist comments (or of sexual harassment)? How do we deal with the lack of a common culture that promotes dialogue, exchange and feedback of this sort among faculty members? Under these circumstances, it is the would-be-confrontor who violates the norms of civility, who potentially tears the fabric of academic freedom, who is seen as acting in a manner disloyal to his/her colleagues and the "club," who stands the risk of arrogantly alleging that she/he knows things that one's colleague does not. The structure and culture of the university mitigates strongly against individual faculty initiatives to challenge racism within the ranks of the faculty itself. When challenged on its own behavior, the faculty tends to adopt a "fortress mentality," to close ranks (and eyes and ears) against the threat from students or from deviants within its own ranks.

All these efforts to alter the infrastructure of the educational organization require new thinking about the place and manner of teaching in the university's system of priorities. Indeed, Richardson and de los Santos point out the need to go beyond the recruitment of faculty of color, but to influence "colleges and universities to value diversity among their faculties and to reward good teaching (including sensitivity to cultural differences, high expectations for all students, and caring and mentoring) through staff development, recruitment procedures, and criteria for tenure and promotion (1988, p. 326)." Unfortunately, deficiencies in the skills required for effective education in a multicultural or anti-racist environment seldom are dealt with via university programs attempting to (re)educate or influence the faculty; rather, the faculty that is already presumed to be fully competent and experienced in teaching students is assumed to be competent in teaching a diverse student body as well. Thus, by default such issues are ignored, and ignorance, denial and the continuation of racism are subtly (and perhaps unconsciously) reinforced.

In universities, like other organizations, social relationships are both formally and informally patterned, and these social patterns affect processes of racial interaction, communication and influence. Patterns of social relationships often exclude faculty of color from (white dominated) informal social networks, or treat them awkwardly when they are included. As social networks go, so go professional networks; thus, these practices of exclusion and awkwardness have major impact on people's professional lives and affect opportunities for promotion, advance and achievement, long after initial hiring decisions. In fact, Smelser and Content (1980) refer to a "succession of exclusions" that carry the "potential at every point for discrimination, both overt and institutionalized, conscious and unconscious (Exum, 1983, p. 394)." As a potential antidote, Blackwell (1989) emphasizes the necessity of expanded mentoring programs to aid the retention, development and achievement of faculty members of color. Perhaps proactive collegiality is a better model than mentoring, since most sustained exchanges of wisdom and caring are reciprocal rather than unidirectional. Such collegial relationships can explore the rules of the faculty game, journals most appropriate or rewarded as publication outlets, information about which colleagues can/should be avoided and which deferred to, the real balance of teaching and research and service in a department, avenues for research funding, assistance in teaching or in contacting teaching assistants, and in general the "politics of tenure" (Blackwell, 1989).

It also is quite common for graduate students of color to "miss out on" important but informally communicated information concerning opportunities for funding, time-tested ways of preparing dissertation proposals and contacts with influential people in their field of specialization. When faculty (or graduate students) of color are unable to participate effectively in or influence formal and informal networks, they may form their own social and professional groups. Frequently, however, there is resistance to racially homogeneous groups of people of color. Such "caucuses" are apparently offensive or threatening to whites, even though they may be important for personal and professional identity, safety and collegiality in a white dominated environment (Blakey, 1989).

The unique situation of faculty of color in white-dominated institutions results in a number of special burdens and responsibilities. The white faculty's ignorance of these "special tasks" presents serious dilemmas for the scholar of color. For instance, it is possible for most white scholars, regardless of their personal values, to do their work and live their lives without paying serious attention to racism and racial discrimination. It is improbable that faculty of color can do the same: one's personal experience, demands from students, community needs, and pressure to "serve the cause" create quite different responsibilities. Brooks reviews some of these special (often defined simply as service) burdens and responsibilities as follows (1986):

> white students' difficult time dealing with minority professors
>
> minority students' desire for problem-solving, advice and counselling
>
> community organizations' search for assistance and role models
>
> pressure to address issues of special interest to Black Americans

Several observers indicate that these and other special tasks create significant conflicts with traditional role definitions and with the multiple audiences who are served by and who evaluate faculty members' work (Elmore and Blackburn, 1983; Exum, 1983; Moore and Wagstaff, 1974). Blakey notes, however, that whites often see the demand/request to deal with such issues, in the definition or reward system for these service, teaching or research roles, as political, non-objective or self-serving, and as an excuse for not meeting traditional academic and organizational expectations (Blakey, 1989). Blackwell states the institutional duality of this situation well: "I don't think there is a campus in this country that will not dump every single thing minority on that particular person. Then we turn around . . . and say, well, you haven't published enough (1989, p. 13)."

A parallel danger, but one standing in sharp contrast to non-recognition or denial of the distinctive status/situation/interests of faculty of color, is the potential for stereotyping these colleagues only as faculty of color. Just as minority students sometimes are expected to be (or are limited to being) expert testifiers on their culture (see Crenshaw, 1989), minority faculty sometimes are expected only to conduct research or teaching on matters related to Black or Hispanic concerns, or only to be interested in alternative scholarly paradigms. Thus, faculty of color may be "tracked" into Ethnic Studies Centers, or hired with funds allocated specifically for these purposes, regardless of their scholarly predispositions or preferences. This sort of automatic coding represents another form of stereotyping. The university organization that seeks both to recognize the unique interests of faculty of color, and to deal sensitively with the unique interests and styles of every one of its faculty members as individuals, often will confront this dilemma. While this may be a very complex dilemma, avoiding it with either polar response (non-recognition of differences or tracking on the basis of assumed differences) engages in sustained stereotyping.

The structure of social and professional relations that dominate the faculty, and the classroom, inevitably permeate the student culture itself. Since the administration and the faculty generally pay little attention to internal processes in the student culture or to the racial intricacies of the student peer system, students learn to ignore these issues as well. Students structure their lives in ways that sustain racially separated and insensitive domains; thus all are protected from discomfort . . . and from contact that might be enriching . . . and from contact that might reduce systematic stereotypes and ignorance. The inevitable outcome of these separated structures of learning and living are both isolated incidents and regular actions that discriminate against students of color. It is easy to see these incidents as isolated acts, as the behaviors of individually insensitive or hateful students.

A more adequate analysis would see these incidents as a natural outgrowth of a culture, power structure and set of social and intellectual relations that teach people who are different from one another not to bother to understand or respect or work well with one another.

An interesting innovation in most university structures at this juncture in history is a special office or offices in charge of minority group affairs. Generally such an office is in charge of the "care and feeding" (recruiting, counselling, financing) of minority students; occasionally it has a broader organizational agenda of achieving affirmative action or of reducing institutional racism. Whatever its charge, its relative priority is indicated by its location in the academic structure, its access to resources, and related factors. If its creation is not reflected in the mission or goal statement of the university, we understand it as an "add-on" rather than a basic change in the organization's direction. If it is a staff office/position rather than a line office/position we understand that there is little authority or power connected to it. If it is located solely in the central administration, and not also represented in each sub-unit of the system, we know it is likely to be isolated from the places where critical decisions are implemented. If it is staffed by other than prestigious faculty members, we understand that it is not likely to have significant impact on the majority of the faculty. If it is charged with dealing with social relationships, and not with pedagogical and curricular change, we understand it strikes at the margin but not at the heart of the academic enterprise. If it cannot influence (through incentives) the institution's research program, and faculty review and promotion processes, we understand it will not carry significant intellectual power. And if students (especially students of color) are not involved in its formation, staffing, and ongoing functioning, we understand it will be unlikely to reflect their unique experiences of racism in the university and their visions of how things might be different.

Finally, an essential part of the organization's structure is its boundary system or interface with other, external, organizations (Brown, 1983). The influence of external social environments on colleges and universities and their interactions with other units across organizational boundaries also involves racism. Whatever their internal focus, higher educational organizations generally are expected to ignore racist practices in other institutions. For example, the recent actions of several law schools to deny the FBI the right to recruit because of court findings of discrimination in this agency was greeted with shock, surprise, and anger. So, too, would university efforts to advocate alteration of discriminatory municipal housing, hiring or policing practices. The university that is not sensitive to issues of racism often fails to attend to the community environment that diminishes and demeans the lives of many faculty and students of color. Societal racism often affects faculty and students of color, in housing opportunities, K-12 educational systems, relations with local police departments, and access to community services. People of color who must fend for themselves in dealing with these issues encounter an alienating community as well as a disinterested university. Similarly, as colleges and universities more aggressively recruit high school students of color, they are likely to become involved in programs of educational assistance or improvement that inevitably draw them into potential conflicts with community and school system practices that support racism. Consistent and effective anti-racist practices necessarily will involve universities in aiding the struggle for justice in community organizations: most are not prepared to undertake such action.

In a reciprocal fashion, federal and state anti-discrimination laws and policies may have substantial impact on the internal dynamics of higher educational organizations. Unfortunately, many colleges and universities have argued that such laws should not apply to them; despite federal judicial and executive decisions that these organizations are not exempt from anti-discriminatory laws, their implementation at the higher educational level still encounters resistance in the form of claims of institutional autonomy and the pursuit of excellence.

In summary, among the most alienating realities of these institutional structures and operations for faculty of color are:

the failure to receive respect from white colleagues

the inability of white colleagues to discuss issues of racism

the unwillingness of colleagues to confront/challenge outrageously racist comments or memos made by other faculty or administrators

the lack of reward for pro-actively anti-racist work

the failure of white colleagues to appreciate different research priorities and a need for active engagement in racism

the unwillingness of colleagues to confront racism in the community

the perception that white faculty are not committed to students of color

In a restatement of the issues dealt with in this section, Payne argues that (1989, p. 21):

> If departments are to send the right "message" to current and prospective faculty, they must learn to ask the hard questions about the quality of interaction, social professional opportunities, cultural integrity, professional respect, common goals, social styles, aspirations, conflict, freedom and independence, entrepreneurial interest, quality of housing, and community support—all those aspects of higher education that make professional life on a campus attractive and self-fulfilling.

To ask these questions, and to discover the answers, would do much to advance the quality of life for faculty of color. The extent to which attention to such issues might improve the life of all faculty emphasizes the degree to which none of us will be free and fulfilled until all of us are.

Resources

The key resources utilized by colleges and universities are financial, physical and human. In the process of garnering these resources higher educational organizations encounter a variety of constraints and dilemmas. Sometimes perceived constraints or dilemmas lead to efforts to shape the organization's or unit's image and program to appeal to wealthy and powerful individuals, private corporations, or public agencies. An emphasis on social change, on altering structures of social privilege and oppression, on challenging racism, may not "sell well" to these constituencies. On the contrary, anti-racist mission statements and programs may be disquieting and alienating to people and organizations whose donations and other financial support might make a difference for key programs. They may see a university's efforts to create a plural culture or an anti-racist program as cavilling to special interests, as "selling out" western civilization, as bending core values under pressure, or as sacrificing excellence.

Indeed, when the University of Michigan's alumni magazine printed a story about campus racial incidents, and on a negotiated agreement reached between the President and leaders of student protest groups, several alumni responded with letters and commentary. Although some letters praised the magazine's "honest and courageous" approach, and even the University administration's commitment to dealing with racism, others adopted the critical perspective and language suggested above (*Michigan Alumnus*, 1987):

> . . . this "problem" does not warrant the attention it has been receiving.

> . . . The regents and the administration . . . succumbed to the pressure.

> I have never seen so much bull printed in a single copy . . . The University's reactions to racial incidents is that of nervous Nellies seeking refuge in phraseology and chasing their own tails.

> It is, in my mind, inconceivable that the administration and the regents could accede to the demands of a group of lawbreakers . . . shows a lack of moral fortitude.

> What we've witnessed on campus by UCAR, BAM III, Jesse Jackson and sadly, *Michigan Alumnus*, is nothing more than an amoral, political partisan purge . . . your publication perpetuate(s) ignorance and bias.

Rarely is there a concerted and committed effort to inform all alumni and potential funders about the university's commitments, policies, and programs designed to combat racism. Thus, the defensive and reactive posture of the university on these matters is "affirmed" by alumni donor patterns, and vice versa.

As universities and colleges appeal to wealthy and powerful people for resources, they often must deal with allegations by conservative media that they pursue politics favorable to left-wing radicals and unfairly penalize conservative scholars and students. A recent *Wall Street Journal* editorial (1989), "The Privileged Class," is a clear example of this biased picture of higher education. This editorial, among other claims, depicts higher education's efforts to combat racism as an example of the operation of a "privileged ideology," and alleges that "radical teachers . . . have insistently dominated discussion in recent years." Similar analyses by conservative media and political activists (see, for example, Finn, 1989) blame radical faculty for curricular changes that enhance student exposure to and knowledge of cultures other than the traditional white Western culture. They see efforts at an anti-racist or multi-cultural curriculum as evidence that colleges are overrun by left-wing "ideological indoctrination." This argument is made in the face of incontrovertible evidence of rapid globalization of the economy, communication systems and policy making, changes which require graduates to understand and deal with cultures other than one's own. Other informed observers and analysts continually have indicated that politically left-wing and actively anti-racist faculty are very much a minority in higher education and, while often outspoken, certainly do not dominate discussions or decisions on the curriculum or on campus policies in general. Nevertheless, such media perspectives and political presentations play on fears and stereotypes, and contribute to privileged groups' desires to resist higher education's efforts to control racism and to continue to develop multi-cultural learning opportunities. At the very least, they make it that much more difficult for colleges and universities to raise funds for these objectives.

Research grants and contracts are an increasingly important source of revenue for both private and public universities. Most such projects are funded by government or corporate interests to achieve goals related to economic prosperity, national defense or medical and educational improvements. Research in the areas of public health, environmental quality, social welfare and poverty occur, but at a much lower level of resources. Although support is available for studies of racial attitudes, rarely are there well-funded efforts to analyse institutional racism in different societal sectors, or policies and programs designed to ameliorate the structures of wealth and power that support racism over time.

The vast majority of research funds are decided upon and allocated by powerful social institutions, most of which suffer from the same enmeshment in systems of institutional racism as universities themselves, and most of which also benefit from the racism of the status quo. Despite this situation, universities can apply pressure to fund basic and applied research in the area of institutional racism. In all likelihood, however, such opportunities will not be successful without deliberate and concerted action and without the application of pressure by collectivities of concerned constituencies in universities and communities.

Student tuition is another important source of a university's financial resources. To a major extent, the ability to pay tuition is dependent upon a family's wealth, and since many students of color come from less wealthy families, they often are not able to pay as large a portion of their own tuition as are students from white families. They also are less likely to have extra resources available for entertainment and other collegiate expenses. Thus, they are more dependent upon the largess of the university in the allocation of funds to cover educational expenses.

Several scholars have pointed to the importance of an adequate financial support package to the collegiate success of students of color. Often, aid packages do not allow students of color to live comfortably and to participate fully in the institutional culture dominated by people from wealthier backgrounds. Thus, racism once again is manifest—this time in definitions of financial need. Fields provides one example from inquiries conducted in the University of California system (1988, p. 25):

> Expanded financial aid, better information about it and simplified financial aid processing were among the more important things that students (at California State-Long Beach) said the campus might do to help them remain in college.

Note that it is not merely financial aid that is important, but notification and processing of applications in ways that are simple and that avoid additional stigma. When the university fails to explain the reasons for such need-based grants, and its commitment to their social necessity on the basis of concerns for justice and institutional excellence, white students' images of "reverse discrimination" and unfair advantages to students of color are heightened.

Public universities' appropriations from state legislatures are to a certain extent dependent upon the university's ability to satisfy the interests of concerned state officials. Because of the ways in which public policies generally favor the interests of white and upper middle class people, and their young who are college students, support for university efforts to combat racism and create a multi-cultural environment are, for the most part, not a priority. When state legislatures or their subcommittees do seek to analyze university race relations and their impacts, or pressure the university to reduce racism, their efforts often are seen as unwarranted intrusions on the academic freedom of the institution, or perhaps as an example of special interest group publicity-seeking. Rather than take advantage of these rare opportunities for legislative support or community collaboration in a broad change effort, the university leadership generally reacts negatively, both to deny its own problems and to resist external influence attempts.

Put simply, because the bulk of financial resources available to institutions of higher education do not come from people of color, or from the institutions they control, these resources are generally not allocated nor sought with an interest in combatting racism.

Colleges and universities are labor intensive organizations, and faculty/staff salaries constitute a major (and unyielding) portion of the overall budget. Most of their faculties are white and male. Most of their top administrative staffs are white and male as well. Their clerical, secretarial, and plant staffs may be more diverse; certainly Black and Hispanic employees are concentrated here. Moreover, most of the student body is likely to be white. Of course, there are exceptions to these patterns in historically Black or Hispanic colleges, and in some urban universities. If people are a crucial resource in the labor-intensive environment of higher education, the recruitment, employment, retention and development (growth and promotion) of people of color must be a crucial issue in the creation/deployment of anti-racist resources for the organization. However, it is common knowledge that despite rhetoric and policies of affirmative action, routing recruitment and hiring practices have generally failed to employ and sustain substantial numbers of people of color in faculty and senior staff roles. When employed, many people of color fail to be affirmed and sustained in a racist environment, and often leave or are pushed out of the organization (in spirit if not in body).

White faculty who are opposed to affirmative action programs, whether on principle, in particular cases, or because of a general resistance to racial change, often make faculty of color "feel uncertain about the reasons for their faculty appointments, consultantships and committee appointments . . . African-Americans are continuously confronted by the racist notion among colleagues that our successes are not achieved or merited, that affirmative action has allowed substandard scholars to rise to positions formerly held by meritorious whites (Blakey, 1989, pp. 18–17)." White faculty and administrators know such conversations occur: mostly in private but not always; mostly with white colleagues but sometimes with students. Faculty of color know it as well. Ironically, this stance does more than demean and humiliate faculty of color; it also ignores the history of preferential hiring of whites, which has itself led to problems in ethnocentrism, incompetence and inadequacy in some spheres of intellectual labor.

Wilson (1987, p. 3) argues that some additional reasons for the failure to make significant progress on the hiring of faculty of color rest in four widely-believed myths that often accompany faculty recruiting efforts:

> the myth that the problem is the "availability" of minorities with the terminal degree (no available data sustains this assumption).
>
> the myth that minority women are "prime hires" because they represent two "protected groups" (in fact minority women often are at the very bottom of the professional ladder).
>
> the myth that minority Ph.D.s in science and engineering are so rare that they can command top salaries and that many colleges cannot afford them (in fact they attain promotion and tenure at a lower rate than do whites).
>
> the myth that there is no necessary correlation between commitment to equity on the part of academic leaders and the number of minorities in those leaders' student bodies and faculties.

One of the reasons frequently cited for not recruiting more students or faculty of color is the lack of a suitable pool of candidates for these respective roles. Seldom is it acknowledged that the definition of the suitability of these students or faculty members affects the boundaries and make up of the candidate pool. The so-called pool is not a given, it is in itself a product of the mission and culture of the organization; and it can be redefined to enable more people of color to be included. Moreover, colleges and universities seldom take responsibility to remedy the social conditions that influence whether or not adequate numbers of people of color are included in a pool of candidates. (e.g., through work in local/regional elementary and secondary schools, job training or economic development programs). Higher educational organizations certainly have the capability (in research and service activities) to help alter those social conditions that lead to the exclusion of minorities from the pool they wish to use in selecting students and faculty members. To cite the absence of people of color in a pool of potential candidates for university positions, without taking some responsibility for the social conditions shaping the make-up of the pool, is obfuscatory at best and self-serving at worst.

It is important to expand the numbers of people of color, but not only from the standpoint of social justice or equity; it also is a matter of excellence. A diverse faculty and staff can exercise valuable modelling and leadership for others—if provided with the opportunity and support for such initiatives. Students and faculty who come from middle and upper middle-class white communities typically bring to their teaching and learning (and research and service) the racial attitudes and behaviors of their families of origin. They reflect the alienation and biases of the communities and class groupings of which they are a part. These "legacies" generally include little experience interacting as peers with people of color, and subtle notions of their inferiority. Whites may be curious about the living patterns of people of color, but they also are awkward with and ignorant of their life styles. Under these circumstances, living and working together is a challenging and difficult enterprise. So is creating a high quality and diverse educational environment. Although many universities seek to counter this awkwardness and ignorance through dormitory and extra-curricular programs, or even in rare circumstances through the curriculum, it cannot be accomplished without the substantial presence of people of color themselves.

Racial diversity also enhances academic excellence by broadening the intellectual content and methods that are part of a teaching and research program. Many people of color in colleges and universities bring with them constituency liaisons, topical interests, pedagogies and epistemologies that differ from many of their white colleagues. This occurs because of sub-cultural influences and because the values and interests of many people of color and many white people are affected by their socialization into different subordinate and superordinate statuses in the society. Intellectual diversity cannot be divorced from social diversity, and academic excellence cannot be achieved without maximum intellectual diversity. In pursuing intellectual diversity it is absolutely necessary to have a faculty and student body that has been socialized in different subcultures and in different socio-economic status groups—and that can and will communicate to and share their perspectives with one another.

Racial ignorance, awkwardness and isolation lead to a waste of key human potential and educational resources. They not only affect white students' views and relationships with students of color in the dormitories and residence halls, they affect their perceptions and expectations of these students' performance in class. They not only affect faculty behavior with students of color in the classroom, they affect faculty behavior with colleagues of color. They not only affect staff members' behavior as they counsel, advise or otherwise serve students of color, they affect their interactions with staff members of color as well. In general, the human capital of the university, the labor and educational resources themselves, are demeaned and limited by the institution's inability to create or take advantage of a diverse community or an anti-racist educational environment.

The physical plants of most colleges and universities are located in or near white neighborhoods and predominantly white communities. These settings carry a history of racial exclusion, and often are uncomfortable environs for people of color to enter and sustain themselves within. It is to be expected, moreover, that the art and architecture of these settings are generally more reflective of white and Western culture than of others. These settings further serve to make students of color feel they are in "strange territory." Even those universities located in the hearts, or on the margins, of communities of color, generally are so heavily invested in land ownership patterns that further the economic exploitation and alienation of poor and minority communities (Jacobs, 1963), that they fare no better on these dimensions.

Because the post-Korean era of growth in higher education is over, resource reallocation rather than resource growth has become the dominant theme in college and university budgeting. New goals have to be pursued by reallocating scarce funds from other programs and priorities. Such changes in financial patterns are notoriously controversial and ridden with conflict, and the conflict is likely to be escalated when reallocated resources appear to benefit people of color. All the ancient stereotypes and concerns about racial inferiority and unfair advantage are likely to surface.

New efforts to recruit and admit minority students, to recruit and hire and promote minority faculty, to recruit and hire and promote minority staff leaders, to achieve changes in instructional and research programs so as to combat racism, and to move toward an anti-racist university will involve significant battles over the reallocation of financial resources.

Summary

Each of these major institutional elements operates in ways that pass on societal racism and that constrain the potential for change. At the same time, within each of these elements conflicts exist, as day-to-day realities are at odds with institutional ideals, as people of color and their allies seek improved opportunities, and as external pressures of internationalization, domestic demographics, improved human resource development systems, and renewed pursuit of social justice impact on institutions of higher education. Universities are not neutral actors in this historic sequence, however; without proactive commitment otherwise, they do not merely pass on societal racism, but they also encourage and promote oppression and domination within their own institutional operations. Figure 6 summarizes this discussion by providing an overview of some of the ways in which racism may be altered in the operation of each element of higher educational organizations. The identification, diagnosis, and assessment of these patterns are necessary steps in planning changes to reduce institutional racism. Each element also carries a key to the change process, to the effort to combat and reduce racism. To the extent we can alter the mission, culture, power, structure or resources of higher educational organizations we can alter the institutional racism that permeates these organizations. In turn, as we alter institutional racism in colleges and universities, we also alter aspects of their organizational missions, cultures, power, structures and resources.

IV. Changing Institutional Racism in Higher Education[5]

In order to create change in the well-institutionalized character of racism in higher education a comprehensive planning process is required. Anything less will lack an integrative vision and design, will lead to piecemeal and sporadic efforts, and will fail to produce lasting results. False starts and minimalist or poorly planned efforts can make a situation worse by failing to anticipate resistance, failing to confront opposition forcefully, escalating stigmatizing reactions to intended beneficiaries of new policies, appearing to solve problems without real substance, etc.

Significant organizational change involves alterations in all components of the collegiate or university organization, including mission, culture, power, structure and resources. Even then, questions of feasibility remain; the kinds and extent of change required to significantly reduce racism may be impossible in the context of current organization forms and procedures. Indeed, some scholars and activists argue that universities, and racism itself, are so embedded in the political and economic structures of our society that no meaningful change is possible short of major societal transformation. Despite this potential, we think that even the limited organizational changes discussed here can have significant positive impact in and of themselves; they also can be key elements in a more sustained and far-reaching effort to alter institutional racism.

When "incidents" of racism surfaced on college and university campuses the primary responses of many local administrators were focused on eliminating conflict to achieve "image management." That is, a major initial concern was to protect the image of the university, sometimes by denying the importance of events, and to indicate a high level of concern when denial could not be maintained. In a recent issue of *Black Issues In Higher Education*, Warren (1988) confirms this impression, arguing that "Too often, attention is directed at crisis situations born out of daily incidents which have been ignored by all except the victims (p. 56)."

When it was clear that some action had to be taken, the usual first efforts were limited and short-range. Typical initiatives that were rapidly deployed included multiple meetings to talk about issues, special campaigns to recruit students and faculty of color, the commissioning of human relations or "sensitivity" training programs, the appointment of a special assistant for minority affairs, and the

MISSION
  Attend to societal/demographic transformations that require reducing racism.
  Attend to racism as a threat to institutional excellence, effectiveness, and goal attainment
  Attend to linkages between racism and other forms of oppression/exploitation
  Generate plural definitions of excellence—in research, teaching and service.
  Provide justification for anti-racism programs

CULTURE
  Recognize and celebrate multicultural norms and practices, and distinct cultural backgrounds and styles
  Advance scholarly epistemologies and curricula that embrace the world views and knowledge of
    different cultures
  Respond to conflict in ways which do not seek to dominate, repress or deny differences but rather to
    learn about problems and cherish differences (and potential commonalities)

POWER
  Provide people of color with access to decisional arenas
  Redistribute power to achieve broader sharing among various stake holders, including increased power
    for people of color.
  Utilize formal and informal power to combat racism
  Demonstrate senior administrative, faculty and staff commitment to change

STRUCTURE
  Alter patterns of interaction to promote collaboration across existing group and organizational boundaries
  Develop task designs and study/work groups that encourage formal and informal multi-racial collaboration
  Develop new priorities in teaching/curriculum and research that improve responsiveness to cultural and
    economic diversity
  Develop new courses, teaching methods, research methods, and topics that seek to understand and
    combat racism
  Develop policies and practices to identify and combat discrimination and harassment generally—and
    racial harassment specifically
  Provide ongoing support for people of color to achieve excellence, as well as to gain access to higher
    education

RESOURCES
  Seek and allocate financial resources to local efforts that promote organizational innovation and change
  Apply financial resources to reducing racism in research and teaching and university life as a priority
  Improve recruitment and enrollment/employment to address both diversity and excellence
  Provide spaces that are comfortable and supportive for the gathering, collaborating, and celebrating of
    under-represented groups

Figure 6   Keys to potential reduction of racism in higher education.

development of study skills' programs for students of color (Ransby, 1987). To the extent that the issues were raised by protesting student groups, first efforts also were likely to include meetings with aggrieved students or the formation of task forces to "study" or "solve" local problems.

Sometimes the gross symptoms of racism, including embarrassing public conflict, can be temporarily alleviated through such piecemeal efforts, programmatic add-ons, and crash initiatives. However, these crisis-focused responses will not reduce institutional racism because they do not address the underlying organizational and institutional factors that are involved. These activities can be valuable components of more comprehensive and longer-range change programs, but by themselves they only raise false hopes for institutional change.

Comprehensive organizational change to reduce racism requires the top leadership of colleges and universities to make explicit decisions that commit the organization to major change. But these changes cannot be decided upon by the senior leadership themselves; the traditional white and male dominance of this leadership cadre must itself be challenged as part of the change process. Thus, major planning efforts and decisions must include: faculty, staff and students as well as administrators; students and faculty of color as well as whites; and women as well as men. Conflict will inevitably occur as a result of such widespread participation, but plural involvement also provides ideas that are more responsive to the needs of different groups of people throughout the organization. It may begin to develop, moreover, a more legitimate and effective multicultural educational environment by its very example. If "lower-level" organizational members have to be relied upon to implement any plan organizational leaders develop, they are more likely to do so to the extent that they and their representatives have been involved in the planning process and have developed programs relevant to their needs, mindsets and resources.

Efforts to reduce racism in organizations often are motivated primarily by the guilt of white administrators and faculty members, and the desire to ameliorate public protests or bad press. While such factors may contribute to initial efforts to reduce racism they are insufficient bases for pursuing long-term and lasting change. Other motivations must be developed for this endeavor. These other motivations can be grounded in several factors, including:

> The costs of institutional racism to the organization, both to whites and people of color.
>
> New potentials open to the organization and all of its members by reducing institutional racism.
>
> New internal organizational rewards for members or units which undertake positive efforts to reduce racism (and/or sanctions for resistance or continued racism).

If people and organizations are operating in racist ways they must be receiving some "benefit" from such activities. It must in some way be in their interest (real or perceived), at least in the short term, to continue such activities in the face of laws and moral codes to the contrary. Whether that self-interest is financial, positional (status), emotional, or cultural, may not matter as much as its existence, per se. Only change in the self-interest basis for behavior, the things that cause people and organizations to seek their own gain, will permanently cause (and support) change. This principle of organizational change is articulated clearly by the Stanford University self-study of campus racism (Stanford University Committee on Minority Issues, 1989):

> Good intentions are not enough . . . At the departmental level, some managers find the University's pluralistic goals important and apply them to their particular office, but when others make half-hearted efforts or no efforts at all to recruit, develop, and retain minority staff, they face no repercussions . . . Until we impose real sanctions for willful failure to implement stated goals for diversity and inclusion in the workplace, the University will not be able to say that it acknowledges and opposes institutional racism—or that "bigotry is out." (pp. 9, 214).

As self-interests are redefined, based on a long term perspective on the future of social relations and institutional success, alternative motivations to reduce institutional racism in higher education may become more compelling. Such redefinition of self-interests also will require effective education and sustained incentives. For instance, if college or university leaders (or staff members or faculty members or students) do not experience rewards or gains for anti-racist behavior they are not likely to sustain that behavior for long. Similarly, if college or university leaders see very clearly the costs of racism for themselves and their institution, they will not (unless simultaneously seeing major gains) continue to engage in or support the operations that generate that cost. At the more micro-level of influencing the behavior of faculty members, Monaghan argues for the self-interest principle in the following terms:

> Colleges and universities should offer incentives and rewards to faculty members who show a commitment to cultural pluralism, and should hold administrators more accountable for advancing institutional goals to improve opportunities for minority scholars. (1989, p. A18)

Certainly there are potential costs to a meaningful change effort, and planning and implementation designs must be cognizant of the pain or threat that will occur to some peoples' values and interests, and their resultant resistance. It is our experience that while members of institutions of higher education often are ignorant of the long-term costs of current racist policies and procedures, and of the potential long-term gains of change, they are very sophisticated (often to the point of paralysis) regarding the short-term costs (and political resistance) involved in an anti-racism effort.

The attempt to plan and carry out a long-term change program can focus on some of the key challenges to institutional racism summarized in Figure 6. These organizational change options are grouped according to the 5 core elements of higher educational organizations outlined in Figure 4 and discussed in detail earlier. Since these 5 core elements, as well as the many individual program suggestions, interact with the are co-dependent upon one another, an integrated strategic plan is absolutely necessary.

Implementing these or other organizational change options also requires making a number of tactical choices, choices that determine the shape and conduct of a local change effort. A detailed discussion of such tactics is beyond the scope of this paper, but the reader is referred to our forthcoming companion piece for elaboration. Briefly, the following issues must be dealt with:

The balance between (or combination of) top-down and bottom-up change approaches.

The number and types of groups or constituencies to be involved in planning and implementing the change effort.

The role of people of color, especially students, in designing responses to their experience of racism.

The role and visibility (and accountability) of senior administrative officers and senior faculty.

The degree and type of involvement of external organizations and individuals in planning, implementing and evaluating the organizational change effort.

The balance between (or combination of) persuasion and coercion as change approaches.

The stance taken toward those passively resisting or actively opposing anti-racism efforts.

The maintenance of a thrust on countering counter organizational/institutional racism in the face of probable efforts to focus on individualistic analyses and solutions.

The linkage of anti-racism efforts to other change programs, such as anti-sexism and general designs to improve student learning and faculty working environs.

These problems and possibilities in the effort to reduce racism in institutions of higher education impress upon us the delicate, complex and immense natures of this task. At the same time, the cries of protesting students, the often muted voices of faculty and staff of color, and the analytic perspective offered earlier impress upon us the necessity of undertaking this task. Decisions made within the university both reflect and influence decisions made by students, faculty and administrators, policy makers and just plain citizens in their daily work and activity outside the university as well. The future of social justice and peace in our entire society and the world, not merely in our systems of higher education, rest on the efforts we can make to acknowledge, understand, and reduce the racism within our universities and colleges.

Notes

1. This working paper is a revised and expanded version of a chapter prepared for ETHICS IN HIGHER EDUCATION, edited by W. May (Macmillan, 1990). We plan to complement it later with another working paper, "Racism in higher education II: Designing and implementing organizational change."
2. This list of proposals from the United Coalition Against Racism is similar to a series of demands/ proposals also made in the Winter of 1987 by the Black Action Movement III and the Hispanic Student Association.
3. From materials prepared and distributed by the Black Action Movement.
4. Of course, it is uniquely visible, accessible and objectionable to us, as faculty of the University of Michigan.
5. A separate paper (in preparation) will draw on the foregoing analysis to create an expanded discussion of some of the possibilities and strategies for changing institutional racism in higher education.

References

Alderfer, C., Aderfer, D., Tucker, L. and Tucker, R. Diagnosing race relations in management. *The Journal of Applied Behavioral Science.* 1980, 16(2): 135–166.

Allen, W. *Gender and Campus Race Differences in Black Student Academic Performance, Racial Attitudes and College Satisfaction.* Atlanta, Southern Educational Foundation, 1986.

Allen, W. Improving Black student access and achievement in higher education. *The Review of Higher Education.* 1988, 11(4), 403–416.

Astin, A. *Minorities in Higher Education.* San Francisco, Jossey-Bass, 1982.

Alvarez, R., & Lutterman, K (Eds). *Discrimination in Organizations*. San Francisco, Jossey-Bass, 1979.

Baldridge, V. and Deal, T. Overview of change processes in educational organizations. In Baldridge and Deal (Eds.), *Managing Change in Educational Organizations*. Berkeley, McCutchan, 1975.

Bayh, B. Let's tear off their hoods. *Newsweek*, 1989, April 17.

Bell, D. The price and pain of racial perspective. *Stanford Law School Journal*. 1986, May 9, 5.

Benjamin, E. Faculty responsibility for enhancing minority participation in higher education. *Academe*. 1989, 75(5), 64.

Birnbaum, R. Administrative commitment and minority enrollments: College president's goals for quality and access. *The Review of Higher Education*. 1988, 11(4), 435–458.

Blackwell, J. Mentoring: An action strategy for increasing minority faculty. *Academe*. 1989, 75(5), 8–14.

Blakey, M. The professional caucus: Place of refuge, source of change. *Academe*. 1989, 75(5), 15–18.

Blauner, R. *Racial Oppression In America*. New York, Harper & Row, 1972.

Brooks, R. Life after tenure: Can minority law professors avoid the Clyde Ferguson syndrome? *University of San Francisco Law Review*. 1986, 20, 419–427.

Brown, D. *Managing Conflict at Organizational Interfaces*. Cambridge, Addison-Wesley, 1983.

Campbell, A. and Schuman, H. *Racial Attitudes in Fifteen American Cities*. Ann Arbor, Institute for Social Research, 1968.

Carmichael, S., & Hamilton, C. *Black Power: The Politics of Racism in America*. New York, Vintage Books, 1976.

Checkoway, B. Unanswered questions about public service in the public university. *The University Record*. 1989, February 6, 10–12.

Clark, B. *The Distinctive College: Antioch, Reed and Swarthmore*. New York, Aldine, 1970.

Clark, K., and Plotkin, L. *The Negro Student at Integrated Colleges*. N.Y., National Scholarship Service and Fund for Negro Students, 1963.

Crenshaw, K. Foreword: Toward a race-conscious pedagogy in legal education. *National Black Law Journal*. 1989, 11(1), 1–14.

Dill, D. The management of academic culture: notes on the management of meaning and social integration. *Higher Education*. 1982, 11, 303–320.

Elmore, C. and Blackburn, R. Black and white faculty in white research universities. *Journal of Higher Education*. 1983, 54, 1–15.

Epps, E. Academic culture and the minority professor. *Academe*, 1989, 75(5), 23–26.

Exum, W. Climbing the crystal stair: Values, affirmative action, and minority faculty. *Social Problems*. 1983, 30(4), 383–399.

Feagin, J., & Feagin, C. *Discrimination American Style: Institutional Racism and Sexism*. Englewood Cliffs, Prentice Hall, 1986.

Fields, C. The Hispanic pipeline: narrow, leaking and needing repair. *Change*. 1988, 20(3), 20–27.

Finn, C. The Campus: "An island of repression in a sea of freedom." *Commentary*. 1989, September, 17–23.

Fiske, E. The undergraduate Hispanic experience: A case of juggling two cultures. *Change*. 1988, 20(3), 28–33.

Fleming, J., Gill, G. and Swinton, D. *The Case for Affirmative Action for Blacks in Higher Education*. Washington, D.C., Howard University Press, 1978.

Friere, P. *Pedagogy of the Oppressed*. New York, Seabury Press, 1970.

Gardner, A., Mason, C. & Matyas, M. Equity, excellence and just plain good teaching. *The American Biology Teacher*. 1989, 51(2), 72–77.

Gross, N. Universities as organizations: a research approach. *American Sociological Review*, 1968, 33, 518–543.

Hurst, F. *Report on University of Massachusetts Investigation*, Amherst, UMass, 1987.

Jackson, B., and Holvino, E. Multicultural organizational development. Ann Arbor, Program in Conflict Management Alternatives (Working Paper #11), 1988.

Jacobs, J. *The Death and Life of Great American Cities*. New York, Vintage, 1963.

Jones, J. *Prejudice And Racism*. Reading, Mass. Addison-Wesley, 1970.

Justus, S., Freitag, S. & Parker, L. *The University of California in The Twenty-First Century*. 1987.

Katz, J. Facing the challenge of diversity and multiculturalism. Ann Arbor, Program in Conflict Management Alternatives (Working Paper #13), 1988.

Katz, J. *White Awareness*. Norman, Oklahoma, University of Oklahoma Press, 1978.

Katz, D. and Kahn, R. *The Social Psychology of Organizations.* New York, Wiley, 1978.

Keller, E. *Reflections On Gender And Science.* New Haven, Yale University Press, 1985.

Kennedy, R. Racial critiques of legal academia. *Harvard Law Review.* 1989, 102(8), 1745–1819.

Kochman, T. *Black and White: Styles in Conflict.* Chicago, University of Chicago Press, 1981.

Knowles, R. and Prewitt, K. (eds.) *Institutional Racism in America.* Englewood Cliffs, Prentice Hall, 1969.

Martin, J., and Siehl, C. Organizational culture and counterculture: An uneasy symbiosis. *Organizational Dynamics.* 1983, Autumn, 52–64.

Maclay, K. Berkeley faculty considers mandatory minority course. *Black Issues In Higher Education.* 1988, 5(20), 15.

Masland, A. Organizational culture in the study of higher education. *The Review of Higher Education.* 1985, 8, 157–168.

McBay, S. *The Racial Climate on the MIT Campus.* Cambridge, MIT, 1986.

Michigan Alumnus. 1987, 94(1).

Monaghan, P. Action, not just policy change, seen needed to improve minority scholars' opportunities. *The Chronicle of Higher Education,* 1989, 35(26), A17–18.

Moore, W. and Wagstaff, L. *Black Faculty in White Colleges.* San Francisco, Jossey-Bass, 1974.

Omi, M. and Winant, H. *Racial Formation in the United States.* London, Routledge and Keegan Paul, 1986.

Payne, H. Hidden messages in the pursuit of equality. *Academe.* 1989, 75(5), 19–22.

Peterson, M., Blackburn, R., Gamson, Z., Arce, C., Davenport, R., & Mingle, J. *Black Students on White Campuses: The Impacts of Increased Black Enrollments.* Ann Arbor, Institute for Social Research, 1978.

Ransby, B. University goes for pushbutton solution. *Agenda,* 1987, October, 7–18.

Richardson, R., & de los Santos, A. The guest editors' introduction: From access to achievement: Fulfilling the promise. *The Review of Higher Education.* 1988, 11(4), 323–328.

Richardson, R., Simmons, H., & de los Santos, A. Graduating minority students: Lessons from ten success stories. *Change.* 1987, 19(3), 20–26.

Ridgeway, J. *The Closed Corporation.* New York, Ballantine, 1968.

Rosenberg, L. A battle far from won. *Yale.* 1988. November, 44–47.

Schuman, H., Steeh, C., and Bobo, L. *Racial Attitudes in America: Trends and Interpretations.* Cambridge, Harvard University Press, 1985.

Schwartz, B. and Disch, R. (eds.) *White Racism.* New York, Dell, 1970.

Smelser, N. and Content, R. *The Changing Academic Market.* Berkeley, University of California Press, 1980.

Stanford University Committee on Minority Issues. *Building a Multiracial, Multicultural University Community.* Stanford University, 1989.

Steele, S. The recoloring of campus life. *Harpers Magazine.* 1989, February, 48–55.

Sudarkasa, N. Black enrollment in higher education: The unfulfilled promise of equality. In Dewart (Ed), *The State of Black America.* 1988. New York, National Urban League, 1988.

Takaki, R. An educated and culturally literate person must study America's multi-cultural reality. *The Chronicle of Higher Education.* 1989, 35(26), B1–2.

Terry, R. The negative impact on white values. In Bowser & Hunt (Ed), *The Impact of Racism on White Americans.* Beverly Hills, Sahe Press, 1981.

Thomas, G. *Black Students in Higher Education: Conditions and Experiences in the 1970s.* Westport, Greenwood Press, 1981.

Tichy, N. *Managing Strategic Change.* New York, Wiley, 1983.

United States Commission on Civil Rights, *Affirmative Action in the 1980s: Dismantling the Process of Discrimination.* 1981 (Clearing House Publication #65).

Vetter, B., Babco, E., and Jensen-Fischer, S. *Professional Women and Minorities.* (3rd edition) Washington, D.C., Scientific Manpower Commission, 1982.

Wall Street Journal. The privileged class. 1989, September 19.

Warren, S. One step forward, two steps back. *Black Issues in Higher Education.* 1988, 5(6), 56.

Wilson, R. and Carter, D. *Minorities in Higher Education.* Washington, D.C., American Council on Education, 1988.

Wilson, R. Recruitment and retention of minority faculty and staff. *AAHE Bulletin.* 1987, February, 2–5.

Zorn, J. Ethics, values best imparted by example. *The University Record.* 1986, July 7, 8.

THE EMPEROR HAS NO CLOTHES: REWRITING "RACE IN ORGANIZATIONS"

STELLA M. NKOMO
UNIVERSITY OF NORTH CAROLINA AT CHARLOTTE

This article analyzes how race has been studied in organization scholarship and demonstrates how our approaches to the study of race reflect and reify particular historical and social meanings of race. It is argued that the production of knowledge about race must be understood within a racial ideology embedded in a Eurocentric view of the world. Finally, a "re-vision" of the very concept of race and its historical and political meaning is suggested for rewriting "race" as a necessary and productive analytical category for theorizing about organizations.

"Now, is not that magnificent?" said both the worthy officials. "Will your Majesty deign to note the beauty of the patterns and the colors?" And they pointed to the bare loom for they supposed that all the rest could certainly see the stuff. "What's the meaning of this?" thought the Emperor. "I can't see a thing! This is terrible! Am I stupid? Am I not fit to be Emperor? That would be the most frightful thing that could befall me." "Oh, it's very pretty, it has my all highest-approval!" said he, nodding complacently and gazing on the empty loom: of course, he wouldn't say he could see nothing. The whole of the suite he had with him looked and looked, but got no more out of that than the rest. However, they said, as the Emperor said: "Oh, it's very pretty!" And they advised him to put on this splendid new stuff for the first time, on the occasion of a great procession which was to take place shortly . . .

So the Emperor walked in the procession under the beautiful canopy, and everybody in the streets and at the windows said: "Lord! How splendid the Emperor's new clothes are. What a lovely train he has to his coat! What a beautiful fit it is!" Nobody wanted to be detected seeing nothing: that would mean that he was no good at his job, or that he was very stupid.

"But he hasn't got anything on!" said a little child. . . . "Why he hasn't got anything on!" The whole crowd was shouting at last; and the Emperor's flesh crept, for it seemed to him they were right. "But all the same," he thought to himself, "I must go through with the procession." So he held himself more proudly than before, and the lords in waiting walked on bearing the train—the train that wasn't there at all. (Excerpt from "The Emperor's New Clothes," by Hans Christian Anderson, 1968: 104–107)

The children's fairy tale, "The Emperor's New Clothes," is an excellent allegory for the primary way in which organization scholars have chosen to address race in organizations. For the most part, research has tended to study organization populations as homogeneous entities in which distinctions of race and ethnicity are either "unstated" or considered irrelevant. A perusal of much of our research would lead one to believe that organizations are race neutral (Cox & Nkomo, 1990).

Although the emperor, his court suitors, and his tailors recognize that he is naked, no one will explicitly acknowledge that nakedness. Even as the innocent child proclaims his nakedness, the emperor and his suitors resolutely continue with the procession. Similarly, the silencing of the importance of race in organizations is mostly subterfuge because of the overwhelming role of race and ethnicity in every aspect of society.

Race in the United States has been a profound determinant of one's political rights, one's location in the labor market, one's access to medical care, and even one's sense of identity (Omi & Winant, 1986). Its immediacy is manifested in everyday life experiences and social interactions (Blauner, 1989;

Essed, 1991; van Dijk, 1987). Most important, race is one of the major bases of domination in our society and a major means through which the division of labor occurs in organizations (Reich, 1981). As I will argue later, race has been present all along in organizations, even if silenced or suppressed.

One might ask, why use a European fairy tale to call attention to the exclusion of race in the study of organizations? I have purposefully used a Eurocentric parable to signify this problem through parody, in the African-American tradition of what Gates (1988: 82) has called "black signifyin(g)"—the figurative difference between the literal and the metaphorical, between surface and latent meaning. In this article, the emperor is not simply an emperor but the embodiment of the concept of Western knowledge as both universal and superior and white males as the defining group for studying organizations. The court suitors are the organizational scholars who continue the traditions of ignoring race and ethnicity in their research and excluding other voices. All have a vested interest in continuing the procession and not calling attention to the omissions.

Who then is most likely to call attention to these omissions? As has been the case in other disciplines, it is most likely to be the *other*, the excluded, who is assumed to be childlike and inferior. Even as these *other* voices point to the omissions and errors and the need for inclusiveness, the dominant group refuses to hear the message and continues with the procession. The real issue for the *others* is getting truly heard, rather than simply "added on." As noted by Minnich (1990), it is difficult to add new knowledge to anything that has been defined as the whole. The challenge must strike directly at the center of the kingdom and its attendant theoretical foundations.

The purpose of this article then is to analyze how race has been written into the study of organizations in incomplete and inadequate ways. It demonstrates how our approaches to the study of race reflect particular historical and social meanings of race, specifically a racial ideology embedded in a Eurocentric view of the world. This view is evident first in the general exclusion of race when organizational theories are developed and, second, in the theoretical and methodological orientation of the limited body of research on race. Finally, suggestions are made for ways of making race a necessary and productive analytical category for theorizing about organizations. Perspectives are drawn from several disciplines including African-American studies and race and ethnic relations. The intent is not to provide a specific theory of race but to suggest ways of "re-visioning" the study of race in organizations.

On the Exclusion of Race in the Study of Organizations

Why do we as organizational scholars continue to conceptualize organizations as race neutral? Why has race been silenced in the study of organizations? One way of explaining this exclusion is to examine what Minnich (1990) has called intellectual errors in the production of knowledge. The root error might be labeled faulty generalization or noninclusive universalization. This error occurs when we take a dominant few (white males) as the inclusive group, the norm, and the ideal of humankind (Minnich, 1990). The defining group for specifying the science of organizations has been white males. Only recently have we begun to study the experiences of women in management, and even this body of literature focuses mainly on white women (Nkomo, 1988). We have amassed a great deal of knowledge about the experience of only one group, yet we generalize our theories and concepts to all groups. We do not acknowledge that these universal theories emanate from an inadequate sample and, therefore, there is the possibility that the range of a theory or construct is limited (Cox & Nkomo, 1990).

According to Minnich (1990), faulty generalization leads to a kind of hierarchically invidious monism. Not only are dominant group members the defining group, but they are taken to be the highest category—the best—and all other groups must be defined and judged solely with reference to that hegemonic category (Keto, 1989). Other racial and ethnic groups are relegated to subcategories; their experiences are seen as outside of the mainstream of developing knowledge of organizations.

This point can be illustrated by examining the use of prefixes in the description of research samples in our work. The prefix "white" is usually suppressed, and it is only other racial groups to which we attach prefixes (Minnich, 1990). "Race" becomes synonymous with *other* groups, and whites do not have "race." A study based on a sample of white male managers is unlikely to state that the results may be valid only for that group. More likely than not the term *manager* will be used. The problem is the usurpation of the category *manager* by the dominant group and the lack of awareness that white managers also have race.

Concomitantly, a study that has a minority group sample will rarely be accepted for developing and generalizing organization theory. The results of the study would be viewed as valid only for that group with minimal or little relevance for organization knowledge. Thus, instead of race being an analytical category critical to the fundamental understanding of organizations, it is marginalized. Unless the study is explicitly about race (e.g., affirmative action or bias in performance ratings) or has a minority-group sample, it is not included as an important variable, even when contextual factors may indicate otherwise.

The faulty generalization error stems mainly from bias in science. The practices of science reflect the values and concerns of dominant societal groups (Harding, 1986). The concepts and approaches used in Western academia help to maintain the political and intellectual superiority of Western cultures and people (Joseph, Reddy, & Searle-Chatterjee, 1990). Kuhn (1962) argued that problem selection and the search for explanations by scholars are influenced by the social and political conditions of the times. To the extent that white males have dominated the production of knowledge, their values and concerns are predominant. The study of race is an especially sensitive issue because scholars must not only be aware of how prevailing societal race relations influence their approach to the study of race but they must also understand the effects of their own racial identity and experiences on their work (Alderfer, 1982).

The tendency toward faulty generalization is further explained by the adherence to the assumption, embedded in Western philosophy from Socrates to the Enlightenment, that there is one ultimate objective truth and the scholar's mission is to search for that truth. This truth cannot come from *other* non-Western views of knowledge (Keto, 1989). Hence, there is a relationship between the desire for universal theories and the suppression of the experience of *others*. Researches who ignore the influence of race in understanding organizations may reflect a veiled hope that, indeed, management theories and constructs are universal. Once there is acceptance of the idea that the major theories and concepts of the field of management do not address all groups, the holding of and search for universal theories is undermined.

It is illusory to think that other views are socially located while one's own are not. We cannot avoid the implicit influence of the scholar's perspective and values in the theories we develop (Morgan, 1983). The research questions that are asked and not asked and the chosen methodology of research on race in organizations parallel the dominant theoretical, political, and social meanings of race.

Theoretical and Ideological Foundations of Research on Race

Before race can be re-visioned as an analytical category in the formulation of organization theory, a first step is to understand the historical and theoretical foundations of research on race and its influence on the ways in which we have studied race in organizations.

According to Omi and Winant (1986), the meaning, transformation, and significance of racial theories are shaped by actual existing race relations in any given historical period. Blanton (1987) added that within any given historical period, a particular racial theory is dominant, despite the existence of competing paradigms. The dominant racial theory provides society with a framework for understanding race relations and serves as a guide for research with implications for the kinds of questions scholars address. The dominant racial paradigm in the field of race and ethnic studies for the last half century has been that of ethnicity (Blanton, 1987; Omi & Winant, 1986; Thompson, 1989).

The Ethnicity Paradigm

The basic premises and assumptions of this paradigm are reflected in much of the research and writing in the management literature. Ethnicity-based theory emerged in the 1920s as a challenge to biological and social Darwinian conceptions of race (Blanton, 1987). Sociological concepts primarily replaced biological ones, and racial and ethnic forms of identification and social organizations were viewed as "unnatural" (Thompson, 1989). Becoming predominant by World War II, the ethnic paradigm has shaped academic research about race and guided policy formation (Omi & Winant, 1986). Despite serious challenges from alternative paradigms during the 1970s and 1980s, the rise of neoconservatism in the United States has led to a resurgence of ethnicity theory in a new guise, which has been labeled the *new ethnicity* (Omi & Winant, 1986; Steinberg, 1981; Thompson, 1989).

Ethnicity theorists' main empirical reference point was the study of immigration and the social patterns and experiences of European immigrants (Omi & Winant, 1986). Dominated by two recurrent oppositional themes, assimilation versus cultural pluralism, ethnicity theory was focused on the incorporation and separation of ethnic minorities, the nature of ethnic identity, and the impact of ethnicity on life experiences (Omi & Winant, 1986). One of the earliest explications of assimilationalism appeared in Park's 1939 essay, "The Nature of Race Relations" (Park, 1950/1939). Park focused on the problem of European migration and what he called *culture contact*. Park's famous *race relations cycle* became the basis for further development of assimilation theory (e.g., Gordon, 1964). Park argued that this cycle "which takes the form of contacts, competition, accommodation and eventual assimilation, is apparently progressive and irreversible" (Park, 1950/1939: 150). Despite Park's (1950/1939) acknowledgment that it was possible that a particular stage might be prolonged, assimilation was viewed as the most logical and natural antidote for racism and ethnocentricism. The widespread view of assimilation as a process of interpenetration and fusion in which persons and groups acquire the mentality, sentiments, and attitudes of dominant groups led to the well-known *melting pot* concept (Omi & Winant, 1986). For example, much of the early research on management was developed during a period of widespread European immigration to the United States. The new immigrants, urban white workers, particularly the Irish and people from Eastern Europe, were often degraded as "children" and "savage" and as being more interested in seeking lower rather than higher pleasures (Takai, 1979: 127). These early factory workers were scolded for their idleness and their lack of punctuality and industry (Gutman, 1977: 20). The theme of assimilation pervaded efforts by industrial capitalists to teach these workers the requisite attitudinal and work ethic skills needed to perform industrial jobs.

Other early proponents of assimilation theory included Myrdal (1944) and Gordon (1964). Gunnar Myrdal's classic work, *The American Dilemma*, called into question the contradiction between continued discrimination against African-Americans and the democratic ideals of equality and justice espoused in U.S. society. Both Myrdal's and Gordon's works attempted to extend ethnicity theory, which has been largely derived from the experience of European immigrants, to the situation of African-Americans (Thompson, 1989). It was assumed that the experience of racial minorities could be theorized in much the same way as the experience of ethnic immigrants. Thus, race in the United States was largely reduced to a question of integration and assimilation of racial minorities into the mainstream of a consensus-based society (van den Berghe, 1967). Within the assimilation framework, legal remedies like the Civil Rights Act of 1964 were viewed as necessary for removing barriers so that racial minorities would encounter the same conditions as white ethnics (Omi & Winant, 1986; Thompson, 1989). However, preferential treatment remedies like affirmative action were not supported (Glazer, 1987; Gordon, 1964). Blauner (1972: 2) pointed out that research on racial minorities (i.e., African-Americans, Latinos, Asian Americans, and Native Americans) from the ethnicity perspective was premised on several assumptions: (a) racial groups were not viewed as central or persistent elements of society; (b) racism and racial oppression were ultimately reducible to other causal determinants—usually economic or psychological; and (c) there were no essential long-term differences between the experience of racial minorities and the European ethnic groups that immigrated to the United States.

Research on race emanating from the ethnic-based paradigm centered on questions of why racial minorities were not becoming incorporated or assimilated into mainstream society. Or directly stated, "What obstructs assimilation?" Much of this research was devoted to problems of prejudice and discrimination and grew out of social psychological approaches to the study of intergroup relations (Oudenhoven & Willemsen, 1989). It was based on the belief that relations between dominant group members and racial minorities resulted from prejudiced attitudes of individuals. For example, Merton (1949) argued that discrimination might be practiced by unprejudiced people who were afraid not to conform to the prejudices of others. Adorno, Frenkel-Brunswick, Levinson, and Sanford (1950: 8) studied the relationship between prejudice and personality. He argued that prejudiced persons differed from tolerant persons in central personality traits—specifically, that they exhibited *authoritarian personalities*. Allport (1954) suggested that there was a direct link between prejudiced people and discriminatory acts. Unlike Adorno et al. (1950), Allport (1954) did not view prejudice as an aberrant cognitive distortion. Allport argued that prejudice was a natural extension of normal cognitive processes (Pettigrew, 1979). Thus, prejudice and discrimination were mainly reduced to either an individual aberration or faulty generalization (Henriques, 1984). Adorno's and Allport's emphasis on prejudice as an attitude also found widespread acceptance because of its amenability to quantification and statistical measurement (Henriques, 1984).

This traditional stress on the expressive function of prejudice by individuals is still manifested in much of contemporary social psychology research on race (Oudenhoven & Willemsen, 1989). For example, dominant contemporary social psychology theories for explaining prejudice include social identity or social categorization theory, social attribution theory, and the contact hypothesis (Dovidio & Gaertner, 1986).

The phenomenological approach of social identity or social categorization theory postulates that an individual's identity depends to a large extent on social group memberships where individuals seek positive social identity (Tajfel, 1969, 1970; Tajfel & Turner, 1979, 1986). The evaluation of one's own group is determined with reference to specific other groups through social comparisons in terms of value-laden attributes and characteristics. This mechanism is basic to the evaluation of one's social identity. These comparisons involve perceptual accentuation of similarities of people belonging to the same group and differences between people belonging to a different social group or category (Tajfel, 1981). Accordingly, if categorization is in terms of a racial or an ethnic criterion, then it is likely that this process is responsible in part for the prejudices found in the judgment of people belonging to different groups. Tajfel (1981) stressed the influence of the social factors of status, power, and material interdependence in the categorization process.

Social attribution theory or intergroup attribution theory refers to "how members of different social groups explain the behavior and social condition of members of their own group (ingroup) and other social groups (outgroups)" (Hewstone, 1989: 25). In this case, research emphasis is placed on explaining the behavior of individuals who act as members or representatives of social groups. An important explanatory concept in this theory is the fundamental attribution error—the phenomenon that one tends to explain the behavior of others by internal factors rather than situational factors (Oudenhoven & Willemsen, 1989). The extreme manifestation of social attribution is what Pettigrew has called the ultimate attribution error—"a systematic patterning of intergroup misattributions shaped in part by prejudice" (Pettigrew, 1979: 464). On the one hand, when blacks or other minority group members behave in a manner perceived to be negative, majority group members, especially those who are prejudiced, are likely to attribute this behavior to the personal character of the group (Pettigrew, 1979). On the other hand, prejudiced majority group members can explain away behavior that is seen as positive by attributing it to (a) the exceptional, special-case individual who is contrasted with his or her group; (b) luck or special advantage, which is viewed as unfair; (c) high motivation and effort, which is ultimately unsustainable; or (d) a manipulated situational context (Pettigrew, 1979: 469). Therefore, the ingroup (majority group) can still hold negative assessments of the outgroup (minority group), despite contrary evidence.

Finally, a third social psychology theory used to explain prejudice is the contact hypothesis. This is best understood as a solution to intergroup conflict which posits that positive contacts between ingroups and outgroups will reduce prejudice (Wilder, 1986). The success of contact is contingent upon the favorability of the interaction, especially the ingroup's perception of the interaction. Proponents of this theory underscore the important role of structuring the situation to promote cooperation rather than competition (Pettigrew & Martin, 1987). A major assumption underlying the contact hypothesis is that frequent positive contact between groups will minimize the information-processing errors (e.g., stereotyping) by ingroup members.

Although social psychologists like Tajfel argued that the major contribution of their work was its focus on the group rather than on individuals, making it more social and progressive, a close reading reveals it also ultimately relies on individual cognitive processing to explain prejudice and discrimination (Henriques, 1984). The results of Tajfel's minimal intergroup laboratory experiments led him to conclude that the mere perception of belonging to two distinct groups (i.e., social categorization per se) is sufficient to trigger intergroup discrimination favoring the ingroup. In other words, ingroup bias is a natural feature of intergroup relations. Therefore, if groups have no real bases for conflict, then discrimination lies in failures in the mechanism of individual cognition (Henriques, 1984).

Additionally, the primary solution offered by these social psychological approaches—the contact hypothesis—falls within the assimilation approach through the assumption that the reduction of the salience of group boundaries will improve intergroup interaction (Oudenhoven & Williemsen, 1989).

The New Ethnicity

During the mid-1970s, the ethnic-based paradigm was reformulated (Thompson, 1989). The upheavals during the Civil Rights movement of the 1960s and the urban riots of the 1970s underscored the fact that for African-Americans assimilation into dominant society was less than forthcoming. The major failure of assimilationists to explain the lack of African-American assimilation spawned a new paradigm, which has been called the *new ethnicity* (Steinberg, 1981; Thompson, 1989; Yinger, 1986). The *new* in *new ethnicity* is not so much a significant shift in theory as an attempt by assimilationists to explain the enduring nature of racial stratification (Thompson, 1989). According to Thompson (1989: 91), this paradigm is based on two interrelated positions: (a) that ethnic and racial criteria have become major forms of group-based sociopolitical behavior because of the changing nature of industrial society and (b) that ethnic and racial groups ought to maintain their separate boundaries and seek their separate interests provided such interests recognize and respect the multitude of other, different ethnic interests (i.e., the cultural pluralism creed). The popular origins of the new ethnicity lie in the revival of the ethnic consciousness of white ethnics in response to the perceived preferential treatment of racial minority groups (Steinberg, 1981).

The theoretical dilemma that existed within the new ethnicity paradigm was how to explain the persistence of racial and ethnic stratification. Two different explanations have been offered. One explanation is that the persistence of racial and ethnic stratification reflects biological tendencies and that people, by nature, have a basic, primordial need for group identification. This explanation is grounded in sociobiology and primordialism. In his more recent work, entitled *Human Nature, Class and Ethnicity*, Gordon (1978), one of the major early proponents of assimilation theory, emphasized the importance of understanding human nature (i.e., biological predisposition) and its interaction with the social and cultural environment. Gordon (1978: 74) wrote, "Some observers, including myself, . . . have begun to wonder whether there are not biological constants or propensities in human behavior which fall short of the instinct category but which predispose the actor to certain kinds of behavior." In a similar vein, van den Berghe (1981: 80) theorized that ethnic and racial sentiments are extensions of kinship sentiments and, as such, express the sociobiological principle of inclusive fitness. In his analysis, van den Berghe (1981) argued that genetic predisposition for kin selection causes people to behave in racist and ethnocentric ways. Accordingly, racism and discrimination in society and culture were viewed as the sum of individually motivated behaviors that were rooted in genetic predisposition. *According to this essentialist explanation, racial and ethnic stratification are viewed as an almost permanent and inevitable part of human society.*

The alternate explanation rejects biological criteria and relies upon social psychological theories that attribute the failure of minority group assimilation to improper attitudes of majority group members or the lack of self-reliance on the part of minorities (Thompson, 1989). The common denominator for all of these explanations is that they stress some essential property of individuals.

Problems With the Ethnic Paradigm

There are several problems with the ethnic-based paradigm and its so-called *new* form for producing knowledge for understanding race in organizations. In this paradigm, the dualistic oppositional categories of assimilation versus pluralism are emphasized as the solution to questions of discrimination and racism (Glazer & Moynihan, 1970; Omi & Winant, 1986; Thompson, 1989).

Assimilationalism is basically individualistic in its ontology, and in this case, race is largely conceptualized as a problem of prejudiced attitudes or personal and cultural inadequacies of racial and ethnic groups (Thompson, 1989). The fact that certain groups have not been successfully assimilated is not due to the structure of U.S. society and institutions but to psychological or personality characteristics of both whites and minorities (Henriques, 1984; Thompson, 1989). Assimilation is conceptualized as a one-way process that requires non-European, non-English-speaking groups to change to fit the dominant culture (Feagin, 1987). Consequently, researchers have tended to focus on other groups as having race, and questions of "why aren't they like us, or how can they become like us?" dominate. Herein lies one of the major deficiencies in the very premise of the assimilation approach. Inequality is accepted as a natural feature of U.S. society or any other complex social structure and, therefore, inequality itself is a "nonissue" and not part of the analysis (Thompson, 1989: 85).

Assimilation represents an inadequate model for understanding racial hierarchy in organizations. Its best answer to why racial and ethnic minorities are underrepresented in higher level positions in organizations would lie in social psychological explanations, which emphasize cognitive causes of prejudice and discrimination. Sole emphasis on microlevel or individualistic remedies are unlikely to affect existing social and power relations in organizations. Billig (1985) noted that the emphasis placed upon explaining cognitive biases by social categorization theory and other cognitive theories winds up confirming the status quo in the sense that changing the cognitions of individuals is often viewed as less amenable to intervention. Users of the individual-focused social psychology approaches are silent on the sociohistorical dynamics of the capitalist system in creating and maintaining inequality in organizations. Such explanations detract from issues of power and domination in racial dynamics and reflect a failure to analyze both the historically specific experience of racial minorities in U.S. society and the influence that this history has had on their status in organizations (Foner & Lewis, 1982; Takai, 1979).

Furthermore, assimilation within the ethnic paradigm often leads to a "blame-the-victim" explanation of why certain groups have not been assimilated as successfully as other groups (Omi & Winant, 1986). According to Thompson (1989), one of the less explicit assumptions of the ethnic paradigm is the acceptance of the neoclassical view of the very nature of a capitalist economy. In this view, individual opportunity is widely available, and the kind of job one has is a function of choice and skill level. People who fail are seen as making bad choices or not exhibiting the appropriate character traits (Sowell, 1975). Minority group members who do not succeed have abnormal cultural patterns or other deficiencies.

The essentialist element of this argument often results in tautological explanations of success whereby a minority group that has not been subjected to the social and historical conditions of another group is seen as a "good group," which has been successfully assimilated. For example, the contemporary view of Asian Americans as the model minority reinforces the notion that only "good groups," whose members do the right thing, become assimilated. Successful achievement and mobility reflect a group's willingness and ability to accept the norms and values of the majority group.

The theoretical alternative to assimilation, cultural pluralism, supposedly allows for the possibility that groups do not assimilate but remain distinct in terms of cultural identity. However, similar to users of assimilation theory, proponents of cultural pluralism still maintain the existence of an allegedly "normal" (understood to mean superior) majority culture, to which other groups are juxtaposed (Omi & Winant, 1986). Further, they suggest that separation of racial and ethnic groups is natural and immutable. Steinberg (1981) pointed out that cultural pluralism is not a viable option in a society where inequality exists because true cultural pluralism would be based on equality among different groups. In the words of Henriques (1984: 63), "It is a case of putting the ideal cart before the real horse."

Unfortunately, cultural pluralism has often been superficially interpreted as an opportunity to celebrate difference (Yinger, 1986). For example, the influence of this school of thought is reflected in the nascent "managing diversity" discourse appearing in management literature (Thomas, 1990). Yet underlying some work in this area are assumptions like, "Minority workers are less likely to have had satisfactory schooling and training. They may have language, attitude, and cultural problems that prevent them from taking advantage of the jobs that will exist" (Johnston & Packer, 1987: xxvi).

The Writing of Race in the Organization Literature

The influence of the ethnic paradigm and its assumptions are reflected in much of the extant research on race found in the organization literature. Thus, not surprisingly, when management researchers have studied race, much of the research is narrowly focused, ahistorical, and decontextualized; in this research, race is mainly treated as a demographic variable. In their review of 20 journals during the period 1965–1989, Cox and Nkomo (1990) identified 201 articles focusing on race. They reported a notable decline in this type of research during the 1980s. For the most part, the topics and approaches in these articles reproduced the standard organization literature with emphasis on five content areas: affirmative action/equal employment opportunity; staffing, including test validation; job satisfaction; job attitudes and motivation; and performance evaluation.

Research designs were dominated by comparative studies of black and white workers to the neglect of other racial and ethnic groups (Cox & Nkomo, 1990). Within these studies, race was treated mainly as a demographic variable whereby blacks and whites were compared on a standard organizational theory or concept. Studies in the area of job satisfaction typically compared job satisfaction levels of black and white workers (e.g., Jones, James, Bruni, & Sell, 1977; Konar, 1981; Milutinovich & Tsaklanganos, 1978; Moch, 1980; Slocum & Strawser, 1972; Veechio, 1980; Weaver, 1978). Results in this area were largely inconsistent—some studies reported that white employees were more satisfied than black employees, and other studies reported the opposite effect. Although a few of these studies attempted to identify the factors that contributed to differences in levels of satisfaction (e.g., Konar, 1981), in general, the research provides little insight into the complexity of the psychological, organizational, and societal variables that may account for such findings. Often, the results appear to be tautological. For example, to explain their finding that whites were more satisfied with their jobs and that whites associated overall satisfaction more closely with promotion than nonwhites, O'Reilly and Roberts (1973) concluded that whites and nonwhites approach their jobs with different frames of reference.

One of the pervasive questions found within all topics was: "Does discrimination exist?" In this research, emphasis was placed on searching for objective and quantifiable evidence of racial discrimination. For example, a majority of the early articles in the area of affirmative action/equal employment opportunity were focused on whether or not discrimination existed in the occupational distribution of jobs (e.g., Franklin, 1968; Kovarshy, 1964; Northrop, 1969; Taylor, 1968). Representative questions included: To what extent are blacks overrepresented in lower socioeconomic jobs? (Franklin, 1968); Where are blacks employed within the aerospace industry? (Northrop, 1969); and Is there discrimination within the governmental apprentice training program? (Kovarshy, 1964). In the area of staffing, research was focused on discrimination and bias in recruitment and selection outcomes for blacks and whites in organizations (e.g., Brown & Ford, 1977; Newman, 1978; Newman & Krzytofiak, 1979; Stone & Stone, 1987; Terpstra & Larsen, 1980). Typically, explanations were centered on the stereotyping of minority groups.

Over the years, a number of studies have been used to examine bias in performance ratings and evaluation. The level of activity in this area is evidenced by the existence of three comprehensive literature reviews on the subject (Dipboye, 1985; Kraiger & Ford, 1985; Landy & Farr, 1980). According to some studies, ratees received significantly higher ratings from evaluators of their own race (e.g., Schmitt & Lappin, 1980), whereas other studies failed to support the existence of significant race effects on performance evaluation (Mobley, 1982). Still other studies reported results that indicated a complex interaction between the race of the ratee and his or her performance (Hamner, Kim, Baird, & Biogness, 1974). In their 1985 meta-analysis, Kraiger and Ford concluded that ratees tend to receive higher ratings from raters of the same race and that these effects were more pronounced in field studies than in laboratory ratings. Only a handful of researchers explored the processes underlying differences (Cox & Nkomo, 1986; Dipboye, 1985; Pettigrew & Martin, 1987). Most often the explanations were based on a social psychology perspective with an emphasis on rater bias, including stereotyping and perceptual error in information processing.

The other prototypical question underlying much of this literature was: Do racial and ethnic minorities have what it takes to succeed in organizations? or more concisely, Why aren't they like us? Illustrative of this theme are studies that were conducted regarding job attitudes, motivation, and affirmative action. A common question in the research on job attitudes was: Do blacks have different attitudes toward their jobs and work environment than whites? (Alper, 1975; Gavin & Ewen, 1974). Several studies were focused on race differences in motivation (e.g., Bhagat, 1979; Bankart, 1972; Brenner & Tomkiewicz, 1982; Greenhaus & Gavin, 1972; Miner, 1977; Watson & Barone, 1976). An unstated assumption in much of this research might be labeled the deficit hypothesis—whether or not minorities possessed the necessary motivational profile and values needed by organizations. Bhagat (1979) created a model to explain how black ethnic values coupled with negative job experiences have prevented a large majority of the black population from identifying strongly with the work ethic. The approach used in these studies included using a well-known theory of motivation and comparing scores of black employees to white employees. In the few studies that addressed the behavioral dimensions of affirmative action, authors emphasized the assimilation of minorities into organizations. Typical questions included: What changes are needed to assimilate the hard-core black into organizations? (Domm & Stafford, 1972) and Can the Afro-American be an effective executive? (Goode, 1970).

The final theme permeating much of this research was an emphasis on the legal, technical, and mechanical aspects of how organizations could comply with affirmative action and Title VII guidelines. Indeed, the highest concentration of research on race was conducted on the topic of affirmative action (e.g., Hitt & Keats, 1984; Marimont, Maize, Kennedy, & Harley, 1976; Marino, 1980). Some of the authors prescribed mathematical and computer simulation models for effectively implementing affirmative action programs (e.g., Hopkins, 1980; Ledvinka & Hildreth, 1984; Solomon & Messmer, 1980). Effectiveness in this area was most often defined by specifying the technical requirements of affirmative action and equal employment opportunity and fitting those requirements to existing organizational systems. Only a few studies were used to examine the behavioral and social ramifications of affirmative action and equal employment (e.g., Goodman, 1969; Lakin, 1966; Rubin, 1967). A similar emphasis on techniques and mechanics is found in the test validation literature where the issue of differential validity dominated personnel/human resource management research for a number of years (e.g., Bartlett & O'Leary, 1969; Bayroff, 1966; Boehm, 1977; Hunter, Schmidt, & Hunter, 1979; Schmidt, Pearlman, & Hunter, 1980). In this area there was very little discussion of theory about why researchers expected differential validity to occur among different racial and ethnic groups or why test score differentials persisted (Arvey & Faley, 1988). Little attention was given regarding the roles that educational opportunities and other societal factors play in explaining differences or that "universal knowledge" may not be value free.

Several observations can be drawn from the way race was considered in management studies. Much of the research lies along the prejudice-discrimination axis, with an emphasis on discovering objective evidence of racial discrimination and racial differences in behavior, primarily between blacks and whites. This is consistent with the premises underlying the ethnicity paradigm that race can largely be understood as a problem of prejudiced attitudes or personal and cultural inadequacies of racial minorities. A notable exception was the work of Alderfer, Alderfer, Tucker, and Tucker (1980). Using an intergroup framework that emphasized the interaction of power differences at the group, organizational, and societal levels, they examined the broad issue of *race relations* within an organizational setting.

What is most striking about the management literature is researchers' fixation on searching for differences. Although this fixation may reflect the positivist approach to research adopted by many management scholars, it raises important issues for how race has been conceptualized. When no significant differences were found, authors were likely to conclude that race had no effect. This might be interpreted as an affirmation of the universality of management concepts. Another interpretation, consistent with the theoretical premises of the ethnicity paradigm, is that there really are no differences between racial minority groups and the European immigrants who successfully achieved assimilation. In contrast, when significant behavioral differences were reported, explanations were often focused on inadequate socialization of racial minorities to the norms and requirements for successful accomplishment or prejudice or stereotyping by majority group members. Conspicuously absent from these articles is any suggestion or recognition of the different sociohistorical experience of African-Americans or other racial minorities in the United States. There was little awareness that racial minorities may have something to contribute to organizations or that perhaps race can inform our understanding of organizations in other ways. For the most part, in this literature, race has been considered an issue or a problem. Or race enters the discussion of organizations only when "minority" employees are studied. Aside from Alderfer and his colleagues (1980), there were no researchers in the studies reviewed who examined the meaning of race for majority group members. This omission reflects an unconscious assumption by organizational researchers that majority group members do not have a racial identity and, consequently, it is a "nontopic" for research.

In summary, the questions that addressed race in the organizational literature echo the assumptions and themes of the ethnicity paradigm. Further, lest we think that the *managing diversity* discourse represents a *new* approach, we should be reminded that it may be only as *new* as the *new ethnicity*. Our conceptualization of race in organizations has been constrained by these theoretical orientations, and, consequently, a necessary step toward rewriting race is recognizing these influences.

Rewriting Race into the Study of Organizations

To rewrite race, we must not continue the emperor's procession by remaining silent about race or studying it within the narrowly defined ethnicity-based paradigm that has dominated much of our research. First, we must acknowledge that the emperor is indeed naked. Organizations are not race-neutral entities. Race is and has been present in organizations, even if this idea has not been explicitly recognized. Second, rewriting race is not a matter of simply clothing the emperor, but the emperor must be dethroned as the universal, the only reality. We need to revise our understanding of the very concept of race and its historical and political meaning. Only then can race be used as a productive analytical concept for understanding the nature of organizations.

Alternative Frameworks

A useful starting point is to examine alternative theoretical frameworks for understanding the complexity and nature of race. For example, power-conflict theories of race and ethnic relations offer ways to move beyond sole reliance on assimilation models.

Power-conflict approaches to race and ethnicity emphasize issues of economic power, inequalities in access to material resources and labor markets, and the historical development of racism (Bonacich, 1980; Cox, 1948; Reich, 1981). One of the earliest proponents of these approaches (Cox, 1948) argued that racial exploitation and race prejudice developed with the rise of capitalism and nationalism. In Cox's analysis, American colonies imported African slaves to fill a particular labor need and simultaneously incorporated the ideology of racism as a justification of slavery. He contended that the idea of racial inferiority didn't precede the use of minority groups as servile labor but that an ideology of racial inferiority developed to maintain Africans and other racial minorities in a servile status. According to Cox, the racial division of labor into white and black workers hindered any positive contact between the white and black masses. Thus, the persistence of racial stratification in society was not a function of atomistic individuals or cultural deficiencies of minorities but was rooted in the class positions of workers.

Reich's (1981) class-conflict theory of racial inequality attempts to explain the meaning of race within the context of an advanced capitalist system. Like Edwards (1979), Reich (1981) conceptualized the workplace as contested terrain wherein workers and capitalists engage in power struggles over income distribution and material resources. White workers do not benefit from racial inequality but capitalists do, and the very organization of jobs in the workplace is structured to exploit the existence of racial and other divisions among workers. Racial antagonism among workers inhibits the collective strength of workers and sustains the power of capitalists.

These and other power-conflict theories attempt to analyze race within the relations of capitalists' production without reducing it to an epiphenomenon (Thompson, 1989; Wilhelm, 1983).

Thus, if applied to organizational analysis, power-conflict theories would focus our attention on understanding how organizations have become racially constructed, the power relations that sustain racial divisions and racial domination, and the important role of capitalist modes of production in maintaining these divisions.

Omi and Winant's (1986) racial-formation theory represents another alternative formulation of race. They argued that race is preeminently a sociohistorical concept whose meanings and categories are given concrete expression by the specific social relations and historical context in which they are embedded. They noted, for example, that in the United States with the consolidation of racial slavery, a racially based understanding of society was set in motion, which resulted in the shaping of a specific racial identity for both slaves and European settlers. Africans with specific ethnic identities became simply "black," and European settlers previously identified as Christian or English and free became "white" (Omi & Winant, 1986: 64).

Race occupies a central position in our understanding of social relations, and in their theory, Omi and Winant (1986: 66) distinguish between two levels of social relations: micro and macro. At the microlevel, race is a matter of individuality, of the formation of identity. The ways we understand ourselves, our experiences, our interactions with others, and our day-to-day activities are all shaped by racial meanings and racial awareness. At the macrolevel, race is a matter of collectivity, of the formation of social structures. These authors conceived of social structures as a series of economic, political, and cultural/ideological sites, which represented a region of social life with a coherent set of constitutive social relations. For example, at the economic level, the very definition of labor and the allocation of jobs among workers have been dependent on race as an organizing principle. Consequently, in this case, the racial order is organized and enforced by the continuity and interaction between the microlevel and macrolevel of social relations. Racial discrimination within the economic structure has consequences for individual identity at the microlevel.

The term *racial formation* in Omi and Winant's (1986: 61) model refers to the process by which social, economic, and political forces determine the content and importance of racial categories and the subsequent process through which these categories are, in turn, shaped by racial meanings. Accordingly, the meaning of race is defined and contested throughout society, in both collective action and personal practice. In the process, racial categories themselves are formed, transformed, destroyed, and reformed. These authors caution not only against the tendency to view race as an essence (i.e., as something fixed or objective) but also against the tendency to view race as a mere illusion that will disappear with the correct social order.

Similarly, Essed (1991) argued that because race is an organizing principle of many social relations, the fundamental social relations of society are *racialized* relations. She conceptualized race as both an ideological and a social construction with structural expressions. Using cross-cultural empirical data, Essed (1991) developed a theory of everyday racism, which attempts to build upon both the micro and macro perspectives of race and ethnicity. Essed defined *everyday racism* as "a process in which (a) socialized racist notions are integrated into meanings that make practices immediately definable and manageable, (b) practices with racist implications become in themselves familiar and repetitive, and (c) underlying racial and ethnic relations are actualized and reinforced through these routine or familiar practices in everyday situations" (1991: 52). The three main practices are marginalization (a form of oppression), containment (a form of repression), and problematization (ideological constructions legitimizing exclusion through hierarchical organization of difference). The integration of racism into everyday situations through these practices activates and reproduces underlying power relations.

Omi and Winant's (1986) theory of racial formation and Essed's (1991) theory of everyday racism emphasize the instability of race as a natural category and the impossibility of maintaining the essentialist position about race that sustains the ethnicity paradigm. At the same time, these theories help in understanding the reproduction of race from its historical to contemporary site in particular forms that occupy every part of society. They suggest that we have left out an important analytical concept for understanding organizations and that if race forms the core of individual, social, and institutional life in the United States, then we need explicit theories of race and ethnicity to overcome this omission.

Other theoretical approaches that have race at the center can be found in the literature and research in African-American and African studies, Asian studies, and Chicano/Latino studies. This literature can also provide a focus for developing theoretical content specifically about race and can help us to ask different questions than those that stem solely from the ethnicity paradigm.

For example, African-American and African studies, or Black studies, are ideologically and philosophically distinct from European social scientific theory because in them Africa is viewed as the genesis and foundation of knowledge and study of black people (Anderson, 1990). *Black studies* has been defined as "an analysis of the factors and conditions which have affected the economic, political, psychological, and legal status of African-Americans as well as the African in the Diaspora from the social reality of their own experience" (Gordon, 1978: 231). The early work of Black studies scholars called attention to the exclusion of the culture and experience of blacks from textbooks and curricula of educational institutions (Karenga, 1984). Despite this exclusion from mainstream academia, a great deal of scholarly work had been previously produced and generated about the experience of black people (e.g., Bennett, 1966; Diop, 1955; Du Bois, 1961; Fanon, 1963). Initial goals of Black studies were to add to the body of knowledge about blacks within the various disciplines. Taylor (1990) noted that most early attempts failed to move theory substantially beyond the extant paradigms of mainstream social science and research centered around relabeling familiar concepts and adapting existing research strategies.

A second strand of Black studies emerged that has been devoted to a critical assessment of traditional social science paradigms and the systematic articulation of a "black perspective," from which the development of new theories and alternative interpretation of the black community and its relation to the larger society could be advanced (e.g., Cheek, 1987; Gates, 1985; Kershaw, 1990). An effort was made to move away from the "pathological behavior" model of the black community. These strands have appeared as black psychology and black sociology, and they can be found in many other social science disciplines.

For example, within black psychology the attempt has been to build conceptual models to organize, explain, and understand the psychosocial behavior of African-Americans. These models are based on the primary dimensions of an African-American world view instead of the traditional psychology concerned mainly with categorization, mental measurement, and the establishment of norms (Azibo, 1990; Guthrie, 1976; White, 1984). Cross (1978) and others (e.g., Parham, 1989) have developed a model of racial identity for African-Americans. The model describes a process of psychological Nigrescence that hypothesizes the kinds of changes that occur in the racial identity of African-Americans at various points in the life cycle. Research addressing specific applications of Nigrescence theories can be found in the areas of value orientations (Carter & Helmes, 1987) and self-actualization (Parham & Helms, 1985). More recently, research has been focused on models of white racial identity (Helms, 1990). Another useful concept for understanding the experiences of racial and ethnic minorities that has been widely used is *biculturalism* (Bell, 1990), or what Du Bois (1961) called *double consciousness*. Users of this concept recognize that African-Americans have both Afrocentric and Eurocentric elements of culture and racial identity.

Within the discipline of history, scholars researching African-American experiences have sought to correct the theoretical and methodological errors that questioned the historical actuality of African societies (Davidson, 1991; Rodney, 1974) and the nature and effect of slavery upon African-Americans. By examining slave narratives, songs, and other historical documents, scholars in the field have offered re-visions that characterize slaves as more than empty vessels who were acted upon, shaped, and dominated by their European American enslavers (Blassingame, 1979; White, 1984). Slaves had cultural, psychological, and technical resources from their African heritage that not only contributed to the development of the United States but also helped them to resist the devastation of slavery. Revisiting the early history of African-American and other minority workers and their exclusion from skilled industrial jobs in organizations also can inform our understanding of their present status (Foner & Lewis, 1982; Takai, 1979).

A third strand of research has developed, which calls attention to the need for theoretical development and construction of ideas toward building a new social science (Taylor, 1990). The aim of such research is to move beyond explanations of black institutional life and behavior toward theoretical formulations that build upon a more expansive lens. That is, how would social science concepts differ if we used race as a core analytical concept? What concepts and constructs have been omitted? Other areas of development include analyses that examine the intersection of race with gender and class (e.g., Hill-Collins, 1990; King, 1988; Wilson, 1984).

Implications of Alternative Frameworks

Although I have expanded upon African-American studies as a body of knowledge from which management studies can draw, analogous work can be found for other racial groups. My purpose is not to suggest the replacement of Eurocentric theories with Afrocentric or Asian-centered ones. Yes, these approaches do imply efforts toward accounting for the absence of or any reference to perspectives from other groups in understanding organizations; they also imply that we not view racial minorities solely as deviants or problems in the study of organizations. Yet, such changes do not simply mean *adding* on studies of these groups. The major point is that we re-vision the very way we "see" organizations. Clearly, the specific historical context of race should be considered in the development and use of concepts. A ready example can be found in Thomas's (1989) study of mentoring in organizations. He explicitly draws on the historical impact of social taboos from our legacy of slavery in order to understand the dynamics of present-day cross-race mentoring relationships. Finally, new approaches would suggest different questions about race in organizations. Table 1 contains a comparison of the questions that have emanated from the ethnicity paradigm and the kinds of questions supported from the alternative theoretical frameworks and bodies of literature discussed in this section.

Rewriting race also suggests recognizing the limitations of positivist research methods. Research strategies determine the kinds of knowledge produced, and a realistic view of the research

TABLE 1

Asked and Unasked Questions About Race

Research Questions From Ethnicity Paradigm
Does discrimination exist in recruitment, selection, etc.?
Can the Afro-American be an effective executive?
Do blacks identify with the traditional American work ethic?
Do blacks' and whites' problem-solving styles differ?
How can blacks/minorities be assimilated into organizations?
How can organizations manage diversity?
How can organizations comply with equal employment opportunity/affirmative action requirements?
Do blacks and whites have the same job expectations?
Are there different levels of motivation between black and white employees?
Is there racial bias in performance ratings?
What is the role of stereotyping in job bias?
Does differential test validity exist?

Silenced Research Questions From Alternative Paradigms
How are societal race relations reproduced in the workplace?
How did white males come to dominant management positions?
To what extent is race built into the definition of a "manager"?
What are the implications of racial identity for organization theories based on individual identity?
How does racial identity affect organizational experiences?
How does the racial identity of white employees influence their status and interaction with other groups?
Why, despite national policies like affirmative action, does inequality still exist in the workplace?
Are assimilation and managing diversity the only two means of removing racial inequality in the workplace?
How do organizational processes contribute to the maintenance of racial domination and stratification?
Are white male-dominated organizations also built on underlying assumptions about gender and class?
What are the patterns of relationships among different racial minorities in organizations?

process encourages us to use these strategies in different ways (Morgan, 1983). A majority of the organizational studies mentioned in this article relied upon comparative designs in which race was categorized as a two-level variable (i.e., black and white). There are two basic problems with this approach. First, comparative designs too often adopt a position of cultural monism that assumes equivalence of groups across race (Azibo, 1990). In such a case, meaningful and valid interpretations of any observed differences are hindered. An awareness of the appropriate use of emic (within culture) and etic (cross-culture) approaches is critical (Triandis, 1972). Azibo (1990) noted that researchers must seek a balance between the assumption that cultures can best be understood in their own terms and the desire to establish universal theories of human behavior. Research efforts in this direction can be found in the works of Marin and Triandis, 1985; Triandis, Marin, Lisanky, and Betancourt, 1984; and Cox, Lobel, and McLeod, 1991.

Second, categorization of subjects is an essentialist view of race as a discrete, demographic variable that can be objectively observed and measured. Reconceptualizing race not as a simple property of individuals but as an integral dynamic of organizations implies a move toward phenomenological and historical research methods that would contribute toward building theories and knowledge about both how race is produced and how it is a core feature of organizations.

Conclusion

I have argued that we should not continue our silence about race, and when we do study it, that we expand our approaches beyond the ethnicity-based paradigm that has implicitly dominated much of our research. This expansion would allow race to become a productive analytical category used in understanding organizations. What does it mean to use race as an analytical category? This use suggests a view of organizations as made up of *race relations* played out in power struggles, which includes the realization that "race" is not a stable category. Then, not only would we not conduct research on "race in organizations" the way we have done it in the past, but we would also need to rethink the very nature of organizations.

Finally, it is important to point out that race is just one part of a more complicated web of socially constructed elements of identity formation such as gender and class. Race, gender, and class can form interlocking bases of domination in social relations (Hill-Collins, 1990; Spelman, 1988). Although each part may be manifested in its own peculiar and distinct way, the common factor is domination based on notions of inferiority and superiority. To the extent that each system reinforces and reproduces the other, an analysis of organizations cannot exclude the importance of these significant elements of identity. Indeed, the challenge before us becomes much more complex than simply clothing the emperor!

References

Adorno, T. W., Frenkel-Brunswick, E., Levinson, D. J., II, & Sanford, R. N. 1950. *The authoritarian personality.* New York: Harper & Row.

Alderfer, C. P. 1982. Problems of changing white males' behavior and beliefs concerning race relations. In P. S. Goodman & Associates (Eds.), *Change in organizations:* 122–165. San Francisco: Jossey-Bass.

Alderfer, C. P., Alderfer, C. J., Tucker, L., & Tucker, R. 1980. Diagnosing race relations in management. *Journal of Applied Behavioral Science,* 16: 135–166.

Allport, G. 1954. *The nature of prejudice.* New York: Doubleday.

Alper, S. W. 1975. Racial differences in job and work environment priorities among newly hired college graduates. *Journal of Applied Psychology,* 60: 120–134.

Anderson, H. C. 1968. *Forty-two stories* (M. R. James, Trans.). London: Faber & Faber.

Anderson, T. (Ed.). 1990. *Black studies: Theory, method, and cultural perspectives.* Pullman: Washington State University Press.

Arvey, R. D., & Faley, R. H. 1988. *Fairness in selecting employees.* Reading, MA: Addison-Wesley.

Azibo, D. A. Y. 1990. Personality, clinical, and social psychological research on blacks: Appropriate & inappropriate research frameworks. In T. Anderson (Ed.), *Black studies: Theory, method and cultural perspectives:* 25–41. Pullman: Washington State University Press.

Bankart, P. C. 1972. Attribution of motivation in same-race and different race stimulus persons. *Human Relations,* 215: 35–45.

Bartlett, C. J., & O'Leary, B. S. 1969. A differential prediction model to moderate the effects of heterogeneous groups in personnel selection and classification. *Personnel Psychology,* 22: 1–18.

Bayroff, A. 1966. Test technology and equal employment opportunity. *Personnel Psychology,* 19: 35–39.

Bell, E. L. 1990. The bicultural life experiences of career-oriented black women. *Journal of Organizational Behavior,* 11: 459–477.

Bennett, L. 1966. *Before the Mayflower: A history of the negro in America, 1619–1964.* Baltimore: Penguin Books.

Bhagat, R. 1979. Black-white ethnic differences in identification with the work ethic: Some implications for organizational integration. *Academy of Management Review,* 4: 381–391.

Billig, M. 1985. Prejudice, categorization and particularization: From a perceptual to a rhetorical approach. *European Journal of Social Psychology,* 15: 79–103.

Blanton, M. 1987. *Racial theories,* Cambridge: Cambridge University Press.

Blassingame, J. 1979. *The slave community: Plantation life in the antebellum south.* New York: Oxford University Press.

Blauner, B. 1989. *Black lives, white lives: Three decades of race relations in America.* Berkeley: University of California Press.

Blauner, R. 1972. *Racial oppression in America.* New York: Harper & Row.

Boehm, V. R. 1977. Differential prediction—A methodological artifact. *Journal of Applied Psychology,* 62: 146–154.

Bonacich, E. 1980. Class approaches to ethnicity and race. *Insurgent Sociologist,* 10: 9–23.

Brenner, O. C., & Tomkiewicz, J. 1982. Job orientation of black and white college graduates in business. *Personnel Psychology,* 35: 89–103.

Brown, H. A., & Ford, D. L., Jr. 1977. An exploratory analysis of discrimination in the employment of black MBA graduates. *Journal of Applied Psychology,* 62: 50–56.

Carter, R. T., & Helms, J. E. 1987. Relationship of black value orientation to racial identity attitudes. *Measurement and Evaluation in Counseling and Development,* 19: 185–195.

Cheek, D. K. 1987. Social science: A vehicle for white supremacy? *International Journal for the Advancement of Counseling,* 10: 59–69.

Cox, O. C. 1948. *Caste, class, and race: A study in social dynamics.* New York: Doubleday.

Cox, T., Jr., & Nkomo, S. M. 1986. Differential appraisal criteria based on race of the ratee. *Group and Organization Studies,* 11: 101–119.

Cox, T., Jr., & Nkomo, S. M. 1990. Invisible men and women: A status report on race as a variable in organization behavior research. *Journal of Organizational Behavior,* 11: 419–431.

Cox, T., Jr., Lobel, S., & McLeod, P. 1991. Effects of ethnic group cultural differences on cooperative versus competitive behavior in a group task. *Academy of Management Journal,* 34: 827–847.

Cross, W. E. 1978. The Cross and Thomas models of psychological nigrescence. *Journal of Black Psychology,* 5: 13–19.

Davidson, B. 1991. *African civilization revisited.* Trenton, NJ: Africa World Press.

Diop, C. A. 1955. *The African origin of civilization: Myth or reality.* Paris: Presence Africaine.

Dipboye, R. L. 1985. Some neglected variables in research on discrimination in appraisals. *Academy of Management Review,* 10: 116–127.

Domm, D., & Stafford, J. 1972. Assimilating blacks into the organization. *California Management Review,* 15(1): 46–51.

Dovidio, J. F., & Gaertner, S. L. (Eds.). 1986. *Prejudice, discrimination, and racism.* Orlando, FL: Academic Press.

Du Bois, W. E. 1961. *The souls of black folk.* Greenwich, CT: Fawcett.

Edwards, R. 1979. *Contested terrain.* New York: Basic Books.

Essed, P. 1991. *Everyday racism.* Newbury Park, CA: Sage.

Fanon, F. 1963. *The wretched of the earth.* New York: Grove Press.

Feagin, J. 1987. Changing black Americans to fit a racist system? *Journal of Social Issues,* 43(1): 85–89.

Foner, P. S., & Lewis, R. L. (Eds.). 1982. *The black worker: A documentary history from colonial times to the present.* Philadelphia: Temple University Press.

Franklin, R. 1968. A framework for the analysis of inter-urban negro-white economic differentials. *Industrial and Labor Relations Review,* 2: 209–223.

Gavin, J., & Ewen, R. 1974. Racial differences in job attitudes and performance—Some theoretical considerations and empirical findings. *Personnel Psychology,* 27: 455–464.

Gates, H. L., Jr. 1985. Editor's introduction: Writing "race" and the difference it makes. In H. L. Gates, Jr. (Ed.), *"Race," writing, and difference:* 1–20. Chicago: University of Chicago Press.

Gates, H. L., Jr. 1988. *The signifying monkey: A theory of Afro-American literary criticism.* New York: Oxford University Press.

Glazer, N. 1987. *Affirmative discrimination: Ethnic inequality and public policy.* Cambridge, MA: Harvard University Press.

Glazer, N., & Moynihan, D. P. 1970. *Beyond the melting pot: The Negroes, Puerto Ricans, Jews, Italians, and Irish of New York City.* Cambridge, MA: MIT Press.

Goode, K. 1970. Can the Afro-American be an effective executive? *California Management Review,* 13(1): 27–30.

Goodman, R. 1969. A hidden issue in minority employment. *California Management Review,* 11(1): 22–26.

Gordon, M. M. 1964. *Assimilation in American life: The role of race, religion, and national origin.* New York: Oxford University Press.

Gordon, M. M. 1978. *Human nature, class, and ethnicity.* New York: Oxford University Press.

Guthrie, R. V. 1976. *Even the rat was white: A historical view of psychology.* New York: Harper & Row.

Gutman, H. G. 1977. *Work, culture, and society in industrializing America.* New York: Knopf.

Greenhaus, J., & Gavin, J. 1972. The relationship between expectancies and job behavior for white and black employees. *Personnel Psychology,* 25: 449–455.

Hamner, W. C., Kim, J. S., Baird, L., & Biogness, W. J. 1974. Race and sex as determinants of ratings by potential employers in a simulated work-sampling task. *Journal of Applied Psychology,* 59: 705–711.

Harding, S. 1986. *The science question in feminism.* Ithaca, NY: Cornell University Press.

Helms, J. G. 1990. *Black and white racial identity: Theory, research, and practice.* Westport, CT: Greenwood Press.

Henriques, J. 1984. Social psychology and the politics of racism. In J. Henriques, W. Hollway, C. Urwin, C. Venn, & V. Walkerdine (Eds.), *Changing the subject: Psychology, social regulations and subjectivity:* 60–89. London: Methuen.

Hewstone, M. 1989. Intergroup attribution: Some implications for the study of ethnic prejudice. In J. P. Van Oudenhoven & T. M. Williemsen (Eds.), *Ethnic minorities: Social psychological perspectives:* 25–42. Amsterdam: Sivets & Zeitlinger.

Hill-Collins, P. 1990. *Black feminist thought: Knowledge consciousness, and the politics of empowerment.* Boston: Unwin Hyman.

Hitt, M., & Keats, B. 1984. Empirical identification of the criteria for effective affirmative action programs. *Journal of Applied Behavioral Science.* 20: 203–222.

Hopkins, D. 1980. Models for affirmative action planning and evaluation. *Management Science,* 26: 994–1006.

Hunter, J. E., Schmidt, F. L., & Hunter, R. 1979. Differential validity of employment tests by race: A comprehensive review and analysis. *Psychological Bulletin,* 85: 721–735.

Johnston, W., & Packer, A. 1987. *Workforce 2000: Work and workers for the 21st century.* Indianapolis, IN: Hudson Institute.

Jones, A. P., James, L. R., Bruni, J. R., & Sell, S. B. 1977. Black white differences in work environment perceptions and job satisfaction and its correlates. *Personnel Psychology,* 30: 5–16.

Joseph, G. G., Reddy, V., & Searle-Chatterjee, M. 1990. Eurocentrism in the social sciences. *Race & Class,* 31(4): 1–26.

Karenga, R. 1984. *Introduction to black studies.* Los Angeles: Kawaida Publications.

Kershaw, T. 1990. The emerging paradigm in black studies. In T. Anderson (Ed.), *Black studies: Theory, method, and cultural perspectives:* 17–24. Pullman: Washington State University Press.

King, D. K. 1988. Multiple jeopardy, multiple consciousness: The context of black feminist ideology, *Signs,* 14: 42–72.

Keto, C. T. 1989. *The Africa centered perspective of history.* Blackwood, NJ: KA Publications.

Konar, E. 1981. Explaining racial differences in job satisfaction: A reexamination of the data. *Journal of Applied Psychology,* 66: 522–524.

Kovarshy, I. 1964. Management, racial discrimination, and apprentice training programs. *Academy of Management Journal,* 7: 196–203.

Kraiger, K., & Ford, J. 1985. A meta-analysis of ratee race effects in performance ratings. *Journal of Applied Psychology,* 70: 56–65.

Kuhn, T. 1962. *The structure of scientific revolutions.* Chicago: University of Chicago Press.

Lakin, M. 1966. Human relations training and interracial social action: Problems in self and client definition. *Journal of Applied Behavioral Science,* 2(2): 139–149.

Landy, F. J., & Farr, S. L. 1980. Performance rating. *Psychological Bulletin,* 87: 72–107.

Ledvinka, J., & Hildreth, W. B. 1984. Integrating planned change intervention and computer simulation technology: The case of affirmative action. *Journal of Applied Behavioral Science,* 20(2): 125–140.

Lefkowitz, J. 1972. Differential validity: Ethnic groups as a moderator in predicting tenure. *Personnel Psychology,* 25: 223–240.

Marimont, R. B., Maize, B., Kennedy, P., & Harley, E. 1976. Using FAIR to set numerical EEO goals. *Public Personnel Management,* 5(3): 191–198.

Marin, G., & Triandis, H. C. 1985. Allocentrism as an important characteristic of the behavior of Latin Americans and Hispanics. In R. Diaz-Guerrero (Ed.), *Cross-cultural and national studies in social psychology:* 85–104. Amsterdam: Elsevier Science.

Marino, K. E. 1980. A preliminary investigation into the behavioral dimensions of affirmative action compliance. *Journal of Applied Psychology,* 65: 346–350.

Merton, R. K. 1949. Discrimination and the American creed. In R. MacIver (Ed.), *Discrimination and national welfare:* 99–126. New York: Harper & Row.

Milutinovich, J. S., & Tsaklanganos, A. 1976. The impact of perceived community prosperity on job satisfaction of black and white workers. *Academy of Management Journal,* 19: 49–65.

Miner, J. 1977. Motivational potential for upgrading among minority and female managers. *Journal of Applied Psychology,* 62: 691–697.

Minnich, E. K. 1990. *Transforming knowledge.* Philadelphia: Temple University Press.

Mobley, W. 1982. Supervisor and employee race and sex effects on performance appraisals: A field study of adverse impact and generalizability. *Academy of Management Journal,* 25: 598–606.

Moch, M. 1980. Racial differences in job satisfaction: Testing four common explanations. *Journal of Applied Psychology,* 65: 299–306.

Morgan, G. 1983. Toward a more reflective social science. In G. Morgan (Ed.), *Beyond method: Strategies for social research:* 368–376. Beverly Hills, CA: Sage.

Myrdal, G. 1944. *An American dilemma.* New York: Harper & Row.

Newman, J. M. 1978. Discrimination in recruitment: An empirical analysis. *Industrial and Labor Relations Review,* 32; 15–23.

Newman, J. M., & Krzytofiak, F. 1979. Self-reports versus unobtrusive measures: Balancing method variance and ethical concerns in employment discrimination research. *Journal of Applied Psychology,* 64: 2–85.

Nkomo, S. M. 1988. Race and sex: The forgotten case of the black female manager. In S. Rose & L. Larwood (Eds.), *Women's careers: Pathways and pitfalls:* 133–150. New York: Praeger.

Northrop, H. 1969. The negro in aerospace work. *California Management Review,* 11(4): 11–26.

Omi, M., & Winant, H. 1986. *Racial formation in the United States: From the 1960s to the 1980s.* New York: Routledge & Kegan Paul.

O'Reilly, C. A., & Roberts, K. M. 1973. Job satisfaction among whites and nonwhites: A cross-cultural approach. *Journal of Applied Psychology,* 57: 295–299.

Oudenhoven, J. P. V., & Williemsen, T. M. (Eds.). 1989. *Ethnic minorities: Social psychological perspectives.* Amsterdam: Sivets & Zeitlinger.

Parham, T. A. 1989. Cycles of psychological nigrescence. *Counseling Psychologist,* 17(2): 187–225.

Parham, T. A., & Helms, J. E. 1985. Relation of racial identity attitudes to self-actualization and affective statements of black students. *Journal of Counseling Psychology,* 32: 431–440.

Park, R. E. 1950. *Race and culture.* Glencoe, IL: Free Press. (Original work published in 1939)

Pettigrew, T. F. 1979. The ultimate attribution error. Extending Allport's cognitive analysis of prejudice. *Personality and Social Psychology Bulletin,* 5: 461–476.

Pettigrew, T. F., & Martin, J. 1987. Shaping the organizational context for black American inclusion. *Journal of Social Forces,* 43(1): 41–78.

Reich, M. 1981. *Racial inequality.* Princeton, NJ: Princeton University Press.

Rodney, W. 1974. *How Europe underdeveloped Africa.* Washington, DC: Howard University Press.

Rubin, I. 1967. The reduction of prejudice through laboratory training. *Journal of Applied Behavioral Science,* 3(1): 29–51.

Schmidt, F. L., Pearlman, K., & Hunter, J. 1980. The validity and fairness of employment and educational tests for Hispanic Americans: A review and analysis. *Personnel Psychology,* 33: 705–724.

Schmitt, N., & Lappin, M. 1980. Race and sex as determinants of the mean and variance of performance ratings. *Journal of Applied Psychology,* 65: 428–435.

Slocum, J., Jr., & Strawser, R. 1972. Racial differences in job attitudes. *Journal of Applied Psychology,* 56: 28–32.

Solomon, R. J., & Messmer, D. J. 1980. Implications of the Bakke decision in implementing affirmative action programs: A decision model. *Decision Sciences,* 11: 312–324.

Sowell, T. 1975. *Race and economics.* New York: David McKay.

Spelman, E. V. 1988. *Inessential woman: Problems of exclusion in feminist thought.* Boston: Beacon Press.

Steinberg, S. 1981. *The ethnic myth.* New York: Atheneum.

Stone, D. L., & Stone, E. F. 1987. Effects of missing application-blank information on personnel selection decisions: Do privacy protection strategies bias the outcome? *Journal of Applied Psychology,* 72: 452–456.

Tajfel, H. 1969. Cognitive aspects of prejudice. *Journal of Social Issues,* 25(4): 79–97.

Tajfel, H. 1970. Experiments in intergroup discrimination. *Scientific American,* 223(5): 96–102.

Tajfel, H. 1981. *Human groups and social categories.* Cambridge: Cambridge University Press.

Tajfel, H., & Turner, J. C. 1979. *An integrative theory of intergroup conflict: The social psychology of intergroup relations.* Monterey, CA: Brooks/Cole.

Tajfel, H., & Turner, J. C. 1986. The social identity of theory of intergroup behavior. In S. Worchel & W. G. Austin (Eds.), *Psychology of intergroup relations:* 7–24. Chicago: Nelson-Hall.

Takai, R. 1979. *Iron cages: Race and culture in nineteenth-century America.* New York: Knopf.

Taylor, D. 1968. Discrimination and occupational wage differences in the market for unskilled labor. *Industrial and Labor Relations Review,* 21: 373–390.

Taylor, Ronald L. 1990. The study of black people: A survey of empirical and theoretical models. In T. Anderson (Ed.), *Black studies: Theory, method and cultural perspectives:* 11–15. Pullman: Washington State University Press.

Terpstra, D., & Larsen, M. 1985. A note on job type and applicant race as determinants of hiring decisions. *Journal of Occupational Psychology,* 53(3): 117–119.

Thomas, D. A. 1989. Mentoring and irrationality: The role of racial taboos. *Human Resource Management,* 28: 279–290.

Thomas, R. R. 1990. From affirmative action to affirming diversity. *Harvard Business Review,* 68(2): 107–117.

Thompson, R. H. 1989. *Theories of ethnicity: A critical appraisal.* New York: Greenwood Press.

Triandis, H. C. 1972. *The analysis of subjective culture.* New York: Wiley.

Triandis, H. C., Marin, G., Lisansky, J., & Betancourt, H. 1984. Simpatia as a cultural script of hispanics. *Journal of Personality and Social Psychology,* 47: 1363–1375.

van den Berghe, P. 1967. *Race and racism.* New York: Wiley.

van den Berghe, P. 1981. *The ethnic phenomenon.* New York: Elsevier.

van Dijk, T. A. 1987. *Communicating racism: Ethnic prejudice in thought and talk.* Newbury Park, CA: Sage.

Veechio, R. 1980. Worker alienation as a moderator of the job quality—job satisfaction relationship: The case of racial differences. *Academy of Management Journal,* 23: 479–486.

Watson, J. G., & Barone, S. 1976. The self-concept, personal values, and motivational orientations of black and white managers. *Academy of Management Journal,* 19: 36–48.

Weaver, C. N. 1978. Black-white correlates of job satisfaction. *Journal of Applied Psychology,* 63: 255–258.

White, J. L. 1984. *The psychology of blacks: An African-American perspective.* Englewood Cliffs, NJ: Prentice-Hall.

Wilder, D. A. 1986. Cognitive factors affecting the success of intergroup contact. In S. Worchel & W. G. Austin (Eds.), *Psychology of intergroup relations:* 49–66. Chicago: Nelson Hall.

Wilhelm, S. 1983. *Black in white America.* Cambridge, MA: Schenkman.

Wilson, W. J. 1984. *The declining significance of race.* Chicago: Chicago University Press.

Yinger, J. M. 1986. Intersecting strands in the theorization of race and ethnic relations. In J. Rex & D. Mason (Eds.), *Theories of race and ethnic relations:* 20–41. Cambridge: Cambridge University Press.

E PLURIBUS UNUM? ACADEMIC STRUCTURE, CULTURE, AND THE CASE OF FEMINIST SCHOLARSHIP

PATRICIA J. GUMPORT

E pluribus unum—out of many, one. Higher education scholars have used this phrase both descriptively and prescriptively. Both as metaphor and motto, the phrase suggests that, despite a plurality of interests and specialties in academic life, there is cohesion within the organization of academic work and that this cohesion corresponds to lines of formal structure based on one's disciplinary and institutional affiliation. In this article, I call into question the utility of this idealized image as a conceptual frame for understanding complex variations in academic culture. Drawing on recent empirical data about the formation of intentional intellectual communities, I analyze feminist scholarship as a contemporary current in academic life.

Two significant findings are: (1) Faculty seek and find intellectual communities beyond lines of formal structure (e.g., department, institution); and (2) The departmental organization of academic work does not necessarily function as an integrating framework for resolving conflicting interests and advancing common ones. This analysis concludes with an invitation to rethink the premises about culture and structure that are implicit in prevailing conceptual frameworks for studying change in higher education organizations.

Frameworks for Understanding Academic Change

The current configuration of departments and disciplines across campuses evolved in an evolutionary process of intellectual and social differentiation, according to functionalist accounts of academic change in American higher education (e.g., Blau 1973; Clark 1983; Rudolph 1981; Trow 1984). From this perspective, disputes over curricula and new academic programs have been handled by additive solutions—that is, expanding to cover a plurality of interests rather than replacing what counts as worthwhile academic pursuits. Regardless of whether this explanation is the definitive historical explanation, it is apparent that differentiation has its limits. Fewer resources and more capital-intensive academic endeavors render infinite expansion an untenable solution for solving conflicting academic visions.

With varying degrees of urgency over the past decade, some scholars have challenged higher education to "pull itself together" against the current proliferation of new fields and the "blurring of genres" (Geertz 1983; Clark 1983, 1987). Other scholars have warned that "faculty are even more sharply divided than in previous years, . . . and the end of this . . . fragmentation is not in sight" (Bowen and Schuster 1986, 152). One assessment of this state of academic affairs is to assure us of *e pluribus unum*, that is an enduring, harmonious system where faculty are held together by a devotion to knowledge, dual commitments to one's discipline and institution, a unified system albeit constituted by a pluralistic landscape of interests, as Clark (1987, 145) has proposed. An alternative assessment is to view the contemporary scene as a site of oppositional discourses, imbued with fundamental conflicts of vision and resistance to new ideas, such that the revision of the current departmental organization may be imminent (Lincoln 1986).

Such divergent assessments of how things are and how they may be in the future compel us to reconsider some assumptions about academia. In the broadest sense, when we speak of the organization of academic work or of the academic profession, we usually presuppose some degree of integration, whether it be cohesion among people around a knowledge base by discipline or by department, or whether it be cohesion around a professional ideal of purpose or service.

Yet, both within and across disciplines as well as within and across departments on any given campus, such cohesion appears to be waning or, if present, is buried under an array of dramatically different visions of the nature and content of academic knowledge. Debates over the value of Euro-centric scholarship and Western culture undergraduate requirements in the curricula, to name two recent examples, illustrate not only different but conflicting interests. Although the metaphor of organizational culture has been implicitly used in higher education for over two decades (e.g., Clark 1970, 1972), the increased popularity and refinement of cultural perspectives among higher education researchers and managers attest to the pervasive interest in understanding the glue that holds academia together. The theoretical and empirical work on organizational culture in higher education is, at least in part, a response to this functionalist concern.

Whether positing structural dimensions of organizations as a foil or merely as an analytical complement, deliberate cultural analysis in higher education settings has provided an alternative set of concepts and methods for studying cultural artifacts (e.g., myths, symbols, and rituals) in higher education organizations. The purpose of such research is to uncover beliefs and values among organizational participants, with the promise of more accurately portraying organizational life (Clark 1983; Dill 1982; Gumport 1988; Harman 1988; Masland 1985; Tierney 1988).

Most of such higher education research has been constructed and disseminated within a functionalist paradigm that implicitly seeks to uncover layers of academic order and mechanisms of integration. For example, Andrew T. Masland proposes that culture be seen as "a force that provides stability and a sense of continuity" (1985, 165). Along similar lines, William G. Tierney suggests that the study of cultural dynamics can help us "to decrease conflict" and "to understand and, hopefully, to reduce adversarial relationships" (1988, 18, 5).

Grounded in an *e pluribus unum* premise of organic solidarity (Durkheim 1933), such frameworks for understanding academic organization may be appealing for their currency as a motto, if not as a metaphor, for the hoped-for, ensuing coordination. However, as a conceptual frame for analyzing academic culture, the approach limits inquiry by assuming equilibrium rather than investigating it as an open empirical question. Conflict among organizational participants is seen as either a transient condition that erupts in an otherwise smoothly running system or as a more substantial difference of interest that nonetheless can and should be remedied or resolved. The solution may be structural (by creating a new organizational unit) or cultural (by accepting a divergence of beliefs). Conflict in academic culture is conceptually rendered part of a trend toward differentiation and pluralism.

An alternative starting point for the analysis of academic culture is to ask a different question than what glue is holding everything together, for it may be that things will fall apart or fall out along different lines. Rather than beginning with integration as an *a priori* analytical strait-jacket, we can examine what faculty do—"not what others think they do or should be doing," as George Kuh and Elizabeth Whitt have proposed (1988, 109). What becomes centrally problematic is to examine the nature of individuals' interests and commitments. In other words, the researcher should try not only to find out whether faculty really have dual commitments to their disciplines and institutions, but also to describe faculty perceptions of how their commitments are constructed in different academic settings. This approach leaves open the possibility for ambiguity, conflict, and disintegration. Moreover, this line of inquiry dovetails with an enduring interest in the sociology of knowledge and of science to determine the interplay between social structures and the development of ideas.

Accordingly, my analysis is framed by two questions: First, how do faculty seek and find intellectual community? And second, how do patterns of association differ in different campus organizational settings? I have found that the emergence of feminist scholarship and its associated academic networks call into question the accuracy of the *e pluribus unum* framework. The analysis is based on interview data from twenty-seven full-time faculty located on two campuses and case study data analyzing how different organizations frame the possibilities for forming intentional communities. These data are drawn from a larger two-year study in which I conducted seventy-five semi-structured, in-depth interviews with administrators and a stratified, random sample of women faculty across ten campuses and three disciplines (Gumport 1987). By supplementing the interviews with case study research and by conceptually anchoring faculty at the center of the analysis, I examined how faculty are constrained by, yet contribute to, their academic settings.

A major substantive line of inquiry in the interviews was examining whether and how these faculty became involved with feminist scholarship and its teaching arm, women's studies. Some of the faculty were located in conventional departments (sociology, history, and philosophy); others were in autonomous women's studies programs. Since they were all women who were in academia at a time of heightened gender consciousness, the contemporary emergence of academic feminism provided a set of intellectual, social, and political interests that they could ignore or embrace. Voluntary association was the major mechanism whereby faculty became participants in this newly emerging, not-yet-legitimate academic specialty. Feminist scholarship is interdisciplinary, potentially of interest to faculty in a wide range of disciplines, and controversial. Some scholars interpret it as having an explicitly political and oppositional agenda. These factors make it a suitable empirical opportunity to examine contemporary lines of academic culture on different campuses.

Analysis

Through an iterative, grounded theory analysis of the interview data (Glaser and Strauss 1967), I discerned patterns that reflected a complex process of finding intellectual affinity and forming intentional networks that cross-cut structural lines of departments. Faculty described individual and group processes as characterized by ambiguity of purpose and conflict of vision as well as by an absence of forethought, conscious planning, or likelihood of academic rewards. In fact, more often than not, the reference group and source of authority were identified as outside the department and sometimes outside academia entirely. Visible communities of feminist scholars emerged across departments as well as across campuses.

Faculty career histories and intellectual biographies enable us to examine what compelled them to associate and what subsequent senses of intellectual and organizational community emerged. First, I address the individual level of how faculty conceive of their intellectual community. Second, I analyze the campus levels for the distinctive informal networks that emerged.

Although individual variations may be interesting in and of themselves, different patterns among individuals provide greater insight for the analysis of social action. The faculty in this sample may be grouped into the following four patterns: (1) scholars whose interests matched their conventional departments and who had no interest or participation in feminist thinking; (2) feminist scholars working primarily in their department and discipline of training but who had some dual or mixed loyalties; (3) feminist scholars in departments yet whose primary loyalty was to women's studies as an autonomous unit separate from the conventional department; and (4) feminist scholar-activists located in women's studies programs who saw themselves as change agents to develop women's studies as an autonomous unit, and whose primary affinity was to the broader national feminist movement.

In this sample, those in the first group were fewer in number, especially among those who entered graduate school in the 1960s. The other three groups reflected some involvement with feminist scholarship and conveyed varying experiences of fragmentation and conflict in academia, both internally and interpersonally. They expressed a sense of conflicting membership within their departments and even internally within an emerging women's studies subculture. I examine each group in turn.

Faculty Identifying with Departments

The scholars who were oriented to their department and discipline agendas did not see their work as intersecting with feminist scholarship in a meaningful way. They did not become involved with feminist research or teach women's studies, deeming them either irrelevant or inappropriate due to the perceived political nature of feminist scholarship.

Four quotations illustrate this sense of detachment. A philosopher commented, "I was conscious of there being a feminist movement; but since there weren't any differences for me as a woman at the time, I more or less ignored all of it."

"I could see it as an area of interest but not something that can stand alone," said a sociologist. "It could get into trouble if it becomes a matter of taking sides rather than material that can be analyzed and looked at critically. It's fine to see women as victims, but that should be separate from the academic milieu. I feel uncomfortable with that."

"I just don't understand it," admitted a second sociologist, and added, "I don't think I agree with it. It worries me a little . . . because I can see people saying we need a Catholic or Jewish sociology; we need a sociology of white supremacy or anti-white supremacy. It gets off into directions I feel real uncomfortable with. . . . I'm not very comfortable with a larger political role. I don't have any problem with people trying to shift the agenda of the discipline as an intellectual activity, but I have problems with combining the roles—using their academic credentials to legitimate a particular political position. . . . I prefer to keep them separate."

"The label is a disservice," a historian charged. "I've had enough ideologies and dogmas. I have not found [feminist scholars] a natural audience. . . . I'm mistrustful. . . . They want something more doctrinaire, much more ideological."

These four scholars conceived of themselves and their sense of community as clearly anchored in their departments and disciplines. Their networks and associations were not problematic, since they followed the formal structure; but they were only a few voices in my sample.

Faculty with Mixed Loyalties

The second group tried to balance the dual loyalties of their department/discipline and their emerging interests in feminist scholarship.

For some, the balancing act worked. These were usually historians who found a niche in the emerging subfield of women's history. For example, one historian explained she "fell into" feminist scholarship "by accident." Initially she was worried about possible consequences and

> . . . toyed briefly with not telling anyone here that I was working on it, because I was afraid of how it might be perceived, especially as I was coming up for tenure at the time. But I decided not to. There was the practical reason that people would wonder what I was working on. . . . Then it also just didn't seem right. Then I presented some of it in the form of a paper to colleagues in my department. It went very well. I was amazed. Some of the issues that I dealt with are at the intersection of sex and power. They are interested in that. . . . They were very supportive and made good suggestions, and I was much relieved.

Recalling her relations with departmental colleagues prior to her feminist research, she realized in retrospect that there was no need to worry: "I had established such a moderate or really a conservative facade in my department that . . . I felt it would not be detrimental." This scholar thus conceived of herself and her community as centered in history, yet able to accommodate a feminist research project.

Others found no convergence between interests in historical and feminist scholarship. They either felt pulled in two different directions or tried to enact a new kind of scholarly identity.

Another historian described herself as "balancing on women's history and French history. Each of them takes me in a direction away from the other. I do pursue women's history outside of France and French history outside of women's history. But in different periods of my life, I'm concentrating either on one or the other."

Her primary professional involvement was the American Historical Association, although she characterized that group as "not exciting." In contrast, she was "attached to" the Berkshire Conference of women's historians and feminist scholars with related interests: "It's special and it's a happening. To go to a place where you know you're going to be indulging your professional interests with other women . . . perks you up in a sense because it takes away a burden you don't even know is there when you're working in a male-dominated place like this." In spite of her identification with those who attend the Berkshire Conference, her sense of her work and community was still problematic. She felt pulled apart, unable to find a home entirely in either location.

In trying to reconcile this kind of tension, some scholars in history, sociology, and philosophy generated a research agenda and tried to establish a new intellectual and organizational identity created from the intersection of disciplinary and feminist interests. Historians were most likely to succeed in making this a viable option, although others made concerted efforts.

One historian, who described herself as a pioneer, characterized her efforts:

> I was putting together the politics and the scholarship and feeling like it had to be done. . . . I still do it that way. You can see all my articles start out with the contemporary political issue and end up with it, too. And I do the history in between. . . . Now I define myself as someone in women's history and a feminist. I have a network of women's historians around the country. It's an intellectual community: we read each others' work and comment on it . . . and go to conferences. We also socialize at those gatherings and other times. It's also active as a political network.

She had a clear sense of belonging in a feminist scholarly community. Rather than feeling pulled in two separate directions or working in two separate worlds, she had constructed a new primary identity as a "feminist historian." Simultaneously she retained a strong disciplinary orientation, which reflected a comfortable congruence with her being located in the history department at a leading research university: "I'm very wedded to history," she described herself. "I read in other fields, but I really believe in history and in having strong disciplinary training, that without it people can float too much. So my primary identity is as a feminist historian."

It is noteworthy that both this historian and the one who described herself as "balancing" between feminism and history were in the same department at the same institution. Yet their experiences differed, one ending up with dual loyalties while the second ended up constructing a new sense of self and community.

Two philosophers also spoke of finding a new scholarly path which united their divergent scholarly interests. However, they characterized this orientation as more problematic, both in the process and in the outcome, than for the historians. Both philosophers described the difficulty of, first, establishing an intellectual and organizational niche and, second, finding an audience for their research.

The first philosopher observed, "In college I was definitely not a feminist," but over the past two decades, she became a self-described "feminist and a philosopher." She described the process: "The challenge for me as my own person and independent thinker was to get the blend that is desirable. I felt that it was too difficult . . . to meet the narrow constraints of the discipline, so I shifted into a women's studies program for a while. That context was invaluable for me [in being] able to develop my thinking freely." Then she took a position in a philosophy department. Her sense of her work was that "it is not straight philosophy." Her most recent paper probably will not be accepted for the American Philosophical Association annual conference because "it's too bizarre in its multidisciplinary approach." In sum, this scholar did not see herself fitting comfortably into her discipline.

A second philosopher also sought to "have something to say to both feminist and philosophical audiences," a task she conceived of as doing something new for her field.

> I take the current [feminist] agenda and ask myself is there something useful a philosopher can do here. . . . When I'm speaking to a feminist audience . . . , I have to make my work relevant in ways that I don't have to when I'm speaking to a philosophical audience. . . . After the initial encounter between the disciplinary work and feminist concerns, then the work develops its own momentum and generates its own sorts of questions, so that it no longer seems appropriate to talk about my work as bridging some gap between my subfield in philosophy and separate [feminist] concerns.

This philosopher still saw negative consequences for not "doing straight philosophy," so she spent time developing a feminist scholarly network and trying to publish in both feminist and philosophy journals.

In sum, the pattern characteristic of this group was mixed loyalties that they tried, with different degrees of success, to balance or blend through different strategies. Historians tended to find more resolution in carving out an intellectual and organizational niche for themselves and their community.

Faculty Identifying Primarily with Women's Studies

A third pattern in this sample was scholars who, although located in conventional departments, found their intellectual and social center outside the department. For the most part, they were extensively involved with a campus women's studies program and read, attended, and published primarily in women's studies forums. They consistently reported feeling "more and more distance" from their departments. (Not surprisingly, these scholars were employed at a comprehensive state university, not at a research university, which is a point I will address later in the analysis.)

As an example of this pattern, a historian described how she has struggled with this dimension of academic life since graduate school in the late 1960s. She stayed in history, even though her identity and interests gradually moved into women's studies. As a graduate student, she recalled, the discipline was more a heavy hand than an intellectual home. "Where there was a question of my values being in direct conflict with the trajectory of the disciplinary career, I got slapped down and I was very well aware of that. I could see that happening. I cried. I wept. I said it was unfair. And I changed."

Years later, her intellectual affinities turned toward women's studies, even though she had a full-time position in a history department. She did not find it feasible to be in both worlds, so she, in effect, "dropped out of the history department." She remembered: "I wouldn't serve on any committees and I wouldn't socialize with anyone. I had nothing to do with the department. . . . All of my orientation was with the women's studies program. Because that was a confrontational program at the time, the separation was absolute. I could be here, or I could be there. But I couldn't be in both places."

In retrospect, she characterized herself as having been "professionally dumb" to make a primary commitment to women's studies without thinking about the consequences. Still, her identification with women's studies was so strong that "if someone had said don't risk it, it would have had to have been the leader of our feminist movement. If the chair of the [history] department had said to me, 'Look, I'm with you and I love what you're doing for women's studies but I'm not going to be able to get you through the department,' I would have said 'screw you.'" She gained tenure in her department, probably because of her outstanding teaching record; her courses, which were cross-listed with women's studies, were popular and consistently well-enrolled.

Naturally faculty located in women's studies programs most frequently expressed the feeling of having an intellectual and organizational home in women's studies. Since they were not located in conventional departments, they would have a greater opportunity to find congruence between their interests, expertise, and organizational niche. However, such positions lacked the security of appointments in more traditional departments. Only some women's studies faculty had "retreat rights" to another department in the event of program dissolution. However, the perceived marginality of women's studies coupled with a lack of common intellectual interests made those future scenarios unsatisfactory. One women's studies program director, who was simultaneously a full professor in a sociology department, explained her own situation: "The loss of collegiality with my 'home' department is something I hadn't anticipated would happen. I no longer go to their meetings—on campus or nationally in the association. I can't do both." The center of her academic life was clearly in women's studies, locally, regionally, and nationally—an orientation shared by some other women's studies scholars who had departmental appointments.

Faculty Identifying with Feminism

Some faculty with positions in women's studies differed from their departmental colleagues in having a distinctive nonacademic orientation, where the faculty member conceived of her work and her community as lying outside the academy. In those cases, the primary loyalty and reference group became more the political movement than the academy.

For example, one faculty member reported having had a series of terminal appointments over the last seven years, part-time on and off, later full-time in a women's studies program. "Basically I've been a gypsy scholar and to me it [politics and academics] is not an internal conflict. If it's a choice between my political convictions and a job, the job can go to hell. . . . I will never make those kinds of compromises. It's not an internal conflict, but it's a conflict with the system." She identifies herself as a feminist scholar and black scholar who believes in women's studies programs as "an essential institutional power base . . . not . . . in it being a safe harbor, but in it being a real space for women . . . scholars and women students." She describes having a primary political agenda.

She is located in a women's studies program on a campus where the program functions much like a department; a handful of other full-time faculty in women's studies ostensibly share her feminist scholarly interests. However, this setting has not become a complete home. As a woman of color, she felt that she was hired to boost enrollments; and the other women's studies faculty felt threatened when she wanted to change things, "threatened enough to complain to the administration." She felt betrayed:

> Most of the tension has come in women's studies because they didn't realize what it'd mean to have a woman of color who is not a clone of traditional feminist theory. . . . They put on file with the administration a criticism saying that I was not collegial because I did not validate the work of the women who went before me, that I moved too fast. And they refused to talk with me about it. . . . So that's saying to me we don't want you here, and if we want you here we want you under our control.

Although this particular case may seem extreme, it is a useful reminder that the basic organizing units of academic life do not necessarily convey cohesion of purpose and loyalty. Both on the individual level and the interpersonal level, fragmentation and conflict may be pervasive. Even in a case where women's studies functions like a department, there may be less cohesion than we presume. In fact, faculty involved with women's studies and feminist scholarship admit to internal lack of consensus on program content, visions for change, and even who qualifies as members in their enterprise (Gumport 1990). As one director of a women's studies program observed: "People differ in what they mean by feminist and feminist scholarship, and some programs have been torn apart over it."

Campus Networks

These four patterns of faculty orientations also coincide with different higher education organizational settings. Individuals oriented toward conventional departments without interest or involvement in feminist work as well as individuals who felt pulled in two directions from conflicting departmental and feminist scholarly associations were located at a leading research university. Those whose primary affinities were in autonomous women's studies programs or who were highly politicized and oriented outside academia entirely were located at a comprehensive state university.

At the common-sense level and in a functionalist framework, this pattern is no surprise. One obvious hypothesis is that either the individual women self-selected organizational settings that matched their interests or the research-oriented and teaching-oriented institutions each selected faculty with orientations that fit their particular campus culture. However, rather than assuming conscious choice on either part, and examining disaggregated individual behaviors, it is more illuminating to examine the kinds of informal networks that developed in each campus setting.

The reward system within research universities for departmental and disciplinary research and the emphasis in comprehensive state universities on teaching suggest that the different organizational settings provide different possibilities for cross-departmental networks among feminist scholars. The case study data from the two campuses point to a distinctive pattern: the comprehensive university had a thriving cross-departmental feminist, scholarly network; the leading research university had a floundering one.

At the comprehensive university, the faculty in general were described as "progressive" and "having a radical bent." The core of the feminist scholarly community revolved around the women's studies program, which was established in the early 1970s and, at the time of this research, boasted fifty undergraduate majors, eighteen courses a semester, and a dozen faculty (including part-timers) with women's studies appointments. The faculty network also included over a dozen more active feminists located in departments.

The faculty network originated in and has been sustained by students' grass-roots efforts to establish a women's studies program. In the early years, there was a student alliance, where students either ran the courses or taught them informally. Since the courses were well-enrolled and highly politicized, the administration took notice. As an administrator remembered: "It scared the administration. The mere size of the thing, the numbers of people involved, the energy generated around it! I think all that was significant enough to carry us ultimately into the women's studies program itself." Years later, the alliance became an ad hoc committee which has been the intellectual, social, and political center for feminist faculty and students ever since. Many departmental faculty became connected formally by cross-listing courses or serving on committees, or informally by socializing. Their efforts are constrained by time; "we're all teaching heavy loads." Their focus shifted to formulating a master's program in women's studies and whether to make women's studies a general education requirement, thereby changing small, personal classes into large required ones.

As faculty described the campus milieu, they often referred to "the administration." "The administration," they said, "does not penalize us for being involved in women's studies." What seemed to count most was generating and sustaining high enrollment programs. Since departmental involvement and women's studies involvement were not differentially valued, participating in a feminist network on campus had a pay-off.

In contrast to the thriving feminist scholarly network at the comprehensive university, the research university has had a small though growing faculty group, whose members tended to keep an intellectual and organizational anchor in their departments. The women's studies program at the research university was small and had no permanent autonomous faculty lines; except for an occasional visitor, the program relied on cross-listed departmental courses. Established relatively late vis-á-vis the national scene, the program did not grant degrees; students petitioned individually to an interdisciplinary majors committee for a bachelor's degree in women's studies.

At the time of this research, the dozen or so most visible feminist faculty in the departments wanted the teaching program to flourish but recognized the constraints in faculty recruitment and hiring practices in the departments. A historian explained: "The reality of the university is so discipline-based that you do a disservice to create something outside the disciplines. . . . Strategically, people need to be based in the disciplines. . . . And it's not just strategically but intellectually as well." However, the women's studies program director acknowledges that the institution was willing to support women's studies, provided that it demonstrated "strong scholarship" and an "assurance of respectability." The willingness came from the competitive drive for excellence—the fact that "entrepreneurs get their way here. . . . It's survival of the fittest. . . . You survive if you get a high level of visibility, if you are judged by your peers as at the top."

Participating in an emerging informal feminist scholarly network on this campus would have little pay-off for faculty, given the strong disciplinary orientations and time constraints from pressure to publish. In addition, according to one observer in the humanities:

> It's a little risky that no matter how committed you are, you have to draw the line somewhere because there is so much to be done. There are considerations of practicality, of what you need to do and can do if you want to stay here. . . . Most people are much more cautious about getting involved in anything besides writing their books. . . . It's getting labeled—not as a feminist or a women's studies person per se. It's getting labeled as a person who will do non-scholarly, collaborative, student-oriented things. . . . It's the kiss of death.

In spite of the risk, participating in a feminist network on a small scale provides intellectual, social, or political support for faculty who are trying to balance or blend feminist with disciplinary interests. Although informal feminist networks connect people who would otherwise be dispersed and isolated in conventional departments, they may also do a disservice. A philosopher explained: "In general there isn't a location for feminist work in the field. . . . The status of feminist work is still fairly fragile. . . . It's mostly women doing it. And so, of course, [since] women are all engaged in this funny kind of work just really confirms people's initial prejudice that women can't do real philosophy . . . [but] are doing this other thing which isn't really philosophy." In any case, despite the scrutiny and stigma, a scholar with this orientation may still seek a feminist scholarly network as an intellectual and organizational home. Another philosopher explained her own decision to do so and remarked on the same inclination of her colleagues:

> If you are working on feminist stuff, you are likely to feel embattled. . . . The women in philosophy who see themselves as feminist scholars will generally be the only person doing feminist work in a department and may sometimes be the only woman period. [They] may feel cut off or deprived of collegial relationships among departmental colleagues and may develop closer relationships with colleagues in women's studies [located] in other departments. . . . Those are the only places where you get both philosophical colleagueship and feminist colleagueship. You get both of them at the same time, in the same place, in the same sentence. And for most women philosophers that is extremely rare.

Thus, both the advantages and disadvantages of associating with a feminist scholarly network are heightened in the constraints of the research university than in the comprehensive university.

The contrast between these two campuses raises questions about the organizational factors that might account for these differences. The inability of the research university to generate—let alone sustain—a thriving feminist scholarly network reflects a distinctive structure and culture which stand in dramatic contrast to that of the comprehensive university.

At the research university, faculty were oriented primarily to their disciplinary colleagues; and departments did the essential work of research and graduate education. In a sense, this peer culture became coercive, guiding faculty behavior and time management as a means of social coordination. In effect, it kept people on their assigned academic tasks, not only junior faculty who faced the "publish or perish" criteria for tenure but senior faculty who earned merit increases in promotion. Since departmental senior faculty held the power, other faculty were not inclined to spend too much time and energy on voluntary associations. Those who chose to do so essentially ran against the grain at their own risk by leaping across the discrete departmental building blocks on which the university organization rests. When it comes to peer review, they ran an even greater risk of not fitting in (Gumport 1990). A feminist scholar who had been denied tenure at a leading research university explained it this way: "It's harder to work when it's not fitting into your discipline in a particular way. You can't expect to get clear judgments and rewards, although you'll get different opinions about it. . . . The problem is the people who could judge it are out there and not in here in my department and my discipline."

In contrast, the locus of power at the comprehensive university lay with administrators, not with a departmental/disciplinary peer culture. Administrators' power was linked to their discretion over academic programs and teaching loads. Enrollment-driven data carried clout. Consequently, there was a greater organizational distance between the faculty and the central administration. Faculty and administrators ended up antagonists, no matter what voluntary associations faculty formed. Since course enrollments were the currency for leverage, it was less important whether a feminist faculty member was participating in women's studies centrally, marginally, or in a conventional department. The issue simply lacked the salience it assumed in the disciplinary peer culture of the research university.

In light of these fundamental differences in organizational settings, it becomes clear that overarching academic beliefs like academic freedom and devotion to knowledge are mediated by local settings. Moreover, each setting coordinates academic work with a different emphasis so that faculty are encouraged to attend to different concerns. Thus, each setting is more likely to raise different possibilities for the formation of a cross-departmental feminist scholarly network. Although these patterns appear to warrant an *e pluribus unum* conclusion, such a conclusion would be overly simplistic and premature. As the first part of this analysis shows, participants interpret and reenact beliefs according to their subjective perceptions and have the potential to reconstitute the settings in which they work.

Conclusion

In an analysis of recent empirical data, I reexamine the functionalist premise of *e pluribus unum*—out of many, one. Rather than beginning with the assumption of past, present, or future cohesion among organizational participants, as other higher education scholars have, I bring the analysis down to the level of individuals to examine how they enter, negotiate, and play out structural and cultural dimensions of their particular organizational settings. The interview data reveal that faculty conceive of their commitments and their sense of community in ways that do not always correspond with idealized conceptions of academic organization in which departmental and institutional affinities reign supreme.

Setting aside the sub-group in this small sample whose orientations did correspond to their departments, the three other groups of women scholars exemplify a kind of intellectual and social incongruence with their organizational locations. There are plenty of academics whose work does not fit neatly into their so-called home departments and disciplines. In fact, many of the quotations cited in the preceding analysis could have been spoken by faculty in such fields as area studies, urban studies, environmental studies, science policy studies, and ethnic studies—to name a few. These are contemporary fields whose scholarly content and practice do not match the current departmental organization. These are fields where, in an effort to reconstitute academic knowledge, people seek and find intentional communities that are cross-departmental and sometimes even nonacademic.

In a fundamental sense, the emergence of faculty with orientations that diverge significantly from their departments/disciplines of training remains a puzzle. Are they self-chosen outliers, deviants, or examples of inadequate disciplinary socialization? Do they reflect the particular dynamics of those with distinctive special interests? Or are their experiences characteristic of academics who are engaged in the formation of new specialties or interdisciplinary fields?

While I am not proposing generalizability from this small sample of women faculty, I am suggesting that the data may illuminate some persistent dynamics of conflict and ambiguity in academic life that are overlooked when one begins in the aggregate by attributing cohesion of purpose to departments and institutions. Whether it be for academics who engage in not-yet-legitimate academic pursuits or even for those who apparently have conventional disciplinary and departmental affiliations, the process of forming a scholarly identity, the nature of interpersonal communication, and positioning oneself within the academic reward system may be central features of academic organizational life that have been understudied and undertheorized.

The nature of academic organization needs to be reconceptualized because departmental units do not necessarily or inevitably determine behavior, interests, and, more profoundly, the pace and direction of knowledge change. That is, the formation of intentional communities may be integral to the process of negotiating the tension between constraints of the academic reward structure and personal ambitions, between the designation of what is cutting edge versus trivial, and between determining what is legitimately innovative versus what is off the map. The consequences for innovation in higher education are significant, as there is a perennial need to consider which administrative frameworks foster scholarly creativity. As Dean MacHenry has noted: "In scholarship, as in farming, the most fertile soil may be under the fences, rather than at the center of long-established fields" (1977, ix). Similarly, Angela Simeone has proposed that "there are some who would argue that these networks constitute the most vital development within the recent history of American higher education" (1987, 99).

Functionalist conceptions do not make problematic how, where, and why faculty seek and find intellectual community, since a premise of overlapping memberships assures that affinities will converge along two primary lines of disciplinary and campus affiliations. Such an orientation assumes that beliefs lead to commitments (Clark 1987, 106–7) and commitments lead to community. Beliefs and increasingly specialized orientations more or less correspond to, or at least complement, one's departmental affiliation; otherwise, a new unit will be differentiated. A further functionalist presupposition is one of coordination, where the organization of academic work and knowledge acts as a "framework for both resolving conflicting interests and advancing common ones" (Clark 1987, 109). In spite of "narrow groups that in turn generate their own separate subcultures," cultural overlap emerges from a common commitment to shared, overarching principles and beliefs (Clark 1987, 109, 140–42).

While my analysis challenges Clark's rationalistic premises, one functionalist proposition finds support in this analysis: beliefs get played out differently in organizational settings (Clark 1987, chap. 5). At research universities, disciplinarity and cutting edge scholarship are valued; whereas in the comprehensive college sector, both faculty and administration, the "they" to whom faculty often refer, turn their attention to teaching and undergraduate enrollments. Using this analytical distinction, I examined how these different organizational settings may inhibit or foster informal, cross-departmental faculty networks.

As the analysis revealed, location was linked with distinctive patterns of association among faculty. Feminist scholarly activity at the comprehensive university most closely approximates a subculture, although this particular subculture seems more likely to subvert the status quo enterprise than enhance it. The research university could not generate and sustain a viable cross-departmental network; instead faculty behavior tended to either correspond to, or complement, lines of differentiation in the formal structure. Both patterns illustrate that structural and cultural features of organizational life may be a coercive force. Yet faculty are active agents who may try to reshape their immediate academic settings; further, faculty's innovative interests may be tied to the wider external culture. Thus, when supposedly shared beliefs are viewed in their respective organizational embodiments, far more variation, fragmentation, conflict, and ambiguity exist than the *e pluribus unum* framework presumes.

For those who study higher education, a theoretical and methodological directive is clear. The kinds of questions we need to ask about academic life need to reflect complexity, not only of structures but of processes; not of distinct levels but of the mechanisms that cross-cut and potentially undermine the levels; not of daily life inside an organization but of how daily life is necessarily situated in wider socio-cultural circumstances. The questions locate both the realities of organizational life and the potentials for change in people's subjective experiences, not solely in *a priori* notions of formal structure, dominant norms, and beliefs as determinative.

Indeed, an even further diversity of perspectives is necessary to understand something as complex as the nature of academic change. As illustrative of one emerging approach, a critical cultural perspective signifies a marked departure from functionalist premises in order to take seriously the interplay between prevailing social structures and individuals' perceptions and agency (Tierney 1991). The intention is to yield a more accurate portrayal, not only of the variation in academic life in its myriad settings, but also of the ways in which research from a functionalist perspective advances a myth of unity in pluralism. The aim is to examine how interests may conflict and come to be differently valued, "not to celebrate organization as a value, but to question the ends it serves" (Smircich 1983, 355). Nor is the intention to remain silent on the unresolved and unacknowledged controversies underlying established departmental categories, but rather "to think about them and to recognize they [themselves are] the product of theoretical choices" (Graff 1987, 8).

Although some proponents of this line of inquiry approach their data with an etic standpoint from the top down, other proponents of a critical cultural analysis advocate inductive inquiry that begins at the local level from the inside out. From either perspective, a cultural analysis makes problematic conventional functionalist analyses of such essential academic processes as curricular change, faculty hiring and promotion, and academic program planning. It forces us to rethink concepts such as hierarchy—an all-important context of academic life. For instance, rather than seeing hierarchy as an ordered arrangement that promotes coordination and excellence, hierarchy may also be examined as a means of social control which is contested between the Weberian bureaucratic interests of central administrators and the faculty's professional interests for self-regulation and autonomy.

From this line of inquiry, empirical study on the problem of social integration generates a wider range of questions worth pursuing, ultimately for revising theoretical explanations of the nature of academic organization. For example, how and under what conditions do academic organizations reflect enduring systemic disequilibria, either in the contemporary era or historically? Are there new types of social and intellectual integration that have emerged beyond the administratively decentralized, rational organizational order; if so, how has the formation of intentional communities played a role in academic change? Are current faculty commitments pointing to a disintegration of the modern academic role, or possibly to a postmodern legitimacy for explicit expression of political and economic commitments, or perhaps to an institutionally mediated academic role in which certain commitments and behaviors—such as political protest or economic entrepreneurship—are deemed acceptable lines of partisanship in certain kinds of campus settings but not in others?

As researchers of higher education define directions for further organizational studies, they will determine whether the various structural and cultural analyses of higher education may be used in a complementary manner or may be judged incompatible on the basis of divergent directives for what to study, how to study it, and to what end. It remains to be seen whether this uncertainty should be interpreted as a sign of knowledge growth and differentiation in a maturing field of study or as a sign of impending fragmentation and cultural ambiguity in a field of study that is itself inescapably embedded in multiple nested contexts.

Bibliography

Blau, Peter. *The Organization of Academic Work.* New York: John Wiley & Sons, 1973.

Bowen, Howard, and Jack Schuster. *American Professors: A National Resource Imperiled.* New York: Oxford University Press, 1986.

Clark, Burton R. *The Distinctive College.* Chicago: Aldine, 1970.

_____. "The Organizational Saga in Higher Education." *Administrative Science Quarterly* 17 (June 1972): 178–84.

_____. *The Higher Education System: Academic Organization in Cross National Perspective.* Berkeley: University of California Press, 1983.

_____, ed. *The Academic Life: Small Worlds, Different Worlds.* Princeton: The Carnegie Foundation for the Advancement of Teaching, 1987.

Dill, David D. "The Management of Academic Culture: Notes on the Management of Meaning and Social Integration." *Higher Education* 11 (May 1982): 303–20.

Durkheim, Emile. *The Division of Labor in Society.* 1933; reprint ed., New York: The Free Press, 1984.

Geertz, Clifford. "The Way We Think Now: Toward an Ethnography of Modern Thought." In his *Local Knowledge: Further Essays in Interpretive Anthropology,* 147–66. New York: Basic Books, 1983.

Glaser, Barney, and Anselm Strauss. *The Discovery of Grounded Theory: Strategies for Qualitative Research.* New York: Aldine, 1967.

Graff, Gerald. *Professing Literature: An Institutional History.* Chicago: The University of Chicago Press, 1987.

Gumport, Patricia J. "The Social Construction of Knowledge: Individual and Institutional Commitments to Feminist Scholarship." Ph.D. diss., Stanford University, 1987.

_____. "Curricula as Signposts of Cultural Change." *Review of Higher Education* 12 (Autumn 1988): 49–61.

_____. "Feminist Scholarship as a Vocation." *Higher Education* 20 (October 1990): 231–43.

Harman, Kay. "The Symbolic Dimension of Academic Organization: Academic Culture at the University of Melbourne." Ph.D. diss., La Trobe University, 1988.

Kuh, George, and Elizabeth Whitt. *The Invisible Tapestry: Culture in American Colleges and Universities.* ASHE–ERIC Higher Education Reports, Washington, D.C.: Association for the Study of Higher Education, 1988.

Lincoln, Yvonna S. "Toward a Future–Oriented Comment on the State of the Profession." *Review of Higher Education* 10 (Winter 1986): 135–42.

MacHenry, Dean. "Preface." In *Academic Departments,* edited by Dean MacHenry and Associates, ix–xvi. San Francisco: Jossey-Bass, 1977.

Masland, Andrew T. "Organization Culture in the Study of Higher Education." *Review of Higher Education* 8 (Winter 1985): 157–68.

Rudolph, Frederick. *Curriculum: A History of the American Undergraduate Curriculum Since 1936.* San Francisco: Jossey-Bass, 1981.

Simeone, Angela. *Academic Women: Working Toward Equality.* South Hadley, Mass.: Bergin and Garvey, 1987.

Smircich, Linda. "Concepts of Culture and Organizational Analysis." *Administrative Science Quarterly* 28 (1983): 339–58.

Tierney, William G. "Organizational Culture in Higher Education: Defining the Essentials." *Journal of Higher Education* 59 (January/February 1988): 2–21.

_____, ed. *Culture and Ideology in Higher Education: Advancing a Critical Agenda.* New York: Praeger, 1991.

Trow, Martin. "The Analysis of Status." In *Perspectives on Higher Education,* edited by Burton Clark, Chap. 5. Berkeley: University of California Press, 1984.

Deconstructing Organizational Taboos: The Suppression of Gender Conflict in Organizations*

Joanne Martin
Graduate School of Business,
Stanford University

This paper begins with a story told by a corporation president to illustrate what his organization was doing to "help" women employees balance the demands of work and home. The paper deconstructs and reconstructs this story text from a feminist perspective, examining what it says, what it does not say, and what it might have said. This analysis reveals how organizational efforts to "help women" have suppressed gender conflict and reified false dichotomies between public and private realms of endeavor, suggesting why it has proven so difficult to eradicate gender discrimination in organizations. Implications of a feminist perspective for organizational theory are discussed.

The schools of Business, Law, Education, and Medicine at a major university recently sponsored a conference focusing on the ways that individuals, businesses, and other organizations can help solve societal problems. Students and faculty from the university, as well as the press and members of the surrounding community, came to hear an anchor man from NBC Nightly News interview several panelists. One of those panelists was the president and Chief Executive Officer of a very large, multi-national corporation. This company has an unusual reputation for being deeply concerned, in a humanitarian fashion, about the personal well-being of its employees. In response to a question about the company's concern for the well-being of women employees with children, the president told the following story. (The appendix includes excerpts from the official conference proceedings, including events that immediately preceded and followed the telling of this story.)

> We have a young woman who is extraordinarily important to the launching of a major new (product). We will be talking about it next Tuesday in its first world wide introduction. She has arranged to have her Caesarean yesterday in order to be prepared for this event, so you—We have insisted that she stay home and this is going to be televised in a closed circuit television, so we're having this done by TV for her, and she is staying home three months and we are finding ways of filling in to create this void for us because we think it's an important thing for her to do.

In this paper, I deconstruct and reconstruct this story from a feminist viewpoint,[1] examining what it says, what it does not say, and what it might have said. This analysis highlights suppressed gender conflicts implicit in this story and shows how apparently well-intentioned organizational practices can reify, rather than alleviate, gender inequalities.

---

*Accepted by Richard L. Daft; received September 9, 1988. This paper has been with the author 7 months for 1 revision.

Recent efforts to alleviate gender inequality have made it socially, and in some contexts legally, inappropriate to express overt gender prejudice. Of course, open and direct expressions of gender prejudice do still occur. However, gender conflict in organizations is often unspoken or hidden "between the lines" of what people say and do, like the more subtle forms of modern racial prejudice (e.g., Pettigrew and Martin 1987). Such suppressed conflict is easier to deny, harder to detect and combat, and more difficult to study. Deconstruction offers one way to address this problem. Because deconstruction is unfamiliar to many organizational researchers (see, as exceptions, Calas and Smircich 1987; Kilduff 1981), a brief introduction may be useful before proceeding.

Introduction to Deconstruction

Developed by philosophers and literary critics, deconstruction can be defined as an analytic strategy that exposes, in a systematic way, multiple ways a text can be interpreted. Deconstruction is able to reveal ideological assumptions in a way that is particularly sensitive to the suppressed interests of members of disempowered, marginalized groups. In a text, dominant ideologies suppress conflict by eliding conflicts of interest, denying the existence of points of view that could be disruptive of existing power relationships, and creating myths of harmony, unity, and caring that conceal the opposite. Deconstruction peels away the layers of ideological obscuration, exposing the conflict that has been suppressed; the devalued "other" is made visible. Thus, deconstruction reveals "power operating in structures of thinking and behavior that previously seemed devoid of power relations" (White 1986, p. 421).

How, then, does this mysteriously powerful deconstruction do its work? One relatively succinct description is:

> It is in the significant silences of a text, in its gaps and absences that the presence of ideology can be most positively felt. It is these silences which the critic must make 'speak.' The text is, as it were, ideologically forbidden to say certain things; in trying to tell the truth in his (sic) own way, for example, the author finds himself forced to reveal the limits of the ideology within which he writes. He is forced to reveal its gaps and silences, what it is unable to articulate. Because a text contains these gaps and silences, it is always incomplete. (Eagleton 1976, p. 34–35).

Deconstruction starts from epistemological premises that are radically different from those held by most organizational researchers. Deconstruction focuses on suppressed conflicts and multiple interpretations of a text in order to undermine all claims to objective "truth." The number of possible interpretations of a text is endless. A deconstruction offers a purposeful selection of some of these interpretations, but it does not and cannot claim to represent the objective truth about which interpretation is correct or what the author intended to say.

Thus, deconstruction is far more than a methodology; it has profound implications for the inescapable ambiguities of theory building and research in any field. For example, deconstruction presents a radical challenge to much of the research in our field which implicitly endorses logical positivist claims of privileged access to objective knowledge. I hope that this paper's exploration of deconstruction will be of interest, even to those (like myself) who are uncomfortable with a full acceptance of deconstruction's epistemological assumptions.

There may be organizational scholars, previously unfamiliar with deconstruction, who would consider experimenting with using this analytic strategy in their own work. To be helpful to these researchers, this paper is written as an introduction to deconstruction. Before I make each different type of deconstructive move, I briefly describe what I am going to do in abstract terms, quoting and citing relevant references to the deconstruction literature. This direct and didactic style is an attempt to demystify deconstruction. It carries the risk of oversimplifying a process that is usually elaborated—eloquently—rather than delineated—prosaically.[2]

There is a second aspect of the style of this paper that merits mention. Organizational research is usually written in a traditional scientific writing style, for example, using a strictly impersonal tone and passive verb constructions ("the subjects were instructed. . ."). These stylistic conventions make the author invisible while enhancing his or her authority (e.g., Van Maanen 1988). In contrast to the impersonal tone of most organizational research, deconstruction requires subjectivity and reflexivity—indeed, that is one of its objectives. It inevitably reveals the I/eye/ideology of the deconstructor as well as the deconstructed. Because the next sections of this paper focus on deconstruction, I will use a more personal voice in order to acknowledge limitations and sources of potential bias in my perspective.

Had I been present when the Caesarean story was told, I would have joined those in the audience who responded with a hiss. As a feminist, I am dismayed that anyone—but particularly a representative of a company with such power and such a humanistic reputation—would be apparently oblivious of this story's negative connotations and actually expect that it shows evidence of concern for the well-being of women or children. Other people, however, react differently to this story, either approving of it or not being able to articulate why it makes them feel uncomfortable. The story, therefore, deserves more than a hiss of dismissal. Its deconstruction can reveal both obvious and subtle reasons for such a hiss—including hidden assumptions about gender that can underlie ostensibly benign organizational practices.

Deconstruction and Feminism: An Unsuppressed Conflict

Deconstruction is a particularly useful approach to studying suppressed gender conflict in organizational contexts. Most organizations are controlled by men and by assumptions, for example about the legitimacy of authority, which in effect favor men. Women's interests, therefore, often appear as contradictions, disjunctions, disruptions, and silences—signs of suppressed conflict:

> The feminine has consequently had to be deciphered as forbidden ("interdit"), in between signs, between the realized meanings, between the lines. (Irigaray 1974, p. 20, quoted in Moi 1985, p. 132).

This paper uses deconstruction to analyze, from a feminist point of view, interpretations which lie between the lines of the Caesarean story.

Deconstruction and feminism are not obvious allies. In contrast to deconstruction, feminism (in all its varieties) makes a truth claim: that women's interests have been unjustly subordinated to those of men. Because deconstruction can be used to undermine, as well as support, any truth claim, it is essential to acknowledge before proceeding that this feminist deconstruction, like any deconstruction, can in turn be deconstructed from an opposing point of view.[3]

A second caveat is also essential. Deconstruction cannot and does not claim to reveal the truth about what the author of a text intended to communicate. This is particularly germane when a speech, rather than a literary or philosophical masterpiece, is being deconstructed.[4] The physical presence of a speaker is sometimes seen as a personal guarantee of his or her intended meaning (Weedon 1987, p.67). Thus, to be fair to the teller of the Caesarean story, it is important to acknowledge that he may well not have intended to convey the meanings outlined below.

Overview

The rest of this paper is divided into two parts. The first section begins the deconstruction of the text of the Caesarean story by dismantling the alleged dichotomy between the public world of work and the private domain of the family. Gender-specific difficulties are isolated from the more general difficulties characteristic of any unequal power relationship. Silences and disruptions in the story text reveal gendered asymmetries, and metaphors point to ideological assumptions that work to the disadvantage of women. The pregnancy of a female employee is seen as breaking organizational taboos concerning nurturance, sexuality, and emotion.

In the second part of the paper, the gender conflicts revealed by this deconstruction are iteratively eased with a series of phrase substitutions. These rewritings—or "reconstructions"—offer increasingly emancipatory visions of how we might work and care for children. These reconstructions show why relatively minor changes in organizational practices will fail to be (even) "small wins." Instead, major changes in the organization of work and family life are essential, if gender inequalities are to be genuinely alleviated.

Deconstructing the Story

Dismantling the Public/Private Dichotomy

Deconstruction dismantles a dichotomy by showing it to be a false distinction. Categories that had seemed to be mutually exclusive opposites are revealed to be inextricably intertwined. Any dichotomy could be a candidate for deconstruction, although the dismantling of any single dichotomy cannot encapsulate or exhaust analysis of all the ramifications of a text. One good starting point is a dichotomy that is so central to a text's unstated, fundamental assumptions that its deconstruction can serve as a fulcrum point for prying open deeply embedded alternate interpretations of the text.

There is a dichotomy that is central both to the Caesarean story and to many organizational theories and practices, particularly those based on an ostensibly humanitarian philosophy of management. This is the public/private dichotomy that contrasts the public domain of the marketplace, the political arena, and the legal system with the "closed and exclusive sphere of intimacy, sexuality, and affection characterizing the modern nuclear family" (Benhabib and Cornell 1988, pp. 6–7).[5]

This alleged dichotomy between the public and private spheres of influence is a false distinction. Concerns and behaviors, said to be characteristic of the public arena (particularly the marketplace), are evident within the family (e.g., Berk 1985). For example, one feminist analysis concludes:

> (Modern nuclear families) are sites of egocentric, strategic and instrumental calculation as well as sites of usually exploitative exchanges of services, labor, cash and sex, not to mention sites, frequently, of coercion and violence. (Fraser 1988, p. 37)

In addition, concerns supposedly relegated to the private domain of the family also surface in organizational contexts. For example, the needs of children and other family members are inseparable from the demands of the workplace (e.g., Frug 1986; Olsen 1983). Because most women carry a disproportionate share of these family responsibilities, they must somehow find time during working hours to take a sick family member to the doctor, meet with a teacher, etc. (e.g., Berk 1985; Hess and Ferree 1987). Unless adequate forms of childcare are consistently available, and unless work is restructured to allow family members' needs to be met, these conflicts take time away from work, forcing many women to operate at a competitive disadvantage with comparable men. In these and other ways, concerns associated with the private domain are constantly intertwined with life at work.[6]

This public/private dichotomy is an ideological assumption, not a social fact. Indeed, other eras and other cultures have used different definitions of what is public and what is private, for example considering production the responsibility of kinship groups (e.g., Collier and Yanagisako 1987; Nicholson 1986; Rosaldo 1974). Even in industrial societies, working class women have long worked in the marketplace as well as the home (e.g., Ferree 1987; Gagnier forthcoming). If this dichotomy is indeed so problematic, why is it reified and perpetuated?

Woman Is to Private as Man Is to Public?

This public/private dichotomy is associated with gender. Supposedly, the public world of politics, economics, and organizations is territory dominated by men, while women watch over the private sphere where children are conceived and family members are nurtured. This gendered characterization of the dichotomy, like the dichotomy itself, is oversimplified:

> This characterization (of the public/private split) tends to exaggerate the differences and occlude the similarities between them. For example it directs attention away from the fact that the household, like the paid workplace, is a site of labor, albeit unremunerated and often unrecognized labor. Likewise, it does not make visible the fact that in the paid workplace, as in the household, women are assigned to, indeed ghettoized in, distinctly feminine, service-oriented and often sexualized occupations. Finally, it fails to focalize the fact that in both spheres women are subordinated to men. (Fraser 1988, p. 37)

When work is conceptualized as separate from family concerns, the conflicts encountered by working mothers are defined as private problems that must be solved individually; the corporation is not responsible.

On an aggregate level, it is clear that working women are occupationally segregated (Barron and Morris 1976; Bielby and Baron 1986; Harlan and Weiss 1982; Malveaux 1982), unfairly evaluated (e.g., Blum and Smith 1988; Kanter 1977; Hartmann 1976; Taylor, Fiske, Etcoff, and Ruderman 1978; Terborg and Ilgen 1975), and paid less than men (e.g., Kahn and Crosby 1985; Larwood, Gutek, and Stromberg 1985; Strober 1982; Treiman and Hartmann 1981; Waite 1981). This gender inequality is explained and legitimated as an inevitable after-effect of a "natural" distinction between public and private concerns. Emphasis on individual solutions to "private" family problems further defuses the potential for collective action by women. This may explain, in part, why the problematic public/private dichotomy is reified and perpetuated—it provides a rationale for gender discrimination:

> 'The separation of public and private,' namely the separation of the official economic sphere from the domestic sphere and the enclaving of childrearing from the rest of social labor . . . (is) an institutional arrangement that is widely held to be one, if not the, linchpin of modern women's subordination. (Fraser 1988, p. 39)

The management of some organizations, such as the corporation described in the Caesarean story, partially acknowledge the inevitable intersections of work and family life, expressing concern for employee well-being as well as the usual desire for productivity at work. In addition, as in the Caesarean story, some organizations have instituted a series of ostensibly humanistic policies designed to "help women." These policies are congruent with human relations theories that advocate humanitarian philosophies of management that express concern for employee well-being (e.g., Hackman, Oldham, Janson, and Purdy 1975; Katz and Kahn 1978; Leavitt 1972; Likert 1967; McGregor 1960; Ouchi 1981), sometimes less as an end in itself than as a means of increasing productivity and efficiency. These human relations theories advocate partial acknowledgment of interconnections between the public and private spheres.

Critics have argued that some of these theories mask conflicts of interest between employers and employees with an apparently benign, humanitarian facade (Braverman 1974; Clawson 1980; Nord 1974; Perrow 1986). Below, I make a similar argument about the kinds of policies and values implicit in the Caesarean story.

Who Is in Control of the Private Domain?

This part of the deconstruction explores what is not said, what is left out of the Caesarean story (for a more general description of this kind of deconstructive move, see Macherey 1978, p. 60). The Caesarean story begins with the phrase, "We have a young woman . . . ," rather than "A young woman works for us." This phrase situates the text at the juncture between the public and the private domains and offers a redefinition of the usual employment contract. Such a contract is generally conceived of as an exchange. Employees surrender, within some ill-defined limits, control of their behavior at work. In exchange, the employees are guaranteed pay, benefits, and certain explicit and implicit rights.

This standard conception of an employment contract implicitly attempts to separate an employee's public and private lives, giving the employer extensive control over the employee's behavior at work. In contrast, the possessive language of the Caesarean text, (e.g., "having"), suggests that the company has access to the whole of the woman—her health and her homelife—as well as her work. The usual boundaries between the public and the private have been transgressed to an unusual degree—far in excess of the usual understandings of what is implicitly and explicitly entailed in an employment contract.

The choice and timing of the Caesarean operation is also problematic. A Caesarean operation is painful, its timing can be crucially important, and current medical practice questions its necessity or helpfulness in many cases. The sentence, "She arranged to have her Caesarean yesterday in order to be prepared for this event," suggests that the employee may have let the choice of this treatment, or its timing, be influenced by the company's product introduction schedule. Since the employee agreed to the Caesarean operation and "she arranged" its timing, it is not clear whether the company forced her, or encouraged her, to make these choices. Either way, the text implies that the product introduction schedule affected the timing of the baby's birth.

It would be highly unusual if such a serious operation were not followed by some period of recuperation away from work. Such phrases as "We insisted she stay home . . ." indicate that the corporate "we" took responsibility for making decisions that are usually the responsibility of a doctor and a patient—not an employer. This use of "we," as in the first sentence of the text, lends the authority of a group to the words of an individual (in this case, the president) while absolving that individual speaker, to some extent, of personal responsibility.

The placement of the closed circuit television in the employee's bedroom was also apparently an initiative of the company: "so we're having this done by TV for her." The employee seems to have lost control over decisions about what goes in her bedroom. Of course, she may have appreciated the chance to keep in touch with her work, perhaps as a welcome distraction from pain. It is also possible that she resented the placement of closed circuit television in her bedroom. Arguably, had she actually chosen to have the television transmissions, the invasion into her privacy could be seen as even greater than if this intrusion occurred against her expressed will. Because the story is not told from the employee's point of view, it includes no mention of how the employee reacted to these events.

Whether she acquiesced to these decisions with alacrity or felt she had little choice, the silences and absences of this text are eloquent, documenting a corporation that has, to an unusual degree, taken control of aspects of an employee's life usually considered "private." Next, I ask who benefits from this attempt to "help" a working mother.

Who Benefits?

In addition to focusing on what is not said, deconstruction also analyzes disruptions. The hidden ideology of a text is revealed at those places where the text is disrupted, where a contradiction or a glimpse of meaninglessness reveals a subtext that may be inconsistent with the text's apparent message:

> How could we ever discover the nature of the ideology that surrounds us if it were entirely consistent, without the slightest contradiction, gap, or fissure that might allow us to perceive it in the first place? (Moi 1985, p. 124)

The most obvious disruption in the Caesarean text is: "we are finding ways of filling in to create this void for us." This incoherence surfaces precisely at the point where the text addresses the organizational costs of the arrangements described in the text. The contradiction, evident in simultaneously "filling" and "creating" this void, reflects the organization's ambivalence about the extent to which the organization and the employee benefit from this acknowledgement of the interconnections between the public and private spheres.

The text suggests that the employer was willing to invest in having the television brought to the sickroom, so that this important employee could keep up to date concerning her work responsibilities. In this regard, the benefits to the company were clear. The employee's need to take an extended leave of absence, however, was of less obvious direct benefit to the company. When the president jumbled his words and contradicted himself, ambivalence about entailing these latter costs became evident.

To summarize, beneath the surface of the company's apparently benign concern with the employee's well-being are a series of silences, discomforts, and contradictions. These difficulties arise because the Caesarean operation exposes conflicts of interest between the organization (for example, to have the product released on time, to have the employee perform her job) and the individual employee (such as, to rest and let her incision heal). Although the president ostensibly was claiming wholistic concern for the employee's well-being, the text's disruptions reveal that concern is expressed, not as an end in itself, but rather as a means of maintaining some level of employee involvement and productivity during a leave. The primary beneficiary of this company's attempt to "help" a working woman is the company, not the woman.

At this point, it is essential to acknowledge that none of the observations offered so far are gender-specific. An employee by definition has entered an unequal power relationship with the employer, and in a roughly comparable surgical situation, the interests of a male employee might well be similarly subordinated to those of the employing organization. Below, this possibility is explored in some detail.

Bypassing the Heart

It is essential that any feminist critique separate gender-specific concerns from those that arise in any unequal power relationship. Since deconstruction focuses closely on the wording of a text, one way to approach this problem is to rewrite the Caesarean story, making the employee a man. Since men do not have Caesarean operations, the nature of the surgery must also be altered. Changing, then, only the sex of the protagonist and the type of operation, the rewritten story is:

> We have a young man who is extraordinarily important to the launching of a major new (product). We will be talking about it next Tuesday in its first world wide introduction. He has arranged to have his coronary bypass operation yesterday in order to be prepared for this event, so you—We have insisted that he stay home and this is going to be televised in a closed circuit television, so we're having this done by TV for him, and he is staying home three months and we are finding ways of filling in to create this void for us because we think it's an important thing for him to do.

No surgical procedure, of course, is strictly comparable to a Caesarean, but a coronary bypass operation is similar in some important ways. Like a Caesarean operation, a bypass operation is painful. Current medical practice questions the necessity and helpfulness of both operations in many cases. In addition, the timing of both operations is crucial. The need for bypass surgery is sometimes unexpected and is usually dictated by a doctor, with the permission of the patient. Similarly, the need for a Caesarean can arise unexpectedly and a doctor's advice about timing is generally followed.

One might argue that an organization has more right to exercise control over a woman having a Caesarean, in contrast to a man having a bypass operation, because a woman has control over the timing of a pregnancy and a Caesarean birth. This is not the case. Assuming her doctor concurs, a woman can control the timing of the Caesarean only within a very small range of days—a degree of latitude often available to bypass candidates. Of course, a woman can take steps to avoid the chance of a Caesarean by avoiding pregnancy, but birth control techniques do fail and short of abstinence or abortion, the tick of the biological clock (menopause) is an uncontrollable factor for women who wish to bear children.

Again the bypass operation is not dissimilar. A person can choose to abstain from smoking, reduce intake of high cholesterol foods, and exercise with fanaticism. Nevertheless, the effects of the biological clock may still be impossible to counteract; a bypass may still be necessary. Thus, both a woman having a Caesarean and a man having a bypass operation have little—sometimes no—control over the long-term need for and timing of the surgery.

When the original Caesarean and the rewritten bypass stories are compared, some similarities are evident. In both stories, the corporate "we" apparently made choices that would, under most circumstances, be made by the employee and the doctor—such as whether and when to have an operation, where and how long to recuperate, and whether to have a closed circuit television in the bedroom. As in the story about the Caesarean operation, the invasion of the employee's bedroom reveals suppressed conflicts of interest between the employer (for example, to have the product released on time, to have the employee present to perform his job) and the employee (such as, to rest and to heal). In both stories, the alleged public/private dichotomy is bypassed.

The Product-Baby Trade-Off: A Caesarean Birth

Although these two operations do have salient similarities, the dissimilarities are even more important, as they reveal gender-specific aspects of this conflict of interest between employer and employee. Differences between the operations become evident when, at the risk of explaining the obvious, we review what a Caesarean operation entails. The Concise Oxford Dictionary offers two definitions of "Caesarean:"

> (1) Delivery of child by cutting walls of abdomen (from the improbable belief that Julius was so delivered); (2) Adherent of Caesar or an autocratic system. (1964, p.167)

Whereas bypass surgery places one life in jeopardy, both a mother and an infant are involved in a Caesarean birth. Although both operations are painful, heart disease is an illness to be endured or cured, while, in spite of the pain, childbirth usually brings a welcome addition to life. A bypass operation literally bypasses a weak heart, the realm of intimate emotions, while a Caesarean brings a baby, the focus of these emotions, into the world. These differences between the two operations point to some aspects of the Caesarean story that are gender-specific.

The choice and timing of a Caesarean operation would usually be dictated by the progress of the infant's gestation and the mother's labor. The Caesarean story suggests that the mother may have jeopardized her child, or at least altered the timing of its birth, to fit the schedule of a product introduction. If this is so, the second of the Oxford's definitions becomes relevant. If the organization implicitly or explicitly influenced the timing of the baby's birth, then this Caesarean operation goes far beyond the usual terms of an employment relationship that "renders unto Caesar the things that are Caesar's."

The Caesarean story pits maternity against a form of corporate paternalism. The Caesarean text makes it clear which side of this opposition "won;" the timing of the product introduction took precedence over the timing of the birth. When a product introduction schedule influences the timing of a bypass operation, only the employee is affected. When the timing of a product introduction influences the timing of a Caesarean operation, two lives are affected and only one of them is an employee.

The gender-specific aspects of the Caesarean story, however, go deeper than a simple conflict between the interests of the organization and the mother and her child. The fact that the employee in the Caesarean story is pregnant exposes intersections between the public and private spheres and reveals a series of sexual organizational taboos.

Gender at the Juncture of Public and Private

Deconstructions often focus on whatever element is most alien to a text because such an element has the greatest potential for revealing hidden ideological assumptions (e.g., Moi 1985, p. 128). In a male-dominated organization, a pregnant employee is just such an alien element, (especially when she is a "token," that is, one of few women holding a relatively high ranking organizational position usually reserved for men, as in the Caesarean story). When a working woman becomes pregnant, her belly becomes clearly visible. Images of infant care carry connotations of nurturance and intimacy—a context in which organizational norms of efficiency and predictability seem less appropriate. The fact that sexual intercourse has occurred becomes salient. For reasons such as these, an employee's pregnancy reveals organizational taboos. These limits of the permissible reinforce an unstated sexual ideology that undergirds current norms of organizational functioning, as detailed below.

A Pregnant Belly Typically Becomes Visible

To the extent that pregnancy and child-rearing interfere with the ways work has been structured, organizations are faced with a conflict. When a working woman announces that she is pregnant, employers have to deal with that conflict. Because a pregnant woman's belly typically becomes visible, denial and an invisible absorption into the usual ways of doing business in a male-dominated organization are not possible. Pregnancy removes the option of ignoring a working woman's gender: "Honorary men" don't become pregnant.

Effective Infant Care Involves Emotion and Nurturance

Emotional expression and nurturance are not completely taboo in organizational contexts. Emotions that are related to ambition, such as aggression and fear, are often evident. A limited form of nurturance of younger employees, referred to as mentoring, is also encouraged. Thus, to the extent that nurturance and emotionality are permitted, they are focused on the organization: its tasks and its employees. Outside of these limits, nurturance and emotional expression are usually taboo.

The emotions involved in caring for an infant are not usually aggressive. They are more likely to be deeply intimate, loving, and playful—emotions that seldom characterize board meetings or the usual business lunch. The nurturance involved in childcare is also drastically different from the mentoring permitted in organizational contexts. Furthermore, while an employee and perhaps an organization benefit from a mentoring relationship, the primary beneficiary of a mother's love is her child.

Pregnancy Is Caused by Sexual Intercourse

Sex, of course, is not taboo—across the board—in organizations. It is the limitations of the sexual taboo in organizations, the ways it is regularly broken, that are germane to the Caesarean story. High ranking men are not usually condemned for having sex with lower ranking women, provided the affair is handled with some discretion. In addition, men's sexual harassment of female employees, in both subtle and not-so-subtle forms, is commonplace (e.g., Gutek ; Kahn and Crosby 1985). In these kinds of sexual and pseudo-sexual activities, men retain a position of power. Male sexual activity is taboo in organizations only when it occurs outside these limits.

Organizational taboos concerning the voluntary sexual behavior of women are more limiting—an organizational intensification of the sexual double standard (e.g., Gutek 1985; Kahn and Crosby 1985; Kanter 1986). Women are frowned upon if they sleep "beneath them," that is with lower ranking men. If a woman has "slept up" with a higher ranking man, and if that woman is subsequently promoted, her advance is likely to be credited to her seductive abilities, rather than her competence on the job.

There is evidence here of a class bias. These taboos seem especially directed toward relatively high ranking women—those who might be promoted or have men subordinates. The sexual availability of lower status women is left intact, perhaps because their lack of formal power may make them less threatening to men and, perhaps, more easily coerced or harassed.

Kanter (1977) captured some aspects of these taboos in her categorization of sex-typed organizational roles for women. The first of these is the Iron Maiden, an asexual, highly competent worker who displays little of the emotional, nurturing behavior usually expected of a female. In a sense, an Iron Maiden is an "honorary male." Other sex-typed roles are the Mother and the Pet, a younger sister figure. These are emotionally nurturing roles. Sex, however, is again forbidden, in these cases by a form of the incest taboo. Finally, there is the Seductress. This is a sexually active, dangerous figure of unclear competence. Although she may act in an emotionally nurturing manner, it is unclear whether this behavior is sincere. Her sexuality is usually directed toward higher ranking men.

Kanter's roles suggest why a pregnant female employee upsets the sexual status quo in an organization. She is sexually active. Unlike the Seductress, however, she has (usually) not chosen an employee. This act fits none of the stereotypes. The Iron Maiden is revealed as sexually active. There is no virgin Mother and even the younger sister is not sexually innocent. The Seductress is plying her seductive talents outside the firm. This, then, is the sexual taboo that a pregnant employee violates: Sex is happening and the high ranking male employee is getting none of it.

For all these reasons, a pregnant employee is an alien element in a male-dominated organizational context. Her pregnant belly draws attention to her gender, carries connotations of intimacy and nurturance, and makes acknowledgment of taboo aspects of sexuality inescapable. This breaking of the sexuality taboo is particularly problematic, as can be seen with further deconstruction of the metaphors/puns in the Caesarean story.

The Sexual Subtext: Who Does What to the Void?

Since Freud exposed the power of the unconscious and, in particular, the pervasiveness of suppressed/repressed sexuality, many psychologists have found exploration of these hidden elements to be potentially informative. That acceptance, however, has seldom extended to organizational theory, where the explicit examination of sexual issues has usually remained as taboo as in actual organizations. The analysis below discusses sexuality in an overt manner quite alien to the usual forms of organizational discourse.

Readers uncomfortable with this approach may find this section of this paper particularly inappropriate or ill-founded. I was tempted, therefore, to delete this material rather than risk dismissal of the entire paper. However, resistance may well be a natural reaction to the discussion of a taboo topic. I decided to include this section because any resistance experienced may be conceptually germane and potentially a useful source of insight into the ways sexual taboos operate in the context of organizational discourse.

When the man's bypass surgery becomes a woman's Caesarean operation, deconstruction reveals suppressed sexuality in undertones and "double entendres" of the president's speech. For example, the phrase, "We have a young woman," is a "double entendre." The sexual meaning of "having a woman" enters the text.

In the context of the Caesarean story, the disruption of the president's language also has sexual undertones. "We are finding ways of filling in to create this void for us" carries sexual meanings. In addition to the void at the office created by the employee's absence, there was a void in the woman's body. That void, once filled by a man, and then by the child, was emptied by the Caesarean.

These interpretations have the linguistic effect of making the woman sexually accessible ("filling in" her void, "having" her). The incest taboo of motherhood has been semantically broken. No wonder, then, that the president's language was disrupted ("filling in to create this void") at this particular point in the text.

The corporate "we" of the Caesarean text is masculine because it is (usually) a man who has a woman and it is a man who fills the void. To explore what is left out here, the relationship between reproduction and production must be examined. Traditionally, reproductive capacities are the aspects of womanhood that have been associated with the private domain. Supposedly, a woman provides physical and emotional nurturance for her family, thereby freeing her husband to devote his energies to the workplace and the broader public domain. Because women experience sexual pleasure independently of reproduction and production, this gendered way of attempting to separate public from private effaces—by ignoring—a woman's potential for sexual pleasure (Spivak 1987).

Thus, the sexual double entendres in the Caesarean story presume a masculine perspective which, in effect, supports men's dominance of production in the public arena, reinforces women's responsibilities for reproduction and nurturance in the private domain, and excludes consideration of a woman's need for sexual pleasure. Such attempts to reify a gendered public/private dichotomy mask the ways organizations structure child care and sexuality by making the birth process, children's needs for nurturance, and some aspects of female sexuality taboo in organizational contexts. These are ways the public/private dichotomy serves as a linchpin of gender discrimination.

Although awareness of the interconnections between work and family life is the first step to dismantling this false dichotomy, a deeper acknowledgment of these interconnections could deeply disrupt and transform the language, premises, and objectives of organizational discourse. How this might be done is the topic of the next section of this paper.

Reconstructing the Story in the Emancipatory Interest

In this section of the paper, the Caesarean story is rewritten, in an attempt to articulate what would have to be changed in order to alleviate the problems discussed above. This is a kind of proactive deconstruction, a "reconstruction," that can be defined as an iterative process of rewriting that alters—using substitutions—only a few phrases of the text at any one time. Because this method stays close to the original text, a small change in wording can make adjacent phrases seem "unnatural." In this way, iterative reconstructions reveal unanticipated repercussions of each small step in a major change effort.

Metaphors: Why a Product Can Be Launched and a Baby Cannot

The Caesarean story partially acknowledges interconnections between the public and private spheres, but it does so in a way that gives precedence to the public rather than the private, the product rather than the baby. Below, the first reconstruction reverses this precedence, changing nothing else. In such a rewriting, the story would begin:

> We have a young woman who is extraordinarily important to the launching of a major new child. We will be talking about her baby next Tuesday in its first world wide introduction. She arranged to have her product introduced early yesterday in order to be prepared for this birth.

Spivak suggests that ". . . it is at those borders of discourse where metaphor and example seem arbitrarily chosen that ideology breaks through" (1987, p. 125). There is an arbitrary use of metaphor in this first reconstruction. Although both products and babies are delivered and, in both cases, it is good to deliver on time, the metaphor of "launching a baby" does not work. Why is it possible to launch a product, but not a baby?

Babies are "brought into" the world with more pain and a different kind of trajectory than is suggested by the metaphor of "launching." The Concise Oxford Dictionary (1964, p. 683) defines "launching" in terms of hurling, discharging, sending forth, and bursting—all images that have the male sexual connotations of ejaculation. The language of the public domain, in this case "launching a product," often has male sexual undertones that make it inappropriate for describing women-related issues such as birth (e.g., Derrida 1976; Spivak 1987). In this way, our habits of language use reinforce a gendered characterization of the public/private dichotomy.

The Unnatural

Other word combinations in this first rewriting of the story seem awkward or "unnatural," a condition that deconstruction points to as informative:

> The hegemonic orientation prevails not by overt domination or resigned acceptance, but by naturalization, by a general recognition that 'this is the way things are, and they cannot be any other way.' (Calas 1987, p. 209)

Although all babies, even at birth, are not created equal, it does not seem "natural" to say "a major new" baby. A new product may be considered "major," but a mother's investment in producing a baby cannot easily make it "major," except in the eyes of the baby's family. Similarly, a "world wide introduction" seems inappropriate, except possibly for a baby with royal or celebrity parents. For these few babies, birth is a transition from the private world of the womb into, quite literally, the public domain. Only in these instances does the language of a product introduction become a "natural" substitute for discussing issues of reproduction and nurturance, usually relegated to the private domain.

Furthermore, it does not seem "natural" that an organization would see a baby as so important. It would indeed be costly to devote this much attention to the babies of even a few employees. And, given the organization's tendency to give precedence to its own interests, rather than the interests of the family, parents might well fear having their baby be so important to an organization.

Altering Who Does What Where

The next step of the reconstruction alters the mother's behavior. The protagonist of this reconstruction is a new mother who wishes to work and to be with her infant—simultaneously. In the president's version of the story, the company "insisted she stay home." Suppose instead that she insisted on coming in to the office—with her baby. Now, the ending of the story would read:

> She has insisted that she come to work and this new baby is going to be brought to the office, so she's having this done for herself, and she is working for three months. She is finding ways of filling in to create this void for us because she thinks it's an important thing for her to do.

In this version, the woman takes responsibility for arranging a merger between her work and childcare responsibilities, locating these activities in the office. In this reconstruction, the woman's attention would be split between work and the infant. The public and private spheres, however, probably have not been symmetrically merged. The office location suggests that work will be given priority most of the time, as organizations are not generally accustomed to accommodating the needs of parents working with children present. Furthermore, the sentence structure of this version of the story, (". . . she thinks it's an important thing for her to do"), makes it seem as if the corporation does not share her perception of the importance of her childcare activities.

Experimental Organizational Forms: A Failure to Thrive

Some might argue that such conflicts of interest between working parents and their employers are inevitable. Other judgments, however, are possible. In the next version of the story, the choice to merge work and childcare remains in the hands of the woman, but the organization sees itself as benefiting as well:

> She has insisted that she come to work and this new baby is going to be brought to the office, so she's having this done for us, and she is working for three months. We are finding ways to create this void for us because we think it's an important thing for us to do.

At this point the limitations of reconstruction by substitution become evident. If an organization really wanted to take responsibility for helping men and women live comfortably with the interconnections between the public and private realms of their lives, then a wide range of organizational policies would have to change. The scope of these changes cannot be anticipated by using simple substitutions to reconstruct the Caesarean text. For example, such an organization might have on-site pediatricians and sick care available, flexible hours, and comfortable, safe, and supervised places for children to play near where their parents work. In contrast to some "humanitarian" theories of management, the objective of these policies would not be to increase parent's productivity, although this might well happen. The organization would be doing this in order to provide a more humane place for adults and children to work and play.

The limitations of this last reconstruction become evident if I go beyond the text to discuss some research on experimental organizational forms. Some organizations and social movements have attempted to institutionalize variants on the ideas described in the reconstruction above, providing a place where work and family, public and private, can be merged (e.g., Ferguson 1984; Kanter 1972; Kreiger 1981; Rothschild-Witt 1979; Smelser 1962; Swidler 1979; Zald and Berger 1978). These organizations usually allow flexible working hours and permit employees/owners to divide their time between childcare and work. In order to avoid the power inequalities inherent in hierarchy, many of these organizations have refrained from using clearly defined job descriptions or long-term divisions of labor. For similar reasons, many of these organizations prefer consensual decision-making. Sanctions for nonperformance are sometimes avoided.

These innovations have costs which make it difficult, but not impossible, for experimental organizations to survive in the long term (e.g., Kanter 1972; Rothschild-Witt 1979; Swidler 1979). For example, the development of consensus is time consuming. Tasks sometimes do not get done. Split attention can mean decreased productivity on the job. As a result of these "inefficiencies," these new organizational forms often take more time than conventional organizations to do the same amount of work.

The long-term benefits of these practices might well outweigh the costs of their "inefficiency," if it were not for the competitive markets characteristic of a capitalist economy. (This is not an observation unique to profit-seeking firms. Organizations also fail to survive in the nonprofit/governmental sectors.) As long as an experimental organization has to compete with organizations that are more productive, its long-term chances of survival will not be good.

Mandating Nurture

It is not enough, therefore, to create an innovative organizational form. Change in the broader public realm is also necessary. An experimental organizational form may seem to be a viable alternative, but it may well fail to survive unless enough organizations change in the same way at the same time. This is a big "unless"—one that requires governmental intervention.

The necessity of this broader scope of change can be argued from a different starting point. Rather than changing the way work is organized, imagine changing childcare. One way to do this is to bring in a person not yet mentioned in the reconstructions of the Caesarean story: the baby's father. If he were willing to stay home and care for the baby (without the immunogenic advantages of breastfeeding), the woman could go back to work as soon as her Caesarean incision heals, with minimal disruption for the company.

As long as the father is willing to take the parenting role traditionally assigned to the mother, the organization does not have to change its ways. Such a "resolution" is a reconstruction by substitution; it simply reverses gender roles. It is insufficient because it leaves the public/private dichotomy intact. To show this, I must again go beyond the text.

Because a man generally earns considerably more than a woman, many families would find it a financial strain to substitute a woman's salary for that earned by her husband. It is possible, of course, to legislate equal pay for men and women, perhaps in the form of a comparable worth law. In that case, the man might still not want to stay at home with his child because he fears subsequent maltreatment when he returns to work. Again, this could be forbidden by legislation.

However, a man might still not want to be at home, perhaps because of the traditional devaluation of housework and childcare, as opposed to paid labor. Again, legislation might be helpful. In Sweden, for example, so few men have taken advantage of opportunities for parental leave, that some have suggested the leaves be made mandatory (Olsen 1983, p. 1559).

In each of these examples, change in the private domain of the family's childcare arrangements requires governmental intervention as well as new organizational policies. This analysis of policy alternatives reveals that the gendered aspects of the public/private dichotomy are critical to the current structure of our organizational, familial, and governmental systems. The eradication of gender discrimination within an organization would require change in all these realms (e.g., Frug 1986; Olsen 1983).

Reconstruction and the Analysis of Reforms

In these reconstructions of the text, I made a series of simple substitutions (baby for product, employee's interests from employers' interests, man for woman) to offer an increasingly radical series of proposed reforms. The small change of a single substitution repeatedly caused language in adjoining sentences to seem unnatural (a "major new baby" and "launching a baby"). As the number of substitutions increased, the sequence of small changes necessary to make the text "make sense" became more complex and interconnected. The complexity of this kind of change analysis provides a far more detailed analysis than a simple list of proposed reforms.

The specificity that comes from staying iteratively close to the original text makes reconstruction a useful way to think about the feasibility, scope, and potential impact of supposedly minor reform efforts. The iterations graphically portrayed the possibility of changing organizational practices that reify the public/private dichotomy. In somewhat utopian terms, the iterations explored ways that personal and organization lives might be differently structured. Perhaps more importantly, the iterations also revealed how current organizational practices have been grounded in assumptions that are more ideologically motivated and less stable than we might have expected.

Reconstruction by substitution also has a clear limitations that became increasingly evident as broader, more radical changes were iteratively considered. This reconstruction relied on substitutions in a text, that is, on relatively small variations in existing forms. The analysis revealed that such small-scale reforms could not succeed within an organization without broader based changes outside of the organization, that is, outside of the public/private boundaries assumed by the original story. Thus, the specificity that is a source of the power of this form of reconstruction is also a critical limitation. The "small wins" of minor changes, reflected in the phrase substitutions of the reconstructions above, do not suffice. Major change, on a broad scale, is essential.

Stopping

Deconstructing My Silences

Deconstruction is potentially an endless process. At this point I will stop and briefly note the silences of this deconstruction. In its focus on a relatively high ranking woman, this paper has tacitly accepted the managerial class bias of most organizational research. More specifically, the costs incurred by the pregnant employee in the Caesarean story are far less than the personal costs that would be incurred by a person with a similar medical condition, but no job or a job that was less important to the organization. Few organizations would be concerned enough about the health of clerical or blue-collar employees to bother to put televisions in their bedrooms. This neglect might seem benign unless job security were threatened, as it well might be if a lower status employee needed a long-term leave of absence to recuperate. Disability insurance, legal constraints, and medicaid/medicare provide only limited protection for those at the bottom of the economic hierarchy.

In addition, the deconstruction does not explore how the organization's reaction might differ, across classes, if the employee were black, handicapped, or a member of some other disempowered group. For example, the alien element that is the focus of this deconstruction is a pregnant woman. This focus draws the analysis into the realm of heterosexual concerns that may not be central, at least in legally recognized ways, to many people. To choose only one of these issues, suppose that the story concerned a man whose life is threatened by AIDs, rather than a failing heart. Deconstruction of the AIDs story would explore the homosexual subtext ignored in this paper (for example, "having a man"). Analysis of these kinds of possibilities would clearly enrich, extend, and challenge the results of the present analysis.

Other reconstructions could analyze the intersections of gender and class with race and ethnicity. This is a much-needed form of feminist analysis, as it is often difficult to determine whether a given difficulty is common to all, a subset, or only one of a nested, overlapping set of disempowered groups. To the extent that a reform would benefit others in addition to women, or a particular subset of women, political strategies could be broadened or targeted appropriately.

A final and most important limitation must be acknowledged. Because any deconstruction can itself be deconstructed—perhaps most easily where its author would wish it were invulnerable—this paper is most silent about its central limitation: the feminist assumptions that are its backbone. Deconstructing these is a task I willingly leave undone, although unfortunately it is not undoable.

An Invitation to Deconstruction

Although the limitations described above are crucial, their importance would be diminished if other deconstructions, lacking these limitations, were performed. The present paper offers examples of a wide variety of deconstruction strategies, summarized in Figure 1. The abstract explanations of these deconstructive moves, the references, and the examples provided in this paper could serve as an introduction to deconstruction for organizational scholars previously unfamiliar with this analytic strategy. I hope a few might be tempted to try using deconstruction in their own research domains.

Theoretical and empirical texts as well as examples of discourse by organizational members could be deconstructed from a variety of ideological viewpoints. For example, a politically leftist deconstruction might dissect the functionalist and adaptive assumptions of population ecology or the assertions about legitimation that lie at the core of institutional theory. A politically more conservative deconstruction, perhaps stressing efficiency explanations for behavior, might usefully question the "nonrational" assertions that pervade research on both institutional theory and cognitive heuristics. If organizational theory development drew on the critical and analytic power inherent in deconstruction, our research might be deeply changed and considerably enriched.

Why Gender Discrimination Is So Persistent

In this paper, I have used deconstruction to achieve a specific objective: to reveal gender conflicts suppressed between the lines of a story about a Caesarean operation. This story was told by a corpo-

1   Dismantling a dichotomy, exposing it as a false distinction (i.e., the public/private opposition).

2   Examining silences—what is not said (i.e., noting who or what is excluded by the use of pronouns such as "we").

3   Attending to disruptions and contradictions, places where the text fails to make sense (i.e., "filling in to create a void").

4   Focusing on the element that is most alien to a text or a context (i.e., a pregnant executive), as means of deciphering implicit taboos—the limits to what is conceivable or permissible.

5   Interpreting metaphors as a rich source of multiple meanings (i.e., "launching a product").

6   Analyzing "double-entendres" that may point to an unconscious subtext, often sexual in content (i.e., "having a woman").

7   Separating group-specific and more general sources of bias by "reconstructing" the text with iterative substitution of phrases (i.e., using the bypass story to isolate gender-specific difficulties).

8   Exploring, with careful "reconstructions," the unexpected ramifications and inherent limitations of minor policy changes (i.e., a woman bringing a baby into the office).

9   Using the limitations exposed by "reconstruction" to explain the persistence of the status quo and the need for more ambitious change programs (i.e., why small-scale organizational reforms will not alleviate gender inequalities at work).

Figure 1   Analytic strategies used in deconstruction.

ration president as evidence of his firm's humanitarian concern for the well-being of women employees with children. Deconstruction revealed that the primary beneficiary of this apparently well-intentioned effort to "help" was the corporation—not the woman or her child. The deconstruction used a comparison of the Caesarean operation with coronary bypass surgery to separate gender-specific difficulties from the problems inherent in other unequal power relationships.

Some of these gender-specific issues included the organizational taboos that make life at work extremely difficult for a pregnant woman. Her visible pregnancy, capacity for sexual pleasure, and involvement with intimate emotions and nurturance all become evident in an organizational context where such aspects of life are considered "inappropriate." In this part of the paper, the deconstruction revealed how apparently well-intentioned efforts to alleviate gender inequality can force it into hiding, leaving it free to surface in more subtle and pernicious forms.

In the second half of the paper, the reconstructions of the Caesarean story explored ways to renegotiate the usual social contract between employer and employees, merging and transforming personal and organizational life. Analysis of the unexpected ramifications of a series of these reconstructions demonstrated the inadequacy of small-scale organizational reforms. The public/private dichotomy was revealed to be a linchpin supporting discrimination against women. The gender segregation of tasks, paid and unpaid, made it impossible to discuss changing gender discrimination in organizations without changing gender roles within the family. These could not be changed without a fundamental realignment of government policies concerning both the family and the marketplace.

Given the scope of the needed changes outlined in the second half of this paper, it is no wonder that gender-based pay inequality and occupational segregation have been so difficult to eradicate. Small-scale organizational reforms—however well-intentioned—reify, rather than alleviate, gender inequality. This is a policy domain where "small wins" won't win.

Breaking the Taboos of Mainstream Organizational Thinking

It is reasonable to ask at this point if this deconstruction of suppressed gender conflict makes a contribution to organizational research. Previous studies have, for example, measured the extent of gender inequality, documented the unfairness of certain organizational practices, and offered women advice about how to fit into a male-dominated organizational world. Much of this research assumes that public/private boundaries are real and that current structural and institutional arrangements are fixed (cf., Blum and Smith 1988; Calas and Smirich 1989).

Instead of asking how women might fit into existing organizational structures, this paper asks how structures will have to be changed—radically—if woman and children are to be genuinely helped. In this respect, this paper fails to offer a direct contribution to mainstream organizational research, in the usual sense that the word "contribution" is used. Such a contribution would, in effect, be using a feminist perspective as "a special-interest glamorization of mainstream discourse" (Spivak 1987, p. 130).

If a feminist perspective is constrained to be a "special interest" enrichment of mainstream organizational theory and research, its disruptive and constructive potentials will have been severely and unnecessarily limited. In this paper I have tried to illustrate how feminist perspectives have the capacity to disrupt the usual terms of organizational discourse, transforming its content, premises, and objectives. For example, in the deconstructions and reconstructions above, customary phrasing appeared "unnatural," a sexual subtext became more overt, and the shortcomings of limited reforms became evident.

A full incorporation of a feminist viewpoint into organizational theory and research would be far more than a "special-interest glamorization of mainstream discourse." A feminist perspective would do far more than reinforce the "common sense" observation that there are disempowered groups of people, such as women, whose interests are not well represented—or sometimes even considered—in organizational theory and practice. Gender-based sensitivity could infuse our thinking in a transformative way, illuminating the gaps in taken-for-granted forms of organizational thinking.

Familiar dichotomies might be abandoned. Some of the most basic categories of organizational theory might need to be rethought. For example, female sexual pleasure, the needs of children, emotions of fear, attraction, sadness, and love—such topics would no longer be taboo territory for organizational theory. Organizational researchers might seek viable alternatives to hierarchy and stable divisions of labor ("jobs"), thereby putting into question the correlation of income with occupational status (e.g., Ferguson 1984; Kanter 1987; Smirich 1985). If feminist perspectives were fully incorporated, the usual emphases on rationality, hierarchy, competition, efficiency, and productivity would be exposed as only a very small piece of the organizational puzzle.

Appendix

Below are some excerpts from the official transcript of the conference proceedings:

> Anchor man: If the family is the woof and warp of American society, and there is a great deal of concern that it is deteriorating before our very eyes, is it a concern to corporate America? Are you doing things like providing, for example, maternal care and paternal care, providing as well, day care centers for the working mothers who may be valuable members of your company so they can come and continue to contribute to (your company) and still not have to worry about their children?

> President: Well, I think we are, of course, concerned about family values. I think they are on the decline, and I think that is a problem . . . As far as the corporation acting as a proxy to the family, I think it's not a great one. Again, I think we provide a whole range of benefits and that kind of thing, but when you're thinking about it from a family values point of view, that really isn't a substitute for what really happens in the strong family relationship.

> Anchor man: That's a nice rhetorical commitment, but let me ask you about some specific things. What about day care centers at (your company)? What about a woman who may be a single mother or they need both incomes in the household to go on? She has a job because they want to have a child in the family, and yet she is making a real contribution not only to her financial well-being, but to her psychic and intellectual well-being and to your company's well-being. Do you try in some fashion to help her with this problem of caring for that child by maybe providing some day care centers, and if you don't, why not?

> President: We have a lot of range of working mothers. Let me give you one example.

At this point the president told the Caesarean story with which this paper began. The official transcript does not note it, but the president's story was greeted with some hisses. Other members of the audience nodded approval of the president. Many of the rest seemed puzzled by extreme reactions of either form. One who hissed later explained her reaction:

> Not only was it an outrageous statement, it was stupid. It didn't occur to him to ask, 'Where are our values here?' . . . Didn't it occur to him that this kid deserves his (sic) own timing?

Notes

1. Feminism is a leftist political ideology that has lead to the development of feminist theory. That theory challenges functionalist assumptions, particularly those that disproportionately serve the interests of men. Feminist theory seeks a fuller understanding of both overt and suppressed gender conflict. Research in this tradition reveals how female interests have been subordinated to those of males, with the ultimate goal of eradicating that subordination and transforming relations between men and women.

2. My direct and simple style is quite different from the fluid, complex, inconsistent, and rhetorical style that characterizes a deconstruction that "intends to defuse—by refusing—reason" (e.g., Derrida 1976; Spivak 1987). A simpler, more direct style is characteristic of those (like critical legal scholars or myself) who use deconstruction to delegitimate ideological bias.

3. I do not want to leave the mistaken impression that all deconstructions are tightly unified around a single theme, such as feminism. Indeed, many feminists are uncomfortable with the use of deconstruction. Two contradictory reasons for this discomfort have been offered (e.g., Flax 1987; Moi, 1985; Spivak 1987; Weedon 1987). Deconstruction is damned, either because it is not a powerful means of advancing political agendas, or because it is. These difficulties are discussed more fully below.

   Those who fail to find deconstruction politically useful, including many feminists, argue that texts chosen as targets for deconstruction tend to be rather esoteric. This lack of focus on everyday concerns is said to be a politically conservative sign. Deconstruction (like much of organizational theory) is often a language-game, played by intellectuals for an audience of intellectuals. Few others would have the time, money, or patience to spend their time deciphering deconstructions where, it sometimes seems, every other phrase is a neologism, enclosed in quotation marks, embedded in multiple dependent clauses, or expressed in one or several foreign languages. Furthermore, although deconstruction can and does challenge existing power structures, it does so with ideas. Thus, these critics argue that deconstructions fall prey to the intellectuals' occupational hazard: overestimating the transformational power of ideas. Because of reasons such as these, some criticize deconstruction as intellectually elitist and politically unimportant.

   Others, including some feminists, disagree. These scholars argue that deconstruction is politically powerful because it can be used to undermine the verbal tactics of legitimization used by advocates of dominant ideologies. The problem with this position, however, is that if deconstruction can be a powerful aid to a political ideology, it can also be used, with equal effectiveness, against that ideology. Given the intensity and perseverance of gender inequality, admitting the deconstructive potential of feminism is a risky strategy.

   I am an advocate of the political utility of deconstruction. The risks are worth it, I believe, because charges of intellectual elitism and political powerlessness can be addressed by focusing on a text that is practical rather than esoteric, writing in a direct style accessible to those as yet uninitiated into the mysteries of deconstruction, and using phrase substitutions as a means of exploring policy-relevant alternatives to current practices. For all these reasons, I hope the deconstruction in this paper will be politically useful.

4. Deconstructions have usually (particularly among literary critics in the U.S.) focused on polished written texts, masterpieces of literary grace or cogent logic. In contrast, this deconstruction focuses on a speech excerpt that obviously lacks both forms of polish. Such a focus on a speech is consistent with the work of those who use deconstruction to critique institutional arrangements (e.g., Derrida 1976), legal theory (e.g., Frug 1986; Olsen 1983), and sexism (e.g., Spivak 1987; Weedom 1987). It is also consistent with Ricoeur's (1981) ideas of "social action as text."

5. Habermas (1984) delineates a second version of the public/private dichotomy, contrasting some shared conception of the public good with the private interests of both individuals and profit-seeking organizations. This second version of the dichotomy is not the focus of the present paper.

6. The second version of the public/private dichotomy is also a false distinction (e.g., Frug 1986; Olsen 1983). For example, government regulations often constrain the behavior of firms in the private sector, requiring them to hire women, refrain from hiring children, or treat pregnancy like any other short-term disability. Conversely, the private sector has an enormous impact on governmental functioning.

References

Barron, R. D and G. M. Morris (1976), "Sexual Divisions and the Dual Labor Market," In D. Barker & S. Allen (Eds.), *Dependence and Exploitation in Work and Marriage*, Longman, New York, 47–69.

Benhabib, S. and D. Cornell (Eds.) (1988), *Feminism as Critique*, Banta Company/George Banta Company, Inc., Menasha, WI.

Berk, S. (1985), *The Gender Factory: The Appointment of Work in American Households*, Plenum, New York.

Bielby, W. and J. Baron (1986), "Men and Women at Work: Sex Segregation and Statistical Discrimination," *Amer. J. Sociology*, 91, 4, 1–42.

Blum, L. and V. Smith (1988), "Women's Mobility in the Corporation: A Critique of the Politics of Optimism," *Signs*, 13, 3, 528–545.

Braverman, H. (1974), *Labor and Monopoly Capital*, Monthly Review Press, New York.

Calas, M. and L. Smircich (1987), "Post-Culture: Is the Organizational Culture Literature Dominant but Dead?" Paper presented at the Third International Conference on Organizational Symbolism and Corporate Culture, Milan, Italy.

_____ (1989), "Using the F-Word: Feminist Theories and the Social Consequences of Organizational Research," Paper presented at the annual meeting of the Academy of Management, Washington, D.C.

Clawson, D. (1980), *Bureaucracy and the Labor Process*, Monthly Review Press, New York.

Collier, J. F. and S. J. Yanagisako (Eds.) (1987) *Gender and Kinship: Essays Toward a Unified Analysis*, Stanford University Press, Stanford, CA.

Concise Oxford Dictionary. (1964), Oxford University Press, London, England.

Derrida, J. (1976), *Speech and Phenomenon*, Northwestern University Press, Evanston, IL.

Eagleton, T. (1976), *Marxism and Literacy Criticism*, University of California Press, Berkeley.

Ferguson, K. E. (1984), *The Feminist Case against Bureaucracy*, Temple University Press, Philadelphia, PA.

Flax, J. (1987), "Postmodernism and Gender Relations in Feminist Theory," *Signs*, 12, 4, 621–643.

Fraser, N. (1988), "What's Critical about Critical Theory? The Case of Habermas and Gender," In S. Benhabib & D. Cornell (Eds.), *Feminism as Critique*, Banta Company/George Banta Company, Inc., Menasha, WI, 31–55.

Frug, G. (1986), "The Ideology of Bureaucracy in American Law," *Harvard Law Rev.*, 97, 1276–1388.

Gagnier, R. (in press), "The Literary Standard, Working-Class Lifewriting, and Gender," *Textual Practice*.

Gutek, B. (1985), *Sex and the Workplace: The Impact of Sexual Behavior and Harassment on Women, Men and Organizations*, Jossey-Bass, San Francisco, CA.

Habermas, J. (1984), *The Theory of Communicative Action*, Beacon Press, Boston, MA.

Hackman, R. J., G. Oldham, R. Janson, and K. Purdy (1975), "A New Strategy for Job Enrichment," *California Management Rev.*, 17, 4, 57–71.

Harlan, A. and C. Weiss (1982), "Sex Differences in Factors Affecting Managerial Career Advancement," In P. Wallace (Ed.), *Women in the Workplace*, Auburn House, Boston, MA, 59–100.

Hartmann, H. (1976), "Capitalism, Patriarchy, and Job Segregation by Sex," In M. Blaxall & B. Reagen (Eds.), *Women and the Workplace*, University of Chicago Press, Chicago, IL, 137–170.

Hess, B. B. and M. M. Ferree (Eds.) (1987), *Analyzing Gender: A Handbook of Social Science Research*, Sage Publications, Newbury Park, CA.

Irigaray, L. (1974), *Speculum de L'Autre Femme*, Editions de Minuit, Paris, France.

Kahn, W. A. and F. Crosby (1985), "Discriminating between Attitudes and Discriminatory Behavior: Change and Stasis," In L. Larwood, B. A. Gutek, & A. H. Stromberg (Eds.), *Women and Work: An Annual Review*, Vol. 1, Sage Publications, Beverly Hills, CA, 215–238.

Kanter, R. M. (1972), *Commitment and Community*, Harvard University Press, Cambridge, MA.

_____ (1977), *Men and Women of the Community*, Anchor Press, New York.

_____ (1986), "The New Workforce Meets the Changing Workplace: Strains, Dilemmas, and Contradictions in Attempts to Implement Participative and Entreprencurial Management," *Human Resource Management*, 25, 4, 515–537.

Katz, D. and R. Kahn (1978), *The Social Psychology of Organizations* (2nd ed.), John Wiley and Sons, Toronto.

Kilduff, M. (1981), "Deconstructing Organizations," Paper presented at the annual meeting of the Academy of Management, New Orleans, LA.

Kreiger, S. (1982), *Mirror Dance: Identity in a Women's Community*, Temple University Press, Philadelphia, PA.

Larwood, L., B. A. Gutek, and A. H. Stromberg (Eds.) (1985), *Women and Work, an Annual Review*, Vol. 3, Sage Publications, Beverly Hills, CA.

Leavitt, H. (1972), *Managerial Psychology*, Vol. 1, University of Chicago Press, Chicago, IL.

Likert, R. (1967), *The Human Organization*, McGraw-Hill, New York.

Macherey, P. (1978), *A Theory of Literary Production*, Routledge and Kegan Paul, London, England.

Malveaux, J. (1982), "Moving Forward, Standing Still: Woman in White Collar Jobs," In P. Wallace (Ed.), *Women in the Workplace*, Auburn House, Boston, MA, 101–133.

McGregor, D. (1960), *The Human Side of Enterprise*, McGraw Hill, New York.

Moi, T. (1985), *Sexual/Textual Politics: Feminist Literary Theory*, Methuen & Company, New York.

Nicholson, L. (1986), *Gender and History*, Columbia University Press, New York.

Nord, W. (1974), "The Failure of Current Applied Behavioral Sciences: A Marxian Perspective," *J. Appl. Behavioral Sci.*, 10, 4, 557–578.

Olsen, F. (1983), "The Family and the Market: A Study of Ideology and Legal Reform," *Harvard Law Rev.*, 96, 7, 1497–1578.

Ouchi, W. (1981), *Theory Z*, Addison-Wesley, Reading, MA.

Perrow, C. (1986), *Complex Organizations: A Critical Essay*, Random House, New York.

Pettigrew, T. and J. Martin (1987), "Shaping the Organizational Context for Black American Inclusion," *J. Social Issues*, 43, 41–78.

Ricoeur, P. (1981), "The Model of the Text: Meaningful Action Considered as a Text," In J. B. Thompson (Ed.), *Hermeneutics and the Human Sciences*, Cambridge University Press, Cambridge, England.

Rosaldo, M. Z. (1974), "Theoretical Overview," In M. Z. Rosaldo & L. Lamphere (Eds.), *Women, Culture, and Society*, Stanford University Press, Stanford, CA, 17–42.

Rothschild-Witt, J. (1979), "The Collectivist Organization: An Alternative to Rational-Bureaucratic Models," *Amer. Sociology Rev.* 44, 509–527.

Smelser, N. J. (1962), *Theory of Collective Behavior*, Free Press, New York.

Smircich, L. (1985), "Toward a Woman Centered Organization Theory," Paper presented at the annual meeting of the Academy of Management, San Diego, CA.

Spivak, G. C. (1987), *In Other Worlds: Essays in Cultural Politics*, Metheun, New York.

Strober, M. (1982), "The MBA: Same Passport to Success for Women and Men?" In P. Wallace (Ed.), *Women in the Workplace*, Auburn House, Boston, MA, 25–55.

Swidler, A. (1979), *Organization without Authority: Dilemmas of Social Control in Free Schools*, Harvard University Press, Cambridge, MA.

Taylor, S., S. Fiske., N. Etcoff., and A. Ruderman (1978). "Categorical and Contextual Bases of Person Memory and Stereotyping," *J. Personality and Social Psychology*, 36, 7, 778–793.

Terborg, J. R. and D. R. Ilgen (1975), "A Theoretical Approach to Sex Discrimination in Traditionally Masculine Occupations," *Occupational Behavior and Human Performance*, 13, 352–376.

Treiman, D. J. and H. I. Hartmann (1981). *Women, Work, and Wages: Equal Pay for Jobs of Equal Value*, National Academy Press, Washington, DC.

Van Maanen, J. (1988), *Tales of the Field*, University of Chicago Press, Chicago, IL.

Waite, L. J. (1981), "US Women at Work." *Population Bulletin*, 36, 2, Population Reference Bureau, Washington, DC.

Weedon, C. (1987), *Feminist Practice and Poststructuralist Theory*, Basil Blackwell, Inc, New York.

White, S. K. (1986), "Foucault's Challenge to Critical Theory," *Amer. Political Science Rev.*, 80, 2, 419–431.

Zald, M. and M. Berger (1978), "Social Movement in Organizations: Coup d'etat, Insurgency, and Mass Movements," *Amer. J. Sociology*, 84, 4.

HARNESSING A DIVERSITY OF VIEWS TO UNDERSTAND MULTICULTURALISM

PATRICIA L. NEMETZ AND SANDRA L. CHRISTENSEN

Formal diversity-training programs have been growing rapidly, but anecdotal literature suggests that many such programs garner negative reactions from participants. Charges of "political correctness" and "white-male bashing" may typify such responses. This article theorizes that fundamental beliefs and multiple sources of influence must be taken into account to predict a participant's reaction. Burrell and Morgan's (1979) work on paradigmatic differences is used to identify polar opposite beliefs about multiculturalism. Ideal states of multiculturalism are then defined and predicted from these fundamental beliefs. These belief systems are compared to sources of influence to predict reaction to a formal diversity-training program. We conclude with some cautionary dialogue about realistic expectations of diversity and the polarizing effects of Balkanizing rhetoric.

Corporate public relations officers and media sources have provided a barrage of information to promote efforts to "value diversity" (Copeland, 1988; Cox, 1991; Cox & Blake, 1991). Often, such information has been accompanied with evidence illustrating the changing demographics of this multicultural society, suggesting diversity is based on racial, ethnic, gender, or physical differences. Yet well-intentioned exhortations to diversify the workplace seem somewhat inadequate, given the confusion of issues surrounding "multiculturalism." Well-intentioned statements may simply serve to attenuate underlying conflicts without adequately addressing the racial tensions and cultural alienation inflicting the nation and its institutions. In media outlets, such as radio talk shows and campus speech events, much of the rhetoric about multiculturalism has been neither honest nor dignified, thus creating the possibility of long-term strained relations. Organizations that want to become more diverse frequently hire consultants to "take care of the problem" (Rossett & Bickham, 1994: 41). However, a review of diversity-training articles turns up such phrases as "white-male bashing or a pointless waste of time" (Lunt, 1994: 53), "punishment for the insensitive" (Rossett & Bickham, 1994: 41), "PC's final frontier" (Lynch, 1994: 32), "sensitivity overload" (Kaufman, 1994: 16), and "confusion, disorder, and hostility" (Thomas, 1994: 61).

We believe much of the controversy arises from two basic issues surrounding multiculturalism. The first issue stems from a failure to understand the most fundamental differences about how individuals view ideal or desirable states of multiculturalism in today's society and how these ideals have evolved or changed during the last 30 years. Whereas integration and equal treatment were once broadly prescribed remedies for the relief of racism, sexism, and other forms of discrimination, today's societal prescriptions have become much more complex and confusing. White separatist movements have been widely criticized as racist, whereas minority separatist movements have been regarded as remedies for racism. Some authors view the "mommy track" as highly supportive of women, whereas others view it as sexist. Similar differences apply to numerous other examples, yet formal programs often fail to take into account the origins of these different views.

A second issue stems from the fact that organizationally sanctioned diversity programs are only one source of influence for individuals. Many individuals also are influenced by sources of their own choosing, which may or may not reflect the view endorsed by the organization. In fact, many of the influences can be quite polarizing and mitigate the effect of formal diversity-training programs. Unless these influences are explored and recognized, we believe that diversity programs will cease to exist, regardless of their honorable intention or efficacy.

The purpose of this article is to provide a theory predicting how individuals react to various sources of influence shaping different views of diversity. We describe multiple dimensions of multiculturalism and predict an individual's ideal state of multiculturalism in society based on Burrell and Morgan's (1979) paradigmatic differences of the view of the nature of society. We continue development of the theory (a) by acknowledging that influencers and target individuals may not necessarily share the same ideal of multiculturalism and (b) by predicting how individuals react to these differences. We then discuss the theoretical, research, and practical implications of the theory before concluding.

View of the Nature of Society and Multiculturalism

The first part of the theory is primarily concerned with defining an individual's predisposition toward a particular ideal state of multiculturalism based on a particular view of the nature of society. The view of the nature of society is based on the work of Burrell and Morgan (1979). In Figure 1, this relationship is illustrated and the various dimensions of multiculturalism are identified. According to the theory, individuals have certain ideals and views that may be expressed or latent. Further, the theory is reflective of late 20th-century thinking in modern democratic societies and would not be appropriate in other circumstances. We begin by defining and explaining key variables in the theory, and then we state hypothesized linkages among the variables. The process is then repeated as we examine multiple sources of influence. The unit of analysis is at the individual level.

View of the Nature of Society

Individuals interpret the world through various lenses or perspectives that form a framework of assumptions about the world. Kuhn (1962) labeled these frameworks *paradigms* and suggested they are changed only rarely through major knowledge revolutions. Burrell and Morgan's (1979) extensive work on various sociological paradigms identified "an individual's view of the nature of society" as an important way of distinguishing differences in how individuals interpret their world. Burrell and Morgan defined the concept as "two broad sociological perspectives in the form of a polarized dimension" (1979: 19). One polarity is labeled *the sociology of regulation* and the other *the sociology of radical change*. The term *sociology of regulation* refers to explanations of society that emphasize its underlying unity and cohesiveness. *Sociology of radical change* refers to explanations of the deep-seated structural conflict and modes of domination characterizing modern society (Burrell & Morgan, 1979). Organization theorists who seek to explain social relations and events objectively through the sociology of regulation have been labeled *functionalists*, whereas those who have taken the *sociology of radical change* perspective have been labeled *radical structuralists* (Burrell & Morgan, 1979). These polar opposites view society from inherently different perspectives. Radical structuralists are interested in dramatic change, whereas functionalists are supportive of the status quo.

Radical Structuralism

Radical structuralism is rooted in the writings of Marx, who viewed capitalism as a new mode of societal organization, spawned by the dissolution of feudalism and beset by repression, oppression, and human bondage. According to radical structuralism, capitalism and its latter-day transmutations are characterized by gross economic inequalities and by vast discrepancies in power, which means that social life inevitably rests upon domination and conflict. The underlying purposes of activists who assume a radical structuralist view are to provide a critique of contemporary society and to propose social change through revolutionary and sometimes violent means (Burrell & Morgan, 1979). Radical structuralists assert that humans cannot assume a common value system built around consensus, but that a plurality of interests exist. Plurality is seen not as a purposeful exercise in democracy, but rather as a collection of central points of conflict (Worseley, 1985). Further, they view conflict resolution as an opiate and a tool of domination whose purpose is to prevent revolution and the shift of power to the oppressed. The growth of conflict between interest groups is a central and necessary feature of the movement for revolutionary change. Much of this ideology was adapted to specific problems in the United States during the 1960s and 1970s, notably the causes of minority groups and feminists, where oppression, domination, and economic inequality are recurring themes (Hughes, 1993). The viewpoint has become deeply embedded in contemporary liberal arts curricula, spawning the *dead white male* label to describe authors of traditional classics (Bloom, 1994; Hughes, 1993; Shulman, 1994). It is a substantial change in university tradition, and its effects on graduates entering the workforce may become increasingly noticeable.

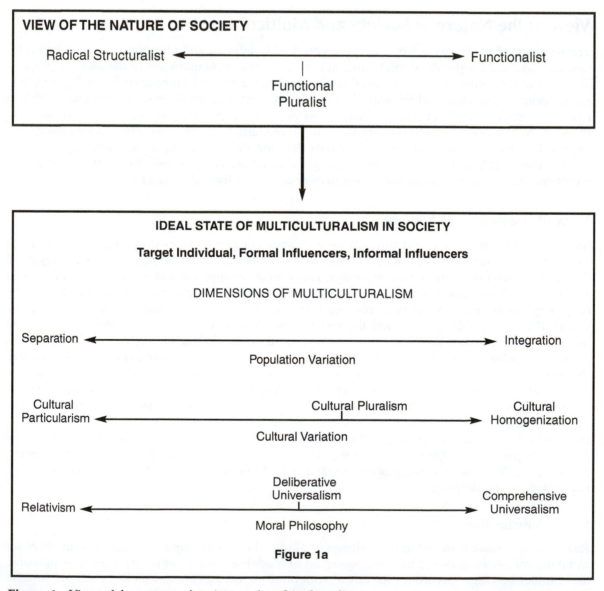

Figure 1   View of the nature of society and multiculturalism.

Functionalism

Functionalism, by way of contrast, is a perspective whose proponents are highly supportive of the status quo, concerned with understanding society in a way that generates knowledge that can be put to practical use. They emphasize the importance of maintaining order in society and inducing social change through problem solving (Burrell & Morgan, 1979). They are essentially satisfied with society as is, though they recognize the need for ongoing activity in building consensus and social order, often within the boundaries of existing authoritative and control structures. Although their primary orientation is not activist in the same way as radical structuralists, their viewpoint may create backlash movements when serious threats to the status quo are created. Burrell and Morgan (1979) noted that most scholars, particularly those in organizational studies, assume this orientation.

Functional Pluralism

Within the functionalist perspective is a view that recognizes *functional pluralism*. Its followers emphasize conflict and power as factors affecting society, but they are primarily concerned with seeking a balance among these factors (Burrell & Morgan, 1979). To them, pluralism and controlled conflict are necessary elements in building democratic institutions through consensus. Conflict resolution is viewed as a useful exercise in creative problem solving. Change is sought primarily through results-oriented debate and consensus. Their pluralist orientation reflects reform, not revolution of oppressed against oppressor. In this respect, their approach to pluralism differs greatly from that of the radical structuralist.

Ideal State of Multiculturalism in Society

A state or condition of multiculturalism can be defined as an environment "designed for a combination of several distinct cultures" (*Webster's Collegiate Dictionary*, 1993: 764). But this definition lacks the clarity necessary to fully describe the concept's complexities in contemporary society. A review of several streams of literature turns up three major dimensions of the multiculturalism construct. In ethnic studies concerning immigrants, two fundamental dimensions—*assimilation* and *acculturation*—have long been recognized as distinct processes underlying multicultural adaptations (Pratt, 1974). However, because multiculturalism often has been associated with groups whose ancestors have been in the country for many generations—blacks, feminists, gays, Native Americans, and so on (Fukuyama, 1993)—we prefer other terms. More inclusive terms for today's applications are *population variation* and *cultural variation*. In addition to these two dimensions, a moral dimension is evident in a variety of multiculturalism literature. A delineation of the distinctions among these dimensions is important to understanding an individual's ideal or desired state of multiculturalism in his or her society. Figure 1a illustrates the three dimensions with their polar labels. The continuum illustrating the state of multiculturalism ranges from an ultimate level of intergroup diversity on the left, to a complete absence of multicultural diversity on the right. Because functional pluralism is a subset of functionalism, functional pluralism and its relationships are shown slightly off-center and to the right.

Population Variation

Population variation can be defined as the extent of subgroup members' interactions and relationships with other subgroups (Pratt, 1974). Degrees of population variation exist on a continuum with complete *separation* at one extreme and complete *integration* at the other extreme. A fully integrated population is one in which relationships are randomly distributed without regard to race, ethnicity, gender, religion, or sexual orientation. Population separation, in contrast, might occur along any of these lines. Furthermore, separation might occur by choice or by imposition of an existing socioeconomic structure. For example, it has long been recognized that first-generation immigrants band together to protect themselves and to share their familiar ways of life (Worseley, 1985). Often, however, subgroups have been forced to live under ghetto conditions as the result of a social structure that affords little opportunity for access to society's goods (Sowell, 1975, 1981). However, separation also might be driven by political movements that seek to isolate majority or minority subgroups from the influence of other subgroups, such as that occurring in Yugoslavia today.

Cultural Variation

Cultural variation refers to the variety and concentration of values, behavior, and attitudes experienced and accepted by various groups within a society. At one end of the continuum is cultural particularism, and at the other end is cultural homogenization. A more centrist position is described by cultural pluralism.

Cultural particularism. *Cultural particularism* is a concept that emphasizes "within-group" similarities and "between-group" differences within a diverse society. It is most positively associated with values like solidarity, a local identity, and a "sense of community" *within a group* (Barber, 1992). According to Quincy Wright,

> A perfect community is objectively one which manifests cultural uniformity, spiritual union, institutional unity, and material unification in the highest possible degree and subjectively one with which the members resemble one another closely in evaluations, purposes, understandings, appreciations, prejudices, appearances, and other characteristics which any of them consider important. They are all in continuous contact with group sentiment, contributing to group policy and group decisions. (1964: 204)

Although providing a sense of pride and attachments to its adherents, cultural particularism in its more negative form can be parochial, isolationist, and prejudicial, "disparaging any common element [of] history, society, and culture" (Ravitch, 1991: 77). Solidarity is often secured through war (in various degrees) against outsiders, fanaticism, obedience to a hierarchy, and obliteration of individual self in the name of the group. Cultural separation is often viewed as a necessary precondition for cultural preservation.

Cultural pluralism. According to the concept, *cultural pluralism*, many cultures can coexist in the same society. It involves a process through which minority and majority culture members adopt some norms of the other group. Pluralism also means that members of a minority culture are encouraged to enact behaviors from an alternative culture as well as from the majority culture. They therefore are able to retain a sense of identity with their minority-culture group (Cox, 1991).

Cultural homogenization. *Cultural homogenization*, in contrast, is the creation of a modern, integrated society through the application of a common language, common currency, and common cosmopolitan behavior. Homogenization is the process of blending diverse elements into a smooth mixture (*Webster's Collegiate Dictionary*, 1993: 555). Homogenized societies minimize between-group differences through structural institutions at the societal level. In such societies, religion, culture, and nationality are marginal elements in a person's working identity (Barber, 1992). Although Sowell (1981) characterized this state as resulting from the give and take of majority and minority subgroups, others emphasize the importance of industrialization and commercialization as the driving force behind homogenization (Barber, 1992: Bloom, 1987). The question of the source of the "dominant" homogenized culture of America remains unresolved. Some critics characterize cultural homogenization as the imposition of a dominant, Eurocentric, technologically driven culture on less-than-vigilant subgroups (Worseley, 1985), whereas other critics point to the free and equal participation of all subgroups in a mass culture that appeals to the basest instincts of human existence (Bloom, 1987; Lasch, 1979). Although an offshoot of cultural homogenization might be an emphasis on the individual over the group, its major pathology is the alienation of some individuals from society at large through the marginalization of cultural and religious identity (Lasch, 1979, 1993).

Approach to Moral Philosophy

The third dimension evident in the multiculturalism literature defines differences in the approach to moral philosophy. The continuum on this dimension extends from relativism to comprehensive universalism, with deliberative universalism as a variant to comprehensive universalism. According to relativism, no common moral guidelines can be applied to all humankind, whereas according to universalism, common guidelines either exist or can be found.

Relativism. The argument from *relativism* has as its premise the well-known variation in moral codes from one society to another and from one period to another; it is also based on differences in moral beliefs between different groups and classes within a complex community (Mackie, 1987). Moral relativists assert that, ideally, tolerance of these differences is essential to openness among people. Finding common ground is not essential to the moral relativist. Moral relativism can create severe practical difficulties in a multicultural society, however, because such a wide variety of conflicts among gender, racial, ethnic, and religious groups can arise during the course of normal interaction (Wolin, 1993). Ideas of Western liberal democracy are subject to attack, even though a liberal democracy is the system most likely to make allowances for giving voice to such conflicts (Hughes, 1993). Furthermore, because moral relativism recognizes no objective moral truth, it gives great liberty to those who define all outcomes according to economic and power relationships (Shweder & Bourne, 1984). This attitude often leads to zero-sum thinking, in which the world is bifurcated into oppressors and victims, that is, a place where there is no chance for victims to better their positions unless at the expense of the oppressors. This argument, in turn, can lead to the so-called oppressors believing that they are victims of powerfully protected vocal subgroups, as in white male claims of victimization by affirmative action programs (Cox, 1991). Such dilemmas have no resolution under relativism because no guiding principle can be applied (Shweder & Bourne, 1984).

Comprehensive universalism. Proponents of universalism believe that an objective moral truth exists at a *fundamental* level and can be applied to all humankind (Taylor, 1987). Furthermore, they may take an evolutionist view and believe that some societies are more enlightened than others (Fukuyama, 1992; Shweder & Bourne, 1984). Often, these proponents support Enlightenment principles associated with the development of Western liberal democracy and argue that history is progressing linearly toward this goal (Fukuyama, 1992; Wilson, 1993). Enlightenment principles include such ideals as freedom, equality, human rights, meritocracy, and the rule of law. An alternative set of principles often is found in universalist religions, such as Christianity and Islam. A current example of such absolutist principles have been found in Pope John Paul II's encyclical, *Veritatis Splendor (The Splendor of Truth)* (Ostling, 1993). He emphasized stricter and more specific moral guidelines and suggested that they apply not only to Roman Catholics but also all humankind. Fundamentalist Protestant religions also endorse a strict and thorough set of moral guidelines based on their interpretation of the Bible. Gutman (1993) labeled such thorough sets of guidelines *comprehensive universalism*. These two examples illustrate quite clearly the problem associated with comprehensive universalist guidelines, that is, a disagreement over whose rules are the objective truth.

Deliberative universalism. Gutman (1993) suggested that a more viable approach in a multicultural democratic society is *deliberative universalism*. Deliberative universalists rely partly on a core of universal principles and partly upon publicly accountable deliberation to address fundamental conflicts concerning social justice. Deliberation is required in those instances of moral conflict where no substantive standard can legitimately claim a monopoly on reasonableness or justification. Deliberation encourages the search for common ground and the understanding of each other's point of view (Gutman, 1993). No guarantee exists that resolution can be found quickly, but some movement toward consensus is encouraged.

Beliefs about these three dimensions—population variation, cultural variation, and moral philosophy—can be combined to define an individual's ideal or desired state of multiculturalism. Many variations exist, not only in how the variables are combined but also in how many are accessed in one's ideals. Some people may prefer integration and hold no strong opinions on other dimensional aspects, whereas others may strongly prefer cultural particularism, separation, and judgment based on moral relativism. The ideal is unique to the individual and may remain unexpressed. Furthermore, an individual may hold to more than one ideal for different contexts, for example, favoring cultural homogenization at the workplace and cultural particularism at church.

The Relationship Between Nature of Society and Ideal State of Multiculturalism

Figure 1 identifies a linkage between *view of the nature of society and ideal state of multiculturalism*. We hypothesize relationships at the polar extremes and in the center based on the assumption that individuals' perceptions and ideals are influenced by their fundamental belief systems. We predict individuals who have extremely strong radical structuralist beliefs will support an ideal of multiculturalism that is consistent with separation, cultural particularism, and relativism, whereas individuals who have extremely strong functionalist beliefs will support an ideal that is consistent with cultural homogenization and comprehensive universalism. We predict that functional pluralists will support an ideal that is consistent with integration, cultural pluralism, and deliberative universalism.

Radical Structuralist View

Radical structuralists use Marxist theory to explain all relationships in terms of *material* (economic) structures. Marx took no account of individual character, moral conviction, or altruistic behavior, which have been viewed as social constructions of existing elites who seek the stabilization of their power base. Using this reasoning, morality and cultural practices are thus determined by who holds power. In Marx's writings, the primary determinant of behavior is membership in an economic class—the *bourgeoisie* is inherently oppressive; the *proletariat* is inherently alienated (Roberts, 1993). However, his theory is not particularly cultural. Adapting his theory to cultural groups leads to the inevitable classification of individuals according to group membership without taking into account individual circumstances or character. Males, whites, European-Americans, and/or heterosexuals, by virtue of their traditionally higher economic status, are seen as dominating existing structures and institutions in the United States; hence, they are oppressive (Hughes, 1993). Whereas Marx and radical structuralists have a utopian, post-revolutionary vision consistent with egalitarianism and social justice through economic equality, *revolutionary* activity today requires the demonization of elitists and oppressors. Radical structuralists are likely to see the greatest threat as coming from the subtle influence of a dominant, all-powerful elite. Therefore, within present-day capitalist America, radical structuralists are most likely to espouse some degree of isolation from these elitist attitudes, consciousness raising to *illuminate* the truth of domination, the establishment of their own power base, and a *revolutionary* movement that includes separatism, an emphasis on between-group differences and moral relativism. Thus, we suggest that individuals who have extremely strong radical structuralist beliefs are likely to support an ideal of multiculturalism that is consistent with separatism, cultural particularism, and moral relativism.

Functionalist View

Functionalists, who prefer unity and social cohesion, are likely to see the greatest threat to society as coming from conflict and a failure to bind society together with common values; therefore, they are more likely to espouse cultural homogenization and comprehensive universalism. To them, the status quo and existing authority structures are the mechanisms for expressing society's common values; the inexorable movement toward homogenization (Barber, 1992) and the authoritative nature of comprehensive universalism are not problematic for them. Rather, those characteristics are seen as solutions to problems.

The functionalist position on population variation (integration-separation) is more complex. A functionalist's source of the common values that bind society together—whether secular or religious—must be examined to predict the relationship for this dimension. Functionalists who do not support certain types of comprehensive universalism or who support moral universalism based on secular Enlightenment principles would undoubtedly endorse integration. It is far more difficult to argue that all those at the functional extreme would support integration, particularly if their moral universalism is based on certain types of religious fundamentalism. For example, Kolchin (1993) indicated that a major tenet among religions of the American South came with the recognition that Christianity applied universally, even to slaves, but it was perfectly acceptable to separate black churches from white churches. Furthermore, some fundamentalist religions are absolute in their position on the role of women and acceptance of sexual behavior, often endorsing limited interaction between the genders and shunning those who deviate from their sexual and religious mores. Because of these fundamental differences over whose universalism is the truth, we cannot predict a correlation between functionalism and integration or between functionalism and separatism. We can, however, predict that individuals who have extremely strong functionalist beliefs are likely to support an ideal of multiculturalism that is consistent with cultural homogenization and comprehensive universalism.

Functional Pluralist View

Functional pluralists also are supportive of a society bound together by common values. However, rather than relying on existing control and authority structures, they seek the use of debate and conflict resolution to build consensus. In a diverse society, this behavior suggests they are essentially open to many differences as long as the ultimate endpoint is a commonality of values. The underlying belief is consistent with the idea that many individuals of different cultures can provide input into building integrated relationships through deliberation. Thus, individuals who have extremely strong functional pluralist beliefs are likely to support an ideal of multiculturalism that is consistent with integration, cultural pluralism, and deliberative universalism.

Multiple Sources of Influence

Formal influencers, informal influencers, and target individuals all have a view of the nature of society and a view of the ideal state of multiculturalism in society (hereafter referred to as *views* and *ideals*). Further, the examination of multiple sources of influence assumes that an individual targeted for a formal diversity program exists in an environment rich with opportunity for interaction with a variety of other people. Influence could originate with informal sources as well as with formal sources. We are concerned primarily with the target's reaction to a formal diversity program through which the formal influencer is motivated to create some change in a group of target individuals. A target individual is an employee, student, or organizational participant who is required or encouraged to attend a formal diversity program.

Formal Influence

Formal influence is defined as organization-sponsored intervention intended to affect a target's attitudes, behaviors, and/or emotions toward multicultural diversity. Organizations engage in two major types of formal influence to promote diversity—training and setting policy.

Training. Diversity training exists in many different forms. Table 1 defines and describes several types and methodologies. Methodologies differ greatly among the different types; some are psychologically intensive and participative (psychotherapeutic approaches), and others are more superficial and less participative (lectures and listening). Some types of training have content that is consistent with a certain view of the nature of society, but most are adaptable to the trainer's view. Psychotherapeutic approaches generally involve functional pluralist views because they seek common ground through participative group therapy. However, other types are highly adaptive. Examples of techniques associated with different views are included in Table 1. For example, cultural awareness training can be used to uncover common stereotypes for the purpose of discrediting them and for building consensus about how to treat other people. This approach represents a functional pluralist view. Alternatively, cultural awareness training can be used to make *oppressive* employees aware of how *oppressed employees feel* (Caudron, 1993). This approach represents a radical structuralist approach. The view of the nature of society expressed in the training program and/or by the trainer is important because it may or may not coincide with the view of those who will be influenced.

TABLE 1

Types of Formal Diversity Training

Types of Training	Description	Sample Functionalist or Functional Pluralist Tactics	Sample Radical Structuralist Tactics
Ethnic, Black, or Feminist Studies	Scholarly academic class using in-depth analysis to review status of minority group in dominant society	Studying the contributions of women and minority members to American society (National Public Radio, 1993)	Criticizing Western civilization using deconstructionist techniques, then promoting ethno-centric studies to dramatically over-haul beliefs about existing institutions (Jaroff, 1994)
Psychotherapeutic Approaches	Group therapy involving groups experiencing conflict. The approach is based on the belief that the roots of ethnic hostility lie in the infantile need to externalize un-welcome self-images; ethnic rival becomes target of projected guilt and self-loathing (Cullen, 1993)	Dwelling on the history of animosity and loss brought on by ethnic hatred. Acknowledging through group therapy with neighbors that wrongs occurred. Acting contrite if appropriate (Cullen, 1993)	—
Sensitivity Training	Sensitizing individuals to feelings provoked by discrimination (Smith, 1990; Spokesman-Review, 1993)	Separating individuals by eye color. Discriminating against one eye color arbitrarily to illustrate the underlying belief that all individuals are hurt by discrimination	Separating men from women. Empowering women to sexually harass men through role play to illustrate the underlying belief that women are victimized by men (Caudron, 1993)
Dissonance Creation	Purposely creating cognitive dissonance with the hope that the target will resolve dissonance by changing attitude (Leippe and Eisenstadt, 1994)	Requiring an individual who shows initial prejudice to write an essay showing the absurdities of stereotyping	Requiring an individual who shows initial prejudice to debate in favor of the idea that whites are oppressive

Organization policy. Cox (1991) noted that organization policy is an important determinant of success when implementing diversity programs. Top management support is manifested through the provision of resources and inclusion of diversity in corporate strategy. In addition to voluntary implementation of such organization policies, affirmative action programs provide legal validation

TABLE 1 (cont.)

Types of Training	Description	Sample Functionalist or Functional Pluralist Tactics	Sample Radical Structuralist Tactics
Cultural Awareness	Exploration of cultural or gender differences (Gordon, 1992)	Discussing stereotypes and unintentional slights. Building consensus on how to avoid them	Separating oppressed individuals from oppressive individuals. Encouraging oppressed individuals to express feelings to oppressive individuals (Caudron, 1993)
Legal Awareness	Explaining discrimination laws	Describing various activities that violate the law and stating the consequences of violation (Thomas, 1994)	Discussing unfairness and bias in laws and the injustice present in a white-male-dominated justice system (Schafran, 1993)

for promoting diversity efforts (Cox & Blake, 1991). However, formal organization policy may be somewhat problematic when policymakers take a unidimensional view of multiculturalism. For example, Gordon (1992) asserted that most organizations use the term *diversity program* as a synonym for equal employment opportunity or affirmative action. Such organizations rely primarily on the integration-separation dimension of multiculturalism to define their programs and disregard the cultural variation and moral philosophy dimensions. Organizations that are truly multicultural are not only interested in hiring workers with various backgrounds but also in accepting some of the norms from the various backgrounds (Cox, 1991).

Informal Influence

Informal influence is that which is not sanctioned by formal authority, organizational policy, or certified expertise (Mintzberg, 1983). It is often conceptualized as a mass of competing power groups, each seeking to influence policy in terms of its own interests (Strauss, 1964). Informal influence can come from a variety of sources, such as reference groups (Bock, Beeghley, & Mixon, 1983; Hall, Varca, & Fisher, 1986; Hooper, 1982; Merton, 1958; Merton & Rossi, 1950; Montgomery, 1980), support groups and career networks (Ibarra, 1993), political activists, media rhetoric (Triandis, 1971), and organization culture (Martin & Siehl, 1983; Mintzberg, 1983; Smircich, 1983; Van Maanen & Barley, 1984). Informal influence often involves the search for a common understanding of acceptable behavior, communication with similar people, and an acknowledgment of roughly the same problems (Van Maanen & Barley, 1984). Although the sources of informal influence can be a consequence of the social circumstances to which an individual was born or directed, they often are chosen on the basis of self-categorization (Turner, 1982; Turner & Oakes, 1989). Also, some types of informal influence may be more influential than others; for example, media has been shown to have only a moderate impact (Becker, McCombs, & McLeod, 1975).

According to a number of theories and empirical studies, informal influence is particularly important in shaping the views of individuals, primarily through social-identity processes. Asch (1952, 1956), Moscovici (1976), and Turner and Oakes (1989) argued that the normative expectation of similar others is more important in shaping views than is information. They argued, along with dissonance theorists (Festinger, 1957; Simon, Greenberg, & Brehm, 1995), that disagreement with people with whom one expects to agree creates uncomfortable uncertainty that acts to align one's views with the other or to trivialize the issue. Furthermore, the influence of similar others is important for polarizing and extremitizing one's initially similar views. This concept is described as *group polarization*, which is the tendency of group discussion or some related manipulation to extremitize the average of group members' responses on some dimension from pre- to postdiscussion in the direction of the prevailing tendency (Moscovici & Zavalloni, 1969; Turner & Oakes, 1989). It arises because people seek to conform to what defines their social group as a whole in contrast to other groups (Turner & Oakes, 1989). This socializing process also is evident in work organizations, where organization leaders frequently achieve their positions by conforming to the *status quo*. Often, individuals in a position of organizational leadership believe their work group to be a primary reference group and are under severe pressure to conform to social norms. Kanter (1977) argued that the pervasiveness of conformity pressures and the development of exclusive management circles stem from the degree of uncertainty surrounding managerial positions. "The greater the uncertainty, the greater the pressures for those who have to trust each other to form a homogeneous group" (Kanter, 1977: 49).

A number of phenomena and empirical studies confirm the theoretical importance of informal influence when it is applied to issues of multiculturalism. Conventional wisdom suggests that an individual's view of other races and ethnic groups is strongly determined by the age of five under the influence of reference groups (Adorno, Frenkel-Brunswik, Levinson, & Sanford, 1950; Frenkel-Brunswik & Havel, 1953; Maddi, 1968; Triandis, 1971). In general, attraction to demographically similar others is strongly supported in empirical studies (Feldman, 1968; Hornstein, 1978; Hornstein, Fisch, & Holmes, 1968; Hornstein, Masor, Sole, & Heilman, 1971; Krebs, 1970; Piliavin, Rodin, & Piliavin, 1969; Stotland, 1969; Tajfel, Billig, Bundy, & Plament, 1971), and similarity exerts strong influence on views (McCroskey, Richmond, & Daly, 1975; McGuire, 1985). Insko, Nacoste, and Moe (1983) found that attraction and persuasive impact increase with ideological and demographic similarity, and ideological similarity has been increasing in importance in the United States. Myers and Bishop (1970) empirically verified a group-polarization effect on racial attitudes by showing that the intensity of initial attitudes increased after discussion with similar others. Stigmatizing language is an everyday manifestation of group-polarization effect, with *politically correct* and *patriotically correct* statements used to establish solidarity among like-minded participants, as in Pat Robertson's characterization of "a feminist agenda, a socialist anti-family political movement that encourages women to leave their husbands, kill their children, practice witchcraft, destroy capitalism, and become lesbian" (Wicker, 1991: A12). These informal-influence processes, in general, are thought to be the primary source of influence for individuals, with more formal informational influence playing a secondary role only in limited circumstances (Rajecki, 1990).

Individual's Commitment to His or Her Own Views and Ideals

The commitment to one's own views and ideals is a measure of the stability of one's initial views in the presence of new information and/or a measure of the lengths to which an individual will go to achieve a desirable state in society. Both political literature in the 1960s and literature on attitudinal change have dwelled extensively on this concept. Bell and Kristol (1965) labeled those who have an extreme commitment to their ideals *ideologues*. Ideologues, according to Bell and Kristol (1965), *preconceive reality* and attempt to engineer a *new utopia* (Bell, 1965). An *ideologue* differs from an *idealist* (one who is guided by one's ideals), in that he or she assumes one can place ideals before practical considerations. Both the idealist and idealogue, nevertheless, have a strong motivation to achieve a more desirable state of society. Lack of commitment, by way of contrast, may be characterized by apathy and/or alienation. An intermittent stage has been defined as *latency* by Mann (1986). The idea of latency is especially important to radical structuralists, who believe revolution will occur if only individuals can be aroused from their latent state (Mann, 1986).

In the literature on attitude change, commitment to one's views is an important component in the integration (Siero & Doosje, 1993) of social judgment theory (SJT; Sherif & Hovland, 1961; Sherif, Sherif, & Nebergall, 1965) and the elaboration likelihood model (ELM; Petty & Cacioppo, 1986). According to SJT, every person has three latitudes of attitudinal commitment: a latitude of acceptance (opinions with which the person agrees), a latitude of noncommitment (opinions with which the person neither agrees nor disagrees), and a latitude of rejection (opinions with which the person disagrees). People are persuaded to change attitude most strongly by messages that are at moderate distance from the recipient's initial attitude (Freedman, 1964; Wittaker, 1965) and that are in the individual's latitude of noncommitment (Siero & Doosje, 1993). It is in the latitude of noncommitment that individuals are most likely to elaborately process new information that might change their views (Siero & Doojse, 1993); regarding other latitudes, individuals will remain committed to their initial views and distort new information (O'Keefe, 1990). Some evidence indicates that attitudes people consider personally important are resistant to change (Fine, 1957; Gorn, 1975) and stable over time (Krosnik, 1988; Schuman & Presser, 1981).

Reactions to Formal Diversity Programs

In defining reaction to a formal diversity program, we select two separate dependent variables to comprehensively define the terms—*behavior and attitude change* and *response to the diversity program itself.*

Behavior and Attitude Change

It has often been noted in the training literature that training evaluation is inadequate because it fails to measure the appropriate dependent variables (Bunker & Cohen, 1977; Latham & Saari, 1979). Training evaluation should assess if the program accomplished what it intended to accomplish; it also should assess how the target individuals responded to the training itself (Latham & Saan, 1979). With this in mind, we begin with the assumption that diversity training is intended to provoke some change in *behavior* or *attitude*. Thus, a measure of such change becomes an important dependent variable.

Response to the Formal Diversity Program Itself

Response to the formal diversity program itself also is important because survival of diversity programs depends on this outcome. The interest in *response* also is clearly expressed in the practitioner literature, particularly when unusually intense organizational conflict has been generated by a program. The intended response to a formal diversity-training program is difficult to define because the goals of the program often are undetermined (Rossett & Bickham, 1994). Without well-defined organizational goals, the intention of the program may become intermixed with the personal intention of the trainer. If the trainer operates from a radical structuralist perspective, the goals may be to increase conflict among interest groups and to raise the consciousness of participants about oppression (as is typical in many university diversity programs). If the trainer operates from a functional pluralist perspective, the goal may be to increase harmony and productivity. Because of these differences, the definition of *response* must rest upon some assumptions about what is the desirable outcome. We define *response* according to anecdotal reports noted in the diversity literature, acknowledging that the literature exhibits a functionalist bias. *Negative response* to a formal diversity program includes emotions, attitudes, and behaviors consistent with confusion, disorder, hostility (Thomas, 1994), punishment (Rossett & Bickham, 1994), resentment, vulnerability, and anger (Caudron, 1993). *Positive response* includes emotions, attitudes, and behaviors consistent with bias reduction (Dovidio, 1993), harmony, inclusion, legal compliance (Rossett & Bickham, 1994), creativity, productivity (Cox, 1991), and approval (Thomas, 1994).

Dynamics That Influence Reactions to Formal Diversity-Training Programs

We predict reaction to formal diversity programs based on SJT (Sherif & Hovland, 1961; Sherif et al., 1965; Siero & Doosje, 1993) and the ELM (Petty & Cacioppo, 1986). According to SJT, the likelihood of change following a persuasive message is dependent on the discrepancy between the position advocated in the message and the target individual's initial view, with moderate discrepancy evoking the most change. However, the degree of discrepancy between a person's views and the message conveyed in a training program is not sufficient to explain reactions to the training program. A person's degree of commitment to an ideal or a view also affects how that person reacts. People who are weakly committed to an ideal or a view are more likely to be in a state that is receptive to new information and reasoning than are those who are strongly committed (Siero & Doosje, 1993; Triandis, 1971). In the case of diversity training, target individuals who agree in principle with the views and ideals of the formal diversity program would likely have a positive response to it. People who initially disagree but have a weak commitment to their own ideals may respond positively if they learn something that causes them to elaborately process the information (Petty & Cacioppo, 1986; Siero & Doosje, 1993). These individuals are the most likely candidates for behavioral and attitudinal change, but where target individuals have an initially strong disagreement with the views of the program, the probability and intensity of a negative response increases as the commitment to their own ideals increases. For example, an individual who regularly agrees with and contributes to conservative radio talk shows probably shows a high commitment to a functionalist point of view. Exposure to a radical structuralist viewpoint in a diversity-training program would likely create a very strong negative response and little or no change.

Another predictor for reaction to a formal diversity program is the predominant view expressed by informal influencers. If an individual has little exposure to informal sources of information on diversity, the issue is likely to have little personal importance (Boninger, Krosnick, & Berent, 1995), and the formal diversity program will be the most influential (Siero & Doosje, 1993). However, because informal sources of influence generally are chosen by the individual rather than recommended by the organization, they tend to be more influential than formal sources (Berent, Krosnick, & Boninger, 1993; Triandis, 1971). Further, informal influencers can offer social support for arguments that refute a formal influencer (Mitchell, 1982). Therefore, we predict that consistently self-selected informal influence takes precedence over formal influence. Where the two are not congruent, the probability of a negative response to a formal diversity-training program increases. For example, if friends and support groups operate from a radical structuralist viewpoint, they are not likely to favor greater productivity and harmony with the *dominant majority*. Programs that promote such goals will receive a negative reaction among target individuals with radical structuralist leanings.

Organizational Influence

Though organizations frequently announce formal organization policies to define their position on an issue, the formal announcement may be perceived as nothing more than a facade. The *real* views of the organization may be expressed more subtly through an organizational culture that negates formal pronouncements (Van Maanen & Barley, 1984). For diversity programs, this may be evidenced by much sloganeering with little or no resources dedicated to diversity (Cox & Blake, 1991). Further difficulties occur when organizations define diversity as forced affirmative action programs (Gordon, 1992), or when there are subtle messages to conform to the norms of exclusive management circles (Kanter, 1977). As a consequence of the mismatch between formal and informal organization practices and values, target individuals may become cynical about formal diversity programs. Little behavior and attitude change is likely to occur when the organization's diversity goals are not perceived as serious (Minizberg, 1983). Attendance at formal diversity-training programs also may be perceived as occasions for appearance's sake only. In such circumstances, negative responses to the formal diversity training are likely. Only when the informal organizational culture corresponds to the formal pronouncements of the organization will target individuals give due consideration to the seriousness of the issue. To summarize, behavioral change, attitudinal change, and positive responses to training are more likely to occur when the organization's informal influence is congruent with formal organization influence compared to when it is not.

Training Methodology

The importance of training methodology has long been recognized in the training literature, and participative methods have been particularly important for changing attitudes and eliciting positive responses (Carroll, Paine, & Ivancevich, 1972). Participation of individuals who have many different views may be even more important. Vinokur and Burnstein (1978) found that some group depolarization is likely to occur when members of a group with heterogeneous opinions participate in discussing an issue. The causal mechanism for this depolarization is believed to be a transition from normative social influences as primary determinant of attitude to informational influence as primary determinant. Normative influence is based on the desire to conform to the expectations of similar others, whereas informational influence is based on the acceptance of information of others as evidence about reality. When similar others are not available for comparison, informational influence has more impact. This is particularly true when multiple arguments and, thus, multiple choices are provided (Rajecki, 1990). From this argument, it follows that formal diversity-training programs that fully engage target individuals and promote open acknowledgment of multiple viewpoints are more likely to elicit a change in views and a positive response compared to those that do not.

Theoretical, Research, and Practical Implications

Theoretical Implications

Our theory is important because it provides a foundation for the concept of multiculturalism and an analysis of how different paradigmatic views create complexities in developing effective formal diversity programs. In public policy and liberal arts literatures, both prominent black scholars (Boynton, 1995) and white scholars (Hughes, 1993; Wilson, 1993) have begun to critically examine the meaning and limitations of multiculturalism, often in the form of essays. This article overcomes the *fuzzy thinking* that may be a part of critical essays because it provides a structured framework for the development of a common body of knowledge on the topic of multiculturalism. Because some of the knowledge generated in other disciplines may not yet have filtered into management literatures, we believe the theory represents state-of-the-art thinking about multiculturalism and cultural diversity.

Well-defined concepts and relationships are necessary for continued critical evaluation and the development of a meaningful dialogue about the consequences of paradigmatic differences when applied to multiculturalism. The challenge or paradox of diversity lies in the fact that diversity today is defined only along cultural lines, rather than according to differences of opinion. For example, it is paradoxical that proponents of *politically correct* speech codes often are active proponents of cultural diversity, yet speech codes restrict a diversity of opinion (as expressed through paradigmatic differences). Our theory offers a vehicle for respecting diversity of opinion while also recognizing the value of cultural diversity.

The theory also provides a balanced approach for assessing the reasons why diversity programs garner support or failure. Because of the highly charged emotions surrounding the issue of cultural diversity, researchers, formal influencers, and participants often interpret results on the basis of their own paradigmatic biases. Negative responses to diversity-training programs may be interpreted as racism or sexism, when, in fact, participants may be confused about programs that emphasize racial or gender differences when they had been taught in the past to be *color blind* or *gender neutral.* Although we do not refute that a negative response may be due to prejudice, in our theory we take into account a broader variety of reasons for the response and some basis for assessing the paradigmatic biases of the trainer or researcher. We also examine the influence target in the full context of multiple sources of influence. Diversity programs often compete with informal influences, both inside and outside of the organization, which present formidable challenges; these influences must be included in assessing the likelihood of success in a diversity program.

We also suggest that Pfeffer's (1993) call to limit future organizational research to a single paradigmatic viewpoint may be premature. Pfeffer (1993) identified lack of consensus about theoretical structures as a serious limitation in advancing knowledge. Although we leave that particular argument to others, we believe that an individual's paradigmatic viewpoint can be a *very powerful* predictor of his or her behavior and attitudes. Failure to acknowledge these different viewpoints would limit a whole range of explanations that deserve merit. Certainly, the most plausible explanation for this decade's irrational international ethnic conflicts lies in the ability of demagogues to influence others to live by their paradigmatic viewpoints. These viewpoints must be thoroughly understood if a rational defense is to be mounted against destructive behaviors.

Several points of contention may arise from the theory. For example, conservative critics often portray Americans as far too entrenched in moral relativism and having little or no regard for universal moral reasoning (Bloom, 1987). Although we respectfully acknowledge this contention, we believe a majority of Americans are not radical structuralists; rather, we suspect that the difference between deliberative and comprehensive universalism has not been adequately addressed in these critiques. The critiques do, however, represent alternative theories that can be tested against this one. Other theorists may argue that radical structuralists have social integration in mind as the ultimate goal of social organization and do not favor separatism. We believe there is merit in this argument, but our theory is limited to American society as it exists today. In capitalist America, radical structuralists must continuously create conflict to relieve perceived oppression. The pursuit of such conflict often requires unrelenting commitment to such an extent that the radical structuralist can lose sight of the ultimate goal. This loss of sight can result in an unintended lifelong struggle as conflict expands for such a person without ultimate end (revolution) or intermediate resolution (Tinder, 1989). Our theory assumes a certain stability of American society that precludes revolution any time soon; in such a sustained condition, conflict becomes the goal in and of itself.

Last, the theory raises the question of whether individuals' different paradigmatic viewpoints can or should be reconciled to improve the viability of diversity programs. Burrell and Morgan (1979) indicated that these viewpoints simply cannot be reconciled. Proponents of each viewpoint harbor suspicion about the hidden agenda of others. Suspicion is not conducive to reconciliation. Further, predictions that paradigmatic or idealogical differences would resolve over time (Bell & Kristol, 1965) have not come to pass. Dionne (1991) noted that Bell's (1965:59) publication of *The End of Ideology* was "followed almost immediately by an intensely ideological period, especially in America." We must conclude, therefore, that theoretical efforts at this time should center on defining different viewpoints and predicting their relationships to behavior and attitudes. Further, this knowledge should be discussed openly, so that individuals can make an educated choice as to their beliefs.

Research Implications

Despite the rapid growth in diversity-training programs (Rossett & Bickham, 1994), little research has been conducted to assess their impact. Anecdotal evidence offers a pot pourri of advice, suggesting that empirical examination must begin before problems are worsened rather than improved (Kaufman, 1994; Lunt, 1994; Lynch, 1994; Rossett & Bickham, 1994; Thomas, 1994). We agree with this assessment but acknowledge that researchers must be especially careful in controlling for response bias when conducting research on this topic. For example, although most direct surveys show that Americans favor integration in general, they quickly alter their responses when questions about integration are applied to their own neighborhoods (Dovidio, 1993).

A substantial amount of instrument development and measurement must be conducted to assess the constructs defined in the theory. A number of unobtrusive techniques may be used to assess certain variables. For example, scenarios with alternative explanations could be used to assess people's agreement with different paradigmatic viewpoints. Laboratory studies are useful for measuring the effect that rhetoric has on attitudes and behaviors. Experimental methods can be used to measure the effect of cultural diversity classes on university students. Most important, field studies can be conducted with the cooperation of organizations undergoing diversity training. In fact, researchers in this area appear to have a number of avenues to pursue and fewer impediments when compared to other subject areas.

A second approach that may yield interesting results is comparing the effects that various training programs have on different outcome variables. For example, if behavior is the outcome of most concern, legal awareness with a functional viewpoint may be the program most likely to yield positive results for the organization. By informing employees of the law and the consequences for breaking the law, the trainer may provide sufficient incentive for employees to engage in appropriate behaviors. Such training would not necessarily be enough, however, to change employees' attitudes about diversity. Psychotherapeutic approaches and dissonance creation may be more useful for changing people's attitudes.

In conclusion, research in this field appears to be reasonably feasible. The theory offers some guidelines for beginning a series of research projects that may enable greater understanding of multiculturalism. Furthermore, the methodologies necessary for adequate evaluation of training programs have received considerable attention in the training literature (Bunker & Cohen, 1977; Campbell, Dunnette, Lawler, & Wieck, 1970; Latham & Saari, 1979), so the research techniques are immediately available for a researcher's use.

Practical Implications

The theory has several important implications for practitioners, but we also should caution practitioners to have realistic expectations about the potential impact of formal diversity programs. First, the theory indicates that formal diversity programs are most likely to induce behavioral and attitudinal change under the following specific conditions: (a) when target individuals have not yet committed to strong paradigmatic views of their own, (b) when conflicting informal influence is absent, and (c) when the organizational culture supports a well-defined ideal of multiculturalism. Many target individuals may, in fact, have a wide latitude of noncommitment or be in a state of latency about multiculturalism, so formal diversity training may have far-reaching potential. Furthermore, formal diversity-training programs may provide useful information that causes target individuals to develop a view of multiculturalism that is congruent with the intent of the program. However, practitioners must be aware that they may be "awakening a sleeping elephant" when they broach the topic of multiculturalism. Informal influencers have as much potential to arouse individuals in the state of latency as do formal influencers. When individuals seek the support of informal influencers to refute the message of formal diversity programs, they may, in fact, become even more "dug in" in a paradigmatic viewpoint at variance with the formal program (Perloff, 1993: 205). Furthermore, this may arouse antidiversity-program activism by eliciting a negative response to the formal diversity program itself. For these reasons, we believe the most appropriate approach to formal diversity training is to use the foundation of knowledge developed in the theory as a basis for discussion of various viewpoints. It may, in fact, be useful to develop a certification process for trainers based on this foundation of knowledge.

Second, it may be unrealistic to assume that many individuals in organizations do not have a functionalist or functional pluralist bias. Trainers who have radical structuralist leanings may speculate on how to change this situation. Radical structuralist training programs have, in fact, been reported in the literature (see Table 1). However, we believe it is extremely difficult to change individuals to a radical structuralist viewpoint in a work organization setting. Radical structuralists question the very nature and purpose of work organizations, particularly in capitalist economies, where they are perceived as a major cause of oppression and domination. According to Mann (1986), the true radical structuralist must operate outside the boundaries of work organizations, encouraging escalating episodes of protest until revolution is ultimately achieved. Radical structuralists cannot rely on the gentle art of persuasion in a training setting to fulfill radical ends. Trainers who take radical structuralism out of its appropriate context and who fail to convey the richness of its literature mistakenly assume that all individuals have a common understanding of concepts like oppression and domination. These concepts should remain in an educational setting where a thorough examination and critique of the viewpoint can be made.

Third, the theory encourages a methodology of open dialogue for formal diversity-training programs. Open discussion creates the possibility for individuals to choose what they believe in an educated manner. Presenting only a single viewpoint may appear to be a "salesmanship" job rather than serious discourse. Open discussion of various viewpoints also reduces the threat of normative sanction within the training session. If the threat is reduced, individuals are less likely to seek social support for their own point of view in a different setting. Long-term change is then more likely to occur.

Last, the theory suggests that practitioners must realistically evaluate their own willingness to undertake the difficult task of "valuing diversity," when the potential for intense criticism exists. In modern times, multiculturalism has been central to most memorable political events. Horrific wars, great acts of moral courage, and difficult civil rights movements have characterized the intensity of the struggle for greater inclusiveness of all peoples. The intensity of these events attests to the difficulty of changing attitudes about and behaviors regarding multiculturalism. Recent attacks on affirmative action provide fresh evidence that diversity programs remain a controversial topic. Practitioners must not be naive in assuming that everyone will accept diversity as a worthy goal.

Reflections and Conclusion

Lack of a well-defined foundation of knowledge about multiculturalism has created a situation whereby much of the information about multiculturalism comes in the form of rhetoric. However, rhetoric that polarizes, rather than informs, has characterized much of the debate accessed by average citizens. We note from history that the impulse toward tribalism, or Balkanization, destroys the civilization in which the impulse toward polarization has free rein. For this reason alone, debaters of multiculturalism must shift course to a more reasoned and civilized dialogue. Our theory provides a basis for such dialogue.

Our theory is not excessively optimistic about diversity; we attempt to firmly ground our expectations in reality. Philosophers have long recognized a tension between the individual and the community or between the smaller organizing unit and the larger society. Researchers must recognize that no utopian solution exists to resolve this tension. The unfortunate consequence of struggling for a utopian ideal is that the ideal turns into a tyranny once in practice (Tinder, 1989). History is also littered with lost civilizations that failed to set high standards for appreciating the uniqueness of others while also recognizing a common humanity. Part of the human condition is struggling for this balance. Our theory attempts to identify the differences that define the struggle.

Researchers and organizational participants must recognize that attachment to "one's own" is not easily abandoned, but as organizational citizens, people must also recognize that attachment to "one's own" is not all that matters. A sense of dissatisfaction and yearning may characterize typical sentiments about the alienating effects of organizational life, not just subgroup members' sentiments. Though people might hope for greater personal attachments and cultural meaning in their work life, the organization is limited in the intensity of diversity it can absorb before Balkanization occurs.

Organizations also have obligations to their citizens. Forced affirmative action plans may be insufficient to resolve the tensions associated with diversity. However, more important, organizations must recognize the performance limitations imposed by "organization-man" social conformity. Repression of unorthodox ideas may be far more damaging to individual initiative and organizational success than is political dissension. Broad-based and informal efforts to eliminate mediocrity by pursuing heterogeneous ideas may go further in relieving tensions than more formalized programs. To the extent that formalized programs are pursued, organizational leaders must be responsible for articulating a vision of diversity, for diligently examining the content of diversity programs, and for empirically evaluating the results of diversity training. Programs that exacerbate tensions surrounding diversity should be abandoned in favor of those that promote tolerance and curiosity.

References

Adorno, T. W., Frenkel-Brunswik, E., Levinson, D. J., & Sanford, R. N. 1950. *The authoritarian personality*. New York: Harper.

Asch, S. E. 1952. *Social psychology*. Engelwood Cliffs, NJ: Prentice Hall.

Asch, S. E. 1956. Studies of independence and conformity: A minority of one against a unanimous majority. *Psychological monographs: General and applied*, 70: 1–70 (Whole No. 416).

Barber, B. J. 1992. Jihad vs McWorld. *Atlantic Monthly*, 269(3): 53–63.

Becker, L. B., McCombs, M. E., & McLeod, J. M. 1975. The development of political cognitions. In S. H. Chattee (Ed.), *Political communication: Issues and strategies for research*: 21–63. Beverly Hills, CA: Sage.

Bell, D. 1965. *The end of ideology*. New York: Free Press.

Bell, D., & Kristol, I. 1965. What is in the public interest? *Public Interest*, 1(1): 3–5.

Berent, M. K., Krosnick, J. A., & Boninger, D. S. 1993. *Attitude importance and memory for attitude-relevant information*. Unpublished manuscript.

Bloom, A. 1987. *The closing of the American mind*. New York: Simon & Schuster.

Bloom, H. 1994. *The Western canon*. New York: Harcourt Brace Jovanovich.

Bock, E., Beeghley, W., & Mixon, A. J. 1983. Religion, socioeconomic status, and sexual morality: An application of reference group theory. *Sociological Quarterly*, 24: 545–559.

Boninger, D. S., Krosnick, J. A., & Berent, M. K. 1995. Origins of attitude importance: Self-interest, social identification, and value relevance. *Journal of Personality and Social Psychology*, 68: 61–80.

Boynton, R. S. 1995. The new intellectual. *Atlantic Monthly*, 275(3): 53–71.

Bunker, K. A., & Cohen, S. L. 1977. The rigors of training evaluation: A discussion and field demonstration. *Personnel Psychology*, 30: 525–541.

Burrell, G., & Morgan, G. 1979. *Sociological paradigms and organizational analysis*. London: Heinemann.

Campbell, J. P., Dunnette, M. D., Lawler, E. E., III, & Weick, K. E., Jr. 1970. *Managerial behavior, performance, and effectiveness*. New York: McGraw-Hill.

Carroll, S. J., Paine, F. T., & Ivancevich, J. J. 1972. The relative effectiveness of training methods—Expert opinion and research. *Personnel Psychology*, 25: 495–509.

Caudron, S. 1993. Training can damage diversity efforts. *Personnel Journal*, 72(4): 51–63.

Copeland, L. 1988. Valuing workplace diversity. *Personnel Administrator*, November: 65–88.

Cox, T. 1991. The multicultural organization. *Executive*, 5(2): 34–47.

Cox, T., & Blake, S. 1991. Managing cultural diversity: Implications for organizational competitiveness. *Executive*, 5(3): 45–56.

Cullen, R. 1993. Cleansing ethnic hatred. *Atlantic Monthly*, 272(2): 30–36.

Dionne, E. J. 1991. *Why Americans hate politics*. New York: Simon & Schuster.

Dovidio, J. 1993. The subtlety of racism. *Training & Development*, 47(4): 51–57.

Feldman, R. E. 1968. Response to compatriot and foreigner who seek assistance. *Journal of Personality and Social Psychology*, 10: 202–214.

Festinger, L. A. 1957. *A theory of cognitive dissonance*. Stanford, CA: Stanford University Press.

Fine, B. J. 1957. Conclusion-drawing, communicator credibility, and anxiety as factors in opinion change. *Journal of Abnormal and Social Psychology*, 54: 369–374.

Freedman, J. 1964. Involvement, discrepancy, and change. *Journal of Abnormal and Social Psychology*, 69: 290–295.

Frenkel-Brunswik, E., & Havel, J. 1953. Prejudice in the interviews of children: I. Attitudes toward minority groups. *Journal of Genetic Psychology*, 82: 91–136.

Fukuyama, F. 1992. *The end of history and the last man*. New York: Avon Books.

Fukuyama, F. 1993. Immigrants and family values. *Commentary*, 95(5): 26–33.

Gordon, J. 1992. Rethinking diversity. *Training*, 29(1): 23–31.

Gorn, G. J. 1975. The effects of personal involvement, communication discrepancy, and source prestige on reactions to communication on separatism. *Canadian Journal of Behavioral Science*, 7: 369–386.

Gutman, A. 1993. The challenge of multiculturalism. *Philosophy & Public Affairs*, 22(3): 171–206.

Hall, R. G., Varca, P. E., & Fisher, T. D. 1986. The effect of reference groups, opinion polls, and attitude polarization on attitude formation and change. *Political Psychology*, 7: 309–321.

Hooper, M. 1982. Explorations in the structure of psychological identifications with social groups and roles. *Multivariate Behavioral Research*, 17: 515–523.

Hornstein, H. A. 1978. Promotive tension and prosocial behavior: A Lewinian analysis. In L. Wispe (Ed.), *Altrusim, sympathy, and helping*: 177–207. New York: Academic Press.

Hornstein, H. A., Fisch, E., & Holmes, M. 1968. Influence of a model's feeling about his behavior and his relevance as a comparison other on observer's helping behavior. *Journal of Personality and Social Psychology*, 10: 222–226.

Hornstein, H. A., Masor, H. N., Sole, K., & Heilman, M. 1971. Effects of sentiment and completion of a helping act on observer helping. *Journal of Personality and Social Psychology*, 17: 107–112.

Hughes, R. 1993. *Culture of complaint*. New York: Oxford University Press.

Ibarra, H. 1993. Personal networks of women and minorities in management: A conceptual framework. *Academy of Management Review*, 18: 56–87.

Insko, C. A., Nacoste, R. W., & Moe, J. L. 1983. Belief congruence and racial discrimination: Review of the evidence and critical evaluation. *European Journal of Social Psychology*, 13: 153–174.

Jaroff, L. 1994. Teaching reverse racism. *Time*, 142(17): 74–76.

Kanter, R. M. 1977. *Men and women of the corporation*. New York: Basic Books.

Kaufman, L. 1994. Painfully aware. *Government Executive*, 26(2): 16–22.

Kolchin, P. 1993. *American slavery 1619–1877*. New York: Hill & Wang.

Krebs, D. 1970. Altruism—An examination of the concept and a review of the literature. *Psychological Bulletin*, 73: 258–302.

Krosnick, J. A. 1988. Attitude importance and attitude change. *Journal of Experimental Social Psychology*, 24: 240–255.

Kuhn, T. 1962. *The structure of scientific revolutions*. Chicago: University of Chicago Press.

Latham, G., & Saari, L. M. 1979. Application of social-learning theory to training supervisors through behavioral modeling. *Journal of Applied Psychology*, 64: 239–246.

Lasch, C. 1979. *The culture of narcissism*. New York: Warner Books.

Lasch, C. 1993. Traditional values: Left, right, and wrong. *Harper's Magazine*, 287(1720): 13–16.

Leippe, M. R., & Eisenstadt, D. 1994. Generalization of dissonance reduction: Decreasing prejudice through induced compliance. *Journal of Personality and Social Psychology*, 67: 395–413.

Lunt, P. 1994. Should you do diversity training? *ABA Banking Journal*, 98(8): 50–55.

Lynch, P. R. 1994. Workforce diversity: PC's final frontier? *National Review*, 48(3): 32–35.

Mackie, J. L. 1987. The subjectivity of values. In G. Sher (Ed.), *Moral philosophy*: 177–200. San Diego: Harcourt Brace Jovanovich.

Maddi, S. A. 1968. *Personality theories*. Homewood, IL: Dorsey Press.

Mann, M. 1986. *Consciousness and action among the Western working class*. London: McMillan.

Martin, J., & Siehl, C. 1983. Organizational culture and counterculture: An uneasy symbiosis. *Organizational Dynamics*, 90(2): 52–64.

McCroskey, J. C., Richmond, V. P., & Daly, J. A. 1975. The development of a measure of perceived homophily in interpersonal communication. *Human Communication Research*, 1: 325–332.

McGuire, W. J. 1985. Attitudes and attitude change. In G. Lindzey & E. Aronson (Eds.), *Handbook of social psychology*, vol. 2: 233–346. New York: Random House.

Merton, R. K. 1957. Continuities in the theory of reference groups and social structure. In R. K. Merton (Ed.), *Social theory and social structure*: 335–440. New York: Free Press.

Merton, R. K., & Rossi, A. S. 1950. Contributions to the theory of reference group behavior. In R. K. Merton (Ed.), *Social theory and social structure*: 279–335. New York: Free Press.

Mintzberg, H. 1983. *Power in and around organizations*. Englewood Cliffs, NJ: Prentice Hall.

Mitchell, T. R. 1982. *People in organizations*. San Francisco: McGraw-Hill.

Montgomery, R. L. 1980. Reference groups as anchors in judgements of other groups: A biasing factor in "ratings tasks"? *Psychological Reports*, 47: 967–975.

Moscovici, S. 1976. *Social influence and social change*. London: Academic Press.

Moscovici, S., & Zavalloni, M. 1969. The group as a polarizer of attitudes. *Journal of Personality and Social Psychology*, 12: 125–135.

Myers, D. G., & Bishop, G. D. 1970. Discussion effects on racial attitudes. *Science*, 169: 778–779.

National Public Radio. 1993. Morning edition. October 23.

O'Keefe, D. J. 1990. *Persuasion: Theory and research*. London: Sage.

Ostling, R. N. 1993. A refinement of evil. *Time*, 142(14): 75.

Perloff, R. M. 1993. *The dynamics of persuasion*. Hillsdale, NJ: Erlbaum.

Petty, R., & Cacioppo, J. 1986. *Attitudes and persuasion: Central and peripheral routes to attitude change*. New York: Springer-Verlag.

Pfeffer, J. 1993. Barriers to the advance of organizational science: Paradigm development as a dependent variable. *Academy of Management Review*, 18: 599–620.

Piliavin, I., Rodin, J., & Piliavin, J. 1969. Good Samaritans: An underground phenomenon? *Journal of Personality and Social Psychology*, 13: 289–299.

Pratt, H. J. 1974. *Ethno-religious politics*. Cambridge, MA: Schenkman.

Rajecki, D. W. 1990. *Attitudes* (2nd ed.). Sunderland, MA: Sinquer Associates.

Ravitch, D. 1991. Pluralism vs. particularism in American education. *Responsive Community*, 1(2): 32–45.

Roberts, J. M. 1993. *History of the world*. New York: Oxford University Press.

Rossett, A., & Bickham, T. 1994. Diversity training: Hope, faith, and cynicism. *Training*, January: 41–46.

Schafran, H. L. 1993. Is the law male? Let me count the ways. *Chicago-Kent Law Review*, 69: 397–416.

Schuman, H., & Presser, S. 1981. *Questions and answers: Experiments on question form, wording, and context in attitude surveys*. New York: Academic Press.

Sherif, M., & Hovland, C. 1961. *Social judgment, assimilation and contrast effects in communication and attitude change*. New Haven, CT: Yale University Press.

Sherif, M., Sherif, C., & Nebergall, R. 1965. *Attitude and attitude change: The social judgement-involvement approach*. Philadelphia: Saunders.

Shulman, K. 1994. Bloom and doom. *Newsweek*, 124(15): 75.

Shweder, R. A., & Bourne, E. J. 1984. Does the concept of the person vary cross-culturally? In R. A. Shweder & R. A. Levine (Eds.), *Culture theory: Essays on mind, self, and emotion*: 158–199. London: Cambridge University.

Siero, F. W., & Doosje, B. J. 1993. Attitude change following persuasive communication: Integrating social judgment theory and the elaboration likelihood model. *European Journal of Social Psychology*, 23: 541–554.

Simon, L., Greenberg, J. & Brehm, J. 1995. Trivialization: The forgotten mode of dissonance reduction. *Journal of Personality and Social Psychology*, 68: 247–260.

Smirchich, L. 1983. Concepts of culture and organizational analysis. *Administrative Science Quarterly*, 28: 339–358.

Smith, A. 1990. Social influence and antiprejudice training programs. In J. Edwards, R. Scott Tindale, L. Heath, & E. J. Posavac (Eds.), *Social influence processes and prevention*: 183–196. New York: Plenum Press.

Sowell, T. 1975. *Race and economics*. New York: McKay.

Sowell, T. 1981. *Ethnic America: A history*. New York: Basic Books.

Spokesman-Review. 1993. German teachers receive training to fight bigotry. October 17: A8.

Stotland, E. 1969. Exploratory studies in empathy. In L. Berkowitz (Ed.), *Advances in experimental social psychology*, vol. 4: 271–314. New York: Academic Press.

Strauss, G. 1964. Workflow frictions, interfunctional rivalry, and professionalism: A case study of purchasing agents. *Human Organization*: 137–149.

Tafjel, H., Billig, M. G., Bundy, R. P., & Plament, C. 1971. Categorization and intergroup behavior. *European Journal of Social Psychology*, 1: 149–178.

Taylor, P. 1987. Ethical relativism. In G. Sher (Ed.), *Moral philosophy*: 146–160. San Diego, CA: Harcourt Brace Jovanovich.

Thomas, V. C. 1994. The downside of diversity. *Training & Development*, 48(1): 60–62.

Tinder, G. 1989. Can we be good without God? *Atlantic Monthly*, 264(6): 68–98.

Triandis, H. C. 1971. *Attitude and attitude change*. New York: Wiley.

Turner, J. C. 1982. Towards a cognitive redefinition of the social group. In H. Tafjel (Ed.), *Social identity and intergroup relations*: 15–40. Cambridge, England: Cambridge University Press.

Turner, J. C., & Oakes, P. J. 1989. Self categorization theory and social influence. In P. B. Paulus (Ed.), *Psychology of group influence* (2nd ed.): 233–275. Hillsdale, NJ: Erlbaum.

Van Maanen, J., & Barley, S. 1984. Occupational communities: Culture and control in organizations. In B. M. Staw & L. L. Cummings (Eds.), *Research in organization behavior*, vol. 1: 209–264. Greenwich, CT: JAI Press.

Vinokur, A., & Burnstein, E. 1978. Depolarization of attitudes in groups. *Journal of Personality and Social Psychology*, 36: 872–885.

Whittaker, J. 1965. Attitude change and communication—Attitude discrepancy. *Journal of Social Psychology*, 85: 141–147.

Wicker, T. 1991. The Democrats as the devil's disciples. *New York Times*, August 30: A12.

Wilson, J. Q. 1993. *The moral sense*. New York: Free Press.

Wolin, S. S. 1993. Democracy, difference, and re-cognition. *Political Theory*, 21(3): 464–484.

Worseley, P. 1985. *Introducing sociology*. New York: Penguin Books.

Wright, Q. 1964. *A study of war*. Chicago: University of Chicago Press.

Patricia L. Nemetz received her Ph.D. from the University of Washington. She is an associate professor of management at Eastern Washington University. Her research interests include the technology-human interface and both domestic and international multiculturalism, with an emphasis on Eastern Europe.

Sandra L. Christensen received her Ph.D. from the University of Washington. She is an assistant professor of management at Eastern Washington University. Her current research interests include ethics and public policy and environmental history.

PART XII

RETHINKING ACADEMIC ORGANIZATION AND INSTITUTIONAL GOVERNANCE

POSTMODERNISM AND HIGHER EDUCATION

HARLAND G. BLOLAND

Postmodern perspectives, terms, and assumptions have penetrated the core of American culture over the past thirty years. Postmodernism's primary significance is its power to account for and reflect vast changes in our society, cultures, polity, and economy as we move from a production to a consumption society, shift from national to local and international politics, commingle high and low culture, and generate new social movements. Postmodernism has captured our interest because it involves a stunning critique of modernism, the foundation upon which our thinking and our institutions have rested. Today, modernist values and institutions are increasingly viewed as inadequate, pernicious, and costly. Postmodernists attack the validity and legitimacy of the most basic assumptions of modernism. Because higher education is quintessentially a modern institution, attacks on modernism are attacks on the higher education system as it is now constituted. The modern/postmodern debate began in the United States in the 1960s in the humanities, gained momentum in the 1970s in the arts and social theory, and by the early 1980s became, as Andreas Huyssen noted, "one of the most contested terrains in the intellectual life of Western society" [59, p. 357]. Today, having swept through the humanities and social sciences, the modern/postmodern debate has ebbed, and in literary studies at least, scholars refer to the current period as "post-theory" [101, p. A9].

In anthropology and other social sciences, postmodernism has had transformational effects, but currently many scholars who have been influenced by it distance themselves from the term, asserting that it identifies others, but not them [70, p. 563]. In literary studies, scholars continue to employ postmodern conceptualization extensively, while they assume that those who use the words also know the theory. No such assumption can be made in higher education studies concerning familiarity with modern/postmodern theory. Despite its significance in the past three decades the modern/postmodern debate has had relatively little direct impact on the study of higher education. The term "postmodern" appears with increasing frequency in the titles of presentations on postsecondary education in American Educational Research Association presentations, but few of the discussions address directly the background of the modern/postmodern divide that provides the vocabulary for the issues addressed.[1]

The paucity of literature in higher education on postmodernism is surprising, because the postmodern debate has been in the foreground for many education scholars who write about the public schools, particularly in the fields of curriculum studies, school administration, and educational theory [3, 37, 68]. Still, we rarely find postmodernism studies in the ASHE Reader series, in the ASHE/ERIC monographs, the *Journal of Higher Education*, the *Review of Higher Education*, or *Change* magazine. Postmodernism does find a place in *The Chronicle of Higher Education* articles, but they are not authored by higher education professors. The meagerness of higher educationists' general engagement with the postmodern is unfortunate, for despite the fact that the high tide of debate seems to be waning, the postmodern/modern discussion continues to have an unsettling but significant impact on the way in which we now think about society, politics, economics, and education. Thus, the terms and concepts of this debate are still with us, and the postmodern critique affects every field of inquiry that deals with human society.

Perhaps nowhere are the issues of the postmodern/modern debate more sharply drawn, more clearly illuminated, and more difficult to acknowledge than in higher education in the United States. For higher education is so deeply immersed in modernist sensibilities and so dependent upon modernist foundations that erosion of our faith in the modernist project calls into question higher education's legitimacy, its purpose, its activities, its very raison d'être. In attacking modernism, postmodernism presents a hostile interpretation of much of what higher education believes it is doing and what it stands for.

This study examines postmodernism and higher education by presenting four seminal postmodernist authors' ideas that provide a framework for discussions for much of the literature on postmodernism:

Jacques Derrida, Michel Foucault, Jean-François Lyotard, and Jean Baudrillard. Derrida and Foucault are viewed as representative of poststructuralist thought from which postmodernism as a perspective is derived, and Lyotard and Baudrillard are reflective of the view of postmodernism as a historical period. The postmodern concepts of these authors are discussed in terms of their implications for merit, community, and autonomy, three crucial characteristics of modernist higher education as it is situated in American society. Twelve reactions to the postmodern are introduced, each of which purports to interpret the consequences and illuminate the uses of postmodern thought. A summary of postmodernism's legacy for higher education concludes the discussion.

Postmodernism as a Perspective

The terms "modern" and "postmodern" occupy no fixed positions; their meanings are imprecise and highly contested. Despite this ambiguity, however, these concepts are critical reference points for discussions that try to make sense of what appear to be disparate cultural, economic, political, and social changes taking place in architecture, art, philosophy, literary criticism, the social sciences, in every day life, in popular culture, in industry, business, technology, and education.

Modernism

Modernism requires faith that there are universals that can be discovered through reason, that science and the scientific method are superior means for arriving at truth and reality, and that language describes and can be used as a credible and reliable means of access to that reality. With its privileging of reason, modernism has long been considered the basis for the emancipation of men and women from the bonds of ignorance associated with stagnant tradition, narrow religions, and meager educations. Championing democracy, modernism promises freedom, equality, justice, the good life, and prosperity. Equating merit with high culture, modernism provides expectations of more rigorous standards for and greater enjoyment of the arts and architecture. Through science and scientific method, modernism promises health, the eradication of hunger, crime, and poverty. Modernist science claims to be progressing toward true knowledge of the universe and to be delivering ever higher standards of living with effectiveness and efficiency. Modernism promises stability, peace, and a graspable sense of the rational unfolding of history. Modernism equates change with progress, which is defined as increasing control over nature and society.

Perhaps the most important means for understanding and carrying out the modernist project is education. Higher education is deeply embedded in the ideals, institutions, and vocabulary of modernism. Higher education trusts that merit should be rewarded through good jobs, promotions, higher status, and prestige. Higher education defends the notion that knowledge and expertise are important for problem solving in the society. Higher education assumes that science, scientific methods, and the science sensibility are better means for discovering and creating truth than tradition. Higher education treats high culture as separate from and better than popular culture. Higher education values differentiation, recognizing that there are different discourse communities in the academy and that there is a difference between the inside and outside of institutions of higher education. While valuing diversity, colleges and universities treasure community and institutional autonomy.

Higher education assumes that middle-class values are good for society and for individuals, that parents and students want middle-class status, and that the road to upward mobility and the way to prevent downward mobility or skidding is through education. Higher education assumes that progress is possible and good, and that the way to move in that direction is through education. Higher education assumes that community is good, that some fundamental set of values, some basic accepted rules of conduct, and some sense of limits are good.

However, over time, modernism has displayed another, quite negative face. Although modernism has been a spectacularly successful and powerful orientation, it has also organized and constructed its own serious failures. For Max Weber (a doubting, skeptical modernist), reason in the form of instrumental rationality has generated the overorganized modern economic order which in turn has imprisoned people in an "iron cage" of work incentives. As Weber writes, "This order is now bound to the technical and economic conditions of machine production which today determine the lives of all the individuals who are born into this mechanism . . . with irresistible force" [97, p. 181]. The highly rationalized world Weber described as our modern fate is characterized as having lost the sense of enchantment that tradition provides for societies [41, p. 155]. The Frankfort school of critical social theory, with such luminaries as Theodore Adorno, Max Horkheimer [1], and Herbert Marcuse [71] offered pessimistic interpretations of modernism, seeing in it the rise of faceless, characterless mass societies. Even Jürgen Habermas, the current generation's premier Frankfort school intellectual who believes in Enlightenment values and goals and whose project is to save modernism, sees rationality as having strayed from its proper direction, resulting in highly dysfunctional institutions in the world society [51, 52]. Many of the Frankfort school's ideas have been incorporated into the postmodern diatribe against modernism. Instrumental rationality in its current postmodern reading is seen as having forged the consumer society, in which commodification, the definition of persons and activities solely in terms of their market value, has become dominant. Science is now associated as much with death through annihilation, environmental problems, and uncontrollable technology as it is with progress and benign innovation.

Richard Bernstein reminds us that the terms, "reason" and "rationality" now "evoke images of domination, oppression, repression, patriarchy, sterility, violence, totality, totalitarianism, and even terror" [12, p. 32]. Thus, fascism, nazism, and communism, as well as democracy, are associated with modernism. As Stephen White writes, "The costs of Western modernization or rationalization are being progressively reestimated upward" [99, p. 5]. In this negative image of modernism, postmodernists deeply implicate higher education.

Postmodernism and Poststructuralism: Derrida and Foucault

Postmodernism may be seen as a perspective [67, p. 14], a means for understanding the conditions we now live in. It may also be viewed as a new epoch, or a new historical era. In either case, the major concepts and ideas of postmodernism provide a devastating attack on modernism. This assault renders as questionable the major assumptions and assertions of our modern culture. That is, it makes problematic what is taken for granted in a wide range of topics. The postmodern problematic zeroes in on hierarchies of any kind—and hierarchies are inherent in modern life—with the view that "there are no natural hierarchies, only those we construct" [57, p. 13].

Postmodernism interrogates the modern system, which is built on continuing, persistent efforts, to totalize or unify, pointing out that totalization hides contradictions, ambiguities, and oppositions and is a means for generating power and control. Institutions of modernity come under critical postmodern scrutiny, and among the primary institutions open to questioning are the college and university. To see postmodernism as a way of understanding the limits of modernism is to view our world in the midst of profound change and to concentrate on the disillusionment we are experiencing with some of our deepest assumptions and cherished hopes relating to our most important institutions. We seek rational solutions in a world that increasingly distrusts reason as a legitimate approach to problem solving. We try to move forward in our lives and through our institutions in a milieu of declining faith in the possibility of progress. We act on dimly apprehended foundational assumptions, for example, faith in science and the scientific method, even as we grow increasingly suspicious of all grand narratives.

Postmodernism as a perspective (often printed "postmodern" rather than "post-modern," defined as an era) borrows extensively from the definitions and concepts of poststructuralism. Thus it focuses upon the indeterminacy of language, the primacy of discourse, the decentering and fragmentation of the concept of self, the significance of the "other," a recognition of the tight, unbreakable power/knowledge nexus, the attenuation of a belief in metanarratives, and the decline of dependence upon rationalism. Poststructuralist thought developed in France in the 1970s as a reaction to the French structuralist attempts to build a rigorous, objective, scientific analysis of social life through the discovery of the underlying, deep structural linguistic and social rules that organize language and social systems [13, pp. 18, 20]. Poststructuralist concepts have been appropriated, broadened, and extended by the international movement of postmodernism, which has applied the poststructural ideas to a much larger number of topics in its wide-ranging attacks on modernism.

What do these poststructural/postmodern concepts mean and what is their significance for society and for higher education? Much of this orientation is related to poststructuralist views of language and of how language is used. Two poststructuralists who have transformed our ideas about language are Jacques Derrida and Michel Foucault.

Derrida

Derrida attacks basic modernist assumptions about languages and reality. The usual assumption is that there are thoughts and realities prior to language and that language is the vehicle for communicating ideas and of describing reality. He asserts, instead, that language comes before knowledge and that the meaning of words is constantly changing. Language becomes indeterminate and difficult to control. For Derrida, the meanings of words are permanently in flux. Word meanings continually escape their boundaries as these meanings are negotiated and renegotiated in social settings. The Derridian strategy is to search out and illuminate the internal contradictions in language and in doing so show how final meaning is forever withheld or postponed in the concepts we use. The means for carrying out this project is deconstruction [29].

Deconstruction involves a close reading of a text,[2] examining and bringing to the surface concealed hierarchies and hidden oppositions, inconsistencies, and contradictions in the language [29]. The method of deconstruction includes "demystifying a text, tearing it apart to reveal its internal, arbitrary hierarchies and its presuppositions" [86, p. 120].

The central arguments of a text are ignored as deconstruction looks to the margins and to that which has been omitted, erased, or withheld. The Derrida position is that "the binary oppositions governing Western philosophy and culture (subject/object, appearance/reality, speech/writing, and so on) work to construct a far-from-innocent hierarchy of values which attempts not only to guarantee truth, but also serves to exclude and devalue allegedly inferior terms or positions. This binary metaphysics thus works to positively position reality over appearance, speech over writing, men over women, or reason over nature, thus positioning negatively the supposedly inferior term" [13, p. 21].

The purpose of deconstruction is not simply to unmask or illuminate hierarchies and demonstrate their arbitrariness, to delegitimate them, but to do so without replacing them with other hierarchies and so create tensions without resolving them. Thus, as Rosenau points out, "deconstruction attempts to undo, reverse, displace, and resituate the hierarchies in polar opposites . . . But the goal is to do more than overturn oppositions, for this would permit new hierarchies to be reappropriated" [86, p. 120].

Deconstruction and higher education. Derrida's powerful attack upon hierarchies of the modernist world can be used with great effect in challenging higher education's hierarchies and illuminating its exclusions. Higher education is composed of hierarchies. The disciplines are arranged within institutions of higher education in a loose hierarchy of discourses[3] that give preference to the physical sciences over the social sciences and humanities and to the arts and sciences over education and other marginal professions.

Research is above teaching, doctoral studies over masters, and bachelors over associate degree studies. Private education is over public education, professors over students, administrators over professors, tenured over nontenured professors. The list is long. To deconstruct these discourses is to indicate first that they are social constructions and did not emerge from some inherent, universalistic rationale or logic. It is to point out the hidden contradictions, inconsistencies, and ambiguities within academia, to show just how much hierarchy is based on what look like arbitrary exclusions, and to illuminate how much they serve to put other ideas and people on the margin or exclude them entirely. Concepts that lend credence to faith in reason, science, progress, and the Enlightenment are privileged in the modernist world, and especially in the university and college. Once their legitimacy is called into question, all sorts of hierarchies become suspect in the university—science over the humanities, high culture over popular culture, literary canons over wider definitions of literature, classical over popular music. This erosion of faith in the legitimacy of the assumptions embedded in the hierarchical academic order provides a series of cracks in the dominant culture of the university, encouraging historically marginal groups, such as persons of color, gay and lesbian groups, and women, to claim space in these institutions, even as this erosion delegitimates the dominant modernist culture for its assumptions of superiority.

The delegitimation goes well beyond simply allowing space for those individuals traditionally thought to be marginal in the universities. Delegitimation encompasses harsh questioning of universities and colleges about their reward structures, the purposes and practices in which they are engaged, and the claims of those now in positions of power and responsibility to their right of office. If the hierarchies of academia are falsely assembled, are arbitrary, and illegitimate, the question becomes why are these particular professors and administrators, rather than others, now sitting in their superior positions benefiting from the modernist academic hierarchies?

Colleges and universities are particularly susceptible to the postmodern critique that denigrates hierarchy because institutions of higher education see themselves as institutions with the responsibility to create and distribute knowledge, civic values, and meaning to new generations. They act as sorting mechanisms and as institutions that maintain the middle class status of students (class being another modernist hierarchical concept), while also creating the means for upward mobility of students. Institutions of higher education are the generators of large numbers of professionals and of the professional sensibility. Expertise, the primary attribute of professionals, is suspect, for it places clients and lay people in an inferior position. These concepts, when directed toward higher education, provide a powerful delegitimating lever that interrogates the purposes, structure, and activities of higher education as it now operates in its modernist context.

Deconstruction provides reasons and arguments supporting the accusations that excluded groups make against institutions of higher education. Some authors are particularly good at providing the ideas and language that speak to marginality. No one is clearer in pointing out the exclusionary character of modern language and institutions than Derrida. As Richard Bernstein says of Derrida, "Few contemporary writers equal him in his sensitivity and alertness to the multifarious ways in which the 'history of the West'—even in its institutionalization of communicative practices—has always tended to silence differences, to exclude outsiders and exiles, those who live on the margins. . . . This is one of the many good reasons why Derrida 'speaks' to those who have felt the pain and suffering of being excluded by the prevailing hierarchies embedded in the text called 'the history of the West'—whether they be women, Blacks, or others bludgeoned by exclusionary tactics" [12, pp. 51, 52].

However, this deprivileging is dangerous and can easily backfire for marginal groups. If there are no legitimate bases for rewarding the privileged in our society, there are also no foundational standards for rewarding marginal groups. There are no grounded assumptions or moral grounds from which marginal groups can claim privilege. From this postmodern perspective there is no compelling reason for controlling groups to give ground to others.

Merit and community. Higher education is a modern institution that has the concept "merit" deeply embedded in its value structure. Derrida's hostility toward hierarchies is an attack on merit, for merit creates standards that separate and hierarchicalize those who meet them from those who do not. Deconstruction can be used to demonstrate that merit or standards are not only capricious and without foundation, but are arbitrarily exclusive in their consequences. They instantly create marginality. Because higher education places high value on scholarly merit—attempting to find a way to keep it, but make it fair—it is constantly structurally creating and justifying exclusions. Derrida would not eliminate merit, although in his thought there are no foundational reasons for claiming that one standard for merit is better than another; rather, he would keep a continuous tension between what is viewed as merit and what is not, thus making the merit boundaries more open and presumably less exclusionary.

Deconstruction celebrates differences, but refers not to the difference of heterogeneity, which is intrinsic to modernism, but to the difference of disruption, tension, and the withholding of closure. The modernist idea of community also celebrates difference, but emphasizes that which unites people, smooths over disruption, and places limits on the depth and intensity of differences. The creation of community generally is a process of setting boundaries, and this means that communities always have those excluded and those created as marginals. An extreme anticommunity perspective is developed by Iris Marion Young, who believes that a politics of difference should be organized which would have as its chief characteristics "inexhaustible heterogeneity" and "openness to unassimilated otherness," a system that would completely eliminate community with its exclusions of others [102, p. 301].

Higher education promotes the idea of community and is interested in community on several levels. Disciplines are conceived of as communities of scholars, and institutions are viewed as communities of scholars, students, and administrators. The promotion of community is a constant in higher education, and one of its assumptions is that it fosters a concept of citizenship that is an idea of community. Higher education teaches and promotes identification with the larger differentiated community.

Foucault

Both Derrida and Foucault give discourse theory a central place in their writings. Foucault deals initially with what he terms an archaeological approach to discourse. Foucault asks, "What rules permit certain statements to be made; what rules order these statements; what rules permit us to identify some statements as true and some false; what rules allow the construction of a map, model, or classificatory system [78, p. 69].

Archaeology. Archaeology seeks out the rules that designate what will be true or false in a discourse and create the possibility of organizing a discipline, a field of knowledge such as physics or psychology. When academic disciplines, especially the human sciences, are looked at in this archaeological way, they have histories that do not resemble mainstream, modernist notions of how history explains things. Instead of smooth continuities and totalizing explanations, one gets discontinuities and disruptions. As Gibson Burrell points out, Foucault's "aim is to attack great systems, grand theories and vital truths, and to give free play to difference, to local and specific knowledge, and to rupture, contingency, and discontinuity. In Foucault, there is no unity of history, no unity of the subject, no sense of progress, no acceptance of the History of Ideas" [15, pp. 223, 229].

Genealogy. Foucault later expanded his archaeological approach to concentrate on the power/knowledge relationships that exist in institutions. For Foucault, knowledge and power are inextricably bound together. That is, there is no knowledge without a power question arising, and no power without knowledge. This power/knowledge connection has a confounding effect on our understanding of knowledge in the academy. If Foucault is correct about the power/knowledge relationship, there can never be anything approaching neutral, objective knowledge. That is, whatever knowledge comes from research in the disciplines is always implicated in power considerations. This is very different from the modernist assumption in higher education that each discipline can be a separate and independent intellectual enterprise that exists above and outside of politics. Rather, Foucault and the postmodernists view disciplines as completely involved with politics, economics, culture, and other external influences. In Foucault's terms, this means there is little interest in the substance of a discipline or in whether it has legitimate rules for determining meritorious from mediocre work. The interest is only in what power relations are permitted and assumed. The power/knowledge relationship is embedded in discourses, and discourses are the locations where groups and individuals battle for hegemony and over the production of meaning. Disciplines become sites for power contests for control of subject matter through language. As Val Rust writes, "Discourse analysis and cultural studies are really fundamentally studies of power. They should reveal who wields power, in whose interest it is wielded, and with what effects" [89, p. 619].

Power and politics in Foucault's thought. Foucault views power not in terms of a commodity that someone or some group uses or has over others, but as a system or network. Power is pervasive, but it is not in the hands of anyone or any institution, such as the state. Thus one does not ask, Who has power? but, What are the consequences of applying power? Foucault is interested in power in terms of its results, or power at the point where it is wielded. This places his interest at the local level. The Foucaultian analysis provides a species of politics at the margin, ineluctably plural, and on the microlevel. "Foucault calls for a plurality of autonomous struggles throughout the microlevels of society, in the prisons, asylums, hospitals, and schools" [13, p. 56].

Negatively, the Foucaultian perspective is disinterested in what politically could build a larger, better society. His micropolitical perspective favors small communities at the margins of institutions, such as those formed through identity politics. Modernist notions of politics are usually couched in terms of what cross-cutting political activism would add to the larger community. Thus, modernist politics uses such categories as class, or class struggle, or the state and political party action, or the unions and union activities, categories that are justified on the basis of their commitment to an improved macrocommunity and to universals.

As Todd Gitlin argues, in a discussion that employs traditional right/left political orientations, "A troubling irony: the right, traditionally the custodian of the privileges of the few, now speaks in the general language of merit, reason, individual rights, and virtue that transcends politics, whereas much of the left is so preoccupied with debunking generalizations and affirming the differences among groups—real as they often are—that it has ceded the very language of universality that is its birthright" [45, pp. 16, 18, 19].

This politics at the microlevel, or the politics of everyday life, is significant for universities and colleges in terms of the idea of community. Institutions of higher education recognize and encourage differences among disciplines in methods, orientations, languages, and scholarly commitments by individual professors. Colleges and universities recognize that disciplinary discourses may be incommensurate. But even incommensurate academic discourses are assumed to identify with a broad, common set of values that include respect and reward for academic rigor, intellectual creativity, academic freedom, peer review, and general respect for the rules of scholarship. Incommensurate social and cultural discourses are much more difficult to encompass within academia, for institutions have trouble reconciling academic values as they are interpreted within the institutions of higher education with the incommensurate cultural values that are apparent between marginal groups and mainstream academia. The usual method for trying to create community in this situation is for colleges and universities to broaden their interpretations of merit and justice in such a way as to include other cultural values and thus preserve community through the traditional common values. But this modernist strategy in colleges and universities is failing.

For marginal groups, such modernist concepts as freedom, equality, and justice provide the vocabulary for legitimating incommensurate cultural discourses, but their meanings are so contested that they do not provide the same sense of having common values that academia assumes it has, and hence they do not provide the foundations for commitment to a larger community. The larger community values of academia and the language in which they are communicated are viewed in the Foucaultian argument as elements of a hegemonic discourse that places minorities and others at the margins of the institution and directly benefits those who created and sustain the discourse of scholarship and community. The knowledge/power nexus cuts in a different direction that also affects higher education. As Sarup points out, for Foucault "knowledge ceases to be liberation and becomes a mode of surveillance, regulation, discipline" [90, p. 73]. This view of knowledge as surveillance and discipline is in contradistinction to the modernist view that knowledge is emancipating and liberating. And it flies totally in the face of what colleges and universities are traditionally about in a modernist world, for they are the master institutions that preach freedom, liberation, and emancipation through knowledge.

Postmodernism as a Historical Period

The concepts embedded in the notion of postmodernism as a perspective feed into and provide a basis for looking at postmodernism as a new historical era. Viewing postmodernism as a new historical phase is a means for approaching a number of important questions that higher education is involved in and must deal with. To see our postmodern condition through the lens of a new era is to focus on the rapid and unfamiliar changes that are taking place in the world. Looking at postmodernism as a new era dovetails with the intense interest we have in societal change generated by the rapid approach of a new century. Postmodernism as a new era concentrates our attention on the impact of the information age, consumer society, commodification, performativity, multinational corporations, and similacra. Perhaps most disconcerting, this new age is characterized by increasingly shattered cultural orders and growing levels of disorganization in such significant institutions as the state, society, and the economy.

Lyotard

Although Lyotard sees postmodernism as a condition or mood, not an epoch [67, p. xiii], he can be viewed as a transitional figure because his analysis takes on characteristics of a historical period. Lyotard picks up the assault upon modernism, particularly in terms of a denigration of rationalism, but concentrates on what he calls "metanarratives"' those large universals that undergird our orientations toward the modern world, the grand stories that provide the foundation for modern life. Metanarratives are the foundational stories that legitimate discourses and are criticized by postmodernists as locking society in a prison of restrictive, totalizing systems of thought. In Stephen K. White's description, metanarratives, "focusing on God, nature, progress, and emancipation, are the anchors of modern life" [99, p. 5]. For Lyotard the postmodern is defined "as incredulity toward metanarratives" [67, p. xxiv]. The erosion of belief in metanarratives fits with the Derridian and Foucaultian notions that language is not a path to truth or a means for describing reality, but simply a series of discourses socially created in varying contexts, none of which have superior truth claims. The disbelief in metanarratives again foregrounds a questioning of hierarchies, including those of higher education.

The questioning of metanarratives is important for higher education, because metanarratives are the foundation of modern university and college life, especially as they undergird the scientific-technological aspects of higher education, but also higher education's assumptions about progress, knowledge, and socialization. Unlike Derrida and Foucault, who avoid the term postmodern in describing their works, Lyotard writes specifically about postmodernism, and his most influential book is called *The Postmodern Condition: A Report on Knowledge* [67].

Lyotard is interested in the changing circumstances of contemporary science and technology in what he sees as a postmodern society. This concern allows him to look at a number of questions about society, many of which are related to university and college organization and circumstances. He specifically discusses the changing university and the future status of the professor. Lyotard predicts a dim future for higher education as it is now constituted. His notion that performativity is the only viable criterion in a postmodern world means that higher education's sole reason for existence is its ability to contribute directly to the performativity of the economic system. For Lyotard, the task of universities and colleges is to "create skills, and no longer ideals. . . . The transmission of knowledge is no longer designed to train an elite capable of guiding the nation towards its emancipation, but to supply the players capable of acceptably fulfilling their roles at the pragmatic posts required by its institutions" [67, p. 48].

Teaching by professors is still necessary, but it is reduced to instructing students in the use of the terminals [67, p. 50]. If you do not have legitimate grand narratives, you do not need professors to teach them, but you can rely upon machines to teach students what they need to know in a performatively driven society. Lyotard is quite explicit about the death of the professorship. In the cases of both the production and transmission of knowledge, he asserts that "the process of delegitimation and the predominance of the performance criteria are sounding the knell of the Professor" [67, p. 53].

Like Foucault, Lyotard is concerned with questions of power and language. Lyotard has an interest in legitimacy and how it is created. He sees discourses as language games in which players' speech is viewed as "moves" directed at legitimating their language game and proving its superiority over other language games. As Keane describes Lyotard's perspective, "players within language games are always embedded in relations of power—power here understood as the capacity of actors wilfully to block or to effect changes in speech activities of others within the already existing framework of a language game which itself always prestructures the speech activities of individuals and groups" [62, p. 86].

The discourse of science and higher education. Modernism is associated with science and the scientific mode of thinking and doing, and science is tightly connected to higher education. For one hundred fifty years, higher education has promoted the concept that science and its forms, science research, scientific methods, and the progress that results from science, are the principal guarantors of the legitimacy of higher education. The belief in science and its assumptions and methods has provided the basis for creating and justifying the prestige hierarchies among and within colleges and universities and the reward structures among academics. Much of higher education's argument for autonomy is premised on scientific values relating to creativity, objectivity, and neutrality. The social sciences strive for legitimacy through claiming that what they do is scientifically grounded. Even where science and the scientific method are not dominant, as in the humanities, there are constant debates concerning whether the humanist disciplines ought to be more scientific, and if they decide that they are not, they are still consumed by notions of discovery, of objectivity, and of cumulative knowledge, notions that are derived from perceptions of how science proceeds in its work. Higher education as it is currently organized, constituted, and structured is committed to a search for truth, is dependent for its legitimacy on a belief in the scientific method and science as a way of obtaining this goal. Such a search has the assumption that as the search becomes more sophisticated and knowledge information accumulates, progress will result. Problems will be solved. Life will become better. Science has operated as an independent sphere with its own rules, much of its own structure, and though not unaffected by the market, government, and the institutions in which it has been housed, it has, nevertheless, been viewed as clearly differentiated from them. It has had a superior position in the academy, has lived by its own standards of excellence and good work, and has been able to impose its perspectives on large areas within the academy.

In the postmodern world this position is jeopardized. Lyotard, who writes extensively on science and technology in *The Postmodern Condition*, denigrates this view of science on two grounds. First, science is just one more metanarrative and has no more legitimacy than any other metanarratives. Second, science in the postmodern world becomes judged by efficiency and effectiveness and turns into technology. Postmodernism thus makes science and the scientific method problematic, less a basis for legitimacy or for determining good work. Science is viewed, not as a value-free, disassociated form of knowledge, above and outside of social and political values, but as a discourse like any other discourse, a political terrain where power struggles take place for the control of meaning. If science is a discourse equal to any other discourse, then there is no meritocratic basis for privileging science over creationism, astrology, or any number of noxious theories about race and gender. It means there is no rational argument for keeping any discourse from finding a place in the curricula of colleges and universities. What is left is a series of power positions and contested viewpoints vying for a place in academe with no real set of standards by which to judge their relative merits and no rules to follow that allow anyone to say yes or no to questions of inclusion and exclusion in the curriculum. This is the extreme consequence of relativism that is involved in extreme readings of the postmodern critique.

Performativity. In the postmodern world described by Lyotard, performativity is viewed as the most powerful criterion for judging worth, taking the place of agreed upon, rational, modernist criteria for merit. Crook, Pakulski, and Waters describe performativity as "the capacity to deliver outputs at the lowest cost, replaces truth as the yardstick of knowledge" [24, p. 31]. That is, efficiency and effectiveness become the exclusive criteria for judging knowledge and its worth in the college and university. Knowledge becomes "technically useful knowledge." The criterion of technically useful knowledge is its efficiency and its translatability into information (computer) knowledge. Therefore, the questions, "'Is it true?', 'Is it just?', 'Is it morally important?' become reduced to 'Is it efficient?', 'Is it marketable?', 'Is it sellable?', 'Is it translatable into information quantities?'" [62, p. 108].

Baudrillard

Baudrillard also identifies himself as a postmodern thinker. His significance lies in what he has to say about the consumerism, fashion, and the media/information society. His ideas about simulation, implosion of boundaries, hyperreality, and simulacra destabilize our sense of the boundaries within institutions of higher education and between them and the external world [6].

His political stance is similar to that of Derrida, Foucault, and Lyotard. That is, he is interested in micropolitics, politics at the margin, with emphasis upon differences. In Baudrillard's case, it is a micropolitics that emphasizes lifestyle and communication changes that would free individuals from a repressive modernist society. For Baudrillard, the postmodern society is a world in which the images or simulations, which are an intrinsic aspect of computerization, media, and information processing generally, replace modern production as the basis for organizing our lives [13, p. 118].

Perhaps the most significant of his concepts is that of implosion. This involves a process that leads to boundary collapses in a wide variety of circumstances. Implosion simply means that the boundary between a simulation and reality is erased, that is, implodes, and the basis for determining the real is gone. A telling example of postmodern implosion is the collapse of the boundary between the political and the image, in which the image of the politician in our society replaces the reality of the political. One of his most startling concepts is "hyperreality," a post modernist state in which models become the basis for determining the real, thereby replacing the real. According to Linda Hutcheon, Baudrillard "has argued that mass media has neutralized reality for us and it has done so in stages: first reflecting, then masking reality, and then masking the absence of reality, and finally, bearing no relation to reality at all. This is a simulacrum, the final destruction of meaning" [57, p. 223].

Higher education implosions in the postmodern era. If we accept Baudrillard's concept of implosion, we see in education that the collapsing of boundaries may be drastically changing the organization, purposes, and activities of higher education. As the metanarratives of progress, rationality, and science are undermined and deprivileged, the boundaries and hierarchies they sustain are weakened and move toward collapse. Thus, academic disciplines based on these metanarratives find their borders dissolving and the bases for their hierarchical structures attenuated. Also threatened are those boundaries that define the difference between the inside and outside of organizations, institutions, groups, and individuals. In the postmodern era, there is danger of the collapse of the distinction between knowledge inside the academy and outside of it, with the result that certain kinds of knowledge that used to be the monopoly of the academy are now shared with institutions outside of the academy. As Geyer writes, "Students no longer get their knowledge about the world from the universities, which are losing their 'paternal authority'. . . . TV entertainment, news and documentary spectacles, radio talk shows, and for that matter, the religious revival and the instruction that comes with it have developed a power commensurate with university education. They are our competition, replacing rapidly the remnants of civic and transcivic education that have survived the past decade" [42, p. 511].

With the collapse of boundaries between the inside and outside of the academy, there is pressure for the inclusion of new subjects waiting to be taught, brought in by groups who believe they should be a part of the curriculum without the impediment of the usual modernist criteria as a restraint. This means that the boundaries between modern differentiating curricula based on rationality, the discipline's standards, and the model that science offers are breaking down. These boundaries have always been contested and in flux. But now, curricular boundaries are contested by religious, racial, ethnic, gender, and new cultural perspectives that seek to establish their own potentially incommensurable criteria for inclusion in higher education curricula. The idea of the canon is a concept from literary studies concerning what the boundaries of a discipline should be. As the canons are contested, the boundaries of various disciplinary discourses become more vulnerable to disintegration. However, this collapsing, like other aspects of the postmodern changes, is occurring slowly and sporadically. For example, in the teaching of literature, where some of the most divisive and rancorous arguments over the canon have been occurring, the 1990 MLA biennial survey of English departments indicates that some changes have taken place, such as the introduction of feminist perspectives and heightened interest in the relationship of race, class, and gender to literature generation and interpretation. The authors go on to say, "These innovations, however, have not displaced traditional classroom goals or approaches to literary study" [39, p. 42].

Implosion of cultures and other boundary collapses. An implosion often noted in postmodern discussion is the collapse of the distinction between high culture and popular culture. What is its significance for higher education? The postmodernist collapse of boundaries entails a mixing together of high and low culture. Intellectuals, including academic intellectuals, enter the world of popular culture and interpret it. As intellectuals become associated with popular culture and identified with it, they begin to lose their hierarchical station as experts [95, p. 4].

Another example of the collapse of the boundary between the college or university and its city environment is that campuses are now viewed as the scenes of crimes that are simply a part of the same density and pattern of crime that any urban center generates. The campus is rapidly losing its identity as an enclave. None of the racial, poverty, health, and environmental problems of the city or the surroundings of the campus can be avoided by institutions of higher education. The boundaries between city and campus continue to weaken.

Postmodernism, Economic Life, and Higher Education

Some of the most striking postmodern changes are associated with economic life viewed in terms of performativity, and these changes profoundly affect the place of higher education in the society. The changes affect what kind of education may be offered by higher education, the methods of delivery, the autonomy of the colleges and universities, and the competitive position of institutions of higher education. The postmodern society is a postindustrial society. The changes taking place are striking. The workforce is moving out of industrial production to service jobs. A primary change for United States citizens is from the centrality of work to the centrality of consumption. We now emphasize the production of information over the manufacturing of goods. Corporations are less constrained by national and state boundaries and are entering a world of multinational manufacturing and trade, relying on telecommunications networks and using foreign local work forces for producing goods and services. Large, industrial conglomerates are giving way to small, highly specialized businesses confined to single sites and run by a relatively small cadre of highly entrepreneurial owners.

Service jobs. When postmodernism is viewed as a new historical era, it illuminates the potentiality for higher education to play a much different and potentially attenuated role in the postmodern society of the future. The changes put considerable strain on the conventional purposes and activities of institutions of higher education. However, institutions of higher education respond by introducing conventional changes in curriculum, under the increasingly questionable assumption that the changes will allow institutions of higher education to continue to educate middle-class managers and professionals in hierarchically arranged, large scale, now global bureaucracies. Thus the optimistic assumption is that educating for service jobs means preparing people for professional careers, and that the information society requires large numbers of professionals at many levels to operate it. In fact, service jobs may turn out to be low-paying, noncareer-producing positions that require vocational and technical education. Although the impact of the information society is very much in a muddle at this point, there may be only a small number of opportunities for autonomous, highly skilled information professionals, what Jencks has called a "cognitariat" [60].

Multinational corporations. There is an assumption that multinational, globally oriented corporations will need many persons fluent in foreign languages, able to understand diverse cultures, willing to move easily to foreign sites which will act as way stations in the corporate ladder. Many higher education institutions are initiating programs of global studies with this scenario in mind.

However, it has become more apparent with time, that multinational corporations find local work forces to have great advantages over imported American experts. Local workers are knowing about the local culture and language, will often work for lower wages and salaries, and have less desire to globe trot in order to move up the corporate ladder.

The aggressive activities of multinational corporations, the great fluidity of capital, and the increasing cross-national mobility of labor mean that multinational corporations with their Eurocentric cultures must incorporate great chunks of the cultural assumptions and, indeed, of the cultural orientations of the Third world. The global system itself may be drastically changing the culture of business. In doing so, Eurocentric culture becomes diffused and the Eurocentric cultures of multinational corporations may be watered down.

Dirlik has a fascinating interpretation of the complex interplay of incentives, actions, and consequences that arise from what are usually perceived to be the contradictory perspectives on the multiculturalism of the academy and business. "Focusing on liberal arts institutions, some conservative intellectuals overlook how much headway multiculturalism has made with business school administrators and the managers of transnational corporations. . . . While in an earlier day it might have been Marxist and feminist radicals, with the aid of a few ethnics, who spearheaded multiculturalism, by now the initiative has passed into the hands of 'enlightened' administrators and trustees who are quite aware of the 'manpower needs' of the new economic situation. . . . Among the foremost and earliest of United States advocates of transnationalism and multiculturalism is the *Harvard Business Review*" [32, 354–55].

Consumer culture. Perhaps most foreign of all, and potentially most disruptive to the higher education curricula, is the notion that the United States is now a consumer culture. The conventional interpretation of this in higher education is that a consumer culture education prepares persons to supply consumer goods and services to a population that is awash in conspicuous displays of television and other electronic devices, a population that seeks an ever greater supply and variety of consumer goods. But the postmodern interpretation is that consumer activity is now "the cognitive and moral focus of life, the integrative bond of the society, and the focus of systemic management" [93, p. 63]. In Baudrillard's perception of postmodern society, commodities through advertising in the media, become "codes, shared systems of meaning . . . without material foundation" [24, p. 132].

Such an orientation, if it is an accurate description, would call for higher education to prepare students, not simply to be producers and sellers of consumer goods, but to be intellectually and philosophically skillful and knowing consumers. But higher education has such formidable competition for attention from the mass media that it is almost unthinkable that it would be viewed as the legitimate institution which teaches consumerism. Learning what a consumer society should or wants to consume comes not from the teachings of professors in a university or college, but from television, the information highway, or another mass media alternative.

Much of what students want to consume that higher education has supplied in the past is either in the process of erosion, for example, high culture, or can be supplied by other sources (science education, education for the professions). To say that students are extremely consumption-oriented at this time is to say that they have choices, can do comparative shopping, and can find much of what they want outside the walls of the traditional colleges or university. Institutions of higher education, over much of our history, have defined to a large extent the nature and shape of an education and have confidently and accurately assumed that the legitimacy that education conferred was not only a societal but a private good. Students as consumers are rapidly reaching a point where they are asking for a different education, and they are willing to look for this education in a variety of locations. As Robert Zemsky writes, "Students today want technical knowledge, useful knowledge, labor related knowledge in convenient, digestible packages" [103, p. 17].

At present, institutions of higher education are still able to offer legitimacy and credentials that promise to give graduates a jump start on middle-class careers. But the changes in the economy and culture make this promise highly problematic for the future. A consumer culture calls into question the assumption that the academy has a monopoly of knowledge. This delegitimates belief in professors as experts, particularly as ultimate authorities on the subjects they teach.

The Loss of State Authority in the Postmodern Era

The changes taking place that increase the power and reach of multinational organizations and the reality of a truly global world mean a potential reduction of the strength and legitimacy of the state, historically the chief financial supplier for higher education. It also means the continuation and expansion of research, but for competitive, consumer, and international interests.

In this postmodern era, institutions rely increasingly on their own efforts to acquire funding in the face of weakened state and federal agencies to grant needed resources. There is more dependence on multinational organizations for funding. A consequence is that research is judged on its ability to aid in the competitive position of the multinational organizations. A totally utilitarian view of research is a logical consequence. Science as a totally commodified enterprise becomes simply technology.

The loss of authority of governments is paradoxical. Centralization, which includes increased regulatory demands by government upon institutions and more means of control, is occurring simultaneously with loss of control by government. Persons within institutions of higher education feel increasingly burdened by the addition of more rules and stringent regulations from the state. This seems to demonstrate that the state is becoming stronger as the institutions of higher education become weaker and lose more of their autonomy. Paradoxically, the increase in regulations can be seen as a loss of authority by the state. The state, through government, has great difficulty in maintaining a taxing capacity that will allow it to do its business. Governments find it harder to make necessary but unpopular decisions. Governments are hampered by the explosion of interest groups with incompatible interests, whose collective weight easily vetoes government decisions. The state finds it more difficult to permit institutions of higher education the autonomy they need to fulfill their purposes.

Changes related to postmodernism must be viewed in a long time frame, such as the time it has taken tradition to give way to modernism. We can expect to see changes occur in fits and starts, discontinuously, with some aspects of the world in accelerated change, and some changing slowly, while in some areas of life there is no change at all. Thus, as we see that both the traditional and the modern are very much alive in today's society, we also become increasingly aware of postmodernism in our world.

What is the impact of the ideas of our four representative authors on the whole field of higher education? How can higher education retain three modern metanarratives, the ideas of merit, community, and autonomy, all three of which are extremely questionable in the poststructuralist, postmodern modes of thought? These essentialist characteristics, community, merit, and autonomy, are sorely tested by the deconstructive and postmodern descriptions of boundary collapse, the celebration of differences, the close connection of power to knowledge, the strength of micropolitics that take the form of identity politics, the rising disbelief in metanarratives, and the destruction of reality that is a part of the similacrum.

Solutions

The postmodern world is a place of contradictions. It is rife with uncertainty, ambiguity, and contradiction. In reaction to the devastating critique of modernism, a number of voices, positive and negative, have been raised that tell us how we might react to the postmodern assault and/or the postmodern world. Some see in postmodernism a return to a kind of right-wing barbarism that seeks to undo all of the progress associated with the Enlightenment. Others see postmodernism as a basis for the organization of a new, freer, more open society, capable of allowing the individual to create his/her own life in ways that have not been conceived of previously, picking and choosing parts of lifestyles that appear everywhere.

Presented next are some voices from among the many who have taken seriously and commented on the consequences of the postmodern sensibility. It is not meant to be exhaustive but to give some perspectives on postmodernism and what its meaning might be for our society.

The Social Conservative Position

This response to a postmodern society is to pull back to an ideal time, a period when the country's values were homogeneous, where hierarchy reigned, distinctions between high and low culture were ironclad and backed by money, government, tradition, and a belief in experts. The politics of nostalgia can be used to promote elements of both a premodern tradition and a modern sensibility. The argument is that we should return to a time that seems in retrospect enchanted, more stable, more predictable, and safer. One modernist source of such enchantment is the romance of technology when viewed optimistically. Attempts to capture the enchantment of a traditional world often emanate from religious fundamentalism and political conservatism.

There is also in this social conservatism, a good deal of talk about how a particular institution previously had been characterized by community, but is now rife with fractiousness and depersonalization. But, as most marginalized persons and groups are aware, such a community was hegemonically white, male, Western European, and exclusive. Such communities marginalized minorities and women in ways that are unacceptable in a postmodern world.

Hardcore Postmodernism

At the other extreme is what Rosenau calls "skeptical postmodernism" [86, p. 15]. Its adherents use postmodernism to attack and delegitimate modernism, but essentially offer no real way to organize a society or a university. They see a collection of autonomous discourse groups operating in a university, responding entirely to their own vocabularies and sets of values, which are assumed not to be commensurable with other discourses, groups of discourses without any hierarchical principles and eschewing the values of merit and the larger college or university community. It is not clear how this apparently anarchic organization would work, because it seems clear that some discourses are going to be more equal than others, and some are going to have more power, more resources, richer vocabularies, and definitions of merit that work better than others. The result will again be hierarchy, but without the values of merit, neutrality, or objectivity. It will be based strictly on power.

Although power seems to be at the center of much of the discussion about postmodernism, in its most extreme form, postmodernism so assaults as foundational any standards for justifying the assertion of power that actual political intervention to change things has only weak reasons to motivate action by anyone. This is one of the reasons why post-post modernists, new historicists, and students of cultural studies find themselves in such an ambiguous relationship to postmodernism. They want to act, to change the modernist world, and in order to do so they need strong reasons to do so, foundational reasons.

The Project of Unfulfilled Modernism

Habermas, the defender of modernism, agrees with much of the critique by postmodernists, but sees postmodernism as a retrogressive conservative force pushing modernism toward a premodern unenlightened stage. In contrast, he seeks to develop a renewed modernism, a rationality based on communication; open, free, and engaged in by all, as a means for preserving and improving democracy, freedom, equality, and progress. Habermas has strongly asserted that "we can never escape the demand to warrant our validity claims, to defend them by the best possible arguments and reasons which are available to us. This is the 'truth' in the Enlightenment tradition that needs to be preserved and defended" [12, p. 26].

Yet Habermas has been strongly criticized for depending too much upon the possibility of building institutions that could and would sustain what sounds like perfect communication. So much dependence upon the communication process seems extremely precarious in a postmodern moment, when we are discovering the extent to which meanings shift and slide and disappear across cultures and time contexts.

Feminist Perspectives on Postmodernism

Feminists have conflicting views on postmodernism. For those who have viewed themselves as marginal and excluded because of gender, postmodern criticism is helpful. Postmodernism is used to attack many of the major philosophical perspectives of modernism, such as essentialism, foundationalism, and the assumption of universals, which have been used to create hierarchies that place women in positions inferior to men and then legitimate that subordination. Best and Kellner assert that modernist discourses since the time of Plato and Aristotle have generated "antithetical sets of characteristics that position men as superior and women as inferior. This scheme includes dichotomies between rational/emotional, assertive/passive, strong/weak, or public/private" [13, p. 207]. Feminists are sympathetic to attacks on modernist academic assumptions about neutrality and objectivity, for these assumptions are associated with the maintenance of the binary oppositions that subordinate women. Feminists find that the postmodern notions of difference, plurality—including plural selves, transience, marginality, otherness, and disjointedness—are compatible with many feminist perspectives [16, p. 108; 39, pp. 34–35]. However, feminists are concerned that the elimination of essentialist assumptions, that is, metanarratives, weakens the possibility of doing theory and of having a strong philosophical basis for political change and change in gender relations [16, pp. 107–8].

Feminists are bothered by postmodernism's potential for a relativist reading of feminist agendas and goals that severely attenuates the basis for political and social action to change the male-dominated status quo in and out of universities. As Best and Kellner point out, "Modern categories such as human rights, equality, and democratic freedoms and power are used by feminists to criticize and fight against gender domination, and categories of the Enlightenment have been effectively mobilized by women in political struggles and consciousness-raising groups; indeed, the very discourse of emancipation is a modern discourse" [13, p. 208]. Also, empiricist and standpoint theories that maintain as legitimate the modernist scientific and academic standards are negated by postmodernist perspectives.

Marxist Responses to Postmodernism

Many Marxists are critical of postmodern thought [17], but others see postmodernism as a new, higher stage of capitalism [61]. Frederick Jameson, in particular, has written extensively about postmodernism, which he sees as a historical period in which culture has penetrated all forms of social life, including economics. The postmodern era is characterized for Jameson by a global capitalism far more extensive than ever before, with considerable cultural fragmentation and differences in how a person experiences time and space [61]. His perspective takes into consideration the impact of media and information and their relationship to an almost total commodification of social and political life.

Jameson's critics see him as one who tries to introduce postmodernist concepts into a traditional foundational Marxist emphasis upon class and economic determinism. Because the concept of a Marxist metanarrative would seem to be incompatible with the anti-metanarrative orientation of postmodernism, he is accused of inconsistency in his position [13, pp. 187–88]. As Cohen writes, "The fundamental charge is that Jameson cannot have it both ways" [21, p. 339]. Nevertheless, he has greatly reinvigorated the Marxist position.

The Post-Marxist Reaction

As Post-Marxists, Ernesto Laclau and Chantel Mouffe embrace postmodernism but are interested in political action as well [65]. They attempt to find a path to change the order of things in the university and in society. This means that they accept the idea of discourse theory and assert that it implies "the commitment to show the world for what it is: an entirely social construction of human beings which is not grounded on any metaphysical 'necessity' external to it—neither God, nor 'essential forms' nor the 'necessary laws of history'" [65, p. 198].

These theorists differ from Marxists in their views on class struggle. As post-Marxists they are no longer convinced that the analysis of classes is relevant in the struggle against capitalism. They emphasize, instead, the need for a variety of forms of resistance.

Cultural Studies

Cultural studies is one of several movements—this one highly interdisciplinary—that attempt to reflect the diversity, the plurality, the diffuseness, and the blurring of boundaries of academic disciplines and between disciplines and the external world. Its orientation is to what has been called the "new politics of difference—racial, sexual, cultural, transnational" [69, p. 393]. It overlaps with postcolonial studies and uses concepts and vocabulary from postmodernism and poststructuralism. It seems to be in a fluid state by choice, and has not gelled into a discipline with its own methodology. It draws from anthropology and tends to be humanistic in its orientation. There is a strong predilection to think in terms of political action in relation to marginal groups [49].

New Historicism

In the aftermath of the powerful impact of poststructuralism and postmodernism upon English departments in the nineteen-seventies, literary studies in the United States began to focus on the historical, political, and cultural contexts in which literary texts are written and read [72, p. 392]. The major figure leading this movement was Stephan Greenblatt, who coined the term "new historicism" to describe this form of literary criticism [9, p. 32]. Retaining many of the concepts from postmodernism, such as Foucault's ideas about power, disbelief in the metanarratives related to objectivity or neutrality, new historicist scholars are particularly concerned about the boundaries that result from the continual struggle for control over meaning in literary studies. New historicists penetrate the borders that separate literary studies from history, anthropology, art, economics, science, cultural studies, and other disciplines. "The boundaries to be reckoned with in literary studies range from national, linguistic, historical, generational, and geographical to racial, ethnic, social, sexual, political, ethical, and religious" [47, p. 4].

New historicists are accused by some feminists of speaking in a "neutral, authoritative, putatively interest-free voice" (10, p. 93]. Conservative critics deplore the new historicist's politicization of literary studies and are hostile to the boundary collapse that seems to eliminate "the distinction between good art, bad art, and non-art" [9, p. 32].

Postcolonialism

The postcolonial perspective has developed from the efforts of third world intellectuals. They want to dismantle Eurocentrism, which has in the past dominated not only the territories of the third world, but also their histories, their perceptions of self, and their political lives. Their aim is to "abolish all distinctions between center and periphery as well as other 'binarisms' that are allegedly a legacy of colonial(ist) ways of thinking and to reveal societies in their complex heterogeneity and contingency" [32, p. 329].

Postcolonialism is related to postmodernism in that metanarratives are repudiated, which means that the premises and concepts of European enlightenment, and therefore of modernism, are deeply criticized. Postcolonialists have a strong affinity for local politics, local histories, and fragmentation of the national into the local. A strong criticism of the postcolonial approach is that "within the institutional site of the First World academy, fragmentation of earlier metanarratives appears benign (except to hidebound conservatives) for its promise of more democratic, multicultural, and cosmopolitan epistemologies. In the world outside the academy, however, it shows in murderous ethnic conflict, continued inequalities among societies, classes, and genders, and absence of oppositional possibilities that, always lacking in coherence, are rendered even more impotent than earlier by the fetishization of difference, fragmentation, and so on" [32, p. 347].

Postmodernism and Chaos Theory

An optimistic perspective on postmodernism links it with chaos theory. Both postmodern and chaos theory give center stage to ideas about disorder, indeterminacy, undecidability, and fragmentation in their emphasis upon complexity. But in its two most frequently argued versions, that is, order hidden in chaos and order rising out of chaotic systems [54, p. 12], chaos theory gives a structure and hope for controlling complexity that is not found in several of the reactions to postmodernism discussed above—for example, hardcore postmodernism, social conservatism, and new historicism.

In an optimistic reading of postmodernism, the affinity with chaos theory is striking. What could be more optimistic for the postmodern emphasis upon the marginal and the local than the concept of nonlinearity, in which small causes result in large consequences (the butterfly effect—that is, the butterfly flapping its wings in China through a long, complex chain of causes and effects results in a hurricane in Guatemala). It would seem to give hope to a number of politically conscious groups whose focus is the micropolitical stage, but who seek large changes in the society, such as postcolonialists, those interested in cultural studies, and post-Marxists. At the same time, however, the idea of the butterfly effect from chaos theory should lead to pessimism for those with specific political agendas, because it emphasizes that those who initiate local actions will have no power to predict or control the consequences that follow on the macrolevel.

But the most important convergence, or relationship, between chaos theory and postmodernism lies in the area where one branch of chaos theory emphasizes the possibility of the creation of order from disorder. This concept when transferred to postmodernist conceptions of society, or of narratives and texts, provides strong reason for using deconstruction to attack seemingly settled metanarratives, to generate discontinuities, and to point to the void that lies beneath language. Chaos theory seems to promise that out of the nothingness that results from deconstructing the language, will arise a new, albeit tenuous, and constantly shifting order that will provide space for new voices and new perspectives to be heard and granted legitimacy.

Border Crossing and Border Pedagogy

Henry A. Giroux combines postmodernism, feminism, postcolonialism, and culture studies to promote a social, cultural, political, educational agenda that invites teachers, students, and cultural workers to critique, then challenge and oppose the institutions, the knowledge claims of disciplines, and the social relationships that now dominate our society. This process he calls "border crossing." The means for helping and effecting this crossing is "border pedagogy," and the purpose of border crossing is to create "borderlands" or "alternative public spaces" [44, p. 22], where the partial, shifting nature of negotiated and constructed realities allows students, among others, "to rewrite their own histories, identities, and learning possibilities" [44, p. 30]. These constructed borderlands are realms where democratic political and ethical revolutionary battles are to be waged, and the values of this crusade are to be firmly grounded in what appear to be modernist readings of such values as freedom, equality, liberty, and justice [44, p. 32].

Postmodern language is invoked when the author discusses how educators might understand marginality, the life world of the Other, and the positive qualities of difference and radical pluralism. While border pedagogy speaks of revolutionary change in society, it takes a long and benign road to that end by focusing first on the transformation of individuals; only later, when radical changes in individuals have occurred, will quick changes in society and its institutions happen.

The Liberal, Pragmatist Approach

Liberal thinking continues to dominate higher education today, and liberalism is quintessentially modernist in its orientation and in its effects. It is clear that this approach does not dismantle the ideas of merit, democracy, progress, science, and rationality, but expands and modifies them so that new ideas and orientations will be accommodated. The strategy in current higher education thinking, in an era of greatly increasing multicultural consciousness, is to redouble efforts to bring marginal persons and ideologies into an expanded modernist college and university. Mainstream educators assume that given educational opportunities and access, ethnic, minority, and religious groups and individuals will be socialized into liberal modernist culture. Administrators and faculty hope that this strategy will change the structure and life of the college and university, but not the metanarratives.

This solution is attractive in that it preserves merit, autonomy, and community, but it does require considerable modification to have credibility with the marginal and excluded groups to whom it is directed. Richard Rorty's distinction between public and private life provides a possible justification for the use of a liberal, pragmatic approach that is postmodern in orientation, strong, but flexible, yet retains room for merit, community, and autonomy. In the Rorty perspective, such modernist Enlightenment concepts should be fostered, not on the basis of any objective or foundational superiority, but because they are historically, traditionally, and habitually shared by enough people in academe to make it worthwhile to preserve them, albeit not in as rigid a basis as before. Rorty takes his justification from Jefferson's view of politics and religion: "Jefferson maintained that religion is essentially 'irrelevant to social order but relevant to, and possibly essential to individual perfection.' The gist of this insight, formulated as the 'Jefferson compromise,' is that any ideas used to shape public policy, which are bound to some larger commitments—whether religious, philosophical, or ideological—must be capable of defense in terms of views and traditions widely shared by a given polity. If such ideas cannot be defended on these grounds, then they must be rebuffed and the individual must sacrifice her conscience on the 'altar of public expediency.' Politics is about common-sensical argument that appeals to the values and traditions shared by a given 'public' and commitment which falls outside this grouping, or cannot be translated to appeal to citizens must be relegated to the private realm. . . . This direction reflects his deep misgivings about philosophy as well as his sense that people could agree about a wide range of problems and share common practices while maintaining vastly different cultural and ethnic backgrounds as well as religious and philosophical convictions" [100, p. 553].

However, the feminist scholar Nancy Frazer is strongly critical of Rorty's separation of the public and private spheres. Feminists argue that the private is the public. From this perspective, practical politics have always emanated from what modernists have thought of as nonpolitical, that is, "the domestic and the personal" [100, p. 555]. Thus, if the private and the public are separated, the result is the retention of the modernist status quo with its built-in superior/inferior oppositions.

Nevertheless, Rorty does address this problem through his version of pragmatism and irony. As Wicks points out, the ironist "acts to negotiate the boundaries of the private and the public" [100, p. 554]. Ironists are especially sensitive to and capable of showing us where we do not understand our biases. "We may expand the logical space of reasons to include, and socially embrace, alternative understanding of practices that do not oppress. It is this capacity for empathetic understanding, vocabulary switching, and metaphor construction which makes the role of the ironist . . . so vital to oppressed groups" [100, p. 557].

This perspective does two things for the maintenance of the college and university and their values of merit, community, and autonomy. It expands the space for having multiple definitions for the three terms, while perhaps indicating limits to what those definitions might contain. At the same time, as with Jefferson's desire to keep religion out of politics, we can justify severely limiting the inclusion as truth in the curriculum, assumptions inherent in fundamentalist religions, for example, or contained in extreme ideological positions.

But for those who have been heavily influenced by the postmodern critique, the foundational premises of liberalism do not have the legitimacy they used to have. This is why Rorty is significant. He believes in the postmodern critique but asks of us that we embrace a liberal stance, knowing full well that it does not provide the foundations that modern notions of liberalism assume but only that its practical consequences are better than other ideologies. But others, particularly Richard Bernstein, add an especially significant caveat: the necessity for dialogue. In fact, Rorty, Bernstein, Derrida, Habermas, all place a heavy burden on listening and dialogue.

The Legacy of Postmodern Thought for Higher Education

An important consequence of postmodern thought is that almost no responsible scholar today is unaffected by the arguments that displace essentialism, or metanarratives. Postmodernism makes us aware of the destabilization and uncertainty that we confront not only in society, but in higher education. We are in a crisis in which the standard categories of modernism fail to account for—that is, to explain and make predictable—the conditions we face in the world today. The specter of relativism hangs over all our institutions. Higher education is not an exception. It cannot act as though it spoke truths; it can argue only that what it does is useful, but not that it is true.

The modernist orientation is to resolve problems; the postmodern perspective not only points to the contradictions in discourses, but makes a virtue of preserving that essential tension. It may be that opposing perspectives need to be kept alive and in tension with the dominant model. This would mean that institutions of higher education must be able to sustain and cope permanently with considerable unresolved conflict and contradiction.

If there is a transformation in higher education, what should it be? Is there a need for a set of values that transcend group values, for a vocabulary that will speak to all groups within the academy? Or should there be a wide open conglomeration of presumably incommensurate values, ethics, standards? Some poststructuralist thought seems to indicate that we already have this incommensurability among discourses. The destruction of the belief in eternal verities and the attenuation of the drive to search for truth mean that higher education's task may be to pay much more attention to values, what they mean, where they come from, what their function is, and how to forge new values that fit the higher education world and its mission.

Because the borders of colleges and universities are becoming more permeable in the postmodern world and the great sustainers of the independence of higher education, the state and governments, are becoming weaker, institutions need to find ways of maintaining autonomy in the face of multinational corporate resources and power, the debilitating effects of the increased proliferation of active interest groups, and the encroachment of extreme local power.

In the world of simulacra and the power that comes from creating images, the universities' task may be to seek and sustain a kind of authenticity of information and knowledge. In this it needs to create a consistent and useful concept of merit; it cannot rely as heavily upon the strictures of science or the rules of a broken canon. But it needs to sustain the value of merit and find with all the contradictions, the plural voices, the lack of a sense of progress, and the continual tension an interest in and pursuit of means for measuring, judging, and rewarding merit. As the boundary between higher education and the market collapses, some means for organizing and sustaining autonomous sanctuaries, oases, or enclaves in universities should be found that do not simply respond to the drive for performativity and the standards of the market. Institutions of higher education need ways to construct and sustain community, and community at several levels: community on the campus and community in the larger society, a commitment to citizenship.

The emphasis upon the other, the marginal, the outsider, in postmodern thought needs to be kept in the foreground in higher education. Colleges and universities need to find ways of encompassing the other, of taking in marginal people and ideas. However, it should not be done in the usual liberal strategy of simply adding courses on multinationalism, women's studies, and cultural studies. These need to be included in academia more on the basis of their own standards. But the argument here is that this inclusion does not mean that the search for and creation of standards of merit is compromised. An important means for ensuring this is to follow the advice that a number of postmodern writers have offered, namely, to listen very hard and openly. As Cornel West has written, "I hope that we can overcome the virtual de facto segregation in the life of the mind in this country, for we have yet actually to create contexts in which black intellectuals, brown intellectuals, red intellectuals, white intellectuals, feminist intellectuals, genuinely struggle with each other" [98, p. 696].

At the same time, we need to pay attention to Richard Bernstein's caution, "There can be no dialogue, no communication unless beliefs, values, commitments, and even emotions and passions are shared in common. . . . Dialogical communication presupposes moral virtues—a certain 'good will' at least in the willingness to really listen, to seek to understand what is genuinely other, different, alien, and the courage to risk one's more cherished prejudgments. But too frequently this commonality is not really shared, it is violently opposed" [12, p. 51].

Just how difficult the process of authentic listening to "others" and creating and sustaining meaningful dialogue is, may be illustrated by U.S. business as it becomes globalized. We must face the fact that moral boundaries may blur as we face a world in which the center, the Eurocentric center, is in transition, perhaps moving to the periphery, while the marginal is becoming central. Thus, a business overseas may encounter the moral dilemma of responding to the situation in Saudi Arabia, in which "it is illegal to hire female managers for most jobs" [33, p. 11]. The lines of morality become very fuzzy indeed. A kind of in-between moral relativism may result. Thus, "If Thai tolerates the bribery of public officials, then Thai tolerance is no worse than Japanese or German intolerance. . . . If Switzerland fails to find insider trading morally repugnant, then Swiss liberality is no worse than American restrictiveness" [33, p. 11].

Although no other institution in our society is as capable of listening and of dialogue as the colleges and universities, institutions of higher education find themselves confronting similar problems as they seek to relate to other cultures, internationalize the curriculum, and enter also into the globalized world. It is not just a matter of responding with open arms to different dress and celebrations of new holidays, or of taking in new languages and literatures; it is dealing fairly but firmly with customs and values that have been morally repugnant to higher education.

Conclusion

The term postmodern is disappearing from the vocabularies of excluded groups, social scientists, humanist intellectuals, scholars of all kinds. But postmodern terms and concepts remain very much alive and in constant use. Postmodernism is disappearing because of its relativistic connotations and because, by accepting the corpus of the postmodern perspective, a group with a political agenda places its own position in jeopardy. For those drawn to the postmodern critique, who have political, cultural, social, and/or economic agendas, including feminists and ethnic and cultural groups, postmodern concepts are an extremely effective weapon to discredit and delegitimate modernism, the status quo, and colleges and universities as they are now constituted. However, if the metanarratives of modernism and higher education have no philosophical foundation, the metanarratives of marginal and excluded groups do not have essentialist foundations either. This is what engenders the profound ambivalence toward postmodernism of those who are most critical of the current modernist world. By avoiding the term "postmodernism" and by declining to identify oneself as a postmodernist, critics may and do continue to use the terminology of postmodernism, while retaining their own necessary metanarratives to justify their political, cultural agendas.

If we accept the implications of postmodernism and see it as a critique that applies both to modernists and to those critical of modernism, we can reach a point where the postmodern stricture to listen and listen very hard and long to the "other" has strong credibility. If neither side has any foundational credentials, there is space for real and continuing dialogue. The result of such listening and the pursuit of dialogue under such conditions could mean the retention in universities and colleges of the values of merit, community, and autonomy, and their justification in Rorty's terms, on the basis of agreement that these are, in some form, even as the particulars are contested, an integral part of our higher education heritage. For the excluded "others" this kind of dialogue could well provide the basis for changing the meaning and terms of merit, community, and autonomy in ways that are satisfactorily inclusive and representative of the plurality of "others'" cultures and politics. Currently, we are precariously poised between a modern/postmodern incommensurable hostility and the conditions for tough authentic dialogue. In higher education our course is clear. We need to increase and sustain the dialogue, even as we acknowledge that the tension will not, and perhaps should not, be resolved.

Notes

1. One set of notable exceptions published in the *Journal of Higher Education* involved an article by Gary Rhoades which used both Derrida and Foucault [81]. This stimulated a lively and provocative exchange (two critiques and a rebuttal) in a subsequent issue [19, 66, 82].
2. In addition to referring to the words of a speech or piece of writing, texts should be understood as events and relationships. Almost anything can be a text. This means that events and relationships as well as words can be deconstructed to indicate contradictions, tensions, oppositions, hierarchies, hidden meanings, withheld meanings, and multiple interpretations [82, pp. 34–41].
3. "Discourses are about what can be said and thought, but also about who can speak, when and with what authority . . . Meanings . . . arise not from language but from institutional practices, from power relations. Words and concepts change their meaning and their effects as they are deployed within different discourses" (5, p. 2).

References

Adorno, T., and M. Horkheimer. *The Dialectic of Enlightenment*. London: Verso, 1979.

Alexander, J., and S. Seidman (eds.). *Culture and Society: Contemporary Debates*. Cambridge: Cambridge University Press, 1990.

Aronowitz, S., and H. A. Giroux. *Postmodern Education*. Minneapolis: University of Minnesota Press, 1991.

Ashley, D. "Habermas and the Completion of 'The Project of Modernity'." In *Theories of Modernity and Postmodernity*, edited by B. S. Turner, pp. 88–107. Newbury Park, Calif.: Sage, 1990.

Ball, S. J. (ed.). *Foucault and Education*. London: Routledge, 1990.

Baudrillard, J. *Simulations*. New York: Semiotext(e), 1983.

_____. *America*. Trans. C. Turner. London: Verso, 1989.

Bauman, Z. "Is There a Postmodern Sociology?" *Theory, Culture, and Society*, 5 (1988), 217–37.

Begley, A. "The Tempest around Stephen Greenblatt." *New York Times Magazine*, 28 March 1993, p. 32.

Bender, J. "Eighteenth-Century Studies." In *Redrawing the Boundaries*, edited by S. Greenblatt and G. Gunn, pp. 79–99. New York: The Modern Language Association, 1992.

Bernstein, R. J. (ed.). *Habermas and Modernity*. Cambridge, Mass.: MIT Press, 1985.

_____. *The New Constellation*. Cambridge, Mass.: MIT Press, 1992.

Best. S., and D. Kellner. *Postmodern Theory*. New York: The Guilford Press, 1991.

Bloland, H. G. "Higher Education and High Anxiety: Objectivism, Relativism, and Irony." *Journal of Higher Education*, 60 (September/October 1989), 519–43.

Burrell, G. "Modernism, Post Modernism, and Organizational Analysis 2: The Contribution of Michel Foucault." *Organization Studies*, 9 (1988), 221–35.

Calas, M. B., and L. Smircich. "Re-Writing Gender into Organizational Theorizing: Directions from Feminist Perspectives." In *Women in Higher Education: A Feminist Perspective*, edited by J. Glazer, E. M. Bensimon, and B. Townsend, pp. 97–117. Needham Heights, Mass.: Ginn Press, 1993

Callinicos, A. *Against Postmodernism: A Marxist Critique*. Cambridge: Polity Press, 1989.

Cherryholmes, C. H. *Power and Criticism: Poststructural Investigations in Education*. New York: Teachers College, Columbia University, 1988.

Cinnamond, J. "Replicating Rhoades: Deconstructing a Deconstructionist." *Journal of Higher Education*, 62 (November/December 1991), 694–706.

Clegg, S. R. *Modern Organizations: Organization Studies in the Postmodern World*. Newbury Park, Calif.: Sage, 1990.

Cohen, W. "Marxist Criticism." In *Redrawing the Boundaries*, edited by S. Greenblatt and G. Gunn, pp. 320–48. New York: Modern Language Association, 1992.

Connolly, W. E. *Political Theory and Modernity*. New York: Basil Blackwell. 1989.

Cooper, R., and G. Burrell. "Modernism, Postmodernism, and Organizational Analysis: An Introduction." *Organization Studies*, 9 (1988), 91–112.

Crook, S., J. Pakulski, and M. Waters. *Postmodernization*. Newbury Park, Calif.: Sage. 1992.

Curti, L. "What is Real and What is Not: Female Fabulations in Cultural Analysis." In *Cultural Studies*, edited by L. Grossberg, C. Nelson, and P. A. Treichler, pp. 134–53. New York: Routledge, 1992.

Davidson, A. "Archaeology, Genealogy, Ethics." In *Foucault: A Critical Reader*, edited by D. C. Hoy, pp. 221–33. Cambridge, Mass.: Basil Blackwell, 1986.

Denzin, N. K., and Y. S. Lincoln (eds,). *Handbook of Qualitative Research*. Thousand Oaks, Calif.: Sage, 1994.

_____. "Preface." In *Handbook of Qualitative Research*, edited by N. K. Denzin and Y. S. Lincoln, pp. ix–xii. Thousand Oaks, Calif.: Sage, 1994.

Derrida, J. *Of Grammatology*. Baltimore: Johns Hopkins University Press, 1976.

_____. *Positions*. Chicago: University of Chicago Press, 1981.

_____. *Writing and Difference*. Trans. A. Bass. Chicago: University of Chicago Press, 1978,

Dirlik, A. "The Postcolonial Aura: Third World Criticism in the Age of Global Capitalism." *Critical Inquiry*, 20 (1994), 329–56.

Donaldson, T. "Global Business Must Mind Its Morals." *New York Times* 13 February 1994, p. 11.

Doyle, K. "The Reality of a Disappearance: Frederick Jameson and the Cultural Logic of Postmodernism." *Critical Sociology*, 19 (1992), 113–27.

Dreyfus, H. L., and P. Rabinow. *Michel Foucault: Beyond Structuralism and Hermeneutics*. 2nd ed. Chicago: University of Chicago Press, 1983.

Esch, D. "Deconstruction." In *Redrawing the Boundaries*, edited by S. Greenblatt and G. Gunn, pp. 374–91. New York: Modern Language Association, 1992.

Foster, W. *Paradigms and Promises: New Approaches to Educational Administration*. Buffalo, N.Y.: Prometheus, 1986.

Foucault, M. *Discipline and Punish*. New York: Vintage Books, 1979.

Franklin, P., B. J. Huber, and D. Lawrence. "Continuity and Change in the Study of Literature." *Change*, 24 (1992), 42–48.

Frazer, N., and L. J. Nicholson. "Social Criticism without Philosophy: An Encounter between Feminism and Postmodernism." In *Feminism/Postmodernism*. edited by L. J. Nicholson, pp. 19–38. New York: Routledge, 1990.

Gerth, H. H., and C. W. Mills (eds. and translators). *From Max Weber: Essays in Sociology*. New York: Oxford University Press, 1958.

Geyer, M. "Multiculturalism and the Politics of General Education." *Critical Inquiry*. 19 (1993), 499–533.

Giddens, A. *The Consequences of Modernism*. Stanford, Calif.: Stanford University Press, 1990.

Giroux, H. A. *Border Crossings*. New York: Routledge 1992,

Gitlin, T. "The Left, Lost in the Politics of Identity" *Harpers*, 287 (1993), 16–20.

Glazer, J. S., E. M. Bensimon, and S. K. Townsend (eds.). *Women in Higher Education*. Needham Heights. Mass.: Ginn Press, 1993.

Greenblatt, S., and G. Gunn. "Introduction." In *Redrawing the Boundaries*, edited by S. Greenblatt and G. Gunn, pp. 1–11. New York: The Modern Language Association. 1992.

_____. *Redrawing the Boundaries*. New York: The Modern Language Association, 1992.

Grossberg, L., C. Nelson, and P. A. Treichler (eds.). *Cultural Studies*. New York; Routledge, 1992.

Habermas, J. "Modernity versus Postmodernity." *New German Critique*, 22 (1981), 3–11.

_____. *The Theory of Communicative Action*. Vol. 1: *Reason and Rationalization of Society*. Trans. T. McCarthy. Boston: Beacon Press, 1981.

_____. *The Theory of Communicative Action*. Vol. 2: *Lifeworld and System*. Trans. T. McCarthy. Boston: Beacon Press, 1987.

Hassan, I. *The Postmodern Turn: Essays in Postmodern Theory and Culture*. Columbus: Ohio State University Press, 1987.

Hayles, N. K. "Introduction: Complex Dynamics in Literature and Science." In *Chaos and Disorder*, edited by N. K. Hayles, pp. 1–33. Chicago: University of Chicago Press, 1991.

_____ (ed.). *Chaos and Disorder: Complex Dynamics in Literature and Science*. Chicago: University of Chicago Press, 1991.

Hazzard, J., and M. Parker (eds.). *Postmodernism and Organizations*. Newbury Park, Calif.: Sage, 1993.

Hutcheon, L. *A Poetics of Postmodernism*. London: Routledge, 1988.

Hoy, D. C. (ed.). *Foucault: A Critical Reader*. Cambridge, Mass.: Basil Blackwell, 1986.

Huyssen, A. "Mapping the Postmodern." In *Culture and Society: Cultural Debates*, edited by J. C. Alexander and S. Seidman, pp. 355–75. Cambridge: Cambridge University Press, 1990.

Jencks, C. *What is Post-Modernism?* 2nd ed. London: Academy, 1987.

Jameson, F. "Postmodernism, or the Cultural Logic of Late Capitalism." *New Left Review*, 146 (1984), 53–93.

Keane, J. "The Modern Democratic Revolution: Reflections on Lyotard's 'The Postmodern Condition'." In *Judging Lyotard*, edited by A. Benjamin, pp. 81–98. London: Routledge, 1992.

Kerrigan, W. "Seventeenth-Century Studies." In *Redrawing the Boundaries*, edited by S. Greenblatt and G. Gunn, pp. 64–78. New York: Modern Language Association. 1992.

Kiziltan, M. U., W. J. Bain, and A. M. Canizares. "Postmodern Conditions: Rethinking Public Education." *Educational Theory*, 40 (1990), 351–69.

Laclau, E., and C. Mouffe. "Post-Marxism without Apology." *New Left Review*, 66 (1987). 79–106.

Lokke, V., and D. Jaeckle. "Plastic Buffalo Humps: Theory as Sludge in the *Journal of Higher Education*." *Journal of Higher Education*, 62 (November/December 1991), 683–94.

Lyotard, J. F. *The Postmodern Condition*. Minneapolis: University of Minnesota Press, 1984.

McLaren, P. "Review Article—Postmodernity and the Death of Politics: A Brazilian Reprieve." *Educational Theory*, 36 (1986), 389–401.

Mani, L. "Cultural Theory, Colonial Texts: Reading Eyewitness Accounts of Widow Burning." In *Cultural Studies*, edited by L. Grossberg, C. Nelson, and P. A. Treichler, pp. 392–405. New York: Routledge, 1992.

Marcus, G. E. "What Comes (just) after 'Post'?: The Case of Ethnography." In *Handbook of Qualitative Research*, edited by N. K. Denzin and Y. S. Lincoln, pp. 563–74. Thousand Oaks, Calif.: Sage, 1994.

Marcuse, H. *One Dimensional Man*. Boston: Beacon Press, 1964.

Montrose, L. "New Historicisms." In *Redrawing the Boundaries*, edited by S. Greenblatt and G. Gunn, 392–418. New York: The Modern Language Association, 1992.

Nelson, C., P. A. Treichler, and L. Grossberg. "Cultural Studies: An Introduction." In *Cultural Studies*, edited by L. Grossberg, C. Nelson, and P. A. Treichler, pp. 1–16. New York: Routledge, 1992.

Nicholson, C. "Postmodernism, Feminism, and Education: The Need for Solidarity." *Educational Theory*, 39 (1989), 197–205.

Nicholson, L. J. (ed.). *Feminism/Postmodernism*. New York: Routledge, 1990.

Nuyen, A. T. "Lyotard on the Death of the Professor." *Educational Theory*. 42 (1992), 25–37.

Parker, M. "Post-Modern Organizations or Postmodern Organization Theory?" *Organization Theory*, 13 (1992), 1–17.

Philp, M. "Michel Foucault." In *The Return of Grand Theory in the Human Sciences*, edited by Q. Skinner, pp. 65–81. Cambridge: Cambridge University Press, 1985.

Rasmussen, D. M. *Reading Habermas*. Cambridge, Mass.: Basil Blackwell, 1990.

Reed, M. I. "Organizations and Modernity: Continuity and Discontinuity in Organization Theory.' In *Postmodernism and Organizations*, edited by J. Hazzard and M. Parker, pp. 163–82. Newbury Park, Calif.: Sage. 1993.

Rhoades, G. "Calling on the Past: The Quest for the Collegiate Ideal." *Journal of Higher Education*, 61 (September/October 1990). 512–34.

_____. "Vive la 'Differance': Poststructural Analysis of Education." *Journal of Higher Education*, 62 (November/December 1991), 706–21.

Rorty, R. *Contingency, Irony, and Solidarity*. New York: Cambridge University Press, 1989.

_____. "Habermas and Lyotard on Postmodernity." In *Habermas and Modernity*, edited by R. J. Bernstein, pp. 161–75. Cambridge, Mass.: MIT Press, 1985.

_____. *Objectivism. Relativism, and Truth*. New York: Cambridge University Press, 1991.

Rosenau, P. M. *Post-Modernism and the Social Sciences*. Princeton, N.J.: Princeton University Press, 1992.

Ross, A. (ed.). *Universal Abandon? The Politics of Postmodernism*. Minneapolis: University of Minnesota Press, 1988.

Rowe, J. C. "Postmodern Studies." In *Redrawing the Boundaries*, edited by S. Greenblatt and G. Gunn, pp. 179–208. New York: Modern Language Association, 1992.

Rust, V. "Postmodernism and Its Comparative Education Implications." *Comparative Education Review*, 35 (1991), 610–26.

Sarap, M. *An Introductory Guide to Post-Structuralism and Postmodernism*. Athens: The University of Georgia Press, 1989.

Skinner, Q. (ed.). *The Return of Grand Theory to the Human Sciences*. Cambridge: Cambridge University Press, 1985.

Smart, B. *Michel Foucault*. London: Tavistock Publications, 1985.

_____. *Postmodernity*. New York: Routledge, 1993.

Tichi, C. "American Literary Studies to the Civil War." In *Redrawing the Boundaries*, edited by S. Greenblatt and G. Gunn, pp. 209–31. New York: Modern Language Association, 1992.

Turner, B. S. "Periodization and Politics in the Postmodern." In *Theories of Modernity and Postmodernism*, edited by B. S. Turner, pp. 1–13. Newbury Park, Calif.: Sage, 1990.

_____. (ed.). *Theories of Modernity and Postmodernity*. Newbury Park, Calif.: Sage, 1990.

Weber, M. *The Protestant Ethic and the Spirit of Capitalism*. Trans. T. Parsons. New York: Charles Scribner Sons, 1958.

West, C. "The Postmodern Crisis of the Black Intellectuals." In *Cultural Studies*, edited by L. Grossberg, C. Nelson, and P. A. Treichler, pp. 689–96. New York: Routledge, 1992.

White, S. *Political Theory and Postmodernism*. Cambridge: Cambridge University Press, 1991.

Wicks, A. C. "Divide and Conquer? Rorty's Distinction between the Public and the Private." *Soundings*, 76 (1993), 551–69.

Winkler, K. "Scholars Mark the Beginning of the Age of 'Post-Theory'." *Chronicle of Higher Education*, 13 October 1993, pp. 9, 16, 17.

Young, I. M. "The Ideal of Community and the Politics of Difference." In *Feminism/Postmodernism*, edited by L. Nicholson, pp. 300–323. New York: Routledge, 1990.

Zemsky, R. "Consumer Markets and Higher Education." *Liberal Education*, 79 (1993), 14–17.

UNDERSTANDING RADICAL ORGANIZATIONAL CHANGE

ROYSTON GREENWOOD AND C. R. HININGS

The complexity of political, regulatory, and technological changes confronting most organizations has made radical organizational change and adaptation a central research issue. This article sets out a framework for understanding organizational changes from the perspective of neo-institutional theory. The principal theoretical issue addressed in the article is the interaction of organizational context and organizational action. The article examines the processes by which individual organizations retain, adopt, and discard templates for organizing, given the institutionalized nature of organizational fields.

The complexity of political, regulatory, and technological changes confronting most organizations has made organizational change and adaptation a central research issue of the 1990s. The ability to cope with often dramatically altering contextual forces has become a key determinant of competitive advantage and organizational survival (D'Aveni, 1994). The purpose of this article is to set out a framework for understanding organizational change from the perspective of neo-institutional theory (Powell & DiMaggio, 1991). Institutional theory is used as a starting point because it represents one of the more robust sociological perspectives within organizational theory (Perrow, 1979), and it makes sense, as Dougherty pointed out, to "integrate some theoretical threads regarding the specific issue of transformation by building on already developed theories" (1994: 110). We use the term *neo-institutional* to capture the developments that have taken over the past decade (Powell & DiMaggio, 1991).

In their review of the state of institutional theory, DiMaggio and Powell (1991: 13) distinguished between the old and the new institutionalism. In the old institutionalism, issues of influence, coalitions, and competing values were central, along with power and informal structures (Clark, 1960, 1972; Selznick, 1949, 1957). This focus contrasts with the new institutionalisrn with its emphasis on legitimacy, the embeddedness of organizational fields, and the centrality of classification, routines, scripts, and schema (DiMaggio & Powell, 1983; Meyer & Rowan, 1977). Scott (1987) suggested that institutional theory was at the stage of adolescence. Later, he saw considerable progress, namely: "I see convergent developments among the approaches of many analysts as they recognize the importance of meaning systems, symbolic elements, regulatory processes, and governance systems" (Scott, 1994: 78). It is this convergence around multiple themes, the coming together of the old and the new institutionalism that we label *neo-institutionalism*. The convergence that Scott (1994) wrote about involves all of the elements of the old and new institutional theory.

Institutional theory is not usually regarded as a theory of organizational change, but as usually an explanation of the similarity ("isomorphism") and stability of organizational arrangements in a given population or field of organizations. Ledford, Mohrman, Mohrman, and Lawler (1989: 8), for example, concluded that institutional theory offers not "much guidance regarding change." Buckho

(1994: 90) observed that institutional pressures are a "powerful force" *against* transformational change. Here we present the opposite view, agreeing with Dougherty that the theory contains "an excellent basis" (1994: 108) for an account of change, first, by providing a convincing definition of radical (as opposed to convergent) change, and, second, by signaling the contextual dynamics that precipitate the need for organizational adaptation (Leblebici, Salancik, Copay, & King, 1993; Oliver, 1991). As formulated, however, neo-institutional theory is weak in analyzing the *internal* dynamics of organizational change. As a consequence, the theory is silent on why some organizations adopt radical change whereas others do not, despite experiencing the same institutional pressures. Nevertheless, neo-institutional theory contains insights and suggestions that, when elaborated, provide a model of change that links organizational context and intraorganizational dynamics.

In this article, then, the central purpose is to provide an explanation of both the incidence of radical change and of the extent to which such change is achieved through evolutionary or revolutionary pacing. The explanation has three themes. First, we establish that a major source of organizational resistance to change derives from the normative embeddedness of an organization within its institutional context. This statement is a central message of institutional theory. Second, we suggest that the incidence of radical change, and the pace by which such change occurs, will vary across institutional sectors because of differences in the structures of institutional sectors, in particular in the extents to which sectors are tightly coupled and insulated from ideas practiced in other sectors. Third, we propose that both the incidence of radical change and the pace by which such change occurs will vary *within* sectors because organizations vary in their internal organizational dynamics. In order to understand differences in organizational responses, organizations are conceptualized as heterogeneous entities composed of functionally differentiated groups pursuing goals and promoting interests. How organizations "respond" to institutional prescriptions, in particular, whether they undergo radical change, and, if they do, how quickly, is a function of these internal dynamics.

By addressing the interplay of organizational context and organizational action, this article is consistent with recent developments in organization theory. The initial polarization of perspectives offered, on the one hand, by population ecologists, with their essential denial of radical organizational change and emphasis upon peremptory environmental determinism (e.g., Hannan & Freeman, 1989) and, on the other hand, by strategic choice theorists, with their emphasis upon the pivotal role of executive action (e.g., Child, 1972; Tichy, 1983; Tichy & Devanna, 1986) has given way to attention to the interaction of choice and context. Hrebiniak and Joyce (1985), Van de Ven and Poole (1988), Astley and Van de Ven (1983), Pettigrew (1987), and Wilson (1994) have lodged pleas for theoretical understanding of how contextual pressures are interpreted and acted upon by organizational actors. To date, however, existing accounts have "not been successful" (Van de Ven & Poole, 1988: 327). Ledford and colleagues (1989: 4) dismissively described them as "of limited help." Here we seek to provide a more complete account for understanding organizational interpretations of, and responses to, contextual pressures, by stressing the political dynamics of intraorganizational behavior and the normative embeddedness of organizations within their contexts.

It is beyond the scope of this article to summarize the extensive literature on organizational change, but it is important to establish two aspects of change of particular concern here: first, the difference between convergent and radical change and, second, the difference between revolutionary and evolutionary change. A distinction is frequently drawn between convergent and radical change (Greenwood & Hinings, 1988; Miller & Friessen, 1984; Mohrman, Mohrman, Ledford, Cummings, & Lawler, 1989: Nadler & Tushman, 1989; Nadler, Shaw, Walton & Associates, 1995: Tushman & Romanelli, 1985). Radical organizational change, or "frame bending" as it is sometimes evocatively known, involves the busting loose from an existing "orientation" (Johnson, 1987; Miller, 1982, 1990) and the transformation of the organization. Convergent change is fine tuning the existing orientation. It is radical, not convergent change in which we are interested.

Revolutionary and evolutionary change are defined by the scale and pace of upheaval and adjustment. Whereas evolutionary change occurs slowly and gradually, revolutionary change happens swiftly and affects virtually all parts of the organization simultaneously. Tushman and Romanelli's (1985) punctuated-equilibrium model describes revolutionary change. Pettigrew's (1985; 1987) model of continuity and change reflects the process of evolutionary change.

The remainder of the article is divided into two sections. We begin the following section by outlining the current contribution of institutional theory to understanding change. We then develop a more complete account of intraorganizational dynamics and their interaction with contextual dynamics. In the final section, we draw attention to a number of key issues and discuss possible directions for research.

Institutional Theory and Change

Scott (1987: 493), in a seminal review of institutional theory, advised that "the beginning of wisdom in approaching institutional theory is to recognize that there is not one but several variants." At the outset, however, we begin by briefly reviewing three salient characteristics of what has become known as neo-institutional theory. The theory of change that can be derived from those characteristics is then elaborated.

The Impact of the Institutional Context

Institutional theorists declare that regularized organizational behaviors are the product of ideas, values, and beliefs that originate in the institutional context (Meyer & Rowan, 1977; Meyer, Scott, & Deal, 1983; Zucker, 1983). To survive, organizations must accommodate institutional expectations, even though these expectations may have little to do with technical notions of performance accomplishment (D'Aunno, Sutton, & Price, 1991; DiMaggio & Powell, 1991; Scott, 1987). For example, an accounting firm may be organized as a professional partnership, not because that form of governance has been analyzed and found to facilitate efficient and effective task performance, but because that form is defined as the appropriate way of organizing the conduct of accounting work. Institutional theory, in other words, shows how organizational behaviors are responses not solely to market pressures, but also to institutional pressures (e.g., pressures from regulatory agencies, such as the state and the professions, and pressures from general social expectations and the actions of leading organizations).

Templates of Organizing, Isomorphism, and Convergence

Institutional pressures lead organizations to adopt the same organizational form. That is, the institutional context provides "templates for organizing" (DiMaggio & Powell, 1991: 27). The idea of templates connects to the growing interest in "configurational" research (for a review, see Meyer, Tsui, & Hinings, 1993). Configurational researchers conceptualize organizations holistically, seeking to recognize archetypal patterns in the display of structures and systems (Drazin & Van de Ven, 1985; Mintzberg, 1983; Miller & Friesen, 1984). Greenwood and Hinings (1993), consistent with the neo-institutionalist emphasis upon values, suggested that the configuration or pattern of an organization's structures and systems is provided by underpinning ideas and values, that is, an interpretive scheme (Barley, 1986; Bartunek, 1983; Ranson, Hinings, & Greenwood, 1980).

Thinking of organizational arrangements in terms of templates or archetypes (Greenwood & Hinings, 1993) provides a robust definition of radical and convergent change. Convergent change occurs within the parameters of an existing archetypal template. Radical change, in contrast, occurs when an organization moves from one template-in-use to another. That is, an accounting firm operating as a professional partnership may institute representative democracy in place of more broadly based democratic involvement in order to accommodate the exigencies of growth and large size. Such a change would be consistent with prevailing core ideas and values of the importance of clan rather than bureaucratic bases of authority (Ouchi, 1980), and it is convergent change. If, in contrast, a firm were to move from one template to another, the change would be radical, because it represents the breaking of the mold defined by an interpretive scheme. For example, if members of a professional partnership hired a nonaccountant as chief executive officer charged with formal responsibility for monitoring and evaluating senior professionals, there would be a discordant structure within the professional partnership and an indication of possible movement toward a new template (e.g., the "corporate" model). The new structures and responsibilities would not fit the clan orientation and would be more consistent with bureaucratic values.

Stressing ideas, beliefs, and values as the basis for identifying templates of structures and systems is not unique to institutional theory. The same idea is found in Miller's (1991: 8) "stable central themes," Blau and McKinley's (1979: 200) "work motifs," and Pettigrew's (1987: 658) "dominating beliefs or ideologies." It is also present in much of the culture literature. Institutional theorists are different because they stress ideational templates as originating outside of the organization and being relevant to a population of organizations within an organizational field. As a consequence, institutional theory draws attention to institutionally derived and created templates of organizing to which organizations converge, rather than to the uniqueness of individual organizational cultures. Organizational convergence, not uniqueness, is implied.

DiMaggio and Powell (1983, 1991b: 63) stressed the convergence of organizations by bluntly framing *the* question as "Why [is there] such startling homogeneity, not variation?" The same authors discussed the primary processes (coercive, mimetic, and normative) by which convergence might occur as organizations seek to become isomorphic with their contexts. Underlying DiMaggio and Powell's (1991a) analysis is that organizations conform to contextual expectations of appropriate organizational forms to gain legitimacy and increase their probability of survival.

The focus of neo-institutional theory is thus not upon the individual organization but upon a category or network of organizations. Even though much of the early empirical work (e.g., Meyer & Rowan, 1977) was based upon individual organizations, or case studies, neo-institutional theorists treat organizations as a population within an organizational field. These theorists stress that the institutional context is made up of vertically and horizontally interlocking organizations[1] and that the pressures and prescriptions within these contexts apply to all of the relevant classes of organizations.

Resistance to Change

According to early contributions to institutional theory, the organizational field and the templates of organizing within it become infused with a taken-for-granted quality, in which actors unwittingly accept the prevailing template as appropriate, right, and the proper way of doing things. DiMaggio and Powell (1983) and Fligstein (1985) noted that a template rationale for an individual organization may not be rational for large numbers of organizations. There is, in short, a normative tone to institutional discussions (Meyer & Rowan, 1977; Oliver, 1991; Zucker, 1977). For this reason, institutional theorists stress the stability of organizational arrangements and the characteristic of inertia rather than change (Tolbert, 1985; Tolbert & Zucker, 1983). Stressing inertia may be slightly misleading in that organizations constantly experience unfolding change. To the institutional school, however, the prevailing nature of change is one of constant reproduction and reinforcement of existing modes of thought and organization (i.e., change is convergent change).

By emphasizing archetypes/templates that originate in the institutional context and around which networks of organizations converge, institutional theorists actually show a likely dynamic of inertia, which can be illustrated from the accounting industry. The accounting profession mimicked the law (and the clergy) and adopted the partnership organizational form, which has endured and become almost synonymous with the very meaning of "professional," with its emphasis on independence, autonomy, and responsible conduct. Development of the profession during the 19th century and structuration of the accounting industry field followed much the same path as DiMaggio (1991) described for the museum profession. Thus, the values of the professional partnership became reinforced by professional associations that worked closely with universities and state agencies to promulgate and protect the self-regulating independence and autonomy of accounting firms. As a result, strong reciprocal exchanges have developed between the accounting field and any one accounting firm, such that the firm both accommodates the expectation of the field by observing appropriate behaviors and practices, and in doing so, acts as a role model within the field to other accounting firms. Thus, there are strong mimetic, normative, and coercive processes at work.

These mimetic, normative, and coercive processes are part of the institutional context. Such contexts differ in the strength of these kinds of pressures (i.e., the degree of embeddedness and in the extent to which change may occur because of deinstitutionalization (Oliver, 1992). Radical change is thus problematic not solely because of weak organizational learning (as emphasized by strategic choice theorists such as Kanter, 1983, and Johnson, 1987) or the constraints of strategy "commitments" (Ghemawat, 1991) or the difficulty of mobilizing internal support (as emphasized by Tichy, 1983, and Fombrun, 1992)—although these forces for inertia may and often do occur—but because of the normative embeddedness of an organization within its institutional context (Baum & Oliver, 1991). Also, the greater the embeddedness, the more problematic is the attainment of radical change. Indeed, Powell and DiMaggio (1991a) noted that the greater the extent to which organizations are tightly coupled to a prevailing archetypal template within a highly structured field, the greater the degree of instability in the face of external shocks. That is, the rigidity of tight coupling and high structuredness produces resistance to change; however, should institutional prescriptions change dramatically, the resultant organizational response would be revolutionary, not evolutionary (in terms of the scale and pace of upheaval and adjustment).

The above starting points may be summarized as follows:

Hypothesis 1: Organizations are structured in terms of archetypes (templates of organizing), which are institutionally derived.

Hypothesis 2: Radical change (movement from one archetype to another) is problematic because of the normative embeddedness of an organization within its institutional context. Convergent change is the more normal occurrence.

Hypothesis 3: The greater the normative embeddedness of an organization within the institutional context, the more likely that when change occurs it will be revolutionary rather than evolutionary (i.e.. the pace of upheaval will be fast, not gradual, and the scale large, not modest).

The Possibility for Change

Institutional theory, in summary, emphasizes convergence around institutionally prescribed templates. Indeed, Powell (1991a: 183) was particularly critical of such theory for its "static, constrainted, and over-socialised views of organizations." DiMaggio and Powell (1991a: 29) asked the question, "If institutions exert such a powerful influence over the ways in which people can formulate their desires and work to attain them, then how does institutional change occur?" Three streams of work within institutional theory give insights into the possible processes and likelihood of radical change, and it is these streams that lead us to a neo-institutional perspective. Early contributions (e.g.. Tolbert & Zucker, 1983) proposed a two-stage dissemination model of change. In the early (youthful) development of an organizational field, technical performance requirements are more important than in later (mature) stages of the field, at which point institutional pressures become more salient (Tolbert & Zucker, 1983; Baron, Dobbin, & Jennings, 1986). Subsequent authors have examined the "mechanisms of imitation" (Haunschild, 1993: 564), paying particular attention to the role of interlocking directorates (e.g., Davis, 1991; Davis & Powell, 1992; Haveman, 1993; Palmer, Jennings, & Thou, 1993) or the object of imitation (e.g., Burns & Wholey, 1993; Galaskiewicz & Wasserman, 1989; Haveman, 1993; O'Reilly, Main, & Crystal, 1988).

A second line of development within institutional theory, which has implications for understanding change, considers the structure of the institutional context (i.e., the *extent of tight coupling* and the *extent of sectoral permeability*). Regarding tight coupling, sectors usually have been perceived as having clearly legitimated organizational templates and highly articulated mechanisms (the state, professional associations, regulatory agencies, and leading organizations) for transmitting those templates to organizations within the sector (Fligstein, 1991; Haveman, 1993; Hinings & Greenwood, 1988a; Kikulis, Slack, & Hinings, 1995; Tolbert, 1985; Wholey & Burns, 1993). Furthermore, much of this work has assumed ideological consensus within an institutional field. Tight coupling, in other words, refers to the existence of mechanisms for dissemination and the monitoring of compliance combined with a focused and consistent set of expectations.

In practice, there can be variation across institutional sectors in the degree of tight coupling. Carroll, Goodstein, and Gyenes (1988), for example, questioned the probability of ideological consensus. Fligstein (1991: 316) noted that the possibility of "innovative behavior" is higher in "ill-formed" organizational fields. Barnett and Carroll (1987) documented how during the founding years of the telephone industry, high political differentiation in the markets enabled several organizational forms to flourish (i.e., high political differentiation was associated with low institutional consensus over templates). DiMaggio and Powell (1991a), Scott (1991), Powell (1991), Oliver (1991). and D'Aunno and colleagues (1991) accepted that institutional fields may have multiple pressures providing inconsistent cues or signals, opening the possibility for idiosyncratic interpretation and either deliberate or unwitting variation in practices.

Mechanisms for dissemination also can vary across institutional fields. In mature sectors, such as accounting and law, there are very clear mechanisms, and thus normative, coercive, and mimetic pressures (for conformity) are high. In governmental sectors, too, regulatory pressures are usually clear and reinforced (Hinings & Greenwood, 1988b; Kikulis, Slack, & Hinings. 1995). In less well-developed sectors such as biotechnology, the existence of leading organizations is less clear and there is no developed network of regulatory agencies comparable to accounting bodies (Powell, 1993). As a consequence, there is no stipulated template for organizing, and thus pressures for conformity are much less pronounced. Thus,

> Hypothesis 4: Radical change in tightly coupled institutional fields will be unusual, but when it occurs, it will be revolutionary.

> Hypothesis 5: Radical change in loosely coupled fields will be more common (than in tightly coupled fields), and when it occurs it will be evolutionary.

Institutional fields vary in their insulation from other fields. Same fields lack permeability (i.e., they are relatively closed to or not exposed to ideas from other institutional arenas). Other fields are more open and thus more likely to permit variation and change. Child and Smith (1987), for example, described the transfer of ideas that happen as contractors service firms in different industries. Similarly, members of accounting firms inevitably work in several fields (by consulting or by conducting audits) and become exposed to and potentially influenced by the ideas prevailing in those fields. Because of the tight coupling within the accounting industry, however, the influence of other fields traditionally has been limited (consistent with Hypothesis 4). Because of looming performance crises, however, members of accounting firms are beginning to consider other fields for possible solutions (e.g., the partnership form of governance is under review, *European Accounting Focus*, 1995). That is, permeable boundaries enable radical change because of the availability of new archetypal solutions. Thus,

> Hypothesis 6: Institutional fields that are impermeable will be associated with low rates of radical change.

> Hypothesis 7: Radical change that occurs in impermeable institutional fields will be revolutionary in pace.

> Hypothesis 8: Institutional fields that are permeable will be associated with a higher incidence of radical change than will occur in impermeable institutional fields.

> Hypothesis 9: Institutional fields that are permeable will be associated with evolutionary change.

These elaborations are significant because through them we admit to the possibility and even the likelihood of *alternative* templates within an institutional context.[2] In tightly structured contexts, the occurrence of such alternatives may be infrequent, and it may be dependent partly on a serious decline in performance (as in the law industry described by Cooper, Hinings, Greenwood, and Brown, in press, and in the municipal sector of the United Kingdom as described by Hinings and Greenwood, 1988a) and partly on the permeability of the sector. In less tightly coupled contexts, the occurrence of alternative templates may be more frequent but less coherently formulated. The central point is that organizations are recipients of prescribed ideas about appropriate templates of organizing whose relative salience and clarity *may change over time*. Particular organizations do not respond to a template of organizing, but they do respond over time to evolving and competing prescriptions. This conclusion leads to two issues: how do individual organizations respond *and why do they differ in their responses*.[3]

Intraorganizational Dynamics

In the old institutionalism (e.g., Selznick. 1949), issues of influence, coalitions, and competing values were central, and the emphasis was placed on the ways in which the formal, rational mission of an organization is diverted by the operation of group interests. Thus, the key forms of cognition are values, norms, and attitudes; conflicts of interest and vested interests are central; and the individual organization is the locus of institutionalization and the primary unit of analysis. Selznick (1957: 17) wrote of institutionalized organizations being "infused with value," becoming ends in themselves, and thus operating within essentially moral frames of reference.

Similarly, Clark (1960) emphasized that actual organizational practices diverge from expressed organizational goals. In further work, Clark (1972) showed how values may be "precarious." That is, newly appointed administrators attempted to signal shifts in values and expectations through changes in structures. However, the organizational implications of the new values and meanings were imperfectly understood, and it took a long time for the new values to be embodied in practice.

Brint and Karabel (1991: 344) related with the "old institutionalism" of Selznick (1949) and Clark (1960, 1972), building primarily "on the insights of the 'conflict' tradition in sociology, rather than on the insights of the Durkheimian tradition which have proven so fruitful for the new institutionalism." They also drew on the insights that Michels (1962) generated about the role of interests in organizations, which allow diversions to occur from original goals. As Brint and Karabel (1991: 352) observed, old institutionalism "emphasizes the details of an organization's interactions with its environment over time" and pays attention to the beliefs and actions of those who have the power to define directions and interests.

New institutionalism emphasizes the regulative, the normative, and the cognitive. In this case, rather than values and moral frames, it is cognition that is important. As Meyer and Rowan (1977: 341) put it, "normative obligations . . . enter into social life primarily as facts." The key units of analysis are organizations-in-sectors and their relation to societal institutions.

From the point of view of understanding change, the old institutionalism suggests that change is one of the dynamics of organizations as they struggle with differences of values and interests. The new institutionalism emphasizes persistence. Combining the two into neo-institutionalism gives the possibility of dealing with the question asked by DiMaggio and Powell (1991: 29): "If institutions exert such a powerful influence over the ways in which people can formulate their desires and work to attain them, then how does institutional change occur?"

Oliver (1992), building upon the work of Zucker (1987), began to provide a way of bringing these two perspectives together in her examination of the antecedents of deinstitutionalization. Oliver suggested (1992: 584) that "the persistence and longevity of institutionalized values and activities may be less common than the emphasis of institutional theory on cultural persistence and the diffusion of enduring change implies." Oliver (1992) introduced the notion of *dissipation,* a gradual deterioration in the acceptance and use of a particular institutionalized practice, which provided an overall conceptual framework for understanding that process. Her framework involves both environmental and organizational features that can produce deinstitutionalization. Among the organizational features are, inter alia, changing values, conflicting internal interests, and increasing social fragmentation.

Our aim is to bridge the old and the new institutionalisms by explaining the response of the individual organization to pressure in the institutional field as a function of the organization's internal dynamics. Oliver (1992) did this partly, but only in outline, and there is no expansion of how the characteristics of the organizational field *interact* with the internal characteristics of an organization. Also, Oliver emphasized how institutionalized practices break down and are replaced by new ones. Our aim is to understand both persistence and change. We do so by focusing upon four aspects of an organization's internal dynamics—interests, values, power dependencies, and capacity for action.

Given the institutionalized nature of organizational sectors, what are the processes by which individual organizations adopt legitimated templates and change them? DiMaggio and Powell (1991a: 27) suspected that "something has been lost in the shift from the old to the new institutionalism" and "the goal must be a sounder multidimensional theory, rather than a one-sidedly cognitive one." They go on to suggest that "power and interests have been slighted topics in institutional analysis" (1991a: 30). This line of thought leads to the conclusion that the role of intraorganizational dynamics in accepting or rejecting institutionalized practices is critical.

The framework for understanding organizational change that we wish to advance is summarized in Figure 1. The Figure encompasses exogenous (market context, institutional context) and endogenous dynamics (interests, values, power dependencies, and capacity for action).

One difficulty with representing a model of change dynamics in a diagram is that the representation itself is essentially cross-sectional and linear. In fact, radical organizational change, which is shown as the outcome of the model in Figure 1, would become the input to market and institutional contexts. For example, an organization that adopted a new organizational form and achieved competitive success in the marketplace would produce pressures on other organizations to adopt the same organizational form. Organizations, as Fligstein (1991: 316) noted, "extensively monitor one another," and successful practices are mimicked and institutionalized.

Exogenous variables have been discussed previously. In order to elaborate the model, first, we summarize the endogenous components of the framework that act as precipitating dynamics and, second, we summarize those that are enabling dynamics.

Precipitating Dynamics

From our perspective, it is necessary to take seriously the internal complexity of organizations (i.e., every organization is a mosaic of groups structured by functional tasks and employment status). Thus, in accounting firms there are separate functional groups for audit work, tax activities, small business practices, insolvency, and management consultancy. Within each of these groups are "students," "managers," and "partners." Blau's (1974) analysis of organizational structuring demonstrated that complex organizations handle growth and/or contextual complexity by differentiation into groups, each of which is focused on specialized tasks. The process of specialization leads to significant differences between groups in terms of structural arrangements (e.g., Lawrence & Lorsch, 1967) and orientation (e.g., Payne & Mansfield, 1973; Payne & Pugh, 1976; Pheysey, Payne, & Pugh, 1971).

However, central to our perspective is the role of "interests" and "value commitments." Functionally differentiated groups are not neutral and indifferent to other groups. Much of the work on differentiation and conflict in organizations (Lawrence & Lorsch, 1967) shows how technical boundaries between departments and sections are reinforced and buttressed by cognitive boundaries. Thus, in any organization are the seeds of alternative ways of viewing the purposes of that organization, the ways in which it might be appropriately organized, and the ways in which actions might be evaluated. This view is very much reflected in the old institutionalism of Selznick (1949).

One outcome of such organizational differentiation is that groups seek to translate their interests into favorable allocations of scarce and valued organizational resources. As Palmer, Jennings, and Zhou (1993: 103) put it: "Organizations are. . . . arenas in which coalitions with different interests and capacities for influence vie for dominance." A potential pressure for change and/or inertia, therefore, is the extent to which groups are dissatisfied with how their interests are accommodated within an organization. A high measure of dissatisfaction becomes a pressure for change (Covaleski & Dirsmith, 1988; Walsh, Hinings, Greenwood, & Ranson, 1981).

We would expect organizations to vary in the extent to which they are characterized by interest dissatisfaction, for two reasons. First, organizations develop portfolios of services that vary in scope and balance. Arthur Andersen, for example, has aggressively promoted management consulting (especially in information technology), and the result has been that consulting income constitutes 45% of the firm's income (*Public Accounting Report*, 1995). In other accounting firms, the proportion is much lower. Arthur Andersen also has a smaller proportion of partners to total members employed, and the result is that income per partner is higher than the industry average. These differences in operating practices influence the relative sizes of different groups within the organization and their position of advantage and disadvantage. Hence, even in the same market context, the extent of interest dissatisfaction can vary from firm to firm (line a in Figure 1).

Dissatisfaction, however, does not provide direction for change. Intense pressure for change arising from dissatisfaction with accommodation of interests will not lead to *radical*

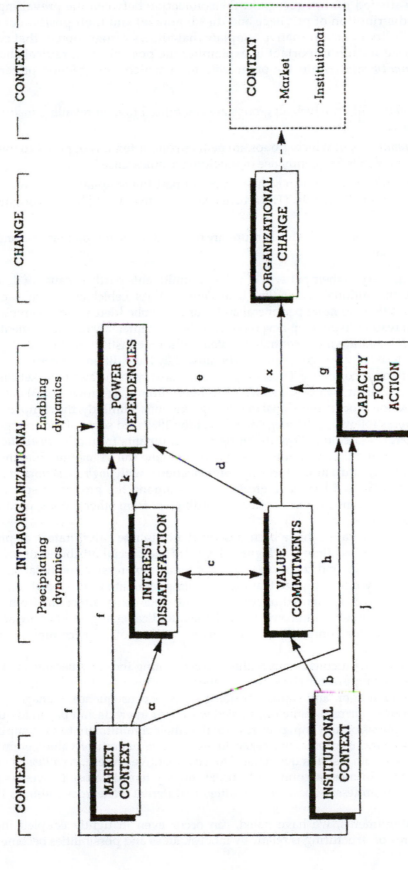

Figure 1 Model for understanding organizational change.

change, unless dissatisfied groups recognize the connection between the prevailing template (which shapes the distribution of privilege and disadvantage) and their position of disadvantage.[4] It is the possibility of an alternative template that allows recognition of that connection. Thus, what becomes critically important in explaining the possibility of radical change is the *pattern of value commitments* within the organization, of which four generic patterns can be identified:

1. *Status quo commitment*, in which all groups are committed to the prevailing institutionalized template-in-use.

2. *Indifferent commitment*, in which groups are neither committed nor opposed to the template-in-use. This situation is frequently one of unwitting acquiescence.[5]

3. *Competitive commitment*, in which some groups support the template-in-use, whereas others prefer an articulated alternative. (The articulated alternative would have its origins in the institutional context.)

4. *Reformative commitment*, in which all groups are opposed to the template-in-use and prefer an articulated alternative.

Organizations will vary in their patterns of value commitments partly because of their different locations within the institutional sector (line b in Figure 1). As Leblebici and colleagues (1991) showed, organizations that are more peripheral and thus less embedded are less committed to prevailing practices and readier to develop new ones. They lack the intensity of commitment to the status quo found in firms that are more centrally located within the institutional field. Organizations also vary in their patterns of value commitments because they have different rates of success in the marketplace and respond accordingly. Thus, the growing maturity in the audit market coupled with the decline in perceived client loyalty (Greenwood, Cooper, Hinings, & Brown. 1993) has caused accounting firms to develop more professional marketing functions. Similarly, the complexity of organizational arrangements following the mega mergers of the 1980s led some of the enlarged firms to strengthen the human resource function. By hiring nonaccountants from *other institutional sectors*, new sets of expectations and thus commitments to ways of doing things are built into the organization (line b in Figure 1). Put more formally, organizations with *high structural differentiation* (Lawrence. & Lorsch, 1967) tend to have greater conflict among the groups of specialists. Each group may adhere to a set of institutional norms that is different from other groups, producing competitive commitment.

Thus far, interests and values have been described as discrete precipitators of pressure for change. In fact, they are linked (line c in Figure 1). One of the crucial attributes of values is that they become taken for granted and can serve to mute or temper expressions of dissatisfaction. That is, dissatisfied groups may not recognize that the prevailing template is a cause of that disadvantage. The role of value commitments is thus critical. because there is no direct link from interests to radical change, only from interests to convergent change. Radical change will occur only if interests become associated with a competitive or reformative pattern of value commitment (line x in Figure 1).

For example, management consultants within the accounting industry became cuckoos in the nest, increasingly producing greater shares of revenues and growth and yet being denied full reward (in terms of remuneration and status) for doing so. As a consequence, management consultants in several accounting firms became dissatisfied with their interests and began to question the organizational assumptions of how things were done (i.e., their commitment to the template-in-use, which favored the accounting profession, began to erode). The pattern of value commitments in these firms thus moved from a status quo pattern to a competitive pattern, *even though institutional pressures were unchanged*. In most accounting firms, an uneasy tension arose between accountants and consultants, as each profession became committed to different archetypes (*Business Week*, 1988; Stevens, 1991).

Competitive commitments, we have noted, can occur even in tightly coupled institutional fields, but if the degree of structuring is relatively modest, ideas and possibilities become more easily expressed and articulated. In situations of inconsistent cues and the absence of reinforcing institutional mechanisms, alternative templates develop and can be promoted by dissatisfied groups (line c in Figure 1). In this way, market and institutional contexts interact with interests and value commitments to create pressures for change. Pressures from the market and institutional contexts, in other words, precipitate the desire for change and, as we have stressed, the intensity of the pressure will likely vary from one organization to the next. The *direction* of change or of inertia is a function of the pattern of value commitments. Thus,

> Hypothesis 10: Radical change will occur if the pattern of value commitments is competitive or reformative, irrespective of market and institutional pressures.
>
> Hypothesis 11: Interest dissatisfaction will lead to radical change only if it is associated with a competitive or reformative pattern of value commitments. Otherwise, interest dissatisfaction will precipitate convergent change.
>
> Hypothesis 12: A reformative or competitive pattern of value commitments is more likely to occur (a) in peripheral rather than core organizations, (b) in organizations with a complex portfolio of product/services, and (c) in institutional contexts that are loosely structured.

In terms of the speed of change, it seems reasonable to suggest that a reformative commitment will be associated with revolutionary change because of the absence of resistance. A competitive change, in contrast, is more likely to be evolutionary in pacing as resistance occurs. Thus,

> Hypothesis 13: A reformative commitment will be associated with revolutionary change.
>
> Hypothesis 14: A competitive commitment will be associated with evolutionary change.

Enabling Dynamics

Internal pressures for change, in summary, derive from interest dissatisfaction and the pattern of value commitments. The intensity of those pressures is the outcome of their links with market and institutional contexts. Radical change, however, will occur only in conjunction with an appropriate "capacity for action" and supportive power dependencies. Capacity for action and power dependencies are the *enablers* of radical change.

A political model of organizational change that starts from groups with different beliefs and interests must incorporate power (Clegg, 1975). Groups use favorable power dependencies to promote their interests (line k in Figure 1): As Fligstein (1991: 313) noted, "Change . . . can only occur when either a new set of actors gains power or it is in the interest of those in power to alter the organization's goals." An interesting twist in recent studies has been recognition that radical change cannot be nakedly prescribed, but it is better accomplished by appeals to normative "visions" (Collins & Porras, 1991).

Organizationally defined groups vary in their ability to influence organizational change because they have differential power. Some groups and individuals are listened to more keenly than others. Some have more potential or less potential for enabling or resisting change. The relations of power and domination that enable some organizational members to constitute and recreate organizational structures according to their preferences thus becomes a critical point of focus (Pettigrew, 1985; Ranson et al., 1980). The operation of values and interests can be conceptualized and understood only in relation to the differential power of groups.

There is a reciprocal relationship between power dependencies and value commitments (line d in Figure 1). Any normative scheme implies differential access to and control over key decision processes within organizations. In this sense, the prevailing archetypal template in an organization "gives" power to some groups and not to others. To the extent that groups recognize this link, it will be to their advantage to promote the norms of that template. Positions of power also can be used to buttress the prevailing archetype (Covaleski & Dirsmith, 1988). Hence, in a situation of a competitive pattern of commitment, radical change would not be the likely outcome, *unless* those in positions of privilege and power were in favor of the proposed change. Power dependencies either enable or suppress radical organizational change (line e in Figure 1).

It is when one explores the role of power that the interaction of market and institutional contexts becomes apparent. The resource dependence model (Pfeffer & Salancik, 1978) expresses one logic of change by tracking the effects that changes in market pressures have on power dependencies within the organization, which then enables change. That is, the precipitator of change (for the resource dependence model) is the market context, which, when the salience of some issues is raised relative to others (e.g.. the need for aggressive marketing of accounting services), alters the relative power of groups (line t in Figure 1) within the organization (e.g., marketing specialists. vis-à-vis audit practitioners) and leads to the executive succession link. The new executive then introduces radical organizational change. That is, the resource dependence model posits a direct link among market changes, power dependencies, and radical change. (This line of reasoning is consistent with Fligstein's, 1991, account of the evolution of the M-Form organization in the United States. Fligstein showed how changes in the market context led to changes in the relative power of functional groups within the American corporation—specifically, from manufacturing, to sales and marketing, to finance—which led to shifts in strategy and organization from the vertically integrated undiversified form, through the related diversification model, to the unrelated diversified corporation.)

We suggest that the resource dependence thesis complements the institutionalist perspective, because market pressures may well reconfigure power relationships within an organization. However, the institutional context also acts to configure the power and status of groups within an organization (line i in Figure 1) and not necessarily in a manner consistent with market exigencies. For example, accounting firms universally have accorded high status and power to professional accountants, compared to both consultants and professional managers (e.g., marketing and human resource) despite the growing importance of these latter professions in generating revenue. In other words, the institutional context might *nullify* pressures from the market context. Alternatively, institutional pressures, even without market pressures, might shift power dependencies in favor of groups that prefer an alternative template to the existing one.

Most important, shifts in power dependencies, whether brought about by market and/or institutional pressures, will produce radical change *only* if the dominant coalition recognizes the weaknesses of existing template arrangements *and* is aware of potential alternatives. That is, users of the resource dependence model *assume* that there exists a competitive value commitment within an organization (which may not be correct) and also assume that as changes in power occur, alternative templates will be introduced. In our model, we propose that there are *several* possible patterns of commitment, which means that changes in power dependencies within an organization may or may *not* lead to radical change. Enabling power dependencies will lead to radical change *only* if alternatives to the prevailing archetypal template are *known*. This is similar to Fligstein's note that "shocks or instability still require that actors develop a set of solutions based on their interpretation of the shock, which will generally reflect their position in the organization and the interests of that position" (1991: 316). Change occurs where power dependencies *combine* with either a competitive or reformative pattern of value commitments. Thus,

> Hypothesis 15: Radical change will not occur without an enabling pattern of power dependencies combined with either a reformative or competitive pattern of value commitments.

The second enabling dynamic—capacity for action—is the ability to *manage* the transition process from one template to another, which has three aspects.[6] Radical change cannot occur without the organization's having sufficient *understanding* of the new conceptual destination, its *having* the skills and competencies required to function in that new destination, *and* its having the ability to manage how to get to that destination. The importance of capacity for action has been alluded to by other authors (Carnall, 1990; Clarke, 1994; Fombrun, 1992; Nadler & Tushman, 1989; Tichy, 1983). Nadler and Tushman (1990), in their discussion of leadership and change, distinguished among three sets of leadership activities: charismatic (envisioning, energizing, and enabling), instrumental (structuring, controlling, and rewarding), and institutional (ensuring changes stick). These activities have to be performed by multiple actors. In our terms, capacity for action embraces both the *availability* of these skills and resources within an organization *and* their *mobilization*. Mobilization, in this sense, is the act of leadership. Capacity for action is also consistent with Amburgey and colleagues' work (1993), which showed that organizations with recent experience of change are more likely to attempt further change. In our terms, experience increases capacity for action. Capacity for action is an enabling dynamic because without it radical organizational change will not occur (line g in Figure 1). By itself, however, capacity for action would not be expected to precipitate change—there has to be a motivation for change driven by the precipitating dynamics. Thus,

> Hypothesis 16: Radical change will not occur without a sufficient enabling capacity for action combined with either a reformative or competitive pattern of value commitments.

Capacity for action may influence the speed by which radical change is accomplished. A clear understanding of the new destination and of how to get to that destination may give an organization the confidence to push ahead rapidly with change. On the other hand, lack of clarity and lack of expertise may promote lack of sureness and slower, almost experimental steps. Thus,

> Hypothesis 17: High capacity for action will be associated with revolutionary change.

Figure 1 shows capacity for action linked to the market context (line h). The recruitment of marketing and human resource management specialists into accounting firms illustrates how the market context is connected to capacity for action. Recruited ostensibly to introduce new marketing and human resource management practices, these employees often brought to the organization the experience of governing and organizing in fundamentally different ways. Their previous employment in corporate organizations (e.g., Proctor and Gamble) introduced within the accounting firm an awareness of alternatives to the professional partnership form of organization and a knowledge of how to operate such alternatives. Similarly, the experience of mega mergers undertaken in response to perceived market pressures (Greenwood, Hinings, & Brown, 1994) provided accounting firms with significant experience of managing change. In other words, developments in the market context can have an impact on the level of capacity for action in the organization, increasing the *possibility* for radical change.

The capacity for action might also be shaped or constricted by the institutional context (line j in Figure 1). Deeply embedded firms may be prevented by the institutional context from developing an action capability. That is, organizations that are centrally located within an institutional context may be less likely to develop the specialties and competencies of an alternative archetype. Peripheral organizations, in contrast, may develop these competencies because they are less fully socialized by the context. In this sense, the institutional context can act to limit the development of capacities for action in some but not all organizations. However, the context itself might fundamentally shift and articulate a new template, as occurred in Hinings and Greenwood's (1988a) study of municipal governments in the United Kingdom. In this scenario, the institutional context serves to articulate the need for new competencies and promotes the development of capacities for action.

Power dependencies and capacity for action are necessary but not sufficient conditions for radical organizational change. By themselves they will not lead to radical change, but they can and do enable or constrain it.

Conclusions

In the introduction to a collection of articles that summarized the current position of institutional theory, DiMaggio and Powell (1991a: 27) stated that "one of the principal goals of this volume is to address head on the issues of change, power, and efficiency." They saw these three issues as neglected in the historical development of institutional theory. Our emphasis has been to develop the contribution of institutional theory in order to understand radical organizational change. In particular, we have focused on the interplay of contextual forces and intraorganizational dynamics.

In making this attempt we also see ourselves dealing with two other points made by DiMaggio and Powell (1991a). The first point relates to the relationship between the "old" and "new" institutionalism (DiMaggio & Powell, 1991a: 11–5, especially Table 1.1). New institutionalism, these authors suggest, is primarily related to organizations-in-sectors, whereas the old institutionalism centers on the individual organization. We have attempted to build something of a bridge over this gap, both posing and trying to answer the question: What are the processes by which individual organizations adopt and discard templates for organizing, given the institutionalized nature of organizational fields (neo-institutionalism)? We have tried to show how the external processes of deinstitutionalization have to be understood (organizations-in-sectors) *together with* the internal dynamics of interpretation, adoption, and rejection by the individual organization.

We have also suggested that the understanding of radical change requires more than an analysis of the institutional arena or sector. There must be a concern with patterns of value commitments, power dependencies, interests, and capacity for action within the organization. Typically, institutional theorists have informed our thinking about the nature of institutional pressures toward conformity and uniformity. They have emphasized the exogenous nature of change, which emanates from the realm of ideas and legitimacy. But understanding change is about understanding variations in response to the same pressures, which can only be done by analyzing the features of organizations that produce adoption and diffusion rather than resistance and inertia. The model of radical change developed here is about such understanding.

Future Directions

A central message of this article is that to understand the incidence and pacing of radical organizational change, in particular the differences between organizations as they respond to apparently similar contextual pressures, it is necessary to understand the play of intraorganizational dynamics. These dynamics have been defined as the pattern of value commitments, dissatisfaction with interests, power dependencies, and capacities for action. These dynamics are largely the product of ongoing studies into the accounting and law industries (Hinings, Brown, & Greenwood, 1991) and earlier work into the municipal sector in the United Kingdom (Hinings & Greenwood, 1988a; Greenwood & Hinings, 1993). An obvious requirement is examination of the applicability of the ideas to other sectors, especially less mature and less homogeneous sectors. Our suggestions at this point, however, concern the role of the dynamics in explaining why organizations respond differently to the same contextual pressures, which implies comparisons between organizations in the same sector. Two questions seem particularly important:

1. What are the determinants of a reformative or competitive commitment (i.e., of normative fragmentation)?
2. How do precipitating and enabling dynamics interact to respond to increasing pressures for change?

What are the determinants of normative fragmentation? Central to the framework is that radical organizational change will occur only if the pattern of value commitments is either reformative or competitive (*and* associated with favorable power dependencies and capacity for action). A key research endeavor, therefore, would be to identify what increases the likelihood of a competitive or reformative pattern of value commitments. In which situations is the researcher likely to find erosion of commitment to a prevailing archetype-in-use and development of either a competitive or reformative commitment? What are the precursors of "deinstitutionalization" (Oliver, 1992) *within* the organization?

Numerous factors might cause such an erosion of commitment, and several are noted in the change literature. In particular, performance problems and crises act to trigger political dissensus over existing arrangements and permit groups less committed to prevailing practices to more legitimately raise and promote alternative perspectives (e.g., Child & Smith, 1987; Oliver, 1992; Pettigrew, 1985; Tushman & Romanelli, 1985). This occurred in the local government sector of the United Kingdom, as groups such as corporate planning units and administrative departments espoused the logic of corporate planning as preferable to traditional professional practices as a means of handling social and urban problems (Hinings & Greenwood, 1988a). The pressure for change was contextual but amplified by groups within the organization. The push of management consultants within accounting firms for a new approach to management, in contrast, was the product of the dissatisfaction with their share of organizational resources (compensation *and* influence) rather than poor organizational performance. Precipitators of change, as we have shown previously, can be contextually or internally driven.

Hinings and Greenwood (1988b) pointed out that it may be quite unusual for the market and institutional contexts to produce strong, consistent signals about the need to change to a new archetype. There may well be conflictive institutional signals. This conflict currently can be seen in the law sector, where there are not only pressures from the market for organizations to become more corporate but also pressures from regulators for organizations to remain groups of autonomous professionals. The result may well be high levels of competitive commitment and the existence of sedimentation of values, structures, and systems (Cooper et al., In press) and unresolved excursions (Hinings & Greenwood, 1988a).

A second possible cause of erosion of commitment to a prevailing archetype would be increasing representation of ideas and views within the workforce, which cause "normative fragmentation" (Oliver, 1992: 575). An increasing representation of ideas and views would follow changes in the composition of the workforce (e.g., increasing diversity, turnover of personnel), changes in the portfolio of activities (e.g., the development of new "products," such as management consultancy within accounting firms), and changes in specializations within the organization (e.g., the growth of forensic accountants). The common theme of these developments is that organizational differentiation, both in the way that Lawrence and Lorsch (1967) and Blau and Schoenherr (1971) used those terms, increases the possibility of normative disagreement.

Even a superficial reflection on the forces that might lead to normative fragmentation indicates that some contemporary organizations are likely to experience fragmentation. Most studies of the future workplace stress increasing workforce diversity (e.g., Boyett & Conn, 1991; Krahn & Lowe, 1993). Similarly, the trend of contemporary society has been toward increased specialization of knowledge and thus of occupational differentiation. (For example, the accounting profession has for some years operated through four major divisions: audit and accountancy, insolvency/corporate recovery, tax, and small/ independent business.) Recently, however, new specializations have developed—forensic accounting, environmental accounting, and so forth (Lawrence, 1993). These trends suggest that more organizations will experience normative fragmentation and dissensus than may have been the case previously.

This line of research would explore the extent to which increasing workforce diversity and structural differentiation is associated with normative fragmentation and thus competitive value commitments. Sites where this might occur would include companies growing through mergers and/or acquisitions or organizations that have recently experienced severe market/funding challenges. In these situations, it would be informative to trace how the changes either "produce" or "do not produce" competitive commitments.

Hinings and Greenwood (1988a), from their studies of municipalities, found that change occurs more quickly where organizational size is small, where there is low structural and task complexity, and where mergers and amalgamations sharpen the search for a relevant organizational form to cope with the new situation.

How do precipitating and enabling dynamics interact in response to pressure for change? Understanding the causes or conditions of normative fragmentation is a preface to the key task of uncovering how precipitating and enabling dynamics interact in response to pressures for change. At present, we know relatively little of these interactions. Probably, both detailed case comparisons and broader examinations are required.

Kikulis and colleagues (1995) and Fligstein (1991) gave indications of how broad surveys might provide insights into the play of intraorganizational dynamics. Kikulis and colleagues examined the adoption by sports organizations in Canada of a more professional approach to management. They showed how some organizations were much earlier movers than others and how some retained more traditional practices. By comparing these three groups (early movers, late movers, and nonmovers) it would be possible to ascertain whether the timing or absence of movement was a function of differences in precipitating and/or enabling dynamics. Given a large enough sample, researchers could gain insights into whether early movers tend to be those with reformative commitments (i.e., no resistance) and that have a high capacity for action, or whether there is a range of configurations conducive to early movement (e.g., competitive commitment plus favorable power dependencies plus capacity for action). Similarly, it would be interesting and not too difficult to observe whether late movers begin either with unfavorable precipitating dynamics (e.g., status quo commitment) or with unfavorable enabling dynamics (inappropriate power dependencies and/or low capacity for action). Furthermore, late movers would provide some understanding of what it is that changes in order that change can occur (is it a shift from reformative to competitive commitments, or reconstitution of power dependencies, or acquisition of capacity for action?).

Fligstein's (1991) study of the adoption of strategies of diversification and associated organizational structures, by the *Fortune* 100, from 1919 to 1979, provides another example of how some of the basic parameters of the intraorganizational dynamics might work. He showed that organizational change followed appointment of a CEO from a different functional background, who provided a "new view of the firm's strategy" (Fligstein, 1991: 334). Appointment of a CEO with a new functional background reflected a redistribution of power dependencies. From our perspective, it is the analysis of historical data of large numbers of organizations and the comparison of early and late movers that enables some insights to be gleaned into the workings of intraorganizational dynamics.

Comparative studies that have the scope of those conducted by Fligstein (1991) and by Kikulis and colleagues (1995) can only go so far in uncovering the role of intraorganizational dynamics. Equally necessary are more detailed studies that permit the careful assessment of nonlinear processes. Previously we suggested that the study of sports organizations could have identified first movers and late movers and traced differences between them. But to fully understand (a) *how* new archetypal templates are uncovered, (b) *which* organizational actors uncover them (e.g., by monitoring other organizations), and (c) how they are *used* within the organization requires the case study method. Is it usually disadvantaged groups (i.e., those with high interest dissatisfaction) that are sensitive to new archetypal possibilities, or is it those with greater exposure to contextual change? For example, are members who cross the organizational boundary and come into contact with new ideas and possibilities more likely to question existing archetypal arrangements, or is it those who are dissatisfied with their share of scarce and valued organizational resources?

There is also the need to understand how new ideas become legitimated within the organization. In situations of a competitive commitment, power dependencies determine which view prevails. However, how do groups that do not have power but prefer change obtain sufficient power to effect change? Do these groups convince others that changes are desirable? From an institutional perspective, changes brought about by the latter method are more likely to be sustainable. But under what circumstances and for what reasons do privileged groups accept radical change and diminished privilege?

Our previous work on the adoption of new archetypes in a highly institutionalized sector, British local government, provides some insight into how these dynamics might play out (Hinings & Greenwood, 1988a). The development of movement away from an archetype depends on the existence of an articulated alternative organizational form and a leadership and power structure that allows alternatives to be expressed in arenas that matter. For an organization to move toward an institutionally novel archetype, a high degree of organizational capacity is needed. That initial movement toward a new archetype is consolidated through a spreading of commitment to change and a gradual tightening of the power structure. However, in an organization, a high value propensity to change and a low resistance to change are sufficient conditions to produce structural change, regardless of context, interests, and power.

In contrast, change can be blocked through a concentrated power structure (elite domination) and/or an active, transformational leadership that continuously reaffirms the importance, efficiency, and effectiveness of the current archetype. Sufficient conditions for no change become a high resistance to change by a dominant coalition with a concentrated power structure, regardless of the values held by the non-elite.

Both of the (big) questions we have raised as future directions generate questions of relationship with two other areas of theorizing, organizational cognition and organizational learning. Scott (1991) suggested that the new institutionalism places more emphasis on cognitive factors than did the old institutionalism, and DiMaggio and Powell (1991a: 29) characterized our previous work as institutional theory with "a cognitive spin." Walsh (1995: 311) reviewed the field of managerial and organizational cognition, examining the "representation, use, and development of the content and structure of knowledge structures." Clearly, in dealing with value commitments and capacity for action, we are dealing with knowledge structures and hypothesizing that radical change involves changes in them. A link can be made to the questions that Walsh (1995: 307) raised, such as "the rate, magnitude, and locus of knowledge structure change" that is involved in radical organizational change and the extent to which institutional redefinition involves changes in knowledge structures. Certainly, the possible overlap of conceptual categories should be examined.

Similarly, organizational change requires organizational learning. Not only is there a link between change and learning but there is also a link between learning and cognition. Change from one archetype to another involves designing new organizational structures and systems, learning new behaviors, and interpreting phenomena in new ways. How do group members acquire and learn these new behaviors and interpretations? How are the values contained in new archetypes diffused to different groups in the organization?

Methodological Assumptions

The previous discussion has touched on a number of methodological themes that require amplification. The first is that archetypes exist and can be observed empirically: indeed, they have to be because they are the basis of the definition of radical change. The means of uncovering and measuring archetypes has been provided in other studies (Greenwood & Hinings, 1993). It involves immersion within an institutional sector such that a detailed understanding is obtained of that sector. In particular, the different interpretive schemes have to be unearthed, and the implications they have for organizational design must be worked through.

Using archetypes as the basis for understanding the dynamics of organizational change means that research has to be based on populations of organizations that are subject to similar institutional pressures. Most likely this will be situated in an industry sector, something which is quite usual in institutional theory. However, it could be based on organizational sets from different sectors, in which there are similar pressures for organizational change, for example, the work exemplified in Fligstein's (1991) study of the *Fortune* 100. Large-scale comparative studies such as those of Tolbert and Zucker (1991), Fligstein (1991), Baum and Oliver (1991), Palmer et al. (1993), and Kikulis et al. (1995) are necessary to establish (a) the changes in structures and systems that have taken place in a population and (b) the ways in which these changes coincide with institutional templates. However, these studies are limited in what they can show regarding the processes and dynamics through which individual organizations either do or do not adopt new institutional prescriptions.

As a result, detailed comparative case studies are required, and, if possible, in real time. There are a number of reasons for case studies. First, the conceptual framework that we have outlined in Figure 1 contains a number of concepts that are difficult to measure (e.g., power, interests, and leadership). These concepts tend to be highly sensitive to context in their operation. Second, radical organizational change takes place over lengthy periods of time. A number of researchers (cf. Nadler & Tushman, 1989; Miller, 1990; Huber & Van de Ven, 1995) suggested that not less than three years is required to gain some indication of how such changes are proceeding. To establish the interactions of precipitating and enabling dynamics in the light of institutional pressures over such time periods requires careful case study research (cf. Barley, 1986).

The third and very important point is that it is likely that radical organizational change is the product of processes that are oscillatory and iterative. Much organization theory operates, at least implicitly, with a linear perspective. That is, outcomes (in the present instance, radical organizational change) are treated as the product of sequential interactions between a given set of variables. In one sense, Figure 1 is laid out in this fashion. However, radical organizational change occurs in ways that are iterative, and close attention to such iterations is required to truly understand the dynamics. It is improbable that a single, simple line of causation will explain the occurrence of radical change. Instead, different combinations of interactions between precipitating and enabling dynamics are possible.

Concluding Remarks

It would be possible to elaborate further possible research directions, each based on some combination of the elements of the intraorganizational dynamics. However, our concluding and key points are somewhat more general. The first is that institutional theory does, in fact, have a contribution to make to understanding organizational change, which goes beyond the ideas of inertia and persistence. But this can only happen when the old and the new institutionalism are combined in a neo-institutionalist framework. As so often happens in the evolution of theoretical areas, there is a period of movement away from starting points, a process of rediscovery of those starting points, and the "reincorporation" of these points into existing theory. We have attempted to start this task.

A second key point is that it is when theorists research the *interaction* of organizational actors with institutionalized contexts that they will find new directions. It is in the intersection of two forces that explanations of change and stability can be found. On the one hand, institutions are shapers of organizational arrangements (Jepperson, 1991; Jepperson & Meyer, 1991). On the other hand, key actors in organizations articulate views of strategy and have the power to implement that view (Fligstein, 1991). As Brint and Karabel (1991: 343) put it, "we wish to make a distinction, then, between the sociology of institutional forms and the sociology of institutional change." This distinction raises questions of why particular archetypal templates are chosen over possible alternatives and why those templates change in particular directions over time.

This observation leads directly to our final key point. The action of values, interests, power, and capacity within an organization must be brought into play. *However,* this action has to be located in the groups that make up any particular organization. Action is not disembodied; it comes from organizational actors who have positions, skills, commitments, and histories that are primarily found in the groups of which those actors are members. Change and stability are understood through the ways in which organizational group members react to old and new institutionally derived ideas through their already existing commitments and interests and their ability to implement or enforce them by way of their existing power and capability.

Notes

1. Scott and Meyer (1991: 108) referred to the institutional context as the *societal sector*, defined "to include all organizations within a society supplying a given type of product or service together with their associated organizational sectors: suppliers, financiers, regulators, and so forth."

2. In our model, we assume that "archetypes" exist within institutional sector. As such the model presented is of archetype diffusion, not archetype creation.

3. Our model and hypotheses are based on the existence of archetypes, so they are about the adoption of those archetypes by individual organizations, which for those organizations is radical, second-order change. Here we do not deal with the creation of archetype within sectors. For a preliminary approach to this latter issue, see Hinings, Greenwood, Brown, and Cooper (In press).

4. We believe that groups often do *not* recognize how the existing organizational design is disadvantageous to their interests. Indeed, the most effective way by which advantaged groups maintain their privileged positions is through an organizational archetype that is regarded by disadvantaged groups as legitimate (Walsh et al., 1981).

5. We deliberately use what may seem like a conceptual oxymoron (indifferent commitment) to represent the situation of group members being neither for nor against particular changes. It also represents the midpoint that occurs on all scales used to measure values.

6. Some institutional studies have shown how organizations may make significant changes to their structures, in order to meet institutional expectations, but without fundamentally affecting the technical processes at the core of the organization (e.g., Meyer & Rowan, 1977). Such changes would not require a capacity for action because the new structures are not intended to accomplish anything (other than legitimacy). In our model, radical changes are intended to be substantive, not a matter of appearance, hence the need for "capacity for action."

References

Amburgey, T. L., Kelly, D., & Barnett, W. P. 1993. Resetting the clock: The dynamics of organizational change and failure. *Administrative Science Quarterly*, 38: 51–73.

Astley, W. G., & Van de Ven, A. 1983. Central perspectives and debates in organization theory. *Administrative Science Quarterly*, 28: 245–273.

Barley, S. R. 1986. Technology as an occasion for structuring: Evidence from observations of CT scanners and the social order of radiology departments. *Administrative Science Quarterly*, 31: 78–108.

Barnett, W. P. & Carroll, G. R. 1987. Competition and mutualism among early telephone companies. *Administrative Science Quarterly*, 32: 400–421.

Baron, J. P., Dobbin, F., & Jennings, P. D. 1986. War and peace: The evolution of modern personnel administration in the U.S. industry. *American Journal of Sociology*, 92: 250–283.

Bartunek, J. M. 1984. Changing interpretive schemes and organizational restructuring: The example of a religious order. *Administrative Science Quarterly*, 29: 355–372.

Baum,J., A. & Oliver, C. 1991. Institutional linkages and organizational mortality. *Administrative Science Quarterly*, 36: 187–218.

Blau, P. M. 1974. *On the nature of organizations*. New York: Wiley.

Blau, P. M., & McKinley, W. 1979. Ideas, complexity and innovation. *Administrative Science Quarterly*, 24: 200–219.

Blau, P. M. & Schoenherr, R. A. 1971. *The structure of organizations*. New York: Basic Books.

Boyett, J. H. & Conn, H. P. 1991. *Workplace 2000: The revolution reshaping American business*. New York: Dutton.

Brint, S. & Karabel, J. 1991. Institutional origins and transformations: The case of American community colleges. In W. W. Powell & P. J. DiMaggio (Eds.), *The new institutionalism in organizational analysis*, 337–360. Chicago: University of Chicago Press.

Buchko, A. A. 1994. Barriers to strategic transformation. In P. Shrivastava, A. Huff, & J. Dutton (Eds.), *Advances in strategic management*, vol. 10: 81–106. Greenwich, CT: JAI Press.

Burns, L R. & Wholey, D. R. 1993. Adoption and abandonment of matrix management programs: Effects of organizational characteristics and interorganizational networks. *Acedemy of Management Journal*, 36: 106–138.

Business Week. 1988. An identity crisis at Arthur Andersen. October 24: 34.

Carnall, C. A. 1990. *Managing change in organizations*. New York: Prentice Hall.

Carroll, G. R, Goodstein, J., & Gyenes, A. 1988. Organizations and the state: Effects of the institutional environment on agricultural cooperatives in Hungary. *Administrative Science Quarterly*, 33: 233–256.

Child, J., 1972. Organization structure, environment and performance: The role of strategic choice. *Sociology*. 6:1–22.

Child, J., & Smith, C. 1987. The context and process of organizational transformation. *Journal of Management Studies*. 24: 585–593.

Clark. B. R. 1960. *The open-door colleges: A case study*. New York: McGraw-Hill.

Clark, B. R. 1972. The organizational saga in higher education. *Administrative Science Quarterly*. 17: 178–184.

Clarke, L. 1994. *The essence of change*. New York: Prentice Hall.

Clegg, S. 1975. *Power, rule and domination*. London: Routledge & Kegan Paul.

Collins, J. C., & Porras, J. I. 1991. Organizational vision and visionary organizations. *California Management Review*. 34(1): 30–52.

Cooper, D. J., Hinings, C. R., Greenwood, R., & Brown, J. L. In press. Sedimentation and transformation in professional service firms. *Organization Studies*.

Covaleski, M. A.. & Dirsmith, M. W. 1988. An institutional perspective on the rise, social transformation, and fall of a university budget category. *Administrative Science Quarterly*. 33: 562–587.

D'Aunno, T., Sutton, R. I., & Price, R. H. 1991. Isomorphism and external support in conflicting institutional environments: A study at drug abuse treatment units. *Academy of Management Journal*. 34: 636–681.

D'Aveni, R. A. 1994. *Hyper-competition*. New York: Free Press.

Davis, G. F. 1991. Agents without principles? The spread of the poison pill through the intercorporate network. *Administrative Science Quarterly*. 36: 583–613.

Davis, G. F., & Powell, W. W. 1992. Organization-environment relations. In M. D. Dunette & L. M. Hough (Eds.), *Handbook of industrial and organizational psychology:* 315–376. Palo Alto, CA: Consulting Psychologists Press.

DiMaggio, P. J. 1991. Constructing an organizational field as a professional project: U.S. art museums, 1920–1940. In W. W. Powell & P. J. DiMaggio (Eds.), *The new institutionalism in organizational analysis:* 287–292. Chicago: University of Chicago Press.

DiMaggio, P. J., & Powell, W. W. 1983. The iron cage revisited: Institutional isomorphism and collective rationality in organizational fields. *American Sociological Review*. 48:147–160.

DiMaggio, P. J. & Powell. W. W. 1991a. Introduction. In W. W. Powell & P. J. DiMaggio (Ed.), *The new institutionalism in organizational analysis:* 1–38. Chicago: University of Chicago Press.

DiMaggio. P. J.. & Powell. W. W. 1991b. The iron cage revisited: Institutional isomorphism and collective rationality in organizational fields. In W. W. Powell & P. J. DiMaggio (Ed.), *The new institution in organizational analysis:* 63–82. Chicago: University of Chicago Press.

Dougherty, D. 1994. Commentary. In P. Shrivastava, A. Huff & J. Dutton (Eds.), *Advances in strategic management*. vol. 10: 107–112. Greenwich. CT: JAI Press.

Drazin, R. & Van de Ven, A. H. 1985. Alternative forms of fit in contingency theory. *Administrative Science Quarterly*. 30: 514–539.

European Accounting Focus. 1994. KPMG Incorporation. October: 1.

Fligstein, N. 1985. The spread of the multidivisional form among large firms, 1919–1979. *American Sociological Review*, 50: 377–391.

Fligstein. N. 1991. The structural transformation of American industry: An institutional account of the causes of diversification in the largest firms, 1919–1979. In W. W. Powell & P. J. DiMaggio (Eds.), *The new institutionalism in organizational analysis:* 311–336. Chicago: University of Chicago Press.

Fombrun, C. 1992. *Turning points: Creating strategic change in corporations*. New York: McGraw-Hill.

Galaskiewicz, J., & Wasserman, S. 1989. Mimetic and normative processes within an interorganizational field: An empirical test. *Administrative Science Quarterly*. 34: 454–479.

Ghemawat, P. 1991. *Commitment: The dynamic of strategy*. New York: Free Press.

Gilson, R. J., & Mnookin, R. H. 1988. Coming of age in a corporate law firm: The economics of associate career patterns. *Stanford Law Review*, 41: 567–595.

Greenwood, R., Cooper, D. J., Hinings, C. R., & Brown, J. L. 1993. Biggest is best? Strategic assumptions and actions in the Canadian audit industry. *Canadian Journal of Administrative Sciences*, 10: 308–321.

Greenwood, R., & Hinings, C. R. 1988. Design archetypes, tracks and the dynamics of strategic change. *Organization Studies*, 9: 293–316.

Greenwood, R., & Hinings, C. R. 1993. Understanding strategic change: The contribution of archetypes. *Academy of Management Journal*. 36: 1052–1081.

Greenwood, R., Hinings, C. R., & Brown, J. L. 1990. The P2-form of strategic management: Corporate practices in the professional partnership. *Academy of Management Journal* 33:725–755.

Greenwood, R., Hinings, C. R., & Brown, J. L. 1994. Merging professional service firms. *Organization Science*. 5: 239–257.

Hannan, M. T., & Freeman, J. H. 1989. *Organizational ecology*. Cambridge, MA.: Harvard University Press.

Haunschild, P. R. 1993. Interorganizational imitation: The impact of interlocks on corporate acquisition activity. *Administrative Science Quarterly*. 38: 564–592.

Haveman, H. A. 1993. Follow the leader Mimetic isomorphism and entry into new markets. *Administrative Science Quarterly*. 38: 564–592.

Hinings, C. R., Brown, J. L., & Greenwood, R. 1991. Change in an autonomous professional organization. *Journal of Management Studies*. 28: 375–393.

Hinings, C. R., & Greenwood, R. 1988a. *The dynamics of strategic change*. Oxford. England: Basil Blackwell.

Hinings, C. R. & Greenwood. R. 1988b. The normative prescription of organizations. In L. Zucker (Ed.), *Institutional patterns and organizations:* 53–70. Cambridge, MA: Ballinger.

Hinings, C. R., Greenwood, R., Brown, J. L., & Cooper, D. In press. Organizational change: The role of archetypes, environmental dynamics and institutional ideas. *Scandinavian Journal of Management*.

Hrebiniak, L. G., & Joyce, W. F. 1985. Organizational adaptation: Strategic choice and environmental determinism. *Administrative Science Quarterly*, 30: 336–349.

Huber, G. P. & Van de Ven, A. H. (Eds.). 1995. *Longitudinal field research methods*. Thousand Oaks, CA: Sage.

Jepperson, R. L. 1991. Institutions, institutional effects, and institutionalism. In W. W. Powell & P. J. DiMaggio (Ed.). *The new institutionalism in organizational analysis:* 143–163. Chicago: University of Chicago Press.

Jepperson, R. L., & Meyer, J. W. 1991. The public order and the construction of formal organizations. In W. W. Powell & P.J. DiMaggio (Eds.), *The new institutionalism in organizational analysis:* 204–231. Chicago: University of Chicago Press.

Johnson, G. 1987. *Strategic change and the management process*. Oxford, England: Basil Blackwell.

Kanter, R. M. 1983. *The change masters*. New York: Simon & Schuster.

Kikulis, L. M., Slack, T., & Hinings, C. R. 1995. Sector-specific patterns of organizational design change. *Journal of Management Studies,* 32: 87–100.

Krahn, H. J., & Lowe, G. S. 1993. *Work, industry and Canadian society* (2nd ed.). Scarboro: Nelson.

Lawrence, P. R., & Lorsch, J. W. 1967. *Organization and environment*. Boston: Harvard Business School Press.

Lawrence, T. 1993. *Institutional entrepreneurs in emerging industries*. Unpublished doctoral dissertation, University of Alberta.

Leblebici, H., Salancik, G. R., Copay, A., & King, T. 1991. Institutional change and the transformation of interorganizational fields: An organizational history of the U.S. radio broadcasting industry. *Administrative Science Quarterly*, 36: 333–363.

Ledlord, G. E., Mohrman, A. M., & Lawler, E. E. 1989. The phenomenon of large-scale organizational change. In A. M. Mohrman, S. A. Mohrman, G. E. Ledford, T. G. Cummings, E. E. Lawler, & Associates (Eds.), *Large-scale organization change*: 1–31. San Francisco: Jossey-Bass.

Meyer, A. O., Tsui, A. S., & Hinings, C. R. 1993. Guest co-editors' introduction: Configurational approaches to organizational analysis. *Academy of Management Journal*, 36: 1175–1195.

Meyer, J. W., & Rowan, B. 1977. Institutionalized organizations: Formal structure as myth and ceremony. *American Journal of Sociology*, 83: 340–363.

Meyer, J. W., Scott, W. R., & Deal, T. 1983. Institutional and technical sources of organizational structure. In H. D. Stein (Ed.), *Organization and the human services:* 151–178. Philadelphia: Temple University Press.

Michels, R. 1962. *Political parties*. New York: Collier Press.

Miller, D. 1981. Towards a new contingency approach: The search for organizational gestalts. *Journal of Management Studies,* 18: 1–26.

Miller, D. 1982. Evolution and revolution: A quantum view of structural change in organizations. *Journal of Management Studies.* 19: 131–151.

Miller, D. 1987. Strategy making and structure: Analysis and implications for performance. *Academy of Management Journal.* 30: 7–32.

Miller, D. 1990. *The Icarus paradox*. New York: Harper Collins.

Miller, D., & Friesen, P. H. 1984. *Organizations: A quantum view*. Englewood Cliffs, NJ: Prentice Hall.

Mintzberg, H. 1983. *Structure in fives: Designing effective organizations*. Englewood Cliffs, NJ: Prentice Hall.

Mohrman, A. M., Mohrman, S. A., Ledford, G. E., Cummings, T. G., & Lawler, E. E., III. 1989. *Large-scale organizational change*. San Francisco: Jossey-Bass.

Nadler, D. A., Shaw, R. B., Walton, A. E., & Associates, 1995. *Discontinuous change*. San Francisco: Jossey-Bass.

Nadler, D. A., & Tushman, M. L. 1989. Organizational frame bending: Principles for managing reorientation. *Academy of Management Executive.* 3(3): 194–203.

Nadler, D. A. & Tushman, M. L. 1990. Beyond the charismatic leader: Leadership and organizational change. *California Management Review.* 32: 77–79.

Oliver, C. 1991. Strategic responses to institutional processes. *Academy of Management Review.* 16: 145–179.

Oliver, C. 1992. The antecedents of deinstitutionalization. *Organization Studies.* 13: 563–588.

O'Reilly, C. A., Main, B. G., & Crystal, G. S. 1988. CEO compensation as tournament and social comparison: A tale of two theories. *Administrative Science Quarterly*, 33: 257–274.

Ouchi, W. G. 1980. Markets, bureaucracies, and clans. *Administrative Science Quarterly.* 25: 129–141.

Palmer, D. A., Jennings, P. D. & Zhou, X. 1993. Late adoption of the multidivisional form by large U.S. corporations: Institutional, political, and economic accounts. *Administrative Science Quarterly.* 38: 100–131.

Payne, R. L. & Mansfield, R. 1973. Relationship of perceptions of organizational climate to organizational structure, context and hierarchical position. *Administrative Science Quarterly*. 8: 515–526.

Payne, R. L. & Pugh. D. S. 1976. Organizational structure and climate. In M. D. Dunnette (Ed.), *Handbook of industrial and organizational psychology*: 1125–1173. Chicago: Rand McNally.

Perrow, C. l985b. Overboard with myth and symbols. *American Journal of Sociology*. 91:151–155.

Perrow, C. 1979. *Complex organizations: A critical essay* (2nd ed.). New York: Random House.

Pettigrew, A. 1985. *The awakening giant*. Oxford, England: Basil Blackwell.

Pettigrew, A. 1987. Context and action in the transformation of the firm. *Journal of Management Studies*. 24: 649–670.

Pfeffer, J. 1981. *Power in organizations*. Boston: Pitman.

Pfeffer, J. 1992. *Managing with power*. Boston: Harvard Business School Press.

Pfeffer, J., & Salancik, C. H. 1978. *The external control of organizations: A resource dependence perspective*. New York: Harper & Row.

Pheysey, D. C., Payne, R. L., & Pugh, D. S. 1971. Influence of structure at organizational and group levels. *Administrative Science Quarterly*. 19: 61–73.

Powell, W. W. 1991. Expanding the scope of institutional analysis. In W. W. Powell, & P. J. DiMaggio (Eds.), *The new institutionalism in organizational analysis*: 183–203. Chicago: University of Chicago Press.

Powell, W. W. 1993. *The social construction of an organizational field: The case of biotechnology*. Paper presented at the Warwick–Venice Workshop on perspectives on strategic change. University of Warwick.

Powell, W. W., & DiMaggio, P. J. (Eds.). 1991. *The new institutionalism in organizational analysis*. Chicago: University of Chicago Press.

Public Accounting Report. 1995. Annual survey of national accounting firms. May 31:1.

Ranson, S., Hinings, C. R., & Greenwood, R. 1980. The structuring of organizational structures. *Administrative Science Quarterly*, 25: 1–7.

Scott, W. R. 1987. The adolescence of institutional theory. *Administrative Science Quarterly*, 32: 493–511.

Scott, W. R. 1991. Unpacking institutional arguments. In W. W. Powell, & P. J. DiMaggio (Eds.). *The new institutionalism in organizational analysis*: 164–182. Chicago: University of Chicago Press.

Scott, W. R. 1994. Institutions and organizations: Toward a theoretical synthesis. In W. R. Scott & J. W. Meyer (Eds.), *Institutional environments and organizations*: 55–80. Thousand Oaks, CA: Sage.

Scott, W. R., & Meyer, J. W. 1983. The organization of societal sectors. In J. W. Meyer & W. R. Scott (Eds.), *Organizational environments, Ritual and rationality*: 129–153.

Scott, W. R., & Meyer, J. W. 1991. The organization of societal sectors: Propositions and early evidence. In W. W. Powell & P. J. DiMaggio (Eds.), *The new institutionalism in organizational analysis*: 108–140. Chicago: University of Chicago Press.

Scott, W. R., & Meyer, J. W. (Eds.). 1994. *Institutional environments and organizations*. Thousand Oaks, CA: Sage.

Selznick, P. 1949. *TVA and the grass roots*. Berkeley: University of California Press.

Selznick, P. 1957. *Leadership in administration*. Evanston, IL: Row, Peterson.

Slack, T. 1994. Institutional pressures and isomorphic change: An empirical test. *Organization Studies*. 15: 803–827.

Stevens, M. 1991. *The big six*. New York: Simon & Schuster.

Tichy, N. M. 1983. *Managing strategic change*. New York: Wiley.

Tichy, N. M., & Devanna, M. A. 1986. *The transformational leader*. New York: Wiley.

Tolbert, P. S. 1985. Resource dependence and institutional environments: Sources of administrative structure in institutions of higher education. *Administrative Science Quarterly*. 30: 1–13.

Tolbert, P. S. & Zucker, L. G. 1983. Institutional sources of change in the femoral structure of organizations: The diffusion of civil service reform. 1880–1935. *Administrative Science Quarterly*, 28: 22–39.

Tushman, M. L., Newman, W., & Romanelli, E. 1986. Convergence and upheaval: Managing the unsteady pace of organization evolution. *California Management Review*. 29: 29–44.

Tushman, M. L. & Romanelli, E. 1985. Organizational evolution: A metamorphosis model of convergence and reorientation. In L. L. Cummings & B. M. Staw (Eds.). *Research in organizational behavior*. vol. 7: 171–222. Greenwich, CT: JAI Press.

Van de Ven, A. H., & Poole, M. S. 1988. Paradoxical requirements for a theory of organizational change. In R. E. Quinn & K. S. Cameron (Eds.), *Paradox and transformation*: 330–341. Cambridge, MA: Ballinger.

Virany, B., Tushman, M. L., & Romanelli, E. 1992. Executive succession and organization outcomes in turbulent environments: An organization learning approach. *Organization Science*. 3: 72–91.

Walsh, J. P. 1995. Managerial and organizational cognition: Notes from a trip down memory lane. *Organization Science*. 6: 280–321.

Walsh, K., Hinings, C. R., Greenwood, R. & Ranson, S. 1981. Power and advantage in organizations. *Organization Studies*, 2:131–152.

Wholey, D., & Burns, L. R. 1993. Organizational transitions: Form changes by health maintenance organizations. In S. Bacharach (Ed.), *Research in the sociology of organizations*: 257–293. Greenwich, CT: JAI Press.

Wilson, D. C. 1994. *A strategy of change*. New York: Routledge.

Zucker, L. G. 1977. The role of institutionalization in cultural persistence. *American Sociological Review*, 42: 726–743.

Zucker, L. G. 1983. Organizations as institutions. In S. B. Bacharach (Ed.), *Research in the sociology of organizations*: 1–42. Greenwich, CT: JAI Press.

Zucker, L. G. 1987. Institutional theories of organizations. *Annual Review of Sociology*, 13: 443–464.

Zucker, L. G. (Ed.). 1988. *Institutional patterns and organizations: Culture and environment*. Cambridge, MA: Ballinger.

Royston Greenwood is the AGT Professor in the Department of Organizational Analysis, Faculty of Business, at the University of Alberta. He received his Ph.D. degree from the University of Birmingham, England. His research interests include the management of professional service organizations, strategic organizational change, and the institutional specificity of design archetypes.

C. R. Hinings is the Thornton A. Graham Professor of Business in the Department of Organizational Analysis, University of Alberta. His research interests include the management and dynamics of strategic organizational change, with particular reference to professional service firms.

THE INVISIBLE WORKERS

JUDY SZEKERES
UNIVERSITY OF SOUTH AUSTRALIA, AUSTRALIA

Where are university administrators placed in texts that are centred around universities? There appears to be either a total confusion in terminology about administration or a complete disregard for administrators' work but in most cases administrative staff in universities are largely invisible.

This paper explores a range of texts (academic, government reports and novels) and provides a picture of how the work of administrators and the staff themselves are represented. It examines how they are positioned in the organisation as people, as workers and as power brokers and provides a starting point for further research into how these workers see themselves. "There has been remarkably little systematic study of the roles and values of university administrative staff" (McInnis, 1998, p. 161). Maybe it is time that this was remedied.

Who Are the Administrators?

It is important to be clear about who the *administrators* are. Blau (1970) states that one of a number of distinctive characteristics of a bureaucracy is that there is a specialised administrative staff whose role it is to maintain the organisation. These staff contribute only indirectly to goal achievement in the organisation. While this is a generalist idea about what administration might be, Gumport and Pusser point out "there is no uniform definition in higher education research of what constitutes administration or administrative functions" (1995, p. 496). The formal distinction that the Australian government makes is that academic staff are "those members of staff employed to perform the functions of teaching-only, research-only or teaching-and-research" while administrative staff are described as "not one of the three types specified for the academic classification, they are classed as having a non-academic classification" (Pickersgill, van Barneveld & Bearfield, 1998, p. 1).

Rather than be described by what they are not, I define administrative staff as being those people in universities who have a role that is predominantly administrative in nature, i.e. their focus is about either supporting the work of academic staff, dealing with students on non-academic matters or working in an administrative function such as finance, human resources, marketing, public relations, business development, student administration, academic administration, library, information technology, capital or property. This paper looks only at white-collar workers and also is not concerned with those who are termed by some as "academic managers".

Why Be Concerned?

In the 1995 Higher Education Management Review conducted by the federal government, the reviewers noted a need to focus on general staff issues:

> Because it is the academic staff who are seen as delivering teaching programs or undertaking research there has been a traditional tendency for universities not to take as seriously as they might the people

management issues facing that group of people currently known, perhaps somewhat unsatisfactorily as general staff. (Hoare, 1995, p. 76)

I am clearly not alone in believing administrative staff are an invisible group. Castleman and Allen are quite blunt about why they think this invisibility has come about:

> General staff have been a neglected part of the higher education workforce. The literature and data on academic staff has vastly overshadowed that on general staff. General staff issues are often overlooked by university managers. Yet general staff are an important and varied category of the higher education workforce. It is also a feminised workforce which perhaps partly explains its lack of visibility. (Castleman & Allen, 1995, p. 65)

More to the point, while women make up the majority of general staff, they are disproportionably in the lower-level positions (Barker & Shatifin, 1995; Castleman & Allen, 1995; McLean, 1996; Turnbull, 1995). There are various writers who perceive an invisibility, such as McLean (1996), Moodie (1995) and Elson-Green (2002). Ian Dobson finds that "the propensity for general staff to be ignored is high" and quotes Maree Conway:

> references to general staff in most government publications appear to be afterthoughts and it is a sobering reminder for administrators and other general staff that their role may be taken for granted or may not be viewed as critical to the work of their employing institutions. (Dobson, 2000, p. 204)

Conway is the greatest public advocate for administrative staff in Australia's universities. In her critique of the Commonwealth government's 2002 "Crossroads" paper she points out that the term "staff" normally means "academic staff".

> There is now more to the teaching and learning experience, and more to the running of universities, than academic staff and their work, but the silence in public forums and reports about the role of administrative staff in universities is deafening. (Conway, 2002)

And I give Conway the final word on this:

> I am not sure whether the issue is that [university administrators] . . . are invisible or whether they have been included in the amorphous "university management" and by inference are therefore part of the problem. (Conway, 2003)

To understand the "problem" Conway refers to here, there needs to be some understanding of the current contexts universities are operating in. What changes have occurred that have affected the work of people within them? And what are the discourses operating in the sector that might affect the representations of administration staff?

The Current Context and Discourses

The university sector in Australia has been beset by changes over the last twenty years which are closely linked to changes in the public sector. As pressure increases on governments to account for the expenditure of public funds, they respond either by privatising government institutions or by increasing the reporting requirements of those few public institutions left. Higher education has seen the effect of both of these as student numbers have increased while government funds have decreased. Universities are essentially being privatised through stealth. At the same time, despite their decreasing dependence on the public purse, the increase in accountability requirements is felt at all levels in the institutions.

In many texts, this increase of surveillance and privatisation is characterised as a *neoliberal agenda*. It exhibits itself through public institutions remodelling themselves along commercial lines and falls into a general discourse, *corporate managerialism*. This discourse has a number of separate elements including: an increase in managerial control (managerialism); competing with each other in the market place (marketisation); being under greater scrutiny while having greater devolved responsibility (audit); and generally modelling their structures and operations on corporate organisations (corporatisation).

Managerialism

As the neoliberal agenda has accountability as one of its most important tenets, the need for managerial control rises in importance. Not only is there a need for constant detailed reporting, but senior managers have to be able to successfully account for all activities in the organisation. One way to achieve this is to have clear reporting lines in the organisation and sophisticated reporting tools that can capture all the necessary data and churn it back out in various combinations. As the latter of the choices seems quite elusive, despite universities spending enormous sums implementing sophisticated IT systems, most institutions have adopted a modicum of both.

To achieve what looks like line management, not only do structures change, but people at the top of the chain of command assume greater importance as they are held responsible for the performance of those reporting to them. The term "managerialism" refers to this increased importance of senior management staff (both academic and general) and decision-making processes that shift from collegiate to hierarchical.

> "New managerialism" represents a way of trying to understand and categorise attempts to impose managerial techniques more usually associated with medium and large "for profit" businesses, onto public sector and voluntary organisations. (Deem, 1998, p. 49)

There are numerous writers who ask whether managerialism is appropriate for universities or who rail against its effect, such as Dearlove (1998), Tourish (2000), Birnbaum (2000), Davis (2002), Meek (1995) and Samier (2002a). There are also some writers who see possibilities; for instance Geoff Sharrock (2000) contends that, while the balance of power between faculty and administration has shifted, arguing for collegiality and against management sets up a false dichotomy. Without a new prescription for the current challenges that face all public sector organisations, Sharrock suggests the critics of managerial-ism are simply rejectionists.

Meyer (2002) suggests that what is happening in universities can be better understood if considered within the context of wider changes in all organisations. In particular, ideas about cultural fit and networks positioned between structure and culture could be helpful. He suggests that the traditional collegial management structures are unsuited to the current climate in higher education.

The managerialist discourse is likely to impact on representations of general staff in a number of ways—if efficiency takes precedence over process, for instance, then administrators would be in the ascendance. Private-sector management practices might be in conflict with the cultural norms of academic staff; however, they would mostly be acceptable and useful in the delivery of administrative services. In this climate, general staff might be seen to have more power and credence than academic staff. Certainly, their day-to-day activity and culture would be more in tune with managerialist behaviours. In this discourse, texts written from the point of view of academics are likely to take a cynical and critical view of the general staff and almost certainly of the senior management.

Corporatisation

"Corporatisation" is closely linked to managerialism. Rather than being about how universities are managed, it refers to how universities are organised. In this discourse the discussions are about universities adopting corporate structures and modes of operation. It focuses on how managers organise work to meet the requirements of government, how they try to make universities look and behave like corporations in the hope of increasing efficiency and accountability and the acceptance and accolades of government.

Erica McWilliam (2000), for instance, suggests that the corporation has become the *approved* model in the Western world for institutional living. The implications of this have been: the need to make up for funding shortfalls by the development of commercial activities (or being *enterprising*); the use of strategic planning; the adoption of quality assurance processes and business re-engineering; and the use of the market as a controlling mechanism. She does not necessarily see these changes as entirely detrimental, although most of the other writers who touch on corporatisation see it as creating serious problems for the university.

Cynthia Hardy perceives that universities have borrowed techniques from the corporate world such as strategic planning, performance indicators and programme evaluation. She thinks that an erroneous underlying assumption is that all players are bound by a common goal. Strategic planning, difficult at the best of times, is even more difficult in a university where "goals are more ambiguous, authority is less hierarchical and power is more decentralised" (Hardy, 1991, p. 129). Kennedy (1995) agrees that some of the corporate values fit uncomfortably into the university environment, where accountability is seen as much less important than independence, individuality and creativity.

Eugenie Samier (2002b) sees the signs of corporatisation in the development of new administrative units in the university such as marketing, business development, human resources, international, IT, etc. Historically, the adoption of corporate principles can be seen as the direct result of the Dawkins reforms. "Operating on the assumptions that the private sector was the ultimate model of efficiency . . . corporate management is the emergent form of organisation" (Coleman, 1995, p. 106). And there is a clear change in language—" 'line managers', 'customers' and 'products' begins to displace the academic language of deans, students and courses" (Parker & Jary, 1995, p. 324).

All of these writers, other than McWilliam, agree that the corporate model fits uncomfortably with universities. However, these writers are focused entirely on the effect on the academic side of the institution. Like managerialism, corporatisation has administrators and managers as its instrumentalists. As administrative departments grow in number and size, this is seen to be using up resources that could better be used by academic departments and is simply increasing evidence of corporatisation rather than possibly better managing the university. The likely effect on representations of administrative staff is similar to the managerialist discourse; to increase the apparent importance of administrative staff.

Marketisation

"Marketisation" is based around the idea that universities are now operating in a *marketplace* where they compete with each other for students, government funding and the corporate dollar. The most obvious of these is the student market, where universities compete both locally and internationally. There is little question that this marketplace arises from the neoliberal agenda that demands mass education but constantly withdraws funds.

There are numerous writers who focus on marketisation and there are a number of subthemes apparent in this discourse. Marginson (1997), Niklasson (1996) and Meek (1995) see universities as operating only in quasi-markets. These markets can be seen as deceptive, based on

> an ideological commitment to a rational and limited neo-liberal notion of the wealth creation value of the market, leading to the individualisation of society and a culture of blame and wastefulness. (Gibbs, 2001, p. 85)

The instrumental view of education that comes with marketisation leads to "the commodification of education in skills packages to be managed through market principles rather than under pedagogical guidance" (Gibbs, 2001, p. 87).

Another subtheme is the student as consumer. In this discourse the student's role in the university shifts from a joint participator in the education process to a consumer of educational goods as described by Marginson (1993), Barnett (2000), Scott (1997) and Sharrock (2000). Yet another subtheme is that of the efficiency of the market as described by Power (1997) and Harper (2000). While these writers are not convinced that markets have improved efficiency, there are some who contend that markets have downright failed in higher education. Watson (2000), Scott (1999), Latham (2001) and Prichard and Willmott (1997) all believe this is the case. Finally, Larry Forbes (2002) suggests that education is too sophisticated a commodity to be treated like a product and left to the vagaries of the market based on a "greengrocer retail business model".

Marketisation is likely to have the following effects in representations of administrative staff: added to the core of administration in most universities is now a marketing unit, staffed by professional marketers, publicists and fundraisers, who are likely to understand the university's activities as *products* in a way foreign to most academics; and, as ideas about customer service take ascendancy, the sort of administrative staff who live at the frontline dealing with students is likely to change. Many universities are now setting up "one-stop shops" where students can get all their administrative needs met. This often takes the service deliverers a step away from where they were previously, embedded in schools and departments. This results in these administrative staff being at arm's length from the academic staff and is likely to result in representations that show a lack of understanding of their work.

Audit (or Total Quality Management—TQM)

The final relevant discourse is that of audit and TQM. The idea of audit has shifted markedly over the last twenty years. It originated from the world of accounting, but all activities are now considered auditable. However, universities have traditionally been self-regulating. Academic staff have behaved as most professions do, having virtually no regulations over their work but rather self-regulating through behavioural norms embedded in their discipline. This is slowly changing as government funding begins to depend on universities achieving particular outcomes and imposing external audits into the system.

The rise of quality assurance and external audit of control systems is a way of enhancing control: "there is a commitment to push control further into organisational structures, inscribing it within systems which can then be audited" (Power, 1997, p. 42). Quality assurance is not necessarily about high standards but rather about uniform and predictable standards. In public institutions where there is no easily measurable product, the management systems become the mark of effectiveness. The rise of an audit culture has had a profound effect on academic life, since it can be seen to rely on "hierarchical relationships and coercive practice" (Shore & Wright, 2000, p. 62) and what is being audited is not the real frontline action but the bureaucratic paper trails imposed on it. Birnbaum (2000) also sees the inapplicability of audit and TQM to universities given that its aim is to reduce variation in output and that customer satisfaction is the essential criterion for quality measurement. The problem here is that students are not only customers, but also producers and product. Therefore outcomes are dependent on them at least as much as teaching staff.

Generally, it can be said that many of the writers focused on corporatisation and managerialism also touch on audit as it pertains to universities. As an idea, audit is so embedded in the neoliberal agenda that it is sometimes difficult to separate out. This discourse is also likely to affect representations of administrative staff, for two reasons. The first is, as with marketisation, that there are now often administrative units in universities which focus on audit and quality assurance, and growing external audit processes foisted on universities take up copious amounts of time and energy for little perceived benefit. The need to expend resources in what is essentially a bureaucratic exercise always raises questions about whether the money could have been better spent elsewhere. The second is the perception of power that audit gives administrators. If it is they who are seen as the instruments of quality assurance, then one might expect to see representations that place them as very powerful in the organisation with the right to praise or condemn.

Themes from the Texts

Out of a number of texts that do comment on administrative staff in universities, there do emerge a few common themes. I would reiterate that in most writing about universities the administrative staff are not mentioned at all or given scant regard. In fact it is clear from the literature scanned above that the vast majority of writers focus on the effects of the discourses on academic work and staff. However, the few representations that do appear fall into the following themes: a confusion of terms; different working conditions; menial workers; and taking over.

Theme 1: Confusion of Terms

In many of the texts there is confusion about the term "administration". This confusion masks the fact that for many of these writers administrative staff are largely invisible. For these writers, "administration" is in fact senior management. In most universities this group of people are mainly made up of academic rather than administrative staff, including the vice chancellor and the next layer of management. Their work at this level is about management and leadership (Coaldrake & Stedman, 1998) rather than teaching or research, but, rather than describing it as such, the majority of writers term it "administration" with pejorative connotations in most cases.

To set the tone for this theme, Michael Wilding's satirical comment on university life, *Academia Nuts*, has as its main characters caricatures of professors among a group of highly ambitious femocrats. Each chapter is a vignette describing a different aspect of university life. Wilding clearly means senior management when he refers to the "administration". He has one chapter entitled "Administrative Matters", which is the only one where the voice of his characters drops out and his own voice takes over. The final section of this chapter is a long and bitter soliloquy about "the administration":

> What sort of academic would become a Dean, a Pro-Vice-Chancellor, a Vice-Chancellor? . . . The people who occupy these administrative roles are self-selected failures from the academy they presume to control. (Wilding, 2002, p. 201)

> They are not even trained administrators, they are not even professional managers. They are the Judases of the profession. (2002, p. 202)

It is also interesting that Wilding himself recognises that a change in terminology has taken place, even though he clearly has not internalised it. After a discussion about what "they" are doing to academics, one character finally asks the question:

> "And this they?" asked Dr Bee.

> "The ministry. The administration."

> "Senior Management you have to call it now," said Lancaster. (Wilding, 2002, p. 112)

Sometimes a confusion in terms appears within single articles. For instance, de Boer and Goedegebuure were trying to understand decision-making processes in higher education and distributed a questionnaire to "top administrators" in seven European countries. It becomes clear that in fact this was a group of vice chancellors. However, later in the same article they point out that the only thing that all institutions could agree on was that "Administrative support staff are little involved in the decision-making process" (de Boer & Goedegebuure, 1995, p. 42).

Mike Shattock (2000) provides an insight into how this terminology is currently in the process of change. University administration, he asserts, has been transformed by government pressures and institutional competition, and the scale of expansion has "turned administration into management" (p. 34). Maree Conway (2000) talks at length about the importance of the naming of administrators. She sees that the terms "administration" and "administrators" are used in such a variety of ways that it is difficult to find a generic definition that everyone might understand and accept.

Finally, one of the only novels based in universities where this confusion of terms never surfaces is Mary-Rose MacColl's *No Safe Place* (1995). This novel has a university registrar as its central character who deals daily with the senior managers of the institution as well as a vast array of other administrators and academics and at no point does the author create confusion about the term "administrator". However, this should be no surprise—MacColl was a senior administrator herself so has a respect for the complexity and importance of administration.

Theme 2: Different Working Conditions

A second construction that appears in a number of texts is that administrative staff have different working conditions to academic staff (in most cases better ones). This can be characterised as administrative staff getting more pay, better parking spots, lower workloads, etc.

MacColl (1995) touches on this in a discussion among senior management about a suggested change in working conditions for senior managers. It is proposed that these staff be offered a five-year contract in lieu of tenure. The vice chancellor says, "the trick is to make sure the [salary] loading is high enough to be attractive to people" (MacColl, 1995, p. 133). Despite the many changes to the higher education sector over the last twenty years and the well-documented casualisation of academic staff, the fact is that permanent academic staff still have a strong expectation of ongoing employment and the university has to take the drastic step of shutting down a discipline to remove academic staff while administrative staff on these sorts of contracts are not only open to similar threats of downsizing but have to win their jobs over again at the end of their five-year contracts.

Wilding (2002) takes a somewhat different view of the differences between academic and general staff conditions. In one vignette he describes how the editor of the university's newspaper gets a year's leave, even though he is not an academic, so that the university can restructure the area and make his job redundant:

> "How can non-academic staff get study leave?" asked Dr Bee.
>
> "Must have signed a good contract." (Wilding, 2002, p. 196)

This reflects Wilding's dismissal of administrative staff. In fact this staff member was being royally shafted by the university management who were making his job redundant while he was on leave. However, instead of sympathising, Wilding's characters can only gripe about the fact that general staff shouldn't have access to the same study leave provisions as academic staff and suggest that the only way general staff can access these conditions is to manipulate their employment contracts in their own favour.

Others see a different sort of disparity between conditions for general and academic staff. Academic staff can be seen to have "better career opportunities and more flexible working arrangements" (McLean, 1996, p. 24), particularly since administrative staff can gain promotion only by leaving their jobs and when they do win a promotion position their duties increase in complexity and responsibility. However, academic staff who move up the hierarchy of levels do not necessarily get increased responsibilities.

From a recent Australian Vice Chancellors Committee (AVCC) data report on staffing from 1994 to 2002 the following statistics show quite a dramatic change in the levels of the majority of administrative staff. In 1994, 54% of general staff were appointed at level 4 and below and only 19% at level 7 and above. In 2002, only 36% were at level 4 and below and 27% at level 7 and above (AVCC, 2003). What this shows is that, as corporate managerialism takes hold and the importance of administrative staff increases, their visibility in the organisation increases. This results in some writers making assumptions about the privileges afforded them. It is clear from the figures above that, indeed, the level of complexity and responsibility of the work of administrative staff has increased (as position levels increase according to these parameters). What is not possible to glean from these statistics is whether the working conditions for administrative staff have improved relative to academic staff. I would argue that both sides have experienced an increase in workload, stress and pressure and the intrusion of what might seem trivial administration into their working lives.

Theme 3: Menial/Women's Work

One of the most common representations of administrative staff is that of menial workers or administration being *women's work*. There are some writers who make this link overtly and others who make it subtly, usually depending on whether they approach the question from a feminist perspective. Sometimes it emerges through a juxtaposition with high-ranking professional males.

The higher education environment can be seen as devaluing the skills of women. In an institution where the emphasis is on academic qualifications,

> female administrative, secretarial, and clerical staff are not perceived as having any status, power or authority: they are only there to support the academics and students. (Barker & Shatifin, 1995, p. 237)

Some see both casual academics and administrative staff as invisible, particularly since both groups are predominantly women: "the reality is that, were it not for the two groups . . . our universities simply could not function" (Coaldrake & Stedman, 1998, p. 155). This recognition is not evident in the following authors. Wilding (2002) only once refers to an administrative staff member in terms of the work they might do, which consists of booking rooms and typing notices. For David Lodge (1988) the sum total of administrative staff are departmental secretaries whose roles are about keeping the head of department organised and taking phone messages for other academics.

Smiley's (1995) more recent picture of American university life, *Moo*, provides a more detailed portrait of an administrator. Lorraine Walker, the provost's secretary, is a major character, with her work role drawn as *just* a secretary engaged in fairly menial work, but involved in quite complex power relationships. Mrs Walker is clearly seen as the person who gets things done. For example, when one academic wants something done, he addresses a memo to the provost's office, but sends it to Mrs Walker:

> Of course, this memo would never reach the provost, nor was it intended to. The Chairman stuck it into a campus envelope and addressed it to Mrs Walker, Provost's office. That was how you got anything done on this campus. (Smiley, 1995, p. 41)

There are some opposite constructions of the menial female worker appearing in later texts. In Mac-Coll's book *No Safe Place* (1995), which is the only novel to have a senior female administrator as a character, all the other senior administrators in it (such as the finance manager, the public affairs director and the university lawyer) are male. Barry Maitland's *Babel*, a detective novel in which an academic is murdered, has as a character the President's Executive Officer, who is described as "a young man in a sharp suit" (2002, p. 15). Similarly as in MacColl's novel, the only male administrators Smiley (1995) describes are very senior—a budget specialist and a human resources manager. They are depicted as high level, well paid and unattached to the decisions they make about budget cutbacks.

This construction of administrative workers—relatively powerless women doing menial tasks—is a rather old-fashioned one. It may have had its place in the 1970s but seems anachronistic today. Administrative roles are, on the whole, more complex, more specialised, more skilled and more responsive to the external environment than these constructions of administrators. Even the secretarial role itself has changed from how it is depicted in many of these texts, now requiring a high level of skill in information management and external liaison. And the construction has its opposite in a few recent texts—powerful males making ruthless decisions. I would suggest that the corporate managerialist discourse results in this latter construction.

Theme 4: Taking Over/Too Powerful

The construction of administrators taking over and increasing in power is the one most closely linked to the current discourses in higher education. It should be no surprise that this construction appears only in the more recent texts (since 1995). The reason for this could be that an emphasis on technical staff is one of the main characteristics of the current corporatisation of the university:

> contributing in large part to the proportional increase in administrative staff, the creation of new administrative units in university organizational structure . . . and the growth of professional programs, usually at the expense of traditional academic faculties. (Samier, 2002b, p. 40)

McInnis suggests that previously "administrative staff were considered powerless functionaries" but they now "increasingly assume high-profile technical and specialist roles that impinge directly on academic autonomy and control over the core activities of teaching and research" (1998, p. 166). He also sees an underlying tension between what he describes as the two groups of professionals in the university:

> with the old (academics) perhaps losing ground in authority and status and the new (administrators) making strong claims for recognition as legitimate partners in the strategic management of the university. (McInnis, 1998, p. 168)

There is certainly a perception among a number of these writers that there has been a substantial growth in numbers of administrative staff relative to academic staff. Some writers perceive "striking increases in the ratio of administrative to academic staff in recent years" (Coady, 2000, p. 17) and "the rapid rise in non-academic staff number relative to academic staff numbers" (Patience, 2000,

p. 33). In fact this is not the case. The true increase in the ratio in fact amounts to a decline in 0.2% from 1993 to 2002 if looking at classification and an increase of 1.3% in the same period if looking at function (DEST, 2002).

Barry Maitland (2002) also has an academic character who voices similar concerns as the detective interviews him. The academic describes himself as the person who asks,

> the questions about where the money's going and how come they can recruit so many bloody administrative assistants when we can't afford tutors and library books. (Maitland, 2002, p. 36)

This perception of the growth in administrative staff, which is clearly not a reality according to the statistics, may be related to the fact that it is the number of senior administrators that has grown. In many universities there would now be senior administrators in faculties who would be fully fledged members of committees with voting rights. While they are valued by their academic managers for their professional administrative skills, as clearly shown in Maddy McMaster's (2002) paper on how deans and their faculty managers work together, they might not be viewed in this light by other academic staff. And as the university tries to address the agendas arising from the discourses discussed earlier in this paper, there are a number of senior roles taken by specialist administrators which become vitally important to the successful management of their institutions. What has increased is visibility.

If this contention about the perception of growing numbers is right, then closely linked is the growing power of administrators. There are two sides to constructions about administrative power—one is about overt or position power, and the other is about tacit power. The tacit power representation is strongest in those texts which construct administrative workers as low-level females. Jane Smiley's *Moo* is full of descriptions of the tacit power of women in secretarial positions. The provost's secretary, Mrs Walker, is pictured as someone who knows the workings of the university better than anyone. However, she would only reveal exactly what was asked for. As a result, the provost "spent a portion of his time meditating over what he might ask Mrs Walker and how he might phrase the question" (Smiley, 1995, p. 21). Here, knowledge is seen as power and withholding knowledge makes Mrs Walker more powerful than she might otherwise seem.

In writing about position power, many writers see that the balance between faculty and administration has shifted:

> This shift entails an encroachment on the assumed freedoms of academic life and fuels resentment toward institutional authority. Even worse, it lends power to non-academics, many of whom are otherwise seen as second-class citizens in their own institutions. (Sharrock, 2000, p. 155)

As an interesting twist Lee and Bowen (1971) found that academics tended to confound the lives of administrators, but at the same time they vastly over-estimated the power that administrators had. The new hybrid institution, part bureaucratic corporation, part traditional university "both threatens academic values and generates significant institutional confusion in relation to the appropriate culture, governance and purposes of the universities" (Miller, 2000, p. 112). In this climate, academic issues become resource, financial and market issues and this results in a shift of power from academics to administrators.

And this, I would contend, is the nub of the matter in the construction of administrators taking over. Their numbers haven't changed markedly in relation to academic staff but their roles and place in the university have. The neoliberal agenda that turns universities into corporations, operating in markets and being constantly audited requires a much more active and professional administration. For many, this increased visibility translates into power. The administrative staff may be just as downtrodden as academic staff, they may feel the burden of the agendas just as acutely, but they are also the instruments of them.

Conclusion

Many of the constructions of administrative workers in the texts above have arisen out of the corporate managerialist discourses. The increase in the number of administrative units in the university has been directly related to the increase in government surveillance and demands for universities to be managed more like the private sector. While this increase in units has not, in fact, resulted in a serious increase in the proportion of administrative staff in universities, it has resulted in a shift of staff away from the departmental or school level where they would have been perceived by the academic community as providing the greatest service. As a result, much of the writing about universities which has emanated from the academic community has displayed erroneous perceptions. Many of these writers have been dismissive of administrative staff and their roles in the institution or have ignored them altogether.

When provided at all, many of the constructions of administrative staff demonstrate false impressions of what administrators actually do, the nature of their work and their relationship to the organisation. The commonly held view of the administrator as a secretary who is at the beck and call of academics to do typing, distribute notices and take phone calls does not capture the complexity of their roles today, the skills required, or the difficulty of where they sit in the organisation. It is a telling statistic that, out of all the texts focused on universities which I have examined, only a small percentage concentrate any serious energy on the life of administrative staff (14 out of over seventy). For most of the authors, administrative staff continue to be pretty much invisible. In the second half of this paper, where I have concentrated on the constructions that do exist in the literature, I can only find 23 authors who write about administrative staff at all and in at least half of these the constructions provided are negative, demeaning or, at the very least, problematic. I think this gap in the literature is calling out to be filled. I would agree strongly with McInnis (1998), Moodie (1995), McLean (1996), Dobson (2000) and, loudest of all, Maree Conway—the stories of administrative staff need to be heard.

References

AVCC (2003). *Non-academic staff by classification and gender, 1994–2002* (http://www.avcc.edu.au/policies _activities/resource_analysis/key_stats/index.htm).

Barker, J., & Shatifin, N. (1995). Lack of recognition for women in traditional female jobs in higher education. Paper presented at the "Women Culture and Universities: A Chilly Climate?" conference, University of Technology Sydney, Sydney, 19–20 April.

Barnett, R. (2000). *Realizing the university in an age of supercomplexity.* Buckingham: Society for Research into Higher Education and Open University Press.

Birnbaum, R. (2000). *Management fads in higher education.* San Francisco: Jossey-Bass.

Blau, P. (1970). Weber's theory of bureaucracy. In D. Wrong (Ed.), *Max Weber*, 141–146. New Jersey: Prentice Hall.

Castleman, T., & Allen, M. (1995). The forgotten workforce: Female general staff in higher education. *Australian Universities Review*, 1, 65–69.

Coady, T. (2000). *Why universities matter.* Sydney: Allen & Unwin.

Coaldrake, P., & Stedman, L. (1998). *On the brink. Australia's universities confronting their future.* St Lucia: University of Queensland Press.

Coleman, K. (1995). Women and corporate management in universities. Paper presented at the "Women Culture and Universities: A Chilly Climate?" conference, University of Technology Sydney, Sydney, 19–20 April.

Conway, M. (2000). What's in a name? Issues for ATEM and administrators. *Journal of Higher Education Policy and Management, 22*(2), 199–201.

Conway, M. (2002, July 24–30). General staff at the crossroads. *Campus Review*, p. 24.

Conway, M. (2003, February 12–18). Same old, same old . . . *Campus Review*, p. 24.

Davis, R. (2002). *The unbalancing of Australian universities.* Retrieved January 9, 2003 from < http://www.ouw.edu.au/arts/sts/bmartin/dissent/documents/sau/Davis.pdf >.

Dearlove, J. (1998). The deadly dull issue of university "administration"? Good governance, managerialism and organising academic work. *Higher Education Policy, 1*(1), 59–79.

De Boer, H., & Goedegebuure, L. (1995). Decision-making in higher education: A comparative perspective. *Australian Universities Review*, 1, 41–47.

Deem, R. (1998). "New managerialism" and higher education: The management of performance and culture in universities in the United Kingdom. *International Studies in the Sociology of Education, 8*(1), 47–69.

DEST (2002). < http://www.dest.gov.au/highered/statpubs.htm > . Table 3, Table 13 and Table 14.

Dobson, I. (2000). "Them and us": General and non-general staff in higher education. *Journal of Higher Education Policy and Management, 22*(2), 203–210.

Elson-Green, J. (2002, October 9–15). How the heirarchies interact. *Campus Review*, p. 24.

Forbes, L. (2002, October 16). Unis are not supermarkets. *The Australian*, p. 24.

Gibbs, P. (2001). Higher education as a market: A problem or solution? *Studies in Higher Education, 26*(1), 85–94.

Gumport, P. J., & Pusser, B. (1995). A case of bureaucratic accretion. *Journal of Higher Education, 66*(5), 493–520.

Hardy, C. (1991). Pluralism, power and collegiality in universities. *Financial Accountability and Management, 7*(3), 127–142.

Harper, H. (2000). New college hierarchies? Towards an examination of organizational structures in further education in England and Wales. *Educational Management and Administration, 28*(4), 433–445.

Hoare, D. (1995). *Higher education management review*. Canberra: AGPS.

Kennedy, D. (1995). Another century's end, another revolution for higher education. *Change, 27*(3), 8–16.

Latham, M. (2001). The network university. *Journal of Higher Education Policy and Management, 23*(1), 7–17.

Lee, E., & Bowen, F. (1971). *The multicampus university, A study of academic governance*. New York: McGraw Hill.

Lodge, D. (1988). *Nice work*. London: Penguin.

MacColl, M.-R. (1995). *No safe place*. Sydney: Allen & Unwin.

Maitland, B. (2002). *Babel*. Sydney: Allen & Unwin.

Marginson, S. (1993). *Education and public policy in Australia*. Cambridge: Cambridge University Press.

Marginson, S. (1997). The limits of market reform. In J. Sharpham & G. Harman (Eds.), *Australia's future universities*, pp. 157–173. Armidale, NSW: University of New England Press.

McInnis, C. (1998). Academics and professional administrators in Australian universities: Dissolving boundaries and new tensions. *Journal of Higher Education Policy and Management, 20*(2), 161–173.

McLean, J. (1996). Hearing from the forgotten workforce: The problems faced by general staff women working in universities. *Australian Universities Review, 2*, 20–27.

McMaster, M. (2002). Partnerships between administrative and academic managers: How deans and faculty managers work together. Paper presented at the ATEM National Conference, Brisbane, 29 September–2 October.

McWilliam, E. (2000). The perfect corporate fit: New knowledge for new times. *International Journal of Leadership in Education, 3*(1), 75–83.

Meek, L. (1995). Introduction: Regulatory frameworks, market competition and the governance and management of higher education. *Australian Universities Review, 1*, 3–10.

Meyer, H.-D. (2002). The new managerialism in education management. *Journal of Educational Administration, 40*(6), 534–551.

Miller, S. (2000). Academic autonomy. In T. Coady (Ed.), *Why universities matter*, 111–131. Sydney: Allen & Unwin.

Moodie, G. (1995). The professionalisation of Australian academic administration. *Australian Universities Review, 1*, 21–23.

Niklasson, L. (1996). Quasi-markets in higher education: A comparative analysis. *Journal of Higher Education Policy and Management, 18*(1), 7–22.

Parker, M., & Jary, D. (1995). The McUniversity: organization, management and academic subjectivity. *Organization, 2*(2), 319–338.

Patience, A. (2000). Beyond the silencing academy. In P. James (Ed.), *Burning down the house. The bonfire of the universities*, 32–45. Melbourne: Arena.

Pickersgill, R., van Barneveld, K., & Bearfield, S. (1998). *General and academic work: Are they different?* Canberra: Department of Employment, Education and Training.

Power, M. (1997). *The audit society*. New York: Oxford University Press.

Prichard, C., & Willmott, H. (1997). Just how managed is the McUniversity? *Organization Studies, 18*(2), 287–316.

Samier, E. (2002a). Managerial rationalisation and the ethical disenchantment of education. *Journal of Educational Administration, 40*(6), 589–603.

Samier, E. (2002b). Weber on education and its administration. *Educational Management and Administration*, 30(1), 27–45.

Scott, P. (1997). The postmodern university. In A. Smith & F. Webster (Eds.), *The postmodern university? Contested visions of higher education in society*, 36–48. Bucking-ham: Society for Research into Higher Education and Open University Press.

Scott, S. V. (1999). The academic as service provider: Is the customer "always right"? *Journal of Higher Education Policy and Management*, 21(2), 193–202.

Sharrock, G. (2000). Why students are not (just) customers (and other reflections on "Life after George"). *Journal of Higher Education Policy and Management*, 22(2), 149–164.

Shattock, M. (2000). Managing modern universities. *Perspectives*, 4(2), 33–34.

Shore, C., & Wright, S. (2000). Coercive accountability. The rise of audit culture in higher education. In M. Strathern (Ed.), *Audit cultures*, 57–89. London: Routledge.

Smiley, J. (1995). *Moo*. New York: Ivy.

Tourish, D. (2000). Management and managerialism: Mis/managing Australian universities? *New Horizons in Education*, 103, 20–42.

Turnbull, M. (1995). Female general staff in universities: Do we matter? Paper presented at the "Women Culture and Universities: A Chilly Climate?" conference, University of Technology Sydney, Sydney 19–20 April.

Watson, D. (2000). Managing in higher education: The "wicked issues". *Higher Education Quarterly*, 54(1), 5–21.

Wilding, M. (2002). *Academia nuts*. Sydney: Wild & Woolley.

RESPONDING TO ORGANIZATIONAL IDENTITY THREATS: EXPLORING THE ROLE OF ORGANIZATIONAL CULTURE

DAVIDE RAVASI
BOCCONI UNIVERSITY

MAJKEN SCHULTZ
COPENHAGEN BUSINESS SCHOOL

In this paper, we present a longitudinal study of organizational responses to environmental changes that induce members to question aspects of their organization's identity. Our findings highlight the role of organizational culture as a source of cues supporting "sensemaking" action carried out by leaders as they reevaluate their conceptualization of their organization, and as a platform for "sensegiving" actions aimed at affecting internal perceptions. Building on evidence from our research, we develop a theoretical framework for understanding how the interplay of construed images and organizational culture shapes changes in institutional claims and shared understandings about the identity of an organization.

To maintain our identity we have to renew it.

—*What?* (Bang & Olufsen house magazine), November 1993

Research on organizational identities indicates that events that call into question members' beliefs about central and distinctive attributes of an organization can challenge collective self-perceptions and self-categorizations (Dutton & Dukerich, 1991; Elsbach & Kramer, 1996; Golden-Biddle & Rao, 1997). Organizational scholars have generally referred to these potentially disrupting events as "identity threats" (Elsbach & Kramer, 1996; Ginzel, Kramer, & Sutton, 1993).

Past research on identity threats has highlighted the interplay between organizational identities and construed or desired organizational images, portraying organizational responses aimed at restoring alignment between who members think they are as an organization (Albert & Whetten, 1985) and how they believe they are perceived—or would like to be perceived—by others (Dutton & Dukerich, 1991; Gioia & Thomas, 1996; Gioia, Schultz, & Corley, 2000). Such emerging representation of identity dynamics, however, seems to emphasize external responsiveness, either through manipulation of external perceptions (Ginzel et al., 1993) or adaptation to external changes (Gioia et al., 2000), over internal coherence.

Although researchers have explicitly acknowledged the role of organizational practices, norms, symbols, and traditions in providing substance to collective self-perceptions (e.g., Albert & Whetten, 1985; Dutton, Dukerich, & Harquail, 1994), how these manifestations of organizational culture affect identity dynamics seems to be largely unexplored. Unlike conceptualizations of identity-image dynamics, ideas about identity-culture interrelations have been based on anecdotal or illustrative evidence only (e.g., Fiol, 1991; Fiol, Hatch, & Golden-Biddle, 1998; Rindova & Schultz, 1998). In this paper, building on findings from a longitudinal field study of three organizational responses to identity-threatening environmental changes in one organization over 25 years, we examine how organizational culture shapes responses to identity threats and, along with external images, drives identity dynamics. Our findings provide an empirically based account of culture-identity dynamics and point to the role of culture in informing and supporting sensemaking and sensegiving processes triggered by external changes that induce members to reevaluate aspects of their organizational identity.[1] Our findings provide evidence of a dynamic relationship between organizational culture, identity, and image that, so far, has been suggested only at a theoretical level, but never systematically grounded in empirical data (Hatch & Schultz, 1997, 2000, 2002).

The broad scope of our study helped us link constructs such as identity claims (Ashforth & Mael, 1996), construed external images (Dutton & Dukerich, 1991), organizational culture (Martin, 2002; Schein, 1992), desired external images (Gioia & Thomas, 1996), and desired identity (Whetten, Mischel, & Lewis, 1992) and examine how their interactions may change members' understandings about central and distinctive attributes of an organization. In this respect, the conceptual model that emerged from our study connects various identity-related constructs and processes described in previous research, and it provides a broad framework for understanding how the interaction between external stimuli and internal sensemaking and sensegiving processes drives organizational dynamics.

In the first section of this article, we discuss the theoretical background of our study, arguing for the inclusion of both identity claims and understandings in a broad definition of organizational identity. Next, we present our research setting—Bang & Olufsen, a Danish producer of audiovisual equipment—and illustrate our methodology. In the following sections, we introduce a conceptual framework emerging from our research, and we provide supporting evidence from our study. Implications for theory are discussed in the final section.

Theoretical Background

Despite generally referencing Albert and Whetten's (1985) original definition of organizational identity, students in the field have developed different views of the phenomenon, and thus different interpretations of dynamism and change in organizational identities (Corley, Harquail, Pratt, Glynn, Fiol, & Hatch, 2006; Gioia, 1998; Ravasi & van Rekom, 2003; Whetten, 2006; Whetten & Godfrey, 1998). Table 1 summarizes the two principal lines of thought about organizational identity.

A Social Actor Perspective on Organizational Identity

Some scholars, building on work in the institutional tradition (e.g., Friedland & Alford, 1991; Selznick, 1957), have emphasized the functional properties of self-definitions in satisfying the basic requirements of individuals and organizations as social actors: continuity, coherence, and distinctiveness (Albert, 1998; Whetten & Mackey, 2002; Whetten, 2003). In other words, these scholars conceive of identity as "those things that enable social actors to satisfy their inherent needs to be the same yesterday, today and tomorrow and to be unique actors or entities" (Whetten & Mackey, 2002: 396). According to this view, organizational identity resides in a set of *institutional claims*—that is, explicitly stated views of what an organization is and represents—that are expected to influence its members' perceptions of central, enduring, and distinctive features of the organization by providing them with legitimate and consistent narratives that allow them to construct a collective sense of self (Czarniawska, 1997; Whetten & Mackey, 2002).

In our view, proponents of this conception tend to emphasize the *sensegiving* function of organizational identities, linking identity construction to the need to provide a coherent guide for how the members of an organization should behave and how other organizations should relate to them (Albert & Whetten, 1985; Whetten, 2003). Through formal identity claims, then, organizational leaders and/or spokespersons attempt to influence how internal and external audiences define and interpret the organization, by locating it within a set of legitimate social categories.

TABLE 1

Perspectives on Organizational Identity: Social Actor versus Social Constructionist

Characteristic	Social Actor Perspective	Social Constructionist Perspective
Theoretical foundations	Institutional theory	Social constructivism
Definition of identity	Organizational identity resides in institutional claims, available to members, about central, enduring and distinctive properties of their organization (e.g., Whetten, 2003).	Organizational identity resides in collectively shared beliefs and understandings about central and relatively permanent features of an organization (e.g., Gioia et al., 2000).
Emphasis on cognitive processes	Sensegiving: Identity claims are organizational self-definitions proposed by organizational leaders, providing members with a consistent and legitimate narrative to construct a collective sense of self.	Sensemaking: Shared understandings are the results of sensemaking processes carried out by members as they interrogate themselves on central and distinctive features of their organization.
Emphasis on endurance or on change	Identity claims are by their own nature enduring and resistant to change; labels tend to change rarely and never easily.	Shared understandings are periodically renegotiated among members
Fundamental work	Czarniawska (1997) Whetten & Mackey (2002) Whetten (2003)	Dutton & Dukerich (1991) Fiol (1991, 2002) Gioia & Thomas (1996) Gioia, Schultz, & Corley (2000) Corley & Gioia (2004)

Advocates of this perspective generally conceive of organizational identity as a set of emotionally laden, stable, and enduring self-descriptions or characterizations. As Ashforth and Mael observed: "A collective identity provides a sense of self and meaning, and places one in a wider social context. . . . given the importance of an organization's soul to its members, a certain degree of inertia is not only inevitable, but desirable" (1996: 52–53). Proponents of a social actor perspective, therefore, observe how deeply held beliefs, embodied in formal claims, tend to change only rarely and never easily (Whetten & Mackey, 2002). External occurrences that challenge an organization's claims are likely to trigger responses aimed at countering identity-threatening events and preserving personal and external representations of what the organization is or stands for (Albert & Whetten, 1985; Ginzel et al., 1993).

A Social Constructionist Perspective on Organizational Identity

Empirical evidence of changing interpretations of the identity of organizations, however, has led other scholars to observe how members' beliefs about central and distinctive characteristics of their organization may indeed evolve in the face of internal and external stimuli (Corley & Gioia, 2004; Dutton & Dukerich, 1991; Fiol, 2002; Gioia & Thomas, 1996). These scholars have shifted attention from formal claims to, as Gioia and colleagues put it, "*collective understandings* of the features presumed to be central and relatively permanent, and that distinguish the organization from other configurations" (2000: 64; emphasis added). In their view, organizational identities reside in shared interpretive schemes that members collectively construct in order to provide meaning to their experience (Gioia, 1998). These shared schemes may or may not correspond to their organization's official narrative (Ashforth & Mael, 1996).

According to Fiol, the adoption of a social constructionist approach emphasizes the *sensemaking* process that underlies the social construction of organizational identities, as "meanings and meaning structures . . . are negotiated among organizational members" (reported in Whetten and Godfrey [1998: 36]). Scholars embracing this perspective have observed how substantial organizational changes tend to require alterations in the way members interpret what is central and distinctive about their organization. In other words, substantial changes require members to "make new sense"—to develop new interpretations—of what their organization is about (Fiol, 1991; Gioia & Chittipeddi, 1991).

Research in this tradition examines how members develop collective understandings of their organization and how these affect organizational changes (e.g., Corley & Gioia, 2004; Fiol, 1991) and strategic decisions (e.g., Gioia & Thomas, 1996). In fact, proponents of a social constructionist perspective expect shared beliefs to be subjected to periodic revision, as organizational members modify their interpretations in light of environmental changes. Accordingly, these scholars generally downplay endurance as a constitutive property of organizational identities and observe how strategic responses to environmental changes may be driven by organizational leaders envisioning and promoting new conceptualizations of an organization (Corley & Gioia, 2004; Fiol, 2002; Gioia & Thomas, 1996). These scholars do not deny the relative endurance of formal claims, or their importance in preserving a sense of self and continuity, yet they observe that the meanings associated with these claims may evolve as organizational members try to adapt to changing environments (Gioia et al., 2000).

By changing the focus of attention from formal claims to meanings and understandings, social constructionist research highlights the dynamism in organizational identities and encourages scholars to investigate organizational responses to severe external changes that induce members to reconsider the sustainability of presumed core and distinctive features (Corley & Gioia, 2004; Gioia et al., 2000).

Organizational Identity as Claims and Understandings

We believe that the respective emphases of the two perspectives—institutional claims and collective understandings—represent different aspects of the construction of organizational identities. Together, the social actor and social constructionist views suggest how organizational identities arise from sensemaking and sensegiving processes through which members periodically reconstruct shared understandings and revise formal claims of what their organization is and stands for. One needs, therefore, to account for both perspectives to fully understand organizational responses to identity-threatening environmental changes.

Although both groups of scholars often use the same term, "organizational identity," without any additional qualification, they seem to focus on complementary aspects of the same phenomenon. On the one hand, proponents of an institutional view tend to focus on the discursive resources, or "identity claims," available for organizational members to use to construct a sense of collective self, implying that the former will influence the latter. On the other hand, adopters of a social constructionist view concentrate on shared emergent beliefs about central and distinctive features of an organization—what we could call "identity understandings." They acknowledge the possible influence of an official organizational narrative on emergent understandings, but they underline the central role of members' interpretations of formal claims. Whereas the first perspective emphasizes institutional constraints channeling and shaping members' interpretations (Czarniawska, 1997), the second emphasizes human agency: the freedom that organizational members enjoy in renegotiating shared interpretations about what their organization is about and what its official identity claims really mean to them (see Gioia et al., 2000).

We believe that the juxtaposition of these perspectives will produce a more accurate representation of organizational identities as dynamically arising from the interplay between identity claims and understandings—or, in other words, between who members say they are as an organization (*identity claims*) and who they believe they are (*identity understandings*). In this respect, we argue that identity claims and understandings represent two interrelated dimensions (or levels) of organizational identity that generate an embedded dynamic, as the former are expected to reflect organizational leaders' interpretations and to influence other members' understandings. Whether claims and understandings will come to coincide and how they may do so is, we contend, an empirical question.

Adapting Identity to Environmental Changes

In their seminal article, Albert and Whetten (1985) advanced the idea that external pressures increase the likelihood that organizational members engage in explicit reflection on identity issues. Later, in a work representing several views and authors (Barney et al., 1998), Huff extended this line of argument, shifting attention from the nature of an event to its interpretation by organizational members as a source of stress demanding substantial alterations in core and distinctive organizational features. In fact, recent studies have indicated that substantial environmental changes may challenge the sustainability of organizational identity (Bouchikhi & Kimberly, 2003; Brunninge, 2004).

Past research has indicated how members' responses to environmental changes and adjustments in collective understandings are affected by construed (Carter & Dukerich, 1998; Dutton & Dukerich, 1991) or desired organizational images (Fombrun & Rindova, 2000; Gioia & Thomas, 1996). Building on this research, Gioia, Schultz, and Corley (2000) offered a conceptual elaboration of identity-image interdependence, arguing that comparisons between internal and (construed) external perceptions occasionally trigger attempts to alter identity or image. Gioia and colleagues, however, observed how various conditions are likely to constrain the image-driven shift of organizational identities. As these authors concluded, "Organizations cannot construct just any arbitrarily chosen identity. Changes in identity are constrained within non-specified, but nonetheless moderating, environmental bounds" (Gioia et al., 2000: 73).

Later research has reinforced the idea that identity changes are not shaped solely by shifting organizational images. A study of a failed attempt to redefine general perceptions of a British institute of higher education to achieve "university status" showed that members are likely to reject new conceptualizations that they perceive as incoherent with organizational history, tradition, and their sense of self, along with the changes they are expected to promote (Humphreys & Brown, 2002). Conversely, in Dutton and Dukerich's (1991) study at the New York Port Authority, managers pushed by a deteriorating organizational image reconsidered their rigid approach to the issue of homelessness and came to perceive the adoption of a more humane and socially responsible line of action as closer to the agency's skills and traditional commitment to the region's welfare. Together, these studies foreshadow a relationship between changing identity claims and understandings, and deeper assumptions and beliefs embodied in organizational traditions, structures, and practices—in other words, a relationship between organizational identity and culture.

Organizational Identity and Culture

In the last few decades, management scholars have proposed various definitions for the concept of organizational culture (see Martin, 1993; Schultz, 1995; Smircich, 1983). In this article, we broadly define organizational culture as a set of shared mental assumptions that guide interpretation and action in organizations by defining appropriate behavior for various situations (Fiol, 1991; Louis, 1983; Martin, 2002). These largely tacit assumptions and beliefs are expressed and manifested in a web of formal and informal practices and of visual, verbal, and material artifacts, which represent the most visible, tangible, and audible elements of the culture of an organization (Schein, 1992; Trice & Beyer, 1984).

In the past, the relationships between organizational identity and culture have been examined mainly at a conceptual level. Advocates of a social actor perspective have observed how organizational culture may serve as an important source of self-other distinction and act as a "signifier" of organizational identity (Whetten, 2003: 30). In other words, for these scholars, unique values, beliefs, rituals, and artifacts may help organizational members substantiate their identity claims and express their perceived uniqueness (Albert, 1998; Albert & Whetten, 1985). As Albert remarked, "From this perspective, the relationship between identity and culture is clear: A particular culture [. . .] may, or may not, be part of the answer to the identity question: Who am I? What kind of firm is this?" (1998: 3).

Theoretical works in a social constructionist tradition, conversely, have emphasized the common nature of these constructs and their reciprocal influence in affecting sensemaking in organizations (Fiol, 1991; Fiol et al., 1998; Hatch & Schultz, 1997). Proponents of this perspective view both organizational culture and identity as collectively shared interpretive schemes. However, while organizational culture tends to be mostly tacit and autonomous and rooted in shared practices, organizational identity is inherently relational (in that it requires external terms of comparison) and consciously self-reflexive (Fiol et al., 1998; Hatch & Schultz, 2000, 2002; Pratt, 2003).

According to Fiol (1991), organizational identities help members make sense of what they do—as defined by tacit cultural norms and manifested in visible and tangible artifacts—in relation to their understanding of what their organization is. Organizational identities, then, provide the context within which members interpret and assign profound meaning to surface-level behavior. Taking seriously the idea that organizational culture acts as a context for sensemaking efforts, later contributions have underlined how these efforts also include attempts at internal self-definitions (Hatch & Schultz, 2002): "Identity involves how we define and experience ourselves, and this is at least partly influenced by our activities and beliefs, which are grounded in and interpreted using cultural assumptions and values" (Hatch & Schultz, 2000: 25).

These contributions have emphasized the interrelatedness of organizational identity and culture that manifests as organizational members draw on organizational culture, as well as on other meaning-making systems (professional culture, national culture, etc.), to define "who we are as an organization" (Fiol et al., 1998; Hatch & Schultz, 2002). With this emphasis, these scholars have converged with proponents of a social actor perspective in advancing the idea that organizational culture supplies members with cues for making sense of what their organization is about—and for "giving sense" of it as well.

Despite some empirical evidence of the influence of shared history, traditions, and symbols on member's reevaluations of self-definitions (e.g., Albert & Whetten, 1985; Brunninge, 2004; Fombrun & Rindova, 2000; Gioia & Thomas, 1996), the issue has never been subjected to systematic investigation. Our research was initially intended to increase our understanding of organizational responses to identity-threatening environmental changes. Evidence gathered in the course of our study directed our attention to the underexplored role of organizational culture in driving identity dynamics and led us to reframe our study as an empirical investigation of how identity, image, and culture interact in driving responses to identity threats.

Methods

Research Setting

Our research was based on a longitudinal study of Bang & Olufsen, a Danish producer of audio-video systems. At the time of our study, in the mid 90s, Bang & Olufsen ("B&O" from now on) employed around 2,600 people worldwide. The company's annual turnover had risen significantly from 2,180 million Danish kroner in 1992 to more than 3,700 million (513 million euros) at the end of 2000. Its geographical scope had gradually expanded beyond Europe and reached 42 countries by the end of the 90s.

B&O was founded as a radio manufacturer in 1925 in the village of Struer in the north of Denmark. Very early in the life of the company, significant technological innovations and the painstaking care of its founders (Peter Bang and Svend Olufsen) for the quality of components and manufacturing earned the company an excellent reputation, as the first corporate motto, "B&O—The Danish Hallmark of Quality," proudly boasted. In the following decades, attention to design and style intensified and led to the fortunate involvement in product design of renowned Danish architects and industrial designers. Between 1972 and 1998, however, three times recurrent competitive threats and environmental changes induced organizational leaders to explicitly address issues of organizational identity and to reevaluate their beliefs about core and distinctive features of the organization. In all three cases, the process culminated in a revision of formal identity claims. This history gave us a rare opportunity to study identity-related processes across three explicit responses to perceived identity threats within the same organization.

Data Collection

The sources of empirical evidence we relied on to analyze responses to identity threats at B&O can be divided into five general categories:

Semistructured interviews. We conducted a total of 50 semistructured interviews with 40 organizational members. Our sampling logic moved from purposeful to theoretical (Locke, 2001): we initially interviewed people who could provide rich and insightful information on the identity-related projects of interest. Later, we theoretically selected our informants on the basis of specific research interests. To deepen our understanding of the environmental and strategic issues the company had faced, we interviewed all members of the top management team running the company during the 90s and some retired executives who could illuminate us on an early attempt to formally define the identity of the company (this definition is described later as "the Seven Corporate Identity Components"). In order to investigate in more detail how the revision of identity claims and understandings was actually carried out, we also interviewed all members of project teams that in 1993 and 1998 formulated or reformulated identity claims, and most team members that participated in the earlier identity-related program mentioned above. Finally, to reduce the risk of capturing only a narrow set of potentially biased interpretations, we also interviewed national and international middle managers involved in "identity seminars" at the firm (see below), as well as company employees at different levels. Overall, our informants included 8 top managers, 24 middle managers, 4 staff members and technicians, and 4 retired executives; 22 of these individuals came from the firm's headquarters, and 18 came from the international network. Interviews ranged from a half-hour to two hours, and most of them were tape-recorded. Whenever this was not possible, we took detailed field notes.

Identity seminars. Both in 1993 and 1998, new identity claims were introduced and debated during company seminars. We had access to transcripts of all the seminars held between December 1993 and January 1994, which included all headquarters employees. In 1998, one of us participated in ten seminars involving the CEO and 450 managers and dealers. Participation in the identity seminars allowed informal conversations (not counted as interviews) with 45 middle managers. These conversations offered an important forum for testing ideas and emergent interpretations with organizational members, and we included issues emerging from them in our field notes. Finally, one of us had the opportunity to interact with 20 top managers of the company during three full-day seminars between 1997 and 1999.

House magazines and other internal communication tools. The first house magazine published by B&O, *B&O Magazine*, was founded in late 1991 and purposefully used by the top managers to sustain change efforts in the early 90s (the "Break Point" project described later). The internal publication *What?* later replaced *B&O Magazine*. Our database included issues of these magazines published between November 1991 and December 1995, comprising a total of 476 pages. In 1996, *What?* was replaced by *Beolink*, initially published in 12 languages and distributed to all the firm's dealers as well as at headquarters. We also gained access to other documents, such as identity manuals, posters, and the like, used to illustrate and diffuse new identity statements internally.

Annual reports and other external communication tools. We carefully analyzed annual reports from 1989 through 2000, the corporate Web site in various stages of development, and other documents intended for external communication. Between 1992 and 1994, the company's annual reports included interviews with managers or other employees and detailed descriptions of corporate strategies, the new vision, and the logic underlying changes.

Corporate histories and other archival material. Archival search helped us track the evolution of B&O's corporate and business strategy, its strategic goals, and links to the evolving identity claims. We had also access to the reports of the internal task forces that in 1997 conducted exploratory work on fundamental values and future strategic directions. Finally, two corporate histories of the firm were of critical importance to our understanding of the evolution of organizational identity at B&O. The first (Poulsen, 1997) reported a detailed analysis of the recent history of the company. The second (Bang & Palshøy, 2000), written by two important leaders of B&O in the 60s and 70s, contained insightful retrospective reflections on early identity management programs.

Data Analysis

Our study started as two separate research projects that converged into a common investigation. Both authors shared an interest in how environmental changes affect organizational identities. In 1992, when the reexamination of organizational identity at B&O was already underway, the first author gained access to members of the task force that had been in charge of redefining the identity claims of the company. Data collection began soon after the completion of the projects leading to the redefinition of identity statements. The researcher was never involved in any internal or external communication activity, and there is no evidence that his work affected the process in any way.

In 1997, the second author was introduced to the company as a speaker to the top management group, and soon afterwards she negotiated permission to conduct a two-year intensive study of how the company responded to new environmental threats. During the identity seminars carried out in 1999, she acted as a nonparticipant observer. She did not have a formal role or responsibility in the process. She was asked to share with top managers observations on the interpersonal dynamics occurring during seminars, but there is no evidence that her feedback had an impact on internal initiatives aimed at diffusing and illustrating the new claims.

In the summer of 1999, we two authors discovered we had both examined the same company adopting similar approaches but focusing on different periods of company history. In the following months, we started a mutual exchange of data in order to integrate, compare, and elaborate our respective databases. Further data collection on an earlier process leading to the development of the first formal identity statement at B&O, dating back to 1972, extended our longitudinal analysis over a time span of more than 25 years and across three different responses to perceived identity threats. Each of the three responses was considered a separate case, although each case provided contextual information for analyzing later events.

Following the merger of the databases, we established a common protocol of analysis. Interview transcripts and other pieces of text produced by organizational members (transcripts from the seminars, articles from the house magazines, retrospective narrations from corporate biographies, etc.) served as primary data for our analysis. We also used internal documents, annual reports, and other archival material to increase our understanding of the processes. Our purpose was to build on existing concepts in organizational identity research to develop a more comprehensive framework for understanding how organizations react to identity-threatening external events. In this respect, our analysis was aimed at elaborating theory, rather than at generating a completely new theoretical framework (Lee, Mitchell, & Sablynski, 1999).

Data analysis followed prescriptions for grounded-theory building (Glaser & Strauss, 1967; Locke, 2001) and relied initially on a coding phase. Databases were searched for identity-related incidents—that is, concepts, actions, and statements that were explicitly related to the investigation, elaboration, definition, and communication of organizational definitions. During this search, which we conducted independently, we identified various terms and concepts that our informants related to the identity of the organization. The literature on organizational identity and on related constructs (image, culture, etc.) offered us a terminology and a conceptual reference that helped us relate each incident (e.g., a market survey of consumers' perceptions of the firm) to a more general category (e.g., analyzing external perceptions). Tables (Miles & Huberman, 1994) and category cards (records of categories including related data incidents [Locke, 2001]) facilitated comparison of each other's interpretations of categories. Discrepancies were usually solved through mutual agreement. In this phase, triangulation of sources (interviews, seminars, house magazines, etc.) helped us refine and strengthen our emerging categories (Glaser & Strauss, 1967).

In this initial stage, categorization brought us to identify a number of identity-related concepts and actions that seemed to underpin organizational responses to environmental changes. Subsequent readings of our data were dedicated to merging concepts and actions into more general conceptual categories—a procedure Locke (2001) labeled "comparing"—in order to gradually move from our informants' account of the process to a more general explanation. Building on insights from our earlier round of analysis, we first divided actions into the externally oriented (primarily aimed at exploring and influencing external perceptions) and the internally oriented (primarily aimed at reflecting on organizational features and influencing internal perceptions). Further attempts to group identity-related actions brought us to categorize some identity-related actions as sensemaking or sensegiving actions, given their roles in the change processes (Gioia & Chittipeddi, 1991). Sensemaking actions included those that underpinned the reevaluation of core members' interpretations of core and distinctive attributes of the company (e.g., interorganizational comparison, exploration of refracted images, etc.). Sensegiving actions referred to managerial actions that supported the presentation and illustration of new identity claims to internal and external audiences (e.g., promoting coherence, rooting in history, etc.). Eventually, most identity-related actions were categorized according to both their orientation (internal vs. external) and role (sensemaking vs. sensegiving) and grouped into four main processes that appeared to drive identity dynamics.

In the next stage of the analysis, we concerned ourselves with how the various conceptual elements we had identified could be linked into a coherent framework explaining organizational responses to identity threats. Initially, within-case analysis helped us link the actions and concepts into a tentative framework explaining how the revision of formal identity claims occurred at B&O over the three periods. At this stage, memos from previous rounds (notes capturing early insights from the first reading of the data [Glaser & Strauss, 1967]) supported our efforts to uncover the relationships between our concepts. Later, comparisons of cases helped us increase the robustness of our model by refining the boundaries of our categories and by dropping conceptual categories or subcategories that appeared to be less relevant to a general account of the process. After some iteration among the different sets of data and between data and theory, we converged on a tentative framework. Positive feedback on our tentative interpretations from different informants reinforced our confidence in the reliability of our constructs and model (Lee, 1999).

We believe that the peculiar structure of our study actually reinforced the validity of our explanatory framework. First, although we started our research with the same general interest, our respective conceptual foundations were only partly overlapping, thus reducing the possibility of a biased interpretation of the collected data. Furthermore, prescriptions for grounded theory building advise subjecting data to the separate analysis of different researchers. In this respect, a substantial convergence on a similar framework for understanding the observed phenomenon increased our confidence in the internal validity of our analysis (Miles & Huberman, 1994). Furthermore, our tentative frameworks were submitted to colleagues involved in research on organizational identities, and their comments often proposed alternative explanations to be examined and helped us refine our provisional interpretations (Locke, 2001).

Finally, in order to corroborate our interpretations and increase the robustness and generalizability of our framework, we compared our findings with available studies of reexaminations of identity claims and understandings (e.g., Brunninge, 2004; Gioia & Thomas, 1996; Fombrun & Rindova, 2000). Evidence from related studies, in fact, indicated that identity dynamics similar to what we observed seemed to occur, albeit less visibly, in other organizations engaged in similar processes, which increased our confidence that what we had observed reflected more general dynamics occurring in organizations facing identity threats.

Findings

A comparative analysis of the way managers at B&O responded to identity-threatening environmental changes at different times revealed similar patterns of behavior. In this section, we describe the theoretical framework emerging from our data and define and illustrate each element. Figure 1 summarizes our theoretical framework.

Table 2 provides an overview of how the various processes described in Figure 1 unfolded.

Following earlier work deriving a process model from a rich, longitudinal study (e.g., Sutton & Hargadon, 1996), we developed a detailed overview of how the core elements of the emerging model were grounded in evidence from each source of data. Table 3 presents this overview.

External Challenges to Organizational Identity

At three different times between 1972 and 1998, environmental changes induced the managers of B&O to interrogate themselves as to the features that were *really* central and distinctive to the organization.

In 1972, increasing competition from Japanese producers motivated CEO Ebbe Mansted's decision to stimulate B&O managers' reflections on core and distinctive features of the company. Japanese producers had entered the European markets with a low-price, high-volume strategy. As one of our informants observed, there was pressure from audiovisual dealers for B&O to be "more like the Japanese"—that is, to alter product design to conform to Japanese standards (modular square shapes, traditional knobs, hi-fi performance, etc.).

The rise of Japanese competitors raised questions about the sustainability of the expensive niche strategy B&O had pursued, which was expressed in the corporate motto, "Bang & Olufsen: for those who discuss design and quality before price." As our informants reported, however, B&O managers doubted that imitating Japanese competitors would be good for the company, or even possible. Furthermore, they felt that conforming to external expectations would have meant the loss of B&O's unique design philosophy, a loss no management team member was even willing to consider. Nevertheless, in order to address external changes and expectations, they felt the need to reevaluate and formalize what really made the company (and hence its products) different from the Japanese companies and products. As a participant reported later:

> The task was not to lay a new foundation, but to formulate values that were already part of Bang & Olufsen's identity and then select the strongest elements for the company's international future. (Bang & Palshøy, 2000: 86)

Eventually, the team's reflections coalesced into the Seven Corporate Identity Components, or the Seven CIC—authenticity, "autovisuality" (self-explanatory design features), credibility, domesticity, essentiality, individuality, and inventiveness—a set of features that, in the eyes of the top managers, distinguished the company and its products from other producers of audiovisual equipment. The Seven CIC were shared with the rest of the organization through various internal communication devices, including a manual that came to be known as "the little red book."

Throughout the 1970s, product development and communication followed the Seven CIC. Over time, however, members' understandings, as expressed in product and market strategies, seemed to drift. With the tacit approval of new CEO Vagn Andersen, product developers designed increasingly sophisticated and expensive equipment. Powerful subsidiaries repositioned products as luxury objects and status symbols. As an internal observer retrospectively reflected:

> For a time, the company tried to create a survival niche by turning B&O into a Rolls-Royce type company which focused only on exclusivity. Whilst concentrating on outer prestige, the product's idea content and qualities were forgotten. (Bang & Palshøy, 2000: 102)

In 1990, however, economic recession and the end of the yuppie culture, which had spurred sales of B&O products during the 80s, abruptly halted the tacit drift towards luxury and led the company into severe financial trouble. The sudden decline in sales, combined with research revealing that a large number of retailers portrayed B&O as a producer of beautiful boxes with average technical quality, brought managers to conclude that changes in the product line and communication policies required a convergence around a new understanding of what Bang & Olufsen was about. A few months later, a new CEO, Anders Knutsen, initiated a program called Break Point '93, which was aimed at refocusing the organization on the "distinctiveness of its product and its spirit." After several informal meetings, the group in charge of revising the identity statement produced a phrase that would later be known as "The New Vision"—"The best of both worlds: Bang & Olufsen, the unique combination of technological excellence and emotional appeal."

Between 1994 and 1996, sales and profits soared. At the end of 1996, however, the high growth rates of the previous years began to slow down. In the following months, some competitors declared their intention of invading the profitable niche for "design products," threatening the unique position of the company. An occasional restyling of its products by well-known designer Philippe Starcke led low-cost producer Thomson to enthusiastically declare that it would soon compete in the same

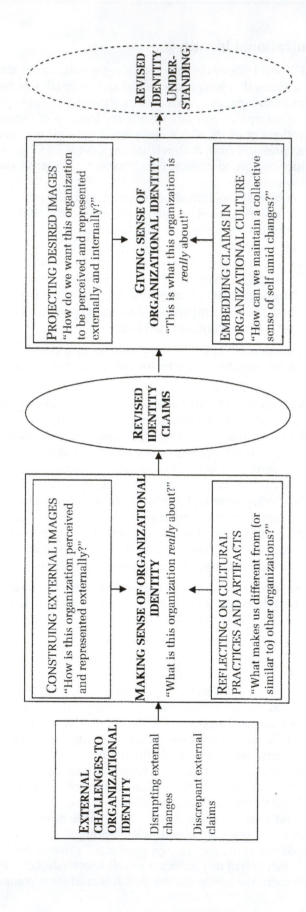

Figure 1 Organizational response to identity threats: a theoretical model[a].

[a] The dotted line indicates relationships and constructs for which we could collect only limited evidence.

TABLE 2

Stages of Response to Identity Threats at Bang & Olufsen, 1972–98

Stages	Identity Threats and Organizational Responses		
	Seven Corporate Identity Components, 1972: Increasing competition from large-scale Japanese competitors Pressures from dealers to adopt Japanese formats	**Break Point, 1993: General recession and loss of market appeal Drifting organizational images (industry analysts, retailers, customers)**	**B&O United, 1998: Competitors enhance the design content of their products Open threat of imitation by competitors like Thomson and Sony**
Construing external images	External recognition reinforces confidence in the corporate design philosophy.	Consumer surveys are carried out to identify distinctive attributes of the company and the product.	Evaluation of perceptions by international brand experts. Examination of consumer stories.
Reflecting on cultural practices and artifacts	Reflection on how products have been designed. Japanese products are used as a negative term of comparison. Identity is defined in terms of design principles and practices.	Reflection on the distinctive traits of the company and the products. Explicit comparison with competitors' claims. Identity is defined in terms of core technologies and product features.	Reflection on the cultural heritage of the company (Bauhaus style, etc.). Positioning against drift toward exclusivity. Identity is defined in terms of members' behavior and product features.
Revision of identity claims	One team formulates The Seven Corporate Identity Components: authenticity, autovisuality, credibility, domesticity, essentiality, individuality, and inventiveness.	One team formulates a synthetic definition: "The best of both worlds— Bang & Olufsen, the unique combination of technological excellence and emotional appeal."	One task force proposes a set of values, later approved by top management: excellence, synthesis, and poetry.
Projecting desired images	Corporate slogan: "Bang & Olufsen: We think differently." The Seven CIC are intended as guidelines for advertising campaigns.	Awareness of organizational identity is spread throughout the dealers' network (Match Point Program) and diffused externally through other initiatives (e.g., "vision forum").	Dialogue is initiated in local seminars with the dealers, and it is later carried out through reshaping external communication, taglines, and visual expression.
Embedding claims in organizational culture	Identity is illustrated in terms of design principles and established practices. Identity is diffused in the organization through a manual, posters, internal seminars, etc.	Identity is presented in terms of core competencies. An exhibition, The Curious Eye, traces the roots of the identity back in the corporate history.	Values are presented and discussed in "value seminars," facilitating further internal dialogue by cascading.

TABLE 3
Sources and Levels of Empirical Evidence[a]

Stages	Semistructured Interviews	Identity Seminars	House Magazines and Other Internal Communication Tools	Annual Reports and Other External Communication Tools	Corporate Histories and Other Archival Material
Construing external images	*Strong evidence* "Dealers were asking us to be more like the Japanese." (1972) "Customers are the judge. If customers reject our values, they are useless." (1998) "Brand experts related us to status symbols, smartness, and trendsetting." (1998)	*Moderate evidence* "B&O became a very expensive brand. . . . We have made potential buyers think our products are much too expensive and 'not for them.'" (1993) "People in our target group regard B&O as an unusual synergy of aesthetics and technology." (1993)	*Moderate evidence* "We make products that are a reflection of our customers. . . . The organization and the culture should therefore reflect their ways of thinking and their perceptions." (1998)	*Sporadic evidence* "Blind tests in the shops indicated that on average 30–40 percent of the retailers around Europe still empha-sized merely the aesthetic aspects of the products." (1993)	*Sporadic evidence* " In 1972 B&O had captured what the Museum of Modern Art had defined as *good design*." (1972) "Whilst concentrating on outer prestige, the product's idea content and qualities were forgotten." (1993)
Reflecting on cultural practices and artifacts	*Strong evidence* "The Seven CIC grew out of the design philosophy that emerged during the sixties." (1993) "We were not happy with our initial definition— The 'Artist in Audio-Video'; it focused on aesthetics and under-emphasized the technology behind the products." (1993) "We had the ability to challenge established boundaries of how you make radios." (1998)	*Strong evidence* "Getting an overall view provides us with a better understanding of the fundamental ideas that have proven to be strong." (1993) "We have a long tradition for product development and design." (1998) "Design is a language. We can use designers because we have something to tell, as opposed to Philips' adventure with Alessi." (1998)	*Strong evidence* "The identity is what we are. What we come from. Our heritage." (1993) "Products are created within a Scandinavian context characterized by values such as pride integrity, reliability, and confidence in dialogue as a form of communi-cation, as opposed to monologue as a form of address." (1998) "An international product has no identity. B&O is and always will be a Danish and Scandinavian company." (1998)	*No evidence*	*Strong evidence* "The Seven CIC aimed at interpreting existing, but unexpressed attitudes." (1972) For the rest of the century, these significant innovations, i.e., movement and highly sophisticated mode of operation, remained a hallmark of B&O's products. More than anything else they differentiated the company from other players in the market." (1972)

1108

TABLE 3 (Cont.)

Stages	Semistructured Interviews	Identity Seminars	House Magazines and Other Internal Communication Tools	Annual Reports and Other External Communication Tools	Corporate Histories and Other Archival Material
Projecting desired images	*Strong evidence* "Today you would call [the Seven CIC] an attempt to make one coherent brand." (1972) "We are communicating the New Vision to all the retailers, asking them if they agree: if they do not, they can as well sell something else." (1993)	*Strong evidence* "In B&O we never doubt for one moment that our identity, seen as a whole, is important to people's views on and acceptance of us and our actions." (1972) "We are communicating the New Vision to all the retailers, asking them if they agree: if they do not, they can as well sell something else." (1993)	*Strong evidence* "If our brochures, advertisements, etc., are directed toward different-ent groups, if we speak in different tongues, in the end, we lose our identity." (1993) "It is important that all our communication activities express the same identity." (1993)	*Moderate evidence* "Our vision is expressed in a new business model: We call it Bang & Olufsen United, because we focus and cohere around the brand. All business areas build on the same core competencies." (1998)	*Sporadic evidence* "Each single component was used in advertisements, brochures, at exhibitions and in shop design, such that the Seven CIC formed an overall and coherent picture of the company's objec-tive, goal, and special character." (1972)
Embedding claims in the organizational culture	*Strong evidence* "In order to diffuse the Seven CIC, we printed what later came to be known as the 'Little Red Book.'" (1972) "The new vision is a confirmation of the past and a guide for the future." (1993) "Synthesis is our everyday life. Poetry reminds us that we are building a cathedral, and are just carving stones." (1998)	*Strong evidence* "B&O has a strong and desirable identity which has been created over a number of years." (1993) "Verner Neertoft's graphic work, brochures and exhibitions, and the Gutenberghus adver-tising campaigns became both identity-creating and identity-carrying elements." (1993) "We are aware of the product design's impor-tance for our identity." (1993) "We have a history, we are more than a name." (1998)	*Strong evidence* "Our ability to maintain the positive aspects of 'the old culture' as to idea, form, and quality is of great value." (1993) "Fundamental values cannot be invented, constructed, dictated, bought, borrowed, copied, suppressed.... Values can be found, discovered, revealed, recognized, exposed, acknowledged." (1998) "Excellence is doing things the right way, down to the smallest detail." (1998)	*Strong evidence* "It is equally important, amid all these changes, that the company maintains its basic identity and is aware of its heritage." (1993) "B&O (...) identity is closely connected with with its products." (1993) "We believe in the power of excellence. Excellence meaning the quality of materials and finish, and the quality of performance—two of our core competencies!" (1998)	*Strong evidence* "[The Seven CIC] were drummed into our heads. We heard about it and we were tested on it." (1972) "The definitive new graphic style . . . together with the product design, communicated the company's new identity." (1972)

[a] "Strong evidence" is used to indicate a dominant theme in this data source; "moderate evidence," a recurring but not prominent theme in this data source; "sporadic evidence," a theme that appeared occasion-ally in this data source. Numbers in parentheses indicate the year of the identity-related program the data refer to; thus, 1972 refers to the Seven CICs; 1993, to Break Point; and 1998, to Bang & Olufsen United.

league as B&O. Eventually, managers felt the need to formulate new plans to counter imitative attempts and support growth on a global scale. An essential part of this strategy was a much stronger reliance on exclusive stores or "shops-in-shops" in upscale department stores. Bang & Olufsen products had previously been distributed through a wide range of multibrand dealers, where they would be displayed and presented along with many other brands. Managers were, however, unsure about the possibility of fully expressing the uniqueness of their products in such a retail environment and felt that their dealers had to possess a profound understanding of the philosophy behind the products. Consequently, they triggered another wave of reviewing and clarifying the identity of the company as part of a new strategy. In their own words, they focused on "restating and debating the fundamental values" of the company, as these values were meant "to provide the foundation for strategic change." This further change effort was labeled "Bang & Olufsen United." From these reflections, top managers developed a new set of identity claims expected to support B&O's future strategy; they labeled these the three "Fundamental Values: Excellence, Synthesis, and Poetry."

A recent conceptualization of identity change in organizations (Barney et al., 1998) rests on the idea that internal or external events that members perceive as sources of stress and pressure may lead the members to consciously reexamine their organization's identity. At B&O, the circumstances that organizational leaders perceived as threatening shared two fundamental features (as indicated in the first box in Figure 1): first, environmental changes seemed to challenge the prospective viability of current conceptualizations of the organization and of the strategies that rested on them; and second, external changes were associated with shifting external claims and expectations about the organization, eventually leading managers at B&O to ask themselves, "Is this who we really are? Is this who we really want to be?"

Making Sense of Organizational Identity

Recent research shows how loss of clarity about the identity of an organization may lead to what Corley and Gioia (2004) referred to as "identity ambiguity." In this condition, multiple possible interpretations of core and distinctive organizational features stimulate organizational leaders to take action to resolve the confusion surrounding identity claims and beliefs and make new sense of "who we are as an organization." Indeed, research on social cognition in organizations has shown how ambiguity regarding issues or events requires members to engage in constructing or reconstructing shared interpretations, allowing coordinated collective action (Gioia, 1986; Weick, 1979, 1995). Building on this notion, a stream of research on strategic and organizational change has emphasized how the initial step of a change process usually involves collective efforts to build or to revise shared understandings of the internal and external environment in order to coordinate collective efforts toward new organizational goals (Gioia & Chittipeddi, 1991; Gioia, Thomas, Clark, & Chittipeddi, 1994).

Building on this literature, we conceptualized B&O managers' initial response to what they perceived as identity threats as a *sensemaking phase* aimed at building new interpretations or, at the very least, revising old conceptions of central and distinctive features of the organization. As they reexamined their organization's identity, they looked both inside and outside the organization (as indicated in the second box in Figure 1), searching for cues that helped them make sense of its identity.

Construing external images. Researchers have observed how construed external images—members' perceptions of how their organization is perceived externally—serve as a gauge against which members evaluate organizational action (Dutton & Dukerich, 1991). At B&O, construed external images provided members engaged in self-examination with cues that helped them interpret changes and evaluate action in the light of perceived identity threats.

In 1972, for instance, the decision to resist external pressures found support in widespread external recognition, manifested in design awards and the praise of critics. Indeed, a tangible sign came in early 1972, when the Museum of Modern Art in New York acquired seven B&O products for its permanent collection. As two members of the team that produced the Seven CIC recalled later, official recognition from MOMA gave the firm's managers a confidence in the soundness of their approach that they had lacked in the previous decade (Bang & Palshøy, 2000).

In 1993, the influence of construed organizational images on the process was even more explicit, as the reevaluation of the identity of the organization was based on information gathered by two teams working in parallel, one of which had the mandate to investigate external perceptions of the company. A field survey with four groups of actual and potential customers reported consistent perceptions of the organizational image. Customers ranked what one informant later called "the immediate perception of technological excellence" as the primary characteristic of the company: quality of sound reproduction, reliability, and so forth. Next, customers pointed to "the emotional side of the product," as reflected in the elegant design and the unusual mechanical movements of products. Feedback from the customer survey was later incorporated in the statement that provided a new self-definition for the organization.

Finally, in 1998, interviews with leading international brand experts alerted the team in charge of reexamining the fundamental values of the organization that the notion of "exclusivity" was still central to external perceptions of B&O. Despite internal efforts to revise understandings and aspirations, externally B&O was still widely perceived as a producer and purveyor of luxury goods, and associated, as one of our informants summarized, with "Balmain, Chateau Margoux, Dior, Mercedes . . . status symbols, trend setting and smartness." According to team members, these perceptions reflected a mistaken understanding of the company's past and did not capture its desired future image.

In summary, evidence from our study confirmed the influence of construed external images on identity dynamics. At Bang & Olufsen, however, members were not merely passive recipients of external feedback: as they engaged in self-examination, they deliberately used consumer surveys, blind tests in shops, expert panels, and other tools to construe external perceptions of the organization. Looking at the organizational images reflected in the mirror of stakeholders' perceptions stimulated further elaboration of environmental changes and comparative reflections about identity features.

Reflecting on cultural practices and artifacts. Reinterpretation of organizational identity at B&O, however, was not underpinned solely by a comparison between internal understandings and external images. On the contrary, members seemed to assign a considerable importance to what some organizational members referred to as the "cultural heritage" of the organization, manifested in distinctive practices and objects that they perceived as a legacy of a shared past. Building on previous works on organizational culture (Martin, 1993, 2002; Schein, 1992), we labeled this process *reflection on cultural practices and artifacts*, emphasizing how organizational members interpreted embedded behavioral patterns and unique physical, linguistic, and material artifacts as manifestations of underlying assumptions and distinctive organizational traits.

In early 1972, the team entrusted with the task of defining the "corporate identity" interpreted the task as a "reflection on what we were doing" and found in product design—the most visible element of differentiation between B&O and its competitors—a natural starting point for their investigation. A review of recently developed products helped members surface the principles that had guided design choices. As chief designer Jacob Jensen retrospectively observed:

> B&O was about simplicity and understandable products. They had no buttons, but were flat and horizontal opposed to the Japanese verticalism. The product had to enrich the experience by having a surprising feature. Products should be self-explanatory and communicate by themselves.

As one of our informants observed, the group gradually discovered that they had really been working according to some common tacit beliefs. Throughout the years, search for simplicity and essentiality was perceived as having inspired milestones like the audio system Beomaster 1900, which had user interfaces designed to facilitate access to music reproduction, and the one-thumb integrated remote control Beolink 1000, which could connect all the video and audio sources in a house (Bang & Palshøy, 2000).

In 1993, the group in charge of finding a new way to define the essence of the company found again in the products a starting point for making sense of what was unique about the organization. Although not denying the accuracy of earlier statements such as the Seven Corporate Identity Components, the group purposefully tried "to go deeper" into the "essence" or "spirit" of the company. As a member of the team, a communication manager, recalled:

We knew we were different from Pioneer, from Sony. We knew we were something else. We started wondering what was so special about us, about the way we do things, about our products, which made us different from them.

Group members went through a painstaking search for a precise definition of what made B&O distinctive. According to the communication manager just cited,

> Every single word was subject to an obsessive search and long discussions. We started with "B&O, the artist in audio-video"; our attention was focused on the artistic-emotional aspects, and we were leaving the technological dimension to a definition of our field of activity (audio-video). But this was not enough: it was necessary to give more emphasis to the technological aspects.

Eventually group members condensed their understandings about the features that made the company unique into an identity statement, the New Vision, that, as top managers explained later, synthesized the distinctive competencies that were the foundation for a new strategy: sound-image integration, mechanical micromovements, the choice of materials, human-system interface, and design. The concept of "emotional appeal," for instance, was linked to distinctive features of the products, such as the silent sliding doors of CD player B&O 2500, which relied on capabilities (design and mechanical micromovements) that, according to group members, no other producer possessed and no competing product featured.

Finally, when in late 1997 CEO Anders Knutsen set up a task force to reflect on the fundamental values of the company, he asked them to "identify the fundamental values of Bang & Olufsen" with "no methodological restrictions." Despite the formal mandate, the team soon redefined its purpose as "rediscovering" rather than "constructing" fundamental values. They explicitly positioned the company's heritage in opposition to what was described as the "drift into an international look-alike luxury brand" of the mid 80s. Team members observed how during the 80s the company had "lost touch with its heritage." The drift towards "exclusivity" was seen as a move away from the company's heritage, which was embedded, according to the group, in the Bauhaus tradition and reflected in a motto of that movement, "Better products for a better world."[2] They found examples of the Bauhaus tradition in early products, like the Beolit 39 radio, which had a Bakelite cabinet, and in the sober elegance of the company's first trademark, readopted in 1994 as part of the Break Point program.

Eventually, the team identified a fundamental challenge in revitalizing the company's heritage, rooted in the Bauhaus-inspired balance of design, aesthetics, and technology. Reference to the Bauhaus tradition, for instance, brought them to associate "excellence" with "simplicity and modesty" and the company's ability to "make choices on the basis of patience and persistence, honesty and decency." One manager took the company's frequent use of anodized aluminum as a practical illustration of the concept: "Aluminum is excellence. Gold is exclusive." Similarly, the concept of "poetry" emerged from team members' attempts to make sense of what really differentiated B&O from relevant competitors such as Sony and Philips and was inspired by observing the unusual features of the company's products. Poetry, as a member of the team described it, is "the unfolding of the product as a flower."

Although conceptually distinct, the two processes described earlier—construing external images and reflecting on cultural practices and artifacts—were tightly intertwined (hence their inclusion in the same box in Figure 1). Both processes drove the careful selection and wording of new identity statements (official documents reporting organizational self-definitions) as members engaged in active debate, retaining or discarding labels, until they converged on what they judged to be a satisfying codification and definition of their perceptions of the essential character of the organization: the Seven CIC in 1972, the New Vision in 1993, and the Fundamental Values in 1999 (see Table 1). Further rounds of reflection, construal, and comparison helped members clarify the meaning and the implications of the labels they had tentatively agreed upon at an earlier stage. The outcome of this sense-making process was a *revision of the official identity claims* summarizing what top managers perceived as central and distinctive features of the organization (see the first oval in Figure 1).

Empirically, we considered the revision of identity claims as the manifestation of adjustments in the shared understandings of organizational leaders. The revised statements expressed a desired future identity (Whetten et al., 1992), a set of features around which leaders hoped to align the rest of the organization in order to address changes in the external environment successfully. The deliberate choice and codification of a set of features that were claimed to define the organizational identity marked a transition from sensemaking action to sensegiving action, and to organizational leaders' engagement in providing a consistent account of the revised claims aimed at affecting collective understandings throughout the organization.

Giving a Sense of Organizational Identity

Given their role as legitimate representatives of an organization and their privileged access to internal communication channels, organizational leaders are in a particularly favorable position to influence official accounts and explanations (Cheney & Christensen, 2001; Whetten, 2003). Furthermore, providing organizational members with a unitary and consistent narrative that helps them attach meaning to events, issues, and actions is a critical administrative activity (Pfeffer, 1981: 9). Recent research indicates that when organizational identities are called into question or surrounded by ambiguity, organizational leaders are increasingly subjected to a "sensegiving imperative" (Corley & Gioia, 2004). As a consequence, rising uncertainties about what is really central to and distinctive about the organization require organizational leaders to fill a "void of meaning" and to reconstruct a credible and consistent narrative for internal and external audiences, helping members rebuild their sense of who they are as an organization.

At B&O, the reformulation of identity claims was then followed by a *sensegiving phase* (summarized in the third box in Figure 1), as top managers engaged in a number of initiatives to circulate the new identity statements to an internal audience. The managers provided an official account of the statements' meaning and practical implications or, in other words, gave a sense of the new claims to the rest of the organization. On the one hand, managers made a concerted effort to project a unitary and coherent organizational image, while on the other hand they strived to imbue the visible outcomes of the sensemaking phases—the Seven CIC, the New Vision, and the Fundamental Values, respectively—with meaning, by embedding the revised identity claims in the culture of the organization.

Projecting desired images. At this stage, image-related actions were formally aimed at influencing external stakeholders' perceptions of the organization and primarily targeted subjects such as retailers, clients and, to some extent, the press, whose construed perceptions were not aligned with internal beliefs and aspirations. What we observed has been described in the past as the deliberate attempt to leave favorable impressions on external audiences in order to realign internal beliefs and aspirations with external perceptions (e.g., Ginzel et al., 1993; Rindova & Fombrun, 1999). At B&O, however, external projections also served a second purpose. Past research indicates that organizational leaders deliberately project desired images in order to stimulate internal redefinition of organizational identity (Fiol, 2002; Gioia & Thomas, 1996), and they produce ideal organizational images to promote a coherent sense of self inside their organization (Cheney & Christensen, 2001).

At B&O, presentations and illustrations of the new corporate slogans embodying the revised identity statements appeared in annual reports as well as on the corporate Web site. However, the fact that these statements were never used in advertising campaigns reinforces the impression that the real receivers of projected images were internal and peripheral members of the organization: employees and dealers.

In 1972, for instance, the top management expected the newly codified identity claims (the Seven CIC) to be reflected in the products and to guide both marketers and designers. Conscious and consistent efforts to communicate the essence of the product were considered as important as technical quality in differentiating B&O in the marketplace. One of our informants retrospectively observed that "today you would call it an attempt to make one coherent brand." The perceived uniqueness of the company was illustrated in detail in a little manual and a poster, later to become a corporate icon. A senior marketing manager was given the responsibility of presenting and discussing the Seven CIC throughout the company, including foreign subsidiaries and dealers.

Even in 1993, top managers emphasized that it was important that actions at every level (design, manufacturing, advertising, retailing, etc.) support a unitary and internally coherent organizational image. As CEO Anders Knutsen publicly declared in the November 1993 issue of *What?*:

> It is just as important that all our communication activities express the same identity. Because a company can have only one identity. . . . We know that a lot of people have strong feelings about B&O, and that they have great expectations of our products. We must always meet these expectations and never accept a compromise as to "the best of both worlds"—neither in our research and development, nor in our communication activities.

Whereas the investigation of perceptions among actual customers had revealed a consistency between their expectations and the central features of the organizational identity, blind tests in shops indicated that on average between 30 and 40 percent of European retailers still merely emphasized the aesthetic aspects of the products. This emphasis reinforced the idea, diffused among potential customers and reflected in the press (e.g., *Forbes*, 1991), that, as one of our informants said, "inside, they are all the same" and "what you really pay for is just a beautiful box."

B&O's communication efforts, therefore, were primarily addressed to the international network of retailers that shaped how customers perceived its products. In 1994 more than 600 dealers visited B&O headquarters to participate in training courses aimed at aligning their perceptions with the intentions of the new top managers. Seminars illustrated attributes of the desired image—the "brand essence" expressed in the New Vision—in terms of product features, design choices, and technological competencies. The content of the seminars was also widely publicized in the internal magazine.

Similarly, in 1998 top managers expected the new identity claims to be meaningful to all stakeholders. It was decided, however, that the revised identity statement would be communicated to and debated only among exclusive B&O dealers and would not be openly used in an advertising campaign. Additional seminars were held locally in order to ensure that new mono-brand shops that the company was founding and supporting would faithfully transfer the desired impressions to customers.

Embedding claims in organizational culture. Projected images seemed to serve the purpose of "energizing" members (Gioia & Chittipeddi, 1991) and stimulating a reconceptualization of the organization, but top managers turned once again to the culture of the organization to imbue revised identity claims with meaning, relying on a web of familiar stories, objects, and practices to facilitate interpretation of the new claims and illustrate their implications for action.

The Seven CIC, for instance, were described in terms of design and communication practices. Autovisuality, for instance, meant designing products so that they were self-explanatory to the user. Similarly, authenticity was illustrated by a decision to test the quality of sound and image reproduction on trained panels of viewers and listeners rather than on sophisticated technological measurement tools. During presentations, recently developed products were cited as concrete manifestations of the Seven CIC.

In fact, revised claims were never presented as radically new, but rather as a rediscovery of values and attitudes that were already part of the collective heritage of the organization. In 1994, every employee in the headquarters and several from the international network participated in a series of seminars aimed at clarifying the organizational identity and its importance for B&O's competitive success. The seminars were linked to an exhibition, The Curious Eye, which showed the evolution of B&O identity through different periods, as reflected in communication, advertising, and so forth. The firm's 1992–93 annual report stated that it was important that "amid all these changes, the company maintains its basic identity and is aware of its heritage." In this respect, the exhibition complemented the corporate seminar, as it showed how the company's identity had been constructed and expressed through self-defining company slogans and external communications. The presentation of the exhibition in the May 1994 issue of the house magazine *What?* read:

> When we know these periods, when we understand how they came into existence and see them expressed in the means of communication, we are better able to understand why and how Bang & Olufsen's identity has developed over the years. And understanding Bang & Olufsen's identity is a precondition for being able to further develop it.

Later, in 1998, the work of the task force provided a platform for so-called value seminars, where the Fundamental Values were first shared within the company as deliberate statements of who B&O was and what it stood for. Top managers intended to stimulate debate about values throughout the entire organization both nationally and internationally. However, the values themselves were not intended to be questioned, as a human resources manager on the top management team remarked during a seminar:

> Values must be found within the company, not defined. . . . Our values cannot be discussed: they are there where we have found them.

Although labels were defined at the top, the CEO intended debate to facilitate the emergence of a shared interpretation that would imbue the values with meaning. Top managers used an in-house video created in 1998 to provide concrete examples of how values manifested in everyday behavior. For instance, the video presented a popular B&O story as an illustration of how "synthesis" was a fundamental feature of the company's product development process:

> Chief designer David Lewis walks in with a cardboard tube that looks like a pencil and says: This is the new B&O loudspeaker. . . . He passes that on to the people in Business Development where people tear it apart and scream: no way! . . . Loads of discussion between them and David, and then they produce a synthesis: a prototype of the speaker. They then pass it on to Operations, who shout and scream: We can't make that! After another new round of yelling a new synthesis emerges: the product. . . . The following round of discussions involves Sales and Marketing: They in turn claim that nobody will buy it. Endless fights result in a new synthesis: The marketing concept. Now marketing has the problem. The dealers bend over backwards claiming that it won't sell. The result is a new synthesis: How to present the product in the stores. . . . Half a day later it has been sold. That's the way we work.

In summary, as new identity claims were illustrated and discussed, a reconstruction of the organizational history and tradition through display of physical and linguistic artifacts (products, advertising, corporate mottos, logos, stories, etc.) substantiated and supported official interpretations. New definitions and conceptualizations, therefore, appeared to be solidly embedded in a claimed cultural heritage and to reflect established patterns of behavior.

Although we have no direct evidence of the effect on the whole organization of the identity-related actions the top managers undertook to revise collective understandings (hence the dotted line in Figure 1), we gathered indirect indications of the success of their efforts. In none of the three cases did we observe resistance to changing conceptualizations of the organization, and our informants reported no such resistance. Furthermore, most of our informants traced explicit links between the revision of identity claims and their impact on activities such as product design or advertising campaigns. B&O managers, for instance, seemed to agree that in the long run the Seven CIC had a significant impact on both employees and dealers across the world. As a manager recalled:

> There was a general acceptance of the fact that the Seven CIC expressed a vision and provided an operational management tool which gave individual efforts a meaning and a purpose. (Bang & Palshøy, 2000: 87)

Our informants made also explicit connections between the new interpretations proposed by the revised identity claims and new products, such as the portable stereo system Beosound Century, and changes in the style of the company's catalogues in the 90s.

Discussion

Past research on how organizations handle identity-threatening issues has emphasized the central role of construed or desired images in stimulating and gauging members' responses (Dutton & Dukerich, 1991; Elsbach & Kramer, 1996). Gioia, Schultz, and their colleagues (e.g., Gioia et al., 2000; Hatch & Schultz, 2002) have suggested that, in doing so, organizational images "destabilize" members' self-perceptions. Construed images provide members with a feedback from external stakeholders about the credibility of their organization's identity claims (Whetten & Mackey, 2002). Although minor inconsistencies between external perceptions and internal beliefs are likely to trigger self-justification and the use of impression management to restore a favorable external image (Elsbach & Kramer, 1996; Ginzel et al., 1993), a serious discrepancy may undermine members' confidence and induce them to reevaluate their understandings of core and distinctive features of the organization (Gioia et al., 2000; Whetten & Mackey, 2002).

At B&O, however, both construed external images and cultural practices and artifacts offered cues for members who were reevaluating their organization's identity. Although construed external images seemed to act as a destabilizing force, the visible and tangible manifestation of the organizational culture seemed to have an opposite effect, inspiring and circumscribing members' responses and preserving their coherence with underlying assumptions and beliefs underpinning the collective sense of self. Cultural practices and artifacts served as a context for sensemaking and as a platform for sensegiving by providing organizational members with a range of cues for reinterpreting and reevaluating the defining attributes of the organization through a retrospective rationalization of the past.

Organizational Culture as a Context for Sensemaking

Extant conceptions of organizational culture tend to converge on the idea that culture is composed of a web of cultural expressions—including rituals, stories, artifacts, language, and more—that reflect an underlying pattern of shared interpretive beliefs, assumptions, and values (Louis, 1983; Martin, 2002; Schein, 1992; Trice & Beyer, 1984). At Bang & Olufsen, as members engaged in reflections and discussions about central and distinctive features of their organization, they seemed to find in these visible and tangible elements of their organization's culture a reservoir of cues supporting and mediating interorganizational comparisons, insofar as these cultural forms were perceived as a legacy of a shared past and interpreted as material manifestations of distinctiveness.

Material practices and interorganizational comparison. Building on psychological theories of identity, Albert and Whetten (1985) observed how organizational identities emerge from comparisons between the self and other entities. Perceived similarity or difference supports members' self-categorizations. Indeed, at B&O, as organizational members discussed the identity of the organization, they widely referred to the way products were designed or components selected, catalogues prepared, or prototypes tested. Material practices and artifacts, such as the sliding doors of the CD player Beosystem 2500, the sober elegance of anodized aluminum finishes, and the understatement of graphic designer Werner Neertoft's advertisements from the late 60s facilitated interorganizational comparison, helping members make sense of the similarity/dissimilarity between B&O and other, comparable organizations.

Research on organizational culture suggests that practices, artifacts, rituals, and other cultural forms visibly manifest idiosyncratic patterns of thought unique to one organization and the product of a collective learning history (Martin, 1993; Schein, 1992; Trice & Beyer, 1984). By their own nature, then, cultural forms, such as stories (Martin, Feldman, Hatch, & Simkin, 1983), sagas (Clark, 1972), corporate architecture (Berg & Kreiner, 1990), and dress (Pratt & Rafaeli, 1997) and other physical artifacts (Pratt & Rafaeli, 2001) tend to reflect—and be interpreted by members as evidence of—an organization's distinctiveness. As Dutton, Dukerich, and Harquail observed:

> Organizations have a broad repertoire of cultural forms such as rituals, symbols, ceremonies, and stories that encode and reproduce shared organizational patterns of behavior and interpretation. . . . Rituals, ceremonies, and stories objectify and communicate the collective organizational identity to organizational members. (1997: 243)

Tangible, material differences in product design or the content of advertising, therefore, may plausibly be interpreted as reflecting deeper, less visible differences in goals, values, and competencies.

At B&O, members' reflections focused largely, although not exclusively, on product design and development practices and on their visible outcomes as product features. As some of our informants observed, however, products had always been central to the culture of the organization. Furthermore, when comparing B&O with its competitors, the originality of the company's products made them one of the most evident elements of differentiation. In this respect, identity-related reflections seemed to converge around those aspects of the organizational culture—its design and development practices—that members considered distinctive traits of their organization.

Organizational culture and retrospective rationalization. Sensemaking can be understood as the imposition of an order a posteriori onto an ambiguous reality (Gioia, 1986; Weick, 1995). In this respect, visible and tangible elements of the culture of an organization may provide cues for retrospective rationalization. At B&O, as managers reexamined organizational identity, elements of the cultural heritage of the organization were interpreted as reflections of past achievements and manifestations of values, attitudes, and competencies that were retrospectively considered as central to the survival of the company.

Whether these interpretations were actually "true" is beside the point: organizational history is periodically reinterpreted by members in light of a current situation (Biggart, 1977). As individuals try to make sense of a complex history and to identify a causal sequence of events leading to a known outcome, accuracy is often less important than plausibility and pragmatism (Weick, 1995). In this respect, cultural practices and organizational artifacts may provide members reevaluating their organization's identity with a less ambiguous starting point than, for instance, values, goals, and mission. As Ashforth and Mael observed:

> Matters of the soul are inherently abstract, nebulous, arational, and potentially divisive; members often feel safer and more confident discussing the manifestations of identity, such as reporting relationships, budgets, operating routines, and recruiting practices. (1996: 29)

As members face a highly ambiguous cognitive task such as answering the question, "What is this organization really about?," familiar manifestations of a shared culture provide them with a starting point for making sense of their organizational identity.

Organizational Culture as a Platform for Sensegiving

Although it is not unreasonable to assume that institutional claims will influence members' understanding of what their organization is and stands for (Czarniawska, 1997; Whetten, 2003), past research indicates that changing identity claims may not always alter collective understandings accordingly (Humphreys & Brown, 2002). Institutional claims tend to express the view of organizational leaders, individuals who are expected to represent and to speak on behalf of their organization (Cheney, 1983; Whetten, 2003) and to mediate between the organization and the external environment (Hatch & Schultz, 1997). Collective understandings, however, may be less malleable and fluid than leaders' aspirations. Whereas changing claims can be plausibly interpreted as an expression of revised interpretations and aspirations on the organizational leaders' side, new claims are only loosely coupled to changes in collective understandings in the rest of the organization. New conceptualizations must be "socially validated" to be internalized by organizational members (Ashforth & Mael, 1996: 39). Therefore, accounting for how revised claims may influence collective understandings and overcome the spontaneous resistance displayed by organizational members is central to understanding change and adaptation in organizational identities.

Past research suggests that projecting new idealized conceptualizations embodied in "desired future images" (Gioia & Thomas, 1996) or "core ideologies" (Fiol, 2002) may induce members to gradually revise their understandings. At B&O, projected images were supplemented by narratives forging explicit connections between new claims and various manifestations of a common organizational culture—a claimed "cultural heritage." Physical or linguistic artifacts were used as concrete illustrations of values, attitudes, and behaviors that should support strategic response to environmental changes. Embedding new claims within the culture of the organization helped managers imbue claims with meaning and illustrate their practical implications and to preserve a sense of self and continuity in the face of changing self-definitions.

Organizational culture and symbolic action. Research on organizational change has highlighted the role of symbols and symbolization in promoting new understandings of an organization (Berg, 1985; Gioia et al., 1994). In order to facilitate members' sensemaking, as organizational leaders strive to "give sense" to organizational changes, they should present the changes in ways that relate them to previous experience (Gioia, 1986). Managing organizational change, therefore, involves considerable "symbolic action" carried out in order to help the rest of the organization develop a new interpretation of the organization, while at the same time preserving a connection with existing knowledge structures (Gioia et al., 1994; Pfeffer, 1981).

Symbols, understood as representative objects, acts, or events that stand for wider or more abstract concepts or meanings (Morgan, Frost, & Pondy, 1983), are central to organizational sensemaking, as they facilitate the interpretation of ambiguous experiences or events by conveying relationships with existing knowledge structures (Donnellon, Gray, & Bougon, 1986; Gioia, 1986). As Gioia remarked, however:

> Attempts to foster change . . . must take explicit recognition of the socially constructed nature of symbols, inasmuch as the overt symbols used to communicate the character of desired change should not have different meanings for different individuals and groups. It is important to develop symbols for change that have consensual bases to them: ones that are likely to engender common (and desired) meaning. (1986: 68)

In organizations, visible, tangible, and audible manifestations of culture, such as language, stories, visual images, material artifacts, and established practices, are among the most powerful symbols members rely upon for constructing meaning and organizing action (Gioia, 1986; Louis, 1983). As organizational leaders engage in sensegiving action, therefore, they can use manifestations of culture as influential discursive resources for crafting a meaningful account of new claims and resolving possible divergence of interpretations about core and distinctive features.

Organizational culture and the preservation of a sense of self and continuity. Institutional identity claims perform an important function in providing organizational members with a sense of self and continuity (Whetten & Mackey, 2002). Changes in identity claims, therefore, are likely to generate distress (Whetten, 2003) and encounter resistance (Fiol, 2002; Humphreys & Brown, 2002). Past research suggests that the proposal of idealized images of an organization may help members gradually overcome their resistance and redefine their beliefs (Gioia & Thomas, 1996; Reger, Gustafson, DeMarie, & Mullane, 1994). Our findings complement this line of research, as they suggest that a revision of collective understandings may be facilitated by embedding new claims in a narrative providing a postreconstruction of organizational history. As Whetten remarked:

> The need for continuity is so compelling that even profound organizational changes are typically portrayed as reaffirmations of higher level identity claims. . . . Another strategy used by organizational change agents to affirm an essential shared sense of organizational continuity is to portray a proposed change as a reinterpretation of an enduring identity claim. (2003: 13)

The narrative function of institutionalized claims, then, leads to the frequent inclusion of references to the history and tradition of an organization (Ashforth & Mael, 1996). An albeit simplified reconstruction of an alleged past, glossing over disruption and temporal inconsistency, helps members preserve a sense of self in the face of proposed changes (Gioia et al., 2000). In this respect, enriching the illustration of identity claims with specific details from a company's history and culture is likely to increase the credibility of the official narrative and support its claim of uniqueness (Martin et al., 1983). As old cultural practices and forms are imbued with new meaning, new claims can be convincingly presented as a rediscovery of shared values, the awareness of which had gradually faded over time. Furthermore, embedding new claims in the cultural heritage of the organization emphasizes the connection with "who we have been" rather than "who we want to become" (Gioia et al., 2000), providing credible support to a claim of continuity in the face of a management-driven attempt to reframe collective understandings in the light of new environmental conditions.

At B&O, the periodic renewal of a collective sense of self involved the projection of "desired images" or "future selves" that were deeply embedded in the organization's past.[3] Selected images of an organizational past—the Bauhaus heritage, the legacy of the founders, milestone products, and excerpts from old advertising campaigns—were used to give new sense to the organizational present and substantiate future aspirations. Revised identity claims did not seem aimed at substantially altering collective self-perceptions. On the contrary, their firm grounding in established practices and cultural forms made them appear to be attempts to return members' attention to features that had already been part of the way they had conceptualized the organization in the past.

Although our findings provide rare longitudinal evidence of actual changes in identity claims, then, they suggest that shared understandings may be less fluid than currently understood. A social actor perspective on organizational identity is centered on the notion that institutional claims provide continuity and consistency to members' collective self-perceptions. Conversely, a social constructionist perspective emphasizes the fluidity of shared understandings, even in the face of unchanging formal claims. Evidence from our study, however, suggests the paradoxical insight that although both perspectives may be correct in their own right, their advocates may have respectively underestimated the generative potential of institutional claims and the resilience of shared understandings under environmental pressures.

Organizational Identity Dynamics

Collectively, our findings suggest that in order to comprehend the processes that unfold in situations of perceived identity threat, researchers need to invoke a simultaneous recognition of the internally and externally directed dynamics of identity. Evidence from our study indicates that redefinitions of "who we are as an organization" tend to be influenced by how members believe the organization is perceived externally (construed external image) and by their beliefs and assumptions about idiosyncratic patterns of behavior (organizational culture).

Our emerging interpretations extend current conceptualizations of organizational responses to identity threats. Table 4 compares the current view of organizational responses to identity threats, and insights from our study. Building on our evidence, we propose a broad conception of identity threats that includes discrepant images as well as identity-threatening environmental changes, insofar as members perceive them as a challenge to the identity of the organization and are induced by them to reevaluate internal claims and understandings about organizational self-definitions. Previous conceptualizations have emphasized how "spoiled organizational images" threaten individual members' social identity and self-esteem (Elsbach & Kramer, 1996), but our conception includes challenges to the integrity and the continuity of members' collective sense of self as an organization (Whetten & Mackey, 2002). Unlike past research, which has focused on impression management

TABLE 4

New Insights on Organizational Responses to Identity Threats

Theoretical Aspect	Past Literature	Insights from Our Study
Nature of identity threats	External events challenging members' definition of central and distinctive attributes of their organization (Elsbach & Kramer, 1996; Ginzel et al., 1993).	Organizational identities may also be challenged by environmental changes that question the viability of what members' perceive as central, distinctive, and enduring features.
Drivers of organizational response	Organizational responses are guided by the attempt to realign construed and aspired external images (Dutton & Dukerich, 1991; Ginzel ct al., 1993). Construed external images act as a destabilizing force and as a trigger for identity-related action (Gioia et al., 2000).	Organizational responses arc constrained by the need to reconcile responsiveness to external changes with preservation of sense of self. The cultural heritage of the organization acts as a context for sensemaking and a platform for sensegiving, helping members maintain a sense of continuity amid formal or substantial changes.
Nature of organizational response	Organizational responses rely primarily on impression management (Sutton & Callahan, 1987; Ginzel et al., 1993) and self-affirmation techniques (Elsbach & Kramer, 1996) aimed at influencing external perceptions and representations of the organization.	Environmental changes induce reevaluation of shared definitions of self in light of identity-threatening events (sensemaking). Revised claims reflect understandings and aspirations of organizational leaders; new conceptualizations support adjustments in collective understandings linking to claimed cultural heritage (sensegiving).

techniques and cognitive tactics intended to realign external perceptions and internal beliefs and aspirations, our study points to the influence of organizational culture on sensemaking and sensegiving processes driving reexamination and revision of collective understandings. More broadly, our findings support a view of organizational responses to identity-threatening events as shaped by the interplay between organizational images and culture.

Hatch and Schultz (2000, 2002) advanced the idea that interplay between construed external images and organizational culture drives the evolution of organizational identities. Hatch and Schultz built their arguments on Mead's theory of identity as a social process, according to which individual identities arise in the interaction between two constructs: the "me," understood as the organized set of attitudes of others assumed by individuals, and the "I," the individual answer to external attitudes (Mead, 1934). Hatch and Schultz (2002) argued that construed external images and organizational culture may be considered the organizational equivalent of Mead's "me" and "I" and proposed a framework for understanding identity formation as emerging from the interaction of image and culture. According to the two authors, the tacit assumptions and beliefs of organizational members constitute the organizational context for the more aware reflections of "who we are as an organization" and can be seen as the conceptual parallel to the "organizational I" (Hatch & Schultz, 2000, 2002).

Conceptually, Hatch and Schultz's arguments are compelling. However, although their framework may provide a theoretical explanation for our findings, our study is the first to provide evidence of a dynamic relationship between culture, identity, and image that, so far, has been suggested at a theoretical level but never really supported empirically.

Methodological Limitations

Our study suffered from the usual limitations associated with case study research, which trades generality for richness, accuracy, and insight into observed processes (Langley, 1999; Yin, 1984). Our framework, however, emerged from comparing three separate instances of organizational responses to identity threats. Observing similar patterns of behavior across different cases reinforced our confidence in the generalizability of our emerging interpretations beyond the limited boundaries of our study.

We cannot exclude the possibility that specific traits of our research setting—a medium-sized business organization with a highly differentiated niche strategy—might have affected how the observed process unfolded. It is not unreasonable to argue that the relatively long history, unique products and positioning, and peculiar values of B&O might have provided members with a heightened sense of self, rooted in a rich organizational culture. We believe, however, that at B&O a strong culture and diffused pride and awareness of cultural heritage may have simply increased the visibility of processes that occur less visibly elsewhere. Comparison with earlier work on organizational identities seems to indicate that similar identity-related processes occur in large global corporations (Brunninge, 2004; Fombrun & Rindova, 2000) as well as in public nonprofit organizations (Dutton & Dukerich, 1991; Gioia & Thomas, 1996).

It is also possible that the emphasis on distinctiveness—as opposed to similarity—that we observed all along might have been affected by the nature of the organization that we studied: a business firm. Most organizations are subjected to conflicting pressures for conformity and differentiation (Deephouse, 1999), but the need for business firms to differentiate themselves from competitors may increase the relative importance of claims of distinction, such as those observed in B&O (Whetten, 2003). Claims of uniqueness may be even more important to consistently support a highly differentiated niche strategy such as B&O's. Future research might investigate more systematically whether variables such as age, type of activity, and organizational form or strategy influence the relative extents to which image and culture affect identity dynamics.

Finally, it may be argued that when environmental changes call for a substantial transformation in goals, values, structures, and practices, it may not be advisable, or even feasible, to have changes emanate from a reinterpretation of the past. To our knowledge, however, the literature holds little evidence of successful radical changes of organizational identity. The New York Port Authority, observed by Dutton and Dukerich (1991), seemed to rediscover traits that were perceived as already part of the identity of the organization. In Gioia and Thomas's (1996) study, whether the new dean's attempt to turn a large university into a "top ten" school actually produced any effect is not clear. A similar attempt described by Humphreys and Brown (2002) failed owing to the resistance of most organizational members. This is not to say that radical identity changes are impossible. We believe, however, that more empirical research on radical identity changes is needed to shed more light on the conditions that affect organizational leaders' willingness and capacity to carry out profound modifications in organizational identity claims and understandings.

Conclusions

Our study explored organizational responses to environmental changes and shifting external representations that induced members to reflect on their organization's recent and prospective courses of action and ask themselves, "What is this organization *really* about?" Although past research has documented the impact of desired images on organizational responses to environmental changes, our findings highlight the influence of organizational culture—and in particular, the influence of its manifestations—on the redefinition of members' collective self-perceptions.

Our findings point to organizational culture as a central construct in understanding the evolution of organizational identities in the face of environmental changes, suggesting that collective history, organizational symbols, and consolidated practices provide cues that help members make new sense of what their organization is really about and give that new sense to others. Further, our findings highlight the role of culture in preserving a sense of distinctiveness and continuity as organizational identity is subjected to explicit reevaluation. Our research, then, suggests that the roles external images and organizational culture play in affecting organizational responses to identity threats may be more complementary than the current literature on organizational identity would suggest.

Notes

1. Following earlier research (Weick, 1995), by "sensemaking" we refer to the act of constructing interpretations of ambiguous environmental stimuli; by "sensegiving" we refer to the deliberate attempt to shape the interpretations of others (Gioia & Chittipeddi, 1991).
2. The Bauhaus movement in architecture and design developed in the early 1920s around the work of architects and designers Walter Gropius, Marcel Breuer, and Mies van der Rohe.
3. We are indebted to one anonymous reviewer for pointing at this paradoxical insight.

References

Albert, S. 1998. The definition and metadefinition of identity. In D. A. Whetten & P. C. Godfrey (Eds.) *Identity in organizations: Developing theory through conversations*: 1–13. Thousand Oaks, CA: Sage.

Albert, S., & Whetten, D. A. 1985. Organizational identity. In L. L. Cummings & B. M. Staw (Eds.), *Research in organizational behavior*, vol. 7: 263–295. Greenwich, CT: JAI Press.

Ashforth, B. E., & Mael, F. 1996. Organizational identity and strategy as a context for the individual. In J. A. C. Baum & J. E. Dutton (Eds.), *Advances in strategic management*, vol. 13: 19–64. Greenwich, CT: JAI Press.

Bang, J., & Palshøy, J. 2000. *Bang & Olufsen, vision and legend*. Copenhagen: The Danish Design Center.

Barney, J. B., Bunderson, J. S., Foreman, P., Gustafson, L. T., Huff, A., Martins, L. L., Reger, R. K., Sarason, Y., & Stimpert, J. L. 1998. A strategy conversation on the topic of organization identity. In D. A. Whetten & P. C. Godfrey (Eds.), *Identity in organizations: Developing theory through conversations*: 99–168. Thousand Oaks, CA: Sage.

Berg, P. O. 1985. Organization change as a symbolic transformation process. In P. J. Frost, L. F. Moore, M. R. Louis, C. C. Lundberg, & J. Martin (Eds.), *Organizational culture*: 281–299. Beverly Hills, CA: Sage.

Berg, P. O., & Kreiner, K. 1990. Corporate architecture: Turning physical settings into symbolic resources. In P. Gagliardi (Ed.), *Symbols and artifacts: View of the corporate landscape*: 41–67. Berlin: de Gruyter.

Biggart, N. W. 1977. The creative destructive process of organizational change: The case of the post office. *Administrative Science Quarterly*, 22: 410–425.

Bouchiki, H., & Kimberly, J. R. 2003. Escaping the identity trap. *Sloan Management Review*, 44(3): 20–26.

Brunninge, O. 2004. *Translating strategic change in companies with strong identities: The dynamics of identity and strategic change at Scania and Handelsbanken.* Paper presented at the 20th Egos Colloquium, Ljubljana, Slovenia, July 1–3.

Carter, S. M., & Dukerich, J. M. 1998. Corporate responses to changes in reputation. *Corporate Reputation Review*, 1: 250–270.

Cheney, G. 1983. The rhetoric of identification and the study of organizational communication. *Quarterly Journal of Speech*, 69: 143–158.

Cheney, G., & Christensen, L. T. 2001. Organizational identity: Linkages between internal and external communication. In F. M. Jablin & L. L. Putnam (Eds.), *New handbook of organizational communication*: 231–269. Thousand Oaks, CA: Sage.

Clark, B. 1972. The organizational saga in higher education. *Administrative Science Quarterly*, 17: 178–184.

Corley, K. G. 2004. Defined by our strategy or our culture? Hierarchical differences in perceptions of organizational identity and change. *Human Relations*, 57: 1145–1177.

Corley, K. G., & Gioia, D. A. 2004. Identity ambiguity and change in the wake of a corporate spin-off. *Administrative Science Quarterly*, 49: 173–208.

Corley, K. G., Harquail, C. V., Pratt, M. G., Glynn, M. A., Fiol, C. M., & Hatch, M. J. 2006. Guiding organizational identity through aged adolescence. *Journal of Management Inquiry*, 15: 85–99.

Czarniawska, B. 1997. *Narrating the organization: Dramas of institutionalized identity.* Chicago: University of Chicago Press.

Deephouse, D. L. 1999. To be different or to be the same? It's a question (and theory) of strategic balance. *Strategic Management Journal*, 20: 147–166.

Donnellon, A., Gray, B., & Bougon, M. G. 1986. Communication, meaning and organizational action. *Administrative Science Quarterly*, 31: 43–55.

Dutton, J., & Dukerich, J. 1991. Keeping an eye on the mirror: Image and identity in organizational adaptation. *Academy of Management Journal*, 34: 517–554.

Dutton, J., Dukerich, J., & Harquail C.V. 1994. Organizational images and membership commitment. *Administrative Science Quarterly*, 39: 239–263

Elsbach, K. D., & Kramer, R. M. 1996. Member's responses to organizational identity threats: Encountering and countering the Business Week rankings. *Administrative Science Quarterly*, 41: 442–476.

Fiol, M. C. 1991. Managing culture as a competitive resource: An identity-based view of sustainable competitive advantage. *Journal of Management*, 17(1): 191–211.

Fiol, M. C. 2002. Capitalizing on paradox: The role of language in transforming organizational identities. *Organization Science*, 13: 653–666.

Fiol, M., Hatch, M. J., & Golden-Biddle, K. 1998. Organizational culture and identity: What's the difference anyway? In D. Whetten & P. Godfrey (Eds.), *Identity in organizations*: 56–59. Thousand Oaks, CA: Sage.

Fombrun, C. J., & Rindova, V. 2000. The road to transparency: Reputation management at Royal/Dutch Shell. In M. Schultz, M. J. Hatch, & M. Holten Larsen (Eds.), *The expressive organization: Linking identity, reputation and the corporate brand*: 77–97. Oxford, U.K.: Oxford University Press.

Forbes. 1991. A beautiful face is not enough. May 13: 105–106.

Friedland, R., & Alford, R. R. 1991. Bringing society back in: Symbols, practices, and institutional contradictions. In W. W. Powell & P. J. DiMaggio (Eds.), *The new institutionalism in organizational analysis*: 232–266. Chicago: University of Chicago Press.

Ginzel, L., Kramer, R., & Sutton, B. 1993. Organizational impression management as a reciprocal influence process: The neglected role of the organizational audience. In L. L. Cummings & B. M. Staw (Eds.), *Research in organizational behavior*, vol. 15: 227–266. Greenwich, CT: JAI Press.

Gioia, D. A. 1986. Symbols, scripts, and sensemaking. In H. P. Sims (Ed.), *The thinking organization*: 49–74. San Francisco: Jossey-Bass

Gioia, D. A. 1998. From individual to organizational identity. In D. A. Whetten & P. C. Godfrey (Eds.), *Identity in organizations: Developing theory through conversations*: 17–31. Thousand Oaks, CA: Sage.

Gioia, D. A., & Chittipeddi, K. 1991. Sensemaking and sensegiving in strategic change initiation. *Strategic Management Journal*, 12: 443–448.

Gioia, D. A, Schultz, M., & Corley, K. 2000. Organizational identity, image and adaptive instability. *Academy of Management Review*, 25: 63–82.

Gioia, D. A., & Thomas, J. B. 1996. Identity, image and issue interpretation: Sensemaking during strategic change in academia. *Administrative Science Quarterly*, 41: 370–403.

Gioia, D., Thomas, J. B., Clark, S. M., & Chittipeddi, K. 1994. Symbolism and strategic change in academia: The dynamics of sensemaking and influence. *Organization Science*, 5: 363–383.

Glaser, B. G., & Strauss A. L. 1967. *The discovery of grounded theory.* New York: Aldine.

Golden-Biddle, K., & Rao, H. 1997. Breaches in the boardroom: Organizational identity and conflicts of commitment in a nonprofit organization. *Organization Science*, 8: 593–609.

Hatch, M. J., & Schultz, M. 1997. Relations between organizational culture, identity and image. *European Journal of Marketing*, 31: 356–365.

Hatch, M. J., & Schultz, M. 2000. Scaling the Tower of Babel: Relational differences between identity, image and culture in organizations. In M. Schultz, M. J. Hatch, & M. H. Larsen (Eds.), *The expressive organization:* 11–36. Oxford, U.K.: Oxford University Press.

Hatch, M. J., & Schultz, M. 2002. The dynamics of organizational identity. *Human Relations*, 55: 989–1018.

Hatch, M. J., & Schultz, M. 2004. *Organizational identity: A reader.* Oxford, U.K.: Oxford University Press.

Humphreys, M., & Brown, A. D. 2002. Narratives of organizational identity and identification: A case study of hegemony and resistance. *Organization Studies*, 23: 421–447.

Langley A. 1999. Strategies for theorizing from process data. *Academy of Management Review*, 24: 691–710.

Lee, T., Mitchell, T., & Sablynski, C. 1999. Qualitative research in organizational and vocational behavior. *Journal of Vocational Behavior*, 55: 161–187.

Lee, T. W. 1999. *Using qualitative methods in organization research.* London: Sage.

Locke, K. 2001. *Grounded theory in management research.* London: Sage.

Louis, M. R. 1983. Organizations as culture-bearing milieux. In L. R. Pondy, P. J. Frost, G. Morgan, & T. Dandridge (Eds.), *Organizational symbolism:* 39–54. Greenwich, CT: JAI Press.

Martin, J. 1993. *Cultures in organizations. Three perspectives.* Oxford, U.K.: Oxford University Press.

Martin, J. 2002. *Organizational culture: Mapping the terrain.* Thousand Oaks, CA: Sage.

Martin, J., Feldman, M. S., Hatch, M. J., & Simkin, S. B. 1983. The uniqueness paradox in organizational stories. *Administrative Science Quarterly*, 28: 438–453.

Mead, G. H. 1934. *Mind, self, and society.* Chicago: University of Chicago Press,

Miles, M. B., & Huberman, M. A. 1994. *Qualitative data analysis.* Thousands Oaks, CA: Sage.

Morgan, G., Frost, P. J., & Pondy, L. R. 1983. Organizational symbolism. In L. R. Pondy, P. J. Frost, G. Morgan, & T. Dandridge (Eds.), *Organizational symbolism:* 3–38. Greenwich, CT: JAI Press.

Pfeffer, J. 1981. Management as symbolic action: The creation and maintenance of organizational paradigms. In L. L. Cummings & B. M. Staw (Eds.), *Research in organizational behavior*, vol. 3: 1–52. Greenwich, CT: JAI Press.

Poulsen, P. T. 1997. *Break-point.* Copenhagen: Jyllands-Postens Forlag.

Pratt, M. G. 2003. Disentangling collective identity. In J. Polzer, E. Mannix, & M. Neale (Eds.), *Identity issues in groups: Research in managing groups and teams:* 161–188. Stamford, CT: Elsevier Science Ltd.

Pratt, M. G., & Rafaeli, A. 1997. Organizational dress as a symbol of multilayered social identities. *Academy of Management Journal*, 40: 862–898.

Pratt, M. G., & Rafaeli, A. 2001. Symbols as language of organizational relationships. In L. L. Cummings & B. M. Staw (Eds.), *Research in organizational behavior*, vol. 23: 93–132. Greenwich, CT: JAI Press.

Ravasi, D., & van Rekom, J. 2003. Key issues in organizational identity and identification theory. *Corporate Reputation Review*, 6(2): 118–132.

Reger, R. K., Gustafson, L. T., DeMarie, S. M., Mullane, J. V. 1994. Reframing the organization: Why implementing total quality is easier said than done. *Academy of Management Review*, 19: 565–584.

Rindova, V. P., & Fombrun, C. J. 1999. Constructing competitive advantage: The role of firm-constituent interactions. *Strategic Management Journal*, 20: 691–710.

Rindova, V. P., & Schultz, M. 1998. Identity within and identity without: Lessons from corporate and organizational identity. In D. A. Whetten & P. C. Godfrey (Eds.), *Identity in organizations: Developing theory through conversations:* 46–51. Thousand Oaks, CA: Sage.

Schein, E. H. 1992. *Organizational culture and leadership.* San Francisco: Jossey-Bass.

Schultz, M. 1995. *On studying organizational cultures: Diagnosis and understanding.* Berlin: Walter de Gruyter.

Selznick, P. 1957. *Leadership in administration.* New York: Harper & Row.

Smircich, L. 1983. Organizations as shared meanings. In L. R. Pondy, P. J. Frost, G. Morgan, & T. Dandridge (Eds.), *Organizational symbolism:* 55–65. Greenwich, CT: JAI Press.

Sutton, R. I., & Callahan, A. 1987. The stigma of bankruptcy: Spoiled organizational image and its management. *Academy of Management Journal,* 30: 405–436.

Sutton, R. I., & Hargadon, A. 1996. Brainstorming groups in context: Effectiveness in a product design firm. *Administrative Science Quarterly,* 685–718.

Trice, H., & Beyer, J. 1984. Studying organizational cultures through rites and ceremonies. *Academy of Management Review,* 9: 653–669.

Weick, K. 1979. *The social psychology of organizing.* Reading, MA: Addison-Wesley.

Weick, K. 1995. *Sense-making in organizations.* Thousand Oaks, CA: Sage.

Whetten, D. A. 2003. *A social actor conception of organizational identity.* Unpublished manuscript, Brigham Young University, Provo, Utah.

Whetten, D. A. 2006. Albert and Whetten revisited: Strengthening the concept of organizational identity, *Journal of Management Inquiry:* In press.

Whetten, D. A., & Godfrey, P. C. 1998. *Identity in organizations: Developing theory through conversations.* Thousand Oaks, CA: Sage.

Whetten, D. A., & Mackey, A. 2002. A social actor conception of organizational identity and its implications for the study of organizational reputation. *Business and Society,* 41: 393–414.

Whetten, D. A., Mischel, D., & Lewis, L. G. 1992. *Toward an integrated model of organizational identity and member commitment.* Paper presented at the annual meeting of the Academy of Management, Las Vegas.

Yin, R. K. 1984. *Case study research.* Beverly Hills, CA: Sage.

THE POWER OF SYMBOLIC CONSTRUCTS IN READING CHANGE IN HIGHER EDUCATION[1]

HASAN SIMSEK

Abstract. Based on interviews with 24 faculty members at a large, public university, this article reports the use of metaphors as a new conceptual strategy to analyze change in higher education organizations. Results of the study indicate that strategic choices guiding the behavior of the organization under study and the metaphorical images held by the faculty members about their organization show a high degree of congruence. Implications for change and maintenance of enacted realities in higher education organizations are discussed.

Introduction

As the base of the organization theory expands (Burrel and Morgan 1983), new terms, concepts, analytical and methodological tools are increasingly used in ways that are consistent with these emerging new themes. In particular, with the emergence of the symbolic or cultural perspective on organizations (Bolman and Deal 1991; Smircich 1983), anthropological concepts such as myths, sagas, symbols, ceremonies, beliefs and values as well as some linguistic concepts such as metaphors have received a great deal of attention. Using these concepts, organizations are analyzed as enacted cultural realities that bind and hold an entire community and its membership.

"A metaphor is a figure of speech in which a term or a phrase with a literal meaning is applied to a different context in order to suggest a resemblance" (Sackmann 1989, p. 465). Besides its transformative power as a language form, metaphor also denotes a way of knowing: For example, scientists view the world metaphorically in developing their framework for analysis (Morgan 1980, p. 611). Furthermore, Lakoff and Johnson argued that less concrete and inherently more vague concepts are restructured in terms of more concrete concepts that have clear meanings, understanding and familiarity in our daily life. Thus, through metaphor, the unknown is explained by known experiences (Lakoff and Johnson 1982, p. 112; reported in Sackmann 1989, p. 465).

According to Morgan, "the creative potential of metaphor depends upon there being a degree of difference between the subjects involved in the metaphorical process" (Morgan 1980, p. 611), one being more concrete than the other when used to explain the target phenomenon. In most cases, while the commonalties are emphasized, differences are suppressed in a selective comparison (Morgan 1980, p. 611). On the other hand, metaphors transmit entire systems or domains of meaning by under-emphasizing individual and isolated concepts or phenomena. They create a mental picture which substitutes for thousands of words in describing an entire situation. This makes metaphors very powerful communication tools with their picture-like nature since they transmit a complete story visually using only one image (Sackmann 1989, pp. 467–68).

Metaphors transfer schema from one area to another, they filter and define reality in a simple fashion such as "Richard is a lion," "the brain is a computer," "capitalist economies are markets"

"Metaphorical Images of an Organization: The Power of Symbolic Constructs in Reading Change in Higher Education Organizations," by Hasan Simsek in *Higher Education*, Vol. 33, No. 3, April 1997.

(Sterman 1985, p. 98), or "organizations are machines," "organizations are organisms," "organizations are flux and transformation," etc. (Morgan 1986). Metaphors are very powerful in describing the most important features of a complex array of variables in a simple form, but they only provide part of a whole picture (Morgan 1980; Sterman 1985).

It is useful in the following ways to employ metaphors to explain tacit background assumptions in organizations:

1. to clarify the enacted reality in organization which emphasizes commonalities between the nature of organization and of the used metaphor,

2. to draw an approximate visual picture of the organization in terms of the dominant strategic orientation guided by the underlying enacted reality,

3. to provide somewhat detailed information about the organization by containing certain linguistic components, specifically adjectives and adverbs used in a metaphorical description (Simsek 1992).

Thus, metaphor is an expressive (language-related) form that facilitates communication in understanding the tacit assumptions widely shared in an organization. These tacit assumptions in turn define the mode and direction of behavior in organizations.

A growing literature has examined the use of metaphors in a variety of social settings ranging from the process of theory construction in science, to the behavior of firms, to procedures by which children in grade school classroom learn (Morgan 1986; Sackmann 1989; Sterman 1985). The value of metaphors come from their rich linguistic character and their relationship with explication of reality: "All languages have deeply embedded metaphorical structures that are reflective of and influential in the meaning of reality . . . become[ing] vehicles of vernacular for expressing one's understanding of one's environment within a specific cultural, historic context" (Bredeson 1985, p. 30). The important reflection of a cultural and historic context through metaphorical linguistic forms has been widely recognized in studies explaining construction and perception of reality in organizational settings (Lakoff and Johnson 1982; Sackmann 1989; Bredeson 1985; Simsek and Louis 1991; Louis and Simsek 1994).

Several authors emphasize the importance of metaphors in knowledge creation and defining ways of knowing the world through a process of interpretation (Smircich 1983; Morgan 1986). By using metaphors, Morgan (1986), for example reinterpreted mainstream organization theories by identifying their metaphorical imagery. Similarly, Sackmann (1989) demonstrated how metaphors were used by executives in a private firm's restructuring process to redefine their changing reality. Her results showed that the metaphors of "gardening" (cutting, pruning, gathering, nurturing) were effectively used to change the firm's overall identity.

Bredeson (1985), on the other hand, analyzed the bases of three metaphorical images held by a number of school principals about their jobs: maintenance, survival and vision. The maintenance metaphor was represented by an image of caretaker or overseer who keeps the school doors open and the process going. The metaphor of survival was depicted by an image of a constant flow of day-to-day and immediate activities. The metaphor of vision, on the other hand, reflected their broad understanding of the future on certain educational issues concerning their schools, surrounding community and the state at large.

This discussion proves two powerful uses of metaphors in organizational analysis: First, there is enough evidence of the uses of metaphorical analysis in reading the present nature of organization. It is like taking the picture of an often implicit and tacit world view that overwhelmingly defines the behavior of an organization. Thus, in this mode of inquiry, metaphors are tools to read the situation. Second, some scholars use metaphors not as a reading tool but as a catalyst for change as reported in Sackmann's study (1989). Sackmann argued that metaphors may be used to inject a particular vision in the organization. Since metaphors have picture-like qualities, they may potentially constitute a powerful medium for communication of an often abstract and tacit future orientation. A simple metaphor may substitute a thousand-word document in prescribing particular actions to be taken or a particular path to be followed. In this study, metaphorical analysis was used in the first sense, that is, in reading the organization.

On the other hand, organization theory in higher education is based on five powerful models: the bureaucratic or structural frame, the collegial or human resource frame, the political frame, the organized anarchy frame and the symbolic frame. The bureaucratic or structural frame involves a hierarchical, rule-based administrative scheme in which change is explained as structural reconfiguration of organizational apparatus as the environment demands (Emery 1969; Katz and Kahn 1978; Lawrence and Lorsch 1967). The collegial or human resource frame considers higher education institutions as a collegium "where differences in status are deemphasized, people interact as equals in a system that stresses consensus, shared power and participation in governance, and common commitments and aspirations" (Bensimon, Neumann and Birnbaum 1989, p. 54). In this frame, change is through community-wide consensus and participative decision-making. The political frame sees the higher education institutions as essentially political entities where there exists more than one interest group or coalition. Change, under the political frame, is a dynamic politicking process among various groups struggling for more control and influence (Baldridge et al. 1978). The organized anarchy frame (Cohen and March 1974), on the other hand, explains higher education organizations as essentially unpredictable entities where change is random because of "politicized nature of the involvement of different actors with different agendas and interests" (Simsek and Louis 1994, p. 671).

Of the symbolic frame, one of the least utilized perspectives to higher education organizations as part of a general trend in the organization theory is that "the symbolic side of modem organizations has been vastly understated in research" (Clark 1983, p. 73). However, starting with Clark's seminal work on organizational sagas (Clark 1972), scholars have devoted attention to the symbolic side of academic organizations in terms of beliefs, ideologies, stories, legends and sagas. In a recent study, for example, Simsek and Louis argued that changes in organizational structure and procedures in higher education institutions may not produce much change in behavior unless there is a genuine shift in the underlying organizational paradigm, namely assumptions and values (Simsek and Louis 1994, p. 690).

Departing from a symbolic orientation, and, by using a case study design, the purpose of this article is to present how metaphors as symbolic constructs can be used in the analysis of change in higher education organizations.

Statement of the Problem

The following questions guided the data collection and analysis process:

1. *Before the Commitment to Focus Plan*

   1a. What metaphor, image or analogy were used by the faculty members to describe the University before the Commitment to Focus Plan?

   1b. What institutional strategies or policies were perceived by the faculty to describe the University before the Commitment to Focus Plan?

   1c. Is there any relationship or contextual congruence between the metaphors, images or analogies and institutional policies or strategies from the perspectives of faculty members concerning the period before the Commitment to Focus Plan?

2. *After the Commitment to Focus Plan*

   2a. What metaphor, image or analogy were used by the faculty members to describe the University after the Commitment to Focus Plan?

   2b. What institutional strategies or policies were perceived by the faculty to describe the University after the Commitment to Focus Plan?

   2c. Is there any relationship or contextual congruence between the metaphors, images or analogies and institutional policies or strategies from the perspectives of faculty members concerning the period after the Commitment to Focus Plan?

Before describing the method of study, it would be relevant to provide background information about the planning and change at the University of Minnesota.

The Case: Strategic Planning in the University of Minnesota

According to Foster (1989–90), the University of Minnesota has a number of unique roles that distinguish it from other higher education institutions in the United States:

- It is the land-grant university for a state that is a center for both agriculture and technology, so that education in 'agriculture and the mechanic arts' is an important responsibility; it is the state's only source for higher education in agriculture and related fields and, until 1983, its only source of engineering education. The university maintains the strong commitment to public service and statewide outreach that such a combination implies.

- The university's Twin Cities campus serves as the urban university for the Minneapolis–St. Paul metropolitan area, with a population of 2.5 million; its evening extension classes serve 37,000 students per year.

- It is the state's only research university (Foster 1989–90, p. 26).

A number of internal and external calamities forced the university to undertake a strategic planning process. Externally, the reasons laid within the state's financial difficulties in the late 1970s and the early 1980s. Internally, on the other hand, many observed an erosion of quality over the previous forty years as a number of departments' national reputation declined. Especially, the university's undergraduate education was criticized in several areas: an impersonal campus climate, large classes, long lines, bureaucratic rules, and very few faculty who showed interest in their students (Foster 1989–90 p. 26).

Although a strong planning orientation was started in the early 1980s, the planning process at the University of Minnesota dates back to the mid 1970s. Clugston (1987, p. 91), for example, divided the strategic planning process of the University into four phases. During the period between 1974–79, the structure and framework for planning was started with the appointment of a planning council by the president. Following this preparation phase, the first cycle of planning occurred between the spring of 1979 and the spring of 1982. Following a centrally developed planning statement, all units, including colleges, were required to submit their goals and objectives under the direction of guidelines defined by the central planning document for the 1980s.

The second cycle covered the period between 1982–84. A severe budget shortfall in the state economy in the early 1980s (1981–83) resulted in a four percent cut in the state's allocation for the university. This unexpected development forced the university to immediately link the already-in-process program prioritization with the budget decisions in terms of internal resource allocation (Clugston 1987, p. 95).

The third cycle, covering the period between 1984–85, let each unit find ways or develop strategies in order to implement set targets in program prioritization. The fourth cycle, on the other hand, was designed to give feedback to the first cycle through which each unit would re-examine its mission in light of the second and third cycles of the planning process (Clugston 1987, p. 96). During this planning process at least seven university committees were dealing with different issues confronting the university [—such as undergraduate and graduate education, research, outreach and technology transfer, and improving the management of the university—]. The result of this committee work was a vast array of diagnoses, prescriptions and recommendations (Foster 1989–90, p. 26).

By the time the university was busy with the planning and committee work, an incidental event occurred which sparked a series of momentous events in the planning and change process of the university:

> In late 1984, while the university was attempting to digest the many committee recommendations and to set a direction for concerted action, an activist governor visited to tell the interim president that the university was trying to do too much and should focus its activities if it hoped for support in the governor's budget recommendations to the legislature (Foster 1989–90, pp. 26–27).

The response to this challenge came from Kenneth Keller, vice president for academic affairs, then interim president and subsequently president. His "Commitment to Focus" proposal announced in 1985 was largely based on the previous committee recommendations, although it was a personal interpretation of those recommendations. The proposal gained the support of the majority of the faculty as well as the governing board (Foster 1989–90, p. 27).

In the report, the foundation of the Commitment to Focus plan was described as the governing board's mission statement and the institution-wide planning activities. The Commitment to Focus plan was put forth as an effort to make the university one of the five top public universities in the nation with emphasis on being an international research university, a land-grant institution, a metropolitan university carrying out the functions of research, teaching and service, and, fundamentally serving a clientele composed of professional, graduate and undergraduate students (Keller 1985).

The Commitment to Focus Plan: A Vision for Change

The plan was basically laid out on the following dimensions:

1. Efforts of higher education institutions in the state should be coordinated, or duplication of efforts should be minimized.
2. Faculty should be released from certain involvements such as heavy load of teaching.
3. The university is out of balance in terms of ratio of undergraduates to graduates.
4. Quality should not be sacrificed in order to preserve the breadth of programs.
5. Various campuses in the system should be coordinated through a number of rearrangements (Keller 1985).

To release faculty from certain involvements and to reduce the undergraduate/graduate ratio, the plan recommended that undergraduate enrollments should be reduced (which would lead to reduced undergraduate class sizes) and the number of graduates should be increased. The cuts in the undergraduate numbers could easily be absorbed by other higher education institutions in the state. By doing so, the principle of equal educational opportunity would not be harmed.

In order to reduce the breadth of programs which had resulted in increasing financial burden and declining quality, the plan proposed eliminating and reducing a number of programs and units.

Of the declining quality, it was proposed that the admission requirements should be increased to recruit high-ability undergraduates, and the quality of undergraduate programs should be improved through increased admission standards and reduced class sizes.

On the issue of coordinating campuses, the plan proposed that the mission of each campus should be focused and sharpened. The University's attention should be focused on the Twin Cities campus, and entrance standards should be increased and unified across all undergraduate colleges on this campus (Keller 1985).

The plan received wide support from inside and outside the university. By the time the plan was announced, the university was in search of its new president. Then, Kenneth Keller was appointed as president by the governing board in 1986, no doubt owing to his Commitment to Focus Plan. This was a "green light" signaling the approval to implement the strategies developed in the plan. Described by many as an intelligent and visionary leader, he managed to convince the legislature on the funding issues. The state's support for the University was going to remain the same even as enrollment declined. This was an unusual and impressive success for the university in general and for the new president in particular. On the other hand, a considerable amount of private funding was provided through a series of successful fund raising campaigns.

However, the president resigned in March 1988 as a result of a public controversy due to alleged financial mismanagement of the University (Foster 1989–90, p. 35). The new president, inaugurated in October 1989, had served on numerous university committees since the initial phases of the strategic planning process. In his inauguration address, he laid out his plan for the University demonstrating his strong commitment to the fundamental spirit of the Commitment to Focus plan. However, the name of the plan was changed to "Access to Excellence" in order to overcome charges of elitism levied against the original plan. Additionally, he emphasized his priority as upgrading the quality of undergraduate education.

Data Collection and Analysis

The Interview Schedule

The interviews were held in the summer of 1992, seven years after the Commitment to Focus proposal was announced. In order to elicit the metaphors that describe the University after and before the Commitment to Focus initiative and their relation to most cited strategic choices with which the University was identified, four types of open-ended interview questions were designed:

Before Commitment to Focus:

- What metaphor, image or analogy would best describe the University as a higher education institution before the Commitment to Focus Plan?[2]
- What particular policies, strategies or organizational actions could best describe the University before the Commitment to Focus Plan?

After Commitment to Focus:

- What metaphor, image or analogy would best describe the University as a higher education institution after the Commitment to Focus Plan?
- What particular policies, strategies or organizational actions could best describe the University after the Commitment to Focus Plan?

Pilot Test, Sampling and Interview

The interview schedule was initially pilot-tested on six randomly selected faculty members representing six departments from different colleges. Then, a "multiple embedded case design" (Yin 1984 pp. 44–47) was used to form the sample which involved five departments from the four largest colleges. These departments and colleges were chosen after the researcher's consultations with knowledgeable members of the faculty. Of particular concern was that the selected departments should not be involved in similar professional circles which might yield a routine interaction as a result of overlapping responsibilities or similar professional and intellectual backgrounds. The sample involved the following departments: Strategic Management (School of Management), Political Science and English (College of Liberal Arts), Mathematics (Institute of Technology), and Food Science (College of Agriculture). In each department, a list of faculty members was obtained. Since the researcher was interested in exploring the degree of shared understanding in terms of symbolic images and subjective perceptions held by the faculty members about their institution, professional experience and length of tenure in the institution was used as a sampling criterion rather than the academic ranks of the faculty. For this, the researcher decided that the faculty member should have been in the institution for at least ten years to ensure that the perception of faculty would reflect the differences (if any) between the two phases of the change process in the institution.

From each department, a list of five primary and three substitute faculty members were selected through a random sampling procedure. As a result, the sample involved faculty members from various academic ranks who were actively teaching. Potential respondents were contacted first by letter and then by telephone. Disinterested or unavailable respondents were substituted by others through similar stages. A total of 24 faculty members from five departments were interviewed. All interviews were tape-recorded and later transcribed verbatim by a professional typist.

Although the researcher is aware of the fact that the universities involve various levels, this study only deals with the perceptions of the faculty members. As was explained elsewhere, "we focused on faculty as informants, because they are viewed as carrying a special status of responsibility for conserving the university and typically have a longer time perspective that administrators, who, at least at the University of Minnesota, often occupy their positions for five or fewer years" (Simsek and Louis 1994, p. 678).

Qualitative Data Analysis and Reporting

To analyze the data, a qualitative method was followed. Particularly, in identifying the strategic choices that the university was most engaged in before and after the Commitment to Focus initiation, the interview transcripts were content analyzed to find out themes and patterns (Patton 1987, p. 149). By using a word processing program, each interview transcript was sorted under four question categories by cutting and pasting without changing the original word structure or phrasing used by respondents, so each piece of information could be accurately grouped under a related category. The procedure was carefully constructed in an effort to avoid any distortion of the information at the primary level of analysis. Then, each pasted item in each category was given a name or a tag describing each intact sentence. Finally, the tags under each category were compared across five interview transcripts for each department, and then they were grouped in their contextual similarity. This analysis procedure is called "open coding" by Strauss and Corbin (1990, pp. 61–74).

Qualitative analysis and reporting may range from pure narrative to statistical forms and graphic presentations (Wolcott 1994, pp. 17–32). The nature of data at hand and the nature of the problem posed may dictate different analysis and reporting strategies, but, in many cases, the same data can be treated in both ways based on the priorities identified by the researcher. In this study, extensive interview data were reduced to thematic categories based on the general categories stated in the research problems. The purpose in doing so was to compare two phases of organizational change at the University of Minnesota from the perspectives of the faculty members, to relate these findings to the planning efforts of the university administration, and to explore the likelihood of any congruence between the metaphorical images and organizational strategies generated by the faculty members. So, an analysis and reporting strategy which was more categorical based on simple frequencies, and less narrative (see Exhibit 2 and Exhibit 4) seemed appropriate for this purpose.

The following points should be made for better understanding of the findings which will be presented later:

1. As mentioned earlier, Nils Hasselmo, the new president replacing Kenneth Keller, who designed the Commitment to Focus Plan, did not alter the fundamental spirit of the Commitment to Focus Plan other than changing the name of the plan to Access to Excellence to overcome negative charges against the original plan and to emphasize the quality of the undergraduate education. For these reasons, interviewees were asked to generate metaphors/images/analogies as well as institutional strategies and policies only about the periods before and after the Commitment to Focus Plan. Since Access to Excellence can not be called a radically different plan per se, the findings that will be presented later only concern two distinct institutional phases, namely pre-1985 (before the Commitment to Focus initiation), and post-1985 (after the Commitment to Focus initiation).

2. Since the interviews were held in the summer of 1992, the post 1985 period covers a seven year time span during which most of the proposed strategies in the Commitment to Focus Plan were already put into action (e.g. program closures to solve the problems of duplication and of quality deterioration, reduction in the undergraduate student population in favor of an increase in the graduate student number). Because of this, and of the way the research questions were designed, the following findings reflect the faculty's perception of the changes at the University of Minnesota in reference to the Commitment to Focus Plan.

3. Although the sampling design was carefully constructed to ensure diversity and representation of the general faculty population, one generic weakness of qualitative research holds true in this study as well: ". . . a lone qualitative researcher, working with inevitable limitations of time and resources . . ." (Wolcott 1994, p. 183) studying large organizations such as the University of Minnesota. In this respect, findings of this study should be considered more of an exploratory effort to bring forth a new analytical tool in higher education organization research such as metaphors rather than to make generalizable descriptive inferences to the larger population.

Findings

Q1. *Results reading the period before the Commitment to Focus Plan*

   1a. *Metaphorical images*

A total of 32 metaphors were produced by 22 respondents (Exhibit 1). More than one-third of them were match: Octopus=5, elephant=3, amoeba=3, and a wildly growing garden or vegetable=2. Some of the images can still be grouped under these four broad categories in terms of their contextual similarity.[3] For example, "cow" and "buffalo" metaphors can be added to the "elephant" metaphor, since all three metaphors emphasize the massive size of the institution. By their contextual similarities, other metaphors such as the following can be grouped together, and linked to the metaphor of "a wildly growing garden or vegetable:" "a tangled up ball of twine," "an enormous size, Chinese menu catalog of offerings," "unruly group of school children," "a feudal-medieval landscape containing many fiefdoms with their own princes and princesses," "a wagon train going different directions for different purposes" and "a beehive going different directions, doing their own separate jobs." From an organizational perspective, these metaphorical images can be interpreted in two ways. On the one hand, they may confirm an organized anarchy in terms of lack of control, lack of coordination and collaboration, and uncontrolled growth in organizational activities. On the other hand, they may simply confirm the fact that the University of Minnesota is one of the largest and most complex universities in the U.S. Both of these interpretations seem to confirm the organization change literature that there is a positive association between the size of the organization, and differentiation and structural complexity, as well as more decentralization (Hage and Aiken 1967; Pugh et. al. 1969; Blau and Schoenherr 1971; Scott 1992).

Thus, by combining the metaphorical images in terms of their contextual similarities, we reach the following picture:

Amoeba=3, Octopus=5, Elephant and related metaphors=5, A wildly growing garden and related metaphors=8

   1b. *Institutional strategies*

Faculty members identified four clusters of dominant strategic behaviors that identified the University before the Commitment to Focus Plan (Exhibit 2):

1. Growth and expansion in program areas, and in program diversity, variety of offerings, opening and creating many small departments and programs.

2. Teaching and service emphasis as rewarded and praised faculty behavior.

3. Large student population and emphasis on quantity, open access and guaranteed admission, and low admission standards.

4. Independent unit activities, freedom to develop programs; autonomy and decentralized/collegial decision making granted to colleges, units and departments.

   1c. *The match between metaphors and institutional strategies*

The following interpretation can be drawn from these four central metaphors in relation to the four clusters of institutional strategies:

1. The amoeba metaphor represented an image of the University as a land grant institution that lacked a solid/strong identity. Many referred to the University as an institution "being all things for all people." Additionally, it was in a constant process of growth similar to the amoeba's multiplication by fission.

2. The elephant and related metaphors (cow and buffalo) provided an image that is significant by its size and massive body. They refer to the institution that has traditionally been one of the largest public universities in the nation.

3. The octopus, however, is easily identified with eight arms on a single body. As several faculty members remarked "the university was like an octopus with its eight arms embracing different constituencies simultaneously." The organization was explained as a single body attempting to satisfy the demands of many constituencies at the same time.

4. The metaphors of "wildly growing garden or vegetable," and other related images listed above, characterize an uncontrolled and continuous growth and expansion in the program areas and activities in the University. As a result, the metaphorical images used by the faculty in describing the most noticeable features of their organization are strikingly linked to the most salient institutional strategies, with each metaphor representing a group of central institutional strategies.

Q2 *Results reading the period after the Commitment to Focus Plan*
   2a. *Metaphorical images*

A total of 24 metaphors were produced by 21 faculty members (Exhibit 3). In this case, there is considerable diversity and less consensus over the metaphors chosen compared to the metaphors used for describing the period before Commitment to Focus, except the "lion" metaphor which was repeated three times. However, respondents see the current organization as being different than the prior one in terms of being more directed, focused, powerful and purposeful in its strategic orientation, smaller and trimmed down in size and structure, and more coordinated in its internal decision making.

A careful examination of metaphors reveals that almost half of the metaphors generated by the faculty in describing the university after the Commitment to Focus plan show a metaphoric continuity. Although a minority, some faculty were not convinced that a real change was evident in the university. Rather, the situation was worsened as revealed by such metaphors as "a great, big, multi-limbed, stumbling animal," "an enormous Chinese menu catalog of offerings," "a sick octopus," "a jungle," "a wounded buffalo," "an amoeba." On the other hand, a number of faculty added a qualitative improvement (often in a positive manner) in the university's overall image. "A grazing bull" implies a still large body but it is more powerful and aggressive to go after things, "a hippopotamus" but little faster, smaller, more trimmed down and directed, "a rhinoceros" but a self sufficient organism, still "an octopus" but smaller in size, still a wagon train but more coordinated, "a large bear" which is still a large body but smaller than an elephant, scaled down, however, still an indiscriminate eater (Exhibit 3).

On the other hand, a third group of metaphors reveal a rather sharp change in the overall image of the university that might be ascribed to the Commitment to Focus plan. The "lion" metaphor which was repeated three times by three faculty members who had quite different disciplinary or departmental orientations indicate a rather focused and powerful image for the university. Perhaps the content of the image was best described by a faculty member from political science: "a better hunter, a bit ruthless, and the head triumph over the heart" which explains a focused and selective attention for vision and organizational goals, a rational and logical emphasis on organizational structure, process and commitments.

Other images such as "fox," "fish," "a pruned tree," "an ant colony," "a hunting dog," and, "a neatly set up garden" describe a context which is close to the qualitative richness of the "lion" metaphor. Various qualities of these metaphors ascribed to the used images by the faculty members provide rich insights into the nature of this new strategic orientation at the university such as clever and faster, more focused movement, but still darting around, focused on a task, seeks, searches and finds (Exhibit 3).

Compared to the images that described the university before the Commitment to Focus plan, the sort of fuzziness and diversity in the content of provided metaphors can be explained in three ways: (1) if an organization is identified with incremental and slow change, metaphorical images may provide a rather strong picture of the organization. Change, on the other hand, distorts this continuity and clarity of the images like taking of picture of a moving target. Thus, fuzziness and diversity in the metaphorical images may prove that change is in order in the organization. (2) Metaphorical fuzziness may, however, also be due to people being able to judge the past more clearly than the present.

   2b *Institutional strategies*

Results show that 7 groups of emerging strategies were identified by the interviewed faculty. The first policy or action, the reallocation plan which was originally defined in the Commitment to Focus proposal, was designed to distribute resources differentially. Following the identification of the priority areas among the programs, the plan proposed that the available resources should be shifted from low-priority to high-priority programs. It seems that this strategy directly addresses an immediate need to remedy the declining resources of the University by offering an internal solution to the problem.

The second group of strategies concerns access issues or reduction in size of the University. As the interviewed faculty perceived, enrollment and class size are reduced by raising admission and preparation standards.

The third group of strategies focused on certain activities designed to reduce already-expanded units, programs and campus diversity in the university. To do this, certain departments, units or programs have either been closed, merged or their budgets cut.

According to the results concerning the fourth policy, there appears to an emphasis on quality, especially at the levels of teaching and undergraduate education.

Along with the quality concern, there seems to be a tendency towards more emphasis on research and publication expected from the faculty, and more priority has been given to graduate level education.

The sixth strategy indicates, as reported by the faculty, that there is a trend towards more centralization in the internal affairs of the university through planned activities and an emphasis on collaborative work among the units.

The seventh group of policies show that the university has more aggressively sought outside funding by creating endowed chairs, increasing fund raising activities and applying for more research grants.

Regarding these results, first, if a comparison is made between the period before and after the Commitment to Focus, the new or proposed policies seem to be constructed to reverse the trend. For example, while the previous policy was praising the quantity that ended up in an inflated size, the new one attempts to reduce it. In order to overcome the financially problematic situation, the new set of policies were created to generate a partial solution by distributing the resources differentially as well as finding ways of generating external funding. In order to solve the problem of massive program diversity, complexity and expansion or a "diseconomized scale," the new policies and strategies are developed to streamline the institutional and program complexity. To do all these, central administration gained more control in the internal affairs. Lastly, as a response to eroding or declining quality, upgrading quality especially in the undergraduate education was given the highest priority after the Commitment to Focus.

These findings lend some support to Miller and Friesen's discussion that revolution in the strategy and structural variables in organizations first attempts to reverse the excesses of the period preceding any discontinuous change initiative (Miller and Friesen 1980).

There appears another important point concerning the order of the proposed policies (Exhibit 4). It seems that the order of strategic choices with respect to their percentage ratios from high to low define the level of concreteness, as perceived by the respondents. The highly-rated ones are those in which the university administration is actively promoting the resolution of the problems inherited by the previous policies.

2c. *The match between metaphors and emerging institutional strategies*

Although the congruence between the provided images and the emerging institutional strategies is not as strong as in the case of the period prior to Commitment to Focus, the images are, however, rich in context in terms of describing the university's overall strategic direction.

1. As discussed earlier in relation to the metaphors describing the period after the Commitment to Focus, whereas the same images were used by the faculty, we observed some qualitative differences in each image. Although the emerging images did not sharply contrast with the previous images, a qualitative improvement was evident as in the following examples: from "a grazing cow" to "a grazing bull" from "an elephant" to "a hippopotamus" (faster, smaller, trimmed down and more directed), from "a coral reef" to "a stabilized coral reef," from a free-flowing "wagon train" to "a coordinated wagon train," from "a kitten" (sits there and loves to be petted) to "a hunting dog" (seeks, searches and finds), from "a wildly growing vegetable" to "a pruned tree," from "a garden without strict gardeners" to "a neatly set up garden."

These metaphors indicate a strategic continuity or an incremental change in the strategic orientation of the university. Change was not seen as radical or discontinuous, rather as focused on trimming the extremities of the previous institutional strategies. This analysis was supported through the analysis of the strategic choices that the new strategies were designed to treat the ills of the prior period. Metaphorical images clearly showed this connection as the faculty members used the same metaphors, but in the second case, with more positive attributes.

2. On the other hand, some metaphorical images sharply contrasted with the dominant metaphors characterizing the university's past and the present. The metaphorical images of bull, lion, fox, fish and hunting dog all resemble a different character for the university, the one that has slimmer, swifter, lean and focused qualities of emerging strategic inclination. For example, the reallocation plan, the program, campus closures and consolidations are well described by the image of a "lion" that is a little bit ruthless and puts the head over the heart. This is contrasting with the university's image of "attempting to satisfy everybody's willy-nilly" with a rationalistic approach of efficiency and effectiveness.

Images that are related to the size of the university were clearly evident in the scaled down versions of the previously used metaphors: from elephant to hippopotamus, from octopus to smaller octopus, from elephant to a large bear, from a jungle to a pruned tree, etc.

The imagery of the emerging strategic orientations related to planned, coordinated and collaborative activities; and, more central direction in the university was hidden in the previously cited metaphors of bull, lion, fox, fish and hunting dog. Such organisms do have more control, coordination and swifter qualities in their movements compared to rather sloppy and slow organisms such as elephant, octopus and cow. The university is no more a "free enterprise, a tangled up ball of twine, an unruly group of school children, a feudal-medieval landscape," but moving towards a more centralized, coordinated and unified configuration.

Discussion and Conclusions

Land grant universities endure on a populist image originated from an agrarian socialism. This populist land-grant philosophy was explained by a University of Minnesota faculty as follows:

> It was highly populous, a belief that the university had to be all things to all people, a general world view that we just serve everybody's demands willy nilly (Simsek and Heydinger 1993, p. 20).

After the Second World War, this populist image transformed into an "entrepreneurial populism" under the influence of the growth years (late 1950s and early 1970s) (Simsek 1992; Simsek and Heydinger, 1993; Simsek and Louis 1994). During these years, institutions engaged in a number of strategies that resulted in an uncontrolled expansion in program areas, diversity in institutional missions, growth in size and decentralization in decision making. The metaphorical analysis in this article shows that dominant images (metaphors) among faculty are matched with sets of institutional strategies provided by the same professionals, and verified by individuals involved in articulating those strategies.

In the case of the University of Minnesota, the era of "entrepreneurial populism" was terminated by the 1985 Commitment to Focus plan. As the reported results show, the institution was trying to reverse the extremities of the entrepreneurial populist strategies as well as providing a vision for the future.

This article draws the following four implications from the study:

(1) *Since metaphors provide simple ways of knowing and seeing the world, organization members' sense of reality and their role accomplishments will be consistent with these implicit images. These images provide the necessary framework that limit or delimit the members' accomplishment of organizational roles.* According to interpretive organization theorists, "the world is, essentially, an ambiguous realm of experience that is made concrete by the people who interpret it, and who act on the basis of these interpretations. People's interpretations construct reality and, through subsequent actions based on those interpretations, actually shape future realities. Realities are not given; they are *made!*" (Morgan 1989, p. 93: emphasis original). From the images provided by the University of Minnesota faculty, a large number of

images show an improvement in the image of the University compared to the previous period. A man-made, constructed reality which defines the University as more coordinated, focused, scaled down, and directed prescribes individual actions and a criterion for role accomplishments by the faculty members consistent with these images. Moreover, a faculty member's image of the University as "a sick octopus," or "a great, big, multi-limbed, stumbling animal," or "an enormous, Chinese menu catalog of offerings" will prescribe a different set of individual actions on the part of these community members. Similarly, if a faculty member sees the University as "a fox who is clever and devious," then he or she will be cynical about the University's, especially about the administration's, agenda of change that will frame this particular faculty member's daily job routine.

(2) *These images are shared across a population of organization members.* As we discussed elsewhere (Simsek 1992; Simsek and Heydinger 1993; Simsek and Louis 1994), an enacted or socially constructed reality in organizational settings can be reframed as an organizational paradigm. An organizational paradigm is a cognitive map that guides and directs organizational activities. As was originally put forward by Kuhn (1970), every paradigm creates its own language pattern, its unique concepts and principles. This language form is disseminated among the members of a community, the process which is called the social matrix. The full use of any paradigm comes into existence when the social matrix is close to the maximum level of membership. At this phase, the image of paradigm reality is shared among the majority of the community members. In the University of Minnesota case, we were able to find out almost the same, sometimes similar, semantic approaches in the faculty's description of the university. Faculty members with quite dissimilar professional and departmental interests articulated similar metaphors in describing the university.

On the other hand, *if the shared reality is orderly, dominating images are strong, clear and agreed. If the constructed reality is chaotic and disorderly, images are correspondingly fuzzy and weak.* As you may recall, the metaphors describing the University of Minnesota prior to the Commitment to Focus plan were stronger and consensus was higher compared to the period after the Commitment to Focus. The diversity and relative lack of consensus on the metaphors related to the period after the Commitment to Focus may indicate that change is underway, and that it is directly reflected by the provided metaphors. This eventually creates a fuzzy imagery or picture of the organization under study.

(3) *Changes in strategic choices create changes in members' image of their organization. Conversely, effective management of images may create a situation where certain desired strategic choices can easily be implemented.* This was evident in the case of the University of Minnesota in such a way that the Commitment to Focus plan altered "the entrepreneurial populist image" in this public university. Any change in strategic choices that are a direct extension of an implicit world view may distort the image of the community members about their organization. Conversely, the process may work the other way. Any alteration in the images may create a situation where certain strategies can be disseminated in the organization. This second case was not the purpose of this study. However, as earlier reported from Sackmann's study (1989), creating a particular vision and articulating new strategic choices may be achieved through alterations of dominant images in an organization.

(4) The results regarding the metaphorical images used by faculty members in describing the period prior to the Commitment to Focus plan (before 1985) are supportive of the three theory bases to higher education organizations as applied to the case under study. *The study provides evidence that theories such as "loose-coupled systems" (Weick 1976), "organized anarchies" (Cohen and March 1974), and "multiversities" explain the most important characteristics of the university organization before the 1980s.* The metaphorical images of "octopus," "amoeba," and "a wildly growing garden or vegetable" are able to define the most salient characteristics of the University of Minnesota before 1985 defined by others as a loosely-coupled system, an organized anarchy, or a multiversity. However, the results of this study show that all these descriptions of the academy of the 1970s were some essential components of one socially enacted image, what Simsek and Louis (1994) called the paradigm of "entrepreneurial populism." The imagery representing the University of Minnesota presented in this article describes the general characteristics of a large university organization of the early 1970s in which these theories were offered: a loosely-linked structural configuration, independent and decentralized decision making, multiple, sometimes conflicting, mission and vision in a single institution. What is important here is the fact that each of these three theories simply focused on only

one dimension of the higher education institutions. At least in the University of Minnesota case, metaphorical images presented in this article provide a perspective that fundamental aspects of these three theories are interconnected. This may lend some proof to the temporal dimension of theories in describing social phenomena of the time in which a particular theory is developed.

On the other hand, the University of Minnesota has traditionally been one of the largest public universities in the U.S. Our findings of metaphorical imagery associated with loose-coupling and organized anarchy are equally important in confirming the findings in organization theory—when translated into the context of higher education organization—that growth in size, leads to differentiation and complexity in structure of organization and decentralization in decision making (Hage and Aiken 1967; Pugh et al., 1969; Blau and Schoenherr 1971; Scott 1992).

Notes

1. An earlier version of this article was presented at the annual meeting of the University Council For Educational Administration (UCEA), Philadelphia. PA, USA (October, 1994). The author would like to thank three anonymous reviewers and editor Grant Harman for their helpful comments.

2. In cases where this direct question did not work in eliciting striking images, the researcher alternatively used the following question, which, in most cases, worked well: "Which animal or living organism would best describe this institution before 1985? After 1985?" This method was suggested by Gareth Morgan at an informal seminar at the University of Minnesota.

3. If you consult Exhibit 1 and Exhibit 3, you will see an extensive list of metaphorical images generated by the faculty about their institution. The discussions under 1a and 2a were limited only to cover the metaphors that are contextually similar or the ones that have, one way or another, relevance to the institutional strategies. The images which seem to be random in the responses list were left untreated.

References

Baldridge, J. V., Curtis, D. V., Ecker, G. and Riley, L. (1978). *Policy Making and Effective Leadership: A National Study of Academic Management*. San Francisco: Jossey-Bass.

Bensimon, E. M., Neumann, A. and Birnbaum, R. (1989). *Making Sense of Administrative Leadership: The "L" Word in Higher Education*. ASHE-ERIC Higher Education Report 1, Washington D.C.: The George Washington University, School of Education and Human Development.

Blau, P. M. and Schoenherr, R. (1971). *The Structure of Organizations*. New York, NY. Basic Books.

Bolman, L. G. and Deal, T. E. (1991). *Reframing Organizations: Artistry, Choice, and Leadership*. San Francisco, CA: Jossey-Bass.

Bredeson, P. V. (1985). 'An analysis of the metaphorical perspectives of school principals', *Educational Administration Quarterly*, 21(1), 29–50.

Burrell, G. and Morgan, G. (1983). *Sociological Paradigms and Organizational Analysis*. London: Heinemann Educational Books.

Clark, B. R. (1972). 'The organizational saga in higher education', *Administrative Science Quarterly*, 17, 178–183.

Clark, B. R. (1983). *The Higher Education System: Academic Organization in Cross-National Perspective*. Berkeley, CA: University of California Press.

Clugston, R. (1987). *Strategic Adaptation in Organized Anarchy: Priority Setting and Resource Allocation in the Liberal Arts College of a Public Research University*. Ph.D. Dissertation, University of Minnesota.

Cohen, M. D. and March, J.G. (1974). *Leadership and Ambiguity: The American College President*. New York, NY: McGraw-Hill.

Emery, F. E. (1969). *Systems Thinking*. Harmondsworth, England: Penguin.

Foster, E. (1989–90). 'Planning at the University of Minnesota'. *Planning for Higher Education*, 18(2), 25–38.

Hage, J. and Aiken, M. (1967), 'Program change and organizational properties: a comparative analysis', *American Journal of Sociology*, 72, 503–519.

Katz, D. and Kahn, R. L. (1978). *The Social Psychology of Organizations*, 2nd ed. New York, NY. Wiley.

Keller, K. H. (1985). *A Commitment to Focus: Report of Interim President Kenneth H. Keller to the Board of Regents*. University of Minnesota.

Lakoff, G. and Johnson, M. (1982). *Metaphors We Live By*. Chicago, IL: University of Chicago Press.

Lawrence, P. R. and Lorsch, J. W. (1967). *Organization and Environment*. Cambridge, MA: Harvard Graduate School of Business Administration.

Louis, K. S. and Simsek, H. (1991). 'Paradigm shifts and organizational learning: some theoretical lessons for restructuring schools'. *Paper presented at the annual meeting of the University Council for Educational Administration*. Baltimore, MD.

Miller, D. and Friesen, P. H. (1980). 'Momentum and revolution in organizational adaptation', *Academy of Management Journal*, 23, 591–614.

Morgan, G. (1980). 'Paradigms, metaphors and puzzle solving in organization theory', *Administrative Science Quarterly*, 25, 605–622.

Morgan, Gareth (1986). *Images of Organization*. Newbury Park, CA: Sage.

Patton. M. Q. (1987). *How to Use Qualitative Research in Evaluation*. Newbury Park, CA: Sage.

Pugh, D., Hickson, H., Hinings, C. R. and Turner, C. (1969). 'The context of organizational structures', *Administrative Science Quarterly*, 14, 91–114.

Sackmann, S. (1989). 'The role of metaphors in organization transformation', *Human Relations*, 42, 463–485.

Scott, W. R. (1992). *Organizations: Rational, Natural and Open Systems*, 3rd ed. Englewood Cliffs, NJ: Prentice-Hall.

Simsek, H. (1992). *Organizational Change as Paradigm Shift: Analysis of Organizational Change Processes in a Large, Public University by Using a Paradigm-Based Change Model*. Ph.D. Dissertation, Minneapolis, MN: University of Minnesota.

Simsek, H. and Heydinger, R. B. (1993). 'An Analysis of the Paradigmatic Evolution of U.S. Higher Education and Implications for the Year 2000', in Smart, J.C. (ed), *Higher Education: Handbook of Theory and Research*, New York, NY: Agathon Press, Vol. 9, 1–49.

Simsek, H. and Louis, K. S. (1994). 'Organizational change as paradigm shift: analysis of the change process in a large, public university', *Journal of Higher Education*, 65(6), 670–695.

Smircich, L. (1983). 'Concepts of culture and organizational analysis', *Administrative Science Quarterly*, 28, 339–358.

Sterman, J. D. (1985). 'The growth of knowledge: testing a theory of scientific revolutions with a formal model', *Technological Forecasting and Social Change*, 28, 93–122.

Strauss, A. and Corbin, J. (1990). *Basics of Qualitative Research: Grounded Theory Procedures and Techniques*. Newbury Park, CA: Sage.

Weick, K. E. (1976). 'Educational organizations as loosely coupled systems', *Administrative Science Quarterly*, 21, 1–19.

Wolcott, H. F. (1994). *Transforming Qualitative Data: Description, Analysis and Interpretation*. Thousand Oaks, CA: Sage.

Yin, R. (1984). *Case Study Research*. Beverly Hills, CA: Sage.

[Exhibit 1]

*Metaphors Describing The University Before Commitment
To Focus Plan*

Strategic Management

1. A grazing cow = sturdy, big, dependable, very slow

   A tangled up ball of twine

   A highly departmentalized hierarchy

2. A great, big multi-limbed, stumbling animal

   (A cross b/w centipede & elephant)

   An octopus

3. A big, non-thinking bureaucracy

   An elephant

   An octopus

   "Communiversity"

4. A dog = takes resources, but returns something to environment
    A good quality, faculty run, democratic inst.
5. An enormous size, Chinese menu catalog of offerings

Political Science
1. Amoeba=constantly dividing,
    "U of Lake Wabegon" = decentralized, unwilling to make hard decisions
    Unruly group of school children, all going & doing separate things
2. An octopus = with all eight arms embracing different constituencies and concerns
3. A ship = sailing in the smoother waters
4. A healthy octopus

English
1. Amoeba
    A free enterprise
2. An octopus
3. A coral reef
4. A feudal-medieval landscape
5. A wildly growing vegetable

Food Science
1. A free enterprise
    A wagon train = going different directions for different purposes
2. A healthy buffalo
3. A beehive = going different directions, doing their own separate jobs
4. A kitten = sits there & loves to be petted

Department Of Mathematics
1. Amoeba = if something comes along that you haven't planned for, just go out and grab it
    = if you push it one place, it pops out in another place
2. An elephant = large, sloppy, slow, ponderous, eats large amounts
3. A garden without strict gardeners

Octopus=5, Elephant=3, Amoeba=3,
A wildly growing garden/vegetable=2
Sturdy, big, very slow, departmentalized, multi-limbed, stumbling, dividing, decentralized, opportunist, unplanned, sloppy, large, ponderous, unruly.

[Exhibit 2]

Dominant Policies, Strategies Or Organizational Actions By The University Before Commitment To Focus Plan

1. Growth/expansion in program areas,
Variety/many offerings,
Growth in program diversity,
Opening/creating many small departments/programs
Diverse/too many programs

StrMan	PolSci	English	FoodSci	Math	Tot. #
4/4	3/5	4/5	4/5	3/4	18/23(78%)

2. Teaching emphasized, praised, rewarded

StrMan	PolSci	English	FoodSci	Math	Tot.#
3/4	3/5	3/5	1/5	1/3	11/22(50%)

3. Large student population
Emphasis on quantity
Open access
Too many admissions
Large/guaranteed admission
Low admission standards

StrMan	PolSci	English	FoodSci	Math	Tot.#
2/4	1/5	3/5	1/5	2/3	9/22 (41%)

4. Independent activities,
Freedom to develop programs
Autonomous, collegial decision making
Unit autonomy
Decentralized decision making

StrMan	PolSci	English	FoodSci	Math	Tot.#
0/4	3/5	2/5	3/5	0/3	8/22 (36%)

5. Service emphasized, praised, rewarded

StrMan	PolSci	English	FoodSci	Math	Tot.#
4/4	0/5	0/5	0/5	0/3	4/20 (20%)

[Exhibit 3]

Metaphors Describing The University After Commitment To Focus Plan
Strategic Management

1. A grazing bull = more powerful & aggressive to go after things & to do things
2. A great, big, multi-limbed, stumbling animal. A cross b/w a centipede & an elephant
3. A hippopotamus = little bit faster, smaller, more trimmed down, more directed
4. A lion = grabs resources from the environment, but contributes little
5. An enormous, Chinese menu catalog of offerings

Political Science

1. A rhinoceros = a self sufficient organism
2. A lion = better hunter, a bit ruthless, the head triumph over the heart
3. A fox = clever, devious, operate w/o being seen, moves faster
4. A centipede
   A sick octopus
   A jungle

English

1. A fish = more focused movement, but still darting around
2. A smaller octopus
3. A stabilized coral reef
4. 19th Century German Uni. model = research, publication, graduate studies oriented
5. A pruned tree

Food Science

1. A coordinated wagon train = wagons rounding up into a circle
   A lion = aggressive, not easy to prey on
2. An ant colony = busy, working hard, focused on a task
3. A wounded buffalo
4. A hunting dog = seeks, searches and finds

Department Of Mathematics

1. Amoeba = no change in the image
2. A large bear = smaller than elephant, scaled down, but still an indiscriminate eater
3. A neatly set up garden

Lion = 3

More (powerful, aggressive, trimmed down, directed, focused, stabilized), faster, smaller, self sufficient, better hunter, bit ruthless, clever, pruned, coordinated, seeks, searches, scaled down.

[Exhibit 4]

Dominant Policies, Strategies Or Organizational Actions By The University After Commitment To Focus Plan

1. Reallocation Plan

StrMan	PolSci	English	FoodSci	Math	Tot.#
4/5	4/5	4/5	1/5	3/4	16/24(67%)

2. Reduced/limited enrollment
Higher preparation/admission standards
Limited course offerings
Smaller classes

StrMan	PolSci	English	FoodSci	Math	Tot.#
2/5	3/5	4/5	3/5	4/4	16/24(67%)

3. Program/campus closings
Program consolidation
Program/unit mergers/cuts

StrMan	PolSci	English	FoodSci	Math	Tot.#
3/5	3/5	4/5	2/5	3/4	15/24(63%)

4. Emphasis on quality
Quality teaching
Quality undergraduate education

StrMan	PolSci	English	FoodSci	Math	Tot.#
2/5	2/5	1/5	2/5	3/4	10/24(42%)

5. More emphasis on research, publication, graduate level

StrMan	PolSci	English	FoodSci	Math	Tot. #
4/5	1/5	0/5	0/5	3/4	8/24(33%)

6. Planned/coordinated/collaborative activities
More central direction
Planned activities for setting priorities, defining areas of strengths

StrMan	PolSci	English	FoodSci	Math	Tot. #
1/5	1/5	2/5	3/5	1/4	8/24(33%)

7. Endowed chairs
Fund raising activities
Orientation towards external funding

StrMan	PolSci	English	FoodSci	Math	Tot.#
2/5	2/5	1/5	1/5	0/3	6/24(25%)

BALANCING CORPORATION, COLLEGIUM, AND COMMUNITY

JAMES DOWNEY

It has been customary, at least since John Henry Newman (1852), to speak of "the idea of the university." Many books have been written bearing that title or alluding to it. Of no other social institution do we converse in quite the same way. We do not speak so naturally of "the idea of the hospital," or "the idea of the school," or "the idea of the corporation," or "the idea of the trade union," or even "the idea of the church." This is because no other social institution is so dedicated to the life of the mind, to thinking, reasoning, and imagining—in other words, to ideas—as the university.

Another reason why we speak of the *idea* of the university is, I think, because the idealized character of the university, which is to say its essence, always seems to elude definitional capture. Dictionary definitions describe the coil but not the current. Consider, for example, this definition from the *American Heritage Dictionary*:

> *University*. 1. An institution of higher learning with teaching and research facilities that awards undergraduate and postgraduate degrees. 2. The buildings and grounds of a university. 3. The students, teaching staff, and governing body of a university, regarded collectively.

That's the enterprise all right; what is missing is the purpose, which is the raison d'être, which is the essence. What is missing is the *idea* of the university.

Still, in an important sense, as Karl Jaspers says in his own book on *The Idea of the University* (1959), "the university exists only to the extent that it is institutionalized" (p. 83). Jaspers continues:

> The idea becomes concrete in the institution. The extent to which it does this determines the quality of the university. Stripped of its ideal the university loses all value. Yet "institution" necessarily implies compromises. The idea is never perfectly realized. Because of this a permanent state of tension exists [in] the university between the idea and the shortcomings of the institutional and corporate reality. (p. 83)

In its institutional form, however, a university is not a unity but a trinity; three simultaneous incarnations in one. It is corporation, collegium, and community. Each contains elements which are essential to the realization of the idea of the university, but each also contains elements and tendencies which are not readily harmonized.

The easiest of the three to describe, and for the lay person to understand, is the university as corporation. Corporations have existed in various forms for many centuries. They have been found so useful and durable that they have survived countless political and economic upheavals. They may be privately owned and managed; they may be publicly owned and managed; they may be a combination of both, as is the case with Canadian crown corporations. They may exist for profit or not for profit; either way they are creations of the state and answerable to it.

For the most part universities in Canada are legal corporate entities of the provincial governments and, like other corporations, have the right to appoint officers, own property, make contracts, sue in the courts, and have perpetual possession. Their administrative powers are held by delegation from the civil authority and are contained usually in an act of parliament which, like other statutes, may from time to time be amended. They are also generally bound by the same laws that apply to all corporations in the conduct of business. Whatever "institutional autonomy" and "academic freedom" may mean, these concepts cannot be used to argue that the corporation, its officers, or employees may operate outside the law.

Corporations have long been a principal legal and economic instrument of democracies, but they are not in their operations particularly democratic. They have a hierarchical structure, with authority vested in a corporate board and delegated to designated officers. Because legal compliance across a range of accountabilities is required of it, the university as corporation cannot afford to operate as a consensual community; it needs the administrative levers to act, and its structure provides them. The corporation doesn't have colleagues: it has officers, employees, and clients, and for its own integrity it must deal with them as such.

In exchange for its compliance in the ways indicated, the state confers on the university as corporation, and through the mechanism of a lay board of directors, a considerable measure of institutional autonomy in the conduct of its affairs. The body corporate therefore is a shield as well as a shell.

It is also a vehicle. It provides an orderly environment in which the business of the academy may be transacted. Through the corporation the state, clients, and donors provide the material resources without which scholarly endeavour is impossible. The corporation's systems of financial accounting, personnel management, plant operation, and resource allocation are essential preconditions for the research, teaching, and service that constitute the principal activities of the modern university. If the academic corporation is not well structured, financed, governed, and managed, the cause of scholarship will be, depending on the degree of deficiency, impeded or imperiled. No one would claim that the corporation is itself the essence of the university. To the extent, however, that it makes possible the institutional autonomy, the material resources, and the administrative order essential for the conduct of the work of the university, it is an indispensable vehicle for that essence.

More people would be prepared to claim, especially among the professoriate, that the second modality of my trinity, the collegium, is indeed the essence of the university. I would argue that while it is essential to, it is not the essence of, the academy. The collegium is the complex network of assumptions, traditions, protocols, relations, and structures within the university which permit the professoriate to control and conduct the academic affairs of the institution, determining, among other things, who shall be admitted, who shall teach and research, what shall be taught and researched, and what standards shall be set for which rewards. The collegium is thus the practical realization of academic freedom.

It may be worth emphasizing what academic freedom is and is not, so important is it to an understanding and the functioning of the collegium. Academic freedom and constitutional free speech are sometimes conflated. They should not be; they may be sisters, but they are not identical twins. Academic freedom does not entitle professors to rights as citizens over those enjoyed by other citizens. To quote Jaspers again: "Academic freedom . . . does not mean the right to say what one pleases. Truth is much too difficult and great a task that it should be mistaken for the passionate exchange of half-truths spoken in the heat of the moment. It exists only where scholarly ends and commitment to truth are involved. Practical objectives, educational bias, or political propaganda have no right to invoke academic freedom" (p. 142).

Academic freedom therefore has both an individual and collective connotation. For the individual faculty member it means the greatest reasonable measure of autonomy in the performance of his or her academic duties. Only through the possession of such a right, it is argued, can the pursuit of truth be guaranteed. For the collectivity it means the right of faculty members conferring together through departmental, faculty, and university councils, to determine the academic content and character of their institution.

If the corporation rests on the principle of hierarchical authority, the collegium rests on the principle of hieratic authority, on the notion that the professoriate constitutes a priesthood when it comes to matters of academic policy and principle. Students and staff and alumni may be invited to offer views, but it is the ordained members of the community who make decisions. While the collegium as part of the community is anything but democratic, within the collegium there is ample scope for the practice of democracy. Any faculty member may speak his or her mind with impunity, any objection may be raised, any argument made, any decision challenged.

It is through this time-intensive process that the consensus is formed which is so essential to concerted action. At the same time, it is also the process which often seems to those outside the university, not to say many within, to inhibit unreasonably institutional responsiveness to social change. When under pressure to respond with dispatch, most universities of course find ways of doing so, especially when institutional self-interest is involved. The recent incident, however, of Yale University's having to return a multi-million dollar gift to a donor after a couple of years' inability to decide whether the donation could be used as intended, illustrates how the interests of corporation and collegium may sometimes collide.

Then there is the university as community. If the vertical axis of this complex organizational graph represents the corporation and the horizontal axis represents the collegium, the community is all of the interstitial space around and between. Among our manifold social institutions none so approximates a complete community as a university. No other institution has such an impressive range of communal attributes. There is first the physical infrastructure of land, buildings, roads, sewers, communication and transportation systems, and cultural and athletic facilities. There is as well the infrastructure of a different sort; this is the impressive range of services provided to citizens—personal, professional, social, recreational, and of course educational. There is finally the professional and demographic diversity of the citizenry, representing the broadest possible range of interest, competence, and ethnicity. It is the least structured, most malleable of the three components of the university. It is also the most encompassing. Everyone belongs to and has equity in the university as community.

Unlike the corporation, there is nothing neat and orderly about the community, nothing straightforward, nothing unambiguous, not much clearly defined. We cannot speak of the community, as we can of the corporation, as a structure. It is a culture in which things grow. It accommodates itself, if it is a good culture, to the gray and grainy nature of our lives as we live them: it makes way for the eccentric, it tolerates the absurd, it protects the vulnerable, it subsumes differences into common cause, it grounds in democratic perspective the elitisms inherent in the corporation and the collegium. Without such a community, neither the corporation nor the collegium will prosper.

All three dimensions of the university are being tested at present in Canada, as I believe they are in the United States, and it might be instructive to reflect for a moment on how and why. For the corporation there are the contractions and adjustments necessitated by declining government support. Ours in Canada is almost exclusively a state-supported system of higher education. For the past generation government has supplied more than 75% of the revenues of universities, with student fees accounting for about 15%. In the 90s, as governments have attempted to do combat with Canada's monstrous public debt, fiscal transfers to universities on a per-student basis have decreased significantly. Now, at least in Ontario, which represents approximately 40% of the higher-education system in Canada, a precipitous drop in government support will occur this year.

With this dramatic reduction in government support will likely come a partial deregulation of tuition fees. These two actions together will place great stress upon the corporation in meeting its obligations to the state, on the one hand, and to students, faculty, and staff, on the other. It now seems clear that in the short run major reductions will have to be made to the numbers of employees, to wages and benefits, and, conceivably, to the range and perhaps quality of courses and programs. For all the short-term dislocation, however, the prospects for the corporation look reasonably good. There seems little doubt that as reliance on bloc grants from government decreases and market-place competition for students increases, boards of governors and university officers will have more scope for strategic management, which is to say, more scope for both fiscal success and failure, than is true at present. In becoming more directly accountable to the client, whether the student who will pay much higher fees or the agency which commissions research or consulting service, the corporate aspect of the university will unavoidably be accentuated.

Will this accentuation of the corporate come at the expense of the collegium? Our tradition is that of a bicameral system, under which an institution has both a board of governors, generally lay persons, and an academic senate. Will the strengthening of corporate governance weaken further the bicameral system of university governance which has been under siege for some time? It is by no means foreordained that bicameralism will wane as corporatism waxes; it will depend in large part on what imaginative power the concept of the collegium still holds for academics. There is, I believe, general agreement that the bicameral system has been considerably weakened over the past quarter-century. There is also agreement about the factors which have contributed to this malaise.

The widespread unionization of faculty in the 1970s has been perhaps the most significant constraint on the powers of both boards of governors and academic senates. For ill-prepared boards, as Professor David Cameron explains so well in his book, *More than an Academic Question* (1991), the nature of the contracts negotiated with well-orchestrated faculty unions left them with very weak management rights. Since boards have been little more than proxies for government in the negotiation of salaries and benefits, and while government was prepared to provide more or less adequate funding on a generally unrestricted basis, this system worked well enough. In the present state of fiscal crisis, however, and contemplating a future where neither adequacy of funds nor equity of their distribution is assured, boards will have to accept greater responsibility for the health and perhaps the very survival of the institutions they govern. I believe that boards will do this; either they will recover through negotiations the tools they need for effective governance in the new environment or they will be given them by government intervention. My own decided preference is for the former; the latter way could be at the expense of the institutional autonomy which boards exist in part to protect.

As for academic senates, the heart of the collegium, I am less sanguine about their prospects. At the same time that faculty unionization limited the discretionary powers of boards of governors, it removed from academic senates several important jurisdictions over the terms and conditions of employment of faculty, promotion and tenure criteria and procedures being only the most obvious example. There is little in the situation evolving in Canada to suggest that faculty are prepared to transfer any jurisdiction from their collective agreements or memoranda of agreement back to their senates. In fact, the current crisis in funding might well have the opposite effect, strengthening the syndical aspects of faculty life and weakening the collegial. In the end, faculty unions tend to strengthen the corporation at the expense of the collegium.

The second powerful factor which has helped to circumscribe the scope and effectiveness of bicameralism is the pronounced tendency of Canadian governments in the past to prefer regulation rather than competition as a means of ensuring accountability. As our most respected cultural critic, Robert Fulford, said recently,

> Canadians love regulation. What rice is to the Japanese, what wine is to the French, regulation is to the Canadians. When any new phenomenon appears on the horizon, whether it is *in vitro* fertilization or superconductivity, our first response is always the same: how do we regulate this sucker? An Ottawa bureaucrat's highest word of praise for an industry is "orderly," meaning well regulated. The BNA Act promises "peace, order, and good government," but the only one we absolutely insist on is order."
> (Toronto *Globe & Mail*, 22 December, 1993)

The tendency of governments to limit through regulation the sphere of decision-making has had a debilitating effect upon boards of governors, making their most important function one of ensuring that their institutions are in compliance with increasingly more intrusive and detailed legislation.

Affecting the bicameral system too, and weakening collegial self-determination, has been the growing litigiousness of Canadian society, which has resulted in many more complaints being referred for resolution outside the university, to adjudicators, tribunals, human-rights commissions, and the courts. No one is prepared, it seems, to take no for an answer, or even a "yes, but," until it comes from the highest authority to which it can be appealed. Unlike Americans, Canadians have had a written charter of rights and freedoms for only little more than a decade, and we are still somewhat in its thrall. Such thralldom sits ill with the more informal, less definitive methods of dispute resolution characteristic of the traditional collegium.

Finally, as the knowledge intensity of the modern university has grown, and with it the technology intensity of modern scientific knowledge, universities have assumed an importance in strategic economic development never before known in Canada. The perishable nature of much scientific and technological knowledge has meant that the slow, consensual decision-making processes of the collegium have been inadequate. Both the corporation and the individual faculty members with marketable intellectual property have had to find faster ways to respond to transfer opportunities. University-owned technology-transfer offices and, in some cases, corporations have been established to facilitate the corporation's responsiveness. Many professors, their academic freedom ensuring their ownership of the intellectual property they have created, incorporate to market their inventions. In themselves these developments are not only not bad but may be essential to the competitiveness of the provincial and national economies. They are, however, a further short-circuiting of the collegial system, and they leave many gifted professors with no time to assume collegial governance responsibilities and little time even for teaching.

The forces just described have also affected the university as community. I spoke earlier of the physical, social, and cultural infrastructures which provide the basis for the university as community. But these are not its essence. There is another meaning of community. It is the spirit of concern and caring, of regard and respect, of cooperation and sharing which is the communal bonding agent. This is the essence which harmonizes divergent interests and creates cohesion. It is this spirit which is being severely tested in our universities at the moment, as it is in our society at large.

As the fiscal belt tightens, the several groups that make up the university become more concerned about their own interests—administration, faculty, staff, students, and occasionally alumni. In a new book, *Troubled Times for American Higher Education* (1994), that wise man Clark Kerr writes: "Additionally, the campus, as also the external society, is becoming more a series of enclaves divided by race/ethnic group, by gender, by political orientation, by 'old guard' citizens versus 'guest workers' whose basic allegiances lie elsewhere" (p. 13). I do not believe that things are that bad at most Canadian universities, just as they are not that bad at many American universities, but the dangerous tendencies of which Kerr speaks are all there to be observed.

Where then does all this leave us in thinking about the modern university and assessing its prospects? What if anything can be done to balance the legitimate claims of corporation, collegium, and community, and to ensure that the university of the 21st century, as it has been for most of the 20th, is an institution characterized by "a fruitful interaction in a dynamic state of tension" (Jaspers, 1959, p. 20)?

In the first place it is important to understand that none of these three modalities of the university is its essence. It is almost as important to understand that each carries within it elements of that essence, elements without which the university is in some respect deficient. There never has been a time perhaps when all of these elements have been fully present and perfectly balanced, but present dangers of imbalance are greater than they have been in a long time. The spirit of the times is corporate, not communal, and certainly not collegial. Corporate is about the production of wealth and the exercise of power; communal and collegial are about the sharing of wealth and power. There is a strong sense in both Canada and the United States that we have for too long been too concerned about the bottom rung and not enough about the bottom line. The governments we have of late elected with unambiguous mandates have assured us they will correct this imbalance. We in the universities are not immune to the political temper of the times, any more than we are to the fiscal and social policies that our governments enact. It seems clear by now that, in Canada at least, universities will participate in a process of corporate restructuring similar to that which has characterized business and, more recently, government. This may be neither fair nor reasonable, given how effectively universities have adapted over the past generation to changing social needs, but the forces at work are powerful and undiscriminating. Corporate restructuring will occur, and as it does it will confer salience on the economic utility and responsiveness of the university.

This is not in itself a bad thing, as long as we recognize and seek to redress its potentially distorting tendencies on the other two cultures of the university. There are, after all, many inside as well as outside the academy who have argued of late that the exercise of faculty control through the collegium has led to abuses, in the neglect of teaching, the pursuit of irrelevant research and scholarship, using tenure to protect the incompetent, and a general failure to make honest and rigorous judgments about each other's work. Whatever the validity of these criticisms, we would be ill-advised to ignore them and well-advised to seize the opportunity presented by the fiscal changes that will be forced on us to ask ourselves the most basic of questions, which is, what is the *idea* of the university on the cusp of a new millennium?

Three ingredients are, I believe, essential. One is responsiveness to the economic and social stresses and challenges facing society and the people, organizations, and institutions that comprise it. It is not enough merely to be good at what we do; we must also be focused and relevant. For universities like Georgia and Waterloo this will not come as anything other than commonplace thinking. But Canada has no land grant tradition to point the way to a more practical and applied approach to higher education, and in much of Canada there has been too sharp a distinction drawn between the role of universities and the role of colleges of applied arts and technology. Universities, even among many who support them, have an image of aloofness and indifference to society's urgent needs, a readiness to criticize but not to help.

Lest the point I am making here be assumed to constitute my entire philosophy of education, let me hasten to affirm that the primary mission of the university, as I embrace it, is not just to train, though training is essential to all learning, but to educate, not just to prepare students for work, but to make them wiser and more civilized people. And this is true for all students, even those learning the technical and mental skills of a profession.

I believe that, while there will always be some tension between the university's role as critic of society and its role as society's servant, there is ultimately no contradiction between the two. We not only can, but we must, prepare our students to live fuller and more capacious lives as individuals and citizens even as we equip them with the skills and knowledge and attitudes necessary for earning a living. We not only can, but we must, continue to pursue fundamental knowledge through research and scholarship even as we look for outreach opportunities for the products of that work. Indeed, I have long since been persuaded that the better we do the one the better we shall do the other.

The second element that will need to be present in our universities is a deeper sense of community, which is to say, a stronger sense of academic citizenship and a greater willingness to participate in and contribute to the *vita communitatis*. For their part, and it is a vital part, professors find their loyalties divided between the institution that employs them and the disciplines they pursue. Not infrequently, the colleagues with whom they most closely confer are in the same disciplines at other universities. Modern means of communication and transportation make those collaborations easier, while pressures to perform research and to publish often leave too little time, energy, or interest for citizenship duties within the university.

In the 22 September 1995 issue of *Science*, William H. Danforth, former president of Washington University in St. Louis and now chairman of the board, writes as follows:

> If it was ever true that faculty members' pursuit of individual interests automatically created a great university, it is certainly not so now. Rather, the loosening of institutional ties has become a major risk, for today's successful university requires effective internal operations aimed at agreed-upon goals. Because faculty do the essential work of teaching and research, their participation and leadership are key. Also, faculty must embody and serve as guardians of the values that should permeate the institutional culture, including, at a minimum, freedom of exploration and expression, commitment to excellence in scholarship and teaching, and tolerance for differences. Promotion of such values requires time, effort, and devotion.

I am glad Danforth put it in terms of values and personal commitment on the part of faculty because that is what it comes down to. For the most part students, staff, and alumni are, I have observed, only too willing to make the commitments of which Danforth speaks. What is often missing is the essential leadership that only a significant cadre of the best faculty can provide. We need it in our departmental and faculty councils, we need it in our senates and on our committees, we need it at the numerous and nuanced interfaces where the several estates of the university—the students, the staff, the alumni, the faculty, and friends—come together to plan, to transact, or merely to enjoy.

Finally, we need in our institutions a fresh infusion of idealism, a renewed affirmation of faith in the central, civilizing purpose of the university. We need to remind ourselves in fresh and uninhibited language of the great ennobling tradition we have inherited. I'm not talking about the survival of the university. An institution that has weathered the vagaries, vagrancies, and vicissitudes of the past eight hundred years has obviously acquired an impressive capacity for adaptation to changing circumstances. And there is no good reason to think that we in our time will lack the wit or the resolve to lead our institutions into a new century. There is, I believe, no cause for despair. What I lament is that there seems too little disposition for celebration.

In his book, *A Free and Ordered Space*, Bart Giamatti (1988) reminds us in many places and many ways of what is too often missing in our collegial life, distracted and preoccupied as we are with the ceaseless ebb and flow of debate about curriculum and course loads and political correctness. Here is one such reminder:

> Intellectual and civic in nature, pluralistic in purpose and composition, hierarchical in structure, the University exists for that play of restrain and release in each of its individual members. Through that creative play of opposites in teaching, learning, and research, the university nourishes at its core the humanizing and spacious acts of the individual imagination. Those acts are found in every area of study, whether lasers, literature, or law, and are proof of the human capacity to make and impose a design. Those designs made by the imagination are the signs of our ability to shape instinct and flux, to find or reveal patterns in the seemingly unplanned. The University is the guardian of the imagination that both defines and asserts our humanity. (pp. 48–49)

Ah, to be able to catch a glimpse of that from time to time, to feel that *this* is the enterprise of which we are a part, to sense our pulses quickened and our spirits lifted by the realization that all around us new fields of understanding are being explored and minds illumined and lives liberated by the knowledge and skills we impart and cultivate.

More than we need strategic planning or new facilities or organizational re-engineering or revised curricula or more resources, we need a reawakening of our sense of the wonder and grandeur of it all. And if that sounds too much like Cardinal Newman, I do not apologize. Though I share neither his religious faith nor his academic philosophy, his reverence for the idea of the university is the kindly light we still need to lead us amid the encircling gloom.

References

Cameron, D. M. *More than an academic question: Universities, government, and public policy in Canada.* Halifax, NS: Institute for Research on Public Policy.

Danforth, W. H. Universities are our responsibility. *Science*, 269 (5231), 1651, 1995.

Giamatti, A. B. *A free and ordered space: The real world of the University.* New York: W. W. Norton, 1988, pp. 48–49.

Jaspers, K. *The idea of the university.* Karl W. Deutsch (Ed.). Boston: Beacon Press, 1959.

Kerr, C., Gade, M. & Kawaoka, M. *Troubled times for American higher education: The 1990s and beyond.* Albany: State University of New York Press, 1994.

Newman, J. H. *The idea of a university defined and illustrated.* I. In nine discourses delivered to the Catholics of Dublin (1852). II. In Occasional lectures and essays addressed to the members of the Catholic University (1858). I. T. Kerr (Ed.). Oxford: Clarendon, 1976.

Toronto *Globe and Mail* (22 December, 1993).

APPENDIX A—THE MAJOR HIGHER EDUCATION ASSOCIATIONS, JOURNALS, AND PERIODICALS

COMPILED BY M. CHRISTOPHER BROWN II

Select Professional Associations for the Field of Higher Education

American Association of Colleges for Teacher Education (AACTE)
American Association of Colleges and Universities (AACU)
American Association of Collegiate Registrars and Admissions Officers (AACRAO)
American Association of Community Colleges (AACC)
American Association of State Colleges and Universities (AASCU)
American Association of University Administrators (AAUA)
American Association of University Professors (AAUP)
American College Personnel Association (ACPA)
American Council on Education (ACE)
American Education Research Association (AERA)
Association of American Colleges and Universities (AAC&U)
Association of American Universities (AAU)
Association of Governing Boards of Universities and Colleges (AGB)
Association of Institutional Researchers (AIR)
Association for the Study of Higher Education (ASHE)
College and University Personnel Association Human Resources (CUPAHR)
Comparative and International Education Society (CIES)
Council for Advancement and Support of Education (CASE)
Council for Higher Education Accreditation (CHEA)
Council for the Study of Community Colleges (CSCC)
Council of Graduate Schools (CGS)
Council of Independent Colleges (CIC)
NAFSA: Association of International Educators (NAFSA)
National Association of College and University Attorneys (NACUA)
National Association of College and University Business Officers (NACUBO)
National Association for Equal Opportunity in Higher Education (NAFEO)
National Association of Independent Colleges and Universities (NAICU)
National Association of State Universities and Land-Grant Colleges (NASULGC)
National Association of Student Affairs Professionals (NASAP)
National Association of Student Financial Aid Administrators (NASFAA)
National Association of Student Personnel Administrators (NASPA)
National Collegiate Athletic Association (NCAA)

Society of College and University Planning (SCUP)
University Continuing Education Association (UCEA)

Higher Education Specific Journals and Monographs

ASHE-ERIC Monographs
College and University
Higher Education Management
Higher Education in Review
Journal of Diversity in Higher Education
Journal of Excellence in College Teaching
Journal of General Education
Journal of Higher Education
Journal of Hispanic Higher Education
Journal of the Professoriate
Liberal Education
New Directions in Higher Education
New Directions in Institutional Research
Planning for Higher Education
Research in Higher Education
Review of Higher Education
Studies in Higher Education
Thought & Action

General Education Journals for the Field of Higher Education

American Behavioral Scientist
American Educational Research Journal
American Journal of Education
Daedalus
Educational Administration Quarterly
Educational Researcher
Gender and Education
Harvard Educational Review
Journal of Education Policy
Journal of Negro Education
Peabody Journal of Education
Review of Educational Research
Teachers College Record
Urban Education

Student Development Journals and Monographs for the Field of Higher Education

College Student Affairs Journal
Community College Review
Journal of College and Character
Journal of College and University Housing
Journal of College Student Development

Journal of College Student Retention: Research, Theory, and Practice
Journal of Student Affairs Research and Practice
National Academic Advising Association (NACADA) Journal
National Association of Student Affairs Professionals Journal
New Directions for Community Colleges
New Directions for Institutional Research
New Directions in Student Services

International/Comparative Journals for the Field of Higher Education

Canadian Journal of Higher Education
Comparative Education Review
Higher Education
Higher Education in Europe
Higher Education Policy
Higher Education Quarterly
Higher Education Research and Development
International Higher Education
Journal of Higher Education Policy and Management
Research in Comparative and International Education
Studies in Higher Education
Universidades

Periodicals for the Field of Higher Education

About Campus
Academe
Change Magazine
Community College Times
The Chronicle of Higher Education
Diverse Issues in Higher Education
The New York Times, Education Supplement
The Presidency
Times Higher Education
University Business

APPENDIX B—100 CITATIONS ON ORGANIZATION AND GOVERNANCE IN HIGHER EDUCATION PUBLISHED BETWEEN 2000–2010

COMPILED BY T. ELON DANCY II

Alexander, F. K. (2000). The changing face of accountability: Monitoring and assessing institutional performance in higher education. *The Journal of Higher Education, 71*(4), 411–431.

Argus, L. (2004). Globalisation and educational change: Bringing about the reshaping and renorming of practice. *Journal of Education Policy 19*(1), 23–42.

Armstrong, L. (2001). A new Game: competitive higher education. *Information, Communication & Society, 4*(4), 479–506.

Bastedo, M.N., Gumport, P.J. (2003). Access to what? Mission Differentiation and academic stratification in U.S. Public Higher Education. *Higher Education, 46*(3), 341–359.

Benjamin R. (2003). The environment of American higher education: A constellation of changes. *The Annals of the American Academy of Political and Social Science, 585*, 8–30.

Bennett, B. (2002). The new style boards of governors: Are they working? *Higher Education Quarterly, 56*(3), 287–302.

Bensimon, E. M. (2005). Closing the achievement gap in higher education: An organizational learning perspective. *New Directions for Higher Education, 2002* (131), 99–111.

Berdahl, R., Altbach, P., Gumport, P. (Eds.). (2005). *American higher education in the twenty-first century: Social, Political, and economic challenges.* Baltimore, MA: The John Hopkins University Press.

Bess, J. L., Dee, J. R. (2008). *Understanding college and university organization*: Theories for effective policy and practice. Sterling, VA: Stylus Publishing.

Birnbaum. R. (2002). *Management fads in higher education.* San Francisco: Jossey-Bass.

Burke, J. C. (2005). *Achieving accountability in higher education: Balancing public, academic, and market demands.* San Francisco: Jossey-Bass.

Burke, J.C. (2002). *Funding public colleges and universities for performance: popularity, problems, and prospects.* Albany, NY: Rockefeller Institute Press.

Burke, J.C., Modarresi, S. (2000). To keep or not keep performance funding: Signals from the stakeholders. *The Journal of Higher Education, 71*(4), 432–453.

Bogue, E.G., Aper, J. (2000). *Exploring the heritage of American higher education: the evolution of philosophy and policy.* Phoenix, AZ: The American Council on Education and Oryx Press.

Bolden, R., Petrov, G., Gosling, J. (2007). *Tensions in higher education leadership: Towards a multi-level model of leadership practice.* Paper presented at the Annual Conference of the Society for Research into Higher Education (SRHE), December 2007.

Cassie, K.M., Sowers, K., Rowe, W. (2007). Ready, willing and able: An assessment of Academic leadership preparation and interest. *Journal of Baccalaureate Social Work, 13*(1), 115–127.

Compora, D.P. (2003). Current trends in distance education: An administrative model. *Online Journal of Distance Learning Administration, 6*(2).

Coughlin, M. A., Hoey, J., Hirano-Nakanishi, M. (2009). Sector differences in the role of institutional research in informing decision making and governance in higher education. *Asia Pacific Education Review, 10*(1), 69–81.

Curri, G. (2002). Reality versus perception: Restructuring tertiary education and institutional organisational change—a case study. *Higher Education, 44*(1), 133–151.

Deem, R., Brehony, K. (2005). Management as ideology: The case of new managerialism in higher education. *Oxford review of Education, 31*(2), 217–235.

Deem, R., Mok, K. H., Lucas, L. (2008). Transforming higher education in whose image? Exploring the concept of the 'world-class' university in Europe and Asia. *Higher Education Policy, 21*, 83–97.

Del Favero, M. (2003). Faculty-Administrator Relationships as Integral to High Performing Governance Systems: New Frameworks for Study. *American Behavioral Scientist, 2003, 46*(6), 901–922.

Dika, S. L., Janosik, S. M. (2003). The role of selection, orientation, and training in improving the quality of public college and university boards of trustees in the United States. *Quality in Higher Education, 9*(3), 273–285.

Dill, D. (2003). Allowing the market to rule: The case of the United States. *Higher Education Quarterly, 57*(2), 136–157.

Doyle, W. R. (2006). Adoption of merit-based student grant programs: An event history analysis. *Educational Evaluation and Policy Analysis, 28*(3), 259–285.

Dunn, D. (2003). Accountability, democratic theory, and higher education. *Educational Policy, 17*(1), 60–79.

Duryea, E., Williams, T. (Eds.). (2000). *The academic corporation: A history of college and university governing boards.* New York, NY: Falmer Press.

Eckel, P. (2003). *Changing course: Making the hard decisions to eliminate academic programs.* Westport, CT: Praeger.

Eckel, P. D. (2000). The role of shared governance in institutional hard decisions: Enabler or antagonist? *Review of Higher Education, 24*(1), 15–39.

Ehrenberg, R. (2004). *Governing academia.* Ithaca, NY: Cornell University Press.

Enders, J. (2004). Higher education, internationalization, and the nation-state: Recent developments and challenges to governance theory. *Higher Education, 47*(3), 361–382.

Ferlie, E., Musselin, C., Andresani, G. (2008). The steering of higher education systems: A public management perspective. *Higher Education, 56*(3), 325–348.

Fish, S. (2007). Shared Governance: Democracy Is Not an Educational Idea. *Change: The Magazine of Higher Learning, 39*(2), 8–13.

Gayle, D. J., Tewarie, B., and White, A. Q. Jr. (2003). Governance in the Twenty-First Century University: Approaches to Effective Leadership and Strategic Management. *ASHE-ERIC Higher Education Report, 30*(1).

Geiger, R.L. (2004). *Knowledge and Money, Research Universities and the Paradox of the Marketplace.* Palo Alto, CA: Stanford University Press.

George, E. (2006). Positioning higher education for the knowledge based economy. *Higher Education, 52*(4), 589–610.

Green, R. (2003). Markets, management and reengineering higher education. *Annals of the American Academy of Political and Social Science, 585*(1), 196–210.

Gumport, P. J. (2000). Academic restructuring: Organizational change and institutional imperatives. *Higher Education, 39*(1), 67–91.

Hanson, M. (2001). Institutional theory and educational change. *Educational Administration Quarterly, 37*(5), 637–661.

Hines, E. (2000). The governance of higher education. In J. C. Smart & W. G. Tierney (Eds.), *Higher Education: Handbook of Theory and Research, XV,* (pp. 105–155). New York: Agathon Press.

Ho, W., Higson, H., Dey, P. (2007). Multiple criteria decision making approach for resource allocation in higher education. *International Journal of Innovation and Learning, 4*(5), 471–486.

Howell, S., Williams, B.P., Lindsay, N.K. (2003). Thirty-two trends affecting distance education: An informed foundation for strategic planning. *Online Journal of Distance Learning Administration, 6*(3), 1–18.

Huisman, J., Meek, L., and Wood, F. (2007). 'Institutional diversity in higher education: a cross-national and longitudinal analysis', *Higher Education Quarterly 61*(4), 563–577.

Jeliazkova, M., Westerheijden, D. F. (2002). Systemic adoption to a changing environment: Towards a next generation of quality assurance models. *Higher Education, 44*(3–4), 433–448.

Jongbloed, B., Vossensteyn, H. (2001). Keeping up performances: an international survey of performance-based funding in higher education. *Journal of Higher Education Policy and Management, 23*(2), 127–145.

Kerr, C. (2001). *The Uses of the University: The Godkin lectures on the essential of free government and the duties of the citizen*, (5th ed.). Cambridge, MA: Harvard University Press.

Kezar, A. (2006). Rethinking Public Higher Education Governing Boards Performance: Results of a National Study of Governing Boards in the United States. *The Journal of Higher Education, 77*(6), 968–1008.

Kezar, A. (2005). Consequences of Radical Change in Governance: A Grounded Theory Approach. *The Journal of Higher Education, 76*(6), 634–668.

Kezar, A. (2004). What is more important to effective governance: Relationships, trust, and leadership, or structures and formal processes. *New Directions for Higher Education, 127*, p. 35–46.

Kezar, A., Eckel, P. (2002). Examining institutional transformation process: The importance of sense making, interrelated strategies, and balance. *Research in Higher Education, 43*(3), 295–328.

Kezar, A., Eckel, P. (2002). The effect of institutional culture on change strategies in higher education. *The Journal of Higher Education, 74*(4), 435–460.

King, R. P. (2007). Governance and accountability in the higher education regulatory state. *Higher Education, 53*(4), 411–430.

Kivisto, J. A. (2005). The government-higher education institution relationship: Theoretical considerations from the perspective of agency theory. *Tertiary Education and Management, 11*(1), 1–17.

Kogan, M. (2006). *Transforming higher education: A comparative study*. New York, NY: Springer.

Lane, J. E. (2007). Spider Web of Oversight: Latent and Manifest Regulatory Controls in Higher Education. *Journal of Higher Education, 78*(6), 1–30.

Leslie, D., Novak, R. (2003). Substance versus politics: Through the dark mirror of governance reform. *Educational Policy, 17*(1), 98–120.

Levy, D. C. (2006). The unanticipated explosion: Private higher education's global surge. *Comparative Education Review, 50*(2), 217–240.

Liefner, I. (2003). Funding, resource allocation, and performance in higher education systems. *Higher Education, 46*(4), 469–489.

Locke, W. (2008). Higher education mergers: Integrating organizational cultures and developing appropriate management styles. *Higher Education Quarterly, 61*(1), 83–102.

Lowry, R. C. (2001). Governmental structure, trustee selection, and public university prices and spending. *American Journal of Political Science, 45*(4), 845–861.

Marginson, S. (2006). Dynamics of national and global competition in higher education. *Higher Education, 52*(1), 1–39.

Massy, W. F. (2003). *Honoring the Trust, Quality and Cost Containment in Higher Education*, Boston, MA: Anker.

McCaffery, P. (2004). *The Higher Education Manager's Handbook: Effective Leadership and Management in Universities and Colleges*. London: Routledge Falmer.

McLendon, M. (2003). Setting the governmental agenda for state decentralization of higher education. *Journal of Higher Education, 74*(5), 479–515.

McLendon, M., Ness, E. (2003). The politics of state higher education governance reform. *Peabody Journal of Education, 78*(4), 66–88.

McLendon, M. K. (2003). The politics of higher education: Toward an expanded research agenda. *Educational Policy, 17*(1), 165–191.

McLendon, M. K., Deaton, R., Hearn, J. C. (2007). The enactment of state governance reforms in higher education. *The Journal of Higher Education, 78*(6), 645–675.

McLendon, M. K., Hearn, J. C., Deaton, R. (2006). Called to account: Analyzing the origins and spread of state performance-accountability policies for higher education. *Educational Evaluation and Policy Analysis, 28*(1), 1–24.

McLendon, M. K., Heller, D. E., Young, S. (2005). State postsecondary education policy innovation: Politics, competition, and the interstate migration of policy ideas. *The Journal of Higher Education, 76*(4), 363–400.

Morey, A. I. (2004). Globalization and the emergence of for-profit higher education. *Higher Education, 48*(1), 131–150.

Morphew, C.C. (2006). Conceptualizing change in the institutional diversity of US colleges and universities. *The Journal of Higher Education, 80*(3), 243–269.

Moskal, P., Ellis, T., Keon, T. (2008). Summary of assessment in higher education and the management of student-learning data. *The Academy of Management and Education, 7*(2), 269–278.

Mumper, M. (2003). The future of college access: The declining role of public higher education in promoting equal opportunity. *Annals of the American Academy of Political and Social Science, 58*(1), 97–117.

Newman, F., Couturier, L., and Scurie, J. (2004). *The Future of Higher Education, Rhetoric, Reality and the Risks of the Marketplace*, San Francisco, CA: Jossey-Bass.

Nicholson-Crotty, J., Meier, K. J. (2003). Politics, structure, and public policy: The case of higher education. *Educational Policy, 17*(1), 80–97.

Ortmann, A., Squire, R. (2000). A game-theoretic explanation of the administrative lattice in institutions of higher learning. *Journal of Economic Behavior & Organization, 43*(3), 377–391.

Payne, A. (2003). The effects of Congressional appropriation committee membership on the distribution of federal research funding to Universities. *Economic Inquiry, 41*(2), 325–345.

Priest, D., St-John, E. (Eds.). (2006). *Privatization and public universities.* Bloomington, IN: Indiana University Press.

Pusser, B. (2003). Beyond Baldridge: Extending the political model of higher education organization and governance. *Educational Policy, 17*(1), 121–140.

Pusser, B., Slaughter, S., Thomas, S. (2006). Playing the Board Game: An Empirical Analysis of University Trustee and Corporate Board Interlocks. *The Journal of Higher Education, 77*(5), 747–775.

Richardson, R., Martinez, M. (2009). Policy and Performance in American Higher Education: An Examination of Cases Across State Systems. Baltimore, MA: John Hopkins University Press.

Rindfleish, J. M. (2003). Segment profiling: reducing risk in higher education Management. *Journal of Higher Education Policy and Management, 25*(2), 147–159.

Rosse, J. G., Levin, R. A. (2003). *The Jossey-Bass Academic Administrators Guide to Hiring* (1st ed.). San Francisco, CA: Jossey-Bass.

Rusch, E., Wilbur, C. (2007). Shaping Institutional Environments: The Process of Becoming Legitimate. *The Review of Higher Education, 30*(3), 301–318.

Salerno, C. (2004). Public money and private providers: Funding channels and national patterns in four counties. *Higher Education, 48*(1), 101–130.

Salter, B., Tapper, T. (2002). The external pressures on the internal governance of universities. *Higher Education Quarterly, 56*(3), 245–256.

Santos, J. (2007). Resource Allocation in Public Research Universities. *Review of Higher Education, 30*(2), 125–144.

Shattock, M. L. (2003). *Managing Successful Universities.* Maidenhead: SRHE/Open University Press.

Spendlove, M. (2007). Competencies for effective leadership in higher education. *International Journal of Educational Management, 21*(5), 407–417.

Stensaker, B., Norgard, J. D. (2001). Innovation and isomorphism: A case study of university identity struggle 1969–1999. *Higher Education, 42*(4), 473–492.

Stromquist, N. P. (2007). Internationalization as a response to globalization: Radical shifts in university environments. *Higher Education, 53*(1), 81–105.

Taylor, J., Machado, M. (2008). Governing boards in public higher education: A perspective from the United States. *Tertiary Education Management, 14*(3), 243–260.

Teichler, U. (2008). Diversification? Trends and explanations of the shape and size of higher education. *Higher Education, 56*(3), 349–379.

Tierney, W. G. (Ed.). (2004). *Competing conceptions of academic governance: Negotiating the perfect storm.* Baltimore, MD: Johns Hopkins University Press.

Tierney, W. G., Lechuga, V. M. (Eds.). (2004). *Restructuring shared governance in higher education.* San Francisco, CA: Jossey-Bass.

Ulrich, T. (2006). Changing structures of the higher education systems: The increasing complexity of underlying forces. *Higher Education Policy, 19*(4), 447–461.

Volkwein, J. F., Tandberg, D. A. (2008). Measuring up: Examining, the connections among state structural characteristics, regulatory practices, and performance. *Research in Higher Education, 49*(2), 180–197.

Vaira, M. (2004). Globalization and higher education organizational: A framework for analysis. *Higher Education, 48*(4), 483–510.

Weerts, D.J., Ronca, J.M. (2006). Examining Differences in State Support for Higher Education: A Comparative Study of State Appropriations for Research I Universities. *The Journal of Higher Education, 77*(6), 935–967.

ABOUT THE EDITOR

M. Christopher Brown II is Executive Vice President and Provost at the historic Fisk University in Nashville, Tennessee where he holds the rank of University Professor. Prior to this appointment he served as Dean of the College of Education at the University of Nevada, Las Vegas, Vice President for Programs and Administration at the American Association of Colleges for Teacher Education, Director of Social Justice and Professional Development for the American Educational Research Association (AERA), as well as Executive Director and Chief Research Scientist of the Frederick D. Patterson Research Institute of the United Negro College Fund. Dr. Brown has held faculty appointments at The Pennsylvania State University, the University of Illinois at Urbana-Champaign, and the University of Missouri-Kansas City.

Dr. Brown earned a national reputation for his research and scholarly writing on education policy, governance/administration, and institutional contexts. He is especially well known for his studies of historically black colleges, educational equity, and professorial responsibilities. Dr. Brown has lectured and/or presented research in various countries on six continents—Africa, Asia, Australia, Europe, North America, and South America.

Dr. Brown is the author/editor of fifteen books and monographs—*The Quest to Define Collegiate Desegregation* (1999), *Organization and Governance in Higher Education* (2000), *Black Sons to Mothers* (2000), *Equity and Access in Higher Education* (2002), *Studying Diverse Institutions* (2003), *Black Colleges* (2004), *Unique Campus Settings* (2004), *Achieving Equitable Educational Outcomes with All Students* (2005), *The Politics of Curricular Change* (2005), *The Children Hurricane Katrina Left Behind* (2007), *School Matters* (2007), *Still Not Equal* (2007), *Ebony Towers in Higher Education* (2008), *The Broken Cisterns of African American Education* (2009), and *The Case for Affirmative Action on Campus* (2009). He is the author or co-author of more than 100 journal articles, book chapters, and publications related to education and society.

A former member of the South Carolina State University Board of Trustees, Dr. Brown lists among his many honors and awards, The 100 Black Men of Charleston 2002 Image Award, and the 2004 Pennsylvania State University Alumni Achievement Award. He received the 2001 Association for the Study of Higher Education's Promising Scholar/Early Career Award, the 2002 AERA Committee on Scholars of Color Early Career Contribution Award, the 2007 Philip C. Chinn Book Award from the National Association for Multicultural Education, and the 2008 Association of Teacher Educators Distinguished Educator Award. His research has been supported by the Lumina Foundation, Spencer Foundation, AT&T Foundation, the Pew Charitable Trusts, the Sallie Mae Fund, as well as other foundations and corporations.

Dr. Brown received his B.S. in Elementary Education from South Carolina State University and the M.S.Ed. in Educational Policy and Evaluation from the University of Kentucky. He received a Ph.D. in Higher Education from The Pennsylvania State University with a cognate in public administration and political science.

ABOUT THE ASSOCIATE EDITORS

Jason E. Lane is an Assistant Professor of Educational Administration and Policy Studies at the University at Albany, State University at New York, where he also holds affiliate appointments with the Comparative and International Education Policy Program (CIEPP) and the Rockefeller School of Public Affairs. In addition, he is the Secretary of the Comparative and International Education Society (CIES), head of the Society's secretariat, and the institutional liaison between the University and Organization for Economic Co-operation and Development's (OECD) Institute for Management in Higher Education. Previously Dr. Lane held a faculty appointment at the University of North Dakota and served as the special assistant to the president at Southeast Missouri State University.

Dr. Lane is recognized internationally for his work in organizational theory, accountability, and public policy pertaining to the development of higher education organizations and their relationship with governments and society. As a Public Policy Fellow with the Western Interstate Commission on Higher Education (WICHE), he authored a national report analyzing the role of public agenda setting to link the goals of higher education systems with the needs of states. As a Fulbright New Century Scholar his interests have focused on investigating the development of cross-border higher education, particularly the organizational design of international branch campuses (IBCs) and their effect on local development. Dr. Lane has conducted extensive fieldwork in more than 10 countries around the globe. This work has culminated in several journal articles, book chapters, and a forthcoming book (with Kevin Kinser): *The Multi-National University: Administration, Governance, and Leadership of International Branch Campuses.* Lane's research has appeared in several journals and books, including *The Journal of Higher Education, Higher Education: Handbook of Theory and Research,* and the *Journal of Comparative Policy Analysis.* He has co-edited (with M. Christopher Brown) two monographs on institutional accountability (*Examining Unique Campus Settings* and *Studying Diverse Students and Institutions*) and is currently working on *The Handbook of Academic Administration in Higher Education.* Dr. Lane previously served as the co-editor of the *Journal of Natural Inquiry,* member of the *Higher Education in Review* editorial board, and a columnist on legal and policy issues in student affairs for the American College Personnel Association (ACPA). He has also lectured and presented his research throughout Asia, Europe, the Middle East, and North America.

Eboni M. Zamani-Gallaher is a Professor and Coordinator of the Graduate Certificate Program in Community College Leadership in the Department of Leadership and Counseling at Eastern Michigan University. Prior to joining the College of Education at EMU, she was a faculty member at West Virginia University and a Fellow of ACT, Inc. and Mathematica Policy Research in Washington, D.C. Dr. Zamani-Gallaher's teaching, research, and service considers the psychosocial adjustment and transition of marginalized college student populations, policies relating to access and matriculation in both two- and four-year institutions of higher education, women in leadership, and institutional practices affecting work and family balance. As the author or co-author of numerous publications, including journal articles and book chapters, her work on policies and practices relating to educational access, affirmative action, and equity across race and ethnicity, gender, socioeconomic status, and institutional contexts have been well received. Her recent scholarship includes co-authoring *The Case for Affirmative Action on Campus: Concepts of Equity, Considerations for Practice* (Stylus Publishing, 2009) and co-editing *The State of the African American Male* (Michigan State University Press, 2010).

Dr. Eboni Zamani-Gallaher was honored for her leadership in delivering girls' mentoring programs and diversity education in K–12 schools, her instructional excellence, innovative research, and community service as a 2010 recipient of the EMU Dr. Martin Luther King Jr. Humanitarian Award. In 2009, she received the Mildred B. Garcia Senior Scholar Award for Exemplary Scholarship from ASHE (Association for the Study of Higher Education) Council on Ethnic Participation. This award recognizes innovative research that attends to underserved populations of color in postsecondary education. Dr. Eboni Zamani-Gallaher balances her scholarly agenda by serving on a number of departmental and campus-wide committees at EMU, including curriculum planning, personnel, and graduate student mentorship and advocacy (ombudsman). In association with national professional organizations, she has participated on several committees on student development and research on Black Education along with planning, proposal review and participation for annual conferences hosted by ACPA (American College Personnel Association), AERA (American Education Research Association), ASHE (Association for the Study of Higher Education), and CSCC (Council for the Study of Community Colleges). Dr. Zamani-Gallaher received her B.S. in Psychology and M.S. in General Experimental Psychology from Western Illinois University. She received a Ph.D. in Higher Education Administration from The University of Illinois at Urbana-Champaign with a cognate in Community College Leadership.